The R

French H

Restaurants

le guide du Routard

English edition

2004

Editor: Philippe Gloaguen

Translation and revision produced by Book Production Consultants plc, Cambridge in association with First Edition Translations Ltd, Cambridge, England

In addition to this guide, Rough Guides publish nine guidebooks on France:

France • Brittany & Normandy • Corsica

The Dordogne & Lot • Languedoc & Roussillon • Loire

Provence & the Côte d'Azur • Paris

The Pyrenees (French and Spanish)

There is also a

Rough Guide French phrasebook

NEW YORK • LONDON • DELHI

www.roughguides.com

Contents

❶ **Alsace** 001
Bas-Rhin, Haut-Rhin

❷ **Aquitaine** 025
Dordogne, Gironde, Landes, Lot-et-Garonne, Pyrénées-Atlantiques

❸ **Auvergne** 081
Allier, Cantal, Haute-Loire, Puy-de-Dôme

❹ **Bourgogne (Burgundy)** 121
Côte-d'Or, Nièvre, Saône-et-Loire, Yonne

❺ **Bretagne (Brittany)** 165
Côtes-d'Armor, Finistère, Ille-et-Vilaine, Morbihan

❻ **Centre** 219
Cher, Eure-et-Loir, Indre, Indre-et-Loire, Loir-et-Cher, Loiret

❼ **Champagne-Ardennes** 263
Ardennes, Aube, Marne, Haute-Marne

❽ **Corse (Corsica)** 291

❾ **Franche-Comté** 301
Doubs, Jura, Haute-Saône, Territoire de Belfort

❿ **Île-de-France** 325
Paris, Seine-et-Marne, Yvelines, Essonne, Hauts-de-Seine, Seine-Saint-Denis, Val-de-Marne, Val-d'Oise

⓫ **Languedoc-Roussillon** 409
Aude, Gard, Hérault, Lozère, Pyrénées-Orientales

⓬ **Limousin** 457
Corrèze, Creuse, Haute-Vienne

⓭ **Lorraine** 481
Meurthe-et-Moselle, Meuse, Moselle, Vosges

⓮ **Midi-Pyrénées** 515
Ariège, Aveyron, Haute-Garonne, Gers, Lot, Hautes-Pyrénées, Tarn, Tarn-et-Garonne

⓯ **Nord-Pas-de-Calais** 567
Nord, Pas-de-Calais

⑯ **Basse-Normandie** 593
Calvados, Manche, Orne

⑰ **Haute-Normandie** 621
Eure, Seine-Maritime

⑱ **Pays-de-la-Loire** 649
Loire-Atlantique, Maine-et-Loire, Mayenne, Sarthe, Vendée

⑲ **Picardie** 695
Aisne, Oise, Somme

⑳ **Poitou-Charentes** 709
Charente, Charente-Maritime, Deux-Sèvres, Vienne

㉑ **Provence-Alpes-Côte d'Azur** 745
Alpes-de-Haute-Provence, Hautes-Alpes, Alpes-Maritimes, Bouches-du-Rhône, Var, Vaucluse

㉒ **Rhône-Alpes** 815
Ain, Ardèche, Drôme, Isère, Loire, Rhône, Savoie, Haute-Savoie

Small print and Index 919

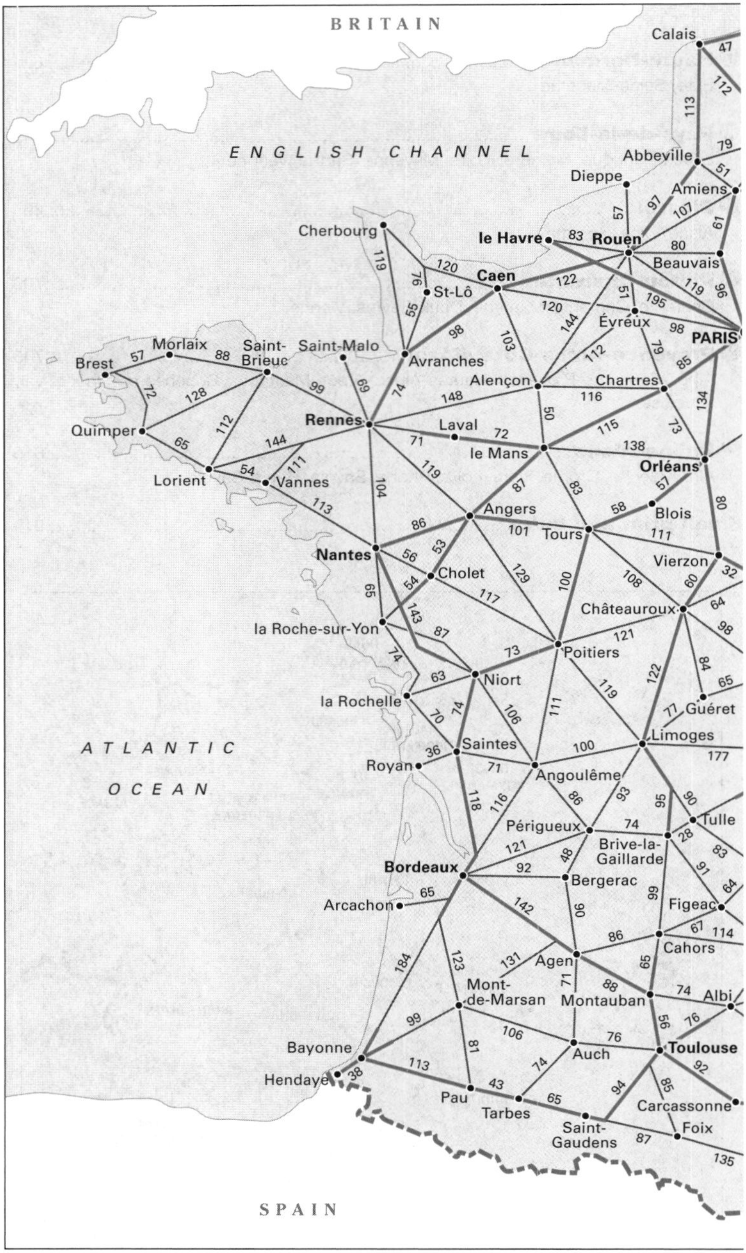

BRITAIN

ENGLISH CHANNEL

Calais
Abbeville
Dieppe
Amiens
Cherbourg
le Havre
Rouen
Beauvais
Caen
St-Lô
Évreux
PARIS
Brest
Morlaix
Saint-Brieuc
Saint-Malo
Avranches
Alençon
Chartres
Quimper
Rennes
Laval
le Mans
Orléans
Lorient
Vannes
Angers
Blois
Tours
Nantes
Cholet
Vierzon
Châteauroux
la Roche-sur-Yon
Poitiers
Niort
la Rochelle
Guéret
Limoges
Saintes
Royan
Angoulême
Périgueux
Tulle
Brive-la-Gaillarde
Bordeaux
Bergerac
Arcachon
Figeac
Cahors
Agen
Mont-de-Marsan
Montauban
Albi
Bayonne
Hendaye
Auch
Toulouse
Pau
Tarbes
Saint-Gaudens
Carcassonne
Foix

ATLANTIC OCEAN

SPAIN

N
BELGIUM
LUX.
GERMANY
SWITZERLAND
ITALY
Dunkerque
Bruxelles
Lille
Arras
Valenciennes
St-Quentin
Charleville-Mézières
Luxembourg
Laon
Reims
Metz
Châlons-en-Champagne
Nancy
Strasbourg
St-Dizier
Troyes
Chaumont
Épinal
Colmar
Nemours
Mulhouse
Basel
Auxerre
Briare
Vesoul
Belfort
Dijon
Besançon
Bourges
Nevers
Beaune
Chalon-sur-Saône
Lons-le-Saunier
Moulins
Montluçon
Mâcon
Genève
Bourg-en-Bresse
Chamonix
Lyon
Clermont-Ferrand
St-Étienne
Chambéry
Modane
Grenoble
Briançon
le Puy-en-Velay
Valence
Aurillac
Gap
Mende
Rodez
Millau
Orange
Digne
Nîmes
Aix-en-Provence
Nice
Cannes
Montpellier
Marseille
Toulon
Béziers
Narbonne
Perpignan
le Perthus
Calvi
Bastia
Ajaccio
Bonifacio

About this book

This is the seventh edition of the **Rough Guide to French Hotels & Restaurants**, a translation of the Routard guide, the best-selling French guide to good-value restaurants and accommodation in France. Revised every year, *French Hotels & Restaurants* is up-to-date, comprehensive and opens up the country in a way that no other guide does. Its listings include everything from simple hostels and family-run bistros to high-comfort rural retreats and city-centre three-stars. All selected are reviewed by Routard's team of locally based writers, who re-assess the entries for each edition.

The hotels and restaurants selected tend to be small, independent establishments – look out for the Routard stickers on their front doors. There may also be a Logis de France sticker, too – a fireplace symbol with one, two or three fires to indicate the level of facilities provided. This denotes membership of a scheme that promotes family-run hotels, often in rural locations well away from major towns.

The guide's layout

The Routard/Rough Guide is divided into twenty-two **chapter regions**, each with a regional map. The regions are listed alphabetically and within each chapter the **main towns** (marked by black circles on the maps) are listed in alphabetical order, their names appearing in large type followed by the postcode:

Quiberon

57170

Small towns and villages within a radius of 30km of a larger town are included after the entries for that town (and marked by white circles on regional maps); these places are listed in the order of their distance from the main town, and their names are displayed in smaller type:

Levernois

21200 (4km SE)

Within each town hotels are listed first, followed by restaurants, and both are listed in ascending order of price. Note that stars indicated are the official ratings of the French hotel industry and not of this guide.

After the address of the establishments, tips on **how to get there** are given wherever possible, plus phone number, fax number, email address, closing times and a summary of facilities where relevant.

In addition to regional maps, certain key cities are covered by detailed **city maps**. Hotels and restaurants in these places are given a two-part map code (eg **Map B2-13**) comprised of a grid reference and the establishment's number in the map key. Sometimes city establishments are located outside the area covered by the map; these are marked **Off map** and correspond to an arrow pointing in the direction you'll need to travel in order to get there.

Symbols

The following symbols have been used:

- hotel
- restaurant
- discount

The **discount symbol** indicates that an establishment offers some sort of benefit to readers of this guide. In the case of hotels, it's usually a discount (generally 10%) on the price of the room. You are usually obliged to stay for a minimum of two nights to qualify but sometimes the period or the amount of the discount can be different. The benefit can also be limited to certain periods of the year. Where possible these conditions have been indicated in the text. In some instances, the concession consists of a free breakfast or free garage space; many restaurants in this guide offer a free coffee, house apéritif or house digestif, but you qualify only when you order a complete meal and, more often than not, the choice of drink will not be up to you.

All establishments will insist that you are entitled to the benefit only if you are carrying the **current year's edition** of this guidebook.

In all cases, show your copy when you check in at the hotel or before you order your meal in a restaurant. Hotels and restaurants are familiar with the French Routard guide, and should you have any difficulties claiming the benefits with this translation, point to the front cover where the Routard logo is clearly displayed.

The French way

It pays to know what's what in French hotels and restaurants and your basic rights as a consumer.

When you're reserving a room by phone or in writing, it's not unusual for the hotel to ask for a **deposit** by way of a guarantee. There's no law to say how much this deposit should be, but don't pay any more than around 25–30% of the total. The French have two words for deposit – *arrhes* and *acompte*. The first is refundable, the second is not. So in the event of cancellation your arrhes can be returned in full if you give the hotel reasonable notice. If it's the hotel that cancels the booking, then under Article 1590 of the Civil Code (which dates back to 1804) you're entitled to double the amount of the *arrhes* you paid. So if you do make a deposit, be very specific in your letter as to whether it's *arrhes* or *acompte*.

Hotels and restaurants are required by law to **display their prices**. You won't get anywhere arguing about extortionate charges if they're clearly marked on a price list.

Hotels are **not permitted to try to sell you something you haven't requested**; for example they can't force you to book for several nights if you only want to stay for one. Similarly, they can't insist you have breakfast or any other meal at the hotel unless it's clearly stated that **half** or **full board** is compulsory. Make sure you find this out before you book into a hotel with a restaurant, and bear in mind that half-board prices often apply to a minimum stay of three nights. This is permitted by law.

In restaurants the cheapest **set meals** are often served at lunchtimes on weekdays only. This should be clearly marked on the board outside. The same menu may cost more at night.

Wine lists aren't always very clear so be sure that you know precisely what you're ordering. For example, you might select a bottle of Burgundy at 18 and be charged 116; when you check the list again, you find (maybe in small print) that the price was for a half-bottle. A bottle of wine must be opened in front of the customer – otherwise you've no way of knowing that you're getting what you ordered. A jug of tap water is free as long as you're ordering a meal.

Occasionally restaurants **refuse to serve** customers if they feel they haven't ordered enough. But no one can force you into ordering something you don't want and refusing to serve you is technically against the law.

Alsace

Altkirch

68130

🏃 ☗ |●| Auberge Sundgovienne**

1 rte. de Belfort; it's 3km out of town on the D419 in the direction of Dannemarie.
Ⓣ03.89.40.97.18 Ⓕ03.89.40.67.73
Closed *23 Dec–1 Feb.* **Restaurant closed** *Tues until 5pm. With booking only Sun and Mon eve.* **High chairs and games available. Disabled access. TV. Pay car park.**

A cross between an American motel (it's near the road), a Swiss chalet (Switzerland isn't far) and a traditional Alsatian hotel. Refurbished rooms with shower/wc or bath cost €50–58, are clean and comfortable and some have a balcony. Even though they are all double-glazed, the ones at the back are quieter. The cooking is a pleasant surprise: it's inspired by the fresh produce in the market, and the chef has some interesting ideas. Typical dishes are sliced duck's liver with caramelized pears, monkfish steak marinated in pepper, veal with port and fresh rhubarb cooked with strawberries and served with vanilla ice cream. There is a weekday menu at €11.50 and others at €20–43. The terrace is a great place to sit over a drink, admiring the Sundgau countryside. *10% discount on the room rate.*

Hirtzbach

68118 (4km S)

|●| Restaurant de la Gare-Munzenberger

Ⓣ03.89.40.93.27
Closed *Mon, Tues evening; Wed.*

This good country inn is part of the official network on the *route de la Carpe frite* (carp and chips route). You can serve yourself to as many helpings as you want of their delicious crispy carp for just €13.50. But the menu lists all sorts of other equally tasty specialities, including delicious calves' liver. And the *spaetzle* are among the best in the region.

Gommersdorf

68210 (12km W)

☗ |●| 🏃 L'Auberge du Tisserand**

28 rue de Cernay; it's on the D103 as you leave the village.
Ⓣ03.89.07.21.80 Ⓕ03.89.25.11.34
Closed *Mon; Tues; 15 Feb–6 March; 22 Dec–6 Jan.* **High chairs available. TV. Car park.**

This is a typical Alsace inn with a long history. Parts date from the seventeenth century when it was a weaver's house, and other parts are even older. On the first floor, reserved for smokers, the wooden floor has buckled with age. Good cooking and enormous portions at reasonable prices. The weekday lunch menu, €7.50, is one of the cheapest around; other menus are €14–25. They offer Alsace specialities including *choucroute*, bake their own bread and serve flambéed tarts every night. A really delightful place with a few rooms for €45 with shower/wc. *10% discount on the price of a room or a bottle of mineral water per room (except during the Bâle fair) offered to our readers on presentation of this guide.*

Barr

67140

🏃 ☗ |●| Hôtel Maison Rouge**

1 av. de la Gare; it's near the post office.
Ⓣ03.88.08.90.40 Ⓕ03.88.08.90.85
Ⓦwww.hotel-restaurant-maisonrouge.com

Bitche
Wissembourg
Four-à-Chaux
Climbach
Parc
naturel régional
des Vosges du Nord
Niederbronn-les-B.
Wœrth
Hinsingen
Sarre-Union
A 4
N 82
la Petite-Pierre
D 919
MOSELLE
Schweighouse-
sur-Moder
Haguenau
Kaltenhouse
Rhin
A 4
Sarrebourg
N 4
Saverne
BAS-RHIN
A 35
D 30
N 4
STRASBOURG
Handschuheim
Achern
Scharrachbergheim
N 4
Molsheim
N 420
Rosheim
Offenburg
Schirmeck
Klingenthal
Ottrot
Obernai
N 83
Fouday
Natzwiller
Heiligenstein
Erstein
le Hohwald
Barr
Andlau
N 59
N 420
Bleinschwiller
Dambach-
la-Ville
Saint-Dié
Sélestat
Rathsamhausen
Sainte-Marie-aux-Mines
Thannenkirch
D 468
Bergheim
GERMANY
Ribeauvillé
Illhaeusern
le Bonhomme
Hunawihr
Riquewihr
VOSGES
Lapoutroie
Kaysersberg
Orbey
Ammerschwihr
Niedermorschwihr
Les Trois-Epis
Turckheim
COLMAR
Stosswihr
D 417
Wettolsheim
Munster
Wihr-
au-Val
Eguisheim
Neuf-Brisach
Freiburg
D 430
Rouffach
Rhin
D 468
Guebwiller
Soultz
St-Amarin
N 66
Moosch
N
Thann
MULHOUSE
TERR.
DE BELFORT
N 83
A 36
A 35
N 83
HAUT-RHIN
Belfort
Gommersdorf
Altkirch
D 419
D 419
A 36
Hirtzbach
D 432
Montbéliard
Ferrette
Basel
SWITZERLAND
DOUBS
0
20 km
A
1
2

Closed *Tues evening; Wed; 1 Jan–15 Feb.* **High chairs and games available. TV. Car park.**

This place is far enough away from the centre not to attract too many tourists and there's a leafy little square with a charming terrace across from the hotel. The hotel has been totally refurbished, with a different style for each room (some of which enjoy views over the Kirschberg vineyard). The restaurant has been redecorated by a famous local artist. There's a dish of the day at €7 (weekday lunchtimes), a menu at €18 and an hors d'œuvre buffet in summer. Alsace specialities include *baeckeoffe*, zander with Riesling, flambéed kidneys and tarts. In the bar, there are over 60 kinds of beer, along with cocktails. Friendly, family atmosphere. Pleasant rooms €45–65 with en-suite bath. *Free apéritif offered to our readers on presentation of this guide.*

Heiligenstein

67140 (1.5km N)

Relais du Klevener**

51 rue Principale.
03.88.08.05.98 03.88.08.40.83
Closed *1Jan–10 Feb.* **Restaurant closed** *Mon; Tues lunchtime.* **TV. Car park.**

This inn has wonderful views over the vineyards, the Rhine and Germany beyond. The rooms are simple with no great appeal but some have views. Doubles at €42–52. There's a brasserie and a separate restaurant. Generous set menus €16.50–29 and à la carte. Specialities include home-made foie gras, terrines, *choucroute*, zander and *baeckeoffe*. Sit out on the terrace and have a glass of Klevener – it's an old grape variety peculiar to Heiligenstein and pretty rare elsewhere in Alsace. *Apéritif on the house offered to our readers on presentation of this guide.*

Andlau

67140 (4km SW)

Le Zinck Hôtel

13 rue de la Marne.
and 03.88.08.27.30
www.zinckhotel.com
Disabled access. TV. Car park.

Charming hotel in a restored water-mill. The eighteen comfortable rooms have been tastefully decorated, each with a distinctive look. They have names rather than numbers – the Vigneron has a bed with a canopy. Doubles from €59 with shower/wc or bath. The hall has been beautifully decorated and they have preserved the mill wheel. The hotel doesn't have its own restaurant but the owner runs the *Relais de la Poste* at 1 rue des Forgerons (closed Mon and Tues). It's a wine cellar with a good reputation. *10% discount on the price of a room (out of season) offered to our readers on presentation of this guide.*

Hohwald (Le)

67140 (9km W)

Hôtel Marchal**

12 rue Wittertalhof; take the D425 and look for the signs out of the village.
03.88.08.31.04 03.88.08.34.05
Closed 3–27 Nov. **Restaurant closed** *Sun eve and Mon (except for hotel guests).* **TV. High chairs available. Car park.**

A family hotel set amongst greenery in this small health and ski resort. The old-style rooms have been freshened up and, although not huge, they have decent services and are very restful. Double rooms with shower/wc or bath €42.70. Excellent welcome and a quiet atmosphere. Good, classic cooking that's lighter than usual and very tasty. Menus €12.20–25.15. *Apéritif on the house offered to our readers on presentation of this guide.*

Blienschwiller

67650

Hôtel Winzenberg**

58 rte. du Vin; on the N422.
03.88.92.62.77 03.88.92.45.22
www.winzenberg.com
Closed *3 Jan–22 Feb.* **Disabled access. TV. Car park.**

The Dreschs believe that it's the division of labour that makes their family tick: mother and daughter run the hotel while father and son take charge of the vineyard. They seem to have got it about right. The comfortable rooms, with pretty Alsace furniture and brightly coloured bedspreads and curtains, prove good value: doubles cost €41–48. The whole family is very welcoming – they will show you the wine cellar, built in 1508, and invite you to taste the wine.

Colmar

68000

Auberge de Jeunesse

2 rue Pasteur; take the #4 bus to the "Pont rouge" stop; or walk 30 min from the train station (behind the station, cross the bridge in the direction of Ingersheim, following the signposts).
Ⓣ03.89.80.57.39 Ⓕ03.89.80.76.16
Closed *mid-Dec to mid-Jan.* **High chairs available. Car park.**

Large, spotless, well-run youth hostel – and quiet, too. New guests are received 7.30–10am and 5pm–midnight. There are eleven rooms with eight beds, one with five, three with four and seven with two. Reckon on €11.65 per person in the larger ones, €16.65 in an individual room and €28.30 in a double room. Breakfast not included. Add €3.50 for rent of sheets. No meals (except for groups, by request). No sporting activities but there's an attractive little park, ideal in fine weather. Very busy from April to June, so it's advisable to book.

Hôtel Colbert**

2 rue des Trois-Épis; footsteps away from the historic centre, next to the station.
Ⓣ03.89.41.31.05 Ⓕ03.89.23.66.75
High chairs and games available. TV. Pay garage.

A reliable, functional hotel with no particular charm; the rooms are air-conditioned, comfortable and clean, with double glazing to keep out the noise from the railway. Doubles with bath or shower/wc €44–48. A small detail that will keep beer drinkers happy: there's a bottle-opener on the wall in the bathroom. There's a disco-bar, *The Toucan*, in the hotel basement, but noise levels aren't too bad. *10% discount on a room offered to our readers on presentation of this guide.*

Hôtel Turenne**

10 rte. de Bâle, a few minutes' walk from the centre of town.
Ⓣ03.89.21.58.58 Ⓕ03.89.41.27.64
Ⓦwww.turenne.com
TV. Pay car park.

A good establishment made up of a collection of buildings with pink, green and cream walls hung with geraniums. The contemporary-looking rooms have been renovated in a functional style, but they're pleasant enough. The ones over the road are noisier than those at the back. Air-conditioning throughout. Doubles with bath or shower/wc €58–66; the buffet breakfast is generous. *5% discount on room rate 11 Nov–14 March.*

Hôtel Beauséjour**

25 rue du Ladhof, ten minutes' walk from the centre.
Ⓣ03.89.20.66.66 Ⓕ03.89.20.66.00
Ⓦwww.beausejour.fr
Closed *Sat lunchtime and Sun out of season.* **High chairs and games available. Disabled access. TV. Car park.**

This hotel has been run by five generations of the Keller family since 1913 and they owned the eighteenth-century post house that stood here before that. They have added lots of annexes with around forty rooms, most of which now have modern facilities (doubles with shower/wc or bath €59–120). In the garden there's a terrace with wisteria clambering over the pergola. The dining room is elegant and the chef gives an inventive twist to classic local dishes. Menus from €20.50 at lunch (from €23 at dinner) to €54. *One breakfast per person per night or an apéritif on the house offered in the restaurant to our readers on presentation of this guide.*

Le Caveau Saint-Pierre

24 rue de la Herse, Petite Venise.
Ⓣ03.89.41.99.33
Closed *Sun evening; Mon; Fri lunchtime; Jan.* **Disabled access.**

Elegant but affordable, this is undoubtedly the best restaurant in the romantic area known as *Petite Venise* (Little Venice). It's up against the old town walls and you can only get to it by walking over a wooden footbridge which crosses a charming canal lined with half-timbered houses and beautiful gardens. It's a lovely spot that strives to be "typically Alsace", and when it's sunny, tables are set out by the water. The dining room has lots of alcoves, painted furniture and checked tablecloths. The prices are reasonable – set menus €13–22 or €24 à la carte. Service is polite without being fussy. Mouthwatering specialities include oxtail with shallots in Pinot Noir and occasionally they offer *baeckeoffe*, a stew of beef, mutton and pork marinated in local wine.

Restaurant Garbo

15 rue Berthe-Molly.
Ⓣ03.89.24.48.55

Closed *Sun; Mon; public holidays; 1st week in Jan; 2nd week in Aug.*

This restaurant, dedicated to the screen goddess, is in one of the town's old mansion-lined streets. The huge dining room is part bistro, part gastronomic restaurant and does good regional cuisine, using seasonal ingredients. Specialities include duck foie gras terrine with Gewürztraminer, zander fillet with lavender and cold *sabayon* with beer. There's a lunchtime menu at €17 and à la carte at €32. The hushed atmosphere makes it ideal for a romantic dinner. *Apéritif on the house offered to our readers on presentation of this guide.*

Chez Hansi

23 rue des Marchands.
03.89.41.37.84
Closed *Wed; Thurs.*

Typical Alsace setting, typical Alsace menu, waitresses in typical Alsace costume – you get the feeling you're in a place for tourists. However, this is one of the most reliable restaurants in town and the regulars are locals. All the same, there is a tourist menu priced at €18.

Wistub Brenner

1 rue de Turenne; it's just beside Petite Venise.
03.89.41.42.33
Closed *Tues; Wed; 11–26 Feb; 22–30 June; 14–26 Nov; 24 Dec–1 Jan.*

Gilbert Brenner is a real character. He's stocky, rosy-cheeked, loves life – and it shows. He does the cooking and the serving, helped by his wife (who always manages to laugh at his jokes). They keep things simple here, with hearty dishes like salad of *choucroute* or deep-fried Munster cheese, fondant of asparagus or leeks, fried goose liver and tripe in Riesling. Gilbert trained as a pastry chef so leave room for dessert. A meal costs around €22. The beer flows into the small hours and students, regulars, wine-growers and tourists all come to have a good time.

Wettolsheim

68920 (6km SW)

Hôtel au Soleil**

20 rue Sainte-Gertrude; take the D417.
03.89.80.62.66 03.89.79.84.45
Closed *Thurs; 17 June–8 July; 22 Dec–13 Jan.* **TV. Car park.**

Run by a young couple, this is a great little place just outside Colmar in a tiny, little-known village on the *Route des Vins d'Alsace*. A good choice if you want to be near but not actually in the town, and, unlike many other hotels in the vineyards, it's reasonably priced. Reception is in a renovated half-timbered building, but you actually stay in a quiet annexe where rooms look out either onto the hotel car park or across acres of vineyards. Double rooms with shower/wc at €41. Half board is compulsory July–Sept, at €42 per person. There's a short weekday lunch menu at €9, at other times there's a menu at €16. Credit cards not accepted.

Ammerschwihr

68770 (7km NW)

L'Arbre Vert**

7 rue des Cigognes.
03.89.47.12.23 03.89.78.27.21
www.arbre-vert.net
Closed *Mon from Nov to April and Tues (open to welcome hotel guests in season 5.30–7pm); 9 Feb–20 March; 12–21 Nov.*
High chairs available. TV.

A very professionally run establishment in a large, pleasant, post-war building. There are a few good specialities on the menu, like *escalope* of goose liver in Pinot Noir, roast rack of lamb with garlic crust and warm soufflé with seasonal fruits. Set menus for €14 weekdays only, otherwise €20.30–46, including the traditional menu at €33, with a glass of wine with each course. Impeccable rooms, regularly renovated, cost €37 with basin, €48–60 with shower/wc or bath. Half board from €48 to 60 per person. *Apéritif or coffee offered for a minimum of two consecutive nights on presentation of this guide.*

Eguisheim

68420 (7km S)

Le Caveau d'Eguisheim

3 pl. du Château St. Léon.
03.89.41.08.89
Closed *Mon; Tues; end Jan to end Feb/early March.*

Two restaurants in one – a gourmet establishment on the first floor, serving delicious Alsace specialities given a modern slant by the creative young chef: *choucroute*, eel *matelote* cooked with Gewürztraminer, black pudding from free-range pork served with cinnamon-scented red cabbage and apple, and a *kugelhopf* cake that's served as bread pudding. Menus €35–55, or around €45 à la carte. In the wine-press room, the menu is much more affordable and the cuisine much simpler but no less tasty; chicken in beer, tripe in Riesling, flambéed tarts. There are no set menus here; expect to pay around €20 à la carte. Unusually, the chef cooks for both restaurants and guests in both dining rooms are afforded the same attentive service and welcome. A lovely place.

Niedermorschwihr

68230 (7km W)

Restaurant Caveau Morakopf

7 rue des Trois-Épis; take the N415 and the D11.
03.89.27.05.10
Closed *Sun; Mon lunch; last fortnight in Jan; last fortnight in June; 3rd week in Nov.* **High chairs available. Disabled access.**

This big pink-and-green house can be found in a charming village tucked away among the vineyards. There is a glorious garden in the summer. The restaurant is all wood with comfortable benches and the window panes have been decorated with a "Morakopf" (the same Moorish head that adorns T-shirts in Corsica). The food is meticulously prepared and served in generous portions. Excellent home-made *presskopf* (brawn) and *baeckeoffe*, layers of different meats and potatoes marinated for twelve hours (for four people minimum and to order in advance). Specialities include tripes in Riesling, *fleischschnaka* and the unmissable duck *confit* on *choucroute*. Good local wines. A main course and a pudding will cost €20–25. Reservations recommended.

Turckheim

68230 (7km W)

Auberge du Brand**

8 Grand-Rue.
03.89.27.06.10 03.89.27.55.51
www.aubergedubrand.com
Closed *1st week in July; 2nd fortnight in Nov.* **Restaurant closed** *Wed; open evenings only.* **TV.**

This is a superb, traditional half-timbered Alsace building. The forest provides the chef with lots of wild mushrooms for autumn dishes. The warm décor of the dining room really complements the food. Set menus €25–48. Nine pretty rooms. Doubles from €60, including breakfast.

Hôtel des Deux Clefs***

3 rue du Conseil; it's in place de l'Hôtel-de-Ville.
03.89.27.06.01 03.89.27.18.07
www.2clefs.com
Disabled access. TV. High chairs and cots available. Pay car park.

The loveliest house in Turckheim has some really wonderful rooms; with a little luck you may spend the night in the same room as Dr Schweitzer, Hortense de Mancini or General de Gaulle. Some forty doubles €69–115 with shower/wc or bath. Buffet breakfast €11.50. A classy place with lots of character. Credit cards not accepted. *50% discount on buffet breakfast offered to our readers on presentation of this guide.*

Trois Épis (Les)

68410 (10km W)

Hôtel-Restaurant Villa Rosa**

4 rue Thierry-Schoéré, on the Turckheim road; it's about 400m from the village.
03.89.49.81.19 03.89.78.90.45
www.villarosa.fr
Closed *8 Jan–19 March.* **Restaurant closed** *lunchtimes; Thurs; Sun.* **High chairs available. Swimming pool.**

A gorgeous house run by a lovely couple who are committedly green and really make their guests feel at home. The rooms are delightful – ask for one with a view of the garden and swimming pool. Doubles with shower/wc or bath are €48–53. The restaurant serves evening meals only, with menus from €20–24 for guests who have booked a table. Produce comes from the garden or local growers, and the cooking has an engaging personal touch. They run all sorts of courses too, including cookery and painting (see the Web site for more details). Credit cards not accepted. *10% discount on the price of a room (weekdays, outside school holidays) or apéritif offered to our readers on presentation of this guide.*

Neuf-Brisach

68600 (16km SE)

La Petite Pallette

16 rue de Bâle; access via the town centre.
03.89.72.73.50
Closed *Sun evening; Mon; Tues evening; a*

week in Feb; 3 weeks in Aug. **High chairs available.**

The yellow décor is attractive and the fairly priced, fine cuisine is prepared by a dedicated young chef who carried off first prize in the Veuve Cliquot 1993 talent competition, which explains a lot: themed menus every month, traditional dishes – house *choucroute* or calves' head – or more original seasonal dishes which change constantly and marry the traditional with the modern. Weekday lunch menu €11 and others up to €58. An excellent place, so it's advisable to book. *Free coffee offered to our readers on presentation of this guide.*

Erstein

67150

Hôtel et Estaminet des Bords de l'Ill**

94 rue du Général-de-Gaulle near the Centre Nautique.
Ⓣ03.88.98.03.70 Ⓕ03.88.98.09.49
Ⓦwww.hotel-bordsill.com
Disabled access. TV. High chairs and games available. Car park.

Small, 1960s hotel just footsteps from the Ill river. Rooms are decorated in contemporary style; doubles with shower or bath at €51 (prices go down after your third night). The restaurant is across the road and has a terrace by the water. The owners serve carefully cooked Alsace dishes using fresh local produce; there are tartes flambées on offer at the weekend. Set menu €7.50 (lunchtimes only), with others from €18 to €22. Wonderful wine from Alsace and elsewhere. *10% discount on the price of a room offered to our readers on presentation of this guide.*

Fouday

67130

Hôtel Julien**

32 rue Principale.
Ⓣ03.88.97.30.09 Ⓕ03.88.97.36.73
Ⓦwww.hoteljulien.com
Closed *Tues; 1st fortnight in Jan; 1st week in Oct.* **Disabled access. TV. Swimming pool. Car park.**

One of the most popular establishments in the Bruche Valley. It's set alongside the main road, but fortunately, most of the rooms look out over the Bruche and the green slopes of Mont Saint-Jean. There's a whole range of them: the smallest are simple yet comfortable and the largest are a princely 60m², with wood panelling and ample balconies. Doubles with shower/wc or bath €52–106, depending on the size. Half board (€69–90 depending on the room) offers the best value for money in the region. The Goetz family provide a warm welcome. The interior design is rustic but cosy – wood panelling, flowers and green pot plants everywhere. Seasonal decorations at Easter and Christmas. Staff wear updated regional costume. The dining rooms are huge, with wooden ceilings, and they're nice and warm. Excellent regional cuisine; weekday lunch menu €11 or others €16–25. The cheapest menu is perfect. The house wines are – unusually – reasonably priced. Terrace ideal for a drink or meal in the sun. There's a swimming pool, sauna and a fitness room. Booking strongly recommended.

Natzwiller

67130 (13km NE)

Auberge Metzger

55 rue Principale; take the D214.
Ⓣ03.88.97.02.42 Ⓕ03.88.97.93.59
Ⓦwww.hotel-aubergemetzger.com
Closed *Sun evening and Mon; 5–26 Jan; 23 June–6 July; 22–25 Dec.* **Disabled access. TV. High chairs and games available.**

A pleasant place to stop in this beautiful valley. Mme Metzger takes her guests' comfort very seriously, and the rooms are huge, comfortable, and decorated with a certain style – particularly the ones that have been renovated. It costs €57–72 for a double room with shower/wc or bath. Good cooking and typical local dishes on the weekday lunch menu, at €12 . Reckon on around €23 à la carte.

Haguenau

67500

Restaurant au Tigre

4 pl. d'Armes; it's in the pedestrian precinct.
Ⓣ03.88.93.69.47
Ⓔjean-paul.fremeau@wanadoo.fr
Closed *Sun evening in winter.* **High chairs available.**

The handsome dining room has high ceilings, wood panelling and lots of wrought iron. This is a classic brasserie serving typical fare: seafood in winter, kebabs and salad in summer. Dish of the day around €7; reckon on €21 or so à la carte. When the sun comes out the large terrace is very popular. *Coffee offered to our readers on presentation of this guide.*

S'Buerehiesel-Chez Monique

13 rue Meyer; it's next to the theatre.
Ⓣ03.88.93.30.90 Ⓕ03.88.06.13.22
Closed *Sun; Mon; public holidays; last week in May; first fortnight in Sept; Christmas–New Year.*

This *winstub*, a typical Alsatian wine tavern, serving only wine from the region (as opposed to a *bierstub*, which serves beer), has a relaxed, cosy feel. Weekday lunch menu €7.50 or around €20–25 à la carte. They concentrate on regional dishes including *choucroute*, of course, *waedele* (hot ham), *quenelles* of liver and so on. *Free coffee.*

Schweighouse-sur-Moder

67590 (3km W)

Aux Berges de la Moder

8 rue de la Gare.
Ⓣ03.88.72.01.09 Ⓕ03.88.72.63.16
Ⓔclarisse.jost@wanadoo.fr
Closed *Sun evening; Mon; first fortnight in Nov.* **Disabled access.**

The view over the industrial park is hardly idyllic but the two dining rooms are typical Alsace, with a lovely dresser, tiled floor, vermilion walls and decorated beams. The specialities – fish, game and rhubarb strudel – are quite delicious. Weekday lunch menu €7, or €10–19. Reckon on €25 à la carte. A place to enjoy.

Kaltenhouse

67240 (5km SE)

La Crémaillère (Chez Kraemer)

32 rue Principale.
Ⓣ03.88.63.23.06 Ⓕ03.88.63.67.48
Closed *Fri evening; Sat lunchtime; last 3 weeks in Aug.* **TV. High chairs available. Car park.**

In the same family for four generations, this inn, located only 5km from the border, is also the village bistro. Locals, pensioners and passing travellers create a convivial atmosphere (there's even dancing on Sat nights). Home cooking; try the lunchtime dish of the day and the local specialities. Menus €12.50 (weekdays only) and €20–35. Doubles at €55 have good facilities, though they're slightly gloomy; it's best to avoid the ones overlooking the road. *Free house apéritif to our readers on presentation of this guide.*

Hinsingen

67260

La Grange du Paysan

8 rue Principale.
Ⓣ03.88.00.91.83 Ⓕ03.88.00.93.23
Closed *Mon.* **High chairs available.**

This little restaurant is something of a local institution. Décor is rustic, with a huge bay window, and there is a large variety of menus at €10 (weekdays) and €17.85–45. reckon on €17 à la carte. Country-style food served in hearty portions that fill you up: braised ox cheek, grilled turbot, *baeckeoffe* (Fri only) and wood-grilled meat (weekends).

Kaysersberg

68240

Auberge de la Cigogne

73 rte. de Lapoutroie.
Ⓣ03.89.47.30.33 Ⓕ03.89.78.16.42
Closed *Fri; Sun evening; the first fortnight in July; between Christmas and New Year.* **Car park.**

A restaurant popular with long-distance lorry drivers and workers from the paper factory next door. This is the type of roadside establishment where you get a good, hearty meal without forking out lots of money. Weekday lunch menu €8.10 and others from €12.30–27.50. The food ranges from brasserie classics to a few house specialities like fillet of zander and *choucroute*. A good place to stop. It has a terrace for outdoor dining.

Restaurant Saint-Alexis

Lieu-dit Saint-Alexis.
Ⓣ03.89.73.90.38
Closed *Fri.* **High chairs available.**

Service noon–8pm. This appealing converted farmhouse, covered in ivy and hidden away in the forest, is very popular with locals. Inside, there's an appetizing smell of soup and *choucroute*. Three set menus, €11–16, are all very filling: good home-made soup, a large ham omelette as starters, followed by delicious free-range chicken and, to round it all off, there's a lovely *tarte alsacienne* (a kind of jam tart). In nice weather you can eat outside. Free coffee.

Lapoutroie

68650 (9km W)

Hôtel les Alisiers

5 rue du Faudé; it's 3km out of the village, follow the signs.
Ⓣ03.89.47.52.82 Ⓕ03.89.47.22.38
Ⓦwww.alisiers.com
Closed *Mon; Tues (except for hotel guests); Jan.* **TV. High chairs available. Car park.**

Way out in the wilds at an altitude of about 700m, this friendly and unusual little place is classified as a "Hôtel au Naturel" by the National Parks administration. It used to be a farm and the old stone sink and bread oven are still visible. There's a stunning view over the valley and the peaks of the Vosges. The bedrooms and the sitting room, with an open fire where they burn whole logs, are charming and cosy. Double rooms €50–66. Appetizing cooking using updated versions of old family recipes – veal kidneys steamed with leeks, old-style *choucroute* and braised shin of veal with potato salad. Weekday menus €15–38. *Free apéritif and 10% discount on the room rate or half board from 15 Nov to 15 March (except 25–31 Dec) offered to our readers on presentation of this guide.*

Hôtel-restaurant du Faudé

28 rue du Général Dufieux.
Ⓣ03.89.47.50.35 Ⓕ03.89.47.24.82
Ⓦwww.faude.com
Closed *2–26 Nov; 1 Feb–19 March.* **Restaurant closed** *Tues; Wed, except for guests on half board.* **TV. Swimming pool. Car park.**

A traditional hotel that has kept up-to-date. Besides the extremely comfortable rooms, facilities include a covered and heated swimming pool, Jacuzzi, steam room and gym. Double rooms with shower/wc or bath €58–67. The quality extends to the restaurant, where they serve authentic local dishes. Menus start at €19 and go up to €60. Various themed meals and excursions. *Coffee offered to our readers on presentation of this guide.*

Orbey

68370 (9km W)

Hôtel Pairis

283 lieu-dit Pairis; it's 2km from Orbey on the way to Lac Blanc.
Ⓣ03.89.70.20.15 Ⓕ03.89.71.39.90
Ⓦwww.hotelpairis.com
Closed *Wed; Nov.* **High chairs and games available. Car park.**

An excellent little hotel, in a superb 1900 house, run by a delightful German woman. The entrance hall is modish and mininiminalist, with designer furniture and white everywhere. Lots of natural materials have been used in the rooms. Doubles with basin from €50, up to €64 with bath. Sumptuous buffet breakfast, with freshly squeezed fruit juices, charcuterie and cheese, is included in the room rate. Half board by arrangement (€15.50 per person). Set menu €18 (vegetarian dishes available). There's a TV room and a wide choice of books and board games. A favourite with German visitors. *Coffee offered to our readers on presentation of this guide.*

Bonhomme (Le)

68650 (18km SW)

Hôtel de la Poste – Restaurant la Béhine**

48 rue du 3e-Spahis-Algérien; take the N415, then the road to the col du Bonhomme; it's next to the post office.
Ⓣ03.89.47.51.10 Ⓕ03.89.47.23.85
Ⓦwww.hotel-la-poste.com
Closed *5–26 Jan and 7–29 March.* **Disabled access. TV. Swimming pool. Car park.**

A good inn with really nice rooms, some with a small sitting room. The ones near the road are noisy. Doubles with shower/wc €46–54 depending on the season. Six rooms (as well as the sauna and the indoor pool) have been specially adapted for disabled visitors. Regional cooking: *spaetzle* (local noodles) and house foie gras are specialities. Menus €10–34. The friendly, professional woman who runs the place will even let you cancel your skiing holiday if there's no snow. *Apéritif on the house or 10% discount on a room offered to our readers on presentation of this guide.*

Mulhouse

68100

Hôtel Saint-Bernard**

3 rue des Fleurs, five minutes' walk from the town hall square.
T03.89.45.82.32 F03.89.45.26.32
Wwww.hotel.saint-bernard.com
TV. Pay car park.

The *Saint-Bernard* is probably the nicest hotel in Mulhouse. The rooms are all impeccable and have high ceilings; no. 16 has a hundred-year-old fresco depicting the four seasons, while nos. 14 and 15 have water beds. Doubles with shower or bath €39–48.50, depending on their size and which floor they're on. Guests also have free access to bicycles, an Internet area and a library. *10% discount on a room offered to our readers from the third consecutive night, on presentation of this guide.*

Le Petit Zinc

15 rue des Bons-Enfants.
T03.89.46.36.78
Closed *Sun; public holidays; first 3 weeks of Aug; Christmas–New Year's Day.*

A chic but cool bar/restaurant that's a gathering place for artists, musicians, writers and their mates. There are loads of photos on the wall and a big bar with a huge old calculating machine. Local dishes with unexpected twists, such as *choucroute* with fish, and more traditional favourites like *haxala* (pork knuckle) or smoked ox tongue. Weekday two-course set lunch for €8; meals à la carte from around €23.

Winstub Henriette

9 rue Henriette, off pl. de la Réunion.
T03.89.46.27.83
Closed *Sun except July–Aug.*

This wine tavern is named after the first woman in the town officially to become a French citizen in 1798. The interior, decorated in typical Alsace style, has seen many years and many gourmets come and go. Classic regional dishes on the menu include *choucroute*; chef's recommendations include pan-fried foie gras with apples or fillet of beef with Munster cheese. At lunchtime, there's a menu at €10, with a children's menu at €7.62. You'll pay about €20 à la carte.

Soultz

68360 (21km NW)

Restaurant Metzgerstuwa

69 rue du Maréchal-de-Lattre-de-Tassigny; take the D430 in the direction of Guebwiller.
T03.89.74.89.77
Closed *Sat; Sun; three weeks in June; a fortnight from Christmas to 5 Jan.*

Veggies be warned: this little restaurant in a green house on Soultz's main road is run by a man who owns the butcher's next door. It serves meat, meat and more meat – boned pig's trotters, skirt with shallots, calves' brains with capers, home-made black pudding, veal sweetbreads and bulls' testicles with cream, all in enormous portions. Big local following. There is an unbeatable *menu du jour* at €7 and others at €15–21. You can also buy home-made products to take away. *Free liqueur offered to our readers on presentation of this guide, if they order a coffee after their meal.*

Munster

68140

Hôtel-restaurant du Chalet*

Col de la Schlucht; from the centre take the D417 to col de la Schlucht (1139m) on the Alsace-Vosges border.
T03.89.77.04.06 F03.89.77.06.11
Whotel-du-chalet.com
Closed *Wed evening and Thurs out of season; 12 Nov–20 Dec.* **TV. High chairs and games available. Car park.**

The hotel is one of the busiest passes over the peaks of the Vosges but being in such a prime location doesn't mean they take their patrons for granted. The rooms have been nicely refurbished. Doubles with shower/bath €45. Half board is compulsory during school holidays and in high season. In the vast dining room, welcoming especially on cold days, they serve simple but good regional dishes: *choucroute*, *baeckeoffe* in winter, chicken with bacon, potatoes with Munster cheese, *spaetzle*. The lunch menu in the brasserie costs €10, and others are €14–22. Reservations recommended. *Free apéritif offered to our readers on presentation of this guide.*

Restaurant à l'Alsacienne

1 rue du Dôme.
T03.89.77.43.49

Closed *Tues lunchtime; Wed; 1–10 March; 1–10 June; 1–10 Sept.* **High chairs available.**

Locals and tourists alike enjoy sitting at the tables on the pavement alongside the church. The décor is typical of the Alsace region, as is the food. They serve individual dishes or set menus at €7.20 (lunchtime only) and €12.50–19. A meal à la carte will set you back around €23. Specialities include *choucroute* garnie, stuffed pig's trotters, *escalope* of veal with Munster cheese – or simply try a plate of local Munster served with a glass of Gewürztraminer.

|●| À l'Agneau d'Or

2 rue Saint-Grégoire.
☎03.89.77.34.08
Closed *Mon; Tues.*

The best table in Munster is also a very welcoming place. Martin Fache and his wife do their utmost to ensure that your visit will be "a hugely enjoyable gourmet stop". Specialities change with the seasons; the chef uses lots of local produce and favours fish. Try the pike-perch on *choucroute* or the equally delicious pigs' cheeks with foie gras. Desserts include iced beer soufflé, Gewürztraminer brandy sorbet and iced *kugelhopf*. Menus from €22 to €38. Deservedly, the chef has received many accolades from his peers. Reservations highly recommended, especially at the weekend. *Apéritif on the house offered to our readers on presentation of this guide.*

Stosswihr

68140 (6km W)

|●| Auberge des Cascades

6 chemin de Saegmatt; as you leave the village, take the left turn towards the war memorial.
☎03.89.77.44.74
Closed *Mon; Tues; mid-Jan to mid-Feb.*

Service until 10pm. A very good inn which hasn't been spoiled by too many tourists (yet). The pretty house is in a flower garden where you can hear the peaceful play of a waterfall nearby. There's a hearty weekday lunch menu at €8, and another on Sunday at €23. Specialities include flambéed tart of frogs' legs prepared under the attentive gaze of Madame Decker and her flights of china ducks on the walls. If you fancy something more classic, there are traditional flambéed tarts baked in a wood-fired stove (served at the weekend), trout fillet with sorrel and an awesome *entrecôte* with ceps. Treat yourself to the house Edelzwicker wine, which isn't expensive but is among the best in the region. Credit cards not accepted. *Free coffee offered to our readers on presentation of this guide.*

|●| Auberge du Schupferen

From Munster take the D417 to the col de la Schlucht and turn right towards Le Tanet ski resort. About 4km down the road, you'll see a sign to the Auberge on a tree. Follow the increasingly poor road (it's OK for cars) for about 3km.
☎03.89.77.31.23
Closed *Mon; Tues; Fri.*

Non-stop service 9am–7pm. Although this place is off the beaten track, it's definitely worth the effort to get here, and is ideally approached on foot. Christophe Kuhlman, the easy-going owner, cooks great dishes like *fleischsnecke*, pastry filled with mince, or a salad with leaves and vegetables from the garden. You'll pay around €15 for a full meal, but unfortunately the quality is variable. Don't forget to order a small jug of house Edelzwicker. The view over the forest and valleys from this high pasture (1,100m) is amazing.

Wihr-au-Val

68239 (11km NE)

|●| La Nouvelle Auberge

9 rte. Nationale; take the D417 in the direction of Colmar.
☎03.89.71.07.70
Closed *Sun eve; Mon eve; Tues; Feb and All Saints half-terms; first week in July; Christmas period.*

The talented chef has worked in some great kitchens but he hasn't let it go to his head. His roadside restaurant packs them in on weekday lunchtimes on account of the €9 menu, which is amazing – you'll be lucky to find a parking space. The other menus, €15–49, list dishes such as cockerel in Riesling and Tricastin lamb with thyme *jus*, and the dishes are remarkable value given the quality of the produce and the chef's skill. The simple dining room is very pretty, and the welcome is unaffected and kindly.

Niederbronn-les-Bains

67110

☗ |●| Hôtel-restaurant Cully**

33–37 rue de la République; it's near the station.
Ⓣ03.88.09.01.42 Ⓕ03.88.09.05.80
Ⓦwww.hotel-cully.fr
Closed *7–28 Feb; 22 Dec–5 Jan.* **Restaurant closed** *Sun eve; Mon.* **Disabled access. TV. Car park.**

The hotel is low-key and comfortable with large rooms, all of them different. You pay no more for those with balconies. Doubles €58–60 with shower/wc or bath. The restaurant serves classic local specialities. Good weekday set menu for €10, another at €19 or around €28 à la carte. Reservations recommended.

|●| Restaurant les Acacias**

35 rue des Acacias.
Ⓣ03.88.09.00.47 Ⓕ03.88.80.83.33
Closed *Fri and Sat lunchtimes; 2nd fortnight in Aug; 27 Dec–15 Jan.* **Disabled access. High chairs and games available. Car park.**

Quaint, flowery place on the edge of the forest with a terrace for the summer. Stylish service. They do a nice set menu at weekday lunchtimes for €11; others cost €15–38. Reckon on €33 à la carte. Traditional Alsace cooking and dishes such as foie gras and *civet* of young wild boar. The view of the valley is sadly marred by a factory. *Free coffee offered to our readers on presentation of this guide.*

Obernai

67210

☗ Hostellerie la Diligence**

23 pl. de la Mairie.
Ⓣ03.88.95.55.69 Ⓕ03.88.95.42.46
Ⓦwww.hotel-diligence.com
Open *all year round.* **Tea room open** *11am–6.30pm, except Tues and Wed.* **TV. Pay car park.**

It would be difficult to find anywhere more central – the rooms at the front look out onto place de la Mairie in the town centre. With such a great location, you'd think the owners would just sit back and wait for the customers to roll in. In fact, they go out of their way to make you feel welcome. The rooms are of an excellent standard, and there is a cosy breakfast room. Rooms with shower/wc or bath €47–73. *10% discount on a room after a minimum of three consecutive nights offered to our readers on presentation of this guide.*

☗ Hôtel du Gouverneur

13 rue de Sélestat.
Ⓣ03.88.95.63.72 Ⓕ03.88.49.91.04
Closed *1 Jan–March.* **Disabled access. Pay car park.**

This building dates from 1566 and was the residence of the town's governor. It's generously proportioned and has an interior courtyard; one wall forms part of the town ramparts. There's a gallery and a Louis XV balustraded staircase. The bright, new rooms are decorated in contemporary style and some are very spacious (sleeping three or four people). Doubles with shower/wc €50–69, including breakfast. Credit cards not accepted. *One free breakfast per room per night offered to our readers on presentation of this guide.*

|●| L'Agneau d'Or

99 rue du Général-Gouraud; it's on the main street.
Ⓣ and Ⓕ03.88.95.28.22
Closed *Sat lunch; Sun evening; Mon; Jan.*

An authentic *winstub*. The painted ceiling, cuckoo clock, prints and decorated plates all make for a cosy atmosphere. All the usual local dishes are listed on a good weekday lunch menu at €9 and others at €19 and €30.

Klingenthal

67530 (6km W)

☗ |●| Hôtel-restaurant au Cygne

23 rte. du Mont-Sainte-Odile; take the D426.
Ⓣ03.88.95.82.94
Closed *end June to mid-July.* **Restaurant closed** *Tues evening; Wed.* **High chairs available. Car park.**

This is a nice little place in a good location on the Mont-Sainte-Odile road. It has a traditional atmosphere with clean simple rooms. Doubles with basin from €22.50. Weekday lunch menu €9, others €14–18; all include good home cooking served in generous portions. The delicious fruit tarts are made in the family bakery next door. *10% discount on a room (Nov–March) offered to our readers on presentation of this guide.*

Scharrachbergheim

67310 (18km N)

Restaurant Lauth & Fils

82 rue Principale; take the Molsheim road then the D422 in the direction of Marlenheim.
T 03.88.50.66.05 F 03.88.50.60.76
Closed *Mon, Tues; lunchtimes; Christmas–New Year.* **Disabled access. TV. Car park.**

The vast dining room used to be a dance hall and is now a popular, relaxed restaurant. The place has the atmosphere of a tavern and the dishes on offer are in appropriate style: *choucroute*, *pot-au-feu*, horse steak with Port. If you have a sweet tooth, save room for the flambéed apple tart – a favourite – and the iced kirsch soufflé. Reckon on €15–20 à la carte. The serving staff wear traditional costume. Across the courtyard in the other part of the building there are seven guest rooms. Number 104 is furnished in Alsace style with a canopied bed and a mirrored ceiling. Double with shower (wc on the landing) €42. *A free bottle of beer (brewed on the premises) offered to our readers on presentation of this guide.*

Ottrott

67530

À l'Ami Fritz***

8 rue des Châteaux.
T 03.88.95.80.81 F 03.88.95.84.85
W www.amifritz.com
Closed *Wed; last 2 weeks in Jan and 1st week in Feb.* **Disabled access. TV. High chairs and games available. Car park.**

This seventeenth-century house is impressive both outside and in, and it's one of the least touristy places in town. It's beautifully decorated and very quiet. Bedrooms are pretty, fresh and colourful; those in the annexe, *Le Chant des Oiseaux*, 600m away, are cheaper but not so nice. The rooms overlooking the street are air-conditioned; the others (nos. 104, 105, 126 and 128) are quiet and attractively decorated. Doubles €62–65 with shower/wc and €80–99 with bath. Pleasant dining room with rustic décor and efficient, attentive service. Patrick Fritz, the owner, prepares some cracking regional dishes using fresh produce – warm pigeon salad, duo of goose foie gras with potatoes, various snail dishes. Set menus €21–39. Breakfast buffet €10 in low season, €11 in high season. *Free coffee offered to our readers on presentation of this guide.*

Petite-Pierre (La)

67290

Hôtel des Vosges**

30 rue Principale.
T 03.88.70.45.05 F 03.88.70.41.13
W www.hotel-des-vosges.com
Closed *Tues; mid-Feb to mid-March; end July to early Aug.* **Disabled access. TV. High chairs available. Car park.**

A large place that retains a family atmosphere. You're bound to find a room to your taste (whether that's pale modern wood or traditional Alsace). Among the less expensive options (small but comfortable), a few look over the château and the village – gorgeous at sunset. Comfortable double rooms, €46–75, with bath or shower/wc, and some luxury suites from €103 to €150. There's even a gym with Jacuzzi, sauna and sunbed. The focus in the restaurant is strictly regional; *coq* with Riesling is the house speciality. Impressive wine list, too. Menus start at €19 (weekdays only), with others at €28–49.

Ribeauvillé

68150

Hôtel de la Tour**

1 rue de la Mairie.
T 03.89.73.72.73 F 03.89.73.38.74
W www.hotel-la-tour.com
Closed *1 Jan–15 March.* **TV. Car park.**

An old wine-grower's house in the middle of a little medieval town – it offers pleasant rooms for €61–77 with shower/wc or bath. Guests can use the sauna, Turkish baths and Jacuzzi for free. There is no restaurant, but try the local wine and specialities in the typical Alsace *winstub*. Very pleasant, even stylish, place.

L'Auberge au Zahnacker

8 rue du Général-de-Gaulle.
T 03.89.73.60.77
Closed *Thurs; Jan; Feb.* **High chairs available. Disabled access.**

Service 9am–10pm. This inn, owned by the local wine co-operative, is a little oasis of calm off a main street jammed with tourists. Even though it's grey and next to a roundabout, in summer, when the sweet-smelling wisteria is in full bloom, you can sit out on the terrace and savour a glass of Pinot Blanc while you wait for your classic regional fare: perhaps *presskopf* (brawn) or onion tart. *Menu touristique* €20.50. Unfortunately, the service is not always up to the standard of the food.

Bergheim

68750 (4km NE)

Auberge des Lavandières

48 Grand-Rue.
Ⓣ03.89.73.69.96
Closed *Mon and Tues lunchtimes; Mon and Tues Oct–May.* **High chairs available.**

Turnover stuffed with ceps and frogs' legs, guineafowl fillet filled with *bibalakas* cheese served with *spaetzle*, braised calves' head, lamb tajine . . . the young chef brims with inventive ideas and talent, presenting the best of Alsace regional dishes with a modern, individual approach that shows off the produce and flavours to best advantage. Weekday lunchtime menu €16, others at €21 and €27 and around €25–30 à la carte. The décor is chic and discreet and suits the house to a T. Best of all is the small terrace just outside on the bank of a small stream where the *lavandières*, or washerwomen, used to do the washing. Excellent value for money, with a good selection of wines by the jug.

Illhaeusern

68970 (11km E)

À la Truite

17 rue du 25-Janvier; coming from Ribeauvillé on the D106, it's on the left before the bridge in the centre of the village.
Ⓕ03.89.71.88.15
Closed *Tues evening; Wed; Thurs lunchtime; end Feb to early March; a week at the end of June.* **High chairs available. Disabled access.**

A nice country inn with a terrace looking onto the river and the weeping willows. The simple, relaxed dining room is full of office and factory workers, farmers, long-distance lorry drivers and many others looking for an inexpensive meal. Here you can eat the best fish stew in all Alsace (you need to order it in advance). Alternatively try the freshly caught trout, fried fillet of carp or home-made foie gras. The bill is always easy on the pocket: weekday lunch menu €11.30, others €15–36. *Free coffee offered to our readers on presentation of this guide.*

Thannenkirch

68590 (11km NW)

Auberge la Meunière**

30 rue Sainte-Anne; take the D1 then the D42.
Ⓣ03.89.73.10.47 Ⓕ03.89.73.12.31
Ⓦwww.aubergelameuniere.com
Closed *Mon and Tues lunchtimes; 20 Dec–25 March.* **TV. High chairs available. Car park.**

From the road it's a classic Alsace inn, festooned with geraniums. From the valley, it's one of a rash of buildings that sprang up in the Alps in the 1970s. The rooms are rustic but contemporary in style, done out in a superb combination of natural materials. Most have a balcony or a terrace and splendid views – you can watch the deer coming for a drink at dusk. Doubles with shower/wc or bath €50–70. Sauna and billiards for guests. The fine, inventive cuisine in the restaurant is reasonably priced, with a set weekday lunch menu at €17 and others €25 and €35 à la carte, you'll find tasty dishes like *baeckeoffe* of snails in Riesling, wild boar with juniper berries and ox tongue with a horseradish sauce. The prices overall are fair, given the quality of the place, the perfect welcome and the attentive service. *Free coffee offered to our readers on presentation of this guide.*

Riquewihr

68340

Hôtel de la Couronne**

5 rue de la Couronne, just off rue du Général-de-Gaulle.
Ⓣ03.89.49.03.03 Ⓕ03.89.49.01.01
Ⓦwww.hoteldelacouronne.com
TV. High chairs and cots available. Car park.

This attractive sixteenth-century hotel is spot-on. It has a delightful gateway, and there are inviting little wooden benches and tables in the porch where you can enjoy a glass of Gewürztraminer before going off to explore the forests. All the rooms have been tastefully refurbished with prettily stencilled walls and wooden beams. The prices are decent for the location – doubles with bath €58–65. *Apéritif on the house offered to our readers on presentation of this guide.*

Hunawihr

68150 (4km N)

|●| Wistub Suzel

2 rue de l'Église.
Ⓣ03.89.73.30.85
Closed *Mon evening (except July–Aug); Tues; Jan–end March.* **High chairs available. Disabled access. Car park.**

The Mittnacht family, who run this wine tavern, make it a warm, welcoming place. There's a view of the church tower and in summer the shady terrace is covered with flowers. The big wooden doors at the back of the restaurant lead to the cellars, where you can sample good Alsatian wine. But the main reason to come here is the food – whatever you have it'll be good. An onion tart with salad is more than enough for smaller appetites, while the *Katel* menu would satisfy a hungry Obélix: you get onion tart, *roulades farcies* (rolled meat or fish with stuffing), sautéed potatoes, green salad and dessert. Menus €15–22, children's menu €7.50. On Sunday evenings they do flambéed tarts.

Rouffach

68150

|●| Caveau de l'Haxakessel

7 pl. de la République; it's next to the tourist office and the Tour des Sorcières.
Ⓣ03.89.49.76.76
Closed *Tues evening (out of season); Wed (all year round); Feb.*

Haxakessel means "the witch's cauldron". Don't panic, though – it's a long time since any sorcery has been practised in Rouffach. For a modest sum you can eat good *choucroute* – the house version is called the *Witch*, naturally – or the highly prized flambéed tarts. On a sunny day you can eat on the terrace. A meal costs about €15. *Free coffee offered to our readers on presentation of this guide.*

Saverne

67700

Auberge de Jeunesse

Château des Rohan (Centre); in the right-hand wing of the splendid Rohan château, above a school.
Ⓣ03.88.91.14.84 Ⓕ03.88.71.15.97.
Ⓔaj.saverne@wanadoo.fr
Closed *23 Dec–22 Jan.*

The interior does not entirely live up to the expectations of the grand exterior, but it is very conveniently situated. New guests are received 8–10am and 5–10pm. €11.80 per night in a dormitory with breakfast (€8.55 without). FUAJ card compulsory (you can buy it in situ). Ask for a key if you're going to be out after 10pm. *One breakfast per room offered to our readers on presentation of this guide.*

|●| Villa Katz

42 rue du Général Leclerc; it's southwest of the centre in the direction of the camp site.
Ⓣ03.88.71.02.02
Ⓔtavernekatz@wanadoo.fr
Closed *Tues; a fortnight in Jan.* **Car park.**

An elegant, bourgeois house in Jugendstil (the German version of Art Nouveau) that stands out from the unassuming houses in the rest of this quiet neighbourhood. It's a charming hotel decorated in an easy, relaxed style: like a family house with older furniture, a scattering of pictures and ornaments, and books in the rooms. The eight rooms are all different but equally charming. Doubles with shower/wc or bath €54–100. The pocket-sized restaurant has the same charm. Weekday menu for €16 or others €24–42. A likeable place.

Hôtel Europe***

7 rue de la Gare.
Ⓣ03.88.71.12.07 Ⓕ03.88.71.11.43
Ⓦwww.hotel-europe-fr.com
Disabled access. TV. Car park.

This is the best hotel in town. The walls and floors have recently been refurbished in the rooms, which have good facilities – a number even have whirlpool baths. €58.50–68.50 for a double with shower/wc and €82.50 with bath. Some are more spacious and have cable TV. The ritzy atmosphere, the first-rate service and the excellent buffet breakfast make sure that guests – including a large number of staff from the European Parliament in Strasbourg – keep coming back. For families there's a flat in an adjoining house. *Apéritif on the house offered to our readers on presentation of this guide.*

|●| Taverne Katz

80 Grand-Rue; it's near the town hall.
Ⓣ03.88.71.16.56 Ⓕ03.88.71.85.85

Closed *Tues evening; Wed.*

This beautiful place was built in 1605 for the archbishop's tax collector, Katz – the house's history is retold on a board outside just above the menu. Beautiful dining room with wood panelling. The first-rate cooking focuses on traditional dishes and excellent desserts – the dishes rarely change and are totally reliable. Lunchtime weekday menus start at €16 and go up to €45. The terrace looks out onto the pedestrianized street. *Free coffee offered to our readers on presentation of this guide.*

Sélestat

67000

⌂ |●| dAuberge des Alliés**

39 rue des Chevaliers.
Ⓣ03.88.92.09.34 Ⓕ03.88.92.12.88
Ⓦwww.auberge-des-allies.com
Closed *Sun evening; Mon; 4–19 July; 25 Dec–11 Jan.* **TV.**

This building, built in 1372, was a bakery in the first half of the nineteenth century when Louis-Philippe ruled France, and has been a restaurant since 1918. In the middle of the dining room is an impressive old Alsatian stove, and there's also a beautiful fresco showing the place aux Choux in the first half of the nineteenth century. The à la carte menu is typical of this kind of restaurant, with local dishes such as ham hock, *choucroute*, zander with Riesling, home-made foie gras and calves' kidneys. Set menus €14–27. Comfortable, modern double rooms with bath €53–58; those at the back are the quietest. *10% discount on a room (from 3rd consecutive night) or free apéritif offered to our readers on presentation of this guide.*

Rathsamhausen

67600 (3km E)

⌂ |●| Hôtel-restaurant à l'Étoile**

Grande-Rue; take the D21 in the direction of Muttersholtz.
Ⓣ03.88.92.35.79 Ⓕ03.88.82.91.66
Closed *Mon and Fri lunchtime; early Feb.* **TV. Swimming pool.**

A young couple have cleverly modernized this old house by adding an extension with a bright foyer and a stairway in wood and glass. Nice doubles with shower/wc cost €40, rooms for four people €65. Half board €35 per person, available even for a single night. The dining room is warm and intimate in the evenings. The à la carte menu is limited but lists good dishes, particularly the fried carp or fried small fry. Expect to pay €16–18, or opt for the cheap set menu at €11 (weekday lunchtimes) or others €14–19. In summer the terrace is covered with flowers and there's an open-air pool. A really nice little place.

Dambach-la-Ville

67650 (10km N)

⌂ Hôtel le Vignoble**

1 rue de l'Église.
Ⓣ03.88.92.43.75 Ⓕ03.88.92.62.21
Closed *end June to early July; Christmas to mid-March.* **Disabled access. TV. Car park.**

Charming hotel, tastefully converted from an eighteenth-century gabled barn. Stylish, comfortable rooms, with doubles €47–51.

Strasbourg

67000

See map on pp.18–19

⌂ |●| Auberge de Jeunesse du Parc du Rhin

Rue des Cavaliers; near the frontier, in the direction of Kehl. Take no. 2 bus in the direction of Pont-du-Rhin to the "parc du Rhin" stop, 1km from the hostel. **Off map D4-2**
Ⓣ03.88.45.54.20 Ⓕ03.88.45.54.21.
Ⓔstrasbourg.parc-du-rhin@fuaj.org
Closed *at end of year.* **Disabled access. Car park.**

Large, modern building, some distance from the centre, but a stone's throw from Germany and the Rhine. Closed to new arrivals 12.30–2pm. FUAJ card compulsory (you can buy it in situ). 246 places in all. €14 (breakfast included) per person in a room with three or five beds and, in most cases, shower/wc. Several are adapted to the needs of disabled people. Meals €8.50. Restaurant and bar-discothèque.

⌂ |●| Auberge de Jeunesse René-Cassin

9 rue de l'Auberge-de-Jeunesse La Montagne-Verte; take no. 2 bus from the train station in the direction of Lingolsheim to the "Auberge de Jeunesse" stop. **Off map A4-1**
Ⓣ03.88.30.26.46 Ⓕ03.88.30.35.16.

Closed *Jan.* **Disabled access. Car park.**

Friendly youth hostel spread over a group of 1970s-style buildings surrounded by green spaces (although the railway is nearby). There are 276 beds. Reckon on €14 per person (including breakfast) in a room with three–six beds, €32 in an individual room and €44 in a double room. Hire of sheets. Lunch, dinner at €8.40. Fully equipped kitchen. Bar-café open in the evenings until 1am. It's advisable to book.

Hôtel de l'Ill**

8 rue des Bateliers-Krutenau. **Map D3-7**
Ⓣ03.88.36.20.01 Ⓕ03.88.35.30.03
Closed *29 Dec–6 Jan.* **TV. High chairs available.**

It's advisable to book at this popular, family-run hotel. Rooms are not very big but they're pleasant and nicely decorated. They're divided between the old building and a new annexe in the courtyard. Some are non-smoking. Doubles €42–44 with shower, €48–50 with shower/wc, €58–65 with bath. There's a lovely sunny terrace on the first floor. *Two breakfasts offered to our readers for a stay of 7 nights in July–Aug on presentation of this guide.*

Hôtel Michelet*

48 rue du Vieux-Marché-aux-Poissons. **Map C3-4**
Ⓣ03.88.32.47.38 Ⓕ03.88.32.79.87
Ⓔhotelmichelet@net.up.com

Well-located right in the middle of town, a few steps from the cathedral. Most of the rooms look out onto the walls of the neighbouring buildings which are very close. On the plus side, however, they have decent facilities, and some, which have been renovated, have nice sunflower-yellow walls (the others still have those depressing, maroon, carpeted walls). Doubles with shower/wc or bath €44. Breakfast, served in your room, lacks appeal. *One breakfast per room offered to our readers on presentation of this guide.*

Hôtel Kyriad-Saint-Christophe**

2 pl. de la Gare. **Map A3-9**
Ⓣ03.88.22.30.30 Ⓕ03.88.32.17.11
Ⓔhotel-kyriad-gare@wanadoo.fr
Disabled access. TV.

In one of the grandest buildings near the station, this well-run hotel (part of a chain) offers comfortable, functional rooms (doubles €54–75 depending on season). The nicest ones are at the back, despite the double glazing in the rooms overlooking the square. *Apéritif on the house offered to our readers on presentation of this guide.*

Hôtel Gutenberg**

31 rue des Serruriers. **Map C3-8**
Ⓣ03.88.32.17.15 Ⓕ03.88.75.76.67
Ⓦwww.hotel-gutenberg.com
Closed *1–14 Jan.* **TV.**

The owner of this eighteenth-century house, whose grandfather was an officer in the Grande Armée, is mad about military engravings from the Napoleonic period and his collection is displayed over all the walls. This passion for the Empire carries through into the rooms which have good pieces of old family furniture. On the two top floors the pretty attic rooms afford delightful views over the rooftops. Overall, this feels more like a three-star hotel than a two-star one. Double rooms €57–77 with shower/wc or bath.

Hôtel Couvent du Franciscain**

18 rue du Faubourg-de-Pierre. **Map B1-5**
Ⓣ03.88.32.93.93 Ⓕ03.88.75.68.46
Ⓦwww.hotel-franciscain.com
Closed *Christmas to 1 Jan.* **Disabled access. TV. High chairs available. Pay indoor car park.**

A centrally located hotel near the covered market. It's a classic two-star, and nice and quiet. Doubles cost €60–62 with shower/wc or bath. Buffet breakfast is served in the basement, decorated with frescoes. Warm welcome. *10% discount on a room (Jan, Feb, July and Aug, outside parliamentary sessions) offered to our readers on presentation of this guide.*

Le Grand Hôtel***

12 pl. de la Gare. **Map A2-10**
Ⓣ03.88.52.84.84 Ⓕ03.88.52.84.00.
Ⓦwww.le-grand-hotel.com
TV.

This hotel in the square by the train station really is grand. You can't miss the Soviet-looking, concrete, 1950s building, with its stark lines and bulky forms. The enormous reception with a high ceiling is equally imposing, but the striking glass lift (a unique 1950s prototype) whisks you up

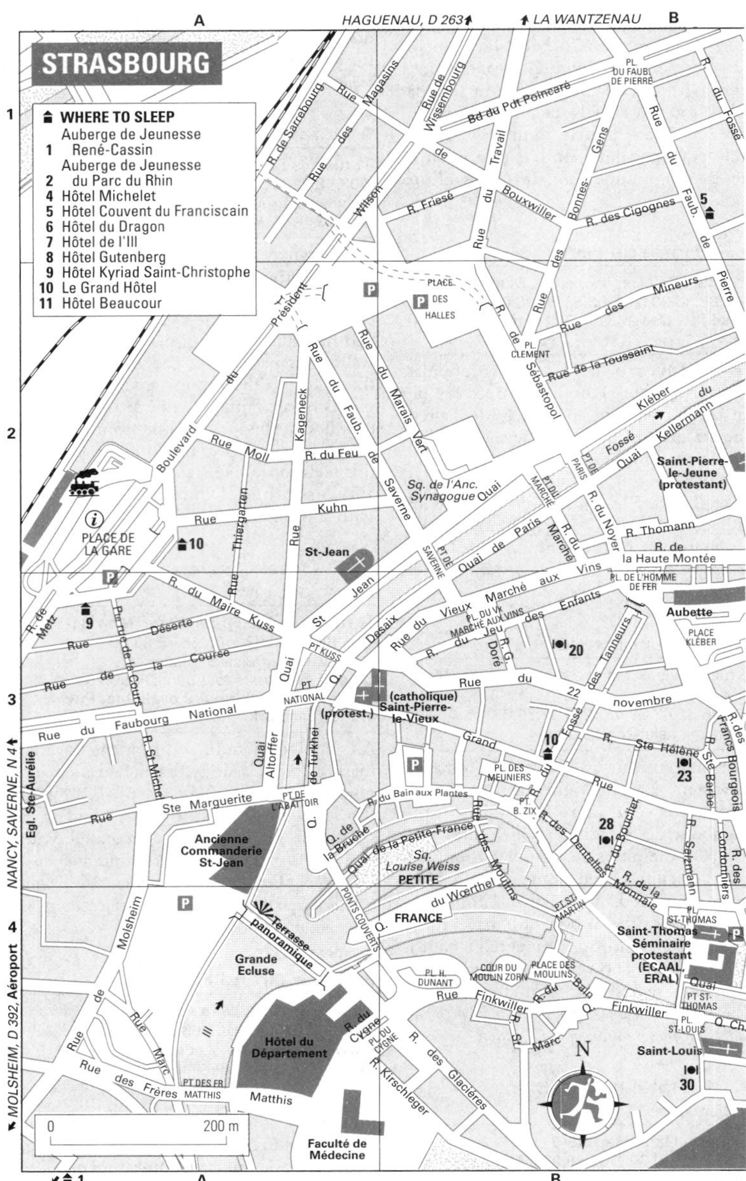
STRASBOURG
WHERE TO SLEEP
1 Auberge de Jeunesse René-Cassin
2 Auberge de Jeunesse du Parc du Rhin
4 Hôtel Michelet
5 Hôtel Couvent du Franciscain
6 Hôtel du Dragon
7 Hôtel de l'Ill
8 Hôtel Gutenberg
9 Hôtel Kyriad Saint-Christophe
10 Le Grand Hôtel
11 Hôtel Beaucour
A
B
1
2
3
4
HAGUENAU, D 263
LA WANTZENAU
NANCY, SAVERNE, N 4
MOLSHEIM, D 392, Aéroport
PLACE DE LA GARE
PLACE DES HALLES
PL. CLÉMENT
PL. DU FAUB. DE PIERRE
Bd du Pdt Poincaré
Boulevard du Président Wilson
Rue du Faub. de Saverne
Rue du Marais Vert
Rue de Sébastopol
Quai Kléber
Fossé du Quai Kellermann
Saint-Pierre-le-Jeune (protestant)
Sq. de l'Anc. Synagogue
Quai de Paris
St-Jean
Quai St Jean
Rue du Maire Kuss
Rue du Faubourg National
PT NATIONAL
Quai Altorffer
Q. de Turkheim
(catholique) Saint-Pierre-le-Vieux
(protest.)
Grand Rue
Rue du 22 novembre
Rue du Vieux Marché aux Vins
Rue des Enfants
Aubette
PLACE KLÉBER
PL. DE L'HOMME DE FER
Rue Ste Hélène
Ancienne Commanderie St-Jean
Terrasse panoramique
Grande Ecluse
Hôtel du Département
Faculté de Médecine
Quai de la Petite-France
Sq. Louise Weiss
PETITE FRANCE
PONTS COUVERTS
PL. DES MEUNIERS
PLACE DES MOULINS
COUR DU MOULIN ZORN
PL. H. DUNANT
Rue Finkwiller
Saint-Thomas Séminaire protestant (ECAAL, ERAL)
PL. ST-THOMAS
Saint-Louis
PL. ST-LOUIS
Rue des Frères Matthis
PT DES FR. MATTHIS
Egl. Ste-Aurélie
0 200 m
N

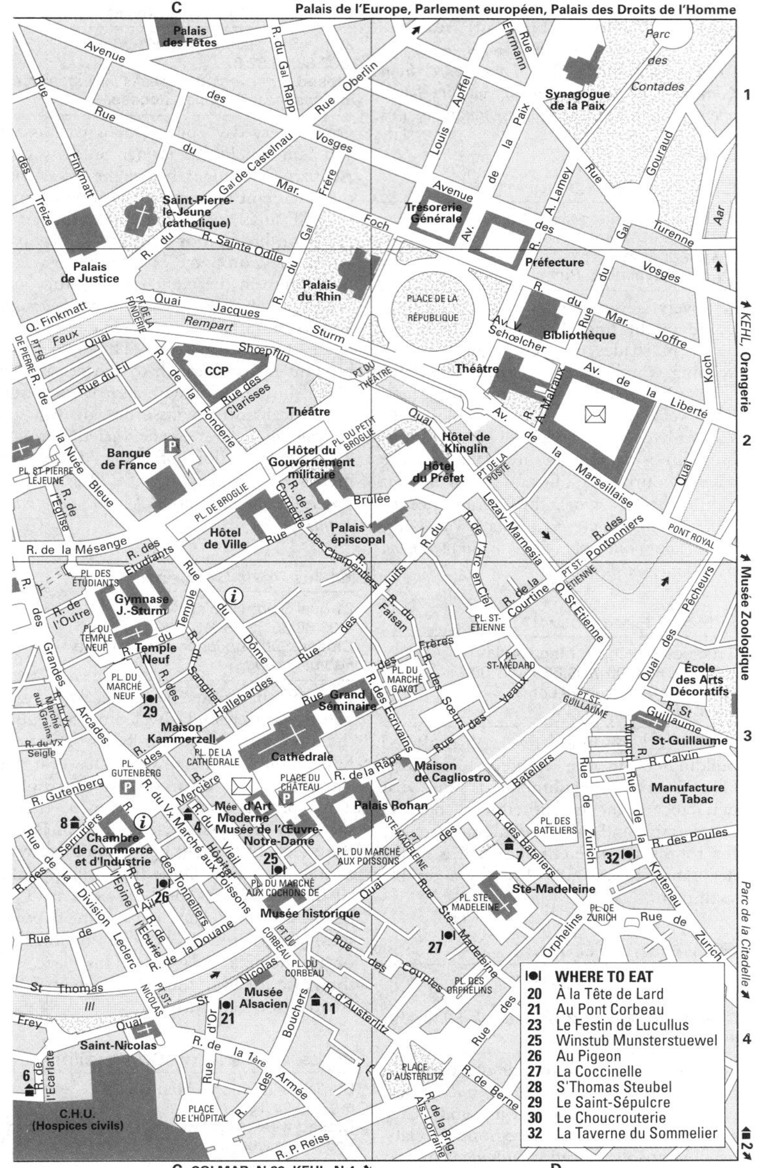
C
Palais de l'Europe, Parlement européen, Palais des Droits de l'Homme
1
2
3
4
C COLMAR, N 83, KEHL, N 4
D
KEHL, Orangerie
Musée Zoologique
Parc de la Citadelle
2
Palais des Fêtes
Avenue des Vosges
R. du Gal Rapp
Rue Oberlin
Rue Ehrmann
Parc des Contades
Synagogue de la Paix
Rue du Faubourg
Rue Finkmatt
Rue des Treize
Gal de Castelnau
Rue Louis Apffel
Rue de la Paix
Rue A. Lamey
Rue Gouraud
Aar
Saint-Pierre-le-Jeune (catholique)
Mar. Foch
Frère
Avenue des Vosges
Trésorerie Générale
Gal Turenne
Palais de Justice
R. du R. Sainte Odile
Gal du
Préfecture
Palais du Rhin
PLACE DE LA RÉPUBLIQUE
R. du Mar. Joffre
Q. Finkmatt
Quai Jacques Sturm
PT DE LA FONDERIE
Rempart
Av. V. Schœlcher
Bibliothèque
PT FG DE PIERRE
Faux Quai
Shoepflin
Koch
Rue du Fil
CCP
PT DU THÉÂTRE
Théâtre
R. de Pierre
R. de la Fonderie
Rue des Clarisses
Théâtre
Av. de la Liberté
Av. de la Marseillaise
R. A. Malraux
Quai
Banque de France
Hôtel du Gouvernement militaire
PL. DU PETIT BROGLIE
Hôtel de Klinglin
Hôtel du Préfet
PT DE LA POSTE
Quai
PL. ST-PIERRE LEJEUNE
R. de la Nuée Bleue
R. de l'Église
PL. DE BROGLIE
R. de la Comédie
Brûlée
Lezay-Marnesia
R. des Pontonniers
PONT ROYAL
Hôtel de Ville
Rue des Charpentiers
Palais épiscopal
R. du
R. de l'Arc en Ciel
R. de la Mésange
R. des Étudiants
PL. DES ÉTUDIANTS
Rue du Temple
R. des Juifs
PT ST-ÉTIENNE
Q. St Étienne
Quai des Pêcheurs
Gymnase J.-Sturm
R. de l'Outre
R. du Faisan
R. de la Courtine
PL. ST-ÉTIENNE
PL. DU TEMPLE NEUF
Temple Neuf
Rue du Dôme
Rue des Frères
PL. ST-MÉDARD
R. des Grandes Arcades
R. du Sanglier
R. des
PL. DU MARCHÉ NEUF
PL. DU MARCHÉ GAYOT
R. des Sœurs
École des Arts Décoratifs
Rue des Hallebardes
Grand Séminaire
R. des Écrivains
PT ST-GUILLAUME
R. St Guillaume
29
R. du Vx Marché aux Grains
Maison Kammerzell
Rue des Veaux
St-Guillaume
R. du Vx Seigle
PL. DE LA CATHÉDRALE
Cathédrale
Maison de Cagliostro
Rue Munch
R. Calvin
PL. GUTENBERG
R. des
PLACE DU CHÂTEAU
R. de la Râpe
Rue des Bateliers
Rue de Zurich
Manufacture de Tabac
R. Gutenberg
R. Mercière
Mée d'Art Moderne
Musée de l'Œuvre-Notre-Dame
Palais Rohan
Rue de la Krutenau
8
4
Serruriers
Chambre de Commerce et d'Industrie
R. du Vx Marché aux Poissons
R. du Vieil Hôpital
PT STE-MADELEINE
R. des Bateliers
PL. DES BATELIERS
R. des Poules
Rue de la Division Leclerc
R. des Tonneliers
25
PL. DU MARCHÉ AUX POISSONS
7
32
26
PL. DU MARCHÉ AUX COCHONS DE
Quai des
Ste-Madeleine
R. de l'Épine
R. de l'Ail
R. de l'Écurie
Musée historique
PL. STE-MADELEINE
PL. DE ZURICH
Rue de Zurich
Rue Ste-Madeleine
Orphelins
R. de la Douane
PT DU CORBEAU
Rue des Couples
27
St Thomas
PT ST-NICOLAS
Quai St Nicolas
PL. DU CORBEAU
PL. DES ORPHELINS
Musée Alsacien
11
Frey
21
R. d'Or
Rue des Bouchers
R. d'Austerlitz
Rue des
Saint-Nicolas
R. de la 1ère Armée
6
R. de l'Écarlate
PLACE D'AUSTERLITZ
R. de Berne
C.H.U. (Hospices civils)
PLACE DE L'HÔPITAL
R. P. Reiss
R. de la Brig. Als.-Lorraine
WHERE TO EAT
20 À la Tête de Lard
21 Au Pont Corbeau
23 Le Festin de Lucullus
25 Winstub Munsterstuewel
26 Au Pigeon
27 La Coccinelle
28 S'Thomas Steubel
29 Le Saint-Sépulcre
30 Le Choucrouterie
32 La Taverne du Sommelier

to comfortable rooms refurbished in modern 3-star style, some fitted with air-conditioning. Double rooms start at €63 with shower/wc to €98 with bath at the weekend (€109 with breakfast). Attentive service. *10% discount on a room (except in May, June, Sept, Oct, Dec apart from Christmas market) or apéritif on the house offered to our readers on presentation of this guide.*

Hôtel du Dragon***

2 rue de l'Écarlate. **Map C4-6**
ⓣ03.88.35.79.80 ⓕ03.88.25.78.95
ⓦwww.dragon.fr
TV. Cots available. Pay car park.

A lovely seventeenth-century building. Some might find the starkly minimalist décor in shades of grey slightly out of keeping – and some of the rooms are not all that big – but it's pleasant enough and in a very quiet location. Doubles with shower/wc or bath €79–112. Generous breakfast – in summer it's served in the paved courtyard. There's a permanent exhibition of work by contemporary artists. *10% discount on a room in July–Aug, 5% the rest of the year offered to our readers on presentation of this guide.*

Hôtel Beaucour***

5 rue des Bouchers. **Map C4-11**
ⓣ03.88.76.72.00 ⓕ03.88.76.72.60
ⓦwww.hotel-beaucour.com
Open *all year round.* **TV.**

This hotel occupies five half-timbered buildings from the eighteenth century. Considerable refurbishment has somewhat detracted from its authenticity, but it's comfortable and has a matchless charm. All the rooms are different and each is nicely decorated. Prices €89–126 for a double with bath.

S'Thomas Stuebel

5 rue du Bouclier. **Map B3-28**
ⓣ03.88.22.34.82
Closed *Sun; Mon; Easter week; first 3 weeks in Aug; Christmas week.*

There's nowhere more friendly than this pocket-sized traditional *winstub*. Local wines by the glass or the jug and plate-groaning portions of the region's specialities: reasonably priced *choucroute*, Munster *gratin*, veal with cream and *bibeleskass* (cream cheese with sautéed potatoes). Lunch menu is €8.30, or expect to pay €23 à la carte. *Free coffee offered to our readers on presentation of this guide.*

La Choucrouterie

20 rue Saint-Louis. **Map B4-30**
ⓣ03.88.36.52.87
Closed *Sun evening; 3 weeks in Aug; a week at Christmas.* **Disabled access.**

Open every day 7pm–1am, as well as Sat and Sun lunchtime. Roger Siffer was an Alsatian folk singer before he went into the restaurant business. From time to time he still sings in his restaurant-theatre – either on his own or with his musical pals when they drop by. The building was a post house in the eighteenth century and was then home to the last *choucroute* makers in Strasbourg – apparently they made the best in town. The owner has brought his own touch to the decoration of the dining room, with a great collection of musical instruments. And you can still get *choucroute here* – seven varieties, in fact – along with lots of other dishes. Set menus €9–15, reckon on €22 à la carte. *Free coffee offered to our readers on presentation of this guide.*

Au Pont Corbeau

21 quai Saint-Nicolas. MAP C4-21
ⓣ03.88.35.60.68 ⓕ03.88.25.72.45
Closed *Sat; Sun lunchtime; 1st week in February; Aug.*

First off, the owner here will always give you a warm, friendly welcome. Secondly, the food is great, and thirdly, it's one of the few *winstubs* in the town centre near the cathedral that's open on Sunday nights. The mineral water and wines (many served by the glass) are from the Bas-Rhin, the excellent draught beer from a brewery across the Rhine. These little things make all the difference. The house speciality (a must), is grilled ham with sautéed potatoes. Menus at €11 (weekday lunchtimes) or around €23 à la carte. This place is a showcase for everything that's great about Alsatian food and drink.

La Taverne du Sommelier

Ruelle de la Bruche. **Map D3-32**
ⓣ03.88.24.14.10
Closed *weekend; 3 weeks in Aug; 1 week at end of the year.*

The ruelle de la Bruche is extremely narrow but widens out just by the tavern to make a bit of space. It's a nice place with lots of regulars. There is typical *winstub* fare on the menu, but the thoughtfully prepared dishes range more widely than the basic regional classics. Dish of the day €8; à la carte around €25. Good little wines, served by the glass.

Le Festin de Lucullus

18 rue sainte-Hélène. **Map B3-23**
Ⓣ and Ⓕ03.88.22.40.78
Closed *Sun, except the 1st two Sun lunchtimes in Dec; Mon; mid-Aug to early Sept.* **Disabled access.**

Four years' training under the eagle eye of the famous chef Michel Guérard is character-forming to say the least, and the chef here was certainly inspired by his time at Eugénie-les-Bains – everything from the well-judged cooking times to the use of fresh herbs and seasonings is thoughtful and the results are excellent. The cheerful, friendly welcome, good service and honest prices mean that you'll want to come back, too. Starter plus main course (or main course and dessert) €11 during the week. Copious three-course weekday lunch menu €13, and a dinner menu at €26; à la carte around €30.

Au Pigeon

23 rue des Tonneliers. **MAP C4-26**
Ⓣ03.88.32.31.30 Ⓕ03.88.28.71.71
Closed *Sun evening; Mon; Tues evening; 3 weeks in Jan; 1 month spread over July and Aug.*

Occupying one of the town's oldest buildings – a glorious, half-timbered, gabled residence built in the sixteenth century – this historic *winstub* has been going for years. Above the door are two carved pigeons. The dining room is sober and classic in style, and serves dishes such as *baeckeoffe*, duckling with orange, *choucroute* and knuckle of pork braised in Pinot Noir. Dish of the day is around €9, menus €13–23.50. *Free house apéritif offered to our readers on presentation of this guide.*

Restaurant à la Tête de Lard

3 rue Hannomg. **Map B3-20**
Ⓣ03.88.32.13.56 Ⓕ03.88.61.12.89
Closed *Sat lunchtime; Sun.*

An unpretentious, popular bistro known for its lively atmosphere. Flambéed tart, goose breast with honeyed apples, *choucroute*, baked potatoes with Munster cheese, winemakers' *tourte* and a menu with seasonal dishes – all the regional specialities, with a few variations, are here. Weekday lunchtime menus, €15 and €25. *Free coffee offered to our readers on presentation of this guide.*

La Coccinelle

22 rue Sainte-Madeleine. **Map D4-27**
Ⓣ03.88.36.19.27 Ⓕ03.88.35.34.80
Closed *Sat lunchtime; Sun; 1–15 Aug.*

Two sisters run this place: one does the cooking and the other looks after the dining room. The restaurant is packed with regulars at lunchtime, drawn by the reasonably priced dish of the day (€8). It's less frenetic in the evenings. Good regional specialities include beef with rock salt and *vigneronne* pie. On Saturday evenings in winter, order the Alsace classic *baeckeoffe*, a stew of beef, mutton and pork. Reckon on around €22 à la carte. *Apéritif on the house offered to our readers on presentation of this guide.*

Le Saint-Sépulcre

15 rue des Orfèvres. **Map C3-29**
Ⓣ03.88.32.39.97
Closed *Sun; Mon; 3 weeks in Aug.*

This is one of the best-known restaurants in Strasbourg. The food is excellent, solid Alsace cuisine – there's confit of pork tongue, potato salad, ham *choucroute*, goose foie gras and a fabulous ham *en croute* which is sliced in front of you. The typical little bistro glasses, carafes of wine, checked napkins, polished floors and the wooden stove in the middle of the room all create the right atmosphere for an unforgettable meal, which will cost about €23 per person.

Winstub S'Munsterstuewel

8 pl. du Marché-aux-Cochons-de-Lait. **Map C3-25**
Ⓣ03.88.32.17.63 Ⓕ03.88.21.96.02
Closed *Sun; Mon; early March; mid-Aug to early Sept.*

The décor is grander and prices are slightly higher – €23 for a set menu, €29 à la carte – than in a traditional *winstub*, but the quality is undeniable. Oxtail *pot-au-feu* with vegetables, marrowbone and crudités with horseradish sauce, pork cheek with *choucroute* and potatoes are typical of the hearty fare on offer. Good selection of wines and spirits. Nice terrace in summer.

Handschuheim

67117 (13km W)

L'Auberge à l'Espérance

5 rue Principale; take the N4 from Strasbourg.
Ⓣ03.88.69.00.52 Ⓕ03.88.69.10.19
Closed *lunchtimes; Mon; Tues; a week in March; second fortnight in Sept.* **High chairs available. Car park.**

Welcoming restaurant in an attractive half-timbered house. You go up the stairs and there's a choice of five pretty dining rooms. *Flammenkéche* (flambéed tart) is a particular speciality, cooked here in the old-fashioned way on wood cinders – which gives it its unique flavour and lightness. The ham is great, too. The place appeals to families and groups of friends, so the atmosphere is warm and friendly. They have some good wines, and they don't push the local vintages too hard. Menus at €7.20 and €9.95. Expect to pay €13.50 à la carte.

Thann

68800

Hôtel-restaurant Kléber**

39 rue Kléber.
Ⓣ03.89.37.13.66 Ⓕ03.89.37.39.67
Closed *1–21 Feb. Restaurant closed Sat and Sun.* **TV. High chairs available. Disabled access. Car park.**

This hotel is in a residential area away from the hustle and bustle of town. It's quite stylish, with fair prices. Rooms 24 and 26 in the annexe are really quiet, with flower-festooned balconies overlooking orchards. Doubles €29.75 with basin, up to €53.50 with shower/wc or bath. The restaurant, which has a good reputation, offers a weekday lunch menu at €11 and others at €17.80 and €32, with dishes like beef with morels, game in season (wild boar or kid), and *kugelhopf* for breakfast. Good value for a two-star. Breakfast free for children under 8. *10% discount on a room (except in July–August) offered to our readers on presentation of this guide.*

Moosch

68690 (7km NW)

Ferme-auberge du Gsang

From Moosch, head for the Mine d'Argent campsite, follow the forest road for 7km, and park in the car park in the Gsang. Then it's a 10–20 minute walk.
Ⓣ03.89.38.96.85
Closed *Fri; Sun evening.*

It's worth making the effort to find this delightful farmhouse, where they have yet to discover electricity. You'll eat very well, for around €12: they do sandwiches at any time of the day, smoked scrag of mutton, roasts, *fleischschnacka*, vegetable stew and the most wonderful soup *fermière*. Accommodation is in clean, basic dorms, but bring a sleeping bag and a torch. Half board only; €23. You have to walk everywhere and the view is fabulous. Great atmosphere. Reservations highly recommended. *Free coffee offered to our readers on presentation of this guide.*

Saint-Amarin

68550 (9km NW)

Auberge du Mehrbächel

Route de Geishouse. Leave the N66 at Saint-Amarin signposted to Geishouse; about 3km along the main road, before the village, turn off left and keep going (where all the pine trees are) until you come to the inn.
Ⓣ03.89.82.60.68 Ⓕ03.89.82.66.05
Ⓔsarl.kornacke@wanadoo.fr
Closed *Mon and Thurs evenings; Fri; Easter school holidays.* **TV. Car park.**

The chalet, with woods on one side and pastures on the other, is set on the side of the mountain dominating the Thur valley. The views of the valley from the bedrooms – which are in a modern annexe – are splendid. Doubles with shower/wc or bath €50–55. The restaurant is well worth the effort of getting here. Cooking is traditional, but the chef has added his own touches. Specialities include Alsatian terrine, duck dishes and trout with almonds. Menus from €16 (except on Sun) to €34. The generous breakfast buffet features smoked bacon, ham, cereal, yoghurt and more.

Wissembourg

67160

Hôtel-restaurant Walk**

2 rue de la Walk.
Ⓣ03.88.94.06.44 Ⓕ03.88.54.38.03
Ⓦwww.moulin-walk.com
Restaurant closed *Fri lunchtime; Sun evening; Mon.* **Disabled access. TV. High chairs available. Car park.**

This place, outside the town's fortifications and surrounded by lots of greenery and the vestiges of an ancient mill, has a relaxing atmosphere. Comfortable rooms are decorated in a contemporary style; the largest are in a small modern annexe. They go for €55 with shower/wc or bath. The cooking is pretty upmarket. Menus at €29 and €37. *Apéritif on the house offered to our readers on presentation of this guide.*

Climbach

67510 (9km SW)

|●| Restaurant au Col de Pfaffenschlick

Col du Pfaffenschlick. Climbach is on the D3; turn left up to the pass (373m).
Ⓣ03.88.54.28.84 Ⓕ03.88.54.39.17
Closed *Mon; Tues; 15 Jan–15 Feb.* **Disabled access. High chairs available. Car park.**

The Séraphin family will give you a genuinely warm welcome to their little inn in the heart of the forest. The dining room, with its hefty beams and wood panelling, has a friendly atmosphere, and there's a terrace for summer. They serve ham, snails, salads, cheeses, quiches, onion tarts and regional specialities including free-range chicken in Riesling, wild boar stew and *baeckeoffe* (order in advance). Weekday lunch menus start at €8 and then go up to €17–30; or pay about €22 à la carte. A good place, and only a few kilometres from Four à Chaux, an important sector of the Maginot Line.

Woerth

67630

|●| restaurant sans Alcool et sans Fumée

11 rue de la Pépinière; it's at the entrance to the town.
Ⓣ03.88.09.30.79 Ⓕ03.88.54.06.42
Closed *Mon; evenings; Feb school holidays.*
Disabled access.

This place dates back to 1944, when the owner at the time, under heavy bombardment, swore that if she ever got out alive she would open an alcohol-free inn. She kept her word but had to cope with the most challenging of times: her traditional customers left in droves and it took a while to build up a new clientele – but the quality of the cuisine ensured that she did. Today, even though the inn has moved from its pretty old building in the centre of town to more modern premises on the outskirts, people come from far and wide (especially on Sun) for the marvellous regional cooking. Weekday lunchtime menu €7.60, other menus €12–22. *Free coffee offered to our readers on presentation of this guide.*

Aquitaine

Agen

47000

Hôtel des Ambans*

59 rue des Ambans; it's near the station.
Ⓣ05.53.66.28.60 Ⓕ05.53.87.94.01
Closed *Christmas and New Year; Ascension weekend.* **TV.**

A well-run, clean and simple little hotel on a quiet street in the old part of town. Eight of the rooms are a little shabby, though there are plans to refurbish them soon and they're attractively priced: doubles €26 and €29 with shower and €30.50 with shower/wc. Note that the hotel reception is closed on Sunday from 11am to 7pm, and after 11pm during the week. *One free breakfast per room offered to our readers on presentation of this guide.*

Hôtel des Iles

25 rue Baudin.
Ⓣ05.53.47.11.33
Ⓕ05.53.66.19.25
TV.

Behind the white stone façade, this lovely hotel is arranged around a central light well. There's every chance the owner himself will check you in, his cheroot clamped in the corner of his mouth. The laid-back feel is deceptive as it's actually a well-organized place. The ten clean rooms are clean and nicely maintained and you'll have peace and quiet in this residential area. Doubles €29 with shower/wc and €32 with bath. Breakfast €4.50. It doesn't have an official star rating but it carries on regardless, unaffected by passing fads or displays of style.

Atlantic Hôtel**

133 av. Jean-Jaurès; 1.2 km from the centre of town, on the N113 towards Toulouse and Montauban.
Ⓣ05.53.96.16.56 Ⓕ05.53.98.34.80
Ⓔatlantic.hotel@wanadoo.fr
Closed *24 Dec–4 Jan.* **Disabled access. TV. High chairs available. Swimming pool. Car park. Basement garage at €5.**

Neither the surroundings nor the '70s architecture of this building are particularly attractive, but the rooms are spacious and quiet, and the air-conditioning – not to mention the swimming pool – helps beat the heat. Six rooms overlook the garden. Doubles with shower/wc go for €45; with bath they're €48. Breakfast €5.50. Very warm welcome. *Free use of garage and 10% discount on a room offered to our readers on presentation of this guide.*

Les Mignardises

40 rue Camille-Desmoulins.
Ⓣ05.53.47.18.62
Closed *Sun; Mon; a fortnight in Aug.*

Though it has no pretentions to being gourmet cuisine, the food here is good value. They do four menus that include soup, starter, main dish and dessert, starting at €10.20 (served on Tues and Wed evenings, and Thurs to Sat lunchtimes) and going up to €24.40. Settle down on one of the plum-coloured benches and get stuck into beef's tongue with a spicy sauce, while enjoying the mouth-watering smells emerging from the kitchen. The place is always packed at lunchtime. *Apéritif on the house offered to our readers on presentation of this guide.*

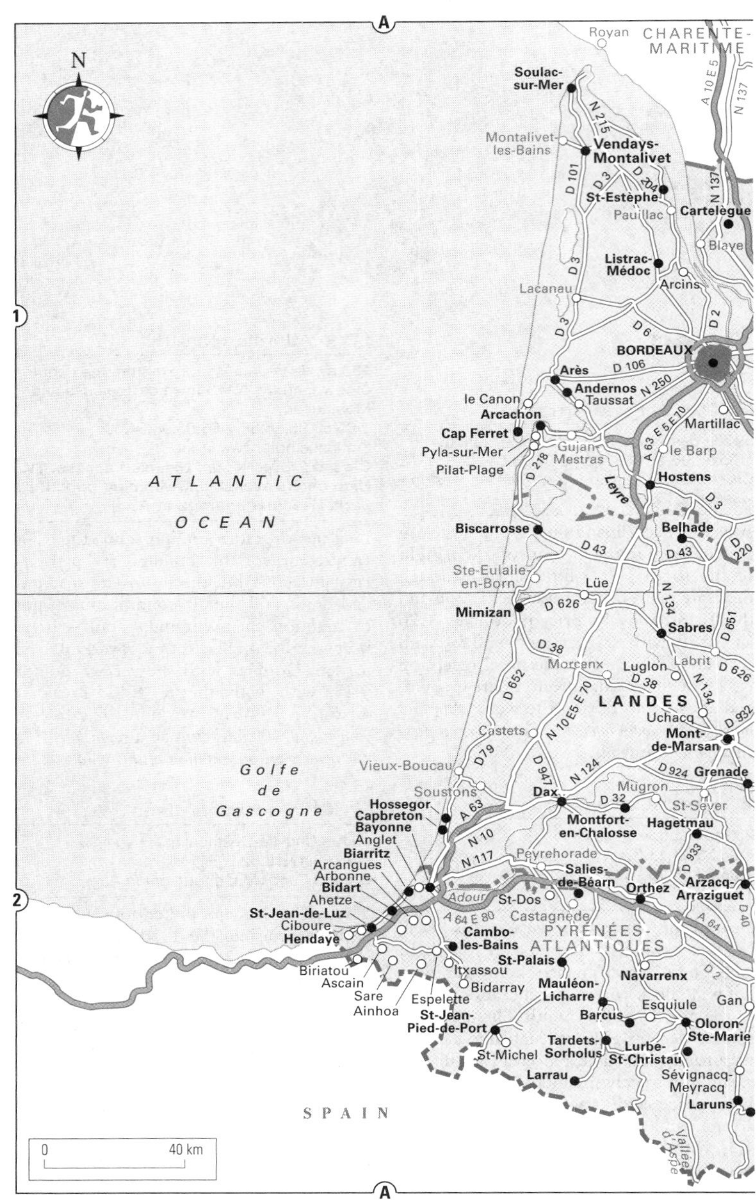

N
ATLANTIC OCEAN
Golfe de Gascogne
SPAIN
LANDES
PYRÉNÉES-ATLANTIQUES
CHARENTE-MARITIME
BORDEAUX
Royan
Soulac-sur-Mer
Montalivet-les-Bains
Vendays-Montalivet
St-Estèphe
Pauillac
Cartelègue
Blaye
Listrac-Médoc
Arcins
Lacanau
Arès
Andernos
Taussat
le Canon
Arcachon
Cap Ferret
Pyla-sur-Mer
Pilat-Plage
Gujan-Mestras
Martillac
le Barp
Hostens
Leyre
Biscarrosse
Belhade
Ste-Eulalie-en-Born
Lüe
Mimizan
Sabres
Morcenx
Luglon
Labrit
Uchacq
Mont-de-Marsan
Castets
Vieux-Boucau
Soustons
Grenade
Mugron
Dax
St-Sever
Hossegor
Capbreton
Bayonne
Anglet
Biarritz
Arcangues
Arbonne
Bidart
Ahetze
St-Jean-de-Luz
Ciboure
Hendaye
Montfort-en-Chalosse
Hagetmau
Peyrehorade
Salies-de-Béarn
Orthez
Arzacq-Arraziguet
Adour
St-Dos
Castagnède
Cambo-les-Bains
St-Palais
Navarrenx
Biriatou
Ascain
Sare
Ainhoa
Espelette
Itxassou
Bidarray
Mauléon-Licharre
Esquiule
Gan
Barcus
Oloron-Ste-Marie
St-Jean-Pied-de-Port
St-Michel
Tardets-Sorholus
Lurbe-St-Christau
Sévignacq-Meyracq
Larrau
Laruns
Vallée d'Aspe
A 10 E 5
N 137
N 215
D 101
D 3
D 204
D 2
D 6
D 106
N 250
A 63 E 5 E 70
D 218
D 43
D 220
D 626
N 134
D 651
D 38
D 652
N 10 E5 E 70
D 932
D 79
D 947
N 124
D 924
D 32
A 63
N 10
N 117
D 933
A 64 E 80
A 64
D 40
0 40 km
A
1
2

B
HAUTE-VIENNE
CHARENTE
Angoulême
Nontron
Vieux-Mareuil
St-Jean-de-Côle
Thiviers
Barbezieux
Monsec
Brantôme
CORRÈZE
Bourdeilles
Sorges
Ribérac
Hautefort
Chancelade
Antonne-et-Trigonant
Tulle
Marsac-sur-l'Isle
Périgueux
Annesse-et-Beaulieu
Brive-la-Gaillarde
Montpon-Ménestrol
Montignac
St-Amand-de-Coly
Mussidan
la Chapelle-Aubareil
Laval-de Jayac
DORDOGNE
Sergeac
Paulin
Libourne
St-Julien-de-Crempse
Tursac
Tamniès
St-Emilion
Ste-Foy-la-Grande
les Eyzies
Marquay
Bergerac
Sarlat-la-Canéda
Trémolat
Castillon-la-Bataille
Lalinde
la Roque-Gageac
Cadouin
GIRONDE
Ste-Radegonde
Issigeac
Beaumont
Domme
Sauveterre-de-Guyenne
Razac-Eymet
Montferrand-du-P.
Duras
Castillonnès
Villefranche-du-Périgord
St-Macaire
la Réole
Villeréal
Langon
Lauzun
Montflanquin
Sauternes
Marmande
Fumel
LOT
Villandraut
LOT-ET-GARONNE
Monclar
Ste-Livrade
Villeneuve-sur-Lot
Tournon-d'Agenais
Cahors
Bazas
Clairac
Tonneins
Pujols
Penne-d'Agenais
Goualade
Aiguillon
Captieux
le Temple-sur-Lot
Casteljaloux
Laroque-Timbaut
Buzet-sur-Baïse
Agen
St-Maurin
Sérignac-sur-G.
Puymirol
TARN-ET-GARONNE
Nérac
Mézin
Astaffort
Francescas
Montauban
St-Justin
Ste-Mauré-de-Peyriac
Gaillac
Villeneuve-de-M.
GERS
TARN
Aire-sur-l'Adour
Eugénie-les-Bains
Auch
TOULOUSE
Lembeye
HAUTE-ET-GARONNE
Pau
Tarbes
AUDE
Lestelle-Bétharram
Lourdes
St-Gaudens
Eaux-Bonnes
HAUTES-PYRÉNÉES
ARIÈGE
Foix
Figeac
Garonne
Dordogne
Adour
N 141 E 603
N 10 E 606
D 731
D 700
D 674
D 675
D 4
D 75
N 21
D 704
A 20
D 979
D 940
D 939
D 710
D 705
N 89 E 70
N 120
A 89
D 708
N 89
D 936
D 660
D 933
N 140
D 670
D 911
D 124
A 62 E 72
D 655
D 932
N 20 E 9
118
D 656
D 926
N 113
D 999
A 68
D 930
D 626
D 6
D 30
N 124
D 935
N 134
D 943
A 61 E 80
A 64 E 80
N 117
D 117
1
2

|●| L'Imprévu

7 rue Camille-Desmoulins.
☎05.53.66.39.31.
Closed *Sun; Mon evening; 1st week in Sept.*

Everybody here seems to know the young owner, who passes cheerily from table to table. The attempt to create a rustic setting is not entirely successful, but the hearty regional dishes, served in generous portions, more than make up for this faux pas. Menus at €10.50 (except Fri and Sat evenings), €16 and €21 include fillet of zander with crayfish, *aiguillettes* of duck with orange and foie gras fried with peaches. Reckon on around €26 à la carte. Excellent bar, too. In short, it's more than just a friendly meeting place, attracting a strong local following for its fine cuisine.

|●| L'Atelier

14 rue du Jeu-de-Paume.
☎05.53.87.89.22
Closed *Sat; Sun; 1st week of Jan.*

Everyone comes to this sparky place in the centre of town, run by a couple of live wires. Monsieur is very skilled in choosing his wines, while Madame is very attentive to her guests. There are quite a lot of fish dishes on the menu and the local speciality, duck, also features strongly. Lunch menus €16–24; evening menus €22–28. *Apéritif on the house offered to our readers on presentation of this guide.*

|●| Las Aucos

33 rue Voltaire.
☎ and ℻05.53.48.13.71
Closed *Sat lunch; Mon evening; Tues; 2 weeks in Jan; Easter holidays; 2nd fortnight in Aug.*

Specializing in dishes featuring goose (*aucos* in Provençal), this restaurant is located in the medieval quarter on a little street that becomes an outdoor café on Thursday, Friday and Saturday evenings from May to September. The interior décor is simple but creates a nice atmosphere with bare brick walls, Basque tablecloths, a grandfather clock and classical music playing in the background. Lunch is a speedy affair but at dinner you have time to savour the local gastronomic delicacies – stuffed goose neck with herbs, goose ham fillets and so on – in carefully crafted dishes. Lunch menu at €16 (except weekends), then €24–39. There's a wide and interesting selection of wines. *Liqueur on the house offered to our readers on presentation of this guide.*

|●| Restaurant Mariottat

25 rue Louis-Vivent.
☎05.53.77.99.77
Closed *Sun evening; Mon; Sat lunchtime; a week in Feb; Christmas week.* **High chairs and games available. Disabled access. Car park.**

Éric and Christiane Mariottat run a good restaurant in a fine mansion surrounded by parkland – just a stone's throw from the Jacobin monastery. The house has a warm atmosphere and a cosy décor with ceiling mouldings, splendid parquet and impressive chandeliers. Duck is the speciality of the region and the chef makes full use of it – his duck pâté *en croûte* is a real treat. Every morning he reinvents his dishes depending on what he's bought fresh at the market that day. Everything is wonderful, from the potato *millefeuille* with warm foie gras and truffle gravy to the suckling lamb medley with basil. Lunchtime menus €20, except Sunday and public holidays, then €30–51. À la carte, reckon on around €55. *Free coffee offered to our readers on presentation of this guide.*

|●| Restaurant Le Nostradamus

40 rue des Nitiobriges; it's on the outskirts, on the way to Colayrac.
☎05.53.47.01.02
Closed *Sun evening; Mon; lunchtimes Tues–Sat.*

The wife of the medieval seer Nostradamus is supposed to have come from around here – hence this restaurant's name. This all-wooden house is on the edge of town and you feel as if you're in the country. In summer you can have a meal on the terrace in the dappled shade of the trees. Inside, the décor is a successful balance between rustic and modern. The €20.50 menu includes a selection from the twenty starters on the buffet and a choice of ten desserts. In between, there's a small selection of tasty main courses: quail with grapes, duckling with orange, grilled meat, tenderloin pork. Reckon on around €35 à la carte. *Apéritif on the house offered to our readers on presentation of this guide.*

Sérignac-sur-Garonne

47310 (8km W)

Hôtel le Prince Noir***

It's on the D199 in the direction of Nérac, after the bridge over the Garonne.
05.53.68.74.30 05.53.68.71.93
Closed *Sun evening.* **Disabled access. TV. Swimming pool. Car park.**

A wonderful place in a seventeenth-century convent. The Black Prince of the hotel's name was the son of Edward III, the Lieutenant-General of Aquitaine who laid waste to the southwest during the Hundred Years' War. You get to the courtyard through a turreted porch. With high ceilings and period furniture, the rooms at ground level and upstairs are all comfortable. Doubles €54–88; half board €60 per person. Menus €17–30, or you can eat carefully prepared regional dishes à la carte. It's worth booking because they often host business seminars, as well as providing accommodation for the Agen rugby team.

Aiguillon

47190

Hôtel-restaurant La Terrasse de l'Étoile**

8 cours Alsace-Lorraine.
05.53.79.64.64 05.53.79.46.48
Disabled access. TV. Swimming pool.

A superb little hotel built in white stone. There are eighteen rooms – all different but equally charming – and they're decorated in a vaguely Provençal style (iron bedsteads and country furniture). Particularly striking are the four rooms on the second floor, set in an old loft, with the brick walls exposed to view. Doubles €48–52. Three separate dining rooms (all with plastic chairs, unfortunately) and a terrace overlooking the swimming pool. The menus start at €12 (except Sunday and public holidays) with others at €15–24, and change with the seasons. Children's menu €7. À la carte, reckon on around €20. They offer traditional fare such as fillets of mullet in cider (simply delicious), duck foie gras au torchon with prunes and ray's fin with grain mustard. Very good local wines, including a fairly dry, syrupy white Tariquet. *Free coffee offered to our readers on presentation of this guide.*

Clairac

47320 (8km NE)

L'Écuelle d'Or

22 rue Porte-Pinte.
05.53.88.19.78 05.53.88.90.77
écuelle.or@wanadoo.fr
Closed *Sat lunchtime; Sun evening; Mon; a week in Feb; Easter.*

A typical village house in rough brick with oak beams. The two dining rooms are relaxing and there's an inviting open log fire in the oldest one. Fresh produce appears in imaginative dishes, for example salmon steak and asparagus from Fargues-sur-Ourboise, in springtime. They make everything in their own kitchens, including the bread, and also do more traditional fare such as duck confit. Weekday lunch menu €14, with others €17 to €47 and a children's menu at €11. Count on €40 à la carte with a plate of fine cheese. *Free apéritif offered to our readers on presentation of this guide.*

Andernos-les-Bains

33510

Hôtel de la Côte d'Argent

180 bd. de la République.
05.56.03.98.58 05.56.03.98.68
Closed *Sun evening.* **Disabled access. TV.**

This newly redecorated roadside hotel, with ten well-equipped rooms, offers the best value in the area. €40–48 with shower/wc or bath. There's a small flowery patio with a small fountain – the two rooms at garden level have the view. Breakfast includes fresh fruit and real orange juice.

Taussat

33148 (3km SE)

Restaurant Les Fontaines

Port de plaisance de Taussat; take the D3.
05.56.82.13.86 05.57.70.23.43
Closed *Sun evening; Mon; 3 weeks in Nov; 1 week in Feb.* **High chairs available. Car park.**

This modern building near the marina doesn't exactly ooze charm, but it has a pleasant terrace where you can sit on a warm evening and enjoy the inspired cooking of chef Jean-Pascal Paubert. Try the scallops with Serraut or the roast langoustines in an aubergine marinade, followed by warm apple tart. Menus €21.50–39.50. Good wine list – not surprisingly, as the owner is chairman of the local cellarmasters' association. *Free apéritif on the house offered to our readers on presentation of this guide.*

Antonne et Trigonant

24420

La Charmille

It's on the N21, in the direction of Limoges.
05.53.06.00.45 05.53.06.30.49
www.lacharmille.fr
Closed *Sun evening and Mon (Oct–June); Fri lunch (July–Sept); Jan; a week in Nov.* TV.
High chairs and games available. Disabled access.

A charming manorhouse covered in Virginia creeper. All the rooms have been refurbished and are very comfortable. Opt for the ones overlooking the garden; those at the front overlook the road, which gets very busy in the morning. Doubles €42–50. You have breakfast on a large wooden mezzanine with hefty beams. There is also a restaurant, with a terrace in summer. The €15 weekday lunctime menu is good value – after that there are menus at €18–33. The kindly Sardinian owners are always ready to give you advice about the activities in the region. *Apéritif on the house offered to our readers on presentation of this guide.*

Arcachon

33120

Hôtel Les Mimosas**

77 [bis] av. de la République; it's near place de Verdun.
05.56.83.45.86 05.56.22.53.40
www.mimosas-hotel.com
Closed *Jan–Feb.* **TV. Car park.**

This hotel is in a fine, large Arcachon house 500m from the ocean. Warm welcome and clean, neat rooms, some of them in a motel-like annexe. Doubles €40–61, depending on the season. *One free breakfast per room offered to our readers on presentation of this guide.*

La Plancha

17 rue Jehenne; it's parallel to boulevard de la Plage, behind the market and the Town Hall.
05.56.83.76.66
Closed *Sat, Sun lunchtimes; Wed; a fortnight in early Nov; 15 Jan–15 Feb.*

One of the best cheap restaurants in town. They offer a selection of tapas and the hake *koskera* is up to the standard of any self-respecting Spanish establishment. The *salade plancha* makes a satisfying lunch (lettuce, tomato, cod, marinated anchovy, mussels and prawns), and, for dinner, the *plateau plancha*, a mixed grill with four types of meat, will satisfy even the heartiest appetites. Menus start at €6.40, then progress to €8.80 and €10.50; à la carte, a meal will cost over €18. The tables are jammed together – there aren't that many – which can get very cosy indeed.

Le Pavillon d'Arguin

63 bd. du Général-Leclerc.
05.56.83.46.96
Closed *Sun evening and Mon out of season.*
Disabled access.

A young team (even the chef is only 26) goes to great lengths to offer both fast service and light, inventive dishes in the large blue-and-white dining room, with a special emphasis on seafood (although the grilled meat is also excellent). Lunchtime menus (except Sun) at €12.50 and €16. Other menus at €23.50 and €32, not forgetting the copious spread at €59, which includes two starters, two main courses, cheese, dessert, wine and a liqueur. A safe bet in Arcachon. *Liqueur on the house offered to our readers on presentation of this guide.*

Pyla-sur-Mer

33115 (5km S)

Hôtel Maminotte**

Allée des Acacias; from Arcachon take the D217 or the D218 and it's 200m from the beach.
05.57.72.05.05 05.57.72.06.06
TV.

This small, twelve-room hotel looks just like all the other houses in this peaceful part of town, lost among the pine trees and 100m from the ocean. Fresh, comfortable and pleasant rooms; some have little balconies. €40–85, depending on the season – pricey but not atypical for this chic resort. Friendly welcome and family atmosphere.

🏠 |●| Hôtel-restaurant Côte du Sud**

4 av. du Figuier.
☎05.56.83.25.00 (restaurant) or 05.56.22.59.16 (hotel) Ⓕ05.56.83.24.13
Ⓦwww.cote-du-sud.fr
Closed *Dec and Jan.* **TV.**

This unpretentious, single-storey, blue-and-yellow hotel faces south (as you might guess), and is right by the sea. Eight comfortable, themed rooms (Moroccan, Asian etc) with shower/wc or bath are €59–115, depending on facilities and the season. All but one have a sea view. The nice restaurant is renowned for its speciality, mussels *Côté du Sud*, prepared Spanish-style. Set menus are €21.50–28, or it'll cost around €38 à la carte.

Pilat-Plage

33115 (8km S)

🏠 |●| Hôtel-restaurant La Corniche**

46 bd. Louis-Gaume.
☎05.56.22.72.11
Ⓦwww.corniche-pyla.com
Closed *Wed except July–Aug; Nov–mid-April.* **TV. High chairs available.**

Wonderfully located between pine trees and the foot of a large dune with steps down to the beach. There's a large communal terrace with deckchairs and hammocks. Doubles with shower/wc €55, and with bath €80. Rooms over the kitchens are noisy; others have balconies overlooking the ocean. The panoramic restaurant offers menus at €15 and €23 and a children's menu for €10. Fish and seafood predominate and only fresh ingredients are used; whelks with aïoli, pollock steak with diced bacon, cuttlefish in their ink. Half board, compulsory in July and August, costs €70–90 per person. Unfortunately, the welcome is not as warm as it could be. Make sure you confirm your hotel reservation by fax. *Apéritif on the house offered to our readers on presentation of this guide.*

Arès

33740

🏠 |●| Le Saint-Éloi

11 bd. de l'Aérium.
☎05.56.60.20.46 Ⓕ05.56.60.10.37
Ⓦwww.nlatour@free.fr
Closed *Mon; Sun evening and Wed evening (out of season); 3 weeks in Jan.*

Situated among the pines 500m from the beach. Clean, spacious double rooms with good beds; €54–85, depending on the comfort and the season. Half board compulsory in July–Aug: €112–143. The elegant restaurant has a particularly good reputation on account of its perfectly prepared dishes. Try the trio of duck liver or lamprey *à la Bordelaise*. Menus €22–37. Good wines and competent service.

Arzacq

64410

|●| La Vieille Auberge

Place du Marcadieu; it's in the centre of the town.
☎05.59.04.51.31

A friendly old house with an old-style dining room and a village bistro with formica tables and a TV beaming the world in. The new chef is full of youthful energy and an equal measure of creativity. Try his stuffed, filleted sardines or his pan-fried mussels – tasty, generously served and inexpensive. Menu for €9.15 (including wine) and others €13–25. Fantastic fry-ups from €13–25. An excellent place.

Astaffort

47220

🏠 |●| Le Square (Michel Latrille)***

5–7 pl. de la Craste.
☎05.53.47.20.40 Ⓕ05.53.47.10.38
Ⓦwww.latrille.com
Hotel closed *Sun evening (except July–Aug).* **Restaurant closed** *Sun evening; Mon; Tues lunchtime.* **Both closed** 1 week in May; 3 weeks in Nov. **Disabled access. TV. Pay car park.**

Michel Latrille is passionate about using high-quality produce for his dishes and experiments with different flavours. The results are excellent: langoustine ravioli with truffles, duck confit pie with thyme sauce and his famous *moelleux au chocolat* dessert. Menus €22 (except Sunday and public holidays) and €34 or €52, with a children's menu at €11. À la carte, reckon on €52. There are also fourteen very comfortable rooms, individually decorated in bright but subtly harmonious Provençal colours by the owner's wife. Doubles €62–120. No. 6, which has a private balcony, costs €110. Breakfast €10. *Free coffee offered to our readers on presentation of this guide.*

Barcus

64130

Chilo***

Centre.
05.59.28.90.79
martine.chilo@wanadoo.fr
Closed *Sun evening, Mon and Tues morning (1 Nov–15 March); Sun evening and Mon (15 June–15 July).* **Disabled access. TV. Swimming pool. Car park.**

A popular place on the borders of the Béarn and Basque country. It has been extended but hasn't lost its soul, and it's still family-run. Attractive, nicely appointed rooms are €50–85 with shower/wc or bath. Unusual, original cooking: fillet of Soule beef with hot foie gras and traditional lamb sweetbreads with white *piperade*. Keep a space for the speciality desserts, *macaron à l'Izarra* and a *charlotte* made with ewe's milk. Menus at €23 and €38. Reckon on €43 à la carte.

Restaurant Chez Sylvain

Place du Fronton.
05.59.28.92.11
Closed *Thurs; 19–26 May.*

You'll get a charming welcome in this family-run restaurant. It's like a country inn, and has a mainly local clientele. The country-style cooking is prepared with a great deal of care and taste. Dishes include roast lamb, lamb sweetbreads with parsley, delicious omelettes and an excellent home-made *garbure* (Béarnaise vegetable broth). Menus €11–19. Worth going out of your way for. Credit cards not accepted. *Free coffee offered to our readers on presentation of this guide.*

Bayonne

64100

Adour Hôtel

13 pl. Sainte-Ursule.
05.59.55.11.31 05.59.55.86.40.

The only hotel of any charm in Bayonne; it is small, with just twelve rooms (although the biggest ones can sleep four people), at €55–80, depending on the size. It has recently been taken over by a new young owner, a former fashion stylist, who has redecorated everything in local style and in vivid colours and created a friendly atmosphere in this doll's house setting. At night he also cooks up dinner for the hotel's guests – he only likes cooking for small numbers. In other words, he comes from the mould of the old-style hotelier, eager to make his guests feel at home. Booking essential.

Hôtel Loustau***

1 pl. de la République; it's near pont Saint-Esprit on the river bank.
05.59.55.08.08 05.59.55.69.36
www.hotel-loustau.com
Restaurant closed *Sat and Sun (15 Oct–30 March).* **Hotel/restaurant closed** *Jan.* **Disabled access. TV. High chairs available.**

On the River Adour, with an uninterrupted view of old Bayonne and the Pyrenees, this 200-year-old hotel offers clean, well-soundproofed, excellent-value rooms. Doubles with bath or shower €76–101; breakfast €8. The restaurant offers specialities such as *piperade* with dried duck breast and Serrano ham, *carpaccio* of beef or duck, scallop stew, roast suckling lamb and Spanish-style cod. Set menus €16–23. Reckon on €31 à la carte. *10% discount on a room (Oct–May) offered to our readers on presentation of this guide.*

Auberge du Petit Bayonne

23 rue des Cordeliers.
05.59.59.83.44
Closed *Tues evening; Wed lunchtime.*

Kattalin, the owner, comes from the Mixe area, a region where tradition is valued and her CV includes a spell cooking in a convent. She must have been sorely missed when she left – she cooks like an angel. The menus are filling, but, as an alternative, opt for the *assiette campagnard* (boudin, ham, *piperade* and house *frites*, with a crisp salad) or the *assiette basquaise* (ham, fried egg, *piperade* and salad). Also good are lamb sweetbreads with ceps and parsleyed eels. The house *piperade* is the best there is, with the peppers and tomatoes almost cooked like preserves – and Kattalin swears that all the vegetables come from her kitchen garden at Lantabat. Menus €9.50 (weekday lunchtimes) and €13. Reckon on €20 à la carte. *Apéritif on the house offered to our readers on presentation of this guide.*

Le Bistrot Sainte-Cluque

9 rue Hughes; it's opposite the train station.
☎05.59.55.82.43
Closed *Mon Oct–July.* **Disabled access.**

The place to eat in Bayonne. David is an excellent English chef who plays around with flavours, coming up with creative combinations and using simple produce. Prices are reasonable. Try the shrimp salad with Serrano ham, the seafood platter, the pan-fried foie gras, or the roasted cod with garlic confit. There's a basic weekday lunch menu for €10, and another at €15; à la carte you can eat for about €20. You are strongly advised to book; the place is always full both inside and on the terrace – it's particularly popular with the gay community. Credit cards not accepted. *Apéritif on the house offered to our readers on presentation of this guide*

Le Chistera

42 rue Port-Neuf.
☎ and ℱ05.59.59.25.93
Closed *Mon, Tues and Wed evenings out of season; a fortnight in May.*

Jean-Pierre manages to combine being a restaurateur and a professional pelota player. The food in this local canteen-style place is typical of Bayonne, with fabulous tripe and fish, and daily specials chalked up on the blackboard. If you see pig's trotters, *louvines* (wild bream) or Basque-style tripe, order them at once. Prices are reasonable – there's a €15 menu (€7.50 for children) or you'll spend around €23 à la carte – and service is friendly. *Free sangria offered to our readers on presentation of this guide.*

Le Bayonnais

38 av. quai des Corsaires.
☎05.59.25.61.19 ℱ05.59.59.00.64
Closed *Mon; Sun evening out of season; 3 weeks in Nov; first fortnight in June.* **TV. Pay Car park. Disabled access.**

Fresh, tasty food, perfectly produced; portions that make "generous" sound mean; quantity that equals quality. Try roast milk-fed lamb, lamb pie or prawns with the perfect amount of garlic. The weekday €15 menu is a filling three courses (but no wine) and you should pay about €30 per person for a meal à la carte. The wine list has a selection from different regions with bottles for €15. It's a friendly neighbourhood favourite, with a pleasant, rustic dining room and a waterside terrace.

Restaurant El Asador

Place Montaut; it's near the cathedral.
☎05.59.59.08.57
Closed *Sun evening (except when there's a bullfight); Mon.*

Set on the Montaut square, this ten-table restaurant specializes in grills over the open fire – *asador* is the Spanish word for a grill chef, and the man in question is Maria-Jésus. The line-caught fish is splendid, particularly the cod with garlic and the sea bream *à l'espagnole*. For starters, ask for a *para-pica*, a selection of tasty morsels. Weekday menu €19.10, or about €25–35 à la carte.

Auberge du Cheval Blanc

68 rue Bourg-Neuf; it's in the Petit Bayonne area near the Bannat and Basque museums.
☎05.59.59.01.33 ℱ05.59.59.52.26
Closed *Sun evening and Mon except Aug; Feb school holidays; first week in July; first week in Aug.* **Disabled access.**

Rather than following the menus, you'll have a much more interesting meal if you allow the chef to guide your gastronomic journey and choose his daily or seasonal dishes; you might be tempted by the cream of chestnut and cep soup with *xingar*, or the *louvine* (wild bream) with salt. He also cooks "peasant" dishes such as ham bone *xamango* served with wholesome mashed potatoes and glamorized with truffle *jus*. Sublime desserts, in particular his grapefruit and grape soup with figs. There are weekday menus at €23 and €32. Reckon €50 à la carte. The setting is cosy and there's a family atmosphere. It's worth putting aside part of your holiday budget to eat here.

Bazas

33430

Restaurant des Remparts

Espace Mauvezin; it's on the cathedral square.
☎ and ℱ05.56.25.95.24
Closed *Sun evening; Mon; Tues, Wed, Thurs evenings (Nov–May); a fortnight in June; a fortnight in Nov.* Disabled access.

Park near the cathedral and walk through the passage to this restaurant. It's superbly situated next to the Mairie, on the *brèche de Bazas*, overlooking the Sultan's garden. You can enjoy these quite exceptional surroundings from the terrace when the weather is fine. The very classic décor is understated, and the cuisine is inspired, using quality produce like Bazas beef or Grignol capon. Set menus, €14 (weekday lunchtimes) and €17–27, feature semi-cooked foie gras, grilled rib-eye steak, cabbage stuffed with duck and prune and Armagnac mousse. À la carte there is always pig's trotter, prepared in various ways. Reckon on €30 à la carte.

Goualade

33840 (16.5km SE)

L'Auberge Gasconne

From Bazas take the D12: it's on the main road opposite the church.
Ⓣ05.56.65.81.77 Ⓕ05.56.65.89.91
Closed *Mon; Sun evening; 16 Aug–5 Sept.*

This inn is in the middle of nowhere, deep in the woods across the road from an old village church. Inside, though, it is unexpectedly smart and comfortable, and air-conditioned too. A group of regulars, including lorry drivers and electricity-board employees, flock here for good cooking and low prices. No one would dream of "reinventing" local dishes here. The simple country food comes from good old recipes and is substantial, filling and unpretentious. Large slices of Bayonne ham, wood-pigeon stew, pressed foie gras with leeks, *confit* of turkey, duck, pork and wild boar casserole. Set menu €10 (including wine and coffee) and around €18 à la carte.

Captieux

33840 (19.5km S)

Hôtel-restaurant Cap des Landes

Rue Principale; from Bazas take the D932 and it's in the centre of town opposite the church.
Ⓣ05.56.65.64.93 Ⓕ05.56.65.64.75
Closed *Sun afternoon; Mon; 11 Nov–5 Dec.* **Disabled access. TV. Car park.**

This hotel is in the middle of a small market town on a noisy road with lorry traffic at night – so try to get one of the simple rooms at the back. Doubles €31 to €36 with shower or bath. Nice family atmosphere. The hotel may be a bit on the noisy side but there are no complaints about the food. Though you can get a meal in the little room by the bar, the dining room next door is more stylish with a weekday lunctime menu at €10 and €15. Choose from local duck specialities, various gourmet salads and *escalope* of foie gras with apples and fresh grapes.

Belhade

40410

L'Auberge du Chêne-Pascal (Restaurant Euloge)

Ⓣ05.58.07.72.01
Closed *Sun evening and Mon out of season.*

A charming little inn with friendly staff, situated oppposite an equally charming church. The quality of the tasty meat and fish dishes makes it worth the detour, the full flavours of the ingredients brought out in the cooking process. Menus from €16 to €45. One of the best restaurants in the Haut-Pays Landais.

Bergerac

24100

Hôtel-restaurant La Flambée***

153 av. Pasteur; it's 2km north of Bergerac on the N21 towards Périgueux.
Ⓣ05.53.57.52.33 Ⓕ05.53.61.07.57
Ⓦwww.laflambee.com
Restaurant closed *Sat lunchtime out of season; Sun evening; Mon.* **TV. High chairs available. Swimming pool. Car park.**

This hotel is on the edge of the Pecharmant hills set in substantial gardens screened by trees with a tennis court and a swimming pool – so it's as quiet as anything. The twenty or so individualized rooms are split between a large Périgord residence and a summer house; each has a small terrace. Doubles are €57–66 depending on the season. The restaurant is the place to be seen on the Bergerac circuit, thanks to its opulent décor and the finely cooked local dishes. It's best to book. Set menus €16–31. À la carte dishes include grilled duck's foie gras and beef-fillet pastry with foie gras. Pleasant terrace near the swimming pool for when the weather is fine. Themed evenings in summer. *10% discount on a room offered to our readers on presentation of this guide.*

|●| Restaurant La Sauvagine

18–20 rue Eugène-Leroy.
Ⓣ05.53.57.06.97
Closed *Sun evening; Mon; a week in June; 2 weeks in Sept.* **High chairs available.**

Modern air-conditioned restaurant that serves traditional, well-prepared cuisine at honest prices. Go for fish such as lamprey from the Bordeaux region, seafood or game in season, and make room for the delicious desserts. Great menus €12.20–40. Classy clientele but a friendly, genuine welcome. *Free coffee offered to our readers on presentation of this guide.*

|●| Restaurant L'Enfance de Lard

Rue Pélissière.
Ⓣ05.53.57.52.88 Ⓕ05.53.57.52.88
Ⓔlenfancedelard@yahoo.fr
Closed *lunchtime; Tues evening (except in summer); 2nd fortnight in April; last week in Sept.*

A charming restaurant on the first floor of a twelfth-century house on one of Bergerac's finest squares. It's small and soon fills up, so it's essential to book. It has a warm, intimate atmosphere and a fantastic view of the medieval church. Classical music plays in the background. The remarkable regional cuisine from the southwest includes quality meats grilled over vines in the superb fireplace, Sarlat-style potatoes which melt in the mouth, rack of lamb with mint, ceps in parsley vinaigrette, grilled sirloin of steak pricked with cloves of garlic and foie gras served with peaches in the summer or lentils in winter. Generous helpings. €26 menu or around €30–35 à la carte.

Saint-Julien-de-Crempse

24140 (12km N)

Le Manoir du Grand Vignoble***

From Bergerac take the N21 then the D107.
Ⓣ05.53.24.23.18
Ⓔgrand.vignoble@wanadoo.fr
Closed *15 Nov–31 March.* **TV. Swimming pool. Car park.**

A very fine seventeenth-century manor house – also an equestrian centre – in beautiful countryside. It's a luxury establishment, with enormous, charming rooms, costing €58–110, depending on the season. The rooms vary in size but all are very well equipped. Breakfast €9. Facilities include tennis courts, heated swimming pool and fitness centre. The restaurant offers set menus for €23–45; reckon on €38 à la carte. Try dishes such as terrine of foie gras with dried fruit, pan-fried veal served with baby vegetables and chocolate soufflé. *10% discount on a room offered to our readers on presentation of this guide.*

Issigeac

24560 (19km SE)

|●| Chez Alain

Outside the town walls, opposite the château.
Ⓣ05.53.58.77.88.
Open *all year round.* **Disabled access.**

A very elegant building, entirely refurbished with great skill, a magnificent terrace centred on an old village water fountain, sophisticated and tasteful interior decoration. Fortunately, the cooking lives up to these high standards. The classically inspired dishes are approached with finesse and originality, although customers used to the copious offerings of other restaurants in this region may find the menu here a little on the short side. The focus, however, is on quality rather than quantity, so all the ingredients are fresh and in season. The owner is often to be found in the dining room, surrounded by his friendly, efficient waitresses. There are plans to provide some luxury accommodation next door; if they're anything like the cuisine you'll need to book well in advance. *Free coffee offered to our readers on presentation of this guide.*

Razac-d'Eymet

24500 (20km SW)

La Petite Auberge**

It's on the edge of the village.
Ⓣ05.53.24.69.27 Ⓕ05.53.61.02.63
Disabled access. Swimming pool. Car park.

Set in a tiny village, this former farm transformed into a charming hotel by an English couple guarantees peace and quiet. There are just six pleasant rooms, some under the eaves, one of them a little suite; €39 for a double with basin, €46 with shower/wc or bath. Breakfast €6. You can also rent self-catering houses: the "Petite Maison" (small house) for two people, the

"Poulailler" (henhouse) for four or the "Ferme" (farm) for six; rates vary according to the season. Delightful swimming pool.

Biarritz

64200

Hôtel Palym*

7 rue du Port-Vieux; it's 100m from the sea.
ⓣ05.59.24.16.56 ⓕ05.59.24.96.12
ⓦwww.le-palmarium.com
TV.

A well-maintained old hotel with a décor that strikes a nice balance between past and present, cosy and modern. A little winding staircase leads to the neat and tidy rooms, some of which have been modernized. Doubles cost €40–54 with shower/wc or bath, depending on season. The rooms at the rear are quieter than those overlooking the nice (but noisy) rue du Port-Vieux. There are also some rooms sleeping three or four. Half board is available; you eat at the *Palmarium*, next door, which is run by the brother of the *patron*.

Hôtel Le Saint-Charles**

21 av. Reine-Victoria.
ⓣ05.59.24.10.54 ⓕ05.59.24.56.74
ⓦwww.hotelstcharles.com
Closed *15 Nov–15 Dec.* **TV. High chairs available.**

A haven just outside the centre of town, very prettily done out in pink. If you like peace and quiet, greenery and flowers, you'll find it hard to leave – especially after breakfast in the lovely garden. Thirteen freshly refurbished rooms with period furniture; doubles are €50–65 with shower/wc and €64–90 with bath/wc. Some single rooms at €43–52 and quadruples €80–110. Breakfast €7. Well worth going out of your way for, although the welcome could be warmer. *One free breakfast per person after the third night, or a fruit juice or fizzy drink, offered to our readers on presentation of this guide.*

Hôtel Maïtagaria**

34 av. Carnot; it's 500m from the sea.
ⓣ05.59.24.26.65 ⓕ05.59.24.27.37
ⓦwww.hotel-maitagaria.com
TV.

You'd do well to book at this place, which attracts a host of regulars. It's a charming town house, opposite the public gardens, offering quiet, comfortable rooms with great bathrooms. Everything is beautifully decorated, and all rooms have a view. Doubles with shower/wc or bath for €52–58. Breakfast €6. There's a very pleasant flower-filled garden. This could well be the best place in Biarritz, especially if you get room 16, which has its own terrace. *One free breakfast per room offered to our readers on presentation of this guide.*

Hôtel La Romance**

6 allée des Acacias; from the centre take avenue du Maréchal-Foch, then avenue Kennedy. It's near the racecourse.
ⓣ05.59.41.25.65 ⓕ05.59.41.25.83
ⓔhotel.la.romance@wanadoo.fr
Closed *15 Jan–1 March.* **TV.**

A perfect romantic hideaway a little off the beaten track in a residential area. The ten rooms of this huge house are attractively decorated with a floral theme and feature painted wood and thick duvets. Half of them look straight out onto the garden. Doubles with shower/wc or bath cost €67–87, including breakfast.

Le Château du Clair de Lune***

48 av. Alan-Seeger; it's near the station on the Arbonne road.
ⓣ05.59.41.53.20 ⓕ05.59.41.53.29
ⓦwww.chateauduclairdelune.com
TV. Cable. Car park.

A secluded early-twentieth-century residence, splendidly decorated in Art Deco style and set in wonderful flower-filled grounds with landscaped gardens. The enormous rooms are stylishly decorated, painted in muted tones and furnished with antiques. Doubles €70–140 in the château, depending on the season. There are other rooms in the hunting lodge and one room sleeping four at €120. Breakfast €10. A dream of a place where you can relax away from the hectic life on the coast. Reservations are advisable.

Maison Garnier***

29 rue Gambetta.
ⓣ05.59.01.60.70 ⓕ05.59.07.60.80
ⓦwww.hotel-biarritz.com
TV. Cable.

The only three-star hotel in the town centre near all the sights. This is where the owner decided to settle after a ten-year odyssey around the world. There are only seven rooms and they've all been smartly decorated and well updated. Go for no.5 if you want a romantic little nook up in the roof, from where you can see the solid metal column that supports the whole house. No. 3, on the other hand, has heaps of space. Rooms range from €80 to €115, depending on the size and space. It's a popular place and essential to book.

|●| Le Crabe-Tambour

49 rue d'Espagne.
Ⓣ05.59.23.24.53
Closed *Mon; mid-Oct to mid-Nov.*

The chef was formerly responsible for the cuisine on board the *Jaureguibery*, a cruiser that featured in a successful French film starring Jean Rochefort. His voyages have left him with a taste for subtle culinary combinations, such as free-range Landes chicken accompanied by grilled Laotian mango, while Spanish influences are discernible in the fish dishes. A restrained use of spices, a love of simplicity and a crew of beaming waitresses are the final touches that make everything shipshape. Booking essential.

|●| Le Saint Amour

26 rue Gambetta.
Ⓣ05.59.24.19.64
Closed *Sun; Mon out of season; second fortnight in Feb; June; Nov.*

A Lyonnais bistro in exile – this place is a real find. Besides which, they serve lots of wines from small Lyonnais vineyards. The *andouille* and sausage come from the town too but there are also inventive Basque specialities on the menu: sautéed scallops with red peppers and bacon, fresh cod with creamed lentils, *andouillette à la ficelle* with creamed potatoes. The *moelleux au chocolat* is a very special dessert. There's a weekday lunchtime menu at €15, or à la carte you'll pay about €30. It's frequented by lots of people who know a good thing when they eat it. *Liqueur on the house offered to our readers on presentation of this guide.*

|●| Campagne et Gourmandise

52 av. Alan-Seeger.
Ⓣ05.59.41.10.11 Ⓕ05.59.43.96.16
Closed *Wed evening and Mon lunch in summer; Wed evening and Sun evening in winter; fortnight in Nov; fortnight in Feb.*

A classic setting with dining rooms that provide a degree of intimacy. On the menu at €38, there's a choice of eight starters (four hot and four cold), eight main courses (four fish and four meat) and eight desserts. The chef has a quiet, inventive flair without going over the top. He uses the local ingredients in his own way – a nice balance between regional, traditional French and nouvelle cuisine. In summer there's a terrace with a view of the Pyrenees. *Liqueur on the house offered to our readers on presentation of this guide.*

Anglet

64600 (3km E)

|●| Auberge de Jeunesse Gazte Etxea

19 rte. des Vignes, Chiberta area (northeast). Take the blue line no. 9 bus outside Biarritz station; it stops right outside.
Ⓣ05.59.58.70.00. Ⓕ05.59.58.70.07.
Ⓦwww.fuaj.org
Closed *Nov to end Feb.* **TV. Car park.**

A large, friendly and comfortable youth hostel, just ten minutes' walk from the sea. Spotless dormitories with four, five or seven beds from €12.70 per person, including breakfast. Guests are received 8.30am–12.30pm and 6–10pm. Booking (by post) is only accepted for full-board stays of at least a week. You can cook your own food in the evening (except May–Oct), and the cafeteria is open 7–9.30pm in the high season; menu at €5. No curfew. The hostel organizes a variety of sporting and cultural activities, particularly watersports. It organizes week-long courses of surfing and free-surf, and there are also facilities nearby for rafting, diving, golf, tennis, rollerskating, horse riding, *fronton* and pelota – as well as a Scottish pub with live music at night.

Arcangues

64200 (4km SE)

|●| Auberge du Trinquet

It's in the village.
Ⓣ05.59.43.09.64 Ⓕ05.59.43.15.10
Closed *Mon; Tues out of season; Feb; March.*

Healthy and solid cuisine using fresh local produce. The dining room, set in a modern building, looks over the *trinquet*, the playing area, where the players test their skills; it's fun to watch them expending so many calories while you eat terrine of foie gras, broiled mussels, stuffed crab, *croustillant* of boned pig's trotter or calf's head. Copious menu for €22; individual dishes €13–15. In the evening, the bar is abuzz with local players. There's a huge terrace which has a view over the golf course and the small pink pelota court.

Arbonne

64210 (5km SE)

Eskualduna**

Take the D255 from Biarritz.
05.59.41.95.41 05.59.41.88.16
Closed *Sun evening.* **TV. Car park.**

Jolly place with a lively bar. Customers, most of them factory workers, are welcomed into the big dining room. Jacky the owner keeps the conversation going between courses, commenting on the latest rugby match or chatting away while cooking up the sauces. He's as robust as the regional cuisine on his set menus (€11–22). The place also has double rooms with shower or bath for €35.50–44; breakfast is €4. *10% discount on a room offered to our readers on presentation of this guide.*

Laminak***

Route de Saint-Pée.
05.59.41.95.40
www.hotel-laminak.com

Disabled access. TV. High chairs available. Car park.

A nice quiet spot which isn't miles away from everywhere. It's comfortably located in a thoroughly renovated Basque house with a terrace and surrounded by a garden. The owner moved here from a health spa, so he's expert at looking after the inner you. Clean rooms, fresh décor and good facilities. Doubles cost €54–95; those at €54 are on the small side; some of the more expensive ones have a private terrace giving onto the garden. Breakfast is served on the veranda or in the garden facing the mountains – sheer heaven. If you fancy a round of golf, the hotel has an arrangement with the local links which offer discounts to guests. A charming place only minutes from the sea. *10% discount on a room (from 2 Jan to 31 March) offered to our readers on presentation of this guide.*

Ahetze

64210 (8km S)

Hiriartia

8 pl. du Fronton; take the D255 in the direction of Arbonne, then turn right onto the D655.
and 05.59.41.95.22
Closed *Mon in season; Wed out of season; mid-Dec to mid-Jan.*

A beautiful inn. You go through a bar which can't have changed for sixty years: dark beams, antique wood and patronized by practically the whole village. The dining room lies beyond and leads through to the terrace and the garden. Typical cuisine without frills and generous (very generous) portions: peppers stuffed with cod and crab, monkfish kebabs with *beurre blanc* and omelettes with ceps. Menus €16–21. Very pleasant service and welcome.

Bidart

64210

La Villa L'Arche***

Chemin Camboenea; 200m from the town centre.
05.59.51.65.95 05.59.51.65.99.
www.villalarche.com
Closed *mid-Nov to mid-Feb.* **TV. Car park. High chairs available.**

A pretty Basque-style house converted into a three-star hotel. The eight rooms (six with large bay windows opening on to the sea) are tastefully decorated and boast large bathrooms. Doubles cost €80–160, depending on the season. Continental breakfast is extra (€12), and there is an additional charge for a pet (€12 per day). The hotel gardens, complete with teak furniture, lead directly down to the beach; there is also a terrace, with deckchairs offering a fine view of the surfers in the ocean. In bad weather, you can still while away the time in comfort, nestled in a sofa beside the log fire on the veranda. Booking highly recommended.

Biscarrosse

40600

Hôtel Le Saint Hubert**

588 av. Latecoere; it's 500m from the centre of the village, near the lake.
05.58.78.09.99 05.58.78.79.37

ⓦwww.biscarrosse.com/saint-hubert/fr
Disabled access. TV. Car park.

It's just outside the village, but you feel as if you're way out in the country – the summer hordes simply don't come here. You can stretch out with a book in the garden, brimming with scented flowers. They put out tables for tea or breakfast. Double rooms €45–63 with bath or shower, according to season. You can order simple food in advance for around €8. The most attractive feature, however, is the owner's expansive welcome, and he'll give you good tips for your meals or on places to see – and, if you've got a bike, the best paths to follow.

Hôtel La Caravelle**

5314 rte. des Lacs, quartier ISPE, lac Nord. On the bank of Lac Cazaux on the way to the golf course.
ⓣ05.58.09.82.67 ⓕ05.58.09.82.18
ⓦwww.lacaravelle.fr
Closed *Mon lunchtime except in July and Aug; Tues lunchtime; 1 Nov to 15 Feb.* TV.
High chairs available. Car park.

A fine, large building in a pleasant setting on the banks of the lake with a small beach. The whole place is painted white, and nearly all the rooms have a little balcony looking out onto the water. Doubles €60 with shower/wc, €76 with bath. There's also a villa to rent in summer, which sleeps four. A lovely restful place – though the frogs may disturb some guests on spring nights. The restaurant serves good local food, with dishes such as veal sweetbreads in Jurançon wine, leg of duck with pepper sauce, eel *fricassée* and prawns in Caravelle sauce. Cheapest menu €15, then others €22–37. Half board is compulsory in summer, at €50–54 per person. *Apéritif on the house offered to our readers on presentation of this guide.*

Restaurant Chez Camette

532 av. Latécoère. 500m from the town centre, going towards the Hydro-aviation Museum.
ⓣ05.58.78.12.78 ⓕ05.58.78.12.78
Closed *Fri evening and Sat out of season; Christmas–1 Jan.* **High chairs available.**

A popular and quaint little inn with white walls and red shutters. Wonderful welcome and generous helpings. The food is simple and unpretentious: set menus €10 (except Sun), and then €14.50 and €21.50. Dishes include thick soup, mussels in white wine and *escalope* in cream sauce. Don't miss out on the house speciality – duck breast grilled over the open fire. Credit cards not accepted.

Bordeaux

33000

See map on pp.40–41

Hôtel Bristol

4 rue Bouffard. **Map B2-3**
ⓣ05.56.81.85.01 ⓕ05.56.81.24.72
ⓦwww.hotel-bordeaux.com
TV.

This is part of a hotel group comprising the *Hôtel de Lyon*, the *Hôtel d'Amboise* and the *Hôtel La Boétie*, each of them in quiet, centrally located streets in a pedestrian zone. Rooms cost €24.40–46 depending on the hotel and the size of the room. They are all clean and well maintained. It's advisable to book because this is the best value in town and attracts a lot of regulars.

Acanthe Hôtel**

12–14 rue Saint-Rémi. **Map C2-6**
ⓣ05.56.81.66.58 ⓕ05.56.44.74.41
ⓦwww.acanthe-hotel-bordeaux.com
Closed *Christmas holidays.* **TV.**

Just twenty metres from the superb place de la Bourse and the riverside, in the picturesque Saint-Pierre area. It's in a quiet street, and there's double glazing. Tasteful, personalized rooms and good facilities. Doubles €42–58 with shower/wc or bath. The owner greets you warmly and knows the region well. Parking is difficult around here, though.

Hôtel Notre-Dame**

36 rue Notre-Dame. **Off map C1-9**
ⓣ05.56.52.88.24 ⓕ05.56.79.12.67
TV.

At the heart of the Les Chartrons district, which used to be full of wine merchants, this stone-fronted nineteenth-century house has been beautifully restored. It's overlooked by the monumental Cité Mondiale du Vin – where you can find anything and everything related to wine. In contrast to the modern and somewhat neutral décor of the rooms, the rue Notre-Dame overflows with antique dealers and bric-à-brac shops. Doubles with shower/wc €44.60; with bath €48.65. Pay

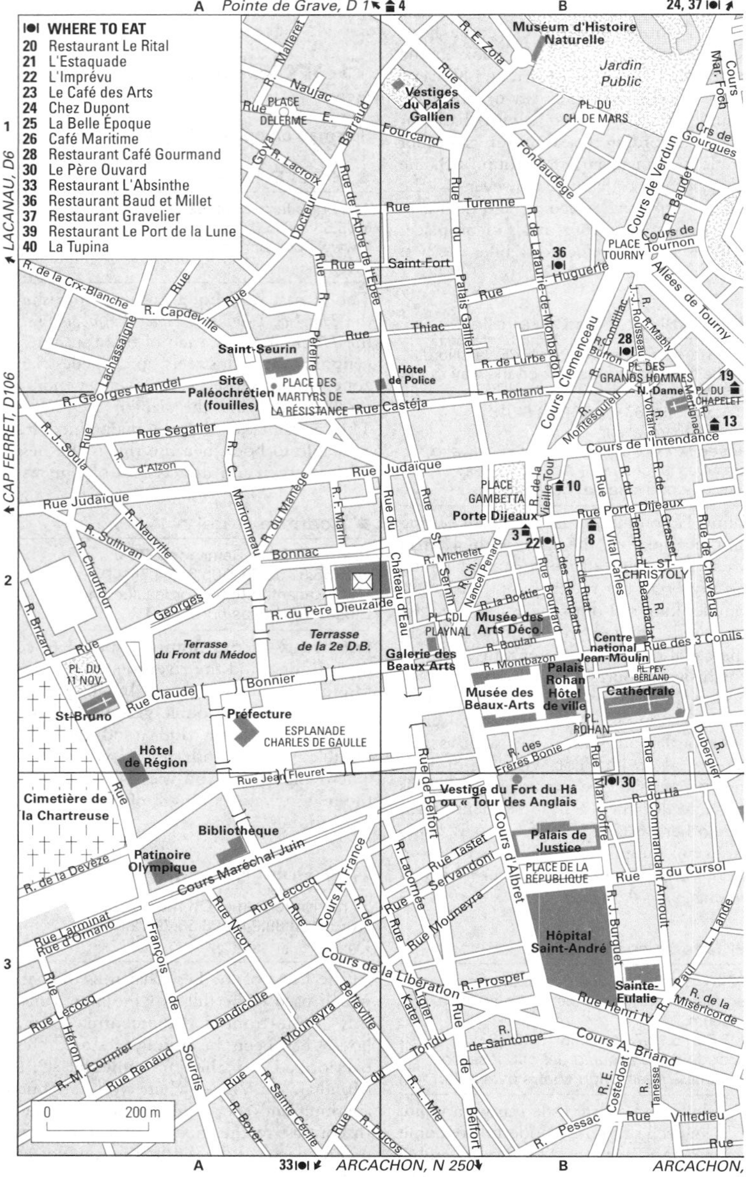
WHERE TO EAT
20 Restaurant Le Rital
21 L'Estaquade
22 L'Imprévu
23 Le Café des Arts
24 Chez Dupont
25 La Belle Époque
26 Café Maritime
28 Restaurant Café Gourmand
30 Le Père Ouvard
33 Restaurant L'Absinthe
36 Restaurant Baud et Millet
37 Restaurant Gravelier
39 Restaurant Le Port de la Lune
40 La Tupina
A
B
1
2
3
Pointe de Grave, D 1
4
24, 37
LACANAU, D6
CAP FERRET, D106
33
ARCACHON, N 250
ARCACHON,
Muséum d'Histoire Naturelle
Jardin Public
PL. DU CH. DE MARS
Vestiges du Palais Gallien
PLACE DELERME
PLACE TOURNY
Allées de Tourny
Cours de Verdun
Cours de Tournon
Crs de Gourgues
Cours Mar. Foch
Saint-Seurin
Site Paléochrétien (fouilles)
PLACE DES MARTYRS DE LA RÉSISTANCE
Hôtel de Police
PL. DES GRANDS HOMMES
N.-Dame
PL. DU CHAPELET
19
13
Cours de l'Intendance
PLACE GAMBETTA
Porte Dijeaux
10
3
22
8
PL. ST-CHRISTOLY
Rue Porte Dijeaux
Rue Judaïque
Terrasse du Front du Médoc
Terrasse de la 2e D.B.
PL. CDL. PLAYNAL
Musée des Arts Déco.
Galerie des Beaux Arts
Centre national Jean-Moulin
PL. PEY-BERLAND
Palais Rohan Hôtel de ville
Musée des Beaux-Arts
Cathédrale
PL. ROHAN
PL. DU 11 NOV.
St-Bruno
Préfecture
ESPLANADE CHARLES DE GAULLE
Hôtel de Région
Cimetière de la Chartreuse
Vestige du Fort du Hâ ou « Tour des Anglais »
30
Palais de Justice
PLACE DE LA RÉPUBLIQUE
Bibliothèque
Patinoire Olympique
Cours Maréchal Juin
Cours d'Albret
Hôpital Saint-André
Sainte-Eulalie
Cours de la Libération
Cours A. Briand
Rue Henri IV
Cours A. France
36
28
0 200 m

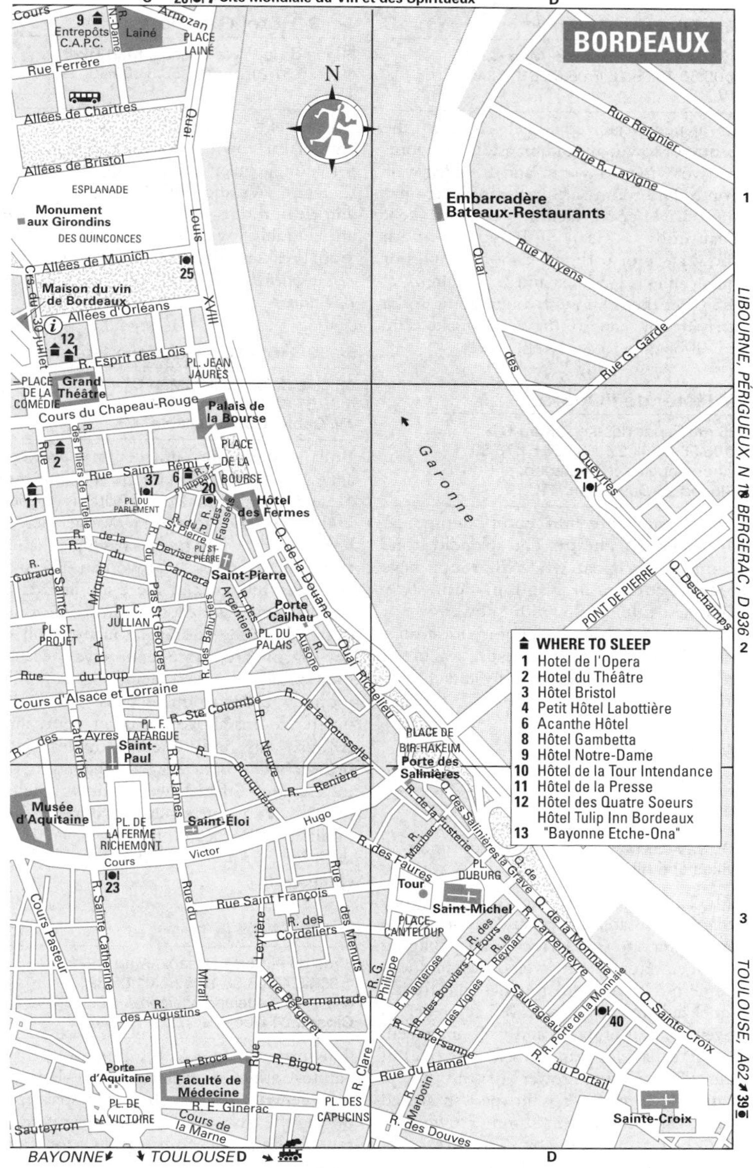

BORDEAUX
C
26 Cité Mondiale du Vin et des Spiritueux
D
N
Cours
9
Entrepôts
C.A.P.C.
R. N.-Dame
Lainé
Arnozan
PLACE LAINÉ
Rue Ferrère
Allées de Chartres
Allées de Bristol
Quai
Louis
XVIII
ESPLANADE
Monument aux Girondins
DES QUINCONCES
Allées de Munich
25
Maison du vin de Bordeaux
Allées d'Orléans
Crs du 30 Juillet
12
1
R. Esprit des Lois
PL. JEAN JAURÈS
PLACE DE LA COMÉDIE
Grand Théâtre
Cours du Chapeau-Rouge
Palais de la Bourse
PLACE DE LA BOURSE
Rue
2
R. des Piliers de Tutelle
Rue Saint Rémi
37
6
20
11
PL. DU PARLEMENT
Hôtel des Fermes
R. F. Philippart
R. des Faussets
R. du P. St Pierre
R. de la Devise
PL. ST-PIERRE
Saint-Pierre
R. du Cancera
R. Guiraude
Sainte
Miqueu
Pas St Georges
PL. C. JULLIAN
R. des Bahutiers
R. des Argentiers
Porte Cailhau
PL. DU PALAIS
R. Ausone
Q. de la Douane
Quai Richelieu
PL. ST-PROJET
R. A.
Rue du Loup
Cours d'Alsace et Lorraine
R. Ste Colombe
R. de la Rousselle
Catherine
PL. F. LAFARGUE
R. des Ayres
Saint-Paul
R. St James
R. Neuve
R. Bouquière
R. Renière
PLACE DE BIR-HAKEIM
Porte des Salinières
Musée d'Aquitaine
PL. DE LA FERME RICHEMONT
Saint-Éloi
Hugo
Cours Victor
R. de la Fusterie
R. Maubec
R. des Faures
Q. des Salinières
la Grave
Q. de
PL. DUBURG
Tour
Saint-Michel
23
R. Sainte Catherine
Cours Pasteur
Rue du Mirail
Rue Saint François
Rue Leytière
R. des Cordeliers
Rue des Menuts
PLACE CANTELOUP
R. des Fours
R. le Reynart
R. Carpenteyre
Q. de la Monnaie
R. G. Philippe
R. Planterose
R. des Bouviers
R. C.
R. des Vignes
Sauvageau
R. Porte de la Monnaie
40
Q. Sainte-Croix
R. des Augustins
Rue Bergeret
R. Permantade
R. Traversanne
R.
du Portail
Rue du Hamel
R. Marbotin
R. Clare
Porte d'Aquitaine
R. Broca
Faculté de Médecine
R. Bigot
Rue
PL. DE LA VICTOIRE
R. E. Ginerac
Cours de la Marne
PL. DES CAPUCINS
R. des Douves
Sainte-Croix
Sauteyron
BAYONNE
TOULOUSE
D
Embarcadère Bateaux-Restaurants
Rue Reignier
Rue R. Lavigne
Rue Nuyens
Quai des
Rue G. Garde
Garonne
Queyries
21
PONT DE PIERRE
Q. Deschamps
1
2
3
LIBOURNE, PÉRIGUEUX, N 10 BERGERAC, D 936
TOULOUSE, A62 39
WHERE TO SLEEP
1 Hotel de l'Opera
2 Hotel du Théâtre
3 Hôtel Bristol
4 Petit Hôtel Labottière
6 Acanthe Hôtel
8 Hôtel Gambetta
9 Hôtel Notre-Dame
10 Hôtel de la Tour Intendance
11 Hôtel de la Presse
12 Hôtel des Quatre Soeurs
Hôtel Tulip Inn Bordeaux
13 "Bayonne Etche-Ona"

car park nearby. *10% discount on a room (July and Aug) offered to our readers on presentation of this guide.*

Hôtel du Théâtre**

10 rue Maison-Daurade. **Map C2-2**
Ⓣ05.56.79.05.26 Ⓕ05.56.81.75.06
TV.

In a pedestrianized street right in the centre of town, this old mansion has rooms in two wings. A warm and friendly welcome. The rooms are rather ordinary but they have good facilities and are kept beautifully clean. Doubles with shower/wc or bath are €45–50; triples or quadruples (2 adults and 2 children) at €55. Let them know if you're going to be arriving by car, so they can make sure you'll be able to access the street.

Hôtel de l'Opéra**

35 rue Esprit-des-Lois. **Map C1-1**
Ⓣ05.56.81.41.27 Ⓕ05.56.51.78.80
Ⓔhotel-opera.bx@wanadoo.fr
Closed *23 Dec–3 Jan.* **TV.**

An elegant eighteenth-century house next to the Grand Théâtre. The splendid stone staircase is original, while the rooms have been decorated in bland modern style. Doubles €48.50–53 with shower/wc or bath. The drawback is the noisy location – it's right on one of the busiest streets in the centre of town. Warm, friendly and charming welcome.

Hôtel de la Tour Intendance**

16 rue de la Vieille-Tour. **Map B2-10**
Ⓣ05.56.81.46.27 Ⓕ05.56.81.60.90
TV. Pay car park (€7), but free for motorbikes and bikes.

Two sisters take turns on reception in this charming establishment, and guests always encounter the same friendly and obliging service. Here the welcome includes numerous thoughtful touches like freshly squeezed orange juice served at breakfast. Everything is efficient and well organized. In the cellar, you can see a few vestiges of the third-century tower of the hotel's name. The rooms on the pedestrianized street can be noisy in summer owing to the chatter of passers-by – but it's completely quiet at the rear where the cheapest rooms (singles) have a nice view over the rooftops. The rooms aren't large but they've done their best with the décor. Doubles with shower/wc from €50. Breakfast €6.

Hôtel Gambetta**

66 rue de la Porte-Dijeaux. **Map B2-8**
Ⓣ05.56.51.21.83 Ⓕ05.56.81.00.40
TV.

This hotel is a good base, located in a lively part of the town centre. It's decent value for money given this and the facilities – there are TVs and mini-bars in the bright and clean rooms – and the owner is pleasant. Doubles with shower/wc and bath €50; breakfast €5.50. *One free breakfast per person offered to our readers on presentation of this guide.*

Hôtel des Quatre Sœurs***

6 cours du 30-Juillet. **Map C1-12**
Ⓣ05.57.81.19.20 Ⓕ05.56.01.04.28
TV. Cable. Cots available.

Built in the eighteenth century, between allées de Tourny, the Grand Théâtre and place des Quinconces, this hotel is steeped in history. The composer Wagner stayed here in 1850 when he was having an adulterous affair with a local woman. The staff are really relaxed and there are attractive, freshly decorated, classy rooms. The ones overlooking the cours de Tourny or allées de Tourny are more expensive because they are bigger – they include some family rooms with two double beds – than the quieter rooms above the inner courtyard. All are air-conditioned. Doubles with shower/wc or bath €60–70 depending on the season. Special weekends for wine lovers, with a tour of châteaux and tasting of different Bordeaux. *Bottle of Bordeaux on the house offered to our readers on presentation of this guide.*

Hôtel de la Presse***

6 rue de la Porte-Dijeaux. **Map C2-11**
Ⓣ05.56.48.53.88 Ⓕ05.56.01.05.82
Ⓦwww.hoteldelapresse.com
Closed 24 Dec–2 Jan. TV.

This place is close to the junction of rue Sainte-Catherine and rue Porte-Dijeaux in a central area which is pedestrianized during the day; some cars are permitted in the evening. The comfortable rooms are soundproofed and air-conditioned. If you really can't stand any noise at all, those on the courtyard side are the quietest. This place offers modest luxury at a reasonable price. Doubles with shower/wc €73, with bath €85. *One free breakfast per room offered to our readers on presentation of this guide.*

Hôtel Tulip Inn Bordeaux "Bayonne Etche-Ona"***

15 cours de l'Intendance. **Map C2-13**
☎05.56.48.00.88 Ⓕ05.56.48.41.60
Ⓔbayetche@bordeaux-hotel.com
TV.

A 63-room hotel, part of which is housed in an eighteenth-century building, very much in keeping with this affluent area. Courteous staff and attractive 1930s-style lounge. On the upper floors the rooms have been completely refurbished in an impersonal, contemporary style. If you can, choose a room in the Etche-Ona building, which is quieter and more comfortable. Doubles with bath €105–121. *10% discount on a room offered to our readers on presentation of this guide.*

Petit Hôtel Labottière

14 rue Francis Martin. **Off map B1-4**
☎05.56.48.44.10 Ⓕ05.56.48.44.14
Car park.

The "must-stay" hotel in Bordeaux, an eighteenth-century private mansion and listed building with a small interior courtyard. It's right in the centre of town, restored to perfection, with stucco-work, wainscoting and period furniture. This jewel has just two double rooms costing €180, breakfast (actually, it's more of a brunch) included. Needless to say, the welcome is unbeatable. Reservations essential. No pets are allowed – not with all those deep-pile rugs and silk-covered armchairs. *Rooms at €160 offered to our readers on presentation of this guide.*

Restaurant Le Rital

3 rue des Faussets. **Map C2-20**
☎05.56.48.16.69
Closed *Sat; Sun; mid-Aug to early Sept.*

In a part of the city where restaurants come and go every few months, this little Italian place has been around for twenty-one years. The food is very good and you get a warm welcome. Tables are in a series of linked rooms, each of which gives a view of the kitchen. The pasta is fresh (fettuccine with seafood or pesto, spaghetti, cannelloni) and they serve old favourites like *osso buco* and good home-made desserts. Lunchtime menu €8.50, and others at €11–18. *Apéritif on the house offered to our readers on presentation of this guide.*

Restaurant L'Absinthe

137 rue du Tondu, opposite Tondu Polyclinic. **Off map A4-33.**
☎05.56.96.72.73 Ⓕ05.56.90.14.23
Closed *Sat lunchtime; Sun; public holidays; Aug.* **High chairs available.**

You can almost imagine Toulouse-Lautrec sitting with a glass of absinthe in his hand at this bistro restaurant with its period décor. The food is good, too. Weekday lunchtime set menu €10, others at €14.50 and €20. Reckon on €20–25 à la carte. Extensive choice of dishes, including *fricassée* of scallops with oyster mushrooms and veal sweetbreads in port. The desserts – chocolate cake and so on – are home-made. Nice terrace, heated in winter, left open on sunny days. *Apéritif on the house offered to our readers on presentation of this guide.*

Le Café des Arts

138 cours Victor-Hugo. **Map C3-23**
☎05.56.91.78.46
High chairs available.

A really popular brasserie in a busy, buzzing part of town, open all year round from 8am to midnight. The terrace is quite wide and the dining room is like an old-style bistro with simple chairs and moleskin benches. Honest, traditional dishes in good-sized portions: herrings in oil, *andouillette*, scallops with ceps, and that rarity, real *frites*! Lunch menu €10.50; reckon on €20 à la carte. This place has been going for years and is a real favourite with the younger crowd.

L'Imprévu

11 rue des Remparts. **Map B2-22**
☎05.56.48.55.43
Closed *Sun; Mon; 2nd fortnight in Feb; 3 weeks in Aug.*

A few bistro tables are set out on the terrace in this pedestrianized street, with a couple of attractive dining rooms inside – one a vaulted cellar decorated with dried flowers and willow baskets. Lots of regulars chatting with the affable owner. Good, quick service and healthy cooking using fresh, market produce: *pot-au-feu*, beef skirt, pork fillet in mustard and home-made *clafoutis*. Menus at €11.50 (weekday lunch); €13.50 (dinner) and €19.50. Splendid sweet crêpes for dessert. It's a good idea to book. Credit cards not accepted. *Apéritif on the house offered to our readers on presentation of this guide.*

I●I La Belle Époque

Quai Louis XVIII. **Map C1-25**
☎05.56.79.14.58
Closed *Mon; Sun evening (Sun lunch and evening July–Aug); 3 weeks in Aug; some long weekends.* **High chairs available. Disabled access.**

New management has brought a breath of fresh air to Bordeaux's most attractive brasserie. The young owner has come up with a simple, short menu based around meat and traditional dishes such as veal chump and roast chicken. Set menu €13; dish of the day €9; other menus from €15 (weekday lunch) to €28. The substantial portions and swift service contribute to its renewed popularity; the gorgeous tiling doesn't hurt, either. *Apéritif on the house offered to our readers on presentation of this guide.*

I●I L'Estaquade

Quai de queyries. **Map D2-21**
☎05.57.54.02.50

Whoever invested in this place must have made a packet. It's on the river bank, right across from the stock exchange, and it offers a wonderful night-time panorama of the illuminated town. The décor and the lighting are low-key – not surprisingly it's popular with couples looking for a romantic night out. Seasonal produce and perfectly judged cooking make for delicious dishes, from the flash-fried squid to the slow-cooked leg of lamb. Weekday lunch menu for €14, or reckon on €35 à la carte. It's essential to book for dinner.

I●I Chez Dupont

45 rue Notre-Dame. **Off map C1-24**
☎05.56.81.49.59 ℻05.56.51.39.19
Closed *Sun and Mon (except private parties).* **Disabled access.**

About the best value for money you'll get in the Les Chartrons district. Attractive bistro-style surroundings and traditional dishes such as *pot-au-feu*, calf's head or sweetbreads chalked up on the blackboard. Menu €14.50; reckon on €30 à la carte. Good-humoured atmosphere and the staff provide a cheery welcome. Occasional live jazz in the evenings. *Apéritif on the house offered to our readers on presentation of this guide.*

I●I Le Père Ouvrard

12 rue du Maréchal-Joffre. **Map B3-30**
☎05.56.44.11.58 ℻05.56.52.32.11
Closed *Sat lunchtime; Sun.*

With the first spring sun tables are set up outside, opposite the École Nationale de la Magistrature. Unsurprisingly, it's popular with judges and lawyers. There's a huge blackboard with an appetizing selection of bistro dishes: grilled sardines *fleur de sel*, *moules marinière*, grilled chicken with cayenne pepper, with a few creative additions. Lunchtime menu at €14.50, an evening one at €20 or around €35 à la carte. *Apéritif on the house offered to our readers on presentation of this guide.*

I●I Restaurant Café Gourmand

3 rue Buffon. **Map B1-28**
☎ and ℻05.56.56.79.23.85
Closed *Sun and Mon lunchtimes.*

In sunny weather, nab one of the tables outside this elegant restaurant and admire the covered market. Bruno Olivier comes from a well-known family of chefs, and photos of them adorn the walls. He produces sound, well-judged dishes – using southwestern and Spanish produce – at bistro prices, with a lunch menu at €14.50. Expect to pay €35 for a dinner à la carte with wine. *Free coffee offered to our readers on presentation of this guide.*

I●I La Tupina

6–8 rue Porte-de-la-Monnaie. **Map D3-40**
☎05.56.91.56.37
Pay Car park. Disabled access.

An unmissable place serving gastronomic Bordelais dishes. It's one of those rare restaurants serving genuine dishes from the southwest, using the finest produce. The décor is attractive, rustic-chic, and the dining room centres on a large fireplace where they roast free-range meats. The prices reflect the quality of the cooking, with a €16 lunchtime set menu and other menus at €32 and €48. Reckon on €46 à la carte.

|●| Café Maritime

Quai Armand Lalande. **Map C1-26**
☎05.57.10.20.40
Closed *Mon evening; Sat lunchtime; Sun.*
Disabled access.

This huge, fashionable restaurant, in a reclaimed warehouse, seats 450. In spite of the vast space, the lighting creates an intimate ambience, enhanced by the teak and bottle-green décor. Dishes are fresh and delicate; the chef reinterprets Japanese and Thai cooking, giving it a Bordeaux twist. The specialities include *sushi*, Spanish-style sea bream and cod *tajine* with cumin. Weekday lunch menu for €18 (including wine and coffee) or around €30 à la carte. You get a lovely view of the harbour from the mezzanine tables.

|●| Restaurant Le Port de la Lune

59 quai de Paludate. **Off map D4-39**
☎05.56.49.15.55 Ⓕ05.56.49.29.12
Disabled access.

Service until 1am, seven days a week. Opposite the abattoirs, in one of Bordeaux's nightlife areas, this is a great place for jazz fans, with live bands most nights. It's an animated, friendly, "lived-in" place, with photos of jazz legends lining the wall. You can eat very well, with bistro dishes – as well chosen as the music – at reasonable prices. Seasonal à la carte dishes (reckon on €25 or so) include baby eels *à l'espagnole*, shad in green sauce, lamprey and so on. Affordable wines. Michel, the boss, creates an easy-going atmosphere with his ready smile and chat.

|●| Restaurant Baud et Millet

19 rue Huguerie. **Map B1-36**
☎05.56.79.05.77 Ⓕ05.56.81.75.48
Closed *Sun and public holidays.*

A specialist cheese restaurant serving 200 kinds of cheese, meticulously selected by M. Baud. He has a great passion for his work and applies strict criteria. The cheeses can be sampled from the cheese board, but are also used in numerous dishes, ranging from *millefeuille*, *raclette* and *tartiflette* to more daring concoctions. The "cheese and dessert" set menu is a surprising but tasty combination of sweet and savoury ingredients. There is an impressive and well-chosen selection of nearly a thousand different wines from all over the world. A very pleasant, air-conditioned restaurant with friendly staff. Menus at €18.50 and €23. *Apéritif on the house or 10% discount on a meal offered to our readers on presentation of this guide.*

|●| Restaurant Gravelier

114 cours de Verdun. **Off map C1-37**
☎05.56.48.17.15 Ⓕ05.56.51.96.07
Closed *Sat; Sun; Feb half-term; 3 weeks in Aug.* **Disabled access.**

Among the new wave of restaurants in Bordeaux, run by the daughter of one of the famous Troisgros brothers. Her husband, Yves Gravelier, is also a creative chef. The surroundings are modern without being flashy, with a covered terrace, and prices are reasonable. Lunch menu €20, with others at €25 and €32. The menus change frequently, but fish, of the highest quality, is a speciality.

Brantome

24310

Restaurant Au Fil de l'Eau

21 quai Bertin. By the riverside, near the Périgueux bridge.
☎05.53.05.73.65
Closed *Tues evening; Wed; mid-Oct to early May.*

This was once a fishermen's bistro. The pictures of fish are no longer on sale behind the bar, but it is still possible to hear customers boasting about their latest catch, and the sophisticated décor of the small dining room still draws on this passion. There is even a small boat moored beside the pretty little terrace on the edge of the Dronne. Not surprisingly, river fish (trout, perch, etc) feature prominently on the menu, along with local specialities. The cooking is unpretentious but skilled: home-made foie gras, zander in red Bergerac, *matelote* of freshwater fish, fried bleaks. Menus €22–27. The place has quite a reputation, so it is advisable to book. Warm welcome and attentive service. Meat lovers may prefer to opt for *Le Fils du Temps*, on the other side of the bridge, with its fine selection of roast meats and charming terrace. *Liqueur on the house offered to our readers on presentation of this guide.*

Monsec

24340 (12km NW)

Hôtel-restaurant Beauséjour**

Rue Principale.
05.53.60.92.45 05.53.60.72.38
Closed *Fri evenings and Sat in low season.* **TV. High chairs and games available. Car park.**

Really friendly welcome and quality food served in a pleasant restaurant with a panoramic view of the garden. Fine range of set menus celebrating local cuisine: duck sausage, oyster mushroom omelette, foie gras and duck breast kebab. The cheapest menu, €10 (not Sun), includes a quarter of a litre of wine and there are others at €15–25, with a children's menu at €5.50. Simple but impeccable rooms cost €35 with shower/wc; breakfast is €4. Half board available at €38 per person.

Vieux-Mareuil

24340 (13km NW)

Hostellerie de l'Auberge de l'Étang Bleu***

It's 2km from the hamlet, and well signposted.
05.53.60.92.63
www.perigord-hotel.com
contact@perigord-hotel.com
Closed *Sun evenings (15 Nov–30 April);5–11 Jan.* **TV. High chairs available. Car park.**

In a huge park at the edge of a private lake, with a small beach where you can bathe. The spacious, nicely furnished rooms are as quiet as can be. Those overlooking the lake (nos. 1–6) have a covered balcony. Doubles €53–62 with shower/wc or bath; half board, €53–61 per person, is compulsory in July–Aug. Good breakfasts, with boiled eggs. The elegant dining room has a lakeside terrace which is inhabited by noisy ducks, and nice views from the window tables. Good, generously flavoured dishes include salmon with ceps, along with a fine selection of salads with foie gras, scallops, crayfish tails or smoked duck. €15.50 weekday lunchtime menu and others €20–45, with a children's menu at €12; à la carte it'll cost around €44. *10% discount on a room offered to our readers on presentation of this guide.*

Saint-Jean-de-Côle

24800 (20km NE)

Hôtel Saint-Jean**

Route de Nontron; take the D78.
05.53.52.23.20 05.53.52.56.10.
Closed *Sun evening and Mon evening (out of season).* **TV. Car park.**

Charming little place, of the kind that helps to keep up the good image of country hotels, thanks to the efforts of its diligent and professional owners. Pretty garden. Traditional-style rooms that are comfortable and meticulously maintained. Doubles €33.55 with shower/wc. Breakfast €4.60. High-quality regional cooking: terrine of foie gras made from ducks bred in situ, scallops with *fricassée* of ceps, duck's breast with orange in truffle and parsley sauce. Weekday lunchtime menu at €11 and others at €14.50–25. Reckon on €22 à la carte.

Buzet sur Baïze

47160

Auberge du Goujon Qui Frétille

Rue Gambetta; it's opposite the church.
and 05.53.84.26.51
Closed *Tues evening; Wed.* **High chairs and games available.**

The village is quiet and pretty – and so is this inn, literally "The Inn of the Wriggling Gudgeon", which stands opposite the church. You sit down in peaceful surroundings to generous helpings of fine food, much of it Provençal, all of it based entirely on fresh ingredients, such as wild fish and beef and vegetables supplied by small local farmers. The wine list is similarly dominated by treasures from the Buvet region. No menu here (apart from a children's menu at €7.50), so you have to eat à la carte; reckon on €15–45. Reservations advised. *Free coffee offered to our readers on presentation of this guide.*

Cambo-les-Bains

64250

L'Auberge de Tante Ursule**

Fronton du Bas-Cambo; 2.5km from the centre of town.
05.59.29.78.23 05.59.29.28.57

Closed *Tues; mid-Feb to mid-March.* **Disabled access. TV. Car park.**

This very old farm building, painted all in white, has an annexe offering decent rooms for €27 with basin and from €42 with shower/wc. Good, home-prepared food, with a range of set menus at €15 (not Sun or hols) and €19.50–35. Look out for specialities such as braised lamb sweetbreads with ceps, salad of home-made black pudding fried with pickled garlic and sautéed cuttlefish.

Espelette

64250 (5km W)

Hôtel-restaurant Euzkadi**

285 Karrika-Nagusia; take the D918 towards Saint-Jean-de-Luz.
05.59.93.91.88
www.hotel-restaurant-euzkadi.com
Closed *Mon; Tues out of season; 2 Nov–20 Dec.* **TV. High chairs available. Swimming pool. Car park.**

This is one of the most popular country hotel-restaurants in the Basque area and it's a good idea to book well in advance. Michèle and André Darraïdou, both completely mad about Basque cooking, search out old recipes and revamp them. In their enormous restaurant you'll discover dishes you would have very little chance of finding elsewhere: *tripotxa* (black pudding made from veal and served with a tomato and capsicum sauce); *axoa* (cubed veal browned with onions and peppers); *merluza en salsa verde* (poached hake with pea and asparagus sauce); cockles and hard-boiled eggs in a sauce made with Jurançon wine and fish stock; *elzekaria* (vegetable soup). Set menus €16–28. The lovely little rooms are €46 for a double with bath; half board at €47–49 per person. Breakfast is €7. Now that there's a bypass, there's no noisy through-traffic. In the back there's a pleasant garden, tennis court and swimming pool. *Apéritif on the house offered to our readers on presentation of this guide.*

Itxassou

64250 (5km S)

Hôtel-restaurant Ondoria**

It's 100m from the Pas de Roland.
05.59.29.75.39 05.59.29.24.99
Closed *Mon; 20 Dec–25 Jan.* **High chairs and games available. Car park.**

A quiet place with lots of flowers out in the countryside. There's an easy-going family atmosphere with nice rooms with shower/wc from €36.60; breakfast €5.30. The dining room has a picture window with a view of the mountains to admire while you enjoy Basque-style chicken at a very reasonable price (menus €12.20–23).

Hôtel-restaurant du Chêne**

Place de l'Église: take the D918 towards Saint-Jean-Pied-de-Port, then the D249 to the Nive valley.
05.59.29.75.01 05.59.29.27.39
Closed *Mon; Tues out of season; Jan; Feb.* **TV. High chairs available. Car park.**

This establishment is superbly situated, and they serve unpretentious but delicious local cuisine. Set menus €15–28. Specialities include a mix of traditional and Basque dishes cod fritters with chilli and garlic in Basque coulis, duck *carpaccio* with ewe's cheese, chicken with rice and red peppers, *escalopes* of foie gras with ceps. Doubles cost €40–46 with bath; ask for one with a pretty view. *Glass of sangria on the house offered to our readers on presentation of this guide.*

Ainhoa

64250 (12km SW)

Ithurria***

Rue Principale; it's at the northern edge of the village when you come from Cambo-les-Bains. Take the D918 to Espelette then the D20.
05.59.29.92.11
www.ithurria.com
Closed *Wed out of season; Thurs lunchtime out of season; 3 Nov–8 April.* **TV. High chairs available. Swimming pool. Car park.**

One of the nicest inns you'll find anywhere, this very fine place is set in a large seventeenth-century house and former coaching inn on the pilgrim route to Santiago de Compostela. The gorgeously furnished rooms go for €115–125. There's an attractive dining room with hand-made floor tiles and a vast fireplace. Dishes include pepper stew, Basque *cassoulet* with red kidney beans and roast pigeon with garlic. Menus from €29 to €44. Fine garden, sauna and swimming pool to the rear. Reservations essential.

Capbreton

40130

Le Bistro

Place des Basques. 300m south of the town centre.
05.58.72.21.98
Closed *Sat lunch; Sun; Tues and Wed evenings (out of season); Oct; Christmas–New Year.* **Disabled access. Car park.**

Innocuous-looking from the outside, but delightful within. The owner, his apron wrapped round his waist, will take your order and cook your food. Chalked up on the blackboard are delicious dishes that are carefully prepared and perfect in their simplicity: shoulder of veal with whisky and hazel nuts, saint-marcellin in brioche or pineapple tart. Menu of the day €10 (weekday lunchtimes) or around €25 à la carte.

Les Copains d'Abord

Port des Mille-Sabords.
05.58.72.14.14
High chairs available.

There's a strong holiday feel to the décor: sea blue, forest green and sunshine gold. The restaurant has a lovely terrace which is at its best on summer evenings – it can get too hot at lunchtime. Menus at €17 (weekday lunchtime) and €29, featuring dishes that use produce straight from the farm or the ocean: pan-fried mussels, cuttlefish with garlic. Or you could go à la carte, which won't cost much more, and try pig's trotters, a speciality of the house. *A bottle of Côtes-de-Gascogne on the house offered to our readers on presentation of this guide.*

Restaurant La Pêcherie Ducamp

Rue du Port-d'Albret; near the beach and the casino.
05.58.72.11.33
Closed *Mon, Tues and Fri lunchtimes in season; Mon–Fri and Sun evenings out of season; fortnight in Feb; end Sept to early Oct.*

Direct from the fishmonger to the consumer – the tables are arranged around the fish counter, and the waitresses wear boots and plastic aprons. Wide range of seafood menus €21–33. You'll find cuisine such as seafood platter and grilled fish; the house speciality is *parillada*, a dish containing seven varieties of fish and seafood. Careful, though: the bill can mount up quickly. A touristy place, but pleasant nonetheless. Booking advised.

Cap-Ferret

33970

Hôtel des Pins**

23 rue des Fauvettes.
05.56.60.60.11 F 05.56.60.67.41
Closed 11 Nov–April.

A delightful early twentieth-century house quietly situated in a flower-filled garden between the bassin d'Arcachon and the ocean. The meticulously planned décor, all classic advertisements and old billiards tables, creates the impression that time has stood still. Spotless rooms are €55–71 with shower or bath, though some of them are tiny. The restaurant specializes in seafood; there are menus at €19 and €25, or you can dine à la carte for about €36.

La Maison du Bassin***

5 rue des Pionniers.
05.56.60.60.63 F 05.56.03.71.47
www.lamaisondubassin.com
Closed Tues (except July–Aug); Jan; Feb. Summer weekdays only open in the evening. **Disabled access. TV.**

A superb colonial-style wooden house in a picturesque district. It reserves a warm welcome for its guests and is undoubtedly the smartest place in Cap-Ferret. Each room has a slightly different feel, with maritime details and lots of pitch pine creating a soothing, timeless atmosphere. Doubles €100–135, depending on the size and the season. There's a restaurant, too, with menus from €38.

Le Muscaret Chez Yvan

17 rue des Goëlands; it's near the lighthouse.
05.56.03.75.74
Closed *Wed; a fortnight in Feb; a fortnight in Oct.* **High chairs available.**

A favourite haunt of locals who couldn't give a fig about the sea view (they see that every day, after all), but who really care about what is served on their plates. Yvan is a great character and his wife, two daughters and son-in-law make up the rest of the team. It's a convivial place, perfect for an evening out with friends. Great food with huge helpings of seasonal dishes. Menus at €11.50 (weekday lunchtime) and €20.

Canon (Le)

33950 (6km N)

Hôtel-restaurant de la Plage

L'Herbe, 1 rue des Marins.
05.56.60.50.15
Closed *Mon out of season; 31 Dec–10 Feb.*

A typical wooden house just by the water's edge, that's thankfully resisted the pressure to modernize. The restaurant is simple and cheap, filled, on Sunday especially, with locals and tourists feasting on *moules marinière*, grilled sea bream and the like. Set menus from €16 to €25. Eight modest double rooms with shower on the landing €40–42; some have sea views.

Cartelegue

33820

Chez Olga**

1 Bel Ormau. It's on the main road.
05.57.64.71.18
Closed *Sat; Sun evening; Aug; Christmas.*
TV.

A typical old-school truckers' restaurant run by Olga's grandson, who's given the place a make-over but kept the *Routiers* atmosphere. So what if the rooms are simple and the road rumbles close by? A double costs just €30. The restaurant, with its drab décor, is full of nice surprises. Simple, tasty cooking, which follows the changing seasons – asparagus in spring, ceps in autumn, and game or fried fish from the Garonne. Lunch menu €10, and others €13–30. It's a popular stop for local wine-growers.

Casteljaloux

47700

Hôtel des Cordeliers (Logis de France)

1 rue des Cordeliers.
05.53.93.02.19. 05.53.93.55.48.
www.hotel-cordeliers.fr
Restaurant closed *Sun; Mon lunch; Fri evening.* **TV. Car park.**

The owners, originally from Normandy, do everything possible to make their guests feel at home – some come a long way to stay here, knowing that the service will be exceptional. Very comfortable rooms (most of them renovated), with an attractive carpet in warm colours (dark blue, scarlet) and décor with a Provençal touch. Double rooms €45–48. Half board possible. The restaurant, which offers many local dishes, displays a similar attention to detail: for example, the croissants and bread at breakfast are served warm. Lunchtime weekday menu €12; other menus at €16 and €25.

La Vieille Auberge

11 rue Posterne.
05.53.93.01.36
www.casteljaloux.com
Closed *Sun evening; Tues evening and Wed out of season; 1 week in Feb half-term; 2 weeks end June; 2 weeks end Nov.*

In one of the oldest streets in town, this inn has a thoroughly local flavour. Pretty yellow dining room with old-fashioned furniture. Enjoy all the delicacies Gascony has to offer with produce skilfully selected according to season, including asparagus in spring. Set menus €18.30–38.10, with one for children at €10.70. Reckon on €37 à la carte. Attentive, if slightly distant, service. A few simple rooms with shower for €27.50. *Free coffee offered to our readers on presentation of this guide.*

Castillones

47330

Hôtel-restaurant des Remparts

26–28 rue de la Paix.
05.53.49.55.85 05.53.49.55.89
lesremparts@wanadoo.fr
Closed *last 3 weeks of Nov; Jan.* **Restaurant closed** *Sun evenings and Mon out of season.*
TV. High chairs available.

A beautiful and sturdy stone house in the middle of the village, sensitively converted into a hotel. The rooms are spacious (nos. 1–4 are the largest) and painted in pale, soothing colours; the ones overlooking the main road are fitted with double glazing. €37 for a double with shower, €44.50 with shower/wc and €50.50 with bath. Breakfast €6. The traditional regional dishes in the restaurant are predictable but well prepared: duck breast with foie gras sauce and prunes preserved in Monbazillac wine, red mullet fillet with thyme butter and a platter of duck. The bread is especially good. €12.20 lunch menu (not Sun), and others up from €15.20 to €40. Children's menu €8. Reckon on €24 à la carte. *Apéritif on the house offered to our readers on presentation of this guide.*

Dax

40100

Hôtel-restaurant Beausoleil**

38 rue du Tuc-d'Eauze.
05.58.56.76.76 05.58.56.03.81
www.hotel-beausoleil-dax.fr
Closed *mid-Dec to early March.* **Restaurant closed** *Mon and Thurs evenings.* **Disabled access. TV. Pay car park.**

This is the most charming and friendly hotel in town, quietly situated near the centre. It's a pretty white house with a terrace and 32 comfortable rooms. Doubles €43–69 with shower/wc or bath. Half board €46–64 per person. The food is conventional but good, all of it prepared with quality produce – make sure you try the foie gras. Menus €12 (except Sun) and €17–35. Your bottle is already set on the table next to your napkin ring. Excellent value. Every three weeks evening entertainment is laid on for guests. *Free house apéritif and, if you stay, one free breakfast per room per night.*

Les Champs de l'Adour**

5 rue Morancy; near the cathedral and the covered market.
05.58.56.92.81 05.58.56.98.61
leschampsdel'adour@club-internet.fr
Restaurant closed *Sun, Mon evenings in season; all day Sun, Tues and Wed evenings out of season; 1 week at Christmas.* **Disabled access (restaurant). TV. High chairs available.**

This little hotel looks more like a private house. The outside walls and the wooden staircase are original, but inside it's been totally rebuilt with seven quiet rooms; doubles €44–47; breakfast €5. The restaurant produces tasty dishes prepared with fresh, natural ingredients and including marinated salmon Scandinavian style, seaweed *à la marinière* and beef skirt with pickled shallots. The wine list features organic wines. Set menus from €13 to €21. *10% discount on a room (Dec–March) or free apéritif or coffee offered to our readers on presentation of this guide.*

La Guitoune

Pl. Roger-Ducos.
05.58.74.37.46
Closed *evenings; Sun; Mon; Feb.* **Disabled access. TV. High chairs available.**

Ideal if you don't want to spend too much. It's best to come on a Saturday when all local life is on show; the place teems with stall-holders from the market and it's a rendezvous for lots of Dax inhabitants. On offer are plates of good food like omelette with asparagus tips or mushrooms, squid cooked in their ink or in a stew, *moules marinière* or a dozen fresh oysters with a glass of local white wine. Dishes of the day €5–10. *Apéritif on the house offered to our readers on presentation of this guide*

Lou Balubé

63 av. Saint-Vincent-de-Paul.
05.58.56.97.92
Closed *Wed; Thurs evening; Christmas–New Year.*

Lou Balubé is named after the new owners' three children: Baptiste, Lucas and Bérénice. This charming, brightly decorated little restaurant not only serves good food but also has the virtue of being open on Sunday (unusual in Dax). Basic dishes include hearty slices of meat or tuna steak with vegetables, but there are more imaginative options if you order à la carte. Weekday lunchtime menus at €10, including wine and coffee, others €16–23. Friendly service.

L'Amphytryon

38 cours Galliéni.
05.58.74.58.05
Closed *Sat lunchtime; Sun evening; Mon; Jan; one week at end of Aug.*

Eric Pujos will delight you with dishes from the Landes and the Basque country in his bright, modern little restaurant, one of the gourmet establishments in the area. Dishes include rustic-style duck foie gras, prawn salad with foie gras, sizzling prawns, grilled lamb, and to finish, a delicious pastis from the Landes region. Very reasonable set menus €20–37. The à la carte menu changes every month. Prompt and pleasant service. *Apéritif on the house*

offered to our readers on presentation of this guide.

El Mesón

18 pl. Camille-Bouvet.
Ⓣ05.58.74.64.26 Ⓕ05.58.74.52.89
Closed *Sat lunchtime; Sun; Mon lunchtime; last fortnight of Aug; Christmas–New Year.*

You're in Spain here. The décor and the cooking tell you so: pan-fried squid, grilled whole turbot, paella, gazpacho, parsleyed eels and juicy grilled lamb chops. If all you want is a snack, lean against the bar and order from the range of tapas, washing the delicacies down with a strong Spanish wine or the house sangria. The portions are generous, but be sure to watch your budget. Reckon on a minimum of €23 for a complete meal.

Duras

47120

L'Hostellerie des Ducs**

Boulevard Jean-Brisseau; it's near the tourist office.
Ⓣ05.53.83.74.58 Ⓕ05.53.83.75.03
Ⓦwww.hostellerieducs-duras.com
Restaurant closed *Mon and Sun evenings (Oct–June); Mon lunch (July–Sept).*
Swimming pool. TV. High chairs available. Car park.

Originally a convent, these two fine semi-detached buildings now house the region's most prestigious hotel and restaurant. It's quietly situated, with pleasant terraces, lovely swimming pool and flower-filled garden. There's a friendly atmosphere in the restaurant, where the food enjoys an excellent reputation. You can choose from a €14.50 weekday lunch menu – glass of wine and coffee included – and others at €25–51. Specialities include terrine of duck foie gras with dried tomatoes, Garonne shad with sorrel cream sauce and omelette with locally-grown asparagus. The chef puts regional produce before originality and the result is good, high-quality cooking. The wine list has a fine selection of Duras vintages. In winter, try to book a table near the fireplace. Comfortable rooms at €51 for a double with shower/wc and €88 with bath (some have air-conditioning). Possibility of half board. No. 7 has a balcony with a view. It's pretty much essential to book in season. *10% discount on a room (except Aug–Sept) offered to our readers on presentation of this guide.*

Eaux-Bonnes (Les)

64440

Hôtel Richelieu**

35 rue Louis-Barthou; close to the spa.
Ⓣ05.59.05.34.10 Ⓕ05.59.05.43.46.
Closed *April; 1 Nov–20 Dec.* **TV. High chairs available. Disabled access.**

Despite its location on one of the corners of the main square, this is a quiet place, taken over and refurbished by a young couple from the Alps. It's a charming cross between a nineteenth-century spa hotel and a modern establishment, with attentive service, vast lounges with high ceilings and large, bright rooms, some with antique furniture. Doubles in high season, with shower/wc or bath, €43–47, depending on the view. The restaurant, on the other hand, serving Alpine specialities such as tartiflettes and fondues, is pretty average; menus at €13 and €16–27. *10% discount on a room offered to our readers on presentation of this guide.*

Eugénie-les-Bains

40320

La Ferme aux Grives

Ⓣ05.58.51.19.08 Ⓕ05.58.51.10.10
Ⓦwww.michelguerard.com
Closed *Tues evening; Wed (open every day in Aug).*

This restaurant is in the hands of famous chef Michel Guérard, who owns several local hotels, a spa and two other restaurants. This place is cheaper than some of his others, with a single menu at €36 – well worth it for perfectly simple dishes based on wonderfully fresh produce. Cured hams hang from the ceiling while a suckling pig turns slowly on the spit in the fireplace. You feel good as soon as you sit down. Dishes include pork pâté of the day, buckwheat pancake with pig's head and pig's trotters, slow-roasted lamb and boiled beef salad with mustard sauce. It's a wonderful celebration of culinary art; you will rarely eat better.

Eyzies-de-Tayac (Les)

24620

Le Moulin de la Beune – Restaurant Le Vieux Moulin**

05.53.06.94.33 05.53.06.98.06
www.souliebeune@perigord.com
Closed *Tues, Wed and Sat lunchtimes (except July and Aug); 1 Nov–1 April.* **Disabled access. Car park.**

This place, which used to be a mill, is on the water's edge at the quiet end of the village. The décor of the rooms is understated, a little austere perhaps for some tastes, but they're comfortable and good value. Doubles €55–58 with shower/wc or bath. Tasty, well-prepared food is served in *Le Vieux Moulin*, which houses the original mill machinery. There is a €22 menu, and others going up to €45. You'll find dishes like *escalope* of foie gras, squab casserole, scallops with ceps and chocolate soufflé. In summer you eat in the garden on a delightful terrace, lulled by the murmuring river.

Hôtel de France – Auberge du Musée**

Rue du Moulin.
05.53.06.97.23 05.53.06.90.97
hotel-de-france24@wanadoo.fr
Restaurant closed *Mon and Sat lunchtimes except for groups and on public holidays; Nov–Easter.* **TV. Swimming pool. Car park.**

Two establishments standing opposite each other at the foot of a cliff. The inn, which serves traditional and regional food, has two dining rooms – or you can eat outside under the wisteria-covered arbour. Set menus €12–37. Reckon on around €20 à la carte. There are a few rooms in the main building and others in an annexe on the banks of the Vézère, where there is a garden and a swimming pool. Doubles with bath €58–68. Half board (€55–60 per person) is recommended 2–15 Aug.

Hostellerie du Passeur**

It's opposite the museum.
05.53.06.97.13 05.53.06.91.63
www.hostellerie-du-passeur.com
Closed *Mon and Tues lunchtime (except in summer); early Nov to early March.* **TV. High chairs available. Car park.**

On a small, peaceful pedestrian square by the river. The white shutters add a touch of charm to the old ivy-covered walls. Very attractively decorated rooms. Doubles €62–100 with bath. Beautifully restored rustic restaurant serves well-prepared, reasonably priced traditional dishes. Weekday menu at €19, then €22.50–46, are good value and list dishes such as *délice périgourdin* with foie gras and rabbit *confit* on a bed of cep mushrooms in truffle juices. À la carte, try three styles of foie gras or scallops with ceps. Half board (€60–82 per person) is compulsory Aug–Sept.

Hôtel-restaurant Le Centenaire***

Rocher de la Penne; it's on the main street.
05.53.06.68.68 05.53.06.92.41
www.hotelducentenaire.fr
Closed *early Nov to early April.* **Restaurant closed** *Mon–Thurs lunchtimes.* **TV. Swimming pool. Car park.**

This exceptional establishment is quite simply the best restaurant in Périgord. Chef Roland Mazère is a culinary artist and his flavours are subtle, intense and original – try salad of asparagus with foie gras, hot wild cep terrine with garlic and parsley, creamy black truffle risotto or fillet of goose "Rossini" (with foie gras) served with macaroni and Cantal cheese gratin. Menus €34 (weekday lunchtimes) and €58–110. Despite its cachet, the dining room is not in the least stuffy. Alain Scholly and his wife offer you a genuine welcome and the service is perfect in its discreet efficiency. The décor is luxurious without being ostentatious, and the rooms are wonderfully furnished. Doubles €138–260 with bath. Half board (€145–230 per person) compulsory in July–Aug.

Tursac

24620 (6km N)

Restaurant La Source

From Eyzies, take the D706.
05.53.06.98.00 05.53.35.13.61
leolerschen@aol.com
Closed *Sat, evenings March–June and Sept–Nov (unless you book a table); early Nov–mid-March.* **High chairs and games available.**

Decent little village inn run by a friendly young couple. It's a rustic-style restaurant, and when the weather is fine you can eat out on the terrace and admire the spring running through the garden. Modern cuisine with a good selection of local dishes: foie gras, gizzards, *confit*, cep mushroom omelette, cod *au gratin* and rabbit terrine with hazelnuts. Menus, €12–22.50, include a vegetarian option (with vegetable pie). Staff are discreet and pleasant. *Free coffee offered to our readers on presentation of this guide.*

Tamniès

24620 (14km NE)

🏠 |●| Hôtel-restaurant Laborderie**

From Eyzies take the D47 and the D48 – it's equidistant between Sarlat and Montignac.
Ⓣ05.53.29.68.59 Ⓕ05.53.29.65.31
Ⓔhotel.laborderie@worldonline.fr
Closed *Wed lunch (except July–Aug); 1 Nov–2 April.* **TV. High chairs available.Swimming pool. Car park.**

Set on a peaceful square in this hillside market town, surrounded by exceptional countryside, *Laborderie* started off as a farm, became a country café and restaurant, and is now a rather chic hotel-restaurant. Lovely rooms at reasonable prices; you'll pay €26–47 for a double with shower/wc and €59–87 with bath, depending on the season. Some rooms are in the turreted main house, which has a great deal of charm, while others are in a garden annexe looking onto open countryside – those on the ground floor face the swimming pool. The large, bright restaurant has become one of the most popular in Périgord. The chef skilfully prepares generous helpings of classics such as Périgord platter, half-cooked foie gras, duck with peaches and iced soufflé with hazelnuts. Menus €18–41; reckon on €30 à la carte. There's a terrace.

Grenade sur Adour

40270

🏠 |●| Pain, Adour et Fantaisie***

14–16 pl. des Tilleuls; it's on the church square.
Ⓣ05.58.45.18.80 Ⓕ05.58.45.16.57
Ⓔpain.adour.fantaisie@wanadoo.fr
Closed *Sun evening (except in summer); Mon; Wed; fortnight in Feb; fortnight in Nov.* **Disabled access. TV.**

This gorgeous old village dwelling stands between the main square and the Adour River. It has comfortable, tastefully decorated rooms with great views. Doubles €64–122; breakfast €11.40. The food is unforgettable, served in the sophisticated surroundings of the restaurant or on the riverside terrace. Dishes include foie gras marinated in Jurançon wine, risotto with glazed prawns, potatoes stuffed with ribbons of pork, pan-fried red mullet in lavender vinegar, braised rabbit with ceps in chestnut *jus* and milk-fed lamb from the Pyrenees with cashew curry sauce. The service is unobtrusive. Menus at €28 (except on public holidays) and €37–83. Unbeatable charm and value for money.

Hagetmau

40700

🏃 🏠 |●| Le Jambon**

27 av. Carnot; it's opposite the covered market.
Ⓣ05.58.79.32.02. Ⓕ05.58.79.34.78
Closed *Sun evening; Mon; Oct.* **TV. Swimming pool. Car park.**

Behind the freshly painted pink-and-white exterior is a nice little place famous for its good cooking: foie gras with spices, scallop stew with ceps, best lamb with thyme, quail stuffed with foie gras, pigeon and hot Grand Marnier soufflé. Menus €17–30. Meal and overnight stay €55 per person. The rooms are also recommended; doubles go for €45–60 with shower/wc or bath. *Apéritif on the house offered to our readers on presentation of this guide.*

🏠 |●| Hôtel-restaurant des Lacs d'Halco

Route de Cazalis. 2 km after leaving the town; it is marked on the Orthez road.
Ⓣ05.58.79.30.79 Ⓕ05.58.79.36.15
Ⓦwww.hotel-des-lacs-dhalco.fr
Open *every day, all year round.* **Swimming pool (indoor).**

Off the beaten track, but well worth a detour. The building stands slightly apart from the traditional local style, yet it has been built with natural materials from the region, by the architect Eric Raffy, who also has other top-class restaurants to his name. It is startlingly modern, if somewhat austere at first sight, but guests soon become accustomed to it, especially after they've sampled the comfort of the rooms overlooking the lake and the sophisticated cooking (including one menu based entirely on foie gras) in the Waterlily Room (one glance will explain the name). Double rooms €58–90, depending on the season. Menus at €30 (fish) and €32.

Hendaye

64700

Hôtel-restaurant Bergeret-Sport**

4 rue des Clématites; it's 150m from the sea and 1km from the centre of town.
05.59.20.00.78 05.59.20.67.30
mariecarmen.bergeret@wanadoo.fr
Closed *Christmas.* **Restaurant open** *every day 1 June–30 Sept.* **Disabled access (restaurant only). TV. Car park.**

The photos on the walls are pictures of long-term guests, which creates a friendly atmosphere. It's a family-run hotel with comfortable rooms – €47–60 with shower/wc – that are well maintained by a charming, chatty woman. Her chef husband is a real pro – his classic, regional dishes are to be recommended and the portions are substantial. Menus €15–22. You can eat in the garden under the shade of the plane trees. Half board is compulsory in July–Aug: €56 per person. Credit cards not accepted. *Apéritif on the house offered to our readers on presentation of this guide.*

Le Parc à Huîtres

4 rue des Orangers.
05.59.20.32.38
Closed *Tues out of season.*

This is a grocer's shop which also serves a fine array of seafood and salads. They're all cold: ultra-fresh oysters are €9–12.10 for a dozen, mixed platters €3–6.40 and there's a variety of salads for €4.60–5.40. Service is inside or on the terrace. Tempting desserts and local wines served by the glass. Reckon on around €13 for a full meal. A really good place. *Free coffee offered to our readers on presentation of this guide.*

La Cabane du Pêcheur

Quai de la Floride.
05.59.20.38.09
Closed *Sun evening (except during school holidays); Mon 15 Oct–31 May.* **Disabled access. Car park.**

Given its name and location, there are no prizes for guessing that fish is king in this restaurant. You'll find the freshest of fish landed on the quayside opposite and cooked simply: either chargrilled, Spanish-style with pickled garlic or in a Basque-style stew. The large, simple dining room has a view of the boats. Menus €13.80–24.40, seafood platter €22. Reckon on €22 à la carte. Children's menu €7. Groups of up to ninety catered for (with booking). Charming welcome by the owner – who learned his trade with some of the best chefs in the region. *Free house digestif offered to our readers on presentation of this guide.*

Biriatou

64700 (4km SE)

Hôtel-restaurant Bakea**

Take the D258 from Hendaye and follow the signs.
Hotel 05.59.20.02.01 05.59.20.58.21
Restaurant 05.59.20.76.36
www.bakea.fr.st
Closed *Mon and Tues lunchtimes April–Sept; Sun evening and Mon 1 Oct–31 March; 20 Jan–15 Feb.* **Disabled access. TV. Car park.**

A gorgeous, isolated place where you'll get complete rest and relaxation. Ten clean and flowery double rooms cost €39–62 – the prettiest have balconies and views over the Bidassoa valley (nos. 7–10) – and there are another 23 in an annexe nearby. Half board July–Aug (not compulsory) from €124 for two people. Excellent restaurant with a dreamy terrace, serving generous portions of imaginative dishes; specialities include lobster salad, warm duck liver, joint of monkfish and fresh anchovy lasagne marinated in basil. Menu at €30 (except Sun and public holidays), and gourmet menus from €55.

Hossegor

40150

Hôtel Barbary Lane

156 av. de la Côte-d'Argent. Between the beach and the canal.
05.58.43.46.00 05.58.43.95.19
www.barbary-lane.com
Closed *Jan to mid-Feb.* **Restaurant open** *mid-June to mid-Sept.* **TV. Pool table. High chairs available. Garage for bikes.**

Barbary Lane is the name of the house

that provided the setting for Amistead Maupin's *San Francisco Chronicles.* Pretty location, with a small swimming pool to the rear and a terrace giving onto a promenade, just ten minutes' walk from the sea. Reasonably priced: pretty little double rooms €45–60. Similar value for money can be found in the restaurant. Great breakfasts, with coconut *crème caramel* and other tidbits. Very friendly service. Booking strongly recommended.

Hôtel-restaurant Les Huîtrières du Lac**

Avenue du Touring-Club. On the edge of the lake, on the Seignosse road.
Ⓣ05.58.43.51.48 Ⓕ05.58.41.73.11
Ⓔleshuirieresdulac@wanadoo.fr
Closed *Jan.* **Restaurant closed** *Sun evening and Mon out of season.* **TV. High chairs available. Garden. Car park.**

Doubles €61–85, depending on the season. Reserve well in advance to be sure of getting a room with a view of the lake. A well-run family business, well worth a stop for a meal overlooking the promenade and the lake: fresh oysters, seafood platter, sea bass in a salt crust or foie gras pan-fried with grapes. Set menus €19 and €33. *Free coffee offered to our readers on presentation of this guide.*

Hostens

33125

Le Café des Sports

9 rte. de Bagas.
Ⓣ05.56.88.55.13
Closed *daily from 3–5pm; in winter, closed Fri evening, Sat lunch and Sun evening.* **Car park.**

The good-humoured boss lords it behind the bar, and his wife keeps the whole place in order with her wry, Gascon humour. There's a large dining room populated by a crowd of regulars who know a thing or two about good food; everyone within a radius of 50km raves about this place. Specialities include seasonal game and pork from the farm next door. Cheapest menu €10, with others at €14–27. You can also rent bungalows in the peaceful garden at the back: they sleep up to four people and go for €34 with bath. *Kir on the house offered to our readers on presentation of this guide.*

Lalinde-en-Périgord

24150

Hôtel-restaurant Le Château***

Rue de la Tour; take rue des Martyrs-du-21-Juillet-1944, then turn down rue de la Poste.
Ⓣ05.53.61.01.82 Ⓕ05.53.24.74.60
Closed *Mon and Tues; mid-Nov to mid-Feb; 3rd week in Sept.* **Hotel also closed** *Sun evenings Nov–March.* **TV. High chairs available. Swimming pool.**

This is a proper little castle with its corbelled turret, pepper-pot towers and balcony overlooking the sleepy Dordogne. Guy Gensou, who has redecorated the entire place, is in charge of the kitchen and gives you a very warm welcome. He adds his own touch to local dishes and uses superb fresh produce. The dining rooms are peaceful and the staff pleasant. Good, traditional cuisine on the menus €23.50–40 (the first menu includes apéritif) or à la carte: pâté with truffle fragments, stuffed trout in white Bergerac, *millefeuille* with raspberry *coulis*. Comfortable double rooms with shower/wc €49–69.50, or with bath €100.50–152.50. The small swimming pool overlooks the Dordogne. Half board, €61–115, is compulsory from May to the end of Sept. Guy is a motorbike enthusiast and gives his fellow bikers a particularly warm welcome: *10% discount on a room and 5% discount on half board offered to bikers for a minimum of two consecutive nights on presentation of this guide.*

Laroque-Timbaut

47340

Le Roquentin

It's opposite the church.
Ⓣ05.53.95.78.78
Closed *Thurs and Sun evenings, Mon; 1st week in July and 1st week in Oct.*

Recently built, and cheerfully decorated in the style of a stone Provençal house. The chef has acquired a good reputation for regional cooking, using the finest quality produce and the traditional methods of the southwest. Dishes include caramelized duck's leg and squabs on a bed of ceps. Weekday lunch menus €10 and €15, except for public holidays; other menus

€19–34. There's a fine wine list, with a good Cahors Clos La Coutale 1999. *Free coffee offered to our readers on presentation of this guide.*

Larrau

64560

🏠 |●| Hôtel-restaurant Etchemaïte**

☎05.59.28.61.45 Ⓕ05.59.28.72.71
Ⓦwww.hotel-etchemaite.fr
Closed *Sun evening and Mon out of season; 5 Jan–2 Feb; 5–14 Dec.* **TV. High chairs available. Car park.**

It's easy to fall in love with this contemplative spot, and the welcome and kindness of the Etchemaïte family help to make it a magical experience. Simple, comfortable doubles go for €42 with shower/wc or €49–58 with bath. Half board, €43 per person, is compulsory in summer. Chef Pierre's aim is to combine tradition with originality; mainly using lamb, duck and mushrooms as a basis, he conjures up dishes such as duck breast and duck foie gras with apples, *parmentier* of *boudin* with apples, cutlets of suckling lamb, cep terrine with foie gras *jus*, monkfish with chicory and grilled hake fillet with herb butter. Set menus €15 (in the week) to €42, or you can eat à la carte. The rustic dining room has a view over the mountains and the wine list is full of pleasant surprises at reasonable prices.

Laruns

64400

|●| L'Arrégalet

37 rue du Bourguet.
☎05.59.05.35.47
Closed *Sun evening; Mon; 10–26 May; 5–26 Dec.* **Disabled access.**

A warmly welcoming restaurant in an old street with a small terrace. The Coudouy family cook typical local dishes using the best ingredients the mountain can produce. The owner's brother makes the charcuterie and the bread is baked in the kitchens. Their *garbure* and duck foie gras with leek fondue are both special, but *poule-au-pot*, with the chicken served whole in a vegetable broth, is the house speciality. Service can be a little bit slow though. Menus at €13.30 (weekday lunchtime) and €18.30–26. *Arrégalet* is the local word for a crust of garlic bread fried in duck fat.

|●| Auberge Bellevue

55 rue Bourguet.
☎05.59.05.31.58 Ⓕ05.59.05.39.08
Closed *Tues evening and Wed except 10 July–31 Aug; 3 weeks in Jan; fortnight in June.* **Disabled access.**

An attractive, friendly place with appetizing set menus at €13.60–27.50, plus a *formule*, in season, for €11.50. The chalet is festooned with flowers and there is an uninterrupted view of the mountains. Try the cep omelette, *salmis* of pigeon or veal stew *à l'ancienne*, *garburade*, duck *confit* with ceps or chicken *fricassée* with freshwater crayfish. And don't overlook their *crème catalane. Liqueur on the house offered to our readers on presentation of this guide.*

Sévignacq-Meyracq

64260 (15km N)

🏠 |●| Hôtel-restaurant Les bains de Secours**

As you come into the vallée d'Ossau, it's signposted after Rébénacq.
☎05.59.05.62.11 Ⓕ05.59.05.76.56
Ⓦwww.hotel-bains-secours.com
Closed *Sun evening; Mon; Thurs lunchtime out of season; Jan.* **TV. High chairs available. Car park.**

A scenic road leads to this restored Béarn farm, now a country inn adorned with flower-filled balconies. Just seven well-appointed rooms go from €50 with shower/wc to €60 for a triple with bath. Delicious food is served by the open fire in winter and on the terrace in summer. Set menus €13 (weekday lunchtime, but also available for hotel guests in the evenings and at the weekend) and €25 (lunch and dinner, except Sun), featuring such dishes as sole salad with ceps, and *garbure Béarnaise*. Sunday lunch menu at €26.50. A very good place to eat, close to the old spa. *10% discount on a room offered to our readers on presentation of this guide.*

Lestelle-Betharram

64800

🏠 |●| Le Vieux Logis***

Route des Grottes; it's on the outskirts of the village, towards the caves.
☎05.59.71.94.87 Ⓕ05.59.71.96.75
Ⓦwww.hotel-levieuxlogis.com

Closed *Sun evening and Mon out of season; Mon lunchtime; 25 Jan–1 March; 25 Oct–4 Nov.* **Disabled access. TV. High chairs and games available. Swimming pool. Car park.**

Sizeable modern roadside hotel at the foot of the mountains, with a swimming pool and extensive grounds. An ideal place to relax. It's excellent value, with impeccable double rooms (several of them refurbished) for €55–60 with shower/wc or bath. Half board €56–60 per person. There are separate wooden chalets in the grounds where the rooms have balconies. Breakfast €8. The restaurant has been restored to create a delightful setting for the top-quality regional cooking – foie gras with fruits, sole with ceps, duck breast – and particularly good desserts. Menus €22–42.

Listrac-Medoc

33480

L'Auberge Médocaine

13 pl. du Maréchal Juin; it's in the centre on the N215.
Ⓣ05.56.58.08.86
Closed *Fri and Sun evening out of season.* **High chairs available.**

The patio, which is set back from the road, is a very pleasant place to eat good local dishes such as eels with parsley. The weekday lunch menu, €10.50, gets you a selection of starters from the buffet, a dish of the day, dessert and wine, and there are others at €15–35, with a children's menu at €8. Rooms are simple and clean, some with beamed ceilings. Rooms 2 and 3 are the quietest and cosiest. Doubles €28 with basin, €34 with shower and €39 with bath/wc; rates include breakfast. *Free coffee offered to our readers on presentation of this guide.*

Arcins

33460 (8km E)

Café-restaurant du Lion d'Or

From Listrac, take the D5 to Mouis, then take the road on the right. It's in the centre of the village.
Ⓣ05.56.58.96.79
Closed *Sun; Mon; July; New Year holiday period.* **Disabled access.**

The owner can be brusque, but the cooking is superb, with game in season and fish from the estuary prepared to local Médoc recipes. The €10.60 menu (not served Sat night) offers starter, main course, cheese, dessert and a half-litre of country wine. Dishes of the day are good: roast lamb, beef *tournedos*, liver *à l'anglaise*, or a simple omelette. À la carte, expect to pay less than €30.

Lurbe-Saint-Christau

64660

Au Bon Coin***

Route d'Arudy; it's about 1km outside the village.
Ⓣ05.59.34.40.12 Ⓕ05.59.34.46.40
Ⓔthierrylassala@wanadoo.fr
Closed *Sun evening; Mon.* **Disabled access. TV. Swimming pool. Car park.**

A good, comfortable, modern hotel set in peaceful countryside in the foothills 300m from a spa. The swimming pool is across the (rarely used) road. Quiet double rooms €48–78; the largest have balconies with tables and chairs. In the restaurant they serve unusual dishes at reasonable prices, making best use of what is good at the market: cep pie, Pyrenees lamb with thyme flower, to name only a couple. Menus €23 (weekday lunchtimes) up to €59. Half board, compulsory in July and Aug, costs €100 per person, €115 for a room with balcony overlooking the pool.

Mauleon-Licharre

64130

Hôtel Bidegain**

13 rue de la Navarre, opposite the château.
Ⓣ05.59.28.16.05 Ⓕ05.59.19.10.26
Ⓔhotel-bidegain@wanadoo.fr
Closed *Sun evening and Mon out of season.* **TV. Pay car park.**

One of the oldest and most beautiful town-centre hotels, once inhabited by the smart set, has undergone a renaissance. Pierre and Martine Chilo have taken this place in hand and have very quickly turned it into the best gourmet restaurant in town. You'll find cod terrine with a spicy pimento paste smeared on good bread, barbecued beef and chocolate soufflé on the €30 menu; on the cheapest at €15 (in the week) there are delicious dishes such as shin of veal and lamb's sweetbreads. Double rooms go for €46–54 with shower/wc or bath, depending on the season.

Mimizan-Plage

40200

Hôtel-restaurant Atlantique

38 av. de la Côte-d'Argent; it's on the north end of the beach, close to the town centre.
☎05.58.09.09.42 Ⓕ05.58.82.42.63
Ⓦwww.hotelatlantique.landes.com
Restaurant closed *Wed lunch (except in summer); 10–30 Jan; 1–15 Oct (hotel remains open).* **Disabled access. TV. High chairs available. Pay car park.**

This modest and friendly family establishment stands on the seafront but enjoys only a limited sea view. The façade of the old wooden building is intact and they've built a thirty-room modern hotel on the back. Double rooms €30–48, according to the degree of comfort. The best rooms are in the main house, and four of them have a sea view. Menus €9–21; there's a children's menu for €8. Simple, nourishing dishes include duck breast with foie gras and balsamic vinegar, scallop salad with mango, grilled fish with garlic butter, and chicken with prawns. Half board, €32–47, is compulsory in July–Aug. *10% discount on the price of a room after two consecutive nights (except July–Aug) offered to our readers on presentation of this guide.*

Hôtel-restaurant L'Émeraude des Bois**

66–68 av. du Courant; take the D626, or it's a ten-minute walk from the centre.
☎05.58.09.05.28
Ⓔemeraudedesbois@wanadoo.fr
Closed *Oct to early April.* **TV. Car park.**

This hotel-restaurant is another good family establishment in a charming house surrounded by large trees and decorated in traditional style. Double rooms €43–59, depending on the season. Half board, compulsory in July and August, costs €46–51 per person – well worth it given the quality of the cooking. Excellent menus €15.30–28. Specialities include home-made foie gras, salmon tartare, cream of courgette soup, fish soup, sea bream soufflé with shellfish *coulis*, monkfish *à la provençale*, duck breast with honey, chocolate mousse and home-made *crême brûlée*. A great deal of care goes into the preparation and cooking. The veranda and terrace provide welcome shade in summer. *Apéritif on the house offered to our readers on presentation of this guide*

L'Airial

6 rue de la Papeterie. On the southern end of the beach.
☎05.58.09.46.54. Ⓕ05.58.09.32.10
Closed Nov–end March.

The building is nothing much to look at on the outside, but the interior is relaxing and quiet (no TV) and the rooms are meticulously kept and tastefully decorated – and you will wake up to the sound of birdsong. Ask for one at the back, with a balcony overlooking the garden. Double rooms €45–49, depending on the season. The owner is very friendly and will be more than willing to fill you in with details about the town and the region.

Le Patio

6 av. de la Côte-d'Argent.
☎05.58.09.09.10 Ⓕ05.58.09.26.38
Ⓦwww.le-patio.fr
Closed *Mon Oct–end March; Jan; Nov.* **TV. High chairs and games available. Swimming pool. Car park.**

It's advisable to book well in advance for this place because the oceanfront location means it gets full. Stunning little rooms, nicely furnished in Provençal style. Doubles with shower/wc are €59–90 depending on the season, or you could choose to stay in the quiet bungalows at the back near the swimming pool. *10% discount on a room (except 15 Sept–15 June) offered to our readers on presentation of this guide.*

L'Île de Malte

5 rue du Casino. Next to the Casino.
☎05.58.82.48.15
Disabled access.

There has long been a restaurant called *L'Île de Malte* on this spot, but this one is sparkling new. Since April 2003 a young team has taken up the challenge of offering sophisticated food all year round. They have attracted an equally young crowd, and the place is very lively at weekends and on fine days. Friendly service, and a large terrace (protected from the wind) with trendy furniture, ideal for having lunch or simply enjoying a drink. Menus from €12.50 (weekday lunchtime) to €30. A restaurant with great potential.

Lüe

40210 (22km NE)

Restaurant L'Auberge Landaise

In the village; take the D626.
☎05.58.07.06.13
Closed *Sun evening; Mon; Oct; 3 weeks in Jan.* **Car park.**

A jolly little inn where they serve a string of eight set menus to suit every pocket, from €9.50 (weekday lunchtimes) and from €17 up to €30. Unless you're a veggie, it's impossible not to find something you fancy: wood-pigeon or game stew, foie gras, duck gizzard salad, duck breast and duck *confit*, baby squid in ink or monkfish *à l'armoricaine*. The quality of Monsieur Barthet's cooking and the range of prices ensure a varied clientele, from VIPs to factory workers, all tucking into the delicious food.

Mont-de-Marsan

40000

Hôtel-restaurant des Pyrénées*

4 rue du 34ème R.I.
☎05.58.46.49.49 Ⓕ05-58-06-43-57
Ⓔhoteldespyrenees@wanadoo.fr
Closed *Sat lunch; Sun; 1st week in July.* **TV.**

You can't miss this wonderful old pink house. At lunchtimes – when there's a €10.50 menu – it's rather like a canteen for local workers. Other menus, €21–35, list good, simple, tasty dishes such as duck breast, foie gras, scallops and stuffed *aiguillettes*. When it's hot, the dining room's large bay windows are opened onto a terrace surrounded by trees and flowers. The rooms are attractive, particularly those which overlook the garden – the ones on the crossroads side are noisier, so make sure to call to reserve. Doubles €21 with hand-basin, €39 with shower/wc.

Hôtel-restaurant Richelieu**

Rue Wlérick; it's behind the theatre.
☎05.58.06.10.20 Ⓕ05.58.06.00.68
Ⓦwww.citotel.com/hotels/richelieu.html
Restaurant closed *Sat; Sun evening.* **TV. High chairs available. Pay car park. Disabled access.**

The only hotel in the town centre with a touch of style. The good-value doubles (€44.50–46) with bath are unremarkable and rather impersonal, but clean and quiet. There's a charming breakfast room and in the restaurant you get some of the best cooking in town. Weekday menu at €15, served for €22 on Sundays, then others at €27 and €29. They include tasty traditional dishes like wild mushroom ravioli, half-cooked duck foie gras terrine, roast milk-fed lamb, roast guineafowl with Armagnac, and iced nougat. *10% discount on a room (except July–Aug) offered to our readers on presentation of this guide.*

Chez Despons - Le Plumaçon

20 rue Plumaçon; it's at the foot of the train station steps. ☎05.58.06.17.56
Closed *evenings; Sun; 3 weeks in Aug.* **Disabled access.**

At weekday lunchtimes, there is a menu at €8, and others from €9.50 to €14; the latter includes a large buffet of salads and cooked meats and wine. Good family food – the kind you dream of finding on your travels through France. The €9.50 menu lists grilled entrecôte steak with house or green pepper sauce served with green beans or *frites*, a salad and dessert. Credit cards not accepted. *Free apéritif or coffee offered to our readers on presentation of this guide.*

Le Bistrot de Marcel

1 rue du Pont-du-Commerce.
☎05.58.75.09.71
Closed *Sun; Mon lunchtime; public holidays.* **Children's games available.**

Despite the name, this isn't an old-style bistro but a good restaurant with tasteful, modern decoration, fine cooking and a rather wonderful setting – there are two terraces with views over the Midouze, too. The cooking is defiantly representative of the Landes region and the chef uses excellent local produce. Try duck breast, foie gras, *confit*, mussels and so on. Weekday lunchtime menu at €8, then others for €14–25, including one at €21 specifically devoted to regional specialities. They've set aside a play area for kids.

Uchacq

40090 (4km NW)

Restaurant Didier Garbage

It's on the RN134, on the way to Sabres-Bordeaux.

Ⓣ05.58.75.33.66
Closed *Sun evening; Mon; Tues evening; 1st week in Jan; last fortnight in June.* **High chairs available. Car park. Disabled access.**

The chef moved to this small village restaurant – and all his customers followed. The dining room is a pleasant place in which to sit and enjoy his fine cooking (don't be put off by the slightly sloppy presentation). Recommended are pan-fried foie gras with figs, lamprey with leeks, duck *confit* and *tournedos* of pig's trotter with truffle oil. Weekday set menus in the bistro corner (which has a host of loyal regulars) at €11.50 and €20, and two others in the restaurant at €25 and €45. If you don't fancy these, you can just have a slice of country ham and a glass of wonderful local wine.

Montferrand-du-Périgord

24440

Hôtel-restaurant Lou Peyrol

La Barrière; it's on the D26.
Ⓣ and Ⓕ05.53.63.24.45
Ⓦwww.hotel-loupeyrol-dordogne.com
Closed *Wed lunchtime in April–June and Sept; 1 Oct–Easter.* **High chairs available. Car park.**

A pretty little country hotel with a restaurant run by Sarah and Thierry, a friendly Anglo-French couple who also run the snack bar across the road. It's a good base for a walking holiday, with simple, clean double rooms (nos. 7 and 8 offer a view of the gorgeous village of Montferrand) going for €35 with basin and up to €42 with shower/wc or bath. Good cooking, too: roast Barbary duck; omelettes with ceps, morels or girolles; chocolate and walnut gâteau. Menus €14–28.30. Reckon on €23 à la carte. *Apéritif on the house offered to our readers on presentation of this guide.*

Cadouin

24480 (7km N)

Auberge de Jeunesse

In part of the abbey, in the town.
Ⓣ05.53.73.28.78 Ⓕ05.53.73.28.79
Ⓦwww.fuaj.org
Closed *mid-Dec to early Feb.* **Car park.**

Stunning setting, inside a lovingly restored abbey with an adjoining park. The one- and two-person rooms are the old monks' cells, giving onto the cloister, and the other rooms are just as delightful. Reckon on €14.95 per person in a single, double or triple room; €12.40 in one with 4–7 beds. All have their own bathroom. Half board, at €20.95, is compulsory for groups. Packed lunch and meals (€8.50) available. A very friendly place.

Montfort-en-Chalosse

40380

Aux Tauzins**

It's on the D2 (the route to Baigts and Hagetmau).
Ⓣ05.58.98.60.22 Ⓕ05.58.98.45.79
Closed *Sun evening; Mon (except the 1st fortnight in Aug); Jan; 1st fortnight in Oct.* **TV. Swimming pool. Car park.**

A fine example of a traditional hotel and restaurant, but with some welcome modern facilities – such as the pool. The owners have been hotel-keepers for three generations, so the establishment has a comfortable family feel with old-style bedrooms overlooking the grounds; it's wonderfully peaceful. Doubles €51–54; breakfast €7. The bright restaurant has a view over the valley. Dishes are from the region: *tournedos* Landais with liver and ceps, liver with apples and grapes, *fricassée* of monkfish and scallops with ceps. Menus €18 (except weekends) and €27–34.50. *10% discount on a room (Nov–Feb) offered to our readers on presentation of this guide.*

Montignac

24290

Hôtel-restaurant Bellevue

Regourdou; it's on the Lascaux road, after the caves at the top of the hill.
Ⓣ05.53.51.81.29
Closed *evenings; Sat; 1 week in June; 1 week in Oct; 3 weeks in Dec–Jan.* **Disabled access. Car park.**

Located close to the Lascaux caves, with superb views from its bay windows and terrace, this place is a restaurant with a few rooms. It serves decent food with a regional bent: chicken *confit* and *enchaud*, baked loin of pork, pig's trotters with garlic and truffles, gizzard salad, cep mushroom omelette. Prices are reasonable – a weekday menu for €10 and others €13–23. Rooms €34–40. Reservations recommended on Sundays.

🏠 |●| Hostellerie La Roseraie***

11 pl. d'Armes.
☎05.53.50.53.92 Ⓕ05.53.51.02.23
Ⓦwww.laroseraie.fr.st
Closed *lunchtime (except weekends in mid-season); 1 Nov–Easter.* **TV. High chairs and cots available. Swimming pool.**

A solid, elegant nineteenth-century town house on the place d'Armes. The staircase is wooden and there are several small sitting rooms. The rooms, costing €70–130, are exquisite; though each is different, all have en-suite bathrooms. It feels more like an old-style guest house or a family *pension* than a stylish three-star establishment – they even cork your unfinished wine and leave it on the table for the next meal. The small, enclosed grounds have high walls so it's easy to imagine you're out of town, and behind the swimming pool you'll find the rose garden the hotel is named after. The restaurant – which has a delightful terrace – serves sophisticated local dishes, adroitly prepared and reasonably priced: foie gras with asparagus and vegetables, glazed free-range guinea-fowl in langoustine broth. Set menus €21–40. Half board is compulsory from July until the end of September, as well as at weekends and on public holidays (€75–100 per person).

|●| L'Auberge de l'Oie Gourmande

La Grande Béchade; take the Lascaux road, turn left after 500m and it's out in the fields.
☎05.53.51.59.40
Closed *Sun evening and Mon out of season; Jan to mid-Feb.*

This place is somewhat off the tourist track. The ample dining room has stone walls and they set tables out on the terrace in summer. Menus at €14 and €22. Try the *aumônière* made with *cabécou*, a sweet and salty turnover with cheese. The delicious desserts are to die for. Fine, creative Périgord cuisine that's a lovely combination of tradition and modern invention. Good prices, too: the €14 menu is particularly good value. Attentive service.

Saint-Amand-de-Coly

24290 (8km E)

🏠 |●| Hôtel-restaurant Le Gardette**

In the village.
☎05.53.51.68.50 Ⓕ05.53.51.04.25
Ⓦhotelgardette.free.fr
Closed *1 Oct to Easter.* **High chairs available. Car park.**

Two pale stone houses overshadowed by a fantastic church. Quiet, modernized rooms at reasonable prices – €29–36 depending on facilities and the season. Some have a balcony with a view of the abbey. The restaurant across the lane has a few small tables in one corner – the owner cooks for the local schoolchildren during term time. For taller customers, set menus are €15–23.50, offering salads and dishes from the southwest including omelette with cep mushrooms or truffles, duck breast and *confit*. In summer, it's advisable to book during the classical music festival. *10% discount on a room (except July–Aug) offered to our readers on presentation of this guide.*

Sergeac

24290 (8.5km SW)

|●| Restaurant L'Auberge du Peyrol

It's on the D65, between Montignac and Les Eyzies.
☎05.53.50.72.91
Ⓦwww.dordogne24.com
Closed *Mon (except July–Aug); Dec–Feb. In high season the restaurant is open weekday lunchtimes and lunch and evenings at the weekend.* **Disabled access. Car park.**

A traditional stone-built inn standing on its own just outside a quaint little village. A large bay window looks out over the lovely Vézère valley. The fine rustic restaurant has a big fireplace where they smoke fillets of duck breast. Jeanine concocts rare country dishes – fresh goose liver, baked loin of pork, pig's trotters with garlic and truffles, duck liver *confit*, duck breast with Périgueux sauce, walnut salad, Sarlat-style potatoes, truffle omelettes. Menus €12–35. It's best to book. Credit cards not accepted. *Apéritif on the house offered to our readers on presentation of this guide.*

Chapelle-Aubareil (La)

24290 (12km S)

Hôtel-restaurant La Table du Terroir**

From Montignac take the road to Lascaux II, from where it's signposted.
05.53.50.72.14 05.53.51.16.23
Open *only at lunch (evenings May–Nov); 20–28 Dec.* **Disabled access. TV. Swimming pool. Car park.**

The Gibertie family have developed a tourist complex around their smallholding, deep in the country. The restaurant is on a hill 100m from the hotel; midway between them there's a swimming pool with views over the countryside. The buildings are new, but in traditional Périgord style, and they blend well with their surroundings. Rooms are pleasant, and the rates €46–61 with shower/wc or bath (depending on the season) include breakfast. Half board, compulsory from 10 July to 31 August, costs €48 per person per night. Set menus, €13.70–33, list regional cooking, based on farm produce: sliced duck, duck *confit* and so on. Reckon on about €22 à la carte. They can even make you a packed lunch. Credit cards not accepted. *Apéritif on the house offered to our readers on presentation of this guide.*

Navarrenx

64190

Hôtel-restaurant du Commerce**

Place des Casernes.
05.59.66.50.16 05.59.66.52.67
www.hotel-du-commerce.fr
Closed *Jan.* **TV. High chairs and games available.**

One of the oldest houses in Navarrenx. They light a fire in the large fireplace in the foyer at the first sign of cold weather. Pleasant rooms – the nicest up in the attic – are €45 with shower/wc or bath. Wonderful Béarn flavours in the restaurant, which has plush surroundings, or there's a large shady terrace for the summer. Menus are very reasonably priced: €11 for the weekday lunch one and others at €16–25. Try the foie gras, salmon steak with *piperade*, duck *confit* and chocolate *fondant*. *Free coffee offered to our readers on presentation of this guide.*

Nérac

47600

Aux Délices du Roy

7 rue du Château; on the place de la Mairie.
and 05.53.65.81.12
Closed *Wed.*

A small, nicely decorated dining room provides the setting for inviting food that has earned a loyal following, based on a winning combination of tradition, subtle flavours and high-quality produce. The menus at €16, 30, 45 and 60 (children's menu at €9.20) include unusual dishes: snails with Vire *andouille* and crisp cabbage, a whole duck's breast with honey and an array of fish and seafood recipes, including a Mediterranean touch, with the Provençal tuna. Attentive, polite service. The wine list features regional wines. *Apéritif on the house offered to our readers on presentation of this guide.*

Francescas

46600 (13km SE)

Le Relais de la Hire

From Nérac take the D930 for 10km towards Condom, then left onto the D112.
05.53.65.41.59
www.perso.wanadoo.fr/la.hire
Closed *Sun evening; Mon; 1st week in Nov.* **High chairs and games available. Disabled access.**

This restaurant, set in a stunning eighteenth-century manor house with a beautiful terrace, has a peaceful atmosphere. After working with Robuchon at the *Ritz* and running the kitchens at the *Carlton*, Jean-Noël Prabonne returned to Gascony. He is fussy about buying from local suppliers when creating his masterful dishes: Albret artichokes with a soufflé of foie gras, zander with a crust of *fines herbes*, roast squab with foie gras, morel with ravioli and *fricassée* of asparagus. Menus €23–53; it costs around €40 à la carte, and there's a children's menu for €13. Pleasant reception from Mme Prabonne and attentive service. *Apéritif on the house offered to our readers on presentation of this guide.*

Saint-Maure-de-Peyriac

47170 (17km SW)

Restaurants Duffau-les 2 Gourmands

Rue Principale; from Nérac take the D656.

Ⓣ and Ⓕ 05.53.65.61.00
Closed *evenings; Sat; early Feb.*

At lunchtime during the week this place is like many others, with a clientele of travelling salesmen, local workers and lost tourists – though the food is better than average and dishes are substantial. The all-inclusive menus at €10 (during the week), €23 and €26 include soup, terrine or omelette as typical starters. But Sunday lunch is a different story: the restaurant is a magnet for gourmands so you have to book in advance. The chef has worked at the *Ritz* and *Lasserre* (two of the very best kitchens in Paris) and on Sundays he and his associates give flight to their skill and imaginations at prices that would be unthinkably cheap in the capital. Dishes change according to the season, but are typical of the best of the southwest.

Nontron

24300

Hôtel-restaurant Pélisson**

3 pl. Alfred-Agard
Ⓣ 05.53.56.11.22 Ⓕ 05.53.56.59.94.
Ⓦ www.hotels-restau-dordogne.org /pelisson
Closed *Sun evening (Oct–May).* **TV. High chairs available. Disabled access. Swimming pool.**

Right in the town centre, this grand-looking hotel, with an elegant if somewhat austere façade, conceals a pretty garden and lovely pool. The old-fashioned rooms are reasonably priced and, round the back at least, very quiet. Doubles €45–53.50, with shower/wc or bath. Family atmosphere (it has been in the hands of the Pélissons for several generations). Huge opulent, rustic dining room with beautiful crockery (from a nearby factory) and a terrace giving onto the garden. The traditional food has earned a great reputation: baby rabbit salad with slithers of foie gras, sole *cassolette* with ceps, *tête de veau* with vinaigrette, *aiguillettes* of beef with *pécharmant*, all at reasonable prices. Menus at €15, except Sun, then €22–47. Interesting wine list. *10% discount on a room (Oct–May, after two consecutive nights) offered to our readers on presentation of this guide.*

Oloron-Sainte-Marie

64400

Hôtel de la Paix**

24 av. Sadi-Carnot; it's opposite the train station.
Ⓣ 05.59.39.02.63 Ⓕ 05.59.39.98.20
Ⓦ www.hotel-oloron.com
Closed *Sun (except 1 July–15 Sept); 15 Oct–15 Nov.* **TV. Car park.**

The new owner has made visible changes to this place: some of the rooms have already had a makeover with double glazing and new beds and linen. All the rooms are huge and light. Doubles €34–38 with shower and €41 with bath. Breakfast €5.

Relais Aspois**

Route du col-du-Somport; take the D55 and the N134, in the direction of Zaragoza and the Aspe valley.
Ⓣ 05.59.39.09.50 Ⓕ 05.59.39.02.33
Ⓦ wwwrelais-aspois.com
Closed *Mon lunchtime; 2nd fortnight in Nov.* **TV. High chairs and games available. Car park.**

The dining room here is full of character, with slate tiles, bare stone and beams and, in cool weather, a fire crackling in the hearth. Set menus are €16–30 – try Béarnaise vegetable broth, foie gras or *confit* of duck leg. They also prepare good regional dishes: ceps with parsley, *garbure* (thick soup), Basque tripe pâté, trout, duck breast with ceps. Double rooms with bath at €50; some of them have fabulous views of the Pyrenees. *Apéritif on the house offered to our readers on presentation of this guide.*

Esquiule

64400 (12km W)

Chez Château

Place du Fronton.
Ⓣ 05.59.39.23.03 Ⓕ 05.59.39.81.97
Closed *Sun evening; Mon; 15 Feb–15 March.* **Disabled access. TV. High chairs and games available.**

This is a fantastic place and the food is something else. Bernard Houçourigaray's cheapest menu lists *garbure*, trout with parsley, duck *confit* and a strawberry soup. Or you can order a *garburade*; as you dig down to the bottom of the dish you uncover duck drumsticks, chunks of ham, duck meat *confit*. If you're in a mind to treat yourself, opt for the marble cake of boiled chicken and liver or bass on braised cabbage and chicory mixed with orange zest. Seasonally changing menus cost €9.15 (weekday lunchtime) and then €14–43, and there's a superb wine list at more than reasonable prices. The dining room is country-inn in style and the hosts are from the area – which explains why the portions are so big. Another option, even better value, is to eat in the bar with the villagers. The innkeeper is young, energetic (like his friendly team), attentive and chatty. This is the place to brush up on your Basque – Esquiule's population is exclusively from that area. Double rooms with shower/wc at €35.10. *Apéritif on the house offered to our readers on presentation of this guide.*

Orthez

64300

Hôtel-restaurant Au Temps de la Reine Jeanne**

44 rue du Bourg-Vieux; it's opposite the tourist office.
☎05.59.67.00.76
Closed *Sun evening (Oct–April); 2 weeks in Feb.* **Disabled access. TV. High chairs available.**

A peaceful and quiet hotel with lovely, tasteful rooms overlooking the patio. Doubles with shower/wc or bath €45–49. The restaurant is a pleasant surprise: the décor is modest but the cuisine is opulent and modestly priced – fresh liver with figs, foie gras terrine with artichokes, joint of monkfish with bacon, duck cassoulet, Béarn black pudding on split bread, and suckling pig. Weekday lunchtime menu at €9 and another at €26. Perfect service. Occasional live jazz. *Liqueur on the house offered to our readers on presentation of this guide.*

Pau

64000

Le Postillon**

10 cours Camou; it's five minutes from the centre, two minutes from the château and just by the place de Verdun.
☎05.59.72.83.00
Ⓦwww.hotel-le-postillon.fr
Closed *Christmas–1 Jan.* **Disabled access. TV.**

A hotel in the neo-Romantic style. There's a little flower garden in the courtyard and a trickling fountain. Doubles with shower/wc or with bath €41–44; breakfast €5.50. A good place, particularly given the value for money. *10% discount on a room (in July–Aug) offered to our readers on presentation of this guide.*

Hôtel-restaurant Le Commerce**

9 rue du Maréchal-Joffre; it's opposite the Préfecture de Police.
☎05.59.27.24.40 Ⓕ05.59.81.83.74
Ⓔhotel.commerce.pau@wanadoo.fr
Restaurant closed *Sun and public holidays, except for groups.* **TV. High chairs available.**

Traditional hotel in the centre of town, with a certain charm and a warm welcome. Comfortable, soundproofed double rooms at €46. with shower/wc or bath; €6 per extra person. Half board at €60.50 per person. No lift. There's a bar and a fine restaurant with rustic décor with walls built from smooth stones. Menu €13.80; reckon on around €20 à la carte. Specialities include fillet *mignon* with morels, sole with ceps and duck breast with prawns. Pleasant courtyard terrace with good service. *10% discount on a room (for two consecutive nights on a weekend) offered to our readers on presentation of this guide.*

Don Quichotte

30–38 rue Castetnau.
☎05.59.27.63.08
Closed *Sat lunchtime; Sun; Mon lunchtime.*

One of the cheapest restaurants of quality in Pau – you can eat well for €8. They list fifteen dishes (including tapas, paella and zarzuela) for derisory prices and three lunchtime *plats du jour* at €7.80, including wine. An €8 menu features pork specialities; chorizo, *boudin blanc*, ham and so on; other options include *parrillada* of fish or pork, *axoa* of veal and undercut of beef. Takeaway dishes at €5.80. *Sangria on the house offered to our readers on presentation of this guide.*

Restaurant La Brochetterie

16 rue Henri-IV; it's near the château, opposite the church.
☎05.59.27.40.33
Ⓔeric.freyer1@lybertysurf.fr
Closed *Sat lunchtime; Mon; 15–30 Sept.*

Service until 11pm. Attractive stone-built

restaurant where they grill duck breast and meats over the fire. The lunchtime clientele consists mainly of people who work nearby. Weekday lunchtime menu at €10.40, then others at €14.50 and €19, with a children's menu for €8. À la carte you'll spend around €16; try grilled hake flambéed with anis, wild boar cutlets, the mixed grill, foie gras and various fresh salads. On Thursday nights don't miss the milk-fed lamb and the pork. A real treat, so it's best to book. *Apéritif on the house offered to our readers on presentation of this guide.*

|●| Le Majestic

9 pl. Royale.
Ⓣ05.59.27.56.83
Closed *Sun evening; Mon.* **Disabled access.**

Locally born chef Jean-Marie Larrère is a little ill-served by the dull surroundings – though the shady terrace on the Place Royale makes up for it on sunny days. In any case, Larrère produces remarkable dishes: hot foie gras with caramelized pears, cannelloni of *confit* or duck foie gras, salad of *croustillant* of pig's trotters with fresh morels, pot-roast pigeon with ceps, saddle of monkfish with a chorizo *jus* and mushrooms. Menus €16 (weekday lunchtimes) to €32. Reckon on €40 à la carte. Mme Larrère is very welcoming, and runs the dining room to perfection.

|●| Au Fin Gourmet

24 av. Gaston-Lacoste; it's opposite the station, about five minutes from the centre.
Ⓣ05.59.27.47.71 Ⓕ05.59.82.96.77
Closed *Sun evening; Mon; 1 week in Feb; 2 weeks end July–early Aug.* **High chairs and games available. Disabled access.**

This place, a firm favourite with the people of Pau, really lives up to its name. Quality cooking is on all the menus, which start at €18 (weekday lunchtimes) then go from €26 up to €58. Children's menu from €10. Dishes are finely prepared – highlights include the terrine of duck foie gras with Piquillo peppers and roast pigeon breast with five spices, apples cooked in duck fat and small caramelized turnips.

|●| Restaurant La Table d'Hôte

1 rue du Hedas.
Ⓣ and Ⓕ05.59.27.56.06
Closed *Sun; Mon; Christmas.*

In one of the oldest parts of Pau, Fabrice and Martine will welcome you like a regular to their impressive restaurant with stained-glass windows and beams. The richly flavoured cuisine is spot-on, and uses lots of quality produce: pan-fried foie gras with wine jam, duck pie with truffles, Gascon black pork and fresh fruit tart. Menus €19 (weekdays only) and €25, or around €30 à la carte. *Free coffee offered to our readers on presentation of this guide.*

Gan

64290 (8km S)

⌂ |●| Hostellerie L'Horizon**

Chemin de Mesplet.
Ⓣ05.59.21.58.93 Ⓕ05.59.21.71.80
Ⓦwww.hostellerie-horizon.com
Closed *Sun evening and Mon out of season; 2–31 Jan; 23–25 Dec.* **Disabled access (restaurant only). TV. High chairs and games available. Car park.**

A pink house with a garden full of flowers and a peaceful terrace, in extensive grounds. Attractive, well-equipped rooms for €60; some have great views. Half board at €68 per person. Sophisticated cuisine à la carte: duck foie gras, braised sole with foie gras, salmon trout with ceps, lamb sweetbreads with girolles and so on. There are menus priced €15–46 (weekday lunchtime). *10% discount on a room offered to our readers on presentation of this guide.*

Penne-d'Agenais

47140

|●| Restaurant L'Air du Temps

Mounet area.
Ⓣ05.53.41.41.34
Closed *Sun evening; Mon; 1 week in Jan; 1 week in Nov.*

While her husband is away working in Paris, Martine Harasymezuk unassumingly but efficiently runs this old farm, brilliantly restored in a neo-rustic style. Delightful restaurant and terrace. Adventurous cooking that marries tradition (duck foie gras) and modern French (bass tartare with pears, sea-trout terrine with spinach). Weekday lunchtime menu (except public holidays) at €12.20, including a quarter bottle of Buzet. Friendly welcome, but the service is a little slack.

Périgueux

24000

Hôtel-restaurant du Midi**

18 rue Denis-Papin, opposite the train station.
Ⓣ05.53.53.41.06 Ⓕ05.53.08.19.32
Closed *Sat 20 Oct–15 April; Christmas–New Year.* **TV. Car park.**

A typical station hotel which has been completely renovated by the friendly young couple who run the place. Nice family atmosphere. Very clean modern rooms at €29 for a double with basin to €44 with bath; rooms at the back are bigger and quieter, although those at the front are fitted with double glazing. The restaurant is peaceful. Set menus €12.50–29; reckon on €20 à la carte. Traditional cooking with local dishes such as truffle omelette, caramelized duck with apples and the house speciality: *tête de veau* with vinaigrette. *Apéritif on the house offered to our readers on presentation of this guide.*

Les Berges de l'Isle

2 rue Pierre-Magne.
Ⓣ05.53.09.51.50 Ⓕ05.53.05.19.08
Closed *Sun evening; Mon. For Sat lunchtime, reserve 48hr in advance.* **High chairs and games available. Disabled access.**

This restaurant is in a picturesque spot – on the shore of the island opposite the cathedral – and they have the only waterside terrace in town. Unusual cuisine such as *cassoulet* with four different meats and walnut oil, soufflé of foie gras with *vigneronne* sauce and lampray with Bordelais sauce. Menus €12.50 (weekday lunchtime) and €15.50, as well as several combinations. Some wines are served by the glass. Friendly atmosphere. Reservations advised. *Free coffee offered to our readers on presentation of this guide.*

Restaurant Le 8

8 rue de la Clarté; it's next to the Saint-Front cathedral.
Ⓣ and Ⓕ05.53.35.15.15
Closed *Sun; Mon; 2 weeks in Feb; 2 weeks in Oct.*

Regional and creative dishes served in a sunny dining room – home-made foie gras or *croustillant* of duck are the star turns. The prices are steepish: set menus €14 (weekday lunchtime), €22.50, or around €22 à la carte. The owner has travelled widely, so the food is tinged with exoticism: grilled cauliflower and prawn pancake, grilled fresh cod and *tête de veau* poached in ginger. There's a courtyard and garden, and the cellar has been turned into a sitting room. Reservations recommended; it's a small place with a good reputation. Exhibitions by local artists and a garden at the back. A wonderful stopover on the way to Compostela. *Liqueur on the house offered to our readers on presentation of this guide.*

Restaurant Hercule Poireau

2 rue de la Nation; it's in a small street opposite the main door of the Saint-Front cathedral.
Ⓣ05.53.08.90.76
Closed *Sat; Sun; Christmas; 31 Dec–3 Jan.*

The name of this restaurant, an impressive sixteenth-century vaulted cellar, is a play on words – Inspector Hercule Poirot was fastidious about what he ate, while *poireau* means leek. The dishes revel in local tradition; the highlights include *andouillette*, veal *blanquette*, and, their speciality, a splendid duck Rossini with foie gras. The wine list is unusual in being divided into three main price bands. Combinations of main course and dessert (€18), starter and main course (€20); menus €22–42; à la carte, reckon on €30. *Apéritif on the house offered to our readers on presentation of this guide.*

Chancelade

24650 (3km NW)

Le Pont de la Beauronne**

4 rte. de Ribérac; it's 3 km from Périgueux, at the crossroads of the D710 and D39, on the way to Angoulême.
Ⓣ05.53.08.42.91 Ⓕ05.53.03.97.63
Closed *Sun evening; Mon lunchtime; Feb half-term; 20 Sept–15 Oct.* **TV. Car park.**

Service until 9.30pm. The crossroads doesn't exactly enhance the charm of the place, but the rooms are reasonable and well kept. Doubles with basin or shower €25, €37 with bath – try to get one at the back, looking onto the garden. There's a half-board option for €38. Family atmosphere. In the rustic-style dining room the cooking is straightforward, with an emphasis on the regional. Menus from €12 to €33. *Apéritif on the house offered to our readers on presentation of this guide.*

Marsac-sur-L'Isle

24430 (4km W)

|●| Restaurant Le Moulin du Golf

Route de Chancelade.
Ⓣ05.53.53.65.90
Closed *evenings, except by reservation.* **Car park.**

On a public golf course overlooked by glowering towers of council blocks. There are two dining rooms – the tiny one has an open fire – with tables covered with pretty linen cloths. The crowd of regulars create a family atmosphere. All the produce is market-fresh; try the pan-fried foie gras with apples or the omelette with ceps. For carnivores, there's an excellent rib of beef for two. And the home-made desserts are so delicious that you're tempted to lick your plate clean. Menu €12.50 or à la carte €15. *Free coffee or liqueur offered to our readers on presentation of this guide.*

Annesse-et-Baulieu

24430 (12km SW)

⌂ |●| Château de Lalande – Restaurant Le Tilleul Cendré***

Take the D3 in the direction of Gravelle then Saint-Astier.
Ⓣ05.53.54.52.30 Ⓕ05.53.07.46.67
Ⓦwww.chateau-lalande-perigord.com
Closed *11 Nov to mid-March.* **Restaurant closed** *Wed lunch.* **TV. High chairs and games available. Swimming pool. Car park.**

Situated in extensive grounds on the banks of the Isle, this is luxury without ostentation. You are welcomed with old-fashioned charm. The quiet and cosy rooms are attractively furnished and most have a river view. Doubles €53–85 with shower/wc or bath. The cuisine is resolutely regional and prepared to the most exacting standards: salmi of pigeon with truffle, liver with hot, spicy bread, lamb's sweetbreads with Marsala. Menus €24–49. There's a swimming pool down by the river. *Apéritif on the house offered to our readers on presentation of this guide.*

Sorges

24420 (23km NE)

⌂ |●| Auberge de la Truffe***

Take the N21.
Ⓣ and Ⓕ05.53.05.02.05
Ⓦwww.auberge-de-la-truffe.com
Closed *Sun evening in winter; Mon lunchtime (all year round).* **TV. High chairs and games available. Swimming pool. Car park.**

Good traditional food in a region famous for truffles. The restaurant is popular with local businesspeople, as well as tourists. Menus €16 (weekdays only) and €23–52. The cheaper ones include a self-service hors d'œuvre buffet and daily specials and are well worth checking out. On the more expensive menus you might find *gratin* of scallops with asparagus, grilled monkfish or stuffed trout *à l'ancienne* with *verjus*. There's a menu devoted to foie gras and another to truffles – *escalope* of warm foie gras with fruit, *marbré* of veal sweetbreads with truffle vinaigrette, *croustillant* of lamb with truffles. Though the inn is right on the road, the rooms look out onto the open countryside and some have a garden view. Doubles €47–62. Good breakfast buffet. *10% discount on a room offered to our readers on presentation of this guide.*

Réole (La)

33190

|●| Aux Fontaines

8 rue de Verdun
Ⓣ05.56.61.15.25.
Closed *Sun; Mon (except public holidays); 2nd fortnight in Nov.*

This restaurant set in an attractive old house on a hill is generally considered one of the best in the region. There are two large, light and airy dining rooms, with vaguely Provençal décor. The menus, at €15–42, offer excellent value for money and are served every day, including the weekend, apart from public holidays. The *escalope* of foie gras, accompanied by seasonal fruit, and duck, prepared in a variety of ways, are the main specialities, along with the poultry and egg dishes (the *brouillade* is delicious).

Sainte-Radegonde

33350 (26km N)

⌂ |●| Château de Sanse***

Ⓣ05.57.56.41.10 Ⓕ05.57.56.41.29.
Ⓔsanse@chateau-hotels.com
Closed *lunchtimes, Sun, Mon and Tues (but opens every day May–Sept for bookings); Feb.* **TV. High chairs and games available. Disabled access. Car park.**

A total of fourteen double rooms,

€90–100 with shower/wc, and €110–185 with bath (depending on the season). If this sounds expensive, just consider that you'll be sleeping in a superbly restored eighteenth-century château with magnificent décor (a successful fusion of traditional materials and high-tech facilities), set in a five-hectare park complete with a swimming pool. What is more, you will receive impeccable service and at night you can enjoy delicate cuisine served on the terrace. Menu at €26; reckon on €44 à la carte. A perfect place for a treat.

Ribérac

24600

Restaurant Le Chevillard

Gayet.
2km from Ribérac, on the Montpon-Bordeaux road (D708).
☎05.53.91.20.88.
Closed *Mon and Tues (except July to end Sept); Jan.* **Disabled access. Car park.**

Set in an old farmhouse, in the middle of a huge garden, this is a warmly welcoming restaurant decorated in tasteful rustic style and run by an effusive owner (a former travelling salesman). Menus at €11 (weekday lunchtime) and €16–31. Reckon on €25 à la carte. Wide range of dishes, particularly meat (grilled outside on the terrace) but also an array of fish. All the menus (apart from the €11 one) feature a superb buffet of oysters and a variety of extremely fresh shellfish. Fresh poultry bred on the farm and a dessert buffet.

Sabres

40630

L'Auberge des Pins***

Rue de la Piscine; take the road going right in the centre (coming from Bordeaux or Bayonne).
☎05.58.08.30.00 Ⓕ05.58.07.56.74
Ⓔaubergedespins@wanadoo.fr
Closed *Sun evening and Mon (out of season); Mon lunch (in season); fortnight in Jan; 1 week in Nov.* **TV. High chairs and games available. Disabled access. Car park.**

Large, traditional Landais house, with wooden walls, a wide roof and balconies laden with flowers. The family that runs it goes out of their way to satisfy their guests, starting with the bedrooms, with their beautiful furniture, charming knickknacks and comfortable beds. Doubles with shower/wc or bath €60–75. The lovingly prepared food lives up to the setting with a similar combination of the rustic and the sophisticated: *croustillant* of duck foie gras, stuffed squab roasted with risotto of baby vegetables, langoustine ravioli with ceps, strawberries marinated in orange skin and fromage blanc. Menus at €19 (except Sun) and €60–63. Children's menu at €12.20. *One breakfast per person or 10% discount on a room offered to our readers on presentation of this guide.*

Luglon

40630 (8km SE)

La Maison

Place de la Mairie.
☎05.58.08.33.34
Closed *Wed.* **Disabled access.**

A small, up-and-coming addition to the the area, run by a couple (Ludovine in the kitchen, Loïc waiting on tables). The cooking is creative, using both regional and more exotic ingredients. Elegant dining room offering exceptional value for money. Delicious pizzas or huge salads at €9. Weekday lunchtime menu at €10, then others at €18 and €19.

Saint-Émilion

33330

L'Auberge de la Commanderie**

Rue des Cordeliers.
☎05.57.24.70.19 Ⓕ05.57.74.44.53
Ⓦwww.aubergedelacommanderie.com
Closed *1 Jan–15 Feb.* **Disabled access. TV. Car park.**

A senior officer of the Order of the Knights Templar used to live here, and during the French Revolution the disgraced Girondins used it as a hiding place. Very little of this rich past is evident today in this comfortable and welcoming family hotel. Rooms in the main building are fairly traditional and pretty, while those in the annexe are starkly modern. Doubles €60–90 with shower or bath. There is also an apartment that sleeps four (€90).

Hôtel Au Logis des Remparts***

Rue Guadet.
☎05.57.24.70.43 Ⓕ05.57.74.47.44

Ⓔ logis-des-remparts@saint-emilion.org
Closed *mid-Dec to end Jan.* **TV. High chairs available. Swimming pool. Pay car park.**

A fine three-star in a very old building which has kept the original stone staircase to the entrance, the terrace and the garden bordering the ramparts. Doubles with shower/wc or bath, €68–150, depending on the season. Some rooms can sleep five people; half of them are being renovated, and an extension project is underway in the Gothic house next to the hotel. When the weather's fine, breakfast (which is substantial and very good – just try the cake) is served on the elegantly paved terrace or in the garden.

Saint-Estèphe

33250

Le Peyrat

It's in the port.
Ⓣ 05.56.59.71.43
Closed *Sun evening; second fortnight in Aug; Christmas.* **High chairs available. Disabled access.**

This restaurant is in the heart of the village. The boss is jovial and the cooking simple – home-made vegetable soup is a speciality – using fresh seasonal produce and eel, sturgeon and shad from the river. In summer, the terrace is a wonderful spot from which to enjoy the sunset. There's such a convivial atmosphere that you completely lose track of time. Menus €10.50, €15 and €32. The owner runs the Fête de l'Anguille (the eel festival) at the beginning of June, when the village comes into its own.

Saint-Jean-de-Luz

64500

Le Petit Trianon**

56 bd. Victor-Hugo.
Ⓣ 05.59.26.11.90 Ⓕ 05.59.26.14.10
Ⓔ lepetittrianon@wanadoo.fr
Closed *Jan.* **TV. High chairs available. Pay car park.**

This hotel is charming, simple, clean and unpretentious, and what's more, reasonably priced. The new owners have retained the family character of the place, while coming up with a few new ideas to make it more up-to-date and comfortable (double glazing in the rooms overlooking the street), and they are refurbishing and redecorating the rooms systematically. The third-floor rooms have sloping ceilings, which makes them rather romantic. Doubles €40–70, depending on facilities and season. Breakfast €6.50. Pretty private terrace. *10% discount on a room (Oct–March) offered to our readers on presentation of this guide.*

Hôtel Ohartzia**

28 rue Garat; it's in a little street between the church and the sea, 40m from the beach.
Ⓣ 05.59.26.00.06 Ⓕ 05.59.26.74.75
Ⓦ www.hotel-ohartzia.com
TV.

The façade is appealing with its Spanish ceramic flowerpots overflowing with pansies, geraniums and petunias. Inside, the peaceful garden seems far from the hubbub of summer crowds and it's perfect for breakfast. Most of the rooms are tastefully decorated. The ones on the first floor have rattan twin beds lacquered in navy blue while those on the third are more rudimentary – but the view of the Rhune is great compensation. Double rooms €56–75 with shower/wc and €62–84 with bath, depending on the season; breakfast included in room rate mid-July to mid-Sept. *Free fresh fruit juice with breakfast (except 12 July–31 Aug) offered to our readers on presentation of this guide.*

Hôtel La Devinière***

5 rue Loquin; it's 100m from the beach.
Ⓣ 05.59.26.05.51 Ⓕ 05.59.51.26.38
Ⓦ www.hotel-la-deviniere.com

A family house right in the middle of the old town. It's a haven of peace which makes you want to stay a while. There's a music room and even the cosily decorated rooms strike the right note. All the rooms are different and furnished with antique furniture, pictures and ornaments. Doubles €100–150 with bath/wc. *Free apéritif or coffee or fruit juice or fizzy drink offered to our readers on presentation of this guide.*

La Buvette des Halles

Boulevard Victor-Hugo; it's in the covered market.
Ⓣ 05.59.26.73.59
Closed *Mon in winter.*

There's a great atmosphere on market days. The oldest (more than 70 years) and smallest (three tables plus the terrace on warm days) restaurant in town. Jean Laborde prepares a fine dish of mussels, and the grilled sardines are delicious, too. Other specialities include grilled line-caught tuna with *piperade*, *axoa* of veal, and anchovy salad with garlic. Reckon on over €12 for a meal à la carte.

|●| Pil-Pil Enea

3 rue Sallagoïty; it's near the covered market and the post office.
☎05.59.51.20.80
Closed *Sun evening (except summer); Mon.*

The small dining room houses a dozen tables and a minimalist décor. The chef is king of line-caught hake – and it's super fresh because his wife, the only woman who owns a fishing boat in the port, is responsible for catching it. Her whole crew is female and off they sail to bring the fish back for Monsieur to cook. The choice of what to eat depends on what she lands. There's a set menu for €23; as well as hake, try salt cod or prawns. Reckon on €25 à la carte. The clientele is local and a mixture of fishermen and fishmongers and the chat is mainly about the price of fish.

Ciboure

64500 (1km S)

|●| Chez Mattin

Place de la Croix-Rouge.
☎05.59.47.19.52 Ⓕ05.59.47.05.57
Closed *Mon; Sun evening out of season; 8 Jan–20 Feb.*

Service until 9.30pm out of season and 10.15pm in season. One of the best-known fish restaurants in the area. The agreeable dining room is bright white with a few good pictures of the region on the wall. The place is famous for the "ttoro", a fish soup costing €19 per portion. It may seem expensive but on its own will do for a whole meal. All the fish landed at the quay make an appearance on the menu unless you fancy deep-fried, breadcrumbed tripe for €8 or pig's cheeks with potato terrine for €12. In summer this place gets very busy. *Apéritif on the house offered to our readers on presentation of this guide.*

Ascain

64310 (7km SE)

|●| Hôtel Oberena***

Route des Carrières; it's on the edge of the village going towards the Saint-Ignace pass.
☎05.59.54.03.60
Ⓦwww.oberena.com
Closed *12 Nov–20 Dec; 3 Jan–3 Feb.* **Disabled access. TV. Swimming pool. Car park.**

The hotel is in huge grounds with views of the mountains. It has 25 rooms and is run by an energetic woman who is systematically doing them up. Doubles with shower/wc or bath €55–87 – the priciest have a balcony. An alternative is to book one of the chalets in the garden for €80–110, depending on the season (they sleep four, but have no kitchen). There's a heated indoor pool, another outside, a Jacuzzi, a sauna and an exercise room. Buffet breakfast €6–10. *Free apéritif or fruit juice or fizzy drink offered to our readers on presentation of this guide.*

Sare

64310 (13.5km E)

|●| Hôtel Pikassaria**

It's just outside Sare in the hamlet of Lehenbiscay and is well signposted.
☎05.59.54.21.51 Ⓕ05.59.54.27.40
Ⓦwww.logis-de-france.fr
Closed *Wed out of season; 1 Jan–1 April; 11 Nov–31 Dec.* **Disabled access. TV. High chairs and games available. Car park.**

Located in breathtaking countryside, this place has built quite a reputation for itself. However, with its success it's lost that touch of intimacy which is the charm of country hotels. Big, bright rooms with shower/wc or bath €42–46; some have terraces. Half board is compulsory from mid-July to mid-Sept; €43–46 per person. The local specialities in the restaurant make the punters come back time after time – try the cep omelette, salt cod *à l'espagnole*, pigeon stew, fruit tart or chocolate *fondant* – and you'll understand why. Menus €20–27. There's a terrace for sunny days. Reservations advised. *Apéritif on the house offered to our readers on presentation of this guide.*

|●| Hôtel Arraya

It's on the village square.
☎05.59.54.20.46 Ⓕ05.59.54.27.04
Ⓦwww.arraya.com
Closed *Sun evening and Mon lunch (4 April–28 June/19 Sept–25 Oct), except public holidays; 2 Nov–27 March.* **TV. High chairs available. Car park.**

This place was originally an old coaching

inn on the pilgrim route to Santiago de Compostela, then it became a presbytery in the nineteenth century before being bought by the Fagoaga-Arraya family. Now it's a hotel again and the rooms are decorated very attractively. Some are very spacious, some are at garden level, while others have balconies. Superb period furniture and hand-sewn bed linen decorated with the Basque symbol of a flaming torch. Doubles €62–92; breakfast €8. The €15 menu (not Sun) is served only in July and August, on the terrace, and there are gastronomic menus at €21–31 with a children's menu at €9.50. *Free house apéritif offered to our readers on presentation of this guide.*

🏃 |●| Restaurant Lastiry

It's on the village square.
Ⓣ05.59.54.20.07 Ⓕ05.59.54.20.07
Closed *Tues; Mon and Tues out of season; Jan; 1st week in July; 1st week in Sept; 2nd week in Nov.* **High chairs available.**

Guillaume Fagoaga is still very young but he has a passion for his craft, his region and its produce. With his brother Jean in charge front-of-house, he opened this restaurant, which in just a few months became the talk of the area – perhaps because both brothers are equally perfectionist in their approach. Guillaume's dishes are prepared with artistry and invention and they change as often as the produce is available – house classics include creamed salt cod, fresh fish, duck foie gras, cep risotto with foie gras and chargrilled squid. Menus €15 and €26. *Liqueur on the house offered to our readers on presentation of this guide.*

Saint-Jean-Pied-de-Port

64220

🏃 ⌂ |●| Central Hôtel**

1 pl. du Général-de-Gaulle.
Ⓣ05.59.37.00.22 Ⓕ05.59.37.27.79
Closed *Tues (out of season); 10 Dec–1 March.* **TV.**

Rooms here are luxurious and impeccably clean; they cost €56 with shower and €64 with bath. Ask for one with a view of the Nive. Breakfast €8. Similarly high standards in the restaurant, which offers set menus at €19–41 plus a children's menu for €9. The dining room has charm and the cooking is first-rate: salmon, roast milk-fed lamb, lamb sweetbreads with *piquillos*, soufflé with Izarra (a liqueur similar to Chartreuse), home-made Basque gâteau. Good welcome and attentive service. *Free coffee offered to our readers on presentation of this guide.*

⌂ |●| Les Pyrénées***

19 pl. du Général-de-Gaulle.
Ⓣ05.59.37.01.01 Ⓕ05.59.37.18.97
Ⓔhôtelpyrénées@wanadoo.fr
Closed *Mon evening Nov–March; Tues excluding July–Aug; 6–28 Jan; 20 Nov–22 Dec.* **TV. High chairs available. Swimming pool. Pay car park.**

On paper, €92–220 might seem a lot to pay, but this is a high-class hotel, the rooms are impeccable and there's a very pleasant indoor pool. The chic restaurant, which has a well-established reputation throughout the Basque country, offers fine cuisine artistically conjured from local produce – delicious *piperade*, peppers stuffed with cod, foie gras, hot oysters with "caviar" of salmon, mullets grilled with peppers, sweetbreads with leeks and ceps, lamb sweetbreads with ceps and remarkable desserts and sorbets. Menus €40–88. Reckon on €78 à la carte.

|●| Restaurant Arbillaga

8 rue de l'Église; it's inside the fortified part of town.
Ⓣ05.59.37.06.44 Ⓕ05.59.37.12.88
Closed *Tues evening and, out of season, Wed; 1st fortnight in June; 1st fortnight in Oct.*

Grand dining room in a stunning location between the fortified walls and the old houses. Delicious food is served in generous portions, both on the set menus €13 and €19.50, plus, in winter only, €25.92) and à la carte – try scrambled eggs with truffle and foie gras, *garbure Béarnaise*, *Txauguro* (stuffed crab), scallops with smoked bacon or spit-roast milk-fed lamb. Spirited welcome and service in an intimate atmosphere.

Saint-Michel

64220 (4km S)

⌂ |●| 🏃 Hôtel-restaurant Xoko-Goxoa**

From Saint-Jean-Pied-de-Port take the D301.
Ⓣ05.59.37.06.34 Ⓕ05.59.37.34.63

Closed *Tues out of season; mid-Jan to early March.* **Car park.**

This is a large traditional house surrounded by greenery. Most of the rooms look straight onto the countryside, but they are rather basic and crying out for refurbishment. Double rooms €32–39 with shower/wc or bath. Half board at €38 in July–Aug. Atmospheric rustic-style dining room and no-nonsense, good-value cooking. Set menus, €11 (not Sun) to €25, feature specialities such as fish soup with prawns, trout *etxekoa*, parsleyed ceps, salad *gourmande* and so on. The à la carte prices are very reasonable. Large terrace with a wonderful panoramic view. *Apéritif on the house offered to our readers on presentation of this guide.*

Bidarray

64780 (15km NW)

Hôtel-restaurant Barberaenea**

Place de l'Église; take the D918.
05.59.37.74.86 05.59.37.77.55
www.hotel-barberaenea.fr
Closed *15 Nov–15 Dec.* **Disabled access. TV. High chairs available. Car park.**

A very old country inn belonging to the Elissetche family, which has been beautifully renovated. Cheery welcome and attractive, charming rooms with white walls, period furniture and shining parquet floors. They look out onto the square and its twelfth-century church; the newer rooms are clean and comfortable with views of the countryside. Doubles €30.50 with basin, €45–55 with shower/wc. In the restaurant you can get appetizing dishes including salad of warm cod with garlic sauce, thick beef stew, and bread-and-butter pudding. *Menu du randonneur* €15.50, *menu du terroir* €21.50, and a children's menu for €7.50. *Apéritif on the house offered to our readers on presentation of this guide.*

Auberge d'Iparla

Place du Fronton; take the D918.
05.59.37.77.21.
Closed *Wed; Jan–Feb.*

Earthquake in Bidarray: the village inn has fallen into the hands of Alain Ducasse, France's most fêted chef. He answered the call of some of his similarly lauded colleagues to bring staff from his best restaurants to… sell sandwiches at €3. It is true that a little can go a long way, but putting Bidarray on a par with New York is a hard act to follow. At first sight, it doesn't look like anything's changed: it is still the same village bar, between the church and the town hall, opposite the *fronton* court, with its card and domino games. Still the same big room opening on to the mountain, even though it has been soberly but attractively redecorated; there's still a menu for €20, individual dishes at €15 and bottles of wine at less than €15. So what of the food? It's typical village inn fare: pepper omelettes, Basque tripe, *chipirones a la plancha*, flambéed woodpigeon in season. But everything has a touch of Ducasse; for example, he has added a few chickpeas to the tripe to eliminate the acidity; the omelettes are wonderfully moist. As for the blood pudding, it's based on a recipe from his friend Parra, while the ham comes from a little village in Aragon and the trout is purchased in Banka. Needless to say, the venture has proved a great success and it is essential to book.

Saint-Justin

40240

Hôtel de France**

Place des Tilleuls.
05.58.44.83.61 05.58.44.83.89
Closed *Sun evening; Mon; Thurs evening; 1 week in mid-April; mid-Oct to mid-Nov.* **TV.**

1930s-style décor in this hotel in the middle of a thirteenth-century fortified town. Peace and quiet reigns here, along with a traditional family atmosphere. Lovely rooms at €38 with shower/wc and €46 with bath. The restaurant is at the back. The chef comes up with delicious flavours and prepares everything from fresh produce: salad of duck gizzards and hearts, prawns with diced cep and ginger with green chilli, suckling pig with ratatouille, duck breast with mushrooms and foie gras. The house speciality is goose simmered in red wine. Set menus €12, except Sun, then €21–45. Friendly welcome and relaxed atmosphere, although the service is a bit slow. Packed in summer.

Saint-Macaire

33490

L'Abricotier

It's on the N113 between Langon and La Réole.

☎05.56.76.83.63 ⓕ05.56.76.28.51
Closed *Mon; Tues evening; 12 Nov–15 Dec.* **TV. Car park.**

This restaurant would be one of the most beautiful in the region were it not on the edge of the N113. At least the little dining room looks out onto the terrace at the back – lovely when the sun is out. The kitchen turns out imaginative dishes including *cassolette* of snails with *confit* of pig's trotters and lamb chops with aioli. Menus at €18 and €25–35. Very good wine list – exclusively Bordeaux. A handful of en-suite rooms for €46. *Free fruit juice or fizzy drink offered to our readers on presentation of this guide.*

Les Feuilles d'Acanthe**

5 rue de l'Église.
☎05.56.62.33.75
ⓦwww.feuilles-dacanthe.fr
Closed *Jan.* **TV. Disabled access. Swimming pool.**

A ravishing, brand-new hotel offering remarkable value for money. It occupies a sixteenth-century building that's been renovated to perfection with rough-hewn stone walls and beams. The large rooms have been intelligently decorated and the bathrooms are sparkling. There are twelve rooms (doubles €60–115), but it's best to reserve in advance because they fill up quickly. The restaurant-crêperie provides simple, local dishes at fair prices.

Saint-Palais

64120

Hôtel-restaurant de la Paix**

33 rue du Jeu-de-Paume.
☎05.59.65.73.15 ⓕ05.59.65.63.83
Closed *Fri evening; Sat lunchtime (except July–Aug); Sun evening; 1st week in July; 27 Dec–27 Jan.* **Disabled access. TV.**

You'd never think from the outside that this hotel has been around for two hundred years – it's been entirely rebuilt and has all mod cons. Rooms €48 with shower/wc or bath; breakfast €5.50. Good regional cooking, with a weekday menu at €11 and others €21–25. Dishes include lamb's sweetbreads with ham and ceps, *ttoro* (fish stew), eel and game in season. Pretty terrace in the summer. *Apéritif on the house offered to our readers on presentation of this guide.*

Salies-de-Béarn

64270

Au Petit Béarn**

Rue Bellecave.
☎05.59.38.17.42 ⓕ05.59.38.65.01
Hotel/restaurant closed *Feb half-term.* **Restaurant closed** *Wed and Sun, except for hotel guests.* **TV. Car park.**

The new, young owners decided to start renovations of this place by upgrading the rooms first so don't be put off by the atrocious wallpaper in the corridors. Especially since there's a labyrinth of corridors and they're all long. The rooms themselves are bright, clean and attractive. Double room with washbasin for €25, rising to €43 with shower/wc. In the restaurant, the dishes on the menus are simple but good quality – the salmon marinated in Salies salt is excellent, as is the duck with ceps and pears or the prawns flambéed in pastis. Set menus €10 (weekday lunchtimes only except out of season), €12 and €23, with a children's menu at €6.

Saint-Dos

64270 (8km W)

Auberge du Béarn

Place de l'Église.
☎05.59.38.40.38 ⓕ05.59.38.44.28
ⓔalain.darc@wanadoo.fr
Closed *Sun evening; Mon.* **TV. High chairs and games available.**

An authentic country inn in a charming little village of a hundred souls. It's on the pilgrim route to Santiago de Compostela. The bar is quite a meeting place for villagers and others from further afield. What a pleasure to sleep in proper sheets that have been dried in the fresh open air. Doubles at €27. Breakfast €4. The local cooking isn't expensive, and only fresh ingredients are used by the innkeeper/chef. Try the salmon or the chicken dishes. Weekday lunch menu €10, or others €19–36. À la carte around €25. Half board €26 per person. *10% discount on a room offered to our readers on presentation of this guide.*

Sarlat-la-Canéda

24200

Auberge de Jeunesse et Gîte d'Étape

77 av. de Selves (North). At the entrance to the town.
☎05.53.59.47.59 Ⓕ05.53.30.21.27
Closed *Jan. Reception of individual guests 6–8pm.*

A windfall just a stone's throw from the town centre. Sixteen beds spread over three dormitories. €10 per person on the first night, €9 on the following ones. It is also possible to put up a tent for €6 on the first night, then €5. Booking essential as it is often full – backpackers from 24 different countries have passed through here. Fully equipped kitchen available, but guests are responsible for its upkeep. Not open to people under age. Credit cards not accepted.

Hôtel les Récollets**

4 rue Jean-Jacques-Rousseau; it's in the middle of the medieval city.
☎05.53.31.36.00 Ⓕ05.53.30.32.62
Ⓦwww.hotel-recollets-sarlat.com
TV. Car park.

This place is in a quiet, picturesque lane away from the cars and the tourist crowds. Sarlat is an old town so it's good to stay in a hotel with a bit of history – this used to be the cloisters of a seventeenth-century convent. Today it's managed by a father-and-son team and you get a convivial welcome. The rooms have been tastefully refurbished; doubles with shower/wc cost €40–50, those with bath €60. A few look out onto a quiet courtyard where you have breakfast. No. 15 is particularly light and has a lovely view over the tiled rooftops in the old town, while no. 8 has elegant stone archways.

Hôtel Le Mas de Castel**

Sudalissant (South); 3 km from the town; take the D704 towards Souillac, then towards La Canéda; it is signposted.
☎05.53.59.02.59 Ⓕ05.53.28.25.62
Closed *11 Nov–Palm Sunday.* **TV. Disabled access. Car park. Swimming pool.**

An ideal base for a trip to the country, very close to Sarlat. Charming hotel at street level surrounded by greenery, built in the local style (pretty white stones, small stone outhouse). Warm welcome and attractive, comfortable rooms, recently refurbished with relaxing, pastel-coloured décor. Double rooms with shower/wc or bath €46–55. Nos. 2, 3, 4, 5 and 14 are bigger and have a terrace or a separate area giving on to the garden. No restaurant. *Apéritif on the house offered to our readers on presentation of this guide.*

Hôtel-restaurant La Maison des Peyrat**

Le Lac de la Plane; a bit out of the way, overlooking the east of the town, but it's well signposted; carry on for about 2km after the gendarmerie.
☎05.53.59.00.32 Ⓕ05.53.28.56.56
Ⓦwww.maisondespeyrat.com
Closed *15 Nov–1 April.* **Disabled access. TV. Swimming pool. Car park.**

A seventeenth-century hermitage that has been converted and refurbished to become a charming hotel. The thoughtful décor makes the most of the old stonework, and the setting is very peaceful. Bright, spacious rooms with pretty bathrooms €47.30–77.30, depending on the season. Half board is also offered. Very charming welcome. Menu at €17.80, evenings only, exclusively for hotel guests. *Free coffee offered to our readers on presentation of this guide.*

Hôtel-restaurant Saint-Albert et Hôtel Montaigne**

10 pl. Pasteur and 11 rue Emile-Faure; behind the main post office.
☎05.53.31.55.55 Ⓕ05.53.59.19.99
TV. Pay car park.

Two hotels and one restaurant, close to the town centre. The staid façade of the *Montaigne* hides some pretty, well-equipped rooms (particularly those on the top floor, with their exposed beams). The décor is modern, but not unpleasantly so. There is a covered terrace where you can have breakfast. On the other side of the road, the *Saint-Albert* hotel-restaurant offers renovated rooms, with double glazing installed in those overlooking the street. Double rooms €48–56. The traditional fare served in the enormous dining room attracts elderly regulars: side of beef, duck sausage, ceps omelette, duck stew with walnut extract. Menus from €19–30. Bistro with dish of the day (around €10) at lunchtime on weekdays.

Hôtel de Compostelle***

64 av. de Selves; near the centre of town on the road to Montignac/Brives.
☎05.53.59.08.53 Ⓕ05.53.30.31.65
Ⓦwww.hotelcompostelle-sarlat.com

Closed *Sun lunchtime until 4.30pm; 11 Nov–30 March.* **Disabled access. TV.**

Excellent, large and pleasant rooms; doubles €54–62 with shower/wc or bath. A few have a glassed-in balcony but they look out onto the street. The quieter rooms at the back overlook a tiny garden. Families can go for the small suites with two bedrooms and bath. This hotel has deservedly just won itself three stars, after an extensive refurbishment: air-conditioning installed in the rooms, reception and lounge overhauled, cosy breakfast room giving on to the garden.

La Hoirie***

La Giragne; take the Souillac road out of Sarlat and it's well signposted.
ⓣ05.53.59.05.62 ⓕ05.53.31.13.90
ⓦwww.lahoirie.com
Closed *lunchtime; Mon out of season; 15 Nov–15 March.* **TV. High chairs and games available. Swimming pool. Car park.**

Some parts of the original thirteenth-century house remain, and a recent refurbishment has brought out the brilliance of the pale stone. There are large grounds with a pool so you can sunbathe and cool down afterwards. The rooms, costing €58–104, are spacious and more like comfortable apartments, and some of them have benefited from the refurbishment. The kitchen cooks everything fresh – look out especially for the *escalope* of foie gras in thin slices with pears in blackcurrant juice and the Rossini-style Aquitaine fillet with French fries in duck's fat. Menus €20–42. *Apéritif on the house offered to our readers on presentation of this guide.*

Le Présidial

6 rue Landry; it's behind the town hall.
ⓣ05.53.28.92.47 ⓕ05.53.59.43.84
Closed *Sun and Mon lunch; 15 Nov–1 April.*

Great gastronomic feats are accomplished in this restaurant, run by a charming couple. This jewel is their new enterprise and already it's become *the* place to eat in Sarlat. The building is classified as a historic monument and is a gorgeous house from 1552, set in a large, quiet garden in the old town. The dining room is very elegant and the terrace is the loveliest around. Menus at €19 at lunchtime, and then from €25 upwards. Reckon on €38–46. The cheapest menu offers great value for money, the others dishes like perfect duck foie gras, a nest of tagliatelle and lamb's sweetbreads with rosemary and beautifully cooked guineafowl supreme in pastry. An extensive wine list with fair prices. No reservations 20 July–25 August.

Roque-Gageac (La)

24250 (9km S)

Hôtel-restaurant La Belle Étoile**

Rue Principale; take the D46.
ⓣ05.53.29.51.44 ⓕ05.53.29.45.63
ⓔhotel.belle-etoile@wanadoo.fr
Restaurant closed *Mon and Wed lunchtimes; Nov–end March.* **TV.**

Charming, stylish hotel in a glorious setting in one of the most beautiful villages in France. The rooms are individually decorated and tastefully furnished. A few have a great view of the slow-moving Dordogne, but these are a bit noisy in the high season. Doubles €48–74. The elegant dining room has a vine-smothered terrace overlooking the river, and the food is excellent – the kitchen concentrates on the classics but adds the odd unexpected modern touch. Set menus from €23.

Domme

24250 (12km S)

Nouvel Hôtel**

Rue Maleville and Grande-Rue.
ⓣ05.53.28.38.67 or 05.53.28.36.81
ⓕ05.53.28.27.13
Closed *Jan–March.* **Restaurant closed** *Sun evening and Mon (except July–Aug).* **TV.**

A pretty stone house ideally situated in the centre of the old fortified town. Good prices for the area. The pleasant rooms cost €42–62. The restaurant, which has set menus starting at €15 up to €40, offers regional cuisine. Specialities include pan-fried scallops with ceps, foie gras, *confit* and breast of duck.

Marquay

24620 (12km NW)

Hôtel des Bories**

About 12km from Sarlat; from there, take the D47 for 2km, then the D6.
ⓣ05.53.29.67.02 ⓕ05.53.29.64.15
ⓔhotel.des.bories@wanadoo.fr
Closed *1 Nov–Easter.* **Restaurant closed** *Wed lunchtime.* **Disabled access. TV. Swimming pool. Car park.**

A delightful hotel in a very good location

– a nice village off the beaten track. It has a big garden, a swimming pool and a superb view. Bright, clean rooms from €31 with shower/wc to €60 with bath. Thirty-two of these have a corner sitting room, a big fireplace and a view, and some have separate rooms for children. Breakfast (€7.50) is served on the two terraces. Friendly welcome. The restaurant next door, now part of this establishment, has a good reputation. They serve dishes such as *aiguillette* of duck with ceps and foie gras. Menus €13–38. *10% discount on the most expensive rooms (March–June and Oct) offered to our readers on presentation of this guide.*

Paulin

24590 (24km NE)

La Meynardie

From Sarlat, go in the direction of Salignac-Eyvignes, then towards Archignac.
T 05.53.28.85.98 F 05.53.28.82.79
@ la-meynardie@wanadoo.fr
Closed *Tues (except July to mid-Sept); Wed; Dec to mid-Feb.* **Car park.**

An old farmhouse set deep in the country. The dining room, with its paved floor and massive fireplace dating from 1603, has been carefully restored and has a certain appeal. Courteous welcome, though the atmosphere's a little on the chic side. Weekday lunchtime menu at €12.20, then others at €19.10–47, are all based on traditional dishes, but include creative variations like *carpaccio* of duck breast and goose stew with Bergerac wine. Good desserts include an iced nougat with red fruit *coulis*. Sit out on the terrace in summer, or stroll through the chestnut tree forest after your meal. Best to book, especially for Saturday evening and Sunday lunch.

Laval-de-Jayac

24590 (25km NE)

Hôtel-restaurant Coulier**

It's in the village; take the D60.
T 05.53.28.86.46 F 05.53.28.26.33
W www.hotelcoulier.com
Closed *Fri evening and Sat out of season; 15 Nov to end Feb.* **Disabled access. TV. High chairs available. Swimming pool. Car park.**

You'll find this hamlet in an almost deserted part of darkest Périgord. The pretty converted farm buildings make a U-shape around a courtyard, on a hillock set well away from the road. The fairly small double rooms with shower/wc are scattered around the building; they go for €48–53. Half board is advised in July and August: €51 per person. The restaurant serves regional dishes like trout stuffed with walnuts, scrambled eggs with truffle, warm semi-cooked foie gras, veal sweetbreads, scallops with balsamic, breast of duck with violet mustard and iced hazelnut soufflé. Menus are €16–38. Reckon on €30 à la carte. If you don't want to spend all day by the pool, there are several short trails nearby – the owners know the area very well so don't hesitate to ask them for advice. *10% discount on a room (except July–Aug) offered to our readers on presentation of this guide.*

Sauternes

33210

Auberge Les Vignes

Place de l'Église.
T 05.56.76.60.06 F 05.56.76.69.97
Closed *Tues evening and Wed (out of season); 15 Jan–15 Feb.* **Disabled access.**

A gorgeous country inn with log fires and tables laid with checked cloths. Warm, homely atmosphere. The unpretentious local cuisine changes with the seasons – try foie gras with apples, rabbit or quail au Sauternes, apple crunch with Armagnac and meat grilled over vine shoots. The puff pastry fruit tart comes straight from the oven to your plate. Menus €11 (weekdays only) and €18–25.50. Superb selection of wines – five or six of them very affordable.

Restaurant Le Saprien

11 rue Principale; it's opposite the tourist office.
T 05.56.76.60.87 F 05.56.76.68.92
Closed *Sun evening; Mon; Wed evening; Feb; Christmas holidays.*

A little house with thick stone walls on the outskirts of the village. It's ever so slightly chic and the elegant interior is a successful blend of old and new. It has a delightful reading room and also a huge terrace that opens out onto the vineyard. They grill food over vine shoots and offer Sauternes by the glass. Primarily they offer dishes that reflect the changing seasons and what the market has to offer: terrine of foie gras in Sauternes jelly, local grilled beef. Various menus, at €23–36. *Free coffee offered to our readers on presentation of this guide.*

Martillac

33650 (15km N)

Les Sources de Caudalie

It's in the centre of the village.
05.57.83.83.83 05.57.83.83.84
www.sources-caudalie.com
TV. High chairs available. Disabled access. Pay car park.

A sumptous health resort – not for anyone on a budget (rooms from €185, €215 in high season). The grounds, garden and barn are all pristine, a river runs through the property, and the peace and quiet is total. Rooms are in small, isolated buildings; they look charmingly rustic, but all have air-conditioning. The must here is the "vinotherapy", where they use wine instead of sea water. Sloshing around in a tub of rough red is some way of fighting the ageing process. But sadly, this isn't Vichy, so the French Social Security system doesn't reimburse the cost – €578–726 for a weekend or €175–240 per night.

Soulac-sur-Mer

33780

Hôtel Michelet**

1 rue Baguenard; it's on the sea port.
05.56.09.82.18 05.56.73.65.25
Closed *Jan; 3 weeks in Nov.* **Disabled access. TV.**

A typical seaside villa. The staff are beyond compare – their thoughtful gestures include giving out little gifts to the kids. The rooms are pleasant and comfortable (if a little noisy); eight have a balcony and four lead out into a sandy garden. Doubles with bath €41–70 depending on facilities and season. It's 50m from the sea and 250m from the town centre.

Tardets-Sorholus

64470

Ühaltia – Hôtel-restaurant du Pont d'Abense*

Abense-de-Haut; it's 1.5km outside the town on the banks of the Saison.
05.59.28.54.60
uhaltia@wanadoo.fr
Closed *Sun evening; Mon; Jan; 1st fortnight in Dec.* **Car park.**

This riverside hotel is a lovely place to stay, with nice quiet rooms. Doubles €42–53 with shower/wc or bath. There's a friendly bar where you can sample the local ales. The restaurant has a good reputation and the chef, who's also the owner, loves preparing simple dishes using the freshest ingredients. Orders are taken, after booking a table, noon–1.15pm and 7.45–9pm. Dishes change often but are in the style of warm cep terrine, pig's trotter and potato pie, stuffed baby pigeon, foie gras, tart of *piperade* and ham, fondue, pan-fried hake, *aiguillettes* of duck with wine, and crêpes as good as any you'll get in Brittany. Menus €16–28. Reckon on €30 on Sundays and public holidays. You can eat on the terrace. They prefer you stay on a half board basis in the summer; add €22 to the price of the room.

Tonneins

47400

Côté Garonne

36 cours de l'Yser.
05.53.84.34.34 05.53.84.31.31
www.cotegaronne.com
Open *all the year round.* **Disabled access. TV. Car park.**

The street doesn't look particularly appealing – neither does the town, for that matter – so this beautiful building really stands out. It's like entering a different world when you step inside. After a lean period in the restaurant, Christian Papillon has completely rethought his menu, rejecting any ideas of cordon bleu to come up with simpler, more affordable local dishes. We haven't been able to try them out yet, but we are confident that this great chef has not lost his magic touch. This is a chance to eat in style at a reasonable cost, in a wonderful atmosphere. Menus from €12 (lunchtime) to 39. Luxurious, extremely comfortable rooms, with a stunning view of the river. Doubles 70–86; breakfast €8. *10% discount on a room offered to our readers on presentation of this guide.*

Trémolat

24510

Le Bistrot d'en Face

It's on the square.
05.53.22.80.69

Open *all year round.* **High chairs available. Disabled access.**

It's essential to book – even the day before – because this bistro has a very good reputation. It's a favourite with the English ex-pats who inhabit the region. The owner also owns the *Vieux Logis* opposite – hence the name. Attentively prepared traditional dishes: *grattons* of duck (something like duck scratchings), chicken pâté with hazelnuts, sautéed chicken thigh with garlic and *verjus*, and brilliant house desserts. Excellent value, with a weekday lunchtime menu at €11.90, others at €18.50 and €25, or about €25 à la carte. *Free liqueur offered to our readers on presentation of this guide.*

Vendays-Montalivet

33930

Hôtel de France**

Place de l'Église.
Ⓣ05.56.41.70.34 Ⓕ05.56.41.74.33
Closed *Sun; Tues evening and Wed (in winter).* **TV. Disabled access.**

This place is principally a restaurant, with a little dining room decorated with images of the sun. The cuisine is light and the talented young chef uses a lot of sweet spices to enhance the flavours of the local produce – cinnamon with partridge, for example. Menu of the day €11 or others €15–35. There's a peaceful atmosphere and the prices are nice and provincial – €40 for a double room.

Villandraut

33730

Hôtel-restaurant de Got**

Place Principale; it's right in the centre of the village.
Ⓣ05.56.25.31.25 Ⓕ05.56.25.30.59
Closed *Sun evening and Mon out of season; Jan.* **Pay car park.**

A pretty village inn with stone walls. The rooms are clean and well cared-for. Doubles from €29 with shower/wc or bath. Decent traditional local dishes include scallops au Sauternes, chicken *confit* and whole breast of duck with peaches. Set menus €10.50 (weekday lunchtimes) and up to €27. In fine weather, sit on the terrace on the square. Motorcyclists are welcome; the owner is mad on motorbikes and can advise you on lots of good itineraries.

Villefranche-du-Périgord

24550

La Petite Auberge**

Les Peyrouillères; 800m to the south of the village, well signposted.
Ⓣ05.53.29.91.01 Ⓕ05.53.28.88.10
Closed *end Nov–end Feb.* **TV. Car park. Swimming pool.**

A haven of tranquillity. Large house, typical of the region, lost in the countryside. A huge garden with inviting sunbeds. Tastefully decorated rooms. Doubles €43–50. Half board available. Local dishes in the restaurant, varying according to the season: Périgord ceps, semi-cooked foie gras, duck breast in walnut liqueur. Weekday lunchtime menu €15, then others €20–35. À la carte is another option. Attractive terrace, ideal for summer. *Free coffee offered to our readers on presentation of this guide.*

Villeneuve-sur-Lot

47300

Hôtel La Résidence**

17 av. Lazare-Carnot; it's near the old station.
Ⓣ05.53.40.17.03 Ⓕ05.53.01.57.34
Ⓔhotel.laresidence@wanadoo.fr
Closed *fortnight from Christmas to early Jan.* **TV. Pay car park.**

A pretty little hotel with a pink façade, green shutters and lots of character, in a very quiet neighbourhood near the old station. As soon as you set foot inside you find a church pew and, at the end of the corridor, the garden where you can have breakfast in fine weather. Cool, tastefully decorated rooms. Doubles €25 with washing facilities, €39 with shower/wc and €46 with bath. Breakfast €4.60. It's ideal if you like things simple and if you're looking for peace and quiet. *10% discount on a room (for a two-night stay, except July–August) offered to our readers on presentation of this guide.*

|●| Chez Câline

2 rue Notre-Dame.
Ⓣ05.53.70.42.08
Closed *Sun and Wed out of season.*

The owner has an impish spirit and has created a two-level restaurant overlooking the Lot River. One floor has a lovely but tiny balcony (two tables), while the other is in an atmospheric cellar. They serve decent local dishes such as duck *confit* with locally grown apples, salmon fillets with sorrel, and cherry soup with mint for dessert. Set menus €13.50 and €20.50 or about €22 à la carte. It's a small place, so it's best to book.

Pujols

47300 (3km S)

🏃 ⌂ Hôtel des Chênes***

Lieu-dit Bel-Air.
Ⓣ05.53.49.04.55 Ⓕ05.53.49.22.74
Ⓦwww.hoteldeschenes.com
Closed *27 Dec–5 Jan.* **TV. High chairs available. Swimming pool. Car park.**

Look out for the restaurant *La Toque Blanche* – the hotel is next door. They stand on their own on the side of the valley so they're both very quiet. Lovely, well-equipped rooms looking onto the medieval village; they're all decorated differently. Doubles with shower/wc at €57, or with bath €68; those with private balconies and direct access to the pool are €8.50 more. Breakfast €7. *Free coffee or apéritif offered to our readers on presentation of this guide.*

Temple-sur-Lot (Le)

47110 (17km SW)

🏃 ⌂ |●| Les Rives du Plantié***

It's on the D13 between Castelmoron and Le Temple-sur-Lot.
Ⓣ05.53.79.86.86 Ⓕ05.53.79.86.85
Restaurant closed *Mon and Sat lunch; Sun evening out of season; early Nov.* **Disabled access. TV. Games available. Swimming pool. Car park.**

This place was a crumbling wreck before a brave young couple took it on and converted the house and some of the outbuildings into a hotel and restaurant. The grounds are planted with ancient trees and they slope down towards the River Lot, leaving space for the swimming pool. The rooms – depending on the size, €58–64 in low season, €61–67 in high season – are spacious and have good facilities, if rather ordinary décor and furniture (inherited from the previous owners). Happily, the view over the park is splendid. The cooking features local ingredients subjected to outside influences, including a Mediterranean accent, with lots of fish alongside the duck and regional meat dishes. Try Aquitaine caviar and the local beef. Weekday *formule* €15 or other menus €25–41 and a children's menu at €11.45. *Apéritif on the house offered to our readers on presentation of this guide.*

Monclar

47380 (18km NW)

🏃 |●| Le Relais

Rue du 11-Novembre; take the D911 to Sainte-Livrade, follow the D667 for 5km, then turn onto the D113.
Ⓣ05.53.49.44.74
Closed *Sun evening; Mon; 2nd fortnight in Sept.*

Locals crowd in here for lengthy lunches on Sunday and public holidays. Simple dishes and generous portions; the service is attentive. The rustic dining room has a beautiful terrace overlooking the valley (ask for table no.16 if you want a panoramic view). The cooking has a strong regional bias, with hot foie gras with apples, *boudin* (a kind of sausage), *millefeuille* and a few fish dishes such as zander fillet with dried tomatoes and salmon stuffed with shrimps. Menus €11 (weekday lunchtimes), with a children's menu at €7 and others €13–23. Reckon on around €30 à la carte. *Free coffee offered to our readers on presentation of this guide.*

Auvergne

Ambert

63600

Hôtel-restaurant Les Copains**

42 bd. Henri-IV; it's opposite the town hall.
Ⓣ04.73.82.01.02 Ⓕ04.73.82.67.34
Ⓦwww.multimania.com/restolescopains
Closed *Sat; Sun evening; 15 Sept–15 Oct; a week in Feb.* **TV. High chairs available.**

The dining room is fresh, flowery and air-conditioned and boasts an unusual pianola from 1935. The traditional cuisine, based largely on local produce, is simple, but Thierry Chelle, the fourth generation of his family to be in charge, picked up some tricks from the time he spent in the Robuchon kitchens. Thus the menu has a touch of class: terrine of trout with lentil salad and raspberry vinegar, fillet of sea bream roasted in its skin with a Maury sauce, frogs' legs in flaky pastry. Set menus €12 (lunch only) then €20–42. Double bedrooms €45–48 with shower/wc or bath. Service noon–1.30pm and 7.30–8.30pm.

Hôtel-restaurant La Chaumière**

41 av. Foch, near the station.
Ⓣ04.73.82.14.94 Ⓕ04.73.82.33.52
Closed *Sun evening; Fri and Sat evening out of season; Jan.* **Disabled access. TV. Car park.**

A reminder that you can eat well at reasonable prices. Nothing fancy – just good plain cooking and substantial set menus at €15 (except public holidays) up to €36. The restaurant has been expanded and there's a south-facing terrace overlooking the garden. The dining room is in classical style, with a fireplace where they do grills, and the cooking similarly sticks to old faithfuls: fresh foie gras, *potée auvergnate*, wood-grilled meats and so on. The bedrooms are clean, modern and fresh; doubles €48 with shower/wc or bath. Coming soon, Jacuzzi, sauna and hammam.

Arconsat

63250

L'Auberge de Montoncel**

Les Cros d'Arconsat; take the N89 then the D86.
Ⓣ04.73.94.20.96 Ⓕ04.73.94.28.33
Ⓦwww.montoncel.com
Closed *Sun evening and Mon except July–Aug; 1–15 Oct; 1–15 Jan.* **Disabled access. High chairs available. TV. Car park.**

An old building in the middle of the Bois Noirs, above Chabreloche, with a simple hotel alongside in a recently built annexe. Rooms €31. Small, old-fashioned restaurant with a copious menu of the day. According to the season, the other mouth-watering menus include grilled crayfish and undercut of beef with Bleu d'Auvergne cheese. Menus €11.50–26. Friendly service and pretty garden. Credit cards not accepted. *One breakfast per person per night (except July–Aug) offered to our readers on presentation of this guide.*

Aubusson-d'Auvergne

63120

Hôtel-restaurant Au Bon Coin

It's between Thiers and Ambert.

A
1
2
N
Châteauroux
Saint Amand-Montrond
NIÈVRE
INDRE
CHER
D 925
D 940
D 951
A 71 E 11
St-Bonnet-Tronçais
Cérilly
Bourbon-l'Archambault
D 1
N 7
Argenton-sur-Creuse
la Châtre
D 943
Ygrande
Coulandon
Souvigny
N 144
D 3
D 94
D 11
Meillers
D 945
N 145
D 990
Tronget
ALLIER
D 940
D 917
A 20 E 9
Montluçon
N 145
D 46
N 9
Montmarault
St-Pourçain-sur-Sioule
N 145 E 62
Néris-les-Bains
Charroux
Lalizolle
Servant
D 942
D 997
D 4
Gannat
D 912
CREUSE
St-Gervais-d'Auvergne
Effiat
D 227
Blot-l'Église
D 210
Bourganeuf
Aubusson
N 141
Châtelguyon
Riom
Tournoël
Volvic
D 940
D 982
D 941
Pontgibaud
Clermont-Ferrand
HAUTE-VIENNE
St-Pierre-le-Chastel
Chamalières
Mazaye
D 979
Eymoutiers
Puy de Dôme
1 465
Royat
Orcival
St-Genès-Champanelle
Bourg-Lastic
N 89
D 30
Nebouzat
D 36
D 982
D 12
A 20 E 9
le Mont-Dore
Saint-Nectaire
A 75 E 11
Ussel
A 89
Super-Besse
D 978
Issoire
la Bourboule
Picherande
Besse-et-St-Anastaise
D 979
D 978
Boudes
Uzerche
Marchal
Bort-les-Orgues
Égliseneuve-d'Entraigues
CORRÈZE
Champs-sur-Tar.
Antignac
Condat-en-Féniers
D 922
Saignes
D 16
St-Bauzire
D 18
Anglards-de-Salers
Riom-ès-Montagnes
Allanche
Massiac
N 89
N 120
Mauriac
D 22
le Falgoux
Dienne
Chalinargues
Drugeac
Brive-la-Gaillarde
D 921
D 980
Salers
Murat
CANTAL
le Lioran
Tournemire
Mandailles
St-Flour
St-Cirgues-de Jordanne
Vic-sur-Cère
Saint-Georges
Viaduc de Garabit
Pailherols
Narnhac
Laroquebrou
Aurillac
Polminhac
D 103
N 120
Chaudes-Aigues
Sansac-de-Marmiesse
St-Martin-sous-Vigouroux
Souillac
Carlat
Vitrac
N 122
D 904
D 921
N 20
A 20 E 9
N 140
D 940
Marcolès
AVEYRON
LOT
D 19
St-Urcize
Maurs
Montsalvy
Calvinet
D 987
Vieillevie
Entraygues-sur-T.
A 75 E 11
Figeac

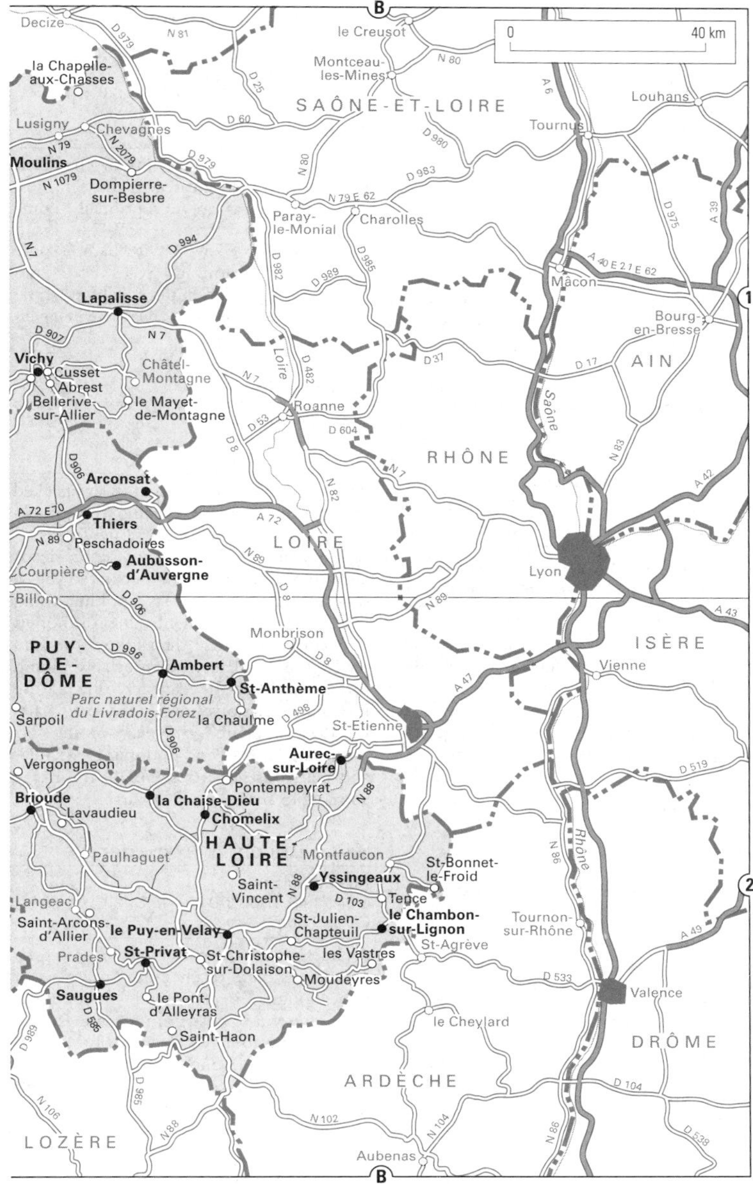
B
0
40 km
Decize
le Creusot
Montceau-les-Mines
SAÔNE-ET-LOIRE
Louhans
Tournus
la Chapelle-aux-Chasses
Lusigny
Chevagnes
Moulins
Dompierre-sur-Besbre
Paray-le-Monial
Charolles
Mâcon
Bourg-en-Bresse
AIN
Lapalisse
Vichy
Cusset
Abrest
Bellerive-sur-Allier
Châtel-Montagne
le Mayet-de-Montagne
Roanne
Loire
Saône
RHÔNE
Arconsat
Thiers
Peschadoires
Aubusson-d'Auvergne
Courpière
Billom
LOIRE
Lyon
ISÈRE
Vienne
Monbrison
PUY-DE-DÔME
Ambert
St-Anthème
Parc naturel régional du Livradois-Forez
Sarpoil
la Chaulme
St-Etienne
Aurec-sur-Loire
Vergongheon
Pontempeyrat
Brioude
la Chaise-Dieu
Chomelix
Lavaudieu
Paulhaguet
HAUTE-LOIRE
Montfaucon
St-Bonnet-le-Froid
Saint-Vincent
Yssingeaux
Tence
Rhône
Langeac
Saint-Arcons-d'Allier
le Puy-en-Velay
St-Julien-Chapteuil
le Chambon-sur-Lignon
Tournon-sur-Rhône
Prades
St-Privat
St-Christophe-sur-Dolaison
les Vastres
St-Agrève
Moudeyres
Saugues
le Pont-d'Alleyras
Valence
le Cheylard
Saint-Haon
DRÔME
ARDÈCHE
LOZÈRE
Aubenas
N 81
D 979
N 80
D 25
A 6
D 60
N 79
N 2079
D 980
D 979
N 1079
D 983
N 80
N 79 E 62
D 975
A 39
D 994
N 7
D 982
D 985
D 989
A 40 E 21 E 62
D 907
N 7
D 37
D 17
D 482
N 7
D 53
D 604
D 8
D 906
N 7
N 82
N 83
A 42
A 72 E 70
A 72
N 89
N 89
D 8
N 89
D 906
A 43
D 996
D 8
A 47
D 498
D 906
D 519
N 88
N 86
N 88
D 103
A 49
D 533
D 585
D 989
D 985
N 106
N 88
N 102
N 104
D 104
N 86
D 538
1
2

3 AUVERGNE

Ⓣ04.73.53.55.78 Ⓕ04.73.53.56.29
Closed *Sun evening and Mon out of season; 20 Dec–20 Jan.* **Car park.**

A little inn decorated in pleasant country style – the only problem being that it can get a bit noisy when the big dining room is opened up for coach parties. The proprietor-chef uses quality ingredients in his cooking and serves generous portions: good house terrines, fillet of char with cream and bacon, pear in flaky pastry with strawberry *coulis*. They have lots of special dishes during crayfish season. Menus €18 (weekdays only) up to €37 or about €30 à la carte. Note that they stop serving at 9pm. There are a few rooms which go for €36.60 with basin or shower. Half board, around €42 per person, is obligatory in July and August.

Aurec-sur-Loire

43110

Les Cèdres Bleus

Route de la Rivière; it's 4km from Aurec on the road to Bas-en-Basset.
Ⓣ04.77.35.48.48 Ⓕ04.71.77.35.04
Closed *Sun evening; Mon lunch; Jan.*
Disabled access. TV. High chairs available.

This pink house among the cedar trees is spacious and modern and is set in grounds with a few comfortable guest chalets. Doubles €53–55, breakfast €7. Refined local dishes listed on weekday menu at €16 and others up to €65. The large terrace has a good view over the town.

Aurillac

15000

Hôtel-restaurant La Thomasse***

28 rue du Docteur-Mallet.
Ⓣ04.71.48.26.47 Ⓕ04.71.48.83.66
Ⓦwww.hotel-la-thomasse.com
Closed *22 Dec–10 Jan.* **TV. Swimming pool. Car park. High chairs and games available.**

In a residential area 1km from the centre, this charming hotel overlooks a large park. Pretty en-suite rooms in rustic style cost €65. Regional dishes and gastronomic cuisine are served in the restaurant. Menus €25–35. More often than not, the owner will serve you a free glass of champagne as you sit down to eat. He's welcoming and talkative, and the club bar gets lively in the evenings. *Free apéritif offered to our readers on presentation of this guide.*

Grand Hôtel de Bordeaux***

2 av. de la République.
Ⓣ04.71.48.01.84 Ⓕ04.71.48.49.93
Ⓦwww.hotel-de-bordeaux.fr
TV. Pay car park.

A charming hotel with lots of character, built in 1812 and located in the centre of town. Bedrooms are exceptionally comfortable and cost €67–74 with shower/wc, or €75–84 with bath – some have air-conditioning. Stylish bar and lounges and a good buffet breakfast. *A free breakfast per room offered to our readers on presentation of this guide.*

Café Jean

17 rue des Carmes.
Ⓣ04.71.64.96.20
Closed *Sun; Mon–Wed evenings.*

The nicest bistro in town is always packed at lunchtime. In the evening the atmosphere is cosier but just as convivial. It's a bright place, with appealing retro décor and two dining rooms separated by a superb brass bar. The tasty cooking, using fresh produce, is excellent value for money. You could do worse than follow the lead set by the regulars who invariably plump for the dish of the day and one of the meltingly delicious home-made fruit tarts for dessert. There's a *formule* of the day with main course and pudding for €8.90, and generous salads for €6.50. You'll pay about €15 maximum à la carte.

Le Bouchon Fromager

Rue du Buis.
Ⓣ04.71.48.07.80 Ⓕ04.71.48.34.20
Closed *Sun.*

A cheese and wine bar where you can grab a delicious plate of cheese with a glass of wine bought direct from the vineyards – Auvergne wines cost from around €2.50. Also a number of reasonably priced regional dishes. Lunchtime menu €9 and large salads for around €7; reckon on around €15 à la carte. There's a nice terrace for sunny days.

L'Arsène

24 rue Arsène-Vermenouze.
Ⓣ04.71.48.48.97

Closed *lunchtime; Sun and Mon evenings; Ist fortnight in July.*

A warm and cosy dining room, with exposed stonework and modern paintings. It's very popular with locals attracted by the cheap, hearty food. The restaurant specializes in fondue; try also the *tartiflette*, raclette, pork fillet with blue cheese or breast of duck with honey (any of which could easily feed two people). Generous set menus at €14–19 and reasonably priced wines; house wine costs around €8. *Free coffee offered to our readers on presentation of this guide.*

Sansac de Marmiesse

15130 (8km W)

La Belle Époque

Lieu-dit Lasfargues; on the Maurs road (N122); it's well signposted.
☎04.71.62.87.87
Closed *Sun evening and Mon (except July–Aug); Jan.* **Disabled access.**

An old restored farm in the heart of the countryside. You can eat in one of three dining rooms: the Belle Époque (with décor that lives up to the name), the Cantou-style or the rustic. Menus €19–40. À la carte (reckon on €28), you can try some classic dishes, such as pig's trotters, fried foie gras and, in season, mushroom specialities like cep omelette (the chef is a great mushroom enthusiast). On fine days, you can take advantage of the charming terrace. Unfortunately, the service is a bit slow and erratic.

Polminhac

15800 (14km E)

Le Berganty

Place de l'Église; take the N122.
☎04.71.47.47.47
Closed *Sat evening and Sun (except by reservation in summer); Christmas and New Year holidays.*

The square is superb, with its church and its crowd of stone-roofed houses. And the dining room is wonderful, too, with an old polished sideboard, a massive table positioned in front of the fireplace and large bouquets of flowers from the garden. The chef prefers to prepare dishes to order and uses only fresh seasonal produce enhanced with herbs from his vegetable plot: trout with bacon, *truffade* (a potato cake with Cantal cheese and ham) are served at any time, but you have to order in advance for the stuffed cabbage, the *pounti* (a mixture of bacon and Swiss chard), and the *potée auvergnate*, the hearty local soup. Other specialities include rabbit with prunes and carrots and shoulder of local beef. Menus €13–40. The young owner has a flair for making people feel welcome.

Besse-et-Saint-Anastaise

63610

Hôtel-restaurant Le Clos**

It's 400m from the medieval centre in the direction of the route du Mont-Dore.
☎04.73.79.52.77 Ⓕ04.73.79.56.67
Ⓦwww.hotel-le-clos.fr
Closed *mid-Oct to end Dec; a week in Jan; a week in March.* **Restaurant closed** *Mon–Fri lunchtimes in Jan, March and April.* **TV. Swimming pool. Car park. High chairs and games available.**

This modern establishment just out of the town centre offers a wide range of facilities – indoor pool, well-equipped gym, Turkish bath and games room. Bedrooms are pleasant and very clean; doubles cost €45–54 with shower/wc or bath and there are a few family rooms too. The owners can provide suggestions for excursions and walks. The food is decent and traditional (*truffade*, sausages with cabbage, trout terrine with lentil sauce). Set menus €14.50–31. *Free apéritif offered to our readers on presentation of this guide.*

Hostellerie du Beffroy**

26 rue de l'Abbé-Blot.
☎04.73.79.50.08 Ⓕ04.73.79.57.87
Closed *Mon and Tues except Feb, July and Aug; a fortnight in Dec.* **TV. Pay car park.**

A fifteenth-century building owned and run by Thierry Legros, who has a fine reputation as a chef: try his *fricassée* of wild salmon, the pan-fried Salers beef with woodland mushroom *jus*, the Cantal turnover or the *pounti* (a mixture of bacon and Swiss chard). Menu at €23; you'll spend about €50 for a full meal à la carte. Rooms are decent but facilities vary. Doubles with shower/wc or bath €46–75.

Super-Besse

63610 (8km W)

Restaurant La Bergerie

Route de Vassivières; take the D149.
ⓣ04.73.79.61.06 ⓕ04.73.79.66.63
Closed *15 Sept–15 Dec; open every day during Christmas and summer seasons for group bookings.*

It would be a crime to come here without trying the *truffade* (potato cake with Cantal cheese). The young owner serves a hearty portion, with local ham, straight from the frying pan; it's cooked to order and probably the best you'll get in the region. Extremely satisfying, well worth the thirty-minute wait. Lots of other local delicacies on menus from €15.50–27.50: terrine of pig's trotters with lentils, zander with a ewe's cheese crust. You'll really feel at home in this country inn with its delightful décor and atmosphere. It's popular in winter and summer alike – on warm days you can eat on the terrace overlooking the lake.

Boudes

63340

Le Boudes la Vigne**

Place de la Mairie.
ⓣ and ⓕ04.73.96.55.66
Closed *Sun evening; Mon; a fortnight in Jan; last week in Aug.* **Disabled access. TV. Car park.**

This popular little hotel-restaurant, in a pleasantly renovated house, is in the centre of a small wine-growing village south of Puy-de-Dôme. The cooking is quite delightful: roast lobster, snail ravioli with garlic cream, *blanquette* of chicken with honey. For dessert, it's hard to resist the iced nougat with walnuts and Boudes honey. Menus €15 (weekday lunchtimes) up to €40. Breakfast costs €6. You're right in the midst of the best vineyards of the Auvergne so the wine list is splendid and wine is also served by the glass. The hotel was built only recently and is very quiet. Doubles €32 with shower/wc. *10% discount on the room rate (except Jun–Sept) or a free apéritif offered to our readers on presentation of this guide.*

Sarpoil

63500 (9km NE)

La Bergerie de Sarpoil

From Issoire, take the D996 then the D999 in the direction of Saint-Germain-en-l'Herm.
ⓣ04.73.71.02.54 ⓕ04.73.71.02.99
ⓦwww.bergerie.ch.sarpoil.com
Closed *Mon evening–Wed evening except June–Oct; Jan; All Saints' Day.*

The best gastronomic restaurant in the region. Laurent Jury and Éric Moutard produce marvels using the finest Auvergne produce: free-range pork, Salers beef, milk-fed lamb, wild ceps and morels from the forest. Menus €17–70 and about €35 à la carte. The *menu campagnard* lists dishes like mouthwatering *andouille* pancake with onion *confit* and house tripe with thyme. On the *menu dégustation* you'll find slightly more elegant dishes like frogs' legs with garlic cream and herb *jus* or roast crayfish. There's a little motto on the menus: "the art of the cook begins where nature's work ceases". So now you know.

Bourbon-l'Archambault

03160

Grand Hôtel Montespan-Talleyrand***

2–4 pl. des Thermes.
ⓣ04.70.67.00.24 ⓕ04.70.67.12.00
ⓦwww.hotel-montespan.com
Closed *end Oct to end March.* **TV. Disabled access. Car park.**

A superb hotel in a fine old-fashioned building facing the spa. It's an oasis of peace and quiet – there are reading rooms and card rooms hung with velvet and tapestries, a bright flower-filled dining room and a pool among the greenery of the garden. Bedrooms are tastefully and stylishly decorated. Doubles cost €51.50–80, which is very reasonable given the standard of accommodation. The restaurant sticks to old favourites and the cooking is worth the trip. There's a simple lunchtime weekday menu at €14.50 and menus up to €27. Friendly staff and excellent service.

Ygrande

03160 (10km W)

Château d'Ygrande***

Le Mont; it's 3km outside the village.
ⓣ04.70.66.33.11 ⓕ04.70.66.33.63
ⓦwww.chateauygrande.fr
Closed *Sun evening; Mon except July–Aug; Jan; Feb.* **TV. High chairs available. Baby**

changing facilities. Swimming pool. Car park.

This remarkable place looks out over a copse which you can admire from your candelit dinner table. Classic architecture with superb parquet floors, glorious décor in all the bedrooms, excellent welcome and service, and a quality restaurant to boot. Understandably, it's widely admired, and when the Formula 1 teams race at Magny-Cours or Lurcy-Lévis, they take over the whole château. It's not cheap, yet it's good value for money and well worth making a dent in your holiday budget. Double rooms €90–160, depending on the size and the view. There's a lunch menu for €20 and others up to €40. Facilities include a pool, a sauna, a billiard room and horse riding.

Cérilly

03350 (11km W)

Hôtel-restaurant Chaumat**

Place Péron.
Ⓣ04.70.67.52.21 Ⓕ04.70.67.35.28
Closed *Mon; Sun evening; early Sept; end Dec.* **TV.**

Eight well-appointed rooms which have been nicely renovated – doubles €32–36 with shower/wc – but the real attraction here is the quality of the cuisine, as the roomful of regulars attests every lunchtime. The dining room has a rustic, country look. They serve interesting dishes with mixtures of sweet and savoury flavours, with delicious game – the house speciality is a terrine of pork tongue. Quality fresh produce is used and helpings are substantial. Weekday lunch menu €10 and others up to €27. Friendly and welcoming. *Free apéritif offered to our readers on presentation of this guide.*

Saint-Bonnet-Tronçais

03360 (23km NW)

Le Tronçais**

Take the N144, then the D978 in the direction of the forest of Tronçais as far as the Rond de Tronçais. It's 3km south of Saint-Bonnet-Tronçais.
Ⓣ04.70.06.11.95 Ⓕ04.70.06.16.15
Closed *Sun evening; Mon and Tues out of season; mid-Nov to mid-March.* **TV. Car park.**

A peaceful, very comfortable lakeside hotel with lots of charm. The forest of Tronçais, one of the oldest and most beautiful in France, becomes every shade of green in spring and every shade of yellow, red and brown in autumn. Spacious yet cosy bedrooms €51–67 with shower/wc or bath/wc. The restaurant is strong on traditional local dishes: snails with walnuts, eel terrine with blackberries, veal cutlet with ceps. Menus €20–33. The two dining rooms are very elegantly and tastefully decorated, with great views of the grounds and surrounding countryside. *Free coffee offered to our readers on presentation of this guide.*

Tronget

03240 (23km S)

Hôtel du Commerce**

D945; take the D1 towards Montet.
Ⓣ04.70.47.12.95 Ⓕ04.70.47.32.53
TV. High chairs available. Disabled access. Car park.

A hotel that contrasts old and new. The building is modern, with comfortable bedrooms (€45 with shower), though they're a bit lacking in character. Compare that with the traditional cooking of Monsieur Auberger, which is heavily based on local produce (terrines, lentils, snails): don't miss the *crème brûlée*. Menus €14 (not Sunday) to €32. *Free apéritif offered to our readers on presentation of this guide.*

Bourboule (La)

63150

Hôtel-restaurant Le Pavillon**

Avenue d'Angleterre.
Ⓣ04.73.65.50.18 Ⓕ04.73.81.00.93
Closed *Nov–March.* **TV.**

In a quiet residential area, this nice little place has a pretty Art Deco façade. There's a warm family atmosphere. Rooms are modern and clean, if a little functional. Doubles €42 with shower/wc, telephone and TV, €51 with bath, or between €38 and €45 except July–Aug and Easter. Simple family cooking using regional ingredients; menus €12–20. *Free apéritif offered to our readers on presentation of this guide.*

Hôtel Le Charlet**

94 bd. Louis-Chousy.
Ⓣ04.73.81.33.00 Ⓕ04.73.65.50.82
Ⓦwww.lecharlet.com

Closed *mid-Nov to Dec.* **TV. High chairs and games available. Swimming pool. Car park.**

An attractive family-run place in a quiet residential area – indeed, the whole town is quiet and residential. The forty bedrooms are pleasant, with modern facilities, though the décor is a little old-fashioned; they go for €42–69 according to the season. There's a nice pool with a wave machine, a Turkish bath and a gym. The cooking is traditional and local, with dishes like *potée auvergnate* (a regional soup), *truffade* and rabbit foie gras. The breakfast buffet includes pastries, cereals, sausage and red wine. Menus €16–28. Credit cards not accepted.

Bourg-Lastic

63760 (20km NW)

La Pomme d'Or

In the town; take the D31 in the direction of Messeix, then the D987.
☎04.73.21.80.18 Ⓕ04.73.21.84.15
Closed *Wed (except July–Aug); early Nov–Easter.* **High chairs available. Disabled access. Car park.**

A beautiful, traditional house in a lush setting. On the first floor, seven spotless rooms, some of which have recently been refurbished. Doubles €32–40 with shower/wc, €50–75 with bath. Some rooms can sleep a whole family. The cosy, rustic dining room (complete with large fireplace and exposed beams) attracts a loyal following that appreciates fine regional cooking. Many of the local classics are on offer: *tripoux*, zander, duck *confit*, sirloin steak with blue-cheese sauce, all prepared with loving care and the freshest of ingredients. Specialities from other parts of France are also sometimes available: *bœuf bourguignon* or *coq au vin*, for example. Menus €15–22.50. Reckon on €25 à la carte. Excellent wine list. On a fine day, you can enjoy the pretty little terrace and garden. *Free coffee offered to our readers on presentation of this guide.*

Brioude

43100

Hôtel de la Poste et Champanne**

1 bd. du Docteur-Devins.
☎04.71.50.14.62 Ⓕ04.71.50.10.55
Closed *Sun evening; Mon lunch; Feb.* **TV. High chairs available. Car park.**

An old country hotel which has been updated to suit modern tastes. The bedrooms facing the street are rather noisy, while those in the annexe at the back are very quiet. Doubles €27 with shower or basin, €44 with shower/wc or bath. There's a bar on the ground floor; the restaurant on the floor above has long had a reputation for good food and does a number of set menus; weekday at €14, others up to €36 and also à la carte. Traditional, unpretentious food: pressed cod with Roseval potatoes and caper vinaigrette, blue cheese mousse with walnuts, lamb's trotters with Fourme d'Ambert cheese and lentils and fillet of zander with ham. The jolly owner serves the food himself. *Free coffee offered to our readers on presentation of this guide.*

La Sapinière***

Avenue Paul-Chambriard; it is signed from the N102, which runs through Brioude.
☎04.71.50.87.30 Ⓕ04.71.50.87.39
Ⓔhotel.la.sapiniere@wanadoo.fr
Hotel closed *Feb.* **Restaurant closed** *Sun evening, Mon and Nov–Easter.* **Disabled access. TV. Swimming pool. Car park.**

An appealing modern building built from wood, brick and glass, located between two old farm buildings. The fifteen spacious rooms look out over the grounds and are decorated in different styles. They're named rather than numbered – "Vulcania" has a bedhead carved from lava. There's a lovely indoor swimming pool with Jacuzzi. Doubles with shower/wc €75, with bath €85. Breakfast €9. The restaurant serves dishes with interesting flavour combinations, such as bitter dandelion with ham and honey-roast radish, Salers beef with ground ceps, salmon with simmered green Puy vegetables, cabbage stuffed with foie gras and poultry *mousseline*. Menus €22 (weekdays only) to €36. *Free coffee offered to our readers on presentation of this guide.*

Vergongheon

43360 (8km N)

La Petite École

Rilhac; take the RN102 then the D14.
☎04.71.76.00.44
Ⓔpetite.ecole@wanadoo.fr
Closed *Sun evening; Mon; Tues evening*

Oct–Easter; the last week in June; 1st week in Sept. **Disabled access.**

The décor takes you straight back to school – blackboards, maps of France, school photos and desks. Françoise and Éric run the place and produce delicious dishes (no school dinners here): grilled zander, veal kidneys and the famous "Récré", a fabulous dessert trolley. You choose from an exercise book full of menus at €15–24 with a children's menu at €11. Best to book. *Free apéritif offered to our readers on presentation of this guide.*

Lavaudieu

43100 (9km SE)

Auberge de l'Abbaye

Centre; take the D19 and the D20.
Ⓣ04.71.76.44.44
Closed *Sun evening and Mon; Mon only in summer.* **Disabled access.**

A charming village inn on the little street opposite the church. It has a rustic interior – complete with log fires in winter – which has been very nicely renovated and decorated. The carefully prepared traditional dishes, based on local produce, include fillet of trout and gnocchi with green lentils, salmon steak with ceps and ice cream with green verbena. Reservations recommended. Set menus €14 (summer lunchtimes only); other menus up to €23.

Saint-Beauzire

43100 (10km W)

Hôtel Le Baudière – Restaurant Le Vieux Four**

Ⓣ04.71.76.81.70 Ⓕ04.71.76.80.66
Closed *end Dec to end Jan.* **Restaurant closed** *Mon.* **Disabled access. TV. High chairs available. Swimming pool. Car park.**

A pleasant modern hotel with sauna, indoor and outdoor swimming pools and very comfy bedrooms. Rooms 17, 18 and 19 offer views over the countryside. Doubles with bath and satellite TV €48–50. Right next door is the restaurant, which has a handsome stone oven in the main dining room. The grilled meat is as good as the *escalope* of veal muzzle with mushrooms, the zander with baby vegetables, the *crépinette* of pig's trotters and the *crème brûlée*. Good wine list, too. Set menus €18–43, with a children's menu for €10. *Free apéritif offered to our readers on presentation of this guide.*

La Marmite

It's in the centre of the village.
Ⓣand Ⓕ04.71.76.80.21
Closed *Sun evening; Wed; by reservation only evenings, weekends and public holidays I Oct– 30 April; Jan; April; last week in June; 2 weeks in Sept.* **Disabled access.**

The copper *marmite* (cooking cauldron) is set on the open fireplace in this adorable and lovingly tended family restaurant. Françoise is in charge of the cooking and Marc takes care of the service – and if you want to know anything about the local area he's your man. Dishes are generously served; try the haddock in pastry or the lamb with tomato. There's a €12 lunch menu or others at €15–26 in the evening. They don't press you to buy wine you don't want. When the weather is fine you can appreciate the ivy-swathed frontage and large lawn. A really lovely place. *Free apéritif offered to our readers on presentation of this guide.*

Chaise-Dieu (La)

43160

Hôtel de la Casadeï**

Place de l'Abbaye; it's at the foot of the steps to the abbey.
Ⓣ04.71.00.00.58 Ⓕ04.71.00.01.67
Ⓦwww.hoteldelacasadei.fr.fm
Restaurant closed *Sun evening and Mon except in summer; Nov–April.* **TV.**

You get to the hotel through a flower-filled terrace and an art gallery. The best rooms have a view of the abbey and are nicely furnished; doubles €38–50 with shower/wc. In the restaurant they serve *potée auvergnate* (a thick local soup), omelette of chanterelle mushrooms, mutton tripe and *truffade* (potato cake with Cantal cheese). Set menu €15; à la carte reckon on around €20. The photos you'll see everywhere are of artists who've stayed at the hotel during the town's sacred music festival. There's a little terrace at the back. *10% discount on a room (except July–Aug) or free coffee offered to our readers on presentation of this guide.*

Hôtel de l'Écho et Restaurant de l'Abbaye**

Place de l'Écho, behind the abbey.

Ⓣ04.71.00.00.45 Ⓕ04.71.00.00.22
Closed *Wed lunch except mid-June to mid-Sept; Jan–April.* **TV. Car park.**

This delightful inn is fully booked during the festival – all the big names have stayed here. The handsome dining room with its antiques and Louis XIII décor is housed in the former monastery kitchens. You'll find tasty, regional dishes using plenty of wild mushrooms, truffles and foie gras: *glacis* of zander with crispy snails and velouté of chanterelles, fillet mignon with Fourme d'Ambert blue cheese, *tarte tatin* with ceps and artichokes, watercress, escalope of fried foie gras, Granny Smith apples and French toast and a trolley of fresh desserts. Fine wine list, too. Menus €17–58, with a children's menu at €11. Eleven bedrooms are available; doubles go for €47–60 with shower/wc or bath. Nos. 7 and 15 have wonderful views of the abbey. Breakfast €9. *10% discount on a room offered to our readers on presentation of this guide.*

Chambon-sur-Lignon (Le)

43290

Hôtel Beau-Rivage*

19 rue de la Grande-Fontaine.
Ⓣ04.71.65.82.77
Closed *Oct to mid-April.* **Car park.**

If you're after peace and quiet, this is the place. The staff greet you with big smiles and everything is done thoughtfully; doubles with shower/wc cost €38. Two terraces give you a view of the river. Although a bit old-fashioned, it's a very nice place with genuine people. *10% discount on the room rate offered to our readers on presentation of this guide.*

Tence

43190 (8.5km N)

Café-restaurant Brolles

Mas-de-Tence; 5km east of Tence, near the village of Mazeaux.
Ⓣ04.71.65.42.91
Restaurant open *Sat and Sun; reservations required Mon–Fri.*

An authentic country inn run by friendly people. The restaurant has been tastefully decorated and the stone floor makes the place feel nice and cool. Sit at the table beside the fireplace and enjoy home-made *saucisson* or omelette made from eggs laid by the owner's hens. Also recommended are the baby potatoes sautéed with lentils, and people come from miles around to taste the ewe's-milk cheese, which is served warm. Set menus €12.20–27.50; children's menu €6.10. Simple but clean rooms with basin at €20; breakfast costs €4. It's a small place, so it's best to book. *Free apéritif offered to our readers on presentation of this guide.*

Vastres (Les)

43430 (18km SW)

Auberge du Laboureur

It's opposite the village church, 2km beyond Fay-sur-Lignon.
Ⓣ04.71.59.57.11 Ⓕ04.71.59.55.23
Disabled access. Baby changing facilities.

This old village bakery has been turned into a country inn. It has been very thoughtfully and tastefully decorated, with quiet, elegant rooms that have a separate entrance. Doubles €30; breakfast €6. The large dining room has lots of style and there's a terrace, too. Delicious local dishes and desserts (iced soufflé with verbena) are prepared by the owner, and even the rye bread is home-made. Menus €10–18. *10% discount on half board (except July–Aug) offered to our readers on presentation of this guide.*

Saint-Bonnet-Le-Froid

43290 (20km NE)

Auberge des Cimes***

Rue Principale.
Ⓣ04.71.59.93.72 Ⓕ04.71.59.93.40
Ⓦwww.regismarcon.fr
Closed *Mon evening, Tues and Wed lunch; Tues and Wed June–Oct; Jan to mid-March.* **Disabled access. TV. Car park.**

One of the culinary high points of the area, run by Régis Marcon, who is constantly scaling new heights with his inventive cuisine. His preparation is meticulous, everything he buys is of the freshest quality and he's well acquainted with the traditional dishes of the Velay and the Vivarais. Subtle, delicate dishes full of unexpected flavours. Menus ranging from €80 up to €130. There are rooms of the same calibre for €140–216 with bath.

Champs-sur-Tarentaine

15270

L'Auberge du Vieux Chêne**

34 rte. des Lacs.
T 04.71.78.71.64 F 04.71.78.70.88
W www.advc.free.fr
Closed *lunchtime; Sun evening and Mon in low season; Nov–March.* **TV. Car park.**

A renovated old farm in northern Cantal. Bedrooms have been nicely done up in bright, cheerful colours and all have bathrooms; doubles cost €56–62. There's an enormous fireplace on the back wall of the restaurant, and though the dining room is large it's laid out in such a way that it actually feels quite intimate. Menu at €22 and children's menu at €10. On offer are regional specialities alongside classic dishes – try the snails in pastry, trout with diced bacon or *entrecôte* steak with Roquefort cheese. There's a pretty terrace where you can dine or take breakfast. *10% discount on the room rate out of season offered to our readers on presentation of this guide.*

Marchal

15270 (5km NE)

L'Auberge de l'Eau Verte

Take the D679 then the D22.
T 04.71.78.71.48
Closed *Wed out of season.* **Car park.**

A traditional little inn on a small hill beside the church. Super-friendly welcome in the restaurant, where you'll find special "taste of Auvergne" menus. These have to be ordered in advance and offer a delicious plate of cold meat, *truffade* (potato cake with Cantal cheese), salad, cheese and dessert. Prices €10.50–20 and about €20 à la carte. There are a few bedrooms with basin (bathroom on the landing) for €35. Half board €33 per person. A good place to appreciate traditional Auvergne cuisine. *Free apéritif offered to our readers on presentation of this guide.*

Châtelguyon

63140

Hôtel-restaurant Castel Régina**

3 av. de Brocqueville.
T 04.73.86.00.15 F 04.73.86.19.44
Closed *Oct–April.* **TV. Car park.**

A stylish spa hotel. The Belle Époque décor gives it a delightful, old-fashioned charm, and the atmosphere is relaxed, if staid – you're hardly going to come to Châtelguyon for the nightlife. Clean, well-kept bedrooms €30 with wc, €34–37 with shower or bath. The €13 *menu du jour* (weekdays only) and others at €15–23 are more substantial than you'd expect for a rest cure. Credit cards not accepted. *Free coffee offered to our readers on presentation of this guide.*

Hôtel Bellevue – Restaurant le Cèdre Bleu**

4 rue Punett.
T 04.73.86.07.62 F 04.73.86.02.56
Closed *Oct–April.* **TV. High chairs available.**

This hotel offers quiet rooms with excellent facilities. Doubles with shower/wc or bath €42–65. They serve local dishes in the restaurant: cod steak with crusty gingerbread. Menu of the day €18, regional menu €20 and menu *Cèdre Bleu* €30. *10% discount on a room (April–May) or free apéritif offered to our readers on presentation of this guide.*

Les Chênes**

15 rue Guy-de-Maupassant.
T 04.73.86.02.88 F 04.73.86.46.60
E leschenes63@aol.com
Open *all year.* **Car park. TV.**

Annexe to the *Hotel Apollo.* The rooms are quiet and pleasant and some have balconies with views over the countryside. Doubles €43 with enormous breakfast of fruit, yoghurt, ham, cheese and pancakes. Credit cards not accepted. *6% discount on a room (after two consecutive nights) offered to our readers on presentation of this guide.*

Restaurant La Potée

34 av. Baraduc.
T 04.73.86.06.60
Closed *Mon; Nov.*

The façade of this restaurant is beautifully timbered, and the dining room is pretty. You sit at nice tables with proper cloths to sample classic dishes: *andouillette* (a type of sausage), mutton tripe, *truffade* (potato cake with Cantal cheese), pork knuckle and trout with bacon. No menus; around €18 à la carte. They stop serving at 9.30pm.

Chaudes-Aigues

15110

Au Rendez-vous des Pêcheurs

Pont-de-Lanau; take the D921.
☎04.71.23.51.68
Disabled access. Car park.

A little inn at the side of the road which has been modernized. The owner's son is carrying on the long tradition of friendly and unpretentious service. Menus from €12.50 (weekdays) up to €15.50 (Sundays), with good, reliable home cooking: rabbit stew, *potée*, tripe, home-made icecreams and sorbets. There's a terrace open in the afternoons. A few basic but clean rooms with handbasin go for €28. No credit cards. *Free coffee offered to our readers on presentation of this guide.*

Chomelix

43500

Auberge de l'Arzon**

Place de la Fontaine.
☎04.71.03.62.35 Ⓕ04.71.03.61.62
Closed *Mon evening and Tues except July–Aug; All Saints' Day to Easter.* **Disabled access. TV. Car park.**

This is a good village inn and the restaurant is extremely popular. It's best to book in summer, especially during the music festival in nearby La Chaise. The bedrooms are impeccable and situated in a quiet modern annexe with shower/wc upstairs and bathroom downstairs; doubles €40–45. The restaurant uses fresh local produce: foie gras, salmon with lentils, and mouthwatering home-made desserts. Set menus €15 (not Sun) and up to €38. *10% discount on the room rate for more than two nights Sept–June.*

Pontempeyrat

43500 (13km N)

Hôtel-restaurant Mistou***

Take the D498, 50km from Craponne-sur-Arzon.
☎04.77.50.62.46 Ⓕ04.77.50.66.70
Ⓦwww.mistou.fr
Closed *Nov to end April.* **Restaurant closed** *lunchtime (except Sun, public holidays and Aug).* **TV. Car park.**

Unbeatable bucolic setting at the bottom of the beautiful Ance valley: the river laps the fir trees and irrigates the delightful garden with a swimming pool. An old water mill, built around 1730, used to stand here, but now a recycled turbine provides the electricity required by this three-star hotel. All the comfortable and extremely quiet rooms are tastefully decorated, and the biggest ones give on to the garden. Doubles with shower/wc or bath €86–114; breakfast €11. In the kitchen, Bernard Roux, one of the country's great advocates of regional cooking, creates succulent seasonal dishes set off by spices from his native Provence. The platter of four foies gras, the young guinea-fowl marinated in spices and the baked strawberries with Szechuan pepper are all delicious – not to mention the touch of vanilla in the butter. Several menus from €28–52. Half board is compulsory in high season. Sauna and Jacuzzi (at extra charge). *Free regional apéritif offered to our readers on presentation of this guide.*

Clermont-Ferrand

63000

See map on pp.94–95

Auberge de Jeunesse du Cheval Blanc

55 av. de l'Union-Soviétique; 100m from the train station. **Map D2-1**
☎04.73.92.26.39 Ⓕ04.73.92.99.96
Closed *31 Oct–1 April.* **Car park.**

The building may not be very attractive but the owner is very friendly and the evenings in the small inner patio can be lively affairs. New arrivals received 5–11pm. Rooms with two, four, six and eight beds. Reckon on €12 for a night in a double room, including breakfast. You can rent sleeping bags.

Hôtel Cartier

19 rue de l'Industrie. **Map D1-9**
☎04.73.92.02.14
Cots available.

An unpretentious little hotel in a quiet street in the commercial district, offering very competitive prices. Don't expect luxury, however – for €15.30 for a double room with basin, €20.60 with shower, you get saggy beds, stark décor and a shower on the second floor. If you want a TV, the owner, who has a room on the first floor, will bring one to your room for a modest price. Avoid room no. 5, which is noisy. The clientele includes white-collar workers and young people on a budget.

Hôtel Foch*

32 rue du Maréchal-Foch. **Map B3-8**
Ⓣ04.73.93.48.40 Ⓕ04.73.35.47.41
TV. Pay car park.

The entrance is easy to miss in spite of the sugar-coloured frontage. Reception is on the first floor but the rooms here are best avoided; opt for the ones on the upper floors, even though they're quite small. Rooms with basin €32, or €40–48 with wc.

Hôtel de Bordeaux**

39 av. Franklin-Roosevelt. **Map A3-3**
Ⓣ04.73.37.32.32 Ⓕ04.73.31.40.56
Ⓦwww.hoteldebordeaux.com
Closed *Sun afternoon.* **TV. Pay car park.**

This hotel is five minutes from the centre in an unprepossessing area, but it's comfortable and convenient for the main tourist attractions, and the welcome and service are great. Doubles €35 with basin/wc, €45–52 with shower/wc or bath. Credit cards not accepted.

Hôtel Ravel**

8 rue de Maringues. **Map D2-7**
Ⓣ04.73.91.51.33 Ⓕ04.73.92.28.48
Ⓦwww.hotelravel63@wanadoo.fr
Closed *23 Dec–2 Jan.* **TV.**

This little family-run hotel is in a quiet neighbourhood tucked away between the station and the town centre. It has a captivating mosaic façade and the proprietress will give you a warm welcome. She runs the place virtually single-handed and creates a nice relaxed atmosphere – if you want more bread at breakfast, she'll nip across to the baker's. The décor in the bedrooms is simple and charming and they're good value at €40 with bath/wc. Breakfast costs €5.

Hôtel Albert-Élisabeth**

37 av. Albert-Élisabeth. **Map D2-4**
Ⓣ04.73.92.47.41 Ⓕ04.73.90.78.32
Ⓦwww.hotel-albertelisabeth.com
TV. Car park. High chairs available.

This place, 100m from the station, is marked by a big red neon sign – you won't miss it. Well-soundproofed rooms, some overlooking the courtyard, though on the whole they lack character. A breakfast buffet is served and costs €6.50. Doubles €46–50 with shower/wc or bath. *10% discount on the room rate at the weekend except July–Aug is offered to our readers on presentation of this guide.*

Hôtel de Lyon***

16 pl. de Jaude. **Map B3-6**
Ⓣ04.73.93.32.55 Ⓕ04.73.93.54.33
Ⓔ hotel.de.lyon@wanadoo.fr
TV. High chairs available. Car park.

You can't get more central than place de Jaude – it's in the very heart of town. Comfortable if conventional rooms with good facilities, double glazing and telephones; doubles with shower/wc or bath €72. Weekday lunch menu at €13.50; reckon on €17 for a meal à la carte. Breakfast is served as a buffet in the pub downstairs or can be brought to your room.

L'Oliven

5 rue de la Boucherie. **Map B2-17**
Ⓣ04.73.90.38.94
Closed *Sat lunchtime, Sun and Mon.*
Disabled access.

This place has pretty décor in orange hues and is run by a bright, friendly team. They offer a fresh look at Provençal and Mediterranean cooking and dishes are light and tasty. Didier, the chef, will take time to present his dishes to you. Specialities include marinated roast aubergines; *cassolette* with polenta; prawns with lime, coriander and tomato croutons; warm smoked salmon with marinated red peppers and aïoli; sea bass with herbs; coconut cake with ricotta and almond liqueur cream. Lunch menu €10.50 and *menus-cartes* at €17–23 in the evening. À la carte will cost around €25.

Restaurant Le Bougnat

29 rue des Chaussetiers. **Map B2-21**
Ⓣ04.73.36.36.98
Closed *Sun; Mon, Wed and Fri lunchtimes; July.*

Set not far from the cathedral, in the pedestrian zone, this place might sound like a tourist trap, but it's not. The restaurant has a rustic feel and offers a wonderful selection of well-prepared regional dishes – mutton tripe, *pounti* (a mixture of

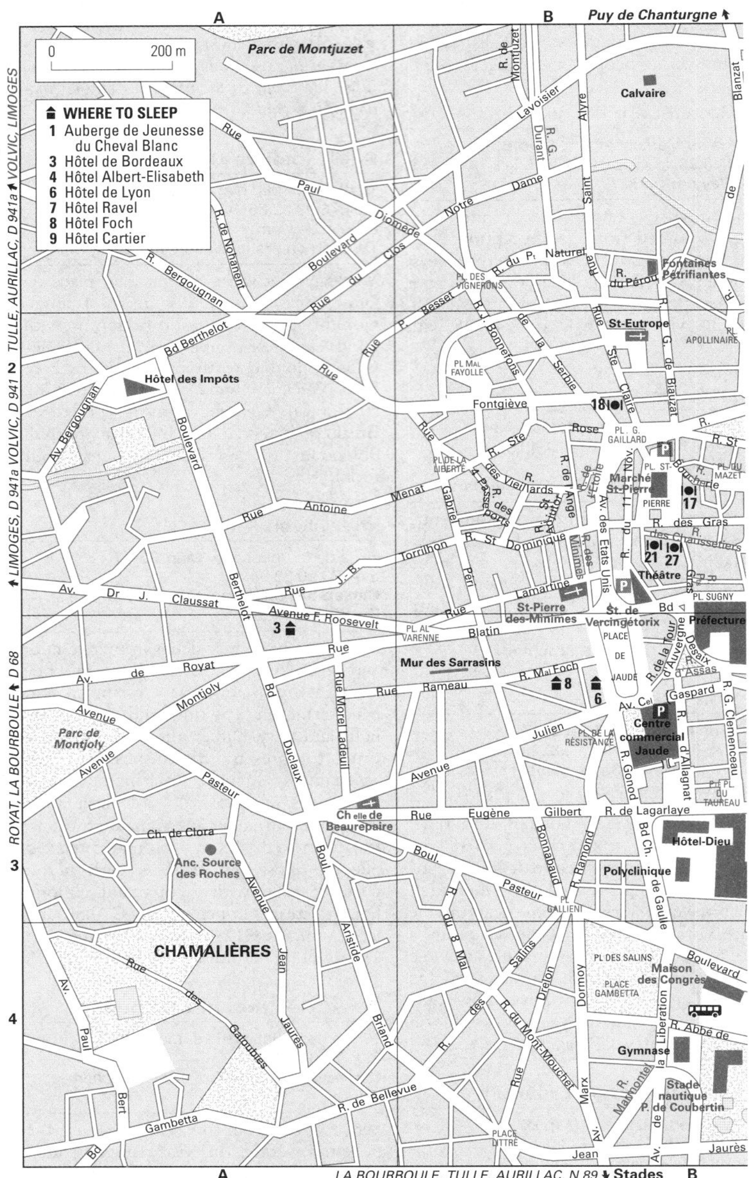
Puy de Chanturgne
LIMOGES, D 941a VOLVIC, D 941 TULLE, AURILLAC, D 941a VOLVIC, LIMOGES
ROYAT, LA BOURBOULE D 68
LA BOURBOULE, TULLE, AURILLAC, N 89 Stades
0 200 m
WHERE TO SLEEP
1 Auberge de Jeunesse du Cheval Blanc
3 Hôtel de Bordeaux
4 Hôtel Albert-Elisabeth
6 Hôtel de Lyon
7 Hôtel Ravel
8 Hôtel Foch
9 Hôtel Cartier
Parc de Montjuzet
Calvaire
Fontaines Pétrifiantes
St-Eutrope
Hôtel des Impôts
Marché St-Pierre
Théâtre
St-Pierre des-Minimes
Préfecture
Mur des Sarrasins
Centre commercial Jaude
Chapelle de Beaurepaire
Hôtel-Dieu
Polyclinique
Anc. Source des Roches
Parc de Montjoly
CHAMALIÈRES
Maison des Congrès
Gymnase
Stade nautique P. de Coubertin
PL. DES VIGNERONS
PL. Mal FAYOLLE
PL. G. GAILLARD
PL. DE LA LIBERTÉ
PL. AL VARENNE
PLACE DE JAUDE
PL. DE LA RÉSISTANCE
PL. GALLIENI
PL DES SALINS
PLACE GAMBETTA
PLACE LITTRÉ
PL. SUGNY
PL. APOLLINAIRE
Pte PL. DU TAUREAU
Boulevard Berthelot
Avenue F. Roosevelt
Av. Dr J. Claussat
Av. de Royat
Avenue Julien
Avenue Pasteur
Rue Blatin
Rue Gabriel Péri
Rue Eugène Gilbert
R. de Lagarlaye
Bd Ch. de Gaulle
Av. de la Libération
R. de Bellevue
Rue des Galoubies
Avenue Jean Jaurès
Boul. Aristide Briand
Av. Bergougnan
Rue Fontgiève
Av. des États Unis
Bd Desaix
R. G. Clemenceau
Av. Paul Bert
Bd Gambetta
Av. Jean Jaurès
Av. Marx Dormoy

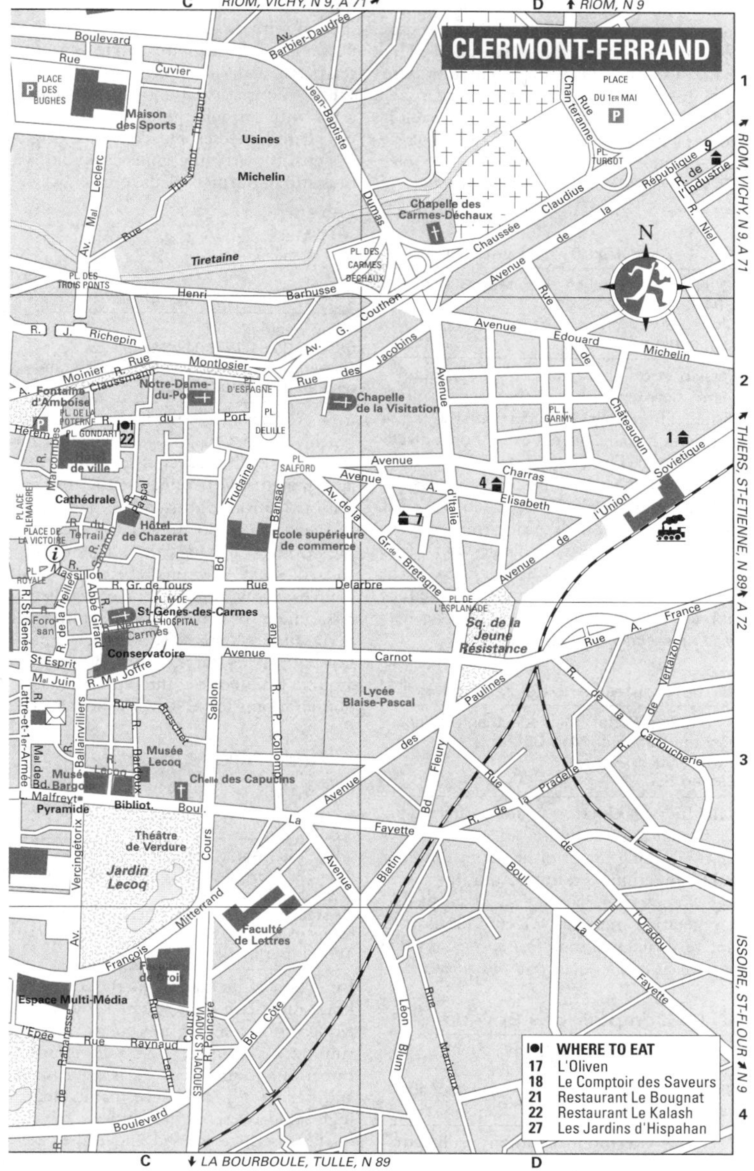
CLERMONT-FERRAND
C
RIOM, VICHY, N 9, A 71
D
RIOM, N 9
RIOM, VICHY, N 9, A 71
THIERS, ST-ETIENNE, N 89, A 72
ISSOIRE, ST-FLOUR, N 9
LA BOURBOULE, TULLE, N 89
1
2
3
4
N
PLACE DES BUGHES
Maison des Sports
Usines Michelin
Tiretaine
Chapelle des Carmes-Déchaux
PL. DES CARMES DÉCHAUX
PLACE DU 1ER MAI
PL. TURGOT
PL. DES TROIS PONTS
Boulevard
Rue Cuvier
Av. Barbier-Daudrée
Jean-Baptiste Dumas
Rue Thévenot Thibaud
Av. Mal Leclerc
Rue Chanteranne
Chaussée Claudius
Henri Barbusse
Av. G. Couthon
Avenue de la République
R. de l'Industrie
R. Niel
Avenue Edouard Michelin
R. J. Richepin
Rue Montlosier
R. Moinier
Rue Claussmann
Rue des Jacobins
Fontaine d'Amboise
Notre-Dame-du-Port
Chapelle de la Visitation
PL. D'ESPAGNE
PL. DELILLE
PL. SALFORD
PL. L. GARMY
PL. DE LA POTERNE
PL. GONDART
Hôtel de ville
Cathédrale
Hôtel de Chazerat
Ecole supérieure de commerce
Avenue Charras
Avenue A. Elisabeth
Av. de la Gr. de Bretagne
Avenue de l'Union Soviétique
Avenue d'Italie
Rue de Châteaudun
PL. DE L'ESPLANADE
Sq. de la Jeune Résistance
PLACE DE LA VICTOIRE
PL. ROYALE
R. Massillon
R. Gr. de Tours
Rue Delarbre
St-Genès-des-Carmes
Conservatoire
Avenue Carnot
Rue A. France
Lycée Blaise-Pascal
Musée Lecoq
Chelle des Capucins
Bibliot.
Pyramide
Théâtre de Verdure
Jardin Lecoq
Boul. La Fayette
Avenue des Paulines
Bd Fleury
Rue de la Pradelle
R. de la Cartoucherie
R. de Vertaizon
Faculté de Lettres
Av. François Mitterrand
Espace Multi-Média
Av. Vercingétorix
Rue Raynaud
VIADUC ST-JACQUES
Bd Côte Blatin
Léon Blum
Rue Marivaux
Boul. de l'Oradou
Boulevard
WHERE TO EAT
17 L'Oliven
18 Le Comptoir des Saveurs
21 Restaurant Le Bougnat
22 Restaurant Le Kalash
27 Les Jardins d'Hispahan

bacon and Swiss chard), pigs' trotters and *potée auvergnate*, the thick local soup which is becoming harder and harder to find in Clermont. There's a splendid wood-burning stove in the foyer, which the chef uses to prepare Auvergne pancakes. The €12.50 set menu is very decent and there are good wines from the Auvergne. Reckon on €15–30 à la carte. If you're on your own, try to get one of the stools at the counter where the regulars sit. *Free coffee offered to our readers on presentation of this guide.*

Les Jardins d'Hispahan

11 ter rue des Chaussetiers. **Map B2-27**
☎04.73.90.23.07
Closed *Sun, Mon and public holidays; Ist fortnight in Aug.*

Persian cooking with subtle, flowery, aromatic flavours rather than heavily spiced dishes. The décor's not particularly exciting, which makes it easier to concentrate on the food. The kebab *bargue*, made with grilled veal marinated in lemon, is perfect, as is anything cooked with a sauce. And if you think you don't like rice, the way they cook basmati here will change your mind forever. Menus from €14 up to €25; around €16 à la carte. Travellers' cheques not accepted. *Free apéritif offered to our readers on presentation of this guide.*

Restaurant Le Kalash

8–10 rue du Port; in the pedestrian precinct near the cathedral. **Map C2-22**
☎04.73.90.19.22
Closed *Sun.*

This Indo-Pakistani restaurant offers typical fare of high quality in an attractive setting. The long list of dishes from different Pakistani ethnic groups is mouth-watering. Menus €16.25 and €21.50, as well as a vegetarian menu at €13.60. Friendly, if not very talkative, staff. *Free apéritif offered to our readers on presentation of this guide.*

Le Comptoir des Saveurs

5 rue Saint-Claire. **Map B2-18**
☎04.73.37.10.31 Ⓕ04.73.36.49.12
Closed *Sun; Mon; Feb and Aug school holidays.*

A typical Clermont restaurant with retro-chic décor and welcoming staff who readily offer information about the food or advice about the wines. It's not the cheapest place in town, but the dishes are tasty and imaginatively prepared. Menu of the day €24 at lunchtime, then others at €29–43 depending on the number of dishes, which can get elaborate – smoked salmon with asparagus béarnaise, creamed peas and asparagus with curried croutons, sea perch with artichokes with a sliver of warm foie gras, veal chop in a parmesan crust with an aubergine and thyme *compote*. Good cheeses and delicious, original desserts, too (try the apple crumble with mustard). Gourmet meals to take away.

Royat

63130 (2km W)

La Pépinière Chalut

11 av. Pasteur.
☎04.73.35.81.19 Ⓕ04.73.35.94.23
Closed *Sun evening and Mon.* **High chairs available. TV. Car park.**

You are warmly welcomed by Madame Chalut when you arrive at her charming inn. Her husband's cuisine is appetizing and imaginative, concentrating on fresh regional produce used in old family recipes, such as potato sausage and boned pig's trotters. But his palette is not limited to traditional Auvergnat cuisine – he also handles fish with great skill; try zander à la pissaladière or ravioli langoustines with herb sauce. Menus €21.50 (except public holidays). À la carte, count on spending around €32. Four completely refurbished double rooms for €40 with shower/wc.

Chamalières

63400 (3km W)

Hôtel Radio***

43 av. Pierre-et-Marie-Curie.
☎04.73.30.87.83 Ⓕ04.73.36.42.44
Ⓦwww.hotel-radio.fr
Restaurant closed *Sat lunchtime; Sun evening; Mon lunchtime; Jan; a week in Nov.*
TV. Car park.

Built as a radio station in the 1930s, this hotel-restaurant was owned by Michel Mioche for many happy years. Now it's run by his daughter, who gave up her career as a journalist in Paris to do so; she and her young team have maintained the high standards set by her father. Only top-quality produce is used and dishes are as skilfully prepared as they are imaginative. Good choices include Breton lobster with truffle *jus*, casserole-roast pigeon and hot Caribbean chocolate soufflé. Menus

€27–79. Beautiful bedrooms with lots of Art Deco style; doubles €69–78 with shower/wc and €78–120 with bath.

Saint-Genès-Champanelle

63122 (9km W)

Auberge de la Moréno

Col de la Moréno; between Puy de Dôme and Puy de Laschamps, on the D941A.
04.73.87.16.46
Closed *Mon (summer); Mon and Tues (winter); 1st fortnight in Jan; 2nd fortnight in Nov.* **High chairs available. Disabled access. Car park.**

Recently acquired by new management, this inn has an interesting history, for it once belonged to the territory of Morlac, a legendary (but all too real) highway robber. Little is known about him – hardly surprising, as apparently nobody who fell into his clutches lived to tell the tale. Now guests receive a warm welcome that dispels all thoughts of such horrors, and the inn has retained its period charm, untainted by any touristy additions: large fireplace, dining table and stone floor worn down with age. The food lives up to these surroundings: the famous *truffades*, stuffed pig's trotter, mountain char fish with green lentils, Salers and Aubac beef. Try washing your meal down with a fine Gamay rosé, for example, and finish off with a *tarte tatin* (unusually, made with pears). Menus €13 (weekday lunchtime) to €26. Reckon on €25 à la carte. It's worth booking, as the inn has earned a well-deserved success. *Free apéritif offered to our readers on presentation of this guide.*

Nebouzat

63210 (28km W)

Auberge de la Fourniale

It's at Récoléine; from the col de la Ventouse, take the N89 in the direction of Nebouzat-Tulle. After Randanne turn right towards Récoléine and it's 4km further.
04.73.87.16.63
Closed *Sun and Mon lunchtimes in season; Mon, Tues and Sun out of season; 3 weeks in Sept.* **High chairs available.**

The Gauthiers gave up the family charcuterie and renovated this old shepherd's house and shed, keeping many of the original features. The chef loves tinkering, so there's an extraordinary décor hung with bells and baskets and a cheese service ingeniously made from horse shoes. Only fresh produce is used in the cooking which majors in traditional, substantial dishes like stuffed, boned pig's trotters. Be sure to try the impressive cheese platter, and for dessert opt for the *tarte tatin* with whipped cream. Weekday lunch menu €10 (charcuterie, scrambled egg with truffles and dessert) or another for €12.50; also a snack *formule* of a plate of Auvergne ham and sausage. *Free liqueur offered to our readers on presentation of this guide.*

Condat-en-Feniers

15190

Hôtel-restaurant Ché Marissou

Le Veysset; it's 3km from Condat on the D62, and well-signposted.
04.71.78.55.45
marissou@aol.com
Closed *Oct–March. Open every day including school holidays April–Sept.*

This hotel, surely the smallest in the world, was born out of the genuine passion of a Laval industrialist – a local boy made good – and helped along by an elaborate marketing campaign. Transformed from a holiday home into an inn, it has a lot of charm. You'll be welcomed by the owner himself in a dining room that looks as much like a living museum as it does a restaurant. Marissou's job is to send you away full, no matter how hungry you were when you arrived. Special one-day package for two people (full board at €240, half board at €190), with free champagne thrown in. The price of your meal depends on your age: children under 7 eat free; €11 for ages 7–10; €22 for 10–65; €20 for over-65s, and free again for guests aged 100 or over. You can help yourself as often as you like to traditional cold meat and *crudités*. That will be followed by the day's special – *potée*, the thick local soup, perhaps, or mutton tripe – then you serve yourself from a table bearing a selection of perfectly matured regional cheeses and dessert. With the cheese you'll get a chance to sample (on the house) a glass of rare wine made from late-harvested local grapes. The one and only bedroom is traditionally decorated. Perfect for a special night away.

Égliseneuve-d'Entraigues

63850

🏠 |●| Hôtel du Nord*

Rue Principale.
☎04.73.71.90.28
Closed *Sun evening; Mon out of season; by reservation only out of season; a fortnight in Sept.*

After a day's walking in the Cézallier, this pretty little country inn is a lovely place to stop for an Auvergnat snack or something a bit more substantial. Menus €10–20, or, if you call in advance, you can choose from menus up to €30. It's local cooking, classic and sure-handed: stuffed cabbage, *truffade* (potato cake with Cantal cheese), pig's trotters, home-made liver terrine. Doubles €25 with outside bathrooms. Credit cards not accepted.

Falgoux (Le)

15380

🏠 |●| Hôtel-restaurant L'Éterlou**

Take the D680 and then the D37.
☎04.71.69.51.14
Closed *13 Nov–30 March.* **Disabled access. TV.**

In a pretty village halfway between Salers and Puy-Mary, this cosy hotel offers bedrooms with kitchenettes. They're clean and modern, if lacking in atmosphere; doubles €42.50–59 with shower/wc or bath. Half board costs €39.50 per person out of season; €49.50 in season. The restaurant serves up hearty portions of tasty local dishes. Set menus €12–26.

Gannat

03800

🏠 |●| Hôtel du Château**

9 pl. Rantian; it's opposite the château.
☎04.70.90.00.88 Ⓕ04.70.90.30.79
Closed *Sat out of season; mid-Dec to early Jan.* **TV. Car park.**

This hotel is charming in a way that only nineteenth-century buildings in provincial towns can be. The kitchen provides traditional cooking from generations back: *andouillette bonne femme*, sautéed veal and chicken with creamed garlic. They also do a wonderful *pâté bourbonnais*, a potato and bacon pie, and a delicious walnut cake. Set menus €11.50 (weekdays only) to €22. Clean simple bedrooms start at €38 with shower/wc, up to €49 with bath.

Charroux

03140 (10km NW)

|●| La Ferme Saint-Sébastien

Chemin de Bourion; take the N9, then turn right onto the D42.
☎04.70.56.88.83 Ⓕ04.70.56.86.66
Closed *Mon and Tues except July–Aug; Jan; last week in June; last week in Sept.*
Disabled access. Car park.

This delightful restaurant, in one of the region's most beautiful villages, has quickly become a local favourite. The renovated farmhouse offers an intimate atmosphere in which to enjoy Valérie Saignie's fresh, creative cooking. Menus (€22–60) make great use of foie gras and local cheeses (Lavor and smoked Lavor) and they have an excellent cellar. It's very popular, so you'll definitely need to book.

Lalizolle

03450 (15km W)

🏠 |●| Hôtel La Croix des Bois**

It's 1km from Wolframines at the intersection of the D987 and 284 in the Colettes forest.
☎04.70.90.41.55
Closed *Dec–Jan; a fortnight in Feb.* **Car park.**

It would be a pity to miss out on lunch in this establishment. Its location, in the middle of the wood, is lovely; add to that the pleasure of good regional cuisine and home-made bread made by the owner who used to be a pastry cook. The typical traditional dishes will make you want to linger over lunch – all the more time to appreciate the view of the valley. Weekday menu €10.50 then others €13–23.63. The rooms are simple and clean. Doubles with shower/wc €38.11.

Lapalisse

03120

🏠 |●| Hôtel-restaurant Galland**

20 pl. de la République.
☎04.70.99.07.21 Ⓕ04.70.99.34.64

Closed *Sun evenings out of season; Mon; end Jan to Feb; last week in Nov and Ist week in Dec.* **Disabled access. High chairs available. TV. Car park.**

A delightful place where you can eat such dishes as fresh oysters, baked langoustines and *escalope* of duck foie gras pan-fried with figs. The cooking is inventive and all ingredients are extra-fresh. Menus €23–47. The spick-and-span bedrooms cost €45 for a double with shower/wc or €50 with bath. Ask for one overlooking the interior courtyard. The breakfast is heavenly. *Free apéritif offered to our readers on presentation of this guide.*

Mandailles-Saint-Julien

15590

Auberge Au Bout du Monde

Ⓣ04.71.47.92.47 Ⓕ04.71.47.95.95
Ⓦwww.auberge-auboutdumonde.com
Closed *Wed afternoons; Sat out of season; 15 Nov–26 Dec.*

A nice place in the Jordanne valley which is a starting point for hillwalkers going up the Puy-Mary. The hotel is quiet, simple and well run; doubles €33 with wc/shower. The restaurant, with its traditional *cantou* (inglenook fireplace) and gleaming copperware, is as cosy as you could wish. The cooking will satisfy even the hungriest hiker. Menus ranging from €10 to €14, with a regional menu at €18, offer charcuterie and regional specialities like *truffade* (potato cake with Cantal cheese), tripe, *pounti* and *potée* (the substantial local soup). Stuffed cabbage is made to order. There's a waterside terrace. Effusive welcome. *10% discount on a room (except school holidays) offered to our readers on presentation of this guide.*

Hôtel-restaurant Aux Genêts d'Or*

Ⓣ04.71.47.94.65 Ⓕ04.71.47.93.45
Open all year. **TV.**

A small hotel with a homely atmosphere, set back from the road down a quiet cul-de-sac. Comfortable doubles €32.50 with shower/wc, plus a few duplexes with kitchenette. Breakfast costs €6 and half board is available. Good cooking, with set menus at €11 (weekday lunchtime) and €13.50–20. Specialities include *tournedos* with gentian sauce, scallops on a bed of *fondant* leeks, sautéed foie gras, duck *confit* and *millefeuille. Free apéritif before a meal offered to our readers on presentation of this guide.*

Saint-Cirgues-de-Jordanne

15590 (8km SW)

Hôtel-restaurant Les Tilleuls**

Take the D17.
Ⓣ04.71.47.92.19 Ⓕ04.71.47.91.06
Ⓦwww.hotellestilleuls.com
Restaurant closed *Sun evening Nov–April.* **Hotel closed** *mid-Nov to April.* **High chairs and games available. TV. Swimming pool. Car park.**

A beautiful building overlooking the road and the Jordanne valley. You can relax in the garden, swimming pool or hot tub when you come back from a walk on the Puy-Mary. The quiet, pleasant bedrooms go for €40–43; half board costs €39–42 per person. The dining room is equally pleasant and the open fire is welcome in winter. Cooking is refined and creative: platter of asparagus, duck breast with dandelion honey, grilled mullet fillets with morels. Menus €11–31.50. *Free apéritif offered to our readers on presentation of this guide.*

Massiac

15500

Grand Hôtel de la Poste**

26 av. du Général-de-Gaulle.
Ⓣ04.71.23.02.01 Ⓕ04.71.23.09.23
Ⓦwww.hotel-massiac.com
Closed *10 days end Nov and 10 days early Dec.* **High chairs and games available. Disabled access. TV. Swimming pools. Car park.**

No sure shortage of facilities here: indoor and outdoor pools, Jacuzzi, steam bath, squash courts, gym. Doubles with all mod cons weigh in at €40–51 with shower/wc or bath. There's a pleasant restaurant at the back; it offers a set menu at €12.20 (not served on Sunday or public holidays), and others €18.20–29.50. Specialities include Auvergne ham, Cantal tripe, potato in flaky pastry, pig's trotters grilled with lentils and warm apple tart. 10% discount on the room rate 1 Oct–31 May. *10% discount on a room (1 Oct–1 June) offered to our readers on presentation of this guide.*

Mauriac

15200

Hôtel des Voyageurs – La Bonne Auberge**

Place de la Poste.
ⓣ04.71.68.01.01 ⓕ04.71.68.01.56
ⓦwww.auberge-des-voyageurs.com
Closed *Sat and Sun evening Nov–April; a week in June; fortnight at Christmas.* **High chairs available. TV.**

The nicest hotel in Mauriac, with twenty pretty rooms. Good bathrooms. Doubles €28 with shower (wc on the landing), €41 with shower/wc or bath. Menus, €11–30, feature regional specialities and traditional dishes. *10% discount on the room rate (except June–Sept) offered to our readers on presentation of this guide.*

Anglards-de-Salers

15380 (9km E)

Ferme-auberge Les Sorbiers

It's in the village on the D22.
ⓣ04.71.40.02.87
Closed *end Sept to April except during All Saints' Day holidays.* **Games available. Car park.**

A beautiful old stone building that's attractively arranged, with a warm atmosphere, pleasant dining room with big wooden tables and a huge open fireplace. Spotless, comfortable rooms with private en-suite bathrooms – two are family rooms with garden views, so they're quiet. Doubles for €36.59 including breakfast. Half board (if you stay three nights or more) at €58 for two. *Table d'hôte* €15, but it's best to book. Set menus, priced at €15–20. An ideal place if you want to enjoy the Cantal area. Credit cards are not accepted.

Drugeac

15140 (12km SE)

L'Auberge des Saveurs

ⓣ04.71.69.15.50.
ⓦwww.chez.com/dessaveurs
Closed *Wed.* **Games available. Disabled access.**

A village inn with a simple, inviting dining room, a sunny terrace and sophisticated cooking. It's run by a husband-and-wife team – David will welcome you warmly front of house, while Nicole is in charge of the kitchen. She worked in a number of restaurants on the Côte before settling here and developing her own style. Menus feature such dishes as Auvergne ravioli with baby vegetables, poussin terrine and house foie gras; they also specialize in fine grilled meats, and home-made desserts and bread. Dishes change with the seasons. Weekday lunch menu €10, and others €16–24. *Free coffee offered to our readers on presentation of this guide.*

Mont-Dore (Le)

63240

Auberge de Jeunesse Le Grand Volcan

Route du Sancy; 3km to the south of the town.
ⓣ04.73.65.03.53 ⓕ04.73.65.26.39
ⓔle-mont-dore@fuaj.org
Closed *10–25 Nov.* **Games available.**

A large, wooden chalet on the edge of the forest and the Dordogne with rooms for two to six people (some with mezzanines), of which ten have been refurbished. FUAJ membership card compulsory (you can buy it on site). €11.70 per person, breakfast included. Single menu at €8.40 in the large refectory, packed lunch at €6 on request. Bar, pool, table football.

Hôtel de la Paix**

8 rue Rigny.
ⓣ04.73.65.00.17 ⓕ04.73.65.00.31
Closed *mid-Nov to 20 Dec.* **TV.**

Built in 1880, this hotel has a lovely old-fashioned décor. Half board €44 per person, compulsory for Christmas Eve and New Year's Eve. Menus €15–49. It's run by a friendly woman who greets you warmly, and the atmosphere is wonderfully nostalgic. Simple, functional rooms go for €40 with shower/wc. Superb Belle Époque dining room and a charming sitting room. Classic cooking, appropriate to the surroundings, using simple, fresh produce: house foie gras, truffles with scrambled eggs, *croustillant de petits gris* with Laqueuille blue cheese, sautéed scallops with cream. *Free apéritif offered to our readers on presentation of this guide.*

Hôtel Le Castelet**

Avenue Michel-Bertrand; it's near the town centre.
04.73.65.05.29 F 04.73.65.27.95
castelet@compuserve.com
Closed *end March to 15 May and 1 Oct–20 Dec.* **TV. High chairs and games available. Swimming pool. Car park.**

There's not so much emphasis on spa cures here as much as in the other hotels in town, but it's a friendly place, with a swimming pool, garden and terrace. There are some thirty double-glazed rooms, with en-suite doubles at €56. Good local cuisine in the restaurant: trout with bacon and Puy lentils, raspberry gratin. Menus from €17 up to €27.

Restaurant Le Bougnat

23 av. Georges-Clemenceau.
04.73.65.28.19
Closed *5 Nov–15 Dec.* **Garden. Car park.**

Traditional cooking with a modern slant – nobody in Mont-Dore does it better. An old stable has been very nicely transformed to make a delightful dining space with little tables and tiny sideboards. The *pounti* (a mixture of bacon and Swiss chard) is one of the best ever, and the *truffade* (potato cake with Cantal cheese) is excellent. The garlic soup, the sautéed rabbit *à la gentiane* and the stuffed cabbage are also good. Set menus €15–23, or around €23 à la carte. This is a great place to come on cold winter evenings after a good day's skiing. Best to book – it's very popular.

Montluçon

03100

Hôtel des Bourbons - Restaurant aux Ducs de Bourbon**

47 av. Marx-Dormoy; it's near the station.
04.70.05.28.93 F 04.70.05.16.92
Restaurant 04.70.05.22.79
Restaurant closed *Sun evening and Mon.* **TV.**

This beautiful eighteenth-century townhouse has been stylishly renovated and offers comfortable, bright bedrooms. Doubles €47 with shower/wc or bath. The restaurant has a great reputation, serving serious, not very original but beautifully executed cuisine; the menus, €13–35, offer dishes such as skate wings with capers, grilled salmon and scorpion fish with two sauces and profiteroles with chocolate sauce. There's a pub, with a menu for €13, which lets you eat the same standard of food in more casual surroundings. *Free apéritif offered to our readers on presentation of this guide.*

La Vie en Rose

7 rue de la Fontaine; it's beside Notre-Dame church.
04.70.03.88.79
Closed *Sun lunchtime; third week in Nov.*

If you find yourself in the old part of Montluçon, unwind in this relaxed, cosy place. The walls are hung with old photos of the town and adverts from the 1930s. The cooking is great – *bourbonnaise* not only in quality but also in quantity. Excellent potato pie in particular. Menus €8 (weekday lunchtimes) and €14.50.

Le Safran d'Or

12 pl. des Toiles; it's in the pedestrian zone of the medieval town.
04.70.05.09.18 F 04.70.05.55.60
Closed *Sun evening; Mon; Tues evening; 15 Aug–15 Sept.*

Behind its yellow marbled façade, this place has the ambience of a Parisian brasserie and the cooking is of the kind you'd get in a high-class bistro. You'll receive a warm welcome from the owner. The service is quick and efficient but you won't feel rushed, and the excellent cooking (simple, traditional dishes using the freshest ingredients) won't cost you a fortune. Set menus €19 (weekdays only) to €23.

Néris-les-Bains

03310 (8km SE)

Hôtel-restaurant Le Garden

12 av. Marx-Dormoy.
04.70.03.21.16 F 04.70.03.10.67
hotel.le.garden@wanadoo.fr
Restaurant closed *Sun evening; Mon 1 Nov–31 March. Annual holidays 26 Jan–6 March.* **High chairs and games available. TV. Pay car park.**

The facade of this attractive house is hung with geraniums and inside there's a very lovely wooden staircase which creaks just enough to give added charm. The more than acceptable rooms open onto the grounds. Doubles €40.50–54.50, depending on size. Classic yet innovative cuisine with lots of seafood, foie gras, offal and perfectly deglazed sauces. Weekday menu €13, others up to €30.50 (three courses). *10% discount on the room rate 1 Nov–31 March offered to our readers on presentation of this guide.*

Montmarault

03390

Hôtel de France**

1 rue Marx-Dormoy.
T *04.70.07.60.26* F *04.70.07.68.45*
Closed *Sun evening; Mon; 3 weeks from 11 Nov; a week in Spring.* **TV. High chairs available. High chairs available. Car park.**

Not a place you'd stop at if you hadn't heard about Patrick Omont's cooking. It's well worth the trip. Try snails with walnuts, skate wing with Charroux mustard or omelette *à la Brayade* with bacon and potatoes. Sheer delight. Menus €15–42. There are rooms, too, at €40.40–45 for a double with shower/wc or bath.

Montsalvy

15120

L'Auberge Fleurie**

Place du Barry.
T 04.71.49.20.02 F 04.71.49.29.65
W www.auberge-fleurie.com
Restaurant closed *Sun evening; Mon at All Saints' Day and Easter; 1 Jan–13 Feb (restaurant only).* **High chair available. TV. Car park.**

Gorgeous place with ivy clambering up the front wall, a fireplace, exposed beams and ancient doors. The cosy restaurant offers delicious menus that change with the seasons and a number of reasonably priced wines. The lunch menu, €11, and others (€17–30), are good value. The hotel has been renovated and offers spacious, comfortable and nicely decorated rooms with shower/wc or bath €39–51; half board is €41.50–47 per person. *Free apéritif offered to our readers on presentation of this guide.*

Inter-Hôtel du Nord**

T 04.71.49.20.03 F 04.71.49.29.00
W www.hotel-du-nord.com
Closed *1 Jan–Easter.* **TV. High chairs and games available. Car park.**

Situated in the heart of the Châtaigneraie, this quiet, plush restaurant has an excellent reputation for its traditional local dishes. Menus at €15 (weekdays only) up to €40, with a regional menu at €22. Specialities include *crépinette* of pig's trotters, trout soufflé with lentil sauce, *falette* (stuffed breast of mutton), stew of suckling pig, pan-fried snails with ceps and walnuts, fresh foie gras in Sauternes, locally grown beef and iced mousse flavoured with gentian liqueur. Plus all the classics: *aligot, confit* and so on. Colourful, comfortable rooms for €50–56 with shower/wc or bath; €55 half board.

Calvinet

15340 (17.5km W)

Hôtel de la Terrasse*

Place Jean-de-Bonnefon; take the D19.
T 04.71.49.91.59
Closed *Nov to end Dec.* **Car park.**

The chatty lady who's been running this hotel since 1936 has a gift for taking care of her guests. She has created a wonderful and homely atmosphere, with lovely rustic décor including copper pans, an old clock and a sideboard. Her specialities are crêpes stuffed with Cantal cheese, stuffed pig's trotters and pear tart. Cheapest menu €10, followed by others at €12.20–26 (with two starters). The bedrooms are furnished with period furniture; doubles are €28 with basin, €40 with bath/wc. Half board €32 per person.

Hôtel Beauséjour**

Route de Maurs.
T 04.71.49.91.68 F 04.71.49.98.63
W www.cantal-restaurant-puech.com
Closed *Mon and Tues lunch in season; Sun evening, Mon and Tues out of season; Jan.* **TV. Car park.**

Michelin has awarded the restaurant a coveted star – it's the only place in Cantal to have one – and it's won regional awards, too. There's a cheery atmosphere and lots of regulars – travelling executives and local farmers who come here for family celebrations. Superb, seasonally changing and reasonably priced menus (€25–55) feature dishes such as black-pudding and duck-liver pie, locally produced pork chop cooked under the rind, potatoes stuffed with pig's trotters. À la carte: duck-liver waffle and caramel with gentian. Good wines at reasonable prices. Comfortable double rooms cost €46.

Moulins

03000

Le Parc**

31 av. du Général-Leclerc; it's near the train station.
Ⓣ04.70.44.12.25 Ⓕ04.70.46.79.35
Restaurant closed *Sat and Sun evening. Annual holidays 9–25 July, 1–10 Oct; 23 Dec–2 Jan.* **TV. Car park.**

The Barret family have been running this hotel since 1956 and they offer a kindly welcome. It's a beautiful building, classic in style and exceptionally well appointed. The bright dining room is relaxing, and the furniture, fabrics and colours are simple and harmonious. The restaurant serves traditional and local dishes with no surprises and no nasty shocks: Charolais fillet with Fourme d'Ambert cheese, duck *aiguillette* with orange. Set menus range from €17 (not Sun) up to €36. Rooms are well soundproofed; doubles with shower/wc or bath cost €35–59. Those in the pretty annexe are simplest and the most peaceful. *Free apéritif offered to our readers on presentation of this guide.*

Hôtel de Paris-Jacquemart***

21 rue de Paris.
Ⓣ04.70.44.00.58 Ⓕ04.70.34.05.39
Ⓔhotel-de-paris-moulins@wanadoo.fr
Closed *Sat lunch except on public holidays; Sun evening; Mon; 2 weeks in Jan; 3 weeks in Aug.* **Disabled access. TV. High chairs available. Car park.**

The chic-est establishment in Moulin. Elegant décor, refined furnishings and courteous welcome – everything to please. And the prices are more than reasonable for the quality. Doubles €54 with shower/wc and €69–100 with bath. The chef specializes in high-quality classic cuisine with a creative twist – weekday menu €25 or others up to €54. *Free apéritif offered to our readers on presentation of this guide.*

Restaurant La Petite Auberge

7 rue des Bouchers; it's near the main post office.
Ⓣ04.70.44.11.68 Ⓕ04.70.44.82.04
Closed Sun *except public holidays; Mon evening; Feb holidays; 4–25 Aug.* **Disabled access.**

Recently renovated restaurant that offers great food. The chef's expertise with first-rate ingredients produces results that are full of flavour – scallop *fricassée* with salad, Charolais steak with Auvergne blue cheese and Saint-Pourçain *andouillette* with Charroux mustard. There's a quick set menu at €10, including wine, in the brasserie. At greater leisure, in the restaurant, weekday menu at €14.50, then others at €20 and €28. Delightful welcome. *Free apéritif or coffee offered to our readers on presentation of this guide.*

Le Grand Café

49 pl. d'Allier.
Ⓣ04.70.44.00.05
Closed *Sun in winter.* **Car park. Disabled access.**

Service until 11pm. This superb 1900s brasserie is a listed building, and it's the most popular place in the area – people come for the atmosphere as much as as the food. Past regulars have included a youthful Coco Chanel. Popular choices include grilled pig's trotters, calf's brawn, oxtail and steak. Menus €18 and €23. *Free coffee offered to our readers on presentation of this guide.*

Coulandon

03000 (6km W)

Hôtel Le Chalet-Restaurant Le Montégut***

It's on the D945.
Ⓣ04.70.46.00.66 Ⓕ04.70.44.07.09
Ⓦwww.hotel-lechalet.com
Closed *1 Dec–31 Jan.* **Disabled access. TV. High chairs available. Swimming pool. Car park.**

If you're on the lookout for a relaxing break, this late nineteenth-century chalet nestling in the depths of the countryside is ideal. Bedrooms have been tastefully decorated and they're all different; doubles €63–74 with shower/wc or bath. From the rooms you'll either have a view of the countryside or the park, which has an ornamental lake. The restaurant is in a separate building, and when summer arrives you can lunch or dine by the pool. The first menu at €18 (weekdays), €22 (weekends), is based on fresh market produce and there are others up to €39. *Free apéritif offered to our readers on presentation of this guide.*

Souvigny

03210 (11km W)

Auberge Les Tilleuls

Place Saint-Éloi.
☎04.70.43.60.70 ℻04.70.44.85.73
Closed *Sun evening; Mon; Tues evening mid-Nov to end June; 30 Aug–6 Sept; 30 Dec–6 Jan.* **High chairs available.**

You're greeted by a riot of geraniums in this country inn, where folk art on the walls portrays village scenes from the 1940s. €11 weekday lunch menu and others €15–37.50. Specialities include three types of foie gras, Salers beef and pork, with a number of more sophisticated dishes. Superb food and a good wine list, too. *Free apéritif offered to our readers on presentation of this guide.*

Meillers

03210 (20km SW)

Au Bon Vieux Temps**

It's in the village.
☎04.70.47.33.36
Closed *Tues; Wed; 20 Dec–20 Feb.* **High chairs available. Disabled access.**

Raymond Tixier is a great chef who has won prizes for his desserts. One day, however, he woke up and realized that chasing Michelin stars was no longer for him. So he left the fancy restaurants behind and reopened this country inn, opting for a menu of quality and carefully prepared traditional dishes. The rustic décor includes an old oven where he cooks his bread and stews his casseroles. The sauces are unbelievable – try the West Indian colombos – and, of course, desserts are perfect. Menus go for €20–24. It's essential to book because the dining room is so small. *Free coffee offered to our readers on presentation of this guide.*

Chapelle-aux-Chasses (La)

03230 (22km NE)

L'Auberge de la Chapelle-aux-Chasses

6km to the north of Chevagnes; take the D31.
☎04.70.43.44.71
Closed *Tues; Wed; fortnight in Feb.*

This inn in a beautiful village seems like a doll's house, or a typical postcard image, complete with a front garden. Inside the tiny dining room, only the chiming of the bells in the nearby church will remind you of the passing of time. The cooking is appropriately traditional, with a choice of exquisite home-made desserts chalked on a blackboard. The menu changes often; weekday lunchtime menu at €12.50, then others at €17.50–32.

Dompierre-sur-Besbre

03290 (30km E)

Auberge de l'Olive**

129 av. de la Gare; take the D12.
☎04.70.34.51.87 ℻04.70.34.61.68
www.auberge-olive.fr
Closed *Fri (except July–Aug); one week at the end of Sept; three weeks end Jan–Feb.* **TV. High chairs and games available.**

A handsome, well-maintained building covered in Virginia creeper. Care is taken with the cooking and the service is faultless. Set menus range from €15 (weekdays only, not public holidays) to €22. A free gift is offered to children. There are seventeen comfortable, quiet rooms; doubles with shower/wc or bath go for €43–46. *Free coffee offered to our readers on presentation of this guide.*

Murat

15300

Aux Globe-Trotters**

22 av. du Docteur-Mallet, opposite the train station.
☎04.71.20.07.22 ℻04.71.20.16.88
Closed *Sun out of season; first week in July.* **TV.**

There are twenty very clean, modern rooms here, costing from €29 to €38. Nicest, and most peaceful, are those overlooking the garden. The attic rooms are delightful, too, though watch your head if you're tall. Very laid-back atmosphere in the downstairs bar restaurant which is popular with young people.

Hôtel Les Breuils**

Avenue du Docteur-Mallet.
☎04.71.20.01.25 ℻04.71.20.33.20
www.hostellerie-les-breuils.com

Closed *mid-Nov to end April; call to check opening periods outside school holidays.* **TV. Swimming pool. Pay car park.**

A substantial nineteenth-century private house which has been turned into a hotel. Decorated with antiques and works of art, it has an old-fashioned, aristocratic charm that's a world away from the sterility of some modern establishments. There's a garden with a nice heated indoor pool. Ten cosy, comfortable rooms, stylishly redecorated. Doubles €61–76. *10% discount on the room rate in low season (excluding July–Aug) offered to our readers on presentation of this guide.*

Chalinargues

15170 (9km NE)

Auberge de la Pinatelle

☎04.71.20.15.92 ℻04.71.20.17.90
Closed *Wed and Sun evenings; a fortnight Sept–Oct.* **Disabled access (restaurant only).**

A pretty, popular inn. The young owners have five comfortable and tastefully decorated rooms; doubles with wc/shower or bath €37. Half board €34 per person. In the convivial dining room you can choose from menus between €12.50 and €30. They offer Auvergne and Mediterranean specialities and good fish – typical dishes include trout with bacon, *coq au vin*, duck breast, salad with truffles and other Périgord delicacies.

Dienne

15300 (11km NW)

Restaurant du Lac Sauvage

Take the D3 from Murat then the D23.
☎04.71.20.82.65
Closed *Oct–June.*

Paradise for fishermen and walkers in a magnificent setting on the banks of a private lake 1230m up. The kitchen uses local produce to prepare tasty regional specialities, served up in generous portions: especially good are trout with bacon, *truffade* (potato cake with Cantal cheese) and *pounti* (a mixture of bacon and Swiss chard). €13 for set menu or around €16 for a full meal à la carte. You can even catch your own trout – no permit needed and there's equipment for rent. *Free coffee offered to our readers on presentation of this guide.*

Lioran (Le)

15300 (12km SW)

Hôtel-restaurant Le Rocher du Cerf**

Take the N122 from Murat then the D67.
☎04.71.49.50.14 ℻04.71.49.54.07
Closed *1 April–1 July and 10 Sept–22 Dec.* **TV. High chairs and games available. Car park.**

A typical family hotel in a ski resort. Located near the slopes, this is the nicest place in the area, a perfect base for skiing in winter and hiking in summer. Bedrooms are simple and well kept; they all have views of the mountains. Half board is obligatory; €30–43 per person. The restaurant has the same kind of homely atmosphere and the set menus (€12–18) change regularly. Specialities include stuffed cabbage, trout with bacon, truffade (the local potato cake with Cantal cheese), *pounti* (a mixture of bacon and Swiss chard), *coq au vin*, steak with bleu d'Auvergne (a local blue cheese) and bilberry tart. *10% discount on the room rate per person for a week's stay July–Aug offered to our readers on presentation of this guide.*

Allanche

15160 (23km NE)

Restaurant au Foirail

Maillargues; it's 1km from the centre of Allanche on the D679.
☎04.71.20.41.15
Closed *evenings; first week in Jan.* **Disabled access. Car park.**

You'll find this place on a little hill in the middle of the summer pastures and near one of the Auvergne's biggest cattle markets. It's a simple place serving flavourful Salers beef and regional specialities such as *truffade* and *pounti*. Hearty dish of the day €7, *menu du jour* €11.50 (weekdays only) and Sunday menus at €13 and €16. There are panoramic views from the dining-room windows. *Free coffee offered to our readers on presentation of this guide.*

Narnhac

15230

L'Auberge de Pont-la-Vieille**

Pont-la-Vieille; take the D990.
☎ and ℻04.71.73.42.60

Closed *Nov to mid-Dec.* **TV. Games available. Car park.**

This is a welcoming and relaxing little hotel with a nice terrace on the riverbank. Quiet and pleasant double rooms with shower/wc or bath are €35–38. Half board €32 per person. Set menus, €10 (weekdays only), and others €14–23, feature regional specialities – choose from dishes like stuffed cabbage, trout with bacon *à l'ancienne*, *rissole Saint-Flour* (a sort of fritter with a cabbage and bacon filling) and tripe. No credit cards. *10% discount on the room rate (in May–June and 1–21 Sept) offered to our readers on presentation of this guide.*

Pailherols

15800

⌂ |●| L'Auberge des Montagnes**

It's southeast of Vic-sur-Cère on the D54.
Ⓣ04.71.47.57.01 Ⓕ04.71.49.63.83
Closed *Tues out of season; 8 Oct–20 Dec.*
Disabled access. TV. High chairs available. Swimming pool. Car park.

A pretty little winding road from Vic-sur-Cère will lead you up to this excellent family hotel on the outskirts of the village. It's been thoughtfully renovated and there's a new building constructed in the traditional style with a beautiful turret. The pond and the wonderful view complete the setting. There's a terrace, indoor and outdoor swimming pools, a climbing wall and a games room in the old barn across the road – it also offers horse-drawn carriage rides. The bedrooms are cosy and well decorated; the bigger ones are in the new building. Doubles €42–49 with wc/shower or bath. Possibility of half board, from €41. There are two very bright dining rooms, one with the traditional *cantou* (inglenook) fireplace. The €13 *menu du jour*, and others €16.50–28, list local dishes such as *pounti* (a mixture of bacon and Swiss chard) and *truffade* (potato cake with Cantal cheese), along with house nut terrine, salmon trout, home-made patisserie and so on. Reservations recommended. *10% discount on a room (in low season, except weekends) offered to our readers on presentation of this guide.*

Picherande

63113

⌂ |●| Auberge du Tarafet

Lieu-dit Chareire; it's 3km from Picherande on the D149 to Superbesse 2.
Ⓣ04.73.22.31.17
Car park. High chairs available.

Christian is a big, friendly soul who has run this gîte-bar-restaurant for the last twenty years. He can tell you everything you need to know about the GR30 walking trail that goes through the area as well as the GR3 and the cross-country ski trails. His gîte is ideally located and very well maintained. For €14 you can sleep on one of thirty mattresses laid out on the ground floor, with separate kitchen and dining room on the first. You'll need to bring your own sleeping bag and food. In addition, there are three rooms with double-beds and bunks for practically the same price as the gîte – €25–40 for a double. Christian also runs a large, rustic inn where he serves regional specialities and sandwiches; menus from €10.40 and children's menu at €6. It's popular with locals who take a glass or two at the bar or at tables with their friends.

Pontgibaud

63230

⌂ |●| Hôtel-restaurant de l'Univers

It's 1km from town on the D578; you'll find it opposite the station.
Ⓣ04.73.88.70.09
Restaurant open *lunchtime only.* **Car park.**

This family guesthouse looks like a picture postcard. Charlot grows the vegetables and milks the cows, and Marie-Antoinette is the highly competent chef – she can feed the local fire brigade on her tripe dish while at the same time beating up a few eggs for an omelette for another customer. Although strictly speaking the restaurant is only open at lunchtime, you can actually eat here at any time of the day as long as you order in advance (and you're not in a hurry): dishes include unforgettable jellied veal, terrific grilled *andouillette* and fine pig's trotters. Menus from €10. Simple double rooms €26 with shower on the landing; and rooms sleeping four for €38.50.

Hôtel de la Poste**

Place de la République.
☎04.73.88.70.02 ℻04.73.88.79.74
Closed *Sun evening; Mon and Tues mornings (except June–Sept); Jan; the first fortnight in Oct.* **TV. Car park.**

A traditional hotel-restaurant with appealing, old-fashioned rooms. Doubles €34 with shower/wc or bath. Half board available for a minimum of three nights at €35 per person. Delicious local and seasonal dishes in the restaurant: salmon with lentils, *crepinette* of pig's trotters, chard with *mousserons* (small white or yellow mushrooms). Menus €14–44. *Welcoming glass of Kir offered to our readers on presentation of this guide.*

Saint-Pierre-le-chastel

63230 (6km S)

Les Genêts Fleuris

Follow the signs from Pontgibaud and it's in the hamlet of Bonnabaud.
☎04.73.88.75.81
✉genets.fleuris@wanadoo.fr
Car park.

Away from the tourist circuit, out in the country on the edge of the Combrailles, this renovated farmhouse has a very pleasing view of the chain of volcanic plugs of the Puys. The young couple who own the place are full of information and can advise you on good rambles nearby. The guest rooms have all facilities and they're well maintained. Doubles €40. Joël is a trained chef and cooks *potée* (local soup) and scrambled eggs with truffles among other delicious traditional dishes. Menus from €14. *Apéritif or liqueur on the house offered to our readers on presentation of this guide.*

Mazayes

63230 (7km S)

Auberge de Mazayes**

Take the D578, the D62, then the D52.
☎04.73.88.93.90 ℻04.73.88.93.80
Closed *Mon and Tues lunchtimes April–Sept; 15 Dec–25 Jan.* **Disabled access. TV. Car park.**

Located at the end of a winding road, this former stable has been fabulously converted into a charming and stylish inn, preserving its authentic rustic air (stone walls, big bunches of fresh flowers, open kitchen). It's the perfect place for a peaceful retreat in the country, and you can watch the sun set while sipping an apéritif from the pleasant terrace. Proper regional dishes, with an excellent *potée auvergnate* and tasty stuffed pig's trotters leading the way. Weekday menu at €14.50, and others €19–32. The attractive rooms cost €53–62 with shower/wc, and breakfast costs €7.50.

Puy-en-Velay (Le)

43000

Dyke Hôtel**

37 bd. Maréchal-Fayolle.
☎04.71.09.05.30 ℻04.71.02.58.66
Closed *Christmas to 1 Jan.* **TV. Pay car park.**

All the advantages of a chain hotel, plus a central location. Everything's clean and new, the décor is low-key and the service is efficient. Bedrooms are decorated in a similar, vaguely Japanese style, though they vary in size; no. 20 has a fine, huge mirror, while no. 31 affords a great view of the street. Doubles €36–45 with shower/wc or bath. Breakfast, €5.35, is served in the bar. "Dyke" refers to the local sugarloaf rock formations which give the area its character. NB: make sure to confirm your reservation before arriving; some of our readers have been disappointed.

Hôtel-restaurant Le Val Vert**

6 av. Baptiste-Marcet; it's around 1.5km from the centre, south of town on the way to Aubenas.
☎04.71.09.09.30 ℻04.71.09.36.49
🌐www.hotelvalvert.com
Restaurant closed *Sat lunchtime; last week in Dec.* **Disabled access. High chairs available. Baby changing and bottle warming facilities. TV. Car park.**

Though it looks rather like a chain establishment from the outside, inside you'll find a friendly, homely atmosphere. The comfortable, modern rooms are well maintained and decorated. Bedrooms with wc/shower or bath €50–54. The restaurant serves carefully prepared classics; the weekday lunch menu, €11, and others up to €36, feature seasonal specialities. Generous buffet breakfast, with home-made pastries and biscuits. *Free coffee offered to our readers on presentation of this guide.*

Hôtel du Parc - Restaurant François Gagnaire

4 av. Clément-Charbonnier; behind the place du Breuil, alongside the Henri-Vinay garden.
Ⓣ04.71.02.40.40 Ⓕ 04.71.02.18.72
Closed *1st week in Jan; restaurant (Ⓣ04.71.02.75.55) closed Sun and Mon and Tues lunch (July–Aug); Sun evening, Mon and Tues lunch the rest of the year.* **TV. High chairs available. Disabled access. Pay car park.**

This unassuming hotel near the historic quarter is being transformed: the foyer and lounges, decorated with a superb collection of labels from cigar boxes, have been tastefully refurbished. The bedrooms have yet to match this refinement, but they are comfortable, spacious and reasonably priced. Doubles €51–69, breakfast €6.50. The restaurant has won over gourmets through the sophistication of the dining room (with a bay window overlooking the park), the (almost excessively) attentive service, the originality of the dishes (using only regional produce) and the unerring elegance of their presentation: fillet of Vourzac trout with Puy lentils, *dodine* of duck foie gras, *millefeuille* of nougatine with pistachio cream. To top it all, a fine wine list, an impressive cheeseboard and excellent home-made bread rolls, including one variety made with lentils. Menus from €27 (weekdays only) to €70. It is advisable to book and turn up smartly dressed. A good place to sample "nouvelle cuisine", where creativity counts for more than quantity.

Hôtel Le Régina***

34 bd. Maréchal-Fayolle.
Ⓣ04.71.09.14.71 Ⓕ04.71.09.18.57
Ⓦwww.hotelrestregina.com
Disabled access. TV. Pay car park.

This hotel, in a beautiful old building right in the centre of town, is something of an institution. Prices are very reasonable for a three-star, especially considering the high standard of the facilities and service: doubles with shower/wc or bath €55–62. If you're a light sleeper, ask for a room at the back rather than one overlooking the street. The ground-floor restaurant offers some of the best cooking in Le Puy, specializing in fish (try the turbot in mint butter); regularly changing menus are €14.50 (lunchtime only) rising to €35. Staff are courteous and friendly.

La Parenthèse

8 av. de la Cathédrale, at the foot of the avenue leading up to the cathedral.
Ⓣ04.71.02.83.00
Closed *Sat and Sun; Christmas to New Year; one week in June; a week in Sept.*

A friendly, rustic restaurant in a quiet paved street at the foot of the imposing cathedral. It serves regional dishes that are simple and tasty: salad of trout from the Vourzac, duck with honey vinegar sauce and *aligot* (potatoes cooked with Tome du Cantal cheese). Desserts include *crème brûlée* with chestnut honey. Menus €16–22. Reservations recommended. *Free coffee offered to our readers on presentation of this guide.*

Restaurant L'Olympe

8 rue du Collège; 20m from the town hall.
Ⓣ and Ⓕ04.71.05.90.59
Closed *Sat lunch except July–Aug; Sun evening and Mon; Sun evening only in Aug; a fortnight around Easter; Nov.* **Disabled access.**

A delightful restaurant in a cobbled alleyway in the town's conservation area. The young chef sticks resolutely to local specialities but interprets them in his own, sometimes exotic, way; lentils, trout, game and verbena play star roles. In just a few years he's made this one of the best eating places in Le Puy. Menus €17–50, in various formats, all exceptional: "Traditional", "Pleasure" and "Discovery". Children's menu at €13. *Free coffee offered to our readers on presentation of this guide.*

Restaurant Tournayre

12 rue Chênebouterie; it's behind the town hall.
Ⓣ04.71.09.58.94
Closed *Sun and Wed evenings; Mon; Jan; Ist week in Sept.* **Disabled access.**

The exterior may be lovely, but the sixteenth-century vaulted dining room decorated with murals is simply magnificent. The service is pleasant and unobtrusive and Eric Tournayre is a first-rate chef who creates imaginative dishes of a very high order: snapper and foie gras on a bed of Puy lentils, *truffade* (potato cake with Cantal cheese) with a Saint-Agur sauce, *galette* of veal sweetbreads, pan-fried foie gras with ceps. A good range of desserts. Menus, at €20–67, include a vegetarian option. Best to book in summer.

Saint-Christophe-sur-Dolaison

43370 (10km SW)

Auberge du Grand Chemin

It's in the village, opposite the church.
04.71.03.18.99
Closed *Mon.*

When the pilgrims set out on the path from Le Puy to Santiago de Compostela, this village was their first overnight stop. The inn is an ideal place to restore your strength, with a nice terrace opposite the pretty village church. The setting is rustic with huge wooden beams and a fireplace at the entrance, and the young staff give you a charming welcome. The chef buys all the produce from local farmers: Ardèche-style potato pancake with garnish, beef with hot goat's cheese, cream cheese. The menu costs €13 or allow about €20 à la carte.

Saint-Julien-Chapteuil

43260 (18km E)

Le Cantamerlou

Place Saint-Robert.
04.71.08.46.83
Closed *Tues evening; Wed; Sat lunchtime.* **Disabled access.**

The restaurant, which opened in 2001, looks like a museum of local arts and folklore. The dining room is decorated with various articles foraged from local junk yards; with its wooden tables and open fire, it has a wonderfully nostalgic atmosphere. The cuisine is generously served; big salads and pastry cases stuffed with blue Auvergne cheese. Weekday menu €11 and others at €16, €19 and €22. The terrace is very peaceful. A genuine village inn with a good helping of style. *Free coffee offered to our readers on presentation of this guide.*

Restaurant Vidal

Place du Marché; take the D15.
04.71.08.70.50
www.restaurant-vidal.com
Closed *Mon evening and Tues out of season; Sun evening except July–Aug; mid-Jan to end Feb.* **High chairs available. Children's room with TV and Play Station. Disabled access. Car park.**

Though he modestly describes himself as "a country cook", Jean-Pierre Vidal is a brilliant and creative chef and one of the most important in the Haute-Loire. "Bistro" menus at €14 and €20 and "gastronomic" menus from €27 to €60 display his exquisite skill, and he makes sure he uses seasonal produce – game, wild mushrooms, green Puy lentils, duck and local beef. Courteous, attentive service in the quiet, pleasant dining room. *Free apéritif offered to our readers on presentation of this guide.*

Saint-Vincent

43800 (18km N)

Restaurant La Renouée

Cheyrac; take the D103 that follows the gorges of the Loire, and it's signed on the left.
04.71.08.55.94
Closed *Sun evening; Mon except July–Aug; Jan–Feb; a week at the end of Oct.* **Disabled access. High chairs available.**

The most delightful place in the area. It's a romantic house in a tiny garden where you'll find a warm welcome and fine, imaginative cooking: zander with crispy onions, morels stuffed with duck foie gras, *fricassée* of pike with *velouté* of green lentils. Set menus €17–35 and children's menu €10. Nice set tea on Sunday afternoons. *Free apéritif offered to our readers on presentation of this guide.*

Moudeyres

43150 (20km SE)

Le Pré Bossu***

It's as you enter the village on the D361.
04.71.05.10.70 04.71.05.10.21
www.leprebossu.fr.fm
Closed *weekday lunchtimes and Nov to Easter.* **Car park.**

A cosy, characterful cottage in the middle of a field; the air is clean and it's very quiet. There are ten smart, comfortable rooms, some of which overlook the field; others have a view of the vegetable garden. Doubles with bath/wc €90, suites with a view €120–130. The copious breakfast costs €12. Half board in high season costs €105–120 per person. The red mullet with *ratatouille* and fruit soup with coconut are particularly tasty, and all vegetables are fresh and good. Menus €38–58. Quick, efficient service. There's a pleasant terrace in summer. *10% discount on a room (Easter–Nov) offered to our readers on presentation of this guide.*

Pont-d'Alleyras

43580 (29km S)

Hôtel-restaurant du Haut-Allier***

Le pont d'Alleyras: take the D33.
Ⓣ04.71.57.57.63 Ⓕ04.71.57.57.99
Closed *Sun evening and Mon and Tues lunchtimes, except high season and public holidays; mid-Nov to mid-March.* **TV. Disabled access.**

This delightful hotel-restaurant, tucked away in a little village in the Haut-Allier valley, has been run by the same family for three generations. The building was renovated recently and the large restaurant has a classical décor. Service is good, and the elaborate cuisine is prepared by Philippe Brun, a fine chef who specializes in regional dishes full of authentic flavours. There's a wide choice on the set menus, which range from €20–78; the trout with mousse of lentils and foie gras is excellent, as is the pigeon deglazed with honey vinegar; the dishes are generously sprinkled with herbs personally gathered by a friend of the chef. Well-stocked cellar. Comfortable, well-maintained and peaceful doubles from €48 with shower/wc or bath; suites with Jacuzzi and balcony start at €85 up to €110. *10% off the room rate except in July–Aug offered to our readers on presentation of this guide.*

Saint-Haon

43340 (29km SW)

Auberge de la Vallée**

Take the N88 in the direction of Pradelles/Langogne, travel 7km on the D33 to Cayres and then take the D31.
Ⓣ04.71.08.20.73 Ⓕ04.71.08.29.21
Ⓦwww.auberge-de-la-vallee.fr
Closed *Mon Oct–May; Jan to mid-March.* **TV. Car park.**

The village is out in the wilds at 970m and just a few kilometres away the Allier cascades down the rocks of a deep gorge. This rustic, welcoming inn stands in a square dominated by a church with an unusual tower. Its ten comfortable rooms, furnished with solid old furniture, afford a peaceful night's sleep; they're €34.50 for a double with shower/wc and €37.50 with bath. Breakfast €6.50. In the restaurant they serve a series of menus, €13.50–32, featuring the chef's specialities which include veal with mushrooms and pear turnover. *10% discount on a room (except July–Aug) offered to our readers on presentation of this guide.*

Riom

63200

Restaurant L'Âne Gris

13 rue Gomot.
Ⓣ04.73.38.25.10
Closed *Sun; Mon; 15–30 Aug.*

Whether you think this place is insane, ghastly or heaven on earth will depend on how you feel about the owner, Casimir. He's slightly mad but ever so nice – forever making jokes at his customers' expense. He used to just call his chef "baboon" but now he uses the nickname for his favourite customers, too. To hear him talk, you might think the food wasn't up to much, but the kitchen produces good traditional dishes: *truffade* (potato cake with Cantal cheese or ham), *aligot* (fried potato cakes with Aligot cheese and sausage), salt pork with lentils and Charolais steaks. Brilliant list of local wines which Casimir chooses with a genuine passion. No set menus; you'll pay around €11 for an Auvergne speciality. A great place if you're prepared for Casimir's outsized personality. Credit cards not accepted. *Free apéritif offered to our readers on presentation of this guide.*

Tournoël

63530 (1.5km W)

Hôtel-restaurant La Chatellenie

It's on the D986.
Ⓣ04.73.33.63.23
Closed *Dec–April.*

Located on the road going up to Tournoël, this hotel is peaceful and the rooms overlook the valley. Simple, spacious doubles with shower/wc or bath €38–40. The dining room is decorated in rustic style and has a panoramic view. In it you'll find wholesome local dishes; menus at €15–26 offer regional specialities and portions are generous. Friendly service. *Free house apéritif offered to our readers on presentation of this guide.*

Effiat

63260 (27km NE)

Le Cinq Mars

16 rue Cinq-Mars.

Ⓣ04.73.63.64.16 Ⓕ04.73.63.64.16
Closed *Sun–Thurs evening; fortnight during Feb school holidays; last fortnight in Aug.*

Behind a deceptively anodyne exterior lies a very good restaurant. The chef has worked with some of the greats, including a Michelin star recipient, and his cooking is excellent. The generous, expertly prepared dishes use the season's best ingredients: highlights include *coq au vin*, salmon *tartare*, frogs' legs, salmon croquettes, Auvergnat soup and fillet of cod with creamed lentils. Modestly priced dishes of charcuterie are served with Auvergne wine. Four menus from €10 (weekday lunchtimes) up to €27 at weekends. Children's menu costs €9. It's best to book. *Free coffee offered to our readers on presentation of this guide.*

Riom-ès-Montagnes

15400

Hôtel-restaurant Le Saint-Georges**

5 rue du Capitaine Chevalier.
Ⓣ04.71.78.00.15 Ⓕ04.71.78.24.37
Ⓔ www.hotel-saint-georges.com
Restaurant closed *Sun evening and 3 weeks in Nov.* **Disabled access. TV.**

This large house with plain stone walls has been well restored and is right in the middle of the town, opposite the church of Saint-Georges. Modern doubles with shower and good facilities €38–45, according to the season. The restaurant menus boast good regional produce and quality "peasant" dishes: *panachée* of pork with green lentils, *confit* of rabbit with prunes and Auvergne wine, fine apple tart with honey caramel. Lunch *formule* €8.40, menu of the day €11.50 and other menus €19–27. *Free apéritif offered to our readers on presentation of this guide.*

Saignes

15240

Hôtel Relais Arverne*

Take the D22.
Ⓣ04.71.40.62.64 Ⓕ04.71.40.61.14
Ⓦwww.hotel-relais-arverne.com
Hotel closed *Feb school holidays and two weeks in Oct.* **Restaurant closed** *Fri and Sun evenings out of season.* **TV. Car park.**

This stone building has a huge corner watchtower and the tables on the terrace are made from ancient stone wheels. The bedrooms are comfortable and accessed via the terrace, so you can come and go as you please. Doubles €38–42.70 with shower/wc or bath. Breakfast costs €4.50. The hotel is full of interesting nooks and crannies. The dining room, where they serve dishes from the Dordogne and elsewhere, has a big clock and a huge fireplace. Specialities include *fricassée* of frogs' legs, red snapper with tarragon, mutton tripe *bonne femme* and trout with bacon. Menus €12 (weekdays only) and €20–38.50. *Free apéritif offered to our readers on presentation of this guide.*

Antignac

15240 (6km E)

Auberge de la Sumène

Take the D236 and it's in the village.
Ⓣ04.71.40.25.87

You can enjoy this traditional inn whether you're staying overnight or just eating. The rooms have limited facilities – doubles with basin €20, with bathroom €25 – but they're well maintained. The restaurant is popular with locals for the huge portions of sturdy, regional dishes; the kind of cooking that leads you to linger long over Sunday lunch. *Menu ouvrier* with starter, main course, cheese and dessert €10; otherwise the system is €8 for one course, €12.50 for two, €15 for three courses and €18 for four. Nicolas, who hails from the Dordogne, is an enthusiastic and warm host. Shady terrace at the back.

Saint-Anthème

63660

Hôtel-restaurant Au Pont de Raffiny**

It's 4km along the Saint-Romain road.
Ⓣ04.73.95.49.10 Ⓕ04.73.95.80.21
Closed *Sun evening and Mon out of season; Jan–15 Feb; weekdays in March.* **TV. Disabled access. High chairs available. Car park.**

If you're looking for a gourmet meal, head for this place, located on the banks of a little river near Saint-Anthème. The main attraction is Alain Beaudoux's light, creative cooking, typified by *andouillette* of fish with shellfish *coulis*, young rabbit *en crépine*, *croustillant* of guineafowl with morels and verbena *parfait*. €15 weekday menu and others up to €30. Excellent, reasonably priced wine list. The hotel is quiet and comfortable, offering rooms with shower/wc or bath for €36–41; some have a terrace. There are also a few chalets sleeping four to six, which are available by the week for €270–410. *10% reduction on the room rate (except July–Aug) or a free coffee offered to our readers on presentation of this guide.*

Chaulme (La)

63660 (10km S)

Auberge du Creux de l'Oulette

Take the D67 then the D258.
Ⓣ04.73.95.41.16 Ⓕ04.73.95.80.83
Ⓦwww.auberge-creux-oulette.com
Closed *Wed (except June–Sept); 15 Nov to early March.* **Disabled access. High chairs and games available. Swimming pool. Car park.**

This village hotel has recently been renovated, and it's an ideal spot if you want to go hiking in the region – the owners are a dynamic pair who have organized discovery trails for you to follow. Double rooms with shower/wc €37. Half board €38 per person. The chef is passionate about cooking and his wholesome family dishes have a good reputation locally; expect to be offered copious salads, snail stew with mushrooms, fish fillet with Fourme cheese sauce or calves' sweetbreads with mushrooms. Choice from five menus from €10 up to €28 which you can eat on the terrace in summer. All-round good value. *10% discount on a room or free apéritif offered to our readers on presentation of this guide.*

Saint-Flour

15100

Hôtel-restaurant des Roches**

Place d'Armes; near the cathedral.
Ⓣ04.71.60.09.70. Ⓕ04.71.60.45.21
Ⓔinfo@hotel-des-roches.com
Closed *Sun out of season.* **TV. High chairs available.**

Very central place with bright, pleasant bedrooms with shower/wc or bath priced at €35.10–40. Classic and regional styles dominate in the first-floor restaurant, which has a pretty terrace where you can take an apéritif. Choose from fillet of beef with blue Auvergne cheese, duck breast with herbs, *truffade*, *aligot* and so on. Dish of the day with dessert €7.35 (weekday lunchtimes only) and menu at €10; other menus €14–20. No credit cards. *Free coffee.*

Auberge de la Providence**

1 rue du Château-d'Alleuze.
Ⓣ04.71.60.12.05 Ⓕ04.71.60.33.94
Ⓦwww.auberge-providence.com
Restaurant open *evenings only.* **Closed** *Mon lunchtime; Fri evening and Sun out of season; 15 Nov to 15 Dec.* **Disabled access. TV. Car park.**

This old inn has been completely refurbished. The décor is generally low key and the ten rooms are decorated in pastel shades; all have good bathrooms. Doubles €42–50. Set menu at €18 offer some of the best value in town: duck breast with blue Auvergne cheese, fillet of beef, morels in season. *Free apéritif offered to our readers on presentation of this guide.*

Saint-Georges

15100 (4km SE)

Hôtel-restaurant Le Bout du Monde**

Take the D250.
Ⓣ04.71.60.15.84 Ⓕ04.71.60.72.90
Ⓦwww.hotel-leboutdumonde.com
Closed *Sun evening out of season.*
Disabled access. TV. Swimming pool. High chairs and games available. Car park.

As its name says, this place is indeed at the end of the world, deep in a valley in the countryside outside Saint-Flour – ideal for anglers and walkers. It's also got a heated swimming pool in a lovely natural setting. The restaurant serves a range of delicious regional specialities. Menus, €10 (weekdays only) up to €26, feature *tourte de caillé* (curds), *pounti* (a mixture of bacon and Swiss chard), *coq au vin*, *truffade* and *aligot*. On the most expensive menu, you can get scallops and prawns with a hazelnut *tuile*, quail in pastry with Armagnac, duck breast with blackberries and *millefeuille* with spiced bread and ice cream. Simple, well-maintained rooms cost €38–45 with shower/wc or bath.

Garabit

15320 (12km SE)

🏃 ⌂ |●| Hôtel-restaurant Beau Site**

Ⓣ04.71.23.41.46 Ⓕ04.71.23.46.34
Ⓦwww.beau-site-hotel.com
Closed *3 Nov to end March.* **Disabled access. TV. High chairs and games available. Swimming pool. Car park.**

The hotel looks down on Eiffel's viaduct (he of tower fame), and you get wonderful views of the lake. It's a huge building with bright, roomy doubles for €40–55 with shower/wc or bath. Half board, compulsory in July and August, is €39–55 per person. Excellent facilities include a heated swimming pool and tennis courts: it makes a good base for fishing, windsurfing and long walks. The restaurant serves classic French dishes and gourmet cuisine. Set menus at €14 (weekdays) and €21–37, list specialities such as *feuillantine* with soft Cantal cheese, veal's head with vinaigrette, scallop kebabs with ceps.

Saint-Gervais-d'Auvergne

63390

⌂ |●| Le relais d'Auvergne**

Route de Châteauneuf-les-Bains.
Ⓣ04.73.85.70.10 Ⓕ04.73.85.85.66
Ⓦwww.relais-auvergne.com
Closed *25 Dec–1 March.* **TV. Car park. Disabled access.**

A good place in the middle of the village. It's run by an energetic and friendly young couple. Bedrooms are decorated in slightly flashy colours, but they're fresh and modern, with lovely feather eiderdowns. Doubles €40 with good facilities including en-suite bath; half board is the same price per person. The dining room is cosy and there's a huge chimney piece where they light an open fire in winter. Honest, traditional food: chicken *aiguillette* with Fourme cheese, stuffed cabbage and pork knuckle with lentils. Menus, €12.50 (weekdays lunchtime) rising to €28, are good value.

⌂ |●| Hôtel-restaurant Castel Hôtel 1904**

Rue du Castel.
Ⓣ04.73.85.70.42 Ⓕ04.73.85.84.39
Ⓔ castel.hotel.1904@wanadoo.fr
Closed *12 Nov–15 March.* **TV. Car park.**

This place has been handed down from generation to generation since 1904 and if you have a taste for the simple pleasures of days gone by, you'll enjoy the genuine atmosphere here. There are two restaurants: the tiny *Comptoir à Moustaches* serves traditional cuisine based on local produce. Menus start at €14. The second serves gourmet cuisine delicately prepared by Jean-Luc Mouty, who trained with Robuchon. It's cooking from a lost age: *pavé* of zander with cider, *fondant* of cabbage with stewed young rabbit, veal sweetbreads. Menus here go for €26–43. The hotel is spacious and very quiet, and the well-equipped rustic rooms are affordable at €61 for a double with shower/wc or bath. Half board €98 for two people.

Blot-L'Église

63440 (25 km NE)

|●| Auberge Les Peytoux

Lieu-dit Les Peytoux; between Charbonnières-les-Vieilles and Blot-L'Église, in an isolated valley by the River Morge.
Ⓣ04.73.97.44.17
Closed *Mon–Thurs, Fri lunch and Sun evening (except public holidays and the night before them); Christmas and New Year.* **Car park.**

You will not be the only one to decide that this inn is worth a detour. Despite a total lack of advertising, word of mouth has made it necessary to book almost one month in advance. Menus €10–20, everything included – not just the coffee but even the liqueur, too. Only fresh farm produce is used: exceptional goat's cheese, wonderful salads and superb poultry. A real treat.

Servant

63560 (27km NE)

🏃 ⌂ |●| Hôtel-restaurant Le Beau Site*

Gorges de la Sioule; take the D227 then the D109; from there head left towards Menat and continue by the D18, taking the N144 for Gorges de Chouvigny.
Ⓣ04.73.85.50.65
Ⓦwww.le-beau-site.com
Closed *Feb.* **Restaurant closed** *out of season; Wed and Thurs (except in July–Aug).* **High chairs and games available. Car park.**

Here's a place that really deserves its name. It's in a really wonderful setting, which you reach on the road that follows the Sioule, and offers a perfect base for exploring the area and doing a bit of fishing. Six pleasant double rooms cost €32–42. In summer you can have a meal or a drink on the terrace overlooking the river. Menus €13.80 (weekdays only) and €18.80–45.20. One of them lists only house specialities: Rocquefort terrine with chestnuts, salad with walnut oil and farm-reared chicken with crayfish, among others. *Free apéritif offered to our readers on presentation of this guide.*

Saint-Martin-sous-Vigouroux

15230

Le Relais de la Forge*

Take the D990; it's west of Pierrefort.
T 04.71.23.36.90 F 04.71.23.92.48
Closed *Wed out of season and during school holidays.* **High chairs and games available. Car park.**

A simple, welcoming country hotel with a restaurant that has a very substantial *menu du jour* for €10. It includes a selection of charcuterie and dishes such as trout with bacon, *pavé* of beef with morels, *truffade* (potato cake with Cantal cheese), and cheese and dessert. Other menus at €12.90 and €18.90. There are ten renovated rooms, available at €30.50 with shower/wc or bath. Half board costs €32 per person. *Free apéritif offered to our readers on presentation of this guide.*

Saint-Pourçain-sur-Sioule

03500

Hôtel-restaurant Le Chêne Vert**

35 bd. Ledru-Rollin.
T 04.70.47.77.00 F 04.70.47.77.39
Closed *first fortnight in Jan.* **Restaurant closed** *Fri lunch, Sun evening out of season; Mon; Jan (first fortnight for the hotel, whole month for the restaurant)* . **TV. Car park.**

A classic, conventional establishment with excellent facilities at decent prices. Pleasant rooms with fresh décor cost from €44.50 for a double with shower/wc up to €53.50 with bath. (Light sleepers should note that the church bells toll throughout the night.) Good traditional cooking with lots of game in season; menus €17 (not Sun) to €42 (three courses). *Free coffee offered to our readers on presentation of this guide.*

Saint-Urcize

15110

Hôtel-restaurant Remise

In the centre of the village.
T and F 04.71.23.20.02
Closed *Mon evening; Dec–Jan.* **Disabled access. Car park.**

A marvellous country inn that's very popular with anglers, hunters, hikers and cyclists. The home cooking is wonderful with dishes such as *aligot*, nettle soup or trout – it all depends on what's good in the market – and the proprietress prepares a lovely jam from local wildflowers. Menus €13–18. Since so many anglers stay here, they make up picnic baskets to see you through a day's fishing. The owner can tell you anything you want to know about the region, from local history to the best walks and places to visit. Friendly, easy-going atmosphere. Doubles €40 with wc/shower or bath; they also have rooms in a wooden lodge for €30 per person half board. Half board (€38 per person) obligatory in July and August. *Free apéritif offered to our readers on presentation of this guide.*

Salers

15140

Hôtel des Remparts**

Esplanade de Barrouze.
T 04.71.40.70.33 F 04.71.40.75.32
W www.salers-hotel-remparts.com
Closed *15 Oct–20 Dec.* **TV. High chairs available. Disabled access.**

Well located, slightly off the tourist trail, with a superb view of the Cantal mountains from some rooms and a delightful, panoramic terrace. Double rooms €44.50–51, depending on the season; some have exposed beams and half-timbering. Menus €12–29. A well-run place. *Free coffee offered to our readers on presentation of this guide.*

Restaurant La Poterne

Rue Notre-Dame.
T 04.71.40.75.11

Closed *2nd and 3rd weeks of March and Oct; Sat (out of season).*

A cosy setting (exposed stone and beams, old fireplace) for regional specialities, carefully prepared with high-quality, fresh ingredients. The traditional dishes on offer include *truffade*, *pounti*, stuffed cabbage, *bourriols* (type of crêpe filled with Auvergne blue cheese) and a delicious bilberry pie. Menu of the day €12.20 and regional menus €14.40–21. Reckon on around €18 à la carte. Friendly service and good value for money.

Saugues

43170

La Terrasse**

Cours Gervais.
Ⓣ04.71.77.83.10 Ⓕ04.71.77.63.79
Ⓔlaterrasse.saugues@wanadoo.fr
Closed *Sun evening and Mon out of season; end Nov to end Jan.* **TV.**

The owner is friendly and particularly attentive to his guests. The twelve rooms have been refurbished, and doubles go for €49–69 with shower/wc or bath; there are also a few suites at €69. The ones at the back are particularly quiet and have an uninterrupted view of the Tour des Anglais. Breakfast €6. The brasserie serves classic dishes but the restaurant is a bit fancier, with specialities such as upside-down tart with foie gras and apple. Set menus €19 and €26 (lunchtime only), €36 and €50 (evenings).

Saint-Arcons-d'Allier

43300 (15km N)

Les Deux Abbesses

In the village; take the D585 in the direction of Prades.
Ⓣ04.71.74.03.08 Ⓕ04.71.74.05.30
Ⓦwww.les-deux-abbesses.fr
Closed *Sun evening; Nov to Easter.* **TV.**

Mme Fustier, the proprietor, had the inspired idea of renovating eight houses to make a sort of hotel village, gathered around the twelfth-century château on an outcrop of rock between the Allier and the Sioule rivers. There are fourteen charming, comfortable and spacious rooms with period furniture; with en-suite facilities they cost €140–300. Breakfast €20. The pretty garden, where you can eat breakfast in summer, is next to a Romanesque church built of volcanic rock. The restaurant (dinner only) offers sophisticated, tasty dishes – profiterole with *petit-pois* ice cream and parsley *coulis*. There's a single menu at €45 evening only that must be pre-booked.

Thiers

63300

Hôtel de la Gare

30 av. de la Gare; it's opposite the train station.
Ⓣ and Ⓕ04.73.80.01.41
Hotel closed *Sat and Sun afternoons; end Sept to early Oct.*

The cheapest and friendliest hotel in town, completely hidden under a covering of wisteria. Simple, clean rooms €15 with basin and €20 with shower (wc on the landing); no. 7 is the quietest. Friendly atmosphere and a small bar which is quite cool but can get noisy. *10% discount on a room (from the fourth consecutive night) and free apéritif, coffee or liqueur offered to our readers on presentation of this guide.*

Hôtel-restaurant Chez La Mère Dépalle**

Pont-de-Dore; take the N89, and it's 2km from the town centre.
Ⓣ04.73.80.10.05 Ⓕ04.73.80.52.22
Ⓦwww.chezlameredepalle.com
Closed *Fri and Sun evenings; Sat out of season; 22 Dec–20 Jan.* **High chairs and games available. TV. Car park.**

Though its roadside location is a slight minus, this establishment is a model of hotel and restaurant-keeping and the owners are unfailingly courteous and helpful. Double rooms with shower/wc or bath for €45–65. Half board, €48 per person, is compulsory during the clay pigeon shooting competitions in June. The weekday lunch menu, €14.50, and others up to €36, list such dishes as a delicious smoked salmon with whisky, Salers fillet with Auvergne blue cheese, the simplest calf's head with *sauce ravigote*, roast leg of venison or an aristocratic medallion of Fallow deer. The cheese trolley is superb, too, and includes a soft goat's cheese with a remarkable depth of flavour. And to finish off, the *crème brûlée* with kumquats is delightful.

|●| Restaurant Le Coutelier

4 pl. du Palais.
Ⓣ and Ⓕ04.73.80.79.59
Closed *Mon evening except July–Aug; Tues; last 3 weeks in June; a fortnight in Oct.*

Thiers is the centre of France's cutlery industry and this restaurant is in a converted cutler's workshop. What with the collection of old implements and knives displayed on the walls it's almost a museum and restaurant in one. Classic dishes like *aligot* with sausage and cabbage, *coq au vin*, *tripoux* – the fish dishes, however, can be disappointing. Good value menus €12–25.

Peschadoires

63920 (4km SW)

|●| La Ferme des Trois Canards

North of the N89, near the village of Pont-de-Dore. Take the D224 towards Maringues and after 1.5km turn left at the sign; the restaurant is 300m further along.
Ⓣ04.73.51.06.70 Ⓕ04.73.51.06.71
Ⓦwww.alainroussingue.com
Closed *Sun and Tues evenings; Wed; fortnight in Jan.* **Garden. Car park.**

The most delightful place in the area. It's a beautifully renovated farmhouse in the heart of the countryside but not far from the motorway exit. Dishes on the set menus, €22–47, are perfectly cooked and presented: pan-fried foie gras with an onion *compote*, roast spiced pigeon and hot chocolate *fondant*. Cheeses are matured to perfection. Terrace in summer.

Tournemire

15310

🏃 ☗ |●| Auberge de Tournemire

Rue Principale; take the D60, the D160 and the D260 – you'll find it about 20km north of Aurillac.
Ⓣ04.71.47.61.28 Ⓕ04.71.47.68.76
Ⓦwww.aubergedetournemire.com
Closed *10 Jan–4 Feb.* **TV. High chairs available.**

In one of Cantal's prettiest villages, you'll find this delightful inn set on the side of a hill; the views of the valley are gorgeous, especially at sunset. The six simple bedrooms are well maintained and one or two have lovely sloping ceilings. Doubles €37–62; half board from €38 per person. There's a *formule brasserie* at €10, otherwise menus at €15–25.50 – all reserved for hotel guests in the evening, but available to all at lunch. Good cooking in the restaurant with Auvergnat dishes such as black pudding with a fondue of onions. The *menu gastronomique* offers foie gras, black pudding with onion and apple fondue, *truffade*, lobster with vanilla and such like. You'll need to call to reserve if you want to eat at the restaurant outside the tourist season; it's also wise to reserve rooms at the hotel. *10% discount on a room (except July–Aug) offered to our readers on presentation of this guide.*

Vichy

03200

🏃 ☗ À l'Hôtel de Naples**

22 rue de Paris; it's opposite the station.
Ⓣ04.70.97.91.33 Ⓕ04.70.97.91.28
TV.

The hotel, located in the most famous (and busiest) street in town, isn't luxurious, but it does have modern facilities. Cosy, well-equipped, refurbished doubles with satellite TV, phone and mini-bar go for €24 with basin/wc, and €28–32 with shower/wc or bath. Ask for a room overlooking the pretty garden, which is full of flowers in summer. *10% discount on a room (except summer) offered to our readers on presentation of this guide.*

🏃 ☗ |●| Hôtel du Rhône**

8 rue de Paris; look for the station, then take the only one way street to the right; it's the last hotel 300m on the left.
Ⓣ04.70.97.73.00 Ⓕ04.70.97.48.25
Ⓔhoteldurhone@hotmail.com
Closed *1 Nov–Easter.* **TV. Disabled access. High chairs and games available. Pay car park.**

No lift here – the owner cheerfully announces that he deliberately hasn't installed one so his guests get a bit of exercise. It's an elegant building with a cosy décor. The rooms are clean and simple – go for one overlooking the patio, which is particularly lovely when the hydrangeas are in flower. Doubles €30 with shower or €75 with shower/wc or bath. Stay three nights and get one night free. Menus range from €12.90 (weekday lunch) to €46 (gastronomic menu), with a vegetarian menu at €14 and a buffet for €9. The cooking features a variety of Auvergne and Normandy dishes: veal *escalope* flambéed with Calvados in a cream and mushroom sauce, sea bass with sorrel and ham on the bone in Saint-Pourçain wine – this isn't the place to begin your diet. *10% discount on the room rate (except April–Oct) or a free apéritif or coffee offered to our readers on presentation of this guide.*

Le Pavillon d'Enghien***

32 rue Callou; it's in the spa area of the town.
Ⓣ04.70.98.33.30 Ⓕ04.70.31.67.82
Restaurant closed *Sun evening and Mon (except for guests).* **Hotel closed** *22 Dec– 1 Feb.* **High chairs available. TV. Swimming pool.**

This hotel-restaurant offers some of the best value for money in town. The spacious double rooms, €42–75, are individualized and soundproofed. Food is good and fresh; they offer a weekday lunch menu at €12, with others from €17 up to €25. The slab of Charolais beef with blue Auvergne cheese sauce is recommended, as are the desserts. Pretty swimming pool. *Free apéritif offered to our readers on presentation of this guide.*

La Brasserie du Casino

4 rue du Casino.
Ⓣ04.70.98.23.06 Ⓕ04.70.98.53.17
Closed *Tues and Wed; second fortnight in Feb; Nov.* **Disabled access.**

This restaurant has got more character than any other in Vichy. Big prewar brasseries have a certain something, and this one, built in 1920, is no exception. The walls are covered in photos of stars who used to dine here after performing at the opera house. The à la carte menu has a long list of classic dishes and set menus are also available. The weekday lunch menu costs €14 and there's another at €24 – they feature oven-roasted goat, calf's liver with onions and a killer chocolate dessert. They serve a special after-show dinner. Fairly priced wines. *Free apéritif offered to our readers on presentation of this guide.*

La Table d'Antoine

8 rue Bournol.
Ⓣ04.70.98.99.71
Closed *Sun evening; Mon except for public holidays and the eve of public holidays; a fortnight in Feb; a week in Sept; a fortnight at the end of Nov.* **Disabled access. High chairs and games available.**

This is one of the nicest restaurants in Vichy, with décor reminiscent of a winter garden of the Second Empire. The dining room is small, the welcome perfect – quiet and smiling and genuinely disappointed if they can't find you a table. And the way they cook the perfectly chosen produce is superb. Fish is line-caught, the Charolais beef is melting, the desserts are perfectly sweetened and the portions are generous. *Menu du marché* €19 and others €27–41. Children's menu costs €12. *Free coffee or liqueur (depending on the menu) offered to our readers on presentation of this guide.*

Cusset

03300 (1km E)

Le Brayaud

64 av. de Vichy; it's as you approach Cusset coming from Vichy.
Ⓣ04.70.98.52.43
Closed *lunchtime; Tues; Wed; end of Aug to early Sept; 10 days in April.*

This is where you come if you want to stay out late in Vichy (it's open from 8pm to 2am), but more importantly it's the best place to eat meat around here. Steaks are exceptional – the *entrecôte* of Charolais beef weighs close on 400g and the *onglet* 300g. A €16 menu is served until 10.30pm, offering a good variety of salads, meat, cheese and dessert. There's enough to satisfy even the biggest appetites, and there's a friendly family atmosphere. *Free apéritif offered to our readers on presentation of this guide.*

Bellerive-sur-Allier

03700 (2km SW)

La Rigon**

Route de Serbannes.
Ⓣ04.70.59.86.86 Ⓕ04.70.59.94.77
Closed *Sun evening out of season; 1 Oct–31 March.* **Disabled access. TV. Swimming pool. Car park.**

A little haven of peace and quiet up in the Bellerives hills above Vichy, just five minutes from the town centre. You'll get the best of both worlds here – the excellent service and hours you'd expect from a hotel and the intimacy of a good-quality guesthouse. It's a beautiful building, with its own extensive grounds, and the bedrooms, decorated in subtle tones, are all lovely. Doubles with shower/wc €54 in the low season; €64 in summer. Hearty breakfast for €6. Brilliant swimming pool in a large 1900s glasshouse.

Abrest

03700 (3km S)

La Colombière

Route de Thiers; take the D906, it's 2km beyond Abrest.
04.70.98.69.15 04.70.31.50.89
lacolombiere@wanadoo.fr
Closed *Sun evening; Mon; mid-Jan to mid-Feb.* **Disabled access. TV. High chairs, booster seats, changing table, feeding-bottle warmer and games available. Car park.**

An old dovecote converted into a restaurant and set high above the Allier. Menus €16 (weekdays only) to €52, range from the simple to the refined. The cuisine is imaginative and dishes change with the seasons, mixing tradition and new ideas. The selection of cheeses is excellent as are the home-made desserts. Four huge, bright, charming bedrooms at €48 with shower/wc and €55 with bath. Nice terrace.

Mayet-de-Montagne (Le)

03250 (23km SE)

La Vieille Auberge

6 rue de l'Église; take the D62.
and 04.70.59.34.01
Closed *Mon evening July–Aug; Wed out of season; three weeks in Jan; the last fortnight in Sept.* **High chairs and colouring books available.**

Time seems to have stood still in this old inn, behind a church in a wonderful little village deep in the Bourbonnais mountains. Décor of stone and wood brighted up by posters. Traditional dishes on the shortish menu, made with fresh local ingredients: hot goat's cheese salad with almonds, duck *confit*, *coq au vin* and wonderful home-made desserts. *Menu campagnard* at €8.70 (weekdays out of season) with a selection of charcuterie, sausage and ham; others at €10.40 (€15.50 at weekends) and €21.40. À la carte also available. Credit cards not accepted. *Free coffee offered to our readers on presentation of this guide.*

Vic-sur-Cère

15800

Hôtel-restaurant Bel Horizon**

Rue Paul-Doumer.
04.71.47.50.06 04.71.49.63.81
www.hotel-bel-horizon.com
Closed *end Nov to end Dec.* **TV. Swimming pool. Pay car park.**

A pleasant place on the edge of town. It attracts crowds at the weekends for the fine traditional regional cooking – and the huge servings. Menus, €14–41, list such dishes as stuffed cabbage, *pounti* (a mixture of bacon and Swiss chard), roast zandre with red butter, *coq au vin*. The chef rings the changes frequently, but his specialities are dishes such as salmon fillet with light-flavoured Cantal cheese, *coq au vin* and foie gras. The home-made ice creams and desserts are delicious. The dining room has a big bay window. Rooms are comfortable and well maintained, and cost €35–45 with shower/wc or bath. *Free apéritif offered to our readers on presentation of this guide.*

Vieillevie

15120

Hôtel La Terrasse**

Rue Principale; take the D141.
04.71.49.94.00 04.71.49.92.23
www.hotel-terrasse.com
Closed *Mon in Oct, May, Sept and Oct; 11 Nov–31 Dec.* **Disabled access. Swimming pool. Car park.**

At 200m, this hotel is apparently at a lower altitude than any other in Cantal. Comfortable rooms priced at €42–49 for a double with shower/wc or bath. Good outdoor facilities: shaded terrace, beautiful swimming pool, garden and tennis courts. You'll enjoy the cooking: specialities include char in wine sauce, pig's trotters *en crépine* and *feuillantine* of caramelized pears. Menus €14.50 (weekdays only) and up to €31. *Free apéritif offered to our readers on presentation of this guide.*

Vitrac

15220

L'Auberge de la Tomette**

It's off the D66, a few km from Marcolès.
04.71.64.70.94 04.71.64.77.11
www.auberge-la-tomette.com
Closed *15 Nov–1 April.* **Disabled access. TV. High chairs and games available. Swimming pool. Car park.**

This is a delightful village inn set in a large

flower-filled garden overlooking the countryside. The hotel is pleasant and has comfortable, modern double rooms at €59–75, or €52–67 per person half board (preferred during high season). A few duplexes are available for families and there's a large, covered, heated pool and spa. The cosy, rustic dining room offers good hearty food and a choice of set menus at €21–35. Try the chef's specialities: calves' sweetbreads in a crust, duck with shallot marmalade. *Free apéritif offered to our readers on presentation of this guide.*

Yssingeaux

43200

Auberge Au Creux des Pierres

It's in Fougères; 5km south of the town on the D152 in the direction of Queyrière.
Ⓣ and Ⓕ04.71.59.06.81
Ⓔchristian.sqperissen@free.fr
Closed *Christmas and Feb*. **Restaurant closed** *Mon except 1 April–31 Oct. Out of season, open Fri evening, Sat and Sun only.* **High chairs and games available.**

A charming inn in a superbly renovated property that's surrounded by a lovely garden. They offer well-appointed rooms with views of the countryside. Doubles with shower/wc for €35. The restaurant offers excellent food, simple and homely with Auvergne and Alsace specialities: seasonal veg, fresh starters, local cheeses and moist home-made tarts. Menus €12–18. It's a favourite with walkers and cyclists, many of whom stay in the ten-bed dorm. *Free apéritif offered to our readers on presentation of this guide.*

Le Bourbon**

5 pl. de la Victoire.
Ⓣ04.71.59.06.54 Ⓕ04.71.59.00.70
Ⓦwww.le-bourbon.com
Restaurant closed *Sun evening; Mon and Fri evening; in July–Aug open Fri evening but closed Tues lunch; Jan.* **TV. Car park.**

Attractive, welcoming and agreeable hotel with comfortable rooms each named after a flower. Doubles with bath or shower and wc go for €58 and €70. The handsome dining room, decorated in English-garden style, serves a lighter version of the regional cuisine. Set menus from €19 (not available Sun) to €43; like the à la carte menu, they change every three months. You'll find a list of local suppliers beside the dishes. Breakfast €9.

Bourgogne

Ancy-le-Franc

89160

Hostellerie du Centre**

Place du Château.
Ⓣ03.86.75.15.11 Ⓕ03.86.75.14.13
Ⓦwww.diaphora.com/hostellerieducentre
Closed *18 Nov–18 March.* **Disabled access. High chairs and games available. TV. Swimming pool. Car park.**

In an old, much-refurbished building in the main street. The hotel looks quite classy but the atmosphere is easy-going.The cosy, restful bedrooms, decorated in pastel tones, are €48–56 with shower/wc or bath, depending on the degree of comfort. The restaurant – the larger of the two dining rooms is the prettier – offers traditional local dishes including snails or ham in a Chablis sauce. Set menus are as varied as the portions are generous. Cheapest menu at €15, then others at €20–43. The terrace is opened when the weather gets fine and there's a heated indoor swimming pool.

Chassignelles

89160 (4km SE)

Hôtel de l'Écluse No. 79

Chemin de Ronde; take the D905 then take the small left turn.
Ⓣ03.86.75.18.51 Ⓕ03.86.75.02.04
Closed *mid-Dec to mid-Jan.* **TV.**

A delightful family-run country hotel on the banks of the Burgundy canal. Grandmother still runs the bar, while her daughter runs the hotel. The bar has a delightful terrace by the waterside, although the plastic furniture is an eyesore. The rooms are charming and tastefully decorated at prices that are very reasonable for the region; one overlooks the canal. Doubles with shower/wc or bath €45–55. Breakfast €6.50. The cooking is done by the granddaughter, who specializes in local dishes: *œufs en meurette*, duck bourguignon, terrine of *andouillete*, ham *à la chablisienne* and blackcurrant tart. Menus €17–30. You can rent bikes to ride along the towpath.

Pacy-sur-Armançon

89160 (6 km NW)

Hôtel-restaurant au Petit Câlin

4 Grande-Rue. 6 km to the northeast of Ancy-le-Franc via the D905 (in the direction of Lézinnes), then a side road to the left; signposted in the village.
Ⓣ and Ⓕ03.86.75.51.17
Closed *Wed (out of season).* **Car park.**

A few no-frills, but huge and comfortable bedrooms, starting at €48, have been installed in the old farmhouse. The food is similarly unpretentious but satisfying, and it is served in a dining room with small partitions or on the flower-filled terrace. The place settings are delightfully old-fashioned and the service is friendly. Highlights include *bougnettes*, home-made potato pancakes accompanied by a Chablis *andouillette* or a typical local fondue. There are interesting fish dishes as well. Weekday lunchtime menu at €14.50 (except Sun) then others at €24–38. Other options are a generous platter or single course for around €13.

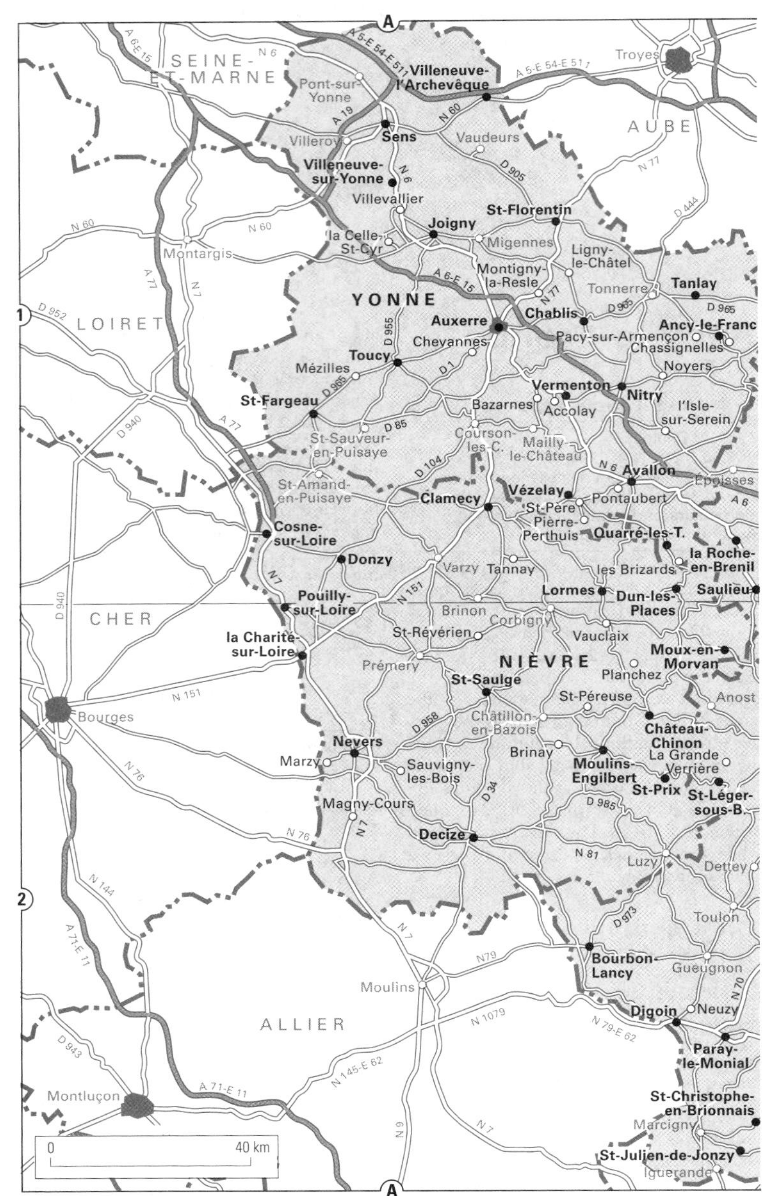
A
SEINE-ET-MARNE
A 6-E 15
N 6
A 5-E 54-E 511
Pont-sur-Yonne
Villeneuve-l'Archevêque
Troyes
AUBE
A 19
Sens
Villeroy
N 60
Vaudeurs
Villeneuve-sur-Yonne
D 905
N 77
Villevallier
St-Florentin
D 444
N 60
Joigny
Migennes
la Celle-St-Cyr
Montargis
Ligny-le-Châtel
Montigny-la-Resle
A 77
N 7
YONNE
Tonnerre
Tanlay
A 6-E 15
N 77
D 965
D 965
1
D 952
LOIRET
Chablis
Auxerre
Ancy-le-Franc
D 955
Chevannes
Pacy-sur-Armençon
Chassignelles
Toucy
Mézilles
D 1
Noyers
Vermenton
Nitry
D 965
St-Fargeau
Bazarnes
Accolay
l'Isle-sur-Serein
D 940
A 77
D 85
Courson-les-C.
Mailly-le-Château
St-Sauveur-en-Puisaye
D 104
N 6
Avallon
Époisses
St-Amand-en-Puisaye
Vézelay
Clamecy
Pontaubert
A 6
St-Père
Pierre-Perthuis
Quarré-les-T.
Cosne-sur-Loire
la Roche-en-Brenil
Donzy
Varzy
Tannay
les Brizards
N 7
Lormes
Saulieu
N 151
Dun-les-Places
Pouilly-sur-Loire
D 940
Brinon
CHER
Corbigny
St-Révérien
Vauclaix
la Charité-sur-Loire
Moux-en-Morvan
NIÈVRE
Prémery
Planchez
St-Saulge
N 151
St-Péreuse
Anost
Bourges
D 958
Châtillon-en-Bazois
Château-Chinon
Nevers
Brinay
La Grande Verrière
Moulins-Engilbert
Marzy
Sauvigny-les-Bois
N 76
St-Prix
St-Léger-sous-B.
D 34
Magny-Cours
D 985
N 7
N 76
Decize
N 81
Luzy
Dettey
N 144
2
Toulon
D 973
N 7
N79
Bourbon-Lancy
A 71-E 11
Gueugnon
Moulins
N 70
Digoin
Neuzy
ALLIER
N 1079
N 79-E 62
D 943
Paray-le-Monial
N 145-E 62
A 71-E 11
Montluçon
St-Christophe-en-Brionnais
N 7
Marcigny
N 9
0
40 km
St-Julien-de-Jonzy
Iguerande
A

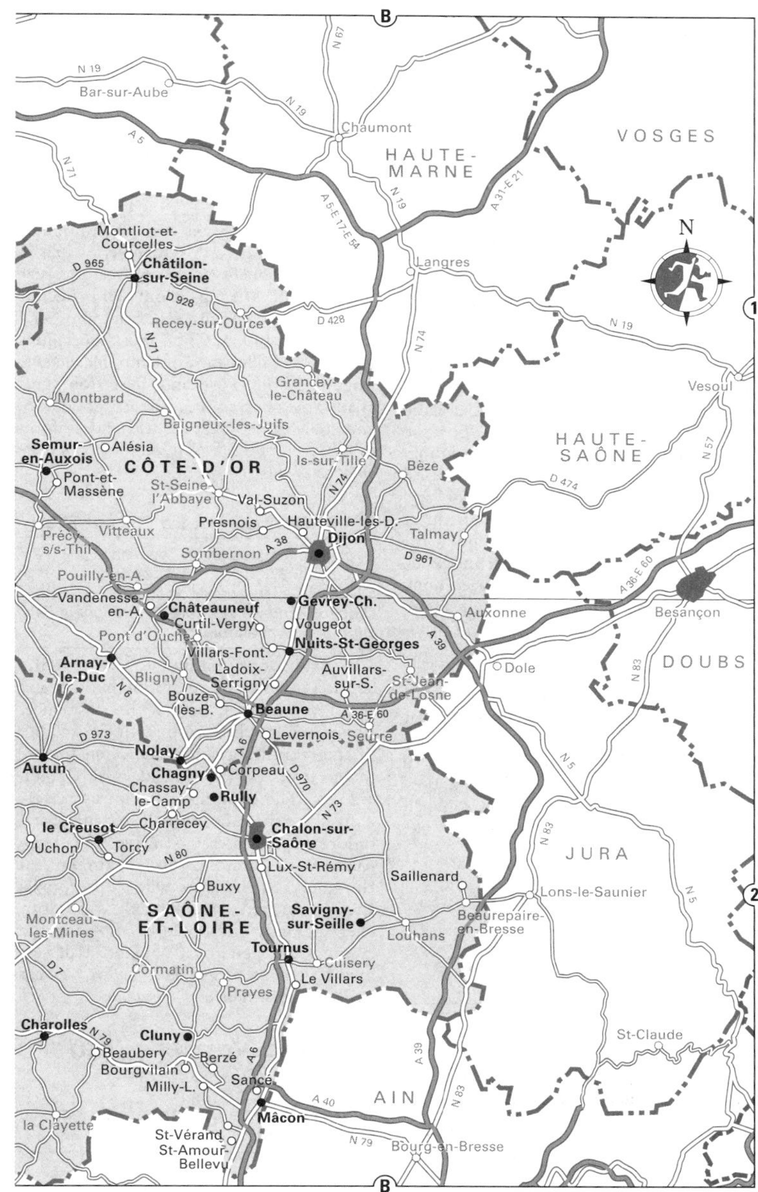
B
N 67
N 19
Bar-sur-Aube
N 19
Chaumont
A 5
N 71
HAUTE-
MARNE
VOSGES
N 19
A 5-E 17-E 54
A 31-E 21
N
Montliot-et-
Courcelles
D 965
Châtilon-
sur-Seine
Langres
1
D 928
Recey-sur-Ource
D 428
N 19
N 71
N 74
Grancey-
le-Château
Vesoul
Montbard
Baigneux-les-Juifs
HAUTE-
SAÔNE
Semur-
en-Auxois
Alésia
CÔTE-D'OR
Is-sur-Tille
Bèze
N 57
Pont-et-
Massène
St-Seine-
l'Abbaye
N 74
D 474
Val-Suzon
Presnois
Hauteville-les-D.
Précy-
s/s-Thil
Vitteaux
Dijon
Talmay
Sombernon
A 38
D 961
Pouilly-en-A.
A 36-E 60
Vandenesse-
en-A.
Châteauneuf
Gevrey-Ch.
Besançon
Auxonne
Curtil-Vergy
Vougeot
Pont d'Ouche
Nuits-St-Georges
A 39
Arnay-
le-Duc
Villars-Font.
Dole
DOUBS
Bligny
Ladoix-
Serrigny
Auvillars-
sur-S.
St-Jean-
de-Losne
N 83
N 6
Bouze-
lès-B.
Beaune
A 36-E 60
D 973
Levernois
Seurre
Nolay
Autun
A 6
Chagny
Corpeau
D 970
N 5
Chassay-
le-Camp
Rully
N 73
le Creusot
Charrecey
Chalon-sur-
Saône
Uchon
Torcy
N 83
N 80
JURA
Lux-St-Rémy
Saillenard
Buxy
Lons-le-Saunier
2
N 5
Montceau-
les-Mines
SAÔNE-
ET-LOIRE
Savigny-
sur-Seille
Beaurepaire-
en-Bresse
Louhans
Tournus
D 7
Cuisery
Cormatin
Le Villars
Prayes
Charolles
N 79
Cluny
St-Claude
Beaubery
Berzé
A 6
A 39
Bourgvilain
Sancé
Milly-L.
A 40
AIN
N 83
Mâcon
la Clayette
St-Vérand
N 79
Bourg-en-Bresse
St-Amour-
Bellevue
B

4

BOURGOGNE

Arnay-le-Duc

21230

🏠 |●| Chez Camille***

1 pl. Édouard-Herriot.
℡03.80.90.01.38 Ⓕ03.80.90.04.64
Ⓦwww.chez-camille.fr
TV. Disabled access. High chairs available. Car park.

This authentically old-fashioned inn with blue shutters, located at the foot of the old town, looks as if it's straight out of an operetta. Waitresses in flowery dresses enter the lounge, serving apéritifs with cheesy choux pastries and home-made ham before conducting you to the conservatory, which has been converted into a dining room. Here you can sit as though in a theatre and watch the ballet of sous-chefs and kitchen staff, which is performed on a kind of stage raised up behind a large window – on one side you've got the pastry kitchen, on the other an awning. The whole scene is enacted beneath a glass roof in a room full of pot plants and wicker armchairs. The cheapest menu at €18.50 offers remarkable value for money; it provides traditional, refined cuisine – satisfying dishes like pan-fried duck foie gras, Burgundy snails in their shells, fillet of Charolais beef and *bœuf bourguignon*. You can also try specialities such as parsleyed ham and zander. Other menus go up to €76; children under 11 eat for free. The wine list is terrific, and the cellar is worth visiting. There are a few plush bedrooms, too; doubles with bath €70 (again, children under 11 go free if they share your room); €104 per person half board.

Autun

71400

🏠 |●| 🏃 Hôtel-restaurant de la Tête Noire**

3 rue de l'Arquebuse.
℡03.85.86.59.99 Ⓕ03.85.86.33.90
Ⓦwww.hoteltetenoire.fr
Closed *15 Dec–31 Jan.* **TV. High chairs available. Disabled access.**

Double rooms with shower/wc or bath at €55–60. Several menus, ranging from €12 to €42. The hotel is comfortable, the rooms are full of charm and have recently been renovated. Good, hearty local cooking that has been delighting customers for a decade. Specialities: Charolais fillet of beef, snail soup, French toast with apples. Wine by the glass or pitcher. Friendly service. Air-conditioning in restaurant. *Free coffee offered to our readers on presentation of this guide.*

|●| 🏃 Restaurant Chateaubriant

14 rue Jeannin.
℡03.85.52.21.58 Ⓕ03.85.52.04.54
Closed *Sun evening; Mon; Wed evening (except Aug); a fortnight in Feb; 3 weeks in July.* **High chairs available.**

Centrally positioned just behind the municipal theatre, this reliable establishment offers quality cooking year in, year out. Classic dining room and decent reception. Set menus €12.50 (on weekdays) and €14–35. Good meat specialities include beef fillet, rack of lamb, *andouillette*, frogs' legs *provençale* and fresh foie gras salad. The *oeufs en meurette* are good too, and there are some nice fish and seafood dishes. *Free coffee offered to our readers on presentation of this guide.*

🏃 |●| Restaurant Le Chalet Bleu

3 rue Jeannin; beside the town hall.
℡03.85.86.27.30 Ⓕ03.85.52.74.56
Ⓔle-chalet-bleu@wanadoo.fr
Closed *Mon evening; Tues; a fortnight in Feb.* **High chairs available.**

The exterior is nothing to write home about – in no way does it look like a chalet – but you can eat here with confidence. Philippe Bouché, who trained in the kitchens of the Elysée Palace, offers five set menus from €14.50 (weekdays only), then €23–43. The cooking is gloriously imaginative: perch and frogs' legs with baby onions; pigeon breast; veal sweetbread rissoles with almond milk; tureen of Burgundy snails with wild mushrooms; Bresse chicken caramelized with sour cherry brandy and broad beans – and the helpings are generous. Wonderful dessert menu. *Apéritif on the house offered to our readers on presentation of this guide.*

Grande-Verrière (La)

71990 (14km W)

🏠 |●| Hôtel de la Poste - Chez Cécile

Take the D3.
℡03.85.82.52.41 Ⓕ03.85.82.55.86
Closed *Sun evening; 21 Dec–4 Jan.*

There are seven charming rooms from

€24 to €44. Menus cost €11–22. A stay with "Pépète Cécile" is an unmissable experience . It is she who decides what you will eat, and she tells you off if you arrive late, hugs you and adopts you as one of her own – and, above all, she prepares you huge meals, more than you can possibly eat. Try to leave some space for the desserts, such as the delicious fromage blanc and crème fraîche.

Auxerre

89000

Hôtel Normandie**

41 bd. Vauban.
03.86.52.57.80
www.acom.fr/normandie
Disabled access. TV. High chairs available. Car park.

Surrounded by a small garden, this large bourgeois house dates from the late nineteenth century. It's named after a famous French liner, and the atmosphere in the elegant, slightly dated hotel (complete with uniformed night porter) is indeed reminiscent of a luxury transatlantic cruise ship.The stylishly furnished rooms are very comfortable and extremely well looked after. Prices range from €55 to €75 for a double room with shower/wc or bath. Breakfast €7. A gym, sauna and billiard room are also at your disposal. There's a lock-up garage for cars and bikes.

Le Jardin Gourmand

56 bd. Vauban; it's on the pedestrian precinct near the town centre, 50m from the Carrefour de Paris.
03.86.51.53.52 03.86.52.33.82
le.jardin.gourmand.auxerre@wanadoo.fr
Closed *15 Feb–2 March; 9 March–23 April; 12–27 Oct.* **Disabled access. High chairs and games available.**

The chef here is an artist and frequently makes sketches of his dishes. His cooking is very inventive, too, and the service is perfection itself – the staff will guide you expertly through an à la carte menu that changes according to the whims of the chef and the produce from his kitchen garden. The cheapest menu costs €30 (weekday lunchtimes) and others are at €40–72, all offering an ideal introduction to what is truly imaginative cooking. Here's a taster: terrine of duck foie gras with spiced bread, hake with orange butter and seafood risotto, rabbit in sage jelly, Charolais beef steak, veal shin with vegetables and morels. Fine selection of wines. The dining room is cosy, and there's a nice terrace for good weather. Reservations highly recommended.

Chevannes

89240 (8km SW)

La Chamaille***

La Barbotière – 4 rte de Boiloup. From Auxerre, take the Nevers-Bourgnes road then the D1; once in the village, second street on the left.
03.86.41.24.80
la-chamaille@wanadoo.fr
Closed *Sun evening; Mon; Wed evening; 1st fortnight in Jan.* **Car park.**

An excellent place located in the middle of wonderful scenery within minutes of Auxerre. It's in an old turreted farm smelling reassuringly of polish. Double rooms €45–56. It has recently changed hands, and the new owners, Florence and Hervé, provide a sophisticated fusion of traditional cooking and creative invention. You can eat in a bay window looking out on the beautiful countryside (complete with a little stream), or on the terrace. Menus at €24 and €26 (weekdays only), then €35–48.

Montigny-la-Resle

89230 (12km NE)

Hôtel-restaurant Le Soleil d'Or**

From Auxerre take the N77.
and 03.86.41.81.21
le-soleil-dor@wanadoo.fr
Disabled access. TV. High chairs and games available. Car park.

The hotel and restaurant are housed in old farmhouses that have been completely renovated. The rather pretty bedrooms with shower/wc or bath cost €52; breakfast €7. The kitchen turns out classical dishes that are consistent in quality and sometimes show a touch of imagination. The weekday lunch menus, €12 and €17, include a quarter litre of wine; various others €24–60. Try the pan-fried foie gras with runny caramel, pigeon with sweet cider, roast lamb cutlet with foie gras and artichoke *millefeuille* or crayfish tails with mandarin. Wine by the glass is rather expensive. Essential to book in the hotel.

Avallon

89200

Hôtel-restaurant des Capucins**

6 av. Paul-Doumer; the road leads to the station.
Ⓣ03.86.34.06.52 Ⓕ03.86.34.58.47
Closed *Tues; Wed; 8 Dec–9 Jan; last week in June.* **TV. Car park.**

The bright dining room is a nice place to enjoy remarkable cooking prepared by a chef who's a real pro. He makes everything himself – try the foie gras – and gets his ingredients and produce from local suppliers. There's a weekday lunchtime menu at €18 and others €26–36. Wines served by the glass. Although the seven bedrooms are somewhat nondescript, they're quiet – even those overlooking the road. Doubles €50; breakfast €6.

Relais des Gourmets

47 rue de Paris; it's 200m from the main square.
Ⓣ03.86.34.18.90 Ⓕ03.86.31.60.21
Ⓔrelais-des-gourmets@wanadoo.fr
Closed *Sun evening and Mon from 1 Nov to 1 May.* **Disabled access. Car park.**

This used to be the *Hôtel de Paris* in the days when Avallon was still a staging post and – unlike its contemporaries, which have long since disappeared – it's found a new lease of life. It's no longer a hotel but you can have a good meal in a pleasant atmosphere. Set menus €15–43. The chef prepares fish (lemon sole with scallops in herb butter) with as much skill as he does the meat from neighbouring Charolais herds, along with dishes such as roast pigeon with hazelnut oil. There's a covered terrace. It's a popular spot, so it's advisable to book.

Isle-sur-Serein (L')

89440 (15km NE)

Auberge du Pot d'Étain

24 rue Bouchardat; take the D557 then the D86.
Ⓣ03.86.33.88.10 Ⓕ03.86.33.90.93
Ⓦwww.potdetain.com
Closed *Sun evening except July–Aug; Mon; Feb; 3rd week in Oct.* **TV. Pay car park.**

This charming and tiny country inn is one of the best places to eat in the entire region. The cooking is a mixture of the traditional and the modern. Try *andouillette* of snails, flan of foie gras and asparagus tips, langoustines poached with artichokes and citrus fruit, or chicken breast in watercress milk. There's a weekday lunchtime menu €18, and others at €23 and €49. They have the most fantastic cellar – the spectacular wine list features over a thousand vintages. Nine pleasant rooms in a recently renovated wing, ranging from €46–53 for a double. The charming ones at the back of the flower-filled courtyard are quieter. *Free coffee offered to our readers on presentation of this guide.*

Beaune

21200

Hôtel Grillon***

21 rte. de Seurre.
Ⓣ03.80.22.44.25 Ⓕ03.80.24.94.89
Ⓦwww.hotel-grillon.fr
Closed Feb. TV. Swimming pool. Car park.

It's difficult to see why people make do with chain hotels when, in a charming place like this, you can fall into bed after a visit to the wine cellar and wake up to the sound of chirping birds. The cosy, air-conditioned rooms in this old family house have style and all are decorated with a modern touch; it's a pity that you can hear the traffic noise. Doubles with shower or bath €50–65. In the summer you can eat breakfast in the garden or on the terrace. Dine at *Le Verger*, in the park opposite. *10% discount on a room (Dec–March) offered to our readers on presentation of this guide.*

Le Home**

138 rte. de Dijon; take the A31 south of Beaune in the direction of Dijon, leave at exit 24.
Ⓣ03.80.22.16.43 Ⓕ03.80.24.90.74
Ⓦwww.lehome.fr
Disabled access. TV. Car park.

It's rather hard to spot this old Burgundian house, nestling in lush greenery – it's tucked away behind a wall on the way into the town. It makes a very pleasant place to stop, and an ideal spot in which to relax. The décor, not surprisingly, is English in style and the welcome is as charming as the location. Some of the rooms overlook the garden and hopefully those on the road will benefit from soundproofing in a promised refurbishment. €54–65 for a double with shower/wc or bath; excellent breakfast. *10% discount on a room (1 Dec–15*

April) offered to our readers on presentation of this guide.

Hôtel Central***

2 rue Victor-Millot; take the outlying boulevard, turn left into rue de l'Hôtel-Dieu, then turn right.
Ⓣ03.80.24.77.24 Ⓕ03.80.22.30.40
Ⓦwww.ot-beaune.fr/sites/loger/hotel-central
Closed *20 Oct–20 Dec. Restaurant closed Wed out of season.* **TV. Car park.**

An aptly named (it's a stone's throw from the Hospices), quiet and comfortable hotel, with spacious bedrooms with good facilities at €65–77 with shower/wc or bath, depending on the season. Some rooms have been completely refurbished and fitted with air-conditioning. The country cooking also enjoys a good reputation. The owner has delved into his history books, unearthing seventeenth- and eighteenth-century dishes which he interprets in his own way. Menus €24–39. *Free bottle of Crémant-de-Bourgogne offered to our readers on presentation of this guide.*

Au Bon Accueil

La Montagne (southwest). Take the D970 in the direction of Auxerre, turn right, and at the Beaune exit head towards La Montagne; after that, it's signposted.
Ⓣ03.80.22.08.80 Ⓕ03.80.22.93.12
Closed *Mon and Tues evenings; Wed; 20 Aug–4 Sept.*

Tourists often outnumber locals in the town centre. But this restaurant, barely a kilometre from the Hospices, is a thoroughly local preserve. It's filled with families at Sunday lunchtime, when the menu includes terrine, *crudités* and pâté (as much as you can manage) and their star dish, roast beef, followed by a cheese platter and home-made tart. Menus €12 (weekday lunchtime) and €14.50–23. Paper tablecloths on the tables but choice of wines at good prices. Bask in the warm reception and, in summer, on the wonderful tree-shaded terrace.

Restaurant Le P'tit Paradis

25 rue Paradis.
Ⓣ03.80.24.91.00
Closed *Mon; Tues; 9–23 March; 10–19 Aug; 16 Nov–3 Dec.* **Disabled access.**

Beaune's road to paradise was a gastronomic purgatory until this restaurant opened opposite the Musée du Vin. It's painted in colours as fresh as the cooking, which is very reasonably priced. Weekday lunch menu at €12.50 and others at €16 and €27.50. Terrace in summer.

Restaurant La Ciboulette

69 rue de Lorraine; it's in the old part of town, opposite the theatre.
Ⓣ03.80.24.70.72 Ⓕ03.80.22.79.77
Closed *Mon; Tues; last 3 weeks in Feb; second and third weeks in Aug.*

The renovated premises are small and the décor is restrained. Two well-priced set menus (€18 and €24) bring in tourists and locals alike, which is reassuring. An ideal spot to gather your strength for a tour of the Hospices or the city's numerous wine cellars. Friendly atmosphere.

Le Benaton

25 rue du Faubourg Bretonnière; it's five minutes from the town centre, heading towards Autun.
Ⓣ03.80.22.00.26 Ⓕ03.80.22.51.95
Ⓔle.benaton@liberty.surf.fr
Closed *Wed and Thurs lunchtime in season; Wed and Thurs out of season.* **Disabled access.**

Though it's not ideally located, this restaurant is worth seeking out. The cooking is of the traditional local variety with modern touches: pan-fried snails, courgette caviar served on a reduced tomato sauce and custard cream. The €20 weekday lunchtime menu is a model of its type (served at weekends and evenings too from Nov–Feb), and there are others at €34 and €48. One way to ensure quality at a reasonable price is by ordering a combination of the cheapest menu with wine chosen à la carte. *Free Kir offered to our readers on presentation of this guide.*

Restaurant Le Verger

21 rte. de Seurre; same entance as *Hôtel Grillon*.
Ⓣ03.80.24.28.05
Closed *Tues; Wed and Thurs lunch; 15 Jan–1 March.* **Disabled access. Car park.**

This superb restaurant stands out for its architectural daring in the context of Beaune. It is run by a friendly couple who are equally adventurous in their cooking and are gradually forging an enviable reputation, which is only enhanced by the reasonable prices: menus €20–40. The dishes, steeped in local tradition, are light and aromatic: Burgundy snails in a tureen of tomato *confit*, crumble of fried duck foie gras, nest of braised chicory. In summer you can eat on the terrace.

Levernois

21200 (4km SE)

Le Parc**

13 rue de Golf: take the D970 in the direction of Verdun-sur-le-Doubs then turn left.
Ⓣ03.80.22.22.51 Ⓕ03.80.24.21.19
Ⓦperso.wanadoo.fr/hotel.le.parc
Closed *1–20 Jan; 25 Nov–31 Dec.* **Disabled access. TV. Car park.**

An old house, now a charming hotel. The trees in the grounds are a hundred years old and full of birds. The bedrooms are full of character, each different; doubles €38 with handbasin, €45 with shower/wc and €45–85 with bath. A friendly, relaxed place – it's best to book.

Bouze-lès-Beaune

21200 (7km NW)

La Bouzerotte

It's on the D970.
Ⓣ03.80.26.01.37 Ⓕ03.80.26.09.37
Ⓦperso.wanadoo.fr/la.bouzerotte
Closed *Mon; Tues; also Sun evening 1 Dec–30 March; 11–19 Sept; 22 Dec–2 Jan.* **Car park.**

A real country inn, ten minutes from the centre of Beaune, with real Burgundians and real Burgundy cooking. Real flowers (so unusual nowadays you have to mention the fact) decorate the old wooden tables, and there's an old-fashioned sideboard and a fireplace where a fire crackles in cold weather. More to the point, they also have good wines from small local vineyards which Christine, who used to be a wine waitress, can recommend. The freshest produce of the highest quality is used in the dishes and the presentation is lovely. Try ravioli of snails and calf's trotters with garlic. Cheap menu at €15 (weekdays only) and others €21–37. It'll cost about €23 à la carte.

Ladoix-Serrigny

21550 (7km NE)

Auberge de la Miotte

4 rue de la Miotte; 1.5 km from Ladoix; follow the road to Corgolain and look out for the signposts.
Ⓣ03.80.26.40.75
Closed *Sun, Mon and Tues evenings.*

An old hunting lodge on the edge of the forest that calls to mind the set of a swashbuckling film: enormous wooden tables on a worn stone floor, with sturdy beams and metal chandeliers in the ceiling. The low prices also seem to belong to another era: weekday lunctime menu €11, with others €13–23. Home cooking with fresh, seasonal ingredients, and an exceptional (and very cheap) wine list, with several vintages provided by the owner's friends from nearby vineyards. Cheerful, unpretentious service. Pretty terrace shaded by trees.

Les Coquines

N74 – Buisson; 10 minutes from Beaune; take the N74, in the direction of Dijon.
Ⓣ03.80.26.43.58 Ⓕ03.80.26.49.59
Closed *Wed; Thurs; 2–21 Feb.* **Car park.**

A charming old house with views of the surrounding countryside. Menus at €29 and €39. You can choose a table under the glass roof or in the cellar, depending on how much privacy you want. Menus in the great gastronomic tradition.

Bourbon-Lancy

71140

Hôtel La Tourelle du Beffroi

17 pl. de la Mairie; at the entrance to the old town, beside the belfry.
Ⓣ03.85.89.39.20Ⓕ03.85.89.39.29
Ⓦwww.latourelle.net

A delightful little hotel in the medieval quarter. Only eight rooms, all different and pretty, and with poetic names; three of them look on to the garden. Reckon on €45–70 for two people; breakfast buffet (€7) served on the veranda or the terrace, with its fine view of the belfry. For other meals, just follow the owner to her former restaurant *La Grignotte du Vieux Bourbon* (see below), which is close by.

Le Grand Hôtel***

Parc Thermal, in the direction of Dijon.
Ⓣ03.85.89.08.87 Ⓕ03.85.89.32.23
Ⓦwww.grand-hotel-thermal.com
Closed *end Oct to end March; restaurant closed Nov–March except weekends.* **TV. Car park.**

Perfect for lovers of charming, old-fashioned spas. Set in a former Visitandine convent, the cloister of which remains intact, the hotel itself is outsize without being overblown. Clean rooms with enormous bathrooms at reasonable prices: doubles €58–75. The austerity of the spa does not extend to the classic cuisine on offer in the *Restaurant du Cloître*: fried duck foie gras, scallops in raspberry vinegar, zander *en croûte* with parsley and chives sauce, pear poached in spices and pink sorbet. €12 menu every day at lunch and dinner, then another at €18. Extensive wine list. Meals served on the terrace under the cloister in fine weather. *Free coffee offered to our readers on presentation of this guide .*

|●| La Grignotte du Vieux Bourbon

12 rue de l'Horloge; in the heart of the old town.
Ⓣ03.85.89.06.53
Closed *Christmas.*

A heart-warming stopover, on account of both the food and the atmosphere. An authentic bistro with lively regulars and a young owner (commonly known as Hervé de la Grignotte), who is kept busy serving the tasty *entrecôtes* and other dishes of the day. Rustic menu at €13. Sale and sampling of wines in the shop alongside, *La Cav'atout.*

Chablis

89800

⌂ Au Relais de la Belle Étoile-Bergerand's

4 rue des Moulins
Ⓣ03.86.18.96.08 Ⓕ03.86.18.96.09
Ⓔbergerand-belleetoile@wanadoo.fr
Closed *Tues.*

The new owner, who is nicknamed "the American", has transformed these premises in the town centre into a charming, highly presentable hotel with bright, colourful rooms; these vary in size and cost €55–75 according to the degree of comfort. Bed and breakfast also available. It is advisable to book.

⌂ |●| Hostellerie des Clos***

Rue Jules-Rathier.
Ⓣ03.86.42.10.63 Ⓕ03.86.42.17.11
Ⓦwww.hostellerie-des-clos.fr
Closed *20 Dec–17 Jan.* **Disabled access. TV. Car park.**

In this hostelry, housed in a former hospital and chapel, the waiters wear tails, the tinkling chandeliers gleam luxuriously, the illuminated gardens are delightful and Madame sports elaborate jewellery. Despite all this, the waiters don't take themselves too seriously and Madame's laugh makes you feel welcome. Her husband uses only the finest ingredients and his best-known dishes are subtly flavoured with Chablis, so take your credit card – menus start at €33 (every day), with others at €50 and €70. If you're eating à la carte, choose just a main course and a dessert and they won't object. Specialities include *fricassée* of snails with a simple herb *coulis*, roast zander or boned ham, and fruit desserts. Double rooms with bath €55–84.

|●| Le Vieux Moulin de Chablis

18 rue des Moulins.
Ⓣ03.86.42.47.30 Ⓕ03.86.42.84.44
Ⓦwww.vieux-moulin-chablis.com
Closed *Christmas holidays.* **Car park.**

A lot of water from the Serein river has flowed under the bridge since this restaurant started up in a house which used to belong to a wine-growing family. The large dining room has walls of local stone, the regional cuisine is well up to standard and the prices are fair. Best dishes are the beef fillet in Pinot noir, *andouillette* and zander in Chablis. Four menus €17–40.

Ligny-le-Châtel

89144 (15km NW)

⌂ |●| Relais Saint-Vincent**

14 Grande-Rue; take the D91 from Chablis.
Ⓣ03.86.47.53.38
Ⓔrelais.saint.vincent@libertysurf.fr
Closed *21 Dec–6 Jan.* **Disabled access. TV. Car park.**

The village and the street are from another age, and the half-timbered house dates back to the seventeenth century. It has been tastefully converted by the welcoming owner and the rooms have all mod cons. Doubles €42–68 with shower/wc or bath. Cheapest menu €13 (every day, dinner and lunch), with others at €16–27. Excellent, authentic local cuisine and there's a remarkable cheese selection including a local Époisses. You can sit out in the quiet flowery courtyard.

|●| Auberge du Bief

2 av. de Chablis; it's next to the church; take the D91.

Ⓣ03.86.47.43.42 Ⓕ03.86.47.48.14
Closed *Sun evening; Mon; Tues evening; Wed–Fri evenings out of season; Christmas school holidays; last week in Aug.* **High chairs available. Car park.**

Very popular locally for lunch on Sunday. There aren't many tables so it's advisable to arrive early or book – otherwise you might find a small space on the terrace. Well-presented dishes and refined cooking: gâteau of artichokes with lemon and herb butter, duck *confit* in a buckwheat pancake with Emmental cheese, ham on the bone with Chablis sauce, Burgundy snails, *andouillette* salad with vinaigrette, and Bavarois with Chablis and a *coulis* trio. Good value for money with the cheapest menu at €14 (during the week) and others at €17–36. Charming, smiling welcome.

Chagny

71150

Hôtel de la Ferté**

11 bd. de la Liberté.
Ⓣ03.85.87.07.47
Ⓦwww.hotelferte.com
Closed *12–26 Dec.* **TV. Car park.**

This substantial house has been attractively refurbished and turned into a welcoming hotel. There are thirteen rooms with open fires, flowery wallpaper and antique furniture. And, without detracting from the period style, all the bathrooms are modern. The rooms are also efficiently soundproofed. Doubles €42–49 with shower/wc or bath. A country breakfast (€5.50) is served in a room overlooking the garden, or outside in good weather. One of the best hotels in the price range in the area.

Lameloise****

36 pl. d'Armes.
Ⓣ03.85.87.65.65 Ⓕ03.85.87.03.57
Ⓦwww.lameloise.fr
Restaurant closed *Tues lunchtime; Wed; Thurs lunchtime; 17–24 Jan.* **Disabled access. TV. Car park.**

The third generation of the Lameloise family runs this establishment, which attracts a varied clientele from local businessmen and committed foodies to well-heeled couples. The decoration in the five small dining rooms is stylish – stone walls, hefty beams, comfortable chairs, fresh flowers and so on. The service is unobtrusive, precise and perfect. The cooking is based on local produce: snail ravioli in sweet garlic broth, roast pigeon and foie gras pasta. In between each course, delicious morsels, both savoury and sweet, appear out of nowhere. The desserts are served in gargantuan portions. Menus €85 and €120. In the hotel, doubles are €120–270. *Apéritif on the house offered to our readers on presentation of this guide.*

Chassey-le-Camp

71150 (5km SW)

Auberge du Camp Romain***

From Chagny take the D974 in the direction of Santenay and turn left; it's down the hill from the ruins of a Roman camp.
Ⓣ03.85.87.09.91
Ⓦperso.wanadoo.fr/camp.romain
Closed *1 Jan–10 Feb.* **Disabled access. TV. Swimming pool. Car park.**

The inn overlooks a lush green valley and you'd think you were in the mountains. It's a sort of mini *Club-Med* with tennis courts, crazy-golf, pools, sauna, Jacuzzi, steam bath and a gym. The inn has 44 spacious rooms with en-suite bathrooms for €61–77. The restaurant offers some ambitious dishes, and there's sufficient talent on hand to bring them off successfully. Set menus €19–43. Nice place for a weekend of sport with the family or for lounging around – though perhaps it's not ideal for a romantic weekend *à deux*. *Free apéritif offered to our readers on presentation of this guide.*

Charrecey

71510 (13 km SW)

Le Petit Blanc

Le Pont-Pilley; signposted from the D978.
Ⓣ03.85.45.15.43
Closed *Sun evening; Mon; Thurs evening and Sun lunch (in winter); a week at Easter; fortnight in Aug; fortnight at Christmas.*

A country inn with chequered tablecloths, slates, enamelled plaques on the walls and, above all, authentic traditional dishes, as promised in the menu: home-made *terrine maison*, *coq au vin* and old-style *blanquette*. The lively dining room is always packed, and customers often spill out on the terrace as well. Weekday lunchtime menu €13, then €19–27. Diligent service, friendly welcome and a wine list with a wide range of Mercurey (a bit on the pricey side, however). *Liqueur on the house offered to our readers on presentation of this guide.*

Chalon-sur-Saône

71100

Hôtel Kyriad**

35 pl. de Beaune.
03.85.90.08.00 03.85.90.08.01
kyriad.chalon@wanadoo.fr
TV. Pay car park.

Small hotel in a renovated old house. Accommodation is in the main building or in two annexes, the more recent of which overlooks an inner courtyard and is quieter. Some rooms have parquet floors, open fireplaces and old furniture; many have been entirely renovated. Doubles €50–58, breakfast €6. There's a sauna, a solarium and a gym. *10% discount on a room offered to our readers on presentation of this guide.*

Hôtel Saint-Jean**

24 quai Gambetta.
03.85.48.45.65
Disabled access. TV. Pay car park.

If you have to spend a night in Chalon, the *Saint-Jean* is the only hotel on the Saône riverbank and it's away from the traffic – so booking is advisable. The mansion has been tastefully decorated by a former restaurateur who gave up cooking in favour of hotel-keeping, and the staff are friendly and professional. A quiet, clean and welcoming establishment with magnificent views, where everything is pleasing and the prices are reasonable. Large double rooms decorated in fresh colours go for €50. You feel there should be some sort of preservation order on the handsome imitation marble staircase, which dates from the late nineteenth century.

Le Saint-Georges***

32 av. Jean-Jaurès; it's opposite the station.
03.85.90.80.50 03.85.90.80.55
www.lesaintgeorges71.fr
Restaurant closed *Sat lunchtime; Sun evening; 1–17 Aug.* **TV. High chairs available. Pay car park.**

A classic station hotel. All the rooms have been refurbished with good facilities – the armchairs will appeal to fans of modern design. All in all, it's value for money with double rooms for €67–120. The gastronomic restaurant may beckon but if you're looking to spend less try your luck at the friendly bistro *Le Comptoir d'à Côté* instead, where you can have a meal of Burgundian specialities – parsleyed ham with Aligoté, foie gras *escalope* with spiced bread – for around €16. Menus in the fine restaurant are €20 (not Sunday) and €28–45; specialities include such dishes as Bresse chicken terrine with foie gras. *Apéritif on the house offered to our readers on presentation of this guide.*

L'Air du Temps

7 rue de Strasbourg.
03.85.93.39.01
Closed *Sun; Mon.*

Sample the cooking of a great chef at extremely accessible prices: incredible lunch menu at €14; other menus at €19 and €24. Cyril Bouchet has acquired an impeccable technique working alongside some of France's greatest chefs (Meneau, Jung, Troigros, Robuchon) before branching out on his own in modest surroundings and building up a loyal following. The budgetary limitations are evident in the somewhat neutral setting with sparse decorations, but the dishes provide a subtle, precise splash of colour and tastes, with fresh ingredients and just the right amount of spices to catch you off guard for a moment. Cheerful and effusive service.

Restaurant Ripert

31 rue Saint-Georges; between the sous-préfecture and the Grande-Rue.
03.85.48.89.20
Closed *Sun; Mon; 1 week early Jan; 1 week early May; 3 weeks end Aug.*

Over the last twenty years Alain Ripert has created something of an institution. The dining room is small with a few touches reminiscent of a 1950s bistro (adverts, enamel signs and so on) and fills up rapidly with locals. Dishes change daily with the fresh produce in the market but might include *escalope* of veal sweetbreads with spices and honey, monkfish stew with saffron, *croustillant* of oxtail, lobster tail *timbale*. Save room for a dessert. Set menus €13.80–23.80. Unusually for this part of the world, they serve some good wines in carafes as well as bottles. *Free coffee offered to our readers on presentation of this guide.*

|●| Restaurant Chez Jules

11 rue de Strasbourg; it's on île Saint-Laurent.
Ⓣ03.85.48.08.34 Ⓕ03.85.48.55.48
Closed *Sat lunchtime; Sun; a fortnight in Feb; 1st 3 weeks in Aug.*

This small restaurant, located in a quiet neighbourhood, is popular with the locals, and the salmon-pink walls, sturdy beams, copper pots, paintings and old sideboard add to the cosy atmosphere. The cooking is inventive and enjoys playing with the colours and tastes of the classic local dishes. *Menu du jour* at €15; others at €18–30. Good wine list available by the glass, bottle and carafe. After all that, a post-prandial stroll along the embankment might well be called for.

|●| Le Gourmand

13 rue de Strasbourg; in the Île Saint-Laurent.
Ⓣ03.85.93.64.61
Closed *Sun evening; Mon; Tues lunch; last fortnight in Jan; 3 weeks in Aug.*

The ever-smiling, ever-helpful owner sets the tone for this chic but down-to-earth restaurant that has built up a loyal following. The food is sophisticated and exquisitely presented, with particularly outstanding sauces with generous quantities of herbs. Menus €15.50–30. Specialities include baked turbot on a bed of ratatouille, roast pigeon or *tournedos* of pig's feet with foie gras, etc.

Lux-Saint-Rémy

71100 (4km S)

|●| Ma Campagne

Quai Bellevue; take the N6 in the direction of Tournus.
Ⓣ03.85.48.33.80 Ⓕ03.85.93.33.72
Closed *Sun evening; Mon evening (and Mon lunch out of season); mid-Jan to mid-March.*
TV. Car park.

This huge country house, set in splendid isolation in the middle of trees on the banks of the Saône, is a bucolic delight, with birdsong and walks by the river. While the hotel is undergoing renovation, rooms (for €39) above the restaurant provide temporary accommodation. Highly accomplished classic cooking, with an emphasis on fish. Menus €17–29. On a fine day you can eat on a large terrace shaded by an awning. *Apéritif on the house offered to our readers on presentation of this guide.*

Buxy

71390 (15km SE)

Hôtel Fontaine de Baranges

Rue de la Fontaine-de-Baranges; take the D977.
Ⓣ03.85.94.10.70 Ⓕ03.85.94.10.79
Ⓦwww.hotelfb.com
Closed *Jan.* **Disabled access. TV. Car park.**

A substantial early-nineteenth-century residence in grounds planted with shady trees, right next to a pretty old stone wash-house. The whole place has been completely restored, and the attractive rooms are spacious and peaceful; some have private terraces overlooking the garden. Doubles €65–135, depending on the size. No restaurant but there is a charming bar. Breakfast, €9, in the cellar or the terrace.

Charité-sur-Loire (La)

58400

Hôtel Le Bon Laboureur**

Quai Romain-Mollot; it's on the île de Loire, 500m from the town centre.
Ⓣ03.86.70.22.85 Ⓕ03.86.70.23.64
TV.

An ancient building, each room of which is a different size and has different facilities. They've all been refurbished; doubles cost €35–48; some can sleep three or four people, at €8 per extra person. Breakfast €5.50. The best rooms overlook an interior garden or the Loire. Reasonable prices and a warm welcome.

|●| L'Auberge de Seyr

4 Grande-Rue.
Ⓣ and Ⓕ03.86.70.03.51
Closed Sun evening; Thurs evening; Sun evening; a week in Feb; 3 weeks end Aug to early Sept.

A simple, unpretentious restaurant serving cuisine with character. Dishes change daily but the fresh fish and home-made pastries are always good. The weekday *menu du jour* at €10.50 includes a starter – various salads or home-made terrine – and a main dish of meat or fish followed by cheese or dessert. Other menus €16–26. *Free coffee offered to our readers on presentation of this guide.*

Charolles

71120

🏃 🏠 🍴 Hôtel-restaurant Le Lion d'Or**

6 rue de Champagny.
☎03.85.24.08.28
Closed *Sun evening and Mon except mid-July to mid-Aug.* **TV. Swimming pool. Car park.**

This seventeenth-century coaching inn is on the banks of a small river. Large double rooms with shower go for €45–54. Nos. 23 and 25 have a view of the river. The top-notch restaurant serves good regional cooking, with exceptional meat dishes, as you would expect in Charolais country. Set menu €15 except Sunday, with others €26 and €34. *Free coffee offered to our readers on presentation of this guide.*

🏃 🏠 🍴 Hôtel-restaurant de la Poste***

2 av. de la Libération.
☎03.85.24.11.32 ℻03.85.24.05.74
🌐www.la-poste-hotel.com
Closed *Sun evening; Mon.* **TV. Pay car park.**

This is a very important establishment in the Charolais – it's run by Daniel Doucet, the ambassador of Burgundy gastronomy, and his cooking is as fresh and tasty as ever. The dining room is richly decorated and the service is faultless and attentive, but this place is definitely not affected. You'll get great advice on wine to suit your taste and an excellent choice of dishes – don't miss the Charolais rib steak with Guérande salt, the *cassolette* of scallops with a leek fondue, the *croustillant* of veal sweetbreads with morels and chanterelle mushrooms, or the hot apple *soufflé*. Magnificent cheese platter and desserts. Set menu at €21 during the week, others at €30–60. Eat out under the maple trees in the interior garden on fine days. Comfy bedrooms €48–69. *Free coffee offered to our readers on presentation of this guide.*

Beaubery

71220 (12km SE)

🏃 🍴 Auberge de Beaubery

La Gare; take the N79 from Charolles, then the D79.
☎03.85.24.84.74
Closed *Wed evening; Sat; Christmas holidays.* **Disabled access.**

Little inns like this offering a complete meal for €11 (not Sun) are few and far between. Basic home cooking, lovingly prepared and served in generous portions, is dished up in a dining room decorated with prints and a kitschy old clock. It's full of regulars and local travelling salesmen. The cheapest menu gets you a sandwich filled with local ham, omelette and soft white cheese. Other menus €16–20, which list dishes such as an excellent *coq au vin*, frogs' legs, guineafowl in red wine sauce and Charolais steak. À la carte will cost you around €16. *Free coffee offered to our readers on presentation of this guide.*

Château-Chinon

58120

🏃 🏠 🍴 Hôtel du Parc - Le Relais Gourmand**

Nevers road; on the left of the Nevers road, just before leaving the town.
☎03.86.79.44.94.℻03.86.79.41.10.
Closed *Feb; restaurant closed Sun evening (15 Nov–15 March).* **TV. Disabled access.**

Despite its name, this modern, functional hotel is not surrounded by a park, although it does fall within the Morvan region Natural Park. Comfortable, air-conditioned rooms at €42. It's a good place to eat, too; the €12 menu is particularly good value (though it is not available on Sundays or public holidays). Other menus €15–38. The food is not only cheap but also well prepared, and to top it all there's a very friendly atmosphere. *Free coffee offered to our readers on presentation of this guide.*

Planchez

58230 (16km NE)

🏠 🍴 🏃 Le Relais des Lacs

Avenue François-Mitterrand; take the D37.
☎03.86.78.49.00
℻03.86.78.49.09
🌐www.morvan.gourmand.fr

Presentable double rooms with shower/wc €39–43, with bath €45–52. Splendid dining room with a terrace, and good cooking to match. The chef is very fussy about the quality of his ingredients, and all the beef and game comes from the immediate area. The trout with Pouilly is delicious, but the *grapiaud de forment* (a local speciality) is disappointing. Menus €14–38. Fine wine list and friendly service. Don't miss the local apéritif, Morvandiau. The chef is a multi-faceted character; he is the mayor of the village and a mine of information about the region.

Châteauneuf

21320

Hostellerie du Château**

Rue de Centre. Take the Pouilly-en-Auxois exit off the A6.
Ⓣ03.80.49.22.00 Ⓕ03.80.49.21.27
Ⓦhostellerie-chateauneuf.com
Closed *Mon and Tues except July–Aug; Dec; Jan.* **Disabled access.**

Despite the fact that it looks as if it hasn't changed for years, nearly all the twelfth- and fourteenth-century houses in this picturesque hilltop village have been bought by outsiders. Similarly misleading is the medieval exterior of this hotel, which stands in the shadow of a twelfth-century castle – inside it's modern and comfortable. The cheapest menu at €23 (daily, lunch and dinner) and others at €23–40 list traditional local dishes such as Charolais beef and snails. Doubles with shower or bath, €45–70; some look out over the countryside.

Vandenesse-en-Auxois

21320 (5km NW)

Restaurant de l'Auxois

It's very close to Châteauneuf-en-Auxois on the banks of the canal.
Ⓣ03.80.49.22.36 Ⓕ03.80.64.68.36
Closed *Sun evening and Mon Oct–June; 20 Dec–1 Feb.* **Car park.**

The whole village has benefited from the reopening of the grocer's and this restaurant, both run by the Wallons. Food served here spices up the local style of cooking: fillet of beef with Époisse cheese sauce, zander in red wine sauce, and *pauchouse* with two types of fish. There's a weekday menu at €13.50 and others at €17–32. The garden is superb in summer, and there's an old-fashioned dining room for greyer days.

Châtillon-sur-Seine

21400

Sylvia Hôtel**

9 av. de la Gare; it's on the outskirts of town, in the direction of Troyes.
Ⓣ03.80.91.02.44 Ⓕ03.80.91.47.77
Ⓦwww.sylvia-hotel.fr
Disabled access. TV. Car park.

The previous owners transformed this enormous old family home, set in parkland, into a delightful hotel and named it after their daughter. Then Sylvia grew up and the family moved on. The present owners decided to keep the name, though, and do their utmost to make you enjoy your stay, offering cosy rooms and wonderful breakfasts which are eaten round a large communal table. Simple doubles €31 with basin and €38–44 with bath/wc.

Le Bourg-à-Mont "Chez Julie"

27 rue du Bourg-à-Mont; in the old town, opposite the old law court, near the Archeological Museum.
Ⓣ03.80.91.04.33
Closed *Mon; Sun evening (out of season); a fortnight in Oct.* **High chairs available. Disabled access.**

A pleasant surprise in this sleepy town, famous for its Vix vase: a house from another era, replete with gaudy old posters and paintings, that is nevertheless particularly popular with young people. In winter, there is a blazing log fire; in summer, the big windows are thrown open on to the courtyard bedecked with lilacs where you can even eat your meal (provided you book on time, as the places are limited). Menus €14.50–33. The dishes, which reflect the old-fashioned atmosphere, include Châtillonnais trout terrine, Bourg-à-Mont beef (a spicy, easily digestible version of the famous *bœuf bourguignon* accompanied by blackcurrant cream) and almond tart with chocolate and custard. *Free coffee offered to our readers on presentation of this guide.*

Montliot-et-Courcelles

21400 (3.5km N)

Chez Florentin

On the N71, at the entrance to the village.
Ⓣ03.80.91.09.70.

Closed *Sun evening; Mon (except for lunch on public holidays, when it closes Tues).* **Disabled access.**

Friendly service and unbeatable prices. Lorry drivers' menu at €10.50 served from Tuesday lunch to Friday dinner: mushroom *timbale* with cream, *blanquette* of veal and mouth-watering pies. Other menus from €12–44. You can eat in the bar with the lorry drivers; the large dining room is reserved for banquets and baptisms and is often occupied. At night the customers are usually local, whereas at lunch they are mainly just passing through.

Clamecy

58500

Hostellerie de la Poste**

9 pl. Émile-Zola.
Ⓣ03.86.27.01.55 Ⓕ03.86.27.05.99
Ⓔhotelposteclamecy@wanadoo.fr
TV.

A substantial building in the centre that looks the part – like a post house that's been there forever. The rooms are clean and comfortable and it's obvious that the hotel is seriously well run. Doubles from €51. The *menu du jour* (not Sun) is pricey at €18, though the cooking is of good quality; there's another menu at €28 and a children's menu at €15. The beef is local Charolais and there are fresh river fish too. *Free coffee offered to our readers on presentation of this guide.*

La crêperie du Vieux Canal

18 av. de la République; it's opposite the museum.
Ⓣ03.86.24.47.93
Closed *Sun (out of season); Mon (in season); 1st fortnight in Feb; a week in Sept.*

One of Clamecy's friendliest spots to eat, a place where you can have a good, quick lunch. The décor is Breton and they serve savoury and sweet pancakes (also to take away) – try the Savoyarde, or the Normande – as well as pasta dishes and bruschetta. A *galette* costs €6 and you'll spend around €10 à la carte. *Free coffee offered to our readers on presentation of this guide.*

L'Angélus

11 pl. Saint-Jean; opposite the collegiate church.
Ⓣ03.86.27.33.98
Closed *Sun evening; Mon; Feb; 1 week at New Year.*

Most locals agree that this Nivernais restaurant is the best in Clamecy. It's a lovely building with wooden sides and is set right in the heart of the old town, close to the town hall that nestles under the beautiful Saint-Martin collegiate church. Sophisticated presentation and efficient service. Menus €14.50–25. The wines are generally a little expensive, but the Irancy from Auxerre, one of the cheapest vintages listed, is good value for money. In fine weather you can eat on the terrace.

Restaurant au Bon Accueil

3 rte. d'Auxerre.
Ⓣ03.86.27.91.67
Ⓔlanglois.fr@wanadoo.fr
Closed *Sat and evenings; winter school holidays; Nov school holidays.* **Disabled access.**

A restaurant with a welcome that lives up to its name. It also has a peaceful dining room that has views of the Yonne and the collegiate church. François Langlois cooks with flair and passion – dishes change as the mood takes him and there are many regional options on the menu. Weekday menu €18, with others €22 and €31. It's not a very big place, so it's best to book. *Free coffee offered to our readers on presentation of this guide.*

Tannay

58190 (16km SE)

Hôtel du Relais Fleuri**

2 rue de Bèze; take the D34 from Clamecy.
Ⓣ03.86.29.84.57 Ⓕ03.86.29.33.88
Ⓔrelaisfleuritannay@libertysurf.fr
Closed *Sun evening; Mon except July–Aug; fortnight in Feb; fortnight in Sept.* **Disabled access. Swimming pool. Car park.**

A comfortable hotel in an attractive period house. Doubles with shower/wc or bath €43–50. The cooking has a good reputation with an emphasis on the regional. Recommended dishes include Tannay-style ham, snail and mushroom pie and praline-flavoured *croustine*. Satisfaction guaranteed. Weekday lunch menu at €10 and others €21.20–30.50. *Free coffee offered to our readers on presentation of this guide.*

Cluny

71250

Hôtel du Commerce*

8 pl. du Commerce.
03.85.59.03.09 03.85.59.00.87
Closed *1st week in Dec.* **TV.**

In this expensive town, this is a small, well-maintained and central hotel that offers basic, clean accommodation at reasonable prices. Wonderfully friendly reception to boot. Doubles cost €24–38.50.

Bourgvilain

71520 (9km S)

Auberge Larochette

From Cluny take the D980 then the D22, and it's on the village square facing the church.
and 03.85.50.81.73
Closed *Tues evening; Wed; Dec–March.*

A welcoming provincial dining room in this large, traditional village inn. There are reproductions of Millet paintings on the wall and a country clock in the corner. The excellent cooking likewise carries on the best French traditions: dishes are finely judged by Monsieur Bonin and generously served. Weekday lunch menu at €14, with others €20–40. À la carte you can get warm foie gras with apples, frogs' legs and *trompette* mushrooms in flaky pastry, zander *millefeuille*, and a tasty Charolais steak. In summer, food is served outside in the fresh air under the trees opposite. The atmosphere is relaxed, so don't be in a hurry and make the most of it. Reservations recommended. *Free apéritif offered to our readers on presentation of this guide.*

La Pierre Sauvage

Col des Enceints. From Cluny take the D980 then the D22.
03.85.35.70.03 03.85.35.74.71
Closed *Tues evening and Wed except July–Aug; Mon–Thurs 1 Oct to Easter; Jan.* **Disabled access. Car park.**

Service until 9.30pm (10pm in summer). This place is on a hilltop 529m high. Some fifteen years ago, it was a ruin which has since been wonderfully restored and is now an appealing place to stop. Start off with a hunk of bread and strong cheese or house terrine before getting onto the main courses. Specialities include *cassolette* of snails *forestière*, guineafowl with vanilla and fresh figs, chicken with seasonal fruits and pigeon with *pêche de vigne*. They also do good vegetarian platters and terrines. Menus €16.50–27. The terrace is superb in summer. Best to book. *Free digestif offered to our readers on presentation of this guide.*

Berzé-la-Ville

71960 (10km SE)

Relais du Mâconnais**

La Croix-Blanche; from Cluny, take the D980 and the N79, then follow the D17.
03.85.36.60.72 03.85.36.65.47
www.lannuel.com
Closed *Sun evening and Mon in low season; Mon lunch July–Sept; 6 Jan–6 Feb.* **TV. Car park.**

The quiet atmosphere here will be to many people's liking and the well-spaced tables mean that you won't overhear your neighbours. Fittingly, Christian Lannuel's cooking has a very personal touch. The small *tartare* of beetroot is so original that it deserves to be upgraded from an appetizer to a starter. Other dishes, based on local produce, are finely flavoured: try *escalope* of foie gras with raspberry vinegar, milk-fed veal cutlets with vegetables *au gratin* or roast pigeon with garlic purée and sautéed mushrooms. Good dessert trolley. The cheapest menu at €26 is served every day; other menus at €36–52, with a children's menu at €11. Ten or so comfy double rooms with shower or bath go for €59–63, with breakfast at €9; half board costs €63–67 per person. *Free coffee offered to our readers on presentation of this guide.*

Cosne-sur-Loire

58200

Hôtel-restaurant Le Saint-Christophe**

Place de la Gare; it's opposite the train station.
03.86.28.02.01 03.86.26.94.28
Closed *Sun evening; Fri; 24 July–22 Aug; 25 Dec–3 Jan.* **TV.**

Comfortable rooms with good facilities. Doubles with shower/wc or bath from €38; breakfast €5.80. The smiling owner seems to be doing things right in the newly renovated restaurant too, which is popular with locals. The weekday *formule* of main course with a choice of starter or dessert costs €14, and there are menus €19–26 and options à la carte.

Straightforward, robust cooking. *10% discount on the room rate (weekends) offered to our readers on presentation of this guide.*

☗ |●| Le Vieux Relais***

11 rue Saint-Agnan.
☎03.86.28.20.21
ⓦwww.le-vieux-relais.fr
Closed *Fri evening, Sat lunch and Sun evening from Sept–May; 25 Dec–10 Jan.* **TV. Car park.**

A coaching inn straight out of the nineteenth century. The double rooms are cosy and spacious, as you would expect for the price range (€76–78), and the cooking is one of the establishment's great strengths. Father and son team up in the kitchen, while mother and daughter-in-law run the dining room. It's a popular place. The cheapest menu is €16.75, with others ranging from €19.50 to €30, and a children's menu at €11.45 which includes fish, vegetables and chocolate mousse – not just the usual *steak frites*. Specialities include Charolais beef or zander. There's a dream of a courtyard with a balcony overgrown with Virginia creeper and a puzzle of higgledy-piggledy roofs. Internal garage.

Creusot (Le)

71200

|●| Le Restaurant

Rue des Abattoirs; coming from Marteau-Pilon, to the south, turn right into rue des Abattoirs; after 500m it's indicated on the left; at the end of a cul-de-sac.
☎03.85.56.32.33
Closed *Sun; Mon evening; 1–20 Aug.*
Disabled access.

In a rather unlikely location near the abbattoirs, an area that's pretty deserted at night, this culinary beacon is well worth seeking out. You'll find a friendly welcome and a convivial atmosphere in the bright, vividly coloured dining room topped with a mezzanine. The decoration is elegant and uncluttered, with some interesting paintings, and the old zinc bar provides a traditional touch. Inspired cooking based on exhaustive research and a balance between the natural taste of fresh ingredients and a skillful use of herbs: eel with onion *confit* sprinkled with parsley, braised red mullet with fennel, veal kidneys with liquorice gravy, rabbit with gingerbread, farm-reared lamb with mint. Menus at €13, on request at dinner, and then €17–29. Reckon on around €25 à la carte. Wonderful selection of wines at a wide range of prices, including some budget-stretching Burgundies. It's advisable to book for dinner. Credit cards not accepted.

Torcy

71210 (3km SE)

|●| Le Vieux Saule

Route du Creusot; take the road from Châlon-sur-Saône.
☎03.85.55.09.53
Closed *Sun evening; Mon.*

A beautiful setting – an old country inn at the entrance to Creusot – a cheerful atmosphere and some of the tastiest cooking in the region. Excellent weekday menu at €17, regional menu at €23 and another impressive one at €40: pastry with frogs' legs and herbs, pheasant pie with leeks and foie gras. The desserts are similarly imaginative. Good wine list. *Liqueur on the house offered to our readers on presentation of this guide.*

Uchon

71190 (16km W)

☗ |●| Auberge La Croix Messire Jean

La Croix Messire Jean; head for Montcenis, then take the D228. It's 1km from Uchon.
☎03.85.54.42.06
Closed *Tues evening; Wed; Christmas–New Year.* **High chairs and games available. Car park.**

Ideal base for walkers and mountain bikers planning to tackle one of the splendid routes up one of the highest mountains (684m) in the *département*. This is a friendly inn and one of only three that have been classified as a "Bistrot Accueil du Parc du Morvan", all of which offer authentic dishes using local ingredients. It offers basic but perfectly adequate doubles with handbasin for €21. Tasteful rustic décor and prices to suit all pockets. There's a half board option for €39. It's best to book in high season; if you yearn for peace and quiet, this won't be your scene. There's a large shaded terrace where you can enjoy the exceptionally reasonable set menus, which range from €9.50 to €21. You'll spend about €15 à la carte. Mountain bikes for rent. *Free coffee or 10%*

discount on half or full board if you stay a minimum of three days.

Decize

58300

|●| Auberge des Feuillats

116 rte. des Feuillats; take boulevard Voltaire from the tourist office. Cross the bridge and then take the Moulins road; after 1km, turn left into route des Feuillats.
Ⓣ03.86.25.05.19.
Closed *Mon; Wed evening.*

The terrace to the rear, on the edge of a canal leading off the Loire, provides a good view of the pleasure boats going to and fro, setting the tone for the holiday atmosphere inside. Lunchtime menu at €10 and others at €15–24. This is the place to enjoy Charolais steak. Slightly sloppy service.

|●| Restaurant La Grignotte

57 av. du 14-Juillet.
Ⓣ03.86.25.26.20
Closed *Sun; Mon evening; a week in March; 1st fortnight in Aug; last week in Dec.*

An unpretentious restaurant unfortunately situated on a busy road. The floral dining room is lovely. You can eat decently and cheaply: the lunch menu (not Sunday) costs €10 and there are others €11–24.50. *Fondue*, shellfish are specialities, also a large selection of salads.

|●| Snack du Stade Nautique

Promenade des Halles. Take the street that goes past the tourist office to the end; it's next to the campsite.
Ⓣ03.86.25.00.99 Ⓕ03.86.77.16.58
Closed *mid-Sept to end April.* **Disabled access.**

This is a waterside café and, when it's sunny, it's the prettiest place in Decize. Happiness is sitting at a table in the shade of the plane trees with a plate of country ham, an omelette with salad or some fresh cream cheese. They do *frites* to take away. A couple of menus at €9.15, or you'll spend around €10 à la carte. You can play volleyball or have a pony ride, and some evenings in summer they have live music. Really friendly welcome.

|●| Le Charolais

33 bis rte. de Moulins.
Ⓣ03.86.25.22.27 Ⓕ03.86.25.52.52
Ⓦwww.decize.net/charolais
Closed *Sun evening; Mon; 1st week in Jan; a week in Feb.* **Disabled access.**

An attractive dining room with quiet service and refined cuisine. The cheapest menu, at €15.50, will allow you to judge, or there's a dish of the day for €13. Other menus are €24.50–51. Covered terrace at the back.

Digoin

71160

⌂ |●| Les Diligences**

14 rue Nationale; it's in a pedestrian street in the centre.
Ⓣ03.85.53.06.31 Ⓕ03.85.88.92.43
Ⓦwww.les-diligences.com
Closed *Mon evening and Tues except July–Aug; 15 Nov–15 Dec.* **TV. High chairs available. Car park.**

In the seventeenth century, travellers arriving in the town by mail coach or boat stayed at this inn. It has recently been restored and the exposed stonework, beams, polished furniture and gleaming coppers make it look very smart. But that doesn't mean the prices in the restaurant are insane: set menus start at €16 and go up to €36. Dining à la carte, you'll find lobster and crayfish tail salad with raspberry vinegar, Charolais fillet steak with five peppers, *fricassée* of ceps Bordeaux-style and John Dory fillet with watercress sauce – all are a bit pricey. Six tastefully furnished and decorated rooms, €42–49 with shower or bath, overlook the quiet banks of the Loire. There's a duplex with a private spa in the vast bathroom. Reservations advisable; you may be heavily encouraged to eat dinner at the restaurant if you stay.

Neuzy

71160 (3km NE)

⌂ |●| Le Merle Blanc***

36 rte. de Gueugnon-Autun; take the D994 going towards Autun.
Ⓣ03.85.53.17.13 Ⓕ03.85.88.91.71
Ⓦperso.wanadoo.fr/lemerleblanc
Closed *Sun evening; Mon lunchtime.*
Disabled access. TV. Car park.

The hotel is set back from the road. Doubles with shower/wc €33, or up to €46 with bath. The substantial set menu at €14 (not Sun) and others at €19–38.50

offer dishes such as pan-fried duck foie gras terrine with grapes, scallops with Noilly-Prat, Charolais sirloin and apple and walnut crumble. *Free house apéritif offered to our readers on presentation of this guide.*

Dijon

21000

See map overleaf

Hôtel du Palais**

23 rue du Palais. **Map B2-2**
Ⓣ03.80.67.16.26
Ⓕ03.80.65.12.16
Ⓔhoteldupalais-dijon@wanadoo.fr
TV.

A superb location in the (surprisingly quiet) old city centre, opposite the municipal library (worth a visit, even if you don't intend to read the books) and the Palace of Justice. Most of the rooms – simple but clean and cheerful – have been refurbished and soundproofed. Doubles with washbasin €20 and with shower/wc or bath €34–50. Beautiful breakfast room with an impressive old ceiling.

Hôtel Le Chambellan**

92 rue Vannerie. **Map C2-1**
Ⓣ03.80.67.12.67 Ⓕ03.80.38.00.39
TV.

This is the place if you're after the splendours of yesteryear combined with the convenience of mod cons. It's an old building and a delightfully old-fashioned establishment with extremely reasonable prices. Doubles with basin €26, and €42–48 with shower/wc or bath. They've all got character, but go for one overlooking the seventeenth-century courtyard.

Hôtel Le Jacquemart**

32 rue Verrerie. **Map B1-3**
Ⓣ03.80.60.09.60 Ⓕ03.80.60.09.69
Ⓦwww.hotel-lejacquemart.fr
TV.

Book to avoid disappointment. A huge old eighteenth-century house, with dauntingly steep stairs and creaky corridors, offers rooms with varying degrees of comfort at a range of prices: doubles with washbasin €29, with shower/wc or bath €45–47; breakfast €5.50. The rooms are quiet and comfortable and all have cable TV. A hotel with old-fashioned charm that is ideal for a well-earned rest after a day spent exploring old Dijon; it is also popular with actors on tour and travelling sales agents. Friendly service. *10% discount on the room rate (Dec–March inclusive) offered to our readers on presentation of this guide.*

Hôtel Victor Hugo**

23 rue des Fleurs. **Map A1-5**
Ⓣ03.80.43.63.45 Ⓕ03.80.42.13.01
TV. Car park.

Located in Dijon's sedate, middle-class neighbourhood, this isn't the place to let your hair down: it's quiet, spotless and has an atmosphere that is ever so slightly staid. There are twenty or so comfortable, welcoming rooms; doubles €36.50–43 with shower/wc, and €43 with bath. Breakfast €5.

Hôtel des Allées**

27 cours du Général-de-Gaulle. **Off map C3-6**
Ⓣ03.80.66.57.50
Ⓕ03.80.36.24.81
Ⓦwww.hotelallees.com
TV. Car park.

Set in an old maternity hospital, opposite the paths (*allées*) in the park that were traditionally used for strolling but have now been invaded by rollerbladers. Double rooms with shower/wc or bath €48–59. The building has a certain charm but the rooms are nothing special (although they are due for refurbishment, and there's a pretty garden full of birds). The hotel closes at 11pm, so you have to ask for the code to get back in.

Le Piano Qui Fume

36 rue Berbisey. **Map B2-15**
Ⓣ03.80.30.35.45
Closed *Wed; Sat lunch.*

The *Smoking Piano* consistently offers seasonal dishes that bring out the taste of the ingredients without any elaborate trickery. The chef returned to his home town after spells working with some of France's most prestigious chefs (Veyrat, Thorel, Tarridec) and seven years of critical acclaim in charge of the *Pot d'Étain* in L'Isle-sur-Serein. There is only a narrow range of dishes on offer, but they are all excellent, reasonably priced and remarkable for their simplicity, professionalism and refusal to

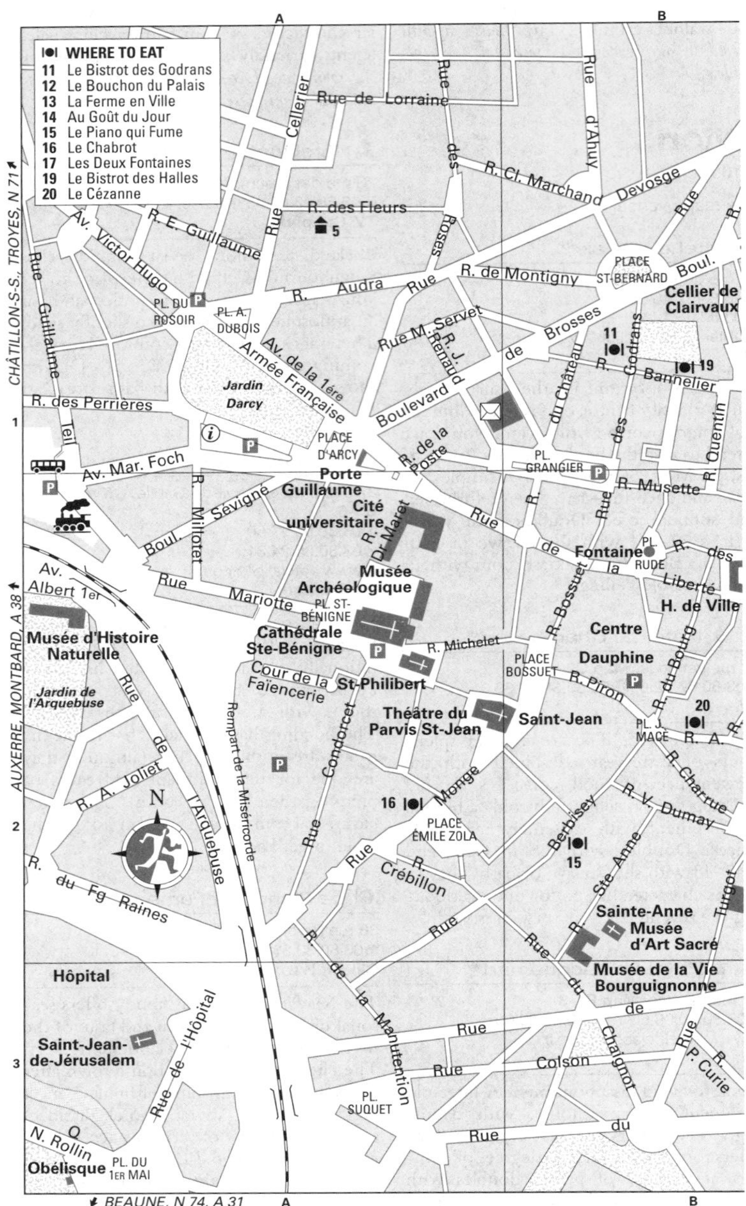
WHERE TO EAT
11 Le Bistrot des Godrans
12 Le Bouchon du Palais
13 La Ferme en Ville
14 Au Goût du Jour
15 Le Piano qui Fume
16 Le Chabrot
17 Les Deux Fontaines
19 Le Bistrot des Halles
20 Le Cézanne
CHÂTILLON-S-S., TROYES, N 71
AUXERRE, MONTBARD, A 38
BEAUNE, N 74, A 31
A
B
1
2
3
Rue de Lorraine
Rue Cellerier
Rue des Roses
Rue d'Ahuy
R. Cl. Marchand
Devosge
R. des Fleurs
5
R. E. Guillaume
Av. Victor Hugo
Rue Guillaume
R. Audra
Rue
R. de Montigny
PLACE ST-BERNARD
Boul.
Cellier de Clairvaux
PL. DU ROSOIR
PL. A. DUBOIS
Av. de la 1ère Armée Française
Rue M. Servet
R. J. Renaud
Boulevard de Brosses
11
19
R. Bannelier
R. du Château
Rue des Godrans
R. Quentin
Jardin Darcy
R. des Perrières
Teil
PLACE D'ARCY
R. de la Poste
PL. GRANGIER
R. Musette
Av. Mar. Foch
Porte Guillaume
R. Millotot
Boul. Sévigné
Cité universitaire
R. Dr Maret
Rue de la Fontaine
PL. RUDE
R. des
R. de la Liberté
H. de Ville
Av. Albert 1er
Rue Mariotte
Musée Archéologique
PL. ST-BÉNIGNE
Cathédrale Ste-Bénigne
Musée d'Histoire Naturelle
Jardin de l'Arquebuse
R. Michelet
R. Bossuet
Centre Dauphine
PLACE BOSSUET
R. Piron
R. du Bourg
Cour de la Faïencerie
St-Philibert
Rempart de la Miséricorde
Théâtre du Parvis St-Jean
Saint-Jean
20
PL. J. MACÉ
R. A.
Rue de l'Arquebuse
R. A. Joliet
Rue Condorcet
Rue Monge
16
R. Charrue
R. V. Dumay
N
PLACE ÉMILE ZOLA
Berbisey
15
R. Ste Anne
R. du Fg Raines
Rue Crébillon
Turgot
Sainte-Anne
Musée d'Art Sacré
Musée de la Vie Bourguignonne
R. de la Manutention
Rue du Chaignot
Hôpital
Rue de l'Hôpital
Saint-Jean-de-Jérusalem
Rue Colson
Rue P. Curie
PL. SUQUET
Rue du
N. Rollin
Obélisque
PL. DU 1ER MAI

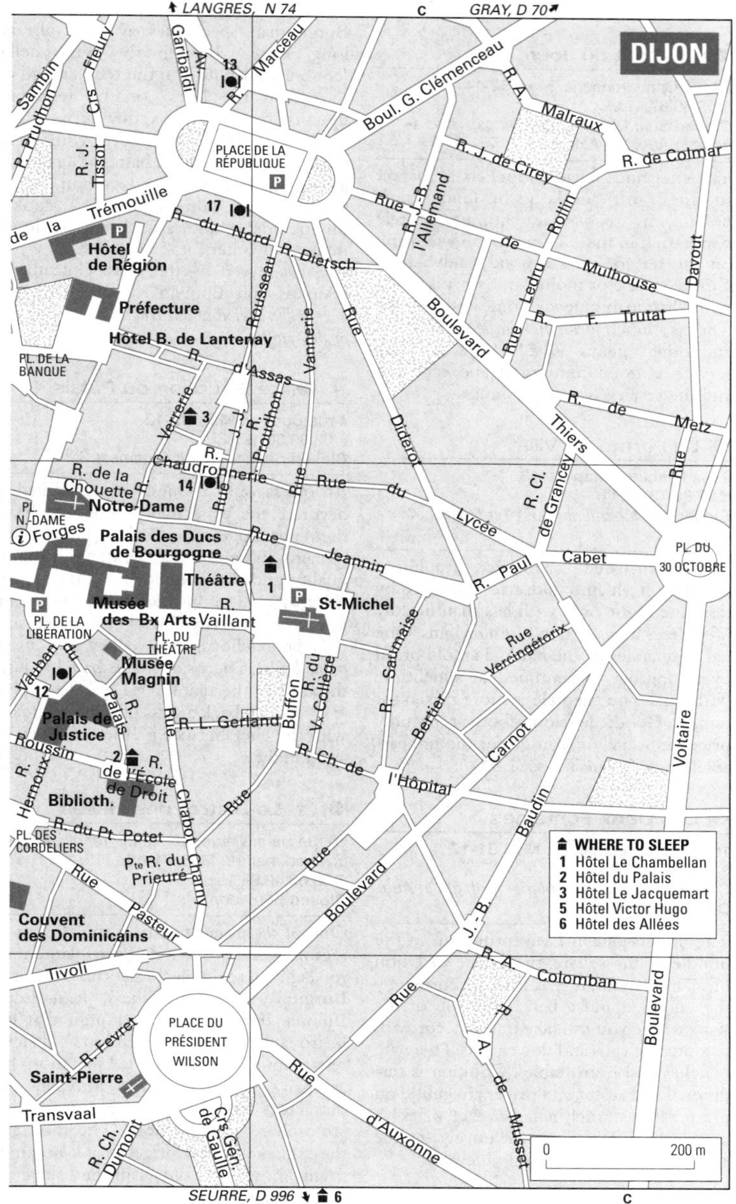
DIJON
LANGRES, N 74
GRAY, D 70
SEURRE, D 996
6
C
1
2
3
PLACE DE LA RÉPUBLIQUE
PLACE DU PRÉSIDENT WILSON
PL. DU 30 OCTOBRE
PL. DE LA BANQUE
PL. N.-DAME
PL. DE LA LIBÉRATION
PL. DU THÉÂTRE
PL. DES CORDELIERS
Hôtel de Région
Préfecture
Hôtel B. de Lantenay
Notre-Dame
Forges
Palais des Ducs de Bourgogne
Théâtre
St-Michel
Musée des Bx Arts
Musée Magnin
Palais de Justice
Biblioth.
Couvent des Dominicains
Saint-Pierre
Boul. G. Clémenceau
R. A. Malraux
R. J. de Cirey
R. de Colmar
Rue de Mulhouse
Boulevard Thiers
R. F. Trutat
R. de Metz
Rue Diderot
Rue du Lycée
Rue Jeannin
R. Dietsch
R. du Nord
Rue de la Trémouille
R. Marceau
Av. Garibaldi
R. Sambin
P. Prudhon
Crs Fleury
R. J. Tissot
Rousseau
Vannerie
R. d'Assas
R. Verrerie
R. J. J. Prudhon
R. Chaudronnerie
R. de la Chouette
R. Vaillant
R. Vauban
R. du Palais
R. L. Gerland
Buffon
R. du Vx Collège
R. Ch. de l'Hôpital
R. Saumaise
R. Paul Cabet
Rue Vercingétorix
Bertier
Carnot
Voltaire
Davout
R. J.-B. l'Allemand
Rollin
Rue Ledru
R. Cl. de Grancey
Rue Chabot Charny
R. de l'École de Droit
Roussin
R. Hernoux
R. du Pt Potet
Pte R. du Prieuré
Rue Pasteur
Tivoli
R. Fevret
Transvaal
R. Ch. Dumont
Crs Gén. de Gaulle
Rue d'Auxonne
Boulevard
Baudin
J.-B.
R. A. Colomban
R. A. de Musset
Rue
0
200 m
WHERE TO SLEEP
1 Hôtel Le Chambellan
2 Hôtel du Palais
3 Hôtel Le Jacquemart
5 Hôtel Victor Hugo
6 Hôtel des Allées
13
17
14
12

bow to passing fads. Weekday lunchtime menus at €9–12, others at €15 (lunch and dinner), €25 and €28, including cheese.

Au Goût du Jour

24 rue Chaudronnerie. **Map B2-14**
03.80.67.47.99
Closed *Sun; Mon–Wed evenings; 1st fortnight in Aug. Sat lunchtime.*

The chef finds reliable suppliers at market (no mean feat) and keeps his lunch prices down. His regular lunchtime clientele come back in the evening to enjoy a drink on the terrace with a good sandwich of Comté cheese or mountain ham, pike balls with shrimp bisque or guineafowl breast. There's a lunch *menu du marché* for €10.60, and other menus at €16.10–22.10. The service is good humoured and efficient, and the terrace is very pleasant.

La Ferme en Ville

9 rue Marceau. **Map B1-13**
03.80.73.39.41
Closed *Sat lunchtime; Sun; 1st fortnight in Aug.*

This town-based "farm" has brought a breath of fresh air to a district inhabited by dissolute night-owls with less than healthy lifestyles. There are two dining rooms. One has cosy tables by the bar and an old bread oven, another is crammed at lunchtime with suits. The clientele is more mixed for dinner. Good, delicious food at friendly prices, especially if you go for the unbeatable lunch *formule* for €11.50.

Les Deux Fontaines

16 pl. de la République. **Map B1-17**
03.80.60.86.45
Closed *Sun; Mon lunchtime; fortnight in Aug.*
Disabled access.

The *Two Fountains* have sprung up in the middle of the square, the centre of Dijon life. This restaurant has a quiet corner by the entrance and a bar at the top of the stairs where you can take in the décor with its watering cans and flower pots. There are benches and bistro tables. Cooking is traditional and rustic, and prices are gentle on the pocket – lunch *formules* €11 or €12, or around €23 for dinner. Lovely service and nice wines from small vineyards.

Le Chabrot

36 rue Monge. **Map A2-16**
03.80.30.69.61 03.80.50.02.35
Closed *Sun; 1st fortnight in Aug.*

Service until 10.30pm. Plates of Burgundian specialities available all day long. Enter through the wine cellar (choose your bottle on the way) and go on to eat in the bistro or the restaurant upstairs; there's even a tiny terrace. The cooking is emphatically local with a few twists: try the parsleyed ham, *coq au vin*, the pressed goat and smoked salmon, or the signature dish, salmon *unilatérale* (cooked on one side). There's a €12 weekday lunch menu and others at €21 and €30. Wines are also served by the glass: Coteaux de l'Auxois and Epineuil red for example. *Free coffee offered to our readers on presentation of this guide.*

Le Bouchon du Palais

4 rue Bouhier. **Map B2-12**
03.80.30.19.98
Closed *Sat and Sun lunchtimes; Sun.*

An old favourite. Guests are still asked to decorate the paper tablecloths which are then put up on the walls. The cooking remains straightforward and of the same quality and the helpings are ample: gratinéed marrow bone, *andouillette*, veal *escalope* with St Marcellin cheese sauce, and tasty lamb chops, followed by *clafoutis* or *crème brûlée*. There's a *formule* based around the dish of the day for €13, and menu at €17. Knock back a glass of wine at the bar with the chef. Service is efficient, attentive and kindly.

Le Bistrot des Halles

10 rue Bannelier; opposite the renovated covered market. **Map B1–19**
03.80.49.94.15
Closed *Sun; Mon.*

One of *the* places to eat in the Burgundy region. A lively old-style bistro (large mirrors, chequered tablecloths) run by one of Burgundy's greatest chefs, Jean-Pierre Billoux. It must be said though that the bistro (an annexe to Billoux's pricier restaurant in the place de la Libération) has as many fervent admirers as vociferous detractors who curse the setting, the atmosphere and the noise. The food and the remarkably low prices brook no argument, however: old-fashioned *pâté en croûte*, ham terrine with parsley, or dishes of the day. In addition, there are superb local specialities and grilled dishes, along with some fine, reasonably priced wines. Lunctime menu at €16; reckon on around €20 à la carte. Attractive terrace giving on to the market. *Apéritif on the house offered to our readers on presentation of this guide.*

|●| Le Cézanne

40 rue Amiral-Roussin. **Map B2-20**
Ⓣ03.80.58.91.92 Ⓕ03.80.49.86.80
Ⓦwww.bienpublic.com
Closed *Sun; Mon lunchtime; 18 Aug–1 Sept; 22 Dec–30 Dec.*

Located in an old pedestrianized street, the restaurant has vintage stonework and beams and an intimate atmosphere brightened up by the Provençal décor. The chef's cooking has become a gastronomic yardstick in the town. You won't be disappointed by the quality even on the cheapest menu chalked up on the blackboard at €17 (except Sat evenings). Other menus go for €26–45, and you'll pay about €38 à la carte. Pleasant little terrace in summer and the service is very attentive.

|●| Le Bistrot des Godrans

28 rue des Godrans. **Map B1-11**
Ⓣ03.80.30.46.07
Closed *Sun.*

This old friend has had a youthful rethink. Out go the drinkers who propped up the bar, in come stylish waitresses and dishes of the day that aren't swamped with unnecessary garnishes. But they've kept the old chairs, so this is less a revolution than an evolution. As well as steak *tartare*, the chef's speciality, dishes include black pudding with apples (only in winter), and plates of sausage and ham. Reckon on €20–25 à la carte.

Hauteville-les-Dijon

21121 (8km NW)

⌂ |●| La Musarde**

7 rue des Riottes; it's on the N71 road to Troyes.
Ⓣ03.80.56.22.82 Ⓕ03.80.56.64.40
Ⓔhotel.rest.lamusarde@wanadoo.fr
Closed *Tues; Sun evening; 20 Dec to mid-Jan.* **Disabled access (restaurant only). TV. Car park.**

Nowadays it's also a restaurant and it's best to book, especially at the weekends, to be sure of a table. The informal, relaxed atmosphere is at the same time sophisticated and professional. It's run by Marc Ogé, a true Breton with his feet planted firmly on the ground. His dishes brighten Breton and Burgundy traditions with a little North African sun: avocado tart with crayfish tails and warm goat's cheese, turbot with basil purée; foie gras cooked in a cloth; pigeon *tajine*; terrine of shellfish with foie gras and *confit* of aubergines; roasted sea trout with *coulis* of mussels. Set menus €19–32.50 and there's a weekday menu (lunch and dinner) at €18 including wine and coffee. Nice terrace. Attractive bedrooms €45–62. Credit cards not accepted.

Prenois

21370 (12km NW)

|●| Auberge de la Charme

It's a turning off the road that goes to Darois aerodrome.
Ⓣ03.80.35.32.84
Ⓔdavidlacharme@aol.com
Closed *Sun evening; Mon and Tues lunchtimes; Feb school holidays.* **Disabled access.**

Even though the chef's reputation has grown considerably, the prices remain very attractive. He uses good-quality local produce from which he concocts interesting dishes, seasoned and presented with a rare attention to detail. This is the best establishment in these parts and not to be missed. Set menu €16 weekday lunchtimes, other menus at €23–69.

Val Suzon

21121 (15km NW)

⌂ |●| Hostellerie du Val Suzon***

It's on the N71.
Ⓣ03.80.35.60.15 Ⓕ03.80.35.61.36
Ⓦwww.logis-de-bourgogne.com/hostellerie-du-val-suzon
Closed *Oct–May Sun evening, Mon lunch and Tues lunch; June–Sept Mon, Tues lunch and Wed lunch; 12 Nov–20 Dec.* **TV. Car park.**

A peaceful, comfy establishment serving good food. It's a bewitching site, just fifteen minutes from Dijon, in a valley surrounded by magnificent parkland and gardens. It is just as inviting in summer – when you can take advantage of the terrace – as on cold days, when you can relax by the fireplace. Spacious Zen-style rooms, ideal for recharging your batteries; they are spread over three buildings, including a curious chalet that dominates the garden. Doubles €68–95 with shower/wc or bath, half board €82 per person (compulsory in high season). The chef likes to use spices and flavours from the Far East, though his cooking remains fundamentally true to tradition. Weekday lunch menu €20 and others €35–85, with a children's menu at €13. Ideal for a romantic weekend. Wonderful terrace. *Free coffee offered to our readers on presentation of this guide.*

Donzy

58220

Le Grand Monarque**

10 rue de l'Étape; it's near the church.
03.86.39.35.44
www.multimania.com/grandmonarque/
Closed *Mon evening and Tues out of season; in Jan.* **TV. Disabled acccess. Car park.**

This is a delightful village with a number of fifteenth-century half-timbered buildings. The hotel is the old stone house practically next door to the Romanesque church, but don't worry – the bells don't ring between 9pm and 8am. Rustic charm with all mod cons and a warm, tastefully decorated interior. Spacious doubles – some have brand-new bathrooms – with shower/wc or bath are €52–54. Set menus at €14 (weekday lunchtimes) and €20–35. Good-quality regional cooking with a number of fish dishes. *10% off the room rate (Nov to end March) offered to our readers on presentation of this guide.*

Dun-les-Places

58230

Le Chalet du Montal

Le pont du Montal: it's 1.5km northeast of the village.
03.86.84.62.77 03.86.84.61.03
chaletdumontal@wanadoo.fr
Disabled access. Car park.

Here's a genuine chalet perched above a river in wild surroundings straight out of *Twin Peaks*; it's a paradise for fly fishermen and hikers. There's a bar and an enormous central fireplace. The cooking is simple but a lot of care goes into the preparation of the dishes. Menus €10–25. If you want to spend the night, they offer four basic but newly refurbished rooms for €45–52.50. *Free coffee offered to our readers on presentation of this guide.*

L'Auberge Ensoleillée

It's on the D6 Lormes to Saulieu road.
03.86.84.62.76 03.86.84.64.57
Closed *Christmas; evenings out of season.* **Car park.**

It's wise to book. A typical Morvan inn run by three women – one at the bar, one in the restaurant and one in the kitchen. Warm welcome and traditional local recipes. Substantial weekday menu at €14 with others €21–38. Simple rooms at €22–43 for a double with shower or bath. *Free coffee offered to our readers on presentation of this guide.*

Gevrey-Chambertin

21220

Aux Vendanges de Bourgogne

47 rte. de Beaune.
03.80.34.30.24 03.80.58.55.44
aux.vendanges.de.bourgogne@wanadoo.fr
Closed *Sun and Mon; fortnight around Christmas.* **TV. Car park.**

Among the gourmet restaurants, world-renowned cellars and inflated prices of the area is this old-fashioned hotel-restaurant. It has a warm Art Deco décor with a stencilled ceiling and stained-glass lampshades and there's an interior terrace. Good local dishes in hearty portions at reasonable prices, all charmingly served. Menus change according to the season and what's good at the market. Weekday lunch menu at €16; others €23 and €26.50. The arrival of the owner's son in the kitchen has steered the menu towards new horizons. Local wines that are usually impossible to find unless you know the grower come at very reasonable prices and can be sampled by the glass. Despite being in the epicentre of great Burgundies, they even serve wine by the glass. Simple rooms with shower/wc €38–52, and with bath €52–58. *10% discount on the room rate for a minimum two-night stay offered to our readers on presentation of this guide.*

Chez Guy

3 pl. de l'Hôtel-de-Ville.
03.80.58.51.51 03.80.58.50.39

Ⓦwww.hotel-bourgogne.com Ⓔaux-vendanges-de-bourgogne@wanadoo.fr
Closed *Tues; Wed; fortnight at Christmas.*

The attempt to be "chic" (and the prices that go with it) are let down by the rather plain décor in the large dining room (choose the terrace in summer). Friendly but rather laid-back service. Traditional Burgundy dishes with innovative touches that win over tourists and locals alike. An attractive choice of Gevrey wines (but not necesssarily cheap). Reservation is strongly recommended. *Free coffee offered to our readers on presentation of this guide.*

Joigny

89300

Le Paris-Nice**

Rond-point de la Résistance.
Ⓣ03.86.62.06.72 Ⓕ03.86.62.56.99
Closed *Sun evening and Mon.* **TV. Car park.**

The N6 from Paris to Nice used to be known as the "Route des Anglais" before the motorway to the Côte d'Azur was built. Those were the glory days of this establishment, though it's recently been done up by its new owners. There are ten simple rooms, all with double glazing; they're yours for €39 with shower or bath. Good restaurant serving traditional fare and regional dishes: roast pork with honey, salmon with frogs' legs, *île flottante* with spiced bread. Menus €9.50 and €12 on weekdays only, then €15.50 and €20. There's a fine, shady terrace.

Le Rive Gauche***

Chemin du Port-au-Bois; it's on the banks of the Yonne, very close to the old town.
Ⓣ03.86.91.46.66
Ⓦwww.hotel-le-rive-gauche.fr
Closed *Sun evening Nov–Feb inclusive.*
Disabled access. TV. Car park.

The Lorains realized that things were changing – so they built a modern building looking just like a chain hotel opposite their famous *Côte Saint-Jacques* (not reviewed here). The new establishment is welcoming and has good-looking, comfortable and functional rooms – doubles with bath €60–76. There's a tennis court and a garden. You can eat outside on the terraces or in the dining room, where the décor and the food both reflect modern tastes. The cooking is bistro-style, with set menus €18 (not weekends or public holidays) and others at €28 and €32. Try buckwheat pancakes with snails and potatoes and finish with the chocolate mousse cake. *10% discount on the room rate except July–Aug offered to our readers on presentation of this guide.*

Celle-Saint-Cyr (La)

89116 (8km W)

Auberge de la Fontaine aux Muses**

Take exit 18 off the motorway and head towards Joigny on the D943; after 3km, turn left when you come to the village of La Motte – the inn is 3km further.
Ⓣ03.86.73.40.22 Ⓕ03.86.73.48.66
Ⓦwww.fontaine-aux-muses.fr
Closed *Mon–Thurs Oct–April (except public holidays); lst fortnight in Jan.* **Disabled access. TV. Swimming pool. Car park.**

Hidden away in the Burgundy hills, this country house inn is covered in Virginia creeper, and the rooms are wonderfully rustic: doubles with shower or bath for €58–98. The cooking is passionately Burgundian: foie gras pan-fried on one side only, duck breast with honey, hot oysters with caramelized endive, Burgundy beef and local wines. Set weekday menu €28, or reckon on €37 à la carte. The Langevin family are musicians (father Claude composed the European anthem, no less), so their friends often turn up at weekends and a jam session frequently results. They also have their own vineyard, the Fontaine aux Muses, which produces white (Chardonnay) and red (Pinot Noir) wines. Tennis court and heated swimming pool. *A special Routard menu for €20 on Wed–Fri lunchtimes (except public holidays) offered to our readers on presentation of this guide.*

Villevallier

89330 (9 km NW)

Le Pavillon Bleu**

31 rue de la République; take the N6, to the south of Villeneuve-sur-Yonne.
Ⓣ03.86.91.12.17 Ⓕ03.86.91.17.74
Closed *Fri evening; Sun evening; 20 Dec–15 Jan; 1st fortnight in Aug.* **TV. Car park.**

With its friendly welcome and big blue shutters, this hotel is worth a detour and, furthermore, it is among the most reasonably priced in the area. Admittedly, the rooms are not very big but they are delightful all the same. Doubles with shower/wc or bath €40–45. Copious portions of home cooking: snail salad, *œufs meurette*, beef fillet *au gratin* with local Époisse cheese, zander, trout, braised pineapple with Ratafia. *Apéritif on the house offered to our readers on presentation of this guide.*

Lormes

58140

Hôtel Perreau**

8 rte. d'Avallon; cross the town via the D944 main road from Avallon to Château-Chinon.
☎03.86.22.53.21 Ⓕ03.86.22.82.15
Closed *Sun evening and Mon (early Oct to end May); 6 Jan–15 Feb.* **TV. Car park.**

The village hotel is a large, imposing and thoroughly restored old house with a large capacity. Spacious double rooms €44–60 with shower/wc or bath. The restaurant is pretty, in a rustic style with a large fireplace, and the food is sophisticated, with a particularly good menu of regional specialities. Cheapest menu at €11, then others at €20 and €26. *10% discount on a room offered to our readers on presentation of this guide.*

Vauclaix

58140 (8km S)

Hôtel de la Poste**

From Lormes take the D944.
☎03.86.22.71.38 Ⓕ03.86.22.76.00
Ⓦwww.hotel-vauclaix.com
Disabled access. TV. Swimming pool. Car park.

Located in deepest, darkest Morvan, this is a popular and friendly hotel. Five generations of Desbruères have run the place and they're constantly doing it up and introducing new ideas – there's a swimming pool in the garden, a giant chess game and ping-pong. The rooms are big but cosy and cost €53 with shower/wc or bath. It's worth the trip here for the cooking alone. The two-page menu changes regularly according to the season and offers traditional dishes. €10 weekday menu and others €16–40. Pay attention to the prices of menus on offer; it's a bit confusing.

Mâcon

71000

Hôtel d'Europe et d'Angleterre**

92 quai Jean-Jaurès.
☎03.85.38.27.94
TV. Pay car park.

This eighteenth-century building has character and, with its original staircase and large public rooms, it offers the charm of a long-past era. The hotel has been tastefully renovated and is well located on the riverside; although it's right on the N6, the rooms are soundproofed, and some of them have river views. Doubles are €50–60. Free garage space, except in July and August.

Charm'hôtel Terminus

91 rue Victor-Hugo.
☎03.85.39.17.11 Ⓕ 03.85.38.02.75
Ⓦwww.charmehotel.com
TV. Pay car park.

Astonishing hotel on the doorstep of the train station that hides a highly original interior design behind an old-fashioned façade. Some rooms retain their classical style, but most have been attractively refurbished along the lines of the murals at the head of each bed, painted by a member of the owner's family. As the mural is reflected in a large mirror, the effect is doubly striking. Doubles €59–74. Charming breakfast room, decorated in warm colours. Garden with swimming pool. Meals are also available.

Inter Hôtel de Bourgogne**

6 rue Victor-Hugo.
☎03.85.38.36.57 Ⓕ03.85.38.65.92
Restaurant closed *Mon lunchtime; Sat lunchtime; Sun; 3 weeks in Jan.* **TV. Pay car park.**

Lovely hotel on a shady, flower-filled square just a step away from the pedestrian area. Delightful interior with a foyer that's straight out of a Chabrol film. Rooms are painted in pastel shades. Lots of twists and turns, half-landings, nooks and crannies. Air-conditioned double rooms with shower/wc are €62–73. Breakfast €8.50. In the restaurant evening menus go for €18–32. Meals can be had in the hotel (€18–32) if you don't feel like venturing out in the evening.

Maison Mâconnaise des Vins

484 av. de-Lattre-de-Tassigny; it's on the bank of the Saône as you come into town from Chalon-sur-Saône.
03.85.22.91.11 03.85.22.91.12
www.maison-des-vins.com
Open *1 Sept–30 June: Mon–Thurs 8am–6.30pm, Fri–Sun 8am–10pm; every day during July–Aug.* **Disabled access. Car park.**

This establishment represents a considerable number of vineyard owners from the Côtes Chalonnaises, Beaujolais and Mâcon. They also serve a selection of regional specialites – you'll spend around €13 à la carte – including *bœuf bourguignon, andouillette Mâconnaise*, salt pork with lentils, and good house Mâconnaise tarts and waffles. Menus go for €10–18. All dishes make the perfect accompaniment to a Saint-Véran, a Pouilly-Fuissé, a Rully or a Givry, many of which are served by the glass. You'll be spoilt for choice. There's a terrace overlooking the Saône (you almost forget the traffic on the N6). *Free apéritif offered to our readers on presentation of this guide.*

L'Amandier

74 rue Dufour; it's near the tourist office.
03.85.39.82.00 03.85.39.82.21
Closed *Sun evening; Mon.*

Salad of pig's trotters *gribiche* is the house speciality, but Florent Segain often rejigs his menus to use what's best in the market. Menus (served every day) go for €19.50–48; dish of the day (except Sat evening and Sun lunch) costs €12. It's easy enough to find the restaurant since it's painted blue – the flowers and the plates are the same colour, complemented by the yellow fabrics in the cosy, comfortable dining room. Specialities include *andouillette gratin* with steamed potatoes, roast herb-crusted lamb, crayfish, lobster roasted with fresh herbs, Burgundy snails with parsley butter, roast *noisette* of lamb, duck foie gras, roast fillet of red mullet with a basil emulsion and stuffed courgettes with tapenade. Flowers adorn the terrace.

Le Poisson d'Or

Port de Plaisance; take the N6 towards Tournus, and it's 1km from the town centre on the banks of the Saône.
03.85.38.00.88 03.85.35.82.55
Closed *Tues evening; Wed; fortnight end of March; fortnight end of Oct.* **Disabled access. High chairs available. Car park.**

Contemplate the glinting lights in the water and the shady river banks from the large picture windows of this plush but informal establishment, which also has a large, shaded terrace. Menus €19–49. It's a refined place with tables covered in thick white cloths and enormous vases of flowers everywhere. Attentive service.

Sancé

71000 (3km N)

La Vieille Ferme**

If you're taking the N6 motorway towards Mâcon, it's well signposted on the right. You can also approach on the A6, exit Mâcon Nord.
03.85.40.95.15
www.hotel-restaurant-lavieilleferme.com
Closed *25 Nov–15 Dec.*
Disabled access. TV. Swimming pool. Car park.

An old farm which has been restored in good taste and turned into a small hotel complex. It is particularly well positioned on the banks of the Saône, surrounded by real cornfields and real cows, patient anglers and peaceful cyclists riding along the tow-path. The modern part is built like a motel and most of the bedrooms, €45, overlook the Saône or the countryside. They are spacious and pleasant and you hardly notice the high-speed train hurtling past. Breakfast €5.50. The lovely dining room has rustic décor and old-fashioned furniture, but on fine days the terrace is everyone's favourite place to be. Dishes are executed with care and are perfectly affordable. Set menu at €11 is served every day (lunch and dinner); others €14–26. Beautiful swimming pool in summer with a generous lunchtime buffet.

Milly-Lamartine

71960 (10km NW)

Chez Jack

Place de l'Église; take the N79 from Mâcon and turn off at Milly-La Roche Vineuse.
03.85.36.63.72
Closed *Mon; Tues evening; Sun evening; a week in Feb; end Aug to early Sept.* **Disabled access.**

A lovely little village restaurant in the shadow of a beautiful church and Lamartine's house, boasting good

Beaujolais cooking. Tables are set outside on fine days. Weekday lunch menu €9; dinner menu €15.50. À la carte a meal will cost €18.30–22 on average. Dishes include calf's foot *remoulade*, veal kidneys in cream, *andouillette* with mustard sauce, *entrecôte* steak, hot sausage with Beaujolais and *tablier de sapeur* (a slab of ox tripe egged, crumbed and fried). Good wine selection by the jug or the bottle: Mâcon rouge, Régnié, Pouilly-Fuissé and so on. *Free coffee offered to our readers on presentation of this guide.*

Saint-Vérand

71570 (13km SW)

L'Auberge de Saint-Véran**

Lieu-dit La Roche; leave the A6 at exit 29 (in the direction of Vinzelles, Juliénas, Saint-Vérand).
Ⓣ03.85.23.90.90 Ⓕ03.85.23.90.91
Ⓦwww.auberge-saint-veran.com
Closed *Tues (out of season).* **TV. Disabled access. Car park.**

A beautiful stone house in a traditional village, with a terrace and garden, a stream nearby, and vineyards and rolling hills all around. A simple hotel, but clean and comfortable. Double rooms €61–75 with shower/wc. Ask about the interesting system of half board. Regional cooking, with a lunch and dinner menu at €20 and others from €28–55.

Saint-Amour-Bellevue

71570 (14km SW)

L'Auberge du Paradis

Lieu-dit Le Plâtre-Durand; a small road in the village of Crêches-sur-Saône leads to Saint-Amour.
Ⓣ03.85.37.10.26
Closed *Mon; Tues; Jan.* **Disabled access. High chairs available.**

Pretty dining room decorated with pale colours and plenty of flowers, with some tables adapted from old sewing machines. The real spectacle, however, lies on the plates. The menu changes every two months, according to the availability of ingredients and the whim of the chef, a globetrotting gourmet, who acquired a love of spices and daring sweet/savoury mixtures in Turkey and Morocco. After spells with some of France's greatest chefs (Blanc, Chibois), he now works entirely alone to concoct his mouth-watering dishes. Small weekday lunchtime menu at €17, and a more extensive evening one at €26 (€29 at the weekend). The service is friendly and the wine list is remarkably cheap for the area.

Moulins-Engilbert

58290

Au Bon Laboureur**

Place Boucaumont.
Ⓣ03.86.84.20.55 Ⓕ03.86.84.35.52
Closed *1st fortnight in Jan. Disabled access (restaurant only).* **TV. Car park.**

One of the most reliable places in the south of the Morvan where you can have a scrumptious meal at an attractive price. The dishes are generously served and carefully prepared: specialities include Burgundy snails with smoked bacon, ceps, poached egg and *meurette* sauce, pan-fried scallops with herbed truffle salad, and lobster salad with crayfish and baby vegetables. Weekday menu €12 and numerous others from €18.50–41.50. The rooms range from simple to quite comfortable – €27–47.50. Those above the restaurant are pleasant but a little noisy.

Brinay

58110 (11km W)

L'Ancien Café

Take the D132 to Limanton, then continue for 5km in the direction of Châtillon-en-Bazois.
Ⓣ03.86.84.90.79
Closed *Sun evening.*

A modest bar-cum-grocery-cum-bread store-cum-garage with a real restaurant attached. Tasty dishes, generously served: Morvan ham, calf's head, fresh fish, Charolais steaks and house terrine. There's a two-course *formule* for €10 and menus €12–23, with a children's menu at €8.50. Run by the owners and their daughter. There's a shaded terrace.

Saint-Péreuse

58110 (14km NW)

Auberge de la Madonnette

In the town centre; take the D978, then the D78 for 2km in the direction of Château-Chinon, then turn left.
Ⓣ03.86.84.45.37

Closed *Tues and Wed evening (except July–Aug); 15 Dec–5 Feb.*

The owner, Marie-Madeleine Grobost, found a new vocation later in life. Formerly a teacher of handicapped children, she re-trained and launched herself into the conversion of this big house covered in beautiful Vichy tiles and adjoined by a magnificent terraced garden with an unbeatable view of the château nearby. Menus €11, then €16–43. Tasty country cooking: traditional-style veal's head, lamb fried with parsley, snail pie.

Moux-en-Morvan

58230

Hôtel-restaurant Beau Site*

Bellevue-Moux-en-Morvan: it's on the D121, 7km from the Settons lake.
03.86.76.11.75 03.86.76.15.84
Closed *Sun evening and Mon 11 Nov to mid-March; Dec; Jan.* **Car park.**

An ordinary-looking place but the name's appropriate – it's in a fantastic setting. Sound home cooking at good prices, specializing in traditional dishes with lots of sauce. The menu at €11.80 is very respectable; others are €15–32. Favourites include snails with creamed garlic and chicken terrine. In the hotel, a five-minute walk away, there are cheap, simple and spacious rooms; doubles with basin €27 and up to €42 with bath.

Nevers

58000

Hôtel Beauséjour**

5 bis rue Saint-Gildard; it's opposite the shrine of Ste Bernadette.
03.86.61.20.84 03.86.59.15.37
Closed *Fri out of season; fortnight in Aug; Christmas school holidays.* **TV . Pay car park.**

Cheap, simple, functional rooms which are kept spotlessly clean. Just out of the town centre in a busy street, but everything is well soundproofed and the garden rooms are very quiet. Doubles with washing facilities €24.50, up to €33 with shower/wc and a garden view. The welcome is really charming and breakfast (€5.50) is available on the veranda from a self-service buffet.

Hôtel de Clèves**

8 rue Saint-Didier.
03.86.61.15.87 03.86.57.13.80
Closed *New Year.* **TV.**

Well placed, not far from the station in a quiet street in the town centre. A small establishment, very well run by an affable woman who's happy to chat while you have breakfast. The rooms have been updated with quality bedding. There's a small, pleasant corner of a garden. Doubles with shower €39, €47 with bath. *10% discount on the room rate offered to our readers on presentation of this guide.*

Hôtel Molière

25 rue Molière. Take the boulevard du Maréchal-Juin; when you get to the BP garage turn right into the rue de Vauzelles and follow the signs.
03.86.57.29.96 03.86.36.00.13
Closed *3 weeks in Aug; 21 Dec–6 Jan.* **TV. Car park.**

A small hotel in a quiet spot near the town centre run by a kindly, welcoming woman. The rooms are bright and cheerful and half of them have views over the garden. Excellent beds. Double rooms €43 with shower/wc and €47 with bath. There are some non-smoking rooms. There's a big, enclosed (and free) car park across the road.

Hôtel-restaurant La Folie

Route des Saulaies.
03.86.57.05.31 03.86.57.66.69
www.hotel-lafolie.com
Restaurant closed *Fri and Sun evening Sept–May; Fri lunchtime June–Aug.*
TV. Swimming pool. Cots available. Car park.

It's well worth choosing this place – its park, tennis court and swimming pools give it an atmosphere of a holiday club. Bedrooms, contemporary in design, cost €47.80–50.20 with shower or bath – no charge for children under 2 and cots are available. You eat either in the dining room or on the terrace, which has a distant view of the Loire. Cheapest menu at €13 (weekday lunch only) and others €15.90–24.90. Ham, duck and steak dishes are all good. It's advisable to book. Credit cards are not accepted. *Free coffee offered to our readers on presentation of this guide.*

|●| 🏃 Le Goémon - Crêperie Bretonne

9 rue du 14-Juillet.
Ⓣ03.86.59.54.99
Closed *Sun; Mon; 1 week in March; end Aug to mid-Sept.*

The setting is nothing special but the service is attentive and the crêpes are good, whether sweet or savoury (the crêpe with Guéméné *andouillette* is exquisite). Weekday lunchtime menu with starter, pancake and dessert at €8.90. Reckon on €14 à la carte. *Apéritif on the house offered to our readers on presentation of this guide.*

|●| Restaurant Aux Chœurs de Bacchus

25 av. du Général-de-Gaulle; near the station.
Ⓣ and Ⓕ03.86.36.72.70
Closed *Mon and Sat lunch; Sun; a week in April; 1st 3 weeks in Aug; 23 Dec–3 Jan.*

Very good little restaurant. Service is slick, fast and friendly. The cuisine has been honed and improved over the years; it's self-confident and delicious, and the dishes strictly follow the seasons. Specialities include the beef and the iced nougat. Enjoy wine carefully chosen to complement each dish, turning your meal into a feast fit for a king – at affordable prices. The €14.10 menu is also served in the evenings and there are others €19.40–29.80, with a children's menu at €7.70.

|●| La Cour Saint-Étienne

33 rue Saint-Étienne; it's behind the church of Saint-Étienne.
Ⓣ03.86.36.74.57 Ⓕ03.86.61.14.95
Closed *Sun; Mon; 1–6 Jan; 24 Feb–4 March; 1–23 Aug.* **Disabled access.**

Menus €15 (not Sat evening) and others at €19–27. The talented chef concocts pleasing dishes using seasonal ingredients, with the high standard of presentation expected around these parts. The only drawbacks are that the portions are slightly small and the service is off-hand. The bells of the nearby church of Saint-Étienne were evoked in *Hiroshima mon amour* by Marguerite Duras as ringing out the liberation of Nevers.

|●| Restaurant Jean-Michel Couron

21 rue Saint-Étienne.
Ⓣ03.86.61.19.28 Ⓕ03.86.36.02.96
Closed Mon; Tues; Sun evening; 2–18 Jan; 13 July–6 Aug.

A Michelin star for the star restaurant of Nevers. Three small, elegant rooms, one in a particularly charming Gothic style. Fine, well-balanced cuisine at good prices: menus start at €19 (weekdays only; includes cheese or dessert), and go up to €43. Particularly recommended are the tomato tart, the Charolais beef and the stewed plaice fillet with a red pepper and sage *compote*. For dessert, the warm spiced chocolate soup is a delight. Reservations advised.

Marzy

58000 (5km SW)

🏃 🏠 |●| Le Val de Loire

From Nevers take the D131, and it's on the edge of the village on the way to Corcelles.
Ⓣ03.86.38.86.21
Disabled access. TV. Car park.

A quiet, cheap place with a nice family feeling. Doubles €20 with basin to €32 with bath. The rooms are in a new annexe and are very well maintained. The only drawback is that it's a bit far from Nevers and there are only two buses a day. Uncomplicated dishes – snails, frogs' legs, steaks – in ambitious portions and a fairly priced menu at €10. Credit cards not accepted. *Free coffee offered to our readers on presentation of this guide.*

Savigny-les-Bois

58160 (10km SE)

🏃 |●| Restaurant Le Moulin de l'Étang

64 rte. de l'Étang. Take the D978 Nevers–Château-Chinon then turn right on the D18. It's just outside the village on the D209.
Ⓣ03.86.37.10.17 Ⓕ03.86.37.12.06
Closed *Mon; Wed evening; Sun evening in winter.* **Car park.**

One of the area's best tables; the €16 menu lists a tasty *mignon* of pork in game marinade and excellent brawn, served with all the fat and a "slimline" *sauce gribiche*. Or you could try the beef in red wine. The desserts are a little disappointing – the *crème brûlée* is heavy and over-sweet – but these are quibbles. Attentive, friendly service in the large, provincial-feeling dining room.

Other menus €24–40. *Free coffee offered to our readers on presentation of this guide.*

Magny-Cours

58470 (12km S)

Hôtel-restaurant La Renaissance****

2 rue de Paris. It's in the village; take the RN7.
ⓣ03.86.58.10.40 ⓕ03.86.21.22.60
ⓔhotel-la-renaissance@wanadoo.fr
Closed *Sun evening; Mon; 3 weeks in Feb-March; a fortnight in Aug.* **TV. Car park.**

A smart hotel-restaurant whose cooking has a good local reputation. It's about 3km from Magny-Cours car-racing circuit, and it's full of guys from the pits who like the chef's tasty cooking. He uses the freshest produce: pan-fried frogs' legs in herb butter with vegetables; sole with foaming butter; roast pigeon with thyme *jus*; duck breast with *jus nerveux*; grilled monkfish with an *escalope* of duck foie gras and Saint-Émilion wine sauce. Good Loire wines at affordable prices, served in a pleasant dining room with attentive service. The first menu (evenings and Sun only) at €30 includes wine; and there are others at €40–60. Bedrooms have good facilities and cost from €84 for a double with shower/wc or bath up to €153 for a luxurious suite with two large double beds. Breakfast €12.20. *Free house apéritif offered to our readers on presentation of this guide.*

Nitry

89310

Auberge La Beursaudière

Chemin de Ronde; it's on the Sacy road.
ⓣ03.86.33.69.69 ⓕ03.86.33.69.60
ⓦwww.beursaudiere.com
Closed *Mon evening Nov–March; 2nd and 3rd week in Jan.* **TV. Car park.**

A superb Morvan building with a medieval dovecote. There's an emphasis on "local" character here: waitresses in regional costume, quaint menu titles and the like, but the terrace is great – it really sizzles in summer. Sturdy local dishes built for robust appetites; specialities include *mosaïque* of crayfish and scallops, *oeufs en meurette*, ravioli with bacon cream and head of veal cooked "*façon grand-mère*". In the week, there's a €12 *formule* of starter and a main course; the first real menu costs €16, with others €30 and €39. Children's menu €8. Brand-new hotel rooms from €60 with shower/wc to €70–99 with bath. Breakfast €8.

Noyers-sur-Serein

89310 (10km NE)

Hôtel Saint-Nicolas

22 rue de la République; 300m from the exit from the village, in the direction of Montbard.
ⓣ03.86.82.83.23
Disabled access.

A pleasant surprise close to the historic centre of Noyers. This old farm with a keep has been intelligently overhauled in a tasteful, modern style. Bedecked with flowers and covered in contemporary paintings, it exudes tranquillity, with the courtyard turned into a terrace garden, clean, breezy rooms, beautiful furniture and a range of magazines at hand. Doubles with a view of the wash house or garden €46–53. Suites for more than two people also available. Effusive welcome and copious breakfast in a lovely rustic room. Modernity in the old style, with high quality and accessibility.

Nolay

21340

Restaurant Le Burgonde

35 rue de la République, 200m from the town hall.
ⓣ03.80.21.71.25
ⓦwww.nolay.net/restaurant.htm
Closed *Tues; Wed; Feb school holidays.*

Unusual dining room set in an old department store, with old windows, the original floor and a certain crazy charm. The tables are even decorated with brightly coloured (and roughly made) art works! The chef will come out in his full regalia to explain the dishes on his menu. If you can't make your mind up, there's a regional menu and the chef uses produce bought from the neighbouring farms and local producers. Menu €27.10; wine at reasonable prices. *Free coffee offered to our readers on presentation of this guide.*

Corpeau

21190 (8km E)

L'Auberge du Vieux Vigneron

Route de Beaune; it's opposite the town hall.
ⓣ03.80.21.39.00 ⓕ03.80.21.38.81

Closed *Mon; Tues; a week in Jan; Feb school holidays; 11–27 Aug.* **Car park.**

This village wouldn't merit a special trip were it not for the inn. In the dining room, the atmosphere feels a bit like it's time for harvest supper: old tables, old furniture and a wide fireplace where lamb cutlets and *andouillettes* are cooked. The must-have dishes include scallops and snails. Menus €15–20. House wines include a Chassagne-Montrachet and a Puligny, both affordable; try a few other vintages grown by the owner in their newly refurbished cellar. It's a simple place and a good one. *Free apéritif offered to our readers on presentation of this guide.*

Nuits-Saint-Georges

21700

Hôtel-bar de l'Étoile*

5 pl. de la Libération.
☎03.81.61.04.68
Closed *Wed.*

This small family hotel may have only one star but it's certainly well deserved. The simple, clean rooms have been refurbished, and those at the back are extremely quiet. Double with washbasin €25, with shower/wc €37. Small restaurant serving regional food: daily dish €8; menus €14 and €14.70. The bar is an ideal place to catch up on local gossip. Wine by the glass and a good selection of real ale. Genuinely cheerful welcome.

Villars-Fontaine

21220 (5km W)

Auberge du Coteau

It's in the centre.
☎03.80.61.10.50 Ⓕ03.80.61.30.32
Closed *Tues evening and Wed, a fortnight in Feb and 15 Aug–5 Sept.* **Car park.**

This is a real country inn, serving home-made terrine, *coq au vin*, snails, beef and lots of other lovely local dishes – not for those on a diet. They'll satisfy your hunger after a walk through the vineyards and your thirst will be more than slaked by the local wines from the Hautes Côtes. There's an open fire, checked tablecloths and old-fashioned prices – the weekday lunch menu costs €10, and there are others at €13.50–21.

Vougeot

21640 (10km N)

Hôtel de Vougeot

18 rue du Vieux-Château.
☎03.80.62.01.15
Ⓦwww.castel-tres-girard.com
Closed *Mon; Tues; 15 Jan–15 March.* **TV. Car park.**

Vougeot is world-famous for the wine festivals organized by the Confrérie du Clos Vougeot, founded to maintain the quality of Burgundy's wines and to promote them across the globe. This odd hotel, with its dreary façade, is not what you'd expect to find here, but the lovely courtyard and the peace and tranquillity make up for that. Rooms, some with a view of the château, are €65 and €75. It has a bar where they serve local wine. Everyone is treated well. *10% discount on the room rate 1 Nov–31 March offered to our readers on presentation of this guide.*

Auvillars-sur-Saône

21250 (15km SE)

Auberge de l'Abbaye

Route de Seurre; take the D35 then the D996.
☎03.80.26.97.37 Ⓕ03.80.26.92.25
Ⓔauberge-abbaye@wanadoo.fr
Closed *Sun and Tues evenings; Wed.* **Car park.**

You simply have to stop here – it's only 1km from Citeaux Abbey, the mother house of the Cistercian order. And the restaurant offers enough reasons of its own: succulent dishes such as pan-fried foie gras with fruits of the season, and crayfish salad with hazelnuts and spiced bread terrine – all at reasonable prices. You can also eat in the delightful bistro corner and opt for the menu of the day – chicken liver terrine, pork with apples and bread-and-butter pudding are typical. The bistro *formule* at lunchtime in the week costs €14, and there are other menus for €19.80–39.90. There's a picturesque terrace, too. *Free coffee offered to our readers on presentation of this guide.*

Curtil-Vergy

21220 (18km NW)

Hôtel Le Manasses

Rue Guillaume-de-Tavanes; as you leave the village, take the side road going up to the Hautes Côtes de Nuits.

Ⓣ03.80.61.43.81 Ⓕ03.80.61.42.79
Ⓦwww.ifrance.com/hotelmanasses
Closed *Dec–Feb.* **TV. Car park.**

There's a splendid view over the vineyards and a remarkable silence to this place. The Chaleys and other winegrowers in the area have built up the reputation of the wines from the Hautes Côtes. In his younger days, grandfather used to deliver his wines himself; his son does the same today, but at least he has a car. They have constructed this charming little hotel and turned a barn into a wine museum where you can sample the goods. Wine tasting every evening from 6pm. Breakfast, €9.50, is Burgundy-style. Very comfortable doubles €70–95.

Paray-le-Monial

71600

Grand Hôtel de la Basilique**

18 rue de la Visitation; it's 100m from the basilica, opposite the chapel of the Visitation.
Ⓣ03.85.81.11.13 Ⓕ03.85.88.83.70
Ⓦwww.hotelbasilique.com
Closed 1 Nov–20 March. TV. Pay car park.

Double rooms go for €42–57, all with new bathrooms, and half board €36–50 per person. Regional dishes are served in the restaurant – menus €12–37. Of the specialities, try the turbot, the Charolais beef steak *label rouge* (which means its origins can be traced) and *œufs en meurette*. Delightful hotel but best behaviour is required – it's a favourite of visiting pilgrims. *10% discount on the room rate offered (except July–Aug) to our readers on presentation of this guide.*

Hôtel Terminus***

27 av. de la Gare; it's opposite the train station.
Ⓣ03.85.81.59.31 Ⓕ03.85.81.38.31
Ⓦwww.terminus-paray.fr
Closed *1–15 Nov.* **Restaurant closed** *lunchtimes; Fri–Sun; 1–15 Nov.* **TV. Car park.**

Big, well-restored hotel. Don't let the austere façade put you off; once inside you'll be warmly greeted and you'll see that the owners pay great attention to detail. The spacious rooms have been revamped and decorated in matching floral fabric. The bathrooms are state of the art, done out in wood and perspex and equipped with power showers. Rooms from €55 with shower/wc to €65 with bath; half board at €51 per person in summer. A limited number of good dishes in the brasserie, with a menu at €15.50. *Free coffee offered to our readers on presentation of this guide.*

Pouilly-sur-Loire

58150

Le Relais de 200 Bornes

1 av. de la Tuilerie; at the entrance to Pouilly via the A7 (signposted).
Ⓣ03.86.39.10.01 Ⓕ03.86.39.18.55

The last survivor of the petrol station-transport cafés that used to dot the N7 every 100 kilometres or so. The owners have a wealth of anecdotes about the holiday route that used to pass by their doorsteps, before the coming of the motorway. Not exactly thrilling stuff it has to be said, but the fine food is far from humdrum. Cheapest menu at €10.50, others from €15. Double rooms €40.

Le Relais Fleuri - Coq Hardi***

42 av. de la Tuilerie; it's 1km southeast of the centre, opposite the wine cellars.
Ⓣ03.86.39.12.99 Ⓕ03.86.39.14.15
Ⓦwww.le-relais-fleuri.fr
Closed *Tues and Wed Oct–April; mid-Dec to mid-Jan. Disabled access.* **TV. Car park.**

Typical *Logis de France* hotel, with rustic furniture and flowers everywhere. The rooms are good, particularly those with a view over the Loire. Doubles with shower/wc or bath €45–78; breakfast €9. The restaurant serves regional cooking worth its salt: smoked salmon pancake with vine stems, roast turbot with meat *jus* and Nivernais pigeon roast with fresh herbs. Menus start at €15 then €20 and €55, with a children's menu at €12. Good, if a little pricey, wine list. A pleasant, reliable establishment.

Quarré-les-Tombes

89630

Hôtel-restaurant Le Morvan

6 rue des Écoles.

ⓣ03.86.32.29.29
ⓕ03.86.32.29.28
Closed *Mon and Tues (except July–Aug); ealy Dec to end Feb.*

Despite a forbidding exterior, this is one of those hotels that makes you feel immediately at home, thanks to an inexpensive detail that is all too often overlooked: a smile. The staff here really know how to look after their guests. Another key factor is the emphasis on simplicity. The rooms are all personalized and the Burgundy cuisine varies according to the availability of fresh ingredients. Double rooms from €47. Weekday lunchtime menu at €13, then €17–28.

Auberge de l'Âtre***

Les Lavaults; take the N6, then the D10 in the direction of Lac des Settons.
ⓣ03.86.32.20.79 ⓕ 03.86.32.28.25
ⓦwww.auberge-de-lattre.com
Closed *Tues evening and Wed (out of season); 1–28 Feb; 2nd fortnight in June.* **TV. Disabled access. Car park.**

Isolated in the heart of Morvan, this inn is a haven for any traveller who has gone astray, especially on cold or foggy nights. A few pleasant bedrooms have been installed for guests: doubles with bath at €84, but the main attraction is the outstanding and reasonably priced food. The smaller dining room recalls an old-style bistro, while the main dining room is decorated in a warm, rustic fashion. The chef loves experimenting with herbs and Morvan mushrooms in the dishes he creates. *Free apéritif or coffee offered to our readers on presentation of this guide.*

Brizards (Les)

89630 (6km SE)

Auberge des Brizards**

Take the D55; follow the signposts.
ⓣ03.86.32.20.12 ⓕ03.86.32.27.40
ⓦwww.aubergedesbrizards.com
Closed *Mon and Tues (except July–Aug); early Jan to mid-Feb.* **TV. High chairs available. Car park.**

What could be more romantic than this delightful inn, lost in the midst of the Morvan forest, which seems to have come out of a fairy tale. Double rooms €38.11–83.85 with shower or bath, depending on the degree of comfort. In the restaurant, cheerful service in a bright, spacious dining room, a world away from the time when grandmother Odette received her customers surrounded by terrines and pickle jars. Outstanding dishes include *matelote* of zander in red wine, pork pie, black pudding with home-grown potatoes, squab with cabbage and traditional gingerbread with liquorice ice cream. Weekday menu at €23, including wine, others at €27–46. Tennis court and a pond for fishing. *10% discount on a room (15 Oct–15 March, except weekends and public holidays) or an apéritif on the house offered to our readers on presentation of this guide.*

Roche-en-Brenil (La)

21530

Aux Portes du Morvan

It's on the RN6.
ⓣ03.80.64.75.28 ⓕ03.80.64.75.28
Closed *Tues evening; Wed; Jan; 2nd fortnight in June.* **Disabled access.**

Tasty, healthy food that won't turn your stomach when you see the bill. The chef's specialities include ham with cream, eggs in wine sauce, *filet mignon* with port, and Morvan tarts at the weekend. Get into the swing before your meal by having a drink at the bar, which is full of local regulars. Menus €11, €16 and €21. Omelettes are available all day.

Rully

71150

Le Vendangerot**

Place Sainte-Marie; leave the N6 after Arnay-le-Duc in the direction of Châlon-sur-Saône, taking the D981 then the D978 in the direction of Rully.
ⓣ03.85.87.20.09 ⓕ03.85.91.27.18
Closed *Tues; Wed; 1–15 Jan; 15 Feb–1 March.* **TV. Car park.**

A large house bedecked with flowers and surrounded by greenery, overlooking the square of this picturesque wine-producing village. It is well kept and fully deserves its two-star classification. Neat, spacious rooms: doubles at €50. The restaurant is a safe bet: foie gras, pig's-foot and oxtail steak, zander fillet with Aligoté, snail pastry, squab stuffed with truffles. Menus at €15 (except Sun), then €22–39.

Saint-Christophe-en-Brionnais

71800

Bar-restaurant du Midi

Grand-Rue; either on the D34 from Paray-le-Monial or from Clayette on the D989.
03.85.25.87.06
Closed *Mon; Jan.*

Thursday is market day and for a good number of years Marielle and Dominique Lauvernier have opened at 6am to feed and water the horse-dealers and traders. They all pile into the big dining room-cum-canteen beyond the bar and the kitchen; dishes include tasty brawn, ham hock, delicious *pot-au-feu* (meat poached with vegetables), good sirloin and skirt – they use only top quality meat. If you don't fancy the bustle, it's quieter the rest of the week. Menus €10 (weekday lunchtimes) and €12–21. Decent Côtes-du-Rhône, Mâcon Village and Saint-Véran. *Free coffee offered to our readers on presentation of this guide.*

Saint-Fargeau

89170

L'Auberge Les Perriaux

La Gare; take the Auxerre road going out of the town.
03.86.74.16.45
Closed *Sat and Sun (Sept–June); open all day, lunch and dinner, in July–Aug.*

Charming décor in an old railway station converted into a friendly restaurant. You will be greeted by the saying for the day written on a blackboard, then go into the cool, white dining room with old-fashioned decorations or on to the terrace lawn to eat under the linden trees. Many of the ingredients, such as the duck and the *confit*, are supplied by six local farms; the cooking is good, if somewhat erratic. Irresistible dessert platter (which saves you the dilemma of what to order). Weekday lunchtime menus at €14, others at €18 (in summer, on nights when there's a performance in the château), €27 and €33. For lunch you need to make sure you arrive no later than 1pm. Fast and efficient service.

Saint-Florentin

89600

La Cruchade

RN7; 3 km from the centre; turn right off the Auxerre road.
03.86.35.19.34 03.86.35.00.19
Closed *Sun.* **Car park.**

La Cruchade is the name of a cake typical of southwest France – although you can't actually buy it here. At first sight it appears to be just another restaurant beside a main road, but in fact the traditional cooking is of high quality and served in abundant portions at reasonable prices: terrine Saint-Florentin, ray's fin *à la dijonnaise*, chocolate duo. Depending on the weather, you can choose the large dining room with walls of exposed stone or the huge terrace (sometimes a little noisy as it is close to the road). For an apéritif, try the cherry Kir with Crémant de-Bourgogne. Menus from €10 (weekday lunchtime) to €25. The rooms are merely intended for stopovers; try to get one overlooking the back. Doubles €31–37; night-time, €38–46 per person. Efficient, attentive service.

Les Tilleuls**

3 rue Decourtive.
03.86.35.09.09
alliances.tilleuls@wanadoo.fr
Restaurant closed *Sun evening; Mon.* **TV. Car park.**

In a quiet side street just outside the centre. You can have a peaceful lunch under the lime trees here, on a pretty terrace surrounded by an equally pretty garden and far from the stress of daily life. Set menus start at €16 and then go from €18 up to €44. Comfortable rooms with good facilities cost €48–56 with shower/wc or bath; breakfast €7.

Saint-Julien-de-Jonzy

71110

Hôtel-restaurant-boucherie Pont Bernard**

It's 8km south of Saint-Christophe-en-Brionnais – from Paray-le-Monial, take the D34 and the D20.
03.85.84.01.95

Closed *Sun and Mon evenings; a fortnight in Feb; a week at the beginning of July.* **TV. Swimming pool. Car park.**

This is Charolais country, 30km north of Roanne, and they don't do things by halves. Monsieur Pont is both butcher and cook so the meat is of superb quality, cooked up in generous portions; this is simple, tasty home cooking. Dishes include *coq au vin*, Charolais steak, fillet of sea bream with champagne sauce, home-made foie gras, *tournedos* and farm-raised veal *escalope* in cream sauce. Excellent desserts. There's a weekday lunch menu at €12 and others €12.50–28. Simple and comfortable rooms with bath at €34–47. *Free digestif.*

Saint-Léger-sous-Beuvray

71990

Hôtel du Morvan*

In the town; take the D3 from Autun.
Ⓣ03.85.82.51.06Ⓕ03.85.82.45.07
Ⓦwww.hoteldumorvan71.com
Closed *Mon and Tues (out of season); 25 Dec–31 Jan.*

A village hotel that has opted to enhance its comfort, create a warm atmosphere and keep the prices within reasonable bounds. A village hotel that sets store by comfort and a warm atmosphere and yet keeps prices within reasonable bounds. There are seven rooms with a rural charm; doubles with washbasin €33, with shower/wc €42. Fine regional cooking: weekday lunchtime menu €10.80; others €15–26.50, including an amusing Gallic-Roman menu at €19 (the major Gallic site of Bibracte is nearby). *10% discount on a room (apart from July–Aug) offered to our readers on presentation of this guide.*

Saint-Prix

71990

Chez Franck et Francine

Ⓣ03.85.82.45.12
Closed *Sun evening; Mon.*

Cooking worthy of the great chefs of Burgundy: fried snails, pig's foot pancake, zander steak cooked under the skin with celery cream and sorrel. Book at least two days in advance to ensure a friendly welcome from Francine who, although a young woman, is already a firmly established local character. The chef works alone in the kitchen, using only the freshest of ingredients. A variety of menus from €25 to €38.

Saint-Saulge

58330

Le Restaurant des Légendes

6 rue du Commerce; 15km to the southwest of Châtillon-en-Bazois.
Ⓣ03.86.58.27.67 Ⓕ03.85.84.01.95
Closed *Sun evening and Wed all day.*

A huge, bright and cheery dining room crammed with curios: a spyglass, pot-pourri, paintings, hats, tools, etc. The show continues on the table, thanks to a master chef from Niverne; many a local has been startled to find his strawberry soup swimming in a strange blue liquid. Nothing is surprising, however, in Saint-Saulge, the stuff of legends, where, so the story goes, a cow was once hauled on top of the church roof to graze the village's last blades of grass. Cheapest menu at €15.50 then menus at €21.40–25.92.

Saint-Révérien

58420 (13km N)

Le Chali

Chez Philippe Chanut; take the D34.
Ⓣ03.86.29.08.10
Closed *Mon and Tues (July–Aug); Mon evening–Wed the rest of the year.*

The pride and joy of Saint-Révérien. A beautiful dining room with a striking ceiling, and a tank with a few fish awaiting the intervention of the chef, whose star turn is undoubtedly Nivernais duck breast soaked in Sezchuan sauce. Audacity in the kitchen is combined with great charm at the table. Cheapest menu €18, then others €26–34.

Saulieu

21210

La Vieille Auberge

15 rue Grillot.
Ⓣ03.80.64.13.74 Ⓕ03.80.64.13.74
Closed *Tues evening and Wed except*

July–Aug; 5–31 Jan; 1st week in July. **Car park.**

Everyone who drove south on the N6 to the coast knew Saulieu well, but when the autoroute opened the old town fell on leaner times. A new generation of restaurateurs have put Saulieu back on the gastronomic and tourist map, however, and two of them took over this inn. Having said that, you could drive past without even noticing; it's tucked away behind a bend in the road. The cooking is well worth seeking out: try the brilliant terrine of Charolais beef, *marbré* of rabbit or roast zander with red wine. Menus €12–30. Absolutely delightful dining room and an attractive hidden terrace. Rooms with shower/wc or bath €33. Half board, compulsory in July–Aug, costs €45–55. *10% discount on the room rate for two nights minimum offered to our readers on presentation of this guide.*

La Borne Impériale**

14–16 rue d'Argentine.
Ⓣ03.80.64.19.76
Ⓦwww.borne-imperiale.com
Closed *Tues evening; Wed (except in July–Aug); 5 Jan–5 Feb.* **TV. Car park.**

Near Pompom's famous sculpture of a bull – a Saulieu landmark – you'll find *La Borne Impériale*, a gastronomic landmark and one of the last old-fashioned inns in Burgundy. It has seven rooms at €37–50, the best of which have a view of the attractive garden. The beautiful dining room has a terrace for fine days. Weekday menu €18 and others at €22 and €42, listing good, regional cooking. *Free apéritif offered to our readers on presentation of this guide.*

Savigny-sur-Seille

71440

Auberge La Rivière

Tiellay; 11km west of Louhans.
Ⓣ03.85.74.99.03
Closed *Tues evening and Wed (16 Sept–14 June); Wed (15 June–15 Sept).* **High chairs available. Disabled access.**

Enchanting inn in a natural setting on the banks of the Seille, formerly the home of a ferryman. Charming interior with a slight slope and a friendly welcome. Regional cooking: *oeuf cocotte* with snails, ham braised with morel, Bresse chicken with morel or crayfish, poultry-liver cake, crayfish supreme and and fish that couldn't be fresher – the owner is a keen fisherman and catches them in the river himself. You may be lucky enough to find silurid (a giant freshwater fish) available. The excellent desserts include raspberries with vanilla ice cream. Cheapest menu at €15.10, served every day at lunch and dinner, then others €18.50–28.20. On fine days you can eat on the idyllic terrace, with a lawn stretching down to the water. *Free coffee offered to our readers on presentation of this guide.*

Saillenard

71580 (26km NE)

Auberge Le Moulin de Sauvagette

Saillenard; pass through Louhans, then take the N78 to Beaurepaire-en-Bresse, then the D87 to Saillenard; from there, follow the direction of Bletterans, 3km away; it's well signposted.
Ⓣ and Ⓕ 03.85.74.17.58
Closed *Sun evening, Mon and Tues (except for staying guests); end Jan; 2 weeks in Oct.*

The ideal place to get away from it all in a bucolic backwater in the heart of Bresse. An old mill lost in the countryside, attractively fitted out and decorated. Pretty rooms with old-fashioned furniture. Cheerful service and excellent regional cooking, served in a beautiful, rustic dining room. Double rooms €40–44. Regional platter €12; menu €20. Credit cards not accepted. Booking essential. *Free apéritif or coffee offered to our readers on presentation of this guide.*

Semur-en-Auxois

21140

Hôtel des Cymaises**

7 rue du Renaudot.
Ⓣ03.80.97.21.44 Ⓕ03.80.97.18.23
Ⓦwww.provais.com/lescymaises
Closed *Mon evening Oct–Easter; Feb school holidays; 3 Nov–7 Dec.* **Disabled access. TV. Car park.**

In the heart of the medieval city, just behind Porte Sauvigny, there's a beautiful eighteenth-century building which has adapted extremely well to life as a twenty-first-century hotel. It's cool, clean and comfortable, with a small, flower-filled garden, and you can come and go as you please. Breakfast, €6.20, is served under the pergola. Nicely furnished rooms at €56–57.50.

|●| Restaurant des Minimes

39 rue Vaux; it's 500m from the town centre.
Ⓣ03.80.97.26.86
Closed *Sun evening; Mon; Christmas–New Year's Eve.* **Disabled access. Car park.**

This "local" bistro below the ramparts has become an absolute must for tourists in search of the soul and the cooking of Semur. There's a pastoral feel to the décor and an informal atmosphere; on offer are a €15 menu and a *menu-carte* at €25. The *patronne* loves good wine and good banter and she's completely unfazed by anyone – from local politicians to people who quibble about the bill.

|●| Le Calibressan

16 rue Feveret.
Ⓣ03.80.97.32.40
Ⓔle.calibressan@wanadoo.fr
Closed *Sat lunchtime; Sun evening; Mon; Jan; 1st week in July.*

A twist of California in this Bresse kitchen – thus the name. An attractive little restaurant combining authentic rustic décor – beams, unadorned brick walls, flowers and pretty curtains – with the vitality and exoticism of America, well-represented by Madame at reception. You'll also detect flavours of the New World in certain sauces and side dishes. Try the roast kangaroo fillet with Grand Veneur sauce, the Hawain pork salad or the house chilli con carne. Plus regional dishes including snails and chocolate pudding. Weekday lunch menu €16 and others €18.50–30.

Pont-et-Massene

21140 (3km SE)

🏃 🏠 |●| Hôtel du Lac**

10 rue du Lac.
Ⓣ03.80.97.11.11
Ⓦwww.hoteldulacdepont.com
Closed *Sun evening and Mon out of season; 8 Dec–14 Jan.* **TV. Car park.**

Just below the lake, this huge building reeks of the 1950s. Some pleasant rooms but others are fairly dreary; €46–69. There's a family atmosphere in the restaurant and the kind of regional cooking you'd eat during a traditional Sunday lunch: dishes like *jambon persillé* made with local ham, chicken *fricassée* with mushrooms, *coq au vin* and calf's head *ravigote*. A set menu at €12.50 is served in the week; others are €14.64–26. Try the local *blanc de l'Auxois*, which is very drinkable and deserves to be more widely known. There's a terrace with a canopy for fine summer days. *Free house apéritif offered to our readers on presentation of this guide.*

Alésia

21150 (20km NE)

|●| L'Auberge du Cheval Blanc

Rue du Miroir.
Ⓣ and Ⓕ03.80.96.01.55
Closed *Sun evening; Mon; 1 Jan–15 Feb.* **Disabled access. Car park.**

Repair here after a morning reviewing the excavations at Alésia, where Vercingetorix and the Gauls fought their last battle against the armies of Julius Caesar. The brasserie menu lists parsleyed ham with salad and other simple dishes, and good regional cooking is served in the bigger dining room. The chef uses vegetables from the garden and the market. Try local snails, fish stew, chicken *fricassée*, scallops, grilled Charolais steak with cream and mushrooms or pineapple *millefeuille*. Weekday lunch menu €16; others €26 and €35. The place has lots of energy with a team of young serving staff. Have a glass of local Chardonnay or Pinot Noir.

Sens

89100

🏃 |●| Restaurant Le Soleil Levant

51 rue Émile-Zola; it's close to the station.
Ⓣ and Ⓕ03.86.65.71.82
Closed *Sun evening; Wed; Aug.* **High chairs available.**

A restaurant, very classic in both décor and cuisine, which is well known for its fish – particularly the signature dish of salmon with sorrel and the fish *bouillabaisse*. They also do good meat dishes such as house duck foie gras and calf's head *gribiche*, along with some heavenly desserts including chocolate charlotte. The cheapest menu costs €13 (weekday lunchtimes); others are €20 and €31 or you'll pay around €40 à la carte. *Free coffee offered to our readers on presentation of this guide.*

|●| Au Crieur de Vins

1 rue Alsace-Lorraine.
☎03.86.65.92.80
Closed *Sun; Mon; Tues lunch.* **Disabled access.**

An annexe to a large house (*La Madeleine*). The space is limited but skilfully laid out (you don't have to put your elbow in your neighbour's plate) and the dishes are very good (although a little expensive à la carte): haddock fillets poached with chives and *merleur* with violet mustard, all served by the owner, Guy. There's a lunch menu at €21.50 and an evening menu at €35. There's also an impeccable selection of wines straight from the growers, but pay attention to the prices before getting carried away. Ask about the suggestions of the day, as these alone are often worth the trip. Attentive service. Booking essential.

Tanlay

89430

|●| Le Bonheur Gourmand

6 Grande-Rue-Basse.
☎03.86.75.82.18
Open *every day April–Oct.* **Disabled access.**

In one of the outhouses of a château, a small, attractively decorated dining room complemented by a modest lounge with a few children's games and some reading matter on the region. The formula is simple: you compile your meal from the three or four choices chalked on the blackboard. The selection changes regularly but you will always be spoilt for choice: melon with Ratafia, poultry with oyster mushrooms, lovers' sorbet and walnut and coffee dessert. Menus at €15 (lunch) and €20 (dinner). Lison, the waitress, is all smiles, while the chef, Régis, genuinely enjoys pleasing his guests. The quality of the service and the results on the plate are considered more important than the number of customers. Unsurprisingly, it is very popular and booking is essential. Credit cards not accepted.

Toucy

89130

⌂ |●| Le Lion d'Or

37 rue Lucile-Cormier.
☎03.86.44.00.76
Closed *Sun evening; Mon.* **TV. Car park.**

Old hotel with a magnificent wooden staircase. The rooms are modest but cosy and spotless, with a lingering scent of beeswax polish. Doubles €35 with washbasin and €50 with shower/wc or bath. The restaurant is charming, as is its manager. Regional specialities: fish *en croûte*, snails with croûtons, *steak au poivre*, Dijon-style veal kidneys. Menu at €12 served every day, then others at €16–26. Credit cards not accepted. *Free coffee offered to our readers on presentation of this guide.*

Mezilles

89130 (10km SW)

|●| La Mare aux Fées

Le Vieux-Pont; take the D965.
☎03.86.45.40.43
Closed *Tues evening; Wed: Feb.*

An enchanting restaurant at one end of an old bridge over the River Branlin. The cooking is classic but subtle: authentic *œufs meurette*, tender undercut with shallots, *andouillette* with white wine and home-made Paris-Brest that melts in the mouth. Menus €17–22. Fine selection of wines. A relaxing, bucolic setting with service that pays attention to detail (and genuine respect to non-smokers). It is advisable to book.

Tournus

71700

⌂ |●| Hôtel-restaurant aux Terrasses**

18 av. du 23-Janvier.
☎03.85.51.01.74
Closed *Sun evening except July–Aug; Mon; Tues lunchtime.* **TV. Car park.**

This place is known primarily for the quality of the cooking in the restaurant – it's one of the best in town. It's set in an enormous roadside establishment, probably a former coaching inn. The lounge separates two large, richly decorated dining rooms. Reception's a bit on the smart side but not overly so, and service is attentive. Set menus start at a good-value weekday lunch menu for €20 and go up to €52. À la carte lists a variety of dishes: zander with Morvan ham, Bresse chicken with morels, parsleyed ham, *escalope* with blackcurrants, and *millefeuille* with pears and gingerbread ice cream. Comfortable rooms with shower/wc €56 or €62 with bath. Breakfast €7.20.

Hôtel Le Sauvage***

Place du Champ-de-Mars.
03.85.51.14.45 03.85.32.10.27
le-sauvage-tournus.com
TV. High chairs available. Pay car park.

You can't miss this Virginia-creeper-smothered house a little set back from the main road. This old establishment has been ticking over quietly for ages. Pleasant rooms €62 with shower/wc, or €65 with bath. The restaurant does a good range of set menus from €14 to €39 – one is dedicated to regional dishes like rabbit with parsley and onion *confit*, gateau of chicken liver with crayfish, *coq au vin* or duck fillet with pears and Marc de Bourgogne. À la carte – reckon on around €30 – you can choose from specialities including parsleyed frogs' legs, snails, Bresse chicken in cream and morel sauce and flambéed fillet of Charolais beef. *Apéritif on the house or 10% discount on the room rate (out of season) offered to our readers on presentation of this guide.*

Villars (Le)

71700 (3km S)

L'Auberge des Gourmets

Place de l'Église; on the Mâcon road.
03.85.32.58.80
Closed *Sun evening; Tues evening; Wed.*

Daniel Rogié, formerly the chef in *Le Rempart* in Tournus, has created this beautiful restaurant in a pretty village overlooking the Saône. It's impossible to miss as it's opposite the double-nave Roman church. The large trees in the square provide shade for the terrace, while the interior is cool and restful. Menus from €16.50 in the week to €39.50. Booking essential if you want to have a chance of experiencing seasonal cooking that has managed to renew a tradition, served in a very convivial atmosphere. *Free coffee offered to our readers on presentation of this guide.*

Vermenton

89270

Auberge L'Espérance

3 rue du Général-de-Gaulle.
03.86.81.50.42
Closed *Mon; Tues evening; Sun evening; in Jan; some evenings end of Oct.* **High chairs and games available. Disabled access.**

However glum you're feeling, the mere mention of this inn's name (*espérance* means "hope") should perk you up. You'll get a delightful welcome, and the kitchen turns out wonderful dishes which change with the seasons – try the house duck foie gras, Burgundy-style prawns, all of which are regulars. Set menus €15–35, including one grill menu. Children's menu costs €8. They've provided a play area for the kids. Everyone will find the air-conditioning a blessed relief in summer. Credit cards not accepted. *Free coffee offered to our readers on presentation of this guide.*

Accolay

89460 (3km W)

Hostellerie de la Fontaine**

16 rue de Reigny.
03.86.81.54.02 03.86.81.52.78
hostellerie.fontaine@wanadoo.fr
Restaurant closed *Mon–Fri lunch; mid-Nov to 31 March.* **Car park.**

A traditional Burgundy house in a lovely little village in the Cure valley. On fine evenings you can relax in the garden while feasting on salad of snails with mustard dressing, red mullet fillet with cucumber cream or *entrecôte* steak with soft creamy Chaource cheese sauce. Set menus at €21, and others at €28.34–43, with a children's menu at €10.20. Doubles €43–47, and there's a good breakfast for €7. *10% discount on the room rate offered to our readers on presentation of this guide.*

Bazarnes

89460 (6km W)

Restaurant La Griotte

3 av. de la Gare; it's opposite the Cravant-Bazarnes station.
03.86.42.39.38
Closed *Mon–Wed; 24 Dec–15 Feb.*

A nice little restaurant with a great chef who's an expert in seeking out fantastic local suppliers. With this fresh produce, his imagination takes him to culinary heights. The dishes really taste of the country – you just have to try the pork *andouille* to know what we mean. The cheapest menu is €11.50, then two others at €18 and

€20. Delightful service. *Free apéritif offered to our readers on presentation of this guide.*

Vézelay

89450

Hôtel La Maison des Glycines

Rue Saint-Pierre; opposite the tourist office.
Ⓣ and Ⓕ03.86.32.35.30
Open *all year round.* **Disabled access.**

In summer it is easy see why this hotel is called the "House of Wisterias", as the patio and terrace are swathed in wisteria, and you can have breakfast or an afternoon tea in their midst. The rooms, all with names like Marie-Madeleine or Saint-Bernard, are sophisticated, with shiny colours, old floor-tiles and, in those highest up, a view of the Basilica. Double rooms €30–74, according to the degree of comfort. Limited choice of food available if required.

Le Compostelle**

Place du Champ-de-Foire.
Ⓣ03.86.33.28.63 Ⓕ03.86.33.34.34
Ⓔle.compostelle@wanadoo.fr
Closed *Jan to mid-Feb.* **Disabled access. TV.**

Vézelay was one of the assembly points for pilgrimages to Santiago de Compostela in northwestern Spain. That fact is commemorated by the name of this pretty house, which has reverted to being an inn – as it was at the beginning of the twentieth century. The service is first-rate and the modern, well-equipped bedrooms have views of the countryside or the garden; doubles €46–55. It's best to reserve.

Restaurant Le Bougainville

26 rue Saint-Étienne.
Ⓣ03.86.33.27.57 Ⓕ03.86.33.35.12
Closed *Tues; Wed; Mon (out of season); mid-Nov to mid-Jan.*

This restaurant, in a beautiful old building overflowing with flowers, is very good value for money (cheapest menu at €14.50, others at €19–39) – a pleasant surprise in a town where low prices are a rarity. Traditional local dishes: chicken thighs in white wine, *œufs en meurette*, ham knuckle *à la morvandelle*. The dining room, with its magnificent old fireplace, is a pleasant place to sit.

Saint-Père-sous-Vézelay

89450 (2km SE)

À la Renommée**

19–20 Grande Rue; it's on the D957, at the foot of Vézelay hill.
Ⓣ03.86.33.21.34 Ⓕ03.86.33.34.17
Ⓦwww.avallonnais-tourisme.com/renommee
Closed *Oct–March.* **Disabled access. TV. Car park.**

This hotel is also a newsagent's and a tobacconist's so there's a relaxed atmosphere. The more expensive rooms are spacious and have a small terrace with a view over the countryside and the Saint-Pierre church. Doubles from €34 with basin, up to €54 with bath.

L'Entre-Vignes

Route de Vézelay.
Ⓣ03.86.33.33.33
Closed *Mon; Tues; Wed evening; Thurs evening; Fri lunch; Sat lunch; Sun evening; out of season, closed some weekdays at lunchtime.* **Disabled access. Car park.**

Single menu at €28 at lunch and €32 for dinner and the copious, original Sunday brunch. When speaking of Saint-Père, it is impossible not to mention the great chef Marc Meneau. His brand-new "annexe" is still searching for its identity. The formula is simple but a little more choice would not go amiss, and the menu, although very fine, still lacks a touch of the creativity that is so dear to the great chef. The plastic furniture on the large terrace compares badly with the more elegant interior dining room. The service is immaculate and the whole setting is adorned with flowers. For those whose budgets can stand it, *L'Espérance,* Marc Meneau's Relais & Château restaurant, is on the other side of the street.

Pierre-Perthuis

89450 (6km SE)

Restaurant Les Deux Ponts

It's signposted from Saint-Pére-sous-Vézelay.
Ⓣ03.86.32.31.31 Ⓕ03.86.32.35.80
Closed *Mon; Tues; Mon only in July and Aug.*

This old village inn has been restored by a couple of love-birds who are brimming with ideas. Double rooms with shower/wc or bath €45. Breakfast €6.10. Philippe has collated a compendium of recipes that reflect his personality but which are anchored in tradition; they all call for fresh, quality ingredients. Marianne welcomes you; she is a natural and instantly puts you at your ease. Summertimes you eat in the shade of the huge chestnut tree, in winter you bundle up by the open fire. There are three set menus €22–60. They will make you up a picnic hamper – to order in advance – which you can take when you rent one of their canoes, horses or bikes. And you can even hire a donkey with a pack saddle, and ride along the river bank. There's a pleasant walk, and from the top of the town, a lovely view of Vézelay in the distance.

Pontaubert

89200 (10km NE)

Le Moulin des Templiers**

Vallée du Cousin; coming from Vézelay, turn right as soon as you cross the bridge and follow the arrows.
☎03.86.34.10.80
www.hotel-moulin-des-templiers.com
Closed *end-Nov to end-Feb.* **Car park.**

This large ochre-coloured house, in the Cousin valley and covered with Virginia creeper, is now a waterside hotel with oodles of charm. It's an old twelfth-century mill that's been wonderfully restored; there are sitting rooms for intimate conversations and a flowery waterside terrace for when the sun shines. Lovely walks and mountain-bike rides in the surrounding woods. Comfortable double rooms at €38 with shower, and €58 with shower/wc or bath, depending on the size, with shower/wc or bath. Breakfast, €6.50, can be taken on the terrace. Charming hotel with a friendly welcome.

Les Fleurs**

69 rte. de Vézelay; take the D957.
☎03.86.34.13.81 Ⓕ03.86.34.23.32
Closed *Wed; Thurs lunchtime (all day Oct–March); Jan; Nov school holidays; Christmas.* **TV. Car park.**

This beautiful hotel is surrounded by a delightful garden overflowing with flowers. It's been tastefully decorated by the owners, with lovely wood panelling in the dining room. The bedrooms are pretty, and bathrooms have shower or bath; they cost €45–54. The restaurant gets things just right and the prices are reasonable – the cheapest set menu is €15 (not served on Sun), with others €22–37 – and there's a wealth of specialities like trout terrine with basil sauce, smoked salmon maison, fillet of beef Morvandiau and *pavé de Pontaubert*. Pleasant terrace and good choice of wines to go with dishes.

Villeneuve-l'Archevêque

89190

Les Vieux Moulins Banaux

18 rte. des Moulins-Banaux; on the Arcès-Dilo road out of the town.
☎03.86.86.72.55. Ⓕ03.86.86.78.94
www.bourgognehotels.fr
Closed *Jan.* **Disabled access.**

This old mill by the banks of the River Vanne used to belong to the village squire, who rented out its services to anybody who wanted to grind their grain. (This practice was known as "banality"). In 1801 it was turned into a paper factory, before becoming a hotel in 1966. It has lost none of its class since it was taken over two years ago by a cosmopolitan team (English and French chefs, a Dutchwoman serving at the tables and a German woman at the reception). The setting has been intelligently conceived, with a terrace by the waterside, a quiet garden for apéritifs and a spacious, wood-panelled dining room that displays the mechanism of the mill that once operated here. The dishes are sophisticated and creative, with touches of the Far East and an impressive selection of wines from all over the world. Weekday menu €15.50, others at €23 and €26, the latter with Kir, wine and coffee. The rooms (ask for one to the rear) have all the mod cons. Doubles at €39 with shower, €49 with bath. Booking is highly advisable, as the value for money here is exceptional. *Coffee offered to our readers on presentation of this guide.*

Villeneuve-sur-Yonne

89500

La Lucarne aux Chouettes

7 quai Bretoche.

Ⓣ03.86.87.19.26 Ⓕ03.86.87.22.63
Ⓦwww.lesliecaron-auberge.com
Closed *Sun evening; Mon; mid-Nov to mid-Dec.*

Double rooms from €90. Four old houses on a picturesque quay by the River Yonne, transformed into a charming hotel by the actress Leslie Caron. The rooms, decorated in an old-fashioned style, all overlook the river. The dining room has an almost Zen-like rusticity. Cooking with local ingredients and a touch of invention. Weekday lunchtime menu €18 and another at €35. At the very least, it is worth dropping into the bar for a drink, even though the service is a bit aloof.

Bretagne

Arzon

56640

Crêperie La Sorcière

59 rue des Fontaines.
Ⓣ02.97.53.87.25
Closed *Mon; Mon lunchtime in season; Jan.*
High chairs available.

You'll be bewitched by this pretty stone house, where they conjure up devilishly delicious recipes. All the crêpes have names: la Pensardine, la Vendéenne, la Périgourdine, l'Irlandaise – and you'll only have to cross their palm with a (small) amount of silver. Quality produce and ingredients are used – such as the black wheat. Around €10 for a meal of good crêpes with interesting fillings. There's a terrace with a view of the old port of Morbihan.

Audierne

29770

Hôtel de la Plage**

21 bd. Emmanuel-Brusq; 2km towards the quay for the île de Sein.
Ⓣ02.98.70.01.07 Ⓕ02.98.75.04.69
Closed *Oct–April.* **TV. Car park.**

A hotel on the sea front that helps its guests get into a holiday mood with its cheerful décor of nautical references in the lounge and the bedrooms: treasure chests, white walls and blue curtains and models of tall ships. Bright, attractive rooms, almost all overlooking the beach. High-quality bedding. Double rooms €45–62, depending on the season. Half board €56–63. Great charm and value for money.

Auray

56400

Hôtel Le Marin

1 pl. du Roland Saint-Goustan.
Ⓣ02.97.24.14.58 Ⓕ02.97.24.39.59
Closed *mid-Jan to mid-Feb.* **TV.**

Very close to the port (although it's out of sight). Pretty, comfortable double rooms €57–72; one room for a family of four, with terrace, at €81. Beautiful bathrooms. On the ground floor, a lounge replaces the old bar-restaurant that was once open to hotel guests. Charming terrace. *10% discount on a room (mid-Nov to mid-March) offered to our readers on presentation of this guide.*

La Belle Bio

4 rue Philippe-Vannier.
Ⓣ02.97.24.26.75
Games available.

A fine organic crêperie hidden away in an unremarkable street. Friendly service in a warm dining room (log fire in winter), beautiful terrace, a space where kids can play, draw and read. All very authentic, just like the smiles of its young owners. The food is also excellent: Roquefort pancake, crêpe with milk and organic cider jam. Reckon on €9–15. Exhibitions of original art works on the old walls.

Restaurant L'Églantine

Place Saint-Sauveur Saint-Goustan, port d'Auray.
Ⓣ02.97.56.46.55
Closed *Wed (only at lunch in high season).*

Lovingly prepared, traditional Breton food in the only really recommendable restau-

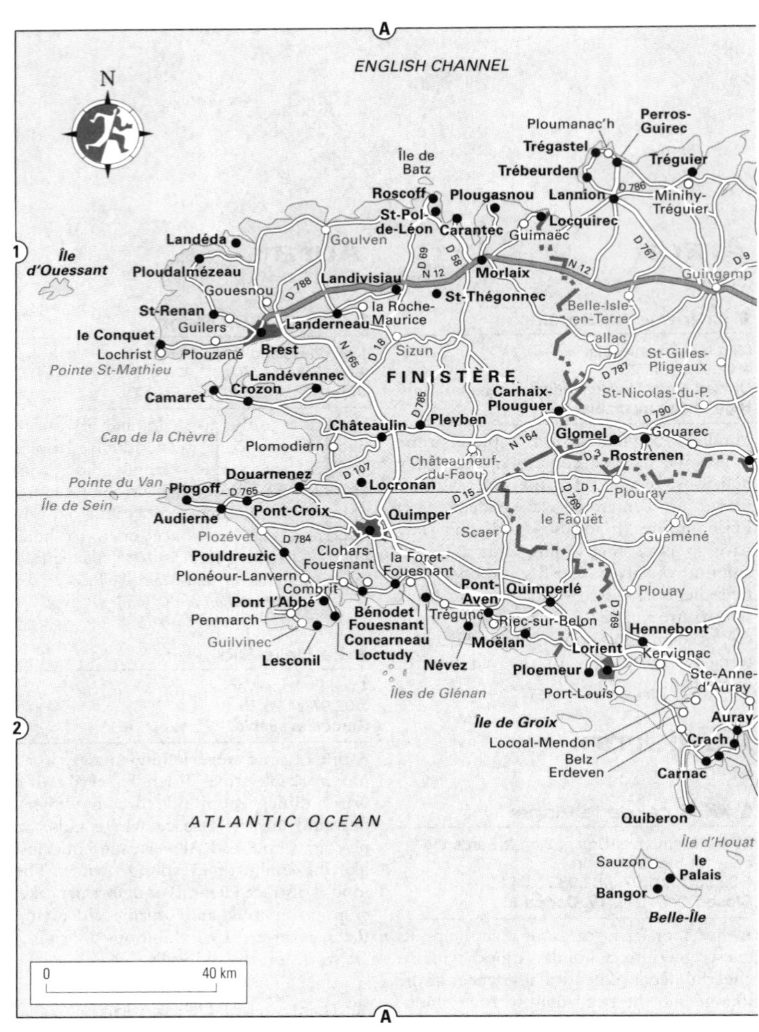
ENGLISH CHANNEL
N
Ploumanac'h
Perros-Guirec
Trégastel
Île de Batz
Trébeurden
Tréguier
Roscoff
Plougasnou
Lannion
Minihy-Tréguier
St-Pol-de-Léon
Carantec
Locquirec
Guimaëc
Landéda
Goulven
Île d'Ouessant
Ploudalmézeau
Landivisiau
N 12
Morlaix
Guingamp
Gouesnou
St-Thégonnec
St-Renan
la Roche-Maurice
Belle-Isle-en-Terre
Guilers
Landerneau
le Conquet
Brest
Sizun
Callac
Lochrist
Plouzané
St-Gilles-Pligeaux
Pointe St-Mathieu
Landévennec
FINISTÈRE
Camaret
Crozon
Carhaix-Plouguer
St-Nicolas-du-P.
Châteaulin
Pleyben
Cap de la Chèvre
Glomel
Gouarec
Plomodiern
Rostrenen
Châteauneuf-du-Faou
Pointe du Van
Douarnenez
Locronan
Plogoff
Plouray
Île de Sein
Pont-Croix
Audierne
Quimper
le Faouët
Scaer
Plozévet
Guéméné
Pouldreuzic
Clohars-Fouesnant
la Foret-Fouesnant
Plonéour-Lanvern
Combrit
Pont-Aven
Quimperlé
Plouay
Pont l'Abbé
Bénodet
Trégunc
Riec-sur-Belon
Penmarch
Fouesnant
Hennebont
Guilvinec
Concarneau
Moëlan
Lorient
Kervignac
Loctudy
Lesconil
Névez
Ploemeur
Ste-Anne-d'Auray
Îles de Glénan
Port-Louis
Île de Groix
Auray
Locoal-Mendon
Crach
Belz
Erdeven
Carnac
ATLANTIC OCEAN
Quiberon
Île d'Houat
Sauzon
le Palais
Bangor
Belle-Île
0
40 km
A
1
2

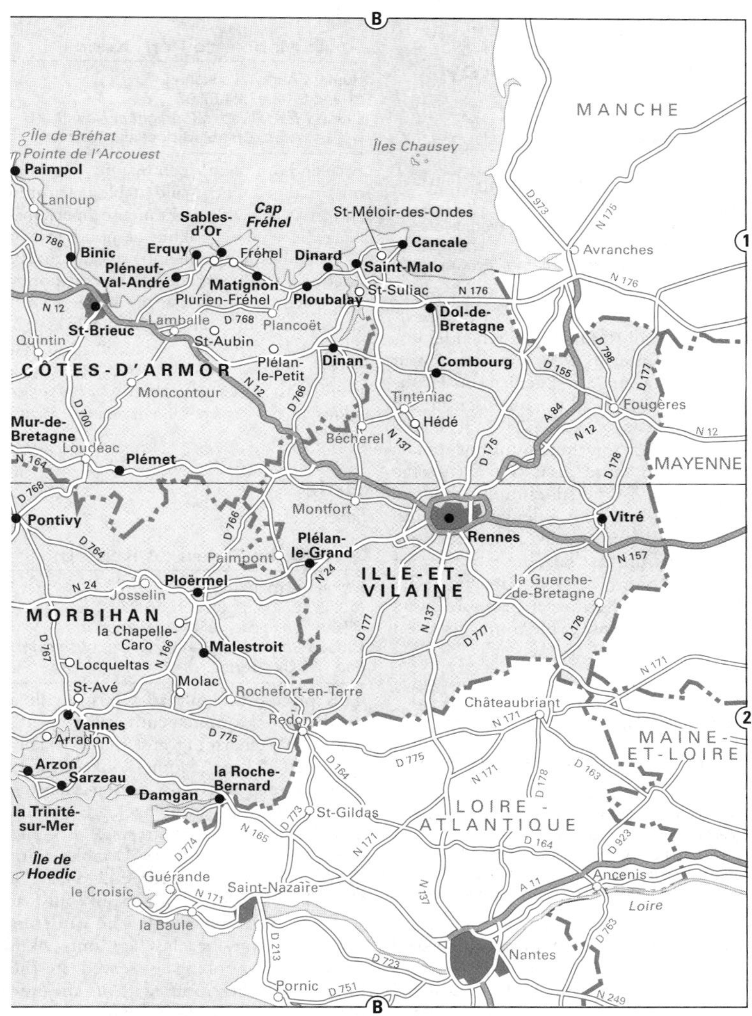
B
MANCHE
Île de Bréhat
Pointe de l'Arcouest
Paimpol
Îles Chausey
Lanloup
Sables-d'Or
Cap Fréhel
St-Méloir-des-Ondes
D 786
Binic
Erquy
Fréhel
Dinard
Cancale
Pléneuf-Val-André
Matignon
Saint-Malo
Plurien-Fréhel
Ploubalay
St-Suliac
N 176
N 12
St-Brieuc
Lamballe
D 768
Plancoët
Dol-de-Bretagne
Quintin
St-Aubin
CÔTES-D'ARMOR
Plélan-le-Petit
Dinan
Combourg
D 973
N 175
Avranches
N 176
D 798
D 155
D 177
Fougères
Moncontour
N 12
D 766
Tinténiac
Hédé
A 84
N 12
D 700
Mur-de-Bretagne
Bécherel
N 137
D 175
N 12
D 178
Loudéac
Plémet
MAYENNE
N 164
D 768
Montfort
Pontivy
Rennes
Vitré
D 766
D 764
Plélan-le-Grand
Paimpont
N 157
N 24
N 24
Ploërmel
ILLE-ET-VILAINE
Josselin
la Guerche-de-Bretagne
MORBIHAN
la Chapelle-Caro
D 767
N 166
Malestroit
D 177
N 137
D 777
D 178
Locqueltas
N 171
St-Avé
Molac
Rochefort-en-Terre
Châteaubriant
Vannes
Redon
N 171
Arradon
D 775
D 775
MAINE-ET-LOIRE
D 164
N 171
D 178
D 163
Arzon
Sarzeau
la Roche-Bernard
Damgan
St-Gildas
D 773
LOIRE-ATLANTIQUE
la Trinité-sur-Mer
N 165
D 164
D 923
Île de Hoedic
D 774
N 171
Guérande
A 11
Ancenis
le Croisic
Saint-Nazaire
N 171
N 137
Loire
la Baule
D 213
D 763
D 723
Nantes
Pornic
D 751
N 249
B

rant in the port; elegant and classical, but not excessively so – you will be warmly welcomed. Specialities include fish sauerkraut and monkfish *blanquette* with cream and *bouillabaisse*. The walls are adorned with portraits of the leaders of the eighteenth-century counter-revolutionary army.

Sainte-Anne-d'Auray

56400 (6km N)

L'Auberge

56 rte. de Vannes.
Ⓣ02.97.57.61.55 Ⓕ02.97.57.69.10
Ⓦwww.auberge-lavou.com
Closed *Tues except July–Aug; Wed; winter school holidays; 12 Nov–9 Dec.* **Disabled access. High chairs available. TV. Car park.**

One of the best restaurants in the locality; John-Paul II dined here when he visited the region in 1996. You can savour the delicacy of Jean-Luc Larvoir's culinary approach on all the menus, from the cheapest at €19 and €24 (not served Sat evening, Sun lunchtime or public holidays) to those at €35–63: try crab *tartare*, home-smoked salmon, chopped oysters, sea bass with Guéméné *andouille*, truffle *coulis* and the like. The extensive wine list proves excellent value for money. Rooms €34–46. Breakfast €6. A place of pilgrimage in more ways than one, as people come from afar to eat here

Erdeven

56410 (15km W)

La Crêperie du Manoir de Kercadio

Lieu-dit Kercadio; from Auray, take the road to Ploërmel then Erdeven.
Ⓣ02.97.24.67.57
Open *daily in July–Aug; Easter to end June weekends, public holidays and school holidays.*

The setting is elegant, with wood-panelled walls, original fireplace and wide hearth – and the bread oven in the kitchen is the real thing. But costs are actually very reasonable; try the simple crêpe with butter or one stuffed with mushrooms or scallops *à l'armoricaine*. Reckon on €9 for a complete meal. They also offer salads, omelettes and so on. On nice days tables are set in the garden, under the shadow of a large magnolia tree. You can rent a bike or set out from here along the hiking paths. *Free apéritif offered to our readers on presentation of this guide.*

Locoal-Mendon

56550 (15km NW)

Manoir de Porh Kerio

Route d'Auray; it's signed.
Ⓣ and Ⓕ02.97.24.67.57
Closed *Tues; Wed; a fortnight in Nov; 3 weeks in Jan.* **Disabled access. Car park.**

A splendid fifteenth-century manor, miles out in the country, with tables elegantly laid in a hall with an immense open fireplace. Very fine cooking at good prices: many dishes have delicious sweet/savoury contrasts, including the duck with honey and spices or pork *noisettes* sautéed with sweet-and-sour beetroot. Menus €15–32. They serve in the garden in summer. Service is efficient and easy-going so it's a pleasure to while away the time. *Free coffee offered to our readers on presentation of this guide.*

Belz

56550 (16km W)

Le Relais de Kergou**

It's on the road from Auray.
Ⓣ02.97.55.35.61 Ⓕ02.97.55.27.69
Ⓔjean.francois.lorvellec@wanadoo.fr
Closed *Sun evening and Mon out of season; Feb.* **TV. Car park.**

This place was built as a farm with a smithy in the nineteenth century. It's thoroughly charming and is remarkably furnished. Three rooms look directly over the road so they're noisier than the others – the ones at the back are quieter. The bathrooms vary in size, also, and some are a real squeeze. Doubles with shower/wc or bath go for €42–54, and a few cheaper ones with basin only at €26–30. Breakfast €4.80. The garden is lovely and the beaches are only 4km away. Good cooking is served in the imposing dining room with its majestic proportions and large bay window. Menus, €11 (not Sun) and €24, feature lots of fish dishes; try the lemon sole and scallops followed by the *tarte tatin*. *10% discount on the half-board rate (except July–Aug) offered to our readers on presentation of this guide.*

Bangor

56360

Hôtel-Village La Désirade***

Le Petit Cosquet; it's outside Bangor on the Port-Colon road.
02.97.31.70.70 02.97.31.89.64
www.hotel-la-desirade.com
Closed *Nov–Easter.* **Restaurant closed** *Sun evening and Mon.* **Disabled access. TV. High chairs available. Swimming pool. Car park.**

A charming hotel with architecture typical of Belle-Île: a series of low buildings with painted walls and shutters. Twenty-six thoughtfully decorated and spacious rooms €96.80–120.50; half board is compulsory in high season and holiday weekends at €79.85–108.15 per person. There's a single menu; allow €45 for a meal. They specialize in fish, shellfish and lamb: the owner-chef offers delicate dishes like roast Dublin Bay prawns with sweet peppers, sea bream with fennel and preserved tomatoes and small crêpes garnished with pears and apples. They have a lot of regulars in high season and since they've enlarged the restaurant it's also open to non-residents. It's best to book.

Crêperie des Quatre Chemins

Marta; it's at the crossroads of the two main roads on Belle-Île.
02.97.31.42.13 02.97.31.45.38
www.4chemins.com
Closed *Wed out of season; Nov–1 Feb.* **Disabled access. High chairs and games available. Car park.**

Service noon–2pm and 7–11pm. Crêpes stuffed with unusual fillings. Try grilled scallops or snail butter. Lots of word-play on the menu and a jovial atmosphere. Brightly decorated, complete with a small children's play area, and there's soft jazz and blues in the background. A meal costs about €15. *Free coffee offered to our readers on presentation of this guide.*

Bénodet

29950

Hôtel Les Bains de Mer**

11 rue de Kerguelen; it's up a steep street 100m from the sea.
02.98.57.03.41 02.98.57.11.07
% wwww.lesbainsdemer.com
Closed *15 Nov–1 March.* **Restaurant closed** *Tues out of season.* **Pizzeria closed** *20 Dec–1 Feb.* **TV. Swimming pool. Pay car park.**

This hotel is very comfortable, even plush, but it's retained a family atmosphere. Very friendly welcome and lovely double rooms with shower/wc €52–70. If the weather is cloudy, dive into the swimming pool or try a relaxing sauna. There are two places to eat: the *Domino* pizzeria-grill, open until 11pm (midnight in summer), offers salads, pasta, pizzas and grilled dishes. The restaurant has set menus at €15–27. House specialities include seafood *choucroute*. Half board, €50–66 per person, is recommended in July–Aug.

Hôtel Kastel

Corniche de la Plage; opposite the sea, next to the seawater therapy centre.
02.98.57.05.01 02.98.57.29.99
www.hotel-kastel.com
Open *all year.* Car park.

A modern and well situated hotel. The twenty-three bright, spacious and extremely comfortable rooms are complemented by lovely bathrooms. Doubles €63–114. Half board €79–81 per person. Special rates for a six-day treatment. Attractive, airy dining room where you can eat fine local cooking, with fish taking pride of place, in a contemporary setting. Menus €17–24. Hearty breakfast buffet. Attentive service.

Le Transat

Quai l'Herminier; in the old port.
02.98.66.29.29
Closed *5 Jan–5 Feb.*

The dining room, decorated in a nautical style, is presided over by the cup won by the famous steamship *Normandie*. Good local cooking, with dishes of the day incorporating produce coming straight from the sea. Menu of the day €19. Huge, tiered terrace overlooking the port. Attentive service. Open daily noon–3pm and 6.45–11.30pm.

Restaurant L'Alhambra

Corniche de l'Estuaire.
02.98.57.16.00
Closed *Mon–Thurs except school holidays (Oct–March). Open daily 11am–1am (April–Sept).*

At the foot of a lush garden that is only separated from the beach by a small road, this bar-restaurant is a friendly, fashionable spot with Moorish décor, including mosaics and a fountain. You can eat fish dishes, seafood platters and oysters at any time of day. Reckon on around €20 for a full meal à la carte. You can also just enjoy a cocktail on the terrace, with its stunning view of the Odet estuary. *Free coffee offered to our readers on presentation of this guide.*

Clohars-Fouesnant

29950 (3km NE)

Restaurant La Forge d'Antan

31 rte. de Nors-Vraz.
Ⓣ02.98.54.84.00
Closed *Mon; Tues lunchtime; Sun evening out of season.* **Disabled access. Car park.**

Way out in the country. Friendly welcome and superb rustic décor, with a stylish atmosphere and clientele to match. The imaginative seasonal cuisine doesn't come cheap: set weekday lunch menu €20 and another at €28. À la carte reckon on around €45.

Combrit

29121 (5.5km NW)

Hôtel-restaurant Sainte-Marine*

19 rue Bac; it's in the little port of Sainte-Marine.
Ⓣ02.98.56.34.79 Ⓕ02.98.51.94.09
Ⓦwww.hotelsaintemarine.com
Closed *Sun evening and Mon except school holidays.* **TV.**

A favourite with ocean-racing seafarers, novelists and film-makers. The wonderful dining room is decorated in a nautical style and has a magnificent view of the River Odet and Pont de Cornouaille; there's also a terrace. Menus €18–50. Specialities include fish *carpaccio* with spices and coriander and grilled fish with *purée maison*. If you want to prolong the pleasure, there are a few quirky rooms also decorated in a nautical style. Doubles with shower/wc or bath €69–80. Breakfast €7. Half board, compulsory July–Aug, costs €69 per person. *Free apéritif offered to our readers on presentation of this guide.*

Plonéour-Lanvern

29720 (18 km NW)

Hôtel-restaurant des Voyageurs**

1 rue Jean-Jaurès; take the D2 from Pont-l'Abbé; it's behind the church.
Ⓣ02.98.87.61.35 Ⓕ02.98.82.62.82
Closed *Fri evening and Sat lunch (Sept–Oct); weekends (Nov–Easter); 1–15 Nov; Christmas.* **TV. Car park.**

Typical, friendly village hotel. Effusive welcome, excellent cooking and reasonable prices. Attractive rooms, although the ones looking out on the street can be a little noisy. Doubles €38–53 with shower/wc or bath with shower/wc or bath. Half board compulsory July–Aug, at €50 per person. Weekday lunchtime menu €11.50, with others going up to €31. Dishes include home-made fish soup and chef's terrine with Port.

Penmarch

29760 (25km W)

Le Doris

Port de Kerity, pointe de Penmarch; take the D785 in the direction of Pont-l'Abbé then pointe de Penmarch.
Ⓣ02.98.58.60.92 Ⓕ02.98.58.58.16
Closed *All Saints' to Easter.*

Right on the harbour of this little port, this place is something of an institution, with a reputation for serving good seafood and fresh fish. It's run by a fishing family so the fish appear direct from the sea and served in traditional ways: seafood platters, grilled lobster, scallops on a skewer, poached turbot with *beurre blanc* and medallions of monkfish cooked to a Cancale recipe. Menus €11 (weekday lunchtimes) and €15.20–60. There are also three simple bed and breakfast rooms for €31. The lively bar is open all year.

Binic

22520

Hôtel Benhuyc***

1 quai Jean-Bart.
Ⓣ02.96.73.39.00 Ⓕ02.96.73.77.04
Ⓦwww.benhuyc.com
Closed *15 Dec–1 Feb.* **Restaurant closed** *Sun evening; Mon lunchtime.* **Disabled access. TV.**

Overlooking the boats moored in the pleasure port, this modern hotel is easy to recommend. The bright, comfortable rooms are well maintained, and most have a view of the harbour or the Banche beach. Doubles with shower or bath/wc €49–75; the smaller ones are the cheapest but they're still pleasant. *10% discount on the room rate (l Jan–1 April and 20 Sept–31 Dec) offered to our readers on presentation of this guide.*

Brest

29200

🏃 ☗ Hôtel Astoria**

9 rue Traverse; it's between the station and the château, close to the rue de Siam.
Ⓣ02.98.80.19.10
Ⓦwww.hotel-brest-astoria.com
Closed *20 Dec–4 Jan.* **TV. Pay car park.**

A hotel that looks like so many other buildings in Brest, but it offers good value considering its excellent position. Bright, cheerful rooms, some with balconies overlooking the quiet street. Doubles with basin €26 and €41–51 with shower/wc or bath. Breakfast €6. In July and August the Brest *jeudis* are just seven minutes' walk away. The car park costs €6 per day or €31.50 for a week. *10% discount on the room rate except in July–Aug offered to our readers on presentation of this guide.*

🏃 ☗ Hotel Abalys**

7 av. Georges-Clemenceau: it's equidistant (100m) from the tourist office and the train station.
Ⓣ02.98.44.21.86 Ⓕ02.98.43.68.32
Ⓦww.abalys.com
Disabled access. TV. Car park.

Very central, with double rooms from €28 with handbasin, and €40–50 with shower/wc or bath. They all have double glazing, though they're a bit small; some have a sea view. Reception is open round the clock. *Free liqueur and 10% discount on a room (15 Dec–15 March except during important festivals) offered to our readers on presentation of this guide.*

🏃 ☗ Hôtel le Pasteur*

29 rue Louis-Pasteur; it's between the rue de Siam and the covered market.
Ⓣ02.98.46.08.73
TV.

An establishment that holds its own in its category. It's clean and pleasant, and though the soundproofing between rooms is not great, the beds are good and at least the windows are double-glazed. It's just a shame the welcome isn't as warm as it could be. Doubles €30 with shower. Breakfast €4.50. *Free coffee offered to our readers on presentation of this guide.*

☗ Citôtel de la Gare**

4 av. Gambetta; it's opposite the station.
Ⓣ02.98.44.47.01 Ⓕ02.98.43.37.07
Ⓔinfo@hotelgare.com
Disabled access. TV.

Practically sited and more appealing than many station hotels, this friendly place offers some lovely views of the harbour from the third floor and above. There's a panoramic room on the fifth floor. Doubles with shower €40 or €48–58 with shower/wc or bath. Reception open around the clock.

🏃 ☗ Mercure - Les Voyageurs***

2 rue Yves-Collet; it's on the corner of av. Clemenceau and rue Yves-Collet.
Ⓣ and Ⓕ02.98.80.31.80
Ⓦwww.mercure.com
TV.

It's rare for a chain hotel to fight its way into this guidebook, but this brilliant three-star is one of the best of its category in town. The hotel has retained its superb 1940s entrance hall. The well-equipped bedrooms have bathrooms with character; doubles €80–90 with shower/wc or bath. Buffet breakfast €8. Reception open around the clock. *One free breakfast per room per night offered to our readers on presentation of this guide.*

🏃 |●| Restaurant La Pensée Sauvage

13 rue d'Aboville and rue de Gasté; behind Saint-Michel church.
Ⓣ02.98.46.36.65
Closed *Sat lunchtime; Sun; Mon; mid-July to end Aug.* **Disabled access.**

You have to hunt a little for this restaurant – it's way off the beaten track. But it has two simple little dining rooms that generate a great atmosphere so it's worth the effort. The cooking is tasty and comes in generous servings: try the home-made *cassoulet*, duck *confit* or the goat's cheese or fig *gratin*. It's excellent value, with a lunchtime *plat du jour* for €8, or you can eat for about €16 à la carte. Portions are huge and they'll give you a doggy bag if you can't finish all the *cassoulet*. Getting a table here can be a challenge. *Free apéritif offered to our readers on presentation of this guide.*

🏃 |●| Restaurant Le Marrakech

44 rue Traverse.
☎02.98.46.45.14
Closed *Wed lunch; Sun lunch; mid-July to mid-Aug.*

Service noon–2.30pm and 7–11pm. Attractive, restrained décor and good-quality cooking. The delicate and aromatic dishes are expertly spiced according to secret recipes that have been passed down from mother to daughter for generations. Lunch menu €8, another at €9.30, and around €15–20 à la carte. Takeaway available. An excellent place. *Free apéritif offered to our readers on presentation of this guide.*

🏃 |●| Crêperie Moderne

34 rue d'Algésiras.
☎02.98.44.44.36
Closed *Sun lunchtime.* **Disabled access. High chairs available. Car park.**

Service 11.30am–10pm. The façade is an arresting strawberry colour, while the ninety-seat dining room is uninspiringly traditional. The crêpes are delicious, however, whether served simply with butter or more elaborately with scallops in vermouth. À la carte costs €10. This establishment has been going since 1922, so they know what they're about. *Free house apéritif offered to our readers on presentation of this guide*

|●| Amour de Pomme de Terre

23 rue des Halles; it's behind the Saint-Louis covered market.
☎02.98.43.48.51 ℻02.98.43.61.88
✉amourpdt@wanadoo.fr
Disabled access. Car park.

Open at lunchtime and in the evening until 11pm, 10.30pm on Sun and Mon. This restaurant is devoted to potatoes, and just the "samba" variety, which was developed for its baking qualities. A multitude of preparations: with parsley, stuffed with different cheeses or grilled meats, with fish and shellfish. Menus €9.15 (weekday lunchtimes) and €11. The lunchtime dishes of the day change daily with one of the excellent (potato-free) desserts. The walls and the menus give you glimpses of the owner's sense of humour. The setting is pretty nice, sort of revisited rustic. And since the tables are rather tightly packed, you may well make new friends.

Guilers

29820 (5km NW)

|●| Crêperie Blé Noir

Bois du Keroual. From Guilers take the D105 south to the red cross; from there it is signed.
☎02.98.07.57.40

Open daily from 11.30am to 9.30pm. Almost hidden by trees and bushes next to a small lake and located in an ancient mill, this crêperie is a dream of a place. Friendly service, delicious crêpes and plenty of opportunity for wonderful country walks after the meal. A meal will cost around €11. Specialities include buckwheat pancakes with medallions of monkfish *armoricaine*, with scallops or smoked salmon.

Gouesnou

29850 (10km N)

|●| Crêperie La Finette

Rue du Bois-Kerallenoc; from Gouesnou it's signposted and 1km along the road to Kerallenoc.
☎02.98.07.86.68
Closed *Mon and Tues lunchtime out of season; Mon lunchtime July–Aug; a week mid-Sept; a week mid-Nov.*

Lydie and Jean-Yves Pirou chose this lovely old house with a beautiful garden to prepare their very tasty, traditional crêpes. The interior is old stone with a huge fireplace; you get a real sense of Brittany and the sea. A meal costs about €12. Best to book.

Plouzane

29280 (10km W)

|●| Les Mille et Une Lunes

Plage du Minou; more or less mid-way between Plougonvelin and Brest; well signposted from the D789.
☎02.98.48.41.81
Closed *weekday evenings; school holidays (except July–Aug).*

Restaurant owned by a scientist from Ilfremer, the French marine research centre, with his students waiting on the tables. He seeks out top-quality ingredients with an appropriately scientific meticulousness (superb local cheeses and tasty organic produce), as well as growing no fewer than 35 different varieties of tomatoes. Dish of the day and *assiette osée* (home-made terrines and charcuterie), served in generous portions, around €10. Lively wines and aromatic coffees round off the fine meals. Small terrace with the sea in the background.

Camaret

29570

🏃 🏠 |●| Hôtel-Restaurant du Styvel**

Quai du Styvel; one of the last restaurants at the end of the quay.
Ⓣ02.98.27.92.74 Ⓕ02.98.27.88.37
Ⓔhotelstyvel@wanadoo.fr
Closed *Fridays out of season; Jan.*

The thirteen well-kept rooms are small but generally comfortable and those overlooking the harbour have been redecorated. Doubles €36–44 with shower/wc. The cooking is reasonable and, as you'd imagine, revolves around the fish landed in the harbour. Menus cost €14.50–36.

|●| Brasserie Côté Mer

12 quai Toudouze; in the port.
Ⓣ02.98.27.93.79
Closed *Nov–Jan; Tues and Wed in Feb, March and Oct; Thurs in April–June.*

A beautiful brasserie painted yellow, with pretty lamps creating a very pleasant atmosphere. The various menus offer something for every taste. Set menus chalked up on the blackboard start at €13 (weekday lunchtimes) and €15 (not Sat evening, Sun). Other menus at €24 and €35 (based on lobster). Food is served throughout the day in July–Aug, but the range of food on offer is more limited. Specialities: seafood stew and *cassolette de Jacques*. The terrace is covered and heated.

|●| 🏃 Les Frères de la Côte

11 quai Toudouze.
Ⓣ02.98.27.95.42
Closed *Mon–Fri (April to end June); Wed–Thurs (Sept).*

The two brothers of Breton origin who own this restaurant came back to their roots after running another establishment in Guadeloupe, and they use the spices they discovered in the Caribbean to flavour Breton produce: fish are cooked with cider and mango, spicy caramel, Indian Marsala or pistil of saffron. Other dishes include ray salad with passion-fruit vinegar, bass with fennel *confit* and baked lobster with vanilla and pineapple. A genuine gastronomic adventure. Menu €25; reckon on €30 à la carte. *Free liqueur offered to our readers on presentation of this guide.*

Cancale

35260

🏠 |●| Hôtel de la Pointe du Grouin**

Take the signs to Pointe du Grouin, and it's about 3km from the centre of town.
Ⓣ02.99.89.60.55 Ⓕ02.99.89.92.22
Ⓦwww.hotelpointedugrouin.com
Closed *10 Nov–31 March.* **Restaurant closed** *Tues and Thurs lunchtimes out of season.* **Disabled access (restaurant only). TV. Car park.**

A solidly constructed building out on the Pointe du Grouin, facing the sea. The site is exceptional and the smart hotel is built of local stone and has a cosy interior. The small, simple rooms have been smartened up. Doubles €78–94 with shower/wc or bath. Four of them have a private terrace. Quiet is guaranteed. Breakfast €7.70. The dining room has a panoramic view of the bay of Mont-Saint-Michel. Traditional cuisine and menus €19–58. Go for the seafood platters, grilled lobster, brill with *beurre blanc*, and the soufflé flambéed with Grand Marnier. It's a good starting-point for walks in the wild countryside hereabouts.

🏠 |●| Le Querrien**

7 quay Duguay-Trouin; it's in the port.
Ⓣ02.99.89.64.56 Ⓕ02.99.89.79.35
Ⓦwww.le-querrien.com
TV.

You find some of the loveliest rooms in Cancale at this place. They're all brand new, huge, bright and equipped with good bathrooms. Doubles with shower/wc or bath €80–110. Breakfast €8. The restaurant is decorated like a smart brasserie with wood panelling, copper pans on the walls and a large fish tank. Good cooking and highly competent service. Menus at €15 (not Sun), €23 and €37.50 list grilled lobster, hot oysters, seafood platters and crêpes in orange butter. A meal à la carte will cost around €38. They take their work seriously here.

🚶 |●| La Cancalaise

3 rue de la Vallée-Porcon; it's 2 mins from the Musée des Arts et Traditions Populaires.
☎02.99.89.71.22
Closed *Mon and Tues out of season; Mon only during July–Aug and school holidays.*
Disabled access. Car park.

A place frequented by locals and tourists alike. The walls are made from dressed stone and adorned with old photographs, and the tables are nicely set. At the back of the dining room there's a long range with a double line of hot plates to cook the crêpes – all the dishes are made to order. The crêpes and galettes are crispy and delicate. There's nothing revolutionary here but everything is very tasty. Good range of Breton ciders; try the Ker Avel. About €12 for a meal; they also do a takeaway service. *Free apéritif offered to our readers on presentation of this guide.*

|●| Le Surcouf

7 quai Gambetta.
☎02.99.89.61.75 Ⓕ02.99.89.76.41
Closed *Wed and Thurs except July–Aug; 3 weeks in Jan; 15 Nov–15 Dec.*

This gourmet restaurant stands out from the rest of the establishments along the port. The produce used is not only wonderful but the ingredients are deftly and creatively prepared and cooked. The setting is carefully designed in quiet good taste. Menus cost from €18 (not served on Sun) to €60. Not cheap, but definitely worth the extra.

|●| Au Pied d'Cheval

10 quai Gambetta.
☎02.99.89.76.95
Closed *15 Nov–Palm Sunday.* **Disabled access.**

Service 9am–9pm (10pm in summer). "Unbeatable oysters" says the slogan, and the oyster-farming family who run this place are not wrong. The seafood and cooked dishes (not available Nov–April) are great too – the ingredients are ultra-fresh. Try the *écuelle du Père Dédé*, a mixture of shellfish in a creamy lemony sauce, the mussels, or the *patouillou* (whelks) *à l'armoricaine*. The tables and stools on the ground floor are rustic but the upstairs dining room is more comfortable. You'll pay between €18 and €50 for a meal depending on how hungry you are. Good wines.

|●| Restaurant Le Saint-Cast

Route de la Corniche; it's a 5-min walk from the centre.
☎02.99.89.66.08 Ⓕ02.99.89.89.20
Closed *Wed; plus Tues and Sun out of season; mid-Nov to mid-Dec and during the Feb school holidays.*

A delicious restaurant in all senses of the word. It's just outside the town in an elegant building overlooking the sea – with Mont-Saint-Michel away in the distance – and an ideal place to spend a delightful evening dining on fresh seafood expertly but simply cooked. The €20 menu served at lunch and dinner during the week is remarkable for quality and balance. Other menus up to €37 feature specialities prepared in the same vein; €50 for à la carte. Reservations recommended.

Saint-Méloir-des-Ondes

35350 (5km SW)

🏠 |●| La Maison Richeux- Le Coquillage, Bistrot Marin

Le Point-du-Jour.
☎02.99.89.25.25 Ⓕ02.99.89.88.47
Ⓦwww.maisons-de-bricourt.com
Closed *Mon; Tues and Thurs lunchtimes; plus Fri lunchtime in winter.* **TV. Car park.**

A ravishing 1920s manor house looking down over the Mont-Saint-Michel bay. The prices in the restaurant are fair when all is said and done, and the wines are affordable, but the lovely bedrooms are very expensive indeed – €160–310 depending on the season. The whole place shows great refinement and good taste, with a country interior with checked and plaid fabrics, leather chairs, a bar and a wide fireplace. The sea views are breathtaking. There are no à la carte options; menus €26–47, with a children's menu for €15.30; *formule grignotage* for two €57 including three cold and three hot dishes. Olivier Roellinger, the darling of Breton cuisine, produces the best dishes from what the sea has to offer. Breakfast is fabulous, based on traditional Breton produce.

Carantec

29660

|●| La Cambuse et Le Cabestan

7 rue du Port.
☎02.98.67.08.92 Ⓕ02.98.67.90.49

Ⓦ www.lecabestan.fr Ⓔ le-cabestan @wanadoo.fr
Closed *Mon except July–Aug; Tues; 5 Nov–15 Dec.* **High chairs available. Disabled access.**

Two restaurants in one here: La Cambuse and Le Cabestan. Choose the one that suits your mood; the chef is the same for both but the serving staff and atmospheres are very different. La Cambuse is a mixture of a brasserie, a bar and an inn. Generous portions of filling brasserie food and Breton specialities are served at reasonable prices. Next door at Le Cabestan the mood is quieter, even hushed. With its smart décor and softly spoken diners, this is the place for a romantic dinner. The cuisine is more refined, too, featuring pan-fried scallops and prawns with thyme. À la carte you will pay about €20 at La Cambuse, and €30–40 at Le Cabestan.

Carhaix-Plouguer

29270

Crêperie les Salines

23 rue Brizeux; it's near the tourist office.
Ⓣ 02.98.99.11.32 Ⓕ 02.98.99.14.65
Closed *Tues–Thurs evenings; Sun out of season and on holidays; June to early July.*

They've created a maritime feel in the dining room. The tasty crêpes are made from Breton organic flour and stuffed with unusual fillings. Various weekday lunch *formules* for €7.50 except public holidays, and other menus up to €14.50. Good choices include salmon in seaweed preserve and a Breton crêpe with apple flambéed in Calvados and cream. À la carte, go for the *fleur grand cru* with Guéméné *andouille* and cider preserve. A quality place for all budgets.

Carnac

56340

Hôtel Le Râtelier**

4 chemin Douët.
Ⓣ 02.97.52.05.04 Ⓕ 02.97.52.76.11
Ⓔ bouvart@infonie.fr
Closed *Tues and Wed Oct–March; Jan.* **Disabled access (restaurant only). TV. Car park.**

A charming little hotel in an attractive house weighed down by ivy, tucked away down an alley in the town centre. Well-kept rooms for €38–51; most have shower/wc but a few have washing facilities only. Breakfast €6. Half board, from €43.50–55 per person, is compulsory for two people staying in July and Aug. First menu at €17 (not Sat evenings or public holidays) and others €26–40. Dishes change every three months, but they specialize in seafood and fish often served with complicated but delicious sauces. Depending on the season you might be offered John Dory pan-fried with baby vegetables, sea bream with fennel and cockles, terrine of house foie gras, or hot chocolate tart. One menu offers nothing but lobster in all shapes, sizes and styles.

Restaurant La Côte

Kermario. Take the Auray road and turn right at the first lights; it's 800m further, near the standing stones of Kermario.
Ⓣ and Ⓕ 02.97.52.02.80
Closed *Sat lunch, Sun evening and Mon out of season; Mon only in July and Aug; 5 Jan–10 Feb; a week in Oct and 3 weeks in Nov.* **Car park.**

Pierre Michaud has transformed the family restaurant into the best restaurant in the district. You will taste dishes of rare subtlety here; a concentration of tastes and colours that will transport you for a couple of hours. A starter that mixes fish and meat sets the tone and whets your appetite: terrine of foie gras with Chinese pepper, veal sweetbreads and sardines. The main courses include fillet of sea bream with ginger *rillette*, buckwheat pancake with red onion, chorizo and tomatoes – a surprising explosion of flavours. The menus change every three months. Extremely pleasant service. There's a menu at €21 (not served Sun) and €31–49. You will pay around €40 à la carte.

Châteaulin

29150

Crêperie Marc Philippe

29 quai Cosmao; it's very close to the tourist office.
Ⓣ 02.98.86.38.00
Closed *Mon out of season; April–Sept.*

A very small, very central crêperie. The crêpes are fairly priced and taste great. A meal will cost around €10. It's a cheerful place where they use quality local produce, including Fouesnant cider and local beer; all the grain is grown in Brittany. *Free coffee offered to our readers on presentation of this guide.*

Plomodiern

29550 (15km W)

Auberge des Glazics

Rue de la Plage; take the D887, then the D47.
02.98.81.52.32
Closed *Mon; Tues; Oct.*

In the early nineteenth-century these premises were used as a blacksmith's foundry. As so many customers came, the blacksmith's wife decided to offer them soup, and her grandchildren have continued this culinary tradition, although in less modest style: Olivier Bellin has been declared the best young chef in Brittany. He has set out to prove that Breton cooking means not only the fine, fresh produce provided by nature but also a creative approach to it; his imagination seems to know no bounds, and his desserts, in particular, are a veritable symphony of tastes and colours. Weekday lunchtime menu €23, with others €35.50–69.50; children's menu €10.70. Reckon on €38 à la carte. Excellent wines. Booking essential. The service and atmosphere could be improved by setting a more relaxed tone.

Combourg

35270

Hôtel du Lac**

2 pl. Chateaubriand; it's on the Rennes road.
02.99.73.05.65
www.hotel-restaurant-du-lac.com
Closed *Fri and Sun evening out of season; Feb.* **TV. Car park.**

This place has a tranquil charm, and it's just a little old-fashioned. On one side there is the château and on the other the lake which was so dear to the writer Chateaubriand. Rooms for €49–80 depending on the facilities; they're fine, though the décor is dated. Ask for a room with a view – it's worth paying extra. Breakfast €8–8.50. Good, traditional dishes in the restaurant. Set menus €16–39; à la carte about €30.

Restaurant L'Écrivain

Place Saint-Gilduin; it's opposite the church.
02.99.73.01.61
Closed *Wed evening; Thurs; Sun evening; Thurs only mid-July to mid-Aug; Feb holidays; All Saints holidays.* **Disabled access. Car park.**

This restaurant has a good reputation, built up over a number of years. The prices are low considering the inventive flavours presented to you, and though there's a limited choice à la carte, that's because the chef uses only the freshest produce: try the home-smoked fish, cod with cockle jus, or *millefeuille* of house foie gras and artichokes. Set menus €14 (weekday lunchtimes) then €20.50, with à la carte costing about €30. The restaurant name means "The Writer" and they sell illustrated books here too.

Hédé

35630 (15km SW)

Restaurant Le Genty Home

Vallée de Hédé; it's on the N137 in the direction of Tinténiac, 500m outside Hédé.
02.99.45.46.07 02.99.45.50.61
Closed *Tues evening; Wed; Sun evening out of season; 3 weeks end Feb–March; fortnight in Oct.* **Disabled access.**

It's hard not to fall for this charming, flower-bedecked hostelry with natural stone walls and a huge fireplace. It's run by a highly talented young chef who has already attracted a following of food lovers. His cooking is excellent and even the most demanding of foodies will be intrigued by the selection of dishes he puts on his menus. Delicious weekday lunch menu at €10.60 and four others €18.50–32. Specialities include asparagus tips with Cancale oysters, *escalope* of foie gras with a scallop kebab, pigeon breast stuffed with foie gras and sea bass with leeks and balsamic sauce. *Free coffee offered to our readers on presentation of this guide.*

Concarneau

29900

Hôtel des Halles

Place de l'Hôtel-de-Ville; in the town centre, near the enclosed town.
02.98.97.11.41 02.98.50.58.54
www.hoteldeshalles.com
Car park.

Small, modern hotel that is constantly being made more comfortable. Although it is right in the town centre, it is a quiet spot. All the rooms are different, but they are equally attractive and regularly refurbished. Doubles €35 with shower, €48–57 with shower/wc or bath. Two single rooms available. Breakfast €6. The hotel has come to an agreement with the restaurant and brasserie *L'Amiral* so that its guests can take advantage of special half-board rates. The owner is a friendly man who'll happily ply you with information about the region. *10% discount on a room (out of season) offered to our readers on presentation of this guide.*

Citôtel de France et d'Europe**

9 av. de la Gare.
☎02.98.97.00.64
Ⓦwww.groupecitotel.com/hotels/fraeur.html
Closed *Sat evening (15 Nov–15 March); New Year.* **Disabled access. TV. Pay car park.**

Well-positioned in the centre of town, this hotel offers the kind of pleasant, comfortable rooms – with telephones, alarm clocks, and efficient double-glazing – that you would expect from a modern hotel. Enjoy a drink in the bar or on the sheltered terrace. Double rooms €50 with shower/wc or €58 with bath; buffet breakfast €6.

Hôtel Kermor**

Les Sables Blancs.
☎02.98.97.02.96
Ⓦwww.kermorlespiedsdansleau.com
TV.

The Kermor is a characterful turn-of-the-(twentieth)-century hotel right on the beach. Inside it's been beautifully decorated with lithographs, etchings and photographs from the 1920s. Rooms are bright and fresh, with wood panelling and, to complete the illusion, some have portholes for windows. Each one has a sea view, and the most expensive have huge bay windows and wooden balconies. Double with shower/wc €64–70. The splendid breakfast room has a fantastic view of the sea too. Breakfast, €9, is served until 11.30am.

Crêperie Aux Remparts

31 rue Théophile-Louarn.
☎02.98.50.65.66
Closed *Nov–Easter.*

Outside, a stone façade with carvings in floral designs and a quiet terrace; inside, a rustic setting complete with fireplace. Effusive welcome. Fine, professional cooking, with plenty of seafood. Menu €11. Our first recommendation in the enclosed town. *Free apéritif offered to our readers on presentation of this guide.*

L'Amiral

1 av. Pierre-Guéguin; in the town centre, opposite the enclosed town and the bridge.
☎02.98.60.55.23
Closed *Mon (July–Aug); Sun evening and Mon (other months); fortnight in Sept.*

The façade of this old building hides a beautiful modern, dining room, with decoration on a nautical theme centred on brown wood panelling, blue benches and elegant lamps. The young chef, Arnaud Lebossé, served his apprenticeship in some of France's top restaurants (*Le Récamier, Troisgros, La Pérouse*), and the fruits of this experience are plain to see in his inventive cooking that varies according to the availability of fresh ingredients. The menu changes every day, but some of his dishes have already become classics: John Dory with herbs, *cassolette* of squid, lobster pancakes with shellfish *coulis*, chocolat gateau, etc. The bread rolls, foie gras and ice creams are all made on the premises. The menus offer excellent value for money: €14 (lunchtime), €17, €21 and €24 (excellent "Simenon" menu); children's menu €7. Reckon on €40 à la carte. Alongside the restaurant, a brasserie with a menu at €11.

Restaurant Chez Armande

15 bis av. du Docteur-Nicolas; it's opposite the marina.
☎02.98.97.00.76
Closed *Tues and Wed out of season; Wed only in summer; during Feb and Christmas school holidays.*

One of the best seafood restaurants in Concarneau and the prices go down well, too. Lovely panelling and pleasant furniture in the dining room, which also has a fishtank brimming with crustaceans. Excellent fresh fish and seafood straight from the quay, which is just a stone's throw away. The cheapest set menu costs €18.60 (not Sat evening and Sun), and there are others at €24.60 up to €34. Reckon on about €50 à la carte. The *cotriade*, a Breton five-fish soup, is the signature dish. You would return to this place for that alone. Good selection of desserts from the trolley.

Conquet (Le)

29217

Le Relais du Vieux Port

1 quai du Drellac'h.
Ⓣ02.98.89.15.91
Disabled access (restaurant). High chairs available.

In times gone by this old harbour inn provided simple rooms and a restaurant. But after substantial alterations it has been upgraded to the standards of a modern hotel. It's a friendly place, run by a family who know how to make you feel welcome. Stripped wooden floors and white walls are gently brightened up with blue stencilling. Five rooms with a view of the estuary go for €38–63 with shower/wc – really excellent prices for the quality but the cheapest room only has a shower. The dining room is a relatively new addition to the building and they've put in an open fireplace – there's a good choice of crêpes, seafood and good quality fish dishes. A meal à la carte will cost around €10–20. Live music on Wednesday evening in summer. *Free apéritif and one free breakfast per room per night offered to our readers on presentation of this guide.*

La Ferme de Keringar

It's in the village.
Ⓣ02.98.89.09.59 Ⓕ02.98.89.04.39
Ⓦwww.keringar.com
Restaurant closed *lunchtimes out of season.*
High chairs available.

The farm is sheltered from the wild sea storms between Le Conquet and the Pointe de Saint-Mathieu and has been in the same family for over two hundred years. The current owner used to teach primary school kids and is a passionate advocate of organic farming: he's turned the farm into a teaching centre and it also provides a welcome stopping place for walkers. Half board only: stay in one of the eight attractively arranged rooms with shower/wc for €40–42 per person per night. In the restaurant there's a massive granite fireplace and wooden tables and benches. The cuisine is a mixture of fish and meat and offers good value for money: *cotriade*, *kig ha farz*, Molène sausage smoked over seaweed, as well as oat broth and bacon *andouille*. Bread is baked on-site. Menus €15–40. There's a shop selling their produce. *Free apéritif offered to our readers on presentation of this guide.*

Crach

56400

Restaurant Crêperie L'Hermine

12 rue d'Aboville.
Ⓣ and Ⓕ02.97.30.01.17
Closed *Mon–Wed out of season; Tues evening and Wed April–June and Sept; end Nov to early Dec.*

You can't miss this lovely house, festooned with flowers. The dining room is bright and pleasant, and there is also a lovely veranda opening onto the rock garden. There's no set menu but a wide choice of galettes, and fish and seafood dishes. Anyone with a sweet tooth will be spoilt for choice between the tempting desserts. A meal will cost around €12. There's a children's play area, too. It's a good idea to reserve. *Free Breton Kir or coffee offered to our readers on presentation of this guide.*

Crozon

29160

Hôtel de la Presqu'île – Restaurant Le Mutin Gourmand

1 rue Graveran; it's on the church square.
Ⓣ02.98.27.29.29 or 02.98.27.06.51
Ⓕ02.98.26.11.97
Ⓦwww.chez.com/mutingourmand
Closed *Sun evening, Mon and Tues lunchtime out of season; Mon lunchtime in season; mid-Jan to Feb.* **Disabled access. TV.**

A charming hotel that radiates the true style of Brittany. The décor is inspired by the yellow and ochre of local costumes, Breton pottery and the sea. Double rooms €44–66 in low season, €47–72 in high season. There are several dining rooms decorated in the same style. Menus €16 (not public holidays) and €23–49. Very good cuisine using fresh market produce: egg *chaud-froid* and sea-urchin coral, fillet of yellow pollack with black wheat pancake and very good desserts. Everything from the bread to the foie gras is prepared in their kitchens.

Damgan

56750

Crêperie L'Écurie

31 Grande-Rue à Kervoyal.

Ⓣ02.97.41.03.29
Closed *Mon–Fri (except school holidays) out of season; early Jan to Feb half-term.* **Disabled access.**

L'Écurie is a local institution that was founded in 1967 and recently changed hands. Crêpes from €5.40–8.40. Reckon on around €15 for a full meal. The crêpes are original and delicious, crispy on top and moist inside, as well as being superbly presented. Highlights include the Kerjeannette, with its mustard cream, or for dessert you could try the Arthurette, with vanilla ice cream, caramel, almonds and Chantilly. Gigantic salads are also available. You can eat under the pergola overrun with vines and ivy or in the cosy wood-panelled dining room; either way, a good time is guaranteed. *Free coffee offered to our readers on presentation of this guide.*

Dinan

22100

Auberge de jeunesse Moulin du Méen

Vallée de la Fontaine-des-Eaux; 600m from the port; from the end of the port, take the Plouer road and then another little one on the left (it's signposted); 2km from the train station: cross the track, then turn right and follow the signposts.
Ⓕ02.96.39.10.83 Ⓕ02.96.39.10.62
Ⓔdinan@fuaj.org

Old windmill in a charming, wooded valley. With an FUAJ card (compulsory, on sale *in situ*), €9.30 per night. Half board (with reservation only) €21.20. Breakfast €3.30. 75 beds in dormitories, rooms with one–eight beds and a few doubles with shower/wc at the same rate. Eight beds in a large tent (€5.30 per night), and you can also camp in your own tent. Fully equipped kitchen, sitting room with fireplace, piano and guitar available. Trekking in the surrounding countryside and photography courses.

Hôtel Les Alleux**

Route de Ploubalay, Tanen; take the D2 in the direction of Ploubalay and it's in a ZAC.
Ⓣ02.96.85.16.10
Ⓔhotel.alleux@wanadoo.fr
Restaurant closed *Sun evening out of season; Nov to end-Feb.* **Disabled access. TV. High chairs available. Car park.**

A modern hotel surrounded by greenery with comfortable rooms. Doubles cost €44–56, breakfast €6.10. On weekdays there's a lunchtime *formule* at €10.50. Menus in the restaurant for €14.90 (not Sun) and €26; specialities include cod with bacon and lentils. It's popular with groups. *One free breakfast per room or 10% discount on the room rate (in March and Oct) offered to our readers on presentation of this guide.*

Interhôtel Les Grandes Tours**

6 rue du Château; it's opposite the château.
Ⓣ02.96.85.16.20
Ⓔcarregi@wanadoo.fr
Closed *mid-Dec to Jan.* **High chairs available. TV. Pay car park.**

Victor Hugo and Juliette Drouet stayed here on 25 June 1836 while they were on a five-week tour of the west of France. "They dined, spent a pleasant night and dined there again the following evening. They found the hotel to their taste." The recommendation still holds good, especially considering the recent updating that's been done – the refurbished rooms on the second floor are more pleasant. It's a quiet place. Doubles with shower/wc or bath €45–48 with bath. Breakfast €5. Half board is available for a minimum stay of three nights. You can dine in the neighbouring restaurant (and arrange half board) where there's a menu for €12. The car park is in the courtyard, though there's a charge in summer. *One free breakfast per room per night offered to our readers on presentation of this guide.*

Hôtel Le Challonge**

29 pl. Du-Guesclin.
Ⓣ02.96.87.16.30 Ⓕ02.96.87.16.31
Ⓦwww.lechallonge.fr.st
Disabled access. TV.

Eleven of the twenty rooms look over the square but don't worry about noise – the double glazing is efficient. Doubles cost €56–67 with shower/wc or bath. Breakfast, €7, includes a basket of pastries. There are some family rooms, with a connecting room with two single beds. There's also a room especially adapted for disabled visitors. All the bathrooms have heated towel rails. Weekday lunch menu €12 and others €15–29.

Hôtel d'Avaugour***

1 pl. du Champ.

02.96.39.07.49 Ⓕ 02.96.85.43.04
Ⓦ www.avaugourhotel.com
Closed *Jan; Nov to end Dec.* **TV. High chairs available. Disabled access.**

Cosy hotel in the centre of Dinan. Very comfortable, recently refurbished rooms; some (principally nos. 19, 28 and 38) overlook the garden and the town's ramparts. Doubles €65–150, depending on the season and the exhibition. A few suites at €130. *Free apéritif offered to our readers on presentation of this guide.*

Crêperie des Artisans

6 rue du Petit-Fort.
Ⓣ 02.96.39.44.10
Closed *Mon; Oct to end–March.*

A beautiful building in a charming street in the old town. It's an ancient residence with a rustic setting, bare stone walls and wooden tables. The relaxed atmosphere is enlivened by the really friendly owners. Excellent traditional crêpes and galettes and cider from the barrel. There are four menus from €7.50 (lunchtime) to €12.50. They play nice music and, in summer, set up a large wooden table in the street.

Restaurant La Courtine

6 rue de la Croix.
Ⓣ 02.96.39.74.41
Closed *Wed; Wed and Sun evening in winter; a weekend of June; fortnight in Nov.*

A warm and cosy dining room in a quiet side street. The fresh, friendly decoration provides a nice setting for the cuisine. Everything comes straight from the market and the fish and seafood are skilfully prepared. Weekday lunchtime formules €11.50 and €13.80; then menus €16–35. Specialities include duck in cider and red mullet *à la provençale. Free coffee offered to our readers on presentation of this guide.*

Le Léonie

17 rue Rolland.
Ⓣ 02.96.85.47.17
Closed *Sun and Mon in July–Aug; rest of year Sun evening, Mon, Thurs evening; a week in Feb; a week in May; last week of Aug; 1st fortnight in Sept.*
Disabled access.

In a good spot in the centre but away from the tourist hordes. This is the first establishment run by a young pair who have built up a faithful, local clientele. The dining room isn't that big but you don't get distracted by the proximity of your neighbours because your attention is focussed on what's on your plate. The young chef produces creative but in no way pretentious dishes using quality, seasonal produce. Just try to resist the dark chocolate *pavé*. At lunchtimes from Tuesday to Saturday, they serve a dish of the day with a coffee for €7.80; add a dessert and it costs €9. Opt for a starter/main course or main course/dessert menu and it will cost €12.50; it's €15.50 for starter/main course/dessert. A really nice place.

Le Bistrot du Viaduc

22 rue du Lion-d'Or, Lanvallay; take the road to Rennes, and you'll see the restaurant on the left at the bend, just beyond the viaduct.
Ⓣ 02.96.85.95.00 Ⓕ 02.96.85.95.05
Ⓦ www.lebistrotduviaduc.com
Closed *Mon; Sat lunch; Sun evening; the 2nd fornight in June; 20 Dec–15Jan.* **Disabled access. Car park.**

Incredible views of the Rance valley from this restaurant, which is in a splendid setting and has a pleasant interior with pastel colours and a stove in the dining room. They serve delicious local cuisine, including *millefeuille* of artichoke and crab, scallops with herb salad, *croustillant* of pig's trotters with morel reduction, *tian* of scallops and salmon with courgettes, grilled fish with fennel, pigeon braised with truffle *jus*, and cod *à la Bretonne*. There's a short weekday lunch menu for €15.50 and others €28.50 and €38.50; à la carte you'll pay somewhere in the region of €58. They offer a range of affordable wines. Booking is essential.

Plélan-Le-Petit

22980 (13km W)

Le Relais de la Blanche-Hermine

Lieu-dit Lourmel; take the N176 towards Jugon-les-Lacs. At the Plélan-le-Petit roundabout take the old road signposted for the zone artisanal. The restaurant is 800m on the left.
Ⓣ 02.96.27.62.19 Ⓕ 02.96.27.05.93
Closed *Tues and Wed evening, plus Mon evening in winter.*

This restaurant has a good reputation in the region and is housed in a long stone building by the road. Spacious, lively dining room. Classy cooking with menus €18–46. Reckon on €25 à la carte. Specialities include couscous (every Fri), roast suckling pig on the spit (first and third Thurs of every month), and spit-roast lamb (Sun). Seafood or shellfish must be ordered in advance.

Dinard

35800

Hôtel Les Mouettes

64 av. George-V; it's 50m from the Yacht Club.
Ⓣ02.99.46.10.64
Ⓦwww.hotel-les-mouettes.com
Closed *Jan.* **TV.**

A pleasant family hotel with ten charming, cosy rooms which are freshly decorated with a hint of the sea – they're €32–37, depending on facilities and season. Breakfast €5. It's friendly, simple and inexpensive, a rarity in Dinard. Ask at reception for information about parking.

Restaurant L'Escale à Corto

12 av. George-V.
Ⓣ02.99.46.78.57
Closed *lunchtimes.*

Service until midnight. A lively little restaurant, popular with young locals. It is also known as *Restaurant des Marins*. Dod is the barman, while Marie runs the kitchen, producing seafood salad, oysters, salmon *tartare* and various other fish dishes. There are no set menus, but you can enjoy a good, healthy meal for around €18. This restaurant is only open in the evening, as Corto likes to take a nap on the beach in the afternoon. *Free apéritif offered to our readers on presentation of this guide.*

Didier Méril

6 rue Yves-Verney.
Ⓣ02.99.46.95.74 Ⓕ02.96.16.07.75
Ⓔdidiermeril@wanadoo.f.

Didier Méril has created one of the best restaurants in Dinard yet he's barely 30 years old. He's full of passion and creativity and has recruited a dynamic young team – the welcome comes with a smile and good humour. The setting is a tad minimalistic but not unappealing. The presentation on the plates is original and meticulous and matches the inventive and delicious cuisine. Seafood dishes predominate à la carte and they change frequently. Weekday lunch menu €20 and others €27–99. One of the great temptations is the home-made bread – there are eight different types of rolls so go easy because the desserts are too good to miss.

Dol-de-Bretagne

35120

Grand Hôtel de la Gare**

21 av. Aristide-Briand.
Ⓣ02.99.48.00.44 Ⓕ02.99.48.13.10
Closed *a week in Feb; 2nd fortnight in Oct.* **TV.**

A small, plain and unpretentious hotel with double rooms at €30–40 depending on facilities and season. Breakfast €4.70. The new owners have refurbished. There's a lively café on the ground floor.

Douarnenez

29100

Le Keriolet

29 rue Croas-Talud; this is the prolongation of rue Jean Jaurès.
Ⓣ02.98.92.16.89Ⓕ02.98.92.62.94
Closed *Mon (out of season); Feb half-term (zone A).*

This slightly eccentric hotel close to the Plomatc'h footpath has recently been redecorated. Eight comfortable rooms, four of which (the most expensive) overlook the bay. Doubles with shower/wc. €40–45. Half board €48 per person. The restaurant serves tasty, traditional dishes prepared with a dash of creativity: flambée of langoustines with pastis, mussels in cider, ray with warm raspberry vignaigrette. Friendly service . *10% discount on a room (Oct–March) offered to our readers on presentation of this guide.*

Hostellerie Le Clos de Vallombreuse***

7 rue Estienne-d'Orves; it's near the Sacré-Cœur church.
Ⓣ02.98.92.63.64 Ⓕ02.98.92.84.98
Ⓔclos.vallombreuse@wanadoo.fr
Disabled access. TV. Swimming pool. Car park.

An elegant, early twentieth-century building very close to the church and overlooking the sea – beautifully decorated inside. The rooms are charming and bright, some with a sea view; they go for €52–116. Charming welcome. Menus €16–53. One of the good restaurants in town.

Crêperie Au Goûter Breton

36 rue Jean-Jaurès.
☎02.98.92.02.74 or 06.62.68.17.80
Closed *Sun and Mon in winter except during school holidays; fortnight end of June; fortnight end of Nov.*

Lots of character here: the proprietor gets around on a Harley-Davidson or in a Cadillac, and inside the décor is very Breton with a soundtrack of Breton bagpipe music mixed with plenty of jazz and rock. It's no surprise to find an American hamburger among the list of crêpes. Crêpe menus from €8–14 and a children's menu for €7.30. Flower-filled terrace to the rear.

L'Athanor

1 rue Henri-Barbusse.
☎02.98.92.88.97
Closed *Tues (except July–Aug); 3 weeks in March; 3 weeks in Oct.*

The tiled décor evokes Spain, and the food on offer will confirm your first impressions: tapas, grilled peppers, Spanish rice dishes (including paella, a meal in itself with different variations, at €16–30). Breton dishes are also served, however. Dish of the day €10; lunch menu €13, except Sunday and public holidays. Other menus €18–31, including a Spanish menu at €26. Children's menu €7.80. Splendid, extensive wine list with vintages from Portugal, Argentina, Chile, Brazil, Mexico, Uruguay and even Bordelais.

Le Saint-Pierre

5 rte. des Roches-Blanches à Tréboul.
☎02.98.74.03.33
Closed *Wed; 5 Jan–10 Feb.*

Didier and Antoinette will welcome you into their little hotel on the Sables-Blancs beach with a panoramic view of the bay. Three double rooms at around €40. Good traditional cooking, with specialities like fried scallops, flambéed langoustines, lobster salad with garden herbs, fish couscous, locally made *tuiles*. You can sample these delicacies on the lovely terrace. Menus €15–38. Reckon on €35 à la carte.

Erquy

22430

Hôtel Beauséjour**

21 rue de la Corniche.
☎02.96.72.30.39
hotel.beausejour@wanadoo.fr
Restaurant closed *Sun evening and Mon Oct–June; during Christmas school holidays.*
Disabled access. High chairs available. TV. Car park.

Only 100m from the port lies this small, traditional holiday hotel. Well-maintained, light and airy doubles with shower/wc €47–62. Breakfast €6.50. Moderately priced restaurant with generously served set menus at €16–30: specialities include seafood *choucroute* and scallop kebabs with crab *coulis*. Substantial fare. Half board, obligatory 10 July–31 Aug, is good value at €50–62 per person.

La Cassolette

6 rue de la Saline.
☎02.96.72.13.08
delanglecassolette@wanadoo.fr
Closed *Tues lunchtime; Thurs and Fri lunchtime out of season; 15 Nov–15 Feb.*
High chairs available.

The locals are lucky enough to have two excellent restaurants in town (the other is *L'Escurial*). This one is run by a nice woman who was smart enough to hire a young chef who trained in some excellent kitchens. He uses the best seafood straight from the sea: scallop ravioli, langoustines with orange sauce, semi-cooked foie gras with cider, *cassolette* of crayfish with orange, *andouille* with cider butter, veal kidneys with Pommeau sauce and, for dessert, a Byzantin with two chocolates. Prices are reasonable – there's a weekday lunch formule at €12, a weekday lunch menu at €14, and menus for €22–40 or €40 à la carte. Eat in the cosy little dining room, with its large chimney, or out in the garden-terrace on sunny days. *Liqueur on the house offered to our readers on presentation of this guide.*

Saint-Aubin

22430 (3km SW)

Restaurant Le Relais Saint-Aubin

At the Super U roundabout, direction St-Aubin.
☎02.96.72.13.22 Ⓕ02.96.63.54.31

Closed *Mon July and Aug; Tues and Wed out of season; during Feb school holidays.* **Disabled access. Games available. Car park.**

Situated in a small hamlet, this peaceful, characterful seventeenth-century priory has its own garden. There's a ravishing dining room with ancient beams, antique furniture and a monumental granite fireplace. In summer you can eat on the terrace. A variety of set menus: one at weekday lunchtimes for €13 and others €19.50–32. There's also a dish of the day written up on the slate. Specialities include *fricassée* of mussels with bacon and cider, a *menu dégustation* with three scallop dishes, fish stew flavoured with cider, and grilled lobster with herb butter. A good selection of wines, including white or red Menetou Salon. Best to book in season and at the weekend.

Fouesnant

29170

Hôtel À l'Orée du Bois**

4 rue de Kergoadig.
Ⓣ02.98.56.00.06 Ⓕ02.98.56.14.17
Ⓦwww.hotel-oree-du-bois.fr.st
TV. Pay car park.

Small, classic family hotel that's been completely renovated. Good rooms at good prices: €31 with basin/wc, €42–49 with shower/wc and bath. Some have a sea view of the Cap-Coz or of the forest of Fouesnant. There are also rooms sleeping three or four. Walking trails start just nearby and the beach is three minutes away by car.

Hôtel Belle Vue**

30 descente Bellevue, Cap-Coz; 3km from the town.
Ⓣ02.98.56.00.33Ⓕ02.98.51.60.85
Ⓦhotel-belle-vue@wanadoo.fr
Closed *Nov–Feb; restaurant closed Mon (except for hotel guests).*

A quiet spot just a stone's throw from the sea. This hotel has stayed in the same family since 1919 but it still retains some of the atmosphere of its previous incarnation as a grocer's shop-cum-café. The rooms have a quaint charm, with flowery but discreet wallpaper and old furniture (although the ones overlooking the garden are more modern). Doubles with washbasin or shower €45–53, with shower/wc or bath €54–66. The restaurant is also old, but the chef is young and extremely talented. His fresh duck foie gras is delicious. Menus €15–32. Booking essential in season.

Hôtel de la Pointe de Mousterlin***

108 rte Pointe-Mousterlin; 6.5km from the town.
Ⓣ02.98.56.04.12 Ⓕ02.98.56.61.02
Ⓦwww.mousterlinhotel.com
Restaurant closed *Sun evening; Mon; Tues lunch.* **TV.**

This 44-room hotel has been in the same family for four generations, and this experience is reflected in the thoughtfulness of the service and the range of facilities: heated swimming pool, sauna, Jacuzzi, weights room, tennis courts, library and daily programme of activities and excursions. Double rooms €58–109. Half board €60–85.50 per person. The restaurant offers excellent, reasonably priced seafood served in a beautiful setting. Just below the hotel, the sand dunes invite guests to explore a natural setting that has remained largely untouched. An ideal place to spend a weekend.

Hôtel de La Pointe du Cap Coz

153 av. de la Pointe-du-Cap-Coz; 3 km from the town.
Ⓣ02-98-56-01-63 Ⓕ02-98-51-53-20.
Ⓦwww.hotel-capcoz.com
Closed *14 Dec–Feb half-term.* **Restaurant closed** *(out of season) Sun evening, Mon lunch and Wed.*

The rooms are gradually being refurbished, with no.10 particularly outstanding, both for its décor and its view. Doubles €59–86. Breakfast €7.50. Half board €61–75 per person. The restaurant has a deservedly high reputation in the area, so it is advisable to book. There are two dining rooms; one, reserved for hotel guests, looks out on the cove of Penfoulic. The dishes change every four months. Menus €20–40. Children's menu €11. Another excellent establishment that will not let you down.

Crêperie Saint-Nicolas

1 descente de Rozembars; on the way out of the town.
Ⓣ02.98.56.50.25
Closed *Wed; Sun lunch.*

This crêperie, set in a beautiful building,

offers an unpretentious selection of crêpes and pancakes, as well as salads and a copious dish of the day. The prices are very reasonable – reckon on €8. It's often packed, so it's best to book in season. Friendly service.

Forêt-Fouesnant (La)

29940 (4km NE)

Auberge du Saint-Laurent

6 rte. de Beg-Menez; on the tourist road from La Fôret-Fouesnant to Concarneau.
02.98.56.98.07
Closed *Tues evening; Wed; Mon evening (winter only).*

This beautiful inn provides exceptional value for money, matched by attentive service from the couple who run it. The setting is rustic but sophisticated, and in summer the French windows are thrown open so that guests can take full advantage of the garden and terrace. The food is a combination of traditional recipes and imaginative, seasonal cooking. Menus from €15 (weekday lunchtime) to €35; the cheapest dinner menu is €18. Highly recommended, but it is advisable to book.

Glomel

22110

La Cascade

5 Grande-Rue; it's on the main street.
02.96.29.60.44.
TV. Disabled access.

A pleasant little country hotel with pretty rooms in the main building and more in a brand new extension; €28 with basin, €32 with shower/wc. Some overlook the garden and are very quiet. Half board €30 per person. They serve a *menu ouvrier* in the restaurant available to hotel guests only at €9.50 (lunchtime) and €10 (evening).

Groux (Île de)

56590

Auberge de jeunesse du Fort du Méné

Fort du Méné; 1.3km from the port and town; take the coastal footpath to La Croix headland; by road, turn to the left of *Ty-Mad* and follow the signs.
02.97.86.81.38 02.97.86.52.43
Closed *15 Oct–31 March.* **Car park.**

The rooms with three to ten beds are a series of converted bunkers, now covered with murals painted by a German university professor, depicting characters like Asterix and the Little Prince. What a good idea to convert all this ill-advised concrete into a seaside youth hostel. Altogether, nearly 80 people can be accommodated here; two of the dormitories sleep nineteen people each, and the conditions are very basic. €7.35 per person, €6.50 in a twelve-bed tent and €5 if you're camping under your own devices. A small studio is also available. Breakfast €3.25. There's a covered dining room and several kitchens that can be used by guests. Clean toilets. New arrivals are received 8.30am–noon and 6–9pm (6–10pm in July–Aug). A youth hostel that has preserved the original spirit of the movement. Credit cards not accepted.

Hôtel de la Jetée**

It's in the port.
02.97.86.80.82
laurencetonnerre@fresbee.fr
Closed *5 Jan–5 March.*

The very last house on the right before you reach the sea, this is a picture-postcard of a place, fronted by a jetty with a lighthouse at the end, with anchored boats bobbing, gulls wheeling and squealing and the sea practically licking the hotel walls. The décor inside is tasteful and the rooms are pretty. Doubles with shower/wc €48 up to €79 with bath and a nice view of the coast. Breakfast €6.50. Credit cards not accepted.

Hennebont

56700

Hôtel-restaurant du Centre

44 rue du Maréchal-Joffre.
02.97.36.21.44
Closed *Sun evening and Mon except July–Aug.* **TV.**

A likeable young couple have taken over this grand old hotel and brought it up-to-date without sacrificing its simple provincial appeal. You will appreciate the patronne's charm and the excellent value. Doubles €26 with shower (wc on the landing) and others €32–36. Breakfast €5.

Half board is compulsory in July and Aug. Above all, though, this place is a very good restaurant, one of the best in town. Set menus – €12.20 in the week and others €20–37.50 – list good, honest dishes, particularly fish and seafood: grilled crayfish with cream, foie gras with fig preserve, *millefeuille* of swordfish and salmon with two sauces. *Free coffee offered to our readers on presentation of this guide.*

Hoëdic (Île de)

56170

Les Cardinaux

Ⓣ02.97.52.37.27 Ⓕ02.97.52.41.26
Closed *3 weeks in Oct; Sun evening and Mon out of season.* **Disabled access.**

Double rooms €50–80. Half board recommended (€45 per person). The three most attractive rooms look on to the garden, a further six are on the first floor; all have shower/wc. Intimate, old-fashioned, purple lounge. Pretty breakfast room, a bar in the front, and a restaurant tucked away to the rear. The house speciality is seafood sauerkraut. Menus €21–31. Booking absolutely essential: it is not only a delightful place, it's also the only hotel on the island. Even at the height of summer, however, the service does not lose its relaxed friendliness.

Landéda

29870

Hôtel La Baie des Anges***

350 rte. des Anges; it's on Aber-Wrac'h port.
Ⓣ02.98.04.90.04 Ⓕ02.98.04.92.27
Ⓦwww.baie-des-anges.com
Closed *Jan to mid-Feb.* **Disabled access. TV. Car park.**

Gorgeous hotel in a lovely, stylish house, dating from the early 1900s, set just across from the beach and overlooking the ocean. The views and sunsets are breathtaking. The place is full of light, and has an Art Deco feel. Spotless, attractively decorated rooms, some with sitting rooms, €68–90 with shower/wc or bath. Breakfast €12 with a choice of coffees, home-made jams, and bread and pastries from the local baker – delicious. There's a terrace and a lovely lounge with huge comfy armchairs and plenty of board games. *A glass of champagne per person (for two consecutive nights from 15 Feb–1 May and 1 Oct–25 Dec), offered to our readers on presentation of this guide.*

Landerneau

29800

L'Amandier**

55 rue de Brest; coming down from the station, turn right at the first set of traffic lights, 500m from the town centre.
Ⓣ02.98.85.10.89
Restaurant closed *Sun evening and Mon.* **TV.**

This hotel offers remarkable value. Very elegant interior, with attractive paintings and refined furniture. The rooms are particularly pleasant and have superior facilities. Doubles go for €48. Breakfast €6.50.

Resto de la Mairie

9 rue de la Tour-d'Auvergne; it's on the quay opposite the town hall.
Ⓣ08.98.85.01.83 Ⓕ08.98.85.37.07
Ⓦwww.restaurantdelamairie.com
Closed *Tues evening.* **Disabled access. High chairs and games available. Car park.**

A long, thin, friendly bar-restaurant. Plush décor with stained glass, red carpet and lush plants. The patronne has been running the place for thirty years with infectious *bonhomie*. For the kids, there's a tortoise called Nono which hides in the patio. Among the specialities try the marmite Neptune, a seriously good fish stew, made with scallops, monkfish, shrimps and prawns expertly cooked with cream and cognac (you'll have to wait thirty minutes for this, because it's prepared to order). Otherwise, depending on the season, try the mussels maison, scallops, monkfish and spring vegetable stew or, for carnivores, the *fricassée* of veal kidneys. Weekday lunchtime menu €9, and others €11.50–29. *A Breton kir on the house offered to our readers on presentation of this guide.*

Roche-Maurice (La)

29220 (4km NE)

Auberge du Vieux Château

4 Grand-Place.
Ⓣ02.98.20.40.52
Ⓦwww.amatable.fr
Closed *evenings in the week.* **Disabled access. Car park.**

A fine inn set in a peaceful village square near a lovely Breton church and in the shadow of a ruined eleventh-century château. It undoubtedly offers the best value for money in the Landerneau region. The first menu, €10, served on weekday lunchtimes, attracts crowds of people from all walks of life who know a good place to eat when they find one. There are others from €12–35, and a children's menu at €8.38. Specialities include a fish stew made with lemon sole and thyme.

5 BRETAGNE

Landevennec

29560

Saint-Patrick

Rue Saint-Guénole; it's next to the church.
ⓣ02.98.27.70.83
Closed *mid-Oct to mid-March*. **Restaurant closed** *Tues evening and Wed out of season*.

A charming little hotel in a peaceful village on the Crozon peninsula, with an unspoilt bistro where old wooden chairs scrape noisily on the tiled floor. There's a parade of aged Irish whiskeys on the shelf behind the cramped bar. Good home cooking in the restaurant with a lot of fish dishes. Specialities include lobster with orange or saffron cream. Menus start at €15 and then go up from €17, or you'll spend around €19 à la carte. The lovely rooms are just like you'd find in a private home: marble fireplaces and scattered ornaments. Rooms 1, 4 and 7 have windows overlooking the Rade de Brest. Doubles with basin €31–34. Breakfast €5.50.

Landivisiau

29400

Restaurant Le Terminus

94 av. Foch; head towards the town centre from the eastern edge of Landivisiau.
ⓣ02.98.68.02.00
Closed *Fri evening; Sat lunch; Sun evening*. **TV. Car park.**

One of the best transport cafés in Finistère. The number of lorries parked outside vouches for its success and unbeatable value for money. Weekday menu €10, others €12.50–22. The former comprises two starters (including seafood), main course with vegetables of choice, salad, cheese, dessert and coffee – plus some house wine to wash it down! There's also a restaurant alongside, with more traditional menus and a seafood platter.

Lannion

22300

Auberge de jeunesse Les Korrigans

6 rue du 73e-Territorial; 200m from the train station and 300m from the town centre.
ⓣ02.96.37.91.28 ⓕ02.96.37.02.06
ⓦwww.fuaj.org
Disabled access.

This youth hostel has recently been done up in pretty colours. Rooms with two and four beds. With an FUAJ card (compulsory, but can be bought in situ): €13.85–15,20 per person in a four-bed room with shower/wc. Possibility of half board. No curfew. Very friendly welcome. Fitted kitchen. The hostel organizes a host of artistic and sporting activities – bird-spotting hikes, a boomerang club, Breton dances, archery, acrobatic kite-flying, etc. – as well as supplying detailed information about what's going on in the area. *Le Pixie* bar-restaurant with concerts, exhibitions, story-telling, theatre. One of the most dynamic youth hostels around. Credit cards not accepted. *Group rates (except July–Aug) offered to our readers on presentation of this guide.*

Le Tire-Bouchon

8 rue de Keriavily.
ⓣ02.96.37.10.43
Closed *Sat lunch; Sun; Mon lunch*. **Disabled access.**

A restaurant with a warm, relaxed atmosphere that is noticeable as soon as you open the door. The menu proudly proclaims "No chips, no ketchup" and indeed the food is fresh, traditional – and very good. A board hanging on the wall announces several dishes of the day. Set menus €10–13 (weekday lunchtime), then €20–30. It is often full (a good sign), so don't arrive too late.

La Ville Blanche

It's 5km along on the Tréguier road, by Rospez.
ⓣ02.96.37.04.28 ⓕ02.96.46.57.82
ⓦwww.la-ville-blanche.com ⓔjaguin@la-ville-blanche.com
Closed *Mon; Wed and Sun evening out of*

season; a week end June to early July; 22 Dec–30 Jan. **Disabled access.**

Great cooking prepared by a pair of brothers who have gone back to their roots. If they offer to show you their aromatic herb garden, don't refuse. Their specialities are seasonal – scallops from October to March, Breton lobster from April to October. Try the pork knuckle pâté with foie gras, the roast brie with rhubarb or the *millefeuille* with caramelized apples. Weekday menu at €28 and others €42–70. You can also buy good wines by the glass, which is rare in a place of this quality.

Lesconil

29730

Grand Hôtel des Dunes**

17 rue Laennec.
Ⓣ02.98.87.83.03 Ⓕ02.98.82.23.44
Ⓔgrand.hoteldesdunes@wanadoo.fr
Closed *mid-Oct to Easter.* **TV. Car park.**

This huge establishment is in a fabulous location: one side looks out over a sand dune which falls away to the sea 100m beyond. There's a lovely walk from the hotel along the shore. The rooms have been refurbished; doubles from €55–66 depending on facilities and season. Breakfast €8.50. Half board, compulsory in July and Aug, costs from €60 per person. They're spacious and well appointed – obviously the ones with sea view are the best. The food is pretty good value, and even on the half-board menu there's lots of choice. Menus at €18.50 (not served Sun lunch) and €24.40–55.40.

Locquirec

29241

Hôtel Les Sables Blancs

15 rue des Sables-Blancs.
Ⓣ02.98.67.42.07 Ⓕ02.98.79.33.25
Closed *Tues; Wed in mid season; Jan–Feb.* **Car park.**

Small, chic hotel and crêperie, tucked away in the dunes facing Lannion Bay. Wild, magnificent setting and warm welcome. Doubles with shower/wc for €48–55. It has recently taken on a new look; its handful of bedrooms has been renovated and a cosy, little lounge added to its cheery dining room. Crêperie and salad menu can be enjoyed on a veranda looking out over the sea.

Guimaëc

29620 (3km W)

Le Caplan and Co

Poul-Rodou; take the Plouganou road out of Guimaëc and turn right at the third crossroads.
Ⓣ02.98.67.58.98 Ⓕ02.98.67.65.49
Open *daily in summer; out of season Sat, Sun and public holidays.* **Games available.**

Service noon–midnight in summer, out of season Sat 3–9pm, Sun and public holidays noon–9pm. Right at the end of a track, at the mercy of the howling winds, Le Caplan stands defiantly against the elements. Push open the door and you'll find a warm, friendly café-bookshop that is almost unique in France – a brilliantly successful combination of reading room and bar. Piles of books are strewn here and there on the tables, selected by Lan and Caprini, where fishermen and book-lovers can while away the hours over a drink or a book – or both. The menu is even more of a surprise in Brittany – it features a platter of Greek specialities at €9.50, served with Greek wine.

Locronan

29180

Crêperie Le Temps Passé

Rue du Four; close to the tourist office.
Ⓣ02.98.91.87.29
Closed *Mon and Tues (except July–Aug); 3 weeks in October.*

A beautiful building, with one room with a fireplace below and another upstairs. The menu lists 58 types of pancakes, ranging in price from €2.60–7; if this is not enough for you, you can always fall back on the salads and omelettes. Excellent service.

Loctudy

29750

Hôtel de Bretagne**

19 rue du Port.
Ⓣ02.98.87.40.21 Ⓕ02.98.66.52.71
Ⓔhoteldebretagne@msn.com

Disabled access. TV. Car park.

The renovation work they've done on this old building is exquisite – the two owners have added excellent facilities yet retained the building's character and charm. Lavishly decorated rooms, all with shower/wc and telephone, €40–60. Breakfast €6. Walkers and cyclists especially welcome. There's a sauna and a Jacuzzi.

|●| Relais de Lodonnec

3 rue des Tulipes, plage de Lodonnec; it's 2km south of Loctudy.
Ⓣ02.98.87.55.34
Closed *Mon July–Aug; Tues evening and Wed out of season; 15 Jan–15 Feb.*

This old granite fisherman's house, just 20m from the beach, is home to one of the region's up-and-coming restaurants. Pleasant ambience, with blond wood and exposed beams. Depending on the menu – they're €12 (weekday lunch) and €19–40 – you get platters of oysters or seafood and gratinéed sea trout or red mullet fillets in a sea urchin sauce. Specialities include scallops rosace with two sauces, hot foie gras and mushrooms in a pastry case, and grilled bass with basil. The wine list has affordable bottles to satisfy most tastes. Booking advised at weekends.

Lorient

56100

|●| Auberge de jeunesse

41 rue Victor-Schœlcher; take no. 2 bus from the town centre, to the "Auberge de Jeunesse" stop; by car, take the Lamor-Plage road and follow the signs.
Ⓣ02.97.37.11.65 Ⓕ02.97.87.95.49
Ⓔlorient@fuaj.org
Closed *New Year's holidays.* **Disabled access.**

Fairly new youth hostel with some degree of comfort (kitchen, small bar, TV room, table football, table tennis, etc.). Rooms with four or five beds and washbasins (be sure to book your bed in summer). €8.85 per person. Breakfast €3.25. Lunch and dinner (€8.40) available, but you must book first. Clean toilets. Internet connection (at extra charge). Superb place, albeit a little far from the town centre.

Hôtel les Pêcheurs*

7 rue Jean-Lagarde.
Ⓣ02.97.21.19.24
TV. Car park.

The rooms here are simple but impeccably clean. The cheapest ones don't have private facilities and there are communal ones along the corridor. Doubles €17 with basin, €28–34 with shower/wc or bath – excellent value for money for this town-centre establishment. Breakfast €5. On the ground floor, there's a brasserie-bar with a very welcoming owner. *Free apéritif offered to our readers on presentation of this guide.*

|●| Hôtel-restaurant Victor Hugo**

36 rue Lazare-Carnot; it's near the ferry terminal for Île de Groix, 5 mins' walk from the centre of town.
Ⓣ02.97.21.16.24 Ⓕ02.97.84.95.13
Ⓔhotelvictorhugo.lorient@wanadoo.fr
TV. Pay car park.

Warm welcome from the cheery patronne. Clean doubles with handbasin go for €27 up to €62 with bath/wc, depending on the season. Those overlooking the street are well soundproofed. Buffet breakfast €6.10. Dishes include house foie gras and fresh fish. 10% *discount on the room rate (Oct to end March) offered to our readers on presentation of this guide.*

|●| Hôtel-restaurant Gabriel**

45 av. de la Perrière; it's on the main road from Keroman fishing port.
Ⓣ02.97.37.60.76 Ⓕ02.97.37.50.45
Ⓦwww.hôtel-le-gabriel.com
Restaurant closed *Sat evening and Sun.* **TV.**

Small, unfussy hotel with an inexpensive, friendly restaurant. Modern, very clean doubles with shower/wc and telephone for €27–45; they add a supplement of €13 during the Interceltic Festival. Room no. 304, on the corner of the top floor, overlooks the'entrance to the harbours and the citadel of Port-Louis. The set menu costs €10 including wine (not served Sat night or Sun); you will pay around €15 for a meal à la carte. There's a nice atmosphere and warm welcome from the owner. *10% discount on the room rate offered to our readers on presentation of this guide.*

|●| Tavarn ar Roue Morvan

17 rue Poissonnière.
Ⓣ02.97.21.67.47 Ⓕ02.97.64.33.42
Ⓔroimorvan@wanadoo.fr

Closed *Sun.*

Service 11am–1am. A genuine Celtic establishment with a typical décor and serving dishes of the day for lunch and dinner – one meat, one fish – priced €5.80, €8 and €9. Reckon on €13 for a meal à la carte. It's tasty food, particularly the scallops with saffron, Breton soup with cabbage and sausage and the Irish mutton stew. They have a good range of red, white and rosé wines with dry cider as an alternative. There's lots of noisy music, creating a young, energetic atmosphere. They hold regular folk concerts and on Monday evenings there are classes in the Breton language. *Free apéritif offered to our readers on presentation of this guide.*

|●| Restaurant Le Pic

2 bd. du Maréchal-Franchet-d'Esperey; it's near the post office and the *médiathèque*.
Ⓣ02.97.21.18.29
Closed *Sat lunchtime; Sun.* **Disabled access.**

A pleasant spot with Parisian bistro décor and a terrace for sunny days. Simple, tasty cooking including roast noisette of lamb with rosemary, cod with aïoli, pig's trotters stuffed with oxtail, and chocolate fondant. Menus €15 (except Sunday evening) up to €40. The restaurant has just been included in the Qualité de France list, and the owner, Pierre Le Bourhis, is a wine connoisseur who was voted Brittany's best wine waiter in 1986. Have a good look in the cellar.

|●| Restaurant Le Jardin Gourmand

46 rue Jules-Simon; it's near the train station.
Ⓣ02.97.64.17.24 Ⓕ02.97.64.15.75
Closed *Sun and Mon; Feb school holidays; first fortnight in Sept.* **High chairs available. Disabled access.**

Delicious dishes concocted from the freshest local produce are served outside under a pergola and in the airy, elegant dining room. Courteous service from the host and skilful, creative cooking by his wife, who uses fresh market produce. Weekday lunch menu €17, with other menus at €21 and €32 at lunch and €18–48 in the evening. They all change daily. You'll spend €32 à la carte for an excellent meal including wine. There's a selection of coffees or teas on a special menu. One little perk for Rough Guide readers: the chef will reveal the recipe of a dish you particularly like. This is one of the best restaurants in Lorient so it's best to book.

Kervignac

56700 (10km E)

|●| Crêperie Hent er Mor

30 av. des Plages; take the N165.
Ⓣ02.97.65.77.17
Closed *Tues; Mon out of season; Oct.*
Disabled access. Car park.

There's such a range of crêpe fillings to choose from that it's hard to decide – the choice is huge. You'll pay between €1.60–5.50 for a savoury one while the sweet ones cost around €4.50. This place has been run by the same man since 1967 and he has a genuine passion for good crêpes; he's also a bit of a painter so the restaurant serves as an art gallery as well. You're invited to do your own painting on a pancake – the possibilities are limitless.

Port-Louis

56290 (20km S)

🏃 ⌂ |●| Hôtel-restaurant du Commerce**

1 pl. du Marché; take the N165 to Port Louis.
Ⓣ02.97.82.46.05 Ⓕ02.97.82.11.02
Closed *Sun evening and Mon out of season; mid-Jan to mid-Feb.* **TV.**

A quiet, comfortable hotel in the centre of town on a tranquil, tree-lined square with a small orchard behind. There are thirty-odd rooms, not all in the first flush of youth, but spacious and well maintained. Doubles €43 for a simple room with shower, €68 for a double with shower/wc up to €71 for a large room with bath/wc and TV. The cheapest menu in the week is €12, and there are others €16–37. You'll pay around €35 à la carte. Dishes to go for include mussels, flambéed scallops or pan-fried bass with saffron, and there's a nice long wine list. Half board, compulsory in July–Aug, is priced at €54.50–66.50 per person. *10% discount on the room rate Nov–March, and free apéritif offered to our readers on presentation of this guide.*

🏃 |●| La Grève de Locmalo

18 bis, rue Locmalo.
Ⓣ and Ⓕ02.97.82.48.41
Ⓔmarc.brunet.sanz@wanadoo.fr

Closed *Wed 3pm till Fri 7pm; All Saints' to end Feb.* **Disabled access. High chairs available.**

The recipe they use for the crêpe batter must have something unusual in it to produce such a light yet firm texture. And there are some unusual fillings, too: *La Grève* is stuffed with bacon, garlic butter and onions cooked in cider. The flambéed crêpe with crayfish is very good. They also do fish and seafood, depending on the catches landed, specializing in mussels and a tasty scallop kebab with Breton sauce. *Formule* (main meal plus dessert) at €12, or around €20 à la carte. The place is a charming stone building with a dining room in bright yellow and blue, on a charming little harbour with bobbing boats. *Free apéritif offered to our readers on presentation of this guide.*

Malestroit

56140

Restaurant Le Canotier

Place du Docteur-Queinnec.
Ⓣ02.97.75.08.69
Closed *Sun evening; Mon.*

You can choose to eat in a romantic dining room divided off by climbing vines or a lush terrace. Copious, fairly complicated dishes revolving around zander fillets, scallops, a wide selection of seafood (all the year round) and specialities from Lanvaux. Weekday lunchtime menu €9, then four others €12.50–26. Parking space is usually available in the place du Marché.

Chapelle-Caro (La)

56460 (12km N)

Le Petit Keriquel**

1 pl. de l'Église.
Ⓣ and Ⓕ02.97.74.82.44
Ⓦwww.lekeriquel.com
Closed *Sun evening out of season; Wed lunchtime July–Aug; the Feb school holidays.* **TV. High chairs and games available. Car park.**

This pretty Logis de France hotel has eight decent, inexpensive rooms mostly facing the church; doubles €37–41 with basin, shower/wc or bath. Breakfast €6. Half board is compulsory in Aug and costs €52 per person. In the restaurant, classic dishes are made from fresh ingredients and are generously served. Menus €10.50 (not served Sun) and €15–20.50. Dishes include salad of artichoke hearts with foie gras, *andouille de Guémené*, and roast belly of pork. *Free apéritif offered to our readers on presentation of this guide.*

Molac

56230 (13km SW)

Hôtel-restaurant À la Bonne Table

Place de l'Église.
Ⓣ02.97.45.71.88 Ⓕ02.97.45.75.26
Closed *Sun evening; Fri evening out of season; during Feb school holidays.* **TV.**

The old coaching house standing on the church square dates back to 1683. It offers clean and simple rooms with good beds above the restaurant for €24 with washing facilities only. The annexe, 100m from the restaurant, provides rooms with shower/wc, common entrance hall but private doors and a small sitting room; these are €29.50. Breakfast €4.90. There's a weekly rota of dishes of the day: fish couscous is Thursday's special, for example, and on Tuesday in winter they serve a hearty Breton soup. Try also the salmon roulé. Weekday lunch menu €8 (served in the evenings to guests only) and others €18–26. Welcoming, busy atmosphere with well-served traditional dishes and attractively laid tables. *Free coffee offered to our readers on presentation of this guide.*

Matignon

22550

Hôtel de la Poste**

11 pl. Gouyon; next to the station overlooking the railway tracks.
Ⓣ and Ⓕ02.96.41.02.20
Ⓦwww.hoteldelaposte.paysdematignon.net
Closed *Sun evening and Mon except July–Aug; 3 weeks in Jan; a fortnight in Oct.* **Disabled access. TV. High chairs available.**

This establishment is an ideal spot for exploring the whole region and a nice, quiet place to come back to in the evening for a good meal in comfortable surroundings. There are attractively priced bed and breakfast or half-board options. There's a family atmosphere and the welcome is kindly. Rooms are classic but pleasant and quiet. Doubles with basin €31 or €45 with shower/wc. The cuisine served in the restaurant is traditional, but shows dashes of real creativity. Specialities include seafood *pot-au-feu* and excellent house smoked salmon and foie gras. Weekday menu €12.50, with others €16–26. A nice, quiet little spot to stop. *Free apéritif offered to our readers on presentation of this guide.*

Crêperie de Saint-Germain

Saint-Germain-de-la-Mer, on the village square; from Matignon, drive 1km on the D786 in the direction of Fréhel, turn right for Saint-Germain and continue 2km.
02.96.41.08.33
Closed *1 Oct to Easter except for school holidays.*

It's worth making the trip to this seaside village for the best pancakes in the area. They're made using local black wheat flour and while the fillings are not unusual, Mme Eudes uses top-quality ingredients. And it's not pricey – expect to pay €9 or so for a meal. The old house is lovely and so is the garden terrace in summer. *Free coffee offered to our readers on presentation of this guide.*

Moëlan-sur-Mer

29350

Manoir de Kertalg****

Route de Riec: from Moëlan take the D24 towards Riec, and after 2km fork off to the right.
02.98.39.77.77
www.manoirdekertalg.com kertalg@free.fr
Closed *mid-Nov to mid-April.* **TV. Car park.**

An impressive building of hewn stone, smothered in ivy and set in grounds in the forest. The rooms are vast and individually decorated. Doubles and duplex rooms €90–180. You can eat breakfast till 10.30am (€11) on the magnificent terrace, which has a panoramic view over the countryside. They hold exhibitions in the tearoom.

Morlaix

29600

Hôtel du Port**

3 quai de Léon; it's 400m from the viaduct on the quayside.
02.98.88.07.54 02.98.88.43.80
www.1hotelduport.com
TV. High chairs available.

With its harbour view and reasonable prices, this little hotel offers value for money. Fresh, pleasant rooms with shower/wc or bath for €46–58 with bath. Breakfast €7. Pleasant welcome. *€6 discount (from second consecutive night's stay Oct–April) offered to our readers on presentation of this guide.*

Le Bains-Douches

45 allée du Poan-Ben; it's opposite the Palais de Justice on the river bank.
02.98.63.83.83
Closed *Sat lunchtime; Sun; Mon evening.*
Disabled access. High chairs available.

One of the most original restaurants in town. They've kept the turn-of-the-century feel, with the railings, tiles and etched glass from the old public baths. Decent bistro food at very reasonable prices. Specialities include a good range of seafood. You could start with the *galette* of roast goat's cheese followed by peppered duck steak or *fricassée* of rabbit in cider with gingerbread. The more adventurous can choose the kangaroo or ostrich. Good desserts. Weekday lunch menu €11 and others €14–23. *Free Kir offered to our readers on presentation of this guide.*

La Marée Bleue

3 rampe Saint-Mélaine.
02.98.63.24.21
Closed *Sun evening and Mon out of season; 3 weeks in Oct.*

A good fish and seafood restaurant. Elegant and intimate surroundings on two levels, with lots of wood and stone. Dishes are seasonal – the menus change every three months – and they're carefully prepared using very fresh ingredients. Set menus start at €13.50, or around €25 à la carte.

Mur-de-Bretagne

22530

Auberge Grand-Maison***

1 rue Léon-le-Cerf; it's near the church.
02.96.28.51.10 02.96.28.52.30
grandmaison@armornet.tm.fr
Closed *Sun evening and Mon July–Aug; Sun evening, Mon and Tues lunch Sept–June.* **TV. High chairs available.**

A smart place that will set you back a bit. Jacques Guillo is one of the best respected chefs in the *département*. Just read his menus: *escalopes* of marinated turbot, aubergine cannelloni with lamb *confit*, foie gras profiteroles with a truffle *coulis*, lobster *fricassée* with crisp vegetables, *tournedos* of pigs' trotters, potato pancakes with *andouille* and hot mandarin crêpes or honey ice cream. This is a serious gastronomic experience, as demonstrated by the prices: weekday lunch menu €28, with others €43–61. The nine magnificent rooms have been confidently redecorated and they're worth the price: doubles €58–108 with shower/wc or with bath. Breakfast, €14, is a meal in itself. This is an exceptional place, and it's well worth considering half board at €110–155 per person. *10% discount on the room rate (except July–Aug) or free coffee offered to our readers on presentation of this guide.*

Gouarec

22570 (17km W)

Hôtel du Blavet**

It's on the N164.
Ⓣ02.96.24.90.03 Ⓕ02.96.24.84.85
Closed *Christmas and Feb.* **Restaurant closed** *Sun evening and Mon out of season.* **TV. Car park.**

A sturdy, stone-built house on the banks of the River Blavet with the relaxed atmosphere you find in remote Brittany. Nice, comfortable rooms for €30 with basin/wc, €36–60 with shower/wc or bath. Breakfast €7. The restaurant offers an interesting range of six menus; weekday lunch menu for €13 and others €25–50. (The last is a *menu gastronomique*.) Traditional dishes are well worked by the owner-chef. Specialities include crayfish tails roasted with Szechuan pepper, zander with chive butter, filet mignon of veal, and hot soufflé with pears. A pleasant dining room with big mahogany cupboards and a lovely view of the River Blavet.

Nevez

29920

Hôtel ar Men Du***

Raguenez-Plage.
Ⓣ02.98.06.84.22
Closed *Oct to end March except during school holidays.* **TV. Car park.**

This is a seasonal holiday hotel. It has a peaceful atmosphere and all the rooms have been decorated in pretty colours. It's luxurious and quiet with a lovely Breton atmosphere. Rooms have teak shelves, maritime furniture and rooms with views of the countryside and the island. Doubles €80–130; breakfast €7. The two most expensive have huge bay windows overlooking the sea. The restaurant is decorated in similar fashion. Dishes use lots of local produce prepared with a Mediterranean twist; menus €22–36, with a children's menu at €10.

Ouessant (Île d')

29242

Crêperie Ti à Dreuz

Lampaul Ouessant.
Ⓣ02.98.48.83.01
Closed *Oct–April except for school holidays.*

Ti à Dreuz means "crooked house", and the leaning stone façade looks as if it was built in a force ten gale. Inside it's painted blue and white. There's a huge choice of delicious crêpes. Crêpes are individually priced and you'll pay €12–16 for a meal.

Paimpol

22500

Le Repaire de Kerroc'h***

29 quai Morand; it's on the marina.
Ⓣ02.96.20.50.13 Ⓕ02.96.22.07.46
Ⓦwww.chatotel.com
Restaurant closed *Mon lunchtime; Tues; Wed lunchtime; 3 weeks in Jan.* **Disabled access. TV.**

Dating back to 1793, this house, in a style originating in St Malo, was built by a privateer who pillaged the seas for Napoleon. Its thirteen stylish, scrupulously clean and spacious rooms cost €44–114. Some of them have port views. Breakfast €10.50. In the elegant dining room, done out in shades of green, the chef offers menus €14–45. Diners and AmEx aren't accepted. *Free apéritif offered to our readers on presentation of this guide.*

Hôtel K'Loys***

21 quai Morano; it's on the harbour.
Ⓣ02.96.20.40.01 Ⓕ02.96.20.72.68
Ⓦpagesjaunes.com

Disabled access. TV. Folding cots available.

The *Hotel K'Loys* is in the nineteenth-century shipfitter's house, now an elegant hotel with an intimate atmosphere. The eleven rooms, €65–120, have been tastefully furnished in keeping with the period; some look over the harbour and one has a sitting room with a bow window. Breakfast €8. The only concession to modernity is the lift, put in to assist disabled access.

|●| Crêperie-restaurant Morel

11 pl. du Martray.
Ⓣ02.96.20.86.34
Closed Sun; Tues evening out of season; Nov.

A genuine traditional Breton crêperie in a welcoming room that is always bustling with a lively crowd of regulars. Delicious crêpes, such as *à l'andouille de Guémené* (a type of sausage). Dish of the day €8, or count on around €12 à la carte. Excellent cider. For an apéritif, try the *pommeau des Menhirs*.

|●| Restaurant de l'Hôtel de la Marne**

30 pl. de la Marne; it's near the train station.
Ⓣ02.96. 20.82.16 Ⓕ02.96.20.92.07
Ⓔrestaurant.hotel.marne@wanadoo.fr
Closed *Sun evening and Mon; the Feb school holidays*. **Disabled access. TV. Car park.**

This restaurant is in the hotel itself, which looks rather like an ordinary provincial establishment. But there's a good reason why it is a favourite with the locals. The chef is inventive: Breton lobster poached in chicken stock, roast sea bream with a stock flavoured with crayfish, fresh foie gras marinated in *verjus* and fresh herbs, *boudin noir* with langoustines. Menus €23 (not Sun) and €27–80; drinks are included in the more expensive ones. An impressive wine list, with at least 360 different wines. You can also buy some of their specialities to take away (salmon, house foie gras, terrines and so on).

Palais (Le)

56360

☗ |●| Auberge de jeunesse

Haute-Boulogne; behind the citadelle du Palais, 15 min from the landing stage.
Ⓣ02.97.31.81.33 Ⓕ02.97.31.58.38
Ⓔbelle-ile@fuaj.org
Disabled access. Car park.

Loïc, the owner, is totally dedicated to his youth hostel, and it shows. It is particularly well known for its hiking courses, with a fascinating tour of the island on a coastal footpath in five–six days (packed lunch, back to the hostel by van at night, then back to the same point the following morning). 100 beds, including bunks, in rooms for two people. €9 per person. Possibility of half board €21.50. Reading room, TV lounge, café, communal dining or use of kitchen. Highly popular, especially in summer, so it's best to book.

☗ Hôtel La Frégate

Quai de l'Acadie; it's opposite the ferry terminal.
Ⓣ02.97.31.54.16
Closed mid-Nov to end Feb.

Nice, cosy little hotel that's pleasantly furnished and excellent value for money. Most of the rooms look out onto the harbour. They cost €29 with basin or €39 with shower/wc. Breakfast €6. The pleasant salon-bar, furnished with family antiques, also has a great view, and there's a big terrace from where you can watch the arrival of the ferries.

|●| Crêperie La Chaloupe

10 av. Carnot; it's near the market place.
Ⓣ02.97.31.88.27 Ⓕ02.97.31.32.48
Ⓦwww.lachaloupe.com
Closed *Jan; mid-Nov to mid-Dec*. **Disabled access.**

Excellent crêpes served in an appealing setting. The batter is made using organic milk, eggs and flour – the pancakes come out light and crispy and stuffed with prawns, seafood, smoked fish and so on. They also do fish soup, big salads and good ice cream. A meal costs about €15, and there's a children's menu. *Free apéritif offered to our readers on presentation of this guide.*

Sauzon

56360 (8km NW)

|●| Le Petit Baigneur

Rampe des Glycines.
Ⓣ02.97.31.67.74
Closed *Mon (outside school holidays); Jan–Feb.*

There are nice photographs on the wall of the pleasant dining room and the dishes of the day are inscribed on the blackboard. The cuisine is tasty, well executed and combines lovely flavours using only fresh produce. The tuna mousse with lemon and oregano is light, the marinated anchovies and sardines are tasty then there's clam *fricassée*, haddock stew, stir-fried prawns with aubergines and grilled lamb chops. There are also more substantial dishes such as veal *escalope* and sea bream with crayfish bisque. Keep some room for a home-made dessert – crêpe with apple charlotte and *caramel maison*. Lunch menu €16; children eat half-price. In summer they put a few tables outside. *Free Kir offered to our readers on presentation of this guide.*

La Maison

In the town; take a sharp left when you enter Sauzon.
Ⓣ02.97.31.69.07 **Service** *daily until 11pm.*

Three distinct sections here: the bistro, popular with Sauzon's last surviving fishermen; the restaurant inside and the completely separate heated terrace. Some of the best cooking going in these parts, thanks to a highly creative chef who has held court in the kitchen for some twenty years. His specialities include an extraordinarily tender lamb *en croûte*, grilled peppers, tortellini with crab flesh and, above all, wonderful desserts (don't miss the fennel *confit* pie). Lunch menu €16. Reckon on €40 à la carte. Reservations highly recommended.

Le Roz-Avel

Rue du Lieutenant-Riou.
Ⓣ02.97.31.61.48
Closed Wed; Jan–Feb.

An elegant venue that is without doubt the best restaurant on the island. There's a single menu for €23, which is very good value, but à la carte can get pricey – you need to allow around €42.50. The food is sophisticated, though: pig's trotter in oyster marinade, lamb *de l'ile*, skate with lemon verbena and monkfish *osso buco* with spices. Lobster to order. The setting and service match the excellence of the food.

Perros-Guirec

22700

Hôtel-Restaurant La Bonne Auberge

Place de la Chapelle; it's in the hamlet of La Clarté, 3km from Perros-Guirec on the road to Plonmanach.
Ⓣ02.96.91.46.05 Ⓕ02.96.91.62.88
Ⓔgouriou.m@wanadoo.fr
Restaurant closed *Sat lunchtime; last 3 weeks in Nov and first week in Dec.* **High chairs available. TV.**

Warm welcome, charming place. There's a huge wood fire, a piano and sofas that you won't want to get up from and they serve very more-ish little canapés. Rooms, €26–33.50, are small and simple. Nos. 1, 2 and 3 have a (distant) sea view. Half board, €33.50–39.50 per person, is compulsory 15 June–15 Sept, for long weekends and on public holiday weekends. Lunchtime menu €13 during the week then €19–31. The food is interesting, and with a modern edge, and the first menu especially proves good value; dishes are based around the best and freshest seafood (the proprietor is also a fisherman). *10% discount on the room rate 16 Sept–14 June (outside school holidays and holiday weekends) for a stay of at least two nights or on a half board basis.*

Le Gulf Stream

26 rue des Sept-Îles; it's at the start of the road that leads to Trestraou beach.
Ⓣ02.96.23.21.86 Ⓕ02.96.49.06.61
Ⓦwww.gulf-stream-hotel-bretagne.com
Closed *Mon lunch; Thurs; Wed except July–Aug.* **TV.**

There is a pleasant turn-of-the-last-century feel to this charming establishment, perched on a hillside above the sea. A few of the simple, pretty and well-maintained rooms have splendid views of the ocean and cost €40–45 with basin, €50–65 with shower/wc or bath. Bikers and hikers welcome, and there's a garage for bikes. In the restaurant there's the same atmosphere. The well-spaced tables are attractively laid and the dining room is brightened up with green plants. The views from here are also spectacular. Menus €16 (not Sun or public holidays) and €25–45. Fish and seafood are the dishes of choice, and the menus change regularly. The cooking holds some pleasant surprises. The local wines are well chosen, too.

Crêperie Hamon

36 rue de la Salle; it's in a steep little street opposite the marina.
Ⓣ02.96.23.28.82
Disabled access. High chairs available.

Service 7.15–9.15pm. This place has been

a local institution since 1960. It would be a secret little hideaway if its reputation didn't go before it – Hamon is known for miles around as much for its rustic setting and good atmosphere as for the spectaclular way the host tosses the crêpes to the waitress to catch. A meal costs about €11. Booking essential. Credit cards are not accepted.

Ploumanac'h

22700 (7km NW)

Hôtel Le Parc Resto La Cotriade**

Place Saint-Guirec; by the Ploumanac'h car park, 100m from the beach and the customs officers' footpath.
Ⓣ02.96.91.40.80 Ⓕ02.96.91.60.48
Ⓔhotel.duparc@libertysurf.fr
Closed *Sun evening and Mon (plus Tues lunch Oct–Nov); 15 Nov–30 March.*

Alright, it has to be admitted that it's next to a car park, but the attractively decorated modern rooms are impeccable and it's very quiet round the back. Double rooms with shower/wc or bath €40–43.50. Half board compulsory in July–Aug, €46.50–49.30 per person. Menus at €12.50, except Sun lunch, and €15–33. The restaurant, in a classical style with inevitable nautical touches, provides excellent food : tagliatelle with seafood, *cotriade* and fresh foie gras with langoustines. Good service. *Kir offered to readers who stay in the hotel on presentation of this guide.*

Plélan-le-Grand

35380

Auberge des Forges

Les Forges. Take the D724 to the Forges lake in the middle of the Brocèlioande forest.
Ⓣ02.99.06.81.07 Ⓕ02.99.06.92.15
Ⓦwww.forges-de-paimpont.com
Closed *Mon evening; Feb school holidays.*

A really pretty country inn – it's been run by the same family since 1850. The traditional cuisine makes the best of the quality of local produce. They place a substantial terrine on the table or you could opt for a 'lighter" pan-fried *andouille* with potatoes. The fish, game, meat and poultry cater for all tastes and budgets – and they serve frogs' legs. There's pretty amazing value for money on the menus €11 (not weekends) and €32. *Free Breton Kir offered to our readers on presentation of this guide.*

Plémet

22210

Le Saint-Antoine

8 pl. Charles-de-Gaulle; 14km to the east of Loudéac via the N164, in the direction of Rennes.
Ⓣ02.96.25.61.62
Closed *Tues evening; Wed evening; Thurs evening; Sun evening.* **Disabled access.**

It is hard to enthuse too much over the cold, unimaginative, modern setting, but the meals make up for it with their sophistication and creativity, and the service is extremely friendly. The excellent bread and charcuterie are home-made. Menus at €10.80 (weekday lunchtime), then €17–35. Undoubtedly one of the best restaurants in the area.

Pléneuf-Val-André

22370

Auberge du Poirier

Rond-point du Poirier at Saint-Alban; it's next to the petrol station.
Ⓣ02.96.32.96.21
Ⓦmonsite.wanadoo.fr/aubergedupoirier
Closed *Sun evening and Mon out of season; late Feb; June; Oct.* **Disabled access. High chairs available.**

Olivier Termet has made such a success of his restaurant that he's had to build a new dining room. The chef trained in some of the most famous kitchens before bringing his talent home. The first menu at €13.50 (weekdays only) includes a main course, dessert, wine and coffee. There are more original dishes on the menus at €16.50–34.50, which change with each season. Each dish is prepared with meticulous care. Reservations advised. *Free coffee offered to our readers on presentation of this guide.*

Au Biniou

121 rue Clemenceau; it's near Val-André beach.
Ⓣ02.96.72.24.35
Closed *Tues evening and Wed out of season; Feb.*

This has long been a favourite locally. It's a

traditional, elegant restaurant with excellent cuisine prepared by the owner-chef. Specialities include fish and meat dishes: *fricassée* of crayfish and scallops with Noilly and cauliflower with coriander, fillet of sea bass braised in fennel-scented milk, pigeon in bread crust and foie gras *escalope* with garden vegetables. Menus €15.50 (weekday lunchtimes), €23, €27.50 and €37.50, or around €42 à la carte. You can walk it all off with a bracing stroll on the wind-blown Val André beach or along the customs officers' tracks.

Pleyben

29190

Auberge du Poisson Blanc

Towards Pont-Coblant, at 4.5km on the old Quimper road in the direction of Briec.
☎ 02.98.73.34.76 Ⓕ 02.98.73.31.21
Closed *Mon evening.*

On the shores of the Nantes-Brest canal, this inn, affiliated to the *Logis de France*, serves fresh, hearty dishes like *andouille* salad with Puy lentils, *cassolette* of scallops with lambic, Père Keru's tripe, mustard *andouillette* and roast free-range chicken. Several dining rooms, one at the water's edge. Menus €13–28. The €24 traditional menu will satisfy even the fussiest eater. Children's menu €7.50. Reckon on €20 à la carte. Double rooms €45. Breakfast €5.50. *Free apéritif offered to our readers on presentation of this guide.*

Crêperie de L'Enclos

51 pl. du Général-de-Gaulle: opposite the parish compound.
☎ 02.98.26.38.68
Closed *11 Nov–15 Dec.* **Open** *daily at lunch, plus Fri, Sat and Sun evening; during the school holidays, open daily lunch and evening, except Mon evening.*

This crêperie is a gourmet's delight. Just reading the menu (all twenty pages of it) is an adventure in itself: 250 varieties of crêpes, made with wheat or buckwheat, served in a pretty blue and yellow setting. Reckon on €6.50 for a crêpe with a mixture of fillings. The menu is not restricted to crêpes, however. Every autumn the owners travel to the South of France in search of new flavours and authentic farmhouse produce and they invariably come back with some veritable treasures. (This explains the presence of specialities from Gascony and Provence.) Excellent cider, made by traditional methods (the same type is served in the presidential palace in Paris, no less). Warm welcome.

Ploemeur

56270

Le Vivier**

Port de Lomener; 4km from the centre, on the coast road.
☎ 02.97.82.99.60 Ⓕ 02.97.82.88.89
Ⓔ levivier.lomener@wanadoo.fr
Closed *Christmas–10 Jan; restaurant closed Sun evening (except July–Aug).* **TV. High chairs available. Disabled access.**

The double rooms (€69–77) all boast a bay window with a splendid view of the island of Groix. The restaurant, one of the best in the area, also enjoys a stunning view of the sea and Groix. Seafood is obviously much in evidence; langoustines, oysters, salmon charlotte with crab, *fricassée* of squids with cider, bass fillet grilled with fennel, etc. Good value: menus at €20 (except weekends and public holidays), then €28–42. Attentive, friendly service, without being overbearing. It's advisable to book. *10% discount on a room (*Oct–March*) offered to our readers on presentation of this guide.*

Crêperie le Grazu

Port de Lomener.
☎ 02.97.82.83.47
Closed *Tues; Wed in winter except in school holidays; Nov.* **Disabled access. High chairs available.**

The young owners are making a real success of this place. They have sorted out a network of local suppliers for their crêpes, so they use buckwheat as well as ordinary wheat and the fillings are fresh and very interesting. They do huge salads as well. Weekday menu €7.90 and there's another at €9.90. *Free coffee offered to our readers on presentation of this guide.*

Ploërmel

56800

Hôtel-restaurant Saint-Marc**

1 pl. Saint-Marc, near the old station.

Ⓣ02.97.74.00.01 Ⓕ02.97.73.36.81
Closed *Sun evening.* **TV. High chairs available.**

Trains rarely call at the neighbouring station so it's quiet here. The well-maintained rooms cost €33–40 depending on facilities. The bar is a popular local watering-hole, while the restaurant is generally regarded as the best in Ploërmel. Menus, €12 in the week then €15–27. Breakfast €5.25. *10% discount on the room rate (1 Sept–30 June) offered to our readers on presentation of this guide.*

Hôtel Le Cobh**

10 rue des Forges.
Ⓣ02.97.74.00.49 Ⓕ02.97.74.07.36
Ⓦwww.au.cobh.com
Disabled access. TV. High chairs and games available. Car park.

The reputation of this hotel, with its brilliant yellow façade, is totally justified – you'll appreciate the convivial and comfortable atmosphere, and there are lovely furnishings in the spacious rooms (€42–60). Half board €40–42 per person. The meal they bring to your room on a tray is excellent, so you won't have to dress for dinner. In the park, a pavilion for two–six people at €50–80. Cheapest menu goes for €14, a traditional menu €21.50, then other menus up to €32. This hotel has been transformed into one of the most astonishing hotels in the whole of Morbihan. It has been completely redecorated by the Celtia design team, a local company that specializes in giving hotels a new look. Here, the chosen theme is the legends and fairy tales of Brocéliande (somewhat akin to our Arthurian legends). Three types of rooms have been created: the first focus on writing and the sacred (blue background); the second on the forest (green background); and the third on Opalescence (red background). This may sound rather daunting but the results are soothing and gently usher guests into the world of dreams. The exterior and the surrounding land are the next areas that will be subject to a drastic overhaul. The restaurant serves good, unpretentious but wholesome food. Effusive welcome and very cheerful service. *10% discount on meals, drinks included (all year), and 10% discount on the room rate (Oct–Easter) offered to our readers on presentation of this guide.*

Le Thy**

19 rue de la Gare.
Ⓣ02.97.74.05.21 Ⓕ02.97.74.02.97
Ⓦwww.lethy.com
TV. Car park.

Each of the seven rooms is dedicated to a painter and decorated in the style of the artist: Klimt is spacious and sensual while Pratt has a travel theme complete with globe and packed trunk. Atelier is bright with light streaming through the windows and sketches on the wall – it's as if the painter has just left. Other rooms are named after Tàpies and van Gogh. Each room is large and the bathrooms are superb; doubles €50–60. On the ground floor, there's a bar and a concert room that looks like a chapel; the apse is flanked by books and hung with purple curtains. The pub is open from Wednesday to Friday – concerts are held here. *Free apéritif offered to our readers on presentation of this guide.*

Plogoff

29770

Hôtel de la Baie des Trépassés**

On the seafront; it's 3km from pointe du Raz and pointe du Van.
Ⓣ02.98.70.61.34 Ⓕ02.98.70.35.20
Ⓦwww.baiedestrepasses.com
Closed *15 Nov–15 Feb.* **TV. Car park.**

This large, prosperous hotel stands in splendid isolation in front of a magnificent surfing beach in an exceptionally wild situation. Doubles €32–58; half board, compulsory in August, is €48–63. Menus in the restaurant cost €18.50–50 and feature lots of fish dishes. AmEx and Diners not accepted. *Free coffee offered to our readers on presentation of this guide.*

Ploubalay

22650

Restaurant de la Gare

4 rue des Ormelets.
Ⓣ02.96.27.25.16 Ⓕ02.96.82.63.22
Ⓦwww.restaurantdelagare.com
Closed *30 Sept–30 June Mon and Tues evenings and Wed; July–Aug Mon and Tues lunch and Wed; 15 Jan–30 Jan; 15 June–30 June; 10 Oct–25 Oct.* **Disabled access. High chairs available.**

They closed the station long since as well

as the ragged bar that used to be here. The three dining rooms are attractively decorated with floral designs. The menu is like some public declaration of intent with the chef explaining his involvement in no uncertain terms: "the scallops are fished locally and placed in the marinade instantly". This is excellent cuisine using fresh Breton produce, prepared with a personal touch; calf's head, turbot in champagne, lamb, fresh duck foie gras, black pudding and wonderful seafood dishes. Menus €20 (not Sun) and €30–40. Around €50 à la carte. Reservations essential for dinner. *Free Kir offered to our readers on presentation of this guide.*

Ploudalmézeau

29830

La Salamandre

Place du Général-de-Gaulle.
Ⓣ02.98.48.14.00
Closed *Tues evening and Wed out of season; weekdays from Oct to Easter except during the school holidays; mid-Nov to mid-Dec.*
High chairs and bibs available. Baby changing facilities.

Grandma opened this pleasant and bright crêperie and grandson is the present owner. The crêpes are tasty – try the one with scallops and baby vegetables, the *bigoudène* (stuffed with *andouille*, fried potatoes and cream), the *forestière* (mushrooms, ham, cream) or the *paysanne* (bacon, potatoes, cheese and cream). For dessert there's the decadent *lichouze* (butter caramel, ice cream and Chantilly cream). Children are very welcome. Weekday lunch menu €8.90 or around €12–13 à la carte. *Free Breton Kir offered to our readers on presentation of this guide.*

Plougasnou

29630

Hôtel Roc'h Velen**

Saint-Samson; 6km from the village on a road that leads down to the sea.
Ⓣ02.98.72.30.58 Ⓕ02.98.72.44.57
Ⓔroch.velen@wanadoo.fr
Closed *Sun evening out of season; Jan.* **TV. High chairs available.**

This hotel is a small place located on the sea road with ten pretty rooms decorated in a maritime style. Each has the name of an island from the area; some look out onto the sea. Doubles with shower/wc or bath for €35–48.50. Breakfast €4.50–5.50. The restaurant offers lots of seafood and fish dishes cooked by the owner's wife. Try the seafood stew or the *cotriade*. Menus range from €11.50 (weekday lunchtime) to €21.50. In summer they have a week-long festival featuring local singers. *10% discount on the room rate except in July and Aug offered to our readers on presentation of this guide.*

Pont-Aven

29930

Hôtel Les Ajoncs d'Or

1 pl. de l'Hôtel-de-Ville.
Ⓣ02.98.06.02.06 Ⓕ02.98.06.18.91
Ⓔajoncsdor@aol.com
Closed *Sun evening and Mon out of season; Jan.*

A breath of fresh air has swept through this old building since Gauguin stayed here on his last trip to Pont-Aven in 1894. The comfortable, refurbished double rooms with shower or bath go for €49.50. The old dining room has also been overhauled to serve fine dishes with a maritime touch, such as farandole of stuffed shellfish and bass *en croûte* with cream of hazelnut and cream of chives. Menus €18.50–38. Children's menu €9. Friendly welcome.

Crêperie Le Talisman

4 rue Paul-Sérusier; at the entrance to the town, on the Riec road.
Ⓣ02.98.06.02.58
Closed *Mon; Sun lunch out of season; June; 2nd fortnight in Nov.*

This crêperie has a beautiful terrace overlooking the garden. The crêpes, and the little dishes that accompany them, are all excellent. Reckon on around €10 à la carte for a meal (three crêpes). Some specialities: the "Talisman" and "seafood" crêpes, and the pancake with flambéed apples.

Restaurant le Tahiti

21 rue Belle-Angèle; it's on the Bannalec road.
Ⓣ02.98.06.15.93
Closed *Mon; Tues; Wed except during school holidays; fortnight in Feb.* **Disabled access.**

This is run by a local man and his Tahitian

wife. The restaurant has been prettily decorated, and the cooking is exotic because Madame is in the kitchen – Tahitian chow mein with chicken, yellow noodles, black mushrooms and vegetables, Tahitian fish marinated in lemon and blanched with onion. Divine desserts start with the *po'e maïa*, a *compote* of banana with vanilla pod cream. There's a weekday lunch menu at €12, and you'll pay about €19 for a full meal à la carte. They also do a takeaway service. The table staff are friendly if sometimes a little too laid-back. *Free liqueur offered to our readers on presentation of this guide.*

Riec-sur-Belon

29340 (4.5km SE)

⌂ |●| Domaine de Kerstinec et restaurant Le Kerland

Ⓣ02.98.06.42.98 Ⓕ02.98.06.45.38
Ⓔrestaurant.kerland@wanadoo.fr
Closed *Sun evening in low season; a week before Christmas.*

Beautiful rooms looking onto the garden and overlooking the Belon, with smaller ones upstairs. Doubles €57–90, depending on the category and season. The restaurant has built up a great reputation in the region, thanks to the talent of the young chef, Yannick Chatelain, the owners' son. The cooking is subtle and, unsurprisingly, based on seafood, with delicious specialities like scallops with five spices, thin buckwheat pancakes with smoked salmon and mango cream, asparagus flan with langoustines and melon *coulis*. Menus €20–68. The dining room, decorated in a rosewood colour, has a panoramic view of the river. All in all, a beautiful place.

Trégunc

29910 (9km W)

⌂ |●| Les Grandes Roches

Well signposted from the town.
Ⓣ02.98.50.10.72 Ⓕ02.98.97.62.97
Ⓦwww.hotel-leszgrandesroches.com
Closed *Jan.* **Restaurant closed** *Tues evening and Wed.* **Disabled access.**

Maud and Nicolas Raday welcome you to this magnificent complex made up of several old, restored buildings and two idyllic cottages, in the middle of a flowery five-hectare park complete with rocks and a menhir classified as a historical monument. Double rooms €55–120. Breakfast €10. Inventive cooking in the restaurant: baked green asparagus and crusty lard, loin of lamb with crusty bread and Provençal tian, stuffed courgette with veal sweetbreads and kidneys and tarragon, baked turbot with croustillant of vegetables, aniseed and sea-urchin sauce. These dishes are served in two beautiful dining rooms with a fireplace. Menus from €21 (weekdays) to €51. Lovely swimming pool and billiards room. Peace and quiet guaranteed in this distinctive setting.

Pont-Croix

29790

⌂ |●| Hôtel-restaurant Ty-Evan**

18 rue du Docteur-Neis; it's on the main square next to the town hall.
Ⓣ02.98.70.58.58
Ⓔtyeva@club-internet.fr
Closed *Sat lunchtime out of season; Jan to mid-March.* **Disabled access.**

Pont-Croix is a delightful, characterful town, definitely worth visiting for its magnificent cathedral portal. If the crashing waves have got too much for you, this is an ideal place to come for some gentle charm. Good double rooms for €39–50. Warm welcome and honest food with set menus at €10 (weekday lunchtimes) and €14.50–32.50. Half board, €43.50–48.50 per person, is obligatory 1–15 Aug. Parking space for motorbikes and cycles.

Pontivy

56300

|●| Crêperie La Campagnarde

14 rue de Lattre-de-Tassigny; it's on the Vannes road on the edge of town.
Ⓣ02.97.25.23.07
Disabled access.

This country restaurant is decorated like a farm with old farm implements, cartwheels, forks and threshers that the owners have gleaned from here and there. Good crêpes made from Breton black wheat, stuffed with everything from cheese and seafood to apples and pears. All the cooking methods are respectful of the quality of the produce used. A good meal will cost about €12. They also serve chistr per – a rare Breton pear cider made locally.

Pont-L'Abbé

29120

Hôtel La Tour d'Auvergne

22 pl. Gambetta.
Ⓣ02.98.87.00.47 Ⓕ02.98.82.33.78
Closed *Sun lunch out of season.*

These premises have recently been taken over by a young couple, who have opened a highly successful gourmet bistro on the ground floor, with cosy décor dominated by wood. In the kitchens, the chef Franck Evin and his colleague Ronan O'Raw, an Irish food journalist enamoured of Brittany, dream up dishes according to the fresh ingredients available – and their own fancy! Their cuisine is based on associations of flavours. No tired routine here; every fortnight or so a new dish is chalked up on the blackboard, and even then it evolves constantly. These dishes of the day are cheap (€9), surprising and available at any time: Morteau-sausage salad, mayonnaise with orange, pears poached in wine with Roquefort and walnuts. There is also a menu at €12.50. À la carte, starters at €8 and main courses at €14. The wine list ranges from carefully chosen local wines, available by the glass, to the most prestigious vintages. Well worth the detour for both the quality of the food and the atmosphere. As for the rooms, they are a bit old-fashioned but are due to be refurbished next year. Doubles €43–46. Breakfast €6.

Pouldreuzic

29710

Hôtel-restaurant Breiz-Armor**

It's on the beach of Penhors.
Ⓣ02.98.51.52.53 Ⓕ02.98.51.52.30
Ⓦbreiz-armor.fr
Closed *Mon; Mon lunchtime in July and Aug; Jan–Feb; Nov school holidays.* **Disabled access. TV. Car park.**

A beautifully located hotel right on the sea shore which, over the years, has spread – it's built of concrete but in the Breton style. It's easy to put up with the building, in any case, because the location and the cuisine make all the difference. You'll find traditional dishes with an oriental streak. Menus €13.20 (lunch in the week) and €17.90–45.30. Lovely rooms, some with fabulous views of the sea. Doubles €55–72; breakfast €6.90. Half board is compulsory in July and Aug for €62–70 per person.

Quiberon

56170

Parc Tehuen*

1 rue des Tamaris; it's 500m from the town centre.
Ⓣ02.97.50.10.26
Ⓦa-parc-tehuen.com
Closed *30 Sept–30 April.* **TV. Disabled access. Car park.**

A really nice family pension. It's got a huge garden and is only 400m from the beach. Half or full board only; full board costs €46.40 per person for a room with basin or shower in July and August. The restaurant serves Breton fare, with a menu for €11.50 (not served Sun). Good value for money.

Hôtel-Restaurant Bellevue***

Rue de Tiviec; it's set back from the beach, by the casino.
Ⓣ02.97.50.16.28 Ⓕ02.97.30.44.34
Ⓦ**www.**bellevuequiberon.com
Closed *Oct to end March.* **Disabled access. TV. Swimming pool. Cots and high chairs available. Car park.**

This is a big, angular 1970s block which, while not having the appeal of a more traditional building, is quiet, comfortable and boasts lots of facilities – heated swimming pool, solarium and gardens. Doubles €57–114. Breakfast €8.50. From 10 July to 25 Aug, half board is compulsory and the price of the room becomes more or less the rate per person. Menus in the restaurant are €15.30–19.10, with a selection of local and other dishes: the lemon sole fillet with cockle cream is particularly good. *10% discount on the room rate April–June offered to our readers on presentation of this guide.*

Crêperie-restaurant du Vieux Port

42–44 rue Surcouf; the street is above the old port of Port-Haliguen.
Ⓣ02.97.50.01.56 Ⓕ02.97.30.53.13
Ⓦwww.crepvxport.nfrance.com
Disabled access.

Non-stop crêpes from noon to 10pm, and from noon–3pm and after 7pm in the restaurant. In a street overlooking the harbour this crêperie is a tad more expensive than others around but in a lovely spot and well worth the money. An all-inclusive menu of crêpes and cider at €11 will limit your cash outlay; you'll spend around €13–15 for a meal à la carte. Their speciality crêpe is served with salt butter and caramel but they also do a great fish and seafood choices. There's a small garden. *Free coffee offered to our readers on presentation of this guide.*

La Chaumine

36 pl. du Manémeur; it's in the village of Manémeur.
Ⓣ and Ⓕ 02.97.50.17.67
Closed *Sun evening except July–Aug; Mon; March; 1 Nov–16 Dec.* **Disabled access.**

The restaurant is in an adorable spot, surrounded by fishermen's cottages. Arrive in time for an apéritif at the bar and join the fishermen and locals sipping Muscadet – it's a million miles from the stress and traffic jams of city life. The set menus have no frills, just good, honest ingredients – mussels, prawns, fish – while specialities include sole with *girolle jus* and soft fruit *au gratin* with almond cream. The menu at €13.50 is served at lunchtime, though not on Sun, and there are others €23–46.50.

Restaurant La Criée

11 quai de l'Océan; it's on the port Maria.
Ⓣ 02.97.30.53.09 Ⓕ 02.97.50.42.35
Closed *Sun evening and Mon; Mon lunchtime only in July–Aug; 1–15 Dec; Jan.*

One of the best seafood and fish specialists of the peninsula – La Criée means "fish market" and it's the restaurant belonging to the Lucas smokehouse. Not surprisingly, the shellfish and seafood are of the freshest. Good value for money and fast service with a smile. There are dishes of the day on the €16 menu and they do shellfish platters, fish couscous and fish *choucroute*, along wtih *sole meunière*, grilled fish and house smoked fish; expect to pay €30 or so à la carte.

Quimper

29000

Hôtel Gradlon***

30 rue de Brest.
Ⓣ 02.98.95.04.39 Ⓕ 02.98.95.61.25
Ⓦ www.hotel-gradlon.com
Closed *mid-Dec to mid-Jan.* **TV. Pay car park.**

Well situated, close to the town centre. Prettily decorated rooms of a good size, with some looking onto the charming, quiet inner garden. Doubles €68–98. Excellent breakfast €10.50. Delightful owner.

Crêperie Au Vieux Quimper

20 rue Verdelet.
Ⓣ 02.98.95.31.34
Closed *Sun lunchtime; Mon evening and Tues out of season; the 1st fortnight in June.*

The little dining room has bare stone walls and Breton furniture and it quickly gets full. There's a friendly family atmosphere and everyone tucks into the delicate and crispy crêpes, swigging down tumblers of cider and milk ribot. You'll pay around €10 for a meal. It's an excellent place so it's good to book.

Le Cosy

2 rue du Sallé.
Ⓣ 02.98.95.23.65
Closed *Sun; Mon; 2 or 3 weeks in May or June; 1 week at Christmas.*

The owner will be offended if you expect chips or crêpes, but she will happily serve you some fine *tartines*, savoury pies, toasted country bread, salmon, smoked duck, well-prepared dishes of the day and excellent desserts. Many dishes are based on fruit, ably combining sweet and savoury flavours: duck *confit* with dates and cumin, free-range chicken with honey and star anis. Everything is home-made. The building is equally striking, and the three upstairs dining rooms are very attractive. Reckon on €10–15 for a *tartine* meal with dessert and €20 for a full meal with one of the dishes of the day. This gourmet bistro really lives up to its name.

Jardin de l'Odet

39 bd. de Kerguelen.
Ⓣ 02.98.95.76.76
Closed *Wed eve; Sat lunch; Sun; Sept.*

This restaurant, well situated between the Odet and the Évêché garden, is set in a stunning 1930s building and also boasts a lovely garden looking onto the ramparts. You can eat a very reasonably priced dish of the day in the shade of an olive tree.

Menus €19 (lunch), €26 and €40. You can combine dishes from these menus if you eat à la carte.

|●| La Fleur de Sel

1 quai Neuf; on the right bank of the Odet.
☎02.98.55.04.71
Closed *Sat lunch; Sun; Mon; during New Year holidays.* **Disabled access.**

Smokers, be warned: tobacco is not permitted in this restaurant. Cosy little dining room, ideal for a sophisticated get together – business meetings are the rule at lunchtime – plus a couple of tables on a terrace, with a glimpse of the river. Local cooking with a dash of invention; the house speciality is salmon marinated with *fleur de sel*. Menus €19–33. The service is slow but charming. *A Breton sangría offered to our readers on presentation of this guide.*

|●| Le Steinway

20 rue des Gentilshommes; it's in the centre of the old town.
☎ and ℻02.98.95.53.70
Closed *Sun lunchtime and Mon except July–Aug; a week in Nov.*

The décor hails from the 1950s, with local ornaments and memorabilia; there's also an old petrol pump, a trombone, lots of old radios and plenty of telephones. The whole place feels warm and welcoming. They do an excellent slab of steak or simple salmon with fresh basil, and servings are ample. Normally they produce good peasant food but occasionally they'll spice it up with Mexican or American dishes. Menus €18.50 and €25.50 or around €20 à la carte. Coffee lovers are in their element here: you have to pay for the first cup, but after that you can have as many as you like for free. A live band plays in the corner in summer.

|●| L'Ambroisie

49 rue Élie-Fréron.
☎02.98.95.00.02
Closed *Mon and Sun evening (except summer); end June to early July.*

The young chef concocts sophisticated dishes with a touch of daring, without ever straying too far from local tradition: Parmentier d'*andouille* with cider, sautéed langoustines in shellfish broth, etc. Menus €22 (weekdays) and then €30–59. Reckon on around €58 à la carte. The dining room is solidly impressive, and the food it serves is undoubtedly some of the best on offer in the whole town. *Free coffee offered to our readers on presentation of this guide.*

|●| Au P'tit Rafiot

7 rue de Pont-l'Abbé; near the quay.
☎02.98.53.77.27
Closed *Mon; Tues out of season.*

Don't be put off by the rather dull exterior: inside is thoughtfully decorated in marine style with portholes. In the middle of the room there's a splendid aquarium full of sea creatures with huge claws – the cook will only work with the freshest ingredients, and all fish and shellfish come from the patron's own tanks. The dishes are excellently served, very tasty and good value. The waiter gives very clear descriptions of the dishes, and you'll pay about €30 for a complete meal, €25 for a Breton bouillabaisse.

Quimperlé

29300

Le Vintage Hôtel

20 rue de Brémond-d'Ars; in the lower town, next to *La Bobine* cinema.
☎02.98.35.09.10 ℻02.98.35.09.29
@bistrotdelatour@wanadoo.fr
TV.

This former savings bank is famous locally for inspiring the hotel in Breton writer Bernard Cariou's *Bistro de la Tour*. Cariou's son is now in charge, and he has successfully introduced original, contemporary design. The ten rooms are all decorated differently, with highly evocative frescoes on the walls. Doubles €55–77.

|●| La Cigale Égarée

5 rue Jacques-Cartier.
☎02.98.39.15.53
Closed *Sun and Mon evening.*

This place feels as though it comes from much further south, with its two delightful dining rooms with colour-washed walls and the terrace. The chef prepares dishes combining original flavours and following the seasons; the menu changes every three months. Specialities include carpaccio of salmon with Breton honey, *fricassée* of scallops with royal jelly and grilled bacon with pesto. Desserts are just as good. There's a *formule* at €14.70 (lunchtime) and €17.90 (evening); menus €22.90 and €31.50. It's a good idea to book.

Le Bistro de la Tour***

2 rue Dom-Morice; it's in the ville basse, by the covered market, opposite Sainte-Croix church.
Ⓣ02.98.39.29.58 Ⓕ02.98.39.21.77
Ⓦwww.perso.wanadoo.fr/bistro-de-la-tour
Closed *Sat lunchtime; Sun evening; Mon.*
Disabled access.

This place is beautifully furnished – two beautiful dining rooms with sophisticated decoration. Traditional cuisine is prepared by the very friendly host, who is a great wine connoisseur. There's a cellar if you feel like a visit. Specialities include fresh fish of the day and seafood dishes such as langoustine *fondant*, baked local sardines and marinated Petit-Chèvre cheese. Menu €17 (not Sat evening or Sun) and others up to €53. Children's menu €13.

Rennes

35000

See map on page 204

Hôtel de la Tour d'Auvergne

20 bd. de la Tour-d'Auvergne. **Map A2-8**
Ⓣ02.99.30.84.16 Ⓕ02.23.42.10.01
TV.

On the upper floor of the nice brasserie *Le Serment de Vin*. Plain but spotless rooms, all with phone, go for €23.50 with basin, up to €36.50 with shower/wc – a bargain. Breakfast €5. Ideal family hotel for limited budgets, run by a very kindly woman. Breakfast is served in your room.

Hotel Garden**

3 rue Duhamel. **Map B2-4**
Ⓣ02.99.65.45.06 Ⓕ02.99.65.02.62
Ⓦwww.logis-de-france.fr
TV. Pay car park.

Charming, tasteful hotel, set between the station and the old town. There's a café decorated in apple-green and a small internal garden. Very nice, individualized rooms in fresh colours; doubles for €43–58 with shower/wc or bath. Some rooms sleep four. Breakfast €6. *10% discount on the room rate Fri–Sun (except July–Aug) offered to our readers on presentation of this guide.*

Hôtel Lanjuinais**

11 rue Lanjuinais. **Map A2-6**
Ⓣ02.99.79.02.03 Ⓕ02.99.79.03.97
Ⓦwww.hotel-lanjuinais.com
TV.

A quiet, well-maintained hotel in a small street leading towards the quai Lamennais. Most rooms look over the street but some look into the (rather dark) courtyard. They have reasonable facilities and cost €49 with shower/wc or €52 with bath. Breakfast €6.50. *10% discount on the room rate Fri–Sun including public holidays out of season.*

Hôtel Astrid**

32 av. Louis Barthou. **Off map B3-11**
Ⓣ02.99.30.82.38 Ⓕ02.99.31.85.55
Ⓦwww.hotelastrid.fr
Disabled access. TV.

Well-located near the station and only a ten-minute walk from the town centre. A pretty, chic hotel where you'll get a friendly welcome. It's spotless and the rooms – modern, large, quiet and well equipped – cost €50.50–66 with shower/wc or bath; 20% reduction at the weekend. Breakfast €6, or €7.10 if taken in your room. The breakfast room looks out onto a small garden. A reliable establishment, run very professionally.

Hôtel de Nemours**

5 rue de Nemours. **Map B2-9**
Ⓣ and Ⓕ02.99.78.26.26
Ⓦwww.hotelnemours.com
Closed *end-July to early Aug.* **TV.**

In reception the walls are covered with autumn leaves, engravings and butterflies. The rooms have undergone a programme of refurbishment and they're pretty and clean; doubles with shower/wc or bath €51–60. The quieter rooms face onto the courtyard. Breakfast €6.10–6.90. All guests, without distinction, are afforded an effusive welcome and served with genuine kindness. *10% discount on the room rate offered to our readers on presentation of this guide.*

Hôtel des Lices**

7 pl. des Lices. **Map A1-7**
Ⓣ02.99.79.14.81 Ⓕ02.99.79.35.44
Ⓦwww.hotel-des-lices.com
Disabled access. TV. Pay car park.

Reliable establishment on one of the most beautiful squares in the old town.

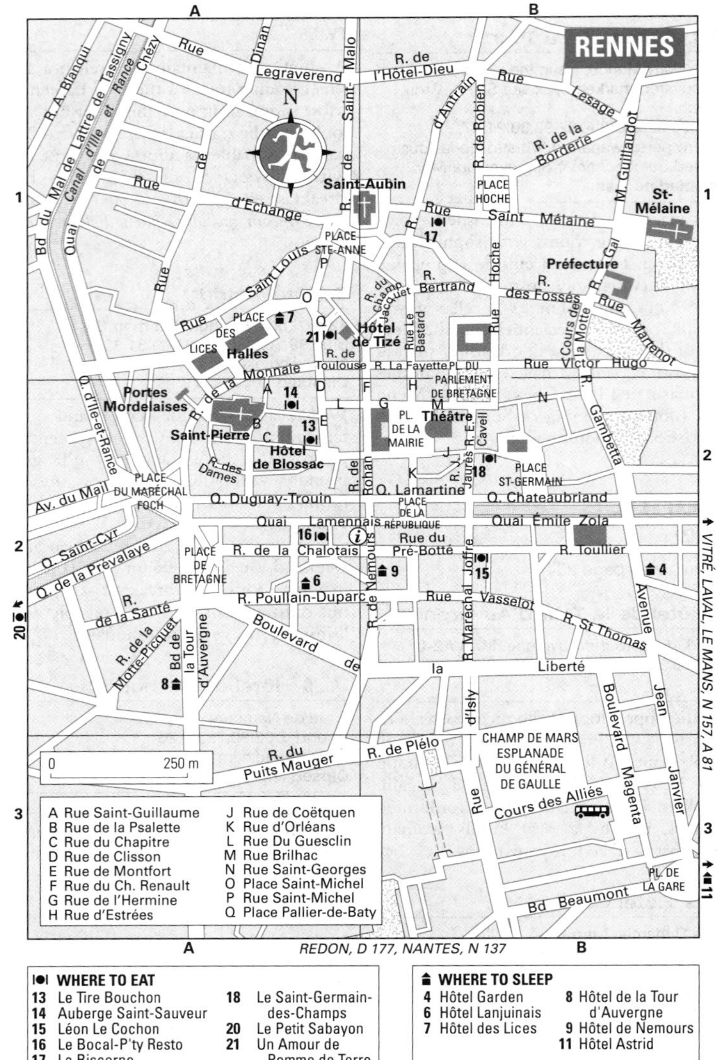
RENNES
A
B
1
2
3
N
Saint-Aubin
St-Mélaine
Préfecture
Halles
Hôtel de Tizé
Portes Mordelaises
Saint-Pierre
Hôtel de Blossac
Théâtre
PLACE STE-ANNE
PLACE DES LICES
PLACE HOCHE
PL. DE LA MAIRIE
PL. DU PARLEMENT DE BRETAGNE
PLACE ST-GERMAIN
PLACE DU MARÉCHAL FOCH
PLACE DE LA RÉPUBLIQUE
PLACE DE BRETAGNE
CHAMP DE MARS ESPLANADE DU GÉNÉRAL DE GAULLE
PL. DE LA GARE
Rue Legraverend
R. de l'Hôtel-Dieu
Rue Lesage
R. de la Borderie
Rue de Dinan
Rue de Saint-Malo
Rue d'Echange
Rue Saint Louis
Rue Saint Mélaine
R. d'Antrain
R. de Robien
Rue Hoche
M. Guillaudot
R. Gal
R. Bertrand
R. des Fossés
Rue Martenot
Rue Victor Hugo
Cours de la Motte
R. Gambetta
R. de la Monnaie
R. de Toulouse
R. La Fayette
R. du Champ Jacquet
Rue Le Bastard
R. des Dames
R. de Rohan
R. J. Jaurès
R. E. Cavell
Q. Lamartine
Q. Chateaubriand
Q. Duguay-Trouin
Quai Lamennais
Quai Émile Zola
R. Toullier
Rue du Pré-Botté
R. de Nemours
R. de la Chalotais
R. Poullain-Duparc
R. Maréchal Joffre
Rue Vasselot
R. St Thomas
Boulevard de la Liberté
Avenue Jean Janvier
Boulevard Magenta
Rue d'Isly
Cours des Alliés
Bd Beaumont
R. de Plélo
R. du Puits Mauger
R. de la Santé
R. de la Motte-Picquet
Bd de la Tour d'Auvergne
Q. de la Prevalaye
Q. Saint-Cyr
Av. du Mail
Q. d'Ille-et-Rance
Bd du Mail de Lattre de Tassigny
R. A. Blanqui
Quai de Chézy
Canal d'Ille et Rance
0 250 m
VITRÉ, LAVAL, LE MANS, N 157, A 81
REDON, D 177, NANTES, N 137
A Rue Saint-Guillaume
B Rue de la Psalette
C Rue du Chapitre
D Rue de Clisson
E Rue de Montfort
F Rue du Ch. Renault
G Rue de l'Hermine
H Rue d'Estrées
J Rue de Coëtquen
K Rue d'Orléans
L Rue Du Guesclin
M Rue Brilhac
N Rue Saint-Georges
O Place Saint-Michel
P Rue Saint-Michel
Q Place Pallier-de-Baty
WHERE TO EAT
13 Le Tire Bouchon
14 Auberge Saint-Sauveur
15 Léon Le Cochon
16 Le Bocal-P'ty Resto
17 La Biscorne
18 Le Saint-Germain-des-Champs
20 Le Petit Sabayon
21 Un Amour de Pomme de Terre
WHERE TO SLEEP
4 Hôtel Garden
6 Hôtel Lanjuinais
7 Hôtel des Lices
8 Hôtel de la Tour d'Auvergne
9 Hôtel de Nemours
11 Hôtel Astrid

They've completely modernized this hotel, which is full of light and well appointed. The very pleasant rooms have balconies and the ones on the upper floors have good views over the rooftops and the old town. Doubles €53.50 with shower/wc or €56 with bath. Breakfast €6.

|●| Un Amour de Pomme de Terre

14 pl. Rallier-de-Baty **Map A1-21**
☎02.99.79.04.91 Ⓕ02.99.79.06.15
Disabled access. Car park.

Service noon–11pm, till 10.30pm on Sun and Mon. The noble tuber stars in all dishes, accompanied by salads, smothered in melted cheese, or served with seaweed-smoked Molène sausage, smoked Camaret trout, and foie gras. The choice seems endless. Lunchtime menus €9.15–11, or reckon on around €20–25 à la carte. Portions are mountainous but a shot of vodka or lambig helps the food slip down just so you can make room for a pud. There are several floors and the decoration is really nice. But the dining room on the ground floor, where you can eat by the open fire, is probably the most appealing. It's best of all on a Thursday which is when they serve kig ha farz.

|●| La Biscorne

8 rue Saint-Mélaine. **Map B1-17**
☎02.99.38.79.77
Closed *Sun evening; Mon; a week at Christmas*. **Disabled access.**

Warm, rustic charm, harmonizing well with the traditional cuisine. There's lots of wood and an enormous fireplace where the young chef displays his awards. They offer à la carte and a range of set menus at €10 (weekday lunchtimes) and €14–25. The nicely realized dishes change every four months, and are always good and fresh. Wine is reasonably priced. *Free Kir offered to our readers on presentation of this guide.*

|●| Le Bocal-P'ty Resto

6 rue d'Argentré. **Map A2-16**
☎02.99.78.34.10
Closed *Sat lunch; Sun; Mon; 1st fortnight in Jan; 1st fortnight in May; Aug.*

This friendly restaurant is overflowing with creative ideas. The décor is lovely: glass jars are filled with all sorts of strange things collected here and there and the lids have been used to decorate the walls and even the doors in the toilet. The dishes of the day – for example a huge muffin with chicken, bacon and black pepper – are scrawled up on a blackboard. There's a particularly delicious sticky *moelleux au chocolat*. Menus €11 and €14. You'll pay about €18 for three courses à la carte. There's a well-chosen, reasonably priced wine list; all are served by the glass. Trendy, young and appealing.

|●| Auberge Saint-Sauveur

6 rue Saint-Sauveur. **Map A2-14**
☎02.99.79.32.56
Closed *Sat lunchtime; Sun; Mon lunchtime; 3 weeks from mid-Aug.*

In a lovely sixteenth-century canon's house behind St-Pierre cathedral, this restaurant has a warm, intimate, sophisticated atmosphere. Good-value weekday lunch *formule* €12 and menus €18–46. You'll pay around €30 à la carte. They offer quality traditional cuisine in dishes such as flambéed veal, *fricassée* of sole with oyster mushrooms, duck breast with honey, roast monkfish with cabbage, grilled lobster and good duck foie gras. *Free coffee offered to our readers on presentation of this guide.*

|●| Le Saint-Germain-des-Champs

12 rue Vau-Saint-Germain. **Map B2-18**
☎02.99.79.25.52
Closed *Sun; Mon; Tues–Fri evenings; Aug.*
Disabled access.

When the cows went mad, chickens were steeped in dioxin and vegetables were genetically modified, this had to be the place to come. A genuine organic vegetarian restaurant where you can have a good meal without eating bits of animal. Interesting ingredients like sprouting grains and seaweed in dishes that are full of colour and generously served. Expect to pay around €12 (weekday lunchtime) and up to €17 for a meal à la carte. Even the wines and fruit juices are organic. One dining room has a plate-glass window onto the street while the second looks onto the courtyard. Delightful welcome. *Free apéritif offered to our readers on presentation of this guide.*

Léon Le Cochon

1 rue du Maréchal-Joffre. **Map B2-15**
Ⓣ02.99.79.37.54 Ⓕ02.99.79.07.35
Closed *Sun July–Aug.* **TV.**

A lot of thinking has gone into creating this restaurant, which is at once modern, refined and authentic – not an easy achievement. Dried flowers, walls hung with chilli peppers and windows full of leaves are the backdrop for unpretentiously prepared local cooking. There's a weekday lunchtime menu for €12.50; à la carte reckon on around €21. Best to book. *Free apéritif offered to our readers on presentation of this guide.*

Le Petit Sabayon

16 rue des Trente. **Off map**
Ⓣ02.99.35.02.04
Ⓔpetit-sabayon@wanadoo.fr
Closed *Sat lunchtime; Sun; Mon; a week in Jan; 2nd fortnight in Aug.*

One of the best tables in town, with simple décor and diligent, smiling service. Try the salad with two kinds of foie gras, the *tournedos* of sardines with rhubarb sauce or the marquise with chocolate and an arabica coffee sauce. Realistic prices: an Ardoise lunch menu for €14.50 (starter, dish of the day and dessert) and others €19–27. Good wine list at reasonable prices. The restaurant is a smoke-free zone.

Le Tire Bouchon

2 rue du Châpitre. **Map A2-13**
Ⓣ02.99.79.43.43
Closed *Sat; Sun and public holidays; Feb school holidays; 3rd week in Aug.* **Disabled access.**

A new approach to the wine bar. You sit side by side at the big counter or at one of the small wooden tables. Reckon on €20 for a meal. There's a choice of only three or four dishes of the day – the kind that are slowly and carefully cooked. Alternatively, opt for a plate of charcuterie or farmhouse cheese, or for a tartine – toasted sandwich – with cheese, fruit or charcuterie. Prices are modest – you'll pay around €9 for a dish, €6 for the toasties and €4 for a dessert. The wine list is thoughtfully chosen and includes some unusual vintages from overseas. They're sold by the glass. Super décor, lovely welcome – it's very popular, and so it's best to book.

Roche-Bernard (La)

56130

Les Deux Magots**

3 pl. du Bouffay.
Ⓣ02.99.90.60.75 Ⓕ02.99.90.87.87
Ⓔaubergelesdeuxmagots.rochebernard@wanadoo.fr
Restaurant closed *Sun evening and Mon; in high season Mon and Tues lunchtime; 20 Dec–15 Jan; a week end of June; a week mid-Oct.* **TV.**

This comfortable hotel has a lovely façade with arched windows and fifteen pleasantly furnished rooms. Doubles €43–55 with shower/wc or bath. Breakfast €6. Seafood dishes predominate – roast langoustine tails, warm crayfish salad, braised sea bream with baby vegetables, roast turbot in cider and onions – though the *tournedos* Rossini and duck foie gras are worth trying, too. Menus start at €13 (not Sun), then there are others €23–70. Lengthy wine list. The bar has an impressive collection of miniature bottles of apéritifs, cognac, whisky and so on. Credit cards not accepted.

Roscoff

29680

Les Chardons Bleus**

4 rue Amiral-Réveillère; on the way to the church from the port.
Ⓣ02.98.69.72.03 Ⓕ02.98.61.27.86
Closed *Thurs and Sun evenings, except July–Aug.* **TV. High chairs available.**

Ten rooms with fairly unremarkable contemporary decoration but a good degree of comfort (high-quality bedding, efficient double glazing on the street), the liveliest in the town centre. Doubles with shower/wc or bath €48–65. Tasty, traditional food. Weekday lunchtime menu €10, then others €16–38. Children's menu €8. *Free coffee offered to our readers on presentation of this guide.*

Hôtel Aux Tamaris**

49 rue Édouard-Corbière; it's next to the Kerléna clinic.
Ⓣ02.98.61.22.99 Ⓕ02.98.69.74.36
Ⓦwww.auxtamaris.com
Closed *early Nov to Easter.* **TV.**

A nearly great location – although this

welcoming hotel looks out towards the Île de Batz it's separated from the sea by the coast road. Bright, comfortable rooms, some with a view, for €50–65 with shower/wc or bath. Breakfast €8. No restaurant, but some of the best hospitality in Finistère.

L'Écume des Jours

Quai d'Auxerre.
02.98.61.22.83
Closed *Tues and Wed out of season.*
Disabled access. High chairs available.

A granite mansion house that formerly belonged to a shipbuilder, with a comfortable, intimate interior and a big fireplace. Menus €17–40. Children's menu €8. Sophisticated and meticulously conceived dishes that skilfully combine local products from both the sea and the countryside.

Batz (Île de)

29253 (5km N)

Auberge de jeunesse

Creach-ar-Bolloch; take one of the launches that leaves Creach-ar-Bolloch every half-hour for Roscoff (last departure 8pm).
02.98.61.77.69 02.98.61.78.85
www.auberges-de-jeunesse.com
Closed *30 Sept–Easter.*

The fixtures and fittings in this youth hostel may be the worse for wear, but its location is stunning, right by the sea; its small buildings house dormitories that resemble the cabins of boats. €7.90 a night, breakfast €3.30 and meals €7.80. Youth hostel card compulsory (LFAJ-FUAJ-IYFH). Kitchen available. Credit cards not accepted.

Rostrenen

22110

Coeur de Breizh

14 rue Abbé-Gibert.
02.96.29.18.33
Closed *Wed out of season; 20 Dec–7 Jan.*
Disabled access.

Orders taken till 9.45pm during the week, 10.30pm at the weekend. Situated in the middle of the hamlet, in a substantial yellow house. The owners raised the money to get started through the support of friends and clients who had been trying to persuade them to transform their bar into a restaurant; and it worked. The setting is totally seductive – stone walls and a Breton décor. Roger is a natural front-of-house and Anne-Laure is a self-taught chef with talent. She cooks local dishes using fresh, good-quality produce – organic for the most part – which she sources through local farmers and producers. Delicious main courses and an array of seductive sweets. Weekday lunch menu for €11 and menus €18–26. À la carte, prices are fair. Occasional exhibitions and concerts with apéritifs.

Sables-d'Or-les-Pins

22240

Hôtel des Pins**

Allée des Acacias; it's 400m from the beach.
02.96.41.42.20 02.96.41.59.02
Close *1 Oct–1 April.*

A holiday hotel with the kind of charm that suits the slightly old-fashioned feel of the resort. Doubles €36–38 with shower/wc and €46–52 with bath. Half board, €42–52 per person, is obligatory July–Aug. Menus, €14–32, feature lots of good seafood and fresh fish. Mini-golf and a garden. *10% discount on the room rate (out of season) offered to our readers on presentation of this guide.*

Plurien-Fréhel

22240 (2km S)

Manoir de la Salle**

Rue du Lac; it's 500m from Sables-d'Or-les-Pins, just before you get to Fréhel.
02.96.72.38.29 02.96.72.00.57
www.manoir-de-la-salle.com
Closed *30 Sept–24 March.* **Disabled access. TV. Car park.**

A stone-built, sixteenth-century manor house which you enter through a beautiful gothic portal built a century earlier. Bright, comfortable rooms furnished with modern pieces; doubles with shower/wc or bath for €47–55 depending on the season. They've converted another old building to make a couple of apartments with kitchens sleeping four to six at €88–109. The hotel is set in two hectares of grounds, and there are lots of things to keep you amused – such as the solarium and ping-pong, along with a golf course nearby – not to mention the beach. They can arrange sea trips for residents, and there are even stalls for horses and ponies if you're on a riding holiday. It's an excellent place, run by a delightful young couple, and is very fashionable in these parts.

Fréhel

22240 (5km SE)

Hôtel Le Fanal**

Lieu-dit Besnard; take the road to Cap-Fréhel and when you get there turn right for Plévenon – the hotel is on the left after 1.5km.
02.96.41.43.19
Closed *1 Oct–31 March.* **Car park.**

A tall chalet, the sort of architecture you'd expect to find in Scandinavia – perfect for this barren Breton wasteland stretching to the ocean. Regulars come here time and again to unwind; there's a lovely big garden. Comfortable rooms with shower/wc or bath for €38–54. Breakfast €5.50. TV is outlawed. Rooms 6–9 are more spacious than the others, with nice old furniture. Children under ten get a free breakfast.

Saint-Brieuc

22000

Auberge de jeunesse-Manoir de la Ville-Guyomard

Les Villages; 3km from the town centre, near the *Géant* shopping centre (well signposted from the train station).
and 02.96.78.70.70
www.fuaj.org
Open *all year round.* **Disabled access.**

Youth hostel situated in a wonderful fifteenth-century manor house. Rooms with one–four beds. From €12.70 per night including breakfast. Meals only served to groups. Booking is highly advisable. Rental of mountain bikes.

Hôtel-restaurant Du Guesclin**

2 pl. du-Guesclin; it's in the pedestrian area.
02.96.33.11.58 02.96.52.01.18
hotelduguesclin.com
TV. High chairs available.

Centrally located and completely refurbished with comfortable rooms which, though they are nothing to shout about, are reliable. Doubles with shower/wc or bath €43–45. Breakfast €6. There's a bar-brasserie on the ground floor and an elegant dining room serving menus at €10 (weekday lunchtime) and €15–27; specialities include *mousseline* of scallops, bream with fennel, home-smoked fish and chocolate *fondant. Free apéritif, and 10% discount on the room rate (Fri–Sun except in July and Aug) offered to our readers on presentation of this guide.*

Hôtel du Champ de Mars**

13 rue du Général-Leclerc.
02.96.33.60.99
hoteldemars@wanadoo.fr
Closed *during New Year.* **Disabled access. TV.**

This well-run, pleasant establishment with all the facilities you expect of a two-star hotel has the merit of being reasonably priced: €48–51 for a double; breakfast €6. Friendly owners who enjoy what they do.

Restaurant Le Sympatic

9 bd. Carnot; it's behind the train station.
02.96.94.04.76 02.96.78.68.91
lesympatic@wanadoo.fr
Closed *Sun; Mon; public holidays; fortnight in Aug.* **Disabled access.**

Open until 10pm. A happy combination of a good atmosphere and good food grilled over vines. The ambience is warm with lots of wood and bare stone. The service is friendly and efficient; dishes using quality ingredients are served on huge plates with a side vegetable, and they're inexpensive. Set menus €11–38, with a children's menu at €8 or around €25 à la carte. *Free apéritif offered to our readers on presentation of this guide.*

Au Petit Bouchon Briochin

10 rue Jules-Ferry; it's behind the train station.
02.96.94.05.34 02.96.75.23.69
Closed *Sat lunchtime; Sun. Disabled access; fortnight end-Feb to early March; fortnight in Aug.*

The cuisine is faithful to the region with a few modern takes on traditional recipes from old-hand local chefs. The set lunch offers dish of the day or a plate of organic hams followed by dessert, and a choice of a glass of wine or a coffee, for €10.60. Menus go for €15–25; coffee and drinks are included in the most expensive one. There's also a menu-carte with starter, a selection of main courses and dessert for the same price. A different glass of wine is offered with each dish. Less impressive is the décor in the dining room – the sepia photographs and old farm implements on the wall clash somewhat with the 1980s monochrome. But that's just quibbling when the service and welcome are a cut above the ordinary. *Free coffee offered to our readers on presentation of this guide.*

Aux Pesked

59 rue du Légué; it's 1km north of the town centre.
Ⓣ02.96.33.34.65 Ⓕ02.96.33.65.38
Ⓦwww.pesked.fr
Closed *Sat lunchtime; Sun evening; Mon; 1–15 Jan; 1–8 May; 1 Sept–8 Sept.* **High chairs available. Car park.**

The gastronomic reputation of this restaurant is highly regarded in Saint-Brieuc. It's got lots going for it – a sober, elegant, modern setting and a terrace which gives superb views of the Légué valley. Delightful light, mouth-watering dishes, with a €19 weekday lunch menu and others at €33–85. Some days they offer a seven-course *menu dégustation*. The extensive cellar contains an impressive collection of 15,000 bottles. Some are rare and expensive, lots are Loire wines, but many are less prestigious and more affordable. *Free apéritif offered to our readers on presentation of this guide.*

Saint-Malo

35400

Hôtel du Louvre**

2 rue des Marins; near the place de la Poissonnerie, in the inner town.
Ⓣ02-99-40-86-62 Ⓕ02-99-40-86-93.
Ⓦwww.hoteldulouvre-saintmalo.com
TV. Pay car park.

Despite its fifty rooms, this is a family hotel, and one of considerable charm. A fair part has been totally refurbished and the results are superb, so the next stage is eagerly awaited. Comfortable double rooms €38 with washbasin, €48 with shower/wc, €55 with bath. There are also some triple rooms, and even one for seven people. *10% discount on a room (50% 15 Nov–15* March*) offered to our readers on presentation of this guide.*

Hôtel Le Nautilus**

9 rue de la Corne-de-Cerf.
Ⓣ02.99.40.42.27 Ⓕ02.99.56.75.43
Ⓦwww.lenautilus.com
TV.

A little hotel inside the old town, just five minutes from the beach. It's newly decorated in bright, young colours. Smallish rooms with good facilities at €40–57 for a double with shower/wc. On the ground floor, there's a lively pub with psychedelic walls – more Yellow Submarine than Nautilus.

Hôtel de l'Univers**

Place Châteaubriand.
Ⓣ02.99.40.89.52 Ⓕ02.99.40.07.27
Ⓦwww.hotel-univers-saintmalo.com
Restaurant closed *Wed.* **TV.**

This establishment is right next to the legendary *Bar de l'Univers* and the hotel stands as testimony to a splendid past. It's one of those local places with style, *je ne sais quoi*, and refined charm. The reception is spacious, the corridors and sitting rooms well proportioned. The atmosphere in the huge bedrooms is lovely – some can sleep three or four. Doubles €58.50–76 depending on the view, facilities and the season. Breakfast €7.30. In the restaurant there are menus at €12–30; good choices include scallops and foie gras. The management have undertaken work to restore the rooms and the stucco in the dining room to their former glory. *10% discount on the room rate except for 10 July–25 Aug offered to our readers on presentation of this guide.*

Le P'tit Crêpier

6 rue Sainte Barbe.
Ⓣ02.99.40.93.19
Ⓦwww.lepetitcrepier.fr
Closed *Tues and Wed except July–Aug.*

The pancakes and girdle cakes here are as good as they are surprising. Cosy, enticing nautical-style dining room, or a lovely terrace in fine weather. A good crêperie, thanks to its subtle flavours, excellent ingredients and astonishing but never reckless combinations. Diligent, attentive service. You'll pay around €14 for a meal.

La Corderie

Saint-Servan, chemin de la Corderie; it's behind the Alet camping site.
Ⓣ02.99.81.62.38
Ⓦlacorderie.com

Closed *Mon out of season.*

La Corderie is off the tourist track and wonderfully lacking in traffic noise. It's an old family house filled with old furniture, books and paintings. From the terrace and dining room, there is a beautiful view of the sea, the Solidor tower, La Rance and Dinard beyond. They serve light, well-presented dishes at reasonable prices, and they change practically every day – you can usually count on seeing a good Greek salad and grilled fish. Menu at €16; à la carte a meal will cost around €25.

|●| La Touline

6 pl.de la Poissonnerie.
☎02.99.40.10.98
Closed *Mon; 3 weeks in March; 3 weeks Nov–Dec.*

One of the best crêperies in Saint-Malo. The ideas for the delicious crêpes are original and well executed, and the fillings, such as sausage and *andouille*, are of the highest quality. There are also fresh, tasty salads on offer. Reckon on around €15 for a full meal. You can eat out on the attractive terrace on the pretty little place de la Poissonnerie. The service could not be more friendly.

|●| Restaurant Borgnefesse

10 rue du Puits-aux-Braies; it's inside the town walls.
☎02.99.40.05.05
Closed *Sat lunchtime; Sun; Mon lunchtime; a fortnight end June–early July; a fortnight at Christmas.*

A restaurant with a pirate theme run by a larger-than-life patron, a poet and seafarer – a legendary character in Saint-Malo. At the drop of a hat he'll weave tales of pirates and derring-do and tell you how the restaurant got its name. On the food front they serve good mussels, oysters, meats and kig ha farz; all produce is local. Menu €19.70.

|●| Le Bénétin

Les Rochers-Sculptés-Rothéreuf.
☎02.99.56.97.64 ℻02.99.56.91.59
Closed *Wed.*

Lunch *formule* (main course and dessert) for €19 and another at €25. Reckon on €55 à la carte without drinks. A fabulous setting, worthy of a design magazine, with teak furniture, sophisticated decoration and a stunning view of the sea. The cooking is equally subtle and refined (as well as being on the expensive side – this is a place for special occasions). If your budget doesn't stretch to a meal, you can always take advantage of the bar-lounge or the terrace for an apéritif at sunset.

|●| Fleurs de Sel

93 bd. de Rochebonne Paramé.
☎02.99.40.09.93
Closed Sat lunchtime; Sun evening and Mon.

A fine restaurant, just ten minutes from the beach of Rochebonne. The walls are decorated with murals depicting the exploits of the yachtsman Eric Tabarly and his various *Pen-Duick* boats. The food is tasty and meticulously prepared, as well as being exquisitely presented on beautifully laid tables. Not surprisingly, it is always full, so it's advisable to book. Menus €20 and €26. Reckon on around €30 à la carte.

|●| Restaurant Chez Gilles

2 rue de la Pie-qui-Boit.
☎02.99.40.97.25
Closed *Wed; Thurs 1 Nov–1 May.*

The gloriously fresh seafood here is cooked with enthusiasm and served in a cosy, comfy, bourgeois dining room with intimate corners. There's a €16.50 lunch *formule* and menus at €22.50 and €31.50. A meal à la carte will cost you €38. The owner/chef cooks fish to perfection in delicate, aromatic sauces: slivers of John Dory with hot oysters and bacon pieces, brill in a chicken stock and foie gras. You get the same quality of cooking on all the set menus.

Saint-Suliac

35430 (10km S)

🏠 |●| Le Galichon

5 La Grande-Cohue; it's on the N17.
☎02.99.58.49.49
Closed *Mon–Thurs from Oct–May.* **TV.**

Service daily 11am–11pm. A really nice place, this. A handful of the rustic, a shake of refinement and a pinch of nostalgia combine to make a delicious venue where they serve good pancakes and dishes using old recipes cooked over the fire. It works a treat. No set menu; dishes around €8 and desserts for €3 or so. In fine weather you can eat in the small courtyard. Best to book.

Saint-Pol-de-Léon

29250

🏨 |●| Le Passiflore

28 rue Penn-Ar-Pont; not far from the station.
Ⓣ and Ⓕ02.98.69.00.52
Closed *Sun evening; 24 Dec–2 Jan.* **High chairs available. TV.**

A small, unpretentious hotel, where guests are given a warm welcome and offered attractive rooms at very reasonable prices. Doubles cost €35–40. Its restaurant, *Les Routiers*, is also good value; it has two rooms: one is a little "cantine" that is packed with locals at lunchtime, the other serves more elaborate meals based on fish and seafood. Weekday lunchtime menu €9.50–18; others at €20–32.

Saint-Renan

29290

|●| La Maison d'Autrefois

7 rue de l'Église.
Ⓣ02.98.84.22.67
Closed *Sun lunch; Mon out of season; end Nov to mid-Jan.* **High chairs available.**

Superbly attractive, half-timbered house. Inside, the natural stone walls are decorated with old farm implements and beautiful furniture. Good, traditional crêpes – the Bretonne is stuffed with scallops, chopped leeks and cream and flambéed with Calvados, while the Sauvage drips with wine caramel and honey ice cream. Weekday lunch menu for €7.20 and a children's menu for €5.50. Reckon on €11 to eat à la carte. *Free apéritif offered to our readers on presentation of this guide.*

Saint-Thégonnec

29410

🏨 |●| Auberge de Saint-Thégonnec***

6 pl. de la Mairie (Centre).
Ⓣ02.98.79.61.18 Ⓕ02.98.62.71.10
Ⓦwww.auberge.saint.thegonnec.com
Closed *Sat lunchtime; Sun (evening only in season); Mon lunchtime; 20 Dec–10 Jan.* **Car park. TV. Disabled access. High chairs available.**

Not only one of the best hotel-restaurants on the "circuit des Enclos", also one of the best in the whole of Finistère. It lies just opposite one of the most beautiful enclosures in the region (although the church has been partially destroyed by a fire). The setting is elegant and refined, but without being overwhelming, and the seasonal food is excellent. The bill climbs up steeply if you eat à la carte (reckon on around €45), but the chef was shrewd enough to balance it with more accessible menus (the cheapest goes at €25). The bedrooms are attractive and extremely comfortable: doubles with shower/wc or bath €80–100. Breakfast is served in a charming lounge.

|●| Crêperie Steredenn

6 rue de la Gare.
Ⓣ02.98.79.43.34 Ⓕ02.98.79.44.45
Closed Mon and Tues except in July and Aug; mid-Nov to 30 Jan. Disabled access.

Christine and Alain offer a friendly greeting and an open fire. A huge choice of delicious, cheap crêpes: the Picardie, with creamed leeks; the Indien, with white sauce, onions, mushrooms and curry, and the sweet Druidique, with marmalade, almonds and Grand Marnier. Three menus at €11–12.20 or about €9-15 à la carte. Wash it down with cider brewed on the premises.

|●| Restaurant du Commerce

1 rue de Paris; it's in the centre of the village.
Ⓣ02.98.79.61.07
Closed *evenings; Sat and Sun; first 3 weeks in Aug.* **Disabled access.**

A roadside restaurant of the Routier variety. Friendly welcome, good cooking, huge portions and cheap prices. For €10 you get soup, starter, dish of the day, cheese and dessert – the menu states that a drink is included for "workers" but not for people "passing through"! They also have a few specialities like *pot-au-feu*, a broth with large chunks of meat and vegetables, *choucroute*, *kig-ha-farz* and couscous. Pleasant dining room with stone walls. It's a lively place.

Sarzeau

56370

|●| Auberge de Kerstéphanie

Route du Roaliguen; at the Sarzeau roundabout take the Roaliguen exit and it is on the right at the end of a cul-de-sac.
Ⓣ02.97.41.72.41 Ⓕ02.97.41.99.15

Closed *Sun evening; plus Tues evening and Wed out of season; Christmas and Feb holidays.* **Disabled access. Car park.**

One of the very best restaurants in Morbihan, in a gorgeous room with elegant, unfussy service. Jean-Paul Jego is a virtuoso chef, ably helped by his wife. There's a €15 lunch menu, for example, and others at €23–38, all change with the seasons. Thanks to the spit, there's a different rôtisserie dish each day, perhaps lamb shank or farm-reared rabbit with mustard. The lobster is grilled fresh from the fish tank. Fabulous food at excellent prices. *Free coffee offered to our readers on presentation of this guide.*

Restaurant L'Hortensia

La Grée-Penvins, around 7km from Sarzeau itself.
Ⓣ02.97.67.42.15 Ⓕ02.97.67.42.16
Closed *Mon and Tues except July–Aug; fortnight in March; fortnight in Nov.*

The restaurant is in an old house where you go through one dining room to get to the next. They're all painted hydrangea-blue, contrasting attractively with the starkness of the granite walls. A good range of seafood, shellfish and meat. There's a lunch menu for €16, others at €26–62 and a lobster one for €55.

Trébeurden

22560

Auberge de jeunesse

60 la Corniche Goas-Trez, lieu-dit Toëno; 2km to the north of the town, on the hills by the sea.
Ⓣ02.96.23.52.22 Ⓕ02.96.15.44.34
Ⓦwww.fuaj.org
Car park.

A modern building that clashes slightly with the landscape – but what a landscape! It has one of the best locations of any youth hostel in Brittany; right by the sea, with a diving club next door and a botanical trail nearby. FUAJ card compulsory (you can buy it in situ): €8.40 a night in a dormitory with four–twelve beds. Breakfast €3.25. Possibility of camping. No curfew.

Hôtel-restaurant Ker An Nod**

Rue de Pors-Termen; it's opposite île Millau.
Ⓣ02.96.23.50.21 Ⓕ02.96.23.63.30
Ⓦwww.kerannod.com
Closed *Mon lunchtime; Tues lunchtime; Thurs lunchtime except July–Aug and public holidays.* **TV. High chairs and games available.**

Peaceful beachside hotel run by a nice couple. Of the twenty rooms, fourteen look out to sea. Doubles with shower/wc €44–66. Breakfast €7.50. They're comfortable and bright with great picture windows. The dining room is equally pleasant; you dine here on fresh fish, seafood and local dishes – gratinéed oysters with Muscadet butter, fisherman's soup, Trégor chicken with crayfish, caramelized apples with vanilla ice. Menus €15–29. *Liqueur on the house offered to our readers on presentation of this guide.*

L'Albatros

14 rue de Trozoul.
Ⓣ02.96.23.53.78
Closed *Mon–Wed; mid-Jan to mid-Feb; fortnight end of June.*

Locals may tell you that this is a charming bistro where fishermen arrive early in the morning to prop up the bar and solve the problems of the world; others may say that this is the most fashionable restaurant in town, serving dinners of traditional meals like fish in *court-bouillon* with fresh vegetables or lobster in algae *papillote* with "grand-mother's pancakes". Which of these versions is true? They both are! After several decades working in big restaurants, Louis de Roy, a son and grandson of fishermen, has come back to his roots to open a restaurant in his own likeness, with a real canvas sail, a nautical ladder and furnishings and school benches. He re-creates timeless Breton recipes, and every weekend cuts up 15kg of abalones with coconuts from Paimpol. Weekday lunchtime menu €15, then others at €20–30 (Sun €25 and €38). *Free apéritif offered to our readers on presentation of this guide.*

La Tourelle

45 rue du Trozoul; it overlooks the port.
Ⓣ02.96.23.62.73
Closed *Tues evening and Wed except mid-July to end Aug; from mid-Nov open weekends only; Jan; Feb school holidays.*

The huge, pleasant dining room has wide bay windows with a view over the port. Good, inventive, modern cuisine with an emphasis on fish or seafood, and lots of nice little attentions to detail. Menus €16–46; the most expensive is a lobster menu. Specialities include *millefeuille* of *andouille* and foie gras with butter of Breton beer, and roast monkfish with bacon.

Trégastel

22730

Hôtel-restaurant de la Corniche**

38 rue Charles-Le-Goffic; it's in the town centre, not far from the beaches.
Ⓣ02.96.23.88.15 Ⓕ02.96.23.47.89
Ⓦwww.hoteldelacorniche.fr
Closed *Jan.* **Restaurant closed** *lunchtimes.* **TV. Car park.**

Service till 11pm. It may not exactly be by the sea (in fact, it faces a roundabout), but this is a bright place where rooms have a range of facilities. They're €39 with shower/wc and up to €60 with bath, depending on the season. Breakfast €6.10. Half board is compulsory from mid-July to 20 Aug; it costs €37–48 per person. The menu at €16 is for hotel guests only. The restored rooms (on the 2nd floor) are more expensive but more attractive, with warm colours and flowery material. The other rooms are in need of a lick of paint. *Third consecutive night (except July–Aug and public holidays) offered to our readers on presentation of this guide.*

Auberge de la Vieille Église

Place de l'Église; it's in the old town.
Ⓣ02.96.23.88.31
Closed *Sun evening; Mon; Tues evening out of season; Mon only July–Aug; March.* **High chairs available.**

This place used to do it all: canteen for local workers, butcher's, fruit and veg shop, mini-market – the lot. But it's been completely transformed since the owner and his family bought the place in 1962. They've turned it into an unmissable restaurant and you won't miss it – the outside is smothered in flowers. There's a weekday lunch menu at €13 and others at €20 and €30; à la carte you'll spend about €30. Tagliatelle with scallops, brill, and John Dory roast with bacon are house specialities, along with a good foie gras. Exceptionally high-quality cuisine, served by attentive staff in delightful surroundings. It's best to book in the evening during the season and at weekends.

Tréguier

22220

Hôtel Aigue Marine et Restaurant des 3 Rivières***

It's on the marina.
Ⓣ02.96.92.97.00 Ⓕ02.96.92.44.48
Ⓦwww.aiguemarine.fr
Closed *out of season Sat lunchtime, Sun evening and Mon; July and Aug closed every lunchtime except Sun; early Jan to end Feb.* **Disabled access. TV. Swimming pool. Car park.**

A recently built establishment on the harbour but also overlooking the car park, with 48 very comfortable rooms for €68–91 depending on the season. Breakfast €8.50. There's a heated swimming pool and a garden, and they've built a sauna and Jacuzzi. The owners have passed on responsibility in the restaurant to a talented young chef who shows his skill with local dishes. Menus at €19 (not Sun) and €28–39. The prices are good for such high-quality cuisine. *10% discount on the room rate except in July and Aug offered to our readers on presentation of this guide.*

La Poissonnerie du Trégor

2 rue Renan.
Ⓣ02.96.92.30.27
Tasting rooms open *daily July–Sept.*

A warm, unusual establishment which has been run by Mme Moulinet for the last thirty or so years. Her son, Jean-Pierre, runs a fishmonger's (open year round) where you can buy fish to cook – or you try fabulously fresh fish, seafood and shellfish dishes in the tasting rooms upstairs. Crab mayonnaise €8.50, *moules marinière* €5.50, and platters of shellfish €18.50 (€27.50 for two people). Marine frescoes line the walls, and the overall atmosphere is such that you could almost imagine you were at sea – minus the seasickness, naturally. No desserts.

Minihy-Tréguier

22220 (1.5km SW)

Kastell Dinech'h**

In a country house on the route de Lannion; take the N786 towards Lannion.
Ⓣ02.96.92.49.39 Ⓕ02.96.92.34.03
Closed *Tues evening and Wed out of season; mid-Nov to end April.* **Restaurant closed** *lunchtimes.*

Disabled access. TV. Swimming pool. Car park.

An elegant Breton manor house that's been turned into a hotel with a restaurant. They've kept all the period furniture and preserved its intimate atmosphere. The rooms are extremely pleasant; doubles with shower/wc or bath €80–84; some rooms sleep three or four. Breakfast €10.40. It's highly advisable to opt for half board, and it's obligatory between 14 July and 20 Aug: €80–84 per person. Excellent cuisine and attentive service. Set evening menus €22 and €38. *10% discount on the room rate (end Sept–mid-Nov) offered to our readers on presentation of this guide.*

Trinité-sur-Mer (La)

56470

L'Azimut - Les Chambres Marines***

1 and 3 rue du Men-Dû; 100m from the yacht club, on the coast road leading to Camac Plage.
Ⓣ02.97.55.71.88 Ⓕ02.97.55.80.15
Ⓦwww.charme-gastronomie.com
Closed *Tues evening; Wed (except for school holidays).* **Car park. TV. High chairs available. Disabled access.**

The best place to eat in town. "Here all the guests are VIPs" declares the owner-chef Hervé Le Calvez, and he puts his money where his mouth is. If you present the current edition of this guide and book in advance, he will serve you an exceptional dinner menu at €39, which includes absolutely everything: apéritif, tidbits, starter, main course, cheese or dessert, with each course accompanied by a specially chosen glass of wine. The food is meticulously prepared with fresh ingredients, mainly from the sea, and the wine list is superb. Other menus €15 (lunch, except weekends and public holidays), then €20–50. All this in a classy but convivial setting, with wood panelling and nautical knick-knacks. The bedrooms are charming and tastefully decorated – the must luxurious even has its own Jacuzzi-style bath. *10% discount on a room (in winter) or free apéritif or free coffee offered to our readers on presentation of this guide.*

Vannes

56000

Hôtel Le Bretagne**

36 rue du Mené; it's 50m from the Prison gateway.
Ⓣ02.97.47.20.21
Ⓔhotel.le.bretagne@wanadoo.fr
Closed *Sun afternoon; lst week in Oct.* **TV.**

This welcoming place has an old-fashioned charm and is often full. The quiet, smallish rooms, some overlooking the town walls, are all well maintained. Doubles €31–40 with shower/wc or bath. Breakfast €4.50. Good value.

Hôtel Le Marina**

Place Gambetta.
Ⓣ02.97.47.22.81 Ⓕ02.97.47.00.34
Ⓔlemarinahotel@aol.com
TV.

Service 7am until 1am. This hotel is above L'Océan bar, one of the drinking holes around the square; it's ideal if you like to be where the action is. Pretty rooms with double glazing have views of the harbour and town walls, and good facilities. Doubles at €35–55 offer good value for money in the heart of the old town. Breakfast €5.40. *Free coffee offered to our readers on presentation of this guide.*

Hôtel Le Richemont**

26 pl. de la Gare.
Ⓣ02.97.47.17.24 Ⓕ02.97.54.27.37
Ⓦwww.hotel-richemont-vannes.com
Closed *Sun noon–6pm.* **TV.**

A station hotel that has found a new lease of life, largely thanks to the bright colours and very professional, friendly service; considering that it is so close to the railway lines, it is surprisingly easy to shut out the outside world and it's remarkably quiet at night. Double rooms €52. The excellent breakfast is served in a room with decoration that recalls the hotel's glory days.

Hôtel La Marébaudière

4 rue Aristide-Briand.
Ⓣ02.97.47.34.29 Ⓕ02.97.54.14.11
Ⓦwww.marebaudiere.com
Car park. TV. High chairs available.

A stone's throw from the town's historic centre, huge rooms with all the mod cons and, for those on the ground floor, a small terrace as well. Double rooms €67–77. Small breakfast buffet. The enclosed private car park is another bonus. *10% discount on a room (15 Oct–15 April) offered to our readers on presentation of this guide.*

|●| La Morgate

21 rue de la Fontaine.
Ⓣ02.97.42.42.39 Ⓕ02.97.47.25.27
Closed *Sun and Mon except public holidays; a fortnight in May.*

A gourmet restaurant in a street that just climbs and climbs. Fine, flavoursome cuisine firmly based in local tradition. It mainly attracts people on business lunches and expense accounts but the menus offer good value: weekday lunch menu for €13, then others from €19.70 to €27.70. Dishes change according to the seasons, but if you see the hot/cold chocolate duo listed, don't hesitate.

|●| Le Rive Gauche

5 pl. Gambetta; in the port, on the corner of place Gambetta.
Ⓣ02.97.47.02.40
Closed *Sat lunchtime; Sun; Mon lunchtime.*

As it was a coastal stopover, Vannes used to import anything from wood to Libourne wine. By opening this pretty, little wine bar-bistro, Nathalie and Stéphane Berrigaud have unknowingly revived an old tradition. Fine choice of Bordeaux wines and some small dishes, such as the mackerel pie with tapenade and fillet of John Dory with aromatic spices. Menus €13 (lunch), €19 (dinner).

|●| Restaurant de Roscanvec

17 rue des Halles.
Ⓣ02.97.47.15.96.
Ⓦwww.roscanvec.com
Closed *Mon except July–Sept; Sun evening; 23 Dec–1 Jan.* **High chairs available.**

This cosy, traditional restaurant occupies two floors of a characterful fourteenth-century house. The owner-chef is full of talent and ambition and he has succeeded in attracting a clientele of informed gourmets. Things get serious from the first menu at €17 (served at lunch and up till 8.15pm, but not on Sun) and right up till the lobster menu at €74; try the turbot in honey crust, pig's trotters and lobster stew, *hochepot de bœuf* (boned oxtail), and in summer, the almond pastry with red fruits. Dishes change regularly to reflect what's good in the market. Reckon on around €38 à la carte. First-rate wine list.

|●| Le Carré Blanc

28 rue du Port.
Ⓣ02.97.47.48.34
Closed *Sun; Mon lunchtime.*

A restaurant in tune with the times, dreamed up by two friends who had worked sufficiently in big establishments to realize that Vannes lacked a really modern eatery. Minimalist décor, trendy colour scheme, dishes mixing traditional ingredients with unusual spices: young and old enjoy the mackerel menhir aux fines herbes, the Szechuan style *croustillant* of pollack and gingerbread with savoury caramel ice cream. Reckon on €20–25 à la carte.

|●| L'Eau à la Bouche

Rue Larmor-Gwened; near the Kerino bridge.
Ⓣ02.97.69.02.02

An evocative name (mouth-watering) sets the tone for this intimate setting at the water's edge. Sophisticated decoration and an elegantly dressed clientèle. Fashionable cooking that is basically Provençal but also takes advantage of the fresh fish from the nearby Gulf of Morbihan: baked bass with anchovy sauce, mullet with vierge sauce. Dishes around €20; desserts €6. Pretty terrace surrounded by poplars (best appreciated at high tide).

Saint-Avé

56890 (5km N)

|●| Le Pressoir

7 rue de l'Hôpital; it's 1km out of Saint-Avé.
Ⓣ and Ⓕ02.97.60.87.63
Ⓦwww.le-pressoir-st-ave.com
Closed *Sun evening; Mon; Tues; 1–8 Jan; 1–15 March; 1–10 July; 1–20 Oct.* **Disabled access. Car park.**

Exceptional surroundings and facilities, a warm welcome and gastronomic delights in an attractive house just outside town. It's quite simply the best restaurant in these parts, serving great fresh fish and specialities like galette of red mullet with potato and rosemary, foie gras ravioli with wild mushroom broth, and baked Granny Smith apples. The cheapest set menu at €28 is served only on weekday lunchtimes, but it's worth going out of your way to try it.

Others €40–80. *10% discount on the second menu (except weekends) offered to our readers on presentation of this guide.*

Arradon

56610 (8km SW)

Hôtel-restaurant Le Stivell***

15 rue Plessis-d'Arradon; take the D101.
Ⓣ02.97.44.03.15 Ⓕ02.97.44.78.90
Closed *15 Nov–15 Dec.* **Restaurant closed** *Sun evening and Mon out of season.* **TV.**

An extremely well-run *Logis de France* in one of the most beautiful parts of the Gulf of Morbihan. Ideal if you want to enjoy the peacefulness of the sea without straying too far from Vannes. Double rooms €48–62, with a tempting offer of half board at €45–54, depending on the season. Gastronomic menu at €41. The chef, inspired by the ocean, uses the fresh ingredients it provides: seafood sauerkraut, warm oysters with champagne, etc. Magnificent seafood platters (order 48hrs in advance). Astonishing gastronomic menu for children, with the dishes on the menu in half portions. Friendly service.

Le Logis du Parc Er Gréo

9. rue Mane-Guen lieu-dit Le Gréo, near Moustoir.
Ⓣ02.97.44.73.03 Ⓕ02.97.44.80.48
Ⓦwww.parcergreo.com
Closed *12 Nov–12 March.*

A hotel best described as intimate, with charming, attentive service and impressive furniture. Delightful south-facing rooms, all different. Doubles €70–130, depending on the degree of comfort and the season. Breakfast (€10), served in a room lined with pictures painted by the owner's father (if you want to see more, he's also got a gallery close by). Breakfast €10. Pretty garden and heated swimming pool, in use from Easter to early Nov.

Locqueltas

56390 (15km N)

Hôtel La Voltige**

8 rte. de Vannes; from Vannes, take the D767 for Pontivy.
Ⓣ02.97.60.72.06 Ⓕ02.97.44.63.01
Ⓦwww.la-voltige.fr
Restaurant closed *Sun evening and Mon out of season; Mon in season (except for hotel guests); a fortnight in March; a fortnight in Oct.* **Disabled access (restaurant). TV. High chairs and games available. Car park.**

Located north of Vannes, a dozen impeccable rooms – €37–55 with shower/wc or bath – check out the great split-level rooms for three or four people. Some overlook the road and can be a bit noisy, despite the double glazing. From 1–25 Aug they prefer you to stay on a half board basis at €37–52. It's an attractive option because of the rather good traditional food that's offered on even the cheapest menu (€13.80 – not served weekends or public holidays). Other menus €18.50–42. Try the Breton seafood platter or the navarin of sole and cod with spices. There's a garden with an area set aside for games. *Free coffee and 10% discount on the room rate 15 Sept–5 April offered to our readers on presentation of this guide.*

Vitré

35500

Hôtel Le Minotel**

47 rue Poterie.
Ⓣ02.99.75.11.11 Ⓕ02.99.75.81.26
Ⓦwww.ot-vitre.fr
TV.

Really pretty hotel in the old town; they've virtually rebuilt the house but have respected the local style while providing modern facilities. Perhaps, if you're being very picky, the result is rather unimaginative. The green and tartan décor makes the place look a bit like a golf clubhouse – and aptly enough they've done a deal with the local golf club and offer packages if you want to play a round or two. Doubles €47 with bath, and there are family rooms for four people. Breakfast €5.50. Diners cards not accepted. You can eat at the crêperie-pizzeria adjoining the hotel; show this guide to get a 10% discount. Credit cards not accepted.

La Gavotte

7 rue des Augustins.
Ⓣ02.99.74.47.74
Ⓔla.gavotte-vitre@wanadoo.fr
Closed *Mon; Tues except July–Aug.*

This restaurant fits in well with the surroundings in this charming village. It's a crêperie with a large pink and green dining room. They serve excellent girdle cakes and pancakes with fillings from the traditional to the unusual: Darley cheese (a Breton variety), *andouille*, various sausages and an apple preparation which is somewhere between purée and chutney. The delicious dishes are accompanied by cider and local beverages There's a lunchtime *formule* at €9.50 and a menu at €12; à la carte you'll pay around €14 for a complete meal. *Free apéritif offered to our readers on presentation of this guide.*

|●| Auberge Saint-Louis

31 rue Notre-Dame.
Ⓣ02.99.75.28.28

Closed *Sun evening; Mon; Tues lunchtime; a week in March; a fortnight in Sept.* **Disabled access.**

An elegant fifteenth-century house which has built up a solid reputation. The wood panelling in the dining room creates a warm, sophisticated yet family-style atmosphere. The young patronne will bring you a small plate of appetizers to nibble while you select your meal. You're in for a feast in a cosy setting. Menus €12.50–26; à la carte you'll spend around €29. There's a good selection of grilled meats and superb fish, accompanied by well-crafted sauces.

Centre

Amboise

37400

Auberge de jeunesse de l'Île d'Or

Centre Charles-Péguy Entrepont.
02.47.30.60.90 02.47.30.60.91
www.ucrif.asso.fr
Open *all year round.* **Disabled access. Car park.**

A lush setting for one of the very few youth hostels that boast a better view than any of the nearby hotels – in this case of the Amboise château. So, if possible, book a room overlooking it (nos. 7, 8, 9, 10 and 14). €6.60–8.60 a night, depending on the season. Breakfast €2.60. Half board €15.90–17.90 per person, depending on the season. Meals around €6.70. The place has recently been renovated, and Didier Giovannelli and his team will give you an effusive welcome.

Hôtel Le Chanteloup**

12 av. Émile-Gounin; it's 1.5km from the château.
02.47.57.10.90 02.47.57.17.52
Closed *1 Oct–31 March.* Car park.

Staying in Amboise tends to be expensive so it's good to find a hotel, open in season only, offering good value for money. This big block of a house, with a private car park front and back, is just outside the centre of town. There's no consistent style to speak of – armchairs are in fake leather, surfaces in Formica. There are three floors (with lift), and very simple rooms; a double with shower/wc costs €40–46 or with bath €46–58. Breakfast €5.50. Rooms up in the roof have skylights. It's very well maintained. There's a small garden and a terrace behind the hotel.

Restaurant L'Épicerie

46 pl. Michel-Debré; opposite the château's car park.
02.47.57.08.94
Closed *Mon and Tues out of season; Nov to mid-Dec.*

A splendid old façade with olive-green half-timbering; behind the curtains, out of sight of the hordes of tourists, you can enjoy some fine food: *rillettes* of smoked Loire eel, veal sweetbreads with morels, *tournedos* of duck *confit* with Chinon wine, roast squab with truffle crumble. Weekday lunch menu €11, then several other menus €18–35. The service is efficient but relaxed, at times even playful, in contrast to the somewhat traditional atmosphere.

Cangey

37530 (12km NE)

Le Fleuray Hotel***

Route Dame-Marie-les-Bois; from Amboise, take the N152 towards Blois, then turn left onto the D74 signposted to Cangey, Fleuray and Dame-Marie, or exit 18 on the A10.
02.47.56.09.25 02.47.56.93.97
www.lefleurayhotel.com
Closed *one week in Feb and Nov; Christmas–New Year.* **Restaurant closed** *lunchtime.* **Swimming pool. Disabled access. High chairs and games available. Car park.**

This nineteenth-century manor house is a cross between a hotel and a guesthouse. Hazel and Peter Newington and family have called their fifteen prettily decorated rooms after flowers such as *bouton d'or*

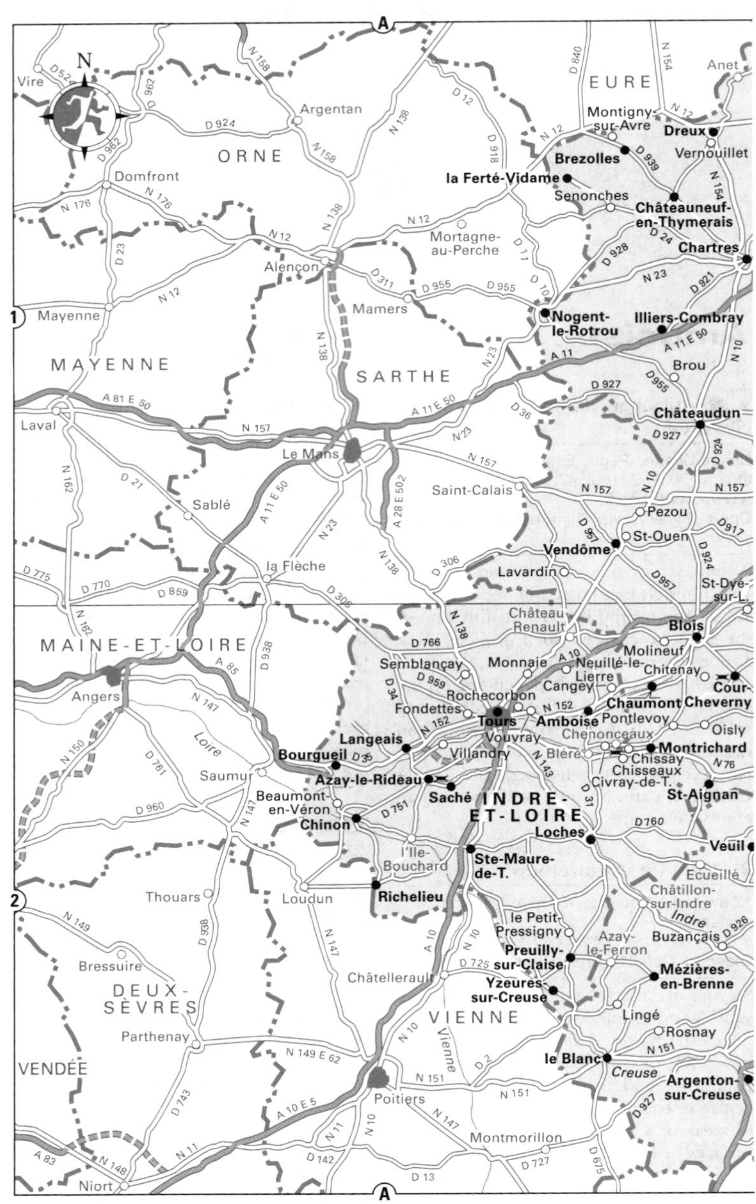
A
N
Vire
Argentan
ORNE
Domfront
EURE
Anet
Montigny-sur-Avre
Dreux
Vernouillet
Brezolles
la Ferté-Vidame
Senonches
Châteauneuf-en-Thymerais
Chartres
Mortagne-au-Perche
Alençon
Mamers
Nogent-le-Rotrou
Illiers-Combray
1
Mayenne
MAYENNE
SARTHE
Brou
Châteaudun
Laval
Le Mans
Saint-Calais
Pezou
St-Ouen
Sablé
Vendôme
la Flèche
Lavardin
St-Dyé-sur-L.
Château-Renault
Blois
MAINE-ET-LOIRE
Molineuf
Semblançay
Monnaie
Neuillé-le-Lierre
Chitenay
Cour-Cheverny
Angers
Cangey
Rochecorbon
Chaumont
Fondettes
Tours
Amboise
Pontlevoy
Oisly
Vouvray
Chenonceaux
Langeais
Villandry
Bléré
Montrichard
Bourgueil
Chissay
Chisseaux
Loire
Saumur
Azay-le-Rideau
Civray-de-T.
St-Aignan
Saché
Beaumont-en-Véron
INDRE-ET-LOIRE
Chinon
Loches
Veuil
l'Ile-Bouchard
Ste-Maure-de-T.
Ecueillé
Richelieu
Châtillon-sur-Indre
2
Thouars
Loudun
Indre
le Petit-Pressigny
Azay-le-Ferron
Buzançais
Preuilly-sur-Claise
Bressuire
Mézières-en-Brenne
Châtellerault
Yzeures-sur-Creuse
DEUX-SÈVRES
Lingé
VIENNE
Rosnay
Parthenay
Vienne
le Blanc
VENDÉE
Creuse
Argenton-sur-Creuse
Poitiers
Montmorillon
Niort
A 81 E 50
A 11 E 50
A 11
A 10
A 28 E 502
A 85
A 10 E 5
A 83
N 12
N 138
N 157
N 10
N 152
N 147
N 149 E 62
N 151
D 927
D 955
D 13
D 142

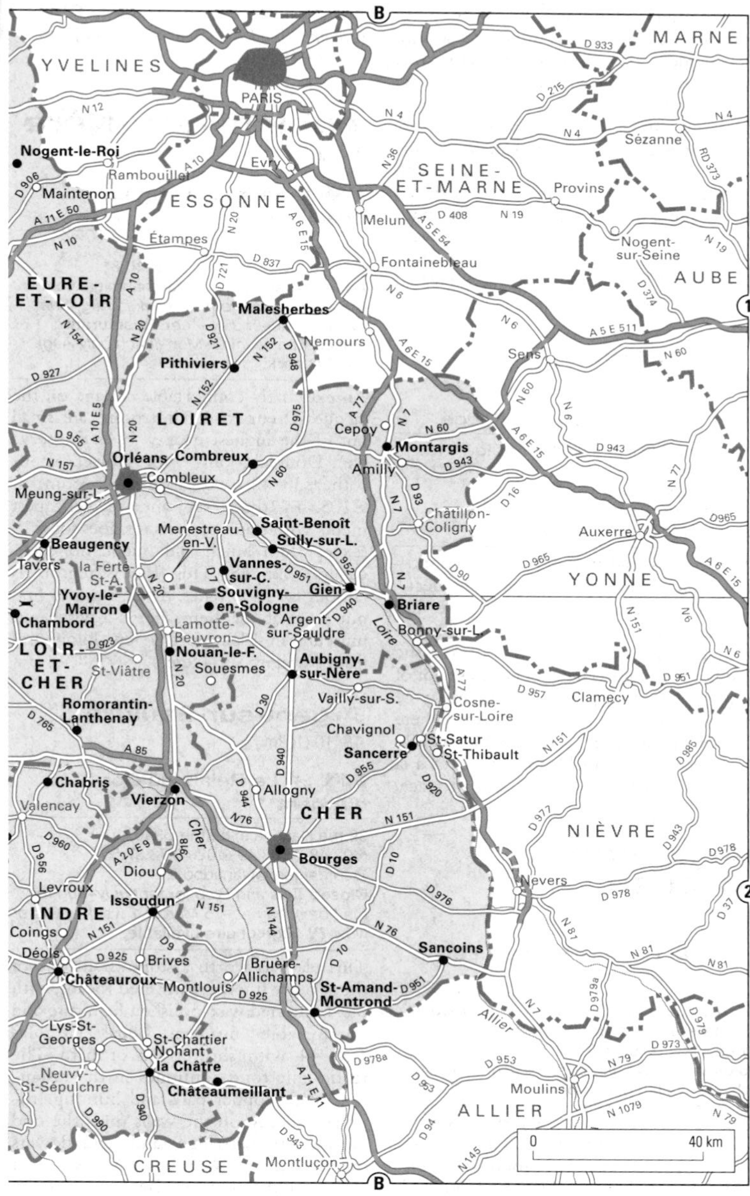

YVELINES
PARIS
MARNE
Nogent-le-Roi
Rambouillet
Maintenon
Evry
ESSONNE
SEINE-ET-MARNE
Sézanne
Provins
Melun
Nogent-sur-Seine
Étampes
Fontainebleau
AUBE
EURE-ET-LOIR
Malesherbes
Nemours
Sens
Pithiviers
LOIRET
Cepoy
Montargis
Orléans
Combreux
Amilly
Combleux
Meung-sur-L.
Châtillon-Coligny
Menestreau-en-V.
Saint-Benoît
Sully-sur-L.
Auxerre
Beaugency
Tavers
la Ferté-St-A.
Vannes-sur-C.
Gien
YONNE
Yvoy-le-Marron
Souvigny-en-Sologne
Briare
Chambord
Lamotte-Beuvron
Argent-sur-Sauldre
Bonny-sur-L.
Loire
LOIR-ET-CHER
St-Viâtre
Nouan-le-F.
Souesmes
Aubigny-sur-Nère
Vailly-sur-S.
Clamecy
Cosne-sur-Loire
Romorantin-Lanthenay
Chavignol
St-Satur
Sancerre
St-Thibault
Chabris
Vierzon
Allogny
Valencay
CHER
Cher
NIÈVRE
Bourges
Diou
Nevers
Levroux
Issoudun
INDRE
Coings
Sancoins
Déols
Brives
Bruère-Allichamps
Châteauroux
Montlouis
St-Amand-Montrond
Allier
Lys-St-Georges
St-Chartier
Nohant
la Châtre
Neuvy-St-Sépulchre
Châteaumeillant
Moulins
ALLIER
CREUSE
Montluçon
0
40 km

(buttercup), *cerisier* (cherry blossom) and *clochette* (bluebell); *capucine* (nasturtium) and *perce-neige* (snowdrop) are larger than the others. Doubles €68–78 with shower/wc or bath, according to season; the garden rooms (from €80) are large, with their own terrace. Gourmet cooking, with set menus €26–36, is served in a pleasant dining room or out on the terrace. Specialities include pan-fried langoustines with garlic butter, chicken with Creole curry sauce, lamb cutlets with red fruits and Loire wine, pears stuffed with goat's cheese. Nice welcome, and a very international clientele, but you must book. Half board from €80 per person. Heated swimming pool in summer.

Chisseaux

37150 (17km SE)

Auberge du Cheval Rouge

30 rue Nationale; it's on the road to Montrichard.
☎02.47.23.86.67
Closed *10–30 Nov; Mon and Tues out of season; Mon only in summer.*

A few steps lead from this lovely country bistro into a charming and tastefully decorated dining room. Mme Feron serves her husband's cooking with great kindness – though when the restaurant is packed she has her hands full. The chef devotes a lot of care to his food, particularly to his wine and cream sauces: this is a place where cooking is taken very seriously. Menus €22 (not served Sun lunch) up to €42, or à la carte. There's a lovely garden and a terrace.

Argenton-sur-Creuse

36200

Hôtel-restaurant Le Cheval Noir**

27 rue Auclert-Descottes; it's on the road to Gargilesse-Dampierre.
☎02.54.24.00.06 Ⓕ02.54.24.11.22
Closed *Sun evening out of season.* **TV. High chairs available. Car park.**

The restoration work done on this nineteenth-century posthouse has been particularly well executed. The rooms are quiet and comfortable. Doubles €52–56 with shower/wc or bath. The elegant, subtle cuisine is prepared by chef Christophe Jeannot, whose specialities include duck foie gras with Guérande sea salt and fillet of zander with leeks. Weekday lunch menu at €10 and other set menus at €16–24. *Free apéritif offered to our readers on presentation of this guide.*

Aubigny-sur-Nère

18700

Hôtel-restaurant La Chaumière**

1 av. du Parc-des-Sports.
☎02.48.58.04.01 Ⓕ02.48.58.10.31
Ⓦwww.hotel-restaurant-la-chaumiere.com
Closed *Feb half-term; 1 week in Aug; Sun evening (except July–Aug).* **Restaurant closed** *Sun evening; Mon (lunch only Aug).* **TV. Car park.**

An extremely comfortable cottage on the Jacques-Cœur road. The rooms are small but of the highest quality (as is the service). Double rooms with shower/wc or bath €38–42; two "top-rank" rooms at €105. In the restaurant, the cheapest menu, with traditional dishes, goes for €18 (except Sun lunch and public holidays), others €25–48. This Berry region is famous for its witches. If you want to find out more about them, there's a witchcraft museum in Blancafort, a few kilometres from Aubigny-sur-Nère.

Argent-sur-Sauldre

18410 (10km N)

Le Relais du Cor d'Argent**

39 rue Nationale; off the D940.
☎02.48.73.63.49 Ⓕ02.48.73.37.55
Ⓔcordargent@wanadoo.fr
Closed *Tues and Wed (except July–Aug for the hotel); 15 Feb–15 March; 1 week in Oct or Nov.* **TV. High chairs available.**

This place is worth a stopover in one of the seventy finely refurbished rooms, with old-fashioned wax-polished furniture and comfortable modern beds. Doubles €34–44 with shower/wc or bath. The rustic-chic tone continues in the restaurant, with copper pans and hunting trophies hanging on the walls (plus the odd pheasant or partridge) and wild flowers on the tables. The cooking is much appreciated all over Berry: game in season, *fricassée* of lobster with Noilly and leek *confit*, fried scallops and langoustines with chicory and *noisette* of rabbit with kidneys. Menus start at €14 (except Sun lunch and public holidays) and go up to €50. *Free apéritif offered to our readers on presentation of this guide.*

Vailly-sur-Sauldre

18260 (17km E)

Le Lièvre Gourmand

14 Grand-Rue; take the D923 in the direction of Sancerre.
02.48.73.80.23 02.48.73.86.13
lelievregourmand@wanadoo.fr
Closed *Sun evening; Mon; Tues.* **Disabled access.**

William Page from Australia displays his art in these two old village houses. His cooking is exceptional and makes inspired use of spices – *roulade* of semi-cooked foie gras and fig *compote*, sea bream with lemon zest. The menu changes with the seasons but the inventiveness is constant. And there are even a few good Australian vintages to help wash down your fillet of kangaroo. Give it a whirl – it's one of a kind. Set menus at €22–45.

Azay-le-Rideau

37190

Restaurant L'Aigle d'Or

10 av. Adélaïde-Richer; head towards Langeais.
02.47.45.24.58
aigle.d'or@wanadoo.fr
Closed *Sun evening; Wed; Tues evening except July–Aug; Mon evening Dec to end March; Feb; 1st week in Sept; 2nd fortnight in Nov.* **Disabled access. Games available.**

One of the best gastronomic restaurants in Touraine, with a welcoming and refined setting – even the beams in the dining room are a relaxing soft green – and reasonable prices. Attentive service. Meals served in the garden in summer. Weekday lunch menu €18; then €26–57 including wines. The à la carte menu changes frequently, but retains a few classics: langoustine salad with foie gras; *blanquette* of zander in Azay wine sauce; and *la griottine* with chocolate. The wine list is most instructive, with maps showing the provenance of numerous wines. *Free glass of Azay-le-Rideau sweet wine (1 Nov–31 March) offered to our readers on presentation of this guide.*

Villandry

37510 (10km NE)

L'Étape Gourmande

Domaine de la Giraudière; from Azay, take the D751 towards Tours. After about 5km, turn left towards Druye, then get to Villandry on the D121.
02.47.50.08.60 02.47.50.06.60
www.etapegourmande.com
Closed *15 Nov–15 March.* **Disabled access. High chairs available. Car park.**

Open every day 12.45–3pm and 7.30–9pm. This is a splendid seventeenth-century farm which, despite the complicated-looking directions, is easy to find. The superb dining room has a huge fireplace and you can also eat outside on the terrace. The chef gave up a career as a diplomat to start the place – expect a courteous welcome and punctillious service. They serve their own goat's cheese and other farm produce. There are plenty of local dishes, complicated salads, omelettes, quiches and lovely Loire wines. Set menus €14–27 or à la carte about €29. On the first Saturday of the summer they give concerts with singers and storytellers (reservations necessary). You can buy goat's cheeses and fruits preserved in wine and they will even show you the goats and take you round the dairy. *Free coffee offered to our readers on presentation of this guide.*

Beaugency

45190

Auberge de jeunesse

152 rte. de Châteaudun lieu-dit Vernon; on the D925 (in the direction of Cravant-Châteaudun); no bus from train station, you must take a taxi.
02.38.44.61.31 02.38.44.14.73
Closed *Jan–Feb.* **Disabled access. Car park.**

This youth hostel, set in the old school of a quiet little village, exudes an irresistible charm, with its courtyard with linden trees and gravel that crunches underfoot, reminiscent of the photos of Robert Doisneau. Guests sleep in the old classrooms or in the more recent annexes, which blend in well with the older buildings. Dormitories with five, six and eight beds, with a total capacity of 120 people. There are also five double rooms with toilets and ten studios with bunks to accommodate families. You can also pitch a tent outside. €8.85 per person (FUAJ card compulsory), €8.40 for meals (groups only), €10.20 with wine and coffee. A kitchen is also available. Credit cards not accepted.

Hostellerie de l'Écu de Bretagne**

5 rue de la Maille d'Or.
Ⓣ02.38.44.67.60 Ⓕ02.38.44.68.07
Restaurant closed *Sun evening; Mon Nov–March.* **High chairs available. TV. Car park.**

There are heraldic shields on the wall and an atmosphere reminiscent of a Chabrol film, but no visible connection with Brittany – in fact, this old staging post gets its name from the Breton family who have owned the place since the fifteenth century. Rooms, most of them refurbished, vary in size, but are all comfortable. Double rooms cost €48. The renovated restaurant is pricey but the quality is superb. Menus €18–27.50 (the last one has a few supplements). *10% discount on the room rate (Nov–March) offered to our readers on presentation of this guide.*

Hôtel de la Sologne**

6 pl. Saint-Firmin.
Ⓣ02.38.44.50.27 Ⓕ02.38.44.90.19
Ⓦwww.hoteldelasologne.com
Closed *mid-Dec to mid-Jan.* **TV. Car park.**

The medieval rue de l'Evêché leads to a delightful little flower-filled square dominated by a statue of Joan of Arc. This is a wonderfully peaceful setting, and the hotel fits in perfectly. The lovely old rooms have been refurbished with taste. Doubles from €43–63 with shower/wc or €63 with bath. There's a patio where you can eat breakfast on fine days. Reservations are advised for this charming place. *20% discount on the room rate (19 Oct–31 March) offered to our readers on presentation of this guide.*

Tavers

45190 (3km SW)

La Tonnellerie****

12 rue des Eaux Bleues.
Ⓣ02.38.44.68.15 Ⓕ02.38.44.10.01
Closed *Sat and Mon lunchtimes; Jan–Feb.* **TV. High chairs available. Swimming pool. Car park.**

An austere-looking building in the centre of the village – but inside it's a different story. By general consent, this is the best place in Beaugency: very chic, with relaxing, comfortable décor. It's so quiet that you can hear the birdsong and the chimes of the church bell, and you can stroll through the grounds, which are full of chestnut trees (and even have a heated swimming pool). The cooking is luxurious and fragrant, putting new spins on old classics: try, for example, the lobster couscous. Menus €27–47. The rooms are super-comfortable. Doubles and suites cost €120–224 depending on facilities and the season. *10% discount on the price of a room (March, Nov and Dec) or a free apéritif offered to our readers on presentation of this guide.*

Blanc (Le)

36300

Domaine de l'Étape***

Route de Bélâbre; drive 5km along the D10 in the direction of Bélâbre.
Ⓣ02.54.37.18.02 Ⓕ02.54.37.75.59
Ⓦwww.domaineetape.com
Disabled access. TV. Car park.

This magnificent nineteenth-century estate is a magical place. It's set in huge grounds, with a lake, woods and fields, and the thirty-five rooms are spread between the château itself, the modern lodge and the rustic farm by the stables. The most splendid are on the first floor in the château: they're immense and beautifully furnished – ideal for a honeymoon or an intimate weekend *à deux*. Doubles €38–105 with shower/wc or bath. There are set menus from €20–54 or you can dine à la carte. The cooking is in keeping with the wonderful environs. *Free apéritif offered to our readers on presentation of this guide.*

Le Cygne

8 av. Gambetta.
Ⓣ02.54.28.71.63 Ⓕ02.54.28.72.13
Closed *Mon; Tues; Sun evening except July–Aug; 1st fortnight in Jan; 2nd fortnight in June; few days in Aug.* **Disabled access. High chairs available.**

On one floor the décor is fresh, with pinkish walls, while on the first floor the dining room is more rustic, with big beams and walls painted straw-yellow. There's also an intimate salon which is perfect for groups of four to nine. The chef comes out of the kitchen to chat to his clients. Menus

€15–45; specialities include *cassolette* of snails Berry-style and ox kidneys cooked whole and flambéed in Marc. Good food and good value.

Rosnay

36300 (15km NE)

Le Cendrille

1 pl. de la Mairie.
Ⓣ02.54.28.64.94 Ⓕ02.54.28.64.93
Closed *Tues; Wed; 15 Dec–15 Jan.* **High chairs available. Disabled access.**

This delightful restaurant, in the middle of a village in the Brenne, has been stylishly done up by Florence and Luke Jeanneau with the aid of a grant from the town hall. They have chosen strong yellows and blues and created a warm atmosphere; they'll welcome you warmly, too. The cooking is simple, tasty and traditional. Menus start at €9.15 (weekday lunchtimes), then go up from €15 to €27. *Free house apéritif offered to our readers on presentation of this guide.*

Linge

36220 (16km NE)

Auberge de la Gabrière**

La Gabrière. From Le Blanc, take the D975 in the direction of Azay-le-Ferron, then the D6; at Lingé follow the signs for La Gabrière.
Ⓣ02.54.37.80.97 Ⓕ02.54.37.70.66
Restaurant closed *Tues evening and Wed except July–Aug.* **Disabled access. TV.**

The inn is beautifully situated on Lake Gabrière. The restaurant is crowded all year because the cuisine is good and you can enjoy the view while you eat. Menus range from €10.50, served on weekdays, to €24. They specialize in Brenne produce: fillet of carp *paysanne*, pike with cream and chive sauce and *fricassée* of frogs' legs provençale. The inn has a number of rather ordinary, but clean rooms, some with a lake view; doubles with shower/wc or bath €33.50. *Free coffee offered to our readers on presentation of this guide.*

Blois

41000

Auberge de jeunesse

18 rue de l'Hôtel-Pasquier; take the #4 bus, in the direction of Les Grouëts, to the "Église" or "Auberge-de-Jeunesse" stops.
Ⓣ and Ⓕ02.54.78.27.21
Ⓦwww.fuaj.org
Closed *mid-Nov to 1 March; 10am–6pm.* **Car park.**

Total of forty-eight beds (one dormitory for men and one for women). Reckon on €7.50 per night. Breakfast €3.50. You can cook your own meals in the fully fitted kitchen.

Hôtel Saint-Jacques*

7 rue Ducoux; it's opposite the train station.
Ⓣ02.54.78.04.15 Ⓕ02.54.78.33.05
Closed *24 Dec–5 Jan.* **TV.**

Small, simple, friendly place with well-maintained rooms. Doubles range from €36 for a big room with shower/wc down to €25 for a simpler, smaller room with handbasin. *Rebate on breakfast offered to our readers on presentation of this guide.*

Hôtel Le Savoie**

6 rue Ducoux; it's opposite the train station.
Ⓣ02.54.74.32.21 Ⓕ02.54.74.29.58
Ⓔhotel.le.savoie@wanadoo.fr
Closed 24 Dec–5 Jan. **TV.**

This is a nice little hotel, reminiscent of a guesthouse, away from the hustle and bustle of the tourist area. Rooms are clean and bright; doubles €40–48. Breakfast buffet €6. You'll get a very nice welcome. Best to book.

Hôtel de France et de Guise**

3 rue Gallois; it's behind the château.
Ⓣ02.54.78.00.53 Ⓕ02.54.78.29.45
Closed *Nov–March.* **TV.**

Very, very *Vieille France*, from the welcome to the atmosphere – and the floral wall coverings and sofas in the hall and the dining room. The rooms are in the same style, but brighter and freshly decorated. Some are particularly attractive, with plaster mouldings and big fireplaces, and a few have a view of the château. All are well maintained. Doubles €47–60.

Hôtel Anne de Bretagne**

31 av. Jean-Laigret; it's 300m from the château and the city centre, near the tourist office.
Ⓣ02.54.78.05.38 Ⓕ02.54.74.37.79
Ⓔannedebretagne@free.fr
Closed *4 Jan–6 Feb.* **TV. Car park.**

A family hotel, stylishly provincial and

situated in the middle of town. The rooms at the rear of the building have double glazing; those at the front have a nice view of the square and the bar terrace, which is set back from the road. Pleasant rooms for €52–58. *Free coffee offered to our readers on presentation of this guide.*

Au Bouchon Lyonnais

25 rue des Violettes; head for place Louis-XII.
Ⓣ02.54.74.12.87
Closed *Sun and Mon except in summer and public holidays; 21 Dec–20 Jan.* **High chairs available.**

A genuine traditional Lyon-style bistro serving authentic Lyon-style specialities: pan-fried snails with wild mushrooms, warm *saucisson*, calf's liver *à la lyonnaise*, calf's head *ravigote*, baked cod and Lyonnais *quenelle* of pike. The prices are really very reasonable given quality and quantity. Set menus €18.30–25.90. The setting is a superb Louis XII house and there's a terrace for sunny days.

Au Rendez-vous des Pêcheurs

27 rue Foix.
Ⓣ02.54.74.67.48
Closed *Sun and Mon except July–Aug; 3 weeks in Aug.*

It must be said that this is not only the most pleasant place to eat in the town, but maybe also in the entire region: relaxed bistro atmosphere, cheerful, keenly attentive service and very good value for money. Enticing market menu at €24, served during the week at lunch and dinner, with another menu at €68 and around €38 à la carte. Superb Loire wines. The chef, Christophe Cosme, is young but has already made a name for himself, and his inspired, personal cooking and frequent appearances in the dining room have attracted an equally young crowd. Booking essential.

Le Bistrot du Cuisinier

20 quai Villebois-Mareuil; it's on the banks of the Loire, 50m from the pont Gabriel.
Ⓣ02.54.78.06.70 Ⓕ02.54.74.00.98
Ⓔbistrot.du.cuisinier@wanadoo.fr
Closed *a fortnight at the end of the year.*
Disabled access.

A restaurant with a wonderful view of the city. Simple, unpretentious dining room with decent, good-value food. There's a *formule* at €24 with main meal and starter or dessert, and a set menu at €30. The regional cuisine is really delicious and portions are big. Very interesting list of wines from the Loire. About once a month the chef takes you on a gastronomic tour, producing dishes from other French regions as well as further afield.

Molineuf

41190 (9km W)

Restaurant de la Poste

11 av. de Blois; from Blois, take the D766 in the direction of Angers.
Ⓣ02.54.70.03.25 Ⓕ02.54.70.12.46
Ⓦwww.poidras.com
Closed *Tues evening out of season; Wed and Sun evenings except July–Aug; 18 Nov–6 Dec; Feb.* **High chairs available.**

This little restaurant on the outskirts of Molineuf is a good place to stop and treat yourself to some of the delicious creations of chef Thierry Poidras. Menus at €16 (weekdays only) to €28.50. An extremely good restaurant, decorated in bright citrus colours. *Free coffee offered to our readers on presentation of this guide.*

Chitenay

41120 (15km S)

L'Auberge du Centre**

Place de l'Église; take the D956 as far as Cellettes and then the D38.
Ⓣ02.54.70.42.11 Ⓕ02.54.70.35.03
Ⓦwww.auberge-du-centre.com
Closed *Mon evening and Tues evening; Feb.*
Disabled access. High chairs and games available. TV. Car park.

The classical frontage doesn't really give any clue to the handsome interior of this hotel and its delightfully peaceful garden. It's a great place to park the car or the bike for a day or two and simply relax. Doubles €56–66. Half board, preferred May to September, costs €53-58. Excellent cuisine, bringing out the full flavour of all the ingredients, is served in a friendly atmosphere – the clientèle is really mixed. There's a good *menu du marché* (not served at weekends or public holidays) for €19.50 and other menus €25–39. Good wine list. *Free apéritif offered to our readers on presentation of this guide.*

Bourges

18000

See map on pp.228–9.

Auberge de jeunesse Jacques-Cœur

22, rue Henri-Sellier; in a park near the palais des congrès and exhibition park. **Off map A3-1**
Ⓣ02.48.24.58.09 Ⓕ02.48.65.51.46
Ⓔbourges@fuaj.org
Open *every day 8am–noon and 5–10pm (24 hour access via a magnetic card system).*
Closed *mid-Dec to early Jan.*

€8.40 per person staying in dormitories with three, five and eight beds; rooms for couples and families. Rental of sheets €2.75. Breakfast costs €3.25. Menu (prebooking required) €8.40 (including deposit). Possibility of cooking your own meals. FUAJ card compulsory. *10% discount on the bed rate offered to our readers on presentation of this guide.*

Hôtel Le Christina**

5 rue de la Halle. **Map A2-4**
Ⓣ02.48.70.56.50 Ⓕ02.48.70.58.13
Ⓦwww.le-christina.com
TV. Pay car park.

Well-located on the edge of the historic town, near the pedestrianized area. Good facilities. All rooms have effective soundproofing; some have attractive rustic furniture and a toilet separate from the bathroom. Doubles €41–75. Nice welcome. It's a shame breakfast is not up to standard. *10% discount on the room rate (Fri–Sun, public holidays and on the eve of public holidays from 1 Nov to 31 March) offered to our readers on presentation of this guide.*

Relais de l'Agriculture**

18 bd. de Juranville. **Map A2-3**
Ⓣ02.48.70.40.84 Ⓕ02.48.65.50.58
TV. Car park.

You'll get a very warm welcome from Madame Maigret, who likes to talk delightedly about how she realized her dream of having a farm in the Sologne. If you arrive by car, use the door opposite the car park on boulevard de Juranville. Rooms are pretty as well as quiet. Doubles €54 with kitchenette. Some are air-conditioned and have exposed beams, but they're on the top floor. *10% discount on the room rate (1 Nov–31 March) offered to our readers on presentation of this guide.*

Inter Hôtel Les Tilleuls**

7 pl. de la Pyrotechnie. **Off map C3-2**
Ⓣ02.48.20.49.04 Ⓕ02.48.50.61.73
Ⓦwww.les-tilleuls.com
Disabled access. TV. Swimming pool. Car park.

This hotel is on a little square just out of the centre; you'll need a car. Doubles with shower/wc or bath go for €56–61 according to season. The annexe rooms, with air-conditioning and nice bathrooms, lead to the flower-filled garden; those in the old building are nothing special to look at, but comfortable nonetheless. There's a gym and a heated pool. Meals can be brought to your room on a tray. *10% discount on the room rate offered to our readers on presentation of this guide.*

Les 3 P'tits Cochons

27 bis av. Jean-Jaurès. **Map B1-16**
Ⓣ02.48.65.64.96
Restaurant closed *Sat lunch; Sun.*

Open until 2am. A switched-on place with a young, local crowd. Join the line at the lengthy bar for a drink or take over the benches for a meal. The cuisine combines local and far-away flavours; *andouillette, filet mignon* with morels or goat terrine with beetroot. Lunch menu €10 or around €20 à la carte. Attractive décor – soft lights, ochre walls decorated with maps, old sewing tables and a lovely spiral staircase. They also host raucous concerts and DJ nights. *Free apéritif offered to our readers on presentation of this guide.*

Le Guillotin

15 rue Jean-Girard. **Map B2-17**
Ⓣ02.38.31.22.29
Closed *Sun and Mon Sept–June; a fortnight after the Printemps de Bourges.*

The walls of this large, friendly restaurant are smothered with posters of the Printemps de Bourges festival and pictures of the artists who appear in the small café-theatre upstairs (*La Soupe aux Choux*). Gilles Brico feeds the whole person – the heart, the stomach and the spirit – and the meat grilled over the open fire is said to be the best in Bourges. Lunch *formule* €11 or around €18 for dinner à la carte.

Le Comptoir de Paris

Place Gordaine. **Map B2-15**
Ⓣ02.48.24.17.16 Ⓕ02.48.24.68.90

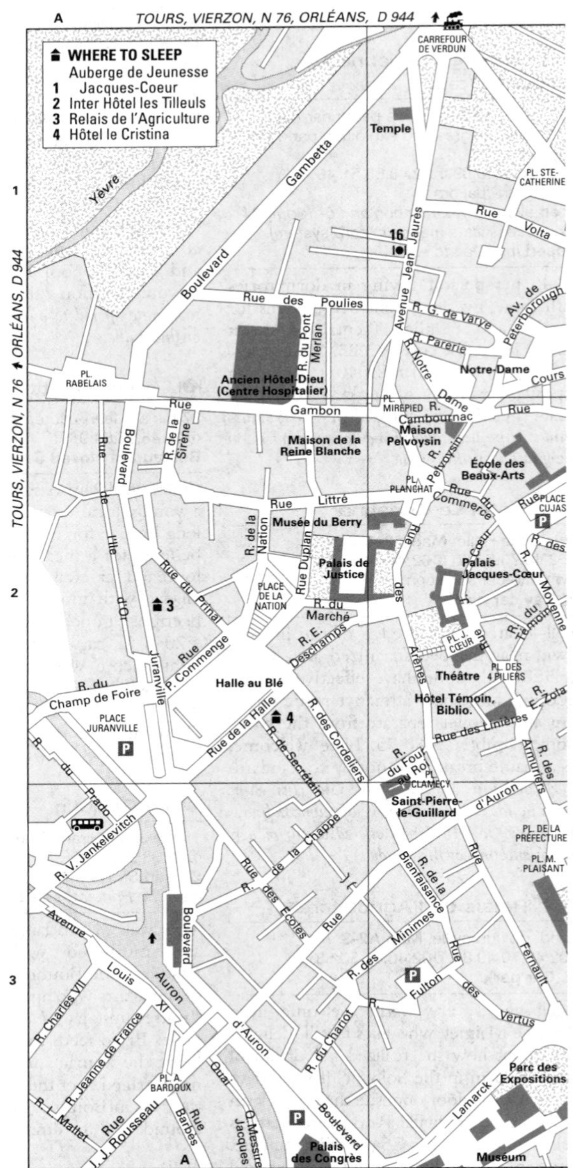
A
TOURS, VIERZON, N 76, ORLÉANS, D 944
WHERE TO SLEEP
Auberge de Jeunesse
1 Jacques-Coeur
2 Inter Hôtel les Tilleuls
3 Relais de l'Agriculture
4 Hôtel le Cristina
CARREFOUR DE VERDUN
Temple
PL. STE-CATHERINE
Yèvre
Boulevard Gambetta
Rue Volta
16
Avenue Jean Jaurès
Rue des Poulies
R. G. de Varye
Av. de Peterborough
R. Parerie
R. du Pont
Merlan
R. Notre-Dame
Notre-Dame
Cours
PL. RABELAIS
Ancien Hôtel-Dieu (Centre Hospitalier)
Rue Gambon
PL. MIREPIED
R. Cambournac
Maison Pelvoysin
R. Pelvoysin
Maison de la Reine Blanche
École des Beaux-Arts
Rue de l'Ile d'Or
Boulevard Juranville
R. de la Sirène
PL. PLANCHAT
Rue du Commerce
PLACE CUJAS
Rue Littré
Musée du Berry
R. de la Nation
Rue Duplan
Palais de Justice
Rue des Arènes
Rue Cœur
R. des
Palais Jacques-Cœur
R. Moyenne
R. du Temoin
Rue du Prinal
PLACE DE LA NATION
R. du Marché
R. E. Deschamps
3
Rue P. Commenge
PL. J. CŒUR
Théâtre
PL. DES 4 PILIERS
R. du Champ de Foire
Halle au Blé
Hôtel Témoin, Biblio.
R. E. Zola
PLACE JURANVILLE
Rue de la Halle
4
R. des Cordeliers
Rue des Linières
R. de Sécrétain
R. du Four au Roi
PL. CLAMECY
R. des Armuriers
R. du Prado
Saint-Pierre-le-Guillard
Rue d'Auron
PL. DE LA PRÉFECTURE
R. V. Jankelevitch
Rue de la Chappe
PL. M. PLAISANT
R. de la Bienfaisance
Rue Fernault
R. des Écoles
Rue des Minimes
Avenue Louis XI
Boulevard Auron
R. des
Rue Fulton
Rue des Vertus
R. Charles VII
R. du Chariot
d'Auron
R. Jeanne de France
Quai
Parc des Expositions
PL. A. BARDOUX
Lamarck
R. L. Mallet
Rue J. J. Rousseau
Rue Barbès
Jacques
Q. Messire
Boulevard
Palais des Congrès
Muséum
A
A 71, N 151 CHÂTEAUROUX MONTLUÇON, LA CHÂTRE 1
TOURS, VIERZON, N 76 ORLÉANS, D 944
1
2
3

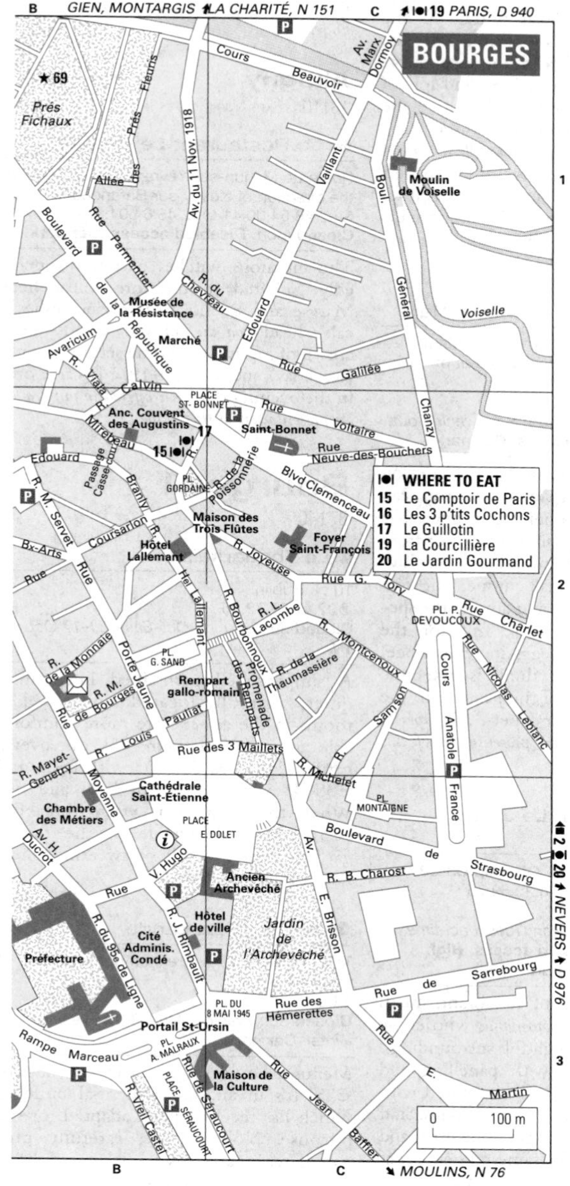
B
GIEN, MONTARGIS
LA CHARITÉ, N 151
C
19 PARIS, D 940
BOURGES
Cours Beauvoir
Av. Marx Dormoy
★ 69
Prés Fichaux
Allée des Prés Fleuris
Av. du 11 Nov. 1918
Vaillant
Boul.
Moulin de Voiselle
1
Boulevard
Rue Parmentier
de la République
R. du Chevreau
Edouard
Général
Voiselle
Musée de la Résistance
Marché
Avaricum
R. Viala
Calvin
Rue Galilée
PLACE ST-BONNET
Rue Voltaire
Chanzy
Anc. Couvent des Augustins
17
15
Saint-Bonnet
Rue Neuve-des-Bouchers
Mirebeau
Edouard
Passage Casse-cou
R. M. Servet
Branly
PL. GORDAINE
R. de la Poissonnerie
Blvd Clemenceau
WHERE TO EAT
15 Le Comptoir de Paris
16 Les 3 p'tits Cochons
17 Le Guillotin
19 La Courcillière
20 Le Jardin Gourmand
Maison des Trois Flûtes
Foyer Saint-François
Coursarlon
Hôtel Lallemant
Bx-Arts
Rue
R. Joyeuse
Rue G. Tory
2
Hel Lallemant
R. Bourbonnoux
R. L. Lacombe
PL. P. DEVOUCOUX
Rue Charlet
R. Montcenoux
Rue Nicolas Leblanc
Cours Anatole France
R. de la Monnaie
Porte Jaune
PL. G. SAND
Rempart gallo-romain
Promenade des Remparts
R. de la Thaumassière
Samson
R. M. de Bourges
Rue
Paullat
R. Louis
Rue des 3 Maillets
R. Mayet-Genetry
Moyenne
R. Michelet
Cathédrale Saint-Étienne
Chambre des Métiers
PLACE E. DOLET
PL. MONTAIGNE
Boulevard de Strasbourg
Av. H. Ducrot
V. Hugo
Av.
2 20 NEVERS D 976
Ancien Archevêché
R. B. Charost
Rue
R. J. Rimbault
Hôtel de ville
E. Brisson
Jardin de l'Archevêché
R. du 95e de Ligne
Cité Adminis. Condé
Préfecture
Rue de Sarrebourg
PL. DU 8 MAI 1945
Rue des Hémerettes
Portail St-Ursin
Rue E.
3
Rampe Marceau
PL. A. MALRAUX
Rue de Séraucourt
Maison de la Culture
Rue Jean Baffier
Martin
R. Vieil Castel
PLACE SÉRAUCOURT
0
100 m
B
C
MOULINS, N 76

Closed *Sun*. **Car park.**

Service until 10.30pm. This place is painted bright red so it stands out from the wonderful medieval houses in the prettiest square in Bourges. Inside the décor is wood, so it's a bit more subdued. There's a friendly atmosphere and lots of animated conversation; this is where the lively and creative people of Bourges congregate. The speciality is *andouillette à l'ancienne*. Good simple meals from €15; also a *formule* at €9 with main meal and either a starter or a dessert. The downstairs dining room is cosier than the one upstairs.

Restaurant La Courcillière

Rue de Babylone; head for avenue Marx-Dormoy and look for a narrow street off to the right. **Off map C1-19**
02.48.24.41.91
Closed *Tues evening; Wed; Sun evening out of season.* **Disabled access. Car park.**

In the heart of the magical marshlands on the banks of the river Yèvre. You can admire the view either from huge bay windows in the cosy dining room or from a waterside terrace. Denis Julien serves lovingly prepared regional cuisine. The terrines are made on site, and among the specialities you should look out for the famous *couilles d'âne* (eggs in wine sauce) and calf's head. Everything is authentic here, from the smile of the *patronne* to the local accent of the gardeners. *Free apéritif offered to our readers on presentation of this guide.*

Restaurant Le Jardin Gourmand

15 bis av. Ernest-Renan. **Off map C3-20**
02.48.21.35.91 02.48.20.59.75
jardingourmand.fr
Closed *Sun evening; Mon; Tues lunchtime; 20 Dec–20 Jan.* **Disabled access. High chairs available. Car park.**

This is a very pleasant restaurant, much appreciated by local *gourmands* who enjoy a good meal in delightful surroundings. Handsome building with panelling and beams; the dining room is decorated with flowers and watercolours on the walls. Staff are pleasant, the service is unobtrusive and the cooking shows the same refinement as the décor. Specialities include fish *pot-au-feu*, game in season and *fondant* with arabica extracts. Set menus €15 and €23–49. From June to September there's also a lobster menu at €49. You can eat in the garden, weather permitting. *Free coffee offered to our readers on presentation of this guide.*

Allogny

18110 (18km NW)

Restaurant Le Chabur

Route de Mehun-sur-Yèvre; take the D944 in the direction of Neuvy-sur-Barangeon.
02.48.64.00.41 02.48.64.04.87
Closed *Mon.* **Disabled access. Car park.**

The infamous witches of Berry supposedly gathered in the forest near here. Maryse and Bruno serve classic dishes – calf's head, *coq au vin* and so on – to a crowd of locals. Lunchtime set menus €10 (weekday) and €14.50–19; à la carte only in the evening. *Free Kir offered to our readers on presentation of this guide.*

Bourgueil

37140

Le Thouarsais

10 pl. Hublin.
02.47.97.72.05
Closed *Sun evening Oct–Easter; l–17 Oct.* **TV.**

A simple, well-maintained hotel in a quiet, centrally-located square. The rooms in the annexe are more comfortable and some of them look out over a garden. Doubles €25–33 with basin and €38–41 with shower or bath and wc. When the weather is warm, breakfast (€5) is served outside in the flower garden, which is full of tweeting birds. Pets are not allowed.

Auberge La Lande

Take the D35 in the direction of the "Cave touristique".
02.47.97.92.41
Closed *Sun evening; Mon; Tues evening in winter.* **Car park.**

Menus from €13.75 (weekdays) up to €25. It's in an old residential building which has recently been adapted for the purpose. No-nonsense, carefully prepared, regional cooking is served here. Regional produce is offered according to the season. Meals can be eaten on the terrace.

Brezolles

28270

⛹ 🏠 |●| Le Relais de Brezolles**

4 rue Berg-op-Zoom; it's on the outskirts of town, in the direction of Chartres.
Ⓣ02.37.48.20.84 Ⓕ02.37.48.28.46
Ⓦwww.lerelais-brezolles.fr.st
Closed *Fri and Sun evenings; Mon lunchtime; 1–20 Jan; 1–20 Aug.* **Disabled access (restaurant). High chairs and games available. TV. Car park.**

Although its surroundings aren't very picturesque, this venerable truckstop's warm welcome, comfortable rooms, attractive restaurant and good range of food make it well worth a stopover. The rooms cost €46 with bath/wc or €34 with shower. The appetizing menus range from €11 (available midweek lunch only) to €30. À la carte, you'll find enough interesting meat, fish and vegetables to satisfy any gourmet, and the specialities change with the seasons. Good options include lentil bread with foie gras, duo of lamb and veal, goose breast, lobster *mousseline* and veal *tournedos* with girolle mushrooms. There's a garden and terrace. *10% discount on the room rate or free coffee with a meal offered to our readers on presentation of this guide.*

Montigny-sur-Avre

28270 (8km NW)

⛹ 🏠 |●| Hôtel-restaurant Moulin des Planches

It's 2km from the village, in the middle of the countryside; from Brezolles take the D102.
Ⓣ02.37.48.25.97 Ⓕ02.37.48.35.63
Ⓦwww.moulin-des-planches.fr
Closed *Sun evening; Mon; Jan.* **Disabled access. TV. Car park.**

This old flour mill, on the banks of the River Avre, looks like something out of a picture book – even the light has a special quality. It's been turned into a very handsome inn by an ex-farming couple, and the whole place has the friendly atmosphere of a B&B. Delightful, comfortable rooms €47–61 with shower/wc or bath. Breakfast €8. Set menus start at €15 (weekday lunchtimes) with others €20–49. The chef specializes in foie gras and veal sweetbreads; the duck breast is good, too. *5% discount on the price of a menu offered to our readers on presentation of this guide.*

Briare

45250

|●| Restaurant Le Bord'Eau

19 rue de la Liberté; it's on the main street.
Ⓣ02.38.31.22.29
Closed *Wed; Mon–Fri evenings in winter; 2–6 Jan.*

With a name like this, you'd be forgiven for expecting a lovely waterside terrace. But no. However, the cuisine and the maritime décor will soon help you swallow any disappointment about the surroundings, or the very ordinary décor. The restaurant's name is more to do with the fresh fish that they serve here, and the food is very good: zander fillet with *beurre blanc* and calf's head with *gribiche* sauce. Menus €15 (not served Sun) to €34.

Bonny-sur-Loire

45420 (10km SE)

🏠 |●| Les Voyageurs

10 Grande-Rue. From Briare take the N7 and then the A77.
Ⓣ02.38.27.01.45 Ⓕ02.38.27.01.46
Closed *Sun evening; 2–11 Jan; 23 Feb–8 March.* **Restaurant closed Sun evening; Mon; Tues lunchtime. TV. Car park.**

Given the prices – menus are listed at €15 (weekdays) and €24.50–38 – you might not realize that this is one of the best gourmet restaurants in the area. Philippe Lechauve is a local, but he was the chief *saucier* for the renowned Troisgros brothers for years; the prices are even more unbelievable given his pedigree. He manages to provide such interesting dishes by simplifying the ingredients and relying on his talent to produce something wonderful. The menus change every three months, but you can count on the wonderful *chocolat fondant* – the chocolate oozes over the pistachio sauce and *crème anglaise* as you cut the cake – on the second menu. There are also some decent wines. Double rooms with shower/wc €33–36.

Chabris

36210

🏠 |●| ⛹ Hôtel de la Plage**

42 rue du Pont; 25 km east of Saint-Agnan, via the D17 then the D35.
Ⓣ02.54.40.02.24 Ⓕ02.54.40.08.59

Ⓔ hoteldelaplage@wanadoo.fr
Closed *Sun; Mon (open Mon evening mid-July to end Aug); Jan.* **Car park. TV.**

On the road from Valençay to Romorantin, going to Sologne, an ideal stopover for a meal or a night's rest. Comfortable rooms, but choose one that overlooks the garden, as those on the first floor are bigger, and those on the second have been modernized. Double rooms at €39 with shower/wc or bath. In the kitchen, Madame d'Agostino prepares traditional food, and her husband proudly serves it in the dining room or, on fine days, in the garden which has a refreshing fountain. Her specialities are duck foie gras and veal kidneys sautéed with port. The menu changes every three months, and the fish varies according to availability. Menus €15–30. *Free apéritif or coffee offered to our readers on presentation of this guide.*

Chambord

41250

Hôtel du Grand Saint-Michel**

Château de Chambord.
Ⓣ 02.54.20.31.31 Ⓕ 02.54.20.36.40
Closed *Wed in winter; 12 Nov–15 Dec.* **TV. Car park. High chairs available.**

This hotel is in an exceptional location opposite the château, and it boasts spacious, comfortable and pleasant rooms – even without the view. Doubles €52–79. The dining room is traditionally decorated, providing an appropriate setting for the cuisine, which includes salmon, zander with fennel seeds and wild boar stew in game season. Menus €19 and €25. Considerate, attentive service and a friendly welcome – not at all the mechanical toil you might expect in such a touristy place. In summer you can eat on the terrace with the château right in front of you – very romantic. Book well in advance. *10% discount on the room rate 1 Oct–1 April offered to our readers on presentation of this guide.*

Saint-Dyé-sur-Loire

41500 (5km NW)

Le Manoir de Bel-Air**

1 rte. d'Orléans.
Ⓣ 02.54.81.60.10 Ⓕ 02.54.81.65.34
Ⓦ www.manoirdebelair.com
Closed *mid-Jan to mid-Feb.* **TV. Car park. Disabled access.**

This old ivy-smothered building is on the banks of the Loire. It has a delightfully provincial feel and there's a lovely smell of beeswax polish. Rooms are reasonably priced given the facilities and cleanliness: doubles go for €54–89. (The ones with a view of the river are the best.) The dining room, which also has the view, is bright and spacious. Set menus, €22–43, list very good regional cooking. There's a track along the riverbank if you fancy a post-prandial walk. *10% discount on the room rate Oct–April offered to our readers on presentation of this guide.*

La Bourriche aux Appétits

65 rue nationale.
Ⓣ 02.54.81.65.25
Closed *Mon–Thurs except public holidays; fortnight in Jan.* **Shop open** *Tues–Sat 10am–noon and 4–7pm.*

Take a stroll along the banks of the Loire at Saint-Dyé, where the sailing barges that brought the hewn stone for Chambord used to tie up. Then make your way to the restaurant run by Gilles Quesneau, an epicurean who has opened a shop selling home-made dishes alongside. The décor is as tasty as the food; specialities include river fish, *gratin* of crayfish tails, Loire eel kebab and fish, couscous. An exceptional place, with old-fashioned cooking at its best and a warm welcome for guests. Menus €23 and €28. You can stock up with terrines or pâtés in jars to take home.

Chartres

28000

Hôtel-restaurant de la Poste**

3 rue du Général-Kœnig; it's between the post office and the Hôtel Grand Monarque.
Ⓣ 02.37.21.04.27 Ⓕ 02.37.36.42.17
Ⓦ www.hotelposte-chartres.com
Restaurant closed *Fri and Sun evenings.* **Disabled access. TV. High chairs available. Pay car park.**

A practical place to stay, given its excellent location. It's not spanking new, but the welcome is pleasant and if it's not exactly a bundle of laughs, at least you can sleep well. Clean, comfortable rooms €56.50 with shower/wc, €61.50 with bath; some have a lovely view of the cathedral. The buffet breakfast, €8, is generous. Brasserie style menus €15–26; dishes include duck with honey and lemon, beef steak *à la Chartres* and zander fillet with pepper *sabayon. Free apéritif, coffee or a breakfast per person (Nov–March) offered to our readers on presentation of this guide.*

|●| Le Pichet

19 rue du Cheval-Blanc; beside the cathedral.
Ⓣ02.37.21.08.35
Closed Wed; Sun; Mon; Tues evening. High chairs available.

Just twenty metres from the forecourt, this restaurant is not called "the pike" for nothing: the fish appears in various guises on the no-frills menus (€11 and €14), often in combination with wine. Other dishes include the standard fair of the region: calf's head *ravigote*, chicken *au pot Henri-IV* and the mysteriously named hen's milk with fruit as dessert.

|●| Brasserie Bruneau

4 rue du Maréchal-de-Lattre-de-Tassigny; it's 30m from the town hall.
Ⓣ02.37.21.80.99
Closed *Sat lunchtime; Sun.*

Open 11.45am–2pm and 7–10.30pm. There's a 1930s atmosphere in this brasserie with its classic zinc-topped bar, bistro tables, benches covered in red velvet and retro posters covering the walls. Traditional food cooked using exclusively fresh produce, speedy yet relaxed service and a pleasant and enthusiastic welcome. There's an €11.80 *formule*, or you can eat à la carte for around €20.

|●| Au P'tit Morard

25 rue de la Porte-Morard.
Ⓣ and Ⓕ02.37.34.15.89
Closed *Sun evening; Wed.*

No middle-class girl from a good family would have ventured into the lower end of town twenty-five years ago, but it's now the liveliest, friendliest, greenest part of Chartres. It's full of attractive cafés, and everyone loves the old doorways and mill buildings. You'll be as happy inside the *P'tit Morard* as out on the terrace – where you pick up a buzz from the cheerful crowds in the street. Set lunch menu €16 during the week, otherwise €24–30.

|●| Restaurant Le Saint-Hilaire

11 rue du Pont-Saint-Hilaire; it's between place Saint-Pierre and pont Saint-Hilaire.
Ⓣ and Ⓕ02.37.30.97.57
Closed *Sat lunchtime; Mon; Sun; 27 July–18 Aug; 24 Dec–5 Jan.* **Disabled access. High chairs available.**

Don't even think of visiting Chartres without eating in this delightful little restaurant (which has just ten tables). Everything is of a piece: the welcome, the service, the cooking and the décor. Benoît Pasquier's family have been in the Beauce for five generations and he makes a point of showing off local produce to its best advantage. The dishes change with the seasons, though favourites such as *petit-gris* snails with a *fondue* of tomato, pan-fried foie gras with lentils, *parmentier* of oxtail *confit* with beer, veal sweetbreads cooked in a haybox, *crème brûlée* and regional cheeses are available all year. Set menus €15 (not served Sun), €23.30 and €38.

|●| Le Moulin de Ponceau

21–23 rue de la Tannerie; it's below the collegiate church of Saint-André.
Ⓣ02.37.35.30.05
Ⓦwww.lemoulindeponceau.fr
Closed *Sat lunchtime; Sun evening; Feb school holidays.* **Disabled access.**

Arguably the most attractive summer table in Chartres. It's in a romantic, charming situation on an arm of the river, just behind the cathedral. There's a covered terrace at the waterside and another summer terrace made from an old wash-house – once numerous in these parts. They serve attentively and laboriously produced dishes that may seem a bit pricey, but the setting adds considerably to the pleasure. Specialities include terrine of foie gras, prawns *royales* and white chocolate ice cream. Menus €20 (weekday lunchtimes) and €24–48. *Free coffee offered to our readers on presentation of this guide.*

Maintenon

28130 (18km NE)

|●| Le Bistrot d'Adeline

3 rue Collin-d'Harleville; it's in the main street, 100m from the chateau.
Ⓣ02.37.23.06.67
Closed *Sun; Mon; 15 July–15 Aug.*

A little restaurant in a rustic style – evidenced by the old iron cooking pot in the entrance. It's one of the best in Maintenon for both its welcome and the family dishes the boss prepares. He's particularly famous for his calf's head *ravigote* and classic sauces. Lunch menu at €11.50; others €15.50–26. Booking is essential. *Free coffee offered to our readers on presentation of this guide.*

Châteaudun

28200

🏃 ⌂ |●| Le Saint-Louis**

41 rue de la République.
Ⓣ02.37.45.00.01 Ⓕ02.37.45.16.09
Ⓦwww.lesaintlouishotel.fr
TV. Car park.

Ben Maamar pulled off quite a stunt in a very few years, first by turning a ruin into a decent, comfortable hotel and then by adding a restaurant and a lively brasserie next door. This is the place to eat in Châteaudun, especially in summer when the piano bar gets going outdoors. It's got the loveliest terrace in town. Mussels, salads, grills – dishes to satisfy all tastes and pockets. Menus go for €14–23, with grills €10–12 and pizzas €5.50. A real success. And the hotel rooms are fairly priced, at €33–42 for doubles with shower/wc or bath.

|●| La Licorne

6 pl. du 18-Octobre; it's on the main square.
Ⓣ02.37.45.32.32
Closed *Tues evening; Wed; 20 Dec–15 Jan.*

The dining room is long and narrow and decorated in salmon pink. You'll find solid cooking in big portions; dishes include pan-fried skirt of beef with shallots, oysters and leeks *au gratin* (in winter), and breast of duck with orange and honey. Service, usually very pleasant, can get a bit rushed when they're busy. Nice terrace on sunny days. Set weekday menu €11, then others €14–27.50.

|●| Aux Trois Pastoureaux

31 rue André-Gillet; it's between pl. du 18-Octobre and espace Malraux.
Ⓣ02.37.45.74.40 Ⓕ02.37.66.00.32
Ⓦwww.aux-trois-pastoureaux.fr
Closed *Sun evening; Mon; Thurs evening; a fortnight in Jan; a fortnight in July–Aug.*
Disabled access.

Open noon–1.45pm and 7.15–9pm. This is the oldest inn in Châteaudun and there's a calm atmosphere – choose between the simply set tables in the green dining room and a seat in the sun on the terrace. There's a wide variety of dishes on offer here, including some very unusual taste combinations – this is sophisticated cooking. There's a €21 weekday menu, then others up to €46; reckon on around €32 à la carte. Pleasant welcome.

Châteaumeillant

18370

⌂ |●| Hôtel-restaurant Le Piet à Terre**

21 rue du Château.
Ⓣ02.48.61.41.74 Ⓕ02.48.61.41.88
ⒺTFINET@wanadoo.fr
Closed *Sun evening; Mon; Tues except July–Aug; 12 Nov–28 Feb.* **High chairs available. TV.**

A two-star hotel with a three-star restaurant. The dining room has blue shutters and a fine chimney place for open fires in winter and there's a new veranda too. Thierry Finet is passionate about cooking and he makes the bread and breakfast rolls on the premises. The cuisine revolves around fresh produce from the market and reflects the mood of the chef and the *menu tradition*, specializing in local dishes. Menus €33.50–86. The vegetables and herbs come from grandfather Piet's garden and will soon come from the jardin des Aydes. The newly renovated bedrooms are named after flowers. Doubles €46–69 with shower/wc or bath. No dogs admitted.

Châteauneuf-en-Thymerais

28170

⌂ |●| L'Écritoire**

43 rue Émile-Vivier; take the Dreux road.
Ⓣ02.37.51.85.80 Ⓕ02.37.51.86.87
Closed Mon; Wed; Sun evening; Feb half-term; early Nov. **Car park.**

This old sixteenth-century staging post has been a restaurant ever since 1743 and is recognized as one of the best in Eure-et-Loir. The chef, Luc Pasquier, is a veteran of gastronomic adventures in Asia and Africa, but he has come back to his roots to create classical dishes inspired by the produce of the region, such as garden snails from

Conie, rabbit from Thymerais and honey from Beauce. Depending on the season, you could find specialities like foie gras and scallop salad (spring), *fricassure* of quail and prawns with five spices and five peppers (autumn) or sautéed rabbit and lobster with sweet pepper and walnuts (winter). Excellent menus, at very reasonable prices, considering the quality: €23 (weekday lunch) to €57. There are also a few simple but clean and comfortable rooms giving on to a little courtyard with balconies bedecked with flowers. Doubles with shower/wc or bath €45. Impeccably attentive service.

Senonches

28250 (13km W)

Auberge La Pomme de Pin**

15 rue Michel Cauty; take the D928 to Digny then the D24.
Ⓣ02.37.37.76.62 Ⓕ02.37.37.86.61
Ⓔlapommedepin@club-internet.fr
Closed *Sun evening; Mon; 2–31 Jan.* **TV. High chairs and games available. Pay car park.**

A half-timbered inn which used to be a posthouse on the edge of the Zandere area. Ten comfortable rooms from €48 with shower/wc, €61 with bath/wc. Half board, €47 per person, is compulsory for a stay of more than three nights. They serve good quality, wholesome food with an emphasis on local specialities: dishes include carp with crayfish, Chartres pâté, oxtail with foie gras or game and wild mushrooms in season. *Formules* (main course, cheese or salad, dessert) for €15, €20 and €25; set menus €15 (weekday lunchtimes), then €22–40. *10% discount on the room rate Dec–Feb offered to our readers on presentation of this guide.*

Châteauroux

36000

Hôtel Le Boischaut**

135 av. de la Châtre.
Ⓣ02.54.22.22.34 Ⓕ02.54.22.64.89
Ⓦwww.citotel.com
Closed *26 Dec–6 Jan.* **Disabled access. TV. Car park.**

This recently built hotel has large, comfortable double rooms at €34.50–39.50 with shower/wc or bath. Ask for one overlooking the garden. No restaurant – but there is a bar, and they can provide a meal on a tray for €12 with a hot main dish, cheese and dessert. Free lock-up parking for two-wheelers.

Élysée Hôtel***

2 rue de la République; it's practically opposite the Équinoxe cultural centre.
Ⓣ02.54.22.33.66 Ⓕ02.54.07.34.34
Ⓔelysee36@aol.com
Closed *25 Dec–l Jan.* **Disabled access. TV. Car park.**

An excellent little hotel run by a Norman couple who used to run a newsagent's. It's in the centre of town, with spotless, pleasant rooms which have been recently renovated; doubles €46–59.50. Breakfast €7.80. There's a salon-bar filled with old Routard guides; you can indulge in a little wine-tasting here or in your room. Though there's no dining room they have a deal with a nearby restaurant and can offer a meal on a tray until 11pm. *10% discount on the room rate (weekends and 1 July–15 Aug) offered to our readers on presentation of this guide.*

Le P'tit Bouchon

64 Rue-Grande.
Ⓣ02.54.61.50.40
Closed *Sun; public holidays.*

The old-fashioned green façade, the little tables inside, the blackboard menu, the old bar jammed with bottles and the waiters in long aprons – all these are redolent of a Lyonnais *bouchon* (bistro). The owner gave up being an insurance salesman; his good humour is as choice as the tasty cuisine which tends more towards the Berry region than to Lyon. Very good value for money. Menus €11–14. There's also a wine bar offering at least a hundred different wines by the glass. Cheese lovers can indulge themselves further in the owners' cheese shop. *Free apéritif offered to our readers on presentation of this guide.*

Le Bistrot Gourmand

10 rue du Marché.
Ⓣ and Ⓕ02.54.07.86.98
Closed *Sun; Mon lunchtime; public holidays; fortnight at the end of Feb to early March; 3 weeks from mid-Aug to early Sept.*

Cheerful dining room decorated bright yellow and soft green. A huge blackboard displays the dishes of the day. They use only the freshest produce: try the beef *Limousin*. There's a menu at lunchtime for €12.50, or you'll pay around €20 à la carte. *Free apéritif or coffee offered to our readers on presentation of this guide.*

Restaurant La Ciboulette

42 Rue-Grande.
Ⓣ02.54.27.66.28
Closed *Sun; Mon; Aug; fortnight at New Year.* **High chairs and games available.**

This is Châteauroux's gourmet restaurant – everybody dines here. It has pleasant décor and friendly service, and the menus have been thoughtfully put together. There's a weekday menu at €16 and others up to €37; they include such local specialities as *couilles d'âne* (eggs poached in red wine and shallot sauce), foie gras and lentil terrine, roast pigeon with balsamic vinegar and vanilla Bavarois. Around fifteen wines are sold by the glass; some are produced by vineyards owned by Gérard Depardieu (who lives nearby). *20% discount on the price of a meal when you show your guide in advance.*

Déols

36130 (2km N)

L'Escale Village

Take the N20 from Châteauroux. It's opposite the entrance to the airport zone; exit 12 on the A20 (in the direction of the airport).
Ⓣ02.54.22.03.77 Ⓕ02.54.22.56.70
Disabled access.

Open noon–2.30pm and 7pm–midnight. This restaurant attracts people of all ages from across the region – whole families crowd in. Good traditional dishes include seafood platter, sole *meunière*, beef with shallots and *moules marinière*. Menus start at €10.30, then go up to €25. Long-distance lorry drivers prefer the brasserie where they can watch TV while they eat. It's open round the clock – you never know who you'll bump into. A lively, vibrant place.

Coings

36130 (8km N)

Le Relais Saint-Jacques***

Take exit 12 off the A20 going in the direction of the airport, then Coings. Turn left before Céré.
Ⓣ02.54.60.44.44 Ⓕ02.54.60.44.00
Ⓦwww.relais.st.jacques.com
Restaurant closed *Sun evening.* **Disabled access. TV. Car park.**

Don't let the dreary setting near the airport put you off: this modern hotel is pleasant, comfortable and quiet. Each of the rooms is decorated differently and looks onto the garden or over the countryside at the rear. Doubles start at €55.10 with basin, and go up to €60.50. But the establishment is best known for the excellent cuisine of the chef/proprietor, Pierre Jeanrot. Menus start at €18.30. The dishes change frequently, but specialities include skate terrine with tapenade. In good weather, there's a less expensive brasserie service available on the terrace.

Levroux

36110 (21km N)

Restaurant Relais Saint-Jean

34 rue Nationale; it's near place de la Collégiale-de-Saint-Sylvain.
Ⓣ02.54.35.81.56 Ⓕ02.54.35.36.09
Ⓦwww.relais.saint.jean.fr
Closed *Wed; Sun evening; last week in Aug; during winter school holidays.* **High chairs available.**

The chef who owns this old coaching inn has made this one of the best restaurants in the Indre region. His skilful use of first-rate ingredients, and the charming welcome you get from his wife, make for a winning combination. The dining room is pleasant, and in summer you can admire the sunsets over the Saint-Sylvain collegiate church from the terrace. There's a menu at €15 (not served on Sat night, Sun or public holidays), and others at €22–38 with an impressive children's menu at €11 including fruit juice. Specialities include lobster tails with herbs. The cooking is judged to perfection and practically sings with flavour. *Free coffee offered to our readers on presentation of this guide.*

Buzançais

36500 (25km NW)

Hôtel-restaurant L'Hermitage**

Route d'Argy-Écueille; take the N143 then follow the signs for Argy.
Ⓣ02.54.84.03.90 Ⓕ02.54.02.13.19
Closed *Sun evening and Mon except*

July–Aug; Ist fortnight in Aug; 2nd week in Sept. **Restaurant closed** *Sun evening and Mon; Ist fortnight in Aug; 2nd week in Sept.* **Disabled access. TV. Car park.**

It really is as peaceful as a hermitage. The hotel is covered in Virginia creeper and overlooks a broad expanse of greenery on the banks of the Indre. There's a big kitchen garden and a really nice terrace. Bedrooms in the main building have been carefully decorated and have a view of the grounds. The ones in the annexe are slightly less attractive, but they too have been redecorated and overlook the courtyard. Comfortable double rooms with basin at €24.50, with bath or shower/wc €48–52 according to season. Set menus €15.50–49. The cooking is fairly sophisticated, featuring specialities from Berry and the Landes with lots of fish. *10% discount on the half-board rate (1 Nov–30 March) offered to our readers on presentation of this guide.*

Châtre (La)

36400

Auberge de jeunesse

Rue du Moulin-Borgnon; take the no. 15 bus (Châteauroux-Montluçon route) to the "Champ-de-Foire" stop; between the town centre and the shores of the Indre.
Ⓣ02.54.06.00.55 Ⓕ02.54.48.48.10
Ⓦwww.fuaj.org

This recently opened youth hostel has sixty beds (two- to six-bed rooms with toilets), a lounge and a kitchen. €8.40, with breakfast and sheets/blankets on top. FUAJ card compulsory. Children's playground and games rooms nearby.

Hôtel Notre-Dame**

4 pl. Notre-Dame.
Ⓣ02.54.48.01.14 Ⓕ02.54.48.31.14
Disabled access. TV. Car park.

A nice place to stay, in a fifteenth-century building with a flower-filled balcony. It overlooks a quiet little square that echoes with birdsong. Bedrooms are spacious and nicely furnished, perfectly in keeping with the style of this pretty town. Some are particularly big and well laid-out, overlooking the square. Doubles €39 with shower/wc, €42 with bath. There's a private garden with a terrace. Hotels like this are rare.

Nohant-Vic

36400 (6km N)

L'Auberge de la Petite Fadette***

Place du Château; it's on the D943.
Ⓣ02.54.31.01.48 Ⓕ02.54.31.10.19
Ⓦwww.auberge-petite-fadette.com
Disabled access. TV. High chairs available. Car park.

This beautiful building, covered in Virginia creeper, is totally in keeping with the world of novelist George Sand, who spent the greater part of her life in Nohant. The bedrooms are very prettily decorated in assorted shades of blue. Doubles with shower/wc from €58 and €90–120 with bath. The dining room features marvellous nineteenth-century wood panelling. Menus €16–45 with tasty, classic dishes.

Saint-Chartier

36400 (8.5km N)

Hôtel-restaurant La Vallée Bleue***

Route de Verneuil. Take the D943 then the D918; it's at the end of the village, towards Verneuil.
Ⓣ02.54.31.01.91 Ⓕ02.54.34.04.48
Ⓦwww.chateauvalleebleue.com
Closed *Sun evening and Mon in March, Oct and Nov.* **Restaurant closed** *lunchtime except Sun and public holidays Nov to end March; Sun evening and Mon in March, Oct and Nov.* **TV. High chairs and games available. Swimming pool and children's pool. Sandpit. Car park.**

This building, once owned by George Sand's doctor, has been wonderfully converted into a hotel, retaining many original features. Everything is in keeping – the dining rooms, the lounge and the bedrooms. You'll have a pleasurable stay here and the restaurant is pretty good, too. Set menus at €25 (not public holidays) and €35. Children's menu €12. A la carte lists specialities such as zander fillet with *Guérande salicorne*, cream of crayfish and *croustillant* of Berry pears. There are two terraces and a swimming pool in four hectares of grounds. Very comfortable rooms €80–200 with shower/wc or bath. Half board is preferred for a stay of more than two consecutive nights at €80–115 per person. *Free house apéritif offered to our readers on presentation of this guide.*

Lys-Saint-Georges

36230 (23km NW)

⛹ |●| La Forge

Take the D927 in the direction of Neuvy-Saint-Sépulcre and then the D74. It's opposite the château.
☎02.54.30.81.68 Ⓕ02.54.30.94.96
Ⓔrestaurantforgelys@club-internet.fr
Closed *Sun evening, Mon and Tues Sept–June; Mon July–Aug; 3 weeks in Jan; a fortnight in Oct.* **Disabled access. High chairs and games available.**

This rather good inn has handsome beams, an open fire in winter and a terrace in summer where you can enjoy the peace and quiet of the Noire valley. The *patronne* is friendly and very witty, and her husband, the chef, prepares tasty classic dishes with strong flavours. Menus, €16–39, change regularly with the seasons – though you may well see specialities such as local snail ravioli. The €23 menu is especially popular with locals on Sunday. Reservations advised. *Free house apéritif offered to our readers on presentation of this guide prior to ordering.*

Chaumont-sur-Loire

41150

|●| ⛹ Restaurant La Chancelière**

1 rue de Bellevue; right by the château, facing the Loire.
☎02.54.20.96.95
Closed *Wed and Thurs; 11 Nov–6 Dec; mid-Jan to mid-Feb.* **Disabled access. High chairs available.**

An ideal stopover before or after visiting the château or Garden Festival. Two dining rooms, one dourly rustic, the other more cheerful, but both serving equally fresh and aromatic dishes. The terrine of duck foie gras and zander with *beurre blanc* are particularly tasty, the meat dishes are tender and the desserts are accomplished. Cheapest menu €15 (except Sun and public holidays), then others €20–33. Reckon on €30 à la carte. A few tables overlook the Loire. Excellent value for money and friendly service. *Free coffee offered to our readers on presentation of this guide.*

|●| Restaurant Le Grand Velum

It's the château farm.
☎02.54.20.99.22
Closed 20 Oct–1 June.

Make your way across the château car park to this restaurant. François-Zavier Bogard's cooking is enjoyed by horticulturalists and gourmets alike. Menus range from €16 to €30. It's probably best to plan a meal here in good weather because they haven't yet installed heaters to cope with cooler days. But overall, the experience is extraordinary.

Chinon

37500

⛹ ☗ Hôtel Diderot**

4 rue Buffon; it's away from the centre, 100m from place Jeanne-d'Arc.
☎02.47.93.18.87 Ⓕ02.47.93.37.10
Ⓦwww.hoteldiderot.com
Disabled access. TV. Car park.

Through the big gateway at the end of the courtyard you'll see a very handsome eighteenth-century house covered in Virginia creeper. Inside there's a fifteenth-century fireplace, an eighteenth-century staircase and beams everywhere. It's all very lovely. The twenty-eight cosy rooms are all decorated differently, and range in price from €50 to €69 with shower or bath and wc. Breakfast, €6.10, comes with wonderful preserves and is served on the terrace on sunny days and by the fire in winter. Very professional and welcoming greeting. *20% discount 1 Nov–31 March offered to our readers on presentation of this guide.*

⛹ ☗ |●| Hôtel de France – Restaurant au Chapeau Rouge***

47–49 place du Général-de-Gaulle.
hotel: ☎02.47.93.33.91 restaurant: ☎02.47.98.08.08 Ⓕ02.47.98.37.03
Ⓦwww.chinon-hoteldefrance-restaurant.com
Closed *15 Feb–8 March; 13–30 Nov.*
Restaurant closed *Sun evening and Mon except July–Aug.* **TV. Pay car park.**

This beautiful sixteenth-century building has been pleasantly renovated and is now a *Best Western* hotel. The rooms are comfortable – some have views of the château and the rue Voltaire, a pedestrianized medieval street. Doubles with shower or bath €65–90. Breakfast €8. The public spaces are pleasant, with little seating areas here and there. Banana, orange, lemon and bay trees grow in the Mediterranean garden in the inner courtyard. Traditional dishes predominate in the restaurant, with specialities such as zander with *beurre blanc*, duck terrine with foie gras, braised lamb's sweetbreads with white truffle and pears with Chinon wine preserve. Menus go for €24–54. *10% discount on the room rate (Oct–March) or free apéritif offered to our readers on presentation of this guide.*

Beaumont-en-Veron

37420 (5km NW)

Manoir La Giraudière - Restaurant Le Petit Pigeonnier**

Beaumont-en-Véron; take the D749 towards Beaumont for about 4km, turn left at Domaine de la Giraudière and the restaurant is 800m further on.
Ⓣ02.47.58.40.36 Ⓕ02.47.58.46.06
Ⓦwww.hotels-france.com/giraudiere
Disabled access. TV. High chairs available. Baby-changing facilities. Baby-bottle warmer. Car park.

This delightful country seat of some seventeenth-century gentleman has been made into an incredibly peaceful hotel; the sixteenth-century dovecote has been turned into a sitting room and library with a piano. Twenty-five rooms with shower/wc or bath go for €39–100. Breakfast €6.50. Good gourmet cooking at affordable prices is served in the restaurant; menus €19–35. They prepare foie gras in a different way according to the season. Half board €42–66 per person. *Free coffee offered to our readers on presentation of this guide.*

Combreux

45530

L'Auberge de Combreux**

35 rte. du Gâtinais. It's on the outskirts of the village.
Ⓣ02.38.46.89.89 Ⓕ02.38.59.36.19
Ⓦwww.auberge-de-combreux.fr
Closed *15 Dec–25 Jan.* **TV. High chairs available. Swimming pool. Car park.**

This magnificent nineteenth-century coaching inn, swathed in ivy and Virginia creeper, has been thoughtfully refurbished. There's a cosy little sitting room with an open fire and a rustic dining room with a veranda overlooking the flower garden. In fine weather you can sit under the trees. Weekday menu €18 and others from €28 up to €35. Well-prepared dishes include *escalope* of hot foie gras and game in season – elaborate and traditional cooking. The bedrooms are in the main building or in one of the little annexes hidden among the trees. They're delightful, with flower-sprigged wallpaper, beams and large wardrobes. Prices from €60 with shower/wc to €63–75 with bath and €79 with Jacuzzi. Half board, requested at weekends and in July and August, costs €64–74 per person. You can rent a bike to explore the Orléans forest nearby and there's a tennis court and a heated swimming pool. It's one of the best hotels around. *10% discount on the room rate except at the weekend and in July–Aug offered to our readers on presentation of this guide.*

Cour-Cheverny

41700

Hôtel-restaurant des Trois Marchands**

Place de l'Église.
Ⓣ02.54.79.96.44 Ⓕ02.54.79.25.60
Ⓦwww.hoteldes3marchands.com
Closed *Mon; mid-Feb to mid-March.* **TV. High chairs available. Car park.**

This half-timbered village inn has a lot of charm. There are 36 rooms, some overlooking the garden. Avoid the ones in the annexe across the way if you can. Doubles €43–56; half board €47–53. The cooking has earned the place a good reputation, especially for frogs' legs with garlic and herbs. There are two dining areas: an upmarket gourmet restaurant and a smaller, rustic-style brasserie. *Formules* at €14 and €18 (in the brasserie), and €20.50 (weekdays). Menus are priced at €43–56. *10% discount on the room rate offered to our readers on presentation of this guide.*

Dreux

28100

Hôtel Le Beffroi**

12 pl. Métézeau.
Ⓣ02.37.50.02.03
Closed *Sun noon–5.30pm; 1–15 Aug.* **TV.**

This is a good place to spend the night when you're just passing through, with its bright, quiet, comfortable rooms overlooking the river or the square. Doubles with shower/wc €55, not including breakfast; some rooms sleep three. Pleasant welcome.

Aux Quatre Vents

18 pl. Métézeau.
Ⓣ02.37.50.03.24
Closed *evenings.* **High chairs available.**

They've given this bistro a good retro look. The best options are the menus – €15, €19 and €23 – where you help yourself to as many hors d'œuvres from the buffet as you like: choose from salmon, shellfish, excellent charcuterie and *crudités*. Follow that with a main course like kidneys in mustard sauce, veal in cream sauce or roast chicken, then finish with dessert. Make the most of the terrace when the weather's good – it faces the belfry. *Free apéritif offered to our readers on presentation of this guide.*

Vernouillet

28500 (3km S)

Auberge de la Vallée Verte**

6 rue Lucien-Dupuis; it's in the centre near the church.
Ⓣ02.37.46.04.04 Ⓕ02.37.42.91.17
Closed *Sun; Mon; 3–26 Aug; 20 Dec–5 Jan.* **TV. Car park.**

This recently refurbished hotel offers cosy rooms with shower/wc for €60. Breakfast €6.10. But the big draw is the cooking: there's a brigade of professionals in the kitchen and they produce classic cuisine using locally farmed produce (veal, lamb and game according to season) and fresh seasonal fish. Cheapest menu at €23 and a fish menu, wine included, for €40.You can dine either in the pretty rustic dining room or under the eaves on the mezzanine.There's an intimate atmosphere and a convivial, smiling welcome. It's best to book at weekends. *Free apéritif offered to our readers on presentation of this guide.*

Ferté-Vidame (La)

28340

La Trigalle*

Ⓣ06.12.97.82.00 Ⓕ02.37.37.51.75
Ⓦwww.cc-la-ferte-vidame.fr
Closed *Mon and Tues except public holidays; 1 Dec–11 Feb.* **Disabled access. Car park.**

This restaurant is a real pleasure: classical music plays in the background but Emmanuel's cooking is far from classical. He invents delicious concoctions, changing the specialities on a regular basis: typical choices include scallops with oysters, pan-fried rump steak, fillets of red mullet with preserved lemon and basil oil, chestnut *truffade* with Armagnac, steamed turbot steak with *andouille de Vire*, bacon and truffles, honey ice cream with almond crackling, Bavarois with sweet wine and raspberry and basil *coulis*. Evening menus, €15–23, are good and generously served. The wine list is exceptional and, if you're feeling flush, there are a number of bottles with three-figure prices. Saint-Simon, the famous eighteenth-century diarist who chronicled events at the court of Louis XIV, had a château here. It's in ruins now but it's worth a visit – the grounds are enormous. NB: for dinner, you must book before 3pm.

Gien

45500

La Bodega

17 rue Bernard-Palissy.
Ⓣ02.38.67.29.01 Ⓕ02.38.67.98.47
Closed *Sun except by reservation; Aug.* **Car park.**

Odd to find such a traditional French hotel with such a Spanish name. Whatever the nomenclature, this is a straight-down-the-line establishment for travellers on a tight budget. It's a small hotel with pretty, old-style rooms that have all been made over with shower rooms added (the wc is still on the landing). Doubles €26–34. Excellent value for money. It has to be said, however, that the two rooms in the courtyard are not well sound-proofed on the road side.The restaurant doesn't go in for complicated cooking, but it's good nourishing fare and the little dining room is pleasant. Thre's a lunch *formule* for €7 (as much hors d'œuvre and pizza as you can eat), along with grills and simple salads, menus at €8 and €11, or dinner à la carte for around €20. They welcome you very naturally, almost as if you were part of the family.

|●| Restaurant Le Régency

6 quai Lenoir; it faces the Loire, near the bridge.
Ⓣ02.38.67.04.96
Closed *Sun evening; Wed; the Feb school holidays, a fortnight 1–15 July; during New Year.*

The restaurant specializes in freshwater fish from the Loire, as well as local dishes cooked simply and with care. Prices are reasonable with menus at €16 (not weekends or holidays), €20 and €22. À la carte, *croustade* of snails with garlic cream, zander fillet with lemon butter, chilled nougat with red-fruit *coulis*. It's a tiny place, so think about reserving.

Illiers-Combray

28120

|●| Le Florent

13 pl. du Marché; it's opposite the church.
Ⓣ02.37.24.10.43 Ⓕ02.37.24.11.78
Ⓔleflorent@aol.com
Closed *Sun evening–Wed evening except on public holidays.* **High chairs available. Disabled access.**

An elegant, unpretentious restaurant – they don't flog the Proust connection to death. The little dining rooms are delightful, and Hervé Priolet is an excellent and imaginative chef. There are tempting set menus at €18 (weekdays, except public holidays) and ranging up to €40 – and, yes, one is named after Proust. There's also a good choice of à la carte dishes, from around €12–21, and wines are sold by the glass. The house specialities include *tournedos*, veal sweetbreads and stuffed brocket breast. Reservations advised. Note that service can be a bit slow.

Brou

28160 (13km SW)

⌂ |●| Le Plat d'Étain**

15 pl. des Halles; on the main square.
Ⓣ02.37.96.05.65
Ⓕ02.37.96.09.29
Ⓦwww.leplatdetain.com
TV.

A spotless setting with a thick carpet, staff members dressed up to the nines and reasonable prices: what more can you want? Spruce double rooms €49–73. The quality extends to the kitchen, even though the chef does not take many risks; the menus revolve around standard but well-prepared dishes like fried foie gras and *entrecôte* with shallots: €14 (weekdays), then €16–40.

Issoudun

36100

⌂ |●| Hôtel de France – Restaurant Les Trois Rois**

3 rue Pierre-Brossolette.
Ⓣ02.54.21.00.65 Ⓕ02.54.21.50.61
Closed *Sun evening; Mon; fortnight in Feb; 3 weeks in Sept.* **TV. Car park.**

Most rooms here are large and spotlessly clean but there are some smaller ones which could do with a makeover. Doubles with shower/wc or bath cost €45–49. The dining room is comfortable and stylish, and the classic cuisine doesn't disappoint. Menu at €14.50 (not served Sun) and another at €18.30. Specialities include calf's head *à l'ancienne* and *andouillette* with Berry green lentils. You'll get an exuberant welcome from the owner, a very efficient woman who keeps an eye on everything. *Free apéritif offered to our readers on presentation of this guide.*

⌂ |●| Hôtel-restaurant La Cognette***

2 bd. Stalingrad; take the N151, go into the town centre and it's near the big market-place.
Ⓣ02.54.03.59.59 Ⓕ02.54.03.13.03
Ⓔlacognette@wanadoo.com
Closed *Sun evening; Mon and Tues lunchtime except I June–3 Sept.* **Disabled access. TV. Car park.**

Balzac gives a very vivid description of this hotel in *La Rabouilleuse*. Then, it was run by a pair called Cognet and a widow from Houssaye who had a reputation as a fine cook. Nowadays the kitchens are in the hands of Alain Nonnet and his son-in-law, Jean-Jacques Daumy, who prepare delicious food that is some of the best in the region. Set menus €24–70. The hotel is perfect; rooms are comfortable and the well-equipped bathrooms are supplied with robe and hairdryer. Some have terraces where you can have breakfast in fine weather and enjoy the scent of roses. Doubles €80–250 with bath. It thoroughly deserves its three stars. *Free apéritif*

offered to our readers on presentation of this guide.

|●| Pile ou Face

11 rue Danielle-Casanova.
Ⓣ02.54.03.14.91
Closed *Sun evening; Mon; Thurs evening in winter; fortnight in May; fortnight in Nov.*

Whether you choose to eat in the conventional dining room or out on the more pleasant covered terrace, the menus are the same. Weekday lunch menu €13, then €20–39. Children's menu €7. Specialities include *cassolette berrichonne* and lobster *croquant*. *Free coffee offered to our readers on presentation of this guide.*

Diou

36260 (12km N)

|●| L'Aubergeade

Rte. d'Issoudun; from Issoudun take the D918, heading for Vierzon.
Ⓣ and Ⓕ02.54.49.22.28
Closed *Wed and Sun evenings.* **Disabled access. Car park.**

A warm welcome, a pretty terrace, a pleasant, comfortable dining room and careful, varied and inventive cooking. Menus run from €16 to €33. Specialities include zander with red cabbage, and Berry pigeon. *Free apéritif offered to our readers on presentation of this guide.*

Brives

36100 (13km S)

|●| Restaurant Le César, Chez Nicole

From Issoudun take the D918; it's beside the church.
Ⓣ02.54.49.04.43
Closed *Mon; 2–9 Aug.*

There are remains of the old dyke built by Caesar's legions close to this restaurant, and it's also near to the village church. The ceiling of the large dining room is supported by enormous beams. Simple tasty cuisine listed on menus from €9.15 (weekdays only) to €30; you'll spend €22 à la carte. Try the house terrine César, calf's head vinaigrette with lentils. Reservations recommended.

Langeais

37130

|●| Hôtel-Restaurant Errard-Hosten

2 rue Gambetta.
Ⓣ02.47.96.82.12 Ⓕ02.47.96.56.72
Ⓦwww.errard.com Ⓔinfo@errard.com
Closed *Sun Oct–April; Mon; Tues lunchtime except public holidays; Dec–Jan.* **TV. Pay car park.**

An old inn right in the centre of the town with ten cosy, comfortable rooms. Doubles with shower/wc are €49, or €61–71 with bath. The ones overlooking the courtyard are the quietest. There's a warm dining room on the ground floor with a small bar just off it. High-quality gastronomic cooking with dishes precisely cooked and seasonings finely judged: typical choices include eel *rillettes*, pigeon with honey and ginger, a classic zander with *beurre blanc*, and Grand Marnier mousse. All delicious. Menus €26–45. Exemplary service and welcome.

Loches

37600

|●| Hôtel-restaurant de France**

6 rue Picois.
Ⓣ02.47.59.00.32 Ⓕ02.47.59.28.66
Closed *Sun evening; Mon; Tues lunchtime except July–Aug; 6 Jan–12 Feb.* **TV. Pay car park.**

This is an old posthouse with a wide courtyard and flower garden where you can have lunch in the summer. Nineteen lovely rooms priced €50–57 with shower/wc or bath. Some are split-level, and they're all very cosily furnished. In the classical dining room they serve inventive and refined cooking prepared with great care and attention: dishes are produced from under domed covers, plates are hot, there are fresh flowers on the table and there's not a paper napkin in sight. After some *amuse-bouches* to get your appetite going, decide between such dishes as pastry-cases filled with langoustine in wine sauce, eel stew, *géline* (local chicken) *de Touraine*, *tournedos* Rossini (fillet steak with foie gras), prune ice cream with Touraine Marc and a Grand-Marnier soufflé. The desserts are prepared on the premises. Menus €15 (not served Sun) and €21–46. Apparently Lodovico Sforza, the duke of Milan, was imprisoned by Louis XI in the dungeons in Loche and had his meals brought in from this hotel – if the quality was anything like this, it can't have been much of a hardship.

Malesherbes

45330

L'Écu de France**

10 pl. du Martroy.
Ⓣ02.38.34.87.25 Ⓕ02.38.34.68.99
Closed *6–19 Aug.* **Restaurant closed** *Thurs and Sun evenings.* **TV. High chairs available. Car park.**

Housed in a seventeenth-century staging post. The courtyard, where the stage-coaches used to turn in, has been transformed into the reception hall. Comfortable, well-maintained double rooms for €48–60 with shower/wc or bath. The restaurant won't blow you away, but the *formule brasserie* served in the bistro is tasty and eating here can prove good value with menus at €18 (not served on Sun) and €28. They offer decent dishes of the day – calf's head is a speciality – and a particularly good dessert with cream and cream cheese beaten together – it's even better with strawberries. A good place to stop if you're driving on the A13, which is just 13km away, and Fontainebleau is also nearby.

Mézières-en-Brenne

36290

Hôtel-restaurant Au Bœuf Couronné**

9 pl. Charles-de-Gaulle (Centre); 20 km south of Châtillon-sur-Indre via the D43 and around 40 km west of Châteauroux.
Ⓣ02.54.38.04.39 Ⓕ02.54.38.02.84
Closed *Sun evening and Mon (except public holidays); 15 Nov–31 Jan.* **TV. High chairs available.**

In the heart of Brenne's lake country, this former staging post, with a front porch dating from the mid-sixteenth century, has established a reputation that has spread far beyond the region. It offers an enticing mixture of warmth and elegance, with a decidedly rural touch. The bedrooms are small but perfectly adequate; the ones overlooking the inner courtyard are the quietest. Doubles with shower/wc €38. Subtle and inventive cooking, prepared and served with loving care. Menus €15.50 (weekdays), then €19–40. Very friendly and attentive service. Credit cards not accepted.

Montargis

45200

Hôtel Le Bon Gîte*

21 bd. du Chinchon.
Ⓣ02.38.85.31.01 Ⓕ02.38.93.28.06
Disabled access. TV. Car park.

Good place for a decent night's sleep at a reasonable price. It's not much to look at from the outside, but inside it's clean and quiet. Simple rooms, some of which look over the inner courtyard – in summer you could almost imagine you were somewhere in the Mediterranean. Doubles cost €28 with shower/wc and go up to €37 with bath. The very nice owners have been here for more than forty years.

Restaurant Les Petits Oignons

81 bis av. du Général-de-Gaulle; it's near the train station.
Ⓣ02.38.93.97.49
Closed *Sun evening; Mon; Feb school holidays; the 1st 3 weeks in Aug.* **Disabled access.**

They've got an effective "two-in-one" formula here. On one side is the bistro with its typical cooking (herring and potatoes in oil, skate wing and so on), while on the other is the gastronomic restaurant, with its bright, uncluttered and rather modern décor and more elaborate dishes, such as zander with saffron and *cendré de Pannes* (goat's cheese coated in grey ash, produced less than 30km away). In the summer you can also dine out in the garden and terrace. Wherever you eat, you can be sure of refined cuisine using only the freshest produce. Cordial welcome and impeccable service. Menus are realistically priced at €12–29.

Amilly

45200 (2km SE)

L'Auberge de l'Écluse

741 rue des Ponts.

Ⓣ02.38.85.44.24
Closed *Sun evening; Mon; Thurs evening; a few days in early Jan.*

From the dining room you can watch while the keeper opens the lock on the nearby canal; there's also a terrace on the waterside. Inside, the classic décor contrasts with the modern and inventive cooking. They specialize in fish – zander, red mullet, cod – and use whatever the day's catch yields. Prices are a little high – menus €22–29 in the week, €29–32 on Sunday – but the dishes are in no way disappointing. You should reserve on sunny days.

Cepoy

45120 (6km N)

Auberge de jeunesse

25 quai du Port; take the no. 2 bus via the N7 to the "Église de Saint-Loup" stop; from there, it's a 200-metre walk to the hostel.
Ⓣ02.38.93.25.45 Ⓕ02.38.93.19.25
Ⓔajcepoy@aol.com
New arrivals *8am–noon and 6–10pm.*
Closed *20 Dec–1 Feb.* **Games available.**

Ideally situated on the banks of the Loing canal, in a charming seventh-century château on the outskirts of the town. Twenty-seven rooms with two to eight beds; doubles with washbasin or shower €24–35. You can also put up your own tent – there's certainly enough space, as the huge garden stretches over 4000 square metres and includes a volleyball court and ping-pong tables. Mainly group bookings, but there's usually room for individual travellers too. FUAJ card compulsory (you can buy it on the spot). Meals €8.80, but a kitchen is also available. Garage for bikes, with the possibility of renting a mountain bike. *Free coffee offered to our readers on presentation of this guide.*

Montrichard

41400

Hôtel de la Croix-Blanche**

64 rue Nationale.
Ⓣ02.54.32.30.87 Ⓕ02.54.32.91.00
Closed *2 Nov–15 March.* **TV.**

This hotel has been completely renovated and is wonderfully clean. It started life as a coaching inn in the sixteenth century and it's right next to the dungeons. The rooms are well appointed, some with a view over the River Cher, and have en-suite bathrooms and phones; doubles around €55. Half board €48 per person per night. There's an attractive patio where they serve breakfast. *10% discount on the room rate (except weekends, public holidays and 7 July–31 Aug) offered to our readers on presentation of this guide.*

Bistrot de la Tour

34 rue du Sully; it's near the tourist office.
Ⓣ02.54.32.07.34
Closed *Sun; Mon out of season.*

A lovely house with a pretty terrace on the town square. The stone and wood décor inside is warm and attractive. Weekday *formule* €10.50, others €15 and €20. Classic, carefully prepared dishes like poached eggs in Gamay sauce, ox kidneys with basil, zander fillet and a particularly good dish of snails and oyster mushrooms. There's also a selection of substantial salads. *Free coffee offered to our readers on presentation of this guide.*

Chissay-en-Touraine

41400 (4km W)

Château de Chissay

It's on the right bank of the Cher. From Montrichard, take the D176 in the direction of Tours.
Ⓣ02.54.32.32.01 Ⓕ02.54.32.43.70
Ⓦwww.chateaudechissay.com
Closed *mid-Nov to mid-March.* **TV. Swimming pool. High chairs available. Car park.**

Historic château built by Charles VIII. It's a wonderful, meticulously restored building, located in the heart of the Cher valley. The terrace is under the arcades, while the splendid dining room is luxuriously decorated with period furniture. Weekday *formule* at €18, and menus €34–52. Double rooms €106–184 (the most expensive are in effect small apartments). *10% discount on the room rate or free apéritif maison offered to our readers on presentation of this guide.*

Pontlevoy

41400 (7km NE)

Hôtel-restaurant de l'École**

12 rte. de Montrichard; it's on the main road coming from Montrichard.

ⓣ02.54.32.50.30 ⓕ02.54.32.33.58
Closed *Sun evening and Mon except public holidays; 20 Nov–12 Dec; 16 Feb–14 March.* **TV. High chairs available. Car park.**

This is a charming little hotel with eleven comfortable rooms with shower/wc at €42 or €45.50–46.50 with bath. The cooking is very traditional but sophisticated and nicely presented. They do several set menus starting at €17 and going up to €46.50. Try their calf's head sauce *gribiche*, the pike balls with crayfish tails, game (in season) and their crackling vanilla dessert with chocolate sauce. In fine weather, you can eat under the pergola in the garden.

Civray-de-Touraine

37150 (9km W)

L'Hostellerie du Château de l'Isle**

Take the D176 1km after Chenonceaux, to the bank of the Cher.
02.47.23.63.60 ⓕ02.47.23.63.62
ⓦwww.chateaudelisle.en-france.com
Closed *mid-Nov to mid-Feb.* **Restaurant closed** *for lunch (except for groups).* **TV. High chairs available. Car park.**

This hotel seems like a family house (not surprisingly, because in fact that's what it is); it is set in a beautiful eighteenth-century residence, in the middle of a huge park bounded by the Cher. Ten comfortable rooms, all refurbished. Ask if you can see a few, as they're all different. Doubles from €53–92 with shower/wc or bath, and a suite at €150. The charming restaurant is spread over two dining rooms with fireplaces; the chef produces high-quality food according to the availability of fresh produce. Menu €31. On fine days you can eat on the terrace, before digesting your meal on a stroll amongst the centuries-old trees in the park. You can also take a boat trip on the Cher. *10% discount on a room offered to our readers on presentation of this guide.*

Oisly

41700 (16km NE)

Restaurant Le Saint-Vincent

From Montrichard take the D764 as far as Pontlevoy then turn right onto the D30.
ⓣ and ⓕ02.54.79.50.04
Closed *Tues; Wed; mid-Dec to end Feb.*

This is quite an exceptional restaurant. It doesn't look like much – the sign is very ordinary and you might mistake it for just another restaurant in just another village square. But step inside and notice the attention to detail: the décor is fresh, there's a decent amount of space between the tables, and the linen and cutlery have been chosen to match the rustic ambience. The menu is varied and full of tempting and original dishes: lobster *boudin* with Thai green curry, lamb braised with chickpeas and lemon *confit*, roast pineapple caramelized with white rum. The creative chef will probably have invented even more culinary delights by the time you read this. Set menus €22 (not public holidays) up to €48. *Free coffee offered to our readers on presentation of this guide.*

Nogent-le-Roi

28210

Le Capucin Gourmand

1 rue de la Volaille; near the church.
ⓣ02.37.51.96.00
Closed Sun evening; Mon; end Aug to early Sept.

In this prettily decorated fifteeth-century house with half-timbering, the chef concocts highly attractive dishes infused with Mediterranean flavours, such as grilled swordfish with tapenade and *croustillant* of langoustines. Before that, though, whet your appetite with the house apéritif, a skilful mixture of champagne and Grand Marnier. Weekday lunchtime menu €15, then others €24–39. A warm welcome is guaranteed.

Nogent-le-Rotrou

28400

Inter Hôtel Sully***

12 rue des Viennes.
ⓣ02.37.52.15.14 ⓕ02.37.52.15.20
ⓔhotel.sully@wanadoo.fr
Closed *23 Dec–4 Jan.* **Disabled access. High chairs available. TV. Pay car park.**

Sure, it's a chain hotel but you get a genuine, smiling welcome that inspires confidence. The prices are affordable for a three-star; doubles with en-suite bathrooms start at €56. Breakfast €6.60. It's quietly located just away from the centre of town in an area that's recently been developed. *Free apéritif offered to our readers on presentation of this guide.*

La Papotière

3 rue Bourg-le-Comte.
☎02.37.52.18.41
Closed *Sun lunchtime; Mon.*

A strange name (it means "the gossiping woman") for this superb early-sixteenth-century stone house with mullioned windows and gargoyles. The snug interior is equally enchanting and the service is friendly, so guests quickly feel at ease. Traditional bourgeois cooking; veal sweetbreads with morels, *noisette* of lamb. As for dessert, you must try the house speciality of chocolate *kanougat*. Delicious bistro-style menu €12.50 served every day at lunch and dinner, with other menus at €26–35.

Nouan-le-Fuzelier

41600

Hôtel Les Charmilles

19 rte. de Pierrefitte-sur-Sauldre; by the exit to the town, on the D122.
☎02.54.88.73.55 ℻02.54.88.74.55
Closed *Feb.* **Disabled access.**

On the edge of a fairly quiet road, a small, modest but charming hotel in a woody park with a little pond, run by a young man with the help of his father. Fifteen very well-kept rooms with shower or bath; nos. 12 and 14 are on the ground floor overlooking the garden. Doubles €45–62. There is no restaurant, but the father used to be a baker and now provides excellent brioches and croissants for breakfast (€7).

Le Raboliot

1 av. de la Mairie; in the main square; the town is between Salbris and Lamotte-Beuvron, a little way off the RN20 and 5 min from the motorway.
☎02.54.94.40.00
Closed *mid-Jan to mid-Feb; Sun evening; Mon.* **Disabled access. Car park.**

Philippe Henry, the owner of this restaurant near the woods and lakes of Malvaux is a local character renowned for his enthusiasm and good humour. His personality has left its mark on this excellent, warm-hearted and reasonably priced restaurant. The specialities include remarkable fresh foie gras, *filet mignon* of Val-de-Loire pork and scallop risotto with lobster *coulis* – and in the hunting season, there is an abundance of game. The desserts are just as mouth-watering: *tarte tatin*, warm *coulant* of Caribbean chocolate. Set menus €15–21, and more extensive menus €28–34. Superb wine list and impeccable service. Regulars know that the owner also serves simpler, but equally exceptional, dishes from the bar at lunchtime: Orléanais free-range chicken with sage, *gratin* of potatoes with Sauvignon.

Le Dahu

14 rue Henri-Chapron; take the N20 in the direction of Ferté-Saint-Aubin.
☎02.54.88.72.88
Closed *Tues; Wed; 2 Jan–13 Feb.* **Disabled access. Car park.**

One of the outstanding restaurants in the region. Marie-Thérèse and Jean-Luc Germain have created an extraordinary garden for *Le Dahu*. Tucked away in an unattractive housing estate, this Solognote farmhouse has shrouded itself in greenery, echoed by the centuries-old beams and posts in the cosy, rustic but chic interior. The food also matches its surroundings admirably: fillet of bass with grapefruit, fillets of sea bream with cream of red pepper, Sainte-Montaine squab with honey and ginger, game in season. Menus at €21 (weekdays), then €28–47. Reckon on €50–55 à la carte.

Souesmes

41300 (16km SE)

Hôtel-restaurant La Croix Verte

Place de l'Église. Take the D122 in the direction of Pierrefitte-sur-Sauldre, then the D126.
☎02.54.98.93.70 ℻02.54.98.88.71
Closed *Tues evening; Wed; Sun evening.* **High chairs available.**

Just simple, traditional, seasonal food, but the chef's artistry has begun to earn it a very high reputation: *croustillant* of goat with bacon, *fricassée* of veal kidneys with pig's fat and mustard, *tarte fine* with potato *confit* and coarse salt. Weekday lunchtime menu €10, then €21–26. A few modest but well-kept rooms that enable you to explore the area more fully. To top it all, art lovers can buy the prints hanging on the walls. *Free apéritif offered to our readers on presentation of this guide.*

Orléans

45000

See map overleaf

Auberge de jeunesse

1 bd. de la Motte-Sanguin; to the east of the town centre (barely 10 min on foot); from the train station, take buses no. 4 or 8 to the "Pont-Bourgogne" stop. **Map D3-4**
Ⓣ02.38.53.60.06 Ⓕ02.38.52.96.39
Ⓔasse.crjs@libertysurf.fr
Open *all year round 8am–7pm (8pm in summer).* **TV. Disabled access. Car park.**

This youth hostel is in a listed building in the heart of a woody park stretching along the quays of the Loire. €7.80 per person. Sheets: €3.20. Breakfast €3.35. There are sixty beds in all, so groups can be accommodated (and they can also buy cooked meals, unlike individual visitors). A kitchen, TV room, ping-pong table and laundry are also available. FUAJ membership card required (on sale in situ). *Free apéritif or coffee offered to our readers on presentation of this guide.*

Hôtel de l'Abeille**

64 rue d'Alsace-Lorraine; it's in a street that flanks the Palais de Justice. **Map C1-3**
Ⓣ02.38.53.54.87 Ⓕ02.38.62.65.84
Ⓔhoteldelabeille@wanadoo.fr
TV. High chairs available.

There's something very special about this hotel. It was opened way back in 1903 and has been run by the same famiily since 1919, which makes it one of the oldest hotels in town. They've put green shrubs and flowers out all over the pavement, and the reception area is wonderfully nostalgic, complete with its own statue. The old wooden staircase gleams from years of polishing and the rooms – all decorated differently – have a quiet, antiquated charm. Prices are fair: €38 for a room with shower, €45–60 for a room with shower/wc or bath. *10% discount on the room rate offered to our readers on presentation of this guide.*

Jackotel**

18 cloître Saint-Aignan; follow quai du Châtelet in the direction of Montargis and turn left before you get to the bridge. **Map D2-5**
Ⓣ02.38.54.48.48 Ⓕ02.38.77.17.59
Closed *Sun afternoon and public holidays 1–6pm.* **Disabled access. TV. Car park.**

This recently built hotel is in a charming location, in a flower-filled courtyard near a lovely little square in the shadow of the church of Saint-Aignan. The rooms, though comfortable, aren't exciting – you come here for the setting. They're mad about parrots, and you'll be greeted by a display of carved parrots in reception. Doubles €46–49 with bath, TV and phone.

Hôtel Marguerite**

14 place du Vieux-Marché; it's 50m from rue Royale, near the main post office. **Map B2-2**
Ⓣ02.38.53.74.32 Ⓕ02.38.53.31.56
Ⓔhotel.marguerite@wanadoo.fr
Closed Sat noon–4.30pm in winter; Sun noon–4.30pm.
TV.

Nice hotel with a pretty brick façade. Prices are good, the welcome is friendly, and you could almost believe this was a three-star. Two types of accommodation – renovated rooms painted in pastel tones, and older, spotless rooms with their own charm. You'll pay €47–57 for a double with shower/wc or bath. Breakfast includes as much coffee as you can drink, fruit juice and honey for only €5 – they'll bring it to your room for no extra charge. *20% discount on the room rate (Fri–Sun and July–Aug) offered to our readers on presentation of this guide.*

Restaurant Les Fagots

32 rue du Poirier; it's near the covered market. **Map C2-6**
Ⓣ02.38.62.22.79
Closed *Sun; Mon; the first week in Jan; 3 weeks in Aug.* **Disabled access.**

You'll see all types here, from romantic couples to convivial groups and chatty locals. The dining room has a huge fireplace, and features old posters on the wall, with enamel and china coffee pots here and there. But you'll come here for the grills, which they do over the open fire – their speciality is donkey meat steak, though you have to order this a day in advance. The lunchtime set menu costs €10.73, there's another at €13.95, and à la carte you'll pay around €22. Friendly welcome and service. It's better in the evening (when reservations are strongly recommended) but on sunny days, the terrace makes it a thoroughly nice place for lunch. *Free apéritif offered to our readers on presentation of this guide.*

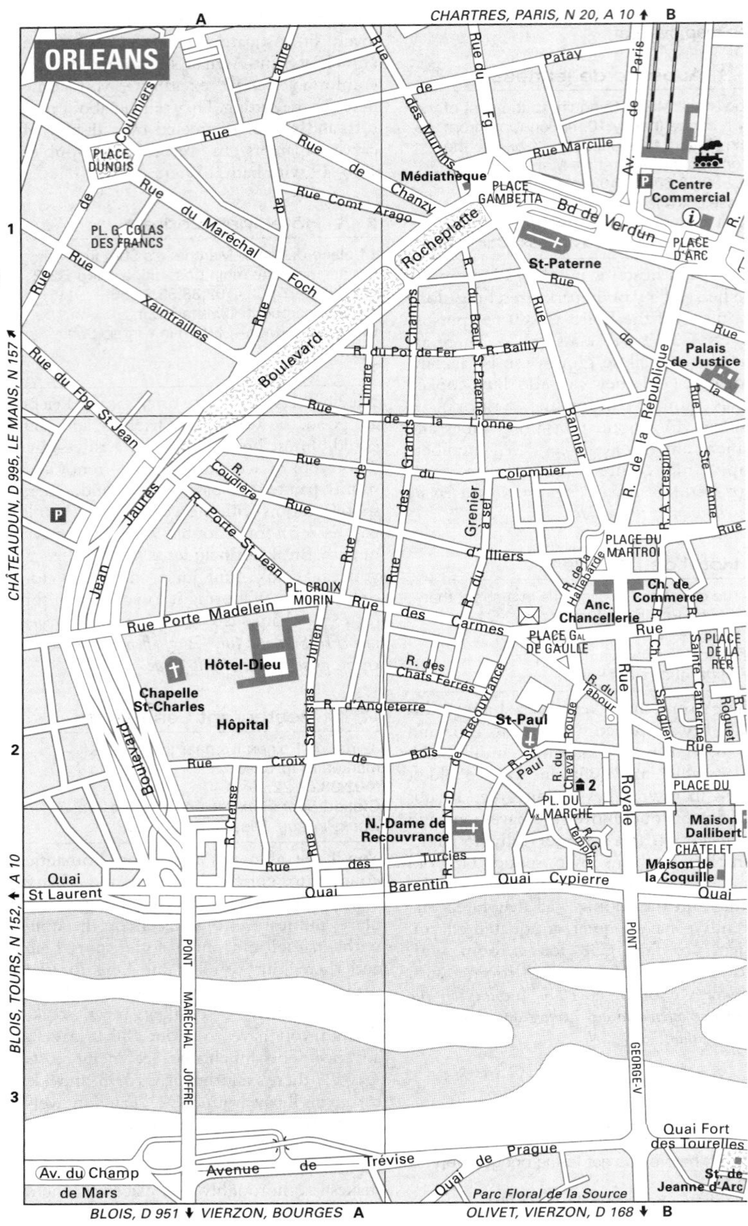
ORLEANS
CHARTRES, PARIS, N 20, A 10
A
B
1
2
3
CHÂTEAUDUN, D 995, LE MANS, N 157
BLOIS, TOURS, N 152, A 10
BLOIS, D 951
VIERZON, BOURGES
OLIVET, VIERZON, D 168
PLACE DUNOIS
Rue Coulmiers
Rue Lahire
Rue de Patay
Rue du Fg
Rue des Murlins
Rue Marcille
Av. de Paris
Médiathèque
PLACE GAMBETTA
Centre Commercial
Rue de Chanzy
Rue Comt Arago
Bd de Verdun
PLACE D'ARC
St-Paterne
PL. G. COLAS DES FRANCS
Rue du Maréchal Foch
Rue Xaintrailles
Rue du Fbg St Jean
Boulevard Rocheplatte
Rue des Grands Champs
R. du Pot de Fer
R. Bailly
Rue Limare
R. du Boeuf St Paterne
Rue Bannier
Rue de la République
Palais de Justice
Rue de la Lionne
Rue du Colombier
R. Coudière
R. Porte St Jean
Jean Jaurès
R. A. Crespin
Rue Ste Anne
Rue de Grenier à sel
Rue d'Illiers
PLACE DU MARTROI
R. de la Hallebarde
Ch. de Commerce
Anc. Chancellerie
PL. CROIX MORIN
Rue Porte Madeleine
Rue des Carmes
PLACE Gal DE GAULLE
Hôtel-Dieu
Chapelle St-Charles
Hôpital
R. des Chats Ferrés
R. d'Angleterre
Stanislas Julien
Rue de Recouvrance
R. du Tabour
Rue Royale
Rue Sainte Catherine
Sanglier
PLACE DE LA RÉP
Roguet
St-Paul
Boulevard
Rue Croix de Bois
R. St Paul
R. du Cheval Rouge
PL. DU V. MARCHÉ
PLACE DU CHÂTELET
Maison Dalibert
R. N.-D. de Recouvrance
N.-Dame de Recouvrance
R. Creuse
R. du Tour Neuve
R. Templier
Maison de la Coquille
Rue des Turcies
Quai St Laurent
Quai Barentin
Quai Cypierre
Quai
PONT MARÉCHAL JOFFRE
PONT GEORGE-V
Quai Fort des Tourelles
Avenue de Trévise
Quai de Prague
Av. du Champ de Mars
Parc Floral de la Source
St. de Jeanne d'Arc

6

CENTRE

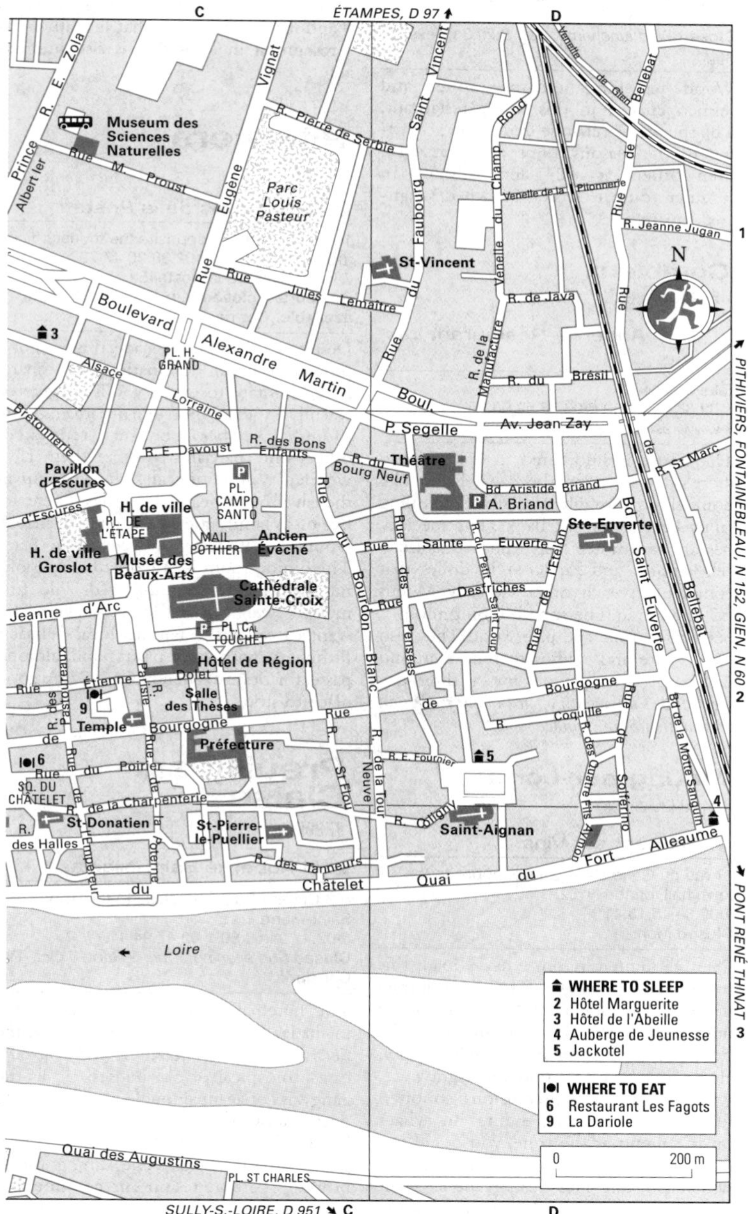

ÉTAMPES, D 97
SULLY-S.-LOIRE, D 951
PITHIVIERS, FONTAINEBLEAU, N 152, GIEN, N 60
PONT RENÉ THINAT
Museum des Sciences Naturelles
Parc Louis Pasteur
St-Vincent
Boulevard Alexandre Martin
Théatre
Pavillon d'Escures
H. de ville
H. de ville Groslot
Musée des Beaux-Arts
Ancien Évêché
Cathédrale Sainte-Croix
Hôtel de Région
Salle des Thèses
Temple
Préfecture
St-Donatien
St-Pierre-le-Puellier
Saint-Aignan
Ste-Euverte
Loire
Quai du Châtelet
Quai du Fort Alleaume
Quai des Augustins
WHERE TO SLEEP
2 Hôtel Marguerite
3 Hôtel de l'Abeille
4 Auberge de Jeunesse
5 Jackotel
WHERE TO EAT
6 Restaurant Les Fagots
9 La Dariole
0 200 m

La Dariole

26 rue Étienne-Dolet. **Map C2-9**
02.38.77.26.67
Closed *Wed lunchtime; Sat; Sun; 3 weeks in Aug.*

Wood panelling, old-rose tones and refined cuisine in this lovely restaurant. The specialities change frequently according to the seasons. Nice menu at €18, then others at €24 and €30.50. In summer you eat outside on a pedestrianized square.

Combleux

45800 (5km E)

Auberge-Restaurant La Marine

Take the N460.
02.38.55.12.69 02.38.52.03.65
www.residence-la-marine.com

The house is smothered in wisteria and there's a terrace on the canal bank. The Loire flows through the village, revealing sandy beaches on the banks. The specialities are freshwater fish from the Loire – eel, lampray and zander – in dishes that complement each other expertly. Menus €20 and €26. The superb dining room is built from stone and pale wood. They also have a gite and studios to rent – around €185 for two people for a three-day weekend. *Free apéritif offered to our readers on presentation of this guide.*

Meung-sur-Loire

45130 (20km SW)

Dix Sept sur Vins

17 rue du Général-de-Gaulle; opposite the town hall, on the N152.
02.38.45.13.41
Closed *Mon.*

Even though it is on a main road, this restaurant is a real gem. The noise of traffic recedes as soon as you enter the simple but cheerful little dining room. The traditional cooking is unfailingly wholesome, always managing to find the right note, without the fussy pretensions so often found elsewhere. Depending on what's on the menu at the time, you could try, for example, *croustillant* of salmon, *magret* with *cassis*, foie gras, sea bream in a salt crust or kidneys in red wine. Lunchtime menu of the day (except Sun) €14; other menus €19–25. The name of the restaurant is a play on words that makes clear, however, the owner's knowledge of wines – and it must be added that his father has a restaurant in Paris that is also unmissable.

Pithiviers

45300

Le Relais de la Poste**

10 Mail-Ouest; it's opposite the tourist office.
02.38.30.40.30. 02.38.30.47.79
www.relais-de-la-poste45.com
Restaurant closed Sun evening. **TV. Cots available. Car park.**

Despite its crumbling façade, this is a good provincial hotel dominating the square. Don't hesitate to enter; you'll be greeted warmly by the Polish-born patron. Some rooms have been entirely renovated, others only partially. Most of them have wooden wainscoting and the ones up in the eaves boast beamed ceilings. There are five or so family rooms with cots available. Doubles €49 with shower/wc or bath. The dining room is rather ordinary looking, but nicely soundproofed. The first menu is well worth a look; you may also want to order the famous local delicacy, Pithiviers with puff pastry and almond paste, for dessert. Menus €16–27. A good place to stop.

Preuilly-sur-Claise

37290

Auberge Saint-Nicolas**

4-6 Grande-Rue; very close to the Abbey of Saint-Pierre.
02.47.94.50.80 02.47.94.41.77
Closed *Sun evening; Mon; 9 Sept–8 Oct.* **TV. Car park.**

This hotel offers nine rooms redecorated in shades of yellow and fitted with all the necessary conveniences. The array of staircases, so typical of old houses, recalls the gangways of a ship. Double rooms €37–43 with shower/wc or bath. Weekday lunchtime menu €10.50, then others going up to €34.50. The dining room, brightly coloured and air-conditioned, serves regional dishes. Friendly service and good value for money.

Petit-Pressigny (Le)

37350 (9km N)

Restaurant La Promenade

11 rue du Savoureulx; take the D41 in the direction of Loches, then the D50.
Ⓣ02.47.94.93.52 Ⓕ02.47.91.06.03
Closed *Sun evening, Mon and Tues except in July and Aug; 5 Jan–4 Feb; 20 Sept–6 Oct.*

Some of the most ordinary-looking villages hide real treasures – this is one. Jacky Dallais was a pupil of Robuchon, and he's converted his father's old smithy into a splendid restaurant with two pretty, contemporary-looking dining rooms. He's a chef with integrity and imagination and creates dishes of great distinction. The choice changes constantly. Set menus, €34–69, are generous; the €69 menu includes four dishes, cheese and dessert. Reckon on €60 à la carte. Specialities include free-range pork chop with beans and black pudding parmentier with mashed potatoes. Don't miss the home-made bread. The wine list is sumptuous and there's efficient service.

Richelieu

37120

Les Mousquetaires

4 av. du Québec (Centre); 20 min from the town centre.
Ⓣ02.47.58.15.17
Restaurant closed *Tues.* **TV. Car park.**

A small, unpretentious but comfortable hotel with a slightly rustic feel. Guests are sure of a warm welcome. Five double rooms with shower/wc giving onto the garden (from €25; 2 quadruples at €35.50). Menu €9.50 for hotel guests only. There's also a small bar.

Romorantin-Lanthenay

41200

Hôtel-restaurant Le Colombier**

18 pl. du Vieux-Marché; it's 150m from the town hall.
Ⓣ02.54.76.12.76 Ⓕ02.54.76.39.40
Closed *Sun evening; Feb.* **TV. Car park.**

Rooms are comfortable, though nothing more; those overlooking the courtyard are quieter. Doubles cost €37. Pleasant garden. The cosy restaurant specializes in cooking from the Sologne and the carefully prepared dishes change with the seasons, using fresh regional produce. A short menu at €17 and others €21.50–32.

Saché

37190

Auberge du XIIe Siècle

Rue principale, opposite the main square.
Ⓣ02.47.26.88.77 Ⓕ02.47.26.88.21
Closed *Sun evening; Mon; Tues lunchtime; 3 weeks in Jan; a week in June; a week in Sept.*

This village is enough to make many a restaurateur green with envy. It's a place of pilgrimage for devotees of Balzac and the splendid restaurant is one of the best in the region – the old beams and wide fireplace can't have changed in centuries. Xavier Aubrun and Thierry Jimenez are the two excellent chefs. They have put together a Balzac menu on which the dessert is loaded with caffeine. Other gastronomic delights include dishes with contemporary combinations of flavour such as pigeon salad, zander with rhubarb, or Géline chicken (a local breed) with capers and hot foie gras. Set menus are priced at €29–63.

Saint-Aignan

41110

Grand Hôtel Saint-Aignan**

79 quai J. J. Delorme.
Ⓣ02.54.75.18.04 Ⓕ02.54.75.12.59
Closed *Sun evening; Mon and Tues lunchtime Nov to end March; 15 Feb–8 March; 2nd fortnight in Nov.* **Disabled access. High chairs and games available. TV. Car park.**

An old coaching inn covered in ivy, standing on the banks of the Cher. Warm greeting, friendly setting and chic atmosphere – the walls are hung with medieval tapestries. Pretty rooms €24–53; some have a view of the river. Specialities in the restaurant include smoked salmon with onion rings, braised ox kidneys with ceps and assiette de trois provinces. All delicious, but portions are a little small. Menus €15 (weekdays only), and €23–34. *10% discount on the room rate (Nov–March) offered to our readers on presentation of this guide.*

|●| Restaurant Chez Constant

17 pl. de la Paix.
Ⓣ02.54.75.10.75
Closed *Mon and Tues out of season except public holidays; during Feb and Nov school holidays.*

This somewhat surprising restaurant, in the centre of town, pulls a cosmopolitan crowd. Chef Sylvain Liboureau creates all sorts of unexpected dishes: *andouillette* turnover with goat's cheese, roast pike-perch fillet on *andouillette* mash. Weekday lunch menu €11, set menu for €16 or around €23 à la carte. The charming owner, Chantal Ragot, has drawn together a list of fairly priced local wines.

Saint-Amand-Montrond

18200

⌂ |●| Hôtel-Restaurant de la Croix d'Or

28 rue du 14-juillet.
Ⓣ02.48.96.09.41 Ⓕ02.48.96.72.89
Closed *Fri evening and Sat lunchtime Nov–March except public holidays.*

The rooms are a bit dreary and ramshackle – doubles €40–53 – but the restaurant is a different story. It's been run for the last thirty years by the twin Moranges brothers, who have created a cuisine in perfect keeping with the small dining room – classic and bourgeois. Traditional dishes include hot foie gras with spiced caramel. Menu €20 (not weekends or public holidays) or others €30–48. *A free glass of Berrichon offered as apéritif to our readers on presentation of this guide.*

⌂ |●| Le Noirlac

How to get there: from Saint-Amand, take the N144 in the direction of Bourges; 2km further on, turn on to the A71. It's about another 5km.
Ⓣ02.48.82.22.00 Ⓕ02.48.82.22.01
Ⓦwww.lenorliac.fr
Closed 24 Dec–9 Jan. Restaurant closed Fri evening, Sat lunch and Sun evening from Nov–April. Disabled access. High chairs and games available. TV (canal +, satellite). Swimming pool.

Situated near the hypermarket in an unprepossessing district on the outskirts of town, this establishment is of most use to travellers with a car. It's an ultra-modern place with good facilities including a pool, tennis court, golf course and also a lake and park. Rooms are comfortable and functional, and some of them have nice views of the countryside. Doubles €62; buffet breakfast €5.95. Menus €13–25.50. The first menu, served daily, is generous. Specialities include *fricassée* of snails and cassolette of veal and petit Noirlac. *10% reduction on the room rate offered to our readers on presentation of this guide.*

|●| Restaurant Le Saint-Jean

1 rue de l'Hôtel-Dieu; it's in the old town near the church.
Ⓣ02.48.96.39.82 Ⓕ02.48.96.46.80
Ⓔlesaintjean@wanadoo.fr
Closed *Sun, Tues and Wed evenings; Mon.*

Great restaurant with a rustic dining room complete with flowers, beams and a wonderful old parquet floor. Chef Philippe Perrichon prepares a quite incredible set menu for €16, with others at €19 and €25. Specialities include home-smoked zander with blinis and seaweed, salmon stuffed with green Berry lentils, and iced nougat. Brilliant value. Booking essential at weekends. *Free coffee offered to our readers on presentation of this guide.*

Bruère-Allichamps

18200 (9km NW)

|●| Auberge de l'Abbaye de Noirlac

From Saint-Amand, take the N144 in the direction of Bourges; 4km further on, turn onto the Noirlac road. It's opposite the abbey.
Ⓣ02.48.96.22.58 Ⓕ02.48.96.86.63
Closed *Tues evening and Wed Sept–March; 15 Nov–20 Feb.* **Disabled access.**

One of the old abbey chapels has been transformed into a restaurant with a bistro where, in summer, you can get cheap snacks – sandwiches, an omelette or a plate of charcuterie at reasonable prices. The restaurant proper, which serves more serious food, has red quarry-tiles on the floor, beams and exposed stonework. Chef Pascal Verdier cooks meat and fish with equal skill; try his fresh salmon with a fish purée, the Charolais steak, the goat's cheese terrine or the flambéed pineapple with chocolate. Prices are good – menus €17–27.

Montlouis

18160 (30 km NW)

☗ Chambres d'hôte du Domaine de Bourdoiseau

Take the N144 and D35 to Châteauneuf-sur-Cher, then the N940; turn right down the D115, then follow the signs.
Ⓣ and Ⓕ02.48.60.06.44

A wonderful place. To start with, the seventeenth-century farm lost in the countryside is stunning; secondly, the owners are genuinely nice people who are steeped in the local cultural life and have turned their house into a veritable meeting place. Isabelle offers guests a fascinating "reading of the landscape", while Eddie enthusiastically explains the details of his organic crops. Double rooms €37. Table d'hôte €11–14. Peace and quiet, generous hospitality, the joys of nature, simplicity – perfection!

Saint-Benoît-sur-Loire

45730

☗ Hôtel du Labrador**

7 pl. de l'Abbaye; it's opposite the basilica.
Ⓣ02.38.35.74.38 Ⓕ02.38.35.72.99
Ⓦwww.hoteldulabrador.fr
Hotel closed *26 Dec–20 Jan.* **Restaurant closed** *Sat lunchtime; Sun evening; Mon; 20 Dec–15 Feb.* **Disabled access. TV. Car park.**

The hotel is in a little square which is wonderfully peaceful; it's a charming place. The rooms in the main building are a little cheaper than the others, and a couple of them have partial views of the abbey. Those in the newer annexe are more comfortable, though they lack the charm of the others. Doubles €56–58 with shower/wc or bath. There's no restaurant but half board (€55 per person per night) can be arranged in conjunction with the Grand Saint-Benoît (see below), which is 200m away.

Le Grand Saint-Benoît

7 pl. Saint-André.
Ⓣ02.38.35.11.92 Ⓕ02.38.35.13.79
Ⓦwww.hoteldulabrador.fr
Closed *Sat lunchtime; Sun evening; Mon; 23 Aug–10 Sept; 20 Dec–15 Jan.* **High chairs available. Disabled access.**

This establishment is one of the best tables in the region – but it's not one of the most expensive. The heavenly cuisine is simple, unusual and stamped with the personality of the chef. The weekday menu, €16, is perfectly adequate, but the €22.20 menu is splendid: snail pancake, roast zander with Chinon wine, and a hot savarin with chocolate and vanilla ice cream. Other menus up to €42. There's a nice terrace on a pedestrian street. It's best to book. *Free coffee offered to our readers on presentation of this guide.*

Sainte-Maure-de-Touraine

37800

☗ Hôtel-restaurant Le Cheval Blanc

55 av. du Général-de-Gaulle N10.
Ⓣ02.47.65.40.27 Ⓕ02.47.65.58.90
Ⓔgauvin.claude@wanadoo.fr
Closed *Thurs evening and Fri lunch (in season); Fri all day and Sun evening (out of season); 3 weeks in March and 3 weeks in Nov.* **Car park.**

This old staging post offers rooms with varying degrees of comfort, although they are all extremely well kept; the reserved but friendly owners, M. and Mme. Gavin, run their establishment with thorough diligence. Double rooms €41–45 with shower/wc or bath. M. Gavin is an excellent cook who serves classic dishes with striking attention to detail. Menus from €7.50. *Free apéritif offered to our readers on presentation of this guide.*

Sancerre

18300

Auberge La Pomme d'Or

1 rue Panneterie. It's in the old town, towards the town hall.
Ⓣ02.48.54.13.30 Ⓕ02.48.54.19.22
Closed *Tues evening and Wed; 10 days early Nov; a fortnight end-Dec–early Jan.* **Disabled access.**

An elegant restaurant in a narrow street in the old part of town. The dining room is cosy and attractive, while the cooking uses fresh, seasonal produce. It's traditional without being too heavy, with a few rustic touches: try the hot goat's cheese wrapped in sheets of brick pasta. The €14 menu (not Sat evening or Sun lunch) is excellent value and there are others at €22–41. The proprietor, Didier Turpin, is the master of his cellar and offers a wonderful selection of wines at very attractive prices. Reservations essential.

Saint-Satur

18300 (3km NE)

Hôtel-restaurant Le Laurier**

29 rue du Commerce; take the D955 and the D4.
02.48.54.17.20 02.48.54.04.54
www.ldf-berry.com/18/laurier
Closed *Sun evening; Mon; Thurs except July–Aug; 3 weeks in March; 3 weeks in Nov.* **High chairs available. TV. Car park.**

You'll find this place swathed in Virginia creeper and a stone's throw from a handsome abbey. The dining room, with its copperware, exposed beams and old wooden furniture, has clearly been decorated by someone with a taste for authenticity. There are six newly refurbished double rooms with shower/wc or bath costing €40–45 – prices are truly reasonable for this very touristy area. The restaurant offers good regional cooking with set menus at €15–40. Its specialities are poached eggs in wine *à l'ancienne* and calf's head and tongue with two sauces. *Free coffee offered to our readers on presentation of this guide.*

Saint-Thibault

18300 (3km E)

Hôtel de la Loire***

2 quai de la Loire in Saint-Thibault, on the road to Cosnes.
02.48.78.22.22 02.48.78.22.29
www.hotel-de-la-loire.com
Closed *18 Dec–8 Jan.* **Disabled access.**

This charming hotel, on the roadside but overlooking the Loire, is well worth the room rate. The comfortable rooms are each decorated on a different theme – you wouldn't be surprised to see them in a modish interiors mag. Their names give you a clue as to their look; Georges Simenon (he wrote two of his novels here), African Queen, Louis XIV, Provençal, Colonial, Indian and so on. Doubles €65–85. *Free tea or coffee in the room, offered to our readers on presentation of this guide.*

Chavignol

18300 (5km W)

Restaurant des Monts Damnés

02.48.54.01.72 02.48.54.14.24
Closed *Sun evening; Tues evening; Wed.* **Disabled access.**

The "damned mountains" give their name both to a highly reputed vineyard in Sancerre and to this inn, a rustic place with beams, patterned curtains and a cosy atmosphere. Local produce plays the central role in robust dishes with a very distinct character. Menus €25–43. The wine list is full of bargains from all parts of France. There's a pergola for sunny days. *Free coffee offered to our readers on presentation of this guide.*

Sancoins

18600

Hôtel du Parc**

8 rue Marguerite-Audoux.
02.48.74.56.60 02.48.74.61.30
Closed *1–15 Jan.* **TV. Car park.**

This classy place looks like a château and is set in extensive grounds. The rooms are lovely, with Baroque mirrors and velvet bedspreads, and they're quiet. Doubles with shower or bath €38, or €48 for rooms sleeping up to four. Very good value.

Souvigny-en-Sologne

41600

La Perdrix Rouge

22 rue du Gâtinais.
02.54.88.41.05
Closed *Mon; Tues; 17 Feb–3 March; 1–9 July; 27 Aug–4 Sept.* **Games available. Disabled access.**

Lovely dining room, both rustic and sophisticated, with an impressive fireplace, shrewdly chosen furniture and prettily laid tables. You will receive a warm welcome, elegant but discreet service and food that is a delight to behold – traditional dishes injected with new life and prepared with only the best and freshest ingredients. First there are some delicious tidbits before the starter itself, then comes the main course – light, savoury and aromatic: *fricassée* of blue lobster with herbs, farm-raised squab with cabbage and zander with *beurre blanc*. Good value for money: menus €15 (weekdays), then others €24–49. *Free liqueur offered to our readers on presentation of this guide.*

Sully-sur-Loire

45600

Hôtel-restaurant de la Poste**

11 rue du Faubourg-Saint-Germain.
Ⓣ02.38.36.26.22 Ⓕ02.38.36.39.35
TV. Car park.

This place is an old staging post, and despite its slightly forbidding exterior it's something of a local institution – the large cage full of parrots is equally renowned. Some of the rooms in the annexe have a limited view of the Loire; in the main building, you'll have to make do with the TV! Doubles from €40 with washing facilities to €46 with shower/wc or bath. A few have been set aside for non-smokers. Menus, €15–33, feature lots of local dishes and fish specialities.

Tours

37000

See map overleaf

Auberge de jeunesse

5 rue Bretonneau. **Map A1-1**; close to the old towers and the Loire.
Ⓕ02.47.37.81.58 Ⓕ02.47.37.96.11

Impressive, brand-new youth hostel in a functional, modern building. It sleeps almost 200 people, spread out in rooms with two–six beds, and in some cases with showers/wc (otherwise they're on the landing). One section houses rooms intended for families. €16 the first night (including sheets and breakfast), €13.25 the following ones. A kitchen is available for use by guests. Garage for bikes and motorbikes; cars can be parked by the quay on the Loire.

Hôtel Saint-Éloi*

79 bd. Béranger **Map A2-2**; less than 10 min from the old towers on foot.
Ⓣ02.47.37.67.34 Ⓕ02.47.39.34.67
Ⓔhotel@saint-eloi.com
Closed *Sun afternoon.* **TV.**

Small, simple hotel set back from the boulevard, at the back of a little courtyard; you can park on the boulevard itself, or on rue Jules-Charpentier, behind the hotel. The atmosphere is warm and subdued. Double rooms €23 with washbasin to €31 with shower/wc. Generally well run, although unfortunately we detected an irregularity when we made our booking, as we were asked to send a deposit that matched the entire price, and this is out of the question. *10% discount on a room (after two consecutive nights) offered to our readers on presentation of this guide.*

Hôtel Régina*

2 rue Pimbert. **Map C1-4**
Ⓣ02.47.05.25.36 Ⓕ02.47.66.08.72
Closed *Christmas school holidays.*

A cheap, cheerful, simple and clean hotel with window-boxes full of flowers. It's really pretty and you quickly feel at home. The soundproofing is good and the cleanliness is evidenced by the nice smell of polish. The rooms are fresh-looking and all different. A double room with hand basin is €23.50, €27 with shower, €31.50 with shower/wc. Breakfast €4.50. Excellent value for money. Free garage for motorcycles and bikes.

Hôtel-restaurant Moderne**

1–3 rue Victor-Laloux. **Map C2-3**
Ⓣ02.47.05.32.81
Ⓔhotel.moderne37@wanadoo.fr
Restaurant closed *lunchtime; Sat; Sun.* **TV.**

This hotel, a fine building in traditional Touraine style, is on a corner in a quiet neighbourhood. There are twenty-three rooms in all (€30–37 with shower/wc, €47–55 with bath); the ones in the attic are cosy and have sloping ceilings, others have mezzanines. Fantastic rustic family cooking. Set menus €13 and €16 are served weekday evenings for hotel guests only. *10% discount on the room rate (Nov–end Feb) or free apéritif offered to our readers on presentation of this guide.*

Hôtel du Musée

2 pl. François Sicard. **Map C1-19**
Ⓣ02.47.66.63.81Ⓕ02.47.20.10.42
TV.

Though some might say that this

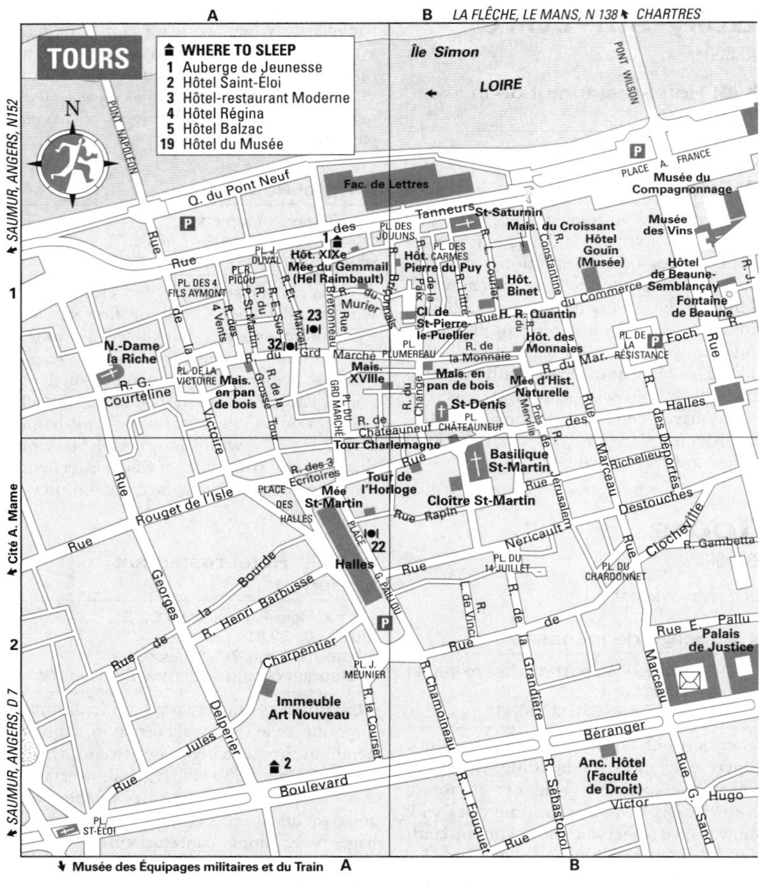
A
B
LA FLÈCHE, LE MANS, N 138
CHARTRES
TOURS
WHERE TO SLEEP
1 Auberge de Jeunesse
2 Hôtel Saint-Éloi
3 Hôtel-restaurant Moderne
4 Hôtel Régina
5 Hôtel Balzac
19 Hôtel du Musée
N
Île Simon
LOIRE
PONT WILSON
PONT NAPOLÉON
SAUMUR, ANGERS, N152
Q. du Pont Neuf
Fac. de Lettres
PLACE A. FRANCE
Musée du Compagnonnage
Musée des Vins
St-Saturnin
Tanneurs
Mais. du Croissant
Hôtel Gouïn (Musée)
Hôtel de Beaune-Semblançay
Fontaine de Beaune
Rue du Commerce
Hôt. XIXe
Mée du Gemmail (Hel Raimbault)
Hôt. Pierre du Puy
Hôt. Binet
PL. DES JOULINS
PL. DES CARMES
PL. J. DUVAL
PL. R. PICOU
PL. DES 4 FILS AYMONT
1
Cl. de St-Pierre-le-Puellier
H. R. Quantin
Hôt. des Monnaies
PL. DE LA RÉSISTANCE
Foch
N.-Dame la Riche
23
32
PL. PLUMEREAU
R. de la Monnaie
R. du Mar.
Mais. XVIIIe
PL. DE LA VICTOIRE
Mais. en pan de bois
Mais. en pan de bois
Mée d'Hist. Naturelle
R. G. Courteline
St-Denis
PL. CHÂTEAUNEUF
R. de Châteauneuf
Halles
Tour Charlemagne
Basilique St-Martin
Richelieu
Tour de l'Horloge
PLACE DES HALLES
Mée St-Martin
Cloître St-Martin
Rue Rapin
Rue Rouget de l'Isle
Destouches
Néricault
Clocheville
R. Gambetta
22
Halles
PL. DU 14 JUILLET
PL. DU CHARDONNET
Cité A. Mame
Rue de la Bourde
R. Henri Barbusse
Rue Georges Delperier
2
Charpentier
PL. J. MEUNIER
Rue E. Pallu
Palais de Justice
Immeuble Art Nouveau
R. Chamoineau
R. de la Grandière
Marceau
Béranger
Anc. Hôtel (Faculté de Droit)
Rue Jules
SAUMUR, ANGERS, D 7
Boulevard
R. J. Fouquet
R. Sebastopol
Victor Hugo
Rue G. Sand
PL. ST-ÉLOI
Musée des Équipages militaires et du Train

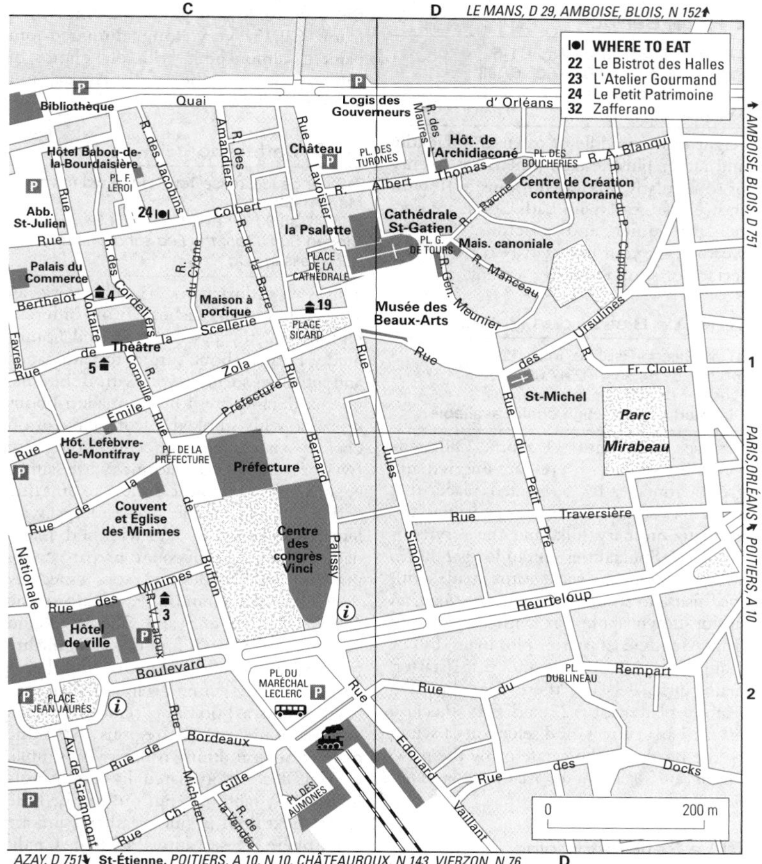
WHERE TO EAT
22 Le Bistrot des Halles
23 L'Atelier Gourmand
24 Le Petit Patrimoine
32 Zafferano
LE MANS, D 29, AMBOISE, BLOIS, N 152
AMBOISE, BLOIS, D 751
PARIS, ORLÉANS POITIERS, A 10
AZAY, D 751 St-Étienne, POITIERS, A 10, N 10, CHÂTEAUROUX, N 143, VIERZON, N 76
Bibliothèque
Hôtel Babou-de-la-Bourdaisière
Abb. St-Julien
Palais du Commerce
Théâtre
Logis des Gouverneurs
Château
Hôt. de l'Archidiaconé
Centre de Création contemporaine
Cathédrale St-Gatien
la Psalette
Mais. canoniale
Maison à portique
Musée des Beaux-Arts
St-Michel
Parc Mirabeau
Hôt. Lefèbvre-de-Montifray
Préfecture
Couvent et Église des Minimes
Centre des congrès Vinci
Hôtel de ville
PL. DU MARÉCHAL LECLERC
PLACE JEAN JAURÈS
PLACE DE LA CATHÉDRALE
PLACE SICARD
PL. DE LA PRÉFECTURE
PL. DES TURONES
PL. DES BOUCHERIES
PL. G. DE TOURS
PL. F. LEROI
PL. DUBLINEAU
PL. DES AUMONES
Quai d' Orléans
Boulevard Heurteloup
Rue Nationale
Rue Colbert
Rue Scellerie
Rue Émile Zola
Rue Jules Simon
Rue Bernard Palissy
Rue Traversière
Rue du Rempart
Rue des Docks
Rue Édouard Vaillant
Rue de Bordeaux
Av. de Grammont
0 200 m
C D 1 2

establishment could do with a face-lift, it would lose its charm in the process. The façade is worn but all the rooms are decorated differently, with lovely wood panelling, and either a terrace or a fireplace, and equipped with old furniture. There's a fine collection of coffee pots in the lounge. Double rooms €45–48.

Hôtel Balzac**

47 rue de la Scellerie. **Map C1-5**
Ⓣ02.47.05.40.87 Ⓕ02.47.05.67.93
Ⓔhotel.balzac@9online.fr
TV.

Right in the middle of town, this friendly and rather plush establishment has twenty or so regularly renovated rooms: €48 with shower/wc, €51 with bath. Some are particularly quiet and spacious. In fine weather, eat your breakfast (€6.10) on the terrace or sit quietly over a drink.

Le Bistrot des Halles

31 pl. Gaston-Paillhou. **Map A2-22**
Ⓣ02.47.61.54.93 Ⓕ02.47.66.19.98
Ⓔedward.bdh@wanadoo.fr
Disabled access. High chairs available.

Service daily until 11.30pm. Old-fashioned brasserie with eye-catching red and green frontage. It's a relaxed place, that attracts everyone from the great and the good to ordinary folk, and the service is faultless. Specialities include *pot-au-feu* with three meats, *bouillabaisse* made with four fish and so on. Try their *tarte tatin*, an upside-down apple tart with caramelized fruit. Menus €12 (starter plus main dish or main dish plus dessert) and €15 (starter, main dish, dessert); there are also two seafood platters at €22 and €28. Reckon on €27 à la carte. Good selection of wines by the bottle, by the carafe or by the glass. *Free digestif offered to our readers on presentation of this guide.*

Le Petit Patrimoine

58 rue Colbert. **Map C1-24**
Ⓣ02.47.66.05.81
Closed *Sun lunchtime.*

A regional restaurant of quality with a dining room decorated in salmon pink. The owner has a real interest in preserving the cuisine of the Touraine, though he's always looking for ways to take it gently forward. The specialities are quite delicious: *tourte tourangelle* with *rillons* and goat's cheese, pike Bourgueil-style, *entrecôte* steak with Saint-Maure sauce, salmon envelope stuffed with Saint-Maure cheese, *andouillette* à la Vouvrillonne (sausage in Vouvray, a white Loire wine), *matelote* of veal with red wine, onions and mushrooms, and a superb selection of cheeses. If you've got room for dessert, try the pears in wine. Menus €11.50 (weekday lunchtime) and €12–26, lunchtime dish of the day €6.20 and good Touraine wines from €9.15. Very long dining room painted salmon-pink, with old photos of the region on the wall. AmEx not accepted. It's best to book.

Zafferano

7–9 rue de la Grosse Tour, in the old town. **Map A1-32**
Ⓣ02.47.38.90.77 Ⓕ02.47.49.26.69
Closed *Sun; Mon; the Feb school holidays; 3 last weeks in Aug.*

This is no ordinary pizzeria. They serve an array of Italian dishes from different regions and the pasta is fresh and homemade. Forget about turgid tomato sauce and let them surprise you with dishes like pasta zafferano (fresh home-made ribbons of pasta with smoked bacon and saffron cream sauce), rigatoni alla bolognese (winter only), or fettuccine with saffron cream. And their meat dishes are amazing – the saltimbocca, the veal escalope with lemon, the lamb noisettes with herb marinade and the osso buco are prepared with precision. Killer desserts, too, especially their ultra-light tiramisù. Pasta dish of the day €9. Menus €15 and €26 or around €28 à la carte. You'll find the same quality on the mainly-Italian wine list, and there's a small grocery counter selling Italian specialities and a bookshop selling titles on cookery, wine, and the regions and music of Italy. Several dining rooms with simple, elegant décor dominated by bright yellows. A few tables are put out on the little square next door in fine weather. Fantastic atmosphere. Reservations advised. Credit cards accepted for bills of more than €15. *Free digestif.*

L'Atelier Gourmand

37 rue Étienne-Marcel. **Map A1-23**
Ⓣ02.47.38.59.87
Closed *Mon lunchtime; Sat lunchtime and Sun.*

In the heart of Tours' old quarter, a pretty little place with solid wooden beams and modern décor. The cuisine is in a similar vein: traditional with a modern twist. Quality ingredients are used, flavoured with choice herbs and spices, creating simple yet tasty dishes. *Plate du jour* €8.50, menu €16. Excellent value and pleasant service.

Rochecorbon

37210 (3km NE)

Hôtel Les Fontaines**

6 quai de la Loire; on the RN52, on the way to Blois.
Ⓣ02.47.52.52.86 Ⓕ02.47.52.85.05
Ⓦwww.tours-online.com/lesfontaines
TV. Car park.

A charming, professionally run hotel; it's a pity it's so close to the main road, although the big trees in the shady park form a relatively effective sound barrier. The bedrooms, spread over three floors, are all different but equally large, comfortable and prettily furnished. The double rooms in the manor house, with shower/wc or bath, go for €37–55; those in the old gardener's lodge are simpler, ideal for families (bunks for children) or limited budgets. Faultless service. Delightful breakfast room.

L'Oubliette

34 rue des Clouets.
Ⓣ02.47.52.50.59 Ⓕ02.47.52.85.65
Closed *Sun evening; Mon; Wed out of season; Feb school holidays; last week in Aug.*

Local people say they serve "modern cooking" here – code for imaginative and inventive cuisine.The chef, Bruno Leroux, uses lots of spices and herbs with great subtlety and finesse, daringly creating inventive sweet-savoury mixtures and not hesitating to combine meat with fish and seafood. And no nouvelle cuisine portions, either: they're perfectly judged, as is the refined presentation. The décor is equally appealing with tapestries on the stone walls. Menus start at €24 (not served Sun) and then go from €37 up to €52.

Fondettes

37230 (5km W)

Auberge de Porc-Vallières

Vallières; take the N152 in the direction of Langeais.
Ⓣ02.47.42.24.04 Ⓕ02.47.49.98.83
Closed *Mon and Tues evenings; Wed; Sun evening; a fortnight in winter; 3 weeks in Aug.*

Because the inn is right on the edge of the N152, you might hesitate to stop. But it's worth it. There are armfuls of wild flowers from the fields in huge vases and a relaxed, pleasant atmosphere; you hardly hear the traffic at all.The welcome is friendly and straightforward and the inventive cuisine brilliantly judged. There's a €16 menu in the week or reckon on €30 à la carte. They list original dishes and various specialities subtly prepared by one of the owners, such as authentic fried fish from the Loire and pig's trotters "Mary-Magdalene". The first dining room is reserved for groups, who usually manage to drown out the noise of the traffic with their festivities. The other room, situated in the back (and therefore quieter), is austere but pretty, with walls painted and decorated by an artist friend of the owners. Friendly service.

Vouvray

37210 (8km E)

Le Grand Vatel

8 rue Léon Brulé.
Ⓣ02.47.52.70.32
Closed *Sun evening and Mon; Christmas; first fortnight in Jan.* **Car park.**

The main reason for coming here is the high-quality food prepared by Frédéric Scicluma, based on fresh ingredients, with everything made *in situ*. It is served in a large, opulent dining room with a high ceiling or, weather permitting, on the terrace (due to be enlarged to escape from the noise of the road); Scicluma's jovial wife will give you sound advice when you choose your meal. One particularly striking dish is the pig's-foot gâteau in lettuce – a light, original reinterpretation of a regional classic; the desserts are no less enticing: try the delicious egg *brouillade* with red fruit. Menus €18 (except public holidays) to €61. Impressive lists of Vouvray wines, served by the glass. There are a few simple, slightly run-down rooms upstairs: doubles with shower/wc or bath €36–39. *Free apéritif offered to our readers on presentation of this guide.*

Semblançay

37360 (12km NW)

Hostellerie de la Mère Hamard**

Place de l'Église; take the N138 in the direction of Le Mans.
02.47.56.62.04 02.47.56.61.67
Closed *Sun evening; Mon; Tues lunchtime; 15 Feb–15 March.* **TV. High chairs available. Car park.**

You'll dine on delicious regional dishes and gourmet cuisine. The dining room is comfortable and welcoming. Menus €16 (not Sun), €26–43. Specialities include duck foie gras with morels, pigeon with truffle jus and potato cakes with foie gras. There are nine lovely double rooms in a delightful annexe from €45–61 with shower/wc or bath. Breakfast €8. *Free coffee offered to our readers on presentation of this guide.*

Monnaie

37380 (14km NE)

Restaurant Au Soleil Levant

53 rue Nationale; it's on the N10.
02.47.56.10.34 02.47.56.45.22
Closed *Sun and Thurs evenings; Mon; 1–15 Jan; 1–21 Aug.* **High chairs available.**

This is among the best gourmet restaurants in the area, with a stylish interior decorated in bright, luminous colours. They produce exceptional dishes imaginatively combining the best ingredients of the season. There's a *formule* at €12.95 and menus at €18 (except Sun) and €27–73; reckon on €26–38 à la carte. Good dishes include fillet steak in Chinon, roast zander with *beurre blanc* and veal sweetbreads with morel mushrooms – all delicious. *Free coffee offered to our readers on presentation of this guide.*

Neuillé-le-Lierre

37380 (15 km NE)

Auberge de la Brenne

19 rue de la République; in the Brenne valley, 10 km north of Vouvray.
02.47.52.95.05
Closed *Tues evening; Wed; Sun evening (Oct–May); 4 Feb–10 March).* **Disabled access.**

This village inn set amidst bucolic scenery offers traditional food at its most rustic. Do not expect anything too subtle or light here. The owner, Ghislaine Sallé, is so devoted to time-honoured practices that she even makes her own rillettes (potted meat). Her pride and joy, however, is her "île flottante" (the "real" version, according to her). Menus €17 (except weekends and public holidays), and then €22–40. Double rooms €55–72 with shower or bath. Unbeatable cooking, charming décor and genuine atmosphere. *Free apéritif or coffee offered to our readers on presentation of this guide.*

Vannes-sur-Cosson

45510

Restaurant Le Vieux Relais

2 rte. d'Isdes.
02.38.58.04.14
Closed *Sun evening; Mon; Tues; 1st fortnight in Aug; mid-Dec to mid-Jan.* **Car park.**

It's obvious that this superb Solognote manor house is pretty old – but you probably wouldn't guess that the original buildings go back to 1462 and that the beams come from a building in the 800s. It's been an inn since 1515 and is one of the six oldest in France. It's an absolutely sumptuous place and the cooking doesn't let the surroundings down. You should certainly go for the chef's foie gras if it's on the menu. He uses seasonal produce for all his dishes so it's hard to list his specialities but the game is superb, as are the langoustine tails – and don't miss out on the *crème brûlée* either. Menus €16 (not served on public holidays), €23.50 and €31. Essential to book. Credit cards not accepted.

Ménestreau-en-Villette

45240 (18 km E)

Le Relais de Sologne

63 pl. du 8-Mai. Take the D120 to Sennely, then the D17.
02.38.76.97.40
Closed *Tues evening; Wed; Sun evening; 3 weeks in Feb.*

This restaurant-caterers is run by the chef Thierry Roger, a virtuoso of French cuisine. The inviting dining room is decorated in the purest local style: red bricks and half-timbering, warm, diffuse lighting, an abundance of fresh flowers and green plants, all in a rich harmony of colours. It is hard to imagine a more pleasant setting for enjoying the sophisticated traditional cooking. The menu changes regularly according to the seasonal produce available. The desserts are exquisite, and you can wash the whole meal down with some splendid wines. Weekday lunchtime menu €15; other menus €30–44.50. All in all, a visit to *Le Relais* is an essential stopover for visitors to the beautiful Sologne countryside. *Free coffee offered to our readers on presentation of this guide.*

Vendôme

41100

Hôtel-restaurant L'Auberge de la Madeleine**

Place de la Madeleine; head in the direction of Blois.
Ⓣ02.54.77.20.79 Ⓕ02.54.80.00.02
Closed *Feb.* **Restaurant closed** *Wed.* **TV.**

An unpretentious place with attractive rooms; nos. 7 and 8 are the largest. Doubles €34.50 with shower/wc and €38.50–47 with bath. Good plain cooking with set menus €14–35.30. Specialities include calf's head, zander with vanilla and rabbit with mushrooms. You can eat out in the garden. Friendly welcome. *Free coffee offered to our readers on presentation of this guide.*

Restaurant Le Paris

1 rue Darreau.
Ⓣ02.54.77.02.71 Ⓕ02.54.73.17.71
Closed *Sun evening; Mon; Aug.*

An excellent gourmet restaurant. It's run by a charming woman, the service is faultless and the chef – who has a particular talent for sauces and for meat and fish dishes – is inspired. Try a good local wine like the Bourgueil Domaine Lalande. Set menus €14–29. *Free coffee offered to our readers on presentation of this guide.*

Saint-Ouen

41100 (2km N)

La Vallée

34 rue Barré-de-Saint-Venant; from Vendôme, take the D92 and head for Paris and the centre of Saint-Ouen.
Ⓣ02.54.77.29.93 Ⓕ02.54.73.16.96
Closed *Mon; Tues; Sun evening Nov–Easter; a week in Jan; fortnight early March; last fortnight in Sept. High chairs available.* **Swings. Disabled access.**

Don't let the uninspiring exterior put you off – go straight in and take a look at the menus. You won't regret it: even the cheapest at €17 (not served Sun) boasts a selection of delights. Other menus €23–35.The specialities change with the seasons, the cooking is sophisticated and the dishes are beautifully presented.

Pezou

41100 (15km NE)

Auberge de la Sellerie

Fontaine; it's on the RN10.
Ⓣ02.54.23.41.43 Ⓕ02.54.23.48.00
Closed *Sun evening; Mon; Wed evening; Jan.* **High chairs available.**

Rustic but chic décor. It's a good inn set back from the main road from Chartres to Vendôme. There's an appetizing menu at €14.20, which changes nearly every day and includes half a bottle of wine and coffee. The cuisine is rich, inventive and of good quality. Other menus up to €43. They serve until a decent time, and even if you show up late they still give you a smile.

Lavardin

41800 (18km SW)

Le Relais d'Antan

6 pl. du Capitaine du Vignau; take the D917, when you get to Saint-Rimay, turn left on the road to Montoire.
Ⓣ02.54.86.61.33 Ⓕ02.54.85.06.46
Closed *Mon; Tues; fortnight in Feb; 3 weeks in Oct.* **High chairs available. Disabled access.**

You're in for a real feast – and at a reasonable price. The choice is deliberately limited so the chef can ensure only the freshest ingredients are used to create his refined, inventive dishes: the menu changes monthly. Two menus at €25 and €33; the last includes a fish and a meat course. Service is friendly and the dining room is pretty; they only have a few tables so you need to book. *Free coffee offered to our readers on presentation of this guide.*

Veuil

36600

Auberge Saint-Fiacre**

It's in the centre of the village.

☎02.54.40.32.78 Ⓕ02.54.40.35.66
Closed *Sun evening and Mon except public holidays. 3 weeks in Jan and 15 days at beginning of Sept.*

A seventeenth-century inn in a flower-filled village with a stream running through it. In summer you dine under the ancient chestnut trees to the accompaniment of the trickling fountain, and in winter around the giant fireplace. The chef changes his menus frequently, inspired by fresh seasonal produce and what is good at the market. Menus €20 (not Sun), and €28.50–34.50.

6 CENTRE

Vierzon

18100

La Maison de Célestin

20 av. Pierre Sémard; it's opposite the station.
☎02.48.83.01.63
Closed *Sat lunch; Sun evening; Mon. 1–20 Jan; 25 Jul–18 Aug.* **High chairs available. Disabled access.**

A modern, stylish restaurant in a semi-circular veranda overlooking a garden and some quite lovely old industrial buildings. Pascal Chaupitre is a young chef who's going places. He uses fresh produce combining inventivenes and convention; he has a talent for putting surprising flavours together but is respectful of Berry traditions as well. Menus €22–58. The dishes on the cheapest menu are really excellent, which is unusual. *Free coffee offered to our readers on presentation of this guide.*

Yvoy-le-Marron

41600

Auberge du Cheval Blanc

1 pl. du Cheval-Blanc; 4.5 km to the north-east of Chaumont-sur-Tharonne via the D35.
☎02.54.94.00.00 Ⓕ02.54.94.00.01
Ⓦwww.aubergeduchevalblanc.com
Closed *1st week in Jan and Aug; 2nd fortnight in March.* **Restaurant closed** *Tues and Wed lunch*; **Disabled access.**

This hotel-restaurant in the heart of the Sologne has a decidedly Parisian feel – unsurprising perhaps, as all the rooms have been superbly refurbished and redecortated by an interior designer from the capital. The result is a chic, tasteful setting, with thick carpets, warm colours and impeccable bedding that even the most coddled city slicker will find comfortable. Double rooms €72–84. Lunchtime menu €16 weekdays, others €25–32. Discreet but friendly service.

Yzeures-sur-Creuse

37290

Hôtel-restaurant La Promenade***

1 pl. du 11-Novembre.
☎02.47.91.49.00 Ⓕ02.47.94.46.12
Closed *Mon andTues; 10 Jan–10 Feb.* **TV. Car park.**

This hotel is in a handsome eighteenth-century building which used to be a coaching inn. The fifteen rooms are decorated in restrained rustic style, some with beams and others with fireplaces; doubles with bath/wc €49. Breakfast €6.50. There's a small sitting room with a piano on the mezzanine. Mme Bussereau creates delicious dishes that bear her own inventive imprint from the best produce she can find on the market – game in season, free-range poultry and excellent fish. She also makes the house terrines and bakes the bread. Set menus €20 (except for public holidays), and then €26.

Champagne-Ardennes

Arcis-sur-Aube

10700

|●| Le Saint-Hubert

2 rue de la Marine; it's signposted from the centre.
☎03.25.37.86.93
Closed *Sat; Tues and Sun evenings; last week in Dec; first week in Jan; last week in July and first fortnight in Aug.*

You'll go a long way to find an owner who puts her guests so quickly at ease and, in the midst of the service, even finds time to set the world to rights. The dining room has a certain elegance, and the traditional cuisine is well prepared and astonishingly good value. Lunch menu €12.50 then others €15–26. The lovely terrace looks over the river.

Bar-sur-Aube

10200

🏠 Hôtel Saint-Pierre

5 rue Saint-Pierre.
☎03.25.27.13.58 Ⓕ03.25.27.24.35
Car park.

A simple, well-run small hotel just opposite the twelfth-century Saint-Pierre church. Rooms 1, 8, 9 and 10 have a view of the church but be warned: the bells start ringing at 7am. Doubles with basin €20, €31 with shower/wc. There's no restaurant, but there is a lively bar where you can eat breakfast (€3.50; not available Sun and public holidays). A nice place at very reasonable prices. *Free apéritif offered to our readers on presentation of this guide.*

🏠 Hôtel Le Saint-Nicholas***

2 rue du Général-de-Gaulle.
☎03.25.27.08.65 Ⓕ03.25.27.60.31
TV. High chairs available. Swimming pool.

A short distance from the centre. This old bourgeois house is on the corner of two streets and has a garden with a swimming pool behind it. All the rooms are soundproofed and air-conditioned and have shower/wc or bath – €59 for a double; €85 for a suite with Jacuzzi. The décor is contemporary but has a charm dictated by the lovely old building. There's also a sauna.

|●| Un P'tit Creux

Place du Corps-de-Garde; entrance 24 rue Nationale.
☎03.25.27.37.75
Closed *Sun and Mon except Whitsun; March; Oct.*

This bright, friendly little restaurant is in a modern shopping centre in the old centre of Bar. Traditional, unpretentious cuisine, with crêpes and pizzas listed on menus €11–16.50. It's great in summer, when you can sit outside on the terrace.

|●| Le Cellier aux Moines

Rue du Général-Vouillemont; it's behind St-Pierre church.
☎03.25.27.08.01 Ⓕ03.25.01.56.22
Closed *Fri and Sat evenings; Tues lunchtime.*

This twelfth-century cellar is remarkable in more than one way. It's the site where local winegrowers chose to meet when the local sparkling wine lost the right to be called "champagne" in 1912; scrawled inscriptions on the walls recount the suffering of the

A
N
BELGIUM
LUX.
Philippeville
Givet
Avesnes
Couvin
Haybes
Fumay
Bastogne
Rocroi
Revin
Monthermé
Vervins
Charleville-Mézières
Sedan
AISNE
Carignan
Signy-l'Abbaye
Bazeilles
Rémilly-Aihicourt
Mouzon
Laon
ARDENNES
Rethel
Buzancy
Pauvres
Vouziers
Reims
Fismes
Verdun
Épernay-Magenta
Val-de-Vesle
Sept-Saulx
Sainte Menehould
Cumières
Épernay
Châlons-en-Champagne
MEUSE
Château-Thierry
Vertus
Chepy
Étoges
Bergère-les-Vertus
MARNE
Bar-le-Duc
Vitry-en-Perthois
Toul
Sézanne
Vitry-le-François
Perthes
Ste-Marie-du-Lac
Saint-Dizier
Eclaron
Giffaumont-Champaubert
Wassy
Arcis
Seine
Lentilles
Montier-en-Der
Joinville
Neufchâteau
Nogent-sur-Seine
AUBE
Piney
Brévonnes
Villiers-sur-Marne
Troyes
Ste-Savine
le Ménilot
Dolancourt
Vignory
VOSGES
St-André-les-Vergers
Mesnil-St-Père
Arsonval
Colombey-les-deux-Eglises
HAUTE-MARNE
Rosières-près-Troyes
Bréviandes
Bar-sur-Aube
Contrexéville
Clairvaux
Chaumont
Chamarandes
Fresnoy-en-Bassigny
Fouchères
Bar-sur-Seine
Marnay-sur-Marne
Ervy-le-Châtel
Chaource
Gyé-sur-Seine
Nogent
les Riceys
Villiers-sur-suize
Bourbonne-les-Bains
Arc-en-Barrois
Langres
Tonnerre
Châtillon-sur-Seine
Auberive
Auxerre
YONNE
Vaux-sous-Aubigny
HAUTE-SAÔNE
Montbard
CÔTE-D'OR
0
20 km
1
2

villages. After a struggle, the wine was reclassified – you'll find it on the pricey end of the wine list. The confident cooking is traditional and unpretentious. Menus €12 during the week and €19–28. The décor is a bit spartan, though the candles on the tables soften the general appearance.

La Toque Baralbine

18 rue Nationale.
Ⓣ and Ⓕ03.25.27.20.34
Closed *Sun evening and Mon except public holidays; 3 weeks in Jan.* **Disabled access.**

After years working in different establishments on the Côte d'Azur, the owner returned to his roots and opened his own gourmet restaurant – and won a loyal local following within months of opening. Sophisticated cooking (spring rolls with langoustines, squab off the bone, warm prune soufflé with Ratafia) in very pleasant surroundings: it's a nice rustic dining room with a small terrace. Menus at €17 (weekdays), €20 (weekends) and €23–44. *Free coffee offered to our readers on presentation of this guide.*

Arsonval

10200 (6km NW)

Hostellerie La Chaumière**

Take the N19 in the direction of Troyes and it's on the left as you're leaving Arsonval.
Ⓣ03.25.27.91.02 Ⓕ03.25.27.90.26
Ⓦwww.lachaumiere.fr
Closed *Sun evening and Mon except in summer and public holidays; 10 Dec–20 Jan.* **Disabled access. High chairs available. TV. Car park.**

This old village inn, run by an Anglo-French couple, has an old red English telephone box to add a bit of *couleur locale*. There are two refurbished rooms in the main building, and others in a modern structure which is somewhat out of keeping with the old half-timbered house – but they're equipped with all mod cons and have views of the grounds and the river. Doubles with shower/wc or bath €53–56. Carefully prepared meals are generously served in a lovely dining room with wooden beams. In fine weather you can eat on the terrace. Menus €20–50. *10% off the price of a room (except April–Nov) offered to our readers on presentation of this guide.*

Dolancourt

10200 (9km NW)

Le Moulin du Landion***

5 rue Saint-Léger; from Bar drive towards Troyes on the N19, then take the left fork 2km after Arsonval and follow the signs in the village.
Ⓣ03.25.27.92.17 Ⓕ03.25.27.94.44
Ⓦwww.moulindulandion.com
TV. Swimming pool. Car park.

This place is ultra-classy and it has all recently been refurbished. The shady garden has a swimming pool and inside the décor is smart – the bright, spacious rooms have small balconies. They are modern in contrast to the rustic dining room in the old mill. The restaurant overlooks the river, while the bay windows open onto the working millwheel; tables are also set at the waterside. Prices reflect the quality of the surroundings: double rooms range from €68 to €85. The cheapest set menu at €18.50 is not served at the weekend; others are €27–54. This is a tranquil spot not far from the mad world of the Nigoland amusement park.

Clairvaux-sur-Aube

10310 (14km SE)

Hôtel-restaurant de l'Abbaye*

18–19 rte. de Dijon; where the D12 and D396 cross.
Ⓣ03.25.27.80.12 Ⓕ03.25.27.75.79
Closed *Mon; 24 Dec–10 Jan.* **TV. Car park.**

Saint Bernard of Clairvaux founded the first Cistercian abbey in these very woods in the twelfth century; the same building is now a prison, with high walls and watchtowers. If you really want to enjoy your freedom, take room 17, which looks directly onto it. Doubles €26–35 with basin, and €28–38 with shower/wc; they could do with updating, but are comfortable nonetheless. It's very quiet at night, despite its position on a crossroads. Honest cooking served in the restaurant; weekday menu €11, then others at €14 and €20. *10% off the price of a room offered to our readers on presentation of this guide.*

Bourbonne-les-Bains

52400

🏃 ⌂ |●| Hôtel d'Orfeuil**

29 rue d'Orfeuil; 80m from the spa.
Ⓣ03.25.90.05.71 Ⓕ03.25.84.46.25
Closed *Mon; 25 Oct–1 April.* **Disabled access. TV. Swimming pool. Pay car park.**

This lovely eighteenth-century house has aged beautifully. It's on a hillside surrounded by a leafy garden in which they've built a very pleasant pool. Very tasteful inside, with antique family furniture, rugs and fireplaces. It's a welcoming place where you get good value for money: €45–51 for a double with shower/wc in the new annexe — the old part is reserved for people taking the waters. Ask for a room with a balcony and a view over the park. Healthy buffet breakfast €5.50. Informal restaurant with set menus €10–20; try salmon *sauce orfeuil* or the langoustine salad. *Free apéritif offered to our readers on presentation of this guide.*

🏃 ⌂ |●| Hôtel des Sources**

Place des Bains; it's next to the baths.
Ⓣ03.25.87.86.00
Ⓔhotel-des-sources@wanadoo.fr
Closed *Wed evening; 30 Nov–1 April.*
Disabled access. TV. Pay car park.

A dynamic young couple run this establishment and offer modern, functional and pleasant rooms. Ask to see a selection, because their size varies considerably – number 34 is big and has a corner sitting room and a garden view. All rooms have en-suite facilities and some have a separate wc; doubles with shower/wc and corner kitchen are €46–51. Breakfast €5.50. Unlike others in town, the restaurant doesn't limit itself to slimmed-down cuisine: specialities include salmon *tartare*, duck with honey and sherry, sole fillet *à la provençale* and an excellent chocolate *trufflon*. Menus €12–25. *Free coffee offered to our readers on presentation of this guide.*

🏃 ⌂ |●| Les Armoises (Hôtel Le Jeanne d'Arc)***

12 rue de l'Amiral-Pierre.
Ⓣ03.25.90.46.00 Ⓕ03.25.88.78.71
Ⓦwww.hotel-jda.fr
Closed *Sun evening; 25 Oct–25 March.* **TV. Swimming pool. Pay car park.**

Not surprisingly, this is the only gourmet restaurant in this health-obsessed spa town. The standard is good: snail jelly with small chanterelles, supreme of chicken with *vin jaune* and morels, foie gras soufflé, and for dessert chocolate marquise. Set menus range from €19 to €32, and children's menu at €10. There's service in the garden in fine weather. The nicest rooms, on the garden side of the building, have been renovated: doubles with shower or bath cost €60 and an extra bed costs €15. Breakfast €7.50. Most people come to the town to take the waters so it's quiet in the evenings; last orders here are at 9pm. *10% off the price of a room (in March, April, Sept and Oct) offered to our readers on presentation of this guide.*

Fresnoy-en-Bassigny

52400 (12.5km NW)

🏃 |●| Restaurant du Lac de Morimond

From Bourbonne take the D139; 2.5km beyond Fresnoy-en-Bassigny, take the little road on the right towards Lac du Morimond and follow the signs.
Ⓣ03.25.90.80.86
Closed *15 Oct–15 March.* **Disabled access. Car park.**

In the depths of the country, close to the ruined Cistercian abbey, there's a little lake encircled by forest where anglers come to tickle carp in the dark of the night. It's the ideal spot to enjoy freshly caught fish or a nice fillet steak with wild girolle mushrooms, which you eat on the terrace overlooking the water. The dining room is also lovely, with an attractive, welcoming fireplace. You get a good selection of dishes on the lengthy menu: zander fillet *meunière*, crayfish tail salad, whitebait, grilled *tournedos*, sirloin steak, calf's head. Menus, €20–22, are served on Sun only. Reckon on €12–20 à la carte. *Free apéritif or coffee offered to our readers on presentation of this guide.*

Châlons-en-Champagne

51000

⌂ Auberge de jeunesse

Rue Kellermann; in the town centre, 1.8km

from the train station. Take bus no. 1, 4, 5 or 7 to place Tissier, then no. 3 to Vallée Saint-Pierre; or walk (10 min).
☎03.26.68.13.56
Car parking. *Check in from 6.30 to 10.30pm (9.30pm in winter).*

An old-fashioned youth hostel near a large, shady square, with forty beds spread over two dormitories. Reminiscent of a dingy boarding house, but the atmosphere is friendly (although the toilets are a bit primitive). €7.50 per person. Breakfast (July–Aug) €3.30. Hire of sheets: €2.80.

Hôtel de la Cité**

12 rue de la Charrière; 800m from the place de la République. From the centre of town, take the sign for Cité administrative; it leads you straight to the hotel.
☎03.26.64.31.20 Ⓕ03.26.70.96.22
Disabled access. TV.

This is a peaceful, provincial place, very much like a family guesthouse, with a regular clientele of businessmen, sales reps and students. Everyone is warmly greeted by the owners, who spare no effort in keeping their hotel nice – it's not high luxury, bit it's very well kept. A few rooms look onto the garden where you can enjoy breakfast (€5) in fine weather or just relax with a book. They cost €25 for a room with basin, €34 with shower, €37 with shower/wc and €40 with bath. *10% discount on the room rate offered to our readers on presentation of this guide.*

Hôtel Pasteur**

46 rue Pasteur; it's about 500m from the place de la République.
☎03.26.68.10.00 Ⓕ03.26.21.51.09
Closed *after Christmas and for New Year.*
Disabled access. TV. Car park.

Part of this hotel used to be a convent which explains the superb, grand staircase. The quiet rooms over the courtyard at the back get the sun. Doubles €28 with shower, €40 with shower/wc and telephone or €47 with bath. Breakfast €5. *5% reduction on the room rate offered to our readers on presentation of this guide.*

Restaurant Jean-Paul Souply

8 faubourg Saint-Antoine; it's 800m from the town centre opposite the young workers' hostel.
☎03.26.68.18.91 Ⓕ03.26.68.97.69
Closed *Fri evening; Sun except certain holidays; first three weeks in Aug.* **TV. Car park.**

A family affair which involves members of three generations. Grandmother runs the bar – she's been in the business more than 65 years – the daughter-in-law manages the restaurant and the son is the owner and chef, who carefully prepares traditional dishes using fresh market produce. He specializes in traditional dishes served in portions which would satisfy a famished giant. Menus €11.50–25.50 and a weekday *formule* at €9.50. They have a few modest rooms for €32, or you can stay half board for €40 or €46 per person. *Free coffee offered to our readers on presentation of this guide.*

Hôtel du Pot d'Étain**

18 pl. de la République.
☎03.26.68.09.09 Ⓕ03.26.68.58.18
Ⓦwww.hotel-lepotdetain.com
TV. Pay car park.

This impressive fifteenth-century house has been beautifully renovated by the family that owns it. There are 27 rooms, quite a few of which can accommodate three or four people. Many have been recently refurbished and are lovely and light. Those on the third floor (no elevator!) have gorgeous views over the square and the rooftops. Doubles with shower/wc or bath and phone €60–65. Monsieur Georges, who used to be a baker, prepares the croissants for breakfast and all the tarts and puddings – he'll bake different things as the mood takes him. You can leave your car parked outside the hotel and explore Châlons on foot.

Le Pré Saint-Alpin

2 bis rue de l'Abbé Lambert, next to the place de la République.
☎03.26.70.20.26
Closed *Sun evening.* **High chairs available.**

This magnificent establishment dates back to 1850 and still has its resplendent stained-glass windows and moulded ceilings. It's a fine example of nineteenth-century architecture, displaying both nobility and elegance. Inventive cuisine: snails in pastry cases with melted Reblochon cheese and a wonderful tart with chocolate and pistachio. The chef, who trained in some of the best kitchens, achieves the perfect balance between tradition and innovation. The cheapest menu costs €16 and there are others at €20–28. A bistro annexe on the parallel street (*La Cuisine d'à Coté*, 1 ruelle St-Alpin) offers a cheaper *formule* with cold starters, main course and dessert. *Free coffee offered to our readers on presentation of this guide.*

Chepy

51240 (7km SE)

Comme Chez Soi

49 rte. Nationale; from Châlons, take the N44 in the direction of Vitry-le-François.
03.26.67.50.21
Closed *Sun and Mon evenings; Tues; a fortnight in Jan; a week in Aug.* **High chairs available.**

Both the setting and the cooking are unreconstructedly provincial. Weekday menu €11 and others €25.50–32. Choices range from a simple *steak-frites* to more elaborate choices such as parsleyed scallops with apples and regional specialities including snails with Chaource cheese and panfried foie gras with Ratafia. Friendly welcome. *Free house apéritif offered to our readers on presentation of this guide.*

Chaource

10210

Hôtel-restaurant Les Fontaines

1 rue des Fontaines.
03.25.40.00.85 03.25.40.01.80
www.perso.wanadoo.fr/champagne-chaource
Closed *Sun and Mon evenings; Tues; 2–23 Jan; last week in July to 1st week in Aug.*

Chaource is located where Champagne borders Burgundy and the classy restaurant serves authentic regional dishes from both *départements*. Menus range from €11, weekdays (€13 weekends), up to €25. The cheapest menu is exemplary; it's a shame about the supplements on the others.

Riceys (Les)

10340 (22km SE)

Hôtel-restaurant Le Magny**

Route de Tonnerre; from Chaource take the D17, and it's on the D453.
03.25.29.38.39 03.25.29.11.72
lemagny@wanadoo.fr
Closed *Tues evening; Wed; Jan; Feb; last week in Aug.* **Disabled access. TV. Swimming pool. Car park.**

Les Riceys is not content with having three churches. It's also the only village in France to produce three AOC wines – one of them a famous rosé that was one of Louis XIV's favourite tipples. The chef uses the wine in a number of dishes, including Chaource cheese pastries or Troyes *andouillette* with mustard. Set menus €12–39. Peaceful rooms; €46–64, depending on the season, for a double with shower/wc or bath. The priciest look out over the garden. There's a heated swimming pool in summer.

Gyé-sur-Seine

10250 (28km E)

Hôtel Les Voyageurs - Le Relais

It's on the old route nationale; from Chaource take the D70, and it's on the far edge of the village on the left.
03.25.38.20.09 03.25.38.25.37
Closed *Wed; Sun evening; the Feb school holidays.* **Disabled access (restaurant). TV. Car park.**

In a village of no little charm, this pretty inn has been revitalized by a nice young couple. It's got a friendly family atmosphere. Tiny renovated doubles with shower/wc €43–65 depending on the season. Good cuisine, simple and generous. Menus €12.50–30.50. *Free apéritif offered to our readers on presentation of this guide.*

Charleville-Mézières

08000

Hôtel de Paris**

24 av. Georges-Corneau; it's opposite the station.
03.24.33.34.38 03.24.59.11.21
hoteldeparis08.fr
Closed *20 Dec–10 Jan.* **TV.**

Rimbaud was born here, and although he cursed the arrival of the railway, his statue stands proudly in the station square. The hotel owner and her cat provide a friendly welcome, and the rooms are classically decorated. The ones on the street side are soundproofed, while those overlooking the inner courtyard couldn't be quieter.

Doubles with shower/wc €44.50, €46.50 with bath. Breakfast €6.30.

|●| Restaurant Le Damier

7 rue Bayard; enter Mézières from Charleville by the avenue d'Arches and take the second on the right after the bridge over the Meuse.
☎03.24.37.76.89
Closed *Mon–Fri evenings; Sun evening.*

This is a unique restaurant run by an association set up to give young and disadvantaged people training and experience, so be patient if the service is sometimes a bit below par. It's nice and bright with a chequered floor, the food is simple but tasty, and eating here good value for money, with menus at €8.85 (weekday lunch only) and €9–16.60. (Prices go up a notch on Sat evening, when the cooking is slightly more sophisticated.) Good dishes include veal *noisettes à l'ardennaise* and iced nougat.

Chaumont

52000

☗ |●| Grand-Hôtel Terminus Reine***

Place Charles-de-Gaulle; it's opposite the train station.
☎03.25.03.66.66 Ⓕ03.25.03.28.95
Ⓔrelais.sud.terminus@wanadoo.fr
Disabled access. TV. High chairs available. Pay car park.

The former residence of the Counts of Champagne. It was rebuilt in the middle of the twentieth century and its turreted, yellow façade and blue shutters give it a modern air. You get all the facilities you'd expect in a three-star hotel. Nearly all the 63 rooms have been refurbished; they're spruce and spacious with modern bathrooms. Doubles with basin €35, with shower €53–60, with bath €70–100. The restaurant serves classic dishes at quite high prices; menus range from €17 to €65 (though there is a €17 lunchtime menu): try the foie gras carpaccio, haddock and potato pie, or the steak, finishing off with the hot soufflé with Grand Marnier. There's also the more modestly priced *Rôtisserie*.

☗ |●| Hôtel-restaurant Le Relais

20 faubourg de la Maladière; it's 1km from the centre of Chaumont, on the N74 to Nancy.
☎03.25.03.02.84
Closed *Sun evening; Mon; a fortnight in Jan; a fortnight end July to early Aug.* **Disabled access. High chairs and games available. TV. Car park.**

A former coaching inn on the outskirts of Chaumont, this is an unpretentious place set between the roadside and the banks of the canal linking the Marne and the Saône. Seven fairly peaceful rooms which have been renovated – numbers 6 and 7 are particularly quiet – and prices are reasonable: €42 for a double with bath. Breakfast €5. Carefully prepared, sophisticated cuisine using the freshest seafood and seasonal produce. Try the warm chicken salad, the calf's head *ravigote* and the house terrine. There's a *formule* for €10 and one at €12; set menus at €13–22. You'll pay around €26 à la carte. Friendly welcome. Credit cards not accepted. *Free coffee offered to our readers on presentation of this guide.*

☗ |●| Hôtel-restaurant des Remparts***

72 rue de Verdun; it's very close to the town walls, and a minute's walk from the railway station.
☎03.25.32.64.40 Ⓕ03.25.32.51.70
Ⓦwww.hotel-des-remparts.fr
Closed *Sun evening 1 Nov–Easter.*
Restaurant closed *Sun evening 1 Nov–Easter; Mon (except public holidays).*
Disabled access. TV.

This place offers the best value for money in Chaumont. The rooms, decorated with posters from the Chaumont Arts Festival, are clean and efficiently soundproofed, and there are newer, more spacious ones in the annexe. Doubles with shower/wc or bath €55–68. Breakfast €7.50. Classic setting in the classy restaurant and first-rate, imaginative cooking: pan-fried foie gras with tart apples, *tournedos* Rossini with truffles, salmon in Pinot Noir sauce and veal sweetbreads in flaky pastry with morels. Set menus €23–45. The *1-2-3* provides a more relaxed atmosphere and brasserie dishes at modest prices. *Free apéritif offered to our readers on presentation of this guide.*

Chamarandes

52000 (2km SE)

☗ |●| Au Rendez-Vous des Amis**

4 pl. du Tilleul. From Chaumont, head towards Langres then Chamarandes on the D162.

Ⓣ03.25.32.20.20 Ⓕ03.25.02.60.90
Ⓦwww.au-rendezvous-des-amis.com
Restaurant closed *Fri evening; Sat; Sun evening; first week in May; 1–20 Aug; 22 Dec–2 Jan.* **TV. Car park.**

The River Marne runs through this unspoilt little village where the old church and school stand near the shady banks. You can glimpse the manor house through the trees of the estate. This is a genuine, quiet country inn with charm, and you get a friendly welcome – all in all, a great place to stop. Rooms have been tastefully renovated and doubles cost €43 with basin/shower or €55–62 with shower/wc or bath. The restaurant is full of hunters, fishermen, businessmen and people travelling through. In summer they serve outside on a lovely terrace shaded by an ancient lime tree. Creative gourmet cooking – duck foie gras with monkfish liver, salmon cooked in leaves, roast duck with a foie gras *fondant*. The wine list has 320 different vintages. Weekday menu €18 and others from €26–46. *10% discount on the room rate (Fri–Sun) offered to our readers on presentation of this guide.*

Marnay-sur-Marne

52000 (18km SE)

Hôtel-restaurant La Vallée

It's on the N19, in the direction of Langres.
Ⓣ03.25.31.10.11 Ⓕ03.25.03.83.86
Ⓦwww.hotel-de-la-vallee.fr
Closed *Sun evening; Mon; a fortnight in Oct; ten days in March; 23 Dec–2 Jan.* **TV. High chairs available. Car park.**

Monsieur Farina produces such good food that it's easy to forget the noise of the main road outside. His place has a great reputation, and rightly so, because his local dishes are skilfully prepared. Try *cassolette* of snails with Marc de Bourgogne or chicken supreme with oyster mushrooms, and finish with a *gratin* of soft fruit. The small, rustic dining rooms are crammed with diners – the overflow goes onto the terrace when the weather is good. Menus €12 (weekdays) or €16.50–37 list dishes such as snail stew with Burgundy Marc, scallops with cream, chives and tongue in a pastry case and red fruit with burned sugar. The half-dozen bedrooms, decorated in provincial style, are fresh and pleasant but quite noisy because of the main road. Doubles with shower/wc €40–45; breakfast €5. Really warm welcome and a family atmosphere. *Free house apéritif offered to our readers on presentation of this guide.*

Vignory

52320 (20km N)

Le Relais Verdoyant**

Rue de la Gare. From Chaumont take the N67 in the direction of Saint-Dizier then follow signs to Vignory gare.
Ⓣ03.25.02.44.49 Ⓕ03.25.01.96.89
Ⓔle-relais-verdoyant@wanadoo.fr
Closed *Sun evening; Mon lunchtime; Mon evening Oct–April; 1 Nov; 20 Dec–15 March.* **Disabled access. High chairs available. TV. Car park.**

This house was built in the early 1900s to provide accommodation for travellers getting off the train at Vignory station. There aren't so many trains nowadays, but the hotel and garden are as elegant as ever. The small, stylish rooms are named after flowers and cost €39 for a double with shower/wc. They're as charming now as they look in the sepia photos of the hotel in the reception area. Breakfast €6. The restaurant serves traditional dishes such as duck breast with shallots, chicken liver terrine with port, and iced nougat with a fruit *coulis*. Set menus €13–24.

Villiers-sur-Suze

52210 (20km S)

Auberge de la Fontaine**

2 pl. de la Fontaine; from Chaumont take the N19 in the direction of Langres, then the D143 to Villiers-sur-Suze.
Ⓣ03.25.31.22.22 Ⓕ03.25.03.15.76
Ⓦwww.aubergedelafontaine.fr
Closed a fortnight in March; a fortnight in Sept. **Restaurant closed** Mon, Tues and Wed. **Disabled access. TV.**

A nice little inn with red shutters smothered in creepers, set in a village surrounded by woods and fields. It's a lovely place to stop for a drink, buy your papers or have a bite to eat. Settle down like the locals in the bar with its shiny ceiling, in the corner sitting room in front of the open fire, in the restaurant with its ancient stone walls, or, in sunny weather, on the terrace. Set menus €11 (weekday lunchtimes) and €16–30 with good, simple, flavoursome dishes that change frequently: try veal with morels, duck foie gras, veal's head with vinaigrette, sole fillet with lobster sauce, rabbit with mustard or *civet* of wild boar in season. Seven or so newly decorated, comfortable rooms in a separate building just a step away. They're €40 for a double with shower/wc or €45 with bath. And if you've forgotten your toothpaste, no worries – the village grocery is in the hotel. Genuine, warm welcome extended by the young owner: this place has brought life back to the village. *Free apéritif offered to our readers on presentation of this guide.*

Arc-en-Barrois

52210 (25 km SO)

Hôtel du Parc**

1 pl. Moreau; take the D10.
03.25.02.53.07 03,25,02,42,84
Closed *Tues and Wed (15 Sept–19 Feb); Mon and Sun eve (April to mid-June); mid-Feb to mid-March.* **TV. High chairs available.**

An unassuming but highly reputed inn with friendly service. Set in a tiny village, opposite a château, it once served as a hunter's lodge, and it is surrounded by woods with abundant game. The rooms are quiet and comfortable – they were all refurbished in 1998 to accommodate the Jamaican footbeall team during the World Cup! Doubles €47–60, with shower/wc or bathroom. Typical local food in generous portions – roe deer and wild boar in season. You can eat on the terrace in fine weather. Menus €16–29. You can go hunting or fishing, play golf or hire a mountain bike. *Free apéritif or coffee offered to our readers on presentation of this guide.*

Colombey-les-deux-Églises

52330

L'Auberge de la Montagne**

17 rue de la Montagne.
03.25.01.51.69 03.25.01.53.20
Closed *Mon; Tues; Jan.* **TV. Car park.**

Small inn, little village, great man – this was General de Gaulle's home. The owner, Gérard Natali, was one of the twelve pallbearers at the general's funeral in 1970. Today people from all over the world come to stay here, from the ex-King of Yemen to the Japanese ambassador, from Breton quarry-owners to French ex-pats. It offers gourmet dining in a chic, rustic setting, and the seasonal dishes feature fresh, local produce. Extensive menus at €26 (weekdays only), and €40–87, as well as à la carte. Specialities include turbot with vanilla, beef *forestière*, boned pigeon with regional truffles, zander cooked in its skin with a crayfish turnover, game in season and the chocolate pyramid with spices and exotic sorbet. The charming rooms are really peaceful; they're €48–54 with shower/wc or bath. Breakfast €8.

Épernay

51200

Hôtel de Saint-Pierre*

14 av. Paul-Chandon.
03.26.54.40.80 03.26.57.88.68
TV. Car park.

The hotel is in a small, quiet street, just away from the city centre (in the direction of the Palais des Fêtes and the swimming pool). It looks like a pleasant family pension and the Jeannels are very welcoming. The rooms are simple yet spacious and very clean. Doubles with basin €26, €31 with shower and €33 with shower/wc.

Hôtel-Restaurant de la Cloche**

5 pl. Mendès-France; it's next to Notre-Dame cathedral.
03.26.55.15.15 03.26.55.64.88
TV. Disabled access.

A nineteenth-century posthouse right in the centre of town. It's recently been updated to suit modern tastes. The rooms are not huge but they're comfortable, attractive and well maintained. Doubles €38–43. Buffet breakfast costs €6. The dining room has an appealing Belle Époque ambience and the cooking is fresh and prepared with care. Set menus start at €17. The nice welcome completes the picture.

Hôtel-Restaurant Les Berceaux***

13 rue des Berceaux; it's near the place de la République.
03.26.55.28.84 03.26.55.10.36
les.berceaux@wanadoo.fr
Closed *3 weeks in Feb; a fortnight in Aug.* **Restaurant closed** *Mon; Tues.* **Wine bar closed** *Sat; Sun.*

An old hotel built in 1889 on the site of the old city walls. Comfortable and very pleasant rooms – each has a different style. Doubles with shower or bath €66–75. Buffet breakfast €11. The restaurant has one star, or you could eat in the wine bar. Weekday menu €27, then €45–59 in Les Berceaux; *menu-carte* in the wine bar €26.

Hôtel de Champagne***

30 rue Eugène-Mercier.
03.26.53.10.60 03.26.51.94.63
www.bw-hotel-champagne.com
Closed *during Christmas holidays.* **TV. Car park.**

The best hotel in the town centre. It's modern and comfortable, and has double glazing. Room prices depend on facilities: €75 with shower/wc and up to €115 with bath. Ten or so rooms are due to be fitted with air conditioning. All-you-can-eat buffet breakfast €9.50.

Epernay-Magenta

51530 (1km N)

Chez Max

13 av. A.-Thevenet; it's 1km from the town centre on the Magenta road.
03.26.55.23.59
Closed Sun and Wed evenings; Mon; 1st fortnight in Jan; 3 weeks in Aug.

This popular restaurant has been going since 1946 and has kept up its good reputation. Weekday set menus €12 and €16 with a choice of four starters, three main courses then salads or cheese and dessert. Other menus at €26–33.50. Dishes change frequently, because they are all cooked using fresh seasonal produce. *Free digestif offered to our readers on presentation of this guide.*

Cumières

51480 (6km NW)

Le Caveau

44 rue de la Coopérative; take the N51 in the direction of Reims, turn on to the D301 and then the D1; it's opposite the wine co-operative.
03.26.54.83.23
Closed *Sun and Tues evenings; Wed; Feb school holidays.*

The restaurant is in vaulted cellars hewn out of chalk. It's a typical Champagne setting, decorated with tools used in vineyards and cellars, and the young staff are dressed in local costume. The local theme continues with the cuisine; the chef has real talent. Weekday lunch menu €15.24 then others €20–35. There is a fine wine list which gives pride of place to the Cumières nectars that have had a fine reputation since the sixteenth century. *Free apéritif offered to our readers on presentation of this guide.*

Bergères-les-Vertus

51130 (24km SE)

Hostellerie du Mont-Aimé***

4 rue de Vertus; take the D3 in the direction of Châlons-en-Champagne then the D9 in the direction of Vertus.
03.26.55.23.59
www.hostellerie-mont-aime.com
Closed *Sun eve and the Feb school holidays.* **Disabled access. TV. Swimming pool. Car park.**

The pleasant air-conditioned rooms look onto the garden or the swimming pool. Doubles €68.50–95. Buffet breakfast €10. Lovely, bourgeois cooking is served in the restaurant and the seasonal produce is efficiently prepared with precision and style. Weekday menu €20 and others €30–64. Not far from the hotel is the famous Mont Aimé, a hillock 240m high which dominates the Champagne plain, and the Côte des Blancs. There's an orientation table which is a big help. *Free house apéritif offered to our readers on presentation of this guide.*

Étoges

51270 (24km S)

Château d'Étoges***

4 rue Richebourg; take the D51 from Épernay to Montmort-Lucy then turn onto the D18.
03.26.59.30.08 03.26.59.35.57
www.etoges.com
Closed *midday Mon–Fri; end Jan to mid-Feb.* **TV. Car park.**

The Château d'Étoges, once a stopping place for the kings of France on their way east, was built in the seventeenth century and is now a classified Ancient Monument. It well deserves all its accolades. There are twenty refined rooms, each different and furnished with antiques. Doubles €110, more for a suite. Breakfast €12. Half board €110–120 per person compulsory in high season. The 18-hectare grounds offer wonderful romantic walks, and there's a billiard room to play a frame or two before dinner. Service in the elegant dining room is as refined as you would expect. Four menus for €30, €40, €50 and €60. Reservations only Nov–April, and it's advisable to book the rest of the year. It's a favourite with English travellers. *10% off the room rate (except Sat and eve of public holidays) offered to our readers on presentation of this guide.*

Ervy-le-Chatel

10130

Auberge de la Vallée de l'Armance

25 av. de la Gare; from the centre of Ervy, take the D374 in the direction of Aix-en-Othe. It's on the outskirts of the village, on the left.
Ⓣ03.25.70.66.36 Ⓕ03.25.70.09.26
Closed *Sun, Mon and Wed evenings.* **Car park.**

An old-style bistro serving good menus. The dining room, behind the pretty garden, has been converted from an old cowshed: part of an old wooden manger has been left in its place and it's decorated with old implements – hay forks and wooden bread paddles hang on the wall. Good regional food includes *gratin d'andouillette* with local cheese, house foie gras and veal sweetbreads with oyster mushrooms. Menus €10.50 (weekdays) and €20–38.

Givet

08600

Hôtel Le Val Saint-Hilaire**

7 quai des Fours; coming from Charleville, it's on the left as you enter the town.
Ⓣ03.24.42.38.50 Ⓕ03.24.42.07.35
Ⓦwww.chez.com/valsthilaire
Closed *Sun evening; Mon lunch; 20 Dec–5 Jan.* **Disabled access. TV. Car park.**

The area is famous for its blue stone – back in the eighteenth century, it was used in the construction of this old printer's. The bedrooms are pleasant and subtly decorated in contemporary style. The ones overlooking the road and the river Meuse have double glazing (triple glazing on the ground floor) but if you're very sensitive to noise, ask for a room overlooking the courtyard. Doubles with shower/wc or bath €53.50. Breakfast €7.52. The restaurant specializes in local dishes – house foie gras, scallops with Vermouth, game in season, calf's head, veal sweetbreads in champagne, turkey, Ardennes meat stew. Weekday menu €18.30 and €30. Reckon on €26 for à la carte. The bar has a terrace on the waterside where the pleasure boats tie up. You get the best welcome in town and the owners are very informative about local walks. *Free house apéritif offered to our readers on presentation of this guide.*

Fumay

08170 (20km S)

Hostellerie de la Vallée

146 pl. Aristide-Briand; it's on the N51.
Ⓣ03.24.41.15.61 Ⓕ03.24.40.39.60
Ⓦwww.hostelleriedelavallee.com
Closed *Sun evening; Mon; Wed evening; Feb school holidays.* **Disabled access.**

The country inn you were looking for. The owner is in charge of the dining room and serves varied local dishes in substantial portions: scallops *de l'hostellerie*, Ardennes charcuterie, scallops and white pudding and onions in flaky pastry with port sauce, beef grilled on a hot stone. Weekday lunch menu €10 and others from €17–35.

Joinville

52300

Le Soleil d'Or***

9 rue des Capucins; it's beside Notre-Dame church.
Ⓣ03.25.94.15.66 Ⓕ03.25.94.39.02
Closed *Sun evening; Mon; 1–15 Feb.* **TV. Pay garage.**

If you're a fan of cosy rooms with stone walls this is the hotel for you. It's spacious and light, and offers good value for money. Doubles €38–70 with shower/wc or €50–75 with bath. The vaulted dining room looks rather gothic with its wooden beams, stained glass, stone and wood. It's warm and refined and provides the perfect setting for the chef's specialities: lacquered roast squab, mixed vegetables, warm polenta with goat, John Dory with scallops. The food doesn't come at give-away prices, though: there's a weekday menu for €20 and a gastronomic menu at €37, and you'll spend around €57 à la carte. *Free use of garage offered to our readers on presentation of this guide.*

🏃 ⌂ |●| Hôtel-restaurant de la Poste**

Place de la Grève; it's at the edge of town on the St-Dizier road.
Ⓣ03.25.94.12.63 Ⓕ03.25.94.36.23
Closed *Sun evening; 10–27 Jan.* **TV.**

They do have rooms here but the main draw is the chef's delicious cooking. Specialities include duck breast with raspberry vinegar, zandre fillet and trout *sire de Joinville*. The weekday set menu for €12.20 is remarkable value, providing starter, meat or fish main course, cheese and dessert. Other menus are €21–55. Impeccable service and comfortable, quiet rooms for €39 with double glazing and shower/wc or bath; breakfast €4.57. Half board €43 per person.

Villiers-sur-Marne

52320 (17km S)

🏃 |●| La Source Bleue

From Joinville take the N67 in the direction of Chauon. At Villiers, take the Doulaincourt road and follow the signs.
Ⓣ03.25.94.70.35
Closed *Sun evening; Mon.* **Disabled access. High chairs available. Car park.**

An ideal country retreat in an old mill by a river way out in the country. It's run by a young couple who have decorated it thoughtfully and created a warm atmosphere. Dynamic service and modest prices. Specialities include trout *tartare* with red peppercorns, duck fillet with blackberries, zander fillet with cream and goat's cheese sauce, and an array of delicate desserts. There's a short weekday lunch menu at €13, others €18–40, or around €20 à la carte. In summer they serve out on the front lawn, or on a terrace footsteps from the water. It's a genuinely charming place and you get good value for money. Take a quick look at the spring that feeds the trout lake, right next to the house – it's a truly remarkable colour. *Free house apéritif offered to our readers on presentation of this guide.*

Langres

52200

🏃 ⌂ |●| Grand Hôtel de l'Europe**

23–25 rue Diderot.
Ⓣ03.25.87.10.88 Ⓕ03.25.87.60.67
Closed *Sun evening in winter.* **TV. Pay car park.**

This hotel displays all the charm of prerevolutionary France: seventeenth-century wood panelling, squeaking floorboards and huge rooms with blue shutters. It has rare provincial style, friendly staff and reasonable prices considering the quality. Doubles €53 with shower/wc and €64 with bath. Breakfast €7. The rooms on the second floor have been refurbished and painted yellow and blue – they're undoubtedly more functional but a little less personal. The older-style rooms are located in the annexe in the courtyard, and they're quieter. The restaurant is splendid, serving nicely priced regional cuisine: weekday set menu at €16 and others up to €46. Good dishes include lemon scallop kebabs. *Free house apéritif offered to our readers on presentation of this guide.*

🏃 ⌂ |●| L'Auberge des Voiliers**

Lac de la Liez; it's 4km from Langres, on Vesoul road.
Ⓣ03.25.87.05.74 Ⓕ03.25.87.24.22
Ⓦwww.hotel-voiliers.com
Closed *Sun evening and Mon except May–Sept; 1 Jan–15 Feb.* **TV.**

This is about the best place in Langres, close to a peaceful lake. Fair prices and great food. Doubles €55 with shower/wc and telephone or €60 with bath. Breakfast €7. Rooms 4, 5, 6 and 8 have views over the lake. Menus €16 then others €20–40. Children's menu €9. Reckon on €25 à la carte. Their fillet of pike with nettles is a speciality, along with house foie gras, veal sweetbreads with morels, and frogs' legs *millefeuille*. And don't miss the *nougat glacé* with fresh fruit. In summer the shady terrace adds to your enjoyment. *Free coffee offered to our readers on presentation of this guide.*

⌂ |●| Le Cheval Blanc**

4 rue de l'Estres.
Ⓣ03.25.87.07.00
Ⓦwww.hotel-langres.com
Restaurant closed *Wed lunch except July–Aug; 15–30 Nov.* **Disabled access. TV. Pay car park.**

The *Cheval Blanc* is a converted medieval abbey and has gothic arches in some rooms, a terrace overlooking the medieval church, rough-hewn stone walls and exposed beams on every floor. The décor is simple yet refined: all the rooms have been refurbished and they are as quiet as monks' cells. The new rooms in the *Pavillon Diderot*, opposite, are equally well equipped but don't have the same charm. Doubles with shower or bath €57–78. Buffet breakfast €9. Half board, compulsory 1 June–30 Sept, costs €63–90 per person. The restaurant offers a panoply of gastronomic delights which change with the seasons: scallops with green apple vinaigrette, morels with egg and ginger, hot foie gras with spiced honey and shallots, and for dessert, bananas caramelized with jasmine tea. Set menus €25–68. One of the best restaurants in the area.

Bananas

52 rue Diderot.
Ⓣand Ⓕ03.25.87.42.96
Closed *Sun Sept–June; Sun lunchtime July–Aug.*

Country music and a bison head hanging on the wall – you could almost imagine yourself in John Wayne country. The atmosphere is great, as is the service and everything on the Tex-Mex menu: tacos, enchiladas, chilli con carne, fajitas, guacamole, burgers and steaks. Evenings are usually very busy. Lunch *formule* €11.60, and a menu at €13.70 (served Sunday lunch in summer). À la carte you'll spend about €12.

Vaux-sous-Aubigny

52190 (25km S)

Auberge des Trois Provinces

Rue de Verdun; it's on the N74.
Ⓣ03.25.88.31.98
Closed *Sun evening; Mon; 12 Jan–3 Feb.* **Car park.**

The wonderful paved stone floor and impressive fireplace are from another era. This décor goes well with the food, which makes good use of local produce with a glimmer of originality. It's not long since the chef was running the kitchen of a top restaurant in Saint-Maxime and it shows. Good set menus at €16 and €25 featuring such dishes as snail ravioli, *oeufs meurette*, home-made country terrine, salmon-trout *pouchouse* in red wine and a selection of cheeses. Desserts include pears poached in wine and *moelleux* of bitter chocolate with roasted sesame seeds. The wine list contains one or two curiosities from the little-known neighbouring vineyard in Montseaugeon.

Auberive

52160 (27km SW)

Hôtel-restaurant du Lion d'Or

From Langres take the Dijon Road then the D428 to Auberive.
Ⓣ03.25.84.82.49
Ⓔliondor.msca@wanadoo.fr
Closed *Tues; 1 Nov to end April.* **Disabled access. Car park.**

This adorable seasonal country hotel is set right beside a twelfth-century Cistercian abbey in a peaceful village near the forest. The Aube is nothing more than an overgrown stream here and it runs directly past the house. The eight rooms are all different and so tastefully decorated they wouldn't look out of place in a magazine: doubles €53. Breakfast €6. There's also a restaurant with a handful of tables around the fireplace. The cooking is based primarily on fresh, seasonal, local produce. Set menu €16 or reckon on €20 à la carte.

Mesnil-Saint-Père

10140

Auberge du Lac - Le Vieux Pressoir***

5 rue du 28-aout-1944; it's at the start of the village as you come from Troyes on the N19.
Ⓣ03.25.41.27.16 Ⓕ03.25.41.57.59
Ⓦwww.auberge-du-lac.fr
Closed *Sun evening 1 Oct–31 March; a week in Jan; 8–29 Nov.* **Disabled access. TV. Car park.**

This is a stylish timber-framed house near the lake in the Orient forest – the ideal place for a romantic weekend. Quiet, air-conditioned doubles with shower or bath are €67–115. The rustic-chic restaurant is a great place to eat refined cusine with a selection of classic regional dishes and modern interpretations. Menus €22 (weekday lunchtimes) and €32–72.

Menilot (Le)

10270 (3km W)

La Mangeoire***

It's to the left of the N19.
Ⓣ03.25.41.20.72 Ⓕ03.25.41.54.67

ⓦwww.la-mangeoire.com
Closed *Sun evening out of season*. Disabled access. **TV. Swimming pool. Car park.**

This village teems with visitors to the lakes of the Orient forest, and the hotel is quite touristy (they organize boat trips and mini-train rides, for example). It's a welcoming place, with appealing, comfortable rooms at €48; they're nice and peaceful. They serve a brilliant €11 *menu routier* in the bar (lunch and dinner, weekdays only), and menus €19.50–32.50 in the restaurant. *Free apéritif offered to our readers on presentation of this guide.*

7

Montier-en-Der

52220

Auberge de Puisie

22 pl. de l'Hôtel-de-Ville.
ⓣ03.25.94.22.94
Restaurant closed *Tues*. **TV. High chairs available. Pay car park.**

There's a twelfth-century abbey in this town, just five minutes from the Lac de Der. This simple hotel, which is a nice place to stop, offers prices that are far from ruinous: doubles €30 with shower/wc, breakfast €4.50. The six rooms are not very big but they're pretty enough and have good facilities; numbers 1 and 2 look over the quiet courtyard. A range of good sweet and savoury crêpes are served in the yellow and blue dining room or out on the shaded terrace. Menus €10–22, or around €14 à la carte. It's probably worth booking, because the area is a magnet for birdwatchers who come to watch the autumn migrations on the lake. *Free coffee offered to our readers on presentation of this guide.*

Au Joli Bois

Route de Saint-Dizier; it's 1km out of the village.
ⓣand ⓕ03.25.04.63.15
Closed *Mon–Fri evenings Oct–June; 1–15 Jan; 1st fortnight of Sept*. **Car park.**

This big building is easy to miss even though it's by the road – it's slightly set back and hidden by a tall hedge. Keep your eyes peeled, because it's worth finding. The dining room is rustic-modern and the terrace on the edge of the wood is very pretty. Try the pan-fried steak with Chaource cheese, zander with beer, calves head vinaigrette, or duck breast with champagne. The €9.80 weekday lunch menu is good value and offers a choice of five starters and six main courses followed by cheese or dessert. Other menus are €17.10 and €23.90 or you'll pay around €25 à la carte. Unusually, they have a list of thirty beers.

Éclaron

52290 (15km NE)

L'Hôtellerie du Moulin**

3 rue du Moulin; from Saint-Dizier, take the D384 in the direction of the Lac de Der-Chantecoq
ⓣ03.25.04.17.76 ⓕ03.25.55.67.07
ⓦhotellerie.moulin.free.fr
Closed *Sat lunch; Sun evening; Mon.; 13–29 April; 5–14 July; 13–29 Dec*. **TV. High chairs available. Car park.**

One of the few romantic spots near the Lac de Der, in an old wooden mill which is typical of the region. There are five quiet, clean rooms; no. 3 has a view of the mill and the woods. Doubles €58 with shower/wc or bath. Breakfast €7. Half board is "strongly advised", and costs from €51 per person. Simple but tasty cuisine: typical dishes include *fricassée* of snails with morels, pig's-foot *fondant* with foie gras, monkfish *blanquette* with langoustines in Chablis cream, loin of lamb marinated with lavender or zander steak browned with leek purée and aniseed and coconut milk with salted butter. Menus €15 (weekday lunchtimes) and €26–46. *Free apéritif offered to our readers on presentation of this guide.*

Perthes

52100 (25km N)

Auberge Paris-Strasbourg

6 rue de l'Europe. As you come from Saint-Dizier, it's the first restaurant on the right when you leave the R94.
ⓣ and ⓕ03.25.56.40.64
Closed *Sun evening; Mon; the last week in Aug*.

A must for gourmets with prices to suit all pockets. Very cosily decorated with faultless welcome and service. The dining room is full of businessmen in the week, tourists and local residents at the weekend. Delicate dishes such as snail salad, salmon in Riesling sauce, duck foie gras with Ratafia, zander with Champagne sauce and so on. Menus €15–40. *Free coffee offered to our readers on presentation of this guide.*

Nogent

52800

🏃 🏠 |●| Hôtel du Commerce**

Place Charles-de-Gaulle, opposite the town hall.
Ⓣ03.25.31.81.14 Ⓕ03.25.31.74.00
Ⓦwww.relais-sud-champagne.com
Restaurant closed Sun from Sept to June; Christmas–New Year. **TV. High chairs available. Pay car park.**

Well-kept and pleasant singles €30 with basin/wc; doubles go for €49–60 with shower/wc or bath. Breakfast €7. The entrance hall is huge and ever so slightly kitsch, as is the restaurant with its exposed beams and eighteenth-century-style décor. Set menus are generous and well thought out; weekday lunch menu €10, and others €16–25. Try the snail soup with Burgundy butter, the salmon with potatoes, the roast lamb with herbs or the spiced fillet of duck with honey. To finish, they do a great *crème brûlée* with apples. The ideal place to stay if you're visiting the cutlery museum. *Free coffee offered to our readers on presentation of this guide.*

Nogent-sur-Seine

10400

🏠 |●| Hôtel-restaurant Beau Rivage**

20 rue Villiers-aux-Choux; it's about 1km from pl.de l'Église.
Ⓣ03.25.39.84.22 Ⓕ03.25.39.18.32
Ⓔaubeaurivage@wanadoo.fr
Closed *Sun evening; Mon; Feb school holidays; mid-Aug to early Sept*. **TV.**

Newish place in a peaceful, almost bucolic environment. There's a large flowery, shaded garden (with a nice terrace in summer) gently sloping towards the river. Ask for one of the rooms with a view. €52 for a double with shower/wc or bath. Excellent cuisine using seasonal produce, seasoned with herbs picked by the patron. Cheapest set menu €19.50 (except public holidays) and others €28 and €36.

Piney

10220

🏃 🏠 |●| Le Tadorne**

1 pl. de la Halle.
Ⓣ03.25.46.30.35 Ⓕ03.25.46.36.49
Ⓦwww.le-tadorne.com
Closed *Sun evening Oct–March; a week around Christmas; the Feb school holidays*. Disabled access. **TV. Swimming pool. Car park.**

Nice old half-timbered building facing the old market. There's a certain style here, and the bedrooms are classic and comfortable, with extra space in a more modern annexe. From €25 for doubles with basin/wc, €43 with shower/wc, and €63 with bath/wc. Regional cuisine in the restaurant, where they serve a weekday lunchtime menu for €10, and others €16–33. Lovely, private swimming pool. *Free coffee offered to our readers on presentation of this guide.*

Brevonnes

10220 (5km E)

🏠 |●| Au Vieux Logis

1 rue de Piney; it's on the D11.
Ⓣ03.25.46.30.17 Ⓕ03.25.46.37.20
Ⓦwww.auvieuxlogis.com
Closed *Sun evening and Mon; March*. **TV. High chairs available. Car park.**

This old Champenois house has kept its style – exposed beams, antique furniture, a large ceramic cauldron hanging in the fireplace. They serve traditional dishes prepared with great care: snails with garlic cream and *chaource*, *andouillette*, rabbit. The service is wonderfully efficient. The €14 menu (not served Sat evening or Sun) is good value, and there are a couple of others for €24 and €35. The rooms are warm and cosy – doubles €39–44 with shower/wc or bath. Half board at €39–48 per person is usually required. Credit cards not accepted. *Free coffee offered to our readers on presentation of this guide.*

Reims

51100

See map overleaf

🏠 |●| 🏃 Centre International de Reims

Parc Léo-Lagrange, chaussée Bocquaine; take bus B or N (Colin stop) or H (Charles-de-Gaulle stop). **Map A2-2**
Ⓣ03.26.40.52.60 Ⓕ03.26.47.35.70
Ⓦwww.cis-reims.com
Open *round the clock, but check in before 6pm*. **Disabled access. Car park.**

A wonderful youth hostel close to the city

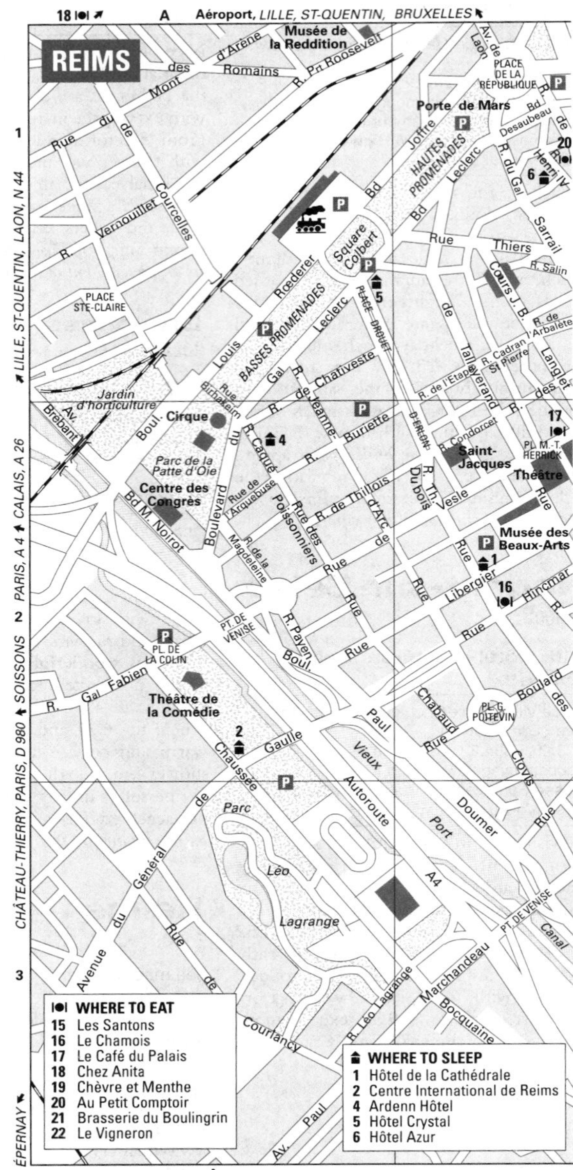
REIMS
WHERE TO EAT
15 Les Santons
16 Le Chamois
17 Le Café du Palais
18 Chez Anita
19 Chèvre et Menthe
20 Au Petit Comptoir
21 Brasserie du Boulingrin
22 Le Vigneron
WHERE TO SLEEP
1 Hôtel de la Cathédrale
2 Centre International de Reims
4 Ardenn Hôtel
5 Hôtel Crystal
6 Hôtel Azur
Aéroport, LILLE, ST-QUENTIN, BRUXELLES
LILLE, ST-QUENTIN, LAON, N 44
CALAIS, A 26
PARIS, A 4
SOISSONS
CHÂTEAU-THIERRY, PARIS, D 980
ÉPERNAY
Musée de la Reddition
Porte de Mars
PLACE DE LA RÉPUBLIQUE
HAUTES PROMENADES
BASSES PROMENADES
Square Colbert
PLACE STE-CLAIRE
Jardin d'horticulture
Cirque
Parc de la Patte d'Oie
Centre des Congrès
Saint-Jacques
Théâtre
Musée des Beaux-Arts
PL. DE LA COLIN
Théâtre de la Comédie
PL. G. POITEVIN
Parc Léo Lagrange
PT. DE VENISE
Canal
A4

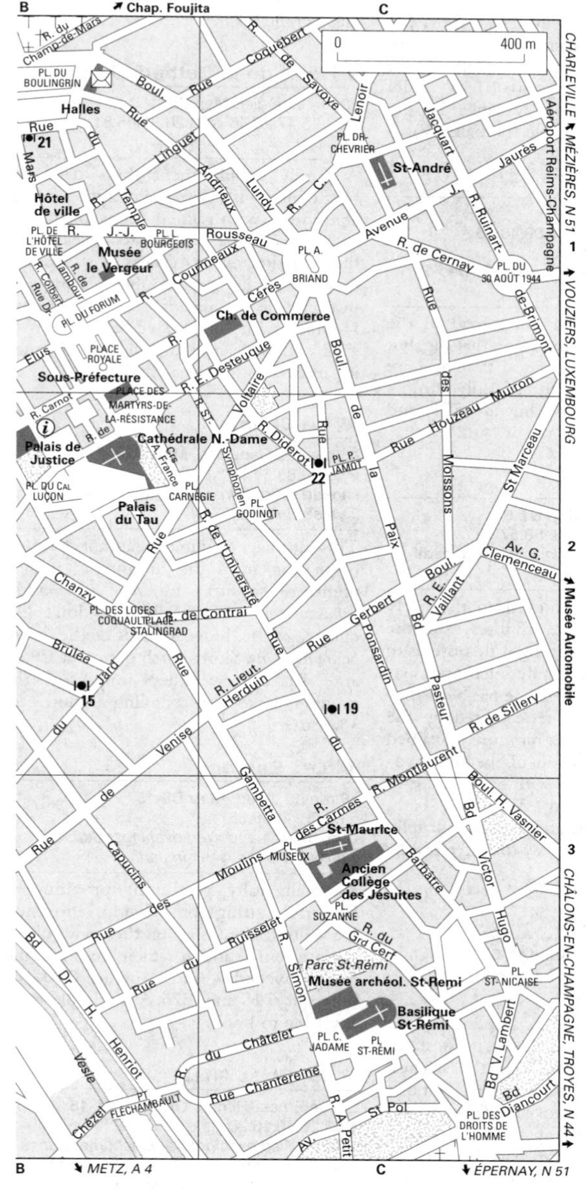

7 CHAMPAGNE-ARDENNES

centre (but quiet, as it's in the middle of a park), with a total of 140 beds spread over rooms with one to five beds. The recently refurbished rooms are modern, attractive and comfortable. They cost €11 per person with washbasin, and €15 with shower/wc. Breakfast: €4. Self-service restaurant: menus €5.50–10.50. Fully equipped kitchen also available. Leisure areas (Internet, pool, table football, TV).

Ardenn' Hôtel**

6 rue Caqué. **Map A2-4**
ⓣ03.26.47.42.38 ⓕ03.26.09.48.56
ⓦwww.ardennhotel.fr
Closed *Sun (reservations only); 20 Dec–7 Jan.* **TV. Pay car park.**

Nice little hotel in a quiet road in the centre of town. Rooms aren't that big, but they're furnished with good taste and are beautifully kept. Warm, friendly atmosphere. Doubles with shower €31 and €47–49 with shower/wc or bath.

Hôtel Azur**

9 rue des Écrevées. **Map B1-6**
ⓣ03.26.47.43.39 ⓕ03.26.88.57.19
Closed *1st fortnight in Jan.* **TV. Cots available. Pay car park.**

Just ten minutes by foot from the lively Place d'Erlon and five minutes from the train station, this charming little hotel is in a quiet street. Rooms are nice and spacious, and much of the place has been renovated and tastefully redecorated by the young owners. It feels a bit more like a bed and breakfast than a run-of-the-mill two-star. Doubles cost €38 with basin/wc, €44 with shower/wc and €50 with bath. Triples cost €57 with bath and quadruples cost €58 with shower. Pay for three breakfasts and get one free.

Hôtel Crystal**

86 pl. Drouet-d'Erlon. **Map A1-5**
ⓣ03.26.88.44.44 ⓕ03.26.47.49.28
ⓦwww.hotelcrystal.fr
TV.

Two good reasons to stay here: its location, in a tranquil situation near the liveliest square in Reims, and its wonderful antique interior, with a beautiful old lift and a glorious *vieille France* dining room. The comfortable and quiet rooms have been renovated and boast good, modern bathrooms; they're €52–66 for a double with shower/wc or bath. There's also a pretty little courtyard where they serve breakfast in warm weather. *10% reduction on the room rate (for two or more consecutive nights Nov–end Feb) offered to our readers on presentation of this guide.*

Hôtel de la Cathédrale**

20 rue Libergier. **Map B2-1**
ⓣ03.26.47.28.46 ⓕ03.26.88.65.81
TV.

A family establishment that's trim and maintained with care. Pretty and comfortable rooms with refined décor. In spite of its location on the main road leading to the cathedral, every step has been taken to ensure a quiet stay: double glazing and insulated doors guarantee peaceful nights. Doubles with shower/wc €56 or up to €62 with bath. Friendly welcome, though it can be a touch over-efficient.

Le Chamois

45 rue des Capucins. **Map B2-16**
ⓣ03.26.88.69.75
Closed *Wed; Sun lunchtime; a week in May; 3 weeks in Aug.*

This intimate, relaxing restaurant draws its inspiration from the mountains, with a menu of *fondues savoyardes* and *raclette valaisanne* or *vaudoise*. If you don't like cheese, go for the geat salads or the *fondue bourguignonne*. Short lunch menus at €8.50 and €13.50 (weekdays only); in the evening, reckon on spending around €20 à la carte.

Les Santons

46 rue du Jarad. **Map B3-15**
ⓣ03.26.47.96.06
Closed *Mon and Wed evenings; Sun; 3 weeks in Aug; a week in Jan.*

A small, jolly restaurant providing a colourful setting for delicious Provençal specialities. The dishes on the menu of the day are remarkable for their freshness and quality. Weekday lunch menus €10 and others at €15 and €25. A lovely place; it's advisable to book.

Chez Anita

37 rue Ernest-Renan. **Off map A1-18**
ⓣ03.26.40.16.20
Closed *Wed evening; Sat lunchtime; Sun; a week in late April; first 3 weeks in Aug; a week at Christmas.* **Disabled access.**

If you like authentic Italian food, *Chez*

Anita is for you. Come here for brilliant oven-baked pizza with a choice of toppings and pasta galore. The portions are generous and very filling – so go easy ordering lunch if you want to stay awake to explore the town in the afternoon. A really popular place with a good local reputation. Lunch *formule* €10.60, lunch menu €14.80; in the evening you'll pay about €20 for a meal à la carte. *Free house apéritif or coffee offered to our readers on presentation of this guide.*

Brasserie du Boulingrin

48 rue de Mars. **Map B1-21**
☎03.26.40.96.22
Closed *Sun.*

A genuine brasserie which has been running since 1925 – it does credit to its kind. The lunchtime din echoes in the vast Art Deco dining room but in the evening it's warm and convivial. The walls are painted with murals and there's an army of uniformed waiters. The excellent €16 weekday *formule* offers a choice of three starters, three main courses, cheese or dessert with a half-litre of wine and coffee included. There's also a menu at €23.

Restaurant Chèvre et Menthe

63 rue du Barbâtre. **Map C3-19**
☎03.26.05.17.03
Closed *Sun; Mon; a week at Easter; Aug; a week between Christmas and New Year.*

This place has had an excellent reputation for years, so you won't be disappointed. The plate-glass windows are decorated with pictures and inside there are two small dining rooms, the nicer one reserved for smokers. The food sounds modest enough but is actually very impressive, and proves good value: try the house tart of goat's cheese with mint or the Jura turkey escalope. A meal à la carte will cost around €16, drinks not included; there are no set menus.

Le Café du Palais

14 pl. Myron-Herrick. **Map B2-17**
☎03.26.47.52.54
Closed *evenings; Sun; public holidays.*

Service 11am to 3pm. This remarkable bistro, founded in 1930, is frequented by the local great and good, including a number of magistrates and lawyers. The superb rococo décor, Art Deco stained-glass dome, photos and decorations on the wall, and the background music, all conspire to create an elegant, relaxed atmosphere. Add to that a genuinely courteous welcome and lively brasserie cuisine that's lovingly prepared. The menu is short but well judged and the desserts are delicious. You'll pay between €20 and €25 for a meal. *Apéritif on the house offered to our readers on presentation of this guide.*

Restaurant Au Petit Comptoir

17 rue de Mars. **Map B1-20**
☎03.26.40.58.58
Closed *Sat lunchtime; Sun; Mon lunchtime; last week in Feb; 1st fortnight in Aug; Christmas to New Year.*

Fabrice Maillot has worked with famous chefs in the past and is enjoying great success with this bistro. He's a clever, creative chef who produces first-rate cooking which looks simple but is finely and precisely judged. The place appeals to people who appreciate good food and the quality of his cuisine is often amazing. The desserts are delicious, too. The menus, €20 (lunchtime only), €26 and €39, change with the seasons, and the impressive wine list features a good selection from the Rhône valley. There's a terrace. *Free coffee offered to our readers on presentation of this guide.*

Le Vigneron

Place Paul-Jamot. **Map C2-22**
☎03.26.79.86.86
Closed *Sat lunch; Sun; the 1st fortnight in Aug; a week at the end of Dec.*

Hervé Liégent's personality is enough to explain the popularity of this place. He's a highly colourful character and totally passionate about his region. Basically, the restaurant is a shrine to champagne-makers. Liégent has re-created the inside of a Champagne winegrower's house and set up a small environmental museum in the middle. There's also a lovely collection of posters advertising champagnes, some of which go back to the nineteenth century. The cuisine is typically Champenois, authentic and appealing. Menus start around €26. Reckon on €20–30 à la carte. And as you'd expect, the remarkable champagne wine list includes some exceptional vintages – the oldest is more than 100 years old. *Apéritif on the house offered to our readers on presentation of this guide.*

Val-de-Vesle

51360 (18km sE)

L'Étrier

From Reims take the N44 and then the D8 in the direction of Châlons.
Ⓣ03.26.03.92.12 Ⓕ03.26.03.29.72
Closed *Sun–Fri evenings.*

Run by a family who make a delightful team. During the week there are two menus: the workers' favourite at €10 includes a starter and charcuterie, dish of the day, cheese, dessert and wine. The €18.30 menu has house terrine, escargots de Bourgogne, smoked salmon or calf's head, cheese and dessert. And the weekend menu (€23) is a real feast: savoury petits fours followed by foie gras of duck with toast or a terrine, then a choice of fish, a choice of meat, finishing with salad, cheese and dessert.

Sept-Saulx

51400 (20km SE)

Le Cheval-Blanc***

Rue du Moulin; take the N44 in the direction of Châlons-en-Champagne then turn left on the D37.
Ⓣ03.26.03.90.27 Ⓕ03.26.03.97.09
Ⓦwww.chevalblanc-sept-saulx.com
Closed *Tues; Wed lunch; Feb; 1 Oct–1 April.* **TV. Disabled access. Car park.**

An old coaching inn with a flower-filled courtyard, set in a large park with the Vesle running through it. The comfortable rooms look onto the courtyard and are peaceful and relaxing. Doubles with shower €64, €77 with bath and up to €155 for a suite. Breakfast €9. There's a tennis court, volley ball court, and fishing equipment. Or you could do nothing at all and simply enjoy the beauty of the surroundings. The restaurant is quite pricey: weekday lunch menu €25 and seven others €29–86.

Fismes

51170 (23km W)

Hôtel-Restaurant La Boule d'Or**

11 rue Lefèvre.
Ⓣ03.26.48.11.24 Ⓕ03.26.48.17.08
Ⓦwww.boule-or.com
Closed *Sun evening; Mon; the last week in Jan and 1st week in Feb.* **TV. Car park.**

Small family place offering sweet little well-kept rooms. Nicest are nos. 4, 5 and 8, at the back. The restaurant is a well-known gourmet stop in the region but it's exceptional value for money. Huge care is taken over the cooking. Weekday menu €11, with others ranging from €15.50 up to €45. Very nice welcome. Double rooms cost €48–55. *Free digestif offered to our readers on presentation of this guide.*

Rethel

08300

Hôtel-restaurant La Champagne**

Bd. de la 2e-D-I; it's opposite the Aisne.
Ⓣ03.24.38.03.28 Ⓕ03.24.38.37.70
Ⓔyves.grustiniam@wanadoo.fr
Restaurant closed *Sun evening.* **Disabled access. TV. Car park.**

Originally built as a block of flats surmounting a parade of shops, this place got turned into a hotel. Not exactly what you'd call charming, but the rooms are nice and clean and it's good value; from €30 for a double with shower/wc, €36 with bath. Half board is €44. There are two restaurants: a cafeteria where you come for the prices rather than the surroundings, and a more attractive dining room with good traditional cuisine – local white pudding, calf sweetbreads, zander with ginger. Set menus €13 at weekday lunchtime, and €17–25 at other times.

Hôtel-restaurant Le Moderne**

Place de la Gare.
Ⓣ03.24.38.44.54 Ⓕ03.24.38.37.84
Ⓦwww.hotel-le-moderne.com
TV. Pay car park.

For over forty years, this place – situated across from the station – has been a favourite with travellers; there aren't many trains now so the rooms are nice and quiet. Despite being renovated they've kept some of their old style, which fits in with the overall look of the solid brick-and-stone building. Well-equipped doubles €37 with shower/wc and €42 with bath. Breakfast €5.50. Decent menus €18 and €26; à la carte you'll get modern classics such as *cassolette* of white pudding and *émincé* of pigeon with foie gras.

Pauvres

08310 (15km SE)

Restaurant Au Cheval Blanc

Route de Juinville. From Rethel take the D946 and it's at the start of the village.
☎03.24.30.38.95
Closed Mon evening; first week in Jan; last week in Aug. Disabled access.

Pauvres may man "poor", but this town is the richer for this gem of a place. There's a sign outside saying they welcome people on foot or on horseback – today you're more likely to see vans and commercial vehicles at lunchtime, when it's full of people who work locally. They generally opt for the €10 *menu du jour*, which includes a litre of red wine, and is served in the evenings (though not at the weekend). The good, hearty portions of family cooking are served with a smile, though the desserts are a little uninspired. At the weekend families flock here for the regional set menus: €17 (gastronomic menu), and three menus at €24, three others at €27, and reckon on €24 à la carte. Specialities include *crousti* of salmon with *julienne* veg, lamb caramelized with honey, pan-fried goose breast, *tourte* of white pudding, veal sweetbreads with cream and saddle of rabbit. *Free coffee offered to our readers on presentation of this guide.*

Signy-l'Abbaye

08460 (23km N)

Auberge de l'Abbaye**

Place Aristide-Briand; take the D985.
☎03.24.52.81.27 Ⓕ03.24.53.71.72
Restaurant closed *Tues evening; Wed.* **TV. Car park.**

This lovely inn has been in the same family since the Revolution. It's in the middle of a small picturesque market town on the edge of a huge forest. You'll get a warm welcome and there's a nice family atmosphere. The stylish rooms, all of them different, are regularly smartened up; room 9 has its own little sitting room. Doubles with basin/wc €32–37, with shower €32, with shower/wc or bath €50. Breakfast €5. In winter they light a fire in the dining room. The Lefebvres are still farmers and you'll find plenty of local produce in the home cooking: the excellent beef comes from their own herd, while the rhubarb for the rhubarb tart is grown in their garden. Menus €10–34 list local specialities; try parsleyed lamb. It's rare to find this sort of place anywhere, let alone in such a wonderful spot. *Free apéritif.*

Revin

08500

Auberge du Malgré-Tout

Chemin des Balivaux; from Revin, go along the Hautes-Buttes road for several km, it's signposted on the left.
☎03.24.40.11.20 Ⓕ03.24.40.18.90
Closed *Sun evening; 3 weeks in Aug.* **Car park.**

The *ferme-auberge* (a farm offering food and lodging) of your dreams, way out in the forest. There are sturdy, wooden tables and a stone fireplace. They serve terrine, house foie gras, charcuterie and game – and in generous quantities, too. Menu at €17.60. The rooms are extremely quiet, as you'd expect, and cost €38.11 with shower/wc. Breakfast €3.05. Lovely warm welcome, but it's essential to book. *Free coffee offered to our readers on presentation of this guide.*

Rocroi

08230

Le Commerce

4 place d'Armes.
☎03.24.54.11.15.Ⓕ03.24.54.95.31
Restaurant closed *Sun eve (Sept to end April).* **TV. High chairs available.**

Right in the centre of the village, a typical country hotel, a bit on the old side but well kept. Small, unremarkable but spotless rooms. Doubles at €40. Menus at €10 (weekday lunchtime), and then €14–36. There is a wide choice of resolutely regional dishes, including the famous "cacasse à cul"(potatoes and lard), slices of Ardennes red turkey hen in oyster-mushroom sauce and calf's head in gribiche sauce. Do not miss the perfectly preserved star-shape fortifications in the village.

Sainte-Ménehould

51800

Hôtel-restaurant de la Poste**

54 av. Victor-Hugo.

Ⓣ03.26.60.80.16 Ⓕ03.26.60.97.37
Closed *Fri evening; Sun evening; Jan.* **TV. High chairs available. Pay car park.**

An unassuming place, not far from the station, run by friendly owners. The rooms aren't very big, but they've been recently refurbished and are comfortable: doubles with shower/wc and telephone go from €36.60. Nos. 7, 8 and 9 are quietest and no. 9 can sleep up to four people. Menus €11–20; try the local speciality, pig's trotters *à la Sainte-Ménehould. Free coffee offered to our readers on presentation of this guide.*

Hôtel-restaurant Le Cheval Rouge**

1 rue Chanzy.
Ⓣ03.26.60.81.04 Ⓕ03.26.60.93.11
Ⓦwww.lechevalrouge.com
Closed *mid-Dec to mid-Jan.* **TV.**

The fabulous €10.50 weekday (except holidays) brasserie menu is reason enough to stay at this place. No boring old *steak-frîtes* and *crème caramel* here. The restaurant menus, €15–52, are equally imaginative. À la carte you'll find the local speciality, pig's trotters – according to those in the know, these are really quite something, given a twist by being served in *galettes* with truffle *jus.* Comfortable double rooms €40–45 with shower or bath.

Auberge du Soleil d'Or

Place de l'Hôtel-de-Ville.
Ⓣ03.26.60.82.49
Closed *evenings except for reservations.*

Yvan de Singly's lovely inn looks like something straight out of the eighteenth century: imposing fireplace, ceramics, coppers and superb Aragonais furniture. Louis XVI is said to have spent his last night here before fleeing to Varennes in 1792. Nowadays the patron has two passions: pedalo (he set the record for crossing the Channel in a pedalo), and pigs' trotters (the speciality of the town). His "pied d'or", which is not boned, is swathed in a cloth and simmered for forty hours in an aromatic *courtbouillon*, then cooled for six hours in a cold room before, finally, being battered and fried and served with apple *compote*. Delicious. Around €38 for a meal. This is a non-smoking restaurant.

Sedan

08200

Le Saint-Michel*

3 rue Saint-Michel.
Ⓣ03.24.29.04.61 Ⓕ03.24.29.32.67
Ⓦwww.lesaintmichel.fr
Restaurant closed *Sun evening.* **TV.**

This is in an ideal spot in a quiet little street beside the high castle walls – the castle is said to be the largest in Europe, and the town is no less than a thousand years old. Decent rooms are €40 with shower and up to €55 with shower/wc. The restaurant is fairly traditional in its approach, with one menu at €12.50 (not Sun), and others €17.50–32.50. They do a few local specialities, like sautéed wild boar, seafood platters and fish dishes. *5% discount on the room rate offered to our readers on presentation of this guide.*

Restaurant La Déesse

35 av. du Général-Margueritte; it's about 200m from the Dijonval Museum of Industry.
Ⓣ03.24.29.11.52
Closed *Sat (except banquets); Aug.* **High chairs available.**

This little bar-restaurant is always full of regulars so you have to grab a table when you get the chance. The atmosphere is warm, friendly and definitely informal. Good set weekday lunch menu at €12. They use only fresh ingredients, even in the desserts – and there's not a microwave in sight. It's authentic, simple and classy – they do game in season. The service is relaxed but efficient, and the owner goes round to make sure everyone's all right. The Sunday (and public holiday) menu, €18.50, is popular with families. *Free coffee offered to our readers on presentation of this guide.*

Bazeilles

08140 (4km SE)

Auberge du Port**

Route de Rémilly; from Bazeilles take the D129 towards Rémilly.
Ⓣ03.24.27.13.89
Ⓦwww.auberge-du-port.fr
Closed *Fri and Sat lunchtimes; Sun evening; 9 Aug–1 Sept; 19 Dec–4 Jan.* **TV. High chairs and games available. Car park.**

This pretty white house stands at the end of a little mooring berth on the River

Meuse. There's a rather polite atmosphere to the place, and the garden and surrounding meadows make it really charming. The characterful bedrooms are in a separate building; those looking out over the river are brighter. They cost €52 for a double with shower or bath. Breakfast €7. There's an excellent menu at €15 (not Sun), and others €22.50–36. The food is beautifully presented and imaginative with lots of fish dishes. Shaded terrace for the summer months. *10% discount on the room rate offered to our readers on presentation of this guide.*

Château de Bazeilles et Restaurant l'Orangerie

It's on the D764, on the edge of the village.
Ⓣ03.24.27.09.68 Ⓕ03.24.27.64.20
Ⓦwww.chateaubazeilles.com
Restaurant closed *lunchtimes except Sun.* **Disabled access. TV. Car park.**

Within the precincts of the château, this lovely establishment offers quiet, spacious rooms with modern décor and great views. There's a special one, no. 201, in a huge separate pavilion with its own open fireplace. They're excellent value at €88 with shower/wc or bath. Breakfast €8.50. The restaurant is of superb quality and is situated in the old orangery in the middle of the grounds. It offers inventive cooking with constantly changing menus costing €22–49: caramelized scallops with chicory *crème brûlée*, roast venison haunch with hazelnuts and brill flambéed with *anise*.

Rémilly-Aillicourt

08450 (6km SE)

Hôtel-restaurant La Sapinière**

1 rue de Sedan. From Sedan take the D6 towards Raucourt-Mouzon.
Ⓣ03.24.26.75.22 Ⓕ03.24.26.75.19
Ⓦwww.lasapiniere08.com
Closed *Jan; 2nd fortnight in Aug.* **Restaurant closed** *Sun evening; Mon.* **Disabled access. TV. Car park.**

This is a traditional country hotel-restaurant which used to be a coaching inn. The rooms are clean and smart with good facilities, and because they look out onto the garden, they're quiet too; doubles €47 with shower/wc, €50 with bath. Breakfast €6. The restaurant has a large dining room which is often used for wedding parties and the like. First menu at €15, except Sundays and holidays, then others at €22–38. Cuisine is traditional and uses a lot of local produce, sometimes with a nice original touch: house foie gras terrine and *tournedos gourmand*. Game is served in season, as are large summer salads. Pleasant terrace. *Free apéritif or 10% discount on the room rate offered to our readers on presentation of this guide.*

Mouzon

08210 (17km SE)

Les Échevins

33 rue Charles-de-Gaulle; from Sedan take the D6, the D4 and then the D27.
Ⓣ03.24.26.10.90 Ⓕ03.24.29.05.95
Closed *Mon; Sat lunchtime; Sun evening; 5–22 Jan; 2–26 Aug.*

The dining room is on the first floor of a glorious seventeenth-century Spanish house. The excellent cuisine combines traditional style with a modern approach and the dishes are meticulously prepared. While you order, a profusion of *amuse-bouches* and other delicacies are served by the smiling, professional waiting staff. First menu at €23 and others from €35–50, which change every couple of months, may list dishes such as asparagus and leeks with *ravigote* sauce and fish *paupiettes*. One of the best restaurants in the area.

Carignan

08110 (20km SE)

Restaurant La Gourmandière

19 av. de Blagny; take the N43 and it's 300m from the centre.
Ⓣ and Ⓕ03.24.22.20.99
Ⓔla-gourmandiere2@wanadoo.fr
Closed *Mon.* **Disabled access. High chairs and games available. Car park.**

The rather fancy dining room is in keeping with the style of this elegant bourgeois residence, and there's still a very homely atmosphere about the place. The talented and daring chef mixes local produce with foreign spices: try the *chiffonnade* of Ardennes ham powdered with garam masala; the pan-fried duck foie gras with seasonal fruit; the braised fillet of smoked haddock with pickled lemons, saffron and cumin; or the pastry case of crab on a salmon cushion. Weekday menu €16 and others €23–50. Lovely terrace in the garden for sunny days. There's a wide choice of wines.

Sézanne

51120

Hôtel-restaurant Le Relais Champenois**

157 rue Notre-Dame; it's on the Troyes road, 500m from the church.
Ⓣ03.26.80.58.03 Ⓕ03.26.81.35.32
Ⓦwww.relaischampenois.com
Closed *Sun evenings; Christmas–New Year.*
Disabled access. TV. Car park.

As you come into the village you enter real Champagne country. This is a friendly old inn with ancient walls. The lovely rooms have been delightfully renovated – from €42 with shower/wc, €63 with bath. Monsieur Fourmi is the chef here, and he prepares superb food inspired by local produce: scallop salad in Reims vinegar, medallion of monkfish with wild nettles and veal. Set menus €18.50 (in the week) to €40. Over more than twenty years, Monsieur and Madame Fourmi have built up a well-deserved reputation for offering quality service and a great welcome. Ask to try a glass of Ratafia de Champagne – it's delicious. *A free glass of Ratafia of Champagne offered to our readers on presentation of this guide.*

Troyes

10000

Hôtel des Comtes de Champagne**

54–56 rue de la Monnaie; it's in an old street between the town hall and the station.
Ⓣ03.25.73.11.70 Ⓕ03.25.73.06.02
Ⓦwww.comtesdechampagne.com
Disabled access. TV. Pay car park.

A twelfth-century building, which was originally the bank of the counts of Champagne. The walls are thick and the wood panelling from the time of Louis XIV creates an authentic feeling of the past. There's also a small, quiet conservatory. Good prices for a two-star hotel: doubles from €25 with basin, and €37–60 with shower/wc or bath. Some rooms are particularly spacious. A very good place. *10% discount on the room rate for a stay of two nights or longer offered to our readers on presentation of this guide.*

Hôtel Arlequin**

50 rue de Turenne; it's near the church of Saint-Pantaléon.
Ⓣ03.25.83.12.70 Ⓕ03.25.83.12.99
Ⓦwww.hotelarlequin.com
Closed *Sun and public holidays from 12.30pm till 6pm; 25 Dec–2 Jan.* **TV. Motorbike garage.**

The *Arlequin* is a brightly coloured hotel where friendliness seems to be the byword. The staff take real pride in looking after guests. They have about twenty bright, spacious rooms at reasonable prices: doubles with shower €37, €46–53 with shower/wc or bath. They also have a number of family rooms that can sleep three to five people. *10% discount on the room rate offered to our readers on presentation of this guide.*

Hôtel de Troyes**

168 av. du Général-Leclerc.
Ⓣ03.25.71.23.45 Ⓕ03.25.79.12.14
Ⓦwww.hoteldetroyes.fr
Disabled access. TV. Cots available. Car park.

For those who prefer somewhere quiet outside the town centre. Immaculate rooms €46.50 with shower/wc, decorated in a contemporary style. You'll get a charming welcome. Buffet breakfast €6.50. There's no restaurant but the owners will gladly guide you to good places to eat nearby. *10% discount on the room rate offered to our readers on presentation of this guide.*

Hôtel Le Champ des Oiseaux****

20 rue Linard-Gonthier; it's near the Saint-Pierre cathedral and the modern art museum.
Ⓣ03.25.80.58.50 Ⓕ03.25.80.98.34
Ⓦwww.champdesoiseaux.com
Disabled access. TV. Pay car park.

In a cobbled street with half-timbered houses, this four-star hotel occupies two fifteenth-century houses. There are twelve rooms and a private courtyard, which is a lovely spot to eat breakfast in the summer. Most of the rooms range between €90 and €210 for a double (breakfast is extra at €15), but if you want the very best, the two enormous suites will set you back an extra €20 or so. They're both gorgeous, with exposed beams, armchairs, period furniture and so on. A delightful place, ideal for a special occasion or a romantic break – it's worth a splurge, if you can afford it.

|●| Aux Crieurs de Vin

4–6 pl. Jean-Jaurès.
Ⓣ03.25.40.01.01
Closed *Sun; Mon; public holidays.*

An old bakery turned into a wine bar, with fashionable décor and a friendly atmosphere. You can sit at wooden tables to enjoy a plate of excellent charcuterie or unfussy bistro dishes, washing them down with a glass of wine from a list that has some interesting finds. *Formules* €10–15, not including drinks.

|●| Le Laganum

34 rue Viardin.
Ⓣ03.25.73.91.34
Closed Sun; Mon lunchtime.

Bernardo, a local character, is the boss in this sixteenth-century half-timbered house. The period dining room has ancient stone walls, beams and a wide chimney – a nice, relaxed place to eat tasty Italian dishes. The pasta is exceptional and the sauces aren't bad either. Between €15 and €20 à la carte.

|●| Au Jardin Gourmand

31 rue Paillot-de-Montabert; it's near the town hall.
Ⓣ03.25.73.36.13
Closed *Sun; Mon lunchtime; a fortnight in Jan; a fortnight in Sept.*

This stylish and intimate little restaurant is right in the old part of Troyes. It has a pretty courtyard, which is heated and sheltered in winter and which looks out onto a sixteenth-century timbered wall that the owner restored himself. There's a menu for €16.50; à la carte costs around €30. But what really makes this place stand out is its speciality: home-made *andouillettes* cooked ten different ways. All their other dishes use only fresh ingredients. Wine by the glass.

|●| Restaurant Le Café de Paris

63 rue du Général-de-Gaulle; it's next to the church of la Madeleine.
Ⓣ03.25.73.08.30 Ⓕ03.25.73.58.18
Closed Sun evening; Tues; 15–22 Feb; 3 weeks end July–mid-Aug.

One of the best restaurants in town, with generous servings of good food dished up in a cosy dining room. Try hot foie gras with apples, Bourgogne snail stew, or Troyes *andouillette* with Chaource cheese. Set menus €21–40. Although it's essentially a lunch spot, it's also a warm and friendly choice for a candlelit dinner.

Sainte-Savine

10300 (2.5km W)

|●| Motel Savinien**

87 rue La Fontaine; from Troyes take the N60, the "Paris par Sens" road, then turn right less than 2km further on.
Ⓣ03.25.79.24.90 Ⓕ03.25.78.04.61
Ⓦwww.motelsavinien.com
Restaurant closed *Sun evening; Mon lunchtime.*
Disabled access. TV. Swimming pool. Car park.

Numerous signposts ensure that this hotel is not hard to find. Though it looks as if it could be part of a chain, it isn't; it is, however, popular with people on the road for business. Facilities include an indoor pool, sauna, tennis, and a gym. The rooms are pretty standard, but prices are attractive considering the quality of service: around €45.15 for doubles with shower/wc or bath. Menus €14.50 (weekdays) and up to €25.50.

Bréviandes

10450 (5km SE)

|●| Hôtel-restaurant Le Pan de Bois**

35 av. du Général-Leclerc; coming from the centre of Troyes, in the direction of Dijon, it's west of the N71 before the intersection on the southbound bypass.
Ⓣ03.25.75.02.31 Ⓕ03.25.49.67.84
Hotel closed *Sun evening out of season.*
Restaurant closed *Sun evening and Mon out of season; Sun and Mon lunchtime in summer; 22 Dec–3 Jan.* Disabled access. **TV. Car park.**

A fairly new, well-designed establishment with all the facilities you'd expect from a chain. The building is designed to suit the local style. The rooms at the back, looking out onto a row of trees, are the most peaceful. Doubles with bath €49. The restaurant is just next door in a similar building; menus at €16 and €17 (not served on public holidays), other menu at €29. They specialize in house terrines and meats and steaks chargrilled over the open fire, and they serve good local wines. The terrace is especially pleasant in summer.

Saint-André-les-Vergers

10120 (5km SW)

Citotel les Épingliers**

180 rte. d'Auxerre; take the N77 in the direction of Auxerre, and it's less than 1km after the Saint-André roundabout.
03.25.75.05.99 03.25.75.32.22
Disabled access. TV. High chairs available. Car park.

A long five minutes from the centre, in an unprepossessing commercial zone crossed by the main road. But this little modern house is covered in flowers, the rooms prettily renovated and well-equipped, and they look out onto a bit of the flower garden. All in all, it's a good place. Doubles €40; buffet breakfast €7.

La Gentilhommière

180 rte. d'Auxerre.
03.25.49.35.64 03.25.75.13.55
gentilhommière@wanadoo.fr
Closed *Sun and Tues evenings, Wed; 3–24 Aug.* **Car park.**

Next to the Citotel les Épingliers, this restaurant suffers from the same unappealing surroundings, and is in a modern building; inside, however, you have a rather chic establishment. The atmosphere, service and food are refined: crab and lobster, sliced veal sweetbreads with Vin de Paille concentrate, and French toast with seasonal fruits. Set menus €18 (not Sun) and €24–53. *Free apéritif offered to our readers on presentation of this guide.*

Rosières-près-Troyes

10430 (7 km S)

Auberge de jeunesse

Chemin de Sainte-Scholastique; take bus no. 6 or 8 from the place des Halles (behind the town hall) right to the terminus.
03.25.82.00.65 03.25.72.93.78
troyes-rosieres@fuaj.org
Car park.

On the site of a twelfth-century priory, of which a chapel and a parlour surrounded by a moat remain; the youth hostel's premises are modern, but they do not spoil the charm and, what it is more, they are surrounded by a two-hectare wooded park, a huge garden and a screen of trees. The hubbub of the town seems a world away. 104 beds, with six in each room, and bathrooms that are each shared by two rooms; €11.70 including sheets, but you must have an FUAJ (French Youth Hostel Association) card (sold in situ). Meals, with booking only, €8.60. Kitchen available.

Fouchères

10260 (23km SE)

L'Auberge de la Seine

1 faubourg de Bourgogne; it's on the N71 between Troyes and Bar-sur-Seine.
and 03.25.40.71.11
cyrillemicard@net-up.com
Closed *Wed; 4 weeks between Jan and Feb; last week in Nov.* **Disabled access. Car park.**

A charming restaurant on the banks of the Seine that looks as if it could be straight out of a de Maupassant story. The dining room has been carefully arranged: the bay windows open onto the river so you can enjoy the cool view, and quacking ducks will serenade you as you dine. The cuisine is delicate and inventive with dishes changing with the seasons. There's a weekday lunch menu for €18, another for €28 or around €35 à la carte. A stylish place where you will be warmly welcomed. *Free apéritif offered to our readers on presentation of this guide.*

Vitry-le-François

51300

Hôtel-restaurant de la Poste***

Place Royer-Collard; it's behind the Notre-Dame cathedral.
03.26.74.02.65 03.26.74.54.71
www.hotellaposte.com
Closed *Sun; 3 weeks in Aug; a fortnight at Christmas.* **Disabled access. TV. Pay car park.**

This comfortable hotel, on a quiet street, is somewhat better value for money than the pricey restaurant, which specializes in fish. Menus €24, €38 and €75 or you can choose à la carte. You'll pay €49 for a double room with shower/wc and telephone, and €53 and €74 for a double with bath. Breakfast €8. Nine rooms have Jacuzzis.

Hôtel-restaurant de la Cloche**

34 rue Aristide-Briand.
03.26.74.03.84 03.26.74.15.52

Closed *Sat lunchtime; Sun evening out of season; last fortnight in Dec.* **High chairs available. TV. Pay car park.**

A peaceful provincial town which was much damaged during World War II – as a consequence, it's not exactly an architectural jewel today. Mme Sautet will make you feel welcome in her establishment and everything is impeccable, be it the napkins in the restaurant, the sheets, the bedspreads or the bathroom towels. The windows have been double glazed so nothing will disturb your sleep. A double room with shower/wc or bath costs €55–58 a night. Jacques Sautet, the chef, was classically trained and certainly knows his stuff – so much so that he's won three stars for the restaurant. He specializes in good traditional French food and has a talent for pâtisseries: trout soufflé with champagne sauce, eel *matelote* "Père Sautet", beef cheek braised in beer with lentils. Menus €21–43. *Free house apéritif offered to our readers on presentation of this guide.*

La Pizza chez Didier

17 Grande-Rue-de-Vaux.
☎03.26.74.17.63
Closed *Sat and Sun lunchtimes; Mon; 24 Aug–7 Sept.*

The pizzas come in a range of sizes to suit all appetites, and with original, tasty toppings. They also offer a nice selection of dishes such as fresh pasta with prawns and asparagus. There's a set menu for €9.50 and a special night-time cinema deal (one dish of your choice = a discount on a cinema ticket). Reckon on around €7–10 à la carte. The menus and the décor change often. *10% discount on the bill offered to our readers on presentation of this guide.*

Restaurant du Marché

5 rue des Sœurs.
☎03.26.73.21.98
Closed Mon.

Without question the best value for money in town. The setting and the cooking are unfussy and the only aim is to feed you decently without ruining you. And that's not a bad ambition. The dishes are simple and very traditional – prepared with fresh produce and generously served. The menus range from €10.90 up to €20.90, and it's a big favourite with the locals who crowd the place. *Free coffee offered to our readers on presentation of this guide.*

Vitry-en-Perthois

51300 (4km NE)

Auberge la Pavoise

26 rue de la Trinité; take the D982 in the direction of Sainte-Ménehould and the D995 towards Bar-le-Duc.
☎03.26.74.59.00
Closed *Sun evening; 31 Dec–15 Jan; 15–31 Aug. Reservations essential at other times.*
High chairs available.

A converted cow-shed, formerly part of the working farm, done up in rustic style. Reckon on €22–35 à la carte. Menus vary according to the seasons and are prepared with fresh local produce. Try chicken with Champagne or duck fillet with Ratafia. Desserts are a hit with everyone. Good wines at reasonable prices. They don't accept credit cards.

Sainte-Marie-du-Lac

51290 (20km SE)

Le Cycloder

Les Grandes Côtes. Take the D13 to Larzicourt, then the D57 to Blaize, then the D60.
☎03.26.72.37.05
Closed *1 Dec–28 Feb.* **Disabled access.**

A lovely *crêperie* where you can get quality *galettes* for €2–5 and crêpes at €1.50–4 – not to mention a friendly welcome. They rent out bikes, which are perfect for exploring the banks of the Der lake nearby. Credit cards not accepted.

Giffaumont-Champaubert

51290 (26km SE)

Hôtel-restaurant Le Cheval Blanc***

21 rue du Lac; take the D13.
☎03.26.72.62.65 ⓕ03.26.73.96.97
ⓔlechevalblanc6@aol.com
Restaurant closed *Sun evening; Mon; Tues lunchtime; 3 weeks in Jan; 3 weeks in Sept.*
TV. Disabled access. High chairs available. Car park.

Set in an adorable village full of half-timbered houses near the Lac du Der, the largest artificial lake in Europe and also a bird reserve. Thierry Gérardin, the young owner, was spurred into rapid action when he took over: all the bathrooms have been renovated and there's a new reception and sitting room. The modern rooms cost €65 for a double with shower/wc or bath. Wonderful welcome. They serve meals in the open air in spring and summer or on the flower-ornamented terrace. The cheapest set menu, €21, is simple and generous. Other menus cost up to €30. *10% discount on the room rate (except July–Aug) offered to our readers on presentation of this guide.*

Vouziers

08400

Argonne Hôtel**

Route de Reims; it's on the way out of town on the Châlons-Retel road, by the first roundabout.
Ⓣ03.24.71.42.14 Ⓕ03.24.71.83.69
Ⓔargonnehotel@wanadoo.fr
Restaurant closed *Sun evening.* **TV. Car park.**

This modern building in the commercial park is neither characterful nor charming, though the welcoming owners certainly are. It's an ideal place for an overnight stop. The rooms are attractively decorated and good value: €43 for a double with shower/wc or bath. Breakfast €5.50. Menus €10.50 (not Sun) and €14.50–23 list classic cuisine with occasional exotic touches — try terrine of foie gras with Armagnac, scallops and prawns with pastis, or duck breast with pears and shallots. *Free coffee offered to our readers on presentation of this guide.*

Buzancy

08240 (22km NE)

Hôtel du Saumon**

Place Chanzy; from Vouziers take the D947.
Ⓣ03.24.30.00.42 Ⓕ03.25.30.27.47
Ⓦwww.hoteldusaumon.com
Restaurant closed *Sat lunchtime.* **High chairs available. TV.**

A charming hotel that it would be easy to fall in love with, right in the middle of the small town. The house has been totally refurbished – each of the nine rooms is decorated differently but with the same good taste throughout, and though they vary in size they all have the same facilities. Some have a garden view. Doubles €42–58 with shower/wc or bath. Breakfast €5. Two dining rooms, one of them a very pleasant bistro offering a *menu-carte* assembled from the fresh produce bought at market. Menus €11 (except Sundays), €14.50 and €19. Particularly friendly welcome. *Free coffee offered to our readers on presentation of this guide.*

Corsica

Ajaccio

20000

Hôtel Marengo**

2 rue Marengo, BP244; it's near the casino and the beaches.
Ⓣ04.95.21.43.66 Ⓕ04.95.21.51.26
Closed *10 Nov–end March.* **TV**.

This is a lovely and very reliable little place at the end of a quiet cul-de-sac. Some rooms look out onto a peaceful courtyard with flowers everywhere. Warm welcome. Double rooms €45–64 with shower or bath. It's basic but well run and has good facilities, including air-conditioning and double glazing. There is parking for six cars. *10% discount on the room rate except July–Sept to our readers on presentation of this guide.*

Hôtel Imperial***

6 bd. Albert-1er.
Ⓣ04.95.21.50.62 Ⓕ04.95.21.15.20
Closed *Nov–March*. **TV.**

A three-star hotel with a lovely Second Empire-style entrance. Take a look at the poster for Abel Gance's film epic, *Napoléon*, in reception. The large rooms are cosy and feel old but they're comfortable and well maintained. Depending on facilities and the season, doubles are €60–85. It's not cheap, but prices include a parasol and sunbed on the private beach just across the way. Rooms in the more modern annexe are smaller and cheaper, but they don't have air-conditioning. *Le Baroko* is the restaurant and the cooking is pretty good – which is just as well, because they like you to stay half board (€54–66 per person) in July–Aug. *Apéritif on the house offered to our readers on presentation of this guide.*

Hôtel Fesch***

7 rue Fesch.
Ⓣ04.95.51.62.62 Ⓕ04.95.21.83.36
Ⓦwww.hotel-fesch.com
Closed *20 Dec–20 Jan.* **TV**.

The *Fesch* is very well located in the centre of town. The rooms are mostly comfortable and the furniture is made of chestnut. The price of a room depends on the facilities and the season: doubles €67–82 with shower/wc or bath. Breakfast €7. If you want a top-floor room with a balcony, it'll cost €8 extra. *One free breakfast per room (except 15 July–15 Sept) offered to our readers on presentation of this guide.*

A Casa

21 av. Noël-Franchini; it's 2km north – go along the coast road towards the airport and turn left at the end of bd. Charles-Bonaparte.
Ⓣ04.95.22.34.78
Closed *Sun; 10 Dec–10 Feb.*

This restaurant is outside the centre, but the originality of the place draws a lot of local people. They've squeezed about ten tables onto the patio/balcony, which is surrounded by plants, flowers and parasols. The cooking is uncomplicated but good: the *menu Corse* is particularly tasty. Weekday menu at €12.20 and others at €19.82 and €32.78. Excellent Sartène or Muscat wine. The real attraction is on a Friday or Saturday night when Frank the boss (also a professional magician) puts on a show. He does all the tricks – cutting people in half, levitation – and even burns

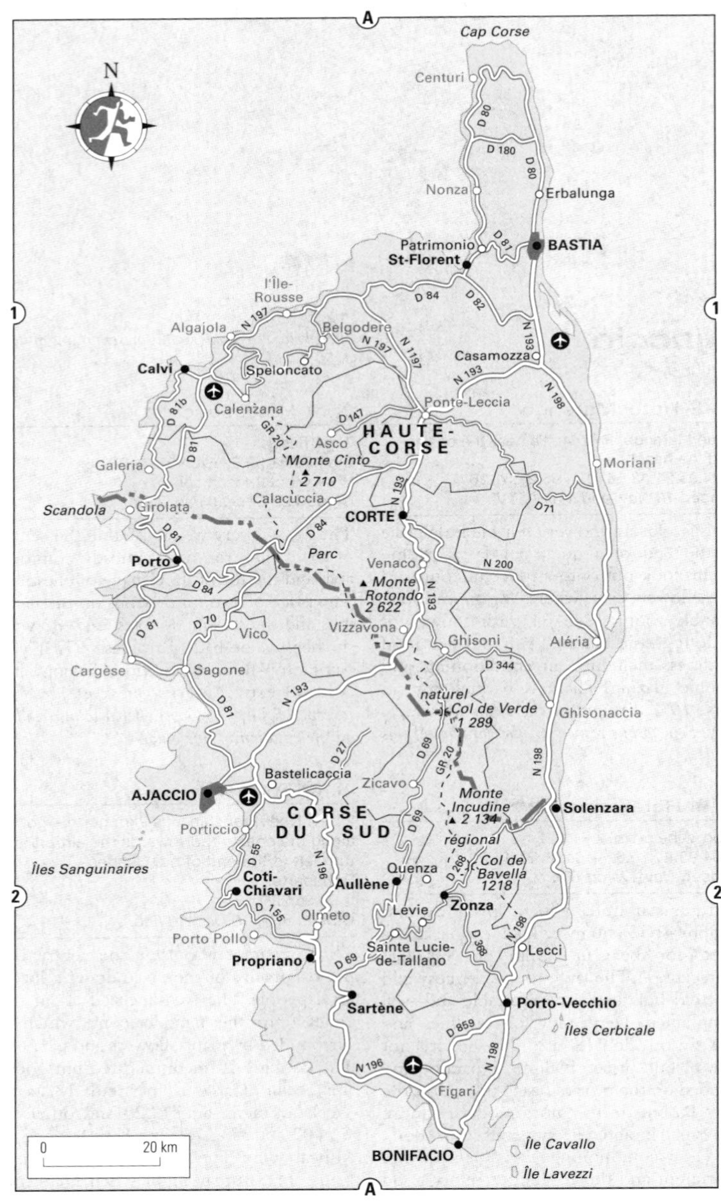
N
A
Cap Corse
Centuri
D 80
D 180
D 80
Nonza
Erbalunga
Patrimonio
D 81
BASTIA
St-Florent
l'Île-
Rousse
D 84
D 82
1
1
Algajola
N 197
Belgodere
N 193
N 197
N 1197
Casamozza
Calvi
Speloncato
N 193
N 198
D 81b
Calenzana
Ponte-Leccia
GR 20
D 147
HAUTE-
CORSE
Asco
D 81
Monte Cinto
Moriani
Galeria
2 710
N 193
Calacuccia
D 71
Scandola
Girolata
CORTE
D 81
D 84
Porto
Parc
Venaco
N 200
D 84
Monte
Rotondo
2 622
N 193
D 81
D 70
Vico
Vizzavona
Ghisoni
Aléria
Cargèse
Sagone
D 344
N 193
naturel
Col de Verde
1 289
Ghisonaccia
D 81
D 27
D 69
GR 20
N 198
Bastelicaccia
Zicavo
AJACCIO
Monte
Incudine
2 134
Solenzara
CORSE
DU SUD
D 69
Porticcio
régional
D 55
N 196
D 268
Col de
Bavella
1218
Îles Sanguinaires
Quenza
Coti-
Chiavari
Aullène
2
2
Zonza
D 155
Olmeto
Levie
N 198
Porto Pollo
D 368
Sainte Lucie-
de-Tallano
Lecci
Propriano
D 69
Sartène
Porto-Vecchio
D 859
Îles Cerbicale
N 196
N 198
Figari
0
20 km
Île Cavallo
BONIFACIO
Île Lavezzi
A

8

CORSICA

his partner alive. (There's a single menu for €30 on these magical nights.) Be sure to book for the show. Credit cards not accepted. *Free coffee offered to our readers on presentation of this guide.*

Le 20123

2 rue du Roi-de-Rome; it's in the old town.
Ⓣ04.95.21.50.05
Closed *lunchtimes; Mon; mid-Jan to mid-Feb.*

This restaurant, which opened in 1987, used to be in Pila Canale, up in the mountains behind Ajaccio, where the postcode was 20123. They moved into a pedestrian street in the old town and set up with the same décor as before. Inside it's almost like a Corsican village with a fountain and little houses; they've even got an old Vespa parked there. There's a small terrace as well. The single menu, €26, lists serious Corsican charcuterie, *brocciu* tart made with sheep's-milk cheese, and a variety of meats – pork, veal, lamb and boar – which are grilled or served as stews. Finish with some genuine local cheese and a simple dessert like flan made with ground chestnuts. Good cooking in a place with character, but they don't accept credit cards. *Free liqueur offered to our readers on presentation of this guide.*

Bastelicaccia

20129 (13km E)

Môtel l'Orangeraie**

It's on the way out of the village towards Porticcio, on the left.
Ⓣ04.95.20.00.09 Ⓕ04.95.20.09.24
TV. Swimming pool. Car park.

The garden, which is filled with palms, arbutus and orange trees, is one of the most amazing in Corsica and it's maintained with passionate care by Monsieur Grisoni. The bungalows are hidden away in glorious Mediterranean vegetation. The setting is wonderful and even though the service gets overwhelmed sometimes, the welcome is warm. You can rent studios for one to three people or two rooms for two to five people; they cost €35–62/€55–85 depending on the season. They're not brand new but they're well equipped, with good bedding, heating, hair-dryers, kitchen, terrace and barbecue. There's a small swimming pool. Remember to book early, as it's often full. Credit cards not accepted.

Aullène

20116

Hôtel-restaurant de la Poste*

Rue Principale.
Ⓣ04.95.78.61.21 Ⓕ04.95.78.61.21
Closed *1 Oct–30 April.*

This attractive stone inn with a lovely view of the mountains was built when people were travelling around in carriages; it's one of the oldest hotels in Corsica, dating back to 1880. Double rooms with basin for €31 or €40 with shower. Half board at €45 per person when you stay for three nights or more. The cooking in the restaurant is simple – in season, try the wild boar, or the house charcuterie at any time. Menus €15.50 and €21. The owner, Jeannot Benedetti, knows all the interesting places to visit and even writes guide books you can borrow. *Free digestif offered to our readers on presentation of this guide.*

Quenza

20122 (6km E)

Auberge Sole e Monti**

Take the D420.
Ⓣ04.95.78.62.53 Ⓕ04.95.78.63.88
Ⓦwww.solemonti.com
Closed *1 Oct–30 April.* **Restaurant closed** *Mon; Tues lunchtime.* **TV.**

Félicien Balesi, a bon vivant who knows how to make his guests feel at home, has run this friendly inn for more than a quarter of a century. The relatively new building has a loggia that would be lovelier still with a sea view; at any rate, it's the perfect spot to admire the beauty of the Corsican mountains, although a bit pricey. There's a huge garden on the other side of the road available for the guests to enjoy. When the weather is inclement regulars gather around the open fire in a cosy salon. The menu changes daily because only fresh produce is used and the delicious dishes are inspired by old Corsican recipes. Set menus €23 (not Sun), €30 and €40. Pleasant, well-equipped rooms. They prefer people to stay half board; the cost per person, sharing a double room with shower/wc or bath, is €70–90. *Free apéritif offered to our readers on presentation of this guide.*

Levie

20170 (15km E)

Ferme-auberge A Pignata

Route du Pianu; from Levie, drive 3km along the Sainte-Lucie road, then turn right as you approach Cucuruzzu; 1.5km further on, after a little hill, turn left through the second gate.
Ⓣ04.95.78.41.90 Ⓕ04.95.78.46.03
Car park.

A very secretive inn: you have to be in the know to find it. No signposts, no arrows, no board – nothing. The restaurant is open from noon–1pm and 7.30–9pm, but you can't just turn up – you have to book. When you get there, though, the hospitality is tremendous. There are only a few rooms but they're clean and spacious and have nice linen. Half board only, at €58–64 per person. According to the locals the authentic Corsican specialities you get here are the best in the region. These include cannelloni with *brocciu* (a mild sheep's milk cheese), stuffed aubergines and wild boar. There's one menu only for €30; it's excellent and the portions are large. Wines are extra but there's a good house wine. A great place. Credit cards not accepted. *Free liqueur offered to our readers on presentation of this guide.*

Bastia

20200

Hôtel Cyrnéa**

Route du Cap; 2km from the centre of Bastia, on the right as you enter Pietranera.
Ⓣ04.95.31.41.71 Ⓕ04.95.31.72.65
Closed *15 Dec–15 Jan.* **Disabled access. TV. Pay car park.**

A long 1970s building, very well maintained, with air-conditioned rooms and fans. Behind, the big garden slopes down to a small pebbly beach 30m from the hotel. Depending on the season and whether you have a view of the road or the sea, doubles with shower/wc cost €50–83, including breakfast. The sea-view rooms all have a balcony – ideal for watching the sun rise over Monte Cristo at breakfast. *Free coffee, and free use of the garage (except 15 June–15 Sept), offered to our readers on presentation of this guide.*

L'Alivi***

Route du Cap; it's 1km from the marina on the right.
Ⓣ04.95.55.00.00 Ⓕ04.95.31.03.95
Ⓦwww.hotel-alivi.com
Closed *Dec.* **Disabled access. TV. Swimming pool. Car park.**

Seen from the sea, this long oblong structure, three storeys high, doesn't do the coastline any favours. But inside, you really appreciate the comfort of the rooms and direct access to the pebble beach. All rooms have a sea view, a balcony and all the facilities you'd expect from a three-star hotel. A double room with shower or bath costs €95–165, depending on the season. A few rooms with shower/wc for slightly less.

Restaurant a Casarella

6 rue Sainte-Croix; it's in the citadel.
Ⓣ04.95.32.02.32
Closed *Sat lunchtime; Sun; Nov.* **Disabled access.**

You have to climb up to the citadel, near the Palais of the Genoese governors, to find this place. Take a seat on the terrace, with views of the old port down below, and enjoy a feast. The inventive chef prepares good authentic Corsican dishes scented with herbs from the maquis. Try the *casgiate*, a fromage frais fritter baked in the oven, the prawns in flaky pastry and the rolled veal with herbs, all of which are excellent. Desserts include the curious *strozzapreti*, a stodgy cake that the people here used to bake for the parish priest on Sundays, and the wonderful *fiadone*, a cheese and orange flan. Lunchtime "discovery" platter €15 and a menu at €28 in the evening; around €28 à la carte.

Erbalunga

20222 (8km N)

Hôtel Castel Brando***

It's in the village.
Ⓣ04.95.30.10.30 Ⓕ04.95.33.98.18
Ⓦwww.castelbrando.com
Closed *1 Nov–13 March.* **Disabled access. TV. Swimming pool. Car park.**

This hotel is in a nineteenth-century Corsican mansion and has great character and charm. It has been tastefully restored and furnished with antiques. The walls are colour-washed in strong pigments and there's an impressive monumental staircase; it all feels slightly Latin American. The garden is planted with palm trees. Near the swimming pool, the pretty rooms in the annexe are quieter than those in the main building. All rooms have air-conditioning, shower or bath, telephone and satellite TV. Doubles €69–134 depending on facilities and season.

Casamozza

20200 (20km S)

Chez Walter***

It's on the N193, about 4km beyond the airport crossroads.
Ⓣ 04.95.36.00.09 Ⓕ 04.95.36.18.92
Ⓦ www.chez-walter.com
Restaurant closed Sun except 15 July–15 Aug and New Year.
Disabled access. TV. High chairs available. Swimming pool. Car park.

A fine, comfortable, professionally-run and reliable establishment. Good facilities in the air-conditioned rooms. Doubles with shower or bath €80–95 depending on the season. Breakfast, with fresh orange juice, €8. There's a pool, tennis court and a lovely garden. It's a place used by ship crews stopping over and visiting football teams come to play Bastia. The restaurant, open noon–2.30pm and 7.30–10.30pm, has a good reputation with tasty fish dishes (sea bream, crayfish and other seafood). Menu at €17. *Free coffee offered to our readers on presentation of this guide.*

Bonifacio

20169

Domaine de Licetto

Route du Phare-de-Pertusato, 2km from the port.
Hotel Ⓣ and Ⓕ 04.95.73.03.59
Restaurant Ⓣ 04.95.73.19.48
Closed *lunchtime.* **Car park. Disabled access.**

There's an unusual view of both the upper and lower towns from the grounds here. The *Domaine* is right in the maquis and the modern hotel is in a separate building 50m from the restaurant. The rooms are smart, and good-value for Bonifacio; doubles €36–67 with shower/wc or €45–79 with bath, depending on the season. Dining in the restaurant, from 8pm, is by reservation only. Single set menu at €30. Typically Corsican cuisine: stuffed squid, milk-fed lamb in sauce, cabbage stuffed with chestnuts and iced charlotte with chestnut cream. Credit cards not accepted. *10% discount on a room for a stay longer than a week in high season. Free coffee, apéritif or digestif, if you take the menu at €30, on presentation of this guide.*

Hôtel des Étrangers*

Avenue Sylvère-Bohn; it's 300m from the port, hidden beneath a cliff, on the right of the road from Ajaccio.
Ⓣ 04.95.73.01.09 Ⓕ 04.95.73.16.97
Closed *1 Nov–15 March.* **TV. Car park.**

Pretty close to the road but the soundproofing is efficient. Good facilities, including shower/wc, telephone and TV. Most rooms have air-conditioning and they're clean. Room prices – €48–79 for a double, depending on the season – include breakfast. Good value for Bonifacio. Lock-up for motorbikes. *10% discount (1–15 April and Oct) on a room offered to our readers on presentation of this guide.*

A Trama

Cartarana, route de Santa-Marza; it's 1.5km from the town centre.
Ⓣ 04.95.73.17.17 Ⓕ 04.95.73.17.79
Ⓦ www.a-trama.com
Restaurant closed *mid-Nov–end Feb.*
Disabled access. TV. Swimming pool. Car park.

In a peaceful setting surrounded by greenery, this new complex has been handsomely built and is well maintained. There are 25 rooms at garden level, each with a private terrace facing the swimming pool – perfect for breakfast. All rooms have modern facilities such as TV, mini-bar and air-conditioning, and the beds are "dorsopedic", apparently. Doubles €80–145 depending on season. It's a nice place and the welcome is courteous and professional. The restaurant, *Le Clos Vatel*, has a good reputation. Menu €28 or à la carte. *Free apéritif or digestif offered to our readers on presentation of this guide.*

Hôtel-restaurant du Centre Nautique***

It's on the north side of the marina across from the quai Jérôme-Comparetti.
Ⓣ 04.95.73.02.11 Ⓕ 04.95.73.17.47
Ⓦ www.centre-nautique.com
Closed *Mon (Oct–March).* **TV. Car park. High chairs available.**

This grand and beautiful building stands on its own quay – quiet compared to the one opposite. It has ten spacious and classy duplex rooms, with contemporary interiors and plenty of facilities such as minibars and air-conditioning. There are sofa beds in the ground-floor sitting rooms; bedroom and shower are upstairs. A duplex with sea view costs €85 Oct–March, €140 April–June and Sept, or €190 in July–Aug. The garden-view rooms are cheaper. Add €34 per person for half board. There's also a restaurant (noon–3pm & 7–10pm), à la carte only, serving excellent and huge plates of fresh pasta; reckon on around €40 for a meal.

Calvi

20260

Hôtel les Arbousiers**

Route de Pietra-Maggiore; from the centre, take the road towards Bastia and L'Île Rousse; after 800m turn right at the start of the pine forest and follow the signs.
Ⓣ04.95.65.04.47 Ⓕ04.95.65.26.14
Closed *end Sept–1 May.* **TV. Car park.**

It can be best to stay just outside Calvi, simply because you get more space. This hotel is in an attractive big house with pink walls and an old wooden staircase leading up to the bedrooms. The décor isn't spectacular, but it's very clean and there are lots of pleasant little terraces overlooking the courtyard. Ask for a south-facing room to maximize the sun. The prices are reasonable: doubles with bath €38–53. The beach is just five minutes' walk away.

Résidence les aloès**

Quartier Donatéo; from the centre of town, take av. Santa-Maria and follow it to the right. It's signposted.
Ⓣ04.95.65.01.46 Ⓕ04.95.65.01.67
Ⓦwww.hotel-les-aloes.com
Closed *15 Oct–15 April.* **TV. Car park.**

This hotel was built in the 1960s on a fabulous site above Calvi – you get a panoramic view of the bay, the citadel and the wild countryside towards Monte Cinto. The surroundings are peaceful and there are flowers everywhere. The décor in the foyer is a bit kitsch but it's reasonably elegant, while the refurbished rooms have TV, telephone and balcony. Prices are €41–49 (high season €50–58) for a double, depending on the view (mountain or sea). *10% discount for a minimum two-night stay (15 April–1 July) offered to our readers on presentation of this guide.*

Hôtel-restaurant Casa-vecchia

Route de Santore; it's 500m from the town centre and 200m from the beach and pine woods.
Ⓣ04.95.65.09.33 Ⓕ04.95.65.37.93
Closed *1 Nov–1 May.* **Restaurant closed** *lunchtimes; open evenings May–mid-Sept.* **Disabled access. Car park.**

The accommodation is in ten simple and attractively priced rooms in a garden full of flowers. Double rooms are €48–60 with shower/wc, €55–70 for extra-large ones. Half board is obligatory July–Aug at €85–110 for two people. Breakfast is served on a shaded terrace. Good, generously served family cooking with €15 and €18 menus.

Le Grand Hôtel***

3 bd. Wilson.
Ⓣ04.95.65.09.74 Ⓕ04.95.65.25.18
Ⓦwww.grand-hotel-calvi.com
Closed *5 Jan–29 Feb.* **TV.**

They don't build places like this early-twentieth-century grand hotel any more: corridors as wide as rooms, a smoking room as large as a ballroom and bedrooms as big as – well, big bedrooms. The tearoom looks a bit dated, and the armchairs need to be re-covered, but they're comfortable; the rooms themselves have been given a lick of paint and the beds are good. Doubles €74.10–108.60, breakfast included, depending on the season and facilities. Nice welcome, a good atmosphere and a spectacular view from the breakfast room: it's high up, so you look down on the rooftops of Calvi to the sea beyond. *10% discount on a room (except May–September) offered to our readers on presentation of this guide.*

L'Abri Côtier

Quai Landry; it's by the harbour.
Ⓣ04.95.65.12.76
Closed *end Nov–early March.* **Disabled access. High chairs available.**

The restaurant is on the first floor, above a bar and tearoom. It's open noon–2pm and 7–10pm (10.30 pm at weekends) out of season, until 10.30pm on weekdays and 11pm at weekends in the high season. There's a big dining room overlooking the marina. The cooking zings with fresh flavours – try their fish grilled with a drizzle of olive oil, starters of fruit and vegetables or their dishes using *brocciu* (mild sheep's milk cheese). Pleasant, efficient service; this is one of the most reliable places in Calvi. Menus €12.50 (lunch) to €27.50. *Free coffee offered to our readers on presentation of this guide.*

Speloncato

20226 (34km N)

A Spelunca**

Place de l'Église; take the N197 heading towards l'Île Rousse.
Ⓣ04.95.61.50.38 Ⓕ04.95.61.53.14
Closed *1 Nov–31 March.*

A hotel with charm in a characterful village set on a rock in the Balagne – this is the real soul of Corsica. Note, however, that it's very near a church – incredibly picturesque, but the bells do toll throughout the night, so if you're after peace and quiet, maybe look elsewhere. This pink house with a little turret and a lovely terrace was built in 1856 as the summer residence of Cardinal Savelli, the Secretary of State to Pope Pius IX. You can see his portrait in the grand drawing room, itself an echo of the island's Napoleonic past. The rooms, some of them with views of the valley, lead off from a superb staircase. Doubles €50–70 with shower or bath, depending on the season. Great value. *One free breakfast per room (except July–Aug) offered to our readers on presentation of this guide.*

Corte

20250

Hôtel de la Poste

2 pl. du Duc-de-Padoue.
Ⓣ04.95.46.01.37
Disabled access.

An old hotel on a shady square, with a dozen totally refurbished and reasonably priced rooms looking onto the *place* or out over the back. Doubles €33 with basin, €44.50 with shower/wc. Breakfast finishes at 9.30am. Good if you're on a budget and want somewhere central. They don't take credit cards, though.

L'Oliveraie

Lieu-dit Perru; head for the university, and when you come to the junction with the main road, take the road to Erbagolo. It's 150m further on the left.
Ⓣ04.95.46.06.32
Closed *Mon evening out of season; Nov.*

This very good restaurant, on the outskirts of town, is in a large stone house with a covered terrace and a garden full of fruit trees. Mme Mattei uses Corsican produce to prepare tasty dishes like *buglidicce* (fromage frais fritters), herb tart, squid stuffed with *brocciu* (mild sheep's-milk cheese), and for dessert, hazelnut and ground chestnut tart – the house speciality. Generous helpings. They take lots of groups at lunchtime and it's popular with students and staff from the nearby campus. Set menus €10–24. Credit cards not accepted. *Liqueur on the house offered to our readers on presentation of this guide.*

U Museu

Rampe Ribanelle; at the foot of the citadel, pl. des Armes.
Ⓣ04.95.61.08.36
Closed *8 Nov–2 April.*

An attractive restaurant where you'll get good food without paying a fortune. Open 10am–2pm and 5–10pm. Very pleasant terrace. €13 for main course + dessert option, or €15 for the menu. There are lots of choices, all of them – herb tart, wild boar stew, *délice* of chestnuts – truly delicious. If you're on a budget you can't go wrong with the salad of two different kinds of goat's cheese, almonds, bacon and potatoes. The jugs of AOC wine go down a treat. Credit cards not accepted.

Coti-Chiavari

20138

Hôtel-restaurant le Belvédère

Take the D55 from Porticcio towards the village of Coti-Chiavari; it's on the left of the Acqua Doria road before you get to the village.
Ⓣ04.95.27.10.32 Ⓕ04.95.27.12.99
Hotel closed *11 Nov–15 Feb.* **Restaurant closed** *evenings in winter; lunchtimes June–Oct.* **Disabled access. Car park.**

A long, low and fairly modern building on its own overlooking the bay of Ajaccio. From the arc of the circular terrace, you get one of the best views of the island.

Caroline, the patronne, really takes care of her guests. Good, generous Corsican dishes. Set menus €16 and €25. The rooms are lovely and have balconies: €50–65 for a double with shower/wc or bath. Breakfast €5. Half board, €90–106 for two, is obligatory in summer. This place is reliable and offers good service – nothing like the rip-off joints you'll find on the coast – but they don't accept credit cards. And it's a good idea to phone before coming, for the hotel as well as the restaurant.

Porto

20150

Hôtel le Colombo**

Porto village; on the right, just by the entrance to the village on the Calvi road.
Ⓣ04.95.26.10.14 Ⓕ04.95.26.19.90
Ⓦwww.porto-tourisme.com/colombo/
Closed *11 November–Easter.* **High chairs available.**

A small hotel in a classical vein, simply oozing charm, with a particularly attractive reception. The whole place is lined with wood and the walls have been painted blue with a sponge. The little garden is equally splendid. Double rooms from €54–110, according to the season and the position, with an excellent breakfast included. Rooms are also available for three or four people. All are decorated according to a different theme, and most of them offer a stunning view (in some cases, from their balcony) of the Gulf of Porto and the mountain. Very attentive service.

Porto-Vecchio

20137

Hôtel le Mistral**

5 rue Jean-Nicoli.
Ⓣ04.95.70.08.53 Ⓕ04.95.70.51.60
Closed *10 Nov–10 March.* **TV. Car park.**

Located in the old town, this attractive and comfortable two-star has doubles with shower/wc or bath for €54–104 depending on the season. (The high-season prices seem steep, but they tend to be in this town, and at least the rooms are meticulously kept.) You can also rent studios by the week. The car park is across the road.

Le Tourisme

12 cours Napoléon; it's in the old town near the church.
Ⓣ04.95.70.06.45
Closed *Sun lunchtime.*

You eat well at *Le Tourisme*, where the cuisine is light and very unusual. They do an excellent dish of spicy mussels *à la porto-vecchiaise*, and great dishes of the day like tagliatelle with asparagus and, for dessert, a soup of strawberries and bilberries. Menus €12 and €15–22. Try the *formule express*, with salad, a choice of pasta or *moules marinière* and *carpaccio* of melon; if you're really in a hurry, try the short menu with main and dessert. A little pricey for what it is but the quality is good and the service is speedy. *Apéritif on the house offered to our readers on presentation of this guide.*

Lecci-de-Porto-Vecchio

20137 (7km N)

Hôtel et Résidence Caranella Village

Route de Cala-Rossa; 3km along the road to Bastia, at La Trinité turn right at the Cala-Rossa signpost, turn left at the next roundabout and head straight on for 4km.
Ⓣ04.95.71.60.94 Ⓕ04.95.71.60.80
Ⓦwww.caranella-village.com
Closed *Jan.* **Disabled access. TV. Swimming pool. Car park.**

Set in flower-filled grounds just 300m from the Cala Rossa beach. About forty self-catering studios, villas and apartments (some with oven, microwave, TV, telephone and dishwasher). Most have a terrace and are set around the heated swimming pool. Facilities include a fitness centre, bike rental, a bar, restaurant, linen hire, a cleaning service and a washing room. Given the prices in Porto-Vecchio this is very good value. Standard rooms at €56–126, depending on the season; studios with shower and corner kitchen cost €560 per week in the high season; you pay more for a bathroom. The villas and apartments sleep four to six people. Friendly welcome and easy-going atmosphere. Reservations recommended.

Propriano

20110

Loft Hôtel**

3 rue Jean-Paul-Pandolfi.

Ⓣ04.95.76.17.48 Ⓕ04.95.76.22.04
Closed *1 Oct–14 April.* **Disabled access. TV. Car park.**

A converted old wine warehouse huddled among a group of houses. As you might expect from the name, the hotel has clean rooms with a modern minimalist look – pale tiles and blond wood. Doubles €41–60 depending on the season; the cheaper rooms are on the ground floor. Nice welcome.

Motel Aria Marina**

Lieu-dit la Cuparchiata. It's in the hills above Propriano; from the centre, take the road to Sartène then turn left towards Viggianello; left again and follow the signs to the motel.
Ⓣ04.95.76.04.32 Ⓕ04.95.76.25.01
Closed *11 Oct–1 April.* **TV. Swimming pool. Car park.**

This is a good motel, some distance from the brouhaha in Propriano and, better still, with a great view of the Gulf of Valinco. The studios or two-roomed apartments are spacious and have good facilities, and cost €60–81, depending on the season. In July and August they rent the studios by the week only at €572–628; the two- and three-roomed apartments cost more so you'll need to check. All the accommodation is sparklingly clean. Nice staff, and the pool is lovely, too.

Restaurant L'Hippocampe

Rue Jean-Paul-Pandolfi.
Ⓣ04.95.76.11.01
Closed *Sun and Mon out of season; Jan; Feb. Open lunchtimes and evenings July–Aug.*

Antoine, aka "The American", runs this place. He loves the sea and freshly caught fish – so what you eat in the evening is what he's pulled out of the Gulf of Valinco that morning. Good cuisine and good value too, served either in warm, simple surroundings or out on the terrace. Set menus €16 and €30 or around €30 à la carte including decent wine. Open noon–2pm and 7–11pm. *Free coffee offered to our readers on presentation of this guide.*

Saint-Florent

20217

Hôtel Maxime**

Route de la Cathédrale, off pl. des Portes.
Ⓣ04.95.37.05.30 Ⓕ04.95.37.13.07
Disabled access. TV. Car park.

A fairly new and very clean hotel, good value for the resort. Each room has a minibar and balcony; some of them overlook the Poggio river, where you can arrange to moor your (small) boat. Doubles €47–69 with shower or bath; prices vary with the season. There's a lock-up for motorbikes, as well as a private car park. Pets are not allowed.

Patrimonio

20253 (5km NE)

Hôtel U Casone

Take the D81 out of Saint-Florent and climb to the centre of Patrimonio, but don't take the left turn towards the church; continue 250m on the D81, then take the right hairpin and you'll see the sign.
Ⓣ04.95.37.14.46 Ⓕ04.95.37.17.15
Closed *1 Nov–1 March.* **Car park.**

Located in the upper village, this is a large house faced with grey rough-cast. It has a pretty garden, where you can have breakfast or enjoy the sun, and huge, well-maintained bedrooms with views over the countryside or the sea. Doubles €40–90, depending on facilities and season. There's a family atmosphere to this unpretentious place, and a friendly welcome from Mme Montemagni. Although there's no restaurant, make sure you try a bottle or two of the Clos Montemagni if you eat elsewhere – the vineyard isn't far. There's a lock-up for motorbikes and the beaches are about 3km away. Credit cards not accepted.

Sartène

20100

Hôtel Villa Piana***

Route de Propriano; it's 1km before Sartène.
Ⓣ04.95.77.07.04 Ⓕ04.95.73.45.65
Ⓦwww.lavillapiana.com
Closed *Nov–April.* **TV. Swimming pool. Car park.**

A pretty, ochre-coloured house amid trees and flowers with a delightful entrance and offering a charming welcome. The rooms have been carefully decorated, and most have a view over Sartène. Avoid the ones overlooking the back because they're not great, particularly those on the ground floor. Doubles €57–95, breakfast €8. Facilities include TV (on request), tennis court, bar and a pool with a superb panoramic view. Lock-up for motorbikes.

Saint-Lucie-de-Tallano

20112 (14km NE)

La Santa Lucia

Place du monument aux morts.
T04.95.78.81.28
Closed *Sun out of season; Jan.* **Car park.**

Excellent Corsican food. The cheaper menu at €15.30 is decent enough – if rather ordinary – but the €21.30 one really showcases the talents of the chefs. The dishes are very attractively presented, the food is tasty and the cooking judged to perfection: the wild boar and rabbit with myrtle are both superb. There's a pleasant terrace with a view of the fountain. *Free coffee offered to our readers on presentation of this guide.*

Solenzara

20145

Hôtel la Solenzara**

It's on the Bastia road as you leave town.
T04.95.57.42.18 F04.95.57.46.84
Wwww.lasolenzara.com
Einfo@lasolenzara.com
Closed *mid-Nov–mid-March.* **Disabled access. TV. Swimming pool. Car park.**

Built two hundred years ago by the Squire of Solenzara, this building has been simply and tastefully redecorated and is now a charming hotel. The old rooms are vast and have newly equipped bathrooms; the high ceilings mean that they're cool in summer, too. If you don't fancy these, there are a few more conventional rooms available in a new annexe. Tall palm trees sway in the garden, and there's a magnificent swimming pool. Direct access to the beach or the port. Reasonable prices for a place of such character. Doubles in the annexe €60–92 with shower/wc including breakfast; they're a little more expensive in the main building or with bath. *Seventh night free on a week-long stay (except May–Sept) offered to our readers on presentation of this guide.*

Zonza

20124

Hôtel-restaurant la Terrasse*

In the centre of the village, but set back from the main road; it's on the right as you come from the Ospédale.
T04.95.78.67.69 F04.95.78.73.50
Closed *31 Oct–1 April.* **Car park.**

The best thing about this place is the terrace – and, even better, you can eat on it. It's the best-positioned place in the village and boasts a view over the roofs of the town and the impressive mountains, so it's fantastic at sunset. Good Corsican food, too: the house charcuterie is particularly tasty and their regional dishes are the genuine article, served in generous helpings. Highlights include wild boar with noodles, cannelloni and chestnut desserts. Menus €15.50–28.50. Open 11.30am–2.30pm and 7–9.30pm. The owners, the Mondolini-Pietris, welcome you with warmth and good humour. The renovated rooms are simple and well maintained; some have a terrace over the valley. There isn't a half-board requirement but they do like you to have lunch or dinner. Since the cooking is good and prices are fair, that's not much of a bind. Double rooms €48.90–60.90 with basin, shower/wc or bath, depending on the season. Half board €48.80–53.30 per person. Credit cards not accepted. *10% discount on a room (April–June and Oct) offered to our readers on presentation of this guide.*

Franche-Comté

Arbois

39600

🏃 🏠 Hôtel des Messageries**

2 rue de Courcelles.
Ⓣ03.84.66.13.43 Ⓕ03.84.37.41.09
Ⓔhotel.lesmessageries@wanadoo.fr
Closed *Wed 11am–5pm out of season; Dec; Jan.* **TV. High chairs available.**

Old post house with a nice stone exterior – all the atmosphere of the old days, and all mod cons. Rooms are comfy, and some have been renovated; €31 with basin or shower, €52 with shower/wc or bath. There's no restaurant, but there is a peaceful bar with a pretty tree-shaded terrace. It's a popular stopping point for foreign travellers passing through, so there's an international feel.

🏃 |●| La Balance - Mets et Vins

47 rue de Courcelles.
Ⓣ03.84.37.45.00
Closed *Sun evening; Tues and Wed except for public holidays (Wed only 14 July–20 Aug); 15 Dec–31 Jan.* **High chairs available. Disabled access. Car park.**

The talented chef at this famed restaurant is onto a winner – the atmosphere is lively and genuinely friendly and there's a lovely terrace. Menus are varied, dishes local with a modern touch and prices modest. The lunch *formule*, €14 (not served Sun), includes dish of the day, dessert, a glass of wine and coffee; there are other menus at €19–36. Many dishes use Jura wines to very good effect. The *sommelier* helps you through the extensive and fairly-priced wine list and many are served by the glass. Reservations highly recommended. *Free glass of Marc du Jura wine offered to our readers on presentation of this guide.*

Salins-Les-Bains

39110 (17km NE)

🏠 |●| Le Relais de Pont-d'héry

It's 3km southeast of Salins on the D266, the Champignole to Chaux-Champagny road.
Ⓣ03.84.73.06.54 Ⓕ03.84.73.19.00
Closed *Mon evening and Tues Sept–May; Mon only in summer; 1st fortnight in Nov; Feb school holidays.* **Swimming pool. High chairs and games available. TV. Car park.**

A nice little place inside a dreary-looking house on the edge of the road. The dining room is pretty and the terrace in the garden lovely in summer, with the added attraction of the pool. There are just two rooms but they're spacious and comfortable. Doubles with bath €45. The cuisine is bang up to date and full of fanciful ideas and flavours. Weekday lunch menu for €12 then others at €16–35; they all include cheese and dessert. *A glass of Coupe de Crémant sparkling wine with dessert offered to our readers on presentation of this guide.*

Baume-Les-Dames

25110

🏃 🏠 |●| Hostellerie du Château d'As***

24 rue du Château-Gaillard.
Ⓣ03.81.84.00.66 Ⓕ03.81.84.59.67

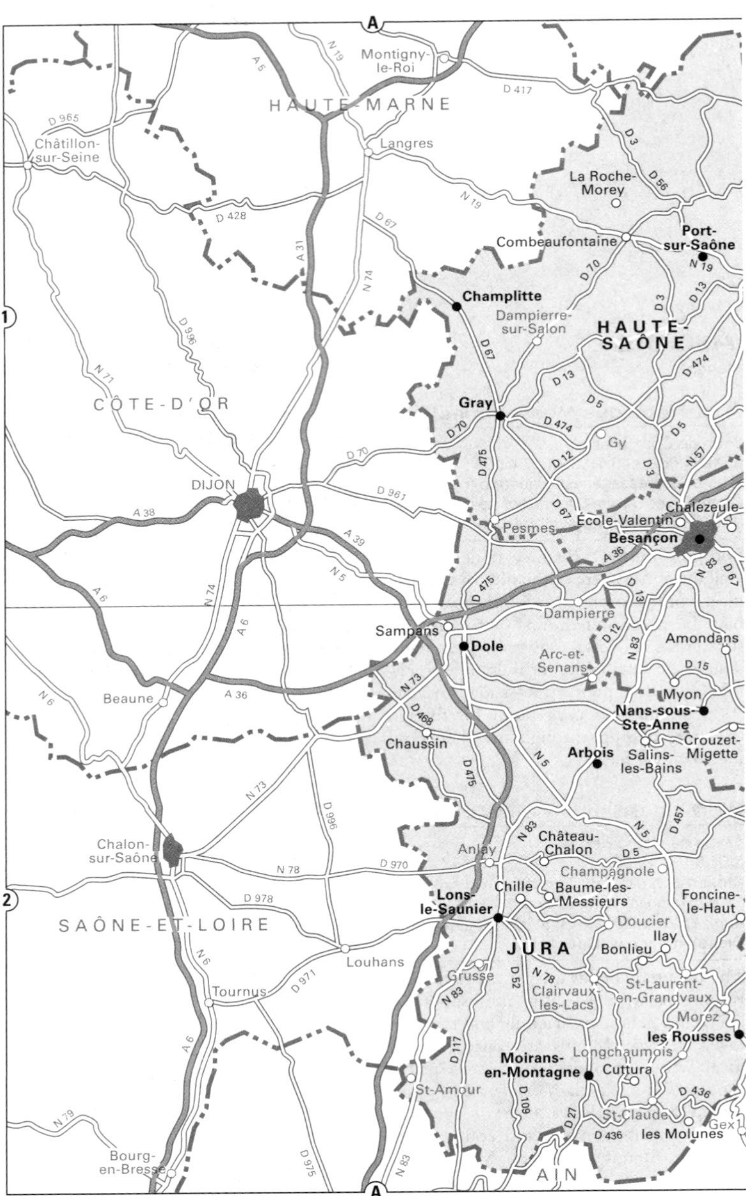
A
1
2
HAUTE-MARNE
CÔTE-D'OR
HAUTE-SAÔNE
SAÔNE-ET-LOIRE
JURA
AIN
Montigny-le-Roi
Langres
Châtillon-sur-Seine
La Roche-Morey
Combeaufontaine
Port-sur-Saône
Champlitte
Dampierre-sur-Salon
Gray
Gy
DIJON
Pesmes
École-Valentin
Chalezeule
Besançon
Dampierre
Sampans
Dole
Arc-et-Senans
Amondans
Myon
Nans-sous-Ste-Anne
Crouzet-Migette
Salins-les-Bains
Arbois
Beaune
Chaussin
Chalon-sur-Saône
Château-Chalon
Anlay
Champagnole
Chille
Baume-les-Messieurs
Foncine-le-Haut
Lons-le-Saunier
Doucier
Ilay
Bonlieu
Louhans
Grusse
Clairvaux-les-Lacs
St-Laurent-en-Grandvaux
Tournus
Morez
les Rousses
Longchaumois
Moirans-en-Montagne
Cuttura
St-Amour
St-Claude
les Molunes
Gex
Bourg-en-Bresse
A 5
N 19
D 417
D 965
D 3
D 56
D 428
N 19
D 67
A 31
N 74
D 70
D 13
D 996
N 71
D 67
D 13
D 474
D 5
D 474
D 70
D 475
D 12
D 5
D 3
N 57
D 70
D 961
D 67
A 38
A 39
A 36
N 83
D 67
N 5
D 475
D 13
A 6
N 74
A 6
D 12
N 83
D 15
A 36
N 6
N 73
D 468
D 475
N 5
N 73
D 996
N 83
N 5
D 457
D 5
N 78
D 970
D 978
N 6
D 52
N 78
D 971
N 83
D 117
A 6
D 109
D 27
D 436
D 436
N 79
D 975
N 83

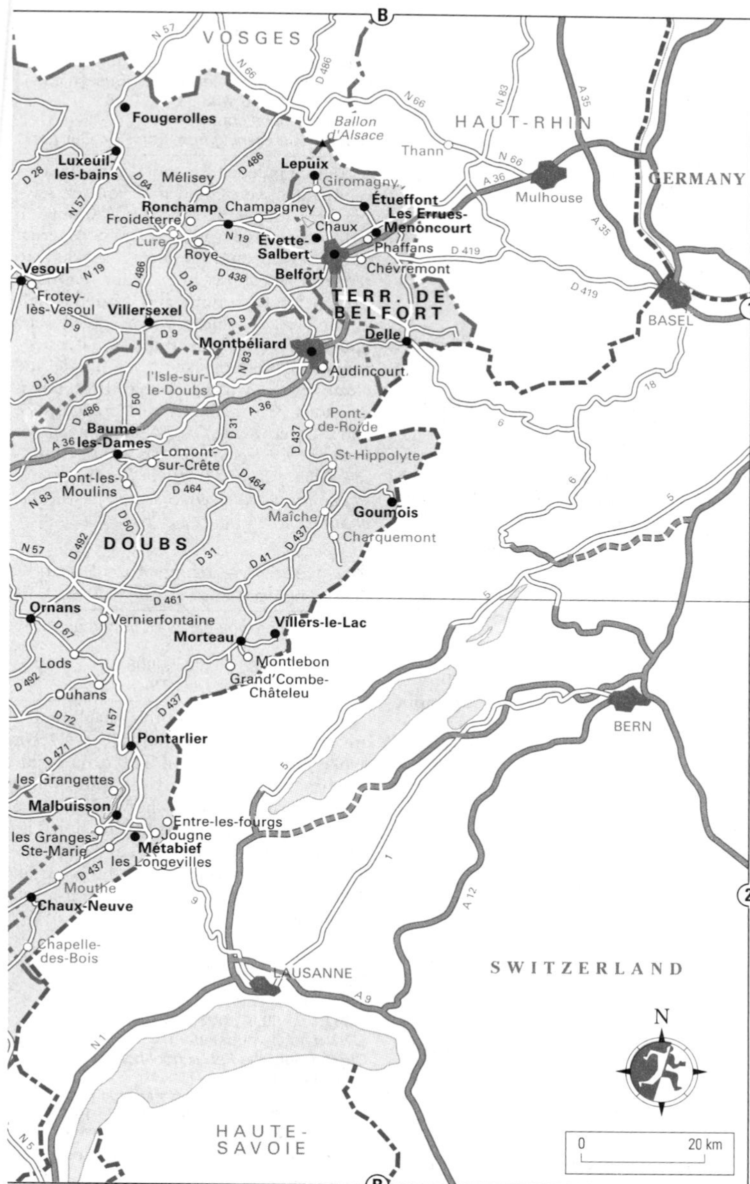

9 FRANCHE-COMTÉ

ⓦwww.chateau-das.fr
Closed *Sun evening and Mon; last week of Jan; 1st week of Feb; last fortnight in Nov; 1st fortnight in Dec.* **TV. Car park.**

A pair of brothers – both gifted cooks – set up this place. The dining room is big and round and somewhat sombre in atmosphere. The weekday lunch menu (€25) offers lots of choice. There are others (€29–68) featuring local dishes with a smattering of individuality; good wine list, too. Doubles €57; half board from €58 per person. Generous breakfast. There's a sauna. *10% discount on the room rate 1 Oct–30 March offered to our readers on presentation of this guide.*

Pont-les-Moulins

25110 (8 km S)

L'Auberge des Moulins**

Route de Pontarlier; take the D50.
Ⓣ03.81.84.09.99 Ⓕ03.81.84.04.44
Ⓔauberge.desmoulins@wanadoo.fr
Closed *22 Dec–28 Jan; restaurant closed Fri; Sat lunch; Sun out of season.*

A cosy spot in the Cusancin valley. Attractive, very comfortable rooms in various sizes and styles. Doubles €49 with shower/wc or bath. There's also an apartment for four people. In the restaurant, a very reasonable menu at €16 (except Sun), then others going up to €29. The chef is fond of using fish, especially trout from farm ponds. *One breakfast per person, in a double room offered to our readers on presentation of this guide.*

Lomont-sur-Crête

25110 (9km E)

Chez La Marthe

23 Grande-Rue.
Ⓣ03.81.84.01.50
Closed Sun evening; end of Aug. Disabled access.

A friendly, simple village café-restaurant. Nice family dishes prepared using good produce. If you want fish, whitebait or trout, you have to order them beforehand because the cook uses fresh (not frozen) fish. They also serve frogs' legs and game in season. Cheapest menu at €11.50. A surprise of a place. *Free coffee offered to our readers on presentation of this guide.*

Belfort

90000

Au Relais d'Alsace**

5 av. de la Laurencie; it's 500m from the centre, north of the town walls (Brisach gate).
Ⓣ03.84.22.15.55 Ⓕ03.84.28.70.48
ⓦwww.arahotel.com
Closed *Sun evening from 9pm.* **TV. Car park.**

This little independent hotel is highly recommended; you could find yourself staying here longer than planned. About ten years ago, a dynamic Franco-Algerian couple, Kim and Georges, decided to reopen this defunct hotel. They renovated it from top to bottom, and created a welcoming place where you're greeted by Kim's infectious cheerfulness. The bedrooms are nothing fancy, but simple and clean; €34–43 for a double. Breakfast is delicious (€5 including real orange juice and hot croissants). *10% discount on the room rate for a minimum stay of two consecutive nights 1 Sept–31 May, or free fruit juice or soft drink, offered to our readers on presentation of this guide.*

Hôtel-restaurant Le Saint-Christophe**

Place d'Armes; you can walk from the château.
Ⓣ03.84.55.88.88 Ⓕ03.84.54.08.77
Closed *last week in Dec.* **TV.**

The dynamic owners of this establishment are always looking to improve it. Décor evokes the Alsace region. The main building has comfortable and spacious double rooms from €60 with shower/wc; some have a view of the town's famous lion. The nearby annexe is very quiet, and has doubles with shower/wc or bath for €54. *10% discount on the room rate offered to our readers on presentation of this guide.*

Hôtel Vauban**

4 rue du Magasin.
Ⓣ03.84.21.59.37 Ⓕ03.84.21.41.67
ⓦwww.hotel-vauban.com
Closed *Sun; the Feb school holidays; Christmas.* **TV.**

The hotel is in a peaceful district just a few minutes' walk from the old town. The owner has covered the walls with his paintings, adding freshness and a party atmosphere to the place. Pleasant bedrooms, some opening onto the lovely garden; doubles with shower or bath start at €51. On fine days, you can breakfast (€6) beside the lily pond and enjoy the birdsong. No pets.

🏠 |●| 🏃 Grand Hôtel du Tonneau d'Or***

1 rue Reiset.
Ⓣ03.84.58.57.56 Ⓕ03.84.58.57.50
Ⓦwww.tonneaudor.fr
Closed Sat; Sun (except first in month); Aug. **Disabled access. TV. Car park.**

The foyer is like the hall of a palace, with an elaborately decorated ceiling, grand staircase and elegant, turn-of-the-century charm. There's a lovely Art Nouveau rotunda – as you'll gather, this small luxury establishment is full of character. Spacious and comfortable rooms are €98 with bath; they're decorated in a modern and tasteful style. There's a well-run restaurant serving traditional cuisine (*andouillette, confit*) with a touch of originality. Single set menu for €22.50. Credit cards not accepted. *A free breakfast per person offered to our readers on presentation of this guide.*

|●| L'Auberge des Trois Chênes

29 rue de Soissons; from the town centre take the Vesoul road (boulevard Kennedy), then follow the signs to the Alstom factory and Cravanche. The restaurant is opposite the factory.
Ⓣ03.84.22.19.45
Closed *evenings Mon–Wed; Aug.* **Disabled access. Car park.**

The comfortable, cosy inn, just outside town, specializes in modern cuisine which is anchored in tradition. There's a decent lunch menu for €12 on weekdays with three others from €25–32, listing super-fresh dishes; many of the veggies come from the garden. Menus are changed four times per year. Reasonably priced wines.

|●| 🏃 L'Ambroisie

2 pl. de la Grande Fontaine.
Ⓣ03.84.28.67.00
Closed *Tues lunchtime; Wed.*

A hushed little restaurant in the centre of town offering a successful new view of traditional cuisine. Nothing is left to chance and the careful presentation only serves to enhance the flavours of the house specialities; tasty morel-filled pastry cases, moist pike soufflé and blueberry *sabayon*. There are several menus ranging from €13.75 (weekday lunchtime) up to €36, to choose from. It's one of the best places around, run by a genuinely likeable couple who pay a lot of attention to the views and comments of their guests. Quality wines, but they're pricey. *Free coffee offered to our readers on presentation of this guide.*

|●| Le Molière

6 rue de l'Étuve.
Ⓣ03.84.21.86.38 Ⓕ03.84.58.01.22
Closed *Tues evening; Wed.* **Disabled access.**

This establishment is in an attractive tree-lined square, surrounded by smart buildings fronted with local sandstone. Only fresh produce is used here and the owner makes a trip to Mulhouse every morning to get his fish. The à la carte choice is almost too extensive, and there's a selection of menus at €21 (weekdays) and up to €45. Here's a taster: scallops pan-fried with honey, baked sea bream, chicken sautéed with pears, and duck in spiced *croûte*. Delicious desserts and impressive wine list (but check what you are being served and the price). The custom of drinking a *digestif* at the end of the meal may be going out of fashion, but here there's a large selection of liqueurs.

Chèvremont

340 (4km E)

|●| 🏃 Les Amis de Georges

14 bis rue du Texas.
Ⓣ03.84.27.50.55
Closed *Sat lunchtime; Sun evening; Mon; Ist fortnight of Jan; Ist fortnight Sept.* **High chairs available. Disabled access.**

The building has the appealing look of a chalet, and the fortifying cooking features *fondues* and *raclette*. Weekday lunch menu at €13 and others up to €23. What really gets you going, though, is the music. Jean-Luc plays French *chansons* all night long featuring all the great Georges – Moustaki, Brassens – and his enthusiastic guests sing along. *Free coffee offered to our readers on presentation of this guide.*

Phaffans

90150 (7km NE)

|●| 🏃 L'Auberge de Phaffans

10 rue de la Mairie. Take the N83, then turn right onto the D46 in the direction of Denney.

Ⓣ03.84.29.80.97 Ⓕ03.84.29.95.24
Closed *Sat lunchtime; Sun; Mon; 22 June–15 July; 20–31 Dec.* **Car park.**

The influence of nearby Alsace is evident in this quaint little village inn. They serve traditional dishes and their speciality is frogs' legs, guaranteed fresh year-round thanks to regular arrivals from the Vendée. The same goes for the farmed eels, served from April to December. They also offer unmissable morel mushrooms *en croûte*, pigeon *paysanne* with prunes, quails with red and white grapes and Arbois wine, marinated leg of venison in season and raw boar ham. Dish of the day €11 during the week; menus €17 and €22. *Free apéritif offered to our readers on presentation of this guide.*

Chaux

90330 (10km N)

Restaurant L'Auberge de la Vaivre

36 Grande-Rue; take the D465.
Ⓣ03.84.27.10.61
Closed *Sat; mid-July to mid-Aug.* **Car park.**

This inn on the Vosges road is run by a mother and daughter who have decorated it most attractively; they really make you feel welcome. It's an old barn with a mezzanine. A lot of care goes into preparing traditional dishes such as terrines, freshly caught trout, *saucisson en brioche*, duck *confit* with cider, and *émincé* of chicken liver with *knoepfle*. They also offer delicious home-made puddings including fresh fruit tarts, *biscuit* with chocolate, and hazelnut dessert. Lunch menu €14.50, with two others at €23 and €30. A nicely presented wine list, served by the glass or jug. *Free coffee offered to our readers on presentation of this guide.*

Besançon

25000

See map opposite

Auberge de la Malate**

Chemin de la Malate. It's 4km out of the centre in the direction of Lausanne; after the Porte Taillée, take the Calèze-Arcier road. **Off map B2-1**
Ⓣ03.81.82.15.16
Restaurant closed *Sun evening; Mon lunchtime; Jan–Feb.* **TV. Car park.**

A picturesque country inn just out of town in the forest facing the Doubs – peace and quiet are assured. Fairly comfortable rooms; doubles €31 or €35. The restaurant is lovely in summer, when you can sit in the shade near the water's edge. Regional dishes with fish as the speciality – small fry or fillets of perch or zander. Menus €12 (weekday lunchtimes) and €19–26.

Hôtel du Nord**

8–10 rue Moncey. **Map B1-2**
Ⓣ03.81.81.34.56 Ⓕ03.81.81.85.96
Ⓦwww.hotel-du-nord-besancon.com
Disabled access. TV. Pay car park.

A pleasant city-centre hotel run by real professionals who are always ready to be of service. Some 44 functional but comfortable and impeccably maintained rooms with good facilities – several have two double beds. Good bathrooms, double glazing and room service. Reasonable prices; doubles with shower/wc or bath €37–53. Parking €5.80. The public areas have been completely refurbished. *10% discount on the room rate July and Aug offered to our readers on presentation of this guide.*

Hôtel Regina**

91 Grande-Rue. **Map B2-4**
Ⓣ03.81.81.50.22 Ⓕ03.81.81.60.20
Ⓦwww.efranxce.fr/hotelregina
Closed *2–10 Aug; 23 Dec–2 Jan.* **TV. Car park and lock-up garage.**

Charming, quiet and comfortable hotel with a pleasant inner courtyard – a haven of peace and tranquillity in the city centre. The rooms are regularly redecorated, and some have balconies or terraces hung with wisteria; doubles €40–44 with shower/wc or bath. There's also a small studio. Nice welcome. Credit cards not accepted. *10% discount on the room rate for a two-night stay offered to our readers on presentation of this guide.*

Le Granvelle**

13 rue du Général-Lecourbe. **Map B2-3**
Ⓣ03.81.81.33.92 Ⓕ03.81.81.31.77
Ⓦwww.hotel-granvelle.fr
TV. High chairs available.Pay car park.

An elegant stone-built hotel located in a wealthy street with many private mansions in a quiet part of the city, not far from the citadel. It's comfortable and characterful, and the owners have created a relaxing atmosphere. All the rooms look out onto an attractive paved courtyard. Doubles

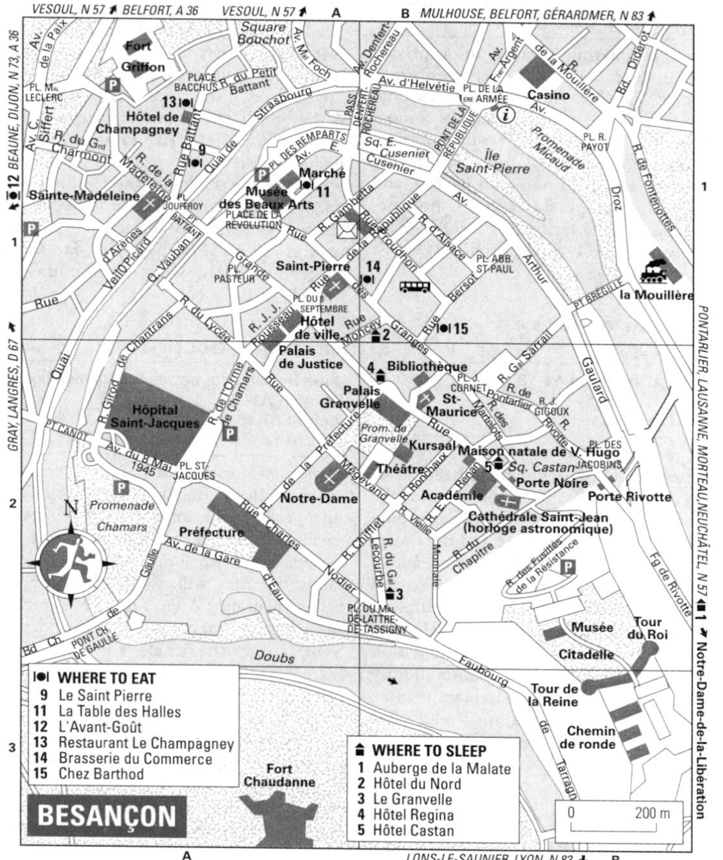
VESOUL, N 57 BELFORT, A 36
VESOUL, N 57
A
B
MULHOUSE, BELFORT, GÉRARDMER, N 83
12 BEAUNE, DIJON, N 73, A 36
GRAY, LANGRES, D 67
PONTARLIER, LAUSANNE, MORTEAU, NEUCHÂTEL, N 57 1 Notre-Dame-de-la-Libération
LONS-LE-SAUNIER, LYON, N 83
1
2
3
Fort Griffon
Square Bouchot
PLACE BACCHUS
R. du Petit Battant
Hôtel de Champagney
13
9
Sainte-Madeleine
Marché
Musée des Beaux Arts
11
PLACE DE LA RÉVOLUTION
Saint-Pierre
14
Hôtel de ville
2
Palais de Justice
4
Bibliothèque
Palais Granvelle
St-Maurice
15
Hôpital Saint-Jacques
Kursaal
Théâtre
Maison natale de V. Hugo
5
Sq. Castan
Porte Noire
Porte Rivotte
Académie
Notre-Dame
Cathédrale Saint-Jean (horloge astronomique)
Préfecture
Promenade Chamars
3
Casino
Île Saint-Pierre
Promenade Micaud
la Mouillère
Musée
Citadelle
Tour du Roi
Tour de la Reine
Chemin de ronde
Doubs
Fort Chaudanne
WHERE TO EAT
9 Le Saint Pierre
11 La Table des Halles
12 L'Avant-Goût
13 Restaurant Le Champagney
14 Brasserie du Commerce
15 Chez Barthod
WHERE TO SLEEP
1 Auberge de la Malate
2 Hôtel du Nord
3 Le Granvelle
4 Hôtel Regina
5 Hôtel Castan
0 200 m
BESANÇON

with wc/shower €42–55; some are set up for families. *10% discount on the room rate offered to our readers on presentation of this guide.*

Hôtel Castan***

6 square Castan. **Map B2-5**
03.81.65.02.00 03.81.83.01.02
www.hotelcastan.fr
Closed *1–20 Aug; 24 Dec–3 Jan.* **Disabled access. TV. Car park.**

Chic and charming hotel in a private mansion dating back to the seventeenth century. Wide fireplaces, wood panelling, period furniture and a luxurious atmosphere. You can choose your room – Versailles, Pompadour, Pompeii (which has a Roman-style bathroom and Jacuzzi) and so on. Doubles are €105–160 – not surprising given the facilities. Breakfast €11. *Free welcome drink offered to our readers on presentation of this guide.*

Restaurant Le Champagney

37 rue Battant. **Map A1-13**
03.81.81.05.71
Closed *Sun.*

This restaurant is in a splendid sixteenth-century town house which has been sensitively renovated – in summer they make use of the old courtyard and set tables outside. Inside, the old fireplace and the beams of the original ceiling have been retained and the décor is a mixture of modern and baroque with lots of style but no stuffiness. The welcome and the service are efficient and cool, and the cuisine is a combination of classic favourites and contemporary inspiration. Jura wines are sold by the glass. Menus €12 (weekdays) and €15–28. *Free apéritif offered to our readers on presentation of this guide.*

Chez Barthod

22 rue Bersot. **Map B1-15**
03.81.82.27.14
Closed *Sun; Mon.*

This is first and foremost a wine bar, but first you come across a shop with many regional products. Then you can relax by a table at the back of the courtyard (but it's advisable to book the table first!). Gourmet dishes, not only from Eastern France but also from the South-West. Wherever their provenance, they are best appreciated when washed down by a good wine – and there's plenty of choice. Reckon on €14–25 à la carte. Friendly service and pleasant terrace.

Brasserie du Commerce

31 rue des Granges. **Map B1-14**
03.81.81.33.11
Closed *Christmas and New Year.* **Open** *daily from 8am (9am Sun) to 1 am (2am weekend).*

This brasserie, founded in 1873, is not only one of the oldest in the town, it's also the most beautiful: huge mirrors and stucco "pâtisseries" in pure Art-Deco style (although there's a more modern room on the mezzanine). Its famous regulars include Colette, who always stopped by when she was staying in the region. Today's clientele still manage to live up to the elegance of its surroundings. À la carte, reckon on €15. Dish of the day €9.50. Open on Sunday, which is something of a miracle in Besançon.

L'Avant-Goût

4 rue Richebourg; beside the train station.
Off map A1-12
03.81.81.48.86
Closed *Sat lunch; Sun; Mon.*

A pleasant surprise, three minutes from the centre of Besançon. Don't be put off by the unappealing exterior, for inside there is a small, friendly bar and a dining room that gets packed with lunchtime regulars who know that they will always find exemplary value for money. After a few years learning with great masters like Girardet in Switzerland, the chef, Thierry Perrod, branched out on its own and now conjures up unfussy but visually elegant dishes entirely on his own. He excels with fish, and his past experience as a pâtissier is put to good use in the desserts. Menus €15 (lunch) and upwards of €28 at dinner. Superb wine list with plenty of foreign vintages. Small terrace for summer evenings.

La Table des Halles

22 rue Gustave-Courbet; very close to the covered market. **Map A1-11**
03.81.50.62.74
Closed *Sun; Mon.*

An old Carmelite convent that became first a scooter shop then a rubber factory before being transformed into this New York-style loft by the interior designer Daniel

Humair: contemporary lamps and pictures, spotlights on the ceiling and on rails and comfortable, modern furniture contrasting with the beautiful vaults and imposing pillars. This trendy setting is matched by tasty experiments with traditional ingredients by the fine Burgundy chef Jean-Pierre Billoux: Morteau sausage with *court-bouillon*, snails with absinthe, poultry with Savagnin. The cooking focuses on the essential, both in its presentation and in the choice of flavours. Lunchtime menu €15; reckon on €25–30 à la carte. There is also a pretty inner courtyard.

Le Saint-Pierre

104 rue Battant. **Map A1-9**
03.81.81.20.20.99 03.81.81.97.33
Closed *Sat lunchtime; Sun; fortnight at Easter; Aug; fortnight at Christmas.*

There's a contrast of styles in this elegant setting – ancient beams, bare stone walls and contemporary pictures. Very good and sensitively prepared dishes, featuring lots of fish. First menu at €35 includes wine and coffee; other menus at €38–50. All are satisfying in every respect and the home-made bread is excellent. The atmosphere is welcoming and very relaxed even though this is one of the smarter places in town. Nice terrace in warm weather. *Free apéritif offered to our readers on presentation of this guide.*

Chalezeule

25220 (2.5km E)

Hôtel des Trois Îles**

1 rue des Vergers; it's on the Belfort road.
03.81.61.00.66 03.81.61.73.09
www.hoteldes3iles.com
Closed *21 Dec–6 Jan.* **TV. Car park.**

Amazing to find such a quiet village only a few minutes' drive from the town centre. It's a recently built hotel in a lovely garden enclosed by high walls; the garden and sitting room are for guests' use. It's part of the *Relais du Silence* group so the peace and quiet come as standard. Double rooms with shower/wc or bath €48–65. They serve evening meals for €16.

École-Valentin

25480 (6 km NW)

Le Valentin

Espace Valentin, Vert Bois Vallon; take the N57.
03.81.80.03.90
Closed *Sun evening; Mon; Feb half-term; first 3 weeks in Aug.* **High chairs available.**

Close to Besançon, a good spot to enjoy superbly fresh produce prepared with a sure touch and an exquisite balancing of flavours. The dishes are also beautifully presented, in a classical style. Outstanding dishes include ragoût of snails au Vieux Pontarlier or duck breast with Morello cherries. Menus €28–68. *Free coffee offered to our readers on presentation of this guide.*

Champlitte

70600

Hôtel-restaurant du Donjon**

46 rue de la République.
and 03.84.67.66.95
hotel.du.donjon@wanadoo.fr
Restaurant closed *Fri evening and Sat lunchtime end Sept to mid-June; Sun evening mid-Nov to mid-April; Mon mid-June to end Sept; 1–8 Jan.* **TV. High chairs available.**

The only remaining medieval element in this old house is the vaulted cellar which is used as the dining room. The cuisine is honest and traditional with a flash of individuality. Weekday menu €10.70 and others €17–21.50. Clean and comfortable rooms; the ten or so that have been redecorated in pastel tones are the lightest. Doubles with shower €30.50, €36.60 with shower/wc or bath.

Chaux-Neuve

25240

Auberge du Grand-Gît**

8 rue des Chaumelles; take the Mouthe road out of the village and then turn right 400m on.
03.81.69.25.75 03.81.69.15.44
Closed *Sun evening and Mon except public holidays; 28 March–4 May; 17 Oct–21 Dec.*
Disabled access. Car park.

Quiet place on the outskirts of the village. It's fairly new, but in keeping with local architecture with a sloping roof and wooden façade. Only eight bedrooms, but they're wood-panelled and cosy – €40–45 for a double with shower/wc and phone. Some have a lovely view of the surrounding countryside; no. 5 has a mezzanine and can sleep five. There are also two large rooms with four and six beds for hikers. Classic regional dishes predominate in the restaurant; menus €12.50 (Mon–Fri except public holidays), and €15.50–€20. The owner is a skiing instructor and uplands guide so he knows all the local long-distance footpaths and cross-country skiing routes intimately – it's the ideal place for sporty types and nature lovers, and gets lively in the evening. Credit cards not accepted. *Free apéritif offered to our readers on presentation of this guide.*

Foncine-le-Haut

39460 (15km SW)

Auberge Le Jardin de la Rivière**

Take the D437.
ⓣ03.84.51.90.59 ⓕ03.84.51.94.69
ⓔeve5@club-internet.fr
Closed *Sun evening out of season; fortnight early Oct.* **TV. Swimming pool. Car park.**

A young couple have taken over the place. The rooms are very classic, but they're comfortable. Doubles with shower/wc or bath €50. The food served in the restaurant is nicely presented and enlivened by an idea or two. Weekday lunch menu €11, then others at €16–25. It's a peaceful place, with a garden flanking the river bank.

Delle

90100

Restaurant Le Galopin

29 Grand-Rue; it's opposite the old town hall.
ⓣ03.84.36.17.52
Closed *Sun; Mon.*

This is where local lovers of good food meet – including many Swiss customers who pop over the border. They immediately make for the restaurant cellar, which is more than a hundred years old, to celebrate the potato – the main component of many dishes, such as *rösh galopin*; other local dishes include *roësti* with Morteau sausage or *à la cancoillotte* – in winter they also do hot cheesy baked potatoes. No set menus so expect to pay €18 or so for a meal. Good, inexpensive and friendly. *Free Kir or coffee offered to our readers on presentation of this guide.*

Dole

39100

Hôtel de la Cloche***

1 pl. Grévy.
ⓣ03.84.82.06.06 ⓕ03.84.72.73.82
ⓦwww.lacloche.fr
Closed *23 Dec–3 Jan.* **TV. High chairs available. Car park.**

A provincial hotel that started life as a coaching inn. It's conventional, with classical and rather bland décor. Nonetheless the rooms are clean and well maintained, the façade is pretty, there's a sauna upstairs, and it's in the middle of town – a big plus in a place where central hotels are a rare commodity. Inevitably, it's often full. Doubles with en-suite facilities from €50–65.

La Chaumière

346 av. du Maréchal-Juin.
ⓣ03.84.70.72.40 ⓕ03.84.79.25.60
ⓔhotelrestaurantlachaumiere@wanadoo.fr
Closed *Mon lunch; Sat lunch; Sun.* **Disabled access. TV. Swimming pool. Car park.**

A huge *faux* cottage by the roadside, hidden behind Virginia creeper and boasting a sweet garden. It's cosy and bourgeois, and the rooms are particularly comfortable, if a little old-fashioned, and maybe slightly overpriced – €60–70 for a double with shower/wc or bath. It owes its reputation to the quality of the cooking in the restaurant. The youthful chef is the latest in a long family line and produces delicious dishes on generous, regularly changing menus; €27–70. Pretty swimming pool.

Le Bec Fin

67 rue Pasteur; it's near the marina.
ⓣ03.84.82.43.43 ⓕ03.84.79.28.07
Closed *Tues and Wed except July–Aug; 1–15 Jan.*

Light, nicely decorated restaurant with some tables in the medieval cellar. The delicious seasonal cuisine prepared by a chef who has trained in some of the finest restaurants in the region. Menus €15 (weekday lunchtimes) and €24–52.

Sampans

39100 (4km NW)

Le Chalet du Mont-Roland**

Take the N5; before Monnières turn right

towards Mont Roland.
ⓣ03.84.72.04.55 ⓕ03.84.82.14.97
ⓦwww.chalet-montroland.com
Disabled access. TV. High chairs available. Car park.

This chalet is on the road to Notre-Dame-du-Mont-Roland, an important pilgrimage site. From the top of the mountain there's a superb view over Chaux Forest. It's definitely the place to spend a relaxing Sunday in the country. Double rooms with shower/wc or bath cost €44.50. The restaurant has its own gastronomic pilgrims from Dole who come to spend a weekend, giving it a chic but bustling atmosphere. There's a glassed-in terrace so you can make the most of the view. Robust regional fare with a weekday lunch menu at €14 and others €21–35, all highly calorific. *Free apéritif offered to our readers on presentation of this guide.*

Chaussin

39120 (20km SW)

Hôtel-restaurant Chez Bach**

4 pl. de l'Ancienne-Gare; take the N73, then turn onto the D468 at La Borde.
ⓣ03.84.81.80.38 ⓕ03.84.81.83.80
ⓦwww.hotel-bach.com
Closed *Sun evening; Mon lunchtime; Fri evening except July–Aug; 20 Dec–6 Jan.* **Disabled access. TV. High chairs and games available. Car park.**

Make a little detour to enjoy the gastronomic cuisine here. The large building doesn't look promising from the outside but its reputation has been established since the 1930s. Weekday menu at €15 and others €21–42; they all list fine regional specialities. The rooms are comfortable and you can keep in touch with friends via the Internet; it'll cost €52 for a double with shower/wc or bath. Half board costs €54 per person. *Free coffee offered to our readers on presentation of this guide.*

Errues-Menoncourt (Les)

90150

La Pomme d'Argent

13 rue de la Noye.
ⓣ and ⓕ03.84.27.63.69
Closed *Mon; Tues evening; Sun evening.* **Disabled access. High chairs available. Car park.**

This lovely place, well off the beaten track, is a real find. It's the welcoming restaurant that's the draw, where the commitment to service has been honed over twenty years. Fine, delicate cooking on menus priced €15 (weekdays only) and €19–45. Chef Stephane is something of a virtuoso, creating a great combination of flavours. The home-smoked salmon is succulent, the foie gras with figs a classic, and the frogs' legs and snail *cassolette* is superb. As for the *crème brûlée* with Bourbon vanilla – it's to die for.

Étueffont

90170

Auberge Aux Trois Bonheurs

34 Grande-Rue; north of Belfort, take the D23 from Valdoie.
ⓣ03.84.54.71.31
Closed *Sun and Tues evenings; Mon; closed every day in winter except Fri evening and Sat evening.* **Car park. Disabled access.**

If this elegant town-house is the *Inn of the Three Happinesses* then the fourth is the journey through flower-filled villages to get to there. It's built in brick and natural stone and occupies a delightful rustic setting. The restaurant is very popular because of the hearty, tasty cooking served in generous portions – it's a place for family gatherings and groups out on a spree. They come for fantastic home-made brawn, fried carp or zander, parsleyed frogs' legs with girolle mushrooms, the special *planchette des Trois Bonheurs*, *tartiflette* and good home-made desserts and fruit tarts. Weekday lunch menu €8.70, or €18.50 at other times. Reckon on around €17 à la carte, where seafood *pot-au-feu* is available.

Evette-Salbert

90350

Gîte de séjour Le Malsaucy

Le Malsaucy; leaving Belfort, go through Valdoie, then take the D24 (follow the direction of "Lac de Malsaucy").
ⓣ03.84.29.21.84ⓕ03.84.29.14.71
Closed *mid-Dec to mid-Jan.* **Car park.**

This is something like a huge youth hostel, with austere but very pleasant rooms and impeccable toilets on the landing. It is open to all comers, but it often has school parties staying so it's best to check availability beforehand. Rooms with two to four beds at €12.80 per night per person, €16.80 with breakfast. Menu €8.70 (with booking only). Nautical and open-air activities (special rates for our readers on presentation of this guide). Credit cards not accepted. *10% discount on a room (July–Aug) offered to our readers on presentation of this guide.*

Auberge du Lac

Lac de Malsaucy.
Ⓣ and Ⓕ03.84.29.14.10
Closed *Mon and Tues lunchtime in season; 1–15 March; 1–15 April; 16–31 Oct.*

This is a big pink house where you'll get a typical Franche-Comté welcome. There's a large, pleasant dining room with well-spaced tables and a terrace on the banks of the lake. Solid regional cooking: fried carp, *parmentier au Morteau* (a kind of shepherd's pie made with Jésus de Morteau, a local sausage), duck breast with bilberries, pan-fried langoustines with whisky and so on. During the week and on Sunday evenings there's a menu for €13, with others at €23–26; you'll pay around €25 à la carte. Good wines at affordable prices.

Fougerolles

70220

Restaurant Le Père Rota

8 Grande-Rue.
Ⓣ03.84.49.12.11 Ⓕ03.84.49.14.51
Ⓔjean-pierre.kuentz@wanadoo.fr
Closed *Sun evening; Mon; Tues evening; Jan.*
Disabled access. Car park.

Jean-Pierre Kuentz is a fantastic advocate of the cuisine of the Haute-Saône. He uses local produce of the highest quality but introduces inspiration from way beyond regional boundaries: duck terrine with sour cherries, poached John Dory, lobster with *vin jaune*, zander with powdered mustard, fillet of beef with red Jura wine sauce. The service is thoughtful and the table settings and modern, bright décor have been put together with care. Weekday menu €17 and others €22–55.

Goumois

25470

Hôtel-restaurant Taillard

3 rte. de la Corniche; at the top of the village.
Ⓣ03.81.44.20.75 Ⓕ03.81.44.26.15
Ⓦwww.hoteltaillard.com
Closed *Mon lunch; Wed lunch (except July–Aug); Nov–March.* **Disabled access. Swimming pool.**

Genuine charm and a serene setting has made this establishment popular for over a century. It seems to have everything: rooms with a beautiful view, a sunny terrace where you can have breakfast, food that is authentic and fresh, a pool and even a gym and sauna. Double rooms €46–84. Menus €22–48.

Auberge Le Moulin du Plain**

Lieu-dit Le Moulin du Plain; at Goumois on the D437b follow the road along the Doubs and look for the signs.
Ⓣ03.81.44.41.99 Ⓕ03.81.44.45.70
Ⓦwww.moulinduplain.com
Closed *1 Nov to end Feb.* **TV. High chairs available. Car park.**

This fairly modern house, built in the local style, is on the banks of the Doubs, which cuts through a fabulous wild valley. Pleasant and comfortable double rooms – all with shower/wc or bath – are €51.15–57.50; some have balconies. In the restaurant there are lots of fish dishes (the trout with shallots is excellent) alongside good country food. Weekday menu €15 and others from €18.50 to €30.50. *10% discount on the room rate (March–April and Oct) or a free apéritif offered to our readers on presentation of this guide.*

Gray

70100

Auberge de jeunesse Le Foyer

2 rue André-Maginot; the street lies perpendicular to the avenue de Verdun.
Ⓣ03.84.64.99.20 Ⓕ03.84.64.99.29
Ⓦwww.foyer-gray.asso.fr
Car park.

Attractively renovated modern building with a number of services, such as laundry. It is essentially a hostel for workers, but some rooms are reserved for FUAJ cardholders. €24 per person in a single or double room with shower/wc; €27 with breakfast. Self-service menu at €7.20. In July and August sports activities such as go-karts, archery, volleyball and fencing are organized (on a daily or weekly basis).

Hôtel-restaurant Le Bellevue**

1 av. Carnot.
03.84.64.53.50 03.84.64.53.69
www.hotel-bellevue-gray.com
Closed *Sat and Sun evenings out of season.* **TV. Car park.**

This hotel near the Saône is ageing gracefully. The rooms are still good and the ones looking onto the public gardens are quiet. Doubles €27.50 with hand-basin to €32.50 with shower/wc or bath. Two approaches in the restaurant: the brasserie does simple but substantial dishes of the day, like *coq au vin* with mashed potato, but you can also get more traditional food like zander with almonds or veal. Menus from €10.55 (weekdays only) and €16–25 with a good, standard choice. Or there's à la carte. Lovely terrace in summer.

Relais de la Prévôté

6 rue du Marché.
03.84.65.10.08
Closed *Sun; Mon; 27 Dec–8 Jan.*

The hushed atmosphere, the elegant room and almost intimidating size of the huge fireplace give you a real sense of privilege. And looking at the quality of the cooking and the price, you get a real sense of value for money. Menus €17–30.50.

Lepuix

90200

Le Saut de la Truite

Take the D465.
03.84.29.32.64 03.84.29.57.42
Closed *Fri; Dec–Jan.* **TV. Car park.**

This place is a mountain refuge that's been open since 1902 and run by the same family for forty years. It's in a superb setting in a forest clearing, facing the waterfall Saut de la Truite. There are some rooms but it's best as a place to eat, with trout freshly caught from the pond and a fine selection of regional specialities such as cockerel in Riesling, pigeon with chanterelles and bilberry tart. Game in season. Weekday menu €15 and others €20–24.

Lons-le-Saunier

39000

Hôtel-Restaurant Terminus**

37 av. Aristide-Briand.
03.84.24.41.83 03.84.26.68.07
www.hotel-terminus-lons.com
Hotel open *Sun 6–8pm out of season.*
Closed *20 Dec–6 Jan.* **TV. Pay car park.**

A solid establishment that was gradually fading as the years passed. Luckily a massive renovation programme has put a stop to the process of decay, without losing too much of the charm of the old building: the relatively large rooms have all been modernized and painted white so they look a lot brighter, if a little sparse. Doubles with shower/wc €40–46, with bath €59–69, according to season. The ones at the back are quieter. *Free apéritif or coffee offered to our readers on presentation of this guide.*

Le Bamboche

23 rue Perrin.
03.84.86.21.25
Closed *Sun; Mon.*

Young, friendly atmosphere and good, original cooking. About five types of *carpaccio* available: not only beef, but also veal, goose and rabbit. If raw meat turns your stomach, there are plenty of salads or grills cooked on the old-fashioned spit – try lamb shank, kebabs or veal kidneys. There's a weekday lunch *formule* for €10.50 and a menu at €16; you'll spend around €19 à la carte. This is the best place in town.

La Comedie

Place de la Comédie.
03.84.24.20.66 03.84.24.12.64
Closed *Sun; Mon; a fortnight at Easter; 3 weeks in Aug.* **High chairs available. Disabled access.**

This stylish restaurant, with a lovely flowery terrace, is the swankiest in town. Modern and traditional cuisine on menus at €15 and €26; it's around €40 à la carte.

Chille

39570 (2km NE)

🏃 🏠 |●| Hôtel-restaurant Parenthèse***

Head for Besançon on the D70, then go 1km on the D157 and look for the signs.
Ⓣ03.84.47.55.44 Ⓕ03.84.24.92.13
Ⓦwww.hotelparenthese.com
Restaurant closed *Sat lunchtime, Sun evening and Mon lunchtime, unless you book first.* **Disabled access. High chairs and games available. TV. Swimming pool. Car park.**

Set in a peaceful little village, this beautiful eighteenth-century residence has been converted into a comfortable hotel and restaurant, with wooded grounds and a superb swimming pool. The rooms deserve their three stars (those with whirlpool baths deserve four) and are decorated in tasteful modern style; €74–130. The restaurant offers a good classic cuisine; there's a weekday menu at €17.50 and others €21–45. Nice terrace. *One free breakfast per room per night offered to our readers on presentation of this guide.*

Château-Chalon

39210 (18km NE)

|●| 🏃 La Taverne du Roc

Rue de la Roche.
Ⓣ03.84.85.24.17
Closed *Mon evening and Tues in season; 15 Dec–15 March.*

A tiny restaurant with stone walls in a timeless house, right in the middle of Château-Chalon. The chef has been concocting delicious dishes for years – try her Bresse chicken with *vin jaune*, which is the best for miles around. Any of her Jura dishes are also worth a try. Menus €22 and €28. *Free coffee offered to our readers on presentation of this guide.*

Baume-les-Messieurs

39210 (20km NE)

🏃 |●| Restaurant des Grottes

Take the D471 to Roches-de-Beaume, then the D70.
Ⓣ03.84.48.23.15 Ⓕ03.84.44.61.59
Closed *evenings; Mon except in July and Aug; 15 Dec–10 March.* **Disabled access. Car park.**

The restaurant is in a little 1900 house opposite a marvellous foaming waterfall cascading down from the high rocks of the Baumes-les-Messieurs amphitheatre. Menus, €15–38, list mainly Franche-Comté specialities. The terrace is open in summer where you can enjoy platters of charcuterie or cheese washed down with a glass of Jura wine. *Free coffee offered to our readers on presentation of this guide.*

Luxeuil-les-Bains

70300

🏠 |●| Hôtel-restaurant Le Rallye

49 rue Edouart-Herriot.
Ⓣ03.84.40.04.92

There's a nice warm welcome here, though the dining rooms are a little tatty. Dishes are tasty and well presented; chicken topped with toasted Comté cheese, crispy-topped potato *au gratin* and divine apple tartlets. *Menu du jour* at €9.90, and others ranging from €11.40 up to the gastronomic menu at €29. Despite being on the main road, this place is a favourite spot for family Sunday lunches. Best to book. The hotel rooms are simple and clean, with doubles from €24.50.

🏃 🏠 |●| Hôtel-restaurant Beau Site***

18 rue Georges-Moulimard; it's close to the spa and the casino.
Ⓣ03.84.40.14.67 Ⓕ03.84.40.50.25
Closed *Fri evening; plus Sat lunchtime and Sun evening mid-Nov to mid-March; Christmas–New Year.* **TV. High chairs and games available. Swimming pool. Car park.**

Near the casino and the spa you find this large, very pleasing establishment surrounded by a green park with a swimming pool. Rooms are spread between the main building and an annexe: doubles with bath or shower/wc €55–65. Things have slipped a little at the restaurant, however; the service is slow and the dishes look lacklustre. That said, a glass of delicious Arbois wine helps deal with the long wait, as does a seat on the terrace. Weekday menu €13 and others €22–40. *Free coffee offered to our readers on presentation of this guide.*

Malbuisson

25160

Hôtel-restaurant Le Lac et Hôtel Beau Site***

31 Grande-Rue.
℗03.81.69.34.80 Ⓕ03.81.69.35.44
Ⓦwww.lelac-hotel.com
Closed *mid-Nov to mid-Dec (except weekends).* **Swimming pool.**

An institution in the area, in an elegant, imposing 1930s building with an annexe for guests on a tight budget. The amazing kitsch decoration is a little overpowering and the service slightly offhand, but the rooms have been attractively refurbished (ask for one with a balcony and a view of the lake). Doubles €32–107, depending on the degree of comfort. Half board €37–74.50. Menus €17–40. Classical cuisine and a fine dessert trolley, with tempting pâtisserie. Charming bar. The pool is in the big garden that slopes gently down to the lake. *Free coffee offered to our readers on presentation of this guide.*

Le Bon Accueil***

Grand-Rue; it's in the centre of the village.
℗03.81.69.30.58 Ⓕ03.81.69.37.60
Ⓔlebonacceuilfaivre@wanadoo.fr
Closed *Sun evening; Mon; Tues lunchtime; mid-Dec to mid-Jan; a week end April; a week around All Saints'.* **TV. Car park.**

The restaurant offers traditional cooking with a modern touch; the chef-owner, Marc Faivre, is committed to using only fresh, quality, local produce. A few specialities: fine tart with Morteau sausage, braised leeks with poached egg, tomatoes stuffed with snails and herbs with a parsley sauce and, for dessert, a gentian sorbet or *macaronade* with grapefruit. It's excellent, characterful cuisine. There's a *formule* (main dish, dessert, glass of wine, coffee) for €22 and menus €35 and €45. A few rooms at €58–68.

Granges-Sainte-Marie (Les)

25160 (3km SW)

Hôtel-restaurant du Coude**

℗03.81.69.31.57 Ⓕ03.81.69.33.90
Closed *Sun evening and Wed (except school holidays); mid-Nov to mid-Dec.* **Disabled access.**

Double rooms at €42 and €45. Menus €16–45. This restaurant has earned a good reputation in the region for its perch fillets, frogs' legs and other delicacies. The atmosphere is informal but the tables are laid out so that you have space to eat in comfort (not always the case in establishments of this kind).

Métabief

25370

Hôtel-restaurant L'Étoile des Neiges**

4 rue du Village.
℗03.81.49.11.21 Ⓕ03.81.49.26.91
Ⓦhoteletoiledesneiges.com
TV. Disabled access. High chairs available. Car park.

A modern building a little way away from the ski resort and above a small river. The fourteen renovated rooms are cosy and comfortable; all have balconies with exceptional views of the Mont d'Or or the countryside. Doubles €49. In the restaurant there's a welcoming family atmosphere. They serve local specialities using the freshest produce. Weekday lunch *formule* €9, with menus €16–22. *Free apéritif offered to our readers on presentation of this guide.*

Longevilles Mont d'Or (Les)

(4km SW)

Hôtel-Restaurant Les Sapins**

58 rue des Bief-Blanc; take the D45.
℗03.81.49.90.90 Ⓕ03.81.49.94.43
Closed *April; 1 Oct to mid-Dec.* **Car park.**

This place is situated in the centre of a little village which hasn't lost any of its character – despite being part of the Métabief resort. The pleasant rooms are the best value for money in the area. Doubles €26.50 with shower/wc up to €30.50 with bath. Worthwhile weekday menu at €10.50, with another at €15. Home-made regional cooking: *franc-comtoise* salad, cheese flan, *entrecôte* of beef and *gratin dauphinois.*

Jougne

25370 (5km E)

Hôtel-restaurant de la Couronne*

Place de l'Église; take the D9 and the N57 then head for the Swiss border.
Ⓣ03.81.49.10.50 Ⓕ03.81.49.19.77
Closed *Mon evenings (except school holidays); Sun evening; Nov.* **Disabled access. TV. Car park.**

Set on a proper village square with a church and fountain, this small country hotel is far enough away from the main road to be nice and quiet. Pleasant rooms €29–43. Reckon on €46–50 per person for half board. Nos. 11, 12 and 14 have a nice view over the Jougnenaz valley and you also get a lovely view from the garden. Classic cuisine with lots of Franche-Comté dishes: duck fillet with wild mushrooms, morels and *petit-gris* snails in flaky pastry, trout fillet in Savagnin. The cheapest menu is €15 (not Sun), and there are others for €23 and €39. *Free apéritif offered to our readers on presentation of this guide.*

Entre-les-Fourgs

25370 (8km NE)

Auberge les Petits Gris

3 pl. des Cloutiers; take the D9 then the N57 to Jougne, then take the D423.
Ⓣ03.81.49.12.93 Ⓕ03.81.49.13.93
Ⓦwww.hotel-les-petits-gris.com
Restaurant closed *Wed; 20 Sept–20 Oct.*

A well-run little inn with comfortable rooms in a quiet, isolated village at the foot of the ski runs (downhill and cross-country). The road goes no further, so you either have to stay here or go back down the mountain. If skiing is not for you, there are plenty of beautiful walks round these parts. Doubles €35–43. The restaurant serves unpretentious but well prepared local dishes. Cheapest menu €14, then others €17.50–27.50. Friendly service.

Moirans-en-Montagne

39260

Le Regardoir

45 av. de Franche-Comté; it's at the Belvédère. Take the D470 northwest of town.
Ⓣ03.84.42.01.15
Closed *Mon, Tues and Wed evenings except 15 June–30 Aug; Sept–April.*

Stop for a snack here just so you can take a seat on the terrace and enjoy the panoramic view over the Lac de Vouglans way below. There's something special about the light at sunset – it's a moment to linger over with an apéritif. Nice, smiling welcome and a straightforward menu, though the cook is serious about his work. Weekday menu €11.50 (wine included) and others €13 and €16. It's always full. *Free apéritif offered to our readers on presentation of this guide.*

Cuttura

39170 (20km E)

L'Auberge du Vieux Moulin

Restaurant du Lac; take the D470; it's between Moirans and St-Claude.
Ⓣ03.84.42.84.28
Closed *Fri evening; Sat lunchtime; Christmas school holidays.* **Car park.**

This is a lovely old water mill and you eat down by the water accompanied by ducks and moorhens. The short weekday lunch menu costs €12 and draws quite a crowd. Then you discover the other menus (€16.50–29) and the à la carte options: generous portions of good local cuisine with dishes such as fried foie gras with Morello cherries from Fougerolles, frogs' legs, crayfish in *vin jaune*, and so on. *Free coffee offered to our readers on presentation of this guide.*

Molunes (Les)

39310 (30km SE)

Le Collège

Take the D470 then the D436 to Saint-Claude then Septmoncel, then the D25 in the direction of Moussières; it's in the middle of the village.
Ⓣ03.84.45.52.34
Closed *Mon evening; Tues; 21 June–2 July; 27 Nov–25 Dec.* **High chairs available.**

In a hamlet 1250m up and so small it doesn't even have a church, this restaurant has a reputation that's spread through the Haut-Jura – it can seat 64 but there's often a fight to get in at the weekend. First-class weekday menu at €10 and several others at €13–24, which are just as good: the food is traditional and full of flavour. Attractively priced wine list. The décor has a genuine country feel.

Montbéliard

25200

Hôtel de la Balance***

40 rue de Belfort; it's in the old town.
Ⓣ03.81.96.77.41 Ⓕ03.81.91.47.16
Ⓦwww.hotel-la-balance.com
Closed *Christmas.* **Restaurant closed** *Sat; Sun.* **Disabled access. TV. High chairs and games available. Pay car park.**

Like a lot of the other buildings in the old town, the façade of this sixteenth-century house has been painted yellow. Inside, the elegant yellow-ochre dining room, the antique furniture and a solid wooden staircase add to the charm of the place – which definitely belies the rather sad image people tend to have of the town. The rooms are stylish, all with bath, and cost €66–80. If you're interested in history, ask for the room where Field Marshal Lattre de Tassigny stayed in 1944. Buffet breakfast €7.50. Classic and regional dishes are listed on the weekday menu at €11, and on the others from €18–22. Credit cards not accepted.

Chez Cass'Graine

4 rue du Général-Leclerc
Ⓣ03.81.91.09.97
Closed *Sat lunchtime; Sun; public holidays; 3 weeks in Aug.*

Reckon on €28 à la carte. It is hard to imagine a more delightful little family restaurant: a mother and daughter team produce all the superb seasonal food and complement it with fine wines and a warm welcome. The décor is highly original and, what is more, it's spruced up several times a year; the overall effect is like a picture from a design magazine, with wonderful tastes and aromas on top. This place has many loyal regulars, and it's easy to see why.

Audincourt

25400 (6km S)

Hôtel des Tilleuls**

51 av. Foch.
Ⓣ03.81.30.77.00 Ⓕ03.81.30.57.20
Ⓦwww.perso.wanadoo.fr/hotel.tilleuls
Disabled access. TV. Swimming pool. Car park.

In a quiet street – be sure to go to the *avenue*, not the *rue* Foch. The rooms are very well equipped with fridge, power shower and hairdryer, and the décor is modern but warm. They're dotted about the main building or in annexes around the garden where there's also a lovely heated swimming pool. Doubles €48–57; suites €57–62. There's no restaurant but they'll get meals brought in for you in the evening. *One free breakfast per room at the weekend offered to our readers on presentation of this guide.*

Morteau

25500

Hôtel des Montagnards**

7 bis pl. Carnot.
Ⓣ03.81.67.08.86 Ⓕ03.81.67.14.57
Disabled access. TV. Pay car park.

This is a small, friendly hotel in the centre of the village looking out onto the surrounding countryside. It offers attractive panelled rooms, some of which have been redecorated in pastel shades. Doubles €42.

Restaurant L'Époque

18 rue de la Louhière; it's on the Besançon road.
Ⓣ03.81.67.33.44 Ⓕ03.81.67.54.94
Ⓔjp.razurel@wanadoo.fr
Closed *Mon evening, Wed evening and Sun (except public holidays); 20 July–20 Aug.* **Car park.**

They know what they're about in this restaurant – the welcome is natural and the service friendly. There are a couple of bistro-like dining rooms where you feel instantly at home. The tasty food is inventive without ignoring its regional origins: sausage *de Morteau* in red Arbois wine, wild mushroom pastry cases and zander fillet with Comté cheese sauce. Set menus €13 (weekday lunchtimes) and €16–32. There's an impressive selection of whiskies. *Free house apéritif offered to our readers on presentation of this guide.*

Montlebon

25500 (2km SE)

Hôtel-restaurant Bellevue*

2 rue de Bellevue; it's on the D48.
Ⓣ03.81.67.00.05 Ⓕ03.81.67.04.74
Closed *Sun and Fri evenings in winter; 1–8 July; 15 Dec–15 Jan.* **TV. Car park.**

This Comptois farmhouse looks over the whole of the Morteau valley – truly a *belle vue*. The weekday lunch menu (€10) is a magnet for locals and the regional dishes are generously served and well prepared. Other menus €14.50–24.50. Rooms €31–40. *Free coffee offered to our readers on presentation of this guide.*

Grand'Combe Châteleu

25500 (4km S)

|●| Restaurant Faivre

Rue Principale.
☎03.81.68.84.63
Closed *Aug.*

A huge chalet with a cosy and very pleasant dining room. The classic, regional dishes betray little in the way of inventiveness but are decent and carefully prepared: trout, fillet of beef with morels and so on. A good place to stop. Lunch menu €17 and others €20–60.

Nans-sous-Sainte-Anne

25330

Hôtel de la Poste**

11 Grande-Rue
☎03.81.86.62.57 Ⓕ03.81.86.55.32
Ⓔhoteldelaposte@aol.com
Closed *Tues evening and Wed out of season; 20 Dec–31 Jan.*

A practical base for exploring the stunning but largely unknown Lison valley. A typical, no-frills, family-run country hotel-restaurant: ivy on the front, a bar-tobacconist's that is the village meeting point, wholesome local dishes at reasonable prices and simple but comfortable rooms with good bedding – not forgetting the terrace for fine days. Doubles with shower/wc €37. Menus €13–19. *Free coffee offered to our readers on presentation of this guide.*

Crouzet-Migette

25270 (4km SE)

|●| Auberge du Pont du Diable

Take the D103, D65, D492 or D9.
☎03.81.49.54.28
Closed *a week in Jan; Nov; Christmas and New York (but it's best to phone).*

Large, shared tables for enjoying cheap, filling and convivial meals. The fine local dishes are available (at around €10) throughout the day at the weekend. Snacks also on offer: menus €13 and €17.50. The friendly owner, Bobo, will enthusiastically guide you through the interesting selection of wines from Jura. In the evening, Marie and her band of helpers welcome you. There's a log fire and sometimes a singer-guitarist performing in the background. You can take horserides from the village next door (reckon on €13 per person, information in the bill). *Free coffee offered to our readers on presentation of this guide.*

Myon

25440 (15km NW)

|●| Auberge Marie

Take the D492, then turn left down the D15.
☎03.81.63.78.47
Closed *Sun evening; 2nd fortnight in Sept.*
Disabled access. Car park.

Charming country inn that is one of the last of a dying breed. Old-fashioned double rooms €35. Generous and unchanging specialities of the house: *croûte forestière*, fillet of zander with hazelnuts, pike sorbet with Savagnin. Half board €38. Menus €19–28. Lovely terrace and small garden, with traditional elements that only add to the charm: pergola, rose garden at the foot of the church. *Apéritif on the house offered to our readers on presentation of this guide.*

Ornans

25290

|●| Hôtel de France***

51 rue Pierre-Vernier.
☎03.81.62.24.44 Ⓕ03.81.62.12.03
Ⓔhoteldefrance@europost.org
Closed *Mon lunchtime; 8–22 Nov; 20 Dec–11 Feb.* **TV. Garden. Pay car park.**

Traditional hotel, very *Vieille France*, friendly and cosy. You can enjoy a lunchtime *formule* at the bar, while the classic restaurant has set menus for €23, €32 and €43, listing good regional cuisine. The rooms are comfortable and old-fashioned; some look out onto the famous Grand Pont, but the road is noisy. You'll get peace and quiet in the rooms at the back, which overlook the courtyard. Doubles €70–80. There's a big terrace and a garden behind the hotel. Private fishing.

Restaurant Le Courbet

34 rue Pierre-Vernier.
T 03.81.62.10.15
Closed *Mon evening (except July–Aug); Tues and Sun evenings (Nov to end March); mid-Feb to mid-March.* **High chairs available.**

Choose your meal from a menu illustrated with a Courbet painting (although the painter himself would have felt out of place in such a quiet, reflective place). The view over the Loue from the two terraces is magnificent, while the cooking is a gourmet's delight, as the masterly chef plays with different tastes and colours to bring out the qualities of the meticulously chosen fresh ingredients. Menus from €16–25 (with two or three courses).

Lods

25930 (12km SE)

Hôtel-restaurant La Truite d'Or**

40 rue du Moulin-Neuf; take the D67.
T 03.81.60.95.48 F 03.81.60.95.73
E latruite-dor@wanadoo.fr
Closed *Sun evening and Mon out of season; 15 Dec–25 Jan.* **TV. High chairs available. Car park.**

An old stone windmill with comfortable rooms at €43. Half board €46 per person. Fine regional dishes, such as trout with wine or local style (stuffed with salmon and chopped morels). Menus €15.50–41.50. *Free apéritif offered to our readers on presentation of this guide.*

Amondans

25330 (14km W)

Le Château d'Amondans***

9 rue Louise-Pommery.
T 03.81.86.53.14
W www.chateau-amondans.com
Closed *Mon evening; Wed; Sun evening; mid-Dec to mid-March.* **Disabled access. TV. Swimming pool. Car park.**

A classy place that isn't oppressive. It's one of the culinary hits of the region – the cooking is remarkable. Chef-owner Frédéric Médique brings a personal interpretation to traditional dishes: don't miss his speciality dessert, *l'Amondanais*. Menus €31 (not served Sun) and two other menus at €52 and €65. The setting is sumptuous, the welcome friendly and the service faultless. The wine list concentrates on the great classics of Burgundy, Bordeaux and Jura. Double rooms €65–75. *Free apéritif offered to our readers on presentation of this guide.*

Vernierfontaine

25580 (17km E)

L'Auberge Paysanne

18 rue du Stade; take the D492 in the direction of Saules, then the D392 to Guyans-Durnes then Vernierfontaine.
T and F 03.81.60.05.21
Closed *Tues evening to Thurs; Mon–Fri between early Nov and early March; 10 days end June to early July; Dec; Jan.* **Car park.**

An old farmhouse in a remote village way out in the country. The décor is cluttered but the cuisine is traditional and full of flavour, utilizing a panoply of wonderful local produce: Morteau sausage, *roësti* (grated potatoes fried in a heavy pan), flaky pastry cases with morels in rich sauce, terrines. First menu at €11.50 and others €14–23. There are four rooms with wood-panelling; doubles €37–40. Gigantic breakfast. Credit cards not accepted. *10% discount on the room rate (mid-Oct–end March) offered to our readers on presentation of this guide.*

Pontarlier

25300

Hôtel-Restaurant le Saint-Pierre*

3 pl. Saint-Pierre.
T 03.81.46.50.80 F 03.81.46.87.80
TV.

This place sits on a square in an area that feels rather quiet and villagey. Nearly all the rooms look out on to the porte Saint-Pierre, the rather elaborate triumphal arch that has become the symbol of the town. The double rooms with shower/wc aren't exactly huge, but they are stylish as well as good value with prices at €27.50–45.50 according to level of comfort. The restaurant serves decent traditional food; menus €11 (weekday lunchtimes), €12.50 and €18. They have the sunniest terrace in town – a great place to linger over an apéritif.

Grangettes (Les)

25160 (12km S)

Hôtel-restaurant Bon Repos**

It's on the lac de Saint-Point on the D129.
Ⓣ03.81.69.62.95 Ⓕ03.81.69.61.61
Ⓦwww.hotelbonrepos.com
Closed *Sun evening and Mon out of season; 17 Oct–21 Dec.* **TV. High chairs available. Car park.**

On the edge of a little village by the lake. An old-fashioned inn – the tablecloths are white and the welcome is inviting. Substantial platters of home-made charcuterie and fine fish specialities. Menus €14.45–30.60. Comfortable, well-maintained rooms; those that have been recently renovated are quite charming. Doubles €36–42.70.

Ouhans

25520 (17km NW)

Hôtel-restaurant des Sources de la Loue**

13 Grande-Rue; take the N57, and at Saint-Gorgon-Main turn left onto the D41.
Ⓣ03.81.69.90.06 Ⓕ03.81.69.93.17
Ⓦwww.hotel-sources-de-la-loue.com
Closed *Fri evening, Sat lunchtime and Sun evenings out of season; 20 Dec–15 Jan.* **TV. High chairs available. Car park.**

A lovely inn in an unspoilt village amidst wonderful countryside. The cooking concentrates on local dishes, as you would expect – they specialize in house smoked salmon and good meats. Weekday lunch menu €11 and others €14.30–33. Pleasant, simple rooms (some in the roof), which at €40–47 are reasonably priced for the area. Half board €47–51.70 per person. They don't accept debit or credit cards. *Free coffee offered to our readers on presentation of this guide.*

Port-sur-Saône

70170

Hôtel-restaurant de la Paix

3 rue Jean-Bogé; it's opposite the church.
Ⓣ03.84.91.52.80 Ⓕ03.84.91.61.21
Closed *Sun evening; Jan.*

In a sixteenth-century priory, this hotel has been refurbished nicely so the decoration is in keeping with the building. Doubles €30 with basin, €36 with shower/wc; they're all quiet, as it's on a pedestrianized street. Unpretentious cooking and traditional dishes: morels in pastry cases, stew of zander and salmon, *coq au vin jaune*. Weekday menu €9.80 and others €12.50–23. There's a pretty, shaded terrace. *Free apéritif offered to our readers on presentation of this guide.*

Restaurant La Pomme d'Or

1 rue Saint-Valère.
Ⓣ03.84.91.52.66 Ⓕ03.84.78.14.16
Ⓦlasaone.com
Closed *Sun evening; Mon; 3 weeks from the end of Aug to early Sept.* **Disabled access.**

You eat in a smart little dining room right on the banks of the Saône. The cuisine is good and dishes change with the seasons: *oeufs en meurette*, pan-fried Jura snails with wild mushrooms and Noilly sauce, fish and meat terrines, zander *au beurre blanc*, *fricassée* of kidneys with mustard, hot duck tart, red mullet fillets in wine – and for dessert don't miss out on the house speciality, golden apples in leaves. Menus €9.20–26. In summer, you might find a table on the tiny terrace overlooking the water.

Combeaufontaine

70120 (12km W)

Hôtel-restaurant Le Balcon**

Take the N19.
Ⓣ03.84.92.11.13 Ⓕ03.84.92.15.89
Closed *Sun evening; Mon; Tues lunchtime; 28 June–7 July; 26 Dec–12 Jan.* **TV. Car park.**

A former coaching inn smothered with ivy and boasting a flower garden. It's a magnificent house with a really warm atmosphere. Pleasant, simple rooms are €39 with shower/wc or €48 with bath – because the hotel is on the main road, the ones at the back are quieter. There are delicious dishes like chicken in *vin jaune* with morels or Montbéliard sausage with lentils, as well as more innovative ones – scallops vinaigrette with hazelnut oil or salmon steak roasted with shellfish *confit*. €11.50 weekday lunch menu and others €23–56.

Roche-Morey (La)

70120 (18 km NW)

Le Point de Vue

La Roche-Morey; take the N19 then, near

Cintrey, the D1; from the village of the Morey, take the little road to the peak of La Roche-Morey, passing through Saint-Julien.
☎03.84.91.02.14
Closed *Sun evening and Mon (except June, July and Aug); Dec and Jan (except groups).* **High chairs and games available. Disabled access.**

The top of the hill has been invaded by a small amusement park (mini-golf, Indian village, little merry-go-round), with this family restaurant in the middle, with a stunning panoramic view. Excellent, copious, meticulously prepared meals at very reasonable prices. The house speciality is *feuilleté* with onions or fresh asparagus. Friendly and diligent service. *Free apéritif offered to our readers on presentation of this guide.*

Ronchamp

70250

Hôtel-restaurant "Le Rhien" Carrer**

Le Rhien; it's 3km from the centre of Ronchamp on the N19 (in the direction of Belfort).
☎03.84.20.62.32 ℻03.84.63.57.08
www.ronchamp.com
Closed *Sun evenings in winter.* **Disabled access. TV. High chairs and games available. Car park.**

Nice country inn in a quiet hamlet in a green valley. The family cooking is very orthodox and they use the best quality fresh produce. The results are delicious: pan-fried *escalope* of foie gras, trout with *vin jaune*, zander in *vin jaune*, fried carp and game in season. Weekday lunch menu at €10.50 and others €18–38; the "four seasons" menus at €15 and €20 according to the *formule*. Rooms are simple and comfortable: doubles at €40 with shower/wc or bath. Mountain bikes available for rent. *Free apéritif offered to our readers on presentation of this guide.*

Champagney

70290 (5km E)

Le Pré Serroux***

4 av. du Général-Brosset. Take the N19 then the D4.
☎03.84.23.13.24 ℻03.84.23.24.33
www.hotel-du-commerce-70.com
Closed *Sun evening 1 Nov–1 May; 22 Dec–12 Jan.* **TV. Disabled access. High chairs and games available. Car park.**

This old house has been entirely transformed, but the family that own it have taken care to retain its original character. There are four dining rooms, each one different: one has a wide fireplace where they serve country dishes, another is more like a sitting room-cum-library. The rooms are either starkly modern or have period furniture; doubles with shower/wc or bath €55. Some things haven't changed, though – the waitresses still wear white aprons and the chef is still committed to preparing sound regional and traditional dishes including casserole of lacquered pork with Champlitte wine, zander fillet with oyster mushrooms and brawn. Weekday menu €12 and a range of others €16–45. There's a fitness room, a sauna and a Turkish bath. *Free liqueur offered to our readers on presentation of this guide.*

Froideterre

70200 (10km W)

Hostellerie des Sources

4 rue du Grand-Bois; take the N19 in the direction of Lure and when you get to La Verrerie, take the road that goes north.
☎03.84.30.13.91 ℻03.84.30.29.87
Closed *Sun evening and Mon except public holidays; Tues; a fortnight in Jan.*

The house looks like a classic farm inn but is completely different inside: the décor is very plush, almost luxurious, and perhaps seems like too much of a contrast with the exterior. The main event is the cuisine, however, which is creative and intelligently conceived. The menus change with the seasons but everthing gets the juices flowing: Jura snails with *maître d'hôtel* butter, braised rack of lamb with parsley and crayfish flambéed in Cognac. It's impossible to resist the *crème brûlée* with vanilla Bourbon. Menus €35–85. Reservations highly recommended. *Free coffee offered to our readers on presentation of this guide.*

Melisey

70220 (10km NW)

Restaurant La Bergeraine

27 rte. des Vosges; take the N19 towards Lure then the D73.
☎03.84.20.82.52 ℻03.84.20.04.47

Closed *Tues evening and Wed (except public holidays).* **Disabled access.**

The chef has created a place which brings people out into the country to eat – but it's so small here that, unless you want to go away hungry, it's advisable to book. He serves appetizing, classic dishes prepared with individualistic flair. Favourites include house-smoked salmon, crayfish salad, veal sweetbreads with morels, and morels in a pastry case with *vin jaune* sauce. The menus change in line with the seasons. Weekday lunch menu €15 with others €20–65. *Chef's surprise offered to our readers on presentation of this guide.*

Roye

70200 (15km SW)

|●| Le Saisonnier

56 rue de la Verrerie; it's on the edge of the village, on the N19.
Ⓣ and Ⓕ03.84.30.46.80
Closed *Sun evening; Wed; a fortnight in Aug.* **High chairs and games available.**

You can stumble on some quite surprising places in the Haute-Saône – and this is one. It used to be a farm, as evidenced by its low ceilings and thick stone walls (which keep it warm in winter and cool in summer). Rather sober décor but pleasant nonetheless, and there's friendly service. Excellent seasonal cooking with a lot of up-to-date dishes, offering good value for money: menus €17.50–46. There's a quiet terrace at the back.

Rousses (Les)

39220

Hôtel du Village**

344 rue Pasteur.
Ⓣ03.84.34.12.75 Ⓕ03.84.34.12.76
Closed *Sun evening out of season; 1–15 June; 1–15 Dec.* **TV. Car park.**

This ten-room hotel in the middle of the resort has been renovated with taste and imagination. The large double rooms, all with shower/wc or bath, are all decorated slightly differently and go for €45–56.

|●| Hôtel Arbez France-Suisse**

La Cure; it's 2km out of town on the D5.
Ⓣ03.84.60.02.20 Ⓕ03.84.60.08.59
Ⓦwww.hotelarbez.fr.st
Closed *Mon evening and Tues out of season; Nov.* **TV.**

With one foot in France and another over the Swiss border, this is an odd place – your room could be in either country, and some of them are even on the border. All the rooms are cosy and comfortable; doubles €53–55 with shower/wc or bath. Half board, requested during the February school holidays and in the summer, costs around €53 per person per night. They offer two ways to dine: a brasserie (with filling portions) and a gourmet restaurant. Menus €13 (lunchtime in the brasserie) and in the restaurant €25–30. *10% discount on the room rate (except in Feb) offered to our readers on presentation of this guide.*

|●| Le Lodge**

309 rue Pasteur.
Ⓣ03.84.50.50.64 Ⓕ03.84.50.04.58
Ⓔlelodge@wanadoo.fr
Closed *Sun evening, Mon and Tues out of season; 12–20 May; first 3 weeks in Nov.* **TV.**

It's rare to find such a charming place in Megève these days. The building is made of stone and wood, with tiled floors and stuffed toy bears hanging from the country-style wardrobes. All the rooms are different, of course, and all are comfortable. Doubles with shower/wc €60–125 according to the season. They serve a few local dishes in the restaurant. *Free apéritif offered to our readers on presentation of this guide.*

Bonlieu

39130 (31km NW)

|●| La Poutre**

25 Grande-Rue; take the N5 as far as Saint-Laurent-en-Grandvaux, then the N78.
Ⓣ03.84.25.57.77 Ⓕ03.84.25.51.61
Closed *Mon; Tues; l Nov–5 May.* **TV. Car park.**

Large house in the heart of the village in this lake-filled region. It's a local institution, run by a new generation, who have added personality and warmth to the enterprise. Lovely creative cooking, using regional specialities, on menus €15–62. Double rooms €45–54 depending on facilities and the season. *Free apéritif offered to our readers on presentation of this guide.*

Ilay

39150 (34km NW)

L'Auberge du Hérisson*

5 rte. des Lacs; take the N5 and the N78; it's 3km after Bonlieu.
03.84.25.58.18 03.84.25.51.11
www.herisson.com
Closed *Mon and Tues in Oct; early Nov to end Jan.* **TV. High chairs available. Car park.**

A good base for local excursions and visits to the nearby waterfalls. Cosy, comfortable double rooms cost €45–50 with shower/wc or bath. Straightforward, honest dishes are served in the restaurant. The ingredients are fresh and the results are good: snails with morels, *boudin* of pink trout. Menus at €17 (not Sun), and €22–40. The cheese selection is exceptional. There are also a few Jura specialities and *fondues*, and an interesting children's menu. *Free apéritif offered to our readers on presentation of this guide.*

Vesoul

70000

Hôtel du Lion**

4 pl. de la République.
03.84.76.54.44 03.84.75.23.31
hoteldulion@wanadoo.fr
Closed *Sat evening in Jan–Feb; 1–16 Aug; 26 Dec–9 Jan.* **TV. Car park.**

Family-run, very traditional hotel in the centre of town. Lovely welcome – the staff know what good service is. The comfortable rooms have modern furnishings and are spacious; doubles cost €45. *10% discount on the room rate for a minimum stay of two consecutive nights (1 Dec–31 March) offered to our readers on presentation of this guide.*

Frotey-lès-Vesoul

70000 (3km E)

Eurotel – restaurant Le Saint Jacques***

Route de Luxeuil. Take the D13.
03.84.75.49.49 03.84.75.55.78
www.eurotel.fr
Closed *Sun evening.* **TV. Car park.**

The outside is very off-putting – it looks exactly like lots of chains throughout France – and the motorway exit is hardly the most joyous view, but you leave all that behind once inside. The rooms are pleasant and contemporary; doubles with bath €55. The bar and dining room are modern, too, as well as being truly elegant. The restaurant offers very good food prepared from seasonal produce. Menus €18–50. *Free apéritif offered to our readers on presentation of this guide.*

Villersexel

70110

Hôtel de la Terrasse**

Route de Lure; it's on the banks of the Ogno.
03.84.20.52.11 03.84.20.56.90
Closed *Sun evening; Fri evening out of season; 7 Dec–2 Jan.* **TV. Car park.**

This hotel is quiet, cosy and very relaxing, and the rooms are prettily and tastefully furnished. Doubles €38–48 with shower/wc or bath. The rustic-style restaurant is warmed by an open fire in winter; in summer you can eat on the terrace surrounded by greenery. Regional dishes are served. Weekday lunch menu at €11.50 and others €14–28. Shame that the value for money factor is not consistent.

Hôtel-restaurant du Commerce**

1 pl. du 13-Septembre; it's near the château museum.
03.84.20.50.50 03.84.20.59.57
www.hotelcommerce-villersexel.fr
Closed *1–15 Jan.* **TV. Car park.**

Classic provincial inn with simple, clean and reasonably priced rooms. Doubles €39 with shower/wc or bath. The owner prepares good regional dishes: smoked ham on the bone cooked in a hay box, terrines, poached trout with morels, fried carp. A range of set menus at €10.50 (except Sat evening and Sun) and €19–34 should satisfy any appetite. There's a huge fireplace where they light a fire on cold nights.

Villers-le-Lac

25130

Hôtel-restaurant Le France

8 pl. Cupillard.
03.81.68.00.06 03.81.68.09.22

Ⓦ www.hotel-restaurant.lefrance.com
Closed *Sun evening; Mon; Tues out of season; Jan; a week in Nov.* **TV. Pay car park.**

The best addresss in this corner of France, thanks to its dynamic chef. Hugues Droz has a reputation for his subtle, inventive cuisine which has humour and passion. He has his own herb garden and a pungent collection of spices brought back from his travels. Tastes and textures contrast beautifully; the food is inventive and simple at the same time. Lunch menu €19, and others at €25 and €65. Interesting wine list. Attractively decorated doubles with shower/wc or bath €65–75. *10% discount on the room rate offered to our readers on presentation of this guide.*

|●| L'Absinthe-restaurant du Saut du Doubs

6km from the town centre, 200 m from the waterfall; you can also go by boat.

Ⓣ 03.81.68.14.15
Closed *Mon and Tues (June, Sept and Oct); early Nov to Easter. Service 10am–7pm in July–Aug.* **Disabled access.**

A building on the river bank with *tavillons* (small wooden planks) on the façade, typical of the Haut-Doubs, is set off by beautiful stone terraces surrounded by absinthe plants and blessed with a fine view of the Doubs lakes. The cooking is simple but excellent. A platter of local dishes at €7. Menus of the day at €8 and €10. You can learn all about the drink that gives the place its name by merely crossing the threshold of the lovely dining room, with its décor from the turn of the twentieth century, as you will be shown posters and utensils associated with the ritual of its consumption. Try to come before it fills up, so that you have time to savour the *free absinthe offered to our readers on presentation of this guide.*

Île-de-France

Angerville

91670

Hôtel de France***

2 pl. du Marché.
Ⓣ01.69.95.11.30 Ⓕ01.64.95.39.59
Ⓦwww.hotelfrance3.com
Hotel closed *Sun evening.* **Restaurant closed** *Sun evening; Mon evening.* **TV. Car park.**

This beautiful old inn, built in 1715, has been restored a number of times without losing its elegance or character – the old beams, fireplace, conservatory and drawing room exude an air of gracious living. There's a sitting room where you can relax over an apéritif before proceeding to the dining room. The cuisine is reassuringly traditional and reliable: cream of watercress soup (this is the region for watercress), terrine with watercress, *salade mérévilloise* and fresh fruit *au gratin*. Set menu €28 or expect to pay around €43 à la carte. There's a pair of ravishing rooms with canopied beds with shower or bath for €80. *Free coffee offered to our readers on presentation of this guide.*

Asnières

92600

Le Petit Vatel

30 bd. Voltaire; M° Asnières-Gabriel-Péri.
Ⓣ01.47.91.13.30
Closed *evenings; weekends; Aug.*

Though you'd be likely to walk past this very ordinary, Formica-table lunch place without a second look, you shouldn't. First, the welcome they extend is genuinely warm; second, the food is very good – and, third, you almost get more than you can eat. They take care in preparing traditional family dishes like ham hock or *provençal* beef stew, and the salads are huge. Weekday lunch menu at €11; you'll spend around €17 à la carte. Reasonably priced wine.

La Petite Auberge

118 rue de Colombes; take the overground train from Saint-Lazare to Asnières or Bois-Colombes.
Ⓣ01.47.93.33.94
Closed *Sun and Wed evenings; Mon; 3 weeks in Aug.* **Open** *12.15–2pm and 7.30–9pm.*

Service until 9pm. The décor is completely over the top, like the set of a Grande Époque operetta – wood panelling and pictures everywhere. You're scooped up by the *patronne* or her daughter and conducted to your table; Dad, in the kitchen, produces wonderful food. There's a *menu-carte* for €27.75 which provides a superb meal, with dishes that change with the seasons. Typical offerings include *croustillant* of pig's trotters with salad or rump steak with truffle sauce. The fish is as fresh as can be – try the bass flambéed in pastis butter – and desserts are great. You should definitely call to book a table.

Aubervilliers

93300

L'Isola

33 bd. Édouard-Vaillant; M°Fort-d'Aubervilliers.
Ⓣ01.48.34.88.76
Closed *Sun; Mon–Wed evenings; Aug.* **Car park.**

This is a genuine Italian restaurant run by

A
1
2
OISE
EURE
VAL-D'OISE
YVELINES
PARIS
VAL DE MARNE
H.-DE-S.
ESSONNE
EURE-ET-LOIR
LOIRET
Oise
Seine
Chantilly
Bray-et-Lû
Magny-en-Vexin
Vernon
Giverny
la Roche-Guyon
Guiry-en-Vexin
l'Isle-Adam
Auvers-sur-Oise
Pontoise
Cergy
Montmorency
Écouen
Rolleboise
Mantes-la-Jolie
Epône
St-Gratien
Deuil-la-Barre
Cormeilles-en-P.
Enghien-les-Bains
St-Denis
Maisons-Laffitte
Asnières
St-Ouen
Bobigny
Aubervilliers
St-Germain-en-Laye
Courbevoie
la Défense
Levallois-P.
Neuilly-s-S.
Montreuil
Port-Marly
Marly-le-Roi
Rueil-M.
Suresnes
Bougival
Thoiry
Saint-Nom-la-Bretèche
St-Cloud
Sèvres
Boulogne-B.
Issy-les-M.
Vincennes
Meudon
Ivry
St-Maur
Créteil
Houdan
Versailles
Élancourt
Montigny-le-Br.
Trappes
Guyancourt
Montfort-l'Amaury
Chevreuse
Gif-sur-Yvette
Chilly-Mazarin
Orly
Yerres
Draveil
Grigny
Évry
Rambouillet
Ste Geneviève-des-Bois
Courcouronnes
Corbeil-Essonnes
Saint-Arnoult-en-Yvelines
le Val-St-Germain
Arpajon
St-Cyr-Sous-Dourdan
Dourdan
St-Sulpice-de-Favières
Soisy-sur-École
la Ferté-Alais
Chartres
Étampes
Morigny-Champiguy
Milly-la-Forêt
Fontaine-la-Rivière
Angerville
Malesherbes
Thoury
Pithiviers
1 - Clamart
2 - Sceaux
3 - Malakoff
4 - Vanves
5 - St-Maurice
6 - Bagnolet
7 - Charenton-le-Pont
8 - St-Mandé
9 - Nanterre
0
20 km

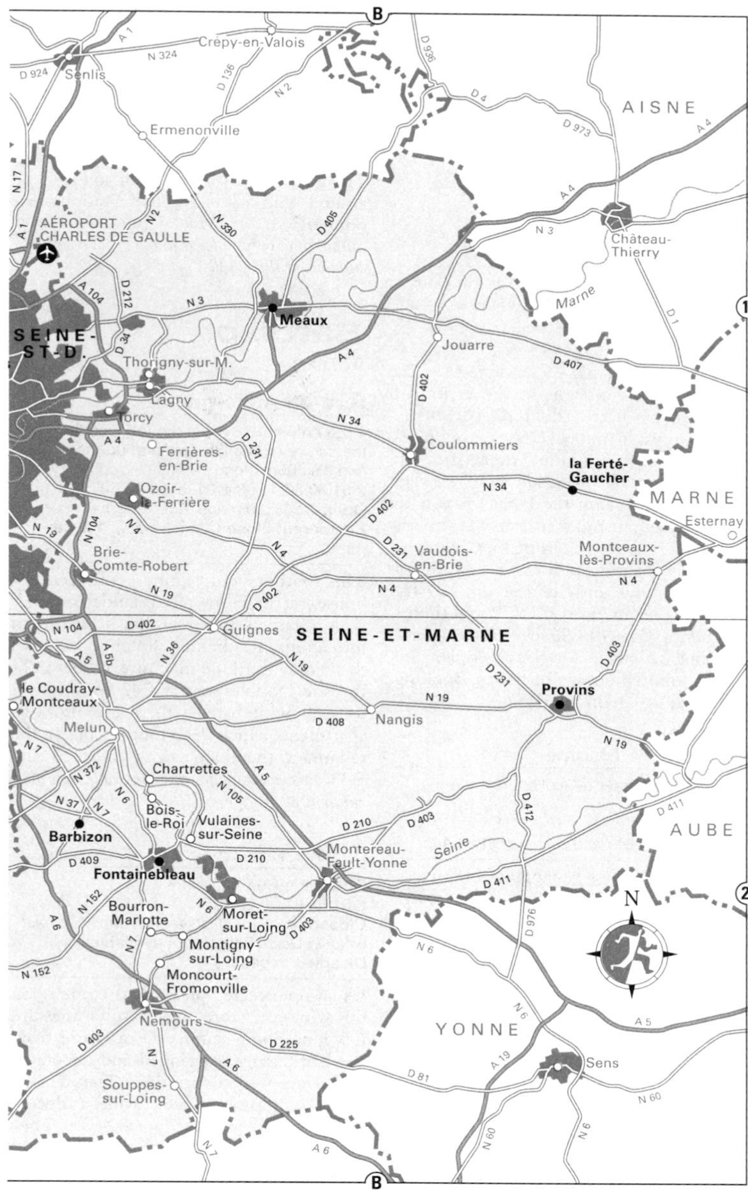
AISNE
Crépy-en-Valois
Senlis
Ermenonville
AÉROPORT CHARLES DE GAULLE
Château-Thierry
Marne
Meaux
SEINE-ST-D.
Jouarre
Thorigny-sur-M.
Lagny
Torcy
Coulommiers
Ferrières-en-Brie
la Ferté-Gaucher
Ozoir-la-Ferrière
MARNE
Esternay
Brie-Comte-Robert
Vaudois-en-Brie
Montceaux-lès-Provins
Guignes
SEINE-ET-MARNE
le Coudray-Montceaux
Provins
Melun
Nangis
Chartrettes
Bois-le-Roi
Vulaines-sur-Seine
Barbizon
AUBE
Montereau-Fault-Yonne
Seine
Fontainebleau
Bourron-Marlotte
Moret-sur-Loing
Montigny-sur-Loing
Moncourt-Fromonville
Nemours
YONNE
Sens
Souppes-sur-Loing
N
B
A 1
N 324
D 924
D 136
N 2
D 936
D 4
D 973
A 4
N 17
N 330
D 405
N 3
A 104
D 212
D 34
D 407
D 402
D 1
N 34
D 231
N 104
N 19
N 4
D 403
A 5
A 5b
N 36
D 408
N 7
N 372
N 6
N 37
N 105
D 210
D 412
D 411
D 409
N 152
A 6
D 976
D 225
D 81
A 19
N 60

a pair of charming sisters who are kindness itself. The décor is pleasant but not ostentatious and dishes are cooked using fresh produce from the market: fresh pasta, veal *escalope*, *osso buco*, ricotta ravioli, lasagne and a delicious Sardinian dish called *coulourgionisi*. Reckon on €25 for a meal. *Free apéritif or coffee offered to our readers on presentation of this guide.*

Auvers-sur-Oise

95430

Le Cordeville

18 rue du Rajon; leave the A15 at exit 7 onto the N184, then take the N322 in the direction of Méry-sur-Oise.
☎01.30.36.81.66
Open *daily 11.30am–2pm.*

This restaurant is right in the centre of the town that attracted so many Impressionist painters. They serve traditional family cuisine and don't stint on the portions. The *patronne* is very sweet and sets the pot on the table for you to help yourself, just like at home. It appeals to a range of people, from local workers to holidaymakers, and has a brigade of regulars. Lunch dish of the day €9.15. The cheapest menu is €13.72 and there's another at €19.40 which includes apéritif, wine (a bottle for four people) and coffee. Limited choice of wines. Booking essential. No credit cards.

Le Verre Placide

20 rue du Général-de-Gaulle; opposite the train station.
☎01.34.48.02.11
Closed *Mon; Wed and Sun evenings; Aug.*

One of the oldest restaurants in Auvers, with a spacious and bright dining room. The weekday menu (€21) gives you starter, main course and dessert, or it's around €31 à la carte. Try the salad of quail *confit*, turbot with a fennel *compote*, or lamb in a pastry case. Wines start at €12 per bottle and service is very polite. Advisable to book at the weekend. *Free coffee offered to our readers on presentation of this guide.*

Auberge Ravoux – Maison de Van Gogh

8 rue de la Sansonne; it's on the town hall square.
☎01.30.36.60.60
Closed *Sun evening; Mon; 10 Nov–10 March.*

Vincent van Gogh lived in this hotel for a while, and died here in 1890 – it's been restored to its original glory and the décor is just as it would have been in the painter's day. The cooking is good, and helpings are substantial. Choose from old-fashioned dishes such as pressed rabbit on a bed of lentils and pickled onions, slow-roast lamb *de sept heures*, and fish stew. There are menus at €26–33; you'll spend around €32 à la carte. Reservations recommended. *Free visit to van Gogh's room (dinnertime only) offered to our readers on presentation of this guide.*

Barbizon

77630

Auberge Les Alouettes**

4 rue Antoine-Barye; at the tobacconist's on the corner of Grande-Rue turn up the street and it's 500m along.
☎01.60.66.41.98 Ⓕ01.60.66.20.69
Open *12.15–2pm and 7.30–9.15pm.*
Restaurant closed *Sun evening.* **TV. Car park.**

This rather chic nineteenth-century house, set in its own substantial grounds with a garden and trees, has been turned into an inn. It's the only hotel in the town that's away from the main street. The décor is rustic. Doubles start at €43 with shower to €59 with bath – there are also two apartments which sleep four people. In the restaurant there are menus at €26 and €33. *Free apéritif offered to our readers on presentation of this guide.*

L'Ermitage Saint-Antoine

51 Grande-Rue.
☎01.64.81.96.96
Closed *Mon; Tues; Ist week in Jan; Aug; last week in Dec.* **High chairs available. Disabled access.**

It's an unexpected pleasure to come upon this wine bar. More unusual still is that this is a nineteenth-century farm house that's been brilliantly rearranged and decorated with trompe-l'œil paintings. The €15.24 menu will provide you with a decent meal; there's another at €24.39. They scribble the dishes of the day on the blackboard – these include gazpacho, parsleyed ham, *andouillette* from Troyes, rabbit salad with green lentils, black pudding with apples and curried spare ribs – or you can get a plate of charcuterie or cheeses served with a glass of wine. If the owner offers advice about which wine to order, take it – he really knows what he's talking about. Most of the wines are served by the glass; even if this is all you order, you'll still get a smile. Free coffee.

Bougival

78380

|●| Restaurant Chez Clément

It's on the N13 about 1km outside the town.
Ⓣ01.30.78.20.00 Ⓕ01.30.78.20.09
Ⓦwww.chezclement.com
Disabled access. Car park.

Service daily until 1am. You come here as much for the décor – a lovely dining room with fireplaces and an interior waterfall – as the food; simple cooking using fresh, seasonal produce. All of this in spacious grounds where you can dine on sunny days. There are two *formules* at €15.90 and €21; otherwise a meal will cost you between €30 and €32 à la carte. This is a very pleasant place, a haven of peace off the main road.

|●| Le Camélia

7 quai Georges-Clemenceau.
Ⓣ01.39.18.36.06
Open *noon–2.30pm and 7.30–10.30pm. Closed Sat lunchtime; Sun evening; Mon; a week in Feb; last week in July and first 3 weeks in Aug.* **High chairs available. TV.**

A welcoming, refined setting. The cuisine is prettily prepared and manages to be both solid and delicate. All the produce used is fresh and the cooking shows off the flavours extremely well. Menus €35 and €65. Swift, efficient service.

Bray-et-Lû

95710

⌂ |●| Le Faisan Doré

12 rte. de Vernon.
Ⓣ and Ⓕ01.34.67.71.68
Closed *Sun evening; Mon.* **TV.**

The balconies here are festooned with an abundance of geraniums and petunias and there's a family atmosphere. In the summer, it's pleasant to sit on the terrace under the flowery parasols. The set weekday menu is €11.43; others, €17–26, include starter, main course, cheese and dessert. À la carte you'll pay about €21: try *fricassée* of veal sweetbreads with morels or veal chops Normandy-style. Good value for money, with attentive service. The rooms are plain; doubles with basin €23–28. Half board costs €42 per person.

Charenton-le-Pont

94220

|●| La Bolée d'Arvor

38 rue de Paris.
Ⓣ01.43.76.85.77
Closed *Sun; Mon.*

In the town's prettiest neighbourhood, this restaurant offers some thirty copious and generous dishes in a restaurant run by Bretons: Tuareg pancake (€5.50), Aubrac pancake (€6.30) and seafood (€7.50).

Chevreuse

78460

|●| Auberge La Brunoise

2 rue de la Division-Leclerc.
Ⓣ01.30.52.15.75
Open *noon–2pm and 7.30–9.45pm.* **Closed** *Mon and Tues evenings; Wed; a week in Feb; a week during the Easter holidays; 3 weeks end July to early Aug.* **High chairs available. Disabled access.**

The village is charming and the walk over the bridges of the Yvette river and the canal is incredibly picturesque. Unpretentious cuisine is on offer here (seafood is the speciality) – honest and good dishes feature on all the menus, which start at €11 (weekday lunch) and then rise from €15 (weekdays only) to €23–30.50. Natural, friendly service; the young owners' eagerness to keep the clients satisfied has earned them a good number of regulars. The dining room has a rustic aspect, though the glorious terrace looks onto the main road. *Free coffee offered to our readers on presentation of this guide.*

Chilly-Mazarin

91380

|●| Thym et Basilic

97 rue de Gravigny; take the Longjumeau exit

off the A6 and continue along the right of the motorway.
Ⓣ01.69.10.92.75
Closed *Sat lunchtime; Sun evening; Mon; end July and 1st 3 weeks in Aug.* **Disabled access.**

There's a hint of Provence in the yellow and blue dining room, and a taste of the same in the dishes: *bouillabaisse* (to order), prawns with pastis, scallop *provençale*, lamb, and cod fillet. The €13.50 lunch *formule* offers a dish of the day plus starter or dessert. Menus €16.50 (not Sun or public holidays), €22.60 and €32. *Free digestif.*

Clamart

92140

Restaurant La Cosse des Petits Pois

158 av. Victor-Hugo; it's outside the centre of town, 300m from the train station.
Ⓣ01.46.38.97.60 Ⓕ01.46.38.08.75
Closed *Sat lunchtime; Sun; Mon; a week in March; a fortnight in Aug.*

The chef creates simple, generous food here, and attracts a good crowd of enthusiastic regulars. The set menu, €28, lists traditional dishes that change with the season. Typical offerings include duck *foie gras, paupiette* of sole and poached haddock in flaky pastry with Roquefort sauce. One caveat: watch out for supplements on the menu, which can create a bit of a surprise when it comes to paying the bill. *Free house apéritif offered to our readers on presentation of this guide.*

Corbeil-Essonnes

91100

L'Épicure

Place de l'Hôtel de Ville; it's opposite the town hall.
Ⓣ and Ⓕ01.60.88.28.38
Open *noon–2pm and 7.30–10pm. Closed Sat lunchtime and Sun except Mothers' Day; a week in mid-May; end July to 25 Aug.*

Epicurean pleasures par excellence in this charming, aptly named restaurant. Soft music plays in the background and the setting is refined-rustic. The chef produces fine, traditional cooking: fish *pot-au-feu, croustillant* of duck (a must), game terrine, calf's head with calf's liver and kidney. Good value on the set menus, at €21 and €25; dishes à la carte are pricey, however. *Free liqueur offered to our readers on presentation of this guide.*

Aux Armes de France

1 bd. Jean-Jaurès; it's on the N7.
Ⓣ01.64.96.24.04 Ⓕ01.60.88.04.00
Ⓦwww.auxarmesdefrance.com
Closed *Sat lunch and Sun except during public holidays.* **Car park.**

Winning cuisine and dishes that change according to the seasons and what's good at the market: wild boar haunch, fresh fish of the day brought straight from the market, soufflés of zander *quenelles*. Menus €33.55–75.50 with wine, €51.10 without wine. Friendly, unobtrusive service. *Free coffee offered to our readers on presentation of this guide.*

Coudray-Montceaux (Le)

91830 (3km S)

Restaurant La Renommée

110 berges de la Seine; it's opposite the train station.
Ⓣ01.64.93.81.09
Closed *Tues evening; Wed; Sun evening.* **Car park.**

A pleasurable place whatever the weather. In summer or winter, you'll feel tranquil on the large veranda, watching the fishermen glide along the Seine. This is a great setting in which to enjoy salmon *parmentier*, bass fillet with vanilla and polenta, a fish platter or snails on a nest of tagliatelle. There are weekday menus at €15 and €16, then others at €26 and €36. It's a good idea to reserve at the weekend. *A free glass of wine champenoise offered to our readers on presentation of this guide.*

Cormeilles-en-Parisis

95240

La Montagne

21 rte. Stratégique; it's in the woods above Cormeilles.
Ⓣ01.34.50.74.04
Closed *Tues; evenings except Fri and Sat 7.30–10pm. 3 weeks in Aug.* **Disabled access. Car park.**

This is the place for robust, straightforward cooking, or so they seem to think locally –

the restaurant is full every lunchtime. A typical *menu du jour* (weekday lunchtimes only) at €9.15 will list egg mayonnaise, seafood salad, steak and *andouillette*, sausages with lentils and *crème caramel*. There are also *formules* for €16.80 and €24.40 listing goose *rillettes*, lamb tripe and *crème brûlée*. You'll pay around €27 à la carte and can choose from dishes such as steak with pepper and Roquefort or *escalope* of foie gras with acacia honey. Terrace in summer. *Free coffee offered to our readers on presentation of this guide.*

Courcouronnes

91080

Le Canal

31 rue du Pont-Amar; it's in the Quartier du Canal, near the Courcouronnes hospital.
☎01.60.78.34.72
Open *noon–4pm and 7pm–midnight.* **Closed** *Sat; Sun; Aug.* **Disabled access.**

Courcouronnes is concrete city and this restaurant is a spark of life in an otherwise desolate wasteland. It's a nice place with an attractive bar and friendly service. The owner cooks robust, colourful dishes as good as you'd get from many of the great-name chefs. There's a new speciality every day: duo of bream and salmon with chives, say, or pig's trotters. First menu at €14.95; others at €19 and €29; children eat free.

Dourdan

91410

L'Auberge de l'Angelus

4 pl. du Chariot; it's 300m from the church, near the library on the banks of the Orge.
☎01.64.59.83.72
Open *noon–1.30pm and 7–9pm. Closed Mon and Tues evenings; Wed.* **Disabled access. Games available.**

In warm weather, you can eat in the flower garden of this old post house in a relaxed, summery atmosphere. Inside the décor is classic, with beige furnishings and tartan fabric stretched across the walls. Delicious cuisine: seafood *pot-au-feu* with baby vegetables, chopped *mignon* of pork with soya sauce, roast pigeon with apples, honey and spices, iced nougat with rose petals and vanilla ice, fine Granny Smith apple tart with a verbena sorbet. Menus €21 (weekdays) up to €37. Around €50 à la carte.

Enghien-les-Bains

95880

Villa Marie-Louise**

49 rue de Malleville; it's behind the spa, near the lake.
☎01.39.64.82.21 ℗01.39.34.87.76
ⓦwww.hotel-marie-louise.com
Restaurant closed *Sat; Sun.* **TV.**

This is a fine turn-of-the-(nineteenth)-century house with a big garden in the centre of town near the lake. The 22 simply furnished, comfortable rooms have been nicely decorated; ask for one with a garden view. Doubles €43–50 with shower/wc or bath – it's probably the cheapest hotel in town. Breakfast €5. If you're looking for a meal, you have a choice of simple, tasty dishes. There's a €10 menu, and another at €16 on Friday evenings. It costs around €12 for a meal à la carte. They take a lot of care of you here. *Free coffee offered to our readers on presentation of this guide.*

Deuil-la-Barre

95170 (1km NE)

Verre chez Moi

75 av. de la Division-Leclerc.
☎01.39.64.04.34
Closed *Sun; Mon; 30 July–25 Aug; 24 Dec–1 Jan.*

This restaurant feels like a Lyonnais tavern and occupies the ground floor of a villa which has been converted into flats. They serve good, well-prepared traditional dishes. There are no set menus, only a daily list on which you'll find *coq au vin*, *miroton* of beef – a typical Lyonnais dish with slices of boiled beef in a rich sauce with onions – or top-quality *andouillette*. Simple starters include herrings and warm steamed potatoes or charcuterie, and they offer a limited range of cheeses (the farmhouse Camembert is excellent) as well as basic but brilliant desserts like *crème brûlée*. The place is lovely and cosy, with a friendly feel and very fair prices: you should pay €21–35 for a meal with a jug of wine.

Saint-Gratien

95210 (2km W)

Le Phare du Forum

14 pl. du Forum; it's in the Forum district in the middle of town.

☎01.34.28.23.07
Open *noon–3pm and 7pm–midnight.* **Closed** *Sun evening.*

Deliveries of fresh fish from the market at Rungis arrive three times a week. All the produce is brilliantly fresh and cooked to order: lots of shellfish and crustaceans, oysters, stuffed mussels, *bouillabaisse* (order 48hr in advance), lemon sole, Dover sole, skate – or you can fill up on pasta or home-cooked pizzas. The restaurant has a maritime décor: model ships, starfish and fishing nets. Weekday menu €9, then others €13 and €20 or €25 à la carte. Musical entertainment on Saturday and Sunday evenings. Smiling, brisk service. *Free house apéritif, house liqueur, fruit juice or soft drink offered to our readers on presentation of this guide.*

Chez Baber

71 bd. Pasteur; it's on the N14, on the edge of Sannois.
☎01.39.89.64.72
Closed *Mon lunchtime.* **Disabled access.**

Service until 11pm. You're welcomed by the gentle music of the sitar and the tabla, and the perfumed air and Indian décor transport you far from the noise of the road outside. Lunchtime menu at €9.50 and two dinner ones at €15.90 and €21.90. Their tandoori specialities feature delicious sauces while other dishes like lamb tikka, chicken tikka masala and fish masala are also good. The chutneys are spicey but well tempered by the cheese naan. You'll pay around €15 à la carte.

Étampes

91150

Hôtel de l'Europe à l'Escargot

71 rue Saint-Jacques. Heading towards the station, go along the road parallel to the rail track for 200m, then turn left then left again; the entrance is down a narrow road.
☎01.64.94.02.96
Closed *July.* **TV. Car park.**

A small, very well-run hotel offering a smiling welcome, comfortable rooms and good value for money. It's in the middle of town yet quiet. Doubles €25 with shower, €28 with shower/wc or €32–38 with bath.

Le Saint-Christophe

28 rue de la République; it's next to the church Notre-Dame-du-Fort.
☎01.64.94.69.99
Closed *Sun evening.*

The speciality of this Portuguese restaurant is, and always has been, cod. It's the national dish, after all, and they're not going to change a winning formula. It's a nice place, attracting a host of regulars who appreciate the simple, tasty cooking. You can eat well for less than €20. There's a weekday menu for €10.

Restaurant Les Piliers

2 pl. Saint-Gilles.
☎01.64.94.04.52
Closed *Sun evening; Mon; Tues evening; a fortnight in Feb; 3 weeks at the end July to mid-Aug.*

The restaurant is in the oldest house in town, and it dates from the twelfth century – go through the paved arcade to find the entrance. Good home cooking with a fair dash of creativity: sole fillet, duck breast, house *confit* and the like. The €17 *formule* gives you a couple of courses, while the one at €28 gives three. A few *appellation* wines at good prices, which is unusual in a place this classy. *Free apéritif offered to our readers on presentation of this guide.*

Morigny-Champigny

91150 (5km N)

Hostellerie de Villemartin

21 allée des Marronniers; it's on the D17.
☎01.64.94.63.54
Open *11.45am–2pm and 7.45–10pm.*
Closed *Tues; Wed; Thurs; 4 days for Christmas; 3 weeks in Feb.* **Swimming pool. Car park.**

An impressive manor house in the middle of a huge estate next to a fortified farmhouse. You'll get a simple, attentive welcome with a family atmosphere that puts you at your ease. The food is a happy surprise; fresh, creative cooking offering a wide choice. The €27 menu and the à la carte choice change with the seasons; typical dishes include pressed summer vegetables with goat's cheese, *millefeuille* of red tuna with ratatouille, rabbit *ballotine* with rosemary *jus* and smoked bacon *tuile*, orange and carrot salad with cinnamon and ice cream or *clafoutis* with apricots and caramel with lavender. Very good value for money. *Free apéritif offered to our readers on presentation of this guide.*

Saint-Sulpice-de-Favières

91910 (8km N)

Auberge de Campagne La Ferronnière

10 pl. de l'Église; take the N20 towards Arpajon.
01.64.58.42.07
Closed *Sat lunchtime; Ist fortnight in Aug.*

A jewel of a village with a country inn that looks like a Wild West saloon. It must have been an old coaching inn originally, with the smithy next door. You won't find a better welcome or service; there's even a shower available for use by walkers. Huge plates of wonderful traditional food with a few authentic regional dishes besides: house terrine, snails, duck breast, steak with shallots. Weekday lunch menu at €12 and another at €22. Terrace in summer.

Val-Saint-Germain (Le)

91530 (18km NE)

Auberge du Marais

1 rte. de Vaugrigneux. Drive towards Dourdan, and it's near the château du Marais.
01.64.58.82.97
Closed *Sun evening; Mon; Christmas.*
Disabled access.

A large rustic house on the edge of the forest, with a terrace that's open in summer. Traditional dishes made with fresh, quality produce; the terrines and the foie gras are particularly fine, as is the game in season, and it's worth following the chef's suggestions. He's a cheery man; if you ask nicely, perhaps he'll give you his recipes for pan-fried foie gras with potato *fondant* or duck stuffed with mushrooms with foie gras and grape sauce. Weekday lunch menu €12, then others €19–29, with a children's menu for €10. The first menu is particularly good, including a starter, dish of the day, cheese plate, salad or dessert, and coffee. Reservations recommended for Sunday lunch. *Free apéritif offered to our readers on presentation of this guide.*

Ferté-Gaucher (La)

77320

Hôtel du Sauvage**

27 rue de Paris.
01.64.04.00.19 01.64.04.02.50
www.hotel-du-sauvage.com
Restaurant Closed *Mon lunch; Fri evening; Sun evening.* **Disabled access. TV. High chairs and games available. Swimming pool.**

This sixteenth-century inn was once a brothel, and its name is said to come from the wild game once abundant in the marshland that used to surround it. The Teinturier family have been innkeepers here for six generations. They've had the courage to refurbish the place, providing attractively modern and comfortable rooms while keeping the place's all-important character. Doubles with shower/wc €49–55, or €60–65 with bath/wc. Breakfast €6.50. Delicious regional dishes made with local produce are on set menus at €18–38. Try poached eggs with Brie, fillet of beef or ham on the bone. Perfect service and smiling welcome. *Free apéritif or 10% discount on the room rate offered to our readers on presentation of this guide.*

Fontainebleau

77300

Hôtel Victoria**

112 rue de France.
01.60.74.90.00 01.60.74.90.10
www.hotel.victoria.com
TV. Pay car park.

George Sand and Alfred de Musset frequented this place in the 1830s. Here and there you'll discern the vestiges of the original master-craftsman's house, even though all nineteen rooms have been renovated. They're clean and pleasant, particularly the ones overlooking the large garden, and it's a real pleasure to be woken by the cooing of the birds. Double rooms with bath cost €58–73. Breakfast €7.

La Petite Alsace

26 rue de Ferrare; next to the Caveau des Ducs.
01.64.23.45.45
Open *daily noon–2pm and 7–10pm.* **Closed** *1st fortnight in Jan; 1st fortnight in Aug.* **High chairs available.**

Pretty décor and setting (complete with storks). Fine Alsatian specialities and succulent onion pies. Weekday lunchtime menu €11 then €15, €25 and €30. Small pavement terrace in fine weather. *Liqueur on the house offered to our readers on presentation of this guide.*

Restaurant Chez Arrighi

53 rue de France.
☎01.64.22.29.43
Open *noon–2pm and 7–10pm.* **Closed** *Mon.*

This place has got an old-fashioned feel about it, with its sturdy, stone façade and luxurious curtains. The two Art Deco dining rooms have been decorated in refined old rose tones, and soft music plays in the background. Menus at €16.50 (not served Sun) up to €31.50 include dishes like frogs' legs in parsley, boned quail in flaky pastry stuffed with foie gras, *goujons* of salmon with creamed spinach, lamb's tongues in sorrel sauce, crêpes suzette, and Grand Marnier soufflé. They're all well prepared and will delight any fan of good traditional cooking. *Free coffee offered to our readers on presentation of this guide.*

Le Caveau des Ducs

24 rue de Ferrare; it's near the château.
☎01.64.22.05.05
Closed *1–15 Jan; 1–15 Aug.* **Disabled access.**

You'll know you're in Fontainebleau in this seventeenth-century vaulted cellar with its period décor and chandeliers. Classical cooking, faultlessly served. Set menus at €20 (except Sat evening), €29 and €38; midday all-inclusive *formule* at €29. The chef uses excellent ingredients to produce great food; the desserts are excellent. The bread is a bit of a let-down, though. *Free digestif offered to our readers on presentation of this guide.*

Bois-Le-Roi

77590 (4km NE)

Le Pavillon Royal***

40 av. du Général-Galliéni; it's near the train station.
☎01.64.10.41.00 ℗01.64.10.41.10
perso.wanadoo.fr/hotel.lepavillonroyal
Disabled access. TV. Swimming pool. Car park.

A new building in neoclassical style, plain and aesthetically pleasing. Quiet, spacious and impeccably clean rooms are €55 with shower/wc or €60 with bath. Breakfast €6.50. Lovely swimming pool and relaxation centre. *10% discount on the room rate Oct–May offered to our readers on presentation of this guide.*

Vulaines-sur-Seine

77870 (5km E)

L'Île aux Truites

Promenade Stéphane Mallarmé; take the D210, cross the Valvins bridge then head left. It's about 1km further on, on the banks of the Seine.
☎06.85.07.01.35
Open *noon–2pm and 7–10pm.* **Closed** *Wed; Thurs lunchtime; 21 Dec–25 Jan.* **Disabled access.**

You're right on the Seine here, in a thatched cottage surrounded by huge willow trees and trout ponds where the children can fish for their lunch – and, as the tables are right by the water's edge, you can keep an eye on them at the same time. Alternatively, in winter you can cosy up by the huge fireplace. Very decent cuisine and perfect service make this restaurant one of the most attractive in the region. They specialize in grilled fish served with baked potatoes. Or try the *assiette de l'Île aux Truites* which includes smoked trout, marinated fillet of trout and fish terrine. In summer they offer nice tarts made with raspberries from the garden. Menus at €22 and €30, with a children's menu at €13. You must reserve in summer to have any hope of getting a table. Trout fishing for children. *Free apéritif offered to our readers on presentation of this guide.*

Bourron-Marlotte

77780 (8km S)

Restaurant Les Prémices

12 bis rue Blaise-de-Montesquiou; take the N7 in the direction of Nemours-Montargis, and at the Bourron-Marlott ZI exit, follow the signs to the village.
☎01.64.78.33.00
Closed *Sun evening; Mon; a week in the Feb school holidays; 1–15 Aug; a week at Christmas.* **TV. Car park.**

The restaurant is in the outbuildings of the superb château Bourron-Marlotte, and they've built a conservatory so you can appreciate the glory of the countryside. Menus €23 and €30, with a gourmet menu at €58: pan-fried foie gras with royal jelly, Kobé beef, grilled lobster with Bourbon vanilla *emulsion*, lamb shank *confit* with potatoes, grilled crayfish with beetroot *coulis*, ice cream scented with lily of the valley. The wine list is unusually good. Reserve well in advance. *Free digestif offered to our readers on presentation of this guide.*

Montigny-sur-Loing

77690 (10km S)

|●| Restaurant de la Vanne Rouge

Rue de l'Abreuvoir; take the D148 along the banks of the Loing river.
☎01.64.78.52.30
Closed *Sun evening; Mon; Tues in winter; 4 weeks spread throughout the year.* **TV. Car park.**

Charming, super-quiet hotel with ten lovely rooms that have views over the River Loing. Doubles €53.36 with bath/wc; half board is compulsory. There's a large sunny terrace where you're lulled by the sound of the waterfalls and you can practically trail your feet in the water while you eat. Chef Serge Granger's speciality is fish. *Menu-carte* €33.54. There's an exceptional wine list. It's wise to book. Credit cards not accepted.

Moret-sur-Loing

77250 (10km SE)

|●| La Poterne

1 rue du Pont-du-Loing; take the N6.
☎01.64.31.19.89
Closed *Mon; Tues (Nov–March); 3 weeks end Aug to mid-Sept; fortnight during New Year.*

This restaurant is in the shortest street in France – it has one building, the gate in the town walls where the restaurant is housed. It's a fine historic dwelling with an alleyway that looks over the Loing. Inventive, local dishes that the manager, Michelle, ferrets out of old recipe books: try that sixteenth-century delight, the *ouin*, sautéed veal like grandma used to make, and *casse-museau* (the favourite dessert of Louis XIII). They also do traditional Moroccan food (couscous, tajines and so on) in summer, along with vegetarian food and salads. There's no set menu but a large number of dishes priced from €7 to €23. An exceptional place. *Free apéritif offered to our readers on presentation of this guide.*

Chartrettes

77590 (11km N)

|●| Restaurant Le Chalet

37 rue Foch; take the D39 and it's the last village on the Seine before you reach Melun. Cross the Seine and the restaurant is on the right, near the marina in a little residential street.
☎01.60.69.65.34
Open *12.15–2pm and 7.30–10pm.* **Closed** *Sun and Mon evenings; Wed.* **Disabled access. High chairs available. Car park.**

This place buzzes with energy and laughter. It's a friendly, popular restaurant in a private mansion that fits in well with the rest in the street. The large rustic dining room decorated in Louis XIII style extends onto an elevated terrace with a pergola, and the cuisine consists of traditional dishes with good sauces: calf's head vinaigrette, duck *confit*, foie gras in flaky pastry, duck terrine, home-made goat's cheese tart, brawn with vinaigrette, *coq au vin*, rabbit *chasseur*. A substantial set menu at €13 (not served Sat evening, Sun or public holidays), then others €21 and €28. *Free apéritif offered to our readers on presentation of this guide.*

Moncour-Fromonville

77140 (13km S)

|●| Le Chaland qui passe

10 rue du Loing. Take the N7 to Montigny-sur-Loing, then the D40.
☎01.64.29.12.95
@chaland.qui.passe@wanadoo.fr
Closed *Sun evening; Mon; during the Nov half term.*

A nice inn on the banks of the canal near the Loing river; the shady terrace gives you a good view of the pleasure boats sliding quietly by. The dining room has a country décor with a wide chimney. The first menu, €13, is great, and there is another at €22. These feature dishes such as house terrine, lambs kidneys *à l'ancienne*, game in season, skate wings and duck *confit*. Easy-going family atmosphere. *Free house digestif offered to our readers on presentation of this guide.*

Fontaine-la-Rivière

91690

|●| Auberge de Courpain

Take the D721 at the junction with the D145, 1km from Fontaine-la-Rivière up the hill. Follow the signs.
Hotel ☎01.64.95.67.04
Restaurant ☎01.69.58.25.09
www.auberge-de-courpain.com
Closed *Mon; Tues; 10 days early Jan; fortnight in Aug.* **Swimming pool. Car park. TV.**

Disabled access. High chairs and games available.

An old post house offering eighteen rooms with good facilities, each with en-suite bathrooms. The décor is charmingly rustic. Doubles €60 and suites €120 for four people. There's a flower garden with a pleasant terrace for summer lunch, with tables made from old cart wheels and shaded by white parasols. Delicate dishes are flavoured with subtle mixtures of spices: sea bream with dill, monkfish and salmon steaks with vanilla, roasted rack of lamb with a herb crust and melon and lime soup for dessert. À la carte, starters go for around €13, main courses €20, and desserts €9. The weekly specials get you two dishes for €20 or three for €28. The hedges and buildings screen you from the road but don't keep out the noise. Attentive service.

Isle-Adam (L')

95290

Le Cabouillet**

5 quai de l'Oise; it's after Cabouillet bridge, on the right as you come from the station.
01.34.69.00.90 01.34.69.33.88
Closed *Sun evening; Mon; Feb.* **Disabled access.**

This big, beautiful bourgeois country house is covered with ivy. Inside, Old Masters hang on the walls and there's a beautiful, polished wooden staircase – the five prettily decorated rooms go from €58 each. The restaurant is the best in L'Isle-Adam. Logis-de-France menu €28; *menu carte* €45. The cooking is refined and tasty and the dishes change with the seasons: *millefeuille* of *foie gras* with gingerbread, *croustade* of pigeon with *andouille*, sauce with *hydromel*. From some tables and from the terrace you get a view of the Oise river.

Au Relais Fleuri

61 rue Saint-Lazare; it's 300m from St Martin's church.
01.34.69.01.85
Open *noon–2pm and 7–9.15pm.* **Closed** *Sun, Mon and Wed evenings; Tues; 1–22 Aug.* **Disabled access.**

The décor is absolutely classic, with blue fabric stretched across the walls and matching curtains. The Roland brothers will give you a courteous welcome and their delicate, sophisticated cooking offers good value for this town. Dishes change with the seasons. Set menu €26 with starter, main dish, cheese, salad and dessert; reckon on around €38.11–45.73 à la carte: snail casserole, roast fillet of Dover sole with a lobster *coulis*, queen scallops with *beurre blanc* and fresh pasta, roast duck with spiced wine, *bouillabaisse* with fish and lobster and superb desserts. There's an enormous shady terrace where you can enjoy a *digestif* after your meal.

Issy-les-Moulineaux

92130

Issy-Guinguette

113 bis av. de Verdun; M° Mairie-d'Issy, then by bus 123 to the Chemin des Vignes stop.
01.46.62.04.27
Closed *Sun evening; Sat (lunchtime only in summer); Sun; a week at Christmas; Aug.*

Yves Legrand, the boss of this place, is the driving force behind the resuscitation of the vineyard in Issy. On sunny days, sit out on the terrace among the vines with a view of lovely old houses – it's hard to believe you're in the suburbs of the capital, and if it gets too hot Yves puts up the parasols. Bistro dishes are carefully cooked and served in generous portions. There's not an extensive choice but the options change all the time: salmon *unilatérale* (cooked on one side), rolled lamb with fresh herbs, pork with cabbage, roast rabbit fillet with sage, stuffed breast of veal, cod with cream sauce, duck *fricassée* and pineapple preserved in red wine and ginger. There's an excellent wine list, as you might expect given the owner's enthusiasm. The service is perfect and the atmosphere relaxed and often quite festive; lunchtime sees lots of businessmen from the area. In winter, they serve in the bright dining room where they light a fire in the hearth. Reservations highly recommended. There's a menu for €23 or you'll pay around €30 à la carte. *Free apéritif offered to our readers on presentation of this guide.*

La Manufacture

20 esplanade de la Manufacture; M° Corentin-Celton.
01.40.93.08.98 01.40.93.57.22
www.restaurantmanufacture.com
Closed *Sat lunchtime; Sun; fortnight in Aug.* **Disabled access.**

The restaurant takes up the ground floor of an old tobacco factory. It's a huge room with a high ceiling painted cream and beige, and it's brightened up with a few modern pictures and green plants. At lunchtime it's full of media execs and exhibitors from the exhibition centre – the huge space makes this a perfect place for private conversations or tricky negotations because you can hear each other without being overheard. The cooking is particularly fine, revelling in subtle flavours. Try the pigs' ears or the lamb shank braised in cider, which literally melts in the mouth. It's the best kind of home cooking rethought and served to suit modern styles and tastes. The menu changes frequently, but there are some staples including calf's brains and tongue *ravigote*, and braised beef cheek. Desserts are excellent, and the bill won't be a shock – especially if you go for one of the *formules* at €25 and €30. Reservations essential.

|●| Les Quartauts

19 rue Georges-Marie; M° Porte-de-Versailles or Corentin-Celton.
Ⓣ01.46.42.29.38
Closed *weekends; evenings except Thurs; Aug.*

It's hard to believe that you could find such a good establishment in a place like this: the street's so quiet that this award-winning bistro can only have made its reputation by word-of-mouth. Simplicity and quality are the watchwords here, with a welcoming warmth generated by the owners, Régine and Christophe. Succulent home cooking is served in substantial helpings, and they do superb meat dishes. There's a good choice of wines from small vineyards at very reasonable prices. The cheese selection is impressive and the desserts are all made on the premises. Dishes of the day cost €10; you'll pay about €26 à la carte.

Maisons-Lafitte

78600

🏃 🏠 |●| Hôtel-Restaurant au Pur-Sang*

2 av. de la Pelouse; go over the Maisons-Lafitte bridge, turn right, and skirt the racecourse until the roundabout, then turn right into avenue de la Pelouse.
Ⓣ01.39.62.03.21 Ⓕ01.34.93.48.69
Open *6.30am–8.30pm.* **Closed** *Sun; 3 weeks in Aug; Christmas holidays.* **TV. Car park.**

Just by the entrance to the racecourse you'll find this thoroughly provincial-looking hotel-restaurant. Simple rooms with shower at €40. This place is hugely popular with anyone to do with the racecourse, all of whom enjoy the simple but carefully prepared cooking. Take a seat in the rustic dining room or on the large sunny terrace, and opt for the €12 set menu – it will offer something along the lines of egg mayonnaise or beef salad with tomatoes, followed by roast beef with cauliflower cheese or duck, and finishing with a classic dessert like *crème caramel*. À la carte will set you back around €24. *Free apéritif offered to our readers on presentation of this guide.*

|●| La Vieille Fontaine

8 av. Grétry.
Ⓣ01.39.62.01.78 Ⓕ01.39.62.13.43
Closed *Sun evening; Mon.*

The building is a fine example of Second Empire architecture and it's situated in the grounds of the château. There's been a restaurant here since 1926, and over the years it's built up a solid reputation. The dining room and interior decoration are very attractive and there's a lovely terrace in the garden. Tasty dishes are produced with great skill: *salade folle*, roast saddle of lamb and warm chocolate tart with raspberry *coulis*. The service is beyond reproach. The *menu-carte* at €34 means you can get a good meal for a fair price, and there are affordable wines too. The place has a certain atmosphere: it has hosted scores of film stars, was used as a movie for a couple of (forgettable) movies – and was also the haunt of some of the Nazi high command during the Occupation.

Malakoff

92240

🏃 🏠 Hôtel des Amis

17 rue Savier; it's in a small street opposite Notre-Dame church.
Ⓣ and Ⓕ01.42.53.57.63
Ⓦwww.hoteldesamis.com
Closed *Sat; Sun evening (except reservations); a fortnight in July.*

It would be impossible to find a quieter place – the owner even says the district is too quiet. And you can't miss it – the roof is outlined in blue neon. The rooms are regularly refurbished and the whole place is spotless. There's a small bar on the ground floor. Doubles €29–40 with wash basin or shower, and €48 with shower/wc. Breakfast €6. Parking is a nightmare, however. It's advisable to book at least a week in advance. *Free apéritif, coffee, fruit juice or soft drink offered to our readers on presentation of this guide.*

Marly-Le-Roi

78160

Les Chevaux de Marly – Restaurant La Tempête***

Place de l'Abreuvoir.
Ⓣ01.39.58.47.61 Ⓕ01.39.16.65.56
Disabled access. TV. Swimming pool. Car park.

Ten faultlessly presented rooms at €79.30 for a double with bath – good value for a three-star hotel in this area. Some of them have a view over the imposing Abreuvoir (the drinking fountain for horses). There's a very high standard in the restaurant, which is presided over by the *sommelier*, the master pastry chef, and the chef, who has won a string of medals. You'll understand why with dishes such as lobster stew, turbot *hollandaise* and foie gras. Excellent fish specialities. There's a menu at €32, but watch out if you order à la carte because many dishes attract supplements. Credit cards not accepted.

Port-Marly

78560 (2km NE)

L'Auberge du Relais Breton

27 rue de Paris.
Ⓣ01.39.58.64.33
Closed *Sun evening; Mon.*

The cuisine is deliciously prepared and served in substantial portions: try the stuffed sole or the chocolate tart to get the picture. Menus €19–38; the most expensive one includes apéritif, wine and coffee. Reckon on €38–45 à la carte. Nice terrace and garden for the summer. It's a shame it's a bit pricey but the service is good.

L'Auberge du Relais de Marly

13 rue de Paris.
Ⓣ and Ⓕ01.39.58.44.54
Closed *Sun and Tues evenings; Wed; Aug.*

The fact that the owners have been successfully running this charming country inn for more than a quarter of a century suggests they're doing something right. Madame produces delicious Normandy dishes but adds a few from other regions as well. Monsieur is debonair and smiling. Most people opt for a dish of the day – around €11 each – or for the menu at €24.50. You'll spend around €35 à la carte. In winter you can cosy up by the fire; in summer the garden is gorgeous. If you fancy fishing, simply wander across the road and drop your line in the Seine. *Free coffee offered to our readers on presentation of this guide.*

Meaux

77100

Acostel**

336 av. de la Victoire. Take the N3 in the direction of Châlons-en-Champagne, and it's on the right just after the Total garage; if you get to Trilport, you've gone too far.
Ⓣ01.64.33.28.58 Ⓕ01.64.33.28.25
Ⓦwww.acostel.fr
Reception open *from 7am to midnight.* **TV. Swimming pool. High chairs and games available. Car park.**

This unadorned concrete building is forbidding, but don't let that put you off – it's the back of the hotel. The front is much more appealing, with a lawn leading from the front door to the banks of the Marne, which is quite beautiful here. Clean rooms at garden level are €53 with shower/wc or €55 with bath. Breakfast €7. *10% discount except Christmas and New Year's Day.*

La Marée-Bleue

8 rue Jean-Jaurès.
Ⓣ01.64.34.08.46
Open *11.30am–3pm and 6.30–11pm.*

This inn, surrounded by a lovely garden, has huge, rustic dining rooms. The specialities are seafood, fish and Alsatian cooking like *baeckoffe*, fish *aïoli* and fish *choucroute* – their star dish. Menus €15, €21.70 and €26.25 (the last is a gourmet menu). *Free apéritif offered to our readers on presentation of this guide.*

Meudon

92190

Le Brimborion

8 rue de Vélizy; it's next to Bellevue station.
Ⓣ01.45.34.12.03

Open *noon–1.45pm and 7.45–10pm.* **Closed** *Sat lunch; Sun evening.*

This is not a modern house – witness the faded sign of the old hotel-restaurant Billard where the railway workers on the Versailles line used to come for a glass or two. Nowadays it's the place to lunch in Meudon. The dining rooms, one of them reserved for non-smokers, both have a certain style, and the family cooking is creative and delicious. They offer a classic tomato, Cantal cheese and mustard tart, salad of *andouille* with apples, saddle of rabbit or scallops with finely sliced chicory. Whatever you do, leave space for the crumble. *Formules* at €19 and €26; menus at €28 and €32. There's the tiniest irritation about the service – the staff start packing up as soon as they stop taking orders – but you can still enjoy the terrace. *Free coffee offered to our readers on presentation of this guide.*

Meudon-la-Forêt

92360

Restaurant La Mare aux Canards

Carrefour de la Mare-Adam; at the Meudon-Chaville exit on the N118, take the first left at the radio mast then head in the direction of Mare Adam.
☎01.46.32.07.16
Open *noon–2.30pm and 8–11pm.* **Closed** *Sun; Mon; fortnight in Aug.*

This restaurant, miles from anywhere, is the perfect place for lunch after a long walk in the Meudon woods. The big family dining room is convivial: they roast chicken, duck and pigeon on a spit in the handsome fireplace, and you're made to feel welcome. The service is fast, and the terrace pleasant in fine weather. There's a €12.50 *formule* of starter plus a quarter of chicken, and another at €17.30; à la carte you'll spend about €27 a head including wine. *Free apéritif offered to our readers on presentation of this guide.*

Le Central

26 rue Marcel-Allégot.
☎01.46.26.15.83
Closed *Sat evening; Sun; fortnight in Aug.*
Disabled access.

Whether you've got a raging hunger or a small appetite, you'll find just what you want here. Try a few Cancale oysters at the bar with a glass or two of Pouilly or sit down in the dining room for plates of duck and potato pie, calf's head or *coq au vin*. The aim of the owners is to send their customers away with a smile on their faces. To this commendable end they serve delicious calf's feet in vinaigrette, herrings in oil with onions, and *andouillette* – and there are two arrivals of fresh fish each day. Reckon on spending around €26; the dishes of the day range from €13–25.

Milly-la-Forêt

91490

Hôtel-restaurant Au Colombier

26 av. de Gamay; it's in the centre of Milly, 200m from the market place.
☎01.64.98.80.74
Closed *Fri evening May–Sept; Sat Oct–April.*
High chairs available.

The small, rustic dining room with sturdy beams has a nice little bar – it's where local workers come for lunch in the week and it's full of families on Sunday. There's a huge array of appetizing crudités set out on the buffet and menus at €10.50 and €15. Their regional dishes are impressive, especially the *coq au vin*. *Free apéritif offered to our readers on presentation of this guide.*

Montfort-L'Amaury

78490

L'Hostellerie des Tours

Place de l'Église.
☎01.34.86.00.43
Ⓔrestaurantdestours@free.fr
Closed *Tues evening; Wed; 5–9 Feb; 14 July–8 Aug.*

They hold the market on the pretty church square near to where this restaurant serves sound, traditional cuisine as it has for decades – they celebrated their 35th anniversary in 2003. The regulars come here because they know the dishes are well prepared. Four menus from €21 to €29 (with a *menu provençale* for €22.50); they do *aioli* and *bourride* on a Friday, the herrings in cream are splendid and the lamb shank is cooked to perfection. The dining room is large and light, and there's a terrace in the summer. *Free coffee offered to our readers on presentation of this guide.*

Chez Nous

22 rue de Paris.
01.34.86.01.62
Open *noon–2pm and 7.30–9.30pm.* **Closed** *Sun evening and Mon except public holidays; during Nov school holidays.*

The best place to eat in town. The dining room is long and decorated in bourgeois style and warm colours. The cooking is good value but sophisticated – marinated raw salmon, duck foie gras, a selection of fried fish and *aiguillettes* of duck with soft fruit sauce. Monsieur cooks, while Madame organizes the service: it's a successul family affair which attracts gourmands in the know. Menus €22 and €28; à la carte reckon on around €46 including drinks. Service is a little slow when the place is full.

Montmorency

95160

La Paimpolaise

30 rue Galliéni; it's on the hill on the way to Champeaux, and signposted off to the left.
01.34.28.12.05
Closed *Sun; Mon; Aug; a week at Christmas.*
Disabled access.

It's like being in Brittany but without the sea – Breton pictures, Breton furniture and Breton cuisine produced by a woman from Paimpol. Her *galettes* are the genuine article. Lunch menus at €8 (green salad, *galette* and dessert) and €10 (starter, *galette* or dish of the day plus dessert). Try the good *trégoroise* (*andouillette* and mustard), a fantastic *galette* with Maroilles cheese, and the creamy flan with pears and whipped cream. Good dry cider, too. There's a quiet terrace. *Free Breton apéritif offered to our readers on presentation of this guide.*

Au Cœur de la Forêt

Avenue du Repos-de-Diane; on the top of the plateau; follow the signs.
01.39.64.99.19
Closed *Mon; Thurs evening; Sun evening.*

You reach this restaurant lost in the middle of trees via a forest track full of potholes. So, if you're thinking of going at night, be warned. Sophisticated décor with pale wood, two cosy fireplaces that are kept alight throughout the winter, a pretty terrace for the summer – and cooking that more than justifies the detour, with unbeatable ingredients: beef from Aubrac, fish from Brittany and foie gras from Périgord. Everything is home-made – from the bread to the *pâtisserie* – and it's all delicious. Menus €24.50 (weekdays) and €31; dish of the day €19.50; reckon on at least €45 à la carte. The wines are searched out by the owner from the Loire and Rhône regions so they are therefore not too pricey. It's advisable to book, especially on Sundays.

Paris

75000

See map on pp.342–3

1st arrondissement

Hôtel de Lille**

8 rue du Pélican; M° Palais-Royal, Louvre or Pyramides.
01.42.33.33.42

This hotel is in a quiet street with a notorious past. In the fourteenth century it was called "rue du Poil-au-Con" because of the brothels situated nearby, but the more respectable residents elected to rename it "rue du Pélican", which caused much less of a sensation on their address cards. It's small, with just fourteen rooms (romantic and slightly old-fashioned), but it's well looked after by a nice family and good value for small budgets. Nos. 1, 4, 7 and 10 are gloomy but quiet. Doubles €40 with basin, €50 with shower. Breakfast €6. *10% discount on the room rate (15 Jan–28 Feb) offered to our readers on presentation of this guide.*

Hôtel de la Vallée*

84 rue Saint-Denis; M° Les Halles.
01.42.36.46.99 01.42.36.16.66
www.mapage.noos.fr/hvallee
TV.

In the middle of Les Halles – you couldn't find a more central location if you tried. It's pretty decent and the price is reasonable, though the sex shops along the street may not be to everyone's taste. Rooms overlooking the street are double-glazed but if you want to be sure of a quiet night, ask for one with a view of the courtyard or on one of the higher floors, although they are not so light. Doubles €48 with basin, €50 with shower and €63 with shower/wc. It would be difficult to find cheaper accommodation in the area. They take credit cards but not cheques and rooms must be paid for in advance.

BVJ Centre International

20 rue Jean-Jacques-Rousseau; M° Louvre-Rivoli or Palais-Royal-Musée-du-Louvre.
01.53.00.90.90 01.53.00.90.91
www.bvjhotel.com

This is a kind of youth hostel, with two hundred beds in rooms for two–six people, but you don't have to be a member of any organization to sleep here. It is open round the clock, but arrive or telephone from 9 to 9.30am to find out about availability, otherwise book two–three days in advance. (If it's full, you can go to a similar hotel in the Quartier Latin, with the same management). If you want to book as a group, say so when you book and the necessary arrangements will be made. Check-out at 10am, although there are some small luggage lockers (€2). A bed for one person costs €25–27, including breakfast, sheets and blankets, sharing in a room for over two people, or €27 per person in a double room. The place is well kept and the communal showers have recently been refurbished.

Hôtel Londres Saint-Honoré**

13 rue Saint-Roch; M° Tuileries or Pyramides.
01.42.60.15.62 01.42.60.16.00
hotel.londres.st.honore@gofornet.com
TV.

Here's a charming hotel with a warm family atmosphere in an area that is not exactly alluring. It's in an old bourgeois house, facing the church of St. Roch. The rooms are spacious and comfortable with double glazing, satellite TV and mini-bar; some are air-conditioned. Doubles €90–107 according to facilities. €15 per day for a dog. There are a number of pay car parks round about the hotel. All credit cards accepted. *10% discount for a minimum three-night stay offered to our readers on presentation of this guide.*

Restaurant Foujita

41 rue Saint-Roch; M° Pyramides or Tuileries.
01.42.61.42.93
Open *noon–2.15pm and in the evening until 10.15pm.* **Closed** *Sun.*

One of the best sushi bars in Paris, with reasonable prices (though it's more expensive in the evening) and a lunchtime menu at €11. There's *sushi*, *sashimi* and *natto*, a bowl of rice topped with raw fish. It's a small place, often full, so try to get there early; lunchtimes are best.

La Fresque

100 rue Rambuteau; M° Étienne-Marcel or Les Halles.
01.42.33.17.56
Open *noon–3.30pm and 7pm–midnight.* **Closed** *Sun lunch; a fortnight in mid-Aug.*

This is a friendly little restaurant in a shop that used to sell snails. The interior is lovely, with very old white tiles on the walls, brilliantly coloured frescoes and long wooden tables. It's very friendly, relaxed and cosmopolitan – you're jammed right up against your neighbour. The lunchtime *formule* offers starter, carefully prepared main course, a quarter-litre of wine and coffee for €11.50. Every day there are good starters, three or four traditional main course dishes, each with an original touch, and a vegetarian dish (a rarity in this town). About €20 à la carte; options vary a little at lunch and dinner. *Free apéritif offered to our readers on presentation of this guide.*

Le Rubis

10 rue du Marché-Saint-Honoré; M° Pyramides.
01.42.61.03.34
Closed *Sun; public holidays; 3 weeks in Aug; 10 days over Christmas.*

Open until 10pm (3pm on Sat). The kind of typical Parisian bistro/wine bar that's on the verge of extinction – great little dishes and wines direct from producers in Beaujolais. You can have a sandwich at the bar with a glass of red. Wines are served by the glass at really decent prices. They do excellent charcuterie and dishes of the day at around €10. In summer, they set up a couple of barrels on the pavement where you can prop yourself up and enjoy a cool glass of wine.

La Mousson

9 rue Thérèse; M° Pyramides or Palais-Royal.
01.42.60.59.46

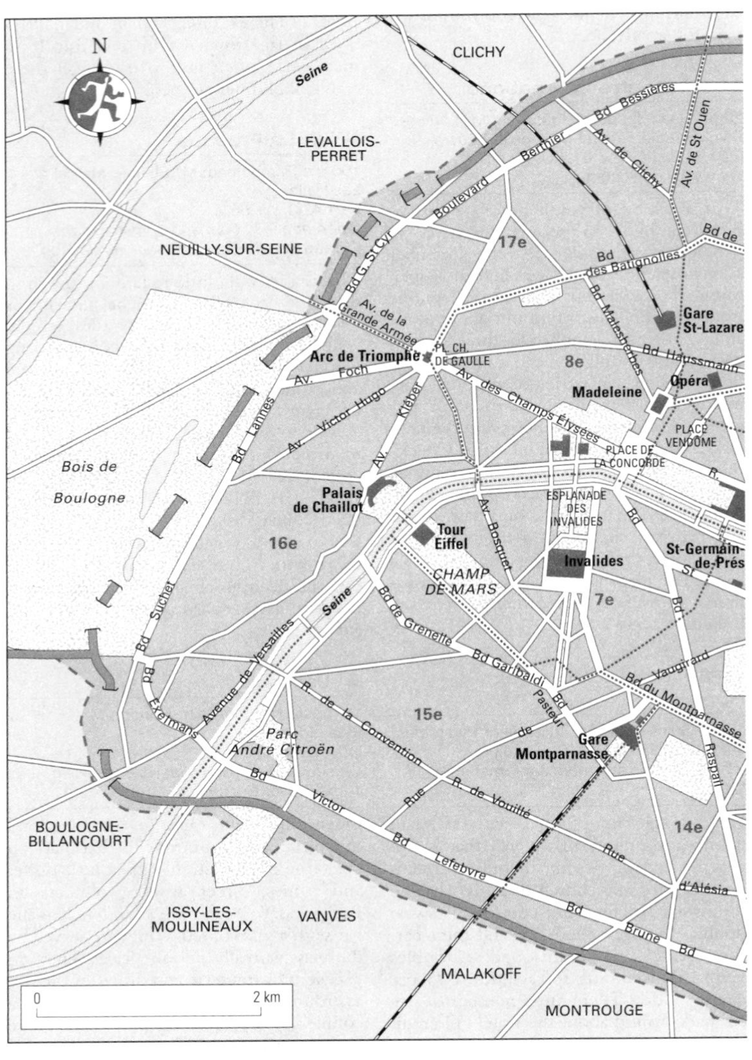
N
CLICHY
Seine
LEVALLOIS-
PERRET
NEUILLY-SUR-SEINE
Bd Bessières
Av. de St Ouen
Av. de Clichy
Berthier
Boulevard
Bd G. St Cyr
17e
Bd de
Bd
des Batignolles
Bd Malesherbes
Gare
St-Lazare
Av. de la
Grande Armée
Arc de Triomphe
PL. CH.
DE GAULLE
8e
Bd Haussmann
Av. Foch
Av. des Champs Élysées
Madeleine
Opéra
Av. Victor Hugo
Kléber
PLACE
VENDÔME
Bd Lannes
Bois de
Boulogne
Av.
PLACE DE
LA CONCORDE
R.
Palais
de Chaillot
ESPLANADE
DES
INVALIDES
Tour
Eiffel
Av. Bosquet
16e
Bd
St-Germain-
de-Prés
Invalides
CHAMP
DE MARS
Seine
7e
Bd Suchet
Bd de Grenelle
Bd Garibaldi
Bd Vaugirard
Avenue de Versailles
Bd Pasteur
Bd du Montparnasse
Bd Exelmans
R. de la Convention
15e
de
Gare
Montparnasse
Parc
André Citroën
Raspail
Bd Victor
Rue
R. de Vouillé
BOULOGNE-
BILLANCOURT
Bd Lefebvre
Rue
14e
d'Alésia
ISSY-LES-
MOULINEAUX
VANVES
Bd Brune
Bd
MALAKOFF
0
2 km
MONTROUGE

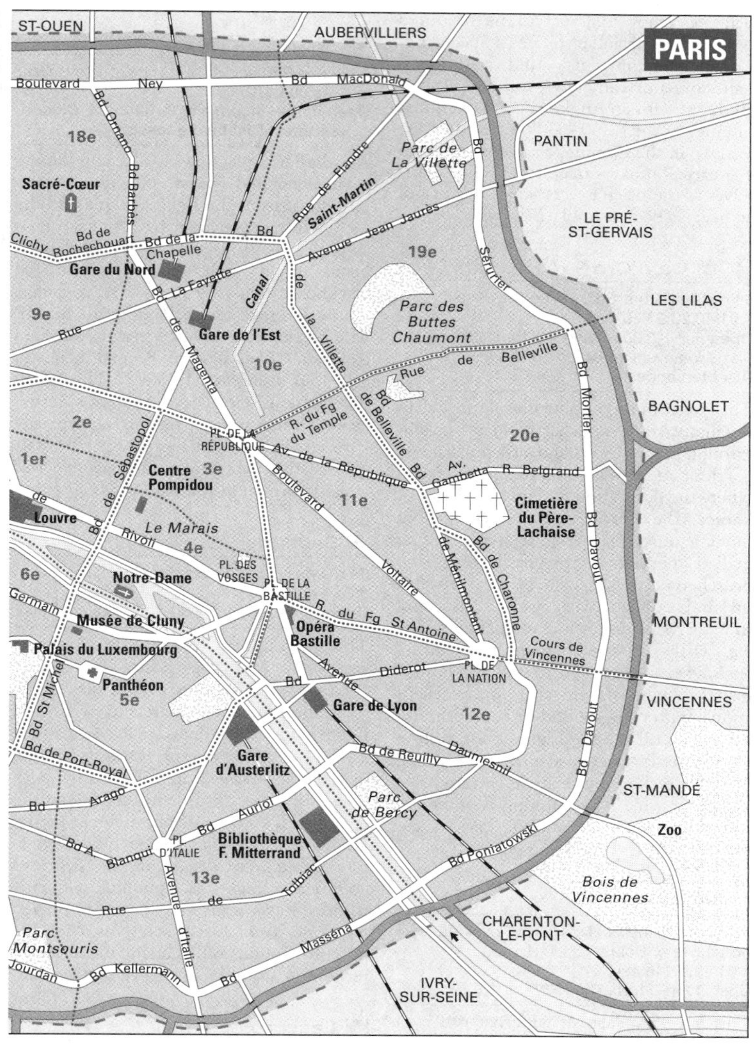
PARIS
ST-OUEN
AUBERVILLIERS
PANTIN
LE PRÉ-ST-GERVAIS
LES LILAS
BAGNOLET
MONTREUIL
VINCENNES
ST-MANDÉ
Zoo
Bois de Vincennes
CHARENTON-LE-PONT
IVRY-SUR-SEINE
Boulevard Ney
Bd MacDonald
18e
Sacré-Cœur
Bd Ornano
Bd Barbès
Parc de La Villette
Rue de Flandre
Saint-Martin
Bd Sérurier
Avenue Jean Jaurès
19e
Clichy
Bd de Rochechouart
Bd de la Chapelle
Bd
Gare du Nord
Bd La Fayette
Canal
Parc des Buttes Chaumont
9e
Rue
Bd de Magenta
Gare de l'Est
Rue de la Villette
10e
Rue de Belleville
Bd Mortier
2e
R. du Fg du Temple
Bd de Belleville
PL. DE LA RÉPUBLIQUE
20e
1er
Bd de Sébastopol
Centre Pompidou
3e
Av. de la République
Av. Gambetta
R. Belgrand
Boulevard Voltaire
11e
Cimetière du Père-Lachaise
Louvre
Rue de Rivoli
Le Marais
4e
Bd de Ménilmontant
Bd de Charonne
Bd Davout
6e
Notre-Dame
PL. DES VOSGES
PL. DE LA BASTILLE
Germain
R. du Fg St Antoine
Musée de Cluny
Opéra Bastille
Palais du Luxembourg
Cours de Vincennes
Avenue Diderot
PL. DE LA NATION
Panthéon
5e
Bd St Michel
Bd
Gare de Lyon
12e
Gare d'Austerlitz
Bd de Reuilly
Daumesnil
Bd de Port-Royal
Bd Arago
Parc de Bercy
Bd Auriol
Bd A. Blanqui
PL. D'ITALIE
Bibliothèque F. Mitterrand
Bd Poniatowski
13e
Avenue d'Italie
Rue de Tolbiac
Parc Montsouris
Bd Masséna
Jourdan
Bd Kellermann
Bd

Open *noon–2.30pm and 7.15–10.15pm.* **Closed** *Sun; Aug.*

In a quiet street, footsteps from Molière's birthplace, this original little restaurant offers tasty Cambodian specialities. The dining room is simple and convivial, a nice place to enjoy fragrant cuisine flavoured with mint, coriander, fennel... Specialities include shrimp curry and pork with lemongrass or caramel – you can wash it all down with an Angkor beer. Lunchtime menus at €12.60–16.80, another at €21.10 in the evening, or around €20–25 à la carte. Smokers need to restrain themselves as the place is very small. A word of advice: it's best to book. *Free coffee.*

Ca d'Oro

54 rue de l'Arbre-Sec; M° Louvre-Rivoli.
☎01.40.20.97.79
Open *noon–2.30pm and 7–11pm.* **Closed** *Sun; Mon evening; Ist fortnight Aug.* **Disabled access.**

This welcoming, unobtrusive little Italian restaurant sticks to what it does best. Go through a tiny room and down a narrow corridor and you'll come to another room where the decoration is gently evocative of Venice, the chef's home town. Before moving on to the pasta, treat yourself to grilled peppers with basil or some bruschetta – a slice of toast fried in olive oil and rubbed with garlic, basil and tomato. Main dishes include penne *disperata* with a sauce including garlic, anchovies, capers and olive oil; home-made ravioli; or, for two, an excellent risotto with ceps, seafood or cuttlefish. You can round off the meal with a hot mousse with marsala. There's a lunchtime menu, €14.50; reckon on €26 à la carte, not including wine. The cooking is authentic and generous. *Free house apéritif offered to our readers on presentation of this guide.*

Juvéniles

47 rue de Richelieu; M° Palais-Royal/Musée-du-Louvre or Bourse.
☎01.42.97.46.49
Open *noon–11pm.* **Closed** *Sun.*

This is a very Parisian wine bar run by a lively Scot. The place is frequented by groups who come to share a bottle of wine and tapas or eat a meal. Lunchtime *formule* at €14.50 and others at €17 and €23; à la carte you'll pay around €28. It's a bit crowded but the warm atmosphere encourages conversation. They sell a good selection of wines and sherries by the glass, and an impressive array of malt whiskies. Service is friendly and attentive. Best to book. *Free house apéritif offered to our readers on presentation of this guide.*

Chez Elle

7 rue des Prouvaires; M° Châtelet-Les Halles.
☎01.45.08.04.10
Open *noon–2.45pm and 7–10.45pm.* **Closed** *at weekends.* **Disabled access.**

Atmospheric place, with a bright dining room decorated with a collection of pin-up photos from the Belle Époque and the 1930s. Terrace, covered by a pretty green awning on sunny days. Well-balanced bistro menu with suggestions on the blackboard that may include steak *tartare*, whole kidneys, *osso buco* or pork brawn. The portions are so huge that they're hard to finish. Classic desserts. Several menus of two–four dishes at €15.50–27. The *Elle* in the name is Cécile, who enjoys herself every Thursday night by singing typically Parisian songs – part raunchy, part nostalgic – with a trio *musette*. *Free apéritif offered to our readers on presentation of this guide.*

Saudade

34 rue des Bourdonnais; M° Châtelet.
☎01.42.36.03.65
Open *noon–2pm and 7.30–11pm.* **Closed** *Sun.*

This sophisticated institution is a veritable ambassador for top-quality Portuguese cooking. Mirrors on the ceiling, tiles on the walls, the sounds of Madredeus or Cesaria Evora in the background (or live *fado* on the 1st Tues of every month). *Pasteis de bacalhau* or *escabeche de sardina* are followed by *carnes* (meat) or *peixes* (fish), with cod being the favourite: it comes in eight different preparations (fried, *gratiné*, grilled, with bread-crumbs, etc). For dessert, try the delicious *arroz doce,* a kind of rice pudding with cinnamon. *Vinho verde*, or a more full-bodied red wine to wash it down, plus a vintage port to round off. Lunch menu €20; reckon on around €30 à la carte. *Obrigado.*

Lescure

7 rue de Mondovi; M° Concorde.
☎01.42.60.18.91
Open *noon–2.15pm and 7–10.15pm.* **Closed** *weekends; in Aug; a week at Christmas.*

A very good restaurant which is often full

with Members of the National Assembly who've popped across the river for lunch. They've been feeding people here since 1919. The cooking is bourgeois, and the prices are popular; you eat squashed up against your neighbour. On the €21 menu you get a starter (the mackerel is delicious), a generously portioned main dish (beef bourguignon, maybe, or poached haddock), cheese, dessert and wine. À la carte, one of the best combinations to go for is hot pâté *en croûte* with stuffed *poule-au-pot* – yours for around €8. All in all you'll pay around €30 à la carte. In the evening, they sit people at the big communal table at the back of the room, creating a relaxed atmosphere. In summer people jostle for tables on the terrace.

L'Ardoise

28 rue du Mont-Thabor; M° Tuileries.
☎01.42.96.28.18
Open *noon–2.30pm and 6.30–11pm.* **Closed** *Aug; Christmas/New Year.*

Pierre Jay may be young, but he's been well trained. His most interesting ideas have made their way onto the €30 menu: fillet of beef with love apples, duck foie gras. The wines are really well priced, too. *Free glass of crème de cassis offered to our readers on presentation of this guide.*

À La Tour de Montlhéry, Chez Denise

5 rue des Prouvaires; M° Louvre-Rivoli, Châtelet or Les Halles.
☎01.42.36.21.82
Open *24 hours.* **Closed** *weekends; mid-July to mid-Aug.*

This is one of the oldest all-night restaurants in Paris. It's kept the atmosphere of an old Halles bistro, but the prices have definitely gone up since those days. The welcome is off-hand but the place is lively. There are moleskin benches, checked tablecloths and hams hanging from the ceiling. Big-hearted cooking includes *andouillette*, tripe, roast lamb with beans, beef *gros sel* and other such traditional fayre. No set menu; dishes cost between €19 and €23; reckon on a minimum of €35 a head with wine.

Macéo

15 rue des Petits-Champs; M° Pyramides, Bourse or Palais Royal.
☎01.42.97.53.85
Open *noon–2.30pm and 7–11pm.* **Closed** *Sat lunchtime; Sun; fortnight in Aug.*

This superb restaurant opened in 1880 and has had a devoted following ever since. Now it's owned by Mark Williamson who also owns *Willi's* wine bar next door; he named this place *Macéo*, after Macéo Parker, one of James Brown's Famous Flames. The décor has a modern British flavour, and the menu is a delight: joint of yellow pollack with a small dish of clams and asparagus, pan-fried swordfish with curry, risotto with vanilla, and pineapple with sweet spices. Lunch menus at €29.50 and €32, €35 and €37 in the evening. It's also a delight for vegetarians. The wine list is very impressive and the *fino* they serve at the bar while you're waiting for your table is excellent.

2nd arrondissement

Hôtel Sainte-Marie*

6 rue de la Ville-Neuve; M° Bonne-Nouvelle.
☎01.42.33.21.61 ℱ01.42.33.29.24
ⓔste.marie.hotel@ifrance.com
Open *24 hours.* **TV. Cots available. Car park.**

This is a pretty little hotel in a quiet street, very close to the shopping area of the Grands Boulevards. It has about twenty rooms, all well equipped. Some have beamed ceilings, but if you're tall and have a room in the attic mind your head because the ceilings slope. They're quite pleasant and even quite bright. Doubles with basin €30–38, with shower/wc €46–54, according to the season. Popular with visitors from overseas.

Tiquetonne Hôtel*

6 rue Tiquetonne; M° Étienne-Marcel or Réaumur-Sébastopol.
☎01.42.36.94.58 ℱ01.42.36.02.94
Open *7.30am–midnight.* **Closed** *Aug and one week Christmas–New Year.*

The pedestrianized streets leading to this one-star hotel are calm and beautiful. The rooms, which vary in size, are very well maintained, though the décor is faintly old-fashioned and the bathrooms pretty ordinary. The ones on the first two floors have double glazing and are quieter. Doubles with shower/wc €41.

Hôtel Bonne Nouvelle**

17 rue Beauregard; M° Bonne Nouvelle or Strasbourg-Saint-Denis.

Ⓣ01.45.08.42.42 Ⓕ01.40.26.05.81
Ⓦwww.hotel-bonne-nouvelle.com
TV. Pay car park.

Doubles €59–72 with shower/wc or bath; triple or quadruple rooms €85–115.They're equipped with TV, direct phone and hairdryer. They're an intriguing blend of old-fashioned and modern. It's a pity that some are small (especially no.17), a few are a bit stuffy and others a little dark. Exceptionally warm welcome. *A free breakfast per person or 10% discount on the room rate offered to our readers on presentation of this guide.*

Hôtel Vivienne**

40 rue Vivienne; M° Rue-Montmartre, Richelieu-Drouot or Bourse.
Ⓣ01.42.33.13.26 Ⓕ01.40.41.98.19.
Ⓔparis@hotel-vivienne.com
TV.

This hotel is in a neighbourhood with lots of tiny streets and lanes filled with shops specializing in coins and medals. It's very close to the *Hard Rock Café*, the Musée Grévin, the wax museum and the Théâtre des Variétés. Warm and informal welcome. The rooms are bright, clean, comfortable and quiet. No. 14 is particularly attractive, and there's a communicating door through to no.15, which makes it good for families. On the fifth and sixth floors you get a lovely view of Paris, and a few rooms have balconies. You can also take breakfast in your room for no extra charge. Doubles €69 with shower, €81 with shower/wc or €84 with bath, and a family room for €114–117.

Hôtel France d'Antin***

22 rue d'Antin; M° Quatre-Septembre or Opéra; RER Auber.
Ⓣ01.47.42.19.12 Ⓕ01.47.42.11.55
Ⓔcarlotta.hotels@wanadoo.fr
TV. Car park.

This pleasant three-star hotel is just 100m from the Opéra Garnier and the Louvre. It is classy yet congenial, and has been completely overhauled and redecorated. Many of the public rooms have exposed stonework and vaulted ceilings. The thirty pretty rooms all have mini-bar and satellite TV, and they're air-conditioned to give you respite from the Paris summer heat. Doubles with shower/wc from €160 with bath. *Free breakfast per person – usually €7 – offered to our readers on presentation of this guide.*

Chez Danie

5 rue de Louvois; M° Bourse or Quatre-Septembre.
Ⓣ01.42.96.64.05
Open *11.30am–3pm.* **Closed** *evenings; weekends; public holidays.*

This tiny restaurant, right next to the Bibliothèque Nationale, is an absolute delight. It serves good traditional dishes that change daily – *bœuf ficelle*, rabbit *en gibelotte*, beef with carrots or tarragon – and all the desserts are home-made. Great value in an area full of expensive, mediocre sandwich shops: the €8 *formule* offers a main course with a choice of starter or dessert, and there's a menu for €9.

Le Tambour

41 rue Montmartre; M° Châtelet, Les Halles or Sentier.
Ⓣ01.42.33.06.90
Open *daily 24 hours.*

The owner, André Camboulas, will immediately make you feel welcome; having built up a group of authentic Parisian bistros similar to this one, he's had plenty of practice. The dining room is decorated with urban detritus – cobblestones, drain covers and road signs. The cooking is very French. Lunchtime *formule* costs €10. Expect to pay €23 for dinner à la carte including drinks.

L'Escalier

80 rue Montmartre; M° Bourse.
Ⓣ01.42.36.95.49
Open *noon–3pm and 7.30–11pm.* **Closed** *Sat lunch; Sun.*

A tiny restaurant with a modern, warm décor. It attracts a 30-something, intellectual, hyperactive crowd – this is where they come to relax over lunch with a few mates or co-workers. There's a chattering, laughing atmosphere. The cuisine is cutting-edge and incredibly fine – unusual for the price. The dishes on the lunch *formules* (€12 and €18) change every day: *croustillant* of goat's cheese with pears on a salad with balsamic vinegar, chicken in a paprika sauce served with rice. Otherwise it's à la carte only; a meal costs around €25. Regular exhibitions of work by young artisits. *Free apéritif offered to our readers on presentation of this guide.*

La Souris Verte

52 rue Saint-Anne; M° Quatre-Septembre.
☎01.40.20.03.70
Closed *Sun.*

Last orders 11.15pm. A warm, friendly restaurant which looks like a small nineteenth-century house with its beams and red fabric stretched on the walls, and the vases of fresh flowers on every table. The cuisine is very French; freshly cooked, refined dishes that are excellent value for money. Menu (lunch and dinner) with starter, main course and dessert for €14, €20 including drinks. À la carte a meal costs about €15. A friendly, intimate atmosphere; the regulars add to the spirit of the place. It's best to book.

La Grille Montorgueil

50 rue Montorgueil; M° Les Halles or Étienne-Marcel.
☎01.42.33.21.21
Open *noon–3pm and 7.30pm–midnight; continuous service on weekends.*

This establishment, which has been around a good hundred years, has been attractively renovated – as has the pedestrianized street it stands on. The menu is full of traditional Parisian bistro fare: hot goat's cheese *amandine*, duck thigh *confit*, *andouillette*, grills and fish dishes and chocolate *fondant*. Straightforward, honest cooking with no frills. There are no set menus but a meal will probably set you back about €23; dishes of the day cost €12 or so. There's a terrace in summer. *Free house apéritif offered to our readers on presentation of this guide.*

Le Petit Vendôme

8 rue des Capucines; M° Opéra or Madeleine.
☎01.42.61.05.88
Open *7am to 8pm; restaurant 11am–4pm.* **Closed** *Sat; Sun; fortnight in Aug.*

This is an Auvergne establishment with a display of local cheeses set out on the bar counter, and Auvergne sausage used in their filling sandwiches. There's a scramble for places at lunchtime, when a dish of the day costs €13–15 or a complete meal around €25 à la carte. Sandwiches cost around €5. Reliable, substantial offerings: pork stewed in Saint-Pourçain wine, grilled pig's trotters, tripe and the like. Efficient, attractive service. Credit cards not accepted. *Free house apéritif.*

Il Buco

18 rue Léopold-Bellan; M° Sentier.
☎01.45.08.50.10
Open *noon–2.30pm and 8–11pm.* **Closed** *Sat lunch; Sun.*

A long, narrow restaurant lined with tables, with ochre walls and the menu written on mirrors. Very convivial but hardly intimate. Reckon on around €25 à la carte. Pasta, salads, *antipasti,* ham and fresh figs. Wine by the glass from €2.30. Nice touches on the tables: three kinds of bread, fresh flowers, flute glasses and candles.

3rd arrondissement

Hôtel du Vieux Saule***

6 rue de Picardie; M° République or Filles du Calvaire.
☎01.42.72.01.14 ℱ01.40.27.88.21
ⓦwww.hotelvieuxsaule.com
TV. Pay car park.

The window boxes and tiny flower garden brighten up the exterior of this lovely hotel; inside, the "high-tech" décor is beginning to date. Modern, comfortable rooms go for €91–106 with shower/wc or €106–121 with bath/wc, according to the season; prices increase during trade fairs. On the fourth floor there are more luxurious rooms with wood flooring and wood panelling on the walls for €151–166. Some rooms are small, but all are comfortable, air-conditioned and equipped with hairdryer, trouser press, iron, telephone, safe and cable TV (thirty channels), and there's free use of the sauna and internet access. Buffet breakfast, €10, is served in a sixteenth-century vaulted cellar. *One free breakfast per person per stay offered to our readers on presentation of this guide.*

Le Sablier

4 rue Dupetit-Thouars; M° République or Temple.
☎01.48.87.38.45
Closed *weekend; Aug; Christmas; New Year's Day; long weekends with public holidays.* **Disabled access.**

A small, spruce little dining room with wood panels and pink-dyed half-timbering and Sophie, the beaming owner, to greet you. She and her husband Jean have been running this romantic, slightly kitsch place in a quiet backstreet opposite the Carreau du Temple for 23 years. Jean sometimes pops his head out of the kitchen to greet regular customers. His cooking adroitly mixes sweet and savoury elements. Old but comfortable Métro benches serve as seats and a collection of hourglasses is displayed in one corner. Lunchtime menu €12.20. At night you have to eat à la carte (around €30 for a full meal without wine). It's best to book. *Free apéritif offered to our readers on presentation of this guide.*

Le Progrès

1 rue de Bretagne; M° Saint-Sébastien-Froissard.
☎01.42.72.37.00
Open *noon–3.30 pm.* **Closed** *Sun; 1 week in Feb; last week in July and first 3 weeks in Aug.* **High chairs available.**

Just what you expect a Parisian bistro to be: set on the street corner, with old chairs, cheerful service, regular customers from the neighbourhood, a Seventies look, an antique clock and metal Banania tins. Make sure to order as soon as you arrive, as the service is slow; consult the blackboard to find out about the two dishes of the day. Generous portions of seasonal food, sometimes including oysters; the preparation of meat is particularly superb. Dishes around €15. Varied and reasonably priced wine list. Good home-made desserts. Dining room upstairs, terrace for fine days.

Au Vieux Molière

12 passage Molière; M° Rambuteau.
☎01.42.78.37.87
Closed *Sat lunchtime; Sun.*

This is an attractive gourmet restaurant. It's located in an untouched part of Paris in the Beaubourg area, and is surrounded by galleries and bookshops. The atmosphere is equally charming inside: there are portraits and photographs on the wall. The menu offers appetizing, bourgeois dishes: veal kidneys, cod, rabbit in Chardonnay sauce, fillet of veal in pastry and good sauces. Fine ingredients and well-judged cooking. Weekday lunch *formules* for €15.25 and €21.10 or around €35 à la carte in the evening.

Chez Nénesse

17 rue de Saintonge; M°Filles-du-Calvairel.
☎01.42.78.46.49
Open *noon–2.30pm and 7.45–10.30pm.* **Closed** *weekends; public holidays; Christmas to New Year; Aug.*

The allure of old Paris is everywhere in this typical, traditional place with tiles on the floor and a lovely Formica bar. Good general atmosphere and a disarmingly smiling welcome. Good, classic well-prepared French cooking with substantial portions to make up for the lack of creative flair. This is a fine example of a successful family business – at lunchtime there's hardly any elbow-room, it's so packed. There are always two or three appetizing dishes of the day for around €9–12. In the evening, the cooking is more elaborate but still in the same spirit. A meal à la carte will cost around €30–38.

La Mule du Pape

8 rue du Pas-de-la-Mule; M°Bastille or Chemin-Vert.
☎01.42.74.55.80
Open *noon–4pm and 7–11pm.* **Closed** *Tues and Sun evenings; 3 weeks in Aug.*

Brunch and salon de thé at the weekend. You could write off this bourgeois-looking restaurant as being prissy and probably bad news for your wallet. But appearances can be deceptive; in fact, the setting is bright and comfortable, and they welcome you with a simple kindness that immediately puts you at your ease. The menu offers dishes to satisfy anyone, whether they're on a zero-calorie diet or looking to pig out: *œufs de la Mule* will do for the slimmers and *assiettes de la Mule* for the hungry; the *plats de la Mule* fit somewhere in between. Desserts are great. There's a menu with main meal and either a starter or dessert for €15; a meal à la carte will cost about €21. *Free apéritif or coffee offered to our readers on presentation of this guide.*

Chez Omar

47 rue de Bretagne; M° Temple.
☎01.42.72.36.26
Open *until around 11.30pm.* **Closed** *Sun lunchtime.*

Omar has been here for a good twenty years, and he serves an eclectic mix of locals and visitors from all over the world in a restaurant where Paris meets North Africa. The ceilings are high, the mirrors have bevelled edges, there's a superb bar counter and the tables are snugly spaced. Waiting staff are smiling and attentive. The couscous is excellent, as are the pastries, but their meat dishes are particularly tender and worthy of note. Expect to pay €25 à la carte. Credit cards are not accepted.

Le Pamphlet

38 rue Debelleyme; M° Filles-du-Calvaire or Saint Sébastien-Froissart.
☎01.42.72.39.24
Open *noon–2pm and 7. 30–11pm.* **Closed** *Sat lunch; Sun; Mon lunch; 1st fortnight in Jan; 2 weeks in Aug.*

An elegant, wood-panelled setting with comfortable seats and a restful atmosphere. The menus (at €30 and €45, lunch and dinner) change constantly. There are four original, mouth-watering choices per course: *aiguillette* of John Dory with purée of *andouillette*, prime cut of beef with tagliatelle and Fourme d'Ambert, *brandade* of squid and snail salad and a subtle banana *clafoutis* for dessert. Apéritif accompanied by tasty dry Laguiole sausage. Good choice of wines to complement the dishes.

4th arrondissement

Hôtel MIJE Fourcy

6 rue de Fourcy; M° Saint-Paul-le-Marais or Pont-Marie.
☎01.42.74.23.45 Ⓕ01.40.27.81.64
Ⓦwww.mije.com
Open *11am–2pm and 5–10pm.* **Closed** *Aug.* **Restaurant closed** *Sat; Sun lunch.*

This veritable palace opposite the Maison Européene de la Photographie was originally a seventeenth-century hotel before becoming one of the city's most famous brothels (this episode was concluded in 1946 by a law banning brothels). Now superbly renovated, it is divided into two wings connected by elegant corridors lined with wood. Small garden on the corner of rue Charlemagne. Rooms with one–eight beds, complete with mezzanine, washbasin and shower; toilets on the first floor. €27 per person in a room for four, €28 in a triple room, upwards of €32 in a double, €42 in a single; breakfast included. Half board compulsory for groups (except Aug). Restaurant in the stunning dining room with vaults and exposed stone; it is shared by the other two MIJE hotels in the neighbourhood. Set meal with dish of the day €8.50. Credit cards not accepted. Annual membership €2.50 *(free for our readers on presentation of this guide).*

Hôtel MIJE Le Fauconnier

11 rue Fauconnier; M° Saint-Paul-le-Marais or Pont-Marie.
☎01.42.74.23.45 Ⓕ01.40.27.81.64
Ⓦwww.mije.com
Closed *Aug.* **Restaurant closed** *weekend lunchtime.*

Magnificently restored seventeenth-century hotel with an imposing front door embellished with wood carvings. Inside, huge old wardrobes, massive chests, long, rustic tables and a splendid wrought-iron staircase with a ramp. All the rooms (one–eight beds) have been refurbished and complemented by excellent little bathrooms with shower/wc. The toilets are in the corridor. €27 per person in a room for four, €28 in a triple room, upwards of €32 in a double, €42 in a single; breakfast included. Half board compulsory for groups (except Aug). In summer you can have breakfast in the paved courtyard. Set menu with dish of the day €8.50. Credit cards not accepted. Annual membership €2.50 *(free for our readers on presentation of this guide).*

Hôtel MIJE Maubuisson

12, rue des Barres; M° Saint-Paul-le-Marais or Pont-Marie.
☎01.42.74.23.45 Ⓕ01.40.27.81.64
Ⓦwww.mije.com
Closed *Aug.* **Restaurant closed** *Sat and Sun lunch.*

Set in a wonderful medieval house with oriel windows, half-timbering and saw-tooth gables, in a pedestrianized area of the Marais that is dotted with café terraces in summer. Tastefully decorated interior, Gothic-style doors, old furniture made of solid wood. View of the neighbouring roofs and the stained-glass windows of the Saint-Gervais church. €27 per person in a room for four, €28 in a triple room, upwards of €32 in a double, €42 in a single; breakfast included. Half board compulsory for groups (except Aug). Set menu with dish of the day €8.50. Credit cards not accepted. Annual membership €2.50 *(free for our readers on presentation of this guide).*

Grand Hôtel du Loiret*

8 rue des Mauvais-Garçons; M° Hôtel-de-Ville.
☎01.48.87.77.00 Ⓕ01.48.04.96.56

Ⓔ hoteloiret@hotmail.com
TV.

Rooms are redecorated here every two years. Some are available with handbasin only for €40; those from the first to the fourth floors are in warm colours and have en-suite shower/wc (€60) or bath (€80). There is one room sleeping four on the seventh floor which has a panoramic view over the Panthéon and the Sacré Coeur – but there's no lift. *One free breakfast per room per night.*

Hôtel Jeanne d'Arc**

3 rue de Jarente; M° Saint-Paul, Chemin-Vert or Bastille; RER Châtelet.
Ⓣ 01.48.87.62.11 Ⓕ 01.48.87.37.31
TV.

You couldn't find a better location than this quiet neighbourhood near place Sainte-Catherine. The hotel is classy and well run, and it's been stylishly decorated – there's an enormous mirror in the foyer made by a local artist. All of the rooms have been refurbished and have shower/wc or bath, phone and cable **TV.** Doubles are €80–95; family rooms cost €112–140. It's essential to book.

Hôtel du 7e Art**

20 rue Saint-Paul; M° Saint-Paul or Sully-Morland.
Ⓣ 01.44.54.85.00 Ⓕ 01.42.77.69.10
Ⓔ hotel7art@wanadoo.fr
TV.

A fairly friendly hotel which is well managed and original. The staircase is black, the walls white, and the rooms are decorated with photomontages and posters of films from the '40s, '50s and '60s. Rooms cost €75–130 with shower or bath and multichannel TV. The top prices are for suites in the attic, which have sloping ceilings. There's a bar on the ground floor, and an unusual display case with plaster figures of Ray Charles, Mickey Mouse, Donald Duck and Laurel and Hardy. Cheques are not accepted. *Free house apéritif or coffee offered to our readers on presentation of this guide.*

Hôtel de Nice**

42 bis rue de Rivoli; M° Hôtel-de-Ville.
Ⓣ 01.42.78.55.29 Ⓕ 01.42.78.36.07
TV.

A very elegant and refined hotel with a small entrance and a multilingual welcome at reception. The owners used to run an antique business – they've kept a large number of attractive pieces to furnish the hotel. Breakfast is served in the television lounge, which has soft-coloured furnishings, eighteenth-century engravings and a portrait of an elegant woman surrounded by her pets. The soundproofed rooms are decorated with sumptuous wallpaper and have good bathrooms. Doubles with bath or shower cost €105, which isn't bad value for money; in summer the rooms overlooking place du Bourg-Tibourg are particularly good.

Hôtel de la Place des Vosges**

12 rue de Birague; M° Saint-Paul or Bastille.
Ⓣ 01.42.72.60.46 Ⓕ 01.42.72.02.64
Ⓔ hotel.place.des.vosges@gofornet.com
TV.

This hotel is in a grand street leading from place des Vosges to the Pavillon du Roi. The entrance is delightful. There are sixteen rooms which, though they're not spacious and have pretty ordinary furniture, are quiet, comfortable and impeccably clean. Doubles cost €120 with bath; family rooms €140. The double rooms with massage shower are normally out of reach at €202; however *on presentation of this guide they can be booked for €140.*

Au Jambon de Bayonne

6 rue de la Tacherie; M° Hôtel-de-Ville. It's just around the corner from the shops on the rue de Rivoli.
Ⓣ 01.42.78.45.45
Open *until 10pm.* **Closed** *weekends; 3 weeks in Aug.*

This establishment offers the best value for money in the arrondissement. You sit down on benches polished by years of use and tuck in to generous portions of regional cuisine. Each day they present a different classic dish – steak with *Marchand de vin sauce*, steak *tartare* and so on. These cost between €8.50 and €14; or you could go for one of the menus at €10.20 and €12.50, served at lunch; in the evening *fondue savoyarde* or *bourguignonne* + dessert + wine will set you back €23. *Menu carte* costs around €23. Convivial atmosphere: you can't fail to like it.

L'Enoteca

25 rue Charles-V; M° Saint-Paul.

☎01.42.78.91.44
Open *daily noon–1am (service until 11.30pm).*
Closed *lunchtimes in Aug; a week in mid-Aug; 1 or 2 days at Easter; a week around mid-Aug; a few days at Christmas; New Year's Day.*

This wine bar, which specializes in Italian wines, is a must. The décor is typical of the Marais, with exposed beams and old stonework. It gets really full and appeals to a very Parisian clientele – it's not unusual to spot the odd TV star. The famous, the not-so-famous and the downright obscure jostle to sample some of the 450 different Italian wines – the ones available by the glass change every week. You can travel north to south, tasting the whites of Trentino and Sicily or giving the reds of Piedmont and Basilicata a go. Accompany them with a few *antipasti misti*, slices of warm aubergine with fresh goat's cheese, *crostini* with Parma ham and mozzarella, fresh pasta with beef stew or chicken livers and tomatoes. Reckon on paying €12 for a dish of the day, or there's a €12.50 weekday lunch *formule* which includes a drink.

|●| La Baracane

38 rue des Tournelles; M° Chemin Vert or Bastille.
☎01.42.71.43.33
Open *noon–2.30pm and 7pm–midnight.*
Closed *Sat lunchtime; Sun.*

Booking advisable. On the one hand, there is the *Oulette,* the chic mother restaurant in the twelfth arrondissement; on the other, there is the *Baracane,* its little down-market annexe. In both cases the cooking looks towards the South-West of France, but here the atmosphere is more convivial. Customers sit elbow to elbow, and this encourages them to exchange comments about the excellent food, give tips when ordering, help finish off each other's meals and practise foreign languages. Lunch *formules* at €12 and €17 (including wine and coffee), and menus at €27 and €37 (including wine). With prices as reasonable as these, consider splashing out on a 1975 Armagnac. *Free house apéritif on presentation of this guide.*

|●| Aux Vins des Pyrénées

25 rue Beautreillis; M° Bastille or Saint-Paul.
☎01.42.72.64.94
Closed *Sat lunchtime; fortnight mid-Aug.*

A friendly cellar-bar-restaurant with a crowd of regulars – though new faces are warmly welcomed. The place is a nice mix of formal city and easy-going provincial, and it's reassuring that a place like this has managed to survive. The recipe is simple: select excellent quality meat and fish, grill it and serve with good side dishes and a decent glass of wine in a wood-panelled dining room with engraved mirrors and moleskin chairs. Finish by issuing a reasonable bill – lunch menu for €12.50 or around €23 for a full meal without wine (€17 at luchtime). One of our favourite restaurants.

|●| Restaurant Le Temps des Cerises

31 rue de la Cerisaie; M° Bastille or Sully-Morland.
☎01.42.72.08.63
Closed *evenings (but you can get a drink until 8pm); weekends; public holidays; Aug.*

This picturesque low-ceilinged eighteenth-century building used to house the office of the Celestine convent's bursar but it's been a bistro since 1900. The décor looks immediately familiar – zinc-topped bar where you can have a drink, marble-topped tables, leather benches – and the day's menu is written up on a blackboard. These, in addition to the photos of old Paris, the cheerful atmosphere and the good-natured customers, are reminders of what a Paris bistro used to be like. You'll find cooking to match: egg mayonnaise, grilled *andouillette* with mashed potato, *pot-au-feu,* lasagne. There's a menu at €12.50, and à la carte dishes from €11. It's essential to arrive before noon to get a table. There's an eclectic selection of wines. Credit cards not accepted.

|●| Le Marché

2 pl. du Marché-Sainte-Catherine; M° Saint-Paul.
☎01.42.77.34.88

A place with a Provençal feel, in the shade of the plane trees on the square. There are bright blue mosaics and yellow tablecloths. The chef prepares simple dishes using fresh produce that celebrate the traditional cuisine of the south; veal cutlet with morel sauce or breast of duck with spiced honey. Side dishes are delicious. There's a two-course lunch *formule* for €14 of starter/main course or main course/dessert, or a three-course dinner *formule* for €22. The wine list has wines from little vineyards and the cellar is awesome. There's a heated terrace in winter. Best to book in season. *Free apéritif offered to our readers on presentation of this guide.*

Le Dôme du Marais

53 bis rue des Francs-Bourgeois; M° Hôtel-de-Ville.
☎01.42.74.54.17
Open *Tues–Sat noon–2.30pm and 7.30–11pm.* **Closed** *15 Aug–10 Sept.* **High chairs available**

All traces of hardship have been banished from this former sales room for the State pawnbroker's, now a chic, refurbished restaurant. Dine under an eighteenth-century frosted-glass dome, surrounded by gold-leaf decorations on the burgundy walls. The chef served his apprenticeship abroad, and he has brought from this experience a subtle understanding of unusual spices, seen to good effect in his baked sea bream and haunch of venison. Cheapest menu €15 (lunchtime), with another at €23. Reckon on €40 à la carte. Friendly, painstaking service. Excellent wine list. If you want a quiet meal, avoid weekends, as it will be crowded and noisy.

Le Coude Fou

12 rue du Bourg-Tibourg; M° Hôtel-de-Ville.
☎01.42.77.15.16
Open *Noon–2.45pm and 7.30pm–midnight.* **Closed** *evenings from 24–31 Dec.*

An extremely successful wine bar-restaurant with a convivial atmosphere that attracts both true connoisseurs and curious beginners. The owner has assembled a highly original wine list, with many vintages from lesser-known vineyards. The slightly tatty walls in the two dining rooms are embellished with pretty, naive murals, and the tables are covered with old wine-bottle crates. Set lunch of starter + first course or main course + dessert, both with a glass of wine, at €16; set dinner €23. Reckon on around €30 à la carte, without drink. Small, traditional dishes, such as sautéed lamb with basil or salmon steak with Guérande salt, or more innovative dishes like ostrich steak with foie gras sauce. *Free apéritif offered to our readers on presentation of this guide.*

L'Endroit

24 rue des Tournelles; M° Bastille.
☎01.42.72.03.07
Open *noon–2pm and 7–10.30pm (midnight Fri and Sat).* **Closed** *Sun; Mon.*

Small restaurant with tasteful decoration that combines the warmth of wood with light sophistication, and white plumes with a *Routard* statuette. The cooking is simple but has some equally original touches: knuckle of lamb caramelized with rosemary: *carpaccio* of scallop with pistachio oil and *tatin* with tomato *confit* (delicious). Set menus at €17 and €29. Good wine list and cheerful, efficient service. *Liqueur on the house offered to our readers on presentation of this guide.*

Le Café de la Poste

13 rue Castex; M° Bastille.
☎01.42.72.95.35
Closed *Sun; public holidays.*

This café is opposite the post office, a brick building from the 1930s. It's a stylish place, with mosaic walls, wide benches, a huge mirror and a splendid wooden bar. Dishes change every day but there's always a pasta dish on the blackboard and a few meat and fish dishes as well – beef Stroganoff or sausage *fricassée*. Expect to pay around €19 for a meal; dishes cost €8.50–15.

Brasserie de l'Île-Saint-Louis

55 quai de Bourbon; M° Pont-Marie.
☎01.46.33.18.47
Open *noon–midnight, 6pm–midnight on Thursday.* **Closed** *Wed; Thurs lunchtime; Aug.*

Nothing's changed at this place for ages – the waiters have worked here for 25 years on average, and they're still enthusiastic and good-humoured. A stuffed stork lords it over the bar, and there's an old clock from the Vosges nearby. Rugby fans gather here in the evening if there's a match on. Star turns include omelette with herbs, *choucroute*, *cassoulet*, ham hock with lentils, fresh skate wings and Welsh rarebit. If you choose a decent Alsace wine to accompany your meal you'll pay about €24.

Brasserie Bofinger

5-7 rue de la Bastille; M° Bastille.
☎01.42.72.87.82
Open *noon–3pm and 6.30pm–1am (weekend non-stop noon–1am)*

This famous brasserie, created in 1864 and transformed in 1919, sports a décor much appreciated by the tourists who flock here to eat – although Parisians prove to be equally impressed by the beautiful stained glass and the upstairs room decorated by Hansi. Whether you eat here or stay downstairs, do not miss the house specialities of *choucroute* and seafood, especially the "*choucroute paysanne*" and the "*Mareyeur*" and the "*Royal*" seafood platters. Weekday lunchtime menu €21.50, with another menu at €31.50; *choucroutes* from €15.50 and seafood platters at €37.50 and €52.90, or €88 for two.

À l'Escale

1 rue des Deux-Ponts; M° Pont-Marie.
℡01.40.46.89.96
Open *noon–3pm.* **Closed** *evenings; Sun; Aug; between Christmas and New Year.*

This pleasant restaurant gets the sun and overlooks the Seine. It's a perfect place to restore your spirits after you've trailed round Notre-Dame or the Île Saint-Louis. There's no set menu, so opt for the dish of the day at €10–11.45: the ox tongue, *pot-au-feu*, roast veal, *coq au vin* and grills are all good. The wine list includes some intelligent choices. You'll pay about €23 for a full meal without a drink.

Bel Canto

72 quai de l'Hôtel-de-Ville; M° Hôtel-de-Ville.
℡01.42.78.30.18
Open *8–10pm.* **Closed** *lunchtimes; Aug.*

Between the Parma ham and the *tiramisù*, the glasses vibrate as Rodolfo and Mimì, the resident vocalists, serenade you while you dine – you come here almost as much for the show. The dishes are straight out of Italy – *carpaccio, osso buco, panna cotta* – and the wine is Italian, too. The menu costs about €50, without drink. Reservations essential. No-smoking restaurant.

5th arrondissement

Young and Happy Hostel

80 rue Mouffetard; M° Monge.
℡01.47.07.47.07 ℻01.47.07.22.24
www.youngandhappy.fr
Closed *11am–4pm and after 2am.*

Basic but clean hostel, undoubtedly the cheapest in this throbbing part of the city centre (the street outside is pretty noisy). It sleeps 70 people, with showers and toilets on the landing. Depending on the season, reckon on €20–23 per person in a dormitory, €23–25 in a double room, with breakfast included. Possibility of cooking in the communal kitchen or eating in the nearby university canteen. Telephone in the hall, soft-drinks machine, Internet area, TV and young, friendly staff. The hostel has been thriving for nearly twenty years, and has become particularly popular with English-speaking travellers. You can book in writing with a night's deposit, or try your luck *in situ* from 8–11am – but you'll be lucky to get in at the weekend without booking first. Credit cards not accepted.

Port-Royal Hôtel

8 bd. du Port-Royal; M° Gobelins.
℡01.43.31.70.06 ℻01.43.31.33.67
www.portroyalhotel.fr.st

This pretty little hotel, run by the same family for nearly seventy years, offers the advantage of a central location and reasonable prices. There is also a discreet charm in the subdued, floral decorations in the bedrooms and the patio where you can have breakfast on a sunny day. Double rooms up to €51 with washbasin, €82 with shower/wc, €87 with bath/wc. The owners go to great lengths to make their guests' stay enjoyable. They even give them a little guide to the area when they arrive, with information about taxis, buses, the Métro, museums, walks, restaurants, etc. It is advisable to book. Credit cards not accepted.

Hôtel Marignan*

13 rue du Sommerard; M° Maubert-Mutualité.
℡01.43.54.63.81
www.hotel-marignan.com

This has been a landing point for travellers for more than three decades. There are lots of common facilities: a dining room for picnics, a microwave, fridges, washing and drying machines, an iron and ironing board. Doubles with basin/wc €55 or €60, with shower/wc €75–80 according to the season, breakfast and taxes included. Out of season, rates go down after three nights. Credit cards not accepted. *A free trip on a bateau-mouche offered to our readers who come as a family.*

Familia Hôtel

11 rue des Écoles; M° Jussieu, Maubert-Mutualité or Cardinal-Lemoine.

Ⓣ01.43.54.55.27 Ⓕ01.43.29.61.77
Ⓦwww.hotel-paris-familia.com
TV. Disabled access. Pay car park.

A comfortable hotel run by the welcoming Gaucheron family, who'll go out of their way to help you. Décor is sophisticated and classic, with medieval-style tapestries and an old library. Doubles €84–113 with shower/wc or bath. Breakfast €6. Some rooms have four posters and frescoes; those on the fifth or sixth floors – some have been recently renovated – have views of Notre-Dame and the Paris rooftops. Reservations essential. *10% discount on the room rate for a stay of at least two consecutive nights (15 Jan–28 Feb, during Aug, and 1–25 Dec) offered to our readers on presentation of this guide.*

Hôtel de la Sorbonne**

6 rue Victor-Cousin; M° Saint-Michel, Cluny-Sorbonne or RER Luxembourg.
Ⓣ01.43.54.58.08 Ⓕ01.40.51.05.18
Ⓔreservation@hotelsorbonne.com
TV.

This charming little hotel is just opposite the venerable Sorbonne and is thus right in the heart of the student district. It has recently been completely refurbished; doubles with shower/wc or bath are €80–90, which is very reasonable considering that the place is so well run and friendly. Breakfast costs €5. The décor is a warm and colourful mixture of the contemporary and the retro, with a vaguely nineteenth-century feel to bring out the cosy atmosphere of the building. To make the pretty lounge even snugger, a log fire is lit as soon as winter starts to set in. *One free breakfast per person offered to our readers on presentation of this guide.*

Hôtel Esmeralda*

4 rue Saint-Julien-le-Pauvre; M° Saint-Michel or Maubert-Mutualité.
Ⓣ01.43.54.19.20 Ⓕ01.40.51.00.68

This small seventeenth-century hotel is a listed monument with a listed staircase. The nineteen rooms are fussily decorated with lots of attention to detail but you should probably ignore the furniture, which is a bit dated. The whole place is really due a redecoration, but because of its location it's always full – some rooms have a glancing view of Notre-Dame or Square Viviani. Doubles €60–85.

Hôtel des Grandes Écoles***

75 rue du Cardinal-Lemoine; M° Cardinal-Lemoine or Monge.
Ⓣ01.43.26.79.23 Ⓕ01.43.25.28.15
Ⓦwww.hotel-grandes-ecoles.com
Disabled access. Pay car park.

The hotel is in a private lane just round the corner from pl. de la Contrescarpe. It's a house of some charm and character, with a small paved courtyard and a leafy garden. The owner and her daughter have long welcomed tourists from around the world and, since this is a favourite with Americans in Paris, it's worth booking well in advance. Rooms are on either side of the lane, and they're carefully maintained and tastefully arranged. They have shower/wc or bath and cost €110–135. Breakfast is extra at €9. In fine weather you can take tea in the garden – even if you're not staying here.

Foyer du Vietnam

80 rue Monge; M° Monge.
Ⓣ01.45.35.32.54
Open *noon–2.30pm and 7–10.30pm.* **Closed** *Sun.*

This restaurant is very plain indeed. It is brightened up only by a poster of Ho Chi Minh and a TV – supposedly for the regulars' amusement but actually of more interest to the waiter. The genuine Vietnamese cooking makes no concessions to Western taste and remains resolutely authentic. They do an excellent pork soup (which, despite its small serving, is very substantial) and delicious steamed dumplings. The other dishes – fish simmered in a spicy sauce, pork kebabs, Hanoi soup – are of the same calibre. There are a few interesting specialities at the weekend, such as rice soup with tripe and grilled prawns with vermicelli. Menus €8.20 and €12.20, with a student menu at €7. à la carte around €15. *Free apéritif offered to our readers on presentation of this guide.*

Rotiss'bar

57 rue Galande; M° Saint-Michel or Maubert-Mutualité.
Ⓣ01.46.34.70.96
Open *daily noon–2.30pm and 7pm–1am; last orders 11pm.* **Closed** *Mon lunchtime.*

The rue Galande follows a route laid down in the thirteenth century and even in those days there was a roasting house barbecuing geese and suckling pig to calm the raging hunger of pilgrims and journeymen. The tradition has been stoutly maintained in this place where the menu lists mouthwatering dishes; you can even watch the gently turning hunks of golden meat basting in their juices before they make their way onto your plate. There are two lunch *formules* at €8 and €11 (starter, main course and dessert). Platters of barbecued meats cost from €9.30 depending on how many types of meat you choose. Desserts from €5. *Free apéritif offered to our readers on presentation of this guide.*

Tashi-Delek

4 rue des Fossés-Saint-Jacques; RER Luxembourg.
☎01.43.26.55.55
Open *noon–2.30pm and 7–11pm.* **Closed** *Sun; 15–27 Aug.*

Lunchtime menu €9, then €10 and €18. This was the first Tibetan restaurant in Paris, run by people who fled their country after the Chinese invasion. The big eye-catching Mandala in the entrance serves as a declaration of national pride, but the rest of the restaurant is more soberly decorated. If you do not opt for the menu, which offers the traditional *momoks* (steamed meat turnovers), take the opportunity of ordering several dishes to familiarize yourself with this remote culinary tradition: *sharil gogtsol* (meat balls with tomato sauce), *baktsa markou* (balls of pasta with melted butter and goat's cheese) and then, for the brave of heart, tea with salted butter. NB: there is an extra charge for the accompaniments. It is essential to book at night, as this place is well-known and justifiably popular. *Free house apéritif offered to our readers on presentation of this guide.*

Au Bon Coin

21 rue de la Collégiale; M° Gobelins or Censier-Daubenton.
☎01.43.31.55.57
Open *noon–2.30pm and 7–11pm (11.30 Fri and Sat).* **Closed** *Sun; first 3 weeks in Aug.*

Generous, hearty French cooking at very reasonable prices, in a classic setting (checked tablecloths). Lunch menu €11 (except Sat and public holidays), dinner €13, and another at €18. House specialities include herring fillets with apple, fried *escalope* of foie gras, *croustillant* of bass and *cassoulet* – and an enticing dessert buffet to round it off. Cheerful service. Arrive early in summer if you want to eat on the terrace – it fills up quickly. Booking advisable. Credit cards not accepted.

Au Coin des Gourmets

5 rue Dante; Maubert-Mutualité or Saint-Michel.
☎01.43.26.12.92
Open *noon–2.30pm and 7–10.30pm.* **Closed** *Mon lunch.*

This very popular restaurant offers "Indochinese specialities" and lives up to its promise by serving delicious dishes from all over the region, with greater subtlety than many Asian restaurants in Paris. The extensive menu includes grated green-papaya salad, *tea khtoeun* (braised duck stuffed with mushrooms – must be ordered 48hrs in advance), *bank xeo* (Vietnamese pancake) and Cambodian *amok*. Weekday lunchtime menu at €11.50. Reckon on around €25 à la carte. Friendly service. Special *soirées* are organized every three months, with a chance to try three or four dishes, each with a different glass of wine (with reservation only); around €45.

Ma Cuisine

26 bd. Saint-Germain; M° Maubert-Mutualité.
☎01.40.51.08.27
Closed *fortnight in Aug.*

Along the way from the Institut du Monde Arabe. The décor has maritime echoes (orange walls, blue beams) and nicely traditional cuisine with a welcoming touch of originality – some dishes have unexpected and subtle flavours. It's a hot favourite with office workers for lunch when there's a €11.50 menu with starter/main course or main course/dessert and a glass of wine. Good value for this part of town. There's another set menu for €25, served at lunch and dinner. The dining room is airy and pleasant and the service efficient. *Free apéritif offered to our readers on presentation of this guide.*

Le Reminet

3 rue des Grands-Degrés; M° Maubert-Mutualité.
☎01.44.07.04.24
Open *noon–2.15pm and 7.30–11pm in the week, later at the weekend.* **Closed** *Tues; Wed; 3 weeks in Aug.*

A restaurant which is situated in this quiet and charming *arrondissement* yet close to the hustling superficiality of Saint-Séverin. The cuisine is refined and the Norman chef prepares many of his region's dishes with certainty and simplicity: mussels, cockles, plaice – heaven for lovers of fresh fish and seafood. There's also rabbit and salt-flat lamb on offer, and the desserts are sublime. Weekday lunch menu €13, two more at €17 and €50; à la carte expect to pay around €35. It's best to book.

Pema Thang

13 rue de la Montagne-Sainte-Geneviève; M° Maubert-Mutualité.
☎01.43.54.34.34
Open *noon–2.30pm and 7–10.30pm.* **Closed** *Sun; Mon lunchtime; Sept.*

The Latin Quarter is still a magnet for the various ethnic groups in the French capital. Take this restaurant, for example, which feels rather like an inn on the high plateaux of Tibet. The cooking, which involves a lot of steaming, is full of delicate, subtle flavours and deserves to be more widely known. While the dishes are pure Tibetan, the flavours might remind you of India, China or Japan – and the cuisine is just as good as any of those. The lunchtime crowd consists of students from the Sorbonne and white-collar workers; they come here to savour *sha momok* (rather like *dim sum*), *thouk* (home-made noodles in clear soup) and *pemathan* (meat balls in a sweet-and-sour sauce with sautéed vegetables). Menus €13–17; one is vegetarian, another offers Tibetan specialities. Reckon on around €17 à la carte. Wines are reasonably priced and the desserts are surprisingly good.

Han Lim

6 rue Blainville; M° Monge.
☎01.43.54.62.74
Open *till 10.30pm.* **Closed** *Mon; Tues lunchtime; Aug.*

Right in the heart of Paris and surrounded by kebab joints, this excellent Korean restaurant is usually full of Korean customers (always a good sign). The lunchtime menu, €14, includes interesting dishes like *pot-au-feu* soup and *sautéed* seafood, rice and a selection of Korean veg, dessert and wine or mineral water. There's also a barbecue menu for €15.90. Both are good value given the exotic cooking. Very tasty grills of marinated beef and delectable garlic chicken. You'll pay about €20 for a meal à la carte. *Free coffee or tea offered to our readers on presentation of this guide.*

Le Mauzac

7 rue de l'Abbé-de-l'Épée; RER B Luxembourg.
☎01.46.33.75.22
Open *8am–midnight. Service noon–2.30pm and 8–11.30pm.* **Closed** *Sun; week of 15 Aug.*

Charming 1950s décor, a terrace that can be heated on fine days and hearty food. The menu rarely changes: *andouillette*, prime cut of beef, *blanquette*, a few less imaginative dishes of the day, and crumble or *crème brûlée* for dessert. Starters €4.75; platters of Auvergne charcuterie €5.10; main courses €11–13; desserts €4.55. A broad selection of wines at reasonable prices, with a particularly outstanding white Mauzac. They are sold by the glass, or in a carafe or bottle. *Free coffee offered to our readers on presentation of this guide.*

Chantairelle

17 rue Laplace; M° Cardinal-Lemoine or Maubert-Mutualité; RER B Luxembourg.
☎01.46.33.18.59
Open *noon–2pm and 7–10pm.* **Closed** *Sat lunch; Sun; week of 15 Aug.*

An embassy of Auvergne run by a radical proselyte for the produce of his homeland (which you can also buy to take away). Copious portions of heart-warming rural specialities, including stuffed cabbage and *pounti auvergnat*, excellent bread and good wine from small vineyards (belying the general belief that Auvergne has nothing to drink except water – although there are some fine mineral waters, such as the *Chateldon*). The attempt to re-create Auvergne even extends to a soundtrack with birdsong and the croaking of frogs! Lunchtime menu €14 (starter, main course and dessert); dinner menus €18 and €25. Lovely, relaxing garden terrace. Unfortunately, the service is sometimes a bit sloppy. *A platter of Auvergne farmyard cheeses offered to our readers who eat à la carte, on presentation of this guide.*

Le Buisson Ardent

25 rue de Jussieu; M° Jussieu.
☎01.43.54.93.02
Closed *weekends; Aug; Christmas and New Year.*

This is a very French place, the kind of

restaurant you'd miss if ever it closed. The décor is as comforting as the cooking, but while they use a lot of good regional produce, the approach is modern and the results tasty and full of colour. Dishes change frequently in response to the fresh market produce available. They do lunch menus for €15 and €28; a full meal à la carte will be about €35.

Le Languedoc

64 bd. de Port-Royal; M° Gobelins; RER Port-Royal.
☎01.47.07.24.47
Open *noon–2pm and 7–10pm.* **Closed** *Tues; Wed; 14 July–15 Aug; 20 Dec–6 Jan.*

They specialize in dishes of the southwest here, and the cooking is excellent. The service is reminiscent of the kind you'd get in a country restaurant. If you order herring, for example, they'll bring the entire dish to your table so you can help yourself. The duck *confit* with garlic potatoes is the star turn, but the meat dishes are well worth a try and the Rouergue wine washes it all down superbly. The poached haddock is also recommended. The white and red Gaillac from the proprietor's own vineyard aren't bad either. Set menu €19, or around €22 à la carte.

L'Équitable

47 bis rue Poliveau; M° Censier-Daubenton or Saint-Marcel.
☎01.43.31.69.20
Open *noon–2.30pm and 7.30–10.30pm.* **Closed** *Sun; Mon; Aug 2–22.*

The setting recalls a slightly rundown, provincial inn, but the cooking is inventive (the young chef served his apprenticeship with some great masters) and has attracted a well-heeled following. Traditional dishes are revitalized by exotic touches (vanilla in the Emperor fish, served on a banana leaf, or celery chips as a garnish for a tasty meat dish). Lunchtime menu €21; other menus €26 and €32. Desserts full of surprises. *Free apéritif offered to our readers on presentation of this guide.*

L'Atlas

10–12 bd. Saint-Germain; M° Maubert-Mutualité.
☎01.46.33.86.98
Open *noon–2.30pm and 7.30–11pm.* **Closed** *Mon.* **Disabled access.**

If you've been nosing round the Institut du Monde Arabe nearby, you can prolong the experience by eating here. Benjamin El-Jaziri, who has worked with some of the really big names, has remained faithful to the cooking of his native Morocco but goes easier on the fat and sugar. Try his incredibly light couscous served with meat and vegetables (it's beyond reproach), or one of sixteen superb *tajines*. As well as these classics, you can feast on grilled gambas, large prawns with paprika, lamb with mallow plant leaves, baked bream Moroccan style or, in season, partridge with mint and lemon. À la carte only; count on €30 without a drink. *Free digestif offered to our readers on presentation of this guide.*

Le Balzar

49 rue des Écoles; M° Cluny-la-Sorbonne or Odéon.
☎01.43.54.13.67 Ⓕ01.44.07.14.91
Open *8am–midnight.*

This fairly plush brasserie has been taken over by the Flo group. It's a pleasant place for supper after the theatre or the cinema, with artificial leather benches, large mirrors and waiters in white aprons. There's a long glassed-in terrace where in winter you can people-watch in the warmth. House specialities include poached eggs in jelly, sole meunière, skate in melted butter and choucroute: good food of the classic variety. A meal à la carte will set you back about €32. *Free apéritif offered to our readers on presentation of this guide.*

Le Petit Pontoise

9 rue de Pontoise; M° Maubert-Mutualité.
☎01.43.29.25.20
Open *noon–2.30pm and 7.30–10.30pm.*

The friendly owner worked in some famous French restaurants and obviously learned a thing or two, to judge by the inventive artichoke *tatin* or the more traditional but equally impressive traditional dishes like oxtail *parmentier* with foie gras. The desserts draw their inspiration from Italy, although the results are quirky: chocolate and gingerbread macaroon filled with ice cream on a bed of cream. Dish of the day €10. Reckon on €35 à la carte. A small, bistro-style dining room with plenty of regular customers. The owner also has a take-away outlet nearby (*Le Canard des Pharaons,* 7 rue de Pontoise, ☎01.43.25.35.93), with a couple of tables too. The dishes are mainly Italian, and some customers say they're even better than those of the main restaurant. *Free coffee offered to our readers on presentation of this guide.*

6th arrondissement

Hôtel des Académies*

15 rue de la Grande-Chaumière; M° Vavin.
Ⓣ01.43.26.66.44 Ⓕ01.43.26.03.72

Small family hotel in a quiet street. It has been going since the 1920s, but the atmosphere is more reminiscent of the 1950s. Doubles range from €51 with shower to €68.50 with shower/wc. You'll need to book in advance for the cheapest rooms, and they'll ask a deposit. The more expensive rooms are slightly overpriced. *One free breakfast per person per night on presentation of this guide.*

Hôtel de Nesle

7 rue de Nesle; M° Odéon.
Ⓣ and Ⓕ01.43.54.62.41
Ⓦwww.hoteldenesle.com
Open *8am till midnight.* Car park.

This hotel, located in a quiet street, is a throwback to the great hippy era. Anglo-Saxon and American accents mingle with Madame's North African one. She and her son shower affection on her guests and reign over their little kingdom with infinite good humour. There's a small interior garden where you can have a quiet read, and when it's not open there's a pretty terrace overlooking the garden. The twenty rooms are simple, clean, well maintained and individually decorated. Doubles range from €75 with basin or shower to €100 with bath and wc. Each room has its own personality: no. 2 has old paintings, slightly faded wallpaper and antique furniture, while no. 9 has been decorated in Egyptian style. The shower is rather awe-inspiring and there's even a little *hammam*, or steam bath, in no. 4. You'll need to reserve at least a week in advance, if you can get through to them by phone. Booking can be problematic.

Hôtel Saint-André-des-Arts*

66 rue Saint-André-des-Arts; M° Odéon.
Ⓣ01.43.26.96.16 Ⓕ01.43.29.73.34
Ⓔhsainand@wanadoo.fr

Superb location in the heart of Saint-Germain, opposite the famous passage Saint-André-des-Arts. There's nothing very luxurious (it has only one star) but it has a certain charm. The rooms are well kept, the bathrooms are spotless and the ceilings are adorned with pretty half-timbering. Double rooms with shower/wc or bath €80, including breakfast; reckon on €100 for three people and €110 for four, including breakfast. No TV, but the local cinemas present eclectic, high-quality programmes day and night. Very friendly service.

Hôtel du Lys**

23 rue Serpente; M° Saint-Michel or Odéon.
Ⓣ01.43.26.97.57 Ⓕ01.44.07.34.90
Ⓦwww.hoteldulys.co
TV.

A pleasant hotel in a seventeenth-century house on a quiet street. There's a nice family atmosphere – you'll get a great welcome. Brightly decorated in pink, blue, with roses or check, the rooms are all different, though they all have cable TV, individual safes and a hairdryer; some have a small balcony and look onto the courtyard, while others have beams. Doubles with shower/wc or bath €95–120 including breakfast; €135 for three people. Reservations advised. A cosy place for lovers.

Hôtel des Canettes**

17 rue des Canettes; M° Saint-Germain-des-Prés or Mabillon.
Ⓣ01.46.33.12.67 Ⓕ01.44.07.07.37
TV.

This establishment, hidden away in a very busy street full of pubs and chain stores, looks old, but inside the décor is rather modern. It was done up in 2001, and the twenty rooms are colourful and clean, though small. Doubles with shower/wc €90, €114 with bath/wc. *10% discount on the room rate offered to our readers on presentation of this guide.*

Grand Hôtel des Balcons**

3 rue Casimir-Delavigne; M° Odéon; RER B Luxembourg.
Ⓣ01.46.34.78.50 Ⓕ01.46.34.06.27
Ⓦwww.balcons.com
TV. Pay car park.

You'd be hard-pressed to find another place in the Latin Quarter, just 100m from the Odéon theatre, offering such value for money: spacious doubles €100–150 depending on facilities. There's an all-you-can-eat buffet breakfast for €10. The reception and public areas of the hotel are Art Deco style, though the rooms are merely functional. Everyone gets a warm welcome. *Free breakfast on the day of your birthday.*

Le Petit Bouillon

3 rue Racine; M° Cluny-Sorbonne or Odéon.
☎01.44.32.15.60
Open *noon–3pm and 7–11pm.* Closed *Sun lunchtime; Mon; Tues; Wed evening; in Aug.*

Just when the Latin Quarter seemed set to be overrun by fast-food joints and clothes shops, this restaurant came on the scene – or, to be more accurate, made a comeback, since it first appeared at the beginning of the twentieth century as the *Bouillon Camille Chartier*. After lots of ups and downs it ended up as a civil service canteen, but luckily the building was listed so the original interior remained – albeit in a rather dilapidated state. Today this magnificent Art Nouveau establishment has been restored to its former elegance. It's all there: bevelled mirrors, stained glass, marble mosaics and gold-leaf lettering. Beer plays a large part in the cooking, and there are lots of varieties to drink, including famous Trappist names like Rochefort, Chimay and Orval. They offer club sandwiches at €8.50, toasted sandwiches at €7.30 and the dish of the day will cost around €13. There are also soups of the day and a selection of wines by the glass and Belgian beers. *Free coffee offered to our readers on presentation of this guide.*

Nouvelle Couronne Thaï

17 rue Jules-Chaplain; M° Vavin.
☎01.43.54.29.88
Open *until 11pm.* **Closed** *Sun; Mon lunchtime.*

An excellent Thai restaurant in a secluded street. Someone has taken a lot of trouble over the setting, with its soft colours, subdued tones and well-spaced tables. And similar care is lavished on the cuisine: fish soup delicately flavoured with coconut milk, casserole of seafood, lacquered chicken with lemongrass, spicy duck sautéed with bamboo shoots and pork spare ribs are among the wonderful things listed on the menu, which also includes Chinese dishes and steamed specialities. The wines are priced very reasonably and they serve Thai and Chinese beer. Set menus €7.90 and €9 at lunchtime; €12 and €16 in the evening. All in all, it's remarkable value.

L'Assignat

7 rue Guénégaud; M° Odéon.
☎01.43.54.87.68
Restaurant open *noon–3pm.* **Closed** *Sun; July.*

Who would have thought you'd find a little neighbourhood restaurant in this crowded narrow street? It's popular with local art dealers, people who work at the Mint and art students – many regulars grab what they want, write down what they've had and settle up at the end of the month. You'll enjoy good, simple food in a lively atmosphere – the owner's mother, who's been doing the cooking for a very long time, clearly revels in her job. Dish of the day costs €6.50; set lunch menu €11 or around the same à la carte. Credit cards are not accepted.

Le Petit Vatel

5 rue Lobineau; M° Mabillon.
☎01.43.54.28.49
Open *noon–2.30pm and 7–10.30pm.* **Closed** *Sun; Mon; 2nd fortnight in Feb.*

This tiny little place has been revamped and is firmly back on track. There's an €11 lunch *formule*; if you opt for individual dishes, a meal will cost about €20. Try the home-made terrine or, if you feel like something more elaborate, kidneys in white wine, sautéed lamb or beef *miroton*. The wines complement the cooking perfectly; they offer quite a few by the glass. This is a non-smoking restaurant. Credit cards are not accepted.

Bouillon Racine

3 rue Racine; M° Odéon or Cluny-Sorbonne.
☎01.44.32.15.60
Open *noon–3pm and 7–11pm.* **Closed** *fortnight in Aug.*

Weekday lunch *formule* at €15.50 including main meal with either a starter or dessert; full menu for €25; or around €30 à la carte. People come here mainly for the décor: the old *Bouillon Camille Chartier*, founded in 1906, ended its days sadly as a common works canteen. However, as it was given a *Monuments historiques* classification, the building retained all its features.

Through the efforts of the *compagnons du Devoir*, bevelled mirrors, opalines and stained-glass windows, marble mosaics and gold-leaf lettering have been returned to their former glory. In this superb Art Nouveau setting – try to get seated on the first floor – you can enjoy *croustillant* of stuffed suckling pig or a nice rib of beef. There's a wine list (a little expensive) and a large selection of Belgian beers. In the afternoon it's a tearoom serving waffles, homemade chocolate and *café liégeois* served by the jug. *Free house apéritif on presentation of this guide.*

Indonesia

12 rue de Vaugirard; M° Odéon; RER B Luxembourg.
☎01.43.25.70.22
Open *noon–2.30pm and 7–10.30pm (11pm Fri and Sat).* **Closed** *Sat lunchtime; lunchtimes in Aug.*

It's best to book for dinner. This is the only Indonesian restaurant in Paris to be set up as a workers' cooperative. The food is good and service comes with a smile. They serve a series of dishes from Java, Sumatra, Bali and Celebes; fish in coconut milk, *nasi goreng* (fried rice), *rendang* (meat in coconut milk with spices) and *balado ikan* (fish in spicy tomato sauce). Great curries and mutton satay. Weekday lunch *formule* €9, then menus at €16–23 or around €20 à la carte.

La Bauta

129 bd. du Montparnasse; M° Vavin.
☎01.43.22.52.35
Open *noon–2pm and 7.30–11pm.* **Closed** *Sat lunchtime; Sun.*

The décor is inspired by Venice and there's a superb collection of masks on the walls. The beautiful people who eat here are on to a good thing: everything is remarkably fresh and cooked with finesse. The pasta will satisfy everyone, and the chef cooks it perfectly *al dente* with all manner of sauces and accompaniments like langoustine, rosemary, cinammon, squid ink and clams. There are lunchtime menus for €16.90 and €23.20; an evening menu for €24.90, or you'll pay around €40 for a meal à la carte. Great service. *Free apéritif offered on presentation of this guide.*

La Rôtisserie d'En Face

2 rue Christine; M° Odéon.
☎01.43.26.40.98
Open *noon–2pm and 7–11pm.* **Closed** *Sat lunchtime; Sun.*

Top chef Jacques Cagna, whose flagship restaurant is just across the way, has every reason to be pleased. He's made this enterprise one of the Left Bank's institutions. Try his guineafowl *en pastilla*, with onion preserve in honey and aubergines, and you'll understand why. There are lots of things cooked on the *rotisserie*, all served with old-fashioned mashed potatoes. The food is definitely the high-point. The wine list isn't very tempting, and it can get noisy. Menus €17.24–27 at lunchtime, and a *menu-carte* for €39; reckon on €53 or so à la carte. *Free apéritif offered on presentation of this guide.*

L'Épi Dupin

11 rue Dupin; M° Sèvres-Babylone.
☎01.42.22.64.56
Open *noon–2.30pm and 7–11.30pm.* **Service** *until 10.30pm.* **Closed** *Sat; Sun; Mon lunch; 1–22 Aug.*

François Pasteau, who trained under Kérever and Faugeron, is a happy man, as you can tell from his beaming smile – his restaurant is full at lunchtime and his customers leave nothing on their plates but the pattern. You'll also get pretty good value for money: there's a lunchtime *formule* for €20 and you'll spend around €30 without wine à la carte. Dishes change according to what's good at the market. You get a daily choice of six starters, six main courses and six desserts; these might include rabbit turnovers with aubergines, scallops with lemons and pears and warm apples in flaky pastry with a mascarpone sorbet. Sheer delight from start to finish. You need to reserve a week in advance for first sitting at dinner.

Le Machon d'Henri

8 rue Guisarde; M° Saint-Germain-des-Prés.
☎01.43.29.08.70
Open *noon–2.30pm and 7–11.30pm.*

This is a good wine bar with stone walls and hefty beams. They serve a rich selection of carefully prepared classic dishes: slow-roast lamb cooked for seven hours with *gratin dauphinois*, courgette terrine, calf's liver with onion *compote*. Dishes of the day cost around €12; you'll spend €24 or thereabouts for a full meal. Reservations advised.

Le Procope

13 rue de l'Ancienne-Comédie; M° Odéon.
01.40.46.79.00
Open *11am–1am.* **Disabled access.**

This is the oldest café in Paris. In 1686, an Italian called Francesco Procopio dei Cotelli came to the city and opened a café serving a then-unknown drink called coffee. His establishment, close to the *Comédie Française*, soon gathered a clientele of writers and artists. In the eighteenth century it was a meeting place for Enlightenment philosophers – the idea for Diderot's famous *Encyclopedia* was spawned here during a conversation between him and d'Alembert. During the French Revolution, Danton, Marat and Camille Desmoulins met here, and it was also a haunt of Musset, Sand, Balzac, Huysmans, Verlaine and many others. It's still a haunt for intellectuals and, incredibly, its prices are still reasonable. The cooking is unabashedly French with meat and fish dishes swathed in sauce, platters of seafood, *coq au vin*, home-made sorbets and ice creams – you haven't been to Paris if you haven't eaten at *Procope*. Set menus €24 (noon–7pm) and €30 or about €45 à la carte. *Free house apéritif on presentation of this guide.*

La Méditerranée

2 pl. de l'Odéon; M° Odéon or RER B Luxembourg.
01.43.26.02.30
Open *noon–2.30pm and 7.30–11pm.*

Time was when the stars of the silver screen and other notables would congregate here. Everyone had their own table – from Orson Welles to Aragon, Picasso to Chagall, Man Ray to Jean-Louis Barrault. It has been delicately renovated to reveal its former glory. À la carte there's a good number of fish dishes and a handful of starters, main courses and desserts: red tuna *tartare*, sautéed calamari with red peppers, house *bouillabaisse,* fine crêpes with orange. There's a *formule* of main course with a choice of starter or dessert for €25, a menu for €29 and à la carte expect to pay around €45. *Free apéritif on presentation of this guide.*

7th arrondissement

Hôtel du Palais Bourbon**

49 rue de Bourgogne; M° Varenne or RER C Invalides.
01.44.11.30.70 01.45.55.20.21
www.hotel-palais-bourbon.com
TV.

Run by the same family for more than thirty years, this hotel has a pleasant reception with lofty beamed ceilings. Some of the rooms are vast – one of the benefits of being in an old building – and all have double glazing, mini-bar, TV, renovated bathrooms and sockets for connnecting a fax or modem. Doubles €75–125, breakfast included. Good prices for the district. *10% discount on the room rate (Jan, Feb, July and Aug 2005) on presentation of this guide.*

Grand Hôtel Lévêque*

29 rue Cler; M° École-Militaire or Latour-Maubourg.
01.47.05.49.15 01.45.50.49.36
www.hotel-leveque.com
TV.

The Eiffel Tower is very close by but you may find the picturesque street market in rue Cler even more appealing – rooms over the street get snapped up first. This is an authentic part of the district and the hotel with its fifty renovated rooms is reasonably priced. Doubles €86–91 with shower/wc. The décor doesn't leave a lasting impression but the rooms are clean and they have safes and hairdryers. The beds and carpets are new. It's a well-known place, so you may have to book. *One free breakfast per person on presentation of this guide.*

Hôtel Muguet**

11 rue Chevert; M° École Militaire or Latour-Maubourg.
01.47.05.05.93 01.45.50.25.37
www.hotelmuguet.com
TV. Pay car park. Disabled access.

This hotel stands out in this quiet little road, away from the traffic noise. The rooms are air-conditioned; doubles with shower or bath €100–107. Three rooms on the sixth floor have a view of the Eiffel Tower; others overlook Les Invalides. It's a good idea to reserve.

Hôtel Bersoly's Saint-Germain***

28 rue de Lille; M° Rue-du-Bac or Saint-Germain-des-Prés.
01.42.60.73.79 01.49.27.05.55
www.bersolyshotel.com

Closed *Aug.* **Disabled access. TV. Pay car park.**

Gorgeous hotel in a proud mansion built in the eighteenth century, in the middle of this historic part of Paris near the antique shops. The rooms may be small, but they're absolutely lovely and perfectly clean. Each bears the name of a painter, and there's a reproduction of one of the artist's pictures on the wall; "Gauguin" and "Turner" are particularly attractive. The hushed atmosphere, period furniture and exposed beams create a nostalgic ambience – but the telephones have Internet points. Rooms cost €107–122 with shower or bath. *Free breakfast from mid-Nov to the end of Feb, except during holiday periods. Free fruit juice or soft drink on presentation of this guide.*

Hôtel d'Orsay**

93 rue de Lille; M° Solférino or Assemblée Nationale, RER Musée d'Orsay.
Ⓣ01.47.05.85.54 Ⓕ01.45.55.51.16
Ⓔhotel.orsay@esprit-de-france.com
TV. Disbled access. High chairs available.

A quiet, comfortable and classy hotel very near the museum in the buildings of the old *Hotel Solférino* and the *Résidence d'Orsay*. Attractive reception. Double rooms €136–155, which is the going rate in this district. It's wise to book.

Chez Germaine

30 rue Pierre-Leroux; M° Duroc and Vanneau.
Ⓣ01.42.73.28.34
Open *noon–2.30pm and 7–9.30pm.* **Closed** *Sat evening; Sun; Aug.*

A simple, clean little dining room with a slightly provincial feel and a truly warm welcome. Dishes might include creamed salt cod or ox tripe, sautéed rabbit *chasseur*, *coq au vin*, haddock fillet salad or pork *colombo*; for dessert you should try the delicious *clafoutis*, an egg custard with apples. There's a lunchtime menu for €9; a menu served all day (except Sat) at €12 and another at €18.

L'Auvergne Gourmande

127 rue Saint-Dominique; M° École-Militaire or RER C Pont-de-l'Alma.
Ⓣ01.47.05.60.79
Open *noon–3pm and 7.30–11pm.* **Closed** *Sun; Aug.*

Two large communal tables take up all the space in what used to be a handkerchief-sized butcher's shop. It's a no-smoking room and as soon as the weather permits, they put out a couple of small tables on the pavement. You'll enjoy a nice, convivial atmosphere and excellent, mouth-watering bistro dishes with a strong Auvergnat accent. Virtually all the produce is trucked up from the region. It's best to book. Dish of the day €11, starters and desserts €5.50. Credit cards are not accepted. *Free coffee on presentation of this guide.*

Le Roupeyrac

62 rue de Bellechasse; M° Solférino.
Ⓣ01.45.51.33.42
Open *noon–2.30pm and 7.30–10.30pm.*
Closed *Sat evening; Sun.*

This is the kind of neighbourhood restaurant you used to find everywhere in Paris; there's none of the flim-flam or the fancy décor that you'll find in lesser (but commoner) places. Monsieur and Mme. Fau have been running this place for more than a quarter of a century, and it's named after the hamlet near Durenque in the Aveyron where they hail from. Wonderful country home cooking, with three or four fresh dishes every day – duck with orange, *haricot de mouton* (leg of lamb with haricot beans), oxtail *pot-au-feu*. Chef's special is marked up on the board daily. There are weekday lunch menus at €17.90 and €22.90 (starter, main meal and desert); à la carte around €26. Excellent value for money for the area. *Free apéritif on presentation of this guide.*

Au Babylone

13 rue de Babylone; M° Sèvres-Babylone.
Ⓣ01.45.48.72.13
Open *lunchtime only.* **Closed** *evenings; Sun; some public holidays; Aug.*

The large dining room is delightfully old-fashioned; the pictures on the walls have yellowed with age and the imitation leather benches are comfortable. The cooking is good, too, with a €18.50 lunch menu that includes three courses and a drink. Dishes of the day cost around €11. The kind of restaurant you always enjoy coming to and which never seems to change. Credit cards are not accepted.

Le Clos des Gourmets

16 av. Rapp; M° Alma-Marceau or RER C Pont-de-l'Alma.
01.45.51.75.61

Open *12.15–2pm and 7.15–11pm.* **Closed** *Sun; Mon; Aug.* **Disabled access.**

This restaurant, five minutes away from the Eiffel Tower, is not particularly inviting from the outside but it is worth a detour to discover the cooking of Arnaud Pitrois. Like many young chefs, Pitrois (who studied with some great masters) has opted for a single menu that changes with the seasons, although there are a few permanent fixtures that set the tone: warm oysters with *ravigote* sauce, fennel *confit* with spices and lemon sorbet. The prices are not exaggerated for gourmet food. At lunchtime you can choose two dishes from the menu for €23 or €27; at dinner, you can eat a full meal, without wine, for €32.

|●| Le Poch'tron

25 rue de Bellechasse; M° Solférino; RER Musée-d'Orsay.
☎01.45.51.27.11
Open *noon–2.30pm and 8–10.30pm.* **Closed** *Sat; Sun.* **Disabled access.**

The restaurant has an outlandish name but the welcoming *patronne* has a popular touch and her husband prepares the dishes with great care. You'll find calf's head with *sauce gribiche, andouillette de Troyes, baeckoffe* and all the traditional fayre you'd expect in a good bistro. You'll spend about €30 à la carte, not including wine – if you're just after a toasted sandwich it will set you back around €10.50–12. They won the Bouteille d'Or "best bistro" award in 1996, so you can rely on the wine list – it has particularly good bottles from Alsace.

|●| L'Ami Jean

27 rue Malar; M° Latour-Maubourg or École-Militaire.
☎01.47.05.86.89
Closed *Sun; Mon; 3 weeks in Aug.*

The décor is old-provincial with a touch of Parisian humour. The young chef, who worked as Camderborde's second in command at the *Régalade*, is going places and producing a cuisine which loudly proclaims its Basque origins. Here is a recipe for success: since Stéphane's arrival in the kitchen, the dining room has been packed out. The word has spread so quickly that it is almost essential to book (admittedly the place was already firmly established as a local institution for several decades). Very convivial surroundings, ideal for dining amongst friends, but a little less so if you want to enjoy an intimate meal. There's a menu for €28, or reckon on around €30–35 à la carte. All the classic Basque specialities are to be found chalked up on the board: cold meats, cod, cuttlefish, black pudding – all prepared according to the chef's whim. First-rate desserts, pleasant wines from the southwest, all in all, a gourmet bistro for food lovers.

|●| L'Œillade

10 rue Saint-Simon; M° Rue-du-Bac.
☎01.42.22.01.60
Service *12.30–2pm and 7. 30–10pm.* **Closed** *Sat lunch; Sun; 15–31 Aug.*

The two rooms in this restaurant run by Pascal Molto are usually full, with a mixture of locals and tourists. He likes to serve his customers as if they were his house guests, and offers hearty dishes that satisfy even the most voracious appetite. À la carte from €30. Reasonably priced wines and cheerful service. *Free apéritif offered to our readers on presentation of this guide.*

|●| Le Basilic

2 rue Casimir-Périer; M° Solferino or Invalides.
☎01.44.18.94.64
Open *noon–2.30pm and 7.30–10.30pm.*

Everyone in the 7th *arrondissement* comes to this chintzy, comfortable brasserie with its welcoming terrace facing the Sainte-Clothilde church. Try the roast lamb in salt, the sole *meunière* or any of the other classics. A complete meal will amount to €30–40.

8th arrondissement

Hôtel des Champs-Élysées**

2 rue d'Artois; M° Saint-Philippe-du-Roule or Franklin-D.-Roosevelt.
☎01.43.59.11.42 Ⓕ01.45.61.00.61
TV.

A clean, comfortable two-star hotel away from the racket of the Champs Élysées. The rooms are soundproofed and air-conditioned, and they're each decorated differently; each one has TV, mini-bar, room safe, hairdryer and direct dial telephone. Doubles with shower/wc or bath €95–103. Breakfast is served in a pretty vaulted room. Consider booking, as it's often full. They offer a dry cleaning service.

|●| Restaurant Chez Léon

5 rue de l'Isly; M° Saint-Lazare.
☎01.43.87.42.77
Closed *Sun; Aug.*

There's a "Relais Routier" sign outside – curious, because this place, right in the centre of town, is near a station, not a main road. But it is the real thing: waitresses in white aprons, transparent plastic table covers to protect the tablecloths, hole-in-the-ground loos and huge 1950s fridges in black and canary yellow. On the food front there are main courses like beef with tomato sauce and noodles and roast beef with mashed potato and cauliflower. The wine comes in 1/4-litre jugs. Starters cost around €4, main dishes €10; expect to pay €15. In case you're still puzzled, the only *Routier* in Paris earned its sign because the Federation of Road Hauliers is across the street.

|●| Tanjia

23 rue de Ponthieu; M° Franklin-D.-Roosevelt.
☎01.42.25.95.00
Open *noon–3pm and 8pm–1am.* **Closed** *Mon, Sat and Sun lunchtimes.*

One of Paris's fashionable restaurants, put together by the "Les Bains" team. The heavy carved wooden doors swing back to reveal an astonishing décor straight out of Marrakesh. Wooden chests, dimmed lanterns, melting cushions and magical candlelight in the evening create a symphony of purple perfumed by rose petal incense. The central room has a mezzanine for dining and there are veiled alcoves for more intimate meals; the basement bar is beautiful. It's generally full of people who come to be seen, but the remarkable cuisine is truly interesting, with a collection of Moroccan specialities: pigeon with almonds, generously flavoured couscous and a variety of starters. All dishes are beautifully presented and swiftly served. They serve a French or Moroccan lunch for €20, and menus in the evening from €43–53. À la carte, the price of a meal starts at €50. The oriental dancers arrive late in the evening. Reservations highly recommended.

|●| Le Bœuf sur le Toit

34 rue du Colisée; M° Franklin-D.-Roosevelt or Saint-Philippe-du-Roule.
☎01.53.93.65.55
Open *daily noon to 3pm and 7pm to 1am (midnight in July and Aug).*

It's not the best of the Flo brasseries, neither is it the cheapest, but its nostalgic air will seduce any Art Deco admirer. It's an age since Cocteau, Picasso, Poulenc, Milhaud and friends gathered in the *Bœuf*. This isn't the original 1940s establishment but it's been rebuilt a few streets away and pays creditable homage to the great inter-war brasserie. The engravings, drawings and sculptures hung on the wall also bear witness to the Années Folles. Typical – even predictable – brasserie menu with a few additions; seafood platters are the speciality. Lunch *formule* €23 and a set menu for €33. À la carte is pricey.

|●| Le Boucléon

10 rue de Constantinople; M° Europe.
☎01.42.93.73.33
Dinner *served until 10.45pm.* **Closed** *Sat; Sun; 1–22 Aug; a week in Dec.*

An easy-going local restaurant named after one of the gates of Constantinople that offers a cuisine from the southwest. The décor is simple but colourful, conjuring up vague images of a mixture of rugby, Basque *pelota* and the bullfight. This complements perfectly the simple but tasty dishes on offer – *parmentier* of black pudding, tender roast pork in beer – accompanied by a large choice of wines by the glass (€4–5). Starters cost €7–12; main meals €14–17; desserts around €7. Starters and desserts are all simple but good and well presented. Service is attentive and the fifteen tables are frequently all taken, sometimes by mysterious characters carrying violin cases. It's not the Cosa Nostra but more likely that these are people who frequent the many music workshops which abound in this area of the Paris Conservatoire. Opposite, at the *P'tit Bouco*, salads, sandwiches, *tapas* and toasted sandwiches. *Free coffee on presentation of this guide.*

|●| La Ferme des Mathurins

17 rue Vignon; M° Madeleine.
☎01.42.66.46.39
Closed *Sat; Sun; public holidays; Aug; 10 days at Christmas.* **Disabled access.**

Georges Simenon, the creator of the fictional French detective Maigret, used to be a regular here in the 1930s – as the plaque tells you. The cooking is straight out of the

Lyonnais area; *andouillette* with mustard, wine sausage, ham with cream sauce, salmon fillet with sorrel, succulent chunks of Charolais steak and pears in wine. Set menus €29 or €39; around €45 à la carte not including wine. They have a good selection of Burgundies – try the Irancy. The boss runs the kitchen and his wife is on duty in the dining room. Easy going welcome; most clients are, like Simenon, long-term regulars.

Spoon, Food and Wine

14 rue de Marignan; M° Franklin-D.-Roosevelt.
Ⓣ01.40.76.34.44
Open *noon–2pm and 2–11pm.* **Closed** *Sat; Sun; mid-July to mid-Aug; Christmas and New Year.*

The minimalist, sober interior creates a peaceful atmosphere; nothing is allowed to interrupt your studious enjoyment of the flavours produced by Alain Ducasse, one of the high priests of modern cooking. It's new-concept world cuisine: a fusion of flavours, spices and fragrances without a hint of fat. Diners can catch glimpses of the kitchen from the dining room, adding to the enjoyment and the spectacle, and the "classic" dishes which emerge have American, Thai and Italian influences – *calamares à la plancha* with satay sauce and sublime vegetables cooked in a wok, pasta with three-tomato marmelade, *ceviche à la grenobloise*. There's a selection of wines which is unique in Paris (just a shame they are quite so expensive). And don't forget the desserts – *malabar*-flavoured ice cream and strawberry ice cream Tagada.

9th arrondissement

Woodstock Hostel

48 rue Rodier; M° Anvers.
Ⓣ01.48.78.87.76 Ⓕ01.48.78.01.63
Ⓦwww.woodstock.fr
Open 8am–2am.

A cheap hotel for students, similar to a youth hostel. No frills but friendly. Double rooms €22, including breakfast; other rooms with bunks are also available. The charming inner patio is a big bonus in summer, but it is closed at 9.45pm (the neighbours complained about the partying!). Several (clean) showers on the landing on each floor. The décor is dotted with rock references, and the reception is presided over by a masked cow called Lily!

Hôtel des Arts**

7 cité Bergère; M° Rue-Montmartre or Cadet.
Ⓣ01.42.46.73.30 Ⓕ01.48.00.94.42
Disabled access. TV. Car park.

A two-star hotel with a pretty, pastel-pink façade in a lovely passageway. There's a confusing array of hotels to choose from around here – this one is the cheapest. It's far enough from the noise to be peaceful, and the rooms are clean. Doubles €65.50–68.50 with shower/wc or bath. The stairway is decorated with old showbills – it is the *Hôtel des Arts*, after all. Why not engage the handsome grey parrot in the lobby in conversation?

Hôtel Chopin**

46 passage Jouffroy; M° Grands Boulevards or Bourse.
Ⓣ01.47.70.58.10Ⓕ01.42.47.00.70
TV.

This jewel of a nineteenth-century town house is in a picturesque setting at the end of a narrow street – a quiet backwater round the corner from the Grands Boulevards. The handsome façade dates from 1850 and features elegant old woodwork. The rooms are quite pretty and the vista over the rooftops is reminiscent of an Impressionist painting – particularly if you're lucky enough to have a view of the setting sun. See if you can get a room on the fourth floor, as these are the brightest. It's best to avoid the ones looking onto the courtyard – all you'll see from these is a massive wall. Doubles with shower/wc or bath €80. Reserve well in advance. *One free breakfast per person per night.*

Hôtel Langlois-Hôtel des Croisés**

63 rue Saint-Lazare; M° Trinité.
Ⓣ01.48.74.78.24 Ⓕ01.49.95.04.43
Ⓦwww.hotel-langlois.com
TV.

This fantastic two-star attracts a host of regulars, so you will have to book. It's in a marvellous location and looks wonderful: the superb reception area has old wood panelling and you just sink into the carpet. The wood-panelled lift with wrought iron gates takes you up to rooms which are sheer magic. They're absolutely huge and each has an individual style with period furniture and marble fireplaces; some have Art Deco wood panelling. No. 25 has an alcove which doubles as a little sitting room and some of the bathrooms are enormous. Doubles with shower/wc or bath €89–90. Breakfast costs €7.50.

Hôtel de la Tour d'Auvergne***

10 rue de la Tour d'Auvergne; M° Cadet.
ⓣ01.48.78.61.60 ⓕ01.49.95.99.00
ⓦwwwhoteltourdauvergne.com
TV.

A pretty three-star in a quiet street near the Sacré-Cœur. The spacious, elegantly decorated rooms have beds with canopies, bath or shower, and hairdryers. There's a bar and 24-hour room service; doubles with bath €130. The fifth floor is exclusively for non-smokers. Breakfast, €10, is good. *10% discount on the room rate or one free breakfast per person.*

L'Auberge du Clou

30 av. Trudaine (on the corner of rue des Martyrs); M° Pigalle or Anvers.
ⓣ01.48.78.22.48
Service *until 11.30pm.* **Closed** *Mon; 24 and 25 Dec.*

You will be welcomed effusively in this charming rustic setting that recalls Normandy and its half-timbering. French classics reinterpreted by a chef with a passion for spices: artichoke hearts with warm foie gras; followed by a *magret* with Jakarta spices, rounded off by the Iranian dessert of saffron ice cream with pistachio pancake and orange supreme. Everything is prepared with finesse and subtlety, with a total respect for the ingredients. Two-dish lunchtime menu €15, dinner menus €18.50 and €24, or a minimum of €30 without drink. Excellent wine list, although a bit expensive for an average budget (although you do not have to drink a whole bottle). Terrace for fine days. Credit cards not accepted. *Free apéritif offered to our readers on presentation of this guide.*

Chartier

7 rue du Faubourg-Montmartre; M° Grands-Boulevards.
ⓣ01.47.70.86.29
Last orders *10pm; no reservations.*

You come in through a huge revolving door and find yourself in an immense turn-of-the-nineteenth-century restaurant with its original décor completely intact – in fact they've made it a listed building. Get there quickly before someone has the bright idea to refurbish it; there are only two or three places like this left and they're not half as wonderful as this one. It's always packed with regulars, local pensioners, students, poverty-stricken artists and tourists: there are 350 covers, 16 waiters and 1500 meals served a day. Menus, €12–18, change daily. The food is passable, though not always as hot as it could be.

Velly

52 rue Lamartine; M° Cadet.
01.48.78.60.05
Open *noon–2pm and 7.30–11pm (last orders 10. 45pm).* **Closed** *weekends; 3 weeks in Aug.*

A shoebox on two floors, with bistro décor and a kitchen open to view. Well-balanced menu that is being permanently renewed, according to the new arrivals in the market; it contains traditional dishes, but with occasional daring additions. Menus €21 (lunchtime) and €28 (with starter, main course and dessert). Wines from small vineyards from €16, also served by the glass. Highly attentive service. Often full, so book in good time.

Au Petit Riche

25 rue Le Peletier; M° Richelieu-Drouot.
ⓣ01.47.70.68.68
Open *noon–2.15pm and 7pm–12.15am.*
Closed *weekends 15 July–31 Aug.*

The restaurant was founded in 1854 – and with its labyrinth of intimate salons and Belle Époque décor, you might as well be dining in an Impressionist painting. They serve dishes like salad of Berry lentils, black pudding *parmentier*, rack of lamb, calf's head *en cocotte*. There's also a strong emphasis on seafood; the Oléron mussels are worth a particular mention. The cooking in this restaurant highlights the qualities of fine old recipes, and long may it continue. Menus €22.50–28.50, excluding drinks; à la carte around €35. The restaurant buzzes with atmosphere and it works with the local theatres to offer special price "theatre-dinner" promotions. *Free house apéritif on presentation of this guide.*

La Petite Sirène de Copenhague

47 rue Notre-Dame-de-Lorette; M° Saint-Georges.
ⓣ01.45.26.66.66

Open *Tues–Fri noon–2.30pm and 7.30–11pm.* **Closed** *Sat lunch; 3 weeks in Aug; Christmas–New Year.*

This Danish restaurant offers specialities somewhat modified to appeal to Gallic gourmands, all served in a bright and pleasant bistro. It's worth making the effort to come because the food is delicious and the prices are appealing. Fish and smoked salmon are regulars on the menus, flavoured with anything from juniper to curry – known to the Danish since the seventeenth century; try the salmon marinated in orange or the mackerel *croustillant*. The guineafowl *fricassée* with ceps with beetroot sauce and juniper berries is inventive and tasty, while the rhubarb soup with cream cheese sorbet is light and delicious. Menu of the day, chalked on the slate, is €24; there's a dinner version, including cheese, for €29. Peter is liable to offer you a shot of *aquavit*.

Restaurant Pétrelle

34 rue Pétrelle; M° Anvers or Poissonnière.
Ⓣ01.42.82.11.02
Service *noon–1.30pm and 8–9.30pm.*
Closed *Mon; Sat lunch; Sun; Aug; a week at Christmas.*

Snug dining room with ten tables, with a maximum of six people each. Customers are treated with the utmost respect; once they're ensconced in their seats, nobody will try to rush them to finish quickly as there's only one serving per session. Similarly, only the freshest ingredients are used for the dishes. Set menu €25, without a drink; reckon on €45–50 à la carte. It's advisable to book. The owners have just opened a shop at no. 28, *Les Vivres,* which also serves *table d'hôte* lunches (around €15) and sells products selected or prepared by the chef. Here also, quality is the watchword.

10th arrondissement

Hôtel Vicq d'Azir

21 rue Vicq d'Azir; M° Colonel-Fabien.
Ⓣ01.42.08.06.70 Ⓕ01.42.08.06.80
Ⓔvicqazir@club-internet.fr
Service *8am–10pm.*

A simple hotel with low-priced rooms which look out onto a charming interior courtyard planted with bushes. You have to pay when you check in: doubles €22–34 depending on facilities. Most of the rooms have been renovated, but due to space restrictions some have wc and shower down the hall. At these prices you can't expect luxury, but it's good value.

Hôtel Moderne du Temple

3 rue d'Aix; M° République or Goncourt.
Ⓣ01.42.08.09.04
Ⓦwww.hotelmodernedutemple.com

This place is a pleasant surprise; you'll find it between the lock on the Saint-Martin canal and the steep section of the faubourg du Temple. It's in a narrow, busy street where the crumbling façades are tinted with bright colours that have faded in the sun. The place is owned by a friendly Slovak who, after rather modest beginnings in 1989, now has 43 rooms with facilities that compare favourably with the nearby youth hostel; some have been improved, and all have direct dial telephone. Doubles €34–46 depending on facilities. There's a simple little bar. Reservations recommended, especially if you want a lower priced room.

Hôtel du Nord – Le Pari Vélo

47 rue Albert-Thomas; M° République.
Ⓣ01.42.01.66.00 Ⓕ01.42.01.92.10
TV.

A wonderful little hotel nestling between the pl. de la République and the canal Saint-Martin. Twenty-odd rooms that all differ in size, colour scheme and inspiration. They are meticulously decorated and create a welcoming atmosphere, with red floor tiles and exposed beams and stonework, plus china knick-knacks, bright colours and house plants that thrive in the overhead light: the effect is one of a guest house rather than a traditional hotel. It is also good value for money: doubles €60–71 and family rooms €91. Breakfast (with home-made jam) is served in the basement, in a vaulted cellar. You can choose between a romantic table for two or a large, communal table – less intimate but more convivial. The owners are avid cycling enthusiasts and they plan to make bikes available to their guests so that they can explore Paris from a different viewpoint. *10% discount on a room (2–15 Jan) offered to our readers on presentation of this guide.*

Hôtel Excelsior République**

4 rue de Lancry; M° République or Jacques-Bonsergent.
01.42.06.23.30 Ⓕ01.42.06.09.80
Ⓔexcelsior.republique@club-internt.fr
TV.

Two-star hotel a stone's throw from the Grands Boulevards, the theatres and the place de la République, recently taken over by a delightful, enterprising couple. Choose one of the newly refurbished rooms (particularly for the quality of the bathrooms). They are all fairly small but they are very clean and have a direct phone line. Double rooms with shower/wc at €69. A word of advice: ask for confirmation of your booking. *10% discount on a room (for a stay of over two nights from 2 Jan–26 Dec for private guests) or free coffee offered to our readers on presentation of this guide.*

New Hôtel**

40 rue Saint-Quentin; M° Gare-de-l'Est.
Ⓣ01.48.78.04.83 Ⓕ01.40.82.91.22
Ⓦwww.newhotelparis.com
TV. Pay car park.

Areas around train stations are notoriously grim, and it would be wrong to pretend that this place is anything other than a cheap hotel – but it does have the advantage of being quiet. The rooms are functional, and most of them have the facilities you'd expect from a two-star: multi-channel TV, hairdryer, and most have air-conditioning. The vaulted basement has been transformed into a cellar with three dining rooms, each decorated in medieval style with rough stone walls; here you can have a generous breakfast, €5. If you turn right when you leave the hotel, you'll come to a terrace at the end of a short street affording a rare view over Paris. Double rooms €70–98 with shower or bath. *One free breakfast per person per night on presentation of this guide.*

Nord-Est Hôtel**

12 rue des Petits-Hôtels; M° Gare-du-Nord or Gare-de-l'Est.
Ⓣ01.47.70.07.18 Ⓕ01.42.46.73.50
Ⓔhotel.nord.est@wanadoo.fr
TV. Pay car park.

This hotel has a delightful provincial charm – fitting in a street with such a name. It's actually in a little garden where you can relax in good weather. There's a good deal of oak for the sitting room, dining room and reception. Small, clean, functional rooms that have recently been refurbished. Doubles €73 with shower/wc or bath. Book well in advance. *10% reduction on the room rate (for a minimum two-night stay Nov–Feb) except during trade fairs and festivals on presentation of this guide.*

Baalbeck

16 rue de Mazagran; M° Bonne-Nouvelle.
Ⓣ01.47.70.70.02
Service *11.30am–2.30pm and 7.30pm–1am Fri and Sat.* **Closed** *Sun; Aug.*

A couple of pointers on how to have a successful time here: one, you absolutely must book; and two, come in the evening. This Lebanese restaurant has some of the best Middle Eastern cooking in Paris. Choose the special *mezze formule* (€56 for two, €112 for four) and you'll get eighteen different dishes. During the week there's a €9 lunch menu and in the evening it's à la carte only – expect to pay around €28 without a drink, €30 with wine or *arak*. Things really begin to hot up after 10pm, when the belly dancers make their appearance – they're the genuine article and could rival those in Istanbul or Cairo. Don't forget to tip them. The rue d'Enghien and the rue de l'Échiquier are home to a number of Turkish restaurants where you can eat rather well for not too much money. Try the *mezze* (starters), grilled meats *adana* and the delicious rice cooked in milk. *Free coffee or mint tea offered on presentation of this guide.*

Restaurant de Bourgogne – Chez Maurice

26 rue des Vinaigriers; M° Jacques-Bonsergent or Gare-de-l'Est.
Ⓣ01.46.07.07.91
Open *noon–2.15pm and 7–11.15pm; Sat evening reservations only.* **Closed** *Sat evening; Sun; public holidays; the last week in July; 1–22 in Aug.*

This little neighbourhood restaurant, not far from the *Hôtel du Nord* and the romantic Saint-Martin canal with its Venetian bridge, hasn't changed for years; it's got a provincial feel and still serves local people. Very inexpensive set menus at €8.50 and €12 for lunch (€1 supplement in the evening). Dishes include beef *bouguignon*, steak with shallots and rabbit in mustard sauce. Round this off with a Côtes du Rhône (€3 for quarter-litre) or a Cheverny.

🍽 Fils du Soleil

5 rue René-Boulanger (opposite no. 70); M° République or Strasbourg-Saint-Denis.
☎01.44.52.01.21
Open *for lunch and dinner.* **Closed** *Sat lunch; Sun; Mon; 1st fortnight in Aug.*

Formerly a Mexican restaurant, now more Colombian, like its friendly owner. It lives up to its name's promise of sunny cooking. The main courses (traditional chilli dishes or delicious Colombian risotto) and exotic desserts (delicious milk jam with figs in syrup) are real talking points. The tequila is also guaranteed to loosen tongues... Lunchtime menu €10.50; reckon on around €23 à la carte.

🍽 La Marine

55 bis quai de Valmy; M° Jacques-Bonsergent or République.
☎01.42.39.69.81
Open *8.30am–2am. Restaurant noon–3pm and 8–11.45pm.* **Closed** *Sun; 1 Jan.*

This restaurant, which is run by three brothers, has a wonderful atmosphere, like a kind of East Parisian *Flore* with an extra dash of cocky humour. It is often packed, and its popularity can be gauged by the tables and chairs – somewhat the worse for wear – and the mouldings on the ceiling – blackened by cigarette smoke. Enticing bistro cooking: *millefeuille* of mullet, rolled larded salmon with lentils. Lunchtime menu €10.70; reckon on around €27 for dinner, excluding drinks. A limited selection of good wines in carafes and some home-made desserts to round off the meal. Friendly and efficient service. *Free coffee offered to our readers on presentation of this guide.*

🍽 SAS Le Chansonnier

14 rue Eugène-Varlin; M° Château-Landon.
☎01.42.09.40.58
Open *noon–3pm and 7–11pm.* **Closed** *Sat lunchtime; Sun; a week from 15 Aug.*

The bistro is on the corner of rue Pierre-Dupont, the songster in question, who wrote a famous drinking song to toast the world. Jean-Claude Lamouroux provides the atmosphere for a truly enjoyable meal; it's warm, the setting is well preserved, the service efficient and the dishes traditional – roast free-range chicken with *confit* of pork cheek, fillet of fish roasted with Provençal herbs. Lunch *formule* at €10.50, and menus at €22 and €23.50. All perfectly prepared and served with jugs of Bergerac. Enough to get you up on the table to raise your glass for a toast. This is a really good place. *Free house apéritif on presentation of this guide.*

🍽 La Vigne Saint-Laurent

2 rue Saint-Laurent; M° Gare-de-l'Est.
☎01.42.05.98.20
Open *noon–2.30pm and 7–10.30pm.* **Closed** *Sat; Sun; 3 weeks in Aug; Christmas–New Year.*

If you've got a train to catch or you're seeing someone off, don't just dive into the nearest brasserie – take a couple of minutes to find this pleasant wine bar instead. Inside there's a long, narrow room with a beautiful spiral staircase. At the far end, the pair of polite chaps with fine moustaches who run the place prepare delicious dishes (a different region of France is represented each day) with great care: rabbit with house *tapenade*, calf's head *sauce ravigote*, beef stewed in red wine. The *menu-assiette*, €12.50, gets you a platter of two types of sausage, a green salad, two cheeses and a glass of wine; a meal will cost about €20 à la carte. If you just want a snack, try a plate of charcuterie or some perfectly ripened cheeses (both €9.50). They offer a good selection of wines by the glass, jug or bottle – Côteaux du Lyonnais, Bourgueil. And to follow up, a home-made dessert perhaps?

🍽 Le Parmentier

12 rue Arthur-Groussier; M° Goncourt.
☎01.42.40.74.75
Open *for lunch and dinner until 11pm.*
Closed *Sat lunch; Sun; Aug.*

A modest but highly successful restaurant a stone's throw from the Sainte-Marthe neighbourhood. Its blue façade and colourful mosaics, its small dining room with shiny yellow walls, its cheerful, attentive service and its fresh gourmet food add up to a winning combination. The menus are chalked up on the blackboard: *hachis parmentier* (home-made, appropriately enough), poached salmon with Maussane olive oil (cooked just as it should be, a little pink in the centre), an orange crêpe for dessert. Weekday lunchtime menu €15; dinner menus €23 and €28, including wine and coffee. If you are not very hungry, you can pick isolated dishes from the menu on an à la carte basis. *Free apéritif offered to our readers on presentation of this guide.*

Le Réveil du Xe

35 rue du Château-d'Eau; M° Château-d'Eau or République.
☎01.42.41.77.59
Open *lunch only, plus Tues evening; Sat open 10am–4pm (last orders 2.30pm).* **Closed** *Sun; public holidays; a few days around 15 Aug.*

Simple but pleasant and authentic bistro run by wine connoisseurs who will give you a warm welcome and some tasty traditional food: tripoux, *pounti*, ox cheek *à l'auvergnate* with steamed potatoes, *aligot-sausage* (lunch on the 1st Tues and dinner on 1st Thurs of each month), succulent charcuterie and creamy cheeses from Auvergne. Lunchtime dishes of the day around €9–13; à la carte €18–20. Only snacks in the evening (except Thurs). Wonderful selection of reasonably priced wines. *Free apéritif or coffee offered to our readers on presentation of this guide.*

Café Panique

12 rue des Messageries; M° Poissonnière.
☎01.47.70.06.84
Open *noon–2.30pm and 7.30–10pm.* **Closed** *weekend; public holidays; Aug.*

A sober, restful setting with walls decorated with contemporary paintings that are regularly changed. The food combines fresh ingredients and subtle, delicious flavours, so just follow your fancy when you order: baked tail of monkfish with artichokes, caramelized sweet and sour veal breast. There is one set menu for dinner (starter, main course and dessert, €29) and a lighter version at lunchtime (main course, glass of wine and coffee,€19); reckon on €31 à la carte. As for the wine, follow the owner's advice, as she is certain to make a good choice. *Free apéritif offered to our readers on presentation of this guide.*

Flo

7 cour des Petites-Écuries; M° Château-d'Eau.
☎01.47.70.13.59
Open *daily noon–3pm and 7pm–1am.* High chairs available.

This is the place to go for *choucroute*. Herr Floederer's old brasserie dates from 1886 and is sparkling. Sarah Bernhardt used to have her meals delivered from here when she was at the Renaissance – others followed suit. Superb décor with stained-glass windows separating the rooms, richly decorated ceilings, leather benches, brass hatstands and period lighting. As well as the *choucroute*, you can enjoy platters of shellfish and seafood, foie gras with apples and grapes, and *sole meunière*. Given the wonderful surroundings, prices are reasonable: menus from €22.90 to €32.90; dish of the day €15, or around €40 à la carte. The place is always buzzing with locals and lots of tourists. *Free apéritif on presentation of this guide.*

Julien

16 rue du Faubourg-Saint-Denis; M° Strasbourg-Saint-Denis.
☎01.47.70.12.06
Open *noon–3pm and 7pm–1am.* **Closed** *Christmas.* **Disabled access. High chairs and games available.**

Another restaurant – one of the oldest in Paris – which has been given a makeover by the talented Monsieur Bücher. The same ingredients continue to work their magic: dazzling Art Nouveau interior, efficient service and a reasonable bill. Skilfully prepared specialities include salad of duck foie gras and morels, warm foie gras with lentils, goose *cassoulet*, grilled sole and *sole meunière*. You'll spend about €30–35 à la carte; there's also a menu at €23 (served at lunchtime and after 10pm, but not Sun) and another, served in the evening, at €33. *Free apéritif on presentation of this guide.*

Chez Michel

10 rue de Belzunce; M° Gare-du-Nord.
☎01.44.53.06.20
Service *noon–2pm and 7pm–midnight.* **Closed** *Mon lunchtime; weekend; Aug.* **Disabled access.**

The countless people who choose to stay in one of the many hotels near the station will be delighted to know that they can now eat in the area as well. The supreme skill of the Breton chef draws attention to this place, which is in a part of the city where greasy spoons abound. The terrine of *andouille* with peppercorns and shortbread biscuits is out of this world, while the guineafowl ravioli with a sauce of ceps and crushed walnuts is so incredibly good that you'll have to loosen your belt. Great desserts include warm *kouign aman* (traditional Breton yeast cake) – worth every calorie. Reckon on paying in the region of €30 à la carte.

11th arrondissement

Hôtel Notre-Dame**

51 rue de Malte; M° République or Oberkampf.
Ⓣ01.47.00.78.76 Ⓕ01.43.55.32.31
Ⓔhotelnotredame@wanadoo.fr
TV.

A well-run two-star hotel in a good location. Everything is grey, down to the business cards and the cat. The tastefully redecorated rooms have direct-dial phones, clock-radios and colour TV. The ones on the street are brighter. Doubles €37–66.50, according to season and facilities. It's best to book. Cheques are not accepted.

Hôtel Mondia**

22 rue du Grand-Prieuré; M° République or Oberkampf.
Ⓣ01.47.00.93.44 Ⓕ01.43.38.66.14
Ⓦwww.hotel-mondia.com
TV.

This well-run hotel in a quiet little street is a good base if you're doing the sights on foot – Belleville, Ménilmontant and the Bastille are not too far away and the Marais-Les Halles area is very close. The comfortable rooms have shower or bath, hairdryer, safe and direct telephone – some even have marble fireplaces and the three on the top floor have sloping ceilings. Doubles €56–67, according to season. Prices may be negotiable if you're planning a long stay, except during trade fairs and festivals. Breakfast €5. *10% discount on the room rate (excluding trade fairs and festivals) on presentation of this guide.*

Hôtel Beauséjour**

71 av. Parmentier; M° Parmentier or Oberkampf.
Ⓣ01.47.00.38.16 Ⓕ01.43.55.47.89
TV.

A hotel with 31 rooms on six floors – with a lift. They all have bath or shower, double glazing, TV and direct telephone, and cost €60–78, some sleeping three or four. Breakfast costs €5. The little bar in the reception area is open 24 hours a day, and they offer room service. *10% discount on the room rate on presentation of this guide.*

Hôtel Daval**

21 rue Daval; M° Bastille.
Ⓣ01.47.00.51.23 Ⓕ01.40.21.80.26
Ⓔhoteldaval@wanadoo.fr
TV.

A nice two-star in the heart of the lively Bastille neighbourhood, near the bars of rue de Lappe and rue de la Roquette. It has modern décor and facilities – TV, double glazing, air conditioning and mini-safe. Doubles with shower €69. *One free breakfast per room per night (it normally costs €8 and is better than average).*

Hôtel Beaumarchais***

3 rue Oberkampf; M° Filles du Calvaire or Oberkampf.
Ⓣ01.53.36.86.86 Ⓕ01.43.38.32.86
Ⓦwww.hotelbeaumarchais.com
TV.

An ideal situation in a lively street full of bars, close to the Bastille, the République and the Marais. It's a modern hotel, decorated in bright sunshine colours and with slicked-up bathrooms. Spacious double rooms €105 with en-suite shower/wc or bath.

Chez Ramulaud

269 rue du Faubourg-Saint-Antoine; M° Faidherbe-Chaligny or Nation.
Ⓣ01.43.72.23.29
Service *noon–2.30pm and 8–11pm.* **Closed** *Sat lunch; Sun evening; a week at Christmas; a fortnight in Aug (in general). Sunday brunch noon–6pm.*

Hearty, copious and often innovative meals in a pretty, gleaming bistro setting (with a terrace for fine days). Classic dishes such as terrine and grilled *andouillette* are complemented by *ballotin* of smoked trout, haddock *mousse* and spicy loin of lamb *en croûte*. Lunchtime menus €9, €12 and €14, depending on the number of dishes ; dinner menu €26. Brunch €19. Reckon on €35 per person à la carte (but be careful, your bill can easily get of hand, although you're bound to get your money's worth). This is first and foremost a bistro, however, so wine takes pride of place, with an emphasis on value for money (bottles from €18–25). So, Bordeaux are out of question and there are only a few Burgundies, but plenty of little-known wines from Languedoc, South-West France, the Rhône and the Loire. No half-bottles, but wine is sold by the glass.

Booking is highly advisable; even on Mondays, it fills up.

🏃 |●| Au P'tit Cahoua

24 rue des Taillandiers; M° Bastille.
☎01.43.00.20.42
Open *noon–2pm and 7.30–11pm (11.30pm Fri and Sat).* **Closed** *24 and 25 Dec.*

Philippe Journoud has created a corner of France which is forever Morocco: ceramic tables, wrought iron, pottery, Berber hangings from the ceiling and on the walls, Arab rhythms in the background. Food-wise you'll find tangy *tajines*, and fluffy, spicy couscous; make sure you try the *kemias*, a selection of starters, or the *pastilla*. In the week, there's a lunch formule for €10; à la carte a meal will cost about €23. *Free coffee or mint tea on presentation of this guide.*

|●| 🏃 La Cale aux Huîtres

136 rue Saint-Maur; M° Goncourt or Couronnes.
☎01.48.06.02.47
Closed *Sat; Sun lunch; Mon; Aug.*

To be honest, the combination of oysters and sushi seemed a strange idea, but it works! If you're not convinced, try the modest €15 set menu (twelve oysters, six *makis*, *crépinette* and *ballon de blanc*); braver (and hungrier) souls can opt for the "Cale" menu, with portions large enough to satisfy even the most voracious appetite. Japanese-style screens, a bar shaped like the hull of a boat, large wooden tables and temporary exhibitions by young artists: in short, a trendy setting typical of this adventurous neighbourhood. Fast, friendly service. You can also buy take-away oysters. Book first if you want to go at the weekend. *Free apéritif offered to our readers on presentation of this guide.*

|●| Au Vieux Chêne

7 rue du Dahomey; M° Faidherbe-Chaligny.
☎01.43.73.23.89
Open *for lunch and dinner until 10pm (11pm Sat).* **Closed** *Sat lunch; Sun; Mon evening; fortnight in Aug.*

This little side-street almost passes unnoticed, but it hides this charming bistro, which is a relic from the days when carpentry was the lifeblood of this area. Amusing advertising signs and toys from the 1950s liven up the well-worn dining room (which even boasts three cast-iron pillars that are classified as a historic monument!). The cooking is similarly old-fashioned: the €10.70 lunchtime menu, which attracts many regular customers, could comprise, for example, *gratin* of aubergines, tomatoes and mozzarella, grilled sirloin steak, and *île flottante* for dessert. Dinner menu €18.30 (it's advisable to book first).

|●| La Vache Acrobate

77 rue Amelot; M° Chemin-Vert.
☎01.47.00.49.42
Open *noon–3pm and 7–11pm.* **Closed** *Sat lunch; Sun.*

Lunch *formule* at €13.50; à la carte expect to pay €20 for a main meal and dessert. A lively little café where the regulars know they'll enjoy warm, inventive cooking: salad of spinach and marinated chicken with raisins, grilled pork in honey and rosemary, regional dishes from the Ardèche. Elegant, hearty dishes – a starter here is equivalent to a main meal. It's just a shame that the surroundings don't quite match the quality of the cooking (small tables jammed in close together); fine for two or three but not for a bigger party. There's a good wine list with particular emphasis on wines from vineyards in the South West. They're all the same price: by the glass, quarter litre or by the bottle. Very friendly welcome.

|●| 🏃 Les Domaines qui montent

136 bd. Voltaire.
☎01.43.56.89.15
Open *noon–2pm.* **Closed** *Sun; the week of 15 Aug.*

You think you're entering a wine cellar until, among the racks of bottles, you notice a few tables with a reserved signs on them and a few more out on the terrace. The smiling owners, who are wine experts, have transformed this old hardware shop into one of the few *tables d'hôte* in the capital. They get deliveries of fresh produce daily and your meal will be accompanied by a bottle from the choice of 300 different wines or a glass from one of the eleven wine fountains. The huge range of dishes ranges from a plate of sausage to accompany your *apéritif* to savoury tarts, big salads, soups, dishes of the day, farmhouse cheeses and simple, tasty desserts. There's a *formule* at €13. Wines are sold by the glass or by the bottle at the shop prices. There are a few surprises, too, like the kiwi juice made in Brittany, the organic beer, or the *bernache* from Touraine. The latter, a sugary drink that's somewhere between cider and wine, is perfect with the home-made *tapenade*. It's best to book. There's another restaurant in the 17th *arrondissement. Free house apéritif or coffee offered on presentation of this guide.*

Cefalù

43 av. Philippe-August; M° Nation.
☎01.43.71.29.34
Open noon–2.pm and 7.30–10pm. **Closed** Sat lunchtime; Sun; Aug.

Mr Cala comes from Mussomeli, famous for its impregnable fortress. His skill does his homeland proud, and his Sicilian restaurant is one of the best places to eat Italian food in Paris: Sicilian antipasti, *spaghetti la sicilienne* (with garlic, tomato, aubergine, capers, anchovies, olives and basil), tagliatelle with a choice of four sauces (cream, gorgonzola, smoked bacon, mint and basil), *spaghetti à l'orange*. Try the *cannolo*, a Sicilian dessert traditionally served on Sunday, something like a brandy snap filled with fresh ricotta, candied fruit and chocolate; it's usually accompanied by a glass of Marsala. There's a €14.50 *formule* at weekday lunchtimes and a *menu dégustation* offering three courses and dessert for €30. Reservations advised for the evenings. *Free house apéritif on presentation of this guide.*

L'Ami Pierre

5 rue de la Main-d'Or; M° Ledru-Rollin.
☎01.47.00.17.35
Service *until 2am.* **Closed** *Sun; Mon; 19 July–19 Aug.* **Disabled access.**

Marie-Jo's been in the Bastille area for years; she's very easy-going and treats her clients like friends. The atmosphere can get a bit heated some evenings if the rugby fans tangle with the regulars – arty types like film-makers and designers. You can have a glass or two of Pouilly, Cahors or Quincy, and fill up on a plate of charcuterie. Dish of the day might be beef *bourguignon*, *pot-au-feu*, oxtail or creamed salt cod. Portions are substantial, which will help prepare you for the long night ahead – things can keep going around here until dawn. Reckon on around €15 à la carte with a drink included. *Free Calva after a meal offered on presentation of this guide.*

Le Villaret

13 rue Ternaux; M° Parmentier.
☎01.43.57.89.76
Open *noon–2pm and 7.30–11.30pm (1am Fri and Sat).* **Closed** *Sun; 10 days in April; Aug; 10 days at Christmas/New Year.*

Joël and the young chef Olivier Gaslain are in charge. Olivier goes to Rungis market for the produce and devises his menus according to what he selects. The prices haven't changed much over the years and the wide-ranging wine list has great vintages at reasonable rates. Starters include dishes such as scallops and thyme *en papillote* (baked in a paper sack), *fricassée* of ceps with garlic and flat-leaf parsley and great fat stalks of green asparagus; for a main course try medallions of monkfish with a sauce made from small crabs, calf's liver in Banyuls vinegar, a terrific sirloin steak with shallots or a *gratin* of Jerusalem artichokes. This is one of the best restaurants in Paris for dinner. Lunch menus at €20 and €25, including main meal and either starter or dessert. In the evening there's a *menu dégustation* for €46.

Les Amognes

243 rue du Faubourg-Saint-Antoine; M° Faidherbe-Chaligny.
☎01.43.72.73.05
Open *noon–2pm and 8–11pm.* **Closed** *Sat lunchtime; Sun; Mon lunchtime.* **Disabled access.**

There's a *menu-carte* at €33; at lunchtime you can choose a dish from the menu for €19. listing delicate flavours and interesting combinations. Try the fine pancakes stuffed with aubergine *compote* and cardamom. There's a very good selection of wines, too, but sadly they're rather pricey. The new owner, Jean Louis Thuillier, who has learnt his trade at *Robuchon,* offers seasonal dishes cooked for just the right amount of time, and accompanied by daring sauces: roast lot with vanilla and rice flavoured with turmeric, cod steak roast on a banana leaf with coconut milk. The wine list offers some great finds - both for the palate and the pocket. Word of mouth means that this is fast becoming a restaurant not to be missed in the 11th *arrondissement. Free house apéritif on presentation of this guide.*

12th arrondissement

Hôtel des Trois Gares**

1 rue Jules-César; M° Gare-de-Lyon.
☎01.43.43.01.70 Ⓕ01.43.41.36.58

Ⓔh3g@tiscali.fr
TV.

This is a well-located two-star in a quiet street between the Gare de Lyon, the Gare d'Austerlitz and Bastille-Plaisance. The façade is smart and the reception is decidedly modern, as are the functional rooms. Doubles €53 with basin or shower, €64–68 with shower/wc or bath, TV and direct dial telephone.

Nouvel Hôtel**

24 av. du Bel Air; M° Nation.
Ⓣ01.43.43.01.81 Ⓕ01.43.44.64.13
Ⓦwwwnouvel-hotel-paris.com
TV.

This establishment is a stone's throw from place de la Nation where you can hook up with any number of buses, the Métro or the RER. The street couldn't be quieter and all the rooms have double glazing. It's as clean as a whistle, and most rooms overlook a delightful garden where you can sit and relax in the shade of a tree. Floral décor, new flooring in all the common areas and excellent facilities. Doubles with shower €71, €81 with bath.

Hôtel Claret***

44 bd. de Bercy; M° Bercy.
Ⓣ01.46.28.41.31
Ⓕ01.49.28.09.29
Ⓦwww.hotel-claret.com
TV. Pay car park.

This unusual but elegant building, formerly a post house, stands out from its concrete surroundings. Now transformed into a charming three-star hotel, it reconciles modern comfort and traditional trappings. The 52 cosy rooms are decorated with painted furniture, thick gingham bedspreads and stained half-timbering to create a vaguely rural feel (evoking the neighbourhood's past as an agricultural and wine-growing area). If you want some real greenery, the Bercy gardens are close by, while the no. 14 bus will take you to Châtelet in four minutes and the Opéra in eight minutes – so you are in a central location. Double rooms €77–150, according to the degree of luxury. *10% discount on a room (subject to availability) offered to our readers on presentation of this guide.*

Hôtel Marceau**

13 rue Jules-César; M° Gare-de-Lyon or Bastille.
Ⓣ01.43.43.11.65 Ⓕ01.43.41.67.70
Ⓦwww.hotel-marceau.com
TV. Pay car park.

It's anyone's guess as to whether General Marceau really slept here. He led the troops in who in 1793 put down the insurrections in the Vendée against the revolutionary government. But the fact that the hotel and the general share a name gives the proprietor a good excuse to display in reception a page in the general's handwriting that he bought at auction. The rooms aren't bad, and some are quite nicely decorated with coordinating fabric, wall lights and wood panelling. Those overlooking the courtyard don't have a great view. Doubles €80–95 with shower or bath.

Le Relais de Paris Lyon Bastille**

35 rue de Cîteaux; Mo Faidherbe-Chaligny or Reuilly-Diderot.
Ⓣ01.43.07.77.28 Ⓕ01.43.46.67.45
ⒺLyon.Bastille@Lesrelaisdeparis.fr
TV. Open *all year round.*

A two-star hotel near the Faubourg Saint-Antoine that is a awash with colours. Choose between pink, blue, green or beige for your room; whatever the colour, it will be modern and comfortable, with a mini-bar and a direct phone line. Basically, it's run on classic lines, however, and it is popular with sales reps who are passing through for a trade fair. Double rooms €82–93, with shower or bath and wc; rooms for families €112–132 (extremely good value). Breakfast buffet €7.50, served in a superb vaulted cellar. *10% discount on a room offered to our readers on presentation of this guide.*

Au Pays de Vannes

34 bis rue de Wattignies; M° Michel-Bizot.
Ⓣ01.43.07.87.42
Open *11.45am–2.45pm.* **Closed** *evenings; Sun; public holidays; Aug.*

A good local eatery with a large Breton flag on the wall – the proprietors are proud of their roots. The €10 menu includes wine and offers a choice of main courses: sautéed pork with cabbage, roast guineafowl with shredded leeks, chicken with rice, breast of veal stuffed with braised celery hearts. Starters include egg mayonnaise and dessert is included. You'll get a good simple traditional French meal and the best value for money in the *arrondissement*. There's another menu at €13. Whole families turn up on Saturday lunchtime for a feast of seafood (oysters, grey and pink shrimps and half a crab) – €19.50 for a platter, including a quarter litre ofValencay white wine. *Free apéritif on presentation of this guide.*

L'Alchimiste

181 rue de Charenton; M° Montgallet.
☎01.43.47.10.38
Service *noon–2pm and 7.30–10pm Mon–Sat.* **Closed** *1st fortnight in Aug.*

Weekday lunchtime menu €13; dinner à la carte, for around €30, excluding drinks. Booking advisable.

Si Señor!

9 rue Antoine-Vollon; M° Ledru-Rollin.
☎01.43.47.18.01
Open *noon–2.30pm and 7.30–11pm.* **Bar closed** *in the afternoon.* **Closed** *Sun; Mon; Aug.*

This Spanish restaurant, run by a group of French and Spanish friends, has nothing to do with those Parisian tapas bars – not least because it isn't a bar. This is honest, robust cooking that is very delicious: great Spanish omelettes and *gambas* grilled *a la plancha* and astonishingly light deep-fried *calamares*. Different specialities from remote regions appear on the menus on a regular basis and there are good desserts. Menus €13.70 at lunchtime, €17.30 and €23 in the evening; reckon on €25 à la carte. They have a few tables on the terrace.

..Comme Cochons

135 rue de Charenton; M° Reuilly-Diderot.
☎01.43.42.43.36
Closed *Sun.*

A newish place that will blow you away first with its look – a modern bistro with a series of interesting paintings on the wall and topiary out front. There's also the remarkably priced lunch *formule* which, for €13, lists starter, main course, dessert and drink. The bill doubles in the evening but at no detriment to the pleasure; it's à la carte only and a meal will cost €23–28. Classic and traditional dishes chalked on the board are prepared with the freshest seasonal ingredients. Everything is tasty, generously served and attractively presented. No surprise that it's always full. It's first-come first-served at lunchtime, but you'd do well to book in the evening.

Cappadoce

12 rue de Capri; M° Michel-Bizot or Daumesnil.
☎01.43.46.17.20
Open *noon–2.30pm and 7–11.30pm.* **Closed** *Sat lunchtime; Sun; Aug.*

Turkish hospitality and kindness are the hallmarks of this establishment and, together with the elaborate cooking, they have helped spread its reputation far beyond the neighbourhood. Small (but not cramped), intricate dining room with soft lighting. The cheese roll and the aubergine caviar are exquisite, while the *pides* (Turkish pizzas), the grilled chicken with aubergines and yoghurt, the stuffed leg of lamb with spices and the kebabs will give your tastebuds a real treat. It's obvious why the restaurant is a success and it's best to book for dinner. Menus €14–23. Don't turn down the home-made desserts – the pumpkin in syrup is extraordinary, a bit like quince paste. Delightful, attentive service. *Free house digestif on presentation of this guide.*

Les Zygomates

7 rue de Capri; M° Michel-Bizot or Daumesnil.
☎01.40.19.93.04
Open *noon–2pm and 7.30–10.45pm.* **Closed** *Sun; Mon; Aug.*

Virtually nothing has changed here since the turn of the twentieth century – the trompe l'œil décor, the varnished wood and the marble were all here when this was a butcher's shop. Best of all, the prices are still reasonable – there's a set lunch menu for €14, and others at €22 and €27 with quite complex dishes: salad of foie gras with pinenuts, pig's tail stuffed with morels, bitter chocolate fondant with a sorbet. It's best to book. *Free coffee on presentation of this guide.*

Square Trousseau

1 rue Antoine-Vollon; M° Ledru-Rollin.
☎01.43.43.06.00
Service *until 11.30pm.* **Closed** *Sun; Mon; 3 weeks in Aug; 10 days in Dec.*

Two layers of curtains – lace and red velvet – shield you from prying eyes as you dine.

In style and atmosphere the restaurant resembles an elegant 1900s bistro: there's a superb antique bar, a mosaic tiled floor, red leather benches and mouldings on the ceiling. The day's specials are chalked up on big blackboards along with a €19 set lunch menu which comprises starter, main course, dessert and coffee. Presentation is pretty and the wine list has been well-researched. Menus at €20 (served lunchtimes only) and €25. The à la carte dishes change weekly; reckon on paying around €35, drink included. A very good restaurant with lots of regulars; reservations are highly recommended. Terrace in summer.

À La Biche au Bois

45 av. Ledru-Rollin; M° Gare-de-Lyon or Ledru-Rollin.
Ⓣ01.43.43.34.38
Open **noon–2.30pm and 7–11pm. Closed** *Sat; Sun; Mon lunch; 25 July–25 Aug; 21 Dec–2 Jan.* **Disabled access.**

If you like an old-style restaurant that does traditional dishes, this is the place for you. Even the décor, which is delightfully old-fashioned, is appealing, with prints and paintings on the walls, a Louis XIV-style clock, artificial flowers and leather benches. It gives good value on its €22.30 set menu, which lists dishes such as *foie gras* with salad, fillet of beef with a cep sauce, fillet of salmon with wild mushrooms, *coq au vin* and game in season – haunch of venison, say, or venison terrine, pheasant *casserole* or wild duck with fruits of the forest. The home-made pastries and reasonably priced wines are a bonus. All in all, this is an excellent restaurant where you can eat well for under €26. It's a good idea to reserve. *Free coffee on presentation of this guide.*

13th arrondissement

Hôtel Tolbiac

122 rue Tolbiac; M° Tolbiac or Pl.-d'Italie.
Ⓣ01.44.24.25.54 Ⓕ01.45.85.43.47
Ⓦwww.hotel-tolbiac.com
TV.

An enormous hotel with 47 rooms just five minutes from place d'Italie. There's a pleasant reception and the rooms are clean; nos. 19, 29, 39 and 49 are the largest and sunniest. Doubles with basin €32, €39 with shower/wc. In good weather, breakfast (€6) is served in a small, flower-filled courtyard. Free internet access for guests 1–9pm. Rue de Tolbiac is quite noisy but a number of the rooms are fitted with double glazing. Be careful not to leave valuable items in your room. Credit cards are not accepted.

Hôtel Coypel**

2 rue Coypel; M° Pl.-d'Italie.
Ⓣ01.43.31.18.08 Ⓕ01.47.07.27.45
TV. Open *all year round.*

The *Coypel*, conveniently situated close to pl. d'Italie, is the kind of hotel that's becoming increasingly hard to find. The rooms may lack imagination but they are well kept and offer all the necessary comfort, including double glazing. All the (recently refurbished) bathrooms are impeccable. Choose a room on the top floor, to take advantage of the view. Double rooms with shower/wc €47–53 depending on the size. Breakfast €5 (it's best to have it in your room as the breakfast room is minute).

Résidence Les Gobelins**

9 rue des Gobelins; M° Gobelins; buses 27, 47, 83, 91.
Ⓣ01.47.07.26.90 Ⓕ01.43.31.44.05
Ⓦwww.hotelgobelins.com
TV.

The rue des Gobelins follows the same route it did in the Middle Ages. The château that belonged to Blanche of Castile, wife of Louis VIII and mother of Louis IX, is just round the corner. The hotel is peaceful and great value for money. Lovely double rooms €70 with shower/wc or bath. The bathrooms are impeccably clean. You can sit outside in the little garden on warm evenings. *10% discount on the room rate for a minimum stay of two nights on presentation of this guide.*

Résidence Hôtelière Le Vert Galant***

41–43 rue Croulebarbe; M° Gobelins or Corvisart.
Ⓣ01.44.08.83.50 Ⓕ01.44.08.83.69
Restaurant closed *Sun; Mon.* **Disabled access. TV. Pay car park.**

A corner of the Basque country in the middle of the 13th *arrondissement*, just across from the Gobelins gardens. It's next to the Auberge Etchegorry restaurant, and belongs to the same people. It's set back from the road with a garden and lawn so it's quiet and has a certain charm. There are ten superb rooms – doubles €87 with shower, and €90 with bath and kitchenette. Delightful buffet breakfast served in a room overlooking the garden. *Free breakfast for your first night on presentation of this guide.*

⛹ ☗ Hôtel La Manufacture**

8 rue Philippe-de-Champaigne; M° Pl. d'Italie.
Ⓣ01.43.35.45.25 Ⓕ01.43.35.45.40
Ⓦwww.hotel-la-manufacture.com
TV. Cots available.

A new and elegant hotel, just next to the local town hall and the old Gobelins tapestry workshop. It's managed by a trio of women who run things like clockwork. The décor is in browns and beiges with splashes of red. The entrance hall has a wooden floor and a corner bar where you can have a drink next to the open fire in winter. Rooms are not huge but go for €99–133 for a double with shower/wc or bath, according to which floor they are on and the season. *One free breakfast per person on presentation of this guide.*

⛹ |●| Bida Saigon

44 av. d'Ivry; M° Porte-d'Ivry.
Ⓣ01.45.84.04.85
Open *daily 11am–10pm (from 10am in summer).*

A huge Vietnamese canteen at the top of an escalator at the entrance to the Terrasse des Olympiades and Paris-Store. The menu consists of the standard twenty or so savoury dishes. The soups, *phô* and Saigon soup come in large and small bowls, and helpings are generous. The spring rolls are crisp and the steamed rice cake is nicely done. Other good choices include pork spare ribs, grilled chicken with lemongrass, and rice with pork and stuffed crab. For dessert, try the white beans with sticky rice or the lotus seeds with seaweed and *longans* – weird, but not unpleasant. It will cost you €8 for soup and dessert; dishes are about €7 each. It's not licensed except for beer, but naturally they have fizzy drinks, fresh fruit juice and tea. *Free coffee on presentation of this guide.*

|●| Virgule

9 rue Véronèse; M° Pl. d'Italie.
Ⓣ01.43.37.01.14
Service *until 11pm.* **Closed** *Wed; Aug.*

Mr Dao is a young chef originally from Cambodia and his restaurant has a lot to recommend it. Main meal and coffe for €8.20 (lunchtimes only); two *formules* at €18.60 and €24.20, and evening menus €12–18. The first menu shows how he has fused the flavours of the Orient and the cuisine of the West. It changes regularly but might list cream of cauliflower soup followed by lacquered roast pork or *choucroute* with ham hock and a fruit tart or cream caramel for dessert. The other menus, €11–17.10, feature some astonishing dishes – sautéed scallops with oyster sauce and celeriac in a mustard mayonnaise, pan-fried scallops with chicken broth and perfumed mushrooms, and *cassoulet* like you find in the southwest of France. It's engaging food served very generously and, on top of all that, the owners are charming.

|●| La Touraine

39 rue Croulebarbe; M° Corvisart or Gobelins.
Ⓣ01.47.07.69.35
Open *daily till 10.30pm.* **Closed** *Sun.* **High chairs available.**

If you want a table on the terrace, you have to book, but in the evenings there's not such a crush. There are two dining rooms, both decorated in subtle rustic style. The cuisine is filling and tasty and the dishes are what you'd expect to find in provincial France: prawns *au gratin*, *tournedos Rossini* and a *panaché* of lamb with pickled garlic. There is a selection of filling menus: first menu €11, others €20.50–29.90, or à la carte around €30 without a drink. *Free house apéritif on presentation of this guide.*

|●| L'Avant Goût

26 rue Bobillot; M° Pl.-d'Italie.
Ⓣ01.53.80.24.00
Closed *Sat; Sun; Mon; 1–8 Jan; 1–8 May; 15–31 Aug; Ist week in Sept.* **Disabled access.**

Christophe Beaufront has spent a lot of thought and energy on this place, from the dishes on the menus to the vintages on the wine list. He offers a triumphant combination of peasant food and elegant preparation. Try the fantastic pork *pot-au-feu*, for instance. There's a lunch *menu du marché* at €12 which includes dish of the day, salad, a glass of wine and coffee; dishes change regularly. Another option is the *menu-carte* at €26, which changes every fortnight but lists a choice of five starters, six main dishes and five desserts. The wine list includes a sparkling Vouvray from Champalou, a Touraine Sauvignon du Père Aug and a red Beaumes-de-Venise domaine de la Fermette-Saint-Martin. À la carte, a complete meal will cost about €28.

Tricotin 1

15 av. de Choisy; M° Porte-de-Choisy.
☎01.45.85.51.52

One of the longest-serving establishments in the district and a veritable institution – at the weekend there's a queue to get in. The big dining room is pretty noisy with efficient waiters, a menu as long as your arm and your neighbour's elbow in your ribs. It's worth it for the *dim sum* – probably the finest and most varied in town – you could easily make a whole meal of it. À la carte only – you'll pay €12–22 or so. Opposite there's another smaller dining room (closed Tuesdays; open 11am–3.30pm) in the same canteen style, always packed out. In here Thai dishes are the speciality.

Les Cailloux

58 rue des Cinq-Diamants; M° Corvisart.
☎01.45.80.15.08
Open *12.30–2.30pm and 7.30–11pm.* **Closed** *Sun; Mon; 3 weeks in Aug; a fortnight at the end of Dec.* **Disabled access.**

Flushed with the pride of its success in Saint-Germain-des-Prés, Casa Bini decided to reinvent itself in a neo-bistro incarnation up on the Butte Montmartre. If you don't like your spaghetti cooked too firm you'd better say when you order. The lunchtime *formule*, €12.50, generously includes a glass of wine, and there's another at €16. The quality of the cooking could be better. Watch out for the coffee – it's expensive! It's popular with regulars, who elbow their way in, so it's best to book.

Etchegorry

41 rue Croulebarbel; M° Pl.-d'Italie or Corvisart.
☎01.44.08.83.51
Open *noon–2.30pm and 7.30–10.30pm.* **Closed** *Sun; Mon; 10–27 Aug.*

On the façade of this building you can still make out the old inscription "Cabaret de Madame Grégoire". Some two hundred years ago, Victor Hugo, Châteaubriand and various poets wined and dined here. The old charm still remains; the décor is rustic and warm and the windows look onto the square. The local clientele enjoy authentic Basque and Béarnaise cuisine: *piperade*, stuffed squid and cod with red peppers, duck and pork *confit* with garlic potatoes, sheep's cheeses and delicious desserts. Everything is cooked fresh on the premises, even the bread. Lunch menu €18.50 and others €24–30. Reservations recommended. *Free coffee offered to our readers on presentation of this guide.*

Anacréon

53 bd. Saint-Marcel; M° Les Gobelins.
☎01.43.31.71.18
Open *noon–2.30pm and 7.30–11pm.* **Closed** *Sun; Mon; Wed lunchtime; Aug.*

Situated in a rather dreary street, this restaurant offers gourmet food. Try the splendid €32 *menu-carte*, which lists well-devised, well-prepared dishes using country produce: rabbit terrine with foie gras and vegetables, *fricassée* of snails with tomatoes, veal kidneys in a mustard sauce, cod with chicory, *parfait* with egg custard. There's also a set lunch menu for €20. Extremely good service and a wine list that matches the cooking.

Le Petit Marguery

9 bd. de Port-Royal; M° Gobelins.
☎01.43.31.58.59
Open *noon–2pm and 7.30–10.15pm.* **Closed** *Sun; Mon; Aug; a week at Christmas.*

Lunch menu €22.20 and others at €25.20 and €33.60. It was a tall order taking over from the Cousin brothers who ran this establishment for two decades: during the season they prepared grouse, pheasant and wildboar to the great delight of their wealthy, joyful guests. The nineteenth-century décor has not changed, and the Parisian brasserie tradition lives on here. The menu lists the same specialities: saddle of scorpion fish with *tapenade*, kidneys with mustard seed still live up to expectations. Film lovers – if they don't happen to bump into Claude Chabrol in the restaurant – can always pop into the *Escurial*, one of the favourite Parisian cinemas. *Free coffee on presentation of this guide.*

Chez Trassoudaine

3 pl. Nationale; M° Nationale.
☎01.45.83.06.45
Open *10am until 10pm.* **Closed** *Sun; Sat lunchtime (except for reservations); Aug.*
Disabled access.

Pop Robert and Mom Asting have run the kitchen for years. A quick look at the menu betrays their Armenian origins. Their sons, Araket and Haigo, and their Dutch and Mexican wives, are also part of the team in this unusual restaurant. Dishes include Limousin beef with white pepper, veal chop with sorrel, grilled bass, scallops with garlic or cream sauce, and plump, pink Senegal prawns with garlic and Cayenne pepper. There are no menus; expect to pay around €14 for a meat main course, or upwards of €9 for fish and seafood. Starters between €5 and €10. There are also some classic French dishes; herring fillets, egg mayonnaise and so on. *Free house apéritif on presentation of this guide.*

Chez Paul

22 rue de la Butte-aux-Cailles; M° Pl.-d'Italie or Corvisart.
☎01.45.89.22.11
Open *daily noon–2.30pm (3pm Sun) and 7.30pm–midnight.* **Closed** *24 Dec–2 Jan.*

Pleasant, low-key bistro decorated with plenty of plants and offering excellent cooking. The menu is quite extensive, offering dishes such as marrowbone, foie gras, *pot-au-feu* and Celtic pork. Wine is reasonably priced with some served by the jug. Desserts are delicious. There are always one or two dishes of the day on the slate. Expect to pay €35. *Free house apéritif on presentation of this guide.*

14th arrondissement

Hôtel des Voyageurs

22 rue Boulard; M° and RER Denfert-Rochereau.
☎01.43.21.08.20 ℱ01.43.21.08.21
ⓔhotel.des.voyageurs2@wanadoo.fr
TV. Disabled access. Open *all year round.*

An enchanting hotel very close to the lively rue Daguerre, one of the best in this price range. The young owner greets his guests warmly, and livens up the ground floor with regular exhibitions of paintings. The furniture in the 26 rooms is basic but they are cool, colourful and spotless. Doubles with shower/wc €50. Breakfast €5. Large garden. Be sure to book. *Free coffee offered to our readers on presentation of this guide.*

FIAP Jean Monnet

30 rue Cabanis; M° Glacière.
☎01.43.13.17.17 ℱ01.45.81.63.91
ⓦwww.fiap.asso.fr

This hostel was co-founded by Jean Monnet (one of the fathers of the European Union) for European students participating in cultural exchanges. It provides beautiful rooms for individual guests (subject to availability) but it gives priority to groups (with compulsory half board). All the rooms (200 in all, with 500 beds) have a shower and toilets (towels provided). €22.70 per person in a six-bed dorm, €29.40 in four-bed room, €32.40 in a double room and €50.20 in a single. Breakfast included. No age limit. Internet area and tourist information centre. Luggage lockers. Doors closed at 2am. *Free coffee offered to our readers on presentation of this guide.*

Hôtel du Parc Montsouris**

4 rue du Parc-Montsouris; M° Porte-d'Orléans; RER Cité-Universitaire.
☎01.45.89.09.72 ℱ01.45.80.92.72
ⓦwww.hotel-parc-montsouris.com
TV. Disabled access.

Great location if you like an early jog – Parc Montsouris is nearby. Everyone can appreciate the peace and quiet of this delightful street. The hotel is resolutely modern and functional. Doubles cost from €60 with shower/wc or €70 with bath; twin rooms cost €79 and apartments €96. All the rooms and bathrooms have been refurbished from top to bottom; despite this prices remain stable. Reserve well in advance.

Cecil Hôtel**

47 rue Beaunier; M° Porte-d'Orléans.
☎01.45.40.93.53 ℱ01.45.40.43.26
ⓦwww.cecilhotel.net_•
Open *all year round.* **TV.**

Double rooms at €70 with shower, and €75 with bath. Hearty breakfast €6.50. Sophie (who comes from the 14th *arrondissement*), Francois (a Savoyard) and Peachy, the labrador, have got the right idea in focusing on the quality of the welcome. Their good taste is evident in the furnishings of the rooms which have been redecorated recently, each with its own theme: "Marrakesh", "Île de Ré", "violet", "romantic" – the choice is yours. Numerous small attentions to detail make all the difference – breakfast is served until 2pm, a spray of lily-of-the-valley is given on 1 May (and chocolates at Easter), a house guidebook detailling everything to be seen and done in the area (including restaurants, walks etc). They even reserve parking spaces in the street for their guests. In the morning the newspapers will be waiting for you on the peaceful, sunny terrace. A wonderful place whose reputation is spreading by word-of-mouth. Please note that the hotel is non-smoking. *One free breakfast per room or 10% discount on the room rate (at weekends excluding trade fairs and in the summer) on presentation of this guide.*

Hôtel des Bains*

33 rue Delambre; M° Vavin or Edgar-Quinet.
Ⓣ01.43.20.85.27 Ⓕ01.42.79.82.78
des.bains.hotel@wanadoo.fr
TV. Pay car park.

This one-star hotel has real character and an elegantly restrained façade. The rooms, overlooking the road or the courtyard, have been tastefully decorated and even the bedspreads and lampshades have been carefully chosen to complement the colour scheme. They're very quiet and comfortable. Doubles with shower/wc or bath €75–79; suites sleeping two to four people €93–141. Breakfast costs €9. Car park charge is around €11. It's really not expensive considering what you get. *10% discount on the room rate Sat and Sun July–Aug on presentation of this guide.*

Hôtel Virginia**

66 rue du Père-Corentin; Porte-d'Orléans.
Ⓣ01.45.40.70.90 Ⓕ01.45.40.95.21
Ⓦwww.123.france.com
TV. Pay car park *(€9.80)*.

This hotel has successfully introduced contemporary design (dark wood, colour scheme of plum, ivory and ochre) into a classical structure (charming wooden lift and Art-Deco stained glass). It is clear from the outset that comfort is one of the main priorities. Double rooms €74–85, depending on the size; there is a €7 supplement when a trade fair is on. Family room €122. Breakfast buffet, €6.80, served in an attractive room. The only drawback is that it is a long way from the city centre.

Hôtel Delambre***

35 rue Delambre; M° Edgar-Quinet or Vavin.
Ⓣ01.43.20.66.31 Ⓕ01.45.38.91.76
Ⓦwww.hoteldelambre.com
Disabled access. TV.

This hotel has changed a good deal since André Breton, Paul Gauguin and other leading lights of the Surrealist movement stayed here. Very reasonable prices for a hotel in this category: doubles with shower/wc or bath €80–95, depending on size of room and whether it looks onto the courtyard or the road. No. 7, which has a large terrace, is particularly recommended for lovers looking for peace and quiet. Buffet breakfast €8. In summer you can sleep with the window open without being disturbed by noise. *One free breakfast per room on presentation of this guide.*

Hôtel Daguerre***

94 rue Daguerre; M° Gaité or Denfert-Rochereau.
Ⓣ01.43.22.43.54 Ⓕ01.43.20.66.84
Ⓦwww.france-hotel-guide.com
Disabled access. TV.

If you have a taste for luxury but not the means, this place is for you. It's treated itself to a facelift of the kind usually reserved for great hotels: the marble, the statues, the trompe l'oeil painting, the co-ordinated fabrics and the exposed beams in the dining room all combine to create the illusion of a much more glamorous era. And all the rooms have been done up, too: everything is clean and shiny, and they've got safes, mini-bars and cable TV. There are even one or two equipped for disabled visitors. And talking of money, the rates really are reasonable considering the level of service. Doubles with shower or bath €83. Breakfast at the buffet or served in your room €8. *Free breakfast in Dec, Jan, July and Aug on presentation of this guide.*

Le Colvert

129 rue du Château; Pernety.
Ⓣ01.43.27.32.56
Service *noon–2pm and 7.30–10.30pm.*
Closed *Sat lunch; Sun; Mon lunch.*

A small, cosy bistro with meals that revolve around duck: *gizzard*, *magret* and *confit*, accompanied by the traditional Sarlaidais apples or innovations like home-made purée of *petits pois* and green beans. There are also fish dishes, looking impressive on a big oval plate. Superb desserts. Lunchtime menu €9, comprising a small starter of charcuterie, a copious traditional dish and a glass of wine; other menus €14, with main course + starter or dessert, and €18.50, served at lunch and dinner. Limited selection of wines, none costing more than €17 a bottle. Friendly service. *Free apéritif offered to our readers on presentation of this guide.*

Aux Produits du Sud-Ouest

21–23 rue d'Odessa; M° Edgar-Quinet.
☎01.43.20.34.07
Open *noon–2pm and 7–11pm.* **Closed** *Sun; Mon; public holidays; mid-July to end Aug.*

This restaurant-cum-shop sells home-made preserves and conserves from the southwest and the prices are unbeatable. It's not gourmet cooking but decent country fare like charcuterie, terrine of rabbit or wild boar, *cassoulet* with goose *confit*, pigeon in a red wine sauce, duck *confit*, goose and duck foie gras, and a terrific apple and Armagnac tart. They also do great salads and sandwiches to take away at €3–4.50. The lunch *formule* at €6.50 includes dish of the day and a coffee or glass of wine; you'll pay around €12–25 à la carte.

Le Château Poivre

145 rue du Château; M° Pernety.
☎01.43.22.03.68
Service *until 10.30pm.* **Closed** *Sun; a fortnight in Aug.* **Disabled access.**

A quiet neighbourhood restaurant that's popular with locals. Dishes like *andouillette*, *cassoulet*, tripe, Hungarian goulash and steak *tartare* are prepared by the proprietor, and the service is extremely pleasant. Excellent menu at €15; à la carte expect to pay about €25.

Restaurant La Coupole

102 bd. du Montparnasse; M° Vavin.
☎01.43.20.14.20
Breakfast served *8–10.30am (8.30am weekends);* **brasserie service** *from 11.30am; last orders at 1am (Sun–Thurs) and 1.30am (Fri/Sat).* **High chairs available.**

This aircraft hangar of a restaurant is the largest in France in terms of square feet, and can house no fewer than 450 diners. Big names have been coming here since it opened in 1927 – people like Chagall, Man Ray and Josephine Baker (complete with lion cub). The bar has been restored to its original location in the middle of the room and the pillars repainted the green they used to be. The dance hall has been preserved, too, and you can trip the light fantastic at one of the early afternoon tea dances or in the evening at weekends. It's now run by Jean-Paul Bücher, of *Flo* fame, and offers the same type of food as in all those bistros: *tartare*, *cassoulet*, curry, hot fudge... Menus €17.50 at lunchtime, others at €22.90 and €32.90; à la carte reckon on around €38, excluding drinks. *Free house apéritif on presentation of this guide.*

L'Auberge de Venise

10 rue Delambre; M° Vavin.
☎01.43.35.54.09
Closed *Mon.*

Montparnasse may no longer have the mystique it once had, but the remaining cinemas and a handful of good restaurants still give an illusion of old Montparnasse. This is one of them – an Italian inn run by Enzo, a jovial host who has the gift of putting you instantly at your ease. You might be surprised to find just the classic dishes of the mainland, but even though the menu holds no surprises, everything is masterfully prepared and well balanced. Enzo's clientele is a mixture of writers and show performers, and his speciality is fillet of beef in balsamic vinegar. Menu at €18 or €35 à la carte.

L'O à la Bouche

124 bd. du Montparnasse; M° Vavin or RER B Port-Royal.
☎01.56.54.01.55
Closed *Sun; Mon; 1–8 Jan; 8–15 April; 1-22 Aug.* **Disabled access.**

Franck Paquier – young and talented yet tried and tested after his time with Troisgrois and Guy Savoy – creates new dishes daily. All the ingredients are fresh and expertly cooked, and the ideas are creative: duck foie gras with fruits of the forest, fillets of duckling with figs and raisins. The desserts – honey crumble with blackcurrants, sweet chestnut flavoured ice cream and liquorice *sabayon* – are fabulous. Lunch menu €19, and there's a *menu dégustation* at €48. À la carte, around €40. The wines are reasonably priced. *Free coffee on presentation of this guide.*

Natacha

17 bis rue Campagne-Première; M° Raspail.
☏01.43.20.79.27
Open *lunch and dinner until 11pm, except Sun and Mon lunch.* **Closed** *a week in Aug.*

A comfortable, relaxing setting that blends red velvet seats with modern paintings. At lunch it attracts mainly businessmen, stylists and publishers, while the evening crowd is more hip. Intelligent lunchtime menus at €19 and €26, with a half-bottle of good red wine at a very reasonable price. Reckon on €40 à la carte. Be sure to book, as the word is already out that a masterly young chef has taken over the reins in this venerable establishment. His cooking is basically classical, but the recipes are modernized and reinterpreted with gusto: succulent *pressé* of snails with a fragrant side-salad, the humble *hachis parmentier* turned into an aristocratic splendour, shin of veal confit whose taste lingers exquisitely in the mouth and an almost-liquid chocolate. *Free coffee offered to our readers on presentation of this guide.*

L'Amuse-Bouche

186 rue du Château; M° Mouton-Duvernet.
☏01.43.35.31.61
Open *noon–2pm and 7.30–10.15pm.* **Closed** *Sun and Mon lunchtimes; Aug.* **Disabled access.**

Gilles Lambert is a consummate artist in the kitchen. If you want proof, try his *menu-carte*. Starters might be langoustine ravioli with tarragon or *mousseline* of pike with saffron mussels, while for a main course you can choose between dishes such as swordfish steak with rosemary, and pig's cheeks with ginger and lemon. Sweet desserts: *millefeuille* of spiced bread, white chocolate mousse and orange sauce. Menu, served at lunch and dinner, for €25; also a *menu-carte* at €27, and another at €31.

Le Vin des Rues

21 rue Boulard; M° Denfert-Rochereau or Mouton-Duvernet.
☏01.43.22.19.78
Open *noon–3pm and 7.30–11pm.* **Closed** *Sun lunch; a week from 15 Aug.*

This is one of those places where you're not sure who's running the show, the owner or the customers. The Lyonnaise cuisine is consistant and well constructed, with, in pride of place, classic *andouillette* dishes and Salers *entrecote* steak with *fourme* d'Ambert. On Thursday evening, it's the big spectacle. With his accordion before him, Danny enters the room escorted by Nini or Jean, or possibly both, to give a colourful recital reminiscent of Boudard. The bench seats are crammed to overflowing and the assembled crowd join in with the old refrains. Monsieur Henri invites you to join as he leads the dance, there's a portraitist whose sketches adorn the walls, and the usual regulars propping up the bar. On Thursdays they make do with platters of cold meats and cheeses (the portions of the latter are a little stingy), but this is the romance of Paris. Excellent Lyon-style cooking, with two or three very substantial dishes that change every day. For starters there's marinated sprats with red peppers or lamb's foot *ravigote*; main dishes include things like calf's liver *à l'étouffée* or braised sweetbreads. Regional cheeses and home-made desserts. Wines and the day's menu are chalked up on a blackboard – which also tells you what saint's day it is. À la carte only; dishes cost around €15, plate of cooked meats €10 or plate of cheese €12, and you'll spend something like €25 for a meal. Thursday night is accordion-chanson night. It's a good idea to reserve, especially at the weekends if you want to eat on the terrace in the evening.

La Régalade

49 av. Jean-Moulin; M° Alésia or Porte-d'Orléans.
☏01.45.45.68.58
Open *noon–2pm and 7–11pm.* **Closed** *Sat, Sun and Mon lunchtimes; Aug; a week at Christmas.*

This is a gem of a place, with a décor that's both low-key and refined and a chef who is inspired. The *menu-carte* at €30 (not including wine) offers as a starter a basket of *charcutailles* from Pau. Try the silky smooth pumpkin soup, the delicate kidneys with pickled shallots, the roast pigeon with bacon, the scallops with shredded celery, the braised cheek of suckling pig with caramelized cabbage, the fillet of sea bass with fennel – the list of wonderful things just goes on. The wine list is astonishing, too, and all at giveaway prices. And so far, success hasn't changed this very special restaurant. You have to book at least ten days ahead, especially for a Saturday night.

Monsieur Lapin

11 rue Raymond-Losserand; M° Gaîté, Pernety or Montparnasse.
01.43.20.21.39
Open *noon–2pm and 7.30–10pm.* **Closed** *Mon; Tues; Aug.*

The setting is attractive with a lot of warm, faded pink, and, surprise surprise, lots of little rabbits used in the decoration. Service is perfection and complements the refined cuisine. The *menu-carte* for €30 and the *menu-dégustation* for €47 give free rein to the chef's imagination. There's plenty of rabbit on the menu: *émincé* of rabbit with tarragon, sautéed rabbit with preserved lemons, rabbit *croustillant* etc... but also roast rack of lamb or fillet of beef with foie gras *escalope*, and a few fish dishes. Tasty starters show off interesting combinations of flavours and ingredients; try the small dish of oysters in champagne. Desserts are lovely, too, with an *île flottante* that's as light as a cloud. And there's a particularly good selection of wines.

15th arrondissement

Aloha Hostel

1 rue Borromée (opposite no. 243 rue de Vaugirard); M° Volontaires.
01.42.73.03.03 01.42.73.14.14
www.aloha.fr
TV.

Regular visitors to this hostel have been astonished by its recent transformation. Absolutely everything has been done up, redecorated and adapted to modern tastes: diffuse lighting, wooden shutters and upbeat colours. As there's no point in changing a winning formula, however, the prices are still appealing and the atmosphere is still friendly. The US flag and the clocks showing the time in Paris, New York and Sydney reflect the high proportion of English-speaking travellers among the guests. Dormitories with four to six beds or double rooms with exposed beams. Depending on the season, reckon on €18–22 per person in a dorm, €22–25 in a double room, including breakfast. Hire of sheets (€3) and towels (€1). Two small showers/wc on each floor. You must be out of your room from 11am–5pm. The doors are closed at 2pm. Kitchen in a pretty vaulted cellar available for use. Internet access. Credit cards not accepted. *One breakfast per person offered to our readers on presentation of this guide.*

3 Ducks Hôtel

6 pl. Étienne-Pernet; M° Félix-Faurre.
01.48.42.04.05 01.48.42.99.99
www.3ducks.fr

No access to rooms 11am to 5pm. Curfew at 2am. It's like a youth hostel but privately run and jammed with Brits. It's all pretty out-dated – just so you know – but the accommodation is some of the cheapest in the *arrondissement*; €22.50–24.50 per person in winter and €17–21 per person in summer, including breakfast. Sheets for hire at €3.50. Rooms have bunk beds or there are dormitories with four or six beds. Bathrooms and loos are on the landing. There's a good atmosphere, and a pub. They put a few tables out in the internal courtyard. *10% discount on the room rate from Nov–Feb or free coffee on presentation of this guide.*

Le Nainville Hôtel

53 rue de l'Église; M° Félix-Faure or Charles-Michels.
01.45.57.35.80 01.45.54.83.00
Closed *6 weeks starting from the Fri before 14 July*. **TV.**

An unobtrusive little hotel with a retro café on the ground floor, a genial proprietor and bedrooms that are old-fashioned in the nicest possible sense. It's incredible to find a place like this in a neighbourhood where they're throwing up blocks of flats everywhere. Clean and cheerful inside. Go for a room which has a view over square Violet. Doubles with basin €39, €57 with shower, €67 with shower/wc. Breakfast costs €6.50. Credit cards not accepted.

Hôtel Amiral

90 rue de l'Amiral-Roussin; M° Vaugirard.
01.48.28.53.89 01.45.33.26.94
www.france-hotel-guide.com/h75015amiral.htm
TV. Disabled access.

This small, discreet hotel is at the back of the area's town hall but has much to recommend it, not least the decent rooms and honest prices. Nos. 7, 25, 26 and 31 all have a balcony and a very Parisian view of the Eiffel Tower in the distance and all have been redecorated in a nautical theme. Doubles with basin €45, with shower/wc

€75–78 or bath. Breakfast at €7. *10% discount on the room rate 15 July–31 Aug on presentation of this guide.*

Hôtel Lilas Blanc Grenelle

5 rue de l'Avre; M° La Motte-Piquet-Grenelle,
Ⓣ01.45.75.30.07 Ⓕ01.45.78.66.65
Ⓔhotellilasblanc@minitel.net
Closed *Aug; a week at Christmas.* **TV.** Cots available.

This hotel, very close to Motte-Piquet-Grenelle, is one of the hidden jewels of the neighbourhood. The service is highly professional and the bedrooms and bathrooms are very comfortable (hair dryer, safe). Go for the ones in series 3, as they're bigger. Doubles at €65–70 with shower or bath offer good value for money. Breakfast €6. Don't miss the fresco painted on the lounge wall by Paul Lomré, who appears in *The Guinness Book of Records* as the world's fastest painter with sponges on canvas. Small patio. *5% discount on a room offered to our readers on presentation of this guide.*

Hôtel de la Paix***

43 rue Duranton; M° Boucicaut ou Convention.
Ⓣ01.45.57.14.70 Ⓕ01.45.57.09.50
Ⓦwww.hotelpaixparis.com
Open *all year round.* **TV. Disabled access.**

Very comfortable, three-star family hotel in a quiet street. The cosy rooms are attractively decorated in vivid, warm colours and they all have air-conditioning. The bathrooms are splendid, with all mod cons (hairdryer, etc.) and marble fittings. Double rooms €66–72 with shower/wc or bath. Breakfast at €6.50 (free for children under ten), is served 6am–noon in a room with wrought-iron tables and a fountain. The reception is equipped with a fireplace. Friendly atmosphere and excellent value for money. *10% discount on the room rate (July–Aug) offered to our readers on presentation of this guide.*

Hôtel Le Fondary**

30 rue Fondary; M° Émile-Zola.
Ⓣ01.45.75.14.75 Ⓕ01.45.75.84.42
Ⓦwww.hotelfondary.com
TV. Disabled.

Good location in a quiet street in one of the liveliest parts of the 15th *arrondissement*. Modern décor and pretty patio with a well. Prices are quite high, but reasonable considering the quality of the service – doubles with direct phone, cable TV and mini-bar cost €72 with shower or €76 with bath. And it's quiet at night. The welcome is variable. *10% discount on the room rate (July–Aug) on presentation of this guide.*

Hôtel Carladez Cambronne**

3 pl. du Général-Beuret; M° Vaugirard.
Ⓣ01.47.34.07.12 Ⓕ01.40.65.95.68
Ⓦwww.hotelcarladez.com
Open *all year.* **TV.**

Carladez is a region in Auvergne where the original owners came from. This is a charming hotel in a little square with a pretty fountain. All the rooms are soundproofed and come with mini-bar, satellite TV, hairdryer and direct-dial telephone. Doubles with shower €73, €80 with bath, family suite for four €128. Breakfast costs €7.50. *10% discount on the room rate in July–Aug, and at weekends, except during trade fairs, on presentation of this guide.*

Hôtel de l'Avre**

21 rue de l'Avre; M° La Motte-Picquet-Grenelle.
Ⓣ01.45.75.31.03 Ⓕ01.45.75.63.26
Ⓦwww.hoteldelavre.com
Disabled access. TV.

The hotel is located in a quiet and narrow street. In summer the amiable owner sets out deckchairs in the pleasant garden where breakfast is served. The prices are fairly reasonable for Paris, with doubles at €74 with shower/wc or €82 with bath; breakfast €7.30. The renovated rooms are decorated in blue or yellow; some overlook the garden. There's also an attractive family room for four people. It's difficult to park in the street but there are two car parks just minutes away. *10% discount on the room rate at weekends on presentation of this guide.*

Hôtel du Parc Saint-Charles

243 rue Saint-Charles (on the corner of rue Leblanc); M° Balard or RER C Boulevard-Victor.
Ⓣ01.45.57.83.86 Ⓕ01.45.53.60.68
Ⓦwww.hotelduparcstcharles.com
TV.

Professionalism and friendliness are the mottos of this hotel, recently taken over by its young owner. It has been spruced up while awaiting a major overhaul to turn it into a three-star establishment. This is a good time to take advantage of it, therefore, as it is already fully equipped and the bedding is all brand new. The rooms are very quiet. Doubles €83–85, one triple €92. A note of warning, however: during some trade fairs the prices go up by €20. The crowning glory is the apartment on the top floor (€120): it sleeps four people, has exposed beams and is fully equipped (kitchen, music centre, pretty bathroom); you can really make yourself "at home". Excellent breakfast. Light meals available (produce and wines from South-West France) until 10.15pm, and it's also possible to share a half-board arrangement with the *Bistrot d'André* (see below), which is just opposite. *One free breakfast per room offered to our readers on presentation of this guide.*

Banani

148 rue de la Croix-Nivert; M° Félix-Faure.
☎01.48.28.73.92
Open *noon–2.30pm and 7.30–11pm.* **Closed** *Sun lunchtime.*

The dining room here is so large that it's divided into two by a low wall and has tables hidden away in bays. A gold statue of Ganesh adorns the entrance; inside there's a wall painting of a Hindu temple, warm wood panelling and low lighting. The Indian dishes come from different corners of the continent and the spicing is skilfully judged: fresh tender tandoori dishes, authentic *byrianis* and excellent *massalas*. The *naan* breads come fresh and hot, and you can have your *lassi* salty or sweet. Portions are generous and the Indian lager is well worth trying. Lunchtime menus €10 and €16 and a substantial evening set dinner at €26. Expect to pay around €20–25 à la carte, without drinks. *Free house apéritif on presentation of this guide.*

Aux Artistes

63 rue Falguière; M° Falguière or Pasteur.
☎01.43.22.05.39
Open *noon–2.30pm and 7.30pm–midnight.* **Closed** *Sat lunchtime; Sun; Aug; Christmas and New Year.*

This restaurant is really something. The price of the set menu has hardly increased in years and the atmosphere and the décor haven't changed much either. The customers are a mixed bunch – students, teenagers from nearby housing estates, professionals, a few artists (Modigliani came here in his time) – who all enjoy their meals in a noisy, lively atmosphere. You'll have to wait for a table on weekend evenings, but the bar serves a mean Kir. Two-course lunch *formule* €8.85, and a menu, €12.20, served all day. Hors d'œuvres are substantial and they can prepare you a steak in many different ways. The surprise of the house is a dessert poetically entitled "young girl's dream".

Le Bistrot d'André

232 rue Saint-Charles; M° Balard.
☎01.45.57.89.14
Closed *Sun; Christmas; New Year's Day.*
Disabled access.

This is one of the few survivors from the (André) Citroën era. It's been updated to cater for today's tastes by the people from the Perraudin (in the 5th *arrondissement*) and given a shot in the arm. "Pre-war" prices for appealing family dishes such as leg of lamb with *gratin dauphinois*, beef *bourguignon*, *andouillette* in a mustard sauce. veal kidneys with wild mushrooms, turbot with sorrel sauce and *canard confit*. Set menu €12.50 served on weekday lunchtimes. It's à la carte in the evening, when you should reckon on a bit more: €22 not including drinks. Wine-lovers take note: there's a tasting of wines from very small vineyards every month. "Wines of the month" are selected because of their superb quality and value for money. It's great to discover such a decent restaurant in an area where there's little else to see.

Le Garibaldi

58 bd. Garibaldi; M° Sèvres-Lecourbe.
☎01.45.67.15.61
Closed *evenings; Sat; Sun; Aug.*

This used to be a working-man's cafe, though nowadays white collars are much more in evidence. It's almost compulsory to have the *museau* vinaigrette or *crudités* as a starter. The €13 set menu features sautéed lamb with flageolet beans, beef *bourguignon* or *blanquette de veau*, and includes wine and service. Expect to pay around €15 à la carte. Service is friendly and there are still traces of the old décor – such as the beautiful counter at the door and a 1900 ceiling in an otherwise plain dining room.

|●| Le Numide

75 rue Vasco-de-Gama; M° Lourmel.
☎01.45.32.13.13
Open *noon–2pm and 7.30–10.30pm.* **Closed** *Sat lunch; Sun; Aug.* **Disabled access.**

On the edge of the 15th *arrondissement*, this restaurant offers tasty Kabyle specialities, such as *anakfou* and *méchoui*, meat from a sheep that is roasted whole, lightly grilled on the outside and deliciously tender inside. The ingredients are of the highest quality but the portions are a little meagre. Weekday lunchtime menu €13 (main course with either a starter or dessert; other menus €13–20.50; reckon on around €23 à la carte for a full meal, excluding drinks; children's menu €8.50. *Free coffee or mint tea offered to our readers on presentation of this guide.*

|●| Les Coteaux

26 bd. Garibaldi; M° Cambronne or Ségur.
☎01.47.34.83.48
Service *12.15–2.15pm and 7.15–10.30 pm.* **Closed** *Sun and public holidays.*

A Lyonnais wine bar the size of a matchbox: just ten tables, covered with check plastic tablecloths and two huge barrels for serving snacks. The menus are all served with a bottle of wine; lunchtime express menu at €17; dinner menu €24. Dishes include Lyon sausage, pig's ear à la lyonnaise and house specialities, such as *œufs meurette*, oxtail *terrine* and *croustillant* of *andouillette*. If all this sounds too filling, your best bet is to perch yourself on a barstool by one of the barrels and have a side-dish or a dish of the day. The wines, which come from small vineyards, are extremely varied and well chosen; they are served by the glass or in a carafe or bottle. *Free apéritif offered to our readers on presentation of this guide.*

|●| Beurre Noisette

68 rue Vasco-de-Gama; M° Lourmel, Balard or Porte-de-Versailles.
☎01.48.56.82.49
Service *noon–2.30pm and 7.15–11pm.* **Closed** *Sun; Mon; 3 weeks in Aug.*

This restaurant in a slightly out-of-the-way little street illustrates how this neighbourhood is acquiring more and more innovative places to eat. In this case, it is thanks to a young chef who skilfully approaches traditional specialities (blood pudding, free-range chicken and braised cabbage, for example) with an inventive touch. As for the desserts, the exquisite chocolate *quenelles* with honey *madeleines* have helped put this new arrival firmly on the map. Lunch menu €20, dinner €29. Reckon on €30 à la carte. Two immaculate dining rooms to choose from.

|●| Le Troquet

21 rue François-Bonvin; M° Sèvres-Lecourbe or Cambonne.
☎01.45.66.89.00
Open *noon–2pm and 7.30–11.30pm.* **Closed** *Sun; Mon; 3 weeks in Aug; a week at Christmas.*

Hidden in a back street, a huge dining room dotted with white tablecloths and Basque waiters bearing dishes with enticing aromas passing between the tables. Their taste lives up to this first impression, as the food is delicious and imaginative. Lunchtime menu €24 and €26 (starter, main course and dessert); these are superb, but fade in comparison with the dinner menus (€29 and €31), comprising four or five dishes (which you can't select – the only blemish – as you have to pay a hefty supplement for any alternatives). Wines from €15. Booking recommended.

|●| Restaurant Stéphane Martin

67 rue des Entrepreneurs; M° Félix-Faure, Charles-Michels or Commerce.
☎01.45.79.03.31
Service *noon–2pm and 7.30–11pm.* **Closed** *Sun; Mon; a week in Feb; 3 weeks in Aug; Christmas.*

There are some suburban restaurants that are OK for filling you up on a Sunday night if you happen to be in the area, and there are others that are worth crossing the city for. This is in the latter category. Its lunch menu (€25) is particularly competitive (three courses, wine and coffee included); another menu with a wider choice at €32. The subtle, creative cooking reflects the availability of fresh seasonal ingredients, but there are some dishes that are served all year round: sliced duck foie gras with herbs, braised pork knuckle with spicy honey and buttered red cabbage, *moelleux* of chocolate *fondant*. All are accompanied by a selection of home-made breads (with thyme, sesame, etc.) that you can eat at will. A classy setting in warm colours, with courteous if slightly slow service.

De la Garde

83 av. de Ségur; M° Ségur or Cambronne.
01.40.65.99.10
Service *noon–2.30pm and 8–10.30pm.*
Closed *Sat lunch; Sun and Mon lunch during school holidays; first 3 weeks in Aug; 25 Dec–2 Jan.*

It takes courage to open a restaurant in such a quiet area, but Yohann Masrracini, a chef from Alain Passard's stable, is clearly up to the challenge. He has attracted an elegant crowd eager to try cooking that boldly strays from the beaten track. His dishes may sometimes lack polish but he is bursting with ideas: *croustillant* of haddock with turmeric, kidneys with Beaumes-de-Venise and ricotta *gnocchi*, pollack with smoked ham flanked by (slightly over-cooked) sweet-onion risotto and rum baba with passion fruit. Two-course lunch menu €25, full menu €29; at night, a three-course menu at €35. Reckon on €33 à la carte. Unfortunately, the atmosphere is often a bit starchy – can't the waiters unwind a little bit?

L'Os-Moelle

3 rue de Vasco-de-Gama: M° Lourmel.
01.45.57.27.27
Open *until 11.30pm (midnight Fri and Sat).*
Closed *Sun; Mon; a month in summer; a week in winter.*

Thierry Faucher, formerly of the *Crillon*, skilfully produces bistro food in the style of a great chef. According to what he finds in Rungis market, you may be able to try cream of langoustine with chorizo or fried veal liver with Banyuls vinegar. Well-chosen wine list, with prices that won't overload your bill. Lunchtime menu €27; dinner menu (samples of four dishes) €32.

L'Épopée

89 av. Émile-Zola; M° Charles-Michels.
01.45.77.71.37
Service *noon–1. 45pm and 8–10pm.* **Closed** *Sat lunch; Sun; 28 July–28 Aug.*

The 15th *arrondissement* may have a host of restaurants, but there are very few where you can dine with any intimacy. This is one of them, as some of its round tables are set slightly apart. The décor is sophisticated but somewhat conventional, but what does it matter if the food is so mouth-wateringly delicious? The menu varies according to the availability of the ingredients; specialities include truly exquisite langoustine ravioli with *saté* and steamed bass with mashed potatoes and olive oil, but all the dishes are of irreproachable quality and extremely well presented. Menu €32; *formule* of main course with either a starter or dessert €27. *Liqueur on the house offered to our readers on presentation of this guide.*

Je Thé...me

4 rue d'Alleray; M° Vaugiraud.
01.48.42.48.30
Service *noon–3pm and 7.15–10.30pm.*
Closed *Sun; Mon; Aug; 23 Dec–3 Jan.*

It is a pleasure merely to enter this old late-nineteenth-century grocery; it is like walking into a doll's house, complete with period tiles and a wonderful array of odds and ends. This intimate setting is ideal for a romantic rendezvous, as the tables are sufficiently far apart to prevent neighbours from overhearing any passionate declarations. The menu, chalked on a blackboard, is particularly strong on fresh seafood, but there are also well-judged variations on traditional meat dishes, such as the tender caramelized ox tongue and fillet *mignon* of pork with red-wine butter. The desserts include a tasty rum baba sprinkled with red fruits. The service is warm and diligent. Menu €33. *Free wine tasting (first weekend of March and Oct) offered to our readers on presentation of this guide.*

16th arrondissement

Au Palais de Chaillot**

35 av. Raymond-Poincaré; M° Trocadéro.
01.53.70.09.09 01.53.70.09.08
www.palaisdechaiullot-hotel.com
TV. Pay car park. High chairs available.

This is a delightful hotel which is fresh and clean-looking. The rooms are decorated in yellow with curtains in red or blue; all have satellite TV, phone and hairdryer. Doubles go for €115–135 according to level of comfort and the season. Continental breakfast is served in a bright little room on the ground floor or they'll bring it to your room. A two-star hotel that easily deserves three – book well ahead. *15% discount on the room rate on presentation of this guide.*

Hôtel Le Hameau de Passy**

48 rue de Passy; M° Passy, La Muette or RER Muette-Boulainvilliers.

☎01.42.88.47.55 Ⓕ01.42.30.83.72
Ⓦwww.hameaudepassy.com
Disabled access. TV.

The entrance is in a small passageway. You come out into a small courtyard full of flowers and ringing with birdsong – a far cry from the luxury designer shops nearby. The hotel is run by an energetic team. Doubles with shower/wc or bath are €115–120, breakfast included; family room €155. There's a room for three people and one for four, and some of the double rooms have communicating doors.

Le Mozart

12 av. Mozart; M° La Muette.
☎01.45.27.62.45
Closed *Sun.*

The best *andouillette* from Duval, meat and mushrooms shipped in from Lozère, ice-cream from Berthillon, bread from the ovens of Michel Moizant and home-made pastries. This kind of quality is coordinated by a man who loves to root out the best produce and good wines. It's hardly surprising that you have to wait for a table – but the Kir they provide you with at the bar while you wait soothes your impatience. Lunch or dinner *formules* €12 (including a platter of foie gras and salad). À la carte you'll pay around €25. *Free apéritif on presentation of this guide.*

Restaurant GR 5

19 rue Gustave-Courbet; M° Rue-de-la-Pompe, Trocadéro or Victor Hugo.
☎01.47.27.09.84
Service *until 11pm.* **Closed** *Sun.* **Disabled access.**

A hiker with a fondness for the GR 5 route from Holland to the South of France hung up his boots to open this modest restaurant right on his doorstep. It is packed for both lunch and dinner but it is worth trying to get in. The little dining room is decorated in a mountain style, with check, red gingham tablecloths, and the menu revolves around a winning trio: *tartiflette* with Reblochon, *fondue* and a superb *raclette savoyarde*. Menus €14 (lunch) and €19.50 (dinner); reckon on around €20 à la carte. Great care is put into the choice of wines, with a wine of the month on offer by the bottle or carafe (large or small) and several fine vintages from the Lyon region. *Free apéritif offered to our readers on presentation of this guide.*

Le Petit Rétro

5 rue Mesnil; M° Victor-Hugo.
☎01.44.05.06.05
Closed *Sat lunch; Sun; Aug; a week between Christmas and New Year.*

The flowery tiles on the walls, beautiful mirrors, round lamps, old-style zinc counter and a practical, long coat rack (reminiscent of a school) all add up to create the illusion that time has stood still. They provide a feast for the eye to prepare the way for the delicacies to come. Typical bistro dishes, given a new twist and varied according to the seasons, to maintain a constant quality and freshness: poached egg with cream of chorizo, oxtail terrine, *croustillant* of black pudding, *papillote* of *andouillette*; the great speciality of the house, however, is *blanquette à l'ancienne*. Lunchtime menus €19 (main course with starter or dessert) and €24 (starter, main course and dessert); reckon on €32 for a full meal à la carte. Good selection of wines (some served by the glass), with a highlighted wine of the month. Very friendly service. *Free apéritif offered to our readers on presentation of this guide.*

Mathusalem

5 bis bd. Exelmans; M° Exelmans.
☎01.42.88.10.73
Service *noon–2.30pm and 8–10.30pm.*
Closed *Sat; Sun.*

Customers come from far and wide to this spot on the outskirts of Paris, and that is a recommendation in itself. The neighbourhood is a bit rundown, but the road leading to *Mathusalem* has been well trod for a long time. The well-established reputation of this restaurant with décor from the 1920s guarantees a packed house every day of the week and, despite the somewhat noisy dining room, its success is fully deserved. The menu is relatively limited and the portions are not over-generous, but the ingredients are fresh and the traditional dishes are tasty, including the enticing desserts. Menu of main course with a choice of either a starter or dessert €20; reckon on €26 à la carte. Terrace for sunny days. *Free apéritif offered to our readers on presentation of this guide.*

Le Beaujolais d'Auteuil

99 bd. de Montmorency; M° Porte-d'Auteuil.
☎01.47.43.03.56

Service *until 11pm*. **Closed** *10 days in mid-Aug*.

Lunch and dinner menu €21, wine included; this provides the basis of the success of this long-standing neighbourhood restaurant. Reckon on around €28 à la carte, excluding drinks; concentrate on the dishes of the day, such as fresh spinach salad, *jarret-choucroute*, poached eggs *meurette* or pig's foot with *ravigote* sauce. Classic desserts: chocolate mousse, *crême caramel*, *île flottante*. Attentive and efficient service. It is advisable to book, and try to get a table on the terrace in summer.

La Marmite

10 rue Géricault; M° Michel-Ange-Auteuil.
01.42.15.03.09
Open *lunch and dinner*. **Closed** *Sat lunch; Sun; Aug*.

A modest restaurant in a nondescript neighbourhood, with equally unremarkable décor inside; not very promising, maybe, but the place comes into its own with the delicious old-fashioned cooking. The dinner menu at €25 is particularly recommended; it's astonishingly good value for money, and whatever you choose, be it veal's liver, scallops or anything else, it will always be of unbeatable quality, as is the service. Reckon on around €27 à la carte. Booking essential.

Restaurant du musée du Vin, Le Caveau des Échansons

5–7 square Charles-Dickens-rue des Eaux; M° Passy.
01.45.25.63.26
Open *noon–3pm*. **Closed** *evenings; Mon; 24 Dec–1 Jan*. **Disabled access.**

The restaurant is in the wine museum and the dining room is in a fourteenth-century vaulted cellar dug out of the Chaillot clay by the monks who used to cultivate the vines. Many of the dishes use wine in their preparation: they include *coq au vin* and perch fillets in Muscadet sauce. The wine list is twelve pages long and lists nearly 250 vintages all the way up to a Château d'Yquem 1908 at €1980 a bottle. Along the way you'll come across *grand crus* from Bordeaux, Burgundy, Alsace and Jura as well as wines from lesser regions in France. Every day there's a selection of fifteen sold by the glass. Dishes cost around €18; menus go for €40 and €50. Free glass of wine offered after visiting the museum or as an apéritif when eating in the restaurant. *A free museum guide for two people who visit the museum.*

17th arrondissement

Hôtel Champerret-Heliopolis**

13 rue d'Heliopolis; M° Porte de Champerret.
01.47.64.92.56 01.47.64.50.44
www.champeret-heliopolis-paris-hotel.com
Disabled access. TV. Cots available.

A very quiet hotel with pretty wooden balconies. Most rooms overlook a delightful patio where you can have breakfast (served 7am–noon) when the weather's nice. The place was beginning to look a little rundown; however it's now under new management and refurbishment is underway, so things are looking up. Rooms have everything you might need – TV, telephone, hairdryer. Doubles with bath or shower €85–93. *One free breakfast per room on presentation of this guide.*

Hôtel Prony***

103 bis av. de Villiers; M° Pereire.
01.42.27.55.55 01.43.80.06.97
TV.

An excellent hotel close to place Pereire and five minutes from Porte Maillot. Facilities include room service, satellite TV and double glazing. Doubles cost €90–130 with bath or shower, depending on the season. Room no. 32 is huge, and ideal for families. *10% discount on the room rate (Jan–Feb, July–Aug and Dec) on presentation of this guide.*

Hôtel Palma**

46 rue Brunel; M° Porte-Maillot or Argentine.
01.45.74.74.51 01.45.74.40.90
www.hotelpalma-paris.com
TV.

This 37-room hotel is a stone's throw from the convention centre and the Air France terminal. It has an attractive frontage and foyer, and offers a degree of comfort at reasonable prices. Service is polite and efficient. The rooms (€85 with shower/wc, €95–120 with bath and all mod cons) have been redecorated in Provençal style, and have a warm, bright feel. Breakfast can be served in your room. The sixth-floor rooms are extremely popular, so it's best to book. *One free breakfast per person on presentation of this guide.*

🏃 |●| La Loggia

41 rue Legendre; M° Villiers.
☎01.44.40.47.30
Open *noon–2pm and 7–11pm.* **Closed** *Sun; Mon lunchtime; Aug.*

This Italian restaurant is as much about fast cars as good food – there's a Ferrari here, another there, and a mural of magnificent machines along the wall. Even the waitresses' T-shirts are emblazoned with that famous rearing horse. The owner-chef produces tasty food: marinated fresh sardine fillets, rigatoni with prawn cream sauce. And let's hear it for the tiramisù. An enjoyable meal won't cost you a bomb, either – there's a lunch menu for €12, and you'll pay around €28 à la carte. Reservations highly recommended. *Free apéritif on presentation of this guide.*

|●| Le Petit Villiers

75 av. de Villiers; M° Wagram.
☎01.48.88.96.59
Open *daily for lunch and dinner until 11pm.* **Closed** *New Year holidays.*

At night this is a beacon that shines in an otherwise deserted street. What is the secret of its success, in such inhospitable surroundings? It is a combination of rural warmth, a convivial and relaxed atmosphere, impressive waxed table linen, romantic candles on the tables, a terrace for sunny days and, last but not least, superb cooking at prices that cannot be matched in the neighbourhood. Foie gras, for example, can be found on the €17 weekday lunchtime menu. There is another lunch menu at €12, and a combination of starter with main course or main course with dessert (there are plenty to choose from – about a dozen items for each course). Excellent salads and lovingly prepared traditional dishes (veal kidneys, poached haddock, duck *confit* and magret, etc), all served in generous portions.

|●| La Table d'O & Co

6 rue de Lévis; M° Villiers.
☎01.53.42.18.04
Open *noon–2.30pm (Mon–Fri); noon–3.30pm (Sat).* **Closed** *evenings; Sun; Aug.*

A big, communal table has been set up in the superb shop of this famous brand of olive oil. They serve light, delicious dishes with strong Mediterranean flavours, but they're not cheap and portions are slight. You choose three of the five *tian* suggestions of the day such as ravioli with *brousse* cheese, stuffed tomato, fish egg-custard, *brandade* of salt cod . . . The sweet *tians* are remarkably delicate and original. The *formule* at €13 gets you three savoury *tians* plus cheese or dessert, and another at €14 includes dish of the day plus cheese or dessert. It's also fun to try different types of olive oil, dipping hunks of home-made bread into the dishes they set out for you. Then you can buy bottles of the stuff on your way out. *Free coffee on presentation of this guide.*

|●| Le Verre Bouteille

85 av. des Ternes; M° Porte-Maillot.
☎01.45.74.01.02
Open *noon–3pm and 7–4.30am.* **Closed** *at Christmas.*

Excellent wine bar where night owls can fill up on robust main dishes like steak *tartare* made with chopped – not minced – steak, or very, very large salads. There's one called *nain jaune*, "the yellow dwarf" (also the name of an old card game), which includes Comté cheese, chicken, raisins and curry sauce. Wines come from around the world and about thirty are available by the glass. Things can get lively on weekends by the time 4am rolls around. *Formules* at €14.50 (lunch only), €20 and €28.50. There's a second *Verre Bouteille* at 5 bd. Gouvion-Saint Cy in the 17th arrondissement – but that one closes at midnight.

🏃 |●| L'Impatient

14 passage Geoffroy-Didelot; M° Villiers.
☎01.43.87.28.10
Closed *Sat lunchtime; Sun; Mon; a fortnight in Aug.*

The entrance is between 92 bd. de Batignolles and 117 rue des Dames. This restaurant is appropriately named – if you haven't booked, some evenings the wait for a table is excruciating. The menus (€17 at lunchtime, €23 in the evening) are excellent value for money – a meal à la carte will cost around €45 not including drink. Dishes include scallops *à la provençale*, ravioli of *langoustine* in a creamy basil sauce, pan-fried *escalope* of foie gras, squid *escabèche* salad, stew of ox cheek with baby vegetables and endive *sabayon* with cocoa sorbet. You can also get delicate vegetarian options like *papillotte* of lightly spiced fresh sweetcorn – it's a delight to find such unusual dishes. Reservations strongly recommended at the end of the week. *Free house apéritif.*

|●| Le Café d'Angel

16 rue Brey; M° Charles-de-Gaulle-Étoile.
Ⓣ01.47.54.03.33
Open *noon–2pm and 7.30–10pm.* **Closed** *Sat; Sun; public holidays; lst 3 weeks in Aug; New Year's holiday.*

In the shadow of the Arc de Triomphe, in a stolidly middle-class street, this bistro packs them in. Its attractions include an inviting dining room with the kitchen open to view in the back, behind the bar; dashing, thirty-something customers from the many nearby offices, who seem to have taken the place to their heart; and finally, attractive cooking that reinterprets tradition in the style of today's great masters (the chef, Jean-Marc Gorsy, served his apprenticeship in the *Jules Verne*), with a touch of fantasy that is all its own. *Croustillant* of pig's foot, veal kidneys, fish of the day and, to finish, home-made chocolate gâteau or orange mousse. The menus are remarkably good value: lunch €19 and €22, dinner €38. Reckon on around €40 à la carte, excluding drinks.

|●| Le Petit Champerret

30 rue Vernier; M° Porte-de-Champerret.
Ⓣ01.43.80.01.39
Closed *Sat lunch; Sun; Mon evening.*
Service *12.30–2pm and 7.30–10.30 pm.*

The couple who have taken over these premises have transformed what was once a humble café into what they call a "gourmet bistro". The old mirror and zinc counter are still there, but the wood panelling has been tinted a raspberry colour and the walls painted cream (a delicious combination). The cornerstones of the new gastronomic adventure are several starters of the day, all supremely fresh; fish and meat dishes cooked to perfection, and a dazzlingly long list of desserts. Lunch and dinner menu €18 (starter with main course or main course with dessert); reckon on around €30 for a full meal à la carte. Wines by the glass or carafe. Efficient, friendly service. It's advisable to book, especially for lunch. *Free coffee offered to our readers on presentation of this guide.*

|●| Graindorge

15 rue de l'Arc-de-Triomphe; M° Charles-de-Gaulle-Étoile.
Ⓣ01.47.54.00.28
Open *noon–2pm and 7–10.30pm.* **Service** *until 11pm.* **Closed** *Sat lunch; Sun.*

Bernard Broux is an inspired chef who uses his expertise to the greater glory of his native Flanders, reinterpreting his culinary heritage: *civet* of *lièvre la Flamande* marinated in brown ale, eel in sauce verte, fish or poultry *waterzoï*, and for dessert, *jam baba* in Gueuze chantilly or dark chocolate *fondant* with coffee and chicory sauce. All the produce is fresh, and dishes are cooked to order. Forget the wine list and stick to beer – any one of the many varieties goes perfectly with the food. Lunch menus at €24 and €28; and another at €32 in the evening. You'll pay around €40 à la carte, not including drinks. Best to book at the weekend. *Free liqueur on presentation of this guide.*

18th arrondissement

Hôtel Bouquet de Montmartre**

1 rue Durantin; M° Abbesses.
Ⓣ01.46.06.87.54 Ⓕ01.46.06.09.09
Ⓦwww.bouquet-de-montmartre.com

A conventional hotel run by a young couple. The rooms are decent if small, and they are all different. Doubles, €60, all have double glazing, their own wc and a choice of shower or bath – but no TV. Excellent location, good reception and a wonderful view over Paris from room 43.

Hôtel Prima Lepic**

29 rue Lepic; M° Blanche.
Ⓣ01.46.06.44.64 Ⓕ01.46.06.66.11
Ⓦwww.hotel-paris-lepic.com
TV. High chairs available. Pay car park.

This is the ideal place to set off for a stroll through the neighbourhood. The impasse Marie-Blanche is close by, and definitely worth a look. The reception is bright and fresh and there's a trompe l'oeil of an English garden, a theme which they've developed by choosing garden furniture. Rooms, which look like something out of a magazine, are well maintained. Doubles €96–110 with shower/wc or bath. Avoid room nos. 11 and 17 – they're very dark. *Breakfast offered at €2 (instead of €8) on presentation of this guide.*

Timhôtel Montmartre**

11 rue Ravignan (place Émile-Goudeau); M° Abbesses, Blanche or Pigalle.
Ⓣ01.42.55.74.79 Ⓕ01.42.55.71.01
Ⓦwww.timhotel.com
TV.

This beautiful hotel is located in a wonderfully pretty square. Doubles with shower or bath €115–145. Each floor is dedicated to a painter: you have a choice of Toulouse-Lautrec, Utrillo, Dalí, Picasso, Renoir or Matisse. All have direct-dial phone and TV, and those on the fourth floor and above have a view of the square or the city; nos. 417 and 517 are especially nice. It's a great place for a romantic weekend which won't break the bank. *10% discount on the room rate (excluding New Year) on presentation of this guide.*

Sonia

8 rue Letort; M° Jules-Joffrin, Simplon and Porte de Clignancourt.
Ⓣ01.42.57.23.17
Open *noon–2.30pm and 6.30–11.30pm.* **Closed** *Sun lunchtime except in summer.*

A small Indian restaurant with a pink and purple dining room seating only 26 people (it's often full). Menus €7.50 and €13 at lunchtime, €16 in the evening. Everything is delicately spiced, beautifully presented and cooked to perfection – from the *naan* to the chicken *Madras* and *vindaloo*, not to mention the lamb *korma* and the aubergine *bhartha*. *Free house apéritif on presentation of this guide.*

L'Étoile de Montmartre

26 rue Duhesme; M° Lamarck-Caulaincourt.
Ⓣ01.46.06.11.65
Open *noon–2.20pm only.* **Closed** *Tues.* **Children's games available.**

In the shadow of the Butte, a little café that evokes a bygone era. High dining room with walls yellowed by age but set off by delightful friezes, a mosaic embedded in the floor and a bar with a Formica counter. This old-fashioned charm attracts regular customers every lunchtime: young and old, office workers in ties and labourers in overalls rub shoulders to enjoy the cheap, unpretentious home cooking. Dish of the day €6.50 and full meal €10. The authenticity of the atmosphere and the conviviality are the responsibility of the Giordano family, which has been running the place for over three decades. Credit cards not accepted.

Le Rendez-Vous des Chauffeurs

11 rue des Portes-Blanches; M° Marcadet-Poissoniers.
Ⓣ01.42.64.04.17
Open *noon–2.30pm (3pm on Sat) and evenings to 11pm.* **Closed** *Wed; Aug.*

This place has a long history, and when Jeannot took it over he was wise enough to change things as little as possible: the old wood counter and mirrors are still there, the tightly packed tables are covered by glazed cotton checked tablecloths and the benches are leather – he's even kept the brownish paint so typical of old restaurants. The menu hasn't changed much either: you might start with celery *remoulade* or egg mayonnaise then follow it with the dish of the day – cottage pie or veal kidneys – ending with a dessert like *crème caramel*. The wines are good and guaranteed to loosen the tongues of both the regulars and passing customers. There's a weekday menu at €14 and a meal à la carte will cost you only a little more than this.

Chez Pradel

168 rue Ordener; M° Guy-Môquet or Jules-Joffrin.
Ⓣ01.46.06.75.48
Open *noon–3.30pm (Mon–Sat) and 7.30–10pm (Thurs and Fri evenings).* **Closed** *Sun; fortnight in Aug.* **High chairs and crayons available.**

This restaurant with décor from the 1920s is extremely popular with the locals of this lively neighbourhood. The owner and his wife prepare classic dishes with no frills but plenty of loving care. The menu includes some specialities from the south-west of France, such as the home-made foie gras, which is an excellent appetizer before tucking into a duck *magret*. Other options are mackerel in white wine, poached eggs with chives and *blanquette* of veal. Dish of the day €9.50, menu €11. Reckon on around €20 à la carte, excluding wine. Sandwiches €2.44–3.80, salads €7. Wide choice of wines served by the glass or in a carafe or bottle, at extremely reasonable prices. *Apéritif on the house offered to our readers on presentation of this guide.*

La Casserole

17 rue Boinod; M° Marcadet-Poissoniers or Simplon.
Ⓣ01.42.54.50.97

Service *at lunch and dinner until 10pm.* **Open** *noon–2pm and 7.30–10pm.* **Closed** *Sun; Mon and Sat lunchtimes; public holidays; 15 July–24 Aug.*

The atmosphere, the service and the cuisine are all so good that it's worth making an effort to go to this restaurant. There's a jovial welcome and smiling service and the chef often chats to you when you've finished your meal. The décor includes postcards, posters and souvenirs brought back by regular customers over the years. Their traditional cuisine respects the changing seasons and the fresh produce from the markets: fish *cassoulet*, duck with honey and ginger, calf's head *ravigote* and fresh fruit desserts. Menu €12.20 (served Tues–Fri lunchtimes only), or à la carte reckon on around €30 with wine on top. They won't let you use the loos unless you're over 18. *Free digestif on presentation of this guide.*

La Preuve par 9

5 rue Damrémont; M° Lamarck-Caulaincourt.
☎01.42.62.64.69
Open *daily noon–3pm and 8.30pm–midnight.* **Closed** *24, 25 and 31 Dec; 1 Jan.* **Disabled access.**

According to one of the blackboards in this restaurant, it is open nine days out of nine. This theme is continued in the menu, where there is a choice of nine starters, nine main courses and nine desserts that all change constantly. The setting has the air of a classroom, and here you can learn about original recipes like goose *magret* with honey and coriander or *sautéed* bison with red fruits. Lunchtime menus €12–17; dinner €24. Even though it's more expensive at night, you must book to be sure of a table. The one drawback is that the wines are rather expensive. *Free apéritif offered to our readers on presentation of this guide.*

Marie-Louise

52 rue Championnet; M° Simplon.
☎01.46.06.86.55
Closed *Sun; Mon; Aug.*

Service from noon for lunch; last orders for dinner 10pm. You'd do well to book – this is a terrific restaurant. When you walk through the door it's as if you've stepped into a *Vieille France* family dining room filled with brass and copper so highly polished you can see your face in it. The cooking is traditional and the portions enormous: wild boar stew, chicken *pot-au-feu*, roast apple in strong cider and honey or bitter chocolate tart. Prices are reasonable with a *formule* for €16, and *menu-carte* available at lunch and dinner for €23.63.

Le Bouclard

1 rue Cavalotti; M° Pl.-de-Clichy.
☎01.45.22.60.01
Open *noon–2.30pm and 7–10.30pm.*

The nicely thought-out rustic setting creates the right atmosphere for traditional, regional cooking and a selection of carefully chosen wines you can drink at the bar. Michel Bonnemort's formula has been running successfully for the last ten years. The boss is a real *bon vivant*, enthusiastic about the simple dishes he creates from quality ingredients: poached eggs *en meurette* Burgundy-style with red wine and bacon sauce, cabbage stuffed with pike-perch, *fricassée* of black pudding and apples with Calvados with mash... all of it is delicious. There's a lunchtime *formule* (starter/main course or main course/dessert) for €17, or reckon on around €40 à la carte. *Free house apéritif on presentation of this guide.*

Taka

1 rue Véron; M° Pigalle or Abbesses.
☎01.42.23.74.16
Open *7.30–10pm.* **Closed** *lunchtimes; Sun; Mon; public holidays; 14–31 July; 15–31 Aug.*

Tiny little Japanese restaurant in a narrow, dingy street at the foot of the Butte. It's often absolutely crammed so it's best to book. Mr Taka is a lovely man and attentive to your needs. Authentic Japanese cooking, perfectly executed: the quality never wavers. You'll find all the Japanese classics – *sushi*, *sashimi*, *miso* soup and so on. Try the *shabu-shabu* (finely sliced beef and vegetables cooked in a seaweed broth), *sukiyaki* (a sort of beef and vegetable *fondue* served in a casserole dish), or the *maku no uchi* (house menu with tasty starters, raw and fried fish, cooked lotus roots) presented in a typically Japanese box. Save room for dessert: warm sweet red beans with green tea flavoured ice cream. Reckon on about €30 a head à la carte, including a bottle of hot *saké*. Typically Japanese décor and ambiance right down to the abacus used by Mr Taka to calculate the bill. It's essential to book one day in advance.

19th arrondissement

🏃 🏠 Hôtel De Crimée**

188 rue de Crimée; M° Crimée.
Ⓣ01.40.36.75.29 Ⓕ01.40.36.29.57
Ⓦwww.hotelcrimee.com
TV. Pay car park.

A simple, comfortable hotel not far from the Parc de la Villet. There's air conditioning and soundproofing in the rooms, as well as good bathrooms and hairdryers. Doubles €63 with shower/wc or €67 with bath; triples cost €70–75. Some rooms for three or four. There's a pay car park nearby (€10 for 24 hrs). *5% discount on the room rate at weekends and July–Aug on presentation of this guide.*

🏃 |●| Cok Ming

39 rue de Belleville; M° Belleville or Pyrénées.
Ⓣ01.42.08.75.92
Open *11am–1.30am.* **High chairs available.**

This place is run by Cambodian staff, who fly and swerve round the tables providing super-efficient service. It's been going for a good 20 years. You can make up your own menu from a selection of seafood for two, arrange a *fondue* or a hot pot for a group of mates, throw back a bowl of soup or take your time over some of their excellent roasts and barbecued meats – Peking duck, chinese *fondue* and *dim sum* – and all for very fair prices. The menu is massive and includes a number of Thai dishes. Menus €7.50 (weekday lunchtimes), €11 (vegetarian) and €13.50. There's also a good choice of teas, wines and beers. *Free apéritif on presentation of this guide.*

|●| Aux Arts et Sciences Réunis

161 av. Jean-Jaurès; M° Ourcq.
Ⓣ01.42.40.53.18
Open *noon–2.30pm and 7–10pm.* **Closed** *Sun.* **Disabled access.**

You'll see compasses and a set square on the façade of this "canteen" for people who work at the headquarters of the carpenters' guild. Go past the bar to an extremely attractive dining room with a parquet floor, ceiling mouldings and lots of photos of guild members on the walls. The food, like the atmosphere, is provincial in style. The weekday lunch menu (€9.70) is good value, with generous helpings and wine included; there's also a *menu campagnard* at €18 and a gastronomic menu at €25.

|●| 🏃 Au Rendez-Vous de la Marine

14 quai de la Loire; M° Jaurès.
Ⓣ01.42.49.33.40
Open *noon–2pm and 8–10pm.* **Closed** *Sun; Mon; a week at Christmas.*

Reservations highly advisable – it's often full. A delightful bistro with flowers on the tables, nautical souvenirs scattered around and photos of film stars. It's the place to come and it's noisy, especially at lunchtime and on every other Saturday evening in the winter when a talented female singer out-Piafs Piaf. In summer, tables are set on the terrace and you have a view of the canal. Food is reasonably priced and helpings are generous, though the cooking, really, is pretty ordinary. Regular dishes include the house chicken liver terrine, mushrooms *à la provençale*, the chef's special prawns, scallops *à la provençale* and duck breast with green peppercorns. If you want paella, you have to order it the night before. For dessert, there's a very good apple tart flambéed with Calvados. Dish of the day costs €11.60, or expect to pay around €26 à la carte. It's a good idea to book. *Free house apéritif on presentation of this guide.*

|●| La Cave Gourmande

10 rue du Général-Brunet; M° Botzaris.
Ⓣ01.40.40.03.30
Service 12.15–2.30pm and 7.30–10. 30pm.
Closed Sat; Sun; a week in Feb; 3 weeks in Aug.

The previous owner, Éric Frechon, has left this restaurant in the extremely capable hands of Mark and Dominique Singer. *Croustillant* of zander with chorizo, *tatin* of sirloin steak with shallots and *aumônière* of oxtail, quail in "*demi-deuil*" (half-mourning) with white summer truffles: all highly original dishes, served with *brio* in a chic, wine-cellar setting. Even when it is full, there is plenty of space for everybody to enjoy their meal at leisure. Lunchtime menu €28; seasonal menu €32.

🏃 |●| Le Pavillon Puebla

Parc des Buttes-Chaumont; M° Buttes-Chaumont.
Ⓣ01.42.08.92.62
Open *noon–3.30pm and 7.30–10.30pm.* **Closed** *Sun; Mon; public holidays.*

It's your wedding anniversary, you've just won the lottery and you've decided to celebrate in style? This is the place to do it. Standing in the middle of the city's most beautiful park, it has a refined setting with fresh flowers everywhere. The terrace is out of this world. You'll be received with style, but there's no bowing or scraping. The cooking is first-rate and chef Christian Verges changes his dishes regularly so they reflect the seasons: squid *à la catalane*, lobster stew with Banyuls wine, *pinata* (braised fish), and oyster ravioli with a curry sauce. And the desserts are to die for. It's expensive – in fact it's very expensive if you go à la carte and have wine too (reckon on around €65) – but the €33 set menu lists, for example, anchovies in flaky pastry, *bouillinade* (an upmarket sort of *bouillabaisse*) and chocolate *tuiles*. It's absolutely terrific and comes complete with canapés, home-made rolls and so on. There's another menu at €48. *Free digestif or glass of champagne with dessert on presentation of this guide.*

20th arrondissement

Tamaris Hôtel*

14 rue des Maraîchers; M° Porte-de-Vincennes or RER A, Nation.
Ⓣ01.43.72.85.48 Ⓕ01.43.56.81.75
Ⓦwww.tamaris-hotel.fr
TV.

Reservations are advisable at this extremely well-run little hotel which has prices you might expect in the depths of the country. The rooms are small and pretty and have flowery wallpaper. Doubles with basin €33, with shower €42, with shower/wc €48; there are also rooms that sleep three or four. It's a bit old-fashioned and altogether delightful – you'll get a warm welcome. *10% reduction on the room rate (during school holidays) or free coffee, fruit juice or soft drink on presentation of this guide.*

Hôtel Paris Gambetta**

12 av. du Père-Lachaise; M° Gambetta.
Ⓣ01.47.97.76.57 Ⓕ01.47.97.17.61
Ⓦwww.parisgambetta.com
TV. Cots available.

A pleasant two-star in a quiet street near Père-Lachaise cemetery. The rooms are perfectly adequate, with large beds pushed into alcoves, and all have TV and mini-bar. Doubles with shower/wc or bath €75–80. It's a good place; quiet and cosy, and in a non-touristy neighbourhood that's worth discovering. The new owner has got everything in hand and is particular about cleanliness. Delightful welcome. *One free breakfast per room or 10% discount on the room rate on presentation of this guide.*

La Boulangerie

15 rue des Panoyaux; M° Ménilmontant.
Ⓣ01.43.58.45.45
Closed *Sat lunch; Sun.*

A delightful place. This is an offshoot of *Lou Pascalou*, the café over the road, as the premises have been bought by its owner's son, Momo, and turned into a restaurant serving traditional dishes livened up by local herbs: roast loin of lamb with lime and lavender, cod poached with balsamic vinegar and pecans, red-tuna *tartare* with lemon grass and a mosaic of grilled vegetables. Cheapest menu €7.50; other lunchtime menus €10.50–12.50; dinner menus €15.50, Mon–Thurs, and €18.50. Reckon on around €23 à la carte. The wonderful food is matched by impeccable service.

Aristote

4 rue de la Réunion; M° Maraîchers or Buzenval.
Ⓣ01.43.70.42.91
Service *at lunchtime and until 11.30pm.*
Closed *Sun; a fortnight in Aug.* **Disabled access.**

This little restaurant, simple but welcoming, may not be much to look at, but you won't have to go to the cashpoint before eating here. It offers generous helpings of Greek and Turkish specialities with lots of kebabs and grills. Try the *hunkar beyendi* (rack of lamb with aubergines and potatoes in a sauce), the *guvec* (veal with vegetables in sauce) or the yoghurt dishes with minced steak or lamb. There are also good fish dishes for non-carnivores. The weekday lunch menu is €8.50; in the evening, à la carte costs €17. Local clientele, background music, pleasant setting and a good atmosphere. *Free digestif on presentation of this guide.*

Pascaline

49 rue Pixérécourt; M° Pl.-des-Fêtes.
Ⓣ01.44.62.22.80
Open *11am–3pm and 6–11.30pm.* **Closed** *Sat lunchtime; Sun; Mon evening; Aug; Christmas/New Year.* **Disabled access.**

This is not the type of Paris restaurant that you'd hunt high and low for, but it's perfectly adequate when you're in the area. Generous portions of good regional dishes: sausage from Cantal, ham hock with lentils, duck *confit*, tripe, *andouillette*, home-made pastries, *clafoutis*. Vegetarians, or anyone on a diet, should give it a miss. Lunch *formule* €9; menu €16; à la carte about €20. Interesting wines start at €15. *Free house apéritif or digestif on presentation of this guide.*

🏃 |●| Au Rendez-Vous des Amis

10 av. du Père-Lachaise; M° Gambetta.
☎01.47.97.72.16
Closed *evenings; Sun; Mon; 14 July–20 Aug.*

There's a good atmosphere in this friendly restaurant where the wine goes so fast it seems to evaporate. Robust dishes: black pudding crowned with apples, shoulder of veal and ratatouille, *escalope* of foie gras with apples and sirloin with blue cheese sauces – it's satisfyingly old-fashioned cooking. The €10.80 menu gives you a starter and main course, there's a *formule* for €9.80 and à la carte will set you back between €22 and €25. *Free apéritif or coffee on presentation of this guide.*

|●| Chez Jean

38 rue Boyer; M° Gambetta or Ménilmontant.
☎01.47.97.44.58
Open *8–11pm.* **Closed** *lunchtimes; Sun; Aug; Christmas to New Year.*

Jean used to be a journalist but a few years ago he decided he'd rather own a restaurant. He now provides home cooking in the best French tradition with a few added touches of his own. The atmosphere is the mixture of working-class and trendy so typical of the neighbourhood. It's always good fun, with an accordion player and singer on Wednesday, Friday and Saturday evenings. *Formule* (daily changing main course plus starter and dessert) €15; €24.50 or so à la carte depending on what you drink.

|●| Le Café Noir

15 rue Saint-Blaise; M° Porte-de-Bagnolet or Alexandre-Dumas.
☎01.40.09.75.80
Open *7pm–midnight; noon to midnight on Sunday.* **Closed** *last week of Aug and 1st week of Sept.*

This was a dispensary at the beginning of the twentieth century, but there's little sign of its medical past – the owners collect coffee pots, hats, enamel signs and posters rather than medicine bottles. They serve generous portions of good food: dishes such as *millefeuille* of artichokes and foie gras, terrine of monkfish liver, veal with violet mustard and fillet of beef with foie gras and spiced bread. And you can indulge in a cigar afterwards – the bar sells single Havanas. You'll pay about €25 for a meal, not including a drink.

|●| Chez Ramona

17 rue Ramponeau; M° Belleville or Couronnes.
☎01.46.36.83.55
Open *7–11pm.* **Closed** *lunchtimes; Mon.*

This little grocer's is always crowded but the restaurant is on the first floor up a steep, narrow staircase. The dining room is astonishing – crammed with Spanish souvenirs, velvet bulls' heads, *banderillas* in cellophane, artificial flowers, photos and posters of flamenco dancers . . . kitsch city. Paella, which you need to order in advance, costs €36.60 for two; though it lacks subtlety the helpings are huge. Otherwise you can choose from a variety of traditional, peasant-style dishes – deep-fried squid rings, mussels, Galicia-style hake – all of them taste good. Reckon on about €23 à la carte.

Neuilly-sur-Seine

92200 (0.5km NW)

🏃 |●| Le Chalet

14 rue du Commandant-Pilot; M° les Sablons; it's near the market square.
☎01.46.24.03.11
Open *noon–2.30pm and 7.30–11pm.* **Closed** *Sun.* **High chairs available.**

A Swiss chalet for those who didn't get away on a skiing holiday last year. There are snowscape photos on the wall to help the illusion and and bits of equipment scattered around. At lunchtime there's a *formule express* at €12.50, and menus at €26 and €28. Specialities include *fondue*, *raclette savoyarde* and *tartiflette*. It's a great place. *Free house apéritif on presentation of this guide.*

🏃 |●| Restaurant Foc Ly

79 av. Charles-de-Gaulle; M° Les Sablons.
☎01.46.24.43.36
Closed *a fortnight in Aug.* **Disabled access. Car park.**

You can't miss this place – it's got a pyramid roof and a pair of lions guarding the entrance. If you cast your eye over the long menu to the right of the front door, you'll see also numerous rave reviews from such figures as Jacques Chirac, Inès de la Fressange and Claude Chabrol. This is undoubtedly one of the best Asian restaurants in the area, with a very refined and varied style of cooking. Weekday lunchtime *formule* €16, menu €18.60, or about €28 à la carte. There's also a children's menu at €12.20 including a drink. *Free apéritif on presentation of this guide.*

Les Pieds dans l'Eau

39 bd. du Parc; it's on the Île de Jatte. M° Pont de Neuilly, then 10 minutes' walk.
01.47.47.64.07
Closed *Sat lunchtime and Sun Oct to end March.*

There's a feeling of times past in this riverside restaurant – an atmosphere of fishing parties and languid summer picnics. The furniture is English-style and there are old engravings on the wall, creating a sort of club-house ambience. The terraces run right down to the edge of the River Seine, under the poplars, fig trees and weeping willows. The chef landed in town from elsewhere and provides flavours from those far-off parts – grilled fish and meats, monkfish *pot-au-feu aïoli*, trout *carpaccio*, raw marinated salmon salad with whipped cream, tuna *aumônière*, chicken breasts with figs. Set menus €21, €23 and €29, or around €40 à la carte. *Free apéritif on presentation of this guide.*

Bagnolet

93170 (1km E)

Indigo Square

7 rue Marceau; M° Gallieni.
01.43.63.26.95
Closed *Sat lunch; Sun; Mon.*

Close to the town hall and opposite the covered market (which isn't an elegant one), this jewel of a restaurant combines French taste and flavours from further afield. You sit on benches with acid-coloured cushions or 1950s chairs. Dishes are delicately prepared – you might see Munster cheese *croustillant* with cumin, or turkey kebab with Jerusalem artichoke flan served with soya sauce – and desserts are fine and original. The €12 *formule* offers a starter/main course or main course/dessert, and there's another *formule* at €15. It's a deservedly popular place.

Boulogne-Billancourt

92100 (1km SW)

Le Quercy

251 bd. Jean-Jaurès; M° Marcel-Sembat.
01.46.21.33.46 01.46.21.72.21
www.hotel-le-quercy.com
TV.

This hotel has been refashioned, and now has a proper reception with a waiting area, and a security guard at night. The décor is still a bit old-fashioned, but who cares, given that this is one of the least expensive places in town. Doubles €44–65 depending on facilities. *One free breakfast per room on presentation of this guide.*

Chez Michel

4 rue Henri-Martin; M° Porte-de-Saint-Cloud.
01.46.09.08.10
Closed *Sat lunchtime; Sun; Aug.*

At lunchtime this place has the atmosphere of a noisy canteen. But in the evening, when friends come and talk more intimately, the noise levels drop. The dishes are chalked up on a blackboard so you can choose your own menu. Try terrine of red mullet with peppers and aubergine or terrine of foie gras with gingerbread. Weekday lunch menu at €13. Reckon on spending around €30 à la carte.

Ivry-sur-Seine

94200 (1km SE)

L'Europe

92 bd. Paul-Vaillant-Couturier; M°Mairie-d'Ivry.
01.46.72.04.64

The welcome is warm and the service efficient. At lunchtime, the two dining rooms are full of noise and overflow with customers. They dish up excellent couscous, €8–11, and also do good grills. Friday's the day for *choucroute* and paella.

Levallois-Perret

92300 (1km NW)

Hôtel du Globe

36 rue Louis Rouquier; M° Louise-Michel or Anatole-France.

Ⓣ and Ⓕ01.47.57.29.39

Small hotel with the appeal of a family pension. The décor is a bit old-fashioned, but not without charm. Pristine rooms. Doubles with basin €32 or €40 with shower.

|●| Au Petit Sud-Ouest

4 rue de Baudin; M° Pont de Levallois.
Ⓣ01.47.59.03.74
Service *to 10pm.* **Closed** *Sat; Sun.*

This is a shop as well as a restaurant that feature food from the southwest. The window has a display of sheep's cheeses and country ham. On the menu, scrambled eggs with ceps, raw foie gras with sea salt, *cassoulet* with *confit* of duck, *daube* of duck in Madiran wine, *garbure*. Gascony by the Seine. Salads for around €8, dishes €10–22. There's a relaxing terrace in a paved courtyard.

|●| Le Petit Poucet

4 rond-point Claude-Monet; it's at the eastern end of the île de la Jatte.
Ⓣ01.47.38.61.85
Service *daily until 11pm.*

There's been a restaurant here for almost a century. Back in the 1900s, it was a country tavern where working-class men used to bring their sweethearts. In the 1980s it became terribly fashionable, before being transformed ten years ago into a cosy place with lots of wood panelling and a warm atmosphere. It has three lovely terraces, one on the bank of the Seine, where elegant women and fashionable young men come to relax as soon as the sun comes out. Good, classic French cooking with a weekday lunchtime *formule* for €19 and a weekend evening menu at €27. Fast, efficient service. It's best to book.

Montreuil

93100 (1km E)

|●| Le Gaillard

71 rue Hoche; M° Mairie-de-Montreuil.
Ⓣ01.48.58.17.37
Closed *Sun evening; Mon lunch; 3 weeks in Aug.*

It's worth braving the boulevard Périphérique to get here. Atop the Guillands hill, in the middle of nowhere, this old residence is a haven of culinary taste and *savoir-vivre*. The starters are delicate and the mains have *panache* – pan-fried foie gras, duck *parmentier* with salad, ox kidneys with puréed potato – while desserts are simple but delicious. Menus €26.70 and €35.80, but à la carte the bill can shoot up – not least because the wines are expensive. There's an appealing open fire in winter and an amazing garden/terrace that comes into its own in the summer (it's best to reserve if you want to sit outside).

Nanterre

92000 (1km NW)

Hôtel Saint-Jean

24-26-33 av. de Rueil; RER Nanterre-Ville on the Saint-Germain-en-Laye line; bus 258/158.
Ⓣ01.47.24.19.20 Ⓕ01.47.24.17.65
Ⓔhotel.stjean@wanadoo.fr

This hotel, 500m from the centre of town in a quiet neighbourhood, has been in the same family for three generations. Each room is different, but they're all clean and well maintained. Some of them look over the pretty garden. Doubles from €26 with basin, €32 with shower or €38 with shower/wc; €40 overlooking the garden. Very pleasant welcome.

Saint-Mandé

94160 (1km E)

|●| Le Bistrot Lucas

8 rue Jeanne d'Arc; M° Saint-Mandé Tourelle.
Ⓣ01.48.08.74.81
Closed *Sun; Mon; 3 weeks in Aug.*

This Lyonnais-style bistro, on the outskirts of Paris, is within striking distance of the Vincennes woods. They treat you very well amid the wooden tables, simple décor and postcards on the walls. Attractive dishes: lentil *rémoulade* with hot Lyon sausage, calf's head *ravigote*, pike dumplings. For dessert, try home-made pastries or the fruit *coulis*. There's one menu at €20, with main courses à la carte for €11–14 and wines around €15 a bottle.

Saint-Ouen

93400 (1km N)

|●| Le Soleil

109 av. Michelet; it's opposite the Biron market; M° Porte-de-Clignancourt.
Ⓣ01.40.10.08.08
Closed *Mon–Wed evenings; Sun evening.*

This restaurant attracts a crowd of regulars,

and the owner scurries between the tables hailing his well-heeled guests. The décor is appealingly elegant – there's a huge sun in the centre of the ceiling and unusual blinds at the windows. The tables are well dressed, with *fleur de sel* salt from the Île de Ré, Saint-Lô butter pats and free-flowing olive oil from the Italian Riviera. Starters €10–14: marinated herring fillets, Andalusian mountain ham, smoked salmon marinated in dill. Main courses €17–22: royal sea bass, roast brill, steak with red wine sauce. Excellent desserts include a huge rum baba, *crème catalan* with Bourbon vanilla, and apple tart. There's a good wine list, too; some are served by the jug, for around €10.50. All this adds up to a substantial bill but, given the quality, that's fair enough. A very, very good place. *Free house apéritif on presentation of this guide.*

Vincennes

94300 (2km SE)

Ristorante Alessandro

51 rue de Fontenay; M° Château-de-Vincennes; RER Vincennes; it's beside the town hall.
☎01.49.57.05.30
Closed *Sun; 3 weeks in Aug.* **Disabled access.**

It's a pity that the décor of this pizzeria is quite so ordinary, as the food itself certainly isn't. These are mainly Italian specialities – aubergine parmigiana, spaghetti with king prawns, tagliatelle with scallops and *saltimbocca alla romana* (a wonderful combination of veal, Parma ham and sage). The *antipasti* – artichokes, olives, sun-dried tomatoes, pickled onions and charcuterie – are fantastic. And the pizzas are the real thing, with delicious crispy bases and generous, classic toppings. Set weekday lunch menu €12, then others at €23 and €30.50. Children's menu at €11. *Free house digestif on presentation of this guide.*

Courbevoie-La-Défense

92400 (3km NW)

Hôtel George-Sand

18 av. Marceau; M° Esplanade-de-La Défense; it's 50m from Courbevoie station.
☎01.43.33.57.04 Ⓕ01.47.88.59.38
Ⓦwww.hotel-paris-georgesand.com

Ask for one of the renovated rooms but, before mounting the stairs, take a look at the collection of George Sand memorabilia on the ground floor: busts, letters, souvenirs. The décor has echoes of the period she lived in. Each room is personalized and furnished by the owner who picks things up at auctions and junk shops. His family have run the place for a couple of generations. It's a quiet hotel that offers good value for money given you're not far from the Défense. Doubles with en-suite bathrooms €130. Breakfast €9. They even provide decent room service; meals on trays, dry-cleaning etc. *One free breakfast per room on presentation of this guide.*

Pasta, Amore e Fantasia

80 av. Marceau; train Saint-Lazare to Courbevoie station or RER line A, La Défense.
☎01.43.33.68.30
Closed *Sun; Mon evening; public holidays; Aug.*

You'll be blown away here by the exuberant colours of Naples – they've even strung washing on a line across the room! The dining room is vast but manages to feel intimate. The cuisine is equally exuberant and colourful: delicious *antipasti*, a huge choice of pizzas, *osso buco à la piémontaise*, Sicilian ravioli, *piccata parmigiana* and so on. Weekday lunch menu at €15 or around €28 à la carte. There's live music after 10.30pm on Friday and Saturday. It's a good idea to book, whenever you come. *Free digestif on presentation of this guide.*

Saint-Denis

93200 (3.5km N)

Les Verdiots

26 bd. Marcel-Sembat; 100m from M° Porte-de-Paris; 400m from the Stade de France.
☎01.42.43.24.33
Open *noon–2.30pm and 7.30–9.30pm.*
Closed *Sun; Mon; 1–8 Jan; Aug.*

Patrick Perney specializes in confident, tasty dishes originating from les Landes on the Atlantic coast – ham from the Aldudes, duck *confit*, guineafowl with figs, crispy pigs' trotters. The service is friendly and charming, the dining room classic and clean, and the prices honest. There's a substantial weekday lunch menu at €12 and another menu at €19.50; otherwise it's about €40 à la carte. A good place with good wines. *Free house apéritif on presentation of this guide.*

Le Wagon

14 [bis] av. Jean-Moulin; M° Porte de Paris; it's near the Baleine swimming pool.
01.48.23.23.41
Closed *Tues, Thurs and Fri evenings; July–Aug.*

This is an amazing restaurant, housed in a railway carriage. It's run by a restaurant school, so the waiters and kitchen staff apply themselves to their tasks with great concentration. You eat cheaply but well; à la carte, reckon on around €14 (there's a children's menu for €5). They specialize in fish and seafood; good dishes include pan-fried scallops with leeks, terrine with red onion marmalade, salmon fillet with grain mustard and excellent house desserts. It's worth booking. *Free apéritif or coffee on presentation of this guide.*

Saint-Maur-des-Fossés

94100 (16km E)

Le Bistrot de la Mer

59 bis av. du Bac; it's a turning off the A4 autoroute.
01.48.83.01.11
www.le-bistrot-de-la-mer.com
Closed *Sun evening.*

Service until 11pm. The dining room is decorated in blue and white, creating just the right atmosphere for a seafood restaurant, and dishes are prepared with style. There's lots of originality and skill in the cooking and the quality is reliable so the place has earned itself a regular following. There's a weekday lunch *formule* at €12. Menus €16 (weekdays lunchtime only) and €26; à la carte reckon on around €35. The lunch *formules* offer excellent value for money. Specialities include scallops, smoked salmon and a superb fish soup. They even do seafood to take away. On certain evenings there's a pianist in the bar. The welcome and service are superb.

Chez Nous comme chez Vous

110 av. du Mesnil.
01.48.85.41.61
cheznouscommechezvous.com
Closed *Sun evening; Mon and Tues lunchtimes; a week early May; Aug.*

There's an old provincial feel about this place. They've got a battery of copper pots on the walls and it would take an earthquake to disrupt the solid traditions in the kitchen, which are rooted deeply in regional cuisine. You're in the hands of real professionals who focus on providing quality rather than originality. Madame has been running front-of-house for a good quarter of a century and the service is first rate; her husband, the chef, keeps his standards similarly high. The menu changes yearly, but specialities include langoustine aïoli, smoked salmon, house duck foie gras, and langoustine and mussel *fricassée* on a bed of tagliatelle. Dishes of the day (around €13) might include *blanquette* of veal, paella or *fondue bourguignonne*. There's a weekday lunch *formule* at €18, and menus ranging from €26 up to €56. *Free coffee or house digestif on presentation of this guide.*

Le Gourmet

150 bd. du Général-Giraud.
01.48.86.86.96
Closed *Sun evening; Mon; end Aug to mid-Sept.* **Disabled access.**

There are decent places to eat and there are good restaurants – and then there's *Le Gourmet*, which offers high-class cuisine at its best. The setting is wonderfully done: the dining room is elegant Art Deco with armfuls of flowers in big vases, and there's a wide bay window looking out onto a lovely terraced garden where you dine in the summer. And that's not all: the proprietor learned his profession in some of the greatest kitchens in the capital and is on absolutely top form. The food is succulent, delicious and prepared with meticulous care – flavours are delicately balanced and each dish is cooked to perfection. The speciality of the chef, Dominique, is duck breast stuffed with lobster. There's a lunch *formule* at €20 (not served Sunday or public holidays) including drink and coffee. Menus go for €30 (excluding public holidays) with wine and coffee included, and €35. *Free house digestif on presentation of this guide.*

Pontoise

95300

Le Pavé de la Roche

30 rue de la Roche; it's a turning off the pl. de l'Hôtel-de-Ville.
01.34.43.14.05
Closed *Sat lunchtime; Sun evening; Mon; 3 weeks in Aug; a week at Christmas.*

You'll find this establishment on a bend of

a road climbing above the Oise. Try the €12.50 weekday lunch menu, with wine included: you start by choosing from the *crudités* buffet, which has at least twenty dishes, and follow with a good main dish and home-made dessert. They also offer a menu at €28, and à la carte you can expect to pay around €30. Specialities include rabbit *à la provençale*, roast Saint-Marcellin cheese with smoked duck breast, Guémené *andouille* with apples, veal *blanquette*, game in season and a fine apple tart with Calvados. There's a terrace for nice weather, and a peaceful courtyard. *Free coffee on presentation of this guide.*

Cergy

95000 (5km W)

Hôtel Mercure Cergy Pontoise Centre***

3 rue des Chênes-Émeraude; from the tourist office, go straight down the rue de Gisors, then take av. Rédouane-Bougara to the roundabout in front of the *Leclerc* shopping centre; from there, turn left and go in the direction of Cergy-centre.
Ⓣ01.34.24.94.94 Ⓕ01.34.24.95.15
Ⓦwww.mercure.com
TV. Disabled access. Pay car park.

One of the best hotels in the Pontoise region as regards value for money. At weekends businessmen make way for travellers looking for a comfortable, sophisticated haven of peace and quiet. It's a great favourite with newly-weds. Double rooms €109–119. Copious breakfast €12. *10% discount on the room rate (Fri, Sat and Sun) offered to our readers on presentation of this guide.*

Provins

77160

Hostellerie Aux Vieux Remparts

3 rue Couverte; in the heart of the medieval city.
Ⓣ01.64.08.94.00 Ⓕ01.60.67.77.22
Ⓦwww.auxvieuxremparts.com
Open *daily noon–2.30pm and 7.30–9.30 pm.*
TV. Disabled access. Car park. High chairs available.

This hotel, set in a beautiful medieval house with a garden ablaze with flowers, has earned an excellent reputation but it is expensive: 32 rooms at €65–140, according to the degree of comfort. These rooms are extremely classy, however: mini-bar, telephone with a direct outside line, luxurious bathroom and any number of mod cons. The restaurant, which has a beautiful shady terrace, offers specialities in the great French tradition, although the chef Lionel Sarre adds modern touches, combining fresh ingredients, interesting combinations and striking presentation. The result is the most sophisticated restaurant in the province *par excellence*. Suggestions menu €26 (weekday), pleasure menu €37 and discovery menu €56. Only black mark: the breakfast is disappointing and fails to justify its high price (€12) – you'll be better off looking for a little bistro in the morning. *Free house liqueur offered to our readers on presentation of this guide.*

La Boudinière des Marais

17 rue Hugues-le-Grand; it's at the lower end of town.
Ⓣ01.60.67.64.89
Closed *Mon and Tues evenings; Wed.* **High chairs available.**

The locals and well-informed sales reps who flock here know that on weekdays for €12.50 you can get a well-cooked, substantial lunch with a quarter-litre of wine included, and that there are other quality menus at €16.50–28.80. It's traditional French cooking: *filet mignon* with brie, rabbit *fondant* with onion marmalade, calf's head, grilled lamb chops with a garlic crust, iced nougat with honey and pistachios. Reservations essential at the weekend.

Rambouillet

78120

Hôtel Saint-Charles**

15 rue de Groussay; from the town hall, follow the road that runs along the park for about 1km.
Ⓣ01.34.83.06.34 Ⓕ01.30.46.26.84
Disabled access. TV. Car park.

A functional hotel near the centre. Most of the rooms are fairly spacious and they're all scrupulously clean. Rooms €49 with shower/wc or bath; breakfast is yours for €6. No surprises here, but no nasty shocks, either.

Restaurant La Poste

101 rue du Général-de-Gaulle.

☎01.34.83.03.01
Closed *Sun evening; Mon.*

If you want to eat here, one of the best restaurants in town, it's best to book. The two dining rooms are extremely pretty, and service is efficient and friendly. Cooking is light and refined, with dishes like house foie gras, lamb *noisette*, chicken *fricassée* with crayfish and house raspberry soufflé. Set menus €20.90 (not served during public holidays) and €27.50–32.20.

Roche-Guyon (La)

95780

Hôtel-Restaurant Les Bords de Seine**

21 rue du Docteur-Duval; it's near the tourist office on the banks of the Seine.
☎01.39.98.32.52

As its name suggests, you can watch the Seine flowing by from this restaurant. The *formule* at €14 is served at weekday lunchtime, and there's a menu for €19. The food is well-cooked, served attractively and you won't go hungry. They serve a wine of the month by the glass. The dinining room is decorated in blue and white, and, like the service, is both elegant and informal. There's a lovely terrace with parasols for the summer and heaters in winter. The hotel is well-run, and although the rooms are small they all have en-suite bathrooms and phones. Doubles €48–64 with shower or bath/wc; some have that river view. *Free house apéritif on presentation of this guide.*

Rolleboise

78270

Le Château de la Corniche

5 rte. de la Corniche; from Paris take the A13 towards Rouen, leaving by exit 13 direction of Rosny-sur-Seine or Vernon; from Rouen take the A13 towards Paris, leaving by exit 15 direction of Bonnières-sur-Seine or Mantes-la-Jolie.
☎01.30.93.20.00 ℻01.30.42.27.44
www.chateaudelacorniche.com
Closed *Sun evening and Mon lunch Sept to end April; 20 Dec–10 Jan.* **TV. Car park.**

The rooms in this nineteenth-century folly have every modern comfort; doubles from €75 with bath/wc. The restaurant is elegant and there's a panoramic view from the terrace. Refined and innovative gourmet cuisine. Lunch menu €25 Tues to Sat; others €36, €46 and €55 – it may not be cheap but it's definitely good value in this category. There are lots of country walks around and it's good base from which to visit Monet's house at Giverny. *One free breakfast per room or free coffee on presentation of this guide.*

Rueil-Malmaison

92500

Le Jardin Clos

17 rue Eugène-Labiche; RER Rueil-Malmaison (ligne A).
☎01.47.08.03.11
Open *noon–2pm and 8–10pm.* **Closed** *Sun; Mon; first 3 weeks in Aug.*

The bland exterior doesn't really give you a clue about what you'll find inside: there's a peaceful garden with a well, and you can eat on the terrace. The cooking is seriously tasty and generously served, and you'll get a good-natured welcome. The good-value €18 lunch menu includes a self-service buffet of hors d'œuvres; others are €25 and €30. Specialities include *salade gourmande* with pine nuts, *fricassée* of scallops and prawns in balsamic vinegar, and roast of lamb with herbs. Main dishes are often accompanied by rissoled potatoes. Reservations advised. *Free house apéritif on presentation of this guide.*

Saint-Cloud

92210

Le Garde Manger

21 rue d'Orléans; go up the hill leading from the Saint-Cloud bridge to the A3 and keep going straight ahead.
☎01.46.02.03.66
Closed *Sun.*

Bottle-green front and cosy little dining room with young, extremely friendly staff. Traditional food from South-West France: fried squids with Espelette peppers, *féroce* of chicken breast and the classic duck *magret*. Weekday lunchtime menus €13 (main course with either starter or dessert) and €16. On the blackboard, eight starters and eight main courses, along with some suggestions of the day.

Saint-Cyr-sous-Dourdan

91410

|●| La Ferme des Tourelles

2 rue de l'Église.
Ⓣ01.64.59.15.29
Open *noon–2pm and 7–9.30pm.* **Closed** *Mon evening; Tues.*

The quality of the cooking and the kindness add to your appreciatiion of this beautiful place. It's one of the most beautiful fortified farms in the Hurepoix. The sixteenth- and seventeenth-century buildings surround a huge, square central courtyard. There are small turrets at each corner (hence the name of the place), with a well in the middle. You can eat in the courtyard where they set tables with red and white checked cloths; from here you glimpse the village church. There's a wide choice of dishes chalked up on a blackboard, and it's delicious, traditional food; rabbit *à l'ancienne*, chicken thigh with cream and cider sauce, monk fish with mushrooms and shellfish. Try the coffee and walnut or chocolate and hazelnut desserts. Set menus from €16. *Free house apéritif on presentation of this guide.*

Saint-Germain-en-Laye

78100

Havre Hôtel*

92 rue Léon-Désoyer; it's on the old road to Chambourcy.
Ⓣ and Ⓕ01.34.51.41.05
Closed *Sun afternoon; lst fortnight in Aug.* **TV.**

Clean, well-run little hotel in the middle of town where a double with shower/wc or bath will cost €47. Some overlook the cemetery, so there are no extraneous noises to wake you, and all are double-glazed. Pleasant, friendly welcome. A good place. *10% discount on the room rate on presentation of this guide.*

|●| L'Ermitage des Loges – Le Saint-Exupéry***

11 av. des Loges.
Ⓣ01.39.21.50.90 Ⓕ01.39.21.50.91
Ⓦwww.ermitage-des-loges.com
Disabled access. TV. High chairs available. Car park.

This place is really smart, and there's a wide view of the avenues of trees leading through the forest to the château. Rooms are extremely comfortable and service is faultless; doubles from €104–135 depending on the season. Fine, classic cuisine is served in the Art Deco dining room. The lunchtime *menu du jour* costs €21 and includes a small bottle of mineral water and coffee; there's another evening menu at €31. Specialities include duck foie gras with dried apricot *compote,* duck breast caramelized with honey, Szechuan pepper and macaroni *gratin* with poached leeks, and orange soufflé with Grand Marnier. *Free house apéritif on presentation of this guide.*

|●| Restaurant La Feuillantine

10 rue des Louviers; it's in the pedestrian area.
Ⓣ01.34.51.04.24 Ⓕ01.34.51.41.03
Closed Sun and public holidays.

Speedy service in a tasteful dining room. You eat very well here: excellent foie gras and omelette with smoked salmon. Lunch *formules* from €18 to €28, and a menu at €28.

|●| Le Tabl'o Gourmand

18 pl. Saint-Pierre.
Ⓣ01.34.51.66.33
Closed *Mon lunchtime; a fortnight in Jan.*
High chairs and games available.

Set on a quiet little square, this is a relaxing restaurant with a Provençal look – beams and dressed stone. The owner is an art lover and fills the dining room with pictures by local artists. He's also a fan of recipes from centuries past and he adapts them for modern tastes – try his *pantoufle de cardinal* stuffed with duck and foie gras, but leave room for the crêpes Suzette. There's a menu at €22; count on around €43 à la carte. Wine list features only a few half-bottles. *Free digestif on presentation of this guide.*

Saint-Maurice

94410

|●| La Pibale

11 rue Paul-Verlaine.
Ⓣ01.42.83.62.35
Closed *Sat lunch; Sun; Mon evening; a week at Easter; a week in Aug.*

There's something typically Spanish-Basque here – it's not the paintings – but rather the ropes of Espelette peppers, the tables with azulejos, and the kitchen open to the dining room. It's also in the way they prepare the food: marinated sardines, anchovy purée with leeks, *axoa* (veal, ham and *piperade*), *pimientos del piquillo* (peppers stuffed with cod)... and what of their eels? Elvers (available in winter only) are highly prized but too expensive (€60 per 80g). For dessert there's *gateau basque* and *tourtière* Marie. Lunch *formule* of main meal and dessert costs €18.50, and the menu-carte goes for €26. *Free children's menu (for children up to five years) on presentation of this guide.*

Sainte-Geneviève-des-Bois

91700

|●| La Table d'Antan

38 av. de la Grande-Charmille-du-Parc; 200m from the town hall, at the roundabout, it's the first road on the right.
☎01.60.15.71.53
Open *noon–1.15pm and 7.30–9pm.* **Closed** *Mon; Sun, Tues and Wed evenings; Aug.*

This place is in a quiet part of the town in a neat, refurbished house. The chef specializes in duck dishes – duck foie gras in particular, cooked in several different ways – but menus also include tasty fish and meat. *Menu tradition* at €26, another at €45. The mistress of the house extends a charming welcome. Essential to book.

Sceaux

92330

|●| L'Auberge du Parc

6 av. du Président-Franklin-Roosevelt.
☎01.43.50.35.15
Closed *in Aug.*

A nice detached house opposite the entrance to the Lycée Lakanal, with a small, sunny terrace at the front. Unsurprisingly, it attracts a regular crowd of students during the week. The dining room has provincial charm and looks down on the garden. The *formules* are of the speedy, efficient type; there's one for students at €5. They offer a selection of reasonably priced Iberian specialities including cod with a range of sauces; certain dishes have to be reserved in advance and are for a minimum of seven people. Weekday menu €9 with starter, main course and cheese or dessert and 25cl of wine, or around €20 à la carte. An ideal stop if you're on a Sunday walk.

Sèvres

92360

|●| La Salle à Manger

12 av. de la Division-Leclerc.
☎01.46.26.66.64
Closed *Sat lunchtime; Sun evening; Mon; Aug.*

The décor is bright and fresh and you immediately feel you're in the country. On the menu you'll find *œufs en meurette* (in red wine sauce), tomato tart with Cantal cheese and mustard, *fricassée* of rabbit with herbs, calf's cheek with orange and cumin and duck breast in honey – a cornucopia of flavours. The place is a hive of activity and the service is quiet, quick and efficient; take your time to enjoy it. It's often full, partly because it's such good value: menus €15.50–28.

Soisy-sur-École

91840

|●| Le Saut du Postillon

On the D948, north of Courances near the fork for Soisy-sur-École.
☎01.64.98.08.12
Open *noon–2pm and 7–9pm.* **Closed** *Sun and Wed eveninsg; Mon; Aug; Christmas and New Year holidays.* **High chairs available.**

Leaded lights, a broad fire place and copper pots on the walls give this inn its authentic rustic look. It's a historic place – good King Henri went to call on his lady friend, Juliette d'Antraygues, in Malesherbes, when a rut in the road caused a carriage wheel to come off. He ordered the *postillon* to jump down to fix it, and that's where the restaurant gets its name, so it's said. The road's in better shape today and there's a car park for your carriage. Excellent classic dishes served with friendliness and efficiency. The plates are hot, the dishes tasty and well presented. Just what you want. Weekday menu served until 9pm for €12.20, standard menu for €22.50 or gourmet menu at €29.50. *Free coffee on presentation of this guide.*

Suresnes

92150

La Cave Gourmande

20 rue des Bourets.
01.42.04.13.67
Closed *Sat lunch; Sun; Mon lunch; Aug.*

This stylish restaurant, right in the centre of Suresnes, has nothing to do with a cellar. So don't panic if you're claustrophobic; the dining room is actually at street level. It's a good place for foodies, serving nicely composed dishes: minced scallops marinated in dill, medallions of monkfish, sautéed crayfish with champagne, panfried *foie gras*. Menus €21, €22 and €35 or around €39 à la carte.

Les Jardins de Camille

70 av. Franklin Roosevelt; take bus no. 244 to the Pont de Suresnes stop or take the train to the Suresnes-Mont-Valérien station.
01.45.06.22.66
Closed *Sun evening.* **Disabled access.**

This big house stands on the hillside of the Suresnes vineyards, way up high with a fabulous view of Paris below. They serve Burgundy wine here, and the cuisine is good – country dishes like *rillettes* of rabbit with Armagnac, snails, *bœuf bourguignon*, game in season and fresh goat from the Morvan. You'll find food like this on their *menus-carte* at €32.50 and €49. The Poinsots know what they're about, greet you well and really take care of you. *Free house digestif on presentation of this guide.*

Vanves

92170

Aux Sportifs

51 rue Sadi-Carnot; it's near the cemetery.
01.46.42.12.63
Service *up to 9pm.* **Closed** *Sat; Sun; a week in Spring; a fortnight in Aug; a week in winter.*

This is a popular bistro-restaurant serving a regular blue- and white-collar clientele. It's as if a bell rings at noon and they all flood in. You could be forgiven for thinking the décor hasn't changed since the '60s – and that's sort of a compliment. The lovely woman who owns the place puts her heart and soul into the traditional home cooking; it's simple and good. There's only one set menu, which will set you back €11.50 for starter, main course and dessert; otherwise you'll pay around €8.80 for a main course.

Versailles

78000

Home Saint-Louis**

28 rue Saint-Louis.
01.39.50.23.55 01.30.21.62.45
TV.

This is a quiet, comfortable, well-looked-after hotel in the heart of the pretty Saint-Louis neighbourhood. Doubles with shower €45, €58 with shower/wc/bath – all have double glazing, TV and hair dryers, but bathrooms are a bit small. It's very good value for money.

Hôtel du Cheval Rouge**

18 rue André-Chénier; it's on the market square.
01.39.50.03.03 01.39.50.61.27
TV. Car park.

This well-located, comfortable hotel – with the atmosphere of a small motel – also has a pretty tearoom (where you take breakfast). Doubles €49 with shower, €66 with shower/wc and €78 with bath/wc – not bad for a town where prices are sky-high, especially near the château. The car park is a definite plus. *10% discount on the room rate (15 Nov–15 March) or free house digestif on presentation of this guide.*

Hôtel Richaud***

16 rue Richaud.
01.39.50.10.42 01.39.53.43.36
TV. Car park.

This must be the most central and yet the most peaceful hotel in town. It has forty very clean rooms with TV and direct-dial telephone – ask for one looking over the buildings of the Hôpital Richaud opposite. The furnishings and decoration are very 1970s – they certainly didn't stint on the carpeting – and make sure you see the bar, which is a monument to kitsch. It doesn't really deserve three stars but it has two-star prices, so that's OK: doubles €51 with shower/wc or €55 with bath. *One free breakfast per room on presentation of this guide.*

Paris Hôtel**

14 av. de Paris; RER Versailles-rive-gauche. It's 400m from the pl. d'Armes.

Ⓣ01.39.50.56.00 Ⓕ01.39.50.21.83
Ⓦwww.paris-hotel.fr
Disabled access. TV.

You will get a very warm welcome in this hotel and the proprietor will give you a friendly handshake when you come down for breakfast. Spacious, clean rooms, the nicest overlooking the courtyard; doubles €68 with shower/wc and €95 with bath. *10% discount on the room rate (not to be used in conjunction with special weekend rates) on presentation of this guide.*

Sister's Café

15 rue des Réservoirs; not far from the château, on the street running along the Neptune pond and the north side of the park.
Ⓣ01.30.21.21.22
Open *daily noon–3pm and 6.30–11pm.*
Children's crayons.

Long, American-style bar restaurant with brash decoration, popular with a young, local crowd for their American or Tex-Mex dishes (chicken wings, *quesadillas*). A few tables on the terrace in fine weather. Menus €13–18. Brunch at the weekend €18. *Free Kir offered to our readers on presentation of this guide.*

Le Baladin Saint-Louis

2 rue de l'Occident.
Ⓣ01.39.50.06.57
Closed *Sun (except for public holidays).*
Disabled access.

Nice terrace where you can appreciate the view of the Saint-Louis district. You'll find expressive and daring cuisine which is often imaginative and always of high quality: jellied rabbit with onion marmalade, fresh cod fillet with *tapenade*, veal kidneys. There's a weekday *formule* (starter/main course/dessert or coffee) for €19, and menus for €24 and €33 (the last includes a half-bottle of wine). *Free house apéritif on presentation of this guide.*

La Cuisine Bourgeoise

10 bd. du Roi.
Ⓣ01.39.53.11.38
Closed *Sat lunchtime; Sun; Mon lunchtime; 1st 3 weeks in Aug.* **Disabled access. Car park.**

This very cosy dining room, decorated in shades of green, is a little more gourmet than bourgeois. You'll see caviar, foie gras and truffles in light, flavoursome dishes. The €21.50 lunch menu is chalked up on the blackboard and there's another at €29.50; menus €39 and €46 in the evening. À la carte you'll pay about €49. There's an excellent list of vintages by the glass. *Free house apéritif on presentation of this guide.*

La Flottille

Ⓣ01.39.51.41.58
Open *daily 8am–5.30pm (9pm in summer).*
Restaurant open *lunchtime only until 3.30pm.* **Disabled access.**

The restaurant is located immediately opposite the landing stage where, on a fine day, small boats can be hired. Undeniably the most agreeable place imaginable: in summer, the terrace flows down to the water's edge. There are two dining rooms and two styles of dining: the brasserie, and the slightly more expensive restaurant. On the whole the cooking is as it should be, and in the brasserie, the dishes and salads are nicely presented. Crêpes and pastries are also on offer. There's a *formule* at €23.50, or you'll pay around €30 à la carte excluding drinks. Otherwise, in the brasserie (serving all day) dishes of the day cost between €9.50 and €12. A word of warning – you'll be charged an entry fee of €4.50 to come here by car.

Montigny-le-Bretonneux

78180 (10km SW)

L'Auberge du Manet***

61 av. du Manet; coming from Paris on the A13 then the A12, take the Montigny exit; follow the signs to Ferme du Manet.
Ⓣ01.30.64.89.00 Ⓕ01.30.64.55.10
Ⓦwww.aubergedumanet.com
Open *noon–2pm and 7–10pm.* **Disabled access. TV. High chairs and games available. Car park.**

The huge farm used to be part of the domaine of the Abbaye de Port-Royal-des-Champs which is about 2km away. They've converted it into a hotel-restaurant in a perfect pastoral setting and they've done it very well. Attractive dining room with a large terrace overlooking a pretty pond. The rooms are faultless and definitely worth the price (€87–96); all have mini-bar, satellite TV and en-suite bathroom with bath or shower/wc, and they're slightly cheaper at the weekend. In the restaurant the cooking is deftly prepared and reasonably priced, starting with the menu for residents at €23 (starter, main course and cheese or dessert), with others from €26–42. Menus change three times a year. Classic dishes cooked with confidence; specialities include tasty lobster "surf and turf", calf's sweetbreads with roes, sea bass with fresh tomatoes and *pistou* sauce cooked *en papillotte*, semi-bitter chocolate soufflé. *10% discount on the room rate or free house apéritif on presentation of this guide.*

Gif-sur-Yvette

91190 (18km SW)

Le Bœuf à Six Pattes

D128 Chemin du Moulon; take the Centre universitaire exit 9 off the N118.
☎01.60.19.29.60

Open *11.30am–2.30pm and 7–10pm. (10.30pm Fri and Sat).* **Disabled access. High chairs and games available. Car park.**

You could well get a crick in the neck as you crane round to look at the cow Slavik has hung up in this restaurant. Unsurprisingly, he specializes in meat dishes, which are first-rate and served with wonderful chips. They also do *confit* of duck thigh and grilled salmon steak, and for dessert they offer a great caramelized rice pudding. *Formule* at €10 with salad and a beef dish; menus, €13.50 and €17, and another at €21.50 which includes *apéritif*, starter, main meal, dessert, drink and coffee. Reckon on €20–22 à la carte. Children's menu (under 12 years) €6.50 – children eat for free at lunchtime on Sat and Sun. There's a terrace. *Free coffee on presentation of this guide.*

Languedoc-Roussillon

Agde

34300

Hôtel Le Donjon**

Place Jean-Jaurès.
Ⓣ04.67.94.12.32 Ⓕ04.67.94.34.54
Ⓦwww.hotelledonjon.com
Closed *2 Dec–4 Jan.* **TV. Pay car park.**

An old stone building practically next door to the ancient cathedral of Saint-Étienne on a pleasant square that buzzes with life in summer. The fresh-looking bedrooms are comfy, exceptionally well maintained and good value. Doubles €49–76 with shower/wc or bath. Breakfast €6. Nice atmosphere, nice prices (given the location).

Hôtel-restaurant La Tamarissière***

Lieu-dit La Tamarissière; go along quai Commandant-Réveille, then follow the D32 for 5km.
Ⓣ04.67.94.20.87 Ⓕ04.67.21.38.40
Ⓦchateauxhotels.com/tamarissiere
Closed *5 Nov–5 March.* **Restaurant closed** *Sun evening and Mon (except public holiday weekends and in high season); Mon, Tues and Fri lunchtimes in season. High chairs available.* **TV.**

This hotel, set on the banks of the Hérault, is the most famous in the region and has a lovely rose garden within a pine wood. Stylish bedrooms cost €66–115 with shower/wc or bath. Breakfast €11.50. The wonderful cooking at the old-fashioned bistro is full of the flavours of the south and successfully combines tradition with style. Choose from dishes such as cuttlefish with parsley, tomato and basil, bourride, fish stew, turbot *a la plancha* and fillet of beef with Banyuls wine sauce. Set menus €27.50 and €39.50. Pleasant hotel with nice rooms overlooking the Hérault river or the rose garden (not forgetting its swimming pool!). Easy-going atmosphere. Lovely terrace by the river under the plane trees. *10% discount on the room rate when you present this guide at your arrival.*

La Fine Fourchette

2 rue du Mont-Saint-Loup; take rue de Richelieu then follow the "Promenade".
Ⓣ04.67.94.49.56
Closed *Sun; every evening;23 Dec–5 Jan.*

A modest-looking restaurant set back from the Grand Boulevards with a shady, flowery terrace. This is the place to enjoy honest regional cooking at fair prices – sardine or mackerel tart, *croustillant* of pigs' trotters. Menus €10.50 and €18.00. The friendly *patronne* takes care of the service.

Numéro Vin

2 pl. de la Marine; very close to the Hérault river and the town.
Ⓣ04.67.00.20.20
Closed *Sat, Sun, Mon lunchtimes, and Mon evening in low season.*

Weekday lunch menu at €11; à la carte menu at €21. A great find and a great asset for Agde, a town located on a volcano. Decorated on a budget but with great effect. An original and tasteful menu, with a touch of gastronomical interest, offering dishes with a definite flavour from the sea and the garrigue. Generous selection of good quality local wines ranging from €17 to €115. Interesting selection of

A
CANTAL
Chaulhac
Aurillac
N 122
Chaudes-Aigues
la Garde
Souillac
St-Chély-d'A.
A 20
N 140
la Chaldette
Laguiole
Nasbinals
Aumont-Aubrac
Javols
Marvejols
Figeac
Aubrac
LOT
N 20
D 920
D 921
D 987
Espalion
N 88
Chanac
Cahors
AVEYRON
Rodez
1
D 911
le Rosier
N 88
TARN-ET-GARONNE
Millau
N 9
A 62
Montauban
D 999
N 113
Albi
A 75
D 999
D 607
D 902
A 68
TARN
Lodève
Lacaune
N 112
Lunas
Villemagne-l'Argentière
Bédarieux
Castres
la-Salvetat-sur-Agout
Lamalou-les-Bains
D 908
Toulouse
St-Pons-de-Thomières
Olargues
Magalas
D 622
Mazamet
HÉRAULT
HAUTE-GARONNE
N 112
Servian
St-Chinian
Roquefère
Caunes-Minervois
Maraussan
Béziers
Siran
Olonzac
Lespignan
A 64
Peyrens
Lastours
Homps
Nissan-lez-Enserune
N 20
Castelnaudary
Lézignan-Corbières
Carcassonne
Escales
Fanjeaux
Narbonne
D 119
A 61
Gaja-la-Selve
Cavanac
Fabrezan
Fontfroide
Pamiers
D 623
D 118
Lagrasse
Gruissan
D 119
Limoux
AUDE
St-Pierre-des-Champs
2
Alet-les-Bains
Villerouge-Termenès
Sigean
Roquefort-des-Corbières
Foix
Fitou
Leucate
D 117
Quillan
Cucugnan
ARIÈGE
D 613
Bugarach
Tautavel
St-Paul-de-Fenouillet
Axat
Port-Barcarès
Gincla
Estagel
Canet-Roussillon
Perpignan
Canet-Plage
N 20
Vinça
A 9
Prades
Villefranche-de-Conflent
PYRÉNÉES-OR.
Argelès-sur-Mer
AND.
Banyuls-dels-Aspres
Collioure
Font-Romeu
Olette
Mont-Louis
Amélie-les-Bains
Sorède
Latour-de-Carol
Céret
Bagnyuls-sur-Mer
Llo
Prats-Balaguer
Bourg-Madame
Prats-de-Mollo
Arles-sur-Tech
SPAIN
Valcebollère
A

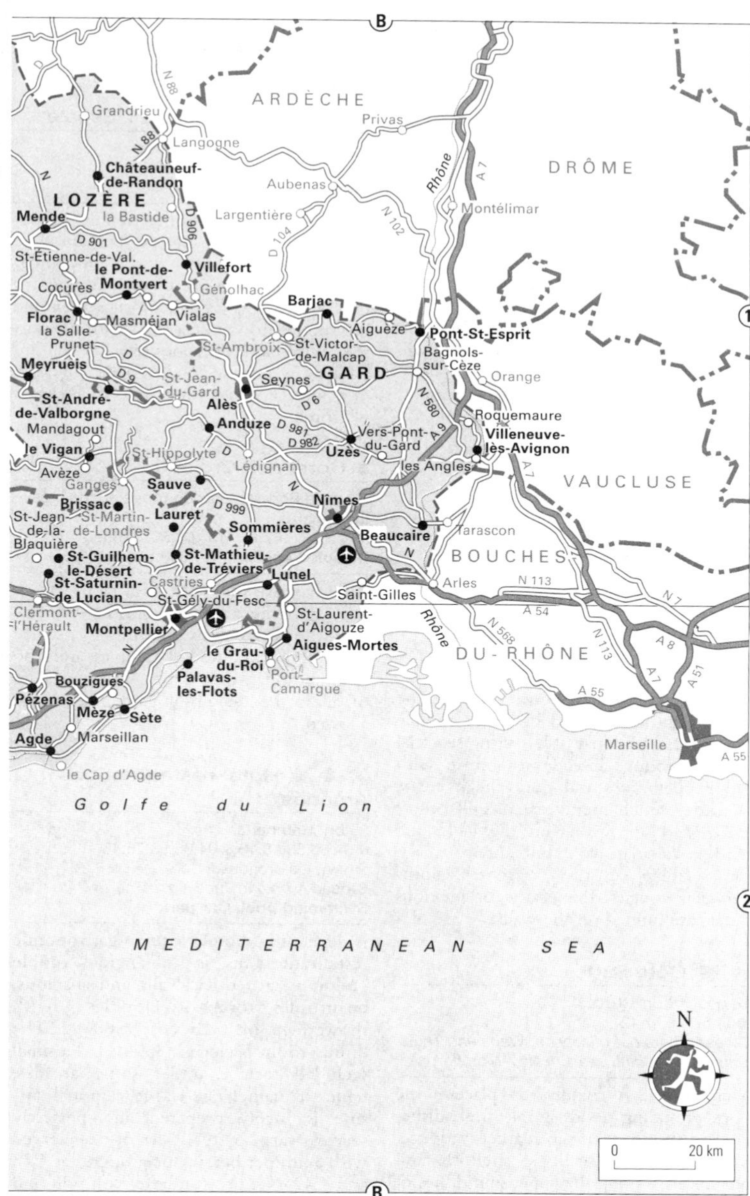
ARDÈCHE
DRÔME
LOZÈRE
GARD
VAUCLUSE
BOUCHES-DU-RHÔNE
Grandrieu
Langogne
Privas
Châteauneuf-de-Randon
Aubenas
Montélimar
Mende
la Bastide
Largentière
St-Étienne-de-Val.
le Pont-de-Montvert
Villefort
Cocurès
Génolhac
Barjac
Florac
Masméjan
Vialas
Aiguèze
Pont-St-Esprit
la Salle-Prunet
St-Ambroix
St-Victor-de-Malcap
Bagnols-sur-Cèze
Meyrueis
St-Jean-du-Gard
Seynes
Orange
St-André-de-Valborgne
Alès
Roquemaure
Mandagout
Anduze
Vers-Pont-du-Gard
Villeneuve-lès-Avignon
le Vigan
St-Hippolyte
Uzès
Avèze
Lédignan
les Angles
Ganges
Sauve
Brissac
Nîmes
St-Jean-de-la-Blaquière
St-Martin-de-Londres
Lauret
Sommières
Beaucaire
Tarascon
St-Guilhem-le-Désert
St-Mathieu-de-Tréviers
St-Saturnin-de Lucian
Castries
Lunel
Arles
Clermont-l'Hérault
St-Gély-du-Fesc
Saint-Gilles
St-Laurent-d'Aigouze
Montpellier
Aigues-Mortes
le Grau-du-Roi
Bouzigues
Palavas-les-Flots
Port-Camargue
Pézenas
Mèze
Sète
Marseille
Agde
Marseillan
le Cap d'Agde
Rhône
N 88
D 906
D 901
D 104
N 102
A 7
D 9
D 6
D 981
D 982
N 580
A 9
D 999
N 113
A 54
N 568
N 7
A 8
A 51
A 55
Golfe du Lion
MEDITERRANEAN SEA
N
0
20 km
B
1
2

wines by the glass too. Friendly welcome from Lionel Albano and his team, in the local style. The courtyard has been kept traditional despite a definite new look for the restaurant.

Le Calamar

La Tamarissière,
33 quai Cornu; on the right bank of the Hérault
04.67.94.05.06
Closed *Tues and Wed in low season; Sat and Mon lunchtimes in the summer.*

Menus at €20–32 ; à la carte menu around €30. Friendly seaside décor for this former fishermen's café that has taken on the appearance of a genuine regional bistro in the glass as well as in the plate. You will love the simply grilled fish or the *parrillada*, while watching the boats or the cars go by, depending on where you're sitting and the time of the day.

Marseillan

34340 (7km NE)

Le Jardin du Naris

24 bd. Pasteur; take the D51.
04.67.77.30.07
Closed *Mon evening and Tues out of season; Tues lunchtime in summer; Feb. High chairs available.*

The walled garden allows you to dine among the flowers and the trees. Simple but good, traditional dishes using seasonal market produce include sea bream with red pepper *coulis* and pork-cheek curry. Weekday lunch menu €9.50 and others €15–27. The crayons on the tables are used to calculate your bill, and you even can scribble on the paper tablecloths between courses; the efforts of previous diners are pinned on the walls.

Côté Sud

18 quai Antonin-Gros.
04.67.01.72.42
Closed *Thurs out of season; Weds and Thurs lunchtimes in high season; Nov–March.*

Menu at €22. A friendly little place on the port, providing good, simple fresh dishes cooked using seasonal market produce. Warm salad of scallops, shellfish and prawns are among the appetising dishes of the day you will find written on a large blackboard, unless you let yourself be tempted by a seafood platter! Good view from the terrace. *Free apéritif on presentation of this guide.*

Aigues-Mortes

30220

Hôtel-restaurant L'Escale*

3 av. de la Tour-de-Constance.
04.66.53.71.14 04.66.53.76.74.
Closed *Sun evenings Nov–Feb.*

A hotel-restaurant with a friendly atmosphere situated opposite the ramparts. The regulars linger over a pastis or lunch. Menus from €10–18; make sure you try the cuttlefish à l'Aiguemortaise. Simple but spotless rooms cost €26 with basin to €32 with bath. The ones over the bar are a bit noisy but air-conditioned, while the ones in the annexe are quieter. Relaxed welcome.

Hôtel des Croisades**

2 rue du Port; it's outside the ramparts, near the canal.
04.66.53.67.85 04.66.53.72.95
Disabled access. TV. Pay car park.

A fairly new hotel with an attractive, tranquil atmosphere. Some rooms have a view over the town walls and the Constance Tower. Air-conditioned doubles are €50 with shower/wc or bath. Most appealing of all is the delightful garden. Pets not allowed.

Hôtel-restaurant Les Arcades***

23 bd. Gambetta.
04.66.53.18.13 04.66.53.75.46
www.les-arcades.fr
Closed *Mon and Tues lunchtime. TV.*
Swimming pool. Car park.

A charming hotel with a gastronomic restaurant. This is an ancient, noble building with thick walls and spacious, beautiful rooms. Doubles with shower/wc or bath cost €88–97. The dining room is elegant. It also has a small secluded terrace under some arcades, hence its name! The classic, regional cuisine is nicely prepared and perfectly served: warm oysters, *pavé* of beef served with a juniper berry sauce. Menus at €33 and €42. Next to the hotel you will find a shop selling local produce, arts and crafts and culinary specialities. *Free apéritif on presentation of this guide.*

Saint-Laurent-d'Aigouze

30220 (7km N)

Hôtel Lou Garbin**

30 av. des Jardins; the village is on the Nîmes road from Aigues-Mortes and the hotel is on the right.
Ⓣ04.66.88.12.74 Ⓕ04.66.88.91.12
Ⓦwww.lougarbin.com
Restaurant closed *lunchtimes 1 July–31 Aug; 15 October–15 March. Reservations only outside July and Aug.* **High chairs and games available. Disabled access. TV. Swimming pool. Car park.**

A really pleasant place to stop between Nîmes and Aigues-Mortes in a typical village of this little corner of the Camargue. It's at the heart of the village, surrounded by a string of cafés with terraces and with the church to one side. The rooms are in the main house or in bungalows around the pool. Doubles with shower/wc or bath €45–52. The restaurant is open only to hotel guests (€45 per person): dishes are reassuringly local with lots of beef on the menu. Unfortunately you can see and hear the main road, which is about 200m away, but pretty soon the bushes will have grown big enough to form a screen. You can play boules and they do barbecues. *Free coffee on presentaton of this guide.*

Alès

30100

Hôtel Orly**

10 rue d'Avéjan.
Ⓣ04.66.91.30.00 Ⓕ04.66.91.30.30
Ⓦwww.orly-hotel.com
TV.

A very central hotel run by a pair of friendly young people who have lots of ideas. The façade dates back to the 1970s but the interior has been completely renovated and styled with taste. No. 108 has two windows, no. 106 is the biggest, and no. 109 is rather zen in style. Doubles €31–53. There's also a studio with a corner kitchen. Excellent value for money, given the location.

Hôtel-restaurant Le Riche**

42 pl. Pierre-Sémard; it's opposite the train station.
Ⓣ04.66.86.00.33 Ⓕ04.66.30.02.63
Ⓦwww.leriche.fr
Closed *Aug.* **TV. Pay car park.**

This is one of the best restaurants in town and something of an institution. The Belle Époque dining room is a great place to eat carefully and creatively prepared dishes in classic style: shellfish salad with fresh basil, fillet of sea bass with a delicate shrimp bisque, good Saint-Nectaire cheese, apricot tart. Menus €15.50–45. The hotel is run with great professionalism and has all the comforts you need. Compared to the dining room the rooms are modern and rather uninteresting, but they have good facilities. Doubles with bath €44. *10% discount on the room rate on presentation of this guide.*

Le Mandajors

17 rue Mandajors.
Ⓣ04.66.52.62.98
Ⓔfrederic-beguin@wanadoo.fr
Closed *Sat lunchtime and Sun; 1st fortnight in Aug.*

Service noon–1.30pm and 7.30–9pm. The décor doesn't seem to have changed since World War II – when the owner helped members of the Resistance disappear out of the back door. The place is now in the hands of a young man, and his wife helps at lunchtime. In the evening, he's on his own to run the kitchen and the dining room. To make it work, he keeps strict opening hours. It's worth it: you'll find delectable, appetizing old-style cuisine at more than reasonable prices. €9.20 lunch menu or €11–23. *Free liqueur on presentation of this guide.*

Le Jardin d'Alès

92 av. d'Alsace; it's on the Aubenas road.
Ⓣ04.66.86.38.82 Ⓕ04.66.86.21.74
Ⓔlejardinales.resto@libertysurf.fr
Closed *Sun evening; Mon; 1st fortnight in Jan; 1st fortnight in July.* **Disabled access. Car park.**

This place is located outside the centre on the edge of an area with a number of looming high-rises – the terrace is almost too close to the roundabout for comfort. But the dining room has been decorated with great taste by the owners. Weekday lunch menu at €11.50 and €16; they change with the seasons. Warm welcome. *Free coffee on presentation of this guide.*

Seynes

30580 (18km E)

La Farigoulette**

It's in the centre of the village. Take the D6 from Alès.
Ⓣ04.66.83.70.56 Ⓕ04.66.83.72.80
Ⓦwww.lafarigoulette.com
Closed *Sun evening in Jan–Feb.* **TV. Swimming pool.**

A lovely, unfussy country establishment with a garden and swimming pool. Ten decent double rooms with shower/wc at €42 (ask for room no. 4, 6 or 10, with a panoramic view or a view over the pool). Customers from far afield come to enjoy the powerfully flavoured home-made dishes prepared by the owner and his family, who run the local charcuterie. Delicious pâtés, terrines, sausage, casseroles and *confits*. Prices are reasonable – set menus from €13, except at weekends and public holidays, others €16–29. Service is in the beautifully simple, rustic dining room. *Free liqueur offered to our readers on presentation of this guide.*

Saint-Victor-de-Macalp

30500 (23km NE)

La Bastide des Senteurs***

It's in the centre of the village; from Alès, take the D904 then the D51 to Saint-Victor.
Ⓣ04.66.60.24.45 Ⓕ04.66.60.26.10
Ⓦwww.bastide-senteurs.com
Closed *Nov–March.* **Restaurant closed** *lunchtimes in July and Aug, except Sun and public holidays; out of season.* **Disabled access. Highchairs available. TV. Swimming pool. Car park.**

In a hill village set in beautiful countryside right on the edge of the Cévennes, this hotel spreads across a collection of houses that have been soberly and tastefully renovated. Pretty rooms, decorated in the local style with bare stone walls, cost €59–70 with bath, depending on the season. Outside there's a glorious swimming pool overlooking the Cèze valley. The superb restaurant is named after the chef, Franck Subileau, who produces dishes of wonderful invention. Menus €26–65. Credit cards not accepted. *10% reduction on the room rate from Oct to March on presentation of this guide.*

Amélie-les-Bains

66110

Le Castel-Émeraude**

Route de la Corniche; follow the signs to the centre sportif Espace Méditerranée.
Ⓣ04.68.39.02.83 Ⓕ04.68.39.03.09
Ⓦwww.lecastelemeraude.com
Closed *15 Nov–15 March.* **Disabled access. Highchairs and cots available. TV. Car park.**

A quiet, tranquil inn on the banks of the river and surrounded by greenery. It's a big castle-like building with two turrets and lots of balconies, but inside the décor is modern. Some 45 double rooms; €48–58. Menus €16–33. Nice welcome from a friendly team led by a gentle, pétanque-loving patron. *Free apéritif on presentation of this guide.*

Anduze

30140

La Régalière**

1435 rte. de Saint-Jean-du-Gard.
Ⓣ04.66.61.81.93 Ⓕ04.66.61.85.94
Ⓦwww.ot-anduze.fr
Closed *Wed lunchtime except July–Aug; 20 Nov–15 Mar.* **TV. Swimming pool. Highchairs and games available. Car park.**

La Régalière is a very old master-craftman's house in a vast estate – a little haven of peace and quiet. The twelve bedrooms have very modern facilities; doubles are €52–57. Half board is compulsory June–Sept (€46–48.50 per person). You can eat on the shaded terrace in summer. House specialities include *aiguillettes* of duck with honey and gentian liqueur, or scallops cooked in various ways. Menus €17–40. On Fridays in high season there are jazz evenings; out of season there's a pianist. *10% discount on the room rate on presentation of this guide.*

La Porte des Cévennes**

Route de Saint-Jean-du-Gard; it's on the D907, 3km out of Anduze.
Ⓣ04.66.61.99.44 Ⓕ04.66.61.73.65
Ⓦwww.porte-cevennes.com
Restaurant closed *lunchtimes, open for lunch and dinner for group bookings only.* **TV. Swimming pool. Highchairs and games available. Car park.**

Located just outside the village of Anduze,

past the bamboo fields, this modern hotel has spacious, clean and comfortable rooms. Doubles with shower/wc or bath are €53–67. The rather grand swimming pool is covered and heated and is used as a restaurant in the evenings. It serves traditional dishes. Menus €17–29. Half board is available for a minimum of three days (€55–57 per person per day). This is a reliable place. *Free apéritif on presentation of this guide.*

Le Moulin de Corbès

Corbès; take the rte. de Saint-Jean du Gard.
Ⓣ04.66.61.61.83 Ⓕ04.66.61.68.06
Closed *Mon and Tues out of season.* **Disabled access. Car park.**

This isn't just any old restaurant. The crunch of gravel underfoot as you approach and the grand staircase inside help to create a special atmosphere. The dining room is painted yellow and flooded with sunlight, and the flower arrangements on the tables add a touch of class. Dishes change with the season but they're always simple and full of cleverly combined, delicate flavours – you can count on the pan-fried liver and liver terrine. Set menus €30–50. Three double rooms with shower/wc or bath at €70, breakfast included.

Aumont-Aubrac

48130

Chez Camillou

10 av. du Languedoc.
Ⓣ04.66.42.80.22 Ⓕ04.66.42.86.14
Closed *early Nov to early April; 10 Jan–16 Feb; 15 Nov–15 Dec.* **TV. High chairs available. Swimming pool. Car park.**

Impressive place being run by the fourth, or maybe the fifth generation. Rooms are well appointed (doubles €46–130), the décor in the restaurant is stunning, and there's a heart-shaped swimming pool. The main attraction, however, is Cyril Attrazic's cooking. Perfectly calibrated preparations, wonderful flavours and tons of creativity. Follow Madame's advice and let yourself be tempted. The desserts are just divine. Friendly service. Menus €16–49. *Free apéritif on presentation of this guide.*

Grand Hôtel Prouhèze***

2 rte. du Languedoc; it's opposite the train station, 300m from the town centre.
Ⓣ04.66.42.80.07 Ⓕ04.66.42.87.78
Ⓦwww.prouheze.com
Closed *Sun evening; Mon and Tues lunch except July–Aug; 1 Nov–31 March.* **TV. Car park.**

Guy Prouhèze's cooking is wonderfully imaginative: his subtle dishes bring out the full flavour of salmon, asparagus, mushrooms and other fresh ingredients. There's an enormous, warm dining room decorated in charming taste. Weekday lunch menu at €33; others are €46–93 with bistro menus at €16 and €22, and good à la carte choices too. Excellent cellar full of vintage wines and fantastic vins de table. Comfy, attractive rooms of varying sizes: the bigger ones have the better facilities, the smaller ones are still quiet, stylish and comfortable. Doubles €66–90 with bath and one with shower/wc at €48.

Javols

48130 (7km SE)

Auberge Le Régimbal

Take the D50.
Ⓣ04.66.42.89.87
Car park.

A newly built inn belonging to the Mazets. It overlooks Gévaudan, which was the ancient Gallo-Roman capital for eight centuries. It's an exceptional archeological site and important excavations have been undertaken. There are eight peaceful rooms with good facilities and views of the village and the surrounding hills. Local cuisine served in the dining room where there's a granite fireplace. Half board only; €44 per person.

Banyuls-sur-Mer

66650

Villa Miramar**

Rue Lacaze-Outhiens; it's 200m from the beach and 400m from the centre.
Ⓣ04.68.88.33.85 Ⓕ04.68.66.88.63
Ⓦwww.villa-miramar@fr.st
Closed *15 Oct–15 March.* **Disabled access. TV. Swimming pool. Car park.**

Set on the hillside just outside the village, the hotel is surrounded by a garden which is full of trees and flowers. It's a peaceful place, packed with Far Eastern souvenirs, many from Thailand. The rooms are comfortable with modern facilities – mini-bar, telephone, TV – and cost €43–59 for a double with shower/wc or bath, depending on the season. There are also some basic bungalows in the grounds for slightly less. Good value for a good location. *10% discount in April.*

Barjac

30430

Hôtel-restaurant Le Mas du Terme***

Route de Bagnols-sur-Cèze; it's 3km from the village, out in the vineyards.
04.66.24.56.31 04.66.24.58.54
www.mas-du-terme.com
Closed *Nov–March.* **Restaurant closed** *out of season – phone to check.* **Disabled access. Highchairs available. TV. Swimming pool. Car park.**

This eighteenth-century silkworm-breeding house has been tastefully converted in the local style by the owners. There's a vaulted sitting room and dining room and a pretty courtyard. The hotel has quiet, attractive bedrooms with modern facilities; they're €60–92 with shower/wc or bath, depending on the season. The restaurant is not bad at all: the price of a menu (half board) is €26.50. The local specialities – *escabèche* of red mullet fillets with garlic, cod steaks with black olive paste, stuffed rack of lamb with sea salt and so on – are carefully prepared. *10% discount on the room rate offered to our readers on presentation of this guide except for July and August.*

Beaucaire

30300

Hôtel-restaurant Le Robinson**

Route de Remoulins; it's signposted on the road to Remoulins.
04.66.59.21.32 04.66.59.00.03
contact@hotel-robinson.fr
Closed *Feb.* **Disabled access. TV. Swimming pool. Highchairs and games available. Car park.**

A good place just on the edge of Beaucaire. On the *menu du terroir* you'll find beef *gardiane*, the local speciality – here they make it like nobody else and serve it up with locally grown rice. It goes well with a wine like a Costières-de-Nîmes. Try donkey and pork sausage as a starter, and a *crème catalane* to finish. Menus €13–36. The bright dining room has huge bay windows overlooking the trees in the garden, and it's run by diligent waiting staff. Rooms are pretty, comfortable and air-conditioned; doubles €62–78 with shower/wc or bath. Smiling welcome and a family atmosphere. They have tennis courts as well as a pool. *A Kir will be offered to our readers on presentation of this guide.*

L'Ail Heurre

Place du Château (Centre).
04.66.59.29.13
Closed *Sat lunch; Sun evening; January.*

This stylish little dining room is decorated with taste, with wrought iron tables and chairs and pictures and works of art on the walls. The chef is jovial and very gifted – he has worked in some great kitchens but decided to come home. Exquisite and creative cuisine, attentively served. Lunch menus €15–39. It's good value for money. *Free apéritif on presentation of this guide.*

Béziers

34500

Le Champ-de-Mars**

17 rue de Metz; it's near the pl. du 14-Juillet.
04.67.28.35.53
Closed *7–15 Feb.* **TV. Pay car park.**

This little hotel in a quiet side street has had its façade thoroughly renovated and it's smothered in geraniums. The meticulous bedrooms overlook the garden. Double rooms €33.50–46 with shower/wc or bath (cheaper in low season) – it's the best value for money in Béziers. Breakfast €5. The cheerful owner can tell you anything you need to know about the town.

Le Grilladin, Le Carnivore et Le Pêcheur

21 rue Française; you get there via the rue de la République.
04.67.49.09.45 04.67.49.20.84
Closed *Sun; Mon; 21 Dec–5 Jan.*

The name tells you what to expect: they do good, tasty grills of meat and fish. Menus €11–23.50. The restaurant is in a cool and charming courtyard with an olive tree in the middle. Nice furniture made from wrought iron outside, while in the dining room the setting is warm and welcoming.

La Raffinerie

14 av. Joseph-Lazare; follow the canal, just outside Béziers, direction Stade de Sauclières.
☎04.67.37.62.50
Closed *Sat lunchtime; Sun; Mon.* **Disabled access.**

Menus €15–21. The former sulphur factory, essential to wine-making (we are right in the middle of the old wine merchants' neighbourhood), has been turned into a contemporary restaurant. In the summer, a terrace near the water allows you to enjoy *alfresco* a refined Mediterranean cuisine. Many inventive dishes at reasonable prices: tajine of cockerel with Morello cherries, squid *a la plancha* served with a black risotto, not forgetting the exquisite *pot au chocolat* for dessert.

L'Ambassade

22 bd. de Verdun; it's opposite the railway station.
☎04.67.76.06.24 ⓕ04.67.76.74.05
Closed *Sun; Mon.*

A vast dining room with a modern look. Patrick Olry is a fine chef with a sure touch; he uses fresh produce and his menus list dishes that change with the seasons – the food is colourful, full of aromas and robustly flavoured. The cheese is out of this world and so are the desserts; the weekday menu costs €24 and others are €32–55. The waiters dress smartly but are informal in their approach and are eager to advise – even the bill is a pleasant surprise.

Maraussan

34370 (7.5km NW)

Parfum de Garrigues

37 av. de la Poste.
☎04.67.90.33.76
Closed *Tues and Wed; end Feb to mid March; mid to end August; All Saints' Day.* **Disabled access.**

Jean-Luc Santuré came here from Béziers and turned this place into the best table in the area. You'll notice the easy-going atmosphere as soon as you arrive, and the cooking is smart and subtle and full of flavour – a real tour de force. Lunchtime menu costs €20 and the other is €25. There isn't a garden as such, but you can stroll around the heath. *Free liqueur on presentation of this guide.*

Lespignan

34710 (10 km SW)

Hostellerie du Château

4 rue des Figuiers.
☎04.67.76.15.90
Closed *Tues and Sun evenings; Wed.* **Disabled access.**

Menus €19–41. An impressive selection of dishes. In the evening, the regulars come back especially from the coast to enjoy a good meal here. At lunch you will enjoy a quiet meal in the coolness of this beautiful old house built with the stones from the old feudal castle of Lord Lespignan that used to overlook the whole countryside. Frank Le Maner is more modest though. After having worked with the best (*Rostang, Le Jardin des Sens*) he now works with his wife, cooks the best ingredients in his own way, puts the finishing touches to his dishes and checks his sauces with the utmost attention. Judicious choice of wines too. Prices very reasonable.

Servian

34290 (10km NE)

Château Laroque

It's 4km from Servian on the N9, half way between Pézenas and Béziers.
☎04.67.39.18.28 ⓕ04.67.32.44.28
ⓔtbraillon@hotmail.com
Swimming pool. Highchairs available. Car park.

The Belgian Braillon family moved here and bought this property as a ruin which, with its acres of land, no one wanted. They set about rebuilding the whole place and decorated it in rococo style, planting a small forest of trees and sinking a dreamy swimming pool. The result is neither a hotel nor a guesthouse, but more like a private home with rooms; doubles cost €65–81 including a generous breakfast. There's a flamingo-themed bar in the entrance and a restaurant where the food is good quality and good value: menu is €27. And with luck, once the motorway link to Béziers is open, the nearby N9 will get less busy. *Free apéritif or coffee offered to our readers on presentation of this guide.*

Nissan-lez-Enserune

34440 (11km SW)

Hôtel Résidence**

35 av. de la Cave; take the N9.

Ⓣ04.67.37.00.63 Ⓕ04.67.37.68.63
Ⓦwww.hotel-residence.com
Closed *Jan.* **Restaurant closed** *lunchtimes.* **TV. Pay car park.**

A beautiful provincial building with bags of charm. There's a relaxed, informal, peaceful atmosphere with flowers everywhere, and several bedrooms have recently been added – you'll find them in the garden annexe. The owners have retained its charm while using slightly off-beat décor. The oppidum and the Midi canal are only a few kilometres away. Doubles €50–66 depending on facilities and season. Half-board €50–56. *Free coffee offered to evening diners at the end of the meal on presentation of this guide.*

Magalas

34480 (22km N)

|●| The Boucherie of Magalas

Place de l'Église. Take the D909 towards Bédarieux.
Ⓣ04.67.36.20.82
Ⓔtheboucherie@aol.com
Closed *Sun (lunchtime only in summer); Mon; Feb; All Saints' Day.* **Disabled access.**

This butcher's shop doubles as a restaurant, and a good one at that. It has two dining rooms, both decorated with odds and ends that look like they were bought in a charity shop, and there's an attractive terrace that leads out onto the village square. Lunchtime menu costs €9; the others at €16 and €21 feature fresh tapas, a selection of cold sausage, stews, steak tartare made in front of you and delicious *carpaccio*. If you like tripe, you'll love the way they do it here. Jazz plays gently in the background and, to cap it all, there are some good wines. It's advisable to book.

Brissac

34190

|●| Le Jardin aux Sources

30 av. du Parc.
Ⓣ04.67.73.31.16
Closed *Mon; Sun evening in low season only; last fortnight in June; Nov.*

Lunchtime menus €20–26 weekdays; others €28–58 ; à la carte around €50. This restaurant offers the most creative cuisine north of the Hérault river, though the décor does not match (yet) its prices. Jérôme Billod-Morel is a Chef traveller who has found inspiration in many a place and his dishes are far from being commonplace. Each dish is a real work of art in itself, and this kind of perfection takes time. Know-how and friendliness make up for a relatively slow service. You will spend indeed a very agreeable time on the terrace facing the garden, or in the small dining room next to the kitchens. Highly recommended for those who like good quality products cooked with passion and originality by a local lad. Quite surprising desserts.

Carcassonne

11000

⌂ |●| Auberge de jeunesse

Rue du Vicomte-Trencavel (Centre); in the medieval city.
Ⓣ04.68.25.23.16 Ⓕ04.68.71.14.84
Ⓦwww.fuaj.org
Closed *15 Dec–15 Jan.*

€13.25 per night, breakfast included. Sheets available on site. Menu at €8.60. Youth hostel card necessary. This is a beautiful hostel, well-kept, in the very heart of the historic city of Carcassonne. 120 beds. Each bedroom accommodates four–six people. All the rooms have been recently updated. Meals available at the bar in the summer. Foyer with fireplace, kitchen, bar, TV room, courtyard. Advance booking recommended.

⌂ |●| Hotel-Restaurant Le Cathare

53 rue Jean-Bringer; in the low city, near pl. Carnot.
Ⓣ04.68.25.65.92 Ⓕ04.68.47.15.02

Doubles with washbasin €18, with showers €27. Full or half-board available. Menus €17–21. Simple but very clean and quiet. The dining room is pretty and very colourful. In fact, it used to be part of a former eighteenth-century monastery. In the summer, tables are brought out onto the street. Specialities of grilled meat; try especially the excellent grilled duck with a pepper sauce. Good place to go. Very friendly welcome.

⌂ Hôtel du Pont-Vieux

32 rue Trivalle; near the medieval city.
Ⓣ04.68.25.24.99 Ⓕ04.68.47.62.71
Ⓔhoteldupontvieux@minitel.net

Doubles €40–74 according to season and

facilities. Buffet breakfast €6.90. Located in a quiet street, a few strides away from the main entrance into the medieval city centre. Simple old-fashioned rooms, but comfortable. Breakfast served until 11.00 am. Fantastic for those who like a lie-in and a good bargain – two meals for the price of one!

Hôtel du Donjon - Les Remparts***

2 rue du Comte-Roger; it's in the heart of the medieval city.
Ⓣ04.68.71.08.80 Ⓕ04.68.25.06.60
Ⓦwww.hotel-donjon.fr
Closed *Sun evening Nov to end March.*
Highchairs available. TV. Pay car park.

This place has everything: it's a medieval building with magnificent beams and an unusual staircase, but it also offers modern facilities such as double glazing, air conditioning, a bar, lounges and a very nice garden. There's good reason for the owner to be proud of the establishment and it's very popular with American visitors. Doubles with shower/wc or bath €79–161; some are in an annexe. Breakfast buffet €10. The restaurant offers a good range of local specialities. Menus €14.50–27. The garage allows you to bring your car right into the middle of the town. Credit cards not accepted. *Free apéritif on presentation of this guide.*

Le Petit Couvert

18 rue de l'Aigle-d'Or.
Ⓣ04.68.71.00.20
Closed *Sun; Mon.* **Disabled access.**

Lunch menu €11 weekdays; others €14–18. A very simple place, run by two lively and friendly young women. Provençal décor with a few tables out on a terrace on a pedestrian street. Good cheap menus that are very satisfactory (1/4 l wine jug included). Large plates of charcuterie, cheese and salad available. For those who are weight-conscious, a light menu is also on offer, still good value for money, with steamed vegetables and aspartam! Otherwise, the chef's specialities are the *cassoulet* and the *confit*. *Free apéritif offered to our readers on presentation of this guide.*

Chez Saskia

Place de l'Église.
Ⓣ04.68.71.98.71
Closed *Dec; Jan.*

Menus €15– 31. Is the *Barbacane* full (their first menu is at €60)? Then come to *Chez Saskia*, the brasserie annexe of Franck Putelat's restaurant. A more subdued décor, but you will still be eating surrounded by pictures of movie stars. The first menu is amusing (it follows for example in the summer an "all tomato" theme), but only the dessert (a strawberry and tomato gazpacho served with rice pudding) is really unusual. If you really want to spoil yourself though, try the menu at €31 or choose à la carte. The Tiger prawn salad served with a mango chutney is worth a try. The service is impeccable and friendly. Good selection of wines at reasonable prices.

Le Jardin de la Tour

11 porte d'Aude; in the heart of the medieval city.
Ⓣ04.68.25.71.24
Closed *lunchtimes.*

Menus €18–26. This restaurant has become a real favourite in the whole town and beyond. A family affair that works. Not surprising: a friendly convivial atmosphere inside, and outside dinner among the trees. In the summer a Berber tent is raised underneath the arbour and you are entertained with live music and tapas! Nice looking dishes, exquisite cooking, trendy waiters and good music. What more could you ask for? Advance booking highly recommended, as it's full every night. Try it, you'll love it!

Le Comte Roger

14 rue Saint-Louis; in the medieval city.
Ⓣ04.68.11.93.40
Closed *Sun and Mon out of season; winter school holidays.*

Pierre Mesa, who had a fine reputation at the Château, took over this restaurant formerly run by his father. Although he changed premises he brought his team and style of cooking with him. The warmth and sincerity of the welcome hasn't changed either. The menus focus on local recipes and local wines. Uncomplicated, flavoursome, well-seasoned dishes are listed on good-value menus from €23 (weekday lunchtimes) up to €34. A la carte menu up to €50. Specialities include *cassoulet* with two *confits* and creamed salt cod with parsley. The setting is modern and really pleasant, though the dining room can get rather noisy. In summer, head for the terrace. Good value for money. *Free apéritif offered to our readers on presentation of this guide.*

Cavanac

11570 (4km S)

Château de Cavanac***

Take the D104 in the direction of St Hilaire.
☎04.68.79.61.04 Ⓕ04.68.79.79.67
Closed *Jan; Feb. Restaurant closed Sun evening; Mon; lunchtimes.* **Disabled access. TV. Swimming pool. Car park.**

An overgrown farmhouse with a very pretty garden in a quiet village. Exquisite rooms with period furniture, lustrous fabrics, canopied beds and elegantly contemporary décor. Doubles €65–150, depending on the size and facilities. The restaurant, in a converted stable, is the bigger draw. There's a genuine country feel – they've kept the mangers and hung some old implements on the walls. Ask to be placed in the room with a fireplace, the most pleasant one. There's a single menu, €36, of delicious local dishes which change regularly: snails *à la carcassonnaise*, foie gras or suckling pig with honey. Apéritif, bread and wine are included. Hotel guests can also choose à la carte. There's a tennis court, a swimming pool, a fitness centre and a sauna – it's a great place. *Free apéritif or liqueur on presentation of this guide.*

Lastours

11600 (12 km N)

Le Puits du Trésor

Route des 4-Châteaux.
☎04.68.77.50.24
Brasserie closed *evenings except Wed and Sun.* **Restaurant closed** *lunchtimes (except Sun); evenings except Mon and Tues.* **Closed** *last week Feb to mid March.*

Brasserie menus €12–14; restaurant menus €30–80. The brasserie offers good fresh dishes made with products from the market. The seasonal neo-classical restaurant menu includes artichoke with rosemary and fried foie gras with cardamom. An establishment that not only has its feet under water but its head up with the castles as well, as it has two separate entrances: a street entrance for the gastronomic restaurant where Jean-Marc Boyer works and a courtyard entrance for its brasserie. Worth a visit!

Roquefère

11380 (22km N)

Le Sire de Cabaret

Take the Mazamet road, turn onto the Conques road, then right onto the D101 to Roquefère.
☎04.68.26.31.89
Closed *Wed and Sun evening except July–Aug; weeknights Nov–Easter; 15 Nov–15 Dec.*

A magnificent house in an attractive village in the middle of the Montagne Noire and the Cabardès. There's an imposing fireplace in the dining room, but it's not just a picturesque feature – it's used to char-grill meat. When you order charcuterie, a huge platter appears laden with sausage, terrines and hams, and you can help yourself to more. They also plonk down a bottle of wine. And why not finish the meal with a liquorice-flavoured *crème brûlée*? It's all handsomely served. Lunch menu €18–31. Children's menu €7.

Castelnaudary

11400

Hôtel du Canal**

2 ter av. Arnant-Vidal; 500m from the city centre, opposite the Gendarmerie.
☎04.68.94.05.05 Ⓕ04.68.94.05.06
Disabled access. TV. Car park.

A recently built hotel on the edge of the Canal du Midi. There's a towpath you can walk along nearby. The rooms are modern, spacious and well-looked-after. €42–50 for a double with bath/wc. Breakfast €5. *One free breakfast per room per night on presentation of this guide.*

Hôtel du Centre et du Lauragais**

31 cours de la République.
☎04.68.23.25.95 Ⓕ04.68.94.01.66
Closed *Jan; lst week in July. TV.*

A huge house on the main square in the town. The rooms are well maintained and comfortable; €40 with shower/wc and €45 with bath/wc. The plush restaurant serves what is probably the best cuisine in town. It's famous for its *cassoulet*, but also serves local specialities and dishes like tripe and pigeon with ceps. Menus €17.50–50. Slightly impersonal welcome but the service is faultless. The "traditional" menu offers good value for money.

Peyrens

11400 (4 km N)

|●| Auberge La Calèche

On the D624 towards Ravel, in the village.
Ⓣ04.68.60.40.13
Closed *Tues evening; Wed; Ist fortnight Nov.*

Menus €15–28.50. The first menu is excellent and very hearty, especially if you choose the *cassoulet* as the main course. It is so generously served that you could order just that! It is definitely one of the best *cassoulets* in the area, so much so that regulars come all the way from Toulouse to sample it. Very friendly welcome and pleasant rural location.

Gaja-La-Selve

11270 (18 km S)

☗ |●| Auberge du Puget

16km from Foueaux, on the D102 towards Belpech.
Ⓣand Ⓕ04.68.60.51.76
Ⓦwww.auberge-du-puget.com
Restaurant closed *Sun evening; Mon.*

Doubles €54. Menus €27–35.50. Located in the middle of an agricultural farm, the inn offers very nice bedrooms that bear exotic names such as Kuala Lumpur, Santiago or Bangkok… Beautiful old farm furniture and comfortable beds. It also has a nice big swimming pool in the garden with even a few hammocks at your disposal. The cuisine is traditional, authentic and refined. It uses local produce from nearby smallholdings and farms. Local wines and apéritifs.

Caunes-Minervois

11160

⛹ ☗ |●| Hôtel-restaurant d'Alibert**

Place de la Mairie; take the D11 for 6km then turn right for Cannes onto the D620 and it's 2.5km further on.
Ⓣ04.68.78.00.54
Ⓔfrederic.dalibert@wanadoo.fr
Closed *Sun evening; Mon; mid Nov to mid March.* **Car park.**

This house, thoroughly lost in the narrow lanes of this Minervois village, looks as if it's suddenly appeared from the sixteenth century. The owners, Monsieur and Madame Guiraud, have run it for years. There are only eight rooms but they're spacious, well maintained and pleasant. Doubles €46–55 depending on facilities and season. The elegant country-manor style restaurant is totally in keeping with the rest of the place, and the open fire adds to the warmth of the atmosphere in cold weather. Good, authentic local dishes like *cassoulet*, calves heads, and stews produced with great skill. Menu €20. The owner will give you advice about the wines – he's a connoisseur of the local *crus* and his enthusiasm is infectious. *Free apéritif offered to our readers on presentation of this guide.*

Céret

66400

☗ |●| Hôtel-restaurant Vidal

4 pl. Soutine; it's in the centre between the town hall and pl. Picasso.
Ⓣ04.68.87.00.85 Ⓕ04.68.87.62.33
www.hotelvidal.com
Closed *Tues in winter; Wed; Nov.* **TV.**

The old bishop's palace dates back to 1735 and is a classified historic monument, with a wonderful sculpted façade. Fairly spacious, clean rooms with good facilities; doubles €28–36. The young owners come from the village so, if you want any hints about where to go and what to see, just ask. On the ground floor, they've opened a Catalan fast-food diner with dishes for €2–3; for the genuine article, head for the bishop's dining room with its polished parquet floors. Menus €23–31.

Châteauneuf-de-Randon

48170

⛹ ☗ |●| Hôtel de la Poste**

L'Habitarelle: take the N88 and it's beside the Mausolée du Guesclin.
Ⓣ04.66.47.90.05 Ⓕ04.66.47.91.41
Ⓦwww.hoteldelaposte48.com
Closed *Fri lunchtime; Sat and Sun evening (except in July and August); Autumn school holidays; Christmas–end Jan.* **Disabled access. TV. Car park.**

Though this establishment is on the main road the traffic noise won't bother you –

most bedrooms overlook the countryside. They've been modernized and are absolutely spotless; doubles cost €43. The large restaurant is in a converted barn which has lost none of its rustic charm. José Laurens prepares tasty traditional dishes. Set menus €14–29 and an attractively priced wine list. Credit cards not accepted. *10% discount on the room rate for a stay of at least two nights (except in July and August) on presentation of this guide.*

Collioure

66190

Les Caranques**

Route de Port-Vendres; it's 300m from the town centre and the beach.
ⓣ04.68.82.06.68 ⓕ04.68.82.00.92
ⓔles-caranques@little-france.com
Closed *1 Nov–1 April.* **Car park.**

This welcoming family-run hotel is right on the sea and has a wonderful view of Collioure and the port of Avall. The 22 peaceful rooms all come with a sea view and a small balcony. Doubles with basin €42, €64–72 with shower/wc or bath. Breakfast €7. No beach, but a terrace where you can sunbathe and private access to the rocks.

Hôtellerie des Templiers**

Quai de l'Amirauté; opposite the castle.
ⓣ04.68.82.98.31 ⓕ04.68.98.01.24
ⓦwww.hotel-templiers.com
Closed *Mon evening and Tues Oct–May; 5 weeks from the Ist Sun in Jan.* **Restaurant closed** *Mon–Fri between Feb and March; Mon evening and Tues Oct–May.* **TV.**

The owner's father, René Pous, used to give painters and sculptors board and lodging in return for works of art. Sounds fair enough, especially when you consider that Matisse, Maillol, Dalí, Picasso and Dufy were among them. He accumulated 2000 original works of art which are on display all over the hotel, including in the bedrooms – even if some of the most precious ones, including a number of Picassos, were stolen a few years ago. Bedrooms are nice, with painted wooden beds, quirky chairs and, of course, the paintings. Doubles with shower/wc or bath cost €38–66 depending on facilities. The service, however, is sometimes quirky. The restaurant has a menu at €19 or you can dine à la carte for around €27. You can eat out on the terrace overlooking the port or in the dining room covered with abstract paintings.

Le Mas des Citronniers**

22 av. de la République.
ⓣ04.68.04.82 ⓕ04.68.82.52.10
ⓦwww.hotel-mas-des-citronniers.com
Closed *11 Nov–10 Feb.* **Restaurant open** 7.15–9.15pm. **TV.**

A generously proportioned 1930s villa with an Art Deco staircase. Well-maintained rooms with good facilities, bathrooms and air-conditioning; doubles €49–82. There are some triple and family rooms. Those in the annexe, the most recent ones, have either a balcony overlooking the garden or a private terrace leading onto the garden. Set menus €21 and €24. Half board is available in summer at €48–65 per person. *10% discount on room rate Feb-April, Nov-Dec, except for bank holidays, on presentation of this guide.*

L'Arpède - Restaurant La Farigole

Route de Port-Vendres; it's 2km from the centre of town.
ⓣ04.68.98.09.59 ⓕ04.68.98.30.90
Closed *1 Dec–end Feb.* **Restaurant closed** *lunchtimes Mon–Fri except public holidays.* **Disabled access. TV. Swimming pool. Car park.**

This place is sturdily built on the rocks above the Mediterranean – the view is wonderful. It's quite near the road, though, and a bit of a trek into town. Attractive rooms decorated in warm colours; most of them have terraces overlooking the sea. Doubles €59–100, depending on the season. You walk down the hill to a lovely swimming pool. The restaurant has a spacious, bright dining room and some tables are set around the pool. Good, tasty local cooking on menus at €17 (weekdays only) and €24–33. *Free coffee on presentation of this guide.*

Hôtel Casa Païral***

Impasse des Palmiers; it's beside pl. du 8 Mai-1945.
ⓣ04.68.82.05.81 ⓕ04.68.82.52.10
ⓦwww.hotel-casa-pairal.com
Closed *2 Nov–1 April.* **Disabled access. TV. Swimming pool. Car park.**

A dream of a place, with a fountain on a patio surrounded by masses of greenery, a Hollywood-style swimming pool, a cosy lounge and absolute peace and quiet: luxury indeed. Comfy spacious bedrooms with period furniture; doubles €70–76 with shower/wc or €90–165 with bath. Reservations taken well in advance, especially for summer holidays. A reliable establishment run by professional staff. *10% discount March, April and Oct, except public holidays, on presentation of this guide.*

Le Trémail

1 rue Arago; it's in the old town.
04.68.82.16.10
Closed *Mon and Tues out of season; 5 weeks from 1 Jan.*

Located in a lively area, with a few tables on a streetside terrace and more in the warmly decorated dining room, this is one of the nicest restaurants in the old town. They serve traditional Catalan specialities: chargrilled squid, grilled fish, shellfish stew, paella (with advance notice). The menu, €22, lists a starter of fresh *boquerones* (marinated anchovies with garlic) with *crème catalane* or home-made pastries for dessert. À la carte expect to pay €30. Wine is by the bottle only – a pity when there are so many good local vintages to try. It's best to book. *Free apéritif or coffee on presentation of this guide.*

Cucugnan

11350

Auberge de Cucugnan

2 pl. de la Fontaine.
04.68.45.40.84
Closed *Jan–Feb.*

Doubles €42–50. Menus €16–40. The first menu fulfils all its promises. It even includes 1/4l bottle of wine. Generous platter of charcuterie and fantastic rabbit. Small terrace in summer. If the hotel is full, you may be offered to stay in a *chambre d'hôte* or in a self-catering flat, very convenient for a large family. Friendly welcome and convivial atmosphere.

L'Auberge du Vigneron**

2 rue Achille-Mir; it's opposite the theatre.
04.68.45.03.00 04.68.45.03.08
www.auberge-vigneron.com
Closed *Sun evening and Mon; 12 Nov–15 Feb.* **TV.**

The inn offers a lovely overnight stop and rustic rooms with rough-hewn stone walls; doubles with shower/wc €39–42. Make your way down to the old wine store – it's been turned into a lovely restaurant. They've decorated it using hogsheads and there's an open fire as well as a terrace. You'll find regional dishes such as crayfish *fricassée*, guinea-fowl and a delicious apple omelette. A shame the service isn't as good. Menus at €19 and €32. Children's menu €12.

Bugarach

11190 (27km W)

L'Oustal d'Al Pech

It's on the D14, 19km from the château de Peyrepertuse.
and 04.68.69.87.59
oustalddalpech@wanadoo.fr
Closed *Wed and Sun evening (except public holidays), evenings Nov–March; Jan.*
Disabled access.

An isolated country inn in a totally unspoilt village. The rustic décor creates a lovely setting for a gourmet meal. Classic, flavoursome dishes using good local produce – foie gras, goose gizzard *confits*, free-range chicken served with a crayfish sauce, wild boar stew and iced nougat with caramel. Everything is made on the premises and the young team running the place are to be congratulated. Menus €15–24. Children's menu €7. Essential to book for Sunday lunch and in winter. *Free coffee on presentation of this guide.*

Florac

48400

Hôtel des Gorges du Tarn - Restaurant l'Adonis

48 rue du Pêcheur.
04.66.45.00.63 04.66.45.10.56
www.lozere.net/gorges-du-tarn.htm
Closed *Wed (except July–August); All Saints' Day; Easter.* **TV. Highchairs available. Car park.**

The name of the restaurant might send your imagination into flights of fancy – but don't be misled. However, if you want a place to rest and a good meal then you won't go far wrong choosing this perfectly run establishment. The quality of the produce and the skill of the chef ensure you won't be disappointed. Menus €17–35.

Rooms are in the same vein. Doubles €36–42. *Free liqueur on presentation of this guide.*

Grand Hôtel du Parc***

47 av. Jean-Monestier (Centre).
☎04.66.45.03.05 Ⓕ04.66.45.11.81
Ⓦwww.grandhotelduparc.fr
Restaurant closed Sunday evening and Mon out of season; Mon lunchtime in high season; 15 Nov–15 March. Disabled access. TV. Car park.

Doubles with shower/wc or bath €43–47. Half-board €43–46 per person. Menus €17–34. This hotel is most likely the oldest and biggest hotel of the region. It's a very big house which may rather remind you of a spa hidden in a very pleasant park. But it's more like a friendly family hotel where the guests of all ages meet in the corridors and at the restaurant. 60 rooms, all comfortable.

Salle-Prunet (La)

48400 (2km SE)

L'Auberge Cévenole-Chez Annie et Serge

Take the Alès road; 2 km away from Florac.
☎04.66.45.11.80
Closed *Sun evening and Mon out of season except public holidays; July–Aug; mid-Nov to mid-Feb.* **TV.**

An old building faced in local stone deep in the Mimente valley. Take your meals on the terrace in summer or, in winter, huddle round the fire – you feel as if you're eating in the family dining room. Set menus €14–21 showcase good local charcuterie, hot Pélardon goat's cheese, Roquefort salad and the house speciality, *noisette* of veal with a cep sauce. Simple rooms; doubles €29–38. It's advisable to book. *10% discount on room rates on presentation of this guide.*

Cocurès

48400 (5km NE)

La Lozerette**

Take the D998.
☎04.66.45.06.04 Ⓕ04.66.45.12.93
Ⓔlalozerette@wanadoo.fr
Closed *Tues (lunchtime only July–Aug); Wed lunchtime; 1 Nov to Easter.* **Restaurant closed** *Mon (except for guests).* **Disabled access. Highchairs and games available. TV. Car park.**

This establishment, set in a quiet little village on the picturesque road up to Mont Lozère, is a family affair. Granny Eugénie once owned an inn herself, but nowadays Pierrette Agulhon's in charge. There's a first menu at €15 (except Sunday lunch) and another at €20.50. Overall the cuisine exhibits a successful combination of imagination, good taste and magnificent flavours, and the wines are carefully chosen. The bedrooms are as stylish as the dining room – floral, pastel-painted and decorated with a keen eye for detail. Expect to pay €50–62 for doubles. Breakfast is good.

Font-Romeu

66120

Hôtel Carlit - Restaurant La Cerdagne - Restaurant Le Foc***

Rue du Docteur-Capelle.
☎04.68.30.80.30 Ⓕ04.68.30.80.68
Ⓦwww.carlit-hotel.fr
Closed *mid-April to early May; Oct; Nov. Grillroom open lunchtimes.* **TV. Swimming pool. Highchairs and games available.**

Though the modern building looks boring, this three-star place is more than adequate and prices are fair. Reception is professional and the rooms have good facilities – though the decoration is perhaps over-bright. There's also a health suite with Jacuzzi, sauna, hammam and weights room. Double rooms with shower/wc €54–70 or bath €64–80. There are two restaurants: chic La Cerdagne, which offers a good mushroom menu, and Le Foc, with a cheaper *formule*. Menus €18–30. If you're planning to stay a day or two, half board is reasonably priced at €53–73 per person, compulsory during winter school holidays. *10% discount (out of season) on the room rate on presentation of this guide.*

Latour-de-Carol

66760 (17km SW)

L'Auberge Catalane

10 av. de Puymorens. Take the D618, then the N20.
☎04.68.94.80.66 Ⓕ04.68.04.95.25
Ⓦwww.auberge-catalane.fr
Closed *Mon except in school holidays; Sun*

evening; a fortnight in May; 12 Nov–10 Dec. **TV. Highchairs available. Car park.**

A good place to stop on the road up to the Puymorens pass. When the inn was taken over by the present owners they did up all the rooms, decorating them in attractive warm colours and fitting good soundproofing. They cost €47 and €49 with shower/wc; some have balconies and TV. There's a little shady terrace and a dining room where they serve honest regional dishes: grilled black pudding with apple, chicken à la catalane and *crème catalane*. Menus €14.50–29.10. *Free house apéritif on presentation of this guide.*

Garde (La)

48200

Le Rocher Blanc**

It's 1km from exit 32 on the A75.
☎04.66.31.90.09 Ⓕ04.66.31.93.67
Closed *1 Nov to Easter. Restaurant closed Sun evening and Mon outside school holidays.* **TV. Swimming pool. Highchairs and games available. Car park.**

Margeride is a wild and beautiful part of the country and the hotel is just 3km from France's smallest museum at Albaret-Sainte-Marie. The rooms here are fairly spacious and they're clean and quiet. Doubles with shower/wc or bath €44–47; half board, compulsory 15 July–20 August, from €45–51 per person. Set menus cost €16 (not served Sun) and up to €34. Credit cards not accepted. *Free apéritif offered to our readers on presentation of this guide.*

Chaulhac

48140 (10km N)

La Maison d'Elisa

Take the D47 towards Lorcières for 10km, then turn left towards Chaulhac.
☎04.66.31.93.32
Closed *Mon (except July–Aug).*

This isolated village, with flowers blooming everywhere, is absolutely idyllic. Originally from Lille, the owners now run a cosy and unassuming inn. They offer decent, nicely presented menus which change daily. The one at €14 includes wine and coffee, and there are others up to €23. Madame exhibits her skill in the kitchen and Monsieur serves with a smile. Truffade and aligot are made to order. *Free coffee offered to our readers on presentation of this guide.*

Grau-du-Roi (Le)

30240

Hôtel Bellevue et d'Angleterre**

Quai Colbert.
☎04.66.51.40.75 Ⓕ04.66.51.43.78
Closed *Christmas school holidays.* **TV.**

There are a good number of rooms in this hotel blessed with a grandstand view over Grau-du-Roi. All the rooms are pretty, well maintained and air-conditioned, and prices are competitive: doubles €32–42 out of season, €43–68 in the summer. Breakfast included in the summer.

Le Gafétou

6 [bis] rue Frédéric Mistral, rive gauche, promenade de la plage.
☎04.66.51.60.99 Ⓕ04.66.51.56.54
Closed *Sun evening, Mon; Nov–end March.* **Highchairs available.**

Fronted by an awning, the large dining room is decorated in aquatic shades – setting the scene for the fish, seafood and shellfish you'll enjoy here. The menus from €12.50 (weekdays lunchtime only) to €39.50 offer good value, and the fish is as fresh as can be. Friendly welcome, perfect service and an ideal seaside location. *Free coffee on presentation of this guide.*

Gruissan

11430

Le Lamparo

I4 rue Amiral-Courbet; it's in the village beside the pond.
☎04.66.49.93.65
Closed *Sun evening out of season; Mon; mid-Dec to end Jan.*

This is a good restaurant specializing in fish and seafood at reasonable prices. The dining room is spruce and the tables are laid with salmon-pink cloths; there are more tables on the terrace, which has a view of the pond (and the car park). Excellent menus €18–30 listing dishes such as roast oysters with duck breast, fillet of sea bream with olive paste, cheese and double chocolate truffle.

Lamalou-les-Bains

34240

🏃 🏠 |●| Hôtel-restaurant Belleville**

1 av. Charcot.
☎04.67.95.57.00
ⓦwww.hotel-belleville.com
Disabled access. TV. Car park.

Typical of a spa town, this is a substantial provincial hotel which has been owned by the same family since 1900. The house has character and has been entirely refurbished. It's spacious and boasts good facilities – doubles with shower/wc or bath €30–50 (many overlooking the garden, the more expensive ones air-conditioned). The restaurant is decorated in Belle-Époque style and they serve a series of set menus at €14.50–34, specializing in local dishes. If you're in a hurry, go for the *menu express*, served on the veranda. Specialities include fish stew, duck with figs and Banyuls wine, and *fondant* with almonds. *10% discount on the room rate from the second consecutive night on presentation of this guide.*

🏃 |●| Les Marronniers

8 av. de Capus; it's on the way out of town after the town hall.
☎04.67.95.76.00
Closed *Sun evening; Mon; Jan.*

A small and rather insignificant house above the town – but the restaurant is currently one of the very best in town. The chef Gilles Aubert approaches local dishes from a fresh perspective and produces seriously good cooking: his roulade of beef oxtail with foie gras is a treat. Market menu at €13.50 (weekdays only) with *menus-carte* for €16.50–39. Efficient service and good seasonal wine by the glass. There's a terrace under an awning. *Free coffee on presentation of this guide.*

Villemagne-l'Argentière

34600 (7km NE)

|●| l'Auberge de l'Abbaye

Place du Couvent. Take the D908 and follow the signs.
☎04.67.95.34.84
Closed *Mon; Tues; Weds Nov–May; 27 Dec–15 Feb.* **Car park.**

Set in the middle of a charming village, this picturesque place has old stone walls and a terrace at the foot of an old tower. It's a very pleasing setting for authentic local cooking, carefully prepared. Specialities include fish platter with spiced caramel, and foie gras *tournedos* with truffle *jus*. Menus €22–48. The latter is a surprise menu that allows you to enter the abbaye's labyrinth of flavours.

Bédarieux

34600 (8km NE)

🏠 🏃 Hôtel Delta

1 rue de Clairac; it's on the street that runs at right angles to av. Jean-Jaurès.
☎and ⓕ04.67.23.21.19
TV.

A lovely young couple have converted this old clinic into a hotel. It may have no stars, but the bedrooms are clean and spacious. Fresh, unusual décor, with Egyptian symbols and Chinese fans here and there. Prices are reasonable, with doubles with shower or shower/wc €26–32. Breakfast €5. It's a nice little place, though the location isn't so nice. *10% discount on the room rate for two consecutive nights on presentation of this guide (except July and August).*

La-Salvetat-sur-Agout

34330

🏠 |●| Hôtel-restaurant La Plage

Les Bouldouires; on the banks of the lake of La Ravière.
☎04.67.97.69.87 ⓕ04.67.97.51.98
Closed *Sun evening out of season.* **Car park. TV.**

Doubles €37–41. Menu of the day at €10.50; others at €17 and €19. Although this is a rather new establishment it has already acquired a certain vintage. The rooms are simple but have a rather nice view over the lake. Quiet, especially out of season. The restaurant is pretty popular as many come a long way to eat the pig's salad or the delicious local speciality with fried egg and bacon. Jean-René Pons' cuisine is traditional, so is his dining room. Better book ahead. Good wines by the glass.

Lauret

34270

☗ |●| L'Auberge du Cèdre

Domaine de Cazeneuve; it's 1km from the village.
Ⓣ04.67.59.02.02 Ⓕ04.67.59.03.44
Ⓦwww.auberge-du-cedre.com
Closed *Dec–15 March. Restaurant closed Mon–Thurs and Fri lunch (but open for hotel guests). Highchairs and games available.* **Swimming pool.**

This old house in an ancient wine area has been converted into a very attractive hotel and restaurant with a swimming pool. Simple but adequate bedrooms are yours for €26–38; some sleep three or four. Half-board €31–36 per person. There's a weekday menu €25–32. Children's menu. Look out for the hiker's platter – sausage, terrine with juniper berries, Serrano ham and other good traditional terroir dishes. There's a wide range of good Mediterranean wines, many of which are available by the glass.

Lézignan-Corbières

11200

🏃 ☗ |●| Hôtel Le Tassigny – Restaurant Le Tournedos**

Rond-point de-Lattre-de-Tassigny; from the centre, take av. des Corbières towards the A9 for about 2km.
Ⓣ04.68.27.11.51 Ⓕ04.68.27.67.31
Closed *Sun evening; last week in Jan; 1st week in Feb; 1–15 Oct. Restaurant closed Sun evening; Mon.* **Disabled access. TV. Car park.**

A great place for an overnight stay if you don't want to spend a fortune. The place is freshly refurbished and modernized, with doubles at €39–43 with shower/wc or bath; the cheaper ones are also the noisiest. Breakfast €5.50. The restaurant is popular locally. Menus €16–33. Hearty specialities include *cassoulet*, *tournedos* with morels, meats and fish grilled over a wood fire. *Free coffee on presentation of this guide. Free car park if rooms have been booked ahead.*

Escales

11200(7km NW)

🏃 |●| Les Dinedourelles

Impasse des Pins; from Lézignan, take the Olonzac road, the D611, for 2km, then turn left onto the D127.
Ⓣ04.68.27.68.33
Closed *evenings (except Mon-Wed July-Aug, Nov-Feb).* **Disabled access.**

A good atmosphere and a pleasant, unusual setting – unusual because you get to eat inside a variety of barrels, including a 10,000-litre one seating six. If that doesn't appeal there's always the lovely terrace under the pine trees with a panoramic view of the Montagne Noire. The cuisine is generously flavoured and original: pan-fried escalope of foie gras, celery ravioli stuffed with goat's cheese and black olive *coulis*. The single menu, €23, offers three choices, which change according to the season. À la carte you'll spend around €26. Out of season on two or three Friday nights a month, they feature entertainment such as French song, jazz, storytelling and even short plays. Two very comfortable chambres d'hôte and one gîte that can accommodate up to six people have recently been opened. *Free digestif on presentation of this guide.*

Fabrezan

11200 (9km SW)

🏃 ☗ |●| Le Clos des Souquets

Av. de Lagrasse; take the D611 towards Lagrasse.
Ⓣ04.68.43.52.61
Ⓔclossouquets@infonie.fr
Closed *Sun; 1 Nov–1 April. TV. Swimming pool.* **Highchairs and games available. Car park.**

This is a jewel of a place on the route to the Cathar châteaux and the Corbières caves. It only has five bedrooms; doubles with bath €46–70. Half board from €76 per person is compulsory in summer. The Julien family spend the winter in the Caribbean, as you'll notice from the exotic touches in the bedrooms and the cuisine. Simple tasty food served around the pool – the first menu lists salad méridionale, mussels *gratinées* and soft cheese with honey. Choose the second menu if you want to sample the grilled fish of the day, which is always superb. Or go for a *carpaccio* of meat or fish. Menus €17–33. *Free apéritif on presentation of this guide.*

Homps

11200 (10km N)

☗ |●| Auberge de l'Arbousier

Route de Carcassonne. Take the D611 towards Olonzac.

Ⓣ04.68.91.11.24 Ⓕ04.68.91.12.61
Closed *Mon all day and Tues lunchtime July–Aug; Wed and Sun evening Sept–June; 15 Feb–15 March; Nov.* **TV. Highchairs and games available. Bicycles racks. Car park.**

The Canal du Midi flows alongside this inn, where old stonework and exposed beams contrast well with the modern art on the walls. It's a nice place, with a shaded terrace in summer and quiet, comfortable rooms. You could almost imagine you were staying in a bed and breakfast. Doubles €40–70 with shower/wc or bath. The kitchen prepares classic but refined dishes: red mullet, rabbit and purple artichokes salad, fig tart (only when in season). Set weekday menu €13 and others €20–34.

|●| Restaurant Les Tonneliers

Port du Canal du Midi.
Ⓣ04.68.91.14.04
Closed *mid-Dec to mid-Feb.* **Disabled access.**

The Canal du Midi runs through the village and only a few metres away from it you'll find this place. It offers good food in rustic surroundings. There's a *formule* for €13 and menus €15–31, listing specialities like *cassoulet* with *confit* of duck, marinated salmon in two kinds of lemon and *tarte tatin*. Tourists come to see the canal in the evening. In summer, sit in the attractive garden or on the shaded terrace.

Limoux

11300

🏃 ⌂ |●| Grand Hôtel Moderne et Pigeon***

Place du Général-Leclerc; it's by the post office.
Ⓣ04.68.31.00.25 Ⓕ04.68.31.12.43
Ⓦwww.grandhotelmodernepigeon.fr
Restaurant closed *Mon, Sat lunch and Sun evening (except July–Aug); 15 Dec–15 Jan.*
TV. Pay car park.

This magnificent building had many lives before being converted into a hotel in the early 1900s. Originally a convent, it became a grand town house and later a bank; make sure you take a good look at the seventeenth-century frescoes on the wall above the splendid staircase. As a hotel it's comfy and well run without being too formal. Lovely doubles with shower/wc or with bath go for €60–130, depending on size and comfort. The dining room has sophisticated décor and a quiet atmosphere. The cheapest set menu is €19.50 with others at €29–53, and they list some delicious dishes: *pot-au-feu* of foie gras in cabbage leaves, lamb with a crust of pressed olives, braised duck in sparkling white wine, followed by cheese and dessert. You can enjoy a glass of sparkling wine in the cellar where the pool players hang out. *Second breakfast free except in July and Aug offered to our readers on presentation of this guide.*

Llo

66800

🏃 ⌂ |●| Auberge Atalaya***

Llo-Haut.
Ⓣ04.68.04.70.04 Ⓕ04.68.04.01.29
Ⓔatalaya66@aol.com
Closed *2 Nov–20 Dec; 15 Jan–Easter.*
Restaurant closed *Mon–Thurs out of season.* **TV. Car park.**

A charming stone house with a courtyard overlooking the village. The walls are covered in vines and there's a small garden. Doubles €90–115. A flat and a large bedroom with a terrace are also available for €136. The restaurant offers seasonal dishes, which vary according to the whim of the chef. Menus €28, à la carte menu also available. *Free apéritif or coffee offered to our readers on presentation of this guide.*

Lodève

34700

🏃 ⌂ |●| La Croix Blanche**

6 av. de Funel.
Ⓣ04.67.44.10.87
Ⓦwww.hotelcroixblanche.com
Restaurant closed *Fri lunchtime; 1 Dec–1 April.* **TV. Highchairs available. Pay car park.**

An impressive collection of copper pots, pans and basins decorate this place and create a welcoming atmosphere. Generations of sales reps and businessmen have stopped by to enjoy the local hospitality and simple accommodation – doubles €36–42. Unfussy cooking and generous portions in the dining room, with specialities such as snails à *la lodevoise* and home-made tripes. Set menus

€13–28. *Free coffee on presentation of this guide.*

Hôtel-restaurant de la Paix**

11 bd. Montalanque.
☎04.67.44.07.46 Ⓕ04.67.44.30.47
Ⓦwww.hotel-dela-paix.com
Closed *Sun evening and Mon (except 1 May–1 Oct); 1 Feb–8 March.* **TV. Swimming pool. Pay car park.**

The same family has been running this place since 1876. It's clean and comfortable and has views of the mountains and the Lergue river. Doubles with bath/wc €53–56 depending on the season. The hearty cooking specializes in regional dishes and uses fresh produce. House dishes include Labeil trout with almonds. In summer they offer chargrilled meats served outside around the swimming pool. Set menus €20 and €30, or à la carte.

Le Petit Sommelier

3 pl. de la République; it's beside the tourist office.
☎and Ⓕ04.67.44.05.39
Closed *Sun evening; Mon; Wed evening in low season; autumn schools holidays.* **Disabled access.**

An informal, unpretentious little place with simple bistro décor. Tasty cooking with dishes like trout with Chardonnay, roast lamb, breast of duck with apples and honey and warm mussels in a cream sauce with Banyuls wine. Set menus €13–29. You'll get a warm, friendly welcome. There's a pleasant terrace.

Lunel

34400

Auberge des Halles

26 cours Gabriel-Péri; it's next to the covered market.
☎04.67.83.85.80
Closed *Sun evening and Mon except public holidays; Feb.*

A well-known restaurant serving honest, traditional cuisine which follows the changing seasons and whims of the owner. You must try the pan-fried foie gras with the local Muscat. Weekday lunch menu €10, others €18–26. There are tables on the terrace outside and the service is friendly.

Mende

48000

Hôtel-restaurant du Pont-Roupt***

2 av. du 11-Novembre.
☎04.66.65.01.43 Ⓕ04.66.65.22.96
Ⓦwww.hotel-pont-roupt.com
Closed *15 Feb–15 March.* **Restaurant closed** *weekends out of season.* **TV. Highchairs and games available. Swimming pool. Car park.**

A nice hotel in a large house on the banks of the Lot on the edge of town. The décor is contemporary and plain but the bedrooms are comfortable, and there's an indoor swimming pool. Doubles with shower/wc or bath €46–65. Gastronomic week-end deals available. The chef draws on a long tradition of cuisine while also creating some modern dishes. Menus €22–46. If you've got to spend the night in Mende, this is fine. But if you're after a romantic weekend, perhaps look elsewhere. *10% discount on the room rate on presentation of this guide.*

Hôtel Le Lion d'Or

12–14 bd. Britexte.
☎04.66.49.16.46 Ⓕ04.66.49.23.31
Ⓦwwwliondor-mende.com
Disabled access. TV. Swimming pool. Car park.

If you're looking for comfortable, quiet rooms in the centre of town, look no further. Doubles €53–75 depending on the season. It's quite luxurious and there's even a swimming pool for you to splash around in. You can dine here, too, if you can't face struggling out. If you do, try the pig's trotters *à la gabale*. Menus €19–29. They have a fine wine list. *Free coffee on presentation of this guide.*

Le Mazel

25 rue du Collège.
☎and Ⓕ04.66.65.05.33
Closed *Mon evening; Tues; 15 Nov–15 March.*

This is one of the few modern buildings in the town centre. Jean-Paul Brun uses first-rate ingredients to create fine, flavoursome dishes such as tripoux with white wine, truffle omelette and duck with wild mushrooms. Menus €13.50–26. It's a popular place for business lunches and the best value for money in town.

La Safranière

Hameau de Chabrits.
Take the N88, cross the Roupt bridge, then straight ahead on the D42.
04.66.49.31.54
Closed *Sun evening; Mon; March; a week in Sept.* **Highchairs available.**

This is where to come if you're in Mende or the surrounding area and want a gourmet experience. The dining room is bright and elegant, and it's in a very old building which has been attractively refurbished. Sebastien Navetch's light, delicate cooking makes clever use of herbs, spices and seasonings like basil, tarragon, cumin, saffron and coconut; try roast pigeon breast with caramelized spices. Weekday menu €18 except Friday evening, others €24–48. Reservations recommended. *Free coffee on presentation of this guide.*

Meyrueis

48150

Hôtel Family**

Rue de la Barrière.
04.66.45.60.02 04.66.45.66.54
hotel.family@wanadoo.fr
Closed *5 Nov to Palm Sunday.* **Disabled access. TV. Highchairs and baby-changing facilities available. Swimming pool. Car park.**

A large building standing by the fast-flowing stream that runs through the village. Well-maintained and redecorated rooms; doubles with shower/wc or bath €35–45. Those on the top floor are the best. The cuisine focuses on local dishes and menus are fairly priced at €12 (weekdays lunchtime only) up to €30. There's a pleasant garden with a swimming pool opposite the hotel which you reach by crossing a little wooden bridge. *10% discount on the room rate in April, May and October on presentation of this guide.*

Hôtel de La Jonte**

Aux Douzes; follow the D996 and the gorges of La Jonte.
05.65.62.60.52 05.65.62.61.62
Closed *mid-Nov to early March.* **Disabled access. TV. Swimming pool. Car park.**

A large establishment by the road which is well known for its good cooking and the warmth of its welcome – and it's cheap too. There are two dining rooms: opt for the one used by workers and travelling salesmen because the cooking is better and the prices are more reasonable, with set menus at €11–24. The rooms are very well maintained and are above the restaurant or in an annexe overlooking the gorge of the river Jonte. Doubles with shower/wc or bath cost €36. Half board €37 per person. The ones with a view of the river are the most expensive. *Free digestif on presentation of this guide.*

Hôtel du Mont Aigoual**

34 quai de la Barrière.
04.66.45.65.61 04.66.45.64.25
www.hotel-mont-aigoual.com
Closed *Tues lunchtime in April and Oct; Nov–end March.* **TV. Swimming pool. Highchairs available. Car park.**

From the outside this place looks ordinary enough, but appearances are deceptive. Stella Robert is energetic and lively and she'll give you a charming welcome. There's a beautiful swimming pool at the back of the hotel in an enormous garden. The rooms are spacious and quiet; they're priced at €46–71 with bath. Half board is compulsory in July/Aug; €46–57 per person. The restaurant is one of the best in the area, offering consistent quality at reasonable prices. Daniel Lagrange uses authentic, tasty local produce to create appetizing local dishes: pan-fried foie gras with creamed lentils, say, or roast saddle of lamb. Local menu at €18, and *menus gourmands* at €27 and €37. *10% discount on the room rate in April and Oct on presentation of this guide.*

Mèze

34140

Le Pescadou

33 bd. du Port; go towards the harbour.
04.67.43.81.72
Closed Tues and Wed in winter; Mon and Tues July–Aug; a week in Jan; a week in June; a fortnight in Oct. **Disabled access.**

Le Pescadou has a pretty terrace on the harbour and a spacious dining room attractively decorated with engravings of ships and lots of green plants. It's a fresh, relaxing place which is very popular with the locals. First menu at €13.50 (not served Sun lunch or public holidays) with others up to €30 – all the fresh fish is good, along with fish soup with toasted croutons, squid with rouille, mussels with garlic butter and sea snails direct from the Thau pond. Advance booking recommended. *Free apéritif on presentation of this guide.*

Mont-Louis

66210

Hôtel-restaurant Lou Rouballou

Rue des Écoles-Laïques; it's on the ramparts, opposite the local primary school.
Ⓣ04.68.04.23.26 Ⓕ04.68.04.14.09
Closed *May; Oct–Nov.* **Restaurant closed** *Wed out of season; lunchtimes in season.* **TV. Car park.**

A family guesthouse with lots of rustic character; it's comfy, delightful and full of charm. You'll be greeted warmly by Christiane Duval, who is Catalan – you can practically feel the sun in her voice when she talks about the Pyrenees. You'll feel perfectly at home in one of the attractive rooms, which go for €38.50 with shower/wc. The restaurant is tastefully decorated and fresh, authentic cooking is offered on set menus, €19.50–30. House specialities include game with hand-picked mushrooms, wild boar stew, duck breast with fruit and honey, and Catalan meatballs. In winter, don't miss the *ollada*, a rustic soup from Cerdagne. Year round there are delicious mushrooms – including the rouballou, which grows locally. *Free apéritif on presentation of this guide.*

Prats-Balaguer

66360 (5 km SE)

Auberge de la Carança

Take the N116 to Fontépouse, then follow directions to Prats-Balaquer.
Ⓣ04.68.97.10.84
Closed *mid-Nov to 20 Dec.*

A little inn at the end of a village, at the end of a lane. There's nothing beyond but the mountain. It's full of walkers who come to restore their strength with the tasty cooking. Specialities include rare Pyrenean veal, omelettes and lots of mushrooms. Menus €12.20–18.30. Simple, clean doubles €34, or €13 for a night in a dormitory. It's essential to book a bed and to order your meal – the nearest baker is an hour away. They can advise you on walks in the area.

Montpellier

34000

See map overleaf

Auberge de jeunesse

Rue des Écoles-Laïques; entrance by La Petite-Corraterie; from the station, take the tramway to Mosson, stop "Louis-Blanc".
Map B1-1
Ⓣ04.67.60.32.22 Ⓕ04.67.60.32.30
Ⓔmontpellier@fuaj.org
Closed *14 Dec–11 Jan.*

One night costs €11.70 (breakfast included). Nineteen rooms with 89 dormitory beds; each room sleeping two–ten people. Generally well-kept. Left luggage facilities. In the summer, nice shaded terrace. Bar open 6 p.m. till midnight. Table football and snooker. Credit cards accepted.

Hôtel Les Fauvettes*

8 rue Bonnard; it's on the no. 7 bus route, tramway also available. Behind the Jardin des Plantes.
Ⓣ04.67.63.17.60 Ⓕ04.67.64.09.09
Closed *Christmas to 7 Jan.*

Probably the cheapest hotel in Montpellier. It's a small establishment in a quiet street, run by a friendly lady. The bedrooms may be basic but they're quiet and clean; most of them look onto the interior courtyard; only two out of eighteen look onto the street. They serve breakfast on the veranda, which is popular in summer. Doubles with basin €24, shower €32, €38 with shower/wc or bath. Breakfast €4.

Hôtel Floride**

1 rue François-Perrier. **Map D3-5**
Ⓣ04.67.65.73.30 Ⓕ04.67.22.10.83
Ⓔhotel.floride@gofornet.com
TV.

Situated in a quiet street near the pl. de la Comédie and the Antigone district. You'll receive a warm welcome. 26 air-conditioned doubles €36–59 depending on the season and facilities; the best ones overlook the terrace, which is a riot of flowers. All the rooms are being gradually updated. Good breakfast at €5. Ask for a room overlooking the terrace.

Hôtel Du Parc**

8 rue Achille-Bège; it's on the other side of Verdanson, 300m from the cathedral.
Off map B1-10

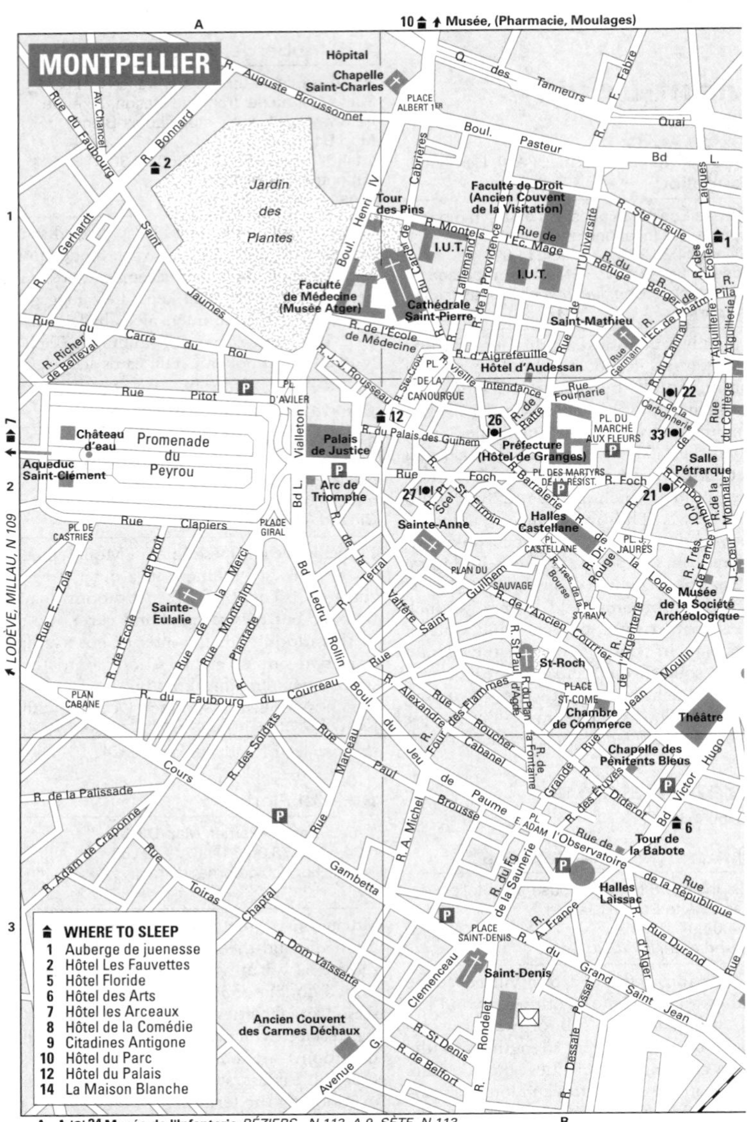
MONTPELLIER
A
10 Musée, (Pharmacie, Moulages)
Hôpital
Chapelle Saint-Charles
PLACE ALBERT 1ER
R. Auguste Broussonnet
Q. des Tanneurs
Boul. Pasteur
Quai
Bd L.
Laïques
Jardin des Plantes
Rue du Faubourg
Av. Chancel
R. Bonnard
2
R. Gerhardt
R. Saint Jaumes
Boul. Henri IV
Tour des Pins
Faculté de Droit (Ancien Couvent de la Visitation)
R. Ste Ursule
1
R. Montels
I.U.T.
Rue de l'Ec. Mage
R. de la Providence
R. Lallemand
R. du Refuge
R. des Écoles
R. Berger de
Faculté de Médecine (Musée Atger)
Cathédrale Saint-Pierre
Saint-Mathieu
R. de l'École de Médecine
Rue du Carré du Roi
R. Richer de Belleval
R. J.-J. Rousseau
PL. DE LA CANOURGUE
R. d'Aigrefeuille
Hôtel d'Audessan
Rue Pitot
PL. D'AVILER
Rue Fournarie
22
Château d'eau
Promenade du Peyrou
Aqueduc Saint-Clément
12
R. du Palais des Guilhem
Palais de Justice
26
Préfecture (Hôtel de Granges)
PL. DU MARCHÉ AUX FLEURS
33
Salle Pétrarque
Arc de Triomphe
Rue Foch
PL. DES MARTYRS DE LA RÉSIST.
R. Foch
21
27
Sainte-Anne
Halles Castellane
PL. CASTELLANE
PL. J. JAURÈS
PL. DE CASTRIES
Rue Clapiers
PLACE GIRAL
PLAN DU SAUVAGE
Musée de la Société Archéologique
Sainte-Eulalie
Rue E. Zola
R. de l'École de Droit
Rue de la Merci
Rue Montcalm
R. Plantade
Bd Ledru Rollin
R. de la Terral
Rue Valfère
Saint Guilhem
R. de l'Ancien Courrier
PL. ST-RAVY
R. St Paul
St-Roch
R. de l'Argenterie
Rue Jean Moulin
PLAN CABANE
R. du Faubourg du Courreau
PLACE ST-COME
Chambre de Commerce
Théâtre
Boul. du Jeu de Paume
R. Alexandre
Rue des Flammes
Rue Roucher
R. Four Cabanel
Chapelle des Pénitents Bleus
Cours Gambetta
R. de la Palissade
R. des Soldats
Rue Marceau
Rue Paul Brousse
Grande Rue
R. Diderot
Bd Victor Hugo
6
R. Adam de Craponne
Rue Toiras
R. A. Michel
PL. E. ADAM
Rue de l'Observatoire
Tour de la Babote
R. du Fg de la Saunerie
Halles Laissac
Rue de la République
R. A. France
R. d'Alger
Rue Durand
PLACE SAINT-DENIS
R. Dom Vaissette
Chaptal
Saint-Denis
R. du Grand Saint Jean
Clemenceau
R. Rondelet
R. Dessalle Possel
Ancien Couvent des Carmes Déchaux
Avenue G.
R. St Denis
R. de Belfort
WHERE TO SLEEP
1 Auberge de juenesse
2 Hôtel Les Fauvettes
5 Hôtel Floride
6 Hôtel des Arts
7 Hôtel les Arceaux
8 Hôtel de la Comédie
9 Citadines Antigone
10 Hôtel du Parc
12 Hôtel du Palais
14 La Maison Blanche
7
LODÈVE, MILLAU, N 109
A 24 Musée de l'Infanterie BÉZIERS, N 113, A 9, SÈTE, N 113
B

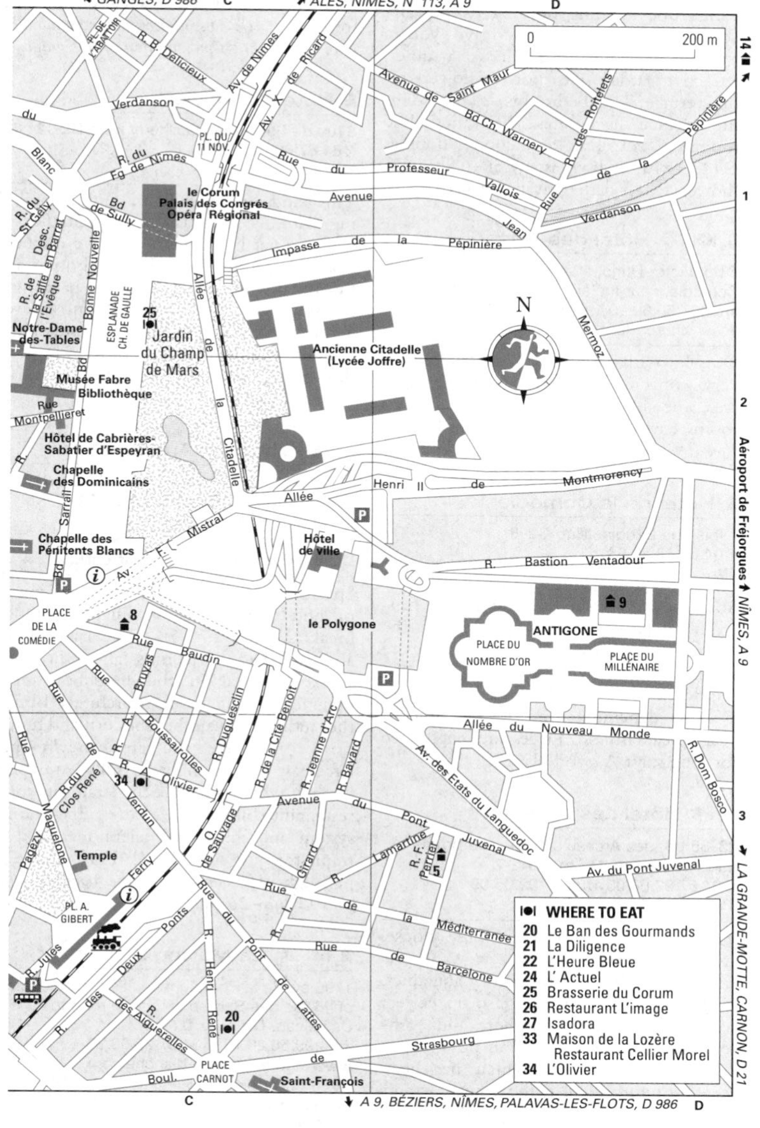
GANGES, D 986
ALÈS, NÎMES, N 113, A 9
C
D
0
200 m
14
1
2
3
Aéroport de Fréjorgues NÎMES, A 9
LA GRANDE-MOTTE, CARNON, D 21
A 9, BÉZIERS, NÎMES, PALAVAS-LES-FLOTS, D 986
PL. DE L'ABATTOIR
R. B. Délicieux
Av. de Nîmes
Av. X de Ricard
Avenue de Saint Maur
Bd Ch. Warnery
R. des Rondelets
Pépinière
Verdanson
PL. DU 11 NOV.
R. du Fg de Nîmes
Rue du Professeur Vallois
Avenue Jean
Rue de la
Bd de Sully
R. du St Gély
le Corum
Palais des Congrès
Opéra Régional
Impasse de la Pépinière
Desc. en Barrat
R. de la Salle l'Evêque
Bonne Nouvelle
ESPLANADE CH. DE GAULLE
Allée de la Citadelle
25
Jardin du Champ de Mars
Notre-Dame-des-Tables
Ancienne Citadelle (Lycée Joffre)
N
Mermoz
Bd
Musée Fabre
Bibliothèque
Rue Montpellieret
Hôtel de Cabrières-Sabatier d'Espeyran
Chapelle des Dominicains
R. Sarrail
Allée Henri II de Montmorency
P
Mistral
Chapelle des Pénitents Blancs
Hôtel de ville
R. Bastion Ventadour
Av. F.
PLACE DE LA COMÉDIE
8
9
le Polygone
ANTIGONE
PLACE DU NOMBRE D'OR
PLACE DU MILLÉNAIRE
Rue Baudin
Rue A. Bruyas
R. Boussairolles
R. Duguesclin
R. de la Cité Benoit
R. Jeanne d'Arc
R. Bayard
Allée du Nouveau Monde
R. Dom Bosco
Av. des Etats du Languedoc
R. du Clos René
34
Olivier
Verdun
Rue de Maguelone
Pagézy
Avenue du Pont Juvenal
Av. du Pont Juvenal
Q. de Sauvage
Girard
Lamartine
R. F. Perrier
5
Temple
Ferry
PL. A. GIBERT
R. Jules
Rue des Deux Ponts
Rue du Pont de Lattes
R. Henri René
R. des Aiguerelles
Rue de la Méditerranée
Rue de Barcelone
20
Strasbourg
PLACE CARNOT
Boul. de
Saint-François
WHERE TO EAT
20 Le Ban des Gourmands
21 La Diligence
22 L'Heure Bleue
24 L' Actuel
25 Brasserie du Corum
26 Restaurant L'image
27 Isadora
33 Maison de la Lozère
Restaurant Cellier Morel
34 L'Olivier

☎04.67.41.16.49 ℻04.67.54.10.0
ⓦwwwhotelduparc-montpellier.com
Disabled access. TV. Car park.

This is a typical eighteenth-century Languedoc building offering twenty air-conditioned rooms. They give you a friendly welcome and there's a quiet, attractive garden with pots of flowers on the terrace. The bedrooms leading onto the terrace have small balconies. The rooms are all clean and comfy; doubles €42 with shower, €56–64 with shower/wc or bath. Private car park.

Hôtel des Arts

6 bd. Victor-Hugo; 50m from pl. de la Comédie, near the station. **Map B3–6**
☎04.67.58.69.20 ℻04.67.58.85.82
ⓦwww.hotel-des-arts.fr

Doubles with shower or bath €43–45. A very convenient place to stay. Friendly welcome and colourful décor. The twenty rooms have all been recently refurbished. *Free coffee on presentation of this guide.*

Hôtel de la Comédie**

1 [bis] rue Baudin. **Map C2–8**
☎04.67.58.43.64
TV.

You'd be hard pushed to find a more central hotel. It's good, quiet and friendly. The rooms have been refurbished. They're simple but clean and welcoming. All the windows are double-glazed. Doubles €52–65 depending on size and time of year. Breakfast €6. Prices are negotiable for long stays. A good place.

Hôtel Les Arceaux**

33–35 bd. des Arceaux; it's behind promenade du Peyrou. **Off map A2-7**
☎04.67.92.03.03 ℻04.67.92.05.09
TV. Car park.

This is an attractive two-storey house, swathed in greenery, with a view on one side of the seventeenth-century aqueduct. The garden is south-facing, so it's perfect to relax. Homely atmosphere and comfortable bedrooms painted in fresh, pretty colours. Ask for one which has been recently refurbished, as the young owners are still in the process of updating the rooms. Some of the bathrooms have retained their trendy seventies tiling. Doubles €52–72 with shower/wc or bath; some have a private balcony and others can sleep three. No. 302 has its own little terrace. Opt for the first floor rooms with high ceilings. The breakfast room is very Mediterranean in style with its wrought-iron tables and sisal chairs. Excellent value for money. *10% discount on the room rate (15 Sept–15 June) on presentation of this guide.*

Hôtel du Palais**

3 rue du Palais-des-Guilhem. **Map B2-12**
☎04.67.60.47.38 ℻04.67.60.40.23
TV.

This handsome nineteenth-century building with its splendid marble entrance is near a quiet little square just five minutes from the centre. The bright bedrooms are furnished with copies of famous paintings, creating a cosy country atmosphere. They're all air-conditioned and have double glazing. Doubles €59–71 with shower/wc or bath. Breakfast at €10. Friendly welcome.

Citadines Antigone***

588 bd. d'Antigone (and pl. du Millénaire); close to pl. de la Comédie. **Map D2-9**
☎04.99.52.37.50 ℻04.67.64.54.64
ⓦwww.citadines.com
Disabled access. TV. Pay car park.

Spacious and clean studios offering a range of hotel services (fresh linen, cleaning, breakfast, etc.); €71–83 for two with bath and sofa-bed. Discounts after the first week. Situated in the neighbourhood designed by the modern architect Bofill, the studios are plain but modern and functional, just like the area they're in. Breakfast €8. Each has a fully equipped kitchen which will ease the strain on your restaurant bill. There's an entry-phone system and direct-dial telephones, and a tram stop just opposite. Parking costs €7 per night. *10% discount on the room rate outside 11 July–26 Aug.*

La Maison Blanche***

1796 av. de la Pompignane; it's on the corner of 46 rue des Salaisons, on the road to Castelnau. **Off map D1-14**
☎04.99.58.20.70 ℻04.67.79.53.39
ⓦwww.hotel-maison-blanche.com
Restaurant closed *Sat lunchtime; Sun; Christmas holidays. Disabled access.* **TV. Swimming pool. Car park.**

This establishment is located in a small park filled with ancient (and now officially protected) trees. The building itself looks somewhat like a mansion from the American Deep South, with spacious light bedrooms elegantly decorated with wood panelling. There's a poster at the reception signed by Alain Delon (he came here in 1991 to film *Casanova*) that shows how popular this hotel used to be with movie stars a few years back! The hotel's exterior is today in need of a make-over to restore its former glory. It is of a good size though with 38 rooms available, so very popular with groups. Small swimming pool. Very quiet. You'll pay €78–90 a night. In the restaurant, menus at €21 (weekdays) to €28. Breakfast for €8. *One free breakfast per room on presentation of this guide.*

L'Actuel

4 rue Bourrely; in a side street off the av. Georges-Clemenceau, level with the local technical secondary school. **Off map A3-24**
☎04.67.58.37.87
Closed *lunchtimes Sat-Sun; evenings Sun–Wed.*

Lunchtime menus €10 and €12, evening menu €20, à la carte around €25. This small gastronomic restaurant located on the premises of a former bar (darkened glass panels in the windows, general outdated décor) is worth a detour. The owners have concentrated their efforts on producing varied and inventive home cooking, where sauces flavoured with exotic spices blend well with the local produce. The lunchtime menus are the most delicious and good value with a good balance between meat (roast beef), fish (fillet of sébaste), and seafood dishes (scallops). Friendly welcome. Advance booking recommended in the evening.

L'Heure Bleue

1 rue de la Carbonnerie. **Map B2-22**
☎04.67.66.41.05
Closed *Sun and Mon.*

Refined teas and delicious savoury and sweet platters for all budgets. At lunchtime, a savoury platter will cost you €9.50. It is situated in a charming city-centre townhouse with a rather oriental décor. If you fancy any of the items on display in the lounge, don't be disappointed as Pierre, the owner and a proud antiques collector, is keen to sell them. All in all, a nice place to go if you enjoy antiques and good food. Also library/tea room. You can even buy tea and coffee there to take home with you.

Brasserie du Corum

Esplanade Charles-de-Gaulle. **Map C1-25.**
☎04.67.02.03.04
Closed *evenings; Sun.*

Several menus on option: bruschetta + salad + dessert of the day €11, bruschetta alone €7.50. Three different functions for one building: art gallery, wine bar and gastronomic restaurant. The latter isn't such good value for money though. The wine bar is light, modern and relaxed, with a view both over the rather futuristic esplanade and over the archeological garden – quite a contrast. Comfortable and quiet dining areas with teak chairs for the terrace and brightly coloured moulded plastic chairs inside. Mouth-watering and well-garnished bruschettas with swordfish and citrus fruit marinated in ginger, chicken kebab with grilled aubergines or thinly sliced beef... not to mention the one topped with the local cheese (pérail saint-pargoire). As for desserts, the fresh fruit compote (the yogurt mousse to be enjoyed mixed with the fruit) is a winner – neither too sour nor too sweet

Isadora

6 rue du Petit-Scel. **Map B2-27**
☎and ℻04.67.66.25.23
Closed *Sat lunchtime; Sun; Mon lunchtime; 1–15 Nov.*

A wonderful thirteenth-century vaulted cellar decorated in Art Deco style. Fine cooking by Gilbert Saugo: hot oysters with braised chicory, foie gras marinated in muscat. Lunch menu €13 with others at €23 and €28, gastronomic menu at €43. A wonderful place to escape from the crushing heat of the summer. Good value for money and very friendly service. *Free coffee on presentation of this guide.*

Le Ban des Gourmands

5 pl. Carnot. **Map C3-28**
☎and ℻04.67.65.00.85
Closed *Sat lunchtime; Sun; Mon; Feb; 3 weeks in Aug; Christmas.*

You get a warm, natural welcome in this fine restaurant, not to mention creative, delicious dishes cooked using fresh produce and served in an intimate setting. Lunchtime *formule* at €13 (starter, dish of the day and coffee) and a menu at €22. À la carte menu around €30. Dishes change according to what's good at the market: try shoulder of pork with figs. It's not a touristy place – more a haven for gourmands and even gourmets. *Free apéritif on presentation of this guide.*

Restaurant L'Image

6 rue du Puits-des-Esquilles. **Map B2-26**
04.67.60.47.79
Closed *Sun; July–Aug. Disabled access. Car park.*

Service 7–10pm only. If you're claustrophobic, head for the dining room upstairs. The simple dishes are suffused with Mediterranean flavours and the portions are generous. Set menus €14–22. A few specialities like the *croustillant* of duck with honey and pears. *Free house digestif on presentation of this guide.*

La Diligence

2 pl. Pétrarque. **Map B2-21**
04.67.66.12.21
www.la-diligence.com
Closed *Sat and Mon lunchtimes; Sun; Aug.*

The restaurant has a splendid dining room with stone walls and a vaulted ceiling – it feels gloriously old. A traditional cuisine with an Asian and Mediterranean twist: sushi of foie gras with a *carpaccio* of aubergines, beef fillet served with a calvados, or a whisky that comes straight from the owner's astonishing cellar. Lunch menu at €18 and others at €31 and €58. The food is good but challenging. It requires a certain open-mindedness. Best to book at the weekend. Patio at the back. *Free house apéritif on presentation of this guide.*

L'Olivier

12 rue Aristide-Ollivier. **Map C3-34**
04.67.92.86.28
Closed *Sun; Mon; July–Aug.*

Modern décor and fine cooking, both popular with local gourmands. The fish is prepared as skilfully as the meat: try the Dover sole and lobster with morels or the braised pig's trotter with a *croustille* of foie gras and ceps. Delicate sauces, good presentation and efficient service. Menus €27 (weekday lunchtimes) and €45 (evenings and lunchtimes), or around €50 à la carte. *Free apéritif on presentation of this guide.*

Maison de la Lozère – Restaurant Cellier Morel

27 rue de l'Aiguillerie. **Map B2-33**
04.67.66.46.36
Closed *Sun; Mon and Wed lunchtimes; a week in Jan; a fortnight in Aug.*

This restaurant and its little sister in Paris are both showcases for Lozère specialities. Éric Cellier's top-of-the-range cooking is served in the superb vaulted dining room down in the basement. Dishes on the €18 lunchtime menu change constantly but there's always aligot and a platter of appetizing, mature cheeses. Other menus at €45 & €58, à la carte menu around €60. Good choice of thoughtfully selected local wines by Pierre Morel. The place is also a high-class grocer's and there's plenty for you to take home. Languedoc wines. *Free house apéritif on presentation of this guide.*

Saint-Gély-du-Fesc

34980 (6 km NW)

Le Clos de l'Olivier

53, rue de l'Aven.
04.67.84.36.36 **Closed** Sun evening; Mon.

Lunchtime menu at €14, others at €24 and €32. Only ten minutes away from Montpellier, you will be surprised to find a quiet terrace here where you will enjoy imaginative and well-prepared dishes in the company of local businessmen. In the evening, as the guests are generally a bit younger, the atmosphere is generally more lively. The cuisine is also more adventurous, with local aromas mixing with more exotic flavours. Very friendly service.

Narbonne

11100

Will's Hôtel**

23 av. Pierre-Sémard; it's in the street opposite the station.
04.68.90.44.50 F 04.68.32.26.28
TV. Pay car park.

There's something solidly reassuring about the beautiful façade of this bourgeois house, an impression reinforced by the owner's friendly reception. The bedrooms are clean and they've been decorated in pastel shades. Doubles at reasonable prices: €30–45 with shower/wc or bath. *10% discount on the room rate (except for July and Aug) on presentation of this guide.*

🏃 🏠 |●| Le Grand Hôtel du Languedoc

22 bd. Gambetta, half-way between the station and the city-centre.
Ⓣ04.68.65.14.74 Ⓕ04.68.65.81.48
Ⓦwww.hoteldulanguedoc.com
Restaurant closed *Sun; Mon. TV. Pay car park.*

A turn-of-the-century mansion with a certain something. It's extremely well maintained, though the corridors are a little dark and gloomy. The recently refurbished bedrooms are bright and have excellent beds and double glazing; some have a view of the cathedral. Doubles with shower/wc or bath €48–65. Breakfast €6.10. In the restaurant there's a weekday lunch menu at €14, and another at €32. They specialize in seafood. *Free fruit juice or soda on presentation of this guide.*

🏃 |●| L'Estagnol

5 [bis] cours Mirabeau (Centre).
Ⓣ04.68.65.09.27 Ⓔlestagnol@net-up.com
Closed *Sun; Mon evening; 15–31 Jan.*
Disabled access.

A friendly brasserie with a Parisian atmosphere but local cuisine. Reasonable prices: lunch *formule* €9.50 and menus €16 and €20. Child's menu at €6.50. Good choices include grilled cod or *fricassée* of prawns with oyster mushrooms. The terrace is open to the sunshine in summer, closed and heated in winter. It overlooks the cathedral and the canal. It's a place to eat quickly and simply, and is popular as an after-show hang-out for actors and performers. The party can go on until the early hours of the morning at the jazz bar, run by the same owners, only a few strides away from the restaurant, and which stays open until 2 a.m. *Free coffee on presentation of this guide.*

|●| Le Petit Comptoir

4, bd. du Maréchal-Joffre (Centre).
Ⓣ04.68.42.30.35.
Closed *Sun mid to June to end Aug; Mon; first week Jan; mid-May to mid-June.*

Lunchtime menu €15, others €23 & €29; à la carte around €35. Best to book as this little bar-restaurant has become very popular thanks to its pleasant location and its cheerful owner who's well-known for choosing the best produce available. Try the tomato and mackerel tart, the fillet of monkfish stuffed with anchovies and the soufflé lemon pancake. The menus change often according to the whims of the chef and what's available at the market. A good little place to go.

|●| La Table Saint-Crescent

Av. du Général-Leclerc; it's on the Perpignan road.
Ⓣ04.68.41.37.37
Closed *Mon; Sat lunchtime; Sun evening; 1–15 Sept; 1–15 March.*

The Palais du Vin was set up to help market local wines and is ideally located just off the motorway. But it also serves a second purpose as the site for this gourmet restaurant. The décor is extraordinary – a mixture of ancient, rough-hewn stone and modern metal sheeting – and the dining room is in an ancient chapel, adding to the feeling of displacement as it is situated in an industrial area. The chef, Claude Giraud, brings you back to this world with his thoughtful cuisine. The lunch *formule*, €17, includes savouries, dish of the day, cheese, dessert, a glass of wine and coffee. The quality of the produce is shown to best advantage in all his dishes, and the astonishing menu "saveurs et terroirs" always changes according to the season and to what's available at the market. Other menus at €28 and €45, or you can eat à la carte (which is a bit pricey).

Nasbinals

48260

🏠 |●| 🏃 Hôtel-restaurant La Route d'Argent**

Route d'Argent; it's the big building beside the church and the village car park.
Ⓣ04.66.32.50.03 Ⓕ04.66.32.56.77
Ⓦwww.nasbinals.com
TV. Car park.

Pierre Bastide's place is something of an institution – everybody in Nasbinals drops in. Guests always get a warm and friendly welcome in the restaurant, and the chef's portions are some of the most generous you'll see. He does cep omelette, duck confit, stuffed cabbage, truffade (potato cake with cheese), and, of course, aligot made to Bastide's special recipe. Set menus €15 (weekdays only) and €18–22. Doubles €38.10 with shower/wc. Breakfast is served at the lively bar. The family has also opened two other hotels: *Le Bastide*, a three-star just outside the town, and *La Randonnée*, a two-star. Credit cards not accepted. *Free house apéritif on presentation of this guide.*

Chaldette (La)

48310 (17km N)

Résidence de Tourisme – Restaurant La Chaldette

La Chaldette.
Hotel ⓣ04.66.48.48.48 ⓕ04.66.31.37.00
Restaurant ⓣ04.66.31.37.00
Closed *Sun evening; Mon; 15 Oct–15 April.*
TV.

A large granite dwelling that's been tastefully renovated, though still a bit soulless, creating a series of well-appointed apartments. To make your reservation, you have to call the thermal baths and pick up your key from there. A week's stay will cost €159–489. *Menu découvert* at €23 (weekday lunchtimes only) and others at €32 and €41.

11

LANGUEDOC-ROUSSILLON

Nîmes

30000

See map on pp.440–441

Auberge de jeunesse***

257 chemin de l'Auberge-de-Jeunesse (off map A2-1); 2km from the city-centre. Signposted from the jardin de la Fontaine. Bus 2 towards Alès from the station. Minibus available from the station after 8pm.
ⓣ04.66.68.03.20 ⓕ04.66.31.37.00
ⓦwww.fuaj.org
Car park.

One night costs €9.30. Meals from €9.20. You must book in advance if you want to stay over the summer. In the heart of a wooded park, this well-maintained youth hostel has recently been entirely refurbished. The dormitories, in the main building or in the small units scattered around the park, sleep 2, 4, 6 or 8 people. Kitchen, launderette, bike park, mountain bikes available, Internet. An electronic key is necessary if you want to come in at any time of the day or the night.

Cat Hôtel**

22 bd. Amiral-Courbet. **Map D2-3**
ⓣ04.66.67.22.85 ⓕ04.66.21.57.51
ⓔcat.hotel@free.fr
TV. Car park.

The owners arrived from the cold, wet north determined to open a hotel in warmer climes, and they've made quite a success of it: the Cat is both pleasant and cheap. They've done everything up, installing double glazing, good ventilation and satellite TV. Everything is just right. Double rooms with shower only €25, or €32 with shower/wc or bath. Breakfast €4.

Hôtel de l'Amphithéatre**

4 rue des Arènes. **Map C3-7**
ⓣ04.66.67.28.51 ⓕ04.66.67.07.79
ⓦwww.perso.wanadoo.fr/hotel.amphitheatre
Closed *Jan.* **TV.**

This is a quiet hotel in a generously proportioned eighteenth-century house. The décor has been spruced up, the place is clean and the beds are comfortable; doubles with shower/wc or bath are €41–59. Good breakfast.

Hôtel Kyriad-Plazza**

10 rue Roussy. **Map D3-5**
ⓣ04.66.76.16.20 ⓕ04.66.67.65.99
ⓦwww.hotel-kyriad-nimes.com
TV. Pay car park.

This place is part of a hotel chain, but you wouldn't think so from its appearance – its a charming old Nîmes house in a quiet street. Its air-conditioned rooms have shower or bath and telephone and cost €55–67. Each floor has a different colour scheme and the corridors are decorated with posters advertising bullfights and opera performances. Rooms on the fourth floor have very attractive little terraces and a view of the old tiled rooftops – they cost €74. *10% discount on the room rate except during Easter, Whitsun and public holidays on presentation of this guide.*

Hôtel Royal***

3 bd. Alphonse-Daudet. **Map B2-4**
ⓣ04.66.67.28.36 ⓕ04.66.58.28.28
Restaurant closed *Sun; Mon.* **TV.**

Most rooms look towards the fountain on the quiet pedestrian pl. d'Assas. The hotel is popular with actors and artists passing through, and the welcome is hospitable. The rooms are individually decorated and are attractive and charming; they don't all have the same facilities but prices are fair for this town: doubles €58 with shower or €66–80 with bath. La Bodeguita, the restaurant, serves tapas and Mediterranean specialities; the terrace is lively in summer (some bedrooms overlook the terrace and can be a bit noisy when the weather's warm). Menus €12 and €14 or around €16 à la carte.

🏠 |●| 🏃 L'Orangerie***

755 Tour l'Évêque. **Off map A4-9**. Take the A9 signposted to the airport, then left at the Kurokawa roundabout onto the N86.
Ⓣ04.66.84.50.57 Ⓕ04.66.29.44.55
Ⓦwww.orangerie.fr
Disabled access. TV. Swimming pool. Highchairs and games available. Car park.

An unusually attractive modern hotel in a big garden with a swimming pool – though the surrounds of the commercial district and the noise from the traffic don't immediately draw you to the area. Professional staff at reception and well-maintained rooms. The prices are reasonable at €64–109 for a double with shower/wc or bath; the nicest have access to a terrace or garden. The restaurant has already established a decent reputation, with a nice dining room and stylish food. Menus from €18. *10% discount on the room rate except during the ferias on presentation of this guide.*

|●| Restaurant La Truye Qui Filhe

9 rue Fresque. **Map C2-11**
Ⓣ04.66.21.76.33
Closed *evenings; Sun; Aug.* **Disabled access.**

The oldest restaurant in town has been an inn since the fourteenth century. Now it's a self-service place with warm service and a lovely patio. There's a €7.60 *formule* consisting of hot main course and dessert; it'll cost you €8.40 with a starter as well. Local dishes such as rouille du pêcheur (fish soup with a spicy mayonnaise), brandade (creamed salt cod in flaky pastry) and paella are dished up on plastic plates in lovely surrounds.

|●| Le Vintage Café

7 rue de Bernis. **Map C2-17**
Ⓣ04.66.21.04.45
Closed *Sat lunchtime; Sun; Mon; 15–31 Aug; 24 Dec–2 Jan.*

Tiny place based around a vintage bistro-style dining room with a fountain. It hosts frequent exhibitions of photographs and paintings. Attractive cooking, delicately seasoned to complement the fresh produce from the market. The dishes change daily, but expect something like Serrano ham, followed by sautéed ravioli with pesto and mixed salad, washed down with one of the interesting southern wines served by the glass. Lunchtime *formule* at €12.35 with a €25 *formule-carte*.

🏃 |●| Restaurant Nicolas

1 rue Poise. **Map C2-13**. In the old Nîmes, near the archeological museum.
Ⓣ04.66.67.50.47 Ⓕ04.66.76.06.33
Ⓔmartin-pascal@wanadoo.fr
Closed *Sat lunchtime; Sun evening; Mon except public holidays; 13 June–6 Aug.*
Disabled access.

The large stone-walled dining room here has been tastefully decorated; inside it you'll be served uncomplicated and reliable home cooking. The menus rarely change because that's how the regulars like it: anchoïade provençale, monkfish bourride (a fish stew with saffron and garlic), creamed salt cod, beef gardiane, and house desserts such as clafoutis. Set menus €12.50–24; all of them include a dish of the day. *Free coffee on presentation of this guide.*

🏃 |●| L'Ancien Théatre

4 rue Racine. **Map B2-14**
Ⓣ04.66.21.30.75
Closed *Sat lunchtime; Sun; 1–15 Jan; last week July; 1–15 Aug.*

They say that there used to be a theatre on the place du Carré nearby, but it was burned to the ground by a singer who went crazy when her son wasn't engaged as a singer. You'll be pleased to hear that you won't find that kind of behaviour in this place: the hospitality and the well-crafted Mediterranean dishes create an altogether more tranquil atmosphere. Menus change every two months. Menus at €13 (weekdays) and up to €24 à la carte. Very good place to go.

|●| Au Flan Coco

31 rue Mûrier-d'Espagne. **Map B2-10**
Ⓣ04.66.21.84.81
Closed *evenings except Sat and by reservation; Sun, last 2 weeks in Feb and Aug.*

A delightful, unusual little restaurant. The two attractive dining rooms are decorated in shades of yellow and red, harmonizing nicely with the granite table tops, and there's a beautiful terrace, perfect for a summer lunch. The imaginative, always fresh dishes vary daily; typical offerings

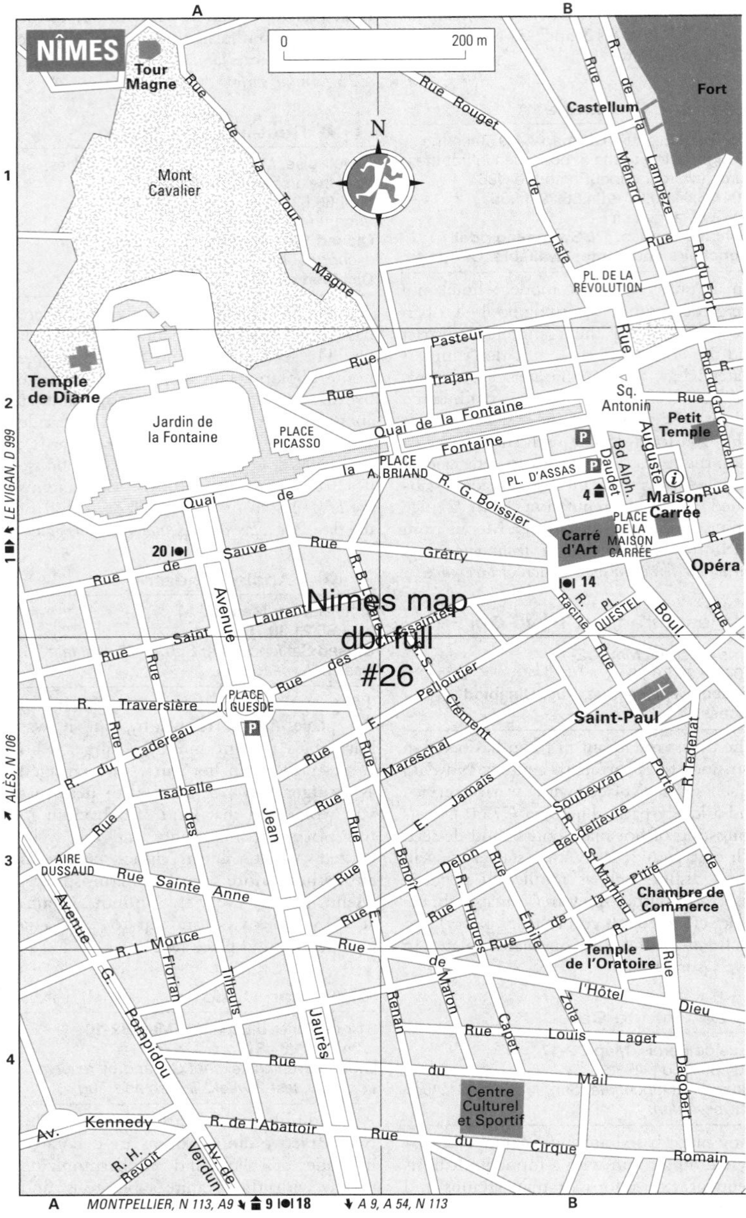

1 LE VIGAN, D 999

ALÈS, N 106

A MONTPELLIER, N 113, A9 9 18 A 9, A 54, N 113 B

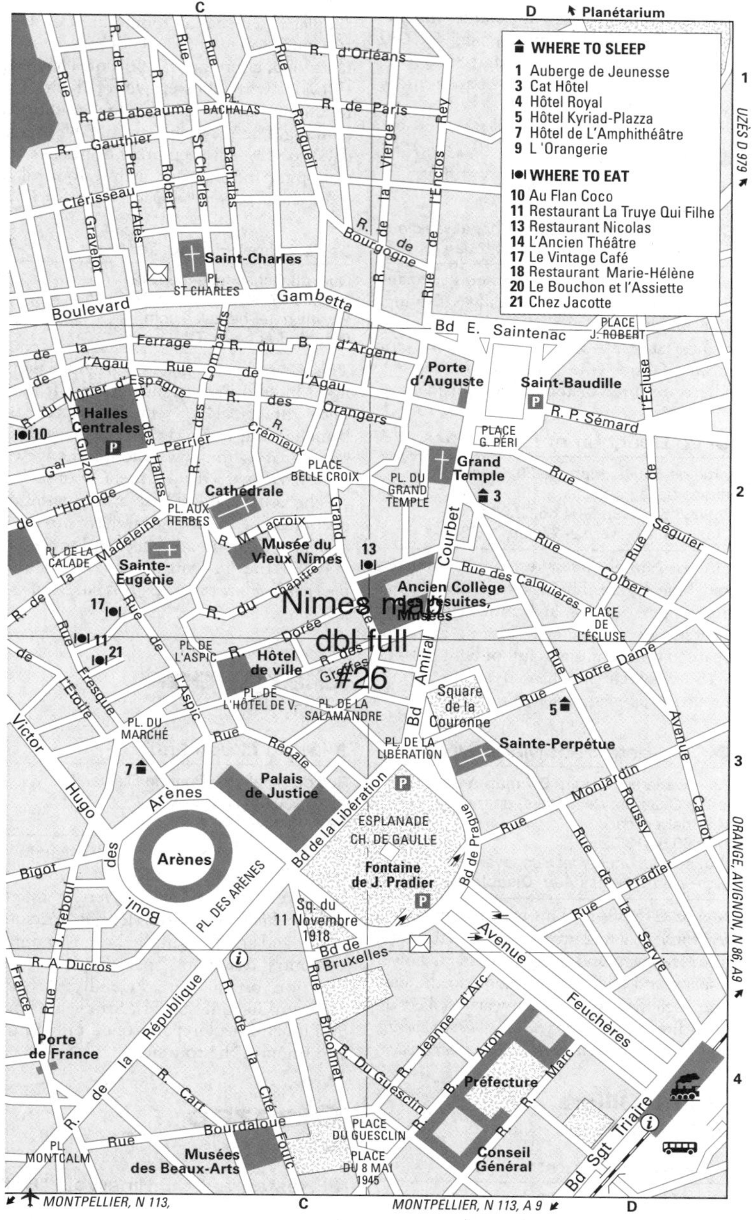
WHERE TO SLEEP
1 Auberge de Jeunesse
3 Cat Hôtel
4 Hôtel Royal
5 Hôtel Kyriad-Plazza
7 Hôtel de L'Amphithéâtre
9 L 'Orangerie
WHERE TO EAT
10 Au Flan Coco
11 Restaurant La Truye Qui Filhe
13 Restaurant Nicolas
14 L'Ancien Théâtre
17 Le Vintage Café
18 Restaurant Marie-Hélène
20 Le Bouchon et l'Assiette
21 Chez Jacotte
Planétarium
UZÈS D 979
ORANGE, AVIGNON, N 86, A9
MONTPELLIER, N 113,
MONTPELLIER, N 113, A 9
Saint-Charles
Halles Centrales
Cathédrale
Sainte-Eugénie
Musée du Vieux Nîmes
Porte d'Auguste
Saint-Baudille
Grand Temple
Ancien Collège des Jésuites, Musées
Hôtel de ville
Square de la Couronne
Sainte-Perpétue
Palais de Justice
Arènes
Esplanade Ch. de Gaulle
Fontaine de J. Pradier
Porte de France
Préfecture
Conseil Général
Musées des Beaux-Arts
Boulevard Gambetta
Bd E. Saintenac
Bd de la Libération
Bd Amiral Courbet
Avenue Feuchères
Bd de Bruxelles
Bd Sgt Triaire
Nimes map dbl full #26

include potato pie, foie gras and creamed salt cod, chicken leg stuffed with prawns and apple crumble with crème fraîche. Menus €14.80 (lunchtime) and €19.80 (Saturday evening), or around €23 à la carte. *Formule* with a main cousrse and a dessert at €12.50 and €18.

|●| Chez Jacotte

15 rue Fresque. **Map C3-21**
Ⓣ04.66.21.64.59
Closed *Sat lunchtime; Sun; Mon; a week in Feb; a fortnight in Aug; 24 Dec–2 Jan.*

Inventive, well-prepared Nîmeois specialities, full of flavour and totally satisfying. The lunch menu at €15 and the evening menus at €30–35 are good value for money. Good wines and attentive service. There are three or four tables outside.

|●| Le Bouchon et L'Assiette

5 rue de Sauve. **Map A2-20**. Close to the jardins de la Fontaine.
Ⓣ04.66.62.02.93 Ⓕ04.66.62.03.57
Closed *Tues; Wed; 2–17 Jan; 1–22 Aug.*

One of Nîmes' nicest restaurants, in a red and blue house. The cooking here has as much personality and finesse as that offered by far fancier places, and the beamed dining room is full of light. Menus €15 (weekday lunchtime) and €20–39. *Free coffee on presentation of this guide.*

|●| Restaurant Marie-Hélène

733 av. Maréchal-Juin. **Off map A4-18**. Next to the Chambre de Métiers, on the Montpellier road.
Ⓣ04.66.84.13.02
Closed *Sat lunchtime; Sun; evenings Mon–Wed; 3 weeks Aug.* **Disabled access.**

Menus €15.50–23. This little restaurant is a real Provençal treasure through and through, from its warm and lively colours, its flower displays and table arrangements to the cuisine itself with its grilled meats cooked on open fires in front of you. *Free house apéritif, fruit juice or coffee on presentation of this guide.*

Saint-Gilles

30800 (19km SE)

⌂ |●| Le Cours**

10 av. François-Griffeuille; take the D42.
Ⓣ04.66.87.31.93 Ⓕ04.66.87.31.83
Ⓦwww.hotel-le-cours.com
Closed *10 Dec–10 March.* **Disabled access. Highchairs available. TV. Car park.**

This white house, shaded by an avenue of tall plane trees, has 33 rooms, most of them air-conditioned but all of them with restrained, contemporary décor. They cost €46–67 with shower/wc or bath. The restaurant offers good-value traditional cooking. The set menus from €11 (weekdays) to €29 – list tempting dishes like the scallop terrine and the warm seafood salad. *5% discount on the half-board rate.*

⌂ Hôtel Héraclée***

Quai du Canal; take the D42.
Ⓣ04.66.87.44.10 Ⓕ04.66.87.13.65
Ⓦwww.hotel-heraclee.com
Disabled access. TV.

This Greek name graces a friendly, pretty hotel housed in a bright building. It looks onto the canal so you can watch the launches, the horse-drawn barges and the houseboats gliding by – though the view is somewhat marred by a metal monstrosity on the other bank. There are 21 tastefully decorated bedrooms; some have a terrace, and all of them are nice and quiet. At €47–55, they're worth it. *10% discount on the room rate (except in Aug) on presentation of this guide.*

Olargues

34390

⌂ |●| Au fil de l'Eau

Rue du Moulin au Pont du Diable.
Ⓣand Ⓕ04.67.97.19.59
Ⓔlefildeleau@free.fr

Doubles €52 (breakfast incl.). Menu at €17. This used to be a former tannery on the river Jaur, nicely converted into a *maison d'hôte* with simple but spacious, bright and and pleasant bedrooms and into a country restaurant. Specialities on open fires or on a spit. Friendly service. Reservations only on Fri, Sat evening and Sun lunchtime. Crêperie open only in the afternoon in the summer.

Olonzac

34210

|●| Restaurant du Minervois "Bel"

Avenue d'Homps.
Ⓣ04.64.91.20.73
Closed *Sat and Sun evening except*

July–Aug; evenings mid-Oct to mid-April.

The first set menu at €10 (weekday lunchtimes) is quite delicious with its house terrine and a perfect omelette aux fines herbes. Other menus are €19–30, the last of which is spectacular. Specialities include duck foie gras with Muscat and crêpes with vanilla ice. The wine list has a particularly rich choice of regional vintages at good prices. A consistently good restaurant that deserves its popularity, perfect to get some strength back before tackling the climb towards Minerve and the Hauts Cantons, or walk back towards the Canal du midi.

Siran

34210 (10km NW)

La Villa d'Éléis***

Avenue du Château; it's in the village.
Ⓣ04.68.91.55.98 Ⓕ04.68.91.48.34
Ⓦwww.villadeleis.com
Closed *Tues and Wed Oct–April; Feb.*
Disabled access. TV. Car park.

An old country house which has been carefully restored. The twelve stylish rooms are quiet and spacious; doubles are €66–160 with shower/wc or bath. Breakfast €9.90. Marie-Hélène will greet you warmly and the cooking is full of southern sunshine. Bernard Lafuente is a talented young chef who has won critical acclaim. Set menus €25.50–39.50. The owners organize musical evenings in summer, including piano and flute recitals, and lead walks to help you learn about the wildlife and history of the area. *10% discount on the room rate in low season on presentation of this guide.*

Palavas-Les-Flots

34250

Hôtel du Midi**

191 av. Saint-Maurice; it's on the left bank.
Ⓣ04.67.68.00.53 Ⓕ04.67.68.53.97
Ⓦwww.hotel-palavas.com
Closed *15 Nov–31 March.* **TV. Car park.**

Don't expect the height of luxury but the rooms are clean, comfortable and they've just been refurbished. And with a bit of luck you might get a room with a sea view or overlooking the lagoon. Doubles €41–77. Half board, compulsory June–Sept, costs €47–66 per person. The restaurant is a pleasant surprise, with inventive, clean cuisine that's very affordable. Menus €12 and €18. Credit cards not accepted. *Free house apéritif or 10% discount on the room rate in low season on presentation of this guide.*

Les Alizés

6, bd. Joffre; on the left bank.
Ⓣ04.67.68.01.80 Ⓕ04.67.50.36.19
TV.

Doubles overlooking the lighthouse or the sea €94–109 (breakfast incl.). A charming and entirely refurbished hotel with a seaside décor right in the middle of town. The rooms are light, air-conditioned, sound-proofed and comfortable. The bathrooms are nicely equipped and decorated.

Au 10

Place du marché, rue Saint-Roch (Centre).
Ⓣ04.67.68.57.41
Closed *Mon out of season.*

Menus €11–21. The owner is Belgian, hence an impressive selection of beers, and an authentic and tasty *moules-frites*. The wine menu is pretty impressive too with a good selection of local wines. A restaurant with a friendly atmosphere where you can relax on a lovely shaded terrace. Every Wednesday morning the market takes over the whole street which adds extra charm.

Le Petit Lezard

63 av. de l'Etang-du-Grec; very close to the embankments.
Ⓣ04.67.50.55.55
Closed *Mon and Tues (lunchtime only in the summer).*

Weekday lunchtime menu at €11 ; others at €17 and €22. A good retaurant for those who like grilled fish *a la plancha*, even though it has also a pizzeria. Lots of different dishes on the menu. The fish of the day is always very fresh and the vegetables cooked in olive oil just delicious. As for deciding between the dining room, the conservatory or the terrace, it's down to you and the time of the day.

La Rotisserie Palavasienne

Rue de l'Église.
Ⓣ04.67.68.52.12
Closed *lunchtimes; Sun; Mon out of season; Jan.*

A place that made its reputation by word of mouth. The restaurant was the brainchild of a local man who wanted to provide cuisine that was typical of his area. The dishes are different each day because he uses only fresh produce; the fish cooked in salt water is particularly good. Menus €19 and around €23 à la carte. *Free house apéritif on presentation of this guide.*

Perpignan

66000

Auberge de jeunesse**

Allée Marc-Pierre parc de la Pépinière; halfway beween the station and the haulage depot, behind the police station.
Ⓣ04.68.34.63.32 Ⓕ04.68.51.16.02
Ⓦwww.fuaj.org
Closed *20 Dec–20 Jan.*

Dormitories of four–eight bunk beds. One night costs €11.90 (breakfast incl.). Youth hostel card compulsory. Set in a big traditional house swathed with a luxurious bougainvillea on its front, it is one of the oldest youth hostels in France. The downside is that there are only 49 places available. Very clean. Kitchen and linen available. A shame the *voie rapide* is at the back..

Avenir Hôtel*

11 rue de l'Avenir.
Ⓣ04.68.34.20.30 Ⓕ04.68.34.15.63
Ⓦwww.avenirhotel.com
Closed *Sun and public holidays noon–6pm.* **Pay car park.**

A pleasing hotel in a quiet street not far from the station. The rooms are simple but well maintained and nicely decorated. Prices are reasonable: doubles with basin €19–21, with shower €28–34. A few very big rooms for families (for up to 5 people) are also available and cost €46. No. 18 has a pretty terrace. Vacationing American students sometimes stay here, as do trainees on work placements. It has a homely atmosphere and there's a sunny terrace on the first floor where you eat breakfast. It's a place to enjoy the sun and the peace and quiet. Use of a garage in the next street costs €4.50 per night.

Hôtel de la Poste et de la Perdrix**

6 rue Fabriques-Nabot; it's between pl. du Castillet and the quai Sadi-Carnot.
Ⓣ04.68.34.42.53 Ⓕ04.68.34.58.20
Closed *7 Feb–16 March. Restaurant closed Sun evening; Mon.* **TV.**

A beautiful, characterful hotel dating from 1832. The sign bears the patina of age, the marble foyer and the gleaming old staircase are delightful and the period stained-glass windows are lovely. The pleasantly old-fashioned bedrooms are well maintained and reasonably priced: doubles with basin €34, with shower/wc or bath €40–43. Simple food is served in a dining room where time seems to have stood still. Weekday lunchtime menu at €10; the other is at €18. You'll spend around €20 à la carte. It has a few good regional specialities: guinea-fowl *à la catalane*, sirloin with old Banyuls wine and crème catalane. *10% discount (except July/Aug) on presentation of this guide.*

Park Hôtel-restaurant Le Chapon Fin***

18 bd. Jean-Bourrat; it's two minutes from the tourist office, opposite square Bir-Hakeim.
Ⓣ04.68.35.14.14. Ⓕ04.68.35.48.18
Ⓦwww.parkhotel-fr.com
Restaurant closed *Sun; Ist fortnight in Jan; last fortnight in Aug.* **Disabled access. TV. Car park.**

The amazing luxury and reasonable prices on offer belie this hotel's dull modern frontage. The bedrooms are decorated in Spanish Renaissance style and have numerous mod cons, including air-conditioning. Double rooms with shower/wc or bath cost €65–95. according to size and facilities. The restaurant is one of the best in town. The chef is especially good at "duos" of meat and fish, and portions are truly huge. There's a good selection of wines. Weekday lunch menu €25 and others up to €48–100. À la carte, dishes are pricey but perfect. *10% discount (week-end) on the room rate on presentation of this guide.*

Hôtel-restaurant Villa Duflot****

Rond-point Albert-Donnezan. It's two minutes from the Perpignan toll booth, towards Argelès.
Ⓣ04.68.56.67.67 Ⓕ04.68.56.54.05
Ⓦwww.villaduflot.com
Disabled access. TV. Swimming pool. Highchairs available. Car park.

If you're planning to stay in Perpignan

itself there are better options (the surroundings here aren't very attractive), but if all you want is a night of luxury on the way to Spain, it's well worth stopping. The rooms (€105–135) have been furnished with enchanting taste – ask for one overlooking the swimming pool rather than the dreary industrial park. The restaurant tends towards modern cooking but also has traditional Catalan dishes, based on fresh seasonal produce. There's a nice selection of Roussillon wines. Weekdays business menu at €31 including wine, weekend gastronomic menu also at €31 (wine incl.). À la carte around €39.

Al Très

3 rue de la Poissonnerie.
Ⓣand Ⓕ04.68.34.88.39
Closed *Sun; Mon lunchtime 15 June–15 Sept; Mon evening rest of the year; a fortnight in Nov; a fortnight in Feb.*

The décor in the dining room has a fresh new look but there's still plenty of old Provence and Catalonia in the sun-drenched cuisine. Good value generally, with a €10 weekday lunch *formule* and a menu for €26; you'll pay around €32 à la carte. Good Catalan specialities and excellent desserts. The wine list features 150 wines from the region. There's a small terrace in the summer. This place is always buzzing with people. *Free house apéritif on presentation of this guide.*

Bistrot Le Saint-Jean

1 cité Bartissol.
Ⓣ04.68.51.22.25
Closed *Sun and Mon evening out of season; Jan.*

The speciality here is substantial filled sandwiches on country bread. Plus good local cuisine at reasonable prices: excalivades, esqueizada of cod, broad beans in Catalan style and so on. Dish of the day €9, *formule* for €10.50 and menus €12–19. The dishes are accompanied by glasses of delicious wine chosen by the boss – he's a bit of an expert. This is the only bistro in Perpignan where you can drink a glass of Mass wine. Out of season, they hold wine tasting evenings. In summer there's a superb terrace flanked by the cathedral and the Campo Santo. *Free apéritif on presentation of this guide.*

Casa Sansa

3 rue Fabrique-Couverte.
Ⓣ04.68.34.21.84 Ⓕ04.68.35.19.65
Ⓦwww.casasansa.com

This local institution has been recently taken over by a young, energetic woman. Students, travellers and intellectuals hang out here in the large dining room, decorated with bright paintings, old photos and posters of the corrida. The cooking is Catalan, generous and simple with a few original touches. Menu €22 except Sun. *Free house apéritif on presentation of this guide.*

Le Sud

12 rue Louis-Bausil; take rue Élie-Delcros from the Palais des Congrès then turn left into the rue Rabelais. Rue Louis-Bausil is a continuation of that street.
Ⓣand Ⓕ04.68.34.55.71
Closed *Mon; lunchtimes; 1 Oct–31 March.*

This place, in Perpignan's Romany quarter, has a patio planted with scented bushes and jasmine flowers. The food is fragrant, too, with cumin, mint, coriander . . . and the delicacies on offer are a delight, combining the best from Provence, the Orient, Mexico, Greece and Catalonia. À la carte only – you'll pay around €30. Some evenings the local guitarists gather here. *Free house apéritif on presentation of this guide.*

Canet-en-Roussillon

66140 (11km E)

La Vigatanne

2 rue des Remparts.
Ⓣ04.68.73.16.30
Closed *Mon in winter.*

There are no set menus in this lovely place, so you should expect to spend around €30 on dinner. An old farm building with thick stone walls, it's near the château and well away from the bucket-and-spade crowds. The décor is madly exuberant, with a miniature yellow train that chugs around the ceiling. There's a blonde on the balcony and a giant sandal, too. . . The food is of high quality and astonishingly fresh – grills are prepared before your eyes on the open fire next to where the old-fashioned fresh loaves are piled up. Taken together these elements create something very special – a kind of gastronomic theatre. Best to book, especially in winter.

Canet-Plage

66140 (12km E)

Le Clos des Pins - Le Bistro Fleuri***

34 av. du Roussillon.
Ⓣ04.68.80.32.63 Ⓕ04.68.80.49.19
Ⓦwww.closdespins.com
Closed *Nov–Feb; Tues in Oct.* **Restaurant closed lunchtime. TV. Swimming pool. Car park.**

In the restaurant the savoury cuisine is light, creative and skilful. There's no cheese on the menu, but you could try asking nicely. There's just one menu at €27. They serve regional wines. In fine weather you eat in the gorgeous garden. Quality air-conditioned rooms also available; doubles are €110–140, breakfast included, or a little cheaper out of season. *10% on the room rate in April, May and Oct, or free house apéritif or free coffee on presentation of this guide.*

La Rascasse

38 bd. Tixador; it's parallel to the seafront.
Ⓣ04.68.80.20.79
Closed *Mon and Thurs April–June; lunchtimes July–Sept (except Sun).*

This is a very well-known fish restaurant as well as a wonderful and untouched example of Vieille France. All the fish, shellfish and seafood are gloriously fresh and the dishes are delicately prepared. Try the crème catalane for dessert. Reasonably priced menus €18–29, and affordable wines. Service is friendly and efficient.

Banyuls-dels-Aspres

66300 (15km S)

Domaine de Nidolières

It's on the N9 Perpignan–Le Boulou road.
Ⓣ04.68.05.81.47 Ⓕ04.68.05.85.80

A lovely little inn among the vineyards. The building doesn't look much from outside and the pseudo-rustic décor won't exactly blow you away. Hold on, though – the cooking and the wine are superb. Try, for example, the roast rabbit with their own red wine. And the helpings are huge. Local speciality menu at €28. *Free house apéritif or free coffee on presentation of this guide.*

Saint-Paul-de-Fenouillet

66220 (33km NW)

Relais des Corbières

10 av. Jean Moulin. Take the D117.
Ⓣ04.68.89.23.89 Ⓕ04.68.59.03.04
Closed *Sun evening and Mon, except July/August.* **Highchairs and games available.**

What a wonderful place – despite its location, right next to the road and the level crossing (there's one train a day at 8.30 in the morning). The rooms are big and well maintained; doubles go for €36–50 depending on facilities. The restaurant serves straightforward regional dishes and the *patronne* can't do enough for you. (And that in itself makes up for the location.) In the evening, indulge yourself with a glass of Maury on the terrace and enjoy the play of the fountains. Menus €14–39.

Pézenas

34120

La Pomme d'Amour

2 [bis] rue Albert-Paul-Allies; it's near the tourist office.
Ⓣ04.67.98.08.40
Closed *Mon and Tues evening except in summer; Jan–Feb.*

This is a pleasant little restaurant in an old stone building in the picturesque old part of town. Good, simple cooking and traditional local dishes. They have a few specialities such as mussels in garlic cream sauce, salmon with saffron and tiramisù. Weekday lunch menu at €8; others at €15 and €20. You'll get a friendly welcome.

Les Marronniers

6 av. de Verdun; from Agde or Béziers, right at the outskirts.
Ⓣ04.67.90.13.80
Closed *Sun and Mon.*

À la carte €17–22. Popular restaurant with a pretty décor and a friendly service. The clientèle is mostly local. The cooking is good and hearty: saucisson or more refined tapas. Relaxed atmosphere in the dining room or on the terrace outside under the chestnut trees. Good local wines €12–30. Generally good value.

Pont-de-Montvert (Le)

48220

La Truite Enchantée

On the main road that goes through the village.
Ⓣ04.66.45.80.03
Closed *11 Nov–15 March; 15 Dec–15 March.* **Car park.**

The hotel, run by Corinne and Edgard, has eight basic rooms which are bright, clean and spacious – they cost €25 with shower (wc on the landing). Half-board €31.50 per person. Choose those overlooking the river Tarn or the garden. Good, hearty, regional cooking is served in the dining room next to the kitchen. Set menus €13.50–22: typical dishes include salmon with sorrel or rabbit *à la royale*. Booking advised for both hotel and restaurant. *Free coffee on presentation of this guide.*

Masméjean

48220 (7km E)

Chez Dedet

Take the D998 Pont de Montvert–Saint-Maurice-de-Ventalon road, then turn left after 5km, just before the bridge, then follow directions to Masméjean.
Ⓣ04.66.45.81.51 Ⓕ04.66.45.80.91
Closed *Wed and evenings out of season; last 10 days June; last 10 days Nov.*

The food here is out of this world. It's a real country restaurant in an old farm building with enormous beams, walls made out of great slabs of stone and a hearth you could roast an ox in. They use pigs, sheep and poultry from the family farm and get their snails, trout and mushrooms from local suppliers; in season, the wild boar and hare are also sourced from the area. Set menus €11 (weekday lunchtimes only) and up to €23. The service is perfect. Credit cards aren't accepted and booking is advisable, especially on Sunday and in winter. *Free coffee on presentation of this guide.*

Vialas

48220 (18km E)

Hostellerie Chantoiseau***

Take the D998.
Ⓣ04.66.41.00.02 Ⓕ04.66.41.04.34
Closed *Tues evening; Wed; Oct–30 April.* **TV. Swimming pool.**

A pleasant combination of smart and rustic décor in this former coaching inn which offers authentic local cuisine of high quality. Patrick Pagès knows and loves this part of the world, its wild valleys, mushrooms, chestnut trees, its fish and its game. The gourmet restaurant is a must, and has one of the region's best wine cellars. Try the *moche* (pork sausage with cabbage, potatoes and prunes), the saucisse d'herbes, the *pompétou* of trout or the *coupétade*. Menus €22–66. Double rooms with shower/wc are €46, or €69 with bath; you'll feel almost as if you are staying in someone's home. Credit cards not accepted. *Free coffee on presentation of this guide.*

St-Étienne-du-Valdonnez

48000 (27km NW)

Auberge des Laubies

Take the D35 to the col du Montmirat, then the N106 for 4km in the direction of Saint-Bauzile.
Ⓣ04.66.48.01.25
Hotel closed *Nov–May. Restaurant closed mid-Dec to Easter.*

A lovely place in an isolated hamlet on the plateau of Mont Lozère, which is magnificent and totally tree-less. The inn is run by a local family. Copious helpings of local dishes (potatoes with bacon), that are cheap as anything. Menus €11–17 (€19.50 on Sundays). Double rooms €25 with basin. Half board for €26 per person. It's an amazing place to talk, to meditate or just dream. You can also fish or go on walks. *Free apéritif on presentation of this guide.*

Pont-Saint-Esprit

30130

Auberge Provençale**

Route de Bagnols-sur-Cèze; take the N86 as you leave the village.
Ⓣ04.66.39.08.79 Ⓕ04.66.39.14.28
Closed *Sun evening Oct–March; 24 Dec–1 Jan.* **Highchairs available. Car park.**

This inn looks far better inside than out. The same family has run it for more than forty years, cheerfully welcoming travellers, long-distance lorry drivers, families and local worthies alike. They serve large portions of honest traditional food in the two large and air-conditioned dining rooms. The cheapest set menu sets the tone: charcuterie, crudités, a dish of the day, seasonal vegetables, cheese platter and fresh fruit or ice-cream. Menus €10–14.50. Gigondas and Tavel are served by the glass and reasonably priced. Rooms with shower/wc or bath cost €27.50; the ones that overlook the courtyard are more peaceful.

Lou Récati

6 rue Jean-Jacques.
04.66.90.73.01
Closed *Sun evening; Mon.*

"Lou Récati" is a local term to describe those little mounds of furniture or clothing thrown together to save them from the floodwaters of the Rhône. It's a rather wonderful name for a restaurant run by a talented young chef who produces delicate, skilfully cooked dishes. The prices are fair considering his professionalism: weekday lunch menu €12 and others at €21 and €31. They list such dishes as snail ravioli, duck with pan-fried artichokes and peas and, for dessert, an unrivalled *crème brûlée* scented with lavender. It's a real treat to dine here. *Free coffee on presentation of this guide.*

Aiguèze

30760 (10km NW)

Résidence Le Castelas**

It's in the village: from Pont-Saint-Esprit, take the N86 for Montélimar then turn left onto the D901.
04.66.82.18.76 04.66.82.14.98
www.residencelecastelas.com
Closed *Jan–Feb.* **Swimming pool. Car park.**

Le Castelas enjoys a remarkable location in a hillside village overlooking the Ardèche. It also has some remarkable qualities of its own: the rooms are all within the ancient castle walls, and are charmingly decorated and fitted with small corner kitchens. You can stay in the main residence near the first swimming pool where the rooms have terraces and views over the gorges of the Ardèche; the annexe, just two streets away, has another pool. The owner is polite and attentive. Double rooms with shower/wc or bath go for €57–70 depending on the season; studios and flats available for rent. Good buffet breakfast. They'll lend you a bicycle and tell you where to go, or advise on hiring a canoe. *Free house apéritif on presentation of this guide.*

Bagnols-sur-Cèze

30200 (15km S)

Hôtel Bar des Sports**

3 pl. Jean-Jaurès; take the N86 from Pont-Saint-Esprit in the direction of Nîmes.
04.68.89.61.68 04.66.89.92.97
TV. Pay car park.

This is a serious place which deserves its two stars: it offers delightful, clean, comfortable double rooms with shower/wc or bath and double glazing for €44. The owner is very kind, and it's quiet at night, even when the bar is open. *Free car park at the week-end (except July/Aug) on presentation of this guide.*

Prades

66500

Le Jardin d'Aymeric

3 av. du Général-de-Gaulle; it's opposite the lorry park.
04.68.96.53.38 04.68.96.08.72
Closed *Sun evening; Mon; Feb school holidays; last week in June; lst week July.*
Disabled access.

A small restaurant with a warm dining room where excellent cuisine is served. It's often full, so consider booking. The generously flavoured regional cooking uses fresh produce, so the menus change regularly. Dish of the day €9.50 (weekday lunchtimes) and menus €17–29. They serve regional wines – and the house wine is as good as some on the wine list. For an apéritif, try a small glass of Banyuls white. Speedy, energetic service from smiling, chatty waiting staff. *Free house apéritif on presentation of this guide.*

Vinça

66320 (9km NE)

La Petite Auberge

74 av. du Général-de-Gaulle; it's on the N116 in the direction of Prades.
04.68.05.81.47 04.68.05.85.80
Closed *Wed; Sun evening; Tues evening Sept–June; Christmas–New Year.* **Highchairs available. Disabled access.**

A nice little inn – as the name suggests.

The chef is chatty, and the cuisine he prepares is as straightforward and generous as he is. Tasty, characterful dishes on menus €14–30. The first menu is reliable, starting with a hors d'œuvre buffet or plate of cooked ham and followed by the dish of the day. It's all simple and good. There are a few basic rooms – €20 with basin, €30 with shower/wc. *Free house apéritif on presentation of this guide.*

Prats-de-Mollo

66230

Hôtel des Touristes**

Avenue du Haut-Vallespir; it's on the right as you arrive in the village on the road from Arles-sur-Teche.
Ⓣ04.68.39.72.12 Ⓕ04.68.39.79.22
Ⓦwww.hotel.lestouristes.free.fr
Closed *31 Oct–1 April.* **Disabled access. TV. Highchairs and games available. Car park.**

This solidly built stone hotel is an ideal spot from which to explore the wild, mountainous Vallespir region. The rooms are well maintained; doubles cost €26–33 with basin/wc or €45–48 with shower/wc or bath. Some have balconies, others little terraces, and the ones at the back have a view of the river. In the huge dining room they serve traditional family-style dishes. Menus €16–33 or à la carte. Breakfast €7.40. *Free house apéritif or one free breakfast per room (in April and October).*

Quillan

11500

Hôtel Le Cartier et Restaurant Les Trois Quilles

31 bd. Charles-de-Gaulle (Centre).
Ⓣ04.68.20.05.14 Ⓕ04.68.20.22.57
Ⓔhot.car@wanadoo.fr

Doubles €41–54. Menus €15–23. Child's menu €8. Comfortable rooms; those overlooking the street are soundproofed. Very good local cuisine right through from the starters to the desserts. Try especially the regional soup *à la rouzole*, made with vegetables, eggs and meatballs...Complete the meal with the mouth-watering chocolate and citrus fruit fudge cake. Friendly service too.

Gincla

11140 (27 km SE)

Hostellerie du Grand Duc

2 rue de Boucheville; take the D117 and follow directions towards Axat and Puilaurens; turn right onto the D22 towards Gincla; the Castle of Puilaurens is 5 km away.
Ⓣ04.68.20.55.02 Ⓕ04.68.20.61.22
Ⓦwww.host.du.grandduc.com
Closed *Wed lunchtime except July–Aug; 3 Nov–1 April.*

Doubles €57–62. Menus €27–57, à la carte around €35. Beautiful mansion set in a lovely garden with a pond. The rooms are decorated in a country style with slightly old-fashioned wallpapers. Good traditional cuisine: duck, pear with cinnamon and good local wines too.

Roquefort-des-Corbières

11540

Le Lézard Bleu

Rue de l'Église.
Ⓣ04.68.48.51.11
Closed *Oct–June. Disabled access.*

The lizard signs outside direct you to this restaurant with the blue door. Inside, the walls are white and hung with modern paintings. The food is lovingly prepared by the owner, a friendly woman who's full of life. Menus from €16.50 (lunchtime only) to €21.50 and €40, though the dessert servings are a bit small for the price. It's best to book.

Saint-André-de-Valborgne

30940

Hôtel-restaurant Bourgade**

Place de l'Église.
Ⓣ04.66.60.30.72 Ⓕ04.66.60.31.25
Ⓔpicoboo@compuserve.com
Closed *Mon-Thur Sept-June; Jan–Feb.*
TV.

This place started as a posthouse in the seventeenth century and has been in the family for generations. The latest lot have shaken out all the cobwebs and offer an enthusiastic welcome. Simple, charming rooms overlook the church square or the stream; doubles with shower/wc or bath €47–53. Flavourful and inspirational cuisine by a chef who did part of his apprenticeship with the great Ducasse. He makes lots of regional dishes using fresh produce, and has kept his grandmother's famous crayfish dish on the menu. Set menus from €17 (weekday lunchtimes).

Saint-Guilhem-le-Désert

34150

|●| L'Auberge sur Le Chemin

38 rue Font-du-Portal, in the heart of the village.
☎04.67.57.75.05
Closed *Wed out of season.*

Menus €23–42. Olivier Crossay has come a long way before opening this village restaurant and he has created a real surprise. The décor of the dining room is imposing with its eleventh and twelfth century vaults. A few touches of colour and a few modern paintings here and there bring it into the twenty-first century. Formerly trained with Bocuse, Olivier now works almost on his own in the kitchens, but the results are very impressive. Try the truffle soup and the cockerel in a puff pastry crust… Good choice of coffees too.

Saint-Mathieu-de-Tréviers

34270

|●| Restaurant La Cour

266 av. Louis-Cancel
☎04.67.55.37.97
Closed *lunchtime (Sun excluded) in the summer; Sat lunchtime, Sun evening and Mon 1 Sept–15 June.* **Highchairs available.**

Weekday lunchtime menu €16; others €38 and €47. After ten years in Mexico, Eric Tapié has come back with a new family and a longing to give a new lease of life to traditional Mediterranean cooking. Like Michel Bras, he likes to use good quality products for his cooking. Try especially the deliciously cooked market vegetables marinated in olive oil and coriander that accompany the roasted monkfish and fried potatoes with aïoli. To complete the meal the pan-fried warm peaches flavoured with vanilla and lavender flowers served with an iced Pic-Saint-Loup *sabayon* is also a nice surprise. Nice terrace in the courtyard. On-site *traiteur* selling home-cooked dishes and local products.

Saint-Pierre-des-Champs

11220

⌂ |●| Hôtel-restaurant La Fargo

☎04.68.43.12.78 Ⓕ04.68.43.29.20
Ⓦwww.chez.com/lafargo
Closed *Mon-Thur out of season.* **Car park.**

Doubles €58–64. Menus €24–24. This former Catalan forge, entirely renovated, enjoys delightful views over mountains, orchards and lavender bushes. Only six rooms that are elegantly decorated and furnished with a mixture of Indonesian and family pieces. On the beds are displayed beautiful batiks from the Asian island of Sonde. Each room is named after a tree in honour of Mother Nature. The cooking has subtle Mediterranean flavours and changes according to season. Pets not admitted.

Saint-Saturnin-de-Lucian

34725

⌂ |●| Ostalaria Cardabela

10 pl. de la Fontaine; take the D130 and it's in the centre of the village.
☎04.67.88.62.62 Ⓕ04.67.88.62.82
Ⓔostalaria.cardabela@wanadoo.fr
Closed *Nov to mid-March.*
TV.

A lovely place if you like your creature comforts – enjoy the gorgeous, cosy rooms and big beds with Egyptian cotton sheets. Great care is taken over everything, starting with the welcome. Rooms €65–85. Breakfast €10. The restaurant is called *Le Mimosa*, and it's to be found in Saint-Giraud 2km away. It's an equally stylish place in a charming old house; one menu only at €48. The cuisine is flavoursome and full of creativity and poetry.

|●| Le Pressoir de Saint-Saturnin

17 pl. de la Fontaine.
☎04.67.88.67.89

Closed *Wed evening; Sat lunchtime; 2 Jan–13 Feb.*

It would be easy to fall in love with this authentic Languedoc inn, which has a great atmosphere in the dining room and on the terrace. You'll find some dishes prepared to very old recipes like the *escoubille* stew simmered in local red wine. Make sure you try the melting cheese croquettes and the free-range lamb or beef grilled over the wood fire. Dish of the day €9; otherwise menus at €16.50 and €25. There's a good selection of regional wines. *Free house apéritif on presentation of this guide.*

Saint-Jean-de-la-Blaquière

34700 (7 km E)

Hôtel-restaurant Le Sanglier

Domaine de Cambourras.
Ⓣ04.67.44.70.51 Ⓕ04.67.44.72.33.
Ⓦwww.logassist.frsanglier
Closed *20 Oct–1 April.* **Car park. TV.**

Doubles €66–86. Breakfast €9. Menus €16–36. Handsome hotel situated in the middle of the heathland. Ten quiet and comfortable rooms on the first and top floors. The dining room is a former sheep pen, quite common around here! Tasty dishes served in the garden or on the terrace in the summer. Wild boar dishes are of course plentiful on the menu. Impressive choice of wines. Lots of walks to do in the area, starting with a walk along the red canyon right next to the hotel.

Sauve

30610

Chez La Marthe

20 rue Mazan; it's near the town hall.
Ⓣ04.66.77.06.72
Ⓦwww.vallee-vidourle.com/heberge /marthe-htm
Closed *Sun evening; Mon.*

Marthe was a woman who ran the local grocery more than two decades ago and the restaurant named after her has been delightfully decorated in local style. Weekday lunch menu €11, with others at €18.50 and €22. Dishes include pieds-paquets (lamb tripe and trotters) and Cévenole salad. They have a habit of closing unexpectedly in winter, so check in advance. In summer you should call in order to guarantee a table! *Free coffee on presentation of this guide.*

Sète

34200

Le P'tit Mousse*

Rue de Provence; it's in the Corniche area, 100m from the beach.
Ⓣ04.67.53.10.66

A bright ochre building in a quiet little street off the Corniche, very close to the sea. The rooms are clean and good value. Doubles around €28 with basin, €33.50 with shower/wc. Breakfast €4.70. Half board is compulsory in July and Aug, and costs around €30 per person per night. Simple cooking and homely atmosphere, with set menus at €12.20 and €21.

Hôtel Venezia

Les Jardins de la Mer La Corniche; near pl. Édouard-Herriot.
Ⓣ04.67.51.39.38 Ⓕ04.67.74.15.05
Ⓦwww.hotel-sete.com
Closed *Dec–Jan.* **Car park. TV.**

Doubles €42–52 depending on the season. A good family hotel with eighteen quiet and well-equipped rooms that have all been refurbished (all with terrace and television). Car park available for each room, quite unusual in the area. Very friendly welcome. And the beach is only 50m away. No restaurant.

Le Grand Hôtel***

17 quai de Lattre-de-Tassigny.
Ⓣ04.67.74.71.77
Ⓦwww.hotel-sete.com
Closed *20 Dec–4 Jan.* **TV. Pay car park.**

This magnificent hotel was built in the 1880s, and it hasn't lost a trace of character. It's spacious and filled with period furniture, and there's a striking patio with a glass roof – a great place to eat breakfast. Rooms with shower/wc €65–85 or bath €85–120. Breakfast €8. Service is faultless, as befits a grand hotel. Its restaurant, *La Rotonde*, is the finest in town and is just around the corner.

Les Terrasses du Lido***

Rond-point de l'Europe-La Corniche.

Ⓣ04.67.51.39.60 Ⓕ04.67.51.28.90
Closed *Sun evening and Mon out of season.*
Disabled access. Swimming pool. TV. Car park.

Everything's just right in this hotel, from the décor of the rooms to the friendly welcome and the creative cooking. There are only nine bedrooms painted in a relaxing pale blue colour, so it's advisable to book well in advance; doubles with bath €70–84. Breakfast €9. Half board is compulsory in high season at €70–82 per person. You will enjoy the terrace by the pool and the hotel is only 300m away from the beach. The goumet cooking is original and includes local specialities as well as creations from the new chef Philippe Mouls, who only uses fresh seasonal ingredients, so the menus change often. Philippe is particularly renowned for his flavoursome and tasty fish and seafood dishes. Try the delicious lasagna of oysters with tomato and basil or the monkish fillets with squid served with a black ink parmesan risotto. Service is faultless too. Advance booking advised.

L'Oranger

5 pl. de la Mairie (Centre).
Ⓣ04.67.51.96.12
Closed *Mon and Tues except public holidays; Jan*

Menus €14–25. Near pl. du Pouffre, with a refined country décor, this restaurant is owned by a couple who know their trade well. While he serves in the dining room in a relaxed and competent manner, she prepares delicious and well-presented octopus bruschettas with aïoli and a tasty monkfish Provençal soup. Good selection of apéritifs and local wines. Advance booking advised.

Le Marie-Jean

26 quai Général Durand.
Ⓣ04.67.46.02.01
Closed *Mon lunchtime; Mon out of season; Feb.*

A really good table which suggests that this quayside, once the pride of the town, might have an interesting future – if only it were possible to get rid of the tourist traps lining the front. Gourmet specialities here: *bouillabaisse*, tuna *carpaccio*, sardine tartare, stuffed squid Sétoise, fresh fish grilled over the coals. Weekday menu €17 and others €22.50–38. The décor is quite smart, the service stylish.

Bouzigues

34140 (15km N)

Chez la Tchèpe

Avenue Louis-Tudesq; it's on the bank of the étang de Thau.
Ⓣand Ⓕ04.67.78.33.19
Closed *Wed; Jan. Disabled access.*

This little terrace catches the eye; apart from anything else, it's often chock-a-block. There are lots of places in this area where everything comes straight from the sea to the table, but this one offers the best value for money. You can get two dozen oysters, a dozen mussels, one violet (a small sea creature from the Mediterranean which is eaten raw and looks rather like scrambled eggs), two warm tielles (a small squid soufflé with tomato sauce) for €20, €28 with wine – and that's for two people. There are no menus – you just choose what you want from the display. Eat in or take away, and service at all hours of the day.

Sommières

30250

L'Olivette

11 rue Abbé-Fabre.
Ⓣ04.66.80.97.71 Ⓕ04.66.80.39.28
Closed *Tues in season; Tues evening and Wed out of season; Jan.*

They certainly know how to make you feel welcome here. The dining room is wonderful, with stone walls and wooden beams and it's air-conditioned. There's a lunch *formule* at €12 (starter plus main or main plus dessert), and menus €16–29. Much of the cuisine is local – snails, salt cod with tapenade – with a few flavours from further afield. *Free tasting of tapenade (home-made olive paste) on presentation of this guide.*

Sorède

66690

La Salamandre

3 rte. de Larroque.
Ⓣand Ⓕ04.68.89.26.67
Closed *Sun evening–Tues lunchtime; Mon and Tues lunchtime only in high season; 7 Jan–15 March; 15 Nov–1 Dec.*

The dining room is on the small side and, curiously, lacks intimacy, but the cuisine simply has to be tried. It's full of originality and combines regional gastronomic recipes with lesser-known ones. The results are delicate and flavoursome. Menus, €16 and €22, change regularly to make the most of seasonal produce. This is a really good place. Incidentally, a "salamandre" is the upper arch of the oven where you place dishes to caramelize them.

Uzès

30700

Hôtel Saint-Géniès**

Quartier Saint-Géniès; it's 1.5 km from the town centre in the direction of Saint-Ambroix.
Ⓣ04.66.22.29.99 Ⓕ04.66.03.14.89
Ⓔsaintgenies2@wanadoo.fr
Closed *mid-Nov–early March.* **Swimming pool. Games available. Car park.**

New hotel in a quiet residential district. There are twenty tastefully decorated bedrooms. The ones up in the roof have sloping ceilings, which makes them feel more intimate. Nos. 20 and 27 have balconies overlooking the garden and pool. Doubles €46–52 with shower/wc or bath. They offer a set meal, €14, if you don't want to venture back into town (not served on Sun). *Free coffee.*

Hôtel d'Entraigues - Restaurant Les Jardins de Castille***

Place de l'Évêché; it's opposite the historic bishop's palace and the cathedral of Saint-Théodorit.
Ⓣ04.66.22.14.48 Ⓕ04.66.22.57.01
Ⓦwww.lcm.fr/savry/
Disabled access. TV. Swimming pool. Car park.

This stylish, charming establishment is spread across a group of town houses from the fifteenth, seventeenth and eighteenth centuries. The 30 air-conditioned bedrooms and apartments are furnished in classic style, and some have a private terrace. Doubles €55–152, depending on the season and facilities. Half-board compulsory in July and August. The restaurant has a panoramic terrace and an elegant dining room. Menus, which change with each season, are €22–49 – though you can always rely on the inspired Provençal cuisine. *10% discount on room rate (except July/Aug) or free house apéritif on presentation of this guide.*

Hôtel-restaurant La Taverne**

4–9 rue Xavier-Sigalon; it's near the cinema.
Ⓣ04.66.22.13.10 Ⓕ04.66.22.47.08
Ⓔlataverne.uzes@wanadoo.fr
Closed *Christmas.* **TV.**

The pleasant garden in the small courtyard provides a quiet setting for your meal, though sometimes it's overrun by groups. The owner knows the town like the back of his hand, so he's a good source of information. Good tasty cooking. Menus €20.50–22. They do *confit*, breast of duck and *cassoulet*, and excellent scrambled eggs with truffles. The hotel is a few metres further on and provides quiet rooms – particularly at the back. They're all different and some have beamed ceilings and stone walls from the original house. €60–85 for doubles with shower/wc or bath, depending on the season.

Le Bistrot du Grézac

Place Belle-Croix.
Ⓣ04.66.03.42.09 Ⓕ04.66.03.62.45
Closed *Mon.*

Just next to the Saint-Étienne church, this brand-new, old-style bistro has been brilliantly done up – when it's aged a little it will be perfect. The simple, delicious cuisine is Provençal in style. Menus from €12 (weekday lunchtime) to €20. Easy-going, efficient service. Sadly, the terrace is just too close to the road for comfort. *Free coffee on presentation of this guide.*

Terroirs

5 pl. aux Herbes.
Ⓣ04.66.03.41.90
Closed *Feb; 11–30 Nov.*

This restaurant is on the loveliest square in town. It's the extension of a food and wine shop selling local specialities (oil, tapenade, herbs, honey). Dominique Becasse, the owner, travelled widely before settling in Uzès, his adoptive home. He serves only quality produce that's meticulously chosen, yet his prices are fair. This is the best of southern cooking, natural and healthy: pesto, pelardon and delicious platters. Around €12–20 per meal.

Vers-Pont-du-Gard

30210 (10km SE)

La Bégude Saint-Pierre

Les Coudoulières; it's on the D98.
Ⓣ04.66.63.63.63 Ⓕ04.66.22.73.73
Ⓦwww.hotel-saintpierre.fr
Closed *Sun evening and Mon Nov–30 March.* **Disabled access. TV. Swimming pool. Car park.**

"Bégude" is the Provençal word for a farm that doubled as a posthouse way back when letters were carried on horseback. Times may have changed but fortunately the road that goes past isn't busy. The beautiful seventeenth-century building has been carefully restored and decorated with Provençal prints. The rooms look onto the coachyard or the swimming pool; they're air-conditioned and individually decorated. Doubles or suites with bath €54–120 depending on the season. The chic restaurant serves cuisine of Provençal pedigree and has menus from €29. *Free house apéritif on presentation of this guide.*

Valcebollière

66340

Auberge Les Écureuils***

Take the N116 and the D30 from bourg Madame.
Ⓣ04.68.04.52.03 Ⓕ04.68.04.52.34
Ⓔauberge-ecureuils@wanadoo.fr
Closed *15 Oct–20 Dec.* **TV. Swimming pool. Highchairs and games available. Car park.**

This cosy inn, built of solid wood and stone, lies deep in the heart of Cerdagne near the Spanish border. Étienne Laffitte's creativity blossoms in the kitchen, where he conjures up hearty dishes based on local produce. Set menus €18 at lunchtime and €25–45 in the evenings. Breakfast €9–11. Dishes include hot duck foie gras with apples and honey, duck breast with ceps or morels, braised lamb fillet and hot *millefeuille* with fresh fruit. Comfortable bedrooms with shower/wc or bath go for €56–95. There's a gym, a sauna and pool tables. You can go on beautiful walks up the mountain, which is 2500m high and towers over the hotel. In the winter there's downhill skiing or snow-shoe hikes.

Vigan (Le)

30120

Hôtel du Commerce*

26 rue des Barris; it's next to the police station.
Ⓣ04.67.81.03.28 Ⓕ04.67.81.43.20
Car park.

This quiet, cheap hotel is just away from the middle of the village and it's a great base from which to explore the area. Bright, simple, spacious and super-clean doubles cost €23 with basin, €30 with shower/wc or bath. There's a small garden.

Avèze

30120 (2km S)

L'Auberge Cocagne**

Place du Château; it's on the road to Cirque de Navacelles.
Ⓣ04.67.81.02.70 Ⓕ04.67.81.07.67
Closed *Dec; Jan.* **Disabled access. Highchairs available. Car park.**

In the south of France "cocagne" means "luck", and this typical country inn, shielded by a clump of trees, couldn't be more aptly named. It's a 400-year-old building with massive stone walls, red shutters and simple yet comfortable bedrooms. Doubles €27.85 with basin, €39.35–44.35 with shower/wc or bath. Half board is compulsory mid-July to mid-Aug and over long weekends and costs €35–44.35 per person. You get a warm welcome as well as cool jazz in the dining room. The place has personality and so has the home cooking which, typical for the Mediterranean, is drenched in olive oil and strewn with spices: terrine with sweet onion chutney, lamb from the Causse and vegetarian dishes. The vegetables are organic and the cheeses bought direct from the farmer. The wines and apéritifs come from local winegrowers. Set menus €12.85–29.85. *Free coffee on presentation of this guide.*

Mandagout

30120 (10km N)

Auberge de la Borie*

Take the D170; 9km along, turn right towards Mandagout, past the village, continue towards Saint-André-de-Majencoules, then follow a sloping street on the left for 250m.
Ⓣand Ⓕ04.67.81.06.03

Closed *Wed out of season; Jan; Feb; Dec.* **Disabled access. TV. Swimming pool.**

An old Cévennes *mas* on a sunny mountainside, with a swimming pool and breathtaking views over the mountains, the chestnut forests and the fig groves. There are ten nicely appointed rooms with old stone walls; doubles with basin are €28 or €50 with shower/wc or bath. Half board is compulsory in season and over long weekends. Nos. 8, 9 and 10 (with wc only), down in the ancient vaulted cellars, are wonderfully cool in summer. In the restaurant they serve home cooking based exclusively on local produce – specialities include foie gras with fig jam, frogs' legs with persillade. Set menus from €14.

Villefort

48800

Hôtel-restaurant du Lac**

Lac de Villefort; take the D906 for 1.5km and it's a white building all by itself on the left by the lake.
Ⓣ04.66.46.81.20 Ⓕ04.66.46.90.95
Closed *Tues evening and Wed except in July–Aug; Jan.* **TV. Highchairs available.**

The bedrooms all have a view of the lake, where you can swim in summer: doubles with shower/wc go for €43 or €58 with bath. Half-board €44 per person. In the restaurant you'll find regional specialities like cep omelette, trout *meunière*, veal *blanquette* and chestnut gâteau. Menus €14.50–23. It's very popular in high season, so it can get noisy. *Free coffee.*

Hôtel-restaurant Balme**

Place du Portalet; take the A75 and A6.
Ⓣ04.66.46.80.14 Ⓕ04.66.46.85.26
Closed *Sun evening and Mon out of season; mid-Nov–mid-Feb.* **TV. Highchairs available. Car park.**

A well-known place which has aged elegantly. It's somewhat reminiscent of a spa hotel – same type of comfort, same English atmosphere. The cuisine is excellent, combining local dishes and specialities from the East, especially Thailand. Menus €21–34; the meals are the best value for money in the region. Good choices include hot foie gras coated with poppy seeds, terrine of calves' head with cep oil or Thai curry with scented rice. The kitchen opens onto the dining room so you can follow what's going on, and since Micheline is a qualified sommelier, they've got a magnificent cellar. In the hotel, doubles go for €46 with shower/wc and €53 with bath. *10% discount on the room rate except in July and Aug.*

Villefranche-de-Conflent

66500

Auberge Saint-Paul

7 pl. de l'Église.
Ⓣand Ⓕ04.68.96.30.95
Ⓦwww.auberge.stpaul.free.fr
Closed *Mon; Sun evening out of season; Tues Oct to Easter; 3 weeks in Jan; a week in June; 10 days end Nov.*

Patricia Gomez has a remarkable culinary imagination: she combines unexpected flavours with top-quality ingredients and produces unforgettable dishes. Set menus €24.50–75; you'll pay around €45 à la carte. Brilliant wines selected by Charly Gomez. One of the best restaurants in the district, with a beautiful terrace to boot.

Olette

66360 (10km SW)

Hôtel-Restaurant La Fontaine

5 rue de la Fusterie.
Ⓣ04.68.97.03.67 Ⓕ04.68.97.09.18
Closed *Tues evening; Wed; Jan.* **TV. Highchairs available. Car park.**

A substantial building painted a brilliant salmon-pink. The rooms are attractive and have good facilities – good-value doubles with shower/wc €39–56. There's a terrace with three or four tables and a pretty dining room on the first floor where you can eat well-executed local dishes. Menus €13 (weekdays only) and €15–35. There's a friendly family atmosphere. *Free coffee on presentation of this guide.*

Villeneuve-lès-Avignon

30400

Centre de Rencontres International YMCA

7 bis, chemin de la Justice; from Avignon at the Royaume bridge, take the av.

Général-Leclerc towards Bellevue-aux-Angles, turn left into Chemin de la Justice after about 300m.
Ⓣ04.90.25.46.20 Ⓕ04.90.25.30.64
Ⓦwww.ymca-avignon.com
Closed *24 Dec–2 Jan.* **Car park.**

Doubles €22–26 with basin, €32–40 with shower/wc, depending on the season. Menu at €10. Set in completely renovated old buildings, the centre contains around 100 beds in rooms of three with wc. The swimming pool, bar and the breathtaking views over Avigon, the Rhône river, the mount Ventoux and Philippe-le-Bel tower make it a worth-while place to stay. Pretty wild atmosphere during the festival season!

Hôtel de l'Atelier**

5 rue de la Foire.
Ⓣ04.90.25.01.84 Ⓕ04.90.25.80.06
Ⓦwww. hoteldelatelier.com
Closed *4 Nov–20 Dec.* **TV. Car park.**

This is a quite delightful sixteenth-century building with 23 bedrooms, all of them different, furnished with antiques. Doubles with shower are €45–60 or €60–90 with bath. Breakfast at €7.50 (compulsory during the Avignon festival) is served in the dining room or on the patio, where plants and flowers proliferate, and there's a rooftop terrace and tea room. It's good value for money – you'd be wise to book in season. *10% discount on the room rate (Oct–March) from two consecutive nights on presentation of this guide.*

Restaurant La Maison

1 rue Montée-du-Fort-Saint-André; it's behind the town hall, overlooking pl. Jean-Jaurès.
Ⓣ04.90.25.20.81
Closed *Tues evening; Wed; Sat lunchtime; Aug.*

This restaurant is attractive to look at, with lace curtains, ceiling fans and a good-looking pottery collection. Simple cooking is served in generous portions: you get a good meal on the €20 menu. Absolutely delightful service.

Angles (Les)

30133 (4km S)

Le Petit Manoir**

15 av. Jules-Ferry; it's on the Nîmes road.
Ⓣ04.90.25.03.36 Ⓕ04.90.25.49.13
Closed *end Jan–early Feb.* **Disabled access. TV. Swimming pool. Highchairs available. Car park.**

This group of modern buildings set around a swimming pool is hardly what you'd call a manor. But the place is not without character or comfort – and most of the quiet, clean rooms have a private terrace. Doubles €42–57 with shower/wc or bath. The restaurant serves traditional, regional cuisine using fresh seasonal produce. Menus €17–46.

Roquemaure

30150 (11km N)

Le Clément V**

6 rue Pierre-Semard; take the D980.
Ⓣ04.66.82.67.58 Ⓕ04.66.82.84.66
Ⓦwww.hotel-clementv.fr.st
Closed *Sat and Sun out of season (except for reservations); 25 Oct–15 March.* **TV. Swimming pool. Highchairs available. Car park.**

A very nice place in a medieval village in the Côtes du Rhône which has so far eluded the tourists. It's in a 1970s-style house in a residential area; the rooms are conventional but they've been renovated with a touch of Provence. The ones overlooking the swimming pool have balconies but those at the back are larger and quieter. Doubles €52–56 with shower/wc. Half board, €45–49, is obligatory in summer. Menus €16–20 are available only to hotel residents. They list typical, simple local dishes. *10% discount on the room rate, except in July and Aug, for a minimum stay of two consecutive nights on presentation of this guide.*

Limousin

Argentat

19400

🏃 🏠 🍽 Hôtel-Restaurant Fouillade**

11 pl. Gambetta.
Ⓣ05.55.28.10.17 Ⓕ05.55.28.90.52
Closed *one week in Feb; 13 Nov–16 Dec.*
Restaurant closed *Mon out of season.*
Disabled access.TV. High chairs and cots available.

A beautiful house that's been running as a hotel-restaurant for two centuries. Scrumptious dishes include duck *confit* with chestnuts, ceps with sorrel butter, *millefeuille* of snails with girolle mushrooms and Grand Marnier soufflé. Menus €11.60 (not served Sun) and €31. Doubles with shower/wc €41. Breakfast €5.80. All the bedrooms have been renovated and there are two new family rooms. *Free coffee offered to our readers on presentation of this guide.*

Saint Julien-aux-Bois

(14km NE)

🏃 🏠 🍽 Auberge de St Julien-aux-Bois

Take the D980 or the scenic rte. des Écoliers.
Ⓣ05.55.24.41.94 Ⓕ05.55.28.37.85
Ⓦwww.auberge-saint-julien.com
Closed *Tues evening and Weds out of season; Weds lunch in July and Aug; 10 Feb–6 Mar.* **TV. High chairs and games available. Play area.**

This lost village on the edge of La Xaintrie and the Dordogne valley offers an unexpectedly pleasant surprise. Neither the village nor the restaurant look that appealing and even the décor in the dining room is ordinary – but it's the food that makes the place different. It's run by a German couple who fell in love with the area and decided to open a restaurant. Madame is the chef, and many of her delicious Limousin specialities have a touch of German cuisine about them: fillet of beef with cep cream, Atlantic matelote with green-corn sauce, daube of wild boar with cornflour pancakes. There are lots of rarely used cereals, herbs and vegetables and most of the ingredients are organic; the choice of cheeses is amazing. There are also some vegetarian dishes, and hearty German desserts. The menus offer excellent value for money: €13, then €16–39. A jug of good wine costs €5. Doubles with basin €27; doubles with bath/wc €35–49; no.5 leads out onto the garden. Breakfast €6. *Free apéritif or one free breakfast per person per night offered to our readers on presentation of this guide.*

Arnac-Pompadour

19230

🏠 🍽 Auberge de la Mandrie**

Route de Périgueux; 5km from Pompadour on the D7 going towards Payzac and Périgueux.
Ⓣ05.55.73.37.14 Ⓕ05.55.73.67.13
Ⓦwww.la-mandrie.com
Closed *Sun evening 1 Nov–31 March; Jan.*
TV. Swimming pool. Games available. Car park.

This place, near the Cité du Cheval and the medieval village of Ségur-le-Château, looks like a holiday club with its little chalets dotted around in a park. There is a

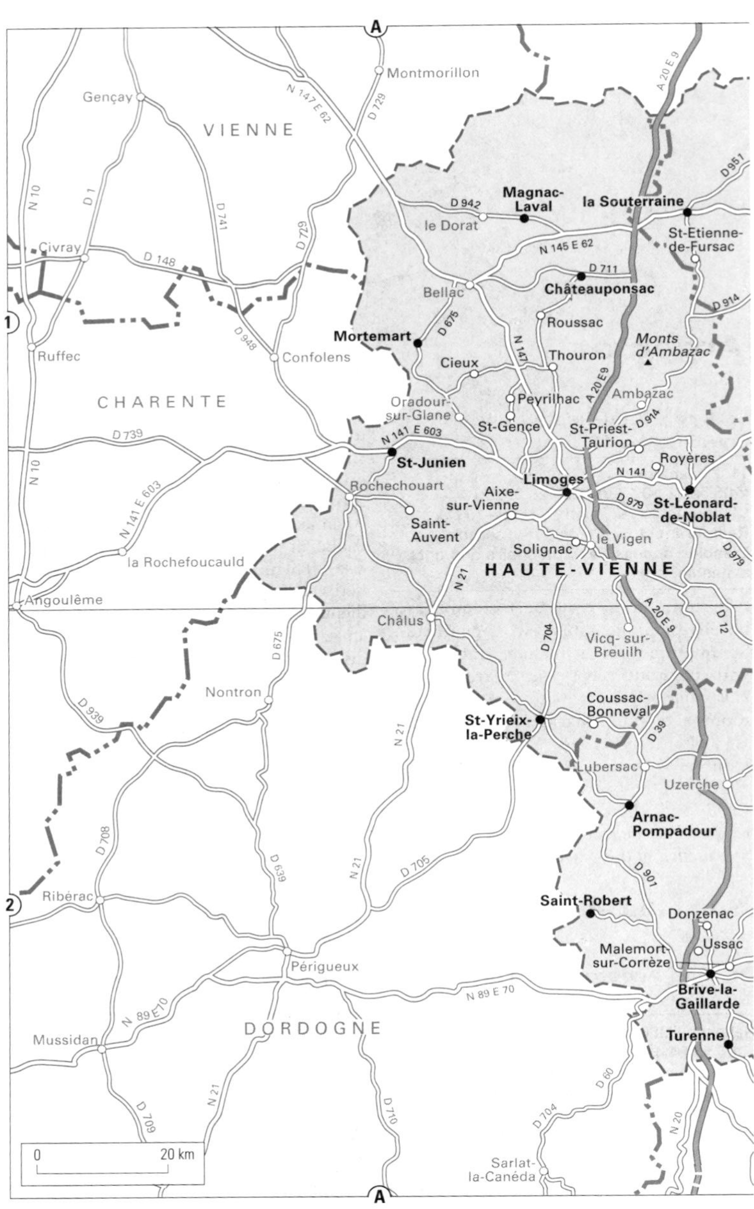
A
Montmorillon
Gençay
VIENNE
N 147 E 62
D 729
N 10
D 1
D 741
Magnac-Laval
la Souterraine
D 951
D 942
le Dorat
Civray
D 148
N 145 E 62
St-Etienne-de-Fursac
D 711
Châteauponsac
Bellac
D 914
D 675
Roussac
Ruffec
D 948
Mortemart
N 147
Monts d'Ambazac
Confolens
Cieux
Thouron
CHARENTE
Peyrilhac
Ambazac
Oradour-sur-Glane
A 20 E 9
D 739
St-Gence
St-Priest-Taurion
N 141 E 603
St-Junien
Royères
N 10
N 141
Limoges
Rochechouart
Aixe-sur-Vienne
D 979
St-Léonard-de-Noblat
N 141 E 603
Saint-Auvent
Solignac
le Vigen
la Rochefoucauld
HAUTE-VIENNE
N 21
Angoulême
Châlus
D 12
D 675
D 704
Vicq-sur-Breuilh
Nontron
Coussac-Bonneval
D 939
St-Yrieix-la-Perche
N 21
D 39
Lubersac
Uzerche
Arnac-Pompadour
D 708
D 901
D 639
N 21
D 705
Ribérac
Saint-Robert
Donzenac
Ussac
Malemort-sur-Corrèze
Périgueux
Brive-la-Gaillarde
N 89 E 70
DORDOGNE
Turenne
Mussidan
D 60
N 21
D 709
D 710
D 704
N 20
0
20 km
Sarlat-la-Canéda
1
2
12
LIMOUSIN

INDRE
ALLIER
CREUSE
PUY-DE-DÔME
CORRÈZE
CANTAL
LOT
AVEYRON
Crozant
Dun-le-Palestel
Genouillac
Boussac
Montluçon
Jouillat
Guéret
Sainte-Feyre
Chambon-sur-Voueize
Evaux-les-Bains
Chénérailles
Fontanières
Bénévent-l'Abbaye
Ahun
Saint-Hilaire-le-Château
Blessac
Bourganeuf
Aubusson
St-Gervais-d'Auvergne
la Villeneuve
Felletin
Crocq
St-Marc-à-Loubaud
Peyrat-le-Château
Lac de Vassivière
Pontgibaud
Augne
Auphelle
Gentioux-Pigerolles
Eymoutiers
Nedde
Peyrelevade
Tarnac
Plateau de Millevaches
Bugeat
le Mont-Dore
la Bourboule
Treignac
Massif des Monédières
Meymac
Ussel
la Serre-de-Mestes
Chamboulive
Egletons
Églisenneuve-d'Entraigues
Seilhac
Corrèze
Neuvic
Gimel-les-Cascades
Clergoux
Saint-Merd-de-Lapleau
Riom-ès-Montagnes
Tulle
Sainte-Fortunade
Saint-Pardoux-la-Croisille
la Roche-Canillac
Mauriac
Lagarde-Enval
Saint-Martin-la-Méanne
les Quatres-Routes-d'Albussac
Collonges-la-Rouge
Meyssac
Argentat
St-Julien-aux-Bois
Murat
Beaulieu-sur-Dordogne
Aurillac
N
B
1
2
A 71 E 11
N 145
N 144
D 943
D 917
D 940
D 997
N 145 E 62
D 915
D 996
D 942
D 912
D 13
N 141
D 982
D 941
D 992
D 36
D 30
D 3
D 979
N 89
A 89 E 70
D 16
D 922
D 978
N 120
D 18
D 10
D 921
N 122
D 103

12

LIMOUSIN

fabulous heated pool and a play area for children. The bedrooms are all at ground level and have a tiny terrace and either a shower or bath; doubles €42. There is a refurbishment programme; some rooms are already finished, while the rest are being done at the moment. The results are generally attractive (although one could quibble about some of the decorative details) and the rooms are certainly value for money. The owners take pride in their work, and you'll get a warm welcome. Breakfast buffet. The regional dishes are particularly tasty and are often prepared with an individual touch. The food is basic regional, but it is sometimes set off by unusual complements: *escalope* of foie gras with season fruit, croustillant of lamb with truffle gravy and Vacherin cheese with walnuts. Menus €11–24 and reckon on €35 à la carte. You can eat in the dining room or on the enormous terrace.

Aubusson

23200

Hôtel de France - Restaurant au Rendez-vous des Gourmets**

6 rue des Déportés.
☎ 05.55.66.10.22 Ⓕ 05.55.66.88.64
Closed *certain public holidays.*
Disabled access. TV. Car park.

An establishment in the best tradition of provincial hotel-keeping. Comfortable and spacious doubles €46–93. In the restaurant there are menus to suit all tastes and budgets at €15–37. There's even a little brasserie on the ground floor, which is great for lunch. *Free apéritif offered to our readers on presentation of this guide.*

Blessac

23200 (4km NW)

Le Relais des Forêts*

41 rte. d'Aubusson. Take D941 towards Pontarion, then right towards Blessac.
☎ 05.55.66.15.10 Ⓕ 05.55.83.87.91
Closed *Fri evening; Sun evening. 3 weeks in Feb; Oct–Nov school holidays.* **TV. Car park.**

A simple, easy-going and honest place – if you like generous portions of home cooking, this is where to come. Menus at €10 (weekdays only), €14 and €31. They offer a balanced selection of regional dishes, such as *entrecôte marchand de vin* and crayfish in season. All the rooms have been refurbished; they're clean and quiet. Doubles €25 with basin/wc (shower along the corridor), €38–65 with shower/wc or bath. Nice welcome, though they don't accept credit cards. *Free coffee offered to our readers on presentation of this guide.*

Villeneuve (La)

23260 (23km E)

Le Relais Marchois

It's on the N141.
☎ 05.55.67.35.78
Closed *Tues evening; Wed; Sunday evening; a week in June; Christmas–mid Jan.*

The description "country inn" suits this traditional little place perfectly, and its décor, with its interesting collection of fans and old coffee pots, creates the right atmosphere. Dishes include grilled rib of beef with potato cake, *millefeuille* of scallops with whisky and an irresistible nougat glacé with coconut milk and petits fours. All the menus, from the regional one at €11 (lunchtime, weekdays only) to the others from €19–35, are good value. The food is generously served and well presented and service is charming. *Free coffee offered to our readers on presentation of this guide.*

Saint-Marc-à-Loubaud

23460 (24km SW)

Restaurant Les Mille Sources

It's in the centre; take the N141 towards Limoges, then the D7 towards Royère, turn left at Vallières in the direction of Saint-Yrieix and follow the signs for Saint-Marc-à-Loubaud.
☎ 05.55.66.03.69
Closed *Mon Feb–April; Sun evening, Mon during school holidays; Dec; Jan.*

Located way up in the north of the Millevaches plateau, this place is very popular, so it's advisable to book. The quality of the cooking is quite astonishing and although the prices are a little high, it shouldn't be missed. Philippe Coutisson is a great chef, as his duck à la ficelle will attest, and his specialities – duck and leg of lamb chargrilled over the open fire – also hit the spot. Set menus €27 and €42. The décor is delightful and the lovingly tended garden is always full of flowers. *Free apéritif offered to our readers on presentation of this guide.*

Beaulieu-sur-Dordogne

19120

Auberge de jeunesse La Riviera Limousine

Place du Monturuc; by the Dordogne.
Ⓣ05.55.91.13.82
Ⓦwww.fuaj.org
Closed *1 Nov to early April.* **Car park.**

This large, charming building by the Dordogne, opposite the Pénitents chapel, is exceptionally luxurious for a youth hostel, and the setting is worthy of a postcard. There are some thirty beds spread over rooms with two–six beds each. €8.70 a night per person; breakfast €3.25. Meals €8.40 (by request only, for a minimum of ten people). The place is a bit chaotic, but good fun. Credit cards not accepted.

Meyssac

19500 (21km NW)

Le Relais du Quercy**

Avenue du Quercy.
Ⓣ05.55.25.40.31 Ⓕ05.55.25.36.22
Ⓦwww.relaisduquercy.com.fr
Closed *3 weeks mid-Nov–early Dec.* **TV. Swimming pool. Car park. High chairs and games available.**

The hotel is in a large building with a stylish dining room that leads onto a terrace overlooking the pool. Duck, a local speciality, figures a lot on the menu, but alongside classic dishes you'll find more inventive ones like chilli *à l'aiguillette* or quail stuffed with walnuts. Menus €12 (weekday lunchtimes) and €13.50 or around €20 à la carte. The friendly, easy-going team are generous with those little extras. The rooms have good facilities and cost €38–50. Half board is compulsory in July–Aug at €46–48 per person per day. *Free coffee offered to our readers on presentation of this guide.*

Boussac

23600

Café de la Place

4 pl. de l'Hôtel-de-Ville.
Ⓣ05.55.65.02.70
Closed *Sun in June.* **Car park.**

Patronne Paulette Roger is a warm and welcoming figure. A typical meal might consist of melon, shellfish, meat en paupiette and potatoes, with pear tart to finish. Menus €11 during the week and €12.50 on Sun. The menu changes daily. It's good value, but they don't accept credit cards. *Free coffee offered to our readers on presentation of this guide.*

Le Relais Creusois

40 La Maison Dieu. Route de la Châtre.
Ⓣ05.55.65.02.20
Closed *Tues evening and Wed except July–Aug; Jan, Feb and 1 week in June; winter evenings by reservation only.*

The cooking is good and the chef prepares lots of local dishes, but he also dreams up his own specialities – menus change according to the seasons, but typical offerings include artichoke stew with marrowbone or lacquered duck thigh and cream beaten with spices. Menus €22–45. He also prepares dishes to take away.

Brive-la-Gaillarde

19100

Auberge de jeunesse

56 av. du Maréchal-Bugeaud parc Monjauze; beside the municipal swimming pool.
Ⓣ05.55.24.34.00 Ⓕ05.55.84.82.80
Ⓦwww.fuaj.org
Closed *15 Dec–15 Jan.* **Car park. Disabled access.**

Only five minutes from the town centre. New arrivals are greeted from 8am–10pm, with a break from noon–6pm on Sat, Sun and public holidays. The reception building also contains two dining rooms (meals €8.40, with booking only). The bedrooms with two, three or four beds are in a long, recently built annexe. Some have the addition of a small balcony and all are clean and well kept, just like the communal shower area. Membership card compulsory, but you can buy it on arrival: €10.70 for guests aged under 26, €15.25 for others. €8.85 a night per person. Tax of € 0.30 per stay per person aged over thirteen. Breakfast €3.25. Hostel guests get a discount in the swimming pool next door; guests have at their disposal: a ping-pong table, a TV room, a kitchen and a garage for bikes. *10% discount on the price of a room (Oct–March) offered to our readers on presentation of this guide.*

Hôtel-restaurant La Crémaillière**

53 av. de Paris; it's 100m from the market.
Ⓣ05.55.74.32.47 Ⓕ05.55.74.00.15
Closed *Sun evening; Mon; the 2nd week in Feb; the 1st week in July.* **TV.**

Pascal Jacquinot, the new owner, had a hard act to follow after Charlou Raynal, but he's definitely succeeded. Although the décor is a bit garish, the cooking is splendid and dishes change regularly: *Tatin* with foie gras and grated truffles, farm-raised pigeon with morels, cream and grilled bacon. Or you could be tempted by his summer truffles with scrambled eggs or the perch with salted butter and fresh sorrel in a light cream sauce. The milk-fed veal cutlet is simple and perfect. Menus €16–40. There are a few decent rooms with bath at €42–45. Breakfast €6.

Bistrot de Brune

13 av. de Paris.
Ⓣ05.55.24.00.91
Closed *3 weeks in April; last week in Dec; Sun.* **Disabled access. High chairs available.**

A new-look brasserie offering tempting, cheap dishes: sardines, magret with honey, duck *andouillette*, salad of gizzards and goat's cheese, omelette with ceps, quality Limousin beef. Menus €13–20 (country menu) or around €22 à la carte. The chatty owner has a good selection of local wines and some fine vintages besides. This is a place that achieves that rare combination of relaxed atmosphere and really excellent food.

Chez Francis

61 av. de Paris.
Ⓣ05.55.74.41.72
Closed *Sun; Mon evening; public holidays except 8 May; 10 days in Feb; 2–19 Aug.*

The flattering comments scribbled on the walls of this delightful place add up to one thing – it's successful and popular, so much so that you have to book. Francis gives free rein to his imagination; his approach to cooking is thoughtful and he produces wonderfully executed dishes, prettily presented. Try hot foie gras cooked over salt and flavoured with rare peppers, suckling calf. All the meats come from the Limousin and they're very tasty. Dish of the day €9 and menus €14–21.

Ussac

19270 (1km N)

Le Petit Clos

Le Pouret; on the northern exit out of Brive.
Ⓣ05.55.86.12.65 Ⓕ05.55.86.94.32
Closed *Sun evening; Mon; 3 weeks in Feb; 3 weeks in Oct.* **Disabled access. TV. Swimming pool. Car park.**

By common consent, this is the best place to eat in Brive – and it has a few fully equipped bedrooms in a modern annexe for €64 and €76 with bath/wc. It's just out of town in a magnificent Corrèze house, originally a coaching inn; there's a lovely terrace and a pretty dining room. The cuisine is excellent and sticks to the classics, and you'll enjoy attentive service. Menus €20–40. It's a place that draws the well-to-do but if you want to talk sport, get the owner talking about rugby – it's his thing.

Malemort-sur-Corrèze

19360 (3km NE)

Auberge des Vieux Chênes**

31 av. Honoré-de-Balzac.
Ⓣ05.55.24.13.55 Ⓕ05.55.24.56.82
Closed *Sun; public holidays.* **TV.Car park. High chairs available.**

This establishment isn't much to look at from the outside, but take a glance at the menus. They range from €12 (except Sat evening) and €30, and list inventive country-style cooking: *escalope* of foie gras pan-fried with soft fruits; veal pan-fried with wild mushrooms; scallop *aumonière* with vegetables in lemon butter; fresh fruit tarts. You'll enjoy both the food and the atmosphere in the bright dining room. The rooms have modern facilities – they're similar to the ones you'd find in a chain hotel but cheaper. Doubles €42–45 with shower or bath/wc. There are some family rooms which have just been done up. *10% discount on the room rate offered to our readers on presentation of this guide.*

Donzenac

19270 (10km N)

Hôtel La Gamade - Restaurant Le Périgord**

Avenue de Paris; take the D920.

Ⓣ05.55.85.72.34 Ⓕ05.55.85.65.83
TV.

There's a rather elegant dining room, a tiny roadside terrace and a nice bar where you can also eat. Mme Salesse keeps a stern but benevolent eye on the regulars who drop in for a drink and a bite. There's a weekday lunch *menu du jour* at €13 and others €18.90–32, listing dishes such as black pudding salad with caramelized apples, calf's head ravigote and duck *confit Périgourdine.* The hotel is in another building, swathed in Virginia creeper, and has nine bedrooms, each of them different. Doubles €29–48. *Free coffee offered to our readers on presentation of this guide.*

Châteauponsac

87290

Hôtel-restaurant du Centre

Place Mazurier; take the D711 and it's opposite the tourist office.
Ⓣ05.55.76.50.19
Closed *Sun; Wed lunch; Sat evening; Christmas holidays.*

This popular, modest hotel with a bar/restaurant has clean, cheap rooms. Doubles €23 with shower/basin, €30 with shower/wc.Dishes in the restaurant include local grills, potato cake and clafoutis. The €13 menu includes cheese and dessert; otherwise à la carte. Good value. *Free coffee offered to our readers on presentation of this guide.*

Roussac

87140 (11km SW)

La Fontaine Saint-Martial

12 rue de la Fontaine.Take the D771.
Ⓣ05.55.60.27.42
Closed *Wed evening.* **Disabled access. High chairs available.**

A very attractive bar-restaurant which also serves as a grocer's and tobacconist's. Marc Foussat, the modest young proprietor-chef, does a marvellous job.You can eat in the spick-and-span dining room or on the terrace. There are four menus, €10–18, which list wholesome dishes: carp mousse with sorrel, roulade of plaice, ling with hollandaise sauce, hare stew, home-made raspberry charlotte. You'll find decent and inexpensive bottles on the short wine list. Classic cooking and friendly professional service. The bar is the meeting place for local football fans, so things really heat up on match nights. It's a convivial, relaxed place.

Chénérailles

23130

Le Coq d'Or

7 pl. du Champ de Foire.
Ⓣand Ⓕ05.55.62.30.83
Closed *Sun evening; Mon; Wed evening; a week at the end of June to early July; a week at the end of Sept; 3 weeks at the beginning of Jan.* **TV. Pay car park. High chairs available.**

Squeezed between Château Villemonteix and Château Mazeau, this place has a reputation for quality cuisine. The chef updates local dishes for today's tastes – go for the potato tart with fromage frais or the fillet of trout with blackwheat spaghetti. Weekday lunch menu €11 and others €17–37. They have a few double rooms which are currently being refurbished (prices not fixed yet).

Clergoux

19320

Hôtel Chammard

At Roche-Canillac get onto the D18 then take the D978 in the direction of Tulle.
Ⓣ05.55.27.76.04
Car park.

Old-style place filled with a lovely aroma of beeswax and home-made jam. Georgette is a delightful woman who'll welcome you into her home – where the cantou, the inglenook fireplace, dominates. The rooms, €26 with basin and €28–35 with shower, are very well maintained and most of the doubles look onto the garden at the back.

Crozant

23160

Restaurant du Lac

Pont de Crozant; it's on the banks of the Creuse, about 12km NW of Dun-le-Palestel.
Ⓣ05.55.89.81.96

Closed *Mon; plus Sun evening out of season; Wed evening; Feb; Ist week in March.*

Don't miss this place. It has an exceptional location on the water's edge, with a splendid view of the cathedral and the bridge that links two départements – and though it's on the Indre bank of the river, it's actually in Creuse. Well-executed, often inventive cooking: specialities include fresh fish (baked zander on leek fondue, cream of shellfish), salad of quail with Berry lentils and foie gras, and beef *tournedos* in a Port sauce. Menus €16–36. It's built a solid reputation so it's best to book. They also offer rooms; €26–46 for a double, breakfast €5.

Évaux-les-Bains

23110

Grand Hôtel**

Les thermes: it's down the hill from the town centre beside the spa.
Ⓣ05.55.82.46.00 Ⓕ05.55.82.46.01
Closed *Nov–March.* **TV.**

This is a grand hotel with old-fashioned charm that's been going since 1900. It has high ceilings and wide blue-carpeted corridors and is full of people who come to take the waters. The guests enjoy the comfort of the large, well-heated rooms, all of which are equipped with a bell to call the staff. The ones which have been done up recently are impeccable. It's peaceful. Doubles €41 with basin/wc, €48 with shower/wc and €53 with bath/wc. Breakfast €5.80. There's also a restaurant with menus at €13.70 (not served Sun), €21.50 and €29.50.

Fontanières

23110 (8km S)

Le Damier

On the main road, on the left-hand side.
Ⓣ05.55.82.35.91
Closed *Mon; Tues; 2 weeks in Feb; 2 weeks in Sept.*

It's not often that you find a pretty little inn like this around here. It has a quiet, stylish atmosphere, with background music and quality regional cuisine. Weekday lunch menu €10.50 and others €16–30, listing house terrine of duck with foie gras, slabs of beef cooked in different ways according to the season. It's a very pleasant place, with a terrace where you can eat snacks in summer.

Gentioux-Pigerolles

23340

La Ferme de Nautas

Pigerolles; take the D982, the D35 and then the D26.
Ⓣ05.55.67.90.68 Ⓕ05.55.67.93.12
Ⓦwww.perso.wanadoo.fr/les.nautas
Closed *weekdays out of season.*

This place, a working farm run by the hospitable François Chatoux, is a winner. He used to be an engineer but took up farming instead, and he runs an original place brimming with warmth and hospitality. His wife does genuine local cuisine, using first-rate ingredients and serving generous helpings of tasty regional dishes – potato pie, cep tarts and superb meat. There's a menu at €15 for hotel residents only and then €21 but you have to book it in advance. The double rooms are rustic in style, comfy and welcoming; they're €43 with shower/wc, breakfast included. *Free coffee offered to our readers on presentation of this guide.*

Guéret

23000

Hôtel de Pommeil

75 rue de Pommeil.
Ⓣand Ⓕ05.55.52.38.54
Closed *Sat evening, Sun Nov-March; 12 June–4 July.* **TV. Car park. High chairs available.**

A very simple, clean and welcoming hotel with good prices. There are just nine rooms, so it's best to book; doubles €27–34 with shower and basin or shower/wc. They have a menu at €11, which lists such dishes as veal *escalope* with a mushroom and cream sauce and scallops with saffron. Friendly atmosphere. *10% discount on the room rate for a two-night stay Sept–June offered to our readers on presentation of this guide.*

Hôtel Auclair**

19 av. de la Sénatorerie; it's nearr pl. Bonnyaud.
Ⓣ05.55.41.22.00
TV. Swimming pool. Pay car park.

About thirty rooms with good facilities and furnished with rattan. Doubles

€38–52 with shower or bath. The small swimming pool adds a hint of luxury. In the restaurant there's a *formule* at €9.20 and a menu at €22. Reckon on around €20 à la carte. Try the *fondue*. You must reserve your parking space in advance.

Le Pub Rochefort

6 pl. Rochefort; it's in a pedestrianized street.
☎05.55.52.61.02
Closed *Sun; Mon lunchtime.*

This place is right in the heart of the town and has an intimate, warm setting with old stone walls and ancestral beams. The food won't get Michelin stars but it's honest and good value and service comes with a smile. Good dishes include salmon and scallops marinated in Avocat, scallops with leek sauce, and hazelnut caramel tart. Weekday lunch menu at €11 and others €14–23. There's a nice covered terrace in the interior courtyard that gets full very quickly. *Free house aperitif offered to our readers on presentation of this guide.*

Sainte-Feyre

23000 (7km SE)

Restaurant Les Touristes

1 pl. de la Mairie; take the D942.
☎05.55.80.00.07
Closed *Sun evening; Mon; Wed evening; Jan.*
Disabled access. High chairs available.

Tasty, classic local cooking prepared by Michel Roux and served in generous portions. There's a quiet atmosphere and the surroundings are lovely. You will get the measure of the excellent cooking from the menus (€14.50–37). His specialities include fresh duck foie gras poached in spicy wine, fried Rossini-style sweetbreads, good local meat and skilfully prepared fish. *Two free apéritifs per table offered to our readers on presentation of this guide.*

Jouillat

23220 (14km NE)

L'Auberge du Château

9 pl. de l'Église; follow rte. de la Châtre, turn right when you get to Villevaleix and it's beside the church.
☎05.55.41.88.43
Closed *Sun evening; Mon; 1–15 Sept; 23 Dec–13 Jan.* **Disabled access.**

Don't expect one of those touristy olde-worlde inns that you often find in the neighbourhood of a château. L'Auberge du Château fulfils an important role in holding the local community together – it serves as a grocer's and tobacconist's as well as a restaurant. There's a rustic dining room and a terrific paved garden with an awning at the back. Menus, €15.60–23, list starter, main course, cheese and dessert; the Sunday menu at €21 lists two main courses. Specialities include coq au vin or zander with meat juices. If you like, call the day before to check what the chef plans and he'll make you something else if you don't like what's available. And think about booking in advance because it's very popular locally.

Limoges

87000

See map overleaf

Hôtel Familia

18 rue du Gal-du-Bessol. **Map C1-1**
☎05.55.77.51.40 Ⓕ05.55.10.27.69
TV.

Just a short walk away from the centre in a quiet street. Though the district has no great appeal, this modest establishment is a find. You get to the rooms across a pretty, shaded courtyard. They are simple, spacious, perfectly maintained and fairly priced: doubles with shower/wc €40. Breakfast €4.60. *10% discount on the room rate at the weekend offered to our readers on presentation of this guide.*

Hôtel de la Paix**

25 pl. Jourdan. **Map C2-2**
☎05.55.34.36.00 Ⓕ05.55.32.37.06
TV. Pay car park.

Well located in the corner of a quiet square – and it's not far from the station or the old parts of town. Between the entrance and the breakfast room there's a small museum displaying the owner's impressive collection of phonographs and mechanical music. The rooms are huge; they're well maintained, regularly redecorated and variously furnished – one has a fireplace, another a big bathroom. You couldn't call it luxury but there's an appealing retro style. It's reliable and offers good value for money: doubles €45–48 with shower/wc or bath. Breakfast €5. There's a €5 fee for use of the garage. *10%*

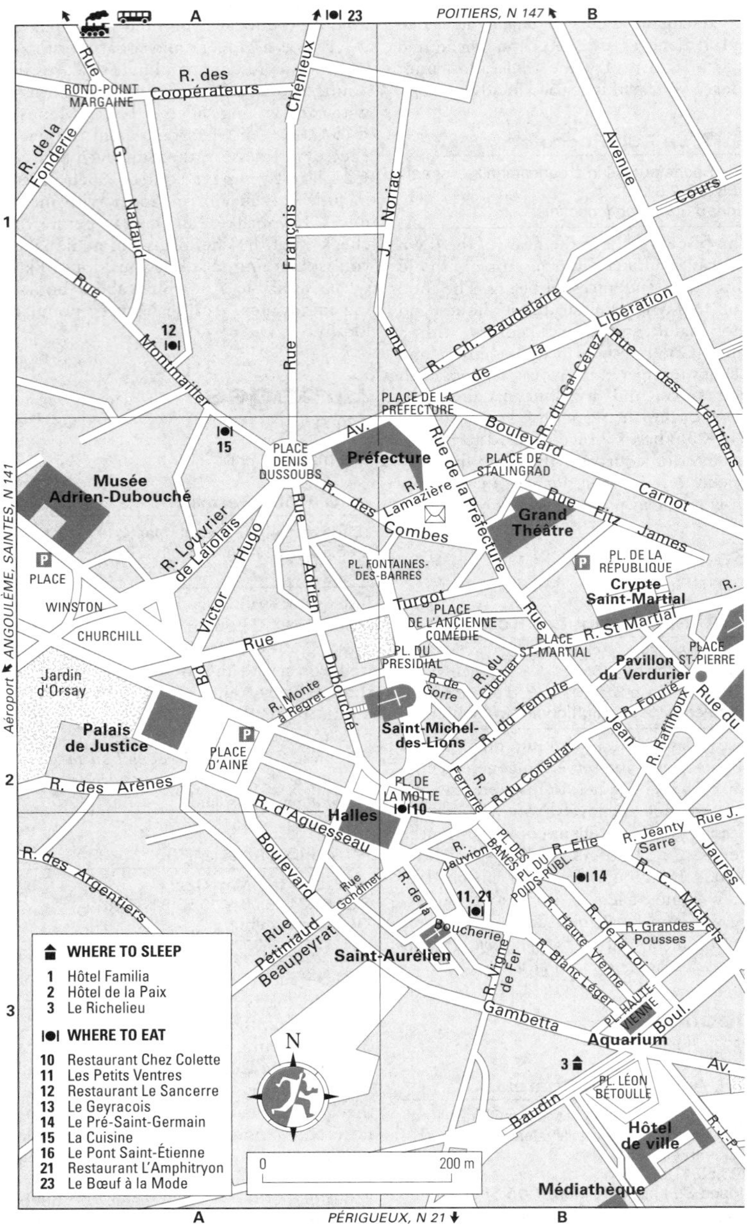

A
23
POITIERS, N 147
B
1
2
3
Aéroport ANGOULÊME, SAINTES, N 141
PÉRIGUEUX, N 21
Rue
R. des Coopérateurs
ROND-POINT MARGAINE
R. de la Fonderie
G. Nadaud
Rue Chénieux
Rue François
J. Noriac
Rue
Avenue
Cours
Rue Montmailler
12
R. Ch. Baudelaire
de la Libération
Rue des Vénitiens
R. du Gal Cérez
PLACE DE LA PRÉFECTURE
15
Av.
Préfecture
Boulevard Carnot
PLACE DENIS DUSSOUBS
PLACE DE STALINGRAD
Musée Adrien-Dubouché
R. des Combes
R. Lamazière
Rue de la Préfecture
Grand Théâtre
Rue Fitz James
R. Louvrier de Lajolais
Victor Hugo
Rue Adrien Dubouché
PL. FONTAINES-DES-BARRES
PL. DE LA RÉPUBLIQUE
Crypte Saint-Martial
R.
PLACE WINSTON CHURCHILL
Turgot
PLACE DE L'ANCIENNE COMÉDIE
Rue
PLACE ST-MARTIAL
R. St Martial
Jardin d'Orsay
Bd
PL. DU PRÉSIDIAL
R. du Clocher
R. de Gorre
PLACE ST-PIERRE
Pavillon du Verdurier
R. Monte à Regret
R. du Temple
R. Fourié
Rue du
Palais de Justice
PLACE D'AINE
Saint-Michel-des-Lions
Jean
R. Raffilhoux
R. des Arènes
PL. DE LA MOTTE
10
R. Ferrerie
R. du Consulat
R. d'Aguesseau
Halles
Rue J. Jaurès
R. des Argentiers
Boulevard
R. Jauvion
PL. DES BANCS
PL. DU POIDS-PUBL.
R. Elie
R. Jeanty Sarre
R. C. Michels
14
Rue Gondinet
R. de la Boucherie
11, 21
R. Haute Vienne
R. de la Loi
R. Grandes Pousses
Rue Pétiniaud Beaupeyrat
Saint-Aurélien
R. Vigne de Fer
R. Blanc Léger
PL. HAUTE VIENNE
Boul.
Gambetta
Aquarium
Av.
N
3
PL. LÉON BÉTOULLE
Baudin
R. J.-P.
Hôtel de ville
0
200 m
Médiathèque
WHERE TO SLEEP
1 Hôtel Familia
2 Hôtel de la Paix
3 Le Richelieu
WHERE TO EAT
10 Restaurant Chez Colette
11 Les Petits Ventres
12 Restaurant Le Sancerre
13 Le Geyracois
14 Le Pré-Saint-Germain
15 La Cuisine
16 Le Pont Saint-Étienne
21 Restaurant L'Amphitryon
23 Le Bœuf à la Mode

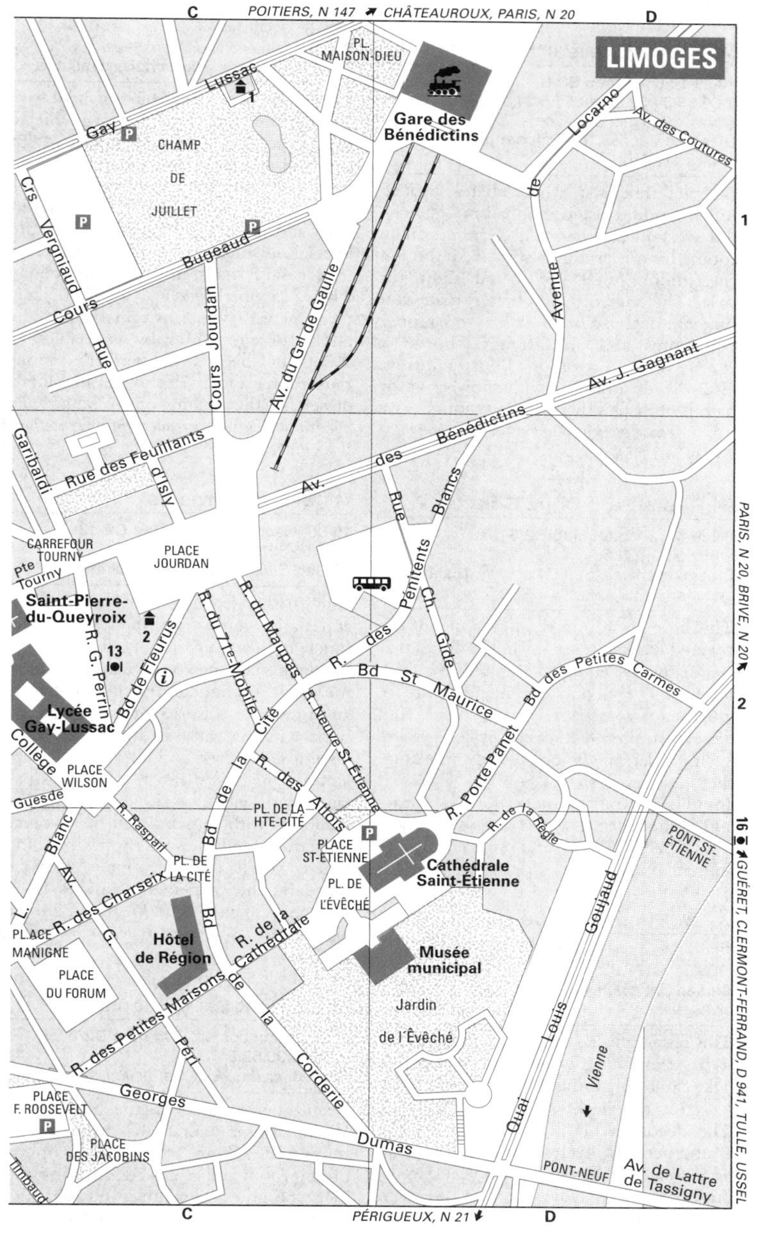
LIMOGES
POITIERS, N 147
CHÂTEAUROUX, PARIS, N 20
PÉRIGUEUX, N 21
PARIS, N 20, BRIVE, N 20
16 GUÉRET, CLERMONT-FERRAND, D 941, TULLE, USSEL
Gare des Bénédictins
CHAMP DE JUILLET
PLACE JOURDAN
CARREFOUR TOURNY
Saint-Pierre-du-Queyroix
Lycée Gay-Lussac
PLACE WILSON
PL. DE LA HTE-CITÉ
PLACE ST-ETIENNE
PL. DE L'ÉVÊCHÉ
Cathédrale Saint-Étienne
Hôtel de Région
Musée municipal
Jardin de l'Évêché
PLACE DU FORUM
PLACE F. ROOSEVELT
PLACE DES JACOBINS
PONT-NEUF
PONT ST-ÉTIENNE
Vienne

discount on the room rate offered to our readers on presentation of this guide.

Le Richelieu***

40 av. Baudin. **Map B3-3**
Ⓣ05.55.34.22.82 Ⓕ05.55.34.35.36
Ⓦwww.hotel-richelieu.com
Disabled access. TV. Pay car park. High chairs available.

A quiet three-star where there's a deep understanding of professionalism – matchless welcome, service and cleanliness. The rooms have everything you need, though the junior suites are a tad tight for space. The facilities are better than you might expect in a hotel such as this: proper bathrooms and an attractive breakfast room with a trompe l'œil painting. €65–97 for a double with shower/wc or bath is perhaps a shade pricey, though. *Free parking space offered to our readers on presentation of this guide.*

Restaurant Chez Colette

Place de la Motte. **Map B2/3-10**
Ⓣ05.55.33.73.85
Closed *evenings; Sun; Mon; July.* **Disabled access.**

This little place is in the lively area of the covered market. It serves simple dishes that are, naturally enough, inspired by fresh produce. There's only one menu at €8.50, which offers starter, main course and dessert – quite a feat for the price. If you're having a late night or an early morning, they also serve snacks 8–10am – now is your chance to try some of the local "peasant" dishes such as *giraud*, a sausage made from sheep's blood and cooked in the animal's intestine.

Restaurant Le Sancerre

18 rue Montmailler. **Map A1-12**
Ⓣ05.55.77.71.95
Closed *Sat lunchtime; Sun; 2 weeks in July or August.*

This restaurant has long been popular, and it has something to suit every appetite. Take a look at the lunch *formule* (€9) served in the week; other menus €14–23. The décor's a bit of a mixture but the atmosphere is lively enough. They do *boudineaux* with chestnuts, veal sweetbreads with ceps, foie gras and sole with orange – especially good with a drop of Sancerre. *Free apéritif offered to our readers on presentation of this guide.*

Le Pré Saint-Germain

26 rue de la Loi. **Map B3-14**
Ⓣ05.55.32.71.84
Closed *Sun evening; Mon; 1–21 Aug.*
Disabled access. High chairs available.

This restaurant tries a bit too hard – the dining room is kitsch rather than chic and the service is rather self-important. But the food makes up for all that: it's fine and light and full of lovely surprises. The young chef delights in colourful ingredients and plays with different textures. Specialities include salad of warm calves, trotters with snails, and chocolate fondant. There's a lunch *formule* for €10 and a menu at €17 which is remarkable value: tartare of chopped baby vegetables followed by beef with perfectly cooked mushrooms and a selection of memorable desserts. Other menus up to €30.50. *Free apéritif offered to our readers on presentation of this guide.*

Le Geyracois

15 bd. Georges-Perrin. **Map C2-13**
Ⓣ05.55.32.58.51
Closed *Sun.* **High chairs available.**

The garish cafeteria-style décor might not appeal, but you eat well here for not very much money. Surprisingly, this is one of the few restaurants to serve local Limousin meat that is stamped for origin and there's an impressive display of certificates for prize-winning cattle in the corridor. The *tournedos*, rib steaks and fillets are all succulent and juicy; try also the foie gras pan-fried with cider, steak tartare, and veal flambéed with mustard. You help yourself to starters and desserts from the buffet where you'll find a wonderful terrine made by the owner and pastries by his wife. Set menus €10.90 and €23. *Free coffee offered to our readers on presentation of this guide.*

Le Pont Saint-Étienne

8 pl. de Compostelle. **Off map D2/3-16**
Ⓣ05.55.30.52.54
Closed *for the New Year holidays.*

Beautifully situated on the banks of the Vienne, this restaurant has been recently renovated. There is a stylish upstairs dining room and a terrace for sunny days. The cooking is inventive and the dishes change with the season. Portions are generous, you'll find local cuisine and the ingredients are fresh. Specialities include the "Admiral" (grilled fillet of mullet on a bed of small vegetables with Thai sauce), the "Porcenet" (sliced shoulder of pork *confit* and vegetable crumble) and the "Orchards of Camelas" (baked apricots with rosemary and almond-milk ice cream. Lunchtime menus €13.50 (except Sunday) and €14.50–33.30 (evenings and Sunday). Wine is a bit pricey. Best to book.

La Cuisine

21 rue Montmailler. **Map A2-15**
Ⓣand Ⓕ05.55.10.28.29
Closed *Sun; Mon; 15–29 Jan; 1–21 Aug.*
Disabled access.

Original, highly personal cooking from a chef who uses only the very freshest ingredients: breast of pigeon in a spiced crust, rolled calf's liver Venetian-style, monkfish in a coconut and coriander broth. Preparation of the meat and fish dishes or the desserts is taken very seriously, but there's an unusual touch of inventiveness. Dishes are generously served and the waiting staff are efficient and kindly. Lunch *formule* €12.50, or reckon on paying €30–35 à la carte. It would be good if the wine list had a few more wines from small vineyards, though. *Free coffee offered to our readers on presentation of this guide.*

Les Petits Ventres

20 rue de la Boucherie. **Map B3-11**
Ⓣ05.55.34.22.90
Closed *Sun; Mon; 1–15 May; 10–25 Sept.*
High chairs and games available.

An attractive, half-timbered house with one of the best restaurants to be found in the old district of the town. Although Petits Ventres means "little stomachs", you can forget the diet when you eat here: pan-fried foie gras, black sausage with mash, *andouillette*, tripe and calf's head. If you like offal, this place is for you – one dish is a feast of calf's head, tongue and mesentery (a membrane that keeps the guts in place). The chef also offers dishes for people who can't stomach tripe – including a vegetarian platter and grilled fish. The menu changes four times a year. They print the name of every supplier, which says everything you need to know about the quality of the produce. Great desserts and attractive rustic setting. Menus €17–30.5, reckon on €20 à la carte. *Free apéritif offered to our readers on presentation of this guide.*

Restaurant L'Amphitryon

26 rue de la Boucherie. **Map B3-21**
Ⓣ05.55.33.36.39
Ⓔamphityron@inext.fr
Closed *Sun; Mon and Sat lunchtimes; 2nd fortnight in Aug.*

You'll find this quality restaurant across from the delightful chapel of Saint-Aurélien, the patron saint of butchers. Try the duck foie gras, tajine of pigeon with dates, roast pigeon with baby vegetables, roulé of langoustine and fresh tomatoes or fillet of Limousin beef – they're all nicely cooked and original without being eccentric. Weekday lunch menu €18–22, then others at €26–33 or €39 à la carte. Not a bad price to pay to eat in an authentic Limoges atmosphere. There's a terrace in summer, which can get a little noisy. *Free house apéritif.*

Le Bœuf à la Mode

60 rue François-Chénieux. **Off map A1-23**
Ⓣ05.55.77.73.95
Closed *Sat lunchtime; Sun; Aug.*

A restaurant in a butcher's shop run by master butcher Claude Lebraud, who's proud of his trade. He's a real pro and knows how to choose his meat and serve it perfectly prepared: sirloin of beef in cider, épigramme of lamb (cooked on one side only) with honey and spices, Chateaubriand with bone marrow. Pleasant décor, with white linen napkins. À la carte only; you'll spend €20–30. *Free coffee offered to our readers on presentation of this guide.*

Aixe-sur-Vienne

87700 (13km SW)

Auberge des Deux Ponts

Avenue du Général-de-Gaulle; take the N21.
Ⓣ05.55.70.10.22
Closed *Sun evening; Mon.*

First-rate, reasonably priced restaurant on the banks of the Vienne. The décor is cheery, with lots of yellow and navy blue, and there are flowers everywhere. They do lots of seafood, including grilled bream, as well as good charcoal-grilled steaks, veal sweetbreads with honey, house foie gras and duck breast with Roquefort sauce. Lunch *formule* €10, and menus €13.50–25.50.

Saint-Gence

87510 (13km NW)

Le Moulin de Chevillou

Take the rte. de Bellac (N147), turn left towards Nieul and Saint-Gence is only 3km away. Go through the village and turn right 300m further on. It's signposted.
05.55.75.86.13
Closed *Mon–Thurs Oct–March.*

Lovely place hidden in a secluded valley beside the Glane, in a park filled with donkeys, goats, ponies and birds. Children can play on the swings and the slide. Enjoy a pancake and a flagon of cider as you're lulled by the splashing sound of the watermill. In the restaurant, go for timbale of fresh goat with leek fondue, trout with country ham and ceps, Limousin beef stew or saddle of rabbit with girolles. Menus €15 (not served Sun) and €20–36. Service is efficient and staff are delightful. Best to book. *Free apéritif offered to our readers on presentation of this guide.*

Saint-Priest-Taurion

87480 (13km NE)

Le Relais du Taurion**

2 chemin des Contamines.
05.55.39.70.14
Closed *Sun evening; Mon; 12 Dec-15 Jan.*
TV. Car park. High chairs available.

This beautiful early-twentieth-century ivy-covered house is memorable for its charm and excellent location on the banks of the Taurion river. The rooms, €45 with shower/wc and €52 with bath, are comfortable and well maintained. There's a restaurant, but it's a bit pricey for what you get: weekday menu for €18 and others at €26 and €34.

Peyrilhac

87510 (15km NW)

Auberge de la Queue de Vache

It's on the N147.
05.55.53.38.11
Closed *Tues.* **TV. Disabled access.**

Sadly this attractive farm is right on the main road. Inside, though, it's pretty and welcoming and the noise isn't too intrusive. You'll get typical local cooking, involving many ingredients from the owners' organic farm. Unusually for the Limousin, it's Scotch beef that appears on the menu – they have a Highland herd. The fruit and vegetables are local, however, and so are the cheeses. Starters include chicken with herbs, warm goat's cheese on green salad and Périgord salad with truffles; main courses include oxtail or beef cheek *confit*, pan-fried sirloin, and an amazing semi-cooked home-made foie gras. Good home-made chips, too, and baked vegetables that change with the seasons. The dessert list includes fruit tarts or melon preserved in honey. Menus €10–24, and reasonably priced wines. There's a small terrace at the back, open in summer. *Free coffee offered to our readers on presentation of this guide.*

Solignac

87110 (15km S)

Le Saint-Éloi

66 av. Saint-Éloi.
05.55.00.44.52 05.55.00.55.56
www.lesainteloi.fr
Closed *Sat lunch; Sun evening; Mon; Jan.*
TV. High chairs available.

A handsome hotel in a peaceful village. The young couple who run it have completely refurbished the place inside and out. The attractive rooms have fine linen and are tastefully decorated in warm tones; some have a terrace and a whirlpool bath. Doubles €45–59. Breakfast €6. The elegant dining room has leaded lights and a splendid fireplace and the tables are perfectly dressed. Cooking is modern and generously served – you'll get practically double what you'd expect in town. Wonderful *carpaccio* of scallops, pork cheek *confit, grenadins* of veal, and scallop *fricassée*; perfectly prepared fish dishes with well-balanced sauces; beautifully presented desserts. Weekday lunch menu €13 and others €40.

Royères

87400 (18km E)

Hôtel Beau Site**

Brignac; take the N141 towards Saint-Léonard-de-Noblat, then turn left onto the D124.
05.55.56.00.56 05.55.56.31.17
www.lebeausite.com

Closed *from 1 Jan to Palm Sunday.* **TV. Swimming pool. Car park. High chairs and games available.**

You can rely on good facilities in this hotel, which is set in peaceful greenery in country surroundings. The comfortable bedrooms are decorated with Madame's hand-painted designs and they're all different. Doubles with shower/wc or bath €50–55; the nicest have a view over the grounds and the pond. There's a nice garden with a wonderful heated pool. The restaurant offers a number of regional specialities such as *fricassée* of snails with ceps, *entrecôte* with bleu d'Auvergne, fillet of zander with champagne and scallops with leeks. For dessert try the marvellous chestnut *sabayon*. Menus from €18.50–28. Attentive service. *Free coffee offered to our readers on presentation of this guide.*

Thouron

87140 (22km NW)

La Pomme de Pin

La Tricherie; take the N147, then turn right onto the D7.
Ⓣand Ⓕ05.55.53.43.43
Closed *Mon; Tues lunchtime; Feb school holidays; 3 weeks in Sept.* **Disabled access. TV.**

One of the best places in Haute-Vienne, in an old mill in the forest near a small lake. Weekday lunch menu €15 with others €23.50–36. Appealing dishes and delicious charcoal grills cooked over the fire; specialities include sweetbread and fresh foie gras salad and chargrilled Limousin beef. There's a remarkable list of excellent wines. The rooms are comfortable and very clean with views of the river; doubles with shower/wc €50–56. *Free house apéritif offered to our readers on presentation of this guide.*

Magnac-Laval

I87190

La Ferme du Logis

Drive as far as Magnac-Laval, and in the centre turn right in the direction of Bellac; the restaurant is 2km along on the left-hand side.
Ⓣ05.55.68.57.23
Closed *Sun evening and Mon except June–Oct.* **Disabled access. Car park. Games available**

This inn is in a converted old building set in two hectares of grounds with a small lake. Generous portions of tasty local dishes are served by accommodating staff. They specialize in beef and venison in season. Appetizing and satisfying menus at €13 (not Sun), €17 and €30; the second menu is particularly good. The wines are fairly priced, too. There's space for ten in their luxury campground and two luxury caravans equipped with shower. *Free apéritif offered to our readers if you show this guide before your meal.*

Mortemart

87330

Hôtel Le Relais*

Ⓣand Ⓕ05.55.68.12.09
Closed *Tues except July–Aug; Wed; Feb.*
High chairs available.

A pleasant and very attractive country hostelry in a beautiful village. There are a few pretty rooms for €47 with shower or shower/wc, and a stylish stone-walled dining room. Attentive service and plenty of flavour in dishes such as foie gras with morel turnovers, duck breast with caramelized pears, roast lamb and *gratin* of wild strawberries. Set menus €16.30 (except Sun) and €23–37. You can also choose à la carte. *Coffee offered to our readers if you show this guide before your meal.*

Cieux

87520 (13km SE)

Auberge La Source**

Avenue du Lac; take the D3 as far as Blond, then turn right for Cieux.
Ⓣ05.55.03.33.23 Ⓕ05.55.03.26.88
Ⓦwww.logis-de-france.fr
Closed *Sun evening; Mon; Tues lunch; 20 Jan–11 Feb; 5–12 Nov.* **Disabled access. TV. Car park. High chairs available.**

A renovated former posthouse which commands a marvellous view of the Cieux lake, the valleys and the Blond mountains. The charming owners are highly experienced and make you feel totally welcome. The restaurant is light and airy and the cuisine, which is classic in style, is confidently and meticulously cooked. The fish is startlingly fresh and if you ask for your meat to be done in a particular way it will be cooked to perfection. Weekday lunch menus at €15 and others from €20–50. The décor in the rooms doesn't have the same charm, though, and the bathrooms look as if they belong in a chain hotel. Even so there's lots of space and they're well maintained. And, of course, there's that wonderful view. Doubles €55 with shower/wc and €70 bath. *Free apéritif offered to our readers on presentation of this guide.*

Neuvic

19160

Château Le Mialaret**

It's on the D991 in the direction of Égletons.
T 05.55.46.02.50 F 05.55.46.02.65
W www.lemialaret.com
TV. Swimming pool. Car park.

This nineteenth-century château, set in a gorgeous park, has been turned into a modestly luxurious hotel with many of its original features. Some bedrooms are in the towers; the largest ones, which are superb, have monumental fireplaces. Their conference centre (built in the grounds and rather a blot on the landscape) brings in the bulk of the income, so they can charge modest prices: doubles €59–84 with full en-suite facilities. The dining room is impressive and the cooking is elegant: warm fish salad, zander with beurre rouge and onion chutney, fillet of beef with green peppercorns. Menus €19.50–45. Hotel guests can use the tennis court. There is also the possibility of camping and there are some chalets to rent. *Free apéritif offered to our readers on presentation of this guide.*

Peyrat-le-Château

87470

Auberge du Bois de l'Étang**

38 av. de la Tour; take the D940 in the direction of Bourganeuf.
T 05.55.69.40.19 F 05.55.69.42.93
W www.boisdeletang.com
Closed *Sun evening and Mon 1 Oct–30 April; 15 Dec–15 Jan.* **Disabled access (restaurant). TV. Car park**

Set in a magnificent, peaceful area a few kilometres from Lake Vassivière. You'll get a very warm welcome. Good clean doubles at €29–48; those in the annexe are nicest and quietest. The restaurant is very nice indeed, and offers inventive dishes like duck foie gras with prawn tails, *cassolette* of baked lobster tails, *émincé* of squab fillets. €12.50 menu (not served Sun) and others €16–32 – there's real innovation on the costlier ones. À la carte can get a bit pricey. Half board, compulsory in July–Aug, costs €29–40 per person (there's a minimum three-night stay with that option). *Free apéritif offered to our readers on presentation of this guide.*

Auphelle

87470 (8km E)

Au Golf du Limousin**

Lac de Vassivière; take the D13 towards Vassivière then the D222 as far as the lake.
T 05.55.69.41.34 F 05.55.69.49.16
W www.hotel-golfdulimousin.com
Closed *1 Nov–31 Mar.*
TV. Car park.

This is one of the few hotels that almost overlook Lake Vassivière. The building is constructed out of stone, surrounded by greenery and just 200m from the beach. The bedrooms are clean and very comfy; doubles go for €39–49 depending on facilities and season. Half board, €45–48 per person per day, is compulsory July–Aug. You'll get good, classic regional cuisine in the restaurant: home-made terrine, fillet of beef with ceps, zander with beurre blanc, sweetbreads with morels, mutton tripe and a fine selection of cheeses. Weekday lunch menu €13.50 and others €19.50–25. *Free apéritif offered to our readers on presentation of this guide.*

Nedde

87120 (10km SE)

Auberge Le Verrou

Le Bourg-Nedde.
T 05.55.69.98.04
Closed *Wed in winter; Jan; Feb.* **Open** *by reservation only out of season.*

A warm, atmospheric establishment with several dining rooms. One has a beautiful old counter where you can prop yourself up while you have an apéritif; another has a pancake corner, and in summer they open up a charming little terrace. It's very popular locally. The short menu offers dishes cooked with fresh market produce, good Limousin meat, a choice of salads and sweet or savoury pancakes. Expect to pay €15–25 for a meal à la carte. There are a few pleasant rooms with shower/wc at €33–38.

Breakfast, with home-made jam and pastries, costs €6. Credit cards not accepted.

Augne

87120 (12km SW)

Le Ranch des Lacs

Take the D14 towards Bujaleuf and go through Chassat. At the next junction go left towards Négrignas; just before the small group of houses take the little road to the left to Vervialle.
☎05.55.69.15.66 Ⓕ05.55.69.59.52
Open *all year but telephone out of season.*

An attractive establishment run by a Belgian couple. It used to be a riding school, and the walls and beams are decorated with old saddles. Nowadays it's a cross between a hotel and a hostel, with a bar-restaurant. They serve about thirty Belgian beers and a selection of national dishes such as coffret du boulanger (a loaf filled with scrambled eggs flavoured with herbs), coucou de Malines (chicken breast stuffed with chicory), veal cutlet with Gouda and, if you order in advance, as many helpings of mussels and chips as you like. There's a €10 *formule* including wine and coffee, and menus from €14.50–30. From the veranda you'll get a view of the unspoiled Vienne valley. If you want accommodation, they have a couple of doubles with bath for €34 and basic hostel rooms with three or four beds in each and communal washing facilities (€12.50 a head). Children, who are particularly welcome, have a special games area all to themselves. *10% discount on the room rate offered to our readers on presentation of this guide.*

Saint-Hilaire-le-Château

23250

Hôtel du Thaurion**

10 Grand-Rue; take the D941 or the N41.
☎05.55.64.50.12 Ⓕ05.55.64.90.92
Closed *Wed; Thurs lunchtime; end Nov–end Feb.* **TV. Car park. High chairs and games available.**

An attractively restored coaching inn owned by Gérard Fanton – the chef by whom all others in the Creuse are judged. His cooking is executed to perfection and he serves a mix of traditional and original dishes. Specialities include braised hock of pork, oxtail pancake, stuffed pig's trotter with Brive mustard sauce and crayfish-tail ravioli. There's a set menu of the day for €15 and others €25–70. Unfortunately, the cheap menu provides very little choice and you may have to resort to a more expensive option. On the hotel side of things, the attractive rooms cost €34–76 for a double; there are also a few guest rooms in the château next door, which go for €95 for two including breakfast.

Saint-Junien

87200

Le Rendez-Vous des Chasseurs**

Lieu-dit Pont-à-la-Planche.
☎05.55.02.19.73 Ⓕ05.55.02.06.98
Closed *Fri; Sun evening; 2–19 Jan.* **Disabled access. TV. Car park. High chairs available.**

This place is renowned for its gourmet menu – but it's not as pricey as you might expect. There's a menu at €12 (not served on Sunday), a *menu terroir* at €17, and others up to €37. The dining room has all the charm of Vieille France and there's a terrace in summer. Well-maintained doubles €32.50 with shower/wc or bath. Breakfast €4.60. *Free digestif offered to our readers on presentation of this guide.*

Le Relais de Comodoliac**

22 av. Sadi-Carnot.
☎05.55.02.27.26 Ⓕ05.55.02.68.79
Restaurant closed *Sun evening Nov-end Feb.* **Disabled access. TV. Car park.**

The building is modern but they've created a very pleasant feel to it. The rooms are huge and well maintained. Doubles with bath €50-56. Half board is compulsory for a stay of more than three nights; it costs €57 per person per night. The restaurant looks onto a little corner of greenery. The cooking is well prepared using the freshest ingredients, and the dishes change with the seasons: pan-fried foie gras, scallops on a bed of endive, salmon, sea bass, local meat and chicken, and wild mushrooms. Prices are fair, with menus at €14–33.

Le Landais

6 bd. de la République.

☎05.55.02.12.07
Closed *Tues*; 15–30 Sept.

As soon as you cross the threshold, you sense you're going to be looked after. The restaurant adjoins the bar and it's easy to get comfortable. Honestly prepared dishes include duck stew, terrine of quail with juniper berries, scallops with ceps, salmis of wood-pigeon, prawns with whisky and *cassoulet*. Menus €14–34.

Saint-Auvent

87310 (14km S)

Auberge de la Vallée de la Gorre

Place de l'Église; it's on the D58.
☎05.55.00.01.27
Closed *Sun; Mon evenings.*

A lovely little inn in a lovely little village. The dishes are devised and prepared by Hervé Sutre, the creative young chef. Try half-cooked foie gras with spiced fruit, sweetbread *tatin*, fillet of Limousin beef with ceps, medallions of veal with crayfish, crayfish salad with sole rouleau, cod steak with morels, or fresh fruit *croustillant*. Menus €12 (except Sunday) and €17–34. There's a pleasant covered terrace for sunny days and it's best to book at the weekend.

Saint-Léonard-de-Noblat

87400

Le Gay-Lussac

18 bd. Victor-Hugo; it's in the old town, about 30m from pl. de la République.
☎05.55.56.98.45
High chairs available.

A tasteful restaurant offering traditional home cooking that reflects the changing seasons. There are welcoming dining rooms on the first floor. The menu changes every month, but specialities might include *marbrée* of foie gras, *tournedos* turf-and-surf, salmon turnover, or veal sweetbreads with ceps and snails. Weekday lunch *formule* €10.50 and other menus from €16–30.50; these prices mean it can be difficult to get a table. There's a little terrace on the square. *Free apéritif offered to our readers on presentation of this guide.*

Les Moulins de Noblat – L'Auberge de Mattre-Pierre

In the lower part of the town, in the direction of Limoges.
☎05.55.56.29.73

There are several water-mills, most of which date from the twelfth century which make a harmonious group and have been restored in order to serve as gallery spaces for local art and crafts; one has been turned into an inn with a terrace on the bank of the Vienne. It's particularly lovely in fine weather, though the noise of the wheel is hard to ignore. Fine, traditional cuisine with some good grills. Menus €14–48. From June to September they organize giant barbecues. Also a hotel. *Free apéritif offered to our readers on presentation of this guide.*

Saint-Martin-la-Méanne

19320

Hôtel Les Voyageurs**

Place de la Mairie; it's in the middle of the village.
☎05.55.29.11.53 Ⓕ05.55.29.27.70
Closed *Sun evening and Mon out of season; All Saints Day–end-Feb.* **Disabled access (restaurant). TV. Car park. High chairs available.**

This typical Corrèze village house has been turned into a family inn with lots of character. Local produce is much in evidence in the cooking, which includes such dishes as pan-fried foie gras with apple *confit*, *fricassée* of frogs' legs and snails with parsley, veal sweetbreads with ceps, fillet of char, veal *escalope* with morels and crêpe soufflé with orange. Set menus €15–33. The rooms are attractive and affordable. Doubles with shower cost €39–42; some have a view over the countryside. Breakfast €5. *Free coffee offered to our readers on presentation of this guide.*

Saint-Merd-de-Lapleau

19320

Hôtel-restaurant Fabry**

Pont du Chambon; it's 8km from Saint-Merd-De-Lapleau via the D13.

Ⓣ05.55.27.88.39
Ⓦwww.medianet.fr/fabry
Closed *Sun evening and Mon out of season; 12 Nov–20 Feb.* **TV. Car park.**

A substantial building in a magnificent setting on the banks of the Dordogne – many rooms have a view of the river. Lots of sea- and freshwater fish on the menus including monkfish and chicory with orange and coriander, zander in beurre blanc, medallion of veal with chanterelles, as well as tasty meat dishes such as venison with bilberries and duck breast with Périgueux truffle sauce. The chocolate fondant with mint ice cream is the star dessert. Menus €16.50–35. The eight rooms (doubles €38) are smart and prettily decorated; five have a river view. Breakfast €6. Half board is compulsory in high season at €41 per person. *Free coffee offered to our readers on presentation of this guide.*

Saint-Pardoux-la-Croisille

19320

Hôtel-restaurant Beau Site***

Take the D131.
Ⓣ05.55.27.79.44 Ⓕ05.55.27.69.52
Ⓦwww.hotel-lebeausite-correze.com
Closed *15 Oct–15 April.* **TV. Swimming pool. Car park. High chairs and games available.**

Hotel and leisure complex with a large garden, fishing pond, swimming pool, tennis courts and mountain bikes for hire – a place for people who like sporty holidays, good food and comfortable surroundings. Doubles with shower/wc or bath cost €56.50–62; the rooms lack soul but they're well maintained. Breakfast €6.80. The country cooking in the restaurant is fine: *parmentier* of house duck *confit*, zander with walnut stock, veal sweetbreads in pastry with truffle *jus* and raspberry soufflé. Menus €14 (weekday lunchtimes) and €17–42.

Saint-Robert

19310

Le Saint-Robert

Route d'Ayen, at the far end of the village.
Ⓣ05.55.25.58.09 Ⓕ05.55.25.55.13
Closed *Sun evening out of season; Mon; 10 Oct–15 April.* **TV. Swimming pool. Car park. Games available.**

A charming place that's as appealing for a family stay as it is for a romantic break. This lovely residence was built on a hillside on the border between the Limousin and Périgord by a rich banker in the nineteenth century and boasts breathtaking views over the valley – enjoy them from the terrace or the swimming pool. The rooms are simple and soberly furnished, retaining all their charm and style; doubles €38–58. Breakfast €6.50. The restaurant offers dishes using local produce and succulent meat. (Telephone first to check on opening days). Specialities include Limousin veal, cep *fricassée* and duck breast with Brive violet mustard. Menus €10–12 (weekday lunchtimes) and *menu-carte* €15 or €23. *10% discount per room for the first night (except for July/Aug) offered to our readers on presentation of this guide.*

Saint-Yrieix-la-Perche

87500

Hostel de la Tour Blanche**

74 bd. de l'Hôtel-de-Ville.
Ⓣ05.55.75.18.17 Ⓕ05.55.08.23.11
Ⓦwww.resto-latourblanche.fr
Closed *Sun; Feb school holidays.* **TV. Car park.**

The bedrooms are nice enough, and although those in the rafters are a bit cramped they're comfortable. Doubles with bath or shower/wc €40. You won't be disappointed by the restaurant. The first of the two dining rooms is the more traditional, serving fresh foie gras either as a terrine or pan-fried, millefeuille of Canadian lobster, good local meat, sea bream with mustard and supreme of Périgord guinea-fowl (menus €19.50–31). Lunchtime dish of the day Mon–Fri at €6.50. The other is more like a New York snack bar: the cooking is simpler but still pleasant and you get big helpings. They do great salads and a reasonably priced dish of the day with vegetables.

Restaurant Le Plan d'Eau

Plan d'eau-d'Arfeuille; it's on the outskirts of town, head for the campsite.
Ⓣ05.55.75.96.84 Ⓕ05.55.08.12.27

Closed *Tues; Wed; Jan.* **Disabled access. Car park.**

This is a very nice restaurant with a view of Lake Arfeuille. Proprietor Jean Maitraud always has time for a chat with his guests and prepares special menus for important dates like Mother's Day. On less festive occasions there's a dish of the day (€6.25) and menus at €8 (weekday lunchtimes) and reckon on €21 à la carte. Traditional home-made cooking and local dishes including Limousin beef and veal, fillet of perch and *tarte tatin. Free soup offered to our readers on presentation of this guide.*

|●| À La Bonne Cave

7 pl. de la Pierre-de-l'Homme; it's near the church.
☎05.55.75.02.12
Closed *Mon; a fortnight in Sept.*

A pleasant restaurant in an old white stone buildling. The cooking is simple and good, prices are reasonable and service comes with a smile. Weekday lunch *formule* for €9.76 and others €9.91–21.80. Dishes include snail profiteroles, veal *tourtière* with ceps and apple croustade with caramel sauce. They have some good bottles of wine, too.

12 LIMOUSIN

Coussac-Bonneval

87500 (11km E)

☗ |●| Les Voyageurs **

21 av. du 11 Novembre.
☎05.55.75.20.24 Ⓕ05.55.75.28.90
Closed *Sun evening; Mon; Jan.*
TV.

Behind this creeper-smothered façade is one of the best establishments in the département. Five of the nine superb rooms look over the garden, and they're all clean and comfortable. Doubles with bath €38.11–44.21. Also a restaurant serving traditional cuisine. Weekday menu at €11 and others €18–26; à la carte things get pricey.

Serre-de-Mestes (La)

19200

|●| Bar-restaurant La Crémaillère

Take the D982.
☎05.55.72.34.74
Closed *evenings; Mon; last week in June; a week end Aug–early Sept.* **Car park.**

Go through the bar to get to the restaurant, where you'll be welcomed by the friendly smile of the owner. The cooking is simple and generously served, with regional specialities and dishes such as duck *confit*, calf's head, coq au vin, *confits* and foie gras. There are terrific home-made fruit tarts for dessert. Weekday lunch menus €11; others €22.. This is a simple-looking place from the outside, but you'll certainly get your money's worth. *Free coffee with a meal offered on presentation of this guide.*

Souterraine (La)

23300

☗ |●| Hôtel Moderne

11 pl. de la Gare.
☎05.55.63.02.33
Closed *Sat lunchtime; Sun.*

A bit outdated, and the facilities are modest, but it is clean and well run. The prices are old-fashioned, too: rooms with washbasiin €19.85. The convivial bar, le Pot de l'Amitié, well deserves its name, which roughly means "A drink among friends". There's one menu only, and it costs €9.45. Great place if you're on a tight budget.

Saint-Étienne-de-Fursac

23290 (12km S)

☗ |●| Hôtel Nougier**

2 pl. de l'Église. Take the D1 in the direction of Fursac.
☎05.55.63.60.56 Ⓕ05.55.63.65.47
Closed *Sun evening; Mon and Tues lunchtime out of season and on public holidays; Mon lunchtime in high season; Dec to mid-March.* **TV. Car park.**

A very appealing, typically Limousin country inn with twelve bedrooms, some looking onto the garden. Doubles with bath €51.The elegant dining room serves local dishes updated for modern tastes: the menu changes twice a year, but typical dishes include terrine of crayfish tails, duck thighs in mushroom sauce, and *croustillant* of pig's trotters. Menus €18 and €30, reckon on €30–38 à la carte. The prices seem a little high for what you get, though, and the welcome is a wee bit frosty. There's a pretty terrace. Swimming pool and table tennis table.

Bénévent l'Abbaye

23210 (20km SE)

Hôtel du Cèdre**

Rue l'Oiseau. Take the D10.
Ⓣ05.55.81.59.99 Ⓕ05-55-81-59-98
Closed *Feb.* **Disabled access. TV. Swimming pool. Car park.**

A magnificent eighteenth-century building which has been carefully restored. The bright rooms are all different and have been decorated with taste; the nicest have a view of the grounds and a majestic cedar tree. Doubles are €40–90, and have good facilities. Breakfast €8. In summer the attractive terrace serves as the setting for the gourmet restaurant. Menus €20–45; dishes change with the seasons but typical choices include salad of crayfish, asparagus and poached eggs, or cod fillet with fennel and smoked crayfish. It's one of the most appealing places in the region.

Tarnac

19170

Hôtel des Voyageurs**

Ⓣ05.55.95.53.12 Ⓕ05.55.95.40.07
Ⓦwww.hotel-voyageurs-correze.com
Closed *Sun evening and Mon out of season; Feb.* **TV. High chairs available.**

A huge stone house in the heart of the village near the church. It's wonderfully maintained by the Deschamps: Madame runs the restaurant with an easy charm while her husband practises his culinary arts in the kitchen. He produces local dishes with a deep knowledge of the region and uses only the freshest produce – fish, Limousin beef, mushrooms picked in the woods in season. Try the calf's feet with ceps, the fillet of char with chive butter or the veal with girolles. Set menus €13.50 (not served Sun) and €21.58–26. The large, bright bedrooms upstairs are very pleasant and cost €42.50 with shower/wc or bath. *Free coffee offered to our readers on presentation of this guide.*

Tulle

19000

Hôtel du Bon Accueil*

8–10 rue Canton.
Ⓣ05.55.26.70.57
Closed *Sat evening and Sun; 23Dec–6 Jan.* **TV.**

A welcoming hotel-restaurant in a quiet street that you probably wouldn't find unless you knew about it. There are several cosy dining rooms where you can eat excellent duck or chicken *confits*, potato pies and, in season, cep omelettes. Set menus €12–23. The menu with two starters should satisfy even the most demanding appetites. The bedrooms are quite large and very well maintained – this place deserves more than one star. Doubles €30–40 with shower or bath. *Free apéritif offered to our readers on presentation of this guide.*

La Toque Blanche**

28 rue Jean-Jaurès, pl. Martial-Brigouleix.
Ⓣ05.55.26.75.41 Ⓕ05.55.20.93.95
Closed *Sun evening; Mon; 10 days end Feb–early Mar; 1 week July–early Aug.* **TV.**

The restaurant is one of the places to eat in the town, but the welcome is much more informal and relaxed than the smart dining room might lead you to expect. You'll find classic cuisine which is wonderfully executed, generously served and attractively presented: hot and cold *escalope* of foie gras, pig's trotter stuffed with duck *confit*, sole cooked on the bone with woodland garnish, iced nougat with Grand Marnier. Wine by the glass. Menus €21–34. Spacious, pretty double rooms with en-suite bathroom, TV and phone go for €40 a night. All in all, it's good value for money.

Hôtel-restaurant de la Gare**

25 av. Winston-Churchill; it's opposite the station.
Ⓣ05.55.20.04.04 Ⓕ05.55.20.15.87
Closed *Sun evening in winter; 1–15 Sept.* **TV.**

A classic station hotel with a restaurant that's popular with the locals. The kitchen has a good reputation: rabbit chasseur, crayfish salad, duck fillet stuffed with morels, zander with sorrel. Menus €11 (not served Sun) and €17–23. The rooms are comfortable and well soundproofed, though the decoration may not be to everyone's taste; doubles €47. *Free coffee offered to our readers on presentation of this guide.*

🏃 |●| Le Passé Simple

6 rue François Bonnelye.
☎ 05.55.26.00.75
Closed *Sun; Mon evening.*

A cosy establishment serving delicious dishes: mosaic of artichokes with tomato *coulis*, warm terrine of beef cheek pickled in red wine, zander with watercress sauce, grilled duck breast with a sweet-and-sour sauce and hot chocolate moelleux for dessert. Weekday lunch menu €16 or three *formules-carte*: €18 with main meal and dessert, €20 with starter and main meal, and €23 with starter, main meal and dessert. The service is sometimes a bit sloppy. *Free coffee offered to our readers on presentation of this guide.*

Sainte-Fortunade

19490 (10km S)

|●| Le Moulin de Lachaud

Take the D940 to Ste-Fortunade then the D1 for Cornil; 4km further turn onto the D94 towards Chastang, Beynat and Aubazin. It's 2km from there.
☎ 05.55.27.30.95
Closed *Mon and Tues excluding public holidays; 1–8 Sept; mid-Dec–mid-Jan.* **Disabled access. High chairs available.**

This old mill is way out in the country. The owners are a delightful young couple from Burgundy. Monsieur works wonders in the kitchen, producing inventive dishes from local produce and local recipes, which he redefines in his own way. Weekday *formules* €13, with menus at €20.50–36. Try the brandade of cold cod with capers or the baked zander with fresh morels. There's a terrace with a lovely view of the lake. You could even fish for trout if you fancy catching your own lunch.

Lagarde-Enval

19150 (11km S)

🏠 |●| Le Central**

It's opposite the church.
☎ 05.55.27.16.12 Ⓕ 05-55-27-13-79
Closed *Sat; Sun; 24 Aug; 8 Sept.* **TV.**

This large house, smothered in Virginia creeper, has been in the same family for four generations. It's across from the church and the pretty manor, both of which are sadly overshadowed by modern buildings. Regional and gourmet dishes – cep omelette, Limousin *escalope*, *confit* and *farcidur* (vegetable dumplings) – listed on the generous menus (€12 at lunch and others at €16 and €23). Very clean, comfortable rooms go for €30.50 with shower/wc and €35 with bath. Breakfast €5.35. It's a pleasant establishment and the staff make sure you enjoy your stay.

Gimel-les-Cascades

19800 (12km NE)

🏠 |●| L'Hostellerie de la Vallée**

☎ 05.55.21.40.60 Ⓕ 05.55.21.38.74
Closed *Sun and Mon evening; Dec–8 March.* **TV.**

A charming hotel. Crowds of people come to see the Gimel waterfalls, and since the sunny dining room has a fine view of them and the terrace is idyllic in warm weather, you'll need to book in summer. Doubles €43–46 with shower or bath; some rooms have views of the valley. Good cuisine in the restaurant, with lots of local produce: sliced beef with ceps and an excellent zander with beurre blanc and small fresh vegetables. Menus from €20; à la carte you'll spend around €25.

Seilhac

19700 (15.5km NW)

🏃 🏠 |●| Hôtel-restaurant La Désirade

42 av. Nationale; take the N120.
☎ 05.55.27.04.17
Closed *Sun out of season.*

This unassuming roadside hotel-restaurant is made more attractive by the friendliness of the owner, who will give you a warm welcome. The dining room has a particularly lovely, unadorned parquet floor. Simple, uncomplicated dishes: Limousin steaks, pizza, mixed salads and meat. Menus €9.50 (except weekends) up to €18.50. The old-fashioned bedrooms have an undeniable charm; doubles €35. Be warned, refurbishment work is planned for 2004. Maybe not the place to spend your entire holidays, but a good stopover. *Free Kir or coffee offered to our readers on presentation of this guide.*

Quatre-Routes-d'Albussac (Les)

19380 (16km S)

Hôtel Roche de Vic**

Les Quatre-Routes; it's at the junction of the N921 and the D940, 26km from Brive.
05.55.28.15.87 05.55.28.01.09
perso.wanadoo.fr/rochedevic
Closed *Mon March-end Sept.; 2 Jan-15 Mar.* **Disabled access. TV. Swimming pool. Car park. High chairs and games available.**

The large stone building is a 1950s-style manor with towers. Most of the bedrooms are at the back, overlooking the extensive grounds, the play area and the swimming pool. Doubles €35–40 – very good value. Even on the cheapest menus the restaurant offers a large choice of regional dishes such as scallops with morels, calves head ravigote, snails with asparagus tips and ceps, foie gras with morels, cod with honey and saffron *jus*, iced nougat and a pancake gâteau with orange. *Formule* €11 and menus €14–30, reckon on €20 à la carte. *Free apéritif (Mar–Dec) offered to our readers on presentation of this guide.*

Corrèze

19800 (22km NE)

Le Pécheur de Lune

Place de la Mairie.
05.55.21.44.93
Closed *Mon except in July and Aug.*

An atypical restaurant, where local dishes are served with a twist – the duck thigh is cooked with bilberries, the skate salad is freshened with asparagus and the cucumber salad has a tang of goat's cheese and pears. The veal's head and the pigeon braised with horn of plenty mushrooms are particularly delicious. €12 weekday *menu du jour* and others €21–23. *Free coffee offered to our readers on presentation of this guide.*

Chamboulive

19450 (24km N)

L'Auberge de la Vézère

Pont de Vernéjoux; take the D26.
05.55.73.06.94 05.55.73.07.05
www.aci.multi.medianet/gastronomie
Disabled access. Car park.

A charming riverside inn popular with local anglers. It's a good idea to book in high season as there are only seven bedrooms under the eaves; they cost €31 for a double with shower/wc. Breakfast €5. On the ground floor there's a friendly, dimly lit bar with a cantou (inglenook fireplace) as its focal point, and also a bright, sunny dining room overlooking the river. Duck features prominently on the menus (as civet, *confit* and foie gras) but there's also good Limousin meat and trout. There's a €10 weekday lunch menu and two others at €15 and €21. You'll get a cheery welcome from the proprietress, and after your meal you can go for a quiet stroll along the banks of the beautiful River Vézère. *Free apéritif offered to our readers on presentation of this guide.*

Turenne

19500

La Maison des Chanoines

Route de l'Église; take the D38 then the D150.
and 05.55.85.93.43
Closed *from All Saints' Day to Palm Sunday. Open every evening including Sun and Mon lunchtime.*

Turenne is a beautiful old town and this hotel is quite delightful. You'll find it at the start of the lane that leads up to the church and the château built by the Knights Templar. The dining room has a vaulted ceiling, or you can eat under the awning on the lovely terrace. Imaginative cooking and nicely presented dishes: *escalope* of foie gras marinated in truffle vinegar served with home-made walnut bread, chargrilled veal with morels and lots of desserts with walnuts. *Menus-carte* €28–34, and a truffle menu (to order; two people minimum) for €55. There are six comfortable, stylish bedrooms for €62–71. Breakfast €8.

La Vicomté

Place de la Halle.
05.55.85.91.32
lavicomte.free.fr
Closed *evenings; Mon; Nov–March.*

Annie runs this place and she serves all the great classics of the local area at modest prices: menus €12–22. The delightful dining room has a parquet floor and windows opening onto the valley. There's a lovely terrace on the village square.

Lorraine

Abreschviller

57560

☗ |●| Hôtel-restaurant Le Donon*

57 rue Pierre-Marie.
Ⓣ03.87.03.74.90 Ⓕ03.87.03.78.64
Closed *Mon; Tues; 3rd week of Sept; 20 Dec to early Jan.* **TV. Car park.**

A small family hotel for walking enthusiasts, within easy reach of the forest trails and mountain tracks. There are five homely bedrooms; doubles with shower/wc or bath go for €30. Half board €45. They serve simple, filling local and traditional dishes in the restaurant: sea trout with *anise*, wild boar haunch with girolles, trout fillet with Riesling, and flambéed tarts on weekend evenings. Menus, ranging from €10 (weekdays lunchtime) to €24, prove good value for money.

Saint-Quirin

57560 (5km SW)

☗ |●| L'Hostellerie du Prieuré**

163 rue du Général-de-Gaulle; take the D96.
Ⓣ03.87.08.66.52 Ⓕ03.87.08.66.49
Closed *Tues evening; Wed; Sat lunch; Feb school holidays; All Saints' school holidays.* **Disabled access. Highchairs available. TV. Car park.**

In the eighteenth century, the Church did not have a reputation for modesty – witness the imposing sandstone priory which now houses this restaurant. The cooking is rich and inventive and has won the restaurant a "*Moselle Gourmande*" award – try *baeckeoffe* of snails in white wine sauce, fish *pot-au-feu* with fresh mushrooms, roast squab, rabbit marinated in white wine with prunes and bacon, *croustillant* of goat's cheese with honey, grilled *escalope* of foie gras with apples and calvados. There's a weekday lunch menu for €10.60, with others from €20–50. You could do worse than stay the night here, too. The new rooms, in an annexe, have modern bathrooms but lack the charm of the restaurant. You'll pay €42–44 for doubles with basin or bath. Half-board €47.50. No. 5 is very spacious and has a pretty balcony where you can eat breakfast. Breakfast €6.50.

Lutzelbourg

57820 (22km NE)

☗ |●| Les Vosges**

149 rue Ackermann; take the RN4, the A4 and then the CD38.
Ⓣ03.87.25.30.09
Ⓦwww.hotelvosges.com
Restaurant closed *Wed; Sun evening; a fortnight in Nov.* **TV. Pay car park.**

In a delightful village in the crook of the pretty Zom valley, this hotel is on the bank of a small canal. The long-established family hotel has lost none of its charm over the years. All the bedrooms are furnished with antiques, and the beds have lace eiderdowns. Doubles with shower/wc €48; with bath €52. The traditional dining room suits the classic cooking. During the hunting season, try the *sautéed* deer with prunes, pheasant with mirabelle plums, or young wild boar with berries. Menus €16–29. Open terrace. *Free house aperitif on presentation of this guide.*

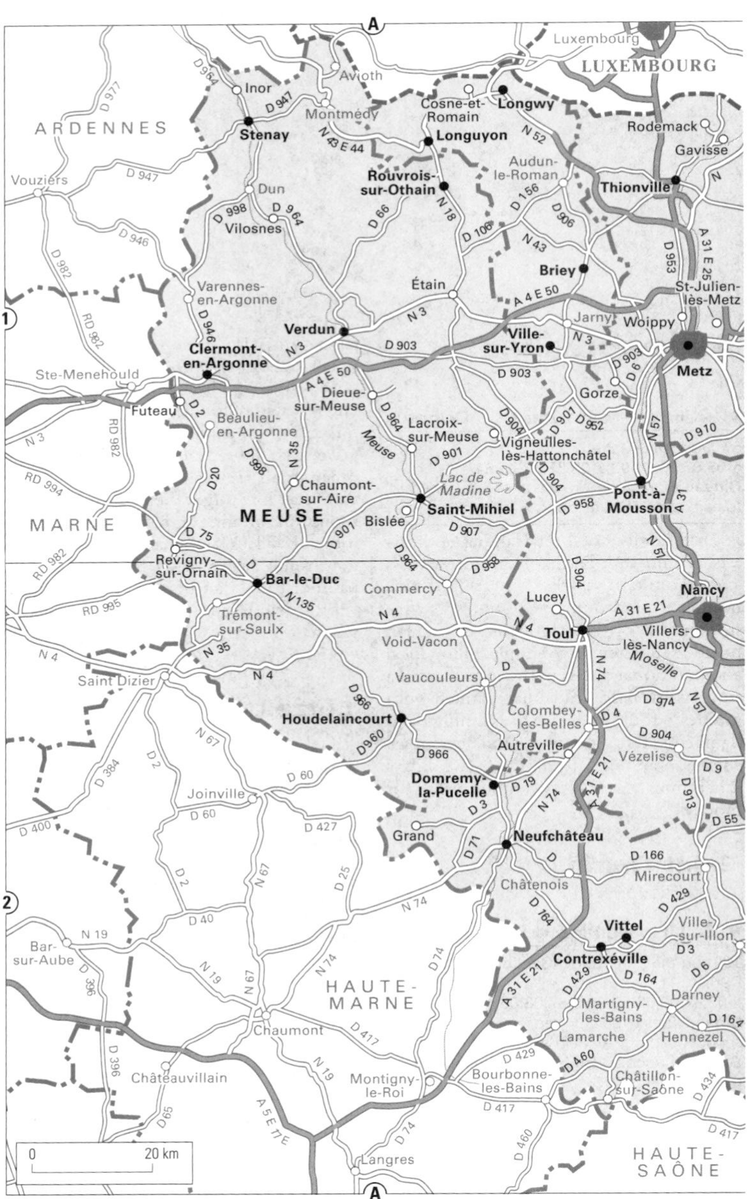
A
Luxembourg
LUXEMBOURG
Avioth
Inor
D 964
D 947
Montmédy
Cosne-et-Romain
Longwy
ARDENNES
Stenay
N 43 E 44
Longuyon
N 52
Rodemack
Gavisse
D 977
Audun-le-Roman
Vouziers
D 947
Rouvrois-sur-Othain
Thionville
Dun
D 998
D 964
Vilosnes
D 66
N 18
D 156
D 906
D 106
N 43
D 946
D 953
A 31 E 25
D 982
Briey
Varennes-en-Argonne
Étain
A 4 E 50
St-Julien-lès-Metz
D 946
Verdun
N 3
Jarny
Woippy
RD 982
Clermont-en-Argonne
N 3
D 903
Ville-sur-Yron
N 3
Metz
Ste-Menehould
A 4 E 50
D 903
D 903
D 6
Gorze
Futeau
D 2
Dieue-sur-Meuse
D 964
Beaulieu-en-Argonne
Lacroix-sur-Meuse
D 904
D 901
D 952
N 57
D 910
N 3
RD 982
Meuse
D 901
Vigneulles-lès-Hattonchâtel
N 35
D 998
Lac de Madine
D 904
RD 994
D 20
Chaumont-sur-Aire
Pont-à-Mousson
Saint-Mihiel
D 958
A 31
MEUSE
MARNE
Bislée
D 901
D 907
D 75
N 57
D 964
RD 982
Revigny-sur-Ornain
D 958
D 904
Bar-le-Duc
Commercy
Nancy
N 135
Lucey
A 31 E 21
RD 995
N 4
Trémont-sur-Saulx
N 4
Toul
Villers-lès-Nancy
Void-Vacon
N 4
N 35
Moselle
N 4
D
Saint Dizier
Vaucouleurs
N 4
N 74
D 966
Colombey-les-Belles
D 974
N 57
D 4
Houdelaincourt
N 67
D 904
D 960
D 966
Autreville
Vézelise
D 2
D 384
A 31 E 21
D 60
Domremy-la-Pucelle
D 19
D 9
Joinville
D 913
D 60
N 74
D 3
D 400
D 427
D 55
Grand
Neufchâteau
D 71
D
D 166
D 2
N 67
D 25
Châtenois
Mirecourt
D 429
N 74
D 164
D 40
Vittel
Bar-sur-Aube
N 19
Ville-sur-Illon
Contrexéville
D 3
D 396
N 19
N 74
D 74
D 429
D 164
D 6
N 67
A 31 E 21
HAUTE-MARNE
Darney
Martigny-les-Bains
Chaumont
D 417
Lamarche
D 164
Hennezel
N 19
D 429
D 396
Châteauvillain
D 460
Montigny-le-Roi
Bourbonne-les-Bains
Châtillon-sur-Saône
D 434
D 417
D 65
A 5 E 17
D 74
D 460
D 417
0
20 km
Langres
HAUTE-SAÔNE
A

13
LORRAINE

GERMANY
Manderen
Sierck-les-Bains
Montenach
Hombourg-Budange
Boulay-Moselle
Freyming-Merlebach
Forbach
Saarbrücken
Oeting
Sarreguemines
Bitche
Wœlfling-lès-S.
St-Avold
Faulquemont
Baerenthal
Niederbronn
MOSELLE
Sarre-Union
Delme
Château-Salins
Dieuze
PNR de Lorraine
Haguenau
Sarrebourg
Lutzelbourg
Saverne
BAS-RHIN
Dabo
Abreschviller
St-Quirin
St-Nicolas-de-Port
Lunéville
Strasbourg
Molsheim
MEURTHE-ET-MOSELLE
Celles-sur-Plaine
Bayon
Magnières
Baccarat
Senones
Raon-l'Étape
Grandrupt
Chamagne
Charmes
Rambervillers
la Petite-Fosse
Saint-Dié
Sélestat
VOSGES
Taintrux
Ban-de-Laveline
GER.
Ribeauvillé
Épinal
Chaumousey
Granges-sur-Vologne
le Valtin
Colmar
St-Étienne-lès-Remiremont
Gérardmer
Xonrupt-Longemer
Bains-les-Bains
Plombières-les-Bains
Remiremont
la Bresse
HAUT-RHIN
Freiburg
Fontenoy-le-Château
Girmont-Val-d'Ajol
le Val-d'Ajol
Bussang
Guebwiller
le Thillot
Thann
Luxeuil
Mulhouse
Rhin
Meurthe
N
B
1
2

13 LORRAINE

Baccarat

54120

🏃 🏠 🍽 Hôtel-restaurant de l'Agriculture

54 rue des Trois-Frères-Clément.
Ⓣ03.83.75.10.44
Closed *Fri evening; Sat; Sun evening.*

You'll see colourful window boxes and bright flowers tumbling down the façade of this irresistible country hotel. It's just outside the centre, with its famous glass museum, and is a perfect place to stop on a long hike through the Santois or the Mortagne valley. Simple rooms €30 with basin shower/wc. Breakfast €5. The convivial family atmosphere in the restaurant attracts a lot of local custom. Menus, €10.50 (weekday lunchtimes) to €21, list good, unpretentious cooking including calf's head and wild mushrooms – you'll spend about €26 à la carte. *Free coffee offered to our readers on presentation of this guide.*

🏠 🍽 Hôtel-restaurant La Renaissance**

31 rue des Cristalleries; it's opposite the glassworks.
Ⓣ03.83.75.11.31 Ⓕ03.83.75.21.09
Ⓦwww.hotel-la-renaissance.com
Closed *Fri and Sun evenings.* **TV.**

This is a convenient place to stay if you want to visit the Baccarat glass museum. The rooms have been simply but tastefully refurbished; doubles with shower/wc or bath €47–58. Half-board €54. The classical cooking uses fresh farm produce, with a weekday lunch menu at €11 and others €15–35. Specialities include calf's head.

Magnières

54129 (15km W)

🍽 🏃 Le Wagon du Pré Fleury

Ancienne gare: take the D47 from Baccarat.
Ⓣ03.83.72.32.58
Closed *Sun evening; 3 weeks Jan/Feb.* **TV.**

This restaurant occupies a genuine old railway carriage, parked at the station of Magnières. The station is also the departure point for draisines, which are like pedalos on rails, and which go for trips up and down the local branch lines. Cooking is a mixture of French and foreign styles, and they sometimes host theme evenings. Menus €13.90–29.30. Around €28 à la carte. *Free coffee on presentation of this guide.*

Bains-les-Bains

88240

🏃 🏠 🍽 Hôtel de la Poste**

11 rue de Verdun; it's next to the spa.
Ⓣ03.29.36.31.01
Ⓦwww.hpost.com
Closed *a week at the end of Oct; mid-Dec to mid-Jan.* **Restaurant closed** *evenings except Mon and Sat.* **TV. Highchairs available. Pay car park.**

This establishment has a somewhat forbidding façade, but it's undoubtedly the best place in the area. There are fourteen attractive rooms at €27.20 with basin, €37.90 with shower/wc, or €39.60 with bath. The hotel has fifteen nicely refurbished bedrooms in a style both rustic and modern. A few of the rooms overlook the flower garden. The cuisine is traditional but can't be faulted. There's an €11.05 menu (weekday lunchtimes only) and others at €13.10 and €15.40; reckon on around €29.50 à la carte. *10% discount on the room rate on presentation of this guide.*

Bar-le-Duc

55000

🏠 🍽 Hôtel-restaurant Bertrand*

19 rue de l'Étoile; it's behind the train station.
Ⓣ03.29.79.02.97 Ⓕ03.29.79.06.98
Ⓦwww.hotel-bertrand.com
Restaurant closed *Sun evening.* **Disabled access. TV. Car park.**

A friendly, warm, no-frills one-star with a family atmosphere. Menu at €8.50. The rooms are ordinary but well maintained; doubles with basin go for €22, with shower €25, with shower/wc €38, with bath €41. Some rooms have a balcony over the garden. The gorgeous Parc Marbeaumont is just a couple of minutes away.

🍽 Patati et Patata

9 rue Ernest Bradfer.
Ⓣ03.29.45.48.03
Closed *Sun; lunchtimes bank holidays; Christmas school holidays.*

Lots of garnished and gratinéed dishes, many of them potato-based (hence the name of the restaurant!), and salads served in this young, cool place where you can eat quickly, cheaply and late into the night. Weekday lunch menu €10, except in high season; à la carte €15–20.

🏃 |●| Grill-restaurant de la Tour

15 rue du Baile; it's in the upper town.
Ⓣ03.29.76.14.08
Closed *Sat lunchtime; Sun; public holidays.*

This sixteenth-century building is quite magnificent. You eat in a tiny room where they grill great *andouillettes* and black puddings over the open fire. The cooking, like the setting, is simple and authentic. Specialities include house duck terrine, grilled meats, and *tarte tatin*. Weekday lunch menu €11.50, others €16.06–20.50. Omelettes from €3.93. Dinner is served only until 8.30pm. *Free coffee on presentation of this guide.*

Revigny-sur-Ornain

55800 (15km NW)

🏃 🏠 |●| Les Agapes-La Maison Forte***

6 pl. Henriot du Coudray; take the D994 in the direction of Reims.
Ⓣ03.29.70.56.00 Ⓕ03.29.70.59.30
Closed *Sun evening; Mon and evenings of public holidays; 8–15 Feb; 1–15 Aug.* **TV. Car park.**

The owners of the Agapes made such a success of their restaurant that they bought the rooms in La Maison Forte and transformed this ancient fourteenth-century building into a charming hotel-restaurant. It's quite splendid and is the only starred place in the département, but all in all, prices are reasonable. The main building, housing the restaurant, is at the end of a tree-lined avenue. It has been thoughtfully decorated and has bare stone walls, old floor tiles and a fireplace. The cuisine is fresh and inventive, using unusual ingredients like dandelions and molasses. Specialities include plum soufflé, foie gras *pot-au-feu* and lobster salad with dandelions. Menus €27–51 or around €50 à la carte. The guest rooms are in the wings to the left and right of the main building; they're all very comfortable with old-style furnishings. Doubles with bath range from €57 to €107; some of those in the towers have beds on a mezzanine floor, and there are a few suites sleeping three. Breakfast €9.15. *Free apéritif on presentation of this guide.*

Chaumont-sur-Aire

55260 (20km N)

🏠 |●| Auberge du Moulin Haut

Take the N35 then the D902.
Ⓣ03.29.70.66.46 Ⓕ03.29.70.60.75
Ⓦwww. moulinhaut.fr
Closed *Sun evening; Mon.* **Disabled access. TV. Highchairs available. Car park.**

The wheel of this eighteenth-century mill turns gently to supply electricity to the restaurant and the noise is masked by the tinkling of a 1910 pianola. It's a peaceful and delightful place, run by a welcoming couple who have travelled widely in Africa, and the cuisine is balanced and full of flavour. The weekday lunch menu costs €15 and there are six others from €23 to €90, variously featuring duck specialities, regional dishes and, at the top of the scale, a gastronomic menu. Keep some space for dessert, especially the *croustillant flambé* of mirabelle plums. There are two double rooms in a charming annexe, costing €45 with shower/wc or bath. Breakfast €6. Half-board €67 for 1 person, €103 for two.

Bitche

57230

🏠 |●| 🏃 Hôtel-Pension de la Gare

2 av. Trumelet-Faber; it's near the station.
Ⓣand Ⓕ03.87.96.00.14
Closed *Sat; Sun; 9–25 Aug; 21 Dec–5 Jan.* **Car park.**

This is the only cheap hotel in town, and though the rooms are modest they're very clean. Doubles with shower €25. Breakfast €3.80. The *patronne* is so kind that you won't notice the slightly fading décor; sometimes the guests even lend a hand behind the bar. You'll eat unpretentious country cooking with a weekday set menu at €8.50; half board is €23 per person. It's advisable to book early. *Free coffee on presentation of this guide.*

|●| L'Auberge de la Tour

3 rue de la Gare; it's close to the Vauban citadel.
Ⓣ03.87.96.29.25

Closed *Mon; July*. **Car park.**

Atmospheric and cosy with its Belle Époque décor, this place has a popular brasserie atmosphere; the local paper, the *Républicain Lorrain*, lies about on the tables, and locals talk politics while they drink and eat. There's a weekday menu for €12.20, and others from €15–45. Interesting food combinations include prawns *marinière* with vegetable broth, or pike-perch and salmon terrine. Try the home-made sorbets for dessert.

Baerenthal

57230 (20km SE)

Le Kirchberg**

8 rue de la Fôret; take the N62 and when you get to Bannstein take the little road on the right.
Ⓣ03.87.98.97.70 Ⓕ03.87.98.97.91
Ⓦwww.le-kirchberg.com
Disabled access. TV. Highchairs available. Car park.

This unpretentious hotel is in a modern, very quiet building where it's easy to get a good night's sleep. Double rooms go for €50–62 with shower or bath; even the smallest are spacious and comfortable. They also have studios sleeping two or four that they rent by the week or weekend. Breakfast €6.80. *5% discount on a stay of three consecutive nights or free house apéritif on presentation of this guide.*

Briey

54150

Hôtel Ancona**

63 rue de Metz; it's near the bridge.
Ⓣ03.82.46.21.00 Ⓕ03.82.20.29.85
TV. Highchairs available.

Benefiting from its efficient double glazing, which effectively blocks out the passing traffic noise, this place offers comfortable rooms that are modestly priced at €45 with bath.The very friendly welcome makes it a pleasure to stay here. Decent, traditional food is served in the restaurant; menus €12 (weekday lunchtimes) up to €32. *Free house apéritif on presentation of this guide.*

Hôtel Aster**

Rue de l'Europe; it's on the edge of the Sangsue lake.
Ⓣ03.82.46.66.94 Ⓕ03.82.20.91.76
Ⓔspitoni@wanadoo.fr
Disabled access. TV. Car park.

A large, modern block that bears no resemblance to that charming inn you could be looking for. But the modern and comfortable rooms are bright and sunny and the surrounding greenery is appealing. Doubles €43 with shower or shower/wc. Breakfast €6. Menus €12 (weekday lunchtimes) and €22–31; try the steak tartare. *Free house apéritif on presentation of this guide.*

Celles-sur-Plaine

88110

Hôtel des Lacs**

2 pl. de l'Église. It's opposite the campsite.
Ⓣ03.29.41.17.06 Ⓕ03.29.41.18.21
Ⓔhotel.des.lacs@netcourier.com
Closed *Tues Oct–May; Sun evening except July/Aug; 23 Dec–26 Jan.* **Disabled access. TV.**

A good old-fashioned country hotel, entirely refurbished but still full of character. In the entrance, the piano and old furnishings immediately create a homely atmosphere. None of the fifteen rooms have a view over the lake but they are nonetheless really nice and comfortable. Doubles €44 with shower/wc or bath. Good cooking in the restaurant, where choices change frequently, and prices are reasonable. The dining room has kept its 1940s feel. Try the snails in flaky pastry with ceps if they're listed. Menus €16–30. Warm family atmosphere and friendly welcome. *Free coffee on presentation of this guide.*

Clermont-en-Argonne

55120

Hôtel-restaurant Bellevue**

14 rue de la Libération.
Ⓣ03.29.87.41.02 Ⓕ03.29.88.46.01
Closed *Sun evening and Wed.* **TV. Highchairs available. Car park.**

Guest rooms are functional and anonymous but the façade and the dining room are ravishing. The dining room, which retains all its original Art Deco features from 1923, leads onto a balcony overlooking the garden and the countryside. The cooking is simple, and portions are generous: in season they offer game dishes such as navarin of wild boar with *fricassée* of wild mushrooms. Other specialities include salad of rabbit liver, crayfish tails with whisky and veal kidneys with violet mustard. The €15 menu is served daily except for Sunday, and there are others at €24 and €32. There are seven rooms, ranging from €46 with shower/wc to €50 with bath. Peace and quiet are guaranteed, especially in the rooms at the back. *Free apéritif on presentation of this guide.*

Futeau

55120 (10km SW)

Hôtel-restaurant L'Orée du Bois***

Take the N3; at Islettes, turn left (south) onto the D2 and it's on the left, 500m beyond Futeau.
Ⓣ03.29.88.28.41 Ⓕ03.29.88.24.52
Ⓦwww.oreedubois.free.fr
Closed *Mon and Tues lunchtimes in season; Nov–March, Mon and Tues; Jan; last week in Oct and All Saints' Day.* **Disabled access. Highchairs available. TV. Car park.**

This place is quietly set on the edge of a wood, so you'll sleep well. The fifteen large bedrooms all have en-suite bathrooms; doubles go for €78–120. Breakfast €10. Half board €83–110 per person. They serve a weekday menu at €20 and others from €25–65. The local pigeon is particularly good, as is the house *fricassée* of crayfish tails. The *patronne* has two passions – cheese and wine – and there's a good selection of fine cheeses and vintages to choose from. Staff are friendly and enthusiastic.

Contrexéville

88140

Hôtel de Lorraine*

122 av. du Roi-Stanislas; it's near the train station.
Ⓣ03.29.08.04.24 Ⓕ03.29.08.09.63
Closed *13 Oct–31 March.* **Highchairs and games available.**

A big, pleasant old place with some style. The cooking is traditional, though special diets can be catered for. Set menus start at €10 (except Sun lunch) and rise to €16 and €21 – the last features Lorraine specialities. Try for example the frogs' legs and snails in pastry. Double rooms €25 with washing facilities and €34 with shower/wc or bath. Half board from €34. The rooms are simple but well-maintained. The hotel has an authentic spa town atmosphere. Really friendly welcome. *Free coffee on presentation of this guide.*

Hôtel des Sources**

Rue Ziwer-Pacha; it's opposite the town hall.
Ⓣ03.29.08.04.48 Ⓕ03.29.08.63.01
Ⓔhsources@club-internet.fr
Closed *Oct–March.* **Disabled access. TV.**

An elegant building very close to the esplanade with its colourful fountains. The atmosphere is just what you'd expect in a spa, with guests playing Scrabble or cards. The rooms are comfortable and have been decorated with care. On the third floor they've got a few attic rooms with basin for €30–33 depending on the season; otherwise doubles with shower/wc or bath cost €48. The restaurant isn't bad at all, with set menus at €11 (not Sun) and €16–24. Specialities include snail flan and fillet of zander with morels and a watercress *coulis*. *Free coffee or one free breakfast per room on presentation of this guide.*

Villa Beauséjour**

204 rue Ziwer-Pacha.
Ⓣ03.29.08.04.89 Ⓕ03.29.08.62.28
Ⓦwww.villa-beausejour.com
Closed *mid-Oct to Easter.* **TV.**

A charming hotel with a cosy salon and reception area. The rooms are individually decorated and furnished with period pieces and old mirrors. Those at the back or looking over the tranquil garden are the nicest. Doubles with basin/wc €39, with shower/wc €43–46. The restaurant provides good food, diet or not. Menus €19–48, including a *saveur minceur* menu at €25.

Hôtel de la Souveraine***

Parc thermal.
Ⓣ03.29.08.09.59 Ⓕ03.29.08.16.29
Ⓦwww.souveraine-hotel.com
Car park. TV.

This elegant building, which used to be the residence of the Duchess Wladimir, aunt of Nicolas II, the last Russian Tsar, looks onto the spa's park. Beautifully renovated rooms, though they've kept most of the old panelling, wooden floor and antique furniture. The prices are reasonable with rooms around €65 with shower/wc or bath. No restaurant.

Dabo

57850

Restaurant Zollstock

11 rte. Zollstock, La Hoube; it's 6km from Dabo on the D45.
03.87.08.80.65
Closed *Mon; Tues evening; end June to early July; Christmas to New Year.* **Highchairs available. Disabled access.**

Looking across a forested valley, this peaceful restaurant doesn't get much passing trade, and most of the customers are regulars. There's a weekday menu for €9 and three others from €14.80–19.50, listing simple but tasty specialities. Plump for venison haunch and fresh charcuterie in season, salmon in champagne sauce and, for dinner, frogs' legs and *mignon* of veal with morels. It's small and extremely pleasant with an appealing family atmosphere, and is especially popular for Sunday lunch.

Delme

57590

Hôtel-restaurant à la XIIe Borne**

6 pl. de la République.
03.87.01.30.18 03.87.01.38.39
www.12eme-borne.com
Disabled access. TV. Pay Car park. Highchairs available.

Delme was once a Roman encampment at the twelfth marker or *borne* on the road from Metz to Strasbourg – hence the establishment's name. The hotel has been refurbished and rooms cost €45 with basin or shower, €64 with bath or shower/wc. Breakfast €7. There's also a sauna, free for all guests. Menus go for €12 (weekday lunchtimes) and €16–68; choose from dishes such as *escalope* of foie gras, roast John Dory with green asparagus butter, beef fillet with morels, mirabelle plum charlotte. There's a good list of local wines. *Free house apéritif on presentation of this guide.*

Domrémy-la-Pucelle

88630

Hôtel Jeanne d'Arc

1 rue Principale; it's next to the church.
03.29.06.96.06
Closed *15 Nov–11 March*. **Car park.**

A welcoming little hotel with seven rooms, very near St Joan's house. Little has changed over the years, and that includes the prices: you'll pay €25 for a quiet, plain but clean double with shower/wc. Breakfast, €4, is brought to your room. Credit cards not accepted, and animals not allowed.

Autreville

88300 (14km NE)

Hôtel Relais Rose**

24 rue de Neufchâteau; take the D19 then the N74.
03.83.52.04.98 03.83.52.06.03
catherine.loeffie@wanadoo.fr
Disabled access. TV. Car park.

The hotel, right on the main road, is not an obvious place to stop, but it's worth it. Over the last two generations, it's been a favourite stop for many holiday makers on their way south. Inside it's a charming old family house with lovely rooms; some (like "Pivoine" or "Dahlia") have balconies or views over the garden and the countryside beyond. With bath or shower they go for €41–66. The weekday lunch menu costs €11.20 and there are others at €21–27. They offer excellent rabbit with *vin gris* from Toul, veal sweetbreads with morels, and a number of dishes from the southwest – where Madame comes from – including foie gras, *cassoulet* and duck *confit*. Excellent wines from the ancient cellar. *10% discount on the room rate for a minimum stay of two consecutive nights on presentation of this guide.*

Épinal

88000

Hôtel Kyriad**

12 av. du Général-de-Gaulle; it's opposite the train station.
03.29.82.10.74 03.29.35.35.14
hotel-kyriad-epinal@wanadoo.fr
Closed *23 Dec–1 Jan.* **TV. Pay Car park.**

The hotel is part of a chain and is located

in a dull neighbourhood, but it has the charm of a family-run station hotel where they make you feel very welcome. They've put in soundproofing, which is essential to block out the noise of the road and passing trains, and there's a bar. Doubles with shower/wc or with bath cost €54–60; there are also three air-conditioned suites for €80. Breakfast €6.50. Good value for money. *Free garage space and 10% discount on the room rate on Fri, Sat and Sun on presentation of this guide.*

Restaurant Le Pinaudré

10 av. du Général-de-Gaulle; it's opposite the train station.
03.29.82.45.29
Closed *Fri evening; Sat lunchtime; Sun; Aug; a week at Christmas.*

A discreet restaurant that's easy to miss. The large, attractive dining room has been done up to look like a modern bistro, and the cooking is traditional with a few modern touches. There's an excellent weekday lunchtime menu at €12, and others at €15–26. Fish and seafood predominate, both on the menus and à la carte, but you'll find a few local dishes too on the menu. Good welcome and good service. *Free coffee on presentaion of this guide.*

Restaurant Les Fines Herbes

15 rue La Maix; it's near pl. des Vosges.
03.29.31.46.70
wwwfines.herbes.fr
Closed *Sun evening; Mon; first fortnight in Sept.*

The décor is streamlined and modern while managing to feel intimate, and the unusual cooking is served with care and attention. Menus change every month and are reasonably priced; the lunchtime menu costs €12.50, with others €17–28.50. A lot of fish dishes on the menus and à la carte. They close at 11pm.

Le Petit Robinson

24 rue Raymond-Poincaré.
03.29.34.23.51
Closed *Sat; Sun; mid-July to mid-August; 24 Dec–1 Jan.*

A very classic restaurant offering classic French cuisine. Menus €19–33. The classic décor – all wood panelling and light colours – is warm and welcoming. Friendly though discreet welcome.

Chaumousey

88390 (10km W)

Le Calmosien

37 rue d'Épinal; take the N460 in the direction of Darney.
03.29.66.80.77
www.vosgeshotels.com/calmsien
Closed *Sun evening; Mon.* **Car park.**

From the outside you might mistake this place for a country station, but inside the dining room is elegant and contemporary. In the summer they set a few tables out in the garden. The imaginative chef comes up with classic cuisine and a few local dishes that change regularly. Menus €19–45. There's a great wine list, with a few pleasant surprises. Since it has such an excellent reputation locally it's best to book.

Forbach

57600

Hôtel Le Pigeon Blanc

42 rue Nationale.
and 03.87.85.23.05
Closed *Sun.* **Disabled access. TV. Car park.**

This establishment is one of the best unstarred hotels in the area – the rooms in the annexe, which are very spacious and quiet, are particularly good. Doubles range from €16 with basin to €26 with shower/wc and €30 with shower/wc/TV. The only drawback is that you have to vacate your room by 10am. No restaurant. TV available in the annexe bedrooms only.

Hôtel de la Poste**

57 rue Nationale.
03.87.85.08.80 03.87.85.91.91
TV. Car park.

This is the oldest hotel in Forbach and it's been providing decent accommodation for a hundred years. Rooms have been fully renovated and decorated in blue, yellow or pink depending which floor they're on. Doubles with basin €28, with shower/wc or bath €43. Breakfast €6. It's set back from the street so you won't be disturbed by noise. *10% discount on the room rate in Jan, July and Aug or one free breakfast per room per night on presentation of this guide.*

Oeting

57600 (2km S)

Restaurant À l'Étang

386 rue de Forbach; it's near the church.
☎ 03.87.87.33.85
Closed *Tues evening; Wed; mid-Aug.*
Highchairs available.

A restaurant in a big, pleasant house with country-style décor and a little pond. The weekday lunch menu, €10, and others, from €20–38, change according to the seasons. Specialities include fish – carp fillet with pepper, pike-perch in Pinot Noir – and game in season. Also good are the Alsace *vol-aux-vents* and the *presskopf*. There's a shady terrace by the pond. *Free coffee on presentation of this guide.*

Freyming-Merlebach

57800

Hôtel-restaurant Au Caveau de la Bière

2 rue du 5-Décembre; it's opposite the music conservatory.
☎ 03.87.81.33.45 Ⓕ 03.87.04.95.95
Closed *Sat; Sun evening.* **Car park.**

A few regulars come to the bar for a beer, but above all this is a business hotel. Rooms are clean and functional; €40 with bath. They prepare simple traditional dishes like quiche lorraine, grilled *andouillette* or tripe in Riesling, which you can wash down with a glass of Amos, one of the few beers that are still brewed locally. Weekday menu €10 and €14, and others from €20–30.

Sainte-Barbe

25 rue de Metz; it's on the edge of town on the way to Metz, opposite the unmissable Houillères du Bassin Lorrain building.
☎ 03.87.81.24.24
Closed *Sat and Sun evenings; 15–30 June.*
Disabled access.

A good local restaurant that's ideal if you want a quick midday meal. Business workers pile into the big, old-fashioned – not to say kitsch – dining room at lunchtime, when they can enjoy huge helpings of hearty family cuisine. Menus €10–22. Service is cheery.

Gérardmer

88400

Aux P'tits Boulas*

4 pl. du Tilleul (centre).
☎ 03.29.27.10.06 Ⓕ 03.29.27.11.91
Ⓦ www.auxptitsboulas.wml.fr
Closed *Wed evening; Thurs; fortnight in March; 3 weeks during the autumn school holidays.* **TV.**

A charming family hotel with four bright, nicely refurbished and well-maintained but small double rooms at €30 with basin, €44 with shower/wc. Half-board €33 per person. Only three bedrooms (incl. our favourite no. 5) have a shower. The restaurant provides good local dishes including sirloin steak with Munster cheese sauce, trout in Riesling, flambéed mirabelle plums and so on. Menus €11.50 (except Sun) and €14.

Hôtel de Paris**

13 rue François-Mitterrand.
☎ 03.29.63.10.66 Ⓕ 03.29.63.16.47
Closed *1st week of March; 1st week of Nov.*
TV. Car park.

A very simple little hotel located in the ski resort's busiest street. It's not a luxurious place, but the rooms are reasonably priced; doubles go from €32 with basin, €40 with shower/wc or bath/wc. The ones overlooking the interior courtyard are the quietest. The hotel fills up at the weekend so you should secure your room by sending a deposit. There's a separate brasserie on the ground floor, and a lively bar with a large selection of beers. *10% discount on the room rate.*

Hôtel Gérard d'Alsace**

14 rue du 152e R.I.
☎ 03.29.63.02.38 Ⓕ 03.29.60.85.21
Ⓦ www.gerardmer.net
Closed *15 Nov–1 Dec.* **TV. Swimming pool.**

This substantial Vosges house, just 150m from the lake on a small track, is a peaceful place. It's got a retro feel – the hotel opened in the early 50s – but it's not unattractive, and it does have a heated swimming pool. The rooms have been refurbished quite nicely; most of them have double glazing, and all of them overlook the garden. You'll pay €38 for a double with basin, €41–58 with shower/wc or bath/wc. Four rooms accommodating up to four persons are also available, all with bath/wc. *10% discount on the room rate except in Feb, July, Aug and Christmas holidays on presentation of this guide.*

🏃 🏠 |●| Hôtel Viry - Restaurant L'Aubergade

Place des Déportés; 200m from the lake.
Ⓣ03.29.6302.41 Ⓕ03.29.63.14.03
Ⓦwww.gerardmer.net/hotel-viry
Restaurant closed *Fri evening out of season.* **TV. Car park.**

The hotel has been around for a good forty years, so it's almost an institution in its own right. The rooms which have been recently refurbished are small but nice. Double rooms €40–44 with basin, €49–60 with shower/wc or bath, satellite TV. Half board, recommended in high season and on holiday weekends, costs €49–54 per person. The rustic-looking dining room offers particularly good value, and in summer you can eat on a covered terrace on the square. They serve sound regional cuisine. There's a decent *menu du marché* at €12 and others up to €39. Friendly welcome and courteous service. *Free house apéritif on presentation of this guide.*

🏠 |●| Hôtel-restaurant Chalet du Lac**

97 chemin de la droite du lac; it's beside the lake, 1km from the town centre on the D147 in the direction of Épinal.
Ⓣ03.29.63.38.76 Ⓕ03.29.60.91.63
Closed *Oct.* **TV.**

Historic wooden chalet overlooking the lake and the road, which is far enough away not to be distracting. Though the rooms have been renovated, they've kept their antique furniture and have a really nice, old-fashioned feel. All of them have shower/wc and a balcony for those overlooking the lake, and they each cost €53.76. Breakfast €7.32. There's an annexe in another chalet a few metres away on the edge of the forest. As for the restaurant, the food is traditional with regional influences. Menus around €18; à la carte €31. There's a lovely garden.

🏠 Le Grand Hôtel***

17–19 rue Charles-de-Gaulle, pl. du Tilleul.
Ⓣ03.29.63.06.31 Ⓕ03.29.63.46.81
Ⓦwww.grandhotel.gerardmer.com
Disabled access. TV. Swimming pool. Car park.

A grand hotel in the old style that has seen many famous guests passing through its doors since its opening in 1870: from Napoleon III who came to open the route over the Schlucht pass to the movie stars of the Fantastic Movie Festival. From its glorious past remain the cosy Louis XIII bar, the huge hall and a large oak staircase. The spacious rooms are however modern and attractively decorated, some on a mountain theme, others with romanticism in mind... Some have balconies or a large terrace where you can have breakfast in summer. Doubles with bath go for €89–127, and they have a few suites, too. Half-board compulsory during school holidays and weekends cost €70–89. There are two swimming pools – the heated indoor one has a wave machine and a Jacuzzi, with a fitness room and beauty salon.

🏃 |●| Le Bistrot de la Perle

32 rue Charles-de-Gaulle.
Ⓣ03.29.60.86.24
Closed *Tues evening and Wed out of season; 1–22 Oct.* **Highchairs available.**

This place, which used to be a butcher's shop, retains its original picturesque façade. The light, pleasant dining room offers a friendly service and eclectic dishes, from fried mussels and *choucroute* to snail clafoutis. Choose the €9.70 *formule* for good, freshly cooked dishes; there are also menus at €14.50 and €20.10. There's a patio planted with flowers at the back. *Free apéritif on presentation of this guide.*

|●| L'Assiette du Coq à l'Âne

Place du Tilleul.
Ⓣ03.29.63.06.31
Ⓦwww.grandhotel.gerardmer.com

Weekday lunch menu at €11; others at €16 and €21. This recently built hotel has successfully re-created the appearance of an old local country house. The floor tiles, high beamed ceiling and fireplace are all pleasantly rustic, and the local cuisine though not worth a detour is good. The service is professional and efficient (this is an annexe of the *Grand Hôtel*).

Xonrupt-Longemer

88400 (7km NE)

🏃 🏠 |●| Hôtel Le Collet - Restaurant Lapôtre***

9937 rte. de Colmar; it's beyond Xonrupt on the D417 in the direction of col de la Schlucht Munster.

Ⓣ03.29.60.09.57 Ⓕ03.29.60.08.77
Ⓦwww.chalethotel-lecollet.com
Closed *12 Nov–12 Dec.* **Restaurant closed** *Wed outside school holidays; Thurs lunchtimes.* **TV. Car park.**

This is a big traditional chalet, set at 1100m in the heart of the Vosges nature reserve; it's near the cross-country ski trails and the ski lifts. The welcome is simple yet special and there's a luxurious feel to the place. Pretty double rooms with shower/wc or bath go for €69; the nicest ones have a balcony with a view of the forest. The very good regional cuisine has been revamped by a young chef bursting with ideas and enthusiasm. Menus, €15 (weekday lunchtimes), €22 and €25, list such dishes as *bibelaskas* (fresh cheese flavoured with horseradish and herbs), *lewerknepfla* (quenelles of liver), *andouillette* and potato pie, and smoked trout *parfait*. The wine list features many Alsace wines along with a few gems from other regions. *10% discount on the room rate on presentation of this guide.*

Bresse (La)

88250 (13km S)

Hôtel-restaurant Les Vallées

31 rue Paul-Claudel.
Ⓣ03.29.25.41.39 Ⓕ03.29.25.64.38
Ⓔhotel.lesvallees@remy-loisirs.com
TV. Highchairs and games available. Car park. Indoor Swimming pool. Tennis courts.

Doubles with bath €42–84, depending on the season. Breakfast €8.50. Weekly lunchtime menu €17; others €21–44. This hotel complex is definitely very contemporary. The rooms are nice and the bathrooms spacious. The breakfast is really good and the helpings generous. A few fully equipped flats with kitchenette are also available. The dining room is very big, hence a bit noisy, but it opens up onto a nice garden. Good traditional cuisine.

Le Clos des Hortensias

51 rte. de Cornimont; just outside Bresse on the road to Remiremont.
Ⓣ03.29.25.41.08
Closed *Sun evening; Mon; 13–20 April; 12–26 Nov.*

Weekly menu at €14; others €19.50–35. Refined but simple regional cuisine (the *andouillette* from Val-d'Ajol is really delicious). The chef is particularly renowned for his fish specialities, such as *rillettes* of salmon or fisherman's pot. Elegant dining room in an old country house. Friendly welcome. *Free coffee on presentation of this guide.*

Valtin (Le)

88230 (13km NE)

Auberge du Val Joli**

12 bis, Le village; from Gérardmer follow the signs to Saint-Dié, turn right onto the D23 in the direction of Colmar, then left at Xonrupt over the mountain road to Le Valtin.
Ⓣ03.29.60.91.37 Ⓕ03.29.60.81.73
Ⓦwww.lorrainehotels.com/val-joli
Closed *Sun and Mon evenings and Tues lunch except school holidays; Mon lunchtime all year (except public holidays); 8–17 April; 15 Nov–8 Dec.* **Disabled access. TV. Car park.**

A superb place in one of the region's prettiest villages, set near pine forests and mountains. This is a real old-fashioned inn, with a warm and friendly atmosphere. Doubles go for €70–75 with shower/wc; with spa bath €77–105. Breakfast €10.50. Half board, at €50–105 per person, is compulsory during the school holidays. The dining rooms are wonderfully rustic with superb old beams on the ceiling and a tiled floor. There is also a conservatory overlooking the mountains. The cooking is good and traditional. There's a weekday menu at €15, with others for €18–50, listing dishes such as pâté lorrain (traditional pure pork meat pie), smoked trout, *blanc de sautret* (Vosges chicken in cream and Riesling sauce) and bilberry tart.

Houdelaincourt

55130

L'Auberge du Père Louis**

8 rue Alainville.
Ⓣ03.29.89.64.14 Ⓕ03.89.78.84
Ⓦwww.aubergeduperelouis.fr
Closed *Sun evening; Mon.* **TV.**

For anyone who likes good food, this is one of the places to eat in the region. The cooking is innovative and exciting, and though the menus change with the seasons you may well see dishes like *carpaccio* of artichoke and parmesan, sweetbreads casserole with truffle and flower and herb sorbet. Menus €18 (weekdays) and €55.

There are six quiet, pleasant rooms with shower/wc, which go for €38. Breakfast €7. *10% discount on the room rate on presentation of this guide.*

Longuyon

54260

Hôtel de la Gare – Restaurant La Table de Napo*

2 rue de la Gare; it's next to the train station.
03.82.26.50.85 03.82.39.21.33
Closed *Fri evening except July–Aug; a fortnight in March; a fortnight in Sept.*
Highchairs available. Car park.

The good-natured owner creates a family atmosphere in her establishment. It feels like an old guest house with pretty pieces of furniture and bright, comfortable rooms; a double will cost €35 with shower, €50 with shower/wc. Breakfast €6.50. The entrance to the hotel is on the station platform, and some rooms look over the tracks – sadly, the double glazing doesn't cut out all the noise. If you're worried about not sleeping well, ask for a room looking onto the street. The three-star restaurant serves superb dishes cooked with fresh market produce, listed on five menus from €12.50–42. *Free coffee on presentation of this guide.*

Hôtel de Lorraine – Restaurant Le Mas***

65 rue Augistrou.
03.82.26.50.07 03.82.39.26.09
www.lorraineetmas.com
Closed *Mon except public holidays; Jan.* **TV. Pay Car park.**

This Belle Époque hotel has an attractive façade and a lovely lounge boasting old beams and ceiling mouldings. The rooms, however, are completely different – though bright, they lack the style of the common areas. Doubles with shower/wc or bath cost €55. In the winter there's a blaze in the open fireplace and in summer they open up the terrace and plant troughs of flowers. The restaurant, with menus at €19 (weekdays) and €38.50, has a good reputation.

Longwy

54400

Hôtel du Nord**

Place Darche; it's right in the middle of the upper town.
03.82.23.40.81 03.82.23.17.73
Closed *last three weeks in Aug.* **Restaurant closed** *Mon evening; Sat lunchtime; Sun; public holidays.* **TV. Car park.**

Many towns in France have a bar-hotel like this, but this one has particular charm because of its unique location on the impressive square. The modern rooms are clean and quiet; they cost €45 with shower/wc or bath. The brasserie offers traditional dishes; reckon on spending €19; dish of the day will cost around €9. *Free house apéritif on presentation of this guide.*

Cosnes et Romain

54400 (5km W)

Le Train Bleu

Rue Béarn; From Longwy-Haut, take the N18 in the direction of Longuyon for 4km, turn right at the sign.
03.82.23.98.09
Closed *Mon; Sat lunchtime.*

They've joined two railway carriages together to create this attractive dining room, and you have to push a button to open the door. Inside, the décor is plush and the cooking is great: try the *cassolette* of sweetbreads and girolles, or sole fillets stuffed with smoked salmon. Menus offer something for every budget, starting with the weekday menu at €12 and ranging up to €36. It's particularly popular at weekends.

Lunéville

54300

Hôtel des Pages***

5 quai des Petits-Bosquets; it's across the river from the château.
03.83.74.11.42 03.83.73.46.63
Disabled access. TV. Car park.

This quiet hotel is enclosed by a large courtyard, not far from the river. A separate building houses the bar, sitting room and breakfast room, along with seven bedrooms. Rooms in the main building have a contemporary feel; the décor is subtle and unusual. Double rooms €50–120 with shower/wc or bath. Half-board €58 per person. Breakfast €6. You can also dine here; there are menus at €15.50 and €20. *One free breakfast per room per night on presentation of this guide.*

Marie Leszczynska

30 rue de Lorraine; it's behind the château.
ⓣ03.83.73.11.85
Closed *Sun evening; Mon; Tues evening.*

This restaurant, named after the wife of King Louis XV, offers a friendly welcome and elegant cuisine: try the pan-fried duck foie gras with spiced bread, the veal steak with cep cream or the turbot in flaky pastry. Menus €13.30–35. The pretty dining room is refined and understated, with an intimate setting, and there's a pleasant terrace in a pedestrianized street – lovely when the sun shines.

Manderen

57480

Le Relais du Château Mensberg**

15 rue du Château; it's on the D64.
ⓣ03.82.83.73.16 ⓕ03.82.83.23.37
Closed *3 weeks in Jan.* **Restaurant closed Tues. Disabled access. Games available. TV. Car park.**

The château of Mensberg – known as the "Château de Malbrouck" – was built in the seventh century and, according to legend, rebuilt in the fifteenth with the help of the devil. Today the impressive building, which dominates the village, offers fifteen comfortable, pretty double rooms €51–60. Half-board €55 per person. Breakfast €7. There's an extremely handsome dining room where you can enjoy a number of carefully prepared Lorraine specialities that change with the seasons; menus €18.50–42. *10% discount on the room rate for a minimum stay of over three consecutive nights on presentation of this guide.*

Metz

57000

See map on pp.496–497

Hôtel La Pergola**

13 rte. de Plappeville. **Off map A1-2**
ⓣ03.87.32.52.94 ⓕ03.87.31.41.60
ⓔe.keil@libertysurf.fr
TV. Car park.

The hotel, with a 1950s-look façade, is 3km from the centre and its sign is not very obvious. It's worth the effort of getting there, though; rooms, which are all furnished differently, feature brass beds and period furniture, and you are woken by the birds singing in the wonderful garden, where afternoon tea is served under the trees. Those up in the eaves have sloping ceilings, and some of the bathrooms are as big as the rooms themselves. Doubles €458. Dogs accepted (€4.50 per night). *10% discount on the room rate on presentation of this guide.*

Hôtel du Centre**

14 rue du Pont-des-Loges. **Map B2-8**
ⓣ03.87.36.06.93 ⓕ03.87.75.60.66
ⓦwwwperso.wanadoo.fr/hotelducentre-metz
Closed *25 Dec–5 Jan; 31 July–22 Aug.* **TV. Pay Car park.**

Ideally located on a pedestrianized street and – hardly surprisingly, given the name – in the centre of the town. An old wooden staircase (no lift) takes you to the attractively arranged, charming rooms; those on the top floor, under the roof, have nice sloping ceilings. Doubles with shower/wc €45. Cots available (€7/night). Breakfast, €5, includes home-baked breads and pastries cooked on the premises. Parking €5 per night. *One free breakfast per room per night on presentation of this guide.*

Hôtel Moderne**

1 rue Lafayette. **Off map B3-4**; opposite the station.
ⓣ03.87.66.57.33 ⓕ03.87.55.98.59
ⓦwww.hotel-moderne-metz.com
TV. Pay Car park.

A classic station hotel with a predominantly business clientèle. Rooms are modern and functional but not impersonal; the ones at the back are the quietest, while those with two double beds, like no. 22, are terrific value. You'll pay €47–54 for a room with shower/wc or bath. Half-board from €40 per person. *15% discount on the room rate during weekends and public holidays on presentation of this guide.*

Cécil Hôtel**

14 rue Pasteur. **Map B3-3**
ⓣ03.87.66.66.13 ⓕ03.87.56.96.02
ⓦwww.cecilhotel-metz.com
Closed *26 Dec–3 Jan.* **TV. Highchairs available. Billard tables. Pay Car park.**

The hotel is in a handsome early twentieth-century building between the station and the centre. Prices for the modern and well-equipped – if slightly soulless – rooms, decorated in a 1970s style, range from €52 for a double with shower/wc to €56 with bath. Breakfast €6. *Free use of garage on presentation of this guide.*

Hôtel de la Cathédrale***

25 pl. de la Chambre. **Map B1-7**
03.87.30.27.25 03.87.75.40.75
hotelcathedrale-metz@wanadoo.fr
Disabled access. TV.

Chateaubriand and Madame de Staël stayed in this coaching inn, which was built in 1627, and various other famous people have slept here since. Monsieur Hocine restored the building himself and Madame undertook to decorate it – they've done it beautifully, and the period beams, iron work, casements and interior courtyard are all amazing. The rooms, too, are full of character and charm; each is decorated differently, but they're all bright with elegant fittings, and some have a view of the cathedral. Doubles €55–80 with shower/wc or €69 with bath. Booking strongly advised. *10% discount on the cheapest room rate on presentation of this guide.*

Hôtel Kyriad – Restaurant du Père Potot**

8 rue du Père-Potot. **Map B3-5**
03.87.36.55.56 03.87.36.39.80
www.kyriad.fr
Disabled access. TV. Pay Car park.

Centrally located but looking a bit out of place in this particular neighbourhood, this hotel offers refurbished rooms. They're all alike but not unpleasant; doubles with shower/wc go for €59. Half-board €41–67. Note that the odd-numbered ones look onto the courtyard of an old abbey. The restaurant is good, too, with a weekday menu for €13 and others at €15 and €18. Good dishes include veal with Munster cheese, snails with Toul Gris wine and mirabelle plum *crème brûlée*. *Free apéritif or 10% discount on the room rate on presentation of this guide.*

Grand Hôtel de Metz**

3 rue des Clercs. **Map B2-6**
03.87.36.16.33 03.87.74.17.04
TV. Highchairs available. Pay Car park.

This hotel, in a pedestrianized street in the old part of town, boasts an ultra-modern entrance with a superb staircase. The clean, comfortable rooms are decorated in pastels and flower-patterned fabrics, and overlook the inner courtyard; doubles €70 with shower/wc or bath. Half-board available for an extra €14 per person. Breakfast €5.80. *Free breakfast on presentation of this guide.*

Aux Petits Oignons

5 rue du Champé. **Map B2-11**
03.87.18.91.33
Closed *Sat lunchtime; Sun; 3 weeks in July/Aug.*

In a small street just off the centre, this restaurant has an intimate dining room that's perfect for a dinner for two. The Provençal cuisine is simple but well-prepared. Menu of the day €10.75. You'll spend about €30 à la carte. It's best to book.

Le Bistrot des Sommeliers

10 rue Pasteur. **Map B3-17**
03.87.63.40.20
Closed *Sat lunchtime; Sun; Christmas to New Year; bank holidays.*

Youthful, good-value place with leatherette-covered benches and wine-bottle candlesticks. There's an interesting selection of wines to drink, too, by the glass or the jug, and traditional dishes that are as simple as they are tasty. The single menu goes for €13, while if you eat à la carte (suggestions of the day are scribbled on the slate) you'll spend about €20. Terrace in summer.

Restaurant Le Dauphiné

8 rue du Chanoine-Collin. **Map B1-13**
03.87.36.03.04
Closed *evenings except Fri and Sat; Aug; Sun by reservation only.*

An unpretentious restaurant and tearoom with exposed beams. There's a €12.50 menu (not Sun), and others at €17 and €20, including a *menu campagnard*. Simple cooking but generous helpings: calf's head with *sauce gribiche*, duck breast with honey and zander fillet with basil.

L'Étude

11 av. Robert-Schuman. **Map B2-18**
03.87.35.36.32
Closed *Sun; 28 July–17 Aug.* **Highchairs available.**

One of the most fashionable restaurants in Metz. The astonishing décor evokes

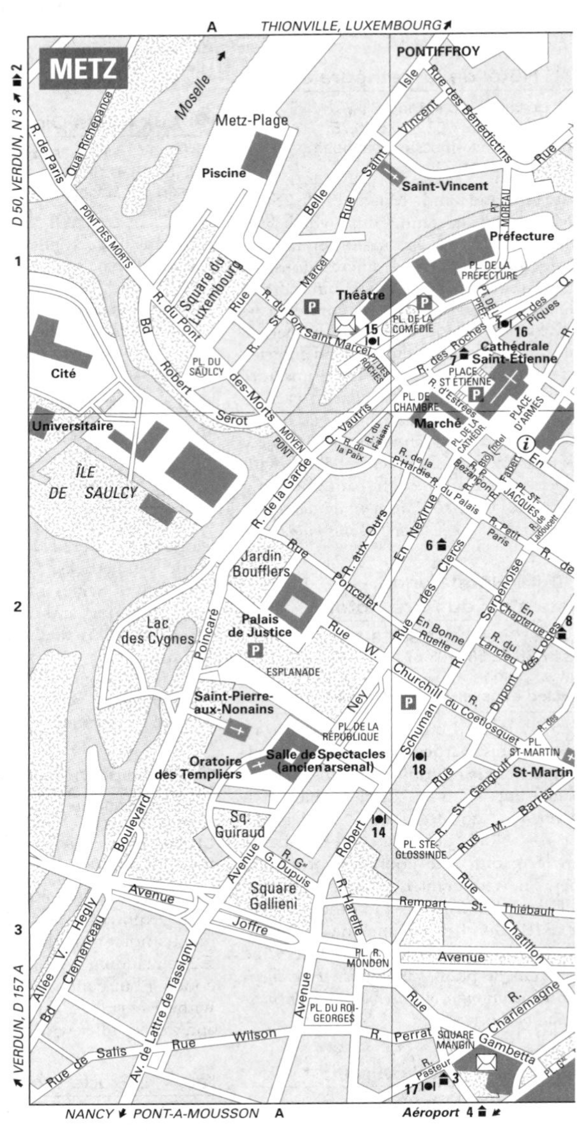
A
THIONVILLE, LUXEMBOURG
METZ
Moselle
Metz-Plage
Piscine
PONTIFFROY
Saint-Vincent
Préfecture
Théâtre
Cathédrale Saint-Étienne
Marché
Cité
Universitaire
ÎLE DE SAULCY
Jardin Boufflers
Palais de Justice
Lac des Cygnes
ESPLANADE
Saint-Pierre-aux-Nonains
Oratoire des Templiers
Salle de Spectacles (ancien arsenal)
St-Martin
Sq. Guiraud
Square Gallieni
PL. DU ROI-GEORGES
SQUARE MANGIN
D 50, VERDUN, N 3 2
VERDUN, D 157 A
NANCY PONT-A-MOUSSON A
Aéroport 4
1
2
3

13

LORRAINE

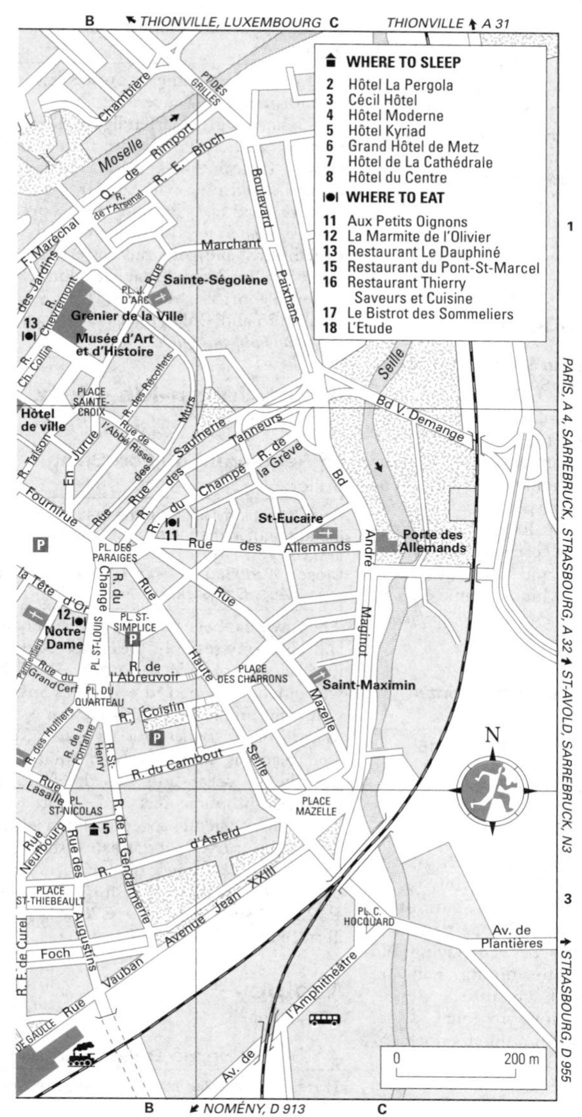

B
THIONVILLE, LUXEMBOURG
C
THIONVILLE A 31
WHERE TO SLEEP
2 Hôtel La Pergola
3 Cécil Hôtel
4 Hôtel Moderne
5 Hôtel Kyriad
6 Grand Hôtel de Metz
7 Hôtel de La Cathédrale
8 Hôtel du Centre
WHERE TO EAT
11 Aux Petits Oignons
12 La Marmite de l'Olivier
13 Restaurant Le Dauphiné
15 Restaurant du Pont-St-Marcel
16 Restaurant Thierry Saveurs et Cuisine
17 Le Bistrot des Sommeliers
18 L'Etude
Moselle
Sainte-Ségolène
Grenier de la Ville
Musée d'Art et d'Histoire
Hôtel de ville
St-Eucaire
Porte des Allemands
Notre-Dame
Saint-Maximin
Seille
PLACE SAINTE-CROIX
PL. DES PARAIGES
PL. ST-SIMPLICE
PLACE DES CHARRONS
PL. DU QUARTEAU
PL. ST-NICOLAS
PLACE MAZELLE
PLACE ST-THIEBEAULT
PL. C. HOCQUARD
Bd V. Demange
Av. de Plantières
Avenue Jean XXIII
R. du Cambout
Rue des Allemands
Boulevard Paixhans
Bd André Maginot
N
0
200 m
PARIS, A 4, SARREBRUCK, STRASBOURG, A 32 ST-AVOLD, SARREBRUCK, N3
STRASBOURG, D 955
NOMÉNY, D 913
1
3

the library of an old English university: the walls are covered with shelves holding some 5,000 books (customers are welcome to sit in one of the cosy armchairs in the lounge area and read to their hearts' content). The food is equally striking; it is basically traditional but infused with new ideas. Weekday lunchtime menu €13.80, then others at €19.50–22.90. On Fridays and Saturdays dinner is accompanied by live music (jazz, chanson, blues); the programme is available on the website. Excellent service. *Free coffee or liqueur on presentation of this guide.*

|●| La Marmite de l'Olivier

9 pl. Saint-Louis. **Map B2-12**
☎03.87.37.05.82
Closed *Mon; Thurs and Sun evenings; fortnight end Aug to early Sept.*

This strategically situated restaurant has three dining rooms (one in a listed wine cellar), as well as an enormous terrace under the arches. Highly convincing renditions of regional specialities are the order of the day: snail *cassolette*, home-made foie gras and terrines, veal sweetbreads, calf's head and fillet of zander with Toul broth. Menus from €13.50 (weekdays) to €21. *Free apéritif on presentation of this guide.*

|●| Restaurant du Pont-Saint-Marcel

1 rue du Pont Saint-Marcel. **Map A1-15**
☎03.87.30.12.29
www.port-saint-marcel.com
Disabled access.

This seventeenth-century building has a terrific location on the banks of the Moselle, with a breathtaking view of the cathedral and the town; there's no other place like it in Metz. The restaurant is decorated with frescoes portraying old city scenes, and the dining staff are dressed in period costume. Menus, €18–29, list delicious regional dishes based on recipes from a nineteenth-century collection: suckling pig in aspic, bacon soup, calf's head, *potée lorraine* and eel *en matelote* in Toul wine sauce. To accompany your meal, try one of the excellent Moselle or Lorraine wines – the wine list features more than 200 vintages. There's a lovely terrace too, with pots overflowing with flowers.

|●| Restaurant Thierry Saveurs et Cuisine

5 rue des Piques. **Map B1-16**
☎03-87-74-01-23.
Closed *Sun; 15 July–15 Aug.* **Disabled access.**

One of our long-time favourites has been transformed into a nice bistro, the *Saveurs et Cuisine*, with a friendly atmosphere, serving authentic cuisine from sunny climes. Typical dishes include tartare of tomatoes and tuna with ginger, *croustillant* of calf's head *ravigotte*, traditional Lorraine *bouchée à la reine* (vol-au-vent filled with sweetbreads) and gorgeous desserts like the tart of caramelized Mirabelle plums. Very reasonable prices. Menus €18.50 (weekdays), €25 and €35. *Free apéritif or coffee on presentation of this guide.*

Saint-Julien-lès-Metz

57070 (3km NE)

|●| Restaurant du Fort Saint-Julien

Route de Thionville; it's in the restored part of the fort right in the middle of the wood.
☎ 03.87.75.71.16
Closed *Wed; Sun evening; 1–10 Jan, and 24 July–8 Aug.* **Car park.**

The town has been traded between France and Germany several times since 1870, so it has a sort of dual nationality. You'll be welcomed by Coco, the owner's mynah bird, who might whistle his version of *The Marseillaise* or *Bridge over the River Kwai*. The place is impressively decorated to resemble a cellar and has the kind of relaxed atmosphere that makes you want to get your friends together for a blow-out. They serve substantial dishes like grilled pork, *baeckeoffe*, quiche lorraine or *choucroute* with Riesling. Menus €12.25–20.60, or around €20 à la carte. Terrace available in summer.

Woippy

57140 (4km N)

|●| L'Auberge Belles Fontaines

51 rte. de Thionville; take the Woippy exit on the A31.
☎ 03.87.31.99.46
Closed *Sat lunchtime; Sun, Mon and Tues evenings; 26 July–19 Aug.* **Disabled access. Highchairs available.**

A restful inn just minutes from the centre

of Metz. It's decorated in classical fashion in the same shades of green as the trees in the park, and there's a terrace. Customers are mainly regulars. Five substantial menus €17–47. *Free coffee on presentation of this guide.*

Gorze

57680 (20km SW)

Hostellerie du Lion d'Or**

105 rue du Commerce; take the Fey exit on the A31.
☎03.87.52.00.90 Ⓕ03.87.52.09.62
Closed *Sun evening; Mon.* **Disabled access. Highchairs and games available. TV.**

You'll find this establishment in the narrow main road of this sleepy town. Once a post house, it still has character and charm, with hand-made floor tiles, timbered walls, a small interior pond, and a huge bay window that lets lots of light into the restaurant. All in all, it's an appropriate setting for the traditional cuisine; the €18 menu (weekday lunchtimes, hotel guests only) and another at €25 list such dishes as calf's head, trout *au bleu*, and house foie gras. Reckon on around €40 à la carte. It's silver service, but you don't need to dress formally. You can stay here too, in renovated rooms; the soundproofing does a pretty good job of cutting down the noise from low-flying jets. Doubles with shower/wc go for €48, or €55 with bath. Half-board €63 per person. *Free apéritif on presentation of this guide.*

Montenach

57480

Hôtel-restaurant Au Val Sierckois

3 pl. de la Mairie.
☎03.82.83.85.20 Ⓕ03.82.83.61.91
Closed *Mon evening; Tues.*

Among the valleys and woods of northern Moselle, where France meets Luxembourg and Germany, this delightful, friendly inn is the ideal place to recharge your batteries. You'll be woken by birdsong and you can go for long walks in the forest. The cooking is unpretentious with menus of Lorraine specialities for €13, €18 and €27. This is hunting country, so try the haunch of venison *Grand Veneur*. They have seven pretty rooms, €30 with basin or shower. Breakfast €4. They are currently installing showers/wc in all the rooms. *10% discount on the room rate on presentation of this guide.*

L'Auberge de la Klauss

1 rue de Kirschnaumen; take the D956.
☎03.82.83.72.38
Closed *Mon; 24 Dec–8 Jan.* **Disabled access.**

This is a friendly place serving quality cooking prepared on the spot using fresh ingredients. You can eat in one of four dining rooms; one is decorated with clocks and old time pieces and another looks like a hunting lodge. Substantial menus €18–46. The owner raises pigs and ducks – you can visit his farm and buy home-made treats – and the game comes from the nearby forest. Specialities include charcuterie (try especially the delicious old-fashioned smoked wildboar and pork hams) and fresh pan-fried foie gras with hot caramelized apples.

Nancy

54000

See map overleaf

Hôtel Carnot**

2 cours Léopold. **Map A2-2**
☎03.83.36.59.58 Ⓕ03.83.37.00.19
TV.

The façade of this hotel had to be rebuilt after the war and is somewhat charmless, but the rooms are decent and the prices attractive; doubles with shower €28–31 and €33–43 with bath. Nos. 24, 25 and 34 are the best: quiet, with nice views of the old town. Breakfast €5. In April, when there is a country fair in the square, make sure to ask for a room at the back. *Free house apéritif on presentation of this guide.*

Hôtel des Prélats**

56 pl. Monseigneur-Ruch. **Map B2-5**; next to the cathedral.
☎03.83.32.11.52 Ⓕ03.83.37.58.74
TV.

This seventeenth-century building, once a convent, offers 44 brand new rooms; some of them are furnished with Art Nouveau pieces and some have four posters. Doubles €40–69. It's good value for money when you consider that pl. Stanislas

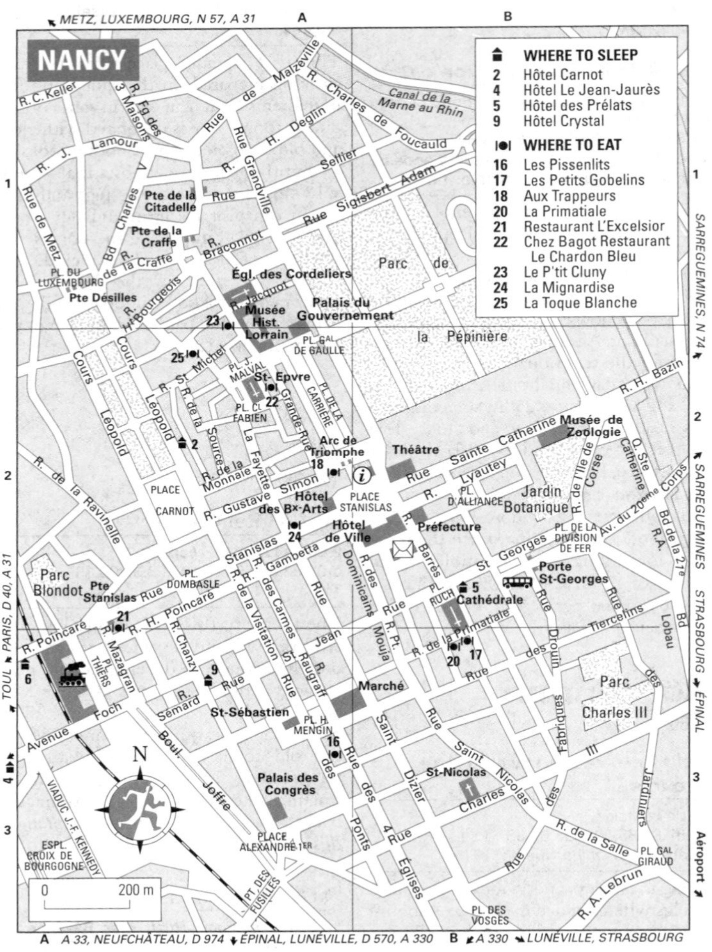
METZ, LUXEMBOURG, N 57, A 31
A
B
NANCY
WHERE TO SLEEP
2 Hôtel Carnot
4 Hôtel Le Jean-Jaurès
5 Hôtel des Prélats
9 Hôtel Crystal
WHERE TO EAT
16 Les Pissenlits
17 Les Petits Gobelins
18 Aux Trappeurs
20 La Primatiale
21 Restaurant L'Excelsior
22 Chez Bagot Restaurant Le Chardon Bleu
23 Le P'tit Cluny
24 La Mignardise
25 La Toque Blanche
Canal de la Marne au Rhin
R. Charles de Foucauld
Rue Sigisbert Adam
Pte de la Citadelle
Pte de la Craffe
Pte Désilles
Égl. des Cordeliers
Musée Hist. Lorrain
Palais du Gouvernement
Parc de la Pépinière
PL. GAL DE GAULLE
St-Epvre
Arc de Triomphe
Théâtre
Musée de Zoologie
Jardin Botanique
PLACE STANISLAS
Hôtel des Bx-Arts
Hôtel de Ville
Préfecture
PLACE CARNOT
Porte St-Georges
Cathédrale
Parc Blondot
Pte Stanislas
Marché
St-Sébastien
Palais des Congrès
St-Nicolas
Parc Charles III
PLACE ALEXANDRE 1ER
ESPL. CROIX DE BOURGOGNE
VIADUC J.-F. KENNEDY
PL. DES VOSGES
PL. GAL GIRAUD
N
0 200 m
SARREGUEMINES, N 74
SARREGUEMINES STRASBOURG
STRASBOURG ÉPINAL
Aéroport
TOUL PARIS, D 40, A 31
A A 33, NEUFCHÂTEAU, D 974 ÉPINAL, LUNÉVILLE, D 570, A 330 B A 330 LUNÉVILLE, STRASBOURG

is so close, and you'll be wakened by the cathedral bells. Friendly welcome too. *10% discount on the room rate in July/Aug on presentation of this guide.*

Hôtel Le Jean-Jaurès**

14 bd. Jean-Jaurès. **Off map A3-4**
03.83.27.74.14 03.83.90.20.94
www.hotel-jeanjaures.fr
TV. Pay Car park.

This place was built as a craftsman's house and has retained a pleasant old-fashioned atmosphere enhanced by the mouldings and tapestries. The rooms over the street have been soundproofed, but you may still prefer the quieter ones over the garden. Whichever you choose, be prepared for a bit of exercise – there are four floors here and no lift. Double rooms with shower/wc €45; breakfast €4.70. *10% discount on the room rate at weekends on presentation of this guide.*

Hôtel Crystal

5 rue Chanzy. **Map A3-9**
03.83.17.54.00 03.83.17.54.30
hotelcrystal.nancy@wanadoo.fr
TV. Pay Car park.

Conveniently located near the station with small, cosy rooms that are very comfortable and tastefully decorated. The quality beds and linen will ensure you have a good night's sleep. Doubles with shower/wc or bath €79–110. *One free breakfast per person on presentation of this guide.*

Aux Trappeurs

SARL Le Vaudémont,
4 pl. Vaudémont **Map A2-18**; next to pl. Stanislas.
03.83.37.05.70

The simple but tasty and copious dishes on offer here provide some of the best value for money in Nancy. Dish of the day €7 and menus at €15–22. Reckon on €20 à la carte. The atmosphere is enticing and the decoration highly accomplished, with a remarkably lifelike maple tree in the dining room (only the trunk is in fact genuine). It also has one of the nicest terraces in town. *Free coffee offered to our readers on presentation of this guide.*

Chez Bagot – Le Chardon Bleu

45 Grande-Rue. **Map A2-22**
03.83.37.42.43
chez.bagot@wanadoo.fr
Closed *Sun evening; Mon; Tues lunchtime; 3 weeks in Aug.*

It's a fair way from the shores of Brittany to the streets of Nancy, but that doesn't deter Breton Patrick Bagot from offering his customers authentic fish and shellfish from back home. *Cotriade* is a speciality. He also serves such dishes as calf sweetbreads with morels and duck breast with oriental spices. The elegant dining room is brilliantly light and the décor has a maritime feel to it. Weekday lunch menu at €16 and others up to €31; you'll spend around €35 à la carte, which is a bit expensive. The wine list is superb, but again the prices are quite high.

La Mignardise

28 rue Stanislas. **Map A2-24**
03.83.32.20.22
www.lamignardise.com
Closed *Sun evening; 15–30 July.* **Disabled access.**

Just round the corner from the pl. Stanislas, this salmon-coloured restaurant has just a few tables. The menus, €13.75 at lunchtime, and €22–40, list refined dishes such as zander with snails and frogs' legs; dishes change with the season. Desserts are always good. There's also a *menu découverte* in the evening at €18.75. There's a shady terrace for sunny days. Efficient, unobtrusive service. *Free coffee on presentation of this guide.*

Les Petits Gobelins

18 rue de la Primatiale. **Map B3-17**
03.83.35.49.03
Closed *Sun; Mon.*

A gourmet restaurant that's not too expensive. There's an assortment of furniture and collectables about the place and paintings and photos by local artists on the walls. At weekday lunchtimes there's a €14 market menu; others range from €18–60. Sadly, the portions aren't always that generous.

La Toque Blanche

1 rue Monseigneur-Trouillet. **Map A2-25**
03.83.30.17.20
Closed *Sun evening; Mon; 1st week in Jan; 1st week of the Feb school holidays; a fortnight end July to early Aug.*

A refined place with a fresh feeling. Though the dining room is not desperately original, this restaurant offers some of the best cooking in town. It's popular locally for the interesting, good-value lunch menu at €16; they also have four others from €21–65. Delicious specialities include *galette* of pig's trotters and potatoes, snail ravioli with basil and zander cooked in *pinot noir*. The excellent wine list offers a carefully chosen selection at fair prices. This is just the place for a celebration. *Free apéritif on presentation of this guide.*

|●| Les Pissenlits

25 [bis] rue des Ponts. **Map A3-16**
☎03.83.37.43.97
@pissenlits@wanadoo.fr
Closed *Sun; Mon; 1–15 Aug.* **Disabled access.**

Les Pissenlits is the younger sibling of *La Table des Mengi* next door and the cooking is just as good. It's a good-looking place, with marble tables in the large dining room and a handsome dresser showing off a collection of Longwy porcelain. As for the food, they do the most wonderful pastry cases with snails and mushrooms, or try the slivers of duck with honey, the pan-fried cod or the memorable calf's head *gribiche*. The dish of the day costs €8.20, while menus range from €17.10–22.10. Danièle Mengin, one of France's best sommeliers, is responsible for the quite exceptional cellar and there is always a specially chosen selection of splendid wines available by the glass. Extremely popular and often full. *Free apéritif on presentation of this guide.*

|●| Restaurant La Primatiale

14 rue de la Primatiale. **Map B3-20**
☎03.83.30.44.03
Closed *Tues evening; Sat lunchtime; Sun.*

On a pedestrianized street and opposite L'Échanson, a wine bar where you can stop for an apéritif, this is a friendly, appealing restaurant. The cooking is original, light and delicate, and they've designed a really attractive wine list with a huge selection by the glass. There's an agreeable terrace on the street. Menus at €20. Around €37 à la carte. *Free house apéritif on presentation of this guide.*

|●| Restaurant L'Excelsior

50 rue Henri-Poincaré. **Map A2/3-21**
☎03.83.35.24.57
Closed Christmas Eve dinner.

An institution in Nancy, known as the "*Excel*", this is something of a historic monument with its Art Nouveau décor; all the greatest names of the Nancy School are represented, with mahogany furniture by Majorelle and stained glass by Gruber. The cooking and service are in the best brasserie style, with menus from €20.90–29.90. Don't miss the fresh oysters, Strasbourg *choucroute* or the pike-perch with snails. *Free house apéritif on presentation of this guide.*

|●| Le P'tit Cluny**

95 Grande Rue. **Map A1/2-23**
☎03.83.32.85.94
Closed *Sun; Mon; Aug.* **Highchairs available.**

A typical rustic Alsace wine cellar with walls of rough-hewn stone and tankards and other drinking utensils suspended from the ceiling. Among the local specialities you should try the tasty *flammenküche* – which are enough to satisfy a big appetite. Standards are high, as you will find if you order the *choucroute*, the barbecued suckling pig or the calf's head. À la carte you'll spend from €23.

Villers-lès-Nancy

54600 (4 km SW)

|●| Auberge de jeunesse – Château de Rémicourt-Nancy

149 rue de Vandœuvre; from the A33 or N74, take the exit "Nancy-Sud-Ouest-Brabois" (av. de la Forêt-de-Haye, av. Paul-Muller); from the city centre, follow the signs to "Brabois-Rémicourt".
☎03.83.27.73.67 Ⓕ03.83.41.41.35
@aubergeremicourt@mairie-nancy.fr
Closed *between Christmas and New Year. New arrivals received 8.30am–9pm. Accommodation from 5.30pm.* **Disabled access. Car park.**

In the middle of a huge 9-hectare park, this château is a youth hostel with more than a touch of class! It is ideal for nature-lovers with a limited budget who want to stay clear of big towns. It costs €13.20 per person per night staying in a dormitory for three–ten people and €15.20 sleeping in a double room. Stopover menu at €6, then weekday menus €8.50–25, for a minimum of six people. You must book for these, but you can share your order with other visitors to the hostel. It's the perfect base for visiting Nancy's National Botanic Conservatory (100 rue du Jardin-Botanique, ⓣ03.83.41.47.47; greenhouses open daily 2–5pm, or 6pm, depending on the season). More than 10,000 species of plants are on display.

Neufchâteau

88300

Le Rialto**

67 rue de France.
ⓣ03.29.06.09.40 ⓕ03.29.94.39.51
ⓦwww.rialto.vosges.com
Closed *Sun except July–Aug; 21 Dec–6 Jan.* **TV. Car park.**

You'll get a pleasant welcome from the young proprietors of this long-standing hotel on the edge of the historic old town. Rooms are clean; those overlooking the river are particularly nice. Doubles cost €43 with shower/wc or bath. Breakfast €6. Good, traditional cooking in the restaurant – nothing fancy – with a €9 weekday lunch menu and others at €15 and €25. There's a nice terrace open on sunny days. *Free house apéritif on presentation of this guide.*

Le Saint-Christophe**

1 av. de la Grande-Fontaine.
ⓣ03.29.94.68.71 ⓕ03.29.06.02.09
ⓦwwwrelais-sud.champagne.com
Closed *Sun evening 1 Dec–30 March.* **Disabled access. TV. Pay Car park..**

Rooms here are on the small side but comfortable nonetheless; doubles range from €45–62 with shower/wc or bath. Go for one that overlooks the River Mouzon or the Saint Christophe church, which is illuminated at night. The breakfast, €7, is very good and there's lots of it. Along with a brasserie, there's a classic restaurant with wood panelling typical of this leafy region. Very decent cooking; menus €13.50–38. Friendly welcome.

Restaurant Le Romain

74 av. Kennedy; it's on the Chaumont road, as you leave town.
ⓣ03.29.06.18.80
Closed *Sun evening; Mon; winter holidays (Zone A); 18 Aug–1 Sept.* **Disabled access. Car park.**

It's the décor rather than the food which recalls ancient Rome. The chef shows considerable flair in his approach to traditional dishes. Cooking times are judged perfectly and he has an intuition for balancing flavours – you'll feel that you're tasting standard dishes for the first time. Try the pig's trotters with potatoes and mushrooms, the country smoked salmon, or pan-fried scallops with parsley. There's a weekday lunch menu for €12.50 and others from €20–32. You can eat on the terrace in summer but it's a bit too close to the road despite a good thick hedge. Good cheeses and desserts, and a great wine list with a few wines by the glass. *Free coffee on presentation of this guide.*

Plombières-les-Bains

88370

Hôtel de la Fontaine Stanislas**

Fontaine Stanislas – it's 4km from Plombières on the rte. d'Épinal via Xertigny.
ⓣ03.29.66.01.53 ⓕ03.29.30.04.31
ⓔhotel.fontaine.stanislas@wanadoo.fr
Closed *15 Oct–1 April.* Disabled access (restaurant). **TV. Highchairs available. Car park.**

The same family has owned this hotel for four generations. It's miles out in the forest overlooking the valley, with a lovely terraced garden and footpaths through the woods. Bedrooms are regularly decorated and have an old-style charm; doubles go for €37 with shower/wc and €46–51 with bath. Nos. 2, 3 and 11 have their own terrace while 18 and 19 have a corner sitting area. Breakfast €6.25. Half board from €46. There's a fantastic view from the restaurant, where they're strong on traditional cuisine and regional dishes: *andouille* from Val d'Ajol, duck leg with mirabelle sauce and home-made ice creams. Menus €16.50–37. Extremely friendly welcome. *10% discount on the room rate (except July/Aug) on presentation of this guide.*

Pont-à-Mousson

54700

Hôtel Bagatelle***

47–49 rue Gambetta; exit 26 from the A31.
ⓣ03.83.81.03.64 ⓕ03.83.81.12.63

Ⓔ bagatelle.hotel@wanadoo.fr
Closed *Christmas to New Year.* **TV. Pay Car park.**

This modern hotel is brilliantly located near the abbey and the banks of the Moselle. It's a bit mournful, but the rooms are functional; a double with en-suite bathroom will cost €51–56. Breakfast €4.50. *Free use of car park on presentation of this guide.*

Remiremont

88200

Hôtel du Cheval de Bronze**

59 rue Charles-de-Gaulle.
Ⓣ 03.29.62.52.24 Ⓕ 03.29.62.34.90
Closed Nov.
TV. Pay Car park.

Once a coaching inn, this old hotel has retained a lot of its charm. The clean rooms are quiet and the ones overlooking the road have all been soundproofed. Others look over the flowery courtyard. Doubles with shower €32, with shower/wc or bath €40–52. Breakfast €6. *10% discount on the room rate at the weekend on presentation of this guide.*

Restaurant Le Clos Heurtebise

13 chemin des Capucins; from the town centre go down rue Charles-de-Gaulle; after the big crossroads turn right and follow the signs.
Ⓣ 03.29.62.08.04
Closed *Sun evening; Mon; Tues; 13–27 Jan.*
Disabled access. Car park.

This rather stylish restaurant stands at the edge of a wood in the hills that circle the town. The décor is chic and classically provincial and the service is impeccable. You'll eat excellent cuisine using fresh ingredients; try house specialities such as pan-fried foie gras with blueberries, *croustillant* of crayfish, whole roast pigeon, twice-cooked bream and frogs' legs in season. There's a trolley of wicked desserts, too. The €16.50 menu is served during the week and on Saturday lunchtimes; others range from €24.50–42.50. The wine list will delight connoisseurs. In summer you can eat outdoors.

St-Étienne-lès-Remiremont

88200 (2km NE)

Le Chalet Blanc**

34 rue des Pêcheurs. From Remiremont, take the road in the direction of Bresse; it's next to the Centre Leclerc.
Ⓣ 03.29.26.11.80 Ⓕ 03.29.26.11.81
Ⓔ lechaletblanc@hotmail.com
Closed *Sat lunchtime; Sun evening; Mon; Feb school holidays (Zone A); 10–25 Aug; 20 Dec–5 Jan.* **Disabled access. TV. Car park.**

Despite its uninviting surroundings, in a shopping centre and a main road in full view, the restaurant serves finely prepared food à la carte and excellent-value menus at €19 (not Sun) and €28–58. The décor inside transports you into the Alps – exactly what you need to forget the grim surroundings outside. The cuisine is contemporary and innovative: salad of langoustine and orange with blue poppy, Dover sole with hazelnuts, rhubarb and herb butter. Good value for money and very good lunch menu. If you don't want to face the motorway to get back into town after a good dinner, they have a few comfortable and contemporary rooms for €66 with bath. Breakfast €6.50. *Free house apéritif on presentation of this guide.*

Girmont-Val-d'Ajol

88340 (10 km S)

Auberge de la Vigotte**

1 la Vigotte; take the D57 (follow the signs).
Ⓣ 03.29.61.06.32 Ⓣ 03.29.61.07.07
Closed *Tues; Wed; 12 Nov–20 Dec.* **TV.**

This old Vosge farmhouse, built in 1750, stands in isolated splendour on one side of a valley but, against all expectations, the interior resembles a modern establishment that would not be out of place in any capital city, without a traditional art or craft in sight All the rooms are different but all are equally enchanting. Doubles with shower/wc or bath from €43–64. Menus €14 (weekdays), then €21and €35. Extremely relaxed atmosphere. Delightful self-taught cooking, similarly in keeping with the times (a mixture of traditional fare and elements from all over the world).

Rouvrois-sur-Othain

55230

La Marmite

It's on the N18.
03.28.85.90.79
Closed *Sun evening; Mon; Tues in winter; 1–15 Jan; 18 Aug–1 Sept.* **Disabled access.**

This bourgeois gastronomic restaurant is typical of its type; quality ingredients are cooked to perfection and servings are very generous. There's an excellent welcome and you get great value for money. Menus €20–46. Dish of the day €11. Good dishes to try include country foie gras, *andouillette* and smoked pork in *choux* pastry. *Free coffee on presentation of this guide.*

Saint-Avold

57500

Hôtel-restaurant de Paris**

45 rue Hirschauer.
03.87.92.19.52 03.87.92.94.32
Closed *Sat & Sun evenings.* **Highchairs available. TV.**

In the sixteenth century, this building belonged to the counts of Créhange, who were Protestants. They built a small chapel at the back of the inner courtyard where they could practise their religion without hindrance. That courtyard is now the dining room and the chapel, now an art gallery, retains its sculpted keystones and a fine vaulted ceiling. The restaurant's not that great (menus €12.50–35) but the rooms are decent and freshly refurbished. Doubles with bath go for €56. Breakfast €7. Half-board €69. *Free apéritif on presentation of this guide. 10% on the room rate (week-ends only) or free coffee on presentation of this guide.*

Saint-Dié-des-Vosges

88100

Hôtel des Vosges**

57 rue Thiers; it's near the cathedral.
03.29.56.16.21 03.29.55.48.71
Disabled access. TV. Car park and pay garage.

A welcoming, well-managed hotel. Doubles with shower €36.30, with shower/wc €38.10–45.75. The ones overlooking the courtyard are quieter and more spacious. Breakfast €5.35. It's open 24 hours – they have a night porter – which is convenient for late arrivals. No restaurant. *10% discount on the room rate for a stay of at least three consecutive nights, and free use of garage.*

Hôtel de France**

1 rue Dauphine; it's next to the post office.
03.29.56.32.61 03.29.56.01.09
Closed *Sun afternoon.* **TV.**

A well-located hotel with a courtyard. The rooms that look out onto it – nos. 3, 6 and 9 – are particularly quiet and also have a view of the cathedral. Don't be put off by the wallpaper in the staircase; most of the rooms have been renovated. They go for €38 with shower/wc or bath. Breakfast €4.57. *10% discount on the room rate (for more than two consecutive nights) on presentation of this guide.*

Restaurant des Voyageurs

22 rue d'Hellieule.
03.29.56.21.56
Closed *Sun evening; Mon; 15 July–1 Aug.* **Disabled access.**

Air-conditioned dining room, classical in style but with a distinctive veranda, from which, if you choose your table right, you can enjoy a view of the Tower of Liberty. Good food that stays strictly within the French tradition and offers probably the best value for money in town. Menus €15–20; reckon on €25 à la carte.

Taintrux

88100 (6 km SW)

Le Haut-Fer**

230 chemin du Port-Rougiville; take the N420 in the direction of Épinal, then turn left on the D31 towards Taintrux.
03.29.55.03.48 03.29.55.23.40
www.lehautfer.fr
Closed *Sun evening and Mon (except July–Aug and public holidays); a week in early Jan.* **TV. Car park.**

A highly attractive, tranquil spot, set in an old sawmill (hence the name: the *haut-fer* was the biggest blade used to cut up wood). There is little danger of getting bored here, as there's a garden, a swimming pool, and some tennis courts. The rooms are conventional but comfortable, and some of them have a balcony overlooking the surrounding fields. Doubles with bath go for €48. Even if you don't stay the night, the restaurant is highly recommended, as it's one of the most outstanding in the region, and the prices are very reasonable too. Menus €10 (weekdays), then €17–31. The cheerful owner goes to great lengths to make her customers feel at ease.

Ban-de-la-Veline

88520 (15 km SE)

Auberge Lorraine

5 rue du 8-Mai; take the N59 in the direction of Sainte-Marie-aux-Mines.
03.29.51.78.17. Ⓕ03.29.51.71.72.
Ⓦwww.auberge-lorraine.com
Closed *Sun evening; Mon; a week end March; a week end Oct.* **TV. Disabled access. Pay Car park.**

A small bistro with old-fashioned floor tiles and a wooden bar that is, in time-honoured fashion, the meeting point for the whole village. Behind this rural *façade*, however, lie brand new bedrooms with contemporary floral decoration and a high degree of comfort. Doubles with bath €46–52. The restaurant is imbued with the same spirit; the food draws purposefully on local tradition but adds some new twists. Weekday lunchtime menu €12.50, then €16–33. Relaxed atmosphere in which guests are received with unforced friendliness.

Saint-Mihiel

55300

Hôtel-restaurant Rive Gauche**

Place de la Gare; it's near the old station bridge.
Ⓣ03.29.89.15.83 Ⓕ03.29.89.15.35
Ⓦwww.rive-gauche.fr
Disabled access. TV. Highchairs available. Car park.

They've done a wonderful job of restoring the old station house. The en-suite doubles have shower/wc or bath, cable TV and phone; they go for €39, which is fair given the facilities and the atmosphere. Half-board €33–49. Breakfast €5.50. You'll get good traditional cooking in the restaurant, and fairly generous portions; the €11 menu is served daily except Sunday lunch, and others €14–28. Try the duck breast with plums. There's a children's play area outside. *10% discount on the room rate (Oct–April) on presentation of this guide.*

Bislée

55300 (5km SW)

La Table des Bons Pères**

Chemin de Pichaumé; take the Bislée turning off the D964 between St. Mihiel and Commercy.
Ⓣ03.29.89.09.90 Ⓕ03.29.89.10.01
Closed *Sun evening; Mon lunch; 3 weeks in winter; a week in Sept. Disabled access.* **TV. Highchairs available. Car park.**

This restaurant, in a restored farmhouse by the River Meuse, is on the side of a road that is not too busy in summer. You dine in a bright airy room overlooking the meandering river, or on a delightful terrace on the bank. The cuisine has a light touch with a few regional specialities. Lots of terrines and freshwater fish – perch, pike and pike-perch often feature. The weekday lunchtime menu, €9, is served in the bar (wine incl.); other menus, €15–27. The cooking uses plenty of seasonal produce including wild mushrooms. Doubles €42.69–53.36 with bath, slightly more in high season. Breakfast €4.27.

Lacroix-sur-Meuse

55300 (10km N)

Auberge de la Pêche à la Truite

Route de Seuzey; take the D964 then the D109 after Lacroix.
Ⓣ03.29.90.10.97 Ⓕ03.29.90.16.88
Closed Tues out of season; 10 Jan–10 Feb. **Disabled access. Car park.**

This is more than a hotel-restaurant – it's a concept. You come here to catch the trout and ling that they let out of the fish ponds at 9am and 2pm daily – rods are available for hire. There are lots of facilities, including out-door games for the children, so it's a good spot for families. The restaurant itself is a converted paper mill and they've built a terrace with an arbour. Naturally, they serve a lot of trout and other fish dishes: trout terrine, trout *rillettes*, trout *à la lorraine* and char with Belle de Meuse beer sauce are typical offerings. Menus €16–29. There are a few rooms; they go for €28 with basin, €32–46 with shower/wc. Breakfast €4.50. *Free house apéritif on presentation of this guide.*

Vigneulles-lès-Hattonchâtel

55210 (17km NE)

L'Auberge Lorraine

50 rue Poincaré; take the D901.
Ⓣand Ⓕ03.29.89.58.00
Closed *Mon; fortnight in Dec.* **Disabled access.**

A quiet restaurant in a peaceful village in the Lorraine regional park, north of the Lac de Madiane. Simple local fare is listed on the weekday lunch menu (€10) and on others from €13.50–21. Some of the appetizing dishes on the menu are crayfish *cassolette*, *croustade* of chicken liver *confit* or pink trout fillet with *flambée* mirabelles. In the evening you can also get pizza and various cheese-topped dishes. Simple rooms with basin €23–28; breakfast €4.50. *Free coffee on presentation of this guide.*

Sarrebourg

57400

Hôtel-restaurant Les Cèdres**

Zone de Loisirs-chemin d'Imling; from the N4 take the exit to Terrasses de la Sarre, then follow the signs to Zone de loisirs; the hotel is right in the middle.
Ⓣ03.87.03.55.55 Ⓕ03.87.03.66.33
Closed *24 Dec–1 Jan.* **Restaurant closed** Sat lunchtime; Sun evening. **Disabled access. TV. Highchairs and games available, Car park.**

The architecture looks good in this rural setting and the spacious dining rooms are bright and peaceful. There's a piano with a see-through lid for the guests to play after a game of snooker. Chef Monsieur Morin cooks good food: calf's head, zander fillet on a bed of *choucroute* and iced *bergamot soufflée*. They do a weekday lunch menu for €10.70, and others €19.40–34.10. Expect to pay €59.50 for a double room with a bath or shower, or €49 per night at the weekends.

L'Auberge Maître Pierre

24 rue Saint-Martin; head in the direction of the motorway, cross the railway bridge at the Sarrebourg exit towards Morhange, then follow the arrows.
Ⓣ03.87.03.10.16
Closed *Mon; Tues*. **Highchairs available.**

Good, family-style Lorraine cooking, with tasty specialities; a past owner, Marguerite Pierre, invented *flammenküche*, an open bacon and cream tart, which is still on the menu along with flambéed tarts and meats grilled on the open fire. Menus €17.50–27.50. Also a Tex-Mex menu on Friday, Saturday and Sunday evenings served at the lower level. There's a convivial atmosphere and late on it can get riotous. *Free coffee or house apéritif on presentation of this guide.*

Sarreguemines

57200

Hôtel-restaurant L'Union**

28 rue Alexandre-de-Geiger; take rue du Maréchal-Foch and take the second on the left.
Ⓣ03.87.95.28.42 Ⓕ03.87.98.25.21
Ⓦwww.hotelunionsarreguemines.com
Closed *Sat; Sun; 2nd and 3rd week in Aug; 23 Dec–1 Jan* **TV. Car park.**

A classic hotel set slightly away from the centre. The decoration in the rooms is nothing to shout about, but the facilities are good. You'll pay €50 for a comfortable room with shower/wc or bath. Breakfast €6. The restaurant has some style, with a display of minerals in the window and Sarreguemines plates on the walls. Food is regional and perfectly judged, with menus from €12.10–28.

Amadeus Hôtel **

7 av. de la Gare.
Ⓣ03.87.98.55.46 Ⓕ03.87.98.66.92
Ⓦwww.amadeus-hotel.fr
Closed *Sun noon–6pm; Christmas to New Year.* **Disabled access. TV. Highchairs available.**

As the station hotel this place was getting very down at heel, but since its face-lift it's looking a lot better. The façade has a vaguely Art Deco appearance, and the rooms are beyond reproach – contemporary and attractive with good facilities including hairdryers. Doubles with shower/wc or bath go for €56.40. Breakfast €6.10. *10% discount on the room rate at the weekend on presentation of this guide.*

Restaurant La Bonne Source

24 av. de la Gare; in the centre.
03.87.98.03.79
Closed *Sat lunchtime; Sun evening; Mon; 15 July–15 Aug.*

A traditional-looking restaurant with wood panelling and a display of Sarreguemines china, proper tablecloths and cloth napkins. You'll be offered good Alsace and Lorraine specialities here – *flammenküche* (bacon, cream and onion flan), *lever knepfle* (liverballs with bacon and cream), home-made charcuterie, terrines, *choucroute* and spare ribs. For dessert try the bread and butter pudding made with mirabelle plums. They serve a lunch menu for €11 on weekdays and three others at €12.50–15.50. Good value.

Restaurant Laroche

3 pl. de la Gare.
03.87.98.03.23
Closed *Fri evening; Sat; 3–24 Aug; 21 Dec–4 Jan.* **Disabled access.**

There are two dining rooms, one of which offers a speedier service than the other. The décor is rustic and a little old-fashioned, but it's as clean as can be. Dishes are nicely presented and good value; there's a weekday menu at €10.50 and set menus €13.20–17.50. Good choices include calf's head, brawn, and home-made terrines and pâtés. *Free coffee on presentation of this guide.*

Le Casino des Sommeliers

4 rue du Colonel-Cazal.
03.87.02.90.41
Closed *Sun evening; Mon; fortnight in Aug; Christmas–New Year.*

Located in the middle of a small park inside the town's old casino, an unusual building from the late nineteenth century, this classy bistro is decorated with wood panelling and porcelain. In summer there's a lovely terrace under the arcade looking towards the river. As for the food, it's tasty and well priced, listed on the €14 menu and à la carte (reckon on €23). There's an attractively priced wine list, too, with a good number of wines by the glass.

Woelfing-lès-Sarreguemines

57200 (12km SE)

Pascal Dimofski

113 rte. de Bitche; it's on the N62 going in the direction of Bitche.
03.87.02.38.21
pascal.dimofski@wanadoo.fr
Closed *Mon; Tues; a fortnight in Feb; 3 weeks in Aug.*

This may look like an ordinary roadside restaurant from the outside, but owner Pascal Dimofski has turned a simply run family establishment into a gastronomic restaurant that's been rated by the "Moselle Gourmande". The dining room has a refined, quiet atmosphere and it's full of business people and regulars. Menus are priced at €20–64: choose dishes such as grilled potatoes stuffed with snails, bass with Japanese spices, lamb chops pan-fried with thyme or milk-fed veal with parmesan. If you're lucky with the weather, eat in the garden. *Free house apéritif on presentation of this guide.*

Senones

88210

Hôtel-restaurant au Bon Gîte**

3 pl. Vaultrin.
03.29.57.92.46 F 03.29.57.93.92
Closed *Sun evening; Mon; winter school holidays.* **TV. Car park.**

This lovely old house has been renovated inside and out and the resolutely modern décor complements the texture of the old walls. Monsieur and Madame Thomas, the owners, are very welcoming. There are about ten attractive rooms which are most comfortable; doubles go for €39 with shower or €42 with bath. Nos. 2, 5, 6, and 7 are the quietest. In the dining room you'll eat reliable regional cooking with lots of imagination. There's a weekday lunch menu at €11, then others from €15–30. It gets busy at weekends, and reservations are recommended.

La Salle des Gardes

7 pl. Clémenceau.
03.29.57.60.06
Closed *Thurs; evenings except Fri–Sun; 1–15 Jan; 3 weeks in June.* **Disabled access. Car park.**

A simple, attractive brasserie run by a friendly woman with a light culinary touch. Prices are reasonable; menus €9–22. She specializes in meats grilled over the open fire. It's a favourite with young people from all around the area. *Free coffee on presentation of this guide.*

Grandrupt

88210 (8km SE)

Hôtel-restaurant La Roseraie**

3 rue de la Mairie. From Senones, take the D24 then the D45.
03.29.41.04.16 03.29.41.04.74
laroseraie88@wanadoo.fr
Closed *Tues evening; Wed; 2–24 Jan; autumn school holidays.* **TV. Highchairs and games available. Car park.**

The perfect place if you're looking for tranquillity and mountain walks in the forest. Simple but comfortable rooms go for €35–48; they also have a bungalow. The pretty dining room is the ideal setting for their tasty traditional food. Menus €10.50 (weekday lunchtimes only) and €15–26. You get a nice welcome, not least from the resident Saint Bernard. There's a terrace. *Free coffee on presentation of this guide.*

Sierck-les-Bains

57480

Restaurant La Vieille Porte

8 pl. Jean-de-Morbach.
03.82.83.22.61
Closed *Tues; Wed.*

Sierck was a refuge for Cistercian monks during the religious wars, and there's an underground tunnel leading from the château to the eleventh-century tower. You reach the restaurant courtyard through an old gate dating from 1604. As for the food, you'll be offered confident dishes from chef Jean-Pierre Mercier who has a good reputation in these parts and further afield. The signature starter, hot trout with almonds, is well worth a try, and the peppered fillet of Charolais beef flambéed in Cognac is a little marvel. Weekday menu €13, others €23–62 (the latter is a terroir menu for two with drinks and coffee incl.). *Free house apéritif on presentation of this guide.*

Gavisse

57570 (9km W)

Restaurant Le Megacéros

19 pl. Jeanne-d'Arc; it's on the D64.
03.82.55.45.87
Closed *Mon; Tues; 26 Dec–6 Jan.* **Disabled access. Highchairs available.**

The *megacéros* is an extinct ancestor of the deer, but there's nothing prehistoric about this restaurant. The cuisine is innovative and the chef creates subtle combinations with local ingredients – try the duck foie gras and the duck joint with its *julienne* of leeks. Menus €16–51. *Free apéritif on presentation of this guide.*

Rodemack

57570 (13km W)

Restaurant La Maison des Baillis

46 pl. des Baillis; take the D64 then the D62.
03.82.51.24.25
Closed *Mon; Tues; a fortnight in Jan.* **Car park.**

The first lords of Rodemack settled in this handsome village in the twelfth century, and at the end of the fifteenth century the Austrians confiscated the estate. In the sixteenth century, the new owner, bored with being so far from the Viennese court, went home and left a bailiff in the house to manage the place. The restaurant is in this magnificent building. They serve good food in the glorious dining rooms. The menus, €16–30, are built around a robust, local dish such as ham cooked in a hay box with two different sauces. You'll spend about €22 à la carte.

Stenay

55700

Hôtel-restaurant Le Commerce**

9 porte de France.
03.29.80.30.62 03.29.80.61.77
Closed *Fri evening, Sat and Sun lunchtimes from 1 Nov–1 May.* **TV.**

Comfortable, spacious rooms with minibar and good bathrooms. Doubles cost €40–46 with shower or bath/wc. The dining room serves simple, generous dishes and an array of starters; there's a weekday menu at €11.45 and others €13–50. À la carte there are a few specialities cooked with beer. *Free house apéritif on presentation of this guide.*

Inor

55700 (7km N)

Auberge Le Faisan Doré**

Rue de l'Écluse; take the D964.
Ⓣ03.29.80.35.45 Ⓕ03.29.80.37.92
Ⓦwww.aubergedufaisandore.com
Closed *Fri.* **TV. Car park.**

This place, by the river in a village in the Meuse forest, is popular with hunters. You will eat well – try sweetbread terrine, duck *confit* with mirabelle plums, monkfish with *girolles*, sirloin with local morels or trout *à la lorraine*. The weekday menu costs €11, and there are themed menus, focusing on Lorraine specialities or tradional dishes, from €20–30. There's a bar, too. The hotel is decent, though the timbers are fake. Doubles €32 with bath. Breakfast €5.35. *Free Kir on presentation of this guide.*

Vilosnes

55100 (20km S)

Hôtel-restaurant du Vieux Moulin

Rue des Petits-Ponts; take the D964.
Ⓣ03.29.85.81.52 Ⓕ03.29.85.88.19
Closed *Tues lunchtime out of season; Jan; Feb.* **TV. Highchairs and games available. Car park.**

This Logis de France hotel is in the very heart of this quietest of quiet villages. The mill wheel stopped turning years ago but you can watch the Meuse flow peacefully by from the lovely terrace and from some of the guest rooms. Rooms with shower or bath go for €50–51. They are all renovated, simple and charming, though some of the beams are fake. Breakfast €7. They serve wholesome family cooking in the restaurant, with good regional dishes listed on menus from €12–35. Specialities include roast duck with mirabelle plums, frogs' leg tart and pike cooked in white wine. *10% discount on the restaurant bill on presentation of this guide.*

Thionville

57100

Hôtel-restaurant des Amis**

40 av. de-Bertier; leave the motorway at exit 40 and turn right at the fifth set of lights.
Ⓣ03.82.53.22.18 Ⓕ03.82.54.32.40
Hotel closed *Sun until 5pm.* **Restaurant closed** *Fri; 21Dec–2 Jan* **TV. Car park.**

A large establishment covered in Virginia creeper and geraniums. The proprietress, who will treat you like an old friend, keeps the hotel extremely clean. Doubles with shower/wc or bath go for €40–45. The dining room has been redecorated and redesigned; Monsieur painted the fresco himself and the place is lit by ornamental Alsatian lamps in highly carved wood. Menus €11.50–23. Go for the *repas campagnard*, which is a real treat; you get *crudités*, smoked country ham, house terrine, garlic sausage, *fuseau lorrain*, roast potatoes, and cream cheese with herbs.

Hôtel L'Horizon***

50 rte. du Crève-Coeur; take exit 40 on the A31 onto the Thionville ring-road then straight on towards Bel Air hospital.
Ⓣ03.82.88.53.65 Ⓕ03.82.34.55.84
Ⓦwww.lhorizon.fr
Restaurant closed *Sat and Mon lunchtimes; Jan.* **TV. Car park.**

The striking façade of this luxurious hotel marks the building out from others nearby. In the restaurant, the dishes are finely prepared with a sure hand. Menus €35 and €48; à la carte around €38. Specialities include chicken *confit* with spring onions and mirabelle plum *Bavarois*. The real luxury is in the rooms; take no. 3, which has the softest feather bed ever. In the bathroom you are spoilt with perfumes, soaps, shampoos and other extras. Doubles with shower/wc go for €78, €120 with bath. Breakfast €12. *Free liqueur on presentation of this guide.*

Les Sommeliers

23 pl. de la République.
Ⓣ03.82.53.32.20
Closed *Sat lunchtime; Sun; Christmas and New Year; public holidays.* **Highchairs available.**

This reasonably priced restaurant has filled a gap in the market. The frontage is impressive (the building used to be a bank) and the dining room is a lovely space, decorated in brasserie style. They offer really tasty little dishes – depending on the season, what's good at the market, and the inspiration of the chef – and a skilfully selected choice of wines, including some served by the glass. Menu €13, or around €20 à la carte. It's simple and good, and the service is just as it should be.

Hombourg-Budange

57920 (15km SE)

L'Auberge du Roi Arthur

48 rue Principale; it's on the D918 to Bouzonville.
03.82.83.97.15
Closed *Sun–Tues evenings; early July or after 15 Aug.* **Highchairs and games available.**

Nothing to do with the legend of King Arthur, but worth a trip anyway. It's a popular place, with lots of regular customers. They have a series of portraits on the walls from the château, and display a splendid porcelain dish made in Sarreguemines. Good country cooking is listed on menus at €11 and €23: try *croustade* of snails with Moselle wine, fillet of beef with Roquefort, *croustade* of frogs' legs with Moselle wine, smoked salmon *binis* or steak *tartare*.

Toul

54200

La Villa Lorraine**

15 rue Gambetta.
03.83.43.08.95 03.83.64.63.64
TV. Pay Car park.

The style of this building was influenced by the École de Nancy. It's central, clean, charming in an old-fashioned way, and inexpensive. Really nice doubles with shower go for €26, €36 with shower/wc, and €39 with bath. Breakfast €5. *One free breakfast per room per night on presentation of this guide.*

Hôtel de l'Europe**

373 av. Victor-Hugo; it's near the station.
03.83.43.00.10 03.83.63.27.67
Closed *a week in mid-Aug; Christmas and New Year.* **TV. Pay Car park.**

This place is paradise for fans of 1930s style; almost everything dates from that period, including the doors, carpets, furniture and the bathrooms. Some rooms have been redecorated, but what they may have lost in authenticity they have maintained in charm. No. 35 is particularly splendid. Doubles with shower or bath/wc €40–43. Breakfast €6. *Free car park space on presentation of this guide.*

Pizza Remi

10 av. Victor-Hugo; it's by the station, practically opposite the Hôtel de l'Europe.
03.83.6318.18
Closed *Sat lunchtime; Sun; fortnight in Aug.* **Highchairs available.**

A friendly and unaffected restaurant looking onto a little garden where you can eat breakfast in summer. The team of young cooks produce really tasty Italian food including home-made pasta and a wide variety of inexpensive pizzas and meat dishes. Menus €8.50 (lunchtimes) to €19. The wines aren't pricey either. A quality place. *Free house apéritif on presentation of this guide.*

Lucey

54200 (9km NW)

L'Auberge du Pressoir

Rue des Pachenottes; it's on the D908 (known as the rte. des Vins et de la Mirabelle).
03.83.63.81.91
Closed *Wed and Sun evening; Mon; 16 Aug–3 Sept.* **Disabled access.**

It's essential to book at this popular place at the weekend and in summer – not least because of its beautiful countryside setting. It's in what used to be the village station, and there's a genuine antique winepress in the courtyard. All the menus, even the cheapest, offer quality food, delightfully presented and generously served. The cooking is regional and eclectic, with a number of specialities, including profiteroles with snails, *filet mignon* with mirabelle plum vinegar, and trout cooked in *vin gris* from Toul. Menus €16.50–26. The wine list features a good variety, including a Côtes de Toul, and you can pick up a few bottles at the wine merchant's next door.

Val-d'Ajol (Le)

88340

Hôtel-restaurant La Résidence***

5 rue des Mousses; at the church take the D20 signposted to Hamaunard.
03.29.30.68.52 03.29.66.53.00
www.la-residence.com
Closed *Sun evening and Mon 1 Oct–30 April except during the school holidays; Jan and March.* **Disabled access (restaurant). TV. Swimming pool. Car park.**

Handsome nineteenth-century master craftsman's house set in a spectacular 2-

hectare park. The rooms are pretty, cosy and very quiet. In addition to the main building there are two modern annexes in the park where you'll also find the pool and the tennis court. Double rooms with shower/wc or bath cost €55–80. Breakfast €7.50. The cooking is equally good, with weekday *formules* at €11 and €20 and menus €22.50–49. You should definitely try the famous Val d'Ajol *andouille*, which is served in its own dish, the pig's trotters stuffed with *andouillette*, and the flambéed chicken flan with Morello cherries. Impeccable service. It's best to book. *10% discount (except July/Aug and bank holidays) on presentation of this guide.*

Verdun

55100

🏃 🏠 |●| Hôtel Le Saint-Paul**

12 pl. Saint-Paul.
Ⓣ03.29.86.02.16 Ⓕ03.29.86.29.38
Closed *15 Dec–15 Jan.* **Restaurant closed** *Sun evening Nov–April.* **TV. Highchairs available. Pay car park**

This well-situated hotel offers moderate prices, a good standard of comfort, peace and quiet, and a pleasant family atmosphere. It's often occupied by people coming to visit the World War I graves. Rooms range from €26.68 with basin to €36.59 with shower/wc or bath; there are also a couple of rooms for families. For half board, add about €20 per person. The restaurant serves good traditional dishes from Lorraine: menus at €11 and €17.84, with a few unusual specialities such as kangaroo steak. *Free apéritif on presentation of this guide.*

|●| Le Poste de Garde

47 rue Saint-Victor.
Ⓣ03.29.86.38.49
Closed *Mon–Thurs evenings; Sat lunchtime; Sun; Aug.* **Disabled access.**

This establishment was set up to employ young disadvantaged people – ironically, it's in an old guard room. It has been brightly restored in pastel shades with green shutters, and the atmosphere is excellent; the guests all seem to be satisfied. Simple, straightforward cooking, which doesn't attempt to be subtle, is served in large portions that will satisfy your appetite. Menus €9–€17.70, and various options à la carte.

|●| Le Forum

35 rue des Gros-Degrés.
Ⓣ03.29.86.46.88
Closed *Wed evening; Sun.* **Disabled access.**

Good value, and with a strong local following, this restaurant has a lovely dining room tastefully decorated with subtle watercolours – the vaulted basement, however, is best avoided if you're claustrophobic. Cooking is simple but fresh and light, adapting traditional regional recipes with a modern twist. There's a lunch menu at €10 during the week, with others from €15.50–23.50. Good choices à la carte include Lorraine salad with poached eggs, roast monkfish with parsley cream and pan-fried veal kidneys flambéed in Cognac.

🏃 |●| Restaurant Le Picotin

38 av. Joffre.
Ⓣ03.29.84.53.45
Closed *Sun evening.*

If you prefer to eat in peace, opt for the dining room, as the terrace can get fairly noisy. Inside, the décor is cheery, very "Montmartre", with a fireplace for when it gets cold. Wherever you eat, you'll get good-quality, inventive cooking. The weekday lunch menu costs €10, and there are others at €17 and €26. Try the goat's cheese pancake, the fish stew, or if you like steak, the excellent *tournedos 1900*. This place is popular with theatre folk and night-owls, because it stays open late. *Free apéritif and Verdun dragées on presentation of this guide.*

Dieue-sur-Meuse

55320 (12km S)

🏃 🏠 |●| Château des Monthairons****

Les Monthairons; take the D34.
Ⓣand Ⓕ03.29.87.78.55
Ⓦwww.chateaudemonthairons.fr
Closed *1 Jan–7 Feb.* **Restaurant closed** *Mon and Tues lunchtimes 2 April–14 Nov; Sun evening and Tues lunchtime 15 Nov–1 Jan and 7 Feb–1 April.* **Disabled access. TV.**

A nineteenth-century château in a walled park with the Meuse meandering gently through it, this hotel is a member of the classy *Châteaux Hôtels et Indépendants* group. It's undeniably stunning to look at, and the comfortable rooms are furnished with antiques. Some are prettier than others, but for €88–168 for a double room you will spend the night in a lovely place where you get lots of little extras such as dressing gowns and luxury toiletries. Breakfast €12–14. Half board is compulsory from June–Sept at €82–120 per person. The restaurant has a good reputation, and attracts people from all over the département; you'll pay €22 for the weekday lunchtime menu and €30–78 for other set menus. Specialities include foie gras and young wild boar terrine, pigeon breast with its truffle soufflé, snail *cassolette* with duck's gizzards and redcurrant soufflé. *10% discount (1 Nov– 15 March) on the room rate or free house apéritif on presentation of this guide.*

Étain

55400 (20km NE)

Hôtel-restaurant La Sirène**

22 rue Prud'homme-Navette.
☎03.29.87.10.32 ℱ03.29.87.17.65
ⓔhotel.sirene@free.fr
Closed *Sun evening; Mon out of season; Jan.* **TV. Car park.**

Apparently, Napoleon III dined in this handsome house after the battle of Gravelotte in 1870. The interior is very rustic in style and it's filled with antiques. You'll get a pleasant welcome, the atmosphere is hushed and the customers are well-to-do. Rooms are quite comfortable, all of them double-glazed; doubles go for €42–59 with shower/wc or bath. Buffet breakfast €8. The cheapest menu, €11, is served daily except Sunday, and there are others up to €39. You'll eat good, bourgeois cooking with dishes like salmon in flaky pastry, house smoked salmon, ham with peaches and foie gras. There are two tennis courts. *Free coffee on presentation of this guide.*

Ville-sur-Yron

54800

La Toque Lorraine

1 rue de l'Yron; it's on the D132.
☎03.82.83.98.13
Closed *every evening except Fri and Sat; July.* **Disabled access.**

This pretty village is undergoing major restoration work. The restaurant, in one of the cottages opposite the carpenter's, has several dining rooms, one of which has a proud fireplace. It's got a farmhouse atmosphere, refined but formal, with stone walls beautifully shown off by discreet lighting. The cooking is full of flavour, and will set you up for a good walk round the village. Weekday lunch menu at €11.50; evening menus €15.50–35.20; try tripe with Toul *vin gris*, snails in pastry cases, kidneys with morels and Lorraine cake. *Free digestif or coffee on presentation of this guide.*

Vittel

88800

Hôtel Les Oiseaux

54 rue de Sugène; it's near the spa.
☎03.29.08.61.93
Closed *25 Dec– 15 Jan.* **TV. Car park.**

This is not so much a hotel as a pretty little house that's been turned into a B&B by an extremely nice woman. Simple rooms with basin cost €22, with shower €37, and with bath €40. Breakfast €5. It's quiet and pleasant, with a tiny garden.

Hôtel-restaurant La Chaumière

196 rue Jeanne-d'Arc.
☎03.29.08.02.87
Closed *Sun in winter.* **Car park.**

A tiny hotel with a bar and restaurant. It's not much to look at, but the proprietress is delightful, and the chef, who's been in the business for thirty years, cares about what he's doing. They give the impression that they are enjoying themselves, which makes a nice change from the health farm-style strictness that pervades the rest of the town. Rooms, €28 a night, are simple and clean, with washing facilities only. Breakfast €4.80. Menus €10.50–15, listing a selection of local, regional or international dishes. *Free Kir on presentation of this guide.*

Hôtel de l'Orée du Bois**

1, lieu-dit L'Orée-du-Bois; it's 4km north on the D18 opposite the race course.
☎03.29.08.88.88 ℱ03.29.08.01.61
ⓦwww.loreeduboisvittel.fr
Closed *Sun evening from Nov to end Feb.* **Disabled access. TV. Swimming pool. Car park.**

A modern hotel and conference centre in a quiet spot. They specialize in getting guests back into shape; sports facilities include a gym, tennis courts, indoor heated swimming pool with sauna and Jacuzzi. The rooms are comfortable; reckon on paying €54–72 for a double with shower/wc or bath. The décor of the rooms varies: some are rustic while others are contemporary. The owners have recently refurbished a few rooms using environmentally friendly materials. The restaurant serves menus from €11.50–32. The cuisine is traditional and the menu changes regularly. *Free coffee on presentation of this guide.*

Hôtel-Restaurant d'Angleterre***

162 rue de Charmey.
03.29.08.08.42 Ⓕ03.29.08.07.48
www.abc-gesthotel.com
Closed *15 Dec–5 Jan.* **Disabled access. TV. Swimming pool. Car park.**

Classic, imposing spa hotel with a pink frontage and an all-pervading air of faded grandeur. In general, and particularly the rooms, everything has been done up. To guarantee peace and quiet, take a room at the back – the railway isn't that far. Doubles with shower/wc €80–90, depending on the season, with bath €92–180 (for the two suites with a spa bath). The restaurant provides traditional, sometimes regional, dishes on menus between €16 and €30. There's a garden.

Le Rétro

158 rue Jeanne d'Arc.
03.29.08.05.28
Closed *Sat lunchtime; Sun evening; Mon; 21 Jun–6 July; 24 Dec–18 Jan.*

Tasty southern dishes served all year round in this easy-going, rustic dining room with stone walls, flowery tablecloths and a rustic fireplace: frogs' legs *à la provençale* or *andalouse*, calf's head, *coq au vin*, and a mild, creamy-sauced chicken *à la poulette*. They also grill meats over the huge wood fire, which is greatly appreciated by the loyal local clientele. Menus €12 (weekdays only) and €14.50–30. Small outdoor terrace in the summer. Friendly welcome and diligent service.

Midi-Pyrénées

Aignan

32290

Le Vieux Logis

Rue des Arts; it's behind the town hall.
05.62.09.23.55
Closed *Sun evening.* **TV.**

An unobtrusive establishment near the town square with period furniture and a cheery dining room. Good food on €10–21 menus which offer soups, salads, shrimps *à la provençale*, lamb kebabs and desserts. The specialities, produced only when the ingredients are available at market, include such things as fresh duck foie gras with peaches, trout with bacon, cep omelette, zander with *beurre blanc* and prawns flambéed with Armagnac. There's a terrace. Rooms with shower/wc or bath €34; breakfast €4. *Free coffee to our readers on presentation of this guide.*

Alban

81250

Restaurant Daurelle Café du Midi**

9 pl. des Tilleuls.
05.63.55.82.24 05.63.55.89.73
Closed *Tues evening; the last week in Aug.*

This unassuming little restaurant on the village square serves high-quality food – the chef trained in some of the great local kitchens before taking over his grandmother's bistro. There's a set menu at €11.50, which is probably the best in the *département* in this price range, and others possible by reservation and consultation with the chef. Quality ingredients and fresh produce go into tasty dishes. *Free house apéritif on presentation of this guide.*

Albi

81000

La Régence**

27 av. Maréchal-Joffre; it's 150m from the train station.
05.63.54.01.42 05.63.54.80.48
www.hotellaregence.com
TV.

This quiet hotel feels like a friendly family guesthouse. There's a nice garden at the back where they serve breakfast (€5.50) in good weather. Bedrooms are decorated in floral style with coordinated prints. Doubles with basin €21–23 and €33–39 with shower/wc or bath: good value for money. Parking spaces (for a fee) on request. *10% discount on the room rate (Oct–May) on presentation of this guide.*

Hôtel Saint-Clair**

8 rue Saint-Clair; it's near the cathedral.
05.63.54.25.66 05.63.47.27.58
micheleandrieu@hotmail.com
Closed *last fortnight in Jan.* **TV. Pay car park.**

A pretty, recently renovated and well-maintained two-star hotel in the old part of town. Doubles with shower/wc €42 or €50–54 with bath. There's a non-smokers' floor – ask when you book – and a pretty little courtyard. It costs €8 to use the car park.

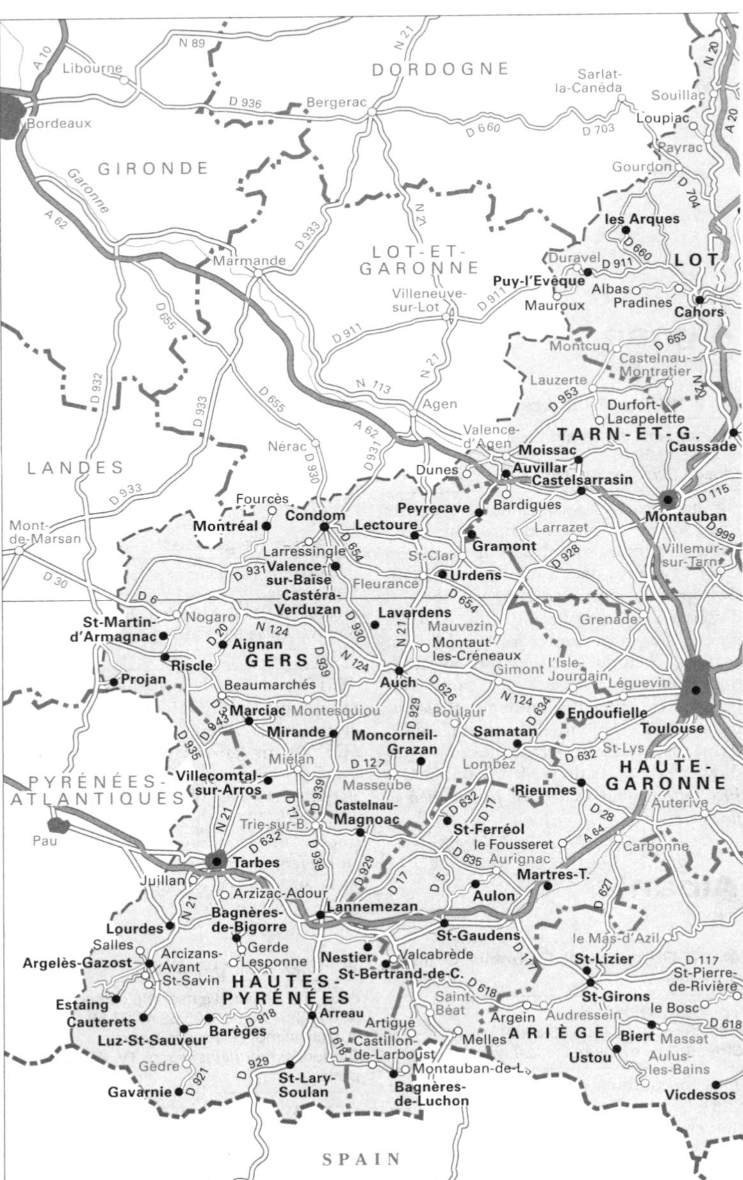

DORDOGNE
GIRONDE
LOT-ET-GARONNE
LOT
LANDES
TARN-ET-G.
GERS
PYRÉNÉES-ATLANTIQUES
HAUTES-PYRÉNÉES
HAUTE-GARONNE
ARIÈGE
SPAIN
Libourne
Bordeaux
Bergerac
Sarlat-la-Canéda
Souillac
Loupiac
Payrac
Gourdon
Garonne
Marmande
les Arques
Duravel
Puy-l'Evêque
Albas
Pradines
Mauroux
Cahors
Villeneuve-sur-Lot
Montcuq
Castelnau-Montratier
Lauzerte
Durfort-Lacapelette
Agen
Valence-d'Agen
Moissac
Caussade
Nérac
Dunes
Auvillar
Castelsarrasin
Montauban
Fourcès
Condom
Montréal
Peyrecave
Bardigues
Lectoure
Larrazet
Mont-de-Marsan
Gramont
Villemur-sur-Tarn
Larressingle
St-Clar
Valence-sur-Baïse
Urdens
Fleurance
Castéra-Verduzan
Nogaro
Lavardens
Mauvezin
Grenade
St-Martin-d'Armagnac
Aignan
Montaut-les-Créneaux
Riscle
Gimont
l'Isle-Jourdain
Léguevin
Projan
Auch
Beaumarchés
Marciac
Montesquiou
Boulaur
Endoufielle
Toulouse
Mirande
Moncorneil-Grazan
Samatan
Miélan
Lombez
St-Lys
Villecomtal-sur-Arros
Masseube
Rieumes
Castelnau-Magnoac
Auterive
Trie-sur-B.
St-Ferréol
Pau
le Fousseret
Carbonne
Tarbes
Aurignac
Martres-T.
Juillan
Arzizac-Adour
Aulon
Lannemezan
Bagnères-de-Bigorre
Lourdes
St-Gaudens
le Mas-d'Azil
Salles
Gerde
Valcabrède
Argelès-Gazost
Arcizans-Avant
Lesponne
Nestier
St-Lizier
St-Pierre-de-Rivière
St-Savin
St-Bertrand-de-C.
St-Girons
Estaing
Saint-Béat
le Bosc
Cauterets
Arreau
Argein
Audressein
Barèges
Artigue
Biert
Massat
Luz-St-Sauveur
Castillon-de-Larboust
Melles
Ustou
Aulus-les-Bains
Gèdre
Montauban-de-L.
St-Lary-Soulan
Gavarnie
Bagnères-de-Luchon
Vicdessos
A 10
A 20
A 62
A 64
N 89
N 21
N 20
N 113
N 124
D 936
D 660
D 703
D 704
D 911
D 933
D 655
D 932
D 931
D 930
D 953
D 653
D 115
D 999
D 928
D 654
D 30
D 6
D 20
D 939
D 626
D 634
D 632
D 943
D 935
D 929
D 127
D 17
D 5
D 635
D 28
D 627
D 117
D 618
D 918
D 921

CANTAL
Saint-Flour
Aurillac
Martel
D 703
Carennac
Meyronne
St-Céré
Latouille-Lentillac
Rocamadour
Leyme
Gramat
N 140
Lacapelle-Marival
Assier
Cardaillac
Labastide-Murat
Figeac
N 122
D 922
D 920
Thérondels
Cassuéjouls
Grand-Vabre
Entraygues-sur-T.
le Fel
Laguiole
D 963
D 920
D 921
Conques
Estaing
Espalion
Mandailles
Mende
N 88
A 75
Tour-de-Faure
D 19
Decazeville
N 140
Marcillac
Ste-Eulalie-d'Olt
St-Geniez-d'Olt
St-Cirq-Lapopie
D 1
D 994
Salles-la-Source
D 988
Gabriac
LOZÈRE
Limogne-en-Q.
Rignac
Belcastel
D 911
Rodez
N 88
Ste Radegonde
Sévérac-le-Château
N 106
Florac
D 19
Villefranche-de-Rouergue
Monteils
Caylus
D 926
Najac
D 922
D 911
Monteils
Sauveterre-de-Rouergue
D 907
St-Antonin-Noble-Val
N 88
Salmiech
Meyrueis
Montricoux
Monestiés
N 88
D 902
AVEYRON
Millau
Brousses
Cordes
Creissels
St-Jean-du-Bruel
Larroque
Cahuzac-sur-Vère
Carmaux
D 999
le Vigan
Castelnau-de-Lévis
Villeneuve-sur-Tarn
D 999
Nant
Castelnau-de-Montmiral
Albi
Plaisance
GARD
Gaillac
A 68
D 999
D 989
Rabastens
TARN
Alban
D 964
Lasgraisses
D 607
St-Sulpice
Réalmont
Giroussens
D 631
Graulhet
Lodève
Lavaur
Lautrec
D 622
A 75
Roquecourbe
Lacrouzette
Lacaune
Burlats
D 922
Puylaurens
Castres
St-Salvy-de-la-Balme
D 909
N 126
St-Julia
St-Avit
N 112
D 2
St-Félix-Lauragais
Dourgne
Mazamet
HÉRAULT
Revel
Sorèze
Villefranche-de-Lauragais
N 9
A 9
Nailloux
N 112
D 118
N 113
Béziers
A 61
Carcassonne
N 9
N 20E
Narbonne
D 623
D 118
AUDE
D 119
Limoux
MEDITERRANEAN SEA
D 625
Foix
Montgaillard
Lavelanet
Nalzen
D 118
N
Montségur
Tarascon-sur-Ariège
A 9
D 117
N 20 E 9
N 9
Ax-les-Thermes
N 116
Perpignan
0
20 km
AND
PYRÉNÉES-ORIENTALES

🏠 |●| Hôtel-restaurant du Vieil-Alby**

25 rue Henri-de-Toulouse-Lautrec; it's 200m from the cathedral in the heart of the old town.
Ⓣ05.63.54.14.69 Ⓕ05.63.54.96.75
Ⓔle-vieil-alby.sicard@wanadoo.fr
Closed *Sun evening; winter school holidays; 27 June–11 July.* **Restaurant closed** *Fri; Sat lunchtime; Sun evening.* **TV. Pay car park.**

This simple, well-run hotel is one of the most reasonably priced in this part of town: double rooms with shower/wc €43, or €52 with bath. Breakfast €6.60. The owner is very congenial, but he doesn't allow smoking anywhere in the hotel. Weekday lunch menu €13, with others €23–35. The cooking is excellent, with house specialities such as tripe, semi-cooked foie gras and *crème brûlée* with figs. Wines from the Gaillac region from €12 a bottle.

🏠 |●| 🏃 Hôtel Mercure Albi Bastides***

41 rue Porta; it's on the left after the bridge over the Tarn in the direction of Paris-Carmaux.
Ⓣ05.63.47.66.66 Ⓕ05.63.46.18.40
Ⓦwww.accorhotels.com
Closed *Fri evening to Sun afternoon (Nov–Feb); Sat and Sun lunchtime March–Oct; 20 Dec–3 Jan.* **Disabled access. TV. Highchairs available. Car park.**

Luxury chain hotel, converted from an eighteenth-century riverside mill, opposite the cathedral. You pay for the comfort, of course, but you also pay for the view, which is probably the finest in Albi. Doubles €80–95 with bath. Breakfast €9. The cooking is wonderful – and if you eat on the terrace you get views of the river and the old town. Set menus €17–38; à la carte you'll pay about €32. The specialities include duck *confit* with ceps, *marbré* of foie gras with duck *aiguillette*, house *cassoulet* and fillet of zander with violet mustard. Wonderful wine list at rock-bottom prices – try the restaurant's own Mercure. The service is amiable and efficient. *One free admission to the Toulouse-Lautrec d'Albi museum on presentation of this guide.*

🏃 |●| Restaurant Le Petit-Bouchon

77 rue de la Croix-Verte.
Ⓣ05.63.54.11.75
Closed *Sat; Sun; public holidays; 9–24 Aug.* **Disabled access. Highchairs available.**

There's a warm atmosphere in this clean, Parisian-style brasserie, which is decorated with the works of great photographers. The weekday menu (€10) consists of a starter, dessert and a choice from the dishes of the day – stuffed mutton tripe, *cassoulet*, sirloin, *coq au vin*, gizzard stew *en daube*. Other menus €12, €18 and €22. Fast, rather brusque service. They specialize in cocktails and have a good regional wine list. *Free coffee on presentation of this guide starting with the €12 menu.*

🏃 |●| Le Lautrec

13 rue Henri-de-Toulouse-Lautrec.
Ⓣand Ⓕ05.63.54.86.55
Closed *Sun evening; Mon; last week Jan; first week Feb; 2 weeks in Sept.* **Highchairs and games available.**

This restaurant, located in the most touristy part of town, is sited in converted stables that belonged to the painter, Henri de Toulouse-Lautrec. Some tables are up on a gallery, while others are more spread out. The regional food is cooked exceedingly well. Try any of the excellent meat or fish dishes; lamb sweetbreads with a walnut wine sauce, scallops with garlic, duck Rossini. €11 weekday lunch menu and others €14–34. *Free apéritif on presentation of this guide.*

|●| Le Tournesol

Rue de l'Ort-en-Salvy; it's in a side street leading to place du Vigan.
Ⓣ05.63.38.38.14
Closed *Sun; Mon; 1–15 May; 15–31 Aug.*

This is the best vegetarian restaurant in the Tarn region, serving good food at realistic prices. The airy dining room is simply decorated and air-conditioned. The cooking is uncomplicated and very tasty. They serve organic apple juice and beer. A meal costs about €13.

|●| L'Esprit du Vin

11 quai Choiseul.
Ⓣ05.63.54.60.44 Ⓕ05.63.54.54.79
Ⓔreslespritduvin@aol.com
Closed *Sun; Mon; Feb.*

The dining room provides a tranquil, sober setting with old stone walls and modern furniture. For summer there's a lovely terrace; for winter, a vaulted cellar. The chef has a penchant for traditional produce – lamb, poultry and fresh baby vegetables – reworked in his own skilful way. He pays great attention to cooking times and produces a dish of milk-fed Pyrenean lamb which is crispy on the outside and gloriously tender inside. The desserts are splendid – try the *crème brûlées*, variously flavoured with mint, tea and lavender. There's a sumptuous cheese trolley. Lunchtime menu €16, other at €25; à la carte up to €89. Lots of superb Gaillacs on the wine list. Best to book.

Castelnau-de-Lévis

81150 (8km W)

La Taverne

Rue Abijoux, Castelnau-de-Lévis; from Albi, take the D600, after 4km turn left onto the D1 and Castelnau is 3km further on. You'll find the restaurant on the right-hand side of the road in the centre of the village.
Ⓣ05.63.60.90.16 Ⓕ05.63.60.96.73
Closed *Mon; Tues; the Feb and All Saints' holidays.*

Heaven on earth for lovers of good food and definitely worth the trip. The "chef's suggestions" include *émincé* of veal with wild mushroom *compote*, superlative roast duckling stuffed with raspberries and grilled lobster. The desserts are out of this world, and the extensive wine list includes a terrific Buzet. Menus €22–44, or around €43 à la carte. You eat either in the dining room, with its country-style décor, or on the covered terrace. The service is as good as the food.

Argelès-Gazost

65400

Hôtel Beau Site**

10 rue du Capitaine-Digoy.
Ⓣ05.62.97.08.63 Ⓕ05.62.97.06.01
Ⓦwww.hotel-beausite-argeles.com
Closed *5 Nov–15 Dec.* **TV.**

A characterful hotel with a stone wall façade brightened up with flowers. Genuine welcome, cosy atmosphere and period furniture, though the look is outdated. The rooms are all different and the ones overlooking the huge and luxuriant garden are particularly appealing. Doubles from €39 with shower or bath. Breakfast costs €6 – though the croissants and bread are perhaps not the best in town. The menu, €15.50, offers two starters, main course, cheese and dessert. And you can enjoy your meal seated on the terrace, which has a splendid view of the gorgeous garden.

Le Miramont***

44 av. des Pyrénées; at the first roundabout, take the road to Cauterets and it's opposite the spa.
Ⓣ05.62.97.01.26 Ⓕ05.62.97.56.67
Ⓦwww.hotelmiramont.com
Closed *Sun evening and Wed Jan–June and Oct; 15 Nov–15 Dec; 3 weeks in Jan.*
Disabled access. TV. Car park.

A fine Art Deco hotel set in a park planted with rose gardens and hydrangeas. The rooms are spacious, elegant and calming, with up-to-date facilities and en-suite bathrooms. They have balconies with views of the old town or over the Pyrenees. Rooms 114, 121 and 122 are larger than standard; doubles with shower/wc or bath €41–70 depending on the season. Breakfast €8. Half board €48–70 depending on the season. The restaurant deserves a mention in its own right, and has won a loyal local following. The chef, Pierre, is the owner's son, and his wife runs the dining room. Dishes, which change with the seasons, include good fish specialities and light versions of regional dishes, along with superb desserts. The cheapest menu at €16 (not available for Sun lunch and public holidays) is fine and generous; others vary from €32 to €42. The second menu is very elaborate, with *amuse-bouches* and cheese. The service is ultra-professional but never stuffy.

Saint-Savin

65400 (3km S)

Le Viscos***

Ⓣ05.62.97.02.28 Ⓕ05.62.97.04.95
Ⓦwww.hotel-leviscos.com
Closed *Sun evening and Mon during school holidays; 1–7 Jan.* **TV.**

A lovely hotel with recently refurbished rooms for €43–68 with shower/wc or bath; half board €51–66 per person. The creative cooking is based on fresh local produce: great fish dishes, *fondant* of duck, pig's trotters and ceps with black pudding from Bigorre and pan-fried foie gras. There's a *formule* for €14 (Mon–Sat), and menus at €20–48. À la carte is rather expensive, but this restaurant justifies its good reputation. *10% discount on the room rate except during school holidays on presentation of this guide.*

Arcizans-Avant

65400 (4km W)

Auberge Le Cabaliros**

16 rue de l'Église. Take the D921then the D13.
☎05.62.97.04.31 📠05.62.97.91.48
Closed *Tues evening and Wed out of season; Oct; Nov.* **TV. Car park.**

This attractive inn has a terrace with views over the valley. You'll get a good-hearted welcome. Some of the rooms are under the eaves and are lovely but others are not that attractive – though they do have decent facilities. Ten doubles with shower/wc or bath €46–52. Breakfast €5.60–8.50. Traditional regional cooking with menus at €15–38.The à la carte menu includes an authentic *garbure*, a broth with pickled goose and stuffed neck of duck (Fri evenings or by reservation only) as well as pigeon in choux pastry with foie gras.

Salles

65400 (4km N)

La Châtaigneraie

It's in the centre of the village. Take the D102.
☎05.62.97.17.84
Closed *Mon in winter; Jan.* **TV. Car park.**

Open only for bookings. A very beautiful dining room in a renovated farm. Grills are a speciality, and they are prepared in front of you: try the grilled Pyrenean lamb with beans. Also good is the braised pigeon *confit*, pan-fried foie gras with grapes and bilberry tart. Menus €23–40. There's a lovely terrace in summer. There are rooms available in the gîte – €40 for a double. Breakfast €6. Half board costs €40 per person. *Free apéritif and 10% discount on the room rate on presentation of this guide.*

Arques (Les)

46250

La Récréation

It's in the village.
☎05.65.22.88.08
Closed *Wed; Thurs lunchtime; weekdays in low season; early Dec to end Feb.*

The village is marvellously situated, perched overlooking a valley surrounded by copses and oak forests; the restaurant is in the refurbished village school. In good weather aim for a table on the little shaded terrace. The cuisine is a delight: lobster ravioli with coral sauce, excellent meat dishes and lots of fish too. Weekday lunch menu €16 and another for €25.

Arreau

65240

Hôtel d'Angleterre**

18 rte. de Luchon.
☎05.62.98.63.30 📠05.62.98.69.66
Closed *Mon and Tues lunch 15 Sept–30 June; Easter–Pentecost; 1 Oct–24 Dec.* **TV. Swimming pool. Car park.**

A seventeenth-century coaching inn which has been tastefully restored to create a warm, comfortable hotel with quality furnishings and service. A bit pricey though. There's a nice family atmosphere and a warm welcome. Doubles with shower/wc €43–50, or €48–60 with bath. Breakfast €7. Half board is compulsory from mid-July to mid-Sept at €50–58 per person. There's a pretty garden and a pool behind the hotel. Good regional cooking in the restaurant: foie gras *au torchon*, beef cuts with subtle woody flavours, country custard with raspberries. Menus €13 (weekday lunchtimes) and €18–35. *Free house apéritif on presentation of this guide.*

Auch

32000

Hotel de France Le Jardin des Saveurs***

2 pl. de la Libération.
☎05.62.61.71.99 📠05.62.61.71.81
Ⓔauchgarreau@intelcom.fr
TV. Pay car park.

This place has a big reputation but you can enjoy the quality of the cooking on the very cheapest weekday lunchtime set menu (€19), which lists the likes of duck terrine with green peppercorns and herbs and farmhouse chicken roasted with bacon. Other menus €25–48 are good but they are somewhat over-priced, especially as the dishes can be a bit stilted. À la carte, prices go off the scale but they don't mind if you order only one dish. There's also a coffee menu. The quality of the welcome and the service are of the standard you'd expect in a place like this. They also have very comfortable rooms at €76 with shower/wc or bath. Breakfast €10. *Free coffee, and one free breakfast per person per night on presentation of this guide.*

|●| La Table d'Hôte

7 rue Lamartine; it's between the cathedral and the Jacobin museum.
☎05.62.05.55.62
Closed *Sun; Wed; Jan; a week in July or Aug; last week of Sept.* **Disabled access.**

A discreet little place between Sainte-Marie Cathedral and the Jacobean Museum, with space for only twenty in the cosy rustic dining room. The *menu du jour* at €15 is particularly good value, and it's best to book if you're determined to taste their famous speciality – "Hamburgers" Gascon (duck and foie gras). There's another menu at €20.50. Terrific welcome from the young owners.

Montaut-les-Créneaux

32810 (10km NE)

|●| Le Papillon

It's on the N21, 6km from the centre of town, in the direction of Agen.
☎05.62.65.51.29 Ⓕ05.62.65.54.33
Ⓔlepapillon@wanadoo.fr
Closed *Sun evening; Mon; a fortnight in Feb; a fortnight Aug–Sept.* **Disabled access. Car park.**

Good restaurant in a modern building. Mainly meat dishes here, though there are also a few good fish specialities. Try the sole stuffed with foie gras, the sword *croustade*, the *cassoulet* with Gascon beans, or the tenderloin with cranberries. The €13 weekday lunchtime menu includes wine, then there are others €15–39.50 – the mid-range ones are particularly good value. Outdoor terrace in the summer. *Free house digestif on presentation of this guide.*

Aulon

65240

|●| Auberge des Aryelets

Take the D30.
☎05.62.39.95.59
Closed *Sun evening to Tues out of season; 15-30 June; mid-Nov to mid-Dec.*

A typical mountain dining room with timbers and beams, a mezzanine floor and a fireplace. The décor has been brightened by Provençal tablecloths and napkins and a few watercolours. The cuisine is rooted firmly in the local tradition: *garbure* (broth with pickled goose), snail stew, lamb steak with shallots, duck with summer fruits, pan-fried *escalope* of foie gras, goat's cheese with ceps in pastry cases, and an upside-down tomato tart. Menus €17, €22 and €27. The place is impeccably clean and the service is friendly and swift. They put a few tables on the terrace in fine weather. It's best to book.

Auvillar

82340

⌂ |●| Hôtel-restaurant L'Horloge**

Place de l'Horloge.
☎05.63.39.91.61 Ⓕ05.63.39.75.20
Closed *Fri and Sat lunchtime except July/Aug; 13 Dec–8 Jan.* **Disabled access (restaurant). TV.**

The pretty village is one of the pilgrimage stops on the way to Santiago de Compostela. The restaurant caters for all appetites and all pockets. It's a charming place and has a superb terrace under the shady plane trees. The young chef has real class – try his southwestern specialities à la carte, washed down with a fine wine from the southwest. Specialities include lamprey *à la bordelaise*, snail stew and a foie gras *dégustation*. Menus €24–55 at the restaurant, and *Au Bouchon* lunchtime menu €15–20. It's also an ideal spot to stay, with very clean doubles at €42 and €50. Breakfast €8. *Free apéritif on presentation of this guide.*

Bardigues

82340 (4km S)

|●| Auberge de Bardigues

Take the D11.
☎05.63.39.05.58
Closed *Mon; 3 weeks in Jan.* **Highchairs available.**

A very nice restaurant in a charming village, run by a young couple called Camille and Cyril. The dining room on the first floor has contemporary décor with splendid stone walls, and there's a beautiful and shady terrace opening onto the village and the surrounding countryside. The cuisine is intelligently prepared, light, tasty and fresh, and dishes change with the seasons: semi-cooked foie gras with onion marmalade, *millefeuille* of salmon and artichoke and veal *blanquette*, tasty chocolate *moelleux*. The weekday lunch *menu du jour* for €10 includes wine and there are *menu-cartes* €17–28. The wine isn't too expensive.

Dunes

82340 (12.5km W)

Restaurant Les Templiers

1 pl. des Martyrs. Take the D12 towards Donzac then the D30.
Ⓣ05.63.39.86.21 Ⓕ05.63.39.56.21
Closed *Sat lunchtime; Sun evening; Mon; Tues evening Nov–April; 15–31 Oct.* **Disabled access. Highchairs available.**

A nice local restaurant prettily set on a lovely village square. The dining room is bright and cosy. The €19 lunch menu (not served weekends and public holidays) offers refined local dishes at very affordable prices; others at €19–49. Seasonal produce and recipes: *toutière* of quail or duck *à l'orange* for the first menu; rabbit terrine with *pruneaux*, *civet de canard* or fish for the second menu. The wine menu includes cheap local wines.

Ax-les-Thermes

09110

Le Châlet**

Avenue Turrel; it's opposite the thermal baths of Le Teich.
Ⓣ05.61.64.24.31 Ⓕ05.61.03.55.50
Ⓦwww.le-chalet.fr
Closed *Sun evening; Mon; Nov to 1st week in March.* **TV. Highchairs available.**

A really nice young couple run this appealing hotel. All the rooms (some of them have recently been updated) are bright and clean and some look over the Oriège that runs alongside the thermal spa of Le Teich. Doubles €40–42; breakfast €5.50. The beautiful restaurant is one of the Ariège's gourmet establishments. Weekly menu at €17; others €20–40. *Free apéritif on presentation of this guide.*

L'Orry Le Saquet**

It's on the N20, 2km from Ax-les-Thermes going towards Andorra.
Ⓣ05.61.64.31.30 Ⓕ05.61.64.00.31
Ⓦwww.auberge-lorry.com
Closed *Tues evening; Wed; Autumn school holidays.* **TV. Car park.**

The steep climb to the top is well worth the effort. The rooms in this hotel have all been refurbished; doubles €50 with bath. Breakfast €8. It's a homely, lived-in kind of place. The restaurant is very good indeed. Menus, €19–42, contain excellent surprises including their speciality, twice-cooked pigeon, along with such dishes as duck cannelloni flavoured with ceps, shoulder of lamb with whisky in a potato crust and *clafoutis* (custard baked with fresh fruit). *10% discount on the room rate (except school holidays) or free apéritif on presentation of this guide.*

Bagnères-de-Bigorre

65200

Hôtel d'Albret**

26 rue de l'Horloge; it's on a corner with place d'Albret.
Ⓣ05.62.95.00.90 Ⓕ05.62.91.19.13
Ⓔeric-coel@wanadoo.fr
Closed *Nov–Jan.*

The hotel has a pretty Art Deco façade and it's on a corner of the quiet and attractive place d'Albret. Old-style rooms, quite large and painted in fresh colours; the bathrooms have old-fashioned shoe-box baths. There's no double glazing but the road is not noisy. Rooms with washing facilities €22 (shower along the landing at a charge of €1.52), or bath €31 with shower/wc or bath. Breakfast €4.60. Good value for money. *10% discount on the room rate on presentation of this guide.*

Hôtel de la Paix**

9 rue de la République.
Ⓣ05.62.95.20.60 Ⓕ05.62.91.09.88
Ⓦwww.hotel-delapaix.com
Closed *10 Dec–10 Jan.* **Disabled access (restaurant). TV.**

With sparkling white and pink fabrics in the hall, it's as kitsch as you like but the facilities are very good and the welcome can't be faulted. The rooms are all different (ask to see more than one) and offer good value for money. They're set around a sunny patio or look onto the garden; nos. 19 and 20 even have small balconies. Doubles cost €24 with basin, up to €50 with bath. Breakfast €5.40. There are three dining rooms serving reassuringly traditional dishes that change with the season. Menus €13, €16 and €23; it's around

€20 à la carte. There's a terrace in summer. The place sometimes hosts business seminars, so it's best to book. *Free apéritif on presentation of this guide.*

Le Bigourdan

14 rue Victor-Hugo.
05.62.95.20.20
Closed *Sun evening; Mon; a week in Nov; a week in the spring.*

This place is on the first floor of an old house in a pedestrianized street, so it's not noisy. Hefty beams, rough-cast walls, floral fabrics and still lifes on the walls. Good regional specialities are cooked using fresh produce – and the menu's as long as your arm. There's a huge choice but quite a lot of supplements. Set menus range from €8.65–31 and list foie gras, scallops and meat. Pizzas available on the children's menu. *Free house apéritif on presentation of this guide.*

Gerde

65200 (1km SE)

L'Auberge Gourmande

4 pl. du 14-Juillet.
05.62.95.52.01
Closed *Mon; Tues; fortnight in Nov.*
Children's games available.

A calculated reworking of the traditional bistro format, with soothing yellow walls and charming floor tiles and a few tables on the terrace next to the village hall. The seasonal dishes concocted by Gilles Béal invite his customers to take a stroll in a kitchen garden complete with aromatic herbs: rabbit with sage, king prawns and vegetables from Provence, snail *ragoût*, pig's foot with Tarbais beans, pork chop *confit* on the bone. The ingredients are fresh and tasty and, unlike some chefs, Béal seems to have applied his imagination more to preparing the food than dreaming up fancy names for it. Menus €18.30 ("gourmet"), €22.11 ("gourmand" or greedy!) and €39 (samples of a variety of dishes). A few wines with AOC (classification of origin), such as Madiran, Buzet rosé, at reasonable prices. Service at the tables is provided by Vincent, in his immaculately white apron. The attention to detail extends to the little basket of games given to children (allowing their parents to eat in peace!).

Lesponne

65710 (10km S)

Domaine de Ramonjuan**

Take the D935 from Bagnères to Baudéan and turn right onto the D29; leaving Lesponne in the direction of Chiroulet, it's on the right.
05.62.91.75.75 05.62.91.74.54
www.ramonjuan.com
Closed *Sun evening; Mon; Easter and All Saints' Day.* **Disabled access. TV. Swimming pool. Car park.**

This farm, at a height of 800m, has been turned into a nice hotel without losing its homely feeling. The pleasant rooms are named after flowers. Doubles with shower or shower/wc €40–60; breakfast €6. Half board (compulsory in the summer) costs €42–54 per person. There are also fifteen holiday apartments for rent. They offer a host of activities including tennis, ping-pong, rafting, ballooning and billiards, and there's a gym with sauna and Jacuzzi in an old riverside barn. The restaurant offers dishes such as *garbure*, wild boar stew, duck and trout with honey; menus €12.50 (not Sun) and €16.90. They hold a good number of conferences so it's advisable to book. *Free house apéritif on presentation of this guide.*

Bagnères-de-Luchon

31110

L'Auberge de Castel-Vielh

Route de Superbagnères; 3km from Bagnères-de-Luchon, take the road on your left towards Superbagnères.
and 05.61.79.36.79
Closed *Wed, except during school holidays; first three weeks Nov.* **TV. Highchairs available. Playground. Car park.**

Spacious doubles with shower/wc overlooking the mountains €39–46. Menus €19–35. Children's menu €8. A nice house in the local style, situated on a hilltop, with a big garden and pretty terrace. Lots of walks to do in the area. Famous for its cooking. À la carte menu includes pan-fried lamb sweetbreads with wild mushrooms and *pan cremat* (burnt bread in the local dialect). *Free house apéritif on presentation of this guide.*

Montauban-de-Luchon

31110 (2km E)

☆ ⌂ |●| Le Jardin des Cascades**

Follow the signs for the Herran forest road and head for the hillside church of Montauban.
Ⓣ05.61.79.83.09 Ⓕ05.61.79.79.16
Closed *Oct–April.* **TV.**

It's advisable to book at this exceptional establishment. The house is a listed building and it's in a wonderful location, clinging on to the mountainside in the middle of an enormous park just 50m from a gushing waterfall. You have to leave your car at the bottom and walk up, but you'll enjoy the scenery and the peace and quiet. Tell them when you arrive so that they collect your luggage. In summer you eat outside and enjoy the superb views over the valley; otherwise it's the elegant dining room. Wonderful traditional cooking, with *pétéram* (stew of sheep's trotters and tripe) and *pistache* (braised leg of mutton with haricot beans). Their meat specialities include beef with ceps and duck breast with pickled shallots. Weekday lunch menu €18.50, with others at €24.40 and €30.50 (on Sunday only). À la carte you can expect to pay around €35 per person. There are a few double rooms; €33.55 with washing facilities and €38.15 with shower/wc. *Free apéritif on presentation of this guide.*

Castillion de Larboust

31110(6km W)

☆ ⌂ |●| Hôtel L'Esquérade**

Take the D618, the road to the Payresourde pass, for about 6km. 500m after Saint-Aventin, the hotel is at the bottom of the road.
Ⓣ05.61.79.19.64 Ⓕ05.61.79.26.29
Ⓦwww.esquerade.com
Closed *Mon and Tues lunchtimes except July–Sept; 15 Nov–15 Dec.* **TV. Car park.**

The village is 954m up in gorgeous green countryside. The hotel itself is comfortable, and the building typical of the locality – it's built of stone with wooden balconies. Most of the rooms overlook the valley. Doubles €40 with shower/wc and €52 with bath/wc. A young and gifted chef recently took the place over and he produces excellent regional dishes. The menus change with each season, because he uses only fresh local produce: frogs' legs with parsley, chocolate *moelleux* and so on. Menus start at €21 (weekdays only, except public holidays) and go up to €58 with a *menu dégustation.* There's an excellent wine list. *Free house digestif or 10% discount on the room rate for a minimum three-night stay on presentation of this guide.*

|●| Les Hauts Pâturages

In the village; take the roads to Juzet, Sode and Artigue.
Ⓣ05.61.79.10.47
Closed *Mon (except public holidays); Nov–March.*

This little restaurant perched on a mountain slope makes no effort to draw attention to itself, so we are thrilled to have discovered it! The location is stunning, with an unbeatable view of the Pyrenees (when there are no clouds); the food is solid, country fare guaranteed to satisfy even the most voracious of appetites and served with loving care in a convivial, welcoming atmosphere. The prices are extremely reasonable: there are no less than eight menus ranging from €8.50–27. It is advisable to book, to make sure that you can enjoy the pleasures of this exceptional spot.

Melles

31440 (30km NE)

⌂ |●| Auberge du Crabère

Take the D618 then the N230.
Ⓣ05.61.79.21.99 Ⓕ05.61.79.74.71
Ⓔpatrick.beauchet@wanadoo.fr
Closed *Tues evening and Wed Sept–June; end Nov to mid Dec.*

The imposing house is right in the middle of the village, on the route of the GR10 walking trail. There are a few spacious, country-style rooms, with half board compulsory all year round at €30 per person. Patrick Beauchet toiled long and hard as a chef on transatlantic cruise liners before going for this post. He's made the mountains his home and his cuisine is bursting with local goodies such as wild mushrooms, crayfish, and game in season. Try mountain soup, crayfish with corander sauce, lacquered pigeon or pigs' trotters with morels. He's become so expert that he's even written two recipe books. Menus €22.90–27.45. There's also a short *menu randonneur* for €11.50 (not served on Sun) – ideal if you're walking – or you can choose à la carte. Open noon–1.30pm and 7–8.30pm.

Barèges

65120

Auberge du Lienz, Chez Louisette

It's 3km from Barèges; travel in the direction of Tourmalet, then turn onto the road to the Plateau de Lienz.
☎05.62.92.67.17 Ⓕ05.62.92.65.15
Closed *2 weeks end April; Nov.*

One of the nicest spots in the valley; it's surrounded by trees and is to be found at the beginning of the route around lakes Gière and Néouvielle. In winter, this is where the ski runs finish. It's a bit like the sort of country inn you might find near a big town, not least because of its glorious summer terrace. The *menu garbure* for two at €28 includes ham *garbure* (stew with ham, cabbage and bacon), pig's trotters stuffed with morels, and stuffed trout with ceps. Desserts are on the pricey side. This auberge has become a real institution in the region. That's a shame as it has now lost some of its original authenticity. The food is still good though. *Free house apéritif on presentation of this guide.*

Le Rozell

39 rue Ramond; go up the main street, towards the tourist office.
☎05.62.92.67.61

Small restaurant with space for just thirty people in a basement with pinewood panelling, roughcast walls and rustic tables. It opts for quality at a reasonable price – all too rare in ski resorts, where expensive food hastily churned out is usually the order of the day. Fish, meat and *fondues*, diligently prepared (you can see the chef at work from your table), provide a tour of France's traditional dishes: *magret fondue*, salad of fried shrimps and queen scallops deglazed with Jurançon wine and grilled swordfish, without forgetting the generously proportioned crêpes. (The restaurant's name even refers to these – a *rozell* is a wooden implement used to spread out pancake dough). Menus €17 and 25. Crêpes €3–8, according to the number of ingredients. Efficient service and classical music in the background. The only complaint is the lack of good ventilation; choose a table near the door!

Belcastel

12390

Hôtel-restaurant du Vieux Pont***

Opposite the bridge.
☎05.65.64.52.29 Ⓕ05.65.64.44.32
Ⓦwww.hotelbelcastel.com
Closed *Sun evening; Mon; Tues lunchtime; 1 Jan–15 March.* **Disabled access. TV. Car park.**

Sisters Michèle and Nicole Fagegaltier have turned their beloved childhood home into a much-admired establishment, serving some of the best cooking around. Their approach is to update old family recipes to show off quality local produce. Some of the dishes come at a price but there's a range of menus at €26–70. The accommodation is as good as the cooking – the rooms are bright and well maintained and full of little extras that make all the difference. Doubles €71–78. Half board €85–92. Reservations essential.

Biert

09320

Auberge du Gypaète Barbu

Place de l'Église; it's 2km from Massat on the road from St. Girons and Tarascon-sur-Ariège.
☎and Ⓕ05.61.04.89.92
Closed *Sun evening; Mon; the last week in June; the last week in Sept; mid-Dec to mid-Jan.* **Disabled access (restaurant). Highchairs available.**

Camille Coutanceau and his wife took over this village bistro on the square, refurbished it beautifully and then gave it the name of a rare scavenging bird which has been recently reintroduced into the wild round here. The three menus, €14–32, are simple and superb: lamb sweetbreads with morels in flaky pastry, tart of duck *confit*, trout with ceps. À la carte around €32. There's a pretty terrace facing the church. Simple double rooms with basin go for €28. Breakfast €5.35.

Cahors

46000

Auberge de jeunesse

20 rue Frédéric-Suisse.
☎05.65.53.97.02 Ⓕ05.65.35.95.92
Ⓦwww.fuaj.org

Restaurant closed *Sat; Sun; public holidays.*

A charming youth hostel that shares an atmospheric seventeenth-century monastery with a hostel for young workers. The imposing façade is bordered by a small garden, while the interior is dominated by a splendid staircase and long corridors paved with worn flagstones. €8.85 a night, in rooms with two–eleven beds. Breakfast €3.25. Restaurant open to all, with meals at €7.80. FUAJ card compulsory. Very friendly welcome. Internet connection and laundry available. Credit cards not accepted.

Hôtel de France***

252 av. Jean-Jaurès; the avenue leads to the station.
Ⓣ05.65.35.16.76 Ⓕ05.65.22.01.08
Ⓦwww.hoteldefrance-cahors.fr
Closed *three weeks around Christmas.*
Disabled access. TV. Car park.

Modern, functional architecture in this eighty-room hotel. Doubles €44–62. The ones overlooking the courtyard are quieter. They all have a direct phone and mini-bar and some have air-conditioning too. *10% on the room rate (15 Oct–15 April) on presentation of this guide.*

Hôtel À l'Escargot**

5 bd. Gambetta.
Ⓣ05.65.35.07.66 Ⓕ05.65.53.92.38
Closed *Sun evening out of season; 2 weeks in Feb; 2 weeks in Oct.* **TV.**

A banal exterior but an attractive interior; the rooms, in an annexe away from the main building, are comfortable and have good facilities. There are beautiful views of the church or private gardens. Doubles €48.50. No. 9 has a mezzanine and a big bay window. Hearty buffet breakfast. Informal and very friendly reception. It's advisable to book. Breakfast €5.90. *10% on the room rate for a minimum 2 nights stay (except July–Aug) on presentation of this guide.*

Le Grand Hôtel Terminus***

5 av. Charles-Freycinet; it's 50m from the train station.
Ⓣ05.65.53.32.00 Ⓕ05.65.53.32.26
ⒺWwww.balandee.com
Restaurant closed *Sun; Mon. Disabled access.* **TV. Highchairs available. Car park.**

This delightful hotel was built at the turn of the last century by the current owner's grandfather and has never been out of the family. It's seen thorough renovation, though they've taken care to preserve its period style. The rooms are large, pleasant and air-conditioned; doubles from €57–95 with bath/wc. There's an award-winning restaurant with menus €40 (weekdays), €55 and €75, and a weekday lunch *formule* for €15, served in the bar.

Bateau-restaurant Au Fil des Douceurs

90 quai de la Verrerie; it's next to the Cabessut bridge.
Ⓣ05.65.22.13.04 Ⓕ05.65.35.61.09
Closed *Sun; Mon; 3 weeks early Jan; a fortnight end June to early July.*

The restaurant looks over the Lot river. The chef has his produce brought in from outlying farms and cooks everything with precision and artistry. Try his delicious truffle *croustade*, or the salmon with candied lime. The desserts are well-balanced and delicious too. Lunch *formule* at €13 and other menus €18–43. Efficient, friendly service.

Restaurant Le Lamparo

76 rue Clemenceau (place de la Halle).
Ⓣ05.65.35.25.93
Closed *Sun. Open 10am–3pm and 7pm–midnight.*

This restaurant, right by the market, is pleasant in all seasons. You can enjoy anything from a home-made pizza to a fillet of beef with foie gras. The dining rooms are always full and the place appeals to all ages because of the range of menus, speed of service and good atmosphere. Weekday menu €14.80 and another at €21. They also offer three appealing mini-apartments (€46–62), which are warmly furnished with bright colours and spotlessly clean. Each has its own entrance. *Free liqueur on presentation of this guide.*

Pradines

46090 (3km NW)

Le Clos Grand**

Laberaudi; take the D8 in the direction of Pradines Luzech.
Ⓣ05.65.35.04.39 Ⓕ05.65.22.56.69
Closed *24 Dec–6 Jan.* **TV. Swimming pool. Highchairs available. Car park.**

A provincial inn with a lush garden and a

lovely swimming pool. The rooms are very pleasant and comfortable: €39–57. Half board €53 per person. Those in the annexe have views over the countryside. The restaurant has a very good reputation; specialities include the fisherman's grilled fish and *Tournedos Rossini*. The cheapest set menu costs €17 (not served Sun), and others are €24 and €36. *Free house apéritif on presentation of this guide.*

Albas

46140 (25km W)

Auberge d'Imhotep

Rivière Haute; between Luzech and Albas, on the left hand side just after you pass Domaine du Château-Eugénie.
05.65.30.70.91
Closed *Sun evening; Mon.*

Wonderfully located on the banks of the Lot, this restaurant serves simple dishes. Menus €13–39. There's a small terrace. You can also buy foie gras to take away. Reservations recommended. *Free apéritif on presentation of this guide.*

Cahuzac-sur-Vere

81140

La Falaise

Route de Cordes; it's 15km north of Gaillac.
05.63.33.96.31
guillaume.salvan@wanadoo.fr
Closed *Sun evening, Mon and Wed evenings.*
Disabled access.

Refined cuisine from Guillaume Salvan, who has a real talent for introducing unexpected flavours to regional dishes. Dishes change with the seasons: foie gras in puff pastry, haunch of veal, *cassoulet* and chocolate *quenelles*. They give well-judged advice about the wine; their list is interesting and features good local Plageoles. The desserts are also excellent. Weekday menu €19 and others up to €36. Best to book.

Carmaux

81400

Restaurant La Mouette

4 pl. Jean-Jaurès.
05.63.36.79.90
Closed *Sun; Mon. Open Mon lunchtime June–Sept; a week in Jan; a week in May; a week in Oct.*

This is without doubt the best gastronomic restaurant in Carmaux. Monsieur Régis has devised a series of interesting menus: a weekday lunch menu at €11.90 and others up to €43. Evening *formule* at €9.90. Specialities include meats grilled over an open fire, calves' feet, ravioli stuffed with smoked duck breast, *petit-gris* snails in flaky pastry and *millefeuille* of spiced-bread ice cream. Practically everything is prepared on the premises. *Free apéritif on presentation of this guide.*

Castelnau-de-Montmiral

81140

Auberge des Arcades

It's on the place des Arcades, the main square.
05.63.33.20.88
www.castelnaudemontmiral.com
Closed *12 Jan–1 Feb.*

Decent, very simple rooms for €30–34; breakfast €5. Half board €44. Full board €54. Some overlook the medieval village square and there are some really spacious ones under the eaves. Downstairs there's a hearty weekday lunchtime *menu du jour* at €11 including cheese, wine and dessert. Or you could opt for a more expensive one; they go from €14 up to €32. The house specialities are wild boar stew and duck *confit*. Service until 9pm. *Free apéritif and 10% discount on the room rate Sept–June.*

Larroque

81140 (14km NW)

Au Val d'Aran

It's on the D964 towards Bruniquel, 3km from Puycelci.
05.63.33.11.15
Closed *Sat (lunchtime only in high season); Christmas to mid-Jan.*

A typical village inn with a comfortable dining room and terrace, and very engaging owners. The weekday lunch menu, €12, starts with a lavish plate of charcuterie and is followed by *crudités*, a main course, cheese and dessert. Other menus €16–25. *Free coffee on presentation of this guide.*

Castelnau-Magnoac

65230

Hôtel Dupont**

Place de l'Église; take the D929 from Lannemezan.
☎05.62.39.80.02 Ⓕ05.62.39.82.20
Disabled access. Swimming pool (July–Aug only).

The hotel has celebrated its 150th anniversary and is a fantastic example of everything that it's worth hanging on to in traditional hotel-keeping. The spacious rooms, €30.50–32 with shower/wc or bath, are very welcoming, scrupulously clean and good value; you'll be woken by church bells. Breakfast €3.60. Generously flavoured local dishes in the large, rustic dining room, with menus €11.50–21. Specialities include grilled scallops, grilled salmon *escalope*, casserole of duck breast, thigh of duck with orange and a delicious mussel soup. *Free apéritif on presentation of this guide.*

Castelsarrasin

82100

Hôtel Marceillac**

54 rue de l'Égalité; it's in a road off the place de la Liberté.
☎05.63.32.30.10 Ⓕ05.62.32.39.52
Ⓦwww.hotelmarceillac.com
TV. Car park.
Closed *5–12 Jan.*

There's a surprise when you walk into this seemingly ordinary hotel, built in the early nineteenth century and run by five generations of the same family. The rooms overlook a small interior courtyard with a glass roof and the reception area is in a kind of glass cage; the whole place is light and airy. The rooms are delightful and the furniture, though it's as old as the hotel, looks cared-for. Doubles with shower/wc or bath €36–50. Breakfast €5.60, or €6.20 in your room. *10% discount on the room rate except July–Aug on presentation of this guide.*

Castera-Verduzan

32410

Le Florida

Rue du Lac.
☎05.62.68.13.22
Closed *Sun evening and Mon except public holidays; Feb school holidays.* **Disabled access.**

A very old establishment which used to be run by the current owner's grandmother. Typical offerings include salad of warm *boudin* with apples, pig's trotter *croustillant*, fig tart with foie gras, *poule au pot*. For dessert, there's the prune soufflé. An excellent weekday lunch menu for €15; others €23–46. *Free coffee on presentation of this guide.*

Castres

81100

Hôtel Rivière**

10 quai Tourcaudière; it's on the banks of the Agout, opposite the old tanners' houses.
☎05.63.59.04.53 Ⓕ05.63.59.61.97
Ⓔhotelriviere@wanadoo.fr
TV. Pay car park.

The attractive décor – reproductions of Impressionist paintings – and the congenial staff make this a pleasant hotel. The pretty rooms smell fresh and clean. You'll pay €26–45 with basin or shower/wc. Buffet breakfast €5.50. The rooms overlooking the embankment can be noisy even though they have double glazing, and the terrace gets very busy in summer.

Resto des Halles

Place de l'Albinque.
☎05.63.62.70.70
Closed *Sun evening; Mon.*

A good brasserie specializing in meat – rib of beef, *pot-au-feu* with marrowbone, *andouillette* with mustard. Weekday lunchtime menu €10.60, or around €22 à la carte. Good wine at fair prices. There's a terrace. *Free apéritif on presentation of this guide.*

Le Pescadou

20 rue des Trois-Rois.
☎05.63.72.32.22 Ⓕ05.63.59.13.08
Closed *Sun; Mon; 15–23 Aug; New Year.*

When there's no space left in this little restaurant they set extra tables in the fish shop – the owner is a fishmonger first and a restaurateur second. There's also a terrace. Though a few dishes are always on the menu – *parillada* (€12.50), *bouillabaisse* (€22) – what you'll be offered depends on the catch of the day. There are no menus but expect to pay around €25 à la carte. Everything is good, fresh and generously served. The service is full of charm and good humour – which explains why the place is always so full. *Free apéritif on presentation of this guide.*

Burlats

81100 (10km NE)

🏠 |●| Le Castel de Burlats

8 pl. du 8-Mai-1945; take the D89 or the D4 then follow the signs to Burlats.
Ⓣ05.63.35.29.20 Ⓕ05.63.51.14.69
Ⓔle.castel.de.burlats@wanadoo.fr
Closed *winter school holidays.* **Disabled access. TV. Highchairs and other baby equipment available. Car park.**

A splendid château built between the fourteenth and sixteenth centuries. The owners have retained the natural charm of the building and the interior, and the extensive gardens are attractive. The ten or so rooms are huge and lovely; some have fireplaces or floors laid with hand-made tiles. Non-smoking doubles €61 with shower/wc or €69 with bath. €8 per night for dogs. There's a huge salon, the perfect place for curling up with a good book, a handsome billiard room, and a tearoom open to non-guests. Menu €20.

Roquecourbe

81210 (10km N)

|●| La Chaumière

14 allée du Général-de-Gaulle; take the D89 from Castres, follow directions to Vabre, turn right at the square with a fountain.
Ⓣ05.63.75.60.88
Closed *Sun evening; Mon; 3 weeks Jan; last week June; first week July.* **Highchairs available. Disabled access.**

A friendly restaurant on a pretty square. You will be welcomed with kindness and the cuisine is excellent. There's a huge, peaceful dining room with a family atmosphere. Menus €16.50–37. Specialities include duck foie gras with apples, zander with shallot butter, *tournedos* with morels and a whole host of good local dishes. *Free apéritif on presentation of this guide.*

Saint-Salvy-de-la-Balme

81490 (16km E)

|●| Le Clos du Roc

Take the D622 in the direction of Brassac for 15km then turn right into the lane to Saint-Salvy.
Ⓣand and Ⓕ05.63.50.57.23
Closed *Mon, Wed and Sun evenings; Christmas–New Year.* **Highchairs available. Disabled access.**

A reliable restaurant in a solid granite house – it's popular locally, so it may be best to book. The spacious dining room is in a converted barn with enormous beams and the décor is stylish and charming. The cuisine has a good reputation and prices are affordable. They do a weekday lunch menu for €11, which includes cheese, dessert and wine, and others at €16–34. Specialities include trout *goujons* with country ham, duck thigh in Banyuls wine, pigeon stuffed with ceps. *Free aperitif on presentation of this guide.*

Caussade

82300

🏠 |●| Hôtel Larroque**

Avenue de la Gare; it's opposite the train station.
Ⓣ05.63.65.11.77 Ⓕ05.63.65.12.04
Ⓦwww.perso.club-internet.fr/hotel.larroque
Restaurant closed *Sat lunchtime and Sun evening out of season; mid-Dec to mid-Jan.* **Disabled access. TV. Swimming pool. Highchairs and games available. Car park.**

A family business that goes back five generations and has a solid reputation. Guests and atmosphere are both rather elegant and the décor is plush; there's a very pleasant swimming pool and a solarium. Double rooms €46–50 with bath – one has a small terrace onto the swimming pool. Breakfast €6. The restaurant offers regional cuisine. Menus €10–30. Newly opened dining area near the swimming pool. *Free apéritif on presentation of this guide.*

Monteils

02300 (2km N)

|●| Le Clos de Monteils

It's 2km from the D17 Caussade exit.

Ⓣ05.63.93.03.51
Closed *Sat lunchtime; Sun evening; Mon; Tues Nov–May; mid-Jan to mid-Feb.*

It's minutes from the motorway to this gourmet restaurant. It's run by chef Bernard Bordaries, who has worked in some of the greatest restaurants in France – and indeed the world – before settling in this lovely priory, swathed in Virginia creeper, out in the country meadows. He and his charming wife have created a place of refined charm. Weekday lunch menus €14 or €22, and evening menus €25 and €35 (also Sun lunchtime). Dishes change with the seasons but may include charlotte with goat's cheese and artichokes, chestnut *velouté* with walnut oil, duo of pork with cabbage and luscious desserts. There's a terrace for sunny days. Credit cards not accepted.

Cauterets

65110

Le Sacca**

11 bd. Latapie-Flurin.
Ⓣ05.62.92.50.02 Ⓕ05.62.92.64.63
Ⓔhotel.le.sacca@wanadoo.fr
Closed *15 Oct–15 Dec.* **Disabled access. TV. Pay car park.**

The clientele here mainly come for the waters. The décor is modern and the chef, Jean-Marc, produces excellent cuisine, the best in Cauterets. He's refined the regional recipes and given pride of place to vegetables – a pretty rare occurrence. Try the asparagus with foie gras or the bream with garlic slivers and chillies. You're served a dish of *amuse-bouches* while you're waiting to order. The plates are hot and the service is very professional. Menus €12–35. The rooms have shower/wc or bath and cost €42–56; some have balconies with a view of the mountains. Breakfast €5. Half board, €38.50–43.50 per person, is compulsory July–Aug.

Hôtel du Lion d'Or**

12 rue Richelieu.
Ⓣ05.62.92.52.87 Ⓕ05.62.92.03.67
Ⓦwww.cauterets.com/hotel-liondor
Closed *1 Oct–20 Dec.* **TV.**

The *Lion d'Or*, run by sisters Bernadette and Rose-Marie, is the oldest hotel in this spa town – the ancient yellow-and-white façade is a bit of a clue. It's gradually been renovated with the utmost attention to detail: the lift is camouflaged by a wooden door and there's a wonderful percolator in the bar. The rooms are plush and cosy, with elegant light fittings, old beds and working antique phones; doubles with shower/wc or bath are €40–64. Half board from €37 per person. Buffet breakfast €7.50. Good home cooking is served in the pleasantly old-fashioned dining room, which is open to residents only. Menu €17 (for residents only). *10% discount on the room rate except during school holidays and weekends.*

La Ferme Basque

It's on the road to Le Cambasque, 2km from Cauterets on the road to Lac d'Ilhéou.
Ⓣ and Ⓕ05.62.92.54.32
Ⓔfermebasque@aol.com
Open *daily in season, by reservation only out of season.*

Lots of crêpes and sandwiches are served in this old farm, which has been going since 1928. The new owners have added some more elaborate dishes, too, using mutton, lamb and vegetables that they grow themselves: *garbure* with wild spinach, black pudding with onions, *blanquette* of lamb, grilled lamb chops, wild boar. Menus €15 and €19. In season meals are served on the huge terrace, which has a fabulous view down to Cauterets. Léon is a shepherd and he likes to talk about his work; Chantal spent twenty years abroad and speaks lots of languages. She's brilliant at managing even the most difficult guests without losing her sense of humour.

Caylus

82160

Hôtel Renaissance**

Avenue du Père-Huc.
Ⓣ05.63.67.06.26 Ⓕ05.63.24.03.57
Closed *Sun evening; Mon; a fortnight in Feb; a week in June; a fortnight in Oct.* **Pay car park.**

The restaurant is in the main street of this very pretty hamlet. The rooms are modern and comfortable – doubles €38 with shower or €44 with bath. Weekday lunch menu €11, others €17–32, and a good selection à la carte. *Free coffee on presentation of this guide.*

Condom

32100

🏠 |●| Hôtel Continental**

20 av. du Maréchal-Foch; on the quay, opposite the Baïse.
Ⓣ05.62.68.37.00 Ⓕ05.62.68.23.71
Ⓔlecontinental@lecontinental.net
TV. Disabled access. Car park.

Charm and comfort are the twin mottos of this hotel, built in the nineteenth century but now completely renovated. The décor is warm and tasteful, with the emphasis on pale wood and madras fabrics. Double rooms €43–64, according to the comfort and season, and a lovely suite with a terrace at €122. The rooms with showers are markedly less expensive, but they are no less attractive, only slightly smaller. The restaurant is also starting to make a name for itself. *Guests receive a discount in the nearby gym.*

Larressingle

32100 (3 km SW)

🏠 |●| L'Auberge de Larressingle**

Take the D15.
Ⓣ05.62.28.29.67 Ⓕ05.62.68.33.14
Ⓦwww.auberge-de-larressingle.fr
Closed *Sun evening and Mon.* **Disabled access. TV. Car park.**

Double rooms at €39. Weekday lunchtime *formule* at €11 (with a main course like a *garbure* or a stew, wine included). Other menus €15–22. Beautiful restaurant with stone walls and its own vegetable garden. Revisited regional cooking with good quality products. The dishes are colourful and tasty. Lovely terrace overlooking the castle. Comfortable doubles, recently updated, in the annexes. Good stop-over.

Conques

12320

🏠 |●| Le Domaine de Cambelong***

It's at the bottom of the village next to the Dourdou.
Ⓣ05.65.72.84.77 Ⓕ05.65.72.83.91
Ⓦwww.moulindecambelong.com
Restaurant closed *Mon–Fri lunchtimes (except July–Aug); Sun; public holidays; 5 Nov–5 Feb.* **Swimming pool. TV. Car park.**

One of the few remaining water-mills on the Dourdou. Very comfortable rooms, some with balconies or private terraces overlooking the river. Doubles €100–170. Half board is compulsory in high season and costs €105 per person. You eat as well as you sleep: try the speciality, duck *tournedos* flavoured with regional spices. Lunch menu at €30 and another at €40. *Free coffee on presentation of this guide.*

Grand-Vabre

12320 (5.5km N)

|●| Chez Marie

Take the D901.
Ⓣ05.65.69.84.55
Closed *Mon–Thurs evenings mid-Sept to mid-May; Dec–end Feb.* **Car park.**

A delightful little inn in this tiny village in the wilds of the Aveyron – Marie, the owner, is the niece of the village grocer. It's decorated simply, with a covered terrace. Staff are amiable and the service is attentive. Quality produce and traditional dishes: chicken with ceps, *aligot* to order, *estofinado* in season. Nothing wildly out of the ordinary, but delicious. Three menus €12.50–22, and an *aligot* menu on Friday nights for €12. It's best to book.

Cordes

81170

🏠 Hôtel de la Cité**

19 rue Raymond-VIII, in the upper town.
Ⓣ05.63.56.03.53
Ⓦwww.thuries.fr
Closed *15 Oct–30 April.* **TV. Car park.**

Eight charming and characterful rooms in this complex of medieval buildings with high ceilings and stout beams. Some have fantastic views over the countryside, and all have modern facilities. Prices are very affordable for a tourist town – €47–52 for a double with bath. Breakfast €5.95.

🏠 |●| Hostellerie du Parc**

Les Cabannes.
Ⓣ05.63.56.02.59 Ⓕ05.63.56.18.03
Ⓦwww.hostellerie-du-parc.fr
Closed *Sun evening and Mon out of season; 15 nov–15 Dec.* **Disabled access. TV.**

Swimming pool. Car park.

This substantial stone country house, which overlooks an old park and garden, has a large rustic dining room. Menus €20–40 with a children's menu for €10; kids under six eat free. Chef Claude Izard is a force to be reckoned with. He chairs an enormous number of associations and is a champion of authentic local cooking. His specialities prove the point – try the rabbit with cabbage, neck of duck stuffed with foie gras. A few simple, quite comfortable rooms for €50–65 with shower/wc or bath, depending on the season.

Dourgne

81110

Restaurant de la Montagne Noire**

15 pl. des Promenades.
☎05.63.50.31.12 Ⓕ05.63.50.13.55
Ⓦwww.montagnenoire.net
Closed *Sun evening; Mon; 3 weeks Jan; a fortnight in Nov; 1–22 Feb.*
Disabled access. TV.

Take a seat on the pleasant terrace overlooking the long village square and enjoy the wonderful creative dishes. Their cooking gets away from the kind of thing you find everywhere in the region and interprets a few traditional dishes with unusual combinations of flavours – a remarkably light *aumônière* of gizzard *confits* and duck breast, salad of deboned pig's trotters with shallot *confit*, quail breasts in a potato crust, pot-roast pigeon, bass with pickled tomatoes. Excellent desserts. Menus €12.50 (not Sat evening or Sunday) and €18–31. A few new double rooms €40–45; breakfast €6. *10% discount on the room rate except in July and Aug on presentation of this guide.*

Saint-Avit

81110 (5km NW)

Les Saveurs de Saint-Avit

La barraque; it's on the D14 between Soval and Massaguel.
☎ and Ⓕ05.63.50.11.45
Ⓔmh_scott@hotmail.com
Closed *Sun evening; Mon; Jan.* **Disabled access.**

The newest gourmet restaurant in the Tarn. Mrs Scott is from the area; her husband Simon was voted the best young British chef in 1991 and worked at the *Ritz* and *Savoy* in London before being persuaded to try his skills out here. For cooking of this quality, the prices are very reasonable; menus €20 (weekday lunchtimes) and €26–68, or around €48 à la carte. *Free coffee on presentation of this guide.*

Endoufielle

32600

La Ferme de Manon des Herbes

It's on the D634 between Lombez and Isle-Jourdain.
☎05.62.07.97.19.
Closed *Wed and Sun evening.* **TV.**

This farm has been lovingly decorated with straw-seated chairs, dried flowers hanging from the beams, flowers and candles on the tables and an open fireplace; it has an intimate, warm ambience. Double rooms with shower/wc €58–74. Breakfast €8. Menus, €20 (weekday lunchtimes), €27 and €42, list regional dishes, fish and house specialities: foie gras, *confits*, salmon *carpaccio* with fresh herbs and a delicious cinnamon cake.

Entraygues-sur-Truyère

12140

Hôtel du Lion d'Or**

Tour de Ville; it's in the main street.
☎05.65.44.50.01 Ⓕ05.65.44.53.43
Ⓦwww.hotel-lion-or.com
Closed *Mon out of season; Jan.* **Disabled access. TV. Swimming pool. Car park.**

Large, solid, stone-built hotel with forty rooms; doubles €44–70 with shower/wc or bath. Décor is a little kitsch for some tastes, but the facilities are pretty good: indoor pool, tennis and crazy golf. There's also a gym, Jacuzzi and sauna. The restaurant is separate from the hotel; in it you enjoy good traditional dishes such as ham, stuffed cabbage or trout. Menus €14 (weekdays) and up to €32.

Fel (Le)

12140 (7km W)

Auberge du Fel

It's in the centre of the village.
☎05.65.44.52.30

Closed *lunchtimes except weekends; school holidays; 3 Nov–31 March.* **Disabled access. Highchairs available. TV. Car park.**

A totally charming mountain inn. The pretty rooms have recently been updated, painted in light colours and arranged with taste. Some have balconies and views of the valley. Double rooms €49–58 with shower/wc or bath. Half board €43–53 per person depending on the season. They prefer you to stay half board, which costs €46 per person. The family cooking has a good reputation, using recipes passed down from mother to daughter; *pounti, truffade*, braised lamb sweetbreads. Menus €18–36. Best to book. *One day half board free for a minimum one week stay, except 5 Aug–19 Sept, and free coffee on presentation of this guide.*

Espalion

12500

L'Eau Vive

27 bd. de Guizard.
05.65.44.05.11
Closed *Sun evening and Mon except July and Aug; the 1st fortnight in Jan; early Nov to early Dec.* **Highchairs available. Disabled access.**

This place is easy to spot with its ochre, half-timbered walls. Jérome has taken over from his father and the quality of his cooking assures him a bright future. He's an enthusiastic fisherman, as you might guess from the décor. Fish dishes have pride of place on the menus – try the *papillotte* of pike-perch with foie gras accompanied by fresh vegetables, pigeon breast brushed with local honey, or the lamb ham joint. Luscious home-made desserts. Menus €12–45. *Free apéritif or fruit juice or soft drink on presentation of this guide.*

Gabriac

12500 (8km S)

Hôtel-restaurant Bouloc

Take the road to Bozouls, after 5km turn left to Gabriac and it's as you come into the village.
05.65.44.92.89 05.65.48.86.74
franckbouloc@wanadoo.fr
Closed *Tues evening; Wed except July/Aug; a week in June; 3 weeks in Oct.* **TV. Swimming pool.**

Despite its position on the roadside, the rooms are comfortable enough and look over the garden and the swimming pool. Doubles €40–45. The dining room is charming, with fresh flowers on the tables. This hotel has been family-run since 1848. Dishes include excellent *fricandeau*, skirt with grain mustard sauce and chocolate *charlotte*. Weekday menu €14.50, others €19 and €27. Good wine list and the good prices. It's best to book. *Free apéritif on presentation of this guide.*

Mandailles

12500 (10km E)

Auberge du Lac

It's opposite the church.
05.65.48.90.27
Closed *evenings May, June, Sept and Oct; 1 May; 1 Nov.*

If you have time to linger, enjoy a drink on the terrace and take in the view over the lake. They serve quality, country cooking: *aligot*, charcuterie and stuffed snails. Menus €12–26. Around €20 à la carte. The kindly service creates a good atmosphere. *Free apéritif on presentation of this guide.*

Estaing

12190

Hôtel-restaurant Aux Armes d'Estaing**

1 quai du Lot; it's across from the Gothic bridge.
05.65.44.70.02 05.65.44.74.54
wwwperso.wanadoo.fr/remi.catusse/home.html
Closed *Mon out of season; 15 Nov–1 March.* **TV. Lock-up car park.**

A traditional hotel with provincial charm. The rooms in the main building have been renovated, and some have views of the Lot; doubles €33–55 with shower/wc or bath. Avoid those overlooking the street; they're noisy in the morning. Half board, which is compulsory in Aug, costs €36.50 per person. In the restaurant they serve local dishes: *croustillant* of goat's cheese with dried fruits, roast zander fillet with bacon and *pavé* of beef with pan-fried foie gras. Set menus €13–38. *Free Kir on presentation of this guide.*

Auberge Saint-Fleuret**

Rue François-d'Estaing.

Ⓣ05.65.44.01.44 Ⓕ05.65.44.72.19
Ⓦperso.wanadoo.fr/auberge.st.fleuret
Closed *Sun evening and Mon out of season; Dec to mid-March.* **TV. Highchairs available. Car park.**

Rooms overlooking the garden are particularly pleasant. Doubles €40–46 with shower/wc or bath. The chintzy dining room is cosy and decorated in shades of blue. The cooking is traditional: *millefeuille* of snails, trout stuffed with pig's trotters. This is no place for frugal eaters. Fair prices with menus from €15 and a gourmet menu with three main courses for €45. Best to book in season.

Figeac

46100

Hôtel Champollion**

3 pl. Champollion.
Ⓣ05.65.34.04.37 Ⓕ05.65.34.61.69
TV.

Ideally located right in the middle of the town, this place is a bit of a change from traditional establishments. Rooms are bright, spacious and attractive with quality beds and linen and tastefully decorated bathrooms; doubles €45. There's a beautiful staircase in a small atrium, a friendly bar and a pleasant terrace. Good value for money. *10% on the room rate on presentation of this guide.*

Restaurant La Cuisine du Marché

15 rue Clermont.
Ⓣand Ⓕ05.65.50.18.55
Closed *Sun.* **Disabled access.**

The open-plan kitchen lets you watch the chefs preparing tasty dishes that are much lighter and more refined than most of the local specialities. The colours, flavours and smells really show off the fresh market produce. There are menus to suit most budgets or appetites, and they change regularly: €27–35. Weekday lunchtime menu €17. *Free apéritif on presentation of this guide.*

Foix

09000

Hôtel Pyrène***

"Le Vignoble", rue Serge-Denis; it's on the N20 about 2km from the centre of town on the Soula-Roquefixade road, going towards Spain.
Ⓣ05.61.65.48.66 Ⓕ05.61.65.46.69
Ⓦhotel.pyrène.com
Closed *Sun 1 Oct–1 March; 20 Dec–30 Jan.* **Disabled access. TV. Swimming pool. Car park.**

This hotel is modern compared to others in town, and it is perfectly placed to catch tourists as they migrate south to the Spanish border. Take a dip in the pool in the garden and you'll forget all about the journey. Doubles with shower/wc or bath €43–56. Breakfast €6. *Free coffee, fruit juice or soft drink on presentation of this guide.*

Hôtel Lons***

6 pl. G.-Duthil; it's in the old town near Pont-Vieux.
Ⓣ05.61.65.52.44
Ⓦwww.hotel-lons-foix.com
Closed *20 Dec–5 Jan.* **Restaurant closed** *Fri evening; Sat lunchtime.* **Disabled access. TV.**

Comfortable double rooms €48.80 with shower/wc or bath. Breakfast €7. Traditional, local dishes in the restaurant – fresh foie gras, *cassoulet* with duck *confit*, duck breast with pepper sauce, steak *tartare*. There's a menu for €13 (with buffet and the local *cassoulet*), or €24. *8% discount on the room rate on presentation of this guide.*

Le Saint-Marthe

21 rue Noël-Peyrévidal.
Ⓣ05.61.02.87.87
Ⓦwww.le-saintemarthe.fr
Closed *Tues evening; Wed out of season; last fortnight Jan.* **Highchairs available.**

Although this is a grand restaurant in a very chic part of town, it's actually relatively affordable: menus €24–36 or around €40 à la carte. You get classic regional dishes for your money – *cassoulet* with duck *confit*, warm goat's cheese with cumin-flavoured whipped cream, stuffed duck breast with foie gras. Serious stuff.

Montgailhard

09330 (1km S)

Le Poëlon

14 av. de Paris.
Ⓣ05.61.03.54.24
Closed *Sun evening; Mon; Wed evening; 1–15 Jan; 1–15 July.*

This restaurant is always packed because of the quality of the tasty cuisine – excellent fish or meat. And with menus at €11 (weekday lunchtimes), €16.50 and €23, it offers good value for money.

Saint-Pierre-de-Rivière

09000 (5km W)

Hôtel-restaurant La Barguillère**

Take the D17.
05.61.65.14.02 05.61.02.62.16
Closed *Wed; end Oct to end Feb; call to reserve out of season.* **Garden. Highchairs available.**

Pleasant little village hotel with a nice garden; doubles with bath from €36. Half board is compulsory in July and Aug. The €11.50 set menu includes cheese, dessert, wine and coffee, and there are others up to €35; a regional menu, a fish menu, country menu and classic menu. Specialities include fresh foie gras with creamed apples flambéed in Hypocras and kid *fricassée* with morels. *Free coffee on presentation of this guide.*

Bosc

(Le)09000 (12km W)

Auberge les Myrtilles**

Col des Marrous; take the D17 from Foix.
and 05.61.65.16.46
www.perso.wanadoo.fr/auberge.les.myrtilles
Closed *Mon and Tues out of season; Nov to end Jan.* **TV. Swimming pool. Highchairs available.**

A lovely chalet 1000m up and just 4km from the ski runs at the Tour Laffont. In summer it's wonderful for walkers – and year round it's good for people who enjoy their food. Double rooms €45–55 depending on the season. Half board is compulsory in high season; €41.50–46.50 per person per night, compulsory during school holidays. In the dining room you'll find delicious dishes including *cassoulet*, duck breast, *confit*, *tartiflette*, foie gras, trout with almonds, omelette with ceps and bilberry tart. Menus €14–24. There's an indoor pool, a sauna and Jacuzzi. *Free apéritif on presentation of this guide.*

Nalzen

09300 (17km SE)

Les Sapins

Route de Foix.
05.61.03.03.85
Closed *Mon; Wed and Sun evenings.*
Disabled access. Highchairs available.

An excellent family-run restaurant offering gourmet cuisine. The dining room is very attractive. Stylishly presented dishes include pigeon with morels or quail salad with spinach *croquettes* – they use exclusively regional produce. Menus €12 (weekday lunchtimes) and €19.50–38. *Free coffee on presentation of this guide.*

Gaillac

81600

La Verrerie**

1 rue de l'Égalité; it's on the road to Montauban and well signposted.
05.63.57.32.77 05.63.57.32.27
www.la-verrerie.com
Closed *Sat lunchtime and Sun evening mid-Oct to mid-April.* **Disabled access. TV. Swimming pool. Highchairs and games available. Car park.**

This is a newish place, but it's housed in a splendid nineteenth-century building which used to be a glass factory. The interior design is remarkably tasteful, retaining the original character while establishing a warm modern style. All the rooms are really pleasant and comfortable and have a personal feel; some have a view over a huge park. Prices are very reasonable considering all of the above; doubles €47 with shower/wc or €62 with bath. You'll find the best in local cooking in the restaurant – there's a *formule* for €13 (not Sun) and menus at €21–35. Good dishes include foie gras, beef and duck liver pan-fried with Port, and iced nougat. *Free apéritif on presentation of this guide.*

Les Sarments

27 rue Cabrol; it's near the tourist office.
05.61.57.62.61
Closed *Sun evening; Mon; Wed evening; mid-Dec to mid-Jan; mid-Feb to mid-March.*
Disabled access.

Located in a narrow medieval street in the old quarter, this restaurant has built a reputation by word of mouth. The setting is splendid – it's an old cellar with fourteenth- and sixteenth-century vaulting which has retained its original character and style. The tables are well spaced and the food is good, taking its inspiration from local produce and combining tastes and flavours in intriguing ways. Try the pan-fried foie gras with puréed leeks or the roast rabbit with whisky cream. Menus €23 (not served Sun) and €28–46.

Gavarnie

65120

Compostelle Hôtel**

Rue de l'Église.
Ⓣ05.62.92.49.43
Ⓦwww.compostellehotel.com
Closed *30 Sept–26 Dec.* **Disabled access. Car park.**

Sylvie, a keen hiker and Velvet Underground fan, travelled a fair bit before taking over this pleasant little family hotel. Rooms are named after mountain flowers; you get the best view from the one called "Lys", which has a balcony. Those on the second floor have skylights. Doubles €34 with shower, €35–46 with shower/wc or €44–45 with bath – unfortunately the soundproofing isn't great, even in the section of the hotel that's been renovated, but it's still a lovely place. Breakfast €6.

14

MIDI-PYRÉNÉES

Giroussens

81500

Hôtel-restaurant L'Échauguette

Ⓣ05.63.41.63.65 Ⓕ05.63.41.63.13
Closed *Sun evening and Mon except in summer; 1–21 Feb; 15–30 Sept.*

An *échauguette* is a corner turret on a house – in this case a thirteenth-century house in wonderful surroundings. Five rooms with bath for €43. Breakfast €5. The restaurant has a good reputation and the dining room is as delightful as the cooking. Menus €15 (weekday lunchtime) to €46, and a splendid list of dishes à la carte, kidney in Gaillac, beef *daube* stew in Madiran and iced pineapple with spices. Wines start at about €10 and you'll get half a bottle of Gaillac for €4. *Free breakfast or apéritif on presentation of this guide.*

Saint-Sulpice-la-Pointe

81370 (9km W)

Le Bersy

It's on the main square opposite the post office.
Ⓣ and Ⓕ05.63.40.09.17
Closed *Sun; Feb school holidays; 3 weeks in Aug; bank holidays.* **Disabled access.**

An excellent bar-restaurant-pizzeria that's always full. They list dishes of the day on the blackboard, and there's quite a good choice à la carte. The speciality is *daube* of gizzards stewed in Gaillac wine. Three weekday lunch menus starting from €10 up to €20. Friendly welcome and swift service, but they don't rush you. *Free apéritif on presentation of this guide.*

Gramat

46500

Le Relais des Gourmands**

2 av. de la Gare.
Ⓣ05.65.38.83.92 Ⓕ05.65.38.70.99
Ⓦwww.relais-des-gourmands.fr
Closed *Sun evening and Mon lunchtime except in July and Aug; bank holidays.* **TV. Highchairs and games available. Swimming pool.**

An enormous house in immaculate condition with a swimming pool, an outside bar and a flower garden. Bright, modern rooms with bathrooms and direct-dial phone go for €49–58. Half board €50–60. You'll get a polite and attentive welcome from Susy, the British owner. The restaurant has a good reputation for light, inventive cooking based on regional produce such as the salad of lamb sweetbreads with sweet and sour sauce. Good cheeses and fine desserts. Weekday menu €15 (€17 on Sun), and others €25–36. Inexpensive local wines. *10% discount on the room rate Sept–June, except bank holidays, on presentation of this guide.*

Le Lion d'Or***

8 pl. de la République.
Ⓣ05.65.38.73.18 Ⓕ05.63.65.38.84.50
Ⓦwww.liondorhotel.com
Closed *15 Dec–15 Jan; closed Mon and Tues lunchtime (varies according to season).* **TV. Car park.**

Excellent reception and service, in the best tradition of French hotel-keeping. Rooms are comfortable and splendidly maintained. Doubles €53–83. The décor is ultra-classic, with cream walls, chandeliers, oil paintings and the finest table linen. The superb chef has extensive experience, and offers some of the best food in the region, with good-value bottles on a marvellous wine list. Menus €22 (weekday lunchtimes) and up to €58.

Gramont

82120

Le Petit Feuillant

It's next to the château.
ⓣ05.63.94.00.08
ⓔcarole.corbiere@wanadoo.fr
Closed *Sun evening; Wed; Mon and Tues in winter; Feb.* **TV.**

The place is wonderfully friendly. No à la carte options, but six menus from €15 (not Sun) to €31 list the likes of roast pork with prunes, *cassoulet*, gizzard salad, tart with garlic and cheese and duck *confit*. Everyone gets a complimentary apéritif, which they can enjoy on the terrace overlooking the château. The good local cuisine is a big draw in the area, so you must book ahead. Five bed and breakfast rooms with mezzanine in a nice village building one minute away. Doubles €42 (breakfast incl.). *10% discount on the room rate except in July and Aug on presentation of this guide.*

Graulhet

81300

La Rigaudié

Route de Saint-Julien-du-Puy; it's 2km east of the town centre.
ⓣ05.63.34.50.07
Closed *Sat lunchtime; Sun evening; Mon.*

This restaurant, in a fabulous setting in a nature park, has an enormous air-conditioned dining room with a magnificent beamed ceiling. The cooking is excellent and the service professional. Weekday lunch menu €14; others €20–38. Start with an appetizer then opt for sole or, even better, cod with *tapenade*. Other dishes include a *chaud-froid* of duck, roast scallops with braised cabbage, pot-roast pigeon with ceps, rib steak with ceps and small tarts of duck with apples and honey sauce. Delicious desserts, too, and good cheeses. *Free apéritif on presentation of this guide.*

Lasgraïsses

81300 (8km NE)

Chez Pascale

It's on the D84, in the direction of Albi.
ⓣ05.63.33.00.78
Closed *weekdays in the evening; Mon July–Aug; the last fortnight in Aug.*

This classic village bistro has old photographs on the walls and trophies in the cabinet. It's a lively place. Weekday menu €11; others up to €28. The cheapest one starts with your own choice of starters from the buffet (including smoked country ham), followed by well-prepared local dishes such as stuffed chicken (Wed, Thurs and Sun lunchtimes in winter only). There's a good cheese board, but leave some space for the house flan. *Free coffee on presentation of this guide.*

Labastide-Murat

46240

Hôtel-restaurant La Garissade

It's in the village.
ⓣ05.65.21.18.80 ⓕ05.65.21.10.97
ⓦwww.garissade.com
Closed *20 Dec–20 Jan.* **TV. Highchairs available.**

A gem of a place where all the rooms have been renovated and decorated in an individualistic colour scheme. They look over the town square at the back. It's the perfect place to stay if you want to explore the limestone plateaux of Le Quercy or La Bouriane. Double rooms from €50 to €58; half board €39–42. The chef offers tasty, authentic dishes and he doesn't cheat on the produce or the flavourings: farm-raised lamb and vegetable stew or scrambled eggs with Lalbenque truffles. Weekday lunch menu €13.50 and another for €18. It's a friendly place; some regulars come from far away to relax and de-stress. The wines are very fairly priced. *10% discount on the room rate (except in July, Aug and on bank holidays) on presentation of this guide.*

Lacaune

81230

Hôtel Calas**

4 pl. de la Vierge.
ⓣand ⓕ05.63.37.03.28
ⓔhotelcalas@wanadoo.fr
Closed *Fri evening and Sat/Sun lunchtimes Oct–Easter; mid-Dec to mid-Jan.* **TV. Swimming pool.**

Four generations of the same family have

run this old house and it's one of the best-known places in the region. The rooms are various sizes but are regularly renovated; doubles €38–40. Breakfast €4.60. It's renowned for a cuisine which is regional but which has an edge of inventiveness: *crepinette* of pig's trotters, twice-cooked pigeon, *boudin* with potato and foie gras. Menus €14.50 (not served Sun) up to €44. It's essential to book for Sunday lunch. The dining room is pleasant and decorated in shades of yellow. *Free coffee on presentation of this guide.*

Lacrouzette

81210

L'Auberge de Crémaussel

The inn is in the forest, north of Lacrouzette, signposted.
Ⓣ and Ⓕ05.63.50.61.33
Closed *Jan.* **Restaurant closed** *Wed; Sun evening.* **Car park.**

Friendly country restaurant with five spotless rooms with parquet floors (€32; breakfast €4). The cosy dining room has stone walls and a fine fireplace, and the cooking has a good reputation. Specialities – cheese soup in winter and crayfish soup in summer – have to be ordered ahead, but they serve a very good Roquefort salad at any time. Menus €15–21; à la carte, prices are fair. Finish with the local pastry known as *croustade*, which is sheer heaven. *Free apéritif on presentation of this guide.*

Laguiole

12210

Grand Hôtel Auguy***

2 allée de l'Amicale.
Ⓣ05.65.44.31.11 Ⓕ05.65.51.50.81
Ⓦwww.chateauxhotels.com/auguy
Closed *Sun evening, Mon and Tues lunchtime except in July and Aug; mid-Nov to end March.* **Disabled access. Highchairs and games available. TV.**

A very good establishment with a solid reputation. Pleasant, well-equipped doubles for €45–85. The large dining room is bright and the cooking first-rate. Most dishes are traditional with some modern twist. Then indulge yourself with one of the wonderful desserts. There's a good wine list, too. Menus €28 (not served at weekends) and up to €65. Terrace and garden.

Cassuéjouls

12210 (10km NW)

Chez Colette

Take the D900 in the direction of the Sarrans dam.
Ⓣ05.65.44.33.71
Closed *Wed out of season.* **Highchairs available.**

Reservations are essential at this lovely little country bistro. Colette will ensure that you fall in love with the region, first by talking about it with passion and warmth and second by serving you simple, invigorating and filling meals. The setting couldn't be less pretentious or the atmosphere more relaxed and friendly. Menus at a modest €10 (weekday lunchtime only) and €12.50: oyster mushroom flan, blue cheese and walnut tart, *truffade. Free coffee on presentation of this guide.*

Lannemezan

65300

Chez Maurette

10 rue des Pyrénées.
Ⓣ05.62.98.06.34
Closed *Sun; early Sept.* **Car park.**

The inauspicious frontage of this restaurant, located in a dreary town, wouldn't make you slam on the brakes to stop – but that would be an error. The house speciality is the prize-winning tripe, and there's excellent *daube* of beef, *confit*, grilled duck and calf's head. The owner and her daughters serve you. *Formule* (dish and dessert) for €8.20, or menus at €9.50 and €14.40. Wednesday is sheep market day – simply everybody piles in for lunch. They also have rooms: doubles with basin for €23, half board €30 per person per night. *Free coffee on presentation of this guide.*

Lavardens

32360

Le Restaurant du Château

At the foot of the château.
Ⓣ05.62.64.58.90
Closed *Mon except July–Aug.*

A delightful place, both inside and out: the interior of stone and wrought iron is swathed in cotton and linen, while the terrace is dominated by a pergola with vines and Liberty prints. The rural tone is further developed in the unpretentious, seasonal dishes like marinated fish and veal medallions with "grand-mother's sauce". Set menus €17 and €22; reckon on €25 à la carte. Friendly service. Don't miss the opportunity to visit the magnificent Lavardens.

Lavaur

81500

Hôtel le Jardin**

8–10 allée Ferréol-Mazas; it's next to the cathedral.
Ⓣ05.63.41.40.30 Ⓕ05.63.41.47.74
Ⓔhotel.du.jardin@wanadoo.fr
Disabled access. TV.

The best hotel in town, beautifully situated in the centre. It's a grand house with comfortable rooms – €37 for a double with shower/wc. Breakfast €5. The restaurant lists classic dishes using fresh produce: fish stew with shallots, duck breast with cherries, pigeon in Gaillac wine, rack of lamb with thyme. They smoke their own salmon and make their own bread. Menus €14, €19 and €28.

Lectoure

32700

Hôtel de Bastard**

Rue Lagrange.
Ⓣ05.62.68.82.44
Ⓦwww.hotel-de-bastard.com
Closed *Sun evening; Mon; 21 Dec–5 Feb.* **TV. Swimming pool. Car park.**

This marvellous hotel is a fine example of eighteenth-century architecture. It's furnished and decorated with taste and is ideal for a romantic weekend. Pleasant welcome and incredible value. Doubles €42–64 with shower/wc or bath; breakfast €9. Half board, €49–62, is compulsory in July and Aug. In summer they serve meals on the terrace, which has a wonderful view over the rooftops, the swimming pool and the cypresses. Menus €15 (weekday lunchtimes), €27 and €59. The exceptional gourmet menu features three special foie gras dishes served with three different regional fruit brandies. *Free coffee on presentation of this guide.*

Leyme

46120

Hôtel-restaurant Lescure**

Route de St-Céré.
Ⓣ05.65.38.90.07 Ⓕ05.65.11.21.39
Closed *Sat and Sun evening out of season; Christmas school holidays.* **TV. Swimming pool. Highchairs available. Car park.**

This characterful hotel-restaurant, which has been run by the same family for more than fifty years, offers comfy accommodation at reasonable prices: doubles €33 with shower/wc or €43 wih bath. Half board €42 per person. The large dining room overlooks a pond; you'll find terrific regional dishes and a nice, varied wine list. Weekday menu €10.70, then others at €12.50–27.50. The decoration is thoughtful and tasteful, with a genuine Picasso and a number of Matisse reproductions. *Free house apéritif on presentation of this guide.*

Lourdes

65100

Hôtel Relais des Crêtes**

72 av. Alexandre-Marqui; it's on the right as you come into Lourdes from Tarbes.
Ⓣ05.62.42.18.56
Closed *early 11 Nov–20 March.*

The location of this small family guesthouse, at the end of a side street behind a pretty hedge, protects it from the noise of the nearby main road. There are eleven tasteful, simple rooms looking out onto the courtyard; they're all spotlessly clean. In warm weather, breakfast is served on the hydrangea-filled terrace. Doubles from €23. Breakfast €3.50. Lovely welcome from the charming *patronne. Free breakfast on presentation of this guide.*

Hôtel Majestic**

9 av. Maransin; it's a ten-minute walk from the shrines, at the corner of the avenue and a cul-de-sac where you can park.
Ⓣ05.62.94.27.23 Ⓕ05.62.94.64.91
Closed *end Nov to Easter.* **Disabled access.**

A classy establishment run by the friendly Cazaux family. The rustic rooms are extremely comfortable with direct-dial phones and en-suite bathrooms with hairdryers; some have balconies. Doubles with shower or bath up to €48. Breakfast €4.60. TV on demand. Family cooking served in the chic dining room: duck breast with morels, salmon *en papillote*. The €8 *formule* is served daily and there's a menu at €15. The *patronne* takes a lot of trouble for her guests; the only drawback, in fact, is the traffic noise during the day. *Free apéritif or coffee and 10% discount on the room rate from April to July on presentation of this guide.*

Hôtel d'Albret**

21 pl. du Champs-Commun.
Ⓣ05.62.94.75.00
Ⓔalbret.taverne.lourdes@libertysurf.fr
Restaurant closed *end Nov to early Jan; Sun evening and Mon out of season.* **Hotel closed** *end Nov to 20 March.* **TV.**

The hotel is opposite the covered market and is in the part of Lourdes which looks most like an ordinary town. It offers old-fashioned but comfortable rooms; those at the back are quiet and have a view of the mountains. Doubles with shower or bath €39–48. Breakfast €5.30. The cuisine in the restaurant is traditional with a regional basis; menus €12 (not served Sun), €16 and €24. Try the *garbure* with duck thigh, the fresh duck foie gras *escalope* with caramelized apples or the iced Grand Marnier soufflé with egg custard. Prompt service. *10% discount on the room rate, except in Aug, on presentation of this guide.*

Hôtel Beauséjour***

16 av. de la Gare.
Ⓣ05.62.94.38.18 Ⓕ05.62.94.96.20
Ⓦwww.hotel-beausejour.com
Disabled access. TV. Car park.

A reasonably priced three-star, conveniently situated near the station. Classy rooms all have direct-dial telephones and safes as well as bathrooms with wc and hairdryer. The ones overlooking the station itself are a bit noisier; the ones at the back are smaller but they have a view over the town and towards the distant Pyrenees. Doubles with shower/wc or bath from €54. Breakfast €6.40. There's a pleasant garden where you can eat in good weather. The brasserie offers a *formule* at €11 and menus at €20 and €30. Good choices include chicken with crayfish and pan-fried morels or salmon *tartare* on a bed of warm apples. *Free apéritif and 10% discount on the room rate 15 Oct–30 March.*

Le Magret

10 rue des 4-Frères-Soulas; behind the tourist office in place Peyramale.
Ⓣ05.62.94.20.55
Closed *Mon; Jan; last 10 days in Aug.*

Beautiful dining room with old red tiles on the floor and gleaming copper pots and pans hanging from the roughcast white walls, setting off the red-and-white tablecloths, diamond-changed plates and strikingly designed carafes containing the fine local water. Hearty food with an original touch: the cheapest menu at €13 (lunchtimes) features dishes such as *garbure paysanne*, a plate of duck and a platter of cheeses from Ossau. The other menus (€24 and €33) include *magret* with *edelweiss* and medallions of whole foie gras with Jurançon. It is impossible to resist the temptation of enticing desserts like the pear *confit* with Madiran and the excellent prune delight with Armagnac. The staff know a smattering of several languages and provide diligent but unfussy service.

Luz-Saint-Sauveur

65120

Auberge de jeunesse - Gîte d'étape Les Cascades

17 rue Sainte-Barbe; close to the GR10 and 150m from the church.
Ⓣ05.62.92.94.14
Ⓦwww.auberges-de-jeunesse.com
Car park.

A first-rate youth hostel run by some particularly dynamic young people – a warm atmosphere is guaranteed! Attractive rooms with two, four, six or eight beds (but you will need a sleeping bag). €10 a night. There are also four double rooms at €22. Half board is compulsory in winter (€22 per person). The excellent meals are served in a large, pretty communal dining room. There is a "hiker's menu" at €10 and thematic dinners revolving around dishes like paella, *garbure* or grilled meat. The staff will also give you all the information you need about hiking in the region.

Hôtel les Templiers**

Place de la Comporte; opposite the church of Saint-André in the old part of town.
Ⓣ05.62.92.81.52 Ⓕ05.62.92.93.05

Closed *May; Oct and Nov.* **TV.**

Rooms are simple but spacious and not without charm – there's some wonderful and highly polished local furniture. Doubles with shower/wc €36; nos. 1 and 2 sleep three people and have shutters opening onto the square. There's a welcoming crêperie at street level. Monday is market day, when the front of the hotel is transformed into a Spanish-style flower stall.

Marciac

32230

Les Comtes de Pardiac**

Place de l'Hôtel-de-Ville; in the heart of the village, close to the *Petit Auberge*.
Ⓣ05.62.08.20.00 Ⓕ05.62.08.28.05
Ⓦwww.hotel-comtespardiac.fr
TV. Car park.

The 25 bedrooms all look out on the back, which is good news in the village jazz festival, as it means you can sleep in peace. The décor is unremarkable, but the rooms have been refurbished with modern conveniences. Doubles €46 with shower and €56 with bath. There is also a suite and two rooms with private gardens that are ideal for families. Friendly service.

Beaumarchés

32160 (11km NW)

Le Relais du Bastidou**

Cayron; take the D3 in the direction of Riscle, then follow the signs.
Ⓣ and Ⓕ05.62.69.19.94
Ⓦwww.le-relais-du-bastidou.com
Restaurant closed *Sun evening and Mon, except in summer.* **TV. Disabled access. Swimming pool.**

A sophisticated haven of peace and quiet – a wonderful old Gascon farmhouse, lost in the countryside. The eight rooms have recently been refurbished and are splendid; they have not only their own TV but also a VCR. Doubles €43–61, depending on the size (but reckon on €95 during the Marciac festival!). The delicious breakfast is included (although there are savoury dishes that cost more). Three menus from €15–25. The "Bastide", for example, offers Gascon charcuterie based on *cul-noir* pork, duck stew or baby cuttlefish with Côtes de Gascogne wine.

Martel

46600

Auberge des 7 Tours

Avenue de Turenne; it's 100m from the centre.
Ⓣ05.65.37.30.16 Ⓕ05.65.37.41.69
Ⓦwww.auberge7tours.com
Closed *Sat evening, Sun evening and Mon 15 Sept–15 July.* **TV.**

A small hotel with eight renovated rooms that have personality. Doubles from €34.50 to €41. The restaurant, set apart from the hotel, is a good new place to eat in the Lot; the couple who run it have travelled extensively and the cooking shows the breadth of their travels. Try slivers of duck in honey and thyme or kangaroo Rossini. Menus €12.20–49; the cheaper ones have more regional dishes. There's a terrace in summer. *Free coffee on presentation of this guide.*

Martres-Tolosane

31220

Hôtel-Restaurant Castet**

Avenue de la Gare.
Ⓣ05.61.98.80.20 Ⓕ05.61.98.61.02
Ⓔhotelcastet@wanadoo.fr
Open *noon–2.00pm and 8.00–9.30pm*
Closed *Sun evening; Mon.* **TV. Swimming pool. Highchairs available.**

A quiet house just opposite the station. Double rooms with bath €36–39; breakfast €5. Menus €15 (except Sat evening and Sun lunchtime) and €22–43. They do duck specialities and a rib of beef cooked in a salt crust alongside other classic dishes using fresh local produce. There's a wonderful shady terrace, but the dining room is a bit gloomy.

Fousseret (Le)

31430 (15km NE)

Restaurant des Voyageurs

Grande-Rue; take exit 23 off the A64 motorway as far as Fousseret and it's on the road up to the central square.
Ⓣ05.61.09.53.06
Open *noon–1.30pm and 7.30–9.00pm.*
Closed *Sat; Sun and Mon evenings; Aug; a week at Christmas.*

A grey house with green shutters. The welcome is as charming as the interior. Family-style cooking and dishes influenced by the region: *pot Gascon*, beef fillet, ravioli with foie gras in cep broth. The menu at €9.50 is excellent value and there are others at €20 and €34. In summer you dine on the terrace behind the house. Credit cards not accepted.

Mazamet

81200

Hôtel Mets et Plaisirs**

7 av. Albert-Rouvière.
Ⓣ05.63.61.56.93 Ⓕ05.63.61.83.38
Restaurant closed *Sun evening; Mon.* **TV.**

Robust, tasty food. On the menus (€14, €21, €40) you'll find specialities like roast zander with mountain ham and lamb fillet lacquered with Armagnac. The restaurant is popular with workers at lunchtime – the atmosphere may be very relaxed but the service is up to scratch, even if there isn't much elbow room. Some of the rooms are a bit cramped, too, but they're clean and air-conditioned. Doubles €43 with shower/wc or €46 with bath. Breakfast €6.

Millau

12100

Hôtel Emma Calvé

1 place de la Tiné.
Ⓣ05.65.60.13.49 Ⓕ05.65.60.93.75
Ⓦwwwemmacalv.ifrance.com
TV.

Pascale receives you like a diva in her glorious bourgeois house (ideally located in the centre of Millau), and the reception looks a little like a boudoir. Each of the thirteen rooms is decorated differently. Those at the back look over the glorious garden but if you like to sleep with the window open, avoid rooms 5, 6 and 7 which look over the road. Doubles with bath €58–80 including breakfast; €75 for three people.

La Mangeoire

8 bd. de La Capelle.
Ⓣ05.65.60.13.16
Closed *Mon except Aug.*
Disabled access. TV. Swimming pool. Highchairs available. Car park.

The establishment creates a superb setting for your meal; vaulted rooms with tasteful decoration and clever lighting. The chef dominates the place in front of the open fireplace where he grills excellent local meat over the glowing coals: lamb with wild mushrooms and roast pigeon. Weekday menu €13; others at €16–43. À la carte around €25. There are some good local wines by the glass, but they can be pricey. In summer they put tables out under the plane trees on the boulevard.

Creissels

12100 (2km S)

Le Château de Creissels

Route de St-Affrique; it's in the middle of the village opposite the church.
Hotel Ⓣ05.65.60.16.59 Ⓕ05.65.61.24.63
Restaurant Ⓣ05.65.61.24.63
Ⓦwww.chateau-de-creissels.com
Closed *Sun evening and Monday lunchtime 30 Sept–30 April; Jan; Feb.* **TV. Highchairs and games available. Car park.**

A quiet candlelit dinner in a chateau... plus a view over Millau and the course of the river Tarn. This is a delicious place with perfect rooms. Tasteful doubles €49–78. Tasty cuisine: foie gras, Roquefort in puff pastry, grilled beef and home-made peach and apricot ice cream. There's a *formule* of the day for €21.50 and other menus up to €46.

Saint-Jean-du-Bruel

12230 (35km SE)

Hôtel-restaurant du Midi-Papillon**

Ⓣ05.65.62.26.04 Ⓕ05.65.62.12.97
Closed *11 Nov to Palm Sunday.* **Swimming pool. Highchairs available. Car park.**

This hotel in the depths of Aveyron welcomed its first guests in 1850 and has since been run by successive generations of the Papillon family. Reservations are recommended. The rooms are exceptionally pleasant, particularly those overlooking the Dourbie, and prices are reasonable: doubles €30.80–55.60. The dining room is decorated with flowers and overlooks the river and there's a pretty and pleasant terrace which is often full. The chef uses only the freshest produce – he grows his own fruit and vegetables, rears his own chickens, fattens his own pigs and gathers his own mushrooms, so the cuisine is full of authentic flavours: home-made charcuterie, Roquefort and walnut tart, duck *confit*, goose fillet with morel sauce and an exquisite gentian jelly accompanied with tuiles and wild blackberries. Menus from

€12.70 (weekday lunchtimes) up to €35.10. Pleasant staff; the service is unobtrusively efficient.

Mirande

32300

🏃 ⌂ |●| Auberge de la Halle

Rue des Écoles.
☎05.62.66.76.81
Closed *Fri evening; Sat.*

A simple place where you feel relaxed right away. Traditional cuisine in handsome portions on a range of appetizing menus from €10 (lunchtime only) to €25 – try the flambéed prawns. There are also a few rooms in a separate building – some overlooking the road, others the garden. They're modest and clean and cost €25 with basin and €30 with shower/wc. Breakfast €4.30. The young owners are lovely. *Free apéritif on presentation of this guide.*

Moissac

82200

⌂ |●| Le Pont Napoléon**

2 allée Montebello; it's just by the bridge.
☎05.63.04.01.55 Ⓕ05.63.04.34.44
Ⓔdussau.lenapoleon@wanadoo.fr
Closed *Sun evening; Mon lunch; Wed.* **TV. Pay car park.**

The hotel is a dream, with fair prices and amazing bathrooms. Redecorated and sound-proofed doubles €35–53; breakfast €7. For all that, the restaurant is better-known. The gastronomic cuisine of Michel Dussau can be sampled on menus at €20 (not Sun) and €30–60: duck foie gras grilled with Moissac fruits, poached eggs with black truffles, *croustade du pays.*

Durfort-Lacapelette

82390 (6km NE)

🏃 ⌂ |●| Hôtel-restaurant Aube Nouvelle**

From Moissac drive towards Lauzerte on the 957, then continue to Durfort on the D16.
☎05.63.04.50.33 Ⓕ05.63.04.57.55
Ⓦwww.chez.com/aubenouvelle
Closed *Sat lunch (except reservations); 23 Dec–20 Jan.* **Disabled access. Car park.**

Owner Marc de Smet's parents moved from Belgium to the Quercy in 1955, and he and his wife Claudine took over their business. It's an idyllic spot surrounded by fields, which you can admire from the lovely terrace and garden. The clean, well-maintained rooms have been renovated to a high standard and cost €49.50 with shower/wc or bath. Breakfast €5. Half board, €42.39 per person, is compulsory April–Sept. The cooking is regional in flavour and Belgian in influence – saddle of rabbit *à la flamande*, shellfish *waterzooi*, beef in brown ale sauce and snail stew with creamed garlic. Portions are generous; menus €11 (weekday lunchtimes) and €15–31. *10% discount on the room rate for a minimum stay of three consecutive nights on presentation of this guide.*

Moncorneil-Grazan

32260

|●| Restaurant L'Auberge d'Astarac

It's between Masseube and Simorre, in the heart of the village.
☎05.62.65.48.81
Closed *lunchtimes (except Sun and bank holidays); Mon; 5 Jan–13 Feb; 15 Nov–15 Dec.*

This inn has been lovingly restored by two exceptional people who fell in love with the area. There's an old bar, a delightful dining room and a glorious terrace. At the bottom of the flower garden you'll see Christian Termote's kitchen garden, full of vegetables and herbs. He taught himself to cook and uses those herbs with great subtlety. Try the apple stuffed with foie gras, the pigeon breast with a reduction of Madeiran wine, the cep and snail stew, the lamb with rosemary, and the gingerbread *crème brûlée.* Set menus €29–46. There's an excellent choice of wine, with a particularly good selection from the south. Lucie is the genial *patronne*; she even lets her clients choose their own bottle from the cellar. You have to book.

Montauban

82000

⌂ Hôtel du Commerce**

9 pl. Roosevelt; you can reach it from the place de la Cathédrale.
☎05.63.66.31.32 Ⓕ05.63.66.31.28
TV. Disabled access.

This hotel right in the centre of

Montauban is a real boon. The owners are sure to give you an effusive and generous welcome. They have totally refurbished the rooms, using floor tiles and fabrics in bright and warm Mediterranean colours. The bathrooms are brand new. Double rooms with maximum comfort €40. You can park just outside.

Hôtel Mercure***

12 rue Notre-Dame.
Ⓣ05.63.63.17.23 Ⓕ05.63.66.43.66
Ⓔmercuremontauban@wanadoo.fr
Disabled access. TV. Pay car park.

Chain hotels don't usually appear in this guide, but this is an exception. The *Mercure* is simply the best hotel in town, very well managed and with real charm. Inevitably it's also the most expensive – double rooms €95 with bath, breakfast €9.50. The décor is bright and warm and the rooms are spacious and decorated in contemporary style with particularly splendid bathrooms. In the eighteenth century, the building was a private mansion. *10% discount on the room rate on presentation of this guide.*

Restaurant Le Ventadour

23 quai Villebourbon; it's on banks of the Tarn, opposite the Ingres museum.
Ⓣ05.63.63.34.58
Closed *Sat lunchtime; Sun; Mon; 1–15 Jan; 1–15 Aug.*

Incredibly popular restaurant with a vaulted brick dining room done up to look like the inside of a castle. The place gets flooded whenever the Tarn bursts its banks, but on the other hand it's always cool whatever the temperature outside. This is cooking at its most refined: bonbons of semi-cooked and cooked foie gras with pears, *rosette* of Mérou and courgette, lamb *confit* and iced Grand-Marnier *soufflé*. The service is first-rate too. Prices are reasonable – weekday lunch menu €17 with others €22 and €42. *Free digestif on presentation of this guide.*

Le Sampa

21 and 21 bis rue des Carmes.
Ⓣ05.63.20.36.46
Closed *Sun; public holidays; 25 Dec–3 Jan.*

The trendy décor with a rustic twist suits the cooking well: salads, chicken curry, duck *aiguillette* with acacia honey, Dover sole fillet or shark steak. À la carte you'll pay around €23 and there's a selection of dishes of the day. It's all good stuff and helpings are enormous. From May to mid-October they serve grills and salads on the lovely terrace. The welcome and service are congenial, and in the evenings the warm, friendly atmosphere at the bar extends to the dining room. *Free digestif on presentation of this guide.*

Montréal

32500

Chez Simone

It's in the village.
Ⓣ05.62.29.44.40 Ⓕ05.62.29.49.94
Closed *Mon; Tues; Sun evening (except during public holidays).*

There are two entrances – one goes into the designer bistro, the other leads via the terrace to a main dining room which has all the attributes of a modish, gourmet restaurant. In the middle there's a display showing off all the bottles on the wine list and an impressive collection of Armagnac flagons – more than thirty vintages. There are three menus at €13, €25 and €45 (the "ronde des tapas"). The cuisine is essentially regional but has quite a lot of sauces and they also do good fish. Goose and duck foie gras is sliced in front of you and served without adornment. The owner has a nice bar under the arcades in the square where you can knock back a glass or two of Armagnac.

Fourcès

32250 (6km N)

Château de Fourcès***

Ⓣ05.62.29.49.53 Ⓕ05.62.29.50.59
Ⓦwww.chateau-fources.com
Closed *Mon; Tues lunch; Oct–April.* **TV. Swimming pool. Car park.**

A smart, charming place in a twelfth-century chateau in the middle of the village. It has been magnificently restored and has all the modern facilities you could wish for. The rooms are in soft colours and elegantly coordinated. There's a river running through the garden and a swimming pool nearby. High-season prices are €130 for doubles with shower or shower/wc and €155 with bath. Breakfast €10. Very good cooking to match, with dishes that change regularly. Menus €22 (weekdays) then €29–35. Formal, stylish welcome and attentive service. *Free house apéritif, coffee or 10% discount on the room rate in April, May and Oct on presentation of this guide.*

Montricoux

82800

🏃 🏠 |●| Le Relais du Postillon *

Le Bugarel.
Ⓣ05.63.67.23.58 Ⓕ05.63.67.27.68
Ⓔrelaispostillon@aol.fr
Closed *Fri and Sat lunchtime except July/Aug.* **TV. Highchairs available. Car park.**

A pleasant inn providing good regional cooking. The dining room is cosy and they do some wonderful house specialities. Weekday lunch menu €15 and others €19–32. À la carte try cep omelette, frogs' legs, civet of hare, *cassoulet*, foie gras, salmon with sorrel in flaky pastry, zander with saffron or the home-made pastries. There's a pleasant shady terrace and a garden. The rooms aren't particularly attractive but they're well maintained; doubles €19.50 with basin, €24 with shower – wc on the landing. Breakfast €4.50. *Free house apéritif on presentation of this guide.*

Montségur

09300

🏠 |●| Hôtel-restaurant Costes**

52 rue Principale.
Ⓣ05.61.01.10.24
Ⓦwww.montsegur.com/costes.ht
Closed *Sat evening; Mon; 11 Nov–1 April.* **Highchairs available.**

The building is covered in Virginia creeper and it's a nice place to stop if you're planning an assault on the peak of Montségur. A dozen simple rooms, fairly priced at €33–47. Breakfast €6.30. There's a family feel to the restaurant where they serve very good home cooking: *civet* of game, duck breast with figs, tenderloin of pork, salad of gizzards, *confit* with chanterelle mushrooms. Menus €17–30. There's a pleasant terrace and garden.

Najac

12270

🏃 🏠 |●| L'Oustal del Barry**

Place du Bourg.
Ⓣ05.65.29.74.32 Ⓕ05.65.29.75.32
Ⓦwww.oustal-del-barry.com
Restaurant closed *Mon except for residents; mid-Nov to Easter.* **Open** *at Christmas.* **Disabled access. Highchairs available. Garden. TV. Pay car park.**

This lovely inn is an appealing place to stop. The décor is plush and the rooms are very elegant while retaining an authentic rustic feel. Doubles with basin €34, with shower/wc and bath €52–70. Half-board €52–70 per person. The restaurant serves largely regional dishes using seasonal ingredients. Menus €18.50–46.50: try the semi-cooked duck foie gras served with warm hazelnut brioche. There's a good wine list, and the desserts are mouthwatering. *Free coffee on presentation of this guide.*

🏃 🏠 |●| Le Belle Rive**

Le Roc du Pont; it's 2km from the village.
Ⓣ05.65.29.73.90 Ⓕ05.65.29.76.88
Ⓔhotel-bellrive.najac@wanadoo.fr
Closed *Sun evening April–Oct; Mon lunchtime.* **Disabled access. TV. Swimming pool. Highchairs available. Car park.**

A pleasant hotel in green, leafy surroundings on a bend in the river. The swimming pool and tennis court make it feel something like a family holiday centre. Rooms are bright and pleasant; doubles with shower/wc or bath cost €52. Half board (compulsory in July–Aug) €52 per person. The cooking is good – house specialities include Roquefort in puff pastry, salad of cured duck fillet, veal steak with garlic vinaigrette or zander fillet with asparagus. Good selection of cheeses and desserts. Menus are €16.50–46; à la carte around €40, and you can eat outside in good weather. *Free coffee on presentation of this guide.*

|●| La Salamandre

Rue du Barriou; it's at the beginning of the street that leads to the chateau.
Ⓣ05.65.29.74.09
Closed *Tues and Wed out of season; mid-Nov to end Jan.*

An unpretentious restaurant offering straight-forward, local dishes: sausages, duck breast, salads, mushroom tart, local cheeses, home-made desserts. The chef, a local boy, has returned to Najac having done his apprenticeship in a number of Parisian brasseries. Lunch menu €10; others at €16 and €20. There is an impressive view of the chateau from the terrace at the back. Magical.

Nestier

65150

Le Relais du Castera**

Centre.
Ⓣ05.62.39.77.37 Ⓕ05.62.39.77.29
Closed *Sun evening; Mon; Tues evening Oct–May; Jan; early June.* **TV.**

The *Relais* looks pretty uninteresting outside but there's nothing remotely dull about the cooking of Serge Latour: he's one of the best chefs in the Hautes-Pyrénées. He assembles and presents dishes with elaborate care. You discover all kinds of new flavours at excellent prices: weekday lunch menu €17 and others €23, €29 and €40. Regional specialities include fresh fish with Jurançon sauce, duck foie gras in many different forms, *cassoulet* with Tarbais beans, crayfish with creamed Tarbais beans, *garbure* with *confit* of duck and a chocolate dessert platter. You can also create your own menu if you order in advance. Lots of local wines. There are a few comfortable rooms, €50 with shower/wc. Breakfast €7. *Free coffee on presentation of this guide.*

Peyrecave

32340

Chez Annie

It's halfway between Lectaure and Castelsarrasin on the Tarn and Garonne border.
Ⓣ05.62.28.65.40
Closed *Sat; Sun; the second fortnight in Sept.*

Annie runs this stunning little roadside inn and she also does the cooking: try her house *cassoulet*, *daube* with prunes, *poule-au-pot*, chicken galantine. Three menus €11 (weekday lunchtimes) up to €18. *Free coffee on presentation of this guide.*

Projan

32400

Le Château de Projan**

It's on the road from Saint-Mont to the N134.
Ⓣ05.62.09.46.21
Ⓔchateaudeprojan@libertysurf.fr
Closed *Fri evening out of season; Jan.* **Car park.**

A genuine château standing alone on a hill. The family who've owned it since 1986 have transformed the place, letting in light and colour and filling the rooms with contemporary art. The salon, which has been decorated in a modern style, looks out over the countryside. Prices are about right for such a wonderful place. Eight double rooms: €60 with bathroom on the landing, €87–110 with shower/wc or bath, and a suite at €150. Breakfast €7.50. It's not a fully fledged restaurant but they offer *table d'hôte* to order in advance, starting at €22–40. Good dishes include duck marinated in Madeira wine and duck liver. *Free apéritif and 10% discount on the room rate except July–Sept on presentation of this guide.*

Puylaurens

81700

Château Cap de Castel***

It's in the village.
Ⓣ05.63.70.21.76 Ⓕ05.63.70.21.76
Ⓦwww.chateau-capdecastel.com
Disabled access. TV. Swimming pool.

This is an admirably run and appealing hotel. The château dates back to 1258 and rooms are in some of the outbuildings. Doubles (all newly updated) €44–66 depending on size; all have large bathrooms. Breakfast €6. There's a swimming pool with a terrace and views over the valley. The cuisine served in the restaurant is typical of the region: beef fillet *en croûte*, duck breast, and, in winter, grills over the open fire. Menus €14.20–25. Extremely friendly welcome. *One free breakfast per room on presentation of this guide.*

Puy l'Evèque

46700

Hôtel Bellevue – Restaurant Côté Lot

Place de la Truffière.
Ⓣ05.65.36.06.60
Restaurant closed *Sun and Mon; mid-Jan to mid-Feb; end Nov.* **Disabled access. TV.**

Doubles €60–85. The restaurant is completely new and has a lovely view over the Lot and the plains. Delicious cooking, and bang up to date; robust local dishes are interspersed with regional recipes that are light and full of flavour.

You'll get the strong flavours of the Mediterranean and the delicacy of Atlantic fish. Menus €26–50. In a separate building, the popular *L'Aganit* brasserie offers simpler fare. It has a veranda and a terrace. *Free house apéritif on presentation of this guide.*

Maroux

46700 (10km S)

Hostellerie Le Vert

It's on the D5.
05.65.36.51.36 05.65.36.56.84
hotellevert@aol.com
Closed *Mon–Fri lunchtimes; Thurs and Sun evenings; mid-Nov to mid-Feb.* **TV. Highchairs and games available. Swimming pool.**

A superb, typical Quercy residence way out in the country, surrounded by landscaped grounds. The orchard and swimming pool offer utter peace. You'll receive a charming welcome, and the staff can give you all sorts of information on local rambles. The seven rooms have been decorated in exquisite taste. One has a beautiful vault in bare stone, while another has a piano and an open fireplace. Doubles with en-suite bathrooms €50–90. The bright, pleasant restaurant well deserves its fine reputation; dishes change with the seasons and what's good at the market. The gastronomic menu costs €40. À la carte will cost around €32. *10% discount on the room rate except during school holidays on presentation of this guide.*

Réalmont

81120

Les Routiers - Chez Richard et Patricia

Boulevard Armengaud; it's on the N112 halfway between Castres and Albi.
05.63.55.65.44
richard-duarte@wanadoo.fr
Closed *Sun; 10–24 Aug.* **Car park.**

A Routier restaurant with a great reputation. There's a huge dining room with attractive stone walls where they serve typical family dishes. The €10.50 menu lists a self-service buffet of *horsd'œuvres*, main course, cheese, dessert and wine; other menus to order. *Free coffee on presentation of this guide.*

Revel

31250

Hôtel-restaurant du Midi**

34 bd. Gambetta.
www.hotelrestaurantdumidi.com
05.61.83.50.50 05.61.83.34.74
Restaurant closed *Sun evening and Mon lunchtime Nov to Easter; mid-Nov to early Dec.* **TV. Car park.**

Elegant early nineteenth-century coaching inn, now a pleasant hotel with smart rooms for €38–61 with bath – the most expensive ones look over the garden. Breakfast €6. The nice dining room is bright and in summer you can eat outside. Weekday lunch menu of the day is €13.50; others €19–45 list many aromatic dishes. The very affordable wines including Corbières, Gaillac and Bordeaux. *Free apéritif on presentation of this guide.*

Rieumes

31370

Hôtel Les Palmiers**

13 pl. du Foirail.
05.61.91.81.01 05.61.91.56.36
www.auberge-lespalmiers.com
Closed *Mon.*

Pretty but subdued décor, with African *bogolan* prints alongside modern paintings in the dining room. Very attractive and quiet courtyard with palm trees – an ideal place for relaxing in fine weather. The inviting rooms combine the charm of the old with the comfort of the new. Doubles €56. The cooking draws its inspiration from regional traditions, with pride of place going to fish dishes. Weekday lunchtime menus €10–20,€19–35 at dinner and on Saturday, €25 on Sunday. Good service.

Riscle

32400

Le Pigeonneau

36 av. de l'Adour.
05.62.69.85.64
Closed *Sun evening; Mon; Tues evening.*

A chic place to eat exquisite traditional food given a subtle, exotic twist, with the chef's English background apparent in the discreet Asian influences: *croustillant* of gizzards with prunes, squab with sweet spices and Pacherenc wine, *croustade* with apples and an unforgettable cardamom. Weekday lunchtime menu €16, including wine, with another menu €25. Wine served by the glass or bottle at reasonable prices. A few tidbits to nibble while waiting for the meal would not go amiss, but that's a quibble – this is one of the best restaurants in the *département*. No smoking.

Rocamadour

46500

Hôtel-restaurant Le Lion d'Or**

It's in the medieval town.
Ⓣ05.65.33.62.04 Ⓕ05.65.33.72.54
Ⓦwww.liondor-rocamadour.com
Closed 2 Nov–3 April. **TV. Highchairs available. Car park.**

A traditional hotel-restaurant which offers a lovely view of the old town. The comfy bedrooms are reasonable value – €35.10–50 for a double with shower/wc or bath. Half board €40.50–52.50 per person. In the restaurant, menus go for €11.50–37.40 and list specialities such as foie gras *tarte tatin* with morel sauce, *confit* of duck and truffle omelette. Brilliant desserts – it's impossible to resist the walnut gâteau with egg custard. Reservations recommended – ask for a table with a view. *10% discount on the room rate (except Aug) on a stay of at least two consecutive nights on presentation of this guide.*

Le Troubadour

Belveyre; it's 800m from L'Hospitalet in the direction of Alvignac.
Ⓣ05.65.33.70.27 Ⓕ05.65.33.71.99
Ⓔtroubadour@rocamadour.com
Closed *mid-Nov to mid-Feb.* **Restaurant closed** *lunchtimes.* **Disabled access. TV. Highchairs and games available. Swimming pool.**

This large white stone house, set back from the road, is a godsend for anyone who wants to avoid the tourist-tussle that is Rocamadour. It's a quiet place surrounded by greenery, and there's a magnificent view of the limestone plain from the pool. The rooms, decorated with floral wallpaper, are delightfully fresh in summer. Doubles €55–85 with bath. The air-conditioned restaurant serves traditional and regional dishes. Menu €23 or à la carte. It's best to book. *Free house apéritif on presentation of this guide.*

Hôtel-restaurant Beau Site***

It's on the only street in the medieval town; access to the hotel permitted by car.
Ⓣ05.65.33.63.08 Ⓕ05.65.33.65.23
Ⓦwww.bw-beausite.com
TV. Highchairs available. Car park.

The *Beau Site* is very appropriately named – it's in the heart of Rocamadour. Some of the well-maintained, attractive bedrooms have a breathtaking view of the abbey perched on the hill; doubles €62–93 in high season or €46–72 in low season. Half board €59–69. Tasty, refined, aromatic dishes are served in a beautiful, flowery dining room; menus €16 (lunchtime) and then from €21.50. The pretty terrace is shaded by lime trees and offers a great view of the château. An excellent establishment in its category. *10% discount on the room rate (except Aug) on presentation of this guide.*

Meyronne

46200 (14km N)

Hôtel-restaurant La Terrasse**

Take the D673 for 4km then turn left onto the D15.
Ⓣ05.65.32.21.60 Ⓕ05.65.32.26.93
Ⓦwww.hotel-la-terrasse.com
Closed *Tues lunchtime; mid-Nov to end March.* **TV. Swimming pool.**

Meyronne is an adorable little village up in the hills and this establishment was at one time the summer residence of the bishops of Tulle. The building is full of charm and character: the stone walls are covered in ivy and it has beams and turrets with sloping roofs. Comfortable doubles go for €60–92 in the hotel or the castle proper; suites from €125. Those in the latter are deliciously cool in summer, which is a considerable plus in this part of the world. The terrace is shaded by a pergola and overlooks the valley, and the restaurant specializes in regional dishes. There's a *formule* for €18 on weekend lunchtimes, and menus €24–45.

Loupiac

46100 (21km NW)

Le Claux de Sérignac

It's on the left, about 10km north of Villeneuve.
Ⓣ05.65.64.87.15 Ⓕ05.65.80.87.66
Ⓔwww.clauxdeserignac.com
Closed *Mon and Tues lunchtime; Sun evening out of season; 15 Dec–15 Jan.* **TV. Highchairs available. Swimming pool.**

The stylish house is in a restful setting surrounded by five hectares of grounds with a swimming pool and tennis court. The rooms are tasteful and spacious and have canopied beds. Doubles €40–62; breakfast €6. There are also four fully equipped chalets that sleep four to six. The fine, original cooking offers rare value for money. Menus €11–36. You can hire mountain bikes. Motorbike parks. *Free house apéritif on presentation of this guide.*

Carennac

46110 (25.5km NE)

Hostellerie Fénelon**

Rue Principale.
Ⓣ05.65.10.96.46 Ⓕ05.65.10.94.86
Closed *Fri and Sat lunchtime out of season; mid-Nov to mid-Dec; Jan to end March.* **TV. Highchairs available. Swimming pool. Car park.**

Service lunchtime, and evening until 9pm. A conventional hotel with very decent, cosy rooms furnished in country style. Doubles €49–59. Half board (compulsory July/Aug) €52–60. The refurbishment of some of the rooms is on the cards for this year. The cooking is good, with menus at €17–47; à la carte can be pricey. The dining room looks over the garden and swimming pool and some tables have views of the river; there's also a nice fireplace. You can eat on the terrace in fine weather. *Free coffee on presentation of this guide.*

Auberge du Vieux Quercy**

Take the D673 as far as Alvignac, then turn left onto the D20; it's on the road that runs through the village.
Ⓣ05.65.10.96.59 Ⓕ05.65.10.94.05
Ⓦwww.vieuxquercy.com
Closed weekday lunchtimes; 15 Nov–15 March. **TV. Highchairs available. Swimming pool. Car park.**

Handsome tourist complex – with hotels, gardens and swimming pool – built around an old coaching inn in an idyllic setting. The main building is pretty ancient and has character; you can have a room there or in one of the annexes around the pool. Pleasant, if maybe slightly pricey, doubles €55–68. Half board (July/Aug) €55–65. The dining room has views of the garden and a maze of rooftops. Set menus, €16–30, list local dishes: *escalope* of poached duck foie gras with roasted figs. Good Cahors wine. *10% discount on the room rate April, May, Sept and Oct on presentation of this guide.*

Rodez

12000

Hôtel de la Tour-Maje***

Boulevard Gally.
Ⓣ05.65.68.34.68 Ⓕ05.65.68.27.56
Ⓦwww.hotel-tour-maje.fr
Closed *Christmas–New Year.* **Disabled access. TV.**

This classic hotel incorporates a fourteenth-century tower, a remnant of the old ramparts. The rooms are pleasant, modern and tastefully decorated; doubles cost €58–66 depending on facilities. Some lovely rooms sleeping two-to-four are available in the tower for €110. Fifth floor completely refurbished. *10% discount on the room rate on presentation of this guide.*

Hôtel Biney

7 bd. Gambetta or rue Victoire Massol; it's between the cathedral and the tourist office. There's a sign at the end of the passage.
Ⓣ05.65.68.01.24 Ⓕ05.65.75.22.98
Ⓔhotel.biney@wanadoo.fr
TV. Pay car park.

This quiet little hotel is right in the middle of Rodez which is most convenient. The interior design is very tasteful, with warm colours and beautiful fabrics, and there's a peaceful flower garden at the back – some rooms overlook it. There are 29 double rooms with modern bathrooms at €29–135, along with a steam room and a sauna (€4). The generous buffet breakfast costs €9 and you can order a tasty TV meal to have in your room for €13. *10% discount on the room rate on presentation of this guide.*

Restaurant La Taverne

23 rue de l'Embergue.
Ⓣ05.65.42.14.51

Ⓦwww.tavernerodez.com
Closed *Sat lunchtime out of season; Sun; public holidays; a fortnight in May; a fortnight in Sept.* **Highchairs available.**

A vaulted basement dining room where you'll be served traditional and regional food – pig's cheek, stuffed cabbage or *aligot*. Prices are very reasonable, though watch out for supplements on the menus: weekday lunch menu €10.50 and an extensive *menu-carte* for €15. There's a terrace at the back, overlooking the garden. *Free apéritif on presentation of this guide.*

Restaurant Willy's

2 rue de la Viarague.
Ⓣ05.65.68.17.34
Closed *Sun; Mon; a week in spring; a week in Sept.*

The building is painted blue and the dining room is in warm, pleasant colours. It's a friendly restaurant specializing in regional cooking with a touch of originality and exoticism. Good fresh produce is used, and fish is a speciality. Menus €13.50 and €20. You'll be welcomed without fuss and the atmosphere is young, informal and relaxed. Reservations advised. *Free house apéritif on presentation of this guide.*

Restaurant Goûts et Couleurs

38 rue de Bonald.
Ⓣ and Ⓕ05.65.42.75.10
Ⓦwww.fau-et-usage-de-fau.com
Closed *Sun; Mon; Jan; 10 days early May; a fortnight in mid-Sept.*

The dining room is painted in pastel shades and there's a warm atmosphere – perfect for an intimate dinner. The chef is a culinary artist, and his cooking from around the Mediterranean seaboard is truly inspired: jellied *tajine* of chicken with pickled lemons and olives, fresh sardine gâteau marinated with fennel. Weekday lunch menu €20, then others €26–65; à la carte around €40. Attentive but relaxed service. Reservations advised.

Sainte-Radegonde

12850 (6km SE)

Saloon Guest Ranch***

Landrevrier-Sainte-Radegonde.
Ⓣ05.65.42.47.46 Ⓕ05.65.78.32.36
Ⓦwww.le-saloon.com
Open *evenings by reservation only; Sun lunchtime.* **TV. Swimming pool. Car park.**

A little corner of the American Wild West right in the heart of the Aveyron countryside, complete with horses and saloon. The latter is authentic down to the smallest detail, with mahogony furniture, red wallpaper and lots of photographs. Not surprisingly, meat looms large on the menu, and it's some of the best in the area; very generous set menus at €19–28. Rooms are spacious and the décor, of course, is cowboy-style – the luxury version, that is. Doubles with shower/wc or bath €50–60. Breakfast €7. The staff are friendly and considerate. You can ride or take part in any of the many other activities if you're staying full board, but don't forget to book. *Free apéritif on presentation of this guide.*

Salles-La Source

12330 (10km NW)

Restaurant de la Cascade

Take the D901 and it's next to the museum.
Ⓣand Ⓕ05.65.67.29.08
Closed *Sun; Mon–Wed evenings; early Jan.* **Disabled access.**

The small dining room is in pinkish tones and has a ravishing view of the surrounding valleys. Honest cuisine with two weekday lunch menus at €11 and €15.90; the cheaper menu changes every day and offers two starters, main course (perhaps *aligot*, or a seasonal dish), cheese and dessert. Week-end menus at €14–23 €13.60 and €20.50. Shady terrace. *Free apéritif on presentation of this guide.*

Saint-Antonin-Noble-Val

82140

Hôtel des Thermes**

1 pl. des Moines; if you're coming from the gorges, it's after the bridge on the left.
Ⓣ05.63.25.06.00 Ⓕ05.63.25.06.06
Ⓦwww.nobleval.com
Restaurant closed *Tues evening and Wed except July–Aug; Jan.* **TV.**

The prices and the waterside location are the best things about this place. Rooms look suspiciously like those you'd find in a chain, but the location and the warmth of the welcome make up for that. Doubles with bath €36. Some have a view of the river and the Anglars cliff-face. Breakfast €5. Weekday lunch menu €9, others €14–29. Try semi-cooked foie gras or foie gras *tournedos*, *cassoulet*, smoked salmon or scallops. There's a wonderful waterside terrace and a cybercafé.

Brousses

82140 (9 km S)

|●| La Corniche

le bourg; take the coast road (D115 bis).
Ⓣ05.63.68.26.95
Closed *Wed and Sun evenings (except July–Aug); Oct–Feb.*

The young chef in this little restaurant tucked away above the Aveyron gorges invites you to a sensual treat. Working alone in his kitchen, he toils away to offer seasonal, traditional food that is really out of the ordinary. Don't be fooled by his shy and modest demeanour – he's a magician, and his best trick is achieving all this with such little expense. Weekday lunchtime menu €15.50, others at €24 and €29. There is a terrace with a view of the Capucins rock, which is very popular with rock climbers. It's best to book at the weekend. Credit cards not accepted.

Saint-Bertrand-de-Comminges

31510

Hôtel du Comminges**

Place de la Cathédrale.
Ⓣ05.61.88.31.43 Ⓕ05.61.94.98.22
Closed *Nov–March.*

The hotel is in a quite delightful old family house opposite the cathedral, swathed in ivy and wisteria with a small internal courtyard: the whole place is utterly charming. Large rooms with period furniture; doubles with shower/wc or bath €29.50–50. Large bedroom for four people at €68. Breakfast €6.

|●| L'Oppidum**

Rue de la Poste; near the cathedral on the road down to the post office.
Ⓣ05.61.88.33.50 Ⓕ05.61.95.94.04
Ⓦwww.hote-oppidum.com
Closed *Sun evening; Mon; 15 Nov–15 Dec.*
Disabled access. Highchairs available. TV.

A small, pretty hotel in an old building. The rooms are comfortable and bright but rather small and priced at €42 with shower/wc or €47.75 with bath – one is big enough to be a honeymoon suite. Breakfast €5.60. Menus from €14 (not Sun) up to €30.50, offering decent cuisine: *émincé* of duck with cep cream, foie gras, stews, and so on. *Free coffee on presentation of this guide.*

Valcabrère

31510 (1.5km E)

|●| Le Lugdunum

After Valcabrère, join the N25, turn right and it's 400m further on.
Ⓣ05.61.94.52.05 Ⓕ05.61.94.52.06
Closed *Sun and Mon evenings; Tues and Wed out of season.* **Car park.**

An unusual restaurant which resembles a Roman villa. It has a terrace overlooking the grazing fields and a fantastic view of Saint-Bertrand. Renzo Pedrazzini, whose family comes from Lombardy, serves traditional local dishes, but the real attraction here are the recipes he has taken from the ancient Romans: sea bream with grapes or lamb with ginger. He mixes honey and vinegar, won't use tomatoes or lemons because they were unknown to the ancients and gets his spices from a local herbalist – he regards himself as an apprentice of Apicius, who wrote a treatise on cooking two millennia ago. The *menu antique* offers a precious haul of forgotten recipes. Take his wife's advice and have a spiced wine with your meal and try the rose or violet apéritif. A meal will cost around €28–47; you must book ahead for the most expensive menu. À la carte around €55.

Saint-Céré

46400

|●| Hôtel-Restaurant Les 3 Soleils

Les Prés-de-Montal.
Ⓣ05.65.10.16.16 Ⓕ05.65.38.30.66
Ⓔlestroissoleils@wanadoo.fr
Closed *Mon lunchtime (July/Aug), Tuesday lunchtime (April, June and Sept), Friday lunchtime; 11 Nov–20 Dec; Jan.* **TV. Highchairs available. Car park.**

On the edge of Saint-Céré, close to the chateau, this is a soothing place that will lift your mood. Frédéric Bizat adds a personal touch to his reinventions of local dishes: *tournedos* of pig's trotters, ham or duck *confit* in a cep crust, duckling cooked twice. Menus €27–68. The building is new and the rooms have been completely refurbished. Doubles with bath €85–100, with a couple of air-conditioned suites for €275 if you want to go a bit mad. *Free coffee on presentation of this guide.*

Latouille-Lentillac

46400 (7 km E)

Restaurant Gaillard**

It's 7km out of town, in Latouille-Lentillac.
Ⓣ05.65.38.10.25 Ⓕ05.65.38.13.13
Ⓦwww.hotel-gaillard.fr
Closed *Nov.* **Disabled access. TV. Car park.**

Rooms here are all pleasantly decorated, simple, clean and air-conditioned; doubles with shower/wc or bath €38–49. The restaurant enjoys an excellent reputation and draws in a regular local crowd. Dishes include trout, *confits* and other regional delicacies. Set menus €14 (not Sun lunch) and €19–30. *Free coffee on presentation of this guide.*

Saint-Cirq-Lapopie

46330

Restaurant L'Atelier

Ⓣand Ⓕ05.65.31.22.34
Ⓔlatelier46@hotmail.com
Closed *Tues evening and Wed in low season; Jan.*

Right at the top of the hill you'll find this old building. There's a warm, cosy atmosphere so you'll quickly feel at home and the hearty cooking will delight gourmands and your average traveller alike. Menus (€12–26) list plenty of courses, with dishes like black Guercy duck, *cassoulet* and good foie gras served with a glass of white wine – excellent value for money.

Tour de Faure

46330 (3km E)

Hôtel Les Gabarres**

Take the D662 towards Figeac.
Ⓣ05.65.30.24.57 Ⓕ05.65.30.25.85
Closed *15 Oct–5 April.* **Disabled access. Swimming pool. Highchairs available. Car park.**

It isn't the most beautiful building but the excellent reception and the bright, clean, spacious bedrooms more than make up for that. Half the rooms overlook the swimming pool and in some parts of the establishment you get great views of the valley. Doubles €47–49. The couple in charge can tell you all about the various walks around. *10% discount on the room rate on presentation of this guide.*

Saint-Félix-Lauragais

31540

Auberge du Poids Public***

Faubourg Saint-Roch.
Ⓣ05.62.18.85.00 Ⓕ05.62.18.85.05
Closed *Sun evening; Jan; a week in Nov.* **TV. Car park.**

Delightful rooms – some with views of the Lauragais hills. Doubles €52–58 with shower/wc or bath and direct phone. They also have two luxurious rooms at €90–125. There are several little sitting rooms and a large, rustic dining room with fine exposed stonework and panoramic views. The atmosphere is classy. Set menus €24–60 which include foie gras cooked in a cloth, milk-fed lamb, Aquitaine sturgeon and summer fruit *croustillant*. You'll find comparatively unknown wines as well as great vintages on the wine list, priced from affordable to astronomical. The terrace is extremely pleasant in summer. One of the best restaurants in the region!

Saint-Julia

31540 (6km N)

L'Auberge des Remparts

Rue du Vinaigre.
Ⓣ05.61.83.04.79
Closed *Sun; Mon and Tues evenings. Open noon–1.30pm and 7–9pm.* **Highchairs available.**

A village inn with a growing reputation. The appetizing €10.50 weekday lunch includes soup, *crudités*, charcuterie, dish of the day, cheese, dessert, wine and coffee. In the evening (when reservations are advised), the young chef shows his colours with more elaborate, refined cooking on menus at €17 and €23. In good weather they serve meals on the shady terrace. *Free coffee on presentation of this guide.*

Saint-Ferréol

31250

Hôtellerie du Lac

Avenue Pierre-Paul-de-Riquet.
T 05.52.18.70.80 F 05.62.18.71.13
W www.hotellerie-du-lac.com
Restaurant closed *Sun evening from Sept to end May; 3 weeks around Christmas and New Year.* **Disabled access. TV. Swimming pool. Car park.**

The hotel has been beautifully renovated since Chabrol used it for shooting most of his film *L'Enfer*: it's plush but colourful. The rooms, €58, are comfortable and some have views of the lake. Breakfast €7. The swimming pool is heated and there's a sauna and a charming conservatory overlooking the garden. The cuisine reaches the same standard on menus at €15 (weekday lunchtimes) and €16: try foie gras or scallops. Friendly welcome.

Saint-Gaudens

31800

Restaurant de l'Abattoir

Boulevard Leconte-de-Lisle; it's opposite the abattoir.
T 05.61.89.70.29 F 05.61.95.23.45
Closed *Sun; evenings from Mon–Wed; public holidays; 12–18 Aug.*

One of the best restaurants in the region. Nowhere else will you get meat that's as fresh, tender and downright delicious as at Christian Gillet's place. He's at the abattoir every morning at dawn, choosing cuts of meat to feed the dealers who arrive from the country to sell their animals at market. The dining room is always packed. Try calf's head with *ravigote* sauce, tripe *à la provençale*, flank of beef, rib of beef with bone marrow or grilled Arbas black pudding. Weekday lunch menu €12.20, others €14.50 and €20 and around €20 à la carte. The large dining room is bright and pleasant and the atmosphere is matey. *Free house apéritif on presentation of this guide.*

Saint-Geniez-d'Olt

12130

Hôtel de la Poste**

3 pl. du Général-de-Gaulle.
T 05.65.47.43.30 F 05.65.47.42.75
W www.hoteldelaposte12.com
Closed *end Nov to mid-March.* **TV. Swimming pool. Highchairs and games available. Car park.**

A traditional village inn with an old section and a modern annexe. The former, furnished with superb antiques, is comfortable and cosy and the rooms are pleasant; €36–48 with shower/wc or bath. The restaurant, across the road in the annexe, is well known for its quality cooking. You can eat in the dining room, on the veranda surrounded by greenery or in the glassed-in terrace on the first floor. Set menus €14 and €16 (weekday lunchtimes) up to €48. The house classics include roasted zander and beef pie with ceps. *10% discount on the room rate for a stay of at least two consecutive nights outside July and Aug on presentation of this guide.*

Sainte-Eulalie-d'Olt

12130 (3km W)

Au Moulin d'Alexandre**

T 05.65.47.45.85 F 05.65.52.73.78
Closed *Sun evening in winter; a fortnight in May; a fortnight in Oct; 22 April–5 May.* **TV. Highchairs available. Car park.**

A delightful country inn in a renovated seventeenth-century water mill. Pretty rooms €42–48. Half board, €43 a head, is compulsory May–Sept. The cooking's good and prices are reasonable, with a €11 menu (not served Sun or public holidays) and others up to €25 as well as good à la carte choices. The restaurant specializes in regional dishes like home-made *tripoux*, chanterelle or cep omelette and stuffed breast of veal – all of which you can eat on the shady terrace. Boats are available for hire to guests. Credit cards not accepted. *Free digestif on presentation of this guide.*

Saint-Girons

09200

Domaine de Beauregard Hôtel-restaurant **

Avenue de la Résistance; it's on the outskirts of town in the direction of Seix-Massat.
T 05.61.66.66.66
W www.domainedebeauregard.com
Closed *Sun evening and Mon Dec–April.* **Disabled access. TV. Swimming pool. Highchairs and games available. Car park.**

A really wonderful place away from the

traffic, camouflaged by a row of trees and a leafy park. Rooms are bright and comfortable and have views of the grounds. Doubles €45–55; breakfast €6. In the pleasant restaurant menus cost €14 at weekday lunchtimes and €20–65 at dinner, listing such things as a delicious shellfish *tartare* with *aïoli* and a very good monkfish stew, along with braised shoulder of Pyrenean lamb with thyme *jus*. In winter the atmosphere changes – they light a fire in the huge fireplace and have menus full of regional dishes. *10% discount on the room rate except in July and Aug on presentation of this guide.*

Argein

09800 (17 km SW)

Hostellerie de la Terrasse**

Take the D618, 3 km after Audressein.
Ⓣ05.61.96.70.11
Closed *early Nov to Easter.* **Restaurant closed** for lunch. **TV. High chairs available.**

Charming little mountain hotel on the Portet-Aspet road. Simple but renovated rooms (ask for one with a view of the mountain) from €36–54 with shower/wc or bath. Excellent service and fine regional cooking; the trout with ceps is particularly recommended. Menu €15 on weekdays. Reckon on €22 à la carte. Credit cards not accepted.

Saint-Lary-Soulan

65170

Hôtel-restaurant La Pergola**

25 rue Vincent-Mir.
Ⓣ05.62.39.40.46 Ⓕ05.62.40.06.55
Ⓔjean-pierre.mir@wanadoo.fr
Closed *a fortnight in May; Nov to mid-Dec.*
Disabled access. TV. Car park.

A pleasant establishment dating from 1957 with a pretty garden and, of course, a pergola. The spacious rooms are comfortable, with wonderful beds, en-suite bathrooms, hairdryers and TV; the ones facing southwest have a view of Le Pla-d'Adet. Doubles €52–72. Breakfast €7.50. Lunch *formule* (not Sun or public holidays) €10.50 and €13; others €22–39. The food is original and very tasty, making good use of herbs and spices. Very good Gascon pork served with slightly acid vegetables. *Free house apéritif or coffee on presentation of this guide.*

Saint-Lizier

09190

Hôtel de la Tour

Route du Pont; it's at the foot of the old town on the banks of the Salat.
Ⓣ05.61.66.38.02 Ⓕ05.61.66.38.01
Ⓦhotel-restaurant.net/hoteldelatour
Closed *Sun evening except in the summer.*
TV.

This, the only historic hotel in the capital of the Couserans, has nine lovely rooms for €33–40; some look over of the river and others have little balconies. Breakfast €6. The chef is creative but also does simple grills. Weekday menu €11 and others €18.25–35.

Saint-Martin-d'Armagnac

32110

Auberge du Bergerayre

Take the D25.
Ⓣ05.62.09.08.72 Ⓕ05.62.09.09.74
Ⓔpierrette.sarrau@wanadoo.fr
Closed *Tues; Weds; lunchtimes in winter (and book in the evening); Jan; Feb.*
Disabled access. TV. Swimming pool. Car park.

A wonderful inn deep in the countryside, complete with garden and swimming pool – you'll revel in the peace and quiet. The extremely comfortable rooms are distributed between two buildings; they're €46–53.50 with shower/wc or €54–107 with bath. The top-price ones are in the old granary and have real character and luxurious facilities. Half board, obligatory in summer, costs €40–77 per person. The restaurant has a very good reputation, and you'll eat in a warm, friendly dining room with rustic décor. Menus €19 and €34. Dishes change through the seasons as and when fresh produce becomes available – *cassoulet*, *salade Gasconne*, chicken cooked in a *caul*, grilled duck breast, grilled duck liver, potatoes *au gratin*, foie gras cooked over vine cuttings. It's best to book. *Free apéritif on presentation of this guide.*

Salmiech

12120

Hôtel-Restaurant du Céor

☎05.65.74.25.88 Ⓕ05.65.46.70.13
Closed *Mon out of season; 12 Jan–9 Feb.* **Highchairs available.**

This nineteenth-century coaching inn offers terrific value. There are thirty pleasant rooms costing €20.80–30.20; breakfast €5.50. Half board €29.10–38.50 per person. Regional dishes dominate in the pretty, rustic dining room: crayfish, duck breast in vine shoots, *aligot* and piglet, just to mention a few. Menus €8 (not Sun) and up to €28. You can sit out on the terrace in good weather and admire the view of the village. Very welcoming owner. *Free house apéritif on presentation of this guide.*

Samatan

32130

Au Canard Gourmand

La Rente; it's on the road to Lombez.
☎05.62.62.49.81
Ⓦwww.canard-au-soulan.com
Closed *Mon evening; Tues; 10 days in Jan; a week in June; a fortnight in Oct.* **Disabled access. Car park.**

Ingenious interpretations of local cuisine. Lots of different foie gras dishes: one with dill, another pan-fried with vanilla sauce and an amazing one with liquorice. Dishes change with the seasons and fresh market produce. For dessert try the *sabayon* with seasonal fruits. Menus €16 (weekday lunchtimes) and €23–34. The dining room is modern and colourful. Very popular, so best to book one week ahead. *Free apéritif.*

Sauveterre-de-Rouergue

12800

La Grappe d'Or

Boulevard Lapérouse; a stone's throw from place des Arcades.
☎05.65.72.00.62.
Closed *15 Oct–early April.* **Restaurant closed** *Wed evening out of season.*

A small, well-run village hotel with double rooms with shower/wc for €29. Half board €42 per person. The restaurant offers simple, robust country cooking. *Menu du jour* at €11.50 and others up to €15.20 (served Sun and public holidays). The garden is very nice and the setting alone is worth stopping for. *10% discount on the room rate in April, May, Sept and Oct on presentation of this guide.*

Auberge du Sénéchal***

It's north, outside the fortifications.
☎05.65.71.29.00
Ⓦwww.senechal.net
Closed *Sun evening, Mon and Tues lunchtimes except in July and Aug; early Jan to mid-March.* **Disabled access. TV. Swimming pool. Car park.**

Local boy Michel Truchon loves this region. He also cares about quality produce, and sets about his cooking like an artist, creating wonderful dishes which are sophisticated and subtle. Set menus €25–100. Try the lentil terrine served with pig's ears or the braised veal and local potatoes drizzled with olive oil and served with aubergine caviar. For dessert go for an iced coffee *parfait* with endive seeds. You also get *amuse-bouches* and a lovely welcome. The rooms are quite magnificent, with terracotta floors and designer décor. Doubles €100–148. Half board €100–120. Service is faultless yet unpretentious and friendly. *Free apéritif on presentation of this guide.*

Sévérac-le-Château

12150

Hôtel-Restaurant des Causses

38 av. Aristide Briand, Séverac-Gare; take exit 42 off the A75 and it's opposite the train station.
☎05.65.70.23.00 Ⓕ05.65.70.23.04
Ⓔles.causses-aveyron@wanadoo.fr
Hotel and restaurant closed *Sun evening Sept–June; 3 weeks in Oct.* **Restaurant closed** *Mon lunchtime.*

A comfortable hotel with slightly faded yet clean rooms which, given the price, are no disappointment. Doubles €25–46, half board €29–40. Good quality cuisine; the meat dishes, including the *pascade* with lamb sweetbreads, are perfectly judged. Try the *flaune*, a local cheesecake, for dessert. Menus €12–26.

Tarascon-sur-Ariège

09400

Hôtel Confort**

3 quai Armand-Sylvestre.
Ⓣ05.61.05.61.90 Ⓕ05.61.05.55.99
Ⓦwww.hotelconfort.fr
Closed *7–20 Jan.* **TV. Pay car park.**

This welcoming place is right in the centre of town but, being on the banks of the Ariège, it's quiet. There are fourteen rooms – some have views of the river, others the patio, others the mountains. Doubles €30 with basin and up to €45 with bath. Half board €35–40 per person depending on the season. There's a €5 charge for use of the garage. Breakfast €5.

Tarbes

65000

Auberge de jeunesse

88 av. Alsace-Lorraine; 2km from the station towards Bordeaux; bus no. 1 at 150m from the station towards Bordeaux (terminus FJT).
Ⓣ05.62.38.91.20. Ⓕ05.62.37.69.81.
Ⓦwww.fuaj.org
Hostel open *all year round.* **Restaurant closed** *Sat eveing; Sun.* **Car park.**

One night in the dormitory will set you back €8.85, and a meal €7 (Mon–Sat lunchtime). You will find a lot of young local workers residing here. The view over the Pyrenees is breathtaking. Friendly staff. Garden, sports facilities with climbing wall. Credit cards not accepted.

Hôtel de l'Avenue**

78–80 av. Bertrand Barère; 50m from the train station.
Ⓣ and Ⓕ05.62.93.06.36
Disabled access. TV.

This is a quiet little hotel, despite being near the station. The rooms are a bit bland but they're good value for money – doubles with shower/wc €28 and €32 with bath – and as clean as can be. The ones looking into the courtyard are the quietest. Breakfast €4. There's a family atmosphere and the owner's father, who retired some time ago, still welcomes the guests occasionally, or serves them breakfast in the bar. *10% discount on the room rate for a stay of at least two consecutive nights on presentation of this guide.*

L'Isard**

70 av. du Maréchal-Joffre; it's 100m from the station.
Ⓣ05.62.93.06.69
Closed *Sun evening. TV.*

A tiny, likeable hotel on a main road, with eight pleasant rooms; doubles with shower/wc or bath €30. Some overlook the garden and are really quiet. The owner is delightful and very accommodating. In the restaurant there are menus and *formules* to suit all budgets – €11–31. Dishes include a duck platter, veal kidneys with mustard, sole fillet with morels, *escalope* of foie gras with lemon, scallops *provençales*, scrambled eggs with fresh liver, *cassoulet* with Tarbes beans and prune ice cream with Armagnac. In fine weather meals are served in the garden under the awning.

Chez Patrick

6 rue Adolphe d'Eichtal; on the corner of rue Saint-Jean.
Ⓣ05.62.36.36.82 Ⓕ05.62.38.19.62
Closed *evenings; Sun; a week in mid-Aug.*

A wonderful local restaurant just out of the centre, with a clientele of regulars who work round the corner or live nearby. It's run by a big family – they keep a cheery atmosphere in the dining room. The cooking is generously flavoured and prices are reasonable: the €9 weekday menu includes soup, starter, dish of the day (tripe or stew), wine and dessert. Dish of the day €5.35. Specialities include a rich stew and foie gras. It's best to arrive early as it quickly gets full. *Free coffee on presentation of this guide.*

Le Fil à la Patte

30 rue Georges-Lasalle.
Ⓣ and Ⓕ05.62.93.39.23
Closed *Sat lunchtime; Sun; Mon; 12–18 Jan; 11–31 Aug.*

A tiny and chic little restaurant looking for all the world like a Parisian bistro. New-style, inventive cuisine with lots of fish and local dishes given fresh interpretations; choices change according to the season and what's good at the market. Weekday lunch menu at €15, the other at €23 – which is also what you'll pay à la carte. Polite, slightly distant service.

Juillan

65290 (5km SW)

L'Aragon**

2 ter rte. de Lourdes; it's on the D921A.
Ⓣ05.62.32.07.07 Ⓕ05.62.32.92.50
Ⓦwww.hotel-aragon.com
Restaurant closed *Sun evening; 20 Dec–6 Jan.* **Bistro open** all year round. **Disabled access. TV. Car park.**

It really is well worth coming to this roadside establishment for its very fine cooking. There's a bistro with a €16 *formule*, and a rather plush dining room with a terrace where the service is impeccable and the cooking rightly enjoys its reputation. Menus at €31.45 and €60. The cuisine combines French classics, bistro dishes and Spanish influences: *gazpacho* with crayfish, scrambled eggs with caviar, duck and goose *confit* with kidney bean stew, a soufflé of pears and fruit brandy. You can stay in double rooms, each decorated on a different theme: €49 with shower/wc or €54 with bath. Breakfast €7.

Arcizac-Adour

65360 (11km S)

La Chaudrée

10 rte. des Pyrénées; it's on the D935 in the direction of Bagnères-de-Bigorre.
Ⓣ05.62.45.32.00
Ⓦwww.pyrenees.tournalet.com
Closed *Sun evening; Mon; 5 days in Feb; Aug.*

A classic little establishment that, despite its unassuming appearance, is one of the best places to eat locally. The dining room has a rustic feel with solid beams, a splendid walnut buffet table and lots of red (curtains, napkins)– very *Vieille France*. There's a €10.20 lunchtime menu (not served Sun), and others €16–26: veal sweetbreads, *cassoulet* of goose *confit*, duck foie gras with apple and bilberry sauce, *garbure* (broth with *confit*).

Thérondels

12600

Hôtel Miguel

It's in the centre of the village.
Ⓣ05.65.66.02.72 Ⓕ05.65.66.19.84
Ⓔhotel-miguel@wanadoo.fr
TV. Highchairs available. Swimming pool.

A pleasant place, in the northernmost village in the Aveyron, which has been run by the same family for three generations. Rooms are simple, clean and quiet. Doubles with bath €37–49. You'll need to call in advance out of season. The dining room has been carefully designed, with lots of green plants, a terrace overlooking the swimming pool, and Sinatra standards playing in the background. Tasty dishes are generously served: duck *confit* with spinach purée, pan-fried foie gras, frog's legs and sweetbreads in a cream sauce, guinea fowl and raspberry dessert from a Dax recipe. Weekday menu €9.80 and others up to €26. Good wine list. *10% discount on the room except July/Aug on presentation of this guide.*

Toulouse

31000

See map overleaf

Hôtel Beauséjour*

4 rue Caffarelli. **Map D1-3**
Ⓣand Ⓕ05.61.62.77.59

A nice, quiet little one-star just like they used to be. It's clean and cheap and you get a friendly, family welcome. Doubles with basin €20, €23 with shower, and €25 with shower/wc. Extra bed for €8. You pay extra for the shower if you don't have one in your room. A really good place.

Hôtel Anatole-France*

46 pl. Anatole-France. **Map B1-2**
Ⓣ05.61.23.19.96 Ⓕ05.61.21.47.66
TV.

Though the façade is nothing to get excited about, you'll get a wonderful welcome in this good-value hotel; reception is on the first floor. All rooms have double-glazing, direct-dial phones and are exceptionally clean; doubles €22 with basin to €33 with shower/wc.

Hôtel des Arts*

Rue des Arts, 1 bis rue Cantegril. **Map C2-4**
Ⓣ05.61.23.36.21 Ⓕ05.61.12.22.37

In a picturesque neighbourhood in the middle of town, this hotel has a maze of corridors leading to pleasant, spacious, renovated rooms. Some of them have fireplaces, some overlook the courtyard and all but three overlooking the street have been

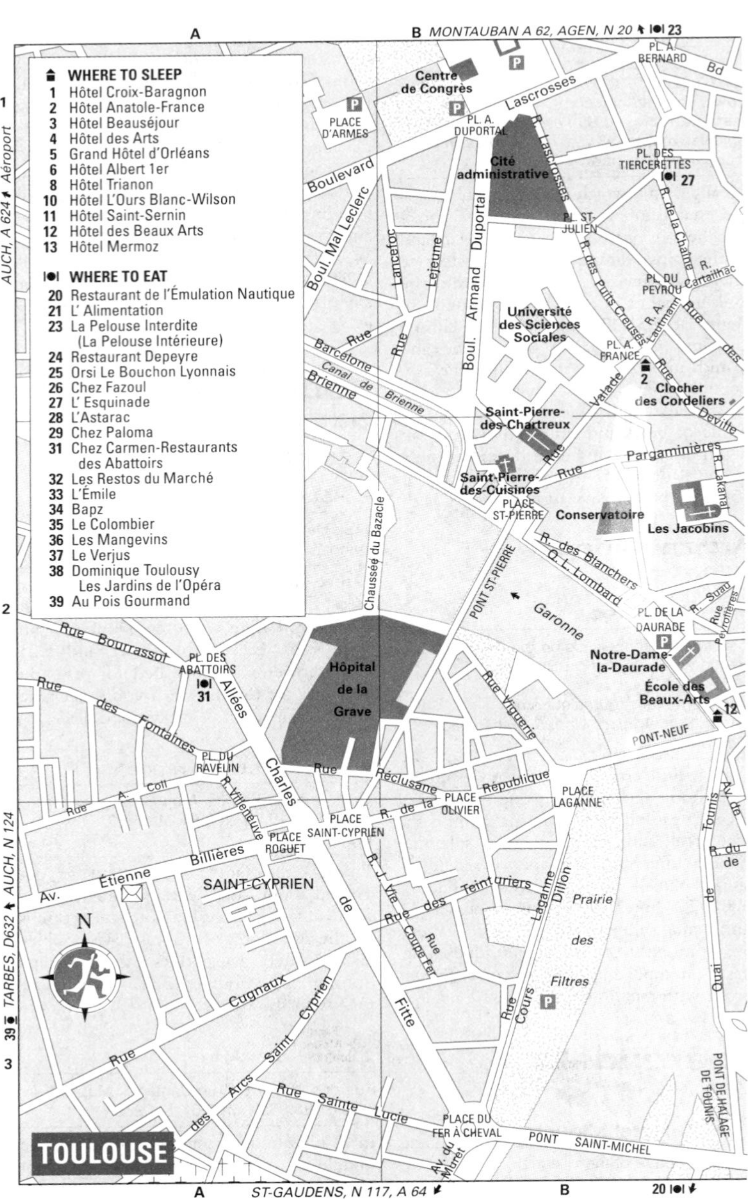

WHERE TO SLEEP
1 Hôtel Croix-Baragnon
2 Hôtel Anatole-France
3 Hôtel Beauséjour
4 Hôtel des Arts
5 Grand Hôtel d'Orléans
6 Hôtel Albert 1er
8 Hôtel Trianon
10 Hôtel L'Ours Blanc-Wilson
11 Hôtel Saint-Sernin
12 Hôtel des Beaux Arts
13 Hôtel Mermoz
WHERE TO EAT
20 Restaurant de l'Émulation Nautique
21 L' Alimentation
23 La Pelouse Interdite (La Pelouse Intérieure)
24 Restaurant Depeyre
25 Orsi Le Bouchon Lyonnais
26 Chez Fazoul
27 L' Esquinade
28 L'Astarac
29 Chez Paloma
31 Chez Carmen-Restaurants des Abattoirs
32 Les Restos du Marché
33 L'Émile
34 Bapz
35 Le Colombier
36 Les Mangevins
37 Le Verjus
38 Dominique Toulousy Les Jardins de l'Opéra
39 Au Pois Gourmand
TOULOUSE
MONTAUBAN A 62, AGEN, N 20
ST-GAUDENS, N 117, A 64
AUCH, A 624 Aéroport
TARBES, D632 AUCH, N 124
Centre de Congrès
Cité administrative
Université des Sciences Sociales
Clocher des Cordeliers
Saint-Pierre-des-Chartreux
Saint-Pierre-des-Cuisines
Conservatoire
Les Jacobins
Hôpital de la Grave
Notre-Dame-la-Daurade
École des Beaux-Arts
SAINT-CYPRIEN
Prairie des Filtres
Garonne
PONT ST-PIERRE
PONT-NEUF
PONT SAINT-MICHEL
PLACE D'ARMES
PL. A. DUPORTAL
PL. DES TIERCERETTES
PL. ST-JULIEN
PL. DU PEYROU
PL. A. FRANCE
PLACE ST-PIERRE
PL. DE LA DAURADE
PL. DES ABATTOIRS
PL. DU RAVELIN
PLACE OLIVIER
PLACE LAGANNE
PLACE SAINT-CYPRIEN
PLACE ROGUET
PLACE DU FER À CHEVAL
Boulevard Lascrosses
Boul. Mal Leclerc
Boul. Armand Duportal
Rue Barcelone
Canal de Brienne
Chaussée du Bazacle
Rue Bourrassol
Rue des Fontaines
Allées Charles de Fitte
Rue Réclusane
Rue de la République
Rue Viguerie
Av. Étienne Billières
Rue Cugnaux
Rue Saint Cyprien
Rue des Arcs
Rue Sainte Lucie
Rue des Teinturiers
Cours Dillon
Quai de Tounis
PONT DE HALAGE DE TOUNIS

14
MIDI-PYRÉNÉES

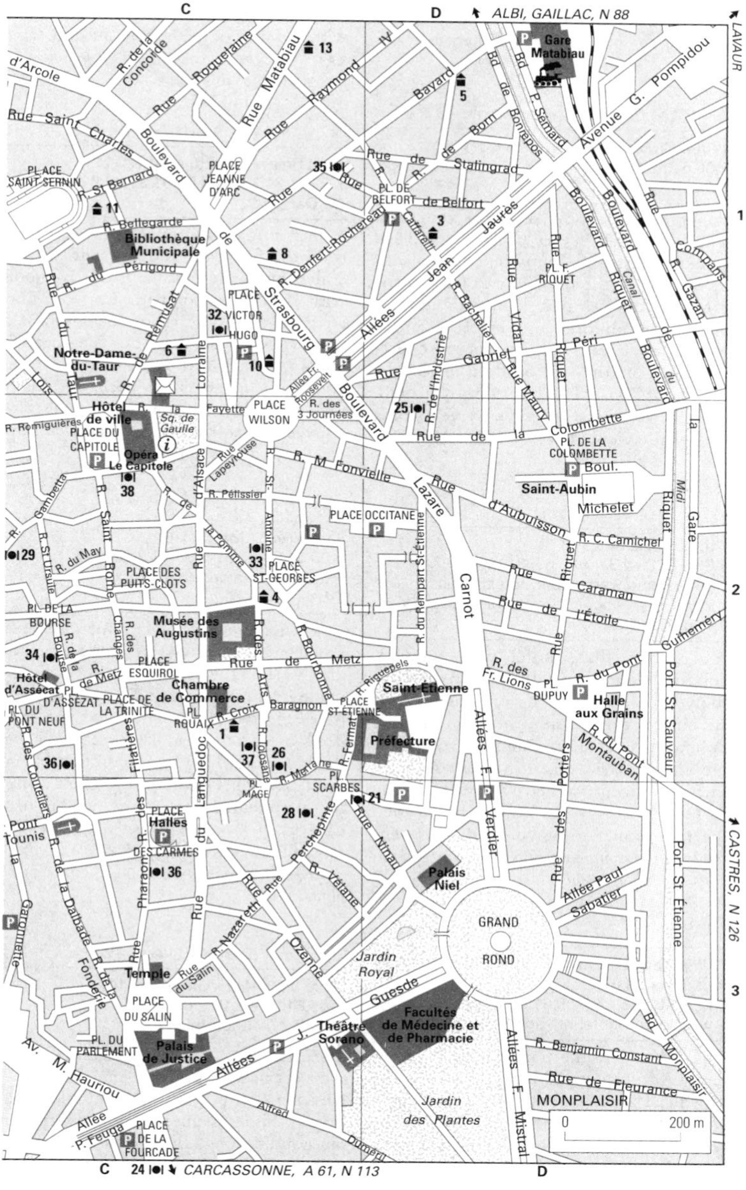

C D ALBI, GAILLAC, N 88

LAVAUR

Gare Matabiau

R. de la Concorde
d'Arcole
Rue Roquelaine
Rue Matabiau
13
Rue Raymond IV
Bayard
5
Bd de Bonrepos
Bd P. Sémard
Avenue G. Pompidou
Rue Saint-Charles
Boulevard
Rue de Stalingrad
PLACE SAINT-SERNIN
R. St-Bernard
PLACE JEANNE D'ARC
35
Rue
PL. DE BELFORT
de Belfort
R. Caffarelli
11
R. Bellegarde
Rue Denfert-Rochereau
3
Allées Jean Jaurès
Boulevard Riquet
Canal de
Boulevard
Rue Compans
R. Gazan
Bibliothèque Municipale
8
Rue du Périgord
Rue R. de Rémusat
PLACE VICTOR HUGO
32
Strasbourg
R. Bachelier
Rue Riquet
PL. F. RIQUET
Rue Vidal
Rue Péri
Notre-Dame-du-Taur
6
10
Lorraine
Rue Gabriel
R. de l'Industrie
Rue Maury
Lois
Rue du Taur
Hôtel de ville
R. la Fayette
PLACE WILSON
Allée Fr. Roosevelt
R. des 3 Journées
Boulevard
25
Rue de la Colombette
R. Romiguières
PLACE DU CAPITOLE
Sq. de Gaulle
PL. DE LA COLOMBETTE
Opéra Le Capitole
38
Rue Lapeyrouse
R. M. Fonvielle
Lazare
Boul.
Saint-Aubin
Michelet
R. Gambetta
Rue Saint-Rome
R. d'Alsace
R. de la Pomme
R. Pélissier
R. St-Antoine
PLACE OCCITANE
R. du Rempart St-Étienne
Rue d'Aubuisson
R. C. Camichel
Riquet
Midi
Gare
la
29
R. Ste-Ursule
R. du May
PLACE DES PUITS-CLOTS
33
PLACE ST-GEORGES
Carnot
Rue Caraman
Rue de l'Étoile
4
PL. DE LA BOURSE
R. de la Bourse
R. des Changes
Musée des Augustins
R. des Arts
R. Bourbonne
Rue de Metz
Rue
Guilhemery
34
PLACE ESQUIROL
R. de Metz
R. Riguepels
R. des Fr. Lions
PL. DUPUY
R. du Pont
Hôtel d'Assézat
PL. D'ASSÉZAT
PLACE DE LA TRINITÉ
Chambre de Commerce
R. Croix Baragnon
PLACE ST-ÉTIENNE
Saint-Étienne
Halle aux Grains
Port St Sauveur
PL. DU PONT NEUF
PL. ROUAIX
1
R. Fermat
Préfecture
R. du Pont Montauban
R. des Couteliers
36
Filatiers
37
26
R. Tolosane
R. Merlane
Allées F. Verdier
Rue des Potiers
R. des Pharaon
Languedoc
PL. MAGE
PL. SCARBES
21
Pont Tounis
PLACE DES CARMES
Halles
28
Rue Ninau
R. Perchepinte
R. de la Dalbade
36
R. Vélane
Palais Niel
Rue des
Rue du
Rue Nazareth
Allée Paul Sabatier
Port St Étienne
la Garonnette
Rue
Ozenne
GRAND ROND
CASTRES, N 126
Fonderie
R. de la
Jardin Royal
Temple
Rue du Salin
Guesde
3
PLACE DU SALIN
Théâtre Sorano
Facultés de Médecine et de Pharmacie
Bd Monplaisir
PL. DU PARLEMENT
Palais de Justice
Allées J.
R. Benjamin Constant
Av. M. Hauriou
Allées F. Mistral
Rue de Fleurance
Jardin des Plantes
MONPLAISIR
Allée P. Feuga
PLACE DE LA FOURCADE
Alfred
Dumeril
0 200 m

C 24 CARCASSONNE, A 61, N 113 D

1
2
3

14

MIDI-PYRÉNÉES

double-glazed. Doubles €28.50–32 with one or two beds. You order your breakfast the night before; it's served in your room – there's no breakfast room – or you can have it in one of the numerous cafés nearby.

Hôtel Croix-Baragnon*

17 rue Croix-Baragnon. **Map C3-1**
Ⓣ05.61.52.60.10 Ⓕ05.61.52.08.60
TV.

Right in the centre, near the cathedral. The hotel itself is very charming and has an external staircase entwined with plants. You go up to the first floor to find reception where a warm welcome awaits. The rooms are comfortable rather than amazing – some have windows over the courtyard – but the atmosphere is lovely. Doubles €33 with one or two beds, shower/wc and a street view; €35 for a courtyard view. There are two family rooms at €40. Best to book.

Hôtel Trianon**

7 rue Lafaille. **Map C1-8**
Ⓣ05.61.62.74.74 Ⓕ05.61.99.15.44
Ⓦwww.perso.wanadoo.fr/hoteltrianon
Closed *1–15 Aug; last fortnight in Dec.* **TV. Pay car park.**

A delightful little hotel with pleasant, comfortable rooms; doubles €46–57 with shower/wc or bath. The ones at the rear are quieter, though some at the front have double glazing. In summer you have breakfast on the patio; in winter you eat in the magnificent vaulted wine cellars. The owner's so keen on wine that he's named the rooms after great vineyards. *10% discount on the room rate for two consecutive nights on presentation of this guide.*

Grand Hôtel d'Orléans**

72 rue Bayard; 5 min from the train station on foot. **Map D1-5**
Ⓣ05.61.62.98.47 Ⓕ05.61.62.78.24
Ⓦwww.grand-hotel-orleans.fr

This hotel near the train station is excellent. Admittedly, there is something provincial about it, but that is offset by a Mediterranean touch, as evident in the covered patio and balconies brimming with plants. There is a family atmosphere, and guests are warmly welcomed; it is spotlessly clean and very well run. Fairly spacious rooms, overlooking either the street or the patio; the latter are smaller, but they are quieter and also air-conditioned, which alleviates the heat in summer. Good value for money: doubles with shower or bath €46.50 and triples €60. *One free breakfast per room offered on presentation of this guide.*

Hôtel Saint-Sernin**

2 rue Saint-Bernard. **Map C1-11**
Ⓣ05.61.21.73.08 Ⓕ05.61.22.49.61
TV. Car park.

A charming, comfortable hotel. Reception is on the first floor and the staff will welcome you with a smile. Attractive rooms with shower/wc or bath €50–68. There are four rose-coloured rooms with a stunning view of the basilica. The local flea market is held in the square at the weekend. It's a lovely little place, despite the regular chiming of the church bells! *10% discount on the room rate for two consecutive nights on presentation of this guide.*

Hôtel Albert-1er**

8 rue Rivals. **Map C1-6**
Ⓣ05.61.21.17.91 Ⓕ05.61.21.09.64
Ⓦwww.hotel-albert-1er.com
TV.

In a quiet street in the commercial centre. Excellent, professional welcome but with a family feel: the owner produces homemade jams for breakfast. The pleasant foyer is decorated with mosaics and pink Toulouse bricks. You'll pay €53–75 for a double room. They're all comfortable and most have air conditioning. They can get you preferential rates in the neighbouring car park. *10% discount on the room rate for a stay of two consecutive nights at weekends and during school holidays on presentation of this guide.*

Hôtel L'Ours Blanc-Wilson**

2 rue Victor-Hugo. **Map C1-10**
Ⓣ05.61.21.62.40 Ⓕ05.61.23.62.34
Ⓦwww.hotel-ours-blanc.fr
TV.

This district is full of mid-range hotels and this one, in a beautiful 1930s building, has good facilities including TV, telephone and air conditioning. Bedrooms all have en-suite bathrooms but the décor is rather disappointing, and they're not all that big: doubles €58–64. Some of them have good views of place Wilson. They've modernized the foyer but have kept the very old wooden lift cage.

Hôtel des Beaux-Arts****

1 pl. du Pont-Neuf. **Map C3-12**
Ⓣ05.34.45.42.42 Ⓕ05.34.45.42.43
Ⓦwww.hotelsdecharmetoulouse.com
TV.

This classy hotel is a favourite with visiting politicians and actors staying in Toulouse. It's in the heart of the historic centre on the edge of the Garonne. The façade is eighteenth-century but the décor inside is up to modern standards. Doubles €77–153; there's one on the top floor with a terrace and a wonderful view of the Garonne. Buffet breakfast €15.

Hôtel Mermoz***

50 rue Matabiau. **Map C1-13**
Ⓣ05.61.63.04.04 Ⓕ05.61.63.15.34
Ⓦwww.hotel-mermoz.com
Disabled access. TV. Pay car park.

This hotel is protected from the noisy street by an interior courtyard; it's a modern, vaguely Neoclassical building with an elegant flight of stairs. The décor makes lots of references to the air-mail service which operated from the city, with Art Deco furniture and drawings of aeroplanes on the walls. Fifty very well-equipped bedrooms; doubles €85–99. Buffet breakfast €9.90. Friendly welcome. *10% discount on the room rate on presentation of this guide.*

Chez Paloma

54 rue Peyrollières. **Map C2-29**
Ⓣ05.61.21.76.50
Closed *Sat; Sun; 3 weeks in July.* **Disabled access.**

A nice local restaurant that's made its reputation by word of mouth. Excellent value for money if you want a really satisfying lunch; there's a *formule* for €7.65. Dinner menus €11 and €14. This is good cooking, using fresh produce and served without frills or fanfares. The wood and brick-walled dining room is decorated with items rescued from junk yards and flea markets and has a pleasant atmosphere. The mezzanine is calmer.

L'Astarac

21 rue Perchepinte. **Map C3-28**
Ⓣ05.61.53.11.15
Closed *Sat lunchtime; Sun; mid-July to mid-Aug.* **Disabled access.**

Service lunchtimes and evenings until 10pm. This excellent restaurant is tucked away in a narrow street in the old town; the tall room has sturdy beams and brick walls hung with attractive paintings. There are discreet booths with comfy benches where you can have an intimate dinner for two. Tremendous Gascon cooking, with dishes such as salad of duck legs with foie gras and *paupiettes* of chicken with a cep cream sauce. Weekday lunch menu €10.70; others €18–26. They also offer two types of foie gras, *tournedos* of duck with a cep sauce and *poêlée Gasconne*. Sensibly priced wines like Fronton and Côtes-de-Saint-Mont. *Free Pruneau à l'Armagnac on presentation of this guide.*

Chez Fazoul

2 rue Tolosane. **Map C2-26**
Ⓣ05.61.53.72.09
Closed *Sun. Open noon–2.00pm and 7.45–10.30pm.* **Disabled access.**

This restaurant has been serving good food for some time in this former seventeenth-century town-house. The €11.50 lunch menu includes wine, service and a self-service buffet of hors d'œuvres – extremely good value for money. Other menus at €18–28 list good regional dishes, particularly *cassoulet* and foie gras cooked old-style. The dining room is elegant with its red brick walls, beautiful old beams and candlelight. *Free house apéritif on presentation of this guide.*

Les Restos du Marché

Place Victor-Hugo. **Map C2-32**
Closed evenings; Mon.

A real Toulouse special. On market days at lunchtime, go up to the first floor of this concrete shed. There you'll find an amazingly lively and colourful scene, with half a dozen small restaurants providing plates of wholesome food cooked using the freshest market produce for the cheapest prices – menus around €12–16 including wine. The names give you a clue to the style of cuisine on offer: *Le Méditerranée*, *Le Magret*, *Chez Attila* (which specializes in fish and *zarzuela*, a sort of Spanish *bouillabaisse*). *Le Louchébem* offers good meats and a broad bean *cassoulet* on the first weekend in the month, while at *Samaran* you can buy your foie gras fresh or cooked. There are a few tables on the long baclony. It's always full. Come early, come late, or be very patient!

🏃 |●| Restaurant de l'Émulation Nautique

Allée Alfred-Mayssonière. **Off map B4-20**
☎05.61.25.34.95
Closed *Sun evening and Mon from May to mid-Sept; every evening mid-Sept–end April; Christmas to mid-Jan.*

This sailing club, one of the oldest in France, has a cosy restaurant. It has a beautiful terrace, shaded by plane trees and looking out over the water, and an elegant dining room. Weekday lunch menu €12, €16 at weekends; à la carte around €30. The grills are enormous, the fish dishes nice and fresh, and they do tasty salads. A wonderful place in summer. *Free house apéritif on presentation of this guide.*

|●| BAPZ (Bakery and tearoom)

13 rue de la Bourse. **Map C3-34**
☎05.61.23.06.63
Closed *Sun; Mon; 10 days in early Aug.*

The décor of this good lunch spot, with its rugs, willow chairs, pictures and old engravings on the walls, creates a relaxing atmosphere. Come here for savoury tarts, quiches and curried pork, or pastries, scones, bread rolls and other sweet delicacies for tea. The excellent cakes and pastries are displayed on a long wooden table. Lunch *formule* – main course, dessert and tea or coffee – €14, or around €6.80 for a dish. There's a sister establishment in place Salengros that's also closed on Sunday and Monday.

|●| 🏃 L'Alimentation

6 bis pl. Saintes-Scrabes. **Map D3-21**
☎05.34.31.61.09
Closed *Sun; Mon evening.*

Only a few years ago all you would have found here would have been packets of pasta and rice . . . to cook yourself. But the local food shop has been turned into a warm restaurant garlanded with multicoloured lights. There's a quiet terrace to enjoy a drink in summer. They serve daring salads at lunchtime – the *Torréfiée* includes Cantal cheese and chocolate chips – which are a hit; lunch *formule* at €10.50; à la carte around €25. At night the flickering candles create an intimate atmosphere and the cooking changes tone, too; regional dishes on the menu. It's run by a friendly, young team. *Free house apéritif on presentation of this guide.*

|●| L'Esquinade

28 rue de la Chaîne. **Map B1-27**
☎05.61.12.12.72
Closed *Sat; Sun; Mon; a fortnight in Aug; a fortnight in Dec.*

Vincent runs a friendly, pocket-handkerchief sized restaurant. Meat and fish are cooked on the open grill and, depending on what day it is, dishes may also include seafood paella, garlicky cod *brandade* with olive oil and so on. Tapas around €5 each, *ración* (dish of the day) €4.50–13 or around €15 for a complete meal. It's best to book.

|●| Les Mangevins

46 rue Pharaon. **Map C3-36**
☎05.61.52.79.16
Closed *Sun; Aug.*

Service until 11pm. Gérard opened this place mainly to sell and enjoy wines. He's a real connoisseur, and chooses excellent dishes, and very good bread, to best show off the taste of the wine. The vast salads, *andouillette*, duck breast, foie gras with sea salt and roast beef are all good. There's a nice cheese selection, too, and fish sold by weight. Count on spending around €15 at lunchtime, or a bit less than twice that in the evening. Reservations recommended.

🏃 |●| Le Colombier

14 rue de Bayard. **Map C1-35**
☎05.61.62.40.05 Ⓕ05.61.99.10.11
Closed *Sat lunchtime; Sun; Aug; a week at Christmas.*

You'll come here for the *cassoulet*, which contains a goose *confit* that's been renowned for several generations – the recipe is top-secret. As well as *cassoulet* (€19.50), they offer a lunchtime *formule* during the week for €16 or menus €19.50–34. You'll also find salad with *lardons* and *confit*, medallion of duck foie gras *au torchon*, duck foie gras in goose fat and *croustade* of apples in Armagnac. *Free cocktail on presentation of this guide.*

🏃 |●| Chez Carmen - Restaurant des Abattoirs

97 allée Charles-de-Fitte. **Map A3-31**
☎05.61.42.04.95 Ⓕ05.61.59.06.59

Closed *Sun; Mon; public holidays; Aug. Open noon–2.00pm and 8–11.00pm.* **Disabled access.**

The local abattoirs have gone – they've been turned into a contemporary art centre – but the meat here is as good as ever. The bistro (it's been going forty years) buzzes with life. Efficient if brusque service under the watchful eye of the owner. Great plates of grilled meat or local dishes à la carte – beef is king here. Try onglet with shallots, steak *tartare*, hearty beef stew, or typical dishes like calf's head and pig's trotters. One menu at €17 or about €25 à la carte. There are a few tables outside in summer. *Free apéritif on presentation of this guide.*

L'Émile

13 pl. Saint-Georges. **Map C2-33**
Ⓣ05.61.21.05.56
Closed *Sun and Mon except in summer; Christmas school holidays.* **Highchairs available.**

Last orders 10pm. The out-of-date décor is knowingly ordinary (terrible pictures), but the cooking is generously flavoured, fine and tasty with lots of fish dishes. The cheapest lunch menu always lists pike-perch fillet, *zarzuela* which is a fish stew, and *rosace* of prawns. Lunch menus €17 and €28 with others for €35 and €45 in the evening. Precise attention is paid to preparation and cooking times.

Orsi Le Bouchon Lyonnais

13 rue de l'Industrie. **Map D2-25**
Ⓣ05.61.62.97.43 Ⓕ05.61.63.00.71
Closed *Sat lunchtime; Sun.*

Service until 11pm. This establishment, with its classy Belle Époque dining room, is run by the younger brother of *the* Orsi, the famous gourmet chef from Lyons. He produces specialities from his adopted region: the four menus list dishes like *tablier de sapeur* (a slab of breaded ox tripe), grilled pig's trotters and sliced *andouillette*. The most expensive menu is dedicated to southwestern cooking and features one of the best *cassoulets* in town. Menus €18.40–30. Great wine list, too. They host occasional theme evenings. *Free apéritif.*

Au Pois Gourmand

3 rue Émile-Heybrard (off avenue Casselardit). **Off map A3-39**
Ⓣ05.34.36.42.60 Ⓕ05.34.36.42.08
Ⓦwww.pois-gourmand.fr
Closed *Sat lunchtime; Sun; Mon lunchtime; a week in Feb; a week at Easter; a fortnight in Aug.* **Disabled access. TV.**

It's not easy to find this place but it's worth the effort. It's a lovely colonial-style house, built in 1870, which stands on the banks of the Garonne. There's a weekday lunch menu at €20 and three others €36–60. The cooking certainly deserves its excellent reputation: just try the foie gras *en papillote de chou* or the deboned pigeon, stuffed and roasted. The dining room is magnificent, and there are green plants all round the terrace. *Free Kir on presentation of this guide.*

Restaurant Depeyre

77 rte. de Revel. **Off map C4-24**
Ⓣ05.61.20.26.56 Ⓕ05.61.34.83.96
Closed *Sun; Mon; 1–22 Aug.* **Disabled access. Highchairs available.**

It's 3km out of town on the edge of a road but both the *Vieille France* décor and the cuisine here are really attractive. Jacques Depeyre is a Maître-Cuisinier de France. Menus reflect the changing seasons: langoustine vol au vent with parsley, pigeon with grapefruit and ginger *confit*, caramelized bread and butter pudding with vanilla ice cream and honey. Menus €21–61 – not bad when you consider the quality of the food. *Free apéritif on presentation of this guide.*

La Pelouse Interdite (La Pelouse Intérieure)

72 av. des États-Unis. **Off map B1-23**
Ⓣ05.61.47.30.40
Closed *lunchtimes; Sun; Mon; 3 weeks in Oct.*

An unusual place – the extraordinary garden is illuminated by numerous candles, furnished with junk-shop tables, chairs and large armchairs, table football and even hammocks and beds. Inside (*La Pelouse Intérieure*) there's a brilliantly coloured bar with a DJ who plays soothing music at the weekend. Delicious, inventive cuisine. There's a *menu-carte* for €17 and a menu for €20 (prices are slightly lower inside). It's essential to book. When you get there, ring the bell and wait. *Free digestif on presentation of this guide.*

Urdens

32500

L'Auberge Paysanne

Place de l'Église.
05.62.06.27.25
Closed *Mon; Tues and Wed evenings; fortnight in March and Oct.* **Disabled access. Car park.**

Authentic rustic inn in converted stables. The terrace is particularly lovely in the summer, and really peaceful. The inn is famous for good local dishes such as *daube*, stuffed chicken, duck thigh with peaches, Gascon salad, duck with wild mushrooms and a lovely Armagnac *croustade* for dessert. The €10 weekday lunch menu includes wine, and there are others €15–27.50. *Free coffee on presentation of this guide.*

Ustou

09140

Auberge Les Ormeaux

Trein; take the D8, 13km north-east of Aulus-les-Bains.
05.61.96.53.22 05.61.66.84.19
www.ariege.com/aubergedesormeaux
Closed *Wed (except school holidays); autumn school holidays.*

An enchanting little hotel in the heart of the Ustou valley with pretty rooms and a lounge-cum-library. The owner creates a lovely atmosphere and welcomes you with genuine friendliness. Double rooms €46, including breakfast. Half board €34.50 per person. Menus €13–15.50. No smoking in the restaurant.

Valence-sur-Baïse

32310

La Ferme de Flaran**

Route de Condom; it's on the outskirts of the village on the D930.
05.62.28.58.22 05.62.28.56.89
www.fermedeflaran.com
Closed *Mon except July–Aug; Sun evening; 1–10 Dec; Jan.* **TV. Swimming pool. Car park.**

This old farm has been successfully converted into a hotel. The small rooms are very comfortable and go for €47–57.50 (depending on the season) for a double with shower/wc or bath. Breakfast €6.10. Fresh produce from the markets and local producers are used for good regional specialities. Menus €17–32, and an affordable wine list. *Free house apéritif on presentation of this guide.*

Vicdessos

09220

Hôtel Hivert

2 rte. de Montréal-de-Sos; just at the exit from Vicdessos, after the crossroad towards Suc-et-Santenac and Auzat.
05.61.64.88.17
www.hotelhivert.com
Closed *Oct.* **Car park.**

A peaceful refuge nestling between two valleys. You can bask in the sunshine and revel in a view of the mountain without even getting out of bed! Doubles €31–35. At night, you can dine on the terrace by the sprawling vines, with the murmur of the river below in the background. Menus with abundant portions €12 (except Sun), and €13 –20. *Free house apéritif on presentation of this guide, when you eat from a menu.*

Villecomtal-sur-Arros

32730

Le Rive Droite

1 chemin Saint-Jacques.
05.62.64.83.08
Closed *Mon–Wed (except mid-July to mid-Aug); Nov half-term.*

This restaurant is superbly located, in an old nineteenth-century bourgeois house nestling in the back of a park. George Sand was seduced by its charm in her day. The décor is sophisticated, while the atmosphere is intimate and relaxed. The dining room is cosy and comfortable; as for the food, it is inventive without being revolutionary. The mouth-watering specialities include *paupiette de porc cul-noir*, *piquillo* stuffed with *brandade*, duck Parmentier with ceps and French toast with apples. Menus at €32 and €39 (a "*Gourmand*" menu). All the essential ingredients for having a great time are on hand here.

Villefranche-de-Lauragais

31290

Hôtel de France**

106 rue de la République.
☎05.61.81.62.17 ℻05.61.81.61.31
Closed *Sun evening and Mon*. **TV. Car park.**

Villefranche-de-Lauragais is one of the best places to eat *cassoulet*, the famous local dish made with dried beans and goose and duck *confit*. Unsurprisingly, it's the house speciality, along with egg flan. Menus €10 (not Sat evening, Sun or public holidays), then €20 (weekends and public holidays) up to €22. The décor of the rooms is outdated, but a complete refurbishment is on the cards. Rooms cost €28. The restaurant has got a good local reputation.

Villefranche-de-Rouergue

12200

Le Relais de Farrou***

It's 3km from the village; head for Saint-Rémy on the Figeac road.
☎05.65.45.18.11 ℻05.65.45.32.59
www.villefranche.com/relaisdefarrou
Restaurant closed *Sat lunch, Sun evening and Mon out of season; autumn, winter and Christmas school holidays.* **Disabled access. TV. Swimming pool. Car park.**

A small tourist complex with a park, pool, Turkish bath and hot tub, along with activities including tennis and mini-golf. The rooms, all comfortable and air-conditioned, cost €48.50–79. Half board €58–68 per person. The décor in the restaurant is a bit showy but the cooking has a good reputation. There's a range of menus: €15 at lunch (except Sun) and others €20–39. Try a glass of plum brandy if you don't fancy dessert. *Free house apéritif on presentation of this guide.*

Restaurant de la Halle - Chez Pinto

Place de la Halle; it's near the cathedral.
☎05.65.45.07.74

This workman's restaurant is one of the few remaining examples of that dying breed. You'll get a cordial welcome and be served substantial helpings of home cooking. There's a set menu for €9.50.

L'Épicurien

8 bis av. Raymond Saint-Gilles; it's between the station and place de la République.
☎05.65.45.01.12
Closed *Mon and Tues out of season.*

This new restaurant, run by a chef from Montpellier, is a turn-up for the books. He uses only fresh produce. Fish, of course, but also beef, and he creates subtle combinations: turbot fillet with fresh vegetables or grills with sauce made from Cahors wine. Menus €13–31.80. There's a good choice of wines, too. The décor has lots of warm wood, and the ancient beams are uncovered.

L'Assiette Gourmande

Place A.-Lescure; it's beside the cathedral.
☎05.65.45.25.95
Closed *Tues–Thurs evenings out of season; Sun; Easter; 1–8 Sept; All Saints' Day.*
Highchairs available. Car park.

The décor is fairly clichéd, all wooden beams and copper pots, but the cooking is good. Set menus €13–29. They grill on an open fireplace fuelled with oak from the Causse chalk plateau, which gives the dishes a distinctive flavour – pan-fried foie gras with apples, *aligot* and *tripou*. The terrace is nice in summer.

Monteils

12200 (22km SW)

Restaurant Le Clos Gourmand

☎05.65.29.63.15 ℻05.65.29.64.98

This substantial master craftsman's house is lovely to look at and you'll get a friendly welcome from Anne-Marie Lavergne, who's well known for the excellent regional specialities she serves her guests. Menus €12–30, listing regional dishes such as the salad of pan-fried foie gras, the zander fillet with sorrel and the beef with Roquefort. She also has a few rooms for €45 with bath/wc; they're large, with fireplaces and pretty views. Half board €44 per person. *Free house apéritif on presentation of this guide.*

Villeneuve-sur-Tarn

81250

Hostellerie des Lauriers**

It's on the D77, 32km east of Albi.

Ⓣ05.63.55.84.23 Ⓕ05.63.55.89.20
Ⓦwww.leslauriers.net
Closed *Sun evening and Mon out of season; 31 Oct–15 March.* **Disabled access. Swimming pool. Car park.**

An absolutely delightful village hotel right next to the church, with a lawn running all the way down to the riverbank. It's brilliantly run by a lovely young couple. Nine good rooms; €44–54 with shower/wc, depending on the season. Breakfast €7. There's a lovely dining room and a bar which is popular with the villagers. Weekday lunch menu €12.50 then others €22–38. The boss really knows his way around the region and is a mine of information. There's a lovely terrace overlooking the grounds, and a heated indoor swimming pool with Jacuzzi (hotel guests only). They offer games for the kids. *Free digestif on presentation of this guide.*

Nord-Pas-de-Calais

Arras

62000

Auberge de jeunesse (FUAJ)

59 Grand'Place; at the very north end of the Grand Place.
Ⓣ03.21.22.70.02 Ⓕ03.21.07.46.15
Ⓦwww.fuaj.org
New arrivals *7.30am–noon and 5–11pm.*
Closed *1 Dec– 1 Feb.*

€8.40 per night; breakfast €3.25; about €2.75 to rent sheets. Holders of FUAJ youth hostel cards (strictly compulsory but you can buy one here) have the good fortune of being able to spend the night in the superb Grand'Place d'Arras. There are only single rooms in the place; all the others have three to eight beds per room (54 in total). Showers and toilets on each floor, and individual wardrobes. Meals for groups only, but there is a kitchen available for guests. Covered bike park.

Café-hôtel du Beffroi*

28 pl. de la Vacquerie; it's behind the bell-tower.
Ⓣ03.21.23.13.78 Ⓕ03.21.23.03.08
Closed *Sun.* **TV.**

You'll find this establishment at the end of a cluster of typical Flemish houses. It's a classic bistro at street-level, jammed with locals, where you can get good food on the €15 menu or on the "dish of the day" and "*petit menu*". The rooms, reached by a steep staircase, are charming and well maintained; with basin, shower/wc or bath in the rooms or on the landing. They cost €33–50. No. 10 overlooks the square, so you have a perfect view of the Golden Lion of Artois on the 75m bell-tower. On the ground floor, a bar opened under a new management of a youthful and dynamic team.

Hôtel-Restaurant aux Grandes Arcades**

8–12 Grand'Place. Situated at the heart of the city centre.
Ⓣ03.21.23.30.89 Ⓕ03.21.71.50.94
Ⓔauxgrandesarcades@wanadoo.fr
High chairs available. Disabled access. TV.

Following a total overhaul, rooms here are comfortable, modern, clean and well soundproofed – and you couldn't possibly be more central. Doubles €52–56 with shower/wc or bath. The main dining room is one of the most beautiful in town, in the style of a 1900s brasserie with a lofty ceiling and gleaming dark wood panelling – there's a second room decorated more traditionally. Menus – served at lunchtime and in the evening (except Sun) – range from €14; other menus from €25 up to €32, including a regional menu. Traditional service, a little starchy but sincere.

Hôtel des Trois Luppars**

49 Grand'Place; take the Lille-Paris bypass.
Ⓣ00.32.16.02.03 Ⓕ03.21.24.24.80
TV. High chairs available.

On the edge of the huge paved esplanade of the Grand'Place – surely one of the most beautiful in Northern France; this building in a pure Flemish Baroque style, listed as a Historic Monument, now houses a delightful hotel. The contemporary decoration in the bedrooms may clash slightly with the surroundings, but they are very restful and

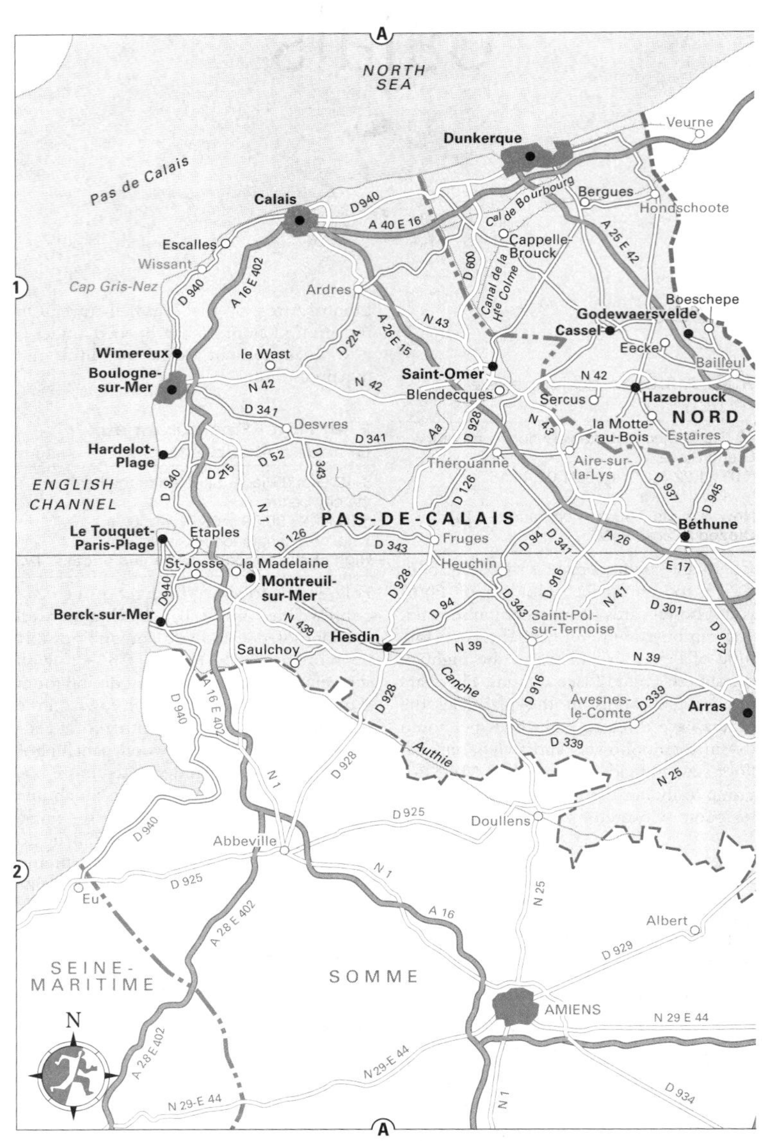

15

NORD-PAS-DE-CALAIS

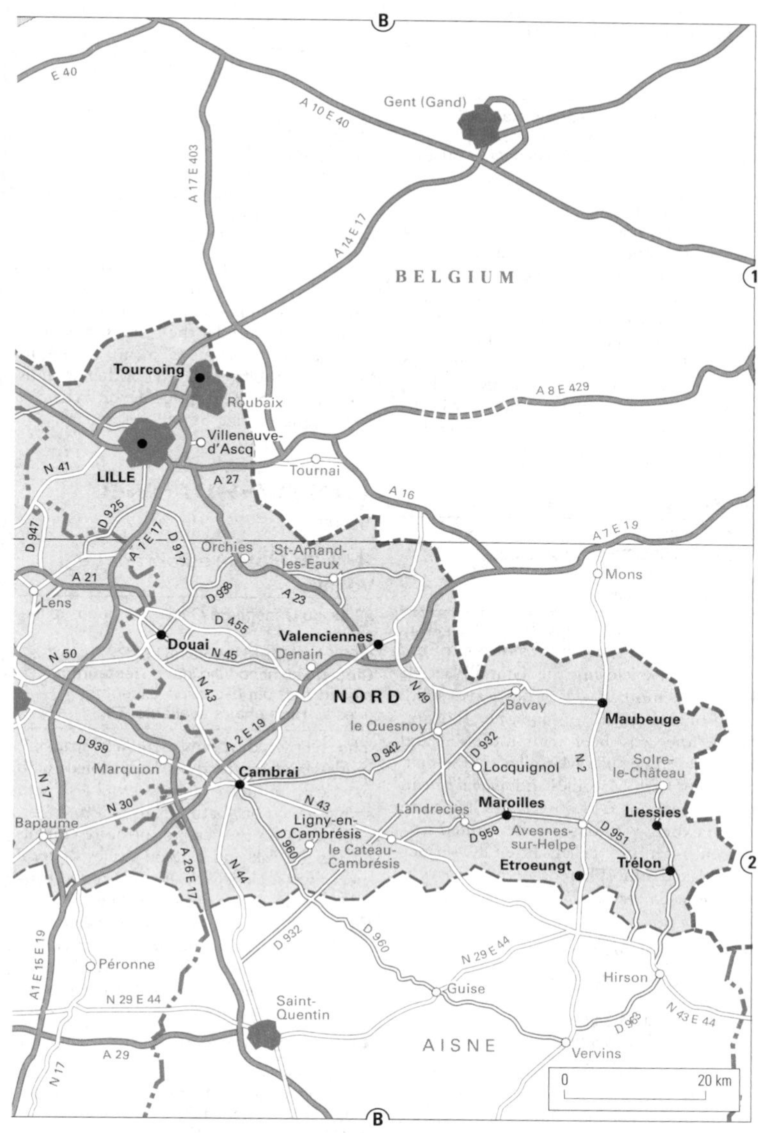

15

NORD-PAS-DE-CALAIS

comfortable. Double rooms with shower/wc or bath €58–63. Enchanting terrace in the inner courtyard. The owners give their guests a really friendly welcome. *One breakfast offered per room per night to our readers on presentation of this guide.*

Le Bouchot

3 rue de Chanzy: it's near the station.
Ⓣ03.21.51.67.51 Ⓕ03.21.71.04.30
Closed *Mon lunchtime. Open until 11.30pm Fri–Sat.*

A bright, freshly decorated canteen-style restaurant with a marine theme – there's a boat in the middle of the dining room – which specializes in huge portions of good mussels prepared in fifteen different ways: with Maroilles cheese, *à la marseillaise*, with cream and dill, and so on. The chips are up to scratch, as they should be, and they also get full marks for their honestly cooked, inexpensive regional dishes. Menus €10–17, or à la carte. *Free coffee offered to our readers on presentation of this guide.*

Restaurant La Rapière

44 Grand'Place.
Ⓣ03.21.55.09.92 Ⓕ03.21.22.24.29
Ⓦwww.larapiere.com
Closed *Sun evening.*

This friendly restaurant is hidden away under the sandstone arcades of one of the 155 houses enclosing the Grand'Place. It has a contemporary décor but serves solid, traditional cuisine – *tournedos* Rossini, house foie gras, beef with morels – and local specialities like Maroilles cheese flan, beef fillet with Maroilles and *andouillette* in pastry. Menus at €14.50–27. You'll need to be on expenses to dine in the vaulted seventeenth-century cellar. Friendly service and relaxed atmosphere. *Free coffee offered to our readers on presentation of this guide.*

Le Troubadour

29 av. du Général-de-Gaulle; it's opposite the casino.
Ⓣ and Ⓕ03.21.71.34.50
Closed *Sun; Mon evening.*

The *bouchon* (Lyonnais restaurant) atmosphere in this place is very appealing; you feel almost as if you're dining with friends in the country. The warm welcome from the *patronne* has something to do with it, as does the cooking. Choices of the day are scrawled up on a blackboard (three lots of starters, main courses and desserts), with traditional dishes such as calf's head sauce *gribiche*, *pot-au-feu* (boiled beef and veg). The dish of the day, served at lunch and dinner, costs €15; expect to pay €26 for à la carte. The desserts are a bit expensive, and so is the wine served by the jug. However, it's worth booking.

La Faizanderie

45 Grand'Place.
Ⓣ03.21.48.20.76 Ⓕ03.21.50.89.18
Closed *Sun evening; Mon; Tues lunchtime; 1–8 Jan; a week during the Feb school holidays; 3 weeks in Aug.*

Joyous dishes, full of flavour and exquisitely prepared in a traditional way. Table settings beautifully laid out amongst sandstone columns under the brick vaults in an ancient cellar. Menus €25 (not Sat night, Sun and public holidays), other menus €40 and €65. Prestigious décor. Friendly, welcoming service of a high standard.

Berck-sur-Mer

62600

Hôtel-restaurant Le Voltaire

29 av. du Général-de-Gaulle; it's opposite the casino.
Ⓣ03.21.84.43.13 Ⓕ03.21.84.61.72
Closed *Feb school holidays.* **Restaurant closed** *Tues out of season (except for guests).* **High chairs available. TV.**

The renovated rooms here are spacious, spotless and efficiently soundproofed, with practical, modern décor. Doubles with shower/wc or bath from €29–44.20, depending on the season. In the restaurant, go for the fish and seafood dishes or local specialities such as *ficelle picarde* (stuffed pancake) and charcoal-grilled beef. Menus €10.55–20.60. *Free coffee and house apéritif (out of season), or 10% discount on the room rate (out of season and excluding public holidays) offered to our readers on presentation of this guide.*

L'Auberge du Bois

149 av. Quetier. Direction Berck-Ville, then left at 1st big roundabout, then right at the traffic light. It's 30m on the left.
Ⓣ and Ⓕ03.21.09.03.43
Closed *Sun evening; Mon out of season; 4 Jan–4 Feb.* **Disabled access.**

Everyone in town calls this convivial place

"*Chez Ben*" because the owner is so well known. His bar-restaurant has a huge, simple and pleasant dining room decorated in warm tones, with menus from €14–30.50. The house speciality, fish *choucroute*, is good and there's plenty of it; if you want one of their impressive seafood platters for two, you'll need to order in advance. *Free second apéritif offered to our readers on presentation of this guide.*

|●| La Verrière

Casino de Berck-sur-Mer, pl. du 18-Juin.
Ⓣ03.21.84.27.25 Ⓕ03.21.84.14.65
Ⓔcasino-62berck@wanadoo.fr
Disabled access. Car park.

There are two entrances to this restaurant – the one that takes you past the rows of jangling slot machines will give you the wrong impression. The other offers the casino's classier face – a spacious, elegant restaurant where they serve the best cooking in town and probably along this stretch of the Opale coast. Weekday lunchtime menu €20, other menus €25–50. The chef uses only fresh produce, so dishes change all the time, and service is perfect. Typical offerings include roast turbot with upside-down tart of caramelized endive.

Béthune

62400

⌂ |●| Hôtel du Vieux Beffroi**

48 Grand'Place.
Ⓣ03.21.68.15.00 Ⓕ03.21.56.66.32
Disabled access. TV. Pay car park.

A vast hotel, with turrets and gables, opposite the fourteenth-century bell-tower. You are woken by the bells in the morning, but thankfully they don't ring at night. Some of the old-fashioned rooms have been renovated and they're not short on charm – doubles €35–55 with shower/wc or bath. Meals are served in a classic dining room or lively brasserie; dishes include *flammenküche* and *choucroute*. You can choose from a range of *formules* at €8–12, menus between €20 and €25, or à la carte. Unfortunately, the restaurant and the brasserie lack interest.

⌂ |●| Restaurant La Taverne

1 pl. de la République.
Ⓣ03.21.56.80.80
Closed *Sat lunchtime; Sun evening; mid-July to mid-Aug.* **TV.**

One of the best places in town, this traditional, unpretentious brasserie serves regional dishes to an appreciative local crowd. Choose from the menus (€15 and €25) or the varied à la carte selection. Specialities include various kinds of *choucroute* and an excellent and substantial fisherman's platter.

|●| La Ripaille

20 Grand'Place.
Ⓣ03.21.56.22.33
Closed *Sun; Mon evening; 1–15 Aug; Christmas holidays.*

Though there's little to see from the outside – just a narrow, very ordinary frontage – this place is usually crammed with regulars who are very obviously enjoying themselves. The portions are big, the sauces and broths are appetizing and the fish and meat invariably splendid; this is a very good place indeed. €12 for the dish of the day and you're looking at around €25 à la carte. The owner gives her guests a really friendly welcome and children are well catered for. It's small, so you'd do best to reserve. *Coffee offered to our readers on presentation of this guide.*

Bully-les-Mines

62160 (12km SE)

⌂ |●| L'Enfant du Pays

152 rue Roger-Salengro. Follow Lens, after Mazingarbe.
Ⓣ03.21.29.12.33
Ⓔm.verbrugge@nordnet.fr
Restaurant closed *Sun evening.* **TV. Car park.**

This place, despite its unprepossessing location at the back of the slag heaps, has got a good reputation for serving generous helpings of straightforward, authentic dishes made with fresh produce. The local and regional dishes change with the seasons; *millefeuille* of Maroilles cheese is always a good bet, as is pork *filet mignon*, lamb in Port, *andouillette* and pigeon with spring onions. Menus €10–23. You can also stay the night, in recently refurbished bedrooms that go for rock-bottom prices: doubles with basin go for €16, or €24 with shower/wc or bath.

Boulogne-sur-Mer

62200

🏠 |●| Auberge de jeunesse

Place Rouget-de-l'Isle; just opposite the train station.
Ⓣ03.21.99.15.30 Ⓕ03.21.99.15.39
Ⓦwww.fuaj.org
New arrivals *received 7.30am–1pm, then 24-hr access code.* **Closed** *weekends 11am–5pm (Sept–March); 22 Dec–31 Jan.* **High chairs, children's games, babies' changing table and plastic sheets available. Disabled access.**

This dynamic youth hostel is very comfortable – the building was formerly part of a hotel chain – and ideally situated if you're travelling by train. Bedrooms with three or four beds and shower/wc. €15.30 a night, including sheets and breakfast (you are obliged to pay for this). Half board €24.50 per person for groups. There is also a bar and cheap restaurant (at €8.40), as well as a fully equipped kitchen. IBN booking service for youth hostels all over the world. The FUAJ card (compulsory, sold *in situ*) gives you the right to several discounts in the town : visits to Nausicaa, bowling, shows, sea sports. *For families, 50% discount on the third night of their next stay (valid for two years) offered to our readers on presentation of this guide.*

🏠 Hôtel Faidherbe**

12 rue Faidherbe.
Ⓣ03.21.31.60.93 Ⓕ03.21.87.01.14
Closed *Christmas and New Year holidays.* **Disabled access. TV.**

Well located near the harbour (though the neighbourhood, rebuilt after the War, is without much charm). If the weather's fine, Victor, the resident mynah bird, might decide to say a few words. There's a small, comfy Victorian-style lounge, and individually decorated rooms with good facilities. Doubles with shower €40, €50 with shower/wc, €55 with bath/wc.

🏠 Hôtel Alexandra**

93 rue Thiers; in city centre, it's near the port.
Ⓣ03.21.30.52.22 Ⓕ03.21.30.20.03
Closed *24 Dec–31 Jan.* **TV.**

A small, unfussy hotel in a central street. Rooms are brightly decorated and have good facilities; some at the back, more spacious and with balcony. Doubles with shower/wc or bath for €49–58. It's best to book in high season, at weekends and during public holidays.

|●| Chez Jules

8–10 pl. Dalton; it's in the heart of the town.
Ⓣ03.21.31.54.12 Ⓕ03.21.33.85.47
Closed *Sun evening (out of season); 15 Sept–10 Oct; 23 Dec–5 Jan.* **Disabled access.**

This is *the* Boulogne brasserie, with a huge terrace on the square. It's been around for aeons so the service is efficient and the cooking tasty and reliable. They have two rooms, one is a brasserie, the other one is a more traditional restaurant/pizzeria. À la carte includes *moules marinière*, *choucroute* (in winter), pizza, stewed fish and calf's head sauce *gribiche*. Menu €13.80 except public holidays and Sun, other menus €22.10–39.60.

|●| Le Châtillon

6 rue Charles-Tellier; in the port area.
Ⓣ03.21.31.43.95
Closed *Sat; Sun.*

Nobody can deny that this place has atmosphere: it nestles among huge metal hangars in the heart of the port, opposite a street as wide as a runway where articulated lorries constantly go to and fro. Inside, the downstairs dining room may be noisier than the one on the first floor, but it's the place to see the heart and soul of this city; you can find fishermen and sea captains, sometimes still in their oilskins and boots, huddled round the bar or one of the cramped tables, knocking down drinks and spinning yarns. All this plus fine home cooking, with unerringly fresh fish taking pride of place. Menus €14 and €16.

Wast (Le)

62142 (15km E)

🏠 |●| Hostellerie du Château des Tourelles**

Take the N42 towards Saint-Omer then take the D127 to Le Wast.
Ⓣ03.21.33.34.78 Ⓕ03.21.87.59.57
Ⓔtourelles.feutry@gofortnet.com
Disabled access. TV. Car park.

As you enter the village you'll see the hotel, which is housed in a very elegant nineteenth-century mansion, hidden behind the trees in a small park. There's a modern annexe next to the tennis courts. Ideally, you should stay in the superb rooms of the "château" with their Louis-Philippe furniture and small balconies. If your funds won't stretch to that, go for an attic room. Doubles with shower/wc or bath €49–75. Half board €42–49 per person per night. Tennis, table tennis and billiards are all free for residents, and the restaurant serves menus at €13 (for half board guests only) and €20–39.

Calais

62100

Hôtel Windsor**

2 rue du Commandant-Bonningue; head for the harbour, and you'll find it on the extension of the place d'Armes.
Ⓣ03.21.34.59.40 Ⓕ03.21.97.68.59
Closed *Christmas and New year.* **TV. Pay car park.**

In a quiet part of town, not far from the marina. Attractive English-style double rooms from €28 with basin to €44 with bath/wc or family rooms €49–57. Friendly atmosphere and staff. Booking is highly recommended.

Hôtel Pacific**

40 rue du Duc-de-Guise; it's near Notre-Dame cathedral.
Ⓣ03.21.34.50.24 Ⓕ03.21.97.58.02
Ⓦwww.cofrase.com/hotel/pacific
Closed *one or two weeks in Winter.* **High chairs available. TV. Pay car park.**

A small, friendly hotel that's centrally located but gratifyingly peaceful. It proves good value for this part of the world, though some rooms are rather small; doubles for €36 or €45 with shower/wc or bath/wc. They also have family rooms that sleep up to four people and some non-smoking rooms. An accommodating, voluble and welcoming staff.

Le Richelieu**

17 rue Richelieu; it's opposite Richelieu park.
Ⓣ03.21.34.61.60 Ⓕ03.21.85.89.28
Ⓦwww.hotelrichelieu-calais.com
Closed *Christmas and New Year's holidays.* **High chairs available. TV. Pay car park.**

Bright, comfortable rooms from €46 for a double with shower/wc or bath. Nine of them have balconies looking over the huge, lush Richelieu park – a soothing contrast to the garish neon signs in the adjacent streets. It's easy to relax here; and the street is very quiet. *One breakfast per room and per night offered to our readers on presentation of this guide.*

Histoire Ancienne

20 rue Royale.
Ⓣ03.21.34.11.20
Closed *Sun; Mon evening; last week in Feb; 1st fortnight in Aug.*

Something for everybody in this pretty bistro with a marked Art-Deco influence in the décor. The chef skilfully manages to combine Lyonnais dishes, meat and fish grilled in the hearth, classic brasserie recipes, time-honoured rural fare and a few appetizing side dishes with a contemporary touch. Combination of main course plus starter or dessert available during the week for €11 at lunch and at night until 8pm; the menus from €17.50–28 are good value, but eating à la carte here will set you back a good deal more. Highly efficient service.

La Pleïade

32 rue Jean-Quéhen; in a street to the east of the place d'Armes.
Ⓣ03.21.34.03.70
Closed *Sun; Mon; Feb half-term; last 3 weeks in Aug.* **Disabled access.**

An unassuming restaurant that has nevertheless established itself in just a few years as one of the best (if not *the* best) restaurant in Calais. The setting suggests the creative, contemporary cooking that is in store, with plenty of enticing discoveries and thrillingly audacious combinations. Menus €22–36. Guests are given a charming welcome and the atmosphere is cosy (perhaps exaggeratedly so).

Escalles

62179 (20 km W)

Hôtel-restaurant L'Escale**

4 rue de la Mer; take the D940 towards Wissant.
Ⓣ03.21.85.25.00 Ⓕ03.21.35.44.22
Ⓦwww.hotel-lescale.com
Restaurant closed *Wed Nov–Dec (except public holidays and school holidays). 12 Jan–13 Feb; 13–26 Dec.* **Disabled access. High chairs and games available. Car park.**

In the annexe – a stone building smothered with ivy – the rooms are tidy and comfortable; other rooms in the main hotel are more modest and noisier due to their proximity to the bar/restaurant. Doubles with basin €32.50, with shower/wc €48, with bath €51. Menus €13.80–35. The garden has outdoor games for children and loungers for the adults. You can play tennis or you can try your hand at mountain biking.

Cambrai

59400

Hôtel de France*

37 rue de Lille; it's 100m from the train station.
Ⓣ03.27.81.38.80 Ⓕ03.27.78.13.88
TV.

A typical station hotel – neat and tidy and quaintly old-fashioned, though many rooms have had a makeover. It's remarkably quiet, even the rooms overlooking the tracks – few trains run at night. Doubles with basin €38, with shower/wc or bath €42–46. You'll get a charming welcome from the owner, who's something of a wine buff.

Le Mouton Blanc***

33 rue d'Alsace-Lorraine; it's about 200m from the train station, in the street opposite.
Ⓣ03.27.81.30.16
Restaurant closed *Sun evening; Mon; a week in Aug (restaurant only).* **Disabled access (restaurant). TV. Car park.**

Solidly built nineteenth-century house with a great deal of charm and a genuine family atmosphere. The rooms exude a certain opulence without going over the top, and cost €55 for a double with shower/wc or €61–90 with bath. They serve good and interesting dishes in the large dining room. Menus €19–42. *10% discount on the room rate offered to our readers on presentation of this guide.*

Le Grill de l'Europe

Place Marcellin-Berthelot; it's in the port district.
Ⓣ03.27.81.66.76
Closed *Sat lunchtime; Sun evening; end July to early Aug.* **High chairs available.**

A popular haunt of truck drivers, sailors and fishermen, this is a simple, warm and lively bar where they serve straightforward home cooking. The €11 menu offers steak, dessert and a quarter-litre of wine; there are other menus at €17 and €23. There's also a self-service hors d'œuvre buffet, dishes of the day and à la carte choices include frogs' legs *provençale*, *fricassée* of sole with port, etc. Terrace and large garden for the summer. *Free coffee offered to our readers on presentation of this guide.*

Le Resto du Beffroi

4 rue du 11-Novembre; city centre; take the avenue opposite the town hall, and it's the second turning on the right.
Ⓣ and Ⓕ03.27.81.50.10
Closed *Sat lunchtime; Sun; 1–15 Jan; 1–22 Aug.*

A friendly, if rather unusual, restaurant tucked away in a little street behind the Grand'Place. The décor is a mixture of traditional bistro and night club, and some of the cuisine takes its influence from the southwest, where chef Yves Galan used to breed ducks. Today he prepares good robust food, including duck breast and *cassoulet* with duck *confit*, veal sweetbreads *toulousaine* and chicken with cream and morel sauce. Menus €15.24–22.90. *Free Kir offered to our readers on presentation of this guide.*

Ligny-en-Cambrésis

59191 (15km SE)

Le Château de Ligny Haucourt****

2 rue Pierre-Curie; take the N43 in the direction of Cateay-Cambrésis, and in Beauvois turn off to Ligny.
Ⓣ03.27.85.25.84 Ⓕ03.27.85.79.79
Closed *a fortnight in Feb.* **Disabled access. TV. Car park.**

This rural hideway is a stylish, tasteful place. The round tower is part of the original twelfth-century château, and the salons have ornamental ceilings. Each guest room has its own personality – you could lose yourself in the biggest one – and prices reflect the quality: you're looking at paying around €100–170 for a double with bath. They also have three suites such as 'La Royale' at €280. The restaurant, which is open to non-residents, has a huge reputation and enjoys a magnificent setting; cooking is tasty, light and inspired, and what you are offered is always dependent on the seasons.

Cassel

59670

|●| La Taverne Flamande

34 Grand'Place; it's opposite the town hall.
Ⓣ03.28.42.42.59 Ⓕ03.28.40.51.84
Closed *Tues evening; Wed. 1–7 Feb; Aug; Oct.*

You'll get an authentic Flemish meal here. Try Flemish *croustillons*, chicken casserole Ghent-style (cooked in a home-made béchamel-type sauce), veal kidneys flambéed with gin, Flemish apple tart sprinkled with brown sugar or crêpes flambéed in Houlle. Menus €11 (not Sun) and others €14–22, with a Flemish menu for €16. Sit on the veranda, which is perched on the slopes of Mont Cassel, and enjoy the same panorama that so delighted the Romantic poet Lamartine.

|●| Estaminet't Kasteel Hof

8 rue Saint-Nicolas; it's opposite the mill; city centre.
Ⓣ03.28.40.59.29 Ⓕ03.28.42.43.23
Closed *Mon–Wed; three weeks in Jan; 1–15 Oct.* **High chairs and games available.**

This tavern, at the top of Mont Cassel, is at the highest altitude in French Flanders – a mere 175.90m. There's a splendid view from upstairs. It's a wonderful little place, stuffed full of spoils from junk shops, with a tiny bar, a few tables, wooden chairs, a fireplace and baskets hanging from the beams. Typical offerings include various kinds of soup with endives, *cœur casselois*, *waterzoï* (fish stew), *potjevfleisch* (a local pâté of veal, chicken and rabbit), beer tart, and apples in flaky pastry. Cheeses include *zermezeelois* or *mont-des-cats*, and even the mineral water is Flemish, hailing from Saint-Amand. This is hop country so there's a list of traditional beers rather than wine. You'll pay around €16 for a meal, or you could settle for one of the filling platters of local cheeses or pâtés. Flemish legends told on Saturday evening and Sunday lunchtime. *Free coffee offered to our readers on presentation of this guide.*

Eecke

59114 (10km SE)

|●| Brasserie Saint-Georges

5 rue de Castre; take the D933 then the D947 and it's halfway between Cassel and Bailleul.
Ⓣ03.28.40.13.71
Ⓦwww.brasseriesaintgeorges.com
Open *Fri evening Sat–Sun out of season; Mon–Thurs evenings July–Aug and the day before public holidays; end Aug.* **Games available.**

This bastion of Flemish culture has its own newsletter. The building started out as a farm in the sixteenth century, after which it became a mill, and then a posthouse, and the jumbled architecture and décor combine elements from this varied past. They began brewing beer here in the 1970s and now sell 63 specialist beers – des Chênes, brewed locally, is the most popular. Good traditional Flemish cooking includes *andouillettes*, grilled pork chitterlings with *standevleech* (potatoes cooked in coals), melted Maroilles cheese with cumin, grilled pork fillet and ham *à la 3 Monts* (ham on the bone marinated in beer with potatoes and Maroilles cheese *au gratin*). Prices are reasonable with a menu at €17, coffee included, or €8.50–19 à la carte. *Free coffee offered to our readers on presentation of this guide.*

Boeschepe

59299 (15km E)

⌂ |●| Auberge du Vert Mont**

Route du Mont-Noir; take the D948 towards Steenvoorde then the N348 to the Belgian border, and finally the D10 towards Bailleul; it's signposted from Boeschepe.
Ⓣ03.28.49.41.26
Closed *Mon lunchtime out of season. 1–15 Jan.* **High chairs and games available. TV. Car park.**

This small tourist complex, next to a hop field, used to be a farm. It retains a rural feel, with ducks splashing about in the pond and goats and sheep bleating in the fields. They offer games for children and there are a couple of tennis courts. The rooms are adorable too; they're €58–80 for a double with shower/wc or bath. There are flowers everywhere in the restaurant, which offers a range of tried-and-tested, well-prepared regional dishes: try fish stew, cheese tart, scallops *à la Hoegarden* or *potjevfleisch* (veal, chicken and rabbit pâté), and wash it down with one of their many Belgian and French beers. Menus €22–35 and you'll pay around €22 à la carte. *Third night (room only) offered to our readers on presentation of this guide.*

Douai

59500

Hôtel Le Chambord**

3509 rte. de Tournai; it's in Frais-Marais, 4km from the centre of Douai on the D917.
03.27.97.72.77 03.27.99.35.14
Hotel closed *3 weeks in Aug.* **Restaurant closed** *Fri evening; Sat lunch; Sun evening; Mon.* **TV. Car park.**

Frais-Marais, a suburb of Douai, still feels like a village, though the main road runs past the hotel – don't take a room on that side of the building. The comfortable, attractive rooms here are reasonably priced for the area – oddly enough, hotels in Douai cost a lot. Doubles with shower/wc or bath €40–46. The restaurant offers a €12.50 weekday menu (except public holidays) with others for €15–40.

Hôtel-Restaurant La Terrasse****

36 terrasse Saint-Pierre.
03.27.88.70.04 03.27.88.36.05
www.laterrasse.fr
TV. Car park.

This is a four-star place and a member of the Châteaux et Hôtels Indépendants organization. It's beautifully situated near the collegiate church in a charming old house. Serious and traditional, run by very professional staff, it nevertheless offers reasonably priced rooms at €48–65 with shower/wc or bath. With its red brick and white stone walls hung with paintings, the dining room evokes traditional France; the ideal setting to enjoy beautifully presented, classic dishes. Fish, including lobster fresh from the tank, dominates, but they also do game in season and good foie gras dishes – and prices are more than honest. Set menus €20.50–66. There's a spectacular wine list of 900 different appellations; the proprietor owns vineyards in Burgundy.

Hôtel Volubilis***

Boulevard Bauban; coming from Tournai, it's where the road comes to the Pont de Lille.
03.27.88.00.11 03.27.96.07.41
contact@hotel.volubilis.fr
Restaurant closed *Sun evening.* **TV. Car park.**

Despite appearances – at first glance it looks like a chain hotel – this is a very pleasant establishment with a fresh, brightly coloured interior and double rooms for €58–68. The restaurant has more than adequate menus at €16.50–30.

Restaurant Au Turbotin

9 rue de la Massue; it's near the Scarpe river, opposite the law courts.
03.27.87.04.16 03.27.87.87.57
Closed *Sat lunchtime; Sun evening; Mon; a week in Feb; Aug.*

Au Turbotin is primarily a fish and seafood restaurant, though they also offer other regional dishes. Try the turbot with champagne, lobster brioche... The weekday menu costs €16, with others at €26–42. With chic yet low-key surroundings, courteous and refined service and customers who don't have to watch the pennies, it's one of the town's classiest establishments. *A free glass of champagne offered after a meal to our readers on presentation of this guide.*

Dunkerque

59240

Trianon Hôtel**

20 rue de la Colline; follow the signs for the Malo-les-Bains and the hotel is signposted.
03.28.63.39.15 03.28.63.34.57
Bicycles available. TV.

In a quiet district inhabited predominantly by retired people, this place is typical of the picturesque seaside villas that were built along this coast in the mid-nineteenth century. The hotel is quite charming and the rooms are pleasant, as is the tiny indoor garden next to the breakfast room. Doubles €44 with shower/wc or bath. The owner, who knows the area well, is always ready to help. *One free breakfast, per room and per night, offered to our readers on presentation of this guide.*

Hôtel-restaurant L'Hirondelle**

46–48 av. Faidherbe; from the centre head towards the Malo-les-Bains, where it's signposted.
03.28.63.17.65 03.28.66.15.43
Restaurant closed *Sun evening; Mon lunch; 1–15 March; end Aug to early Sept.* **TV. Disabled access. Pay car park.**

Right next to a lovely little square – sadly marred by the thunder of the traffic – and not far from the sea, this is a faultless establishment with modern décor. The functional rooms, priced from €57.60, doubles with shower/wc or bath. Reassuringly conventional dishes are served in the restaurant: poached turbot with Hollandaise sauce, seafood platters and *potjevleesch* (veal, rabbit and chicken in aspic cooked in white wine and vinegar). Menus from €11 during the week; you'll spend around €40 à la carte. The small bar is a nice place to drink. *Free apéritif maison offered to our readers on presentation of this guide.*

🏃 |●| Le Péché Mignon

11 pl. du Casino; across the square from the casino.
☎03.28.66.14.44
Closed *Sat lunchtime; Sun evening; Mon.* **High chairs available.**

A cosy little dining room in pastel shades with soft armchairs. If you've lost your shirt in the casino, you will probably still be able to afford the cheapest menu, modestly priced at €14. If you're dining before making for the gaming tables, however, there are others up to €32. Generously flavoured dishes include splendid house foie gras, smoked duck breast, good fish and regional desserts such as spiced bread ice cream. When it's sunny, make for the little terrace in the garden – a consolation for the lack of sea view. The welcome is also excellent. *Free apéritif maison or coffee offered to our readers on presentation of this guide.*

🏃 |●| Au Petit Pierre

4 rue Dampierre.
☎03.28.66.28.36 ⓕ03.28.66.28.49
ⓦwww.aupetitpierre.com
Closed *Sat lunchtime; Sun evening.*

This is one of the town's very few eighteenth-century residences that wasn't shelled in World War II. The owners have lovingly renovated it, creating an elegantly sober setting with varnished wooden furniture and salmon-pink walls. The cooking is some of the best along the coast, with inspired regional dishes. The meat and fish dishes are splendid and particularly fresh, delicious desserts. Menus €14.98–28. *Free coffee offered to our readers on presentation of this guide.*

Bergues

59380 (10km SE)

🏃 ⌂ |●| Hôtel-restaurant Au Tonnelier**

4 rue du Mont-de-Piété.
☎03.28.68.70.05 ⓕ03.28.68.21.87
Closed *Sun evening; Mon lunchtime; 23 Dec–9 Jan.* **TV. High chairs available. Disabled access. Car park.**

An attractive, quiet, ochre-yellow brick inn at the heart of the medieval village. It's opposite the Mont-de-Piété, a superb seventeenth-century building which has been converted into a museum. Doubles go for €52–58 with shower/wc or bath. The rooms looking onto the lovely little paved courtyard are the quietest, and get the most light – in summer this is where they serve meals. The good, regional cooking seems very in keeping with the opulent surroundings of the dining room. There are a number of regional specialities, including *carbonade* with gingerbread and a terrific *potjes vleesch* (veal, rabbit and chicken in aspic cooked in white wine and vinegar). Menus from €13 (weekdays lunchtimes), others to €16–28. you'll pay around €30 à la carte. *Free coffee offered to our readers on presentation of this guide.*

Cappelle-Brouck

59630 (23km SW)

🏃 |●| Le Campagnard

Les Dondaines; it's at the N316 then D600, turn left to Pont-l'Abesse then follow the signs
☎03.28.29.56.09
Closed *evenings (except for groups); in Dec.* **Games available. Disabled access.**

A nice restaurant run by a young local couple who are passionate about the region but also love to travel. They serve excellent country cooking amid a friendly atmosphere with eclectic music playing in the background in a pretty dining room decorated with images of old windmills. The weekday menus at €9–13 and €18 on Sunday prove good value; dish of the day weekdays and Sunday at €7.70. Credit cards are not accepted. *Free coffee offered to our readers on presentation of this guide.*

Etroeungt

59219

🏃 |●| Ferme de la Capelette

La Capelette; it's 7km south of Avesnes.
☎03.27.59.28.33
Closed *Wed. Open weekdays by reservation only.* **Disabled access.**

Naf and Dany Delmée converted their farmhouse into a country inn with splendid results. There's a pleasant dining room, and a vast terrace high above the Helpe valley. Best of all is the superb local cuisine, prepared with passion and professionalism. Nothing but fresh produce is used – the delicious oyster mushrooms are grown right here on the farm. The terrines are always good, particularly the one with duck and shiitake mushrooms. Other hits include the suckling pig *civet* prepared with dry cider, duck with sweet and sour sauce and baby onions, roast lamb with caramelized honey and guineafowl flambéed with apple brandy. The apple tart is made with crisp pastry and fruit picked from the orchard. Dishes change with the seasons. Lunchtime weekday menus from €14.50, others €25–30. Booking essential out of season and highly recommended in summer. *Free apéritif maison, coffee or liqueur offered to our readers on presentation of this guide.*

Godewaersvelde

59270

Het Blauwershof

Rue d'Eecke; it's between Steenvoorde and Bailleul on the D18.
☎03.28.49.45.11
Closed *Mon; 1–15 Jan; a fortnight in Aug.*

The most famous tap-room in Flanders, and one of a dying breed. The bar and dining room have enormous charm – old furniture, rustic pots and long wooden tables where a happy group of patrons sit round enjoying the convivial atmosphere. You can also play traditional bar games. If you're hungry, it's well worth ordering here: herring fillets, leek tart, mustard tart, *potjevleesh* with chips and beef *carbonade* are all good. For pudding, there's *clafoutis* with apples or ice cream. Menus €10 and €15.

Le Roi du Potje Vleesch

31 rue du Mont-des-Cats. City centre;
☎03.28.42.52.56
Closed *Mon; evenings Sept–May; Jan.*

The dining room here is warm and welcoming; odd to think that it used to be the family-run abattoir (you can still see the tethering rings on the walls). It's a characterful place, decorated with old domestic objects, plates, tools and photographs, and the cuisine is resolutely Flemish. Try pâté with garlic, *carbonade* or cockerel in beer. You'll eat excellent meals at very modest prices, starting at €8.50 for a Flemish platter and rising to around €25 for a meal à la carte. They also have a shop selling regional delicacies made on-site – delicious terrines with *potjevleesch*. Reservations recommended at the weekend.

Hardelot-Plage

62152

Le Régina**

185 av. François 1er; it's 1.5km from the town centre.
☎03.28.41.98.79 ℱ03.21.87.44.01
www.lereginahotel.fr
Closed *Sun evening and Mon except Whitsun; Easter; July–Aug. 11 Nov–13 Feb.*
TV. High chairs and games available. Car park.

A handsome, two-storey, modern establishment in a quiet residential district surrounded by wooded countryside. It's quiet, and not bad value given the facilities; doubles with shower/wc or bath are €62. The restaurant, *Les Brisants*, has a bright, elegant dining room and offers fresh, assured cooking; good value for money. Menus €19–32. Half board available from the third night is good value. Tennis, golf and stables are all close by, and the beach is 1km away. *10% discount on the room rate (14 Feb–19 March and 20 Sept–28 Oct), or free apéritif or coffee offered to our readers on presentation of this guide.*

Hazebrouck

59190

Hôtel Le Gambrinus**

2 rue Nationale; it's between the Grand'Place and the train station.
☎03.28.41.98.79 ℱ03.28.43.11.06
Closed *Sun evening; 2nd and 3rd week of Aug.* **TV.**

This is Hazebrouck's only hotel, so it's here or in the car. Inside, the substantial nineteenth-century house is bright and well decorated; pleasant doubles with shower/wc cost €50. The owners really know how to make you feel welcome.

Restaurant-Estaminet La Taverne

61 Grand'Place.
☎03.28.41.63.09

Closed *Sun evening; Mon; a week in Feb; 3 weeks in Aug.* **High chairs available.**

This convivial restaurant has a warm atmosphere, elegant Flanders décor and good, local cooking: Maroilles cheese and leek quiche, tart with rhubarb or chicory, *potjevfleisch* (a veal, rabbit and chicken *pâté*), veal kidneys flambéed with juniper and *carbonade flamande* (beef braised in beer). You'll get generous portions, dished up by good-natured staff. They offer occasional specials, too – mussels and chips on Friday, say, or *fondues* in the evening. Menus €13 (not Sun) and €14.50–23, and à la carte.

Motte-au-Bois (La)

59190 (5km SE)

Auberge de la Forêt**

It's five minutes from Hazebrouck on the D946 heading towards Merville.
☎03.28.48.08.78
Closed *Sat lunchtime (except in season); Sun evening; Mon; 26 Dec–20 Jan; 17–23 Aug.* **TV. Car park.**

This 1950s hunting lodge, almost buried under foliage, is situated in the heart of a village deep in the vast Nieppe forest. The panelled rooms are simple but pleasant, particularly those with latticed windows opening onto lovely little gardens. Doubles €38–43 with shower/wc, €53–58 with bath. The restaurant offers regional specialities along with some exceptionally inventive cooking that justifies the rather high prices. Good options include *fricassée* of veal kidneys with ceps, turbot, roast sole with crayfish. Weekday menu €23.50 and others up to €48. There's a good wine list – the cellar is one of the best in the region. Customers are well-heeled.

Sercus

59173 (6km SW)

Estaminet-auberge Au Saint-Érasme

18 rte. de Blaringhem; take the D106 or the N42 and turn off at Wallon-Capel.
☎03.28.41.85.43
Closed *Mon; evenings (except Fri and Sat); a week Feb, a fortnight end Aug.* **Disabled access. High chairs and games available.**

A spruce country inn with a pretty façade. Inside, it's snug and convivial, with a terrace open in summer. They serve home cooking in generous portions, with local dishes including *flamiches* with Maroilles cheese, a tasty chicken in beer and chips as crispy as can be. Go for the sugar tart for dessert. Prices are very reasonable: dish of the day €8 (weekdays) and you'll pay around €15 for a menu à la carte. *Free coffee offered to our readers on presentation of this guide.*

Hesdin

62140

Hôtel des Flandres**

20–22 rue d'Arras.
☎03.21.86.80.21
Closed *mid Dec to early Jan.* **TV. High chairs available. Car park.**

No-fuss hotel with a family atmosphere in the midst of the "Seven Valleys" area. The rooms are straightforward and comfortable; doubles with shower/wc or bath €50. It's the same story in the restaurant, which serves traditional local dishes like chicken terrine or cockerel cooked in a red wine sauce. Menus may vary from €17–31. *Free coffee offered to our readers on presentation of this guide.*

Saulchoy

62870 (22.5km SW)

Le Val d'Authie

60 La Place; take the D928 towards Abbeville, then turn right onto the D119, which follows the River Authie.
☎03.21.90.30.20
Closed *Thurs out of season.*

A friendly old country inn with character. You'll get good home cooking here; tried and tested recipes include vol au vents, coq au vin, duck breast and leg of lamb. Weekday menu €13, then others €20.50–29. In season they serve copious portions of game: hare casserole, wild boar stew, venison in cream sauce, pheasant in port.

Liessies

59740

Le Château de la Motte**

Take the D133 towards the lac du Val-Joly.
☎03.27.61.81.94 Ⓕ03.27.61.83.57
Ⓦwww.chateaudelamotte.fr

Closed *Sun evening and Mon lunch out of season; 21 Dec–9 Jan.* **TV. High chairs and games available. Car park.**

Backing onto the Bois-l'Abbé national forest, this château was built in 1725 as a place of retreat for the monks of Liessies Abbey. It's a good-looking place, made from unusual pink brick and slate. The rooms, which offer the peace and silence the monks sought, cost €63 for a double with shower/wc or bath. Weekday menus, €19–66, include such specialities as lamb cutlets, foie gras with Sauternes, and *flamiche* with Maroilles. There's also an all-inclusive *formule* (with apéritif, wine and coffee) for €34.50. You'll pay around €45 for a menu à la carte. They host gastronomic evenings and weekends. *A free glass of champagne offered to our readers on presentation of this guide.*

Chez Louis

25 rue Roger Salengro; it's on the D133 on the road from Avesnes.
Ⓣ and Ⓕ03.27.61.82.38
Closed *Mon (except public holidays); mid-Dec to mid-Jan.* **High chairs and games available.**

Despite the sign, which calls it a friterie, this is in fact a good restaurant with a pretty dining room. The building is an old farmer's house with hefty beams, tiled or stone floors and a wide hearth, and you eat communally at long wooden tables. Everything is home-made and tasty – including the wonderful chips – and they use only the freshest local produce to prepare devilishly good terrines, *andouillette*, *carbonade* stews, tripe, white pudding and Maroilles cheese tart. A meal here won't break the bank, either – you can get a dish of the day for around €7, and only the *entrecôte* steak costs more than €8. You'll pay around €15 for a menu à la carte. There's a splendid terrace in summer, and children are well catered for with a playground and special buggy rides. Credit cards not accepted. *Coffee offered to our readers on presentation of this guide.*

Le Carillon

It's in the centre of the village, opposite the church.
Ⓣ03.27.61.80.21 Ⓕ03.77.61.84.38
Ⓦwww.le-carillon.com
Closed *Sun–Tues evenings; Wed; 18 Feb–10 March; 16 Nov–1 Dec.*

A beautiful Avesnois house which has been tastefully restored. It's run by a couple of young professionals who have enhanced the gastronomic reputation of this region with their simple, skilled cooking. Try the grilled zander with beer, *chocolat moelleux* flavoured with Earl Grey tea, lemon in a crispy filo pastry case. All the dishes change with the seasons and their desserts are spectacular. There's a weekday menu for €14.50, and others at €19.50–34. They also offer regularly changing theme menus (paella, couscous, *bouillabaisse,* etc) for one week in a month. The wine cellar next door sells a selection of *vins de pays* and vintages at all sorts of prices, as well as a good range of whiskies. They also have a store with regional products.

Lille

59000

See map on pp.582–583

Hôtel Flandre-Angleterre**

13 pl. de la Gare; facing the train station, city centre. **Map D2-3**
Ⓣ03.20.06.04.12 Ⓕ03.20.06.37.76
Ⓦwww.hotel.flandre.angleterre.fr
TV. Pay car park.

Double bedrooms €63–74 with shower/wc or bath. Despite being opposite the station, the rooms are well-soundproofed with nice bathrooms and modern décor. It's used mainly by businesspeople. *10% discount on the room rate at the weekend and school holidays offered to our readers on presentation of this guide.*

Le Grand Hôtel**

51 rue Faidherbe; midway between the Lille-Flandres train station and the centre. **Map C2-6**
Ⓣ03.20.06.31.57 Ⓕ03.20.06.24.44.
Ⓦwww.legrandhotel.com
Closed *1st three weeks in Aug.* **TV.**

Typical of the sort of hotels France is famous for, this comfortable establishment near the station has attractive rooms decorated with a feminine touch. Very nice female owner and efficient staff. Doubles from €65 with shower/wc or bath. They also have a few family rooms sleeping three or four. *One free breakfast per room per night offered to our readers on presentation of this guide.*

🏃 ☗ Le Brueghel**

5 parvis Saint-Maurice. **Map C2-5**
Ⓣ03.20.06.06.69 Ⓕ03.20.63.25.27
Ⓦwww.hotel.brueghel.com
TV. Pay car park.

This hotel, in an enormous brick building near the St-Maurice church, has personality and – better still – soul. The décor shows excellent taste, with antique furniture everywhere and nice prints on the wall; doubles go for €70–79 depending on facilities. (Rooms with basin are even cheaper.) The rooms at the rear are very pleasant and quiet. The welcome couldn't be better – the staff love their work and the night porter practically has a fan club. It's a favourite meeting place for actors performing in shows in town so it's best to book. *One free breakfast per room per night offered to our readers on presentation of this guide.*

🏃 ☗ Hôtel de la Paix**

46 bis rue de Paris; access city centre. **Map C2-7**
Ⓣ03.20.54.63.93 Ⓕ03.20.63.98.97
Ⓔhotelpaixlille@aol.com
Internet available.

Beyond the grand reception of this hotel there's an eighteenth-century staircase that's so superb it's a shame to use the lift. The rooms are tastefully furnished and spacious; doubles with shower/wc €72 or €77 with bath. The owner gave up painting when she entered the hotel business, but it has remained a passion. She has devoted each room to a different contemporary artist and put reproductions on the walls. No. 12 has a terrace and a garden.

|●| Restaurant La Pâte Brisée

65 rue de la Monnaie; close to Hospice-Comtesse museum in the old Lille. **Map C1-15**
Ⓣ03.20.74.29.00 Ⓕ03.20.13.80.47
Disabled access.

In the face of stiff competition, this restaurant is still the place for sweet and savoury tarts – Roquefort, Maroilles cheese or *tarte tatin* – and regional baked cheese dishes like *tartiflette* with potatoes, diced bacon, braised onion and melted Maroilles cheese. The reasonably priced *formules*, €7.80–15.70, include drinks, and portions are generous. There's a relaxed atmosphere, with a mainly student clientèle; it's packed at lunchtime so it's best to arrive early. After 2.15pm, it also doubles as a tearoom. *Free coffee offered to our readers on presentation of this guide.*

|●| Restaurant Les Brasseurs

18 pl. de la Gare. **Map D2-25**
Ⓣ03.20.06.46.25 Ⓕ03.20.06.46.29
Closed *Christmas Day.*

If only there were more places like this lively, friendly pub. You can choose from several brews including amber, Scotch, Lille white and a pale ale, all brewed on the premises using the best barleys and hops – count on €2–10 for a pitcher containing 1.6l. There's an extensive menu, too, from *tartines hollandaises* to more substantial grills and brasserie dishes including *flammenküche* – you'll be hard pressed to finish the ham hock *choucroute*. *Formules* start at €10 lunch and dinner time; you'll pay around €15 for a meal, if you're famished go for the *formule* "*Choucroute Brasseurs*" with beer.

|●| Les Faits Divers

44 rue de Gard. **Map C1-24**
Ⓣ03.20.21.03.63 Ⓕ03.20.31.48.53
Closed *Sat, Sun and Mon lunchtimes; public holidays.*

There's a convivial, dynamic atmosphere in this brightly coloured, vaguely retro restaurant and welcoming, attentive service – you'll have a great evening. The customers may be cool and youthful, but the food is classic bourgeois fare: scallops in pastry cases with baby vegetables and curry-cream sauce, smoked salmon with scrambled eggs, a selection of fish with a cream and saffron sauce, duck leg *confit* with Salard potatoes, *croustillant* of banana and chocolate *fondue*. Menus €11 (lunchtimes) to €24. There's a choice of exotic coffees.

🏃 |●| Restaurant La Renaissance

29 pl. des Reignaux; train station Lille-Flandres area. **Map D2-16**
Ⓣ03.20.06.17.56
Closed *Mon and Tues evenings, Sun; 15 July–15 Aug.*

Cheap and cheerful place with the atmosphere of a Parisian bistro, serving excellent family cooking and regional specialities. Try their mussels, ox kidneys, *potjevfleisch* (a veal, rabbit and chicken pâté), Maroilles cheese tart, Flemish *carbonade*, *andouillette*

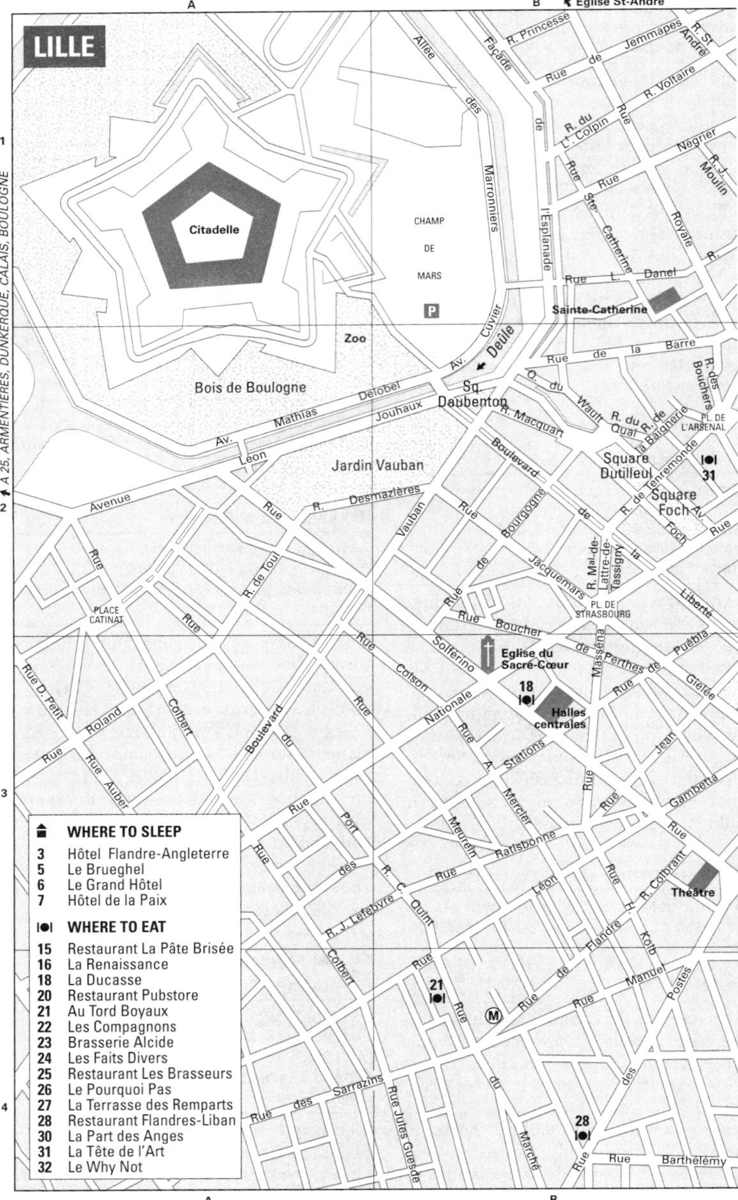
LILLE
A
B
Église St-André
1
2
3
4
A 25, ARMENTIÈRES, DUNKERQUE, CALAIS, BOULOGNE
Citadelle
Zoo
Bois de Boulogne
CHAMP DE MARS
P
Jardin Vauban
Sq. Daubenton
Sainte-Catherine
Square Dutilleul
Square Foch
PL. DE L'ARSENAL
PL. DE STRASBOURG
PLACE CATINAT
Eglise du Sacré-Cœur
Halles centrales
Théâtre
Deûle
Allée des Marronniers
Av. Cuvier
Av. Mathias Delobel
Av. Léon Jouhaux
Avenue
R. Princesse
Façade de l'Esplanade
Rue de Jemmapes
R. St André
R. Voltaire
R. du L. Colpin
Rue Royale
Rue Ste. Catherine
Rue Négrier
R. J. Moulin
Rue L. Danel
Rue de la Barre
R. des Bouchers
Q. du Wault
R. du Quai
R. de la Baignerie
R. Macquart
Boulevard Vauban
R. Desmazières
R. de Tenremonde
Av. Foch
Rue de Bourgogne
Rue de Jacquemars
R. Mal-de-Lattre-de-Tassigny
Rue Liberté
R. de Toul
Rue Solférino
Rue Boucher de Perthes
Rue Colson
Rue Nationale
Rue Masséna
Rue Puébla
Rue Gielée
Rue Jean
Rue D. Petit
Rue Roland
Rue Colbert
Boulevard du
Rue Auber
Rue A. Mercier
Rue des Stations
Rue Meurein
Rue Ratisbonne
Rue Gambetta
R. Colbrant
Rue Port
Rue des
R. C. Quint
R. J. Lefebvre
Rue Léon
Rue H. Kolb
Rue de Flandre
Rue Manuel
Rue des Postes
Rue du Marché
Rue des Sarrazins
Rue Jules Guesde
Rue Barthélemy
M
18
21
28
31
WHERE TO SLEEP
3 Hôtel Flandre-Angleterre
5 Le Brueghel
6 Le Grand Hôtel
7 Hôtel de la Paix
WHERE TO EAT
15 Restaurant La Pâte Brisée
16 La Renaissance
18 La Ducasse
20 Restaurant Pubstore
21 Au Tord Boyaux
22 Les Compagnons
23 Brasserie Alcide
24 Les Faits Divers
25 Restaurant Les Brasseurs
26 Le Pourquoi Pas
27 La Terrasse des Remparts
28 Restaurant Flandres-Liban
30 La Part des Anges
31 La Tête de l'Art
32 Le Why Not

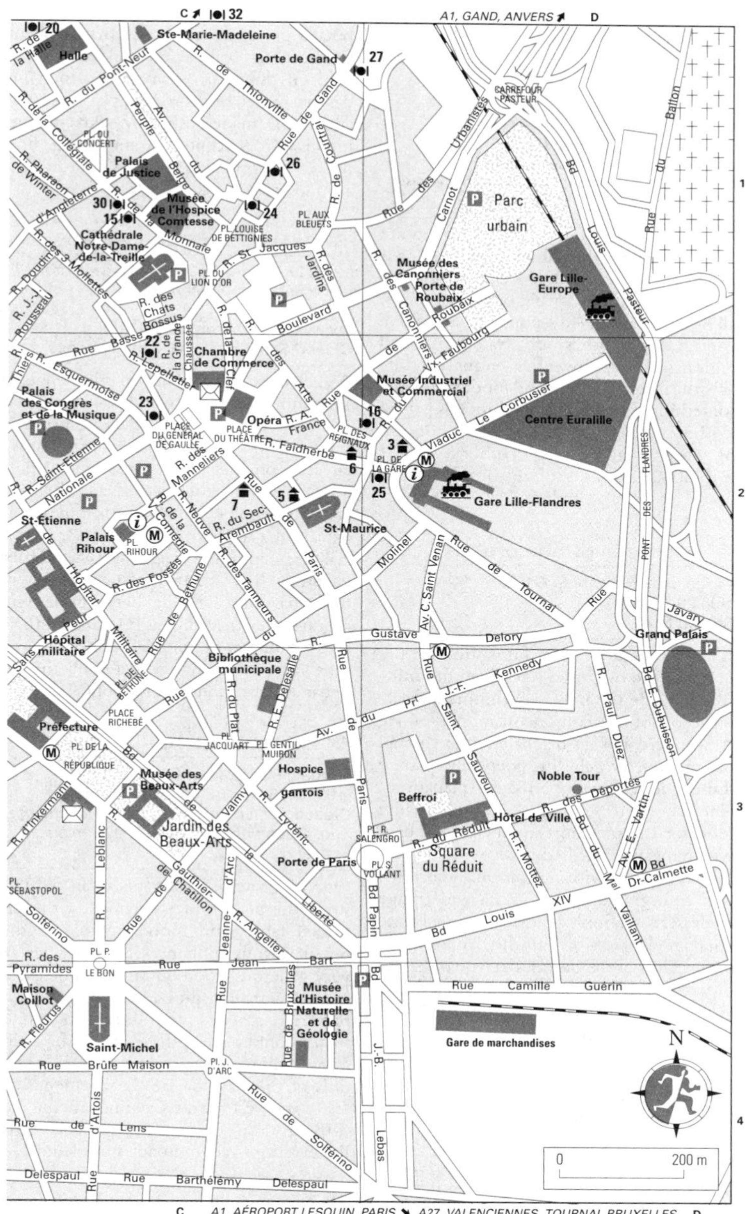

C
32
A1, GAND, ANVERS
D
20
Halle
Ste-Marie-Madeleine
Porte de Gand
27
CARREFOUR PASTEUR
Palais de Justice
26
Musée de l'Hospice Comtesse
30
15
24
Cathédrale Notre-Dame-de-la-Treille
PL. AUX BLEUETS
PL. LOUISE DE BETTIGNIES
Parc urbain
Musée des Canonniers
Porte de Roubaix
Gare Lille-Europe
22
Chambre de Commerce
Musée Industriel et Commercial
Palais des Congrès et de la Musique
23
Opéra
16
Centre Euralille
PLACE DU GÉNÉRAL DE GAULLE
PLACE DU THÉÂTRE
3
6
25
7
5
Gare Lille-Flandres
St-Étienne
Palais Rihour
St-Maurice
Hôpital militaire
Bibliothèque municipale
Grand Palais
PLACE RICHEBÉ
Préfecture
PL. DE LA RÉPUBLIQUE
Hospice gantois
Musée des Beaux-Arts
Noble Tour
Beffroi
Hôtel de Ville
Jardin des Beaux-Arts
Porte de Paris
Square du Réduit
PL. SÉBASTOPOL
PL. P. LE BON
Maison Coillot
Musée d'Histoire Naturelle et de Géologie
Gare de marchandises
Saint-Michel
PL. J. D'ARC
N
0
200 m
1
2
3
4
C
A1, AÉROPORT LESQUIN, PARIS
A27, VALENCIENNES, TOURNAI, BRUXELLES
D

flambéed with gin and any of the home-made desserts. Menus €12.50 and €14. You'll pay around €15 for a menu à la carte. *Free Kir offered to our readers on presentation of this guide.*

Le Why Not

9 rue Maracci. **Off map C1-32**
T 03.20.74.14.14 F 03.20.74.14.15
Closed *Sat lunchtime; Sun (open by reservation only).*

The affable and attentive welcome is quite in keeping with the authentic, warm décor in this beautiful vaulted cellar. There are small tables for two or big ones for groups, all arranged higgledy-piggledy around a central bar. Dishes are traditional and regional, though inventive enough to satisfy the most exacting of foodies. There's something for all budgets on menus priced €12.50 with starter/dish of the day or dish of the day/dessert, other menus €15.50–28.50. Lots of reasonably priced options on the wine list.

Restaurant Pubstore

44 rue de la Halle. **Map C1-20**
T 03.20.55.10.31
Closed *Sun.*

A busy restaurant on a busy street in the north of the old town – it's even full mid-week. Inside the lights are dimmed, creating a sort of old-fashioned gangster-movie atmosphere, but it's bright enough to read the menus, which list poetically named dishes and their more prosaic explanations. They've been serving the same quality food for the past thirty years: grilled ham with pineapple, grilled steak with vegetables, veal chop with mushrooms and noodles with grated cheese, and a wide range of desserts to finish you off. At lunchtime you can choose a dish of the day for €8, a starter/dish of the day/dessert/quarter litre of wine for €13. You'll pay around €22 à la carte. Decent wine, too, with a house red for around €10.

La Terrasse des Remparts

Rue de Gard. **Map C1-27**
T 03.20.06.74.74 F 03.20.06.74.70
W www.lecocq.fr/remparts

This place combines a softly lit seating area with red brick walls and a veranda on two levels that opens onto a terrace in good weather. Warm welcome and efficient, attentive service. The menus list appetizing dishes which change with the seasons, and there are plenty of regional specialities: potato pie with crab and horn of plenty mushrooms, brill with pickled chicory, venison haunch with aubergine. The dessert buffet offers a panoply of pastries and home-made sorbets. Weekdays lunch menu €15 (except Sun and public holidays), with others up to €24.50. You'll pay around €30 à la carte.

Restaurant Flandres-Liban

125–127 rue des Postes. 5min away from place Sébastopol. **Map B4-28**
T 03.20.54.89.92
W www.flandresliban.com
Closed *Sun evening.* **Disabled access.**

A Lebanese restaurant on the edge of Wazemmes, the last working-class part of Lille. The décor, with its delicate panels of carved wood, fountains and hangings, is a far cry from the usual places around here. They do a very good *mezzé*, and the waiters, whose polite demeanour is impeccable, explain the secrets of the twenty or so specialities: hummus, *shwarma*, *kofte* kebabs, cucumber and yoghurt, chicken kebab with three flavours, *kebbé* (a beef rissole with ground wheat). Menus at €16 and €20; à la carte you'll pay around €15. These are reasonable prices for what is definitely the best Lebanese restaurant in or around Lille.

Le Pourquoi-Pas

62 rue de Gard. **Map C1-26**
T 03.20.06.25.86 F 03.20.31.68.35
Closed *Sat lunchtime; Sun; Mon lunchtime; Aug.* **Open** *until 11pm weekdays, midnight weekends.*

One of a row of restaurants in an old Lille street, this place is nicely refined, with well-spaced tables and mood lighting. Dishes reveal various influences and servings are very generous; good options include *émincé* of veal with foie gras and fresh tagliatelle, pan-fried scallops with Bourbon vanilla, snail profiteroles with garlic and parsley cream, and perfectly cooked steak. There's a dish of the day for €8, lunch menus for €11 and €14 and evening menus for €18–28. You could also go à la carte. Reservations recommended weekends.

Au Tord Boyaux

11 pl. Nouvelle-Aventure; close to the market in Wazemmes. **Map B4-21**

Ⓣ and Ⓕ03.20.57.73.67
Closed *Sat and Sun evenings.*

Based in Wazemmes, this family place serves good, substantial and tasty food – if pheasant *choucroute* is on the menu, order it. Monique, the lovely owner, uses fresh seasonal produce, depending on what is good at the market, and the food is always great. Meat dishes cost about €11.90–16.80, while the dish of the day (not offered at weekends) will cost between €9 and €12, salad €6.90. À la carte you'll spend around €19. It's particularly popular for Sunday lunch when you may have to book.

Brasserie Alcide

5 rue des Débris-Saint-Étienne; close to the Grande-Place. **Map C2-23**
Ⓣ03.20.12.06.95

Come here to experience the discreet charm of the bourgeois brasserie; uniformed waiters standing in line, an oak bar, large mirrors – and an equally discreet middle-aged clientele. Menus €20–38 and dishes of the day around €11; *carbonade* with three beers, monkfish *tournedos* wtih bacon and beer sauce, stuffed pig's trotters, *waterzoï*, *cassoulet* with meat *confit*, salmon and leek *andouillette*, fisherman's stew and so on.

Les Compagnons de la Grappe

22 rue Lepelletier. **Map C2-22**
Ⓣ03.20.21.02.79
Closed *Sun.* **Open** *all year, noon–3pm and 7pm–midnight.*

Hidden in a narrow passage, this is one of the nicest restaurants in Lille. The terrace is crammed in sunny weather while the two dining rooms have lovely wood panelling and designer lighting. They're great places to eat handsome portions of well-cooked bistro classics with a modern twist. The bread deserves a special mention, too. There's a menu at €20 and a lunchtime dish of the day for €8. You'll pay around €25 à la carte .There's an extensive wine list, with many offered by the glass. *Free house liqueur offered to our readers on presentation of this guide.*

La Ducasse

96 rue Solférino. **Map B3-18**
Ⓣ03.20.57.34.10
Closed *Sat lunchtime; Sun. 3–24 Aug.*

An old-style local restaurant recently taken over by a new team. Wisely, they have left things well alone – the long carved benches, the traditional tables and a truly lovely counter. In a corner there's a mechanical music player dated 1910 that is activated once in a while, but the huge wooden jukebox seems to be there just for show. The authentic bistro cuisine features veal kidneys, *cassolette* of seafood, chicken *fricassée*, shrimp *croquettes*, prawns cooked in Gueuze, huge salads and a Flemish platter featuring three specialities. Good desserts, too, and Flemish beers. Dish of the day €7.50, you'll pay around €22 for a menu à la carte without any drinks. *Free house apéritif offered to our readers on presentation of this guide.*

La Tête de l'Art

10 rue de l'Arc. **Map B2-31**
Ⓣ and Ⓕ03.20.54.68.89
Ⓦwww.latetedelart.com
Closed *Sun; Mon–Thurs evenings. Aug.*

It's worth booking a table at this quiet little restaurant in a quiet little street. They serve excellent *formules* for €21.50 and €23.50 wine included (weekdays lunchtimes, Fri and Sat evening), with a menu for €25. You'll pay around €25 à la carte. Reservations recommended.

La Part des Anges

50 rue de la Monnaie; centre of the old city. **Map C1-30**
Ⓣ03.20.06.44.01
Ⓦwww.europe-shopping.com
Closed *Sun evening.* **Disabled access.**

A noisy Parisian-style wine bar in the busiest street in the middle of the old town. There's a selection of at least twenty wines, some of which come from unusual shippers, and a few foreign wines including a Pinot Blanc from Egypt. The split-level dining room, all paint effects and voluminous green plants, buzzes with business people, yuppies and students enjoying decent bistro food. A blackboard lists the dishes of the day. At lunchtime on Sundays, you can have a charcuterie or cheese platter, and snacks are always served at the bar. Expect to pay €23 for a meal.

Villeneuve-d'Ascq

59650 (8km E)

Restaurant Les Charmilles

98 av. de Flandre.

Ⓣ and Ⓕ03.20.72.40.30
Closed *Wed and three weeks in Aug.*

A very spacious dining room, painted pale and olive green, ideal for intimate meals for two. The cooking is creative, with menus €12–13.50 lunchtime weekdays, €20 evenings, €27–31 Sunday lunchtime. You'll pay around €22 à la carte. Creative and original food. Good value for money.

Maroilles

59550

L'Estaminet

83 Grand'Rue; it's opposite the church.
Ⓣ03.27.77.78.80
Closed *Sun evening.* **High chairs available.**

A typical village restaurant in the town that produces the famous local cheese. Over the years this place has established a solid reputation for good, reliable local and regional dishes. The €11 weekdays menu offers two courses, and there's another at €16.80, along with à la carte choices. The dishes of the day are listed on a blackboard. You might get steak with Maroilles cheese sauce, mushroom tart, *andouillette* or a good selection of cheeses. Wines are reasonably priced. It's best to phone for a weekend or evening reservation out of season. *Free liqueur offered to our readers on presentation of this guide.*

Locquignol

59530 (6km NW)

Auberge du Croisil

Route de Maroilles; from Maroilles or Le Quesnoi, follow the D233, and it's signposted 3km from Maroilles.
Ⓣ03.27.34.20.14 Ⓕ03.27.34.20.15
Closed *Sun and Tues evenings except public holidays; 22 Dec–14 Feb.* **High chairs and games available.**

This inn, way out in the Mormal forest, serves splendid traditional dishes, prepared by the boss, in a tranquil atmosphere. The terrines and goose *cassoulet* are winners, not to mention the scallops *à la provençale*, pigeon *chasseur* and calf's liver *à la lyonnaise*. The menus, €11 weekdays, other menus €17.50–23, change every week; in the hunting season they do a lot of game, including wild boar cutlets with green peppercorns and delicious venison steak with raspberry. They also offer a couple of double rooms, €23, with shared washing facilities. *Free apéritif offered to our readers on presentation of this guide.*

Maubeuge

59600

Le Grand Hôtel – Restaurant de Paris**

1 porte de Paris; it's near the station.
Ⓣ03.27.64.63.16 Ⓕ03.27.65.05.76
Ⓦwww.grandhotelmaubeuge.fr
TV. High chairs and games available. Disabled access. Pay car park

The best restaurant in the area, a place for family celebrations and business lunches. Menus from €13–55 list lots of local produce: fish, seafood and game in season. Renovated rooms go for €49 with basin, €53–60 with shower/wc or bath. *Free house apéritif offered to our readers on presentation of this guide.*

Montreuil-sur-Mer

62170

Le Darnétal

Place Darnétal.
Ⓣ03.21.06.04.87 Ⓕ03.21.86.64.67
Closed *Mon; Tues; end June to early July; end Dec.*

Traditional hotel on a lovely little square in the old town. The restaurant, which boasts a collection of great antiques, serves lots of delicate, delicious fish dishes: try the poached turbot with hollandaise sauce, lobster in pastis or warm oysters in champagne. Menus at €16 (weekdays), €23 and €30. The four spacious, if rather bare, guest rooms are decorated in late nineteenth-century style. Ask to see them before handing over your money, because they're very different. Doubles €35–50 with shower/wc or bath.

Le Clos des Capucins**

46 pl. du Général-de-Gaulle.
Ⓣ03.21.06.08.65 Ⓕ03.21.81.20.45
Closed *Sun evening; Mon; Thurs evening in winter.* **Disabled access. TV.**

A neat, pretty dining room and a lovely welcome – you just know you're going to have a good meal. It's a particular favourite of English foodies who've popped across the channel for a gourmet experience. Good options include house smoked salmon or Saint-Vaast oysters, half-cooked duck foie gras, grilled crayfish with herbs from Provence or *pot-au-feu* of pork shoulder with cabbage. They have a choice of good, well-matured cheeses to finish. Menus €18–36.50, and good wines from €15 a bottle. Above the restaurant, there are a few rooms for €53 with shower/wc or bath.

Madelaine-sous-Montreuil (La)

62170 (3km W)

Auberge de la Grenouillère*

It's in the centre of the village by the river.
Ⓣ03.21.06.07.22 Ⓕ03.21.86.36.36
Ⓦwww.lagrenouillere.fr
Closed *Tues; Wed except July/Aug; Jan.*
Disabled access. High chairs available. Car park.

This old coaching inn, down in the Canche valley, has several rooms where you can have a drink and a dining room with real charm – low beams, a fire, copper pots and decorative frogs (have a look at the murals). In summer you dine in a pretty flower garden. The chef has reinvented local dishes to create delicate, interestingly seasoned food, and has been awarded a Michelin star for his trouble. Menus €26 (not served Sat evening or public holidays), €45 and €70, with affordable wines. There are four perfectly charming rooms in the old stable block for €75–95 with shower/wc or bath.

Auberge du Vieux Logis

Place de la Mairie; take the D139 or the D917 and it's at the foot of the walls.
Ⓣ and Ⓕ03.21.06.10.92
Closed *Tues evening; Wed.*

Rustic country inn serving traditional dishes using quality produce: house *cassoulet* with goose fat, veal kidneys Vieux Logis and excellent grilled beef. There are a few modish selections, too, including *carpaccio* of raw fish. They have four menus called *Solo* (one dish), *Duo*, *Trio* and *Quatuor* (the last consisting of starter, main course, cheese and dessert) for €11–26 or you'll pay around €25–30 for a menu à la carte. In fine weather you can eat on the terrace.

Saint-Omer

62500

Hôtel-Restaurant le Vivier

22 rue Louis Martel. Near place Foch and place Victor-Hugo.
Ⓣ03.21.95.76.00
Ⓔlevivier@wanadoo.fr
Closed *Sun evening.* **TV.**

A charming hotel situated in the pedestrianized centre of this attractive town. Good-looking, clean rooms with all facilities; doubles cost €52 with shower/wc or bath, hairdryer, mini-bar, TV and phone. Appetizing dishes and regional specialities are served in the pleasant dining room: try fresh fish or any of the numerous shellfish and seafood platters including grilled lobster. Menus at €16 (not Sat evening or Sun), then €22 and €34. Friendly, efficient service. *Free coffee offered to our readers on presentation of this guide.*

Hôtel Saint-Louis – Restaurant Le Flaubert**

25 rue d'Arras.
Ⓣ03.21.38.35.21 Ⓕ03.21.38.57.26
Ⓦwww.hotel-saintlouis.com
Closed *Sat and Sun lunchtimes; 22 Dec–4 Jan.* **Disabled access. TV. High chairs available. Car park.**

The hotel has been around since the 1920s, though it has been attractively renovated since. Calm, comfortable rooms from €59.80 with shower/wc to €60.80 with bath/wc. There's a €13 weekday menu; those at €16.60–28 list more elaborate and upmarket dishes. Specialities include fish *choucroute*, duck *confit* and *cassoulet*. Friendly, retro bar. *10% discount on the room rate (Jan–Feb) or free coffee offered to our readers on presentation of this guide.*

Auberge du Bachelin

12 bd. de Strasbourg.
Ⓣ03.21.38.42.77
Closed *Sun evening; Mon; Tues, Wed and Thurs evenings (except for reservations for a minimum of 15).*

A friendly restaurant decorated in sunny colours. Menus €12.60–21.70. On Friday they make couscous; other specialities include perch fillet with garlic, fish stew and beef *carbonade* with beer. The service is pleasant and efficient.

Blendecques

62575 (4km SE)

Le Saint-Sébastien**

2 Grand'Place; take exit at 4 or 5km off the A26.
Ⓣ03.21.38.13.05 Ⓕ03.21.39.77.85
Ⓔsaint-sebastien@wanadoo.fr
Closed *Sun evening; Mon.* **Disabled access. TV.**

Stone-built inn on a pretty square, with pleasant, comfortable rooms; doubles €45 with shower/wc or bath. In the nice rustic restaurant you'll find dishes like *andouille* salad, chicken *fricassée* with vinegar, *croustillant* of pigs' ears, pan-fried pigs' tripe, veal kidneys with Houlle juniper and local ale pie. Menus €14 or €32 à la carte. *Free coffee offered to our readers on presentation of this guide.*

Touquet (Le)

62520

Hôtel Le Chalet**

15 rue de la Paix; take the A16. It's 60m from the sea.
Ⓣ03.21.05.87.65 Ⓕ03.21.05.47.49
Ⓦwww.lechalet.fr
TV.

This hotel offers spick and span rooms at prices that are more than reasonable for Le Touquet. Doubles with basin and shower go for €30–42 or €48–60 with shower/wc or bath. Some rooms look onto a small patio. You'll pay the top price if you want a balcony and a view of the sea – it's more of a glimpse than a view. *One breakfast per room per night offered to our readers on presentation of this guide.*

Hôtel Blue Cottage**

41 rue Jean-Monnet; it's behind the market place.
Ⓣ03.21.05.15.33
Ⓔbluecottage@wanadoo.fr
Open *daily for lunch and Fri–Sat evenings.* **Closed** *Mon from mid-Nov to end March.* **TV. High chairs available. Car park.**

Reasonably priced hotel with pretty blue and yellow rooms. Doubles €30–78 with basin, depending on season, €45–85 with shower/wc. It's one of the few places in pricey Touquet to offer half board, which costs €34 per person and is preferred July–Aug. In the restaurant there are menus at €10 weekdays, others €12–30. Good dishes include grilled fish, seafood platters and vegetarian specialities.

Hôtel Les Embruns**

89 rue de Paris. Access A16.
Ⓣ03.21.05.87.61 Ⓕ03.21.05.85.09
Ⓦwww.letouquet-hotel-les-embruns.com
Closed *15 Dec–15 Jan.* **Disabled access. TV.**

In a quiet situation set back from the road and not far from the sea. The simple, comfortable rooms are clean and attractive; some look onto the garden, others have terraces. Doubles €40–59 with shower/wc or bath; they also have rooms for three or four. The breakfast room is charming. You can park bikes or motorbikes in the garden. *10% discount on the room rate offered to our readers on presentation of this guide (for a minimum stay of two nights, out of high season).*

Hôtel Le Nouveau Caddy**

130 rue de Metz; it's opposite the covered market and 100m from the beach.
Ⓣ03.21.05.83.95 Ⓕ03.21.05.85.23
Ⓦwww.lenouveaucaddy.com
Reception closed *1–3.30pm, 1–9pm on Sun. Jan.* **Disabled access. TV. Pay car park.**

Tastefully decorated, welcoming hotel with four floors (and a lift), each painted a different colour to represent a different season. All the rooms are pleasant and comfortable with en-suite bathrooms; doubles €50–80. Eveything is pleasant and charming, breakfast room, reception, interior decoration…

Auberge L'Arlequin

91 rue de Paris; it's near rue Saint-Jean and the seafront.
Ⓣ03.21.05.39.11 Ⓕ03.21.06.13.06
Ⓦwww.restaurantarlequin.com
Closed *Wed May to end Sept; Wed and Thurs Oct to end April; 20 Dec–31 Jan.* **High chairs available.**

A classic, small restaurant where the owner cooks straightforward dishes: monkfish kebab with cabbage, rabbit with mustard, *coq au vin* and skate with raspberry vinegar. The cheap weekday menu, €14, is well balanced, and there are others at €17 and €23.

Restaurant Au Diamant Rose

110 rue de Paris.

☎03.21.05.38.10 ℻03.21.05.89.75
Closed *Tues except July–Aug; Wed. Jan.*
Disabled access.

This pastel pink restaurant attracts a loyal crowd of regulars and quiet holidaymakers who lap up the traditional, honest French cuisine. Typical dishes include salmon marinated in lemon, grilled prawns with garlic, frogs' legs, poached monkfish with sorrel, duck thigh *confit* in goose fat, foie gras and *fruits de mer* – and they've got a good wine list. They have menus for €17–23 and à la carte.

|●| Les Deux Moineaux

12 rue Saint-Jean.
☎03.21.0509.67
Closed *Mon and Tues.*

This brick-walled dining room has a warm, intimate atmosphere, with gentle jazz playing in the background. The owner will welcome you pleasantly and the staff are equally kind. Try the *fricassée* of mussels, the prawns pan-fried in pastis, the poached turbot in white sauce or the beef goulash, finishing with an array of well-matured regional cheeses or chocolate *fondant* with lavender caramel. Menus from €18 except Sunday and up to €27. You'll pay around €30 à la carte. The wine list has a few reasonably priced bottles.

Étaples

62630 (5km E)

|●| Aux Pêcheurs d'Étaples

Quai de la Canche (boulevard de l'Impératrice).
☎03.21.94.06.90
Closed *Sun evening; end Dec to end Jan.*

The ground floor is occupied by a fishmonger's run by the maritime cooperative of this lively little fishing port – and it is this fishmonger's that supplies the restaurant upstairs, so the the ingredients could not be fresher. There is the inevitable seafood platter, simply prepared, with contents that vary according to the latest catch. A bit expensive overall, but the quality cannot be faulted. Menus €15–25. Reckon on €30 à la carte. The dining room is decorated in appropriately nautical blue and white, and there's a pretty view of the Canche if you get the right table. The service is efficient, not to say hyperactive.

Saint-Josse

62170 (7km SE)

|●| L'Auberge du Moulinel

116 chaussée de l'Avant Pays, in Moulinel; take the road to Moulinel, go under the motorway and 2km further there's a sign where you turn left.
☎03.21.94.79.03 ℻03.21.09.37.14
Closed *Mon and Tues except for school holidays; 10 days in Jan; 1st week in June.*

One of the best restaurants along the Opal coast, housed in a restored farmhouse way out in the countryside between Le Touquet and Montreuil-sur-Mer. It's run by Alain Lévy who produces deftly prepared dishes. The chef likes to use strong flavours and unusual but intriguing flavour combinations. Good choices and affordable wines. Menus €25–51. Book to avoid disappointment.

Tourcoing

59200

|●| Restaurant Le Rustique

206 rue de l'Yser; from the town centre follow rue de Gand for 3km as it leads into rue de l'Yser.
☎03.20.94.44.62
Open *lunchtime only; Fri and Sat evenings by reservation.* **Closed** *Mon.* **High chairs available. Car park.**

The surroundings have a rustic feel – logs burn in the fireplace and copper pans hang from the walls – but the service and food are rather more refined. Dishes include steak with Carré du Vinage cheese, ham on the bone, scallops on the shell, house foie gras, rack of lamb with herbs and some regional specialities. This is gourmet food at modest prices. Weekday lunch menu €10.52 (Tues–Fri), with other menus at €22.60–41, drinks included, or around €24 à la carte. You can eat on the terrace when the weather is fine. *Free house apéritif offered to our readers on presentation of this guide.*

Trélon

59132

|●| Le Framboisier

1 rue F-Ansieau.
☎03.27.59.73.34

Closed *Sun evening and Mon except during public holidays; a fortnight end Feb; 3 weeks Aug–Sept.* **Disabled access. High chairs available.**

A rare oasis of quality in a culinary desert, run by a couple who wanted to improve the region's gastronomic reputation. The dining room is fresh and pleasant, with sturdy beams, pink paint, pictures on the walls and classical music playing in the background. Service is quietly efficient. The dishes are full of new flavours and often inspired, changing depending on what's available in the markets. Try home-smoked salmon, fresh fish – sardines, skate, turbot, scallops – game in season, pan-fried foie gras with caramel, or the regional platter. The home-made desserts are great too. You'll pay for menus from €13–37 and for a main course "Assiettes de pays" €10–12 drinks included. They host theme evenings twice a month. It's best to book at the weekend. *Free house apéritif offered to our readers on presentation of this guide.*

Valenciennes

59300

Le Bristol**

2 av. de-Lattre-de-Tassigny; it's near the train station.
Ⓣ03.27.46.58.88 Ⓕ03.27.29.94.51
Closed *15–22 Aug.* **TV.**

There's nothing original about this hotel, but it's quiet and clean, the pleasant staff have ready smiles and there's a bar. Some of the light, spacious rooms overlook a courtyard and others the street – fortunately you don't hear the trains. Good-value doubles with basin go for €29, €38 with shower, €44 with shower/wc or bath.

Hôtel Le Clemenceau**

39 rue du Rempart; it's 300m from the Grand'Place and 200m from the train station.
Ⓣ03.27.30.55.55 Ⓕ03.27.30.55.56
TV. Disabled access. High chairs available.

Right near the station, this is a solid red-brick hotel with about twenty rooms, all with double glazing, fully equipped bathroom, hairdryer and safe. Doubles €45.75–51.85, which is good value for money; breakfast buffet €5.50. *10% discount on the room rate at weekends offered to our readers on presentation of this guide.*

Hôtel Notre-Dame**

1 pl. de l'Abbé-Thellier-de-Poncheville; it's opposite the basilica of Notre-Dame.
Ⓣ03.27.42.30.00 Ⓕ03.27.45.12.68
Ⓦwww.hotelnotredame.fr
Open *all year 24hrs a day.* **TV. Car park.**

Charming little hotel in a converted convent. The interior decoration is chic but not flashy, and staff are pleasant. Doubles with shower/wc or bath €56–62. No. 36, on the ground floor, looks out onto the indoor garden and is superb. *10% discount on the room rate (20 May–20 Sept) offered to our readers on presentation of this guide.*

Le Grand Hôtel – Restaurant du Grand Hôtel***

8 pl. de la Gare.
Ⓣ03.27.46.32.01 Ⓕ03.27.29.65.57
Ⓦwww.grand-hotel.de.valenciennes.fr
TV. Pay car park.

In a superb 1930s building just opposite the station, this thoroughly refurbished hotel boasts an elegant interior and spacious, attractive rooms. Doubles with shower/wc or bath are from €82 and a supplement of €8 for the third person is asked. The splendid dining room has a lofty ceiling, a Tiffany stained-glass dome, columns, heavy curtains, old-fashioned lighting and long banquettes – totally beguiling. Great cooking, too. They offer a splendid selection of regional dishes and classic family favourites: home-made *potje vleesh*, pig cheek *confit* in a stew served with lentils, calf's tongue *à la flamande*, beef *carbonade*, shepherd's pie, *mousselline* of pike with Riesling, barbecued pigeon, flambéed veal kidneys and a trolley of home-made desserts. Menus €20–41.50, including a special *choucroute* menu, and good wines at all prices. Buffet breakfast €9.50. Good weekend offers, with up to 20% discount on the normal rates.

Auberge du Bon Fermier****

64 rue de Famars.
Ⓣ03.27.46.68.25 Ⓕ03.27.33.75.01
Ⓦwww.home-gastronomie.com
Closed *on 24 Dec.* **TV. High chairs available. Pay car park.**

An old coaching inn in a splendidly preserved listed building. Inside, the corridors are skewed and tilted, and the staircases are narrow; the place resembles a museum, with ornaments and trinkets displayed in the smallest nooks and crannies. The rooms are equally charming, decorated in medieval or classical style. Doubles €100–126 with shower/wc or bath. The restaurant offers menus from €23 (except Sun) then €27.50 and up to €47, with a number of local dishes: *millefeuille* with Maroilles cheese, *carbonade flamande* and local pear *du hainaut. 10% discount on the room rate (Fri, Sat and Sun if meal taken at the Auberge) offered to our readers on presentation of this guide.*

La Planche à Pain

1 rue d'Oultreman; it's 2min walking distance to the city centre.
03.27.46.18.28 03.27.30.98.01
Closed *3–26 Aug.* **High chairs available.**

A solid establishment in a quiet street. The dining room is cosy, and you feel cosseted as soon as you arrive. Everyone comes here for the quality traditional cooking – they prepare dishes from the region and from the Mediterranean, including pan-fried scallops with celery cream or warm king prawn salad with oyster mushrooms and foie gras. Lunchtime menu €13 and others €23–28. Reservations recommended. *Free house apéritif offered to our readers on presentation of this guide.*

Le Bistrot d'en Face

5 av. d'Amsterdam.
03.27.42.25.25
Closed *Sun evening.*

This is the bistro belonging to the gastronomic restaurant *Rouet* opposite. It's cheaper and more relaxed and the décor is fresh and pleasant. They serve wholesome home cooking, and there's a huge choice: navarin of lamb with spring vegetables, bowls of mussels, frogs' legs, fresh scallops, *blanquette de veau à l'ancienne, cassoulet, gratin* of *andouille* with Chablis, duck legs with wine and blackcurrants, beef steak and oysters... Menu €14 (not Sun or public holidays); around €25 à la carte.

Restaurant La Tourtière

32 rue E.-Macarez; it's just out of the town centre, near the tax office.
03.27.29.42.42
latourtiere@europost.org
Closed *Mon and Wed evenings; Sat lunchtime; 20 July–15 Aug.*

The outside is dreary, but it's much more friendly inside, with a relaxed, lively atmosphere. There's a menu du Nord and a menu d'Italie, and in general the food is a mixture of regional favourites and Italian specialities – sometimes they're even combined, as in the macaroni with Maroilles cheese. Good bets include Avesnois veal, steak with Maroilles, onion tart, and *tarte à la cassonade.* À la carte you'll find pizza and pasta, cheese and onion quiches and so on. Everything is served in vast portions. Menus €14 and €17.

Le Rouet

8 av. d'Amsterdam. In the city centre.
03.27.46.44.52
Closed *Mon; a fortnight in Aug.*

Well-established gastronomic restaurant that just keeps on going. The faded, classic décor shows its age, but no one minds. It's a classy crowd – business people, well-off retired folk, local dignitaries and the like – but everyone is treated the same and the service is so friendly that occasionally the waiters spend more time chatting than serving. The seafood – turbot, sea bream and king prawns – is wonderfully fresh, and all the dishes are brilliantly prepared. Menus €17–32 and great seafood platters.

L'Orangerie

128 rue du Quesnoi.
03.27.42.70.70
Closed *Sat lunchtime; Sun; Mon evening.*

Old local restaurant that's been transformed into a popular, lively, modern place. It has an easy-going, relaxed atmosphere with a warm setting and soft lighting. They serve fresh bistro dishes at affordable prices; the all-inclusive menu, €18, lists such dishes as *veal blanquette à l'ancienne*, grilled shoulder of lamb with thyme, salmon *escalope* with leek *fondue* and various salads and terrines. You'll pay around €20–25 à la carte. On Thurs, Fri and Sat nights they hold dances after dinner.

Wimereux

62930

Hôtel Du Centre

78 rue Carnot.
03.21.32.41.08 03.21.33.82.48
www.hotelducentre-wimereux.com
Closed *20 Dec–20 Jan.* **Restaurant closed** *Mon.* **TV. Pay car park.**

A well-established, Belle Époque, seriously run establishment in the centre of the town, just two minutes from the beach. Recently renovated bedrooms, clean and comfortable. Double rooms go for €48–75 with shower/wc or bath. The dining room is cheery and traditional; they offer a *formule* with two dishes for €14 and menus at €17 and €27 of traditional dishes. Faultless welcome.

⌂ |●| L'Atlantic***

Digue de Mer. 5 min walking distance to city centre.
Ⓣ03.21.32.41.01 Ⓕ03.21.87.46.17
Ⓦwww.atlantic-delpierre.com
Closed *Feb.* **Restaurant closed** *Sun evening; Mon lunchtime.* **TV. Car park.**

An impressive seafront place in one of the prettiest resorts on the Opal coast. There are eighteen spacious, bright rooms, fourteen of which look over the pedestrianized esplanade and the sea; doubles start at €70, or €84–117 with a sea view. Just the place for a truly relaxing weekend – but it's best to book. There are two restaurants – *La Liégeise* is the more stylish, with a good reputation – one of which is a brasserie with an airy dining room and a terrace serving good, decent fish dishes like fish soup and seafood platters. Menus start at €16.50 in the brasserie; in the restaurant they're priced at €31 to €61.

Basse-Normandie

Aigle (L')

61300

Toque et Vins

35 rue Pasteur.
02.33.24.05.27
Closed *Sun; Mon and Tues evenings.*

The cooking is done by an experienced chef who opened this small wine bar with a colleague who takes care of the wine. He serves wholesome dishes at reasonable prices in a bright dining room. Fresh seasonal produce is used and dishes are full of flavour. Good choices include Camembert fritters, caramelized apples with Calvados, homemade foie gras, *andouillette*, and smoked salmon with egg in aspic. There's a *formule* – dish of the day with a glass of wine – at €10.80; then menus €15.80–26.80. It's a good idea to reserve.

Saint-Michel-Tubeuf

61300 (3km E)

Auberge Saint-Michel

3km from L'Aigle, on the Paris road (N26).
02.33.24.20.12
Closed *Tues and Wed evenings; Thurs (open Thurs lunch on public holidays); 1st fortnight in Jan; lst 3 weeks in Sept.* **High chairs and games available. Car park.**

The charm of this country inn is barely diminished by its proximity to the main road. The tables are spread over several intimate, personalized rooms. The hearty food combines tradition with fresh ingredients, so this is a good place for authentic French cooking: poultry liver terrine, excellent veal kidneys with Calvados, *croustillant* with apples and a whole ladleful of *fromage blanc*. Menus €14.50–32. Diligent, friendly service. *Free coffee offered to our readers on presentation of this guide.*

Chandai

61300 (8.5km E)

Auberge L'Écuyer Normand

23 rte. de Verneuil; it's on the N26.
02.33.24.08.54
www.auberge-ecuyer-Normand.com
Closed *Mon; Sun and Wed evenings. Annual holiday out of season (eg fortnight in March).*

A stone and brick building fronted by evergreens. There's an inviting atmosphere in the hushed dining room with its open fire, beams and whitewashed walls. The gifted chef adds a personal, modern touch to good regional dishes: prawn *charlotte*, *galette* with boned pig's trotters, lacquered duckling with apples caramelized in Calvados. Home-made bread and ice-cream. His fish dishes are always good. Menus €22–35. Very warm welcome and attentive service.

Ferté-Frênel (La)

61550 (14km NW)

Le Paradis**

10 Grande-Rue.
02.33.34.81.33 02.33.84.97.52
wwwperso.wanadoo.fr/hotel.paradis/
Closed *Mon; Sun evening out of season; 3 weeks in Feb; a fortnight in Oct.* **Disabled access. TV.**

This attractive little village inn lives up to its name and has a homely, friendly atmosphere. The most romantic room is nestled under the roof. Doubles €30 with basin, €40–46 with shower/wc or bath. The

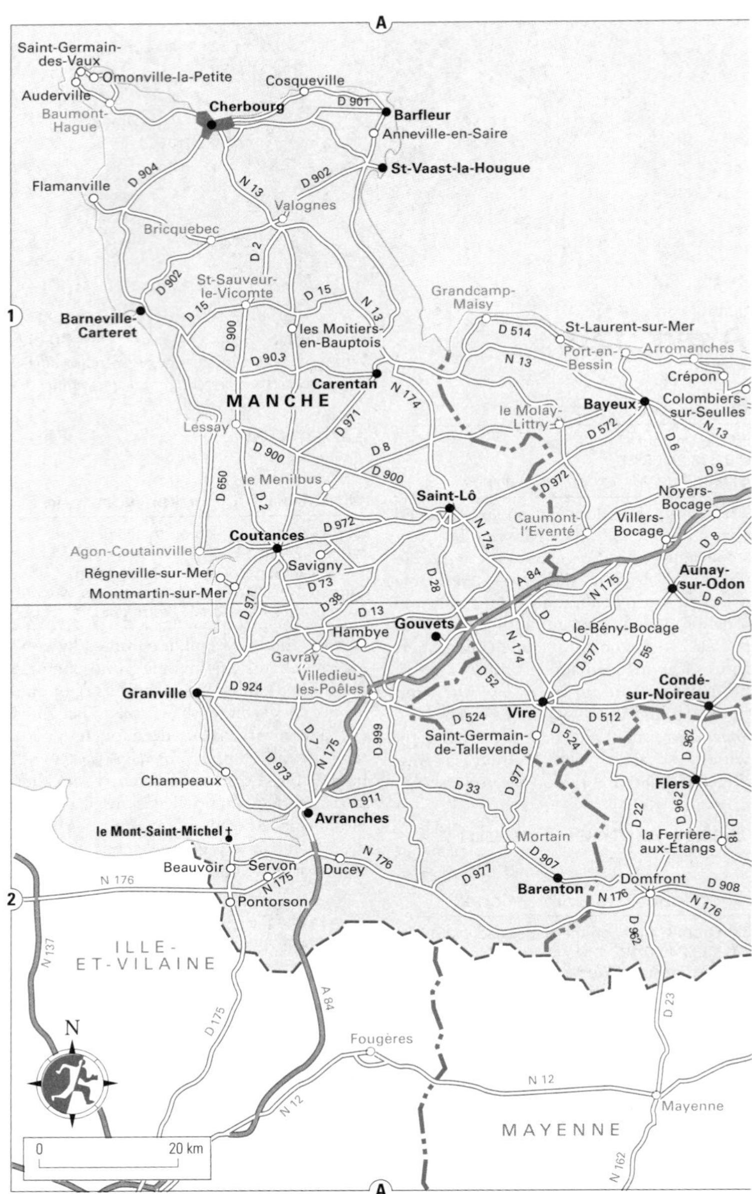
A
Saint-Germain-des-Vaux
Omonville-la-Petite
Auderville
Baumont-Hague
Cosqueville
Cherbourg
D 901
Barfleur
Anneville-en-Saire
St-Vaast-la-Hougue
Flamanville
D 904
N 13
D 902
Valognes
Bricquebec
D 2
D 902
St-Sauveur-le-Vicomte
D 15
N 13
Grandcamp-Maisy
1
Barneville-Carteret
D 15
D 900
les Moitiers-en-Bauptois
D 514
St-Laurent-sur-Mer
N 13
Port-en-Bessin
Arromanches
D 903
Carentan
Crépon
N 174
MANCHE
Bayeux
Colombiers-sur-Seulles
le Molay-Littry
Lessay
D 971
D 572
N 13
D 900
D 8
D 6
D 9
le Menilbus
D 900
D 972
D 650
D 2
Saint-Lô
Noyers-Bocage
Caumont-l'Eventé
Villers-Bocage
Coutances
D 972
N 174
D 8
Agon-Coutainville
Savigny
D 28
A 84
Aunay-sur-Odon
Régneville-sur-Mer
D 73
N 175
Montmartin-sur-Mer
D 971
D 38
D 6
D 13
Gouvets
D
Hambye
le-Bény-Bocage
N 174
Gavray
D 52
D 577
D 55
Villedieu-les-Poêles
Condé-sur-Noireau
Granville
D 924
Vire
D 524
D 512
Saint-Germain-de-Tallevende
D 524
D 7
N 175
D 999
D 962
D 973
Champeaux
D 33
D 977
Flers
D 911
Avranches
D 22
D 962
D 18
le Mont-Saint-Michel
Mortain
la Ferrière-aux-Étangs
N 176
D 907
Beauvoir
Servon
Ducey
D 977
N 175
Barenton
Domfront
D 908
N 176
2
N 176
N 176
Pontorson
D 962
N 137
ILLE-ET-VILAINE
A 84
D 23
D 175
N
Fougères
N 12
N 12
Mayenne
MAYENNE
0
20 km
N 162
A

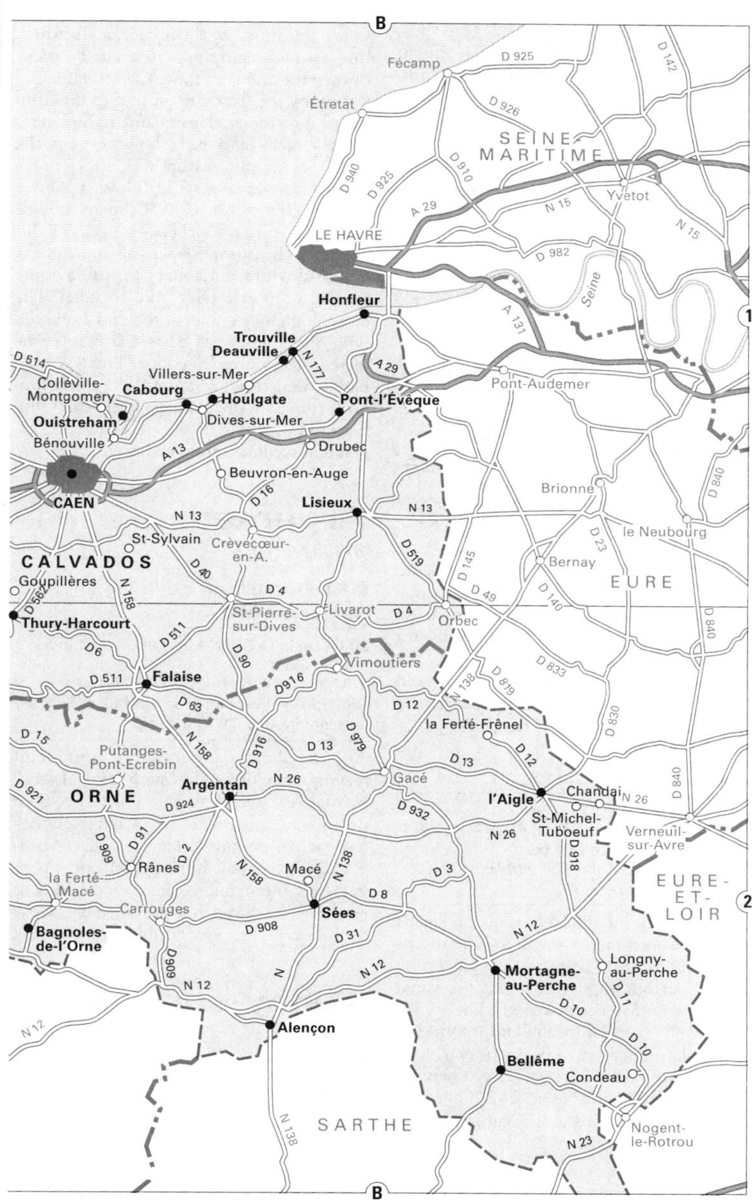

16 BASSE-NORMANDIE

restaurant serves generous portions of lovingly prepared, traditional dishes: mussels in cream sauce, young guinea fowl served with apples, sole flambéed in Calvados, *tarte tatin*. There's a €10 weekday menu and others €13.50–40. A meal à la carte will cost from €22. It's a very pleasant place to spend a summer or autumn evening. *Free apéritif, and 10% discount on the room rate offered to our readers on presentation of this guide 1 October–30 May.*

Alençon

61000

Le Chapeau Rouge

3 bd. Duchamp; 3 min from town centre via rue de Bretagne (turn left at the traffic lights), leaving town in the direction of N12 and Saint-Céneri.
Ⓣ02.33.26.20.23 Ⓕ02.33.26.54.05
TV. Car park.

A small, immaculately clean hotel, superbly run by a couple who offer friendly service, attention to detail and reasonable prices. Double rooms €32 with washbasin, €40 with shower, €45 with bath/wc. All are decorated in a Louis-XV style, with a thick carpet, rustic furniture, a large mirror, a small painting and... a red hat – a souvenir of the distinctive headgear worn by the coachmen who used to stop over in this old staging post. *10% discount on a room offered to our readers on presentation of this guide.*

Le Grand Cerf**

21 rue Saint-Blaise.
Ⓣ02.33.26.00.51 Ⓕ02.33.26.63.07
Ⓦwww.hotelgrandcerf-61.com
Closed *Sat lunchtime; Sun; public holidays; Christmas–New Year.* **TV.**

With its splendid 1843 Neoclassical façade this hotel has a faded grandeur. The rooms are spacious and fairly priced depending on the period, the comfort and the view; they're €47–59. Breakfast €6. The cooking is well regarded locally and is vying to be the best in town. The set menu costs €15; reckon on €25 à la carte. There's a business break available at €62. There are several dining rooms and a garden where they serve in summer.

Au Petit Vatel

72 pl. du Commandant-Desmeulles: near the Museum of Fine Arts and Lace.
Ⓣ02.33.26.23.78
Closed *Wed; Sun evening.* **High chairs and games available.**

Once the most stylish restaurant in town, this is re-emerging as a place to be reckoned with under its new owners. Don't be put off by the gaudy neon sign in the front – the interior is elegant and stylish, with silver cutlery and little bouquets on the table. Set menus €18.50–37, including a *Normandie* menu at €29. There is also a *Gourmand* meal at €69. Diligent service and highly professional cooking. Highlights include delicious nibbles, small apple cocktail, salad with Camembert *beignets* (a house speciality), perch fillet and cockerel. The crowning glory comes at the end, however, with the traditional dessert trolley, complete with impressive copper bowls, which has sealed the restaurant's reputation. Unfortunately, the place is a little stuffy, but it would probably be an ideal place to celebrate a wedding anniversary.

Argentan

61200

Hostellerie de la Renaissance**

20 av. de la Deuxième 2e-D-B; it's on the road to Flers.
Ⓣ02.33.36.14.20 Ⓕ02.33.36.65.50
Closed Sun evening; Mon; a week in Feb; a fortnight in Aug. **TV. Car park.**

An excellent contemporary restaurant serving delicious dishes with a novel slant: braised veal sweetbreads, sea bream cooked on its skin and a *moelleux* of bitter chocolate with coconut ice cream. Menus €15.24 (weekday lunchtimes) and up to €45. It's often full, so it's a good idea to reserve. The hotel has comfortable, well-soundproofed rooms; doubles are €56–60.

Aunay-sur-Odon

14260

Hôtel-restaurant Saint-Michel**

6–8 rue de Caen.
Ⓣ02.31.77.63.16 Ⓕ02.31.77.05.83
Closed *Sun evening and Mon (except July–Aug and public holidays); 15 Jan–15 Feb.* **Disabled access. High chairs available. TV. Car park.**

A pleasant country hotel with a modern

dining room that contrasts nicely with the traditional cooking they serve. The chef uses all the good things that Normandy produces. Menus €12–36, with a children's menu for €8. Decent, double bedrooms with basin or shower €30, shower and wc€38. Half board, €40, is compulsory over long weekends. *10% discount on the room rate offered to our readers from the third consecutive night on presentation of this guide.*

Avranches

50300

Hôtel de la Croix d'Or**

83 rue de la Constitution.
Ⓣ02.33.58.04.88 Ⓕ02.33.58.06.95
Closed *Sun evening mid-Oct to end March; Jan.* **High chairs available. TV. Car park.**

This delightful seventeenth-century coaching inn sits beside the monument to General Patton. It has a superb garden with a stone urn and an old cider press. Inside, it's like a museum with its stone walls, beams, enormous fireplace and walls hung with copper, pewter and earthenware pots – all very charming. Doubles with shower/wc €55 to €65 with bath. Service is impeccable in the attractive dining room. Try the *millefeuille* of crab with basil and peas, the small lobster casserole with sweetbread ravioli, the *moelleux* of pink trout with bacon or the turbot fillet in a potato crust. The lunch menu is priced at €15 and they have others €22.50–48. *Free coffee offered to our readers on presentation of this guide.*

Le Littré

8 rue du Dr-Gilbert; it's opposite the town hall.
Ⓣ02.33.58.01.66
Closed *Sun and Mon; last week in June; 1–8 July.* **Disabled access.**

This place doesn't look like much from the outside, but it's one of the nicest restaurants around and has a beautiful dining room. The traditional cuisine is consistently good – you could order the dish of the day with your eyes shut and depend upon it being great. Fish *choucroute* is the house speciality, or go for the eggs *en meurette* and the veal chops with artichokes. Menus €13.50 (weekday lunchtimes) and up to €16.50. Tasty desserts, including apple *clafoutis* (baked apple custard) and *pavé au chocolat*. Menus vary according to the season.

Ducey

50220 (10km SE)

Auberge de la Sélune**

2 rue Saint-Germain; take the the Ducey exit off the N176, and you'll find it on the left just before you get to the bridge.
Ⓣ02.33.48.53.62 Ⓕ02.33.48.90.30
Ⓦwww.selune.com
Closed *Mon 1 Oct–31 March; 20 Jan–10 Feb.* **Disabled access. High chairs available. TV. Car park.**

Originally a hospice, this huge inn is located on the old road to Mont-Saint-Michel. The comfortable bedrooms are attractively decorated with a personal touch. Double bedroom with bath costs €51.90. A lucky few will get a view of the garden that runs down to the slow-moving Sélune, one of the best trout and salmon rivers in France – it draws lots of fishermen, so pack your fishing rod. Carefully planned and executed menus at €14.70 (weekdays) up to €35.70. They serve specialities such as salmon with perry, trout soufflé, stuffed saddle of rabbit with cider vinegar, fillet of sole with Vermouth and crab pie. *Free digestif offered to our readers on presentation of this guide.*

Bagnoles-de-l'Orne

61140

La Potinière du Lac**

Rue des Casinos.
Ⓣ02.33.30.65.00 Ⓕ02.33.38.49.04
Ⓦwww.hoteldelapotiniere.com
Closed *Mon and Tues 1 Nov–31 March; fortnight end of March; mid-Dec to mid-Jan.* **TV. High chairs available.**

It's hard to miss this place because the façade, with its turret, is one of the prettiest and most striking in town. There's a view of the lake from the dining room and most of the bedrooms – the others look onto a main road which is very quiet at night. This is a nice place and prices are modest: double rooms €21–46. The turret room is rather special. The home cooking is simple and perfectly prepared, with many Normandy specialities; hot Camembert, skate salad, ham in cider. Menus €14–27.90. *Free coffee offered to our readers on presentation of this guide.*

Le Celtic**

14 rue Pierre-Noal; it's on the outskirts of Tessé-la-Madeleine, opposite the château.
☎02.33.37.92.11 Ⓕ02.33.38.90.27
Ⓦwww.leceltic.fr
Closed *Sun evening and Mon out of season; 19 Jan–4 March*. **TV. Disabled access. High chairs and games available.**

Michèle and Erick Alirol make you feel very welcome in this seaside house, which is typical of the region. The pleasant bedrooms, which have been renovated, all have telephone. Doubles with shower and wc or bath €39–43. Half board for a minimum of three nights stay costs €74 for two people. Lots of fresh local ingredients and seasonal produce are used in the rustic dining room. Menus €15.50–27.50 or you can dine à la carte. There's also a snooker table.

Manoir du Lys***

Route de Juvigny-sous-Andaine, la croix-Gauthier; take the D235 and it's 3km from Bagnoles.
☎02.33.37.80.69 Ⓕ02.33.30.05.80
Ⓦwww.manoir-du-lys.fr
Closed *Sun evening; Mon; 1 Nov–31 March; early Jan to mid-Feb*. **Disabled access. TV. Swimming pool. High chairs and games available. Car park.**

A delightful manor deep in the Andaines forest, built as a hunting lodge by a fervent royalist. You'll hear cuckoos in the springtime and glimpse deer straying into the orchard. The rooms are bright and tastefully decorated; some have balconies overlooking the garden. Doubles €58–185 with shower/wc or bath; suites €190–240. The staff and the cooking are as wonderful as the setting. The restaurant uses fresh local produce and revives traditional flavours – *andouille* tart, *croquant* of Camembert with apples, zander smoked over beech, squab in a garlic cream, cappuccino of black pudding with truffles, and divine desserts. Menus €26–65. *10% discount on the room rate on presentation of this guide 1 Nov–31 March (except during public holidays).*

Domfront

61700 (16km W)

L'Auberge du Grandgousier

1 pl. de la Liberté; in the heart of the town, opposite the post office and law courts.
☎02.33.38.97.17
Closed *Mon evening; Wed evening; Thurs; Feb; Oct*.

Rustic touches (some genuine, some contrived) in a house built with stone and half-timbering. Elegant, aromatic Normandy cooking based on fresh produce, with several fish and seafood specialities. Considering the quality, the prices are remarkably low (let's hope they stay that way): menus €14–27. The attractive dining room is large, remarkably clean and flooded with light. The service is charming.

Rânes

61150 (20km NE)

Hôtel Saint-Pierre**

6 rue de la Libération; it's on the D916.
☎02.33.39.75.14 Ⓕ02.33.35.49.23
Ⓦ www.hotelsaintpierreranes.com
Restaurant closed *Fri evening*. **High chairs and games available. TV. Car park.**

This place, housed in a substantial stone building, has been going strong for some thirty years. You can relax in their deep sofas and the dining room is painted in blue and red. The cooking is excellent and prices are reasonable – the house speciality is tripe, which has won countless prizes and awards (check out the certificates on the walls). Other hits include the roast chicken, which is perfectly cooked and seasoned, the *bœuf à la ficelle* (where the meat is tied with string, cooked in stock and served with a Camembert sauce), veal escalope with artichokes and frogs' legs. There's a weekday menu at €12 and others €13–33. Pleasant bedrooms €40–55 with shower and wc or bath. Ask for one overlooking the courtyard; you'll get absolute peace and quiet. *10% discount on the room rate (1 Nov–1 April) offered to our readers on presentation of this guide.*

Barenton

50720

Restaurant Le Relais du Parc

46 rue Pierre-Crestey.
☎02.33.59.51.38
Closed *Mon; Christmas–New Year; Feb school holidays*. **Disabled access.**

If you get here early enough, you'll be able to listen to the Swedish chef issuing orders in the kitchen in jovial but commanding tones. He prepares attractive dishes using local produce with imagination, like a *fricas-*

sée of cockerel with cider vinegar and a range of typical Normandy dishes featuring apples and cream. Menus €11.50–27.20. The dining room centres on a very attractive fireplace and an antique clock.

Barfleur

50760

Le Moderne

1 pl. du Général-de-Gaulle; it's opposite the post office, 50m from the harbour.
☎02.33.23.12.44 Ⓕ02.33.23.91.58
Closed *Tues evening and Wed except mid-July to mid-Sept; Jan to mid-Feb.*

A colourful, pretty place with lots of flowers – it's only a shame that there's no sea view from the clean rooms. Doubles with shower and wc €40–54 depending on the room size. In the restaurant they serve carefully prepared dishes on a range of menus: a weekday lunch option from €17.50 and up to €34. Seafood will cost you €28; lobster €54. The house speciality is fish *choucroute* with *beurre blanc* and there's also a good grilled seafood cocktail. The salmon and duck breast are smoked on the premises and the bread and foie gras are also home-made. Marvellous desserts. One of the nicest places in the region. *Free coffee offered to our readers on presentation of this guide.*

Le Conquérant**

16–18 rue Saint-Thomas-Becket; it's 50m from the port.
☎02.33.54.00.82 Ⓕ02.33.54.65.25
Hotel closed *15 Nov–15 March.* **Restaurant closed** *lunchtimes (residents only).* **TV. Pay car park.**

A handsome seventeenth-century building with a sizeable formal garden at the back. The rooms range from simple to comfortable and go for €54–80 with shower/wc or bath – the best ones overlook the garden, though none has a sea view. There are four set breakfasts on offer at €5.40–9.60. You'll pay €14–23 for a meal in the stylish dining room: good fish soup, *galettes* and crêpes.

Anneville-en-Saire

50760 (5km S)

Café du Cadran GPLM

Take the D902 in the direction of Quettehou.
☎02.33.54.61.89
Closed *evenings; Sat; Sun; 1–15 June; mid-August to Sept.* **Car park.**

This place is almost hidden by the crowd of tractors and juggernauts on their regular round of delivering and collecting the fruit and veg produced in the Val de Saire. The talk is all of cabbages and cauliflowers, yields and set-asides. If a glass of white wine at 11am is tempting, so is the menu of the day: steak and mash, lamb stew – solid classics and cheap as you like. Menu €9, drink included.

Cosqueville

50330 (12km W)

Au Bouquet de Cosqueville

Hameau Remoud; it's on the coast road to Cherbourg.
☎02.33.54.32.81 Ⓕ02.33.54.63.38
Ⓦwww.bouquetdecosqueville.com
Closed *Tues and Wed out of season; Jan.* **TV. Disabled access.**

A big house in a little hamlet where you'll find one of the best tables in the Nord-Cotentin area. Chef Éric Pouhier specializes in carefully judged fish and seafood: cod fillet with tomato cream sauce, oyster and prawn soup with herbs, lobster with dry cider. Stylish, unobtrusive service and menus €18–34; à la carte €45. In the same establishment there's another restaurant, the *Petit Gastro*, which is run by the same team. The atmosphere is less self-important and prices are more accessible with menus €10–14 but the chef takes equal care over the quality of the dishes – mussels with sorrel *au gratin*, russet apples with cider sauce. Doubles go for €44–50. *Free coffee offered to our readers on presentation of this guide.*

Barneville-Carteret

50270

L'Hermitage

Promenade Abbé-Lebouteiller; it overlooks the port.
☎02.33.04.46.39 Ⓕ02.33.04.88.11
Ⓔbienvenu@hotelrestauranthermitage.com
Closed *Sun evening and Mon in winter; 7–31 January, 12 November–20 December.* **TV. Pay car park.**

There's a delightful view of the sea and

Carteret's little fishing port from the dining room and the terrace. Seafood is a speciality: foie gras stuffed with langoustines, fish kebabs. Menus €16–30. Doubles cost €30–75 with shower/wc or bath and a harbour view. *One free breakfast (per room, per night) or free coffee to our readers on presentation of this guide.*

Hôtel de la Marine***

11 rue de Paris.
Ⓣ02.33.53.83.31 Ⓕ02.33.53.39.60
Closed *Mon and Thurs lunchtimes (April–June and Sept); Sun evening and Mon (March and Oct); 12 Nov–1 March.* **TV. Car park.**

There are breathtaking views from this large white building overlooking the harbour. Some bedrooms have a balcony, others a tiny terrace, and the décor throughout is fresh and stylish. Doubles €78–140. The good reputation of this establishment is due mostly to its restaurant, where the cooking is sophisticated, imaginative – and very elaborate. The elegant dining room has a rather chic atmosphere, and a series of appetizing and imaginative menus – starting at €28 (served everyday except Sat, evenings and public holidays); *menu dégustation* €80. They feature dishes such as oysters *en nage* glazed with gherkins, plaice lacquered with honey and thyme with an onion and apple preserve, fillet of duck with shallots, terrine of goat's cheese with pickled aubergines and iced *mousse* with orange liqueur.

Bayeux

14400

Hôtel Mogador**

20 rue Alain-Chartier, pl. Saint-Patrice.
Ⓔhotelmogador@wanadoo.fr
Ⓣ02.31.92.24.58 Ⓕ02.31.92.24.85
Closed *Christmas–New Year; Feb school holidays.* **TV. Pay car park.**

A discreet hotel on the edge of the touristy centre of town. The rooms are elegant and comfortable, and those around the courtyard are very quiet. Doubles with shower/wc €43–48 with bath. Some of the bedrooms have recently been refurbished. Breakfast €6. Welcoming, friendly owner. *10% discount offered on the room rate (Dec–Feb) to our readers on presentation of this guide.*

Hôtel d'Argouges**

21 rue Saint-Patrice.
Ⓣ02.31.92.88.86 Ⓕ02.31.92.69.16
Ⓔdargouges@aol.com
Closed *1st fortnight Jan; 24th Dec.* **TV. Pay car park.**

A lovely eighteenth-century mansion, built for the Argouges family with a delightful, large courtyard. The dining room is majestic and, behind the house, there's a big tree-filled garden where it's wonderful to have breakfast when the weather's good. All rooms have bath, TV and mini-bar and cost €65–90.

La Table du Terroir

42 rue Saint-Jean; it's in the pedestrianized area.
Ⓣ02.31.92.05.53
Closed *Sun and Mon mid-Oct to mid-Nov.* **Disabled access. High chairs available.**

A *table d'hôte* run by an ex-butcher. He has set out a few tables in a beautiful room with stone walls and serves traditional, local, uncomplicated dishes: house terrines, Caen-style tripe and so on. There are four menus from €11 (weekdays) up to €26. This is a good, friendly little place which appeals to tourists and locals alike – anyone who wants a decent lunch. *Free coffee offered to our readers on presentation of this guide.*

Le Petit Bistrot

2 rue du Bienvenu; it's beside the cathedral.
Ⓣ02.31.51.85.40
Closed Sun and Mon out of season; Jan.

This is a genuine little bistro, chic yet very pleasant. The cooking is fresh-tasting and flavoursome, emphasizing the taste of the local ingredients: the veal kidneys are fabulous, as are the scallops in flaky pastry. Set menus – €16 (up to 9pm) and €28 – change with the seasons.

Crépon

14480 (13km NE)

La Ferme de la Rançonnière**

Route d'Arromanches; take the D12 towards Creully – 14km on, turn left onto the D65.
Ⓣ02.31.22.21.73 Ⓕ02.31.22.98.39
Ⓦwww.ranconniere.com
Restaurant closed Jan. **High chairs available. TV. Car park.**

The oldest parts of this beautiful and

imposing fortified farmhouse date from the thirteenth century. The place is charming and not at all stuffy, offering a friendly, sincere, family welcome. All the rooms are individually decorated and tastefully furnished in traditional style. Some look onto a large, peaceful garden. Doubles with shower/wc or bath €45–165. Breakfast €10. Half board, compulsory in high season, costs from €55 per person. The dining room has vaulted ceilings and the cuisine is typical of the region: terrine of Isigny beef, duck breast with tarragon, fish and shellfish stew, *mignon* of pork with lemon, Calvados *parfait* with apricot sauce. Menus €15 (weekdays) up to €24–38; there's a children's menu for €9. *Free room upgrade (Nov–Feb) offered to our readers on presentation of this guide.*

Colombiers-sur-Seulles

14480 (14km E)

Château du Baffy**

Take exit 7 from the Caen ring-road in the direction of Creully; turn right after Pierpont.
Ⓣ02.31.08.04.57 Ⓕ02.31.08.08.29
Restaurant closed *1 Nov–1 Feb*. **Disabled access. High chairs and games available. Car park.**

A perfectly charming place, ideal for a romantic weekend. The bedrooms are comfortable – doubles with shower/wc or bath/wc go for €73.20–85.30 including breakfast. In the restaurant there's a €22 weekday menu, with others up to €29. They offer typical home cooking and some more refined dishes – homemade foie gras, langoustines *croquantes* flavoured with vanilla. You can play games, tennis or you can try your hand at mountain biking. *10% discount on the room rate offered to our readers on presentation of this guide.*

Saint-Laurent-sur-Mer

14710 (18km NW)

Hôtel-restaurant La Sapinière

Le Ruquet; take the D514, then continue in the direction of the beach.
Ⓣ02.31.92.71.72 Ⓕ02.31.92.92.12
Ⓦwww.chez.com/lasapiniere
Closed *early Nov to Easter*. **TV. High chairs available. Disabled access. Car park.**

This is an enchanting place right by the beach, with bedrooms in little wooden chalets, complete with their own terrace. All the rooms are large and breezy, soberly decorated and equipped with a brand-new bathroom or shower. To top it all, the beds are exceptionally comfortable. Doubles €60–75. The restaurant is a beautiful room with bay windows, and a terrace (with heating, if necessary) for fine days. Its walls are covered with exuberant paintings by the artist John Pepper (evidently a fan of *Toy Story*!). Small menu with simple, brasserie-style dishes like fried mussels or superb salads, as well as interesting suggestions of the day. Reckon on around €20 for a meal. The restaurant is used by locals as much as by hotel guests, and take-away sandwiches and waffles (far better than the run of the mill) are also on offer for the bathers on the beach. The owner is extremely friendly and laid-back – he wanders around everywhere in bare feet – and is sure to give you an effusive welcome. Book for dinner.

Bellême

61130

Domaine du Golf de Bellême

Les Sablons.
Ⓣ02.33.85.13.13 Ⓕ02.33.85.13.14
Ⓦwww.belleme.com
Disabled access. High chairs and games available. Swimming pool with health suite. TV. Car park.

Despite being part of a golf club, this restaurant is actually located in the old convent of the sixteenth-century priory of Saint-Val. Bathed in light and with its magnificent woodwork and old stone walls, it could not be more appealing. Menus (€20–34) are served up to 9.30pm. There are a few comfortable rooms in the outbuildings which have modern facilities: doubles €70–99 with bath. Winter terrace.

Condeau

61110 (15km E)

Moulin de Villeray****

Ⓣ02.33.73.30.22 Ⓕ02.33.73.38.28
Ⓦwww.moulindevilleray.com
Disabled access. TV. Swimming pool. Car park.

A charming establishment with several

little mill buildings – and the wheel – dotted around the garden, terrace and swimming pool. There are ten elegant rooms, which are pricey (doubles €75–250) but the place is terribly romantic. Half board is compulsory in high season. And you can enjoy it just as much if you come for a meal. All the dishes are original and flavourful – good choices include marrowbone with snails and mushrooms, calf's cheek stew, potato squab pie, sole fillet with baby vegetables and apple tart. Half board, compulsory in high season. Menus €23 (weekday), others €34–69. The chef's obsession is mushrooms and in the autumn he arranges special mushroom weekends that include picking, cooking and tastings. *Free coffee offered to our readers on presentation of this guide.*

Cabourg

14390

Hôtel Le Cottage**

24 av. du Général-Leclerc; it's opposite the church.
Ⓣ02.31.91.65.61 Ⓕ02.31.28.78.82
TV. High chairs available. Car park.

It's easy to fall under the spell of this delightful hotel in a charming, traditional Normandy house with a pretty flower garden. The owner will greet you like an old friend, and the bedrooms are cosy and charming with their floral décor. Doubles with shower or bath €60–77; with spa bath €86–88 for two people and €100–115 for four people. Although it's beside the road, the double glazing is good and the bedrooms are quiet. Facilities include a gym and a sauna. So there's something to do even when it rains.

Hôtel Castel Fleuri**

4 av. Alfred-Piat; in the centre, 200m from the beach.
Ⓣ02.31.91.27.57 Ⓕ02.31.91.31.81
Ⓦwww.castel-fleuri.com
Closed *5–24 Jan.* **TV.**

A very pleasant hotel, in what was once a family *pension*, surrounded by a pretty garden. The rooms are comfortable and inviting; doubles €63–68. The decoration is gradually being renewed by the new owner, and the results so far reveal good taste and a sure touch.

Dives-sur-Mer

14160 (2km S)

Restaurant Chez le Bougnat

29 rue Gaston-Manneville.
Ⓣ02.31.91.06.13
Closed *Sun–Wed evenings; Jan.*

Filled with trinkets that would turn a junk dealer green with envy, this old place serves excellent food, traditional and simple. Specialities include *pot-au-feu* and veal kidneys. There's a good weekday menu at €14.50 (€18.50 at weekends); it offers starter, main dish, cheese and dessert. You can also choose à la carte, which will set you back about €25. This is the best value for money locally so it's a good idea to book. *Free liqueur offered to our readers on presentation of this guide.*

Beuvron-en-Auge

14430 (14km SE)

Auberge de la Boule d'Or

Place Michel Vermughen.
Ⓣ02.31.79.78.78
Closed *Tues evening and Wed (except July–Sept); Jan.*

Right in the middle of one of the loveliest villages in the Auge, this superb half-timbered house was built in the eighteenth century. The beautiful façade is such a fine example of local architecture that it was photographed for a full-page publicity shot in *Le Monde*. The dining room is stylishly rustic, intimate yet friendly. They serve good local cooking, with tasty dishes at honest prices. Menus €19–26. *Free coffee offered to our readers on presentation of this guide.*

Caen

14000

See map on pp.604–5

Hôtel Saint-Étienne*

2 rue de l'Académie. **Map A2-3**
Ⓣ02.31.86.35.82 Ⓕ02.31.85.57.69
Ⓔcontact@hotel-saint-etienne.com
Closed *Sun 1–6pm.* **TV.**

Awarded a Normandy Quality Tourism certificate, this is a characterful hotel in a peaceful street. It was built before the Revolution and much of the stonework and wood panelling is original. The bedrooms are pretty; doubles €23 with basin and €35–38 with shower/wc and telephone. It's the cheapest hotel in Caen, and often full, so reservations are strongly recommended. *10% discount on the room rate Nov–March offered to our readers on presentation of this guide.*

Hôtel des Quatrans**

17 rue Gémare; right in the centre, near the château and the pedestrian area. **Map B2-4**
Ⓣ02.31.86.25.57 Ⓕ02.31.85.27.80
Ⓦwww.hotel-des-quatrans.com
TV.

In a neighbourhood that was rebuilt after World War II, the unappealing façade hides quiet, well-equipped, comfortable rooms decorated in pastel colours. Attentive service. This hotel has been awarded a Normandy Quality Tourism certificate. *One free breakfast per room offered to our readers on presentation of this guide.*

Hôtel-restaurant Le Dauphin***

29 rue Gémare. **Map B2-6**
Ⓣ02.31.86.22.26 Ⓕ02.31.86.35.14
Ⓦwww.bestwestern.fr
Closed *Feb half-term; 1st week in Nov.*
Restaurant closed Sat evening; Sun. **TV. Disabled access. Car park.**

Set in an old priory, this charming 3-star hotel has just added another fifteen rooms. Most are delightful, but the remainder are nondescript (although comfortable). Doubles €65–75 with shower/wc, €90–95 with bath. Five suites at €130; no. 11 seems specially designed for honeymoon couples, with its exposed beams and sitting room. Breakfast buffet of the highest quality at €10: cheese, charcuterie, yoghurt, unlimited jam. The elegant but slightly starchy restaurant serves some of the best food in town, with skilful reinterpretations of traditional local dishes and reasonably priced menus at €18 (except public holidays), then €28–50. Gym and sauna with power shower.

Crêperie Les Canotiers

143 rue Saint-Pierre. **Map B2-14**
Ⓣ02.31.50.24.51
Closed *after 7pm; Sun (July–Aug); Mon lunch (winter); 3 weeks in Sept.* **High chairs and babies' changing table available.**

The decoration here is as warm as the welcome, with flowery tablecloths and curtains, pale-wood furniture and ornate trinkets. At lunchtime it is packed with locals who appreciate the cosy atmosphere and the fine selection of crêpes, omelettes, salads and crumbles. Menus €8.38–9.90. In the afternoon it becomes a tea room (although it is the exquisite hot chocolate that takes pride of place).

Restaurant Maître Corbeau

94 rue Buquet. **Map B1-11**
Ⓣ02.31.93.93.00
Closed *Sat and Mon lunchtimes; Sun; last 3 weeks in Aug.*

A restaurant entirely devoted to cheese, with a bizarre, dairy-obsessed décor. Among other tasty dishes they serve *fondues* using local cheese or goat's cheese and *escalopines* of Roquefort flambéed with Calvados. Weekday lunch menu €9.60 and others up to €19. Reckon on around €16 à la carte. Informal, enthusiastic welcome and service; the diners are mainly students. It's busy in the evening, so you'd do well to reserve.

La Petite Auberge

17 rue des Équipes d'Urgence. **Map C2-17**
Ⓣ02.31.86.43.30.
Closed *Sun and Mon; first 3 weeks in Aug; a fortnight around Christmas/New Year.*
Disabled access.

The dining room is small and cosy; it's extended by a glassed-in terrace. Low-key welcome, peaceful atmosphere and professional service. The good local dishes change with the seasons. Highlights include tripe *à la mode de Caen*. There's an impeccable *formule du jour* at €11.50 (not Sat night) and an interesting *menu-carte* for €18.

Le Gastronome

43 rue Saint-Sauveur. **Map A2-18**
Ⓣ02.31.86.57.75
Closed *Tues evening; Sun; 10 days in early Aug.*

The chef interprets classic dishes with a very individual touch, using local ingredients: try the delicious tripe *croustillant* with cream and Calvados. Very decent menus €13.50 (not Sat night) and €17–33. The dining room is sober and rather chic, and service is attentive, efficient and unobtrusive.

Restaurant Alcide

1 pl. Courtonne. **Map C2-13**

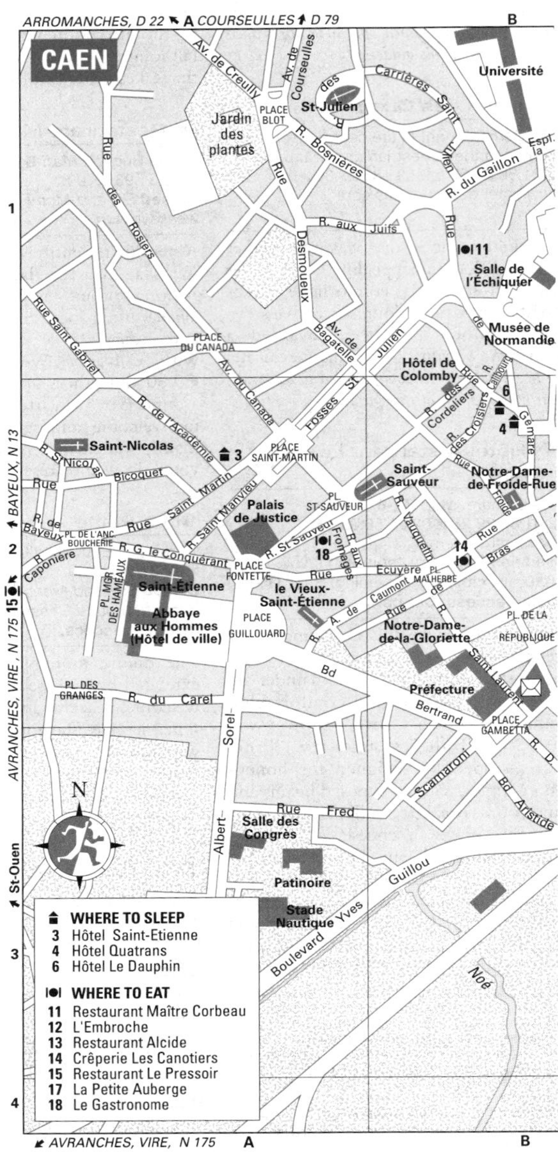
ARROMANCHES, D 22 A COURSEULLES D 79
B
CAEN
Université
Jardin des plantes
St-Julien
PLACE BLOT
Salle de l'Échiquier
Musée de Normandie
Hôtel de Colomby
Saint-Nicolas
PLACE SAINT-MARTIN
Saint-Sauveur
Notre-Dame-de-Froide-Rue
Palais de Justice
PLACE DU CANADA
Saint-Étienne
Abbaye aux Hommes (Hôtel de ville)
le Vieux-Saint-Étienne
PLACE GUILLOUARD
Notre-Dame-de-la-Gloriette
Préfecture
PLACE GAMBETTA
PL. DE LA RÉPUBLIQUE
Salle des Congrès
Patinoire
Stade Nautique
BAYEUX, N 13
AVRANCHES, VIRE, N 175
St-Ouen
WHERE TO SLEEP
3 Hôtel Saint-Etienne
4 Hôtel Quatrans
6 Hôtel Le Dauphin
WHERE TO EAT
11 Restaurant Maître Corbeau
12 L'Embroche
13 Restaurant Alcide
14 Crêperie Les Canotiers
15 Restaurant Le Pressoir
17 La Petite Auberge
18 Le Gastronome
AVRANCHES, VIRE, N 175
A
B

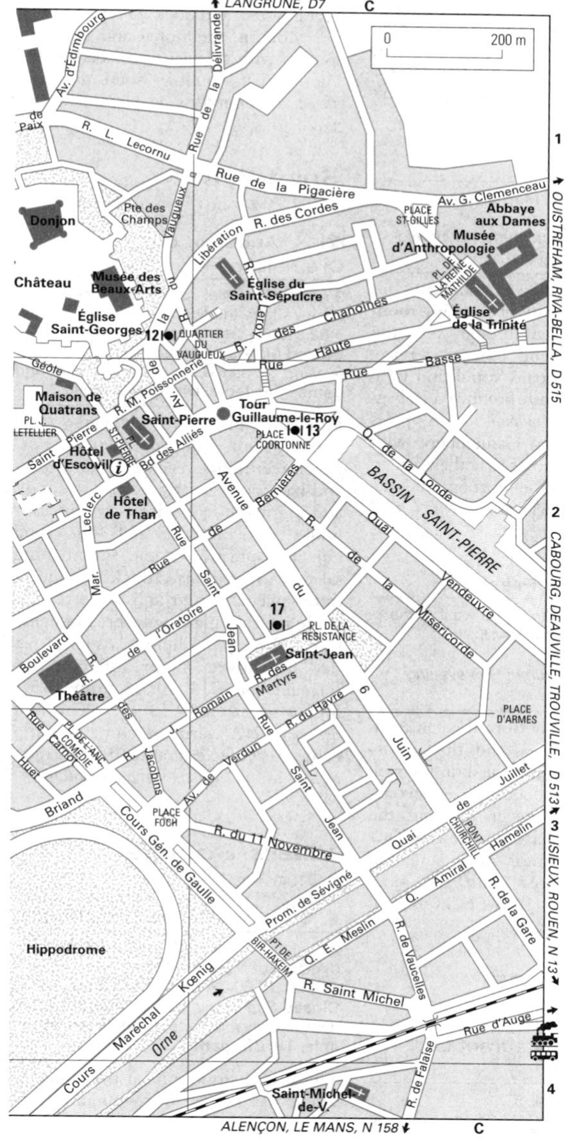
LANGRUNE, D7
C
0
200 m
1
2
3
4
OUISTREHAM, RIVA-BELLA, D 515
CABOURG, DEAUVILLE, TROUVILLE, D 513
LISIEUX, ROUEN, N 13
ALENÇON, LE MANS, N 158
Donjon
Château
Musée des Beaux-Arts
Église Saint-Georges
Maison de Quatrans
Saint-Pierre
Hôtel d'Escoville
Hôtel de Than
Tour Guillaume-le-Roy
Église du Saint-Sépulcre
Abbaye aux Dames
Musée d'Anthropologie
Église de la Trinité
Saint-Jean
Théâtre
Hippodrome
Saint-Michel-de-V.
BASSIN SAINT-PIERRE
Orne
12
13
17

☎02.31.44.18.06
Closed *Sat; 20–31 Dec.*

Behind the sky-blue façade the décor isn't exactly earth-shattering, but the warm atmosphere makes up for it. This is not the place to come if you're on a diet – they serve honest, robust local cuisine including calf's head and tripe *à la mode de Caen*. Menus €13.80–21.90. One of the town's classics.

L'Embroche

17 rue Porte-au-Berger. **Map B1-12**
☎02.31.93.71.31
Closed *Sat and Mon lunchtimes; Sun; mid-Sept to 5 Oct; 24 Dec–6 Jan.*

In a district that boasts lots of restaurants, this is really very good. Pretty little dining room – where you can see through into the kitchen – and charming, efficient service. Chalked up on the board you'll find local dishes cooked with fresh produce and bags of imagination – try *andouilles* with apples and cider vinegar or Camembert with Calvados. Lunch menu €16, others up to €20. All the wines on the short but interesting list are the same price. *Free house liqueur offered to our readers on presentation of this guide.*

Restaurant Le Pressoir

3 av. Henry-Chéron; 2km to the west of the town centre. **Off map by A2-15**
☎02.31.73.32.71
Closed *Mon; Sat lunchtime; Sun evening; Feb school holidays; 3 weeks in Aug.*

This may be some way from the centre, in a pretty charmless area, and the atmosphere may be a bit formal, but it's well worth a detour. The cooking is accomplished and precise, never masking the flavour of the products and avoiding any fancy tricks. Fish, meat and game (in season) are all treated with the same respect. Menu €25 (Tues–Fri evenings); other menus €39 and €60.

Noyers-Bocage

14210 (12km SW)

Hôtel-restaurant Le Relais Normand**

Take the D675 or the N175.
☎02.31.77.97.37 Ⓕ02.31.77.94.41
Closed *Tues; Wed; 25 Jan–8 Feb; 15 Nov–15 Dec.* **TV. Car park.**

The proprietor-chef is a Grand Master of the *Confrérie de fins Goustiers du Pré-Bocage*, an association which defends "real" food. Unsurprisingly, he's a perfectionist when it comes to preparing local dishes. Set menus €12–44 or à la carte – dishes include warm oysters and duck *à l'orange*. Breakfast €8. Modern, functional and comfortable doubles with shower/wc or bath €40–50. The perfect country hotel. *Free apéritif offered to our readers on presentation of this guide.*

Saint-Sylvain

14190 (20km SE)

Auberge de la Crémaillère

2 rue du 18-Juillet-1944; it's in the town centre – take the N58 then the D132A.
☎02.31.78.11.18
Closed *Mon (except public holidays); Sun evening; 25 July–12 Aug.* **High chairs and games available. Disabled access.**

From the outside, this looks like a simple country inn, but appearances can be deceptive. It has recently changed hands and has consequently been redecorated – and to great effect, with a combination of white and raspberry-red. The food is equally sophisticated and enticing: mullet salad with *tapenade*, duck terrine with bitter-sweet mango and desserts such as apple pie that manage to breathe new life into old recipes. There is a special weekday lunchtime menu for commercial travellers at €15. Apart from that, the menus start at €19.50 (excellent) and go up to €42. A warm welcome and impeccable service guaranteed. *Free liqueur offered to our readers on presentation of this guide.*

Villers-Bocage

14310 (26km SW)

Auberge Les Trois Rois**

2 pl. Jeanne-d'Arc; it's on the A84 in the direction of Mont St Michel.
☎02.31.77.00.32 Ⓕ02.31.77.93.25
Closed *Sun evening; Mon; Tues lunchtime; Jan; last week in June.* **High chairs available. TV. Car park.**

This classic stone inn on the large village square has an elegant restaurant. The chef has run the kitchens for thirty years – his *tripe à la mode de Caen* is award-winning. He uses top-quality ingredients in every dish: specialities include fish, shellfish and tripe. Breakfast costs €8. Menus at €20 (weekdays, except public holidays), others at €31–50. The rooms are well maintained and regularly refurbished. Doubles €34 with basin and shower and €48.50–60 with bath.

Carentan

50500

Hôtel du Commerce et de la Gare*

34 rue du Docteur-Caillard; it's opposite the train station.
Ⓣ02.33.42.02.00 Ⓕ02.33.42.20.01
Closed *30 Nov–1 March.* **High chairs available. TV. Car park.**

The hotel has a beautiful, ivy-covered façade. The restaurant is attractive too: it's an intimate place with low lighting, a soothing colour scheme, and a polished parquet floor. There's even a piano bar. You'll get very good home cooking on the set menus at €13–22. Specialities include meat and fish kebabs grilled on a wood fire, Camembert fritters, *moules marinière* and a fine selection of elaborate salads. There's a sign encouraging customers to tell the chef what they thought of the food. Double rooms €31 with shower/wc or €37 with bath.

Moitiers-en-Bauptois (Les)

50360 (20km NW)

Auberge de l'Ouve

Village Longuérac; it's 16km southwest of Sainte-Mère-Église.
Ⓣ02.33.21.16.26
Closed *Oct-March (reservation only).* **Disabled access.**

This lovely inn stands on the banks of the Ouve; it's miles from anywhere, surrounded by a cluster of old farms, with a few horses frolicking about and a line of trees at the water's edge. Great welcome. The restaurant has an attractive décor and a warm atmosphere. The cuisine is wonderful and the menus – very cheap at €10–20 – typically feature as much terrine as you can eat, potato stew with cream, eel *à la Normande* and duck with potatoes. *Free liqueur offered to our readers on presentation of this guide.*

Cherbourg

50100

Auberge de Jeunesse

55 rue de l'Abbaye; half-way between the Arsenal and the town centre.
Ⓣ02.33.78.15.15 Ⓕ02.33.78.15.16
Ⓔcherbourg@fuaj.org
Closed *21 Dec–4 Jan.* **Disabled access. Car park.**

This youth hostel opened in 1998, and its short life is evident in the impeccable rooms and fittings and the modern furniture. €12.70 per night, including breakfast (FUAJ card compulsory), plus €2.75 for renting sheets. You can have breakfast on the terrace in sunny weather; other meals are available, but you can also use the kitchen yourself. Friendly, efficient service. Possibility of taking a course in the nearby sailing centre.

Hôtel de la Croix de Malte**

5 rue des Halles; it's near the harbour, the theatre and the casino.
Ⓣ02.33.43.19.16 Ⓕ02.33.43.65.66
Ⓔhotel.croix.malte@wanadoo.fr
Closed *20 Dec–5 Jan.* **Disabled access. TV. Car park.**

The hotel has been totally refurbished; its quiet rooms have been spruced up and are extremely comfy. You'll get a very warm welcome from the owners. Doubles with shower/wc cost €25 and €46 with bath. If you book in advance, ask for room no. 3, 6, 8 or 15 – they're the biggest. Excellent value for money.

Hôtel de la Renaissance**

4 rue de l'Église; it's opposite the church of La Trinité.
Ⓣ02.33.43.23.90 Ⓕ02.33.43.96.10
TV. Pay car park.

This hotel has a great location in front of the wonderful church of La Trinité – if you're into frothy, frivolous architecture, you'll love the sugar-candy façade. All the comfortable bedrooms are pleasant; every one has a view of the port. Doubles €45–65 with shower/wc or bath, according to size and comfort; suite for two people €60. The smiling owner provides a lovely welcome and looks after her guests.

🏃 |●| Le Cotentin

30 quai de Caligny.
☎02.33.43.51.80
Closed *1–8 Jan*. **Car park**

An ample brasserie-restaurant located near Cherbourg's pleasure port. No surprise to find that fish and seafood are the specialities. Service is good-natured and efficient and the waiting staff are friendly. There's plenty of choice à la carte and three menus ranging from €15.60 to 29.60; also a *formule* at €11 which offers a choice of two main courses or seafood dishes from the main menu. The cooking and dishes are unusually interesting and use good local ingredients; menus change every three months to take account of the seasonal availability of produce. If you're making a booking, be sure to ask for a table on the first floor to get an impressive view over the port. *Free Kir offered to our readers on presentation of this guide.*

|●| Le Faitout

25 rue Tour-Carrée; it's 100m from church of La Trinité. ☎02.33.04.25.04
Closed *Sun; Mon; a week in Feb, fortnight in May; a week over Christmas.*

The attractive basement dining room is built of wood and stone and has a relaxed atmosphere. It's the archetype of a small, reliable restaurant that does precisely what it's supposed to – consequently it's often full. Good traditional cooking at prices that won't give you indigestion: the *formule* of the day "Faitout" €19, gives you starter, dish of the day, cheese and dessert of the day. The dish of the day on its own costs €9.50. À la carte you can expect to pay €20–25; good choices include duck *croustillant*, calf's head *gribiche*, *andouillette* with Calvados and grilled salmon. *Pot-au-feu* is the house speciality, which you should accompany with a bottle of dry cider. It's best to book for dinner and at weekends.

Omonville-la-Petite

50440 (20km NW)

🏃 ☗ La Fossardière**

Hameau de la Fosse; take the D901 or the quieter, coastal, D45.
☎02.33.52.19.83 ℻02.33.52.73.49
Closed *mid-Nov to mid-March*. **Disabled access. Car park.**

You'll find this lovely hotel in a hamlet just 500m from the sea, and you'll be treated to a warm welcome from owner Gilles Fossard. The bedrooms are comfortable and reasonably priced at €40–63 – some have a whirlpool bath (which costs a little more). There's a tiny sauna. *Free breakfast offered to our readers on presentation of this guide after the second night except in July–Aug.*

Auderville

50440 (28km NW)

|●| L'Auberge de Goury

Port de Goury; it's 1km from Auderville on the D901.
☎02.33.52.77.01
Closed *Mon; 3 weeks in Jan*. **Disabled access. High chairs available. Car park.**

The restaurant is located at the very tip of La Hague. It's a fishermen's inn and there's a wide fireplace in the old dining room; the new one has enormous windows that give you a marvellous vista of the sea. The owner is a robust character, and it's hardly surprising that this place is popular in high season – appreciative comments from movie and theatre stars decorate the visitors' book. The specialities are fish and meat grilled over an open wood fire and lobster. Menus €15–51; the most expensive one includes lobster and will do for even the largest appetites.

Flamanville

50340 (28km SW)

🏃 ☗ Hôtel Bel Air***

Rue du Château. Take the D4 and you'll find it 300m from the château.
☎ and ℻02.33.04.48.00 Ⓦwww.hotelbelair.biz
Closed *20 Dec–15 Jan*. **Disabled access. TV. Car park.**

An attractive hotel in the countryside near the magnificent Flamanville headland. The friendly welcome will instantly make you feel at home. Rooms – either overlooking the fields or the garden – are comfortable and have a certain charm for €55–90. *Free room upgrade (except high season and subject to availability) offered to our readers on presentation of this guide.*

Saint-Germain-des-Vaux

50440 (29km NW)

|●| 🏃 Restaurant le Moulin à Vent

Hameau de Danneville; it's on the D90 Port-Racine road.
☎02.33.52.75.20
Closed *Sun evening and Mon from Easter to*

All Saints (except public holidays July–Aug). **Disabled access. High chairs available. Car park.**

A gastronomic restaurant high above the bay beside the ruins of an old mill. The large, pleasant, softly coloured dining room overlooks a little garden full of exotic plants, and beyond to Saint-Martin's cove. Superb cooking using the freshest produce. The good-value €15 menu, served during the week, includes eight oysters; there's another menu at €25. A la carte dishes are pricier: boned roast pigeon, duck breast with sage, salmon fillet *à l'unilatérale* (grilled on one side only) and lobster stew with fresh pasta. Reservations strongly recommended. *Free apéritif is offered to our readers on presentation of this guide.*

Condé-sur-Noireau

14110

Hôtel-restaurant Le Cerf**

18 rue du Chêne; it's 500m from the centre on the Aunay-sur-Odon road.
Ⓣ02.31.69.40.55 Ⓕ02.31.69.78.29
Ⓦwww.le-cerf.com
Closed *Sun evening; Mon.* **High chairs available. TV. Car park.**

A traditional country hotel which has moved with the times. You'll be greeted like an old friend by the *patronne*; she's the vice-president of the local tourism office and knows all there is to know about the area. Traditional local cooking is served in the restaurant. Breakfast €5. The €11 menu – not served on Sun – is fine as far as it goes, but the better dishes are on the more expensive ones (up to €29): try perch fillet, *andouille émincé* with cider butter, honey *délice* with Pommeau. Doubles €31–38 with shower/wc or bath; make sure you ask for a room overlooking the garden.

Coutances

50200

Crêperie Le Râtelier

3 bis rue Georges-Clemenceau; it's near the cathedral.
Ⓣ02.33.45.56.52
Closed *Sun; Mon out of season; Feb school holidays.* **High chairs available. Disabled access.**

A nice little crêperie with a bright and pleasant dining room with a few attractive engravings and decorative plates on the wall. There's a choice of at least fifty different pancakes made with black wheat at €3.10–7.40 and almost as many made with rye. Menus €7.40–15.20.

Montmartin-sur-Mer

50590 (10km SW)

Hôtellerie du Bon Vieux Temps**

7 rue Pierre-des-Touches; it's opposite the post office.
Ⓣ02.33.47.54.44 Ⓕ02.33.46.27.12
Closed *Sun evening and Mon out of season; 10 days end Jan; 10 days end Sept.* **TV. Car park**

This inn, just a couple of kilometres from the sea, is appropriately named. There's a definite feeling of old times in the spacious wood-panelled dining room, hung with paintings. They serve good country cooking using lashings of cream and cider: grilled lobster to order, warm *andouille* with Pommeau sauce, seafood speciality, *tarte tatin*. Weekday lunch menu €12.50, and others €18.50–35, à la carte €29. Well-maintained double rooms €29 with basin/wc and €45–55 with shower/wc or bath. *Free coffee offered to our readers on presentation of this guide.*

Regnéville-sur-Mer

50590 (10km SW)

Le Jules Gommès

Take the D20 towards Granville, then 7km further turn onto the D49.
Ⓣ02.33.45.32.04
Closed *Mon and Tues (except during school holidays); Feb; Nov.* **High chairs available.**

The drive along the D49 gives you splendid views of the sea. Part-restaurant, part-crêperie and part-Irish pub, this is one of the cosiest places in the area and it has magnificent sea views. The first-class décor includes beautiful furniture and walls covered in gorgeous watercolours of the region. It's run by a nice young couple. They serve terrific crêpes and *galettes* – try the crêpe flambéed with Calvados. Reasonably priced menus ranging from €10 (lunchtime weekday) up to €23. The pub is convivial. *Free coffee offered to our readers on presentation of this guide.*

Savigny

50210 (10km E)

La Voisinière

8 rte. des Hêtres; it's signposted on the Saint-Lô-Coutances road. Take the D52 or the D380.
ⓣ02.33.07.60.32 ⓕ02.33.46.25.28
Closed *Sun evening; Mon; Tues morning; 1–15 Jan; Feb school holidays; a fortnight end Oct to early Nov*. **TV. Car park.**

A large, charming building right out in the country. They've planted superb Brazilian plants in the large garden. The four bedrooms, €38.50 for a double with shower/wc, are attractive and traditionally furnished, and the cooking has quite a reputation locally. Menus at €16 (not served on public holidays) and up to €36 list dishes such as pan-fried crayfish with orange, *escalope* of salmon with leek *fondue*, sole fillets with potatoes, and *fricassée* of guineafowl with grapes or mushrooms; they also grill meat over the open fire and prepare lots of good seafood. Booking is essential for Sunday lunch. *Free liqueur offered to our readers on presentation of this guide.*

Hambye

50450 (20km SE)

Auberge de l'Abbaye d'Hambye**

Route de l'Abbaye.
ⓣ02.33.61.42.19 ⓕ02.33.61.00.85
Closed *Sun evening; Mon; the Feb school holidays; 1–15 Oct*. **TV. High chairs and games available. Car park.**

In a beautiful country setting you'll find this quiet little hotel with charming and comfortable bedrooms. Doubles with shower/wc €50. The place is meticulously run, and Micheline and Jean Allain welcome you in a friendly, courteous fashion. The menus, ranging from €20 to €54, list appetizing and delicious dishes from different regions: Burgundy or Alsace snails, fish soup, seafood platters, lamb kebabs grilled over the coals and good crêpes.

Deauville

14800

Le Patio**

180 av. de la République; it's between the beach and the racecourse.
ⓣ02.31.88.25.07 ⓕ02.31.88.00.81
ⓔclaude.may@wanadoo.fr
Closed *Jan*. **Disabled access. TV.**

The bedrooms in this large, white hotel are comfortable and pleasant; some overlook the shaded flower-filled patio. Prices are reasonable for Deauville, with doubles at €35–72 depending on facilities and the season. Breakfast €7. There's a gym.

Hôtel de la Côte Fleurie**

55 av. de la République; 500 m from the train station, opposite the *Hôtel Le Chantilly*.
ⓣ02.31.98.47.47 ⓕ02.31.98.47.46
Closed *Jan*. **TV. High chairs available.**

This hotel has been completely refurbished; its lovely, bright rooms have brand-new bathrooms and a flower on their door. Doubles with shower/wc €61–74; the most expensive one looks on to a pretty garden – it's exquisite, and well worth the extra cost. Rooms for four people €91–116. Friendly, unfussy service. *10% discount on a room (except weekends and school holidays) offered to our readers on presentation of this guide.*

Hôtel Le Chantilly**

120 av. de la République; it's 500m from the train station.
ⓣ02.31.88.79.75 ⓕ02.31.88.41.29
ⓔhchantilly@aol.com
TV.

This hotel, renovated throughout and with modern facilities, radiates a certain charm. Doubles are €61–75 depending on the season. Breakfast €7.50. It's advisable to book. *One breakfast per room offered to our readers on presentation of this guide (except high season).*

Villers-sur-Mer

14640 (7km W)

Hôtel et Salon de Thé Outre-Mer***

1 rue du Maréchal-Leclerc; right in the town centre, opposite the sea.
ⓣ02.31.87.04.64 ⓕ02.31.87.48.90
ⓦwww.hoteloutremer.com
Closed *Jan*. **TV. Cots available. Car park.**

This looks like a classical hotel, but open the door and you are greeted by shrill colours (pink, green and orange) and thoughtfully arranged furnishings (wicker chairs, garlands). The explosion of colours continues in the rooms, which are all different but all brilliantly executed. Doubles €82–115. There's also a jazz bar and tea room: home-made cakes and an extensive range of teas and coffees. Be warned, however, that if you go into the tea room in the afternoon you're more than likely to end up staying the night, as the place is so enticing that you won't want to leave!

Falaise

14700

Hôtel-restaurant de la Poste**

38 rue Georges-Clemenceau.
☎02.31.90.13.14 Ⓕ02.31.90.01.81
ⓔhotel.delaposte@wanadoo.fr
Closed Sun evening; Mon; Fri evening 1 Oct–30 Apr; Sat lunchtime May–30 Sep; 2–24 Jan. **High chairs available. TV. Car park.**

This is a pleasant inn. Many of the rooms have been refurbished and look as good as new. Doubles with shower/wc or bath €48–50. Breakfast €6.50. Simple, traditional food in the restaurant: fish *panaché* in cider sauce or lamb *noisette* in a goat's cheese sauce. Menus ranging from €15 (not Sun) up to €35 change regularly. *10% reduction on the room rate offered to our readers on presentation of this guide, except May to end Aug.*

La Fine Fourchette

52 rue Georges-Clemenceau.
☎02.31.90.08.59
Closed *Tues evening out of season; 19 Feb–8 March.* **Disabled access. High chairs available. Car park.**

Bright, cheerful restaurant. Every year the chef goes off to work with great chefs in different parts of the country, so his cooking is always innovative and dynamic. You get a good idea of the cooking even on the €13.80 menu and a better one on the others up to €34. Tasty options include duckling with honey and spices or duck *confit* with apples. Efficient service by genuinely friendly staff. *Free apéritif or liqueur offered to our readers on presentation of this guide.*

Flers

61100

Auberge des Vieilles Pierres

Le Buisson Corblin; take the Argentan road and it's 3km from the centre.
☎02.33.65.06.96
Closed *Mon and Tues; the Feb school holidays; 1–24 Aug.* **High chairs and games available. Disabled access.**

Bright, attractive restaurant, owned by a team of talented young people who give it an informal, natural feel. The cooking is superb and dishes are skilfully prepared; the chef has a particular way with fish and grilled lobster. There's a brilliant €15 weekday menu and the other menus, €22–37, are equally good.

Restaurant Au Bout de la Rue

60 rue de la Gare.
☎02.33.65.31.53
Closed *Wed evening; Sat lunchtime; Sun; public holidays; a month around Aug.* **Disabled access.**

The jazzy retro décor works well in this excellent place, and the attentive staff make you feel welcome. The cooking is as imaginative as the surroundings, featuring dishes such as marinated raw salmon with herbs, salad with warm *andouille*, salmon with Camembert cream sauce, steak *tartare* finely chopped (not minced), strawberries in a crispy filo pastry case, meringue and ice-cream cake and chocolate *moelleux*. Menus €19–32. Good selection of wines at reasonable prices, and interesting coffees from Costa Rica, Ethiopia and Guatemala.

Ferrière-aux-Étangs (La)

61450 (10km S)

Auberge de la Mine

Le Gué-Plat; take the D18, then the D21 to Domfront and turn left 1.5km further on.
☎02.33.66.91.10
Closed *Tues; Wed; 1–22 Jan; 3 weeks end Aug/early Sept.* **High chairs available. Disabled access. Car park.**

Apparently this large ivy-covered brick house was once a miners' canteen – as the nearby slag heaps attest. But times have moved on and this delightful little place with its stylish décor is now a chic, intimate restaurant. The chef is an artist and his dishes are as beautiful to look at as they are delicious to eat: *fricassée* of prawns served in a buckwheat crêpe with cider butter, pan-fried duck foie gras coated with spiced breadcrumbs, caramelized apple on a sponge base. Menus €19 and €23 (not Sun), others €27–45. Children's menu €10. Cheerful, friendly staff.

Gouvets

50420

Restaurant Les Bruyères

It's on the RN175.
☎02.33.51.69.82
Closed *Sun.* **Open** *lunchtime and evening July–Aug; lunchtime and Fri, Sat evenings Sept–June.* **Disabled access. Car park.**

A fairly new building sitting by the side of the road. It's not especially attractive from the outside, but the welcome, the springtime décor and the value for money make it worth stopping. The chef changes the dishes on the menu every week to take account of the fresh produce or the fish that's been landed. The array of pastries is immensely tempting. The lunch menu costs €11 served lunchtime and evening, except on Saturday evening. The €13 *formule rapide* comprises a main dish and dessert, and there are other menus €13–22. *Free coffee offered to our readers on presentation of this guide.*

Granville

50400

Le Michelet**

5 rue Jules-Michelet; it's on the seashore, near the casino.
☎02.33.50.06.55 ⓕ02.33.50.12.25
TV. Car park.

Near the sea, a few minutes from the casino and the thalassotherapy centre, this little hotel has an attractive white façade. It's run by a charming young couple. The bedrooms are simple, bright and well maintained. Some of the rooms face the city centre and the sea and have balconies and terraces (nos. 1, 2 and 8). Doubles €29 with washing facilities, €34.50–47 with shower/wc or bath. *10% discount offered to our readers on presentation of this guide (for a minimum of two nights, outside school holidays).*

Restaurant Le Phare

11 rue du Port; it's on the harbour.
☎02.33.50.12.94
Closed *Tues; Wed out of season; 20 Dec–10 Jan.* **Disabled access. High chairs available.**

The panoramic view of the harbour from the first-floor dining room is splendid, and the fish market, just footsteps away, supplies the restaurant with ultra-fresh seafood. The medley of fish with a butter sauce is typical of the freshness of the chef's approach, just like the fish *pot-au-feu*, the stuffed yellow pollack with Cardinal sauce and the seafood platter. The cheapest menu costs €11.50 (not served Sun): it includes *moules marinière* or nine oysters with a jug of wine. If you're feeling hungry – and flush – go for the €59 menu, which includes a huge lobster. All the desserts are home-made.

Champeaux

50530 (15km S)

Hôtel Les Hermelles - Restaurant Au Marquis de Tombelaine

Take the D911 that runs along the Channel coast between Carelles and Saint-Jean-le-Thomas.
☎02.33.61.85.94 ⓕ02.33.61.21.52
ⓦwww.marquisdetombelaine.com
Closed *Tues evening and Wed (except July–Aug); Jan; 10 days at the end of Nov.* **Disabled access. TV. Car park.**

You'll find this lively hotel atop the Champeaux cliffs and across the bay from Mont-Saint-Michel. Comfortable double rooms €48–53. The intimate dining room is a successful combination of stonework, panelling and beams. The chef is a disciple of Auge Escoffier, the classic French cook, so the dishes are rich: fillet of cod with hot *andouille*, oysters cooked in cider, lobster Thermidor. Menus €19–59.

Honfleur

14600

Motel Monet**

Charrière du Puits; on the Côte de Grâce.
☎02.31.89.00.90 ⓕ02.31.89.97.16
ⓦwww.motelhotel.fr
Closed *Dec–Feb.* **TV. Disabled access. Pay car park. Cots available.**

In a lush, romantic setting on the heights of Honfleur, this small family hotel offers ten pretty, independent and comfortable rooms that were recently refurbished. Doubles €50–66 with shower/wc or bath. Breakfast €6. Terrace. The owners, who are vintage-car enthusiasts, are sure to give you a warm welcome. *One free breakfast offered to our readers (after 3rd consecutive night) on presentation of this guide.*

Hôtel du Cheval Blanc***

2 quai des Passagers; on the Vieux Bassin.

Ⓣ02.31.81.65.00 Ⓕ02.31.89.52.80
Ⓦwww.hotel-honfleur.com
Closed *Jan.* **TV.**

A building dating from the fifteenth century in a wonderful location, stretching along the harbour, opposite the Lieutenance. Most of the rooms overlook the port. Doubles €52.18–92.18 with shower/wc; €97.18–172.18 with bath (some even have a Jacuzzi); two suites €300–425, depending on the season. According to the time of year and the availability, it is possible to negotiate the price with the owner and choose your own room – she will happily show them to you. Normandy Quality Tourism certificate. *One free breakfast per person offered to our readers on presentation of this guide.*

Hôtel du Dauphin**

10 pl. Pierre-Berthelot; near the Church of Sainte-Catherine.
Ⓣ02.31.89.15.53 Ⓕ02.31.89.92.06
Ⓦwww.hotel-du-dauphin.com **TV.**

A small hotel set in a seventeenth-century house with the half-timbered façade typical of Honfleur. Some rooms (with Jacuzzi) are in the house itself; the rest are in an annexe, offering a pretty view of the church. Doubles with shower or bath and wc €59–124. Breakfast €6.20. *One free breakfast per room (after second consecutive night) offered to our readers on presentation of this guide.*

Hôtel des Loges***

18 rue Brûlée; close to the Church of Sainte-Catherine.
Ⓣ02.31.89.38.26 Ⓕ02.31.89.42.79
Ⓦwww.hoteldesloges.com
TV. Disabled access. High chairs and cots available.

A veritable love nest in a picturesque alley close to the church. It has recently been refurbished. The owner worked in the cinema as a young woman and has since unleashed her dramatic instincts on the décor, while not neglecting the standards of modern comfort. She is more than willing to share her passion with you, and if you like an object she will even sell it to you. Rooms with shower/wc or bath €90–115, according to the size and season. Breakfast €10.

La Tortue

36 rue de l'Homme-de-Bois; it's near the church of Sainte-Catherine.
Ⓣ02.31.89.04.93
Ⓦwww.latortue.net
Closed *Mon evening; Tues.* **High chairs available.**

This is a friendly place – though when they get busy at the weekend the welcome and the speed of service suffer. Other than that, this is an excellent restaurant. Pretty dining room and traditional cuisine: prawn salad, pan-fried foie gras on a bed of spinach in a cider vinegar *jus*, fillets of seabass in a *tapenade*, apple turnover with caramel sauce. Menus €16–30, including a vegetarian one. *Free coffee offered to our readers on presentation of this guide.*

Le Bouillon Normand

7 rue de la Ville; on the place Arthur-Boudin, behind the Saint-Étienne quay.
Ⓣ02.31.89.02.41
Closed *Wed; Sun evening; end Dec to end Jan.* **Children's comics and games available.**

This old yellow, wood-lined bistro reflects the traditional food on offer: *brandade* of fish and shrimps, *croquant* with Camembert and *tarte tatin* with Normandy sauce. One small detail: here you add salt and pepper to your own taste. You can eat on the terrace or in the delightful, recently refurbished dining room. Menus €16–23. Cheerful, unassuming Normand service.

Au P'tit Mareyeur

4 rue Haute.
Ⓣ02.31.98.84.23
Closed *Mon; Tues; Jan.* **Disabled access.**

Inviting restaurant with stylish, chic décor, without being pompous; the stone, half-timbering, greenery and fabrics combine to perfection. The chef, Julien Domin, already a seasoned professional at the age of 24, creates a culinary festival that is a pleasure to both the eyes and stomach: marinated smoked salmon with lentils, fried mullet fillets with *pistou* sauce and *bouillabaisse honfleuraise* (€19). Set menu based on selected à la carte dishes at €20. If you are not satisfied, don't hesitate to tell the chef, as he will really value your opinion. Fast, cheerful service. Consider booking in season, as the dining room is not very big.

Houlgate

14510

Santa Cecilia**

25 allées des Alliés; it's 100m from the beach
Ⓣ02.31.28.71.71 Ⓕ02.31.28.51.73

ⓦwww.hotel-santa-cecilia.com
TV.

A pretty nineteenth-century villa with an atmosphere to match. You'll get a wonderful welcome from the owner. Doubles €54–63 with shower/wc or bath. Breakfast €6.50. *Free coffee offered to our readers on presentation of this guide.*

Lisieux

14100

Hôtel de Lourdes**

4 rue au Char; it's near the town hall and the theatre.
ⓣ02.31.31.19.48 ⓕ02.31.31.08.67
Closed *Sun in winter. Annual holidays during winter* **TV.**

In one of Lisieux's typical, rather dull-looking brick buildings, this welcoming little hotel is popular with pilgrims. The rooms are on three floors (there's a lift) and have all been renovated. They're bright and well maintained. Doubles €35–45 with shower/wc or bath. There's a terrace which is lovely and sunny at the end of the day. *10% discount offered to our readers on presentation of this guide, 1 Nov to end March.*

La Coupe d'Or**

49 rue Pont-Mortain.
ⓣ02.31.31.16.84 ⓕ02.31.31.35.60
ⓦwww.la-coupe-d-or.com
Closed *Fri; the Feb school holidays.* **TV. High chairs available. Cots and changing tables.**

A convivial, well-run hotel. The bedrooms are clean, simple and comfortable, with classic décor. Doubles €47 with shower/wc or bath. Half board, €42–55 per person, is compulsory at long weekends. The cooking is reliable, with seafood-based dishes such as foie gras with crayfish or turbot with ceps, and regional specialities including *vallée d'Auge* calves' kidneys and iced soufflé with Calvados. Weekday lunch menu €11 and others up to €30. *Free apéritif offered to our readers on presentation of this guide.*

Azur Hôtel***

15 rue au Char.
ⓣ02.31.62.09.14 ⓕ02.31.62.16.06
ⓦwww.azur-hotel.com
TV.

A fresh three-star hotel with pleasant well-equipped bedrooms; doubles €60–65.85 with shower/wc or bath. The breakfast room is very pretty; breakfast €8.40. *One free breakfast offered per room to our readers on presentation of this guide.*

Restaurant Aux Acacias

13 rue de la Résistance.
ⓣ02.31.62.10.95
Closed *Sun evening and Mon (except for public holidays); Thurs out of season; the last fortnight in Nov.*

An appealing, centrally located restaurant with a cosy décor – spring colours, vases of dried flowers and little ornaments. It's fresh and pleasant, just like the cooking: roast salt-crusted bass, beef fillet pan-fried with truffle *jus*, apple tart with ice-cream, caramelized apple *brioche*. Menus from €15 (not served Saturday evening or public holidays) to €45. Children's menu €8.50. Efficient service with a smile. *Free coffee offered to our readers on presentation of this guide.*

Mont-Saint-Michel (Le)

50170

Hôtel Du Guesclin**

Grande-Rue; it's one of the first hotels you come to as you climb the main street.
ⓣ02.33.60.14.10 ⓕ02.33.60.45.81
ⓔhotelduguesclin@wanadoo.fr
Closed *Tues evening; Wed; early Nov to end March.* **TV.**

A well-maintained hotel offering reasonable value for money when you compare it to the local competition. Comfortable, very clean doubles at €55–80 with shower/wc or bath. There are two dining rooms; if you want quick service and *formules* for €9.50–11, head for the brasserie downstairs. Upstairs you get a breathtaking view over the bay, and they serve classic regional and fish dishes. Set menus €16–35.

Beauvoir

50170 (4km S)

Hôtel Le Gué de Beauvoir*

Route de Pontorson: it's next to the Gué de Beauvoir campsite.
ⓣ02.33.60.09.23
Closed *1 Oct–Easter.* **Car park.**

This place is in complete contrast to the

dull hotels that proliferate around here: it's a handsome house standing in flower-filled grounds. The bedrooms are simple but have great charm and go for €26 with basin and €43 with shower/wc or bath. Breakfast is served in the pleasant conservatory. *10% discount on the room rate (Easter–June) offered to our readers on presentation of this guide.*

Pontorson

50170 (9km S)

Hôtel-restaurant Le Bretagne**

59 rue Couesnon; it's on the main street.
Ⓣ02.33.60.10.55 Ⓕ02.33.58.20.54
Ⓔdebretagne@destination.bretagne.com
Restaurant closed *Mon, Sun evening–Tues lunchtime out of season; 5 Jan–10 Feb.* **TV. Disabled access. High chairs available. Car park.**

A lovely eighteenth-century coaching inn where you'll be welcomed warmly. The bedrooms are all very pleasant and cost €39–64 with shower/wc or bath. A crowd of regulars inhabits the restaurant, where the dishes are prepared with care and the chef uses only fresh ingredients. Classical, local and simple food: rack lamb with rosemary, oysters with grated Camembert, salmon *tartare* with grapefruit, ox-cheek with a foie gras sauce and fresh noodles, duck breast with spiced pear, *andouille millefeuille* with two kinds of apple, nougat with two chocolates and coffee cream. Menus €14.50–38. Very good value. *Free apéritif offered to our readers on presentation of this guide.*

Hôtel Montgomery**

13 rue Couesnon.
Ⓣ02.33.60.00.09 Ⓕ02.33.60.37.66
Ⓦwww.hotel-montgomery.com
Restaurant closed *lunchtime (open for hotel guests only).* **Closed** *one day a week. 8–19 Feb; 14–24 Nov.* **TV. Pay car park.**

This sixteenth-century house was the seat of the Counts of Montgomery; nowadays it provides the setting for 32 rooms with exceptional furniture. Doubles with bath or shower/wc €55–77.90 depending on the season; there's a luxury room with four-poster and Jacuzzi €100–145. Buffet breakfast €9. Half board available from the third night. The restaurant is exclusively open to hotel guests and serves dinner only (not Saturday), €15–25.

Servon

50170 (10km SE)

Auberge de Terroir**

It's on the road from Pontaubault to Pontorson; take the D107.
Ⓣ02.33.60.17.92 Ⓕ02.33.60.35.26
Ⓔaubergeduterroir@wanadoo.fr
Closed *Wed; Sat lunchtime; Feb school holidays; mid-Nov to early Dec.* **TV. High chairs and cots available. Disabled access. Car park.**

A charming hotel with pretty grounds in a tranquil village. The friendly young owners have created a peaceful, tasteful atmosphere. All the rooms have been attractively refurbished and they're named after famous musicians and composers. In the old presbytery there are six lovely doubles and one room that sleeps four, or you can stay in the annexe; €50–58 with shower/wc or bath. They serve wonderful Périgord specialities in the pleasant dining room – semi-cooked foie gras and breast of duck with honey – along with seafood stew, salmon with green cabbage and monkfish with vanilla. Menus €16–40. Booking is essential.

Mortagne-au-Perche

61400

Hôtel du Tribunal**

4 pl. du Palais.
Ⓣ02.33.25.04.77 Ⓕ02.33.83.60.83
Ⓦwwwperso.wanadoo.fr/hotel.du.tribunal.61.Normandie
TV. Disabled access.

The oldest parts of this handsome, traditional Percheron house date from the thirteenth century, though most of it is younger than that. The square and the façade have hardly changed since the end of the nineteenth century, when the inn was called "John who laughs, John who weeps", perhaps in reference to the fate of those processed by the law courts which stood next door. Renovations have not diminished the character of the interior and there's a lovely annexe at the back where the rooms are even quieter and overlook a tiny flower-filled courtyard. Doubles €45–98 with shower or bath. The food is very good and features interesting cuisine alongside classical dishes: *croustillant* of black pudding, *millefeuille* of sole and wild mushrooms, fine apple tart. Menus €17–32. A delightful, quite chic place where the welcome is warm. *Free apéritif maison offered to our readers on presentation of this guide.*

Longny-au-Perche

61290 (18km E)

|●| Le Moulin de la Fenderie

Route de Bizou; from Mortagne, take the D8 through the forest of Rénovaldieu.
Ⓣ02.33.83.66.98
Closed *Mon and Tues evenings in summer, Sun evening to Wed lunch from Oct; mid-Jan to mid-Feb.* **Disabled access. Car park.**

A restaurant housed in a superb watermill which has been patiently restored by the two owners. You are pleasantly welcomed and there is a terrace by the water's edge. The cuisine is delicate, perfumed and original, and the chef gives local dishes a touch of exotic spice. Menus €19–41 include langoustines, goose foie gras, monkfish, cockerel cooked in a red wine sauce. It's best to reserve. *Free apéritif offered to our readers on presentation of this guide.*

Ouistreham-Riva-Bella

14150

|●| Hôtel-restaurant Le Normandie - Le Chalut**

71 and 100 av. Michel-Cabieu; it's near the harbour.
Ⓣ02.31.97.19.57 Ⓕ02.31.97.20.07
Ⓦwww.lenormandie.com
Closed *Sun evening and Mon from Nov to March; 20 Dec–15 Jan.* **TV. Car park.**

Two classic, and slightly old-fashioned, hotels opposite each other. Doubles cost €58–60 with shower/wc or bath and telephone; some of the bathrooms could do with updating. You'll find wonderful food in the dining room. Choose from delicate, refined versions of traditional dishes such as peppered John Dory fillet with apples and pears. The service can be a tad uptight, though. Weekday menu €17 and others up to €58. Rated "Normandie Qualité Tourisme".

|●| Restaurant Le Métropolitain

1 rte. de Lion; it's near the post office.
Ⓣ02.31.97.18.61
Closed *Mon evening and Tues from Oct to April; a week end Jan; a week end Nov.* **Car park**

Decorated to look like a 1930s Parisian métro station, this place offers local produce and seafood cooked to perfection and attractively presented – try the fresh salted cod with cider or the sole with chives. Menus €10.67 (weekdays) up to €23.50. Children's menu €7. Credit cards not accepted.

Bénouville

14970 (5km S)

|●| Hôtel-restaurant La Glycine**

11 pl. du Commando no.4.
Ⓣ02.31.44.61.94 Ⓕ02.31.43.67.30
Closed *Sun evening out of season; 20 Dec–15 Jan.* **Disabled access. TV. Car park.**

This is a beautiful stone building covered in wisteria. Refurbished bedrooms with shower/wc and telephone go for €53; breakfast is €6.50. The smart-looking restaurant is a perfect setting for good food, imaginatively and carefully prepared – the young chef is in a class of his own. Dishes such as lobster in coral sauce and seafood gratin. Menus €22–39. *Free sorbet Normand offered to our readers on presentation of this guide.*

Colleville-Montgomery

14880 (5km W)

|●| Restaurant La Ferme Saint-Hubert

3 rue de la Mer; take the D35.
Ⓣ02.31.96.35.41
Closed *Sun evening and Mon except in season and on public holidays.* **Disabled access. High chairs available. Car park.**

A large Normandy house where you can lunch either in the cosy rustic dining room or the bright conservatory. Generous portions of well-executed local food: duck foie gras or lemon sole with cider. Weekday lunch menu €16, with others up to €40. *Free coffee offered to our readers on presentation of this guide.*

Pont-L'Évêque

14130

Hôtel de France

1 rue de Geôle.

Ⓣ02.31.64.30.44 Ⓕ02.31.64.98.90
Closed *Feb; Christmas.* **TV.**

A small hotel in a quiet street close to the town centre. The rooms are decorated in country style, with individuality, personality and charm; some have a view over fields of grazing cows. Doubles with basin go for €28 or up to €46 with shower/wc or bath. The breakfast jams and preserves are home-made.

Auberge de la Touques

Place de l'Église; it's 1km from the autoroute exit.
Ⓣ02.31.64.01.69
Closed *Mon lunchtime, Tues and Sun evenings except in Aug; Jan; Dec.* **Car park.**

This is a handsome Normandy building on the bank of the Touques river near the village church. The chef prepares all the Norman classics: cod with apples and cider, tripe *à la mode de Caen*, veal cutlet *à la normande*. €21.50 weekday menu with others up to €32. Reckon on about €42 à la carte. Attentive service. *Free glass of Calvados offered to our readers on presentation of this guide.*

Auberge de l'Aigle d'Or

68 rue de Vaucelles.
Ⓣ02.31.65.05.25
Closed *Tues evening, Wed and Sun evenings out of season; Feb half-term.*

A beautiful old staging post dating from 1520, complete with stained-glass windows and half-timbering, so there's no shortage of atmosphere. Highly accomplished, classic Norman bourgeois cooking, with a few dishes that are hard to find these days: fattened, farm-raised chicken cooked in the style of the Auge country, roast pigeon with foie gras and Sauternes sauce. The prices are pretty high, but this is one of the best restaurants in the whole of Normandy; you might even bump into a few film stars on a visit to the sticks, taking a break from their partying in Deauville. Menus €26–46. Reckon on €60 à la carte.

Drubec

14130 (8km SW)

La Haie Tondue

Take exit 29A of the A13, then D58 and it's 2km south of Beaumont-en-Auge at the N175 junction.
Ⓣ02.31.64.85.00
Closed *Mon evening except in Aug; Tues; 3 weeks in Jan; a week in June; a week in Oct.* **High chairs available. Car park.**

This restaurant, in a beautiful old house covered in vines, offers very good food at reasonable prices. The setting is most agreeable, the service is faultless and there's a good wine list. As for the cuisine, it's perfectly prepared, even on the cheapest of the menus (€21–38). Children's menu €11. Dishes change regularly but are likely to include snail *gratin*, pan-fried crayfish, fish or country style terrine.

Saint-Lô

50000

Armoric Hôtel*

15 rue de la Marne.
Ⓣ02.33.05.61.32 Ⓕ02.33.05.12.68
TV. Car park.

You'll get a very warm welcome in this quiet, out of the way, good-value hotel – though it can cool off in the hectic tourist season. The comfy bedrooms are tastefully decorated and all have phone and TV (even if some are on the small side); doubles €31 with basin, €38 with shower/wc, €49 with spa bath. If you've had a tiring journey, you'll love nos. 16 and 21 which have a whirlpool bath. Even considering the rather frugal breakfast, which costs €6, this is one of the best places in the Manche.

Le Bistrot de Paul et Roger

42 rue du Neubourg; it's halfway between the town hall and the church of Sainte-Croix.
Ⓣ02.33.57.19.00
Disabled access.

This little restaurant, a favourite gathering place for Caen football fans, has a genuine bistro look and atmosphere. Food is quick and good. There's lots of home cooking – shepherd's pie, oxtail, *poule-au-pot*, calf's head *gribiche* and *tarte tatin*. There are three weekday menus: €9.50 for a starter and dessert, €11 for a main course and dessert, or €12 for a starter and main course. Reckon on about €18 à la carte. It's good value for money but watch out for the price of the drinks, which can send the bill soaring.

Le Péché Mignon

84 rue du Maréchal-Juin; go towards Bayeux. It's well away from the town centre.

Ⓣ02.33.72.23.77 Ⓕ02.33.72.27.58
Closed *Mon; Sat lunchtime; Sun evening; 20 July–10 Aug.* **Disabled access.**

The service in this comfortable restaurant is impeccable and the food is marvellous – top-class gourmet cuisine prepared by a talented young chef. Stellar dishes include medallion of lobster and creamy camembert, zander with saffron and cocoa beans, veal sweetbreads with morels and *sabayon* of apples and cinnamon. Five menus €14.50–50. *Free apéritif maison offered to our readers on presentation of this guide.*

Saint-Vaast-la-Hougue

50550

Hôtel de France – Restaurant Les Fuchsias**

20 rue du Maréchal-Foch; it's less than two minutes from the harbour.
Ⓣ02.33.54.42.26 Ⓕ02.33.43.46.79
Ⓦwww.france-fuchsias.com
Closed *Mon except in July–Aug; Tues Nov–Dec; Tues lunchtime in March, April and Sept; Jan–Feb.* **TV. High chairs available. Disabled access.**

Most of the pretty bedrooms overlook a little garden – the fuchsia there gave its name to the restaurant and is a hundred years old. Double rooms with phone €39 with shower, €49–59 with shower/wc, €69–96 with bath and there's also a family room with terrace for €96. Half board, requested in July–Aug, costs €50–76 per person. This is also one of the best restaurants in the area. Ask for a table on the veranda, which is decorated with trompe l'oeil murals. The weekday lunchtime menu (€17) and others (€24–42) list delicious dishes: seafood specialities, hot oysters with *beurre rouge*, roast brill with crab *coulis* and apples in puff pastry with Calvados cream sauce. Every year towards the end of July and August they host chamber music concerts in the garden.

Sées

61500

The Garden Hôtel**

12 [bis] rue des Ardrillers; it's 400m from the cathedral.
Ⓣ02.33.27.98.27 Ⓕ02.33.28.90.07
Closed Sun lunch to Mon morning in winter. **High chairs and cots available. TV. Car park.**

Things are remarkably quiet around here; there's a convent next door. As a mark of respect, none of the bedrooms looks onto it; they overlook a flower garden instead. The basic bedrooms are excellent value: doubles €26 with basin, and up to €40 with bath. Breakfast €5. The staff are perfectly lovely. In keeping with the spiritual atmosphere, there's an amusing collection of religious knick-knacks. *10% discount on the room rate offered to our readers on presentation of this guide.*

Macé

61500 (5km N)

L'Île de Sées**

It's well signposted on the D258.
Ⓣ02.33.27.98.65 Ⓕ02.33.28.41.22
Ⓦwww.ile-sees.fr
Closed *Sun evening; Mon; end Oct to end Feb.* **TV. High chairs available. Car park.**

This big house, in the heart of the countryside, is hidden by a curtain of ivy. Rooms look onto the garden so they're nice and quiet – but those in the extension don't have the charm of the ones in the old house. Doubles €52–55 with shower/wc or bath; breakfast €7. Good, regional dishes, not necessarily from Normandy – the *patronne* is a Breton, while her husband's up from Marseille. Specialities include excellent tripe, beef with Camembert, *turban* of fillet of sole with vanilla and duck foie gras. Weekday lunch menu €15, and others €22–33. *Free coffee offered to our readers on presentation of this guide.*

Thury-Harcourt

14220

Hôtel du Val d'Orne

9 rte. d'Aunay-sur-Odon.
Ⓣ02.31.79.70.81 Ⓕ02.31.79.16.12
Closed *Sat lunchtime in season; Fri evening and Sat out of season.* **Car park.**

Everyone's image of a country hotel – even down to the ivy clambering up the walls. Courteous welcome and simple rooms at €21 with basin up to €30 with shower/wc or bath. In tune with the style, the rustic dining room has paintings of rural scenes on the wall. Simple, straightforward local dishes: calf's head sauce *ravigote* and ox-cheek with Camembert sauce. Weekday lunch menu €9 and others up to €18.

Goupillères

14210 (7km N)

Auberge du Pont de Brie**

La Halte de Grimbosq; take the D 562. Acces via D562.
Ⓣ02.31.79.37.24 Ⓕ02.31.79.84.22
Ⓦwww.pontdebrie.com
Closed *Mon–Tues, Sun evening from 1 Oct–30 March*. **Open** *weekends only Nov–Dec; 15 Dec–8 Feb*. **TV. High chairs available. Car park.**

This well-presented establishment stands alone, surrounded by beautiful countryside. Rooms are spacious and comfortable; doubles €43 with shower/wc or bath. Excellent food; menus go for €16.50–39.50. Authentic Norman cuisine: chicken legs with *fondue* of apples, fillet of bass in cider sauce and delicious homemade three-flavoured apple *marmelade*. The staff are perfectly lovely and the service is really good. A good starting point to discover the region and the Grimbosq forest. Rated "Normandie Qualité Tourisme". *10% discount on the room rate offered to our readers on presentation of this guide (except 14 Jul–15Aug).*

Trouville-sur-Mer

14360

La Maison Normande**

4 pl. de Lattre de Tassigny.
Ⓣ02.31.88.12.25 Ⓕ02.31.88.78.79
Ⓦwww.maisonnormande.com
TV. Cots available.

In a quiet corner of the centre of town, this Norman half-timbered house is fronted by carved stone columns. The rooms have been refurbished in keeping with the charming ambience; doubles €35–61 depending upon facilities and the season. Breakfast €6. *10% discount on the room rate offered to our readers on presentation of this guide (1 Oct–1 Apr, outside zone C school holidays).*

Les Sablettes**

15 rue Paul-Besson; it's near the casino.
Ⓣ02.31.88.10.66 Ⓕ02.31.88.59.06
Ⓦwww.trouville-hotel.com
Closed *Jan*. **TV.**

The frontage of this place is perfect and the hotel itself is as pretty as can be. It has a very cosy atmosphere, almost like a guesthouse, with a comfortable lounge and a lovely old wooden staircase. The whole place is sparklingly clean. Recently renovated doubles go for €40–53 with shower/wc, €48–60 with bath. Breakfast €6. *10% discount on the room rate after the second night offered to our readers on presentation of this guide (except during school holidays or weekends).*

Le Bistrot sur le Quai

68 bd. Fernand-Moureaux; in the town centre, near the tourist office.
Ⓣ02.31.81.28.85
Closed *Wed; 15 Dec–1 Feb*.

This bistro is always full, even out of season. For this, all credit is due to the effusive welcome of the Finnish owner and the delicious house specialities: prawns grilled with garlic, flambéed shrimps with aniseed, *court-bouillon* of three fish, etc. Menus €10–25. Reckon on €30 à la carte. A really convivial place that we recommend without hesitation.

Les Vapeurs

160 bd. Fernand-Moureaux; it's next to the town hall, opposite the fish market.
Ⓣ02.31.88.15.24
Disabled access.

This, the best-known brasserie in Trouville, opened in 1927. All the American actors who come to the Deauville film festival eat here – Jack Nicholson is a regular. Try the house specialities – steamed local mussels with cream and freshly cooked prawns. Everything is fresh as can be; after all, the fishing boats land their catch only minutes away. The tripe's particularly good, too, especially with a nice glass of Saumur. Menus €11.80–19.90. Reckon on about €25–30 à la carte. You'll have to book at the weekend.

Restaurant Les Mouettes

11 rue des Bains; close to the fish market.
Ⓣ02.31.98.06.97
High chairs available.

A fish restaurant in a busy little street. The

décor is reminiscent of a Parisian bistro and there are two terraces – one of them on the pedestrianized street. Pleasant welcome and enjoyable cooking. Particularly good choices include salmon, fish *choucroute* and fish *pot-au-feu*. Menus €12–23.50. Children's menu €7.50. *Free digestif offered to our readers on presentation of this guide.*

Restaurant La Petite Auberge

7 rue Carnot; it's in a little street off pl. du Maréchal-Foch, in front of the casino.
02.31.88.11.07
Closed Tues and Wed except in school holidays.

À la carte menu is about €55 and the reasonably priced menus, €25–42, change with the seasons. They list such dishes as seabass seved with langoustines and aubergines, foie gras with apple and celeriac in puff pastry, raspberry macaroon in a vanilla bourbon *jus*. Nice welcome and efficient service. *Free coffee offered to our readers on presentation of this guide.*

Bistrot Les Quatre Chats

8 rue d'Orléans.
02.31.88.94.94
Closed *Mon and Tues lunchtimes; Wed; Thurs; 15 Nov–15 Dec.*

This place is favoured by Parisians and celebrities alike. The dining room has little bistro tables and rose-coloured walls – it's packed with books, postcards, photos and newspapers. The chef has spiced up a range of classical dishes by adding a few unexpected flavours – try the breast of duck with ginger. Their speciality, however, is the *gigot de sept heures* – a leg of lamb that's cooked for seven hours. Good home-baked bread, too, and a great wine list. Expect to pay €30–40 à la carte.

Vire

14500

Hôtel de France**

4 rue d'Aignaux.
02.31.68.00.35 02.31.68.22.65
Closed *20 Dec–20 Jan*. **Disabled access. High chairs available. TV. Pay car park**

Bedrooms here are all different, decorated in slightly sombre colours, but they're nice and light; doubles cost €38–58 with shower/wc or bath. Rooms at the back are quieter and have marvellous views of the wooded valleys. Half board is compulsory in high season €42–44 per person. Breakfast €6.50. In the restaurant, which specializes in honest, classic cuisine, try the local *andouille*, which is made in Vire. Set menus €12–40; à la carte €32. *10% discount on room rate (15 Nov–15 March) or free coffee offered to our readers on presentation of this guide.*

Saint-Germain-de-Taillevende

14500 (5km S)

L'Auberge Saint-Germain

Place de l'Église; take the D577.
02.31.68.24.13 02.31.68.89.57
le.castel.Normand@wanadoo.fr
Closed *Sun evening; Mon; end Jan to early Feb; 15–30 Sept*. **Disabled access.**

A pretty granite house, typical of the architectural style of the Virois marshes. The dining room is warm and welcoming with its low-slung beams and open fire and you'll experience smiling, speedy service. The chef puts a lot of local dishes on the menu: upside-down tart of Vire *andouille* with cider cream. These are attentively prepared and offer good value for money: menus €15 (weekdays) and up to €28. À la carte €32. They open a small terrace in summer.

Bény-Bocage (Le)

14350 (14.5km N)

Le Castel Normand**

Take the D577 Caen road for about 9km, then turn left onto the D56 for 2km.
02.31.68.76.03 02.31.68.63.58
www.lecastelnormand.com
Closed *Mon; Tues lunchtime; 15–31 Aug*. **TV. Car park.**

A lovely stone building near the handsome covered market on the town square. Refined rustic décor and first-class service. The cooking is full of flavour and the chef combines unusual ingredients to produce dishes that would flatter a grander establishment: *andouille* with Pommeau or lemon sole with bacon. Menus €21–50. If you want to linger, the rooms are as charming as the restaurant: doubles €41–50 with shower/wc or bath. *10% discount on the room rate offered to our readers on presentation of this guide.*

Haute-Normandie

Andelys (Les)

27700

🏃 🏠 |●| Hôtel de Paris - Restaurant Le Castelet**

10 av. de la République; from the main square follow the signs to Le Petit Andely.
Ⓣ02.32.54.06.33 Ⓕ02.32.54.65.92
Ⓦwww.giverny.org
Restaurant closed *Wed; Thurs lunchtime.*
TV. Car park.

A young, dynamic owner has taken over this small castle hotel with pointed roofs. Some evenings he plays his accordion or hosts poetry readings. The rooms are very comfortable. Those over the garden are quieter, though even the ones at the front don't get much traffic noise at night. Doubles €52–59 depending on the level of comfort. The restaurant, which has a huge terrace in summer, specializes in good regional cuisine made with fresh ingredients: duck foie gras cooked in a cloth, say, or *croustillant* of duck breast with honey, monkfish *blanquette* and zander steak. Menus €15 (weekday lunchtimes) and €21–41. *Free house apéritif offered to our readers on presentation of this guide.*

🏠 |●| Hôtel de Normandie**

1 rue Grande, Le Petit Andely.
Ⓣ02.32.54.10.52 Ⓕ02.32.54.25.84
Ⓦwww.hotelnormandie-andelys.com
Closed *Wed evening; Thurs; Dec.* **TV. Car park.**

Run by the same family for several decades, this large hotel, in a traditional Normandy building, has a pretty garden on the banks of the Seine. Doubles €55–58. You'll get a warm welcome and enjoy good cooking. Menus, €17.50 (weekdays) and €24–46, list dishes such as monkfish stew with Pommeau, duck with apples, frogs' legs and other regional specialities, with a Calvados sorbet presented as a variation on the *trou normand* (a shot of Calvados served between courses).

🏠 |●| Hôtel de la Chaîne d'Or***

Place St-Saveur; it's opposite the church on the banks of the Seine.
Ⓣ02.32.54.00.31 Ⓕ02.32.54.05.68
Ⓔchaineor@wanadoo.fr
TV. Car park.

This solidly constructed hotel has a quiet riverside location. Built in 1751, it gets its name from the chain that once stretched from the riverbank to the nearby island. Anyone wishing to pass the chain had to pay a toll; it became known as the "Chaîne d'Or" because it made a fortune. The hotel is luxurious but the easy-going staff make you feel welcome. Doubles, €78–122, have all facilities. Those overlooking the Seine are tastefully decorated and classically furnished, while others are more modern. You get a view of the barges on the river from the wonderful dining room where a fire is lit when it gets cold. It's one of the best restaurants in this part of the world, serving generous menus at €27–56, featuring traditional and gastronomic cooking. Unfortunately some of the prices are prohibitive, especially on the wine list.

Aumale

76390

🏠 |●| La Villa des Houx**

Avenue du Général-de-Gaulle; the street is opposite the station. N29.

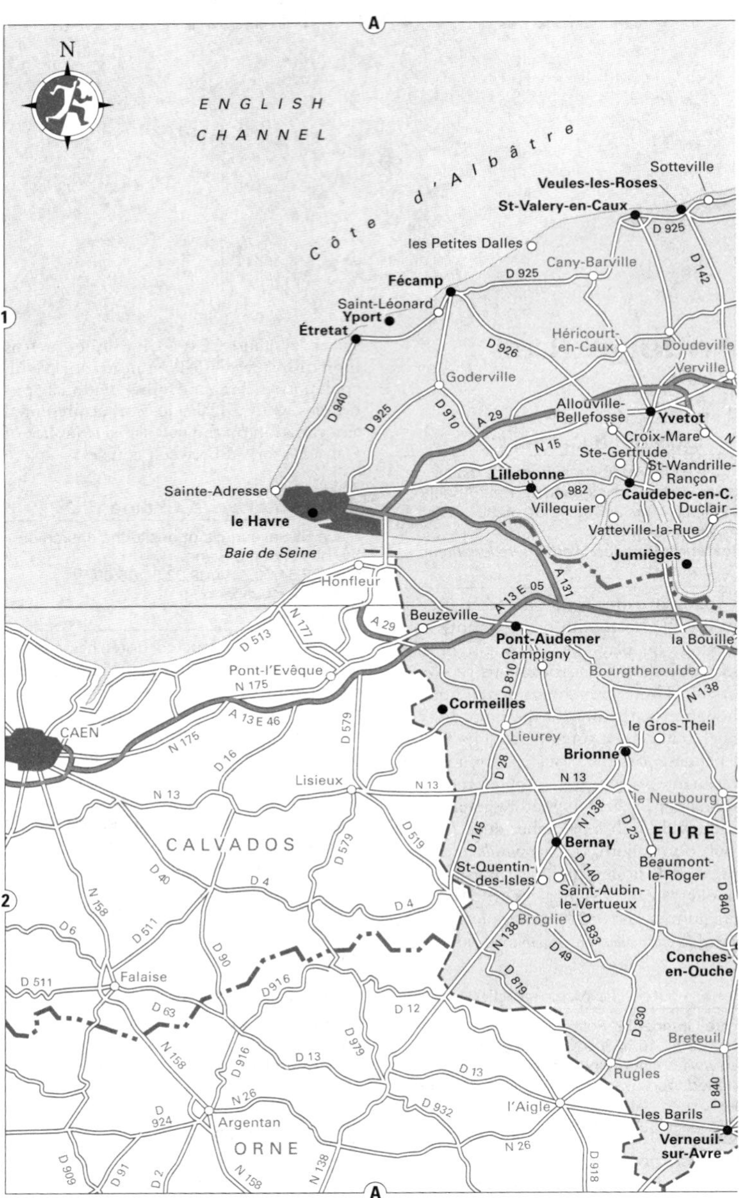

17

HAUTE-NORMANDIE

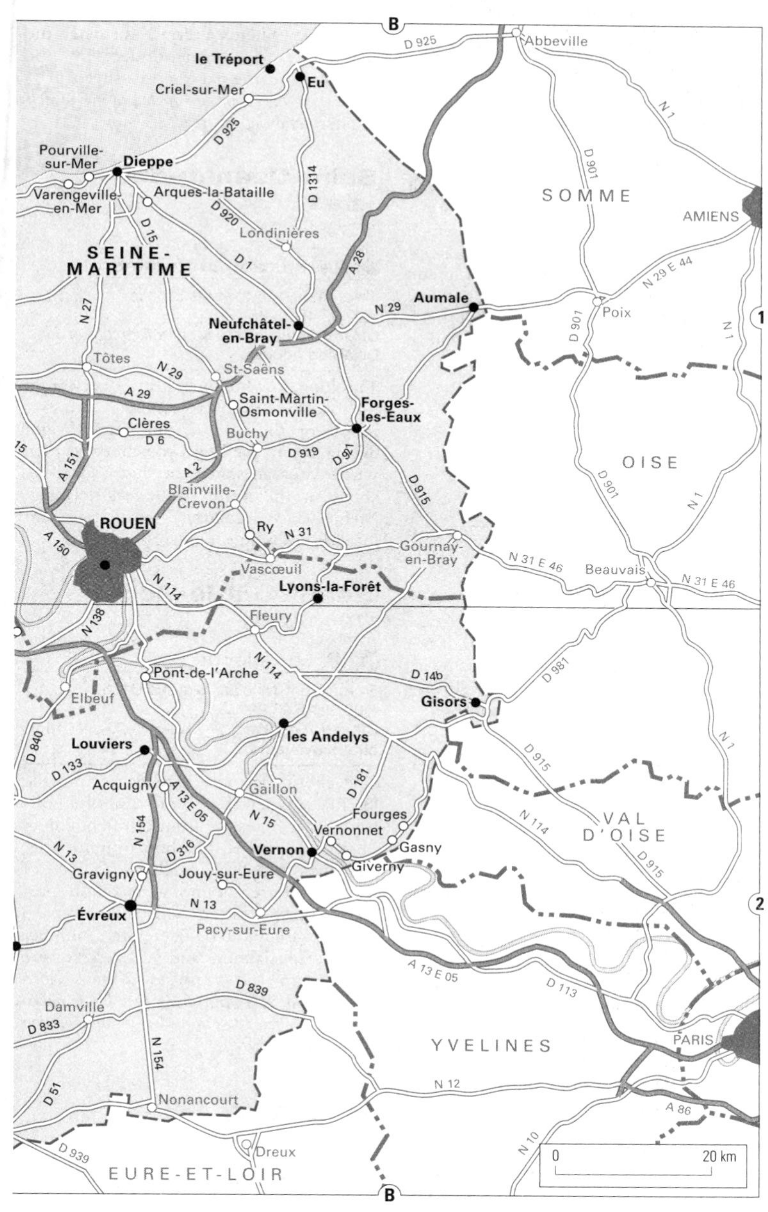

17 HAUTE-NORMANDIE

☎02.35.93.93.30 ℱ02.35.93.03.94
ⓦwww.lavilladeshoux.com
Closed *Sun evening 15 Oct–15 March; Mon lunchtime except Jun–Sept and public holidays; 1–25 Jan.* **Disabled access. TV. High chairs available. Car park.**

This two-star hotel is run so well that it really deserves three. It's in an Anglo-Norman house with 22 rooms. Doubles €58–75 with bath/wc – one has a four-poster bed and costs a little more. Half board, €60–65 per person, is compulsory at the weekend. The stylish restaurant, which has a good view of the garden, lists attractive dishes on its weekday lunch menu €15.50; another *menu terroir* ("regional menu") at €20. Tasty dishes include duck foie gras with apricots, scallops with endive and quail stuffed with foie gras and cooked in a salt crust. It's good value for money.

Bernay

27300

Le Lion d'Or**

48 rue du Général-de-Gaulle; it's in the main street.
☎02.32.43.12.06; ℱ02.32.46.60.58
Disabled access. TV. Car park.

Extremely clean hotel with tasteful, if not desperately original, rooms at €38 with shower/wc and €40 with bath. The breakfast is a buffet. Professional welcome.

Saint-Aubin-le-Vertueux

27300 (3km S)

L'Hostellerie du Moulin Fouret

Take the D140 then the D42.
☎02.32.43.19.95 ℱ02.32.45.55.50
ⓦwww.moulin-fouret.com
Closed *Sun evening and Mon except July–Aug and during public holidays.*
Disabled access (restaurant). Car park.

This sixteenth-century windmill stands in spacious grounds on the banks of the Charentonne. It's a gorgeous setting, and you can go fly-fishing nearby. François Deduit creates imaginative dishes and sauces using fresh local produce and offers very simple choices alongside more elaborate options. Specialities include hot *escalopes* of foie gras, traditional casserole-style pigeon. Top-class service. Menus €29–40. You'll pay around €54 à la carte. The rooms are quite simple, not too big and are mainly reserved for the restaurant's customers. Double rooms €45 with shower/wc. There's a terrace for when the weather is fine, surrounded by the Charentonne, the park and its sheep. *10% discount on the room rate offered to our readers on presentation of this guide.*

Saint-Quentin-des-Isles

27270 (4km SW)

Restaurant La Pommeraie

It's on the N138 towards Broglie.
☎02.32.45.28.88
Closed *Sun evening; Mon; a fortnight in Jan.*
Disabled access.

This long, low building, just set back from the road, has a Neoclassical façade and stylish décor throughout. The huge, bright dining room overlooks the pretty garden where you can watch the ducks splashing about in the pond – all very relaxing. Menus, €13 (weekdays) and €25–46, list local dishes with some exotic accents.

Beaumont-le-Roger

27170 (17km E)

La Calèche

54 rue Saint-Nicolas; take the D133.
☎02.32.45.25.99
Closed *Tues; Wed; 2–20 Jan; 1–20 July.* **High chairs available.**

The chef's creativity extends beyond the kitchen – when there's a festival or a holiday, he decorates the front of the building. His cooking revels in a host of influences, and includes dishes such as *fricassée* of seafood, house terrine with onion preserve, chicken fritters with *pousse* spinach and house apple tart. There are a number of fish specialities, and all desserts are cooked on the premises. Menus €13 (weekdays), €16 and €26. *Free house apéritif or coffee offered to our readers on presentation of this guide.*

Brionne

27800

L'Auberge du Vieux Donjon**

Place Fremont-des-Essarts; it's the market square.

Ⓣ02.32.44.80.62 Ⓕ02.32.45.83.23
Ⓦwww.auberge-vieux-donjon.com
Closed *Sun and Tues evenings; Mon in winter; a fortnight in March; 15 Oct–1 Nov.*
TV. Car park.

A large half-timbered inn with rooms overlooking the garden; doubles €40 with basin/bidet, €46 with shower/wc and €52 with bath. Have breakfast, an apéritif or a meal on the terrace in the courtyard. There's a classic menu at €13 during the week and another at €21.90. Regional dishes include foie gras with onion preserve, seafood platter, duck breast with peaches or apples and beef fillet with morels. *Free coffee offered to our readers on presentation of this guide.*

Hôtel Aquilon**

9 rte. de Calleville; it's at 500m to the centre.
Ⓣ02.32.44.81.49 Ⓕ02.32.44.38.83
Disabled access. TV. Car park.

You'll find this large brick-built building by the eleventh-century keep. No two rooms – doubles €50–72 with shower/wc or bath – are alike: those in the main building are lovely (especially no. 3, which has a double aspect of the valley and the grounds), and there's a nice mini-suite with sloping ceilings. Family atmosphere and attentive staff. Menus are served (€15–20) on weekday evenings, to hotel guests only. *Free coffee offered to our readers on presentation of this guide.*

Le Logis***

1 pl. Saint-Denis. Take N138 Rouen-Bernay, then follow city centre until the last traffic lights.
Ⓣ02.32.44.81.73 Ⓕ02.32.45.10.92
Ⓦwww.lerapporteur.fr/logis
Closed *Sat lunchtime (except reservations); Sun evening; Mon; a fortnight during Feb school holidays; a fortnight early Aug.*
Disabled access. TV. High chairs available. Car park.

This hotel building has been completely refurbished and offers up-to-date comfort. You'll pay €58 for a double with shower/wc, €65 with bath. Half board is compulsory in high season, €65 per person. The cooking is fresh and full of flavour, and dishes change with the season. They have weekday menus for €18–25, and others at the weekend €37–65.

Gros Theil (Le)

27110 (13km NE)

Le Vieux Brabant

Take the D26, opposite to the church.
Ⓣ03.32.35.51.31
Closed *Wed; Feb school holidays.*

A fairly ordinary village that you might drive through without bothering to notice. However let your gaze settle on this appealing inn and stop to look at the menu. The glorious odours of wine sauces, *coq au vin*, home-made pâtés and tarts make your mouth water; and you won't be disappointed. Cheapest menu €11 and others €19.90–39. The setting is rustic, and in summer they put tables out in the flower garden. There are also three double rooms if you're stuck for a bed for €36.

Caudebec-en-Caux

76490

Le Cheval Blanc*

4 pl. René-Coty; from the town hall on the banks of the Seine, go towards Saint-Arnoult-Lillebonne; pl. René-Coty is a few metres further on.
Ⓣ02.35.96.21.66 Ⓕ02.35.95.35.40
Ⓦwww.le-cheval-blanc.fr
Open *until 9pm.* **Closed** *Christmas–New Year.* **Restaurant closed** *Sun evening.* **TV. Disabled access. High chairs available. Car park.**

Friendly staff, tasty cooking and attractive décor. Pretty, comfortable double rooms go from €50 up to €53 with shower/wc or bath. Regional dishes are served in the restaurant, like ox tripe *à la normande*, foie gras with apple jelly, salmon ravioli and *millefeuille* of preserved grapefruit with vanilla. There's a weekday menu at €14 then others €21.50–33. *10% discount on the room rate (minimum of 2 consecutive nights, except in July–Aug) offered to our readers on presentation of this guide.*

Saint-Wandrille-Rançon

76490 (3km E)

Restaurant Les Deux Couronnes

Opposite the church.
Ⓣ02.35.96.11.44

Open *until 9pm.* **Closed** *Sun evening and Mon except public holidays.*

A seventeenth-century inn virtually in the precincts of the famous abbey. Tempting dishes include veal *escalope* served with apples or grilled bass served with smoked *andouille*. There's a €15 *formule* served at the week, and menus at €22 (two-course meal) and €26.50 (three-course meal); à la carte you're looking at €40.

Sainte-Gertrude

76490 (3km N)

Restaurant Au Rendez-Vous des Chasseurs

It's opposite the church.
☎02.35.96.20.30
Closed *Wed; Sun evening; 15–30 Aug.*
Disabled access. High chairs available.

This quiet little restaurant nestling between the forest and the small village church serves good regional cooking at prices to suit all pockets. Hunters and travellers have been coming here for more than 150 years. Menus, €15–25, might feature pork cheek salad, salmon ravioli with basil, calf's head sauce *gribiche*, while in winter the chef makes a delicious game stew with pheasant, venison and hare. You can eat out on the terrace in the garden in fine weather.

Villequier

76490 (4.5km SW)

Hôtel du Grand Sapin

Quai de Seine; it's on the outskirts of Villequier going towards Caudebec.
☎02.35.56.78.73 ⓕ02.35.95.69.27
Closed *Tues evening and Wed except July–Aug; Feb school holidays, 1–15 Nov.* **TV. Disabled access. Car park.**

Magnificent Normandy house on the banks of the Seine, with a lovely flower garden featuring an enormous magnolia – unusual in these parts. Throughout, the place is friendly and cosy, with a terrace for summer. Five double rooms €42 with bath; all of them overlook the river. In the large rustic dining room menus go for €20–34; there's also a short €11.50 menu served during the week and Saturday lunchtime. Specialities include foie gras, scallops and zander with *andouille*. Very good value for money. It's essential to call and make a reservation. Variable welcome.

Vatteville-la-Rue

76490 (8km S)

Auberge du Moulin

Take the D65 from the bridge over the Brontonne. Don't go into Vatteville, but take the road to Aizier; the hamlet of Quesnay is on the left.
☎02.35.96.10.88
Closed *evenings; Wed; 15 Aug to early Sept.*
Disabled access.

Other villages still have places like this multi-purpose establishment – restaurant-bar-tobacconist's-grocer's – but they're not usually as nice. The dining room offers a rustic setting with checked tablecloths, hunting trophies and wild boars' heads on the wall, and a wide, open fire. The few tables are usually taken. Food here is just what you might expect from the setting – lots of rugged, hearty, traditional dishes at inexpensive prices: go for scallops *à la provençale*, rabbit *chasseur*, snails or trout *meunière*. Menus €10.80 (weekday lunchtimes) and €14–25.

Conches-en-Ouche

27190

Hôtel-restaurant le Cygne**

36 rue du Val. At the bottom of Rue Sainte-Foy.
☎02.32.30.20.60 ⓕ02.32.30.45.73
Restaurant closed *Sun evening; Mon; Feb school holidays; Oct.* **Disabled access.**

This hotel has a few comfortable rooms with classic décor. Doubles cost €43–50 depending on facilities. The restaurant, meanwhile, is refined but rustic – the ideal backdrop for traditional, well-flavoured cooking. Dishes change with the seasons: try rabbit in cider, medallions of pork with apricots, and red fruit soup. Good-value menus range from €15 to the *menu terroir* at €28. Extremely nice welcome. *Free coffee offered to our readers on presentation of this guide.*

Cormeilles

27260

Auberge du Président**

70 rue de l'Abbaye.
☎02.32.57.88.37 ⓕ02.32.57.88.31

Ⓔ aubergeduprésident@wanadoo.fr
Closed *Sun evening; Mon (lunchtime only during summer).* **Disabled access. Car park.**

A large, half-timbered house at the entrance to the town, next to the Busnel distillery. This is classic Normandy cooking, though the chef comes from Arras. Lots of dishes with cider sauces or Camembert; the *Saveurs Normandes* is a menu with nothing but apple dishes (and lashings of cream). Menus €13 (lunchtime), others €17–26. The hotel has been completely renovated and double rooms go for €50. Welcoming atmosphere.

Le Florida

21 rue de l'Abbaye; it's opposite the town hall.
Ⓣ 02.32.57.80.97
Closed *Mon; Sun–Fri evenings 15 Oct–31 March; 1–15 June.*

Nice family atmosphere and high-quality, good-value cuisine. Specialities include rabbit in cider. Weekday lunch menu €10.50, and others at €15 and €23. *Free coffee offered to our readers on presentation of this guide.*

Dieppe

76200

Auberge de jeunesse

48 rue Louis-Fromager; a long way out; take the no. 2 bus in the direction of Val Druel to the "Château-Michel" stop.
Ⓣ 02.35.84.85.73 Ⓕ 02.35.84.89.62
Closed *early Oct to end May.*

The building is a little forbidding – it used to be a school – but the warm welcome dispels all doubts. It sleeps 42 people, spread over dormitories or rooms with four beds for €8 per person. Breakfast €3.20. FUAJ card compulsory. Kitchen and barbecue available for preparing your own meals.

Hôtel Au Grand Duquesne*

15 pl. Saint-Jacques; it's in the street opposite the church of Saint-Jacques.
Ⓣ 02.32.14.61.10 Ⓕ 02.35.84.29.83
Ⓦ www.augrandduquesne.fr
TV.

This hotel, which is decorated in a tasteful, modern style, offers pretty, well-equipped bedrooms. Doubles starts at €29 and up to €40 depending on the facilities.

Les Arcades de la Bourse**

1–3 arcades de la Bourse; it's on the marina.
Ⓣ 02.35.84.14.12 Ⓕ 02.35.40.22.29
Ⓦ www.lesarcades.fr
TV.

Modern, comfortable rooms – nothing over the top – some of which have wonderful views over the marina. Doubles €43 with shower/wc or bath, €76 with a view. It also has a restaurant.

Le Bistrot du Pollet

23 rue de Tête de Bœuf; it's on the quai, between Ango bridge and Colbert bridge, opposite the post office.
Ⓣ 02.35.84.68.57
Closed *Sun; Mon; a fortnight in March; Aug.*

A small, friendly restaurant with a cosy interior – lots of old photographs on the walls and old-fashioned music in the background. It may be wise to book, especially at lunchtime, when it fills up with loyal regulars. Fish is a speciality here – the grilled bass and sea bream are wonderful – along with foie gras *du pêcheur*, a typical Dieppois recipe of marinated, puréed monkfish liver. Prices are more than reasonable, with a lunch menu at €11.43 during the week, or around €22 à la carte.

À la Marmite Dieppoise

8 rue Saint-Jean; it's just by quai Duquesne.
Ⓣ 02.35.84.24.26 Ⓕ 02.35.84.31.12
Closed Sun and Mon Nov–March; Sun evening, Mon and Tues evening April–Oct.

A classic Dieppoise restaurant serving fine food. Menus revolve around fish dishes prepared with cream; their superb signature dish is *marmite dieppoise*, a tasty stew of monkfish, ling, brill, sole and scallops, with mussels and crayfish, all cooked together in a pan. You could also go for the lobster or the sole, both of which are delicious. Menus €18 (weekday lunchtimes), others €27–39. *Free coffee offered to our readers on presentation of this guide.*

Pourville-sur-Mer

76550 (4.5km W)

L'Huîtrière

Rue du 19-Août; it's 4km west of Dieppe on the seashore.
Ⓣ 02.35.84.36.20
Open *daily 10am–8pm, tasting session Easter–Sept.* **Car park.**

A seafood restaurant, open all year, above

the store where oysters are sold direct from the oyster beds. It specializes in oysters, of course, along with clams, whelks, winkles, cockles and crêpes. The décor is appealing, with sea-blue walls, oyster baskets hung from the ceiling and an ancient diving suit in the corner, and the bay windows open right onto the beach. In summer, they set up a huge terrace. Though the food is good, prices are high for such a simple place. Credit cards not accepted.

Varengeville-sur-Mer

76119 (8km SW)

Hôtel-restaurant La Terrasse**

Route de Vasterival. Take the D75.
Ⓣ02.35.85.12.54 Ⓕ02.35.85.11.70
Ⓦwwwhotel-restaurant-la.terrasse.com
Closed *mid-Oct to mid-March.* **High chairs and games available. Car park.**

This cosy family hotel snuggling among the pine trees is a regular favourite with British visitors. It's in a remarkable location on the cliffs and the terrace is a superb spot to admire the Channel over a drink. The 22 attractive rooms, all with shower/wc or bath, go for €46–51. Half board is compulsory and costs €45–50 per person per night. The restaurant serves lots of fish, however the view seems nicer than the food quality. Menus €16–30. In fine weather, there are always lots of people so it's best to reserve.

La Buissonnière

Route du Phare-d'Ailly.
Ⓣ02.35.83.17.13
Closed *Sun evening; Mon; Jan–Feb.*

This beautiful private house, flooded with light and bedecked with flowers, is an ideal place for prolonging a visit to the Moutiers wood. The food is a perfect match for the setting; the ingredients, mainly derived from the sea, are superbly fresh and managed with sensual skill. Menu €29, or eat à la carte. A lovely spot.

Arques-la Bataille

76880 (9km SE)

Le Manoir d'Archelles

It's on the D1, Neuchâtel road, on the edge of town, next to *L'Auberge d'Archelles*.
Ⓣ02.35.85.50.16 Ⓕ02.35.85.47.55
Closed *Sat lunchtime and Sun evening, Fri evening in Winter. 1–15 Feb, last week Aug; Christmas.* **TV. Disabled access. Car park.**

This stunning sixteenth-century manor house, built of a mosaic of brick and flint stones, offers doubles for €30 with shower, €40–46 with shower/wc or bath; they also have a suite that sleeps four. The décor is more rustic than chic but that doesn't diminish its charm. The rooms in the fortified gatehouse, reached by a spiral stone staircase, are particularly attractive, giving good views of the château. Have a wander round the orchard and carefully tended vegetable garden. *Free coffee offered to our readers on presentation of this guide.*

L'Auberge d'Archelles

Archelles; it's on the D1, Neuchâtel road, on the edge of town, next to *Le Manoir* (above).
Ⓣ02.35.83.40.51
Closed *Fri evening; Sat lunchtime; Sun evening.* **TV. Car park.**

This good-value restaurant, owned by the same people as *Le Manoir*, is housed in beautifully converted old stables. The cuisine is as attractive as the setting, featuring regional and gastronomic dishes. A nice weekday menu at €13.80, other menus €18–32.50. Try the Camembert *croquettes*, duck in cider sauce, bass with fennel and homemade pastry.

Étretat

76790

Hôtel d'Angleterre

35 av. George-V; it's 100m from the sea on the Le Havre road that starts at the tourist office.
Ⓣ02.35.28.84.97 Ⓕ02.35.28.05.57
TV.

A clean, welcoming, reasonably priced hotel, well away from the touristy part of town and newly refurbished – in other words, something of a find. Doubles €40 with shower/wc.

L'Escale**

Place Foch; it's opposite the old market.
Ⓣ02.35.27.03.69 Ⓕ02.35.28.05.86
TV.

This hotel-brasserie is a really nice place.

The wood-panelled bedrooms are a bit small but pleasant enough; doubles with shower/wc go for €47. The lively ground-floor restaurant-brasserie serves simple dishes – mussels and chips, omelettes, salads, pizzas and crêpes – along with a few gourmet options. You'll pay about €10 for a main course. Sit on the terrace and watch the world hurry by in the square.

L'Huitrière

Rue Traz-Perrier; it's on the seafront, towards Aval cliffs.
Ⓣ02.35.27.02.82
Closed *Jan.*

An extraordinary circular dining room with a sensational panoramic view over the beaches and cliffs. They specialize in seafood and fish and take great care over the preparation of each dish. The €18 menu proves very good value, other menus up to €38; you'll spend around €46 for a seafood tray for two people. *Every diner receives a complimentary trou normand – a shot of Calvados – between courses.*

Restaurant Le Galion

Boulevard René-Coty.
Ⓣ02.35.29.48.74 Ⓕ02.35.29.74.48
Ⓦwww.etretat.net
Closed *Tues and Wed out of season except during school holidays; 15 Dec–15 Jan.*

Cosy restaurant with seventeenth-century décor – enormous fireplace, little tinted window panes, old beams – and high-class service. The €22 menu is beautifully balanced, listing velvety smooth fish soup, *escalope* of salmon with Muscadet, other menus up to €35. *Free coffee offered to our readers on presentation of this guide.*

La Salamandre

4 bd. René-Coty; on the ground floor of the splendid Salamandre manor house.
Ⓣ02.35.27.02.87

This place has really won us over. No need for a sea view here, the food provides sufficient spectacle of its own. The establishment takes pride in offering only ingredients that are organically grown or bred on a farm (apart from the seafood, obviously), not just to show off but because they taste better. Menus €29–38, but you can also eat economically à la carte, with mussels at €8 and large platters at €16. Whatever you choose, it will be presented elegantly and served gracefully, and you're bound to leave contented.

Eu

76260

Centre des Fontaines – Auberge de jeunesse

Rue des Fontaines; in the royal kitchens of the castle.
Ⓣ02.35.86.05.03 Ⓕ02.35.86.45.12
Ⓔcentre-des-fontaines@wanadoo.fr
Reception open *2–9pm (6–9pm Sun and public holidays).* **Closed** *over Christmas and New Year holidays.*

Rooms with four to twelve beds and washbasin or shower (wc in the corridor); a bed costs €12.10 a night, including sheets. Meals available for groups. You can come back any time after 9pm, but you must ask for the key first.

Hôtel-Restaurant Maine**

20 av. de la Gare. 5mn from city centre.
Ⓣ02.35.86.16.64 Ⓕ02.35.50.86.25
Ⓦwww.hotel-maine.com
Restaurant closed *Sun evening; 17 Aug–9 Sept.* **Hotel open** *all year.* **TV. Car park.**

Bright and peaceful establishment in a master-craftsman's house opposite the old station. Though some have been refurbished more recently than others, the bedrooms have all facilities, with en-suite bathrooms, TV and telephones. Doubles with shower/wc cost €47.26, with bath €53.30. Half board is compulsory over public holiday weekends and from Easter to September; the quality of the cuisine is good value. Indeed, it's worth coming just for a meal. The Maine has been serving food since 1867, and the dining room is an exceptional example of Art Nouveau. Dishes are modern yet firmly rooted in local and traditional cuisine. Fish dishes include an *assiette* of marinated fish and *picatta* of salmon with parsley cream and artichoke *fondant*, while carnivores will enjoy the rabbit in cider jelly and the half-chicken grilled with lemon *confit*. There's a weekday menu at €14.95 and two others menus, the "*boucher*" and "*pêcheur*" at €23.70. *10% discount on the room rate offered to our readers on presentation of this guide.*

Évreux

27000

|●| Restaurant La Croix d'Or

3 rue Joséphine.
☎02.32.33.06.07
High chairs available. Disabled access.

Fine food intelligently prepared by people who care about what they do. The restaurant is convenient for the administrative quarter, and is often full of local civil servants enjoying a good lunch. They specialize in fish – and particularly *bouillabaisse*. Other great dishes include Queen scallop *clafoutis*, *millefeuille* of haddock, and fish *choucroute*. Carnivores aren't forgotten, either. Superb weekday lunch menu at €10.90 and others from €14 to €25.

Gravigny

27930 (4km N)

|●| Le Saint-Nicolas

38 av. Aristide-Briand; it's on the D155 towards Louviers, on the right.
☎02.32.38.35.15
Closed *Sun evening.* **Car park.**

This unobtrusive house conceals a number of lovely little dining rooms decorated in a simple, sophisticated style – intimate ones for candlelit dinners, larger ones for lively groups and a terrace for outside dining. The boned pig's trotters with truffles are delicious, as are the perch fillets with Saint-Nicolas butter and the warm oysters with cream and shallot sauce. Superb wine list. Menus €18–30. *Free coffee offfered to our readers on presentation of this guide.*

Jouy-sur-Eure

27120 (20km N)

|●| Le Relais Du Guesclin

Place de l'Église; take the N13 in the direction of Pacy-sur-Eure, then the D57.
☎02.32.36.62.75
Closed *Wed. Open lunchtime; evenings by reservation only.* **Car park.**

A little Normandy inn with a church on one side and fields on the other. Peace and quiet are guaranteed, so you can have an undisturbed lunch outside. The daily *formule*, €15, gets you a main course plus starter or dessert, and there are other menus €25–30; dishes include *bonhomme normand*, foie gras, ox kidneys and warm tarts – the best of Normandy cuisine and good dry cider to boot.

Fécamp

76400

Hôtel de la Plage**

87 rue de la Plage (Centre).
☎02.35.29.76.51 Ⓕ02.35.28.68.30
Ⓦwwperso.wanadoo.fr/hoteldelaplage
TV. Disabled access. Pay car park.

Charming, well-equipped hotel, a stone's throw from the beach. Most of the rooms are refurbished and quiet, and some have a sea view. Doubles €35–50, depending on the comfort and the season. Very pretty breakfast room (although you can also have breakfast in bed). Guests are given a really delightful welcome and plenty of tips on how to take full advantage of their stay.

|●| Hôtel Normandy

2 bis av. Gambetta.
☎02.35.29.55.11 Ⓕ02.35.27.48.74
Ⓦwww.normandy-fecamp.com
TV.

A *Logis de France* with an alluring, totally renovated façade. Double rooms at €45; some are particularly spacious. A good place to stay in the town centre. Very attractive, old-fashioned restaurant. Excellent service.

|●| Le Vicomté

4 rue du Président-Coty; it's 50m from the port, behind the Palais Bénédictine.
☎02.35.28.47.63
Closed *Wed evening; Sun; public holidays; a fortnight end Aug; a fortnight end Dec.*

A very welcoming, and rather unusual, retro bistro with checked tablecloths and posters from the *Petit Journal* adorning the walls. They serve just one set menu at €14.90, but the dishes – regional cooking, based on fresh produce – change every day. Children's menu €6.50. Excellent value for money and impeccable service.

|●| Chez Nounoute

3 pl. Nicolas-Selle; in Bout-Menteux, in the port.
Closed *Sun evening; Wed.*

Nounoute is a real character. She greets customers with cheeky, maternal attention and soon makes them feel at ease. The restaurant used to be a fishmonger's, and

Nounoute similarly stresses the quality of the local fish by serving marinated mackerel, smoked herring, fresh cod and many more besides. Menus €14–25, conviviality and good humour included. Many of our readers are already devoted customers, and a visit to *Chez Nounoute* alone will make any trip to Fécamp worthwhile.

Saint-Léonard

76400 (2km S)

Auberge de la Rouge**

Route du Havre; on the outskirts of Fécamp.
02.35.28.07.59 02.35.28.70.55
www.auberge-rouge.com
Closed *a fortnight in Feb.* **TV. Car park.**

One of the best restaurants in the *département*. The décor and service obey classical rules, but in contrast the cooking takes some risks. The flavours and cooking techniques are skilfully controlled to bring out the qualities of the high-quality ingredients. Menus €17 and €27 (except Sun), then €33 and €49. Double rooms €58; there are also a few soberly decorated duplex rooms at the end of the garden.

Forges-les-Eaux

76440

Le Continental***

110 av. des Sources; it's near the casino, 50m.
02.32.89.50.50 02.35.90.26.14
www.casinoforges.com
Disabled access. TV. Car park.

An impressive half-timbered building that's been thoroughly renovated. With its large foyer and balconies it still has the nicely old-fashioned atmosphere of old casino hotels, and offers well-equipped bedrooms for between €60 and €64. Guests can use the nearby Club Med facilities by arrangement (02.32.89.50.40) and the Casino's restaurant is very close.

Saint-Martin-Osmonville

76680 (23km W)

Auberge de la Varenne

2 rte. de la Libération; take the D919 to Buchy, then the D41.
02.35.34.13.80
Closed *Sun and Wed evenings; Mon.*

They stick firmly to traditional, local cooking in this pleasant roadside inn – the menu changes twice a year, but typical offerings might include *croustillant* of *andouille* with apple and beef cheek with cider. Weekday menu at €16.05 and others €19.10–33.55. With very attentive service and a warm welcome, it's a good place to eat after visiting the old market in Buchy. There's an open fire in the winter, and a lovely terrace in good weather.

Gisors

27140

Le Cochon Gaulois

8 pl. Blanmont; it's opposite the château.
02.32.27.30.33
Closed *Sun.*

They serve only pork dishes; charcuterie, pork cheek salad, ham hock terrine, grilled spare ribs and all sorts of grills. They have a weekday lunchtime menu at €10.70 and another menu for €14.90. But their roast suckling pig is the sensation (€11.90); it's served in its own juice or with any sauce you choose. It's tender, crumbling and delicious. Strangely, only the suckling pig is free range. Karaoke on Friday evening. *Free house apéritif offered to our readers on presentation of this guide.*

Le Cappeville

17 rue Cappeville.
02.32.55.11.08
Closed *Wed evening; Thurs; a fortnight early Jan; a fortnight early Sept.* **Disabled access. High chairs available.**

A good place to pause in this little town where you can get a quality meal that absolutely follows the region's traditions. Specialities include artichoke and crab *millefeuille*, sea bass with pepper, and calves' kidneys flambéed in Calvados (prepared before your very eyes). Menus from €17 (except Sun) up to €37. The interior is as refined as the cuisine and there is a warm welcome.

Havre (Le)

76600

See map overleaf

Hôtel Séjour Fleuri

71 rue Émile-Zola; 500m from the beach and 500m from the ferries. **Map B3-3**
02.35.41.33.81

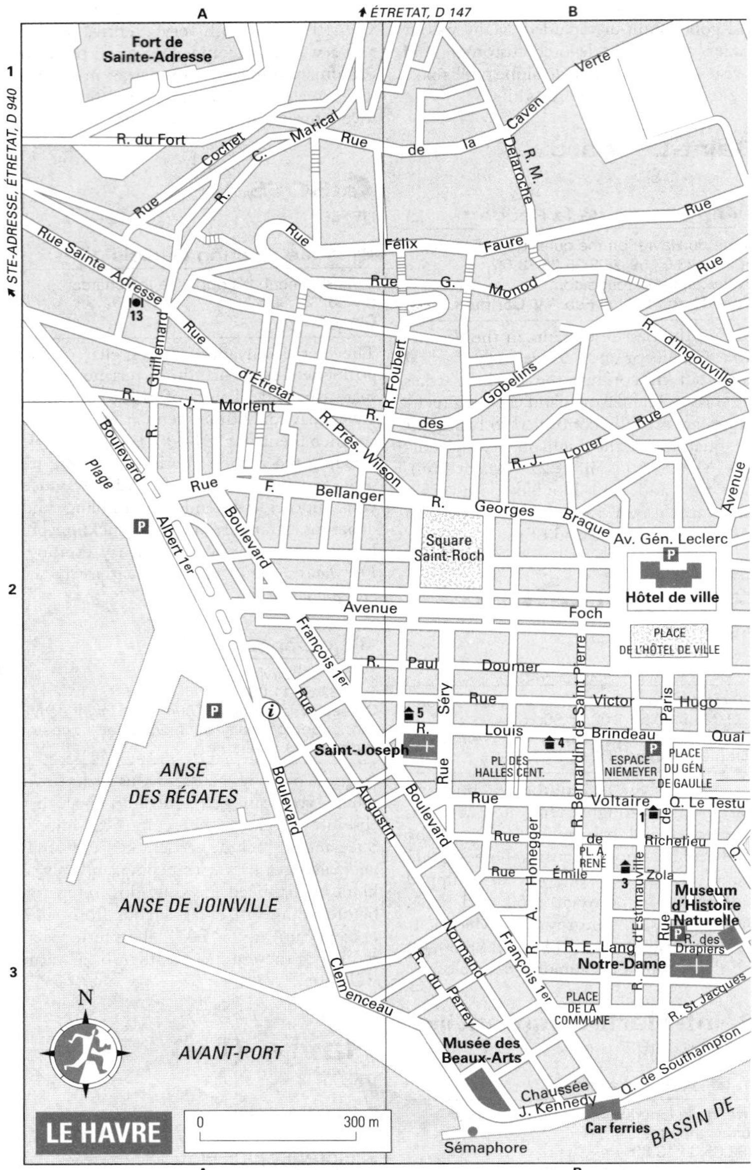

A
ÉTRETAT, D 147
B
STE-ADRESSE, ÉTRETAT, D 940
Fort de Sainte-Adresse
R. du Fort
Rue Cochet
R. C. Marical
Rue de la Cavée Verte
R. M. Delaroche
Rue Félix Faure
Rue G. Monod
Rue Sainte Adresse
Rue d'Étretat
R. Guillemard
R. J. Morlent
R. Foubert
R. des Gobelins
R. d'Ingouville
R. Prés. Wilson
Rue J. Louer
Boulevard Albert 1er
Plage
Rue F. Bellanger
R. Georges Braque
Avenue
Av. Gén. Leclerc
Boulevard
Square Saint-Roch
Hôtel de ville
Avenue Foch
PLACE DE L'HÔTEL DE VILLE
François 1er
R. Paul Doumer
Rue Victor Hugo
R. Bernardin de Saint Pierre
Paris
Quai
Rue Séry
R. Louis Brindeau
Saint-Joseph
PL. DES HALLES CENT.
ESPACE NIEMEYER
PLACE DU GÉN. DE GAULLE
Rue Voltaire
Q. Le Testu
ANSE DES RÉGATES
Boulevard
Augustin
Boulevard
Rue de Richelieu
R. A. Honegger
PL. A. RENÉ
Rue Émile Zola
d'Estimauville
ANSE DE JOINVILLE
Museum d'Histoire Naturelle
R. des Drapiers
R. E. Lang
Notre-Dame
Normand
François 1er
R. du Perrey
Clemenceau
PLACE DE LA COMMUNE
R. St Jacques
N
AVANT-PORT
Musée des Beaux-Arts
Chaussée J. Kennedy
Q. de Southampton
LE HAVRE
0
300 m
Car ferries
BASSIN DE
Sémaphore
1
2
3
13
5
4
1
3

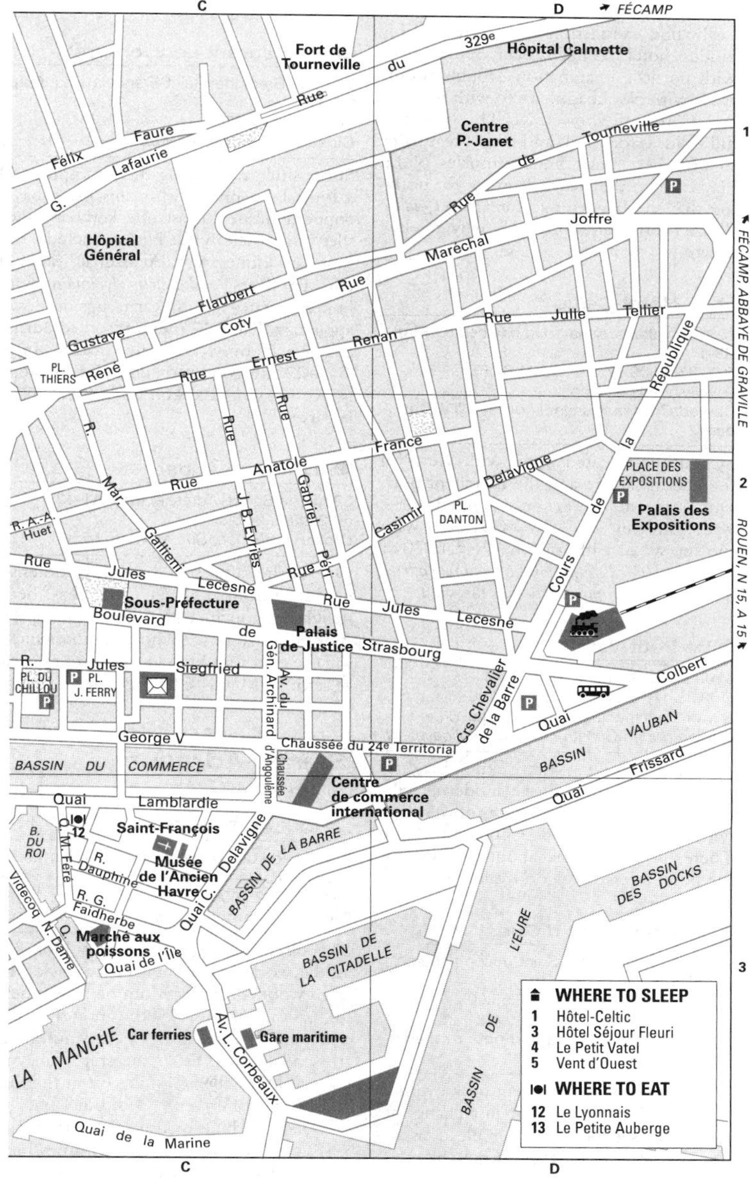
C
D
FÉCAMP
Fort de Tourneville
Rue du 329e
Hôpital Calmette
Centre P.-Janet
Rue de Tourneville
Rue Félix Faure
G. Lafaurie
Hôpital Général
Rue Maréchal Joffre
Rue Gustave Flaubert
Rue René Coty
PL. THIERS
Rue Ernest Renan
Rue Jules Tellier
Rue de la République
FÉCAMP, ABBAYE DE GRAVILLE
Rue Anatole France
Rue J. B. Eyriès
Rue Gabriel Péri
R. Mar. Galliéni
R. A.-A. Huet
Rue Casimir Delavigne
PL. DANTON
PLACE DES EXPOSITIONS
Palais des Expositions
ROUEN, N 15, A 15
Cours de la République
Rue Jules Lecesne
Sous-Préfecture
Palais de Justice
Boulevard de Strasbourg
R. Jules Siegfried
PL. DU CHILLOU
PL. J. FERRY
Av. du Gén. Archinard
Crs Chevalier de la Barre
Quai Colbert
George V
Chaussée du 24e Territorial
Chaussée d'Angoulême
BASSIN DU COMMERCE
BASSIN VAUBAN
Quai Frissard
Centre de commerce international
Quai Lamblardie
12
Saint-François
B. DU ROI
Q. M. Féré
R. Dauphine
Musée de l'Ancien Havre
Quai C. Delavigne
BASSIN DE LA BARRE
R. G. Faidherbe
Videcoq
Q. N.-Dame
Marché aux poissons
Quai de l'Île
BASSIN DES DOCKS
BASSIN DE LA CITADELLE
BASSIN DE L'EURE
LA MANCHE
Car ferries
Gare maritime
Av. L. Corbeaux
Quai de la Marine
1
2
3
WHERE TO SLEEP
1 Hôtel-Celtic
3 Hôtel Séjour Fleuri
4 Le Petit Vatel
5 Vent d'Ouest
WHERE TO EAT
12 Le Lyonnais
13 Le Petite Auberge

Ⓕ02.35.42.26.44
TV. Car park.

A godsend for travellers on a small budget, although more prosperous visitors can easily find satisfaction here as well. This modest hotel has been totally refurbished, with no little imagination. Double rooms €24 with washbasin, €26 with shower and €30 with shower/wc. The owner is full of ideas for strolls and takes great pains to give her guests fine memories of Le Havre when they leave. It is not for nothing that she has won a *Normandy Quality Tourism* certificate. So, frankly, why go elsewhere to pay more?

Hôtel-Celtic**

106 rue Voltaire; situated in city centre. **Map B3-1**
Ⓣ02.35.42.39.77 Ⓕ02.35.21.67.65
Ⓦwww.hotel.celtic.com
Closed *Christmas school holidays.* **TV. Car park.**

Delightfully located hotel with views of the Volcan theatre and the merchant port. Double rooms are brightly painted; those with shower go for €31.30; with shower/wc or with bath they're €42.70 or €47.30. *10% discount on the room rate offered to our readers on presentation of this guide.*

Le Petit Vatel**

8 rue Louis Brindeau. **Map B2-4**
Ⓣ02.35.41.72.07 Ⓕ02.35.21.37.86
Ⓦwww.multimania.com/lepetitvatel
Closed *during Christmas school holidays.* **TV.**

A central hotel where the brightly painted, clean rooms have modern facilities and bathrooms; €37 with shower, €42 with shower/wc and €46 with bath. There's nothing special about the view but the hotel offers very good value.

Hôtel Vent d'Ouest***

4 rue de Caligny; near Saint-Joseph church. **Map B2-5**
Ⓣ02.35.42.50.69 Ⓕ02.35.42.58.00
Ⓦwww.ventdouest.fr
TV. High chairs, games and cots available. Pay car park.

When the new management took over the old *Hotel Foch* they didn't just change its name, they set about the Herculean task of complete refurbishment. It's now a three-star place. Each of the three floors has its own style and the 33 rooms are individually decorated with a country, seaside or mountain look. The little details and ornaments give the rooms a personal touch. Doubles with bath from €80 up to €90, depending on the size of the room.

Restaurant Le Lyonnais

7 rue de Bretagne; Saint-François area. **Map C3-12**
Ⓣ02.35.22.07.31
Closed *Sat lunchtime; Sun.*

Successfully re-creating the atmosphere of a typical Lyonnais bistro, this place has a copper chimney breast, checkerboard floor tiles and brick walls. Dishes include fish stew, veal kidneys with Armagnac, *gâteau* of chicken livers, *andouillette lyonnaise* with boiled potatoes, and warm upside-down apple tart. The €12 menu is served during the week only, but the others, from €14–22, are good too and the €17 menu is worth trying. Reckon on around €25 à la carte.

La Petite Auberge

32 rue de Sainte-Adresse. **Map A1-13**
Ⓣ02.35.46.27.32
Closed *Sat lunch; Sun evening; Mon.*

One of the safest bets for trying authentic cooking from Le Havre; it has been delighting gourmets for generations and it is not unusual to see whole families enjoying the exquisite food in this most classical of settings. Menus €19, €26 and €38. It is advisable to book.

Sainte-Adresse

76310 (2km NW)

Les Trois Pics

Promenade des Régates; it's at the northernmost end of Le Havre beach.
Ⓣ02.35.48.20.60
Closed *Sun evening; Mon.*

This place, standing on the quay, looks for all the world like a liner in dry dock. The large wooden dining room has a wonderful, panoramic view of the mouth of the Seine and the maritime décor is imaginative and refined. From the ship's rail you can see Deauville, ten miles off in the distance. They offer very good dishes but the wine list is a bit expensive. Menus start at €18, served weekday lunchtimes and including a starter or a main course and a dessert, rising to €23 or €35; à la carte will set you back €35 per head. Have a drink on the terrace in the summer (or even in the winter as it's a heated terrace)– when dusk falls and the lights are turned on across the bay, you can almost imagine you're out at sea. *Free house apéritif offered to our readers on presentation of this guide.*

Jumièges

76480

|●| Auberge des Ruines

Place de la Mairie; it's opposite the monastery.
Ⓣ02.35.37.24.05
Closed *Sun and Tues evenings; Wed; Mon and Thurs evenings 1 Nov–15 March.*

The best restaurant in town, where you can snuggle up in front of the fire in winter or relax under the awning in summer. If you regard yourself as a foodie, try the chicken *tartare* with peppers and chorizo, pork chop with juniper berries or the puffed-up chocolate. The weekday menu goes for €15 and €21, with others €31–50.

Duclair

76480 (9km NE)

|●| Restaurant Le Parc

Take the D982.
Ⓣ02.35.37.50.31
Closed *Wed in winter.* **Disabled access.**

Away from the road, and therefore from the cars, an unbeatably romantic setting with décor that would have appealed to Flaubert or Maupassant. It offers unquestionably the best view of the Seine in these parts, with a magnificent terrace and garden overlooking the water. Exquisite, old-fashioned atmosphere, with porcelain tableware in pretty floral designs, lace tablecloths and charming fireplaces. Traditional cooking. Menus from €15 (weekdays) to €44. The welcome you receive is as enchanting as everything else.

Lillebonne

76170

🏃 🏠 |●| La P'tite Auberge

20 rue du Havre; it's beside the church.
Ⓣ02.35.38.00.59 Ⓕ02.35.38.57.33
Ⓦwww.la-ptite-auberge.com
Closed *Sat lunchtime; Sun evening; Fri; 19 July–9 Aug.* **High chairs available. Disabled access. TV.**

This hotel is in a large, half-timbered house. Most of the bright rooms have had new bathrooms fitted; doubles go for €29 with basin (the wc is along the landing) and €43 for shower/wc or bath. The rustic dining room is a good place to eat traditional cuisine such as house foie gras, veal sweetbreads Rossini and chocolate *moelleux*, with two weekday lunch menus for €14 and €17 and others €19–27. There's a shady flower-filled terrace open during warm weather. *Free coffee offered to our readers on presentation of this guide.*

Louviers

27400

🏃 🏠 |●| Le Pré-Saint-Germain***

7 rue Saint-Germain; it's northeast of place Ernest-Thorel.
Ⓣ02.32.40.48.48 Ⓕ02.32.50.75.60
Ⓦwww.le-pre-saint-germain.fr
Restaurant (and bistro) closed *Sat lunchtime; Sun.* **Disabled access. TV. Car park.**

Built in the middle of an old orchard, this Neoclassical-style hotel boasts all the facilities you should expect from a three-star establishment, with doubles at €78–93 with bath/wc. You can be sure of eating well, too, with dishes such as *fricassée* of lobster and King prawns with curry and coconut, duck with apple brandy and cinnamon and a fine apple tart with vanilla ice cream flambéed in Calvados. Menu €15, or around €30 à la carte. Nice terrace in summer. *10% discount on the room rate (weekends Nov–March) or free coffee offered to our readers on presentation of this guide.*

🏃 |●| Le Jardin de Bigard

39–41 rue du Quai; it's on the corner of rue du Coq.
Ⓣ02.32.40.02.45
Closed *Wed and Sun evenings.* **Disabled access.**

A centrally located, unpretentious restaurant with a bright, airy dining room offering simple but carefully prepared dishes at reasonable prices. The weekday lunch menu costs €9.80, and there are others from €12.80 to €22.50. Specialities include scallops in cider, calf's head sauce *gribiche*, fillet of trout with Camembert and cockerel in cider. *Free house apéritif offered to our readers on presentation of this guide.*

Le Clos Normand

Rue de la Gare–chaussée du Vexin; cross the Eure by rue des Anciens-Combattants d'AFN and it's right there.
Ⓣ02.32.40.03.56
Closed *Mon; mid-Aug to early Sept.*

Rustic décor and traditional, though imaginative, cooking. They do a number of fish specialities and lots of dishes using cream and locally grown produce – try the trout with Camembert or the salmon in cream sauce, finishing off with a charlotte of apples and Calvados. Lunch menu €12 during the week, with others at €19–35. *Free coffee offered to our readers on presentation of this guide.*

Acquigny

27400 (5km SE)

La Chaumière

15 rue Aristide-Briand; it's opposite the town hall.
Ⓣ02.32.50.20.54
Closed *Tues; Wed; Feb holidays; a few days around Christmas.*

A really nice restaurant with rustic décor and a relaxed atmosphere. The chef produces new dishes every day, but typical offerings might be ceps on toast, veal chops *à la normande*, *andouillette*, game in season and chocolate terrine. When it's chilly, they grill meat and fish over the fire. No menus, but the à la carte prices are reasonable at €20–48. There's a very good selection of wines available by the glass.

Pont-de-l'Arche

27340 (11km N)

Hôtel de la Tour**

41 quai Foch; take the N15 over the bridge and it's on the left on the Eure riverbank.
Ⓣ02.35.23.00.99 Ⓕ02.35.23.46.22
Ⓦwww.hoteldelatour.net
TV. Car park.

The old façade is perfectly in keeping with the pretty houses along the quay, but the interior has been expertly refurbished by the charming owners. Everything about it – the colours, the décor, the little details that make for a comfortable stay and the friendly welcome – gives this place a quality not normally found in a hotel in this category. If they're not full, you can tour the empty rooms and choose the one you want. Doubles cost €55, and whether you opt for one overlooking the ramparts and the church of Notre-Dame-des-Arts or one with a view of the lush riverbank, they're all equally quiet.

Lyons-la-Forêt

27480

Hostellerie du Domaine Saint-Paul**

It's 800m out of the village on the D321.
Ⓣ02.32.49.60.57 Ⓕ02.32.49.56.05
Ⓦwww.domaine-saint-paul.fr
Closed *1 Nov–1 April.* **Swimming pool. High chairs and games available. Car park.**

A substantial house, built as a hunting lodge in 1815, with various annexes around the main building. It's been in the same family since 1946. The grounds are quiet, planted with flower beds, and there's an open-air swimming pool. Simply decorated rooms go for €49–72. Half board is compulsory at the weekend, May–Sept, for €51–63 per person. The restaurant serves typical regional cooking with a few original touches: Camembert *croquettes*, prawn cocktail, salmon with creamed garlic, duck *fricassée* with cider and Pommeau and delicious house desserts. There's a weekday lunchtime menu at €20 and others from €24 to €36, including a *menu terroir*. Reservations are recommended, especially at the weekend. *Free house digestif offered to our readers on presentation of this guide.*

Neufchâtel-en-Bray

76270

Hostellerie du Grand Cerf**

9 Grande-Rue-Fausse-Porte; go down the main street and it's beyond the church.
Ⓣ02.35.93.00.02 Ⓕ02.35.94.14.92
Ⓔgrand-cerf.hotel@wanadoo.fr
Closed *Fri; Sat lunchtime; a fortnight end Dec.* **TV. Car park.**

You'll be spoiled rotten here, and you'll need a good excuse ready for the waitress if you don't eat every scrap. This is traditional Normandy cooking, with a variety of menus ranging from €13.50 on week-day to €29. Children's menu €7.50. Good choices include cheese crêpes, duck breast and fresh mackerel. The rooms are well maintained, with doubles for €42 with shower/wc. Half board from €50 per person. *Free house apéritif and coffee offered to our readers on presentation of this guide.*

Pont-Audemer

27500

Hôtel du Palais et de la Poste - Restaurant Le Canel

8 rue Delaquaize; it's near the post office.
☎ 02.32.41.50.74
Closed *Mon; Sun evening; 1–5 Sept.*
Disabled access. High chairs available. TV. Car park.

The retro dining room is a perfect setting for quality local dishes: skate terrine, fillet of duck *à l'eunoise, méli-mélo* of fish with *tartare* sauce. The weekday menu, €11, is served lunchtime and evenings until 8.30pm, and there are others at €19–43. À la carte is also available. The hotel is less remarkable, though the rooms are good value; doubles go for €25–29 with basin or €41–45 with shower/wc. *Free coffee offered to our readers on presentation of this guide.*

Campigny

27500 (6km SE)

Restaurant L'Andrien - Hôtel Le Petit Coq aux Champs****

La Pommeraie sud. Take the D29.
☎ 02.32.41.04.19 Ⓕ 02.32.56.06.25
Ⓦ www.lepetit.coqauxchamps.fr
Closed *3 weeks in Jan.* **TV. Heated swimming pool. High chairs available. Car park.**

Beautifully located in glorious Normandy countryside, this welcoming restaurant has a relaxed atmosphere. That said, it's fairly sophisticated, and the food is excellent. Chef Jean-Marie Huard is constantly inventing new dishes that delight both the palate and the eye. His speciality is a terrific foie gras *pot-au-feu* with crunchy cabbage, but it doesn't come cheap. They have a choice of different menus, which change with the seasons, €39 with apéritif, wine and coffee, two other menus for €30.60 and €64. Double rooms with bath cost from €110 up to €141. *10% discount on the room rate to our readers on presentation of this guide.*

Beuzeville

27210 (12km W)

Auberge du Cochon d'Or**

Place du Général-de-Gaulle. Take the N175 towards Pont-l'Évêque or the A13 exit 28; it's opposite the town hall.
☎ 02.32.57.70.46 Ⓕ 02.32.42.25.70
Ⓦ www.le-cochon-dor.fr
Closed *Mon; also Sun evening Oct–March; 15 Dec–15 Jan.* **TV. Car park.**

This inn, which has been well known for a couple of centuries, owes its continuing reputation to the chef who's been marshalling his forces in the kitchen since 1962. He specializes in Normandy dishes like eels stewed in cider, chicken quenelles with a Camembert sauce and skate wings with cabbage, all of which you can enjoy in the large rustic dining room. There's a weekday menu at €14 and others €19, except Sunday lunchtime €40. There's an annexe across the road called the *Petit Castel*; here the quiet rooms overlook a garden where you can have breakfast. Doubles €39–53 with with shower/wc or bath.

Le Relais-Hôtel de la Poste**

60 rue Constant-Fouché; it's opposite the town hall.
☎ 02.32.20.32.32 Ⓕ 02.32.42.11.01
Restaurant closed *Sun evening (except July–Aug); Thurs; 11 Nov–1 April.* **TV. Car park.**

This authentic coaching inn, which dates back to 1844, has a garden and a terrace at the back. Bedrooms €43 with shower/wc or go for €49 up to €63 with bath; if you're there at the weekend or public holidays, half board, €54–64 per person, is compulsory. It's a good deal, with a large choice of menus. Menus at €18 (weekday lunchtime) and €23–36. The chef cooks a good number of regional speacialities, and has a particular weakness for *andouille*, which he prepares in several ways. Also foie gras, smoked salmon and smoked duck, veal kidneys flambéed in Calvados, lamb *noisette* and cream-cheese mousse with cider jelly. *10% discount on the room rate for a minimum two-night stay offered to our readers on presentation of this guide.*

Rouen

76000

See map on pp.640–641

Hôtel du Palais**

12 rue du Tambour. **Map B2-8**
02.35.71.41.40
Closed *Sun noon–7pm.* **TV.**

In a tiny street between the law courts and the Gros Horloge, right across from the underground station, this hotel has two trump cards – its central location and its modest prices. Don't go expecting any great luxury, but the make-believe courtyard and the slightly random décor will appeal to the young at heart. Double bedrooms, the most expensive ones, are €38 with shower/wc.

Hôtel Bristol

45 rue aux Juifs. **Map B2-6**
02.35.71.54.21 02.35.52.06.33
Closed *Sun; public holidays; 2nd week in April; 3 weeks in Aug.* **TV.**

A beautifully restored half-timbered building with nine bedrooms, €36–46 for a double with bath and phone; some have a view of the Palace of Justice. Bedding not always up to scratch. Fantastic welcome.

Hôtel Céline**

26 rue de Campulley; near the train station. **Off map B1-1**
02.35.71.95.23 02.35.89.53.71
hotelceline@wanadoo.fr
TV.

A large white building in remarkably peaceful surroundings. The bedrooms are modern and clean; some of those on the top floor are particularly big, but they can get a little too hot in the height of summer. Reasonably priced doubles with shower/wc €37–42.

Hôtel Beauséjour**

9 rue Pouchet. 200m from the train station. **Map B1-2**
02.35.71.93.47 02.35.98.01.24
www.hotelbeausejour76.com
Closed *15–30 July; 24–31 Dec.* **TV.**

One of the best places near the station, this quiet hotel has a smart exterior with freshly renovated, well-equipped rooms, a charming garden and a salon-bar. Prices are fair for the category, with doubles at €39.50. *10% discount on the room rate for a minimum two-night stay at the weekend, except July and Aug, offered to our readers on presentation of this guide.*

Hôtel des Carmes*

33 pl. des Carmes. **Map C2-5**
02.35.71.92.31 02.35.71.76.96
www.hotelceline@wanadoo.fr
TV.

A very attractive place on one of the liveliest squares in the middle of town. The décor is bright and new, full of circus imagery, and the young team welcomes you with a smile. Rooms are pleasant, colourful and refurbished, with doubles at €42–60 with shower/wc or bath. Breakfast costs €5.50 – the butter and yoghurt come direct from the farm and the jams (try the apple and Calvados preserve) are made by the best Rouen companies using old methods. Excellent value.

Hôtel Andersen*

2 bis and 4 rue Pouchet; near the train station. **Map B1-3**
02.35.71.88.51 02.35.07.54.65
www.hotelandersen.com
TV.

An old house that's been turned into a lovely hotel, conveniently near the station. The bright rooms are delightful, and the décor, which evokes the turn of the eighteenth and nineteenth centuries, has been assembled with taste. All the bathrooms are completely modern. Doubles €45–55 with shower/wc. *10% discount on the room rate at weekends (Fri/Sat or Sat/Sun), including July and Aug, offered to our readers on presentation of this guide.*

Le Cardinal**

1 pl. de la Cathédrale; city centre. **Map B3-7**
02.35.70.24.42 02.35.89.75.14
www.cardinal-hotel.fr
Closed *19 Dec–9 Jan.* **TV. Pay car park.**

This place has got the best location in town. Almost every room overlooks the cathedral – a splendid sight, particularly when floodlit at night – and there's a terrace where they serve breakfast in fine weather. The owner is perfectly charming and the rooms are well maintained – three of them have their own terraces. Doubles are good value at €52.50 with shower/wc and €65.50 with bath. *10% discount for a minimum two-night stay Sept–June offered to our readers on presentation of this guide.*

Hôtel du Vieux Carré**

34 rue Ganterie; city centre. **Map C2-10**
02.35.71.67.70
www.vieuxcarre.fr
Disabled access. TV.

There are a few characterful rooms in this pretty, half-timbered house in the centre of the old town. They're inevitably quite small given the size and age of the building, but they're pretty, with soothing décor, and some of them overlook a delightful courtyard ablaze with colourful flowers. Prices are reasonable: doubles with shower/wc go for €53, €57 with bath. The tearoom offers savoury tarts, salads and cakes, with a menu for €12; in good weather you can take tea out in the courtyard. Friendly welcome. *Free coffee offered to our readers on presentation of this guide.*

Hôtel de la Cathédrale**

12 rue Saint-Romain; near the cathedral. **Map C3-9**
02.35.71.57.95 02.35.70.15.54
www.hotel-de-la-cathedrale.fr
TV. Pay car park.

In a good, quiet location, on a pedestrianized street that runs alongside the cathedral, this is a delightful little hotel with an internal courtyard. The rooms range from €59 with shower/wc up to €69 with bath; some have views of the cathedral. There's a tearoom offering a wide choice of unusal teas.

Hôtel de Dieppe***

Place Bernard-Tissot; near the train station. **Map C1-4**
02.35.71.96.00. 02.35.89.65.21
hotel.dieppe@wanadoo.fr
TV.

A large hotel run with style by a family who've been in the business longer than anyone else in town.The rooms, comfortable but a little impersonal and old-fashioned, cost €77 or you might enjoy a two night stay at the weekend for €102. The restaurant is famed for pressed Rouen duck and good grills; the sole "Michel" is good, too. Good grilled food and menus from €19 up to €35. If you like to eat late, try the hotel bar, which is open until 1am.

La Toque d'Or - Le Grill

11 pl. du Vieux-Marché. **Map B2-22**
02.35.71.46.29
Open *daily.*

This attractive Normandy building is on the very square where Joan of Arc was burned at the stake. The stylish beamed dining room on the ground floor is dignified and peaceful, with two *formules* at €9 and €11 and à la carte you're looking at spending around €30. The dishes in the informal grill upstairs are less sophisticated than on the ground floor, but they prove good value for money.

Au Temps des Cerises

4–6 rue des Basnage. **Map B2-21**
02.35.89.98.00
Closed *Sat and Mon lunchtimes; Sun.* **High chairs available.**

The décor – a kitsch dairy theme – tells you immediately what this place is about. No other restaurant in Rouen offers such a wide range of cheese dishes. Don't miss the poached eggs normand, grilled Camembert with sour cherry preserve, veal *escalope* with Pont l'Évèque cheese, fondue du Pays d'Aube or cream cheese ice cream with caramel sauce. Lunch menu for €10, others €14–20. The low prices and good food make this a popular haunt for young locals. There's a nice terrace. *Free house apéritif offered to our readers on presentation of this guide.*

Brasserie Paul

1 pl. de la Cathédrale. **Map C3-25**
02.35.71.86.07
Open *daily until 2am.*

Menus €10.50 and €17.10.This place has been a brasserie since 1911. Many famous figures have sat down to eat here, Apollonaire and Marcel Duchamp among them. Simone de Beavoir was a regular, and if today's food is anything to go by, she had good reason. Huge salads, sandwiches, small tasty dishes – and the speciality of the house, parcels of Camembert with apples and cider sauce. It's lovely to dine on the terrace in the evening, facing the illuminated cathedral. *Free house apéritif offered to our readers on presentation of this guide.*

Le P'tit Bec

182 rue Eau-de-Robec. **Map C2-26**
02.35.07.63.33
Closed *Sun; Mon-Thurs evenings.*

Lovely, bright tearoom that also does delicious home-made lunches, including *gratins*, coddled eggs, terrines and pastries.

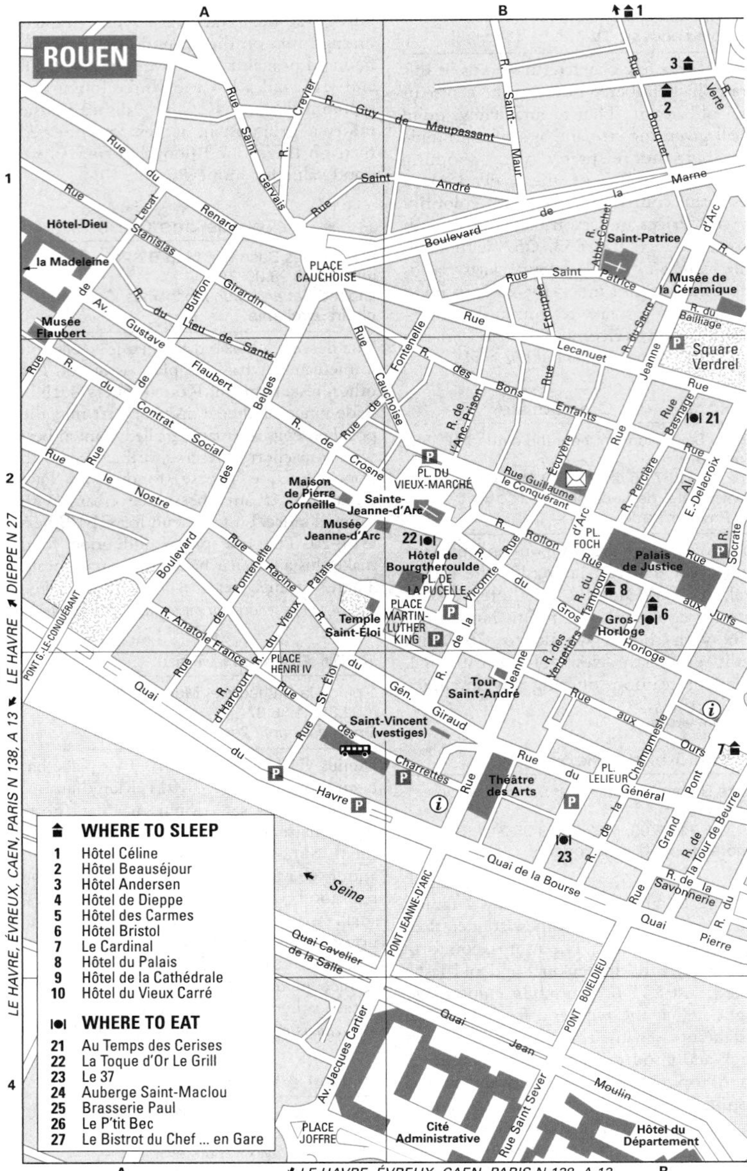

17

HAUTE-NORMANDIE

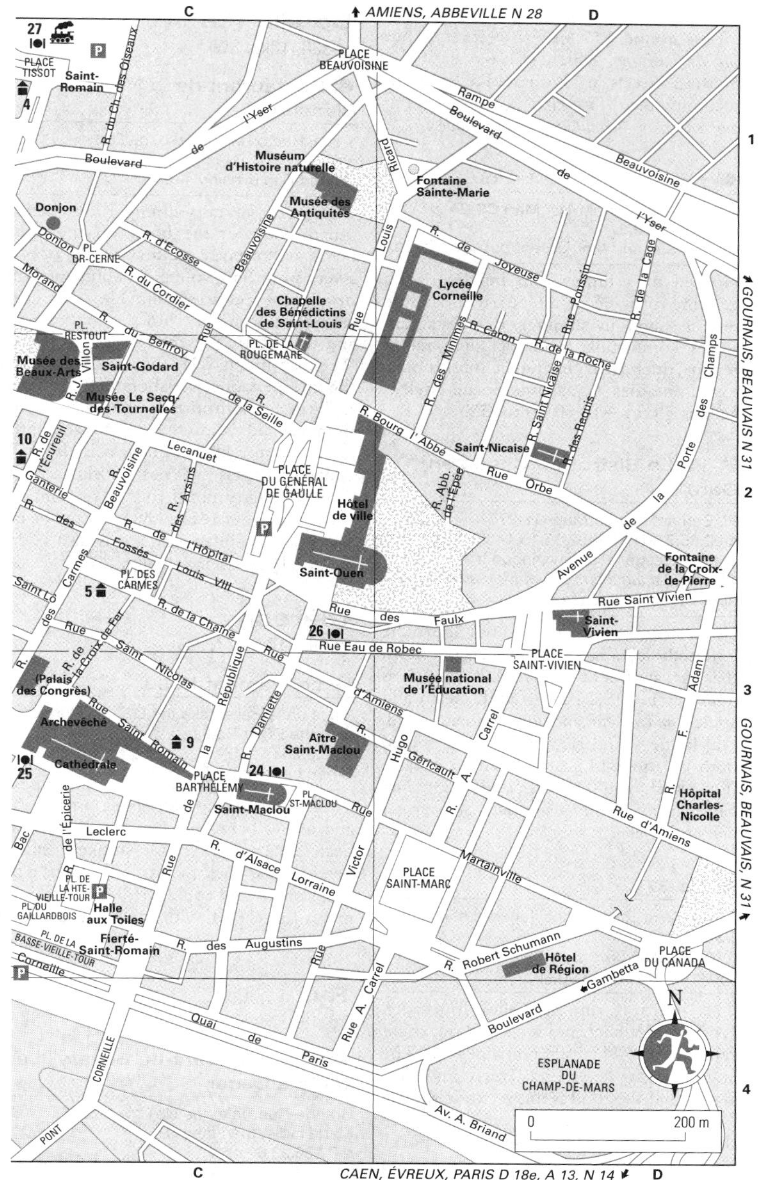

HAUTE-NORMANDIE

Delightful service from the waitresses who race about to keep the regulars happy. Lunch menus, €11 and €13, are well put together and satisfying; à la carte you can eat for around €17. In fine weather, sit out on the terrace, which is on one of the prettiest streets in Rouen. Reservations recommended. *Free house apéritif offered to our readers on presentation of this guide.*

|●| Auberge Saint-Maclou

224–226 rue Martainville. **Map C3-24**
Ⓣ02.35.71.06.67
Closed *Sun and Mon except public holidays.*

Housed in a timber-clad building, with genuine rustic décor, a nice bar and a little terrace open in summer, this restaurant serves comforting food including rabbit terrine, duck with chanterelle mushrooms, roast potatoes in a frangipane style... Menus go for €13.50 up to €23.

|●| Le Bistrot du Chef... en Gare

Pl. Bernard-Tissot. **Map C1-27**
Ⓣ02.35.71.41.15 Ⓕ02.35.15.14.43
Ⓔmedia-restauration@wanadoo.fr
Closed *Sat lunchtime; Sun; Mon evening; Aug.* **Disabled access.**

Good station food. On the floor above the buffet, there's a large, hushed dining room that's always full of regulars. Dishes such as duck terrine, veal *escalope* with cream and apples, *andouillette* and warm potato salad, veal kidneys, and rice pudding are served both on the €14.50 menu and à la carte (for which you'll pay around €23). *Free house apéritif offered to our readers on presentation of this guide.*

|●| Le 37

37 rue Saint-Étienne-des-Tonneliers. **Map B3-23**
Ⓣ02.35.70.56.65
Closed *Sun; Mon; Aug.*

This bistro is run by Gilles Tournadre, Rouen's best chef, and is an offshoot of his renowned *Gill* restaurant, nearby. The ambience is very Elle Deco, modern, warm, and the food is more exotic than at *Gill*. They have dishes which change throughout the seasons, including pork's head sauce sweet and sour, codfish with onion chutney and caramel tart. The prices aren't at all bad, with a €16.50 *formule* served all day from Tues lunchtime to Fri lunchtime. À la carte, reckon on around €33 without wine.

Bouille (La)

76530 (12km SW)

|●| Restaurant de la Maison-Blanche

1 quai Hector-Malot; take the D51.
Ⓣ02.35.18.01.90
Closed *Sun evening; Mon.*

The pretty upstairs dining room with a superb view of the boats on the Seine below has recently acquired the services of a very promising young chef bursting with originality and *savoir-faire*. He takes great care over both the choice of ingredients and the artistic presentation of his dishes. Weekday menu €18, then €27–37. Even the cheapest one is elaborate: oysters and shellfish in saffron-flavoured zabaglione, fresh fish and exquisite desserts. One of the highlights for bigger budgets is the half-cooked foie gras with pears or figs, accompanied by tasty bread rolls fresh from the oven. This chef is already a master of the art of using spices, and he is also a dab hand at baby-tomato *confits*...

Clères

76690 (18.5km N)

|●| Le Flamant Rose

Place de la Halle; take the D27 and turn off onto the D6 at Boulay.
Ⓣ02.35.33.22.47
Closed *evenings; Tues; Nov.*

This simple place serves regional dishes and a few brasserie classics such as calf's head sauce *ravigotte*, home-smoked salmon, perch fillets, duck breasts with cider, tripe in Calvados and apple tart. There's a lunch menu for €9.80, with others at €13 and €19.90.

Ry

76116 (20km E)

|●| Restaurant Le Bovary- La Table d'Oscar

Grande-Rue. Take the N31 towards Martainville, then take D13.
Ⓣ02.35.23.61.46

A venerable establishment that welcomes travellers who have lost their way... For a long time the owners ran the restaurant

Casino de Forges, before coming to this cosy and peaceful place. They offer weekday lunch menus for €9.50 and €12, with other menus at €16.50, €22 and €30. Staff are welcoming and the service is hard to fault, which is pretty amazing at these prices. *Free house apéritif offered to our readers on presentation of this guide.*

Saint-Valéry-en-Caux

76460

Hôtel Henri IV**

16 rte. du Havre; from the centre take the Fécamp–Cany-Barville road; it's several hundred metres along on the left.
Ⓣ02.35.97.19.62 Ⓕ02.35.57.10.01
TV. Disabled access.

Owner Michèle loves taking care of her guests, and she creates a cheerful atmosphere in this large, ivy-covered, brick-built hotel with patio. Comfortable bedrooms start at €30 with basin, and from €40 up to €47 with shower/wc or bath; those at the back are the quietest. Michèle also loves flying; if you'd like a trip along the coast, she can arrange it with her friends at the flying club. There's a nice flowery terrace.

Hôtel-restaurant La Marine

113 rue Saint-Léger; from the bridge go past the Maison Henri IV, the tourist office; it's on the first road on the left.
Ⓣ and Ⓕ02.35.97.05.09
Closed *Tues evening; Wed; 3 weeks in Jan; a fortnight in March.* **TV.**

You'll be made to feel very welcome in this quiet family-run hotel and restaurant. There are no fancy trimmings, but facilities are perfectly adequate. You'll spend from €36 up to €40 for a room with shower/wc or with bath. Weekday menus at €10.50, and others from €16–29, are served in two charming, old-fashioned dining rooms where regional specialities include skate in cider and Norman apple tart. All the fish and seafood dishes are good.

Le Restaurant du Port

18 quai d'Amont.
Ⓣ02.35.97.08.93
Closed *Sun evening; Mon and Thurs evenings except July–Aug.*

As you can guess from the name, this seafood restaurant stands right by the harbour. It's the most refined establishment in town, and the prices reflect that. The €19 menu is simple and classic, while the more interesting one at €33 features *bouillabaisse* using fish from the Channel, mackerel tart and smoked salmon terrine. They also do a seafood platter, warm fish salad with sherry vinegar, mussels with sweet peppers, and a few meat dishes. Everything is freshly cooked and the service can't be faulted, though the portions may be a little too small for some tastes. Ask for a table by the wide window with a view over the port.

Sotteville-sur-Mer

76740 (10km NE)

Hôtel des Rochers**

Place de l'Église.
Ⓣ02.35.97.07.06 Ⓕ02.35.97.71.73
Closed *Jan–Feb. Disabled access.* **TV. Swimming pool. Car park.**

A big building, which used to be a presbytery, with a delightful walled garden. They have ten or so quiet, comfortable rooms with shower/wc or bath €43–46. Excellent welcome. *Free coffee offered to our readers on presentation of this guide.*

Restaurant Les Embruns

Place de l'Église; go towards Dieppe and turn left onto the D68 at Veules-les-Roses.
Ⓣ02.35.97.77.99
Closed *Sun evening; Mon; Tues from Oct to end March; 3 weeks end Jan to mid-Feb; a fortnight end Sept to early Oct.* **Disabled access.**

This used to be a bar and tobacconist's, but has since been transformed into a gourmet restaurant. *Menu-carte* from €12.50 at lunchtime, and between €23–39 in the evening. Specialities, drawn from the local region and further afield, include lamb *noisette* in Provençal style, *escalope* of veal with citrus fruits…

Petites-Dalles (Les)

76540 (17km SW)

Hôtel-restaurant de la Plage

92 rue Joseph-Heuzé; take the D925 towards Fécamp and it's in the main street 50m from the beach.
Ⓣ02.35.27.40.77
Closed *Sun and Mon evenings, Wed out of*

season; Mon only in season; during Feb and Christmas school holidays.

Monsieur and Madame Pierre will welcome you warmly to this handsome brick establishment with its wooden balconies and delightful turrets. The whole place is very quiet, with cosy, inexpensive rooms; doubles €38 with shower/wc or €41 with bath. It's rare to find such a reasonably priced hotel of such quality on the coast. The little dining room, meanwhile, a mixture of traditional and modern styles, is also a good bet. It's great food, prepared with the best produce; they specialize in seafood, including delicious warm oysters wrapped in lettuce – or try *civet* of winkles and oysters with cider and *coulis* of beetroot with apples. Menus €15.80 served every day, lunch and dinertime, other menus from €25 up to €32.50.

Tréport (Le)

76470

Hôtel de Calais**

1 rue de Paris; from the quay, head up towards the church.
Ⓣ02.27.28.09.09 Ⓕ02.27.28.09.00
Ⓦwww.hoteldecalais.com
Open *daily between 7.30/8.00am and 9.30/11pm, depending on the season.* **TV. Car park.**

This former coaching inn, perched above the harbour, was built almost two centuries ago. Previous guests have included Victor Hugo. Rooms are nice and bright, and the bathrooms have been refitted. Only some of the rooms overlook the harbour, and they're not all the same size, so it's worth asking for what you want. Doubles €42–68 with shower/wc or €55–65 with bath. They also have apartments. *One free breakfast per room offered, except public holidays and July–Aug, to our readers on presentation of this guide.*

Mon P'tit Bar

3–5 rue de la Rade; it's in the port.
Ⓣ02.35.86.28.78

A nice, authentic, unstuffy little place that's less a conventional restaurant than a bar which serves food all day until late. They have three different menus at €10.40, €11.90 and €15.20. Dishes are cooked using fresh market produce, prices are low and you get a friendly reception. Good seafood platters.

Criel-sur-Mer

76910 (8.5km SW)

Hostellerie de la Vieille Ferme**

Mesnil-Val-Plage; take the cliff road, and it's in the main street, 300m from the beach.
Ⓣ02.35.86.72.18 Ⓕ02.35.86.12.67
Closed *Sun evening and Mon out of season; mid-Dec to mid-Jan.* **TV. Car park.**

An enormous, traditional Normandy building with a terrace, manicured lawn, a large garden with twittering birds and an old cider press. Very comfortable, quiet bedrooms go for €52–81 with bath. Half board is requested in season. The dining room is decorated in a beautiful, traditional style and the menus, €17–35.

Verneuil-sur-Avre

27130

Hôtel Le Saumon**

89 pl. de la Madeleine; it's on the church square.
Ⓣ02.32.32.02.36 Ⓕ02.32.37.55.80
Ⓦwww.hoteldusaumon.fr
Closed *Sun evening Nov–Easter; end Dec to early Jan.* **Disabled access. TV.**

A good, reliable provincial hotel. Rooms have a view of the old city walls of the square and the magnificent church tower – they're all quiet. Doubles €42–52 with shower/wc or bath. The restaurant is very good, serving dishes typical of this part of Normandy such as salmon, scallops with orange, lobster, veal sweetbreads, calf's head sauce *ravigote* and leg of duck *à la normande*. Menus at €11 (weekdays only) and €15–50.

Barils (Les)

27130 (8km W)

L'Épicier Normand

2 rue de Verneuil; take the N26.
Ⓣ02.32.60.05.88
Closed *Mon evening; Tues; 15–31 Jan.* **High chairs available.**

A charming, triple-purpose place that is restaurant, grocer's and entertainment hall. Warm welcome and tasty cooking: black pudding with apples, *jambon d'York* with cider sauce and a marvellous chicken *Vallée d'Auge* with cream and apple sauce. Menus €15.50–25.50. Musical shows and plays are held from time to time; phone ahead for the schedule. *Free coffee offered to our readers on presentation of this guide.*

Vernon

27200

Hôtel d'Évreux – Restaurant Le Relais Normand***

11 pl. d'Évreux; it's opposite the post office.
☎02.32.21.16.12 Ⓕ02.32.21.32.73
Ⓔhoteldévreux@libertysurf.fr
Restaurant closed *Sun except Easter and Whitsun.* **TV. High chairs available. Car park.**

This hotel may look like a typical Normandy house from the outside, but inside, where the Austrian owner has decorated the place to remind her of home, it's slightly different – witness the rustic bar, collection of Bavarian beer mugs and imposing fireplace. The French chef, passionate about good food, has a number of specialities – roast Normandy oysters, *saucisson* of pig's trotters with truffle *jus*, pan-fried foie gras with apples and a thin-crusted apple tart with an iced Pommeau soufflé. Menus €20 and €26. Rooms, which are well maintained, clean, and rustic, will set you back €33 with shower, €45 with shower/wc or €54 with bath. In the summer they open the conservatory. Reservations are recommended. *Coffee offered to our readers on presentation of this guide.*

La Halle aux Grains

31 rue de Gamilly; it's near the pl. de la République.
☎02.32.21.31.99
Closed *Sun evening; Mon; 1–15 Aug; Christmas school holidays.* **Disabled access.**

The welcome at this restaurant is warm, the setting attractive and the service diligent – no wonder it's packed year-round. Everything – including the pizza dough – is prepared from the freshest produce on the premises. The grilled meat is first-rate, as are the snails in pastry cases, the soufflé with scallops, the fisherman's platter and the orange and Grand Marnier soup. Dishes of the day average at around €7.50 lunctime except weekends and public holidays, and on Sunday you'll pay €23 for a menu including apéritif, €15 for a meal à la carte. The wine list is attractively priced and varied, with some vintages offered by the glass.

Vernonnet

27200 (2km NE)

Le Relais des Tourelles

Rue de la Chaussée; it's opposite Vernon on the other side of the Seine.
☎02.32.51.54.52
Closed *all day Wed and Sun evening.*
Disabled access. Car park.

This charming restaurant serves a range of regional specialities along with classic dishes including sweetbreads with morels, veal kidneys in mustard and warm oysters on a leek. Menus €12 (weekdays only) and €21.50–29.50. They host regular jazz evenings.

Giverny

27620 (5km E)

Hôtel La Musardière**

123 rue Claude-Monet; it's just beyond the Monet museum.
☎02.32.21.03.18 Ⓕ02.32.21.60.00
Closed *Mon lunchtime.* **TV. Car park.**

A large house with a veranda and a huge garden, near Monet's house. The little restaurant, which does good salads, can get very full, so you may have to wait a long time to be served. They have three different menus at €12, €15 and €25. Spacious double rooms go for €51–72 with shower/wc or bath.

Les Jardins de Giverny

1 rue du Milieu; take the D5 from Vernon and it's on the left 1km beyond the petrol station.
☎02.32.21.60.80
Open *lunch only and Sat evening.* **Closed** *Mon.* **High chairs and games available. Car park.**

This typical Normandy building isn't quite as idyllic as the name suggests, but it's not lacking in charm – and Monet did eat here, as did a host of other famous people including Clemenceau and Aristide Briand. Here you can get classic Normandy dishes served in a Louis XVI dining room: roast organic chicken, organic duck, sole fillet with prawns and iced *diplomate normand* with spiced bread. They have different menus at €14 and

€20 weekdays only, others €26–35, all feature an unusual *trou normand* – this is usually a shot of Calvados served to aid digestion, but here you get a refreshing cider and Calvados sorbet. Excellent local specialities and fish dishes, some of them delicately infused with the flavour of seaweed. They're happy to advise on which wine to choose. *Free coffee offered to our readers on presentation of this guide.*

Gasny

27620 (10km NE)

Auberge du Pieuré Normand

1 pl. de la République; take the D313 or the D5 via Giverny.
☎ 02.32.52.10.01
Closed *Tues evening; Wed.* **Disabled access.**

A gourmet stop. The cheapest menu, €14.50 weekday lunchtime, is tempting, but then from €22.50 to €35 menu are a real feast, featuring local specialities: *canapés*, small roast monkfish served on salad leaves, turbot with *andouille*, cheese, *petits fours* and *crème brûlée*. There's a judicious selection of wines at very reasonable prices, and the whole experience proves to be excellent value. One or two gripes: the bread rolls could be better, and although the setting is meticulous it's rather bland. But that won't spoil your enjoyment of the wonderful food.

Fourges

27630 (15km NE)

Le Moulin de Fourges

38 rue du Moulin; take the D5 towards Magny-en-Vexin and follow the signposts in Fourges.
☎ 02.32.52.12.12
Closed *1 Nov–1 April.* **Disabled access. High chairs available.**

It's worth coming to this splendid mill on the banks of the fast-flowing Epte for the romantic setting alone. There's a good-value *formule* served on weekday lunchtimes €22, and a *menu-carte* at €32. The food is simple, full of flavour and traditional, and there's a good wine list. The shaded terrace is enjoyable in summer, but try to avoid coming at the weekend when the tour buses and cars fight over the parking spaces – the groups themselves are catered for in a separate dining room in a restored barn. *Free house apéritif offered to our readers on presentation of this guide.*

Veules-les-Roses

76980

Résidence Douce France***

13 rue du Docteur Girard.
☎ 02.35.57.85.30 Ⓕ 02.35.57.85.31
Ⓦ www.doucefrance.fr
Closed *Tues evening out of season; Jan.*
Disabled access. High chairs available. TV.

This exceptional place is an absolute winner. It's become a hotel only recently after considerable refurbishment of the original seventeenth-century coaching inn. An immense fortified building built of brick and pale-coloured wood, with the coach yard in the middle, it's a quiet, restful and romantic place. The extremely spacious and comfy rooms, more like mini-suites, go for €85–120; they have five family flats for 4/5 people at €190. Their *campagnard* breakfast, €10, includes all sorts of charcuterie, breads and sweet buns, and they serve a brunch for €15. If the weather is good, you can eat in the garden, which is delightful. *10% discount on the room rate, except school holidays, offered to our readers on presentation of this guide.*

Yport

76111

La Sirène**

7 bd. Alexandre-Dumont.
☎ 02.35.27.31.87 Fax: 02.35.29.47.37
Ⓦ www.hotel-sirene.com

This charming seaside hotel has recovered from a lean patch, thanks to the efforts of a local who was perturbed to see it deteriorating and decided to take it over herself. She has renovated the place from top to bottom, no mean achievement. Now *La Sirène* can once again stand tall on the seafront with its impressive half-timbered façade and magnificent view of the cliffs. The new décor is in a tasteful nautical style, in both the rooms and the restaurant. Double rooms at €55, a few triples at €80. Menus €17 and €25. You can enjoy a panoramic view as you eat the carefully selected fresh produce and seafood. A platter of local dishes is available all the year round. The owner's younger brother has opened a pub on the ground floor. All in all, an ideal spot for a romantic getaway.

Yvetot

76190

|●| La Fontaine Gourmande

70 rue Bellanger.
☎02.35.96.11.01
Closed *Mon; Sat lunch.*

An adorable, convivial little restaurant hidden in a little street behind the town hall. Both the décor and the food are traditional, but with the odd modern touch: pig's-trotter tart, ox-cheek lasagne, *mille-feuille* of Livarot cheese. Lunchtime menus at €9 and €12; other menus €20–30. We think this is the best restaurant in Yvetot, and we are not alone in our opinion – so booking is well advised.

Croix Mare

76190 (5km SE)

⌂ |●| Auberge du Val au Cesne

It's 3km beyond Yvetot, on the D5 or D22 towards Fréville, then D5 towards Val-au-Cesne.
☎02.35.56.63.06 Ⓕ02.35.56.92.78
Ⓦwww.val-au-cesne.fr
Closed *Mon and Tues; 20 days in Jan; 15–31 Aug.* **Disabled access. TV. High chairs available. Car park.**

The ducks and beautiful doves outside this cosy old Normandy inn create a perfect pastoral setting. You can eat outside in summer, and the bantams will come and peck up the crumbs. The food is excellent; try the sole stuffed with prawn mousse, the *escalope* of turkey made to a peasant recipe, or the juicy steak. They offer a €25 menu with starter, main course and dessert, another at €45 or you'll pay at least €40 à la carte. The delicious food and the unusual setting make the prices a bit easier to swallow. There are a few rooms with en-suite bathrooms at €76.

|●| Auberge de la Forge

It's on the N15 towards Rouen.
☎02.35.91.25.94
Closed *Tues; Wed.* **Disabled access. Car park.**

A discreetly decorated country restaurant serving traditional regional dishes. The service is friendly and professional. There's a lunchtime weekday menu at €13.80; other menus go for €17.50–29. Though menus change according to the seasons, there are always lots of tasty treats on offer: warm terrine of *andouillette* and lentils, *fricassée* of fish with red pepper and anchovy cream, pan-fried veal stuffed with mushrooms and hazelnuts, warm biscuit with *compote* of apples and honey.

Allouville-Bellefosse

76190 (6km W)

|●| Au Vieux Normand

Take the N15 or the D34.
☎02.35.96.00.00
Closed *evenings (except Fri and Sat).*

You'll find this country inn next to a grand old oak tree on the village square and most of the local population sitting at the tables. There's a great atmosphere around the fire. They offer a huge choice of dishes which change constantly: duck in cider, black pudding gâteau, skate with caper cream, steak, *marmite dieppoise* (fish stew), seafood platters, cheese tart and house tripe, which is a must. Substantial menus €10 weekday lunchtime, others €16–20. They serve red wine by the jug and cider on tap. *Free house apéritif offered to our readers on presentation of this guide.*

Pays-de-la-Loire

Ancenis

44510

La Toile à Beurre

72 rue St Pierre; it's next to the church.
02.40.98.89.64
Closed *Sun and Wed evenings; Mon; Feb school holidays; 15 Sept–1 Oct.*

A superb, vaulted dining room with a tiled floor, an imposing fire place, and a little salon. Seasonal Breton and Nantais cuisine with carefully prepared dishes; *croustillant* of warm sardines, pan-fried sea bass with artichokes. Lunch *formule* for €12, a good-value menu at €15, and others up to €31. There's an attractive list of local wines. *Free house apéritif or coffee on presentation of this guide.*

Angers

49000

See map on pp.652–653

Centre d'accueil International du Lac de Maine

49 av. du Lac-de-Maine, about 2 km from the centre; take no. 6 or 16 bus in the direction of Bouchemaine to "Lac de Maine" or "Perussaie" stop. **Off Map B3-1**
02.41.22.32.10 02.41.22.32.11
www.lacdemaine.fr
Disabled access. Car park.

A lively hostel with nearly 150 beds that is particularly popular with young people in the summer. It is well equipped and surrounded by a park with a lake. €16 per person in a room for four, and €18 in a room for two, breakfast included. Self-service cafeteria lunch and dinner for a minimum of €8. Nautical activities (with a charge), visits to the Environment Centre, free use of sports fields, swimming from mid-June to mid-Sept, a TV room and good (and free) Internet access.

Hôtel Marguerite d'Anjou

13 pl. Kennedy; opposite the castle and the tourist office. **Map B3-4**
02.41.88.11.61 02.41.87.37.61
Closed *Mon morning; a fortnight in Feb.* **TV. Pay car park.**

Brilliantly located opposite the impressive château of Angers. It's essential to book and they ask for a deposit. There are ten rooms, all of which are spotlessly clean and have double glazing and en-suite bathrooms – doubles €38–42. Breakfast, served in the bar, is the real thing, with as much bread as you like. You can also get snacks for around €10.

Hôtel Iéna**

27 rue Marceau; near the train station. **Map B3-2**
02.41.87.52.40 02.41.86.01.58
ienahotel@wanadoo.fr

A fine provincial hotel, neither too big nor too small, set on the corner of a quiet street not far from the château. The rooms are not very spacious but they are modern and comfortable (with shower or bath), and the owners go to great lengths to make you feel at home. Double rooms €42–47.

Hôtel Continental **

12–14 rue Louis-de-Romain. **Map B2-8**
02.41.86.94.94 02.41.86.96.60
www.hotelcontinental.com

A
MANCHE
Dinan
CÔTES-D'ARMOR
D 700
N 137
Fougères
N 1
Ernée
N 164
N 12
N12
Rennes
N 157
Le Genest-St-Isle
ILLE-ET-VILAINE
1
N 24
N 24
D 41
Cossé-le-Vivien
Ballots
MORBIHAN
N 166
D 177
N 137
N 171
Vannes
Châteaubriant
N 171
Pouancé
D 775
D 775
D 775
St-Nicolas-de-Redon
Segré
D 923
D 163
N 165
N 171
Candé
D 178
Guenrouët
D 963
Pontchâteau
N 165
Blain
N 137
Mesquer
St-Germain-des-Prés
Piriac-sur-Mer
St-Joachim
N 171
LOIRE-ATLANTIQUE
A 11
la Turballe
Saillé
Guérande
St-Lyphard
Sucé-sur-Erdre
Ancenis
Batz-sur-Mer
la Baule
Carquefou
Loire
St-Florent-le-Vieil
le Pouliguen
Champtoceaux
Pornichet
St-Nazaire
Paimbœuf
N 165
D 213
Nantes
Basse-Goulaine
D 752
Messan
la Plaine-sur-Mer
D 723
La-Haie-Fouassière
Pte de St-Gildas
D 751
N 249
Pornic
Bourgne
D 117
D 937
Clisson
N 149
Cholet
l'Herbaudière
Noirmoutier-en-l'Île
Machecoul
Tiffauges
Île de Noirmoutier
Paulx
Montaigu
D 753
D 38
Bouin
Mortagne-sur-S.
St-Gervais
St-Laurent-sur-S.
le Puy-du-Fou
D 753
D 763
Challans
les Herbiers
A 83
2
Saint-Jean-de-Monts
D 753
Maché
le Poiré-sur-Vie
Pouzauges
Port-Joinville
Commequiers
N 160
D 948
D 937
Île d'Yeu
Chantonnay
St-Gilles-Croix-de-Vie
D 38
VENDÉE
D 948
la Roche-sur-Yon
N 160
Ste-Hermine
N 148
D 746
Pissotte
ATLANTIC OCEAN
les Sables-d'Olonne
Fontenay-le-Comte
D 949
Luçon
St-Vincent-sur-Jard
Marais Poitevin
Velluire
la Tranche-sur-Mer
CHARENTE-MARITIME
A

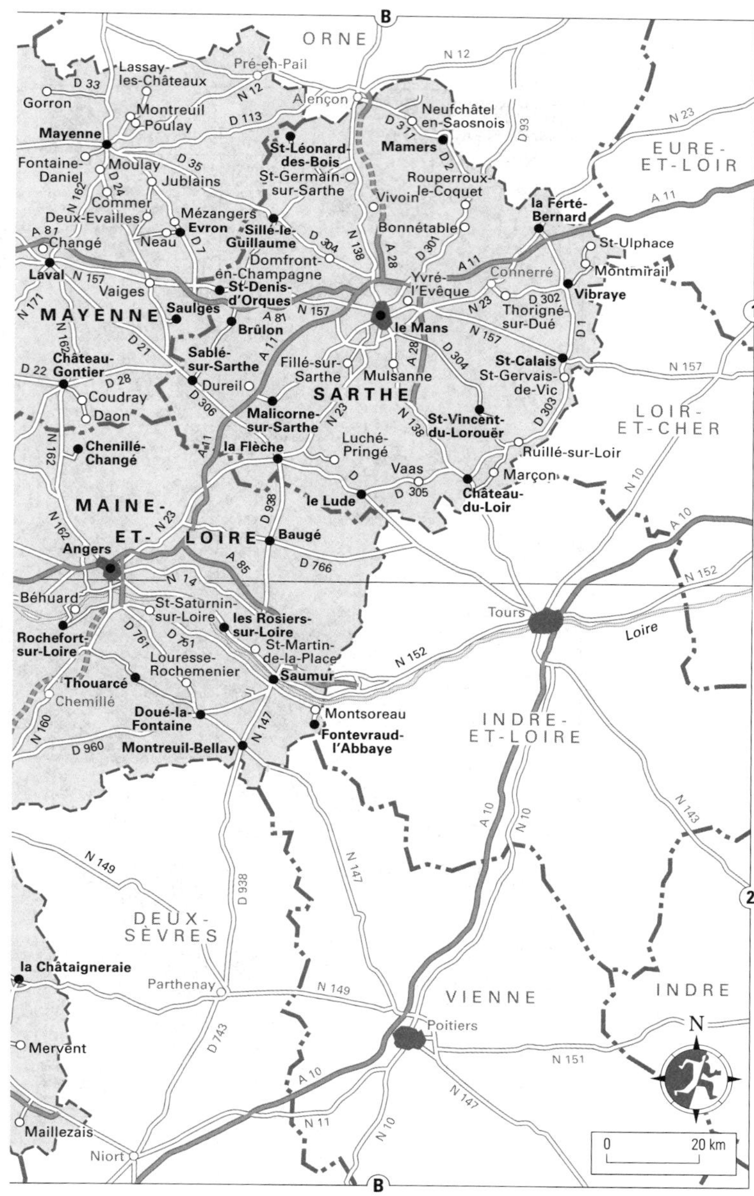

18

PAYS-DE-LA-LOIRE

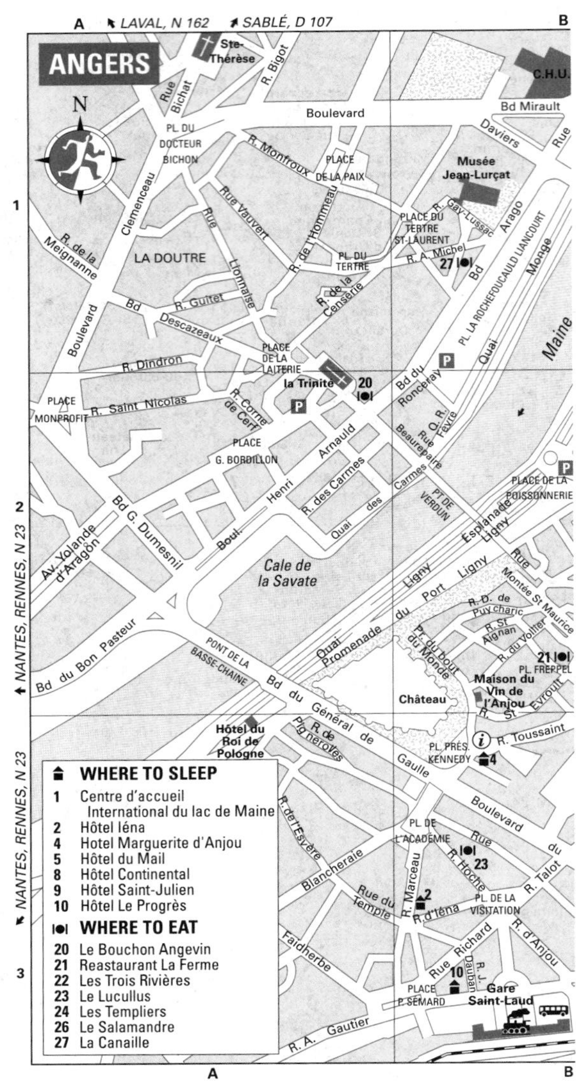
A
LAVAL, N 162
SABLÉ, D 107
B
ANGERS
N
Ste-Thérèse
C.H.U.
R. Bigot
Rue Bichat
Boulevard
Bd Mirault
Daviers
Rue
PL. DU DOCTEUR BICHON
R. Monfroux
PLACE DE LA PAIX
Musée Jean-Lurçat
Clemenceau
Rue Vauvert
R. de l'Hommeau
R. Gay-Lussac
Arago
PLACE DU TERTRE ST-LAURENT
PL. LA ROCHEFOUCAULD LIANCOURT
Monge
1
R. de la Meignanne
LA DOUTRE
Rue Lionnaise
PL. DU TERTRE
R. A. Michel
27
Bd
R. Guitet
R. de la Censerie
Boulevard
Bd Descazeaux
Maine
PLACE DE LA LAITERIE
R. Dindron
la Trinité
20
Bd du Ronceray
P
Quai
PLACE MONPROFIT
R. Saint Nicolas
R. Corne de Cerf
P
Q. R. Fèvre
Rue Beaurepaire
PLACE G. BORDILLON
Arnauld
P
PLACE DE LA POISSONNERIE
Henri
R. des Carmes
Carmes
PT DE VERDUN
Quai des
2
Bd G. Dumesnil
Boul.
Esplanade Ligny
Av. Yolande d'Aragon
Cale de la Savate
Rue
Ligny
Port
Ligny
Montée St Maurice
R. D. de Puycharic
R. St Aignan
Bd du Bon Pasteur
Quai
Promenade
du
Pr. du bout du Monde
R. du Voliier
21
PL. FREPPEL
PONT DE LA BASSE-CHAINE
Bd du Général de Gaulle
Château
Maison du Vin de l'Anjou
R. St Evroult
← NANTES, RENNES, N 23
Hôtel du Roi de Pologne
R. de Pigneroles
PL. PRÉS. KENNEDY
4
R. Toussaint
Boulevard du
PL. DE L'ACADÉMIE
Rue R. Hoche
23
R. de l'Esvère
Blancheraie
R. Marceau
2
Rue du Temple
R. d'Iéna
PL. DE LA VISITATION
R. Talot
↙ NANTES, RENNES, N 23
Faidherbe
Rue Richard
R. d'Anjou
R. J. Dauban
10
3
PLACE P. SÉMARD
Gare Saint-Laud
R. A. Gautier
A
B
WHERE TO SLEEP
1 Centre d'accueil International du lac de Maine
2 Hôtel léna
4 Hotel Marguerite d'Anjou
5 Hôtel du Mail
8 Hôtel Continental
9 Hôtel Saint-Julien
10 Hôtel Le Progrès
WHERE TO EAT
20 Le Bouchon Angevin
21 Reastaurant La Ferme
22 Les Trois Rivières
23 Le Lucullus
24 Les Templiers
26 Le Salamandre
27 La Canaille

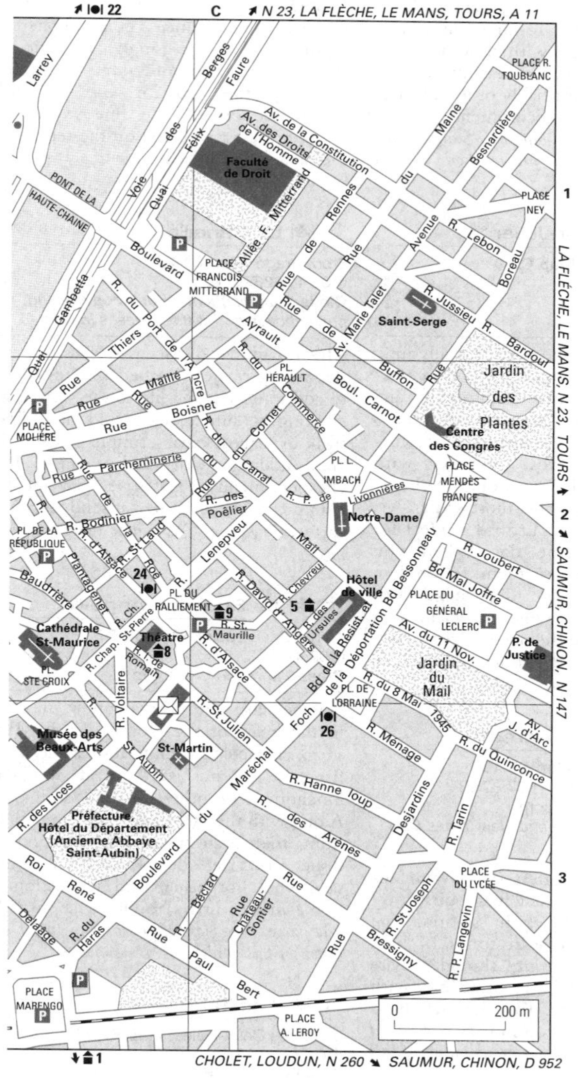

18

PAYS-DE-LA-LOIRE

Closed *Sun 12.30–5pm.* **Cots available. Disabled access. TV.**

The pretty frontage has an old-style sign outside. The communal areas are warm and bright and the whole place has been refurbished; there's a pleasant little lounge and breakfast room. Comfortable rooms cost €44–58 with shower/wc or bath. There's a friendly welcome by the owners, who are justifiably proud of their hotel. Reservations recommended. *10% discount on the room rate Fri–Sun for two consecutive nights on presentation of this guide.*

Hôtel Saint-Julien**

9 pl. du Ralliement. **Map C2-9**
ⓣ02.41.88.41.62
ⓔs.julien@wanadoo.fr
TV.

You'd be hard pushed to find anything more central, and you'll get a nice welcome here. The thirty comfortable air-conditioned rooms are pleasantly decorated – and most have been nicely refurbished. Doubles cost €46–58 with shower/wc or bath. The rooms overlooking the square are the most expensive. The small interior courtyard is ideal for breakfast on a fine day. When you book, you could ask them to book a table at the *Provence Café* next door (ⓣ02.41.87.44.15), which specializes in tasty cooking from the south. Credit cards are not accepted. *10% discount on the room rate on presentation of this guide.*

Hôtel Le Progrès**

26 av. Denis-Papin. **Map B3-10**
ⓣ02.41.88.10.14 ⓕ02.41.87.82.93
ⓦwww.hotelleprogres.com
Closed *Christmas Day and New Year's Day.*
TV.

This comfy hotel offers good value for money in a district which is a bit dreary but handy for the train station. The rooms are decorated in tones of blue with identical furnishings, though they're of varying size; doubles around €49 with shower/wc or bath. Excellent facilities and very friendly reception. *10% discount at weekends July–Aug on presentation of this guide.*

Hôtel du Mail**

8 rue des Ursules. **Map C2-5**
ⓣ02.41.88.56.22 ⓕ02.41.86.91.20
ⓦwww.destination-anjou.com/mail
Closed *Sun noon–6.30pm; public holidays.*
Disabled access. TV. Pay car park.

There isn't another hotel quite like this in Angers – it's a seventeenth-century townhouse in a very quiet street with a definite touch of Vieille France. The atmosphere is sophisticated and pleasingly conventional. Refurbished bedrooms are decorated tastefully; they go for €49–61 with shower/wc or bath. In fine weather, a buffet breakfast is served on the terrace in the shade of an ancient lime tree. It's essential to book.

La Canaille

8 bd. Arago. **Map B1-27**
ⓣ02.41.88.56.11
Closed *Sat lunchtime; Sun; Mon evening; public holidays; 1st three weeks in Aug.*

This run-down district is revitalizing and the young owners opened this restaurant to add some sun and life to the scene. The cooking is simple, tasty and appealing: steak or scallop kebabs, simple grilled fish, and puddings with playful names. The cheapest menu is €10 (weekday lunch), rising to €25; you'll pay around €25 à la carte. *Free glass of Crémant de Loire after your meal.*

Le Bouchon Angevin

44 rue Beaurepaire. **Map A2-20**
ⓣ02.41.24.77.97
Closed *Sun; Mon; 1–7 Aug.*

A wine cellar with a restaurant at the back in the heart of the Doutre district. Two small, characterful dining rooms and a big fireplace. Menus €10.50 at weekday lunchtimes, or others at €14 and €17. Along with the 500 or so wines to choose from, there's an interesting selection of dishes à la carte – deep-fried Camembert, salad with hot *rillauds* and a selection of home-made pastries. You'll pay about €20 à la carte. *Free glass of house wine on presentation of this guide.*

Les Templiers

5 rue des Deux-Haies. **Map B2-24**
ⓣ02.41.88.33.11
Closed *Sun; Mon lunchtime; a fortnight in July.*

A bright dining room with medieval décor. Lances, old swords and pennants ornament the walls, which are illuminated by torchlight. It's best to book, because the tasty, traditional cooking has a lot of local fans. Dishes are classics, well prepared using fresh produce from the daily market. Weekday lunch menu €10, *menu du templier* at €17 and *menu du Roy* at €25. There's not a dress code exactly, but they're not keen on jeans. *Free house apéritif on presentation of this guide.*

Restaurant La Ferme

2–4 pl. Freppel. **Map B2-21**
02.41.87.09.90
Closed *Sun evening; Wed; 22 Dec–10 Jan; 20 July–12 Aug.* **Disabled access.**

One of the most popular restaurants in town, with a terrace in the quiet shadow of the cathedral and a stunning dining room. It's stayed successful over the years by offering reliable cooking and generously flavoured dishes – but when it's crowded the service can get slapdash. Weekday lunch menu at €11.30, then others €15–22.50. They specialize in poultry: *poule-au-pot* and the warm *rillauds d'Anjou. Free coffee on presentation of this guide.*

Restaurant Les Trois Rivières

62 promenade de Reculée. **Off map B1-22**
02.41.73.31.88
Closed *mid-Jan to mid-Feb.* **Disabled access. Car park.**

This famous riverside fish restaurant with its panoramic dining room is always full, even on weekdays, so it's best to book. The welcome and service are efficient but not formal. They specialize in fish and the cooking is excellent; try the platter of the three rivers. Weekday lunch menu €13 with others up to €27. Lots of good dry white wines – try the Domaine de Brizé.

Le Lucullus

5 rue Hoche. **Map B3-23**
02.41.87.00.44
Closed *Sun and Mon (except Mother's Day and Christmas); Feb; last week July; three weeks Aug.* **Disabled access.**

A very good restaurant in fifteenth-century cellars. Faultless service and carefully prepared dishes. The €18 weekday *formule* is a good way of investigating the region's specialities and the dishes are accompanied by local wines. You'll find a weekday lunch menu at €13.50 and gastronomic menus from €19.30 to €52; there's a minimum charge of €21 at weekends.

La Salamandre

1 bd. du Maréchal Foch, near the garden of Mail. **Map C3-26**
02.41.88.99.55
Closed *Sun; Mon and Sat lunchtimes in Aug.*

This restaurant, on the premises of the *Hôtel d'Anjou*, has a reputation for consistently good cuisine. The well-proportioned dining room has an elegant, classic décor, with a portrait of François I on a wooden medallion. Smart clientele and perfect service. The dishes speak for themselves: langoustines for starters followed by John Dory. Lunch menu €23, or around €40 à la carte. Excellent wine list.

Saint-Saturnin-sur-Loire

49320 (17km SE)

Auberge de la Caillotte

2 rue de la Loire; it's on the banks of the Loire.
02.41.54.63.74
Closed *Mon and Tues in winter; Mon only in summer; Nov.* **Disabled access. Car park.**

In autumn and winter you eat in the ravishing rustic dining room; for summer there's a spacious, shady terrace. Hospitable welcome with a touch of humour. Best of all, though, are the cooking and the appealing wine list. Menus, €21–30, list an ever-changing selection of dishes and include a regional dessert, *crème d'Anjou*. À la carte you'll pay €30 – and it's worth it. You'll feel very relaxed here. *Free apéritif on presentation of this guide.*

Béhuard

49170 (18km SW)

Restaurant Les Tonnelles

Rue Principale.
02.41.72.21.50
Closed *Mon and Sun evenings; Wed evenings in low season; 23 Dec–31 Dec.*

The terrace is delightful in summer, when you sit under the arbour and enjoy the wonderful food. Weekday lunch *formule* €23, menus €32–96. The specialities are principally fish dishes from the Loire river, rabbit and pigeon. Very tasty.

Saint-Germain-des-Prés

49170 (23km SW)

|●| La Chauffeterie

Take the D15 between Saint-Germain-des-Prés and Saint-Augin-des-Bois or the A11, leaving at the Beaufreau-Chalonnes exit.
☎02.41.39.92.92
Closed *Mon–Wed (except group bookings).*
Disabled access. Car park.

This little farmhouse, deep in the country, was taken over by a Parisian couple a few years ago. There are two gorgeous dining rooms with fireplaces and the chairs are decorated in antique style. They offer good, simple cooking. Menus €18–27. You'll get attentive service from the owner – who's a trained astrologer – while his wife runs the kitchen.

Baugé

49150

☗ |●| Hostellerie de la Boule d'Or**

4 rue du Cygne.
☎02.41.89.82.12 Ⓕ02.41.89.06.07
Closed *Sun evening; Mon; around the New Year.* **Disabled access. TV. Car park.**

A friendly little hotel with ten attractively decorated rooms overlooking an internal courtyard. Doubles with shower/wc or bath €52–68. The restaurant specializes in good regional cooking including fresh fish, foie gras, veal kidneys and frogs' legs; menus at €17–28. It's best to book.

Baule (La)

44500

☗ Hôtel Marini**

22 av. Clémenceau; it's between the tourist office and the railway station.
☎02.40.60.23.29 Ⓕ02.40.11.16.98
Ⓦwww.lemarinihotel.com
TV. Swimming pool. Highchairs available. Car park.

Pleasantly fresh, youthful hotel with an indoor heated swimming pool. The comfortable, tastefully furnished rooms are particularly good value: doubles with shower/wc or bath €49–82 depending on the season. Restaurant for residents only in the evening. *10% discount, except July–August, spring bank holidays and excluding other offers, on presentation of this guide.*

☗ Hostellerie du Bois**

65 av. Lajarrige; 300m from the beach.
☎02.40.60.24.78 Ⓕ02.40.42.05.88
Ⓦwww.hostellerie-du-bois.com
Closed *15 Nov–15 March.* **TV. Pay car park.**

Set back from a lively street, this hotel is shaded by pine trees and has a flower garden. Bedrooms go for €55–65 with shower/wc or bath, depending on the season. Half-board compulsory in July/Aug €54.50–62 per person. It's a delightful and pleasantly cool place filled with souvenirs of Southeast Asia – the owners are keen travellers who have finally hung up their backpacks in order to greet other globetrotters. *One free breakfast per room on presentation of this guide.*

|●| Restaurant Chez L'Écailleur

37 av. des Ibis; it's near the market.
☎02.40.60.87.94
Closed *evenings; Mon out of season; March; 10 days in Nov/Dec; 10 days end Jan; 10 days around Easter.*

Undiluted pleasure here: treat yourself to a dozen plump Brittany oysters or clams with a half-litre of Gros-Plant wine. Reckon on around €6.90 for a half-dozen oysters and €2 for a glass of white on presentation of this guide.

|●| La Ferme du Grand Clos

52 av. de Lattre-de-Tassigny; it's opposite the riding school.
☎02.40.60.03.30
Closed *Tues; Wed; Tues lunchtime only in season.* **Highchairs and games available. Disabled access.**

The poshest crêperie in town – it's delightful and not at all stuffy. The wheat and buckwheat crêpes are equally delicious and the farm itself is really attractive. They also produce delicious, home-cooked dishes – mussels, *cassoulet* with duck *confit* or calf's head sauce *gribiche* – with *formules* from €15. There's a terrace in summer. *Free apéritif or coffee on presentation of this guide.*

|●| Restaurant Le Rossini

13 av. des Evens; it's near the town hall.
☎02.40.60.25.81

Closed *Sun evening; Tues lunchtime; plus Mon out of season; Jan.* **TV. Highchairs available. Car park.**

An elegant restaurant which is a real classic, with a dining room decorated in 1930s style. You'll get a welcoming smile from *la patronne*, while her husband, the chef, creates stylish, fresh dishes – try fillet of beef Rossini with duck foie gras, fish cooked in a salt crust or roast salmon in *beurre rouge*. The desserts are delicate and unusual, such as fig *au gratin* with almond cream. There's a €20 weekday menu; others up to €41. *Free coffee on presentation of this guide.*

Pouliguen (Le)

44510 (3km W)

Restaurant L'Opéra de la Mer

Promenade du Port.
☎ 02.40.62.31.03
Closed *Wed; Mon–Thurs Nov–March (except during school holidays, July–Aug); fortnight end Nov.* **Highchairs available.**

Families strolling by the harbour stop under the trees to watch the relaxed crowd and pirouetting staff at this popular restaurant – the terrace is chock-a-block in summer. They serve fish salads, nice fish soup, five varieties of mussels and good oysters. Menus €18–25.

Saillé

44350 (5 km NW)

Crêperie La Salorge

12 rue Croix-Sérot.
☎ 02.40.15.14.19
Closed *Wed and Thurs except in season.*

This good-value place is on the peninsula in a pretty village, and everyone knows it. The pancakes are huge – one will be more than enough for a main course. Expect to pay €27 for two savoury pancakes, a sweet one and a drink. The décor is as delicious as the pancakes. Inevitably it's often full, and in summer and over public holiday weekends you have to book a week to ten days in advance.

Pornichet

44380 (6km E)

Villa Flornoy

7 av. Flornoy.
☎ 02.40.11.60.00 Ⓕ 02.40.61.86.47
Ⓦ www.villa-flornoy.com
Closed *Nov–Feb.* **TV.**

A charming hotel in a quiet street just 300m from the beach. It feels like a family house and has been decorated with taste. The sitting room is pleasant and comfortable and attractively furnished with period furniture, and there's a lovely garden where you can relax with a book. Doubles with shower/wc or bath €66–90 with shower/wc or bath. *Free apéritif on presentation of this guide.*

Hôtel-restaurant Le Régent**

150 bd. des Océanides; it's on the seafront.
☎ 02.40.61.05.68 Ⓕ 02.40.61.25.53
Ⓦ www.le-regent.fr
Closed *Sun evening and Mon in winter; Dec; Jan.* **TV. Highchairs available. Car park.**

A family hotel facing the sea. It's bright and colourful, if a little bland, and the prices have gone up dramatically. Doubles €70–90 with bath/wc depending on the season. The restaurant specializes in inventive fish and seafood. Menus €18 (weekday lunchtimes) up to €32. Seven new rooms in an old building which has been renovated.

Batz-sur-Mer

44740 (8km W)

Restaurant Le Derwin

Côte Sauvage; it's on the seafront between Batz and Le Pouliguen.
Closed *Tues; Wed and Thurs (except July–Aug); Nov–1 April.* **Car park.**

This place is popular with the sailing fraternity. The ideal place for a plate of mussels, seafood and crêpes while you gaze out to sea. Expect to pay €18 per person. *Free coffee on presentation of this guide.*

Saint-Lyphard

44110 (16km NE)

Auberge de Kerhinet

☎ 02.40.61.91.46 Ⓕ 02.40.61.97.37
Closed *Tues and Wed except during school holidays; mid-Dec to mid-Jan.* **Highchairs and games available. Car park.**

One of the nicest places in the area, charming and simple, with rooms in little cottages. The décor is chic but country-style and there's a beautiful collection of old photographs. Doubles with shower/wc or bath €40–50. The restaurant serves solid, authentic cooking with a light refinement about it. Specialities include eel, frogs' legs, a casserole including both with curry sauce, duck and game. They put a whole dish of terrine down on the table for you to help yourself. Menus €21–38. In summer you can eat out in the courtyard.

Bouin

85230

Hôtel Le Martinet**

1 pl. de la Croix-Blanche; it's beside the church.
Ⓣ02.51.49.08.94 Ⓕ02.51.49.83.08
Ⓦwww.lemartinet.com
Disabled access. TV. Swimming pool. Car park.

This large and beautiful eighteenth-century house offers a choice of bedrooms – old-fashioned ones overlooking the square or newer rooms at ground level that give direct access to the garden and swimming pool. Doubles €50–60 depending on facilities and season. Françoise has redecorated the place and takes care of reception. Her sons also have a role: Emmanuel looks after the kitchen garden and does the cooking while Jean-François supplies the fish and seafood. Meals, including breakfast, are served in the old dining room, which smells delightfully of beeswax, or on the veranda overlooking the swimming pool. In the evening, typical choices include a dozen oysters, terrine of foie gras, *panaché* of eel and frogs' legs, grilled sea bream and *carpaccio* of marinated salmon. Menu €19. *Free apéritif on presentation of this guide.*

Restaurant Le Courlis

15 rue du Pays-de-Monts; it's on the edge of town.
Ⓣ02.51.68.64.65
Closed *Mon and Wed evening out of season.* **Car park.**

A white, rather squat building which is typical of the area. The flower-filled dining room is a nice place to enjoy the mouth-watering cuisine and a range of specialities that change with the seasons and whichever fresh fish has been landed – hot oysters, sea bream with *beurre blanc, sole meunière* with five spices, turbot with bacon and oyster and foie gras turnover with samphire. Weekday lunch menu €12 and others €18–38. *Free coffee or apéritif on presentation of this guide.*

Challans

85300

Hôtel de l'Antiquité

14 rue Gallieni.
Ⓣ02.51.68.02.84 Ⓕ02.51.35.55.74
Ⓦwww.hotelantiquite.com
Disabled access. TV. Swimming pool. Car park.

This hotel is very ordinary from the outside but inside it's charming, with refined period furniture shown off to best advantage. The rooms are spacious and most of them have been tastefully renovated. The rooms – €49–65 with shower or bath/wc – are all set around the swimming pool which is where you have breakfast. It's a blissful place, run by a nice, energetic couple. *10% discount on the room rate Sept–June on presentation of this guide.*

Restaurant La Gite du Tourne Pierre

Route de Saint-Gilles; it's 3km on the D69, between Challans and Soullans.
Ⓣ02.51.68.14.78
Closed *Fri out of season; 3 weeks in March; 3 weeks in Oct.* **Swimming pool. Car park.**

The décor is outdated, but Marie Ferrand's regional cuisine is certainly worth a try. Menus €32–48. Faultless, unpretentious service. A good place if you're feeling flush and appreciate fine food. *Free coffee on presentation of this guide.*

Commequiers

85220 (12km SE)

Hôtel de la Gare

66 rue de la Morinière; take the D754.
Ⓣ02.51.54.80.38 Ⓕ02.28.10.41.47
Closed *1 Oct–31 May. Restaurant closed Mon out of season.* **Swimming pool. Car park.**

In the early twentieth century, when the railway network extended into the remotest parts of France, this substantial Victorian house was built. No trains now – but at least the nights are quiet. The rooms here are inviting, pleasant and attractively decorated; doubles are €34 with shower and €42 with shower/wc. The dining room is fresh and bright, too, with lots of green and a railway theme – old photographs, station lanterns, ticket punchers. Good, original dishes are served in ample portions. Menus €12 (not Sun), €15 and €22. There's a shady garden where you can relax after a swim. *Free apéritif on presentation of this guide.*

Saint-Gervais

85230 (12km NW)

Restaurant La Pitchounette

48 rue Bonne-Brise; it's on the D948 in the direction of Beauvoir and Noirmoutier.
ⓣ02.51.68.68.88
Open *noon–1.30pm and 7.30–9.30pm.*
Closed *Mon and Tues out of season; a week in June; a week in Jan; a fortnight in Sept.*

A really welcoming and pretty house with flowers everywhere – but Gérard Thoumoux's cooking outshines the décor. There are many tempting specialities, based around foie gras, frogs' legs, snails and eels. Weekday lunch menu €9.15 and others €15.25–26.50. *Free coffee on presentation of this guide.*

Champtoceaux

49270

Hôtel-restaurant Le Champalud**

Promenade du Champalud; it's in the centre of town.
ⓣ02.40.83.50.09 ⓕ02.40.83.53.81
ⓦwww.lechampalud.fr.st
Restaurant closed *Sun evening 1 Oct–30 March.* **Disabled access. TV.**

The hotel is in a charming village on the banks of the Loire. There are twelve comfortable rooms for €49–64 with shower/wc or bath. The restaurant has a good reputation; the *menu du jour* (€11.50) includes wine, and there are others at €15–36. À la carte features regional specialities. There's also a brasserie that serves a worldwide selection of beers and cheaper menu options. They offer various sports facilities – tennis courts nearby, a gym and mountain bikes – and a sitting room filled with board games. Friendly, very energetic owner and a place which is good value for money. *10% discount on the room rate (1 Oct–31 March) on presentation of this guide.*

Châtaigneraie (La)

85120

L'Auberge de la Terrasse**

7 rue de Beauregard.
ⓣ02.51.69.68.68 ⓕ02.51.52.67.96
Closed *Fri evening 15 Sept–31 May; Sun evening; Sat lunchtime; autumn school holidays.* **TV. Disabled access.**

This hotel, which occupies a well-restored, substantial house in a quiet road, has a family atmosphere and a quality restaurant. Double rooms are €53–56 with shower/wc, breakfast included. The owner provides a culinary voyage through the Vendée marshes and across the sea – specialities include eel with butter and bacon, and snails prepared in many different ways. Menus €10–32. There's a shady square opposite, which has a lovely view. *Free Kir on presentation of this guide.*

Châteaubriant

44110

Le Poêlon d'Or

30 bis rue du 11-Novembre; it's near the post office and the town hall.
ⓣ02.40.81.43.33
Closed *Sun evening; Mon; a fortnight in Feb; 1–22 Aug.*

This place is great for gourmands who don't want to spend too much. The service is nicely formal and the rustic décor feels very French. Dishes are prepared using seasonal fresh produce, and change regularly, but there are a few constants including Châteaubriant with port and prunes or sea bass with potato. Menus €15.50–46.

Château-du-Loir

72500

Hôtel-restaurant Le Grand Hôtel**

59 av. Aristide-Briand.
ⓣ02.43.44.00.17 ⓕ02.43.44.37.58
TV. Car park.

This old coaching inn has stood the test of time. It offers doubles with shower or bath/wc for €45–58 and the superb cuisine adds to the establishment's reputation. Meals are served in a charming old-style dining room with a painted ceiling, and include dishes such as calf's head *ravigotte*, duck foie gras, terrine of young rabbit in aspic and *marmite sarthoise* (a stew of chicken, rabbit, ham and mushrooms). Menus €18–39.

Vaas

72420 (8km SW)

Hôtel-restaurant Le Védaquais**

Pl. de la Liberté; take the D305.
☎02.43.46.01.41 Ⓕ02.43.46.37.60
Ⓔvedaquais@aol.com
Closed *Fri and Sun evenings; Mon; winter and Christmas school holidays.* **Disabled access. Highchairs available. TV. Car park.**

This old-fashioned village hotel occupies the old schoolhouse. Daniel Beauvais is a very good chef who doesn't talk much, while his wife Sylvie is a very good hostess who chats away quite happily. They offer a weekday *menu du marché* for €10, and others at €13–25 or à la carte. The food here is a real treat – fresh-tasting, straightforward and brimming with creativity. Typical dishes include roast zander with *petit trou* and chicken breast with morels, with a few little treats such as fine apple tart with rosemary honey for dessert. The rooms – €42 with shower/wc or €55 with bath – are every bit as pleasant. *Free apéritif or coffee on presentation of this guide.*

Marçon

72340 (8.5km NE)

Restaurant du Bœuf

21 pl. de l'Église; take the N138, then head onto the D305.
☎02.43.44.13.12
Closed *Sun evening and Mon outside high season; Mon lunchtime July–Aug; 21 Jan–7 March.*

Creole dishes take pride of place on the menus here; menus €11.50–34. Dishes include chicken with crayfish, prawn *fricassée* with coconut milk, pork stew and lamb colombo, as well as duck breast with raspberry vinegar. Have some punch and a few fritters to start with and round things off with a house liqueur. *Free coffee on presentation of this guide.*

Ruillé-sur-Loir

72340 (16km NE)

Hôtel-restaurant Saint Pierre

42 rue Nationale; take the D305, it's 6km from La Chartre-sur-le-Loir.
☎02.43.44.44.36
Restaurant closed *evenings except for guests; Dec school holidays.*

This appealing little village hotel, with an unassuming façade and a cosy, friendly atmosphere, is one of a dying breed. The proprietress fusses over all her customers and nobody around these parts can rival her €8.50 *menu ouvrier* – the dozens of plates of hors-d'œuvres are even served out ahead of time to deal with the rush. A bottle of red wine is included in the price. Other menus at €12.50 and €19 – on Sunday there is a choice of leg of lamb, fillet of beef or duck with pepper, with salad, cheese platter and dessert. They offer a few simple doubles with basin for €26.70, with shower for €25. *Free coffee on presentation of this guide.*

Château-Gontier

53200

Hôtel du Cerf**

31 rue Garnier; it's opposite the Champion supermarket on the N162, the Laval-Angers road.
☎02.43.07.25.13 Ⓕ02.43.07.02.90
Closed *3 weeks end July/beginning of Aug.* **Hotel closed** *Sun evening.* **Restaurant closed** *Fri–Sun; public holidays*. **TV. Car park.**

The frontage of this hotel, which is in the centre of town and near the river, has had a facelift. As you would expect, the rooms overlooking the garden are quieter than the others: €36–40 for a double with shower/wc or bath. They serve a special evening stop-over menu in the garden in the summer.

Le Parc Hôtel***

46 av. Joffre; at the entrance to Château-Gontier, coming from Angers.
☎02.43.07.28.41 Ⓕ02.43.07.63.79
Ⓔcontact@parchotel.fr
TV. Car park.

A wonderful place to get away from it all: a beautiful nineteenth-century mansion house in a wooded park complete with a tennis court and swimming pool. The rooms are bright, colourful and thoughtfully furnished; they are all different, and each is designed around a foreign country; for example, there is a red-and-green Chinese room. Doubles €55–71. The service is as hospitable as the setting.

|●| Restaurant L'Aquarelle

2 rue Felix-Marchand, in Pendu-en-Saint-Fort. It's 400m from the centre; follow the road that runs along the north bank of the Mayenne towards Sablé, and at the roundabout take the Ménil road.
☎02.43.70.15.44
Closed *Wed; Feb.* **Car park.**

Situated outside town on the banks of the Mayenne, this place will set you dreaming. The terrace is beautiful on summer days, and the panoramic dining room, air-conditioned in summer, offers a magnificent view of the river. The light, creative cooking includes dishes like red mullet terrine with *confit* of tomatoes, crab in a saffron cream sauce or the salmon steak with creamy corn. Weekday lunchtime menu €10; others €14–37.50.

Coudray

53200 (7km SE)

|●| Restaurant L'Amphitryon

2 rue de Daon; take the D22 and it's opposite the church.
☎02.43.70.46.46
Closed *Tues evening, Wed; Sun evening; the Feb school holidays; 1 May; the 1st fortnight in July; a week at All Saints'; 23–25 Dec.* **Disabled access. Car park.**

This place might look like any other inn, but it's gained a reputation as one of the most delightful places in the *département*. There's something invigorating about both the cooking and the décor. Dishes are light and colourful: calf's head and tongue in cider-perfumed *bouillon*, fillet of trout with potatoes, *millefeuille* of Camembert and apple tart. Set menus €16 and €24. There's a terrace and a garden.

Daon

53200 (11.5km SE)

⌂ |●| Hôtel-restaurant À l'Auberge

10 rue Dominique-Godivier; take the D22.
☎ and ℱ02.43.06.91.14
Closed *Sat.* **Hotel closed** *Oct–March.* **Restaurant closed** *a week in Feb; a week in Oct.*

A good country inn specializing in fish and seafood dishes. It's popular with fishermen because the menus are good and cheap – €8.50 (Mon–Sat) and up to €22. Dishes include zander fillet *beurre blanc*, or duck breast with *pommeau*. Basic bedrooms with basin go for €26.50. Best to book ahead in the winter as the restaurant closes sometimes, especially in the evening.

Ballots

53350 (30km NW)

|●| Restaurant L'Auberge du Mouillotin

9 rue de Paris; it's 9.5km northwest Craon on the D25 towards La Guerche-de-Bretagne.
☎02.43.06.61.81
Closed *Tues; Wed; Thurs and Sun evenings; a week in March; a fortnight in Aug.* **Disabled access.**

This restaurant serves delicious omelettes with all sorts of rich and tasty fillings – foie gras and snails – along with crêpes, *galettes* and good gourmet dishes. Weekday lunch menu €10, with others at €14 and €25. The pretty dining room overlooks the garden. *Free coffee on presentation of this guide.*

Chenillé-Changé

49220

⌂ |●| Auberge La Table du Meunier

Le Moulin. Take the N162 north from Lion-d'Angers, then the D78.
☎02.41.95.10.98
Closed *Sun evening, Mon, Tues and Wed in March, Nov & Dec; Mon evening, Tues and Wed from 1 April–30 June and 1 Sept–31 Oct; Jan; Feb.* **Disabled access. Car park.**

Situated in a village full of flowers with a gentle river running nearby, this dreamy place offers guaranteed peace and quiet. There are five charmingly decorated dining rooms and a huge panoramic terrace. Really tasty local cuisine with a good reputation: house foie gras, Loire valley fishes and nougat *glacé* with a raspberry *coulis*. Menus from €17 (except Sun lunchtime and public holidays) and up to €33. They have a few rooms on a boat nearby, where you'll be lulled to sleep by the sound of the flowing water; doubles with shower/wc €34–39.

Cholet

49300

|●| Restaurant Le Croquignolet

13 rue de la Vendée; just outside the centre, to the northwest.
Ⓣ02.41.58.77.00

A traditional restaurant with rather banal décor; the food has character, however, with seafood, snails and locally grown asparagus. A variety of menus starting from €13, but the cheap menu is sufficient for most appetites, as the portions are gargantuan. Round tables, which make for a more convivial atmosphere. Charming service.

Doué-la-Fontaine

49700

|●| Restaurant-Bar La Halte

108 rue de Cholet; opposite the zoo.
Ⓣ02.41.59.14.16
Closed *Tues, Wed and Thurs evening (except July–Aug).* **Car park.**

This restaurant is by the side of the road; it's nondescript inside but the cooking is sophisticated and uses the finest local ingredients, such as mushrooms and fish from the Loire. There's even a pink *crême brûlée* – made without any artificial colourings! Menus €11–32. If you notice any strange noises, they are probably not being made by fellow customers with poor table manners but by the guests of the zoo over the road.

|●| Le Caveau

4 bis pl. du Champ-de-Foire; it's signposted from the town centre.
Ⓣ02.41.59.38.28
Open *daily lunchtime and evening Easter to Oct; Thurs evening to Sunday lunchtime out of season.*

A warm, welcoming place in the heart of the village, which started life a medieval cellar before becoming a famous dance hall. People head here for their *fouaces*, or hearth-cakes – a sort of unleavened bread traditionally cooked in cinders. Try them with *rillettes*, goat's cheese or smothered with sweet local butter. Several *formules* are on offer (generously served and easy on the pocket), as well as a €13 "Express" lunch menu and another at €19 including wine and coffee. The place is run by three smiling young people who will fill you in on all manner of activities in the region; once in a while they have a theatrical evening. *Free digestif on presentation of this guide.*

Louresse-Rochemenier

49700 (6km NW)

|●| Les Caves de la Génévraie

13 rue du Musée-Rocheménier; take the D761 or the D69 north from Doué-la-Fontaine.
Ⓣ02.41.59.34.22
Open *daily July–Aug; closed Mon Sept–June; 24 Dec–15 Jan.* **Disabled access. Car park.**

This gallery, hewn out of the rock, was used as a hiding place during the Wars of Religion. Nowadays there are several small dining rooms and, when it's hot outside, the stone keeps them cool. They offer the local speciality *fouaces* (wheat cakes cooked in cinders), which they stuff with *rillettes*, beans or mushrooms and serve with hors d'œuvres and Layon wines. There's one menu only, at €20, which includes wine and coffee. Reservations only – and smoking is not permitted. *L' Ammonite* nearby (an annexe) offers the same menus.

Évron

53600

🏠 |●| Hôtel-restaurant Brasserie de la Gare**

13 rue de la Paix; it's opposite the station.
Ⓣ02.43.01.60.29 Ⓕ02.43.01.58.28
Ⓔhoteldelagareevron@yahoo.fr
Restaurant closed *Sun; public holidays.*
TV.

This establishment looks like something out of another era and you'd probably hesitate before deciding to give it a go. It's a good place, however, and offers quiet, comfortable bedrooms with shower/wc €37 or €42 with bath. They serve generous portions of good regional cooking in the restaurant – the €11 menu (Mon–Sat only) lists dishes like house terrine, rib steak *façon vallée de l'Erve* and rhubarb tart. There are others at €15–18.

Mezangers

53600 (3km NW)

⌂ |●| Relais du Gué de Selle***

Route de Mayenne; it's on the D7.
Ⓣ02.43.91.20.00 Ⓕ02.43.91.20.10
Ⓦwww.relais-du-gue-de-selle.com
Closed *Fri and Sun evenings, and Mon 1 Oct–31 May; Mon lunchtime 1 June–1 Oct; 1st May; winter and Christmas school holidays.* **Disabled access. TV. Swimming pool. Car park.**

Though this farmhouse – which is located in the middle of the country with the forest at its back and a pond at the front – has lost nearly everything of its original atmosphere, it's been restored and converted into a welcoming inn. It offers great menus from €13.50 (weekdays only); others €19–42. Try the Mayenne specialities such as the foie gras terrine, zander fillet in cider or langoustines kebabs drizzled with honey. You'll get absolute peace and quiet in the pleasant, comfortable bedrooms (€80–112), which overlook either the garden, the swimming pool or the countryside.

Neau

53150 (6km W)

⌂ |●| Hôtel-restaurant La Croix Verte**

2 rue d'Évron; from Évron, head towards Laval.
Ⓣ02.43.98.23.41 Ⓕ02.43.98.25.39
Ⓦwww.croixverte.com
Restaurant closed *Fri evenings Oct–Easter; Sun evenings all year round; winter school holidays.* **TV.**

Your heart might sink when you catch sight of this place – it's set on an unattractive junction and sports a dreary façade. But you'll be pleasantly surprised when you step inside, and might even be tempted to stay longer than you planned. Superbly refurbished bedrooms with shower/wc or bath are €38–47, and there's a nice bar. The à la carte menu is full of tasty specialities – delicious foie gras steak with candied ginger chesnuts. Weekday menu €11, and €18.

Deux-Évailles

53150 (12km NW)

|●| La Fenderie

Site de la Fenderie; it's on the D129 between Jublains and Montsurs, at the edge of the village.
Ⓣ02.43.90.00.95
Closed *Mon; autumn school holidays. Reservation only in the evenings.* **Highchairs and games available. Disabled access.**

This place stands in forty acres of grounds; normally the birds have the place to themselves but at the weekends picnickers crowd in – so avoid the scrum by relaxing on the terrace opposite the pond. Weekly lunch menus at €10 and €15; others €17.50–33. They list local dishes that change daily. Good bets include fillet of beef with morels, duck breast with melon and *pommeau*, scallops in cider with caramelized apples, warm apple tart flambée with calvados and numerous other mouth-watering dishes. When skies are grey, enjoy the dining room with its fireplace and exposed beams; in good weather you can gaze out of the bay windows at the surrrounding countryside. *Free coupette served with your dessert on presentation of this guide.*

Jublains

53160 (17km NW)

|●| Crêperie-grill l'Orgétorix

9 rue Henri-Barbe.
Ⓣ02.43.04.31.64
Closed *evenings out of season, except by reservation.* **Disabled access.**

Here, Monsieur takes command of the stove and Madame oversees the dining room. They're obviously doing something right – after 12.30pm there's hardly a seat left. The menus are delicious and very cheap: two-course *formule* for €5.90, three-course menu at €9.20 including drink. À la carte, the *galettes* and crêpes are good. Perhaps follow your meal with a stroll around this old Gallic village.

Ferté-Bernard (La)

72400

⌂ |●| Hôtel-restaurant du Stade

21–23 rue Virette.
Ⓣ02.43.93.01.67 Ⓕ02.43.93.48.26
Closed *Fri and Sun evenings.* Disabled access (restaurant). **TV. Highchairs available. Car park.**

A small establishment in a little side road –

and stuck in something of a time warp. It's clean and well maintained. Doubles €41–46.50. Nice family-style cooking on a good weekday menu at €10 (including coffee); others go up to €31.50. Good choices include scallops, frogs' legs and prawns flambéed in whisky. *Free coffee on presentation of this guide.*

Hôtel-restaurant La Perdrix**

2 rue de Paris.
☎02.43.93.00.44 Ⓕ02.43.93.74.95
Ⓦwwwperso.wanadoo.fr/restaurantlaperdrix
Closed *Mon evening; Tues; Feb.* **TV. Pay car park.**

Serge Thibaut's establishment is as pleasing to the eye as it is to the palate. Menus ranging from €18 (except Sat evening, Sun and bank holidays) to €38, list masterpieces such as veal kidneys with balsamic vinegar, roast langoustine with tagliatelle, pigeon in red wine sauce with potato pancakes and *carpaccio* of warm pineapple with *sabayon*. The wine cellar boasts almost six hundred vintages. Doubles are €42–52 with shower/wc, and there's a duplex that sleeps five. The talent here goes hand in hand with great modesty and hospitality. *Free coffee on presentation of this guide.*

Le Bocage fleuri

14 pl. Carnot.
☎02.43.71.24.04
Closed *Sun; Tues evening; 3 weeks in Aug.*

A little place in the middle of town, much praised by the locals. The terrace is ideal when the weather's fine. Really professional cuisine and they don't stint on the helpings; menus €8–22. There's a lovely interior garden. *Free coffee on presentation of this guide.*

Le Dauphin

3 rue d'Huisne; it's in a pedestrianized street.
☎02.43.93.00.39
Closed *Sun evening; Mon; a week in March; a week in Aug.* **Disabled access. Highchairs available.**

This delightful restaurant is dominated by a huge fireplace. It's located in a historic building near the port, Saint-Julien, and is popular with couples and gourmands alike. Menus €15 (weekdays only) and €23–38. The dishes, including such choices as veal medallions with Serrano ham, fillet of beef with foie gras or chocolate *moelleux* with pistachios, change with the seasons and according to the chef's inspiration.

Saint-Ulphace

72320 (14km SE)

Le Grand Monarque

5 pl. du Grand-Monarque; it's right in the heart of the village.
☎02.43.93.27.07
Closed *Tues; Wed; early July. By reservation only on weekday evenings.* **TV.**

This restaurant is a hit with the locals – who enjoy long, convivial Sunday lunches here. Menus are priced from €8.50 (weekday lunchtimes) to €28.50 and offer good solid cuisine: house *foie gras*, fish *choucroute*, lamb *muzzle*, scallop and Dublin Bay prawn salad, pan-fried caramelized bananas, warm chocolate profiteroles. There's a covered terrace in summer and in winter they have themed evenings – based around dishes such as paella, *choucroute*, seafood and so on. They also have a few furnished rooms; €30–45 depending on facilities. *Free coffee on presentation of this guide.*

Montmirail

72320 (15km SE)

Crêperie de L'Ancienne Forge

11 bis pl. du Château.
☎02.43.71.49.14
Closed *Mon and Tues, except in summer.* **Disabled access.**

A pretty little restaurant with a terrace overlooking a château. The good food includes wonderful salads and *galettes*, delicately flavoured *taboulé*, rib steak and ice cream with strawberries. It'll cost you around €13 for a meal.

Bonnétables

72110 (20km W)

Hôtel-Restaurant Le Lion d'Or

1 rue du Maréchal-Leclerc.
☎ and Ⓕ02.43.29.38.55
Closed *Sun.* **TV. Car park.**

This charming building, which dates

back to the eleventh century, is situated in the centre of the town. It has fifteen delightful rooms, which cost from €38. There's a restaurant and a *crêperie*, too: in the former the cooking is from the Sarthe region and dishes are sophisticated. Weekday lunch menu €9.50, other at €23. Specialities include gizzard *confit* and goose liver terrine with Port. They also make all their own pastries – try the *tarte tatin. Free apéritif on presentation of this guide.*

Flèche (La)

72200

Relais Henri IV

Route du Mans. It's 2km northeast of town, towards Paris-Le Mans.
☎02.43.94.07.10 ℻02.43.94.68.49
www.logis-de-france.fr
Closed *Sun evening; Mon; the Feb and All Saints' school holidays.* **TV. Highchairs and games available. Car park.**

The inn is on the edge of the town and set back from the road. The rooms are bright, clean and soundproofed; doubles €42–45. Good food, also: the duck breast in a salt crust is excellent, and – since the chef is really passionate about chocolate – make sure you try his *millefeuille*. The walls in the dining room are plastered with 200 chocolate moulds and figurines. Menus €13.50–€31. *Free jar of onion preserve on presentation of this guide.*

Relais Cicero***

18 bd. d'Alger; it's near place Thiers, close to the Prytanée.
☎02.43.94.14.14 ℻02.43.45.98.96
www.cicero.fr
Closed *Sun evening; 1–15 Aug; 20 Dec–3 Jan.* **TV. Car park.**

A beautiful residence in a sixteenth-century building (modified in the eighteenth century), well away from the crowds and noise of the town. There's an English bar, a reading room, a comfortable breakfast room and an open fire. Bedrooms in the main house are so stylish and comfortable that they're well worth splashing out on, but the hotel proper is actually on the other side of the flower garden. There you get cosy doubles with shower or bath for €69–110. Breakfast at €9. This place oozes charm. *10% discount on the room rate for a stay of at least two consecutive nights except July–Aug on presentation of this guide.*

Le Moulin des Quatre Saisons

Rue Gallieni; it's opposite the town hall.
☎02.43.45.12.12 ℻02.43.45.10.31
Closed *Sun and Wed evenings; Mon; a fortnight in Jan; a week in March; autumn school holidays.* **Highchairs available. Disabled access.**

This restaurant has a great riverside location opposite the Château des Carmes, and with the country inn décor and the syrupy background music you could almost imagine yourself on the banks of the Danube. There's a wonderful terrace, too. Tasty, good-value food on menus from €20.10 (weekday lunchtime only), including coffee and wine, and others €25–29. Dishes change regularly but might include *pastilla* of oxtail with horseradish sauce and salmon with fresh noodles. *Free coffee on presentation of this guide.*

Luché-Pringé

72800 (13km E)

Auberge du Port-des-Roches**

Le Port-des-Roches.
☎02.43.45.44.48 ℻02.43.45.39.61
Closed *Sun evening; Mon; Tues lunchtime; 26 Jan–9 March.* **TV. Car park.**

This inn is run by an energetic, hardworking young couple who are bringing the place back to life. Brightly coloured bedrooms cost €40–50 for a double. In the cosy dining room they serve skilfully prepared dishes at good country prices – set menus are €20–39. There's an impressive selection of dishes and they change three times a year: typical offerings might include zander with *beurre blanc* and hazelnuts. The superb flowery terrace overlooks the river, as do some of the bedrooms. *Free apéritif on presentation of this guide.*

Fontenay-Le-Comte

85200

Hôtel Fontarabie - Restaurant La Glycine**

57 rue de la République.

ⓣ02.51.69.17.24 ⓕ02.51.51.02.73
ⓦwww.hotel-fontarabie@aol.com
Closed *Christmas period.* **Disabled access. TV. Car park.**

A long time ago, it was traditional for Basque merchants to travel to Fontenay to trade horses during the Feast of St John. They stayed in this very coaching inn – though the handsome white stone building with its slate roof has been restored somewhat since then. The new décor is tasteful, if a touch too modern, and the bedrooms are clean with adequate facilities. Try to avoid the ones overlooking the street – they're smaller and noiser. Doubles €44–52 with shower/wc or bath. The restaurant, which is named after the wonderful wisteria over the front door, offers good regional cooking and generous portions of dishes like grilled *andouillette*, grilled calf's liver with bacon and a mouthwatering chocolate mousse. Menus €7.80–24. *Free apéritif on presentation of this guide.*

Aux Chouans Gourmets

6 rue des Halles.
ⓣ02.51.69.55.92
Open *noon–2pm and 7–9.30pm.* **Closed** *Sun evening; Mon; Thurs evening except July–Aug; a week in Jan; a fortnight in March; a fortnight Aug–Sept.*

A solidly built house with a noble façade; the dining room has splendid rough-hewn stone walls and there's a covered terrace overlooking the Vendée. You'll find traditional and gourmet cuisine that uses fresh ingredients bought from the market on the doorstep. There are lots of local specialities: Vendée ham, roast farm-raised pigeon with *confit*, iced *parfait* with Kamok. Menus €13.50–34.60. *Free coffee on presentation of this guide.*

Pissotte

85200 (4km N)

Crêperie Le Pommier

9 rue des Gélinières; take the D938.
ⓣ02.51.69.08.06
Closed *Mon and Tues (Mon only in July); 15–30 Sept.* **Disabled access. Car park.**

This serene old building is next to an ancient wine cellar. It has a garden and a conservatory, and is covered in wisteria and Virginia creeper. They do crêpes served with a generous side dish – try the Bretonne with *andouillette*, apples and salad, the Caprine with goat's cheese and thyme or the Syracuse with smoked breast of duck, pan-fried apples and orange sauce. Wash it all down with a nice bottle of local rosé. Weekday lunch menu at €7.50 and another at €11.

Mervent

85200 (11km NE)

Crêperie du Château de la Citardière

Les Ouillères; take the D99 from Mervent.
ⓣ02.51.00.27.04
Open *daily July to mid-Sept; weekends only mid-Sept to end June.*

Pretty place in a rather strange seventeenth-century castle. Parts of it have been converted in order to welcome walkers. There's a gorgeous rustic dining room which smells of wood smoke and pancake batter, or you can enjoy the fresh air out on the terrace in summer. They serve the most wonderful crêpes filled with everything from duck breast to mushrooms; there's a sweet one with flambéed apples. Expect to pay about €13 for a complete meal. There's a cellar where they hold exhibitions and musical evenings. *Free coffee on presentation of this guide.*

Velluire

85770 (11km SW)

L'Auberge de la Rivière**

Take the D938 as far as Nizeau, then the D68.
ⓣ02.51.52.32.15 ⓕ02.51.52.37.42
Closed *Mon all year round; Sun evening out of season; 20 Dec–2 March.* **Disabled access. TV. Car park.**

This place is ideal if you're after quiet, luxury and fine cooking. The attractive dining room, all yellow tablecloths, beams, pot plants and tapestries, makes a great setting to eat hot oysters, bass with artichokes, crayfish in flaky pastry, beef in wine sauce or young pigeon with morels. Weekday menu €19; others €35 and €46. The charming country-style bedrooms cost €73–91 with bath; no. 10 is the only one without a river view. You can hire bicycles. Credit cards are not accepted. *One free breakfast per room for a stay of at least two consecutive nights on presentation of this guide.*

Maillezais

85420 (15km SE)

Hôtel Saint-Nicolas**

Rue du Docteur-Daroux.
T 02.51.00.74.45 F 02.51.87.29.10.
Closed *15 Nov–15 Feb.* **TV. Lock-up garage.**

The young owner of this friendly little hotel looks after everything – from the simple rooms (€38–55 with shower or bath) to the terrace with its tiny gardens. He knows the area like the back of his hand and will show you his own walks through the Poitou marshlands; it's an excellent base from which to explore the area. Breakfast €7. *10% discount on the room rate on presentation of this guide except during school holidays and on long weekends.*

Le Collibert

Rue Principale.
T 02.51.87.25.07
Closed *Sun evening; Mon.*

The rustic setting and hearty food make this an ideal refuge from the rigours of winter, but any time of year is suitable for appreciating the fine dishes created by the chef from Poitou, who is clearly enamoured of his region and its culinary traditions. (The owner, on the other hand, is a mine of information about the cooking of Vendée.) Menus €11–32. The regional menu at €22 is particularly worthy of note, with *farci poitevin*, frogs' legs with eels, Mizotte (a local cheese) and gâteau with angelica. À la carte, you can find ham with *mojhettes* (dwarf runner beans), *lumas* (snails) and crayfish. You are guaranteed a meal as steeped in local knowledge as it is in flavour.

La Grande aux Roseaux

Le Grand-Port; by the waterside, at the foot of the abbey.
T 02.51.00.77.54
Open *daily April to mid-Nov.*
Disabled access.

A romantic setting with a bower outside that attracts both tourists and locals (a recommendation in itself). Good *farcis poitevins*, eels and snails from the vicinity. Menus €11.50–21. Friendly service.

Fontevraud-L'Abbaye

49590

Hôstellerie La Croix Blanche**

7 pl. des Plantagenêts; it's beside the abbey.
T 02.41.51.71.11 F 02.41.38.15.38
W www.fontevraud.net
Closed *Sun evening and Monday out of seasaon; Jan; 17–27 Nov.* **TV. Car park.**

A delightful hotel in an elegant building, right next to the abbey of Fontevraud. They have 21 bedrooms set around a quiet, flower-filled courtyard. Doubles with shower/wc or bath are €53–70. Some have a fireplace made of local stone. The restaurant, well known for its good cooking, offers menus from €19.50 (vegetarian) up to €39.90. Dishes might include foie gras and salad of black pudding. On the most expensive menus – which include two main courses – you might see wild mushrooms with asparagus, *goujons* of sole, beef *tournedos* with truffle sauce and duck foie gras with figs and Calvados. Nice welcome. *10% discount on the room rate on presentation of this guide.*

Guenrouet

44530

Le Jardin de l'Isac

31 rue de l'Isac; it's 6km east of Saint-Gildes-les-Bois.
T 02.40.87.66.11
Open *daily July and Aug. Closed Sun evening and Mon out of season ; 12–25 Nov; 2nd week in Jan.* **Disabled access.**

Sitting below a gastronomic restaurant run by the same people, this cheaper place offers unbeatable prices. In summer you eat on the flower-filled terrace in the shade of a magnificent wisteria. Menus €11 (weekday lunchtimes) and €15.50, or you can dine à la carte. You could easily be satisfied with the *hors-d'œuvre* buffet, which offers a wide selection including fish *terrine*, *charcuterie* and all sorts of *crudités*. For a main course, opt for grilled meat or fish of the day and then head straight back to the buffet for dessert. There are two dining rooms, the best of which looks onto the river – the other one, where the buffets are, is somewhat gloomy. Professional service and welcome. *Free coffee on presentation of this guide.*

Herbiers (Les)

85500

Hôtel-restaurant du Centre**

6 rue de l'Église.
T 02.51.67.01.75 F 02.51.66.82.24
Restaurant closed *Fri evening and Sat out of season; Sun in summer; 1–12 Aug; Christmas school holidays.* **TV.**

This place is located in the middle of the town, but it's quiet enough and warmly welcoming – ideal as a base from which to explore the region. Doubles €45 with shower/wc or bath. Half board is compulsory from June to the end of August and over the weekend. This is no hardship because the owner is a good chef and produces dishes using fresh produce and a lot of fish. Menus €11–24.50.

Hôtel-restaurant Le Relais – La Cotriade**

18 rue de Saumur.
T 02.51.91.01.64 F 02.51.67.36.50
Closed *Sun evening; Mon lunchtime.* **TV.**

This good hotel, with its beautiful, well-renovated façade, offers 26 luxurious bedrooms; doubles are €52. Although it's by the roadside, the double glazing is effective. There's a brasserie, which offers traditional dishes, and a swanky dining room, *La Cotriade*, where you can enjoy gourmet cuisine – portions at each are more than generous. Menus €19–52.

Saint-Laurent-sur-Sèvre

85290 (20km NE)

Hôtel-restaurant L'Hermitage**

2 rue de la Jouvence; take the D752 and it's on the river Sèvre, by the bridge opposite the basilica.
T 02.51.67.83.03 F 02.51.67.84.11
TV. Car park.

A nice family inn, run by a young couple, with a terrace overlooking the river. Half-board isn't compulsory even during the Puy-du-Fou film festival. The menus, €13–26, list good traditional dishes, and you'll get generous portions: Vendée ham, zander with sorrel, chocolate charlotte. The dining room has changed little since the 1960s. Rooms are comfortable; the nicest ones look over the river Sèvre. Doubles €34–40.

Laval

53000

Marin Hôtel**

100–102 av. Robert-Buron; it's opposite the train station.
T 02.43.53.09.68
E decouacon@wanadoo.fr
Disabled access. TV. Pay car park.

This establishment, which belongs to the Inter-Hôtel chain, is modern, functional and an ideal place to stop if you've just got off the TGV. Doubles €42–48 with shower/wc or bath. There are lots of restaurants in the area. *10% discount on the room rate (Fri, Sat and Sun).*

L'Avenio

38 quai de Bootz.
T 02.43.56.87.51
Closed *Sat; Sun; Aug.* **Pay car park.**

This is a haunt of local fishermen. The place is decorated with old fishing lines, reels and hooks and conversations often focus on the ones that got away. You get good home cooking here, including home-baked bread: everything is delicious and served in gargantuan portions – just try the beef. The *formule* at €12 includes a drink. There's a covered, flower-filled terrace. Credit cards not accepted.

L'Antiquaire

5 rue des Béliers; it's behind the cathedral.
T 02.43.53.66.76
Closed *Wed; Sat lunchtime; a week in the Feb school holidays; 9–31 July.*

The food here is simply magnificent. The cheapest menu is a bargain at €16 and there are others up to €35.50. They list dishes like foie gras terrine with apple and cider preserve, zander *escalope* with cider butter, pork steak with Camembert *au gratin*, and iced *marquise* with green apple custard. *Free coffee on presentation of this guide.*

La Braise

4 rue de la Trinité; it's in the old town, near the cathedral.

Ⓣ02.43.53.21.87
Closed *Sat lunchtime; Sun; Mon; a week at Easter; a week around 15 Aug.*

A cute little place with beautiful furniture, wooden beams and hand-made hexagonal floor tiles. You receive a wonderful welcome. The simple, authentic dishes are skilfully cooked, many of them over charcoal. Grilled fish and meat are the specialities, as you would expect – try the scallop kebabs, the knuckle of pork with Armagnac or the red mullet kebab. Menus from €19. If it's sunny, sit on the terrace.

|●| Restaurant Le Bistro de Paris

67 rue du Val-de-Mayenne; it's on the banks of the Mayenne.
Ⓣ02.43.56.98.29
Closed *Sat lunchtime; Sun evening; Mon; 5–26 Aug.* **Disabled access.**

This is the best restaurant in town and can be the most expensive – unless you choose the *menu-carte*, which costs €22 in the week. There's another menu at €27 and a *menu dégustation* for €41. Lots of wonderful dishes are served: *boudin* of lobster and turbot, sole fillet with lobster *jus*, roast saddle of lamb with nettles and a selection of home-made desserts. Guy Lemercier comes up with creative ideas to delight his regulars, who get a good-natured but not overly effusive welcome. Old-fashioned brasserie décor with rows and rows of mirrors, good service and fine wines.

Changé

53810 (4km N)

|●| La Table Ronde

Place de la Mairie; it's near the church.
Ⓣ02.43.53.43.33
Closed *Sun, Tues, Wed and Thurs evenings; Mon.* **Disabled access.**

The upstairs restaurant is impressive and expensive; downstairs there's an attractive bistro with '30s décor, smiling waitresses and low prices. On a fine day you can sit on the terrace, which faces the town on one side and the park on the other. There's a weekday *menu du jour* for €15 and others up to €38, listing dishes like zander and shrimp *ballotin*, cockerel with cider vinegar and pear terrine with caramel. Everything is skilfully prepared, rich in flavour and colourful – it's well worth leaving Laval to get here. *Free apéritif on presentation of this guide.*

Genest-Saint-Isle (Le)

53940 (12km NW)

|●| Restaurant Le Salvert

Route d'Olivet.
Ⓣ02.43.37.14.37 Ⓕ02.43.37.70.48
Closed *Sun evening; Mon; early Jan.*
Disabled access. Highchairs available. Car park.

Just ten minutes from Laval on the Olivet lake, this restaurant has a terrace open in summer and an open fire when the weather is cooler. It's classy, too – this isn't a place to come wearing shorts or hiking boots. Menus (€16–30.50) change twice a year and list local dishes scrupulously prepared using seasonal vegetables. Their bread is home-made, just like everything else. *Free coffee on presentation of this guide.*

Cossé-Le-Vivien

53230 (18km SW)

|●| Hôtel-restaurant L'Étoile**

2 rue de Nantes; take the N171.
Ⓣ02.43.98.81.31 Ⓕ02.43.98.96.64
Closed *Sun evening; Mon; a week Feb; a fortnight in Aug. Open Fri evening by reservation only.* **TV. Car park.**

The seven bedrooms here are pretty and bright. Doubles €28 with shower/wc or bath. The restaurant serves good traditional cooking, with a weekday menu at €8.40 and others (€12–22.11), listing dishes like *croustillant* of pigs' ears, *fondant* of oxtails and *craquant* of starfruit. Best to book at weekends. *10% discount on the room rate (1 Oct–31 March) on presentation of this guide.*

Vaiges

53480 (22km E)

|●| Hôtel du Commerce***

Rue du Fief-aux-Moines; take exit 2 off the A81.
Ⓣ02.43.90.50.07 Ⓕ02.43.90.57.40
Ⓦwww.hotelcommerce.fr
Closed *Fri and Sun evenings Oct to end of April; 1 May; 26 Dec–9 Jan.* **Disabled access. TV. Car park.**

Since 1882, when the Oger family first started running this successful hotel, their only concern has been that their guests should sleep soundly and eat well. You can quite happily spend a night or two in one of their quiet bedrooms – €53–85 with shower or bath – and dine in the conservatory where they serve good food based on local produce: fresh duck foie gras, kidney stew, rabbit thigh in cider, cheeses, apple tart and hot Grand Marnier soufflé. Menus €21–45.

Ernée

53500 (30km NW)

Le Grand Cerf**

17–19 rue Aristide-Briand; it's on the N12 in the direction of Mayenne.
02.43.05.13.09
hotelrestaurantlegrandcerf@wanadoo.fr
Closed *Sun evening and Mon out of season; 15–31 Jan.* **TV. Highchairs available. Car park.**

The establishment is known for its facilities and good food. The dishes are intelligently planned around seasonal produce and offered on various menus: cream of courgette and cucumber, crayfish tails roasted with cubes of pig's trotter, fillet of beef in a potato *galette*, salmon in an olive crust with aubergine caviar and rosemary, and fresh fruit soup with ginger sorbet. Weekday lunch *formule* (starter, dish of the day, dessert) at €14, then others €19–30. Beautiful bedrooms with all comforts cost €40 with bath/wc. The only downfall: the welcome can be so and so… Credit cards are not accepted. *Free apéritif on presentation of this guide.*

18

PAYS-DE-LA-LOIRE

La Table Normande

3 av. Aristide-Briand; it's on the N12 in the direction of Mayenne.
02.43.05.16.93
Closed *Sun; a week in Feb; 1–15 Aug.*

The owners are deeply committed to what they do, and their restaurant has a nice atmosphere. Serving delicious home-made dishes, it's popular with local workers, travelling salesmen and passing tourists. The cheapest menu is €10 during the week – good value; others €13–20.

Luçon

85400

Hôtel-restaurant Le Bœuf Couronné**

55 rte. de La-Roche-sur-Yon.
02.51.56.11.32 02.51.56.98.25
Closed *Sun evening; Mon; 15–30 Sept.*
Disabled access. TV. Car park.

Though it's a little close to the road, this is an attractive place, with a flower-laden pergola, a delightfully cosy lounge and several dining rooms. Good cooking: fresh fish in sauces, duck foie gras in port, *paupiettes* of sole with langoustine. Set menus €12.60–30.15. It's a delight to watch them preparing the flambéed dishes. Four rather plush bedrooms at €47.10 with shower/wc or bath. *Free coffee on presentation of this guide.*

Lude (Le)

72800

La Renaissance**

2 av. de la Libération.
02.43.94.63.10
Closed *Sun evening; Mon; Feb holidays; All Saints' holidays.* **TV. Highchairs available. Car park.**

Though this is a pretty grand place, the atmosphere is in no way formal and men don't even have to wear ties. There is a bewildering choice of dishes on the menu, but the chef is happy to help you decide. He uses the freshest produce and monitors the cooking of each dish meticulously. A typical offering might be beef pan-fried with Camembert cream, or a rich lobster soup. Weekday menu at €10 and others €13.50–35.50. Double rooms €45–55 with shower/wc or bath. *Free house apéritif on presentation of this guide.*

Malicorne-sur-Sarthe

72270

Restaurant La Petite Auberge

5 pl. Du-Guesclin.
02.43.94.80.52
Closed *Sun–Fri evenings out of season; Mon.* **Highchairs available. Disabled access. Car park.**

Set on a riverbank, this restaurant has a rather attractive terrace where you can treat yourself to pike *terrine*, fillet of sea trout, cheese and dessert for €14. There's a choice of menus from €15 (weekdays only) and €20–30. À la carte, dishes change according to what's in season and which fish is available at the market. The elegant flower-filled dining room has a fireplace and is ideal for grey days. *Free apéritif, coffee, fruit juice or soft drink on presentation of this guide.*

Mamers

72600

Hôtel-restaurant Le Dauphin**

54 rue du Fort.
Ⓣ02.43.34.24.24 Ⓕ02.43.34.44.05
Closed *Fri and Sun evenings.* **TV. Car park.**

Pay a visit to this unpretentious little hotel if you want to try *rillettes* – a delicacy made from shredded pork cooked in its own fat – at their best. À la carte you'll come across specialities such as omelette with *rillettes* and *marmite du Dauphine*; menus €10–18.50. They also have perfectly adequate bedrooms: €27–40 with shower, shower/wc or bath. *Free apéritif on presentation of this guide.*

Neuchâtel-en-Saosnois

72600 (10km NW)

Relais des Étangs de Guibert

In the village turn right by the church into rue Louis-Ragot and it's 800m further on.
Ⓣ02.43.97.15.38 Ⓕ02.43.33.22.99
Ⓦwww.saosnois.com.
Closed *Mon; winter school holidays.*
Disabled access. Car park.

Set at the edge of the Perseigne forest near the pond, this place comes to life as soon as the sun shows its face. It's got it all – pleasant décor, wonderful welcome and good prices – and you may find it difficult to get a room at the weekend. Rooms are decorated with sailing or hunting themes. Doubles €49–95, depending on the facilities. In the restaurant they serve lots of fish and house foie gras; there's a weekday lunch menu for €13 and others up to €29. Credit cards not accepted.

Rouperroux-Le-Coquet

72110 (18km SE)

Le Petit Campagnard

It's on the D301.
Ⓣ02.43.29.79.74
Closed *Mon; Tues, Wed and Thurs evenings; 3 weeks in Aug.* **Disabled access. Car park.**

A pretty little place, especially popular on Sundays. The unbeatable €11 menu offers *rillettes* (shredded pork cooked in its own fat), chicken with cider, cheese and dessert. The €9.50 weekday menu is also a good deal, as is the other at €17.10. Around €23 à la carte. The menus list good regional and more exotic dishes. *Free coffee on presentation of this guide.*

Mans (Le)

72000

Auberge de jeunesse Le Flore

23 rue Maupertuis; take the no. 12 bus in the direction of Californie to the "Erpell" stop; or no. 4, in the direction of Gazonfier, to the same stop.
Ⓣ02.43.81.27.55 Ⓕ02.43.81.06.10
Ⓦwww.mapage.noos.fr/florefjt
Closed *Christmas school holidays.* **Disabled access.**

A youth hostel with 22 beds (40 in July–Aug); several rooms with two or three beds, one with four and a flat that sleeps seven. €11.50 per night, including breakfast. Meals €4.85–6.05. Half board (€17.55) compulsory for a stay of more than three nights. FUAJ card required. Free parking of bikes and motor bikes inside the hostel. Credit cards not accepted. *Free Internet connection on presentation of this guide.*

Hôtel La Pommeraie**

314 rue de l'Éventail; follow signs for the N23 to Paris, turn into rue de Douce-Amie at Auberge Bagatelle.
Ⓣ02.43.85.13.93 Ⓕ02.43.84.38.32
Disabled access. TV. Car park.

Though just a short car journey from the city centre, this entirely renovated hotel, which is set in a large, flower-filled garden, is wonderfully peaceful. Concentrate on the garden, the hospitality and the feeling of luxury and you might even be able to forget the bland post-war architecture. Doubles €31–46 depending on facilities and season. The energetic young hotelier offers a number of activities including ping-pong, gym, pétanque and badminton. *Free coffee on presentation of this guide.*

Anjou Hôtel**

23 bd. de la Gare; it's opposite the train station.
Ⓣ02.43.24.90.45 Ⓕ02.43.24.82.38
TV. Car park.

A well-located hotel opposite the station. The young couple who have taken it over really care for their guests and give you a warm welcome. They have redecorated the rooms and put in double glazing: doubles go for €45 with shower or bath. *One free breakfast per room per night on presentation of this guide.*

Hôtel Green 7**

447 av. Georges-Durand; it's in the south of the town on the road to Tours.
Ⓣ02.43.40.30.30 Ⓕ02.43.40.30.00
Ⓦwww.hotelgreen7.com
Disabled access. TV. Car park.

A pleasant hotel less than 2km from the 24-hour Le Mans circuit. Comfortable, well-decorated rooms with shower or bath cost €50. Though the restaurant is not brilliant, it produces more than adequate traditional dishes using fresh produce if you don't want to go into town for a meal: pan-fried scallops with herbs, saddle of lamb with rosemary. Menus €15–32.

Hôtel Chantecler***

50 rue de la Pelouse; it's between the train station and the conference centre.
Ⓣ02.43.14.40.00 Ⓕ02.43.77.16.28
Ⓦwww.hotelchantecler.fr
TV. Highchairs available. Car park.

Just a short distance from the station, this hotel offers peace and comfort within easy reach of the old part of Le Mans. The welcome is sincere, the parking easy and the breakfast, which is served in the conservatory, rather good. Decent doubles with shower or bath, €63–66. *10% discount on the room rate in Aug on presentation of this guide.*

L'Atlas

80 bd. de la Petite Vitesse.
Ⓣ02.43.61.03.16
Closed *Mon and Sat lunchtimes; Aug.*
Disabled access.

Open until 11.30pm. Close to the station, in an area otherwise lacking in good restaurants, this Moroccan restaurant is a real find. The proprietor has done his country proud with both the opulent décor and the cuisine – try the excellent *tajines* and fresh Moroccan pastries. Menus €11.45 and €22.90. Live music at weekends.

Auberge des 7 Plats

79 Grande-Rue; it's in the old town.
Ⓣ02.43.24.57.77
Closed *Sun; Mon.*

The large half-timbered house has real style – there are several in the street but this is one of the best you'll find in the old part of Le Mans. Their gimmick, as you'll guess from the name, is that they offer seven hot dishes on the same menu. The youthful, relaxed welcome adds considerably to the appeal. There's a brigade of staff in the kitchen producing such dishes as beef Rossini-style with foie gras and cep sauce, duck breast with peppercorns, duck *confit* and *paupiettes* with a great deal of care and attention. To top it all, it's good value: €11.80 for a main course and a dessert, with a menu at €14.50. *Appellation* wines are sold by the carafe and all the *apéritifs* cost €2.80. It's advisable to book.

Le Nez Rouge

107 Grande-Rue.
Ⓣ02.43.24.27.26
Closed *Sun; Mon; a week in Feb; mid-Aug to 5 Sept.*

This old-town gourmet restaurant is the place to come for a *mongolfière* of mussels, *fricassée* of langoustines in *beurre rouge*, *escalope* of foie gras and chilled white chocolate soufflé. Weekday menu at €18.50, with others €26–38.

Le Flambadou

14 bis rue Saint-Flaceau; it's near the town hall.
Ⓣ02.43.24.88.38
Closed *Sat lunchtime; Sun; 2nd fortnight in Aug.*

The owner-chef of this highly recommended restaurant prepares specialities from his native region of the Landes and Périgord: *cassoulet*, *fricassée* of duck wings, rabbit with red onions. The main courses are so generous that you may not be able to manage a dessert. Allow around €27.50 à la carte. You can dine in the sweet little dining room or out on the shady terrace.

Warm, hearty welcome. *Free apéritif on presentation of this guide.*

Yvré-L'Évêque

72530 (5km E)

Hôtel-Motel Papea**

Bener; leave Le Mans on the N23 and follow signs to Papea.
Ⓣ02.43.89.64.09 Ⓕ02.43.89.49.81
Ⓦwww.hotelpapea.com
Closed *Sun evening Oct–Feb; Christmas to New Year.* **TV. Car park.**

This motel is set in lovely grounds near the abbey of Epau. Some twenty comfortable chalets, separated from each other by bushes and trees, cost €30–44 with bath/wc. Lower prices for weekends, long stays and commercial travellers are on offer. Ideal if you want to stay in the country but also be very close to the city. *One free breakfast per room per night on presentation of this guide.*

Mulsanne

72230 (8km S)

Hôtel-restaurant Arbor – Auberge de Mulsanne**

Route de Tours; it's 10 minutes from town near the race circuit.
Ⓣ02.43.39.18.90 Ⓕ02.43.39.18.99
Ⓦwww.aubergemulsanne.fr
Restaurant closed *Fri evening; Sat lunchtime; Sun; 1–22 Aug.* **Disabled access. TV. Highchairs available. Swimming pool. Car park.**

This hotel, used by the competing teams during the 24-hour Le Mans race, is worth visiting any time of the year. The impeccable rooms cost €55 with bath, and there's a swimming pool. Weekday menu €16 and others €21–36.

Fillé-sur-Sarthe

72210 (15.5km SW)

Restaurant Le Barrage

Rue du Passeur; it's the last house past the church.
Ⓣ02.43.87.14.40
Closed *Sun evening; Mon.*

This restaurant is very popular locally, so if you want a table on the terrace looking directly onto the towpath and the Sarthe river, you should reserve. It's a serene, rural setting, and a perfect place to enjoy the good food – red mullet salad with olive oil, roast lamb, foie gras flan with port sauce, salmon *escalope* roasted with Merlot sauce, and iced *parfait* with blackcurrants and raspberries. Weekday menus €9 and from €14 (except Sun) to €32. *Free coffee on presentation of this guide.*

Domfront-en-Champagne

72240 (18km NW)

Restaurant du Midi

33 rue du Mans; it's on the D304, towards Mayenne.
Ⓣ02.43.20.52.04
Closed *Mon; Tues; Wed evening to Thurs evening; Sun evening; Feb.* Highchairs available.

The dining room is comfortable, the surroundings are classy and the service is attentive. The cuisine has an excellent reputation, too – the weekday lunch menu, €12.90, lists mixed meat stew braised with Chinon wine, zander with smoked bacon, cheese and dessert. On the other menus, €18.30–35, and à la carte, you'll see such dishes as perch in Champagne sauce, duck breast *à l'ancienne*, mussel stew, swordfish steak with lamb *jus*, beef with Mexican spices, foie gras ravioli with morel cream, lobster stew with *anis* and *croustillant* of langoustines with potatoes and saffron. Reasonably priced wines on a generally good list. *Free coffee on presentation of this guide.*

Vivoin

72170 (25km N)

Hôtel-restaurant du Chemin de Fer**

Place de la Gare, Vivoin. Turn off the N138 onto the D26 towards Vivoin.
Ⓣ02.43.97.00.05 Ⓕ02.43.97.87.49
Ⓦwww.hotel-du-chemin-de-fer.fr
Closed *Fri and Sat Nov–March; Fri and Sun evenings April–Oct; winter and autumn school holidays.* **TV. Car park.**

Cheerful staff welcome you and mouth-watering aromas waft from the kitchens. With the garden behind the house and the pastoral atmosphere in the large dining room you could almost be in the country. Treat yourself – scallops flambéed in whisky, *marmite sarthoise* (local hotpot), rib of beef, and apple *feuillantine* flambéed in Calvados. Weekday *menu du jour* €13.50, and others 17.60–30. Fifteen pleasant rooms €36–46 with basin, shower/wc or bath. *Free apéritif on presentation of this guide.*

Thorigné-sur-Dué

72160 (28km NE)

Hôtel-restaurant Saint-Jacques***

Place du Monument; take the N23 and D302.
Ⓣ02.43.89.95.50 Ⓕ02.43.76.58.42
Ⓔhotel-st-jacques.thorigne@wanadoo.fr
Closed *Sun evening; Mon; Jan; last fortnight in June.* **Disabled access. Highchairs available. TV. Car park.**

This family hotel celebrated its 150th anniversary – in the same family! – in 2000, and the comfort, courtesy and good food it offers are an excellent example of traditional hotel-keeping. Doubles with shower/wc or bath €54–70. Menus €15–54. Specialities include roast prawns on a bed of leeks, chicken with morel cream sauce, scallops with vanilla butter, whole steamed ox kidney with sweet garlic cream and iced nougat with raspberry *coulis*. *10% discount on the room rate on presentation of this guide.*

Saint-Germain-sur-Sarthe

72130 (35km N)

Restaurant Le Saint-Germain

La Hutte. Take the N138; it's at the crossroads.
Ⓣ02.43.97.53.06
Closed *Mon, Tues and Wed evenings; winter school holidays; 3 weeks in Aug.* **Disabled access.**

In spite of the traffic rushing past on the main road this is a lovely place. Madame makes sure there are fresh flowers in the dining room and Monsieur keeps up the high standards of French sauce-making in the kitchen. Try the calf's head *ravigote*, rabbit terrine, a splendid *cassolette* of fish, grilled rib of beef *béarnaise*, *salade gourmande*, fresh oysters, *gratin* of lobster or *fondant* of veal with morels. Dish of the day €10, with menus at €12 (weekdays) and €17–36. *Free apéritif on presentation of this guide.*

Mayenne

53100

Hôtel La Tour des Anglais**

13 bis pl. Juhel.
Ⓣ02.43.04.34.56 Ⓕ02.43.32.13.84
Ⓦwww.latourdesanglais.com
Closed *Aug; Christmas period.* **Restaurant closed** *Fri evening; Sat; Sun; public holidays.* **Restaurant open** *Mon–Thurs evenings by reservation only.* **Disabled access. TV. Car park.**

Very close to Château de Mayenne, this hotel has one wonderful room in a fortified tower with a dramatic view of the Mayenne river. The other rooms are comfortable but more modern; they're €46–63 with shower or bath. Weekday menu €13. Children's menu at €10. There's an English-style bar with a billiard table and impressive wooden beams.

Le Grand Hôtel**

2 rue Ambroise-de-Loré; it faces the Mayenne river.
Ⓣ02.43.00.96.00 Ⓕ02.43.00.69.20
Ⓦwww.grandhotelmayenne.com
Hotel closed *Sat Nov to mid-March; Sat, and Sun evening Nov–April; a fortnight at New Year, a fortnight in Aug.* **Restaurant closed** *Sat and Sun lunchtimes May–Oct; Sat and Sun Nov–April; a fortnight at Christmas/New Year.* **TV. Car park.**

If only the rest of the town could be renovated and maintained as well as this hotel. Tourists arriving by car, bike and even boat are greeted with a cheery smile. Well-appointed rooms are €54–81 depending on facilities. In the restaurant you get Breton or Norman cuisine in a quaint ambience, with menus at €18–39.50; expect house foie gras with Muscat, red mullet fillets with aubergine caviar, duck breast with Coteau Layon sauce and apples with Calvados ice cream. Round off the evening with a good whisky in the bar. *10% discount on the room rate on presentation of this guide.*

Fontaine-Daniel

53100 (4km SW)

Restaurant La Forge

La Place; in the middle of the village.
Ⓣ02.43.00.34.85
Closed *Tues; Wed; Sun evening.*

This lovely restaurant on the main square of this pretty village boasts a very nice terrace where you can enjoy excellent cuisine – dishes change regularly but typical offerings include fried camembert and smoked duck breast salad with a spiced coffee sauce, liver gâteau with scallops, zander steak with buttery cooked cabbage, upside down apple macaroons. Menus €17–32. It's best to book.

Moulay

53100 (4km S)

La Marjolaine**

Le Bas-Mont; it's on the way out of Moulay heading towards Laval.
ⓣ02.43.00.48.42 ⓕ02.43.08.10.58
ⓦwww.chateauxhotels.com
Closed *Sun evening, Mon lunchtime; Ist week in Jan; a fortnight in Feb.* **TV. Car park.**

A hotel with seventeen very comfortable and elegant rooms, five of which are brand new. Doubles €49–72 with shower/wc or bath. In the restaurant, the quality of the cuisine and freshness of the ingredients is exemplary; go for the fish of the day and the chef's suggestions. Menus from €16.50 (weekdays, but not Fri evening) to €49.

Hôtel-restaurant Beau Rivage

Route de Saint-Baudelle; It's on the N162 between Mayenne and Moulay.
ⓣ02.43.00.49.13 ⓕ02.43.00.49.26
ⓔfbeaurivage@9online.fr
Closed *Sun evening; Mon.* **TV. Highchairs available. Car park.**

This lovely hotel-restaurant, set on the bank of the Mayenne river, is quite a sight. The dining room and the terrace (which stretches right down to the water), are often full, so make sure you reserve a table. The €12 menu (not served Sun) and others €14.50–27 list such dishes as calf's head *ravigote* served with a spicy vinaigrette, roast quail *à la périgourdine*, fish casserole, cheese and *crème brûlée*. Eight cosy rooms with all facilities; €53. *Free house apéritif on presentation of this guide.*

Commer

53470 (9km S)

Chambre d'Hôte La Chevrie***

It's 5km south of Mayenne on the N162 towards Laval; follow the signposts to La Mayenne.
ⓣ02.43.00.44.30
ⓔagdlt@aol.com
TV. Car park.

This farmhouse is at least a hundred years old. You'll receive a natural, kind welcome. Two rooms only at €32 and €35, breakfast included. There's a wonderful view over the countryside and neighbouring organic farm. The towpath is close by and a good place for an outing on foot, bike or horseback. Horse-riders are welcome; the overnight accomodation for the horse is free! Credit cards not accepted. *20% discount on the room rate for a stay of more than one night on presentation of this guide.*

Montreuil-Poulay

53640 (12km NE)

L'Auberge Campagnarde

Le Presbytère.
ⓣ02.43.32.07.11
Closed *Sun evening; Mon; a week in March; a week in Aug.* **Disabled access. Games available. Car park.**

You'll get a kind welcome in this restaurant, and the service is friendly without being over-familiar. They serve *apéritifs* and coffee on the terrace even when the weather isn't quite fine enough to eat a full meal outside. You'll find an astonishing selection of local dishes, traditionally made. Weekday lunch menu €9.50, with others €17–28. It's best to book.

Lassay-Les-Châteaux

53110 (16km NE)

Restaurant du Château

37 rue Migoret-Lamberdière.
ⓣ02.43.04.71.99
Closed *Sun (reservations only); Mon evening; 2nd and 3rd weeks in Aug; a week in winter.*

Béatrice and Hervé have a mixed clientele made up of regulars and British tourists passing through. They've set aside a special dining room for the locals, who lunch on the €8.50 or the €9.50 *menu ouvrier* (including a quarter litre of wine). There's another menu at €14. The dishes are all freshly cooked in the kitchens: they're simple, tasty and prepared by a real pro. Best to book. *Free coffee on presentation of this guide.*

Gorron

53120 (25km NW)

🏃 🏠 |●| Hôtel-restaurant Le Bretagne**

41 rue de Bretagne; take the D12 to Saint-Georges-Buttavent and then the D5.
Ⓣ02.43.08.63.67 Ⓕ02.43.08.01.15
Ⓔphbto@aol.com
Closed *Sun evening; Mon.* **TV. Car park.**

A good village restaurant where you can get a hearty meal and gourmet cooking. Menus, €13–25, offer such dishes as *mousseline* of zander with crab sauce, mussel casserole with Noilly, honey-glazed roast breast of duck with Perry and iced nougat with raspberry *coulis*. The décor is spruce in pastel colours, and the dining room looks over the river Colmont. Double rooms €42. *10% discount on the room rate on presentation of this guide.*

Montaigu

85600

🏠 |●| Hôtel-restaurant Les Voyageurs**

9 av. Villebois-Mareuil; it's in the centre of town.
Ⓣ02.51.94.00.71 Ⓕ02.51.94.07.78
Ⓦwww.hotel-restaurant-les-voyageurs.fr
Disabled access. Swimming pool. TV. Car park.

A long pink hotel with a flag flying above it, made up of three buildings constructed around a swimming pool – each facing wall is painted in a different colour and there's definitely a Mediterranean feel. The rooms are comfortable and of varying sizes; doubles €42–54. Choose to have a bath rather than a shower as the rooms with bath are bigger and more modern. Buffet breakfast €5. In the basement there's a fitness room. The dining room is on the ground floor and looks over the swimming pool. It's huge and bright and the cooking is very tasty. Menus €10 (lunchtime only) and up to €30.

🏃 |●| Le Cathelineau

3 bis pl. du Champ-de-Foire.
Ⓣand Ⓕ02.51.94.26.40
Closed *Sun evening; Mon.* **Disabled access. Car park.**

Michel Piveteau's cooking is original, combining unusual flavours, and his menus change every three weeks. Expect dishes like grilled lobster with *beurre blanc*, oysters cooked with liquorice, veal medallions with morels and a *gratin* of seasonal fruit. Menus €17.60–46. *Free coffee on presentation of this guide.*

Montreuil-Bellay

49260

🏠 |●| Splendid'Hôtel**

139 rue du Docteur-Gaudrez; it's near the château.
Ⓣ02.41.53.10.00 Ⓕ02.41.52.45.17
Ⓦwww.splendid-hotel.fr
Closed *Sun evening out of season.* Disabled access. **TV. Swimming pool. Car park.**

This convivial establishment has everything you could ask for. The beautiful building comprises adjoining fifteenth- and seventeenth-century wings with a wide range of conventional, clean rooms – doubles with shower/wc or bath/wc are €47–52. In the mornings the only sound you'll hear is the fountain, while in the evening you can join locals at the lively bar. There's a pleasant dining room where they serve freshly prepared dishes in copious portions. Menus €12.50 (lunch) to €35. There's a big choice of fish dishes; the house speciality is pike black pudding. Rates include free use of the fitness facilities at the *Hôtel-Relais du Bellay* (below). *10% discount on the room rate on presentation of this guide.*

🏃 🏠 Hôtel-relais du Bellay**

96 Rue Nationale; it's behind the château.
Ⓣ02.41.53.10.10 Ⓕ02.41.38.70.61
Ⓦwww.splendid-hotel.fr
Closed *Sun evening Oct–Easter.* **Disabled access. TV. Swimming pool. Car park.**

Owned by the same people as the *Splendid'Hôtel* and sharing its reception area, this hotel – which used to be the local girls' school – has a similarly relaxed, friendly welcome. In the main building, the comfortable and spacious rooms go for €48–70 with shower/wc or bath. Some look out onto the château and the fortifications. There's no restaurant – residents can dine at the *Splendid* – but a buffet breakfast costs €8. There's a large, pleasant garden with swimming pool, as well as a fitness room, sauna, Turkish bath and Jacuzzi. *10% discount on the room rate Oct–April on presentation of this guide.*

Mortagne-sur-Sèvre

85290

Hôtel-restaurant de France et La Taverne**

4 pl. du Docteur-Pichat; it's at the crossroads of the Nantes-Poitiers/Paris-Les Sables roads.
Ⓣ02.51.65.03.37 Ⓕ02.51.65.27.83
Closed *Sat lunchtime and Sun 15 Oct–1 April; evenings 15 Oct–31 March.* **TV. Swimming pool.**

The *Hôtel de France*, built in 1604, was renovated in 1968, and since then, nothing has changed. You can't miss this beautiful and noble building as you arrive in the main square – it's smothered in ivy. Inside, endless corridors and odd little corners lead to plush, comfortable rooms. Doubles €45 with shower/wc, €57.50 with bath and covered terrace with garden view. *La Taverne* has a sumptuous medieval-style dining room with period-looking furniture and collections of copper pans around the fireplace. The food is a festival of delicate, surprising flavours: crayfish in *verjus*, turbot with nettles, slivers of veal kidneys with green peppercorns. Other than the €13 menu of the day, prices are quite high, but justifiably so – menus are €26.70–49.70. During the week, the *Petite Auberge* next door offers three affordable menus. There's a swimming pool in the old curé's garden. Impeccable service.

Nantes

44000

See map overleaf

Hôtel Saint-Daniel*

4 rue du Bouffay. **Map C2-2**
Ⓣ02.40.47.41.25 Ⓕ02.51.72.03.99
Ⓔhotel.st.daniel@wanadoo.fr
Pay car park.

A remarkable little hotel in the Bouffay district, clean and well-run. Doubles €26 with shower or €29 with shower/wc or bath. The nineteen rooms all have telephones and alarm clocks, though you'll pay a €3 surcharge if you want a TV. Some rooms face the pedestrianized street; others look onto the garden and the charming Sainte-Croix church. The prices attract younger travellers especially, so it's essential to book.

Hôtel Fourcroy*

11 rue Fourcroy. **Map B2-3**
Ⓣ02.40.44.68.00 Ⓕ02.40.44.68.21
Closed *20 Dec–4 Jan.* **TV. Car park.**

Plain but quiet and central, this simple one-star offers a two-star level of comfort. Doubles €32 with shower/wc. Some look onto a private courtyard. Opt for one that has just been renovated. Make sure to confirm your reservation. Credit cards not accepted. *10% discount on the room rate on presentation of this guide for a stay of more than one night between 15 July–15 Aug.*

Hôtel Duchesse Anne**

3–4 pl. de la Duchesse Anne. **Map D1-8**
Ⓣ02.40.74.78.78 Ⓕ02.40.74.60.20
Restaurant closed *Sat lunchtime; Sun.* **TV. Pay car park.**

Located in a palatial building behind the château, this hotel has around sixty rooms. Doubles with shower/wc from €52 or up to €93 with bath/wc. Prices vary according to comfort and facilities. *10% discount on the room rate for a stay of at least two consecutive nights on presentation of this guide.*

Hôtel Amiral**

26 bis rue Scribe. **Map B2-5**
Ⓣ02.40.69.20.21 Ⓕ02.40.73.98.13
Ⓦwww.hotel-nantes.fr
Disabled access. TV. Pay car park.

This brand-new chain hotel has everything a business person could want: pleasant rooms, double glazing, mini-bars and so on, and it still has appeal for the leisure traveller. Doubles €57.80 (cheaper at the weekend). *10% discount for a two-night stay on presentation of this guide, except at weekends.*

L'Hôtel***

6 rue Henri-IV. **Map D1-7**
Ⓣ02.40.29.30.31 Ⓕ02.40.29.00.95
Ⓦwww.nanteshotel.com
Disabled access. TV. Pay car park.

A pleasant, easy-going three-star hotel that's very comfortable and perfectly located opposite the château of Anne de Bretagne. Well-soundproofed doubles go for €66–76 with bath – some have private terraces with view over the garden, others overlook the château. *Free parking on presentation of this guide.*

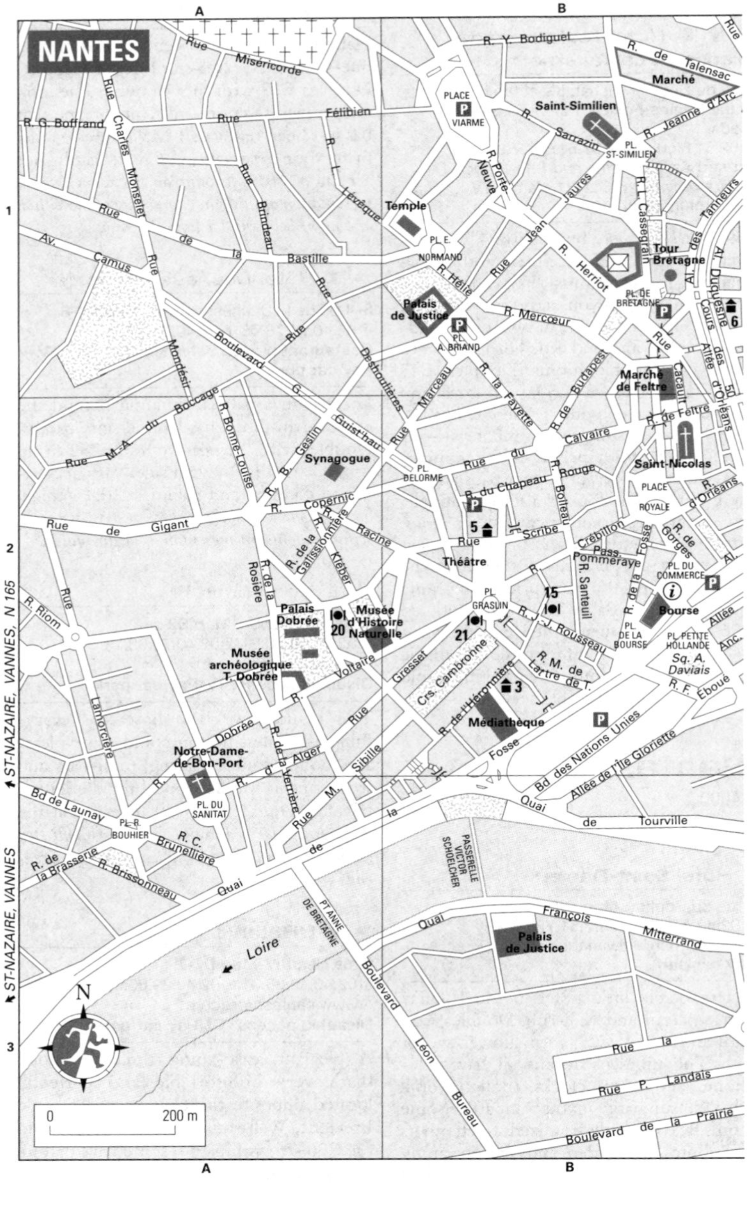

NANTES

A
B
1
2
3
R. Y. Bodiguel
R. de Talensac
Marché
Rue Miséricorde
PLACE VIARME
Saint-Similien
R. Jeanne d'Arc
R. Sarrazin
PL. ST-SIMILIEN
R. G. Boffrand
Rue Charles Monselet
Rue Félibien
R. L. Lévêque
Rue Brindeau
R. Porte Neuve
Jaurès
Rue des Tanneurs
R. L. Cassegrain
Temple
Rue de la Bastille
Av. Camus
PL. E. NORMAND
Rue Jean
R. Herriot
Tour Bretagne
PL. DE BRETAGNE
Al. Duquesne
Cours des 50
6
R. Hélie
Palais de Justice
PL. A. BRIAND
R. Mercœur
Rue Cacault
Allée d'Orléans
Boulevard G. Guist'hau
Rue Deshoulières
Rue Mondésir
R. Marceau
R. la Fayette
R. de Budapest
Marché de Feltre
R. de Feltre
Rue M.-A. du Boccage
R. Bonne-Louise
R. B. Geslin
Synagogue
PL. DELORME
Rue du Calvaire
Rue Rouge
Saint-Nicolas
R. du Chapeau
R. Boileau
PLACE ROYALE
R. d'Orléans
R. Copernic
Rue de Gigant
R. de la Galissonnière
R. Racine
5
Rue Scribe
Crébillon
Pass. Pommeraye
R. de Gorges
Théâtre
R. Santeuil
R. de la Fosse
PL. DU COMMERCE
R. de la Rosière
Kléber
PL. GRASLIN
15
Bourse
R. Riom
Rue
Palais Dobrée
20
Musée d'Histoire Naturelle
21
R. J.-J. Rousseau
PL. DE LA BOURSE
PL. PETITE HOLLANDE
Sq. A. Daviais
Allée
Anc.
Musée archéologique T. Dobrée
Voltaire
Gresset
Crs. Cambronne
R. de l'Héronnière
R. M. de Lartre de T.
3
R. F. Éboué
Lamoricière
R. Dobrée
Rue
Médiathèque
Bd des Nations Unies
Allée de l'Île Gloriette
Notre-Dame-de-Bon-Port
R. de la Verrière
R. d'Alger
Sibille
Fosse
Bd de Launay
PL. DU SANITAT
Rue M.
Quai de la Fosse
Quai de Tourville
PL. R. BOUHIER
R. C. Brunellière
R. de la Brasserie
R. Brissonneau
Quai
PASSERELLE VICTOR SCHOELCHER
PT ANNE DE BRETAGNE
Quai François Mitterrand
Palais de Justice
Loire
Boulevard Léon Bureau
Rue la
Rue P. Landais
Boulevard de la Prairie
N
0
200 m
ST-NAZAIRE, VANNES, N 165
ST-NAZAIRE, VANNES

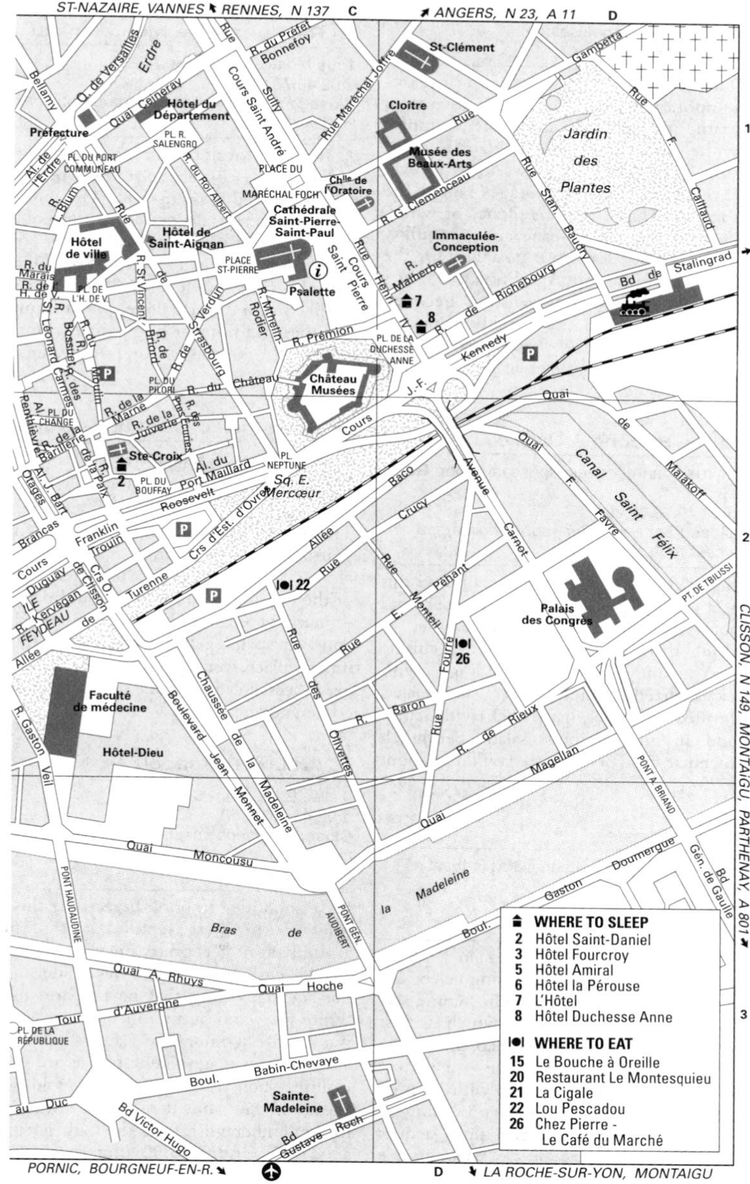
ST-NAZAIRE, VANNES
RENNES, N 137
C
ANGERS, N 23, A 11
D
1
2
3
CLISSON, N 149, MONTAIGU, PARTHENAY, A 801
PORNIC, BOURGNEUF-EN-R.
D
LA ROCHE-SUR-YON, MONTAIGU
St-Clément
Cloître
Musée des Beaux-Arts
Jardin des Plantes
Chlle de l'Oratoire
Cathédrale Saint-Pierre-Saint-Paul
Immaculée-Conception
Préfecture
Hôtel du Département
Hôtel de ville
Hôtel de Saint-Aignan
Psalette
Château Musées
Ste-Croix
Sq. E. Mercœur
Canal Saint Félix
Palais des Congrès
Faculté de médecine
Hôtel-Dieu
Bras de la Madeleine
Sainte-Madeleine
PLACE DU MARÉCHAL FOCH
PLACE ST-PIERRE
PL. DE LA DUCHESSE ANNE
PL. DU BOUFFAY
PL. NEPTUNE
PL. DE LA RÉPUBLIQUE
ILE FEYDEAU
PONT HAUDAUDINE
PONT GÉN. AUDIBERT
PONT A. BRIAND
PT. DE TBILISSI
Quai Moncousu
Quai A. Rhuys
Quai Hoche
Quai Magellan
Boul. Gaston Doumergue
Boul. Babin-Chevaye
Bd Victor Hugo
Bd Gustave Roch
Bd de Stalingrad
Boulevard Jean Monnet
Chaussée de la Madeleine
Cours Saint André
Cours Saint Pierre
Cours F. Roosevelt
Cours J.F. Kennedy
Allée Baco
Rue de Richebourg
WHERE TO SLEEP
2 Hôtel Saint-Daniel
3 Hôtel Fourcroy
5 Hôtel Amiral
6 Hôtel la Pérouse
7 L'Hôtel
8 Hôtel Duchesse Anne
WHERE TO EAT
15 Le Bouche à Oreille
20 Restaurant Le Montesquieu
21 La Cigale
22 Lou Pescadou
26 Chez Pierre - Le Café du Marché

Hôtel La Pérouse***

3 allée Duquesne; cours des 50 Otages; in the city-centre. **Map B1-6**
Ⓣ02.40.89.75.00 Ⓕ02.40.89.76.00
Ⓦwww.hotel-laperouse.com
Disabled access. TV.

There's no middle ground with this contemporary hotel – you either love it or loathe it. A large block of heavy, compact white granite, echoing a Nantais mansion, it has large windows looking over the cours des 50-Otages and the rooftops. Inside there is plenty of wood, designer furniture, space and tranquility – not a place for those nostalgic for the hotels of yesteryear. A tad noisy. Doubles €79–94. There's free parking between 7pm and 9am in the neighbouring car park. *One free breakfast per room, or 10% discount on the room rate on presentation of this guide.*

Le Bouche à Oreille

14 rue Jean-Jacques-Rousseau. **Map B2-15**
Ⓣ02.40.73.00.25
Closed *Sat lunch; Sun; public holidays; 3 weeks in Aug.*

Situated very close to the opera house, this is a gathering place for theatre-goers and sports fans alike. It's more of a place to drink than a restaurant, and the cuisine isn't fancy: black pudding with caramelized apples, *tabliers de sapeurs* (grilled ox tripe), ham hock with lentils and, in summer, huge salads. Set lunch menu at €11, or à la carte you'll pay about €20.

La Cigale

4 pl. Graslin. Opposite the Graslin theatre. **Map B2-21**
Ⓣ02.51.84.94.94
Open *7.30am–12.30am.*

The restaurant to be seen in – from tourists and students to visiting celebrities and high-society types who come for supper after the theatre (which is just opposite). The cuisine isn't bad, but it's the decor of this 1895 brasserie – a perfect example of Art Nouveau, with painted ceilings, wood panelling and coloured ceramics – that is the real pull; Jacques Demy used the place in his classic movie Lola, and actor Jean-Louis Trintignant called it the most beautiful brasserie in the world. It's not too expensive to dine – weekday lunch menu €11.50, with others €15.20–23.80. You can come here for breakfast or tea, too.

Restaurant Le Montesquieu

1 rue Montesquieu. **Map A2-20**
Ⓣ02.40.73.06.69
Closed *Fri evening; Sat; Sun; public holidays; 20 July–31 Aug.*

A friendly local restaurant and student haunt in a quiet spot beyond the pedestrianized Graslin area. The dining room walls are decorated with Rouen and Moustier plates and the tables covered with checked cloths. Specialities include tuna with *aïoli*, leek terrine with onion marmalade, Dauphinois potatoes and home-made pastries. Lunch menu €11.50; the evening equivalent is €15.

Chez Pierre-Café du Marché

1 rue de Mayence. **Map D2-26**
Ⓣ02.40.47.63.50
Closed *evenings; weekends.*

The formula has worked for nigh-on fifty years: they serve a single menu with a choice of at least three starters then a dish of the day, followed by cheese and dessert – yours for €15. Add a decent bottle and you can spend a lovely afternoon. It's a superb place, very popular with business executives escaping from seminars at the conference nearby.

Lou Pescadou

8 allée Baco. **Map C2-22**
Ⓣ02.40.35.29.50
Closed *Sat lunchtime; Sun; Mon evening; a fortnight in early Jan; 3 weeks in Aug.*
Disabled access.

It's a good idea to book here, since this is one of the best seafood restaurants around and it gets pretty busy. The chef is a real enthusiast and a Muscadet *aficionado* – anything that he prepares in a white wine and butter sauce (*beurre blanc*) is a surefire winner. The sea bass baked in a salt crust is magnificent, too, as are specialities such as sole *meunière*, wild sea bream in salt and, if you can afford it, lobster and crayfish from the tank. Menus at €14.50 and €19.50 (not weekends) and €30–58. The most expensive one includes drinks. *Free Nantillais on presentation of this guide.*

Basse-Goulaine

44115 (5km SE)

Villa Mon Rève

Route des Bords de Loire; it's on the D751.
02.40.03.55.50
Closed *a fortnight in Nov; Feb.* **Disabled access. Highchairs and games available. Car park.**

A regional institution that's been run by Cécile and Gérard Ryngel for the last twenty years. It's pleasantly situated among the trees and has a terrace that's particularly lovely in summer. Traditional cuisine: sea bass with *girolles*, frogs' legs with Gros Plant wine sauce and meat juices, fish of the day with *beurre blanc* sauce. The *formule* at €24 (not served Sun or public holidays) includes *apéritif*, wine and coffee; other menus €26.50–38, and an excellent children's menu for €11. They have a good selection of Muscadets. *Free coffee and house digestif on presentation of this guide.*

Haie-Fouassière (La)

44690 (7km SE)

Auberge Chez Pipette

Route de Clisson; take the N249 on the direction of La Chapelle-Heulin and it's at Tournebride.
02.40.54.80.47
Closed *Mon evening*

This old country inn is now a hugely popular lunch spot for travelling salesmen and workers and managers from the LU factory. Grilled sausages are the thing to try here. The menu of the day is very good – €14.99 gets you a starter, main course (such as salmon with *beurre blanc*), cheese or dessert. Other menus €22.90 and €26.80 with wine. The name, incidentally, refers to the two huge barrels at the entrance; each has a small hole into which a small pipette could be inserted to deliver your wine straight into down your gullet.

Carquefou

44470 (10km N)

Restaurant L'Auberge du Vieux Gachet

Le Gachet.
02.40.25.10.92
Closed *Sun evening; Mon; Wed evening; a fortnight Jan; 3 weeks after 15 Aug.*

An attractive country inn with a terrace on the banks of the Erdre. Their inventive, delicious poultry and fish dishes present you with the best of France, and your food is still served under a cloche. Try the stuffed quail with foie gras and onion chutney, it's excellent. Menus €26–43. To walk here from Nantes, simply follow the path along the Erdre – it'll take about two hours. The *Château de la Gacherie* is just opposite.

Sucé-sur-Erdre

44240 (16km N)

Chez Vié

117 quai de l'Erdre.
02.40.77.70.06
Closed *Sun and Tues evenings; Wed.*

A local institution, popular with families, couples and groups of colleagues who come here for a nice lunch on the river bank. The local specialities are the draw; eel, frogs' legs and Loire fish. Menus €13.60–30.45. There's a terrace shared by a small bar-*crêperie* if you're after a quick, light snack.

Messan

44640 (20km W)

Le Tisonnier

It's on the D723 Saint Brévin-Painbœuf road on the way into Messan.
02.40.64.29.83
Closed *evenings; Mon; 15–31 Aug; New Year/Christmas holidays.*

Plain restaurant-café (also a tobacconist's and newsagent's) where the €8.80 first menu gets you a tasty meal including sausage in Muscadet; other menus up to €30 offer dishes such as scallops, frogs' legs or eels. It would be hard to find better value for money and swifter service. *Free apéritif on presentation of this guide.*

Noirmoutier-en-L'Île

85330

Hotel Autre Mer**

32 av. Joseph-Pineau; half-way between the town centre and the Chaise wood.
02.51.39.11.77 02.51.39.11.97
www.autremerhotel.fr
TV.

Doubles €51–71 depending on facilities

and season. This hotel has been completely redecorated, in an unfussy, modern style of nautical inspiration, to match the façade with its immaculate white walls and sea-green shutters. Good value for money and extremely friendly service.

🏃 🏠 |●| Hôtel-restaurant Fleur de Sel***

Rue des Saulniers, BP 207; follow the signs from the château.
Ⓣ02.51.39.09.07 Ⓕ02.51.39.09.76
Ⓦwww.fleurdesel.fr
Closed *1 Nov–2 April. Restaurant closed Mon and Tues lunchtimes (except public holidays).* **Disabled access. Highchairs available. TV. Car park. Swimming pool.**

A magnificent place now classified as a Châteaux, *demeures de tradition* hotel, built some twenty years ago in a style which is typical of the island. It's set apart from the town in the middle of a huge estate with Mediterranean landscapes, and has a lovely swimming pool. All 35 rooms are well equipped; the ones overlooking the pool are cosy and have English pine furniture, while those with private flowery terraces have yew furniture and a maritime feel. Doubles €75–145 with bath/wc. Half board (compulsory) is available for a two-night minimum stay at €70–109 depending on the season. The restaurant is one of the best on the island if not in the Vendée. Lunchtime menus €24.50, or €32.36–43 in the evening. The wine list has some reasonable cheap wines. You can rent bikes or go on excursions, play tennis or practice your golf. All in all, ideal for a relaxing stay. *Free house apéritif on presentation of this guide.*

🏃 🏠 |●| Hôtel du Général-d'Elbée***

Place d'Armes; it's at the foot of the château near the canal port.
Ⓣ02.51.39.10.29 Ⓕ02.51.39.08.23
Ⓦwwwgeneraldelbee.com
Closed *Oct to early April.* Disabled access. **Swimming pool.**

A marvellous hotel in an historic eighteenth-century building. VIP-types stay here but it's quite unspoilt and still affordable to people who prefer refined places with a bit of character. The rooms in the historic part of the building are a bit pricey, but the décor is magnificent, so well worth it. Doubles are €95–180 depending on facilities and season. There's also a cosy bar-sitting room. *10% discount in low season for a two-night stay, except at weekends and bank holidays, on presentation of this guide.*

|●| Le Petit Bouchot

3 rue Saint-Louis
Ⓣ02.51.39.32.56
Closed *Tues evening; Wed; Mon (July–Aug).*

This small restaurant in the heart of the town reflects Noirmoutier's character, both smart and relaxed at the same time. It attracts a loyal following among the locals, and the extremely friendly owner gives everybody his personal attention. Menus at €12, €16 and €23. The specialities revolve around fish and seafood, particularly mussels. Some tables in the cool courtyard dotted with flowers.

|●| Restaurant Côté Jardin

1 bis rue du Grand-Four; it faces the château at the top of the old town.
Ⓣ02.51.39.03.02
Closed *Mon; Thurs and Sun evenings in low season; 15 Nov to early Feb.*

This elegant restaurant in a splendid building has a beautiful dining room with stone walls and hefty beams. It offers good local specialities such as the white kidney bean *croustillant* or the *chaudrée* of potatoes. There's a €12 two-course *formule* and menus for €16–36.

Herbaudière (L')

85330 (2km NW)

🏠 Hôtel Bord à Bord

6 rue de la Linière
Ⓣ02.51.39.27.92 Ⓕ02.51.35.74.17
Open *all year round.* **Heated swimming pool.**

A pretty modern building with comfortable rooms overlooking the sea, decorated in cheery nautical colours. Double rooms €55–78 with shower, wc and TV; also two duplex sleeping four to five people at €105. Some of the rooms are small but they are fitted with big mirrors which make them look more spacious. No restaurant, but if you feel like cocooning yourself inside, the rooms are equipped with a kitchen unit for a supplement of €12. The owner is guaranteed to give you a warm welcome.

|●| La Marine

In the port.

☎02.51.39.23.09
Closed *Tues evening; Wed; Sun evening; Oct.*

One of our top spots in the *département*. The menu varies according to the seasons, and 95 per cent of the produce comes from the island; the suppliers, such as the fish auctioners and the market gardeners, are even listed. Weekday lunchtime menu at €13, then others at €22 and 34. The cheap menu is superb, but it is in the others that the young chef really excels himself: *remoulade* of beans and Granny Smith with cauliflower cream and crusty beetroot, monkfish tail baked with local ham, risotto of cereals and foam of maize and, for dessert, red-fruit shortbread and rosemary sorbet. All in all, the cooking is eye-catching, inventive and really delicious, with an exquisite array of fragrances, fresh herbs, flowers and spices. Nautical-style dining room with a view of the port – and the local priest's garden.

Paulx

44270

Restaurant Les Voyageurs

1 pl. de l'Église; it's opposite the church.
☎02.40.26.02.76
Closed *Mon and Tues (except public holidays); 1–15 March; 3 weeks in Sept.*
Highchairs available. Car park

Call up the day before and they will create carefully prepared dishes to order. Dishes change frequently with the seasons – lobster flambéed, *émincé* of duck with *beurre rouge*, snails with *lardons*, iced soufflé with Mandarin Impériale. The produce is selected with meticulous care – free-range chicken, locally raised meat and exceptionally fresh fish. Menus €14.50–46. There's also an express menu at €10.50 that includes a main course and a dessert. *Free coffee on presentation of this guide.*

Piriac-sur-Mer

44420

Hôtel-restaurant de la Pointe

1 quai de Verdun; it's by the sea wall.
☎02.40.23.50.04 Ⓕ02.40.15.59.65
Closed *Wed and Thurs out of season; 1 Nov–15 March.*

A relaxed hotel. Doubles with basin €31, with shower/wc €40. They're not exactly the last word in style but some have a view of the harbour and beach. Half board, €45, is compulsory July–Aug. The dining room, decorated like a traditional bistro, offers substantial salads, fish and seafood. Weekday menu €9; others €15.50 and €24. *10% discount on the room rate for a minimum two-night stay Sept–June on presentation of this guide.*

Crêperie Lacomère

18 rue de Kéroman.
☎02.40.23.53.63
Open *weekends only in Feb, March, Sept and Oct; during winter and autumn school holidays.* **Closed** *Tues lunchtime only in July–Aug.*

This restaurant is a little more inventive than the standard crêperie, with a menu inspired by the owner's travels around the world. Try the fish *tajine*, the red mullet *escabèche* or the fish *choucroute*. Dishes of the day cost around €10, and there's a menu at €15. There are only ten tables so it's best to book. Pirates theme on Friday evening. *Free apéritif on presentation of this guide.*

Pornic

44210

Auberge La Fontaine aux Bretons

Rue des Noëlls; Fontaine aux Bretons.
☎02.51.77.07.07 Ⓕ02.51.74.15.15
Ⓦwww.auberge-la-fontaine.com
Closed *Sun and Mon evenings Nov–March except during school holidays.* **Disabled access. TV. Highchairs available. Car park. Swimming pool.**

A huge, renovated old farm with studios and apartments decorated in a contemporary maritime style. Each is as charming as the next, and most of them have a sea view. Doubles €64–101 depending on the season. They roast chickens and cook their stews in the wide fireplace which reminds you of the olden days. Most of the produce is organic; you can visit the kitchen garden where forgotten fruits, vegetables and edible plants are used in authentic dishes. The wine is also grown here, the meat comes from local farms, and the bread is cooked in their own oven. Menus €17–30.

|●| Restaurant Beau Rivage

Plage de la Birochère.
☎02.40.82.03.08
Closed *Sun and Wed evenings; Mon; Jan; 15 Dec–31 Jan.*

A friendly, colourful restaurant in a beautiful spot looking right over the beach. Seafood is the speciality here, and the chef thoughtfully crafts excellent dishes from fresh ingredients: Atlantic *bouillabaisse*, sea bream grilled in its skin with olive oil, lobster salad with herbs. There's a €15.50 *formule* served in the bistro, good menus €23–46, and an excellent wine list.

|●| Restaurant L'Estaminet

8 rue du Maréchal-Foch. ☎02.40.82.35.99
Closed *Sun evening; Mon.*

This restaurant in a busy street doesn't look out of the ordinary, but once you're inside, the *patronne's* delightful manner and the chef's fresh cuisine will convince you that it is. Menus €15–25. Try scallops with baby vegetables or skate with nut butter and cider vinegar.

Plaine-sur-Mer (La)

44770 (9km NW)

🏃 ☗ |●| Hôtel-Restaurant Anne de Bretagne***

Port de la Gravette.
☎02.40.21.54.72 Ⓕ02.40.21.02.33
Ⓦwww.annedebretagne.com
Closed *Mon; Tues (open Tues lunchtime in summer).* **Disabled access. TV. Swimming pool. Car park.**

A charming hotel with lovely rooms that have garden or sea views. The location is splendid and it's very quiet. Doubles €66–133 depending on facilities, view and season. There's a fancy little bar and a gourmet restaurant with a good reputation and a sea view. You'll experience a large selection of menus €21–76, including themed ones based on seasonal ingredients. Superb cellar with 15,000 bottles. Excellent welcome. *Free coffee on presentation of this guide.*

Port-Joinville (Île d'Yeu)

85350

🏃 ☗ Hôtel L'Escale**

Rue de la Croix-du-Port.
☎02.51.58.50.28 Ⓕ02.51.59.33.55
Ⓦwww.site.voila.fr/yeuescale
Closed *18 Nov–15 Dec.* **Disabled access. TV. Car park.**

Painted white with yellow shutters, this is the prettiest place on the Île d'Yeu. Despite having thirty rooms, it retains a guesthouse atmosphere, with cool marine décor. Doubles €30 (€36 high season) with basin, and €47 (€63 high season) with bath. Breakfast, €6.50, is served around the old well in the middle of the bright dining room – you can see the garden through French windows. The owner gives good advice about where to visit and what to see in the area. *10% discount on the room rate in low season on presentation of this guide.*

🏃 ☗ Atlantic Hôtel***

3 quai Carnot.
☎02.51.58.38.80 Ⓕ02.51.58.35.92
Ⓦwww.hotel-yeu.com
Closed *3 weeks in Jan.* **TV.**

Fifteen comfortable little rooms. Half of them face the fishing harbour, the focus of local activity, while the others look out over the village – both views are pleasant. You'll pay €39.50 out of season for the latter, and up to €61 in summer for the former. Breakfast €6. They're currently undergoing expansion work. *10% discount on the room rate (except July–Aug and bank holidays) on presentation of this guide.*

🏃 ☗ |●| Flux Hôtel - Restaurant La Marée**

27 rue Pierre-Henry.
☎02.51.58.36.25 Ⓕ02.51.59.44.57
Closed *Sun evening; Fri evening and Sat lunchtime out of season.* **Disabled access. TV. Car park.**

Away from the bustle of Port-Joinville, this hotel's peaceful grounds, bordering the seashore, give it a delightful aspect. Well-kept double rooms overlooking the garden cost €41–56; no. 15, set away from the main hotel, is especially spacious and has a fireplace. The restaurant, *La Marée*, is in an enormous dining room with a huge fireplace for winter evenings and a lovely terrace for dining out beneath the shade of the trees in summer. Creamy soups are a speciality, as are flambéed crayfish, fish in *beurre blanc* and mussels sauce *poulette*. Set menus €13–37. *10% discount on the room rate Sept–June (excluding public holidays) on presentation of this guide.*

Les Bafouettes

8 rue Gabriel Guist'hau; it's 100m from the port, past the tourist office.
☎02.51.59.38.38
Closed *Wed; Tues out of season; 3 weeks Jan; fortnight end Sept to early Oct.*

The dining room is freshly decorated with pictures by local artists, and the cuisine is delicious and served by really enthusiastic staff. Menus start at €14 and go up to €45; dishes include mussel soup with saffron and croutons, fish *choucroute*, pan-fried crayfish with curry and other seafood goodies. In summer there's a lobster menu for €70.

Restaurant du Père Raballand – L'Étape Maritime

6 pl. de la Norvège; it's on the harbour.
☎02.51.26.02.77
Closed *Mon except in July/Aug; 30 Nov–15 March.*

A bar-brasserie decorated to look like the inside of a boat.The cuisine is refined and they serve seafood accompanied by wines bought direct from the vineyards. If you want more intimacy, go for the "gastronomic" dining room upstairs, but the food is the same – blanquette of cuttlefish *à l'ancienne*, scallop stew, mussels prepared house-style and so on. The lunchtime menu at €14.50 is excellent value for money. There's also a cheaper *formule* menu at €11.80. Père Raballand is well known in town and the atmosphere in his bistro in summer or at the weekend is unmatched.

Pouzauges

85700

Restaurant Patrick

Rue de la Baudrière; it's on the D752, at Puzauges-Gare just after Fleury-Michon on the left.
☎02.51.65.83.09
Closed *Sun and Mon evenings; first 3 weeks in Aug; a week in March.* Car park.

A long modern house, painted pink. Everyone round here knows the place because the Patrick in question is a talented chef who has made a great name for himself. Menus from €10 (not at weekends) to €27.50; they're all good.

Rochefort-sur-Loire

49190

Le Grand Hôtel**

30 rue René-Gasnier; in the main street.
☎02.41.78.80.46 Ⓕ02.41.78.83.25
Ⓦwww.le-grand-hotel.net
Restaurant closed *Wed; Sun evening; Tues evening out of season; Feb school holidays.*

A nice old house with a garden, located in the main street. It's ideal as a base for exploring the Layon area. The ground-floor dining room is decorated in shades of yellow and green. Carefully prepared dishes feature lots of local specialities with dishes changing regularly. Menus €17–38. The *patronne* is a passionate wine-lover which explains the well-researched wine list. The rooms are fairly big but quite simple and cost €31 with shower or €37 with shower/wc; the nicest are on the first floor overlooking the garden. *Free coffee on presentation of this guide.*

Roche-sur-Yon (La)

85000

Marie Stuart Hôtel**

86 bd. Louis-Blanc; it's opposite the station.
☎02.51.37.02.24 Ⓕ02.51.37.86.37
Ⓦwww.mariestuarthotel.com
Restaurant closed *Sat lunchtime and Sun except in high season.* **TV.**

This hotel overflows with Scottish trappings, including tartans, coats of arms and a portrait of Mary, Queen of Scots. The spacious rooms are each decorated differently; doubles €53 with shower/wc or bath. The restaurant serves good, simple food with some quasi-Scottish specialities: Highland steak, Scotch eggs and dumplings but also fisherman's stew. Menus are €15 at the bar (starter and main course), €21 and €25. They have a good selection of malts. *Free apéritif on presentation of this guide.*

Le Logis de la Couperie***

Route de Cholet. It's five minutes from the town centre – take the main road to Cholet

and then the D80.
Ⓣ02.51.24.10.18 Ⓕ02.51.46.05.59
Ⓦwww.logiscouperie.com
TV. Car park.

In a stately fourteenth-century mansion hidden away in the depths of the countryside, this is one of the most appealing hotels in the Vendée. The atmosphere is a combination of refinement and simplicity. There are just five cosy rooms, each named after a flower and decorated in English style with canopy beds and antique furniture. Doubles €58–76 with shower/wc or bath, depending on the season. The only sounds to wake you are the ducks and the frogs in the pond. *Free apple juice on presentation of this guide.*

Le Clémenceau

40 rue Georges-Clémenceau.
Ⓣ02.51.37.10.20
Ⓦwww.brasserie-le-clemenceau.fr
Open *daily noon–midnight.* **Disabled access.**

This is a genuine brasserie with an attractive terrace. It's well known for the freshness of its shellfish, seafood and fish – the names of the suppliers are even inscribed on the menu. Very tasty fish soup and generously served seafood platter. Menus €13–25.

Saint Charles Restaurant

38 rue du Général-de-Gaulle.
Ⓣ02.51.47.71.37
Ⓦwww.restaurant-stcharles.com
Closed *Sat lunchtime; Sun.*

Photos of jazz musicians and instruments adorn the walls, jazz plays softly in the background and even the menu features jazz references. In this relaxed atmosphere the chef produces creations such as *carpaccio* of duck with foie gras and sea bream steamed over seaweed. Menus, €16–33, offer good value for money. *Free house apéritif on presentation of this guide.*

Le Rivoli

31 bd. Aristide-Briand
Ⓣ02.51.37.43.41
Closed *Sat lunch; Sun; Mon; 3 weeks in Aug.*

It certainly cannot be said that this charmingly refurbished bistro lacks colour or a sense of humour: it is decorated with a combination of zebra stripes, leopard spots and apple green. The food is a light blend of local cooking and Mediterranean touches. Weekday lunchtime menu €18, with another at €26. The service is friendly enough, but rather impersonal.

Poiré-sur-Vie (Le)

85170 (13.5km NW)

Hôtel-restaurant Le Centre**

19 pl. du Marché; take the D6.
Ⓣ02.51.31.81.20 Ⓕ02.51.31.88.21
Ⓦwww.hotelducentre-vendee.com
Closed *Mon–Fri out of season; Sun evening in season.* **Disabled access. Swimming pool. TV. Car park.**

This welcoming hotel, right in the middle of the village, has clean, comfortable rooms. Doubles are €36 with basin, €55 with bath. The restaurant offers simple authentic regional cooking at reasonable prices. Menus €10.50–39. *Free coffee on presentation of this guide.*

Maché

85190 (22km NW)

Auberge du Fougerais

Take the D948; after Aizenay turn left beyond the river Vie bridge and follow the signposts.
Ⓣ02.51.55.75.44
Closed *Mon, Tues and Wed evenings except July–Aug.* **Car park. Disabled access.**

A lovely converted barn covered in ivy and with a shady terrace. It's a peaceful place, where unfussy, tasty food is served at simple tables. The chef adds a few vine stems to the open fire when he grills eel, salmon, rib of beef or quail and roasts monkfish with citrus fruit. Weekday lunch menu at €10 and others up to €37, offering good value for money. *Free apéritif on presentation of this guide.*

Rosiers-sur-Loire (Les)

49350

La Toque Blanche

2 rue Quarte; it's on the way out of the village on the Angers road, after the bridge.
Ⓣ02.41.51.80.75
Closed *Tues evening; Wed; end Jan; end Nov.* **Highchairs available. Car park.**

It is becoming increasingly necessary to book a table at this up-and-coming restaurant – and it's absolutely essential for Sunday lunch. Inventive cuisine is served in an elegant, air-conditioned dining room. Menus €12–42 include wine. Dishes are cooked using fresh produce chosen from the market by the chef himself; the fresh sea or river fish are consistently good. Specialities include hot oysters, home-smoked salmon, red mullet mousse with caviar sauce, casserole of calf sweetbreads. Friendly welcome. *Free coffee on presentation of this guide.*

Saint-Martin-de-la-Place

49610 (7 km NW)

Domaine de la Blairie

5 rue de la Mairie; 7km away from Rosiers, towards Saumur, along the Loire valley.
ⓣ02.41.38.42.98 ⓕ02.41.38 .41.20
ⓔlablairie@wanadoo.fr
Closed *mid-Nov to mid-Feb.* **Car park.**

Doubles €42–48. This eighteenth century building was once a convent and an old people's home, but the conversion has been pretty successful and this hotel offers a good retreat for families. It has a lovely park, a swimming pool and a good restaurant. Relaxed welcome.

Sables-d'Olonne (Les)

85100

Hôtel de la Tour**

46 rue du Docteur-Canteteau.
ⓣ02.51.95.38.48 ⓕ02.51.95.89.84
ⓦwww.hotel-lessablesdolonne.com
Closed *Feb school holidays; Easter; Christmas.*

This nice little place is in a typical street in the Chaume district, and it's run by a young couple who make guests feel like friends. Madame has decorated each room in a different theme, with colours inspired by the sea. Doubles with shower or shower/wc or bath €38–48, depending on the season; some rooms have a view of the port. You can ask for a TV to be brought to your room. There's also an interior garden full of flowers where you can have breakfast, or you can eat in the pretty dining room next to the wood stove. Very good value for money. *10% discount on the room rate for a minimum stay of three consecutive nights, except public holidays and school holidays, on presentation of this guide.*

Hôtel Les Embruns**

33 rue du Lieutenant-Anger.
ⓣ02.51.95.25.99
ⓦwww.hotel-lesembruns.com
Closed *Sun evening Oct–May; 9–24 Jan; 7 Nov–5 Dec.* **TV. Pay car park.**

You can spot the yellow frontage of this building with its green shutters from the other side of the harbour. The rooms are very pretty and painted in attractive colours, and they're brilliantly maintained by the welcoming young pair who run the place. Some of the rooms overlook the port, while the ones looking onto a small side street are cooler in summer. Doubles €39–55. Dogs not allowed. *10% discount Sept–June (except at weekends, during holidays and the Vendée Globe race) on presentation of this guide.*

Hôtel Antoine**

60 rue Napoléon.
ⓣ02.51.95.08.36 ⓕ02.51.23.92.78
ⓦwww.antoinehotel.com
Closed *mid-Nov to mid-March. Restaurant open evenings (residents only).* **TV. Pay car park.**

A delightful haven right in the centre of town. Quiet rooms, some of which look out over the garden, cost €44–49 with shower/wc in the annexe or in the main hotel. Prices are a little lower out of season. Half board, compulsory July–Aug, is €43–50 per person. The food is excellent and prepared from the freshest market produce. *Free house apéritif to half-board guests on arrival on presentation of this guide.*

Hôtel Les Hirondelles**

44 rue des Corderies.
ⓣ02.51.95.10.50 ⓕ02.51.32.31.01
ⓦwww.perso.wanadoo.fr/leshirondelles
Closed *lunchtime.* **TV. Pay car park.**

This hotel doesn't look particularly attractive from the outside but the rooms have a fresh, modern décor, and the atmosphere is warm and friendly. Some rooms have balconies which are ideal for breakfast and others lead onto a pretty white patio planted with exotic, perfumed plants. Doubles €53–60 with shower/wc. Half board, compulsory in July and Aug, costs

€55–58. Menus, €17–26, list fish, shellfish and seafood dishes. *Free coffee on presentation of this guide.*

🏃 |●| L'Affiche

21 quai Guiné; it's near the port, opposite the dock for the boats to the Île d'Yeu.
☎02.51.95.34.74
Closed *Sun and Thurs evenings; Mon; 12 Dec–20 Jan.*

The outside is painted yellow and beckons you in. The chef uses fresh local produce and the dishes are deliciously exotic and flavoursome. Menus, €11.20–26.50, offer good value for money. *Free house apéritif on presentation of this guide.*

🏃 |●| Restaurant George V

20 rue George-V.
☎02.51.95.11.52
Closed *Sun evening; Mon out of season; Jan; Nov.*

Both elegant dining rooms look out to the harbour entrance. Chef Olivier Burban prepares excellent food – not surprisingly, fish is the main ingredient, but it's imaginatively prepared. Unexpected flavours pop up in dishes such as gateau of crayfish, pan-fried scallops with baby vegetables and oysters with foie gras sauce. Leave room for the *pain perdu* (France's answer to bread-and-butter pudding) or the hot apple tart. Menus €13–30. *Free coffee on presentation of this guide.*

La Fleur des Mers

5 quai Guiné; on the quay opposite the port.
☎02.51.95.18.10
Closed *Mon; Tues (out of season).*

Open the door and enter what seems to be a spotless, elegant chic ship; pass through the various spacious levels until you reach the "deck", with its view of the port. The good taste of the bright interiors are reflected in the delicate cooking, which focuses on seafood and grilled fish. Weekday lunchtime menu €15, then others from €21–35. The cheap menu is generous, with hot tidbits followed by *gratin* of seafood with Mareuil wine, then by grilled sardines and *gâche vendéenne* with red fruits for dessert. Good selection of wines from the region. Everything is indeed shipshape onboard this charming restaurant.

Sablé-sur-Sarthe

72300

🏃 |●| Les Palmiers

54 Grande-Rue.
☎02.43.95.03.82
Closed *Tues; Sat lunchtime.* **Highchairs and changing tables available. Disabled access.**

The Moroccan hospitality and cuisine you'll encounter here offers quite an antidote to the *rillette* and fish stew that otherwise abounds in these parts. Abdou mans the kitchens while his French wife greets the guests. There is little passing trade in this run-down street in the old part of town, and the owners depend on the restaurant's reputation for its survival. Fortunately, that seems safe. The two large dining rooms are smart and very well decorated, offering comfortable surroundings in which to enjoy the best of Moroccan cuisine. They offer large helpings of aromatic stews, vegetables and excellent meat: superb *tajines* cost €10–11, couscous with a selection of meats is €10–15, and there are delicious home-made pastries. You'll pay €12–18 for a meal à la carte. *Free coffee on presentation of this guide.*

|●| L'Hostellerie Saint-Martin

3 rue Haute-Saint-Martin; it's in a small street leading off the town hall square towards the château.
☎02.43.95.00.03
Closed *Mon; Sun and Wed evenings.*

This town-centre restaurant seems to be in a clement microclimate – or so the palm tree across the street would suggest. The high-ceilinged dining room has an antiquated charm and traditional décor, with a dresser, Normandy clock, heavy red velvet curtains, copper pots and pans and fresh flowers on every table; the parquet floor creaks underfoot. You'll find good local food; menus €15–31. You can also eat on the attractive, flower-filled terrace.

Dureil

72270 (16km E)

|●| L'Auberge des Acacias

Take the D309 to Parcé-sur-Sarthe or the D23 to Malicorne, then turn down the small road that follows the Sarthe river.

ⓣ02.43.95.34.03
Closed *Sun evening; Mon; week nights Nov–March.*

It may not be smothered in Virginia creeper these days but it's still worth a visit. Menus change seasonally, but specialities include duck breast with elderflower and zander in cider sauce – there's a good wine list, too. The terrace is delightful, and in winter you can eat beside the cosy fireplace. Menus €11–25.

Saint-Calais

72120

À Saint-Antoine

8 pl. du Marché-aux-Porcs.
ⓣ02.43.35.01.56
Closed *Sun and Wed evenings; Mon (in winter).* **Car park.**

The Achard brothers – wine waiter at Maxim's and chef at Plazza Athénée – caused quite a stir when they took over an old bistro in place Saint-Antoine and turned it into a "real" restaurant. I's a good, unfussy place, where locals meet for lunch at the bar before returning to their occupations; the small dining room soon fills up. Expect colourful, tasty dishes including pig's trotters and foie gras. Weekday menu €12 or others €16–40. Good, affordable local wines.

Saint-Gervais-de-Vic

72120 (4km S)

Le Saint-Éloi

1 rue Bertrand-Guilmain; it's near the church.
ⓣ02.43.35.19.56
Closed *Sun evening out of season; 1–15 Feb; 1–15 Aug.*

The proprietors of this restaurant used to be pork butchers, but now their dining room is full every Sunday. The €9.50 weekday menu (available at evenings by reservation) gets you a buffet of starters, *blanquette* or *coq au vin*, cheese, tart, coffee and wine. There's another menu at €23, which offers three dishes – a starter, a fish course and breast of duck with green peppercorns. You can also eat à la carte; don't miss the duck *pot-au-feu*. *Free apéritif on presentation of this guide.*

Saint-Denis-d'Orques

72350

L'Auberge de la Grande Charnie

Rue Principale; it's on the N157, halfway between Laval and Le Mans.
ⓣ02.43.88.43.12
Closed *Mon; Sun–Thurs evenings; winter school holidays.* **Disabled access. Car park.**

An exquisite dining room and excellent local cuisine at prices that won't break the bank. They offer a dish of the day – such as chicken breast stuffed with foie gras, *croustillant* of crayfish with a fish *coulis* or fish stew – but always take the advice of the patronne who will tell you what's best. Menus €15–36. *Free coffee on presentation of this guide.*

Saint-Florent-le-Vieil

9410

L'Hostellerie de la Gabelle**

12 quai de la Loire.
ⓣand ⓕ02.41.72.50.19
Closed *Sun evening; Mon lunchtime; Fri evening Oct–May; 23 Dec–1 Jan.* **TV. Highchairs available.**

A traditional provincial hotel, well located on the banks of the Loire – it's a good spot to stop if you're travelling between Nantes and Angers. The twenty or so rooms have been decorated on various different themes; doubles €40–43 with shower/wc or bath. The cuisine is simple but tasty: Loire eels *à la Provençale*, zander in *beurre blanc* and house *foie gras*. Menus €13 in the week, with others at €20–38. *Free coffee on presentation of this guide.*

Saint-Jean-de-Monts

85160

Hôtel-restaurant Le Robinson**

28 bd. Leclerc.
ⓣ02.51.59.20.20 ⓕ02.51.58.88.03
ⓦwww.hotel-le-robinson.com

Closed *Dec–Jan.* **Disabled access. TV. Swimming pool. Car park.**

This family business has become a substantial tourist complex over the years. The original hotel has changed considerably with many extensions and additions, but quality has been maintained. There are several types of room, all comfortable – some overlook the leafy avenues, others have a view of the road. Doubles €40–63. Half board compulsory in high season. Traditional, pleasant, carefully prepared cuisine: scallop kebabs and other seafood dishes, duck breast with honey and apples. There's a €12.50 menu (not Sun) and others at €19–38.30. *Free coffee on presentation of this guide.*

Saint-Léonard-des-Bois

72590

Touring Hôtel***

Follow the Alpes Mancelles route.
Ⓣ02.43.31.44.44 Ⓕ02.43.31.44.49
Ⓦwww.letouring.com
Closed *20 Dec–31 Jan.* **Disabled access. TV. Swimming pool. Car park.**

A good place to stay, near the Sarthe river in the heart of the hills known as les Alpes Mancelles. Although the building is constructed from concrete, the atmosphere, hospitality, cuisine and swimming pool soon make you forget the dull architecture – it's the only outpost of the English Forestdale chain in France. Quiet, well-appointed rooms with shower/wc or bath/wc cost €85–120. Menus €22–40. Dishes are tasty – upside-down tart of black pudding and apples, haddock fillet with sage, smoked salmon, duck breast, charlotte with goat's cheese and seasonal fruit turnover. *10% discount on the room rate on presentation of this guide.*

Saint-Nazaire

44600

Hôtel de Touraine*

4 av. de la République; it's near the town halll.
Ⓣ02.40.22.47.56 Ⓕ02.40.22.55.05
Ⓔhoteltouraine@free.fr
Closed *19 Dec–5 Jan.* **TV.**

It's hard enough to find a reasonably priced and pleasant hotel in Saint-Nazaire – let alone one that offers a substantial breakfast (served in the garden in good weather) and a free ironing service to boot. Doubles €30–38, depending on facilities. *10% discount on the room rate for a minimum two-night stay 1 Oct–31 March on presentation of this guide.*

Korali Hôtel**

Place de la Gare.
Ⓣ02.40.01.89.89 Ⓕ02.40.66.47.96
TV. Disabled access.

This welcoming establishment is in a modern building and all the rooms have good facilities. Doubles are €48.90–63 with shower/wc or bath. Breakfast is served, rather incredibly, from 2am to noon. *10% discount on the room rate on presentation of this guide.*

Saint-Joachim

44720 (10km N)

L'Auberge du Parc - La Mare aux Oiseaux

162 île de Fédrun.
Ⓣ02.40.88.53.01 Ⓕ02.40.91.67.44
Ⓦwwwauberge-du-parc.com
Closed *Sun evening and Mon Sept–June; Mon lunchtime only July and Aug; March.* **Highchairs available. Car park.**

The inhabitants of Île de Fédrun have adopted Éric Guérin – an alumnus of the famous Tour d'Argent in Paris – as their favourite chef. He's full of ideas and produces inspired dishes: snails and cuttlefish with wild nettles, lacquered zander, *croquant* of frogs' legs on a bed of Breton seaweed. Menus €32–65. Five rooms with bath/wc are under the reed-thatched roof – in keeping with the local Brièronne atmosphere – cost €65.

Saint-Vincent-du-Lorouër

72150

L'Auberge de l'Hermitière

Sources de l'Hermitière; it's 4.5 km south of Saint-Vincent-du-Lorouër.
Ⓣ02.43.44.84.45 Ⓕ02.43.79.10.04
Closed *Mon evening, Tues and Wed Oct–April; Mon and Tues May–Sept; 20 Jan–2 Feb.* **Disabled access.**

The setting of this house is splendid: it's in

a wood, just by the river, and there's a terrace under the trees. It's one of the great tables in the Sarthe, yet it still serves a menu for €17 – others are €24–48. Specialities include pork kidneys sautéed with cider and apples, lightly smoked and salted foie gras, *chiffonade* of wild mushrooms. *Free apéritif on presentation of this guide.*

Saint-Vincent-sur-Jard

85520

Hôtel-restaurant de l'Océan**

49 rue Anatole-France; 50m from the centre of town, facing the beach.
02.51.30.30.09 02.51.27.70.10
www.hotel-restaurant-ocean.com
Closed *Nov to mid-Feb.* **Disabled access. TV. Swimming pool. Car park.**

The Guicheteau family have been running this hotel for more than seventy years. It's an old-fashioned villa, with 45 rooms overlooking the sea, and attracts a loyal clientèle of regulars. Doubles €41–70.75 with shower or bath. Half board, compulsory 10 June–10 Sept, is €55.64–67.84 per person. The restaurant is in a huge dining room with parquet floors. Menus from €13.45 (except Sun and bank holidays), €18.30 or €39.50. *Free Kir (Oct–May) on presentation of this guide.*

Saulges

53340

Hôtel-restaurantL'Ermitage***

Place Saint-Pierre.
02.43.64.66.00 02.43.64.66.20
wwwhotel-ermitage.fr
Closed *Fri evening, Sun; Mon evening Oct to mid-April; Feb; autumn school holidays.* **Disabled access. TV. Swimming pool. Car park.**

A modern hotel with bright, spacious, comfortable rooms overlooking the park, swimming pool and countryside (€53–89 with shower/wc or bath). The restaurant serves traditional dishes with a modern twist: red mullet roasted on a fire with warm balsamic vinaigrette, home-smoked zander with green lentils, lobster stew, orange *croustillant* with almonds. There's a wide selection of menus at €19.50–46.

Saumur

49400

Hôtel Le Volney**

1 rue Vonley; it's near the post office.
02.41.51.25.41 02.41.38.11.04
www.le-volney.com
Closed *7–22 Dec.* **TV.**

The rooms are spotless, homely and comforting in this simple, cosy place. The prices have been remarkably stable over recent years – €28 for a double with basin, €47 with bath, phone and TV. Excellent welcome from the mistress of the house.

Hôtel de Londres**

48 rue d'Orléans.
02.41.51.23.98
www.lelondres.com
TV. Car park.

Friendly hotel in a busy location, but don't worry – the soundproofing cuts out the noise of the street. It's been redecorated in a charming English style and is well maintained. There are a few family rooms. Doubles €35–47 with shower, shower/wc or bath/wc. Copious buffet breakfast €6. *One free breakfast per room per night on presentation of this guide.*

Central Kyriad**

23 rue Daillé; from quai Carnot take rue Fidélité and it's the first on the left after rue Saint-Nicolas.
02.41.51.05.78 02.41.67.82.35
www.multi.micro.com/kyriad.saumur
TV. Pay car park.

This modern building, in a quiet street, offers pleasant, rather refined décor with exposed beams. The 27 rooms are spacious and some surprise with their flights of stairs, sloping ceilings and stylish furniture. There are some family rooms with spacious bathrooms. Doubles with shower/wc or bath cost €45–70. Affable, welcoming host. *10% discount on the room rate in low season (5% discount in high season) on presentation of this guide.*

Hôtel Anne d'Anjou***

32–33 quai Mayaud; it's below the château, beside the Loire.

Ⓣ02.41.67.30.30 Ⓕ02.41.67.51.00
Ⓦwww.hotel-anneanjou.com
Disabled access. TV. Pay car park.

An elegant and charming eighteenth-century building with a flower-filled internal courtyard and a superb (listed) staircase. Comfortable doubles with antique furniture go for €83 with shower/wc or €96 with bath. Some are under the eaves; there's also an opulent, Empire-style bedroom ideal for a special treat or a honeymoon. Breakfast €10. The restaurant serves good local dishes: Loire zander with asparagus *fondant*, carpaccio of scallops with vinaigrette and pigeon with cocoa seeds. Menus €19–48. *10% discount 1 Nov to mid-March on presentation of this guide.*

|●| La Pierre Chaude

41 av. du Général-de-Gaulle (North-East); on the island of Offard, between the two bridges. Cross the Loire in the direction of the train station; it's on the left, behind the trees.
Ⓣ02.41.67.18.83
Closed *Tues evening (in winter); Wed evening; Sat lunch; Sun evening; 1st fortnight in Aug; a week at Christmas.*

Weekday lunchtime menu €10, "saloon" menu at 13.60 and "*dilligence*" (stagecoach) menu at €18.90. The house speciality, "*the hot butcher's stone*", is extremely filling: a mixture of meat and poultry (pork, duck, etc.) cooked on a stone and accompanied by delicious sauces. Other traditional dishes are also on offer and, what is more, the service is charming. *Free apéritif offered on presentation of this guide.*

|●| L'Auberge Reine de Sicile

71 rue Waldeck-Rousseau; it's on île d'Offard, between the two bridges.
Ⓣ02.41.67.30.48
Closed *Sat lunchtime; Sun evening; Mon; 1–22 Aug.* **Disabled access. Car park.**

This welcoming and quiet restaurant, situated beside a charming medieval building, is away from the usual tourist circuit. They specialize in Loire valley specialities, such as home-made foie gras, duck *confit* and many others. Menus €17–31. It's worth booking. *Free apéritif on presentation of this guide.*

|●| Les Ménestrels

11–13 rue Raspail; it's in the gardens of the Hotel Ann d'Anjou, at the bottom of the castle.
Ⓣ02.41.67.71.10
Closed *Sun.*

Without doubt the best restaurant in Saumur, boasting a rustic setting, original beams and exposed stonework. As for the food, the set menus at €19.50 (lunchtimes Mon–Sat) to €50 offer fine combinations of complex flavours. Specialities change frequently, but a lot of chicken specialities and local produce.

Montsoreau

49730 (11km SE)

|●| Restaurant le Saut-aux-loups

Route de Saumur; coming from Saumur on the D947, it's on the edge of the village.
Ⓣ02.41.51.70.30
Closed *evenings; mid-Dec to mid-Jan.*
Disabled access.

This was the first restaurant in the region to relaunch an almost-forgotten local speciality called the *galipette*. It's made by stuffing three big mushrooms with *rillette* or *andouillette* and *crème fraîche*, snails or goat's cheese. Then they're browned gently in a bread oven fuelled by vine cuttings and served with a light, fruity Gamay. Reckon on €20 for a meal (wine and coffee included). Excellent welcome delivered by the young owner; in summer he puts tables outside. Credit cards not accepted. *Free coffee on presentation of this guide.*

Sillé-Le-Guillaume

72140

⌂ |●| Le Bretagne**

1 pl. de la Croix d'Or; it's near the station.
Ⓣ02.43.20.10.10
Ⓦwwwlebretagne.ifrance.com
Closed *Fri and Sun evening April–Sept; Fri evening, Sat lunchtime and Sun evening Oct–March; 24 July–10 Aug.* **TV. Car park.**

Inside this newly renovated family hotel, there's a superb restaurant offering fresh-tasting and exciting dishes that change with the seasons: leek terrine, hot foie gras with fruit chutney, lightly smoked salmon, green lentils, *fondant* of oxtail, scorpion fish with lemongrass, and a delicious Paris-Brest filled with butter icing. Weekday menu €14, and others €22–44. Decent rooms €45–52. *10% discount on the room rate on presentation of this guide.*

Thouarcé

49380

|●| Le Relais de Bonnezeaux

Take the D24 for about 2km from Thouarcé heading towards Angers; it's in the old train station.
Ⓣ02.41.54.08.33
Closed *Sun and Tues evenings; Mon; 1–22 Jan.* **Disabled access. Car park.**

Though this restaurant is housed in a nineteenth-century station, there's little of the old atmosphere left. Nevertheless, the dining room, with its panoramic view, is an elegant setting for the refined cuisine. There's a €16 menu served on weekdays and others €23–42. They specialize in delicious, original fish dishes. Some of the menus offer a different wine with each course. The wine list includes some amazing old vintages. There's a shady terrace and playground for the children.

Tiffauges

85130

|●| Le Gilles de Retz

Place de l'Église
Ⓣ 02.51.65.72.26
Closed *Tues; a fortnight in Oct.*

It's hard to imagine that one of the most enchanting restaurants in Nord-Vendée is tucked away above this simple village bar. The dining room, with impressive stone walls, has been simply but charmingly decorated. The same qualities apply to the food, with unpretentious dishes imaginatively presented on pretty china. The menu €14.50 offers dishes like small salmon rolls with goat's cheese and spinach, spare ribs of pork with honey and spicy strawberry soup. The bar downstairs is the life and soul of the village; its delightful owner is a leading light in a local cultural organization and regularly puts on concerts.

Tranche-Sur-Mer (La)

85360

|●| Restaurant Le Nautile

103 rue du Phare.
Ⓣ02.51.30.32.18
Closed *Sun evening and Mon out of season; Feb.*

Anonymous-looking restaurant with a terrace, hidden away in the residential part of La Tranche. The setting may be characterless, but this is one of the region's most fashionable venues. Cyril Godard's fine, flavoursome cuisine makes it worth a visit – as do the grounds and the veranda. Try the mussels, the langoustines flambées with *pineau* or the fisherman's casserole. Menus €16–35.

Vibraye

72320

🏃 ☗ |●| Hôtel-restaurant Le Chapeau Rouge**

Place de l'Hôtel-de-Ville.
Ⓣ02.43.93.60.02 Ⓕ02.43.93.60.20
Ⓦwww.le-chapeau-rouge.com
Closed *Sun evening (except by reservation); 1–15 Jan; last week in Nov.* **Disabled access. TV. Highchairs available. Car park.**

Reliable and appealing hotel covered in Virginia creeper. The chef prepares good traditional and classic dishes – smoked salmon, *foie gras*, duck *confit*, classic *crème brûlée* – which are served in a dining room packed with hunting trophies. Weekday menu €16 and others €20–49. Everything they serve is made in their own kitchens – from the bread to the desserts. The sixteen bedrooms are very quiet. They cost €46–54 with shower/wc or bath. *Free house apéritif on presentation of this guide.*

🏃 ☗ |●| L'Auberge de la Forêt**

Rue Gabriel Goussault.
Ⓣ02.43.93.60.07 Ⓕ02.43.71.20.36
Ⓦwww.auberge-de-la-foret.fr
Closed *Sun evening; Mon; 15 Jan–15 Feb.* **TV. Car park.**

Peaceful, central hotel with comfortable rooms around €55 with shower/wc or bath. In the restaurant you can take your time over good, tasty food: there's a menu du terroir for €16.50 and others up to €45. They list mainly local dishes, using the poultry, fish and meats of the region. There's a nice terrace. *Free apéritif on presentation of this guide.*

Picardie

Albert

80300

Hôtel de la Paix**

43 rue Victor-Hugo; it's near the basilica.
ⓣ03.22.75.01.64 ⓕ03.22.75.44.17
Closed *Sun evening; Feb school holidays.*
TV.

This hotel's period wood panelling and bar do a lot to retain the distinguished atmosphere of the 1925 building it's situated in. The rooms have been prettily refurbished and are comfortable. Doubles with handbasin €40, or €55–60 with shower or bath. The dining room is pleasant and simple, with appealing family cooking on the menu: potatoes with snails and Camembert cream sauce, calf's head *sauce gribiche*, steak with shallots. Menus €15–28. *Free apéritif offered to our readers on presentation of this guide.*

Hôtel de la Basilique**

3–5 rue Gambetta.
ⓣ03.22.75.04.71 ⓕ03.22.75.10.47
ⓦwww.hoteldelabasilique.fr
Closed *Sun evening; Mon; 3 weeks in Aug; Christmas school holidays.* **TV. High chair available.**

This hotel near the basilica offers a friendly welcome, comfortable rooms and good regional cooking. Doubles with shower/wc or bath at €50. The conventional dining room makes a matching set with the rooms; weekday *formule* €11 or menus €13–30. Try the home-made duck pâté *en croûte* and the rabbit with prunes. *Free coffee offered to our readers on presentation of this guide.*

Amiens

80000

See map on p.701

Hôtel de Normandie

1 bis rue Lamartine. **Map C2-2**
ⓣ03.22.91.74.99 ⓕ03.22.92.06.56
ⓦwww.hotelnormandie-80.com
TV. Pay car park.

Thirty simple but recently refurbished rooms; doubles with basin, shower or bath/wc €32–50. In contrast, the 1930s breakfast room has splendid stained glass and the Parisian couple who own the place are lovely and welcoming.

Hôtel Victor Hugo**

2 rue de l'Oratoire. **Map C2-3**
ⓣ03.22.91.57.91 ⓕ03.22.92.74.02
TV.

This very old establishment, in a lovely quarter of town, has retained some of its original charm and its natural wood staircase, despite extensive renovations. There are ten or so rooms; each one is different and some of them are more comfortable than others. The one in the basement – the only one with bath – can get a bit noisy. The smaller attic rooms have a romantic view over the roof tops. Doubles €38 with shower/wc or €43 with bath. Best to book.

Hotel Alsace-Lorraine**

18 rue de la Morlière. **Map 1-6**
ⓣ03.22.91.35.71 ⓕ03.22.80.43.90
ⓔalsace.lorraine@wanadoo.fr
Closed *Sunday afternoon.* **TV.**

Just away from the centre in a quiet area, there's a delightful little hotel behind a

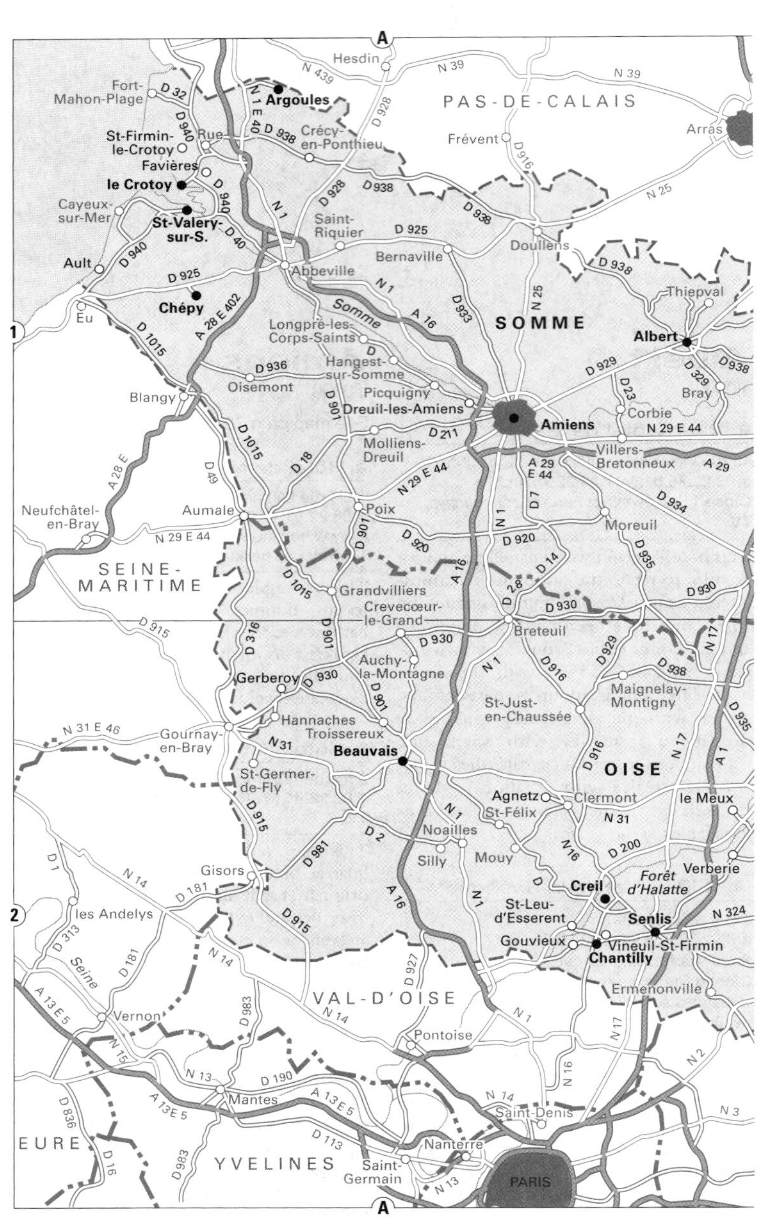
A
Hesdin
N 439
N 39
N 39
Fort-Mahon-Plage
D 32
Argoules
N 1 E 40
PAS-DE-CALAIS
D 928
St-Firmin-le-Crotoy
D 940
Rue
D 938
Crécy-en-Ponthieu
Frévent
D 916
Arras
Favières
le Crotoy
D 940
D 928
D 938
N 25
Cayeux-sur-Mer
St-Valery-sur-S.
D 40
N 1
Saint-Riquier
D 925
D 938
Doullens
Ault
D 940
Abbeville
Bernaville
D 938
D 925
N 1
Thiepval
Chépy
Somme
D 933
N 25
Eu
A 28 E 402
A 16
SOMME
Albert
1
D 1015
Longpré-les-Corps-Saints
D 929
D 938
D
Hangest-sur-Somme
D 936
Oisemont
D 329
Bray
Blangy
Picquigny
D 23
D 901
Dreuil-les-Amiens
Corbie
Amiens
N 29 E 44
D 1015
D 211
Molliens-Dreuil
Villers-Bretonneux
A 29
A 29 E 44
D 18
A 28 E
D 49
N 29 E 44
D 934
Neufchâtel-en-Bray
Aumale
Poix
D 7
N 1
Moreuil
N 29 E 44
D 901
D 920
D 920
SEINE-MARITIME
D 14
D 935
D 1015
A 16
Grandvilliers
D 28
D 930
D 930
Crevecœur-le-Grand
D 915
D 901
Breteuil
N 17
D 316
D 930
D 929
Auchy-la-Montagne
N 1
D 916
D 938
Gerberoy
D 930
Maignelay-Montigny
D 901
St-Just-en-Chaussée
N 31 E 46
Hannaches
Troissereux
D 935
Gournay-en-Bray
N 31
N 17
A 1
Beauvais
D 916
OISE
St-Germer-de-Fly
Agnetz
Clermont
le Meux
D 915
N 1
St-Félix
N 31
Noailles
D 2
N16
D 200
Silly
Mouy
D 981
D 1
Gisors
N 14
Forêt d'Halatte
Verberie
D 181
D
A 16
Creil
N 1
St-Leu-d'Esserent
Senlis
N 324
2
les Andelys
D 915
D 313
Gouvieux
Vineuil-St-Firmin
Chantilly
D 181
N 14
Seine
D 927
Ermenonville
A 13 E 5
VAL-D'OISE
D 983
Vernon
N 14
N 1
N 17
Pontoise
N 15
N 2
N 16
N 13
D 190
Mantes
A 13 E 5
N 14
A 13 E 5
D 836
Saint-Denis
N 3
EURE
D 113
Nanterre
D 16
D 983
YVELINES
Saint-Germain
N 13
PARIS
A

19
PICARDIE

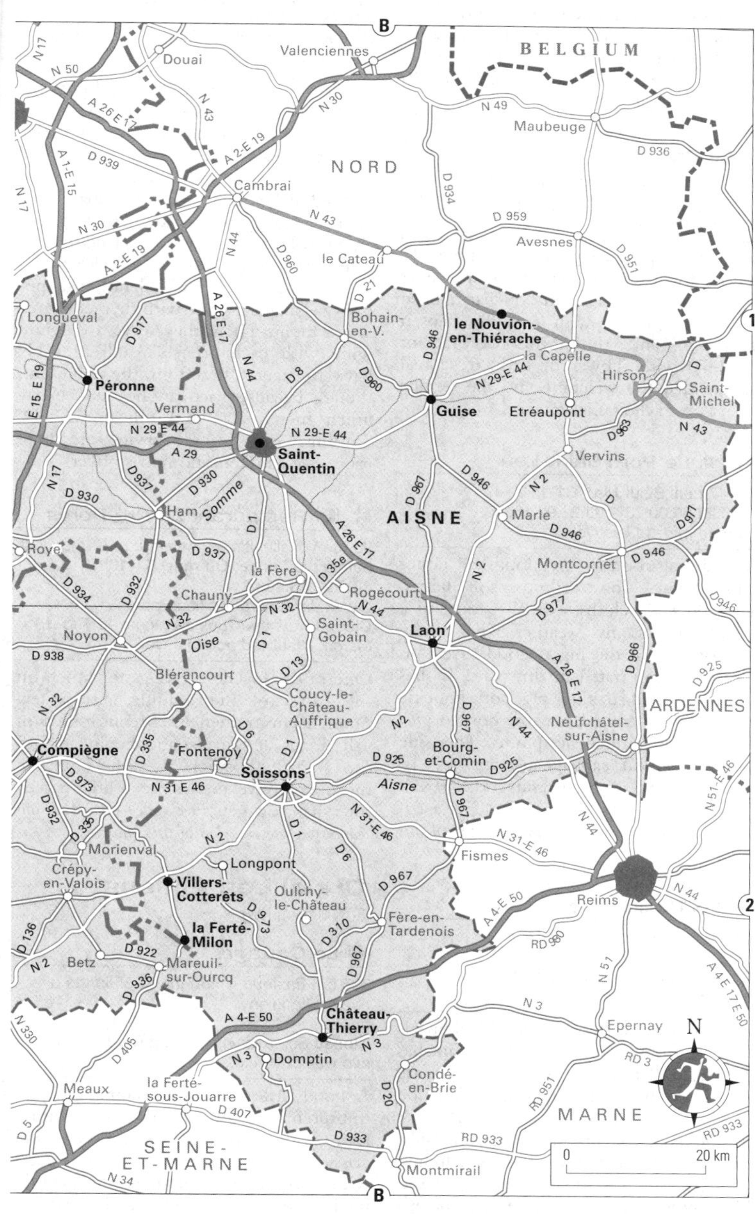
B
BELGIUM
NORD
AISNE
ARDENNES
MARNE
SEINE-ET-MARNE
Douai
Valenciennes
Maubeuge
Cambrai
le Cateau
Avesnes
Longueval
Bohain-en-V.
le Nouvion-en-Thiérache
la Capelle
Hirson
Saint-Michel
Péronne
Vermand
Guise
Etréaupont
Saint-Quentin
Vervins
Ham
Somme
Marle
Roye
Montcornet
la Fère
Rogécourt
Chauny
Noyon
Saint-Gobain
Laon
Oise
Blérancourt
Coucy-le-Château-Auffrique
Neufchâtel-sur-Aisne
Compiègne
Fontenoy
Soissons
Bourg-et-Comin
Aisne
Morienval
Fismes
Crépy-en-Valois
Longpont
Villers-Cotterêts
Oulchy-le-Château
Reims
Fère-en-Tardenois
la Ferté-Milon
Betz
Mareuil-sur-Ourcq
Château-Thierry
Epernay
Domptin
Condé-en-Brie
Meaux
la Ferté-sous-Jouarre
Montmirail
N
0
20 km
1
2

19

PICARDIE

lovely blue door. Thirteen rooms are painted brilliant white and simply but thoughtfully decorated. Some rooms are accessible from the interior courtyard. Doubles with shower/wc or bath €50–63. *Free breakfast offered to our readers on presentation of this guide.*

Le Prieuré**

6 and 17 rue Porion. **Map B1-4**
Ⓣ03.22.71.16.71 Ⓕ03.22.92.46.16
Closed *1–21 Nov.* **TV.**

Situated in a quiet, picturesque street, *Le Prieuré* (main building at no. 17, annexe at no. 6) has a certain amount of charm. Each room is different with carefully chosen furniture and thoughtful decoration; €52–70 with shower or bath. It's a real shame that the welcome and the service aren't up to the same standard.

Le Porc Saint-Leu

45–47 quai Bélu. **Map C1-11**
Ⓣ03.22.80.00.73 Ⓕ03.22.92.13.75
Closed *mid- to late Dec.*

The dining room is very long and rather cabin-like – low ceilings, soft lights, checked table cloths, a small patio and a terrace for sunny weather. The phrase "everything in the pig is good to eat" is clearly demonstrated in this place. Dishes include grilled suckling pig, pork knuckle with trotter attached, marrow bone or *filet mignon* with mirabelle plums. The side dishes are ideal: cabbage peasant style or good mashed spuds. Menus €12.50–26. Best to book – it's very popular. *Free apéritif offered to our readers on presentation of this guide.*

Le T'chiot Zinc

18 rue de Noyon. **Map C2-14**
Ⓣ03.22.91.43.79
Closed *Sun; Mon lunchtime.* **High chairs available.**

The frontage of this Art Deco building is typical of the town and the restaurant has been a local favourite for ages. There are several dining rooms; specialities include suckling pig, *caqhuse* (a sort of stew), duck terrine and, in summer, rabbit in jelly. There's a *formule* with couscous (including wine) served on Friday evening and Monday lunchtime. It's more of a Spanish inn than an authentic French one. *Formule rapide* €11 and menus €14.50–27.70.

Le Bouchon

10 rue Alexandre-Fatton. **Map C2-13**
Ⓣ03.22.92.14.32
Closed *Sun evening; afternoon and evening July–Aug; certain public holidays.*

Service until 10.30pm, later at the weekend. Lovely, old-style bistro with red benches and a zinc-topped bar. It's a stylish little place with an atmosphere and cooking to match. As you might have guessed, it's modelled on a Lyonnais bouchon, basically a brasserie, where the fare is always robust: hot sausage, *andouillette* and other offal dishes. Here you'll also find a seasonal menu and an excellent house speciality – snail casserole with thyme. There's also a menu where they serve a different wine with each course. You'll probably have to steer away from the wine list, though, because prices are heady. Weekday lunch menu €12 and others €22–42. Smiling, easy-going service; separate rooms for smokers and non-smokers.

Restaurant Le Pré Porus

95 rue Voyelle; it's on the edge of Camon just before the bridge. **Off map C1-16**
Ⓣ03.22.46.25.03
Ⓦwww.lerapporteur.fr/lepréporus
Closed *Mon and Tues evenings; 15 Feb–15 March.* **Disabled access. Car park.**

One of the loveliest settings for lunch on the banks of the Somme, just a few moments from the fields. Menus list lots of fish dishes and grills, and begin at €15 (not Sun) with others at €29–34.50. The more expensive menus are a little pricey for what you get. *Free coffee offered to our readers on presentation of this guide.*

Dreuil Les Amiens

80730 (6km NW)

Le Cottage

385 bd. Pasteur; it's on the N235 in the direction of Picquigny.
Ⓣ03.22.54.10.98
Closed *Sun evening; Mon; a week in Feb; two weeks in Aug.*

A good little roadside restaurant. It's an unpretentious Normandy-style dining room with exposed beams and they serve classic, refined cuisine. Lunch menu €13 with others from €20–34. Specialities include roast king prawns with cream of Calvados, roast calf's kidney with wild mushrooms. The welcome and atmos-

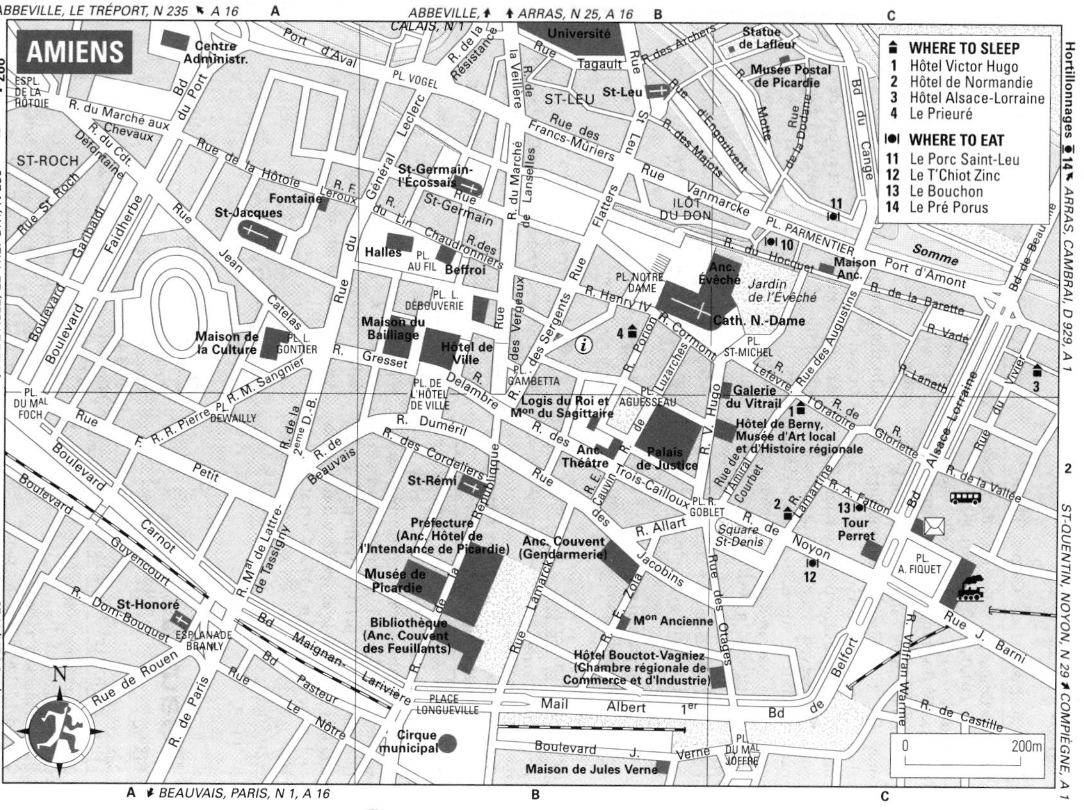
AMIENS
WHERE TO SLEEP
1 Hôtel Victor Hugo
2 Hôtel de Normandie
3 Hôtel Alsace-Lorraine
4 Le Prieuré
WHERE TO EAT
11 Le Porc Saint-Leu
12 Le T'Chiot Zinc
13 Le Bouchon
14 Le Pré Porus
ABBEVILLE, LE TRÉPORT, N 235, A 16
ABBEVILLE, CALAIS, N 1
ARRAS, N 25, A 16
Hortillonnages 14 ARRAS, CAMBRAI, D 929, A 1
ST-QUENTIN, NOYON, N 29 COMPIÈGNE, A 1
BEAUVAIS, PARIS, N 1, A 16
LE HAVRE, ROUEN, N 29
Zoo
Centre Administr.
Université
Statue de Lafleur
Musée Postal de Picardie
ST-LEU
St-Leu
ST-ROCH
St-Germain-l'Écossais
Fontaine
St-Jacques
Halles
Beffroi
ÎLOT DU DON
Anc. Évêché
Jardin de l'Évêché
Cath. N.-Dame
Maison Anc.
Somme
Maison du Bailliage
Hôtel de Ville
Maison de la Culture
Logis du Roi et Mon du Sagittaire
Galerie du Vitrail
Hôtel de Berny, Musée d'Art local et d'Histoire régionale
Palais de Justice
Anc. Théâtre
St-Rémi
Préfecture (Anc. Hôtel de l'Intendance de Picardie)
Anc. Couvent (Gendarmerie)
Musée de Picardie
Bibliothèque (Anc. Couvent des Feuillants)
Mon Ancienne
Hôtel Bouctot-Vagniez (Chambre régionale de Commerce et d'Industrie)
Tour Perret
Square St-Denis
St-Honoré
Cirque municipal
Maison de Jules Verne
PL. VOGEL
PL. AU FIL
PL. L. DÉBOUVERIE
PL. NOTRE DAME
PL. ST-MICHEL
PL. GAMBETTA
PL. AGUESSEAU
PL. DE L'HÔTEL DE VILLE
PL. L. GONTIER
PL. DEWAILLY
PL. DU MAL FOCH
PL. R. GOBLET
PL. A. FIQUET
PL. PARMENTIER
PLACE LONGUEVILLE
PL. DU MAL JOFFRE
ESPL. DE LA HOTOIE
ESPLANADE BRANLY
Mail Albert 1er
Boulevard J. Verne
Bd de Belfort
Rue J. Barni
R. Vulfran Warme
R. de Castille
Bd Alsace Lorraine
Rue de Noyon
Rue des Otages
Rue des Jacobins
Rue des Trois-Cailloux
Rue de la République
Rue Gresset
R. Delambre
R. Duméril
R. des Cordeliers
Rue de Beauvais
R. Mal de Lattre-de-Tassigny
Bd Maignan-Larivière
Bd Pasteur
Rue Le Nôtre
R. de Paris
Rue de Rouen
R. Dom-Bouquet
Guyencourt
Carnot
Petit
Bd du Port
Port d'Aval
Port d'Amont
Rue Jean Catelas
Rue de la Hôtoie
R. du Marché aux Chevaux
R. du Cdt. Defontaine
Rue St-Roch
Garibaldi
Faidherbe
R. de la Résistance
R. de la Veillère
Rue Tagault
Rue St Leu
Rue des Francs-Mûriers
Rue Vanmarcke
R. des Majots
Rue d'Engoulvent
R. des Archers
Motte
Rue de la Dodane
Bd du Cange
Bd de Beauvillé
R. du Hocquet
R. de la Barette
R. Vadé
R. Lanetti
Rue du Vivier
Rue des Augustins
R. Lefèvre
R. de l'Oratoire
R. de la Vallée
R. Gloriette
R. A. Fatton
R. Lamartine
Rue de l'Amiral Courbet
R. V. Hugo
R. Cormont
R. Porion
R. Henry IV
R. des Sergents
R. Luzarches
Rue Flatters
R. du Marché de Lanselles
Rue des Vergeaux
R. du Lin
R. des Chaudronniers
Rue St-Germain
Général Leclerc
R. F. Leroux
R. de la 2ème D.-B.
R. M. Sangnier
R. R. Pierre
R. E. Cauvin
R. Allart
R. E. Zola
Rue Lamarck
N
0 200m
A B C
1 2

phere are a little more formal than they need be.

Argoules

80120

Auberge du Gros Tilleul***

Place du Château; it's 2km from the abbey.
Ⓣ03.22.29.91.00 Ⓕ03.22.23.91.64
Closed *Mon except May–Oct; Jan.* **Disabled access. TV. Swimming pool. Car park.**

This inn is listed in all the guide books, not only for its delightful surroundings, but also due to its history – Sully is said to have planted the lime tree it is named after, and it also served as a branch of a Siennese bank. Rooms go for €58–84 for a double (a word of warning: some problems with reservations; send a written confirmation and make sure it's been received). Half board is compulsory at the weekend, at €53–58. The cuisine is traditional with heavy, rich sauces; weekday *formule* express €11 and gourmet menu for €30. There's a heated pool, golf course and gym.

Auberge Le Coq en Pâte

Route de Valloires; it's 500m from the abbey.
Ⓣ03.22.29.92.09
Closed *Sun evening; Mon; Jan; a fortnight at the end of Sept.* **Disabled access.**

They serve excellent local dishes in this pretty establishment. There's only one menu but dishes change regularly with the seasons and depending on what's fresh at the market; cod pricked with pink garlic, chicken with *vin jaune* or, in winter, cockerel in beer sauce or a pastry crust. Menus €14 (weekdays) and €19; it costs around €30.50 à la carte. By far the best cooking in the area.

Beauvais

60000

Hôtel La Résidence**

24 rue Louis-Borel; it's on the N1.
Ⓣ03.44.48.30.98
Ⓦwww.hoteldelaresidence.fr
Closed *1-23 Aug.* **TV. Car park.**

This hotel is on a very quiet street in a residential area twenty minutes' walk from the town centre, where the only thing disturbing the silence is the sound of the odd passing bicycle. You'll get a jokey, good-natured welcome, a modern, well-equipped room and good value for money. Doubles with shower €40, or €50 with bath. *10% discount on the room rate for a stay of at least two consecutive nights offered to our readers on presentation of this guide.*

Restaurant Le Marignan

1 rue de Malherbe.
Ⓣ03.44.48.15.15
Closed *Sun evening and Mon except public holidays; 25 July–20 Aug.* **High chairs available.**

On the ground floor there's a typical bar-brasserie where they serve a decent weekday menu. But if you want to get the most out of this place, head instead for the plush first-floor dining room. Here you can sample well-prepared Picardie specialities, including fish dishes, coddled eggs, veal *fricassée*, seafood *gratin* and *crème brûlée*. Menus €14–34 and à la carte. *Free house apéritif on presentation of this guide.*

Agnetz

60600 (20km SE)

Auberge de Gicourt

Forêt de Hez-Gicourt; head for Gicourt and take the Gicourt Zone Hôtelière turning.
Ⓣ03.44.50.00.31
Closed *Sun evening; Mon; Wed evening.* **Disabled access.**

This pleasant inn is popular with locals, especially at the weekend. There's a *menu* terroir at €17 and two more at €24 and €42. Reservations recommended. *Free apéritif offered to our readers on presentation of this guide.*

Gerberoy

60380 (21km NW)

L'Ambassade de Montmartre

2 allée du Jeu de Tamis; take the D133 in the direction of Abbeville.
Ⓣ03.44.82.16.50
Closed *Sun evening; Mon; Tues evening; Dec to mid-Feb.*

This place is sited at the foot of the old city walls right at the end of this wonderful village – which is listed as one of the most beautiful in France. Both it and the restaurant are worth making the effort to visit. The pretty half-timbered house is owned by Jean-Pierre, the President of the République de Montmartre, and he makes you feel welcome. The spacious, rustic dining room has a mezzanine where he holds art exhibitions. Decent local dishes with menus €18–25. Specialities include marbré of duck foie gras with apples and Loupiac jelly. When the weather gets warm you can sit on the terrace out front.

Chantilly

60500

Restaurant Le Goutillon

61 rue du Connétable; it's near the château.
☎03.44.58.01.00

This restaurant has an old-fashioned décor with exposed beams and stone walls covered with vintage advertisements. The waiter brings a blackboard to the table and places it on a chair and you make your choice from the dishes listed on it. A variety of tasty starters and house specialities including top-quality *andouillette*, steak *tartare au poivre à l'ancienne*, Lyonnais sausage, and lamb shank *confit*. There's a three-course lunch *formule* for €14; à la carte reckon on €23. *Free house apéritif on presentation of this guide.*

Aux Goûters Champêtres

Hameau du parc du Château; it's inside the grounds of the château where you have to pay to get in.
☎03.44.57.46.21
Closed *evenings; mid-Nov to mid-March.*

A lovely place to eat when it's fine but at the weekend you have to book to have any hope of getting a table. You eat outside in nicely maintained little gardens, under sun-shades – utterly charming. Take a peek at the murals in the Prince de Condé's tea room. Friendly welcome and service. The filling €15.40 menu offers a dish and a dessert; there are two more at €25.40 and €33.20. Specialities include various *gratins*, a "crown" of duck breasts, duck or pork *confit*, and crème Chantilly. *Free apéritif offered to our readers on presentation of this guide.*

Vineuil-Saint-Firmin

60500 (4km NE)

Restaurant Les Grands Prés

Route d'Avilly.
☎03.44.57.71.97
Closed *Sun evening; Mon (lunchtime only June–Aug).* **Disabled access.**

This place is out in the country, a five-minute drive from Chantilly. The straightforward, traditional cuisine includes dishes like marbled *foie gras* and duck *confit*, poached scallops and mussels with *anise*, and ox kidneys with oyster mushrooms. Menus at €16 (not weekends) and €25, with one for the kids at €9. There's a terrace, where you can enjoy the fresh country air. *Free coffee offered to our readers on presentation of this guide.*

Gouvieux

60270 (5km W)

Hôstellerie du Pavillon Saint-Hubert**

Chemin de Marisy.
☎03.44.57.07.04 ⓕ03.44.57.75.42
Closed *15 Jan–15 Feb.* **Restaurant closed** *Sun evening and Mon Nov–Easter.* **TV. Car park. High chairs and games available.**

This old fisherman's house is set in a charming spot on a bend in the Oise river and it's a lovely place to bring family, friends or a special person. From the terrace you can watch the barges slip by or simply listen to the birds. The cooking is traditional, with a weekday menu at €24.50 and €32 at weekends and public holidays. listing a choice of six starters, à la carte dishes such as snail profiteroles with Roquefort, hot *escalope* of duck foie gras and the house speciality, veal kidneys with mustard, to be followed by cheese and a choice of ten desserts. Double rooms from €53 come with shower/wc. The rooms overlooking the river are the most popular and they're often booked at the weekend. *Free coffee offered to our readers on presentation of this guide.*

Saint-Leu-d'Esserent

60340 (5.5km NW)

Hôtel de l'Oise*

25 quai d'Amont; take the N16 then follow the D44.
☎03.44.56.60.24 ⓕ03.44.56.05.11
ⓔhoteldeloise@wanadoo.fr
Restaurant closed *Fri and Sun evenings; Sat; 1–22 Aug.* **TV. Car park.High chairs available.**

A dream of a riverside hotel with two-stars: it's quiet, peaceful and offers friendly hospitality. Double rooms at €52 with shower/wc or bath. The restaurant offers a three-course menu, €12.50 (not Sun), and others at €24 and €37. Dishes vary according to the seasons, and the pastries are all home-made. *10% discount on the room rate Fri, Sat and Sun nights from Oct to March.*

Château-Thierry

02400

Hôtel-restaurant Hexagone**

50 av. d'Essômes; take the Paris road from the centre of town then follow the signs for Charly-sur-Marne.
Ⓣ03.23.83.69.69 Ⓕ03.23.83.64.17
Closed *Sun except for groups; 21 Dec–4 Jan.* **Disabled access. TV. Car park. High chairs available.**

You'll get a warm welcome in this modern hotel, and you will also be well looked-after. Comfortable doubles with shower or bath €42. There is a hearty buffet-style breakfast – cereals, cheese, charcuterie and so on. The restaurant's cheapest menu, €13, is perfectly adequate, and there are four others at €16–30. Good traditional home cooking includes scallops in champagne sauce, pepper steak and a notable *tarte tatin.* The River Marne flows past the bottom of the garden. *10% discount on the room rate on presentation of this guide.*

Domptin

02310 (12km SW)

Hôtel-restaurant Le Cygne d'Argent

24 rue de la Fontaine; take the N3 west from Château-Thierry, then the D11 and it's in the main street.
Ⓣ03.23.70.79.90 Ⓕ03.23.70.79.99
Ⓦwww.otsichateauthierry.com
Closed *Mon evening.* **Disabled access. TV. Car park.**

Lovely country hotel on the Champagne wine route. Fine local cuisine – house terrines, pan-fried scallops with preserved leeks, duck breast roasted with local grapes, champagne sorbet with home-made Ratafia (a fortified wine) and game in season, and also home-made sorbets. There's a weekday menu for €13 and others €18–36. The bedrooms have fully equipped bathrooms (shower or bath/wc), TV and minibar, all priced at €44. One of the best places in the area. *Free apéritif offered to our readers on presentation of this guide.*

Chépy

80210

L'Auberge Picarde**

Place de la Gare; it's opposite Chépy-Valines train station.
Ⓣ03.22.26.20.78 Ⓕ03.22.26.33.34
Ⓔauberge.picarde@wanadoo.fr
Restaurant closed *Sat lunchtime; Sun evening; a week in Feb; a fortnight in Aug.* **Disabled access. TV. Car park.**

The large, modern building is more motel than charming inn, but it has one of the best restaurants in the region. The dining room has ample proportions and is decorated in traditional style. They serve good seafood and typical local dishes using seasonal produce: ficelle Picarde, salmon and asparagus tips in vinaigrette, fried fish with seaweed butter. There's a weekday menu at €14 and others €20–34. It's best to book at weekends. The rooms are standard but comfortable, with doubles for €44–47.

Compiègne

60200

Hôtel de Flandre**

16 quai de la République.
Ⓣ03.44.83.24.40 Ⓕ03.44.90.02.75
Closed *20 Dec–5 Jan.* **TV.**

An enormous classical building on the banks of the Oise. The hotel offers good facilities at reasonable prices: €32 for a double with basin, €51–54 with shower/wc or bath. Rooms are spacious and the double glazing guarantees peace and quiet. *10% discount on the room rate for a stay of at least two consecutive nights, on presentation of this guide.*

Restaurant Le Bouchon

4 rue Austerlitz.
Ⓣ03.44.20.02.03
Closed *Christmas; New Year.* **Disabled access.**

This restaurant is situated in a charming little pedestrianized street in the old quarter, lined with half-timbered houses. Inside, you get good regional cooking in a pleasant atmosphere created by the jovial owner. Two-course lunch *formule* €10.50, with others at €19 and €25. Good regional dishes include Lyon sausage, duck *confit* and sea bream with saffron. Team your food with a glass of first-rate wine – there are more than forty to choose from. They host regular wine-tasting evenings, when you get to sample six diifferent wines with your meal. *Free Kir offered to our readers on presentation of this guide.*

🏃 |●| Le Palais Gourmand

8 rue Dahomey.
Ⓣ03.44.40.13.13
Closed *Sun evening; Mon; 3 weeks in Aug.*

An old baker's transformed into a modern restaurant with lots of corners and little dining rooms. The sky filters through the stained glass and sets off the attractive décor, which strikes a nice balance between bold colour and restrained design. Lovely old hand-made floor tiles. The cuisine offers both seasonal dishes and modern interpretations; *formules* and menus €12.50–20.50. Wine by the jug is sold at fair prices. Overall, it's excellent value for money. *Free apéritif offered to our readers on presentation of this guide.*

|●| Le Bistrot des Arts

30 Cours Guynemer; it's on the riverbank.
Ⓣ03.44.20.10.10
Closed *Sun.*

The easy-going, professional service perfectly suits the setting of this bistro, which is where the gourmands in town come to eat. The weekday lunch *formule* costs €18, including drinks, and the set menu €22, which is fair given the quality. À la carte, a meal costs around €26. Typical brasserie fayre and local dishes – wholesome and generously served. Sadly there are no wines by the jug so it's hard to keep the price down. Best to book.

Meux (Le)

60880 (10km SW)

|●| La Maison du Gourmet

1 rue de la République; it's on the D13.
Ⓣ03.44.91.10.10
Closed *Sat lunchtime; Sun evening; Mon; 10 days end Jan to early Feb; 15 days end July to early Aug.* **Disabled access. Car park. High chairs available.**

The owner-chef isn't new to this game – seven years at *Maxim's* in Paris and a few at the *Château de Raray*. The €15 menu alone makes it worth a visit; a typical selection might be pan-fried foie gras with honey, duck breast with Morello cherries, *filet mignon* with cider sauce, strawberry *croustillant* and warm soufflé with soft fruit. There's more choice on the €24 menu and a wide range of dishes à la carte. It's great value, and you'll be greeted and served in a friendly, efficient manner. It's worth booking.

Verberie

60410 (15km SW)

🏠 |●| Auberge de Normandie

26 rue de la Pêcherie; take the D200 or the D932 near the Oise river.
Ⓣ03.44.40.92.33 Ⓕ03.44.40.50.62
Ⓦwww.auberge-normandie.com
Closed *Sun evening; Mon; 14 July–4 Aug.*
TV. High chairs available.

A nice country inn with a classic dining room furnished with imitation rustic furniture and a pleasant terrace festooned with flowers. Double rooms with washbasin at €35 and with bath at €52. The unexpectedly interesting cuisine uses quality produce which is produced with art and craft. From the meat specialities, try the stuffed pig's trotters. The desserts are delicious. Menus at €20–29.

Creil

60100

🏠 Auberge de jeunesse - Le Centre des Cadres Sportifs

1 rue du Général-Leclerc; 10 min from town centre by no. 1 bus, from the train station, or use the hostel's own shuttle service.
Ⓣ03.44.64.62.20 Ⓕ03.44.64.62.29
Ⓦwww.fuaj.org
Car park. TV. Games available.

A well-equipped youth hostel that offers a host of sporting activities. €13.60 a night per person in a dormitory, including breakfast. You must book in advance for food: full meal €8.70; one hot dish €4.60; children's menu €6.40. FUAJ card compulsory (you can buy it *in situ*). The rooms are in immaculate condition. Relaxed atmosphere and efficient service.

Crotoy (Le)

80550

Les Tourelles*

2–4 rue Pierre Guerlain; take the A16; it's by the beach.
☎03.22.27.16.33 ℻03.22.27.11.45
www.lestourelles.com
Closed *6–30 Jan.* **Disabled access. High chairs and games available.**

This red-brick turreted building, erected on the Somme estuary, was once the mansion of perfumier Pierre Guerlain. Perhaps appropriately, everything is done meticulously, from the charming bedrooms with their wonderful views of the estuary to the relaxing lounge-bar and the children's playroom. There are only 24 rooms so book well in advance. Doubles €54–71; no. 33 is in the tower. The welcome, setting, décor and cuisine are all top quality. Local specialities are served in the smart dining room – star dishes include fish *matelote*, seafood platter, *ficelle picard* and snail *croustade*. Menus €19.80 and €27.80. *Free apéritif on presentation of this guide.*

La Grignotine

5 rue Porte-du-Pont.
☎03.22.27.07.49
Closed *Mon–Fri out of season; Dec–Jan.*

A plain-looking restaurant which is always overflowing with people because the food is so good. The lunchtime *formule*, €9, is as simple as could be, offering mussels with 25 different sauces – garlic, Hungarian-style or simply *marinière*. They're served in a huge pot with fresh chips. Very filling, brilliantly cooked and cheap. They also offer dishes à la carte; a meal will cost around €15. Note that because the place is so small, push-chairs and pets are not allowed.

Favières

80120 (4km NE)

Restaurant La Clé des Champs

Place des Frères-Caudron; take the D140.
☎03.22.27.88.00
Closed *Mon; Tues; week preceding the return to school in Sept.* **Disabled access. Car park.**

If you want to get away from it all, come to this well-known inn situated among the salt meadows. It provides a refined, comfortable setting. The specialities are fish, landed at the local harbour, and dishes based around fresh produce from the market. Madame makes you feel very welcome. Weekday menu €13.73 and others €23–38.11. *Free coffee offered to our readers on presentation of this guide.*

Saint-Firmin-lès-Crotoy

80550 (7km N)

Auberge de la Dune**

Rue de la Dune; take the D104 in the direction of Saint-Firmin, at the D204 turn-off take the signs to the Marquenterre bird sanctuary.
☎03.22.25.01.88
Closed *3–14 March; 7–26 Dec.* **TV. Car park.**

This small farmhouse has been nicely restored and belongs to the nearby bird sanctuary. The eleven brightly-painted bedrooms are cosy as you like and, though they're not big, they're comfortable; all come with shower/wc, TV and phone. Doubles €54. They serve decent food in the restaurant and a menu of Picardy specialities: *ficelles picardes*, pork *filet mignon* with cider and so on. Weekday menus €15 and then €20-26. *Free apéritif offered to our readers on presentation of this guide.*

Ferté-Milon (La)

02460

Hôtel Racine**

Place du Port-au-Blé.
☎03.23.96.72.02 ℻03.23.96.72.37
iap@club-internet.fr
TV. Car park. High chairs available.

A superb little hotel in a seventeenth-century building. The eight rooms have been tastefully decorated and they're reasonably priced: doubles with shower/wc €49, €54 with bath. Outside there's a garden with a paved courtyard and a pretty corner tower overlooking the banks of the Ourcq. The owners organize art courses. *One free breakfast per room offered to our readers on presentation of this guide.*

Restaurant Les Ruines

2 pl. du Vieux-Château.
☎03.23.96.71.56
Closed *Mon; Aug.* **Garden. Car park.**

A good inn owned by a landscape gardener; you dine outside in a lovely garden next to the ruined château, so you get to admire his handiwork. Traditional, good-value cooking; there's an €12 *formule rapide*, served during the week, and other menus at €20–30. They specialize in grilled meat and fish, and game in season. Good dishes include jugged rabbit with chanterelle mushrooms, monkfish steak with spiced prawns, game in season.

Guise

02120

Restaurant Le Petit Manoir**

83 rue Camille-Des-Moulins.
☎03.23.61.38.24
Closed *Sun evening; Mon; a week in Feb; a week in Aug.* **Car park.**

This is a beautiful residence, encircled by a little park and overlooked by the château belonging to the duc de Guise. Service in the restaurant is pleasant and the food is delicious. Menus €17.85–23.65. Specialities include foie gras *escalope* in cider, duck leg with morels. *Free digestif on presentation of this guide.*

Laon

02000

Hôtel Les Chevaliers**

3–5 rue Sérurier; it's in the middle of the medieval town.
☎03.23.27.17.50 ⓕ03.23.23.40.71
ⓔhotelchevaliers@aol.com
Closed *Sun, Mon and Tues except on public holidays and in the tourist season.* **TV.**

Attractively decorated bedrooms with low ceilings and exposed beams in a stylish old building. Doubles €30 with basin, €50 with shower and €60 with shower/wc or bath (including breakfast). Some have an extraordinary view over the surrounding countryside. *10% discount on the price of the room (except in July, Aug and Sept) offered to our readers on presentation of this guide.*

Bar-Restaurant Le Rétro

18 bd. de Lyon; it's the main street in the lower town.
☎03.23.23.04.49
Closed *Sun.*

A friendly, busy place that is particularly popular with local businessmen at lunchtimes. Marie-Thérèse, the owner, has a loyal following. The cheapest menu (€12.50) offers superb traditional cuisine: dishes of the day change every day, depending upon what's good at the market, but typical fare includes red meat, Marennes oysters, and *maroilles* cheese tart. There's also a list of freshly made salads. *Free apéritif offered to our readers on presentation of this guide.*

Restaurant La Petite Auberge

45 bd. Brossolette; it's near the train station.
☎03.23.23.02.38
Closed *Sat lunchtime; Sun except public holidays; Mon evening; a week in Feb; a week at Easter; fortnight in Aug.* **High chairs available.**

Laon's gourmet restaurant. The cooking is modern and the owner's son, Willy Marc Zorn, introduces a touch of originality to tasty dishes such as sea bass with pumpkin *coulis*, *crème au lard* and pan-fried veal sweetbreads in pale ale with a chicory *fondue*. Menus – €24.50–39 – are appropriately priced. The same team runs *Le Saint-Amour* (☎03.23.23.31.01), next door, which offers home-style Lyonnais cooking and excellent Beaujolais.

Nouvion-en Thiérache (Le)

02170

Hôtel de la Paix**

37 rue Mont-Vicary.
☎03.23.97.04.55 ⓕ03.23.98.98.39
ⓦwww.hotel-la-paix.fr
Closed *Sat lunchtime; Sun evening; Feb school holidays; the last fortnight in Aug.* **TV. Car park. High chairs available.**

This is a good country hotel with friendly staff. The restaurant is a delight and the cooking out of the ordinary. They offer regional dishes such as steak with Maroilles *fondue*, seafood specialities including prawn ravioli with a shellfish *coulis* and turbot soufflé with basil and saffron, and tasty desserts to satisfy even the most demanding palate. Weekday menu €15, then two more at €22 and €29.50. The large, comfortable bedrooms cost €46 with shower/wc and €61 with bath. No. 1 faces south and has a private terrace. *Free apéritif, and 10% discount on the room rate (weekends) to our readers on presentation of this guide.*

Étréaupont

02580 (19km SE)

Le Clos du Montvinage et l'Auberge du Val de l'Oise**

8 rue Albert-Ledent; it's on the N2.
Ⓣ03.23.97.91.10 or 03.23.97.40.18
Ⓕ03.23.97.48.92
Ⓦwww.clos-du-montvinage.fr
Restaurant closed *Sun evening; Mon lunch.* **Hotel closed** *Sun evening.* **Closed** *a week in Jan; a week in Aug; a week at Christmas.* **Disabled access. TV. Car park.**

A huge nineteenth-century bourgeois residence in relaxing grounds with tennis courts. The rooms are spacious and comfortable; those on the second floor have exposed beams. Doubles €59–77.50 with shower/wc or bath. Very tasty cooking: *feuillantine* of fish with herbs, calf's sweetbreads *vieille* prune, *clafoutis* with maroilles cheese, hot chocolate soufflé with a Grand Marnier *coulis*, and iced Vacherin with soft fruit. Menus €11.80–35.35 with a weekday lunchtime *menu express* for €11.80. *Free apéritif offered to our readers on presentation of this guide.*

Péronne

80200

Hostellerie des Remparts**

23 rue Beaubois; it's 100m off the main street.
Ⓣ03.22.84.01.22 Ⓕ03.22.84.31.96
Ⓦwww.logisdefrance.fr
Disabled access. TV. Pay car park.

A country inn with a post-war feel in peaceful grounds on a quiet street. Doubles with shower/wc and bath €43–77. They serve traditional local dishes with a creative touch in the cosy dining room; specialities include snail *cassolette* and duck breast. There's a €11.13-15.50 weekday menu (except public holidays), including drinks, then others at €18–45. Extension works are in progress. *10% discount on the room rate (1 Nov–30 April) offered to our readers on presentation of this guide.*

Saint-Quentin

02100

Hôtel de la Paix**

3 pl. du 8-Octobre; it's near the train station.
Ⓣ03.23.62.77.62 Ⓕ03.23.62.66.03
Ⓔhoteldelapaix@worldonline.fr
TV. Car park.

An impressive 1914 building which has been pleasantly modernized. Doubles with shower/wc €46 and €50.50 with bath. There are two restaurants on the ground floor. *Le Brésilien* serves traditional specialities, while *Le Carnotzet* (open evenings until midnight) serves Savoy dishes. There's a menu at €12 and another at €15. Both places offer reasonably priced pizzas and a good chilli con carne. *Free apéritif or coffee offered to our readers on presentation of this guide.*

Hôtel des Canonniers***

15 rue des Canonniers.
Ⓣ03.23.62.87.87 Ⓕ03.23.62.87.86
Ⓦwww.hotel-canonniers.com
Closed *Sun evening except for reservations; 2-16 Aug except for reservations.* **TV. Car park.**

Originally a private residence built in the eighteenth and nineteenth centuries, this hotel is located in the quiet central area of Saint-Quentin. The spacious rooms are extremely comfortable, and feature many personal touches. Double rooms with shower/wc at €50; with bath at €75 and suites with kitchen at €125. Breakfast is served in the pretty internal garden. The female owner will greet you very kindly. *Breakfast at half price for children under twelve on presentation of this guide.*

Restaurant Le Glacier

28 pl. de l'Hôtel-de-Ville.
Ⓣ03.23.62.27.09
Closed *Sun and Mon evenings; 1–8 Jan.*
High chairs available.

Service until 11pm. This small, nicely decorated restaurant has a fresco on the wall, checked tablecloths and opalescent glass lamps. It opens onto the pretty, pedestrian l'Hôtel-de-Ville square, and in summer you can sit on the terrace. They serve ice cream, of course, along with house specialities such as mussels Picardie-style, steak *tartare* and *choucroute* with ham hock or fish. Menus €12.50–22.10; reckon on €13 à la carte. *Free coffee offered to our readers on presentation of this guide.*

Saint-Valéry-sur-Somme

80230

Le Relais Guillaume de Normandie**

46 quai Romerel.
ⓣ03.22.60.82.36 ⓕ03.22.60.81.82
ⓦwww.guillaumedenormandy.com
Closed *Tues except mid-July to end Aug; 21 Dec–17 Jan.* **TV. Car park.**

This tall, narrow manor house, set in a garden by the water's edge, is a bit of an architectural mish-mash. Quite stylish, but some bedrooms feel a bit tired – though they're comfortable enough. Doubles €52–57 with shower/wc or bath. Ask for a room with a sea view or go for no. 1, which has a delightful little terrace. The beautiful dining room breathes *Vieille France*, and serves appropriately traditional fare which is filling but not hugely exciting. Menus, €15–40, list regional specialities. Credit cards refused. *Free apéritif offered to our readers on presentation of this guide.*

Hôtel du Port et des Bains***

1 quai Blavet; it's in the lower town, on the river mouth.
ⓣ03.22.60.80.09 ⓕ03.22.60.77.90
ⓔhotel-hpb@wanadoo.fr
Closed *1–15 Jan.*

A nice little place with a freshly painted façade, situated in a town that features lots of different architectural styles and which is surrounded by varied landscapes. Rooms aren't huge but they're well decorated and painted in bright colours. They all overlook the Somme. Doubles with shower/wc €60–125 (the most expensive come with Jacuzzi). The seafood is good – try the stews or the *choucroute*. Menus €15–32.

Hôtel Picardia***

41 quai du Romerel; it's opposite the Guillaume de Normandy.
ⓣ03.22.60.32.30 ⓕ03.22.60.76.69
ⓦwww.picardia.fr
Closed *6–31 Jan.*

This is a place that will appeal to families or those with a bit of cash. It's a pretty village house which has been thoroughly refurbished so the rooms are bright and the furnishings are stylish – if anything, it feels just a tad overdone. Fairly luxurious bathrooms. Doubles €68 not including taxes. Breakfast €8.

Ault

80460 (21km SE)

Restaurant l'Horizon

31 rue de Saint-Valéry; in upper Ault-Onival on top of the cliffs.
ⓣ03.22.60.43.21
Closed *Wed evening and Thurs out of season; Jan.*

A little restaurant with a vaguely maritime theme; six tables offer a fabulous view of the beach. Menus €12.50–27.50; all dishes are freshly made, but you'd do best to go for the seafood, including a good fish *choucroute* and a seafood stew.

Senlis

60300

Hostellerie de la Porte Bellon**

51 rue Bellon; it's just off rue de la République.
ⓣ03.44.53.03.05 ⓕ03.44.53.29.94
ⓦwww.portebellon.com
Closed *Christmas holidays.* **Restaurant closed** *Sun evening.* **TV. High chairs available.**

A superb old house, set back from the road, with eighteen comfortable and spacious double rooms, €58–72. You can eat in the shady garden in good weather, and there's an eighteenth-century cellar where you can enjoy an apéritif. Weekday menu €21 (€23 on Sun) with others €27–38. *Free apéritif offered to our readers on presentation of this guide.*

Soissons

02200

La Cavéa

1 rue Pétrot-Labarre; it's around the corner from the town hall square.
ⓣ03.23.93.02.01
Closed *Sun evening; Mon; Fri; 1-21 Aug; Christmas holidays.*

The dining room is in the cellar of a nineteenth-century convent; no hint of a chill, though, in its warm and convivial atmosphere. The menus are being redone so you need to ask. However, everything should remain perfectly affordable. *Free apéritif offered to our readers on presentation of this guide.*

Fontenoy

02290 (10km W)

Auberge du Bord de l'Eau

1 rue Bout du Port.
☎ and Ⓕ03.23.74.25.76
Closed *Wed; 16–30 Sept; 14–31 Jan.* **TV.**

A charming hotel on the banks of the Aisne. Weekday lunch menu at €15 and others €19–31. They bake their own bread, smoke their own salmon and make their own foie gras – everything is absolutely fresh. There are seven bedrooms with shower/wc at €40 and some have a lovely, peaceful river view. *Free apéritif offered to our readers on presentation of this guide.*

Bourg-et-Comin

02160 (25km E)

Auberge de la Vallée**

6 rue d'Oeuilly; take the N31 in the direction of Reims then turn left at Fisme in the direction of Laon. It's in the centre of the village.
☎03.23.25.81.58 Ⓕ03.23.25.38.10
Closed *Tues evening; Wed; 2–22 Jan; 31 March–6 April; 22–27 Sept.* **TV.**

Evelyne is the owner and she will welcome you warmly. Her establishment is near the local tourist sites such as the Chemin des Dames, the Caverne du Dragon and the Ailette pleasure park. Rooms are clean and tidy and you'll pay €45 for a double with shower/wc – if you need an extra bed it will cost €5. She provides traditional cuisine using good local produce. Weekday lunch menu €12 then others €15 and €20 or à la carte. Tasty dishes include terrine of grilled rabbit, trout *picardie* and *chaud-froid* with caramelized apples. *Free digestif on presentation of this guide.*

Villers-Cotterêts

02600

Hôtel Le Régent***

26 rue du Général-Mangin.
☎03.23.96.01.46 Ⓕ03.23.96.37.57
Ⓦwww.hotel-leregent.com
Closed *Sun evenings Nov–March, except public holidays.* **Disabled access. TV. Car park.**

There's an authentic sixteenth-century coaching inn behind the eighteenth-century façade and it's run by a distinguished and charming owner. The twenty rooms are all different – some of them have been classifed as historic monuments, in fact. Doubles with shower or bath/wc €48–72. A charming, good-value little hotel.

L'Orthographe

63 rue du Général-Leclerc.
☎03.23.96.30.84
Closed *Sun evening; Mon.* **Disabled access. Car park.**

A restaurant that sets the local standard. The chef prepares mouth-watering dishes from the freshest of ingredients. Try scallops with bacon or duck Rossini if they're on offer. The €20 menu, which includes drink, changes weekly.

Longpont

02600 (11.5km NE)

Hôtel de l'Abbaye**

Rue des Tourelles; turn off the N2 onto the D2.
☎ and Ⓕ03.23.96.02.44
TV. High chairs available.

Gorgeous ivy-covered inn in a romantic setting on the edge of the Retz forest. Rooms cost €47–48 for a double with shower/wc or bath; you get a generous breakfast for €7. No. 111 has a view over the fortified port. Excellent, fresh local produce is served in the restaurant. Menus €19 and €30. In the afternoons they serve delicious pancakes. *Free apéritif offered to our readers on presentation of this guide.*

Poitou-Charentes

Aix (Île de)

17123

Hôtel-restaurant Le Napoléon et des Bains Réunis**

Rue Gourgaud.
05.46.84.66.02 05.46.84.69.70
www.hotelnapoleon-aix.com
Closed *Sun evening and Mon Oct–March; Nov; Dec.*

This comfortable establishment, which has fifteen attractive rooms, is the only hotel on the island. Doubles go for €60 with shower/wc, €62 with bath. There's a pleasant sitting room where you can have a drink, and the restaurant serves fish dishes like *marbré* of salmon with peppers, bass with tarragon or roast cod and red wine stew. Menus €17 and €25. As the island has no other open restaurant during the out of season, clients have to eat there and half board is compulsory in July and August. You'll pay around €96 for two. The good quality service is not always there.

Angles-sur-l'Anglin

86260

Le Relais du Lion d'Or***

4 rue d'Enfer. 50m from the town centre.
05.49.48.32.53 05.45.84.02.28
www.lyondor.com
Open *daily in summer.* **Closed** *Jan; Feb.*
Disabled access. TV. Car park.

Guillaume and Heather met when he worked as a banker in London; since then they've made their home in this fifteenth-century inn and restored it with great style. The ten welcoming guest rooms are individually decorated and comfortable, with nice furnishings and a fresh, period feel. Doubles €55–80 with shower/wc or bath/wc. Meals are served in the regal surroundings of the restaurant where there's a weekday lunch menu for €17 and *menu-carte* at €25. Specialities include foie gras flan with shellfish *coulis*, duck breast with preserved lemons and garlic and, for dessert, apple *croustillant* or chocolate *fondant*. The wine cellar is stocked by Augé, a highly reputed supplier; fine wines cost less than €15. There's also a steam bath or, if you feel more active, they even run short courses in interior design. *The third night free (Oct–April, except Christmas and New Year) and a free Kir offered to our readers on presentation of this guide.*

Angoulême

16000

Auberge de jeunesse

Île de Bourgines; near the train station, walk towards the Houmeau area (the old port of Angoulême), then take the footbridge, it's on the island; or take bus no. 7 or 9 – the stop is 200m from the hostel.
05.45.92.45.80 05.45.92.27.50
www.fuaj.org
Closed *21 Dec–21 Jan.* **Disabled access. TV. Car park.**

Spacious, well-maintained hostel, run by a dynamic team. Pleasant accommodation in dormitories; one double bedroom with shower/wc and two doubles with basin; some overlook the Charente. €9.30 per night or half board at €17.90. Meals are eaten on the large terrace overlooking the river where the family atmosphere is

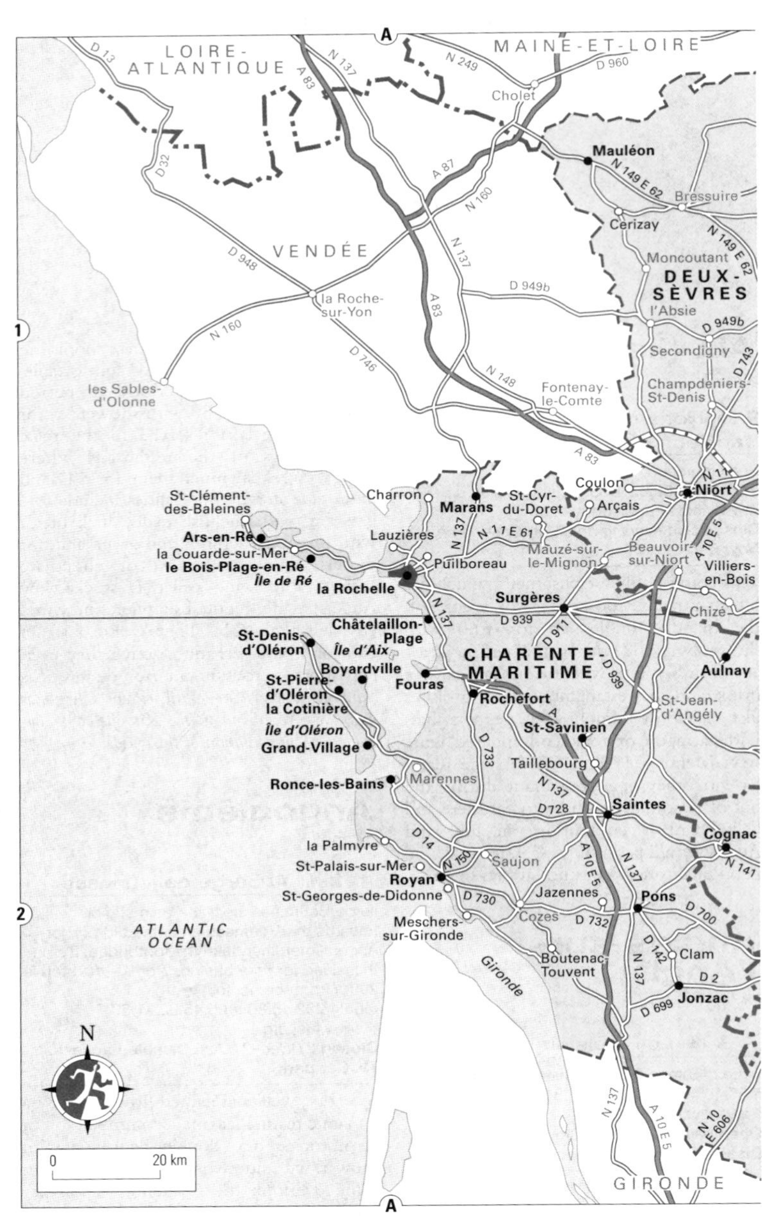
LOIRE-ATLANTIQUE
MAINE-ET-LOIRE
VENDÉE
DEUX-SÈVRES
CHARENTE-MARITIME
GIRONDE
ATLANTIC OCEAN
Cholet
Mauléon
Bressuire
Cerizay
Moncoutant
l'Absie
Secondigny
Champdeniers-St-Denis
la Roche-sur-Yon
les Sables-d'Olonne
Fontenay-le-Comte
Coulon
Niort
Arçais
St-Cyr-du-Doret
Marans
Charron
St-Clément-des-Baleines
Ars-en-Ré
la Couarde-sur-Mer
le Bois-Plage-en-Ré
Île de Ré
Lauzières
Puilboreau
la Rochelle
Mauzé-sur-le-Mignon
Beauvoir-sur-Niort
Villiers-en-Bois
Surgères
Chizé
Châtelaillon-Plage
Île d'Aix
St-Denis-d'Oléron
Boyardville
St-Pierre-d'Oléron
la Cotinière
Île d'Oléron
Grand-Village
Fouras
Rochefort
Aulnay
St-Jean-d'Angély
St-Savinien
Taillebourg
Ronce-les-Bains
Marennes
Saintes
Cognac
la Palmyre
St-Palais-sur-Mer
Royan
St-Georges-de-Didonne
Saujon
Jazennes
Cozes
Pons
Meschers-sur-Gironde
Boutenac-Touvent
Clam
Jonzac
Gironde
D 13
D 32
D 948
N 160
D 746
N 137
A 83
N 249
D 960
A 87
N 149 E 62
D 949b
D 743
N 148
N 11 E 61
A 10 E 5
D 939
D 911
D 733
D 728
D 14
N 150
D 730
D 732
D 700
N 141
D 142
D 2
D 699
N 10 E 606
0
20 km
N
A
1
2

20 POITOU-CHARENTES

friendly and cosmopolitan. Good food on offer; dish of the day at €4.90 and menu at €8.60. Situated on the island, this youth hostel offers all kinds of activities: canoeing, kayaking, motor boat trips, mountain biking, tennis... There's a superb walk – the "Coulée verte" – along the banks of the river Charente leading to a stretch of water, which is open to bathers.

Le Palma

4 rampe d'Aguesseau; it's between the train station and the town centre.
Ⓣ05.45.95.22.89 Ⓕ05.45.94.26.66
Ⓔlepalma16@.com
Closed *Sat lunchtime; Sun; a fortnight at Christmas.* **High chairs available.**

Located on the edge of old Angoulême in a rather ordinary-looking area, this hotel has an attractive frontage, and the classic local food makes it worth seeking out. The restaurant is pleasant, with a corner bodega, and offers good value, too, with a menu at €13 and others at €17 and €26. Good dishes include salad of crayfish, saffron and ceps, prawns with ginger and lamb chops in a herb crust. Rooms are pleasant enough, at €28 for a double with basin and €34 with shower/wc – the best ones are at the back.

Le Flore**

414 rte. de Bordeaux; it's 1km from the town centre.
Ⓣ05.45.25.35.35 Ⓕ05.45.25.34.69
Ⓔle-flore@wanadoo.fr
Closed *Sat; Sun; 1–22 Aug.* **High chairs available. TV. Pay car park.**

A short distance from the centre, this hotel offers comfortable rooms for €32.80 with shower/wc or bath. Half board at €49.90 per person. There's a *formule* (two dishes) for €9 and other menus at €13, €19 and €25. Good choices include the *papillotte* of salmon with baby vegetables, braised guinea fowl with tarragon, scallops with port, pan-fried foie gras with figs and iced nougat with raspberry *coulis. Free house apéritif offered to our readers on presentation of this guide.*

Hôtel du Palais**

4 place Francis-Louvel; it's near the cathedral and next to the law courts.
Ⓣ05.45.92.54.11 Ⓕ05.45.92.01.83
Closed *22 Dec–2 Jan.* **TV. Pay car park.**

One of the few hotels in the old town, looking onto a pretty square. The seventeenth-century façade is one of the most beautiful of its kind in the southwest, while the interior has an air of faded grandeur with its wide staircase, high-ceilinged breakfast room, wood panelling and worn carpets. Decent doubles go for €43 with basin and €58 with shower/wc or bath. Some have big balconies with views of the old town.

Le Saint-Antoine**

31 rue Saint-Antoine. Near the train station.
Ⓣ05.45.68.38.21 Ⓕ05.45.69.10.31
Ⓦwwhotel.saint.antoine.com
Closed *24 Dec–2 Jan.* **Restaurant closed** *Sat and Sun, except for group reservation.* **Disabled access. TV. Car park.**

Newish place on the edge of a commercial district – the pleasant terrace looks onto a roundabout – offering soundproofed bedrooms with basin for €37 or with shower/wc or bath for €47. It's got a good restaurant with menus at €13 (not weekends) and €20–33, and a number of choices à la carte. Specialities include a trio of fish grilled with *beurre blanc* and the dark chocolate *délice* with a chocolate *coulis. One free breakfast per room or free house apéritif offered to our readers on presentation of this guide.*

Chez Paul

8 place Francis-Louve; it's opposite the law courts.
Ⓣ05.45.90.04.61
Open *noon to midnight.* **Disabled access.**

A large and very long dining room, which has been successfully decorated to keep you cosy even when the weather is bad. On warmer days, you can choose from the veranda, a terrace on the square and a cool garden with a stream. They specialize in gourmet *tartines*, with foie gras, salmon, smoked duck and such like. The food is nicely prepared, with a weekday menu for €10.50 and another at €22.90. It's a great spot for a drink, and they even have a café theatre.

Restaurant La Cité

28 rue Saint-Roch.
Ⓣ05.45.92.42.69
Closed *Sun; Mon; Feb school holidays; last week in July; first fortnight in Aug.* **High chairs available.**

The smiling owner is very efficient, the tables are attractively set and all the fish is exceptionally fresh. Try the seafood platter, shellfish, home-made squid fritters, fish *choucroute*, or *brochette la cité*, a kebab of mussels, prawns and scallops. There's a meat menu, too; try the foie gras pan-fried with apples and grapes. The weekday lunch menu costs €12.50, and there are others at €16–25. *Free coffee offered to our readers on presentation of this guide.*

Gond-Pontouvre (Le)

16160 (2km N)

L'Entrecôte

45 rte. de Paris; it's on the N10.
☎05.45.68.04.52
Closed *Mon evening; Sun.* **Disabled access.**

This cosy, friendly tavern houses the best meat restaurant in the area, with a wood-fired grill. They'll show you your slab of meat before it's cooked, in case you think it's too big, and will prepare it exactly as you request. The mega-rib of beef is a good choice for families. They'll also bring you as many plates as you need if you want to share a dessert – a rare touch. Menus €15–20.

Puymoyen

16400 (7km S)

L'Auberge des Rochers

It's opposite the church.
☎ and Ⓕ05.45.61.25.77
Car park.

Friendly country house hotel next to a deer farm. It's simple, peaceful and inexpensive, with doubles at €28 with basin, €32 with shower. Half board is €32.80 per person. You get generous portions in the restaurant, where the menu at €11.50 offers starter, main course, cheese and dessert. Other menus at €18 and €25. *Choucroute* is a speciality.

Champniers

16430 (9km NE)

Restaurant Le Feu de Bois**

It's on the RN10 in the direction of Poitiers.
☎05.45.68.69.96
Closed *Sun evening.* **Disabled access. Car park.**

Large octagonal dining room where they grill meat and fresh fish over a fire fuelled by vine cuttings. They offer a hors d'oeuvres buffet and a few local dishes such as grilled ham with shallots. Menus €14.50–32.

Mouthiers-sur-Boëme

16440 (13km S)

Café-restaurant de la Gare

Place de la Gare; take the N10 in the direction of Bordeaux then take the fork to Blanzac.
☎05.45.67.94.24
Closed *Sun and Mon evenings.*

This is the type of easy-going, popular place you might have found here fifty years ago. There's a gravel terrace under the plane trees, an old zinc-topped bar and a beautiful old-school dining room. The food is of a high standard, with an astonishingly good-value €10.50 menu (not Sun) which gets you soup, starter, main course, cheese, dessert, coffee and a quarter litre of wine. Other menus €14–25. *Free coffee offered to our readers on presentation of this guide.*

Vibrac

16120 (22km W)

Les Ombrages**

Route Claude-Bonnier; take the N141, and 3.5km from Hiersac, turn left to Vibrac.
☎05.45.97.32.33 Ⓕ05.45.97.32.05
Ⓦwww.monsite.wanadoo.fr/lesombrages
Closed *Sun evening; Mon; 15 Dec–15 Jan.*
TV. Disabled access. High chairs and games available. Swimming pool. Car park.

Though the building itself is pretty charmless, it does boast a fantastic location. In a shady garden in the countryside near Bassac abbey – and close to a delightful beach – it also has an outdoor pool, tennis courts and table tennis facilities. Rooms, which are quiet and comfortable, cost €47 with shower/wc and €49 with bath. In the restaurant – which has a veranda overlooking the garden – you can't go wrong with the fish: try monkfish fillet with citrus fruit or scallops. There's a €12.50 weekday lunch menu and others from €20–32, and a range of choices à la carte. Half board at €40 per person. *Free house apéritif offered to our readers on presentation of this guide.*

Villebois-Lavalette

16320 (28km SE)

Hôtel-restaurant du Commerce

Take the D939.

®05.45.64.90.30
Closed *Wed afternoon in winter.* **Car park.**

An attractive old hotel in a nice hillside village, run by a hard-working couple. Rooms are very simple but well maintained, going for €30 with basin, €35–40 with shower or shower/wc. Half board at €38.50 per person. The menus are straightforward, too: you'll get for a lunchtime menu: a starter, main course, cheese, dessert, coffee and a quarter litre of wine – all for €11 (€15 in the evening; not served Sun). Other menus €20 and €28. Try the pan-fried foie gras. There's a nice enclosed terrace, with lots of greenery and flowers.

Verteuil-sur-Charente

16150 (30km N)

La Paloma**

14 rue de la Fontaine. Take the N10 towards Ruffec.
®05.44.29.04.49 ®05.45.29.51.31
Closed *Sun evening and Mon out of season; 1–15 March; 15 Oct–5 Nov.* **High chairs and games available. TV. Car park.**

There's a goat and some Vietnamese pigs roaming around the garden, a talking parrot and an iguana in a corner of the bar. The rooms have been pleasantly and sensitively renovated by the young couple who own the place. Doubles with shower €32, or €40–48 with bath/wc. The cooking is tasty, too; menus prove good value at €14 and €23, served every day. Specialities include hot *croustillant* of goat's cheese and foie gras with figs. *Free house liqueur offered to our readers on presentation of this guide.*

Ars-en-Ré

17590

Hôtel le Sénéchal**

6 rue Gambetta; it's in the town centre by the church.
®05.46.29.40.42 ®05.46.29.21.25
®hotel.le.senechal@wanadoo.fr
Closed *5 Jan–17 Feb; 11 Nov–20 Dec.* **TV. Games available.**

The owner Christophe, architect, and Marina gave a modern spirit to the place. All fifteen rooms in this serene, welcoming place have been superbly renovated with natural floors, stone walls and wooden ceilings, old furniture and sleek, modern lighting. Doubles range depending on size and season from €40 to €150 for the suite with a terrace. There's also a flower-filled patio where you can read in peace, and board games available in the sitting room, which has an open fire. Reservations are essential.

Côté Quai

9 quai de la Crée; it's on the port.
®05.46.29.94.94
Closed *Wed out of season except for the school holidays; Jan; mid-Nov to mid-Dec.* **Disabled access.**

Well-deserving of its good reputation, this small dining room is simplicity itself, exuding a seaside ambience and with a small terrace overlooking the port. The menu, unsurprisingly, features a lot of fish dishes, all of which are delicately judged and tasty. The chef's inventions will keep you guessing – which herb does he use in the cuttle fish *fricassée*? How on earth does he make the hot chocolate *fondant* truffles? There's a menu at €25 or main dishes from €15 up to €25.

Saint-Clément-des-Baleines

17590 (4km NW)

Hôtel Le Chat Botté**

Place de l'Église.
®05.46.29.21.93 ®05.46.29.29.97
®www.hotelchatbotte.com
Closed *early Jan to early Feb; end Nov to 21 Dec.* **Disabled access. TV. Car park.**

A quiet, charming hotel on the church square. The bright rooms feature lots of natural wood and some are panelled throughout. Traditional breakfast is served on the flowery patio. There's a health complex, which offers mineral baths and various treatments, a couple of tennis courts and a number of sun-loungers dotted around the vast, beautiful grounds. Double rooms cost €69–102 with shower or €85–115 with bath. You'll need to book in advance. Friendly welcome. Credit cards are not accepted.

Restaurant Le Chat Botté

20 rue de la Mairie; it's 30m from the church.
®05.46.29.42.09
Closed *Mon out of season; 1–21 Dec; 1 Jan–1 Feb.* **Disabled access.**

The huge dining room is decorated with lots of natural wood, and they light a fire in the open hearth in winter; in summer there's a south-facing terrace to enjoy. As for the food, the quality is good and the prices are reasonable given the location and you're looking at top-notch fresh fish dishes such as sea bass in pastry with *beurre blanc* or hot oysters with Pineau *sabayon*. They're classical, but prepared with flair. The cheapest menu costs €21, served daily at lunch and dinner, and there are others at €30.50–60. Children's menu at €12.

Aubeterre-sur-Dronne

16390

Hostellerie du Périgord**

It's in the pleasure port area on the Ribérac road.
Ⓣ and Ⓕ 05.45.98.40.46
Ⓦ www.hpmorel.com
Closed *Sun evening and Mon out of season; Sun evening in season.* **Disabled access. TV. Swimming pool. Car park.**

This is an old establishment that was saved from ruin by an Anglo-French couple – take a look at the "before" photographs in reception. The rooms have been very nicely renovated and are as lovely as you could wish for. Doubles cost €38.50 with shower/wc, or €46–54 with bath/wc. There's a quiet sitting room where you can read peacefully, and a pleasant dining room with a veranda opening onto the garden (with a pocket-size pool). The cuisine is modern, and bursting with ideas; the weekday lunch menu goes for €16 (not Sun) with others from €25 to €36.

Aulnay

17470

Hôtel du Donjon**

4 rue des Hivers; 12km to the northeast of Saint-Jean-d'Angély, on the D950. It's in the town centre (just off the main square).
Ⓣ 05.46.33.67.67 Ⓕ 05.46.33.67.64
Ⓦ www.hotel-du-donjon.com
TV. Disabled access.

Dominique and Pierre Hervé's skilful restoration of this old house has revealed the charm of old stone and exposed beams. Comfortable, old-fashioned furniture gives the place a lived-in look, creating an atmosphere of warmth in the ten bright, cosy rooms. Doubles cost €54–68.60. The setting is very intimate, with a lovely little garden for whiling away the hours. The service is exceptionally attentive.

Bois-Plage-en-Ré (Le)

17580

Hôtel-restaurant L'Océan**

172 rue Saint-Martin; it's 50m from the church.
Ⓣ 05.46.09.23.07 Ⓕ 05.46.09.05.40
Ⓦ www.re-hotel-ocean.com
Restaurant closed Wed lunchtime and evening (lunchtime only during school holidays); 5 Jan–5 Feb. **TV. Car park.**

This wonderful hotel is in a typical island house, on a quiet street away from passing traffic. There's a string of delightful little sitting rooms furnished with antiques, and the charmingly decorated guest rooms are set round a huge flower-filled patio with an ancient pine tree growing in the middle. Doubles go for €61.50–120 with shower/wc or bath. The dining room is equally delightful, with a terrace on the patio. Half board is from €61.50 up to €75 person. Children's menu at €10. Dishes, prepared from fresh market produce, change seasonally. Try the *chaudrée charentaise* (the local fish soup) and the cod with thyme butter for their finely balanced flavours. Menus €22–32. Typical welcome on the island – stylish and very relaxed.

Les Bois Flottais

Chemin des Mouettes; perpendicular to the avenue de la Plage.
Ⓣ 05.46.09.27.00 Ⓕ 05.46.09.28.00
Ⓦ www.lesboisflottais.com
Open *all year round.* **Car park. Heated swimming pool.**

Hidden away in a quiet back street, this unassuming building with green shutters is an outstanding hotel. The owners' expansive welcome will put you at ease immediately. Every detail of the ten rooms has been treated with consummate care, from the red, tiled floor to the teak washbasin and ceramic wall tiles in the bathroom. Doubles €76.50–91.50. Equal attention goes into the presentation of breakfast. The pool is set off by a wooden terrace. All in all, a fine place for a relaxed, intimate break.

|●| La Bouvette Grill de Mer

Moulin de Morinand; take the Saint-Martin-de-Ré bypass, then the road to Le Bois-Plage, and it's about 1km further.
Ⓣ05.46.09.29.87
Closed *Mon and Tues out of season.*
Disabled access. High chairs available.

One of the island's most interesting restaurants, partly because it's housed in an old garage in magnificent surroundings (with a terrace and barbecue) but also because the seafood is wonderfully fresh. Suggestions are chalked up on the board – *salade terre-mer*, langoustine *fricassée*, monkfish on skewers, grilled bass and, for afters, fresh pineapple and meringue. Star choices include the fish *cassoulet*, the mouth-watering *salade bouvette*, with salmon, scallops and cuttlefish, the *éclade* of mussels served on pine needles with a dash of raspberry vinegar, and the glorious stuffed crab. There's a weekday lunch menu for €20, and other menus for €25–40. It's best to book several days in advance in season.

Couarde-sur-Mer (La)

17670 (3km N)

🏠 |●| Hôtel-restaurant La Salicorne

16 rue de l'Olivette; it's near the main street.
Ⓣ and Ⓕ05.46.29.82.37
Open *daily Jul–Aug and Easter holidays; weekend only in mid-season.* **Closed** *early Nov to Easter.*

Long dining room with a terrace that runs the full length of the establishment. The menu, €22, offers just a glimpse of the chef's great talent. To experience the best, order à la carte: the *clafoutis* of prawns with mushrooms, lobster stew with shellfish, bass with vanilla and crayfish with foie gras show his deft use of spices and flavours. You'll end up paying about €40 a head, which isn't all that bad for this pricey island. The modest rooms cost €31 for a double with basin. *Free coffee offered to our readers on presentation of this guide.*

🏠 |●| Hôtel-restaurant Les Mouettes**

28 Grande-Rue. Opposite the church.
Ⓣ05.46.29.90.30 Ⓕ05.46.29.05.41
Closed *Sun afternoon Oct–March.* **TV. High chairs available.**

One of the most charming places on the island, yet one of the least expensive. Some ten rooms look over the interior terrace, with another twelve in an annexe on a very quiet street. Doubles with shower/wc cost €41–64. Book early if you want to stay in summer, as there are regulars who return every year. The terrace is open all day, with affordable menus at €15, €18 and €22. One of the best value for money on the island. Try the bass with fennel, duck breast with honey and spices, or the cod with peppers; all the fish is freshly caught, of course. *10% discount on the room rate for a minimum two night stay, offered to our readers on presentation of this guide.*

🏠 |●| Hôtel Le Vieux Gréement

13 place Carnot; it's behind the church.
Ⓣ05.46.29.82.18 Ⓕ05.46.29.50.79
Ⓦwww.levieuxgreement.com
Hotel open *all year*; **Bar closed** *on Wed except Jul–Aug.* **Closed** *mid-Nov to mid-March.* **Disabled access. TV.**

This hotel has been tastefully restored, drawing inspiration from the colours of the sea. The well-appointed rooms with shower/wc or bath go for €46–69 out of season and €74–96 in season; those overlooking the square are charming. Be sure to book in advance. They no longer have a proper restaurant but they do serve oysters and tasty filled sandwiches at the bar. Eat them out the terrace or in the courtyard, which is shaded by a vine-covered arbour.

|●| Au Jardin du Pélican

Impasse du Diable; at the end of the Grande-Rue de la Raigon, on the corner of the impasse.
Open *daily July–Aug.* **Closed** *Sun evening to Thurs lunch in May, June and Sept; early Nov to Easter.*

The owner's father is a highly reputed fishmonger, so fish of the highest quality is guaranteed here. His wife will greet you warmly and offer you oysters, grilled sardines with a pinch of salt or a delicious *mouclade*. Everything is cooked simply to allow its flavours to express themselves freely. Dishes around €10. The wines, served by the glass, are more than passable. A popular spot with cyclists, as there is a bike trail nearby.

|●| Restaurant La Cabine de Bain

33 Grande-Rue; at the beginning of the pedestrian street.
Ⓣ 05.46.29.84.26

Closed *Tues lunch (April to mid-Sept); Tues all day until mid-Nov; open on weekends only the rest of the year.* **Disabled access.**

Run by a dynamic young couple who focus on the fish from the area. Lunchtime menu €16, or reckon on around €30 à la carte. Original décor and attractive terrace giving onto the pedestrian street.

Boyardville

17190

La Roue Tourne

It's on the left of the road from Boyardville to Sauzelle, practically opposite the fishponds of the Surine.
05.46.47.21.47
Closed *Oct to end April.*

An unusual and delightful out-of-the-way place, run by the same family for more than thirty years. It's a stone house with beams and a huge open fireplace, and big communal tables with benches (plus cushions). Menus go for €28.50 and €29.50. Seafood is the speciality here, along with fish caught directly from the ponds across the road. Around 11pm in season, when you've struggled your way through a vast seafood platter, the atmosphere hots up as the owner gets out his guitar and leads the gathering in a chorus of *Viva España* and other cheesy classics. There's no other place like it on the island. You should book for dinner, but it's not necessary at lunchtime, when the atmosphere is quieter.

Chalais

16210

Le Relais du Château

15 rue du Château Talleyrand.
05.45.98.23.58
Closed *Sun evening; Mon.* **Car park.**

The restaurant occupies the old guard room of the enormous fourteenth-century château of the Talleyrands, which dominates the Tude and the Vivonne rivers. You reach it across a working drawbridge. There's a period interior, with a vaulted ceiling that gives the dining room real style. The chef, committed to using only fresh produce, adopts an innovative approach to typical local dishes. Specialities include roast turbot, lobster ravioli with truffles and foie gras. Weekday lunch menu €16.50, and others at €21.50–28.50. *Free house liqueur offered to our readers on presentation of this guide.*

Charroux

86250

Hostellerie Charlemagne**

7 rue de Rochemeaux; it's next to the ruined abbey, opposite the covered market.
05.49.87.50.37
Closed *Sun evening and Mon except in July–Aug.* **TV. Car park.**

The décor of this inn, built from stone from the ruined abbey, takes you back to a romantic past. The rooms are comfortable – no. 8, with its bathroom of dressed stone, is very special. Doubles go for €35 with shower/wc or bath. As for dining, tasty dishes include grilled snail *tartines*, goat's cheese salad in honey and lavender sauce, rack of lamb with unpeeled garlic cloves, and apple *galettes* with Calvados caramel. Prices are fair, with menus from €16 to €34.

Châtelaillon-Plage

17340

Hôtel d'Orbigny**

47 bd. de la République; it's between the town hall and Fort Saint-Jean.
05.46.56.24.68 05.46.30.04.82
www.hotel-dorbigny.com
Closed *early Dec to end Feb.* Swimming pool. High chairs available. **TV. Car park.**

This reliable hotel began life as a holiday home at the start of the twentieth century. It's a large, typical seaside building just 100m from the beach – and there's a swimming pool so you can take a dip when the tide goes out (it can recede a good kilometre hereabouts). The rooms, decorated simply but attractively, prove fair value, though those with carpeted walls are inevitably rather dull and dark. Doubles go for €40–51 with shower/wc or bath. Though the rooms over the street have good double glazing, those on the swimming pool side are quietest. Note that there's a charge for the car park in July and August. *One free breakfast per room offered to our readers on presentation of this guide.*

Hôtel Victoria**

13 av. du Général-Leclerc.
Ⓣ05.46.30.01.10 Ⓕ05.46.56.10.09
Ⓔhotel.victoria@fresbee.fr
Closed *Dec.* **TV. Pay car park.**

Typical late eighteenth-century seaside building that has been vigorously brought back to life by the owners. They've refurbished the pleasant rooms in good taste, and offer doubles at €54–58 with shower/wc or bath. Half board at €63 per person. The station is just across the road but there are very few trains at night and the place is large enough for you to find a quiet room.

Les Flots**

52 bd. de la Mer; it's on the seashore.
Ⓣ05.46.56.23.42 Ⓕ05.46.56.99.37
Closed *Tues; Dec–Jan.* **Disabled access. TV. Car park.**

A quietly charming restaurant with a lovely parquet floor and attractive wooden furniture. Savour the aromas of high-class bistro cuisine, with a preponderance of fish dishes and traditional recipes, and try the wonderfully fresh skate wings with *beurre blanc* or one of their seafood platters. Pastries are cooked in-house, and they serve wine by the glass. There's a €23 menu; à la carte you can expect to pay around €40. They also offer double rooms with shower/wc or bath but half board is compulsory and go for €60–72 per person.

Bains des Fleurs

76 bd. de la Mer; opposite the beach.
Ⓣ05.46.56.00.58
Closed *Wed out of season; mid-Nov to end Jan.* **Disabled access.**

At last, an authentic crêperie that is not in Brittany. The word has gone around and booking is essential in season (particularly if you want a table on the lovely terrace overlooking the sea). We must admit that we haven't tried all the crêpes, but then there are nearly 125 of them, all based on fresh ingredients. There really is something for everybody, from classical recipes to audacious creations, from humble snacks to elaborate delicacies. Reckon on around €15 for a whole meal. The crêpes are churned out all day long, but the diligent staff never loses its good humour. *Free coffee offered to our readers on presentation of this guide.*

Chauvigny

86300

Hôtel-restaurant Le Lion d'Or**

8 rue du Marché; it's on the N151. Beside the church.
Ⓣ05.49.46.30.28 Ⓕ05.49.47.74.28
Closed *24 Dec–2 Jan.* **Disabled access. TV. Car park.**

A traditional hotel in the heart of town next to the church. The bedrooms – some in the main building, others situated in an annexe overlooking the quiet car park at the back – have all been done up, and there's one family room. They charge €42 for doubles with shower/wc or bath. In the good-looking dining room, you'll eat tasty dishes like lamb *noisette* with warm goat's cheese, sole with chipped courgettes and *gâteau de crêpe soufflé* with raspberry *coulis*. They have a choice of five menus €16–34.

Le Chalet Fleuri**

31 av. Aristide-Briand; take the Poitiers road out of Chavigny then first left after the bridge over the Vienne.
Ⓣ05.49.46.31.12
Restaurant closed *Mon lunchtime except public holidays.* **TV. High chairs available. Car park.**

This hotel is a fairly modern building surrounded by gardens and trees on the banks of the River Vienne, just outside the village. It's very peaceful, and the spacious interior is nice and bright. Guest rooms are impeccable, with comfortable beds and views either of the river or of the medieval town. Doubles €43 with shower or bath/wc. Half board at €38.50 per person. They serve appealing, traditional cuisine in the large, attractive dining room: try veal *blanquette* or frogs' legs *à la provençale*. Weekday menu at €13 and others €16–33.60.

Les Choucas

21 rue des Puys, Ville Haute; it's in the medieval town.
Ⓣ05.49.46.36.42
Closed *Tues and Wed Oct–March; Jan.* **Games available.**

The setting is welcoming with lots of character, and as you go up the splendid medieval staircase to the first floor you'll smell glorious aromas emanating from the kitchens. Try *farci poitevin* (green vegetables and herbs mixed with pork fat, cream and eggs, wrapped in cabbage leaves and poached in ham and pork stock), pan-fried foie gras, rabbit stew. Menus €13–32. They also offer good local wines by the jug and an apéritif known as "courtisane", made to a medieval recipe using rosé wine steeped with cinnamon and ginger. *Free house apéritif or coffee offered to our readers on presentation of this guide.*

Cognac

16100

L'Étape**

2 av. d'Angoulême; it's on the N14 on the way to Jarnac, take D945 Châteaubernard.
05.45.32.16.15 05.45.36.20.03
www.hotel-letape.com
Closed *Sat lunchtime; Sun evening.* **TV. Car park.**

With its informal welcome and homely atmosphere, this is an ideal base if you want to visit the Hennessy or Martell Cognac houses. Comfy doubles with basin and shower go for €39, €45 with shower/wc or bath. There are two dining rooms here; the one on the ground floor is a brasserie offering a €10 *menu rapide* (weekdays only), while in the basement a more traditional dining room features a range of sophisticated menus, €12–22, with local dishes such as chicken *confit* with Pineau or steak with Cognac.

Restaurant La Boune Goule

42 allée de la Corderie. It's in the town centre.
05.45.82.06.37
Closed *Sun and Mon out of season.* **High chairs available.**

Typically Charentes – a quiet cosy atmosphere, characterful country-style décor and good home-made food. Portions are generous – try the local snails, house terrine with Cognac, tripe in Pineau or rib of beef in Cognac. The cheapest menu costs €12 with a carafe of Bordeaux (not Sun) while others cost €16—22 (wine not included). Musical evenings Fri and Sat in summer, or Sat only in winter. *Free house apéritif or liqueur offered to our readers on presentation of this guide.*

Le Coq d'Or

33 pl. François 1er. In town centre.
05.45.82.02.56
Open *all year, noon–midnight.* **Disabled access. High chairs available.**

This is a Parisian-style brasserie right in the middle of town. Quick service, friendly welcome, a good range of prices and lots to choose from à la carte: salads, *choucroute*, shellfish, grills, calf's head, and so on. There are also some very delicious specialities such as scallops steam-cooked in Cognac; veal chops with ceps deglazed with Cognac or *moules marinière* with Pineau. Go for the Charentais desserts: *jonchet* (cream cheese, drained on rush mats) or *caillebotte* (sour milk served with sugar and a Cognac chaser). Portions are large. Menus €12.20–38. *Free coffee offered to our readers on presentation of this guide.*

Restaurant La Boîte à Sel

68 av. Victor-Hugo. Towards Angoulême.
05.45.32.07.68
Closed *Mon; 20 Dec–5 Jan.* **Disabled access.**

The chef in this converted grocer's store is committed to promoting regional produce and he changes his menus with the season. He's kept the shop's original shelves and windows, using them now to display a range of fine wines and cognacs, many of which can be served by the glass. Excellent cooking: snails, rolled sole fillets stuffed with Dublin Bay prawns, three chocolate *fondants*. Menus at €14 (weekdays) up to €40, or €30 à la carte. Whatever you eat, start with a glass of iced Cognac.

Segonzac

16130 (14km SE)

La Cagouillarde

18 rue Gaston-Briande; take the D24 towards Barbezieux.
05.45.83.40.51
Closed *Sat lunchtime; Sun evening; Mon.*

The unusual décor in this old hotel combines rustic and modern styles. To judge by the décor the first dining room was probably the old bistro, but it's so large it really needs a crowd to achieve any kind of atmosphere. The second, more intimate room has a large fireplace fuelled with vine cuttings for the grills. There's also a terrace for the summer. Food is good – though portions aren't over-generous – with lots of regional specialities like stuffed Cagouille snails (a local variety), ham with shallots and vinegar or grilled lamb cutlets with walnut oil. They also offer a nice selection of Pineau wines. Weekday lunch menu at €12, with others at €18.30 and €25.15, or around €23 à la carte.

Confolens

16500

La Mère Michelet**

19 allée de Blossac.
Ⓣ05.45.84.04.11 Ⓕ05.45.84.00.92
Ⓔmere.michelet@wanadoo.fr
TV. Car park.

A dynamic family-run business that's become something of a local institution. In the restaurant try any of the local dishes – duck breast with Pineau, veal escalope à la Charentaise, Saint-Barthélemy veal sweetbreads – and the tempting homemade pastries. Menus €12–35 and à la carte. Classic, clean bedrooms go for €29 with basin, €32–40 with shower/wc or with bath.

Dangé-Saint-Romain

86220

Le Damius**

16 rue de la Gare. Coming from Chatellerault, 3rd traffic lights on the right; coming from Tours, 2nd traffic lights on the left.
Ⓣ05.49.86.40.28 Ⓕ05.49.93.13.69
High chairs and games available. TV. Car park.

A little family hotel, lovingly run by Michel and Martine Malbrant, with a restaurant overlooking the terrace and a garden especially designed for kids. The cooking is good, with menus from €14.50–32. Try the zander with *beurre blanc*, the chicken with Sauvignon or pig's trotter. Double rooms cost €45 with shower/wc or €51 with bath. The hotel is soundproofed but light sleepers should note that the TGV line does run past. Credit cards not accepted. *Free house apéritif offered to our readers on presentation of this guide.*

Font-d'Usson (La)

86350

Auberge de l'Écurie**

It's on the D727, 3.5km from Usson-du-Poitou.
Ⓣ05.49.59.53.84 Ⓕ05.49.58.04.50
Closed *Sun evening except public holidays; a fortnight in Oct*. **Disabled access. TV. Car park.**

In a wonderfully remote rural location, this place is in a beautifully converted stable that's been decorated in rustic style. The simple dishes, cooked using quality ingredients, include scallops, lamb noisette with herbs, *civet* of kid with wild garlic. Menus at €13 except Sunday, €24 and €34.30. In summer there's a tearoom where you can enjoy home-made pastries and cakes. The ten comfortable double rooms, all with shower/wc, go for €39. *Free coffee offered to our readers on presentation of this guide.*

Fouras

17450

Grand Hôtel des Bains**

15 rue du Général-Brüncher; it's 50m from the Vauban fort and the beach.
Ⓣ05.46.8403.44 Ⓕ05.46.84.58.26
Ⓦwww.perso.wanadoo.fr/grand.hotel.des.bains
Closed *1 Nov–15 March*. **TV. Pay car park.**

Attractive old coaching inn right in the middle of Fouras. The classic rooms have some style, and most of them look out onto the pretty garden where you eat breakfast in the summer. Doubles with shower/wc cost €40–60, or €45–80 with bath/wc. Menus €18.15–28.50.

Hôtel La Roseraie**

2 av. du Port-Nord; follow the signs for port de la Fumée.
Ⓣ05.46.84.64.89
Open *all year*. **Disabled access. TV.**

Monsieur and Madame Lacroix lavish lots of attention on their little hotel, a detached house with an unlikely-looking entrance hall done up to look like a 1950s nightclub. Prices are reasonable for the area: bright, clean doubles, all of which overlook the sea or garden, cost €48–58 with shower/wc or bath. Credit cards not accepted but dogs are. The welcome varies.

Grand-Village

17370

Le Relais des Salines

Port des Salines. Take the D126, it's at 11km South of Château-d'Oléron.
☎05.46.75.82.42
Closed *Sun evening and Mon out of season; mid-Oct to mid-March.* **Disabled access.**

You'll find this attractive restaurant in one of a cluster of brightly painted wooden huts beside the canals in the marshes. Wherever you dine, be it inside or at one of the tables on a boat moored on the quay, the food is delicious and good value, with superb fish and seafood specialities including warm oysters with *fondue* of leeks or red mullet fillets with Pineau. The short lunch menu (not Sunday) lists half a dozen oysters, pan-fried *céteaux* (which resembles sole) and a delicious *crème brûlée*, all for €15. Going à la carte will set you back around €25.

Jarnac

16200

Restaurant du Château

15 pl. du Château.
☎05.45.81.07.17
Closed *Sun and Wed evenings; Mon; 2–17 Jan; 6–27 Aug.*

With a cosy dining room painted yellow and blue, this is the best restaurant in the area, and the cooking is taken very seriously indeed. Dishes change with the seasons and what's fresh at the market, but specialities include foie gras *mille-feuille*, pan-fried langoustine tails with orange, *tournedos* Rossini, and iced soufflé with Cognac. They offer a weekday lunchtime menu at €17.50, with others from €26–39.50 and various options à la carte. The wine list is as impressive as the cooking and includes more than one hundred Bordeaux vintages. *Free house apéritif offered to our readers on presentation of this guide.*

Jonzac

17500

Hôtel Le Club**

8 pl. de l'Église.
☎05.46.48.02.27 Ⓕ05.46.48.17.15
Closed *Sat–Sun evening out of season; Dec.* **High chairs available. TV. Car park.**

This little hotel, which stands on the church square, offers large, clean, well-equipped bedrooms. Nos. 1, 2, 3 and 4 are the biggest. Doubles with shower/wc are €40 or €47 with bath – excellent value for the location. The dining room serves good-quality brasserie and bistro food; à la carte only, you'll pay around €20. Good value for money. *Free coffee offered to our readers on presentation of this guide.*

Clam

7500 (6km N)

Hôtel-restaurant Le Vieux-Logis**

Take the D142 in the direction of Pons.
☎05.46.70.20.13 Ⓕ05.46.70.20.64
Ⓔinfo@vieuxlogis.com
Closed *Sun evening; Mon lunchtime; 5 Jan–5 Feb.* **Disabled access. High chairs available. Swimming pool. TV. Car park.**

You'll feel as if you've been invited to a friend's house when you walk into this welcoming country inn. The owner used to be a photographer and his prints decorate the walls. Madame's cooking is first-rate, with lots of traditional family dishes and regional specialities. Try the pan-fried veal sweetbreads flambéed in Cognac, the *gratinée* of oysters with foie gras or the house foie gras. They offer a €15 menu (not served Sun), and another at €32. Guest rooms, which all overlook a small garden, are in a separate, modern style chalet with private terrace; doubles cost €41–44 with shower/wc and €50–53 with bath. There's a small swimming pool and you can even borrow mountain bikes. Reservations are recommended.

Loudun

86200

Le Ricordeau

Place de la Boeuffeterie. Town centre; by the church.
☎05.49.22.67.27 Ⓕ05.49.22.53.16
Closed *Sun evening; Sat lunchtime in July and Aug; Mon out of season; Feb school holidays.* **TV. High chairs available.**

An enthusiastic young couple own this characterful establishment right in the middle of old Loudun. They offer just three simple, spruce rooms, each of which

is very spacious – though not perfectly soundproofed. Doubles are €35 with shower/wc or bath. The large, bright dining room is an attractive setting for a meal, and in summer you can eat on a flowery terrace right next to the Saint-Pierre church. It's very high-class cuisine here, with tasty, subtle dishes like rump steak with snails and cream, beef cheek *millefeuille* with tomato *confit*, zander fillet with saffron, chocolate *île flottante*. Half board at €45 per person. The *formule* express, €11.40, gets you a main course, choice of starter or dessert and a drink, while other menus range from €14.45 to €31.90. The prices for the wines are a little high but, all in all, given the quality of the welcome, the tasty dishes and the good value, that's a mere quibble.

Hostellerie de la Roue d'Or**

1 av. d'Anjou.
☎ 05.49.98.01.23 Ⓕ 05.49.22.31.05
Closed *Sat; Sun evening Oct–Easter.*
Disabled access. High chairs available. TV. Car park.

This cosy former coaching inn stands at a quiet crossroads, its pink walls swathed in Virginia creeper. In the restaurant, really good regional dishes include calf's head in a warm vinaigrette, ravioli stuffed with foie gras... There's a €13 menu served during the week, with others up to €34.60. The bedrooms are in the same provincial vein as the restaurant; the more characterful ones have beamed ceilings, while those on the side of the building are quietest. Half board is at €43 per person. All doubles cost €42.70. *Free house apéritif offered to our readers on presentation of this guide.*

Marans

17230

La Porte Verte

20 quai Foch. Take the N137, then the main street and rue de la Maréchaussée.
☎ 05.46.01.09.45
Ⓦ www.la-porte-verde.com
Closed *Wed; Nov to end Feb.* **TV.**

This place, in the most attractive part of Marans, has a pocket-handkerchief garden overlooking the Pomère canal – a nice place to dine on a warm evening. Inside, there are two charming, cosy dining rooms; the larger one has a magnificent fireplace with a roaring fire in winter. The cuisine is of a high standard, putting an inventive spin on the best regional dishes: choose rabbit terrine with Vix or the eel with parsley. Menus €15–28. There's a good wine list, too. As for the guest rooms, they're rather magnificent, with enormous bathrooms, rugs and regional style's furniture. The rooms prove good value at €50–72 including breakfast.

Saint-Cyr-du-Doret

17170 (14km SE)

La Pommerie

Take the D116 in the direction of Taugon; 150m after the lieu-dit Margot, look out for the sign to turn left.
☎ 05.46.27.85.59
Open *Thurs–Sun lunchtime; Sat evening.*
Closed *Feb.* **Disabled access.**

To open a restaurant in the countryside is a real challenge..However, Catherine and Gilles were proved to be right with this peaceful place surrounded by an apple orchard. This nice country restaurant presents a rustic look and offers lovingly prepared local food: try the house terrine, snail stew, parsleyed eels or zander *paupiettes*. Portions are massive, and it's excellent value for money.

Mauléon

79700

Hôtel-restaurant L'Europe**

15 rue de l'Hôpital; it's the continuation of la Grand'Rue.
☎ 05.49.81.40.33 Ⓕ 05.49.81.62.47
Ⓦ www.hotelrestaurantleurope.com
Closed *Fri–Sun evenings (Oct–April); Sun evening to Mon lunchtime (May–Sept); Christmas–New Year.* **Disabled access. TV. Car park.**

This former coaching inn has been operating for more than a hundred years, but its combination of modern décor and Jacques Durand's generous portions of elaborate dishes has given it a new lease of life. Menus, €11.45–28.50, list such dishes as fresh foie gras with oyster mushrooms, salmon terrine, oysters cooked in cider, pear with goat's cheese, sautéed farm chicken with crayfish and a lovely apple turnover. Elegant bedrooms from €36.50

with shower/wc or €38.10 with bath. *Free apéritif offered to our readers on presentation of this guide.*

Cerizay

79140 (14km NW)

Hôtel du Cheval Blanc**

33 av. du 25-Août; on the D744, in the direction of Cholet.
05.49.80.05.77 05.49.80.08.74
Closed *Sat and Sun out of season (unless you book in advance); 17–23 May; 20 Dec–9 Jan.* **Restaurant closed** *Sun in season.* **TV. High chairs available. Disabled access. Car park.**

Comfortable, well-equipped rooms, some of them recently refurbished; ask for numbers 21 to 26 – these are quieter as they overlook a small, mossy garden. Doubles €40.40–47.The enormous dining room is dominated by an impressive fireplace, used to grill the house specialities of fish and game. The portions could be bigger, but the meat is particularly delicious. Menus €10.60–19.80. Good wine list.

Melle

79500

Hôtel-restaurant Les Glycines**

5 pl. René-Groussard.
05.49.27.01.11 05.49.27.93.45
www.paysmellois.com/lesglycines/index.htm
Closed *Sun evening –Mon except July–Aug.* **High chairs available. TV.**

Housed in an impressive nineteenth-century building, this hotel takes its name from the wisteria that smothers it. Expect to pay €42 for a double with shower/wc or €47 with bath. The kitchen has a great reputation locally, and the warm, traditional dining room is a nice place to eat dishes such as eel stew, salad of pan-fried pigeon and crayfish, roast rabbit with wild garlic, *farci poitevin*, shortcake with caramelized apples and rosemary ice-cream. Half board goes for €37.50–40.50 per person. There's a €13.50 menu served during the week only, then others from €15–34. You'll pay around €48.50 for a meal à la carte The cooking may be refined, but you'll get an informal, relaxed welcome and service.

Celles-sur-Belle

79370 (8km NW)

Auberge de l'Hostellerie**

1 place des Époux-Laurant; it's opposite the church.
05.49.32.93.32 05.49.79.72.65
www.hotel-restaurant-abbaye.com
Closed *Sun evening; 15 Feb–3 March; 22 Oct–3 Nov.* **Disabled access. TV. High chairs available. Car park.**

Offering good value and attentive service (maybe overly so), this inn enjoys a nice setting and a peaceful little terrace from where you can watch them preparing your food in the kitchens. The elegant, original dishes show off fascinating flavours while keeping in the traditional mould; try the salmon with langoustine's tail or the codfish with warm vinegar. Menus start at €8.84 weekday lunchtime, then go for €12–40. The cocktails are excellent, too, and they offer a good wine list. Guest rooms are spotless, with a warm, refined décor; they go for €40–60. It's essential to book in advance.

Montmorillon

86500

Hôtel de France - Restaurant Le Lucullus**

4 bd. de Strasbourg; it's opposite the Sous-Préfecture.
05.49.84.09.09 05.49.84.58.68
www.lelucullus.com
Brasserie closed *Sat evening and Sun lunchtime May–Sept; Sat evening and Sun Oct–April.*
Restaurant closed *Sun evening and Mon except public holidays; 12 Nov–1 Dec.*
Disabled access. TV. Pay car park.

Air-conditioned doubles with shower/wc or bath from €43–53, room number 205 is the most spacious one. In the bistro, they serve a three-course lunch *formule* for €13 including wine and coffee, along with a range of salads and grills, while the restaurant offers five menus ranging from €18 to €43. This is a place for anyone who takes their food seriously; the chef takes great care in preparing the elaborate, seasonal dishes, and everything, even the bread, is made in-house. Star dishes include a trio of foie gras with *saveurs* Poitou-Charentes, and in spring, suckling lamb *montmorillonnais*.

Le Roman des Saveurs

2 rue Montebello. 5min to the town centre.
05.49.91.52.06
Closed *Sun evening; Jan.* **Disabled access.**

The young couple who run this restaurant fell in love with the area and decided to sell their restaurant in Paris to settle here. They've done a good job of restoring the eighteenth-century mansion, part of which was once a prison; different staircases lead to four small dining rooms with venerable wooden beams and tasteful pictures all around the stone walls. There's nothing fussy to distract you from your food, which is simple, fresh and ungimmicky, listed on menus ranging from €13.50 to €25. Ask for a table in the bay window that looks down on the Gartempe. *Free house apéritif offered to our readers on presentation of this guide.*

Niort

79000

France Hôtel**

8 rue des Cordeliers; it's in the town centre.
05.49.24.01.34 05.49.24.24.50
wwwfrancehotelniort.ht.st
Open *all year.* **Closed** *Sun afternoon.* **TV. Pay car park.**

The rooms are regularly renovated, they're all quiet and many of them overlook the charming interior courtyard. Doubles €38 with bath. There's a cupboard full of comics in the lobby. *Parking space offered (15 Sept–1 June) to our readers on presentation of this guide.*

Hôtel du Moulin**

27 rue de l'Espingole; it's on the riverbank on the Nantes road.
05.49.09.07.07 05.49.09.19.40
Disabled access. TV. Car park.

This recently built hotel, overlooking the River Sèvre, offers very comfortable bedrooms with bath, telephone and radio. Doubles €43 with double bed, doubles €48 with twin beds, shower/wc or bath. Two of them are designed especially for disabled visitors and nine have a balcony overlooking the neighbouring gardens. This is where the performers stay when they're appearing at the cultural centre across the river; if you want to know if anybody famous has stayed in your room, you can check the list pinned up at reception. Good value for money.

Hôtel de Paris**

12 av. de Paris.
05.49.24.93.78 05.49.28.27.57
www.hotelparis79.com
Closed *24 Dec–2 Jan.* **TV. Pay car park.**

This is a nice-looking, welcoming building with identical guest rooms which have all been repainted. Doubles €48–50 with shower/wc or bath. It's near the centre, with lots of restaurants nearby. *Free parking offered to our readers on presentation of this guide.*

Le Grand Hôtel-Best Western***

32 av. de Paris; it's near place de la Brèche and well signposted.
05.49.24.22.21 05.49.24.42.41
Closed *a week at the end of the year.* **TV. Pay car park.**

This hotel has been refurbished and returned to its former glory with a charming dining room, a nice bar leading onto a patio, and a pretty garden with terrace. The owners go to a great deal of trouble for their guests – offering sweet or salt butter at breakfast, say – and the prices are good, with doubles at €70–80 with shower/wc or bath. Rooms with numbers ending in a 5, 6 or 7 overlook the internal garden, where you can have breakfast. *The prices quoted here are special rates for Routard/Rough Guide readers (representing a 15% discount), so you'll need to show this guide or mention it when booking.*

Restaurant Les Quatre Saisons

247 av. de La Rochelle. Outskirts of the town, towards La Rochelle.
05.49.79.41.06
Closed *Sun; 1–16 Aug.* **Disabled access.**

A family-run restaurant offering sound, traditional, and often regional, cooking – dishes like stuffed snails, eel stew with wine from the Haut-Poitou, pork *filet mignon* with Pineau des Charentes, goat's cheeses and angelica soufflé. The cheapest menu costs €10 during the week, with others €11–30. *Free coffee offered to our readers on presentation of this guide.*

La Tartine du Pressoir

2 rue de la Boule d'Or.
05.49.28.20.14
Closed *Sat lunchtime; Sun.*

Just off Niort's noisy main square, this

charming place is housed in the old stables of a nineteenth-century coaching inn. They serve a huge choice of salads, tarts, meat and fish dishes, along with tasty sandwiches made using country bread; menus start at €12.50 (weekdays only), and then others €18.40–23.80. Good specialities include bass in a salt crust and grilled fillets of red mullet with Parmesan risotto. Watch out for the desserts, though, which can be pricey. There's a fine wine list – hardly surprising, since the restaurant is next door to the most famous wine merchant in town. It's safest to book a table. *Free house apéritif offered to our readers on presentation of this guide.*

|●| La Table des Saveurs

9 rue Thiers. Between Les Halles and the town hall.
Ⓣ05.49.77.44.35
Closed *Sun except public holidays.* **Disabled access. High chairs available.**

An efficient, refined place in the centre of town, where classic food – lots of fish – is served with good wines. Menus, €14.50–43, list such dishes as foie gras with nine flavours, chicory tart, pan-fried monkfish. You'll pay around €40 for a meal à la carte.

|●| Restaurant La Créole

54 av. du 24-Février; it's near the tourist office.
Ⓣ05.49.28.00.26
Closed *Sat-Mon lunchtimes; evenings (except Thurs); Aug.*

An exotic restaurant for this rural part of the country – it's brightly coloured and fun, with spicy dishes that smack of the Caribbean. You'll spend about €20 à la carte. Good dishes include blaff of fish, *Creole boudin* and *massalé* of pork from Réunion. *Free Accras cocktail offered to our readers on presentation of this guide.*

Coulon

79510 (13km W)

Hôtel au Marais***

46–48 quai Louis-Tardy; it's on the towpath.
Ⓣ05.49.35.90.43 Ⓕ05.49.35.81.98
Ⓦwww.hotelaumarais.com
Closed *15 Dec–1 Feb.* **Disabled access. TV.**

A classic riverside hotel where you can really relax. Bright cheerful doubles go for €65–75 with shower/wc or bath; some have river views. The owners organize enjoyable walks through this intriguing area of lakes and marshes. It's best to book.

Arçais

79210 (20km W)

|●| Auberge de la Venise Verte

14 rte. de Damoix. Take the D3 towards Saint-Georges-de-Rex, Arçais is at 4km.
Ⓣ05.49.35.37.15
Closed *Tues and Sun evenings; Wed; otherwise Sun evening only in summer; mid-Nov to end March.* **Disabled access. Car park.**

Nicely renovated restaurant with a family atmosphere and muted décor. They offer a wealth of regional dishes, including *farci poitevin*, *choucroute*, eel *millefeuille* and good sliced country ham, with menus from €11 for a lunchtime weekday menu; other menus go for €15–23. They also have a nice (rather pricey) wine list. There's a grassy play area for the kids and they serve up to 10pm. Try the house apéritif, the *troussepinette* – it's delicious.

Villiers-en-Bois

79360 (23km SE)

L'Auberge des Cèdres

Take the N150 Beauvoir-sur-Niort, then towards Zoorama road in Chizée.
Ⓣ05.49.76.79.53 Ⓕ05.49.76.79.81
Ⓔpascale-regis@wanadoo.fr
Closed *Sun evening; Mon; end Feb.* **Disabled access. TV. High chairs and games available. Car park.**

The rooms here are peaceful, sizeable and comfortable, though a few details need attention – tired décor, neon lights and snowstorms on the TV when it rains. Doubles €35–40 with shower/wc or bath. Menus €15–30.50. Credit cards not accepted. *Free coffee offered to our readers on presentation of this guide.*

Parthenay

79200

|●| La Truffade

14 place du 11 Novembre.
Ⓣ05.49.64.02.26
Closed *Tues; Wed; 3 weeks in spring; 3 weeks in autumn.* **Disabled access. Car park.**

This place has a strong taste of the Auvergne, from the décor and the cuisine

right down to the cubes of Tome de Laguiole cheese and the apéritif. There's accordion music in the background and an occasional shout from the boss, all tempered by the good-natured serving staff. Specialities are full of flavour and precisely prepared – try the *truffade* (garlic, potato and cheese bake), tripe, aligot (potato mash with *tomme* cheese and garlic) or cabbage stuffed with duck *confit*, and round it off with one of the home-made desserts. Menus €13–30. They have a nice terrace on the square.

Poitiers

86000

Auberge de jeunesse

1 allée Roger-Tagault; from the train station, take the no. 3 bus in the direction of Pierre-Loti to the "Cap Sud" stop. By car, take the road to Bordeaux and turn right towards Bellejouanne.
Ⓣ05.49.30.09.70 Ⓕ05.49.30.09.79
Ⓦwww.fuaj.org
Disabled access. Car park.

As more than a quarter of Poitiers' population is made up of students, it is bound to have a youth hostel worthy of the name. The spruce rooms, decorated in pale colours, have four beds each. €9.30 a night per person. All-in package of night's accommodation plus meal: €10.70 for ages under 26 and €15.25 for those over 26. Dish of the day €4.90. €2.80 for hire of sheets. Camp site available at €5.30 a night per person. Leisure park spanning 8000 sq. m, offering activities like archery, football and badminton. You can also rent a mountain bike. Inside: hi-fi system, pool table and a big dining room overlooking the park. You can also do your own cooking, as a kitchen complete with crockery is available to guests. The municipal library and swimming pool are close by.

Hôtel Le Paris*

123 bd. du Grand-Cerf; it's opposite the train station.
Ⓣ05.49.58.39.37
Restaurant closed *Sat evening and Sun.*
Hotel open *all year.* **TV.**

The 1960s architecture may be dated, and the location a touch noisy, but this place is one of the better examples of old-school hotel-keeping. You'll be pampered by the staff, who know the area well, and you can eat good food at reasonable prices. Try the *fricassée* of small eels caught in the marsh, duck fillet with pears or the local lamb. Menus €10–35. Doubles €23 with basin, €30 with shower and TV.

Inter Hôtel Continental**

2 bd. Solférino; it's opposite the train station.
Ⓣ05.49.37.93.93 Ⓕ05.49.53.01.16
Ⓦwww.continental-poitiers.com
Open all year. **Disabled access. TV.**

Classic hotel with clean, well-planned bedrooms; rooms 204, 209 and 304 are the most spacious. Doubles with shower/wc or bath €42–50, depending on season; the rates drop slightly at the weekend. Buffet breakfast €6.

Hôtel du Chapon Fin**

Place du Maréchal-Leclerc; it's near the town hall.
Ⓣ05.49.88.02.97 Ⓕ05.49.88.91.63
Ⓔhotel.chaponfin-poitiers@wanadoo.fr
Closed *Sun afternoon until 7pm; 29 Dec–12 Jan.* **TV. Pay car park.**

The quiet bedrooms here are spacious and each one is decorated differently. They cost €44–48 with shower/wc and from €49–53 with bath. *10% discount on the room rate offered to our readers on presentation of this guide.*

Le Plat d'Étain**

7–9 rue du Plat-d'Étain; it's next to the town hall, behind the theatre.
Ⓣ05.49.41.04.80 Ⓕ05.49.52.25.84
Ⓔhotelduplatdetain@wanadoo.fr
TV. Pay car park.

A restored coaching inn hidden away in a narrow side street in the centre. The rooms are comfortable, quiet and spotless, and each one is given a name rather than a number. "Basilic", "Absinthe" and "Aneth" in the eaves have lovely views of the bell tower of Saint-Porchaire, and some look into the interior courtyard. Those on the third floor are non-smoking. Doubles with basin €26, shower/wc €45, bath €50.

Le Terminus**

3 bd. Pont-Achard. Opposite the train station.
Ⓣ05.49.62.92.30 Ⓕ05.49.62.92.40
TV. Pay car park.

A large hotel, lovingly run by a charming couple. The quiet bedrooms – some of them rustic, with sloping ceilings, and others more modern – have all been soundproofed to block out the noise of the station opposite. Doubles €48 with shower/wc and €53 with bath. There's a bar for guests. *10% discount on the room rate offered to our readers on presentation of this guide.*

🏠 Hôtel de l'Europe**

39 rue Carnot; it's opposite the Carnot car park.
Ⓣ05.49.88.12.00 Ⓕ05.49.88.97.30
Ⓦwww.hoteldeleuropepoitiers.com
Disabled access. TV. Pay car park €4 per day.

Attractive, individual and well-equipped rooms. Opt for those in the small courtyard, where some look onto a garden. Doubles with shower/wc or bath cost €52–57, and the buffet breakfast will set you back €6.50.

🏠 Le Grand Hôtel***

28 rue Carnot; it's opposite the Carnot car park.
Ⓣ05.49.60.90.60 Ⓕ05.49.62.81.89
Ⓦwww.grandhotelpoitiers.fr
Disabled access. High chairs available. TV. Pay car park.

A quiet, decent hotel in the heart of the city, with Art Deco-style interior and spacious, well-equipped rooms with air conditioning. Doubles with shower/wc are €72.50, €80.50 with bath, and the buffet breakfast costs €9. *One free breakfast per person offered to our readers on presentation of this guide.*

IOI Restaurant Les Bons Enfants

11 bis rue Cloche-Perse; it's near the town centre.
Ⓣ05.49.41.49.82
Closed *Mon; 1–7 Feb.* **Disabled access.**

This place, in Poitiers' delightful sixteenth-century walled city, is straight out of a fairy tale. The walls are decorated with a large fresco of *Alice in Wonderland*, there are angel clocks and old photographs of school children dotted around. The food's good too, with €8 and €10.50 lunchtime formulas, and menus at € 18 and €22. Try the semi-cooked foie gras, calf's head with chive sauce or the fish stew, and round it off with a scrummy chocolate soufflé.

IOI Le Poitevin

76 rue Carnot; it's near the Carnot car park.
Ⓣ05.49.88.35.04
Closed *Sun; Easter school holidays; a fortnight in mid-July.* **Disabled access.**

This intimate restaurant has a pleasing décor with criss-cross beams. It's popular with businesspeople at lunchtime and with couples who want some quiet, intimate time together in the evening. There's a choice of five different dining rooms, all lit by candles. Menus, starting at €10 for the lunch *formule* and rising to €28, list classic regional dishes including beef fillet with foie gras or the *bouilleture* (eel cooked with wine, mushrooms, prunes, onions and herbs). *Free tasting of the house speciality rabbit dish on presentation of this guide.*

IOI Restaurant Chez Cul de Paille

3 rue Théophraste-Renaudot.
Ⓣ05.49.41.07.35
Closed *Sun; public holidays; Aug.*

The walls of this institution, yellowed with age, have scrawled messages from famous people all over them and strings of garlic and chilli peppers hanging from the beams. You sit on straw-seated stools and eat at wooden tables where they serve authentic regional cooking ranging from grilled kidneys *en brochette* to the local *farci poitevin*, a tasty variation of stuffed cabbage. Pork is a speciality. There's a weekday menu at €18.50, or you'll spend around €26 à la carte. It's open till late, but order before 11pm when prices shoot up.

IOI Restaurant Maxime

4 rue Saint-Nicholas. It's beside the Carnot-Préfecture-town hall in the town centre.
Ⓣ05.49.41.09.55
Closed *Sat lunchtime in winter; Sun; 14 July–20 Aug.*

Serving the best food in Poitiers, this fine restaurant is a gourmand's dream. There's a warmly decorated dining room where you can eat inspired, inventive food prepared with fresh produce. Specialities include hot oyster ravioli with herb butter, beef fillet Béarnaise, and hot soufflé with Grand Marnier. The *menu fraîcheur* goes for €19, while others range from €26–45. The convivial atmosphere just goes to show you don't have to lock yourself in an ivory tower to appreciate quality food, while the perfect service manages to be at once attentive and unobtrusive. *Free house apéritif offered to our readers on presentation of this guide.*

Saint-Benoît

86280 (2km S)

Le Chalet de Venise***

6 rue du Square; it's not far from the ruins of the Roman aqueduct.
Ⓣ05.49.88.45.07 Ⓕ05.49.52.95.44
Restaurant closed *Sun evening; Mon; Feb.* **Disabled access. High chairs available. TV. Car park.**

Wonderful, chic hotel with a lovely garden dotted with riverside fountains and vast, spreading trees, and a bright, uncluttered restaurant boasting a large bay window. The modern bedrooms go for €55 with terrace and shower/wc or bath. As for the food, every dish is skilfully prepared by Serge Mautret, a talented chef who's always searching for new flavours and combinations. Depending on the season, try the fine tart with rabbit and foie gras laced with Cognac, the Poitou snail ravioli or sweetbreads of veal. There's a weekday lunch menu for €25 and others at €32.50 and €40.55.

Coulombiers

86600 (12km SW)

Le Centre Poitou**

39 rte. Nationale; take the N11 towards Lusignan.
Ⓣ05.49.60.90.15 Ⓕ05.49.60.53.70
Ⓦwww.centrepoitou.com
Restaurant closed *Sun evening and Mon except July–Aug; autumn school holidays.* **Hotel open** *daily.* **Disabled access. TV. Car park.**

This large, charming restaurant is a gourmet's dream, serving subtle, refined cuisine – duckling with spiced caramel, poached chicken, warm foie gras *tartelettes* with sautéed truffles, Poitou lamb, and turbot cooked on the open grill and autumn fruit tart flavoured with vanilla. The menus, €19.50–60, are named after queens – "Clothilde", "Diana" and "Aliénoir" – and you eat like a king. Guest rooms have been enlarged and impressively renovated; doubles go for €40–84 with shower/wc or bath and depending on the season.

Vivonne

86370 (14km SW)

Le Saint-Georges**

12 Grande-Rue; it's beside the church.
Ⓣ05.49.89.01.89 Ⓕ05.49.89.00.22
Ⓦwww.hotel-st-georges.com
Open *daily until 10pm.* **Disabled access. TV.**

A very old hotel in the centre ofVivonne. It's slightly lacking in character since being entirely refurbished, but time will do its job, and the owner is extremely friendly and welcoming. There are 32 modern doubles with trouser press, hairdryer and TV; they go for €41–43 with shower/wc, €46–48 with bath. Buffet breakfast costs €5.50. It's very near Futuroscope, so if you want a room you should book in advance. Gourmet food in the restaurant; menus €9.50 (weekdays) and €14–27. *10% discount on the room rate (Nov to end March) offered to our readers on presentation of this guide.*

Restaurant La Treille

10 av. de Bordeaux; take the N10; it's opposite the park de Vonnant.
Ⓣ05.49.43.41.13
Closed *Wed evening; Feb school holidays.* **Car park.**

Napoleon paused long enough on his long march south to Spain to dine in this inn. Panic broke out as staff tried to prepare a dinner fit for the emperor. They served *farci poitevin*, a local variation on stuffed cabbage, and apparently he loved it. Today the inn is as welcoming as ever, though service can be slow, and the cooking is invariably good, rich in traditional flavours. There's a €13 menu (not served on Sunday), which includes wine; if you want to try the famous *farci poitevin*, you'll have to go for the €21 *saveurs régionales menu*. Those with giant appetites will appreciate the two other menus at €25 and €30 – menus list such dishes as *cassolette* of scallops with cream and chives, and duck *compote* in white sauce with mushrooms. *Free house liqueur offered to our readers on presentation of this guide.*

Dissay

86130 (15km NW)

Hôtel-restaurant Binjamin**

It's on the N10, towards Châtellerault, then D15.
Ⓣ05.49.52.42.37 Ⓕ05.49.62.59.06
Ⓦwww.binjamin.com
Closed *Sat lunchtime, Sun evening; Mon; fortnight during Feb school holidays.* **Disabled**

access. TV. High chairs and games available. Swimming pool. Car park.

The unusual architecture – a slightly uneasy marriage between a cube and a round building – houses a nice establishment with a pretty dining room where you can enjoy appealing, subtle cuisine. Try the pan-fried foie gras with apples, the zander with honeyed, sliced potato and shallot *confit*, or the prawn fritters with sesame. There's also an impressive wine list with a good selection of clarets, Burgundies and Loire wines. Weekday menu €19.50, others at €22–46, and various options à la carte. If you want to stay the night, doubles with good soundproofing and shower/wc go for €43; some overlook the pool. *Free coffee or breakfast offered to our readers for a minimum two-night stay on presentation of this guide.*

Restaurant Le Clos Fleuri

474 rue de l'Église; it's on the road to Saint-Cyr.
☎05.49.52.40.27
Closed *Sun evening; Wed*. **Disabled access. Car park.**

Across the road from the fairytale château de Dissay, this restaurant has been run by Jean-Jack Berteau for some three decades. Scouring the region for genuine Poitou produce, he prepares a famously good calf's head with two sauces; along with such delicious classics as eel stewed in Chinon wine and lamb stew with vegetables. There's a weekday menu at €17, with others from €22–33. The wine list has a careful selection of local vintages. *Free house apéritif offered to our readers on presentation of this guide.*

Neuville-de-Poitou

86170 (15km NW)

L'Oasis**

2 rue Daniel-Ouvrard.
☎05.49.54.50.06 Ⓕ05.49.51.03.46
Ⓔoasis-hotel@wanadoo.fr
Restaurant closed *lunchtimes; Sun evening; 15 Dec–15 Jan*. **TV. Disabled access. High chairs available. Pay car park.**

A good place, not too far from Futuroscope, with bright, spring-like rooms. Those looking onto the street are soundproofed – in any case, the street is quiet at night. Doubles cost €47 with shower/wc including breakfast. The restaurant offers simple, unpretentious dishes like *colombo* of frogs' legs, *farci poitevin* and steak with foie gras. Menus are €13 (weekdays only), €15 and €18.

Restaurant Saint-Fortunat

4 rue Bangoura-Moridé.
☎05.49.54.56.74
Closed *Sun and Tues evenings; Mon; 5–25 Jan; 15–30 Aug*. **Disabled access.**

A rustic building with exposed stonework, a veranda and a well-laid-out courtyard. The saint after whom the inn is named was an epicurean – doubtless he would have approved of the good food and excellent regional wines here. The cooking combines simplicity and sophisticated flavours. Try the crayfish salad with preserved apple, the kid with wild mushrooms or the veal kidneys with fresh herbs and spices. There's a €11 menu, served daily, and others at €16–30. Faultless service, though the atmosphere can be a bit solemn. *Free house apéritif or coffee offered to our readers on presentation of this guide.*

Vouillé

86190 (17km NW)

Hôtel-restaurant Le Cheval Blanc**

3 rue de la Barre; take the N149 towards Parthenay.
☎05.49.51.81.46 Ⓕ05.49.51.96.31
Ⓔlechevalblancclovis@wanadoo.fr
Disabled access. TV. High chairs and cots available. Car park.

A family-run waterside hotel overlooking the river with a terrace on the bank. The restaurant specializes in regional dishes and has a fine list of Loire, Burgundy and Bordeaux wines. Specialities include eel stewed in wine, kid cooked Poitou-style and veal sweetbreads in a puff pastry with morels. Weekday lunch menu at €12, others €15–41, and à la carte. It's good value. Doubles with basin €29, with shower/wc €42.50, with bath/wc €45.50. *10% discount on the room rate, except July–Aug, offered to our readers on presentation of this guide.*

Le Clovis**

Place François-Albert.
☎05.46.51.81.46 Ⓕ05.49.51.96.31
Ⓔlechevalblancclovis@wanadoo.fr
Open *all year*. **Disabled access. TV. High chairs and cots available.**

Owned by the people who run the

Cheval Blanc, 50m up the street, and sharing the same restaurant, this place offers modern rooms with good facilities. Doubles go for €42.50–45.50 with shower/wc or bath. Menus at €13, weekday lunchtime, other menus go for €16–43. *10% discount on the room rate except in July and Aug offered to our readers on presentation of this guide.*

Pons

17800

Hôtel-restaurant de Bordeaux**

1 av. Gambetta; from Saintes, take the N137 in the direction of Bordeaux or exit 36 from the A10, signposted to Pons.
Ⓣ05.46.91.31.12 Ⓕ05.46.91.31.12
Ⓦwww.hotel-de-bordeaux.com
Restaurant closed *Sun evening; Mon and Sat lunchtimes Oct–April.* **Hotel closed** Sun evening only. **TV. High chairs available. Car park.**

The austere façade may not promise much, but appearances are misleading. It's actually a welcoming place, with a classy dining room and immaculate service. The young owner has returned to his home town after working in some of the great kitchens of France, and the food he prepares is outstanding, using only the freshest ingredients. The wine waitress recommends good aromatic wines to heighten the dish flavours. Menus, €15–42, list a range of fine dishes that change with the seasons. Children's menu €8. There's an English-style bar where you can extend your evening and in good weather you can dine out on the rose-bordered patio. The rooms are simple but elegant, and some look onto the patio. Doubles with shower/wc or bath go for €42–48. Half board is compulsory in summer at €41–47 per person per night. All in all, you'll get everything you'd expect to find in a luxury establishment – except for the prices. *10% discount on the room rate, Oct to end March, offered to our readers on presentation of this guide.*

Jazennes

17260 (9km W)

La Rozé

La Foy; it's on the D732 about 1km from Gemozac.
Ⓣ05.46.94.55.90
Closed *Sun and Mon evenings except July–Aug; 1–7 Jan; autumn school holidays.* **Disabled access. Games available.**

Charming restaurant in a wonderful old Charentais house with a glorious courtyard – a fabulous place to dine in summer, with a play area for the kids. Inside there's a gentle family atmosphere. Good gourmet dishes appear on the menus – duck breast, for example, and duck *confit* – with a variety of options using fresh, seasonal ingredients. There's a *formule* for €10 lunchtime weekday, other menus go for €12–22.

Rochefort

17300

Auberge de jeunesse

20 rue de la République.
Ⓣ05.46.82.10.40 Ⓕ05.46.99.21.25
Ⓦwww.fuaj.org
Open *July–Aug 8–10am and from 5.30 pm (rest of the year, reception at 97 rue de la République).*

A small, well-situated youth hostel a stone's throw from the centre but in a quiet street. It is set in an old, narrow building, typical of the neighbourhood, with a small communal dining room and a kitchen available for use. Around 50 places distributed in rooms with two, three, four or eight beds that share showers and wc. €8.80 a night per person, with hire of sheets at €3 and breakfast at €3.50. Double rooms €25.60. Menu €9, packed lunch €5. There is room for a few tents in the small courtyard-garden. Credit cards not accepted. It is advisable to book.

Hôtel Roca Fortis**

14 rue de la République.
Ⓣ05.46.99.26.32 Ⓕ05.46.99.26.62
Closed *20 Dec to mid-Jan.* **TV.**

A charming, peaceful place situated on a historic street. Most of the rooms look over a flower-filled courtyard or an internal garden. Rooms are huge and a little old-fashioned; all of them are comfy, and there's a pretty breakfast room. Doubles €40–44 with shower, or €43–55 with bath.

La Belle Poule

Route de Royan; take the road to the Arsenal industrial estate just after the Charente bridge.

Ⓣ05-46-99-71-87 Ⓕ05-46-83-99-77.
Ⓔbelle-poule@wanadoo.fr
Closed *Fri and Sun out of season; Ist fortnight in December.* **TV.**

It may seem strange to recommend a hotel-restaurant on the outskirts of the town; f urthermore, the conventional interior is nothing special and the garden by the terrace is unassuming. The food, however, is in a different class, as the chef skilfully juggles aromatic ingredients like chives, rosemary, ginger, coconut milk, aniseed and fennel to create subtle, delicate dishes; the *jonchée* with almond milk is outstanding. Excellent value for money, with menus from €18.50–32 and a children's menu at €7.60. Double rooms €48; half board €66.50 per person. The place is run by a family, and the owner's son has proudly put his model boats on display. *Free apéritif offered to our readers on presentation of this guide.*

Le Cap Nell

1 quai Bellot; it overlooks the pleasure port.
Ⓣ05.46.87.31.77
Closed *Tues evening and Wed out of season; 3 weeks in Oct; a week in Feb.* **Open** *daily in July–Aug.* **Disabled access. High chairs available.**

A bunch of friends banded together to open this wine bar-cum-fisherman's tavern, where the decent local cooking – lots of seafood – isn't fettered by finesse. There's a *formule* for €8.60, which includes the dish of the day and dessert of the day, and menus from €14.90 to €21, with a children's menu at €5.30. If you're after a drink, make for the terrace; it's the perfect place to relax with a glass of something cold. The tavern's mysterious name refers to a legend that's revealed in the pages of the menus. *Free house liqueur offered to our readers on presentation of this guide.*

Rochefoucauld (La)

16110

La Vieille Auberge de la Carpe d'Or***

1 rte. de Vitrac. Look for Logis de France signs.
Ⓣ05.45.62.02.72 Ⓕ05.45.63.01.88
Disabled access. TV. Car park.

This quiet old inn is an attractively converted sixteenth-century coaching stop in the centre of town. The bedrooms have been done up without losing the style of the house: doubles are €35–47. In the dining room, which is rustic and cosy with relatively formal service, you'll eat generous servings of traditional cuisine. Specialities include fresh foie gras *escalope* pan-fried with seasonal fruits, and *fricassée* of lemon sole with scallops. Menus start at €9 (not on weekends) with others at €15.05–32.

Chasseneuil-sur-Bonnieure

16260 (11km NE)

Hôtel de la Gare*

9 rue de la Gare; take the D141.
Ⓣ05.45.39.50.36 Ⓕ05.45.39.64.03
Closed *Mon; Sun evening; 1–21 Jan; 1–22 July.* **TV. High chairs available. Car park.**

A no-nonsense, good-value place. In the restaurant, go for the specialities — *noisette* of lamb or scallops cooked with Cognac. Menus at €10.50 (not Sun) and €16–24.50. If you're staying, reckon on €24 for a double with basin, and €40 with shower/wc or bath. Half board at €36 per person. *Free house apéritif offered to our readers on presentation of this guide.*

Rochelle (La)

17000

See map overleaf

Auberge de jeunesse

Avenue des Minimes. In the port des Minimes, around 20min from town centre on foot. **Off map C3-1**
Ⓣ05.46.44.43.11 Ⓕ05.46.45.41.48
Ⓦwww.fuaj.org/aj/la-rochelle
Closed *Christmas school holidays. New arrivals 8am–noon and 2–10pm.* **TV. High chairs available. Disabled access.**

More than a youth hostel, this is a modern, very large international meeting point – if you want to practise a foreign language, just hang out in the upstairs bar that extends on to the terrace overlooking the pleasure port. The long zinc counter is a perfect place to make friends, and the background music and TV corner only enhance the lively atmosphere. Simple but adequate rooms and clean toilets and showers. €12.60 or €15.10 per person in a room with six or four beds respectively, including breakfast and sheets. Double

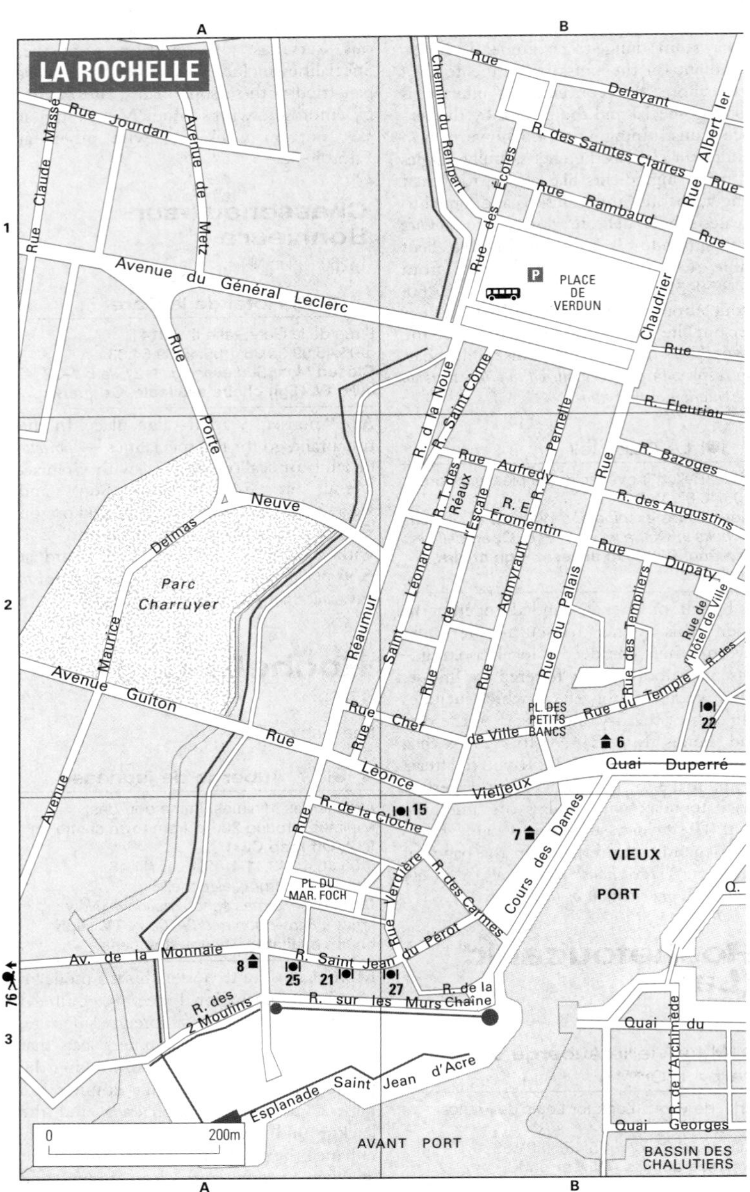

20 POITOU-CHARENTES

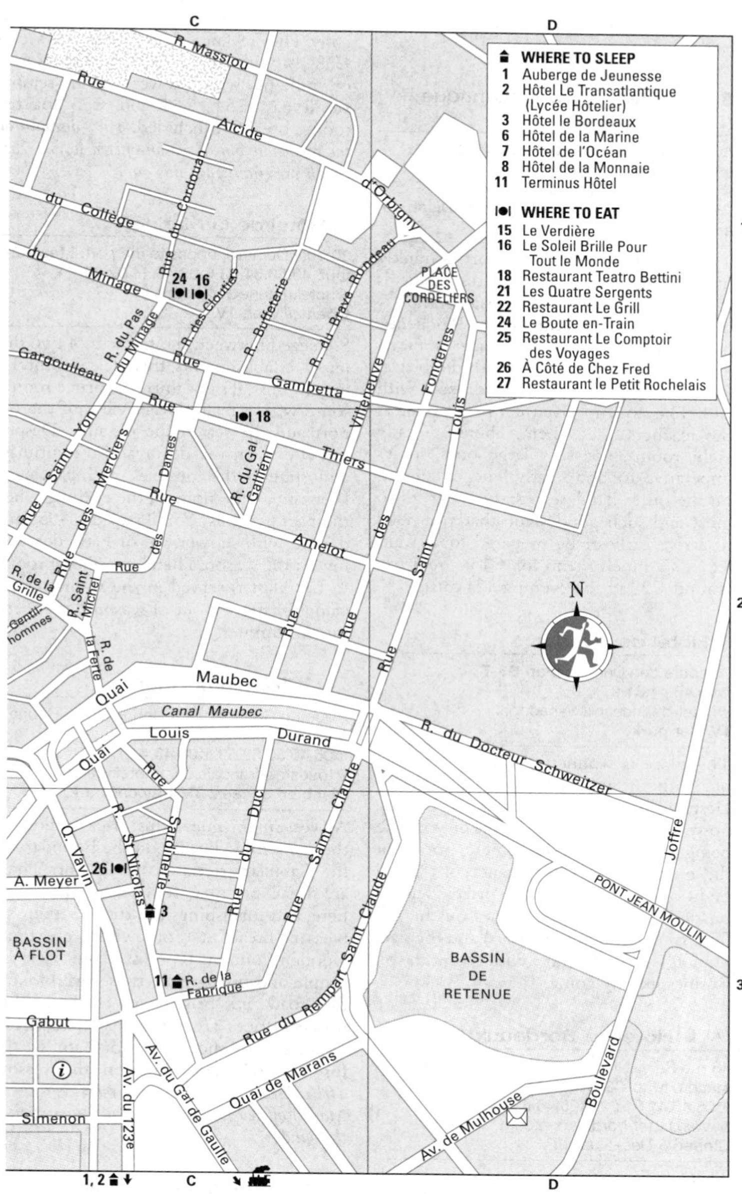

20

POITOU-CHARENTES

rooms with washbasin €30.70. Menu €8, or eat à la carte. Luggage lockers and bike rental in season. *One free breakfast per person offered to our readers on presentation of this guide.*

Hôtel Le Transatlantique (Lycée Hôtelier)

Avenue des Minimes. **Off map C3-2**
05.46.44.90.42 05.46.44.95.43
www.lycee-hotelier.com
Closed *weekends; school holidays.* **Disabled access. TV. Car park.**

The district, near Minimes port, is frankly unappealing, but the hotel-restaurant is extremely attractive and beats all competition hands down. Run by La Rochelle's hotel school and staffed by eager trainees, it offers unbeatable prices, with doubles at €23.50 with shower/wc and €30 with bath. The students give their best service as the teachers assess them. There are only eight rooms, not very large ones, so it's imperative to book early. The restaurant, on the other hand, seats sixty – but it's so great and such good value that you need to arrive early or be prepared for a wait. There's a lunch menu for €15; you'll pay around €22 in the evening à la carte.

Hôtel de l'Océan**

36 cours des Dames. **Map B3-7**
05.46.41.31.97
hotel-de-locean@wanadoo.fr
TV. Car park.

This place is wonderfully situated on the old harbour with a view of the towers. Despite the double-glazing, it can be very noisy at night – which is fine if you like being in on the action. Quieter rooms at the back offer a better chance of a good night's sleep; therefore the prices depend on the location (cheaper ones on the 4th floor or overlooking the port) and the size. Doubles €30–60, all with shower/wc. Businesslike welcome.

Hôtel Le Bordeaux**

43 rue Saint-Nicolas. 500m from the train station. **Map C3-3**
05.46.41.31.22 05.46.41.24.43
www.hotel-bordeaux-fr.com
Closed *5 Dec–5 Jan.* **TV.**

This small, pretty hotel, decorated with colourful window boxes, is in the fisherman's district of the old town. It's like a quiet village during the day but gets very lively at night. The rooms are colourful and well maintained, each one different, with a variety of sizes. Those in the attic get a lot of light, and some even have a balcony. They're fair value, too: doubles cost €38–44 with basin, €42–55 with shower or €48–64 with shower/wc. In season, you'll pay €54, €64 and €73 for the rooms, breakfast included. *10% discount on the room rate out of season offered to our readers on presentation of this guide.*

Hôtel de la Marine**

30 quai Duperré; opposite the port. **Map B2-6**
05.46.50.51.63 05.46.44.02.69
hotel.marine@wanadoo.fr
Open *all year.* TV.

Squeezed between the terraces of two different establishments, this pleasant hotel is easy to miss. It's got thirteen spruce rooms, some with a really lovely view of the old port and the sea in the distance. Despite the efforts on the décor and the intimate atmosphere, the double glazing doesn't keep out all the noise in the evening when the port gets busy. You'll pay €46–95 for a double with shower/wc or bath, depending on the season. There's no dining room, so breakfast is served in the rooms. Good value for money out of season but expensive in summer.

Terminus Hôtel

Place du Commandant-de-La-Motte-Rouge. **Map C3-11**
05.46.50.69.69 05.46.41.73.12
tourisme-francais.com/hotels/terminus
Disabled access. TV. Pay car park.

As you might guess, this place is close to the rail station, but it's on the boundary of the Gabut district and the old port. There are small personal touches in the décor here, and furnishings are rustic – there's a pleasant breakfast room with a charming wooden counter. Rooms at the back are simple and quiet while those overlooking the road are bright and spacious but noisier. Prices are more than reasonable, doubles with shower/wc or bath/wc go for €47–67, depending on the season. *10% discount on the room rate (1 Oct–31 March) offered to our readers on presentation of this guide.*

Hôtel de la Monnaie***

3 av. de la Monnaie; near the port. **Map A3-8**
05.46.50.65.65 05.46.50.53.19

ⓦwww.hotel-monnaie.com
Open *all year*. **Disabled access. TV. Pay car park.**

This seventeenth-century Mint was saved from ruin in 1988 and converted into a hotel. Facilities – attractive bathrooms, air conditioning and efficient sound insulation – are top-notch, and the modern-looking rooms are arranged round a lovely paved courtyard with a pocketsize garden. Double rooms €90–108 depending on the season. *10% discount on the room rate (1 Oct–30 April) for a minimum two-night stay offered to our readers on presentation of this guide.*

Le Soleil Brille pour Tout le Monde

13 rue des Cloutiers. **Map C1–16**
ⓣ05.46.41.11.42
Closed *Sun; Mon; public holidays*. **High chairs available.**

In addition to the small dining room, which has mosaic-encrusted walls and tables tightly packed around the open kitchen, there's a sunny terrace with two to three tables in summer. Everything is made in-house with fresh, organic ingredients and subtle mixtures of herbs and spices, and portions are more than generous. Delicious desserts such as *tiramisù* and crumble. The *formule* — starter and dish of the day accompanied by fresh vegetables — is good value at €10.50, while the small à la carte menu offers tasty, well-seasoned dishes, including a few vegetarian options. Reckon on paying €15 à la carte. Credit cards not accepted.

Le Verdière

6 rue de la Cloche. **Map B3-15**
ⓣ05.46.50.56.75
Closed *Mon; Sun evening in winter; a fortnight in March; 8 days in Oct.*

If you happen upon this place, you'll find it hard to drag yourself away. The décor might be tired, but the cooking more than makes up for it; the owner is always on the go and creates invariably fine food that extends to even the cheapest *formules* and menus. Intelligently prepared dishes use only the freshest produce, with lots of fish; the cuttlefish stew is a speciality, as is the foie gras deliciously prepared with fresh fruit and the roast duck breast with acacia honey. Desserts are no letdown, either. Weekday menu €12 (before 9.30pm), with two others at €21 and €29. *Free house liqueur offered to our readers on presentation of this guide.*

Restaurant Le Grill

10 rte. du Port. It's at the old port of La Rochelle. **Map B2-22**
ⓣ05.46.41.95.90
Closed *Sat and Mon lunchtimes; Sun; end March to mid April; early Oct.*

If you're not lucky enough to get one of the very few tables at this local favourite, sit at the bar (which itself has only ten places) and sink your teeth into a thick steak, fresh from the grill. This is a great place for tasty Basque and Spanish dishes; main dishes between €10–15. Wines by the glass and scrumptious desserts. *Free house liqueur offered to our readers on presentation of this guide.*

Les Quatre Sergents

49 rue Saint-Jean-du-Pérot; beside the port. **Map A3-21**
ⓣ05.46.41.35.80
Closed *Mon*. **Disabled access. High chairs available.**

In a townhouse dating from 1842, this dining room is in a wonderful winter garden with a glass roof. A gallery on the top floor looks down on green plants and trees in pots. It's a superb setting and the formal service perfectly in keeping. The chef doesn't limit himself to classic brasserie food, and enjoys adding contemporary twists to some dishes. Try the crayfish with two sauces, duck breast stew with ceps, trout with Calvados and apples, snail profiteroles in wine sauce or the *blanquette* of hake with pistachios and orange zest. The €14 menu is good value, and there are others at €20–34, with a children's menu for €6. Expect to pay €30–35 à la carte. Wine is served by the glass. Good traditional cuisine with a hint of the sea. Reservations advised. *Free house apéritif offered to our readers on presentation of this guide.*

Restaurant Teatro Bettini

3 rue Thiers. **Map C2–18**
ⓣ05.46.41.07.03
Closed *Sun; Mon; autumn and Christmas school holidays.* **Disabled access.**

Pizza might not be the first thing that springs to mind in La Rochelle, but they're well above average at this popular joint, cooked in a real wood-fired oven. It's worth trying the pasta, too, and the *escalope corrado* – whatever you choose; you'll want to wash it down with one of the large selection of Italian wines. You'll pay around €10 for a pizza, €6 for children's menu, €18 for a meal à la carte. *Free house apéritif offered to our readers on presentation of this guide.*

Le Boute-en-Train

7 rue des Bonnes Femmes. **Map C1-24**
05.46.41.73.74
Closed *Sun; Mon; 25 Aug–8 Sept; 24 Dec–1 Jan.* **Games available. Disabled access.**

A really attractive bistro which, painted in shades of blue with bronzed, aged wood, manages to be bright and intimate at the same time. It's as good for a hasty lunch as it is for a family supper – they provide crayons, felt-tips and paper to keep the children happy and there's a collection of this infant art on the walls. You'll eat good hearty home cooking such as marrowbone on toast with Guérande sea salt, *tian* of red mullet, Dublin Bay prawn stew and chocolate *moelleux*. The *menu-carte* is €21, à la carte around €26, and there are a variety of house specialities for around €12.50. *Free coffee offered to our readers on presentation of this guide.*

Restaurant Le Comptoir des Voyages

22 rue Saint-Jean-du-Pérot; in the old port. **Map A3-25**
05.46.50.62.60

The reference to voyages in this unusual restaurant's name is not amiss; open since 2001, it is fired by a youthful enthusiasm that takes its customers on a veritable culinary world tour, with spicy stopovers like curried cod. Menu around €23, or reckon on about €25 à la carte. Chic, laid-back atmosphere.

Restaurant Le Petit Rochelais

25 rue Saint-Jean-du-Pérot. **Map B3-27**
05.46.41.28.43
Closed *Sun.*

A friendly bistro with waxed cotton tablecloths and good Lyonnais cuisine. The kitchen produces seasonal dishes using the freshest local produce, and traditional dishes, changing regularly, include calf's head sauce *ravigote* and seven-hour lamb. Desserts are delightful, featuring such treats as chocolate soup with banana and orange, and vanilla *millefeuille* with a caramel sauce. Some wines served by the carafe at good prices. They don't do set menus, but the dishes of the day are chalked up on the board. A meal costs around €23, not necessarily hearty but good value for money. Friendly welcome.

À Côté de chez Fred

30–34 rue Saint-Nicolas. **Map C3-26**
05.46.41.65.76
Closed *Sun; Mon. Christmas school holidays.*

Fred, a well-known local character, runs the neighbouring fishmonger's as well as the restaurant; what's on the menu depends on what has been landed that day. It's best to opt for the simplest, seasonal dishes. There are no set menus, but you can expect to pay around €25 for a good meal à la carte. As the years go by the prices have increased but the formula is as successful as ever. It gets very full, so reservations are recommended whether you want to eat in the simple, unadorned dining room or the terrace.

Puilboreau

17138 (5km E)

Auberge de la Belle Étoile

12 rue de la Belle Étoile; take the N11 in the direction of Nantes, take the Chagnolet exit and follow the signs.
05.46.68.01.43 05.46.68.06.10
wwwlabelletoile17.free.fr
Closed *Sat lunchtime; Sun.* **Disabled access. TV. Car park.**

A nice family affair installed in an old sugar beet store. The wife rules the dining room, the children welcome the guests during school holidays and the husband, who used to be a pastry cook, now follows the seasons for his inspiration: you might try foie gras cooked in a cloth, salmon with Pineau des Charentes sauce or fine-sliced deer. Good, simple and traditional food from meat to fish. Main dish around €11 and menu €20, children's menu for €6.10. The guest rooms, in the seventeenth-century outbuildings, vary; some are simple, bright and colourful, while others bask in the muted charm of the old stonewalls. Each of them looks onto the beautifully maintained garden. Doubles with shower/wc or bath cost around €38 out of season and around €80–90, from July to end-Sept as half board is compulsory. *Free house apéritif offered to our readers on presentation of this guide.*

Lauzières

17137 (10km N)

Bar Port Lauzières

Port du Plomb; it's at the seafront facing the île de Ré.
05.46.37.45.44
Closed *Tues except July–Aug; 1 Oct–15 March.* **Disabled access.**

An old fisherman's hut converted into a shellfish bar. Local oyster farmers gather at the old-fashioned zinc-topped bar; on the other side, the dining room has a sea view and a cosy fireplace ideal for wintry evenings. Choose from shellfish, mussels and grilled sardines or fish platters with oysters, langoustines, prawns and sardines. Add a splash of wine and you're looking at not much more than €15–20 for a meal. Children's menu at €4. *Free apéritif offered to our readers on presentation of this guide.*

Charron

17230 (16km N)

Restaurant Theddy-Moules

72 rue du 14-Juillet; take the D105, north of La Rochelle, on the port road known as Le Pave.
05.46.01.51.29
Closed *Oct–April.*

People come to Charron for one reason —to eat mussels at *Theddy-Moules*. Theddy, a mussel farmer, came up with the bright idea of arranging a few tables in a kind of large shed, putting a terrace out front and serving the freshest seafood you can imagine. It's right on the edge of the road and the setting is rudimentary, but customers flock here for the quality seafood at affordable prices. Try the mussels *spécial Theddy* with Pineau and cream at €4.50 or €6. They serve fish à la carte, too: sole, perhaps, or sea bass, or a simple plate of grilled sardines. A full meal will set you back around €18–25, depending on the catch, Theddy also proposes a generous seafood platter. Reservations are recommended in the evening.

Roche-Posay (La)

86270

Hôtel de l'Europe

19 av. des Fontaines.
05.49.86.21.81 05.49.86.66.28
www.hotel-l-europe.fr
Closed *1 Oct–1 April.* **TV. Car park.**

This large building with a garden in the back has thirty rooms that are simple but completely renovated and spotlessly clean. Double rooms €26–37 with shower and wc or bath. The delightful, welcoming owner has created a convivial family atmosphere. An unpretentious but pleasant and easily affordable hotel.

Leigné-les-Bois

86450 (9km W)

Hôtel-restaurant Bernard Gautier

Place de la Mairie; take the D14 and the D15.
05.49.86.53.82 05.49.86.58.05
Closed *Sun evening; Mon–Tues except public holidays; 20 Feb–8 March; 11 Nov–1 Dec.* **Car park.**

In an extremely secluded spot in the remotest part of northern Vienne, this modest-looking establishment offers some of the best food in the region. Here you'll enjoy subtle flavours and exciting combinations: typical offerings include fresh cod with herbs, foie gras, *tartare* of fresh salmon, zander with a light *beurre blanc* and *tournedos*. If you like *andouillette à la ficelle* you're in for a real treat, and the *crème brûlée* is fabulous. Menus cost between €21 and €40; the last menu is so huge that you'll struggle to finish. There's a good wine list, too. If you want to stay, there are a few clean, simple bedrooms, costing €25 for a double with basin. Good food, good rooms and a cheerful owner – you'd be pushed to find better.

Ronce-les-Bains

17390

Hôtel Le Grand Chalet – Restaurant Le Brise-Lames**

2 av. de la Cèpe.
05.46.36.06.41 05.46.36.38.87
frederic.moinardeau@wanadoo.fr
Restaurant closed *Sun evening–Tues out of season; Mon lunchtime and Tues mid-season;*

Tues in summer; normally mid-Nov to early Feb. **Disabled access. Car park.**

An attractive, classic seaside hotel on the edge of the ocean, near the fine sandy beaches that run all the way to Royan. Nice rooms which lead onto the garden with terrace, or come with balconies with sea view; all of them have shower/wc or bath; rates range from €38–48, facing the village, to €53–63, overlooking the sea. The superb chef adapts the menus according to season and whatever's fresh at the market, but you can count on being offered lots of fish and seafood. There's a lunch menu for €16, and others at €21–41 with nice but pricey wine list. Children's menu for €8. The bread and pastries are all home-made. Professional welcome and service. *Free house apéritif offered to our readers on presentation of this guide.*

Royan

17200

Villa Trident Thyrsé

66 bd. Frédéric-Garnier.
Ⓣ05.46.0512.83 Ⓕ05.46.36.16.92
Closed *Sun afternoon out of season*. **TV. Car park.**

There have been a few alterations since this place was built, but that doesn't stop it looking like something from a time warp. Vivid colours, a set of bongo drums next to the Formica bar and salsa music wafting out onto the terrace that looks out to sea – blink and you could be in an Art Deco hotel in Miami Beach. All the rooms are simple and pleasant, with vintage 1950s décor; you'll pay €32–40 for doubles with basin, €40–48 with shower or €48–56 with shower/wc or bath. They also have a few self-contained studios available for rent by the week or for an out-of-season weekend. The sandy beach is just across the road. *10% discount on the room rate offered to our readers on presentation of this guide.*

Hôtel Belle-Vue**

122 av. de Pontaillac; it's on the D25 from Saint-Palais.
Ⓣ05.46.39.06.75 Ⓕ05.46.39.44.92
Ⓔbell-vueroyan@wanadoo.fr
TV. Car park.

Starting out as a family guesthouse in the 1950s, this place has grown into a cosy hotel with antiques in the comfortable rooms and, as the name suggests, a lovely view over Pontaillac bay. Some rooms have a balcony while others look onto the garden. Doubles €35–65 with shower/wc or bath, depending on the size, comfort and view.

Hôtel Abysse - Restaurant l'Anjou**

17 rue Font-de-Cherves; near the market, 200m from the beach.
Ⓣ05.46.05.30.79 Ⓕ05.46.05.30.16
Ⓔfrancoise.branco@wanadoo.fr
Restaurant closed *Sun evening and Mon out of season; Mon lunch in summer*. **TV. Disabled access.**

The restaurant here serves generous portions of good traditional food, and naturally they do lots of fish. The dining room is decorated rather fussily but the owner welcomes you enthusiastically and the service is efficient and unpretentious. Menus go for €11 (weekday lunchtimes) and €16–35; the children's menu is €8. Brightly decorated rooms, some with balcony, cost €46–59 with shower/wc or bath. There are also a few apartments, perfect for families. *Free house apéritif and 10% discount on the room rate for a minimum two-night stay offered to our readers on presentation of this guide.*

Restaurant Le Chalet de Royan

6 bd. de la Grandière. it's at the eastern end of the seafront opposite the tourist office.
Ⓣ05.46.05.04.90
Closed *Tues evening and Wed except July–Aug.*

A towny version of a country inn with rustic décor, local cuisine and slick service. It's built up its reputation over the years with dishes like eel *fricassée* with olives and cod joint with sweet pepper sauce. Weekday lunch menu €15 and others €19–54. *Glass of champagne at the end of the meal offered to our readers on presentation of this guide.*

Saint-Georges-de-Didonne

17110 (4km S)

Hôtel-restaurant Colinette et Costabéla*

16 av. de la Grande-Plage.
Ⓣ05.46.05.15.75 Ⓕ05.46.06.54.17

Ⓦwww.colinette.fr
Restaurant closed *Sun lunchtime and evenings (except for hotel guests); 1 Dec–1 Feb.* **Disabled access. TV.**

Located in the Vallières pine forest, the Colinette has had a face-lift. In the next street, the Costabéla is more like an anonymous 1970s villa with flowery wallpaper and chenille bedspreads, (ten rooms are being refurbished). Moderate but comfortable rooms, some with balconies. Doubles €49–69 with shower/wc or bath depending on the season. The menus, €16 and €23 or €6 for children, list favourites such as flambéed crayfish, terrine, *mouclade* and seafood stew in white sauce. Half board, €50–60 per person per night, is compulsory in July–Aug. A nice stopping point for peaceful holidays, two strides from the beach. Credit cards not accepted.

L'Escapade

7 rue Autrusseau.
Ⓣ05.46.06.24.24
Restaurant closed *Mon and Tues except July and Aug; mid Oct to end March.* **Disabled access.**

Seafood bistro with really nice décor, a terrace and a sweet little patio with vines climbing all over the awning. The quality of the food is well appreciated, however it can sometimes vary slightly in high season. Specialities include fish *choucroute* and beautifully presented seafood platters. Menus €15–30. Nice wine list. Children's menu around €7.

Saint-Palais-sur-Mer

17420 (6km W)

Le Petit Poucet

La Grande Côte; it's on the coast road to La Palmyre.
Ⓣ05.46.23.20.48
Closed *Wed Oct–March; 15 Nov–20 Dec; Jan.* **Disabled access.**

This concrete 1950s block used to be a real eyesore, but it's since been camouflaged by Virginia creeper and ivy, and the trees and shrubs planted around it make it much more attractive. Inside, in the spacious dining room, you get a magnificent view of the Grande Côte beach and the ocean beyond. The decent cooking is good value; it's best to plump for the seafood – pan-fried scallops with apples and cider, snails with garlic cream, Dublin Bay prawns with Pineau, hot oysters with leek *fondue*. First menu goes for €15 (weekdays only); other menus at €20–28, and a children's menu at €7. Good value for money.

Meschers-sur-Gironde

17132 (12km S)

Les Grottes de Matata**

Boulevard de la Falaise.
Ⓣ05.46.02.70.02 Ⓕ05.46.02.78.00
Ⓦwww.grottes-de-matata.com
Restaurant closed *Sun evening out of season, Nov–Feb.* **Hotel open** *all year.* **High chairs available.**

Touristy place on the pathway through the Matata grottoes. It's a modern, cliff top building, with a few rooms: doubles with shower/wc cost €60, €65 with bath. The terrace, which affords breathtaking views of the turbulent grey-blue waters of the Gironde estuary, is a great place for breakfast; you get the same view from the crêperie, which is set up in one of the troglodyte dwellings in the cliffs – check out the walls, made of compacted rock packed full of fossils. There's a menu at €15. *10% discount on the room rate Sept–June offered to our readers on presentation of this guide.*

Palmyre (La)

17570 (18km NW)

Palmyrotel**

2 allée des Passereaux; it's near the zoo, 10mn away from the beach.
Ⓣ05.46.23.65.65 Ⓕ05.46.22.44.13
Ⓦwww.palmyrotel.com
Open *every day in season;* **Closed** *Nov to end March.* **High chairs and games available TV. Disabled access. Car park.**

This vast hotel offers good value for money for the region. It's a contemporary, alpine-style building surrounded by a Mediterranean-style garden on the edge of the pine forest. There are 46 functional and comfortable rooms, some with balconies, terrace or even with garden room (if facing the entrance), all with en-suite shower/wc or bath; doubles cost between €50 and €88 depending on the season. The restaurant specializes in fish and seafood; menus €22 and €28. Children's menu €10. *10% discount on the room rate for a stay of at least two consecutive nights, and 5% for one night, offered to our readers on presentation of this guide.*

Boutenac-Touvent

17120 (28km SE)

Le Relais de Touvent**

4 rue de Saintonge; it's on the D730. 4km NW from Montagne.
Ⓣ05.46.94.13.06 Ⓕ05.46.94.10.40
Closed *Sun evening and Mon except in summer*. **Disabled access. TV. Car park.**

This dreary building, plonked down on a roundabout, doesn't immediately appeal, but it has an absolutely enormous garden and nice, newly decorated rooms. Better still, the prices are attractive for the region. Bedrooms are classic in style though the colours can be garish; they're €41 for a double with shower/wc and €47 with bath. Half board, compulsory in July–Aug, costs €49 per person. They serve good, honest cooking, with plenty of regional dishes; try the *mouclade*, oysters *tartare*, lobster salad. The cheapest menu goes for €15, with others at €24–34. Check out the interesting wine list. *Free coffee offered to our readers on presentation of this guide.*

Saint-Denis-d'Oléron

17650

Hôtel-restaurant Le Moulin de la Galette**

8 rue Ernest-Morisset; it's on the town square, near the church.
Ⓣ05.46.47.88.04 Ⓕ05.46.47.69.05
Ⓦwww.oleron.com/loiselay
Closed *Oct–March*. **Disabled access.**

You can't miss this florid seaside villa on the town square. It's a genuine family guesthouse with simple but large and comfortable rooms decorated in period style or in a more modern annexe with terrace; doubles are €36.40–55.50 with shower/wc, while half board, compulsory in July–Aug, costs €38.70–53 per person. You'll find the same old charm in the dining room, where a few tables are laid on the terrace facing the market square. The first menu served every day is at €13.50, other menus range from €17.50–32. The exacting owner-chef won't use anything but the freshest ingredients. Specialities include lemon sole with garlic cream, seafood platters and salmon with sauce *vierge*. Every guest is welcome and treated as an old friend. *10% discount on the room rate Sept–June offered to our readers on presentation of this guide.*

Saint-Maixent-l'École

79400

Hôtel-restaurant Le Logis Saint-Martin***

Chemin de Pissot; head for Niort, turn left at the last set of lights in the town, and follow the signs.
Ⓣ05.49.05.58.68. Ⓕ05.49.76.19.93
Ⓦwww.logis-saint-martin.com
Closed *Sat lunchtime; Mon; Tues lunchtime. Jan*. **TV. Car park.**

A huge seventeenth-century riverside residence set in its own grounds. Peace and quiet are guaranteed, even though you're just a few hundred metres from the town centre. The rooms have been decorated in keeping with the style and charm of the building, featuring fine fabrics and furniture, with glass from Bohemia and Murano. Doubles €90–120 with bath. Half board, compulsory in July and Aug, costs €100–120. In the restaurant most dishes involve fish or seafood, though the foie gras and beef are good, too; there's a lunch menu at €30 and others €42–68. You'll pay around €60 à la carte. Given the environment, the welcome is splendidly relaxed. *10% discount on the room rate, mid-Oct to mid-April, offered to our readers on presentation of this guide.*

Soudan

29800 (7.5km E)

L'Orangerie

It's on the N11 towards Poitiers, exit 31, it's 5min away.
Ⓣ05.49.06.56.06 Ⓕ05.49.06.56.10
Closed *Sun evening and Wed 1 Oct–31 March; 3 weeks mid-Nov*. **Disabled access (restaurant). TV. Car park.**

Tasty and refined regional cooking at really affordable prices. The dining room is cosy, bright and spacious, with windows opening onto a small garden, and service is swift, attentive and friendly. Menus €14.50–39; choices change according to the seasons, but don't miss the delicious homemade desserts. Original vegetarian weekday menu for €13.50. Should you need to stay, their double rooms are not at all bad for €40 with bath.

Mothe-Saint-Héray (La)

79800 (11km SE)

Hôtel-restaurant Le Corneille**

13 rue du Maréchal-Joffre.
05.49.05.17.08
www.perso.wanadoo.fr/lecorneille
Hotel closed *20 Dec–10 Jan.* **Restaurant closed** *Fri and Sun evenings (and Sat out of season).* **High chairs available. TV. Car park.**

Based in the home of Dr Pierre Corneille, who was the last descendant of the famous seventeenth-century tragedian, this charming old family hotel provides a pleasing rustic setting for a series of small dining rooms. Quality local dishes are listed on all the menus, €13.50 weekdays, then €16.50–28, which you can enjoy inside or out in the garden. Specialities include scallops with asparagus, *farci poitevin* and delicious meats. Comfortable doubles €41–45 with shower/wc or bath. Half board at €35–40 per person. Don't miss breakfast – it's unusually delicious. *Free house liqueur offered to our readers on presentation of this guide.*

Saint-Pierre-d'Oléron

17310

Le Square**

Place des Anciens-Combattants.
05.46.47.00.35 05.46.75.04.90
Open *every day.* **Closed** *Jan, end Feb, 15 Nov–15 Dec.* **TV. Swimming pool. Car park.**

An unpretentious little hotel with a certain style, newly renovated with all the necessary comfort. It's far enough away from the centre to be peaceful, and it has some real attractions, among them a pretty courtyard, a swimming pool surrounded by flowers and a sauna. Doubles €35–66 with shower/wc or bath.

Le Petit Coivre

On departmental road 734, opposite the Claircières area (use the famous windmill as a landmark).
05-46-47-44-23;
Closed *Sun evening; Mon and Tues evenings out of season; Mon lunch only during Aug.*

This is definitely one of the finest restaurants on the island, although its position on the side of the road, in the heart of a dreary commercial area, is hardly promising. The interior, however, is charming, with a décor dominated by wood (scrubbed parquet, grey and white walls and beams), a warm welcome from the lady of the house and exquisite cooking from her husband, who has notched up experience in some of the finest restaurants in Paris. Three-course menu from €22 (some dishes carry a supplement), served at lunch and dinner. The menu changes regularly, according to seasonal availability and the tides – unsurprisingly, the ingredients are dominated by seafood. Some of the mouthwatering dishes you may find are: a superb *mouclade* with Pineau, grilled fillets of swordfish with courgette fritters, cabbage stuffed with shellfish, ice creams and other light desserts.

Cotinière (La)

17310 (3km S)

L'Assiette du Capitaine

It's on the port.
05.46.47.38.78
Closed *Mon evening and Tues out of season; Nov–Jan.* **Disabled access.**

Overlooking the port where fish are sold direct from the boats, and decorated with old sea charts and a lovely collection of mussel baskets, *L'Assiette* serves seafood which is fresh as can be. Dishes are creative, original and change with the seasons: highlights include *mouclades* and shark with banana, and, unusually for a seafood restaurant, their desserts are great – try the chocolate dessert with *confiture de lait.* Menus €13.50–29.

Saint-Savinien

17350

Auberge du Quai des Fleurs

53 quai des Fleurs; it's the continuation of the main street.
05.46.90.12.59
Open *every day June–Sept (except Mon in June), Thurs–Sat evenings and Sun.* **Closed** *Jan.* **Disabled access.**

An unexpected establishment in an old riverside house with two terraces. Old pedal sewing machines are used as table bases and hastily knotted sackcloth covers the chairs; meanwhile Billie Holiday croons in the background. It's run by a Swedish woman so most of the mouth-watering dishes hail from her homeland – choose from a summer lunch menu at €15 or others at €19 and €36; à la carte you'll spend about €30. Specialities include cod cooked Swedish-style and *gratin* of raspberries with white chocolate. They also host occasional live jazz or blues, two to three times a week in summer and a few days in winter, when menus run from €20 to €30, and in August there's a week-long festival of eclectic music. *Free house apéritif offered to our readers on presentation of this guide.*

Saint-Savin-sur-Gartempe

86310

Hôtel de France

38 place de la République.
Ⓣ05.49.48.19.03 Ⓕ05.49.48.97.07
Ⓦwww.hoteldefrance86.fr
Closed *16 Nov–23 Nov.* **Restaurant closed** *Sun evening and Mon lunchtime except in July–Aug.* **Disabled access. TV. Car park.**

A pleasantly traditional hotel behind a welcoming façade, with fifteen good rooms. The three in the eaves are charming and cheaper than the others. Doubles with shower/wc cost €46, €48 with bath/wc. Good traditional cuisine is served in the flowery dining room, where you can choose from a variety of menus (€11–23) or à la carte. Friendly welcome.

Saintes

17100

Auberge de jeunesse

2 pl. Geoffroy-Martel; beside the Abbaye aux Dames.
Ⓣ05.46.92.14.92 Ⓕ05.46.92.97.82
Ⓦwww.fuaj.org/aj/saintes/index.htm
Closed *during Christmas school holidays.* **Disabled access. Car park.**

Ideally situated in the town centre, just five minutes from the train station, this spotless youth hostel can sleep 70 people in simple but comfortable rooms with brick or panelled walls that contain four to six beds. €11.60 a night, including breakfast. Hire of sheets €3. Menu at around €8. The only thing that's missing is a dash of imagination in the décor.

Hôtel de l'Avenue**

114 av. Gambetta; it's near the Abbey aux Dames.
Ⓣ05.46.74.05.91 Ⓕ05.46.74.32.16
Ⓦwww.hoteldelavenue.com
Closed *Christmas school holidays.*

A friendly, colourful hotel with some fifteen pleasant rooms. They're all different, but none of them looks over the street, so they're all quiet, and there's a peaceful calm in the breakfast room to ease you into the day. Doubles range from €34 with basin to €49 with bath/wc. Good value for money.

Hôtel des Messageries**

Rue des Messageries.
Ⓣ05.46.93.64.99 Ⓕ05.46.92.14.34
Ⓦwww.hotel-des-messageries.com
Closed *Christmas school holidays.* **TV. Pay car park.**

Very comfortable, classic hotel in a quiet street in the old town. It started its days as a coaching inn, but today only a few of the stones from the original building are visible in the very old staircase. It has two wings, which enclose a pretty paved courtyard, and the rooms are very quiet. Air-conditioned doubles €48–54 with shower/wc or bath.

Le Pistou

3 place du Théâtre.
Ⓣ05.46.74.47.53
Closed *Sat lunchtime and Sun; a weekend June; a week mid-Sept, a weekend Dec to early Jan.*

A centrally located Provençal-style restaurant with a terrace laid out on the pedestrian part of the square, where the prices won't break the bank. Some of the dishes have a Mediterranean flavour: mussels with *pistou* (the French version of Italian pesto), lemon sole with langoustine *coulis* flambéed in Cognac, salad of foie gras and scallops, paella. There's always a fish dish of the day and lots of salads in summer. The chef gives his students carte blanche to prepare a different dish of the day each week. You'll spend around €20 à la carte. Children's menu at €7.

Restaurant La Ciboulette

36 rue Pérat; go down cours National and cross the Charente, follow av. Gambetta and, after the bridge, turn into the third street on the left.

Ⓣ05.46.74.07.36
Closed *Sat lunchtime; Sun.*

The restaurant, one of the best in town, has a pretty dining room. The chef, who comes from Brest, prepares lots of fish and shellfish – his successes include a tasty mixed "fisherman's platter" and fish smoked over beech chippings. He also pays culinary homage to the Charente with dishes such as jaud (chicken marinated in Cognac), sea bass flambéed *à l'anise*, *fricassée* of eel *à la charentaise* and *mouclade*. Menus vary according to the inspiration of the chef. He makes all the bread and the desserts, too. The €20 menu is served daily except Saturday night and public holidays, and there are others at €25–63 with a children's option at €12. There's a reasonably priced wine list with lots of regional choices, or even wine by the glass for the ascetics. Credit cards not accepted. *Free coffee offered to our readers on presentation of this guide.*

Taillebourg

17350 (12km N)

Auberge des Glycines

It's by the riverside on the Saint-Savinien road coming from Saintes.
Ⓣ05.46.91.81.40
Open *every day 15 May–15 Sept.* **Closed** *Tues evening and Wed out of season; a fortnight in Feb; Nov.*

An absolutely delightful riverside town. This inn stands on the banks of the Charente and is well known. On warm days you eat in the old flower garden or on the shady first-floor terrace which is especially nice in springtime. Menus €13.80 (weekday lunchtimes out of season only), €17 and €22.50, or about €32 à la carte. Children's menu at €10.50. Smiling welcome and friendly atmosphere. Reservations are recommended at the weekend.

Surgères

17700

Hôtel-restaurant Gambetta*

49 rue Gambetta; its on the Niort road.
Ⓣ05.46.07.03.64 Ⓕ05.46.07.37.32
Closed *Sun lunchtime, July–Aug; Sat evening and Sun, Sept–June; 22 Dec–2 Jan.* **TV. Car park.**

This place, popular with sales reps and travelling businesspeople, offers clean and well-maintained, standard doubles for €28 with basin and around €40 with shower/wc. Those on the garden side are quietest. There is a simple menu at €13 and another at €20. À la carte choices include Burgundy specialities as well as local dishes. The proprietress comes from Beaujolais country and the wine list features good wines from her region, all at very decent prices. Half board €39 per person.

Thouars

17300

Restaurant du Logis de Pompois

Sainte-Verge.
Ⓣ05.49.96.27.84
Closed *Sun evening; Mon; Tues; 1–8 Jan.*
Disabled access. Car park.

A remarkable restaurant housed in a magnificent old wine house. You dine in a huge room with beams and unadorned stone. The cuisine is top of the range and the welcome is outstanding. Weekday lunch menu €15, and others go for €24–40 – try the mousse of foie gras with chicken *compote*, the rabbit with ginger and lime, the asparagus charlotte or the caramelized crab and lobster.

Vigeant (Le)

86150

Hôtel Val de Vienne***

Port de Salles; it's 5km south on the D110.
Ⓣ05.49.48.27.27 Ⓕ05.49.48.47.47
Ⓦwww.hotel-valdevienne.com
Closed *20 Dec–9 Jan.* **Disabled access. High chairs and games available. TV. Swimming pool. Car park.**

In the hollow of a green valley, on the banks of the Vienne, this hotel stands in three hectares of grounds and provides twenty functional rooms. The modern architecture gives it the look of a stylish motel, which works well, and there's a private terrace opening onto a heated swimming pool. The setting is enchanting and quiet as can be – it's been awarded a Relais du Silence badge. Doubles with bath range from €63 to €71. *10% discount on the room rate*

offered to our readers on presentation of this guide.

|●| Restaurant La Grimolée

Port de Salles. Take the D110, it's 5km South of Vigeant.
05.49.48.75.22

Closed *Wed; mid Dec to mid Jan.* **High chairs available**.

Imaginative cuisine with a good reputation: foie gras cooked in Sauternes, wild bass in caramel sauce. Menus €17–38. A charming and peaceful atmosphere. Warm and attentive welcome. *Free coffee offered to our readers on presentation of this guide.*

Provence-Alpes-Côte d'Azur

Aix-en-Provence

13100

See map on p.748

☗ Auberge de jeunesse - CIRS

3 av. Marcel-Pagnol, Le Jas-de-Bouffan; 2km from the city centre, near the Vasarely Foundation; from Aix, take the N7 in the direction of Le Jas-de-Bouffan; via the A7, A8 or A51, take Aix-Ouest or Le Jas-de-Bouffan exit and follow signs to youth hostel. **Off map A2-1**
Ⓣ04.42.20.15.99 Ⓕ04.42.59.36.12
Ⓦwww.fuaj.org
Closed *20 Dec–8 Feb.* **Reception open** *7am–noon and 5pm–midnight; new arrivals before 10pm.* **TV. Games available.**

This international meeting place is made up of a set of modern buildings surrounded by green spaces (although it's maybe slightly too close to the bypass). It has been completely refurbished, so it is very comfortable and functional. FUAJ card compulsory (you can buy it *in situ*). €16 a night, including breakfast. Set menu €9.15, packed lunch €6. Lounge.

☗ Hôtel Le Prieuré**

It's on the N96. **Off map B1-5**
Ⓣ04.42.21.05.23 Ⓕ04.42.21.60.56
Car park.

This was once a seventeenth-century priory. All of the cosy rooms look out onto the ornate Pavillon Lanfant park – a fabulous view. Doubles €56–72 with bath. Small terrace at the front.

☗ 🏃 Hôtel Cardinal**

24 rue du Cardinal. **Map B2-7**
Ⓣ04.42.38.32.30 Ⓕ04.42.26.39.05
TV.

There's an appealing atmosphere in this quiet, comfortable hotel. Most of the rooms have been refurbished – people who know the place opt for the bigger ones in the annexe. Doubles €60 with bath. Relaxed, friendly welcome. *10% discount on the room rate after your third consecutive night on presentation of this guide.*

☗ Les Quatre Dauphins**

54 rue Roux-Alphéran. **Map B2-6**
Ⓣ04.42.38.16.39 Ⓕ04.42.38.60.19
TV.

A quiet, charming hotel named after the nearby fountain. The small, tastefully furnished rooms, spaced across three floors, all have telephone. Doubles €60–70 with shower/wc or bath. There's no lift. Advanced booking advised.

☗ 🏃 La Bastide du Roy René

31 av. des Infirmières, 2km from the city centre. **Off map B2-4**
Ⓣ04.42.37.83.00 Ⓕ04.42.27.54.40.
Ⓦwww.bastideduroyrene.com
TV. Disabled access.

This *bastide* (country house) was originally built in the fifteenth century for King René; it later became the property of the canons of Aix cathedral, before being used as a hospice for victims of epidemics in the seventeenth century. It has now been superbly restored and converted into a charming hotel-residence. Splendid, comfortable rooms decorated in a modern Provençal style. Double rooms with bath €70–75, according to the season, as well as studios and duplex. An ideal way to be in

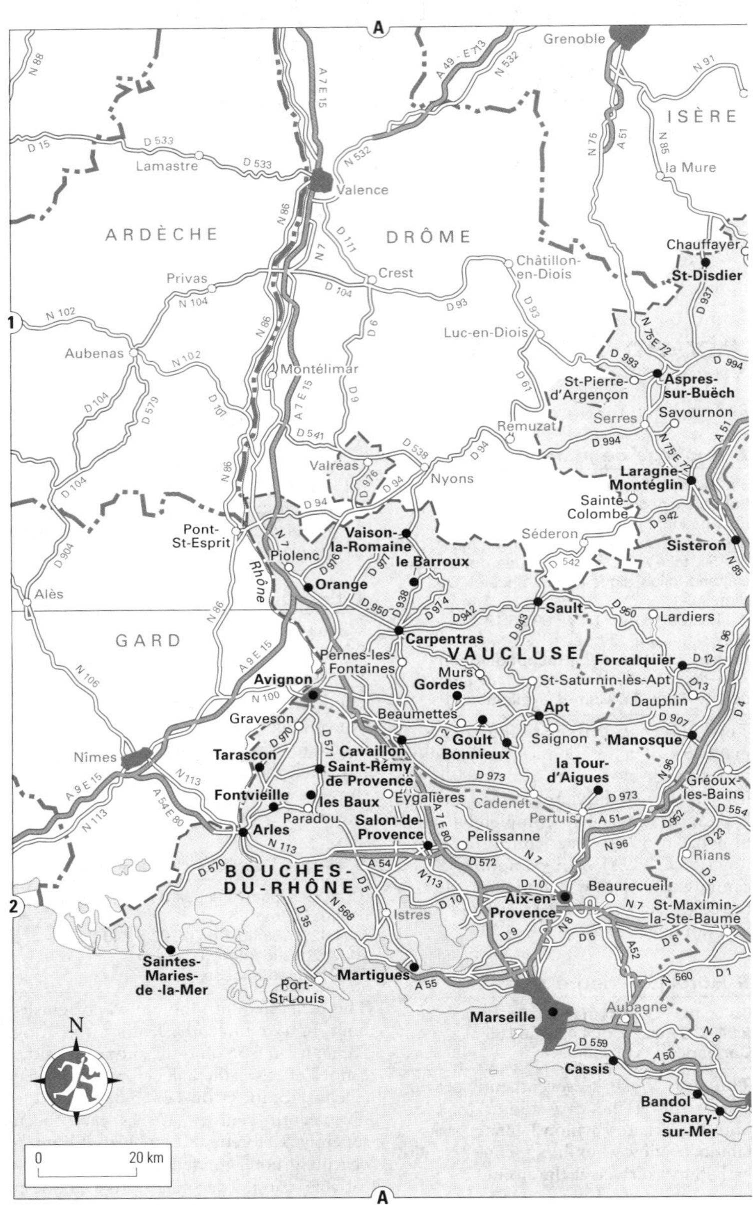
ARDÈCHE
DRÔME
ISÈRE
GARD
VAUCLUSE
BOUCHES-DU-RHÔNE
Grenoble
Valence
Lamastre
Privas
Crest
Châtillon-en-Diois
Luc-en-Diois
Aubenas
Montélimar
St-Disdier
Chauffayer
la Mure
Aspres-sur-Buëch
St-Pierre-d'Argençon
Serres
Savournon
Remuzat
Valréas
Nyons
Laragne-Montéglin
Sainte-Colombe
Séderon
Sisteron
Pont-St-Esprit
Vaison-la-Romaine
Piolenc
le Barroux
Orange
Alès
Sault
Lardiers
Carpentras
Pernes-les-Fontaines
Forcalquier
Murs
Gordes
St-Saturnin-lès-Apt
Dauphin
Avignon
Apt
Graveson
Beaumettes
Goult
Saignon
Manosque
Bonnieux
Tarascon
Cavaillon
Saint-Rémy de Provence
la Tour-d'Aigues
Nîmes
Gréoux-les-Bains
Fontvieille
Eygalières
les Baux
Cadenet
Paradou
Arles
Salon-de-Provence
Pertuis
Pelissanne
Rians
Beaurecueil
Aix-en-Provence
St-Maximin-la-Ste-Baume
Istres
Saintes-Maries-de-la-Mer
Martigues
Port-St-Louis
Marseille
Aubagne
Cassis
Bandol
Sanary-sur-Mer
Rhône
N
0
20 km
A
1
2

PROVENCE-ALPES-CÔTE D'AZUR

21

AIX-EN-PROVENCE

WHERE TO SLEEP

1 Auberge de Jeunesse
4 La Bastide du Roy René
5 Hôtel Le Prieuré
6 Les Quatre Dauphins
7 Hôtel Cardinal
8 Hotel Saint Christophe Brasserie Léopold

WHERE TO EAT

11 Restaurant Le Carillon
12 Chimère Café
13 La Rotonde
14 Restaurant La Brocherie
15 Icône
17 Lauranne et sa Maison
18 L'Amphytrion

MANOSQUE, N 96 5
ARLES, AVIGNON, N 7
ARLES, AVIGNON, N 7 1
MARSEILLE, A 51, N 7
TOULON, BRIGNOLES, A 8, N 7 4

Boul. Aristide Briand
Boul. Jean Jaurès
Cathédrale St-Sauveur
Anc. Archevêché
Musée
PL. BELLEGARDE
R. J. de la Roque
PL. DE L'UNIV.
PL. DES MARTYRS DE LA RÉSISTANCE
R. P. et M. Curie
Pavillon de Vendôme
R. du Bon Pasteur
Av. des Thermes
Thermes Sextius
R. de la Treille
Musée du Vieil Aix
R. G. de Saporta
R. Boulégon
R. Constantin
Rue Mignet
R. Matheron
R. P. Bert
R. Granet
R. de Montigny
Ste-Marie-Madeleine
R. Portalis
PL. DES CARDEURS
Hôtel de ville
PL. DE L'HÔTEL DE VILLE
R. des Cordeliers
PL. RICHELME
R. Mar. Foch
R. Méjanes
Chapelle des Pénitents
St-Jean-Baptiste
Cours Sextius
Pal. de Justice
PL. DES PRÊCHEURS
Boul. Carnot
Rue Manuel
Rue David
R. Lacépède
PL. DES TANNEURS
PL. RAMUS
R. Aude
Musée d'Histoire naturelle
PL. ST-HONORÉ
PL. DE VERDUN
R. Thiers
R. Brueys
R. Lisse des Cordeliers
R. des Tanneurs
St-Esprit
R. Espariat
R. Clemenceau
R. Fabrot
Opéra
PL. MIOLLIS
R. de l'Opéra
R. V. Leydet
PL. B. NIOLLON
PL. JEANNE D'ARC
Av. Bonaparte
Clocher des Augustins
Cours Mirabeau
PL. FORBIN
R. d'Italie
Rue Joffre
Casino
PL. GÉN. DE GAULLE
Musée Arbaud
R. du 4 Septembre
R. F. Mistral
Rue Mazarine
Rue E. Dol
Palais des Congrès
St-Jean-de-Malte
R. Laroque
R. Goyrand
PL. DES 4 DAUPHINS
Rue Cardinale
Musée Granet
Ave. des Belges
Av. V. Hugo
Rue Malherbe
Boul du Roi René
0 200m

the country but to remain in close contact with the city. *10% discount on a room (not to be used in conjunction with other offers) on presentation of this guide.*

🏠 |●| Hôtel Saint-Christophe - Brasserie Léopold**

2 av. Victor Hugo. **Map A2-8**
☎04.42.26.01.24 Ⓕ04.42.38.53.17
Ⓦwww.francemarket.com/stchristophe
Restaurant closed *Mon*. **Disabled access. TV. Pay car park.**

Slap-bang in the centre of town, this is one of *the* places in Aix because of its Art Deco design. Doubles, €73–86, are air-conditioned and have en-suite bathrooms; some even have small terraces. The trump card is the brasserie on the ground floor – a real institution crammed with tables and with waiters in long aprons. Menus €17 (weekday lunchtimes) and €23–35. *Free house apéritif on presentation of this guide.*

|●| Restaurant Le Carillon

10 rue Portalis. **Map B1-11**
Closed *Sat evening; Sun; Aug.* **Disabled access.**

They don't have a telephone here, so you can't reserve: you have to turn up early and take a seat with the regulars, many of them pensioners, who appreciate the home cooking. A completely unpretentious place which is ideal for lunch or dinner. Menus €10 and €12.50. Credit cards not accepted.

|●| Icône

3 rue Frédéric-Mistral. **Map B2-15**
☎04.42.27.59.82.

Mahogany furniture, a fibre-optic bar and cooking that is open to a host of influences (although the basis is Italian); all this adds up to a supremely trendy restaurant that's very popular with the "in crowd" of Aix. It's fairly quiet at lunch, but at night the lighting changes and the conversations become more animated – and the prices soar. Lunchtime dish of the day around €14.

|●| Lauranne et sa Maison

16 rue Victor-Leydef. **Map A2-17**
☎04.42.93.02.03
Closed *Sun; Mon (lunchtime only May–Sept); 15–30 Jan; 15–30 Sept.* **Highchairs available.**

An enticing-looking, friendly place in a lovely and sunny setting. Fresh, inventive cooking, showing off the flavours of the south. Dishes change all the time. Lunch menu for €14, and another at €32. *Free house digestif on presentation of this guide.*

|●| Restaurant La Brocherie

5 rue Fernand-Dol. **Map B2-14**
☎04.42.38.33.21
Ⓦwww.brochaix.com
Closed *Sat; Sun; Aug.*

Pleasant, rustic atmosphere, with a huge Renaissance fireplace where they cook whole chickens on the spit. Lunchtime *formule* (self-service hors d'œuvre buffet and *plat du jour*) €12.50 and a tasty dinner menu for €15. Credit cards not accepted.

|●| L'Amphytrion

2 rue Paul Doumer. **Map A2-18**
☎04.42.26.54.10
Closed *Sun; Mon lunchtime; 15–31 Aug.*

The chef, Bruno Ungar, loves Provençal cuisine – and you certainly experience it in his cooking, which lists local dishes which are colourful and richly flavoured. Menus €17 (weekday lunchtimes) and €29–45. There's plenty of space to be comfortable on the terrace and the *menu du marché* is an ideal option for lunch.

|●| La Rotonde

13 place Jeanne-d'Arc; beside the Rotonde. **Map A2-13**
☎04.42.91.61.70.
Open *8am–2am.*

This restaurant-café-lounge has reconciled a *clientele nostalgique* for the city's good old days with this fast-changing neighbourhood, while also attracting a crowd that no longer knew where to go to make an impression on the local scene. It would be hard to find a more beautiful setting for a rendezvous than the terrace under the shade of plane trees. The interior, decorated by Gilles Gleize, is no less striking. The food is just as chic; try the risotto or the prawns cooked in a wok. Lunchtime dish of the day around €14 and menus at €18 or €23; reckon on €40–45 at night.

|●| Chimère Café

15 rue Bruyès. **Map A2-12**
☎04.42.38.30.00.
Open *Mon–Sat.*

A theatrical setting for gourmets: this old nightclub has retained its décor and seems to be inviting customers to take part in a play among the stucco cherubs (and men dressed up as waiters). Despite appearances, however, this is not a Parisian cabaret, and the real star of the show is the food. Highly accomplished seasonal cooking that brings out the flavour of its ingredients without any fancy tricks, and good, relatively inexpensive wines. There is only one menu, at €21. Booking essential; wearing a suit and tie or a piercing is not essential, but neither would go amiss here.

Beaurecueil

13100 (10km E)

Relais Sainte-Victoire***

Ⓣ04.42.66.94.98 Ⓕ04.42.66.85.96
Ⓦwww.relais-ste-victoire.com
Closed *Mon; Fri lunchtime (Fri evening in winter); Sun evening; 1–8 Jan; the All Saints' school holidays.* **Disabled access (restaurant). TV. Swimming pool. Car park.**

This establishment, out in the countryside near Mont Sainte-Victoire, is one of the best restaurants in the region. The décor is brightly coloured and there's a collection of unusual paddles on the walls. René Berges' cooking is full of sun-drenched, southern flavours: poached eggs with truffle cream, preserved tomato tart served with grilled sardine fillets, rack of lamb glazed with local honey. Menus €39–65. Rooms, €77–122 with shower/wc or bath, are all different. The more expensive have whirlpool baths. *Free house apéritif on presentation of this guide.*

Annot

04240

Hôtel de l'Avenue

Avenue de la Gare; it's in the centre of town.
Ⓣ04.92.83.22.07 Ⓕ04.92.83.33.13
Closed *1 Nov–1 April.* **Restaurant closed** *Wed and Friday lunchtime.* **TV.**

Here, Provence meets the Alps. The hotel building was constructed to withstand the rigours of winter but the cooking is decidedly from sunny Provence. The pair who run the place are local; he's in charge of the kitchen and she welcomes you with a smile, front of house. Fresh flowers adorn the tables. There are eleven pleasant and modern rooms that have been nicely decorated. Doubles €51 with shower/wc or bath. The dining room is elegant and so is the cooking – fine tart of red mullet or veal hock braised with spices. Menus €15–24.

Antibes

06600

Hôtel de l'Étoile**

2 av. Gambetta; it's 5 minutes from the station.
Ⓣ04.93.34.26.30 Ⓕ04.93.34.41.48
Ⓦwwwhoteletoile.com
TV. Pay car park.

The only hotel of this category in the centre of Antibes. Although modern and comfortable, it's better for an overnight stop than as a place to spend a holiday. Spacious rooms with good sound insulation; doubles with shower/wc or bath €54–58 depending on the season. Reservations recommended. *10% discount on the room rate Sept–June for two consecutive nights on presentation of this guide.*

Le Mas Djoliba***

29 av. de Provence.
Ⓣ04.93.34.02.48 Ⓕ04.93.34.05.81
Ⓦwww.hotel.djoliba.com
Closed *4 Nov–4 Feb.* **TV. Swimming pool. Car park.**

A pretty Provençal house surrounded by greenery. The delightful rooms, decorated in the local style, cost €85–120. Half-board is compulsory 1 May–30 Sept; it costs €78–96 per person. There's a relaxing swimming pool so you don't have to fight your way to the crowded beach. Credit cards not accepted. *Free house apéritif on presentation of this guide.*

La Table Ronde

5 rue Frédéric-Isnard; it's in the old town.
Ⓣ04.93.34.31.61
Open *evenings in season only.*

Good humour and good cooking make for a good time in this small restaurant where pictures hang on the wall and cooking pans swing from the ceiling. Dishes range from ostrich to swordfish or more local meat creations. Provençal menu €15, *menu gourmand* €22 and the gastronomic menu €35. There's even a scrap of a terrace for the faithful. *Free house apéritif on presentation of this guide.*

Le Bastion Caffé

1 av. Général-Maizière; it's in the old town at

the end of the city walls.
Ⓣ04.93.34.59.86
Closed *Sun evening and Mon in winter; Sat, Sun and Mon lunchtime in summer; Jan.*
Highchairs available.

An establishment that's well supported by local businesses – the butcher, the baker, the candlestick maker. Original, carefully prepared dishes combining Italian and Provençal flavours are chalked up on the board and change according to whatever's good at the market. Menu €16 (€17 on Sun). There's a lovely, flower-filled terrace with a well and an old fig tree. Not to be missed. *Free house digestif on presentation of this guide.*

Cap d'Antibes

06160 (1km W)

La Jabotte*

13 av. Max-Maurey: it's off bd. James-Wyllie which borders Cap d'Antibes.
Ⓣ04.93.61.45.89 Ⓕ04.93.61.07.04
Ⓦwww.jabotte.com
Closed *Sun afternoon; 5–30 Nov; a week at Christmas.* **Disabled access. Car park.**

This hotel offers good value for money: spotless rooms with shower or bath at €49–76. The bungalows looking onto the terrace are particularly nice. Friendly welcome, but you should avoid arriving between 1pm and 6pm on a Sunday, when they take a break. Relaxing atmosphere and a gentle pace. *10% discount on the room rate in Jan (except for the first week), March and Dec on presentation of this guide.*

Juan-les-Pins

06160 (1km SW)

Hôtel Sainte-Valérie***

Rue de l'Oratoire.
Ⓣ04.93.61.07.15 Ⓕ04.93.61.47.52
Ⓦww.juanlespins.net
Closed *30 Sept–15 April.* **TV. Swimming pool. Car park.**

A stylish – rather pricey – hotel, ideal for a romantic holiday. Book well in advance. Set in a quiet part of Juan-les-Pins just a short distance from the Gould pine woods and the sea, it has a pool and a pretty, shady garden where you can take refuge from the heat. Meals are served in the garden – there's one menu at €32. Modern, tastefully decorated double rooms €114–250, depending on the season and the facilities. *10% discount on the room rate from mid-April to the end of June on presentation of this guide.*

Apt

84400

Hôtel Le Ventoux**

785 av. Victor Hugo; it's opposite the station, roughly 1km from the centre of the road to Cavaillon.
Ⓣand Ⓕ04.90.04.74.60
TV. Highchairs available. Car park.

A small hotel with a popular – a bit noisy, a bit smoky – café on the ground floor. The rooms are excellent for the price at €32–40 with private washing facilities. They are bright, quiet, comfortable and prettily decorated. Ask for one at the back with a view of the valley. *Free coffee on presentation of this guide.*

Le Platane

13 pl. Jules-Ferry.
Ⓣ04.90.74.04.36
Closed *Sun; Mon evening; Tues lunchtime.*

Located in a quiet square where no tourists venture. The intimate, thoughtfully decorated dining room is on the first floor of a tall, old house, above a shaded terrace. The cooking, while simple, betrays an attractive turn of hand and good ideas. Fresh, tasty dishes with the odd exotic touch: fillet of sole with scallops flavoured with vanilla, duck with ginger or vegetable lasagne. Lunch *formules* €10–12.80 or set dinner menus €22.50–32. Well worth a try.

Saignon

84400 (4 km SE)

Auberge de jeunesse Regain

2.5 km above Saignon; take the D48 towards Auribean and look out for the (not very prominent) sign to the entrance.
Ⓣ04.90.74.39.34 Ⓕ04.90.74.50.90.
Closed *mid-Jan to mid-Feb.* **Car park.**

This old Provençal house on a clifftop has been a youth hostel since 1936, no less. It is now run by François Morenas, who is not only an indefatigable hiker and author of some fine travel guides but also used to run a travelling cinema; he still has a fascinating collection of old films and he occasionally organizes screenings for his guests. An international youth hostel card (FUAJ, LFAJ) is compulsory, but you can buy a weekend one if you're just passing through. Half board €25, including wine. Outside, the scenery is wild and rugged; inside, the décor is cosy and rustic, with a fireplace and big harnesses for mules hanging on the walls.

Saint-Saturnin-lès Apt

84490 (9km N)

L'Hôtel des Voyageurs

2 pl. Gambetta; it's on the D943.
☎04.30.75.42.08
Closed *Wed; Thurs lunchtime; 31 Jan–1 March; 31 Oct–30 Nov.*

This "hotel" is actually a restaurant. The setting is hardly mind-blowingly original – a few tables on a terrace and a country-ish dining room with whitewashed walls – and it certainly doesn't prepare you for the quality of the cooking. The simple dishes are prepared with extraordinary skill and intriguing use of herbs and spices that flatter the palate. Menus €15–27. There's also a lunch menu in the summer at €12.50. It's not a place to come if you're in a hurry; service is relaxed... *Free coffee on presentation of this guide.*

Arles

13200

Auberge de jeunesse

20 av. Foch; 5min from the centre; by bus from the train station via the Starlette line (to the Clemenceau stop in the town centre), then take bus no. 4 to the Fournier stop.
☎04.90.96.18.25 Ⓕ04.90.96.31.26
Ⓦwww.fuaj.org
Closed *1 Dec–15 Feb.*

This building near the stadium is by no means new but it is well kept. It sleeps 100 people in dormitories of 8 beds. FUAJ card compulsory (you can buy it *in situ*). €14.50 a night, including sheets and breakfast. Meals (only in season and at night for individuals) at €8.50. Luggage lockers, Internet connection and mountain bikes for hire.

Hôtel Le Cloître**

16 rue du Cloître; it's between the amphitheatre and Saint-Trophime.
☎04.90.96.29.50 Ⓕ04.90.96.02.88
Ⓔhotel_cloitre@hotmail.com
Closed *1 Nov–15 March.* **TV. Pay car park.**

A charming, really tranquil hotel which is supported by thirteenth-century vaulted arcades. The largest rooms, which date from the thirteenth and seventeenth centuries, have big beams and are decorated with gleaming tiles. Simple doubles €44 with shower, €48–60 with shower/wc or bath. Remarkably kind owner.

Hôtel Calendal**

5 rue Porte de Laure.
☎04.90.96.11.89 Ⓕ04.90.96.05.84
Ⓦwww.lecalendal.com
Closed *5–25 Jan.* **Disabled access. TV. Pay car park.**

This hotel, situated in the middle of the town, is decorated with local fabrics and dotted with huge vases of stunningly coloured flowers. Arles is famous for photography and the stairwell is hung with lots of unusual photographs. There's a cool patio where you can shelter from the sun. Small, air-conditioned rooms €45–67 with shower/wc and €67–87 with bath; three have a terrace. By way of food, they offer a buffet *formule* for €14 (lunchtime only in season, dinner out of season), snacks and salads are served in the garden, and there's a tearoom. A lovely place. If you want a parking space it's essential to book. *10% discount on the room rate Jan–March on presentation of this guide.*

Hôtel Saint-Trophime

16 rue de la Calade.
☎ 04.90.96.88.38 Ⓕ04.90.96.92.19

This building was once a clinic for mental patients, but its sad history has been totally dispelled by the striking sculpture in the entrance and the colourful décor reflecting the surrounding landscape: lavender, olive green and raspberry. Double rooms €47–55, with lounge €65–70. The place is a delightful cocoon where you can sleep undisturbed, even overlooking the courtyard (the only noise comes from the clock nearby chiming the hours).

Hôtel de l'Amphithéâtre**

5 rue Diderot.
☎04.90.96.10.30 Ⓕ04.90.93.98.69
Ⓦwww.hotelamphitheatre.fr
TV.

Renovated hotel, full of charm, near the Roman theatre. All the bedrooms have been decorated in Provençal style; they're not huge, but they are bathed in light. Each one has air-conditioning, safe, hair-dryer and internet access. Doubles €49–77 with bath or shower/wc. The charming owner serves an unusually good breakfast. *10% discount 1 Nov–31 March on presentation of this guide.*

Hôtel Mireille***

2 pl. Saint-Pierre; it's the other side of the Rhône in the Trinquetaille district.
Ⓣ04.90.93.70.74 Ⓕ04.90.93.87.28
Ⓦwww.hotel-mireille.com
Closed *Nov–March*. **TV. Highchairs available. Swimming pool. Car park.**

A curtain of trees screens off the swimming pool, which is presided over by a watchful old statue. Doubles overlooking the garden and pool cost €79–119. Half board is compulsory during the *feria* at Easter. There's a huge and pleasant dining room. Lovely seafood (including *bouillabaisse provençale*) and quality meat dishes on menus €20–30. *10% discount (except summer or bank holidays), or free house apéritif on presentation of this guide.*

Le Jardin de Manon

14 av. des Alyscamps; it's a little way from the town centre, at the bottom end of bd. des Lices, beyond the police station.
Ⓣ04.90.93.38.68
Closed *Wed; autumn and winter school holidays.*

A friendly restaurant with a small garden at the back (watch out for mosquitoes in the evening). Excellent, creative regional cuisine. There's a €13 lunch menu and others €18.50–27.50; they all change with the seasons. The extensive wine list offers good value for money.

La Paillotte

28 rue du Docteur-Fanton.
Ⓣ04.90.96.33.15
Closed *Wed and Sat lunch (except in summer).*

This local institution has been taken over by a young chef, Stéphane Bognier, who, working almost alone in the kitchen, produces a variety of dishes to cater for different tastes. A selection of fresh, tasty starters (aubergine *papeton*, vegetable *tian*) precede more traditional main courses like suckling-pig stew or fish casserole. Menus €15–20. Attractive terrace.

La Charcuterie

51 rue des Arènes.
Ⓣ04.90.96.56.96
Closed *Sun and Mon, except public holidays; 20 July–20 Aug.*

A genuine Lyon-style bistro right in the centre of Arles. The owner drives all the way to Lyon to supply the kitchen with authentic produce like the *andouillette de Bobosse* – a must. His restaurant is on the premises of an old charcuterie dating back to the 1940s (note the butchers' hooks!), and Regouya cooks very tasty dishes in front of you on an old marble counter. The *patron* is also a painter: his canvasses cover the walls. In summer, the menu lists salads, grills and tapas and there's a welcoming terrace seating about ten or so customers. Menu €15; à la carte reckon on between €20 and €30.

Au Brin de Thym

22 rue du Docteur-Fanton.
Ⓣ04.90.49.95.96
Closed *Tues; Wed (in season).*

A small restaurant where nothing escapes the attention of the owner, a real character who fusses over her guests. Authentic, sensual traditional cooking in a warm setting. Reckon on €25–30 for a full meal; otherwise, you can have just a main course for €13, such as grilled tuna with pepper sauce, or a starter for €8 and/or a dessert for € 6. If you like the food, drop into the shop next door on the way out (open 10am–11pm). It is highly original, with exclusive creations like the extremely kitsch *Cakes de Bertrand*.

Arvieux

05350

La Ferme d'Izoard***

Hameau de la Chalp; it's 30km northwest of Saint-Véran in the direction of Brançion over the col de l'Izoard or via Guillestre in winter when the col is closed.
Ⓣ04.92.46.89.00 Ⓕ04.92.46.82.37
Ⓦwww.laferme.fr
Closed *Mon–Fri lunchtimes in May, except weekends and publich holidays; 20 Sept–15 Dec.* **Disabled access. TV. Highchairs and games available. Swimming pool. Car park.**

A family-run establishment with good facilities including a heated pool. The building is rustic, but the décor is elegant and stylish. Prices are fair considering the high standards: they range from €52 to €140 for doubles, studios or self-contained two-roomed apartments with kitchenette and bathroom. Half board €51–95. Simple but tasty cooking, with lots of regional dishes and grills on the open fire, and menus €14–32. À la carte around €19. There's also a tea room serving less expensive crêpes. It's a lovely place to relax in superb countryside. *7% discount on the room rate during the first week in July on presentation of this guide.*

Aspres-sur-Buëch

05140

Hôtel du Parc**

Route de Grenoble.
04.92.58.60.01 04.92.58.67.84
www.hotel-buech.com
Closed *Sun evening and Wed out of season; public holidays; 6 Dec–6 Jan.* **TV. Highchairs available. Car park.**

It's very pleasant to lunch on the terrace near the rose garden or the patio – in spite of the main road that passes in front. Lunch menu €20 and others up to €35. Specialities include regional lamb, pork and salads, *pieds-paquets* and pear cake with caramel sauce. Doubles €32–45. All the rooms have recently been updated. They are clean, comfortable and have good facilities.

Saint-Pierre-d'Argençon

05140 (5km SW)

Auberge de la Tour

Near the entrance to the village.
04.92.58.71.08
Closed *Mon–Thurs (apart from school holidays); Nov.* **Highchairs available. Disabled access.**

An outstanding place, set back from the road in this charming, peaceful village, whose heart and soul is provided by the owners of this old staging post. They organize a host of activities (concerts, storytelling, weekend hikes, self-catering accommodation and camping) and effectively constitute an unofficial tourist office. It is here that the locals come to meet, chat and eat (very well too!): fresh seasonal products (trout in *feuilleté* with tarragon), sweet-and-savoury mixtures (goat with honey) and house specialities (order the "*frout-frout*", a cake with a secret recipe). Menus €14–24. The atmosphere is warm, jovial and full of *joie de vivre*, and the décor is colourful, imaginative and elegant. Eat on the terrace or in the dining room; there is even a special little table for children. *Free house apéritif on presentation of this guide.*

Auron

06660

Hôtel Las Donnas**

Grande-Place; it's next to the ice-rink.
04.93.23.00.03 04.93.23.07.37
Closed *1 April–20 July; 1 Sept–19 Dec.* **TV. Highchairs available.**

A pleasant, peaceful hotel with some forty sunny rooms, €38–105, half of which have balconies overlooking the ski runs. Half board €45–68 during school holidays. In winter the restaurant serves good wholesome food – menus, €16–25, offer beef *fondue* and *raclette, mousseline* of fish, rillettes of young rabbit and so on. Lovely glassed-in terrace. *Free apéritif on presentation of this guide.*

Avignon

84000

See map on pp.756–757

Hôtel Mignon*

12 rue Joseph-Vernet. **Map B2-4**
04.90.82.17.30 04.90.85.78.46
www.hotel-mignon.com
TV.

Though the décor in this well-kept and welcoming place is a little busy, it's not unattractive. The rooms have double glazing; doubles €38 with shower/wc. Each room has a telephone, cable TV and a whole host of services you wouldn't expect in a one-star hotel. *10% discount on the room rate, 1 Nov–28 Feb, on presentation of this guide.*

Hôtel Le Splendid*

17 rue Agricol Perdiguier. **Map B3-5**
04.90.82.17.30 04.90.85.78.46
www.avignon-splendid-hotel.com

Closed *15 Nov–15 Dec*. **TV.**

A small family hotel with very pleasant rooms that are bright, well appointed and painted yellow and red. Excellent value for money at €47–50 with shower/wc. Breakfast €6. *One free breakfast per room per night from Nov to March on presentation of this guide.*

Hôtel Bristol***

44 cours Jean-Jaurès. **Map B3-7**
Ⓣ04.90.16.48.48 Ⓕ04.90.86.22.72
Ⓔbristol.avignon@wanadoo.fr
Disabled access. TV. Pay car park.

A modern, rather stylish hotel. All 67 rooms have air conditioning, mini bar and efficient double glazing. Doubles with shower or bath €48–81. Breakfast €10. You'll need to book a parking space in advance. *10% discount on the room rate except in July/Aug on presentation of this guide.*

Hôtel de Blauvac**

11 rue de la Bancasse. **Map B2-8**
Ⓣ04.90.86.34.11 Ⓕ04.90.86.27.41
Ⓦwww.blauvac-hotel.com
Closed *a fortnight in Jan; a week in Nov; a week in Dec*. TV.

A good hotel in an elegant seventeenth-century mansion, ideally located in a narrow street in the historic centre close to place de l'Horloge. It's retained some of the original features of the house, which was the residence of the Marquis de Blauvac – the elegant wrought-iron staircase and some of the arched stone doorways. Well-appointed doubles, all of them different, cost €51–65 with shower/wc or bath. The décor is a happy combination of old stone and modern design. Attentive service.

Citôtel de Garlande**

20 rue Galante. **Map B2-9**
Ⓣ04.90.85.08.85 Ⓕ04.90.27.16.58
Ⓦwww.avignon-et-provence.com/hotel-garlande
Closed *Sun out of season*. TV.

An old house, beautifully situated near the Saint-Didier bell tower. It's a comfortable and welcoming place with eleven rooms; they vary widely in size and style, so do try to have a look at a few if possible. Nos. 3 and 9, along with "Tulip" and "Anemone", are recommended. Doubles €58–90. *10% discount on the room rate after two nights, except during the festival, on presentation of this guide.*

La Fourchette

17 rue Racine. **Map B2-20**
Ⓣ04.90.85.20.93
Closed *Sat; Sun; Feb school holidays; 15 Aug–10 Sept.*

This gastronomic restaurant is fast becoming an institution. Good prices, an elegant setting and, above all, well-worked dishes: marinated sardines, *daube à l'avignonnaise*, meringue with hazelnuts. Lunch menu €22, or €24–27 in the evening. Reasonably priced wines, particularly those served by the carafe. It's essential to book.

Bandol

83150

L'Oulivo

19 rue des Tonneliers; it's 100m from the port beside the church.
Ⓣ04.94.29.81.79
Closed *Sun–Wed evenings out of season; Mon; a fortnight in spring; a fortnight in Dec.*

Very simple, very good restaurant, where a wonderfully kind *patronne* serves fresh, authentic Provençal cuisine. They offer a weekday lunch menu at €12.50 and another at €24. Recommended dishes include aubergine turnovers, lamb tripe and trotters and a notable dish called *alouettes sans tête*. There's a pleasant terrace, which is heated in winter. *Free coffee on presentation of this guide.*

Barcelonnette

04400

Hôtel du Cheval Blanc**

12 rue Grenette.
Ⓣ04.92.81.00.19 Ⓕ04.92.81.15.39
Ⓔgbarneaud@free.fr
Restaurant closed *lunchtimes; Oct to end Dec*. **TV. Highchairs available. Car park.**

This hotel-restaurant has been in the Barneaud family for generations. Double rooms with shower/wc and TV €47–49. Half-board €49 per person. People come here nowadays more for the food than the rooms, though the dining room is for guests only and offers menus at €13–18. The traditional cooking features game,

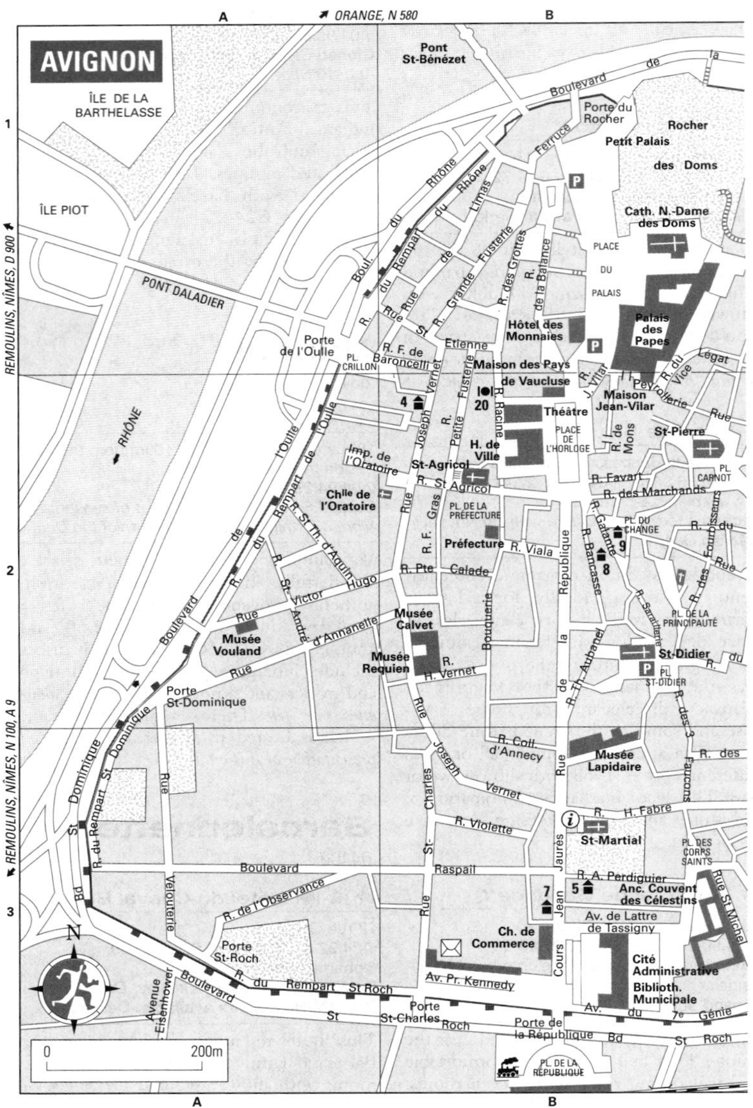
AVIGNON
ORANGE, N 580
REMOULINS, NÎMES, D 900
REMOULINS, NÎMES, N 100, A 9
ÎLE DE LA BARTHELASSE
ÎLE PIOT
RHÔNE
PONT DALADIER
Pont St-Bénézet
Porte du Rocher
Rocher
Petit Palais
des Doms
Cath. N.-Dame des Doms
PLACE DU PALAIS
Palais des Papes
Hôtel des Monnaies
Porte de l'Oulle
PL. CRILLON
Maison des Pays de Vaucluse
Maison Jean-Vilar
Théâtre
PLACE DE L'HORLOGE
H. de Ville
St-Pierre
St-Agricol
PL. CARNOT
Chlle de l'Oratoire
PL. DE LA PRÉFECTURE
Préfecture
PL. DU CHANGE
PL. DE LA PRINCIPAUTÉ
St-Didier
PL. ST-DIDIER
Musée Calvet
Musée Vouland
Musée Requien
Porte St-Dominique
Musée Lapidaire
St-Martial
PL. DES CORPS SAINTS
Anc. Couvent des Célestins
Av. de Lattre de Tassigny
Ch. de Commerce
Cité Administrative
Biblioth. Municipale
Porte St-Roch
Porte St-Charles
Porte de la République
PL. DE LA RÉPUBLIQUE
Av. Pr. Kennedy
Boulevard Raspail
Cours Jean Jaurès
Rue de la République
Avenue Eisenhower
Bd du Rempart St Roch
Boulevard St Dominique
R. de l'Observance
Rue Joseph Vernet
Rue des Teinturiers
0 200m
N
A
B
1
2
3

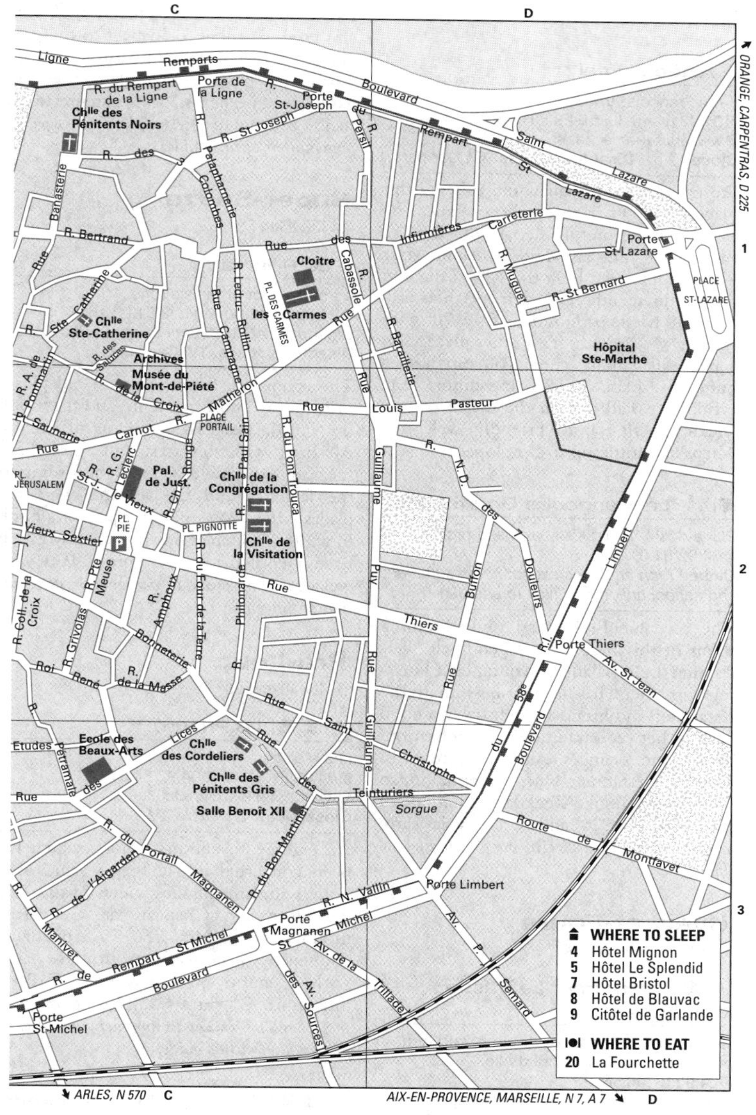
C
D
ORANGE, CARPENTRAS, D 225
1
2
3
Ligne
Remparts
R. du Rempart de la Ligne
Porte de la Ligne
Porte St-Joseph
R. St Joseph
Boulevard
Rempart
Saint
St
Lazare
Chlle des Pénitents Noirs
R. des
Banasterie
Colombes
Peyrollerie
R. du Persil
Infirmières
Carreterie
Porte St-Lazare
PLACE ST-LAZARE
R. Bertrand
Rue des Cabassole
Cloître
les Carmes
PL. DES CARMES
R. Ledru-Rollin
Rue Campagne
R. Muguet
R. St Bernard
R. Bariatterie
Hôpital Ste-Marthe
Ste-Catherine
Chlle Ste-Catherine
R. des Sauras
Archives
Musée du Mont-de-Piété
R. de la Croix
R. A. de Pontmartin
Pl. Saunerie
Rue Carnot
Matheron
PLACE PORTAIL
Rue Louis Pasteur
R. du Pont Trouca
R. Paul Saïn
R. N.D. des 7 Douleurs
PL. JERUSALEM
R. St J. le Vieux
R. G. Leclerc
Pal. de Just.
R. Ch. Rouge
Chlle de la Congrégation
Chlle de la Visitation
PL. PIGNOTTE
PL. PIE
P
Vieux Sextier
R. Pte Meuse
R. Amphoux
R. du Four de la Terre
R. Philonarde
Rue Guillaume Puy
Buffon
Rue Thiers
Porte Thiers
Av. St Jean
R. Limbert
R. Coll. de la Croix
R. Grivolas
Bonneterie
R. de la Masse
Roi René
Rue Saint Christophe
Boulevard du 58e
R. Pétramale
Etudes
Ecole des Beaux-Arts
Lices
Chlle des Cordeliers
Chlle des Pénitents Gris
Rue des Teinturiers
Sorgue
Salle Benoît XII
Route de Montfavet
R. du Portail Magnanen
R. de l'Aigarden
R. du Bon Martinet
R. N. Vallin
Porte Limbert
R. P. Manivet
Porte Magnanen
St Michel
R. de Rempart St Michel
Av. de la Trillade
Av. des Sources
Av. P. Semard
Boulevard
Porte St-Michel
ARLES, N 570
AIX-EN-PROVENCE, MARSEILLE, N 7, A 7
WHERE TO SLEEP
4 Hôtel Mignon
5 Hôtel Le Splendid
7 Hôtel Bristol
8 Hôtel de Blauvac
9 Citôtel de Garlande
WHERE TO EAT
20 La Fourchette

fresh noodles and spinach pie. It's popular with cycle tourists; you can store bikes in the stables, and they prepare special "sporty" breakfasts and packed lunches on request. *Free breakfast for children under ten on presentation of this guide.*

Aztéca Hôtel***

3 rue François-Arnaud.
Ⓣ04.92.81.46.36 Ⓕ04.92.81.43.92
Ⓦwww.hotel-azteca.fr.st
Closed *Nov.* **Disabled access. TV.** Car park.

From the outside you could mistake this place for a rather chic private clinic. The 27 rooms are prettily decorated, three of them in an unusual Mexican-Alpine style – the people who built the villa at the end of the nineteenth century made their fortune in Mexico. Doubles €49–70 with shower/wc or bath. It's a quiet place with a peaceful garden where you can have a buffet breakfast for €8. In summer the breakfast is laid out on the dresser in the Mexican-style salon. Friendly welcome. There's a shuttle up to the slopes.

La Mangeoire Gourmande

Place des 4-Vents; it's near the church.
Ⓣ04.92.81.01.61
Closed *Mon and Tues except in the summer and school holidays; 7 Nov to end Jan.*

The seventeenth-century vaulted dining room of this restaurant is genuinely welcoming. Loïc Balanec, a young chef bursting with talent, has brought new life to the restaurant, and his tasty food strikes a good balance between tradition and innovation. The menu changes every four months. This is a restaurant with a reputation, so you should book. Weekday lunch menu €15, others €26 and €39. À la carte around €40. *Free digestif on presentation of this guide.*

Uvernet-Fours

04400 (4.5km SW)

Restaurant Le Passe Montagne

Take the D902 towards Pra-Loup, and turn before the junction for col d'Allos.
Ⓣ04.92.81.08.58
Closed *Tues and Wed except during school holidays; 15–30 June; 15 Nov–15 Dec.* **Car park.**

This place has the warm atmosphere of a wooden chalet, and you can admire the peaks of Pain de Sucre and Chapeau de Gendarme from the terrace. It's a relaxed place with a peaceful atmosphere heightened in winter when they light a roaring fire in the huge fireplace. The chef has rediscovered traditional Provençal cooking and used his talent to adapt it to the present day – dishes include ham with warm vinaigrette, fresh ewe's milk cheese with garlic and fine herbs, local charcuterie and snails. Set menus €16–24. *Free coffee on presentation of this guide.*

Super-Sauze

04400 (5km SE)

Le Pyjama**

It's at the foot of the ski runs.
Ⓣ04.92.81.12.00 Ⓕ04.92.81.03.16
Closed *15 April–25 June; Sept to mid-Dec.*
Disabled access. TV. Car park.

The rooms are furnished with old pieces of furniture and ornaments, and they look out onto a peaceful panorama of larches. All have wide terraces, and some have mezzanines; doubles €45–80 according to the facilities and the season. There are places where you can curl up with a book in winter and tables outside where you can have a cool drink in summer. Pets very welcome. *Free breakfast per room on presentation of this guide.*

Pra-Loup

04400 (6km SW)

Le Prieuré***

Les Molanes.
Ⓣ04.92.84.11.43 Ⓕ04.92.84.01.88
Ⓦwww.hotel.leprieure.fr
Closed *May; Oct–Nov.* **TV.**

An eighteenth-century priory which has been converted into a very warm, rustic hotel with breathtaking views of the Pain de Sucre and Chapeau de Gendarme mountains. Doubles €50–75. Appetizing cooking – *charbonnade*, or trout or lamb with Génépy butter. Menus €12 at lunchtime, €19 and €35. *10% discount on the room rate, except in summer and Dec, on presentation of this guide.*

Auberge du Clos Sorel**

Les Molanes; it's next to the train station entrance.
Ⓣ04.92.84.10.74 Ⓕ04.92.84.09.14
Ⓦwww.clos-sorel.com

Closed *April–15 June; 1 Sept–15 Dec.* **Restaurant closed** *lunchtimes in winter except during school holidays.* **TV. Swimming pool.**

A charming mountainside inn in a very old farmhouse. It's very close to the ski slopes and there's a lovely pool. Cosy rooms with beams and stone walls €64–140 according to the facilities. Half-board €61–97. You can have tea by the fireside, and they serve honest dishes in the candlelit restaurant, where there's a *menu-carte* for €26; dishes change every day. Friendly welcome. *Free house apéritif on presentation of this guide.*

Bargemon

83830

Restaurant La Taverne

Place Philippe-Chauvier; it's on the village square.
ⓣ04.94.97.89.82
Closed *Thurs out of season and open in the winter according to reservations; mid-Nov to mid-Jan.*

Charming, old-fashioned inn in an amazing village which clings tenaciously to the hillside. Fresh produce gathered from small local growers is used for Provençal cooking infused with a few fresh ideas: snail stew in pastry, lamb *confit* with dried tomatoes, local *caillette* from the Haut Var. It's where the locals come for Sunday lunch. Menus €22–27. Shaded terrace. *Free digestif on presentation of this guide.*

Barroux (Le)

84330

Hôtel-restaurant Les Géraniums**

Place de la Croix.
ⓣ04.90.62.41.08 ⓕ04.90.62.56.48
Closed *5 Jan–5 March.* **Disabled access (restaurant). Highchairs available. Car park.**

A village hotel in a handsome white stone building which has been beautifully renovated. Some rooms have sweeping views of the plains; it's a quiet spot where only the cicadas disturb the silence. Doubles €45–50 with shower/wc or bath. Menus, €16 (weekdays only) and up to €46, list traditional Provençal cooking with innovative twists. Breakfast €7.50. It's a pleasure to dine on the flower-filled terrace.

Bauduen

83630

L'Auberge du Lac**

Rue Grande.
ⓣ04.94.70.08.04 ⓕ04.94.84.39.41
ⓔauberge.lac@wanadoo.fr
Closed *mid-Nov to mid-March.*

This rustic inn is located in a charming little village on the banks of lake Sainte-Croix. The owner has been pampering his guests here for more than forty years. The rooms are attractive and pleasant, particularly those which look onto the lake; they cost €72 with bath. Half board, €67 per person, is preferred during the school holidays. In summer, you can eat on a little terrace wreathed with vines, while in the winter the warm dining room is very welcoming. Good local cuisine, game in season, fish and local wine. Menus €23.50–59. *Free coffee on presentation of this guide.*

Baux-de-Provence (Les)

13520

Hostellerie de la Reine-Jeanne**

ⓣ04.90.54.32.06 ⓕ04.90.54.32.33
Closed *Jan; 15 Nov–20 Dec.* **TV.**

When the main street is heaving with tourists in the summer, all you want to do is get out of town – but this is a charming refuge. The old house has been lovingly and astutely renovated. The rooms are pleasant and individual. Doubles €54–64 with shower, shower/wc or bath; the most expensive one is like an apartment with an amazing view and incredible terrace at €92. In the restaurant they serve quality local dishes. Menus, which start at €16, list quality local cuisine. *Free coffee on presentation of this guide.*

Paradou (Le)

13520 (4km S)

Du Côté des Olivades

Lieu-dit de Bourgeac; outside the village.

Ⓣ04.90.54.56.78 Ⓕ04.90.54.56.79
Closed *Mon (Nov to mid-March).* **TV. Highchairs available. Disabled access. Swimming pool.**

This is owned by a Belgian, André Bourguignon, who, having had enormous success with a brasserie in Brussels, decided to change the northern fogs for the sunshine of the Alpine foothills. He came here with his wife and small daughter to create the hotel of his dreams in the midst of an olive grove. He now has an international clientele, some of whom come back year after year to this idyllic landscape in order to relax in his old farmhouse. Ten cosy rooms complete with beautiful terraces and top-rate cooking, courtesy of his wife, that brings out the best of the local produce without any fancy pretensions. Good, simple dishes of exemplary freshness and precision. Double rooms with shower/wc €95–134, including breakfast. Menus €30–45.

Beaulieu-sur-Mer

06310

Hôtel Riviera*

6 rue Paul-Doumer; between the town centre and the port; 150m from the sea.
Ⓣ04.93.01.04.92 Ⓕ04.93.01.19.31
Ⓦwww.hotel-riviera.fr

Small hotel in a quiet street, with a typically spruce Provençal façade set off by wrought-iron balconies. The interior has been refurbished but retains a certain old-world charm. The redecoration of the rooms is stunning, and the prices are a bargain for this area: doubles with shower/wc or bath €41–48, depending on the season. Some of the rooms give on to the shady patio where breakfast is served in the morning. The welcome is so warm that you won't want to leave. This is maybe our best hotel in Beaulieu.

Hôtel Le Havre Bleu**

29 bd. du Maréchal-Joffre.
Ⓣ04.93.01.01.40 Ⓕ04.93.01.29.92
Ⓦwww.hotel-lehavrebleu.fr
Closed *a fortnight in Nov.* **TV. Car park.**

A nineteenth-century hotel with a quiet family atmosphere. The clean, simple décor, white paintwork and blue shutters are very Mediterranean. Doubles €49–70 (breakfast included) depending on facilities and season; some have a sunny balcony or terrace. The rooms at the back are quieter. *10% discount on the room rate out of season on presentation of this guide.*

Hôtel Comté de Nice***

25 bd. Marinoni; on the main artery, next to the main square.
Ⓣ04.93.01.19.70 Ⓕ04.93.01.23.09
Ⓦwww.hotel-comtedenice.com
TV. Pay car park.

You immediately feel good when you walk into this hotel, five minutes from the beach and the harbour. The façade is very 50s or 60s, but the rooms are well appointed, with air-conditioning, telephone, mini-safe and hairdryer. Most of them have sea views. Doubles with shower/wc or bath €68–130, depending on the season. Good breakfasts for €8.50, and you pay €8.50 for a space in the garage too. There's also a sauna and fitness centre.

Beauvezer

04370

Hôtel Le Bellevue**

Place du Village; 13 km South of Allos.
Ⓣ04.92.83.51.60 Ⓕ04.92.83.51.60
Ⓦwww.verdon-provence.com/bellevue.htm
Closed *mid-Oct to April.* TV.

A charming place to stop between Provence and the Alps – a haven of peace and tranquillity behind an ochre façade. The comfortable double rooms, tastefully decorated in warm colours and Provençal prints, go for €42.50–49.50 with basin, shower or bath. Six rooms have views of the mountains, and there's a suite sleeping four to six. Reservations recommended. You eat heartily in the restaurant – lunch menu €13.50, other menus at €18–25. Delicious regional dishes: aubergine and garlic flan, bass *en papillote*, duck with olives. There's a pretty, shady terrace. Free apéritif and *10% discount on the room rate in low season on presentation of this guide.*

Bonnieux

84480

Restaurant de la Gare

Quartier de la Gare; it's on the D145 in the direction of Goult.

☎04.90.75.82.00
Closed *Mon; Jan.*

The old station was turned into an art gallery, but the restaurant, founded by the grandmother of today's owner, is still there. The huge dining room has an old-fashioned charm and there's a gorgeous terrace overlooking the garden. The lunch menus, €11–22, list hors d'œuvres from the buffet and a freshly cooked dish of the day. Other menus €23–25. The cuisine is distinctly Provençal: good fresh fish, Lubéron lamb and so on. Easy-going welcome. Credit cards not accepted.

Le Fournil

5 pl. Carnot.
☎04.90.75.83.62
Closed *Sat lunchtime; Mon; Tues lunchtime (all day Tues Oct–March); Dec; Jan.*

This establishment has a terrace on the pretty square, with its fountain, and an intriguing stone-built interior. It also has a solid reputation, so you might need to book. Good-value traditional cooking: minestrone with prawns, roast piglet. Menus €24 at lunchtime and €35 in the evening.

Bormes-les-Mimosas

83230

L'Hôtel de la Plage**

Rond-point de la Bienvenue-La Favière; take the road in the direction of the port, then turn off to La Favière.
☎04.94.71.02.74 Ⓕ04.94.71.77.22
Ⓦwww.perso.wanadoo.fr/hoteldelaplage
TV. Highchairs available. Car park.

Other than a few concessions to fashion and some improved comforts, this place has barely changed since opening in 1960, and it still has the same regular guests – there are games of *pétanque* in the evening after dinner. Rooms €46–56 with shower/wc or €60–70 with bath depending on the season. Half board, €55–62 per person, is requested 15 June–15 Sept. Good selection of menus at €17–23. The only blots on the landscape are the concrete blocks on the way to the beach. *Free apéritif on presentation of this guide.*

Lou Poulid Cantoun

6 pl. Lou Poulid Cantoun.
☎04.94.71.15.59
Closed *lunchtimes July–Aug; Mon out of season.*

It's not everyone that has the luck of running a restaurant on the most photographed square in Bormes. In summer there are tables on the terrace and at dusk the place is illuminated by twinkly lights, creating an intimate, relaxed atmosphere. Refined, honest cuisine with Provençal flavours – balsamic vinegar, basil and fennel. Leave room for dessert. Menu for €28, or expect to pay €30–35 à la carte. Best to book.

Briançon

05100

L'Auberge de l'Impossible**

43 av. de Savoie.
☎04.92.21.02.98 Ⓕ04.92.21.13.75
Ⓔauberge.impossible@wanadoo.fr
Closed *lunchtimes in winter.* **TV. Highchairs and baby accessories available. Car park.**

An unpretentious hotel-restaurant with thirty or so decent rooms. Doubles €45 with shower/wc or bath – reasonable prices for the area. Simple, nourishing family cooking is served in the restaurant: barbecue, *fondue* with morels and ceps, *tartiflette*. Menu €22, or €20 à la carte. In summer you dine on the terrace. There's a good atmosphere in the evenings, and in the winter they host occasional crêpe parties or karaoke evenings for the residents. They also offer half board, weekly rates and ski packages. *10% discount on the room rate, except during school holidays or free apéritif on presentation of this guide.*

Hôtel Edelweiss**

32 av. de la République.
☎04.92.21.02.94 Ⓕ04.92.21.22.55
Ⓔhotel.edelweiss.briancon@wanadoo.fr
Closed *15–30 April; 15 Nov–15 Dec.* **TV. Highchairs and games available. Car park.**

A small non-smoking hotel, located very near Vauban's magnificent fortress, opposite the cultural centre and the conference centre. The east-facing rooms have a lovely view of the local woods; those facing west overlook the town. It's clean and quiet. Doubles €50–57 with bath.

L'Auberge du Mont Prorel**

5 rue René-Froger; it's at the foot of the ski lift.

Ⓣ04.92.20.22.88 Ⓕ04.92.21.27.76
Ⓦwww.skisunrosbif.com
Closed *May*. **TV.** Car park.

At the lower end of Vauban fortress, this chalet is at the foot of the Prorel ski lift, which leads up to the Serre-Chevalier area, and there's easy access to the town. Rooms are clean and cosy, and about half of them have a balcony. Doubles €50–70 with shower or bath/wc. Half board costs from €49. The restaurant serves classic regional cooking on menus at €14 (lunchtime) and €18. They host live music on Sunday evenings, when there's a great atmosphere.

|●| Le Péché Gourmand

2 rte. de Gap.
Ⓣ04.92.21.33.21
Closed *Mon; last week in April*. **Disabled access.** Car park.

Though it's set on a corner of a huge junction, this restaurant has a shaded terrace well away from the streams of cars, and two elegant dining rooms. The excellent menus list such delicious things as goat's cheese ravioli with green pea *purée* and roast guineafowl breast with rosemary *jus*. There's a respectable selection of cheeses, good desserts and an extensive list of coffees. Weekday lunch menu €13, then others €21–42.

|●| Le Pied de la Gargouille

64 Grande-Rue; it's in the old town opposite the municipal library.
Ⓣ04.92.20.12.95
Closed *Mon–Thurs, and Fri–Sun lunchtimes out of season; lunchtimes in season*.

This restaurant centres on an open fire where the host keeps an expert eye on the delicious grilled dishes. The walls are adorned with antique skis and snowshoes. Excellent sweet and savoury *tourtons*; other specialities include mountain dishes and steak grilled over the embers. One menu at €16; à la carte around €21. Enthusiastic welcome. *Free apéritif or coffee on presentation of this guide.*

|●| Restaurant Le Rustique

Rue du Pont-d'Asfeld; coming down from the Grande Gargouille take the first left after the fountain and it's 300m further on.
Ⓣ04.92.21.00.10 Ⓕ04.92.21.40.06
Closed *Mon and Tues except public holidays; 2nd fortnight in June; 2nd fortnight in Nov*. **Highchairs available. Disabled access.**

Country décor, good quality cooking and a warm welcome. The speciality is fresh trout served with all manner of sauces – try it with apples flambéed in Calvados, leek coulis, garlic and cream or Roquefort cheese. The generous salads are good, too, and they do a tasty *fondue savoyarde* with morels. Menus €19–26.50, and à la carte around €29. *Free apéritif on presentation of this guide.*

Vachette (La)

05100 (4km NE)

|●| Le Nano

Route d'Italie, Val des Prés; it's on the N94, in the direction of Montgenèvre and Italy.
Ⓣ04.92.21.06.09
Closed *Sun and Mon except July–Aug; Tues in July/Aug; in Nov around All Saints' Day; a few days in May.*

The warm, pleasant setting, the quietly efficient service and above all the quality of the cooking make this one of the best places to eat in the area. The fine, classical dishes are skilfully seasoned – duck foie gras with spices, *roulade* of rabbit with basil, boned cockerel with spiced sauce, fine orange tart with caramel – and there are very good desserts. Menus €23–45. Their wine list is expertly chosen with quality vintages. It's a good idea to book, and to not turn up too late.

Chantemerle

05330 (7km NW)

|●| La Boule de Neige**

15 rue du Centre.
Ⓣ04.92.24.00.16 Ⓕ04.92.24.00.25
Closed *end April to end June; end Aug to mid-Dec*. **TV.**

Prices aren't the cheapest, but this is a wonderfully comfortable establishment and you won't want to leave. Doubles with shower/wc or bath €72–118; half board (compulsory during the Feb holidays) costs €54–77. The restaurant is very pleasant and the cooking is delicate – try parsleyed rabbit cooked with Chardonnay, fillet of pork mignon with endive sauce or rack of lamb with garlic cream sauce. Menu €25. The ski-lift for the Serre-Chevalier slopes is 100m away.

Salle-lès-Alpes (La)

05240 (8km NW)

|●| La Marotte

36 rue de la Guisane; it's in the main street.
Ⓣ04.92.24.77.23
Ⓔpierreaubert@wanadoo.fr
Closed *lunchtimes; Sun; Oct–Nov; May–June.*

A really nice restaurant which has been here for years. The boss prepares delicious dishes; there's a menu at €16.50, or à la carte expect a bill of around €20. Try the terrines, which are the house speciality, made from vegetables, meat or fish. The herring and shallot bread and the apple *tarte tatin* also deserve a mention. Credit cards not accepted. It's best to book.

Cagnes-sur-Mer

06800

Le Mas d'Azur

42 av. de Nice, Cros-de-Cagnes.
Ⓣ04.93.20.19.19
TV. Car park.

At first sight, this hotel, set on the edge of the main road, doesn't look very promising. But inside you travel back in time. It's a charming old Provençal house with a courtyard and an appealing garden, and you're welcomed warmly by the kindly owners. On top of that, it's just three minutes' walk from the beach. Quiet doubles with shower/wc €42–55.

Le Val Duchesse**

11 rue de Paris; it's 50m from the beach.
Ⓣ04.92.13.40.00 Ⓕ04.92.13.40.29
Closed *25 Nov–15 Dec.* **TV. Swimming pool. Car park.**

Set in a quiet street, away from the traffic and the impersonal high-rises down by the sea, this place has a pretty garden planted with palm trees, a swimming pool, a ping-pong table and games for the children. The décor is full of southern colour. You can rent studios from €48–67 and apartments from €66–92.

|●| Le Renoir

23 pl. Sainte-Luce; it's opposite les Halles.
Ⓣ04.93.22.59.58
Closed *Sun and Thurs evenings; Mon; 15 Dec to end of Jan.*

It's a warm, appealing place serving good, flavoursome food: rabbit with tapenade, daube with ceps and *fricassée* of fish. The *patronne*, who is wonderfully kind, will help you choose. Menus €16–26.

|●| Fleur de Sel

86 montée de la Bourgade.
Ⓣ04.93.20.33.33
Closed *Wed and Thurs lunchtime; lst fortnight Jan; lst week June; fortnight during autumn school holidays.*

Pretty little restaurant with typical Provençal stone walls. Philippe Loose had worked for lots of other restaurants until he and his wife decided to give others pleasure by working for themselves. Their guests are glad of it. Authentic, well-presented local dishes that are unfussily and simply served. *Menu saveur* for €21 or €29 with wine and coffee.

Cannes

06400

Hôtel Chanteclair

12 rue Forville; it's near the Palais des Festivals and the Midi beach.
Ⓣand Ⓕ04.93.39.68.88
Closed *Nov; Dec.*

Though it's ideally located (100m from the liveliest part of town), this hotel is nonetheless perfectly quiet. Functional rooms with white walls and simple pine furniture cost €40–42. There's a charming patio where you can have breakfast. You'll get a warm welcome from the chatty host, who will tell you where you can park for free nearby. Credit cards not accepted. *Free coffee on presentation of this guide.*

Hôtel de France***

85 rue d'Antibes.
Ⓣ04.93.06.54.54 Ⓕ04.93.68.53.43
Ⓦwww.h-de-france.com
TV. Closed *22 Nov–26 Dec.*

This place has been completely refurbished without losing its Art Deco style. It's in the busiest part of town, right on the main thoroughfare, and has thirty rooms with modern facilities – air conditioning, safe, hairdryer and the rest – for €82–139 depending on the season. Rooms 501–508 have a view of the sea. *10% discount on the room rate except during the congress on presentation of this guide.*

🏃 ☗ Hôtel Molière**

5–7 rue Molière; it's 100m from La Croisette.
Ⓣ04.93.38.16.16 Ⓕ04.93.68.29.57
Ⓦwww.hotel-moliere.com
Closed *17 Nov–25 Dec*. **Disabled access. TV.**

This friendly nineteenth-century hotel with a pretty façade is furnished in the appropriate style. Lovely rooms €85–110, breakfast included. Although the hotel is very close to the town centre, the location is quiet and there is a large garden in which to enjoy breakfast. *10% discount on the room rate for a stay of at least two consecutive nights, except in July/Aug, on presentation of this guide.*

🏃 ☗ Le Splendid***

4–6 rue Félix Faure.
Ⓣ04.97.06.22.22 Ⓕ04.93.99.55.02
Ⓦwww.splendid-hotel-cannes.fr
Disabled access. TV. Highchairs available.

It's not a palace such as you find on La Croisette but it's pretty close. Behind the majestic turn-of-the-century façade, there's one of the town's loveliest hotels, wonderfully run by Annick Cagnat and her family. The beautiful rooms have antique furniture and great bathrooms – and if you reserve in advance they provide a welcoming fruit basket. Some of the rooms have a balcony and a big terrace overlooking the sea. The prices – €90–214 for a double, depending on the season – are fair. *Free buffet breakfast on presentation of this guide.*

🏃 |●| Le Bouchon d'Objectif

10 rue Constantine.
Ⓣ04.93.99.21.76
Closed *Sun evening and Mon out of season except when there are conferences; 20 Nov–15 Dec.*

Each month this friendly restaurant stages an exhibition of a different photographer's work. The simple, original food includes salad of red mullet with *anchoïade*, duck breast casserole, ceps *parmentier* and piglet with a soya caramel sauce. Menus €15.50 and €25. There's a pretty terrace facing a modern pedestrianized area. *Free house apéritif on presentation of this guide.*

|●| Restaurant Aux Bons Enfants

80 rue Meynadier; it's opposite Forville market.
Closed *Sat evening except in season; Sun; August; between Christmas and the New Year.*

There's no telephone, so regulars pop in during the morning to reserve a table while the staff are still peeling the vegetables bought in the Forville market. Home cooking and regional dishes: Dover sole, sweet and sour peppers, goat's cheese terrine with a *coulis* of tomatoes, rabbit with rosemary, aubergine and sardine fritters, *aïoli*, tarts and home-made iced nougat. Menu €17.

🏃 |●| Restaurant Au Bec Fin

12 rue du 24-Août; it's between the train station and the rue d'Antibes.
Ⓣ04.93.38.35.86
Closed *Sat evening and Sun out of season; Mon lunch in summer; a week in July; a fortnight in Nov*. **Disabled access.**

This restaurant gets very full, so don't arrive too late. The menus, €18 and €22, offer a staggering choice with nearly twenty starters and almost as many mains. Around €28 à la carte. Mostly local cuisine: *daube provençale* (a slowly braised beef stew), vegetable *soupe au pistou*, scorpion fish *à la pêcheur*. Good daily specials, too – you won't even notice the bland décor. *Free apéritif on presentation of this guide.*

🏃 |●| Le Comptoir des Vins

13 bd. de la République.
Ⓣ04.93.68.13.26
Closed *Mon–Wed evenings; Sun; Feb.*

You enter via the cellar, selecting your wine first, then choose food to suit. It took the owner some time to get the local Cannois used to the idea of a bistro-cellar, but he succeeded. It's busy and buzzy, especially in the evening. Good, wholesome dishes: sausage with pistachios, *tartiflette*, and a range of Savoyard specialities. Menu at €22.50 or €23 à la carte. Wine, by the glass or the bottle, is good value. *Free coffee on presentation of this guide.*

🏃 |●| Restaurant Lou Souleou

16 bd. Jean-Hibert; it's on the road to Mandelieu.
Ⓣ04.93.39.85.55
Closed *Mon, and Wed evening out of season; Nov*. **Highchairs available.**

This restaurant is behind the old harbour

in a district where few tourists venture. The menus are excellent value for money, listing dishes such as *blanquette* of monkfish with mussels, fillet of sea bass with watercress and *bourride du pêcheur*, a rich fish soup. Menus at €25 and €35; the *bourride*, paella and fish stew go for €20.50; à la carte around €27. Sip a Kir as you admire the view of the Estérel hills. *Free apéritif on presentation of this guide.*

Golfe-Juan

06220 (4km NE)

Hôtel California*

222 av. de la Liberté; it's on the N7, 800m from the station, close to the seashore.
Ⓣand Ⓕ04.93.63.78.63
Ⓦwww.californiagolfe.fr.st
Closed *Nov school holidays*. **TV. Games available. Car park.**

This 1920s house, set back from the main road, has been converted into a hotel with pretty double rooms available for €23.50–43 with basin or €34–50 with shower/wc; depending on the season. There's a nice old garden. Cards not accepted. *10% discount on the room rate for a stay of at least two nights, except July–Aug, on presentation of this guide.*

Le Palm-Hôtel**

17 av. de la Palmeraie.
Ⓣ04.93.63.72.24 Ⓕ04.93.63.18.45
Ⓦwww.palmotel.fr
Car park. **TV.**

Unfortunately, the N7 passes close by (a definite minus), but this beautiful old house has lots of charm and the owners have a real sense of hospitality. Spruce rooms which have been done up cost €74–80 each, a little less out of season.

Vallauris

06220 (6km NE)

Le Manuscrit

224 chemin Lintier; it's in the centre of town off the boulevard du Tapis-Vert.
Ⓣ04.93.64.56.56
Closed *Mon in season; Sun evening, Mon and Tues evening out of season; 18 Nov–4 Dec.*

The interior of this fine stone building, which used to be a perfume factory, is exceptional, and the food is pretty good too. You can eat in the dining room (where there's a wonderful display of prints and canvasses), in the conservatory (full of subtropical flowers) or on the terrace beneath the hundred-year-old magnolia tree. Menus at €22 and €29, offer a nice range of fish and meat dishes. Affordable wines.

Carpentras

84200

Hôtel Forum**

24 rue du Forum.
Ⓣ04.90.60.57.00 Ⓕ04.90.63.52.65
Ⓦwww.hotel-forum.fr
Closed *Ist fortnight in Feb; Christmas school holidays*. **Disabled access. Highchairs available. TV. Pay car park.**

A hotel to charm you, decorated in pretty, neo-Provençal style. A total of 28 modern rooms that are well equipped with TV, desk and computer connection. Doubles €53.50–58, all with en-suite bathrooms. The dining room has a surprising, glass-fronted bookshelf and the terrace on the roof is wonderful in the heat. *10% discount on the room rate 1 Oct–31 March on presentation of this guide .*

Chez Serge

90 rue Cottier.
Ⓣ04.90.63.21.24
Closed *Sun*. **Disabled access. Highchairs available.**

A very lovely restaurant with a modern decor that really works – New York loft meets timeless Provence. They serve very good pizzas, along with dishes such as *fricassée* of scallops with truffles, farm-raised chicken breast, Armenian platters (Thurs) and delicious desserts. Weekday lunch menu €12.80 and others up to €25. Children's menu €6.50. Not at all bad. *Free house apéritif on presentation of this guide.*

Pernes-les-Fontaines

84210 (6km S)

Dame l'Oie

56 rue Troubadour; it's on the D938.
Ⓣ04.90.61.62.43
Closed *Mon; Tues; autumn and winter school holidays*. **Highchairs available.**

There's a fountain in the middle of the dining room, where the décor is English country style and very Beatrix Potter. The cuisine, however, is typically southern –

simple but nicely prepared, with stunning flavours and delicious desserts. It's good value, with a weekday lunch menu at €14 and others up to €28. Children's menu €11. *Free coffee on presentation of this guide.*

Cassis

13260

Auberge de jeunesse

La Fontasse; by road from Marseille, turn right after about 15km towards Col de la Gardiole (3km of good road, then 2km of stony road); on foot, climb up from Cassis, taking the avenue de l'Amiral-Ganteaume, then the avenue des Calanques until you reach the calanque (creek) of Port-Miou and then start climbing (around 1hr).
Ⓣ04.42.01.02.72
Ⓦwww.fuaj.org
Closed *6 Jan–14 March. New arrivals 8–10am and 5–9pm.* **Car park.**

The only lodging available on the massif des Calanques. A very pretty Provençal house in what is obviously an exceptional setting. You really get back to nature here: there's a tank to collect the rain water (and pools for washing yourself), and solar panels and windmills for electricity. The hostel sleeps 60, in shared rooms with 10 beds. €9e a night (FUAJ card compulsory, but you can buy it *in situ*). Kitchen available (bring your own provisions) . The manager is very friendly and knows the area backwards. A host of activities: hikes (the GR98 passes alongside), climbing, swimming, botanical observation (450 varieties of plants), *pétanque*, etc. Come early in the morning in July–Aug, as otherwise you may find it full (although walkers and cyclists are never turned away). Children are accepted from the age of 7, but there are no bedrooms specifically for families. Credit cards not accepted.

Le Clos des Arômes**

10 rue Paul-Mouton; it's a two-minute walk from the town centre.
Ⓣ04.42.01.71.84 Ⓕ04.42.01.31.76
Closed *5 Jan–20 Feb.* **Restaurant closed** *Mon–Wed lunchtimes except public holidays.* **TV.**

Old village house prettily renovated in a peaceful street. The dining room is cute, with a fireplace and a shady, flower-filled courtyard. Menus at €20 and €28 list refined local cuisine. Charming rooms with subtle Provençal décor; doubles €60–70 with shower/wc or bath. *Free apéritif on presentation of this guide.*

Le Jardin d'Emile

Plage du Bestouan.
Ⓣ04.42.01.80.55 Ⓕ04.42.01.80.70
Ⓔprovence@lejardindemile.fr
Closed *Wed out of season; Jan; a few days in mid-Nov.* **TV. Car park.**

A charming, enjoyable place with a great view. Seven ravishing rooms – including a honeymoon suite and two attic rooms – go for €80–130 with shower/wc or bath. The chic but relaxed restaurant serves creative Mediterranean cooking. There's a weekday lunch menu at €25 and others up to €45. Dine in the garden if at all possible, under ancient pines, olives trees, fig trees and cypresses.

La Poissonnerie

6 quai Barthélémy.
Ⓣ04.42.01.71.56
Closed *Mon; every evening Nov to late March.*

You are among genuine fishing folk here. The eldest son, Laurent, a boatman and fisherman, gets up at 6am. While his mother takes charge of the fishmonger's, the rest of the family makes sure that everything is shipshape in this house that has now been home to five generations of fishermen. Beware of Éric, Laurent's brother, who will shut the restaurant at the first sight of tourists in flip-flops... Fisherman's menu at €20, or reckon on €13–26, or even more. On Tues, there's *aioli*, on Wed *bourride*, on Thurs cod, served in the style of Christmas Eve (*raïto*), and on Fri and Sat there's fish couscous. If you want something else, just point it out in the fishmonger's. There are also snacks (€13) of fresh baby cuttlefish or sardines with a glass of wine.

Fleurs de Thym

5 rue Lamartine.
Ⓣ04.42.01.23.03
Open *every evening, all year round.*

An unusual but really appealing little restaurant. Here also, you have to show your credentials, and do not even consider wearing shorts. Once you pass the initial test, however, it's a relaxed place where you'll be treated like royalty. The décor aspires to sophistication but cannot take itself seriuosly enough to really bring it off. The mother of the family works in the kitchen, producing tasty dishes of remarkable precision: various small *farcis*, *purée* of sardines, aubergine and tomato with basil, fillet of bass with ceps risotto. Her menu varies according to the season, and her whims. Menus €26 and 39. In fine weather you can also eat on the terrace.

Castellane

04120

Nouvel Hôtel du Commerce***

Place Centrale.
Ⓣ04.92.83.61.00
Ⓕ04.92.83.72.82
Ⓦwww.hotel-fradet.com
Closed *Tues; Wed lunch; Nov–Feb.* **TV. Disabled access.** Car park.

This large house by the post office and town hall is decorated like a Provençal family home. It is much appreciated by tourists passing through the town. Spacious, comfortable double rooms with shower/wc or bath from €57–65, depending on the season. You can choose between a view of the town square or one of a 184-metre-high cliff. The food is meticulously prepared with fresh ingredients: a feast of wonderful flavours in a friendly if rather stuffy atmosphere. Menus €18–40. Very polite service.

Garde (La)

04120 (3km SE)

Auberge du Teillon**

Route Napoléon; it's on the N85 towards Grasse.
Ⓣ04.92.83.60.88 Ⓕ04.92.83.74.08
Closed *Sun evening Oct–Easter; Mon except July–Aug; Dec to early March.* **TV. Highchairs available. Car park.**

People come here from all along the coast at the weekend. You feel cocooned in the rustic little dining room, where chef Yves Lépine uses Provençal ingredients to produce flavoursome dishes on menus at €18–40: smoked lamb, veal kidneys with morels and such like. Prolong the pleasure by staying the night; doubles cost €39–49 with basin or shower depending on the season. Half board is requested in summer and at the weekends, at a cost of €45–50 per person. Rooms facing the main road can be noisy, so ask for ones at the back if you want a lie-in. *10% discount on the room rate on presentation of this guide.*

Rougon

04120 (17km SW)

Auberge du Point-Sublime**

It's on the D952 at the entrance to the Verdon Gorges.
Ⓣ04.92.83.60.35 Ⓕ04.92.83.74.31
Ⓔpoint.sublime@wanadoo.fr
Closed *Wed except July–Aug; mid-Oct to early April.* **TV. Highchairs available. Car park.**

There are two small dining rooms here, one of them non-smoking. Whichever you choose, you've got quite a treat in store. Décor is pleasant, with checked tablecloths, tiled floors, green plants and photographs of the Verdon around the rooms. Menus €20.50–38.50. Fresh local dishes are flavoured wth countryside herbs: pesto soup, *pieds-paquets*, lamb kebabs and regional classics like scrambled eggs with truffles. The desserts alone are worth a visit – particularly the fig *crème brûlée*. Doubles, €48–54, are blissfully peaceful. Half board, €47.50–51.50, is compulsory at the weekends, public holidays and during the school holidays. It's best to reserve in July and Aug. *10% discount on the room rate except during weekends, bank holidays and school holidays, on presentation of this guide.*

Palud-sur-Verdon (La)

04120 (25km SW)

Hôtel-restaurant Le Provence**

Rte. La Maline; take the D23, it's 50m from the village.
Ⓣ04.92.77.38.88 Ⓕ04.92.77.31.05
Ⓔhotelleprovence@aol.com
Closed *Nov to end March.* **Restaurant closed** *lunchtimes.* **Disabled access. TV. Highchairs and games available. Car park.**

This hotel has wide views of the rte. des Crêtes. Simple rooms, clean and recently refurbished: doubles with shower/wc or bath go for €41–55. Half board is requested in July and Aug. In the restaurant, specialities include duckling in honey, rabbit *à la provençale*, and salmon with sorrel. Menus €17–30. There's a relaxing lounge, or you can sip a cool drink on the terrace and savour the peace and quiet. *Free apéritif on presentation of this guide.*

Hôtel des Gorges du Verdon***

Take the D952, the road north of the gorges.
℡04.92.77.38.26 Ⓕ04.92.77.35.00
Ⓦwww.hotel-des-gorges-du-verdon.fr
Open *7.30–9.00pm only*. **Closed** *All Saints' to Easter*. **Disabled access. Highchairs available. TV. Swimming pool. Car park.**

This hotel is in the heart of the Verdon Gorges, on a hillside facing the village and the surrounding countryside. The spectacular scenery helps you forget the hotel's rather brutal architecture. The rooms are similarly modern, but they're well equipped, clean and comfortable and decorated in Provençal style. Doubles with shower/wc €92–130 or €100–300 with bath. They serve very decent food, mostly traditional Provençal dishes: *anchoïade*, artichokes *en barigoule* (stuffed with mushrooms and ham), lamb chops with tarragon, fillet of salmon with olive oil and savoury scrambled eggs with truffles. There's one menu at €30. Half board is recommended in season.

Cavaillon

84300

Hôtel du Parc**

183 pl. François-Tourel; it's near the tourist office.
℡04.90.71.57.78 Ⓕ04.90.76.10.35
Ⓦwww.hotelduparccavaillon.com_
TV. Pay car park.

A huge nineteenth-century house opposite the Roman arch. Good hospitality and family atmosphere, with nice communal spaces (especially the patio). The rooms are classically decorated and fit in well with the architecture. Doubles with shower/wc or bath €56–58, depending on the season. Breakfast €6.50.

La Cuisine du Marché

Place Gambetta.
℡04.90.71.56.00
Closed *Tues evening and Wed; Tues evening and Sun lunchtime in July–Aug*. **Highchairs and games available.**

Climb the stairs to the first floor and you'll find an attractive, unfussy dining room with a view over the main square. Excellent fresh dishes with a strong Provençal accent: cod with olive paste crust, rack of lamb, duck breast with Marchand de Vin sauce and lamb tripe and trotters *à la provençale*. Weekday lunch menu €13, then others up to €29.50. Children's menu €8. *Free apéritif on presentation of this guide.*

Chapelle-en-Valgaudemar (La)

05800

Hôtel-restaurant du Mont-Olan**

℡04.92.55.23.03 Ⓕ04.92.55.34.58
Closed *15 Sept to Easter holidays*. **TV.** Car park.

Chalet-style hotel where all the rooms look out towards the soaring peaks that dominate the village. Monsieur and Mme Voltan's large dining room has a panoramic view of the fast-flowing Navette river. You'll consume huge quantities of robust food – potato pie and ravioli with honey – perfect to build up your strength for an assault on the mountains. Menu at €11; à la carte around €25. Doubles €40–42 with shower/wc or bath.

Chauffayer

05800 (22km SW)

Le Bercail**

It's on the N85, the rte. de Napoléon, on the right on the road to Gap.
℡04.92.55.22.21 Ⓕ04.92.55.31.55
Closed *Sun evening; 1 Nov–1 Dec*. **TV. Car park.**

This hotel-restaurant offers good value for money, with prettily decorated, comfortable rooms – doubles €30–46 with shower/wc or bath. The large dining room has a lovely Provençal feel and there's a shaded terrace filled with glorious geraniums. The cuisine is regional and classic, with menus at €17–34; scallops and balsamic vinegar, pan-fried lamb, duck terrine with green pepper, trout *meunière* and raviolis are the specialities. *Menu terroir* at €22. *Free coffee on presentation of this guide.*

Le Château des Herbeys***

It's on the N85, the rte. de Napoléon.
℡04.92.55.26.83 Ⓕ04.92.55.29.66

Closed *Tues except in school holidays*. **TV. Highchairs and games available. Swimming pool. Car park.**

Looking out over the route that Napoleon took on his return from Elba, stands this noble and beautiful residence surrounded by substantial grounds. The rooms are high-ceilinged and luxurious, with parquet floors, plush and tasteful fabrics and splendid bathrooms. The "Roy" room is a truly royal suite with a canopied bed, sitting room and Jacuzzi; it's also the most expensive. Doubles with bath €61–115. Half board from €64–90. In the park there is a tennis court and a swimming pool. The restaurant offers such dishes as lamb roasted with garlic, lobster, scallops, pigeon breast, pan-fried foie gras and goose. Menus €19.50–36. *Free coffee or digestif on presentation of this guide.*

Château-Arnoux

04160

Au Goût du Jour

It's on the N85, opposite the château.
✆04.92.64.48.48
Closed *Mon and Tues lunchtime out of season; early Jan to mid-Feb; a fortnight end Nov to early Dec.*

Relaxed bistro; the cheaper sibling of the upmarket *Bonne Étape* next door. The sunny décor creates an elegant, refined atmosphere, but the food is very reasonably priced: menus €14 and €22. The main courses, displayed on a slate, change with the seasons and what's good in the market. Try fresh anchovies marinated in fennel, duck leg with olives or the delicious *tarte alsacienne* with strawberries. There are some nice wines. *Free coffee, apéritif, digestif, fruit juice or soft drink on presentation of this guide.*

L'Oustaou de la Foun

It's 1.5km north on the N85.
✆04.92.62.65.30
Closed *Sun evening; Mon; a week in Jan; a week in June; a week in early Nov.*

This restaurant, which occupies a Provençal hacienda, manages to be chic yet relaxed. The chef, who comes from a family of farmers and *charcutiers*, really knows his stuff, and he organizes cookery courses. His dishes balance fine ingredients and create delightful flavour combinations. The side dishes are unusual while remaining simple. Menus €20–49.

Aubignosc

04200 (3km NW)

La Magnanerie

Les Fillières; it's on the N85, 3 km from Château-Arnoux.
✆04.92.62.60.11 Ⓕ04.92.62.63.05
Closed *Sun evening; Mon; Thurs evening; Jan*. **TV. Car park.**

An old silk house has been turned into a quality hotel-restaurant by the Paroche family. There are eight quiet and elegant rooms named after flowers of the region. Doubles €43–58. Alain and Stéphane create original dishes with flavoursome ingredients harvested from the kitchen garden: snail mousse, pepper *gazpacho*, Roquefort and walnut *parfait*, salmon trout with cream sauce and custard tart. Menus €22–42. Anchovy toast is served with house cocktails, and there's a lovely wine list. The veranda is decorated bright yellow. A professional place with lots of charm. It's a pity about the main road outside, but the noise doesn't impinge too much.

Collobrières

83610

Hôtel-restaurant des Maures

19 bd. Lazare-Carnot.
✆04.94.48.07.10

A genuine family restaurant that's popular with the locals – everyone crowds in to watch the football on weekday evenings. The simple rooms cost €19 with shower (toilets on the landing) – at that price you can't argue. Nicely cooked Provençal cuisine served in gargantuan portions – the mushroom omelette spills ceps all over the plate and the chestnut ice cream is a challenge to finish. Menus €9–28. There's a charming terrace by the river.

La Petite Fontaine

Place de la République.
✆04.94.48.00.12
Closed *Sun evening; Mon; Tues, Wed and Tursday evenings, Oct–March; winter school holidays; 15–30 Sept.*

One of the best places for miles around, in a peaceful village in the Maures mountains. This rustic restaurant is decorated with old farming implements and the cooking is delicious: *fricassée* of chicken with garlic, rabbit in white wine, beef *daube à la provençale*, duck breast with ceps. Weekday menu €22 and a dinner version at €26. They serve wine from the local cooperative by the glass. Reservations essential. Free digestif *on presentation of this guide.*

Comps-sur-Artuby

83840

Grand Hôtel Bain**

It's between Draguignan and Castellane.
☎04.94.76.90.06 Ⓕ04.94.76.92.24
Ⓦwww.grand-hotel-bain.fr
Closed *mid-Nov to Christmas.* **TV. Highchairs available. Pay car park.**

The Bain family has owned this hotel since 1737. Today it's frequented by local hunters, who relish the hearty local dishes: truffle pâté, omelettes with truffles, trout with basil in pastry, rabbit with tarragon, *daube à la provençale*, roast rack of lamb and goat's cheese. Menus €13–34. Nice rooms cost €45–48 with shower/wc or with bath. Half-board € 64 per person. *Free coffee on presentation of this guide.*

Digne-les-Bains

04000

L'Origan

6 rue Pied-de-Ville; in the pedestrianized area.
☎and Ⓕ04.92.31.62.13
Ⓦwww.hotel-restaurant.net/origan
Closed *Sun; Feb.*

A restaurant in the heart of the old quarter of the spa town. Chef Philippe Cochet prepares delicious food such as John Dory fillets with basil, scrambled egg with truffle, *pieds et paquets* (lamb tripe and trotters). Menus €19–42. They have some simple rooms from €22 with shower. *Free house apéritif on presentation of this guide.*

Hôtel & Pension Villa Gaïa***

Route de Nice; it's 3km from the centre on the Nice road.
☎04.92.31.21.60 Ⓕ04.92.31.20.12
Ⓔhotel.gaia@wanadoo.fr
Open *evenings only from 8.00 p.m.* **Closed** *early Nov to mid-April; Sun evening except in July and August.* **Disabled access. Car park.**

This quiet hotel, an impressive building set in shady, green grounds, was converted from an old convalescent home and still keeps to some of the old rules. Dinner is served at the same time every night, and there's a single menu (€24; reservations essential) featuring superb regional dishes: lamb with lemon, pesto soup and pear tart with goat's cheese. They use vegetables from the garden, local cheeses and meat and fish direct from the market. You dine on the terrace, in the library or the salon. Rooms €65–95 with shower or bath; half board, which is recommended in summer, costs €75 per person. *Free apéritif or coffee on presentation of this guide.*

Hôtel du Grand Paris****

19 bd. Thiers.
☎04.92.31.11.15 Ⓕ04.92.32.32.82
Ⓦwww.chateauxhotels.com/grandparis
Closed *1 Dec–1 March.* **TV. Car park.**

Stylish hotel that has been converted from a seventeenth-century convent. The welcome is slightly formal but the place oozes discreet charm. The chef prepares classic dishes using good ingredients: try the pigeon, the *brandade* of peppers or the delicious *mignonette* of lamb. Menus €23–64 or around €41 à la carte. Lovely, comfortable double rooms with shower/wc for €75–79 or bath for €80–150.

Draguignan

83300

Le Domino

28 av. Carnot; it's on the main street.
☎04.94.67.15.33
Closed *Sun; Mon; 1–16 Nov.*

This building has a lot of character and so does the stylish Tex-Mex restaurant inside. À la carte you'll pay around €20–25 per person for salads, spiced-up meat dishes and Mexican specialities such as chicken and beef fajitas and spare ribs. You can dine on the veranda or out under the palm trees. Kindly welcome and attentive service.

Embrun

05200

🏃 ⌂ |●| Hôtel de la Mairie**

Place de la Mairie or pl. Barthelon.
☎04.92.43.20.65
ⓦwww.hoteldelamairie.com
Closed *Sun evening and Mon in winter; 1–20 May; Oct; Nov.* **Disabled access. Highchairs available. TV.**

This hotel is a model of its type, with a convivial brasserie, high-quality food and competent, charming staff. It's a favourite with locals for an evening drink or Sunday lunch. Specialities include ravioli with morel sauce, sautéed prawns *à la provençale* and an excellent duck *confit*. Menus €16–23. Clean, bright rooms are €46–49 for a double – choose one which looks out onto the square. Reservations recommended for a meal or a room. *Free coffee on presentation of this guide.*

🏃 ⌂ |●| Hôtel Notre-Dame**

Avenue Général-Nicolas – coming from Guillestre, turn right before the post office then right again.
☎04.92.43.08.36 Ⓕ04.92.43.58.41
Closed *Sun evening and Mon except for school holidays; Jan; a week at Easter; a week at All Saints'.* **TV. Highchairs available.**

Just five minutes' walk from the centre of town, this family hotel is a peaceful haven set at the far end of a large garden. After receiving a warm welcome you will be shown to extremely clean rooms with excellent beds. Doubles with shower/wc €46–48. Quality cuisine using only local produce – snails, duck breast, trout, lamb tripe and trotters – is served on menus at €18–26. Half board, compulsory in summer, costs €47. *Free coffee on presentation of this guide.*

🏃 |●| Restaurant Pascal

Hameau de Caléyère.
☎04.92.43.00.69
Closed *Sept.*

It's not the place for a romantic *tête-à-tête*, but the family atmosphere is convivial and infectious – you'll leave in a good mood. The *patronne* greets all her customers by shaking their hand. There's only one menu, at €10, and it's substantial. The vegetables, eggs and meats all come from local farms. The local *digestif* is called *vipérine* – it bites like a snake. Credit cards not accepted. *Free digestif on presentation of this guide.*

Saint-André-d'Embrun

05200 (6km NE)

🏃 ⌂ |●| Restaurant La Grande Ferme

Les Rauffes; it's on the Crévoux road.
☎04.92.43.09.99
Closed *Sun evening to Fri lunchtime; 1 Oct–15 Dec.* **Highchairs available.**

Owners Nicole and Thierry will welcome you into a magnificent vaulted dining room that they restored themselves. This restaurant has a well-deserved reputation in the region and it serves excellent traditional cuisine – try the baked eggs with Queyras blue cheese and the pear *gratin* with brandy from the Hautes-Alpes. Menu at €20. Good selection of wines. Gîtes available for rent. *10% discount on the room rate for a stay of two consecutive nights outside the school holidays, on presentation of this guide.*

Saint-Sauveur

05200 (10km SE)

|●| Restaurant Les Manins

Les Manins; take the road to Les Orres and it's sign-posted off to the left – don't take the ones for St-Sauveur.
☎04.92.43.09.27
Open *noon–9.00pm from early July to mid-Sept; the rest of the year by reservation only.* **Highchairs available.**

Fantastic restaurant with breathtaking views from the terrace looking down at Lac de Serre-Ponçon and Embrun. Architect Eric Boissel built this elegant wooden structure with his own hands, and designed all the furniture. Try *grand mézé*, a complete Middle Eastern meal with individual dishes of red peppers, tzatziki, hummus, köfte, feta cheese, fresh onions, tapenade and the like. They also do mixed salads, substantial pizzas and good crêpes, and there's a splendid crumble for dessert. Pizzas are about €9; expect to pay €21 à la carte. Credit cards not accepted.

Crévoux

05200 (15km E)

🏃 ⌂ |●| L'Auberge

Le Chef-lieu; it's at the top of the village opposite the teleski.

☎04.92.43.18.18
Closed *Wed and Thurs April–June (except public holidays); Sept– Dec.* **Car park.**

An excellent spot at the foot of the ski runs run by two young local brothers. The clean rooms are freshly decorated and warm, though they're not all huge; €33 per person half board or €41.50 full board. The dining room is very spacious and the dishes are typical of the area: egg fondue with blue cheese sauce, cheese turnovers, trout with creamed peppers, pork *filet mignon* with blue cheese crust. Menus €11.50–20. If you want information about the walking trails, don't hesitate to ask. *Free coffee on presentation of this guide.*

Entrecasteaux

83570

La Fourchette

Le Courtil; it's next to the church.
☎04.94.04.42.78
Closed *Sun evening; Mon; Tues; Jan–Feb.*

In the shadow of the famous château, this place attracts gourmet travellers who enjoy delicious food while admiring the wonderful view from the terrace. Chef Pierre Nicolas runs the kitchens while his American wife greets you. Simple, quality cooking and honest prices: menus €16 (weekday lunchtimes) and €25, or €35 à la carte. Dishes include foie gras cannelloni and sautéed king scallops with truffles. *Free coffee on presentation of this guide.*

Èze

06360

Hermitage du Col d'Èze**

Grande Corniche; from Èze, take the D46 and then the Grande Corniche; it's 500m on the left.
☎04.93.41.00.68 Ⓕ04.93.41.24.05
Ⓦwww.eze.riviera.com
Open *7.30–8.30pm for residents only.* **TV. Highchairs and games available. Swimming pool. Car park.**

A place in which to relax in peace and quiet. The swimming pool will ease your aching limbs after a mountain walk – the location is at the start of a lot of trails. There is a splendid view of the southern Alps and the cooler air at this altitude provides relief from the heat of the coast. Doubles €32–55 with shower/wc or bath. Half board from €40–48 per person, compulsory in summer. Choose the newly renovated rooms. *Free house apéritif on presentation of this guide.*

Fayence

83440

Hôtel La Sousto

4 rue du Paty.
☎04.94.76.02.16
Ⓔguy.corteccia@wanadoo.fr
Closed *a week in June; All Saints'.*

You get the best of Provence in this attractive little hotel in the centre of an old village above the valley. The simply furnished rooms have a hotplate, fridge and basin; some also have a shower. Each room has personality – no. 5 has a sunny little terrace overlooking the valley. Doubles with shower/wc €42.60. *10% discount on the room rate for a stay of at least two nights out of season on presentation of this guide.*

Fontvieille

13990

Hôtel Le Daudet***

7 av. de Montmajour; it's on the way out of the village on the road to Arles.
☎04.90.54.76.06 Ⓕ04.90.54.76.95
Closed *1 Oct–1 April.* **Swimming pool.** Car park.

This new hotel is named after the writer Alphonse Daudet, whose mill is nearby. Built around a patio, it offers straightforward rooms with terrace. There's a swimming pool among the pine trees. Doubles €57–65 with shower/wc or bath. *Free apéritif or coffee on presentation of this guide.*

La Peiriero

34 av. des Baux.
☎04.90.54.76.10 Ⓕ04.90.54.62.60
Ⓦwww.hotel-peiriero.com
Closed *Easter; early Nov.* **TV. Disabled access. Car park. Swimming pool.**

This hotel has a forbiddlingly austere façade but inside it's exceptionally welcoming. It is has recently been superbly refurbished and redecorated in pure Provençal style to offer unstandardized rooms and a lovely pool. A great atmosphere (both laid-back and chic) and good value for money. Double rooms with bathroom €82–118. Dinner menu €18.60. You can also order refreshing snacks when you are lounging outside under a parasol. The free car park has a security system. *Free apéritif on presentation of this guide.*

La Cuisine au Planet

144 Grand'Rue; it's in the old village.
Ⓣ and Ⓕ 04.90.54.63.97
Closed *Mon lunchtime (and evening in winter); Feb; Nov.*

This charming, creeper-covered restaurant is run by a couple who are crazy about the area and prepare local cuisine with a light touch all their own. Menus, €25 and €31, list superb dishes. There's also a lunch menu at €15 in the summer. Impressive wine list. *Free coffee on presentation of this guide.*

Forcalquier

04300

Auberge Charambeau**

Route de Niozelles; it's 3.5km out of town on the N100 in the direction of Niozelles.
Ⓣ 04.92.70.91.70 Ⓕ 04.92.70.81.83
Ⓦ www.charambeau.com
Closed *mid-Nov to mid-Feb.* **Disabled access. TV.** Highchairs and games available. Swimming pool. Car park.

This hotel occupies a converted eighteenth-century farm in the middle of a seven-hectare expanse of hills and meadows. It's a lovely place to stay, looking down over the valley. Ten freshly decorated, attractive rooms; some have balconies, others wide terraces and all have good facilities. One room has been converted for disabled visitors. Doubles €53.50–55.50 with shower/wc or €77–84.50 with bath, depending on the season. Self-catering apartments at €400–765. *Free half-day bike rental for the Luberon trek on presentation of this guide.*

Dauphin

04300 (6km SE)

La Pie Margot

Rue du Barri.
Ⓣ 04.92.79.51.94
Closed *Wed; Thurs lunchtime; mid-Dec to end Jan.*

This restaurant is in a side street in a pretty village and is the simplest, warmest and most convivial place possible. The bay window looks over the valley and down to the river below and the dining room is decorated with old posters and advertisements. Nostalgic French music from the 30s plays in the background. The bill of fare lists such things as fish terrine, sautéed pork with honey and walnuts, scallops with raspberries and chocolate *fondant*. Menus €21–27. The place is named after the owner's daughter but it's also a species of magpie that inhabits the region. *Free apéritif on presentation of this guide.*

Lardiers

04230 (18km NW)

Le Café de la Lavande

Take the D950 towards Banon, and at Notre Dame turn right onto the D12 towards Saumane.
Ⓣ 04.92.73.31.52
Closed *Tues evening; Wed; Feb school holidays; mid-Nov to 10 Dec.*

Old-fashioned country café in a village that looks out to the Lure mountains. Regulars drop in for a morning glass of white wine or a pastis in the evening, but its worth taking the time for a meal. It's simple food, all fresh and good: duck with cherries, lamb stew, creamed salt cod. Menu €19. Reservations essential.

Fréjus

83600

Auberge de jeunesse

627 chemin du Counillier; 2km from the old town; by train, get off at Saint-Raphaël station, then go to the bus station, from where bus will take you to the hostel from platform no. 7 at 6pm.
Ⓣ 04.94.53.18.75 Ⓕ 04.94.53.25.86
Ⓦ www.fuaj.org
Open 8–10am and 6–8pm. **Closed** Nov–Feb.

A very pleasant hostel, situated in a seven-hectare park. It's 4.5km from the beach but only a few minutes from old Fréjus; there's a bus every morning to take you to either the train station or the beach. A night in a four or five-bed dormitory (men and women separate) costs €14.20, including breakfast. FUAJ card compulsory (you can buy it *in situ*). Unfortunately, there's a strict curfew at 10.30pm.

Hôtel Oasis**

Impasse J.B. Charcot, Fréjus Plage.
Ⓣ04.94.51.50.44 Ⓕ04.94.53.01.04
Ⓦwww.hotel-oasis.net
Closed *11 Nov–31 Jan.* **TV. Car park.**

A small, quiet 1950s building in a cul-de-sac five minutes from the beach. It's run by a young couple who welcome you like family friends. The rooms are varied – old-fashioned wallpaper in some, pretty Provençal décor in others – and though not big, they're more than adequate. Doubles €39–64. Breakfast is served on the terrace under an awning.

Hôtel Arena***

139 rue du Général-de-Gaulle; it's next to place Agricola.
Ⓣ04.94.17.09.40 Ⓕ04.94.52.01.52
Ⓦwww.arena-hotel.com
Closed *mid-Dec to mid-Jan.* **Restaurant closed** *Sat and Mon lunchtimes.* **Disabled access. TV. Highchairs available. Swimming pool. Car park.**

A lovely place if you're not on a tight budget. It's an old establishment that's been attractively and tastefully renovated, and the décor is pure Provence: warm colours on the walls, mosaic floors and painted furniture. The rooms aren't huge but they're very pretty, air-conditioned and efficiently soundproofed. They go for €80–160 with shower/wc or bath. There's a lush garden with luxuriant greenery and a swimming pool. The flavoursome cuisine consists of mainly Mediterranean dishes with a dash of individuality. Menus €23 (weekday lunchtimes) and up to €54. *Free coffee on presentation of this guide.*

Saint-Raphaël

83700 (3km E)

Le Thimothée**

375 bd. Christian-Lafon; it's 1.5km from the centre in the Plaines district.
Ⓣ04.94.40.49.49 Ⓕ04.94.19.41.92
Ⓦwww.thimothee.com
Closed *Jan.* **TV. Car park.**

A nineteenth-century bourgeois villa in a quiet, residential district that's several minutes from the sea. It's surrounded by grounds with lots of ancient trees. All rooms have TV and mini-bar and some have air-conditioning. Rooms 20 and 21 have balconies and view over the sea. Doubles €35–75. A charming place. *10% discount on the room rate out of season on presentation of this guide.*

Côté Jardin

Rue du 11-Novembre-1943; in Agay, some 10 km from Saint-Raphaël via the N98 in the direction of Cannes.
Ⓣ04.94.82.79.98
Closed *3 Nov–2 Feb.*

It is easy to see that in this restaurant things are done thoroughly, from the delightfully inviting little Provençal-style dining room to the glorious garden, which has been selected as the best flower garden in the whole town. What about the cooking? It's a feast for the eyes, firstly, and then proves to be delicious, creative and prepared with love, or even passion. Weekday lunchtime menu €18, then others from €24–49. There's a huge choice, so there is bound to be something for every taste. Charming service. This restaurant has earned a great reputation, and it is fully justified. It's advisable to book.

Gap

05000

La Ferme Blanche***

Route des Romettes; from the station take the col Bayard road, turn right onto the Romettes road then turn first left, and it's at the end of the road.
Ⓣ04.92.51.03.41 Ⓕ04.92.51.35.39
Ⓔla.ferme.blanche@wanadoo.fr
Closed *Tues–Sat lunchtimes.* **TV. Car park.**

This charming hotel, away from the main road, has a nice sunny terrace. In the public areas, lovely furniture complements the vaulted rooms and the elegant fireplace, and they've used an old bank counter as the bar. Rooms are bright and comfortable, though the decoration is looking a little tired; doubles with shower €43, €49 with bath. Breakfast is served until noon. The cooking is typical of the region and elegantly prepared. Menus €20–50: grilled beef, kid stew and potatoes *Dauphinois* with ceps, crayfish ravioli, *marbré* of rabbit with prunes. The welcoming owner is a mine of information about walks and cultural events. *10% discount on the room rate on presentation of this guide.*

Hôtel-restaurant Porte-Colombe**

4 pl. Frédéric-Euzières.

Ⓣ04.92.51.04.13 Ⓕ04.92.52.42.50
Restaurant closed *Fri; Sat; 2–18 Jan; 30 April–23 May*. **TV. Highchairs available. Pay car park.**

Don't let the electric shutters and cable TV distract you from the beautiful view of Gap and its cathedral. This hotel is in a modern, unappealing building but the rooms are individualized and comfortable with double-glazing. Doubles €44–47 with shower/wc or bath. Fine cuisine includes salmon *mousseline* with crab *coulis*, chicken liver and pistachio terrine, ravioli *en tourtons* and iced *vacherin*. Menus €16–28. *10% discount 1 Oct–30 June on presentation of this guide.*

|●| Les Olivades

Malcombe on the Veynes road. Take the Veynes/Valence road; at the second roundabout, look for the signs to Les Olivades on the right.
Ⓣ04.92.52.66.80
Closed *Sun evening; Mon*. **Disabled access.**

This place overlooks Gap and the neighbouring mountains. It has a huge terrace in dark brown wood, and the tall trees provide shade. If the weather gets bad, you can take refuge in the old sheep shelter with its vaulted ceilings. The regional dishes are deliciously prepared and infused with Provençal flavours: fillet of beef in pastry with morels, cheese-filled ravioli with honey butter, cod with *anise*, peach salad with a mint *coulis*. Simple, elegant fare which isn't too rich nor too heavy – just delicious. Menus €12.50–20.

|●| Le Tourton des Alpes

1 rue des Cordiers.
Ⓣ04.92.53.90.91
Closed *lunchtimes*. **Highchairs available.**

A well-established, successful restaurant which serves the region's best *tourtons* – potato fritters, served here with green salad and raw ham. They're included in the menus at €14.30–19.40, or available to order à la carte. The setting is a large, vaulted dining room with bare stone walls. The simple décor is freshened by a fountain and enlivened by the smiles of the waiting staff. If you're tempted, there's a shop where they sell local specialities. *Free coffee on presentation of this guide.*

|●| La Musardière

3 pl. du Revelly.
Ⓣ04.92.51.56.15
Closed *Tues evening; Wed; 15–30 June; 2–10 Nov.*

Many of the dishes at this spruce, pretty restaurant are traditional Alsatian specialities – the owners come from that part of the world. The substantial *menu Alsacien* includes knuckle of pork braised in beer, fish *choucroute* and zander in Riesling. Menus €18–26. Courteous service.

|●| Restaurant Le Pasturier

18 rue Pérolière.
Ⓣ04.92.53.69.29
Closed *Sun and Mon (lunchtime only in July–Aug); Ist fortnight in July; 2nd week Sept.*

The elegant, intimate atmosphere at this restaurant makes it ideal for a romantic dinner. The owners are lively and welcoming, and chef Pascal Dorche changes his menus frequently, sometimes producing unusual dishes. His honest cooking is more than satisfying – goat's cheese nougat with pistachios and lavender, wild boar ham, a *madeleine* with pike and prawns, artichoke bottoms and Banyuls wine vinegar, ravioli stuffed with leeks and morels, and unmissable white chocolate and coconut desserts. Menus €21–54; à la carte around €49. There's a small terrace open in summer.

Laye

05500 (11.5km N)

|●| Le Petit Renard

It's in the ski resort.
Ⓣ04.92.50.06.20
Closed *Wed from spring to autumn; 15 Nov–15 Dec*. **Disabled access. Highchairs and games available.**

The locals flood in to this restaurant which offers the best value for money in town. Speedy, friendly service. Classic regional dishes including *tourtons*, ravioli and fish *choucroute*, along with roast pigeon and house foie gras. The raclettes and *fondues* are good – the Savoyard cheese variety includes ceps. Menus €17.50–35. The large dining room has a lovely atmosphere: it's like a room in an ample chalet and it has a mezzanine. In summer, the terrace offers a ravishing view and there's a children's games corner. *Free digestif on presentation of this guide.*

🚶 |●| Restaurant La Laiterie du Col Bayard

Take the N85 from Gap to Grenoble and follow the signs.
☎04.92.50.50.06
Closed *Mon; Wed and Thurs evenings except school holidays and public holidays; 11 Nov–20 Dec.* **Disabled access. Highchairs and games available.**

The farmer, the farmer's son and the farmer's grandson run this place – and they've been running it since 1935. They serve platters of charcuterie, salads with blue cheese sauce, cheese kebabs, the *plateau Champsaurin* (which offers a selection of ten different cheeses) and a variety of generous salads. Menus €15–35. *Free coffee on presentation of this guide.*

Montgardin

05230 (12km E)

⌂ |●| L'Auberge du Moulin

Take the N94 in the direction of Embrun and it's on the right in the village.
☎04.92.50.32.98
Closed *Sun evening and Mon; open by reservation only during the rest of the week.* **TV.**

Known locally as the Three Sisters, this place is run by three women who are wonderful cooks. Many of the superb local dishes feature duck or goose. The single menu at €23 is satisfying and skilfully prepared; it lists such dishes as gâteau of spleen and duck liver, *fricassée* of whole duckling cooked *coq au vin* style, fresh cheese with honey and a good *bavarois*. Self-catering studios at €45 per person (maximum four persons). There's a family atmosphere. Credit cards not accepted.

Saint-Julien-en-Champsaur

05500 (20km NE)

🚶 ⌂ |●| Les Chênets

Take the Grenoble road to Fare, then turn right towards Saint-Bonnet and Saint-Julien.
☎04.92.50.03.15 Ⓕ04.92.50.73.06
Closed *Wed and Sun evening out of season; April; 12 Nov–27 Dec.* **Highchairs available.**

A mountain chalet with a warm family feeling. Simple double rooms with shower/wc or bath go for €35.50–41.50. The cuisine is better than good and focuses on regional dishes. Try the *tourtons* (potato fritters with ham and salad), goat's cheese ravioli and *crème brûlée* for dessert. They also do a mean upside down tart of hot foie gras. Perfectly ripened cheeses, excellent home-made desserts and a good wine list. Weekday menu €17 or others €25 and €33. Credit cards not accepted. *Free coffee on presentation of this guide.*

Gordes

84220

⌂ |●| Auberge de Carcarille**

Les Gervais; it's 2km below Gordes on the D2.
☎04.90.72.02.63 Ⓕ04.90.72.05.74
Ⓦwww.auberge-carcarille.com
Closed *Fri (lunchtime only April–Sept); Dec; Jan.* **Disabled access. TV. Highchairs and games available. Swimming pool. Car park.**

A welcoming inn. The dining room is quite elegant and the cuisine is fine: saddle of rabbit with sage, lamb's trotters and tripe and so on. Menus €17–40. Very appealing rooms with terrace or balcony; doubles €60–70 with bathroom. It's good value for this part of the world.

⌂ Hôtel Le Mas de la Sénancole***

Imberts; 5km outside Gordes on the D2.
☎04.90.76.76.55 Ⓕ04.90.76.70.44
Ⓦwww.mas-de-la-senancole.com
Disabled access. TV. Swimming pool. Highchairs available. Car park.

Exceptionally comfortable doubles, decorated with splashes of local colour, go for €77–207 with shower/wc or bath depending on the season. Half board compulsory in July/Aug at € 147 per person. There are also family rooms with small terrace. Restaurant, nice garden and a swimming pool surrounded by greenery.

Murs

84220 (8.5km NE)

⌂ |●| Le Crillon

It's in the middle of the village.
☎04.90.72.60.31 Ⓕ04.90.72.63.12
Ⓦwww.lecrillon.com
Closed *Thurs (lunchtime in season); 5 Jan–8 March.* **TV. Highchairs available. Car park.**

Sweet doubles, nicely painted and furnished with tasteful pieces, cost €50–52 with shower/wc or bath. Weekday lunch menu for €15, then others up to €22. Breakfast at €7. There are some lovely country-style dishes which are made using wild mushrooms, truffles or game in season: *tournedos* with morels, truffle omelette, stewed hare.

Goult

84220

La Terrasse

Rue de la République.
☎04.90.72.20.20
Closed *Tues; 1 Nov–28 Feb.*

The terrace is on the first floor and overlooks the square car park. World décor with Indian and Thai fabrics on the walls, hammocks swinging from the ceiling, and Indonesian fans. It works really well, as does the fine, carefully prepared cooking. Dishes, served with vegetables, €8–12. Around €24 for a meal. Unsurprisingly, there are lots of tourists.

Auberge Le Fiacre

Quartier Pied-Rousset; it's 3.5km out of the village on the N100 in the direction of Apt.
☎04.90.72.26.31
Closed *Sun evening out of season; Thurs lunchtime in season; 11 Nov–15 Dec.* Car park.

An excellent restaurant serving light, inventive Provençal cooking using local produce. The crayfish ravioli, rack of lamb, salt cod *tian* and iced nougat are fabulous; they also do game in autumn. In summer you can dine outside under the lime trees, where you're serenaded by a chorus of cicadas. Menus – €17 (weekday lunchtimes), or €28 and €30 at dinner – offer good value for money. Children's menu €9.50.

Beaumettes

84220 (3km W)

Restaurant La Remise

It's in the middle of the village.
☎04.90.72.23.05
Closed *Wed; Tues evening out of season; 20 Dec–20 Feb.* **Disabled access.**

A nice, unpretentious country restaurant with a number of specialities including *pieds-paquets à la marseillaise* and monkfish fillet with tarragon. Menus €15–35. Children's menu. *Free coffee on presentation of this guide.*

Gourdon

06620

Au Vieux Four

Rue Basse; it's a turning off the main street.
☎04.93.09.68.60
Closed *evenings; Sat.*

A pleasant place for a spot of lunch. Start with a plate of local charcuterie or shepherd's salad, then follow that with rabbit with thyme or meat grilled over the coals. Finish off with *clafoutis*. Menu €17, or à la carte around €20–23. *Free apéritif on presentation of this guide.*

Grasse

06130

Le Café des Musées

1 rue Jean Ossola.
☎04.92.60.99.00
Closed *Sun Oct–March.*

In summer, open 8.30am to 6.30pm. This café, in the historic centre, has a surprisingly ultra-modern décor. It's not far from the Musée Provençal du Costume et du Bijou. The very Mediterranean cooking is warm and strongly flavoured, involving light, tasty salads, fresh savoury tarts and home-made pastries. Expect to pay between €10 and €15 for a meal à la carte. *Free coffee on presentation of this guide.*

Mouans-Sartoux

06370 (6km SE)

Le Relais de la Pinède

Route de La Roquette, the D409.
☎04.93.75.28.29
Closed *Wed; Sun evening out of season; 15–30 Nov; 15–30 June.*

Surprising to find a Canadian cabin in the land of the cicadas. Lavish decoration, professional service, dishes for every pocket and to meet all tastes. Menus €16–26. The wine list is pricey. Lovely terrace under the pines. *Free coffee on presentation of this guide.*

Valbonne

06560 (9km E)

La Fontaine aux Vins

3 Rue-Grande; it's in the old town.
☎04.93.12.93.20

Closed *Sun and Mon out of season; Mon only in season.*

Predominantly a wine bar, this place also serves "Provençal tapas" – little dishes of tasty morsels – along with original sandwiches and attentively prepared dishes. Around €17 à la carte. Wines are carefully selected and affordable, and they also offer a good pale ale. *Free coffee on presentation of this guide.*

L'Auberge Fleurie

1016 rte. de Cannes; it's 1km outside the centre of Valbonne.
Ⓣ04.93.12.02.80
Closed *Mon; Tues; Dec.* **Disabled access.**

A very good restaurant in a pretty, wisteria-covered building with huge mirrors in the dining rooms. Inventive, sunny dishes are made from the best ingredients with the simplest flavours. Menus €23–42. Lots of regular patrons.

Grave (La)

05320

L'Edelweiss**

Ⓣ04.76.79.90.93 Ⓕ04.76.79.92.64
Ⓦwww.hotel-edelweiss.com
Closed *lunchtimes in winter; 5 May–5 June; 1 Oct–10 Dec.* **TV. Highchairs available. Car park.**

This enjoyable hotel is owned by the organizers of the world-famous annual Mieje ski race. The modern hotel stands well away from the noise of the road. The clientele is international and sporty and there's always a riotous atmosphere late into the evening. You can relax on the terrace and gaze upon the summits of the 4000m Écrins, or enjoy the sauna and Jacuzzi. Rooms are on the small side; they cost €52–58. Menus €16–25. *Free coffee, apéritif, fruit juice or soft drink on presentation of this guide.*

Grimaud

83310

Le Ginestel

Chemin des Blaquières; it's 3km outside Grimaud village and 1.5km from Port-Grimaud on the D61.
Ⓣand Ⓕ04.94.43.48.45
Ⓦwww.legenistel.hypermart.net
Closed *Oct–Easter.* **Swimming pool. Car park.**

When the dust has settled from the dirt track you'll negotiate in order to get here, you'll find yourself looking at an unpretentious hotel with eighteen rooms, each with a private terrace overlooking the park and swimming pool. If you want to arrive by boat, there's a pontoon on the River Giscle to tie up. Doubles with shower/wc €46–75 depending on the season.

Hôtel La Pierrerie***

Quartier du Grand Pont; it's 2km from Port-Grimaud on the D61.
Ⓣ04.94.43.24.60 Ⓕ04.94.43.24.78
Ⓦwww.lapierrerie.com
Closed *mid-Nov to 1 April.* **TV. Swimming pool. Games available. Car park.**

An attractive little hotel way out in the countryside above the gulf of Saint-Tropez. It's built like a typical Provençal *mas*, with lots of small stone buildings in the greenery and among the flowers. Rooms with shower/wc or bath €75–102. It's wonderfully quiet. *Seventh consecutive night free, 1 April–25 June and 15 Sept–10 Nov, on presentation of this guide.*

Athénopolis***

Quartier Mouretti; it's 3km outside Grimaud on the road to La Garde-Freinet.
Ⓣ04.98.12.66.44 Ⓕ04.98.12.66.40
Ⓦwww.siteathenopolis.com
Closed *Wed except July/Aug; 1 Nov–1 April.* **Disabled access. TV. Swimming pool. Car park.**

Attractively decorated, airy rooms with balconies or terraces. The swimming pool is inviting and the atmosphere peaceful – ideal if you want to relax. Doubles with shower/wc or bath €79–105. They also provide dinner for residents for €20, or €30 à la carte. The garden and the surroundings are delightful.

Guillestre

05600

Le Chalet Alpin**

Route du Queyras; as you leave Guillestre, turn left onto the Queyras road.
Ⓣ04.92.45.00.35 Ⓕ04.92.45.43.41
Closed *Sun evening and Mon outside the school holidays; a fortnight after Mother's*

Day; 15 Nov–25 Dec. **Highchairs and games available. Car park.**

A family-run establishment with decent rooms at honest prices: doubles €35–41 with shower/wc or bath. The ones facing south over the park have a splendid view. Traditional, well-prepared cooking in the restaurant, on menus at €17–32: scallops with fresh fruit, terrine of duck foie gras, *crépinettes* of salmon with a saffron infusion, duck breast with sour cherries and Génépi wine. Doubles €36–44 with shower or bath/wc. Half board available from €44 per person, compulsory 15 July–31 Aug. *Free apéritif or digestif for hotel guests on presentation of this guide.*

Mont-Dauphin

05600 (4km N)

L'Auberge de l'Echauguette**

Rue Catinat; it's on the main street.
Ⓣ04.92.45.07.13 Ⓕ04.92.45.14.22
Ⓦwww.echauguette.com
Restaurant closed *Mon out of season; 15 Oct–15 Dec; 10–30 April.* **TV.**

The building used to be the school for the children of the soldiers stationed here. The place was restored two years ago and has been impressively done. The welcome is very warm and at the weekend the staff wear local costume. There's a tavern, a restful garden at the back where you can eat or have a drink and an elegantly decorated dining room. Dishes include scallop tart, veal sweetbreads in pastry cases with Roquefort sauce and lots of local specialities. Menus €15 and €30.20. The spacious rooms all have en-suite bathrooms and they've been charmingly decorated. Doubles €37–47; half board €44. *Free coffee on presentation of this guide.*

Saint-Crépin

05600 (8km NW)

L'Amistous

It's in the centre of the village.
Ⓣ04.92.45.25.30
Closed *Mon in July–Aug; end June; Nov.*

This restaurant is popular with locals and tourists alike. Their wood-fired pizzas are particularly good. You should also try the chestnut *charlotte*, trout stuffed with herbs, stuffed crab, and the house speciality, the *potence*, which is grilled lamb with a special sauce. Weekday lunch menu €9, others €12.50–22, and around €20 à la carte. There's an extensive, varied and affordable wine list.

Vars

05560 (13km SE)

La Montagne

Résidence Le Grizzli.
Espace Rodde; it's on the right when you come into the resort, opposite the tourist office.
Ⓣ04.92.46.58.53
Closed *lunchtimes in season and outside the school holidays; May–June; Sept–Nov.*

Emilie and Jacquot put the world to rights with their customers over the bar while Luc, who's a ski instructor during the day, gets busy in the kitchen. His specialities are big salads, *fondues*, *tartiflette* and grills. À la carte only; a meal costs around €24. Charming, smiling service. There's a great atmosphere in the dining room with its fireplace; the bay windows give views of the town and the mountain. *Free apéritif on presentation of this guide.*

Hyères

83400

Hôtel du Soleil**

Rue du Rempart.
Ⓣ04.94.65.16.26 Ⓕ04.94.35.46.00
Ⓦwww.hotel-du-soleil.fr
TV.

A hotel absolutely engulfed by ivy in a very peaceful spot next to the medieval town. The rooms of this old building are haphazardly furnished and smell of lavender. Doubles €38–73 with shower/wc and €44–82 with bath. *10% discount on the room rate for a minimum two-night stay on presentation of this guide.*

Le Jardin

19 av. Joseph Clotis; it's opposite the town hall.
Ⓣ04.94.35.24.12

Service noon to midnight. All the tables are set out in the lovely, shady garden. The setting is elegant and relaxed, and the cuisine is relaxed, with a lot of fish and seafood – fish kebabs, octopus stew etc. Fair prices with dishes at €6–12.50.

Porquerolles

83400 (2km SE)

Les Glycines**

Place d'Armes.
04.94.58.30.36 04.94.58.35.22
www.porquerolles.net
TV.

A charming hotel which has been renovated in the spirit of Provence. The time to come is in March when the "glycines" (wisteria) are in bloom, or in autumn; avoid it in high summer if you want to be pampered. They only do their cosy rooms on a half-board basis – €59–159 depending on the season. The patio is the best place to eat and the cuisine leans heavily in the direction of fish and seafood. Menus €15.90–29. *Free digestif on presentation of this guide.*

Lalonde-les-Maures

83250 (8km E)

Le Jardin Provençal

15–18 av. Georges-Clemenceau.
04.94.66.57.34
Closed *Mon and Tues lunchtimes; 15 Dec–20 Jan.* **Disabled access.**

The dining room has a stylish Provençal décor – with a fireplace and a pleasant terrace in the garden. Charming welcome with equally good service and local dishes: *tartines*, mussels with garlic cream, free-range cockerel gently stewed in local wine. Menus €27–40. *Free apéritif on presentation of this guide.*

Lantosque

06450

L'Auberge du Bon Puits**

Le Suquet de Lantosque; it's 5 km south of Lantosque on the D2565.
04.93.03.17.65 04.93.03.10.48
Closed *Tues except July–Aug; 1 Dec–20 April.* **TV. Highchairs and games available. Car park.**

Though all the rooms are soundproofed, it's still best to ask for a room with a garden view. Renovated doubles, all of them different, from €58–62. The restaurant serves substantial, tasty, family-style dishes prepared with care: live trout from the tank, ravioli with sauce *daube* and mushrooms, duckling *à la brioche flambée*, home-made ice creams. Menus from €19–27. There's a shady terrace which provides welcome shade in the heat of summer. Across the road there's a large play area for children: ping-pong, slides and so on. Credit cards not accepted. *Free coffee on presentation of this guide.*

Laragne-Montéglin

05300

Hôtel Chrisma**

25 rte. de Grenoble; it's 300m from the town centre on the Serres road.
04.92.65.09.36 04.92.65.08.12
www.hotelchrisma.multimania.com
Closed *11 Nov–10 Dec; Feb.* **TV. Swimming pool. Car park.**

If you're simply looking for somewhere to stop for the night, this is a good place. Neat rooms with shower/wc or bath €39.50–45.50. The rooms overlooking the garden – where they do frequent barbecues – are lovely. You'll get a warm welcome. *Free coffee on presentation of this guide.*

L'Araignée Gourmande

8 rue de la Paix.
04.92.65.13.39
Closed *Tues evening; Wed; Feb; Oct.*
Disabled access.

Located in the centre of the town, this unpretentious place is pleasant and clean. Good traditional cooking and a range of set menus: *formule rapide* €10, weekday lunch €12 and others at €19 and €29. Dishes include chicken with pastis, terrine with juniper, lamb's tongue with *sauce gribiche* and fillet of red mullet on leek *fondue*. Attentive service. *Free coffee on presentation of this guide.*

Sainte-Colombe

05700 (17km SW)

Le Céans**

Les Bégües; take the N75 in the direction of Serres, then the D30 towards Orpierre, then take the Laborel road out of the village to Bégües.
04.92.66.24.22 04.92.66.28.29
www.leceans.fr.st/
Closed *Wed 15 March–15 April and in Oct; 1 Nov–15 March.* **Disabled access. TV. Highchairs and games available. Swimming pool. Car park.**

A family-run establishment halfway up

the mountains in the Buech area, surrounded by orchards and lavender fields. *Menu du jour* €15.20 and others up to €32. Specialities include snail profiteroles, lamb chops with honey, *fricassée* of chicken with morels and iced soufflé with orange. The rooms are small but quiet; doubles with shower/wc or bath €42–50. Garden, swimming pool, sauna, Jacuzzi – there's everything for a pleasant stay. *Free coffee on presentation of this guide.*

Savournon

05700 (18km NW)

L'Auberge des Rastel*

Take the D21 towards col de Laye.
Ⓣand Ⓕ04.92.67.13.05
Ⓔauberge.lesrastel@wanadoo.fr
Closed *Wed out of season; school Christmas holidays.* **Highchairs available. Car park.**

A cheap, friendly inn away from it all in a village midway up the mountains. It's a perfect spot for walkers wishing to explore the area. Simple, functional double rooms €30 with shower/wc. The young owner-chef prepares delicious, no-frills dishes using only the freshest local produce; lunchtime menu €13 (also Sun in July–Aug), others €16 and €20. There's a terrace and a bright, large dining room. Credit cards are not accepted.

Larche

04530

Auberge du Lauzanier

It's on the D900, just before the Larche pass.
Ⓣand Ⓕ04.94.84.35.93
Car park.

An enticing hideaway in Haute Ubaye, between Barcelonnette and the Italian border. The substantial, tasty cooking is ideal for skiers and walkers – they offer platters of charcuterie, *tourtons* (potato fritter, local speciality), omelettes, roast lamb with a morel crust and fruit tarts with raspberries or bilberries. Menu €13. Children's menu €10. There's a gîte with comfortable rooms for €15 a night. Breakfast at €5. Half-board at €34 per person.

Lavandou (Le)

83980

Hôtel Le Rabelais**

2 rue Rabelais; it's opposite the old port.
Ⓣ04.94.71.00.56 Ⓕ04.94.71.82.55
Ⓦwww.le-rabelais.fr
Closed *mid-Nov to mid-Jan.* **Disabled access. TV. Car park.**

A small hotel close to the centre and not far from the beaches either. Comfortable, pretty rooms with shower/wc at €37–71 depending on the season. On warm days breakfast is taken on the terrace overlooking the fishing harbour.

Hôtel California**

Avenue de Provence.
Ⓣ04.94.01.59.99 Ⓕ04.94.01.59.28
Ⓦwww.hotelcalifornia.com
TV.

The young couple who own the hotel – just eight minutes from the beach – have completely refurbished it. The husband is an architect who has put his talents to good use, while the wife is wonderfully welcoming. You'll feel immediately at ease, and you can spend hours gazing out at the bay and the islands. The rooms aren't huge, but they have been thoughtfully arranged. Doubles with shower/wc €38–65; the cheaper rooms look over the garden. *One free breakfast per room on the first morning for a minimum two-night stay, out of season, on presentation of this guide.*

Azur Hôtel

Domaine de l'Araguil at Cavalière.
Ⓣ04.94.01.54.54 Ⓕ04.94.01.54.55
Ⓦwww.provenceweb.fr/83/lavandou
Closed *Nov to mid-March.* **TV. Swimming pool. Car park.**

The 23 rooms are situated in several separate buildings. Each has a terrace with sensational views from the heights down to the sea. In the distance you can see the Îles d'Hyères. Quite superb. Some of the rooms have TV and fridge. If you can't be doing with the stress of the beach, just climb up to the top of the little hill and crash out by the pool in complete silence, broken only by the cicadas. Doubles €50–75. Breakfast is served in the shade of the eucalyptus. Nice family welcome. A little corner of paradise. *One free breakfast per room on presentation of this guide.*

Hôtel-restaurant Beau Soleil**

Aiguebelle-plage; it's 5km from the centre on the St-Tropez road.
T 04.94.05.84.55 F 04.94.05.70.89
W www.beausoleil-alcyons.com
Closed *Oct–Easter*. **Disabled access. TV.**

A quiet little hotel, which on summer nights makes a peaceful respite from the cacophony in Lavandou. The dynamic young owners, Monsieur and Mme Podda, offer a kind and considerate welcome to tourists. Simple but pleasant rooms, all with sea view and air conditioning; they go for €50–60. Half board, compulsory in high season, is €65–69 per person. Menus, from €23, list a wide choice of local specialities, including stuffed capon, *bouillabaisse* and fish stew.

Le Relais du Vieux Sauvaire

Route des Crêtes.
T 04.94.05.84.22
Closed *Oct to end May*. **Swimming pool.**

This four-hundred-year-old coaching inn is on a pretty road up to the mountain peaks and there's a lovely view over Lavandou below. You can have a dip in the pool before heading to your table. The dishes are typical of the region – sardines *provençales*, fish in salt crust and so on – with a range to satisfy all tastes and all pockets. Menus €18.50–34. *Free Kir on presentation of this guide.*

Rayol-Canadel

83820 (13km NE)

Maurin des Maures

Avenue du Touring-Club; it's on the main street in the centre of the village.
T 04.94.05.60.11
Closed *lunchtimes; mid-Nov to mid-Dec*. **Highchairs and games available.**

The owner, Dédé Del Monte, paces up and down behind his bar while the locals, perched on their stools, exchange gossip over a pastis (drunk undiluted in these parts). Dishes in the restaurant include *bouillabaisse*, *millefeuille* of aubergines, a trio of grilled vegetables, mixed grills and grilled fish. Weekday lunch menu at €11, then others at €20.50 and €25.50. Reserve a table by the window so that you can admire the view of the bay. *Free apéritif on presentation of this guide.*

Île du Levant

83400 (20km SE)

Hôtel Le Ponant

It's on the island that's 30min by boat off Le Lavandou.
T 04.94.05.90.41 F 04.94.05.93.41
W www.ponant.fr
Closed *end Sept to 1 June*.

It's a thirty-minute crossing to get to the island from here – for information call T 04.94.71.01.02. The 1950s building stands out like the prow of a ship on a crest of coastal cliffs. There are balconies or huge, wide terraces leading out from the rooms; each is personally decorated by Frets, the unusual boss of this unusual place. They're all different – a chunk of rock emerges in one bathroom while another is done entirely in wood. Rooms have shower/wc. Half board only, costing €85 per person. *Free house apéritif or digestif on presentation of this guide.*

Manosque

04100

Restaurant Le Luberon

21 [bis] pl. Terreau.
F 04.92.72.03.09
Closed *Sun evening and Mon except mid-July to end Aug; fortnight in Oct*.

The intense flavours of Provence are found in the food here – even though the chef comes from the north of France. He's got a creative imagination, and offers dishes such as snails, grilled pigeon with rosemary and lamb *daube*, and uses lots of olive oil and basil. Weekday lunch menu €12.50 and others €18–42. Tasteful rustic décor, and a terrace with a pergola.

Restaurant Dominique Bucaille

43 bd. des Tilleuls.
T 04.92.72.32.28
E dombucaille@aol.com
Closed *Wed evening and Sun; a week in Feb; mid-July to mid-Aug*. **Disabled access.**

This place has a very good reputation. The chef adds his own touch to classic dishes: poached egg with foie gras and crushed potato; roast John Dory with pepper served in a casserole of pickled tomatoes and gnocchi; vegetables pickled in olive oil in a pastry case. Menus €16 at lunchtime then others from €25–69. The wine list has a selection of excellent local vintages, particularly the Coteaux-de-Pierrevert from the Blaque domain. Decent prices. *Free digestif on presentation of this guide.*

St-Martin-de-Brômes

04800 (10km SE)

Hôtel-restaurant La Fontaine

It's on the D952.
Ⓣ04.92.78.02.05 Ⓕ04.92.78.02.21.
Ⓔhotel-rest-lafontaine@wanadoo.fr
Closed *Jan; Feb.* **Pay car park. Highchairs available. TV.**

The only establishment in this charming village. The ten rooms are simple and well maintained. Doubles €32–41 with basin, shower/wc or bath. Half-board €42–51 per person. When you arrive in the restaurant, you will be welcomed by the smiling couple who seat you and immediately offer you *tapenade* (olive paste) wth toast. From there you can choose from lots of local dishes including home-made black pudding with ratatouille, snails, a fine cheese platter and lots of desserts including rhubarb *clafoutis* and pineapple tart. Menus are attractively priced at €13.20–19.30. The house apéritif is made from lemon, vanilla and cinnamon and is very tasty. The small terrace is near the cool of the fountain and looks over the village. Best to book in high season.

Marseille

13000

See map overleaf

1st arrondissement

Hôtel Béarn

65 rue Sylvabelle; M° Préfecture. **Map C3-3**
Ⓣ04.91.37.75.83 Ⓕ04.91.81.54.98
Ⓦwww.bestofprovence.com
Closed Jan.

A family hotel in an old apartment building that's been renovated by the new owner. The rooms are €24–42, with basin, shower, shower/wc or bath/wc. Breakfast €6. There's also a room that sleeps five. Rooms with a garden view are quieter. They organize scuba training and dives for trained divers. *10% discount on the room rate on presentation of this guide.*

Hôtel Beaulieu-Glaris*

1 & 3 pl. des Marseillaises; M° St-Charles. **Map D1-15**
Ⓣ04.91.90.70.59 Ⓕ04.91.56.14.04
Ⓦwww.hotel-beaulieu-marseille.com
Closed *between Christmas and New Year.* TV.

A stone's throw from the monumental steps of Saint-Charles station, where you get a breath-taking view of the city. The hotel is handy if you're travelling by train and while it's not the height of luxury, it's clean and well maintained. The rooms at the back are huge and quiet, and get lots of sun. Doubles €25 with basin, €49 with shower/wc.

Hôtel Azur**

24 cours Franklin-Roosevelt; M° Réformés-Canebière. **Off map D1-2**
Ⓣ04.91.42.74.38 Ⓕ04.91.47.27.91
Ⓦwww.azur-hotel.fr
TV.

A pleasant hotel with friendly owners on a steep, quiet street lined with handsome buildings. The rooms have been renovated and have air-conditioning; doubles with shower/wc cost €52 or €55 with bath. The nicest look out onto little gardens at the back. Lovely breakfast with pastries. *Free coffee on presentation of this guide.*

Saint-Ferréol's Hôtel***

19 rue Pisançon; M° Vieux-Port. **Map C2-5**
Ⓣ04.91.33.12.21 Ⓕ04.91.54.29.97
Ⓦwww.hotel.stferreol.com
TV.

This hotel is in a good location, close to the old port. The glitzy rooms are named after famous painters – Van Gogh, Picasso, Monet, Cézanne. Ten of them have TV and double-glazing. Doubles with bath €84–92. Breakfast €7. Rooms nos. 10 and 12 have a Jacuzzi. *10% discount on the room rate on presentation of this guide.*

La Part des Anges

33 rue Sainte; M° Vieux-Port. **Map C3-40**
Ⓣ04.91.33.55.70
Open *9am–2am; Sun 6pm–2am.*

A friendly restaurant-wine bar where you come to buy your table wine from the barrel or a good bottle as a treat. There's a little dining room at the back where you can eat salads for around €7. A full meal costs around €7–12. Lovely atmosphere.

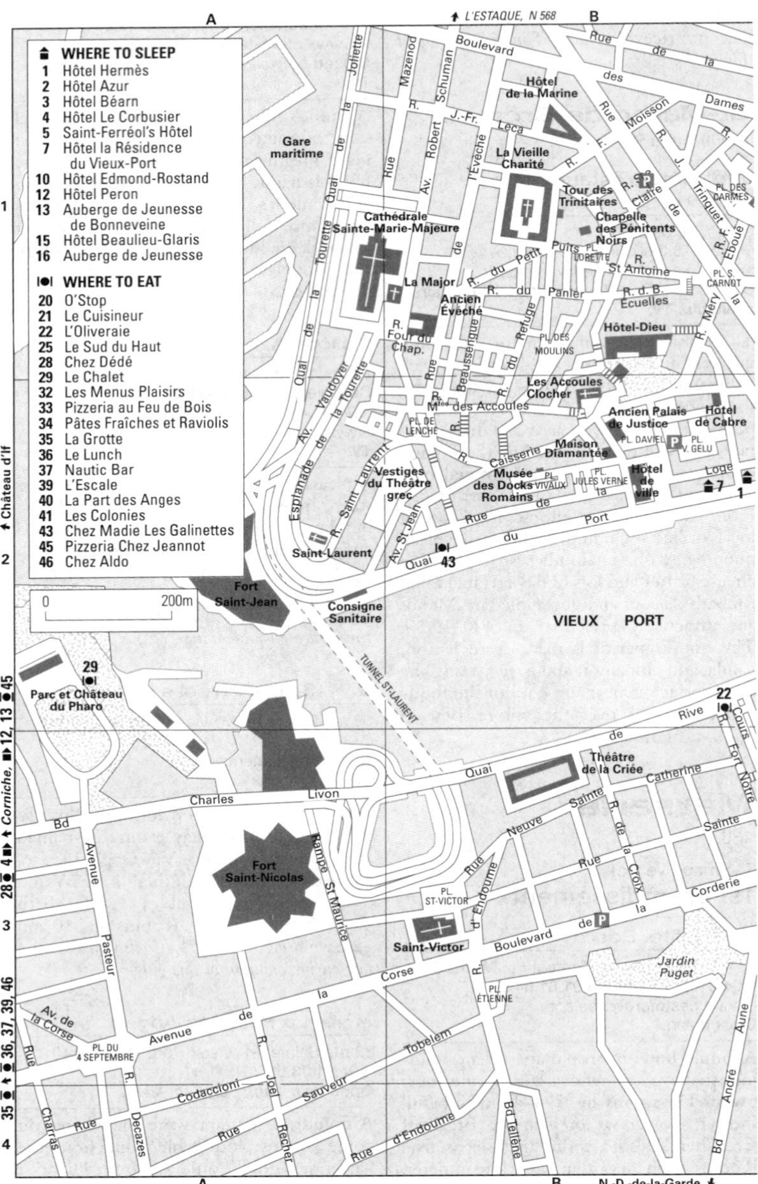
WHERE TO SLEEP
1 Hôtel Hermès
2 Hôtel Azur
3 Hôtel Béarn
4 Hôtel Le Corbusier
5 Saint-Ferréol's Hôtel
7 Hôtel la Résidence du Vieux-Port
10 Hôtel Edmond-Rostand
12 Hôtel Peron
13 Auberge de Jeunesse de Bonneveine
15 Hôtel Beaulieu-Glaris
16 Auberge de Jeunesse
WHERE TO EAT
20 O'Stop
21 Le Cuisineur
22 L'Oliveraie
25 Le Sud du Haut
28 Chez Dédé
29 Le Chalet
32 Les Menus Plaisirs
33 Pizzeria au Feu de Bois
34 Pâtes Fraîches et Raviolis
35 La Grotte
36 Le Lunch
37 Nautic Bar
39 L'Escale
40 La Part des Anges
41 Les Colonies
43 Chez Madie Les Galinettes
45 Pizzeria Chez Jeannot
46 Chez Aldo
0 200m
A
B
1
2
3
4
L'ESTAQUE, N 568
N.-D.-de-la-Garde
Château d'If
Corniche, 12, 13
45
4
28
35, 36, 37, 39, 46
Gare maritime
Cathédrale Sainte-Marie-Majeure
La Major
Ancien Évêché
Hôtel de la Marine
La Vieille Charité
Tour des Trinitaires
Chapelle des Pénitents Noirs
Hôtel-Dieu
Les Accoules Clocher
Ancien Palais de Justice
Hôtel de Cabre
Maison Diamantée
Musée des Docks Romains
Hôtel de ville
Vestiges du Théâtre grec
Saint-Laurent
Fort Saint-Jean
Consigne Sanitaire
VIEUX PORT
TUNNEL ST-LAURENT
Parc et Château du Pharo
Théâtre de la Criée
Fort Saint-Nicolas
Saint-Victor
Jardin Puget
PL. DES CARMES
PL. LORETTE
PL. S. CARNOT
PL. DES MOULINS
PL. DE LENCHE
PL. DAVIEL
PL. V. GELU
PL. VIVAUX
PL. JULES VERNE
PL. ST-VICTOR
PL. ÉTIENNE
PL. DU 4 SEPTEMBRE
Boulevard des Dames
Rue de la Joliette
Quai de la Tourette
Av. Vaudoyer
Esplanade de la Tourette
R. Saint Laurent
Av. St-Jean
Quai du Port
Rue de la Loge
Quai de Rive Neuve
Cours Fort Notre
Rue Sainte
Rue Neuve Sainte Catherine
Rue de la Corderie
Boulevard de la Corse
Bd Charles Livon
Rampe St-Maurice
Rue d'Endoume
Avenue Pasteur
Av. de la Corse
Avenue de la Corse
R. Codaccioni
Rue Tobelem
Rue Sauveur
R. Joel Recher
R. Decazes
Rue Charras
Bd Tellène
Bd André Aune
Rue du Petit Puits
R. du Panier
R. Caisserie
R. Mtée des Accoules
R. Four du Chap.
Rue de l'Évêché
R. Beaussenque
R. du Refuge
R. J.-Fr. Leca
Av. Robert Schuman
R. Mazenod
R. d. B. Ecuelles
R. Méry
R. St Antoine
R. F. Moisson
R. Ste Claire
R. J. Trinquet
R. F. Eboué
Rue de la République

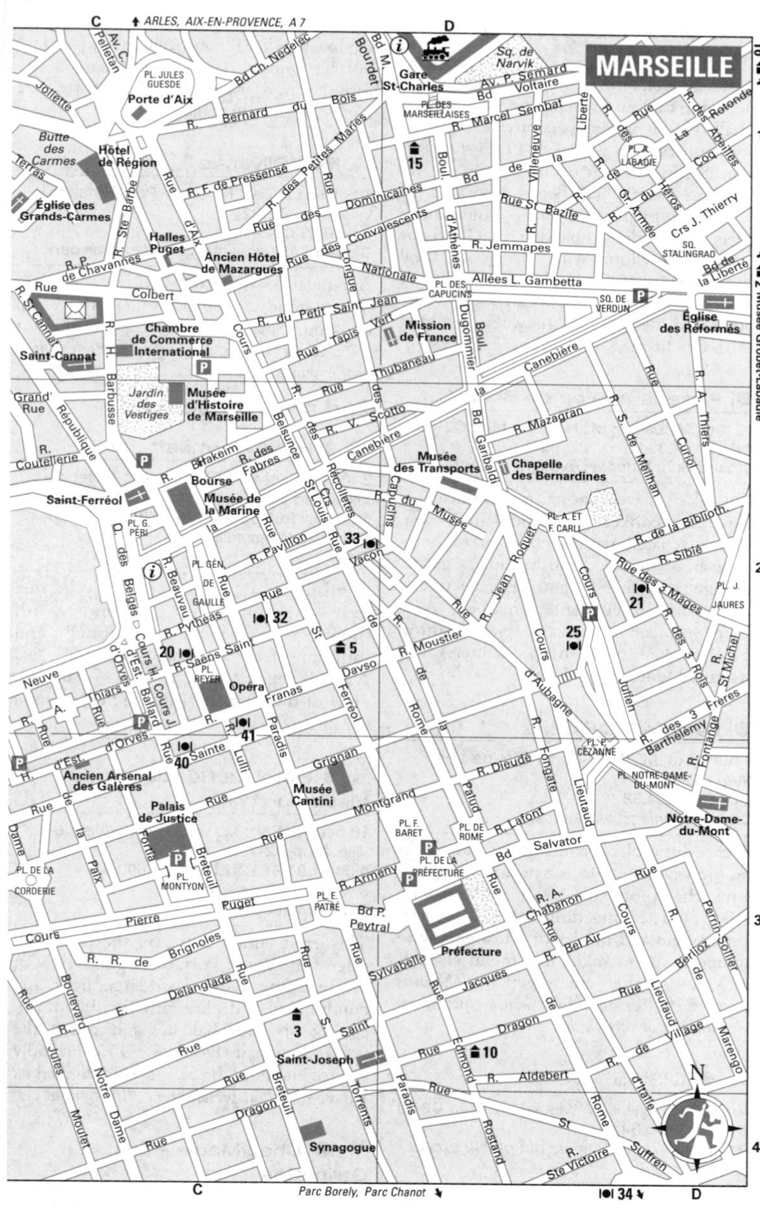

PROVENCE-ALPES-CÔTE D'AZUR

21

Les Colonies

26 rue Lulli; M° Vieux-Port. **Map C2-41**
04.91.54.11.17
Open *8am–7pm*. **Closed** *Sun; public holidays, Aug.*

A warm, welcoming, original place where they don't allow smoking because it's too small. This is where you buy tea, chocolates and biscuits baked by "*Le Petit Duc*" from Saint-Rémy. It occupies an old bank building which has been decorated to within an inch of its life – voluminous curtains, elaborate chandeliers. Good for lunch: cannelloni with *brousse* (a local cheese), tarts, or cream cheese with honey and spiced bread. Weekday menu €16.95; otherwise dishes cost between €4 and €10. Credit cards not accepted.

Pizzeria Au Feu de Bois

10 rue d'Aubagne; M° Noailles. **Map C2-33**
04.91.54.33.96
Closed *Sun; Monday; fortnight in Sept.*

This place is well known for its outstanding pizzas cooked in a wood-fired oven. They're coated with a range of toppings including *royale* (mushrooms, garlic, sausage and cheese) and *orientale* (meat, cream cheese, egg and tomatoes). À la carte you can get *pieds-paquets* (mutton tripe cooked with sheep's trotters) and lasagne. Menus from €8.50.

Les Menus Plaisirs

1 rue Haxo; M° Vieux-Port–Hôtel-de-Ville.
Map C2-32
04.91.54.94.38
Closed *evenings; weekends.*

A nice little place with lots of old clocks on the wall. The boss is a proud Marseillais who champions his town while taking orders and serving dishes. A really warm atmosphere and hordes of customers who appreciate good value. The menu changes daily and dishes are appetizing. Menus from €10. Terrace. *Free house apéritif on presentation of this guide.*

O'Stop

16 rue Saint-Saens; M° Vieux-Port. **Map C2-20**
04.91.33.85.34
Open *8am–7am (23 hours out of 24), except Christmas day.*

The snack bar opposite the opera is an institution; it attracts everyone from the well-dressed gentleman to local shopkeepers, and it's not uncommon to bump into an opera singer or stagehand. The house specialities – *alouettes* (or meatballs), pasta with pesto and *daube à la provençale* – are very decent. The sandwiches have good fillings and should not be ignored. Great atmosphere in the early hours. Meals from €14 à la carte. *Free Kir on presentation of this guide.*

L'Oliveraie

10 pl. aux Huiles; M° Vieux-Port–Hôtel de Ville. **Map B2-22**
04.91.33.34.41
Closed *Sat lunchtime; Sun; Jan.* **Car park.**

A typical local bistro with a welcoming owner, good service and superb Provençal cooking. Lunch menu €16, with others at €22–26 at dinner. *Free coffee on presentation of this guide.*

2nd arrondissement

Hôtel Hermès**

2 rue Bonneterie; M° Vieux-Port–Hôtel-de-Ville. **Map B2-1**
04.96.11.63.63 F 04.96.11.63.64
www.hotelmarseille.com
TV.

A small, renovated hotel superbly located near the Old Port. Rooms (with shower/wc) are air-conditioned and soundproofed; doubles €45–65. "*La Nuptiale*" has a terrace with a fantastic view of the port. *10% discount on the room rate on presentation of this guide.*

Hôtel La Résidence du Vieux Port***

18 quai du Port; M° Vieux-Port–Hôtel-de-Ville. **Map B2-7**
04.91.91.91.22 F 04.91.56.60.88
www.hotelmarseille.com
Disabled access. TV.

This great family hotel, on the town hall side of the Vieux Port, has a good view of Notre-Dame. Rooms are large, light, air-conditioned and pleasantly furnished. You can sit on your balcony and watch the boats chug past. Doubles €115. Friendly service and good breakfast. *10% discount on the room rate on presentation of this guide.*

Chez Madie - Les Galinettes

138 quai du Port; M° Vieux-Port–Hôtel-de-Ville. **Map B2-43**
04.91.90.40.87

Closed *Sat lunchtime May–Sept; Sun.*

You'll find this restaurant on the quay – it's a great place to come for robust, authentic Provençal cooking. It's now run by Madie's granddaughter and, although she still serves the excellent chicken *meunière*, her real speciality is meat (her father was a wholesale butcher). Authentic *pieds et paquets* – lamb tripe and trotters. The clams with thyme are also good. Lunch menu €15 and others up to €25. *Free apéritif on presentation of this guide.*

6th arrondissement

Hôtel Edmond-Rostand**

31 rue Dragon; M° Estrangin-Préfecture. **Map D3-10**
Ⓣ04.91.37.74.95 Ⓕ04.91.57.19.04
Ⓦwww.hoteledmondrostand.com
Closed *20 Dec–8 Jan.* **TV.**

A well-kept family hotel in a quiet street. It is named after the dramatist who wrote *Cyrano de Bergerac* – he was born in a house close by. The bright, modern rooms all have bathrooms and direct-dial phone. Doubles with shower or bath from €54; some rooms sleep four. Ask for one with a view of the garden, which is pretty and quiet. Good value.

Le Sud du Haut

80 cours Julien; M° Noailles. **Map D2-25**
Ⓣ04.91.92.66.64
Closed *Sun–Wed lunchtimes; 15 Aug–6 Sept.*

The setting is like a bric-à-brac shop with its assorted holiday souvenirs. Outside, there's a terrace where you can admire the wonderful fountain in *cours Julien*, and the good atmosphere is enhanced by the Afro-Cuban-Caribbean music that plays in the background. Old recipes are revamped here, and a touch of finesse added to dishes – stuffed vegetables, chicken with basil, duck *confit* with a walnut crust, rack of lamb with herbs. Prices are reasonable: between €14 at lunchtime and €27–30 in the evening. *Free apéritif on presentation of this guide.*

Le Cuisineur

2 rue des Trois-Rois; M° Notre-Dame-du-Mont. **Map D2-21**
Ⓣ04.96.12.63.85
Closed *Tues; Wed; lunchtime.*

One of our favourite places in Marseille. Two intimate little dining rooms separated by an arch, decorated in a mixture of Baroque and garish colours. The atmosphere is genuinely friendly, as is the jovial young owner; sometimes his mother lends a hand waiting at the tables – in short, this is a family affair. Reckon on around €20 for a meal. It is popular with small groups who come to enjoy the good meat, *pieds-paquets* (lamb tripe and trotters), copious salads and desserts made with thyme. Short wine list, dominated by vintages from the Rhône. On fine evenings, you can dine on the cool terrace. It closes at 10.30pm.

7th arrondissement

Hôtel Peron**

119 corniche Kennedy; take bus no. 83 from the Vieux Port and get off at the Corniche-Frégier stop. **Off map A3-12**
Ⓣ04.91.31.01.41 Ⓕ04.91.59.42.01
Ⓦwww.bestofprovence.com
TV. Car park.

Irresistibly kitsch 1960s hotel, where each room is decorated in the style of a different French region with moulded plaster murals and dolls in traditional dress. The bathrooms teem with ceramic fish and sea creatures. Doubles with shower or basin €58, or with bath €67. As it's right beside the sea, you get a nice view from the balconies at the front and the rooms are soundproofed – which keeps out some of the traffic flashing past on the Corniche. Rooms at the back, though lacking the view, are quieter. Cheerful welcome and attentive service.

Le Chalet

Jardin Émile-Duclaux (palais du Pharo). **Map A2-29**
Ⓣ04.91.52.80.11
Open *noon–6pm.* **Closed** *Nov–March.*

Outdoor café in the gardens of the palace built by Napoléon III for the Empress Eugénie. You'll pay around €20 for a complete meal. In summer, when the centre of town can be unbearably hot, the shaded terrace gets a light, refreshing sea breeze. A lovely place for a quiet afternoon drink, with a very beautiful view of the old port.

Pizzeria Chez Jeannot

Vallon des Auffes. **Off map A3-45**
Ⓣ04.91.52.11.28
Closed *Mon; Tues lunchtime.*

Nestling in the bottom of the Vallon des Auffes, this big pizzeria has a significant reputation. As well as succulent pizza and pasta they serve the best of Marseillaise and Provençal cooking: mussels, sea urchins, clams, periwinkles. Everything is incredibly fresh and it'll cost you around €20 a head. *Free apéritif on presentation of this guide.*

8th arrondissement

Auberge de jeunesse de Bonneveine

Impasse du Docteur-Bonfils; M° Rond-Point-du-Prado, then bus no. 44 to "Place Bonnefon" stop; opposite 47 av. J.-Vidal. **Off map A3-13**
04.91.17.63.30
www.fuaj.org/aj/marseille/
Open *5pm–1am*. **TV. Car park.**

A modern and fairly charmless hostel, but it's not far from the beach and the neighbourhood is quiet (but there's a night watchman, just in case). 150 beds. Reckon on around €13 per person in a dormitory, €17 in a double room with washbasin, including sheets and breakfast. Membership card compulsory. Luggage lockers available. There are also snacks if you're feeling peckish. *Free coffee on presentation of this guide.*

Hôtel Le Corbusier

280 bd. Michelet; M° Rond-Point-du-Prado. **Off map A3-4**
04.91.16.78.00 04.91.16.78.28
hotelcorbusier@wanadoo.fr

The largest look out towards the sea in the distance and the smallest look over the garden. Refurbishment in the pipeline for all the rooms. Doubles with bath €70. Buffet breakfast €8. Sunday brunch available. There's a small snack bar near reception. The area is quiet except on match nights in the Vélodrome stadium nearby.

Pâtes Fraîches et Raviolis

150 rue Jean-Mermoz, on the corner of rue Émile Sicard; M° Rond-Point-du-Prado. **Off map D4-34**
04.91.76.18.85
Open *lunchtime; Thurs, Fri and Sat evenings*; **Closed** *Sun and public holidays; 3 weeks in Aug.*

You have to go through the kitchens of this Italian deli to get to the veranda, where all the windows open out onto a gravel courtyard. Start with San Daniele ham or a mozzarella kebab before devouring one of the great pasta or ravioli dishes. Expect to pay around €15–18 for a meal. It's in a very quiet, middle-class area. *Free coffee on presentation of this guide.*

Chez Dédé

32 bd. Bonne Brise. **Off map A3-28**
04.91.73.01.03
Closed *Sun evening to Wed evening Oct–March; Christmas holidays.*

The terrace juts out over the water, while the dining room is decorated with model boats. You'll eat simple food here: oven-baked pizzas, pasta, mussel kebabs and grilled fish. It's one of the few places to offer grilled sardines – truly delicious. Around €23–27 à la carte.

Chez Aldo - La Madrague de Montredon

28 rue Audemar-Tibido. **Off map A3-46**
04.91.73.31.55
Closed *Sun evening; Mon; mid-Feb to mid-March; Christmas holidays.*

An insignificant-looking place, you might think, but it's packed day and night. The pizza and the fresh fish should explain why. The grilled fish is brilliant, or try fresh prawns, mussels and squid cooked over the embers. Around €28 à la carte. Friendly welcome and a lovely terrace with a gorgeous view over the bay. *Free apéritif on presentation of this guide.*

La Grotte

Calanque de Callelongue; M° Castellane. Take a no. 20 bus from the Métro station to Callelongue, the starting point for the Cassis–Calanques walk. **Off map A3-35**
04.91.73.17.79
Disabled access.

Installed in a nineteenth-century factory, this lovely restaurant has a décor fully in keeping with its history. The terrace, shaded by an awning, is much beloved by locals at lunchtime; in the evening they prefer to book a table on the superb interior patio. Excellent pizza and very tasty grilled fish. Between €30 and €40 à la carte.

L'Escale

2 bd. Alexandre Delabre – Les Goudes. **Off map A3-39**
04.91.73.16.78
Closed *Mon and Tues in low season; mid-Jan to mid-Feb.* **Disabled access.**

This restaurant is on the edge of the fishing village. It's run by a man who used to be a fishmonger, so the quality and freshness of the fish can't be bettered. The setting is lovely, with a big terrace overlooking the sea and the fishing port, and a beautiful dining room with a big wooden bar. They offer excellent *bouillabaisse* and seafood paella. À la carte reckon on €40. *Free digestif on presentation of this guide.*

9th arrondissement

|●| Le Nautic Bar

Calanque de Morgiou; M° Rond-Point-du-Prado. At the métro stop, take a no. 23 bus and get off at the Morgiou-Beauvallon stop; it's a bit of a walk. **Off map A3-37**
Ⓣ04.91.40.06.37
Closed *Jan.*

This place, known as "Chez Sylvie" to the locals, has a nice terrace that makes an ideal place to feast on seafood or whitebait. Menus €25–31. Sip some chilled wine and enjoy the cool sea breeze in wonderful surroundings. It's got everything you could want after a morning's swimming and diving, but take some water with you if you're walking because there's no drinking water in the creeks. You have to phone in advance to arrange a pass – the area is closed to unauthorized vehicles June–Sept. Credit cards not accepted. Best to call for opening times in low season.

|●| Le Lunch

Calanque de Sormiou; M° Rond-Point-du-Prado. At the métro stop take a no. 23 bus to La Cayolle and then hop on the free shuttle (7.30am–7pm). **Off map A3-36**
Ⓣ04.91.25.05.37
Closed *end Oct to mid-March.*

In summer, when the road is closed to cars and motorbikes, you have to phone the day before to sort out your pass. Going down towards the creek you get a magnificent view of the blue sea dotted with little spots of turquoise. All you have to do then is to sit on the terrace with a glass of chilled local Cassis and order a plate of sea bream or red mullet. Fish is sold by weight; expect to pay about €35–50 for a meal without wine. Good *bouillabaisse* – order it a day in advance.

12th arrondissement

☗ |●| Auberge de jeunesse

Château de Bois-Luzy, allée des Primevères; around 5km from the centre, but with a (distant) view of the sea. Take bus no. 6 via the Montolivet neighbourhood to the "Marius-Richard" stop: take the métro from Saint-Charles station in the direction of La Rose (line 1) and get off at the "Réformés-Canebière" stop; from there, take bus no. 6 to the "Marius-Richard" stop. **Off map D1-16**
Ⓣand Ⓕ04.91.49.06.18
Ⓦwww.fuaj.org
Hostel closed *from noon–5pm, like all official YHs, and open until 10pm.* **Closed** *20 Dec–6 Jan.* **Car park.**

Situated in a magnificent bastide (country house) built in 1850, with an impressive hall dominated by two gangways. 90 beds in dormitories with four to six beds. Reckon on €12 per person in a dorm, including sheets and breakfast. There are also some double rooms at €13. Meals around €8. Kitchen available.

Martigues

13500

|●| L'Auberge des Saveurs

8 pl. Mirabeau; it's in the middle of the Île district.
Ⓣ04.42.42.13.24
Closed *Sat lunchtime; Sun evening; Mon.*

The inn has a terrace on a pretty, pedestrian square and a small, tranquil dining room with stone walls and good background music. The cuisine is strong on flavours, with tasty traditional and local dishes. You can take the advice of the young and welcoming owner with confidence – he appears to have tried everything they offer, and has definite views. Menus €15–40. *Free coffee on presentation of this guide.*

Menton

06500

☗ |●| Auberge de jeunesse

Plateau Saint-Michel; from the town hall, follow the signs to *Camping Saint-Michel* on the Ciappes and Castellar roads. Cross the campsite, the hostel is on the left. You can also go on foot, but it's a steep climb; better to choose the shuttle from the bus station.
Ⓣ04.93.35.93.14 Ⓕ 04.93.35.93.07
Ⓦwww.fuaj.org
Reservation *exclusively on the Internet.* Ⓦ*www.hihostels.com.*
Closed *10am (noon in summer) to 5pm.*

The owner, a pioneer of youth hostels, is an important figure in the local community;

he also runs his hostel brilliantly, and makes sure that it's absolutely spotless. Dormitories with eight beds; reckon on €12 per person with sheets and breakfast. Half board €21. Meals €9. FUAJ card compulsory. Dinner is served in a refectory with bay windows that offer a stunning view of Menton and the surrounding areas. As you can't book by phone, make sure you arrive early in the morning.

Hôtel Beauregard*

10 rue Albert 1er; it's west of the city centre, about 300m from the train station.
Ⓣ04.93.28.63.363 Ⓕ04.93.28.63.79
Ⓦwww.hotelmenton.com/hotel-beauregard
TV.

The garden surrounding the hotel is planted with palms, lemon trees and bougainvillea; the building has charm and character and is over a hundred years old. It's a remarkable place well away from the bustle of the town. The rooms are fresh and quiet and offer good facilities; doubles with shower/wc €34–39 depending on the season. Warm welcome. *Free drink on presentation of this guide.*

Hôtel Chambord***

6 av. Boyer; it's next to the tourist office and the casino.
Ⓣ04.93.35.94.19 Ⓕ04.93.35.30.55
Ⓦwww.hotel-chambord.com
Closed *4 Nov–6 Dec*. **TV. Pay car park.**

A friendly family hotel on the main street in the centre of Menton. Spacious, really comfortable rooms with bath go for €93–103. The doubles are at the rear of the building; twin rooms have a view of the gardens. All just a stone's throw from the sea. *10% discount on the room rate except July–Sept, and free parking on presentation of this guide.*

A Braïjade Méridiounale

66 rue Longue.
Ⓣ04.93.35.65.65
Closed *lunchtimes in summer; Tues and Wed out of season*. **Highchairs available.**

The rustic dining room has exposed stonework and behind the bar there's a big wood-fired oven that gives a good flavour to the meat dishes. You know exactly what you're getting here – there's a good range of menus from €22 (weekday lunchtimes) up to €45. Lots of marinated and grilled meats along with Provençal favourites such as fish *aïoli* and flambéed kebabs. Everything is served in generous portions by nice, friendly staff.

Roquebrune-Cap-Martin

06190 (3km S)

Les Deux Frères

Place des Deux Frères.
Ⓣ04.93.28.99.00 Ⓕ04.93.28.99.10
Ⓦwww.lesdeuxfreres.com
Restaurant closed *Tues in season; Sun evening and Mon out of season; 2nd week in March; 15 Nov–15 Dec*. **Highchairs and games available. Disabled access. TV.**

This special place, which stands on the outskirts of the old village, is housed in a belvedere that gives a marvellous view of the whole area. The young Dutch owner has restored and redecorated the house charmingly; you'll pay €91–101 for a double with sea or mountain view. The lovely dining room is the perfect setting to savour dishes that are full of flavour and prepared with imagination from high-quality produce. Lunch menu €20 and others up to €45. Credit cards not accepted.

Beausoleil

06240 (8km SW)

Hôtel Diana**

17 bd. du Général-Leclerc.
Ⓣ04.93.78.47.58 Ⓕ04.93.41.88.94
Ⓦwww.monte-carlo.c/hotel-diana-beausoleil
TV. Pay car park.

This hotel has an amazing green Belle Époque façade, and is less expensive than a hotel on the other side of the street – this side is France, the other is Monte Carlo. You get to the rooms using an old lift; they're all air-conditioned and cost €33 for a double with basin, €50 with shower/wc or €56 with bath. Good welcome. They don't accept credit cards.

Molines-en-Queyras

05350

La Maison Gaudissard**

Gaudissard. As you come into town, turn left after the post office; the hotel is 600m further on.
Ⓣ04.92.45.83.29 Ⓕ04.92.45.80.57

Ⓦwww.gaudissard.queyras.com
Closed *5 April–15 June; 15 Sept–20 Dec.*
Games available. Car park.

This establishment has been a tourist centre since 1969 when Bernard Gentil transformed his home into France's first cross-country ski centre. He's constantly introducing new services and facilities. In winter, they offer courses in cross-country skiing and other ski-related activities, including treks through the mountains; in summer, hiking and paragliding bring the crowds in. After your exertions, relax on the terrace high above the village, where you get a wonderful view of the mountains. There's also a sitting room and a Finnish sauna. Doubles with en-suite facilities €50–60. Half board €48–53 per person, compulsory during school holidays. The restaurant offers a single menu at €17 – the salmon with fennel is good. Gîtes are also available. *10% discount on the room rate (except school holidays) or free apéritif on presentation of this guide.*

Abriès

05460 (15km NE)

Restaurant Grain de Lune

Le Roux; take the D441 from Abriès for 3km.
Ⓣ04.92.46.70.05
Closed *winter except during school holidays.*
Restaurant closed *evenings; March–June; Sept–Jan.*

A lovely place in a tiny hamlet run by two women who are passionate about cooking. They prepare your dish in front of you and cook it fresh in the old bread oven; flavours have a strong Italian accent. Their cold dishes are wonderfully fresh and the bread itself is delicious. There's a mix of sweet-savoury dishes – the house terrines are great and the toasted goat's cheese salad with diced bacon and chestnut *coulis* is divine. Take your time here – you'll have to anyway because service isn't the speediest. There's a sunny little garden. À la carte only; a meal will cost around €14, or you can simply enjoy a drink and a dessert in the afternoon. Credit cards not accepted.

Montclar

04140

Les Alisiers

It's on the D207, the road to Seyne, on the way out of St-Jean-Montclar.
Ⓣ04.92.35.34.80
Disabled access.

The Alisier is the service tree, which has red fruit and is found widely in these parts. Genuine French cuisine: house terrine, *coq au vin*, *blanquette* of veal and fruit tarts. Menus €12–28. Nice, serviceable welcome – it can sometimes take a while to get served, but that at least gives you time to appreciate the quiet of the valley; there's a panoramic view over the region from the wide terrace. If you're with someone special, order a little glass of their Amour aperitif, which comes in a choice of flavours: griotte (sour cherry), blueberry or wild strawberry. The house next door (Ⓣ04.92.35.30.88) is a chalet-style farm with a big lawn. It's open all year round and has six rooms, all of which are suitable for the disabled. Doubles with en-suite facilities for €38.20.

Mougins

06250

Le Manoir de l'Étang***

Les Bois de Fontmerle, route d'Antibes – it's not signposted.
Ⓣ04.92.28.36.00 Ⓕ04.92.28.36.10
Ⓦwww.manoir-de-letang.com
Hotel closed *end Oct to early March.*
Restaurant closed Mon. **TV. Car park**

Jean Cocteau dreamed of turning this magnificent site, on the road from Antibes to Mougins, into a "cinema city". The project fell apart but the remarkable building was put to different use as a unique hotel. The huge rooms look onto the vast garden and the lake; doubles €92–153. The restaurant serves sophisticated, delicate cuisine which you can eat indoors or out on the terrace; €25 weekday lunch menu and another at €30.

Resto des Arts

Rue du Maréchal-Foch.
Ⓣ04.93.75.60.03
Closed *Mon and Tues (lunchtime only in the summer); 11 Nov–22 Dec.* **Disabled access.**

An appealing, homely place in a town full of glitzy establishments catering for celebs and millionaires. The cooking is traditional and good: only the freshest ingredients are used to prepare dishes such as *daube provençale*, *stouffi* of lamb with polenta and stuffed baby vegetables. Gregory, formerly hairstylist to the stars, now waits at table, having decided to settle in Mougins. He's easy-going and very relaxed. The €11 lunch menu is a steal and the other one costs only €17.

Moustiers-Sainte-Marie

04360

Hôtel Le Clos des Iris

Chemin de Quinson; it's at the foot of the village, 50m from the Bastide de Moustiers.
Ⓣ04.92.74.63.46 Ⓕ04.92.74.63.58
Ⓦwww.closdesiris.fr.fm
Closed *1–26 Dec; Tues evening mid-Nov to mid-March*. **Disabled access. Car park.**

A charming Provençal *mas*, with pink walls and violet shutters, surrounded by chestnuts, cherry and fig trees and lots of flower beds. It's magnificently managed by Alexia. Each room is different and decorated with a lot of care, with fresh flowers and lots of little extras. Doubles with shower or bath/wc €60–65. Peace and tranquillity reign and it's ideal for a romantic weekend – but don't forget to book.

Hôtel de la Ferme Rose***

Chemin Embourgues; it's at the foot of the town, on the road to Sainte-Croix-du-Verdon.
Ⓣ04.92.74.69.47 Ⓕ04.92.74.60.76
Ⓦwww.lafermerose.fr.fm
Closed *mid-Nov to Christmas; Jan to end March*. **Disabled access. TV. Car park.**

This is a gem of a place, a typical Provençal farmhouse deep in the country. You'd expect traditional rustic décor, but not a bit of it. The owner, a real fan of the '50s and '60s, has decorated the bar and the bedrooms with a jukebox, bistro tables, coat-stands and lots of bric-à-brac dating from that era. Even the kitchen, where they prepare breakfast, continues the theme. It could so easily look a bit tacky, but everything fits in perfectly. The rooms are really quiet and the ones on the ground floor have a pretty terrace. Doubles €100–125 with shower/wc or bath. The copious breakfast will definitely set you up for the day. *10% discount on the room rate in low season on presentation of this guide.*

Nice

06000

See map on pp.794–795

Auberge de jeunesse

Route forestière du Mont-Alban; from the train station, take the no. 17 bus to the "Sun Bus" station, then take no. 14 bus to the hostel In Mont-Boron. **Off map D3-1**
Ⓣ04.93.89.23.64 Ⓕ04.92.04.03.10
Ⓦwww.fuaj.org
Open *6.30am–noon and 5pm–midnight*. **Closed** *Dec*.

Small Provençal house by the Mont-Boron forest. Fantastic view of Nice, with its port and the Baie des Anges. It is easy to understand why this hostel attracts travellers from all over the world. Dormitories with six to eight beds (men and women sleep separately). €14.10 a night, breakfast included. FUAJ card compulsory (sold *in situ*). Kitchen available. Friendly welcome and good atmosphere. Superb thirty-minute walk to the fort, with a view of Villefranche-sur-Mer harbour and Saint-Jean-Cap-Ferrat. Be warned that bookings are not accepted – the number of places available is posted up in the entrance.

Relais International de la jeunesse Clairvallon

26 av. Scuderi; take bus no. 15 from the train station to the "Scuderi" stop. **Off map C1-2**
Ⓣ04.93.81.27.63
Ⓕ04.93.53.35.88
Ⓔclajpaca@cote-dazur.com

Group of buildings set around an old middle-class house and surrounded by a superb park with a swimming pool in a quiet, residential neighbourhood on the outskirts of Cimiez. It's not far from the arenas (jazz festival, etc) and the Matisse and Chagall museums. €15 a night in a room with four, six or eight beds, including sheets and breakfast. Half board €24.50–25.50, depending on the season. Menu at €9 served at lunch and dinner. In summer, meals in the park on the beautiful shady terrace. You can leave your luggage in the morning, before being warmly admitted to your room at 5pm (which is the time when they open).

Hôtel Star**

14 rue Biscarra. **Map C2-3**
Ⓣ04.93.85.19.03 Ⓕ04.93.13.04.23

Ⓦwww.hotel-star.com
Closed *Nov.* **TV.**

"The cheapest 2-star hotel in Nice" is how the extremely welcoming and exuberant owner describes her establishment. Whether this is true or not, it certainly offers excellent value for money, and a fine location. Rue Biscarra is immediately attractive, as it's lined with low houses and bistro terraces. The rooms are decorated in classical style (apart from a few over-the-top bedheads and wall lamps) and are really comfortable. Double rooms with shower/wc from €35–55, depending on the season; €50–75 with bath.

Hôtel Danemark*

3 av. des Baumettes. **Map A3-4**
Ⓣ04.93.44.12.04 Ⓕ04.93.44.56.75
Ⓦwww.hotel-danemark.com
Pay car park.

A quiet and discreet 1950s house, hidden in a residential neighbourhood of Nice. The rooms are simple, but tastefully decorated and clean, and you can take breakfast on the terrace. Doubles €43–51 with shower (toilets on the landing), €48–65 with shower/wc or bath. The clientele is made of regulars, so best to book ahead. *Free parking, if spaces available, offered to our readers on presentation of this guide.*

Hôtel Amaryllis

3 rue Alsace-Lorraine. **Map B2-6**
Ⓣ04.93.88.20.24 Ⓕ04.93.87.13.25
Ⓦwww.hotelamaryllis.com
TV.

Doubles €62–76 with shower/wc or bath. The rooms are plain, but they're comfortable and the windows are double-glazed, so they're quiet. Some rooms lead onto the quiet courtyard. Accommodating, friendly welcome.

Hôtel Vendôme

26 rue Pastorelli. **Map C3-5**
Ⓣ04.93.62.00.77 Ⓕ04.93.13.40.78
Ⓦwww.vendome-hotel-nice.com
Open *all year round.*

Impossible to miss this large, cosy hotel dating from the late nineteenth century, as it is a massive square shape. It has retained all its elegance (wrought-iron staircase, a big lounge with mouldings). Although the décor may hark back to another age, the fittings reflect modern standards of comfort. The attractive rooms are flooded with light and well equipped (air-conditioning, TV and bathrooms in most of them); they are painted a sober, relaxing blue. Double rooms €67–75 in low season and around €110 in high.

Hôtel Durante

16 av. Durante. **Map B2-7**
Ⓣ04.93.88.84.40 Ⓕ04.93.87.77.76
Ⓦwww.hotel-durante.com
Car park (limited space).

This is set in a neighbourhood that is not the most obvious place to spend one's holidays, but it is a delightful building, hidden behind Italian-style shutters at the end of a private drive. It is decorated in warm colours and, although the rooms are small, they are inpeccable and functional, as well as being pretty and quiet. Doubles €69–91.50 with shower/wc or bath, depending on the size and if it has a terrace. The small, delightful courtyard has a few tables and is shaded by a few palm, orange and olive trees.

Hôtel Armenonville**

20 av. des Fleurs. **Map A3-8**
Ⓣ04.93.96.86.00 Ⓕ04.93.44.66.53
Ⓦwww.hotel-armenonville.com
Open *all year round.* **TV. Car park.**

A charming hotel (if you can ignore some of the buildings around it) with very reasonable prices for the city. Pretty early nineteenth-century villa with colonnades and stained glass windows, flanked by a flower garden. The décor in the rooms matches the spirit of the building, although a refurbishing process is gradually eliminating the outdated details. Doubles with shower/wc or bath €71–93. The most expensive ones are spacious, air-conditioned and overlook the garden. Very attentive service.

Hôtel Windsor***

11 rue Dalpozzo. **Map B3-10**
Ⓣ04.93.88.59.35 Ⓕ04.93.88.94.57
Ⓦwww.hotelwindsornice.com
Restaurant closed *Sun.* **TV. Swimming pool.**

WIth its marvellous Oriental-looking foyer, its tropical garden planted with brilliantly coloured bougainvillea, palms and bamboos and its little swimming

WHERE TO SLEEP

1 Auberge de Jeunesse
2 Relais inernational de la jeunesse Clairvallon
3 Hôtel Star
4 Hôtel Danemark
5 Vendôme
6 Hôtel Amaryllis
7 Durante
8 Hôtel Armenonville
9 Hi Hôtel
10 Hôtel Windsor
11 Hôtel de la Fontaine

WHERE TO EAT

20 L'Auberge de Théo
21 Chez Pipo
22 L'Auberge des Arts-la-Cave
23 Restaurant Acchiardo
24 Restaurant Voyageur Nissart
25 Lou Mourelec
26 La Table Alziari
27 Restaurant Aphrodite
28 La Part des Anges
29 Au Moulin Enchanté
30 L' Escalinada
31 Le Grand Café Turin
32 Don Camillo
33 Il Vinaino
34 La Zucca Magica
35 Chez Simon
36 Les Viviers et le Bistrot des Viviers
37 La Merenda

A 8, ANTIBES, CANNES, N 7

35 *ANTIBES, CANNES*

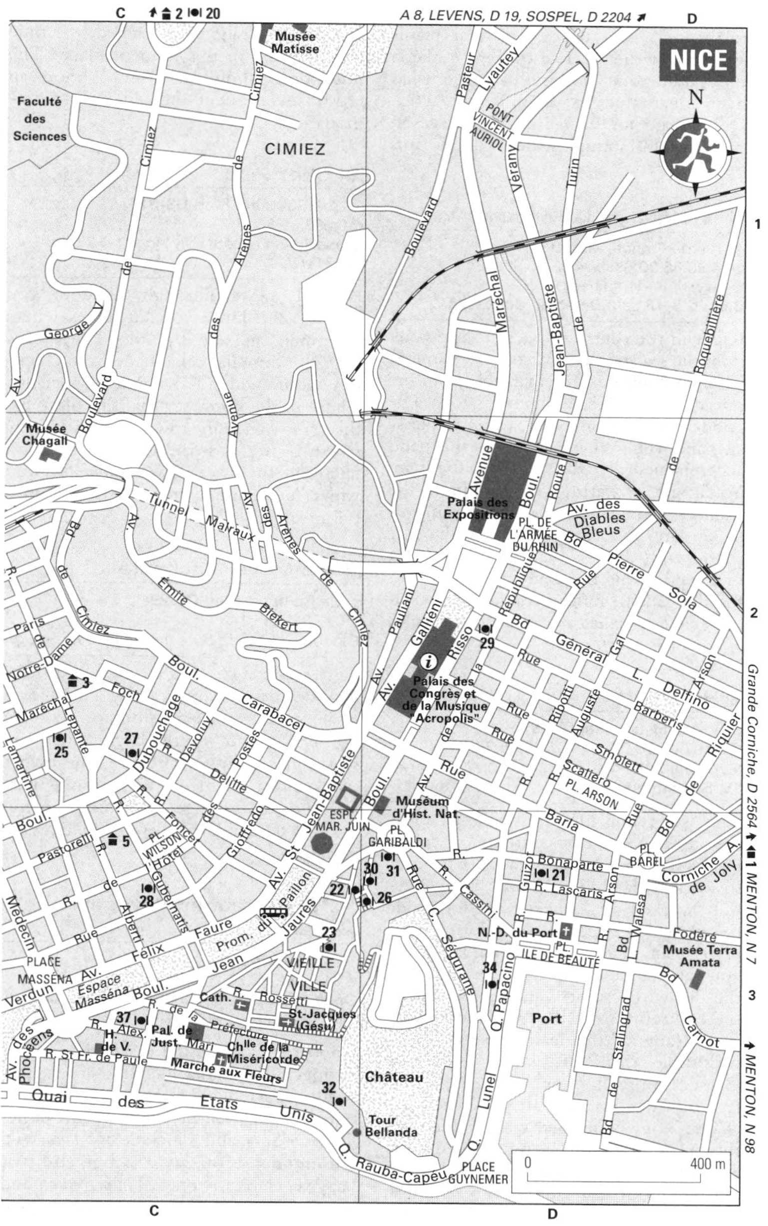
NICE
N
C
D
A 8, LEVENS, D 19, SOSPEL, D 2204
Musée Matisse
Faculté des Sciences
CIMIEZ
Musée Chagall
Tunnel Malraux
Palais des Expositions
PL. DE L'ARMÉE DU RHIN
Av. des Diables Bleus
Palais des Congrès et de la Musique "Acropolis"
Muséum d'Hist. Nat.
ESPL. MAR. JUIN
PL. GARIBALDI
PL. ARSON
PL. BAREL
N.-D. du Port
PL. ILE DE BEAUTÉ
Musée Terra Amata
Port
PLACE MASSÉNA
Espace Masséna
VIEILLE VILLE
Cath.
St-Jacques (Gésu)
Pal. de Just.
H. de V.
Chlle de la Miséricorde
Marché aux Fleurs
Château
Tour Bellanda
Quai des Etats Unis
Q. Rauba-Capeu
PLACE GUYNEMER
0 400 m
Grande Corniche, D 2564 1 MENTON, N 7
MENTON, N 98
1
2
3

pool, this place is truly something special. Guests can use the sauna, Turkish baths and massage rooms, and there's a relaxation room decorated with plants and Thai statuettes. The owners are keen on contemporary art and each room has been decorated by a different artist. Doubles go for €75–105 in low season or €100–140 in high season. Credit cards not accepted.

🏃 🏠 Hôtel de la Fontaine***

49 rue de France. **Map B3-11**
Ⓣ04.93.88.30.38 Ⓕ04.93.88.98.11
Ⓦwww.hotel-fontaine.com
Closed *8–13 Jan*; **Disabled access. TV.**

Right in the centre of Nice, a short walk from the sea and the pedestrianized streets. Though it appears unremarkable from the outside, inside it's a different story. The good-looking rooms are clean and pleasant, and you can breakfast on the patio accompanied by the rushing fountain. You'll get a warm welcome from the friendly owner, who does everything to make sure you enjoy your stay. Double rooms with shower/wc €95–120; ask for one overlooking the courtyard. Top marks for the €8.50 buffet breakfast. *10% discount on the room rate in winter on presentation of this guide .*

🏠 Hi Hôtel***

3 av. des Fleurs. **Map A3-9**
Ⓣ04.97.07.26.26 Ⓕ04.97.07.26.27
Ⓦwww.hi-hotel.net
TV. Swimming pool.

This is certainly the most singular of all the city's hotels. It was entirely conceived by the designer Matali Crasset, who used to work with Philippe Starck. Nine carefully worked-out concepts for forty-odd rooms which beggar description and are crying out to be experienced. However, you can get an idea from the examples of the plaited chestnut branches that divide the bathroom from the "Up and Down" room (one of the least expensive), the irresistible thrill of playing Robinson Crusoe in the "Indoor" room, the serenity of the immaculate "White and White", only disturbed by the discovery that what appears to be a canopied four-poster bed is in fact a bathtub. Minimalist but colourful, intriguing, very modern but fun. Double rooms with shower/wc or bath and broad-band Internet connection €145–350. There is also a rooftop pool in the form of a giant flower pot, a bar overhanging from a gondola that seems to be floating in air, a quiet atmosphere and a slightly detached welcome (not unusual in this kind of place). The hotel breaks boundaries and is more an artistic experiment than luxury accommodation.

|●| Chez Pipo

13 rue Bavastro. **Map D3-21**
Ⓣ04.93.55.88.82
Closed *Mon except July/Aug; 1–15 Dec; 15–31 Jan.*

A lovely place. Through the door, you glimpse the long wooden tables where customers sit side by side. They serve *socca*, the thin, flat cake made from chick-pea flour which is a Nice speciality. Those in the know say that this place has the best *socca* in town; it's definitely worth trying, as is the *pissaladière* (onion tart) and the sweet Swiss *chard* pie. You won't spend much more than €8 on a full meal.

|●| Au Moulin Enchanté

1 rue Barberis. **Map D2-29**
Ⓣ04.93.55.33.14.
Closed *Sat lunch; Sun; mid-July to mid-Aug.*

Tasty, seasonal cooking at prices that make you wonder if you're really in Nice. A small, quiet terrace in front of a dining room that's not overly large either and seems like a Provençal bistro. The owner will explain his menus as if he was performing on a stage. Lunchtime menu €11.50, dinner €13.50 and €20. Enticing wine list.

🏃 |●| Restaurant Voyageur Nissart

19 rue Alsace-Lorraine. **Map B2-24**
Ⓣ04.93.82.19.60
Open *11.30am–2pm and 6.30–10pm*. **Closed** *Mon; Aug.*

Good regional cuisine served in a rustic setting. Restaurants like this are rapidly vanishing. Menus €11.50 and €19; there's one offering well-prepared Niçois dishes for €15. Specialities include *osso buco*, wild mushrooms in oil, ravioli, courgette tart, baby vegetables, peppers *à la provençale* and *soupe au pistou* (vegetable soup with pesto). Different menus daily, according to what's good at the market. *Free apéritif if you take the Niçois menu, on presentation of this guide.*

L'Auberge des Arts - La Cave

9 rue Pairolière; in the old Nice. **Map C3-22**
☎04.93.62.95.01
Open *4pm–1am.* **Closed** *Sun; Mon.*

Lovely wine bistro where you choose your wine straight from the barrel, and can then take it away or drink on the premises with a quick bite. Better still, go downstairs to the glorious, vaulted, seventeenth-century dining room for a more formal meal. The menu exclusively lists bistro dishes; you'll pay €9 for the dish of the day, €14 for the "Soleil" menu, and €6–12 for sample dishes at lunch; à la carte around €20 for a main course with dessert and wine. The waiter offers excellent advice about the wines. Good service, fair prices and great cooking all contribute to the success of this place.

La Zucca Magica

4 [bis] quai Papacino. **Map D3-34**
☎04.93.56.25.27
Closed *Sun; Mon.*

A quirky, hugely popular place run by Marco, the vegetarian cousin of Luciano Pavarotti. The dining room is decorated with Halloween pumpkins and illuminated by a small forest of candles. There's no menu as such, and you simply eat what you're given – lasagne, red peppers stuffed with pasta, pumpkin and gorgonzola tart and the like. The dining room is so dark that it is sometimes hard to see what's on your plate, but you can depend upon it being tasty and inventive, and everything is prepared from the freshest market produce. He uses a lot of chickpeas, lentils and beans, and employs seasonings that pay homage to his Roman background. A meal costs €16 at lunchtime and €25 for dinner. Children under 12 eat for free. Credit cards not accepted. *Free coffee on presentation of this guide.*

Lou Mourelec

15 rue Biscarra. **Map C2-25**
☎04.93.80.80.11
Closed *Sun; Mon evening; 3 weeks in Aug; a week end of Dec.*

Lou Mourelec is local dialect for "fine palate". The cuisine is rooted in local tradition. At lunchtime they serve only freshly cooked dishes of the day, all of which are listed on the blackboard – ravioli with meat sauce, sardines stuffed with Brousse cheese, *pissaladière* or octopus *à la Niçoise* – and which cost around €17 each. Dinner dishes are more elaborate. Evening menus €20–28. *Free house apéritif on presentation of this guide.*

Restaurant Acchiardo

38 rue Droite. **Map C3-23**
☎04.93.85.51.16
Closed *Sat; Sun; Aug.*

This very popular restaurant caters more for local people than for the tourist trade. It's in the old town, and the surroundings are very informal: the big tables are covered with red oilcloths and the atmosphere is cheery. Dishes of the day are always good (€10.50 and €12.50) – tripe *à la Niçoise*, *soupe au pistou* (vegetable soup with basil sauce), *daube*, ratatouille and ravioli with bolognaise sauce, pesto or Gorgonzola. €18–25 à la carte. Wine from the barrel. Cash only. *Free coffee on presentation of this guide.*

L'Auberge de Théo

52 av. Cap-de-Croix. **Off map C1-20**
☎04.93.81.26.19
Open *until 10.30 pm.* **Closed** *Mon; Sun out of season; 20 Aug–10 Sept.*

An inn with a delightful patio up in the hills of the Cimiez area. The dishes betray a strong Tuscan influence: fresh pasta with prawns, Sicilian *maccaronata*, chargrilled meat or fish and a choice of tasty pizzas so large that they hardly fit on the plates. Menus €19 (weekday lunchtimes), and up to €29.50. *Free digestif on presentation of this guide.*

Restaurant Aphrodite

10 bd. Dubouchage. **Map C2-27**
☎04.93.85.63.53
Closed *Sun; Mon.* **Highchairs available.**

One of the finest tables in Nice. David Faure, who started out at the Auberge des Arts, has opened a stylish and warm place with a superb flower-filled terrace. The water playing in the fountain helps mask the street noise. Well-established cooking, as flavourful as it is creative, is available on the lunch menu (€19). Other menus at €24–60 or à la carte around €30. *Free house digestif on presentation of this guide.*

L'Escalinada

22 rue Pairolière. **Map D3-30**
☎04.93.62.11.71.
Closed *15 Nov–15 Dec.* **Open** *daily lunch and dinner.*

Menu at €21.50 and dishes €12–15. More than 45 Niçois specialities are served here: stuffed suckling pig (*porchetta*), home-made ravioli and gnocchi, and even sliced sheep testicles. Customers eat at the foot of the steps in the old city. *Free apéritif with portion of pissaladière on presentation of this guide.*

La Part des Anges

17 rue Gubernatis. **Map C3-28**
☎04.93.62.69.80
Open *10.30am–8pm.* **Closed** *Fri and Sat lunchtimes; Sun.*

A small bistro which draws local wine-lovers. There are only 20 seats but it's the ideal place to enjoy a dish of mushrooms or a *pot-au-feu* with a good glass of wine. Menus around €7–12. Olivier Labarde likes organic wines and he'll advise you which of the ones served by the glass will suit your mood and your meal. It's so popular that it's best to book.

Il Vinaino

33 rue de la Buffa. **Map B3-33**
☎04.93.87.94.25.
Closed *Sun; Mon.*

An Italian restaurant run by Italians and numbering Italians among its customers – a good sign, from the outset. The side dish of Seranno ham and other tidbits that are spontaneously offered before ordering confirm the initial impression. The menu is short and the dishes are simple, but they are all good: Italian charcuterie, mixed salads, pasta. Reckon on €25 à la carte. The service is as delightful as the décor: large murals paying tribute to vegetables and painted wall tiles on the little counters that open onto the street and kitchen.

La Table Alziari

4 rue François-Zanin. **Map D3-26**
☎04.93.80.34.03
Closed *Sun; Mon; 18 Jan–9 Feb; 8–23 Aug; 5–13 Dec.*

In a narrow, climbing street in old Nice, this restaurant has typical Côte d'Azur decor – yellow walls hung with pictures and a few tables outside. Set on each table is a bottle of Alziari olive oil, a family brand that's reputed for its quality. The short menu is scrawled up on the blackboard; all dishes are freshly prepared and produce bought fresh from the market on the Cours Saleya. Favourful local dishes: stuffed vegetables, deep-fried courgette flowers, stuffed sardines. A complete meal, including wine, costs €25–30.

Chez Simon

275 rte. de Saint-Antoine-de-Ginestière; take av. de la Borlana then turn left down rte. de Saint-Antoine (follow the signs to the Archet hospital); it's at the foot of the Church of Saint-Antoine-de-Ginestière. **Off map A3-35**
☎04.93.86.51.62
Closed *Sun evening; Mon evening out of season.*

A village tavern in a... village, even if it's been swallowed up by the agglomeration of Nice. It has been run by the same family for five generations and it doesn't seem to have changed since the time when – legend has it – Queen Victoria used to come here: terrace under the chestnut trees, large banquet hall, pétanque area. Menu at €27 per person for a minimum of two people. Reckon on €25–30 à la carte. Genuinely friendly service. Tasty cooking, firmly rooted in the traditions of Nice. Booking (highly) advisable.

Les Viviers et Le Bistrot des Viviers

22 rue Alphonse-Karr. **Map B3-36**
☎04.93.16.00.48.
Closed *Aug.* **Bistro closed** *Sun.* **Restaurant closed** *Sat lunch; Sun; Mon lunch.*

Two different rooms with two different atmospheres: convivial, nautical décor in the bistro (with wood panelling and glass paintings evoking the Roaring Twenties); the setting is more bourgeois and airy in the adjoining restaurant, but the food is equally irreproachable on either side. Some people claim that this is the best fish restaurant in Nice, and it could well be! In any case, the owners, Renaud and Marilène Geille, have put all their confidence in an extremely young chef, David Baqué, who has served his apprenticeship with Boyer in Reims and with Guérard. This rising star won us over. Beautifully presented dishes with delicate flavours, like the house specialities of monkfish, Breton lobster and scallops, or the memorable raspberry soufflé. There is no mystery –

the ingredients are supremely fresh and cooked with great precision – and the portions are extremely generous. Lunch menu in the bistro €15; lunch and dinner menu in the restaurant €29. Reckon on around €50 à la carte. Not that expensive, if you take into account the quality of the food and of the service (you will not be rushed). There are some extra bonuses, too, such as the tidbits, which are quite exquisite.

La Merenda

4 rue de la Terrasse. **Map C3-37**
Closed *Sat; Sun; public holidays; Ist fortnight in Aug.*

No menu here; reckon on around €30 à la carte. *Merenda* means "snack" in the local dialect, and they prove extremely popular. To such an extent that the tiny dining room (24 seats in all) is constantly packed. You should pass by first in order to book (there's no telephone), or wait patiently, as there are two services. The queue on the street outside is an everyday sight. If you do manage to get a table, you will enjoy authentic, superbly executed, seasonal cooking, full of delicate flavours, created by Dominique Le Stanc, one of the major culinary figures in the region. One day you might find Niçois tripe, the next stockfish, but the excellent stuffed sardines and the soup with pistou are permanent features. Cheques and credit cards accepted.

Le Grand Café Turin

5 pl. Garibaldi. **Map D3-31**
Ⓣ04.93.62.29.52
Open *10am–11pm.* **Closed** *Wed June/July.*

This seafood restaurant is an institution in Nice, serving copious platters of oysters daily (5–11pm in summer), prawns and whelks, and sea urchins in season. The two dining rooms and the terrace are always full but you can simply stop by for a drink if you want. Menu €15 or €23–30 à la carte. There's also *Le Petit Turin* (the annexe) if it's packed. Cheques not accepted.

Don Camillo

5 rue des Ponchettes. **Map C3-32**
Ⓣ04.93.85.67.95
Closed *Sun; Mon lunchtime.*

In an attempt to steer clear of the crowds while still remaining central, Stéphane Viano chose a quiet spot between the cours Saleya and the seafront to site his restaurant. The large dining room is attractively decorated in light colours, and the food is of high quality, using lots of local recipes and fresh fish: gran Emma's *borsotti*, vegetable risotto with crispy bacon, or rabbit *porchetta*. The lunch *formule* at €19 includes main course, dessert, coffee and wine, others €32–56 or €50 à la carte. Friendly service. *Free house apéritif on presentation of this guide.*

Villefranche-sur-Mer

06230 (7km E)

La Fiancée du Pirate**

8 bd. de la Corne-d'Or; towards the top of the town, on the N7.
Ⓣ04.93.76.67.40 Ⓕ04.93.76.91.04
Ⓦwww.fianceedupirate.com
TV. Disabled access. Car park. Swimming pool.

This hotel is a relic from the 1950s, when the N7 was still a major European artery leading to Rome and beyond. Its nondescript façade is deceptive because inside there is a huge dining room (with exotic decoration) that extends on to a terrace with a pool and garden, and a dizzying view of the harbour. Dinner menu €22 in summer. There's also a tea room (open all the year round) that serves not only selected teas but also home-made cakes, coffees from all over the world and cold snacks in summer. Attractive double rooms with shower/wc or bath from €60–125, depending on the season. Some of the rooms give directly on to the garden (although a couple also overlook the road). The young owner has managed to create the cheerful, relaxed atmosphere of a family house.

Restaurant Michel's

Place Amélie-Pollonnais; it's on the big square between the port and the old Villefranche.
Ⓣ04.93.76.73.24
Closed *Tues.*

This is the "in" place at the moment, and the atmosphere's pretty laid-back. The large terrace comes into its own on summer evenings. There are no set menus, but the à la carte menu is full of wonderful dishes – fish and seafood, mostly, prepared with seasonal produce. You'll pay about €25–30 à la carte. Friendly attentive service.

|●| La Mère Germaine

Quai Courbet; it's on the port.
☎04.93.01.71.39
Closed *15 Nov–24 Dec.* **Highchairs available.**

This restaurant is in a perfect situation on the port and is undoubtedly one of the best places between Nice and Monaco. It has a magnificent view of Villefranche's natural harbour, a lovely dining room, and a terrace. There's an army of smart waiters. Dishes are prepared using only the freshest ingredients and the fish and seafood are nothing less than wonderful: *escabèche* of sardines, fillets of sole cooked to perfection. Like everything else, the desserts are prepared in-house. Menu €37. À la carte, prices climb steeply – from €50. *Free coffee on presentation of this guide.*

Levens

06670 (20km N)

☗ |●| Le Mas Fleuri

19 quartier des Grands-Prés; around 2km from Levens, on the right when you reach the valley by the D19; around 200m after crossroads with the road from Saint-Martin-du-Var.
☎ and Ⓕ04.93.79.70.35
Restaurant closed *Tues and Wed from early Oct to April (except for house guests).*
Disabled access. Large car park alongside.

Small inn on the side of a road, shaded by plane trees and bordered by a lawned garden. The ten or so rooms have been refurbished; they are simple but very clean and bright. Doubles €45; there are also some bigger ones for families. There is also an excellent chef in the kitchen: menus from €17; gastronomic menu €37. Very friendly service. Highly recommended. Free *apéritif on presentation of this guide.*

Orange

84100

☗ Hôtel Le Glacier**

46 cours Aristide-Briand.
☎04.90.34.02.01 Ⓕ04.90.51.13.80
Ⓦwww.le-glacier.com
Closed *Sat and Sun Jan–March; 18 Dec–31 Jan.* **TV. Car park.**

This comfortable hotel has been run by three generations of the Cunha family. All the rooms are decorated differently. Doubles with shower/wc or bath €45–65. Musicians performing in the festival often stay here; it's doubtless the best value in town. *10% discount on the room rate except in July and Aug on presentation of this guide.*

☗ Hôtel Arène***

Pllace de Langes; it's in the historic centre, near the town hall.
☎04.90.11.40.40 Ⓕ04.90.11.40.45
Ⓦwww.avignon-et-provence.com/hotelarene
Closed *8–30 Nov.* **TV. Pay car park.**

A quiet, delightful hotel in the pedestrianized area. The air-conditioned rooms are prettily decorated. A few of them have a terrace, where you can eat breakfast, €8, with Provençal pastries and jam made locally. Doubles €67–93 with shower/wc or bath. *10% discount on the room rate Jan–March (except Easter), Oct and Nov, on presentation of this guide.*

|●| Le Forum

3 rue Mazeau.
☎04.90.34.01.09
Closed *Sat lunch in winter; Mon; winter school holidays; 15 Aug–3 Sept.* **Disabled access.**

A really nice place, close to the theatre, with a pleasant yet small dining room. Cuisine is Provençal with gastronomic dishes that show off seasonal produce: black truffles in January, asparagus from March to May. A few classics are always on the menu: liver terrine with figs or scallops with creamed garlic. Menus €16–52 and a children's menu for €10. The wine list includes regional vintages at very fair prices and generally the establishment offers very competitive value for money. In season, it's advisable to book. *Free house apéritif on presentation of this guide.*

|●| La Roselière

4 rue du Renoyer; it's to the right of the town hall.
☎04.90.34.50.42
Closed *Sun; Mon; Aug.* **Games available.**

The décor is a mish-mash and rather funky. If the weather's not good enough to eat outside, come inside and listen to the music, which ranges from Jacques Brel to Mahler. Fred changes the menu each week depending on the seasonal produce: regulars include pig's trotters, duck breast or Indonesian *nasi goreng istimewa*. Reckon on spending about €20 à la carte. The cellar is full of good, inexpensive wines.

Piolenc

84420 (7km NW)

Auberge L'Orangerie

4 rue de l'Ormeau; take the N7.
Ⓣ04.90.29.59.88 Ⓕ04.90.29.67.74
Ⓦwww.orangerie.net
Closed *Mon lunch in summer; Sun evening and Mon out of season; fortnight in Nov.*
Disabled access. TV. Car park.

For almost twenty years Gérard and his wife Micky have been running this beautiful inn surrounded by trees. The six very nice rooms with rustic-style furniture go for €65–74 with shower/wc or bath; the one with a secluded private terrace is particularly lovely. Half board, compulsory Easter to Oct, is €68–70 per person. The whole house is decorated with copies of masters painted by Gérard himself. In the restaurant you'll find a lunch menu at €18 and others up to €39 – stuffed crab, ostrich steak Mexican-style, *osso buco*, fresh pasta with crayfish and all manner of Provençal dishes. Gérard's cellar, which has more than 350 different vintages, is unbelievable. *Free coffee on presentation of this guide.*

Orcières

05170

Auberge-restaurant de Pont-Peyron

Pont-Peyron; below the station, on the right, before going up towards Orcières-Merlette.
Ⓣ04.92.55.75.20
Open *end June to early Sept; by reservation only in winter.*

This farmhouse is set in the heart of the countryside and its only link with civilization is a suspension bridge. It is surrounded by animals who wander to and fro as they please. Inside the atmosphere is homely and relaxed, with a log fire when the weather demands. The owner, Jean-Louis, is a great sportsman. He was one of the organizers of the Croisière Blanche rally that criss-crosses the *département*. (The bridge was built for this event.) He will serve you delicacies typical of the valley: aubergine with Parmesan, home-made absinthe and chocolate *charlotte*. Menus at €15 and 20. Reckon on €22 à la carte. There is also a sunny terrace, a small wall specially designed so that children with aspirations to rock-climbing can practise and a variety of walking routes that start here. There are also plans to acquire a tracked vehicle which visitors will be able to use. All in all, this is an experience that's not to be missed. Credit cards are not accepted. *Free digestif on presentation of this guide.*

Peille

06440

Auberge Le Belvédère

3 pl. Jean-Miol; it's on the edge of the village.
Ⓣ04.93.79.90.45 Ⓕ04.93.91.93.47
Closed *Mon; Dec.* **Disabled access.**

Just five rooms, with a splendid view of the Esterel mountain and the village, in this old building which was once a school and later the town hall. Doubles €40 with shower on the landing. There's a very welcoming dining room with bay windows overlooking the valley. Everything is fresh and tasty. Nice local dishes like pesto soup, stockfish and gnocchi. Menus at €20 and €27.50. *Free digestif on presentation of this guide.*

Peillon

06440 (3km S)

Auberge de la Madone

Peillon-village.
Ⓣ04.93.79.91.17 Ⓕ04.93.79.99.36
Closed *Wed; 7–31 Jan; 20 Oct–20 Dec.* **TV.**

If you want peace and quiet, this is the place to come. Comfortable rooms, completely refurbished in Provençal style, with balconies and an astonishing view of Peillon and the valley. Doubles €92–190 (in high season). Half board €136–160 per person, depending on the season. As for the food, the Millo family has been here for three generations staunchly defending an authentic Provençal cuisine based on supremely fresh ingredients. Their tradition is imbued with sunshine and they have succeeded in adding a few magic touches of their own. The results are truly remarkable, and particularly enjoyable if you have lunch on the pretty terrace with its flowers, mimosas and centuries-old olive trees. Weekday lunchtime menu €30 (main course, dessert and wine); other menus €42–56. If you prefer a snack, you can always go the Millo family's bistro in the village square (*La Table du Pourtaï*).

Pelvoux

05340

Le Saint-Antoine**

On the Briançon–Embrun road, turn off onto the D994 into the Vallouise valley and it's 11km on.
Ⓣ04.92.23.36.99 Ⓕ04.92.23.45.20
Ⓦwww.hotel-st-antoine.com
Closed *Sun evening out of season; 1 May–10 June; 30 Sept–15 Dec.* **Highchairs and games available.**

The valley is on the edge of the Écrins national park and it's still wild. The hotel is a reliable, efficiently run establishment with a friendly atmosphere. Rooms are simple and clean and some have balconies overlooking the stream. Doubles with basin €29–33; €36–45 with shower/wc or bath. Honest, tasty traditional dishes – including the local "donkey's ears", ravioli, and a Savoy *fondue*. Cheapest menu €13.50 then €17 and €23. Half board €38–42 per person. *Free coffee or 10% discount on the room rate March–April, June and Sept, or one day full board for a stay of more than ten days, on presentation of this guide.*

Plan-de-la-Tour

83120

Mas des Brugassières**

Ⓣ04.94.55.50.55 Ⓕ04.94.55.50.51
Ⓦwww.mas-des-brugassieres.com
Closed *mid-Oct to mid-March.* **Swimming pool. Car park. TV. Games available.**

A charming hotel in a pleasant village at the heart of the Massif des Maures, just 5km from the sea and 12km from Saint-Tropez. It's run by a couple of ex-globe-trotters who have decorated the place with oddments that they've picked up on their travels. Rooms €76–91. They do a special pool-side breakfast. Easy-going welcome and ambience. *Free apéritif, or if you stay three nights Sept–June you get two breakfasts free, on presentation of this guide.*

Pontevès

83670

Le Rouge Gorge**

Quartier les Costs; take the D560 2km east of Barjols, go over the bridge and drive up the hill to the village.
Ⓣ04.94.77.03.97 Ⓕ04.94.77.22.17
Ⓦwww.var-provence.com
Closed *Tues out of season; Jan to end Feb.* **Disabled access (restaurant). TV. Swimming pool. Car park.**

Lively inn in a village that is typical of many between the Gorges du Verdon and the coast. The welcome is as warm as the climate. In the evening, you dine by the pool on good local dishes like pork terrine with foie gras, duck breast *paupiettes* with morels or scrambled eggs with truffles. Menus €19–40. Comfortable, unpretentious rooms with shower/wc or bath €54–58. Half board is compulsory in July–Aug and costs €48–51 per person. There are dozens of walks in the surrounding countryside. *5% discount on the half-board rate for a stay of more than three consecutive nights (15 March–15 April and 20 Sept–31 Dec) on presentation of this guide .*

Quinson

04500

Relais Notre-Dame

It's near the Musée de la Préhistoire.
Ⓣ04.92.74.40.01 Ⓕ04.92.74.02.10
Restaurant closed *lunchtimes 1 Feb–1 April and 1 Nov–15 Dec; Mon evening; Tues; 15 Dec–1 Feb.* **Swimming pool. Highchairs and games available.**

The recent renovation of the fifteen rooms has freshened the whole place up and brought in a new clientele. Good, clean doubles €34–55 depending on the season and the facilities. Tasty *pieds et paquets* (lamb's tripe and trotters), trout, local sausage, Valensole truffles, *aïoli*, ratatouille and home-made pastries. Menus €13.50–38. There's a nice terrace under the plane trees, along with a swimming pool, swing and small garden. *Free apéritif on presentation of this guide.*

Saint-Dalmas-de-Tende

06430

Le Terminus**

Rue des Martyrs-de-la-Résistance; it's opposite the station.
Ⓣ04.93.04.96.96 Ⓕ04.93.04.96.97
Closed *lunchtimes 15 Sept–15 June.*
Restaurant closed *Thurs; 20 Oct–27 Dec.*
TV. Car park.

The friendly welcome makes you immediately feel at ease in this old family home. The nights are cool and restful in the mountains, and it'll most likely be the birds that wake you. Very pretty, simple rooms for €37–57, depending on the season and the facilities. There's a pleasant pergola at the front and an attractive dining room with a fire-place and a wood-fired oven. Menus €15–30 list dishes which are prepared on the spot by the *patronne* – her ravioli is unforgettable. *Free coffee on presentation of this guide.*

Brigue (La)

06430 (3km E)

La Cassolette

20 rue du Général-de-Gaulle; it's between place Saint-Martin and place de Nice.
Ⓣ04.93.04.63.82
Closed *Sun evening and Mon; evenings Oct–April; March.*

This tiny, pretty, family-run restaurant serves good home cooking. The dining room is full of models and trinkets of chickens in all shapes and sizes. If they run out of things, the boss will go next door to the butcher to fetch an extra *tournedos* or breast of duck. Menus from €15.50; reckon on around €30 à la carte.

Saint-Disdier

05250

Auberge La Neyrette**

It's where the Saint-Étienne-en-Dévoluy road crosses the road to Veynes.
Ⓣ04.92.58.81.17 Ⓕ04.92.58.89.95
Ⓦwww.laneyrette.com
Closed *13–30 April; 8 Nov–17 Dec.* **TV. Car park. Highchairs and games available.**

Impeccable rooms in an old water mill standing in solitary splendour at the bottom of a little valley. There are only twelve rooms, and they fill quickly, so it's best to book. No. 1 has a splendid view. Doubles with shower/wc or bath €59. Half board is compulsory in winter at a cost of €52 per person. The restaurant is very good, offering trout from the nearby lake, potato *tourtons* (rather like potato fritters) and hazelnut tart. Menus €19–38 or à la carte. *Free house apéritif on presentation of this guide.*

Saint-Jean-Cap-Ferrat

06230

Hôtel Le Clair Logis**

12 av. Centrale; it's in the centre of the peninsula, on the corner of allée des Brises.
Ⓣ04.93.76.51.81 Ⓕ04.93.76.51.82
Ⓦwww.hotel-clair-logis.fr
Closed *6–28 Jan; 12 Nov–15 Dec.* **Disabled access. TV. Car park.**

Situated in a quiet residential area, this haven of peace and tranquillity has an exotic garden and all eighteen rooms have a balcony or a little terrace. General de Gaulle came here to relax back in 1952. It's not cheap, though it is reasonable for the peninsula – a millionaires' haunt. Doubles €85–165 depending on facilities and season. Ideal for a romantic weekend on the Côte d'Azur – but you should reserve at least three weeks in advance.

Saint-Martin-Vésubie

06450

La Bonne Auberge**

Allée de Verdun; turn left as you leave Saint-Martin and head for Colmiane and Boreon.
Ⓣ04.93.03.20.49 Ⓕ04.93.03.20.69
Closed *mid-Nov to mid-Feb.* **TV.**

This beautiful stone hotel is comfortable and well run. Well-maintained doubles go for €47–50. Try to avoid the ones that look out onto the avenue – it gets particularly busy at the weekend. Half board €42–46. Menus, €16–23, list traditional, delicious food. Pleasant terrace, surrounded by a hedge. Credit cards not accepted. *Free house apéritif on presentation of this guide.*

Saint-Maurice-en-Valgaudemar

05800

Hôtel-restaurant Le Val des Sources**

Les Barrengeards; before the village of Le Roux, turn right over the bridge then right again; it's on the left 300m on.
Ⓣ and Ⓕ 04.92.55.23.75
Ⓔ le.val.des.sources@wanadoo.fr
Closed *1 Nov–1 April*. **Swimming pool. Highchairs and games available. Car park.**

Comfortable hotel located in a wild valley. Simple doubles €29.50–32.50 with basin, €48.50–63 with shower/wc or bath. The tasty food is nourishing and many of the dishes are local specialities: *oreilles d'âne* (a pastry case made in the shape of donkey's ears and filled with spinach and chard), ravioli with honey, *flozon* (potato tart with smoked bacon and shallots). Weekday menu €14.50 then others €18 and €25 – it's best to book. Half board, which costs €45–49.50 per person, is compulsory in July/Aug. There are gîtes in the grounds and a covered, heated swimming pool. *Free apéritif or coffee on presentation of this guide.*

Saint-Paul-de-Vence

06570

Auberge Le Hameau***

528 rte. de la Colle; 1km from the village on the D7.
Ⓣ 04.93.32.80.24 Ⓕ 04.93.32.55.75
Ⓦ www.le-hameau.com
Closed *mid-Nov to mid-Feb*. **TV. Swimming pool. Pay car park.**

Set deep in the countryside, this place has a superb view of the village of Saint-Paul. There's a pleasant terraced garden and a pool. Comfortable air-conditioned rooms with nice furniture go for €94–102 with shower/wc or €118–140 with bath. Apartments go for €159. Ask for a room in the main building; the annexe has less character. *10% discount on the room rate (mid–Feb to mid-March and mid-Oct to mid-Nov) on presentation of this guide.*

Saint-Rémy-de-Provence

13210

Le Chalet Fleuri**

15 av. Frédéric-Mistral, route de Maillane.
Ⓣ 04.90.92.03.62 Ⓕ 04.90.92.60.28
Closed *15 Nov–15 March*. **Restaurant closed** *Tues evening*. **Car park. Highchairs available.**

An old-style family guesthouse with a little garden where you can take a pre-prandial stroll among the topiary. Good, wholesome local dishes such as rabbit with olive paste and cuttlefish with parsley; menu €21 in the evening. Refurbished doubles go for €44–48 with shower/wc or bath; they're simple and functional, and they look over the garden. Half board is requested from June to the end of Sept; it costs €52 per person per night. *Free apéritif on presentation of this guide.*

Hôtel du Soleil**

35 av. Pasteur.
Ⓣ 04.90.92.00.63 Ⓕ 04.90.92.61.07
Ⓦ www.hotelsoleil.com
Closed *early Nov to early April*. **TV. Swimming pool. Car park.**

The hotel is set around a large courtyard. The fifteen rooms are not big but well-equipped. Those with a bath are a bit bigger and have a terrace. Doubles €52–72 with shower/wc or bath. You'll be asked for a deposit with your reservation.

Le Cheval Blanc**

6 av. Fauconnet.
Ⓣ 04.90.92.09.28 Ⓕ 04.90.92.69.05
Closed *Nov–March*. **Disabled access. TV. Car park. Enclosed garages available to rent.**

Classic family hotel. Rooms are regularly renovated and prices are reasonable for the area. Doubles with shower/wc or bath and direct-dial telephone €52–60. There's a terrace and a veranda. The private car park is a considerable asset in the centre of Saint-Rémy. Dogs accepted without a charge. *10% discount on the room rate for a stay of more than three consecutive nights on presentation of this guide.*

Hôtel l'Amandière**

Avenue Théodore-Aubanel; it's 700m from the town centre, in the direction of Noves.

®04.90.92.41.00 ®04.90.92.48.38
Closed *Nov to end of March.* **Disabled access. TV. Swimming pool. Car park.**

A vibrant, appealing hotel just outside Saint-Rémy. Comfortable, spacious rooms €52 with shower/wc up to €62 with bath. With its wonderful breakfast, pretty garden, nice pool and warm welcome, this place is one of the best of its type.

L'Hôtel des Ateliers de l'Image***

36 bd. Victor-Hugo.
®04.90.92.51.50 ®04.90.92.43.52
®www.hotelphoto.com
Restaurant closed *Mon and Tues.* **Hotel closed** *in Jan.* **Disabled access. TV. Highchairs available. Swimming pool. Car park.**

A "hotel concept" around photography. It's astonishingly tranquil, given its central location near the old town. Designer rooms with stylish photos all over the place go for €150–380, breakfast included. The bar has been set up in the old cinema. There are also two swimming pools, a big garden and a Franco-Japanese restaurant with a lovely sunny terrace. À la carte around €45.

Restaurant La Gousse d'Ail

6 bd Marceau.
®04.90.92.16.87
Closed *Thurs and Sat lunchtimes; 15 Nov–5 March.*

Service until 11pm. Intimate atmosphere and food that offers value for money. Lunch menu €15 and *menus-cartes* at €30 and €35, with different dishes each day. House specialities include *bouillabaisse* (Tues; by reservation), snails *à la provençale* and, for vegetarians, aubergines stuffed with veg and mozzarella. Great wine list. Jazz on Thursdays. On fine days you can eat on a terrace.

Sette Mezzo

34 bd. Mirabeau; go down the alleyway in front of the Florame perfume museum-boutique.
®04.90.92.59.27
Closed *out of season.*

A hidden secret, greatly treasured by those in the know. On fine days you can eat on the terrace, in the shade of the chestnut trees in the place Moati. The food, a mixture of Provence and Italy, is fresh and satisfying, and it's served in a restful atmosphere, far from the hubbub of the town centre. The menu varies according to seasonal availability, and the whims of the chef. Lunchtime menu €15, and another at €27.

XA

24 bd. Mirabeau.
®and ®04.90.92.41.23
Closed *evenings; Wed; Thurs; end Oct to end March.*

This place looks like a prettily decorated flat with its bistro chairs, mirrors and spotlights, not to mention its appealing terrace. There's only one menu for €24. The food is imaginative – parfait of aubergine or sardines Sicilian-style.

Graveson

13690 (9km NW)

Le Cadran Solaire**

5 rue du Cabaret-Neuf.
®04.90.95.71.79 ®04.90.90.55.04
®www.hotel-en-provence.com
Closed *Nov–March (except by reservation).* **Disabled access. Car park.**

An enchanting old posthouse in a quiet place. The rooms are comfortable and painted in contemporary colours; doubles €52–76 with shower/wc or bath. There's a shady garden and a terrace.

Le Mas des Amandiers**

112 impasse des Amandiers; route d'Avignon.
®04.90.95.81.76 ®04.90.95.85.18
®www.hotel-des-amandiers.com
Closed *Wed and Thurs lunchtimes; 15 Oct–15 March.*
Disabled access. TV. Swimming pool. Highchairs and games available. Car park.

This modern hotel offers attractive, reasonably priced rooms for €57 with bath, and there's a little restaurant where you can have dinner – menus €17–29. Out of season, when they have more time, the owners might take you to the farmers' market with them or to visit the perfume museum; they know how to look after their guests. You may also wish to go on the botanical walk just around the hotel.

Hôtel du Moulin d'Aure**

Quartier Cassoulen; it's just outside the village on the Tarascon road.

☎04.90.95.84.05 Ⓕ04.90.95.73.84
Ⓦwww.hotel-moulindaure.com
Restaurant closed *15 Oct to Easter*. **TV. Games available. Swimming pool. Car park.**

A haven of peace surrounded by vast grounds with pines and olive trees. The cicadas sing, the swimming pool awaits and the proprietress has a friendly smile. Comfortable, air-conditioned doubles cost €70–130. There's a holiday atmosphere in the restaurant; in summer you can eat grills, pasta and Italian specialities outside by the pool. Menu for €35 in the evening, served to guests or by reservation. *Free apéritif on presentation of this guide.*

Eygalières

13520 (10km SE)

Le Petit Bru

Avenue Jean-Jaurès; on the corner of the route D'Orgon.
☎04.90.90.60.34
Closed *Thurs; 15 Nov–15 Jan.*

Formerly the *Bistrot d'Eygalières*, this is the trendiest restaurant in the area (with hefty prices to match). Menu €30, including wine. The atmosphere is reminiscent of a family house in the foothills of the Alps. The expert chef, Wout Bru, was born in Bruges but has applied his prodigious technique, creativity and dynamism to Mediterranean cuisine, much to the delight of well-heeled locals.

Saint-Tropez

83990

Lou Cagnard**

18 av. Paul-Roussel; it's a couple of minutes from the port and 250m from the place des Lices.
☎04.94.97.04.24
Closed *1 Nov–26 Dec*. **TV. Car park.**

A large, typically Provençal house with nicely updated rooms for €44–53 with shower and €55–97 with shower/wc or bath, depending on the season. Pleasant terrace and flower garden. If you want a good night's sleep on summer nights you should reserve a room that looks onto the garden.

Cantina El Mexicano

16 rue des Remparts; go up rue de la Mairie under the gateway and it's about 100m along on the right.
☎04.94.97.40.96
Closed *lunchtimes; Oct–1 April.*

One of the few fashionable places in St-Tropez where the prices won't send a shiver down your spine. Out front there's a little mosaic-lined pond and a statue of the Virgin. They serve real Mexican dishes indoors – tacos, quesadillas, tortillas – and fantastic margaritas. It's delicious, generously served and the place has real atmosphere. Lots of local people come here regularly in high and low season. You'll pay about €20 à la carte.

Ramatuelle

83350 (6km S)

Le Will

Route des Plages; around 3 km from Ramatuelle.
☎04.94.79.81.45
Closed *Mon evening; 15 Oct to Palm Sunday.*

You're far from the madding crowds of tourists here; it is not by the beach or even in the village – it's right in the middle of a vineyard. It's a wonderful place to relax, in the shade of palm trees, and children love it as they can run around to their heart's content. The menu is not very extensive, but the fish and meat are good. Single *menu unique* at €22. Reckon on just under €30 à la carte.

Saint-Véran

05350

Auberge-gîte d'Étape Le Monchu

La Chalp-Sainte-Agathe.
☎04.92.45.83.96 Ⓕ04.92.45.80.09
Ⓦwww.lemonchu.fr
Closed *mid-April to mid-June; 15 Sept–20 Dec*. **Car park.**

In the highest village in France, at an altitude of 2040m, Nathalie and Philippe Babinet have converted their big farmhouse into a welcoming gîte with the comforts of a decent hotel. The cooking is traditional, and meals are served in a handsome dining room faced with larch and with a vaulted ceiling. Specialities include *fondue*, *tartiflette*, *raclette* (to order in advance), ravioli and home-made pastries. Menu €15.50 or €25 à la carte. All the rooms are bright and comfortable and are let out only on a half board basis at €29–47.50 per person. Facilities include sauna, billiard room and table tennis. *10% discount Jan, June and Sept on presentation of this guide.*

Les Chalets du Villard***

Quartier Le Villard.
Ⓣ04.92.45.82.08 Ⓕ04.92.45.86.22
Ⓦwww.leschaletsduvillard.fr
Closed *Tues lunchtime; 10 April–10 June; 20 Sept–20 Dec.* **TV. Highchairs and games available.**

Exceptional place built entirely out of wood, with super-comfortable, spacious studios and two-roomed apartments with south-facing balconies. Each has a hi-fi, dishwasher and luxury bathroom, and some have whirlpool baths. There are even some studios adapted for people with allergies. Doubles with bath €50–120. The restaurant-grill *La Gratinée* is on the ground floor; menus are €17–25 with dishes such as grilled meats and the house speciality, *queyraflette. 10% discount on the room rate Jan, April, June and Sept on presentation of this guide.*

La Maison d'Élisa

Le Raux; it's in lower Saint-Véran.
Ⓣ04.92.45.82.48
Closed *lunchtimes; Easter to mid-June; Sept–23 Dec.*

Marie, Parisian by birth but two decades as Saint-Véranienne, is an artistic woman who has invested the place with her strong personality – there's more than a hint of 1968 in the air. The terrace has a superb view of the valley to the majestic peak of Roche Brune in the distance, and the dining room has a splendid wooden floors. The place is stuffed with old photographs, hats, children's games and knick-knacks. The cuisine is creative, elegant and original: nettle soup, home-made tarts, spicy *fricassée* of veal and a chocolate *moelleux* dessert that melts in the mouth. It really doesn't matter that the service is slow. Meals are served only in the evening by reservation; you'll spend about €26 à la carte. She doesn't accept credit cards.

Sainte-Maxime

83120

L'Ensolleillée**

29 av. Jean-Jaurès; it's on the corner of rue F-Martin, 50m from the beach.
Ⓣ04.94.96.02.27 Ⓕ04.94.49.06.21
Closed *Oct–Easter.* **TV. Car park.**

Lovely welcome and décor in this old-fashioned hotel – rooms are unpretentious, comfortable and clean. Rooms €41–45 with basin, €45–48 with shower/wc, or €55–62 with bath. And the place is only 50m from the beach.

Hôtel-Restaurant-Montfleuri

3 av. Montfleuri.
Ⓣ04.94.55.75.10 Ⓕ04.94.49.25.07
Ⓔmontfleuri.ste.maxime@wanadoo.fr
Closed *mid-Nov to 1 March.* **Restaurant closed** *lunchtimes.* **TV. Highchairs available. Pay car park.**

From the outside this place looks like a deeply traditional seaside hotel. Inside, though, it's full of energy, run by a young couple who create a terrific atmosphere. All the rooms are different, and all are equally pleasant. Doubles with shower/wc €45–95, with bath €70–170 – the most expensive have a terrace and sea view. Good, family cooking served at tables set out around a Hollywoodesque swimming pool. One menu only at €19.50, or €32 à la carte. *Free house apéritif on presentation of this guide.*

Le Jas Neuf

112 av. du Débarquement; it's 2km from the Nartelle beach in the direction of the Gulf of Sainte-Maxime.
Ⓣ04.94.55.07.30 Ⓕ04.94.49.09.71
Ⓦwww.hotel-jasneuf.com
Closed *Nov to mid-March.* **TV. Highchairs and games available. Swimming pool. Car park.**

A genuinely charming hotel run by a nice couple who go to great lengths to look after their guests. Very comfortable air-conditioned rooms, deftly decorated in Provençal style; doubles for €70–172. There's a wonderfully bright veranda and a smiling team. Life here is good, with the swimming pool, sun-loungers in the garden – miles from the turmoil and the crowds.

Restaurant La Maison Bleue

24 bis rue Paul-Bert; it's in the pedestrianized area on the seafront.
Ⓣ04.94.96.51.92
Closed *Wed in Oct; Nov–March.* **Highchairs available.**

A little house decorated in blue, ochre and yellow. The terrace, with its comfortable bench seats, is a lovely spot for a good meal. Menus €19 and €25. This is a very good place.

Issambres (Les)

83380 (4km NE)

Le Provençal***

Take the N98 towards Saint-Raphaël.
Ⓣ04.94.55.32.33 Ⓕ04.94.55.32.34
Ⓦwww.hotel.le.provencal.com
Closed *Wed lunchtime in low season; Nov to early Feb.* **TV. Cots available. Car park.**

Just the place for an old-fashioned holiday, this charming hotel has a view over the gulf of Saint-Tropez and the beach. It's run by the Sauvan family, who are all smiles when you arrive – they are happy to advise you on what to do in the local area. Their traditional cooking is superb, and you dine in the shade of the restaurant's terrace. Menus €24–41. Rooms €53–103.

Saintes-Maries-de-la-Mer

13460

Hôtel Méditérranée**

4 rue Frédéric-Mistral; it's in the middle of town near the arena.
Ⓣ04.90.97.82.09 Ⓕ04.90.97.76.31
Ⓔhotel-le-mediterranee@worldonline.fr
TV. Highchairs available.

A tiny hotel which is both clean and well-run. There are flowers and plants everywhere. Doubles €40–43 – some of them overlook the little courtyard.

Hôtel de Cacharel

Route de Cacharel; 5km from the centre via the D85A.
Ⓣ04.90.97.95.44 Ⓕ04.90.97.87.97
Ⓦwww.hotel-cacharel.com
Disabled access. Car park. Swimming pool.

You arrive via a track full of potholes, thereby ensuring that you won't be accompanied by hordes of tourists. This old house, far from the road, is very peaceful, and its comfortable and well-converted rooms invite you to linger. Double rooms €103. Country platters (ham, sausage, goat's cheese) €10, served until 8pm. The dining room has tables covered with old tiles and an impressive fireplace, along with a beautiful view of the Camargue and the lake; several of the bedrooms also offer stunning vistas. Horses are available. You should book well in advance. *Free coffee on presentation of this guide.*

Manade des Baumelles

Les cabanes de Cambon; take the rte. d'Aigües-Mortes.
Ⓣ04.90.97.84.37

Lunchtime menu only (but you must book) at €27 all in, including an apéritif, wine and a tour of the estate, which all requires a good deal of time. You climb on to a cart to see the livestock and have a drink with the herdsmen in front of the restored stables, seated around a big table or, if the weather permits, on the terrace. Small Provençal starters (tomato pie, Arles sausage, *feuilleté à la bandade*...) followed by a beef rib or a *feuilleté* of grey mullet *en papillote* and then copious desserts. And if a special event occurs in the herd (selection for a race or vaccination), you have the chance to witness it.

Salon-de-Provence

13300

Grand Hôtel de la Poste**

1 rue des Frères-Kennedy; it's at the end of the cours Carnot across from the Fontaine Moussue.
Ⓣ04.90.56.01.94 Ⓕ04.90.56.20.77
Ⓔgrandhotelprovence@wanadoo.fr
Closed *a week in Feb.* **TV.**

A good place to stay in the centre of town, with well-soundproofed rooms for €37–47 with shower or bath.

Hôtel Vendôme**

34 rue du Maréchal-Joffre.
Ⓣ04.90.56.01.96 Ⓕ04.90.56.48.78
Ⓦwww.ifrance.com/hotelvendome
TV.

The rooms in this hotel, decorated in intense Provençal colours, go for €42–50 with shower or bath. All have huge, slightly retro bathrooms, and wonderful beds. Ask for one overlooking the cool, delightful patio. Professional welcome. *10% discount on the room rate on presentation of this guide.*

L'O à la Bouche

1 pl. Crousillat.

☎04.90.44.70.82
Closed *Sun.*

Every day shellfish are served, in accordance with that day's catch, along with grilled sea fish that has also come straight from the sea. This place is far removed from an unadorned fishmonger's, however, as it's a beautiful two-storey building, typical of the hidden jewels tucked away in this town. One dining room is decorated in an Art-Deco style, the other is modern; as for the terrace on top, it's simply wonderful. Platters at €14 and €40 (for two people). Reckon on around €30 à la carte.

|●| La Salle à Manger

6 rue du Maréchal-Joffre; it's between the Fontaine Moussue and the Town Hall.
☎04.90.56.28.01
Closed *Sun evening; Mon.* **Highchairs available. Disabled access.**

The Miège family took over this nineteenth-century residence and transformed it into a vibrant, lively place which is renowned for gourmet cuisine. It's a real pleasure to sit on the terrace under the chestnut trees or in the Rococo salons. Weekday lunch menu €15 (starter and main course) and another at €23; reckon on paying €28 à la carte. Interesting local wines.

Pélisanne

13330 (4km E)

|●| ☗ Le Moulin de Dodé

41 rue Georges Clemenceau; it's behind the church.
☎04.90.55.44.93
Closed *Sun evening; Mon; Wed; 15–31 July.*

This converted seventeeth-century mill is now a good restaurant offering superb value for money. Dodé is the chef who, despite the air of simplicity, uses quality produce for his dishes and pays meticulous attention to flavourings. Weekday lunch *formule* €13.50 and menus €20–30. It has a crowd of local regulars who flood in – it's best to book on the weekend. *Free coffee on presentation of this guide.*

Sanary-sur-Mer

83110

|●| L'Océan Jazz

74 rte. de la Gare; it's 500m from the town centre.
☎04.94.07.36.11
Closed *Sat lunchtime; Sun except in season and public holidays; Christmas school holidays.* **Disabled access.**

An excellent little restaurant with a weekday lunch *formule* at €11 including a quarter litre of wine and others €12.50–25. They put a dish of olive paste and hunks of bread on the table to start you off; carefully prepared regional dishes made with fresh local produce and presentation worthy of a much grander place follow. Efficient, easy-going service and a truly friendly welcome. The dining room is charming and the terrace is splendid. There's music in the background, and live duos and trios on Saturday evening. *15% discount (Fri evening 1 Sept–30 June by reservation only) or free house digestif on presentation of this guide.*

Sault

84390

☗ |●| Hostellerie du Val de Sault***

Ancien chemin d'Aurel; it's 2km from the centre of the village on the route de Saint-Trimit – follow the signs.
☎04.90.64.01.41 Ⓕ04.90.64.12.74
Ⓦwww.valdesault.com
Closed *Nov to end March; weekday lunchtimes in April, May, Sept and Oct.*
Disabled access. TV. Swimming pool. Car park.

Lost in the countryside dominated by Mont Ventoux, this little hotel complex is a haven of peace. Spacious, simply decorated wooden rooms all have a small sitting area and a terrace. Half board, compulsory May–Sept, is €95–150 in high season, €75–130 in low season. There's a gym and a Jacuzzi in a lavender-scented room. In the kitchen, Yves is always improvising and changing his menus. There's one constant, however: the truffle menu (which the entire party has to order). Menus €33–63. *Free apéritif on presentation of this guide.*

Seyne-les-Alpes

04140

☗ |●| Le Vieux Tilleul**

Les Auches; it's a ten-minute walk from the centre of the village.
☎04.92.35.00.04 Ⓕ04.92.35.26.81
Ⓦwww.vieux-tilleul.fr

Closed *10 Nov–26 Dec*; **Car park. Highchairs and games available. Swimming pool.**

Near-perfect hotel near the ski slopes in a sweet village in the Vallée de la Blanche. In summer you can lounge around in the shade of the huge trees in the grounds or by the pool. The rooms in the old farmhouse have been attractively and originally renovated; doubles €32 with basin, to €40–47 with shower/wc or bath. Honest cuisine with some mountain dishes and others from further afield: lamb haunch with cream, farm chicken with morels, cod with lemon zest, sheep's cheese salad, pork with Roquefort and the like. Weekday lunch menu €13, with others up to €22. *10% discount on the room rate on presentation of this guide.*

Sisteron

04200

Hôtel du Rocher

It's at the foot of the town walls, 5 minutes from the centre of town, across the Durance and facing the bridge.
Ⓣ04.92.61.12.56 Ⓕ04.92.62.65.59
Ⓦwww.hotel.rocher.wanadoo.fr
Closed *mid-Oct to end of March; Sun except July–Aug*. **Highchairs and cots available.**

OK, it's right on the main road, which is busy during the day (especially in summer). But it's quiet at night and the view of the citadel and the banks of the Durance below is fantastic – particularly from numbers 2 and 5. And the interior is far more attractive and lively than you might imagine from the outside. Doubles with basin €27, with shower/wc €35 and with bath €43. You have breakfast (€5) in the large dining room set with wooden tables. An unexpected surprise. It's best to book in summer. *10% discount on the room rate except July/Aug on presentation of this guide.*

Grand Hôtel du Cours***

Allée de Verdun.
Ⓣ04.92.61.04.51 Ⓕ04.92.61.41.73
Ⓔhotelducours@wanadoo.fr
Closed *mid-Nov to mid-March*. **TV. Highchairs available. Car park.**

A chic hotel with fifty rooms. Provincial atmosphere, courteous welcome and attentive service. The rooms are all very clean but some are noisier than others – avoid those that look out onto the main road and plump instead for one with a view of the château or the cathedral. Doubles €55–76 with shower/wc or bath. Breakfast €8. *Free apéritif on presentation of this guide.*

Les Becs Fins

16 rue Saunerie; it's in the centre of the lower town, parallel to the tunnel.
Ⓣ04.92.61.12.04
Closed *Sun evening and Mon except July/Aug; a week in June; a fortnight at the beginning of Dec*. **Highchairs available.**

A gourmet restaurant in a town that has a reputation for rearing excellent lamb. They're pretty serious about their cooking, but the atmosphere is relaxed, warm and friendly. The menus are well judged and in the best traditions of Provence – pan-fried *escalope* of foie gras, snail stew in white wine, sautéed lamb, duck breast prepared nine different ways and Châteaubriand prepared eight different ways. And as you would expect, lamb features in many dishes. Menus €15 (weekday lunchtimes) and €21–49.50.

Tarascon

13150

Auberge de jeunesse

31 bd. Gambetta; 15min on foot from the train station.
Ⓣ04.90.91.04.08 Ⓕ04.90.91.54.17
Ⓦwww.fuaj.org
Closed *Dec–Feb*.

On the outskirts of the old town, a youth hostel in an old Provençal house. It sleeps 55 people in small, basic but well-kept dormitories. FUAJ card compulsory (you can buy it *in situ*), €8.50 a night, breakfast €3.50. The red floor tiles and exposed beams in the dining room always delight foreign visitors. Kitchen available. Excellent service and pleasant family atmosphere.

Hostellerie Saint-Michel

Abbaye de Frigolet; it's 12km from the centre of town.
Ⓣ04.90.90.52.70 Ⓕ04.90.05.75.22
Ⓦwww.frigolet.com
Car park.

A former abbey offering rooms with a variety of facilities; spacious doubles

€43.50–53.50 with shower/wc or bath. Meals are served in an old refectory – it's got a fantastic entrance – or in the garden. Appetizing *aïoli* with rabbit and sautéed veal with honey. And you have to try the ice cream served with Frigolet liqueur. Menus €12.50–22.

Hôtel de Provence

7 bd Victor-Hugo.
☎04.90.91.06.43 Ⓕ04.90.43.58.13
Ⓔhoteldeprovence@wanadoo.fr

Eleven spacious rooms in the former residence of the Marquis of Tarascon, which has been given a new lease of life by its new owners. Double rooms €58–70; suite €84. Some rooms give on to the terrace. Gourmet breakfast €7. Possibility of brunch on Sunday, and a splendid afternoon tea is also served. More of a guest house than a traditional hotel, and you get a personalized welcome to match.

Théoule-sur-Mer

06590

Auberge de jeunesse

Route de la Véronèse; around 2 km from the train station, going up to the Trayas neighbourhood.
☎ 04.93.75.40.23 Ⓕ04.93.75.43.45
Ⓦwww.fuaj.org_
Disabled acces. Car park.

The location is really wonderful, with a view of the sea and Estérel; the only problem is getting there. €10 a night, without breakfast. It's worth booking for a stay of more than three nights in summer. FUAJ card compulsory. There's space for a few tents in the garden. Courses in windsurfing, water-skiing, etc.

Thorenc

06750

Hôtel des Voyageurs**

Avenue Belvédère.
☎04.93.60.00.18 Ⓕ04.93.60.03.51
Closed *Thurs out of season.* **TV. Car park.**

Twelve faultlessly clean rooms, €38–45. Half board, compulsory in season, costs €43–45 per person. The good restaurant offers a weekday menu at €14.50 and another at €24; they list dishes such as calf's head sauce *ravigote* and sautéed rabbit *chasseur*. There's a pleasant terrace and garden with a view of the village.

Andon

06750 (4km SW)

Le Christiana

L'Audibergue.
☎04.93.60.45.41
Closed *evenings; Mon except in summer and winter seasons; Dec.*

Set at the foot of the Audibergue ski runs, this restaurant sees a lot of regulars from Cannes. There's a menu at €20; you can help yourself to the five starters – country ham, fried garlic bread, *crudités*, terrines and calf's head – as often as you like, following them with tripe *à la Niçoise*, roast lamb, wild boar or hare stew, cheese and dessert. Dish of the day €11. Booking essential at weekends and on public holidays.

Toudon

06830

La Capeline

It's on the road to Roquestéron at Vescous.
☎04.93.08.58.06
Closed *evenings; Wed March to end Oct; Feb.* **Open** *week-ends only Nov to end Jan.*

The old tram garage, formerly a coaching inn and local school, has been turned into a really nice restaurant. Cosy up to the fireplace out of season or take the air on the shaded veranda in summer; you get a lovely view of the valley below. Laurent Laugier, the chef, originates from Gilette but the dishes on the menus are specialities from the Vallée de l'Estéron. He ensures authenticity by getting his produce and supplies from local producers: *bavarois* with verbena, juicy chicken with ceps, *pissaladière*, ratatouille and so on. Market menus in the week €17–22, a *menu terroir* served at weekends for €24 and another at €26 served on public holidays. *Free coffee on presentation of this guide.*

Toulon

83000

Hôtel Molière*

12 rue Molière; it's in the pedestrianized area next to the theatre.
☎04.94.92.78.35 Ⓕ04.94.62.85.82

Closed *Jan.* **TV.**

A very simple family hotel with unbeatable prices. The owners really know how to make you feel welcome and do their best to make sure you have a pleasant stay. Comfortable, clean, soundproofed doubles €27 with basin up to €33 with shower/wc and TV. Nos. 18, 19 and 20 have a great view of the harbour. An excellent place of its kind. *10% discount for a two-night stay, Sept–June, on presentation of this guide.*

Grand Hôtel Dauphiné**

10 rue Berthelot.
Ⓣ04.94.92.20.28 Ⓕ04.94.62.16.69
Ⓦgrandhoteldauphine.com
Disabled access. Pay car park.

Lots of regulars here, notably the opera singers and fans who attend performances at the Théâtre Municipal close by. The attractive and comfortable rooms all have mini-bar, air-conditioning and soundproofing. Doubles with bath (including hairdryers) go for €41–52. Good value for money. Parking at 50m from the hotel. *10% discount on the room rate except July/Aug on presentation of this guide.*

Le Confetti

40 rue Castillon; in the neighbourhood of Le Mourillon.
Ⓣ04.94.42.54.56
Open *every evening, except Wed; at lunch, by reservation only and for a minimum of four people.* **Disabled access.**

In this tiny restaurant Madame does the cooking while her young son Bruno provides a charming service to the guests. It is worth visiting for both its friendly atmosphere and its regional, family cooking; the dishes change regularly but the Provençal daube with its trio of gnocchi, pasta and polenta always takes pride of place. Dishes €6; menus €10–12.50 with a choice of three starters, main courses and excellent desserts. It's advisable to book. Credit cards not accepted. *Free digestif on presentation of this guide.*

Les Enfants Gâtés

7 rue Corneille.
Ⓣ04.94.09.14.67
Closed *Sat and Sun in summer; in low season Sun–Fri evenings and Sat lunch.*

The décor is fresh and quietly contemporary – walls are given over to local artists – and there's a terrace, too. Olivier injects a personal touch into the highly flavoured dishes, adding a few ideas picked up on his travels to old family recipes from the Sète area. Dishes €15–25 à la carte. *Free coffee on presentation of this guide.*

L'Eau à la Bouche

54 rue Muiron, Le Mourillon.
Ⓣ04.94.46.33.09
Closed *lunchtime; Sun; Mon.*

This is a small unpretentious restaurant with an outdoor terrace that opens on to a little square in Le Mourillon, which is like a village inside the city. Everything here recalls the sea, which you can see gleaming in the distance – from the food to the dining room, lined with painted wood and adorned with nautical paintings and knick-knacks. It is run by a charming couple (he stays in the kitchen while she waits the tables, with great diligence). Menu €28. *Free coffee on presentation of this guide.*

Le Jardin du Sommelier

20 allée Courbet; beside place d'Armes, behind the arsenal.
Ⓣ04.94.62.03.27
Closed *Sat lunchtime; Sun.*

The *sommelier* and chef who run the place believe that what's on your plate and what's in your glass are equally important. Their sunny restaurant is full of wonderful aromas and pretty colours; mouthwatering smells waft from the kitchens, where they prepare fabulous dishes. Menus €28–35; it's around €32 à la carte.

Tour-d'Aigues (La)

84240

Auberge de la Tour

51 rue Antoine-de-Très; it's opposite the church.
Ⓣ04.90.07.34.64
Closed *Mon; Sat lunchtime; Sun evening; 15–28 Feb; 15–30 Nov.*

This restaurant has character, with its grey stone vaults and appealing shady terrace. Menus, €11 (weekday lunchtime) up to €23, feature fish and traditional Provençal dishes like lamb tripe, meatballs *à la provençale*, kid *blanquette* and crayfish *fricassée. Free apéritif on presentation of this guide.*

Utelle

06450

Aubergerie del Campo

Route d'Utelle.
℡04.93.03.13.12
Open *evenings all year round.* **Closed** *a week in July.*

Just below the road climbing steeply up to Utelle, there's a lovingly restored shepherd's house dating from 1785. In the rustic dining room, with its handsome fireplace and olive-wood floors, you're served classic dishes like ravioli with duck and cep filling, king scallop *fricassée* with raspberry vinegar, trout braised with tarragon and splendid desserts. Lunchtime *formule* €14 and set menus €19–33. The beautiful terrace looks over the Gorges de la Vésubie. Friendly atmosphere. Dinner by reservation. Credit cards not accepted. *Free digestif on presentation of this guide.*

Vaison-la-Romaine

84110

Hôtel Burrhus**

1 pl. Montfort; take the Bollène exit off the A7.
℡04.90.36.00.11 Ⓕ04.90.36.39.05
Ⓦwww.burrhus.com
Closed *15 Dec–20 Jan.* **TV. Pay car park.**

Attractive hotel, all ochre walls and wrought iron, with a billiard room. The bedrooms are distributed around a warren of corridors and they're all different – some are decorated in Provençal style, others are more basic. Doubles €46–64 with shower/wc or bath. Breakfast €7. The owners are into contemporary art and hold regular exhibitions. *10% discount on the room rate for the second consecutive night (except 1 July–30 Sept) on presentation of this guide.*

L'Hostellerie Le Beffroi***

Rue de l'Évêché.
℡04.90.36.04.71 Ⓕ04.90.36.24.78
Ⓦwww.le-beffroi.com
Closed *end Jan to end March.* **Restaurant closed** *weekday lunchtimes; Tues; 1 Nov–1 April.* **TV. Highchairs and games available. Swimming pool. Car park.**

Based in the upper town, this hotel is housed in two residences from the sixteenth and seventeenth centuries. All the ancient charm remains – old wood and stone, furniture in keeping – along with comforts of today. Doubles with shower/wc or bath €70–125 depending on the season. Great Provençal cooking: salmon steak with sorrel, *feuilleté* of livers *à la provençale* – and a salad bar on the terrace and superb garden in summer. Menus €26–41. There's a great view of town from the swimming pool. *Free apéritif on presentation of this guide.*

Valberg

06470

Hôtel Le Chastellan**

Rue Saint-Jean; it's behind the tourist office off the main square, up the road to the left.
℡04.93.02.57.41 Ⓕ04.93.02.61.65
Closed *April; May.* **TV. Highchairs and games available. Car park.**

This is a family-run hotel for families to stay in. It boasts 37 lovely rooms, a large, airy dining room and a games room for the children. Doubles with shower/wc or bath €60–70 with breakfast included, and six suites for €110. They all have shower/wc or bath and direct-dial telephone, and prices include buffet breakfast.

Côté Jardin

It's behind the main square.
℡04.93.02.64.70
Closed *April; Nov.*

You rarely think of gourmet food when you think about ski resorts, but here's the exception to the rule. True, you can get *tartiflette*, *raclette* and *fondue*, but it would be a pity to opt for dishes that are more typical of Savoy than of Provence. The dishes on the menus (€14–28) taste good and the presentation is exceptional. Expect to pay around €40 à la carte. The dining room faces the garden. Friendly service. *Free house digestif on presentation of this guide.*

Vence

06140

Auberge des Seigneurs**

Place Frêne.
℡04.93.58.04.24 Ⓕ04.93.24.08.01

Restaurant closed *Mon; Tues, Wed and Thurs lunchtimes; Nov to mid-March.*

This beautiful fifteenth-century building is situated on the ramparts at the entrance to the old town. The rooms, which are more like suites, are named after painters; some have mountain views. Prices are more than reasonable – €70–85 with shower or bath. The restaurant offers sophisticated, imaginative cooking on menus €29–42. *Men are offered a free digestif and women are given a rose, on presentation of this guide.*

|●| Le P'tit Provençal

4 pl. Clemenceau.
Ⓣ04.93.58.50.64
Closed *Wed and Thurs out of season (lunchtimes only in season); a fortnight in March; mid-Nov to mid-Dec.* **Highchairs available.**

A restaurant with a relaxed informal atmosphere in the centre of the old town. The food is extremely imaginative and typically Provençal. Dishes change frequently. Reckon on paying between €8 and €14 for the dish of the day; menus in the evening €20–26. If you eat on the terrace you can admire the view of the lively, historic town.

|●| La Farigoule

15 av. Henri-Isnard.
Ⓣ04.93.58.01.27
Closed *Tues; Wed and Sat lunchtimes in summer; Tues and Wed in winter; the autumn and Christmas school holidays.*

You come here as much for the atmosphere as the authentic Provençal cooking. The chef, who trained with the great Alain Ducasse in Juan-les-Pins, works with the best market produce, combining texture, colour and flavour. The little dining rom is convivial, and there's a large terrace. Menus €22 (lunchtime) and from €28–43.

Saint-Jeannet

06640 (8km NE)

⌂ |●| Hôtel l'Indicible*

Rue du Saumalier.
Ⓣ04.92.11.01.08 Ⓕ04.92.11.02.06
Ⓦwww.saint-jeannet.com
Closed *15 Jan–15 Feb.* **TV.** Highchairs available.

A little hotel in the middle of the village run by Michel originally from Ghent in Belgium. Their hotel is in an old house which has been very attractively renovated and it provides rooms with views over Le Baou, the hills and the sea in the distance. Doubles €54–65. Snacks served in the summer on the terrace. *10% discount on the room rate (1Nov–1 April) or free coffee on presentation of this guide.*

Rhône-Alpes

Aix-les-Bains

73100

🏠 |●| Auberge de Jeunesse

Promenade du Sierroz; take town centre, bus no. 2 towards Grand Port, bus stop Camping.
Ⓣ04.79.88.32.88 Ⓕ04.79.61.14.05
Ⓔaix-les-bains@fuaj.org
Open *6–10pm.* **Closed** *from autumn school holidays to Feb school holidays.* **Disabled access. Car park.**

This youth hostel is relatively far from the town centre but closed to the "Lac du Bourget". It's only a few minutes away from the port and the beaches. It's in a nice countryside area, which unfortunately is beginning to be surrounded by buildings. The youth hostel has three floors; each bedroom contains four beds and an en-suite bathroom. To stay the night is €13.50 per person, breakfast included. Menu at €8.40. FUAJ card is compulsory but you can buy it there. Reservations recommended from May to Sept.

🏠 |●| Hôtel Broisin*

10 ruelle du Revet.
Ⓣ04.79.35.06.15 Ⓕ04.79.88.10.10
Closed *22 Nov–15 March.* **TV.**

A little hotel in a quiet side street in the centre of town, just a short walk from the spa. It's a very typical spa town hotel with the atmosphere of a family guesthouse; many guests have been coming here for years. The rooms have been freshened up and prices are modest: depending on the season, they go for €27–30 for a double with basin, €36–40 with shower/wc. The restaurant doesn't merit a special visit; it offers one menu at €11. *10% discount on the room rate (except July–Aug) offered to our readers on presentation of this guide.*

🏠 |●| Hôtel-restaurant Au Petit Vatel**

11 rue du Temple. Beside Saint-Swithum church.
Ⓣ04.79.35.04.80 Ⓕ04.79.34.01.51
Ⓦwww.petit-vatel.com
Closed *Mon; Tues; Jan.* **TV. High chairs available. Pay car park.**

Charmingly old-fashioned establishment with an elegant atmosphere. The rooms at the back, complete with balcony, overlook a little garden with walls swathed in ivy. Doubles €38–52 with shower/wc or bath, depending on the season. The dining room has a pleasant atmosphere and there's a delightful terrace in the garden. Tasty, classical cooking – the freshwater fish, particularly the trout, is good, as are the *osso buco* and the Savoyard specialities of *fondues* and *raclette*. Weekday menu €15 and others €19 and €27. You'll pay around €30 à la carte.

🏠 |●| Hôtel-restaurant Les Platanes**

173 av. du Petit-Port; it's near the lake.
Ⓣ04.79.61.40.54 Ⓕ04.79.35.00.41
Closed *Sun evening except out of season; mid Nov to end Jan.* **TV. Car park.**

Set in a residential area near the lake, this hotel has a lovely shaded terrace. The firmly classic cuisine features many Savoy specialities, and the chef also has a deft touch with fish dishes. Menus €19–44. Live jazz on Friday and Saturday nights. The décor in the bedrooms has seen better

A
SAÔNE-ET-LOIRE
ALLIER
AIN
RHÔNE
LOIRE
PUY-DE-DÔME
ISÈRE
HAUTE-LOIRE
ARDÈCHE
DRÔME
LOZÈRE
GARD
VAUCLUSE
Digoin
Paray-le-Monial
Marcigny
Lapalisse
Vichy
Pouilly-sous-Charlieu
Noailly
Ambierle
St-Haon-le Châtel
Renaison
Roanne
Villerest
Bully
Juré
Cervières
Thiers
les Salles
Noirétable
Boën
Sail-sous-Couzan
Champdieu
Montbrison
Andrézieux-B.
St-Romain-le-Puy
Ambert
St-Just-St-Rambert
St-Bonnet-le-Château
St-Victor-sur-L.
Usson-en-Forez
St-Paul-en-C.
St-Genest-Malifaux
Mâcon
St-Laurent-sur-Saône
Cormoranche-sur-Saône
Juliénas
Chiroubles
Beaujeu
Belleroche
Quincié-en-Beaujolais
Belleville
Cours-la-Ville
Marnand
Vaux-en-Beaujolais
Ars-sur-Formans
Liergues
Theizé
Marcy-s.-A.
Alix
Anse
Trévoux
Tarare
Sarcey
Violay
Panissières
Montrottier
Feurs
Chazelles-sur-Lyon
Marclopt
Aveize
St-Martin-en-Haut
St-Galmier
Veauche
Lyon
St-Martin-la-Pl.
Rive-de-Gier
St-Priest-en-J.
St-Étienne
Ste-Croix-en-Jarez
le Bessat
Condrieu
Vienne
Chonas-l'Amballan
Serrières
Arbigny
Vonnas
St-Denis-les-Bourg
Meillonnas
Bourg-en-Bresse
l'Abergement-Clémenciat
Châtillon-sur-Chalaronne
Pont d'Ain
Bouligneux
Chalamont
Villars-les-Dombes
Ambérieux
Joyeux
Meximieux
Ste-Croix
Crémieu
St-Hilaire-de-B.
Vignieu
St-Savin
Bourgoin-Jallieu
Domarin
Cessieu
Estrablin
la Côte St-André
Bressieux
Hauterives
Marnans
Brioude
St-Sauveur-en-Rue
Annonay
Satillieu
Yssingeaux
le Puy-en-Velay
St-Agrève
le Crestet
Lamastre
Crozes-Hermitage
Tain-l'Hermitage
Tournon-sur-R.
Granges-les-Beaumont
Romans
Choranche
Bouvante
St-Agnan-en-Vercors
Valence
Omblèze
la Voulte
les Ollières
Sainte-Eulalie
Coucouron
Sagnes-et-G.
Antraigues-sur-Volane
Burzet
Langogne
Privas
Baix
Alissas
Cliousclat
Grane
Crest
Die
Saillans
Mirmande
Saou
Barnave
Vals-les-Bains
Aubenas
St-Pons
Valgorge
Largentière
Sanilhac
Balazuc
Alba-la-Romaine
Viviers
Montélimar
Félines-sur-R.
Bourdeaux
Dieulefit
le-Poët-Laval
St-Ferréol-Trente-Pas
Joyeuse
Vallon-Pont-d'arc
Valaurie
Grignan
Condorcet
les Vans
Orgnac-l'Aven
la Garde-Adhémar
St-Restitut
Nyons
Buis-les-Baronnies
Vagnas
St-Martin-d'Ardèche
Mirabel-aux-B.
Plaisians
Mende
Florac
Meyrueis
Alès
Bagnols-sur-Cèze
Orange
Rhône
Loire
Ardèche
N 1079
N 79 E 62
D 994
D 982
D 985
N 7
D 907
N 209
D 906
D 53
D 8
N 82
A 72
N 89
D 997
D 996
D 999
D 498
A 6 E 15
N 79
A 40 E 21 E
D 975
D 996
A 39
N 83
A 42
D 65
N 75
D 517
N 6
A 46
A 7
N 522
N 85
A 48
D 538
D 518
D 519
D 1
N 102
D 105
D 503
D 82
D 501
D 500
N 88
D 15
D 532
D 534
N 86
N 532
A 49
D 533
D 589
D 989
D 578
D 2
N 104
D 111
N 7
D 93
D 6
N 106
D 104
D 579
D 94
D 907
D 904
D 996
A 7 E 15
N 92
D 6

RHÔNE-ALPES

22

days, but the facilities are good, and they're very quiet. Doubles with shower/wc €39–45.

🏃 🏠 |●| Hôtel-restaurant Le Manoir***

37 rue Georges-1er; it's behind the spa, 500m from town centre.
Ⓣ04.79.61.44.00 Ⓕ04.79.35.67.67
Ⓦwww.hotel-lemanoir.com
Closed *early Dec.* **TV. Swimming pool. High chairs available. Pay car park.**

The "manoir" is actually a series of outbuildings belonging to two Belle Époque mansions. The cosy, well-equipped rooms are decorated in a style that's in keeping with the building. Doubles €78–150 with shower/wc or bath, depending on the season. The sitting rooms are comfortable, the garden pleasant and the indoor swimming pool very 1930s Hollywood; there are also a sauna, hammam, Jacuzzi and a fitness room. Excellent regional cuisine, delicate freshwater fish and a good wine list. Menus €25–53. The young, relaxed staffs create an easy-going atmosphere. *10% discount on the room rate (1st Oct–31 March) offered to our readers on presentation of this guide.*

🏃 |●| Restaurant L'Auberge du Pont Rouge

151 av. du Grand-Port. Towards the lake.
Ⓣ04.79.63.43.90
Closed *Mon evening; Tues; Wed; 21 Dec–9 Jan.*

A little out of the way (there are few good places to eat in the centre), this restaurant is always busy. You can dine on a simple veranda or in the gravel courtyard. The owners are friendly and the cooking is wonderful. Menus include a combination of south-western dishes and fresh fish – which depends on what's landed from the lake – and there are specialities from Périgord. Weekday lunch menu €14, others €23–30. Friendly welcome. *Free house apéritif offered to our readers on presentation of this guide.*

Brison-Saint-Innocent

73100 (9km N)

|●| 🏃 Les Oliviers

212 rte. de Paris Brison-les-Oliviers; take the D991.
Ⓣ04.79.54.21.81
Closed *Tues (except July–Aug); mid-Jan to mid Feb.* **Car park. High chairs available.**

This restaurant is set in a little hamlet by the side of Lake Bourget but is right by the road and not very far from the railway line. The owner uses the fish from the lake to create a seasonal menu full of spirit and good ideas, all at very reasonable prices. Menus €14–43. *Free coffee offered to our readers on presentation of this guide.*

Alba-la-Romaine

07400

🏃 |●| Restaurant La Petite Chaumière

Quartier de la Roche; it's signposted from the main square in Vieil Alba; take the road at the bottom, it's 400m to the hamlet of La Roche,
Ⓣ04.45.52.43.50
Closed *Tues and Wed April–Sept; Mon–Fri in Oct and March; Sun evening to Sat lunchtime.* **High chairs available.**

The setting is very unusual and the welcome is delightful. There are only a few tables inside, as most are on a lovely terrace overlooking an imposing tower of crumbling rocks. Traditional, old-fashioned, family cuisine – cream of carrot soup, sautéed lamb with spices and a real *crème caramel* – is served in handsome portions. There is a special evening menu when there is a concert at the Cavajazz. Menus €10.50–14; they don't have set specialities, though the savoury tart, cream of vegetable soup, lamb sautéed with spices and chocolate tart make a pretty regular appearance. Credit cards not accepted. Booking advisable. *Free Kir, fruit juice or soft drink offered to our readers on presentation of this guide.*

Albertville

73200

🏃 🏠 |●| Auberge Costaroche**

1 chemin Pierre-du-Roy; take the pont du Mirantin – it's near the medieval town of Conflans and the château in Costaroche.
Ⓣ04.79.32.02.02 Ⓕ04.79.31.37.59
Ⓦwww.costaroche.fr.st
Restaurant closed *Wed; 10 days in Sept; 10 days in Jan.* **TV. High chairs and games available. Car park.**

A large, rather dull building in a residential area surrounded by a tree-filled garden.

The owners give you a charming welcome, and the rooms have been gently renovated. Doubles with bath €39–48. The dining room is not very intimate but the cooking is decent: ravioli *de Royans au gratin* (with Tamié cheese from the abbey), king prawns flambéed *à la Provençal*, scallops *au noilly* (Vermouth), caramelized *pain perdu* (French toast). Weekday lunch menu €12; others €16–35. *10% discount on the room rate (except weekends in winter) offered to our readers on presentation of this guide.*

Plancherine

73200 (8km W)

Chalet des Trappeurs

Col de Tamié; from Albertville, follow the signs for Gilly-sur-Isère and then col de Tamié.
Ⓣ04.79.32.21.44
Closed *Wed.* **TV.**

The heliport and the faux antique statues are a little worrying, but inside things are different. This characterful, attractive chalet is sturdily built of wood; huge logs burn in the hearth, hunting trophies line the walls and animal skins are draped on the benches. They serve Savoy specialities like *tartiflette* and *fondue*, substantial omelettes and some remarkable local dishes: *fricassée* of rabbit with *trompette de la mort* mushrooms, country-style fillet of lake whitefish. Weekday lunch menu €13 and others €24–28. There's a large terrace. While you're in the area, buy some of the cheese made by the monks in the nearby abbey of Tamié. Telephone out of season to check if they're open.

Allevard

38580

Les Terrasses**

29 av. de Savoie; it's opposite the old train station.
Ⓣ04.76.45.84.42
Ⓦwww.hotellesterrasses.com
Closed *Wed out of season; Sun evening; Easter school holidays; All Saint's day.* **TV. Disabled access (restaurant). High chairs and games available.**

A rather dull building from the outside, but it's been attractively renovated inside and decorated in shades of blue and white with posters of great artists' works on the walls. The corner bar in the veranda at the entrance is bright and the dining room is fresh and smart. Good dishes include hot goat's cheese salad with honey, duck with gingerbread, fillets of lake whitefish with sesame and Chartreuse iced soufflé. Menus in the week from €13, on Sunday from €15, and up to €27. Doubles €37 depending on the facilities – some have a view over the garden (numbers 3, 8, 12 and 14). *Free house apéritif or coffee offered to our readers on presentation of this guide.*

Goncelin

38570 (10km SW)

Restaurant Le Clos du Château

Take the D525 from Allevard.
Ⓣ04.76.71.72.04
Closed *Sun and Mon evenings; Wed; a fortnight in Aug.* **Disabled access. Car park.**

An extremely nice English couple runs this thirteenth-century house, in the mountains of Chartreuse and Belledonne. It's not easy to see it from the road because it's set in very extensive grounds. You dine in the shade of the hazels and ancient cedars with a view over the mountains, or in the restaurant, which has a French-style ceiling. Bag a table by the fire in winter, outside under the hazel trees in summer. Suzie Glayser is in charge of the service while her husband creates wonderful flavours in the kitchen: specialities include crayfish ravioli in a creamy broth, and beef Wellington with foie gras. Menus €28.50–40.

Annecy

74000

See map overleaf

Aléry Hôtel**

5 av. d'Aléry. **Map A2-6**
Ⓣ04.50.45.24.75. Ⓕ04.50.51.26.90
Ⓔhotel.alery@wanadoo.fr
TV. Car park.

Characterful, traditional hotel in a good spot between the station and the old town. All the rooms are decorated in typical mountain style with pictures painted on wood, and they all have air-conditioning. Doubles €42–59 with shower/wc or bath, depending on the season. The owners welcome you charmingly, the facilities are perfect and you'll have a quiet night in the rooms at the back. Good breakfast.

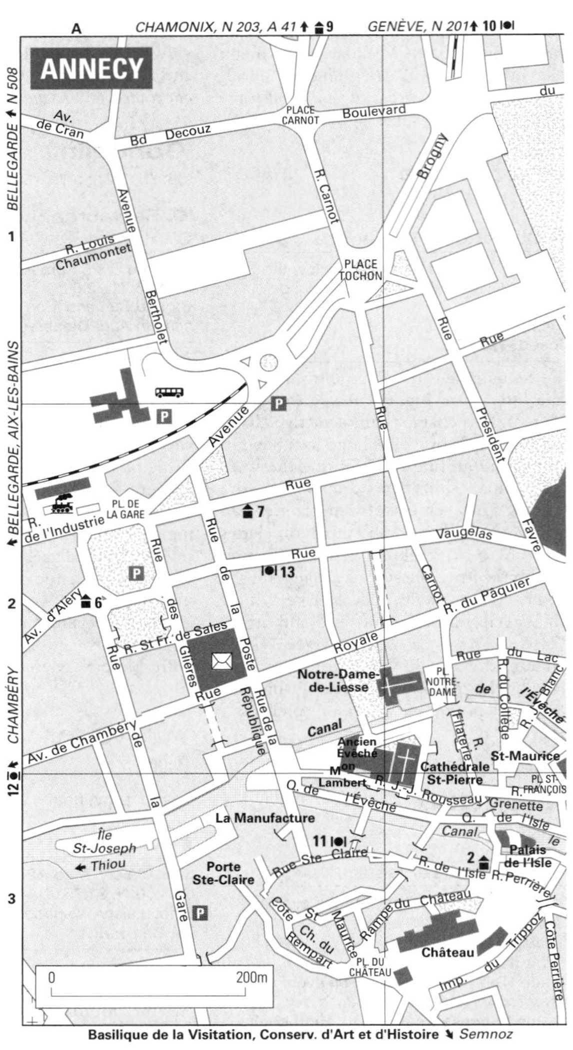
A
CHAMONIX, N 203, A 41 9
GENÈVE, N 201 10
ANNECY
BELLEGARDE N 508
BELLEGARDE, AIX-LES-BAINS
CHAMBÉRY
12
1
2
3
Av. de Cran
Bd Decouz
PLACE CARNOT
Boulevard
du
R. Carnot
Brogny
Avenue
R. Louis Chaumontet
Berthollet
PLACE TOCHON
Rue
Rue
Président
Favre
Avenue
Rue
PL. DE LA GARE
R. de l'Industrie
7
Rue
Rue
Vaugelas
Rue
Rue
13
de
Carnot
R. du Pâquier
6
Av. d'Alery
des
la
R. St Fr. de Sales
Poste
Royale
Rue
Glières
Rue
Rue du Lac
Notre-Dame-de-Liesse
PL. NOTRE-DAME
de
l'Évêché
R. du Collège
R. Blanc
Rue
Rue de la République
Av. de Chambéry
de
Canal
Ancien Évêché
Mon Lambert
Filaterie
R.
Cathédrale St-Pierre
St-Maurice
PL. ST-FRANÇOIS
R.
R. J.-J. Rousseau
Grenette
Q. de l'Évêché
Q. de l'Isle
la
La Manufacture
Canal
Île St-Joseph
Thiou
11
Rue Ste Claire
2
Palais de l'Isle
Porte Ste-Claire
R. de l'Isle
R. Perrière
Gare
Côte St Maurice
Rampe du Château
Ch. du Rempart
PL. DU CHÂTEAU
Château
Imp. du Trippoz
Côte Perrière
0
200m
Basilique de la Visitation, Conserv. d'Art et d'Histoire
Semnoz

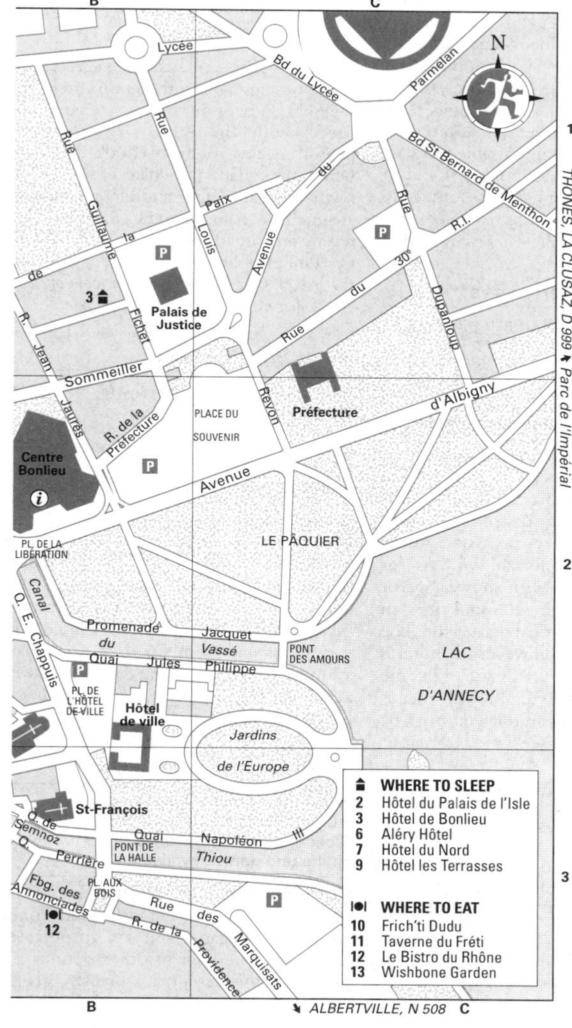
B
C
Lycée
Bd du Lycée
Parmelan
N
1
Rue
Rue
Guillaume
de
la
Paix
du
Louis
Avenue
Bd St Bernard de Menthon
Rue
R.I.
30e
du
Rue
Dupanloup
THÔNES, LA CLUSAZ, D 999 ↗ Parc de l'Impérial
3
Palais de Justice
Fichet
R.
Jean
Sommeiller
Jaurès
R. de la Préfecture
PLACE DU SOUVENIR
Revon
Préfecture
d'Albigny
Centre Bonlieu
Avenue
LE PÂQUIER
PL. DE LA LIBÉRATION
2
Canal
Q. E. Chappuis
Promenade
du
Quai
Jacquet
Vassé
Jules
Philippe
PONT DES AMOURS
LAC
D'ANNECY
PL. DE L'HÔTEL DE VILLE
Hôtel de ville
Jardins
de l'Europe
St-François
Q. de Semnoz
Q. Perrière
Quai
Napoléon
PONT DE LA HALLE
Thiou
3
PL. AUX BOIS
Fbg. des Annonciades
Rue
des
Marquisats
R. de la
Providence
12
WHERE TO SLEEP
2 Hôtel du Palais de l'Isle
3 Hôtel de Bonlieu
6 Aléry Hôtel
7 Hôtel du Nord
9 Hôtel les Terrasses
WHERE TO EAT
10 Frich'ti Dudu
11 Taverne du Fréti
12 Le Bistro du Rhône
13 Wishbone Garden
B
↘ ALBERTVILLE, N 508
C

🏃 🏠 Hôtel du Nord**

24 rue Sommeiller. Between the train station, the lake and the town centre. **Map A2-7**
Ⓣ04.50.45.08.78 Ⓕ04.50.51.22.04
Ⓦwww.annecy-hotel-du-nord.com
TV. Car park.

This hotel is in a great location. The place has a certain charm with its panelled reception and loggia. The rooms are pastel-pretty, with lovely bathrooms; air-conditioning and some have lovely views of old Annecy. Doubles with shower/wc or bath €45–58. The breakfast room provides a pleasurable setting in which to start the day with its parquet floor and modern furniture. Free parking 6.30pm–9am. *10% discount on the room rate (except July–Aug) offered to our readers on presentation this guide.*

🏠 |●| Hôtel Les Terrasses**

15 rue Louis Chaumontel. 10min walking distance to the town centre. **Off map A1-9**
Ⓣ04.50.57.08.98 Ⓕ04.50.57.05.28
Ⓦwww.lac-annecy.com
Restaurant closed *Sat and Sun except July–Aug*. **Disabled access. High chairs available. Car park.**

A stunning old house, which has been transformed into a spruce, modern little hotel with a charming garden. The rooms are plain (white walls, pale wood furniture), quiet and comfortable rooms for €49–65 for a double with shower/wc or bath. Half board is compulsory in July–Aug, at €45 and €52 per person. The area has little to offer; however the hotel is good value for money and the welcome excellent. There's a restaurant with menus at €10 and €14 – it's fine if you can't be bothered to go into town.

🏠 🏃 Hôtel de Bonlieu***

5 rue de Bonlieu; it's beside the Palais de Justice. **Map B1-3**
Ⓣ04.50.45.17.16 Ⓕ04.50.45.11.48
Ⓦwww.annecybonlieuhotel.fr
Disabled access. TV. High chairs available. Pay car park.

A good, dependable little hotel near the lake and the old town, ideal if you're looking for peace and quiet and with all mod cons. It's targeted more at young business execs than travellers, but you'll get a friendly welcome and prices are sensible: double rooms €72–80 with shower/wc or bath, depending on the season. There's a charge to use the car park of €6 per night from May to end Sept. *10% discount on the room rate offered to our readers on presentation of this guide.*

🏠 🏃 Hôtel du Palais de l'Isle***

13 rue Perrière; towards Chappuis and Semnoz. **Map B3-2**
Ⓣ04.50.45.86.87 Ⓕ04.50.51.87.15
Ⓦwww.hoteldupalaisdelisle.com
TV.

An imposing eighteenth-century residence, superbly located in narrow, winding old streets with the River Thiou running beneath. A few rooms overlook the palace, while others face the château and the old town. Soundproofing and air conditioning are gradually being introduced. The modern rooms are superb, with furniture designed by Philippe Starck. Doubles with bath €70–100. *One free breakfast per room offered to our readers on presentation of this guide.*

|●| 🏃 Frich'ti Dudu

9 rue Louis-Armand; it's in the pedestrianized precinct. **Off map B1-10**
Ⓣ04.50.09.97.65
Open *11.30am–3pm*. **Closed** *evenings; weekends, except for group bookings of 15 people or more; 1–15 Aug*. **Disabled access.**

A very popular – non-smoking – restaurant in an area that's seriously short of good places to eat. This bizarrely named place fills that gap and is well worth a visit. Dishes change every day and prices are incredibly low. The cooking is simple, with various *formules* from €6.40 to €10. Takeaway available: dish of the day to take away at €5.50. *Free coffee offered to our readers on presentation of this guide.*

🏃 |●| Wishbone Garden

29 bis rue Vaugelas. **Map A2-13**
Ⓣ04.50.45.25.96
Closed *Sun–Mon*. **Disabled access. High chairs and games available.**

Chicken is king here, served with a variety of sauces – Mexican, mushroom, honey, raspberry vinegar – and superb potatoes. There are a number of other options à la carte (*tartiflette*, duck breast, grilled salmon), along with great home-made desserts. The dining room is on two floors, and there's a peaceful terrace. The jovial British owner creates a relaxed atmosphere. There's a weekday lunch *formule* for €9.50, including drink, and a menu at €15. You'll spend around €17 à la carte.

Free house apéritif offered to our readers on presentation of this guide.

|●| 🏃 Le Bistro du Rhône

13 av. du Rhône. Train station area. **Off map A2-12**
☎04.50.45.53.34
Closed *Mon and Tues evenings; Sat lunchtime; Sun; Aug.* **Disabled access.**

In a somewhat soulless area of the old town, this bistro has a really lovely dining room, almost Provençal with its saffron yellow walls. Very well prepared and tasty dishes use the freshest market produce. Weekday lunch menus €11.30 and €12.80, or €14.95 and €20.60 for dinner. The relaxed atmosphere is underpinned by experienced service. *Free Kir offered to our readers on presentation of this guide.*

|●| Taverne du Fréti

12 rue Sainte-Claire. **Map A3-11**
☎04.50.51.29.52
Open *evenings 7–11.30pm and Sun lunchtime. Closed a fortnight in June.*

The Fréti is one of the few places on this touristy street that still offers quality at reasonable prices. It's a cheese shop, and naturally enough they specialize in dishes that use it: sixteen types of *fondue, raclette, tartiflette* and potatoes with blue or goat's cheese. À la carte you'll pay around €15–20. There's a pretty dining room upstairs – a 1970s version of rustic – where you can eat if the weather's not good enough to sit outside under the arcade.

Sevrier

74320 (5km S)

🏠 |●| 🏃 Auberge de Chuguet-Restaurant l'Arpège

823 rte. d'Albertville.
☎04.50.19.03.69 Ⓕ04.50.52.49.42
Ⓦwww.hotel-de-chuguet.com
TV. Disabled access. High chairs available. Car park.

A roadside inn close to the lake. All the rooms have been renovated and are very pretty; one has been converted for the disabled. The most expensive have a lake view. Doubles €38.10–45.80 with shower/wc, €53.40–56.50 with bath. They also have studios and duplexes. The chef likes working with river and lake fish; on good days you can dine on the terrace. Menus €22–41, business weekday lunch menu (*menu affaires*) at €21, includes starter, main course, dessert, quarter-litre of wine or half-litre of mineral water, and coffee. A young, enthusiastic team runs the whole place. *Free house apéritif offered to our readers on presentation of this guide.*

|●| Auberge du Bessard

525 rte. d'Albertville; on the N508.
☎04.50.52.40.45
Closed *20 Oct–20 March.* **Disabled access. Car park.**

If you dream of sitting on the banks of the lake with the water lapping at the terrace while you dine on fine fresh fish, here's just the place. It's something of a local institution and has been run by the same family for the last fifty years. The atmosphere is warm and friendly. There's a €16 weekday menu, another for €21 at the weekends and on public holidays, or you'll pay about €25 à la carte. *Free house liqueur offered to our readers on presentation of this guide.*

Saint-Jorioz

74410 (9km SE)

🏃 🏠 |●| Hôtel Auberge de la Cochette**

Lieu-dit La Magne-à Saint-Eustache; go to St-Jorioz and follow the signs.
☎04.50.32.03.53 Ⓕ04.50.32.02.70
Ⓦwww.hotel-la-cochette.com
Hotel closed *1 Nov–15 March.* **Restaurant closed** *weekdays end Sept to end April.* **High chairs available. Car park.**

Friendly country inn in a hamlet that offers a magnificent view over the lake of Annecy, 6km away as the crow flies. Nicely renovated rooms with lots of light wood cost €38–44 with shower/wc or bath, family rooms for three to four people go for €46–58. The food is delicious and traditional, with great menus at €17–28. You'll pay around €30 for a menu à la carte. The home-made bread and patisserie are scrumptious. They occasionally host weddings and other large parties. *Free house liqueur or 10% discount on the room rate (except July–Aug) offered to our readers on presentation of this guide.*

Chapeiry

74540 (11km SW)

|●| Auberge La Grange à Jules

Le Pelvoz; leave the A41 motorway at the

Rumilly exit and take the N201 in the direction of Annecy. After Alby, turn left towards Chapeiry and you'll find it after the bridge on the right.
☎04.50.68.15.07
Closed *Mon, Tues and Thurs evenings; Wed.* **Car park.**

Though the façade isn't that alluring – more farm hangar than ancient grange – everything changes once you get inside. It's a cosily rustic place that feels miles away from the motorway. In summer, you can eat barbecues in the garden, under the trees and among the flowers; in winter, the open fire takes the chill off the air. They create good, contemporary dishes using fresh ingredients: potato tart with foie gras, lamb muzzle *confit* with honey and spices, chocolate *fondant*. Menus go for €22–29. Theme evenings are organized at weekends.

Gruffy

74540 (17.5km SW)

Aux Gorges du Chéran**

Pont de l'Abîme; take the N210 and 1km after Chaux turn onto the D5 – once you've passed Gruffy, it's a further 1.5km.
☎04.50.52.51.13 Ⓕ04.50.52.57.33
Closed *15 Nov–15 March.* Restaurant closed *Sun evening (except in July and Aug).* **TV. Car park.**

This peaceful chalet, surrounded by forest, practically clings to the cliff above the Chéran, opposite the bridge over the abyss. Spacious, comfortable, classically designed and refurbished rooms, go for €40–52 with shower/wc or €55–60 with bath. Half board is preferred in summer, at a cost of €41–51 per person. The restaurant offers traditional and regional food with menus at €16–25. Traditional cooking including: beef fillet with morels, almond trout. Faultless, attentive welcome. *Free house apéritif offered to our readers on presentation of this guide.*

Semnoz (Le)

74320 (18km S)

Chalet Hôtel Semnoz - Alpes 1,704 metres **

Le Semnoz; take the D41.
☎04.50.01.23.17Ⓕ 04.50.64.53.05
Closed *April or May; 30 Sept–25 Dec.* **Restaurant closed** *Sun evening and Mon out of season.* **Car park.**

A large late-nineteenth-century chalet, almost alone on Le Semnoz and with a view of the Alps in Cinemascope! Since the 1950s it has been run by the family of the famous guide and ski champion Alfred Couttet (they will tell you his life story at the drop of a woolly hat) and they give their guests a very warm welcome. The rustic/mountain-style rooms are gradually being refurbished. Doubles €32 with washbasin, €44–48 with shower/wc or bath. Menus €15–25. Classical, regional cuisine. A word of advice: if you want the peak of Le Semnoz to yourself, or almost, avoid the high season. *Free house apéritif offered to our readers on presentation of this guide.*

Annonay

07100

Hôtel du Midi**

17 pl. des Cordeliers; it's in the lower town.
☎04.75.33.23.77 Ⓕ04.75.33.02.43
TV. Pay car park.

Set in a good location on a very lively square, this hotel is a sturdy building of remarkable dimensions, with wide corridors, large rooms (especially those overlooking the square) and thick, plush carpets. There are pictures and engravings of hot-air balloons all over the place – the Montgolfier brothers were born in Annonay. Doubles go for €32–49.50, depending on the comfort. *10% discount on the room rate (for a two-night stay Oct–April) offered to our readers on presentation of this guide.*

Restaurant Marc et Christine

29 av. Marc-Seguin; it's opposite the old station.
☎04.75.33.46.97
Closed *Sun evening; Mon; the Feb school holidays; mid-Aug to 1 Sept.* **Disabled access. High chairs available.**

The inventive cooking here is appreciated by an essentially local clientele. Christine gives her guests a warm welcome and ushers them into a sitting room decorated in peach tones. Marc does the cooking, and prepares dishes that combine classic and local ingredients. The menus change monthly: crayfish and sweet onion soup, snails with pig's trotters, sea bream *royale*, grilled tenderloin of beef. Menu at €17 except Sun, other menus €23–42; you'll spend around €35 à la carte. A large selection of wines is available. In summer you can eat outside in the pleasant garden.

Satillieu

07290 (14km SW)

Hôtel-restaurant Sapet**

Place de la Faurie; from Annonay, follow the signs first for the centre of town and then for Lalouvesc D578A.
Ⓣ04.75.34.95.42 Ⓕ04.75.69.91.13
Ⓦwww.chaletsapet.com
Closed *22 Dec–5 Jan*. **TV. Swimming pool. High chairs available.**

This place, situated in the centre of the village, has an excellent reputation. The welcome is really nice and the cooking first-rate. One of the specialities is *crique ardéchoise*, made with grated potatoes sprinkled with garlic, onions and parsley. The frogs' legs with parsley, scallop *fricassée* and tripe are also good. Menus €15–23. The bedrooms are clean and comfortable; doubles with shower/wc or bath cost €41. Arrangements can be made for mountain biking or hiking, and there's an open-air pool. *Free house apéritif offered to our readers on presentation of this guide.*

Serrières

07340 (15km NE)

Hôtel-restaurant Schaeffer**

It's on the R86.
Ⓣ04.75.34.00.07 Ⓕ04.75.34.08.79
Ⓦwww.hotel-schaeffer.com
Closed Sat *lunchtime; Sun evening; Mon; Tues in July–Aug; Jan; autumn school holidays*. **TV. High chairs available. Pay car park.**

A substantial house on the banks of the Rhône. It's a gourmet restaurant which uses the best seasonal produce; menus start at €22 (weekday lunchtimes), with others €33–80. Salivate over dishes such as envelopes of ravioli stuffed with mushrooms topped with pigeon livers and served in a rich, aromatic broth or pan-fried venison steak served with a bitter chocolate *jus*. The cheese board is impressive and their desserts – such as bitter chocolate *au gratin* with pistachio ice cream and sorbet – are delicious. The more expensive menus include appetizers and *petits fours*. The fine wine list includes a range of good Côtes-du-Rhônes and Hermitages but there are also some more modest bottles. Modern, functional, air-conditioned and soundproofed rooms go for €60 with bath; some have views of the river and the bridge. A high-quality place to stay, but one where you don't have to spend a fortune. *Free coffee or liqueur offered to our readers on presentation of this guide.*

Anse

69480

Hôtel-restaurant Le Saint-Romain**

Route de Graves; it's signposted, 200m off the main road.
Ⓣ04.74.60.24.46 Ⓕ04.74.60.24.46
Ⓦwww.hotel-saint-romain.fr
Closed *Sun evening 26 Nov–25 April*. **TV. High chairs and games available. Car park.**

Traditional, classic *Logis de France* hotel with honest cooking in the restaurant – calves liver *confit*, roast pigeon breast with celery gratin, game stew, numerous ripe cheeses and home-made desserts. The dining room has sturdy beams and there's a pleasant terrace for summer. Menus from €19 (except Sun) up to €46. Rooms are sizeable and simple, with good beds; they cost €50 with shower/wc or bath/wc.

Marcy-sur-Anse

69480 (7km SW)

Le Télégraphe

Take the D79 for Lachassagne and turn left onto the D70.
Ⓣ04.74.60.24.73
Closed *Sun evening; Mon*. **Car park.**

You can order any of the menus with confidence – they cost €11 (weekday lunchtimes) and five other menus €17–40. In the first menu, the house terrine and *andouillette* with mustard sauce are delicious, while the *croustille* of St Marcellin goat's cheese has a real tang. Great desserts and flavourful Beaujolais. The pleasant terrace is well away from the road, so it's quiet.

Alix

69380 (10km SW)

Le Vieux Moulin

Chemin du Vieux Moulin; take the D39 in the direction of Lachassagne, turn left for Marcy, and Alix is signposted to the right.

Ⓣ04.78.43.91.66 Ⓕ04.78.47.98.46
Closed *Mon and Tues (except some of the public holidays and for group reservation); 17 Aug–16 Sept.* **Disabled access. Car park.**

This mill built of pale gold stone has been converted into a charming restaurant with three cosy dining rooms and a barn for families or large groups. Menus at €21–47 list good, reliable dishes: sea-trout with sorrel, guinea fowl with morels, duck foie gras, frogs' legs, *andouillette*, monkfish with cream and curry sauce and leek *fondue*. Portions are huge. Afterwards you can have a game of *boules (pétanques)* or relax on the terrace. *Free coffee offered to our readers on presentation of this guide.*

Theizé

69620 (13km W)

Hôtel-restaurant Le Theizerot*

Take the D39 Lachassagne road and it's signposted to the right.
Ⓣ and Ⓕ04.74.71.22.26
Restaurant open *lunchtimes Tues–Sun; evenings for guests only. Closed Sun; Mon evening; 20 Dec–10 Jan.* **TV. Car park.**

This old village café has a few cheap, simple rooms from €20 with basin and €25 with shower. It's not the height of luxury but ideal if you've done too many miles on your bike or walked through one too many vineyards. Weekday menu €10.50 and others up to €17. Filling regional dishes: Lyonnais salad, *andouillette*, pike *quenelles* and *choucroute* in winter. *Free house apéritif offered to our readers on presentation of this guide.*

Antraigues-sur-Volane

07530

Restaurant La Remise

Pont de l'Huile; on the Volane, on the right as you enter the village.
Ⓣ04.75.38.70.74
Closed *Fri; Sun evening (except July–Aug); mid-Dec to early Jan. Mainly open only for bookings, particularly for dinner.*

An enticing, supremely rustic dining room and some of the best food in the Volane valley. It is often full, both in the week and on Sunday. Menus €19 and €28, both with apéritif and liqueur included. Seasonal dishes, with fresh ingredients and delicious flavours – what more can one ask? Well, the service could be less surly, but nothing's perfect, and this restaurant is definitely hard to beat in the vicinity, and in almost the whole *département*!

Arbigny

01190

Le Moulin de la Brevette**

Take the D37, then the D933, and turn right off the road from Arbigny to Pont-de-Vaux.
Ⓣ03.85.36.49.27 Ⓕ03.85.30.66.91
Ⓔmoulin.brevette@wanadoo.fr
Closed *Nov–Feb except by reservation.*
Disabled access. Car park.

This old mill – minus its wheel – stands deep in the countryside. The bedrooms, in a converted farmhouse, are large, bright, comfortable and quiet. Doubles €53–64 with shower/wc or bath; nos. 15–19 and 29–32 have the best views. Possibility to rent flats for €64–100. They do simple meals in the restaurant –*coq au vin*, snails.

Aubenas

07200

Hôtel des Négociants*

Place de l'Hôtel-de-Ville; it's in the old part of town opposite the château.
Ⓣ04.75.35.18.74
Closed *Sun, a fortnight in March; a fortnight in Oct.* **TV.**

Good central location and cheap prices. The clean rooms, most with TV, have decent beds. Doubles €22 with basin, €26 with shower, and €34–38 with shower/wc. The cuisine in the restaurant isn't especially refined. Menus €10–19.50.

Auberge des Pins

95 rte. de Vals.
Ⓣ04.75.35.29.36 Ⓕ04.75.89.00.15
Closed *a fortnight in Feb; a fortnight in Oct.*
Restaurant closed *weekends Jan–Feb.* **TV. Car park.**

A charming, sprawling building in a pleasant setting with lots of pine trees. Some of the rooms are big, others rather small, but they're all clean and most have air-conditioning; doubles with shower/wc or bath/wc €40–49. Try to get a room at the back as the hotel is on the main road and the traffic can be heavy. The restaurant serves dishes including country pâté with chestnuts and onion marmalade, *caillette*, omelette with ceps, and Lyonnais specials. Weekday lunch menu €12, then others €17–21. *Free house apéritif offered to our readers on presentation of this guide.*

La Pinède**

Route du camping Les Pins; it's on the road to Lentillère, the D235, 1.5km from the town centre.
Ⓣ04.75.35.25.88 Ⓕ04.75.93.06.42
Ⓦwww.la-pinede.fr
Closed *Fri lunchtime and Sat evening from mid-Oct to March (except school holidays); Dec–Jan.* **TV. Swimming pool.**

A traditional holiday hotel in a very peaceful location – it's probably best to book in summer. Doubles €44–52 with shower/wc or bath. Half board, compulsory July–Aug, costs €46–48 per person. The restaurant offers decent value for money, with menus €17–29 (except Sun). There's a swimming pool with a panoramic view, a tennis court, and a climbing wall.

Restaurant Le Fournil

34 rue du 4-Septembre; it's near Saint-Benoît cathedral.
Ⓣ04.75.93.58.68
Closed *Sun; Mon; the Feb, autumn and Christmas school holidays; 21 June–8 July.* **Disabled access. High chairs available.**

This handsome fifteenth-century building with its patio and vaults is the ideal setting to try the exquisite dishes prepared by Michel Leynaud. His establishment is stylish, from the welcome to the gourmet food – *cassolette* of crayfish tails with morels, rabbit with herbs and olive paste. Menus €18–32, and à la carte about €23. Extensive wine list.

Sanilhac

07110 (25km SW)

Auberge de la Tour de Brison**

Take the D104, then the D103 in the direction of Largentière then follow the road to Montréal.
Ⓣ04.75.39.29.00 Ⓕ04.75.39.19.56
Ⓦwww.benilbrison.com
Closed *Tues evening and Wed except July–Aug; Nov–March.* **Disabled access. TV. High chairs and games available. Swimming pool. Car park.**

This pleasant hotel, run by a nice couple, has twelve air-conditioned rooms, some with whirlpool bath and (on a clear day) a view of the Alps. Doubles €61 with shower/wc or bath. There are some family rooms with fireplaces. Half board is compulsory in July and Aug, and costs €54 per person. The menu, at €24, is very generously served. Dishes include chicken liver mousse with chestnuts and traditional *caillette*. There are tennis courts and a swimming pool on the spot and lots of other activities in the area. *Free house apéritif or coffee offered to our readers on presentation of this guide.*

Saint-Pons

07580 (26km E)

Hostellerie Gourmande Mère Biquette***

Les Allignols; turn left off the N102 onto the D293, at Saint-Pons you should start to see signs for the inn – it's 4km further.
Ⓣ04.75.36.72.61 Ⓕ04.75.36.76.25
Ⓦwww.logis-d-ardeche.com/merebriquette
Closed *Mon lunchtime; Tues and Fri lunchtime from mid-Oct to April; mid-Nov to mid-Feb.* **TV. High chairs and games available. Swimming pool and tennis court. Car park.**

The natural setting for this old farmhouse is quite spectacular: the grounds are extensive and there are breathtaking views of the mountains and the valley. The country-style bedrooms are very handsome with lots of wood panelling. Prices reflect the quality – doubles €51–75 with shower/wc or bath, depending on the comfort. There's also a welcoming, refined restaurant serving good classics: house charcuterie, foie gras in a pastry case, house *caillette*, snail stew with shallots, duck breast with honey and Calvados and local dishes. Three menus €17.50–35. They can lend you a mountain bike.

Autrans

38880

Hôtel de la Poste***

Place de l'Église.
Ⓣ04.76.95.31.03 Ⓕ04.76.95.30.17
Ⓦwww.hotel-barnier.com
Closed *Sun evening and Mon out of season; 20 April–7 May; 20 Oct–1 Dec.* **TV.**

Swimming pool. High chairs available. Car park.

A local institution that's been run by the same family since 1937. The thirty rooms all have good facilities; some have sitting rooms and balconies looking out over the front. Doubles €50–79; three types of rooms from two to four people. There are splendid sporting facilities – take a look at the superb covered swimming pool with its exotic décor, which you reach via a private underground passageway. There's also a Jacuzzi, a fitness room and a sauna (fee applies). Good cuisine with a *formule rapide* for €12, a weekday lunch menu for €15, and other menus at €18–39. Try the ravioli with crayfish tails or the calf's head. There's a nice terrace and garden.

Méaudre

38112 (6km S)

Le Pertuzon**

Avenue du Vercors.
Ⓣ04.76.95.21.17 Ⓕ04.76.95.26.00
Ⓦwww.perso.club-internet.fr/locana/
Closed *Sun and Tues evenings; Wed.* **TV. High chairs available. Car park.**

An establishment with nine pleasant rooms, some of which have a garden view. Doubles €43. Smart yet warm dining room and cuisine of excellent reputation. The first menu is a weekday lunch menu at €13, then the regional menu at €17 served lunch and dinner times, except on Sun, which varies according to the seasons; typically it might include a salad Vercors, ravioli de Royans, *escalope* caramelized with Clairette de Die, *fromage blanc* and *clafoutis*. Other menus, €26–51, also vary depending upon what's fresh at the market; specialities include duck foie gras with Muscat, pigeon with spices and iced nougat. The chef worked in Réunion and Egypt after qualifying from hotel school then came to Vercors. There's a nice garden and terrace in summer. *Free house apéritif offered to our readers on presentation of this guide.*

Beaufort-sur-Doron

73270

Hôtel-restaurant Le Grand Mont**

Place de l'Église; take the Albert-Beaufort road.
Ⓣ04.79.38.33.36 Ⓕ04.79.38.39.07
Closed *Fri evening out of season and excluding school holidays; 25 April–8 May; Oct; 1–8 Nov.* **TV. High chairs available.**

An old house, with a spotless exterior, on the outskirts of the ancient village. The refurbished rooms are comfortable; doubles with shower/wc €49–54. In the restaurant, which is a traditional bistro with an old-style dining room, they serve primarily regional dishes: *diots* with *crozets* (local vegetable and pork sausages cooked in white wine and served with square-shaped noodles), omelette with Beaufort cheese, fish terrine or rabbit terrine. Menus €17–28. *Free house apéritif offered to our readers on presentation of this guide.*

Beaujeu

69430

Hôtel-restaurant Anne de Beaujeu**

28 rue de la République.
Ⓣ04.74.04.87.58 Ⓕ04.74.69.22.13
Closed *Sun evening; Mon; Tues lunchtime; 20 Dec–20 Jan; 12 days in Aug.* **TV. Car park.**

Though the hotel is named after the daughter of Louis XI (who lived in the late fifteenth century), the building is not of that era. It has a garden, a plush foyer and an impressive dining room. Doubles €52–64 with shower/wc or bath, some can sleep three. They serve classic dishes such as chartreuse of pigeon braised with cabbage, grenadine of veal with morels, and monkfish with apples and vinegar. Menus €19–49. *Free coffee offered to our readers on presentation of this guide.*

Belleroche

42670

Auberge "Le Bel' Roche"

In the centre of the village, opposite the post office, beside the church.
Ⓣ04.74.03.68.63
Closed *Mon evening; Wed.*

An attractive setting in the heart of a sleepy village for excellent food served with a warm smile: rabbit with broad beans and lemon *confit*, ox cheek parmentier. Menu of the day €10, then other menus €13–25. You can eat on a small terrace bedecked with flowers on fine days; otherwise, in the dining room decorated in warm colours.

Belleville

69220

🏃 |●| Le Buffet de la Gare

Place de la Gare; it's near the train station.
☎04.74.66.07.36
Closed *evenings except for reservations; weekends; 1–25 Aug; a week at Christmas.* **Car park.**

It's sometimes said that French train stations and their surroundings aren't as appealing as they once were. This restaurant is an exception: a cute little house full of flowers and plants, it's decorated with old posters, Art Deco light fixtures and quirky old mirrors. Hélène Fessy, the owner, always has a smile and a kind word for her customers. Dish of the day at €10.50, menus at €12.50 and €16. Dishes might include *tapenade*, house terrine, leeks vinaigrette, or stuffed tomatoes and courgettes. Her husband supplies the wine. During the grape harvest, the place is still pretty busy at one o'clock in the morning. *Free house apéritif, fruit juice or soft drink offered to our readers on presentation of this guide.*

Vaux-en-Beaujolais

69460 (15km SW)

🏃 🏠 |●| Auberge de Clochemerle**

Rue Gabriel-Chevallier; take the D43 in the direction of Odenas, and at Saint-Étienne-des-Oullières, turn left in the direction of Vaux.
☎04.74.03.20.16 ℻04.74.03.28.48
🌐www.georgeslegarde.com
Closed *Tues; Wed; 27 July–14 Aug.* **Disabled access. TV.**

All the rooms in this village inn have been freshly refurbished, though they have kept their charm because of the period furniture. Doubles €43–51 with shower/wc or bath. The restaurant serves excellent food, which is in evidence on all the menus (€18.50–45), and the prices are justified. As time goes on, the cuisine is favouring gourmet dishes yet still offers good value for money. Try the deboned pigeon stuffed with foie gras and truffles. Lovely shaded terrace for the summer. *Free house apéritif offered to our readers on presentation of this guide.*

Liergues

69400 (24km SW)

🏃 |●| Auberge de Liergues

Take the D35 in the direction of Tarare.
☎04.74.68.07.02
Closed *Tues evening; Wed; 13–30 Aug.*

The owner likes to have a good laugh and will practically insist on your having a glass of Beaujolais as soon as you arrive – and it's hard to resist in a place like this, where there are more local winegrowers about than tourists. There's a lunchtime menu, which costs €11 and includes terrine, braised ham, cheese and dessert. Other menus €14–22. There are lots of specialities from Lyon such as *andouillette*, *coq au vin* in Beaujolais wine, home-made terrines and seasonal dishes like game. *Free house apéritif offered to our readers on presentation of this guide.*

Besse-en-Oisans

38142

🏃 🏠 |●| Hôtel Alpin

Take the N91, then the D25.
☎04.76.80.06.55 ℻04.76.80.12.45
Open *all year.*

This chalet hotel is in one of the most beautiful villages in the Oisan area. The simple, no-frills rooms are beautifully maintained and cost €47 for a double with shower/wc. It's well worth paying €39 per person and going half-board – and it's compulsory in season. Gîtes (studios or apartments) are also available for rent. The pleasant dining room has huge beams hewn from pine trunks and walls built from local stone. The good family cooking is generously served. Menus go for €11–20. À la carte you can choose snacks such as omelettes or *tartiflette*. Out of season it's best to ring and check on opening times.

Venosc

38520 (19km S)

🏠 |●| Hôtel-restaurant Les Amis de la Montagne*

Le Courtil; towards Grenoble, take Briançon N91 then the D530.
☎04.76.11.10.00 ℻04.76.80.20.56
🌐www.hotel-venosc-deux-alpes.com
Closed *lunchtime in winter except weekends;*

25 April–18 June; 5 Sept–20 Dec. **TV. High chairs available. Swimming pool.**

What the Durdan clan don't know about Venosc, a little mountain village 1000m up, isn't worth knowing. They run hotels, gîtes, restaurants, shops and boutiques, give skiing lessons and rent out rooms. Most of their efforts, however, are focused on this hotel, which is sheer delight if you're after peace and quiet. Rooms €50–85 with shower/wc or bath, some with balconies; half board costs €50–68 per person. You dine in the grill-room, which has lots of atmosphere. Menus from €17 list regional food: the speciality is *grenaillade* (potatoes with Saint-Marcellin, a mild goat's cheese) but you'll also find scrambled eggs with morels, trout with walnuts, duck thigh with bilberry *fondue*, *raclette* and so on. The desserts look good and taste even better. The hotel has a pool, a Turkish bath and a sauna.

Garde (La)

38520 (29km W)

Les Gorges de Sarenne

Take the N91 then the D211.
04.76.80.07.85
www.lesgorgesdesarenne.com
Closed *Sun evening and Mon in mid-season; Tues–Thurs evenings, May; Oct*. **TV. Car park.**

There are 21 bends in the road up to Alpe-d'Huez and this restaurant is the perfect rest stop, with a wonderful view of the gorges and the forest. Rose-Marie and Jacky greet you warmly. Service is swift, the atmosphere's friendly and the place is sparklingly clean. Weekday lunch menu €12.50. Specialities include salmon *escalope* with queen scallops and sorrel sauce and scallop salad. They also do delicious *raclette*, *fondue* and *gardette*, their own style of *fondue*. There's a little terrace for sunny days. They have a few guest rooms – all year, half board is compulsory €46 per person. They also offer two-day/one-night ski packages for around €90 per person. *Free coffee offered to our readers on presentation of this guide.*

Ornon

38520 (39km SW)

Restaurant Le Potiron

La Palud; take the D526 in the direction of La Mure.
04.76.80.63.27
Closed *Sun evening out of season*. Restaurant closed *1Nov–1 March*. **Disabled access. Car park.**

You'll find this restaurant on a bend in the road; it has a warm décor and is always pretty busy. Good snacks are served all day – *casse-croûte campagnard*, raw ham, bacon omelette, fresh cream cheese, soup, salad, terrine. The omelette soufflé with crayfish tails is recommended. Menus €15.50–30 and around €28 à la carte. Perhaps a plate of raw ham and the dish of the day (trout stuffed with wild mushrooms, say, or veal with ceps) served with vegetables prepared in Dany's own special way – in the form of a celery flan, maybe, or as courgette fritters with coriander. For dessert, the violet *crème brûlée* is a revelation. In winter, it's best to call in advance or you might find it's closed. *Free house apéritif offered to our readers on presentation of this guide.*

Boën

42130

Le Cuvage

La Goutte des Bois; it's 1km out of Boën in the direction of Leigneux, on a narrow road overlooking the D8.
04.77.24.15.08
www.s.granger.free.fr
Closed *Mon; Tues*. **High chairs available.**

Whether you eat on the veranda or the terrace, you'll feast your eyes on the superb panoramic view. The menus are built for big appetites: there are menus for €13.60–19.10 listing charcuterie, house terrine, house foie gras, meats grilled over the embers and spit-roast suckling pig. On Saturday evenings they hold live burlesque and comedy shows, with menus at €15.60 and €20.10.

Sail-sous-Couzan

42890 (6km SW)

Les Sires de Semur*

Les Promenades; take the N89.
04.77.24.52.40 04.77.24.57.14
henri1983@aol.com
Closed *Sat lunchtime; Sun evening*. **TV. Disabled access. High chairs available. Car park.**

Situated on a village square dominated by the ruins of a medieval castle, this hotel is run by a very nice Burgundian man and his wife. The cooking is absolutely authentic but prepared by a chef who is always on the lookout for new ideas. One inspiration is ancient cookery – try his guineafowl in flaky pastry with a sauce from a recipe by Apicius, the Roman gourmet. Menus €10.50 (weekday lunchtimes) then €15.50–37. The wine cellar is well stocked. The hotel is a decent one-star with seven rooms, three of which have shower and WC on the landing. Doubles €24–34. You'll enjoy the homely atmosphere. *Free house apéritif offered to our readers on presentation of this guide.*

Bonneval-sur-Arc

73480

Hôtel La Bergerie**

It's 100m from the tourist office and the slopes.
Ⓣ04.79.05.94.97 Ⓕ04.79.05.93.24
Closed *lunchtime in summer except weekends; May; 1 Oct–20 Dec.* **Car park.**

A startling concrete block of a building hidden amongst the trees some distance from the rest of the village. The owners are friendly and offer excellent value for money. Classic rooms, most of which have south-facing balconies with views of the Evettes mountains, at €52 with shower/wc or bath. Half board, which costs around €55 per person, is requested in winter and between 10 July and 20 Aug. Local dishes feature prominently on the menus, €12–22. *Free house apéritif offered to our readers on presentation of this guide.*

Auberge Le Pré Catin

Ⓣ04.79.05.95.07
Open *evenings in winter except Sun and Mon. Closed Mon, Sun evening and Thurs lunchtime in summer; 1 May–25 June; 1 Oct–19 Dec.* **TV. High chairs and games available.**

A lovely stone house with a roof made of *lauzes*, flat stones which weigh about 70kg each. It was built only recently but it blends in well with the other buildings. The chef is mainly self-taught so while the cuisine is genuinely local it's very different from the standard *tartiflette* and *raclette*. He creates dishes based entirely around the best produce he can find – he cooks his *diots* in Cignin wine and does good ravioli. While the portions are adequate, prices are fairly high but rather normal considering its location. The first price menu is at €18 and you'll pay around €27 à la carte. *Free coffee offered to our readers on presentation of this guide.*

Bourg-en-Bresse

01000

Hôtel-restaurant du Mail**

46 av. du Mail; from the centre of town, follow the signs for Villefranche-sur-Saône on the D936.
Ⓣ04.74.21.00.26 Ⓕ04.74.21.00.26
Closed *Sun evening; Mon; 18 July–9 Aug; 22 Dec–8 Jan.* **TV. High chairs available. Pay car park.**

The rather smart restaurant is popular with the locals, who flock here for Sunday lunch. Set menus at €18–50 list traditional local cooking such as frogs' legs sautéed with herbs, fresh fish and chicken of Bresse, and there's an impressive dessert trolley. Essential to book. The comfortable rooms are decorated in contemporary style, and you'll appreciate the air-conditioning in summer. Good-value doubles €42 with shower/wc and up to €52 with bath/wc. Nice terrace. *Free coffee offered to our readers on presentation of this guide.*

Le Logis de Brou**

132 bd. de Brou; it's just before the monastery, on the right.
Ⓣ04.74.22.11.55
Ⓦwww.logisdebrou.com
TV. Car park.

A bleak 1960s building that's hardly brightened up by its blue balconies. But inside it's a comfortable, attractive hotel. The hall is full of flowers and the owner greets you with a winning smile. The bright, clean rooms in soft colours are well soundproofed. Doubles €53 with shower/wc, or €59–65 with bath.

Hôtel de France***

19 pl. Bernard.
Ⓣ04.74.23.30.24 Ⓕ04.74.23.69.90
Ⓦwww.grand-hoteldefrance.com
TV. Pay car park.

Mid-nineteenth-century hotel in the centre of town, in a charming little square with a village atmosphere. The entrance is very grand, and you almost hesitate to walk on the beautiful mosaic floors.

Modern facilities and a warm décor which has retained the hotel's character. Stylish and comfortable double rooms with shower/wc or bath go for €70–75 in low season and €84–87 in high season; the nicest are on the second floor. It's a good idea to reserve. *10% discount on the room rate (in low season) offered to our readers on presentation of this guide.*

🏃 🏠 Le Terminus***

19 rue Alphonse-Baudin; it's 50m from the train station.
Ⓣ04.74.21.01.21 Ⓕ04.74.21.36.47
Ⓦwww.hotel-terminus-bourg.com
TV. Pay car park.

This classic terminus hotel has a grand Napoleon III hall and a wonderful antique lift. It is set in superb grounds with a rose garden and ornamental ponds, and all the rooms are quiet. They vary in style – some have period furniture, others are modern. Doubles with shower/wc or bath €70. Breakfast €8. *Free house apéritif offered to our readers on presentation of this guide.*

|●| Chez Blanc

Place Bernard; it's on the main square.
Ⓣ04.74.45.29.11
Car park.

Like all the "Blanc" establishments attached to the great chef, the cooking here is refined, tasty, unusual and handsomely served. Lots of dishes feature local Bresse chicken but there's also zander fillet, pike fish balls, cream of lentils and kidneys *à la Mâconnaise*. There's a menu of the day for €17 (€19 in the evening), with others €27–40; à la carte you'll pay around €35. There's little to add other than to remark that the swift service comes with a smile and that the modern decoration is light and fresh. If you really want to be picky, it's perhaps a little noisy.

|●| La Brasserie du Français

7 av. Alsace-Lorraine; it's near the tourist office.
Ⓣ04.74.22.55.14
Closed *Sat evening; Sun; the first 3 weeks in Aug, a week between Christmas and New Year.* **Disabled access. High chairs available.**

This splendid Second Empire dining room attracts a clientele of lawyers, journalists and Bourg notables. The ceiling mouldings and bevelled mirrors are lovely, and the service is as classy as the cooking. Excellent, honest regional cuisine and traditional brasserie dishes: *choucroute,* Bresse chicken or beef fillets with morels, scallops Saint-Jacques, marinated salmon. Menus €21.50–48.50. You'll pay around €45 à la carte. Terrace in summer. *Free coffee offered to our readers on presentation of this guide.*

Saint-Denis-lès-Bourg

01000 (5km W)

🏠 |●| Hôtel-restaurant du Lac*

1981 rte. de Trévoux; it's between Saint-Denis and Corgenon.
Ⓣ04.74.24.24.73
Restaurant closed *Wed; 16 Aug–10 Sept. Hotel closed 1 Nov–1 April.* **Car park.**

A roomy family house on the edge of the lake, set back from the road. Rooms are clean and modern with doubles for €27–30 depending on facilities. Breakfast at €5. The restaurant is full of the flavours of the region – menus €14–32. Specialities include *croustillant* of blue cheese, frogs' legs Dombes-style, chicken with cream, and home-made desserts. There's a little bar, a wide terrace, a lake and a field behind that's full of animals. It's ideal for families because the whole atmosphere is easy-going and unfussy. Credit cards not accepted.

Meillonnas

01370 (15km NE)

🏃 |●| Auberge au Vieux Meillonnas

Take the N83 in the direction of Lons-le-Saunier, then the A40 to Meillonnas.
Ⓣ04.74.51.34.46
Open *noon–1.30pm and 7–8.30pm. Closed Tues evening; Wed; Sun evening except in summer; a week during Feb school holidays; last week of summer school holidays, autumn school holidays.* **Disabled access.**

This little village inn, a rustic stone house, is typical of this peaceful part of the world. It's worth making the trip for the chef's cooking. Dishes include mushrooms stuffed with crayfish, ham from the Tarn, veal *escalopes* in lime juice, rabbit with rosemary in flaky pastry, medallions of monkfish with saffron, Bresse chicken with cream and morels, frogs' legs with parsley, and roast pears with spices, duck fillet and foie gras with maple syrup. Weekday lunch menu €10.40, and five other menus

€15–33. In fine weather you can eat in the delightful garden with its weeping willows, pine trees and banana plants. *Free coffee offered to our readers on presentation of this guide.*

Bourget-du-Lac (Le)

73370

☗ |●| Hôtel-restaurant Atmosphères**

618 rte. des Tournelles; it's 2.5km from Bourget, on the D42 in the direction of Les Catons.
☎04.79.25.01.29 Ⓕ04.79.25.26.19
Closed *Tues; Wed; Feb; All Saints' Day*. **TV. Car park.**

This peaceful hotel stands in the heart of the countryside at the foot of the Dent du Chat Mountain. Some rooms have a splendid view of the Bourget Lake which so inspired Lamartine, one of France's greatest poets. Doubles €47 with shower/wc (ask for nos. 1 to 5 if you want to be lakeside). Food is contemporary, full of ideas and flavours. Menus €17 (not served Sun) and €28–50.

☗ |●| Hôtel du Lac

Boulevard du Lac.
☎04.79.25.00.10
Closed *Tues evening; Wed; 1 Dec–1 March*. **High chairs available. Car park.**

Something of an institution, open since 1900. The dining room is very classic, and the food is nicely prepared. The menus for the most part concentrate on fish; in summer, you can sit on the flower-filled terrace and watch the comings and goings at the lakeshore. Set menus €20 (except Sat and Sun lunchtime) and €23–35. Simple rooms in the main building, and more modern rooms with balcony in the annexe and some new studios to spend the night.

Viviers-du-Lac

73420 (3km E)

|●| Restaurant La Maison des Pêcheurs

611 Les Rives du Lac; follow the lakeshore in the direction of Aix-les-Bains.
☎04.79.54.41.29
Closed *Mon evening; Tues; Wed; Jan*.

If you wander into the garden of this waterside restaurant, you'll see all the fishing boats that have been hauled out of the water to dry. In the bar, fishermen compare the size of their catch over a drink. And fish dishes are the mainstay of the kitchen's reputation: fillets of perch and *lavaret*, fried freshwater fish, trout cooked in all kinds of way and frogs' legs. Weekday menu €11.50, with others at €17.50 (during the week) and €20.50–36.

Bourgoin-Jallieu

38300

|●| L'Aquarelle

19 av. des Alpes; it's 100m from the train station on the left.
☎04.74.18.15.00
Closed *Sat lunchtime; Sun evening; Mon; Wed; 1–15 Jan; 1–15 Sept*.

This place has really made a name for itself. It's inside a walled garden in a large, late nineteenth-century mansion; the décor is Art Nouveau with a collection of lovely oil paintings and a large oak staircase. Delicate and inventive cuisine; on the €19 menu (weekday lunchtimes) typically you'll find appetizers, Roquefort and spiced bread terrine, roast rabbit with a cream and mustard reduction and a chocolate Marquise with preserved cherries and *petits fours*. Other menus €26–45. Specialities include pigeon stuffed with truffles and *galette croustillant* of foie gras. There's a separate sitting room for smokers. Reservations preferred. *Free house apéritif offered to our readers on presentation of this guide.*

Domarin

38300 (0.5km SW)

☗ Hôtel des Dauphins

8 rue François Berrier; it's a road to the left opposite the station.
☎04.74.93.00.58 Ⓕ04.74.28.27.39
Ⓔhotel.desdauphins@wanadoo.fr
Closed *26 April–11 May*. **Disabled access. TV. Car park.**

A very quiet place not far from the centre offering non-smoking rooms with all facilities. They are in the main building and on the ground floor of an annexe, looking over the garden. Doubles €31–37 with shower/wc or bath; buffet breakfast €4. There's a terrace next to the lawn. *One free breakfast per room offered to our readers on presentation of this guide.*

Saint-Savin

38300 (4km NE)

Restaurant Le Demptézieu

Place du Château; take the N6 in the direction of Bourgoin-Jallieu, then the D143 on the right.
☎04.74.28.90.49
Closed *Mon; Tues; 1–15 Jan*. **Car park.**

Yves and Corinne Bello have turned this old village café into a wonderful gourmet restaurant. They'll give you a very natural welcome and unpretentious service with a smile. Dishes are elaborate and tuned to today's tastes: scallops, *fondue* of leeks, duck foie gras in Saint-Savin wine, lobster cannelloni with *espelette* peppers. Weekday lunch menu €10.80, including a quarter-litre of wine and coffee; other menus €14–30. You're guaranteed a delicious meal. *Free coffee offered to our readers on presentation of this guide.*

Cessieu

38890 (13km SE)

L'Auberge des Saint-Bernard**

3 rue de Revol. Take the N6 towards Bourgoin-Jallieu and La Tour-du-Pin.
☎04.74.88.30.09 Ⓕ04.74.88.32.61
Ⓦwww.aubergedesstbernard.fr
Pub open *Thurs, Fri and Sat 7pm–1am. Closed Sun evening; Mon; 1–8 Jan; autumn school holidays.* **Disabled access (restaurant). TV. High chairs and games available. Car park.**

A huge ochre house with ivy climbing all over the front. Osange and Rubis, the Saint Bernard dogs, welcome you. Rooms, priced at €43 for a double, have good facilities and en-suite showers; most look out over the tree-filled grounds where there's a swing and lounges. There are also a couple of pretty chalets that go for €54 per night. In the restaurant, good choices include *gratin* of ravioli with ceps or goat's cheese, foie gras pan-fried with Armagnac, and charcuterie; on Friday you can get parsleyed frogs' legs and small-fry. Menus of the day at €12.50 (not served Sun lunch) and €15 (not Sat night or Sun lunch), wine and coffee included; others €17–38. Danish beers and whiskies are their speciality. *Free coffee offered to our readers on presentation of this guide.*

Saint-Didier-de-la-Tour

38110 (19km SE)

Aux Berges du Lac

58 rte. du Lac.
☎04.74.97.32.82
Closed *weeknights Sept–May; the Christmas school holidays.* **Disabled access. High chairs and games available. Car park.**

This place has got it right. You can have a nice meal and enjoy yourself in an atmosphere so good that you scarcely notice the occasional noise from passing trains. There's a huge bay window with a view of the lake and a terrace in summer. Menus are cheap at €7.80–27; among other things, the chef prepares excellent frogs' legs and fried fish. It's perfect for Sunday lunch; think about reserving. *Free Kir offered to our readers on presentation of this guide.*

Vignieu

38890 (22km NE)

Château de Chapeau Cornu***

Take the D16 in the direction of Saint-Chef-Morestel.
☎04.74.27.79.00 Ⓕ04.74.92.49.31
Ⓦwww.chateau-chapeau-cornu.fr
Closed *Dec to end Jan. Restaurant closed Sun evening except July/Aug.* **TV. Swimming pool. Car park.**

An unusual name for a fantastic place which occupies a thirteenth-century castle. It's now a charming hotel-restaurant offering bright, comfortable double rooms furnished with antiques and contemporary art; rooms for two to four people from €72 with shower/wc or bath. Meals are served in the vaulted dining rooms or on the terrace; all dishes are prepared using local produce. The weekday lunch menu of the day, which includes a 1/4-litre of wine and coffee, costs €16; other menus €27 (lunchtimes, Sat included), €45 and €54. Specialities include pan-fried foie gras served hot. Out of season they offer an "Escapade" deal – one night, two meals including apéritif and wine and two breakfasts served in your room for €135 in a standard room, €150 in a suite. *Free house apéritif offered to our readers on presentation of this guide.*

Montferrat

38620 (13km SE)

|●| Auberge Féfette

Le Vernay; towards Les Abrets, follow the lake road from Montferrat.
Ⓣ04.76.32.40.46
Closed *Mon evening; Tues; 15–30 April; 10–30 Oct.* **Car park.**

A nice little house way out in the countryside. It's a family affair run by the Groseilles; the son is the chef while his father runs the dining room. Good menus from €19.60 up to €28, with dishes that change with the seasons: *papillotte* of foie gras with raspberries, roast monkfish with sea salt, potted lamb with apricots, *fricassée* of lobster in Banyuls wine, *cassolette* of scallops, sole and ravioli. You'll pay around €30.50 for a menu à la carte. Dine on the terrace in good weather. It's best to book.

Bourg-Saint-Maurice

73700

🏃 ⌂ |●| Hôtel-restaurant La Petite Auberge*

Le Reverset; it's 1km from the centre of town on the N90 in the direction of Moûtiers.
Ⓣ04.79.07.05.86 Ⓕ04.79.07.26.51
Ⓔhotel.lapetiteauberge@wanadoo.fr
Hotel closed *May; Oct; Nov.* *Restaurant closed Sun evening and Mon; May.* **High chairs and games available. Car park.**

This quiet little inn is away from the main road. Unpretentious if rather elderly rooms go for €35 with shower and €40–44 with shower/wc or bath. The restaurant, separate from the hotel, offers simple, pleasant food of consistent quality and fast and friendly service. You can eat in the low-ceilinged dining room in winter, or the tree-shaded terrace in summer. Set weekday menu €13, and others €18–22. *Free house apéritif or 10% discount on the room rate (except winter and July–Aug) offered to our readers on presentation of this guide.*

🏃 ⌂ Hôtel Autantic***

69 rte. d'Hauteville. It's 2km from the centre of town; take the N90 in the direction of Moûtiers, then turn left onto the small road to Hauteville.
Ⓣ04.79.07.01.70 Ⓕ04.70.07.51.55
Ⓦwww.hotel-atlantic.com
TV. Disabled access. Car park.

This is a fairly recent stone building, but it's hard to believe that it hasn't been here forever. Though it's a chic little place, out near the countryside, you receive a genuinely warm welcome from the two sisters who own it. It is spacious and bright throughout, from the reception area to the rooms. Doubles with shower/wc €40 and €60 with bath; some, at €70, come with balconies and a mountain view. *One free sauna session offered to our readers on presentation of this guide.*

Séez

73700 (3km E)

⌂ Auberge de Jeunesse-La Verdache

4km after Séez, in the direction of Tignes; turn down the little road to the right opposite Longefoy.
Ⓣ04.79.41.01.93 Ⓕ04.79.41.03.36
Ⓔseez-les-arcs@fuaj.org
Closed *fortnight in early May; 20 Sept–20 Dec (except for groups).* **Disabled access. Car park.**

Small group of buildings in the heart of the countryside, on the edge of the forest and on the banks of the River Isère. A very practical setting for organizing a sporting holiday: skiing, surfing, kayaks, rafting, hydrospeed, canyoning, hang-gliding, mountain bikes, hiking, etc. The pleasant bedrooms (with two to six beds) are brand new, or almost so in some cases. In summer, the price of a stopover, including breakfast, is €12.50; for more than three days, you must pay for half board at €21.80 per day. FUAJ card compulsory (you can buy it *in situ*).

⌂ |●| Relais des Villards**

Villard-Dessus; it's 4km from the centre – take the N90 that goes up to the Petit-Saint-Bernard pass.
Ⓣ04.79.41.00.66 Ⓕ04.79.41.08.13
Ⓦwww.relais-des-villards.com
Closed *May; 1 Oct–20 Dec.* **Restaurant closed** *lunchtimes in winter.* **TV. Car park.**

You're just 20km from Italy here, and this typical chalet provides the last stop before the border for many travellers. Ten pleasant, attractive rooms with shower/wc cost €42.70–57.70 depending on the season, or €60–65 with bath. You'll get a warm welcome and service with a smile. Cooking is traditional with a few Savoy specialities. Menus €11–18.50. They can also offer a number of outdoor activities.

Buis-les-Baronnies

26170

Les Arcades – Le Lion d'Or**

Place du Marché.
Ⓣ04.75.28.11.31 Ⓕ04.75.28.12.07
Ⓦwww.hotelarcades.fr
Closed *Dec–Feb*. **TV. Swimming pool. Car park.**

Well-located hotel in the centre of town on a ravishing arcaded square. There's a family atmosphere. The furnishings in the hall are higgledy-piggledy but the rooms are smart with modern bathrooms and good beds. Doubles €42–60 with shower/wc or bath, depending on the comfort and the season. In summer, they open the garden to guests. Best to reserve and to come before 9pm.

Escapade Cloître des Dominicains

Rue de la Cour-du-Roi-Dauphin. It's in the town centre.
Ⓣ04.75.28.06.77 Ⓕ04.75.28.13.20
Ⓦwww.escapade.vacances.com
Reception open *9am–noon and 4–8pm*.
Closed *Dec–March*.

Housed in a sixteenth-century Dominican convent in the centre of town, this is a good option if you want to be centrally located without paying a fortune. It's very well run. Ask for a room looking out onto the cloisters; doubles with shower/wc for €50. Apartments for two to five people can be rented by the week. There's no restaurant but you can order a meal for €13. Bikes can be parked in the courtyard.

La Fourchette

Les Arcades, place du Marché.
Ⓣ04.75.28.03.31
Ⓔfourchette@faxvia.net
Closed *Sun evening; Mon; Oct*.

The chef started here more than twenty years ago, and still approaches his work with the same serious professionalism. Delicious regional cuisine and a smiling, friendly welcome. Pleasant dining room hung with watercolours. The specialities include ravioli *de Royans au gratin*, lamb shank with herbs, *croustade* with morels and very tender meat. If you're lucky enough to find crayfish with cream and tarragon sauce on the menu, don't think twice about ordering it. Menus €13.50 weekday lunchtimes, then €21 and €34. A good selection of local wines at honest prices €6.50 and €9. *Free coffee offered to our readers on presentation of this guide.*

Le Grill du Four à Pain

24 av. Boissis d'Anglas; coming into town, it's before you reach the Mensonges bridge.
Ⓣ04.75.28.10.34
Closed *Mon and Tues lunchtimes in summer; Mon and Tues out of season; Nov–Feb*.
Disabled access. Car park.

A nice little restaurant where the service is pleasant and the sophisticated food is good and inexpensive. There's a weekday lunch *formule* at €14, with a choice of three main courses plus a dessert; other menus at €19–29. Specialities include foie gras, lamb *rillettes*, *cassolette* of scallops with pastis, and duck breast with apricots. The wines are very reasonably priced. There's a shaded terrace in the garden. Reservations essential.

Plaisians

26170 (8.5km SE)

Auberge de la Clue

Take the D72 then the D526.
Ⓣ04.75.28.01.17
Closed *Mon–Fri and Sun evening, from Nov–March; Mon, April to end Sept; Oct*.
Disabled access. High chairs available. Car park.

Hordes of gourmands stream up the mountain to this place, especially at the weekend. The restaurant serves hefty portions of good, cheap food concocted by two brothers. Their mother, who's got a terrific laugh and a great line in conversation, looks after the dining room. She'll set a terrine on your table for you to help yourself until your meal arrives, then you have the choice between home-made mutton tripe, rabbit with olive paste, a delicious haggis-like preparation of baked pork and vegetables with herbs, sheep's trotters, small apricot spelt pastry and lamb's sweetbreads. For dessert, try the quince sorbet with quince liqueur – it's out of this world. Menus €22 and €28. You can see Mont Ventoux from the window. Nice terrace surrounded by greenery. Credit cards not accepted.

Cervières

42440

Les Trois Compères

Le bourg; between Noirétable and Les Salles, on the D2404.
☎04.77.24.92.18

Menu at around €25 (there is no fixed price, because it varies according to the dishes and the ingredients used). At the foot of the very beautiful village of Cervières, you can eat delicious food in the convivial, rustic dining room or on the flowery terrace with its unbeatable view of the Forez mountains. The owner enthusiastically concocts a different menu every day, according to his mood and the seasonal ingredients to hand; he has great respect for culinary tradition and offers a number of very old recipes, such as gratin of frogs. His specialities include duck *magret* with myrtles and chestnuts, as well as game and even fish. Before settling down here three years ago, the owner had travelled widely: allow yourself to be surprised by his cooking – you will not be disappointed.

Chalamont

01320

Restaurant Clerc

Grande-Rue.
☎04.74.61.70.30
Closed *Tues; Wed; 10 days early Jan; 1–8 July*. **Car park.**

The menu informs you that the restaurant has specialized in frogs' legs for three generations – in other words, the cooking is traditional. The chef is gradually introducing changes but doing so slowly so as not to upset the local people who've been coming here for years. There's a menu at €26, or you'll spend about €44 à la carte. Typical dishes include frogs' legs sautéed in butter with herbs, salad of fried carp *goujons* and chicken with morels. *Free coffee offered to our readers on presentation of this guide.*

Meximieux

01800 (11km S)

Hôtel-bar du Lion d'Or**

16 pl. Vaugelas; on the central square (Centre).
☎04.74.61.00.89 ℱ04.74.61.43.80
TV. Pay car park.

This hotel-bar was completely rebuilt after World War II. A German tank ploughed into it during the battle for the liberation of France that raged fiercely in this area. Exceptionally warm welcome. The large rooms, overlooking the quiet courtyard, have been recently refurbished. Double rooms €40. The ground-floor bar fills up with regulars but there will be space for you to have lunch. Dish of the day €7.50. A good little place to sleep at the foot of Pérouges without going broke.

Chambéry

73000

Hôtel de la Banche*

Place de l'Hôtel-de-Ville; it's near the old town.
☎04.79.33.15.62
Closed *Sun; public holidays; 1–10 May; 1–15 Sept.*

A popular place, well located on a pedestrianized square near the old town centre. The rooms are from another era and prices are attractive; doubles €31 with shower, €34 with shower/wc. Nos. 18, 19 and 20 look onto an extraordinary colonnaded alleyway. The restaurant is good, too, serving generous family cooking: menus at €12 (weekday lunchtimes) and €15–24 list *tartiflette*, frogs' legs and, on Fridays from Nov to the end of April, cod Lyonnaise with potatoes. *Free coffee offered to our readers on presentation of this guide.*

Hôtel Le Revard**

41 av. de la Boisse; it's opposite the train station.
☎04.79.62.04.64 ℱ04.79.96.37.26
ⓦwww.ifrance.com/hotel-le-revard
Closed *weekends in June, Sept and Oct–Dec; May except for group reservations.*
Disabled access. TV. High chairs available. Pay car park.

Very welcoming staff greet you in reception. The rooms are rather cold and functional – like you'd find in a chain – but some, happily, look onto the pretty garden. Doubles with shower/wc €42–57, €46–59 with bath. Half board is requested Friday evening in Feb at a cost of €53–59 per person. The restaurant serves traditional and regional dishes.

Menus €11–26. *One free parking space per room offered to our readers on presentation of this guide.*

City Hôtel**

9 rue Denfert-Rochereau; it's between carré Curial and Saint-François cathedral.
Ⓣ04.79.85.76.79 Ⓕ04.79.85.86.11
Ⓦwww.acom.fr/cityhotel
TV. Disabled access. Pay car park.

The hotel is right in the centre of town, so the rooms overlooking the street are noisy. Even though the street has been pedestrianized the bars get lively, especially on Friday and Saturday nights. The rooms are functional and decorated in very contemporary style – which is a bit of a surprise in an eighteenth-century building. You'll get a friendly welcome and prices are decent. Doubles €44 with shower or shower/wc and €50 with bath. *One free breakfast per room offered to our readers on presentation of this guide.*

Hôtel-restaurant Savoyard**

35 pl. Monge; it's on the square next to the carré Curial.
Ⓣ04.79.33.36.55 Ⓕ04.79.85.25.70
Ⓔsavoyard@noos.fr
Closed *Sun except public holidays or for groups.* **TV. Car park.**

This is a big, friendly establishment with ten or so soundproofed rooms with geranium-filled window boxes. Doubles with shower/wc €45. Half board is requested from mid-July to the end of Aug, and costs €41 per person. The owner is descended from a long line of restaurateurs. Menus, €13–24, feature Savoy specialities, fish and regional dishes.

L'Hypoténuse

141 carré Curial.
Ⓣ04.79.85.80.15
Closed *Sun; Mon; public holidays; a week at Easter; end July to end Aug.* **Disabled access.**

Lovely dining room in an old building; the modern, tasteful décor is a successful contrast, and makes a good backdrop for regular exhibitions. The cooking is sophisticated and flavourful, and the menus offer good value. Weekday lunch menu €16.50, and others €21–42. In the summer, they open up the small terrace on a huge courtyard. *Free Kir offered to our readers on presentation of this guide.*

Restaurant La Vanoise

44 av. Pierre-Lanfrey; it's near the main post office.
Ⓣ04.79.69.02.78
Closed *Sun evening and Mon except May–Sept; 21 Aug–10 Sept.*

The décor is bright, young and modern and the restaurant has a clientele of loyal regulars. In contrast, the cooking is traditional, but it does display brilliant, inventive touches. Dishes change regularly. The chef likes to cook all kinds of fish. Ask for your preferred cooking method: steamed, cooked in an aromatic stock, floured and fried. Dishes include *bouillabaisse* of sea fish, char lakefish with olive oil, red mullet grilled *a la plancha*, scallops with truffles. Menus €21 (not Sun), €25 and €38; reckon on paying about €38 à la carte. The wine list is huge, listing both prestigious Burgundies and little-known Savoy wines. It's best to book. *Free coffee offered to our readers on presentation of this guide.*

Chamonix

74400

La Boule de Neige*

362 rue Joseph-Vallot.
Ⓣ04.50.53.04.48 Ⓕ04.50.55.91.09
Ⓦwww.hotel-la-boule-de-neige.fr
Closed *15 Nov–15 Dec.* **Car park.**

Small family hotel with the ambience, and the young international clientele, of a guesthouse. It's a very relaxed place. Rooms aren't luxurious, but they're comfy and recently renovated. Doubles with basin at €40–45, with shower/wc €50–55, depending on the season. Nos. 3 and 4 have south-facing terraces. You can help yourself to as much breakfast as you like from the buffet, and there are hearty breakfast dishes à la carte. *Free coffee offered to our readers on presentation of this guide.*

Hôtel des Lacs**

992 rte. des Gaillands; it's five minutes from the centre of town in the Gaillands area.
Ⓣ04.50.53.02.08 Ⓕ04.50.53.66.64
Closed *15 April–15 June; 1 Oct–15 Dec.*
High chairs available. Car park.

This hotel, which faces Mont Blanc, is an old house with an old-fashioned bar – but it's a different story in the rooms. They're tasteful, functional and good value for money. Some even have a balcony and a view of the mountain. Doubles with shower or bath €46–50 depending on the season. Polite, friendly welcome. *Free coffee offered to our readers on presentation of this guide.*

Hôtel du Faucigny**

118 pl. de l'Église; it's opposite the tourist office.
04.50.53.01.17 04.50.53.73.23
www.hotel.faucigny-chamonix.com
Closed *Nov.* **TV. High chairs available. Car park.**

A little hotel with a homely atmosphere in a quiet street. It's a family-run place with refurbished and comfortable rooms with perfectly adequate facilities. Rooms from the second floor have all been renovated. Doubles €60–68 with shower /wc, depending on the season. There's a small, interior courtyard and a garden.

Hôtel La Savoyarde***

28 rue des Moussoux; it's beside the Brévent cable car station.
04.50.53.00.77 04.50.55.86.82
www.lasavoyarde.com
Restaurant closed *Tues and Thurs lunchtimes; end May to early June; mid-Nov to mid-Dec.* **Disabled access. TV. Car park.**

A peaceful, flower-filled chalet facing Mont Blanc. It's a nineteenth-century building, renovated throughout but with plenty of original features: parquet, tiling, woodwork, fireplaces. The rooms are contemporary, with little touches of mountain style, and their facilities and comfort levels justify the prices: doubles €94–137 depending on the season. Half board, requested during school holidays, costs €60–82 per person. Menus, €16 and €31, offer good-value local dishes. À la carte, try the fillet of lake whitefish with hazelnuts. *Free house apéritif offered to our readers on presentation of this guide.*

Le Panier des Quatre Saisons

24 galerie Blanc-Neige. Take Rue Paccard, then Galerie.
04.50.53.98.77
Closed *Wed; Thurs lunchtime; 15 May–26 June; 15 Nov–5 Dec.* **Disabled access.**

A flight of stairs off la rue Paccard leads to this small, charming restaurant (very "back to nature") offering excellent cooking. For freshness and inventiveness it's unmatched by any of the touristy places – and it's good value for money. The menus go for €22–35. The friendly, personal welcome is refreshing in a town where so many restaurants herd you in and out as fast as possible.

Argentière

74400 (6km NE)

La Crèmerie du Glacier

766 rte. de la Glacière; in summer, take the dirt road after the Lognan cable car; in winter take the chemin de la Rosière.
04.50.54.07.52
Open *noon–3pm and 7–10pm in summer; all day in winter.* **Closed** *Tues evening and Wed in winter, except school holidays; Oct to end Dec.* **Car park.**

A newly built chalet, way out in the forest, where you can eat well from noon to 10pm: simple omelettes with big salads, *fondue* with ceps and morels in pastry. For a truly regional treat, and if you reserve in advance, you can try *farcon* with salad and dessert. There's a lunch menu at €10 and you can expect to pay €20 à la carte. Warm, welcoming atmosphere. *Free house apéritif offered to our readers on presentation of this guide.*

Houches (Les)

74310 (8km SW)

Auberge Le Montagny**

Lieu-dit Le Pont; as you come into the village from Chamonix, it's 450m further along on the left.
04.50.54.57.37 04.50.54.52.97
www.perso.wanadoo.fr/hotel.montagny
Closed *May; 1Nov–15 Dec.* **TV. Car park.**

This farm was built in 1876 in the centre of a tranquil mountain hamlet. You'd hardly realize that now because of all the changes that have been made, but it still has a cosy charm and the wood panelling hasn't been tampered with. The rooms are huge and pretty, and all have superb, bright bathrooms; doubles €70. The ski slopes are nearby. *10% discount on the room rate (out of school holidays) offered to our readers on presentation of this guide.*

Chamousset

73390

Hôtel-restaurant Christin**

La Lilette; take the N90 from Albertville in the direction of Chambéry, and when you reach

Pont-Royal, follow the signs for Chamousset.
ⓣ04.79.36.42.06 ⓕ04.79.36.45.43
Closed *Sun evening; Mon; a week in early Jan; a week in early May; a fortnight end Sept.* **TV. Car park.**

A perfect country inn on a tiny square shaded by chestnut trees. You can hear a little brook flowing somewhere nearby, but you can't see it through the thick vegetation. The pleasant dining room has huge bay windows. The classic cuisine uses excellent ingredients and, given the huge portions, proves good value. There's a €11 lunchtime menu (not served Sun) and others at €14–32. The rooms are in the annexe and, though somewhat lacking in charm, they're spacious and comfortable; doubles €31–39 with shower/wc or bath. If you're a light sleeper, the trains going by at night may disturb you.

Champagny-en-Vanoise

73350

Les Chalets du Bouquetin****

Le Planay; head in the direction of Champagny-le-Haut.
ⓣ04.79.55.01.13 ⓕ04.79.55.04.76
ⓦwww.bouquetin.com
Closed *15 Sept–18 Dec.* **Restaurant closed** *Mon and Sat lunchtimes; Sun.* **Disabled access. TV. Car park.**

This restaurant is hidden away in a small house, decorated in a typical local style with lots of wood and stone. The menus – €22–30 – change every day and you eat good, wholesome, local dishes à la carte for around €30. Specialities include *raclette*, *pierrade* (where your food is cooked on a hot stone), *fondue*, *pela* (potatoes, onions and Reblochon cheese) and *croûte savoyarde* (ham on a base of flaky pastry with cheese sauce). On the other side of the (small) street large chalets hold various types of accommodation; rooms and flats for two to twenty people. Doubles €65–75 with bath. *Free house apéritif offered to our readers on presentation of this guide.*

Châtel

74390

Hôtel-restaurant Les Fougères**

Route du Petit-Châtel.
ⓣ04.50.73.21.06 ⓕ04.50.73.38.34
Restaurant open *evenings 7–8.30pm; in winter for hotel guests only.* **Closed** *20 April–10 July; 1 Sept–20 Dec.*
TV. High chairs available. Garage and car park (free in summer).

This authentic old farm has been restored without losing its original style. It's a cheerful establishment run by a dynamic young couple. In summer it's a perfect place to unwind for a bit, while in winter everyone gets to know each other over *fondue*. The restaurant's not open in summer, though a good buffet breakfast is served. Doubles with shower/wc €45–55, breakfast included. In winter, half board is compulsory at €45–53 per person. In winter there's a weekly charge of €30 for the garage and €15 for the car park.

Hôtel-restaurant La Perdrix Blanche**

Pré-de-la-Joux; it's 2.5km from the centre in the direction of le Linga, at the bottom of the cable lifts.
ⓣ04.50.73.22.76 ⓕ04.50.73.35.21
ⓦwww.laperdrixblanche.com
Closed *27 April–28 June; 6 Sept–1 Dec. Disabled access (restaurant).* **TV. High chairs and games available. Car park.**

This delightful chalet stands among the fir trees. Rooms are simple and cosy, and some have a balcony. Doubles €58–68 with shower/wc or bath. Half board, requested in winter, costs €40–65 per person. The typical local cooking – *tartiflette*, *raclette*, *berthoud* (marinated cheese baked in the oven) and *fondue* – is just the thing after a day's skiing or hiking, and the menus, €13 –22, satisfy even the biggest of appetites. *Free house apéritif offered to our readers on presentation of this guide.*

Restaurant La Bonne Ménagère

It's one street north of the tourist office.
ⓣ04.50.73.24.45
Closed *lunchtimes in summer; Sun lunchtime only the rest of the year; end May to June; mid-Sept to mid-Dec.*

You'll get a delightful welcome here. The two dining rooms, decorated with old enamel plaques and little bunches of dried flowers, are popular with the local ski crowd. They serve starters like charcuterie and main dishes like *berthoud*, *fondue*, and *croûte aux champignons* (mushrooms on a layer of flaky pastry covered with cheese and then grilled), *tartiflette*. The prices are fair; menus from €13, and you'll pay around €13–27 à la carte. Credit cards not accepted. *Free house apéritif offered to our readers on presentation of this guide.*

Restaurant L'Abreuvoir-Chez Ginette**

Hameau de Vonnes; head for Switzerland and you'll find the restaurant 1km out of town, very near Lac de Vonnes.
☎04.50.73.24.89
Car park.

Berthoud de la vallée d'Abondance, the local speciality, is prepared very well at this authentic, country place. It's an absolutely delicious dish in which cheese is diced and marinated in white wine vinegar, Madeira and garlic before being put into the oven. They do other Savoy specialities and on holiday nights Louky gets his accordion out and everyone has a great time. Menus €13.50–25. From the garden, you get a great view of the mountain and the lake, which is lit up at night.

Chapelle d'Abondance (La)

74360 (5.5km NW)

L'Ensoleillé**

Rue Principale.
☎04.50.73.50.42 Ⓕ04.50.73.52.96
Ⓦwww.hotel-ensolleille.com
Closed *Tues; early April to end May; mid-Sept to end Dec.* **TV. Swimming pool. Disabled access. High chairs and games available. Car park.**

The hotel, in a huge family house, thoroughly deserves its good reputation. Most rooms have been renovated and have rustic, wooden furniture. Doubles with shower/wc or bath €60–80. Half board, from €50 up to €80 per person, is requested during the February and Christmas school holidays. There's a heated swimming pool, sauna, hammam and Jacuzzi. Madame and her husband look after the dining room and the guests, one son runs the bar and the *Carnotzet* (where the *fondue* lovers gather) and the other is the chef. He uses only the finest ingredients. Weekday lunch menu €18 and others from €21 up to €45. *Free house apéritif or 10% discount on the room rate offered to our readers on presentation of this guide.*

Les Gentianettes**

Route de Chevennes.
☎04.50.73.56.46 Ⓕ04.50.73.56.39
Ⓦwww.gentianettes.fr
Open *noon–1.30/2.00pm. Closed Easter to 20 May; 27 Sept–20 Dec.* **TV. Disabled access. High chairs and games available. Swimming pool. Car park.**

In the centre of the village, away from the noisy road and just footsteps from the cross-country ski trails. Thirty bright, comfortable rooms cost €70–100 with shower/wc or bath, depending on the season. Half board, priced at €46–86 per person. The restaurant, decorated like a mountain chalet, serves sophisticated cuisine that's unusually inventive for the region. Menus €18–45. Pretty little indoor swimming pool. *Free house apéritif or coffee offered to our readers on presentation of this guide.*

Châtillon-en-Diois

26410

Hôtel-restaurant du Dauphiné

Place Pierre Dévoluy; it's opposite the tourist office.
☎04.75.21.13.13
Ⓔhoteldudauphine@wanadoo.fr
Closed *Tues evening; Wed and Sun evenings, Sept–June; autumn and Christmas school holidays.* **TV. High chairs available.**

An old hotel-café-restaurant right in the heart of the village. Its eight rooms are nicely old-fashioned but painted in fresh colours; the old furniture adds lots of charm and the floorboards creak. Room 5 has an iron bedstead and the bathroom is discreetly hidden in an alcove. Doubles €39–53 with shower/wc. There's a shaded terrace overlooking the road and an attractively decorated dining room (old mirror, bistro tables and friezes on the walls). The changing seasons and the whims of the chef are responsible for the frequent changes in the menus: fresh goat's cheese with pesto and pickled tomatoes, *bouillabaisse provençale*, *aiguillette* of guineafowl with blackcurrants. The €12.50 *menu du jour* and the *menu terroir* at €22 both include a glass of wine. You'll pay around €26 for a menu à la carte. Even if you're not eating you should try the home-made plant syrups – thyme, sage and lime – and the unusual "café du barman". *Free house apéritif or 10% discount on the room rate (Dec–Feb) offered to our readers on presentation of this guide.*

Châtillon-sur-Chalaronne

01400

La Tour - Cocooning et Gastronomie***

Place de la République.
04.74.55.05.12 04.74.55.09.19
www.hotel-latour.com
Closed *Sun evening; Wed.* **Disabled access. TV. High chairs and cots available. Pay car park.**

A delightful establishment that stands out in a beautifully preserved medieval town. The hotel has exposed white stonework, half-timbering and a pepper-pot turret in pink brick; it was built in the fourteenth century and turned into a hotel three centuries later. The place has been renovated with great style. In the restaurant, with its sunny décor and zebra-print chairs, menus start at €18 (not served Fri evening and weekend) and continue at €23–58. They list such things as stuffed mushrooms, vegetable ravioli, Bresse chicken stuffed with foie gras and crayfish risotto. Spacious, stylish doubles with shower or bath €68–100. *Small glass of champagne offered to our readers on presentation of this guide.*

Abergement-Clémenciat (L')

01400 (6km NW)

Restaurant Le Saint-Lazare

Take the D2 as far as Châtillon-sur-Chalaronne and go on another 5km.
04.74.24.00.23
Closed *Wed; Thurs; Sun evening except in Aug; Feb school holidays; 15–31 July.* **Disabled access.**

This is one of the best tables in the region and the setting in a large, bright dining room is ideal. Attentive service and inventive, delicate dishes with a good number of imaginative fish dishes: zander in season, sardines stuffed with minced chard, crayfish tails with grapefruit flesh and avocado *sabayon*. Also on offer are dishes using local, farm-raised chickens and meat. For dessert, try the pear *orientale*. The weekday menu, €28, and the other menus, €32–70, are good value for money. The wines are selected from local growers but there are also some from further afield. Credit cards not accepted.

Chonas l'Amballan

38121

Domaine de Clairefontaine**

Chemin des Fontanettes.
04.74.58.81.521 04.74.58.80.93
www.domaine-de-clairefontaine.fr
Closed *Mon; Tues; 15 Dec–16 Jan; 3rd week in Aug.* **TV. Car park.**

A mansion in a magnificent estate which is more than three hundred years old. The very spacious rooms in the Domaine are furnished with taste. There are plans to update them so hurry to make the most of the prices before they go up: doubles from €48 in the Domaine; from €100 in the Jardins de Clairefontaine. The cuisine is very stylish and prepared by Philippe Girardon (voted the best trainee chef in France) but the menus are in the upper price bracket – weekday menu for €30 with others from €42. You'll receive the professional welcome you should expect in such a place. Tennis courts and *boules*.

Clusaz (La)

74220

Les Airelles**

Place de l 'Église. Town centre.
04.50.02.40.51 04.50.32.35.33
www.clusaz.com
Closed *Tues; 17 Nov–13 Dec.* **TV.**

A dream of a hotel in the centre of the village. It's been carefully renovated and offers bright, colourful doubles with all mod cons and shower/wc at €45–100. Half board, €50–90, is requested during the winter school holidays. Guests have use of the Jacuzzi, sauna and swimming pool in the hotel *Les Sapins*, a bit further up, which belongs to relatives. Genuine, simple welcome, just like the food. Menus, €18–28, list all the regional specialities. *Free house apéritif offered to our readers on presentation of this guide.*

Manigod

74230 (15km SW)

Hôtel-restaurant de la Vieille Ferme**

Col de Merdassier; from Thônes, take the D909 then the D16 towards Manigod, go through La Croix-Fry and head for the resort of L'Étale.
04.50.02.41.49 04.50.32.65.53
Closed *15 April–15 June; 30 Oct–20 Dec.* **TV. Car park.**

An archetypal Alpine chalet at the foot of the Étale ski slopes. They have five contemporary rooms from €46 with shower or bath. Half board, requested during the Feb and Christmas school holidays, costs €46–51. The menus, €14–22, list food that's as typical and authentic as the place itself – try the farcement and leeks au gratin. *Free coffee offered to our readers on presentation of this guide.*

Combloux

74920

Les Granits**

1409 rte. de Sallanches; it's 1.5km from the centre on the Sallanches road.
04.50.58.64.46 04.50.58.61.63
www.lesgranits.com
Closed *lunchtime in summer; early April to mid-June; mid-Sept to Christmas.* **Disabled access. TV. High chairs and games available. Car park.**

Nice family hotel that's been going since the 1940s. Sober double rooms €57 with shower/wc or bath; some have a view of Mont Blanc. Half board, requested during the Feb and Christmas school holidays, costs €45–50 per person. It's quite close to a road – not a very busy one, but if you want to ensure a quiet night, ask for a room in the annexe or at the rear. In the attractive dining room you can choose from menus at €14.90–16.50 or à la carte, around €18. Typical Savoy dishes: *diots*, *tartiflette* and *fondue*. *Free coffee offered to our readers on presentation of this guide.*

Hôtel-restaurant Le Coin Savoyard**

300 rte. de la Cry; it's opposite the church.
04.50.58.60.27 04.50.58.64.44
www.coin-savoyard.com
Closed *Mon out of season; 15 April to early June; 15 Sept–8 Dec.* **TV. Swimming pool. Car park.**

Lots of people come to this prettily modernized nineteenth-century farm building year after year, so it's best to book well in advance. The simple doubles, with shower/wc or bath, cost €73. Half board €55–64 per person. You can have a drink or something light for dinner – they do a good *fondue* with ceps – in a traditional, cosy Savoy setting. No set menus, so expect to pay about €20–25 à la carte. There's a sunny terrace facing Mont Blanc and the pool is great in summer. *Free house apéritif offered to our readers on presentation of this guide.*

Condrieu

69420

Hôtel-restaurant La Réclusière**

14 Rte. Nationale.
04.74.56.67.27 04.74.56.80.05
Closed *Tues; Wed lunchtime; Feb school holidays.* **Disabled access. TV. Car park.**

Chef Martin Fleischmann enlarged this restaurant and added a few rooms, which are very comfortable and stylish. Doubles with shower/wc €51 or €69 with bath. In the restaurant, the menus – €28–84 – change seasonally, but may list such things as minestrone with shellfish and saffron, duck breast with apples fried with smoked bacon and spiced *jus* and Armagnac ice cream. Good wine list and attentive service. *Free house apéritif offered to our readers on presentation of this guide.*

Contamines-Montjoie (Les)

74170

Le Mont-Joly*

La Chapelle, 2564, rte. du Plan du Moulin BP-1.
04.50.47.00.17 04.50.47.91.40
www.montjoly.com
Closed *Oct–Nov.* **High chairs and cots available. Car park.**

This pretty gingerbread hotel on the outskirts of town is friendly and quiet and just 2km from the ski slopes. It offers simple, freshly decorated rooms and a few chalets next to the main building. Doubles cost

€33–39 with basin, €42–47 with shower and €49 with shower/wc. Menu at€14. There's a nice terrace surrounded by trees with a view of the mountains. *Free house apéritif or 10% discount on the room rate for a minimum three night stay (Jan, 15–31 March, April, June, Sept, excluding school holidays) offered to our readers on presentation of this guide.*

La Clef des Champs*

Route de la Frasse; it's above the village, in the street opposite the tourist office.
Ⓣ04.50.47.06.09 Ⓕ04.50.47.09.49
Ⓔdaniel.mattel@wanadoo.fr
Closed *20 April–20 June; 8 Sept–20 Dec.*
High chairs available. Car park.

An old restored farmhouse up the slopes in the resort. Reservations are essential during the winter and summer seasons, when half board costs €35–38 per person. At other times, doubles with shower/wc go for €40.20 – nos. 2, 3, 4 and 9 have balconies with views over the valley. They offer special rates for children under eight. The restaurant is open to residents only.

Hôtel-restaurant Le Gai Soleil**

288 chemin des Layers; it's above the church.
Ⓣ04.50.47.02.94 Ⓕ04.50.47.18.43
Ⓦwww.gaisoleil.com
Closed *mid-April to mid-June; mid-Sept to mid-Dec.* **High chairs and games available. Car park.**

Set in an old wooden farmhouse, built in 1823, this is a beautifully decorated hotel that's maintained with great care. You'll get a tremendous welcome. Handsome rooms, some with a mezzanine floor and all with direct-dial telephones and en-suite bathrooms, go for €50–67 depending on the season. Half board at €47–60 is requested during the school holidays. Menus €17–24.

Contrevoz

01300

L'Auberge de Contrevoz – La Plumardière

Take the N504.
Ⓣ04.79.81.82.54 Ⓕ04.79.81.80.17
Closed *Sun evening in winter; Mon; 24 Dec–30 Jan.*

A charming inn in a countryside village. This huge farmhouse has retained some of its original features, including the big fireplace and an enormous pair of blacksmith's bellows. There's a wonderful garden full of fruit trees where you can eat in good weather. Regional cuisine with an original twist is featured on the €15.50 weekday lunch menu – country salad, roast chicken with thyme and potatoes *dauphinoise*. But the cooking is so good that you might be tempted by the costlier menus at €23–38. Try the foie gras, the home-smoked salmon and duck fillets. Menus change regularly. *Free liqueur offered to our readers on presentation of this guide.*

Cormoranche-sur-Saône

01290

Hôtel-restaurant Chez la Mère Martinet

Take the N6 in the direction of Villefranche as far as Crêches-sur-Saône and then the D51; alternatively, take the D51 from Saint-Laurent-sur-Saône.
Ⓣ03.85.36.20.40 Ⓕ03.85.31.77.19
Closed *Tues evening; Wed; Feb.* **TV. Car park.**

A nice little village inn where you'll receive a very warm welcome. Menus, from €14 (not Sun) up to €42, change every two months, but always list delicious local cuisine: chicken breast with cream, fresh frogs' legs with parsley and garlic, Charolais beef steak with Bresse blue cheese sauce, hot sausage, home-made pastries. In fine weather you can sit out on the little terrace in the garden. A few double rooms with bath for €40.

Saint-Laurent-sur-Saône

01750 (8km N)

Le Saint-Laurent

1 quai Bouchacourt; take the D51 and it's on the riverbank leading to the old bridge.
Ⓣ03.85.39.29.19
Disabled access.

This is another restaurant in the proliferating empire of the great chef Georges Blanc. You get the usual efficiency, kindness, originality and skill, and for only a little more than you might normally pay. Inspiring dishes such as Bresse chicken with cream and *vin jaune* (white wine from Jura), Burgundy snails ravioli, big spicy prawns, caramelized apple. There's a weekday lunch menu at €16.50 and others ranging from €18.50 up to €40. There's a fine list of wines. The decoration is simple with a few old ornaments dotted elegantly around the dining room; black-and-white photographs and old adverts cover the walls. You won't be disappointed – unless you forget to book, that is.

Corps

38970

La Marmotte

Rue des Fossés. Town centre. Take the N85.
Ⓣ and Ⓕ 04.76.30.01.02
Closed Mon; 15–31Dec. **Car park.**

An unpretentious little restaurant with some rooms that, though simple, are bright and comfortable. They're well maintained and some are attractively housed in the eaves. Doubles from €30 with shower/wc or bath and half board for €33 per person. Regional cuisine with a personal touch at very reasonable prices in the restaurant. It's a comfortable setting and there's a small terrace in summer. Substantial dishes on menus €11–15. A few old faithfuls are generally available: *pot-au-feu* with ravioli, home-made *caillette*, pastry parcels stuffed with vegetables, suckling pig stew, *fondue* with goat's cheese and walnuts. *Free coffee offered to our readers on presentation of this guide.*

Hôtel de la Poste**

Place de la Mairie. Take the N85.
Ⓣ 04.76.30.00.03 Ⓕ 04.76.30.02.73
Ⓦ www.hotel-restaurant-delas.com
Closed *3 Jan–14 Feb.* **TV. Disabled access. High chairs available. Car park.**

This hotel, in the centre of the village on the "route Napoléon", is one of the best-known places in the region. The heavy, fussy, old-fashioned interior décor may not be to all tastes, but the rooms are comfortable and cost €38.50–69 with shower/wc or bath. The cooking has a well-established reputation. Menus €19.50–25.50. You get a wide choice à la carte: queen scallops with morels, joint of lamb cooked on a spit, wild boar stew, calf's sweetbreads with cream, trout braised with crayfish, wild duck *grand-mère*. There's a fight for tables on the terrace in good weather, even though the road goes past right in front. *Free coffee or liqueur or one breakfast per room offered to our readers on presentation of this guide.*

Coucouron

07470

Hôtel-restaurant Au Carrefour des Lacs**

Ⓣ 04.66.46.12.70 Ⓕ 04.66.46.16.42
Closed *Dec–Feb.* **TV. Car park.**

An attractive mountain inn near a lake in the middle of the Ardèche plateau. Clean rooms €30–44 depending on the level of comfort. The handsome dining room offers good food prepared from fresh ingredients, including fine charcuterie, delicious local cheeses and home-made desserts. Set menus €11 (weekday lunchtimes) and €13–23.

Cours-la-Ville

69470

Hôtel Le Pavillon**

Col du Pavillon; it's 3km from Cours-la-Ville on the D64 heading in the direction of Écharmeaux.
Ⓣ 04.74.89.83.55 Ⓕ 04.74.64.70.26
Ⓦ www.hotel-pavillon.com
Closed *Fri and Sun evenings; Sat (except July/Aug); Feb.* **Disabled access. TV. High chairs available. Car park.**

This hotel, surrounded by fir trees and an animal park, stands absolutely alone at an altitude of 755m. The modern, comfortable rooms with internet access go for €52–55 with shower/wc or bath, and the ground-floor ones have a private terrace and a view over the grounds. Breakfast at €7.50. The pleasant restaurant offers menus such as the weekday menu at €22, and others go up to €41: haddock fillet, saffron-cream soup, quail terrine with morels and *brioche*, pan-fried Charolais beef, roast pigeon with foie gras, halibut *cassolette*. They also offer various platters – mushrooms, Chinese, seafood, from €18 with dessert. Credit cards not accepted. *Free home-made jam offered to our readers on presentation of this guide.*

Marnand

69240 (10km S)

Hôtel-restaurant La Terrasse**

☎04.74.64.19.22 ℻04.74.64.25.95
www.laterrasse-marnand.com
Closed *Sun evening; Mon (hotel open in the evening); the Feb and autumn school holidays*. **Disabled access. TV. High chairs and children's playroom available. Car park.**

Occupying a converted industrial building, this well-designed hotel looks great, and it's in a good location, with lovely views over the Beaujolais hills from each room. Brightly decorated doubles with bath go for €41. The restaurant is just as attractive, and features unusual dishes alongside traditional choices: pan-fried scallops with puréed leeks, fish fillets with chorizo, fresh fruit ice cream with chocolate sauce. Menus €12–60. Easy-going welcome. *Free house liqueur offered to our readers on presentation of this guide.*

Crémieu

38460

L'Auberge de la Chaite**

Cours Baron-Raverat.
☎04.74.90.76.63 ℻04.74.90.88.08
Closed *Sun evening; Mon; Tues lunchtime Oct–May; Easter and Christmas school holidays*. **TV. High chairs available. Car park.**

A beautiful setting, in a medieval village with ruined fortifications. Doubles €40 with shower, €44 with shower/wc, €48 with bath – those overlooking the garden have had a lovely make-over. You'll be treated like a king in the restaurant or on the terrace. Menus start at €14 (not Sunday), €22.50 and €31.50: typical dishes include roast pigeon with garlic or roast duck with peaches, and vanilla *blancmange*.

Les Castors

41 rue Porcherie.
☎04.74.90.02.49
Closed *Thurs and Sun evenings; Mon; a week in March; a week in June; a fortnight end Sept; a week at Christmas*. **Disabled access. High chairs available.**

One of those places that doesn't look much outside but the pleasant dining room offers the best food in town. Good, tasty dishes: ostrich fillet with green peppercorns, fresh pan-fried foie gras, veal chops with morels, and excellent savoury and sweet crêpes. The weekday lunchtime menu at €10 offers the choice of two main courses, cheese or dessert, and coffee; other menus go for €18–31; the one at €18 changes monthly. *Free coffee offered to our readers on presentation of this guide.*

Saint-Hilaire-de-Brens

38460 (6km SE)

Au Bois Joli

La Gare; coming from Crémieu, it's at the junction of the Morestel and Bourgoin-Jallieu roads.
☎04.74.92.81.82
Open *lunchtimes only. Closed Mon; evenings; mid-Aug to mid-Sept*. **Car park.**

This renowned restaurant has been run for generations by the Vistalli family. It has two large dining rooms, decorated with cowbells, that can accommodate about a hundred people. Try gâteau of chicken livers with crayfish sauce, frog's legs *provençale*, zander fillet with sorrel or game including wild boar in season. The €11 lunch menu (not Sun) includes cheese and dessert, and there are others €16–26. Delicious wines such as Gamay, €10, or Roussette-de-Savoie blanc, €13.

Crest

26400

Le Kléber*

6 rue Aristide-Dumont; it's in the centre of town by the town hall.
☎04.75.25.11.69 ℻04.75.76.82.82
Closed *Sun evening; Mon; Tues lunchtime; a fortnight early Jan; a fortnight end Sept*. **TV. Pay car park.**

This smart-looking little restaurant is decorated in ochre colours. It's known for its gourmet food and specializes in fish and regional dishes. It's the famous gastronomic chef, Maurice Pellier who takes the orders. There's a weekday menu at €17 and others up to €42: ceps salad with slivers of duck, lobster stew with a verbena infusion, *aiguillette* of beef with *bordelaise* sauce. A few prettily decorated rooms at affordable prices: doubles cost €31–52, depending on the comfort. This is the most attractive place in town.

🏃 |●| La Tartine

10 rue Peysson/13 rue de la République; it's near the church of Saint-Sauveur.
☎04.75.25.11.53
Closed *Mon, Wed evening, Sat lunchtime, Sun (except July–Aug); Easter and autumn school holidays; a fortnight end June to early July.* **High chairs and games available. Children's playroom.**

The restaurant occupies the whole of the first floor of a very old house which is typical of the ones you find in old Crest. There's a piano in the large, lofty dining room – this place is popular with musicians, and your visit may well coincide with an impromptu jazz jam. Véronique the owner makes imaginative snacks and serves simple food – there's a dish of the day and various grills. *Menu du jour* €10 then others €12–23. It's very busy at lunchtime and at the weekend so it's advisable to book. *Free coffee offered to our readers on presentation of this guide.*

Grane

26400 (8km W)

🏠 |●| Restaurant Giffon**

Place de l'Église.
☎04.75.62.60.64 Ⓕ04-75.62.70.11
Ⓦwww.hotelrestaurant-giffon.com
Open *daily 1May–1 Oct. Hotel closed Mon and Tues Oct to end April.* **TV. High chairs available. Swimming pool. Car park.**

You get a choice of rooms: the older (and cheaper) ones are over the restaurant, the more individualized and spacious ones are around the swimming pool. Doubles €44–58. The food explains why the chef has made this restaurant such a local favourite: foie gras with honeyed pears and pink peppercorns, *noisette* of lamb with truffle medallions cooked in their juices, *char* with truffle butter and morels. Desserts are excellent and there's a good wine list. Menus €22 (not served Sun) and up to €56. Impeccable welcome and service. *5% discount on the room rate offered to our readers on presentation of this guide.*

Saillans

26340 (16km E)

🏃 |●| La Pantoufle Rieuse

43 Grande-Rue; it's the main street.
☎04.75.21.59.60
Closed *Tues in summer; Mon–Fri lunchtimes out of season; 15 Nov–15 Jan.*

A charming restaurant in a pretty village. The owner brings flavours from distant lands to her cuisine – there's a nice *formule assiette découverte* providing a dish from a different place every two days (every week out of season), and a monthly changing *assiette du monde* – a culinary journey overseas to destinations such as China, Portugal and Armenia. The dishes are tasty and often surprising and always prepared using fresh ingredients. There's a menu for €13; a meal à la carte costs around €17. Out of season, the opening hours are not always respected. *Free coffee offered to our readers on presentation of this guide.*

Omblèze

26400 (29.5km NE)

🏠 |●| Auberge du Moulin de la Pipe

From Crest follow the road to Die, at Mirabel et Blacons, turn onto the D70 as far as Plan-de-Baix, then take the D578 for a further 5km.
☎04.75.76.42.05 Ⓕ04.75.76.42.60
Ⓦwww.moulindelapipe.com
Restaurant closed *Tues and Wed out of season.* **Closed** *end Dec to early Feb.* **Disabled access. High chairs and games available. Car park.**

The owner will take great delight in telling the story of this old restored mill that lies at the far end of a valley with views of the gorges, a river and the waterfalls. It attracts outdoorsy people of all ages who come to Omblèze for the climbing school, flying trapeze and circus courses and the rock, blues and reggae concerts. The various *formules* include dishes such as foie gras ravioli, *caillette* with onion preserve, *Dauphinoise* potatoes *au gratin* and chocolate *fondant* with lavender. Homemade bread and attractive dishes are on offer all day, in the dining room or on the terrace. There's a weekday lunch menu at €14.50, and others up to €25, including one vegetarian menu. A few rooms around €40, depending on the season; plus three gîtes for groups and three furnished apartments to rent. *10% discount on the room rate (except in summer) offered to our readers on presentation of this guide.*

Die

26150

🏃 🏠 Hôtel des Alpes**

87 rue Camille-Buffardel.

Ⓣ04.75.22.15.83 Ⓕ04.75.22.09.39
Ⓦwww.hoteldesalpes.fr
Open *daily all year round*. **TV. Disabled access. High chairs available. Pay car park.**

The wide staircase is all that remains from this former fourteenth-century coaching inn. Nonetheless the hotel offers 24 comfortable rooms with good facilities – the second-floor ones have a splendid view of the Glandasse mountains and are very quiet. Doubles €40–45 and some family rooms. Some might find that the pink everywhere in the house is too much, though, and Madame's passion for puzzles adds to the kitsch. That said, the welcome is pleasant and it's a good base for exploring the town and the countryside. *10% discount on the room rate for a minimum seven-night stay (Oct–April) offered to our readers on presentation of this guide.*

|●| Restaurant des Batets

Quartier des Batets; it's 3km from the centre of town on the D518 road to Crest.
Ⓣ04.75.22.11.45
Closed Sun evening; Wed; 15–30 Oct. **Car park.**

If you're footsore and weary from walking in the Vercors, this old farmhouse – the arched dining room converted seventeenth-century sheep pen and its terrace will come as a welcome sight. Try the guineafowl with thyme, trout fillets or the boned quail with juniper and a glass of local wine like a Châtillon-Champassias from Cornillon. There's an all-inclusive *formule*, the menu éco' for €16, and other menus €20–34, including a vegetarian menu. It can get very busy.

Barnave

26310 (13km S)

|●| L'Aubergerie

Grande-Rue.
Ⓣ04.75.21.82.13 Ⓕ04.75.21.84.31
Ⓔlaubergerie@wanadoo.fr
Restaurant closed *Tues in season; Mon–Fri in winter*. **High chairs and games available. TV.**

You know you're here when you see the sheep sign. The large dining room occupies a converted stable, and upstairs there's an informal café where villagers come to play cards. They serve dishes such as savoury pie, goat's cheese pastries, guinea fowl with oyster mushrooms and rabbit in Clairette de Die, a local sparkling wine. Menus €13–20. The oldest house in the village has been converted to provide five tasteful, simply decorated rooms with kitchenettes; they go for €32. You can also rent them for the weekend or by the week. *Free house apéritif offered to our readers on presentation of this guide.*

Dieulefit

26220

|●| Auberge Les Brises

Route de Nyons; it's 1.5km from the centre of town.
Ⓣ04.75.46.41.49
Closed *Mon evening, Tues and Wed out of season; 15 Jan–15 March; a week in March.*

This restaurant has quickly made a name for itself for its good food and friendly reception. Chef Didier and his wife Marie-Anne have created a little corner of their native Brittany in the Drôme, though they've swapped the flavours of the Atlantic for local ones – try the duck ham salad or the egg custard with picodon cheese. Very appealing menus such as the weekday lunch 'menu express' €13, and others at €19–33, list dishes such as snail profiteroles with garlic butter, *croustillant* of whiting stuffed with garlic, fish *blanquette* with morels and many home-made desserts including a *crème brûlée* with thyme. Eat on the shady terrace in summer or in the rustic dining room. *Free house apéritif offered to our readers on presentation of this guide.*

Poêt-Laval (Le)

26160 (6km W)

|●| Les Hospitaliers***

It's halfway between La Bégude and Dieulefit.
Ⓣ04.75.46.22.32 Ⓕ04.75.56.49.99
Ⓦwww.hotel-les-hospitaliers.com
Open *daily July to mid-Sept. Closed Mon and Tues out of season (except for hotel guests); 1 Jan–15 March; 9 Nov–31 Dec.* **TV. High chairs available. Swimming pool.**

The hotel looks down over one of the loveliest villages in the Drôme; it's an idyllic place for a romantic weekend. There are some twenty rooms at €48–65, prices depending on the season and on the comfort. The salon and dining room are superb – pale wood, ancient beams and cosy furnishings... It seems to come from another era. The terrace looks over marvellous countryside and is a great place for dinner as the sun goes down. It's advisable to stick to the menus (€25–52), because à la carte can be pricey.

Félines-sur-Rimandoule

26160 (12km NW)

Restaurant Chez Denis

At the village. Take the D540 then the D179.
Ⓣ04.75.90.16.73
Closed *Mon and Tues evenings, and Wed out of season; Jan–Feb.* **Car park.**

Denis is actually the present chef's father, but there haven't been any drastic changes since he retired and the whole place quietly carries on just as it ever did. On Sunday and sunny days people flock to this handsome restaurant up in the hills to eat on a cool terrace in a relaxed atmosphere to the sound of a running stream. The weekday lunchtime menu at €17, others €19–26, offer good value for money and specialities include *escalopes* of foie gras with blackcurrant sauce, snails *au gratin* with noodles and duck with olives. It's best to book at weekends. *Free house apéritif offered to our readers on presentation of this guide.*

Divonne-les-Bains

01220

La Terrasse Fleurie**

315 rue Fontaine; it's very near the casino.
Ⓣ04.50.20.06.32 Ⓕ04.50.20.40.34
Restaurant open *to hotel guests only. Closed early Oct to mid-March.* **TV. High chairs available.**

A very quiet and aptly named hotel with a flowery terrace and balcony. It's remarkably peaceful, despite being so close to the centre of town. The modern rooms have some charm; doubles with shower/wc or bath €55–58. The restaurant offers simple, inexpensive home cooking. Menus start at €13.50 in the evening; €14 at lunchtime. Excellent value for Divonne. Half board available for a minimum seven night-stay.

Évian

74500

Hôtel Continental**

65 rue Nationale.
Ⓣ04.50.75.37.54 Ⓕ04.50.75.31.11
Ⓦwww.hcontinental-evian.com
Closed *Jan.* **TV.**

The owners of this hotel, who spend a lot of time in the USA, have made it lively and welcoming. Each room has personality and the atmosphere is genuinely friendly. Courteous welcome and great prices, considering the charm of the place and the size of the rooms: doubles €45–65 with shower/wc or bath, depending on the season. *10% discount on the room rate (except July–Aug) offered to our readers on presentation of this guide.*

Publier

74500 (3.5km W)

Hôtel Le Chablais-Restaurant L'Eau à la Bouche**

Rue du Chablais; it's on the D11.
Ⓣ04.50.75.28.06 Ⓕ04.50.74.67.32
Ⓦwww.hotel-chablais.com
Closed *Sun and Sat lunchtime in winter; 21–28 Dec.* **TV. High chairs available. Car park.**

Classic family hotel. Rooms vary and are in the process of being renovated; those that are finished have a clean, contemporary style. A good half of them have a superb view of the lake. Doubles €32–40 with basin or shower, €46–55 with shower/wc or bath. The dining room, where you eat traditional cuisine, also has a view. Brasserie lunchtime menu €12; restaurant menus €16–35. *Free house apéritif or 10% discount on the room rate offered to our readers on presentation of this guide.*

Thollon-les-Memises

74500 (10km E)

Hôtel Bon Séjour**

Centre.
Ⓣ04.50.70.92.65 Ⓕ04.50.70.95.72
Ⓦwww.bon-sejour.com
Open *noon–1.15pm and 7–8.30pm.* **Closed** *28 Oct–20 Dec.* **TV. High chairs and games available. Table tennis and tennis court. Car park.**

This is a family hotel where everyone

helps out. The younger Duponts are refurbishing the bedrooms one by one; doubles with shower/wc or bath cost €45–52. Good, tasty mountain cuisine in the restaurant, prepared with care and served generously. Prices are attractive, too, with menus at €14 (not Sun) and €15–25. There's a terrace and a garden. *Free house apéritif offered to our readers renting rooms at the hotel, on presentation of this guide.*

Evosges

01230

L'Auberge Campagnarde**

It's 1km from town on the D34.
Ⓣ04.74.38.55.55 Ⓕ04.74.38.55.62
Ⓔauberge-campagnarde@wanadoo.fr
Closed *Jan; 1–8 Sept; 15–30 Nov.*
Restaurant closed *Tues evening; Wed.* **TV. Swimming pool. Car park.**

The winding road up is gorgeous, threading through steep vineyards and past huge white rocks that erupt from the bushes. The inn is like a holiday complex offering games for the children and mini-golf. Most rooms have been renovated and they're comfortable and quiet: €30 with basin, €40 with shower/wc, €50 with bath. Be sure to reserve from mid-May to mid-Sept. In the cosy dining room you can enjoy dishes made with top-quality produce: guinea fowl *fricassée* with balsamic vinegar, snail stew, rabbit stuffed with mushrooms, chicken *suprême* and hazelnut tart. Menus from €22 for the weekday lunchtime menu up to €43 for others. The cuisine is full of flavour and some of the dishes are very subtle. *A free game of mini-golf offered to our readers on presentation of this guide.*

Pezières-Resinand (Les)

01110 (6km NE)

Le Boomerang

Take the N504 to Saint-Rambert and then turn left onto the D34; it's signposted from the village of Oncieu.
Ⓣ04.74.35.58.60
Closed *Sun evening; Mon; whenever the boss goes shopping in Australia; 16 Sept–22 Oct.*

Just one of a few scattered houses huddled in one of Bugey's superb isolated valleys, this unusual inn is owned by Brent Perkins, originally from Adelaide, who settled here with his kangaroo after marrying a French woman. You'll get a genuine barby – even a vegetarian one – along with steak and British and Australian sauces, ostrich fillets and roast emu with bush herbs. Menus €14–25. The wine list is divided between Australia and Bugey. They open a tearoom in the afternoon. Credit cards not accepted. *Free liqueur offered to our readers on presentation of this guide.*

Feurs

42110

Chalet de la Boule d'Or

42 rte. de Lyon; it's near the Feurs east exit.
Ⓣ04.77.26.20.68
Closed *Sun evening; Mon; a fortnight in Jan, 3 weeks in Aug.* **Disabled access.**

A gourmet restaurant that's not too expensive on weekdays. The staff are attentive without being intrusive, the food is delicate and the wines have been carefully selected (though prices are quite high). All the dishes are good: cod and parsley tart, poached bass with cream, kidney *fricassée* with grain mustard, zander with creamed green lentils and terrine with artichoke hearts and herb vinaigrette. The appetizers are full of subtle flavours and the desserts are out of this world. In fine weather, eat outside in the yard by the chestnut tree. Weekday menu €17, with others at €27–53.

Panissières

42360 (12km NE)

Hôtel-restaurant de la Poste**

95 rue J-B Guerpillon; take the D89 then the D60 in the direction of Tarare.
Ⓣ04.77.28.64.00 Ⓕ04.77.28.69.94
Ⓔmireille.collas@worldonline.fr
Restaurant closed *Fri; Sat lunchtime.* **TV.**

A popular hotel in a restored old house. The rooms are simple but good value; doubles €34. Superb views over the Forez mountains, and an elegant dining room serving decent, good cooking. Specialities include foie gras, house rabbit terrine, and hot sausage salad. Weekday lunchtime *for-*

mules at €9 and €11, and other menus €10.50–24.50.

Violay

42780 (22km NE)

Hôtel-restaurant Perrier**

Place de l'Église; from Feurs, head for Balbigny then take the D1 in the direction of Tarare.
04.74.63.91.01 04.74.63.91.77
Closed *Sat from Nov to end March.*
Disabled access (restaurant). TV. High chairs and games available. Car park.

Jean-Luc Clot and his wife will make you feel very welcome when you arrive. The village is a popular centre for cross-country skiing and there's a pretty church over the road from the hotel. It's well run and prices are affordable: €26 for a double with basin or shower, or €34–39 for a room with bath. Much of the cooking in the restaurant is inspired by the cuisine of southwest France. Prices are reasonable – menus €10.60–34, among them a *menu terroir* which includes wine and coffee. Try the *confits* of duck or chicken, grilled sea bream with fennel, frogs' legs à la provençale. *Free house apéritif or 10% discount on the room rate offered to our readers on presentation of this guide.*

Flumet

73590

Hostellerie Le Parc des Cèdres***

04.79.31.72.37 04.79.31.61.66
Closed *mid-March to early June; early Sept to mid-Dec.* **TV. Car park.**

The family who have run this establishment for more than a century belong to the old school of hotel-keeping. The building is surrounded by substantial grounds planted with cedar trees, there are club chairs in the sitting room and a snooker table in the bar. Some of the rooms were redecorated in the 1970s while others are more traditionally rustic. Doubles €45–60 with shower/wc or bath, depending on the season – some have terraces or balconies. In the restaurant, good-quality produce makes for good cooking. The terrace under the cedar trees is wonderful in summer.

Notre-Dame-de-Bellecombe

73590 (5km S)

La Ferme de Victorine

Le Planay; take the N218 in the direction of Les Saisies and 3km before Notre-Dame-de-Bellecombe, take the left towards Le Planay.
04.79.31.63.46
Closed *Sun evening and Mon from April to mid-June; mid-June to early July; mid-Nov to mid-Dec.* **Disabled access.**

The dining room has a huge fireplace for cold winter days and, in the summer, they open a bright, sunny terrace with a great view of the mountain. Menus – €19 at lunchtime in the week and €28–37 – list nicely prepared traditional Savoy dishes. Good Savoy wines also available.

Saisies (Les)

73620 (14km SE)

Le Météor*

1440 rte. de Bisanne. (SW) In the village, follow the signs to the Village Vacances.
04.79.38.90.79 04.79.38.97.00
le.meteor@wanadoo.fr
Closed *May–June; early Sept to end Nov.* **TV. High chairs and games available. Car park.**

This typical, wooden chalet built in a mountain meadow is quietly set apart from the ski resort but just 100m from the slopes. The rooms, nothing special but perfectly acceptable, cost €41 with shower/wc; in winter half board is requested and costs €42–50 per person. Lunch menu €12.50; it's €18 in the evening. They serve Savoy specialities such as *fondue*, *raclette* and *tartiflette*.

Restaurant Le Chaudron

Take the D218, and it's beside the police station.
04.79.38.92.76
Closed *1May–1 July; end Sept to 15 Dec.*

Though the decoration at this friendly restaurant is typical of hundreds of places in the mountains, the food is good. The regional dishes are amply served and fortifying after a day's skiing: *diots*, *fondue*, *potence*, *reblochonnade*, fillets of lake whitefish (a type of salmon), and beef topped with cheese. Menus €13–29 or around €25 à la carte. There's a nice terrace where you can get a good view of the pistes.

Garde-Adhémar (La)

26700

Logis de l'Escalin***

Quartier Les Martines, rte. de Donzère. Take the Montélimar-Sud exit off the A7 then go 1.5km along the road to Donzère.
ⓣ04.75.04.41.32 ⓕ04.75.04.40.05
ⓦwww.lescalin.com
Closed *Sun evening; Mon; 1–8 Jan.* **TV. Car park.**

A little hotel on the side of a hill overlooking the Rhône Valley. The motorway is a couple of kilometres away as the crow flies, but seems much, much further. The hotel, a handsome building in local style painted white with blue shutters, provides fifteen fresh, refurbished rooms in the main building, and seven more in a newer annexe; doubles €45–80, depending on the comfort and the season. There's a weekday menu at €21 and others go up to €46. Dishes include hot *escalopine* of foie gras, pan-fried red mullet, garlic braised ham and veal with cream and tarragon sauce. There are more than 200 vintages on the wine list and a pleasant shady garden in which to sample them.

Gex

01170

Hôtel du Parc**

Avenue des Alpes.
ⓣ04.50.41.50.18 ⓕ04.50.42.37.29
Closed *Sun; 4 Jan–5 Feb.* **TV. Car park.**

This traditional, characterful hotel has been run by the same family for over seventy years. The park it's named after is across the road and the hotel itself has a huge, prize-winning garden full of geraniums, roses, begonias and all sorts of colourful flowers. Rooms go for €56–65 with shower/wc or bath. On a clear day you can see Mont Blanc from no.19! Book in advance. *10% discount on the room rate offered to our readers on presentation of this guide.*

Cessy

01170 (2km SE)

Hotel La Bergerie

805 rte. Plaine; it's on the N5, Geneva–Paris road.
ⓣ04.50.41.41.75 ⓕ04.50.41.71.82
ⓦwww.hotel-la-bergerie.com
TV. Car park.

This place lies between the N5 and the fields, far away from the noise of the road. The rooms are all large, with en-suite bath; doubles €35 and triples €50. It's far from luxurious but it offers value for money and the owner is friendly. They do a substantial breakfast with home-made preserves for €6, served until noon.

Segny

01170 (6km SE)

La Bonne Auberge**

240 rue du Vieux-Bourg (Centre). Take the N5.
ⓣ04.50.41.60.42 ⓕ04.50.41.71.79
Closed *20 Dec–30 March.*
TV. Car park.

An authentic country inn hidden from the road by the trees in the garden. Attractive, well-maintained rooms cost €37–41 with shower/wc or bath – good value for a hotel near Gex. Warm welcome and family atmosphere. There's no restaurant. They do serve breakfast, though, complete with home-made jams. *Free coffee, fruit juice or soft drink offered to our readers on presentation of this guide.*

Crozet

01170 (8km SW)

Hôtel-restaurant Bois Joly**

Route du Télécabine; take the D984 in the direction of Bellegarde and turn right onto the D89 as far as Crozet; it's 500m from the gondola.
ⓣ04.50.41.01.96 ⓕ04.50.42.48.47
Closed *Fri.*
TV. Disabled access. High chairs and games available. Car park.

This is a big establishment on the lower slopes of the Jura. There is a splendid view of the Alps from the terrace, where you can eat in fine weather. The rooms have good facilities – some of them with balconies – and are reasonably priced for the area: €46 with shower/wc or bath. The restaurant provides generous portions of regional dishes such as frogs' legs, duck breast with green peppers or sea perch. Menus €13–16.

Grand-Bornand (Le)

74450

Hôtel-restaurant Les Glaïeuls**

It's at the foot of the slopes, where the cable cars start from.
Ⓣ04.50.02.20.23 Ⓕ04.50.02.25.00
Ⓦwww.hotel-lesglaieuls.com
Closed *mid-April to mid-June; mid-Sept to 20 Dec.* **TV. Car park.**

A very well-run hotel. Though the façade is pretty ordinary, in summer the flowers at every window and on the terrace make it look lovely. It's a very traditional place, with cosy sitting rooms and classic décor. The owners are polite and friendly. Rooms have good facilities and cost €42–57 with shower/wc or bath. Good classic cooking in the restaurant. Menus €15–38.50. You'll pay around €29 for a menu à la carte. There's a sunny terrace. *Free house apéritif offered to our readers on presentation of this guide.*

Hôtel Les Cimes***

Le Chinaillon.
Ⓣ04.50.27.00.38 Ⓕ04.50.27.08.46
Ⓦwww.hotel-les-cimes.com
Closed *1 May–20 June, 5 Sept–1 Dec.* **TV. Car park.**

A stone's throw from the old village of Chinaillon and 100m from the pistes, this is a traveller's dream come true. The couple who run the place have converted an ordinary establishment above a chic boutique into a friendly inn which is full of the fragrance of wood and polish. Bedrooms are wonderfully quiet, with comfortable feather beds. Doubles cost €84–145 with shower/wc or with bath, depending on the season; the price includes a superb breakfast. Half board can be arranged with a restaurant nearby. And the owners look after their guests very well.

La Ferme de Lormay

Vallée du Bouchet; it's 7km from the village, in the direction of the col des Annes – turn right when you get to the little chapel.
Ⓣ04.50.02.24.29
Closed *Tues; weekday lunchtimes in winter; 1 May–20 June; 8 Sept–15 Dec.*

Lovely restaurant in an old farm building. In summer, when they serve food on the terrace, try the chicken with crayfish, the trout or the house *quenelles*. When the weather gets cold the tables are put close together round the fireplace, and there is more charcuterie and pork on the menu – the roast pork and bacon soup are both delicious, as are the tarts and the *clafoutis*. It's cooking you want to linger over. Reckon on about €30 à la carte. Credit cards not accepted. *Free house apéritif offered to our readers on presentation of this guide.*

Grenoble

38000

See map overleaf

Hôtel de l'Europe**

22 pl. Grenette; in town centre. **Map C3-1**
Ⓣ and Ⓕ04.76.46.16.94
Ⓔhotel.europe.gre@wanadoo.fr
TV.

The hotel is in a lively pedestrianized area right in the centre of Grenoble, but the rooms – some 50 of them – are well-soundproofed and noise isn't a problem. It's a comfortable place, the welcome is genuine and the prices are unusually modest for the town: €38–59, depending on the comfort. Rooms are all regularly renovated. There's also a gym and a sauna.

Hôtel des Patinoires**

12 rue Marie-Chamoux; it's 500m south of the Palais des Sports, off avenue Jeanne-d'Arc; 10min from town centre. **Off map D3-2**
Ⓣ04.76.44.43.65 Ⓕ04.76.44.44.77
Ⓦwww.hotel-patinoire.com
TV. Pay car park €5.

One of the best hotels in town, and good value for money. The owners are genial, attentive, and there's a warm atmosphere and décor. It's superbly maintained and extremely quiet. Rooms cost €45 with shower/wc and €50 with bath. *10% discount on the room rate (July–Aug) offered to our readers on presentation of this guide.*

Café de la Table Ronde

7 pl. Saint-André. **Map C2-17**
Ⓣ04.76.44.51.41
Closed *Sun; 1–8 Jan.*

Service until midnight. Located about as centrally as you can get, this café is an institution in Grenoble. Established in 1739, it's the second oldest café in France after *Le Procope* in Paris, and tradition,

WHERE TO SLEEP
1 Hôtel de l'Europe
2 Hôtel des Patinoires

WHERE TO EAT
11 La Frise
12 À la Fortune du Pot
13 Le Loup Bleu
15 Chez Margo
16 Le Bistrot Lyonnais
17 Café de la Table Ronde
18 Le Mal Assis
20 Caffè Forté
21 La Panse

Musée de l'Automobile
Fort de la Bastille
Téléphérique
Jardin Guy Pape
Fort Rabot
Inst. de Géologie
Route de Lyon
ESPLANADE
PLACE A. BRIAND
Jardin des Dauphins
Quai de France
Isère
PT. DE LA PORTE DE FRANCE
PT. M.
GONTARD
Quai Claude Bernard
Quai Créqui
Voie
PL. HUBERT DUBEDOUT (PL. DE LA BASTILLE)
PL. DE PHILIPPE VILLE
Rue Émile Gueymard
R. Jean Macé
R. A. Berges
Egl. du Sacré-Cœur
Rue Casimir Brenier
R. Barbillon
Avenue Félix Viallet
R. du Doct. Mazet
Boulevard Jaurès
Rue Belgrade
Rue de Rey
R. St
PLACE ROBERT SCHUMAN
PL. DE LA GARE
Europole
Avenue Alsace Lorraine
Rochereau
R. Pierre Sémard
R. Clot Bey
Imm. du Griffon
R. Molière
R.F.
St-Louis
Bd
PLACE VICTOR HUGO
Rue Denfert
Péri
Thiers
Crs Berriat
Cours Berriat
Crs Lafontaine
R. Béranger
Lycée Champollion
Gabriel
Cours Jean Jaurès
Rue Génissieu
Rue des Bergers
Gambetta
Lakanal
PLACE ST-BRUNO
12
St-Bruno
Avenue Joseph de Vizille
Rue Nicolas Chorier
Rey
PL. CONDORCET
Rue Condorcet
PL. CHAMPIONNET
R. de Turenne
PL. J. MARVAL
R. Fr.
Rue
0 200 m

11, 16

A B
1 2 3 4

GAP, SISTERON, N 75
VALENCE, N 532, VIZILLE, D 5

RHÔNE-ALPES
22

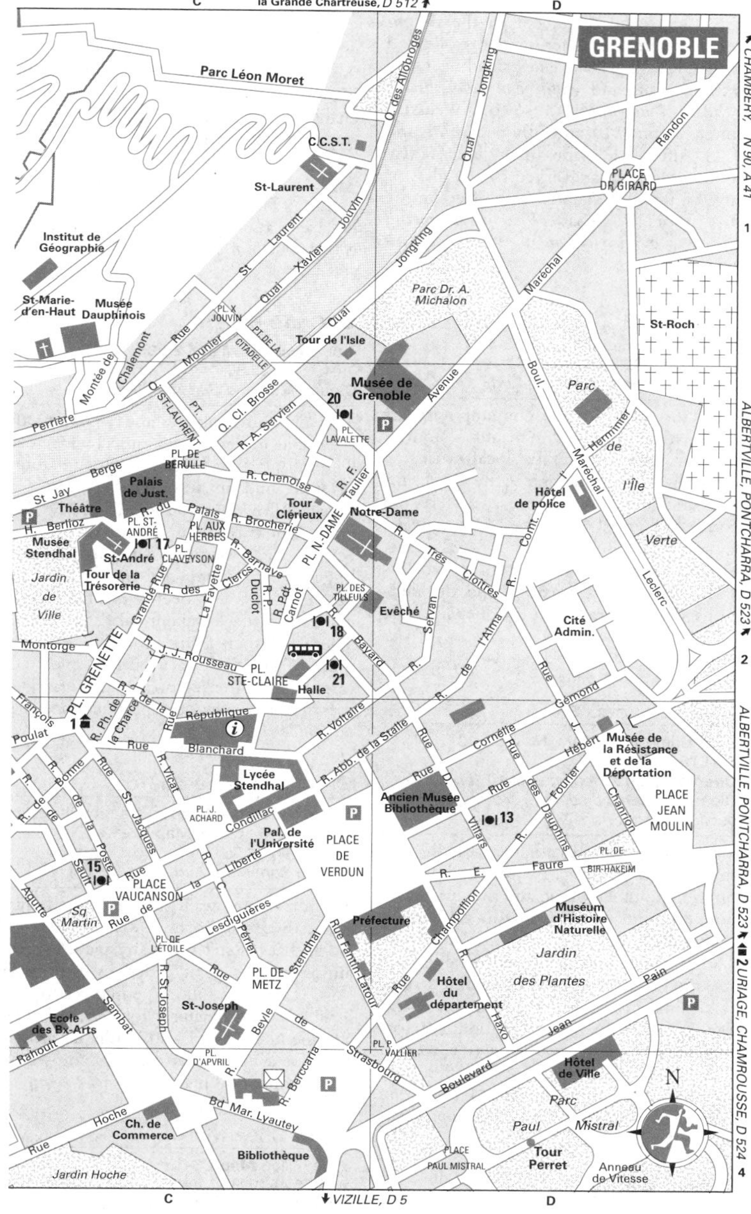
GRENOBLE
la Grande Chartreuse, D 512
CHAMBÉRY, N 90, A 41
ALBERTVILLE, PONTCHARRA, D 523
ALBERTVILLE, PONTCHARRA, D 523
2 URIAGE, CHAMROUSSE, D 524
VIZILLE, D 5
Parc Léon Moret
C.C.S.T.
St-Laurent
Institut de Géographie
St-Marie-d'en-Haut
Musée Dauphinois
Tour de l'Isle
Musée de Grenoble
Parc Dr. A. Michalon
St-Roch
PLACE DR GIRARD
Palais de Just.
Théâtre
Musée Stendhal
St-André
Tour de la Trésorerie
Jardin de Ville
Tour Clérieux
Notre-Dame
Evêché
Hôtel de police
Parc de l'Île Verte
Cité Admin.
Halle
Lycée Stendhal
Ancien Musée Bibliothèque
Musée de la Résistance et de la Déportation
PLACE JEAN MOULIN
Pal. de l'Université
PLACE DE VERDUN
PLACE VAUCANSON
Préfecture
Muséum d'Histoire Naturelle
Jardin des Plantes
Hôtel du département
St-Joseph
Ecole des Bx-Arts
Ch. de Commerce
Bibliothèque
Jardin Hoche
Hôtel de Ville
Parc Paul Mistral
Tour Perret
Anneau de Vitesse
PLACE PAUL MISTRAL
N

hospitality and conviviality are its watchwords. The terrace is a great vantage point from which to watch the world go by on the square, and the décor in the dining room is splendid. There are lots of good dishes: ravioli, *andouillette*, grilled beef, *diot* with shallots and *gratin dauphinois*, calf's head *à l'ancienne* and so on. Weekday lunch menu €10 and others at €21 and €28. Affordable wines include a Gamay de Savoie; some are served by the glass or jug. 'Le Grenier' cabaret takes place on the first floor (Wed–Sat). *Free house apéritif offered to our readers on presentation of this guide.*

|●| La Frise

150 cours Berriat. **Off map A3-11**
☎04.76.96.58.22
Closed *evenings; Sat; Sun; Aug.*

Near the Magasin, the contemporary art centre, this place has a bright, colourful interior with pictures by local artists on the walls. Tasty dishes at €9; the *formule* for €12 includes a main course, dessert and coffee, and you'll pay just €14 for a meal à la carte including a glass of red wine. Dishes are prepared using fresh ingredients and served in big portions, and the delicious desserts are home-made. *Free coffee offered to our readers on presentation of this guide.*

|●| Le Loup Bleu

7 rue Dominique-Villars. **Map D3-13**
☎04.76.51.22.70
Open *noon and evening until 10.15pm.*
Closed *Sat lunchtime; Sun; Mon evening; public holidays; Aug.*

This unobtrusive restaurant, with the old shutters still in place, is quiet and atmospheric, and the cooking and the service are both first-rate. Dishes on the €12 lunch menu change with the seasons. But if you want a slightly more refined meal, go for the menus at €18 and €31, which offer traditional dishes and excellent meat and fish. Some are worth a mention: sea bass with walnut wine, pork *filet mignon* roasted with acacia honey, duck breast stuffed with foie gras, scallops with roasted ceps. *Free house apéritif offered to our readers on presentation of this guide.*

|●| La Panse

7 rue de la Paix. **Map C2-21**
☎04.76.54.09.54
Closed *Sun; public holidays; 20 July–15 Aug.*

The minimalist décor at this place will be a bit too fashionable for some tastes, though it's brightened up by colourful pictures. The welcome's a bit cool, too. But the cooking is reliable and highly distinctive with a touch of sophistication. Dishes change all the time, but might include herring *pâté* with whisky, hot oysters or veal *escalope* with bilberries. Menus €13 on weekday lunchtimes and €15–27 in the evening. There's a wide range of wines. Relaxed atmosphere. *Free house apéritif offered to our readers on presentation of this guide.*

|●| Caffè Forté

4 pl. Lavalette. **Map C2-20**
☎04.76.03.25.30
Closed *Mon and Sun lunchtimes.*

This delightful place stands opposite the Grenoble museum in a quiet, wide road. The lofty dining room is vaguely baroque in style, and in summer the terrace is always full. The atmosphere is pretty easy-going but busy. The choice of dishes is eclectic and everything is freshly prepared: huge steak *tartare*, real *frites*, flambéed prawns, *émincé* of beef with five spices, chicken curry, excellent salads and pasta. There's a lunch *formule* for €13.70, other menus from €18 up to €45; a meal à la carte costs in the region of €23. *Free house apéritif offered to our readers on presentation of this guide.*

|●| À la Fortune du Pot

34 rue de l'Abbé-Grégoire. Near by the Saint-Bruno market place. **Map A3-12**
☎04.76.96.20.05
Closed *Sun; Mon; Aug.*

The dry-stone walls are hung with pictures, there's a Formica bar and an old clock that doesn't work any more and the atmosphere is great, aided by the genial host. It's always full of people recounting local tales and having a good time. There's a single menu at €14.50. You'll pay around €20 for a menu à la carte. Nice owners, fresh food, good place to go to.

|●| Chez Margo

5 rue Millet. **Map C3-15**
☎04.76.46.27.87
Closed *Sat lunchtime; Sun.*

This restaurant, in a quiet little street, is

often busy. Even on weekday evenings there's a reliable stream of regulars who drop in. The dining room is split-level, decorated in a smart-rustic style and the atmosphere is very informal. The cooking is traditional, prepared with care and the regional dishes are quite substantial. There's a €16.50 lunch menu, and others at €20 and €25. You get lots of choice: house foie gras, *fricassée* of scampi with ravioli, sliced veal sweetbreads with ginger and lime, *caillette* served on a potato cake, monkfish medallions with wild mushrooms, *confit* of duck thigh, *fondant* of two chocolates. Dishes of the day use fresh market produce. Short but good wine list. *Free house apéritif offered to our readers on presentation of this guide.*

|●| Le Bistrot Lyonnais

168 cours Berriat. **Map A3-16**
☎04.76.21.95.33
Closed *Sat; Sun; 23 Dec–8 Jan.*

Just opposite the Magasin, the contemporary art centre, this restaurant has a warm interior charmingly decorated in period style. In summer, there's a little terrace that's well protected from the road by a fragrant wisteria and lots of greenery. Good Lyonnais dishes on the menus (€20–34). If you've got time for an extended lunch, this is the perfect place to linger over such dishes as *cassolette* of morels stuffed with foie gras, crayfish ravioli with morels, *millefeuille* of red mullet with baby vegetables or scrambled eggs with truffles. Wine prices are reasonable and they serve Côtes-du-Rhône and Beaujolais by the jug. *Free house liqueur offered to our readers on presentation of this guide.*

|●| Le Mal Assis

9 rue Bayard. **Map C2-18**
☎04.76.54.75.93
Closed *Mon; Sun; public holidays; 14 July–20 Aug.*

This place, a local favourite, has wood panelling and a fireplace and charming service. There's a menu for €22; à la carte will cost you around €25. Dishes include, duckling in peaches and sweet spices, saddle of rabbit with tomatoes, fillet of bass in grapefruit butter sauce. Credit cards not accepted. *Free house apéritif offered to our readers on presentation of this guide.*

Meylan

38249 (4km NE)

|●| La Cerisaie Club

18 chemin de Saint-Martin; leave Grenoble on bd. Jean-Paris, then follow av. de Verdun and av. des Sept-Laux. Before arriving in Montbonnet, turn right into le chemin de Saint-Martin.
☎04.76.41.91.29
Closed *Sat lunchtime; Sun; 23 Dec–6 Jan.*
Swimming pool.

A lovely private mansion in a big park just minutes from Grenoble. The dining room has a high ceiling and the décor is luxurious. On sunny days you get a fabulous view from the superb terrace, which is surrounded by flowers. The place well deserves its good reputation, which has largely spread by word of mouth. There's a weekday lunchtime formule at €22, other menus at €28–47 offering sophisticated dishes. Good wine list. It's best to book. *Free house apéritif offered to our readers on presentation of this guide.*

Uriage-les-Bains

38410 (10km SE)

|●| Auberge du Vernon

Les Davids, 1274 rte. du Vernon; follow the signs for Chamrousse via col du Luitel.
☎04.76.89.10.56
Closed *Sun evening.* **Car park.**

This country inn looks like something from a fairy story; it's a little farm with a pond, a huge tree, flowers all over the place and a phenomenal view of the mountains. The Girouds, who have run the place for thirty years, serve good home cooking in generous portions – this is real country food – including charcuterie and omelette paysanne, and veal sweetbreads with ceps to order. You'll pay €15 for the weekday lunch menu, with others from €20. Six very pretty, tiny doubles go for €35–48 with basin or shower/wc. Half board at € 35–45 per person. Peace and quiet guaranteed. *Free coffee offered to our readers on presentation of this guide.*

|●| Les Mésanges**

Route des Mésanges, Le Vacher: 1km along the Saint-Martin-d'Uriage road, turn right onto the Bouloud road.
☎04.76.89.70.69 Ⓕ04.76.89.56.97

Ⓦwww.hotel-les-mesanges.com
Restaurant closed *except to residents Sun evening, Mon and Tues from Feb–April; Mon lunchtime and Tues from 1May–20 Oct. Closed 20 Oct–31 Jan.*
TV. Disabled access. High chairs and games available. Swimming pool. Car park.

The Prince family, who have owned this place since 1946, have established a solid reputation. All the rooms have been refurbished; the loveliest ones have big balconies from which you can see down the valley as far as Vizille, while the smaller ones look across the fields. Doubles €51–63 with shower/wc or bath. In the restaurant, menus cost €20–47 including a *menu terroir* of local dishes for €25. Specialities include veal with morels, saddle of pigeon with caramelized spices, strawberry soup, pig's trotters, duo of lamb with garlic *confit* and iced *pavé* with Chartreuse. It's all very rich in flavours and calories. *Free house apéritif offered to our readers on presentation of this guide.*

Sappey-en-Chartreuse (Le)

387000 (15km N)

Relais Fort Saint-Eynaud

It's at Fort Saint-Eynard; take the D512 from Grenoble.
Ⓣ04.76.85.25.24
Open *Thurs–Sun in May, June, Sept and Oct; daily, except Sun evening and Mon, in July/Aug; 1 Nov–1 May.* **Disabled access. High chairs available.**

Service 11am–10pm. The restaurant is on the Saint-Eynard summit at an altitude of 1340m. The belvedere is incorporated into the cliff face with an impressive view over Grenoble and the Grésilvaudan valley. There are two vaulted dining rooms with rough-hewn stone walls softened by a selection of pictures and wooden bistro tables swathed in tablecloths. Simple, uncomplicated fare: sandwiches, crêpes and cakes all at modest prices. The €12 menu lists a plate of charcuterie, omelette with chives, salad and dessert. Then there's another for €15 which includes *gratin dauphinois*, a home-made speciality. The Grenoblois swarm here for dinner in summer, when they put tables outside. It's also a bar. *Free house apéritif offered to our readers on presentation of this guide.*

Grignan

26230

Le Clair de la Plume***

Place du Mail; it's below the château, close to the town hall.
Ⓣ04.75.91.81.30 Ⓕ04.75.91.81.31
Ⓦwww.chateauxhotels.com/clairplume
Open *daily, all year.* **TV. High chairs available. Car park.**

Well situated in the old town across from one of the most beautiful washhouses in the Midi. It's a very elegant eighteenth-century house with a serene atmosphere and a small, relaxing garden. The whole place emanates good taste, comfort and refinement. Urbane, polite welcome. All the rooms (€90–165, breakfast included) are different, but each one is air-conditioned. You have breakfast in the old kitchen, which is full of original character. *10% discount on the room rate, Sun evening to Thurs, Nov–March (except during school holidays) offered to our readers on presentation of this guide.*

La Piccolina

It's below the château, close to the town hall.
Ⓣ04.75.46.59.20
Closed *Mon; also Sun out of season; Dec to mid Jan.* **Disabled access.**

This pizza place rivals many a gourmet restaurant. They serve good salads and tasty pizzas cooked in a proper wood-fired oven. There's also a choice of excellent grills. The dining room is small and, because it's good, it gets full quickly. Menus €10.50 and €15.50. Modestly priced wines.

Hauterives

26390

Le Relais**

Place du Général-de-Miribel; it's opposite the church.
Ⓣ04.75.68.81.12 Ⓕ04.75.68.92.42
Closed *Sun evening and Mon out of season; mid Jan to end Feb.* **Restaurant closed** *Mon in summer.* **TV.**

The thick, sturdy walls of this handsome nineteenth-century building are lined with photos and engravings by Ferdinand Cheval – a local postman who constructed an extraordinary sculpture from stones he collected on his rounds. The large, rustic bedrooms cost €30–40 with washing facilities, €50 with shower/wc or bath, and the restaurant offers regional menus at €15–30. Lots of passing customers. Best to book.

Marnans

38980 (25km NE)

L'Auberge du Prieur

2 pl. du Prieuré; from La Côte-Saint-André, take the D51 in the direction of Le Roybon, near the Forêt de Chambaran.
☎04.76.36.28.71
Closed *Tues; Wed; Sun and Tues evenings, and Mon in July/Aug*. **Disabled access. High chairs available.**

A young couple run this place; Cécile does the cooking and her nice husband handles the service. The cooking style is an eclectic mix, using more than a few medieval recipes. Everything is home-made (except the cheese and ice cream) and the menus change every couple of months. Menus €15 (not served Sunday lunch or public holidays) and €20–30 (the last needs to be ordered in advance). There's a medieval menu which includes such things as Saint-Marcellin terrine with beetroot in walnut oil, mustard duck stew, cheese. The terrace overlooks the superb, twelfth-century, Romanesque church. It's best to book.

Joyeuse

07260

Hôtel de l'Europe**

It's on the D104.
☎04.75.39.51.26
www.ardeche-hotel.net
Open *all year*. **TV. Disabled access. High chairs and games available. Swimming pool** *May–Sept.* **Car park.**

You get fair value for a place that's on the way to the gorges of the Ardèche and the Cévennes. The vast, refurbished and standardized bedrooms go for €35–43 with shower/wc or bath. They serve tasty, simple dishes such as omelettes with ceps, quail with tarragon, pork cheek *confit*, trout *meunière*, charcuterie, chestnut custard and pizzas of impressive size. Menus €10–17.50. The large heated indoor pool has a great view over the Cévennes. There's also a *boules* area. *10% discount on the room rate (out of season) offered to our readers on presentation of this guide.*

Restaurant Valentina

Place de la Peyre.
☎04.75.39.90.65
Closed *Mon; mid Sept to 31 March.*

This is the only restaurant in the old town, and since it's well away from traffic, the terrace overlooking the nice little square is a pleasant place to sit. The owners are a nice Italian couple who are keen travellers – there's a Lambretta they brought back from Italy. Authentic Italian cooking – charcuterie, antipasti, *osso buco*, pasta with pine nuts, tortellini with ceps, tagliatelli with smoked salmon and vodka sauce, also meat dishes. The home-made desserts are seriously good. You'll pay around €8.50 for a main course or €21 for a menu. Good Italian wines.

Balazuc

07120 (9km NE)

La Granja Delh Gourmandas

In the village, 50 m from the church; take the D104 to Uzer, then the D294.
☎04.75.37.74.26
Open *daily mid-June to end Aug (bookings only at weekends from May to mid-June).*

This is a restaurant that stands out from the crowd. There's no dining room, just a few tables set in the open air and under a little porch. The food is not only guaranteed to be fresh (there's no freezer here), it is also organically grown. Fine, original salads, generous but light, made from local produce, including seasonal fruit. Salads around €9.50; menus €10 and €21. The desserts and ice creams are also home-made and are equally delicious. Sometimes there are storytelling evenings (you can choose the story you want from a menu) or magic shows guaranteed to delight children; you might even run into a fortune teller. A really inviting place.

Juliénas

69840

Chez la Rose**

☎04.74.04.41.20 Ⓕ04.74.04.49.29
www.chez-la-rose.fr
Restaurant closed *Mon; Tues, Thurs and Fri lunchtimes (except on public holidays); 10–26 Dec; Feb school holidays*. **TV. High chairs available. Car park.**

With its elegant façade, this building has

the look of an old posthouse. The main building houses comfortable, rustic bedrooms while those across the road are genuine suites with a sitting room – one even has a private garden. Doubles with shower/wc or bath cost €38–60. Suites cost €68–100. The magnificent dining room is a perfect setting for famously tasty regional cooking produced by a seriously good chef: terrine of pressed duck breast, foie gras, *coq au vin* and lobster stew. Menus €24–44. They also prepare dishes for takeaway and they are open for light meals Monday to Friday (11am–6pm) in season. *20% discount on the room rate if you dine in the restaurant or free coffee offered to our readers on presentation of this guide.*

Laffrey

38220

☆ ⌂ |●| La Pacodière

Route du Lac; it's on the N85 a dozen kilometres from Vizille.
Ⓣand Ⓕ04.76.73.16.22
Closed *Mon–Thurs; evenings Oct–30 April; Jan.* **High chairs and games available. Car park.**

Three thoughtfully decorated doubles with bath or shower go for €49; the one at the back is particularly pretty, painted in yellow and blue. There's a reading room in the roof space. The dining room is also pleasant, its tables laid with checked cloths, and in summer you can eat on the terrace that leads to the lawn. Good, classic cuisine includes dishes like trout and pike pâté with morels, chicken with duck foie gras, and zander with crayfish *coulis*. Menus €21 and €32. *Free house apéritif offered to our readers on presentation of this guide.*

Lamastre

07270

⌂ |●| Hôtel du Midi - Restaurant Barattéro

Head for Le Puy; it's 2km further on the right.
Ⓣ04.75.06.41.50 Ⓕ04.75.06.49.75
Closed *Mon; Fri and Sun evenings; end Dec to mid-Feb.* **TV. Car park.**

A gourmet restaurant that has enjoyed a good reputation for several decades. The dining room is classy and cosy. You get the measure of the cooking from the cheapest menu at €32, though the pricier ones – €48–76 – include dishes with more unusual and luxurious ingredients: Bresse chicken cooked in a bladder, a divine iced chestnut soufflé. The service is meticulous and old-style French: you feel rather as if you have to sit straight at your table and not clatter your cutlery. Rooms in the hotel are equally cosy and perfectly maintained; doubles €78–95 with shower/wc or bath.

Crestet (Le)

07270 (8km NE)

☆ ⌂ |●| La Terrasse**

Take the D534 in the direction of Tournon; Crestet is on the left.
Ⓣ04.75.06.24.44 Ⓕ04.75.06.23.25
Closed *Sat in winter; Jan.* **Disabled access. TV. Swimming pool. Car park.**

There's an air of serenity in this classic establishment – you get the feeling that the people here really know how to live. Acceptable rooms cost from €33 for a double with basin or shower and from €37 with shower/wc. Menus, €10–21.50, list a good selection of regional dishes; it's worth trying *picodon*, the local goat's cheese, which has a slightly piquant flavour. The dining room has a lovely view of the Doux valley and, in summer, when the swimming pool area is ablaze with flowers, a rampant vine provides shade for the terrace. *Free house apéritif offered to our readers on presentation of this guide.*

Lanslebourg

73480

⌂ ☆ |●| Hôtel de la Vieille Poste**

Grande-Rue.
Ⓣ04.79.05.93.47 Ⓕ04.79.05.86.85
Ⓦwww.lavieilleposte.com
Closed *mid-April to mid-June; 26 Oct–26 Dec.* **TV. High chairs and games available.**

This fine hotel in the middle of the biggest ski station in Maurienne has been run by the same owners for a good 30 years. Guests are so warmly welcomed that they are made to feel part of the family. The rooms have recently been refurbished in a fairly neutral modern style and are quite comfortable; most have a balcony. Doubles with shower/wc or bath around €43 (depending on the season). The restaurant serves simple but satisfying local fare. Menus €12.50–24. All in all, it offers remarkable value for money for this region, so it's easy to see why so many customers keep on coming back. *Free telephone index notebook offered to our readers on presentation of this guide.*

Lyon

69000

See map overleaf

1st arrondissement

Hôtel Saint-Vincent**

9 rue Pareille; M° Hôtel-de-Ville. **Map B1-1**
04.78.27.22.56 04.78.30.92.87
www.hotel-saintvincent.com
TV.

This hotel is freshly redecorated and definitely not lacking in character – all the rooms have parquet floors and some boast beautiful fireplaces. The hotel is made up of four different buildings with internal courtyards; you reach the rooms through a maze of corridors. Doubles cost €38–47 with shower/wc or bath. There are also a few triples. An excellent welcome is guaranteed. *10% discount on the room rate (except Sept–Oct and 8 Dec) offered to our readers on presentation of this guide.*

Hôtel de Paris***

16 rue de la Platière; M° Hôtel-de-Ville. **Map C2-6**
04.78.28.00.95 04.78.39.57.64
www.hoteldeparis-lyon.com
TV.

Very lovely hotel with a nineteenth-century frontage. Note the superb ink fresco in the entrance, created by a Japanese artist. A grand, serpentine staircase leads to the upper floors, where each of the 30 rooms is decorated in a different style. The furniture is antique, with Voltaire armchairs or Art Nouveau wardrobes. Doubles from €53–68 with shower/wc or bath. Breakfast €6.50. An unusual, appealing place right in the heart of the town centre.

Alyssaar

29 rue du Bât-d'Argent; M° Hôtel-de-Ville. **Map D2-43**
04.78.29.57.66
Open *evenings only. Closed Sun; Mon; 1–22 Aug.*

Alyssaar is a Syrian whose genuine kindness makes his customers feel special. He will happily explain the various specialities served on the *assiette du Calife*, a selection of Syrian delicacies, and in which order you should eat them. The beef with cherries is amazing, as is the lamb kebab with aubergines. And the "Thousand-and-one-nights" dessert is a revelation. Menus €12–19, you'll pay around €20 for a menu à la carte. Credit cards not accepted. *Free house liqueur offered to our readers on presentation of this guide.*

Restaurant Vert Olive

9 rue Saint-Polycarpe; M° Hôtel-de-Ville; at the foot of the slopes of Croix-Rousse, behind the place des Terreaux. **Map C1-31**
04.78.28.15.31
Closed *Sun; Mon–Wed evenings.*

Dish of the day €9; dinner menu €21. Both the food and the welcome are equally generous and delightful. Good dishes of the day, lovingly prepared poultry and copious, tasty and colourful salads. Convivial atmosphere and moderate bills. Attentive, enchantingly feminine service. One of our favourites.

Restaurant Chez Georges – Au P'tit Bouchon

8 rue du Garet; M° Hôtel-de-Ville or Louis-Pradel. **Map D1-20**
04.78.28.30.46
Closed *Sat; Sun; Aug.*

Set this down alongside an old Paris bistro and you wouldn't be able to tell them apart – it's got the checked tablecloths, the imitation leather benches, the mirror-lined walls and the original, zinc-topped bar. The attentive but unobtrusive owner serves at table while his wife is busy in the handkerchief-sized kitchen. Well-balanced Lyonnais menus list sausage with lentils, *andouillette* in mustard sauce (pork sausage), pike *quenelles*, tripe *au gratin*, an astonishingly good Saint-Marcellin (a mild cheese from the Dauphiné) and a great upside-down apple tart. Set menus €15.50 lunchtimes and €20.50, or around €25 à la carte.

L'Étage

4 pl. des Terreaux; M° Hôtel-de-Ville. **Map C1-44**
04.78.28.19.59
Closed *Sun; Mon; public holidays; 27 July–27 Aug; a week in winter.*

Push open the door and you find yourself

LYON

A B

25 VILLEFRANCHE-S-S, D 433 VILLEFRANCHE-S-SAÔNE, N 6

MÂCON, A 6

St-Bruno-des-Chartreux
PL. DES CHARTREUX
Rue Pierre Dupont
Cours
R. de la Poudrière
Montée de la Butte
Jardin des Chartreux
Général Giraud
PL. ROUVILLE
22
Rue Rivet
R. de Flesselles
R. de l'Annonciade
1
PL. ST-VINCENT
PL. PORT NEUVILLE
Quai Saint Vincent
Saône
Quai Pierre Scize
R. St Paul
PL. GERSON
Saint-Paul
16
Rue O. Mey
PL. ST-PAUL
St-Paul
Archives départementales
Montauban
Mée des Carmes Déchaussés
Montée de la Sarra
Rue
Montée Nicolas de Lange
Rue Juiverie
R. Lainerie
R. F. Vernay
14
Temple
Mée du Change
PL. DU CHANGE
Tour Métallique
Mée de Gadagne
R. de Gadagne
Mtée du Garillan
PL. DU GOUVERNEMENT
Mairie du 5e (annexe)
PL. DE LA BALEINE
FOURVIÈRE
VIEUX LYON
Archevêché
Notre-Dame-de-Fourvière
Gare
47
27
PL. NEUVE ST-JEAN
Palais de Justice
Musée de l'Œuvre
R. de la Bombarde
46
Radisson
Montée du C. Decourtray
Funiculaire
Fontaine
Cathédrale St-Jean
PL. ST-JEAN
Musée de la Civilisation gallo-romaine
Rue Cléberg
SAINT-JEAN
Bibliothèque
Théâtre Romain
Hôpital de l'Antiquaille
Gare
Av. A. Max
PL. DE LA TRINITÉ
PONT BONAPARTE
15
Montée du Chemin Neuf
Montée du Gourguillon
39
Rue Tramassac
R. Doyenné
PL. B. CRÉPU
Fulchiron
Odéon
PLACE DES MINIMES
Montée
BERTRAS
St-Georges
Rue des Farges
Saint-Just
PLACE DE L'ABBÉ LARUE
Rue Saint Georges
Quai Fulchiron
Quai de Tilsitt
Rue de la Quarantaine
PL. A. VOLLON
R. Ste Hélène

	WHERE TO SLEEP
1	Hôtel Saint-Vincent
2	Hôtel de Bretagne
3	Hôtel d'Ainay
4	Hôtel Normandie
6	Hôtel de Paris
7	Hôtel Bayard
8	Hôtel La Résidence
9	Hôtel Globe et Cécil
10	Best Western
11	Le Lacassagne
12	Grand Hôtel Château-Perrache
13	Hôtel de la Poste
14	Hôtel Saint-Paul
15	Auberge de Jeunesse du Vieux Lyon
16	Phénix Hôtel
17	Hôtel Foch

	WHERE TO EAT
20	Restaurant Chez Georges – Au P'tit Bouchon
23	Café des Fédérations
24	Maison Villemanzy
26	Le Petit Grain
27	Happy Friends Family
28	Le Pâtisson
29	Restaurant Chez Mounier
30	Chez Hugon
31	Restaurant Vert Olive
32	Chez Abel
33	Le Théodore
34	Arizona Grill
35	Brasserie des Brotteaux
36	Restaurant Thomas
37	Le Comptoir du Vin
38	Pure Voyage
39	Alicante el Bario
40	Bar du XXIe siècle
42	Brasserie Georges 1836
43	Alyssaar
44	L' Etage
46	Les Lyonnais
47	Les Adrets
48	En mets, fais ce qu'il te plaît

A ST-ÉTIENNE, N 86 32, 42 12 Perrache B

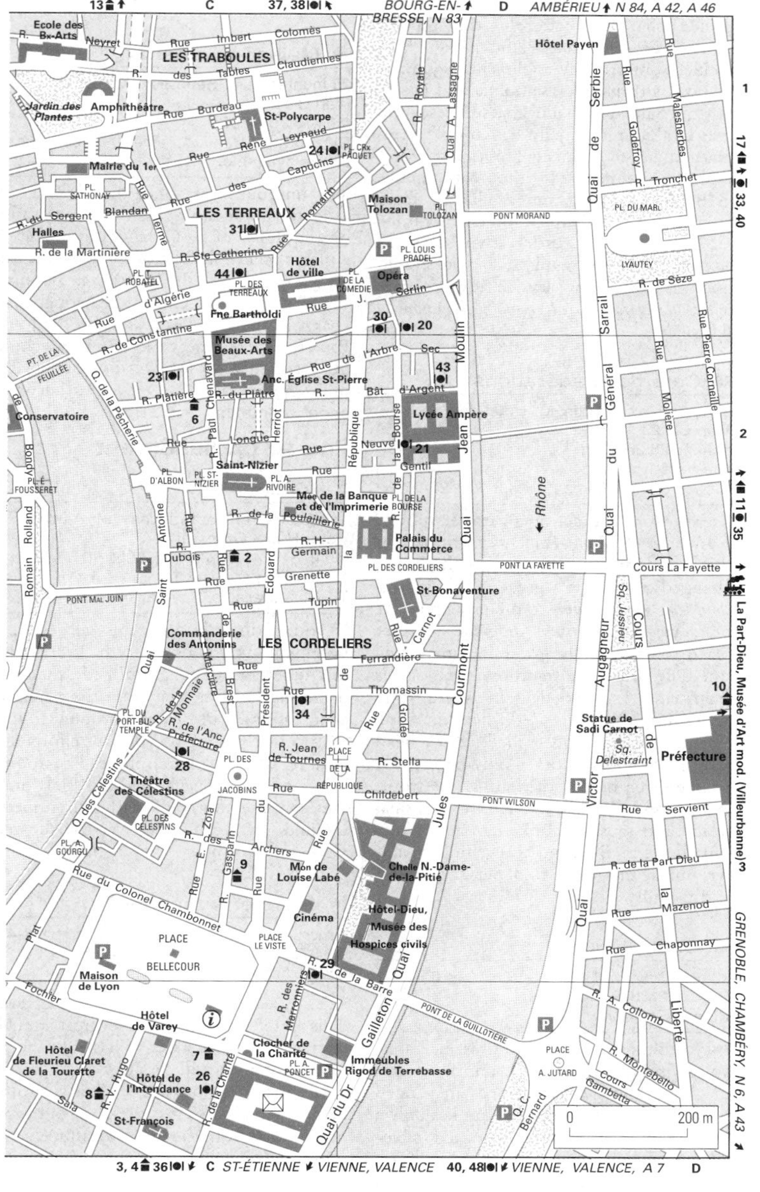
LES TRABOULES
LES TERREAUX
LES CORDELIERS
Ecole des Bx-Arts
Jardin des Plantes
Amphithéâtre
St-Polycarpe
Mairie du 1er
Halles
Maison Tolozan
Hôtel de ville
Opéra
Fne Bartholdi
Musée des Beaux-Arts
Anc. Église St-Pierre
Conservatoire
Lycée Ampère
Saint-Nizier
Mée de la Banque et de l'Imprimerie
Palais du Commerce
St-Bonaventure
Commanderie des Antonins
Théâtre des Célestins
Mon de Louise Labé
Chelle N.-Dame-de-la-Pitié
Hôtel-Dieu, Musée des Hospices civils
Cinéma
PLACE BELLECOUR
Maison de Lyon
Hôtel de Varey
Hôtel de Fleurieu Claret de la Tourette
Hôtel de l'Intendance
St-François
Clocher de la Charité
Immeubles Rigod de Terrebasse
Hôtel Payen
Statue de Sadi Carnot
Préfecture
Rhône
PONT MORAND
PONT LA FAYETTE
PONT WILSON
PONT MAL JUIN
PONT DE LA GUILLOTIÈRE
PLACE A. JUTARD
BOURG-EN-BRESSE, N 83
AMBÉRIEU N 84, A 42, A 46
ST-ÉTIENNE VIENNE, VALENCE
VIENNE, VALENCE, A 7
La Part-Dieu, Musée d'Art mod. (Villeurbanne) 3
GRENOBLE, CHAMBÉRY, N 6, A 43
0 200 m

in a wood-panelled salon draped in red. From the tables by the windows you get a good view of the fountain. The cooking is elegant, fine and precise, and though the dishes change frequently the quality remains the same: marbré of chicken with pickled onions and apple chutney, roast salmon with paprika, semolina and hazelnut oil, Saint-Marcellin goat's cheese, foie gras in a Beaujolais jelly, figs in milk marmalade, lightly cooked freshed scallops. Dish of the day €11 (not Sat); menus €18–26. If you want a change from Lyonnais dishes, there's a lobster menu for €51 (you must order two days in advance). Lots of regulars, so you should book at least a few days in advance. *Free coffee offered to our readers on presentation of this guide.*

|●| Café des Fédérations

8 rue du Major-Martin; M° Hôtel-de-Ville.
Map C2-23
Ⓣ04.78.28.26.00
Ⓦlesfedeslyon.com
Closed *Sat lunchtime; Sun; 25 July–25Aug.*

Scenes from the classic Tavernier movie, *L'Horloger de Saint-Paul*, were filmed in this local institution – and it hasn't changed a bit. It is a great Lyonnais *bouchon* (the name given to the city's popular brasserie-restaurants) and the perfect place to taste really good Lyonnais cuisine. The dishes are traditional: *gras-double* (marinated for two days in white wine and mustard), *tablier de sapeur* (ox tripe egged, crumbed and grilled), calf's head *ravigote*. Splendid hors d'œuvres include charcuterie, bowls of lentils, beetroot, brawn and calf's feet, mixed seasonal salads and sausage cooked in red wine. Lunch menu €19, and an evening *formule* with more choice at €23. Service is swift and friendly.

|●| Chez Hugon

12 rue Pizay; M° Hôtel-de-Ville. **Map D1-30**
Ⓣ04.78.28.10.94
Closed *Sat; Sun; Aug.*

As you wander around the town hall area, you'll find this authentic Lyonnais *bouchon* in a little alley. It's remained unchanged over the years. The dining room has only a few tables, covered with checked tablecloths, where you can eat excellent Lyon specialities veal stew, white pudding with apples, *tablier de sapeur* (ox tripe egged, crumbed and grilled), and *gâteau de foies de volaille* (chicken livers mixed with foie gras, eggs and cream). Menu €22; à la carte reckon on paying €25. There's a nice atmosphere, with lots of locals.

|●| Maison Villemanzy

25 montée Saint-Sébastien; M° Croix-Pâquet.
Map C1-24
Ⓣ04.78.39.37.00
Closed *Sun; Mon lunchtime; 2–16 Jan.* **High chairs available.**

This unspoilt house, once the residence of a doctor-colonel, sits high above the city on the slopes of La Croix-Rousse. There's a magnificent terrace from where you can survey the town – the view's very popular, so it's best to book. Guillaume Mouchel, in charge in the kitchens, was a pupil of Jean-Paul Lacombe, one of Lyon's great chefs. To eat lightly, go for the dish of the day plus green salad for €11; otherwise, choose the menu at €21.50.

2nd arrondissement

Hôtel d'Ainay*

14 rue des Remparts-d'Ainay; M° Ampère-Victor-Hugo. **Off map C4-3**
Ⓣ04.78.42.43.42 Ⓕ04.72.77.51.90
Ⓔhotel-ainay@online.fr
TV. *Cots available.* **Pay car park.**

If you're on a budget, this very simple hotel will suit you down to the ground; it's in a quiet, rather delightful pedestrianized neighbourhood not far from the magnificent basilica. The friendly young couple who run it put a good deal of effort into creating a restful atmosphere. The rooms have good double glazing and look onto the road, the courtyard or the pl. Ampère. Doubles €29–35 with basin or shower, €38–40 with shower/wc or bath.

Hôtel Normandie**

3 rue du Bélier; M° Perrache. **Off map C4-4**
Ⓣ04.78.37.31.36 Ⓕ04.78.40.98.56
Ⓦwww.hotelnormandie.com
TV.

This hotel, named after the great French liner, is in a quiet street. It has about forty rooms for €29 with basin, €43.50–49.50 with shower/wc or bath, €53.50 for three people. The double glazing keeps out most of the noise from the railway station. Some rooms have been spruced up, and more are due for the same treatment. Pleasant staff. *One free breakfast per person offered to our readers on presentation of this guide.*

Hôtel de Bretagne*

10 rue Dubois; M° Cordeliers. **Map C2-2**
Ⓣ04.78.37.79.33 Ⓕ04.72.77.99.92
Ⓦwww.hoteldebretagne-lyon.com
TV.

In a quiet little street in the heart of town. The thirty rooms are clean, smart and soundproofed – particularly handy for the ones overlooking the street, which are big and bright. Those over the courtyard are very gloomy. Doubles with shower/wc cost €45, and there are also rooms that sleep three or four. *10% discount on the room rate offered to our readers on presentation of this guide.*

Hôtel Bayard**

23 pl. Bellecour; M° Bellecour. **Map C4-7**
Ⓣ04.78.37.39.64 Ⓕ04.72.40.95.51
Ⓦwww.hotelbayard.com
TV. Car park.

There are only fifteen rooms in this hotel, and the place has a lot of regulars, so it's a good idea to book. No two rooms are alike. Some have lots of personality, and several have canopied beds, polished parquet floors and a great view of the pl. Bellecour. No. 5 has an enormous bathroom; no. 15, which overlooks the courtyard, can sleep four. Doubles €60–90, breakfast included. The little breakfast nook has a very rural feel. Follow the signs up the stairs to the reception on the first floor.

Hôtel La Résidence***

18 rue Victor-Hugo; M° Bellecour or Ampère-Victor-Hugo. **Map C4-8**
Ⓣ04.78.42.63.28 Ⓕ04.78.42.85.76
Ⓦwww.resitel.com
Disabled access. TV.

Halfway between Perrache and Bellecour in a lively pedestrianized street with lots of shops. They practise old-style hotel-keeping here and it's one of the cheapest three-stars in town. The rooms have all had a makeover and are cosy and air-conditioned – they're €68 with shower/wc or bath.

Grand Hôtel Château-Perrache*****

12 cours Verdun-Rambaud; M° Perrache. **Off map B4-12**
Ⓣ04.72.77.15.00 Ⓕ04.78.37.06.56
Ⓦwww.accorhotels.com
Disabled access (restaurant). TV. Disabled access. Car park.

Formerly the Terminus hotel, built in 1906 by the PLC company. It's an edifice on a monumental scale; the entrance, protected by a wrought iron canopy, is said to be the only genuine example of Art Nouveau in Lyon. Devanne and Curieux were the architects and their style is picked up throughout the beautiful interior; corniches are decorated by sculptured, floral friezes and, exceptionally, the iron-work, window panes and furniture have been carefully preserved. The Majorelle panels turn the restaurant into a place of beauty, too, with its fine paintings and sculptures. Spacious and bright rooms from €110, with superior rooms at €140–155 and suites for €229. It's a quiet place, ideally located near the station and a good walk to pl. Bellecour.

Hôtel Globe et Cécil***

21 rue Gasparin; M° Bellecour. **Map C3-9**
Ⓣ04.78.42.58.95 Ⓕ04.72.41.99.06
Ⓦwww.globeetcecilhotel.com
TV.

A top-notch three-star in the city centre. Each room has been decorated in a style appropriate to its size and has its own character – some have handsome marble fireplaces, balconies and air-conditioning. The rooms that overlook the street are brighter than the others. The service can't be faulted, and it comes with a smile. Doubles €135 with shower/wc or bath, including breakfast. Dogs are accepted at €8 per day. *10% discount on the room rate offered to our readers on presentation of this guide.*

Le Petit Grain

19 rue de la Charité; M° Ampère or Bellecour. **Map C4-26**
Ⓣ04.72.41.77.85
Open *10am–6pm (4pm on Mon).* **Closed** *Sun; 15–30 Aug.*

A simple little snack bar in an old milliner's shop near rue Auguste-Comte, the street with all the antique shops. It's prettily decorated with a scattering of objects picked up from street markets by the cheerful Vietnamese owner. You can have a substantial *bo bun* (stir-fried beef or chicken with rice noodles and lots of herbs), Saigon pancakes, chicken with ginger – and a host of fresh salads. Terrific tarts, too: pear and chocolate or apple. *Formules* and menus from €8; dishes of the day around €10.

|●| Restaurant Chez Mounier

3 rue des Marronniers; M° Bellecour. **Map C3-29**
☎04.78.37.79.26
Closed *Sun evening and Mon, 1–8 Jan, the week of the 8 May; 15 Aug–7 Sept.*

Lyon is famous for its puppets; the one in this restaurant window, smiling at passers-by and inviting them in, is the comic character Guignol. This is the most authentic of the *bouchons* in this touristy street, with two bare little dining rooms. There's a good atmosphere created by Christine Moinier, and the regional cooking has character: *gnafrons* (little sausages), *tablier de sapeur* (ox tripe egged, crumbed and grilled). For €7.40 on weekday lunchtimes you get dish of the day plus cheese or dessert; this goes up to €10 at night. Also two menus for €14 and €16. Credit cards not accepted.

|●| Arizona Grill

8 rue Ferrandière; M° Cordeliers **Map C3-34**
☎04.78.42.35.02
Closed *Sun; Mon.*

This place proves that a hamburger does not have to be a rubbery lump of minced meat shoved between two pieces of cardboard passing as bread by rescuing this American speciality from the indignities it has suffered for so long. Here a hamburger is served on a plate: 200 or 300g of excellent, fresh beef, minced and fried, then served with chunky fries. Lunchtime menu €10; reckon on upwards of €15 à la carte. This restaurant thumbs its nose at all the fast-food joints and meat factories that infest tourist centres. It's a friendly place, ideally suited to families.

|●| Le Pâtisson

17 rue du Port-du-Temple; M° Bellecour. **Map C3-28**
☎04.72.41.81.71
www.lepatisson.com
Closed *Fri evening; Sat (April–Sept); Sun; a week around 15 Aug; Oct to end Feb.*

Yves Perrin, owner of the only organic and vegetarian restaurant in the city, has been a finalist in two prestigious culinary competitions – his diplomas are proudly displayed on the walls. Try *seitan escalope* with mustard, medallions of tofu with a *julienne* of saffron-flavoured vegetables or the millet and aubergine Provençale. Menus €11 and €12.50 at lunchtime and €15.50 and €18.50 in the evening. No smoking. It's a pity the décor is so gloomy. *Free house apéritif offered to our readers on presentation of this guide.*

|●| Chez Abel

25 rue Guynemer; M° Ampère. **Off map B4-32**
☎04.78.37.46.18
Closed *Sat; Sun; Aug; a week at Christmas; New Year.*

This place, just a stone's throw from the Saône and 200m from the basilica, has very old wainscoting and a creaky parquet floor. It looks like a folk museum, full of oddments, hefty wooden tables and a beer pump from 1925. House specialities include grilled pig's trotters, house terrine, chicken with rice, tripe and *quenelles* of pike. Lunch menus €15 and others €22 and €30. There's a terrace, seating twenty, overlooking rue Bourgelade.

|●| Restaurant Thomas

6 rue Laurencin; M° Ampère. **Off map C4-36**
☎04.72.56.04.76
Closed *Sun; Mon.*

Lunch menu €15, dinner €26. For these prices, the quality is remarkable. The young chef here really appreciates his extremely fresh ingredients, bringing out their flavour and seasoning them with precision, without drowning them in any fancy excesses. From the starters to the desserts, the results are exquisite. The wines seem to have been chosen with as much care as the dishes. Impeccable, friendly service. The setting is also worthy of note – it's discreet, tasteful and very pleasant.

|●| Brasserie Georges 1836

30 cours de Verdun; it's next to Perrache station. **Off map B4-42**
☎04.72.56.54.54
Open *11.30am–11.15pm (open till 12.15am Fri and Sat).* **High chairs and games available. Disabled access.**

This cosmopolitan Art Deco brasserie, which has been open since 1836, is a barn of a place – it seats 1000 diners served by 200 staff. The cuisine is in the same grand tradition: sausage in *brioche*, *quenelle* of pike and, inevitably, *choucroute*. Menus from

€18.50 up to €24; ham with mashed potatoes is served free to children under three. They serve good beer and the atmosphere is cheery, with a lively jazz evening on Saturday. Sadly, the ugly Perrache car park mars the view. *Free house apéritif offered to our readers on presentation of this guide.*

3rd arrondissement

Le Lacassagne***

245 av. Lacassagne; M° Grange-Blanche; it's 10mn walking distance, near the hospitals and the town of Bron; bus no.28. **Off map D2-11**
Ⓣ04.78.54.09.12 Ⓕ04.72.36.99.23
Ⓦwww.hotel-lacassagne.fr
TV. *High chairs and cots available.* **Car park.**

You'll need a car to get to this pleasant hotel on the edge of town. It has big rooms; some overlook a garden. Nice welcome and reasonable prices. Doubles €45–59 with shower/wc or bath. Light meals provided on request – salad, *croque-monsieur*, cream cheese and so on – for €10–12. *10% discount on the room rate offered to our readers on presentation of this guide.*

Best Western** Créqui Lyon Part-Dieu

37 rue de Bonnel; it's not far from the TGV station, 10mn walking distance. **Off map D3-10**
Ⓣ04.78.60.20.47 Ⓕ04.78.62.21.12
TV. Disabled access. Pay car park.

A spruce hotel near the law courts, a ten-minute walk from the town centre. The 52 bedrooms are comfortable, with cheerful décor, but they're a bit of a squeeze. Rooms go for €60–115 with bath. Smiling, professional staff. *10% discount on the room rate (except during trade fairs) offered to our readers on presentation of this guide.*

4th arrondissement

Hôtel de la Poste

1 rue Victor Fort; M° Croix-Rousse. **Off map C1-13**
Ⓣand Ⓕ04.78.28.62.67

One of the least expensive hotels in town, located in the heart of the marvellous Croix-Rousse neighbourhood. It's housed in a working-class block of flats and though the building doesn't exactly ooze charm, it's very well maintained. The lovely proprietress has a friendly smile for everybody, but reserves half of her twenty rooms for her regulars. Rooms €17–25 with basin and €32 with shower. *10% discount on the room rate offered to our readers on presentation of this guide for a stay of at least two nights in July–Aug.*

Le Comptoir du Vin

2 rue de Belfort; M° Croix-Rousse. **Off map C1-37**
Ⓣ04.78.39.89.95

This little bar-restaurant is surely the lifeblood of the Croix-Rousse neighbourhood, light years away from the conceptual eateries and marketing campaigns that are now all the rage. Here there's an old-style bistro atmosphere with jovial owners and copious, unpretentious home cooking. The meat is particularly good, whether fried or served with sauce. Dishes €7–10. Wines at very reasonable prices that go down well with the regulars who pack the place and fill it with laughter. As they say in Lyon, "it's better to get hot from eating than cold from working".

Pure Voyage

8 rue Pailleron; M° Hénon. **Off map C1-38**
Ⓣ04.72.07.75.79
Closed *Sat lunch; Sun; Mon.*

A laid-back place tucked behind the Croix-Rousse theatre: laid-back décor, laid-back music, laid-back comfort (you get the idea). The food and service, however, are much better than in most restaurants of this type. The menu is made up of dishes from overseas, such as Creole-style stuffed shellfish with rum and lime and lamb *confit* rubbed with *raz el-hanout* and served in a reduction of sherry. The presentation is meticulous and the prices are extremely reasonable. Lunchtime menu €18; at night, reckon on €30–35 à la carte for a full meal with drinks.

5th arrondissement

Auberge de Jeunesse du Vieux Lyon

41-45 montée du Chemin-Neuf; M° Saint-Jean, then a 5mn climb; from La Part-Dieu station, take no. 28 bus; from Perrache, take no. 31 bus; from place Saint-Jean, take the funicular to Minimes station. **Map B3-15**
Ⓣ04.78.15.05.50 Ⓕ04.78.15.05.51
Ⓦwww.hostelbooking.com

New arrivals *7am–noon and 2pm–1am, but the hostel is open round the clock.* **Disabled access.**

To enjoy the most extraordinary view that the city has to offer, you have two choices: check into *La Villa Florentine*, a four-star luxury hotel, or rush to this youth hostel and save yourself at least €150 a night. It opened in 1998 in this renovated building looking down on the city, a mere five minutes from the Renaissance neighbourhood of old Lyon. 180 beds in all (two to six per room, most with a toilet). €12.70 a night, including tax and breakfast. Sheets can be hired for €2.70. Obviously, an FUAJ card is compulsory: €10.70 and €15.50, for visitors aged under or over 26, respectively. Bar, garage for bikes, laundry, internet connection (€6.85 per hour) and even a tiered garden, literally dug into the hillside. There's no cafeteria, but a kitchen is available for residents. All the mod cons with a genuinely friendly welcome and atmosphere; to top it all, there are a host of activities that make it a really vibrant place; exhibitions of photos, jazz and classical concerts. And then there's that view..

Hôtel St Paul**

6 rue de la Lainerie; M° Vieux Lyon. **Map B2-14**
Ⓣ04.78.28.13.29 Ⓕ04.72.00.97.27
Ⓦwww.hotelstpaul.fr
Closed *Wed except July– Aug; 11 Nov–11 Feb.* **TV. Cots and bottle warmer available. Internet available. Pay car park.**

The only two-star in Vieux Lyon, close to the spot where Bertrand Tavernier made his film *L'Horloger de Saint Paul*. Its twenty rooms are spread across a group of Renaissance buildings; Seventeen have double beds, three have twins. Doubles with shower €42, shower/wc or bath €45–59. All of them are soundproofed. The staff do everything they can to make you feel very welcome, and can provide information about what's on in town.

Phénix Hôtel***

7 quai de Bondy; M° Hôtel-de-Ville. **Map B2-16**
Ⓣ04.78.28.24.24 Ⓕ04.78.28.62.86
Ⓦwww.hotel-le-phenix.fr
Disabled access. TV. Car park.

The hotel, in a splendid seventeenth-century building, offers big, tastefully decorated rooms. It's also the only hotel in town to offer a view of the Saône. Rooms are beautifully appointed and impeccably maintained. Very professional welcome and an international clientele. Doubles €145–155. Breakfast at €10. They host real jazz evenings on Thursdays, Oct–April. *Free house apéritif offered to our readers on presentation of this guide.*

Les Lyonnais

1 rue Tramassac; M° Vieux-Lyon. **Map B3-46**
Ⓣ04.78.37.64.82
Closed *Sun evening; Mon; 1–8 Jan; 1–15 Aug.* **Disabled access.**

An imitation Lyon Bouchon, since it opened ten years ago, this friendly place has drawn regular crowds for its efficient service, good food and affordable prices. Weekday lunch *formule* €11; in the evening menus at €19, including a *menu du marché* which changes with the seasons and a *menu Lyonnais*. Dishes include *tabliers de sapeur*, hot sausages, calf's head with *sauce gribiche*, etc. *Home-made liqueur offered to our readers on presentation of this guide.*

Les Adrets

30 rue du Bœuf; M° Vieux-Lyon. **Map B2-47**
Ⓣ04.78.38.24.30
Closed *Sat; Sun; Aug.* **High chairs available.**

This typically Lyonnais place isn't at the forefront of fashion but it's always full of people. The lunch menu (€13) is brilliant: excellent dishes including as good a fish soup as you'll eat in Marseille, scallop and prawn salad, grilled ravioli, pressed herrings with Jerusalem artichokes, marinated salmon and *croustillant* of zander fillet with spiced bread. It's perfectly accompanied by a jug of wine which, like the coffee, is included in the price. Other menus €19.25–38. *Free house apéritif offered to our readers on presentation of this guide.*

Alicante el Barrio

16 rue Saint-Georges; M° Vieux-Lyon. **Map B3-39**
Ⓣ04.78.37.99.11
Open *Wed–Sat, evenings only.* **Closed** *Aug.*

Tapas are often considered mere tidbits and, let's face it, they're rarely very good. Here, though, they are delicious, and it is easy to make up a whole meal with them, from starters to a dessert. Reckon on around €23 à la carte; menus are available (but only for groups) at €25.50 and €28.50. You can also choose fish a *la plancha* (grilled), or the house speciality, paella *valenciana*. Friendly and attentive service. There's often flamenco music in the background, and the gaudy décor seems to have come straight out of an Almodovar film. A really good place.

|●| Happy Friends Family

29 rue du Boeuf; M° Vieux-Lyon. **Map B2/3-27**
☎04.72.40.91.47
Open *evenings only; Sun lunchtime by booking only*. **Closed** *Mon*. **Disabled access.**

Lots of delicate and unusual ingredients used in inventive combinations here: *millefeuille* of lamb cutlets in a spice crust, pan-fried Jerusalem artichokes with grapes, cream of chestnut-pumpkin soup scented with cardamom, mushrooms stuffed with snails and Saint-Marcellin cheese *gratin*. Weekday lunch menu €27, other menu at €33. You'll spend around €35 à la carte if you include a bottle of wine such as a Pécharmant. It's best to book.

6th arrondissement

Hôtel Foch***

59 av. Foch; M° Foch. 5mn walking distance to the peninsula and in the centre of the 6e arrondissement. **Off map D1-17**
☎04.78.89.14.01 ℱ04.78.93.71.69
ⓦwww.hotel-foch.fr
TV. Car park.

A charming, discreet hotel on the second floor of an old building. The reception has a salon with leather sofas, and there's carpet on the breakfast room floor. It's a quiet place with spacious, well-appointed rooms, and it feels luxurious but not ostentatious. Friendly, personal welcome. Doubles €77–100 with shower/wc or bath, depending on the season. *Free house apéritif offered to our readers on presentation of this guide.*

|●| Le Théodore

34 cours Franklin-Roosevelt; M° Foch. **Off map D1-33**
☎04.78.24.08.52
Bar open *8am–midnight*. **Restaurant open** *noon–2pm and 7–10.30pm (7–11pm Fri and Sat)*. **Closed** *Sun; public holidays; the week including 15 Aug*. **Disabled access. High chairs available.**

The terrace of this lovely establishment is great in summer. Quality produce goes into making refined dishes that are colourful and full of flavour; home-made duck pâté *en croûte* and foie gras, ravioli stuffed with morels, calves' kidneys. Dish of the day €10, a *formule* at €14 (main course with starter or dessert), and menus at €16 (lunchtime), €18, €25, €30.50 and €39.50. The nice wine list lets you try a variety of lesser known reds or whites from the Rhône valley; the Saint-Perray made from the Viognier grape is ideal with the fresh pike fish balls. *Free house apéritif offered to our readers on presentation of this guide.*

|●| Brasserie des Brotteaux

11 pl. Jules Ferry; M° Brotteaux. **Off map D2/3-35**
☎04.72.72.03.98
Café open *from 7.30am*. **Restaurant open** *11.30am–2.30pm and 7.30–10pm*. **Closed** *Sun*.

A marvellous place that's remained unchanged since 1913. There's a large dining room seating 90, with another 60 places on the terrace opposite the old Les Brotteaux station. The décor involves etched mirrors, colourful ceramics and draped red curtains – a theatrical setting in direct contrast with the simple, serious cooking. Laurent Morel worked with the famed chef Point, and Emmanuel Faucon, the boss, is a straight-talking Lyonnais. Menus cost €16–27. Various platters: *pêcheur* for €15, Italian for €15.50 or brasserie for €16. Dishes are handsomely served but also originally presented: *émincé* of beef with Saint Marcellin sauce for €14.50, pressed foie gras with apples caramelized in cider for €14. Everything is made in house. It's very good value, and a must for both the cuisine and the setting. *Free house apéritif offered to our readers on presentation of this guide.*

7th arrondissement

|●| Bar du XXIe siècle

3 av. Berthelot; M° Jean-Macé. **Off map D4-40**
☎04.78.72.00.66
Open *lunchtime only; bar open until 5.30pm*. **Closed** *Sun; 3 weeks in Aug*.

After an overwhelming visit to the Museum of the Resistance and Deportation, this little bistro is an ideal place to recover your spirits and strength. Annick and Élisabeth extend the same warm welcome to both newcomers and regulars. Delicious home cooking that is hard to find these days (everything is home-made, even the desserts); lentil salad, veal *marengo*, *blanquette*, etc. Menu of the day €11.50, with starter, main course and dessert. *Free coffee or apéritif offered to our readers on presentation of this guide.*

En mets, fais ce qu'il te plaît

43 rue Chevreul; M° Jean-Macé. **Off map D4-48**
04.78.72.46.58
Closed *Sat; Sun; Aug.* **Disabled access.**

A really good restaurant with two dining rooms; you can see into the kitchen from the first one, which has a bar, while the second has metal grilles at the windows and tables lit by modern, colourful lamps. It's a relaxing place, with easy-going, attentive service. The menu changes every three weeks but typical offerings include fresh vegetables with olive oil, good succulent duck, fresh sea trout served on a bed of spinach and excellent seafood. The produce and ingredients are the freshest, and the attention paid to precise cooking is impressive. Weekday lunch menu €23, and menu *dégustation* in the evening €36, or around €40 à la carte. There's a selection of good wines served by the glass.

Megève

74120

Hôtel-Chalet des Ours**

Chemin des Roseaux.
04.50.21.57.40 04.50.93.05.73
chaletdesours@aol.com
Closed *Thurs evening; May; Oct; Nov.* **Car park.**

Owned by an English woman, this lovely place is a haven of refinement, simplicity and kindness with a bed and breakfast atmosphere. The panelled rooms are decorated simply with soft feather beds. Doubles €57–72 with shower/wc; half board at €65–78 per person is requested in winter. There's a reading room with a beautiful fireplace and a TV, and a small dining room in the basement. They offer one menu at €16 and a rather exotic Thai version to order for dinner. It's sheer pleasure to have five different kinds of tea to choose from at breakfast.

Praz-sur-Arly

74120 (5km SW)

La Griyotire***

Route de la Tonnaz; take the N212.
04.50.21.86.36 04.50.21.86.34
www.griyotire.com
Restaurant closed *lunchtimes.Closed Easter to mid June; mid-Sept to Christmas school holidays.* **TV. High chairs and games available. Swimming pool. Car park.**

A dream of an Alpine chalet in the middle of a family resort not far from Megève, set well away from the main road that runs through the middle of the village. The rooms have been decorated in exquisite taste and each is different. There's lots of wood everywhere and the feather beds are gloriously soft; doubles with shower/wc or bath €80–105. Half board, requested during the Feb and Christmas school holidays, €75–97 per person. Charming welcome and a family atmosphere – there's even a games room for the children. *Fondue* and *raclette* are served on winter evenings. Set menu €25. There's a lovely garden, a sauna, a hammam and a massage room, and the swimming pool is open in summer. *Free house apéritif offered to our readers on presentation of this guide.*

Mens

38710

Auberge de Mens***

Place du Breuil.
04.76.34.81.00 04.76.34.80.90
Restaurant closed *early Nov to mid-March, except for half board bookings.* **Disabled access. TV. Car park.**

This huge renovated house offers comfortable rooms at €45 for a double with shower/wc or bath. Half board €41 per person. The décor is fresh and colourful and there's a lovely garden where you can relax on quiet evenings. They serve traditional home cooking, with a menu of the day (not Sun) at €15 including cheese and dessert. Other menus €17 and €23.

Café des Arts

Rue Principale; from Grenoble take the N85 then the D526.
04.76.34.68.16
Restaurant closed *Sun evening; Wed Sept–June.* **TV.**

This charming place is the most famous

café in the Trièves and it's listed as a historic monument. In 1896, Gustave Riquet, a painter from Picardy, decorated the ceilings and walls with beautiful allegorical frescoes and views of the countryside. The self-taught chef-owner prepares superb dishes that vary according to what's good at market. The choice is limited, but you can be sure that whatever is on offer will be inspired. Try the house terrine of foie gras and the fresh fish if they're available. Menus €11.50 at lunch then €13–16.80 at dinner (which is by reservation only).

Tréminis

38710 (15km S)

Hôtel des Alpes

Hameau de Château-Bas: take the D66 from Mens then the D216.
☎04.76.34.72.94
Closed *Sun evening and Mon out of season; 1 Nov–1 March.*

This is the type of hotel you'd expect to see on an old sepia postcard of the mountains. Set in marvellous countryside, it's been wonderfully run for generations. There's a vaulted café-bar and a grandfather clock ticking away in the dining room next to the buffet. In these comforting surroundings you can eat good family cooking from low-priced menus: €12 (not Sunday) to €16–23. Specialities include calf's head and gâteau of foie gras *Dauphinois*. Doubles €33.80 with basin and €46.30 with shower. Half board €38–44 per person. *Free coffee offered to our readers on presentation of this guide.*

Chichilianne

38930 (16km W)

Au Gai Soleil du Mont-Aiguille**

La Richardière; take the N75 then the D7, it's 2.5km from the village at the foot of Mont Aiguille, where the walking trails start.
☎04.76.34.41.71 Ⓕ04.76.34.40.63
Ⓦwww.hotelgaisoleil.com
Closed *25 Oct–20 Dec.* **TV. Games and cots available.**

Surrounded by a fantastic ring of mountains, this hotel is at the foot of Mont Aiguille among the woods, copses and wheat fields. The house, built in 1720, has its original stone staircase, and there has been a hotel here for fifty years. The *patronne* is warm-hearted and welcoming. Rooms priced at €48–49 with shower/wc or bath. Half board €39–47, depending on the comfort. Good classic dishes are served in the restaurant: foie gras, house terrine, country-style tart, chicken liver soufflé, and pork stew. Menu €12.50 (not Sun). Cheaply priced wines. It's lively in high season. *10% discount on the room rate (2 Jan–30 April) offered to our readers on presentation of this guide.*

Château de Passières**

Take the D526 from Mens to Clelles, then the D7 to the foot of Mont Aiguille.
☎04.76.34.45.48 Ⓕ04.76.34.46.25
Closed *Sun evening in winter; Dec–Jan.* **TV. Swimming pool. Car park.**

A fifteenth-century château in a magnificent location. Attractive rooms, all have up-to-date facilities and cost €49 with shower/wc or bath. Nos. 1, 4 and 5, with their original wood panelling, cost €66. You can sit and chat in the charming sitting room – a veritable picture gallery – well into the small hours. There's a good bar, and imaginative cooking is served in a large dining room. Menus from €19–32 list specialities such as *compote* of duck and trout with walnuts, turnovers studded with truffles on a creamed leek *fondue*, salmon steak with dandelion honey, *fricassée* of ceps and snails on a bed of ravioli. There's a nice swimming pool in the grounds, and tennis courts.

Mirmande

26270

Restaurant Margot

It's near the post office. Down the village.
☎04.75.63.08.05
Closed *Tues, Oct–Dec and March–May; Jan–Feb.*

This restaurant, like the listed village, is a mixture of stylishness and rustic simplicity. It's a place for people who love old-style cooking. In summer you can go inside to cool off in the tastefully decorated dining room with an old wooden table , or sit out on a bench on the terrace in the shade of the climbing vines. There's a weekday lunch menu at €14 and others up to €25. You get a good choice of regional specialities but dishes constantly change: terrine of *pot-au-feu* with onion marmalade, braised veal *à la provençale*, lamb Tonton Firmin, chocolate *fondant*. They host occasional jazz evenings. *Free house apéritif offered to our readers on presentation of this guide.*

Cliousclat

26270 (2km N)

🏃 🏠 🍽 La Treille Muscate**

It's 1km from Mirmande on the D57.
Ⓣ04.75.63.13.10 Ⓕ04.75.63.10.79
Ⓦwww.latreillemuscate.com
Closed *Wed; 15 Dec–1 March*. **Disabled access. TV. Car park.**

A large, pretty house with green shutters and walls half-covered in ivy. Inside, the rooms have a sophisticated charm and some have a terrace with a view over the countryside; they cost €60 with shower/wc and €80 with bath. There's a lovely enclosed garden and the dining room is bright and roomy with a corner fireplace and a few stylish tables. The cuisine, which uses local produce, is typical of this sunny region: grilled red mullet with broccoli, veal *piccata* with lemon and ginger, pressed chicken in a *pot-au-feu* with mustard, pork cheek with lemon and ginger, *aioli* fish stew. The weekday lunch menu at €15 offers great value, and there's another at €25. *Free coffee offered to our readers on presentation of this guide.*

Modane

73500

🏠 🍽 Hôtel-restaurant Le Perce-Neige**

14 av. Jean-Jaurès; it's opposite the station. Take the A43 exit 30.
Ⓣ04.79.05.00.50 Ⓕ04.79.05.12.92
Ⓔauperceneige@wanadoo.fr
Closed *Sun, 27 April–22 June and 19 Oct–5 Nov; 1–19 May.* **Disabled access. TV.**

This is an ideal place for an overnight stop in a town that is not sufficiently appealing for a longer stay. The rooms are simple; doubles €42 with shower/wc and up to €55.50 with bath. They're all well soundproofed, which is just as well since the hotel is on the road and opposite the railway track. The nicest ones are at the back, overlooking the river. Traditional local cooking listed on menus from €14–19.20.

Montbrison

42600

🏠 🍽 Le Gil de France**

18 bis bd. Lachèze; it's just beyond the centre.
Ⓣ04.77.58.06.16 Ⓕ04.77.58.73.78
Ⓔgil-de-france@wanadoo.fr
Restaurant closed *Fri and Sun evenings 1 Oct–1 May*. **TV. Disabled access. High chairs available. Car park.**

A modern hotel on the outskirts of town, situated in front of a big park. The rooms are bright and fresh with modern facilities and go for €45 with shower/wc or bath. Menus €11 (weekday lunchtimes) and €14–25. Good welcome.

Champdieu

42600 (5km NW)

🍽 Hostellerie du Prieuré

Route de Boën; it's on the D8, away from the centre.
Ⓣ04.77.58.31.21
Open *lunch and dinner time Tues, Wed, Thurs (except Thurs evening, by bookings only).* **Closed** *Aug*. **Car park.**

A nice place, on the border of the *département* that is run by a chef who's absolutely expert at traditional cooking techniques. He offers a simple weekday lunch menu for €11.50 and more complex choices on the other menus (€16.50–22). Try the frogs' legs with garlic and herbs, or perch fillet in a mushroom sauce.

Saint-Romain-le-Puy

42610 (8km SE)

🏃 🏠 🍽 Auberge Les Trabuches**

Take the D8 from Sury-le-Comtal to Montbrison, turn left before the Parot spring and follow the signs to the right.
Ⓣ04.77.97.79.70 Ⓕ04.77.97.79.74
Restaurant open *Wed–Sun lunchtimes*. **Hotel closed** *Mon–Tues*. **TV. Car park.**

Three simple rooms with basin (€34) share common bathing and toilet facilities; the five others have en-suite shower/wc and cost €42. In the restaurant, they serve simple menus: frogs' legs, rabbit terrine, meat dishes with sauce, and home-made desserts. You'll pay €11 for the weekday menu, with others at €15.50 and €21.50. Cheery welcome. *Free house apéritif offered to our readers on presentation of this guide.*

Montélimar

26200

Hôtel Pierre**

7 pl. des Clercs; it's near the church of Sainte-Croix in the old Montélimar town, next to a little square.
Ⓣ04.75.01.33.16
Closed *Feb.* **TV.**

This prettily renovated sixteenth-century town house on a small square is delightful. Its porch, candelabra-studded corridor, paved courtyard, ivy-covered terrace and dressed stone staircase create a striking atmosphere. The twelve rooms – €27 with basin, €41 with bath – are fairly ordinary compared to the rest of the place, though some have been refurbished. The best is no. 2, which has a balcony swamped in Virginia creeper. There's space to park bikes.

Hôtel du Parc**

27 bd. Charles-de-Gaulle.
Ⓣ04.75.01.00.73 Ⓕ04.75.51.27.93
Ⓦwww.i-s-f.com/tourim/hdcparc
TV. Cots available. Pay car park.

Classic hotel, opposite the park, modernized and well-situated, near the town centre. Bright, comfortable rooms with double glazing cost €44–60 with shower/wc or bath; choose the rooms at the back which are very quiet. The owners keep it spotless and welcome you most civilly.

Hôtel Beausoleil**

Place d'Armes-Allées Provencales.
Ⓣ04.75.01.19.80
Ⓔhotelbeausoleil@hotmail.com
TV. Pay car park.

A characterful hotel offering sixteen pleasant rooms at €45 with shower/wc or bath. It's well away from the traffic but close to the centre of the town. Breakfast is served in a lovely garden. The new owners are in command of this well-situated place. *10% discount on the room rate offered to our readers on presentation of this guide.*

Sphinx Hôtel**

19 bd. Marre-Desmarais.
Ⓣ04.75.01.86.64 Ⓕ04.75.52.34.21
Ⓦwww.sphinx-hotel.fr
Closed *Christmas to mid-Jan.* **TV. Pay car park (€3).**

Exceedingly well-located away from the traffic noise, this is a lovely seventeenth-century private mansion with an ivy-swathed exterior and wood panelling and antique furniture inside. The salon has a tranquil atmosphere. You get an appropriately stylish welcome. The rooms are adorable and have good facilities and comfort. Doubles €48–61 with shower/wc or bath, depending on the season. When it's sunny, breakfast is served on the terrace.

Le Chalet du Parc

Boulevard Marre Desmarais, allées Provençales; it's behind the kiosk and the tourist office.
Ⓣ04.75.51.16.42
Closed *Mon evening; Tues; a fortnight in Feb; a fortnight end Sept.* **Disabled access.**

A dynamic young couple took over this place with the express aim of turning it into a top-class gourmet restaurant. And the cooking is indeed inspired, produced by a chef who's bursting with ideas and enthusiasm. He puts together remarkable combinations of flavours and uses only fresh produce: *tartare* of crayfish tails and fresh salmon, beef with morels, grilled *sûpreme* of guinea fowl with fresh herbs and luscious *dôme de chocolat* with iced vanilla. Menus €17–30. The downstairs dining room is still a little bare but they've put all the effort into what really counts – the cooking. And on nice days, you can sit on the terrace overlooking the park. The sort of place you would like to come across more often.

Valaurie

26230 (18km SE)

Domaine Les Méjeonnes***

Take the RN7, then the D133 in the direction of Grignan-Noyons; it's 1km from the village.
Ⓣ04.75.98.60.60 Ⓕ04.75.98.63.44
Closed *Wed.* **Disabled access. High chairs available. Swimming pool. TV. Car park.**

If you want to see this old farmhouse at its best, arrive in the mellow glow of late afternoon or in the evening when the floodlights illuminate the vines and the old stones. Lovely, spacious, comfortable rooms go for €63 for a double with shower/wc or bath. Menus at €20–30 list good, appetizing food. Service a bit slow, but who's in a hurry? You'll get a courteous welcome – and the swimming pool is superb.

Montrottier

69770

L'Auberge des Blés d'Or**

La Curtillat – route de Saint-Julien-sur-Bibost. Take the N89, then the D7; after Saint-Bel, head for Bibost, then take the D246 and keep going until 2km before Montrottier.
Ⓣ and Ⓕ 04.74.70.13.56
Closed *evenings (except by reservation); Tues.* **Disabled access. TV. Car park.**

It's best to book in season to be sure of a room or a table; out of season, check that they're serving meals. This country inn, which stands alone among the fields and is surrounded by flowers, has been superbly restored. The rooms with shower/wc (€49.55) are in an annexe and look over the valley. They boast all mod cons and total silence. Half board at €54.88 per person. The lovely, rustic dining room has a creaking parquet floor and vast beams. Flavoursome cuisine with a regional slant on menus, €16 and €22, with a children's menu at €10. You can sit on your terrace watching the sun go down behind the hills, with the church of Montrottier illuminated in the distance. *Free house apéritif, liqueur or coffee offered to our readers on presentation of this guide.*

Morzine

74110

Les Prodains**

Prodains; it's 4km from the centre of Morzine at the foot of the Avoriaz ski-lift.
Ⓣ 04.50.79.25.26 Ⓕ 04.50.75.76.17
Ⓔ hotellesprodains@aol.com
Closed *21 April–25 June; 10 Sept–7 Dec.* **TV. Disabled access. High chairs and games available. Swimming pool. Car park.**

You'll get a very warm welcome at this friendly family establishment at the foot of the ski runs. The chalet has pretty rooms, some of which are renovated; some have balconies with a fantastic view of the slopes. Doubles with shower/wc or bath from €46 in summer, €60 in winter. The huge terrace gets swamped by skiers as soon as the sun comes out. Menus €18–22; although you can certainly get a tasty *tartiflette*, the inventive cooking is not limited to mountain dishes. There's a swimming pool in summer, which is also when the boss offers trips to a nearby mountain hut where he serves tasty mountain dishes.

Hôtel Les Lans***

Village des Prodains; it's 300m from the cable car that goes to Avoriaz.
Ⓣ 04.50.79.00.90 Ⓕ 04.50.79.15.22
Ⓦ www.leslans.com
Open *evenings 7–8pm.* **Closed** *early April to early July; end Aug to mid-Dec.* **TV. High chairs and games available. Car park.**

He used to be a ski instructor, she's mad about local history and culture – today, along with their two daughters, they put life into this huge newly built chalet. The prices are unbeatable considering what you get. Half board is compulsory, costing €55–90 per person. Monsieur Mallurez happily takes care of the cooking but escapes from the kitchen once a week to take people on wildlife discovery trips, while Madame conducts guided tours. During some periods of the summer, trips are free for children under ten. *10% discount on the room rate offered to our readers on presentation of this guide.*

Restaurant La Grangette

It's near the Nyon cable car.
Ⓣ 04.50.79.05.76
Closed *Mon evening; 20 April–1 June; 25 Sept–25 Oct; 15 Nov–15 Dec.* **High chairs available.**

A little family business at the foot of the ski slopes where you can enjoy a tasty meal in a friendly atmosphere. The €11.50 lunch menu gets you the dish of the day – stew or roast veal with mushrooms, *gratin dauphinois*, chips or vegetables – and home-made tart for dessert. Other menus €18.50–34. The house speciality is frog's legs in cream sauce. Lots of walking trails start (and finish) here. *Free coffee offered to our readers on presentation of this guide.*

La Chamade

Centre; it's near the tourist office.
Ⓣ 04.50.79.13.91
Closed *Tues and Wed out of season; May; 11 Nov–10 Dec.* **High chairs available.**

This is a local institution. First impressions might lead you to dismiss it as touristy and kitsch, offering little but salads and pizzas. Venture in, however, to experience delicious local specialities prepared by the young chef. He adores pork in all its guises, and offers, among other things, pâté of pig's head, *atriaux* (a type of patty) and mountain suckling pig with apple fritters. There's one menu at €42, or expect to pay €33 à la carte. *Free coffee or house liqueur offered to our readers on presentation of this guide.*

Montriond

74110 (6km NW)

Auberge La Chalande

Lieu-dit Ardent.
04.50.79.19.69
Closed *Mon; 20 April–30 June; 15 Sept–15 Dec.* **High chairs available.**

This old chalet feels like it's way out in a lost mountain hamlet – though it's actually at the foot of the ski lifts going up to Avoriaz. It used to belong to the owner's mother, and he hasn't changed the warm, rustic surroundings a bit. He turns out delicious dishes, whether you choose from the menus (€21–43), or go à la carte: cheese *croûte*, braised sausage with leeks and potato fritters. Reservations essential. *Free house liqueur or coffee offered to our readers on presentation of this guide.*

Moûtiers

73600

Hôtel Welcome's**

33 rue Greyffié-de-Bellecombe; it's near the station.
04.79.24.00.48 04.79.22.99.96
www.perso.wanadoo.fr/hotel.welcome
Restaurant *closed Sun.* **Disabled access. TV. Pay car park.**

A comfortable station hotel where they pride themselves on giving a nice welcome. The pleasant rooms cost €52.80–55 for a double with bath – the ones at the rear are very quiet. Half board is compulsory Friday and Saturday in winter season at €46–51 per person. You get traditional cooking in the restaurant, where they serve a few brasserie dishes and some good fish courses. Weekday lunch menu (brasserie) for €12, and restaurant menus €16–28. Free parking spaces for motorcycles and bikes. Credit cards not accepted. *Free house apéritif offered to our readers on presentation of this guide.*

Léchère (La)

73260 (12km NW)

Restaurant La Vieille Forge

Bellecombe; take exit 37, signposted Valmorel.
04.79.24.17.97
Open *evenings only; 7pm–midnight, except Fri–Sat until 4am.* Closed *lunchtimes; Tues (except July–Aug); Feb.* **Disabled access. Car park.**

You won't find the usual stultified spa town atmosphere in this restaurant. It used to be a blacksmith's, and the décor features some of the old smithy equipment. Tasty, traditional cooking, Savoy specialities, meat dishes in sauce, mushrooms and duck breast are listed on the set menus at €10.50–30; some of these include wine. You'll pay around €18 for a menu à la carte. There's live music every Friday and they're open very late – until 4am in summer. *Free house apéritif offered to our readers on presentation of this guide.*

Valmorel

73260 (14km SW)

Château du Crey**

Les Avanchers, hameau du Crey; take the D95 and it's at the lower end of the resort.
04.79.09.87.00 04.79.09.89.51
www.chalet-du-crey.com
Closed *20 April–31 May; 30 Sept–20 Dec.* **TV. Disabled access. High chairs available. Swimming pool. Car park.**

A classic family-run chalet in an authentic mountain hamlet. Everyone knows how to give you a warm welcome. Rooms are well appointed; doubles with shower/wc or bath cost €38–45 in summer. Half board, compulsory during the February schools holidays, costs €39–53 per person per night. There are family rooms, for four to five people, available too. In the restaurant, menus, which list mountain dishes, cost €12 and €18. À la carte, you choose from a range of Savoy specialities, and you'll spend about €30. The vast swimming pool, open in summer, is rather unusual – it's inflatable. *10% discount on the room rate (in summer) offered to our readers on presentation of this guide.*

Restaurant Le Ski Roc

It's in a pedestrianized street off the main street.
04.79.09.83.17

Open *until midnight*. **Closed** *25 April–20 June; 5 Sept–15 Dec.*

This is the place to eat in Valmorel. The wine bar is decorated in a discreetly baroque style, and they dish up good food, with mountain specialities and some modern choices. Take a nice glass of local wine with a toasted sandwich. Covered and heated terrace. Weekday menu for €14 and others at €19 and €23. *Free house liqueur offered to our readers on presentation of this guide.*

Nantua

01130

🏃 |●| Restaurant Belle Rive

23 rte. de la Cluse; take the N84 from La Cluse and it's just before you get to Nantua.
Ⓣ04.74.75.16.60
Open *all day, every day in summer*. **Closed** *Tues and Thurs evenings, Wed in winter*. **Car park.**

This place, right by the lake, is popular with families doing big get-togethers and local workers for lunch. You'll need to book or get there early if you want a table on the pleasant veranda overlooking the lake. The €10.10 lunch menu is pretty decent, and there are others at €15–31. They specialize in the famous *quenelles de* Nantua (meatballs served with a crayfish butter sauce). You have to wait a full fifteen minutes for them; they're freshly cooked and well worth it. They also offer house foie gras, house smoked salmon, terrines and so on.

Charix

01130 (10km SE)

⌂ |●| Auberge du Lac Genin

Take the N84 in the direction of Bellegarde, then turn left at Le Martinet onto the D95.
Ⓣ04.74.75.52.50 Ⓕ04.74.75.51.15
Ⓦwww.lacgenin.com
Closed *Sun evening; Mon; 15 Oct–1 Dec*. **TV. High chairs and games available. Car park.**

The magnificent lake and the setting in the beautiful dark Jura forests make the trip up here worthwhile. In summer, it's a paradise for fishermen and walkers, but be sure to have the right equipment and chains on your car tyres in winter – the weather can be really severe. Unsurprisingly, the best rooms have windows onto the lake. They aren't exactly luxurious, but prices aren't high: €20 with basin, €31 with shower/wc and €40 with bath. The €11 menu is pretty ordinary, but there are three others up to €18 listing mountain ham, meats grilled on the open fire, wine sausage and veal cutlet with mustard. It's substantial rather than gourmet cooking and there's a real family atmosphere. Nice welcome; in summer the place gets very full.

Châtillon-de-Michaille

01200 (12km SE)

⌂ |●| 🏃 Auberge de la Fontaine**

Ochiaz; take the N206, then the N84, turn off at the Ochiaz exit and take the D101 to Châtillon.
Ⓣ04.50.56.57.23 Ⓕ04.50.56.56.55
Ⓦwww.multimania.com/fontaine01
Closed *Sun and Tues evenings, Mon; 7–29 Jan; 8–18 June; 29 Sept–6 Oct*. **Disabled access. High chairs and games available. Car park.**

This pretty stone inn, festooned with flowers in summer, is just next to a bubbling fountain in a delightful village. It is a smart little place without being formal. The rooms are comfortable and quiet and you'll get a restorative night's sleep at reasonable prices – doubles €31 with basin, €37 with shower/wc or bath. You can eat very well, too – duck foie gras terrine, turbot in champagne, Bresse chicken with morels, pike *quenelles* – though dishes are perhaps a little conventional. Weekday menu at €15, then continue at €20–46. *10% discount on the room rate (except July–Aug) offered to our readers on presentation of this guide.*

Lalleyriat

01130 (14km E)

🏃 |●| Les Gentianes

Take the N84 in the direction of Bellegarde as far as Neyrolles and then the D55.
Ⓣ04.74.75.31.80
Closed *Tues; Wed; Sun evening; 6–31 Jan*. **Disabled access. High chairs and games available.**

Given that it's named after a mountain flower, you'd expect to find that this lovely stone-walled village inn specializes in traditional mountain food. The Parisian chef does serve regional cuisine, but he also offers unexpected dishes such as free-range chicken with crayfish and langoustines sauce Nantua, beef fillets with morels. Prices are fair: weekday menu at €23, other menus €38. *Free house apéritif offered to our readers on presentation of this guide.*

Lancrans

01200 (17km S)

Le Sorgia**

Grande-Rue; take the D991 to Lélex and Mijoux.
04.50.48.15.81 04.50.48.44.72
Closed *Mon; Sat lunchtime; Sun evening; 1–5 Jan, 20 Aug–15 Sept, 20–31 Dec.* **TV. High chairs and games available. Car park.**

An old village bar-restaurant named after the mountain in front of it. Over the last century it has grown to become a hotel-restaurant with a balcony and veranda overlooking the valley. The rooms are comfortable and pleasant and filled with period furniture. Doubles €43 with shower/wc and €45 with bath. They serve simple, local dishes in generous portions: lake whitefish (freshwater salmon) cooked in Savoy wine, pan-fried scallops with oyster mushrooms, snails and baby mushrooms in flaky pastry. €14 weekday menu and others €23 and €29. Pleasant welcome. *Free house apéritif offered to our readers on presentation of this guide.*

Noirétable

42440

Hôtel-restaurant Au Rendez-vous des Chasseurs**

Route de l'Hermitage; it's about 1km from the centre of the village on the D53 (in the direction of Vollore-Montagne).
04.77.24.72.51 04.77.24.93.40
Closed *Sun evening and Mon out of season; Sun in Jan–Feb; 22 Feb–3 March; 12 Sept–6 Oct.* **TV. Car park.**

Though the thundering motorway is just 6km away, all you can see from the dining room of this hotel are the Forez mountains. The inn has fourteen rooms – €24.45 with basin and €35.85 with bath. The cheapest menu in the week is at €10, and there are others at €16.80–31.50. All the scents and flavours of Forez can be found in the dishes here, which might include home-made charcuterie, grilled trout, *parfait* of chicken liver with bilberries, pigeon *pot-au-feu*, chicken legs stuffed *à la fourme* (cheese) and game in season. *Free coffee offered to our readers on presentation of this guide.*

Salles (Les)

42440 (5 km NE)

Domaine de la Plagnette

Via the A72-E70 motorway, take the Noirétable exit then go in the direction of Saint-Julien-la-Vêtre; after the village of Chaumette, turn left in the direction of La Plagnette; via the N89 from Boën, turn right towards Les Salles in Saint-Jules-la-Vêtre; after Le Verdier, turn right in the direction of La Plagnette.
04.77.97.74.10 04.77.97.74.11
domaine@plagnette.com
Closed *Wed (except July–Aug); Jan.* **TV. Disabled access. Car park.**

This establishment is distinguished by the comfort of its high-quality accommodation, the beauty of its unspoilt natural surroundings, its convivial service and its peaceful restlessness. You will be warmly welcomed into the old, restored farmhouse, near a three-hectare lake replete with fish surrounded by a wood. Double rooms €42. Apart from the seven spacious, well-equipped rooms, there are also two self-catering cottages, Ideal for families (they sleep eight people). The restaurant is a more recent addition that adjoins the farm and offers simple, regional food at reasonable prices: Fourmiflette (*tartiflette* with Fourme cheese) and *pannequets* with Fourme from Montbrison. Weekday menu €10, then others €13–19.

Juré

42430 (20km NE)

Auberge Le Moulin

Take the D53 and turn right onto the D86 before you get to Saint-Just-en-Chevalet.
04.77.62.55.24
Open *Sat; Sun; public holidays March–Nov from 11.30am–8.30pm; Tues–Sun July–Aug.* **Closed** *mid Nov–early March.* **Disabled access.**

This little inn in an old mill has an idyllic setting. Its electricity is supplied by the stream running underneath, and apparently, the Lumière brothers made their first moving pictures here. It's a shame it's not open more. The country menus, €11–18, are delicious, and offer excellent home-made terrines cooked in a wood-fuelled oven, rissoles, charcuteries, omelettes, free-range poultry, and home-made pastries.

Very affordable wines. *Free house apéritif or liqueur offered to our readers on presentation of this guide.*

Nyons

26110

☗ |●| La Picholine***

Promenade de la Perrière; it's on the hilltop as you come into the town.
Ⓣ04.75.26.06.21 Ⓕ04.75.26.40.72
Closed *Feb; end Oct to mid-Nov. Restaurant closed Mon and Tues (Oct–April); Mon (May–Sept).* **TV. Swimming pool. Car park.**

The décor in the foyer and the restaurant is a bit chi-chi, but the owners make a real fuss of their guests. Big, light and pleasant rooms €50–66. Ask for a room that has breathtaking view looking south to the valley and the garden or to the swimming pool. Half board, €50–62 per person, is compulsory July–Aug. Decent food – the menus at €21.50, €26 and €37 offer extremely satisfying regional dishes. The swimming pool is surrounded by olive trees.

|●| Le Petit Caveau

9 rue Victor Hugo; it's in the street at right angles to the Pavillon du Tourisme.
Ⓣ04.75.26.20.21
Closed *Sun evening; Mon.*

Good wine, experienced chef and excellent cuisine – you get the best of both worlds at reasonable prices. An ingenious *formule* allows you to try different wines depending on your mood. Try the roast saddle of rabbit with hazelnuts, roast lamb, *confit* of lamb chops, sweetbread and kidney kebabs or red pepper risotto. Lunch menu €18 (not Sun or public holidays), others €29–45.

Condorcet

26110 (7km NE)

|●| La Charrette Bleue

Route de Gap. Take the D94.
Ⓣ04.75.27.72.33
Closed *Tues; Wed; Sun evening Oct–March; autumn school holidays; mid-Dec to end Jan.*

Word of mouth is always the best publicity – just follow the trail and you'll get here. Very professional, honest cooking: tradition with an individual twist. Fresh herbs from the hills and the heath are deliciously combined. Great dishes include deboned pigeon stuffed with roast foie gras, roast lamb in a garlic crust, and guineafowl *confit* with a light smoked tomato sauce. Menus €17 (weekday lunchtimes), others €35. Lots of Côtes-du-Rhône wines on the list. Glass of wine from €2.70. The dining room is prettily arranged and there's a terrace for sunny days – the best tables are under the olive trees. Delectable cuisine, warm welcome and efficient service.

Mirabel-aux-Baronnies

26110 (7km SW)

|●| La Coloquinte

Avenue de la Résistance; take the D538 in the direction of Vaison-la-Romaine.
Ⓣ04.75.27.19.89
Closed *Wed out of season; Christmas to early Jan.* **Disabled access.**

When the sun's out it's nice to sit on the lovely shaded patio; otherwise you dine in the colourful dining room with hefty beams and well-spaced tables. The food is good and only fresh seasonal produce is used. Menus €20–32.50; à la carte reckon on €35. The colourful dishes are full of flavour, very carefully prepared and seasoned – the fish is cooked to perfection, and the terrines are great, too. To finish, they offer a fine choice of perfectly ripe cheeses and various desserts. The wine list includes a good selection of Côtes-du-Rhones.

Saint-Ferréol-Trente-Pas

26110 (10km NE)

☗ |●| Auberge de Trente Pas

It's in the village; from Nyons, take the D94, then the D70 in the direction of Bourdeaux.
Ⓣ and Ⓕ04.75.27.71.39
Ⓦwww.guideweb.com/provence/hotel/trente-pas
Closed *mid-Nov to mid-March.* **Restaurant closed** *lunchtimes; open evenings by reservation only.* **Reading area for children.**

The village is typical of those found in the mountains of the Drôme. This straightforward establishment has very simple, clean rooms and family cuisine prepared with soul. You're served in the convivial dining room. There's just one menu at €14.50, or €19 on Sunday lunchtimes. Véronique makes you feel welcome; she's enjoying her country retreat after years in polluted Paris. Rooms start at €34 with basin and rise to €41 with shower/wc. Credit cards not accepted.

Oyonnax

01100

Nouvel Hôtel**

31 rue René-Nicod; 150m from the train station, 5min walking distance to the town centre.
Ⓣ04.74.77.28.11 Ⓕ04.74.77.03.71
Ⓦwww.nouvelhotel.fr
TV. Pay car park.

Despite its name, this place is getting on a bit – but it's not without individuality, as you'll see when you get to reception. The refurbished rooms are good value. Doubles cost €31–40, depending on facilities. It's the little things they do that make all the difference: you can have breakfast brought to your room for no extra charge. *Free car park space offered to our readers on presentation of this guide.*

Hôtel-restaurant Buffard**

Place de l'Église; it's in the middle of town, 100m from the train station.
Ⓣ04.74.77.86.01 Ⓕ04.74.73.77.68
Ⓦwww.hotelbuffard.com
Restaurant closed *Fri and Sun evenings; Sat; 25 July–15 Aug.* **TV. High chairs available. Car park.**

This hotel-restaurant has maintained its excellent reputation for more than a hundred years – it celebrated its centenary in 1998. Rooms with period furniture cost €38–55, depending on the comfort and the season. In the restaurant they serve rich home cooking in generous portions. Menus €12–28. Specialities include *quenelles Nantua, gratin* of crayfish tails, chicken *fricassée* with *vin jaune, délice* of duck liver, *escalope franc-comtoise. Free house liqueur offered to our readers on presentation of this guide.*

Peisey-Nancroix

73210

Restaurant Chez Félix

Plan-Peisey; it's between Les Mélèzes and Val Landry.
Ⓣ04.79.07.92.41
Closed *Mon; mid-April to mid-Dec.* **High chairs available. Car park.**

This nineteenth-century Alpine chalet with a lovely annex for the summer is situated on the edge of the Vanoise park. This place serves crêpes and regional specialities including *diots* with polenta, *berthoud, tartiflette* and so on. The dish of the day costs around €9, the *menu campagnard* €13; à la carte, if you opt for crêpes you'll spend about €13, or around €23 for a Savoyard meal. *Free coffee offered to our readers on presentation of this guide.*

Pont-d'Ain

01160

Restaurant-bar Le Terminus

71 rue Saint-Exupéry; take exit 9 off the A42, then take the N75 in the direction of Bourg-en-Bresse.
Ⓣ04.74.39.07.17
Closed *Sun evening; Mon; evenings before public holidays.* **Car park.**

This restaurant has two pretty little dining rooms and a terrace for warm weather. The real effort goes into the cooking rather than the décor; you get generous portions of regional food at decent prices. Try the Bresse chicken with cream, the parsleyed veal kidneys or the frogs' legs. Menus start at €11.50, with others at €15–27. Friendly welcome and efficient service.

Privas

07000

Hôtel la Chaumette Porte des Suds***

Avenue du Vanel; 10min from the centre on foot.
Ⓣ04.75.64.30.66 Ⓕ04.75.64.88.25
Ⓦwww.hotelchaumette.fr
Closed *Sat lunch.* **Disabled access.**

This hotel dates from the 1970s but it has managed to take on a new lease of life. The comfortable rooms, complete with air-conditioning, are decorated in the warm colours of the South, just like the restaurant. Double rooms €56.70–75.90, depending on the degree of comfort. Original, seasonal cooking that draws on the local produce. Weekday lunchtime menu €16, then others going up to €38.

The atmosphere is more than charming, for this hotel exudes a serenity all its own.

🚶 |●| Le Gourmandin

Cours de l'Esplanade; it's on the corner of rue Pierre-Fillat.
☎04.75.64.51.52
Closed *Sun evening; Mon.*

This is the best place to eat in Privas – you could genuinely call it a fine table. Philippe Bourjas has a way of modernizing local dishes and refining old recipes with delicate and creative adjustments. And he doesn't stint on the portions, generously served. Weekday lunchtime formule €11.50, there are four other menus €15–36.50. The setting is sober, the service conscientious and pleasant but without fuss. There's a good wine list. Good value for money. *Free coffee offered to our readers on presentation of this guide.*

Alissas

07210 (4km SE)

🚶 |●| Restaurant Lous Esclos

Quartier Rabagnol; it's beside the D2, which bypasses Alissas.
☎04.75.65.12.73
Closed *Sun evening; Mon; 3 weeks in Aug; 3 weeks between Christmas and New Year.* **Disabled access. High chairs available. Car park.**

A rather stylish place in a slip-road. The air-conditioned dining room is quiet and the bay windows look out over the bare hills. The weekday lunch menu for €10.70, and at least eight others from €14–38, include such dishes as pan-fried snails with *sauce Esclos*, chicken tart with crayfish tail *jus*, beef with morels, house charcuterie and *mignon* of pork with Madeira sauce. It's all nicely prepared and you can appreciate the quality of the seasonal produce. Incidentally, *esclos* is local dialect for "clogs". *Free coffee offered to our readers on presentation of this guide.*

Baix

07210 (24km E)

⌂ |●| 🚶 L'Auberge des Quatre Vents**

Route de Chomérac; it's on the D2, then right on the N86, 3km from Baix.
☎and ℗04.75.85.84.49
Closed *Sat lunchtime and Sun evening out of season; 3 weeks in Jan.* **TV. Disabled access. Car park.**

There's a soothing atmosphere in the large and light but soberly decorated dining room. Good, local dishes are listed on the *menu du jour* at €11 and on the others from €17–36. Fairly priced wines, too. The smart, quiet rooms cost €28–40 depending on facilities – they're all clean and modern. *Free house apéritif offered to our readers on presentation of this guide.*

Quincié-en-Beaujolais

69430

🚶 |●| Restaurant Au Raisin Beaujolais

Take the D37 from Beaujeu in the direction of Saint-Vincent and it's on the right about 4km along the road.
☎04.74.04.32.79
©cabannes-gerard@wanadoo.fr
Closed evenings; *Sat; 1–22Aug; last week in Dec.* **Disabled access. High chairs available. Car park.**

The food at this unpretentious bistro is just what you need to soak up all those wine tastings. The chatty proprietor looks after the dining room while his wife runs the kitchen, preparing the tasty, slowly cooked dishes. There's a weekday menu at €12.40 and others €14.90–22.10; dishes include chicken liver terrine, snails in garlic butter and *andouillette Bobosse* (a type of sausage) in Mâcon-Villages and local cream cheese. Frogs' legs available if previously ordered. When it comes to the wine, you have a huge choice of Beaujolais *appellations*. There's an enclosed, air-conditioned terrace, which is great in summer. *Free Kir offered to our readers on presentation of this guide.*

🚶 |●| Auberge du Pont des Samsons

Le-Pont-des-Samsons; take the D37 in the direction of Beaujeu.
☎04.74.04.32.09
Closed *Wed evening; Thurs; 2–12 Jan.* **Car park.**

The crossroads is hardly an ideal location, and the restaurant doesn't look much from the outside. But the décor is nice and it's spotlessly clean. Better still, the excellent dishes are served in huge portions: frogs' legs *à la provençale*, foie gras, salad of scallops or squid, half cockerel with cider and prunes, zander with butter sauce, fan of red mullet fillets with almonds and basil sauce, duck breast with red fruits, *brioche* with morel sauce, steak with green peppercorns. Menu served every day except public holidays at €17, others at €23 and €27 and around €30 à la carte. Attentive service from start to finish. *Free coffee offered to our readers on presentation of this guide.*

Chiroubles

69115 (10km NE)

La Terrasse du Beaujolais

Route d'Avenas; take the D9 to Villié-Morgon, then turn left onto the D86.
☎ and ℻ 04.74.69.90.79
Closed *Mon evening and Tues (from early March to end Nov); Mon–Fri (early Dec–end Feb).* **Disabled access. High chairs and games available. Car park.**

A gorgeous place on the winding road that leads you to the major Beaujolais vineyards. Blessed by a cool breeze year round, it also has a playground for children with swing and slide, and attracts lots of famililes at weekends. They do good mixed salads, great terrines and tarts and pastries with all manner of fillings. Menus €20.50–48; the first is interesting, with, for example, a house terrine and nicely cooked Beaujolais *andouillette. Free house apéritif or coffee offered to our readers on presentation of this guide.*

Rive-de-Gier

42800

Restaurant Georges Paquet

Combeplaine; take the La Madeleine exit off the A47.
☎ 04.77.75.02.18
Closed *Sun lunchtime (except public holidays); Sun–Thurs evenings; a week in Feb; 20 July–20 Aug.* **Disabled access. Car park.**

Set in a desolate area of factories and industrial wasteland between the motorway and the main road, this restaurant serves good food. It's got a hushed atmosphere and is decorated in bright, warm colours. The speciality is seafood and there are all sorts of fish served with tasty sauces. The weekday lunch menu, €14.50, offers a choice of three starters and three main courses followed by cheese or dessert; other menus at €22–39. Gastronomes could also go to the "Hostellerie de la Renaissance", 41-rue Marrel ☎ 04.77.75.04.31, the largest Rive-de-Gier's restaurant. *Free coffee offered to our readers on presentation of this guide.*

Saint-Martin-la-Plaine

42800 (8km NW)

Le Flamant Rose

Take the D37, and follow the signs to the Parc Zoologique.
☎ 04.77.75.91.13
Closed *Sun and Mon evenings, 1–15 Aug.* **Disabled access. High chairs available.**

The beautiful terrace is the only lovely thing about this big building, which stands in front of a stretch of water opposite the zoo. Inside, however, the two dining rooms get lots of light. Weekday lunch menu €9.50 and others €17.50–36.50. The chef takes some risks, successfully combining sweet and savoury flavours. They can also prepare you a picnic for about €8.50. *Free house apéritif offered to our readers on presentation of this guide.*

Sainte-Croix-en-Jarez

42800 (10km SE)

Le Prieuré*

Take the D30, towards Sainte-Croix-en -Jarez.
☎ 04.77.20.20.09 ℻ 04.77.20.20.80
Closed *Mon; 2 Jan–28 Feb.* **TV.**

The road leading up to this delightful and beautiful place runs along the Couzon and past the dam. Here you get bed and board in the former guest quarters of a thirteenth-century monastery – most of it dismantled during the Revolution, when its stones were used to build the village. The four rooms, €48 with bath, are simple but well equipped and wonderfully quiet. The restaurant has a beamed ceiling; here you eat unpretentious, traditional cuisine and regional dishes including home-made terrines, chicken stuffed with morels, *tripe au gratin*, charcuterie and fresh cheeses. Weekday menu €15, others €19–34. The bar has a lovely vaulted ceiling and in summer there's a terrace on the village square – you'll appreciate the freshness of the air up here.

Roanne

42300

🏠 Hôtel de la Grenette

12 pl. Maréchal-de Lattre-de-Tassigny.
Ⓣ04.77.71.25.59 Ⓕ04.77.71.29.69
Closed *Christmas*. **TV.**

A little hotel taken over by a lovely lady who is refurbishing it. Rooms are basic but well maintained; €37 with shower, €41 with shower/wc. The reception is shut on Friday, Saturday and Sunday, so you'll need to phone in advance.

🏠 Hôtel Terminus**

15 cours de la République (place de la Gare); it's opposite the train station.
Ⓣ04.77.71.79.69 Ⓕ04.77.72.90.26
Ⓦwwwhotel-terminus-roanne.com
TV. High chairs available. Pay car park.

A good hotel of its kind, and well-located. It has about fifty rooms with bath (€40.50–46) – they're pretty standard. Ask for one overlooking the courtyard, where it's quieter. The terrace is nice in summer. Nice welcome.

🏠 Grand Hôtel***

18 cours de la République; in the town centre, opposite the train station.
Ⓣ04.77.71.48.82 Ⓕ04.77.70.42.40
Ⓦwww.grand-hotel.fr
Closed *1st week in Jan; first 3 weeks in Aug; last week in Dec*. **Pay car park. TV.**

A very comfortable hotel with elegant rooms that have recently been refurbished. The breakfast room, bar and lounges are enticing and the service is excellent. Double rooms €59–80.

|●| Le Central

20 cours de la République; it's opposite the train station.
Ⓣ04.77.67.72.72
Closed *Sun; Mon; 1–22 Aug*. **High chairs available. Disabled access.**

The Troisgros family – the nationally and internationally renowned chefs – have opened up this less expensive restaurant next door to their gourmet flagship, *Troisgros*. Rigged up to look like an old-fashioned grocery store, it sells smartly packaged pots of goodies, mustard with wine, duck *rillettes* and balsamic vinegar. There are photographs of the suppliers on the walls of the two dining rooms. Wonderfully inventive menus at €17 (weekday lunchtimes) and €22–25. Try cod *aïoli* with baby vegetables and the fabulous chocolate dessert. The wine is affordable and served bistro-style, with the bottle uncorked.

|●| L'Aventure

24 rue Pierre-Despierre. Towards Roanne, coming from Coteau.
Ⓣ04.77.68.01.15
Closed *Sun; Mon; a fortnight in Jan; 1–15 Aug.*

Jean-Luc Trambouze is a young chef from Roanne who's on the way up. You'll find his restaurant in a small street near the Loire. The frontage is bistro-blue but inside there's a cosy dining room decorated in pale colours. The kitchen opens out into the dining room – not to be showy but to add to the friendly atmosphere. The chef's dishes are full of imagination and fresh ideas. There are no particular specialities: it's the dynamism of the cooking and the audaciousness of the seasonings that make the dishes so distinctive. Excellent lunch menu for €20 which includes wine, and four others €22–35, including menu *dégustation* with five courses at €55. Affordable wine list.

Coteau (Le)

42120 (1km S)

|●| L'Auberge Costelloise

2 av. de la Libération; on the banks of the Loire, near the bridge going from Roanne to Coteau.
Ⓣ04.77.68.12.71
Closed *Sun; Mon; 1st week in May; 10 Aug–8 Sept; 26 Dec to early Jan.*

A cosy atmosphere and discreet but attentive service set the tone for the high-quality cooking of Christophe Souchon: gâteau of *foies blonds* with lobster *coulis*, risotto of veal sweetbreads with asparagus, fried foie gras with vinegar caramel and celery *confit*. Weekday lunchtime menu €15, weekday lunch and dinner €21.50, then others from €33–60. A real haven for gourmets.

Villerest

42300 (5 km S)

🏠 Hôtel du Domaine de Champlong**

From Roanne, go in the direction of Clermont-Ferrand straight on to the suburbs

of Clermont, ignoring the signs to Villerest centre, then take the first left after the sign for "The Cabaret de l'âne"; from the A72, take the Saint-Germain-Laval exit at 24km in the direction of Roanne.
Ⓣ04.77.69.78.78 Ⓕ04.77.69.35.45
Ⓦwww.hotel-champlong.com
Closed *Feb.* **TV. Car park.**

This hotel boasts a remarkable location in the countryside, just a few minutes from Roanne but also within easy distance of a boating centre, a golf course, a gourmet restaurant, four tennis courts and a riding club. So, although the rooms are comfortable and have their own terrace or balcony and the service is excellent, this establishment can also be recommended for its peaceful setting and the host of activities on offer nearby. Double rooms €53.50–71.50.

|●| Château de Champlong

100 chemin de la Chapelle; from Roanne, go in the direction of Clermont-Ferrand straight on to the suburbs of Clermont, ignoring the signs to Villerest centre, then take the first left after the sign for "The Cabaret de l'âne".
Ⓣ04.77.69.69.69

This fourteenth-century château with a 238-hectare estate provides an unbeatable setting for the delicious seasonal dishes prepared by Oivier Boizet. Customers savour his regional cuisine amid the splendour of a dining room adorned with seventeenth-century paintings. The cheapest menu goes for €19 (weekdays), then others from €27–55. You will leave this wonderful place with only one thought in mind: to come back soon!

Renaison

42370 (12km W)

⌂ |●| Hôtel-restaurant Central**

8 rue du 10-Août-1944; in the centre of the village, on the main square.
Ⓣ04.77.64.25.39 Ⓕ04.77.62.13.09
Closed *Wed.* **TV. Pay car park.**

A small hotel with eight comfortable rooms. Doubles €25–42. Its restaurant offers regional menus. Very good service.

Saint-Haon-le-Châtel

42370 (12km W)

|●| Au Natur'elles

In the centre of the village, opposite the council building.
Ⓣ04.77.62.12.01
Open *daily.* **Closed** *5–25 July.*

A delightful country bistro with a warm, family atmosphere in the pretty village of Saint-Haon-le-Châtel. The cooking is simple but tasty and very reasonably priced. Menu at €10. The rustic dining room is attractively decorated, right up to the ceiling, which is embellished by pitchforks and hessian sacks.

Pouilly-sous-Charlieu

42720 (14km N)

|●| Auberge du Château de Tigny

Take the D487, at the village's exit between Pouilly-sous-Charlieu and Charlieu.
Ⓣ04.77.60.09.55
Closed *Mon; Tues; Wed and Thurs evenings (5 Oct–5 May); 1–15 Jan; 15 Sept–7 Oct; 25–30 Dec.*

This is undoubtedly a favourite spot in the Roanne region. Jacques Rivière, a sometime market gardener who supplied the region's top restaurants, gave it all up to restore a magnificent little manor house and turn it into this delightful inn. There's also an exposition for the lovers of painted porcelains. The menus are exceptional, both for the wide choice offered and for the freshness of the innovative cooking, especially the fish. It's also the best value for money in the region. Weekday lunch menu €17 and gourmet menus €23–36; the €23 menu is particularly good value. When the weather's nice, you can dine on the pleasant terrace or in the cool interior. The river and lake add to the wonderful setting.

Noailly

42640 (15 km NW)

⌂ Château de La Motte***

La Motte; take the N7 to Saint-Germain-Lespinasse, then the D4 in the direction of Charlieu; it's between Noailly and La Benisson-Dieu.
Ⓣ04.77.66.64.60 Ⓕ04.77.66.68.10
Ⓦwww.chateaudelamotte.fr.st
TV. Car park. Swimming pool.

This romantic château may be beyond the price range of modest travellers, but if you want to go on a spree this is a good enough place to do it, due to the charm of its imaginatively decorated and tastefully furnished rooms, its eighteenth-century salon, its park with paths running through the trees and its evocative pond complete with a pergola. Double rooms €66–97 according to the degree of comfort. Communal dinner shared with the owner at €19; it is based on fresh, local products.

Ambierle

42820 (18km NW)

Le Prieuré

In the centre of the village.
☎04.77.65.63.24
Closed *Tues and Sun evenings; Wed; 3 weeks in Jan–Feb; a fortnight in Sept.*

In this well-known restaurant, pride of place goes to the fresh, local ingredients: vegetables, ducks, crayfish, etc. They are supplied by producers from the region and then treated with daring and talent by the chef, who creates surprising but delicious blends of cheese, fruit and vegetables: fresh goat's cheese with walnut oil and leek *confit*, and Fourme cheese with baked pear on a bed of Guaranjá chocolate. He is also extremely skilful in his addition of spices and herbs to meat and fish: *magret de canard* Pacaudois with spiced honey, and grilled bass with herb butter and hyssop. Weekday lunchtime menu €20, then others €24–47. During July and August there is a market in the village every Friday from 5 to 9pm; to coincide with this, the chef offers a special menu featuring the products he buys there.

Bully

42260 (20km S)

Port de Bully

Pont de Presle; between Saint-Polgues and Cordelle, on the D45.
☎04.77.65.23.36

Irène and Stéphane Mouterot had the idea of establishing this charming bar-restaurant above the harbour of Port de Bully. The terrace offers a wonderful view of the hundred-odd boats that are anchored in this curve on the Villerest Lake. You can come and revel in the beauty of the place over a drink or a reasonably priced meal. Weekday lunchtime menu €10, with other menus at €13 and €22 at the weekend. One of the main culinary attractions is "Irène's mystery frogs" (served at weekends or weekday dinners, by prior booking) – the recipe is a closely guarded secret.

Romans-sur-Isère

26100

Hôtel Magdeleine

31 av. Pierre Sémard; the road runs at right angles to the station.
☎04.75.02.33.53 Ⓕ04.75.72.78.38
Ⓦwww.magdeleinehotel.fr.st
Closed *Sun except for reservations; 1–15 Jan; autumn school holidays.* **TV.**

A strategically placed hotel right near the station, the historic centre and the factory shops. The owner originates from the Vosges and he runs the place expertly. He does everything himself – reception, cleaning, breakfasts and even the ironing. The 15 rooms are being renovated one by one; they're quite big and have new bedding and efficient double-glazing. Doubles with shower or bath €38. It's spotlessly clean and you get a genuinely warm welcome. *10% discount on the room rate (except school holidays) offered to our readers on presentation of this guide.*

Hôtel des Balmes**

Hameau des Balmes; it's about 4km from the centre; take the D532, Tain road for 2km, then turn right in the direction of Les Balmes.
☎04.75.02.29.52 Ⓕ04.75.02.75.47
Ⓦwww.hoteldesbalmes.com
Restaurant closed *Mon lunchtime. Closed Sun out of season; a week in Jan.* **TV. High chairs available. Car park. Swimming pool.**

This hotel, in a sleepy little village, has twelve pretty rooms with bath and balcony €44–50. In the restaurant, *Au Tahiti*, the owners have created an exotic décor with glass beads and shells. The cooking is strictly regional French – Drôme guinea fowl, lamb from the Préalpes. Menus are affordable at €13–24.50. Bikers are welcome to use the garage. *Free house apéritif, liqueur, coffee, fruit juice or soft drink offered to our readers on presentation of this guide.*

Restaurant La Cassolette

16 rue Rebatte; it's in a pedestrianized street near tour Jacquemart.
☎04.75.02.55.71
Closed *Sun; Mon; end July to mid-Aug.*

An intimate restaurant in a charming, thirteenth-century building, where the three dining rooms have vaulted ceilings. There's a range of menus, €12.50–34, listing such dishes as monkfish medallions with peppers, snail *cassolette*, *tournedos* with morels, scallop ravioli with warm vinaigrette, aubergine caviar with asparagus tips, duck in Côtes-du-Rhône and saddle of lamb with thyme. Dish of the day €8. Extensive wine list. *Free coffee offered to our readers on presentation of this guide.*

🏃 🍽 Le Café des Arts

49 cours Pierre-Didier.
☎04.75.02.77.23
Closed *Sat lunchtime; Sun.* **Disabled access.**

The round dining room is encircled by a veranda. It's a bit smart but not formal because it's softened by lots of green plants and you can watch the chefs behind the glass. The dishes are substantial, with lots of fresh fish – try tuna and salmon *tartare*, roast sea bream with dill *jus*, or pan-fried king prawns on a bed of red peppers. Local dishes figure on the menus too, and carnivores are well catered for – duck breast with orange, foie gras, steak *tartare*. *Formules* go for €14–25 and dish of the day €10. Wine by the glass. The staff are efficient and friendly; the owner will extend a businesslike welcome. They open the terrace under the plane trees when the sun shines; it's cut off from the road (which can be noisy in the daytime) by a thick green hedge.

Granges-lès-Beaumont

26600 (7km W)

🏃 🏠 🍽 Les Vieilles Granges**

Granges-lès-Beaumont; in the village. Take the D53 Tain road, it's at 6km from Romans, then turn left at the sign, opposite the "lycée horticole".
☎04.75.71.50.43 Ⓕ04.75.71.59.79
Closed *Sun evening; Mon; Tues lunchtime.* **Disabled access. TV. Car park.**

This collection of old buildings overlooking the Isère, surrounded by mature fruit trees, has been renovated and turned into a romantic hotel-restaurant with a terrace shaded by lime trees. Comfortable double rooms go for €37–50 with shower/wc or bath – the more expensive ones have a river view. In the dining room you can eat tasty food, with menus at €17–27. It's easy to decide on the main course – ravioli, regional specialities such as *caillette* (pork and vegetable faggots) and frogs' legs – but more difficult to choose a wine from the extensive list. Luckily the staff are patient and helpful. *Free house apéritif offered to our readers on presentation of this guide.*

Saint-Agnan-en-Vercors

26420

🏃 🏠 🍽 Auberge Le Collet

It's on the D518, 1km outside the Chapelle-en-Vercors.
☎04.75.48.13.18 Ⓕ04.75.48.13.25
Ⓔaubergelecolle@dub-internet.fr
Closed *Sun evening, Mon and Tues except during school holidays; a week in June; 3 weeks in Oct.* **High chairs and games available.**

This substantial mountain house is in the heart of the Vercors and provides an ideal spot for a well-earned rest. The son's owner, Guillaume, also offers his service as an instructor and takes you fishing or for walks on the region's plateau. Lovely dining room, traditionally decorated – sturdy wooden beams, wooden floors and roughcast on the walls ornamented by old photos. The warming log fire chases away the winter chill. Meals are simple, filling, economic and most welcome. The weekday lunch menu for €13 (starter, main course, cheese or dessert) is excellent value; they offer Landes specialities on other menus, €22–27. The owners spent some time in the southwest and brought back a batch of good recipes: *confits*, foie gras, *garbure,* Salard potatoes and so on. It makes a nice change from local mountain food. The welcome is genuinely warm. The simple, well-arranged rooms are meticulously maintained. Doubles €39.50 with shower/wc. *One free breakfast per person offered to our readers on presentation of this guide.*

Saint-Agrève

07320

🏠 🍽 Domaine de Rilhac***

Lieu-dit Rilhac; from Saint-Agrève, follow the road to Le Cheylard for about 1km; take the D21 fork off the D120 and follow the arrows.
☎04.75.30.20.20 Ⓕ04.75.30.20.00
Closed *Tues evening; Wed; Thurs lunchtime; 20 Dec to early March.* **Disabled access. TV. Car park.**

A sixteenth-century farm that has been tastefully restored and converted into a delightful hotel-restaurant. It's a luxury place at affordable prices, set deep in the countryside in a stunning spot facing monts Mézenc and Gerbier. It has a dressed-stone façade, blue shutters and finely engraved wrought ironwork inside, which goes well with the ochre plaster and the exposed beams. Six double rooms from €79–109, depending on the comfort and the season. Breakfast is served until 10.30am. Half board is compulsory, July–Aug, at a cost of €96–117 per person. There's a three-course weekday lunch menu at €23 and others €36–68. The à la carte menu changes with the seasons; specialities include oxtail with Cornas wine, trout salad, *carpaccio* of beef, duck breast with chestnut flower honey and iced nougat with *marrons glacés*.

Saint-Auban-sur-l'Ouvèze

26170

Auberge de la Clavelière

It's in the main street of the village; on the D546, halfway between Buis-les-Baronnies and Séderon.
Ⓣ04.75.28.61.07 Ⓕ04.75.28.60.30
Ⓦwww.guideweb.com/provence/hotel/claveliere
Closed *Sat lunchtime; may be closed In winter (but call to check); a week in June; a fortnight in Sept; a fortnight at Christmas.* **Car park. Swimming pool.**

Charming village way off the beaten track. In its centre stands this simple, warm and welcoming hotel in a solid stone house. Comfortable double rooms €45. In summer, half board is compulsory at €34.50 per person. The cooking offers stalwart family-style and regional dishes. Regular customers head here on weekday lunchtimes to make the most of the €11 menu. The menus at €17 and €22 are more elaborate: Provençale prawn salad, sardines *escabèche*, *croustillant* of duck breast, salad of king prawns à la Provençale, and honey and lavender flan. *Free coffee offered to our readers on presentation of this guide.*

Saint-Étienne

42000

Continental Hôtel

10 rue François-Gillet; in the town centre, near the municipal tourist office; coming from Lyon, take rue de la Montat, then place Fourneyron and rue de la République, then turn left before place Dorian into rue François-Gillet.
Ⓣ04.77.32.58.43 Ⓕ04.77.37.94.06
TV. Car park.

You will receive a warm welcome in this colourful, recently refurbished family hotel. Its central location in a quiet street, its enclosed garage and its accessible prices all add up to a place that we can highly recommend. Double rooms €27–36.

Hôtel Le Baladin**

12 rue de la Ville; it's in a busy pedestrianized street.
Ⓣ04.77.37.17.97 Ⓕ04.77.37.17.17
Closed *20 July–20 Aug. Snack bar closed Sun.* **TV.**

This place fills up very quickly, especially during the theatre season when the actors appearing at the Comédie de Saint-Étienne stay here. It's a pleasant hotel placed in an animated area with fourteen small but nice rooms for €33–40 with shower/wc or bath, or €47 with added bed. They serve food in the snack bar on the ground floor. Warm welcome.

Hôtel Le Cheval Noir**

11 rue François-Gillet.
Ⓣ04.77.33.41.72 Ⓕ04.77.37.79.19
Closed *Aug.* **TV. Pay car park.**

Spacious, pastel tone rooms, slightly faced but clean. Prices are modest considering its central location: doubles €44.50 with shower/wc and €50 with bath.

Hôtel Terminus du Forez***

31 av. Denfert-Rochereau; it's opposite the Châteaucreux station, five minutes from the centre.
Ⓣ04.77.32.48.47 Ⓕ04.77.34.03.30
Ⓦwww.logisdefrance2.com
Closed *Mon and Sat lunchtimes, Sun; 27 July–24 Aug; 21–28 Dec.* **TV. Car park.**

Charming, classic three-star hotel, with stylish rooms with original paintings on the walls. Doubles €58 with shower/wc and €67 with bath. The rooms have an Egytian style and if you walk down the stairs you can pick up a guide to the local tourist attractions in the region. On the ground floor, the restaurant *La Loco*, where they serve seasonal dishes is more than satisfactory. Cheapest menu €12, then others €18.50–36. Excellent welcome. *10% discount on the room rate (Fri–Sun, except during events) offered to our readers on presentation of this guide.*

L'Albatros***

67 rue Saint-Simon; turn left after the arms factory, opposite the golf course.
☎04.77.41.41.00 Ⓕ04.77.38.28.16
Restaurant closed *Sat–Sun in winter. Closed a fortnight in Aug; a fortnight end Dec to early Jan.* **Disabled access. TV. Car park. Swimming pool.**

This *Best Western* offers all mod cons, and it's a nice place to enjoy peace and quiet, overlooking the golf course, in the upper part of the town. Modern, comfortable rooms €72–130, and menus €16–25.

Le Cercle

15 pl. de l'Hôtel-de-Ville.
☎04.77.25.27.27
Closed *Sun and Mon evenings; Aug.*

This restaurant occupies part of the former premises of the Saint-Étienne bridge club, in a superb building opposite the town hall. The owners have kept the panelling and the gilding in one of the most beautiful rooms, which is pure Napoleon III in style. The restaurant attracts local worthies but prices are nevertheless very reasonable, with a weekday lunch *formule* at €12 and menu at €16. Decent food, pleasantly presented, and friendly service.

Bar à Vins "Aux Copains d'abord"

7 rue François-Gillet; in front of place Dorion, on the left, near the town hall.
☎04.77.46.27.31
Closed *Sat lunch; Sun; Mon.*

The entrance is adorned with a sign that says "Here, you come in, enjoy yourself and talk about it afterwards". This is just one of the countless maxims, proverbs and quotations from Georges Brassens that are chalked on the walls, spilling over onto the door frames and beyond. This convivial wine bar offers a winning combination of delicious food and excellent wines. Dish of the day €8; lunchtime menu €12 and another menu at €19. The wines are divided into lists corresponding to France's different wine-growing regions.

Cornes d'Aurochs!

18 rue Michel-Servet; it's 150m from the town hall.
☎04.77.32.27.27
Closed *Sat and Mon lunchtimes; Sun; 20 July–25 Aug.* **Car park by booking.**

A fun bistro offering Lyonnais cooking and traditional specials including dishes with wild mushrooms – *andouillette, tablier de sapeur*, a "Gargantua" platter (which gives you a bit of everything), steak *tartare*, fillet steak with ceps, duck *confit*, Lucullus sweetbreads of veal with morels. The €13 lunch menu is a good deal, with others at €18–35. The owner is jovial, his wife is smiling and welcoming. *Free house liqueur offered to our readers on presentation of this guide.*

Restaurant La Rissolée

23 rue Pointe-Cadet; it's on the edge of the pedestrianized area.
☎04.77.33.58.47
Closed *Mon lunchtime; Sun.*

What's unusual about this restaurant, which is in a district that boasts lots of them, is that it serves Belgian specialities – and, aptly, the menus are written on recycled Tintin albums. They do huge plates of food: mounds of rissoled potatoes, substantial helpings of mussels cooked in 33 different ways and served with chips. In the evening, they offer superb *carbonade*. Menus €14–21, beer included. Try an "SB", the house cocktail – it'll blow your head off. Terrace in summer.

Aux deux Cageots

3 pl. Grenette; in the town centre, near the pl. des Ursules.
☎04.77.32.89.85
Closed *Sat lunch; Sun; Mon.*

This is the most fashionable bar-restaurant in town, the place where would-be jet-setters come to be seen. There is always a party atmosphere and the attentive, jovial owner, Jacques Dargnat, makes sure that everybody has a good time. The food is equally exciting, with daringly original sweet-savoury mixtures and an excellent use of herbs and spices. Lunchtime menu €15, then another at

€30. The menu changes several times a month, which gives you a good excuse to come here more often! Booking highly advisable.

|●| La Mandragore

15 rue des Martyrs-de-Vingré; in the town centre, between pl. Dorian and pl. Chavanelle.
☎04.77.38.50.70
Closed Sun.

A newcomer in a street already enlivened by a number of restaurants. It has chic, sunny décor and offers extremely fresh food at very reasonable prices. Weekday lunchtime menu €15, then others at €26–36. On fine days you can eat on the terrace, under the large white parasols.

|●| Chez Marco

8 pl. Chavanelle; it's near the fire station.
☎04.77.33.92.47
Closed *lunchtimes; Sat; Sun; Aug.* **Disabled access.**

A well-known restaurant where actors and sundry night-owls meet up. Photos of the regulars cover the walls of the cosy little dining room. When you've finished a lovingly prepared meal you'll want to be told the recipe for the *diable au corps*, the explosive house cocktail – they actually set light to it. Menus €20–34. The upper class cooking is the sort you get in a classic Lyonnais bistro: chicken with prawns, *tablier du sapeur*, cheese soufflé. Best to book. *Free coffee offered to our readers on presentation of this guide.*

|●| Nouvelle

30 rue St-Jean.
☎04.77.32.32.60
Closed *Sun; Mon; 2nd and 3rd week of Aug.*

The very best place to eat in Saint-Étienne, right in the centre of town. It's got everything a gourmet restaurant should have – subtle décor, professional staff and the kind of menu you dream about – but it doesn't charge the prices you might expect. There's a wide choice of menus from €25 (weekday lunch) and €38–60. You'll have to travel a long way to taste better tripe *à la mode de Caen* or potato *gratin*. Don't miss the oysters Gillardeau with spinach, accompanied with citrus fruits and almonds. Portions are generous, and it's all very imaginative. It's best to book.

Saint-Pries-en-Jarez

42270 (2km N)

|●| Restaurant du Musée

Lieu-dit La Terrasse; follow the signs to the museum of modern art.
☎04.77.59.24.52
Closed *Mon; Wed evening; Sun evening.*
Disabled access.

Stéphane Laurier (who runs the *Nouvelle* restaurant in town), has taken over this restaurant inside the modern art museum. His cooking is very inventive, skilfully using spices and mixing unusual flavours – try the *croustillant* of fish. There's a lunch menu at €15, others at €17–27, or you'll spend about €25 à la carte. Excellent value for money and efficient service. And there's a lovely terrace that opens in warm weather.

Saint-Genest-Malifaux

42660 (12km S)

⌂ |●| Auberge de Campagne La Diligence**

Le Château du Bois; take the N82 to Bicètre then the D501 and it's 3km from the village and 2km from the "Col du Grand-Bois".
☎04.77.39.04.99 ℻04.77.39.01.80
Closed *Mon; Tues and Wed (except July–Aug); Jan.* **Pay car park.**

This was originally a farmhouse belonging to the thirteenth-century castle, which is still inhabited. Now it's a really nice restaurant and is part of the agricultural college of Saint-Genest. Good food and pleasant service with a seasonal menu at €11 (except Sun lunchtime), others €16.50–21.50. Flavoursome dishes such as free-range guinea fowl with watercress, or *verveine parfait glacé* with crispy bitter chocolate. The handsome dining room has a fireplace and there's a terrace in the farm courtyard. Half board €26 per person, or camping in the grounds for next to nothing. It's a horse farm, so you can go riding. It's advisable to book. *Free coffee offered to our readers on presentation of this guide.*

|●| Restaurant Montmartin

18 rue du Velay; take the N82, then the D501

to Plafony. In town centre, 100m from the church, opposite the 'lycée', sixth form college.
☎04.77.51.21.25
Closed *evenings; Wed; Fri; mid-Jan to mid-Feb.*

Located in one of the less attractive villages in this part of the world, this place was established after World War II by the grandmother of the present owners – they've kept the warm atmosphere and the creaking parquet. No nouvelle cuisine here; this is the place for generous portions of rich food including morels, frogs' legs and *quenelles*. Weekday menu €12.50, and others €15–29. It's very popular with families for Sunday lunch.

Saint-Victor-sur-Loire

42230 (15km W)

Le Croque Cerise

Base Nautique de Saint-Victor; take the D3A.
☎04.77.90.07.54
Closed *Sun and Wed evenings; Mon; Jan.* **Disabled access.**

The big building is not particularly elegant, but the dining rooms with their large windows and the terrace by the harbour are really pleasant. Attentively prepared, simple dishes such as whitebait, but they also come up with inventive offerings like seafood *cassoulet*, *magret de canard* with blackcurrant. Weekday lunch menu €12.20 and others €17–28. The food, service and welcome are pot-on.

Saint-Paul-en-Cornillon

42240 (17km SW)

La Cascade

Travel towards Firminy, take the D3 and turn left onto the D108 before the bridge.
☎04.77.35.70.02
Closed *Mon evening.* **Disabled access. Car park.**

No views of cascades, as it happens, but you do get the Loire instead. The classic dining room gets lots of light, and there's a very pleasant terrace shaded by plane trees and an impressive sequoia. It's a pity that the car park is so badly placed between the terrace and the river. Thoughtfully prepared, simple food, served with care; specialities include small deep-fried whitebait and frogs. Weekday lunch menu €12, and others €16–22.

Bessat (Le)

42660 (18km SE)

Auberge de la Jasserie

La Jasserie; it's 6km after Le Bessat – follow the arrows from the village.
☎04.77.20.40.16 ℱ04.77.20.45.43
Closed *Wed in winter except during school holidays.* **Disabled access. High chairs available. Car park.**

This old farmhouse, with its little bell tower, is a bit of an institution. It's one of those simple country inns that hasn't changed for generations, where you sit at wooden tables and chairs in a huge old dining room. It's at the bottom of the ski runs so it's an ideal place to warm up over a hot chocolate and a slice of bilberry tart. Savoury specialities include morels with cream, morel omelettes and frogs' legs. The only drawback is that it's rather crowded and noisy at the weekend. Menus €10 (except Sun lunchtime), others €12–30. *Free house apéritif offered to our readers on presentation of this guide.*

Hôtel La Fondue – Restaurant Chez le Père Charles**

Grande-Rue.
☎04.77.20.40.09 ℱ04.77.20.45.20
ⓦwww.pere-charles.com
Closed *Sun evening; Mon lunchtime; mid-Nov to mid-March.* **TV. Car park.**

A good restaurant way up at 1170m in the middle of the Pilat regional park, where the people of Lyon and Saint-Étienne come to get a bit of fresh air. Splendid gourmet dishes: goose foie gras, *tournedos* with paprika cream or the home speciality: trout stuffed with ceps. Dish of the day €9, and lots of menus at €13–44. Doubles €43–58 with shower/wc or bath. The bathrooms are big but the rooms with shower have a rather strange arrangement – a revolving cupboard which hides the toilet and the shower.

Saint-Just-Saint-Rambert

42170 (20km NW)

Restaurant du Rempart

2 rue de la Loire; going in the direction of St-Genest-Lerpt, take the west turning off the D8.

Ⓣ04.77.52.13.19
Closed *Sun and Wed evenings; Mon; a week in the Feb school holidays; 3 weeks in Aug.*

A couple of rustic dining rooms up on the first floor of a very old house built in the town walls. There's a gifted, inventive chef at work with excellent veal meat and fish dishes such as sea bream pan-fried on the skin with green beans or the *bouillabaisse* with thyme. Weekday lunchtime *formule* €11, wine and coffee included, other menus €15–32. Smiling, pleasant service. In summer, meals are served on the flowery terrace at the foot of the town walls. *Free coffee offered to our readers on presentation of this guide.*

Saint-Sauveur-en-Rue

42220 (25km SE)

Château de Bobigneux**

Bobigneux; take the N82 to Bourg-Argental, then take the D503 towards Le Puy for about 4km.
Ⓣ04.77.39.24.33 Ⓕ04.77.39.25.74
Ⓔchateau-de-bobigneux@wanadoo.fr
Closed *Wed; from All Saint's Day to Easter.* **High chairs available. Car park.**

After eighteen years in Greenland the owners moved here and took over this sixteenth-century stone manor house, which is right next to a farm belonging to Madame's brother. They've created a delightful place to stay and prices are reasonable. The farm provides them with all the fresh produce they need, and Monsieur, who is a talented chef, creates great dishes. Try the oyster mushrooms in flaky pastry. There's a *menu "Campagnard"* served in the week for €12 and others at €15 and €22. The dining rooms have been pleasantly renovated, and the terrace and the garden are both lovely. Bright, spacious country-style rooms €37–40. *Free house apéritif offered to our readers on presentation of this guide.*

Saint-Galmier

42330

La Charpinière***

Lieu-dit la Carpinière.
Ⓣ04.77.52.75.00 Ⓕ04.77.54.18.79
Ⓦwww.lacharpiniere.com
TV. Disabled access. High chairs and games available. Car park. Swimming pool.

A splendid establishment in substantial grounds that guarantee quiet. Pleasant and functional rooms €83–95. They have a range of facilities including a health and fitness centre, tennis courts and a swimming pool. The restaurant is in a conservatory and offers high-quality cooking that's both original and refined. Try the pressed red mullet with *fleur de sel* salt, crispy Parma ham, *millefeuille* with grilled aubergines. Weekday menu at €11.48, others €20.50–42. *Free house apéritif offered to our readers on presentation of this guide.*

Le Bougainvillier

Pré-Château; it's signposted from the Badoit source on the banks of the Coise.
Ⓣ04.77.54.03.31
Closed *Sun and Wed evenings; Mon; Feb school holidays; Aug.* **Disabled access.**

A pretty building swathed in Virginia creeper in the rather stylish little town which is the source of Badoit mineral water. In the evening, the local inhabitants form a queue to collect their free fizzy water. The restaurant has three dining rooms, one of them a veranda overlooking a walled garden by the water's edge. Gérard Charbonnier is one of the most interesting young chefs in the area. He spent two years in Gagnaire's well-known restaurant, where he was encouraged to be creative. His fish dishes are delicate and skilfully prepared. Menus €20 (not Sat) and €30–52. Charming, low-key welcome.

Veauche

42340 (6km S)

Hôtel-restaurant de la Gare

55 av. H.-Planchet; take the D12 – it's next to the train station and a huge factory.
Ⓣ04.77.54.60.10 Ⓕ04.77.94.30.53
Closed *3.30–6pm daily; Fri and Sun evenings; 1–15 Aug.* **Disabled access. High chairs available. Car park.**

A reliable neighbourhood restaurant providing good food at sensible prices. There's a weekday menu at €9 and others €12–38. The menus list fine, delicately prepared dishes: home-made foie gras, terrine and fish dishes. Pleasant, conventional décor and a warm friendly welcome. The hotel has ten basic rooms for €25 with basin, up to €35 with shower/wc. A place to bear in mind if you're stuck for somewhere to stay – under general circumstances, however, the view of the station and the factory is probably not quite what you're looking for. Good welcome. *Free coffee offered to our readers on presentation of this guide.*

Andrezieux-Bouthéon

42160 (8km S)

Les Iris***

32 rue Jean-Martouret. On the motorway, exit Andrezieux-centre, follow town centre then train station.
Ⓣ04.77.36.09.09 Ⓕ04.77.36.09.00
Hotel open *daily*. **Closed** *Sat lunchtime; Sun evening; Mon; 1–20 Jan; a week in Aug*. **TV. Car park. Swimming pool.**

This handsome residence, which you reach by ascending two elegant flights of steps, stands on the outskirts of a rather industrial town near Saint-Étienne airport. The ten functional but pleasant and redecorated bedrooms, named after flowers, are in the annexe. They overlook the swimming pool and the garden with its gigantic cedar trees; €69–76 with bath. The restaurant serves conventional cuisine and has a décor to match. Flowers and fresh herbs blend beautifully with fish, meat and vegetables to produce cooking that surprises as well as being delicious and refined. Menus, which change weekly, go for €21–57.

Chazelles-sur-Lyon

42140 (10km NE)

Château Blanchard**

36 rte. de Saint-Galmier; very near the hat museum.
Ⓣ04.77.54.28.88 Ⓕ04.77.54.36.03
Closed *Sun evening; Mon; 15–30 April; 10–25 Aug*. **TV. Disabled access. High chairs and games available. Car park.**

This so-called castle, in France's millinery capital, is actually a 1930s folly that was once the home of a hat-maker. It lay neglected for forty years but has since been restored to its original splendour. The garish frontage is decorated with friezes, while inside the décor is a glorious confusion of neo-greco-classical-kitsch. Very well equipped doubles from €55 with bath; no. 6 has its original décor. Half board at €60 per person. The restaurant fits into its surroundings very nicely. You'll get a warm welcome and classic, well-presented menus at €20–29; around €25 à la carte. They specialize in fresh fish; try the *marbré* of red mullet, sea bream and lobster. You can dine on the terrace.

Saint-Jean-de-Maurienne

73300

Hôtel-restaurant du Nord**

Place du Champ-de-Foire.
Ⓣ04.79.64.02.08 Ⓕ04.79.59.91.31
Ⓦwww.hoteldunord.net
Closed *Sun evening (except Feb and July–Aug); Mon lunchtime; April school holidays; autumn school holidays*. **Disabled access. TV. Car park.**

A former coaching inn with a little tower. The restaurant, which has a vaulted ceiling and stonewalls, is in the old stables. It's the best place to eat in town; the cooking is well judged, and although it's classic the chef has some original ideas. There's a €14.50 (except public holidays) menu, and others €18–36. The rooms are spacious and offer good value for money. Doubles €44 with shower/wc. *Free house apéritif offered to our readers on presentation of this guide.*

Saint-Martin-de-Belleville

73440

Le Lachenal**

50m from the ski-lifts.
Ⓣ04.79.08.96.29 Ⓕ04.79.08.94.23
Ⓔlelache-nal@wanadoo.fr
Closed *May–June; Sept–Nov*.

A lovely doll's house of a place, with cosy rooms with flower-painted shutters and panelled walls. Just three double rooms: €55 with shower/wc or bath. Simple, generous, family-style dishes, with a number of Savoyard specialities. Menus €20–38. The Lemattre family are wonderful hosts. It's often full, so it's best to book.

La Bouitte

Quartier Saint-Marcel; take the D117 towards Les Ménuires (about 2km).
Ⓣ04.79.08.96.77 Ⓕ04.79.08.96.03
Ⓦwww.la-bouitte.com
Closed *early May to early July; early Oct to mid-Dec*. **TV. Disabled access. Pay car park.**

Old stone and wood chalet that combines tradition with elegance. Without doubt, this is the best restaurant in the valley. It's local cooking with a finesse that belies its apparent simplicity. Save room for the marvellous desserts. Menus €37–115 – a little pricey, but well worth it for the wonderful food. To prolong your pleasure, they have a few charming rooms, decorated in mountain style; doubles with bath €160–186, breakfast included.

Saint-Martin-en-Haut

69850

Restaurant Les Quatre Saisons

Place de l'Église.
①04.78.48.69.12
Closed *Tues.* **Car park.**

A surprising restaurant on the pretty square of a hilltop village at the edge of the Monts du Lyonnais. Generous portions of seasonal dishes are served in the fresco-lined dining room. Weekday lunchtime menu €10.90, then others €17.50–28.50. Good dishes include parsleyed frogs' legs, beef with morels, Bourgogne snails, and iced *parfait. Free house apéritif offered to our readers on presentation of this guide.*

Aveize

69610 (9km NW)

Hôtel-restaurant Rivollier

Take the D34.
①04.74.26.01.08 Ⓕ04.74.26.01.90
Closed *Sun evening; Mon.*

It's a wonder how a place this size can survive in such a small village. But once you've experienced the sheer professionalism, first-class welcome and service, and eaten a superb meal in the pleasant airy dining room, you'll be less surprised. They offer delectable menus at €11 (weekdays) and €15–25, along with a wide selection of dishes of the day such as salmon with dill, terrine of duck with prunes, pike soufflé with shrimps, *soufflé glacé au Grand Marnier*... If you're stuck for accommodation, they also have eight very basic rooms at €34 with shower/wc. *Free coffee offered to our readers on presentation of this guide.*

Saint-Paul-lès-Monestier

38650

Au Sans Souci**

At Monestier-de-Clermont, take the D8 Gresse-en-Vercors road.
①04.76.34.03.60 Ⓕ04.76.34.17.38
Ⓦwww.perso.wanadoo.fr/au-sans-souci
Closed *Sun evening and Mon out of season; 20 Dec–30 Jan.* **TV. Disabled access. High chairs and games available. Car park. Swimming pool.**

This family-run hotel, surrounded by greenery at the foot of the Vercors regional park, has been running smoothly for four generations. It's a pleasure to be here, and you'll feel even better after a meal in the welcoming restaurant. They offer a €16 weekday menu, and others up to €40. Excellent specialities include morels stuffed with foie gras, *croustillant* of pigeon with truffles or the char lake fish with truffles. You can play *boules* or pool, or have a swim. Double rooms €52–55 with shower/wc or bath. *Free coffee offered to our readers on presentation of this guide.*

Saint-Pierre-de-Chartreuse

38380

Hôtel du Nord**

Rue principale.
①04.76.88.61.10 Ⓕ04.76.88.64.07
Restaurant open *lunchtime all year.* **Car park.**

A lovely atmospheric place with fresh, spruce rooms decorated with period furniture. Doubles €24 with basin up to €40 with shower/wc or bath/wc. All the rooms are different and especially two that are on split-level. Half board €34–44. The dining room has a fireplace and lots of ornaments and paintings on the wall. Classic specialities: *fondue, tartiflette,* trout with almonds, coconut tart. Menus €12.50 (not Sun) and up to €27. Decent Côtes-du-Rhone at modest prices. Shady garden. *Free house apéritif or coffee offered to our readers on presentation of this guide.*

L'Auberge du Cucheron*

Col du Cucheron; it's 3km north of the town centre, on the D512.
①04.76.88.62.06 Ⓕ04.76.88.65.43
Closed *Sun evening and Mon except during school holidays.* **Car park.**

This nice old inn, surrounded by trees, is one of a dying breed. The views are magnificent and the *patronne* is charming. There are seven rooms at €28–37. Half board at €38 per person is compulsory in the winter holidays. Menus €16–27, or around €20 à la carte. Specialities include terrines of duck, salmon and scorpion fish, trout stuffed with nuts, quail with sour cherries, Chartreuse tart and iced nougat. You're just 50m from the ski runs in winter, and it's deliciously peaceful in summer. Reservations recommended in high season. *10% discount on the room rate (except school holidays) offered to our readers on presentation of this guide.*

Saint-Hugues-de-Chartreuse

38380 (4km S)

|●| La Cabine

It's next to the church-museum.
☏04.76.88.67.13
Open *daily 10am–midnight (Jan to mid-March and July–Sept); weekends only the rest of the year.* **Closed** *Nov.* **Disabled access. Car park.**

The restaurant is in a converted school. There's a nice combination of white wood and rough-hewn stone, with sculptures, tools, domestic implements and dried flowers to decorate the place. The pleasant terrace overlooks the forest and the beginning of the cross-country ski trails. Dishes include *tartiflette* (to order an hour in advance), *fondues*, lots of salads, savoury tarts, omelettes, crêpes and ice creams. Menus, €9.90–15, are served until 9.30pm. Reckon on paying €15 or so à la carte. They have live music in the evening – jazz, blues and French songs. Credit cards not accepted. *A little Chartreuse offered to our readers on presentation of this guide.*

Saint-Restitut

26130

|●| Restaurant Les Buisses

Leave Saint-Restitut by the Suze-la Rousse road, go past the statue of the Virgin Mary, and follow the D218. In the village.
☏04.75.04.96.50
Closed *Mon, Sat lunchtime and Sun evening, in winter; Sat, Mon and Tues lunchtimes, in summer; a fortnight mid-March.* **Disabled access.**

A beautiful country house way out in the forest with a Provençal garden. In summer the crickets sing, and you sit out on the terrace to enjoy robustly flavoured cooking from the south. There's also a spacious, newly decorated dining room with a working fireplace. Lovely welcome and a nice relaxed atmosphere. Lunch menu at €18 and another at €25, with a choice of six flavoursome starters and main courses. Cheese and desserts included. Specialities include lamb *fondue*, *assiette des Buisses* (a platter of aubergine, peppers, pickled tomatoes and courgettes drizzled with local olive oil), and deep-fried courgette flowers. Remarkable wine list. *Free house apéritif offered to our readers on presentation of this guide.*

Sainte-Eulalie

07510

⌂ |●| Hôtel du Nord**

It's opposite the church.
☏04.75.38.80.09 Ⓕ04.75.38.85.50
Ⓦwww.ardeche-tourisme.com/hotel-du-nord
Closed *Tues evening and Wed (except July–Aug); 11 Nov to mid Feb.* **Disabled access. High chairs available. Car park.**

Two sitting rooms, one with a veranda; both have magnificent views over the Loire plain. Double rooms €40–49 with shower/wc or bath. Menus at €16.50–32 list interesting specialities such as duck thigh *confit* with bilberry sauce, trout soufflé with *beurre blanc* and pork *estouffade* in Ardèche wine. For dessert you absolutely must try the *crème brûlée* with bilberries and raspberries. This place is a magnet for fans of fly-fishing – the chef is smitten by the sport. *Free house apéritif offered to our readers on presentation of this guide.*

Sagnes et Goudoulet

07450 (8km SW)

⌂ |●| Hostellerie Chaneac**

It's in the edge of the village, on the Buzet road.
☏04.75.38.80.88 Ⓕ04.75.38.80.54
Ⓦwww.ardeche-tourisme.com
Open *weekends; evenings only in July–Aug; otherwise by reservation only.* **Closed** *last week in Aug.* **Disabled access. TV. Car park.**

Instead of leaving the country for the town, the young chef decided to stay and take over the family business – he's the fourth generation to run the place. The climate is harsh and the winters are long which doesn't make things easy, so business is seasonal – sometimes when the snow is deep, it's hard even to get deliveries up here. Inside the thick walls, the rooms are comfortable and the walls are built of stone and wood. Comfortable doubles with shower/wc or bath/wc for €39. Half board is compulsory in July and August at €37 per person. The chef uses carefully selected local produce and he makes the charcuterie and bread himself, as well as the terrines of wild plants and local trout. Menus €16 and €23. Credit cards not accepted. *Free house liqueur offered to our readers on presentation of this guide.*

Sallanches

74700

Auberge de l'Orangerie**

3 carrefour de la Charlotte; it's 3km east of the city centre on the D13 in the direction of Passy.
04.50.58.49.16 04.50.58.54.63
perso.wanadoo.fr/auberge-orangerie
Closed *5–27 Jan; 2–24 June. Restaurant closed Mon; Tues, Wed and Thurs lunchtimes; Sun evening.* **TV. High chairs and games available. Car park.**

Though the hotel is right on a roundabout, its rooms are well soundproofed. The décor is basic but it does have a little something, and most of all it's very comfortable. Prices are very fair for the region: doubles with shower/wc or bath €40–55. The dining room is a random mixture of rustic and kitsch, but the cuisine has a clear, contemporary identity. The chef works with delicacy and cares for every detail. Expect to pay between €31–46 à la carte.

Samoëns

74340

Le Moulin du Bathieu**

Vercland: take the D4 in the direction of Morillon, then turn left to Samoëns 1600.
04.50.34.48.07 04.50.34.43.25
www.bathieu.com
Closed *May; 4 Nov–20 Dec.* **TV. Car park.**

Traditional house in the heart of the countryside. The only thing to break the silence here is the babbling brook that used to turn the millwheel. The bedrooms, with their wood-clad walls, have a warm, soothing feel. Several of them are split-level, making them ideal for families. Doubles with shower/wc or bath €55–100, depending on the comfort. You have to book to eat in the restaurant. Menus, €18–30, feature Savoyard specialities. *Free coffee offered to our readers on presentation of this guide.*

La Fandolieuse- La Cour

04.50.34.98.28
Open *noon–2pm and 4.30–11pm. Closed Wed (except during school holidays); May–June; Sept–Oct.*

In the fifteenth century, the people of this valley spoke a poetic, sing-song dialect called Mourmé; *fandolieuse* is their word for "dancer". This pleasant little crêperie, in a sixteenth-century house with wainscoted walls, has given all its crêpes a Mourmé name: *Tapotu* means "drum", *violurin* means "musician", *crépioti* describes the crackling ice and *soufflache* the biting wind. They also do *fondues* and a very substantial soup made with bread, Tomme cheese and onions – it's a local speciality, traditionally eaten on the feast of Saint Christopher. À la carte only; expect to pay around €15.

Saou

26400

L'Oiseau sur sa Branche

La Placette.
04.75.76.02.03
Closed *Mon and Tues out of season; Jan.* **Disabled access.**

Converted by a restaurateur-poet who settled here after years of travelling, this red and yellow bistro has an old packing case and a map of the world in the hall. Dishes are an array of colours and flavours, and your choice arrives at the table labelled with its name. Dish of the day at €9.50. There's a *menu du bistro* at €15 (weekday lunchtimes) and other menus at €20–25. Not surprisingly, it attracts a lot of regular customers. To cap it all, there's a lovely terrace in the shade of the plane trees – for breakfast in fine weather – very romantic in the moonlight.

Sutrieu

01260

Auberge du Col de la Lèbe*

It's 6km from Champagne-en-Valromey, 8km from Hauteville.

☎04.79.87.64.54 Ⓕ04.79.87.54.26
Restaurant closed *Mon evening and Tues in July–Aug. Closed Mon; Tues; mid-Nov to mid-April; 20–30 June.* **TV. High chairs available. Car park. Swimming pool.**

Right out in the country, on the way up to the pass, this restaurant has a cosy dining room with lots of wood and houseplants. The service is stylish but not in the least pretentious, and the sophisticated cooking includes duo foie gras, free-range chicken with morels, *empereur* with sesame seeds. Dish of the day at €11 during the week and other menus €21–28. They also do grills over the coals. Rooms are fairly modest but their old-fashioned air gives them a degree of style and you're guaranteed lots of peace and quiet. Doubles €42–44. Half board at €45 per person. You get a wonderful view of the Valromey valley from the swimming pool.

Tain l'Hermitage

26600

Hôtel Les 2 Coteaux**

19 rue Joseph Pála; it's on the bank of the Rhône by the pedestrian bridge.
☎04.75.08.33.01 Ⓕ04.75.08.44.20
Closed *Sun evening mid Nov to end Jan.* **TV. Pay car park.**

A family hotel in a superb location on the banks of the Rhône just by a bridge to the Ardèche. They have all been refurbished, the west-facing rooms have a magnificent view of the river and the Château de Tournon; one even has a small terrace. That said, those at the back also have a lovely view, this time over the Hermitage hills. Doubles with hand basin €27, with shower €32, €52 with shower/wc or bath. The breakfast terrace also has a gorgeous view of the Rhône flowing by.

Des Terrasses du Rhône-au-Sommelier

13 rue Joseph Peala.
☎04.75.08.40.56
Open *11am–3pm and 6pm–midnight.* **Closed** *Sun; Mon.*

An ideal place if you're after a tasty snack and a glass of good wine. Excellent sandwiches with a wide variety of fillings. Fabien Louis is a trained *sommelier*, so the honest wines are carefully chosen. Sandwich menu €10 including two glasses of wine; platters of charcuterie and a glass of Saint-Joseph for €8. On a summer's evening, the *bonhomie* spills out onto the road. They organize walks through the vineyards. *Free coffee offered to our readers on presentation of this guide.*

Crozes-Hermitage

26600 (8km N)

Le Bistrot des Vins

Take the D153 and it's in the village.
☎04.75.07.18.03
Closed *Mon–Wed.*

This is serious wine country and this charming village is in the Hermitage vineyard hills. It's a bistro-style dining room with a small terrace, run by a very welcoming young couple. Tasty cuisine using fresh market produce and, naturally enough, you accompany your meal with a jug of the local vintage at knockdown prices. There's one menu only at €17, offering a choice of starters, dish of the day, cheese and dessert. It's doing well and has established a regular clientele so it's best to book.

Tarare

69170

Restaurant Jean Brouilly

3 ter rte. de Paris. Take the N7 exit Roanne
☎04.74.63.24.56
Closed *Sun; Mon; Feb school holidays; 8–31 Aug.* **Car park.**

The Brouillys have been running things here for more than twenty years. The house, built by an industrialist, is pretty typical of the region and has beautiful grounds. Jean Brouilly is a considerable chef and a welcoming man. Whether you choose the fresh garden salad, the pan-fried foie gras with rhubarb, the quartet of scallops with caviar on salt cod mousse, the veal fillet with a magnolia flower, the red mullet with olives or the *millefeuille* with Bourbon vanilla, you'll appreciate his skilful handling of fresh produce and delicate balancing of flavours. He combines herbs, spices and wild produce to most original effect. Menus €32–62. You'll pay around €50 à la carte. On warm days you can eat on the veranda and admire the grounds.

Sarcey

74490 (12km E)

Le Chatard**

1 allée du Mas; take the N7 in the direction of Lyon, turn left onto the D118.
Ⓣ04.74.26.85.85 Ⓕ04.74.26.89.99
Ⓦwww.le-chatard.com
Closed *Sun evening to Tues; 1–22 Jan*. **TV. Disabled access. Car park. Swimming pool.**

A reliable, peaceful hotel-restaurant with a nice swimming pool. The restaurant attracts businesspeople and local families because of the prices and the top-quality traditional cuisine – menus at €15.50 (weekday lunchtimes), other €38. Try the duck foie gras or the smoked salmon. Doubles €57 with basin, shower, shower/wc or bath/wc; they don't have huge charm but they do have all mod cons. Half board available for a three night-stay at €44.50 per person. *Free house liqueur offered to our readers on presentation of this guide.*

Thonon-les-Bains

74200

Restaurant Le Victoria

5 pl. des Arts.
Ⓣ04.50.71.02.82
Closed *between Christmas and New Year's Day*. **High chairs and games available.**

The lovely Belle Époque glass frontage is overrun by greenery, which makes the dining room pleasantly private. They serve good, traditional cooking using fine ingredients, and prepare tasty dishes of both freshwater and sea fish – try the sea bass in a salt crust. In summer they offer huge crispy salads. Menus €12.40 (not Sun) and €19.60–27.80. *Free house apéritif offered to our readers on presentation of this guide.*

Margencel

74200 (5km SW)

Hôtel-restaurant Les Cygnes**

Port de Séchex; when you get to Margencel, head for the port of Séchex on the D33.
Ⓣ04.50.72.63.10 Ⓕ04.50.72.68.22
Ⓦwww.restaurant-les-cygnes.fr
Closed *Wed out of season; mid-Nov to early Feb*. **TV. Car park.**

Known simply as *Chez Jules*, this is a local institution in a small port by the side of Lake Geneva. It's been going since the 1930s. The restaurant is famous for fresh fish – try the soup of freshwater fish, fillets of perch, lake whitefish (a type of salmon) *à l'ancienne*, or fish *pot-au-feu*. Menus €21.50–42. The rooms are delightful and some have a lake view; €50 with shower/wc. *10% discount on the room rate (Feb–April and Oct–Nov) offered to our readers on presentation of this guide.*

Armoy

74200 (6.5km SE)

Hôtel-restaurant Le Chalet**

L'Ermitage; it's on the D26.
Ⓣ04.50.71.08.11 Ⓕ04.50.71.33.88
Ⓦwww.hotel-le-chalet.com
Closed *Dec; Jan*. **Restaurant closed** *out of season except by reservation*. **TV. Car park. Swimming pool.**

This building, which does indeed resemble a Swiss chalet, stands at the top of a wooded slope high above the village and Lake Geneva. You get lots of peace and quiet and a superb view from most of the rooms, some of which have their own terrace. If you're here in summer, ask for one of the wooden chalets around the swimming pool. Doubles €30 with basin, €39–44 with shower/wc or bath, depending on the season. Menus €15–24. The cuisine is carefully prepared: home-made charcuterie, salmon with tarragon. There's a big garden and a fine view of the lake.

Yvoire

74140 (16.5km W)

Le Bateau Ivre

Grande Rue. Take the N5 towards Sciez, then D25.
Ⓣ04.50.72.81.84
Open *daily mid-June to mid-Sept. Closed Thurs and Fri out of season; Jan; 1–8 Feb.*

A fresh little dining room in an old house in this charming – touristy – village. The young chef works equally enthusiastically on fish dishes or desserts, and you'll get smiling service even when the place is full. Menus €15.50 (except Sat evening and Sun lunchtime), with others at €21–28. It's a genuinely lovely place.

Tournon-sur-Rhône

07300

Hôtel Azalées**

6 av. de la Gare.
Ⓣ04.75.08.05.23 Ⓕ04.75.08.18.27
Ⓦwww.hotel-azalees.com
Closed *Sun evening from 15 Oct–15 March; 23 Dec–5 Jan*. **TV. Disabled access. High chairs available. Car park.**

You can sit on the terrace and watch the steam train puffing its way through Haut-Vivarais *en route* to Lamastre. Comfortable, modern doubles €41 with shower/wc or bath. Menus, €15–27, list mainly regional cooking with a good goat's cheese flan, tasty pork cheek and, for dessert, iced chestnut soufflé. *10% discount on the room rate offered to our readers on presentation of this guide.*

Restaurant L'Estragon

6 pl. Saint-Julien; it's opposite the church.
Ⓣ04.75.08.87.66
Closed *Wed except in summer; mid-Feb to mid-March*.

In a great location, in the middle of a pedestrianized area very close to the Rhône, this place offers good, simple food at reasonable prices. Menus €10.50–16.50. There's a *pierre chaude* (hot stone) menu, comprising a salad, veal or steak, cheese and dessert. The salads are huge and the zander with red wine and pickled shallots is very tasty. Efficient, attentive service. *Free house apéritif offered to our readers on presentation of this guide.*

Restaurant Aux Sablettes

187 rte. de Lamastre; go 3km along the Lamastre road, turn left, and it's opposite the Acacias campsite.
Ⓣ04.75.08.44.34
Closed *Wed except July–Aug*. **Car park.**

This restaurant and bar, which specializes in beer, is a bit out of the way, but it's popular with young locals and people from the nearby campsite. The décor doesn't have particular character, but the menu lists a few original specialities: meats and even desserts like mousses and tarts cooked with beer. Teetotallers will be well satisfied with the grills, the ravioli, a delicious regional speciality, the salad of scallops and mushrooms, the ostrich steak or any of the pizzas baked in a wood-fired oven. Menus €11–23. *Free coffee offered to our readers on presentation of this guide.*

Trévoux

01600

Hôtel des Voyageurs**

28 rue du Palais; it's near the Parliament building.
Ⓣ04.74.00.12.343 Ⓕ04.74.00.64.24
Closed *Aug*. **TV. Car park.**

It's the only hotel in town but it doesn't rest on its laurels. It's been nicely and cleanly decorated. Doubles €32 with shower/wc or bath. They have an arrangement with the café-bar on the ground floor so you can have a meal delivered during the week.

Chez Bruno

8 Grande-Rue; it's opposite the church.
Ⓣ04.74.00.20.75
Closed *Sun; Tues and Thurs evenings; 10 days at Easter; a fortnight in Aug; 10 days at Christmas*.

On the face of things this is an ordinary-looking place but it has a lot going for it: a lovely smiling welcome, tasty dishes with menus that change all the time and lots of quick meals for not much money. Specialities are not necessarily local – *bouillabaisse* Sétoise and *fondue* Savoyarde – but they're all full of flavour. There's a huge buffet table of starters and home-made desserts. Buffet *formule* for €13, weekday lunch menu €10, others €15–20. The plates and serving dishes are made by Bruno's father-in-law, and the décor is bright with lots of paintings by Bruno's wife. It's simple, efficient and a real pleasure.

Usson-en-Forez

42550

Hôtel Rival*

Rue Centrale.
Ⓣ04.77.50.63.65 Ⓕ04.77.50.67.62
Ⓔhotelrival@caramail.com
Closed *Mon (Oct–June); last week in June; 12 Nov–11 Dec*. **TV. High chairs and games available. Car park.**

A typical family hotel in a little mountain village up in the Forez. The restaurant serves large portions of traditional dishes, with a weekday menu for €11 and others €19–32. Try the *forézienne* salad and the Fourme *fondue*. You can eat in the dining room with its huge fireplace, or, on good days, on the terrace. The rooms are clean and affordable, if lacking in character. Doubles €24 with basin and €40 with bath. Very friendly proprietress. *10% discount on the room rate (except July–Aug) offered to our readers on presentation of this guide.*

Saint-Bonnet-le-Château

42380 (14km NE)

Le Befranc**

7 rue d'Augel; it's on the edge of town, just before the exit of Usso-en-Forez, take the small road, down on your left by the petrol station.
Ⓣ04.77.50.54.54 Ⓕ04.77.50.73.17
Closed *Sun; Mon; last fortnight in Jan.* **Disabled access. TV. Car park.**

This beautiful town with a medieval centre is the capital of *pétanque*. The hotel is a short distance from the centre and offers spruce rooms that have been attractively decorated. Doubles €38 are comfortable, simple but clean. Regional dishes are the order of the day in the restaurant and menus are priced €12 (weekday lunchtimes) and €16–32. Try the rabbit with fig *compote*.

La Calèche

2 rue du Commandant-Marey (Centre).
Ⓣ04.77.50.15.58
Closed *Tue evening; Wed; Sun evening; Feb half-term; 1st week in July; Nov half-term.* **Disabled access.**

A mansion house where you will be received with a smile before you relish the owner's cooking. The variety and originality of the dishes served and the quality of their ingredients have earned this restaurant a solid reputation, so it's advisable to book. Menus €15.50–40 and à la carte. You also book in advance a special "all-lobster" menu at €36. *Free liqueur on the house offered to our readers on presentation of this guide.*

Valence

26000

Hôtel Continental**

29 av. Pierre-Sémard.
Ⓣ04.75.44.01.38 Ⓕ04.75.44.03.90
TV.

Don't be misled by the impersonal and cramped look of this hotel; it has large rooms and a retro charm. All the rooms are different, but nearly all of them have been updated in a simple, pleasant way. Some have lovely furniture and large bathrooms, particularly in nos. 104 and 206. Doubles with shower and/wc or bath €33–39. Not bad for a two-star hotel.

Hôtel de l'Europe**

15 av. Félix-Faure; it's near the tourist office and the station.
Ⓣ04.75.82.62.65 Ⓕ04.75.82.62.66
Closed *Sun 2–6pm.* **TV. High chairs available. Pay car park.**

A conveniently located hotel with reasonably priced air-conditioned rooms. The double-glazing is very effective at keeping out the noise from the street below. Doubles €41–52 with shower/wc or bath. Special break at €54. *One breakfast per room per night (in low season) offered to our readers on presentation of this guide.*

Le Bistrot des Clercs

48 Grande-Rue.
Ⓣ04.75.55.55.15
Open *noon–2.30pm and 7–11pm (midnight Fri and Sat).* **Closed** *Sun.*

A great bistro offering solid regional dishes prepared with creativity. Chabran, one of the best chefs of the region, offers honest cuisine that's tasty and generously served. Menus €15 and €23. The wine list is very well balanced, offering a number of good quality bottles. *Free coffee offered to our readers on presentation of this guide.*

Restaurant One Two...Tea

37 Grande-Rue.
Ⓣ04.75.55.96.31
Closed *Sun; public holidays, a fortnight mid-Aug.* **Disabled access.**

The interior is a combination of brick and wood, there are pictures on the walls and vases full of flowers – all to create a "British look". It's crammed at lunchtime and for dinner, though a small terrace takes the overflow in summer. You'll get a substantial meal for a modest €18, or €9 for a dish of the day. Dishes include chicken liver gâteau, *caillette* (a sort of haggis) with shallots and wine sauce, ravioli with cream and absinthe sauce, salmon fillet with anchovy butter, huge salads, steak with shallots. It's tasty and filling, but leave room for a portion of the apple pie, crumble or *tarte tatin*. Good value for money and the staff are welcoming.

🏃 |●| Restaurant L'Épicerie

18 pl. Saint-Jean; it's next to Saint-Jean church.
Ⓣ04.75.42.74.46
Closed *Sat lunchtime; Sun; public holidays; Aug; Christmas to early Jan*. **Disabled access.**

It's some time since the grocer's shop closed, but the restaurant that took over the premises continues to flourish. Good, regional dishes: cream of lentil soup with diced foie gras, salad of grilled ravioli, roast mountain lamb with morels, monkfish with watercress, red mullet with Syrah wine sauce, Roseval potatoes with wind-dried ham. Menus €22–55. When the weather's nice, you can sit on the terrace on a little square opposite an old covered market and be at peace with the world. *Free coffee offered to our readers on presentation of this guide.*

|●| Auberge du Pin

285 bis av. Victor Hugo. Take the A7, exit Valence Sud, towards town centre, it's not far from the train station.
Ⓣ04.75.44.53.86
Open *daily all year*. **Disabled access.**

The *Maison Pic* is a four-star establishment with a Relais & Châteaux sign and prices to match; the next door *Auberge* is much more affordable. There's a *menu-carte* at €30 – dishes change very frequently and the flavourful cooking includes local and more traditional choices – Vichyssoise of asparagus, half-cockerel with aromatic herbs, fish *au gratin*. The bright yellow dining room is small, so you ought to reserve in autumn and winter when the terrace isn't open.

Valgorge

07110

🏠 |●| Hôtel Le Tanargue**

Chez Coste.
Ⓣ04.75.88.98.98 Ⓕ04.75.88.96.09
Ⓦwww.hotel-le-tanargue.com
Closed *Sun evening and Mon, Oct–Dec (except during the autumn school holidays); Tues mid-Nov to end Dec; end Dec to mid-March*. **TV. Disabled access. High chairs available. Car park.**

Huddling at an altitude of 500m at the foot of the Tanargue massif on the edge of the Ardèche, this cosy hotel offers large pretty doubles for €39.50–54 with shower/wc or bath/wc. Ask for one with a view of the valley. There's a weekday lunch menu for €10.50 then others €13.90–26.50. Specialities include *roulade* of smoked trout, parsleyed frogs' legs, guinea fowl *sûpreme* with cream and bacon, and salmon terrine with Puy lentils. Portions are generous and particular care is paid to preparing the vegetable dishes. The dining room is vast, attractive, and decorated with attention to detail. *Free house apéritif offered to our readers on presentation of this guide.*

Valloire

73450

🏠 |●| Hôtel Christiania**

Ⓣ04.79.59.00.57 Ⓕ04.79.59.00.06
Ⓦwww.christiania.hotel.com
Closed *21 April–1June; 15 Sept–10 Dec*. **TV. High chairs and games available. Pay car park.**

Everyone in Valloire seems to drop in for a drink at the lively bar at some point during the day. They're all sports fans and express forthright views on stories in *L'Équipe*, the French daily sports paper. There's a relaxed, friendly, family atmosphere. The rooms are stylish with good facilities; €35–45 with basin or shower and €49–58 with shower/wc or bath. Half board, requested in winter, costs €55–68 per person. The big dining room next to the bar offers home cooking and great traditional dishes. Menus €15–29.

🏠 |●| Hôtel La Setaz - Restaurant Le Gastilleur***

Ⓣ04.79.59.01.03 Ⓕ04.79.59.00.63
Ⓦwww.la-setaz.com
Closed *Mon lunchtime in summer; 20 April to early June, 20 Sept–20 Dec*. **TV. High chairs and games available. Car park. Swimming pool.**

Despite its unprepossessing exterior, this is a very classy place. The chef prepares the kind of dishes that take his French customers back to their childhood but adapts them to suit modern tastes. You will find some of his specialities on the menus – €22 (weekday menu) and €26–37. Service is flawless and you'll get a pleasant welcome. In summer they open the heated swimming pool and often have barbecues in the peaceful garden. The hotel rooms are starkly contemporary, but they face due south and some have balconies or terraces. Doubles with shower/wc or bath €65–88. Half board is requested in winter and costs €55–82 per person. *Free coffee offered to our readers on presentation of this guide.*

|●| L'Asile des Fondues

Rue des Grandes Alpes; it's near the church and the tourist office.
☎04.79.59.04.71
Closed *1 May–26 June; 1 Sept–18 Dec.* **High chairs available.**

The restaurant has a charming country dining room with lots of style. The welcome you get is so lovely that you'll be tempted to come back time and time again – if you can cope with the touristy bits, that is. They offer at least ten types of *fondue*, *raclette* (to order) and *diots*, the local pork and vegetable sausages in white wine. You can eat for €19–27 à la carte.

Vallon-Pont-d'Arc

07150

Hôtel des Sites**

In Salavas, very close to Vallon; follow the road to Salavas-Barjac; it's 2km after the bridge, on the left.
☎04.75.88.00.85 Ⓕ04.75.88.44.60
Closed *mid-Sept to Easter.*

This hotel, recently taken over by a friendly young couple, has rapidly taken on a new lease of life. The refurbished rooms are attractive, with sponge-painted walls, individualized friezes and tasteful furniture; they also offer good value for money. Doubles €42–58, depending on the degree of comfort. The most expensive ones have a terrace. Ask for a room overlooking the countryside rather than the street. A restaurant is available to the guests of this spruce, inviting hotel. *Free coffee offered to our readers on presentation of this guide.*

|●| Hôtel Clos des Bruyères – Restaurant l'Olivette

Route des Gorges; it's just on the outskirts of Vallon, at 100m from the roundabout, on the left, towards Saint-Montan.
☎04.75.37.18.85 Ⓕ04.75.37.14.89
Ⓦwww.closdesbruyeres.net
Closed *Tues; Wed lunchtime (except July and Aug); 1 Oct–31 March.* **Disabled access. Car park. Swimming pools.**

A modern-looking, standardized type of building by the side of the road, this hotel offers good facilities. Behind it there are nice green spaces with trees. Though the rooms are functional they have a touch of individuality. Doubles, depending on the facilities and the season, cost €46–56. Some have a view of the garden and the four swimming pools; avoid those that overlook the rte. des Gorges.

|●| Restaurant Le Chelsea

Boulevard Peschère-Alizon; it's on the main street.
☎04.75.88.01.40
Closed *Oct–April.*

An Ardèche version of a trendy young restaurant. The little dining room, which leads out onto the garden, is decorated with pictures of cartoon characters. Salads (€6.80–9.40) and pastas are obviously the Chelsea's thing, but they've added a few cooked dishes to their repertoire: duck breast with honey and mint, *croustillant* of salmon with curry. There's a menu at €18. A reliable place.

Vagnas

07150 (11 km SW)

La Bastide d'Iris

300m after Vagnas, on the right, going in the direction of Barjac.
☎04.75.88.44.77 Ⓕ04.75.38.61.23
Ⓦwww.labastidediris.com
Closed *Jan.* **Car park.** *Swimming pool.*

Elegance, calm, space and serenity: these are the watchwords in this recently opened hotel with a hint of Provence about it. The attractively coloured rooms (yellow, ochre, mauve, green, etc.) all have their own distinctive décor and atmosphere, which the cordial owner will not hesitate to modify whenever he receives a flash of inspiration. Double rooms €57–80, according to the season and the degree of comfort. Suites €84–120. You can have breakfast or admire the sunsets on the attractive terrace overlooking the vineyards.

Saint-Martin-d'Ardèche

07700 (22km SE)

Hôtel-restaurant Le Bellevue**

Quai de l'Ardèche; it's opposite the port.
Ⓣ04.75.04.66.72. Ⓕ04.75.04.61.37
Ⓦwww.hotel-bellevue-restaurant.com
Closed *15 Oct–1 April.* **TV. High chairs available. Car park.**

The Bellevue has an elevated dining room and the terrace overlooks the port. The atmosphere is easy-going and they serve Ardèche specialities without frills – terrine, various fish dishes, *caillette* with boiled potatoes and *crème caramel*. It's a nice, popular place. Menus €16–23. The rooms are of superior quality, clean, with warm colours and air conditioning. Doubles €41 with shower/wc. *Free house apéritif offered to our readers on presentation of this guide.*

Orgnac-l'Aven

07150 (23km SE)

Hôtel de l'Aven***

Place de la Mairie. Take the D579 then the D217.
Ⓣ04.75.38.61.80 Ⓕ04.75.38.66.69
Ⓦwww.aven-sarrazin.com
Closed *Mon (except in season); Feb; mid-Nov to Easter.* **TV. High chairs available. Car park.**

The attentive owner welcomes you to his simple establishment. The corridors and rooms smell fresh; some of the rooms are colourful, others kept their mural carpet, those facing south have balconies. Doubles with shower/wc €43–46. Half board can be worth it. Straightforward and unaffected regional cooking: charcuterie, omelette with ceps and truffles, guinea fowl and local desserts. Service is in a rustic-style dining room or on the terrace. Menus €15–25. *10% discount on the room rate (in low season) offered to our readers on presentation of this guide.*

Vals-les-Bains

07600

Hôtel Saint-Jean**

112 [bis] rue Jean-Jaurès; it's just set back from the road, on the banks of the river Voltour.
Ⓣ04.75.37.42.50 Ⓕ04.75.37.54.77
Ⓦwww.guideweb.com/ardeche/hotel/saint-jean
Closed *Nov to mid-April.* **TV. Car park.**

A tall nineteenth-century building with a slightly sad exterior but an exuberant welcome and comfortable rooms. They have all been renovated and are lovely, though some of them are quite small. Doubles €46–58 with shower/wc or bath/wc. There's a big dining room with wide bay windows – menus €13.90–18.80. It's a classic-style place that offers peace and quiet. Nice welcome.

Grand Hôtel de Lyon***

11 av. Paul Ribeyre.
Ⓣ04.75.37.43.70 Ⓕ04.75.37.59.11
Ⓦwww.sud.ardeche.com/tourism/ohi
Closed *Oct to end April.* **TV. High chairs available. Swimming pool.**

A solid, serious hotel built at the beginning of the twentieth century – a place that won't let you down. The rooms are big, painted in pastel shades and well maintained. The bedding is cosy and smells of roses. Doubles €54–70. The swimming pool has a wave machine and a waterfall – plus it's heated. There's a TV room, a billiards room and a pretty little dining room. Honest, fortifying dishes of quality food – trout, foie gras, *caillette*, truffles – with menus €20–40, or try the weekday lunchtime *formule* at €14. *Free house apéritif offered at the restaurant to our readers on presentation of this guide.*

Hôtel-restaurant Le Vivarais

5 rue Claude Expilly.
Ⓣ04.75.94.65.85 Ⓕ04.75.37.65.47
Closed *Feb.* **TV. Swimming pool. Car park.**

Easy to find: it's the most beautiful building in town and it's painted pink. Since 1930, they have been perfecting the art of providing good beds and good food for their guests. The décor is Art Deco, from the wallpaper and the colours to the furniture and even some of the baths. A high degree of comfort and luxury, with excellent service. Doubles €55–120. The standard at table is just as high and Madame is a wonderful advocate for her region's cuisine. There's a two-course *formule* at €19 including a glass of wine and coffee and menus at €30–50. *Free chestnut Kir and a chestnut and onion pancake offered to our readers on presentation of this guide.*

Restaurant Chez Mireille

3 rue Jean-Jaurès; it's at the end of the main road.

☎04.75.37.49.06
Closed *Tues and Wed evenings out of season; a fortnight in Oct.* **High chairs available.**

Chez Mireille is run by Colette, whose cuisine is highly recommended. Everything is cooked in her kitchen – it may seem odd to have to say this, but it's not always the case. The filling *menu ardéchois* has two starters, and is simply superb. While the cooking is certainly respectful of tradition, there's something individual about it, too: poached eggs with smoked salmon, frogs' legs *à la provençale*, and iced nougat with chestnut pancake. Menus €10 (served lunch and dinnertime as a main course and a dessert) and €14–30.

Vans (Les)

07140

Hôtel Les Cévennes

Place Ollier; it's in the main square.
☎04.75.37.23.09
Closed *Mon; 1–15 May, 1–15 Oct.* **Car park.**

From the minute you walk in, you're aware of a very special atmosphere – a sort of gentle madness that's infected the place for nigh-on forty years, tempered with the straight talking of the *patronne* Marie-Renée. The highly individual décor is a real jumble, with flowers, paintings, photos and old documents all jostling for space. The restaurant serves generous portions – crêpes from the Cévennes, *coq au vin*, and many regional dishes. Half board is compulsory in summer at €32 per person. Set menus €16–30. It is undoubtedly better-known for its cooking than as a hotel, but its double rooms with basin go for €25, with shower and wc on the landing.

Hôtel Le Mas de l'Espaïre**

Bois de Païolive; it's 5km from Les Vans.
☎04.75.94.95.01 Ⓕ04.75.37.21.00
Ⓦwww.hotel-espaire.com
Closed *mid-Nov to mid-March.* **Disabled access. TV. Swimming pool. Car park.**

There's a sense of calm in this sturdy, imposing building in a splendid setting, and you're put at your ease by the excellent welcome. All the facilities you need for a good stay are here: lots of space inside and out, a swimming pool and even cicadas chirruping in the background. Doubles with en-suite bathrooms €52–82, depending on the comfort and the season. The dining room is open to residents only, and offers a daily changing menu for €23. You can go on wonderful walks through the magical Païolive forest, which adjoins the property. *Free house apéritif offered to our readers on presentation of this guide.*

Restaurant Le Grangousier

Rue Courte; it's opposite the church.
☎04.75.94.90.86
Closed *Wed, except July–Aug; Tues out of season; 1 Jan–14 Feb; 1–15 Dec.*

This stylish restaurant serves daily menus and gourmet menus which will delight even the most ardent foodie. The cooking is imaginative – foie gras with cream and nettle sauce, salad of pan-fried foie gras with chestnuts, vacherin with chestnuts. The dining room, with its vaulted ceiling and dressed stone walls, is the perfect setting for these wonderful delicacies and although the place is smart, prices are fair: menus €18–52. Lunch dishes (€10–15) change daily. The wine list includes a number of very affordable bottles.

La Rose des Vans

11 rue des Bourgades.
☎04.75.37.38.05
Closed *Wed lunch, in season; Tues evening and Wed, out of season.* **Open** *for lunch only in autumn and in winter.*

This is a pleasant restaurant that pays tribute to local produce while also adding a few Oriental touches. Menus €12.50–15; platters €12. The dining room may be a bit spartan, but there's a little courtyard hidden in the back that more than makes up for it – not to mention the striking toilets, where the owners have really splashed out.

Vienne

38200

Restaurant L'Estancot

4 rue de la Table-Ronde.
☎04.74.85.12.09
Closed *Sun; Mon; public holidays.* **Disabled access.**

Situated in a quiet side street in the old town near the Saint-André-le-Bas church, *L'Estancot* has a pretty façade with window boxes laden with flowers and a long, beautiful dining room. Dishes of the day go for €7 (including a starter); menus cost €11.50 (weekday lunchtimes), €15 and €21. The house specialities are *criques* (made with potatoes, chopped parsley and eggs – only served Sat), and *paillassons* (plain potatoes) accompanied by all sorts of delicious things. Other delights include sea-urchin flan with shellfish sauce, veal kidneys with walnut wine and pears poached in vanilla with caramel sauce. Super-fast service. Reservations only.

Estrablin

38780 (8km E)

La Gabetière***

Take the D502 and it's on the left after the crossroads that lead you to Estrablin.
Ⓣ04.74.58.01.31 Ⓕ04,74.58.08.98
Closed *1–10 Jan.* **TV. High chairs and games available. Car park. Swimming pool.**

You'll want to hide away forever in this lovely, luxurious sixteenth-century stone manor house – especially if you get a room with a view of the grounds. The décor is exquisitely tasteful and the welcome is simple, warm and attentive. Rooms €45 with shower/wc, €56–62 with bath; a suite in the tower sleeps four. There's a welcoming bar-cum-TV room, a heated pool and tables in the garden where you can have your picnic. This really is an unusually lovely place and the charming *patronne* will give you all sorts of information about what to see.

Villard-de-Lans

38250

Villa Primerose**

147 av. des Bains.
Ⓣ04.76.95.13.17
Ⓦwww.hotel-villa-primerose.com
Closed *15–30 April; 1 Oct–20 Dec.* **High chairs and games available. Car park.**

Here's a place where they really make you feel welcome. The quiet rooms in this beautiful building look out onto the Gerbier mountain range. You'll pay for a double €24–32 with basin, €33–42 with shower/wc; they have some communicating rooms ideal for families. There's no restaurant, but the owner lets residents use the kitchens to cook meals which they are invited to eat in the dining room. Breakfast €5. *Free use of the kitchen offered to our readers on presentation of this guide.*

À la Ferme du Bois Barbu**

It's 3km from the centre in the direction of Bois-Barbu.
Ⓣ04.76.95.13.09 Ⓕ04.76.94.10.65
Ⓦwww.planete.vercors.com/fermeboisbarbu
Restaurant closed *Wed; Sun evening. Closed 13–21 April, 3rd week of June; 15 Nov–8 Dec.* **TV. High chairs and games available. Car park.**

A real mountain inn on the edge of a forest and next to a – not very busy – road. You can sit on the lovely terrace or relax in a nice comfy armchair while Nadine, your hostess, plays the piano. Eight small rooms €42–50 with shower/wc; they've all been recently renovated. They prefer you to stay half-board in high season at €42–48. It's ideal for cross-country skiers, since the trails are just nearby, as well as for hikers and mountain bikers. Menus, €15.50–26, list delicious local dishes that change according to the seasons: terrine of Bleu du Vercors cheese and hazelnuts, trout *rillettes*, bacon and oyster mushrooms in flaky pastry, local pork with onion marmalade and hazelnut *confit*, semi-cooked foie gras with wine, veal stuffed with nuts. *10% discount on the room rate (out of season) offered to our readers on presentation of this guide.*

Malaterre

Lieu-dit Malaterre; from Villars, take the D215C, shortly after Bois-Barbu turn onto the forest road signposted to Malaterre.
Ⓣ04.76.95.94.34
Open *daily noon–6pm (July–Aug and Dec–March); Fri evening (July–Aug); Sun only (Sept–Oct and April–June).*

An excellent restaurant in an old wooden house in the forest. The building dates from the 1900s; there's no electricity and water is still brought up by tanker. Lydia and Bernard, who run a farm nearby, decided to revive this place by providing good food and drink for cross-country skiers and walkers. There's a fantastic variety of foresters' implements ornamenting the walls, and the atmosphere is genuinely warm. When the weather's fine it's wonderful to sit out on the terrace, and when it's cold you can warm your hands around a bowl of good vegetable soup and munch on home-made bread baked in the wood-fired oven. Menus, €10.50 (lunchtimes) and €16, list genuine regional cuisine which relies on fresh produce from the farm – try the Vercors platter, ravioli de Royans, *caillette*, blue Vercors cheese, mushroom omelette, charcuterie, *gratiné* of ravioli with oyster mushrooms and ceps or fillet of smoked trout. And leave space for pudding – there's home-made spice cake with honey and *tarte tatin*. At teatime they offer delicious ice creams. To drink, you can choose between the local *rataplane* (sold by the litre jug), cider and local apple juice. On Friday evenings in summer, your hosts recount the legends of the Vercors around the fire. Credit cards not accepted. *Free house liqueur offered to our readers on presentation of this guide.*

Corrençon-en-Vercors

38250 (6km S)

Le Caribou

Le Clos de la Balme. Take the D215C; it's 2km after the golf course, practically at the foot of the ski runs.
Ⓣ04.76.95.82.82 Ⓕ04.76.95.83.17
Ⓦwww.caribou-vercors.com
Closed *15 Sept–1 Dec; 31 March–15 May.* **High chairs and games available. Car park. Swimming pool.**

The rooms are painted in yellow, green or red and all have en-suite bathrooms and telephone. Doubles €45 with shower/wc or bath for two to three people. Half board is at €49 per person. The restaurant has a lovely wooden floor and is decorated with souvenirs from Africa and Indonesia. Menus, which change frequently, go for €10–16. You'll pay around €25 for a menu à la carte. The owners are lovely and they create a good-humoured atmosphere. There's lots to do – swimming pool, sauna, kids' games, ping-pong and painting class, and even a cabaret at apéritif time. It's great for young families.

Hôtel du Golf – Restaurant du Blois Fleuri***

It's on the D215C between the golf course and the village.
Ⓣ04.76.95.84.84 Ⓕ04.76.95.82.85
Ⓦwww.planete-vercors.com/hotel-du-golf
Closed *Mon–Thurs lunchtimes (except in July/Aug); April; Nov.* **TV. High chairs and games available. Car park. Swimming pool.**

This old farmhouse was restored by the present owners' grandparents and they've recently had it renovated. There's nothing to match it in the luxury category in town. It offers a dozen rooms, two with balconies and some sleeping up to five. They're individually decorated and cosy with the bathroom and separate wc off the spacious entrance hall. Wood panelling and dried flowers complete the picture. And those added extras are provided – mini-bar and dressing gowns. You'll pay €98–120 for a double room with bath. The restaurant opens up onto the terrace in good weather. There's a menu at €29. Specialities include pan-fried crayfish tails in a piquant sauce, and sole in flaky pastry. In the grounds there's a heated swimming pool and sauna. *One free breakfast per room per night or 10% discount on the room rate (in low season) offered to our readers on presentation of this guide.*

Rencurel

38680 (15km NW)

Hôtel le Maronnier**

Take the D531 for 12km, then turn right onto the D35.
Ⓣ04.76.38.97.68 Ⓕ04.76.38.98.99
Ⓦwww.hotellemarronnier.com
Closed *1 Nov–20 Dec.* **TV. High chairs and games available. Swimming pool.**

A typical Vercors house belonging to a Dutch couple. All the rooms, which are located either in the main building or in the more sombre annexe, have en-suite bathrooms; nos. 1 and 2 have large terraces overlooking the solar-heated swimming pool. The bedding is quality, though the doubles have single mattresses with individual duvets. Doubles €45–50. There's also a sauna, and a sitting room with a fireplace, library and TV. The cuisine is typical of the region, with a touch of the Mediterranean. Good choices include trout fillet with ravioli, duck breast in port sauce, and sugar tart. Lunch menu €17.50, with another at €21.50. *Free house apéritif offered to our readers on presentation of this guide.*

Choranche

38680 (24km W)

Restaurant Le Cournier

Grottes de Choranche; it's on the road to Pont-en-Royans, 2km before you get to the village on the right of the road that goes to the top of the cliff.

Ⓣ04.76.36.09.88
Open *lunchtimes 11.45am–2pm*. **Closed** *1 day per week; 1 Nov–31 March*. **Disabled access.**

The panoramic view over the Cirque de Choranche is fantastic. Peregrine falcons live in the cliffs above, and the unforgettable Choranche caves, which are unique in Europe, are nearby. Good food served here, with menus €16–24; typical offerings include warm *caillette* with salad and a list of snacks and sandwiches. The first menu includes a starter, a main course and a dessert.

Villars-les-Dombes

01330

Restaurant L'Écu de France

Rue du Commerce; it's on the main street, near to the church.
Ⓣ04.74.98.01.79
Closed *Sun–Tues evenings; Wed; Jan.*

A traditional restaurant serving regional dishes – lots of Bresse chicken but also parsleyed frogs' legs and duck breast. It's an affordable place to eat in this somewhat touristy town: menus €16–36. Old photographs of the town hang on the wall.

Bouligneux

01130 (4km NW)

Le Thou

Take the D2 Chatillon-sur-Chalaronne road.
Ⓣ04.74.98.15.25
Closed *Mon; Tues; 4–24 Feb; 1–14 Oct.*
Disabled access.

An appealing restaurant. The dining room walls are hung with a variety of pictures, and there's a mature garden with a terrace. The chef's speciality is carp served in many delicious guises: salad of smoked carp and quail eggs, flaky pastry with carp and lobster's *bisque*. The cheeses and the desserts are perfect and the wine list is splendid. It's a good idea to reserve, especially in summer. Menus €27–49 or around €42 à la carte. *Free coffee offered to our readers on presentation of this guide.*

Joyeux

01800 (8km SE)

La Bicyclette Bleue

Take the D904 from Villars in the direction of Chalamont then turn right onto the D61 for 2km and it's in the centre of the village.
Ⓣ04.74.98.21.48
Closed *Tues evening and Wed (except July–Aug); mid-Dec to mid-Jan. Disabled access. Games available.*

An isolated country restaurant in a renovated farmhouse. It's fresh and friendly and smoothly run by a family and their donkey d'Artagnan. It's a lovely place to have lunch – fine in the dining room but even better under the awning. Lots of unpretentious local dishes attentively prepared and thoughtfully cooked: farmhouse chicken with cream sauce, carp fillet with sorrel, fresh frogs' legs. Lunch menu at €18, and other menus €20–29. Try the house cocktail made with sparkling Bugey wine. You can hire a bike and take off through the countryside. Kids especially will love it.

Ambérieux-en-Dombes

01330 (11km W)

Auberge des Bichonnières**

Take the D904 at the edge of town off the road to Ars.
Ⓣ04.74.00.82.07 Ⓕ04.74.00.89.21
Ⓦwww.aubergedesbichonnieres.com
Closed *Mon and Tues lunchtimes in season; Sun evening and Mon (Oct–June); mid-Dec to mid-Jan.* **Car park. TV.**

A very pleasant family hotel-restaurant in a lovely farm. Agreeable, cosy rooms with beams. Doubles €50–60 with shower/wc or bath. The dining room is decorated in woody tones and there's a patio that's festooned with flowers in summer. Genuine gourmet cuisine is generously and elegantly served: classic dishes include parsleyed frogs' legs, *croustillant* of calf's head, and chicken with cream or pimentos. Menus, €24 and €33, change with the seasons.

Sainte-Croix

01120 (14km se)

Chez Nous**

It's in the village; take the D22 as far as Pizay, then turn right onto the D61.
Ⓣ04.78.06.60.60 Ⓕ04.78.06.63.26
Closed *Sun evening; Mon.* **Disabled access. High chairs available.**

Set well back from the road in the countryside, this comfortable establishment offers very quiet rooms in a modern annexe; doubles with bath €46. Menus start at €18 (weekday lunchtimes), with others €24–45. Though you can get traditional cuisine, they also list interesting variations on the regional theme. Specialities include fresh frogs' legs, free-range poultry with morels and cream, home-made duck foie gras and sea fish.

Ars-sur-Formans

01480 (19km W)

Hôtel-Restaurant La Bonne Étoile

Rue J.-M.-Vianney. Take the D904, opposite the car park.
☎ 04.74.00.77.38 Fax 04.74.08.10.18
Closed *Mon evening; Tues; Jan.*

This village is where the relics of Saint Curé are to be found and it attracts many pilgrims. When the Pope visited, he had a meal in this very restaurant – the plate he used is hung up outside the door. It's a welcoming establishment, and the clean rooms smell delicious. Doubles €40 with shower/wc. The owner collects all sorts of knick-knacks – dolls and coffee pots in particular. Simple, unpretentious dishes – fish stew, zander with vanilla – with menus at €12–28. Reserve in advance. *10% discount on the room rate offered to our readers on presentation of this guide.*

Viviers

07220

Restaurant de l'Horloge

Faubourg le Cire; it's on the N86.
☎ 04.75.52.62.43
Closed *Sun evening; Mon.* **Disabled access.**

When you see the neon signs, it's hard to believe what awaits inside. The dining room is vast and decorated by huge murals from the nineteenth century, painted by passing artists. The robust, tasty Ardèche cooking is prepared using fresh market produce. You eat well and cheaply: dish of the day served lunch and dinnertime, €6.90, and three menus from €9.50 (a steal; it's €11 on Sun) up to €18.

Vonnas

01540

L'Ancienne Auberge

Place du Marché.
☎ 04.74.50.90.50
Closed *Jan.* **Disabled access. TV. Swimming pool. Car park.**

Vonnas is the home town of star chef Georges Blanc – his own restaurant is across the road from this old inn, still run by his family. It's full of old family photographs and collections of bottles, and is opposite a romantic little wooden bridge over the Veyle. In summer you can enjoy the terrace and patio at the back. The service is polite, efficient and swift. You start with an appetizer and delicious cocktail, setting you up for your meal and the local regional wines. The recipes and produce used come from the region: chicken liver and morels in pastry, pan-fried king prawns with lemongrass, sautéed frogs' legs "comme en Dombes", *poulet de Bresse* and chicken liver gâteau cooked to Grandmother Blanc's recipe. And the prices are reasonable: the menu of the day costs €17 and the others (€19–40) are simply amazing for what they cost. It's a tad over-commercialized – lots of "Blanc" produce on sale – but it's still superb. They also offer hotel rooms, with doubles for €110.

Rough Guides

advertiser

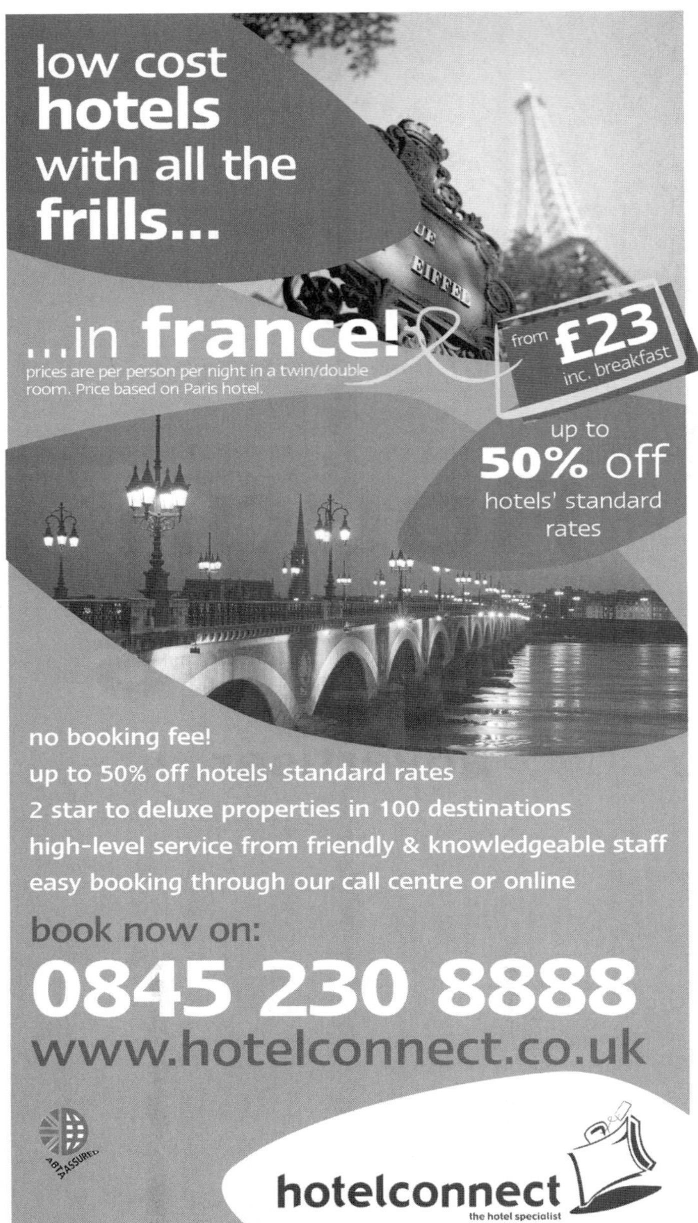
low cost
hotels
with all the
frills...
...in france!
prices are per person per night in a twin/double room. Price based on Paris hotel.
from £23 inc. breakfast
up to
50% off
hotels' standard rates
no booking fee!
up to 50% off hotels' standard rates
2 star to deluxe properties in 100 destinations
high-level service from friendly & knowledgeable staff
easy booking through our call centre or online
book now on:
0845 230 8888
www.hotelconnect.co.uk
ABTA ASSURED
hotelconnect
the hotel specialist

DIRECTIONS

PUBLISHED MAY 2004

1843533146

1843533154

1843530937

1843533170

1843533189

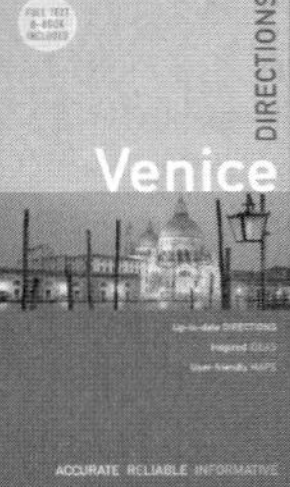

1843533537

PUBLISHED AUGUST 2004

1843533065

1843533197

1843533200

1843533219

1843533227

1843533235

US$10.99 · Can$15.99 · £6.99

Rough Guide Maps, printed on waterproof and rip-proof Yupo™ paper, offer an unbeatable combination of practicality, clarity of design and amazing value.

CITY MAPS

Amsterdam · Barcelona · Berlin · Boston · Brussels · Dublin
Florence & Siena · Frankfurt · London · Los Angeles
Miami · New York · Paris · Prague · Rome
San Francisco · Venice · Washington DC and more...

COUNTRY & REGIONAL MAPS

Andalucía · Argentina · Australia · Baja California · Cuba
Cyprus · Dominican Republic · Egypt · Greece
Guatemala & Belize · Ireland · Mexico · Morocco
New Zealand · South Africa · Sri Lanka · Tenerife · Thailand
Trinidad & Tobago Yucatán Peninsula · and more...

US$9.99 Can$13.99 £5.99

small print and
Index

A Rough Guide to Rough Guides

In the summer of 1981, Mark Ellingham, a recent graduate from Bristol University, was travelling round Greece and couldn't find a guidebook that really met his needs. On the one hand there were the student guides, insistent on saving every last cent, and on the other the heavyweight cultural tomes whose authors seemed to have spent more time in a research library than lounging away the afternoon at a taverna or on the beach.

In a bid to avoid getting a job, Mark and a small group of writers set about creating their own guidebook. It was a guide to Greece that aimed to combine a journalistic approach to description with a thoroughly practical approach to travellers' needs – a guide that would incorporate culture, history and contemporary insights with a critical edge, together with up-to-date, value-for-money listings. Back in London, Mark and the team finished their Rough Guide, as they called it, and talked Routledge into publishing the book.

That first *Rough Guide to Greece*, published in 1982, was a student scheme that became a publishing phenomenon. The immediate success of the book – with numerous reprints and a Thomas Cook prize shortlisting – spawned a series that rapidly covered dozens of destinations. Rough Guides had a ready market among low-budget backpackers, but soon also acquired a much broader and older readership that relished Rough Guides' wit and inquisitiveness as much as their enthusiastic, critical approach. Everyone wants value for money, but not at any price.

Rough Guides soon began supplementing the "rougher" information about hostels and low-budget listings with the kind of detail on restaurants and quality hotels that independent-minded visitors on any budget might expect, whether on business in New York or trekking in Thailand.

These days the guides – distributed worldwide by the Penguin group – offer recommendations from shoestring to luxury and cover more than 200 destinations around the globe, including almost every country in the Americas and Europe, more than half of Africa and most of Asia and Australasia. Our ever-growing team of authors and photographers is spread all over the world, particularly in Europe, the USA and Australia.

In 1994, we published the *Rough Guide to World Music* and *Rough Guide to Classical Music*; and a year later the *Rough Guide to the Internet*. All three books have become benchmark titles in their fields – which encouraged us to expand into other areas of publishing, mainly around popular culture. Rough Guides now publish:

- Travel guides to more than 200 worldwide destinations
- Dictionary phrasebooks to 22 major languages
- History guides ranging from Ireland to Islam
- Maps printed on rip-proof and waterproof Polyart™ paper
- Music guides running the gamut from Opera to Elvis
- Restaurant guides to London, New York and San Francisco
- Reference books on topics as diverse as the Weather and Shakespeare
- Sports guides from Formula 1 to Man Utd
- Pop culture books from *Lord of the Rings* to Cult TV
- World Music CDs in association with World Music Network

Visit **www.roughguides.com** to see our latest publications.

Rough Guide Credits

Layout: Ajay Verma
Cartography: Katie Lloyd-Jones and Miles Irving
Proofreader: Ken Bell
Design: Diana Jarvis
Production: Julia Bovis
Editorial: London Martin Dunford, Kate Berens, Helena Smith, Claire Saunders, Geoff Howard, Ruth Blackmore, Gavin Thomas, Polly Thomas, Richard Lim, Lucy Ratcliffe, Clifton Wilkinson, Alison Murchie, Fran Sandham, Sally Schafer, Alexander Mark Rogers, Karoline Densley, Andy Turner, Ella O'Donnell, Keith Drew, Andrew Lockett, Joe Staines, Duncan Clark, Peter Buckley, Matthew Milton; **New York** Andrew Rosenberg, Richard Koss, Yuki Takagaki, Hunter Slaton, Chris Barsanti, Steven Horak
Design & Pictures: London Simon Bracken, Dan May, Diana Jarvis, Mark Thomas, Jj Luck, Harriet Mills; **Delhi** Madhulita Mohapatra, Umesh Aggarwal, Ajay Verma, Jessica Subramanian
Production: Julia Bovis, John McKay, Sophie Hewat
Cartography: **London** Maxine Repath, Ed Wright, Katie Lloyd-Jones, Miles Irving; **Delhi** Manish Chandra, Rajesh Chhibber, Jai Prakesh Mishra, Ashutosh Bharti, Rajesh Mishra, Animesh Pathak, Jasbir Sandhu, Karobi Gogoi
Cover art direction: Louise Boulton
Online: **New York** Jennifer Gold, Cree Lawson, Suzanne Welles, Benjamin Ross; **Delhi** Manik Chauhan, Narender Kumar, Shekhar Jha, Rakesh Kumar
Marketing & Publicity: **London** Richard Trillo, Niki Smith, David Wearn, Chloë Roberts, Demelza Dallow, Kristina Pentland; **New York** Geoff Colquitt, Megan Kennedy
Finance: Gary Singh
Manager India: Punita Singh
Series editor: Mark Ellingham
PA to Managing Director: Julie Sanderson
Managing Director: Kevin Fitzgerald

Le guide du Routard

Directeur de Collection et auteur: Philippe Gloaguen
Cofondateurs: Philppe Gloaguen et Michel Duval
Rédacteur en chef: Pierre Josse
Rédacteurs en chef adjoints: Amanda Keravel et Benoît Lucchini
Directrice de la Coordination: Florence Charmetant
Directeur de routard.com: Yves Couprie
Rédaction: Olivier Page, Véronique de Chardon, Isabelle Al Subaihi, Anne-Caroline Dumas, Carole Bordes, Bénédicte Bazaille, André Poncelet, Marie Burin des Roziers, Thierry Brouard, Géraldine Lemaruf-Beauvois, Anne Poinsot, Mahtilde de Boisgrollier, Gavin's Clemente-Ruïz, Fabrice de Lestang, Alain Pallier et Fiona Debrabander.

Publishing Information

The Rough Guide to French Hotels and Restaurants le guide du Routard
English edition
2004
Le Guide du Routard
Editor: Philippe Gloaguen
Translation and revision produced by Book Production Consultants plc, Cambridge in association with First Edition Translations Ltd, Cambridge, England
This seventh edition published November 2004 by **Rough Guides Ltd**,
80 Strand, London WC2R 0RL.
345 Hudson St, 4th Floor,
New York, NY 10014, USA.
Distributed by the Penguin Group
Penguin Books Ltd,
80 Strand, London WC2R 0RL
Penguin Putnam, Inc.
375 Hudson Street, NY 10014, USA
Penguin Books Australia Ltd,
487 Maroondah Highway, PO Box 257,
Ringwood, Victoria 3134, Australia
Penguin Books Canada Ltd,
10 Alcorn Avenue, Toronto, Ontario,
Canada M4V 1E4
Penguin Books (NZ) Ltd,
182–190 Wairau Road, Auckland 10,
New Zealand
Typeset in Bembo and Helvetica to an original design by Henry Iles and Diana Jarvis.
Printed in Italy by LegoPrint S.p.A

944pp includes prelims and index
A catalogue record for this book is available from the British Library

ISBN 1-84353-255-7

1 3 5 7 9 8 6 4 2

Help us update

We've gone to a lot of effort to ensure that the seventh edition of **The Rough Guide to French Hotels & Restaurants** is accurate and up-to-date. However, things change – places get "discovered", opening hours are notoriously fickle, restaurants and rooms raise prices or lower standards. If you feel we've got it wrong or left something out, we'd like to know, and if you can remember the address, the price, the time, the phone number, so much the better.

We'll credit all contributions, and send a copy of the next edition (or any other Rough Guide if you prefer) for the best letters. Everyone who writes to us and isn't already a subscriber will receive a copy of our full-colour thrice-yearly newsletter. Please mark letters: "**Rough Guide to French Hotels & Restaurants Update**" and send to: Rough Guides, 80 Strand, London WC2R 0RL, or Rough Guides, 4th Floor, 345 Hudson St, New York, NY 10014. Or send an email to **mail@roughguides.com**

Have your questions answered and tell others about your trip at **www.roughguides.atinfopop.com**

Acknowledgements

Thanks to Karen Weaver, Monique Lantelme and all those at Lexus who worked on the first edition: Jane Goldie, Céline Reynaud, Peter Terrell, Sophie Curien, Alice Grandison, Leslie Harkins, Sarah Cartwright, David Alun Jones and Anita Leyerzapf.

Thanks also to Ajay Verma and Diana Jarvis for typesetting, Katie Lloyd-Jones and Miles Irving for maps and Ken Bell for proofreading.

Cover credits

Front main © John Miller
Front small top: restaurant sign © Robert Harding
Front small lower: bread © Robert Harding
Back top: Calvi, Balagne Region: © Robert Harding
Back lower: La Cigale, Nantes © Corbis

Index

Map entries are in **colour**.

A

Abergement-Clemenciat (L') 842
Abreschviller 481
Abrest 118
Abries 791
Accolay 160
Aclron 276
Acquigny 636
Agde 409
Agen 25
Agnetz 700
Ahetze 38
Aigle (L') 593
Aignan 515
Aigues-Mortes 412
Aiguèze 448
Aiguillon 29
Ainhoa 47
Aix (Île d') 709
Aix-en-Provence 745
Aix-en-Provence 748
Aixe-sur-Vienne 469
Aix-les-Bains 815
Ajaccio 291
Alba-la-Romaine 818
Alban 515
Albas 527
Albert 695
Albertville 818
Albi 515
Alençon 596
Alès 413
Alésia 158
Alissas 880
Alix 825
Allanche 105
Allevard 819
Allogny 228
Allouville-Bellefosse 647
Altkirch 1
Alsace 2
Ambérieux-en-Dombes 905
Ambert 81
Ambierie 884
Amboise 219
Amélie-les-Bains 414
Amiens 695
Amiens 699
Amilly 243
Ammerschwihr 5
Amondans 319
Ancenis 649
Ancy-le-Franc 121
Andelys (Les) 621
Andernos-les-Bains 29
Andlau 3
Andon 811
Andrezieux-Bouthéon 891
Anduze 414
Angers 649
Angers 652–653
Angerville 325
Anglards-de-Salers 100
Angles (Les) 456
Angles-sur-L'Anglin 709
Anglet 37
Angoulême 709
Annecy 819
Annecy 820–821
Annesse-et-Baulieu 67
Anneville-en-Saire 599
Annonay 824
Annot 750
Anse 825
Antibes 750
Antignac 111
Antonne et Trigonant 30
Antraigues-sur-Volane 826
Apt 751
Aquitaine 26–27
Arbigny 826
Arbois 301
Arbonne 38
Arcachon 30
Arçais 725
Arcangues 37
Arc-en-Barrois 271
Arcins 57
Arcis-sur-Aube 263
Arcizac-Adour 557
Arcizans-Avant 520
Arconsat 81
Arès 31
Argein 554
Argelès-Gazost 519
Argentan 596
Argentat 457
Argentière 839
Argenton-sur-Creuse 222
Argent-sur-Sauldre 222
Argoules 700
Arles 752
Armoy 896
Arnac-Pompadour 457
Arnay-le-Duc 124
Arques (Les) 520
Arques-la-Bataille 628
Arradon 216
Arras 567
Arreau 520
Ars-en-Ré 714
Arsonval 265
Ars-sur-Formans 906
Arvieux 753
Arzacq 31
Arzon 165
Ascain 70
Asnières 325
Aspres-sur-Buëch 754
Astaffort 31
Aubenas 826
Auberive 275
Aubervilliers 325
Aubeterre-sur-Dronne 715
Aubignosc 769
Aubigny-sur-Nère 222
Aubusson 460
Aubusson-d'Auvergne 81
Auch 520
Auderville 608
Audierne 165
Audincourt 317
Augne 473
Aullène 293
Aulnay 715
Aulon 521
Ault 707
Aumale 621
Aumont-Aubrac 415
Aunay-sur-Odon 596
Auphelle 472
Auray 165
Aurec-sur-Loire 84
Aurillac 84
Auron 754
Autrans 827
Autreville 488
Autun 124
Auvergne 82–83
Auvers-sur-Oise 328
Auvillar 521
Auvillars-sur-Saone 152
Auxerre 125
Avallon 126
Aveize 892

Avèze 454
Avignon 754
Avignon................756–757
Avranches 597
Ax-les-Thermes 522
Azay-le-Rideau 223

B

Baccarat 484
Baerenthal.....................486
Bagnere-de-Luchon......523
Bagnères-de-Bigorre 522
Bagnoles-de-l'Orne 597
Bagnolet........................397
Bagnols-sur-Cèze 448
Bains-les-Bains.............484
Baix 880
Balazuc 859
Ballots 661
Ban-de-la-Veline 506
Bandol...........................755
Bangor 169
Banyuls-des-Aspres 446
Banyuls-sur-Mer 415
Barbizon........................328
Barcelonnette................755
Barcus.............................32
Bardigues......................521
Barèges.........................525
Barenton 598
Barfleur 599
Bargemon 759
Barils (Les) 644
Barjac............................416
Bar-le-Duc 484
Barnave.........................848
Barneville-Carteret........599
Barr 1
Barroux (Le) 759
Bar-sur-Aube.................263
Basse-Goulaine 681
Basse-Normandie
..........................594–595
Bastelicaccia.................293
Bastia 294
Batz (ile de)...................207
Batz-sur-Mer.................657
Bauduen 759
Baugé............................656
Baule (La)......................656
Baume-les-Dames........301
Baume-les-Messieurs...314
Baux-de-Provence (Les)
....................................759
Bayeux 600
Bayonne..........................32
Bazarnes.......................160
Bazas 33
Bazeilles........................284
Beaubery.......................133
Beaucaire......................416
Beaufort-sur-Doron.......828
Beaugency 223
Beaujeu.........................828
Beaulieu-sur-Dordogne 461
Beaulieu-sur-Mer 760
Beaumarches................541
Beaumettes...................777
Beaumont-en-Veron 239
Beaumont-le-Roger 624
Beaune..........................126
Beaurecueil 750
Beausoleil 790
Beauvais 700
Beauvezer 760
Beauvoir....................... 614
Bédarieux......................426
Béhuard 655
Belcastel 525
Belfort 304
Belhade...........................34
Bellême 601
Bellerive-sur-Allier.........117
Belleroche 828
Belleville........................829
Belz 168
Bénévent L'Abbaye.......477
Bénodet 169
Benouville 616
Bény-Bocage (Le) 620
Berck-sur-Mer...............570
Bergerac 34
Bergères-lès-Vertus 272
Bergheim.........................14
Bergues.........................577
Bernay...........................624
Berzé-la-Ville.................136
Besançon......................306
Besançon 307
Bessat (Le)....................889
Besse et St Anastaise.....85
Besse-en-Oisans 829
Béthune 571
Beuvron-en-Auge 602
Beuzeville.....................637
Béziers 416
Biarritz.............................36
Bidarray 72
Bidart 38
Biert 525
Binic 170
Biriatou............................54
Biscarrosse 38
Bislée 506
Bitche............................485
Blanc (Le) 224
Blendecques 588
Blessac 460
Blienschwiller 3
Blois 225
Blot-L'Eglise..................113
Boen 830
Boeschepe....................575
Bois-le-Roi 334
Bois-Plage-en-Ré (Le) ...715
Bonifacio.......................295
Bonnétables..................664
Bonneval-sur-Arc 831
Bonnieux.......................760
Bonny-sur-Loire 231
Bonomme (Le) 9
Bordeaux 39
Bordeaux 40–41
Bormes-les-Mimosas ...761
Bosc (Le).......................535
Boudes............................86
Bougival 329
Bouille (La) 642
Bouin.............................658
Bouligneux 905
Boulogne-Billancourt 397
Boulogne-sur-Mer.........572
Bourbon-Lancy 128
Bourbon-L'Archambault...86
Bourbonne les-Bains 266
Bourboule (La) 87
Bourg-en-Bresse 831
Bourges.........................227
Bourges 228–229
Bourg-et-Comin 708
Bourget-du-Lac (Le) 833
Bourg-Lastic 88
Bourgogne............122–123
Bourgoin-Jallieu 833
Bourg-Saint-Maurice 835
Bourgueil.......................228
Bourgvilain 136
Bourron-Marlotte 334
Boussac 461
Boutenac-Touvent 740
Bouze-lès-Beaune 128
Bouzigues 452
Boyardville 717
Brantome 45
Bray-et-Lû.................... 329
Bresse L(a) 492
Brest 171
Bretagne 166–167
Bréviandes 287
Brevonnes 277
Brezolles 231
Briançon........................761
Briare 231
Briey..............................486
Brigue (La)....................803
Brinay 148

Brionne 624
Brioude 88
Brison-Saint-Innocent ... 818
Brissac 418
Brive-la-Gaillarde 461
Brives 242
Brizards (Les) 154
Brou 241
Brousses 551
Bruere-Allichamps 252
Bugarach 423
Buis-les-Baronnies 836
Bully 884
Bully-les-Mines 571
Burlats 529
Buxy 132
Buzançais 236
Buzancy 290
Buzet sur Baize 46

C

Cabourg 602
Cabriac 533
Cadouin 60
Caen 602
Caen 604–605
Cagnes sur Mer 763
Cahors 525
Cahuzac-sur-Vere 527
Calais 573
Calvi 296
Calvinet 102
Camaret 173
Cambo-les-Bains 46
Cambrai 574
Campigny 637
Cancale 173
Canet-en-Roussillon 445
Canet-Plage 446
Cangey 219
Cannes 763
Canon (Le) 49
Cap d'Antibes 751
Capbreton 48
Cap-Ferret 48
Cappelle-Brouck 577
Captieux 34
Carantec 174
Carcassonne 418
Carennac 549
Carentan 607
Carhaix-Plouguer 175
Carignan 285
Carmaux 527
Carnac 175
Carpentras 765
Carquefou 681
Cartelegue 49
Casamozza 295
Cassel 575
Cassis 766
Cassuéjouls 538
Casteljaloux 49
Castellane 767
Castelnaudary 420
Castelnau-de-Levis 519
Castelnau-de-Montmiral 527
Castelnau-Magnoac 528
Castelsarrasin 528
Castera-Verduzan 528
Castillion de Larboust ... 524
Castillones 49
Castres 528
Caudebec-en-Caux 625
Caunes-Minervois 421
Caussade 529
Cauterets 530
Cavaillon 768
Cavanac 420
Caylus 530
Celle-Saint-Cyr (La) 145
Celles-sur-Belle 723
Celles-sur-Plaine 486
Centre 220–221
Cepoy 244
Ceret 421
Cergy 401
Cérilly 87
Cerizay 723
Cervieres 837
Cessieu 834
Cessy 852
Chablis 129
Chabris 231
Chaffayer 768
Chagny 130
Chaise-Dieu (La) 89
Chalais 717
Chalamont 837
Chaldette (La) 438
Chalezeule 309
Chalinargues 105
Challans 658
Châlons-en-Champagne 266
Chalon-sur-Saône 131
Chamalières 96
Chamarandes 269
Chambéry 837
Chambon-sur-Lignon (Le) 90
Chambord 232
Chamboulive 479
Chamonix 838
Chamousset 839
Champagney 264
Champagney 321
Champagny-en-Vanoise 840
Champdieu 872
Champeaux 612
Champlitte 309
Champniers 713
Champs-sur-Tarentaine 91
Champtoceaux 659
Chancelade 66
Chandai 593
Changé 669
Chantemerle 762
Chantilly 701
Chaource 268
Chapeiry 823
Chapelle d'Abondance (La) 841
Chapelle-Aubareil (La) 62
Chapelle-aux-Chasses (La) 104
Chapelle-Caro (La) 190
Chapelle-en-Valgaudemar 000
Charenton-le-Pont 329
Charité-sur-Loire (La) 132
Charix 876
Charleville-Mézières 268
Charolles 133
Charrecey 130
Charron 737
Charroux 717
Charroux 98
Chartres 232
Chartrettes 335
Chasseneuil-sur-Bonnieure 731
Chassey-le-Camp 130
Chassignelles 121
Châtaigneraie (La) 659
Chateau-Arnoux 769
Châteaubriant 659
Chateau-Chalon 314
Chateau-Chinon 133
Château-du-Loir 659
Châteaudun 234
Château-Gontier 660
Châteaulin 175
Châteaumeillant 234
Châteauneuf 134
Châteauneuf-de-Randon 421
Châteauneuf-en-Thymerais 234
Châteauponsac 463
Châteauroux 235
Château-Thierry 702
Châtel 840

INDEX

Châtelaillon-Plage.........717
Châtelguyon.....................91
Chatillon-en-Diois 841
Châtillon-en-Michaille...876
Châtillon-sur-Chalaronne 842
Châtillon-sur-Seine 134
Châtre (La) 237
Chaudes-Aigues 92
Chaulhac.......................425
Chaulme (La)..................112
Chaumont 269
Chaumont-sur-Aire 485
Chaumont-sur-Loire......238
Chaumousey.................489
Chaussin 311
Chauvigny 718
Chaux............................306
Chaux-Neuve................309
Chavignol......................254
Chazelles-sur-Lyon 891
Chénérailles 463
Chenillé-Changé 661
Chepy 268
Chépy 702
Cherbourg.....................607
Chevannes....................125
Chèvremont 305
Chevreuse.....................329
Chichilianne 871
Chille.............................314
Chilly-Mazarin...............329
Chinon 228
Chiroubles.....................881
Chissay-en-Tourraine....245
Chisseux 222
Chitenay........................226
Cholet 662
Chomelix........................92
Chonas L'Amballan.......842
Choranche 904
Ciboure 70
Cieux............................471
Civray-de-Tourraine 245
Clairac............................29
Clairvaux-sur-Aube 265
Clam 721
Clamart 330
Clamecy........................135
Clères............................642
Clergoux........................463
Clermont-en-Argonne...486
Clermont-Ferrand 92
Clermont-Ferrand.....94–95
Climbach.........................23
Cliousclat 872
Clohars-Fouesnant 170
Cluny.............................136
Clusaz (La) 842
Cocurès 424
Cognac 719
Coings...........................236
Colleville-Montgomery 616
Collioure........................422
Collobrières...................769
Colmar 4
Colombey-les-Deux-Églises........................271
Colombier-sur-Seulles 601
Combeaufontaine 320
Combleux 250
Combloux 843
Combourg.....................176
Combreux 239
Combrit 170
Commequiers 658
Commer 675
Compiègne 702
Comps-sur-Artuby 770
Concarneau 176
Conches-en-Ouche 626
Condat-en-Feniers..........97
Condeau 601
Condé-sur-Noireau 609
Condom 531
Condorcet 878
Condrieu 843
Confolens......................720
Conques 531
Conquet (Le) 178
Contamines-Mont Joie (Les) 843
Contrevoz 844
Contrexéville 487
Corbeil-Essonnes 330
Cordes 531
Cormeilles.....................626
Cormeilles-en-Parisis....330
Cormoranche-sur-Saône 844
Corpeau 151
Corps 845
Corrençon-en-Vercors 904
Corrèze 479
Corsica 292
Corte 297
Cosnes et Romain 493
Cosne-sur-Loire 136
Cosqueville 599
Cossé-le-Vivien.............669
Coteau (Le) 882
Coti-Chiavari.................297
Cotinière (La)................741
Couarde-sur-Mer (La) ...716
Coucouron 845
Coudray 661
Coudray-Montceaux (Le) 330
Coulandon 103
Coulombiers 728
Coulon 725
Courbevoie-la-Défense 399
Cour-Cheverny.............239
Courcouronnes 331
Cours-la-Ville 845
Coussac-Bonneval 476
Coutances.....................609
Crach 178
Creil..............................703
Creissels 542
Crémieu 846
Crepon 600
Crest 846
Crestet (Le) 860
Creusot (Le) 137
Crévoux 771
Criel-sur-Mer.................644
Croix Mare 647
Crotoy (Le) 704
Crouzet-Migette............318
Crozant 463
Crozes-Hermitage.........895
Crozet 852
Crozon 178
Cucugnan 423
Cumières.......................272
Curtil-Vergy 152
Cusset...........................117
Cuttura 316

D

Dabo 488
Dambach-la-Ville 16
Damgan 178
Dange-Saint-Romain 720
Daon 661
Dauphin.........................773
Dax..................................50
Deauville 610
Decize 138
Delle..............................310
Delme............................488
Déols.............................236
Deuil-la-Barre................331
Deux-Évailles 663
Die................................847
Dienne...........................105
Dieppe 627
Dieue-sur-Meuse 512
Dieulefit.........................848
Digne-les-Bains 770
Digoin............................138

Dijon....139
Dijon....140–141
Dinan....179
Dinard....181
Diou....242
Dissay....728
Dives-sur-Mer....602
Divonne-les-Bains....849
Dolancourt....265
Dol-de-Bretagne....181
Dole....310
Domarin....833
Domfront....598
Domfront-en-Champagne....673
Domme....75
Dompierre-sur-Besbre...104
Domptin....702
Domrémy-la-Pucelle....488
Donzenac....462
Donzy....144
Douai....576
Douarnenez....181
Doué-la-Fontaine....662
Dourdan....331
Dourgne....532
Draguignan....770
Dreuil-les-Amiens....698
Dreux....239
Drubec....617
Drugeac....100
Ducey....597
Duclair....635
Dunes....522
Dunkerque....576
Dun-les-Places....144
Duras....51
Dureil....688
Durfort-Lacapelette....543

E

Eaux-Bonnes (Les)....51
Ecole-Valentin....309
Eecke....575
Effiat....110
Égliseneuve-d'Entraigues....98
Eguisheim....5
Embrun....771
Endoufielle....532
Enghien-les-Bains....331
Entraygues-sur-Truyère....532
Entrecasteaux....772
Entre-les-Fourgs....316
Épernay....271
Epernay-Magenta....272
Épinal....488
Erbalunga....294
Erdeven....168
Ernée....670
Erquy....182
Errues-Menoncourt (Les)....311
Erstein....7
Ervy-le-Chatel....273
Escales....427
Escalles....573
Espalion....533
Espelette....47
Esquiule....63
Estaing....533
Estrablin....903
Étain....513
Étampes....332
Etaples....589
Étoges....272
Étréaupont.... 706
Étretat.... 628
Etroeungt....577
Etueffont....311
Eu....629
Eugénie-les-Bains....51
Évaux-les-Bains....464
Evette-Salbert....311
Évian....849
Evosges....850
Évreux....630
Évron....662
Eyzies-de-Tayac (Les)....52
Èze....772

F

Fabrezan....427
Falaise....611
Falgoux (Le)....98
Favieres....704
Fayence....772
Fécamp....630
Fel (Le)....532
Félines-sur-Rimandoule....849
Ferrière-aux-Étangs (La)....611
Ferté-Bernard (La)....663
Ferté-Frênel (La)....593
Ferté-Gaucher (La)....333
Ferté-Milon (La)....704
Ferté-Vidame (La)....240
Feurs....850
Figeac....534
Fillé-sur-Sarthe....673
Fismes....282
Flamanville....608
Flèche (La)....665
Flers....611
Florac....423
Flumet....851
Foix....534
Foncine-le-Haut....310
Fondettes....259
Fontainebleau....333
Fontaine-Daniel....674
Fontaine-la-Rivière....335
Fontanières....464
Font-d'Usson (La)....720
Fontenay-le-Comte....665
Fontenoy....708
Fontevraud-l'Abbaye....667
Font-Romeu....424
Fontvieille....772
Forbach....489
Forcalquier....773
Foret-Fouesnant (La)....184
Forges-les-Eaux....631
Fouchéres....288
Fouday....7
Fouesnant....183
Fougerolles....312
Fouras....720
Fourcès....544
Fourges....646
Fousseret (Le)....541
Francescas....62
Franche-Comte....302–303
Fréhel....208
Fréjus....773
Fresnoy-en-Bassigny....266
Freyming-Merlebach....490
Froideterre....321
Frotey-les-Vesoul....323
Fumay....273
Futeau....487

G

Gaillac....535
Gaja-La-Selve....421
Gan....65
Gannat....98
Gap....774
Garabit....113
Garde (La)....767
Garde (La)....425
Garde (La)....830
Garde-Adhémar (La)....852
Gasny....646
Gavarnie....536
Gavisse....509
Genest-Saint-Isle (Le)...669
Gentioux-Pigerolles....464
Gérardmer....490
Gerde....523
Gereboy....700
Gevrey-Chambertin....144

Gex 852
Gien 240
Giffaumont-Champaubert 289
Gif-sur-Yvette................407
Gimel-les-Cascades 478
Gincia..............................449
Girmont-Val-d'Ajol 504
Giroussens....................536
Gisors..............................631
Giverny...........................645
Givet..............................273
Glomel............................184
Godeswaervelde...........578
Golfe-Juan 765
Gommersdorf....................1
Goncelin........................819
Gond-Pontouvre (Le) 713
Gordes 776
Gorron...........................676
Gorze 499
Goualade 34
Gouarec 192
Gouesnou 172
Goult 777
Goumois 312
Goupilleres...................619
Gourdon........................777
Gouvets 612
Gouvieux.......................701
Gramat 536
Gramont........................537
Grand'Combe Châteleu 318
Grand-Bornand (Le)......853
Grande-Verriere (La)......124
Grandrupt 509
Grand-Vabre 531
Grand-Village................721
Grane 847
Granges-lès-Beaumont 885
Granges-Sainte-Marie (Les) 315
Grangettes (Les) 320
Granville 612
Grasse...........................777
Grau-du-Roi (Le)...........425
Graulhet 537
Grave (La) 778
Gravigny........................630
Gray 312
Grenade sur Adour 53
Grenoble 853
Grenoble 854–855
Grignan 858
Grimaud 778
Gros Theil (Le)...............625
Groux (Île de) 184
Gruffy 824
Gruissan........................425
Guenrouet 667
Guéret 464
Guilers...........................172
Guillestre.......................778
Guimaëc........................187
Guise.............................705
Gye-sur-Seine 268

H

Hagetmau 53
Haguenau 7
Haie-Fouassière (La).....681
Hambye 610
Handschuheim................22
Hardelot-Plage.............578
Haute-Normandie..622–623
Hauterives.....................858
Hauteville-les-Dijon.......143
Havre (Le)......................631
Havre (Le) 632–633
Hazebrouck...................578
Hédé 176
Heiligenstein 3
Hendaye.........................54
Hennebont 184
Herbaudiere (L')............682
Herbiers (Les)...............668
Hesdin...........................579
Hinsingen 8
Hirtzbach 1
Hoedic (ile de)...............185
Hohwald (Le)....................3
Hombourg-Budange.... 511
Homps 427
Honfleur 612
Hossegor 54
Hostens...........................55
Houches (Les)..............839
Houdelaincourt 492
Houlgate 613
Hunawihr.........................15
Hyères 779

I

Ilay 323
Ile-de-France........326–327
Île du Levant 782
Illhaeusern.......................14
Illiers-Combray 241
Inor................................510
Isle-Adam (L') 336
Isle-sur-Serein (L').........126
Issigeac...........................35
Issoudun 241
Issy-les-Moulineaux......336
Itxassou 47
Ivry-sur-Seine...............397

J

Jarnac 721
Javols............................415
Jazennes.......................730
Joigny 145
Joinville 273
Jonzac 721
Jougne 316
Jouillat...........................465
Jouy-sur-Eure 630
Joyeuse.........................859
Joyeux 905
Juan-les-Pins 751
Jublains.........................663
Juillan 557
Juliénas.........................859
Jumièges 635
Jure 877

K

Kaltenhouse 8
Kaysersberg......................8
Kervignac......................189
Klingenthal 12

L

Labastide-Murat 537
Lacaune 537
Lacroix-sur-Meuse........506
Lacrouzette 538
Ladoix-Serrigny 128
Laffrey 860
Lagarde-Enval...............478
Laguiole 538
Lalinde-en-Périgord 55
Lalizolle 98
Lalleyriat.......................876
Lalonde-les-Maures......780
Lamalou-les-Bains........426
Lamastre 860
Lancrans 876
Landéda........................185
Landerneau...................185
Landivisiau 186
Landvennec 186
Langeais 242
Langres 274
Languedoc-Roussillon 410–411
Lannemezan 538
Lannion 186

Lanslebourg 860
Lantosque 780
Laon 705
Lapalisse.........................98
Lapoutroie.........................9
Laragne-Montèglin........780
Larche 781
Lardiers 773
Laroque-Timbaut 55
Larrau.............................56
Larressingle..................531
Larroque........................527
Laruns 56
Lasgraïsses..................537
Lassay-les-Châteaux....675
Lastours 420
Latouille-Lentillac..........552
Latour-de-Carol 424
Lauret 427
Lauzières.......................737
Laval 668
Laval-de-Jayac 76
Lavandou (Le) 781
Lavardens 538
Lavardin 261
Lavaudieu 89
Lavaur 539
Laye 775
Lecci-de-Porto-Vecchio
..................................298
Lèchére (La) 875
Lectoure........................539
Leigne-les-Bois.............737
Lepuix 313
Lesconil.........................187
Lespignan 417
Lesponne 523
Lestelle-Betharram 56
Levallois-Perret.............397
Levens 800
Levernois 128
Levie 294
Levroux 236
Leyme 539
Lézignan-Corbières.......427
Liergues 829
Liessies 579
Ligny-en-Cambrésis 574
Ligny-le-Châtel 129
Lille...............................580
Lille 582–583
Lillebonne 635
Limoges 465
Limoges................466–467
Limousin 458–459
Limoux 428
Lingé 225
Lioran (Le) 105
Lisieux..........................614
Listrac-Médoc.................57
Llo 428
Loches 242
Locoal-Mendon 168
Locqueltas 216
Locquignol 586
Locquirec 187
Locronan 187
Loctudy 187
Lodève 428
Lods 319
Lomont-sur-Crete 304
Longevilles Mont d'Or (Les)
..................................315
Longny-au-Perche 616
Longpont 708
Longuyon 493
Longwy 493
Lons-le-Saunier 313
Lorient 188
Lormes 146
Lorraine 482–483
Loudun..........................721
Loupiac 549
Lourdes 539
Louresse-Rochemenier
..................................662
Louviers 635
Lubre-Saint-Christau 57
Lucey 511
Luché-Pringé 665
Luçon 670
Lude (Le) 670
Lüe 59
Luglon 68
Lunel 429
Lunéville 493
Lutzelbourg 481
Luxeuil-les-Bains 314
Lux-Saint-Remy 132
Luz-Saint-Sauveur 540
Lyon 861
Lyon 862–863
Lyons-la-Forêt 636
Lys-Saint-Georges 238

M

Macé 618
Maché 686
Mâcon 146
Madelaine-sous-Montreuil
(La) 587
Magalas 418
Magnac-Laval 471
Magnières 484
Magny-Cours 151
Maillezais 667
Maintenon 233
Maisons-Lafitte 337
Malakoff 337
Malbuisson 315
Malemort-sur-Corrèze...462
Malesherbes 243
Malestroit 190
Malicorne-sur-Sarthe....670
Mamers 671
Mandagout....................454
Mandailles.....................533
Mandailles-Saint-Julien...99
Manderen......................494
Manigod 843
Manosque 782
Mans (Le) 671
Marans 722
Maraussan 417
Marchal 91
Marciac 541
Marçon..........................660
Marcy-sur-Anse 825
Margencel 896
Marly-le-Roi 338
Marnand........................846
Marnans 859
Marnay-sur-Marne 270
Maroilles........................586
Maroux 547
Marquay 75
Marsac-sur-L'Isle 67
Marseillan......................412
Marseille........................783
Marseille 784–785
Martel 541
Martigues 789
Martillac 77
Martres-Tolosane 541
Marzy 150
Masméjean 447
Massiac...........................99
Matignon 190
Maubeuge.....................586
Mauléon 722
Mauleon-Licharre............57
Mauriac 100
Mayenne 674
Mayet-de-Montagne (Le)
..................................118
Mazamet 542
Mazayes 107
Méaudre........................828
Meaux 338
Megève 870
Meillers..........................104
Meillonnas.....................832
Melisey..........................321
Melle 723
Melles............................524
Mende...........................429

INDEX

Menestreau-en-Villette...260
Menilot (Le) 275
Mens 870
Menton...........................789
Mervent..........................666
Meschers-sur-Gironde
..................................739
Mesnil-Saint-Père 275
Messan 681
Métabief.........................315
Metz 494
Metz 496–497
Meudon..........................338
Meudon-la-Forêt...........339
Meung-sur-Loire 250
Meux (Le) 703
Meximieux.....................837
Meylan 857
Meyronne.......................548
Meyrueis 430
Meyssac.........................461
Mezangers 663
Mèze 430
Mezieres-en-Brenne
..................................243
Mezilles.........................159
Midi-Pyrénées 516–517
Millau 542
Milly-la-Forêt.................339
Milly-Lamartine 147
Mimizan-Plage 58
Minihy-Tréguier 213
Mirabel-aux-Baronnies
..................................878
Mirande.........................543
Mirmande......................871
Modane.........................872
Moëlan-sur-Mer 191
Moirans-en-Montagne
..................................316
Moissac 543
Moitiers-en-Bauptois (Les)
..................................607
Molac 190
Molines-en-Queyras 790
Molineuf 226
Molunes (Les)................316
Monclar 79
Moncorneil-Grazan 543
Moncour-Fromonville....335
Monnaie 260
Monsec 46
Montaigu.......................676
Montargis......................243
Montauban....................543
Montauban-de-Luchon
..................................524
Montaut-les-Créneaux
..................................521
Montbéliard...................317
Montbrison....................872
Montclar........................791
Mont-Dauphin...............779
Mont-de-Marsan.............59
Mont-Dore (Le)..............100
Monteils 529
Monteils 565
Montélimar....................873
Montenach....................499
Montferrand-du-Périgord
....................................60
Montferrst 835
Montfort-en-Chalosse 60
Montfort-l'Amaury.........339
Montgailhard.................534
Montgardin....................776
Montier-en-Der 276
Montignac 60
Montigny-la-Resle 125
Montigny-le-Bretonneux
..................................406
Montigny-sur-Avre 231
Montigny-sur-Loing 335
Montlebon.....................317
Montliot-et-Courcelles
..................................134
Montlouis 253
Montlouis 205
Mont-Louis....................431
Montluçon.....................101
Montmarault..................102
Montmartin-sur-Mer......609
Montmirail 664
Montmorency................340
Montmorillon.................723
Montpellier....................431
Montpellier 432–433
Montréal........................544
Montreuil.......................398
Montreuil-Bellay............676
Montreuil-Poulay...........675
Montreuil-sur-Mer 586
Montrichard 244
Montricoux....................545
Montriond 875
Montrottier 874
Mont-Saint-Michel (Le)...614
Montsalvy 102
Montségur.....................545
Montsoreau...................692
Moosch 22
Moret-sur-Loing............335
Morigny-Champigny 332
Morlaix 191
Mortagne-au-Perche 615
Mortagne-sur-Sèvre......677
Morteau.........................317
Mortemart 471
Morzine 874
Mothe-Saint-Héray (La)
..................................741
Motte-au-Bois (La)........579
Mouans-Sartoux 777
Moudeyres 109
Mougins 791
Moulay 675
Moulins 103
Moulins-Engilbert..........148
Moustiers Sainte Marie
..................................792
Mouthiers-sur-Boëme...713
Moûtiers........................875
Moux-en-Morvan 149
Mouzon 285
Mulhouse 10
Mulsanne 673
Munster...........................10
Mur de Bretagne...........191
Murat.............................104
Murs..............................776
Myon 318

N

Najac.............................545
Nalzen...........................535
Nancy............................499
Nancy 500
Nans-sous-Sainte-Anne
.... 318
Nanterre 398
Nantes...........................677
Nantes 678–679
Nantua 876
Narbonne 436
Narnhac 105
Nasbinals 437
Natzwiller 7
Navarrenx........................62
Neau 663
Nebouzat 97
Nedde 472
Nérac 62
Néris-les-Bains 101
Nestier...........................546
Neuchâtel-en-Saosnois
..................................671
Neuf-Brisach.....................6
Neufchâteau 503
Neufchâtel-en-Bray 636
Neuille-le-Lierre.............260
Neuilly-sur-Seine...........396
Neuvic 472
Neuville-de-Poitou 729
Neuzy 138
Nevers...........................149
Nevez 192

Nice...792
Nice...794–795
Niederbronn-les-Bains...12
Niedermorschwihr...6
Nîmes...438
Nîmes...440–441
Niort...724
Nissan-lez-Enserune...417
Nitry...151
Noailly...883
Nogent...277
Nogent-le-Roi...245
Nogent-le-Rotrou...245
Nogent-sur-Seine...277
Nohant-Vic...237
Noirétable...876
Noirmoutier-en-L'Île...681
Nolay...151
Nontron...63
Nord-Pas-de-Calais...568–569
Notre-Dame-de-Bellecombe...851
Nouan-le-Fuzelier...246
Nouvion-en Thiérache (Le)...705
Noyers-Bocage... 606
Noyers-sur-Serein...151
Nuits-Saint-Georges...152
Nyons...878

O

Obernai...12
Oeting...490
Oisly...245
Olargues...442
Olette...455
Olonzac...442
Oloron-Sainte-Marie...63
Omblèze...847
Omonville-la-Petite...608
Orange...800
Orbey...9
Orcieres...801
Orgnac-L'Aven...901
Orléans...247
Orléans...248–249
Ornans...318
Ornon...830
Orthez...64
Ottrott...13
Ouessant (Ile d')...192
Ouhans...320
Ouistreham-Riva-Bella...616
Oyonnax...879

P

Pacy-sur-Armancon...121
Pailherols...106
Paimpol...192
Palais (Le)...193
Palavas-Les-Flots...443
Palmyre (La)...739
Palud-sur-Verdon (La)...767
Panissieres...850
Paradou (Le)...759
Paray-le-Monial...153
Paris... 340
Paris... 342–343
Parthenay...725
Patrimonio...299
Pau...64
Paulin...76
Paulx...683
Pauvres...283
Pays-de-la-Loire...650–652
Peille...801
Peillon...801
Peisey-Nancroix...879
Pélisanne...809
Pelvoux...802
Penmarch...170
Penne-d'Agenais...65
Périgueux...66
Pernes-les-Fontaines...765
Péronne...706
Perpignan...444
Perros-Guirec...194
Perthes...276
Peschadoires...116
Petite-Pierre (La)...13
Petites Dalles (Les)...643
Petit-Pressigny (Le)...251
Peyrat-le-Château...472
Peyrecave...546
Peyrens...421
Peyrilhac...470
Pézenas...446
Pezieres-Resinand (Les)...850
Pezou... 261
Phaffans...305
Picardie...696–697
Picherande...106
Pierre-Perthuis...161
Pilat-Plage...31
Piney...277
Piolenc...801
Piriac-sur-Mer...683
Pissotte...666
Pithiviers...250
Plaine-sur-Mer (La)...684
Plaisians...836
Plancherine...819
Planchez...133
Plan-de-la-Tour...802
Plelan-le-Grand...195
Plélan-le-Petit...180
Plemet...195
Pléneuf-val-André...195
Pleyben...196
Ploemeur...196
Ploërmel...196
Plogoff...197
Plombières-les-Bains...503
Plomodiern...176
Ploneour-Lanvern...170
Ploubalay...197
Ploudalmézeau...198
Plougasnou...198
Ploumanac'h...195
Plouzane...172
Plurien-Frehel...207
Poêt-Laval (Le)...848
Poiré-sur-Vie (Le)...686
Poitiers...726
Poitru-Charentes...710–711
Polminhac...85
Pons...730
Pont-à-Mousson...503
Pontarlier...319
Pontaubert...162
Pont-Audemer...637
Pont-Aven...198
Pont-Croix...199
Pont-D'Ain...879
Pont-D'Alleyras...110
Pont-de-l'Arche...636
Pont-de-Montvert (Le)...447
Pontempeyrat...92
Pont-et-Massene...158
Pontevès...802
Pontgibaud...106
Pontivy...199
Pont-L'Abbe...200
Pont-l'Évêque...616
Pont-les Moulins...304
Pontlevoy...244
Pontoise...400
Pontorson...615
Pont-Saint-Esprit...447
Pornic...683
Pornichet...657
Porquerolles...780
Port-Joinville (Île d'Yeu)...684
Port-Louis...189
Port-Marly...338
Porto...298
Porto-Vecchio...298
Port-sur-Saône...320
Pouilly-sous-Charlieu...883

Pouilly-sur-Loire............153
Pouldreuzic...................200
Pouliguen (Le)...............657
Pourville-sur-Mer..........627
Pouzauges....................685
Prades..........................448
Pradines........................526
Pra-Loup.......................758
Prats-Balaguer..............431
Prats-de-Mollo..............449
Praz-sur-Arly.................870
Prenois..........................143
Preuilly-sur-Claise.........250
Privas...........................879
Projan...........................546
Propriano......................298
Provence.............746–747
Provins..........................401
Publier..........................849
Puilboreau.....................736
Pujols.............................79
Puy l'Evèque.................546
Puy-en-Velay (Le)..........107
Puylaurens....................546
Puymoyen.....................713
Pyla-sur-Mer...................30

Q

Quarre-les-Tombres......153
Quatre-Routes-d'Albussac (Les)..........................479
Quenza..........................293
Quiberon.......................200
Quillan..........................449
Quimper........................201
Quimperlé.....................202
Quincié-en-Beaujolais 880
Quinson........................802

R

Ramatuelle....................806
Rambouillet...................401
Rânes...........................598
Rathsamhausen..............16
Rayol-Canadel..............782
Razac-d'Eymet...............35
Réalmont.......................547
Regnéville-sur-Mer........609
Reims...........................277
Reims...................278–279
Rémilly-Aillicourt...........285
Remiremont..................504
Renaison.......................883
Rencurel.......................904
Renédale.......................270
Rennes..........................203
Rennes.........................204
Reole (La)........................67
Rethel...........................282
Revel.............................547
Revigny-sur-Ordain.......485
Revin............................283
Rhône-Alpes.........816–817
Ribeauvillé.......................13
Riberac............................68
Riceys (Les)..................268
Richelieu.......................251
Riec-sur-Belon..............199
Rieumes........................547
Riom.............................110
Riom-ès-Montagnes.....111
Riquewihr........................14
Riscle............................547
Rive-de-Gier.................881
Roanne.........................882
Rocamadour.................548
Roche-Bernard (La)......206
Rochecorbon................259
Roche-en-Brenil (La).....154
Rochefort......................730
Rochefort-sur-Loire.......685
Rochefoucauld (La).......731
Roche-Guyon (La).........402
Rochelle (La)................731
Rochelle (La).........732–733
Roche-Maurice (La)......185
Roche-Morey (La).........320
Roche-Posay (La).........737
Roche-sur-Yon (La).......685
Rocroi..........................283
Rodemack....................509
Rodez...........................549
Rolleboise.....................402
Romans-sur-Isère.........884
Romorantin-Lanthenay 251
Ronce-les-Bains...........737
Ronchamp....................321
Roquebrune-Cap-Martin 790
Roquecourbe...............529
Roquefère....................420
Roquefort-des-Corbières 449
Roque-Gageac (La).........75
Roquemaure.................456
Roscoff.........................206
Rosieres-pres-Troyes 288
Rosiers-sur-Loire (Les) 686
Rosnay.........................225
Rostrenen....................207
Rouen..........................637
Rouen..................640–641
Rouffach.........................15
Rougon.........................767
Rouperroux-le-Coquet...671
Roussac........................463
Rousses (Les) Bonlieu...322
Rouvrois-sur-Othain......505
Royan...........................738
Royat..............................96
Roye.............................322
Royères........................470
Rueil-Malmaison...........402
Ruillé-sur-Loir...............660
Rully.............................154
Ry................................642

S

Sables-d'Olonne (Les)...687
Sables-d'Or-les-Pins....207
Sablé-sur-Sarthe...........688
Sabres............................68
Saché...........................251
Sagnes et Doudoulet....893
Saignes.........................111
Saignon.........................751
Saillans.........................847
Saillenard......................157
Sail-Sous-Couzan.........830
Saint Fargeau................155
Saint Julien-aux-Bois....457
Saint Vincent.................109
Saint-Agnan-en-Vercors 885
Saint-Agrève.................885
Saint-Aignan.................251
Saint-Amand-de-Coly.....61
Saint-Amand-Montrond 252
Saint-Amarin...................22
Saint-Amour-Bellevue...148
Saint-André-d'Embrun 771
Saint-Andre-de-Valborgne 449
Saint-André-les-Vergers 288
Saint-Anthème.............111
Saint-Antonin-Noble-Val 550
Saint-Arcons-d'Allier.... 115
Saint-Auban-sur-l'Ouveze 886
Saint-Aubin..................182
Saint-Aubin-le-Vertueux 624
Saint-Auvent................474
Saint-Avé.....................214
Saint-Avit.....................532
Saint-Avold..................505

INDEX

Saint-Beauzire 89
Saint-Benoît 728
Saint-Benoît-sur-Loire
...................................253
Saint-Bertrand-de-
Comminges................551
Saint-Bonnet-le-Chateau
...................................898
Saint-Bonnet-le-Froid 90
Saint-Bonnet-Tronçais....87
Saint-Brieuc 208
Saint-Calais 689
Saint-Céré.....................551
Saint-Chartier................237
Saint-Christophe-en-
Brionnais 155
Saint-Christophe-sur-
Dolaizon 109
Saint-Cirgues-de-Jordanne
.....................................99
Saint-Cirq-Lapopie 552
Saint-Clément-des-
Baleines 714
Saint-Cloud 402
Saint-Crépin..................779
Saint-Cyr-du-Doret 722
Saint-Cyr-sous-Dourdan
...................................403
Saint-Dalmas-de-Tende
...................................803
Saint-Denis 399
Saint-Denis-d'Oléron 740
Saint-Denis-d'Orques
...................................689
Saint-Denis-les-Bourg
...................................832
Saint-Didier-de-la-Tour
...................................834
Saint-Dié-des-Vosges...505
Saint-Disdier 803
Saint-Dos 73
Saint-Dyé-Sur-Loire 232
Sainte-Adresse 634
Sainte-Anne-d'Auray 168
Sainte-Colombe............780
Sainte-Croix 905
Sainte-Croix-en-Jarez...881
Sainte-Eulalie 893
Sainte-Eulalie-d'Olt...... 553
Sainte-Feyre..................465
Sainte-Fortunade..........478
Sainte-Geneviève-des-Bois
...................................404
Sainte-Marie-du-Lac.....289
Sainte-Maxime..............807
Sainte-Menehould 283
Saint-Émilion...................68
Sainte-Radegonde..........67
Sainte-Radegonde........550
Saintes 742
Saintes-Maries-de-la-Mer
...................................808
Saint-Estephe 69
Saint-Étienne 886
Saint-Étienne-de-Fursac
...................................476
Saint-Étienne-du-
Valdonnez 447
Saint-Félix-Lauragais....552
Saint-Ferreol 553
Saint-Ferreol-Trente-Pas
...................................878
Saint-Firmin-les-Crotoy
...................................704
Saint-Florent 299
Saint-Florentin 155
Saint-Florent-le-Vieil 689
Saint-Flour 112
Saint-Galmier 890
Saint-Gaudens..............553
Saint-Gely-du-Fesc 436
Saint-Gence 470
Saint-Genes-Champanelle
.... 97
Saint-Genest-Malifaux
...................................888
Saint-Geniez-d'Olt 553
Saint-Georges...............112
Saint-Georges-de-Didonne
...................................738
Saint-Germain-des-Près
...................................656
Saint-Germain-des-Vaux
.... 608
Saint-Germain-de-
Taillevende 620
Saint-Germain-en-Laye
...................................403
Saint-Germain-sur-Sarthe
...................................674
Saint-Gervais 659
Saint-Gervais-d'Auvergne
...................................113
Saint-Gervais-de-Vic 689
Saint-Gilles 442
Saint-Girons..................553
Saint-Gratien.................331
Saint-Guilhem-le-desert
.... 450
Saint-Haon....................110
Saint-Haon-le-Chatel
...................................883
Saint-Hilaire-de-Brens
...................................846
Saint-Hilaire-le-Chateau
...................................473
Saint-Hughes-de-
Chartreuse 893
Saint-Jean-Cap-Ferrat...803
Saint-Jean-de-Cole 46
Saint-Jean-de-la-Blaquiere
.... 451
Saint-Jean-de-Luz 69
Saint-Jean-de-Maurienne
...................................891
Saint-Jean-de-Monts....689
Saint-Jean-du-Bruel 542
Saint-Jeannet................814
Saint-Jean-Pied-de-Port
.....................................71
Saint-Joachim...............690
Saint-Jorioz...................823
Saint-Josse...................589
Saint-Julia 552
Saint-Julien-Chapteuil
...................................109
Saint-Julien-de-Crempse
.....................................35
Saint-Julien-de-Jonzy...155
Saint-Julien-en-Champsaur
...................................776
Saint-Julien-lès-Metz....498
Saint-Junien..................473
Saint-Justin.....................72
Saint-Just-Saint-Rambert
...................................889
Saint-Lary-Soulan.........554
Saint-Laurent-d'Aigouze
...................................413
Saint-Laurent-sur-Mer
...................................601
Saint-Laurent-sur-Saône
...................................844
Saint-Laurent-sur-Sèvre
...................................668
Saint-Leger-sous-Beuvray
...................................156
Saint-Leonard 631
Saint-Léonard-de-Noblat
...................................474
Saint-Léonard-des-Bois
...................................690
Saint-Leu-d'Esserent....701
Saint-Lizier....................554
Saint-Lô 617
Saint-Lucie-de-Tallano
...................................300
Saint-Lyphard 657
Saint-Macaire..................72
Saint-Maixent-l'École
...................................740
Saint-Malo 209
Saint-Mandé 398
Saint-Marc-à-Loubaud
...................................460
Saint-Martin-d'Ardèche
...................................901

INDEX

Saint-Martin-d'Armagnac 554
Saint-Martin-de- Marseille 783
Saint-Martin-de-Belleville 891
Saint-Martin-de-la-Place 687
Saint-Martin-en-Haut....892
Saint-Martin-la-Méanne 474
Saint-Martin-la-Plaine 881
Saint-Martin-Osmonville 631
Saint-Martin-sous-Vigouroux 114
Saint-Martin-Vésubie....803
Saint-Mathieu-de-Treviers 450
Saint-Maur-des-Fossés 400
Saint-Maure-de-Peyriac 62
Saint-Maure-de-Tourraine 253
Saint-Maurice 403
Saint-Maurice-en-Valgaudemar 804
Saint-Meloir-des-Ondes 174
Saint-Merd-de-Lapleau 474
Saint-Michel....................71
Saint-Michel-Tubeuf 593
Saint-Mihiel 506
Saint-Nazaire 690
Saint-Omer 587
Saint-Ouen....................261
Saint-Ouen....................398
Saint-Palais.....................73
Saint-Palais-sur-Mer 739
Saint-Pardoux-la-Croisille 475
Saint-Paul-de-Fenouillet 446
Saint-Paul-de-Vence.....804
Saint-Paul-en-Cornillon 889
Saint-Paul-Lès-Monestier 892
Saint-Père-sous-Vézelay 161
Saint-Pereuse 148
Saint-Pierre-d'Argencon 754
Saint-Pierre-d'Oléron 741
Saint-Pierre-de-Chartreuse 892
Saint-Pierre-de-Rivière 535
Saint-Pierre-des-Champs 450
Saint-Pierre-le-Chastel 107
Saint-Pol-de-Leon 211
Saint-Pons 827
Saint-Pourçain-sur-Sioule 114
Saint-Pries-en-Jarez 888
Saint-Priest-Taurion 470
Saint-Prix 156
Saint-Quentin................706
Saint-Quentin-des-Isles 624
Saint-Quirin...................481
Saint-Raphael 774
Saint-Rémy-de-Provence 804
Saint-Renan 211
Saint-Restitut................893
Saint-Reverien 156
Saint-Robert 475
Saint-Romain-le-Puy 872
Saint-Salvy-de-la-Balme 529
Saint-Satur....................254
Saint-Saturnin-de-Lucian 450
Saint-Saturnin-les Apt 752
Saint-Saturnin-sur-Loire 655
Saint-Saulge 156
Saint-Sauveur 771
Saint-Sauveur-en-Rue 890
Saint-Savin 519
Saint-Savin 834
Saint-Savinien...............741
Saint-Savin-sur-Gartempe 742
Saint-Suliac...................210
Saint-Sulpice-de-Favieres 333
Saint-Sulpice-la-Pointe 536
Saint-Sylvain.................606
Saint-Thégonnec 211
Saint-Thibault 254
Saint-Tropez..................806
Saint-Ulphace 664
Saint-Urcize 114
Saint-Vaast-la-Hougue 618
Saint-Valéry-en-Caux....643
Saint-Valéry-sur-Somme 707
Saint-Véran 806
Saint-Verand 148
Saint-Victor-de-Macalp 414
Saint-Victor-sur-Loire....888
Saint-Vincent-du-Lorouër 690
Saint-Vincent-sur-Jard 691
Saint-Wandrille-Rancon 625
Saint-Yrieix-la-Perche...475
Saisies (Les)..................851
Salers 114
Salies-de-Béarn 73
Salins-Les-Bains 301
Sallanches 894
Sallé 657
Salle-les-Alpes (La).......763
Salle-Prunet (La) 424
Salles (Les)....................877
Salles 520
Salles-la-Source 550
Salmiech 555
Salon-de-Provence.......808
Salvetat-sur-Agout (La) 426
Samatan........................555
Samoëns.......................894
Sampans.......................310
Sanary-sur-Mer 809
Sancé............................147
Sancerre........................253
Sancoins 254
Sanilhac 827
Sansac de Marmiesse 85
Saou..............................894
Sappey-e-Chartreuse (Le) 858
Sarcey 896
Sare...............................70
Sarlat-la-Canéda.............74
Sarpoil............................86
Sarrebourg 507
Sarreguemines..............507
Sartène 299
Sarzeau 211
Satillieu 825
Saugues 115
Saulchoy 579
Saulges 691
Saulieu 156
Sault..............................809
Saumur 691
Sauternes.......................76

Sauve 451
Sauveterre-de-Rouergue 555
Sauzon 193
Saverne 15
Savigny 610
Savigny-sur-Seille 157
Savournon 781
Sceaux 404
Scharrachbergheim 13
Schweighouse-Sur-Moder 8
Sedan 284
Sées 618
Séez 835
Segny 852
Segonzac 719
Seilhac 478
Sélestat 16
Semblançay 260
Semnoz (Le) 824
Semur-en-Auxois 157
Senlis 707
Senonches 235
Senones 508
Sens 158
Sept-Saulx 282
Sercus 579
Sergeac 61
Serignac-sur-Garonne 29
Serre-de-Mestes (La) 476
Serrières 825
Servant 113
Servian 417
Servon 615
Sète 451
Sévérac-le-Château 555
Sevignacq-Meyracq 56
Sèvres 404
Sevrier 823
Seyne-les-Alpes 809
Seynes 414
Sézanne 286
Sierck-les-Bains 509
Signy-l'Abbaye 283
Sillé-le-Guillaume 692
Siran 443
Sisteron 810
Soissons 707
Soisy-sur-École 404
Solenzara 300
Solignac 470
Sommières 452
Sorède 452
Sorges 67
Sotteville-sur-Mer 643
Soudan 740
Souesmes 246
Soulac-sur-Mer 77
Soultz 10
Souterraine (La) 476
Souvigny 104
Souvigny-en-Sologne 254
Stenay 509
St-Etienne-les-Remiremont 504
Stosswihr 11
Strasbourg 16
Strasbourg 18–19
Sucé-sur-Erdre 681
Sully-sur-Loire 255
Super-Besse 86
Super-Sauze 758
Suresnes 405
Surgères 743
Sutrieu 894

T

Taillebourg 743
Tain L'Hermitage 895
Taintrux 505
Tamniès 53
Tanlay 159
Tannay 135
Tarare 895
Tarascon 810
Tarascon-sur-Ariège 556
Tarbes 556
Tardets-Sorholus 77
Tarnac 477
Taussat 29
Tavers 224
Temple-sur-Lot (Le) 79
Tence 90
Thann 22
Thannenkirch 14
Theizé 826
Theoule-sur-Mer 811
Therondels 557
Thiers 115
Thionville 510
Thollon-les-Memises 849
Thonon-les-Bains 896
Thorenc 811
Thorigné-sur-Dué 674
Thouarcé 693
Thouars 743
Thouron 471
Thury-Harcourt 618
Tiffauges 693
Tonneins 77
Torcy 137
Toucy 159
Toudon 811
Toul 511
Toulon 811
Toulouse 557
Toulouse 558–559
Touquet (Le) 588
Tour de Faure 552
Tourcoing 589
Tour-d'Aigues (La) 812
Tournemire 116
Tournoël 110
Tournon-sur-Rhône 897
Tournus 159
Tours 255
Tours 256–257
Tranche-sur-Mer (La) 693
Trébeurden 212
Trégastel 213
Tréguier 213
Trégunc 199
Trélon 589
Tréminis 871
Trémolat 77
Tréport (Le) 644
Trevoux 897
Trinite-sur-Mer 214
Trois Épis (Les) 6
Tronget 87
Trouville-sur-Mer 619
Troyes 286
Tulle 477
Turckheim 6
Turenne 479
Tursac 52

U

Uchacq 59
Uchon 137
Urdens 564
Uriage-les-Bains 857
Ussac 462
Usson-en-Forez 897
Ustou 564
Utelle 813
Uvernet-Fours 758
Uzès 453

V

Vaas 660
Vachette (La) 762
Vagnas 900
Vaiges 669
Vailly-sur-Sauldre 223
Vaison-la-Romaine 813
Val Suzon 143

Valaurie 873
Valberg 813
Valbonne 777
Valcabrère 551
Valcebollière 454
Val-d'Ajol (Le) 511
Val-de-Vesle 282
Valence 898
Valence-sur-Baïse 564
Valenciennes 590
Valgaudemar (La) 768
Valgorge 899
Vallauris 765
Valloire 899
Vallon-Pont-d'Arc 900
Valmorel 875
Val-Saint-Germain (Le) 333
Vals-les-Bains 901
Valtin (Le) 492
Vandenesse-en-Auxois 134
Vannes 214
Vannes-sur-Cosson 260
Vans (Les) 902
Vanves 405
Varengeville-sur-Mer 628
Vars 779
Vastres (Les) 90
Vatteville-la-Rue 626
Vauclaix 146
Vaux-en-Beaujolais 829
Vaux-sous-Aubigny 275
Veauche 890
Velluire 666
Vence 813
Vendays-Montalivet 78
Vendôme 261
Venosc 829
Verberie 703
Verdun 512
Vergongheon 88
Vermenton 160
Verneuil-sur-Avre 644
Vernierfontaine 319
Vernon 645
Vernonnet 645
Vernouillet 240
Versailles 405
Vers-Pont-du-Gard 454
Verteuil-sur-Carente 714
Vesoul 323
Veuil 261
Veules-les-Roses 646
Vézelay 161
Vialas 447
Vibrac 713
Vibraye 693
Vicdessos 564
Vichy 116
Vic-sur-Cère 118
Vieillevie 118
Vienne 902
Vierzon 261
Vieux-Mareuil 46
Vigan (Le) 454
Vigeant (Le) 743
Vigneulles-les-Hattonchatel 507
Vignieu 834
Vignory 270
Villandraut 78
Villandry 223
Villard-de-Lans 903
Villars (Le) 160
Villars Fontaine 152
Villars-les-Dombes 905
Villebois-Lavalette 713
Villecomtal-sur-Arros 564
Villefort 455
Villefranche-de-Conflent 455
Villefranche-de-Lauragais 565
Villefranche-de-Rouergue 565
Villefranche-du-Perigord 78
Villefranche-sur-Mer 799
Villemagne-l'Argentiere 426
Villeneuve (La) 460
Villeneuve-l'Archeveque 162
Villeneuve-lès-Avignon 455
Villeneuve-sur-Lot 78
Villeneuve-sur-Tarn 565
Villeneuve-sur-Yonne 162
Villequier 626
Villerest 882
Villers-Bocage 606
Villers-Cotterêts 708
Villersexel 323
Villers-le-Lac 323
Villers-sur-Mer 610
Ville-sur-Yron 513
Villevallier 145
Villiers-en-Bois 725
Villiers-sur-Marne 274
Villiers-sur-Suze 270
Vilosnes 510
Vinca 448
Vincennes 399
Vineuil-Saint-Firmin 701
Violay 851
Vire 620
Vitrac 118
Vitré 216
Vitry-en-Perthois 289
Vitry-le-François 288
Vittel 513
Viviers 906
Viviers-du-Lac 833
Vivoin 673
Vivonne 728
Vonnas 906
Vougeot 152
Vouillé 729
Vouvray 259
Vouziers 290
Vulaines-sur-Seine 334

W

Wast (Le) 572
Wettolsheim 5
Wihr-au-Val 11
Wimereux 591
Wissembourg 22
Woelfing-lès-Sarreguemines 508
Woerth 23
Woippy 498

Y

Ygrande 86
Yport 646
Yssingeaux 119
Yvetot 647
Yvoire 896
Yvoy-le-Marron 262
Yvré-l'Évêque 673
Yzeures-sur-Creuse 262

Z

Zonza 300